SportingNews

2006 EDITION

BASEBALL

the ultimate baseball almanac

GUIDE

EXPLANATION OF STATISTICAL ABBREVIATIONS

A: assists. **AB:** at-bats. **Avg.:** batting average (hits divided by at-bats). **BB:** bases on balls. **Bk.:** balks. **CG:** complete games. **CS:** caught stealing. **E:** errors. **ER:** earned runs. **ERA:** earned-run average (earned runs times nine divided by innings pitched). **G:** games. **GB:** games behind. **GF:** games finished. **GDP:** grounding into double plays. **GS:** games started. **H:** hits. **HB:** hit batsmen. **HP:** hit by pitches. **HR:** home runs. **IBB:** intentional bases on balls. **IP:** innings pitched. **L:** losses. **LOB:** runners left on base. **OBP:** on-base percentage (hits plus bases on balls plus hit by pitches divided by at-bats plus bases on balls plus hit by pitches plus sacrifice flies). **Pct.:** winning percentage. **PO:** putouts. **Pos.:** position. **R:** runs. **RBI:** runs batted in. **Rel.:** relief appearances. **SB:** stolen bases. **SF:** sacrifice flies (run-scoring flyouts). **SH:** sacrifice hits (bunts that advance one or more runners but result in the batter being retired at first base or reaching first on an error). **ShO:** shutouts. **Slg.:** slugging percentage (total bases divided by at-bats). **SO:** strikeouts. **Sv.:** saves. **Sv. Op.:** save opportunities. **TB:** total bases (hits plus doubles plus two times the number of triples plus three times the number of home runs). **TBF:** total batters faced. **TC:** total chances (putouts plus assists plus errors). **TPA:** total plate appearances (at-bats plus bases on balls plus sacrifice hits plus sacrifice flies plus hit by pitches plus times reaching base on catcher's interference). **W:** wins. **WP:** wild pitches. **2B:** doubles. **3B:** triples.

EDITORS: Joe Hoppel, Sarah Gietschier, David Robb.
COVER DESIGNED BY: Chad Painter.
PAGE LAYOUT BY: Chad Painter, David Niehaus.

PHOTO CREDITS: Albert Dickson/Sporting News – 23, 118, 138, 153; **Jay Drowns/Sporting News** – 18, 28, 43, 73, 83, 88, 93, 123, 128, 133; **Sean Gallagher/Sporting News** – 33; **Bob Leverone/Sporting News** – 8, 63, 78, 143, 148; **Robert Seale/Sporting News** – 108; **John Cordes for Sporting News** – 38, 58, 98, 103, 113; **John Dunn for Sporting News** – 48; **David Durochik for Sporting News** – 13, 68; **M. David Leeds for Sporting News** – 53.

Major league statistics compiled by STATS Inc., a News Corporation company, 8130 Lehigh Avenue, Morton Grove, IL 60053. STATS is a trademark of Sports Team Analysis and Tracking Systems, Inc.

Minor league statistics provided by MLB Advanced Media.

ISBN: 0-89204-813-1   10 9 8 7 6 5 4 3 2 1

CONTENTS

2006 Season

Major League Baseball directories

Team by team

NL/AL DS 2006

(W)
OAK - MINN (C)

1. OAK 3 Minn 2 @ Minn 1-0
2. OAK 5 Minn 2 @ Minn 2-0

(E)
NYY - Detroit (WC)

1. NYY 8 Det 4 @ NY 1-0
2. Det 4 NYY 3 @ NY 1-1

(C) STL - SD (W)

1. STL 5 SD 1 @ SD 1-0
2. STL 2 SD 0 @ SD 2-0

(WC) LAD - NYM (E)

1. NYM 6 LAD 5 @ NY 1-0
2. NYM 4 LAD 1 @ NY 2-0

MAJOR LEAGUE BASEBALL

Address
245 Park Avenue
New York, NY 10167
Telephone
212-931-7800
FAX
212-949-5654
Website
www.mlb.com
Commissioner of baseball
Allan H. "Bud" Selig
President and chief operating officer
Robert DuPuy
Executive vice president, business
Timothy Brosnan
Executive v.p., administration
John McHale Jr.
Executive v.p., labor relations and human resources
Robert Manfred
Executive vice president, finance
Jonathan Mariner
Executive v.p., baseball operations
Jimmie Lee Solomon
Senior v.p., international business operations
Paul Archey
Senior v.p., corporate sales/marketing
John Brody
Senior v.p. and general counsel, labor relations
Frank Coonelly
Senior v.p., scheduling/club relations
Katy Feeney
Senior v.p., baseball operations
Joe Garagiola Jr.
Senior v.p., security and facilities
Kevin Hallinan

Senior vice president, public relations
Richard Levin
Senior vice president, club relations
Phyllis Merhige
Senior vice president, special events
Marla Miller
Senior v.p. and general counsel, legal business affairs
Ethan Orlinsky
Senior v.p. and general counsel, legal
Thomas Ostertag
Senior vice president, licensing
Howard Smith
Senior vice president, broadcasting
Christopher Tully
Vice president, licensing operations
Steve Armus
Vice president, community affairs
Thomas Brasuell
V.p., baseball operations and administration
Ed Burns
Vice president, information systems
Julio Carbonell
V.p., accounting and treasurer
Bob Clark
Vice president, public relations
Patrick Courtney
V.p. and executive producer, MLB productions
David Gavant
Vice president, licensing operations
Colin Hagen
Vice president, publishing
Don Hintze

V.p., international licensing
Shawn Lawson-Cummings
V.p., diversity and recruiting
Wendy Lewis
Broadcasting
Bernadette McDonald
V.p., international baseball operations
Lou Melendez
Vice president, creative services
Anne Occi
Vice president, umpiring
Mike Port
V.p., western operations
Laurel Prieb
V.p., programming and business affairs, MLB productions
Elizabeth Scott
Vice president, human resources
Ray Scott
Vice president, finance
Kathleen Torres
Vice president, on-field operations
Bob Watson
V.p., international broadcast sales
Italo Zanzi

OTHER ORGANIZATIONS

LABOR RELATIONS COMMITTEE
Address
245 Park Avenue
New York, NY 10167
Telephone
212-931-7401
212-949-5690 (FAX)
Exec. vice president, labor relations and human resources
Robert Manfred
Sr. v.p. & gen. counsel, labor relations
Francis Coonelly
Deputy general counsel, labor
Jennifer Gefsky
Counsel, labor
Paul Mifsud
Director, salary and contract admin.
John Abbamondi

BASEBALL ASSISTANCE TEAM INC.
Address
245 Park Avenue
New York, NY 10167

Telephone
212-931-7800
President/CEO
Ted Sizemore
Chairman
Bobby Murcer
Vice presidents
Frank Torre
Greg Wilcox
Executive director
James L. Martin
Secretary
Thomas Ostertag
Treasurer
Jonathan Mariner
Vice president
Mark Letendre
Consultant
Sam McDowell

ASSOCIATION OF PROFESSIONAL BASEBALL PLAYERS OF AMERICA
Address
1820 W. Orangewood Ave., Suite 206
Orange, CA 92868
Telephone
714-935-9993
714-935-0431 (FAX)
President
Roland Hemond
Vice presidents
Tal Smith
Dick Wagner
Secretary/treasurer
Dick Beverage

NATIONAL BASEBALL HALL OF FAME AND MUSEUM
Address
25 Main Street
Cooperstown, NY 13326

Telephone
888-425-5633
607-547-7200
607-547-2044 (FAX)
Chairman
Jane Forbes Clark
President
Dale Petroskey
V.p., marketing
Sean Gahagan
V.p., development
Greg Harris
V.p., communications and education
Jeff Idelson
Vice president, chief curator
William T. Spencer Jr.
Curator of collections
Peter P. Clark
Controller
Frances L. Althiser
Librarian
James L. Gates
Director, communications
Brad Horn

MAJOR LEAGUE SCOUTING BUREAU
Address
3500 Porsche Way, Suite 100
Ontario, CA 91764
Telephone
909-980-1881
909-980-7794 (FAX)
Director
Frank Marcos

MAJOR LEAGUE BASEBALL PLAYERS ASSOCIATION
Address
12 E. 49th St., 24th Floor
New York, NY 10017
Telephone
212-826-0808
212-752-3649 (FAX)
Exec. director and general counsel
Donald M. Fehr
Special assistants
Bobby Bonilla
Phil Bradley
Steve Rogers
COO
Eugene D. Orza
General counsel
Michael Weiner
Assistant general counsel
Jeff Fannell
Doyle R. Pryor
Counsel
Robert Leneghan
Director of licensing
Judy Heeter
Director of communications
Chris Dahl

MINOR LEAGUE BASEBALL
NATIONAL ASSOCIATION OF PROFESSIONAL BASEBALL LEAGUES
Address
P.O. Box A
St. Petersburg, FL 33731
Telephone
727-822-6937
727-821-5819 (FAX)
President/CEO
Mike Moore
Vice president
Stan Brand
Vice president, administration/COO
Pat O'Connor
General counsel
Scott Poley
Special counsel
George Yund
Exec. director/business operations
Misann Ellmaker
Executive director/Professional Baseball Umpire Corp.
Mike Fitzpatrick
Director/media relations
Jim Ferguson
Director/baseball operations
Tim Brunswick
Director of Professional Baseball Employment Opportunities
Ann Perkins

MAJOR LEAGUE BASEBALL PLAYERS ALUMNI ASSOC.
Address
1631 Mesa Ave., Suite B
Colorado Springs, CO 80906
Telephone
719-477-1870
719-477-1875 (FAX)
President
Brooks Robinson
Vice presidents
Bob Boone
George Brett
Mike Hegan
Chuck Hinton
Al Kaline
Carl Erskine
Rusty Staub
Robin Yount
Vice chairman
Fred Valentine

WORLD UMPIRES ASSOCIATION
Address
P.O. Box 760
Cocoa, FL 32923-0760
Telephone
321-637-3471
321-633-7018 (FAX)
President
John Hirschbeck

Vice president
Joe Brinkman
Secretary/treasurer
Tim Welke
Labor counsel
Joel Smith

MAJOR LEAGUE BASEBALL ADVANCED MEDIA
Address
75 Ninth Avenue
New York, NY 10011
Telephone
212-485-3444
212-485-3456 (FAX)
President and CEO
Bob Bowman

BASEBALL WRITERS' ASSOCIATION OF AMERICA
President
Peter Schmuck, Baltimore Sun
Vice president
Paul Hoynes, Cleveland Plain Dealer
Secretary/treasurer
Jack O'Connell, Hartford Courant

ELIAS SPORTS BUREAU
Address
500 Fifth Avenue
New York, NY 10110
Telephone
212-869-1530
212-354-0980 (FAX)
President
Seymour Siwoff
Executive vice president
Steve Hirdt
Vice presidents
Peter Hirdt
Chris Thorn

SPORTSTICKER ENTERPRISES, L.P.
Address
Building B
ESPN Plaza
Bristol, CT 06010
Telephone
860-766-1899
800-367-8935
800-336-0383 (FAX)
General manager
Jim Morganthaler
Director, minor league operations
Jim Keller
Assistant director, minor league operations
Michael Walczak

BALTIMORE ORIOLES
AMERICAN LEAGUE EAST DIVISION

2006 SEASON

Orioles Schedule
Home games shaded.
All-Star Game July 11 at Pittsburgh. Schedule subject to change.

APRIL

SUN	MON	TUE	WED	THU	FRI	SAT
2	3 TB	4	5 TB	6 TB	7 BOS	8 BOS
9 BOS	10 TB	11 TB	12 TB	13 TB	14 LAA	15 LAA
16 LAA	17 LAA	18 CLE	19 CLE	20 CLE	21 NYY	22 NYY
23 NYY	24	25 TOR	26 TOR	27 TOR	28 SEA	29 SEA
30 SEA						

MAY

SUN	MON	TUE	WED	THU	FRI	SAT
	1 TOR	2 TOR	3 TEX	4 TEX	5 BOS	6 BOS
7 BOS	8	9 DET	10 DET	11 DET	12 KC	13 KC
14 KC	15 BOS	16 BOS	17 BOS	18	19 WAS	20 WAS
21 WAS	22 SEA	23 SEA	24 SEA	25 SEA	26 LAA	27 LAA
28 LAA	29	30 TB	31 TB			

JUNE

SUN	MON	TUE	WED	THU	FRI	SAT
				1 TB	2 NYY	3 NYY
4 NYY	5 TOR	6 TOR	7 TOR	8 TOR	9 MIN	10 MIN
11 MIN	12 TOR	13 TOR	14 TOR	15 TOR	16 NYM	17 NYM
18 NYM	19	20 FLA	21 FLA	22 FLA	23 WAS	24 WAS
25 WAS	26	27 PHI	28 PHI	29 PHI	30 ATL	

JULY

SUN	MON	TUE	WED	THU	FRI	SAT
						1 ATL
2 ATL	3 CHW	4 CHW	5 CHW	6 CHW	7 CLE	8 CLE
9 CLE	10	11 ALL-STAR	12	13 TEX	14 TEX	15 TEX
16 TEX	17 OAK	18 OAK	19 OAK	20	21 TB	22 TB
23 TB	24	25 KC	26 KC	27 KC	28 CHW	29 CHW
30 CHW	31 SEA					

AUGUST

SUN	MON	TUE	WED	THU	FRI	SAT
		1 SEA	2 SEA	3	4 NYY	5 NYY
6 NYY	7 TOR	8 TOR	9 TOR	10	11 BOS	12 BOS
13 BOS	14	15 NYY	16 NYY	17 NYY	18 TOR	19 TOR
20 TOR	21	22 MIN	23 MIN	24 MIN	25 TB	26 TB
27 TB	28	29 TEX	30 TEX	31 TEX		

SEPTEMBER

SUN	MON	TUE	WED	THU	FRI	SAT
					1 OAK	2 OAK
3 OAK	4 LAA	5 LAA	6 LAA	7	8 NYY	9 NYY
10 NYY	11 NYY	12 BOS	13 BOS	14 BOS	15 DET	16 DET
17 DET	18 TB	19 TB	20 TB	21	22 MIN	23 MIN
24 MIN	25	26 NYY	27 NYY	28 NYY	29 BOS	30 BOS

OCTOBER

SUN	MON	TUE	WED	THU	FRI	SAT
1 BOS	2	3	4	5	6	7

Home games are shaded. All-Star Game is July 11 at Pittsburgh. Schedule is subject to change.

Mora

CLUB DIRECTORY

Chairman of the board/CEO
Peter G. Angelos
Vice chairman/COO
Joseph E. Foss
Executive vice president
John P. Angelos
Vice president/CFO
Robert A. Ames, CPA
Vice president/special liaison to chairman
Lou Kousouris
Executive v.p., baseball operations
Mike Flanagan
Vice president, baseball operations
Jim Duquette
Director/baseball administration
Scott Proefrock

Director/scouting
Joe Jordan
Director/minor league operations
David Stockstill
Asst. director/minor league operations
Tripp Norton
Traveling secretary
Philip E. Itzoe
Executive director/communications
Spiro Alafassos
Director/meda relations and publications
Bill Stetka
Dir./special events & community outreach
Kristen Schultz
Senior director/fan and ticket services
Donald E. Grove Jr.
Director/ballpark operations
Roger Hayden

MINOR LEAGUE AFFILIATES

Class	Team	League	Manager
AAA	Ottawa	International	Dave Trembley
AA	Bowie	Eastern	Don Werner
Advanced A	Frederick	Carolina	Bien Figueroa
A	Delmarva	South Atlantic	Gary Kendall
Short-Season A	Aberdeen	New York-Pennsylvania	Andy Etchebarren
Advanced Rookie	Bluefield	Appalachian	To be announced

BROADCAST INFORMATION

Radio: To be announced.
Cable TV: Comcast SportsNet.

SPRING TRAINING

Ballpark (city): Fort Lauderdale Stadium (Fort Lauderdale, Fla.).
Ticket information: 954-776-1921.

For more on the Orioles, go to **www.sportingnews.com/baseball/teams/orioles/**

SPRING TRAINING ROSTER

Manager—Sam Perlozzo (2).
Coaches—Dave Cash (30), Terry Crowley (48), Rick Dempsey (24), Lee Elia (3), Leo Mazzone (54), Tom Trebelhorn (26).

No.	PITCHERS	B/T	Ht./Wt.	Age*
45	Erik Bedard	L/L	6-1/189	27
	Chris Britton	R/R	6-3/230	23
40	Tim Byrdak	L/L	5-11/190	32
35	Daniel Cabrera	R/R	6-7/250	24
27	Bruce Chen	L/L	6-1/210	28
28	Eric DuBose	L/L	6-3/235	29
	Brian Finch	R/R	6-4/195	24
	LaTroy Hawkins	R/R	6-5/215	33
	James Johnson	R/R	6-5/215	22
50	Jorge Julio	R/R	6-1/232	27
	Ryan Keefer	L/R	6-3/200	24
	Adam Loewen	L/L	6-5/220	21
13	Rodrigo Lopez	R/R	6-1/190	30
61	John Maine	R/R	6-4/205	24
36	John Parrish	L/L	5-11/200	28
49	Hayden Penn	R/R	6-3/195	21
47	Aaron Rakers	R/R	6-3/220	29
37	Chris Ray	R/R	6-3/200	24
	Sendy Rleal	R/R	6-1/165	25
	Marino Salas	R/R	6-0/175	25
53	Todd Williams	R/R	6-3/220	35

No.	CATCHERS	B/T	Ht./Wt.	Age*
9	Geronimo Gil	R/R	6-2/234	30
	Ramon Hernandez	R/R	6-0/210	29
18	Javy Lopez	R/R	6-3/230	35
	Eli Whiteside	R/R	6-2/208	26

No.	INFIELDERS	B/T	Ht./Wt.	Age*
	Brandon Fahey	L/R	6-2/185	25
14	Chris Gomez	R/R	6-1/188	34
	Kevin Millar	R/R	6-0/210	34
6	Melvin Mora	R/R	5-11/200	34
1	Brian Roberts	B/R	5-9/176	28
10	Miguel Tejada	R/R	5-9/209	29
	Walter Young	L/R	6-5/322	26

No.	OUTFIELDERS	B/T	Ht./Wt.	Age*
	Jeff Conine	R/R	6-1/220	39
16	Jeff Fiorentino	L/R	6-1/188	22
25	Jay Gibbons	L/L	6-0/205	29
	Val Majewski	L/L	6-2/225	24
	Nicholas Markakis	L/L	6-2/225	22
32	Luis Matos	R/R	6-0/208	27
11	David Newhan	L/R	5-10/180	32
	Corey Patterson	L/R	5-9/180	26

*Age as of April 1, 2006.

BALLPARK INFORMATION

Ballpark (capacity, surface)
Oriole Park at Camden Yards (48,190, grass)
Address
333 W. Camden St.
Baltimore, MD 21201
Official website
www.orioles.com
Business phone
410-685-9800
Ticket information
410-481-SEAT
Field dimensions (from home plate)
To left field at foul line, 333 feet
To center field, 400 feet
To right field at foul line, 318
First game played
April 6, 1992 (Orioles 2, Indians 0)

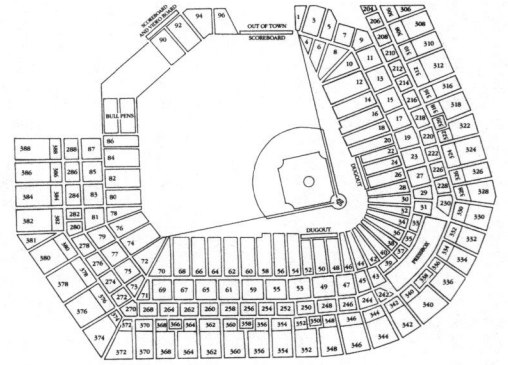

2005 REVIEW
DAY BY DAY

Date	Opp.	Res.	Score	(inn.*)	Hits	Opp. hits	Winning pitcher	Losing pitcher	Save	Record	Pos.	GB
4-4	Bos.	W	7-2		11	11	Ponson	Martinez	Ryan	1-0	1st	+0.5
4-6	Bos.	L	1-4		6	5	Schilling	DuBose	Foulke	1-1	T2nd	0.5
4-7	Bos.	L	3-10		10	14	Lowe	Ainsworth		1-2	4th	1.0
4-8	Bos.	W	3-2	(13)	7	6	Lopez	Jones		2-2	T2nd	0.5
4-9	At T.B.	L	3-4	(10)	9	7	Baez	Parrish		2-3	T3rd	1.0
4-10	At T.B.	W	11-3		16	7	Bauer	Gonzalez		3-3	T1st	...
4-11	At T.B.	L	1-10		8	11	Zambrano	DuBose		3-4	4th	1.0
4-15	At Bos.	W	12-7	(11)	14	11	Groom	Arroyo		4-4	T2nd	0.5
4-16	At Tor.	W	11-2		12	2	Riley	Batista		5-4	T1st	...
4-17	At Tor.	W	5-3		12	6	Ryan	Speier	Julio	6-4	T1st	...
4-18	At Tor.	W	7-0		12	4	DuBose	Hentgen		7-4	1st	+1.0
4-20	T.B.	W	9-1		14	4	Ponson	Hendrickson		8-4	1st	+0.5
4-21	T.B.	L	3-7		4	12	Abbott	Riley		8-5	2nd	0.5
4-22	T.B.	W	7-6		9	7	Parrish	Gaudin	Julio	9-5	1st	+0.5
4-23	Tor.	W	11-3		15	8	DuBose	Towers		10-5	1st	+0.5
4-24	Tor.	L	4-5	(12)	11	14	Ligtenberg	DeJean		10-6	2nd	0.5
4-25	Tor.	L	3-15		7	17	Halladay	Ponson		10-7	2nd	1.5
4-27	Sea.	L	5-7		12	13	Villone	Lopez	Guardado	10-8	2nd	2.0
4-28	Sea.	W	3-1		7	4	Parrish	Hasegawa	Julio	11-8	2nd	2.0
4-29	Sea.	W	9-5		15	5	DuBose	Pineiro		12-8	2nd	2.5
4-30	At Cle.	L	2-11		7	15	Lee	Ponson		12-9	2nd	3.0
5-1	At Cle.	L	2-3	(13)	10	10	Durbin	DeJean		12-10	2nd	2.5
5-3	Chi.	L	4-5		6	8	Schoeneweis	DeJean	Koch	12-11	3rd	2.0
5-4	Chi.	W	10-3		13	5	Lopez	Loaiza		13-11	3rd	1.0
5-5	Chi.	L	5-6		12	11	Takatsu	Ryan	Koch	13-12	3rd	2.0
5-7	Cle.	W	3-2	(10)	7	10	Julio	Durbin		14-12	3rd	2.5
5-8	Cle.	W	10-7		14	7	Parrish	Stewart	Julio	15-12	3rd	2.5
5-9	Cle.	W	12-11		16	15	Lopez	Riske	Julio	16-12	3rd	1.5
5-11	At Chi.	L	0-15		4	19	Buehrle	Ponson		16-13	3rd	2.0
5-13!	At Chi.	W	1-0		6	3	Cabrera	Garland	Julio	17-13		
5-13&	At Chi.	L	5-6		8	7	Jackson	Bedard	Koch	17-14	3rd	1.5
5-14	Ana.	L	9-10	(10)	11	15	Percival	Julio	Shields	17-15	3rd	2.5
5-15	Ana.	L	4-7		6	11	Washburn	DuBose	Percival	17-16	3rd	3.0
5-16	Ana.	W	4-0		9	5	Ponson	Escobar		18-16	3rd	2.5
5-18	At Sea.	W	7-2		10	6	Cabrera	Garcia		19-16	3rd	2.0
5-19	At Sea.	W	5-2		10	7	Bedard	Franklin	Julio	20-16	3rd	2.0
5-20	At Sea.	L	0-11		8	13	Moyer	Lopez		20-17	3rd	2.5
5-21	At Ana.	L	3-5		11	12	Shields	DeJean	Percival	20-18	3rd	3.0
5-22	At Ana.	L	2-3		6	9	Escobar	Ponson	Percival	20-19	3rd	4.0
5-23	At Ana.	L	3-8		11	12	Sele	Cabrera		20-20	3rd	5.0
5-25	N.Y.	L	3-11		7	14	Lieber	Bedard		20-21	3rd	6.0
5-26	N.Y.	L	9-12		14	16	Sturtze	Ryan	Rivera	20-22	3rd	7.0
5-27	N.Y.	L	5-18		14	21	Contreras	Ponson		20-23	3rd	7.0
5-28	At Det.	W	7-5		13	10	DuBose	Johnson	Julio	21-23	3rd	7.0
5-29	At Det.	W	8-4		13	9	Cabrera	Bonderman	Parrish	22-23	3rd	6.5
5-30	At Det.	W	7-3		13	9	Groom	Urbina		23-23	3rd	6.0
5-31	At Bos.	W	13-4		16	9	Lopez	Lowe		24-23	3rd	5.0
6-1	At N.Y.	L	7-8		14	13	Mussina	Ponson	Rivera	24-24	3rd	6.0
6-2	At N.Y.	L	5-6		9	3	Prinz	DuBose	Rivera	24-25	3rd	7.0
6-3	At N.Y.	L	2-5		5	10	Vazquez	Parrish	Rivera	24-26	3rd	8.0
6-4	T.B.	L	7-8	(11)	6	14	Carter	DeJean	Baez	24-27	3rd	9.0
6-6	T.B.	W	5-4		11	12	Lopez	Bell	Julio	25-27	3rd	8.5
6-8	Ari.	L	1-8		5	14	Johnson	Ponson		25-28	3rd	9.5
6-9	Ari.	W	8-2		10	7	Parrish	Randolph		26-28	3rd	9.5
6-10	Ari.	L	0-3		7	4	Fossum	Cabrera	Valverde	26-29	3rd	10.5
6-12#	S.F	L	6-9	(11)	10	12	Herges	Julio		26-30		
6-12$	S.F	W	5-4	(12)	14	5	Parrish	Eyre		27-30	3rd	10.5
6-13	S.F	L	3-7		6	15	Williams	Ponson	Walker	27-31	3rd	11.5
6-14	At Cle.	L	0-14		4	15	Westbrook	DuBose		27-32	3rd	12.0
6-15	At L.A.	L	1-5		5	10	Lima	Cabrera	Gagne	27-33	3rd	13.0
6-16	At L.A.	L	3-6		8	10	Perez	Riley	Gagne	27-34	4th	14.0
6-17	At L.A.	L	3-4		10	9	Mota	Lopez	Gagne	27-35	4th	14.0
6-18	At Col.	L	3-5		9	9	Estes	Ponson	Chacon	27-36	5th	14.0
6-19	At Col.	L	6-11		14	13	Fassero	DuBose		27-37	5th	15.0
6-20	At Col.	W	4-2		6	6	Ryan	Chacon	Julio	28-37	5th	14.0
6-22	N.Y.	L	4-10		5	8	Mussina	Riley		28-38	5th	15.0
6-23	N.Y.	W	13-2		17	7	Bedard	Lieber		29-38	5th	14.0

Date	Opp.	Res.	Score	(inn.*)	Hits	Opp. hits	Winning pitcher	Losing pitcher	Save	Record	Pos.	GB
6-24	N.Y.	L	2-5		9	10	Vazquez	Ponson	Rivera	29-39	5th	15.0
6-25	Atl.	W	5-0		10	4	Cabrera	Byrd		30-39	5th	14.5
6-26	Atl.	L	0-5		10	9	Ortiz	Lopez	Smoltz	30-40	5th	14.5
6-27	Atl.	L	7-8		13	14	Cruz	Grimsley	Smoltz	30-41	5th	16.0
6-28	At K.C.	W	10-1		13	7	Bedard	May		31-41	5th	15.5
6-29	At K.C.	L	3-4		8	10	Wood	Ponson	Camp	31-42	5th	16.5
6-30	At K.C.	W	13-4		15	5	Cabrera	Anderson		32-42	5th	16.5
7-1	At K.C.	W	3-2		10	4	Lopez	Greinke	Julio	33-42	5th	16.5
7-2	At Phi.	W	7-6	(16)	15	10	Rodriguez	Powell	Cabrera	34-42	4th	15.5
7-3	At Phi.	L	6-7		9	10	Cormier	Grimsley	Wagner	34-43	5th	15.5
7-4	At Phi.	L	2-5		8	10	Milton	Ponson	Worrell	34-44	5th	15.5
7-5#	T.B.	W	4-2		11	4	Ryan	Brazelton	Julio	35-44		
7-5$	T.B.	W	8-2		15	6	Borkowski	Gonzalez		36-44	4th	15.0
7-6	T.B.	L	1-3		8	12	Hendrickson	Lopez	Baez	36-45	5th	15.0
7-7	T.B.	L	3-13		6	14	Bell	Parrish		36-46	5th	15.0
7-9	K.C.	L	0-7		5	11	May	Bedard		36-47	5th	16.5
7-10	K.C.	W	7-2		13	5	Cabrera	Wood		37-47	5th	16.5
7-11	K.C.	L	7-11		12	17	Gobble	Lopez		37-48	5th	17.5
7-15	At T.B.	W	5-4		9	10	Cabrera	Harper	Julio	38-48	5th	17.5
7-16	At T.B.	L	0-2		3	9	Halama	Bedard	Baez	38-49	5th	17.5
7-17	At T.B.	W	3-2		7	7	Lopez	Brazelton	Julio	39-49	4th	17.5
7-18	At T.B.	L	2-7		4	11	Hendrickson	Borkowski		39-50	4th	17.5
7-19	At K.C.	W	7-4		12	10	Ponson	Anderson		40-50	4th	16.5
7-20	At K.C.	W	12-3		16	12	Cabrera	Greinke		41-50	4th	16.5
7-21	At Bos.	W	10-5		15	8	Bedard	Martinez		42-50	4th	16.5
7-22#	At Bos.	W	8-3		11	11	Lopez	Alvarez		43-50		
7-22$	At Bos.	L	0-4		10	7	Wakefield	Borkowski		43-51	4th	17.0
7-23	Min.	L	3-7		10	12	Silva	Maine		43-52	4th	18.0
7-24	Min.	W	4-2		5	4	Ponson	Roa	Julio	44-52	4th	17.0
7-25	Min.	L	4-8		9	15	Lohse	Cabrera		44-53	4th	17.0
7-26	Bos.	L	5-12		9	13	Martinez	Bedard		44-54	4th	18.0
7-28	Bos.	W	4-1		7	4	Borkowski	Schilling		45-54	4th	17.5
7-29	At N.Y.	W	9-1		12	4	Ponson	Contreras		46-54	4th	16.5
7-30	At N.Y.	L	1-2		7	8	Brown	Cabrera	Rivera	46-55	4th	17.5
7-31	At N.Y.	L	4-6		7	10	Vazquez	Bedard	Rivera	46-56	4th	18.5
8-1	At N.Y.	L	7-9		14	9	Hernandez	Lopez	Rivera	46-57	4th	19.5
8-3#	Sea.	W	9-7		10	16	Grimsley	Nageotte	Julio	47-57		
8-3$	Sea.	W	5-4		11	15	Julio	Sherrill		48-57	4th	18.0
8-4	Sea.	W	6-3		10	9	Williams	Hasegawa	Julio	49-57	4th	18.0
8-6	Tex.	W	9-1		8	7	Bedard	Regilio		50-57	4th	18.5
8-7	Tex.	W	3-1		10	4	Lopez	Erickson	Julio	51-57	4th	18.5
8-8	Tex.	W	11-5		13	9	Ponson	Rogers		52-57	4th	18.5
8-9	Tex.	W	7-3		9	8	Borkowski	Bacsik		53-57	4th	17.5
8-10	At Ana.	W	11-3		20	6	Cabrera	Sele		54-57	3rd	16.5
8-11	At Ana.	L	2-4		9	6	Escobar	Grimsley	Percival	54-58	3rd	17.5
8-12	At Ana.	W	6-1		14	6	Lopez	Colon		55-58	3rd	17.5
8-13	At Tor.	W	4-0		11	5	Ponson	Batista		56-58	3rd	17.5
8-14	At Tor.	L	2-7		6	14	Towers	Borkowski		56-59	3rd	18.5
8-15	At Tor.	W	11-7		17	11	Groom	Chulk		57-59	3rd	17.5
8-16	Oak.	L	1-3		7	9	Redman	Bedard	Dotel	57-60	3rd	18.0
8-17	Oak.	L	0-11		5	13	Hudson	Lopez		57-61	3rd	18.0
8-18	Oak.	L	4-5		6	11	Mulder	Ryan	Dotel	57-62	3rd	18.0
8-20	Tor.	L	4-14		10	14	Towers	Borkowski		57-63	3rd	18.5
8-21	Tor.	L	4-10		10	15	Bush	Cabrera		57-64	3rd	18.5
8-22	Tor.	L	5-8		13	12	Miller	Bedard	Frasor	57-65	3rd	18.5
8-23	At Oak.	L	3-4		8	12	Hudson	Groom	Dotel	57-66	3rd	19.5
8-24	At Oak.	L	2-6		5	9	Mulder	Ponson		57-67	4th	20.5
8-25	At Oak.	L	0-3		5	5	Dotel	Ryan		57-68	4th	20.5
8-26	At Oak.	L	4-9		8	9	Zito	Cabrera		57-69	4th	21.5
8-27	At Tex.	L	4-6		10	9	Wasdin	Bedard	Cordero	57-70	4th	22.5
8-28	At Tex.	L	3-4		6	7	Francisco	Ryan	Cordero	57-71	4th	23.5
8-29	At Tex.	W	7-6		10	15	Ponson	Young	Julio	58-71	4th	22.5
8-31	At T.B.	W	10-6	(12)	17	11	Groom	Carter		59-71	3rd	21.5
9-1	At T.B.	W	8-0		16	2	Cabrera	Hendrickson		60-71	3rd	21.5
9-2	At T.B.	W	13-2		14	6	Bedard	Brazelton		61-71	3rd	21.5
9-3	At N.Y.	W	3-1		6	6	Lopez	Brown	Julio	62-71	3rd	20.5
9-4	At N.Y.	W	7-0		14	2	Ponson	Mussina		63-71	3rd	19.5
9-5	At N.Y.	L	3-4		9	7	Rivera	Julio		63-72	3rd	20.5
9-6	Min.	W	4-1		10	4	Cabrera	Mulholland	Julio	64-72	3rd	20.5
9-7	Min.	L	1-3		5	4	Romero	Julio	Nathan	64-73	3rd	21.5

Date	Opp.	Res.	Score	(inn.*)	Hits	Opp. hits	Winning pitcher	Losing pitcher	Save	Record	Pos.	GB
9-8	Min.	L	0-9		6	12	Santana	Bedard		64-74	3rd	22.0
9-10	N.Y.	W	14-8		14	13	Lopez	Vazquez		65-74	3rd	22.0
9-11	N.Y.	L	2-5		7	10	Hernandez	Ponson	Rivera	65-75	3rd	23.0
9-12	N.Y.	L	7-9		13	11	Gordon	Julio	Rivera	65-76	3rd	24.0
9-13	At Tor.	W	9-1		12	5	Chen	Miller		66-76	3rd	23.0
9-15	At Tor.	L	0-3		8	5	Lilly	Riley	Speier	66-77	3rd	24.5
9-16	At Tor.	W	9-5		12	13	Lopez	Batista		67-77	3rd	24.0
9-17	At Min.	W	11-2		12	6	Ponson	Mulholland		68-77	3rd	23.0
9-18	At Min.	W	12-3		18	6	Cabrera	Radke		69-77	3rd	23.0
9-19	At Min.	L	1-5		9	8	Santana	Chen		69-78	3rd	24.0
9-20	At Bos.	W	9-6		8	10	Grimsley	Wakefield	Julio	70-78	3rd	23.0
9-21	At Bos.	L	2-3		5	7	Foulke	Ryan		70-79	3rd	24.0
9-22	At Bos.	L	6-7	(12)	12	13	Leskanic	Bauer		70-80	3rd	24.0
9-23	At Bos.	W	9-7		15	11	Williams	Mendoza		71-80	3rd	24.0
9-24	Det.	W	7-5		13	7	Parrish	Yan		72-80	3rd	24.0
9-25	Det.	W	3-0		6	5	Riley	Bonderman	Ryan	73-80	3rd	23.0
9-26	Det.	W	5-0		11	3	Lopez	Maroth		74-80	3rd	22.0
9-27	Tor.	L	1-4		7	11	League	Ponson	Batista	74-81	3rd	22.5
9-29!	Tor.	W	7-6		9	9	Ryan	Speier		75-81		
9-29&	Tor.	W	4-0		8	4	Bauer	Chacin		76-81	3rd	22.5
9-30	Tor.	W	9-3		14	6	Riley	Towers		77-81	3rd	22.5
10-1	Bos.	L	3-8		9	11	Wakefield	Lopez		77-82	3rd	22.5
10-2#	Bos.	L	5-7		10	8	Adams	Cabrera	Foulke	77-83		
10-2$	Bos.	L	5-7		9	11	Kim	Grimsley	Leskanic	77-84	3rd	23.0
10-3	Bos.	W	3-2		7	7	Chen	Williamson	Ryan	78-84	3rd	23.0

Monthly records: April (12-9), May (12-14), June (8-19), July (14-14), August (13-15), September (18-10), October (1-3).
*Innings, if other than nine. ! First game of a doubleheader. & Second game of a doubleheader. # Day separate admission. $ Night separate admission.

RECORDS

2005 regular-season record: 74-88
Position: 4th in A.L. East
Home: 36-45   **Road:** 38-43
A.L. East: 36-37   **A.L. Central:** 13-22
A.L. West: 17-19   **N.L.** 8-10
Vs. LH starters: 25-30
Vs. RH starters: 49-58
Grass: 62-78   **Artificial:** 12-10
Day: 23-30   **Night:** 51-58
1-Run: 14-25   **X-inn.:** 2-6
Doubleheaders: 0-0-0
Team record past five years: 353-456 (.436, ranks 11th in league in that span)

TEAM LEADERS

Batting average: Brian Roberts (.314).
At-bats: Miguel Tejada (654).
Runs: Brian Roberts (92).
Hits: Miguel Tejada (199).
Total Bases: Miguel Tejada (337).
Doubles: Miguel Tejada (50).
Triples: Brian Roberts (7).
Home runs: Melvin Mora (27).
Runs batted in: Miguel Tejada (98).
Stolen bases: Brian Roberts (27).
Slugging percentage: Jay Gibbons (.516).
On-base percentage: Brian Roberts (.387).
Wins: Rodrigo Lopez (15).
Earned-run average: Bruce Chen (3.83).
Complete games: Bruce Chen, Sidney Ponson (1).

Shutouts: None.
Saves: B.J. Ryan (36).
Innings pitched: Rodrigo Lopez (209.1).
Strikeouts: Daniel Cabrera (157).

GAMES BY POSITION

Catcher: Javy Lopez 75, Geronimo Gil 62, Sal Fasano 60, Eli Whiteside 9.

First base: Rafael Palmeiro 93, Chris Gomez 42, Jay Gibbons 22, B.J. Surhoff 18, Alejandro Freire 16, Walter Young 10, Sal Fasano 1, Javy Lopez 1.

Second base: Brian Roberts 141, Chris Gomez 18, Bernie Castro 11.

Third base: Melvin Mora 148, Chris Gomez 17, David Newhan 8.

Shortstop: Miguel Tejada 160, Chris Gomez 10, Ed Rogers 1.

Outfield: Luis Matos 120, David Newhan 73, Jay Gibbons 71, Sammy Sosa 66, Larry Bigbie 62, B.J. Surhoff 60, Eric Byrnes 51, Eli Marrero 16, Jeff Fiorentino 12, Keith Reed 6, Ramon Nivar 4, Napoleon Calzado 2, Bernie Castro 1, Midre Cummings 1, Alejandro Freire 1.

Designated hitter: Jay Gibbons 42, Sammy Sosa 35, Javy Lopez 28, Rafael Palmeiro 15, Bernie Castro 9, Alejandro Freire 9, David Newhan 7, B.J. Surhoff 7, Chris Gomez 6, Sal Fasano 3, Walter Young 3, Ed Rogers 2, Miguel Tejada 2, Melvin Mora 1.

TOP DRAFT CHOICES

1a. **Brandon Snyder**, C, Westfield H.S., Centreville, Va.
1b. **Garrett Olson**, LHP, Cal Poly San Luis Obispo.
2. **Nolan Reimold**, OF, Bowling Green State.
3. **Brandon Erbe**, RHP, McDonough School, Baltimore.
4. **Kieron Pope**, OF, East Coweta H.S., Gay, Ga.
5. **Reid Hamblet**, RHP, Biola.
6. **Blake Owen**, RHP, Belmont.
7. **Bobby Andrews**, OF, Cal State Fullerton.
8. **Chorye Spoone**, RHP, CC of Baltimore County, Catonsville.
9. **Paco Figueroa**, 2B, Miami.
10. **Ryan Stadanlick**, RHP, St. Joseph's.

BOSTON RED SOX
AMERICAN LEAGUE EAST DIVISION

2006 SEASON

Red Sox Schedule
Home games shaded.
All-Star Game July 11 at Pittsburgh. Schedule subject to change.

APRIL

SUN	MON	TUE	WED	THU	FRI	SAT
2	3 TEX	4 TEX	5 TEX	6	7 BAL	8 BAL
9 BAL	10	11 TOR	12 TOR	13 TOR	14 SEA	15 SEA
16 SEA	17 SEA	18 TB	19 TB	20 TB	21 TOR	22 TOR
23 TOR	24	25 CLE	26 CLE	27 CLE	28 TB	29 TB
30 TB						

MAY

SUN	MON	TUE	WED	THU	FRI	SAT
	1 NYY	2 NYY	3 TOR	4 TOR	5 BAL	6 BAL
7 BAL	8	9 NYY	10 NYY	11 NYY	12 TEX	13 TEX
14 TEX	15 BAL	16 BAL	17 BAL	18	19 PHI	20 PHI
21 PHI	22 NYY	23 NYY	24 NYY	25 TB	26 TB	27 TB
28 TB	29 TOR	30 TOR	31 TOR			

JUNE

SUN	MON	TUE	WED	THU	FRI	SAT
				1	2 DET	3 DET
4 DET	5 NYY	6 NYY	7 NYY	8 NYY	9 TEX	10 TEX
11 TEX	12	13 MIN	14 MIN	15 MIN	16 ATL	17 ATL
18 ATL	19 WAS	20 WAS	21 WAS	22	23 PHI	24 PHI
25 PHI	26	27 NYM	28 NYM	29 NYM	30 FLA	

JULY

SUN	MON	TUE	WED	THU	FRI	SAT
						1 FLA
2 FLA	3 TB	4 TB	5 TB	6 TB	7 CHW	8 CHW
9 CHW	10	11 ALL-STAR	12	13 OAK	14 OAK	15 OAK
16 OAK	17 KC	18 KC	19 KC	20	21 SEA	22 SEA
23 SEA	24 OAK	25 OAK	26 OAK	27	28 LAA	29 LAA
30 LAA	31 CLE					

AUGUST

SUN	MON	TUE	WED	THU	FRI	SAT
		1 CLE	2 CLE	3 CLE	4 TB	5 TB
6 TB	7	8 KC	9 KC	10 KC	11 BAL	12 BAL
13 BAL	14 DET	15 DET	16 DET	17	18 NYY	19 NYY
20 NYY	21 NYY	22 LAA	23 LAA	24 LAA	25 SEA	26 SEA
27 SEA	28 OAK	29 OAK	30 OAK	31 TOR		

SEPTEMBER

SUN	MON	TUE	WED	THU	FRI	SAT
					1 TOR	2 TOR
3 TOR	4 CHW	5 CHW	6 CHW	7	8 KC	9 KC
10 KC	11	12 BAL	13 BAL	14 BAL	15 NYY	16 NYY
17 NYY	18	19 MIN	20 MIN	21 MIN	22 TOR	23 TOR
24 TOR	25 TOR	26 TB	27 TB	28	29 BAL	30 BAL

OCTOBER

SUN	MON	TUE	WED	THU	FRI	SAT
1 BAL	2	3	4	5	6	7

Home games are shaded. All-Star Game is July 11 at Pittsburgh. Schedule is subject to change.

Ortiz

CLUB DIRECTORY

Principal owner
John W. Henry
Chairman
Tom Werner
President/chief executive officer
Larry Lucchino
Co-general manager
Ben Cherington
Co-general manager
Jed Hoyer
Senior adviser/baseball projects
Jeremy Kapstein
Special adviser/baseball operations
Bill Lajoie
Special asst./player dev., int'l scouting
Craig Shipley
Chief operation officer
Mike Dee
Senior v.p., planning and development
Janet Marie Smith
Executive vice president/public affairs
Dr. Charles Steinberg
Vice president, publications and archives

Dick Bresciani
Senior vice president/sales and marketing
Sam Kennedy
Vice president and chief financial officer
Bob Furbush
Chief legal officer
Lucinda Treat
Vice president and club counsel
Elaine Steward
Vice president/media relations
Glenn Geffner
Senior vice president/Fenway affairs
Larry Cancro
Senior vice president/corporate relations
Meg Vaillancourt
V.p./finance and human resources
Steve Fitch
Vice president/business operations
Jonathan Gilula
V.p./Fenway Enterprises/broadcast services
Chuck Steedman

MINOR LEAGUE AFFILIATES

Class	Team	League	Manager
AAA	Pawtucket	International	Ron Johnson
AA	Portland	Eastern	Todd Claus
Advanced A	Wimington	Carolina	Chad Epperson
A	Greenville	South Atlantic	Luis Alicea
Short-Season A	Lowell	New York-Pennsylvania	Bruce Crabbe
Rookie	Red Sox	Gulf Coast	Dave Tomlin

BROADCAST INFORMATION

Radio: WEEI-AM (850).
Cable TV: New England Sports Network.

SPRING TRAINING

Ballpark (city): City of Palms Park (Fort Myers, Fla.).
Ticket information: 877-REDSOX9.

For more on the Red Sox, go to **www.sportingnews.com/baseball/teams/redsox/**

SPRING TRAINING ROSTER

Manager—Terry Francona (47).
Coaches—DeMarlo Hale (35), Bill Haselman (37), Ron Jackson (22), Brad Mills (2), Al Nipper, Dave Wallace (17).

No.	PITCHERS	B/T	Ht./Wt.	Age*
59	Abe Alvarez	L/L	6-2/190	23
61	Bronson Arroyo	R/R	6-5/190	29
	Timothy Bausher	R/R	6-4/200	26
	Josh Beckett	R/R	6-5/222	25
30	Matt Clement	R/R	6-3/210	31
57	Manny Delcarmen	R/R	6-3/195	24
55	Lenny DiNardo	L/L	6-4/195	26
29	Keith Foulke	R/R	6-0/210	33
56	Craig Hansen	R/R	6-6/210	22
	Jon Lester	L/L	6-2/190	22
	Edgar Martinez	R/R	6-0/222	24
	Cla Meredith	R/R	6-0/180	22
	Guillermo Mota	R/R	6-4/205	32
58	Jonathan Papelbon	R/R	6-4/230	25
	David Pauley	R/R	6-2/185	22
38	Curt Schilling	R/R	6-5/235	39
	Rudy Seanez	R/R	5-11/200	37
50	Mike Timlin	R/R	6-4/210	40
	Jermaine Van Buren	R/R	6-1/220	25
	James Vermilyea	R/R	6-4/195	24
49	Tim Wakefield	R/R	6-2/210	39
16	David Wells	L/L	6-4/248	42

No.	CATCHERS	B/T	Ht./Wt.	Age*
	John Flaherty	R/R	6-1/200	38
48	Kelly Shoppach	R/R	6-1/210	25
33	Jason Varitek	B/R	6-2/230	33

No.	INFIELDERS	B/T	Ht./Wt.	Age
23	Alex Cora	L/R	6-0/180	30
10	Tony Graffanino	R/R	6-1/190	33
	Mark Loretta	R/R	6-0/186	34
	Mike Lowell	R/R	6-3/210	32
40	Alejandro Machado	R/R	6-0/185	23
	Andy Marte	R/R	6-1/185	22
27	David Ortiz	L/L	6-4/230	30
13	Roberto Petagine	L/L	6-1/170	34
	J.T. Snow	L/L	6-2/209	38
20	Kevin Youkilis	R/R	6-1/220	27

No.	OUTFIELDERS	B/T	Ht./Wt.	Age
	Brandon Moss	L/R	6-0/180	22
	David Murphy	L/L	6-4/190	24
7	Trot Nixon	L/L	6-2/211	31
24	Manny Ramirez	R/R	6-0/213	33
39	Adam Stern	L/R	5-11/180	26

*Age as of April 1, 2006.

BALLPARK INFORMATION

Ballpark (capacity, surface)
Fenway Park (38,805, grass)
Address
4 Yawkey Way
Boston, MA 02215-3496
Official website
www.redsox.com
Business phone
617-226-6000
Ticket information
877-REDSOX9
Field dimensions (from home plate)
To left field at foul line, 310 feet
To center field triangle, 420 feet
To right field at foul line, 302 feet
First game played
April 20, 1912
(Red Sox 7, New York Highlanders 6)

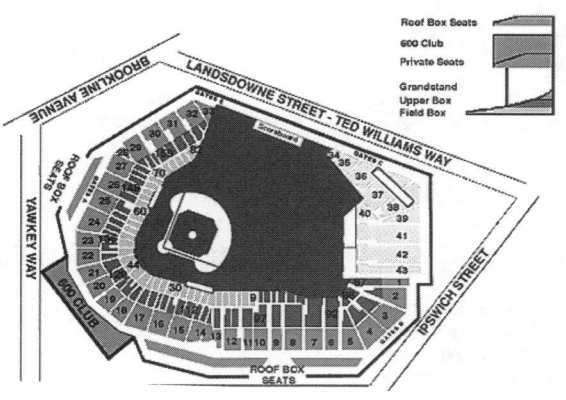

Boston Red Sox | 2006 SEASON

Date	Opp.	Res.	Score	(inn.*)	Hits	Opp. hits	Winning pitcher	Losing pitcher	Save	Record	Pos.	GB
4-3	At N.Y.	L	2-9		6	15	Johnson	Wells		0-1	5th	1.0
4-5	At N.Y.	L	3-4	11	7	Rivera	Foulke		0-2	T4th	2.0
4-6	At N.Y.	W	7-3		14	4	Timlin	Rivera		1-2	T4th	1.0
4-8	At Tor.	W	6-5		9	8	Arroyo	Bush	Foulke	2-2	T1st	...
4-9	At Tor.	L	5-12		8	16	Frasor	Wells		2-3	T4th	1.0
4-10	At Tor.	L	3-4		10	9	Batista	Timlin		2-4	5th	2.0
4-11	N.Y.	W	8-1		9	6	Wakefield	Mussina		3-4	T4th	2.0
4-13	N.Y.	L	2-5		7	12	Wright	Schilling	Rivera	3-5	T4th	2.5
4-14	N.Y.	W	8-5		8	10	Foulke	Gordon		4-5	T3rd	2.5
4-15	T.B.	W	10-0		10	7	Wells	Nomo		5-5	3rd	1.5
4-16	T.B.	W	6-2		7	10	Clement	Brazelton		6-5	3rd	1.5
4-17	T.B.	W	3-1		7	4	Wakefield	Kazmir	Foulke	7-5	3rd	1.0
4-18	Tor.	W	12-7		15	18	Schilling	Bush		8-5	T1st	...
4-19	Tor.	L	3-4		6	13	Halladay	Foulke	Batista	8-6	3rd	1.0
4-20	At Bal.	W	8-0		9	3	Wells	Chen		9-6	T1st	...
4-21	At Bal.	W	1-0		5	9	Clement	Lopez	Foulke	10-6	1st	+1.0
4-22	At T.B.	L	4-5		8	10	Baez	Embree		10-7	T1st	...
4-23	At T.B.	L	5-6		11	10	Fossum	Schilling	Carter	10-8	2nd	1.0
4-24	At T.B.	W	11-3		13	11	Arroyo	Nomo		11-8	2nd	1.0
4-25	Bal.	L	4-8		12	13	Chen	Wells		11-9	2nd	2.0
4-26	Bal.	L	8-11		12	20	Julio	Foulke	Ryan	11-10	2nd	3.0
4-29	At Tex.	L	2-7		3	10	Park	Wakefield	Mahay	11-11	3rd	4.0
4-30	At Tex.	W	9-2		14	6	Arroyo	Astacio		12-11	2nd	4.0
5-1	At Tex.	W	6-5		13	6	Clement	Drese	Foulke	13-11	2nd	4.0
5-2	At Det.	L	3-8		11	12	Bonderman	Neal	Urbina	13-12	3rd	4.0
5-3	At Det.	W	5-3		6	6	Halama	Maroth	Foulke	14-12	3rd	3.0
5-4	At Det.	W	4-3		10	11	Wakefield	Farnsworth	Foulke	15-12	2nd	3.0
5-5	At Det.	W	2-1		12	3	Arroyo	Urbina	Foulke	16-12	2nd	2.5
5-6	Sea.	W	7-2		10	7	Clement	Moyer		17-12	2nd	2.5
5-8#	Sea.	W	6-3		10	6	Gonzalez	Pineiro	Foulke	18-12		
5-8$	Sea.	L	4-6		9	9	Franklin	Halama	Guardado	18-13	2nd	2.5
5-9	Oak.	W	13-5		12	11	Wakefield	Haren		19-13	2nd	2.5
5-10	Oak.	W	3-2		5	3	Mantei	Dotel		20-13	2nd	1.5
5-11	Oak.	W	6-5		11	9	Foulke	Dotel		21-13	2nd	1.5
5-13	At Sea.	L	7-14		13	15	Mateo	Gonzalez		21-14	2nd	1.0
5-14	At Sea.	W	6-3		8	7	Myers	Villone	Foulke	22-14	2nd	1.0
5-15	At Sea.	L	4-5		10	12	Meche	Wakefield	Guardado	22-15	2nd	2.0
5-16	At Oak.	L	4-6		12	9	Yabu	Myers	Dotel	22-16	2nd	2.5
5-17	At Oak.	W	7-5		4	9	Embree	Cruz	Foulke	23-16	2nd	2.5
5-18	At Oak.	L	6-13		8	19	Etherton	Wells		23-17	2nd	3.5
5-20	Atl.	W	4-3		8	6	Miller	Hudson	Foulke	24-17	2nd	2.0
5-21	Atl.	L	5-7		11	9	Davies	Wakefield		24-18	2nd	3.0
5-22	Atl.	W	5-2		14	4	Clement	Colon		25-18	2nd	2.0
5-24	At Tor.	L	6-9		10	11	Batista	Embree		25-19	2nd	3.0
5-25	At Tor.	L	1-6		4	8	Lilly	Arroyo		25-20	2nd	4.0
5-26	At Tor.	L	1-8		9	9	Chacin	Miller	Walker	25-21	4th	5.0
5-27	At N.Y.	L	3-6		11	7	Johnson	Wakefield	Rivera	25-22	4th	5.0
5-28	At N.Y.	W	17-1		27	8	Clement	Pavano		26-22	3rd	4.0
5-29	At N.Y.	W	7-2		14	6	Wells	Mussina		27-22	2nd	3.0
5-30	Bal.	L	1-8		6	14	Lopez	Arroyo		27-23	T2nd	4.0
5-31	Bal.	W	5-1		8	5	Miller	Cabrera		28-23	2nd	3.0
6-1	Bal.	L	3-9		9	11	Ponson	Wakefield		28-24	2nd	4.0
6-2	Bal.	W	6-4		10	10	Foulke	Ryan		29-24	2nd	3.0
6-3	L.A.	W	7-4		7	13	Myers	Shields	Foulke	30-24	2nd	2.0
6-4	L.A.	L	6-13		11	17	Colon	Embree		30-25	2nd	3.0
6-5	L.A.	W	6-3		8	10	Myers	Woods	Foulke	31-25	2nd	3.0
6-6	At StL.	L	1-7		4	9	Morris	Wakefield		31-26	2nd	4.0
6-7	At StL.	L	2-9		9	9	Suppan	Clement		31-27	2nd	4.0
6-8	At StL.	W	4-0		9	6	Wells	Carpenter		32-27	2nd	3.0
6-10	At Chi.	L	6-14		10	20	Maddux	Arroyo		32-28	2nd	4.0
6-11	At Chi.	L	6-7		9	12	Wellemeyer	Miller	Dempster	32-29	2nd	4.0
6-12	At Chi.	W	8-1		17	5	Wakefield	Rusch		33-29	2nd	3.0
6-13	Cin.	W	10-3		16	6	Clement	Milton		34-29	2nd	3.0
6-14	Cin.	W	7-0		10	1	Wells	Hudson		35-29	2nd	3.0
6-15	Cin.	W	6-1		10	8	Arroyo	Harang		36-29	2nd	3.0
6-17	Pit.	W	6-5		11	8	Foulke	White		37-29	2nd	2.0

Date	Opp.	Res.	Score	(inn.*)	Hits	Opp. hits	Winning pitcher	Losing pitcher	Save	Record	Pos.	GB
6-18	Pit.	L	0-2		6	10	White	Embree	Mesa	37-30	2nd	3.0
6-19	Pit.	W	8-0		10	4	Clement	Wells		38-30	2nd	3.0
6-20	At Cle.	W	10-9		13	15	Wells	Sabathia	Foulke	39-30	2nd	2.0
6-21	At Cle.	W	9-2		11	7	Arroyo	Millwood		40-30	2nd	2.0
6-22	At Cle.	W	5-4		12	11	Foulke	Wickman		41-30	2nd	1.0
6-24	At Phi.	W	8-0		12	3	Wakefield	Lieber		42-30	1st	+0.5
6-25	At Phi.	W	7-1		12	8	Clement	Padilla		43-30	1st	+1.5
6-26	At Phi.	W	12-8		15	14	Timlin	Cormier		44-30	1st	+2.5
6-27	Cle.	L	0-7		3	8	Millwood	Arroyo		44-31	1st	+2.5
6-28	Cle.	L	8-12		13	15	Miller	Foulke		44-32	1st	+1.5
6-29	Cle.	W	5-2		11	7	Wakefield	Elarton	Timlin	45-32	1st	+2.0
7-1	Tor.	L	2-15		9	13	Lilly	Clement		45-33	1st	+2.5
7-2	Tor.	W	6-4		13	12	Timlin	Walker	Foulke	46-33	1st	+2.5
7-3	Tor.	L	2-5		8	10	Halladay	Arroyo	Schoeneweis	46-34	1st	+2.5
7-4	At Tex.	L	5-6		8	10	Benoit	Foulke		46-35	1st	+2.5
7-5	At Tex.	W	7-4		7	8	Wakefield	Young	Timlin	47-35	1st	+3.5
7-6	At Tex.	W	7-4		10	9	Clement	Park	Embree	48-35	1st	+4.0
7-7	At Bal.	L	1-3	(6)	3	5	Cabrera	Wells	Byrdak	48-36	1st	+3.0
7-8	At Bal.	W	7-2		15	7	Arroyo	Ponson		49-36	1st	+3.5
7-9	At Bal.	L	1-9		7	14	Chen	Miller		49-37	1st	+3.0
7-10	At Bal.	L	1-4		4	9	Lopez	Wakefield	Ryan	49-38	1st	+2.0
7-14	N.Y.	L	6-8		9	14	Gordon	Schilling	Rivera	49-39	1st	+1.0
7-15	N.Y.	W	17-1		15	5	Wells	Redding		50-39	1st	+1.0
7-16	N.Y.	L	4-7		8	11	Johnson	Clement	Rivera	50-40	1st	+1.0
7-17	N.Y.	L	3-5		7	5	Leiter	Wakefield	Rivera	50-41	1st	+0.5
7-18	T.B.	L	1-3		3	8	Kazmir	Miller	Baez	50-42	T2nd	0.5
7-19	T.B.	W	5-2		9	8	Arroyo	Fossum	Schilling	51-42	1st	+0.5
7-20	T.B.	W	9-4		11	9	Wells	Hendrickson		52-42	1st	+0.5
7-21	At Chi.	W	6-5		14	9	Schilling	Vizcaino		53-42	1st	+1.5
7-22	At Chi.	L	4-8		9	10	Garland	Wakefield		53-43	1st	+1.5
7-23	At Chi.	W	3-0		5	7	Miller	Hernandez	Schilling	54-43	1st	+2.5
7-24	At Chi.	L	4-6		10	10	Contreras	Arroyo	Hermanson	54-44	1st	+1.5
7-25	At T.B.	L	3-4	(10)	11	14	Colome	Schilling		54-45	1st	+1.0
7-26	At T.B.	W	10-9	(10)	16	15	Schilling	Baez		55-45	1st	+1.0
7-27	At T.B.	W	4-1		6	7	Wakefield	McClung	Schilling	56-45	1st	+2.0
7-29	Min.	W	8-5		8	7	Arroyo	Silva	Schilling	57-45	1st	+2.5
7-30	Min.	W	6-2		14	7	Wells	Lohse		58-45	1st	+2.5
7-31	Min.	W	4-3		8	7	Timlin	Rincon	Schilling	59-45	1st	+2.5
8-2	K.C.	W	6-4		10	8	Wakefield	Burgos	Schilling	60-45	1st	+3.5
8-3	K.C.	W	8-5		12	6	Miller	Snyder	Schilling	61-45	1st	+4.5
8-4	K.C.	W	11-9		9	10	Clement	Nunez	Schilling	62-45	1st	+4.5
8-5	At Min.	L	0-12		4	16	Radke	Arroyo		62-46	1st	+3.5
8-6	At Min.	L	3-4		10	9	Nathan	Timlin		62-47	1st	+3.5
8-7	At Min.	W	11-7		17	9	Wakefield	Mays	Schilling	63-47	1st	+3.5
8-8	Tex.	W	11-6		12	16	Gonzalez	Karsay		64-47	1st	+3.5
8-9	Tex.	W	8-7	(10)	11	11	Schilling	Gryboski		65-47	1st	+4.5
8-10	Tex.	W	16-5		15	10	Arroyo	Rogers		66-47	1st	+5.5
8-12	Chi.	W	9-8		13	12	Bradford	Buehrle		67-47	1st	+5.0
8-13	Chi.	W	7-4		13	9	Wakefield	Garland		68-47	1st	+5.0
8-15	At Det.	L	6-7		8	16	Walker	Schilling		68-48	1st	+3.5
8-16	At Det.	W	10-7	(10)	10	9	Bradford	Dingman		69-48	1st	+4.5
8-17	At Det.	L	5-6		13	14	Bonderman	Wells	Rodney	69-49	1st	+4.5
8-18	At L.A.	L	4-13		9	15	Colon	Wakefield		69-50	1st	+4.0
8-19	At L.A.	W	4-3	(10)	14	8	Schilling	Shields		70-50	1st	+4.0
8-20	At L.A.	L	2-4		7	7	Santana	Arroyo	Rodriguez	70-51	1st	+3.0
8-21	At L.A.	W	5-1		9	8	Timlin	Byrd		71-51	1st	+4.0
8-23	At K.C.	W	5-2		9	8	Wells	Greinke		72-51	1st	+3.5
8-24	At K.C.	L	3-4	(11)	10	9	Sisco	Arroyo		72-52	1st	+3.5
8-25	At K.C.	L	4-7		7	12	Lima	Schilling	MacDougal	72-53	1st	+2.5
8-26	Det.	W	9-8		10	13	Wakefield	Johnson	Timlin	73-53	1st	+2.5
8-27	Det.	L	8-12		13	17	Colon	Papelbon		73-54	1st	+1.5
8-28	Det.	W	11-3		14	10	Wells	Robertson		74-54	1st	+1.5
8-29	T.B.	W	10-6		13	11	Clement	McClung		75-54	1st	+1.5
8-30	T.B.	W	7-6		11	13	Timlin	Borowski		76-54	1st	+2.5
8-31	T.B.	W	7-6		8	7	Wakefield	Fossum	Timlin	77-54	1st	+2.5
9-1	T.B.	W	7-4		10	11	Arroyo	Waechter	Timlin	78-54	1st	+3.5
9-2	Bal.	L	3-7		4	12	Maine	DiNardo		78-55	1st	+3.5
9-3	Bal.	W	7-6		9	8	Clement	Bedard	Timlin	79-55	1st	+3.5
9-4	Bal.	W	5-1		7	7	Wells	Lopez		80-55	1st	+3.5

Date	Opp.	Res.	Score	(inn.*)	Hits	Opp. hits	Winning pitcher	Losing pitcher	Save	Record	Pos.	GB
9-5	Chi.	L	3-5		5	11	McCarthy	Schilling		80-56	1st	+3.0
9-6	L.A.	W	3-2		9	8	Wakefield	Shields		81-56	1st	+4.0
9-7	L.A.	W	6-3		6	9	Arroyo	Santana	Timlin	82-56	1st	+4.0
9-8	L.A.	L	0-3		5	8	Byrd	Clement	Rodriguez	82-57	1st	+4.0
9-9	At N.Y.	L	4-8		11	14	Small	Wells		82-58	1st	+3.0
9-10	At N.Y.	W	9-2		16	6	Schilling	Chacon		83-58	1st	+4.0
9-11	At N.Y.	L	0-1		3	3	Johnson	Wakefield	Rivera	83-59	1st	+3.0
9-12	At Tor.	W	6-5	(11)	12	8	Papelbon	Walker		84-59	1st	+3.5
9-13	At Tor.	L	3-9		9	9	Downs	Clement		84-60	1st	+2.5
9-14	At Tor.	W	5-3		7	7	Wells	Towers	Timlin	85-60	1st	+2.5
9-15	Oak.	L	2-6		7	14	Blanton	Schilling		85-61	1st	+1.5
9-16	Oak.	W	3-2	(10)	7	8	Timlin	Cruz		86-61	1st	+1.5
9-17	Oak.	W	2-1		7	4	Arroyo	Haren	Timlin	87-61	1st	+1.5
9-18	Oak.	L	3-12		11	15	Saarloos	Clement		87-62	1st	+1.5
9-19	At T.B.	L	7-8		11	18	Hendrickson	Harville	Baez	87-63	1st	+0.5
9-20	At T.B.	W	15-2		21	6	Schilling	McClung		88-63	1st	+0.5
9-21	At T.B.	L	4-7		9	11	Miller	Timlin	Baez	88-64	2nd	0.5
9-23	At Bal.	W	6-3		9	8	Arroyo	Cabrera	Timlin	89-64	2nd	1.0
9-24	At Bal.	W	4-3		8	10	Papelbon	Ryan	Timlin	90-64	T1st	...
9-25	At Bal.	W	9-3		12	7	Wells	Maine		91-64	T1st	...
9-27#	Tor.	W	3-1		6	5	Wakefield	Bush	Timlin	92-64		
9-27$	Tor.	L	5-7		12	13	Frasor	Bradford	Batista	92-65	T1st	...
9-28	Tor.	L	2-7		8	8	Lilly	Arroyo		92-66	2nd	1.0
9-29	Tor.	W	5-4		10	10	Papelbon	Batista		93-66	2nd	1.0
9-30	N.Y.	W	5-3		4	7	Wells	Wang	Timlin	94-66	T1st	...
10-1	N.Y.	L	4-8		7	12	Johnson	Wakefield		94-67	2nd	1.0
10-2	N.Y.	W	10-1		11	11	Schilling	Wright		95-67	T1st	...

Monthly records: April (12-11), May (16-12), June (17-9), July (14-13), August (18-9), September (17-12), October (1-1).
*Innings, if other than nine. ! First game of a doubleheader. & Second game of a doubleheader. # Day separate admission. $ Night separate admission.

RECORDS

2005 regular-season record: 95-67
Position: 1st in A.L. East
Home: 54-27   **Road:** 41-40
A.L. East: 39-35   **A.L. Central:** 22-13
A.L. West: 22-13   **N.L.** 12-6
Vs. LH starters: 29-22
Vs. RH starters: 66-45
Grass: 87-54   **Artificial:** 8-13
Day: 30-19   **Night:** 65-48
1-Run: 27-15   **X-inn.:** 6-2
Doubleheaders: 0-0-0
Team record past five years: 463-346
(.572, ranks 3rd in league in that span)

TEAM LEADERS

Batting average: Johnny Damon (.316).
At-bats: Johnny Damon (624).
Runs: David Ortiz (119).
Hits: Johnny Damon (197).
Total Bases: David Ortiz (363).
Doubles: David Ortiz (40).
Triples: Johnny Damon (6).
Home runs: David Ortiz (47).
Runs batted in: David Ortiz (148).
Stolen bases: Johnny Damon (18).
Slugging percentage: David Ortiz (.604).
On-base percentage: David Ortiz (.397).
Wins: Tim Wakefield (16).
Earned-run average: Tim Wakefield (4.15).
Complete games: Tim Wakefield (3).
Shutouts: None.

Saves: Keith Foulke (15).
Innings pitched: Tim Wakefield (225.1).
Strikeouts: Tim Wakefield (151).

GAMES BY POSITION

Catcher: Jason Varitek 130, Doug Mirabelli 43, Kelly Shoppach 7, Shawn Wooten 1.
First base: Kevin Millar 110, John Olerud 80, Dave McCarty 12, David Ortiz 10, Roberto Petagine 10, Kevin Youkilis 9.
Second base: Mark Bellhorn 83, Tony Graffanino 51, Alex Cora 35, Bill Mueller 5, Ramon Vazquez 4, Alejandro Machado 3, Kevin Youkilis 2.
Third base: Bill Mueller 142, Kevin Youkilis 24, Ramon Vazquez 8, Alex Cora 5.
Shortstop: Edgar Renteria 153, Ramon Vazquez 12, Alex Cora 11, Hanley Ramirez 2, Mark Bellhorn 1, Alejandro Machado 1.
Outfield: Manny Ramirez 149, Johnny Damon 147, Trot Nixon 118, Jay Payton 53, Gabe Kapler 36, Kevin Millar 34, Adam Stern 21, Adam Hyzdu 12, Alejandro Machado 6, Jose Cruz Jr. 4, Roberto Petagine 2, Dave McCarty 1.
Designated hitter: David Ortiz 148, Doug Mirabelli 5, Roberto Petagine 3, Trot Nixon 2, Manny Ramirez 2, Kelly Shoppach 2, Johnny Damon 1, Ramon Vazquez 1.

TOP DRAFT CHOICES

1a. **Jacoby Ellsbury**, OF, Oregon State.
1b. **Craig Hansen**, RHP, St. John's.
1c. **Clay Buchholz**, RHP, Angelina JC (Texas).
1d. **Jed Lowrie**, 2B, Stanford.
1e. **Michael Bowden**, RHP, Waubonsie Valley H.S., Aurora, Ill.
2a. **Jon Egan**, C, Cross Creek H.S., Hephzibah, Ga.
4. **Scott Blue**, RHP, Morro Bay (Calif.) H.S.
5. **Reid Engel**, OF, Lewis-Palmer H.S., Monument, Colo.
6. **Jeff Corsaletti**, OF, Florida.
7. **Yahmed Yema**, OF, Florida International.
8. **J.T. Zink**, RHP, Everett (Wash.) CC.
9. **Mark Wagner**, C, UC Irvine.
10. **Kevin Guyette**, RHP, Arizona.

CHICAGO WHITE SOX
AMERICAN LEAGUE CENTRAL DIVISION

2006 SEASON

White Sox Schedule
Home games shaded.
All-Star Game July 11 at Pittsburgh. Schedule subject to change.

APRIL

SUN	MON	TUE	WED	THU	FRI	SAT
2 CLE	3	4 CLE	5 CLE	6	7 KC	8 KC
9 KC	10 DET	11	12 DET	13 DET	14 TOR	15 TOR
16 TOR	17 KC	18 KC	19 KC	20	21 MIN	22 MIN
23 MIN	24 SEA	25 SEA	26 SEA	27	28 LAA	29 LAA
30 LAA						

MAY

SUN	MON	TUE	WED	THU	FRI	SAT
	1 CLE	2 CLE	3 SEA	4 SEA	5 KC	6 KC
7 KC	8	9 LAA	10 LAA	11 LAA	12 MIN	13 MIN
14 MIN	15 MIN	16 TB	17 TB	18 TB	19 CHC	20 CHC
21 CHC	22 OAK	23 OAK	24 OAK	25	26 TOR	27 TOR
28 TOR	29 CLE	30 CLE	31 CLE			

JUNE

SUN	MON	TUE	WED	THU	FRI	SAT
				1 CLE	2 TEX	3 TEX
4 TEX	5	6 DET	7 DET	8 DET	9 CLE	10 CLE
11 CLE	12 TEX	13 TEX	14 TEX	15 TEX	16 CIN	17 CIN
18 CIN	19	20 STL	21 STL	22 STL	23 HOU	24 HOU
25 HOU	26	27 PIT	28 PIT	29 PIT	30 CHC	

JULY

SUN	MON	TUE	WED	THU	FRI	SAT
						1 CHC
2 CHC	3 BAL	4 BAL	5 BAL	6 BAL	7 BOS	8 BOS
9 BOS	10	11 ALL-STAR	12	13	14 NYY	15 NYY
16 NYY	17	18 DET	19 DET	20 DET	21 TEX	22 TEX
23 TEX	24 MIN	25 MIN	26 MIN	27	28 BAL	29 BAL
30 BAL	31					

AUGUST

SUN	MON	TUE	WED	THU	FRI	SAT
		1 KC	2 KC	3	4 TOR	5 TOR
6 TOR	7	8 NYY	9 NYY	10 NYY	11 DET	12 DET
13 DET	14 KC	15 KC	16 KC	17 KC	18 MIN	19 MIN
20 MIN	21 DET	22 DET	23 DET	24 DET	25 MIN	26 MIN
27 MIN	28	29 TB	30 TB	31 TB		

SEPTEMBER

SUN	MON	TUE	WED	THU	FRI	SAT
					1 KC	2 KC
3 KC	4 BOS	5 BOS	6 BOS	7 CLE	8 CLE	9 CLE
10 CLE	11 LAA	12 LAA	13 LAA	14	15 OAK	16 OAK
17 OAK	18 DET	19 DET	20 DET	21 SEA	22 SEA	23 SEA
24 SEA	25 CLE	26 CLE	27 CLE	28	29 MIN	30 MIN

OCTOBER

SUN	MON	TUE	WED	THU	FRI	SAT
1 MIN	2	3	4	5	6	7

Home games are shaded. All-Star Game is July 11 at Pittsburgh. Schedule is subject to change.

Crede

CLUB DIRECTORY

Chairman
Jerry Reinsdorf
Vice chairman
Eddie Einhorn
Executive vice president
Howard Pizer
Senior vice president, general manager
Ken Williams
V.p., free agent & major league scouting
Larry Monroe
Executive adviser to Ken Williams
Roland Hemond

Assistant general manager
Rick Hahn
Senior director of player personnel
Duane Shaffer
Director of player development
Dave Wilder
Vice president, communications
Scott Reifert
Director of community relations
Christine O'Reilly
Director of media relations
Bob Beghtol

MINOR LEAGUE AFFILIATES

Class	Team	League	Manager
AAA	Charlotte	International	Razor Shines
AA	Birmingham	Southern	Chris Cron
Advanced A	Winston-Salem	Carolina	To be announced
A	Kannapolis	South Atlantic	To be announced
Advanced Rookie	Bristol	Appalachian	Nick Leyva
Advanced Rookie	Great Falls	Pioneer	Tommy Thompson

BROADCAST INFORMATION

Radio: WSCR-AM (670).
TV: WGN-TV (Channel 9).
Cable TV: Comcast SportsNet.

SPRING TRAINING

Ballpark (city): Tucson Electric Park (Tucson, Ariz.).
Ticket information: 520-434-1111.

For more on the White Sox, go to www.sportingnews.com/baseball/teams/whitesox/

2006 SEASON *Chicago White Sox*

Manager—Ozzie Guillen (13).
Coaches—Harold Baines (3), Don Cooper (21), Joey Cora (28), Art Kusnyer (53), Man Soo Lee (59), Tim Raines (30), Greg Walker (29).

No.	PITCHERS	B/T	Ht./Wt.	Age*
57	Jeff Bajenaru	R/R	6-1/200	28
56	Mark Buehrle	L/L	6-2/220	27
52	Jose Contreras	R/R	6-4/245	34
46	Neal Cotts	L/L	6-2/205	26
34	Freddy Garcia	R/R	6-4/250	29
20	Jon Garland	R/R	6-6/215	26
	Charles Haeger	R/R	6-1/205	22
32	Dustin Hermanson	R/R	6-2/200	33
45	Bobby Jenks	R/R	6-3/270	25
55	Brandon McCarthy	R/R	6-7/190	22
	Arnie Munoz	L/L	5-9/175	23
18	Cliff Politte	R/R	5-10/200	32
	Paulino Reynoso	L/L	6-3/215	25
	Sean Tracey	L/R	6-3/210	25
33	Javier Vazquez	R/R	6-2/215	29

No.	CATCHERS	B/T	Ht./Wt.	Age*
12	A.J. Pierzynski	L/R	6-3/240	29
	Chris Stewart	R/R	6-4/205	24
36	Chris Widger	R/R	6-2/215	34

No.	INFIELDERS	B/T	Ht./Wt.	Age*
24	Joe Crede	R/R	6-1/195	27
17	Ross Gload	L/L	6-0/200	29
15	Tadahito Iguchi	R/R	5-10/185	31
14	Paul Konerko	R/R	6-2/215	30
	Pedro Lopez	R/R	6-1/160	21
10	Rob Mackowiak	L/R	5-10/190	29
38	Pablo Ozuna	R/R	5-10/185	31
	Casey Rogowski	L/L	6-3/230	24
25	Jim Thome	L/R	6-4/245	35
5	Juan Uribe	R/R	5-11/215	26

No.	OUTFIELDERS	B/T	Ht./Wt.	Age*
44	Brian Anderson	R/R	6-2/205	24
	Joe Borchard	B/R	6-5/220	27
23	Jermaine Dye	R/R	6-5/220	32
	Jerry Owens	L/L	6-3/195	25
22	Scott Podsednik	L/L	6-0/190	30

*Age as of April 1, 2006.

BALLPARK INFORMATION

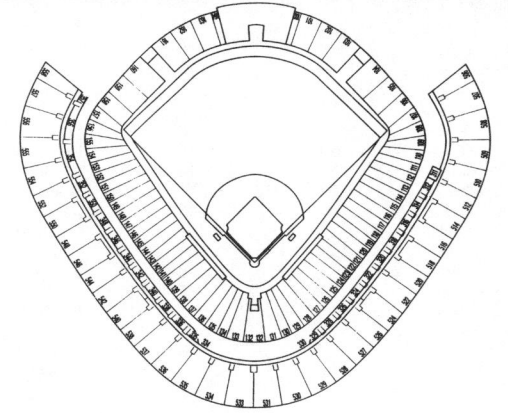

Ballpark (capacity, surface)
U.S. Cellular Field (40,615, grass)
Address
333 W. 35th St.
Chicago, IL 60616
Official website
www.whitesox.com
Business phone
312-674-1000
Ticket information
312-674-1000
Field dimensions (from home plate)
To left field at foul line, 330 feet
To center field, 400 feet
To right field at foul line, 335 feet
First game played
April 18, 1991 (Tigers 16, White Sox 0)

2005 REVIEW
DAY BY DAY

Date	Opp.	Res.	Score	(inn.*)	Hits	Opp. hits	Winning pitcher	Losing pitcher	Save	Record	Pos.	GB
44-4	Cle.	W	1-0		4	2	Buehrle	Westbrook	Takatsu	1-0	T1st	...
4-6	Cle.	W	4-3		9	8	Marte	Wickman		2-0	1st	+0.5
4-7	Cle.	L	5-11	(11)	11	14	Rhodes	Vizcaino		2-1	T1st	...
4-8	At Min.	W	5-1		11	8	Hernandez	Lohse		3-1	1st	+1.0
4-9	At Min.	W	8-5		8	14	Garland	Radke	Takatsu	4-1	1st	+1.0
4-10	At Min.	L	2-5		8	7	Santana	Buehrle	Nathan	4-2	1st	+1.0
4-11	At Cle.	W	2-1		6	4	Garcia	Millwood	Takatsu	5-2	1st	+1.5
4-13	At Cle.	W	5-4	(10)	9	6	Vizcaino	Howry	Hermanson	6-2	1st	+1.0
4-14	At Cle.	L	6-8		12	10	Betancourt	Hernandez	Wickman	6-3	T1st	...
4-15	Sea.	W	6-4		9	5	Garland	Pineiro	Hermanson	7-3	T1st	...
4-16	Sea.	W	2-1		4	3	Buehrle	Franklin		8-3	T1st	...
4-17	Sea.	L	4-5		8	10	Meche	Garcia	Guardado	8-4	T1st	...
4-18	Min.	W	5-4		7	9	Vizcaino	Lohse	Takatsu	9-4	1st	+1.0
4-19	Min.	W	3-1		11	14	Hernandez	Radke	Marte	10-4	1st	+2.0
4-20	At Det.	W	9-1		12	5	Garland	Ledezma		11-4	1st	+2.0
4-21	At Det.	W	4-3		9	7	Buehrle	Bonderman	Takatsu	12-4	1st	+2.0
4-22	At K.C.	W	8-2		12	4	Garcia	Hernandez		13-4	1st	+3.0
4-23	At K.C.	W	3-2	(10)	10	7	Marte	MacDougal		14-4	1st	+3.5
4-24	At K.C.	W	4-3		6	5	Cotts	Camp	Takatsu	15-4	1st	+4.0
4-25	At Oak.	W	6-0		9	4	Garland	Zito		16-4	1st	+5.0
4-26	At Oak.	L	7-9		14	13	Duchscherer	Marte	Dotel	16-5	1st	+4.0
4-27	At Oak.	L	1-2		5	7	Duchscherer	Marte		16-6	1st	+3.0
4-29	Det.	L	2-3	(11)	7	8	Walker	Takatsu	German	16-7	1st	+1.5
4-30	Det.	W	4-3		6	9	Hernandez	Johnson	Hermanson	17-7	1st	+1.5
5-1	Det.	W	8-0		9	4	Garland	Ledezma		18-7	1st	+2.5
5-3	K.C.	W	5-4		11	8	Buehrle	Sisco	Takatsu	19-7	1st	+3.5
5-4	K.C.	W	4-2		6	9	Garcia	Hernandez	Hermanson	20-7	1st	+4.5
5-5	K.C.	W	2-1		2	4	Contreras	Greinke	Takatsu	21-7	1st	+4.5
5-6	At Tor.	W	5-3		9	7	Hernandez	Frasor	Hermanson	22-7	1st	+4.5
5-7	At Tor.	W	10-7		11	10	Garland	Lilly		23-7	1st	+4.5
5-8	At Tor.	W	5-4		10	10	Buehrle	Chacin	Marte	24-7	1st	+4.5
5-9	At T.B.	L	2-4		8	10	Carter	Garcia	Baez	24-8	1st	+4.5
5-10	At T.B.	L	6-7		9	9	Colome	Takatsu		24-9	1st	+3.5
5-11	At T.B.	W	5-2		8	5	Hernandez	Brazelton	Hermanson	25-9	1st	+4.5
5-12	Bal.	W	3-2		6	8	Garland	Chen	Hermanson	26-9	1st	+5.0
5-13	Bal.	W	5-3		12	5	Buehrle	Williams	Hermanson	27-9	1st	+6.0
5-14	Bal.	L	6-9		9	15	Cabrera	Garcia	Ryan	27-10	1st	+6.0
5-15	Bal.	L	2-6		5	11	Bedard	Contreras		27-11	1st	+5.0
5-16	Tex.	L	6-7		7	11	Regilio	Marte	Cordero	27-12	1st	+4.5
5-17	Tex.	W	5-2		9	6	Garland	Astacio	Hermanson	28-12	1st	+5.5
5-18	Tex.	W	7-0		11	9	Buehrle	Drese		29-12	1st	+5.5
5-20	At Chi.	W	5-1		10	6	Garcia	Maddux		30-12	1st	+5.0
5-21	At Chi.	W	5-3		9	8	Contreras	Wuertz	Hermanson	31-12	1st	+6.0
5-22	At Chi.	L	3-4		6	8	Prior	Vizcaino		31-13	1st	+5.0
5-23	At L.A.	L	0-4		5	13	Santana	Garland		31-14	1st	+5.0
5-24	At L.A.	W	2-1	(11)	5	4	Marte	Yan		32-14	1st	+5.0
5-25	At L.A.	W	4-2		7	8	Garcia	Washburn	Hermanson	33-14	1st	+6.0
5-26	At L.A.	L	2-3		6	5	Lackey	Contreras	Shields	33-15	1st	+5.0
5-27	At Tex.	L	2-6		9	9	Young	McCarthy	Cordero	33-16	1st	+4.0
5-29	At Tex.	L	4-12		9	16	Park	Garland		33-17	1st	+3.5
5-30	L.A.	W	5-4		10	10	Politte	Shields		34-17	1st	+4.0
5-31	L.A.	W	5-4		11	9	Politte	Donnelly		35-17	1st	+5.0
6-1	L.A.	L	7-10		8	13	Byrd	Walker		35-18	1st	+4.0
6-3	Cle.	W	6-4		11	7	Hernandez	Westbrook	Hermanson	36-18	1st	+3.5
6-4	Cle.	W	6-5		10	12	Garland	Davis	Hermanson	37-18	1st	+4.5
6-5	Cle.	L	4-6	(12)	11	12	Riske	Hermanson		37-19	1st	+3.5
6-6	At Col.	W	9-3		15	2	Garcia	Kennedy		38-19	1st	+4.0
6-7	At Col.	W	2-1		5	5	Contreras	Kim	Hermanson	39-19	1st	+4.0
6-8	At Col.	W	15-5		22	8	Hernandez	Francis		40-19	1st	+4.0
6-10	At S.D.	W	4-2		9	7	Garland	Williams	Hermanson	41-19	1st	+5.5
6-11	At S.D.	L	1-2		6	11	Linebrink	Hermanson		41-20	1st	+4.5
6-12	At S.D.	W	8-5	(10)	13	10	Politte	Hoffman		42-20	1st	+5.5
6-13	Ari.	L	1-8		8	11	Estes	Contreras		42-21	1st	+5.0
6-14	Ari.	L	4-10		8	13	Vazquez	Hernandez		42-22	1st	+4.0
6-15	Ari.	W	12-6		10	7	Garland	Ortiz		43-22	1st	+5.0
6-17	L.A.	W	6-0		6	8	Buehrle	Houlton		44-22	1st	+5.5

Date	Opp.	Res.	Score	(inn.*)	Hits	Opp. hits	Winning pitcher	Losing pitcher	Save	Record	Pos.	GB
6-18	L.A.	W	5-3		6	7	Politte	Brazoban		45-22	1st	+6.5
6-19	L.A.	W	4-3		6	7	Politte	Sanchez	Hermanson	46-22	1st	+7.5
6-20	K.C.	W	11-8		17	10	Cotts	Jensen	Hermanson	47-22	1st	+8.0
6-21	K.C.	W	5-1		10	4	Garland	Greinke		48-22	1st	+9.0
6-22	K.C.	W	5-1		8	5	Buehrle	Howell		49-22	1st	+10.0
6-24	Chi.	W	12-2		13	5	Garcia	Mitre		50-22	1st	+10.5
6-25	Chi.	L	2-6		5	10	Maddux	Contreras		50-23	1st	+10.5
6-26	Chi.	L	0-2		1	5	Prior	Garland	Dempster	50-24	1st	+9.5
6-28	At Det.	W	2-1		6	9	Buehrle	Robertson	Hermanson	51-24	1st	+9.0
6-29	At Det.	W	4-3	(13)	12	15	Takatsu	Rodney		52-24	1st	+10.0
6-30	At Det.	W	6-1		9	5	Garcia	Maroth		53-24	1st	+10.5
7-1	At Oak.	L	2-6		4	7	Harden	Contreras		53-25	1st	+9.5
7-2	At Oak.	W	5-3		10	5	Garland	Saarloos	Hermanson	54-25	1st	+9.5
7-3	At Oak.	L	2-7		6	16	Zito	Buehrle		54-26	1st	+8.5
7-4	T.B.	W	10-8		11	14	Vizcaino	Nomo	Hermanson	55-26	1st	+8.5
7-5	T.B.	W	6-4		12	8	Politte	Carter	Hermanson	56-26	1st	+9.5
7-6	T.B.	W	7-2		12	7	Contreras	Fossum		57-26	1st	+10.5
7-8	Oak.	L	2-4		9	13	Saarloos	Garland	Street	57-27	1st	+10.0
7-9	Oak.	L	1-10		3	11	Zito	Buehrle		57-28	1st	+10.0
7-10	Oak.	L	8-9	(11)	17	15	Street	Vizcaino		57-29	1st	+9.0
7-14	At Cle.	W	1-0		7	4	Contreras	Millwood	Hermanson	58-29	1st	+10.0
7-15	At Cle.	W	7-1		11	6	Garcia	Sabathia		59-29	1st	+11.0
7-16	At Cle.	W	7-5		11	6	Buehrle	Westbrook	Marte	60-29	1st	+11.0
7-17	At Cle.	W	4-0		8	8	Garland	Elarton		61-29	1st	+12.0
7-18	Det.	W	7-5		10	7	Vizcaino	Spurling	Politte	62-29	1st	+13.0
7-19	Det.	L	1-7		3	12	Bonderman	Contreras		62-30	1st	+12.0
7-20	Det.	L	6-8		6	15	Robertson	Garcia	Dingman	62-31	1st	+11.0
7-21	Bos.	L	5-6		9	14	Schilling	Vizcaino		62-32	1st	+10.0
7-22	Bos.	W	8-4		10	9	Garland	Wakefield		63-32	1st	+11.0
7-23	Bos.	L	0-3		7	5	Miller	Hernandez	Schilling	63-33	1st	+10.5
7-24	Bos.	W	6-4		10	10	Contreras	Arroyo	Hermanson	64-33	1st	+11.5
7-25	At K.C.	W	14-6		22	16	Garcia	Greinke		65-33	1st	+12.0
7-26	At K.C.	L	1-7		8	8	Lima	Buehrle		65-34	1st	+12.0
7-27	At K.C.	L	5-6	(13)	8	12	Camp	Vizcaino		65-35	1st	+11.0
7-29	At Bal.	W	7-2		12	9	Hernandez	Bedard		66-35	1st	+12.5
7-30	At Bal.	W	9-6		13	8	Cotts	Ray	Hermanson	67-35	1st	+13.5
7-31	At Bal.	W	9-4		13	12	Garcia	Lopez		68-35	1st	+14.5
8-1	At Bal.	W	6-3		11	10	Buehrle	Cabrera	Hermanson	69-35	1st	+15.0
8-2	Tor.	L	3-7		8	13	Towers	Garland		69-36	1st	+14.0
8-3	Tor.	L	3-4		9	5	Bush	Hernandez	Batista	69-37	1st	+13.0
8-4	Tor.	W	5-4		7	8	Vizcaino	Speier	Hermanson	70-37	1st	+14.0
8-5	Sea.	L	2-4		8	7	Pineiro	Garcia	Guardado	70-38	1st	+13.0
8-6	Sea.	W	4-2		4	9	Buehrle	Moyer	Hermanson	71-38	1st	+13.0
8-7	Sea.	W	3-1		5	5	Garland	Harris	Hermanson	72-38	1st	+13.0
8-8	At N.Y.	L	2-3		9	4	Mussina	Hernandez	Rivera	72-39	1st	+12.5
8-9	At N.Y.	W	2-1		6	5	Contreras	Chacon	Hermanson	73-39	1st	+12.5
8-10	At N.Y.	W	2-1	(10)	5	7	Cotts	Rivera	Hermanson	74-39	1st	+12.5
8-12	At Bos.	L	8-9		12	13	Bradford	Buehrle		74-40	1st	+12.0
8-13	At Bos.	L	4-7		9	13	Wakefield	Garland		74-41	1st	+12.0
8-15	Min.	L	2-4		9	9	Lohse	Contreras	Nathan	74-42	1st	+12.0
8-16	Min.	L	4-9	(16)	12	20	Romero	Adkins		74-43	1st	+11.0
8-17	Min.	L	1-5		6	10	Santana	Buehrle		74-44	1st	+11.0
8-19	N.Y.	L	1-3		6	8	Mussina	Garland	Rivera	74-45	1st	+9.5
8-20	N.Y.	L	0-5		4	7	Chacon	Hernandez		74-46	1st	+8.5
8-21	N.Y.	W	6-2		10	11	Contreras	Johnson		75-46	1st	+8.5
8-23	At Min.	L	0-1		3	1	Santana	Garcia	Nathan	75-47	1st	+7.0
8-24	At Min.	W	6-4		13	10	Buehrle	Mays	Hermanson	76-47	1st	+8.0
8-25	At Min.	W	2-1	(10)	8	7	Hermanson	Crain	Jenks	77-47	1st	+8.0
8-26	At Sea.	W	5-3	(12)	13	7	Vizcaino	Nelson	Hermanson	78-47	1st	+8.0
8-27	At Sea.	W	4-3		9	7	Contreras	Pineiro	Marte	79-47	1st	+9.0
8-28	At Sea.	L	2-9		8	14	Moyer	Garcia		79-48	1st	+8.0
8-29	At Tex.	L	5-7		11	10	Dominguez	Buehrle	Brocail	79-49	1st	+7.0
8-30!	At Tex.	L	6-8		12	7	Wilson	Garland	Cordero	79-50		
8-30&	At Tex.	W	8-0		14	3	McCarthy	Volquez		80-50	1st	+7.0
8-31	At Tex.	L	2-9		6	10	Loe	Hernandez		80-51	1st	+7.0
9-1	Det.	W	12-3		18	5	Contreras	Johnson		81-51	1st	+7.5
9-2	Det.	W	9-1		9	3	Garcia	Douglass		82-51	1st	+7.5
9-3	Det.	W	6-2		12	11	Buehrle	Robertson		83-51	1st	+8.5
9-4	Det.	W	2-0		5	4	Garland	Bonderman		84-51	1st	+9.5

Date	Opp.	Res.	Score	(inn.*)	Hits	Opp. hits	Winning pitcher	Losing pitcher	Save	Record	Pos.	GB
9-5	At Bos.	W	5-3		11	5	McCarthy	Schilling		85-51	1st	+9.5
9-6	K.C.	W	6-5		11	9	Hernandez	Lima	Hermanson	86-51	1st	+9.5
9-7	K.C.	W	1-0		6	6	Contreras	Wood	Hermanson	87-51	1st	+9.5
9-8	K.C.	L	2-4		2	10	Howell	Garcia	MacDougal	87-52	1st	+8.5
9-9	L.A.	L	5-6	(12)	8	13	Donnelly	Hermanson	Rodriguez	87-53	1st	+7.5
9-10	L.A.	L	5-10		13	10	Colon	Garland		87-54	1st	+6.5
9-11	L.A.	L	1-6		8	11	Lackey	Hernandez		87-55	1st	+5.5
9-13	At K.C.	W	6-4		14	7	Contreras	Wood	Jenks	88-55	1st	+6.0
9-14	At K.C.	L	9-10		14	15	Demaria	Hermanson		88-56	1st	+5.0
9-15	At K.C.	L	5-7		12	14	Burgos	Buehrle	MacDougal	88-57	1st	+4.5
9-16	At Min.	W	2-1	(10)	6	6	Jenks	Crain		89-57	1st	+4.5
9-17	At Min.	L	0-5		4	11	Santana	Hernandez	Nathan	89-58	1st	+3.5
9-18	At Min.	W	2-1		8	5	Contreras	Rincon	Jenks	90-58	1st	+3.5
9-19	Cle.	L	5-7		11	10	Betancourt	Marte	Wickman	90-59	1st	+2.5
9-20	Cle.	W	7-6	(10)	11	14	Hermanson	Riske		91-59	1st	+3.5
9-21	Cle.	L	0-8		5	12	Elarton	Garland		91-60	1st	+2.5
9-22	Min.	L	1-4	(11)	7	8	Crain	Jenks	Nathan	91-61	1st	+1.5
9-23	Min.	W	3-1		9	6	Contreras	Lohse		92-61	1st	+1.5
9-24	Min.	W	8-1		14	5	Garcia	Mays		93-61	1st	+1.5
9-25	Min.	W	4-1		5	4	Buehrle	Liriano		94-61	1st	+2.5
9-26	At Det.	L	3-4		7	10	Rodney	Politte		94-62	1st	+2.0
9-27	At Det.	L	2-3		8	9	Robertson	McCarthy	Rodney	94-63	1st	+2.0
9-28	At Det.	W	8-2		15	10	Contreras	Douglass		95-63	1st	+3.0
9-29	At Det.	W	4-2		10	10	Garcia	Grilli	Jenks	96-63	1st	+3.0
9-30	At Cle.	W	3-2	(13)	10	9	Politte	Cabrera	Jenks	97-63	1st	+4.0
10-1	At Cle.	W	4-3		10	8	Garland	Westbrook	Jenks	98-63	1st	+5.0
10-2	At Cle.	W	3-1		7	7	McCarthy	Elarton	Hernandez	99-63	1st	+6.0

Monthly records: April (17-7), May (18-10), June (18-7), July (15-11), August (12-16), September (17-12), October (2-0).
*Innings, if other than nine. ! First game of a doubleheader. & Second game of a doubleheader.

RECORDS

2005 regular-season record: 99-63
Position: 1st in A.L. Central
Home: 47-34   **Road:** 52-29
A.L. East: 20-13   **A.L. Central:** 52-22
A.L. West: 15-22   **N.L.** 12-6
Vs. LH starters: 23-20
Vs. RH starters: 76-43
Grass: 89-58   **Artificial:** 10-5
Day: 37-20   **Night:** 62-43
1-Run: 35-19   **X-inn.:** 11-8
Doubleheaders: 0-0-1
Team record past five years: 432-378
(.533, ranks 7th in league in that span)

TEAM LEADERS

Batting average: Scott Podsednik (.290).
At-bats: Aaron Rowand (578).
Runs: Paul Konerko (98).
Hits: Paul Konerko (163).
Total Bases: Paul Konerko (307).
Doubles: Aaron Rowand (30).
Triples: Tadahito Iguchi (6).
Home runs: Paul Konerko (40).
Runs batted in: Paul Konerko (100).
Stolen bases: Scott Podsednik (59).
Slugging percentage: Paul Konerko (.534).
On-base percentage: Paul Konerko (.375).
Wins: Jon Garland (18).
Earned-run average: Mark Buehrle

(3.12).
Complete games: Mark Buehrle, Jon Garland (3).
Shutouts: Jon Garland (3).
Saves: Dustin Hermanson (34).
Innings pitched: Mark Buehrle (236.2).
Strikeouts: Jose Contreras (154).

GAMES BY POSITION

Catcher: A.J. Pierzynski 128, Chris Widger 42, Raul Casanova 6.

First base: Paul Konerko 146, Ross Gload 24, Geoff Blum 12, Pablo Ozuna 2, Timo Perez 2, Jamie Burke 1, Jermaine Dye 1, Chris Widger 1.

Second base: Tadahito Iguchi 133, Willie Harris 32, Pablo Ozuna 6, Geoff Blum 2, Pedro Lopez 1.

Third base: Joe Crede 130, Pablo Ozuna 32, Geoff Blum 12, Chris Widger 1.

Shortstop: Juan Uribe 146, Pablo Ozuna 15, Geoff Blum 6, Willie Harris 5, Joe Crede 1, Jermaine Dye 1, Pedro Lopez 1.

Outfield: Aaron Rowand 157, Jermaine Dye 140, Scott Podsednik 127, Timo Perez 50, Carl Everett 22, Brian N. Anderson 12, Pablo Ozuna 10, Ross Gload 3, Joe Borchard 2.

Designated hitter: Carl Everett 107, Frank Thomas 28, Paul Konerko 11, Timo Perez 11, Willie Harris 9, Pablo Ozuna 4, Joe Borchard 3, Joe Crede 1, Jermaine Dye 1, Chris Widger 1.

TOP DRAFT CHOICES

1. **Lance Broadway** RHP, TCU.
3. **Ricky Brooks,** RHP, East Carolina.
4. **Chris Getz,** 2B, Michigan.
5. **Ryan Rote,** RHP, Vanderbilt.
6. **Aaron Cunningham,** OF, Everett (Wash.) CC.
7. **Daniel Cortes,** RHP, Garey H.S., Pomona, Calif.
8. **Clayton Richard,** LHP, Michigan.
9. **Joe Winn,** RHP, Delgado CC (La.)
10. **Israel Chirino,** LHP, Miami.

CLEVELAND INDIANS
AMERICAN LEAGUE CENTRAL DIVISION

2006 SEASON

Indians Schedule
Home games shaded.
All-Star Game July 11 at Pittsburgh. Schedule subject to change.

APRIL

SUN	MON	TUE	WED	THU	FRI	SAT
2 CHW	3	4 CHW	5 CHW	6	7 MIN	8 MIN
9 MIN	10	11 SEA	12 SEA	13 SEA	14 DET	15 DET
16 DET	17 DET	18 BAL	19 BAL	20 BAL	21 KC	22 KC
23 KC	24	25 BOS	26 BOS	27 BOS	28 TEX	29 TEX
30 TEX						

MAY

SUN	MON	TUE	WED	THU	FRI	SAT
	1 CHW	2 CHW	3 OAK	4 OAK	5 SEA	6 SEA
7 SEA	8 KC	9 KC	10 KC	11	12 DET	13 DET
14 DET	15 KC	16 KC	17 KC	18 KC	19 PIT	20 PIT
21 PIT	22	23 MIN	24 MIN	25	26 DET	27 DET
28 DET	29 CHW	30 CHW	31 CHW			

JUNE

SUN	MON	TUE	WED	THU	FRI	SAT
				1 CHW	2 LAA	3 LAA
4 LAA	5	6 OAK	7 OAK	8 OAK	9 CHW	10 CHW
11 CHW	12	13 NYY	14 NYY	15 NYY	16 MIL	17 MIL
18 MIL	19 CHC	20 CHC	21 CHC	22	23 CIN	24 CIN
25 CIN	26 STL	27 STL	28 STL	29	30 CIN	

JULY

SUN	MON	TUE	WED	THU	FRI	SAT
						1 CIN
2 CIN	3 NYY	4 NYY	5 NYY	6 NYY	7 BAL	8 BAL
9 BAL	10	11 ALL-STAR	12	13 MIN	14 MIN	15 MIN
16 MIN	17 LAA	18 LAA	19 LAA	20	21 MIN	22 MIN
23 MIN	24 DET	25 DET	26 DET	27	28 SEA	29 SEA
30 SEA	31 BOS					

AUGUST

SUN	MON	TUE	WED	THU	FRI	SAT
		1 BOS	2 BOS	3 BOS	4 DET	5 DET
6 DET	7	8 LAA	9 LAA	10 LAA	11 KC	12 KC
13 KC	14	15 MIN	16 MIN	17 MIN	18 TB	19 TB
20 TB	21	22 KC	23 KC	24 KC	25 DET	26 DET
27 DET	28 TOR	29 TOR	30 TOR	31		

SEPTEMBER

SUN	MON	TUE	WED	THU	FRI	SAT
					1 TEX	2 TEX
3 TEX	4 TOR	5 TOR	6 TOR	7 CHW	8 CHW	9 CHW
10 CHW	11	12 KC	13 KC	14 KC	15 MIN	16 MIN
17 MIN	18 OAK	19 OAK	20 OAK	21 OAK	22 TEX	23 TEX
24 TEX	25 CHW	26 CHW	27 CHW	28 TB	29 TB	30 TB

OCTOBER

SUN	MON	TUE	WED	THU	FRI	SAT
1 TB	2	3	4	5	6	7

Home games are shaded. All-Star Game is July 11 at Pittsburgh. Schedule is subject to change.

Martinez

CLUB DIRECTORY

Owner and chief executive officer
Lawrence J. Dolan
President
Paul Dolan
Executive vice president, general manager
Mark Shapiro
Vice president, public relations
Bob DiBiasio
Vice president, ballpark operations
Jim Folk

Assistant general manager
Chris Antonetti
Assistant general manager
John Mirabelli
Director of player development
John Farrell
Director of player personnel
Steve Lubratich
Director of media relations
Bart Swain

MINOR LEAGUE AFFILIATES

Class	Team	League	Manager
AAA	Buffalo	International	Torey Lovullo
AA	Akron	Eastern	Tim Bogar
Advanced A	Kinston	Carolina	Mike Sarbaugh
A	Lake County	South Atlantic	Lee May Jr.
Short-Season A	Mahoning Valley	New York-Pennsylvania	Rouglas Odor
Advanced Rookie	Burlington	Appalachian	Kevin Higgins

BROADCAST INFORMATION

Radio: WTAM-AM (1100).
Television: WKYC TV3.
Cable TV: Fastball Sports Productions.

SPRING TRAINING

Ballpark (city): Chain Of Lakes (Winter Haven, Fla.).
Ticket information: 863-293-3900.

For more on the Indians, go to www.sportingnews.com/baseball/teams/indians/

SPRING TRAINING ROSTER

Manager—Eric Wedge (22).
Coaches—Jeff Datz (29), Ruben Felix (96), Luis Isaac (4), Luis Rivera, Derek Shelton (27), Joel Skinner (35), Dan Williams (43), Carl Willis (57).

No.	PITCHERS	B/T	Ht./Wt.	Age*
63	Rafael Betancourt	R/R	6-2/200	30
	Andrew Brown	R/R	6-6/230	25
	Paul Byrd	R/R	6-1/190	35
	Fernando Cabrera	R/R	6-4/225	24
	Fausto Carmona	R/R	6-4/220	22
50	Jason Davis	R/R	6-6/225	25
	Jake Dittler	R/R	6-4/220	23
	Jeremy Guthrie	R/R	6-1/200	26
	Jason Johnson	R/R	6-6/220	32
31	Cliff Lee	L/L	6-3/190	27
59	Matt Miller	R/R	6-3/215	34
	Edward Mujica	R/R	6-2/220	21
	Rafael Perez	L/L	6-3/184	23
53	Arthur Rhodes	L/L	6-2/210	36
54	David Riske	R/R	6-2/180	29
52	C.C. Sabathia	L/L	6-7/290	25
47	Scott Sauerbeck	R/L	6-3/200	34
	Brian Slocum	R/R	6-4/200	25
	Jason Stanford	L/L	6-2/200	29
	Kazuhito Tadano	R/R	6-0/180	25
37	Jake Westbrook	R/R	6-3/200	28
26	Bob Wickman	R/R	6-1/240	37

No.	CATCHERS	B/T	Ht./Wt.	Age*
44	Josh Bard	B/R	6-3/215	28
25	Ryan Garko	R/R	6-2/225	25
41	Victor Martinez	B/R	6-2/195	27

No.	INFIELDERS	B/T	Ht./Wt.	Age*
	Michael Aubrey	L/L	6-0/195	23
20	Ronnie Belliard	R/R	5-8/195	30
17	Aaron Boone	R/R	6-2/200	33
23	Ben Broussard	L/L	6-2/220	29
48	Travis Hafner	L/R	6-3/240	28
2	Jhonny Peralta	R/R	6-1/210	23
	Eduardo Perez	R/R	6-4/240	36
7	Brandon Phillips	R/R	5-11/190	24
15	Ramon Vazquez	L/R	5-11/170	29

No.	OUTFIELDERS	B/T	Ht./Wt.	Age*
1	Casey Blake	R/R	6-2/210	32
10	Coco Crisp	B/R	6-0/180	26
9	Jason Dubois	R/R	6-5/220	27
38	Franklin Gutierrez	R/R	6-2/180	23
24	Grady Sizemore	L/L	6-2/210	23
	Brad Snyder	L/L	6-3/215	23

*Age as of April 1, 2006.

BALLPARK INFORMATION

Ballpark (capacity, surface)
Jacobs Field (43,368, grass)
Address
2401 Ontario St.
Cleveland, OH 44115
Official website
www.indians.com
Business phone
216-420-4200
Ticket information
216-420-HITS, 1-866-48-TRIBE
Field dimensions (from home plate)
To left field at foul line, 325 feet
To center field, 405 feet
To right field at foul line, 325 feet
First game played
April 4, 1994
(Indians 4, Mariners 3, 11 innings)

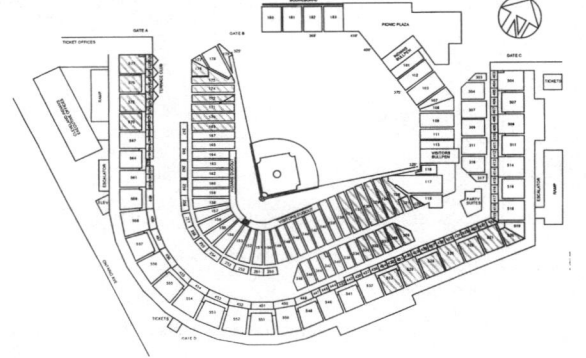

Date	Opp.	Res.	Score	(inn.*)	Hits	Opp. hits	Winning pitcher	Losing pitcher	Save	Record	Pos.	GB
4-4	At Chi.	L	0-1		2	4	Buehrle	Westbrook	Takatsu	0-1	T3rd	1.0
4-6	At Chi.	L	3-4		8	9	Marte	Wickman		0-2	5th	2.0
4-7	At Chi.	W	11-5	(11)	14	11	Rhodes	Vizcaino		1-2	T4th	1.0
4-8	At Det.	W	4-3		7	6	Riske	Urbina	Wickman	2-2	T2nd	1.0
4-9	At Det.	L	1-11		8	11	Ledezma	Westbrook		2-3	T3rd	2.0
4-10	At Det.	W	7-6		9	10	Davis	Bonderman	Wickman	3-3	T2nd	1.0
4-11	Chi.	L	1-2		4	6	Garcia	Millwood	Takatsu	3-4	T4th	2.0
4-13	Chi.	L	4-5	(10)	6	9	Vizcaino	Howry	Hermanson	3-5	T3rd	3.0
4-14	Chi.	W	8-6		10	12	Betancourt	Hernandez	Wickman	4-5	3rd	2.0
4-15	Min.	L	2-3		7	3	Santana	Westbrook	Nathan	4-6	T3rd	3.0
4-16	Min.	L	4-6		7	10	Gassner	Millwood	Nathan	4-7	T3rd	4.0
4-17	Min.	W	2-1		7	5	Howry	Romero	Wickman	5-7	T3rd	3.0
4-18	At K.C.	W	5-1		8	3	Lee	Greinke		6-7	T3rd	3.0
4-19	At K.C.	L	5-6		14	15	MacDougal	Rhodes		6-8	T3rd	4.0
4-20	At L.A.	L	0-2		4	5	Colon	Westbrook	Rodriguez	6-9	T3rd	5.0
4-21	At L.A.	L	5-6	(10)	13	12	Rodriguez	Davis		6-10	T3rd	6.0
4-22	At Sea.	W	6-1		9	6	Sabathia	Meche		7-10	T3rd	6.0
4-23	At Sea.	W	5-2		8	7	Lee	Sele	Wickman	8-10	T3rd	6.0
4-24	At Sea.	L	1-9		6	5	Moyer	Elarton		8-11	3rd	7.0
4-27	Det.	L	3-10		4	12	Bonderman	Westbrook		8-12	4th	7.0
4-28	Det.	L	2-3		7	7	Maroth	Millwood	Percival	8-13	4th	7.5
4-29	K.C.	W	6-0		11	3	Sabathia	Greinke		9-13	4th	6.5
4-30	K.C.	L	1-8		6	12	Bautista	Lee		9-14	4th	7.5
5-1	K.C.	L	5-6		4	8	Wood	Betancourt	Burgos	9-15	4th	8.5
5-3	At Min.	W	4-2		10	10	Westbrook	Mays	Wickman	10-15	4th	8.5
5-4	At Min.	W	5-4		13	13	Howry	Romero	Wickman	11-15	4th	8.5
5-5	At Min.	L	0-9		3	13	Radke	Sabathia		11-16	4th	9.5
5-6	At Tex.	W	8-6		14	11	Lee	Astacio	Wickman	12-16	T3rd	9.5
5-7	At Tex.	L	1-6		6	9	Drese	Elarton		12-17	4th	10.5
5-8	At Tex.	L	2-7		10	12	Rogers	Westbrook	Cordero	12-18	4th	11.5
5-9	At L.A.	W	3-0		8	2	Millwood	Lackey	Wickman	13-18	4th	10.5
5-10	At L.A.	L	4-5		9	11	Byrd	Sabathia	Rodriguez	13-19	4th	10.5
5-11	At L.A.	W	9-3		13	7	Lee	Escobar		14-19	4th	10.5
5-13	Tor.	W	6-4		8	5	Davis	Lilly	Wickman	15-19	4th	11.0
5-14	Tor.	W	3-2		5	7	Rhodes	Frasor	Wickman	16-19	4th	10.0
5-15	Tor.	L	2-5		6	8	Halladay	Sabathia		16-20	4th	10.0
5-16	L.A.	L	1-3		5	7	Byrd	Lee	Shields	16-21	4th	10.0
5-17	L.A.	W	13-5		19	15	Elarton	Santana		17-21	4th	10.0
5-18	L.A.	L	1-2		4	5	Colon	Westbrook	Shields	17-22	4th	11.0
5-20	At Cin.	L	1-2		6	7	Harang	Millwood	Graves	17-23	4th	12.0
5-21	At Cin.	W	5-3		8	9	Sabathia	Ramirez	Wickman	18-23	4th	12.0
5-22	At Cin.	W	9-2		16	8	Lee	Ortiz		19-23	4th	11.0
5-23	Min.	W	2-1		7	8	Rhodes	Lohse	Wickman	20-23	4th	10.0
5-24	Min.	L	3-6	(11)	7	9	Crain	Riske	Nathan	20-24	4th	11.0
5-25	Min.	W	3-2	(10)	8	9	Howry	Rincon		21-24	3rd	11.0
5-26	Min.	L	4-5	(11)	16	8	Crain	Riske	Nathan	21-25	3rd	11.0
5-27	Oak.	W	4-1		6	4	Lee	Zito	Riske	22-25	3rd	10.0
5-28	Oak.	W	6-3		12	8	Elarton	Saarloos	Howry	23-25	3rd	9.5
5-29	Oak.	W	6-2		6	8	Westbrook	Etherton	Miller	24-25	3rd	8.5
5-31	At Min.	W	4-3		9	8	Sabathia	Silva	Wickman	25-25	3rd	9.0
6-1	At Min.	L	2-6		7	13	Radke	Lee		25-26	3rd	9.0
6-2	At Min.	L	3-4	(13)	6	9	Romero	Betancourt		25-27	4th	9.5
6-3	At Chi.	L	4-6		7	11	Hernandez	Westbrook	Hermanson	25-28	4th	10.5
6-4	At Chi.	L	5-6		12	10	Garland	Davis	Hermanson	25-29	4th	11.5
6-5	At Chi.	W	6-4	(12)	12	11	Riske	Hermanson		26-29	4th	11.0
6-7	At S.D.	W	2-0	(11)	9	8	Betancourt	Hoffman	Wickman	27-29	T3rd	11.0
6-8	At S.D.	W	6-1		7	7	Elarton	Peavy	Howry	28-29	3rd	11.0
6-9	At S.D.	L	2-3		9	3	Eaton	Westbrook	Hoffman	28-30	3rd	11.5
6-10	At S.F.	W	10-2		14	5	Sabathia	Tomko		29-30	3rd	11.5
6-11	At S.F.	W	7-6		10	12	Davis	Schmidt	Wickman	30-30	3rd	10.5
6-12	At S.F.	W	5-3		7	6	Lee	Rueter	Wickman	31-30	3rd	10.5
6-14	Col.	W	11-2		15	9	Westbrook	Francis		32-30	3rd	9.0
6-15	Col.	W	7-6	(11)	11	11	Howry	Neal		33-30	3rd	9.0
6-16	Col.	W	2-1		6	7	Millwood	Wright	Wickman	34-30	3rd	8.5
6-17	Ari.	W	13-6		13	11	Lee	Halsey		35-30	3rd	8.5
6-18	Ari.	W	3-1		5	8	Elarton	Webb	Wickman	36-30	3rd	8.5

Date	Opp.	Res.	Score	(inn.*)	Hits	Opp. hits	Winning pitcher	Losing pitcher	Save	Record	Pos.	GB
6-19	Ari.	W	3-2		9	5	Westbrook	Estes	Wickman	37-30	3rd	8.5
6-20	Bos.	L	9-10		15	13	Wells	Sabathia	Foulke	37-31	3rd	9.5
6-21	Bos.	L	2-9		7	11	Arroyo	Millwood		37-32	3rd	10.5
6-22	Bos.	L	4-5		11	12	Foulke	Wickman		37-33	3rd	11.5
6-24	Cin.	L	4-5		8	10	Mercker	Howry	Weathers	37-34	3rd	12.5
6-25	Cin.	W	12-7		21	13	Westbrook	Hudson		38-34	3rd	11.5
6-26	Cin.	W	4-3		9	8	Howry	Weathers	Wickman	39-34	3rd	10.5
6-27	At Bos.	W	7-0		8	3	Millwood	Arroyo		40-34	3rd	10.0
6-28	At Bos.	W	12-8		15	13	Miller	Foulke		41-34	3rd	10.0
6-29	At Bos.	L	2-5		7	11	Wakefield	Elarton	Timlin	41-35	3rd	11.0
6-30	At Bal.	W	9-3		15	7	Westbrook	Penn		42-35	3rd	11.0
7-1	At Bal.	W	3-1		9	3	Sabathia	Lopez	Wickman	43-35	3rd	10.0
7-2	At Bal.	L	0-4		5	4	Cabrera	Millwood		43-36	3rd	11.0
7-3	At Bal.	W	9-4		13	10	Lee	Ponson		44-36	3rd	10.0
7-4#	Det.	W	9-3		14	6	Elarton	Johnson		45-36		
7-4$	Det.	W	6-0		12	6	Davis	Verlander		46-36	3rd	9.5
7-5	Det.	L	2-3		6	7	Maroth	Westbrook	Percival	46-37	3rd	10.5
7-6	Det.	L	3-7		8	15	Bonderman	Sabathia	Percival	46-38	3rd	11.5
7-7	At N.Y.	L	2-7		7	9	Mussina	Millwood		46-39	3rd	12.0
7-8	At N.Y.	L	4-5		10	8	Wang	Lee	Rivera	46-40	3rd	12.0
7-9	At N.Y.	W	8-7		12	11	Elarton	May	Wickman	47-40	3rd	11.0
7-10	At N.Y.	L	4-9		11	9	Johnson	Westbrook	Rivera	47-41	3rd	11.0
7-14	Chi.	L	0-1		4	7	Contreras	Millwood	Hermanson	47-42	3rd	12.0
7-15	Chi.	L	1-7		6	11	Garcia	Sabathia		47-43	3rd	13.0
7-16	Chi.	L	5-7		6	11	Buehrle	Westbrook	Marte	47-44	3rd	14.0
7-17	Chi.	L	0-4		8	8	Garland	Elarton		47-45	3rd	15.0
7-18	K.C.	W	6-2	(5)	10	4	Lee	Carrasco		48-45	3rd	15.0
7-19	K.C.	L	0-4		5	7	Greinke	Millwood		48-46	3rd	15.0
7-20	K.C.	L	3-5		10	11	Lima	Sabathia	MacDougal	48-47	3rd	15.0
7-21	K.C.	W	10-1		11	11	Westbrook	Howell		49-47	3rd	14.0
7-22	Sea.	L	3-4		10	4	Putz	Elarton	Guardado	49-48	3rd	15.0
7-23	Sea.	W	4-3		9	10	Lee	Meche	Wickman	50-48	3rd	14.0
7-24	Sea.	W	6-3		12	4	Millwood	Sele		51-48	3rd	14.0
7-25	At Oak.	L	4-13		6	14	Zito	Sabathia	Yabu	51-49	3rd	15.0
7-26	At Oak.	W	2-0		8	4	Westbrook	Blanton	Wickman	52-49	3rd	14.0
7-27	At Oak.	L	4-5	(10)	14	14	Street	Riske		52-50	3rd	14.0
7-28	At Sea.	W	6-5		11	10	Howry	Putz	Wickman	53-50	3rd	13.5
7-29	At Sea.	W	10-5		17	12	Millwood	Sele		54-50	3rd	13.5
7-30	At Sea.	L	2-3		10	4	Franklin	Sabathia	Guardado	54-51	3rd	14.5
7-31	At Sea.	W	9-7		10	14	Westbrook	Pineiro	Wickman	55-51	3rd	14.5
8-2	N.Y.	W	6-5		8	7	Elarton	Leiter	Wickman	56-51	2nd	14.0
8-3	N.Y.	W	7-4		11	9	Lee	Mussina	Wickman	57-51	2nd	13.0
8-4	N.Y.	L	3-4		9	11	Gordon	Wickman	Rivera	57-52	2nd	14.0
8-5	At Det.	W	9-6		16	6	Sabathia	Robertson	Howry	58-52	2nd	13.0
8-6	At Det.	W	4-2		14	5	Westbrook	Bonderman	Wickman	59-52	2nd	13.0
8-7	At Det.	W	6-5		8	9	Riske	Rodney	Wickman	60-52	2nd	13.0
8-9	At K.C.	W	13-7		17	10	Sauerbeck	MacDougal		61-52	2nd	12.5
8-10	At K.C.	W	6-1		13	7	Sabathia	Greinke		62-52	2nd	12.5
8-11	At K.C.	W	4-2		6	9	Millwood	Carrasco	Wickman	63-52	2nd	12.0
8-12	T.B.	L	6-8		17	12	Hendrickson	Westbrook	Baez	63-53	2nd	12.0
8-13	T.B.	L	2-8		10	14	McClung	Elarton		63-54	2nd	12.0
8-14	T.B.	L	0-1		7	8	Borowski	Wickman	Baez	63-55	2nd	12.5
8-16	Tex.	W	8-2		9	8	Sabathia	Rogers		64-55	2nd	11.0
8-17	Tex.	L	0-3		2	4	Young	Millwood	Cordero	64-56	2nd	11.0
8-18	Tex.	W	9-4		13	10	Westbrook	Wilson		65-56	2nd	10.5
8-19	Bal.	W	5-4	(10)	8	7	Cabrera	Kline		66-56	2nd	9.5
8-20	Bal.	W	6-1		12	5	Lee	Lopez		67-56	2nd	8.5
8-21	Bal.	W	5-1		6	3	Sabathia	Chen		68-56	2nd	8.5
8-22	At T.B.	W	11-4		15	5	Millwood	Miller		69-56	2nd	8.0
8-23	At T.B.	W	5-4		9	14	Westbrook	Miller	Wickman	70-56	2nd	7.0
8-24	At T.B.	L	3-13		10	16	McClung	Elarton		70-57	2nd	8.0
8-25	At T.B.	W	12-4		19	6	Lee	Kazmir		71-57	2nd	8.0
8-26	At Tor.	W	9-3		15	8	Sabathia	McGowan		72-57	2nd	8.0
8-27	At Tor.	L	1-2		5	6	Downs	Millwood	Batista	72-58	2nd	9.0
8-28	At Tor.	W	4-1		6	8	Westbrook	Towers	Wickman	73-58	2nd	8.0
8-29	Det.	W	10-8		12	12	Cabrera	Bonderman	Wickman	74-58	2nd	7.0
8-31	Det.	L	3-4		6	10	Maroth	Betancourt	Rodney	74-59	2nd	7.0
9-2	At Min.	W	6-1		11	5	Sabathia	Radke		75-59	2nd	7.5
9-3	At Min.	L	2-3		3	12	Nathan	Howry		75-60	2nd	8.5

Date	Opp.	Res.	Score	(inn.*)	Hits	Opp. hits	Winning pitcher	Losing pitcher	Save	Record	Pos.	GB
9-4	At Min.	L	5-7		7	12	Crain	Westbrook	Nathan	75-61	2nd	9.5
9-5	At Det.	W	2-0		5	8	Elarton	Maroth	Wickman	76-61	2nd	9.5
9-6	At Det.	W	6-1		9	5	Lee	Johnson		77-61	2nd	9.5
9-7	At Det.	W	4-1		7	4	Sabathia	Colon		78-61	2nd	9.5
9-8	Det.	W	4-2		5	9	Betancourt	Robertson	Wickman	79-61	2nd	8.5
9-9	Min.	W	4-2		9	7	Westbrook	Santana	Wickman	80-61	2nd	7.5
9-10	Min.	W	7-5		12	8	Elarton	Baker	Wickman	81-61	2nd	6.5
9-11	Min.	W	12-4		17	9	Lee	Silva		82-61	2nd	5.5
9-12	Oak.	L	0-2		4	6	Haren	Sabathia	Street	82-62	2nd	6.0
9-13	Oak.	W	5-2		8	8	Millwood	Duchscherer	Wickman	83-62	2nd	6.0
9-14	Oak.	W	6-4		10	3	Westbrook	Zito	Wickman	84-62	2nd	5.0
9-16	K.C.	W	3-1		6	6	Elarton	Gobble	Wickman	85-62	2nd	4.5
9-17	K.C.	W	5-4		11	6	Lee	Hernandez	Wickman	86-62	2nd	3.5
9-18	K.C.	W	11-0		16	5	Sabathia	Lima		87-62	2nd	3.5
9-19	At Chi.	W	7-5		10	11	Betancourt	Marte	Wickman	88-62	2nd	2.5
9-20	At Chi.	L	6-7	(10)	14	11	Hermanson	Riske		88-63	2nd	3.5
9-21	At Chi.	W	8-0		12	5	Elarton	Garland		89-63	2nd	2.5
9-22	At K.C.	W	11-6		15	12	Lee	Sisco	Betancourt	90-63	2nd	1.5
9-23	At K.C.	W	7-6		10	8	Howry	MacDougal	Wickman	91-63	2nd	1.5
9-24	At K.C.	W	11-4		16	9	Millwood	Wood		92-63	2nd	1.5
9-25	At K.C.	L	4-5		8	9	MacDougal	Howry		92-64	2nd	2.5
9-27	T.B.	L	4-5		9	11	Kazmir	Elarton	Baez	92-65	2nd	2.0
9-28	T.B.	L	0-1		5	6	McClung	Lee	Baez	92-66	2nd	3.0
9-29	T.B.	W	6-0		10	5	Sabathia	Fossum		93-66	2nd	3.0
9-30	Chi.	L	2-3	(13)	9	10	Politte	Cabrera	Jenks	93-67	2nd	4.0
10-1	Chi.	L	3-4		8	10	Garland	Westbrook	Jenks	93-68	2nd	5.0
10-2	Chi.	L	1-3		7	7	McCarthy	Elarton	Hernandez	93-69	2nd	6.0

Monthly records: April (9-14), May (16-11), June (17-10), July (13-16), August (19-8), September (19-8), October (0-2).
*Innings, if other than nine. ! First game of a doubleheader. & Second game of a doubleheader. # Day separate admission. $ Night separate admission.

RECORDS

2005 regular-season record: 93-69
Position: 2nd in A.L. Central
Home: 43-38   **Road**: 50-31
A.L. East: 19-17   **A.L. Central**: 40-35
A.L. West: 19-14   **N.L.** 15-3
Vs. LH starters: 26-24
Vs. RH starters: 67-45
Grass: 84-62   **Artificial**: 9-7
Day: 24-29   **Night**: 69-40
1-Run: 22-36   **X-inn.**: 6-8
Doubleheaders: 0-0-0
Team record past five years: 406-404
(.501, ranks 8th in league in that span)

TEAM LEADERS

Batting average: Victor Martinez (.305).
At-bats: Grady Sizemore (640).
Runs: Grady Sizemore (111).
Hits: Grady Sizemore (185).
Total Bases: Grady Sizemore (310).
Doubles: Coco Crisp, Travis Hafner (42).
Triples: Grady Sizemore (11).
Home runs: Travis Hafner (33).
Runs batted in: Travis Hafner (108).
Stolen bases: Grady Sizemore (22).
Slugging percentage: Travis Hafner (.595).
On-base percentage: Travis Hafner (.408).
Wins: Cliff Lee (18).
Earned-run average: Kevin Millwood

(2.86).
Complete games: Jake Westbrook (2).
Shutouts: None.
Saves: Bob Wickman (45).
Innings pitched: Jake Westbrook (210.2).
Strikeouts: C.C. Sabathia (161).

GAMES BY POSITION

Catcher: Victor Martinez 142, Josh Bard 31.
First base: Ben Broussard 138, Jose Hernandez 45, Jeff Liefer 5, Casey Blake 4, Travis Hafner 1.
Second base: Ronnie Belliard 141, Alex Cora 15, Ramon Vazquez 8, Jose Hernandez 4, Brandon Phillips 2.
Third base: Aaron Boone 142, Jose Hernandez 21, Casey Blake 6.
Shortstop: Jhonny Peralta 141, Alex Cora 24, Ramon Vazquez 2, Jose Hernandez 1, Brandon Phillips 1.
Outfield: Grady Sizemore 155, Coco Crisp 145, Casey Blake 138, Jody Gerut 38, Ryan Ludwick 15, Jason Dubois 7, Jose Hernandez 6, Jeff Liefer 3, Franklin Gutierrez 2, Alex Cora 1, Juan Gonzalez 0.
Designated hitter: Travis Hafner 130, Jeff Liefer 9, Jason Dubois 7, Jody Gerut 3, Franklin Gutierrez 3, Ryan Ludwick 3, Ben Broussard 2, Victor Martinez 2, Aaron Boone 1, Ryan Garko 1, Jose Hernandez 1, Brandon Phillips 1.

TOP DRAFT CHOICES

1a. **Trevor Crowe**, OF, Arizona.
1b. **John Drennen**, OF, Rancho Bernardo H.S., San Diego.
2. **Stephen Head**, 1B, Mississippi.
3a. **Nick Weglarz**, 1B, Lakeshore Catholic H.S., Stevensville, Ont.
3b. **Jensen Lewis**, RHP, Vanderbilt.
4. **Jordan Brown**, 1B, Arizona.
5. **Kevin Dixon**, RHP, Minnesota State-Mankato.
6. **Joe Ness**, RHP, Ball State.
7. **James Deters**, RHP, Calvin College.
8. **Ryan Edell**, RHP, College of Charleston.
9. **Roman Pena**, OF, Montgomery H.S., San Diego.
10. **Jason Schutt**, RHP, Central Missouri State.

DETROIT TIGERS
AMERICAN LEAGUE CENTRAL DIVISION

2006 SEASON

Tigers Schedule
Home games shaded.
All-Star Game July 11 at Pittsburgh. Schedule subject to change.

APRIL

SUN	MON	TUE	WED	THU	FRI	SAT
2	3 KC	4	5 KC	6 TEX	7 TEX	8 TEX
9 TEX	10 CHW	11	12 CHW	13 CHW	14 CLE	15 CLE
16 CLE	17 CLE	18 OAK	19 OAK	20 OAK	21 SEA	22 SEA
23 SEA	24 LAA	25 LAA	26 LAA	27	28 MIN	29 MIN
30 MIN						

MAY

SUN	MON	TUE	WED	THU	FRI	SAT
	1 KC	2 KC	3 LAA	4 LAA	5 MIN	6 MIN
7 MIN	8	9 BAL	10 BAL	11 BAL	12 CLE	13 CLE
14 CLE	15	16 MIN	17 MIN	18 MIN	19 CIN	20 CIN
21 CIN	22 KC	23 KC	24 KC	25 KC	26 CLE	27 CLE
28 CLE	29 NYY	30 NYY	31 NYY			

JUNE

SUN	MON	TUE	WED	THU	FRI	SAT
				1 NYY	2 BOS	3 BOS
4 BOS	5	6 CHW	7 CHW	8 CHW	9 TOR	10 TOR
11 TOR	12 TB	13 TB	14 TB	15 TB	16 CHC	17 CHC
18 CHC	19 MIL	20 MIL	21 MIL	22	23 STL	24 STL
25 STL	26 HOU	27 HOU	28 HOU	29	30 PIT	

JULY

SUN	MON	TUE	WED	THU	FRI	SAT
						1 PIT
2 PIT	3 OAK	4 OAK	5 OAK	6	7 SEA	8 SEA
9 SEA	10	11 ALL-STAR	12	13 KC	14 KC	15 KC
16 KC	17	18 CHW	19 CHW	20 CHW	21 OAK	22 OAK
23 OAK	24 CLE	25 CLE	26 CLE	27	28 MIN	29 MIN
30 MIN	31 TB					

AUGUST

SUN	MON	TUE	WED	THU	FRI	SAT
		1 TB	2 TB	3 TB	4 CLE	5 CLE
6 CLE	7 MIN	8 MIN	9 MIN	10	11 CHW	12 CHW
13 CHW	14 BOS	15 BOS	16 BOS	17 TEX	18 TEX	19 TEX
20 TEX	21 CHW	22 CHW	23 CHW	24 CHW	25 CLE	26 CLE
27 CLE	28	29 NYY	30 NYY	31 NYY		

SEPTEMBER

SUN	MON	TUE	WED	THU	FRI	SAT
					1 LAA	2 LAA
3 LAA	4 SEA	5 SEA	6 SEA	7 MIN	8 MIN	9 MIN
10 MIN	11	12 TEX	13 TEX	14	15 BAL	16 BAL
17 BAL	18 CHW	19 CHW	20 CHW	21	22 KC	23 KC
24 KC	25	26 TOR	27 TOR	28 TOR	29 KC	30 KC

OCTOBER

SUN	MON	TUE	WED	THU	FRI	SAT
1 KC	2	3	4	5	6	7

Home games are shaded. All-Star
Game is July 11 at Pittsburgh.
Schedule is subject to change.

Rodriguez

CLUB DIRECTORY

Owner/director
Michael Ilitch
President, CEO, general manager
David Dombrowski
Special assistants to the president
Al Kaline, Willie Horton
Senior vice president
Jim Devellano
Senior v.p., baseball operations
Duane McLean
V.p., assistant general manager
Al Avila
Vice president, amateur scouting
David Chadd
Vice president, corporate sales
Steve Harms
Vice president, park operations
Michael Healy
V.p., corporate suite sales and service
Charles P. Jones

V.p., public affairs & strategic planning
Elaine Lewis
V.p., finance & administration, CFO
Stephen Quinn
Vice president, ticket sales
Bob Raymond
Vice president, player personnel
Scott Reid
Vice president, baseball legal counsel
John Westhoff
Dir., minor league and scouting admin.
Cheryl Evans
Director, player development
Glenn Ezell
Director, minor league operations
Dan Lunetta
Director, baseball operations
Mike Smith

MINOR LEAGUE AFFILIATES

Class	Team	League	Manager
AAA	Toledo	International	Larry Parrish
AA	Erie	Eastern	Duffy Dyer
Advanced A	Lakeland	Florida State	Mike Rojas
A	West Michigan	Midwest	Matt Walbeck
Short-Seasom A	Oneonta	New York-Pennsylvania	Tom Brookens
Rookie	Tigers	Gulf Coast	Kevin Bradshaw

BROADCAST INFORMATION

Radio: WXYT-AM (1270).
Cable TV: Fox Sports Net Detroit.

SPRING TRAINING

Ballpark (city): Joker Marchant Stadium
(Lakeland, Fla.).
Ticket information: 863-686-8075.

For more on the Tigers, go to www.sportingnews.com/baseball/teams/tigers/

SPRING TRAINING ROSTER

Manager—Jim Leyland (10).
Coaches—Rafael Belliard, Chuck Hernandez, Gene Lamont, Lloyd McClendon, Don Slaught, Andy Van Slyke.

No.	PITCHERS	B/T	Ht./Wt.	Age*
38	Jeremy Bonderman	R/R	6-2/220	23
43	Roman Colon	R/R	6-6/225	26
57	Craig Dingman	R/R	6-4/230	32
62	Franklyn German	R/R	6-7/260	26
49	Jason Grilli	R/R	6-5/210	29
59	Todd Jones	L/R	6-3/230	37
39	Preston Larrison	R/R	6-4/235	25
41	Wilfredo Ledezma	L/L	6-4/210	25
46	Mike Maroth	L/L	6-0/190	28
40	Troy Percival	R/R	6-3/235	36
	Nate Robertson	R/L	6-2/220	28
56	Fernando Rodney	R/R	5-11/210	29
	Kenny Rogers	L/L	6-1/190	41
	Humberto Sanchez	R/R	6-6/230	22
	Kyle Sleeth	R/R	6-5/205	24
48	Chris Spurling	R/R	6-5/230	28
	Justin Verlander	R/R	6-5/200	23
32	Jamie Walker	L/L	6-2/185	34
50	Mark Woodyard	R/R	6-2/195	27
	Joel Zumaya	R/R	6-3/210	21

No.	CATCHERS	B/T	Ht./Wt.	Age*
7	Ivan Rodriguez	R/R	5-9/195	34
26	Vance Wilson	R/R	5-11/190	33

No.	INFIELDERS	B/T	Ht./Wt.	Age*
39	Tony Giarratano	B/R	6-0/180	23
9	Carlos Guillen	B/R	6-1/215	30
20	Omar Infante	R/R	6-0/180	24
15	Brandon Inge	R/R	5-11/190	28
	Donald Kelly	L/R	6-4/190	26
	Kody Kirkland	R/R	6-4/200	22
12	Carlos Pena	L/L	6-2/210	27
14	Placido Polanco	R/R	5-10/190	30
31	Chris Shelton	R/R	6-0/215	25
25	Dmitri Young	B/R	6-2/245	32

No.	OUTFIELDERS	B/T	Ht./Wt.	Age*
	Brent Clevlen	R/R	6-2/190	22
	Eulogio de la Cruz	R/R	5-11/175	22
28	Curtis Granderson	L/R	6-1/185	25
19	Nook Logan	B/R	6-2/180	26
27	Craig Monroe	R/R	6-1/220	29
30	Magglio Ordonez	R/R	6-0/215	32
	Jordan Tata	R/R	6-6/220	24
33	Marcus Thames	R/R	6-2/205	29

*Age as of April 1, 2006.

BALLPARK INFORMATION

Ballpark (capacity, surface)
Comerica Park (41,070, grass)
Address
2100 Woodward
Detroit, MI 48201
Official website
www.detroittigers.com
Business phone
313-471-2000
Ticket information
313-471-2255
Field dimensions (from home plate)
To left field at foul line, 345 feet
To center field, 420 feet
To right field at foul line, 330 feet
First game played
April 11, 2000 (Tigers 5, Mariners 2)

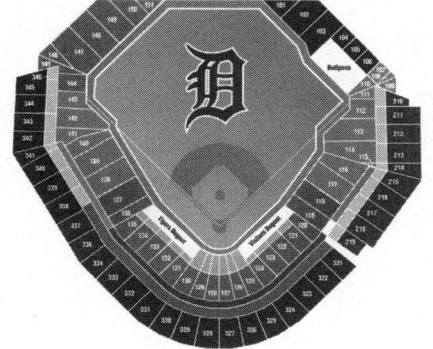

Detroit Tigers

2006 SEASON

Date	Opp.	Res.	Score	(inn.*)	Hits	Opp. hits	Winning pitcher	Losing pitcher	Save	Record	Pos.	GB
4-4	K.C.	W	11-2		13	7	Bonderman	Lima		1-0	T1st	...
4-6	K.C.	L	2-7		6	15	Hernandez	Maroth		1-1	T3rd	1.0
4-7	K.C.	W	7-3		14	9	Johnson	Wood		2-1	T1st	...
4-8	Cle.	L	3-4		6	7	Riske	Urbina	Wickman	2-2	T2nd	1.0
4-9	Cle.	W	11-1		11	8	Ledezma	Westbrook		3-2	2nd	1.0
4-10	Cle.	L	6-7		10	9	Davis	Bonderman	Wickman	3-3	T2nd	1.0
4-12	At Min.	L	4-5		7	9	Rincon	Percival		3-4	T3rd	2.0
4-13	At Min.	L	4-8		11	12	Lohse	Johnson		3-5	T3rd	3.0
4-14	At Min.	L	4-10		9	11	Radke	Robertson		3-6	T4th	3.0
4-15	At K.C.	L	5-6		7	10	Cerda	Urbina	MacDougal	3-7	5th	4.0
4-16	At K.C.	W	7-1		12	6	Bonderman	Anderson		4-7	T3rd	4.0
4-17	At K.C.	W	6-1		12	5	Maroth	Hernandez		5-7	T3rd	3.0
4-18	At Bal.	W	13-3		16	8	Johnson	Bedard		6-7	T3rd	3.0
4-19	At Bal.	L	4-8		9	12	Ponson	Robertson		6-8	T3rd	4.0
4-20	Chi.	L	1-9		5	12	Garland	Ledezma		6-9	T3rd	5.0
4-21	Chi.	L	3-4		7	9	Buehrle	Bonderman	Takatsu	6-10	T3rd	6.0
4-22	Min.	W	5-4	(10)	11	8	Percival	Mulholland		7-10	T3rd	6.0
4-25	Min.	W	6-4		14	6	Farnsworth	Rincon	Percival	8-10	3rd	7.0
4-27	At Cle.	W	10-3		12	4	Bonderman	Westbrook		9-10	3rd	5.5
4-28	At Cle.	W	3-2		7	7	Maroth	Millwood	Percival	10-10	3rd	5.0
4-29	At Chi.	W	3-2	(11)	8	7	Walker	Takatsu	German	11-10	3rd	4.0
4-30	At Chi.	L	3-4		9	6	Hernandez	Johnson	Hermanson	11-11	3rd	5.0
5-1	At Chi.	L	0-8		4	9	Garland	Ledezma		11-12	3rd	6.0
5-2	Bos.	W	8-3		12	11	Bonderman	Neal	Urbina	12-12	3rd	5.5
5-3	Bos.	L	3-5		6	6	Halama	Maroth	Foulke	12-13	3rd	6.5
5-4	Bos.	L	3-4		11	10	Wakefield	Farnsworth	Foulke	12-14	3rd	7.5
5-5	Bos.	L	1-2		3	12	Arroyo	Urbina	Foulke	12-15	3rd	8.5
5-6	At L.A.	L	3-4		7	7	Escobar	Ledezma	Rodriguez	12-16	T3rd	9.5
5-7	At L.A.	W	2-1		8	5	Bonderman	Colon	Percival	13-16	3rd	9.5
5-8	At L.A.	W	10-1		13	3	Maroth	Washburn		14-16	3rd	9.5
5-9	At Tex.	W	2-0		8	7	Robertson	Cordero	Urbina	15-16	3rd	8.5
5-10	At Tex.	L	4-5		13	8	Brocail	Johnson	Cordero	15-17	3rd	8.5
5-11	At Tex.	W	6-5		11	7	Walker	Mahay	Urbina	16-17	3rd	8.5
5-14!	L.A.	L	2-4		9	11	Donnelly	Walker	Rodriguez	16-18		
5-14&	L.A.	W	3-2		9	7	Maroth	Washburn	Urbina	17-18	3rd	9.0
5-15	L.A.	L	3-9		10	11	Lackey	Robertson		17-19	3rd	9.0
5-17	T.B.	W	4-3	(11)	10	8	German	Harper		18-19	3rd	8.5
5-18	T.B.	W	6-4		11	6	Ledezma	Waechter	Urbina	19-19	3rd	8.5
5-19	T.B.	L	2-6		6	13	Kazmir	Maroth	Baez	19-20	3rd	9.0
5-20	Ari.	L	2-6		6	13	Webb	Walker	Bruney	19-21	3rd	10.0
5-21	Ari.	W	3-2	(11)	11	7	German	Bruney		20-21	3rd	10.0
5-22	Ari.	L	0-1		5	5	Vazquez	Johnson		20-22	3rd	10.0
5-24	At N.Y.	L	3-12		10	14	Mussina	Ledezma		20-23	3rd	10.5
5-25	At N.Y.	L	2-4		6	8	Wang	Maroth	Rivera	20-24	4th	11.5
5-26	At N.Y.	L	3-4		12	11	Brown	Bonderman	Rivera	20-25	4th	11.5
5-27	At Bal.	W	4-3		10	9	Robertson	Ponson	Urbina	21-25	4th	10.5
5-28	At Bal.	W	5-3		8	7	Johnson	Julio	Urbina	22-25	4th	10.0
5-29	At Bal.	W	8-6		13	9	Spurling	Reed	Urbina	23-25	4th	9.0
5-31	Tex.	L	2-8		5	15	Rogers	Maroth		23-26	4th	10.5
6-1	Tex.	W	6-4		11	10	Bonderman	Drese	Urbina	24-26	4th	9.5
6-2	Tex.	W	6-5	(10)	10	12	Urbina	Regilio		25-26	3rd	9.0
6-3	Bal.	W	5-3		8	7	Johnson	Chen	Farnsworth	26-26	3rd	9.0
6-4	Bal.	L	7-14		12	16	Reed	Walker		26-27	3rd	10.0
6-5	Bal.	L	2-6		5	10	Cabrera	Maroth		26-28	3rd	10.0
6-6	At L.A.	L	3-5		5	8	Lowe	Bonderman	Gagne	26-29	T3rd	11.0
6-7	At L.A.	W	8-4		13	5	Spurling	Sanchez		27-29	T3rd	11.0
6-8	At L.A.	L	1-3		2	9	Weaver	Johnson	Gagne	27-30	4th	12.0
6-10	At Col.	L	0-2		7	7	Wright	Maroth	Fuentes	27-31	4th	13.0
6-11	At Col.	W	6-4		12	9	Bonderman	Jennings	Percival	28-31	4th	12.0
6-12	At Col.	L	3-7		6	11	Kim	Robertson		28-32	4th	13.0
6-14	S.D.	W	8-4		9	8	Rodney	Peavy		29-32	4th	11.5
6-15	S.D.	W	8-2		11	7	Maroth	Eaton		30-32	4th	11.5
6-16	S.D.	W	3-1		6	4	Bonderman	Williams	Percival	31-32	4th	11.0
6-17	S.F.	L	0-4		7	9	Schmidt	Robertson	Walker	31-33	4th	12.0
6-18	S.F.	W	8-2		14	12	Johnson	Rueter		32-33	4th	12.0
6-19	S.F.	W	10-8	(10)	11	12	Walker	Eyre		33-33	4th	12.0

Date	Opp.	Res.	Score	(inn.*)	Hits	Opp. hits	Winning pitcher	Losing pitcher	Save	Record	Pos.	GB
6-21	At Min.	W	7-2		12	5	Bonderman	Lohse		34-33	4th	12.5
6-22	At Min.	W	8-1		11	5	Robertson	Mays		35-33	4th	12.5
6-23	At Min.	L	2-6		9	11	Silva	Johnson		35-34	4th	13.0
6-24	At Ari.	L	1-2		8	9	Estes	Maroth	Bruney	35-35	4th	14.0
6-25	At Ari.	W	5-1		11	6	Douglass	Vazquez		36-35	4th	13.0
6-26	At Ari.	L	7-13		10	14	Vargas	Bonderman		36-36	4th	13.0
6-28	Chi.	L	1-2		9	6	Buehrle	Robertson	Hermanson	36-37	4th	14.0
6-29	Chi.	L	3-4	(13)	15	12	Takatsu	Rodney		36-38	4th	15.0
6-30	Chi.	L	1-6		5	9	Garcia	Maroth		36-39	4th	16.0
7-1	N.Y.	W	10-2		12	8	Bonderman	Johnson		37-39	4th	15.0
7-2	N.Y.	L	4-8		7	13	Gordon	Percival		37-40	4th	16.0
7-3	N.Y.	L	0-1		6	9	Wang	Robertson	Rivera	37-41	4th	16.0
7-4#	At Cle.	L	3-9		6	14	Elarton	Johnson		37-42		
7-4$	At Cle.	L	0-6		6	12	Davis	Verlander		37-43	4th	17.5
7-5	At Cle.	W	3-2		7	6	Maroth	Westbrook	Percival	38-43	4th	17.5
7-6	At Cle.	W	7-3		15	8	Bonderman	Sabathia	Percival	39-43	4th	17.5
7-7	At T.B.	W	6-4		9	7	Douglass	McClung	Percival	40-43	4th	17.0
7-8	At T.B.	W	7-3		10	8	German	Kazmir		41-43	4th	16.0
7-9	At T.B.	L	4-5		13	10	Baez	Percival		41-44	4th	16.0
7-10	At T.B.	W	9-4		15	10	Maroth	Hendrickson		42-44	4th	15.0
7-14	K.C.	L	9-12		15	13	Greinke	Bonderman	MacDougal	42-45	4th	16.0
7-15	K.C.	W	4-1		11	8	Robertson	Lima	Farnsworth	43-45	4th	16.0
7-16	K.C.	W	5-3		10	7	Johnson	Wood	Farnsworth	44-45	4th	16.0
7-17	K.C.	L	0-5		6	10	Hernandez	Maroth		44-46	4th	17.0
7-18	At Chi.	L	5-7		7	10	Vizcaino	Spurling	Politte	44-47	4th	18.0
7-19	At Chi.	W	7-1		12	3	Bonderman	Contreras		45-47	4th	17.0
7-20	At Chi.	W	8-6		15	6	Robertson	Garcia	Dingman	46-47	4th	16.0
7-21	Min.	L	5-10		12	13	Santana	Johnson		46-48	4th	16.0
7-22	Min.	W	12-6		18	9	Maroth	Mays		47-48	4th	16.0
7-23#	Min.	W	2-1		9	6	Douglass	Silva	Farnsworth	48-48		
7-23$	Min.	L	2-5		6	11	Baker	Verlander	Nathan	48-49	4th	15.5
7-24	Min.	W	5-2		13	7	Bonderman	Lohse	Farnsworth	49-49	4th	15.5
7-25	At Sea.	L	3-5		6	11	Putz	Robertson	Guardado	49-50	4th	16.5
7-26	At Sea.	W	8-5		14	9	Johnson	Mateo	Farnsworth	50-50	4th	15.5
7-27	At Sea.	L	3-9		10	13	Moyer	Maroth		50-51	4th	15.5
7-29	At Oak.	L	4-8		15	8	Harden	Douglass		50-52	4th	16.5
7-30	At Oak.	L	5-9		10	13	Zito	Robertson	Witasick	50-53	4th	17.5
7-31	At Oak.	L	2-5		7	9	Saarloos	Bonderman		50-54	4th	18.5
8-2	Sea.	L	1-4		6	6	Mateo	Johnson	Guardado	50-55	4th	19.0
8-3	Sea.	W	10-7		13	10	Maroth	Meche	Rodney	51-55	4th	18.0
8-4	Sea.	W	3-1		7	3	Douglass	Hernandez	Rodney	52-55	4th	18.0
8-5	Cle.	L	6-9		6	16	Sabathia	Robertson	Howry	52-56	4th	18.0
8-6	Cle.	L	2-4		5	14	Westbrook	Bonderman	Wickman	52-57	4th	19.0
8-7	Cle.	L	5-6		9	8	Riske	Rodney	Wickman	52-58	4th	20.0
8-8	At Tor.	W	9-8	(12)	15	20	Darensbourg	Schoeneweis	Dingman	53-58	4th	19.0
8-9	At Tor.	L	4-6		11	7	McGowan	Douglass	Batista	53-59	4th	20.0
8-10	At Tor.	L	3-4		5	9	Speier	Dingman		53-60	4th	21.0
8-11	At Tor.	L	1-2		2	4	Downs	Bonderman	Batista	53-61	4th	21.5
8-14!	At K.C.	W	8-7		11	12	Dingman	Burgos	Rodney	54-61		
8-14&	At K.C.	W	1-0		5	5	Maroth	Lima	Rodney	55-61	4th	19.5
8-15	Bos.	W	7-6		16	8	Walker	Schilling		56-61	4th	18.5
8-16	Bos.	L	7-10	(10)	9	10	Bradford	Dingman		56-62	4th	18.5
8-17	Bos.	W	6-5		14	13	Bonderman	Wells	Rodney	57-62	4th	17.5
8-19	Tor.	W	9-5		12	12	Maroth	Bush	Dingman	58-62	4th	16.5
8-20	Tor.	W	3-2	(13)	11	5	German	Batista		59-62	4th	15.5
8-21	Tor.	W	17-6		15	11	Douglass	McGowan		60-62	4th	15.5
8-23	Oak.	W	4-1		10	2	Robertson	Haren	Rodney	61-62	4th	14.5
8-24	Oak.	L	2-9		10	15	Saarloos	Bonderman		61-63	4th	15.5
8-25	Oak.	L	1-11		7	15	Zito	Maroth		61-64	4th	16.5
8-26	At Bos.	L	8-9		13	10	Wakefield	Johnson	Timlin	61-65	4th	17.5
8-27	At Bos.	W	12-8		17	13	Colon	Papelbon		62-65	4th	17.5
8-28	At Bos.	L	3-11		10	14	Wells	Robertson		62-66	4th	17.5
8-29	At Cle.	L	8-10		12	12	Cabrera	Bonderman	Wickman	62-67	4th	17.5
8-31	At Cle.	W	4-3		10	6	Maroth	Betancourt	Rodney	63-67	4th	16.5
9-1	At Chi.	L	3-12		5	18	Contreras	Johnson		63-68	4th	17.5
9-2	At Chi.	L	1-9		3	9	Garcia	Douglass		63-69	4th	18.5
9-3	At Chi.	L	2-6		11	12	Buehrle	Robertson		63-70	4th	19.5
9-4	At Chi.	L	0-2		4	5	Garland	Bonderman		63-71	4th	20.5
9-5	Cle.	L	0-2		8	5	Elarton	Maroth	Wickman	63-72	4th	21.5

Date	Opp.	Res.	Score	(inn.*)	Hits	Opp. hits	Winning pitcher	Losing pitcher	Save	Record	Pos.	GB
9-6	Cle.	L	1-6		5	9	Lee	Johnson		63-73	4th	22.5
9-7	Cle.	L	1-4		4	7	Sabathia	Colon		63-74	4th	23.5
9-8	At Cle.	L	2-4		9	5	Betancourt	Robertson	Wickman	63-75	4th	23.5
9-9	K.C.	L	2-12		10	18	Greinke	Douglass		63-76	4th	23.5
9-10	K.C.	W	4-3		14	9	Spurling	Sisco	Rodney	64-76	4th	22.5
9-11	K.C.	W	14-4		18	13	Johnson	Lima		65-76	4th	21.5
9-12	Min.	L	1-2		7	13	Lohse	Spurling	Nathan	65-77	4th	22.0
9-13	Min.	L	3-9		6	14	Radke	Robertson		65-78	4th	23.0
9-14	Min.	W	4-2		9	8	Dingman	Rincon		66-78	4th	22.0
9-15	At L.A.	W	8-6		12	8	Maroth	Colon	Dingman	67-78	4th	21.0
9-16	At L.A.	L	6-7	(12)	9	17	Escobar	Darensbourg		67-79	4th	22.0
9-17	At L.A.	L	1-3		4	4	Santana	Spurling	Rodriguez	67-80	4th	22.0
9-18	At L.A.	L	3-5		11	11	Byrd	Ginter	Rodriguez	67-81	4th	23.0
9-19	At K.C.	L	4-10		5	18	Wood	Bonderman		67-82	4th	23.0
9-20!	At K.C.	L	4-5		9	11	MacDougal	Dingman		67-83		
9-20&	At K.C.	L	2-4		7	7	Greinke	Robertson	MacDougal	67-84	4th	24.5
9-21	At K.C.	L	3-4		8	8	Snyder	Rodney		67-85	4th	24.5
9-23	Sea.	L	1-2		7	7	Franklin	Spurling	Guardado	67-86	4th	25.0
9-24	Sea.	W	7-1		10	5	Grilli	Moyer		68-86	4th	25.0
9-25	Sea.	W	8-1		11	5	Maroth	Hasegawa		69-86	4th	25.0
9-26	Chi.	W	4-3		10	7	Rodney	Politte		70-86	4th	24.0
9-27	Chi.	W	3-2		9	8	Robertson	McCarthy	Rodney	71-86	4th	23.0
9-28	Chi.	L	2-8		10	15	Contreras	Douglass		71-87	4th	24.0
9-29	Chi.	L	2-4		10	10	Garcia	Grilli	Jenks	71-88	4th	25.0
9-30	At Min.	L	3-7		7	11	Liriano	Maroth		71-89	4th	26.0
10-1	At Min.	L	0-3		7	6	Baker	Johnson	Nathan	71-90	4th	27.0
10-2	At Min.	L	4-6		7	11	Santana	Robertson	Nathan	71-91	4th	28.0

Monthly records: April (11-11), May (12-15), June (13-13), July (14-15), August (13-13), September (8-22), October (0-2).
*Innings, if other than nine. ! First game of a doubleheader. & Second game of a doubleheader. # Day separate admission. $ Night separate admission.

RECORDS

2005 regular-season record: 71-91
Position: 4th in A.L. Central
Home: 39-42   **Road:** 32-49
A.L. East: 19-19   **A.L. Central:** 29-46
A.L. West: 14-17 **N.L.** 9-9
Vs. LH starters: 21-21
Vs. RH starters: 50-70
Grass: 65-80   **Artificial:** 6-11
Day: 26-31   **Night:** 45-60
1-Run: 22-26   **X-inn.:** 8-3
Doubleheaders: 1-1-1
Team record past five years: 307-502 (.379, ranks 14th in league in that span)

TEAM LEADERS

Batting average: Placido Polanco (.338).
At-bats: Brandon Inge (616).
Runs: Brandon Inge (75).
Hits: Brandon Inge (161).
Total Bases: Brandon Inge (258).
Doubles: Ivan Rodriguez (33).
Triples: Brandon Inge (9).
Home runs: Dmitri Young (21).
Runs batted in: Craig Monroe (89).
Stolen bases: Nook Logan (23).
Slugging percentage: Chris Shelton (.510).
On-base percentage: Placido Polanco (.386).
Wins: Jeremy Bonderman, Mike Maroth (14).
Earned-run average: Nate Robertson

(4.48).
Complete games: Jeremy Bonderman (4).
Shutouts: None.
Saves: Fernando Rodney, Ugueth Urbina (9).
Innings pitched: Jason Johnson (210.0).
Strikeouts: Jeremy Bonderman (145).

GAMES BY POSITION

Catcher: Ivan Rodriguez 123, Vance Wilson 60.
First base: Chris Shelton 84, Carlos Pena 51, Dmitri Young 30, Ramon Martinez 2, Jason Smith 1.
Second base: Placido Polanco 84, Omar Infante 69, John McDonald 8, Jason Smith 6, Ramon Martinez 4, Kevin Hooper 1.
Third base: Brandon Inge 160, Jason Smith 3, Ramon Martinez 1, John McDonald 1, Placido Polanco 1.
Shortstop: Carlos Guillen 75, Omar Infante 50, John McDonald 22, Jason Smith 15, Tony Giarratano 13, Ramon Martinez 12, Kevin Hooper 2.
Outfield: Craig Monroe 156, Nook Logan 123, Magglio Ordonez 81, Rondell White 65, Curtis Granderson 45, Marcus Thames 31, Dmitri Young 20, Alexis Gomez 9, Bobby Higginson 7, Kevin Hooper 3, Brandon Inge 2, Chris Shelton 1.
Designated hitter: Dmitri Young 71,

Rondell White 30, Carlos Pena 24, Chris Shelton 15, Carlos Guillen 10, Marcus Thames 4, Nook Logan 3, Ivan Rodriguez 3, Bobby Higginson 1, Craig Monroe 1, Magglio Ordonez 1, Jason Smith 1.

TOP DRAFT CHOICES

1. **Cameron Maybin**, OF, T.C. Roberson H.S., Arden, N.C.
3. **Chris Robinson**, C, Illinois.
4. **Kevin Whelan**, RHP, Texas A&M.
5. **Jeff Larish**, 1B, Arizona State.
6. **Clete Thomas**, OF, Auburn.
7. **P.J. Finigan**, RHP, Southern Illinois.
8. **Brendan Wise**, RHP, Pratt (Kan.) CC.
9. **Paul Coleman**, LHP, Pepperdine.
10. **Kevin Ardoin**, RHP, Louisiana-Lafayette.

KANSAS CITY ROYALS
AMERICAN LEAGUE CENTRAL DIVISION

2006 SEASON

Royals Schedule

Home games shaded.
All-Star Game July 11 at Pittsburgh. Schedule subject to change.

APRIL

SUN	MON	TUE	WED	THU	FRI	SAT
2	3 DET	4	5 DET	6	7 CHW	8 CHW
9 CHW	10	11 NYY	12 NYY	13 NYY	14 TB	15 TB
16 TB	17 CHW	18 CHW	19 CHW	20	21 CLE	22 CLE
23 CLE	24	25 MIN	26 MIN	27 MIN	28 OAK	29 OAK
30 OAK						

MAY

SUN	MON	TUE	WED	THU	FRI	SAT
	1 DET	2 DET	3 MIN	4 MIN	5 CHW	6 CHW
7 CHW	8 CLE	9 CLE	10 CLE	11	12 BAL	13 BAL
14 BAL	15 CLE	16 CLE	17 CLE	18 CLE	19 STL	20 STL
21 STL	22 DET	23 DET	24 DET	25 DET	26 NYY	27 NYY
28 NYY	29 OAK	30 OAK	31 OAK			

JUNE

SUN	MON	TUE	WED	THU	FRI	SAT
				1	2 SEA	3 SEA
4 SEA	5 SEA	6 TEX	7 TEX	8 TEX	9 TB	10 TB
11 TB	12 LAA	13 LAA	14 LAA	15 LAA	16 HOU	17 HOU
18 HOU	19	20 PIT	21 PIT	22 PIT	23 MIL	24 MIL
25 MIL	26	27 CIN	28 CIN	29 CIN	30 STL	

JULY

SUN	MON	TUE	WED	THU	FRI	SAT
						1 STL
2 STL	3 MIN	4 MIN	5 MIN	6 TOR	7 TOR	8 TOR
9 TOR	10	11 ALL-STAR	12	13 DET	14 DET	15 DET
16 DET	17 BOS	18 BOS	19 BOS	20 LAA	21 LAA	22 LAA
23 LAA	24	25 BAL	26 BAL	27 BAL	28 TEX	29 TEX
30 TEX	31 CHW					

AUGUST

SUN	MON	TUE	WED	THU	FRI	SAT
		1 CHW	2 CHW	3 MIN	4 MIN	5 MIN
6 MIN	7	8 BOS	9 BOS	10 BOS	11 CLE	12 CLE
13 CLE	14 CHW	15 CHW	16 CHW	17 CHW	18 OAK	19 OAK
20 OAK	21	22 CLE	23 CLE	24 CLE	25 TOR	26 TOR
27 TOR	28	29 MIN	30 MIN	31 MIN		

SEPTEMBER

SUN	MON	TUE	WED	THU	FRI	SAT
					1 CHW	2 CHW
3 CHW	4 NYY	5 NYY	6 NYY	7	8 BOS	9 BOS
10 BOS	11	12 CLE	13 CLE	14 SEA	15 SEA	16 SEA
17 SEA	18	19 LAA	20 LAA	21	22 DET	23 DET
24 DET	25 MIN	26 MIN	27 MIN	28 MIN	29 DET	30 DET

OCTOBER

SUN	MON	TUE	WED	THU	FRI	SAT
1 DET	2	3	4	5	6	7

Home games are shaded. All-Star Game is July 11 at Pittsburgh. Schedule is subject to change.

DeJesus

CLUB DIRECTORY

Chairman/owner
David Glass
President
Dan Glass
Senior v.p. & g.m./baseball operations
Allard Baird
Senior v.p./baseball operations
Mark Gorris
V.p. and asst. g.m./baseball operations
Muzzy Jackson
Vice president/baseball operations
George Brett
V.p./finance and administration
Dale Rohr
V.p./communications and marketing
David Witty
V.p./ballpark operations and development
Bob Rice
Senior adviser to the general manager
Art Stewart

Assistant to the general manager
Brian Murphy
Director/baseball operations
Jin Wong
Sr. director/team travel and assistant to baseball operations
Jeff Davenport
Senior director/player personnel
Donny Rowland
Senior director, scouting
Deric Ladnier
Director/player development
Shaun McGinn
Director/media relations
Aaron Babcock
Director/public relations
Lora Grosshans
Director/community relations
Ben Aken

MINOR LEAGUE AFFILIATES

Class	Team	League	Manager
AAA	Omaha	Pacific Coast	Mike Jirschele
AA	Wichita	Texas	Frank White
Advanced A	High Desert	California	To be announced
A	Burlington	Midwest	Jim Gabella
Advanced Rookie	Idaho Falls	Pioneer	Brian Rupp
Rookie	Royals	Arizona	Lloyd Simmons

BROADCAST INFORMATION

Radio: WHB-AM (810).
Cable TV: Royals Television Network, LLC.

SPRING TRAINING

Ballpark (city): Surprise Stadium (Surprise, Ariz.).
Ticket information: 623-594-5600.

For more on the Royals, go to www.sportingnews.com/baseball/teams/royals/

– 33 –

SPRING TRAINING ROSTER

Manager—Buddy Bell (25).
Coaches—Andre David (26), Billy Doran (13), Fred Kendall (18), Bob McClure (57), Brian Poldberg (49), Luis Silverio (17).

No.	PITCHERS	B/T	Ht./Wt.	Age*
48	Jeremy Affeldt	L/L	6-4/220	26
	Brian Bass	R/R	6-0/200	24
27	Denny Bautista	R/R	6-5/180	25
50	Ambiorix Burgos	R/R	6-3/235	21
	Juan Cedeno	L/L	6-1/160	22
	Elmer Dessens	R/R	5-10/200	35
	Scott Elarton	R/R	6-8/240	30
41	Jimmy Gobble	L/L	6-3/200	24
23	Zack Greinke	R/R	6-2/175	22
40	Runelvys Hernandez	R/R	6-1/250	27
53	J.P. Howell	L/L	6-0/175	22
54	Mike MacDougal	B/R	6-4/185	29
	Bobby Madritsch	L/L	6-2/220	30
	Joe Mays	B/R	6-1/200	30
43	Leo Nunez	R/R	6-1/160	22
	Joel Peralta	R/R	5-11/170	30
	Mark Redman	L/L	6-5/245	32
51	Andrew Sisco	L/L	6-10/270	23
46	Mike Wood	R/R	6-3/210	25

No.	CATCHERS	B/T	Ht./Wt.	Age*
	Paul Bako	L/R	6-2/215	33
2	John Buck	R/R	6-3/220	25
11	Paul Phillips	R/R	5-11/200	28

No.	INFIELDERS	B/T	Ht./Wt.	Age*
4	Angel Berroa	R/R	6-0/180	28
7	Andres Blanco	B/R	5-10/180	21
	Esteban German	R/R	5-9/165	28
30	Ruben Gotay	B/R	5-11/175	23
	Mark Grudzielanek	R/R	6-1/190	35
16	Justin Huber	R/R	6-2/200	23
	Doug Mientkiewicz	L/R	6-2/205	31
31	Donnie Murphy	R/R	5-10/200	23
	Angel Sanchez	R/R	6-2/180	22
29	Mike Sweeney	R/R	6-3/235	32
24	Mark Teahen	L/R	6-3/210	24

No.	OUTFIELDERS	B/T	Ht./Wt.	Age*
18	Chip Ambres	R/R	6-1/190	26
35	Emil Brown	R/R	6-2/200	31
15	Shane Costa	L/R	6-0/220	24
9	David DeJesus	L/L	6-0/185	26
45	Aaron Guiel	L/R	5-10/200	33
	Reggie Sanders	R/R	6-1/205	38
12	Matt Stairs	L/R	5-9/215	38

*Age as of April 1, 2006.

BALLPARK INFORMATION

Ballpark (capacity, surface)
Kauffman Stadium (40,793, grass)
Address
P.O. Box 419969
Kansas City, MO 64141-6969
Official website
www.royals.com
Business phone
816-921-8000
Ticket information
816-504-4040, 800-6ROYALS
Field dimensions (from home plate)
To left field at foul line, 330 feet
To center field, 410 feet
To right field at foul line, 330 feet
First game played
April 10, 1973 (Royals 12, Rangers 1)

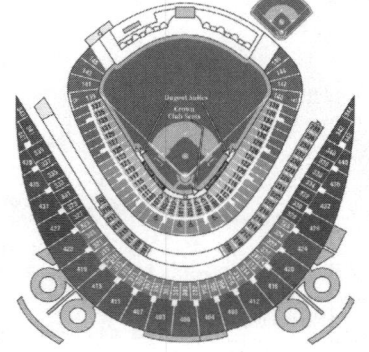

Date	Opp.	Res.	Score	(inn.*)	Hits	Opp. hits	Winning pitcher	Losing pitcher	Save	Record	Pos.	GB
4-4	At Det.	L	2-11		7	13	Bonderman	Lima		0-1	T3rd	1.0
4-6	At Det.	W	7-2		15	6	Hernandez	Maroth		1-1	T3rd	1.0
4-7	At Det.	L	3-7		9	14	Johnson	Wood		1-2	T4th	1.0
4-8	At L.A.	W	6-2		10	5	Bautista	Byrd		2-2	T2nd	1.0
4-9	At L.A.	L	3-8		3	10	Gregg	Lima		2-3	T3rd	2.0
4-10	At L.A.	W	8-3		17	6	Anderson	Colon		3-3	T2nd	1.0
4-11	Sea.	L	2-8		6	13	Franklin	Hernandez		3-4	T4th	2.0
4-13	Sea.	L	1-2		4	7	Sele	Cerda	Guardado	3-5	T3rd	3.0
4-14	Sea.	L	2-10		11	10	Moyer	Bautista		3-6	T4th	3.0
4-15	Det.	W	6-5		10	7	Cerda	Urbina	MacDougal	4-6	T3rd	3.0
4-16	Det.	L	1-7		6	12	Bonderman	Anderson		4-7	T3rd	4.0
4-17	Det.	L	1-6		5	12	Maroth	Hernandez		4-8	5th	4.0
4-18	Cle.	L	1-5		3	8	Lee	Greinke		4-9	5th	5.0
4-19	Cle.	W	6-5		15	14	MacDougal	Rhodes		5-9	5th	5.0
4-20	At Min.	L	4-5		6	9	Rincon	Cerda	Nathan	5-10	5th	6.0
4-21	At Min.	L	9-10	(10)	13	16	Nathan	Camp		5-11	5th	7.0
4-22	Chi.	L	2-8		4	12	Garcia	Hernandez		5-12	5th	8.0
4-23	Chi.	L	2-3	(10)	7	10	Marte	MacDougal		5-13	5th	9.0
4-24	Chi.	L	3-4		5	6	Cotts	Camp	Takatsu	5-14	5th	10.0
4-26	Min.	L	1-2		5	7	Santana	Burgos	Nathan	5-15	5th	10.5
4-27	Min.	L	4-9		8	9	Mays	Anderson		5-16	5th	10.5
4-28	Min.	L	5-6	(11)	10	10	Crain	Wood		5-17	5th	11.0
4-29	At Cle.	L	0-6		3	11	Sabathia	Greinke		5-18	5th	11.0
4-30	At Cle.	W	8-1		12	6	Bautista	Lee		6-18	5th	11.0
5-1	At Cle.	W	6-5		8	4	Wood	Betancourt	Burgos	7-18	5th	11.0
5-3	At Chi.	L	4-5		8	11	Buehrle	Sisco	Takatsu	7-19	5th	12.0
5-4	At Chi.	L	2-4		9	6	Garcia	Hernandez	Hermanson	7-20	5th	13.0
5-5	At Chi.	L	1-2		4	2	Contreras	Greinke	Takatsu	7-21	5th	14.0
5-6	At Bal.	L	1-3		5	7	Ponson	Bautista	Ryan	7-22	5th	15.0
5-7	At Bal.	L	3-5		7	8	Chen	Lima	Ryan	7-23	5th	16.0
5-8	At Bal.	W	10-8		9	11	Burgos	Williams		8-23	5th	16.0
5-9	At Tor.	L	1-6		7	9	Towers	Hernandez		8-24	5th	16.0
5-10	At Tor.	L	1-3		8	6	Halladay	Greinke		8-25	5th	16.0
5-11	At Tor.	L	9-12		16	12	Batista	Burgos		8-26	5th	17.0
5-12	T.B.	W	7-5	(7)	7	7	Wood	Carter		9-26	5th	17.0
5-13	T.B.	L	2-3		4	8	Baez	Burgos		9-27	5th	18.0
5-14	T.B.	W	6-5		6	9	Hernandez	Colome	Wood	10-27	5th	17.0
5-15	T.B.	W	4-3		9	9	MacDougal	Hendrickson	Wood	11-27	5th	16.0
5-17	Bal.	L	8-12		12	15	Parrish	Cerda	Ryan	11-28	5th	16.5
5-18	Bal.	L	4-7		9	14	Chen	Carrasco	Ryan	11-29	5th	17.5
5-19	Bal.	W	7-4		5	6	Nunez	Lopez	MacDougal	12-29	5th	17.0
5-20	StL.	L	6-7		10	13	Mulder	Greinke	Isringhausen	12-30	5th	18.0
5-21	StL.	L	5-6		9	7	Morris	Cerda	Isringhausen	12-31	5th	19.0
5-22	StL.	W	9-2		12	4	Jensen	Suppan		13-31	5th	18.0
5-24	At Tex.	L	3-4		10	7	Drese	Hernandez	Cordero	13-32	5th	18.5
5-25	At Tex.	L	3-7		7	14	Astacio	Greinke		13-33	5th	19.5
5-26	At Tex.	L	1-8		6	7	Rogers	Lima		13-34	5th	19.5
5-27	At L.A.	L	8-9	(10)	12	12	Shields	MacDougal		13-35	5th	19.5
5-28	At L.A.	L	1-14		6	16	Escobar	Jensen	Bootcheck	13-36	5th	20.0
5-29	At L.A.	L	6-7		16	10	Colon	Hernandez	Shields	13-37	5th	20.0
5-31	N.Y.	W	5-3		10	5	Greinke	Brown	MacDougal	14-37	5th	20.5
6-1	N.Y.	W	3-1		9	7	Carrasco	Johnson	MacDougal	15-37	5th	19.5
6-2	N.Y.	W	5-2		9	7	Jensen	Pavano	Burgos	16-37	5th	19.0
6-3	Tex.	W	2-1		7	4	Sisco	Astacio	MacDougal	17-37	5th	19.0
6-4	Tex.	L	9-14		17	19	Park	Lima		17-38	5th	20.0
6-5	Tex.	L	1-8		5	13	Rogers	Greinke		17-39	5th	20.0
6-7	At S.F.	W	8-1		13	5	Carrasco	Rueter		18-39	5th	20.5
6-8	At S.F.	W	4-1		9	6	Hernandez	Fassero	MacDougal	19-39	5th	20.5
6-9	At S.F.	L	7-9		13	14	Munter	Nunez	Walker	19-40	5th	21.0
6-10	At Ari.	L	11-12	(10)	13	20	Bruney	MacDougal		19-41	5th	22.0
6-11	At Ari.	W	8-5		18	11	Howell	Halsey		20-41	5th	21.0
6-12	At Ari.	W	9-4	(12)	15	12	Jensen	Lopez		21-41	5th	21.0
6-14	L.A.	W	3-2		7	9	Hernandez	Weaver	MacDougal	22-41	5th	19.5
6-15	L.A.	W	3-1		8	5	Lima	Penny	MacDougal	23-41	5th	19.5
6-16	L.A.	W	9-6		15	11	Wood	Lowe		24-41	5th	19.0
6-17	Hou.	L	0-7		9	9	Clemens	Howell		24-42	5th	20.0

Date	Opp.	Res.	Score	(inn.*)	Hits	Opp. hits	Winning pitcher	Losing pitcher	Save	Record	Pos.	GB
6-18	Hou.	L	2-6		9	10	Oswalt	Carrasco		24-43	5th	21.0
6-19	Hou.	W	7-1		11	2	Hernandez	Backe		25-43	5th	21.0
6-20	At Chi.	L	8-11		10	17	Cotts	Jensen	Hermanson	25-44	5th	22.0
6-21	At Chi.	L	1-5		4	10	Garland	Greinke		25-45	5th	23.0
6-22	At Chi.	L	1-5		5	8	Buehrle	Howell		25-46	5th	24.0
6-24	At Col.	L	4-12		9	13	Kim	Carrasco		25-47	5th	25.0
6-25	At Col.	L	2-4		6	7	Francis	Hernandez	Fuentes	25-48	5th	25.0
6-26	At Col.	L	4-9		10	12	Kennedy	Lima		25-49	5th	25.0
6-27	At Min.	L	1-3		6	8	Mays	Greinke	Nathan	25-50	5th	25.5
6-28	At Min.	L	8-11		14	15	Crain	Sisco	Nathan	25-51	5th	26.5
6-29	At Min.	W	3-1		11	6	Carrasco	Radke	MacDougal	26-51	5th	26.5
7-1	L.A.	L	0-5		2	10	Byrd	Hernandez		26-52	5th	27.0
7-2	L.A.	L	3-5		5	14	Colon	Lima	Rodriguez	26-53	5th	28.0
7-3	L.A.	L	0-5	(6)	4	12	Washburn	Greinke		26-54	5th	28.0
7-4	Sea.	L	0-6		6	11	Franklin	Howell		26-55	5th	29.0
7-5	Sea.	W	8-6		7	14	Carrasco	Meche	MacDougal	27-55	5th	29.0
7-6	Sea.	W	5-1		12	10	Hernandez	Sele	MacDougal	28-55	5th	29.0
7-7	Min.	W	8-5		12	12	Lima	Lohse		29-55	5th	28.5
7-8	Min.	L	4-5		11	11	Radke	Greinke	Nathan	29-56	5th	28.5
7-9	Min.	W	12-8		21	12	Nunez	Crain		30-56	5th	27.5
7-10	Min.	L	2-3	(12)	7	15	Romero	Wood	Crain	30-57	5th	27.5
7-14	At Det.	L	12-9		13	15	Greinke	Bonderman	MacDougal	31-57	5th	27.5
7-15	At Det.	L	1-4		8	11	Robertson	Lima	Farnsworth	31-58	5th	28.5
7-16	At Det.	L	3-5		7	10	Johnson	Wood	Farnsworth	31-59	5th	29.5
7-17	At Det.	W	5-0		10	6	Hernandez	Maroth		32-59	5th	29.5
7-18	At Cle.	L	2-6	(5)	4	10	Lee	Carrasco		32-60	5th	30.5
7-19	At Cle.	W	4-0		7	5	Greinke	Millwood		33-60	5th	29.5
7-20	At Cle.	W	5-3		11	10	Lima	Sabathia	MacDougal	34-60	5th	28.5
7-21	At Cle.	L	1-10		11	11	Westbrook	Howell		34-61	5th	28.5
7-22	Tor.	W	5-3		6	9	Hernandez	Walker	MacDougal	35-61	5th	28.5
7-23	Tor.	L	4-9		10	10	Bush	Snyder		35-62	5th	28.5
7-24	Tor.	W	6-5		9	10	Carrasco	Gaudin	MacDougal	36-62	5th	28.5
7-25	Chi.	L	6-14		16	22	Garcia	Greinke		36-63	5th	29.5
7-26	Chi.	W	7-1		8	8	Lima	Buehrle		37-63	5th	28.5
7-27	Chi.	W	6-5	(13)	12	8	Camp	Vizcaino		38-63	5th	27.5
7-28	At T.B.	L	5-10		7	14	Kazmir	Snyder		38-64	5th	28.0
7-29	At T.B.	L	3-6		9	11	Fossum	Carrasco	Baez	38-65	5th	29.0
7-30	At T.B.	L	3-7		7	11	Waechter	Greinke		38-66	5th	30.0
7-31	At T.B.	L	2-6		5	13	Hendrickson	Lima		38-67	5th	31.0
8-2	At Bos.	L	4-6		8	10	Wakefield	Burgos	Schilling	38-68	5th	31.5
8-3	At Bos.	L	5-8		6	12	Miller	Snyder	Schilling	38-69	5th	31.5
8-4	At Bos.	L	9-11		10	9	Clement	Nunez	Schilling	38-70	5th	32.5
8-5	Oak.	L	4-5		8	8	Kennedy	Affeldt	Street	38-71	5th	32.5
8-6	Oak.	L	1-16		7	18	Blanton	Lima		38-72	5th	33.5
8-7	Oak.	L	0-11		8	15	Haren	Hernandez		38-73	5th	34.5
8-9	Cle.	L	7-13		10	17	Sauerbeck	MacDougal		38-74	5th	35.0
8-10	Cle.	L	1-6		7	13	Sabathia	Greinke		38-75	5th	36.0
8-11	Cle.	L	2-4		9	6	Millwood	Carrasco	Wickman	38-76	5th	36.5
8-14!	Det.	L	7-8		12	11	Dingman	Burgos	Rodney	38-77		
8-14&	Det.	L	0-1		5	5	Maroth	Lima	Rodney	38-78	5th	36.5
8-15	At Sea.	L	3-11		6	13	Hernandez	Hernandez		38-79	5th	36.5
8-16	At Sea.	L	3-4		6	10	Pineiro	Affeldt	Guardado	38-80	5th	36.5
8-17	At Sea.	L	5-11		7	14	Moyer	Carrasco		38-81	5th	36.5
8-19	At Oak.	L	0-4		5	9	Harden	Lima	Street	38-82	5th	36.5
8-20	At Oak.	W	2-1		4	6	Wood	Zito	MacDougal	39-82	5th	35.5
8-21	At Oak.	W	5-4	(12)	11	10	Gobble	Calero		40-82	5th	35.5
8-23	Bos.	L	2-5		8	9	Wells	Greinke		40-83	5th	35.5
8-24	Bos.	W	4-3	(11)	9	10	Sisco	Arroyo		41-83	5th	35.5
8-25	Bos.	W	7-4		12	7	Lima	Schilling	MacDougal	42-83	5th	35.5
8-26	At N.Y.	L	1-5		6	8	Johnson	Wood		42-84	5th	36.5
8-27	At N.Y.	L	7-8		12	9	Embree	Camp		42-85	5th	37.5
8-28	At N.Y.	L	3-10		5	15	Leiter	Greinke		42-86	5th	37.5
8-29	Min.	L	1-3	(10)	5	8	Rincon	Camp	Nathan	42-87	5th	37.5
8-30	Min.	L	4-7		11	11	Silva	Lima	Nathan	42-88	5th	38.0
8-31	Min.	W	1-0		5	13	MacDougal	Guerrier		43-88	5th	37.0
9-1	Tex.	L	4-5		12	7	Rogers	Howell	Cordero	43-89	5th	38.0
9-2	Tex.	L	7-8	(10)	14	13	Cordero	MacDougal	Wasdin	43-90	5th	39.0
9-3	Tex.	L	3-5		5	10	Dominguez	Carrasco		43-91	5th	40.0
9-4	Tex.	W	17-8		18	12	Nunez	Volquez		44-91	5th	40.0

Date	Opp.	Res.	Score	(inn.*)	Hits	Opp. hits	Winning pitcher	Losing pitcher	Save	Record	Pos.	GB
9-6	At Chi.	L	5-6		9	11	Hernandez	Lima	Hermanson	44-92	5th	41.5
9-7	At Chi.	L	0-1		6	6	Contreras	Wood	Hermanson	44-93	5th	42.5
9-8	At Chi.	W	4-2		10	2	Howell	Garcia	MacDougal	45-93	5th	41.5
9-9	At Det.	W	12-2		18	10	Greinke	Douglass		46-93	5th	40.5
9-10	At Det.	L	3-4		9	14	Spurling	Sisco	Rodney	46-94	5th	40.5
9-11	At Det.	L	4-14		13	18	Johnson	Lima		46-95	5th	40.5
9-13	Chi.	L	4-6		7	14	Contreras	Wood	Jenks	46-96	5th	41.5
9-14	Chi.	W	10-9		15	14	Demaria	Hermanson		47-96	5th	40.5
9-15	Chi.	W	7-5		14	12	Burgos	Buehrle	MacDougal	48-96	5th	39.5
9-16	At Cle.	L	1-3		6	6	Elarton	Gobble	Wickman	48-97	5th	40.5
9-17	At Cle.	L	4-5		6	11	Lee	Hernandez	Wickman	48-98	5th	40.5
9-18	At Cle.	L	0-11		5	16	Sabathia	Lima		48-99	5th	41.5
9-19	Det.	W	10-4		18	5	Wood	Bonderman		49-99	5th	40.5
9-20!	Det.	W	5-4		11	9	MacDougal	Dingman		50-99		
9-20&	Det.	W	4-2		7	7	Greinke	Robertson	MacDougal	51-99	5th	40.0
9-21	Det.	W	4-3		8	8	Snyder	Rodney		52-99	5th	39.0
9-22	Cle.	L	6-11		12	15	Lee	Sisco	Betancourt	52-100	5th	39.0
9-23	Cle.	L	6-7		8	10	Howry	MacDougal	Wickman	52-101	5th	40.0
9-24	Cle.	L	4-11		9	16	Millwood	Wood		52-102	5th	41.0
9-25	Cle.	W	5-4		9	8	MacDougal	Howry		53-102	5th	41.0
9-26	At Min.	W	5-0		7	3	Howell	Baker		54-102	5th	40.0
9-27	At Min.	L	1-3		6	6	Santana	Hernandez	Nathan	54-103	5th	40.0
9-28	At Min.	L	3-6		8	8	Crain	Sisco	Nathan	54-104	5th	41.0
9-29	At Min.	W	10-6		11	11	Carrasco	Bowyer		55-104	5th	41.0
9-30	At Tor.	L	1-10		9	15	Towers	Greinke		55-105	5th	42.0
10-1	At Tor.	W	7-6		12	6	Burgos	Walker	MacDougal	56-105	5th	42.0
10-2	At Tor.	L	2-7		7	14	Chacin	Hernandez		56-106	5th	43.0

Monthly records: April (6-18), May (8-19), June (12-14), July (12-16), August (5-21), September (12-17), October (1-1).
*Innings, if other than nine. ! First game of a doubleheader. & Second game of a doubleheader.

RECORDS

2005 regular-season record: 56-106
Position: 5th in A.L. Central
Home: 34-47   **Road:** 22-59
A.L. East: 13-22   **A.L. Central:** 26-49
A.L. West: 8-26   **N.L.** 9-9
Vs. LH starters: 17-38
Vs. RH starters: 39-68
Grass: 52-91   **Artificial:** 4-15
Day: 22-32   **Night:** 34-74
1-Run: 18-30   **X-inn.:** 4-8
Doubleheaders: 1-1-0
Team record past five years: 324-486
(.400, ranks 12th in league in that span)

TEAM LEADERS

Batting average: Mike Sweeney (.300).
At-bats: Angel Berroa (608).
Runs: Emil Brown (75).
Hits: Angel Berroa (164).
Total Bases: Emil Brown (248).
Doubles: Mike Sweeney (39).
Triples: David DeJesus (6).
Home runs: Mike Sweeney (21).
Runs batted in: Emil Brown (86).
Stolen bases: Emil Brown (10).
Slugging percentage: Mike Sweeney (.517).
On-base percentage: Matt Stairs (.373).
Wins: Runelvys Hernandez (8).
Earned-run average: Mike Wood (4.46).

Complete games: Zack Greinke (2).
Shutouts: None.
Saves: Mike MacDougal (21).
Innings pitched: Zack Greinke (183.0).
Strikeouts: Zack Greinke (114).

GAMES BY POSITION

Catcher: John Buck 117, Alberto Castillo 34, Paul Phillips 20.
First base: Matt Stairs 64, Mike Sweeney 49, Tony Graffanino 22, Joe McEwing 20, Justin Huber 19, Eli Marrero 9, Ken Harvey 5.
Second base: Ruben Gotay 81, Donnie Murphy 29, Andres Blanco 24, Tony Graffanino 22, Denny Hocking 13, Joe McEwing 11.
Third base: Mark Teahen 128, Joe McEwing 29, Tony Graffanino 17, Denny Hocking 1.
Shortstop: Angel Berroa 159, Andres Blanco 7, Joe McEwing 6, Donnie Murphy 2, Tony Graffanino 1, Denny Hocking 1.
Outfield: Emil Brown 139, Terrence Long 121, David DeJesus 119, Chip Ambres 47, Aaron Guiel 30, Matt Diaz 21, Shane Costa 20, Eli Marrero 20, Matt Stairs 15, Joe McEwing 5.
Designated hitter: Mike Sweeney 73, Matt Stairs 40, Emil Brown 10, Matt Diaz 7, Ken Harvey 7, Calvin Pickering 7,

Joe McEwing 6, Shane Costa 4, Justin Huber 4, Terrence Long 4, Chip Ambres 2, Ruben Gotay 2, Eli Marrero 2, Paul Phillips 2, Tony Graffanino 1, Aaron Guiel 1, Donnie Murphy 1.

TOP DRAFT CHOICES

1. **Alex Gordon,** 3B, Nebraska.
2. **Jeff Bianchi,** SS, Lampeter-Strasburg H.S., Lancaster, Pa.
3. **Chris Nicoll,** RHP, UC Irvine.
4. **Joe Dickerson,** OF, Esperanza H.S., Yorba Linda, Calif.
5. **Shawn Hayes,** SS, Franklin Pierce College.
6. **Ryan DiPietro,** LHP, Eastern Connecticut State.
7. **Brent Fisher,** LHP, Tolleson Union H.S., Goodyear, Ariz.
8. **Nick Doscher,** C, Moore Catholic H.S., Staten Island, N.Y.
9. **Kiel Thibault,** C, Gonzaga.
10. **Jeff Howell** C, Florida Southern.

LOS ANGELES ANGELS OF ANAHEIM
AMERICAN LEAGUE WEST DIVISION

2006 SEASON

Angels Schedule
Home games shaded.
All-Star Game July 11 at Pittsburgh. Schedule subject to change.

APRIL

SUN	MON	TUE	WED	THU	FRI	SAT
2	3 SEA	4 SEA	5 SEA	6	7 NYY	8 NYY
9 NYY	10 TEX	11 TEX	12 TEX	13	14 BAL	15 BAL
16 BAL	17 BAL	18 MIN	19 MIN	20 MIN	21 OAK	22 OAK
23 OAK	24 DET	25 DET	26 DET	27	28 CHW	29 CHW
30 CHW						

MAY

SUN	MON	TUE	WED	THU	FRI	SAT
	1 OAK	2 OAK	3 DET	4 DET	5 TOR	6 TOR
7 TOR	8 TOR	9 CHW	10 CHW	11 CHW	12 SEA	13 SEA
14 SEA	15	16 TOR	17 TOR	18 TOR	19 LAD	20 LAD
21 LAD	22 TEX	23 TEX	24 TEX	25	26 BAL	27 BAL
28 BAL	29 MIN	30 MIN	31 MIN			

JUNE

SUN	MON	TUE	WED	THU	FRI	SAT
				1	2 CLE	3 CLE
4 CLE	5 TB	6 TB	7 TB	8	9 SEA	10 SEA
11 SEA	12 KC	13 KC	14 KC	15 KC	16 SD	17 SD
18 SD	19 SF	20 SF	21 SF	22	23 ARI	24 ARI
25 ARI	26 COL	27 COL	28 COL	29	30 LAD	

JULY

SUN	MON	TUE	WED	THU	FRI	SAT
						1 LAD
2 LAD	3 SEA	4 SEA	5 SEA	6 OAK	7 OAK	8 OAK
9 OAK	10	11 ALL-	12	13	14 TB	15 TB
16 TB	17 CLE	18 CLE	19 CLE	20 KC	21 KC	22 KC
23 KC	24 TB	25 TB	26 TB	27	28 BOS	29 BOS
30 BOS	31 OAK					

AUGUST

SUN	MON	TUE	WED	THU	FRI	SAT
		1 OAK	2 OAK	3 TEX	4 TEX	5 TEX
6 TEX	7	8 CLE	9 CLE	10 CLE	11 NYY	12 NYY
13 NYY	14 NYY	15 TEX	16 TEX	17 SEA	18 SEA	19 SEA
20 SEA	21	22 BOS	23 BOS	24 BOS	25 NYY	25 NYY
27 NYY	28 SEA	29 SEA	30 SEA	31		

SEPTEMBER

SUN	MON	TUE	WED	THU	FRI	SAT
					1 DET	2 DET
3 DET	4 BAL	5 BAL	6 BAL	7	8 TOR	9 TOR
10 TOR	11 CHW	12 CHW	13 CHW	14 TEX	15 TEX	16 TEX
17 TEX	18	19 KC	20 KC	21	22 OAK	23 OAK
24 OAK	25 TEX	26 TEX	27 TEX	28 OAK	29 OAK	30 OAK

OCTOBER

SUN	MON	TUE	WED	THU	FRI	SAT
1 OAK	2	3	4	5	6	7

Home games are shaded. All-Star
Game is July 11 at Pittsburgh.
Schedule is subject to change.

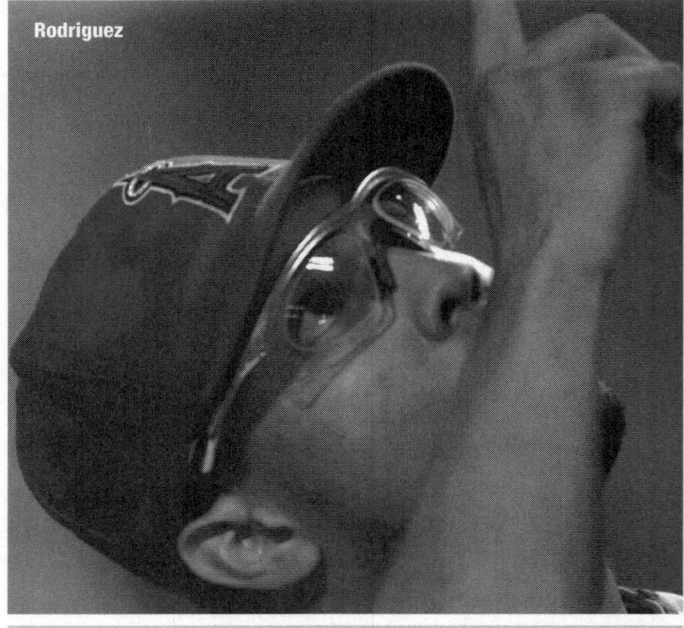

Rodriguez

CLUB DIRECTORY

Owner
Arturo Moreno
President
Dennis Kuhl
Vice president and general manager
Bill Stoneman
Vice president, communications
Tim Mead
Assistant general manager
Ken Forsch
Special assistant to the general manager
Gary Sutherland

Director, scouting
Eddie Bane
Director, player development
Tony Reagins
Manager, baseball operations
Abe Flores
Director, communications
Nancy Mazmanian
Communications/media relations mgrs.
Larry Babcock
Eric Kay
Manager, community development
Matt Bennett

MINOR LEAGUE AFFILIATES

Class	Team	League	Manager
AAA	Salt Lake	Pacific Coast	Brian Harper
AA	Arkansas	Texas	Tyrone Boykin
Advanced A	Rancho Cucamonga	California	Bobby Mitchell
A	Cedar Rapids	Midwest	Bobby Magallanes
Advanced Rookie	Orem Owlz	Pioneer	Tom Kotchman
Rookie	Angels	Arizona	Ever Magallanes

BROADCAST INFORMATION

Radio: ESPN-AM (710).
TV: To be announced.
Cable TV: FSN West.

SPRING TRAINING

Ballpark (city): Tempe Diablo Stadium
(Tempe, Ariz.).
Ticket information: 714-940-2000.

For more on the Angels, go to www.sportingnews.com/baseball/teams/angels/

Manager—Mike Scioscia (14).
Coaches—Bud Black (24), Dino Ebel (21), Alfredo Griffin (4), Mickey Hatcher (7), Orlando Mercado (48), Ron Roenicke (10), Steve Soliz (12).

No.	PITCHERS	B/T	Ht./Wt.	Age*
	Jose Arredondo	R/R	6-0/170	22
	Chris Bootcheck	R/R	6-5/200	27
	Hector Carrasco	R/R	6-2/225	36
40	Bartolo Colon	R/R	5-11/250	32
53	Brendan Donnelly	R/R	6-3/240	34
	Scott Dunn	R/R	6-3/200	27
45	Kelvim Escobar	R/R	6-1/230	29
62	Kevin Gregg	R/R	6-6/235	27
	Greg Jones	R/R	6-2/195	29
41	John Lackey	R/R	6-6/235	27
57	Francisco Rodriguez	R/R	6-0/180	24
	J.C. Romero	B/L	5-11/205	29
54	Ervin Santana	R/R	6-2/160	23
	Joe Saunders	L/L	6-3/210	24
	Steven Shell	R/R	6-5/190	23
62	Scot Shields	R/R	6-1/170	30
59	Esteban Yan	R/R	6-4/255	30

No.	CATCHERS	B/T	Ht./Wt.	Age*
44	Jeff Mathis	R/R	6-0/180	23
28	Jose Molina	R/R	6-2/220	30
	Michael Napoli	R/R	6-0/205	24

No.	INFIELDERS	B/T	Ht./Wt.	Age*
	Edgardo Alfonzo	R/R	5-11/210	32
	Erick Aybar	B/R	5-10/187	22
18	Orlando Cabrera	R/R	5-9/180	31
	Alberto Callaspo	B/R	5-10/175	22
17	Darin Erstad	L/L	6-2/215	31
9	Chone Figgins	B/R	5-7/180	28
6	Maicer Izturis	B/R	5-8/150	25
	Howie Kendrick	R/R	5-10/195	22
2	Adam Kennedy	L/R	6-1/185	30
35	Casey Kotchman	L/L	6-3/215	23
23	Dallas McPherson	L/R	6-4/230	25
22	Kendry Morales	B/R	6-1/220	22
39	Robb Quinlan	R/R	6-1/200	29

No.	OUTFIELDERS	B/T	Ht./Wt.	Age*
16	Garret Anderson	L/L	6-3/225	33
	Nicolas Gorneault	R/R	6-3/220	26
27	Vladimir Guerrero	R/R	6-3/225	30
	Thomas Murphy	B/R	6-0/185	26
20	Juan Rivera	R/R	6-2/205	27
	Reggie Willits	B/R	5-11/185	24

*Age as of April 1, 2006.

BALLPARK INFORMATION

Ballpark (capacity, surface)
Angel Stadium of Anaheim
(45,050, grass)
Address
2000 Gene Autry Way
Anaheim, CA 92806
Official website
www.angelsbaseball.com
Business phone
714-940-2000
Ticket information
714-634-2000
Field dimensions (from home plate)
To left field at foul line, 330 feet
To center field, 400 feet
To right field at foul line, 330
First game played
April 19, 1966 (White Sox 3, Angels 1)

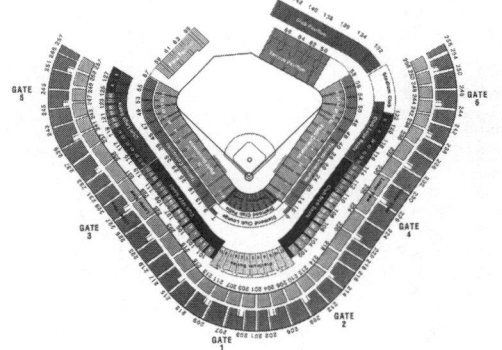

Los Angeles Angels

2006 SEASON

2006 SEASON Los Angeles Angels

Date	Opp.	Res.	Score	(inn.*)	Hits	Opp. hits	Winning pitcher	Losing pitcher	Save	Record	Pos.	GB
4-5	Tex.	W	3-2		6	7	Colon	Drese	Rodriguez	1-0	1st	+0.5
4-6	Tex.	L	2-3	(12)	7	13	Shouse	Prinz		1-1	T1st	...
4-7	Tex.	W	7-6		12	6	Shields	Shouse		2-1	T1st	...
4-8	K.C.	L	2-6		5	10	Bautista	Byrd		2-2	T1st	...
4-9	K.C.	W	8-3		10	3	Gregg	Lima		3-2	1st	+1.0
4-10	K.C.	L	3-8		6	17	Anderson	Colon		3-3	1st	...
4-11	At Tex.	W	7-6	(10)	13	14	Shields	Dickey	Rodriguez	4-3	1st	+1.0
4-12	At Tex.	W	13-8		14	13	Lackey	Young	Shields	5-3	1st	+1.5
4-13	At Tex.	L	5-7		9	11	Park	Byrd	Cordero	5-4	1st	+0.5
4-15	At Oak.	W	6-1		8	2	Colon	Zito		6-4	1st	+1.0
4-16	At Oak.	L	0-1	(10)	4	6	Calero	Shields		6-5	1st	+1.0
4-17	At Oak.	L	6-7		8	11	Street	Lackey	Dotel	6-6	T1st	...
4-18	Sea.	W	6-1		13	12	Byrd	Sele		7-6	T1st	...
4-19	Sea.	L	3-5		9	8	Moyer	Gregg	Guardado	7-7	T1st	...
4-20	Cle.	W	2-0		5	4	Colon	Westbrook	Rodriguez	8-7	T1st	...
4-21	Cle.	W	6-5	(10)	12	13	Rodriguez	Davis		9-7	1st	+1.0
4-22	Oak.	L	3-4		9	10	Yabu	Rodriguez	Dotel	9-8	T1st	...
4-23	Oak.	W	9-5		11	8	Woods	Haren		10-8	1st	+0.5
4-24	Oak.	W	1-0		6	4	Shields	Blanton	Rodriguez	11-8	1st	+1.5
4-26	At N.Y.	L	4-12		8	12	Pavano	Colon		11-9	1st	+1.0
4-27	At N.Y.	W	5-1		12	9	Washburn	Mussina		12-9	1st	+1.5
4-28	At N.Y.	W	3-1		9	8	Lackey	Brown	Rodriguez	13-9	1st	+2.0
4-29	At Min.	L	4-7		12	11	Silva	Byrd	Nathan	13-10	1st	+1.0
4-30	At Min.	L	2-4		7	11	Radke	Escobar	Nathan	13-11	1st	+1.0
5-1	At Min.	W	2-1		2	4	Colon	Santana	Rodriguez	14-11	1st	+1.0
5-2	At Sea.	W	5-0		5	4	Washburn	Franklin		15-11	1st	+2.0
5-3	At Sea.	W	5-2		8	8	Lackey	Meche	Shields	16-11	1st	+2.5
5-4	At Sea.	W	5-2		10	10	Byrd	Sele	Rodriguez	17-11	1st	+2.5
5-6	Det.	W	4-3		7	7	Escobar	Ledezma	Rodriguez	18-11	1st	+3.5
5-7	Det.	L	1-2		5	8	Bonderman	Colon	Percival	18-12	1st	+2.5
5-8	Det.	L	1-10		3	13	Maroth	Washburn		18-13	1st	+1.5
5-9	Cle.	L	0-3		2	8	Millwood	Lackey	Wickman	18-14	1st	+1.5
5-10	Cle.	W	5-4		11	9	Byrd	Sabathia	Rodriguez	19-14	1st	+1.5
5-11	Cle.	L	3-9		7	13	Lee	Escobar		19-15	1st	+1.5
5-14!	At Det.	W	4-2		11	9	Donnelly	Walker	Rodriguez	20-15		
5-14&	At Det.	L	2-3		7	9	Maroth	Washburn	Urbina	20-16	1st	+0.5
5-15	At Det.	W	9-3		11	10	Lackey	Robertson		21-16	1st	+1.5
5-16	At Cle.	W	3-1		7	5	Byrd	Lee	Shields	22-16	1st	+1.5
5-17	At Cle.	L	5-13		15	19	Elarton	Santana		22-17	1st	+1.5
5-18	At Cle.	W	2-1		5	4	Colon	Westbrook	Shields	23-17	1st	+2.5
5-20	At L.A.	W	9-0		9	6	Washburn	Erickson		24-17	1st	+2.5
5-21	At L.A.	W	3-1		8	7	Donnelly	Carrara	Shields	25-17	1st	+2.5
5-22	At L.A.	L	2-6		9	11	Lowe	Byrd		25-18	1st	+1.5
5-23	Chi.	W	4-0		13	5	Santana	Garland		26-18	1st	+2.0
5-24	Chi.	L	1-2	(11)	4	5	Marte	Yan		26-19	1st	+1.0
5-25	Chi.	L	2-4		8	7	Garcia	Washburn	Hermanson	26-20	T1st	...
5-26	Chi.	W	3-2		5	6	Lackey	Contreras	Shields	27-20	T1st	...
5-27	K.C.	W	9-8	(10)	12	12	Shields	MacDougal		28-20	1st	+0.5
5-28	K.C.	W	14-1		16	6	Escobar	Jensen	Bootcheck	29-20	1st	+0.5
5-29	K.C.	W	7-6		10	16	Colon	Hernandez	Shields	30-20	1st	+0.5
5-30	At Chi.	L	4-5		10	10	Politte	Shields		30-21	2nd	...
5-31	At Chi.	L	4-5		9	11	Politte	Donnelly		30-22	2nd	1.0
6-1	At Chi.	W	10-7		13	8	Byrd	Walker		31-22	2nd	...
6-3	At Bos.	L	4-7		13	7	Myers	Shields	Foulke	31-23	1st	+0.5
6-4	At Bos.	W	13-6		17	11	Colon	Embree		32-23	1st	+0.5
6-5	At Bos.	L	3-6		10	8	Myers	Woods	Foulke	32-24	2nd	0.5
6-6	At Atl.	W	4-2		13	8	Donnelly	Smoltz	Rodriguez	33-24	2nd	...
6-7	At Atl.	L	2-3		5	9	Ramirez	Byrd	Reitsma	33-25	2nd	...
6-8	At Atl.	W	8-4		12	4	Donnelly	Foster		34-25	1st	+1.0
6-10	At N.Y.	W	12-2		13	7	Colon	Ishii		35-25	1st	+2.5
6-11	At N.Y.	L	3-5	(10)	8	9	Looper	Donnelly		35-26	1st	+2.5
6-12	At N.Y.	W	4-3		8	7	Shields	Looper	Rodriguez	36-26	1st	+2.5
6-13	Was.	W	11-1		20	5	Byrd	Loaiza		37-26	1st	+2.5
6-14	Was.	L	3-6		11	7	Majewski	Shields	Cordero	37-27	1st	+2.5
6-15	Was.	L	0-1		4	8	Drese	Colon	Cordero	37-28	1st	+1.5
6-17	Fla.	W	3-2	(11)	9	11	Shields	Mecir		38-28	1st	+1.5

Date	Opp.	Res.	Score	(inn.*)	Hits	Opp. hits	Winning pitcher	Losing pitcher	Save	Record	Pos.	GB
6-18	Fla.	W	2-1	(10)	14	6	Rodriguez	Jones		39-28	1st	+1.5
6-19	Fla.	L	5-7		11	12	Leiter	Santana	Jones	39-29	1st	+1.5
6-20	Tex.	W	5-1		15	6	Byrd	Young		40-29	1st	+2.5
6-21	Tex.	W	8-6		15	11	Colon	Park		41-29	1st	+3.5
6-22	Tex.	W	6-0		13	6	Washburn	Rogers		42-29	1st	+4.5
6-24	L.A.	W	7-0		8	5	Lackey	Weaver		43-29	1st	+5.5
6-25	L.A.	W	3-1		4	9	Santana	Penny	Rodriguez	44-29	1st	+5.5
6-26	L.A.	W	5-3		10	5	Donnelly	Wunsch	Rodriguez	45-29	1st	+6.5
6-27	At Tex.	W	13-3		20	8	Colon	Wilson		46-29	1st	+7.5
6-28	At Tex.	W	5-1	(11)	9	9	Donnelly	Loe		47-29	1st	+8.5
6-29	At Tex.	L	6-7	(11)	9	13	Loe	Shields		47-30	1st	+7.5
6-30	At Tex.	L	5-18		10	15	Young	Santana		47-31	1st	+6.5
7-1	At K.C.	W	5-0		10	2	Byrd	Hernandez		48-31	1st	+6.5
7-2	At K.C.	W	5-3		14	5	Colon	Lima	Rodriguez	49-31	1st	+6.5
7-3	At K.C.	W	5-0	(6)	12	4	Washburn	Greinke		50-31	1st	+7.5
7-4	Min.	L	5-7		9	13	Silva	Lackey	Nathan	50-32	1st	+6.5
7-5	Min.	W	2-1		6	7	Santana	Baker	Rodriguez	51-32	1st	+7.5
7-6	Min.	W	7-6		12	12	Peralta	Santana	Rodriguez	52-32	1st	+8.5
7-7	Sea.	L	2-10		6	10	Pineiro	Colon		52-33	1st	+8.0
7-8	Sea.	L	4-10		11	15	Moyer	Washburn		52-34	1st	+7.0
7-9	Sea.	L	3-6		7	12	Franklin	Lackey		52-35	1st	+6.0
7-10	Sea.	L	4-7		8	10	Meche	Santana	Guardado	52-36	1st	+5.0
7-14	At Min.	W	3-2		9	6	Washburn	Lohse	Rodriguez	53-36	1st	+6.0
7-15	At Min.	W	3-2		5	4	Byrd	Radke	Rodriguez	54-36	1st	+7.0
7-16	At Min.	L	4-5		7	9	Santana	Colon	Nathan	54-37	1st	+6.0
7-17	At Min.	W	2-1		5	5	Lackey	Mays	Rodriguez	55-37	1st	+7.0
7-18	Oak.	W	5-2		8	5	Santana	Saarloos	Rodriguez	56-37	1st	+8.0
7-19	Oak.	L	1-3		4	7	Harden	Washburn	Street	56-38	1st	+7.0
7-20	Oak.	L	0-3		7	8	Zito	Byrd	Street	56-39	1st	+6.5
7-21	N.Y.	W	6-5		8	9	Colon	Gordon	Rodriguez	57-39	1st	+6.5
7-22	N.Y.	W	6-3		10	7	Lackey	Leiter	Rodriguez	58-39	1st	+6.5
7-23	N.Y.	W	8-6		11	12	Santana	Brown	Rodriguez	59-39	1st	+6.5
7-24	N.Y.	L	1-4		9	6	Mussina	Washburn	Rivera	59-40	1st	+5.5
7-26	At Tor.	L	0-8		8	14	Chacin	Byrd		59-41	1st	+5.0
7-27	At Tor.	L	2-3	(10)	10	10	Batista	Donnelly		59-42	1st	+4.0
7-28	At Tor.	L	1-2	(18)	9	9	Walker	Shields		59-43	1st	+3.5
7-29	At N.Y.	W	4-1		10	7	Santana	Mussina	Rodriguez	60-43	1st	+3.5
7-30	At N.Y.	L	7-8		9	12	Rivera	Rodriguez		60-44	1st	+2.5
7-31	At N.Y.	L	7-8	(11)	9	13	Gordon	Gregg		60-45	1st	+1.5
8-2	Bal.	W	10-1		14	13	Colon	Ponson		61-45	1st	+1.0
8-3	Bal.	W	8-4		10	11	Lackey	Bedard		62-45	1st	+2.0
8-4	Bal.	L	1-4		4	5	Lopez	Santana	Ryan	62-46	1st	+1.0
8-5	T.B.	W	5-4		9	5	Shields	Waechter	Rodriguez	63-46	1st	+1.0
8-6	T.B.	L	4-6		12	11	Hendrickson	Bootcheck	Baez	63-47	T1st	...
8-7	T.B.	W	10-4		10	10	Colon	McClung		64-47	1st	...
8-9	At Oak.	W	9-2		12	8	Lackey	Harden		65-47	1st	+1.0
8-10	At Oak.	L	3-4		5	8	Duchscherer	Shields	Street	65-48	1st	...
8-11	At Oak.	L	4-5		8	14	Duchscherer	Shields		65-49	2nd	1.0
8-12	At Sea.	W	9-4		13	7	Donnelly	Putz		66-49	T1st	...
8-13	At Sea.	W	9-1		15	4	Colon	Franklin		67-49	T1st	...
8-14	At Sea.	W	7-6		14	10	Donnelly	Sherrill	Rodriguez	68-49	1st	+1.0
8-15	Tor.	W	5-4	(11)	13	9	Shields	Walker		69-49	1st	+2.0
8-16	Tor.	L	3-4		6	7	League	Rodriguez	Batista	69-50	1st	+2.0
8-17	Tor.	L	1-4		8	11	Towers	Washburn	Batista	69-51	1st	+2.0
8-18	Bos.	W	13-4		15	9	Colon	Wakefield		70-51	1st	+2.5
8-19	Bos.	L	3-4	(10)	8	14	Schilling	Shields		70-52	1st	+1.5
8-20	Bos.	W	4-2		7	7	Santana	Arroyo	Rodriguez	71-52	1st	+2.5
8-21	Bos.	L	1-5		8	9	Timlin	Byrd		71-53	1st	+2.5
8-23	At Bal.	W	7-6		16	14	Washburn	DuBose	Rodriguez	72-53	1st	+3.5
8-24	At Bal.	W	3-1		8	5	Colon	Bedard	Rodriguez	73-53	1st	+3.5
8-25	At Bal.	L	0-2		10	9	Lopez	Lackey	Ryan	73-54	1st	+2.5
8-26	At T.B.	L	8-12		14	18	Fossum	Santana		73-55	1st	+1.5
8-27	At T.B.	L	3-6		8	14	Waechter	Byrd	Baez	73-56	1st	+0.5
8-28	At T.B.	L	1-2		6	5	Hendrickson	Washburn	Baez	73-57	2nd	0.5
8-30	Oak.	L	1-2	(11)	4	7	Calero	Rodriguez	Street	73-58	2nd	2.0
8-31	Oak.	W	2-1		6	7	Lackey	Blanton	Rodriguez	74-58	2nd	1.0
9-1	Oak.	W	3-0		10	6	Santana	Kennedy	Rodriguez	75-58	T1st	...
9-2	Sea.	W	4-1		10	6	Byrd	Moyer	Rodriguez	76-58	T1st	...
9-3	Sea.	L	3-6		9	9	Putz	Shields		76-59	T1st	...
9-4	Sea.	W	5-3		9	8	Colon	Harris	Rodriguez	77-59	1st	+1.0

Date	Opp.	Res.	Score	(inn.*)	Hits	Opp. hits	Winning pitcher	Losing pitcher	Save	Record	Pos.	GB
9-6	At Bos.	L	2-3		8	9	Wakefield	Shields		77-60	1st	+1.5
9-7	At Bos.	L	3-6		9	6	Arroyo	Santana	Timlin	77-61	1st	+0.5
9-8	At Bos.	W	3-0		8	5	Byrd	Clement	Rodriguez	78-61	1st	+1.0
9-9	At Chi.	W	6-5	(12)	13	8	Donnelly	Hermanson	Rodriguez	79-61	1st	+1.0
9-10	At Chi.	W	10-5		10	13	Colon	Garland		80-61	1st	+1.0
9-11	At Chi.	W	6-1		11	8	Lackey	Hernandez		81-61	1st	+2.0
9-12	At Sea.	L	1-8		4	14	Pineiro	Santana		81-62	1st	+1.0
9-13	At Sea.	L	1-2		8	9	Putz	Byrd		81-63	1st	+1.0
9-14	At Sea.	L	9-10		16	15	Guardado	Rodriguez		81-64	1st	+1.0
9-15	Det.	L	6-8		8	12	Maroth	Colon	Dingman	81-65	T1st	...
9-16	Det.	W	7-6	(12)	17	9	Escobar	Darensbourg		82-65	1st	+1.0
9-17	Det.	W	3-1		4	4	Santana	Spurling	Rodriguez	83-65	1st	+2.0
9-18	Det.	W	5-3		11	11	Byrd	Ginter	Rodriguez	84-65	1st	+2.0
9-20	Tex.	W	2-1		7	5	Colon	Dominguez	Rodriguez	85-65	1st	+1.5
9-21	Tex.	W	6-5		10	8	Yan	Feldman	Rodriguez	86-65	1st	+2.5
9-22	Tex.	W	7-4		9	7	Santana	Volquez	Escobar	87-65	1st	+3.0
9-23	T.B.	W	7-5		8	11	Shields	Borowski	Rodriguez	88-65	1st	+4.0
9-24	T.B.	W	7-3		10	6	Washburn	Waechter		89-65	1st	+4.0
9-25	T.B.	L	4-8		9	13	Hendrickson	Colon		89-66	1st	+4.0
9-26	At Oak.	W	4-3		6	6	Lackey	Blanton	Rodriguez	90-66	1st	+5.0
9-27	At Oak.	W	4-3		10	8	Santana	Kennedy	Rodriguez	91-66	1st	+6.0
9-28	At Oak.	L	1-6		6	7	Haren	Byrd		91-67	1st	+5.0
9-29	At Oak.	W	7-1		10	9	Colon	Zito		92-67	1st	+6.0
9-30	At Tex.	W	7-1		12	5	Lackey	Dickey		93-67	1st	+7.0
10-1	At Tex.	W	7-6		15	11	Shields	Dominguez	Rodriguez	94-67	1st	+7.0
10-2	At Tex.	W	7-4		9	8	Santana	Loe	Rodriguez	95-67	1st	+7.0

Monthly records: April (13-11), May (17-11), June (17-9), July (13-14), August (14-13), September (19-9), October (2-0).
*Innings, if other than nine. ! First game of a doubleheader. & Second game of a doubleheader.

RECORDS

2005 regular-season record: 95-67
Position: 1st in A.L. West
Home: 49-32 **Road:** 46-35
A.L. East: 19-22 **A.L. Central:** 30-17
A.L. West: 34-22 **N.L.** 12-6
Vs. LH starters: 25-25
Vs. RH starters: 70-42
Grass: 91-58 **Artificial:** 4-9
Day: 24-22 **Night:** 71-45
1-Run: 33-26 **X-inn.:** 9-10
Doubleheaders: 0-0-1
Team record past five years: 438-372 (.541, ranks 5th in league in that span)

TEAM LEADERS

Batting average: Vladimir Guerrero (.317).
At-bats: Chone Figgins (642).
Runs: Chone Figgins (113).
Hits: Chone Figgins (186).
Total Bases: Vladimir Guerrero (294).
Doubles: Garret Anderson (34).
Triples: Chone Figgins (10).
Home runs: Vladimir Guerrero (32).
Runs batted in: Vladimir Guerrero (108).
Stolen bases: Chone Figgins (62).
Slugging percentage: Vladimir Guerrero (.565).
On-base percentage: Vladimir Guerrero (.394).
Wins: Bartolo Colon (21).
Earned-run average: Jarrod Washburn (3.20).

Complete games: Paul Byrd, Bartolo Colon (2).
Shutouts: Paul Byrd, Ervin Santana, Jarrod Washburn (1).
Saves: Francisco Rodriguez (45).
Innings pitched: Bartolo Colon (222.2).
Strikeouts: John Lackey (199).
Strikeouts: Kelvim Escobar (191).

GAMES BY POSITION

Catcher: Bengie Molina 105, Jose Molina 65, Josh Paul 29, Jeff Mathis 3.
First base: Darin Erstad 147, Casey Kotchman 20, Robb Quinlan 9, Jose Molina 4, Lou Merloni 1.
Second base: Adam Kennedy 127, Chone Figgins 42, Zach Sorensen 5, Maicer Izturis 1, Dave Matranga 1.
Third base: Dallas McPherson 60, Chone Figgins 56, Maicer Izturis 45, Robb Quinlan 33, Lou Merloni 4, Zach Sorensen 1.
Shortstop: Orlando Cabrera 140, Maicer Izturis 29, Chone Figgins 4.
Outfield: Vladimir Guerrero 120, Garret Anderson 106, Steve Finley 104, Juan Rivera 74, Chone Figgins 72, Jeff DaVanon 63, Robb Quinlan 6, Curtis Pride 4, Josh Paul 2, Chris Prieto 2, Maicer Izturis 1.
Designated hitter: Garret Anderson 36, Jeff DaVanon 30, Juan Rivera 28, Casey Kotchman 20, Vladimir Guerrero 19, Bengie Molina 11, Chone

Figgins 7, Darin Erstad 5, Steve Finley 5, Jose Molina 5, Curtis Pride 3, Jeff Mathis 2, Josh Paul 1, Zach Sorensen 1.

TOP DRAFT CHOICES

1. **Trevor Bell,** RHP, Crescenta Valley H.S., La Crescenta, Calif.
2a. **Ryan Mount,** SS, Ayala H.S., Chino Hills, Calif.
2b. **P.J. Phillips,** SS, Redan H.S., Stone Mountain, Ga.
3. **Sean O'Sullivan,** RHP, Valhalla H.S., El Cajon, Calif.
4. **Brian Matusz,** LHP, St. Mary's H.S., Cave Creek, Ariz.
5. **Thomas Mendoza,** RHP, Monsignor Pace H.S., Miami.
6. **Jeremy Moore,** OF, North Caddo H.S., Vivian, La.
7. **Robert Romero,** RHP, Grayson County College (Texas).
8. **Matt Hall,** SS, Horizon H.S., Scottsdale, Ariz.
9. **Bobby Mosebach,** RHP, Hillsborough CC (Fla.)
10. **Peter Bourjos,** OF, Notre Dame H.S., Scottsdale, Ariz.

MINNESOTA TWINS
AMERICAN LEAGUE CENTRAL DIVISION

2006 SEASON

Twins Schedule
Home games shaded.
All-Star Game July 11 at Pittsburgh. Schedule subject to change.

APRIL
SUN	MON	TUE	WED	THU	FRI	SAT
2	3	4 TOR	5 TOR	6 TOR	7 CLE	8 CLE
9 CLE	10	11 OAK	12 OAK	13 OAK	14 NYY	15 NYY
16 NYY	17	18 LAA	19 LAA	20 LAA	21 CHW	22 CHW
23 CHW	24	25 KC	26 KC	27 KC	28 DET	29 DET
30 DET						

MAY
SUN	MON	TUE	WED	THU	FRI	SAT
	1 SEA	2 SEA	3 KC	4 KC	5 DET	6 DET
7 DET	8 TEX	9 TEX	10 TEX	11	12 CHW	13 CHW
14 CHW	15 CHW	16 DET	17 DET	18 DET	19 MIL	20 MIL
21 MIL	22	23 CLE	24 CLE	25	26 SEA	27 SEA
28 SEA	29 LAA	30 LAA	31 LAA			

JUNE
SUN	MON	TUE	WED	THU	FRI	SAT
				1 OAK	2 OAK	3 OAK
4 OAK	5	6 SEA	7 SEA	8 SEA	9 BAL	10 BAL
11 BAL	12	13 BOS	14 BOS	15 BOS	16 PIT	17 PIT
18 PIT	19	20 HOU	21 HOU	22 HOU	23 CHC	24 CHC
25 CHC	26 LAD	27 LAD	28 LAD	29	30 MIL	

JULY
SUN	MON	TUE	WED	THU	FRI	SAT
						1 MIL
2 MIL	3 KC	4 KC	5 KC	6	7 TEX	8 TEX
9 TEX	10	11 ALL-STAR	12	13 CLE	14 CLE	15 CLE
16 CLE	17 TB	18 TB	19 TB	20 TB	21 CLE	22 CLE
23 CLE	24 CHW	25 CHW	26 CHW	27	28 DET	29 DET
30 DET	31 TEX					

AUGUST
SUN	MON	TUE	WED	THU	FRI	SAT
		1 TEX	2 TEX	3 KC	4 KC	5 KC
6 KC	7 DET	8 DET	9 DET	10 TOR	11 TOR	12 TOR
13 TOR	14	15 CLE	16 CLE	17 CLE	18 CHW	19 CHW
20 CHW	21	22 BAL	23 BAL	24 BAL	25 CHW	26 CHW
27 CHW	28	29 KC	30 KC	31 KC		

SEPTEMBER
SUN	MON	TUE	WED	THU	FRI	SAT
					1 NYY	2 NYY
3 NYY	4 TB	5 TB	6 TB	7 DET	8 DET	9 DET
10 DET	11 OAK	12 OAK	13 OAK	14 CLE	15 CLE	16 CLE
17 CLE	18	19 BOS	20 BOS	21 BOS	22 BAL	23 BAL
24 BAL	25 KC	26 KC	27 KC	28 KC	29 CHW	30 CHW

OCTOBER
SUN	MON	TUE	WED	THU	FRI	SAT
1 CHW	2	3	4	5	6	7

Home games are shaded. All-Star Game is July 11 at Pittsburgh. Schedule is subject to change.

Santana

CLUB DIRECTORY

Owner
Carl R. Pohlad

President, Twins Sports Inc.
T. Geron Bell

President, Minnesota Twins
Dave St. Peter

Vice president, general manager
Terry Ryan

Vice president, asst. general manager
Bill Smith

Vice president, operations
Matt Hoy

Assistant general manager
Wayne Krivsky

Director of minor leagues
Jim Rantz

Director of baseball operations
Rob Antony

Director of scouting
Mike Radcliff

Director of team travel and baseball accommodations
Remzi Kiratli

Manager of baseball communications
Sean Harlin

Manager of media and player relations
Mike Herman

Publications and baseball communications coordinator
Molly Gallatin

MINOR LEAGUE AFFILIATES

Class	Team	League	Manager
AAA	Rochester	International	Stan Cliburn
AA	New Britain	Eastern	Riccardo Ingram
Advanced A	Fort Myers	Florida State	Kevin Boles
A	Beloit	Midwest	Jeff Smith
Advanced Rookie	Elizabethton	Appalachian	Ray Smith
Rookie	Twins	Gulf Coast	Nelson Prada

BROADCAST INFORMATION

Radio: WCCO-AM (830).
TV: WFTC-TV (Channel 29).
Cable TV: Fox Sport Net North.

SPRING TRAINING

Ballpark (city): Lee County Sports Complex (Fort Myers, Fla.).
Ticket information: 800-33-TWINS.

For more on the Twins, go to www.sportingnews.com/baseball/teams/twins/

SPRING TRAINING ROSTER

Manager—Ron Gardenhire (35).
Coaches—Rick Anderson (40), Steve Liddle (9), Rick Stelmaszek (43), Scott Ullger (46), Joe Vavra (66), Jerry White (13).

No.	PITCHERS	B/T	Ht./Wt.	Age*
	Scott Baker	R/R	6-4/220	24
	Boof Bonser	R/R	6-4/220	24
28	Jesse Crain	R/R	6-1/205	24
31	J.D. Durbin	R/R	6-0/210	24
	Willie Eyre	R/R	6-1/200	27
59	Dave Gassner	R/L	6-2/190	27
54	Matt Guerrier	R/R	6-3/185	27
	Adam Harben	R/R	6-5/210	22
	Justin Jones	L/L	6-4/200	21
47	Francisco Liriano	L/L	6-2/185	22
49	Kyle Lohse	R/R	6-2/201	27
	Jose Mijares	L/L	5-10/220	21
36	Joe Nathan	R/R	6-4/220	31
	Patrick Neshek	B/R	6-2/200	25
22	Brad Radke	R/R	6-2/184	33
39	Juan Rincon	R/R	5-11/215	27
57	Johan Santana	L/L	6-0/206	27
52	Carlos Silva	R/R	6-4/250	26
	Errol Simonitsch	L/L	6-4/225	23

No.	CATCHERS	B/T	Ht./Wt.	Age*
44	Rob Bowen	B/R	6-3/225	25
41	Chris Heintz	R/R	6-1/210	31
7	Joe Mauer	L/R	6-4/220	22
55	Mike Redmond	R/R	5-11/200	34

No.	INFIELDERS	B/T	Ht./Wt.	Age*
18	Jason Bartlett	R/R	6-0/190	26
	Tony Batista	R/R	6-0/208	32
	Luis Castillo	B/R	5-11/190	30
7	Juan Castro	R/R	5-11/195	33
5	Michael Cuddyer	R/R	6-2/222	27
	Garrett Jones	L/L	6-4/245	24
27	Justin Morneau	L/R	6-4/228	24
8	Nick Punto	B/R	5-9/190	28
38	Luis Rodriguez	B/R	5-9/180	25
32	Terry Tiffee	B/R	6-3/210	26

No.	OUTFIELDERS	B/T	Ht./Wt.	Age*
20	Lew Ford	R/R	6-0/195	29
48	Torii Hunter	R/R	6-2/220	30
1	Jason Kubel	L/R	5-11/200	23
	Jason Pridie	L/R	6-1/188	22
	Alex Romero	L/R	6-0/190	22
23	Shannon Stewart	R/R	5-11/210	32
24	Rondell White	R/R	6-1/225	34

*Age as of April 1, 2006.

BALLPARK INFORMATION

Ballpark (capacity, surface)
Hubert H. Humphrey Metrodome (45,423, artificial)
Address
34 Kirby Puckett Place
Minneapolis, MN 55415
Official website
www.twinsbaseball.com
Business phone
612-375-1366
Ticket information
1-800-338-9467
Field dimensions (from home plate)
To left field at foul line, 343 feet
To center field, 408 feet
To right field at foul line, 327 feet
First game played
April 6, 1982 (Mariners 11, Twins 7)

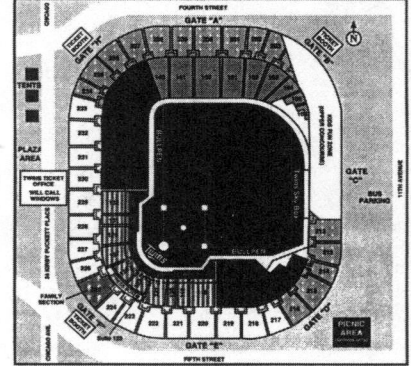

Date	Opp.	Res.	Score	(inn.*)	Hits	Opp. hits	Winning pitcher	Losing pitcher	Save	Record	Pos.	GB
4-4	At Sea.	L	1-5		5	5	Moyer	Radke		0-1	T3rd	1.0
4-5	At Sea.	W	8-4		14	7	Santana	Thornton		1-1	3rd	0.5
4-6	At Sea.	W	4-1		7	10	Silva	Madritsch	Nathan	2-1	2nd	0.5
4-8	Chi.	L	1-5		8	11	Hernandez	Lohse		2-2	T2nd	1.0
4-9	Chi.	L	5-8		14	8	Garland	Radke	Takatsu	2-3	T3rd	2.0
4-10	Chi.	W	5-2		7	8	Santana	Buehrle	Nathan	3-3	T2nd	1.0
4-12	Det.	W	5-4		9	7	Rincon	Percival		4-3	2nd	1.0
4-13	Det.	W	8-4		12	11	Lohse	Johnson		5-3	2nd	1.0
4-14	Det.	W	10-4		11	9	Radke	Robertson		6-3	T1st	...
4-15	At Cle.	W	3-2		3	7	Santana	Westbrook	Nathan	7-3	T1st	...
4-16	At Cle.	W	6-4		10	7	Gassner	Millwood	Nathan	8-3	T1st	...
4-17	At Cle.	L	1-2		5	7	Howry	Romero	Wickman	8-4	T1st	...
4-18	At Chi.	L	4-5		9	7	Vizcaino	Lohse	Takatsu	8-5	2nd	1.0
4-19	At Chi.	L	1-3		14	11	Hernandez	Radke	Marte	8-6	2nd	2.0
4-20	K.C.	W	5-4		9	6	Rincon	Cerda	Nathan	9-6	2nd	2.0
4-21	K.C.	W	10-9	(10)	16	13	Nathan	Camp		10-6	2nd	2.0
4-22	At Det.	L	4-5	(10)	8	11	Percival	Mulholland		10-7	2nd	3.0
4-25	At Det.	L	4-6		6	14	Farnsworth	Rincon	Percival	10-8	2nd	5.0
4-26	At K.C.	W	2-1		7	5	Santana	Burgos	Nathan	11-8	2nd	4.0
4-27	At K.C.	W	9-4		9	8	Mays	Anderson		12-8	2nd	3.0
4-28	At K.C.	W	6-5	(11)	10	10	Crain	Wood		13-8	2nd	2.5
4-29	L.A.	W	7-4		11	12	Silva	Byrd	Nathan	14-8	2nd	1.5
4-30	L.A.	W	4-2		11	7	Radke	Escobar	Nathan	15-8	2nd	1.5
5-1	L.A.	L	1-2		4	2	Colon	Santana	Rodriguez	15-9	2nd	2.5
5-3	Cle.	L	2-4		10	10	Westbrook	Mays	Wickman	15-10	2nd	3.5
5-4	Cle.	L	4-5		13	13	Howry	Romero	Wickman	15-11	2nd	4.5
5-5	Cle.	W	9-0		13	3	Radke	Sabathia		16-11	2nd	4.5
5-6	At T.B.	W	7-1		14	6	Santana	Brazelton		17-11	2nd	4.5
5-7	At T.B.	W	8-1		11	7	Lohse	Kazmir		18-11	2nd	4.5
5-8	At T.B.	W	9-6		11	9	Mays	Waechter	Nathan	19-11	2nd	4.5
5-9	At Bal.	L	0-3		3	10	Cabrera	Silva	Ryan	19-12	2nd	4.5
5-10	At Bal.	W	6-4	(10)	7	11	Crain	Kline	Nathan	20-12	2nd	3.5
5-11	At Bal.	L	4-7		7	11	Ponson	Guerrier	Ryan	20-13	2nd	4.5
5-13	Tex.	L	6-9	(11)	12	13	Brocail	Nathan	Cordero	20-14	2nd	6.0
5-14	Tex.	L	0-5		6	11	Rogers	Silva		20-15	2nd	6.0
5-15	Tex.	W	5-2		11	7	Radke	Mahay	Nathan	21-15	2nd	5.0
5-17	Tor.	L	3-10		9	14	Towers	Santana		21-16	2nd	5.5
5-18	Tor.	W	3-2		7	7	Lohse	Bush	Nathan	22-16	2nd	5.5
5-19	Tor.	W	4-0		10	7	Mays	Chacin		23-16	2nd	5.0
5-20	Mil.	W	7-1		16	5	Silva	Glover		24-16	2nd	5.0
5-21	Mil.	L	0-6		7	10	Davis	Radke		24-17	2nd	6.0
5-22	Mil.	W	6-5	(11)	10	12	Crain	Wise		25-17	2nd	5.0
5-23	At Cle.	L	1-2		8	7	Rhodes	Lohse	Wickman	25-18	2nd	5.0
5-24	At Cle.	W	6-3	(11)	9	7	Crain	Riske	Nathan	26-18	2nd	5.0
5-25	At Cle.	L	2-3	(10)	9	8	Howry	Rincon		26-19	2nd	6.0
5-26	At Cle.	W	5-4	(11)	8	16	Crain	Riske	Nathan	27-19	2nd	5.0
5-27	At Tor.	W	7-2		16	5	Santana	Towers		28-19	2nd	4.0
5-28	At Tor.	W	4-3		6	9	Lohse	Bush	Nathan	29-19	2nd	3.5
5-29	At Tor.	L	0-4		2	13	Halladay	Mays		29-20	2nd	3.5
5-31	Cle.	L	3-4		8	9	Sabathia	Silva	Wickman	29-21	2nd	5.0
6-1	Cle.	W	6-2		13	7	Radke	Lee		30-21	2nd	4.0
6-2	Cle.	W	4-3	(13)	9	6	Romero	Betancourt		31-21	2nd	3.5
6-3	N.Y.	W	6-3		11	9	Lohse	Mussina	Nathan	32-21	2nd	3.5
6-4	N.Y.	L	3-4	(10)	6	7	Gordon	Nathan	Rivera	32-22	2nd	4.5
6-5	N.Y.	W	9-3		14	9	Silva	Brown		33-22	2nd	3.5
6-7	At Ari.	W	9-8		13	13	Rincon	Valverde	Nathan	34-22	2nd	4.0
6-8	At Ari.	W	10-0		15	4	Santana	Vargas		35-22	2nd	4.0
6-9	At Ari.	L	3-4		5	7	Vazquez	Lohse	Bruney	35-23	2nd	4.5
6-10	At L.A.	L	5-6		9	9	Gagne	Mulholland		35-24	2nd	5.5
6-11	At L.A.	W	5-3		10	7	Silva	Lowe	Nathan	36-24	2nd	4.5
6-12	At L.A.	L	3-4		7	9	Houlton	Radke	Gagne	36-25	2nd	5.5
6-14	S.F.	W	4-3	(11)	8	7	Crain	Fassero		37-25	2nd	4.0
6-15	S.F.	L	4-8		8	14	Lowry	Lohse		37-26	2nd	5.0
6-16	S.F.	L	7-14		12	18	Christiansen	Nathan		37-27	2nd	5.5
6-17	S.D.	W	5-4	(11)	12	14	Rincon	Reyes		38-27	2nd	5.5
6-18	S.D.	L	2-7		7	16	Lawrence	Radke		38-28	2nd	6.5

Minnesota Twins

Date	Opp.	Res.	Score	(inn.*)	Hits	Opp. hits	Winning pitcher	Losing pitcher	Save	Record	Pos.	GB
6-19	S.D.	L	1-5		4	7	May	Santana		38-29	2nd	7.5
6-21	Det.	L	2-7		5	12	Bonderman	Lohse		38-30	2nd	9.0
6-22	Det.	L	1-8		5	11	Robertson	Mays		38-31	2nd	10.0
6-23	Det.	W	6-2		11	9	Silva	Johnson		39-31	2nd	9.5
6-24	At Mil.	L	1-3		7	7	Capuano	Radke	Turnbow	39-32	2nd	10.5
6-25	At Mil.	L	6-7		9	9	Wise	Santana	Turnbow	39-33	2nd	10.5
6-26	At Mil.	W	5-2		12	13	Lohse	Santos		40-33	2nd	9.5
6-27	K.C.	W	3-1		8	6	Mays	Greinke	Nathan	41-33	2nd	9.0
6-28	K.C.	W	11-8		15	14	Crain	Sisco	Nathan	42-33	2nd	9.0
6-29	K.C.	L	1-3		6	11	Carrasco	Radke	MacDougal	42-34	2nd	10.0
7-1	T.B.	W	7-4		6	10	Crain	Brazelton	Nathan	43-34	2nd	9.5
7-2	T.B.	W	4-1		8	4	Lohse	McClung	Nathan	44-34	2nd	9.5
7-3	T.B.	W	3-2		4	7	Mays	Kazmir	Nathan	45-34	2nd	8.5
7-4	At L.A.	W	7-5		13	9	Silva	Lackey	Nathan	46-34	2nd	8.5
7-5	At L.A.	L	1-2		7	6	Santana	Baker	Rodriguez	46-35	2nd	9.5
7-6	At L.A.	L	6-7		12	12	Peralta	Santana	Rodriguez	46-36	2nd	10.5
7-7	At K.C.	L	5-8		12	12	Lima	Lohse		46-37	2nd	11.0
7-8	At K.C.	W	5-4		11	11	Radke	Greinke	Nathan	47-37	2nd	10.0
7-9	At K.C.	L	8-12		12	21	Nunez	Crain		47-38	2nd	10.0
7-10	At K.C.	W	3-2	(12)	15	7	Romero	Wood	Crain	48-38	2nd	9.0
7-14	L.A.	L	2-3		6	9	Washburn	Lohse	Rodriguez	48-39	2nd	10.0
7-15	L.A.	L	2-3		4	5	Byrd	Radke	Rodriguez	48-40	2nd	11.0
7-16	L.A.	W	5-4		9	7	Santana	Colon	Nathan	49-40	2nd	11.0
7-17	L.A.	L	1-2		5	5	Lackey	Mays	Rodriguez	49-41	2nd	12.0
7-18	Bal.	L	2-3	(11)	9	10	Julio	Rincon		49-42	2nd	13.0
7-19	Bal.	W	4-3		9	13	Crain	Ryan		50-42	2nd	12.0
7-20	Bal.	W	3-2		7	6	Nathan	Grimsley		51-42	2nd	11.0
7-21	At Det.	W	10-5		13	12	Santana	Johnson		52-42	2nd	10.0
7-22	At Det.	L	6-12		9	18	Maroth	Mays		52-43	2nd	11.0
7-23#	At Det.	L	1-2		6	9	Douglass	Silva	Farnsworth	52-44		
7-23$	At Det.	W	5-2		11	6	Baker	Verlander	Nathan	53-44	2nd	10.5
7-24	At Det.	L	2-5		7	13	Bonderman	Lohse	Farnsworth	53-45	2nd	11.5
7-26	At N.Y.	L	0-4		2	9	Johnson	Radke		53-46	2nd	12.0
7-27	At N.Y.	W	7-3		14	9	Santana	Leiter	Nathan	54-46	2nd	11.0
7-28	At N.Y.	L	3-6		7	11	Small	Mays	Rivera	54-47	2nd	11.5
7-29	At Bos.	L	5-8		7	8	Arroyo	Silva	Schilling	54-48	2nd	12.5
7-30	At Bos.	L	2-6		7	14	Wells	Lohse		54-49	2nd	13.5
7-31	At Bos.	L	3-4		7	8	Timlin	Rincon	Schilling	54-50	2nd	14.5
8-1	Oak.	L	1-2		2	5	Blanton	Santana	Street	54-51	3rd	15.5
8-2	Oak.	L	2-5		9	9	Haren	Romero	Street	54-52	3rd	15.5
8-3	Oak.	W	4-3		5	5	Nathan	Duchscherer		55-52	3rd	14.5
8-4	Oak.	L	2-5		4	12	Zito	Crain	Street	55-53	3rd	15.5
8-5	Bos.	W	12-0		16	4	Radke	Arroyo		56-53	3rd	14.5
8-6	Bos.	W	4-3		9	10	Nathan	Timlin		57-53	3rd	14.5
8-7	Bos.	L	7-11		9	17	Wakefield	Mays	Schilling	57-54	3rd	15.5
8-8	At Sea.	L	4-5		6	9	Sherrill	Silva	Guardado	57-55	3rd	15.5
8-9	At Sea.	L	0-1		5	4	Hernandez	Lohse	Guardado	57-56	3rd	16.5
8-10	At Sea.	W	7-3	(14)	17	12	Nathan	Nelson		58-56	3rd	16.5
8-12	At Oak.	W	1-0		3	3	Santana	Haren		59-56	3rd	15.5
8-13	At Oak.	L	2-5		8	9	Saarloos	Mays	Street	59-57	3rd	15.5
8-14	At Oak.	W	2-1		4	7	Rincon	Duchscherer	Nathan	60-57	3rd	15.0
8-15	At Chi.	W	4-2		9	9	Lohse	Contreras	Nathan	61-57	3rd	14.0
8-16	At Chi.	W	9-4	(16)	20	12	Romero	Adkins		62-57	3rd	13.0
8-17	At Chi.	W	5-1		10	6	Santana	Buehrle		63-57	3rd	12.0
8-18	Sea.	W	7-3		15	11	Mays	Franklin		64-57	3rd	11.5
8-19	Sea.	W	7-4		9	9	Silva	Sherrill	Nathan	65-57	3rd	10.5
8-20	Sea.	L	3-8	(10)	7	10	Sherrill	Guerrier		65-58	3rd	10.5
8-21	Sea.	W	8-3		16	4	Radke	Pineiro		66-58	3rd	10.5
8-23	Chi.	W	1-0		1	3	Santana	Garcia	Nathan	67-58	3rd	9.5
8-24	Chi.	L	4-6		10	13	Buehrle	Mays	Hermanson	67-59	3rd	10.5
8-25	Chi.	L	1-2	(10)	7	8	Hermanson	Crain	Jenks	67-60	3rd	11.5
8-26	At Tex.	L	0-6		6	10	Loe	Lohse	Wilson	67-61	3rd	12.5
8-27	At Tex.	W	7-2	(11)	15	11	Nathan	Shouse		68-61	3rd	12.5
8-28	At Tex.	L	1-2		5	6	Brocail	Crain		68-62	3rd	12.5
8-29	At K.C.	W	3-1	(10)	8	5	Rincon	Camp	Nathan	69-62	3rd	11.5
8-30	At K.C.	W	7-4		11	11	Silva	Lima	Nathan	70-62	3rd	11.0
8-31	At K.C.	L	0-1		13	5	MacDougal	Guerrier		70-63	3rd	11.0
9-2	Cle.	L	1-6		5	11	Sabathia	Radke		70-64	3rd	12.5
9-3	Cle.	W	3-2		12	3	Nathan	Howry		71-64	3rd	12.5

Date	Opp.	Res.	Score	(inn.*)	Hits	Opp. hits	Winning pitcher	Losing pitcher	Save	Record	Pos.	GB
9-4	Cle.	W	7-5		12	7	Crain	Westbrook	Nathan	72-64	3rd	12.5
9-5	Tex.	L	0-7		5	9	Loe	Silva		72-65	3rd	13.5
9-6	Tex.	L	7-10		10	11	Wasdin	Nathan	Cordero	72-66	3rd	14.5
9-7	Tex.	W	8-6		9	14	Romero	Brocail	Nathan	73-66	3rd	14.5
9-9	At Cle.	L	2-4		7	9	Westbrook	Santana	Wickman	73-67	3rd	14.0
9-10	At Cle.	L	5-7		8	12	Elarton	Baker	Wickman	73-68	3rd	14.0
9-11	At Cle.	L	4-12		9	17	Lee	Silva		73-69	3rd	14.0
9-12	At Det.	W	2-1		13	7	Lohse	Spurling	Nathan	74-69	3rd	13.5
9-13	At Det.	W	9-3		14	6	Radke	Robertson		75-69	3rd	13.5
9-14	At Det.	L	2-4		8	9	Dingman	Rincon		75-70	3rd	13.5
9-16	Chi.	L	1-2	(10)	6	6	Jenks	Crain		75-71	3rd	14.0
9-17	Chi.	W	5-0		11	4	Santana	Hernandez	Nathan	76-71	3rd	13.0
9-18	Chi.	L	1-2		5	8	Contreras	Rincon	Jenks	76-72	3rd	14.0
9-19	At Oak.	L	6-7		9	11	Zito	Radke		76-73	3rd	14.0
9-20	At Oak.	L	3-8		6	12	Blanton	Liriano		76-74	3rd	15.0
9-21	At Oak.	W	10-4		12	6	Baker	Kennedy		77-74	3rd	14.0
9-22	At Chi.	W	4-1	(11)	8	7	Crain	Jenks	Nathan	78-74	3rd	13.0
9-23	At Chi.	L	1-3		6	9	Contreras	Lohse		78-75	3rd	14.0
9-24	At Chi.	L	1-8		5	14	Garcia	Mays		78-76	3rd	15.0
9-25	At Chi.	L	1-4		4	5	Buehrle	Liriano		78-77	3rd	16.0
9-26	K.C.	L	0-5		3	7	Howell	Baker		78-78	3rd	16.0
9-27	K.C.	W	3-1		6	6	Santana	Hernandez	Nathan	79-78	3rd	15.0
9-28	K.C.	W	6-3		8	8	Crain	Sisco	Nathan	80-78	3rd	15.0
9-29	K.C.	L	6-10		11	11	Carrasco	Bowyer		80-79	3rd	16.0
9-30	Det.	W	7-3		11	7	Liriano	Maroth		81-79	3rd	16.0
10-1	Det.	W	3-0		6	7	Baker	Johnson	Nathan	82-79	3rd	16.0
10-2	Det.	W	6-4		11	7	Santana	Robertson	Nathan	83-79	3rd	16.0

Monthly records: April (15-8), May (14-13), June (13-13), July (12-16), August (16-13), September (11-16), October (2-0).
*Innings, if other than nine. ! First game of a doubleheader. & Second game of a doubleheader. # Day separate admission. $ Night separate admission.

RECORDS

2005 regular-season record: 83-79
Position: 3rd in A.L. Central
Home: 45-36   **Road:** 38-43
A.L. East: 18-12   **A.L. Central:** 40-35
A.L. West: 17-22   **N.L.** 8-10
Vs. LH starters: 24-24
Vs. RH starters: 59-55
Grass: 33-42   **Artificial:** 50-37
Day: 25-25   **Night:** 58-54
1-Run: 27-30   **X-inn.:** 15-8
Doubleheaders: 0-0-0
Team record past five years: 444-365
(.549, ranks 4th in league in that span)

TEAM LEADERS

Batting average: Joe Mauer (.294).
At-bats: Shannon Stewart (551).
Runs: Jacque Jones (74).
Hits: Shannon Stewart (151).
Total Bases: Jacque Jones (229).
Doubles: Lew Ford (30).
Triples: Lew Ford, Jacque Jones, Justin Morneau, Nick Punto (4).
Home runs: Jacque Jones (23).
Runs batted in: Justin Morneau (79).
Stolen bases: Torii Hunter (23).
Slugging percentage: Torii Hunter (.452).
On-base percentage: Joe Mauer (.372).
Wins: Johan Santana (16).
Earned-run average: Johan Santana

(2.87).
Complete games: Brad Radke, Johan Santana (3).
Shutouts: Johan Santana (2).
Saves: Joe Nathan (43).
Innings pitched: Johan Santana (231.2).
Strikeouts: Johan Santana (238).

GAMES BY POSITION

Catcher: Joe Mauer 116, Mike Redmond 45, Chris Heintz 8, Corky Miller 4, Matthew LeCroy 1.
First base: Justin Morneau 138, Matthew LeCroy 23, Terry Tiffee 13, Michael Cuddyer 8.
Second base: Nick Punto 73, Luis Rivas 53, Luis Rodriguez 40, Brent Abernathy 17, Bret Boone 14, Michael Cuddyer 11, Juan Castro 5.
Third base: Michael Cuddyer 95, Luis Rodriguez 27, Terry Tiffee 24, Juan Castro 22, Nick Punto 12, Glenn Williams 12, Michael Ryan 1.
Shortstop: Juan Castro 73, Jason Bartlett 68, Nick Punto 34, Luis Rodriguez 10, Luis Rivas 6.
Outfield: Jacque Jones 132, Shannon Stewart 125, Lew Ford 95, Torii Hunter 93, Michael Ryan 25, Michael Cuddyer 20, Jason Tyner 15, Brent Abernathy 5, Nick Punto 3.
Designated hitter: Matthew LeCroy 63, Lew Ford 44, Joe Mauer 13, Michael Ryan 13, Terry Tiffee 10, Jacque

Jones 9, Jason Bartlett 5, Torii Hunter 5, Nick Punto 5, Shannon Stewart 5, Luis Rodriguez 3, Jason Tyner 3, Brent Abernathy 2, Corky Miller 1, Justin Morneau 1, Luis Rivas 1.

TOP DRAFT CHOICES

1a. **Matt Garza**, RHP, Fresno State.
1b. **Henry Sanchez**, 1B, Mission Bay H.S., San Diego.
2a. **Paul Kelly**, SS, Flower Mound (Texas) H.S.
2b. **Kevin Slowey**, RHP, Winthrop.
2c. **Drew Thompson**, SS, Jupiter Community H.S., Tequesta, Fla.
3a. **Brian Duensing**, LHP, Nebraska.
3b. **Ryan Mullins**, LHP, Vanderbilt.
4. **Caleb Moore**, C, East Tennessee State.
5. **Steven Tolleson**, SS, South Carolina.
6. **J.W. Wilson**, OF, Midland (Texas).
7. **Greg Yersich**, C, Andrean H.S., Merrillville, Ind.
8. **Danny Powers**, RHP, Central Missouri State.
9. **Erik Lis**, 1B, Evansville.
10. **Matt Betsill**, 3B, Furman.

NEW YORK YANKEES
AMERICAN LEAGUE EAST DIVISION

2006 SEASON

Yankees Schedule
Home games shaded.
All-Star Game July 11 at Pittsburgh. Schedule subject to change.

APRIL
SUN	MON	TUE	WED	THU	FRI	SAT
2	3 OAK	4 OAK	5 OAK	6	7 LAA	8 LAA
9 LAA	10	11 KC	12 KC	13 KC	14 MIN	15 MIN
16 MIN	17	18 TOR	19 TOR	20	21 BAL	22 BAL
23 BAL	24	25 TB	26 TB	27 TB	28 TOR	29 TOR
30 TOR						

MAY
SUN	MON	TUE	WED	THU	FRI	SAT
	1 BOS	2 BOS	3 TB	4 TB	5 TEX	6 TEX
7 TEX	8	9 BOS	10 BOS	11 BOS	12 OAK	13 OAK
14 OAK	15 TEX	16 TEX	17 TEX	18 TEX	19 NYM	20 NYM
21 NYM	22 BOS	23 BOS	24 BOS	25	26 KC	27 KC
28 KC	29 DET	30 DET	31 DET			

JUNE
SUN	MON	TUE	WED	THU	FRI	SAT
				1 DET	2 BAL	3 BAL
4 BAL	5 BOS	6 BOS	7 BOS	8 BOS	9 OAK	10 OAK
11 OAK	12	13 CLE	14 CLE	15 CLE	16 WAS	17 WAS
18 WAS	19 PHI	20 PHI	21 PHI	22	23 FLA	24 FLA
25 FLA	26 ATL	27 ATL	28 ATL	29	30 NYM	

JULY
SUN	MON	TUE	WED	THU	FRI	SAT
						1 NYM
2 NYM	3 CLE	4 CLE	5 CLE	6 CLE	7 TB	8 TB
9 TB	10	11 ALL-STAR	12	13	14 CHW	15 CHW
16 CHW	17 SEA	18 SEA	19 SEA	20 TOR	21 TOR	22 TOR
23 TOR	24 TEX	25 TEX	26 TEX	27	28 TB	29 TB
30 TB	31					

AUGUST
SUN	MON	TUE	WED	THU	FRI	SAT
		1 TOR	2 TOR	3 TOR	4 BAL	5 BAL
6 BAL	7	8 CHW	9 CHW	10 CHW	11 LAA	12 LAA
13 LAA	14 LAA	15 BAL	16 BAL	17 BAL	18 BOS	19 BOS
20 BOS	21 BOS	22 SEA	23 SEA	24 SEA	25 LAA	26 LAA
27 LAA	28	29 DET	30 DET	31 DET		

SEPTEMBER
SUN	MON	TUE	WED	THU	FRI	SAT
					1 MIN	2 MIN
3 MIN	4 KC	5 KC	6 KC	7	8 BAL	9 BAL
10 BAL	11 BAL	12 TB	13 TB	14 TB	15 BOS	16 BOS
17 BOS	18 TOR	19 TOR	20 TOR	21	22 TB	23 TB
24 TB	25 TB	26 BAL	27 BAL	28 BAL	29 TOR	30 TOR

OCTOBER
SUN	MON	TUE	WED	THU	FRI	SAT
1 TOR	2	3	4	5	6	7

Home games are shaded. All-Star Game is July 11 at Pittsburgh. Schedule is subject to change.

Jeter

CLUB DIRECTORY

Principal owner
George M. Steinbrenner III
President
Randy Levine
Special advisers
Yogi Berra, Reggie Jackson, Clyde King
Senior vice president, general manager
Brian Cashman
Senior vice president, baseball operations
Mark Newman
Senior vice president, player personnel
Gordon Blakeley
Vice president, assistant general manager
Jean Afterman

Vice president and senior adviser
Gene Michael
Vice president, scouting
Lin Garrett
Vice president, player personnel
Billy Connors
V.p., corporate and community relations
Brian Smith
Vice president, major league scouting
Damon Oppenheimer
Director of media relations and publicity
Rick Cerrone

MINOR LEAGUE AFFILIATES

Class	Team	League	Manager
AAA	Columbus	International	Dave Miley
AA	Trenton	Eastern	Bill Masse
Advanced A	Tampa	Florida State	Luis Sojo
A	Charleston (S.C.)	South Atlantic	Bill Mosiello
Short-Season A	Staten Island	New York-Pennsylvania	To be announced
Rookie	Yankees	Gulf Coast	Oscar Acosta

BROADCAST INFORMATION

Radio: WCBS-AM (880).
TV: WWOR-TV (Channel 9).
Cable TV: Yankee Entertainment and Sports Network.

For more on the Yankees, go to www.sportingnews.com/baseball/teams/yankees/

SPRING TRAINING

Ballpark (city): Legends Field (Tampa, Fla.).
Ticket information: 813-879-2244, 813-287-8844.

Manager—Joe Torre (6).
Coaches—Larry Bowa, Ron Guidry (49), Joe Kerrigan, Don Mattingly (23), Lee Mazzilli (53), Tony Pena.

No.	PITCHERS	B/T	Ht./Wt.	Age*
	Jason Anderson	L/R	6-0/188	26
	T.J. Beam	R/R	6-7/215	25
	Colter Bean	L/R	6-6/255	29
39	Shawn Chacon	R/R	6-3/220	28
	Jorge DePaula	R/R	6-1/160	27
	Matt Desalvo	R/R	6-0/170	25
	Octavio Dotel	R/R	6-0/210	32
	Kyle Farnsworth	R/R	6-4/240	29
58	Sean Henn	R/L	6-4/200	24
41	Randy Johnson	R/L	6-10/231	42
	Jeffrey Karstens	R/R	6-3/175	23
35	Mike Mussina	L/R	6-2/190	37
	Mike Myers	L/L	6-3/219	36
45	Carl Pavano	R/R	6-5/241	30
43	Scott Proctor	R/R	6-1/198	29
42	Mariano Rivera	R/R	6-2/185	36
31	Aaron Small	R/R	6-5/225	34
	Matthew Smith	L/L	6-5/225	26
56	Tanyon Sturtze	R/R	6-5/225	35
	Ron Villone	L/L	6-3/245	36
40	Chien-Ming Wang	R/R	6-3/200	26
33	Jaret Wright	R/R	6-2/230	30

No.	CATCHERS	B/T	Ht./Wt.	Age*
	Wil Nieves	R/R	5-11/190	28
20	Jorge Posada	B/R	6-2/205	34
	Kelly Stinnett	R/R	5-11/235	36

No.	INFIELDERS	B/T	Ht./Wt.	Age*
	Miguel Cairo	R/R	6-1/210	31
22	Robinson Cano	L/R	6-0/170	23
29	Felix Escalona	R/R	6-0/190	27
25	Jason Giambi	L/R	6-3/230	35
2	Derek Jeter	R/R	6-3/195	31
14	Andy Phillips	R/R	6-0/205	28
13	Alex Rodriguez	R/R	6-3/225	30

No.	OUTFIELDERS	B/T	Ht./Wt.	Age*
39	Melky Cabrera	B/L	5-11/170	21
	Bubba Crosby	L/L	5-11/185	29
18	Johnny Damon	L/L	6-2/205	32
55	Hideki Matsui	L/R	6-2/230	31
	Kevin Reese	L/L	5-11/195	28
11	Gary Sheffield	R/R	6-0/215	37
	Kevin Thompson	R/R	5-10/185	26
51	Bernie Williams	B/R	6-2/205	37

*Age as of April 1, 2006.

Ballpark (capacity, surface)
Yankee Stadium (57,478, grass)
Address
Yankee Stadium
E. 161 St. and River Ave.
Bronx, NY 10451
Official website
www.yankees.com
Business phone
718-293-4300
Ticket information
212-307-1212, 718-293-6000
Field dimensions (from home plate)
To left field at foul line, 318 feet
To center field, 408 feet
To right field at foul line, 314 feet
First game played
April 18, 1923 (Yankees 4, Red Sox 1)

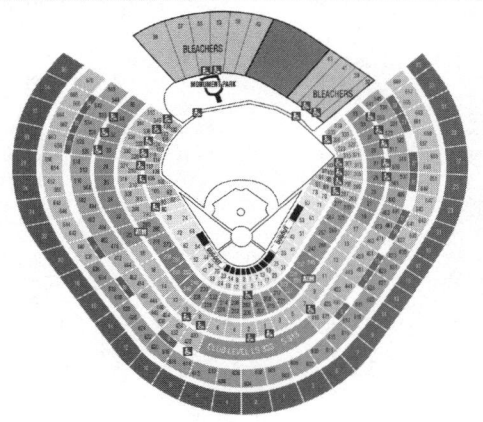

2006 SEASON New York Yankees

New York Yankees · **2006 SEASON**

Date	Opp.	Res.	Score	(inn.*)	Hits	Opp. hits	Winning pitcher	Losing pitcher	Save	Record	Pos.	GB
4-3	Bos.	W	9-2		15	6	Johnson	Wells		1-0	1st	+0.5
4-5	Bos.	W	4-3		7	11	Rivera	Foulke		2-0	T1st	...
4-6	Bos.	L	3-7		4	14	Timlin	Rivera		2-1	T1st	...
4-8	Bal.	L	5-12		10	18	Ponson	Wright		2-2	T1st	...
4-9	Bal.	W	8-5		12	11	Sturtze	Reed	Rivera	3-2	T1st	...
4-10	Bal.	L	2-7		8	14	Lopez	Pavano		3-3	T2nd	1.0
4-11	At Bos.	L	1-8		6	9	Wakefield	Mussina		3-4	T4th	2.0
4-13	At Bos.	W	5-2		12	7	Wright	Schilling	Rivera	4-4	3rd	1.5
4-14	At Bos.	L	5-8		10	8	Foulke	Gordon		4-5	T3rd	2.5
4-15	At Bal.	L	1-8		4	9	Chen	Pavano		4-6	T4th	2.5
4-16	At Bal.	L	6-7		8	13	Kline	Gordon	Ryan	4-7	T4th	3.5
4-17	At Bal.	L	4-8		11	13	Cabrera	Brown		4-8	T4th	4.0
4-18	T.B.	W	19-8		20	14	Wright	Bell		5-8	4th	3.0
4-19	T.B.	L	2-6		9	8	Nomo	Johnson		5-9	T4th	4.0
4-20	At Tor.	W	11-2		14	7	Pavano	Lilly		6-9	4th	3.0
4-21	At Tor.	W	4-3		9	13	Mussina	Chacin	Rivera	7-9	4th	3.0
4-22	Tex.	L	3-5		7	12	Young	Brown	Cordero	7-10	T4th	3.0
4-23	Tex.	L	2-10		5	19	Park	Wright		7-11	5th	4.0
4-24	Tex.	W	11-1		14	3	Johnson	Astacio		8-11	T4th	4.0
4-26	L.A.	W	12-4		12	8	Pavano	Colon		9-11	4th	4.5
4-27	L.A.	L	1-5		9	12	Washburn	Mussina		9-12	4th	5.0
4-28	L.A.	L	1-3		8	9	Lackey	Brown	Rodriguez	9-13	4th	5.5
4-29	Tor.	L	0-2		3	7	Halladay	Johnson		9-14	4th	6.5
4-30	Tor.	W	4-3		10	8	Rivera	Chulk		10-14	4th	6.5
5-1	Tor.	L	6-8		8	16	Walker	Stanton	Batista	10-15	4th	7.5
5-2	At T.B.	W	6-2		13	6	Mussina	Kazmir		11-15	4th	6.5
5-3	At T.B.	L	4-11		6	16	Waechter	Brown		11-16	4th	6.5
5-4	At T.B.	L	8-11		10	15	Fossum	Henn	Baez	11-17	4th	7.5
5-5	At T.B.	L	2-6		7	9	Hendrickson	Wang		11-18	T4th	8.0
5-6	Oak.	L	3-6	(10)	6	8	Dotel	Rivera	Calero	11-19	T4th	9.0
5-7	Oak.	W	5-0		5	4	Mussina	Blanton		12-19	4th	9.0
5-8	Oak.	W	6-0		8	7	Brown	Harden		13-19	4th	8.0
5-9	Sea.	W	4-3		8	7	Johnson	Nelson	Rivera	14-19	4th	8.0
5-10	Sea.	W	7-4		12	6	Wang	Sele	Rivera	15-19	4th	7.0
5-11	Sea.	W	13-9		16	14	Quantrill	Thornton		16-19	4th	7.0
5-13	At Oak.	W	9-4		7	8	Mussina	Harden		17-19	4th	5.5
5-14	At Oak.	W	15-6		18	11	Brown	Blanton		18-19	4th	5.5
5-15	At Oak.	W	6-4		13	7	Johnson	Rincon	Rivera	19-19	4th	5.5
5-16	At Sea.	W	6-3		13	7	Wang	Hasegawa	Rivera	20-19	4th	5.0
5-17	At Sea.	W	6-0		10	5	Pavano	Mateo		21-19	4th	5.0
5-18	At Sea.	L	6-7		11	10	Nelson	Gordon	Villone	21-20	4th	6.0
5-20	At N.Y.	W	5-2		8	5	Brown	Zambrano	Rivera	22-20	T3rd	4.5
5-21	At N.Y.	L	1-7		5	15	Benson	Johnson		22-21	4th	5.5
5-22	At N.Y.	W	5-3		8	8	Pavano	Hernandez	Rivera	23-21	T3rd	4.5
5-24	Det.	W	12-3		14	10	Mussina	Ledezma		24-21	T3rd	4.5
5-25	Det.	W	4-2		8	6	Wang	Maroth	Rivera	25-21	T3rd	4.5
5-26	Det.	W	4-3		11	12	Brown	Bonderman	Rivera	26-21	T2nd	4.5
5-27	Bos.	W	6-3		7	11	Johnson	Wakefield	Rivera	27-21	2nd	3.5
5-28	Bos.	L	1-17		8	27	Clement	Pavano		27-22	2nd	3.5
5-29	Bos.	L	2-7		6	14	Wells	Mussina		27-23	T3rd	3.5
5-31	At K.C.	L	3-5		5	10	Greinke	Brown	MacDougal	27-24	4th	4.0
6-1	At K.C.	L	1-3		7	9	Carrasco	Johnson	MacDougal	27-25	4th	5.0
6-2	At K.C.	L	2-5		7	9	Jensen	Pavano	Burgos	27-26	4th	5.0
6-3	At Min.	L	3-6		9	11	Lohse	Mussina	Nathan	27-27	4th	5.0
6-4	At Min.	W	4-3	(10)	7	6	Gordon	Nathan	Rivera	28-27	4th	5.0
6-5	At Min.	L	3-9		9	14	Silva	Brown		28-28	4th	6.0
6-6	At Mil.	L	3-4		4	9	Davis	Johnson	Turnbow	28-29	4th	7.0
6-7	At Mil.	L	1-2		4	6	Sheets	Pavano	Turnbow	28-30	4th	7.0
6-8	At Mil.	W	12-3		16	6	Mussina	Capuano		29-30	4th	6.0
6-10	At StL.	L	1-8		6	10	Marquis	Wang		29-31	4th	7.0
6-11	At StL.	W	5-0		10	5	Johnson	Mulder	Rivera	30-31	4th	6.0
6-12	At StL.	L	3-5		9	10	King	Sturtze	Isringhausen	30-32	4th	6.0
6-14	Pit.	W	9-0		12	5	Mussina	Wells		31-32	4th	6.5
6-15	Pit.	W	7-5	(10)	15	9	Rivera	Mesa		32-32	T3rd	6.5
6-16	Pit.	W	6-1		9	5	Johnson	Perez		33-32	3rd	6.0
6-17	Chi.	W	9-6		15	12	Stanton	Ohman	Rivera	34-32	3rd	5.0

Date	Opp.	Res.	Score	(inn.*)	Hits	Opp. hits	Winning pitcher	Losing pitcher	Save	Record	Pos.	GB
6-18	Chi.	W	8-1		13	5	Wang	Rusch		35-32	3rd	5.0
6-19	Chi.	W	6-3		9	8	Mussina	Mitre	Rivera	36-32	3rd	5.0
6-20	T.B.	L	4-5		6	10	Fossum	Henn	Baez	36-33	3rd	5.0
6-21	T.B.	W	20-11		23	18	Groom	Harper		37-33	3rd	5.0
6-22	T.B.	L	3-5		6	6	Kazmir	Pavano	Baez	37-34	3rd	5.0
6-23	T.B.	L	4-9		11	11	Hendrickson	Wang	Baez	37-35	3rd	5.0
6-24	N.Y.	L	4-6		8	8	Martinez	Mussina		37-36	3rd	5.5
6-25	N.Y.	L	3-10		11	14	Glavine	Henn		37-37	3rd	6.5
6-26	N.Y.	W	5-4		8	7	Rivera	Looper		38-37	3rd	6.5
6-27	At Bal.	W	6-4		7	10	Sturtze	Kline	Rivera	39-37	3rd	5.5
6-28	At Bal.	L	4-5	(10)	9	9	Ryan	Stanton		39-38	3rd	5.5
7-1	At Det.	L	2-10		8	12	Bonderman	Johnson		39-39	4th	6.0
7-2	At Det.	W	8-4		13	7	Gordon	Percival		40-39	3rd	6.0
7-3	At Det.	W	1-0		9	6	Wang	Robertson	Rivera	41-39	3rd	5.0
7-4	Bal.	W	13-8		14	8	Anderson	Ryan		42-39	3rd	4.0
7-5	Bal.	W	12-3		17	9	Johnson	Lopez		43-39	3rd	4.0
7-7	Cle.	W	7-2		9	7	Mussina	Millwood		44-39	3rd	3.5
7-8	Cle.	W	5-4		8	10	Wang	Lee	Rivera	45-39	3rd	3.5
7-9	Cle.	L	7-8		11	12	Elarton	May	Wickman	45-40	3rd	3.5
7-10	Cle.	W	9-4		9	11	Johnson	Westbrook	Rivera	46-40	3rd	2.5
7-14	At Bos.	W	8-6		14	9	Gordon	Schilling	Rivera	47-40	3rd	1.5
7-15	At Bos.	L	1-17		5	15	Wells	Redding		47-41	3rd	2.5
7-16	At Bos.	W	7-4		11	8	Johnson	Clement	Rivera	48-41	3rd	1.5
7-17	At Bos.	W	5-3		5	7	Leiter	Wakefield	Rivera	49-41	2nd	0.5
7-18	At Tex.	W	11-10		13	12	Sturtze	Brocail	Rivera	50-41	1st	+0.5
7-19	At Tex.	L	1-2		7	7	Loe	Franklin	Cordero	50-42	2nd	0.5
7-20	At Tex.	W	8-4		10	8	Small	Benoit		51-42	2nd	0.5
7-21	At L.A.	L	5-6		9	8	Colon	Gordon	Rodriguez	51-43	2nd	1.5
7-22	At L.A.	L	3-6		7	10	Lackey	Leiter	Rodriguez	51-44	2nd	1.5
7-23	At L.A.	L	6-8		12	11	Santana	Brown	Rodriguez	51-45	2nd	2.5
7-24	At L.A.	W	4-1		6	9	Mussina	Washburn	Rivera	52-45	2nd	1.5
7-26	Min.	W	4-0		9	2	Johnson	Radke		53-45	2nd	1.0
7-27	Min.	L	3-7		9	14	Santana	Leiter	Nathan	53-46	2nd	2.0
7-28	Min.	W	6-3		11	7	Small	Mays	Rivera	54-46	2nd	1.5
7-29	L.A.	L	1-4		7	10	Santana	Mussina	Rodriguez	54-47	2nd	2.5
7-30	L.A.	W	8-7		12	9	Rivera	Rodriguez		55-47	2nd	2.5
7-31	L.A.	W	8-7	(11)	13	9	Gordon	Gregg		56-47	2nd	2.5
8-2	At Cle.	L	5-6		7	8	Elarton	Leiter	Wickman	56-48	2nd	3.5
8-3	At Cle.	L	4-7		9	11	Lee	Mussina	Wickman	56-49	2nd	4.5
8-4	At Cle.	W	4-3		11	9	Gordon	Wickman	Rivera	57-49	2nd	4.5
8-5	At Tor.	W	6-2		11	9	Small	Chacin	Rivera	58-49	2nd	3.5
8-6	At Tor.	L	5-8		10	14	Walker	Johnson		58-50	2nd	3.5
8-7	At Tor.	W	6-2		12	7	Leiter	Towers	Rivera	59-50	2nd	3.5
8-8	Chi.	W	3-2		4	9	Mussina	Hernandez	Rivera	60-50	2nd	3.5
8-9	Chi.	L	1-2		5	6	Contreras	Chacon	Hermanson	60-51	2nd	4.5
8-10	Chi.	L	1-2	(10)	7	5	Cotts	Rivera	Hermanson	60-52	2nd	5.5
8-11	Tex.	W	9-8		13	10	Sturtze	Baldwin	Rivera	61-52	2nd	5.0
8-12	Tex.	W	6-5		12	9	Leiter	Wilson	Sturtze	62-52	2nd	5.0
8-13	Tex.	W	7-5	(11)	12	13	Small	Loe		63-52	2nd	5.0
8-14	Tex.	W	10-3		11	11	Chacon	Benoit		64-52	2nd	4.5
8-15	At T.B.	W	5-2		7	5	Wright	Fossum	Rivera	65-52	2nd	3.5
8-16	At T.B.	L	3-4	(11)	9	8	Orvella	Embree		65-53	2nd	4.5
8-17	At T.B.	L	6-7		7	7	Miller	Sturtze	Baez	65-54	2nd	4.5
8-19	At Chi.	W	3-1		8	6	Mussina	Garland	Rivera	66-54	2nd	4.0
8-20	At Chi.	W	5-0		7	4	Chacon	Hernandez		67-54	2nd	3.0
8-21	At Chi.	L	2-6		11	10	Contreras	Johnson		67-55	2nd	4.0
8-22	Tor.	W	7-0		12	5	Wright	Downs		68-55	2nd	3.5
8-23	Tor.	W	5-4		9	10	Rivera	Batista		69-55	2nd	3.5
8-24	Tor.	L	5-9		13	12	Bush	Mussina		69-56	2nd	3.5
8-25	Tor.	W	6-2		11	6	Chacon	Chacin		70-56	2nd	2.5
8-26	K.C.	W	5-1		8	6	Johnson	Wood		71-56	2nd	2.5
8-27	K.C.	W	8-7		9	12	Embree	Camp		72-56	2nd	1.5
8-28	K.C.	W	10-3		15	5	Leiter	Greinke		73-56	2nd	1.5
8-29	At Sea.	W	7-4		8	7	Small	Thornton	Rivera	74-56	2nd	1.5
8-30	At Sea.	L	3-8		6	10	Harris	Chacon		74-57	2nd	2.5
8-31	At Sea.	W	2-0		5	4	Johnson	Hernandez	Rivera	75-57	2nd	2.5
9-1	At Sea.	L	1-5		6	8	Sherrill	Sturtze		75-58	2nd	3.5
9-2	At Oak.	L	0-12		7	13	Haren	Leiter		75-59	2nd	3.5
9-3	At Oak.	W	7-0		9	5	Small	Saarloos		76-59	2nd	3.5

Date	Opp.	Res.	Score	(inn.*)	Hits	Opp. hits	Winning pitcher	Losing pitcher	Save	Record	Pos.	GB
9-4	At Oak.	W	7-3		13	7	Chacon	Zito		77-59	2nd	3.5
9-6	T.B.	L	3-4		11	9	Orvella	Rivera	Baez	77-60	2nd	4.0
9-7	T.B.	W	5-4		8	8	Sturtze	Borowski	Rivera	78-60	2nd	4.0
9-8	T.B.	L	4-7		6	13	Hendrickson	Wang	Baez	78-61	2nd	4.0
9-9	Bos.	W	8-4		14	11	Small	Wells		79-61	2nd	3.0
9-10	Bos.	L	2-9		6	16	Schilling	Chacon		79-62	2nd	4.0
9-11	Bos.	W	1-0		3	3	Johnson	Wakefield	Rivera	80-62	2nd	3.0
9-13	At T.B.	W	17-3		20	5	Wright	Waechter		81-62	2nd	2.5
9-14	At T.B.	W	6-5		11	9	Wang	Orvella	Rivera	82-62	2nd	2.5
9-15	At T.B.	W	9-5		15	8	Small	McClung	Rivera	83-62	2nd	1.5
9-16	At Tor.	W	11-10		12	14	Proctor	Bush	Rivera	84-62	2nd	1.5
9-17	At Tor.	W	1-0		10	6	Chacon	Chacin	Gordon	85-62	2nd	1.5
9-18	At Tor.	L	5-6		8	11	Lilly	Wright	Batista	85-63	2nd	1.5
9-19	Bal.	W	3-2		8	7	Rivera	DuBose		86-63	2nd	0.5
9-20	Bal.	W	12-9		16	18	Small	Maine		87-63	2nd	0.5
9-21	Bal.	W	2-1		7	4	Johnson	Lopez	Rivera	88-63	1st	+0.5
9-22	Bal.	W	7-6		8	8	Mussina	Chen	Gordon	89-63	1st	+1.0
9-23	Tor.	W	5-0		8	4	Chacon	Lilly		90-63	1st	+1.0
9-24	Tor.	L	4-7		8	10	Downs	Wright	Batista	90-64	T1st	...
9-25	Tor.	W	8-4		12	9	Wang	Towers	Rivera	91-64	T1st	...
9-26	At Bal.	W	11-3		12	8	Johnson	Lopez		92-64	1st	+0.5
9-27	At Bal.	L	9-17		12	14	Rakers	Leiter		92-65	T1st	...
9-28	At Bal.	W	2-1		9	5	Chacon	Cabrera	Rivera	93-65	1st	+1.0
9-29	At Bal.	W	8-4		8	6	Small	Bedard		94-65	1st	+1.0
9-30	At Bos.	L	3-5		7	4	Wells	Wang	Timlin	94-66	T1st	...
10-1	At Bos.	W	8-4		12	7	Johnson	Wakefield		95-66	1st	+1.0
10-2	At Bos.	L	1-10		11	11	Schilling	Wright		95-67	T1st	...

Monthly records: April (10-14), May (17-10), June (12-14), July (17-9), August (19-10), September (19-9), October (1-1).
*Innings, if other than nine. ! First game of a doubleheader. & Second game of a doubleheader.

RECORDS

2005 regular-season record: 95-67
Position: 1st in A.L. East
Home: 53-28   Road: 42-39
A.L. East: 41-33   A.L. Central: 18-13
A.L. West: 25-14   N.L. 11-7
Vs. LH starters: 30-23
Vs. RH starters: 65-44
Grass: 83-58   Artificial: 12-9
Day: 33-22   Night: 62-45
1-Run: 27-16   X-inn.: 4-4
Doubleheaders: 0-0-0
Team record past five years: 495-312
(.613, ranks 1st in league in that span)

TEAM LEADERS

Batting average: Alex Rodriguez (.321).
At-bats: Derek Jeter (654).
Runs: Alex Rodriguez (124).
Hits: Derek Jeter (202).
Total Bases: Alex Rodriguez (369).
Doubles: Hideki Matsui (45).
Triples: Derek Jeter (5).
Home runs: Alex Rodriguez (48).
Runs batted in: Alex Rodriguez (130).
Stolen bases: Tony Womack (27).
Slugging percentage: Alex Rodriguez (.610).
On-base percentage: Jason Giambi (.440).
Wins: Randy Johnson (17).
Earned-run average: Randy Johnson (3.79).

Complete games: Randy Johnson (4).
Shutouts: Mike Mussina (2).

GAMES BY POSITION

Catcher: Jorge Posada 133, John Flaherty 45, Wil Nieves 3.
First base: Tino Martinez 122, Jason Giambi 78, Andy Phillips 19, Russ Johnson 7, Felix Escalona 1, John Flaherty 1.
Second base: Robinson Cano 131, Tony Womack 24, Rey Sanchez 9, Mark Bellhorn 2, Felix Escalona 1, Russ Johnson 1.
Third base: Alex Rodriguez 161, Russ Johnson 8, Mark Bellhorn 4, Felix Escalona 3, Andy Phillips 1, Rey Sanchez1.
Shortstop: Derek Jeter 157, Rey Sanchez 10, Felix Escalona 5, Alex Rodriguez 3, Mark Bellhorn 2.
Outfield: Hideki Matsui 142, Gary Sheffield 131, Bernie Williams 112, Bubba Crosby 67, Tony Womack 66, Matt Lawton 19, Ruben Sierra 18, Melky Cabrera 6, Russ Johnson 3, Kevin Reese 2, Mike Vento 2, Andy Phillips 1.
Designated hitter: Jason Giambi 60, Ruben Sierra 30, Gary Sheffield 23, Bernie Williams 23, Hideki Matsui 19, Tony Womack 11, Andy Phillips 4, Bubba Crosby 4, Russ Johnson 3, Jorge Posada 3, Rey Sanchez 2, Derek Jeter 1, Tino Martinez 1, Alex Rodriguez 1.

TOP DRAFT CHOICES

1. **C.J. Henry**, SS, Putnam City H.S., Oklahoma City.
2. **J. Brent Cox**, RHP, Texas.
3. **Brett Gardner**, OF, College of Charleston.
4. **Lance Pendleton**, RHP, Rice.
5. **Zach Kroenke**, LHP, Nebraska.
6. **Doug Fisher**, RHP, Fresno State.
7. **Garrett Patterson**, LHP, Oklahoma.
8. **Austin Jackson**, OF, Ryan H.S., Denton, Texas.
9. **James Cooper**, OF, Loyola Marymount.
10. **Kyle Anson**, 3B, Texas State.

OAKLAND ATHLETICS
AMERICAN LEAGUE WEST DIVISION

2006 SEASON

Athletics Schedule

Home games shaded.
All-Star Game July 11 at Pittsburgh. Schedule subject to change.

APRIL

SUN	MON	TUE	WED	THU	FRI	SAT
2	3 NYY	4 NYY	5 NYY	6 SEA	7 SEA	8 SEA
9 SEA	10	11 MIN	12 MIN	13 MIN	14 TEX	15 TEX
16 TEX	17	18 DET	19 DET	20 DET	21 LAA	22 LAA
23 LAA	24 TEX	25 TEX	26 TEX	27	28 KC	29 KC
30 KC						

MAY

SUN	MON	TUE	WED	THU	FRI	SAT
	1 LAA	2 LAA	3 CLE	4 CLE	5 TB	6 TB
7 TB	8	9 TOR	10 TOR	11 TOR	12 NYY	13 NYY
14 NYY	15	16 SEA	17 SEA	18 SEA	19 SF	20 SF
21 SF	22 CHW	23 CHW	24 CHW	25 TEX	26 TEX	27 TEX
28 TEX	29 KC	30 KC	31 KC			

JUNE

SUN	MON	TUE	WED	THU	FRI	SAT
				1 MIN	2 MIN	3 MIN
4 MIN	5	6 CLE	7 CLE	8 CLE	9 NYY	10 NYY
11 NYY	12	13 SEA	14 SEA	15 SEA	16 LAD	17 LAD
18 LAD	19 COL	20 COL	21 COL	22	23 SF	24 SF
25 SF	26	27 SD	28 SD	29 SD	30 ARI	

JULY

SUN	MON	TUE	WED	THU	FRI	SAT
						1 ARI
2 ARI	3 DET	4 DET	5 DET	6 LAA	7 LAA	8 LAA
9 LAA	10	11 ALL-STAR	12	13 BOS	14 BOS	15 BOS
16 BOS	17 BAL	18 BAL	19 BAL	20	21 DET	22 DET
23 DET	24 BOS	25 BOS	26 BOS	27 TOR	28 TOR	29 TOR
30 TOR	31 LAA					

AUGUST

SUN	MON	TUE	WED	THU	FRI	SAT
		1 LAA	2 LAA	3	4 SEA	5 SEA
6 SEA	7 TEX	8 TEX	9 TEX	10	11 TB	12 TB
13 TB	14 SEA	15 SEA	16 SEA	17	18 KC	19 KC
20 KC	21 TOR	22 TOR	23 TOR	24	25 TEX	26 TEX
27 TEX	28 BOS	29 BOS	30 BOS	31		

SEPTEMBER

SUN	MON	TUE	WED	THU	FRI	SAT
					1 BAL	2 BAL
3 BAL	4 TEX	5 TEX	6 TEX	7	8 TB	9 TB
10 TB	11 MIN	12 MIN	13 MIN	14	15 CHW	16 CHW
17 CHW	18 CLE	19 CLE	20 CLE	21 LAA	22 LAA	23 LAA
24 LAA	25 SEA	26 SEA	27 LAA	28 LAA	29 LAA	30 LAA

OCTOBER

SUN	MON	TUE	WED	THU	FRI	SAT
1 LAA	2	3	4	5	6	7

Home games are shaded. All-Star Game is July 11 at Pittsburgh. Schedule is subject to change.

Harden

CLUB DIRECTORY

Owners
Lewis Wolff
John Fisher
President
Michael P. Crowley
Vice president and general manager
Billy Beane
Assistant general manager
David Forst
Special assistants to general manager
Randy Johnson
Matt Keough

Director of player development
Keith Lieppman
Coordinator of scouting
Bryn Alderson
Director of minor league operations
Ted Polakowski
V.p., broadcasting and communications
Ken Pries
Director of public relations
Jim Young
Baseball information manager
Mike Selleck

MINOR LEAGUE AFFILIATES

Class	Team	League	Manager
AAA	Sacramento	Pacific Coast	Tony DeFrancesco
AA	Midland	Texas	Von Hayes
Advanced A	Stockton	California	Todd Stevenson
A	Kane County	Midwest	Aaron Nieckula
Short-Season A	Vancouver	Northwest	To be announced
Rookie	Athletics	Arizona	Ruben Escalera

BROADCAST INFORMATION

Radio: To be announced.
TV: KICU-TV (Channel 36).
Cable TV: Fox Sports Net Bay Area.

SPRING TRAINING

Ballpark (city): Phoenix Stadium (Phoenix, Ariz.).
Ticket information: 602-392-0074.

For more on the Athletics, go to www.sportingnews.com/baseball/teams/athletics/

SPRING TRAINING ROSTER

Manager—Ken Macha (39).
Coaches—Brad Fischer (35), Bob Geren (52), Rene Lachemann (15), Gerald Perry (48), Ron Washington (38), Curt Young (41).

No.	PITCHERS	B/T	Ht./Wt.	Age*
55	Joe Blanton	R/R	6-3/225	25
50	Kiko Calero	R/R	6-1/185	31
51	Juan Cruz	R/R	6-2/165	27
58	Justin Duchscherer	R/R	6-3/190	28
47	Ron Flores	L/L	5-11/190	26
46	Jairo Garcia	R/R	6-0/164	23
	Chad Gaudin	R/R	5-11/165	23
40	Rich Harden	L/R	6-1/180	24
24	Danny Haren	R/R	6-5/220	25
37	Joe Kennedy	R/L	6-4/245	26
	Shane Komine	R/R	5-9/175	25
	Esteban Loaiza	R/R	6-3/215	34
54	Chris Mabeus	R/R	6-3/210	27
45	Dan Meyer	R/L	6-3/210	24
36	John Rheinecker	L/L	6-2/215	26
	Matt Roney	R/R	6-3/240	26
31	Kirk Saarloos	R/R	6-0/180	26
20	Huston Street	R/R	6-0/185	22
45	Jay Witasick	R/R	6-4/235	33
75	Barry Zito	L/L	6-4/215	27

No.	CATCHERS	B/T	Ht./Wt.	Age*
5	Jeremy Brown	R/R	5-10/210	26
18	Jason Kendall	R/R	6-0/195	31
17	Adam Melhuse	B/R	6-2/200	34

No.	INFIELDERS	B/T	Ht./Wt.	Age*
49	Freddie Bynum	L/R	6-1/180	26
3	Eric Chavez	L/R	6-1/206	28
7	Bobby Crosby	R/R	6-3/195	26
14	Mark Ellis	R/R	5-11/180	28
11	Dan Johnson	L/R	6-2/220	26
	Antonio Perez	R/R	5-11/175	26
8	Mike Rouse	L/R	5-11/185	25
19	Marco Scutaro	R/R	5-10/170	30

No.	OUTFIELDERS	B/T	Ht./Wt.	Age*
	Milton Bradley	B/R	6-0/190	27
	Javier Herrera	R/R	5-11/190	20
23	Bobby Kielty	B/R	6-1/225	29
21	Mark Kotsay	L/L	6-0/201	30
16	Jay Payton	R/R	5-10/185	33
	Nick Swisher	B/L	6-0/195	26
26	Charles Thomas	L/L	6-0/190	27
12	Matt Watson	L/R	5-11/200	27

*Age as of April 1, 2006.

BALLPARK INFORMATION

Ballpark (capacity, surface)
McAfee Coliseum (34,179, grass)

Address
Oakland Athletics
7000 Coliseum Way
Oakland, CA 94621

Official website
www.oaklandathletics.com

Business phone
510-638-4900

Ticket information
510-638-4627

Field dimensions (from home plate)
To left field at foul line, 330 feet
To center field, 400 feet
To right field at foul line, 330 feet

First game played
April 17, 1968 (Orioles 4, Athletics 1)

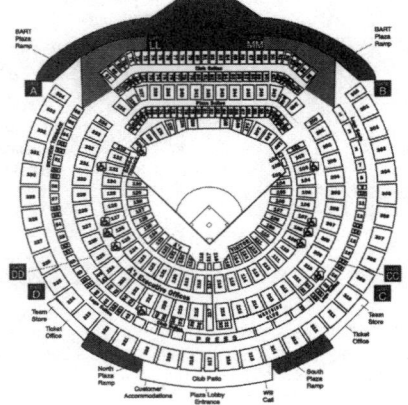

2006 SEASON · Oakland Athletics

Date	Opp.	Res.	Score	(inn.*)	Hits	Opp. hits	Winning pitcher	Losing pitcher	Save	Record	Pos.	GB
4-4	At Bal.	L	0-4		8	7	Lopez	Zito		0-1	4th	1.0
4-6	At Bal.	W	9-0		12	3	Saarloos	Cabrera		1-1	T1st	...
4-7	At Bal.	W	5-1		7	4	Rincon	Kline		2-1	T1st	...
4-8	At T.B.	L	2-3	(10)	11	9	Baez	Cruz		2-2	T1st	...
4-9	At T.B.	L	2-11		3	12	Nomo	Zito		2-3	T2nd	1.0
4-10	At T.B.	W	6-1		9	8	Harden	Brazelton		3-3	T1st	...
4-11	Tor.	L	3-10		9	12	Chacin	Saarloos		3-4	T2nd	1.0
4-12	Tor.	L	2-5		7	6	Towers	Haren	Batista	3-5	T3rd	2.0
4-13	Tor.	W	6-3		8	7	Calero	Frasor		4-5	T3rd	1.0
4-15	L.A.	L	1-6		2	8	Colon	Zito		4-6	4th	2.0
4-16	L.A.	W	1-0	(10)	6	4	Calero	Shields		5-6	T2nd	1.0
4-17	L.A.	W	7-6		11	8	Street	Lackey	Dotel	6-6	T1st	...
4-18	At Tex.	W	8-5		13	7	Haren	Park	Dotel	7-6	T1st	...
4-19	At Tex.	L	0-3		6	7	Astacio	Blanton	Cordero	7-7	T1st	...
4-20	At Sea.	L	6-7		12	13	Pineiro	Street	Guardado	7-8	4th	1.0
4-21	At Sea.	W	3-0		5	6	Harden	Franklin	Dotel	8-8	T2nd	1.0
4-22	At L.A.	W	4-3		10	9	Yabu	Rodriguez	Dotel	9-8	T1st	...
4-23	At L.A.	L	5-9		8	11	Woods	Haren		9-9	3rd	1.0
4-24	At L.A.	L	0-1		4	6	Shields	Blanton	Rodriguez	9-10	T3rd	2.0
4-25	Chi.	L	0-6		4	9	Garland	Zito		9-11	4th	2.5
4-26	Chi.	W	9-7		13	14	Duchscherer	Marte	Dotel	10-11	T3rd	1.5
4-27	Chi.	W	2-1		7	5	Duchscherer	Marte		11-11	T3rd	1.5
4-29	Sea.	L	2-4		9	8	Sele	Haren	Guardado	11-12	4th	2.0
4-30	Sea.	W	6-5	(10)	13	13	Yabu	Villone		12-12	T2nd	1.0
5-1	Sea.	W	3-2		8	6	Zito	Pineiro	Dotel	13-12	2nd	1.0
5-2	Tex.	L	2-3		5	6	Rogers	Harden	Cordero	13-13	2nd	2.0
5-3	Tex.	L	1-6		9	7	Young	Saarloos		13-14	3rd	3.0
5-4	Tex.	L	7-16		10	18	Shouse	Haren		13-15	3rd	4.0
5-6	At N.Y.	W	6-3	(10)	8	6	Dotel	Rivera	Calero	14-15	3rd	4.0
5-7	At N.Y.	L	0-5		4	5	Mussina	Blanton		14-16	3rd	4.0
5-8	At N.Y.	L	0-6		7	8	Brown	Harden		14-17	3rd	4.0
5-9	At Bos.	L	5-13		11	12	Wakefield	Haren		14-18	3rd	4.0
5-10	At Bos.	L	2-3		3	5	Mantei	Dotel		14-19	3rd	5.0
5-11	At Bos.	L	5-6		9	11	Foulke	Dotel		14-20	3rd	5.0
5-13	N.Y.	L	4-9		8	7	Mussina	Harden		14-21	T3rd	5.5
5-14	N.Y.	L	6-15		11	18	Brown	Blanton		14-22	T3rd	6.0
5-15	N.Y.	L	4-6		7	13	Johnson	Rincon	Rivera	14-23	4th	7.0
5-16	Bos.	W	6-4		9	12	Yabu	Myers	Dotel	15-23	T3rd	7.0
5-17	Bos.	L	5-7		9	4	Embree	Cruz	Foulke	15-24	T3rd	7.0
5-18	Bos.	W	13-6		19	8	Etherton	Wells		16-24	T3rd	7.0
5-20	At S.F.	W	8-4		12	9	Yabu	Rueter		17-24	3rd	7.0
5-21	At S.F.	L	2-3		5	10	Fassero	Haren	Walker	17-25	T3rd	8.0
5-22	At S.F.	L	1-3		8	6	Lowry	Zito	Walker	17-26	4th	8.0
5-24	At T.B.	L	4-5		9	9	Harper	Saarloos	Baez	17-27	4th	8.5
5-25	At T.B.	L	6-14		9	15	Kazmir	Blanton		17-28	4th	8.5
5-26	At T.B.	L	1-2		5	4	Nomo	Haren	Baez	17-29	4th	9.5
5-27	At Cle.	L	1-4		4	6	Lee	Zito	Riske	17-30	4th	10.5
5-28	At Cle.	L	3-6		8	12	Elarton	Saarloos	Howry	17-31	4th	11.5
5-29	At Cle.	L	2-6		8	6	Westbrook	Etherton	Miller	17-32	4th	12.5
5-30	T.B.	W	5-4	(11)	11	10	Street	Harper		18-32	4th	11.5
5-31	T.B.	W	10-1		10	5	Haren	Nomo		19-32	4th	11.5
6-1	T.B.	W	11-2		15	9	Zito	Hendrickson		20-32	4th	10.5
6-2	Tor.	W	5-3		8	9	Saarloos	Towers	Street	21-32	4th	10.0
6-3	Tor.	L	2-6		8	9	Halladay	Glynn		21-33	4th	10.0
6-4	Tor.	W	5-2		7	5	Blanton	Lilly	Street	22-33	4th	10.0
6-5	Tor.	W	12-4		16	6	Haren	Gaudin		23-33	4th	9.5
6-7	At Was.	L	1-2		8	5	Armas	Zito	Cordero	23-34	4th	9.5
6-8	At Was.	L	2-7		5	12	Loaiza	Glynn		23-35	4th	10.5
6-9	At Was.	L	3-4		10	8	Hernandez	Blanton	Cordero	23-36	4th	11.0
6-10	At Atl.	W	6-4		10	9	Haren	Colon	Street	24-36	4th	11.0
6-11	At Atl.	L	3-5		5	9	Smoltz	Duchscherer		24-37	4th	11.0
6-12	At Atl.	W	11-5		13	7	Zito	Boyer		25-37	4th	11.0
6-14	N.Y.	W	5-0		12	4	Blanton	Glavine	Street	26-37	4th	10.5
6-15	N.Y.	W	3-2		6	5	Duchscherer	Ring		27-37	4th	9.5
6-16	N.Y.	L	6-9		11	9	Benson	Glynn	Looper	27-38	4th	10.0
6-17	Phi.	L	1-6		5	11	Tejeda	Zito		27-39	4th	11.0

Date	Opp.	Res.	Score	(inn.*)	Hits	Opp. hits	Winning pitcher	Losing pitcher	Save	Record	Pos.	GB
6-18	Phi.	W	2-1		5	9	Saarloos	Lidle	Duchscherer	28-39	4th	11.0
6-19	Phi.	W	5-2		11	6	Blanton	Lieber	Duchscherer	29-39	4th	10.0
6-20	At Sea.	W	6-2		11	7	Haren	Villone		30-39	4th	10.0
6-21	At Sea.	W	4-2		8	7	Harden	Pineiro	Duchscherer	31-39	4th	10.0
6-22	At Sea.	L	4-5	(12)	13	11	Guardado	Glynn		31-40	4th	11.0
6-23	At Sea.	W	5-0		16	4	Saarloos	Franklin		32-40	4th	10.5
6-24	S.F.	W	4-3		11	6	Blanton	Fassero	Duchscherer	33-40	4th	10.5
6-25	S.F.	W	6-3		6	7	Haren	Lowry		34-40	3rd	10.5
6-26	S.F.	W	16-0		24	1	Harden	Tomko		35-40	3rd	10.5
6-28	Sea.	W	8-1		12	7	Zito	Moyer		36-40	3rd	11.0
6-29	Sea.	W	6-2		9	3	Blanton	Franklin		37-40	3rd	10.0
6-30	Sea.	W	6-2		6	8	Haren	Meche		38-40	3rd	9.0
7-1	Chi.	W	6-2		7	4	Harden	Contreras		39-40	3rd	9.0
7-2	Chi.	L	3-5		5	10	Garland	Saarloos	Hermanson	39-41	3rd	10.0
7-3	Chi.	W	7-2		16	6	Zito	Buehrle		40-41	3rd	10.0
7-5	At Tor.	W	10-7	(11)	18	15	Duchscherer	Batista		41-41	3rd	9.5
7-6	At Tor.	L	0-8		7	12	Lilly	Blanton		41-42	3rd	10.5
7-7	At Tor.	L	2-4		7	6	Chacin	Harden	Batista	41-43	3rd	10.5
7-8	At Chi.	W	4-2		13	9	Saarloos	Garland	Street	42-43	3rd	9.5
7-9	At Chi.	W	10-1		11	3	Zito	Buehrle		43-43	3rd	8.5
7-10	At Chi.	W	9-8	(11)	15	17	Street	Vizcaino		44-43	4th	7.5
7-14	Tex.	W	6-0		8	2	Harden	Park		45-43	3rd	7.5
7-15	Tex.	W	7-2		8	4	Zito	Wasdin		46-43	3rd	7.5
7-16	Tex.	L	8-10		12	12	Rogers	Blanton	Cordero	46-44	3rd	7.5
7-17	Tex.	W	5-4	(14)	13	13	Kennedy	Loe		47-44	3rd	7.5
7-18	At L.A.	L	2-5		5	8	Santana	Saarloos	Rodriguez	47-45	3rd	8.5
7-19	At L.A.	W	3-1		7	4	Harden	Washburn	Street	48-45	3rd	7.5
7-20	At L.A.	W	3-0		8	7	Zito	Byrd	Street	49-45	2nd	6.5
7-21	At Tex.	W	6-4		11	9	Witasick	Loe	Street	50-45	2nd	6.5
7-22	At Tex.	W	11-10		15	11	Haren	Young	Duchscherer	51-45	2nd	6.5
7-23	At Tex.	W	5-4		6	9	Saarloos	Rodriguez	Street	52-45	2nd	6.5
7-24	At Tex.	W	8-3		13	7	Harden	Park		53-45	2nd	5.5
7-25	Cle.	W	13-4		14	6	Zito	Sabathia	Yabu	54-45	2nd	5.0
7-26	Cle.	L	0-2		4	8	Westbrook	Blanton	Wickman	54-46	2nd	5.0
7-27	Cle.	W	5-4	(10)	14	14	Street	Riske		55-46	2nd	4.0
7-29	Det.	W	8-4		8	15	Harden	Douglass		56-46	2nd	3.5
7-30	Det.	W	9-5		13	10	Zito	Robertson	Witasick	57-46	2nd	2.5
7-31	Det.	W	5-2		9	7	Saarloos	Bonderman		58-46	2nd	1.5
8-1	At Min.	W	2-1		5	2	Blanton	Santana	Street	59-46	2nd	1.0
8-2	At Min.	W	5-2		9	9	Haren	Romero	Street	60-46	2nd	1.0
8-3	At Min.	L	3-4		5	5	Nathan	Duchscherer		60-47	2nd	2.0
8-4	At K.C.	W	5-2		12	4	Zito	Crain	Street	61-47	2nd	1.0
8-5	At K.C.	W	5-4		8	8	Kennedy	Affeldt	Street	62-47	2nd	1.0
8-6	At K.C.	W	16-1		18	7	Blanton	Lima		63-47	T1st	...
8-7	At K.C.	W	11-0		15	8	Haren	Hernandez		64-47	T1st	...
8-9	L.A.	L	2-9		8	12	Lackey	Harden		64-48	2nd	1.0
8-10	L.A.	W	4-3		8	5	Duchscherer	Shields	Street	65-48	T1st	...
8-11	L.A.	W	5-4		14	8	Duchscherer	Shields		66-48	1st	+1.0
8-12	Min.	L	0-1		3	3	Santana	Haren		66-49	T1st	...
8-13	Min.	W	5-2		9	8	Saarloos	Mays	Street	67-49	T1st	...
8-14	Min.	L	1-2		7	4	Rincon	Duchscherer	Nathan	67-50	2nd	1.0
8-15	Bal.	L	2-6		9	7	Lopez	Zito		67-51	2nd	2.0
8-16	Bal.	L	3-4		8	10	Chen	Witasick	Ryan	67-52	2nd	2.0
8-17	Bal.	L	3-5		5	9	DuBose	Haren	Williams	67-53	2nd	2.0
8-19	K.C.	W	4-0		9	5	Harden	Lima	Street	68-53	2nd	1.5
8-20	K.C.	L	1-2		6	4	Wood	Zito	MacDougal	68-54	2nd	2.5
8-21	K.C.	L	4-5	(12)	10	11	Gobble	Calero		68-55	2nd	2.5
8-23	At Det.	L	1-4		2	10	Robertson	Haren	Rodney	68-56	2nd	3.5
8-24	At Det.	W	9-2		15	10	Saarloos	Bonderman		69-56	2nd	3.5
8-25	At Det.	W	11-1		15	7	Zito	Maroth		70-56	2nd	2.5
8-26	At Bal.	W	4-1		7	9	Blanton	Chen	Street	71-56	2nd	1.5
8-27	At Bal.	W	12-3		15	11	Kennedy	DuBose		72-56	2nd	0.5
8-28	At Bal.	W	10-3		11	7	Haren	Maine		73-56	1st	+0.5
8-29	At Bal.	W	10-5	(12)	9	9	Calero	Julio		74-56	1st	+1.0
8-30	At L.A.	W	2-1	(11)	7	4	Calero	Rodriguez	Street	75-56	1st	+2.0
8-31	At L.A.	L	1-2		7	6	Lackey	Blanton	Rodriguez	75-57	1st	+1.0
9-1	At L.A.	L	0-3		6	10	Santana	Kennedy	Rodriguez	75-58	T1st	...
9-2	N.Y.	W	12-0		13	7	Haren	Leiter		76-58	T1st	...
9-3	N.Y.	L	0-7		5	9	Small	Saarloos		76-59	T1st	...

Date	Opp.	Res.	Score	(inn.*)	Hits	Opp. hits	Winning pitcher	Losing pitcher	Save	Record	Pos.	GB
9-4	N.Y.	L	3-7		7	13	Chacon	Zito		76-60	2nd	1.0
9-5	Sea.	L	0-2		5	7	Hernandez	Blanton	Guardado	76-61	2nd	1.5
9-6	Sea.	L	2-3		7	8	Pineiro	Kennedy	Guardado	76-62	2nd	1.5
9-7	Sea.	W	8-7		15	13	Street	Guardado		77-62	2nd	0.5
9-9	At Tex.	W	9-8		13	8	Zito	Dominguez	Street	78-62	2nd	1.0
9-10	At Tex.	W	5-4		8	8	Blanton	Loe	Street	79-62	2nd	1.0
9-11	At Tex.	L	4-7		10	9	Rogers	Kennedy	Wasdin	79-63	2nd	2.0
9-12	At Cle.	W	2-0		6	4	Haren	Sabathia	Street	80-63	2nd	1.0
9-13	At Cle.	L	2-5		8	8	Millwood	Duchscherer	Wickman	80-64	2nd	1.0
9-14	At Cle.	L	4-6		3	10	Westbrook	Zito	Wickman	80-65	2nd	1.0
9-15	At Bos.	W	6-2		14	7	Blanton	Schilling		81-65	T1st	...
9-16	At Bos.	L	2-3	(10)	8	7	Timlin	Cruz		81-66	2nd	1.0
9-17	At Bos.	L	1-2		4	7	Arroyo	Haren	Timlin	81-67	2nd	2.0
9-18	At Bos.	L	12-3		15	11	Saarloos	Clement		82-67	2nd	2.0
9-19	Min.	W	7-6		11	9	Zito	Radke		83-67	2nd	1.5
9-20	Min.	W	8-3		12	6	Blanton	Liriano		84-67	2nd	1.5
9-21	Min.	L	4-10		6	12	Baker	Kennedy		84-68	2nd	2.5
9-23	Tex.	L	1-3		5	9	Rogers	Haren	Cordero	84-69	2nd	4.0
9-24	Tex.	W	7-6		10	9	Duchscherer	Wasdin	Street	85-69	2nd	4.0
9-25	Tex.	L	2-6		10	12	Dominguez	Saarloos		85-70	2nd	4.0
9-26	L.A.	L	3-4		6	6	Lackey	Blanton	Rodriguez	85-71	2nd	5.0
9-27	L.A.	L	3-4		8	10	Santana	Kennedy	Rodriguez	85-72	2nd	6.0
9-28	L.A.	W	6-1		7	6	Haren	Byrd		86-72	2nd	5.0
9-29	L.A.	L	1-7		9	10	Colon	Zito		86-73	2nd	6.0
9-30	At Sea.	L	1-4		6	9	Moyer	Saarloos	Guardado	86-74	2nd	7.0
10-1	At Sea.	W	4-3		8	9	Blanton	Mateo	Street	87-74	2nd	7.0
10-2	At Sea.	W	8-3		14	5	Kennedy	Sherrill		88-74	2nd	7.0

Monthly records: April (12-12), May (7-20), June (19-8), July (20-6), August (17-11), September (11-17), October (2-0).
*Innings, if other than nine. ! First game of a doubleheader. & Second game of a doubleheader.

RECORDS

2005 regular-season record: 88-74
Position: 2nd in A.L. West
Home: 45-36   **Road:** 43-38
A.L. East: 21-27   **A.L. Central:** 25-15
A.L. West: 32-24   **N.L.** 10-8
Vs. LH starters: 28-18
Vs. RH starters: 60-56
Grass: 83-66   **Artificial:** 5-8
Day: 35-20   **Night:** 53-54
1-Run: 26-24   **X-inn.:** 10-4
Doubleheaders: 0-0-0
Team record past five years: 480-330
(.593, ranks 2nd in league in that span)

TEAM LEADERS

Batting average: Mark Ellis (.316).
At-bats: Eric Chavez (625).
Runs: Eric Chavez (92).
Hits: Eric Chavez (168).
Total Bases: Eric Chavez (291).
Doubles: Eric Chavez (40).
Triples: Mark Ellis (5).
Home runs: Eric Chavez (27).
Runs batted in: Eric Chavez (101).
Stolen bases: Jason Kendall (8).
Slugging percentage: Mark Ellis (.477).
On-base percentage: Mark Ellis (.384).
Wins: Danny Haren, Barry Zito (14).
Earned-run average: Rich Harden (2.53).
Complete games: Danny Haren (3).

Shutouts: Rich Harden, Kirk Saarloos (1).
Saves: Huston Street (23).
Innings pitched: Barry Zito (228.1).
Strikeouts: Barry Zito (171).

GAMES BY POSITION

Catcher: Jason Kendall 147, Adam Melhuse 24, Alberto Castillo 1.

First base: Dan Johnson 101, Scott Hatteberg 53, Nick Swisher 21, Mark Ellis 2, Erubiel Durazo 1.

Second base: Mark Ellis 115, Marco Scutaro 30, Keith Ginter 25, Freddie Bynum 3, Jermaine Clark 2.

Third base: Eric Chavez 153, Keith Ginter 12, Marco Scutaro 5, Hiram Bocachica 2.

Shortstop: Bobby Crosby 84, Marco Scutaro 81, Mark Ellis 7.

Outfield: Mark Kotsay 137, Nick Swisher 121, Bobby Kielty 96, Jay Payton 69, Eric Byrnes 54, Charles Thomas 27, Matt Watson 17, Hiram Bocachica 6, Freddie Bynum 2, Keith Ginter 2, Marco Scutaro 2, Jermaine Clark 1.

Designated hitter: Scott Hatteberg 79, Erubiel Durazo 39, Bobby Kielty 17, Keith Ginter 9, Adam Melhuse 8, Eric Chavez 6, Dan Johnson 5, Eric Byrnes 4, Jason Kendall 3, Mark Kotsay 2, Hiram Bocachica 1, Mark Ellis 1.

TOP DRAFT CHOICES

1a. **Cliff Pennington,** SS, Texas A&M.
1b. **Travis Buck,** OF, Arizona State.
2a. **Craig Italiano,** RHP, Flower Mound (Texas) H.S.
2b. **Jared Lansford,** RHP, St. Francis H.S., Santa Clara, Calif.
3. **Vincent Mazzaro,** RHP, Rutherford (N.J.) H.S.
4. **Jimmy Shull,** RHP, Cal Poly San Luis Obispo.
5. **Scott Deal,** RHP, Curtis H.S., University Place. Wash.
6. **Justin Sellers,** SS, Marina H.S., Huntington Beach, Calif.
7. **Kevin Bunch,** RHP, Serrano H.S., Victorville, Calif.
8. **Jason Ray,** RHP, Azusa Pacific.
9. **Trey Shields,** RHP, Alabama.
10. **John Herrera,** RHP, Lubbock Christian.

SEATTLE MARINERS
AMERICAN LEAGUE WEST DIVISION

2006 SEASON

Mariners Schedule
Home games shaded.
All-Star Game July 11 at Pittsburgh. Schedule subject to change.

APRIL

SUN	MON	TUE	WED	THU	FRI	SAT
2	3 LAA	4 LAA	5 LAA	6 OAK	7 OAK	8 OAK
9 OAK	10	11 CLE	12 CLE	13 CLE	14 BOS	15 BOS
16 BOS	17 BOS	18 TEX	19 TEX	20 TEX	21 DET	22 DET
23 DET	24 CHW	25 CHW	26 CHW	27	28 BAL	29 BAL
30 BAL						

MAY

SUN	MON	TUE	WED	THU	FRI	SAT
	1 MIN	2 MIN	3 CHW	4 CHW	5 CLE	6 CLE
7 CLE	8 TB	9 TB	10 TB	11	12 LAA	13 LAA
14 LAA	15	16 OAK	17 OAK	18 OAK	19 SD	20 SD
21 SD	22 BAL	23 BAL	24 BAL	25 BAL	26 MIN	27 MIN
28 MIN	29 TEX	30 TEX	31 TEX			

JUNE

SUN	MON	TUE	WED	THU	FRI	SAT
				1	2 KC	3 KC
4 KC	5 KC	6 MIN	7 MIN	8 MIN	9 LAA	10 LAA
11 LAA	12	13 OAK	14 OAK	15 OAK	16 SF	17 SF
18 SF	19	20 LAD	21 LAD	22 LAD	23 SD	24 SD
25 SD	26	27 ARI	28 ARI	29 ARI	30 COL	

JULY

SUN	MON	TUE	WED	THU	FRI	SAT
						1 COL
2 COL	3 LAA	4 LAA	5 LAA	6	7 DET	8 DET
9 DET	10	11 ALL-STAR	12	13	14 TOR	15 TOR
16 TOR	17 NYY	18 NYY	19 NYY	20	21 BOS	22 BOS
23 BOS	24 TOR	25 TOR	26 TOR	27	28 CLE	29 CLE
30 CLE	31 BAL					

AUGUST

SUN	MON	TUE	WED	THU	FRI	SAT
		1 BAL	2 BAL	3	4 OAK	5 OAK
6 OAK	7 TB	8 TB	9 TB	10 TEX	11 TEX	12 TEX
13 TEX	14 OAK	15 OAK	16 OAK	17 LAA	18 LAA	19 LAA
20 LAA	21	22 NYY	23 NYY	24 NYY	25 BOS	26 BOS
27 BOS	28 LAA	29 LAA	30 LAA	31		

SEPTEMBER

SUN	MON	TUE	WED	THU	FRI	SAT
					1 TB	2 TB
3 TB	4 DET	5 DET	6 DET	7	8 TEX	9 TEX
10 TEX	11 TOR	12 TOR	13 TOR	14 KC	15 KC	16 KC
17 KC	18 TEX	19 TEX	20 TEX	21 CHW	22 CHW	23 CHW
24 CHW	25 OAK	26 OAK	27 OAK	28	29 TEX	30 TEX

OCTOBER

SUN	MON	TUE	WED	THU	FRI	SAT
1 TEX	2	3	4	5	6	7

Home games are shaded. All-Star
Game is July 11 at Pittsburgh.
Schedule is subject to change.

Suzuki

CLUB DIRECTORY

Chairman and chief executive officer
Howard Lincoln
President and chief operating officer
Chuck Armstrong
Executive v.p., baseball operations
Bill Bavasi
Assoc. g.m./v.p., baseball administration
Lee Pelekoudas
V.p., player development and scouting
Benny Looper
Vice president, scouting
Bob Fontaine

Special assistants
John Boles, Dan Evans
Director, player development
Frank Mattox
Director, professional scouting
Ken Compton
Vice president, communications
Randy Adamack
Director, baseball information
Tim Hevly

MINOR LEAGUE AFFILIATES

Class	Team	League	Manager
AAA	Tacoma	Pacific Coast	Dave Brundage
AA	San Antonio	Texas	Daren Brown
Advanced A	Inland Empire	California	Gary Thurman
A	Wisconsin	Midwest	Scott Steinmann
Short-Season A	Everett	Northwest	James Horner
Rookie	Mariners	Arizona	Dana Williams

BROADCAST INFORMATION

Radio: KOMO-AM (1000).
TV: KSTW (Channel 11).
Cable TV: Fox Sports Net Northwest.

SPRING TRAINING

Ballpark: Peoria Stadium (Peoria, Ariz.).
Ticket information: 480-784-4444.

For more on the Mariners, www.sportingnews.com/baseball/teams/mariners/

Manager—Mike Hargrove (21).
Coaches—Rafael Chaves, Carlos Garcia (13), Mike Goff, Ron Hassey (9), Jeff Pentland, Jim Slaton (41).

No.	PITCHERS	B/T	Ht./Wt.	Age*
	Yorman Bazardo	R/R	6-2/202	21
	Travis Blackley	L/L	6-3/190	23
	Marcos Carvajal	R/R	6-4/175	21
	Renee Cortez	R/R	6-4/180	23
	Jesse Foppert	R/R	6-6/220	25
	Emiliano Fruto	R/R	6-3/170	21
	Luis Gonzalez	L/L	6-0/190	23
18	Eddie Guardado	R/L	6-0/205	35
59	Felix Hernandez	R/R	6-3/225	19
	Cesar Jimenez	L/L	5-11/180	21
	Robert Livingston	L/L	6-3/195	23
40	Julio Mateo	R/R	6-0/220	28
55	Gil Meche	R/R	6-3/215	27
50	Jamie Moyer	L/L	6-0/175	43
37	Clint Nageotte	R/R	6-3/225	25
38	Joel Pineiro	R/R	6-1/200	27
20	J.J. Putz	R/R	6-5/225	29
52	George Sherrill	L/L	6-0/245	28
39	Rafael Soriano	R/R	6-1/220	26
53	Matt Thornton	L/L	6-6/230	29
	Jarrod Washburn	L/L	6-1/195	31
	Jake Woods	L/L	6-1/190	24

No.	CATCHERS	B/T	Ht./Wt.	Age*
	Kenji Johjima	R/R	6-0/200	29
30	Rene Rivera	R/R	5-10/190	22

No.	INFIELDERS	B/T	Ht./Wt.	Age*
29	Adrian Beltre	R/R	5-11/220	26
46	Yuniesky Betancourt	R/R	5-10/190	24
16	Willie Bloomquist	R/R	5-11/185	28
4	Jose Lopez	R/R	6-2/200	22
12	Mike Morse	R/R	6-4/220	24
	Oswaldo Navarro	B/R	6-0/155	21
44	Richie Sexson	R/R	6-8/235	31

No.	OUTFIELDERS	B/T	Ht./Wt.	Age*
	Wladimir Balentien	R/R	6-2/180	21
	T.J. Bohn	R/R	6-5/205	26
	Shin-Soo Choo	L/L	5-11/178	23
	Carl Everett	B/R	6-0/215	34
28	Raul Ibanez	L/R	6-2/220	33
	Matt Lawton	L/R	5-10/195	34
7	Jeremy Reed	L/L	6-0/185	24
32	Chris Snelling	L/L	5-10/165	24
51	Ichiro Suzuki	L/R	5-9/172	32

*Age as of April 1, 2005.

Ballpark (capacity, surface)
  Safeco Field (47,447, grass).
Address
  1250 First Avenue South
  Seattle, WA 98134
Official website
  www.seattlemariners.com
Business phone
  206-346-4000
Ticket information
  206-346-4001
Field dimensions (from home plate)
  To left field at foul line, 331 feet
  To center field, 405 feet
  To right field at foul line, 326 feet
First game played
  July 15, 1999 (Padres 3, Mariners 2)

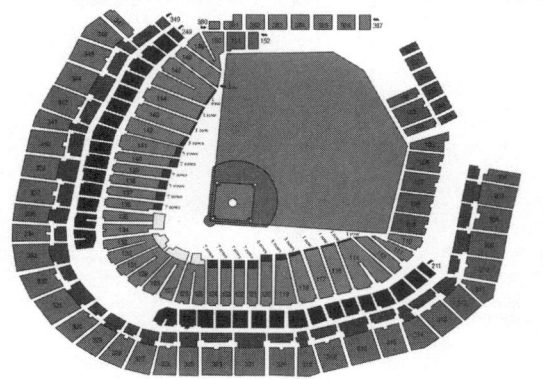

2006 SEASON Seattle Mariners

2006 SEASON *Seattle Mariners*

Date	Opp.	Res.	Score	(inn.*)	Hits	Opp. hits	Winning pitcher	Losing pitcher	Save	Record	Pos.	GB
4-4	Min.	W	5-1		5	5	Moyer	Radke		1-0	1st	+0.5
4-5	Min.	L	4-8		7	14	Santana	Thornton		1-1	2nd	0.5
4-6	Min.	L	1-4		10	7	Silva	Madritsch	Nathan	1-2	4th	0.5
4-8	Tex.	W	9-6		11	9	Putz	Regilio	Guardado	2-2	T1st	...
4-9	Tex.	L	6-7		11	10	Brocail	Guardado	Cordero	2-3	T2nd	1.0
4-10	Tex.	L	6-7		8	11	Riley	Thornton	Cordero	2-4	4th	1.0
4-11	At K.C.	W	8-2		13	6	Franklin	Hernandez		3-4	T2nd	1.0
4-13	At K.C.	W	2-1		7	4	Sele	Cerda	Guardado	4-4	2nd	0.5
4-14	At K.C.	W	10-2		10	11	Moyer	Bautista		5-4	T1st	...
4-15	At Chi.	L	4-6		5	9	Garland	Pineiro	Hermanson	5-5	2nd	1.0
4-16	At Chi.	L	1-2		3	4	Buehrle	Franklin		5-6	T2nd	1.0
4-17	At Chi.	W	5-4		10	8	Meche	Garcia	Guardado	6-6	T1st	...
4-18	At L.A.	L	1-6		12	13	Byrd	Sele		6-7	3rd	1.0
4-19	At L.A.	W	5-3		8	9	Moyer	Gregg	Guardado	7-7	T1st	...
4-20	Oak.	W	7-6		13	12	Pineiro	Street	Guardado	8-7	T1st	...
4-21	Oak.	L	0-3		6	5	Harden	Franklin	Dotel	8-8	T2nd	1.0
4-22	Cle.	L	1-6		6	9	Sabathia	Meche		8-9	4th	1.0
4-23	Cle.	L	2-5		7	8	Lee	Sele	Wickman	8-10	4th	2.0
4-24	Cle.	W	9-1		5	6	Moyer	Elarton		9-10	T3rd	1.0
4-26	At Tex.	W	7-4		15	8	Pineiro	Drese	Guardado	10-10	2nd	1.0
4-27	At Tex.	L	2-8		6	11	Rogers	Franklin		10-11	4th	2.0
4-28	At Tex.	W	4-1		7	5	Meche	Young	Guardado	11-11	T2nd	2.0
4-29	At Oak.	W	4-2		8	9	Sele	Haren	Guardado	12-11	2nd	1.0
4-30	At Oak.	L	5-6	(10)	13	13	Yabu	Villone		12-12	T2nd	1.0
5-1	At Oak.	L	2-3		6	8	Zito	Pineiro	Dotel	12-13	3rd	2.0
5-2	L.A.	L	0-5		4	5	Washburn	Franklin		12-14	4th	3.0
5-3	L.A.	L	2-5		8	8	Lackey	Meche	Shields	12-15	4th	4.0
5-4	L.A.	L	2-5		10	10	Byrd	Sele	Rodriguez	12-16	4th	5.0
5-6	At Bos.	L	2-7		7	10	Clement	Moyer		12-17	4th	6.0
5-8#	At Bos.	L	3-6		6	10	Gonzalez	Pineiro	Foulke	12-18		
5-8$	At Bos.	W	6-4		9	9	Franklin	Halama	Guardado	13-18	4th	5.0
5-9	At N.Y.	L	3-4		7	8	Johnson	Nelson	Rivera	13-19	4th	5.0
5-10	At N.Y.	L	4-7		6	12	Wang	Sele	Rivera	13-20	4th	6.0
5-11	At N.Y.	L	9-13		14	16	Quantrill	Thornton		13-21	4th	6.0
5-13	Bos.	W	14-7		15	13	Mateo	Gonzalez		14-21	T3rd	5.5
5-14	Bos.	L	3-6		7	8	Myers	Villone	Foulke	14-22	T3rd	6.0
5-15	Bos.	W	5-4		12	10	Meche	Wakefield	Guardado	15-22	3rd	6.0
5-16	N.Y.	L	3-6		7	13	Wang	Hasegawa	Rivera	15-23	T3rd	7.0
5-17	N.Y.	L	0-6		5	10	Pavano	Mateo		15-24	T3rd	7.0
5-18	N.Y.	W	7-6		10	11	Nelson	Gordon	Villone	16-24	T3rd	7.0
5-20	S.D.	L	1-6		5	4	Peavy	Franklin		16-25	4th	8.0
5-21	S.D.	W	5-3		8	5	Meche	Lawrence	Guardado	17-25	T3rd	8.0
5-22	S.D.	W	5-0		10	4	Sele	Stauffer		18-25	3rd	7.0
5-24	At Bal.	L	2-3		9	9	Williams	Putz	Ryan	18-26	3rd	7.5
5-25	At Bal.	L	1-3		5	5	Lopez	Moyer	Ryan	18-27	3rd	7.5
5-26	At Bal.	L	2-5		6	10	Cabrera	Franklin		18-28	3rd	8.5
5-27	At T.B.	L	4-5		8	11	Hendrickson	Meche	Baez	18-29	3rd	9.5
5-28	At T.B.	W	3-2		5	4	Sele	Fossum	Guardado	19-29	3rd	9.5
5-29	At T.B.	W	10-9		14	11	Villone	McClung	Guardado	20-29	3rd	9.5
5-30	Tor.	W	4-3		7	8	Moyer	Lilly	Guardado	21-29	3rd	8.5
5-31	Tor.	L	7-9		16	13	Gaudin	Franklin	Batista	21-30	3rd	9.5
6-1	Tor.	W	3-0		10	6	Meche	Chacin	Guardado	22-30	3rd	8.5
6-3	T.B.	L	1-6		5	14	Waechter	Sele		22-31	3rd	8.5
6-4	T.B.	W	6-5		6	10	Mateo	Baez	Guardado	23-31	3rd	8.5
6-5	T.B.	W	6-5		14	11	Villone	Orvella		24-31	3rd	8.0
6-7	At Fla.	W	4-3		9	6	Hasegawa	Mecir	Guardado	25-31	3rd	7.0
6-8	At Fla.	L	4-5		11	8	Willis	Meche	Jones	25-32	3rd	8.0
6-9	At Fla.	W	8-0		11	5	Sele	Beckett		26-32	3rd	7.5
6-10	At Was.	L	3-9		10	10	Ayala	Hasegawa		26-33	3rd	8.5
6-11	At Was.	L	1-2		6	7	Patterson	Putz	Cordero	26-34	3rd	8.5
6-12	At Was.	L	2-3		10	6	Armas	Franklin	Cordero	26-35	3rd	9.5
6-14	Phi.	W	3-1		10	3	Meche	Lieber	Guardado	27-35	3rd	9.0
6-15	Phi.	W	5-1		10	8	Sele	Padilla		28-35	3rd	8.0
6-16	Phi.	L	2-3	(13)	9	12	Geary	Mateo	Wagner	28-36	3rd	8.5
6-17	N.Y.	W	5-0		9	6	Moyer	Ishii	Nelson	29-36	3rd	8.5
6-18	N.Y.	W	4-1		10	6	Franklin	Martinez	Guardado	30-36	3rd	8.5
6-19	N.Y.	W	11-5		17	10	Meche	Glavine		31-36	3rd	7.5

Date	Opp.	Res.	Score	(inn.*)	Hits	Opp. hits	Winning pitcher	Losing pitcher	Save	Record	Pos.	GB
6-20	Oak.	L	2-6		7	11	Haren	Villone		31-37	3rd	8.5
6-21	Oak.	L	2-4		7	8	Harden	Pineiro	Duchscherer	31-38	3rd	9.5
6-22	Oak.	W	5-4	(12)	11	13	Guardado	Glynn		32-38	3rd	9.5
6-23	Oak.	L	0-5		4	16	Saarloos	Franklin		32-39	3rd	10.0
6-24	At S.D.	W	14-5		17	9	Meche	May		33-39	3rd	10.0
6-25	At S.D.	L	5-8		9	9	Peavy	Sele	Hoffman	33-40	4th	11.0
6-26	At S.D.	L	4-5		8	8	Seanez	Mateo	Hoffman	33-41	4th	12.0
6-28	At Oak.	L	1-8		7	12	Zito	Moyer		33-42	4th	13.5
6-29	At Oak.	L	2-6		3	9	Blanton	Franklin		33-43	4th	13.5
6-30	At Oak.	L	2-6		8	6	Haren	Meche		33-44	4th	13.5
7-1	Tex.	L	2-6		5	10	Park	Sele		33-45	4th	14.5
7-2	Tex.	L	5-6		6	12	Loe	Putz	Cordero	33-46	4th	15.5
7-3	Tex.	W	2-1		6	4	Moyer	Rogers	Guardado	34-46	4th	15.5
7-4	At K.C.	W	6-0		11	6	Franklin	Howell		35-46	4th	14.5
7-5	At K.C.	L	6-8		14	7	Carrasco	Meche	MacDougal	35-47	4th	15.5
7-6	At K.C.	L	1-5		10	12	Hernandez	Sele	MacDougal	35-48	4th	16.5
7-7	At L.A.	W	10-2		10	6	Pineiro	Colon		36-48	4th	15.5
7-8	At L.A.	W	10-4		15	11	Moyer	Washburn		37-48	4th	14.5
7-9	At L.A.	W	6-3		12	7	Franklin	Lackey		38-48	4th	13.5
7-10	At L.A.	W	7-4		10	8	Meche	Santana	Guardado	39-48	4th	12.5
7-14	Bal.	L	3-5		2	8	Cabrera	Sele	Ryan	39-49	4th	13.5
7-15	Bal.	L	3-6		9	13	Lopez	Pineiro	Ryan	39-50	4th	14.5
7-16	Bal.	W	3-2		9	11	Putz	Ray		40-50	4th	13.5
7-17	Bal.	W	8-2		10	9	Meche	Ponson		41-50	4th	13.5
7-19	At Tor.	L	10-12		16	17	Lilly	Sele	Batista	41-51	4th	14.0
7-20	At Tor.	L	4-9		10	14	Chacin	Franklin		41-52	4th	14.0
7-21	At Tor.	L	3-6		7	11	Towers	Pineiro	Batista	41-53	4th	15.0
7-22	At Cle.	W	4-3		4	10	Putz	Elarton	Guardado	42-53	4th	15.0
7-23	At Cle.	L	3-4		10	9	Lee	Meche	Wickman	42-54	4th	16.0
7-24	At Cle.	L	3-6		4	12	Millwood	Sele		42-55	4th	16.0
7-25	Det.	W	5-3		11	6	Putz	Robertson	Guardado	43-55	4th	15.5
7-26	Det.	L	5-8		9	14	Johnson	Mateo	Farnsworth	43-56	4th	15.5
7-27	Det.	W	9-3		13	10	Moyer	Maroth		44-56	4th	14.5
7-28	Cle.	L	5-6		10	11	Howry	Putz	Wickman	44-57	4th	14.5
7-29	Cle.	L	5-10		12	17	Millwood	Sele		44-58	4th	15.5
7-30	Cle.	W	3-2		4	10	Franklin	Sabathia	Guardado	45-58	4th	14.5
7-31	Cle.	L	7-9		14	10	Westbrook	Pineiro	Wickman	45-59	4th	14.5
8-2	At Det.	W	4-1		6	6	Mateo	Johnson	Guardado	46-59	4th	14.5
8-3	At Det.	L	7-10		10	13	Maroth	Meche	Rodney	46-60	4th	15.5
8-4	At Det.	L	1-3		3	7	Douglass	Hernandez	Rodney	46-61	4th	15.5
8-5	At Chi.	W	4-2		7	8	Pineiro	Garcia	Guardado	47-61	4th	15.5
8-6	At Chi.	L	2-4		9	4	Buehrle	Moyer	Hermanson	47-62	4th	15.5
8-7	At Chi.	L	1-3		5	5	Garland	Harris	Hermanson	47-63	4th	16.5
8-8	Min.	W	5-4		9	6	Sherrill	Silva	Guardado	48-63	4th	16.0
8-9	Min.	W	1-0		4	5	Hernandez	Lohse	Guardado	49-63	4th	16.0
8-10	Min.	L	3-7	(14)	12	17	Nathan	Nelson		49-64	4th	16.0
8-12	L.A.	L	4-9		7	13	Donnelly	Putz		49-65	4th	16.5
8-13	L.A.	L	1-9		4	15	Colon	Franklin		49-66	4th	17.5
8-14	L.A.	L	6-7		10	14	Donnelly	Sherrill	Rodriguez	49-67	4th	18.5
8-15	K.C.	W	11-3		13	6	Hernandez	Hernandez		50-67	4th	18.5
8-16	K.C.	W	4-3		10	6	Pineiro	Affeldt	Guardado	51-67	4th	17.5
8-17	K.C.	W	11-5		14	7	Moyer	Carrasco		52-67	4th	16.5
8-18	At Min.	L	3-7		11	15	Mays	Franklin		52-68	4th	17.5
8-19	At Min.	L	4-7		9	9	Silva	Sherrill	Nathan	52-69	4th	17.5
8-20	At Min.	W	8-3	(10)	10	7	Sherrill	Guerrier		53-69	4th	17.5
8-21	At Min.	L	3-8		4	16	Radke	Pineiro		53-70	4th	17.5
8-23	At Tex.	L	4-6		9	12	Young	Moyer	Cordero	53-71	4th	18.5
8-24	At Tex.	L	1-8		4	15	Dominguez	Franklin	Wasdin	53-72	4th	19.5
8-25	At Tex.	W	8-2		6	6	Harris	Benoit		54-72	4th	18.5
8-26	Chi.	L	3-5	(12)	7	13	Vizcaino	Nelson	Hermanson	54-73	4th	18.5
8-27	Chi.	L	3-4		7	9	Contreras	Pineiro	Marte	54-74	4th	18.5
8-28	Chi.	W	9-2		14	8	Moyer	Garcia		55-74	4th	18.0
8-29	N.Y.	L	4-7		7	8	Small	Thornton	Rivera	55-75	4th	19.0
8-30	N.Y.	W	8-3		10	9	Harris	Chacon		56-75	4th	19.0
8-31	N.Y.	L	0-2		4	5	Johnson	Hernandez	Rivera	56-76	4th	19.0
9-1	N.Y.	W	5-1		8	6	Sherrill	Sturtze		57-76	4th	18.0
9-2	At L.A.	L	1-4		6	10	Byrd	Moyer	Rodriguez	57-77	4th	19.0
9-3	At L.A.	W	6-3		9	9	Putz	Shields		58-77	4th	18.0
9-4	At L.A.	L	3-5		8	9	Colon	Harris	Rodriguez	58-78	4th	19.0
9-5	At Oak.	W	2-0		7	5	Hernandez	Blanton	Guardado	59-78	4th	18.5

Date	Opp.	Res.	Score	(inn.*)	Hits	Opp. hits	Winning pitcher	Losing pitcher	Save	Record	Pos.	GB
9-6	At Oak.	W	3-2		8	7	Pineiro	Kennedy	Guardado	60-78	4th	17.5
9-7	At Oak.	L	7-8		13	15	Street	Guardado		60-79	4th	17.5
9-9	Bal.	W	3-2		6	10	Moyer	Bedard	Putz	61-79	4th	18.0
9-10	Bal.	L	3-5		8	13	Lopez	Harris	Ryan	61-80	4th	19.0
9-11	Bal.	L	3-6		7	7	Chen	Hernandez	Ryan	61-81	4th	20.0
9-12	L.A.	W	8-1		14	4	Pineiro	Santana		62-81	4th	19.0
9-13	L.A.	W	2-1		9	8	Putz	Byrd		63-81	4th	18.0
9-14	L.A.	W	10-9		15	16	Guardado	Rodriguez		64-81	4th	17.0
9-15	At Tex.	L	3-4		9	5	Loe	Harris	Cordero	64-82	4th	17.0
9-16	At Tex.	L	3-5		11	9	Rupe	Hernandez	Cordero	64-83	4th	18.0
9-17	At Tex.	L	6-7		11	16	Shouse	Guardado		64-84	4th	19.0
9-18	At Tex.	L	6-8		8	9	Dickey	Franklin	Cordero	64-85	4th	20.0
9-19	At Tor.	W	7-5		13	8	Sherrill	Batista	Guardado	65-85	4th	19.5
9-20	At Tor.	L	4-6		10	7	Towers	Harris	Frasor	65-86	4th	20.5
9-21	At Tor.	W	3-2		5	4	Hernandez	Bush	Guardado	66-86	4th	20.5
9-22	At Tor.	L	5-7		10	10	Speier	Pineiro	Batista	66-87	4th	21.5
9-23	At Det.	W	2-1		7	7	Franklin	Spurling	Guardado	67-87	4th	21.5
9-24	At Det.	L	1-7		5	10	Grilli	Moyer		67-88	4th	22.5
9-25	At Det.	L	1-8		5	11	Maroth	Hasegawa		67-89	4th	22.5
9-27	Tex.	L	2-3	(11)	9	7	Wasdin	Mateo	Cordero	67-90	4th	24.0
9-28	Tex.	L	3-7		7	11	Young	Pineiro	Cordero	67-91	4th	24.0
9-29	Tex.	W	4-3		9	6	Franklin	Rogers	Guardado	68-91	4th	24.0
9-30	Oak.	W	4-1		9	6	Moyer	Saarloos	Guardado	69-91	4th	24.0
10-1	Oak.	L	3-4		9	8	Blanton	Mateo	Street	69-92	4th	25.0
10-2	Oak.	L	3-8		5	14	Kennedy	Sherrill		69-93	4th	26.0

Monthly records: April (12-12), May (9-18), June (12-14), July (12-15), August (11-17), September (13-15), October (0-2).
*Innings, if other than nine. ! First game of a doubleheader. & Second game of a doubleheader. # Day separate admission. $ Night separate admission.

RECORDS

2005 regular-season record: 69-93
Position: 4th in A.L. West
Home: 39-42   **Road:** 30-51
A.L. East: 17-25   **A.L. Central:** 21-26
A.L. West: 21-34   **N.L.** 10-8
Vs. LH starters: 22-27
Vs. RH starters: 47-66
Grass: 64-84   **Artificial:** 5-9
Day: 23-31   **Night:** 46-62
1-Run: 26-23   **X-inn.:** 2-5
Doubleheaders: 0-0-0
Team record past five years: 434-376
(.536, ranks 6th in league in that span)

TEAM LEADERS

Batting average: Ichiro Suzuki (.303).
At-bats: Ichiro Suzuki (679).
Runs: Ichiro Suzuki (111).
Hits: Ichiro Suzuki (206).
Total Bases: Richie Sexson (302).
Doubles: Adrian Beltre, Richie Sexson(36).
Triples: Ichiro Suzuki (12).
Home runs: Richie Sexson (39).
Runs batted in: Richie Sexson (121).
Stolen bases: Ichiro Suzuki (33).
Slugging percentage: Richie Sexson (.541).
On-base percentage: Richie Sexson (.369).
Wins: Jamie Moyer (13).
Earned-run average: Jamie Moyer (4.28).
Complete games: Ryan Franklin, Joel Pineiro (2).

Shutouts: Ryan Franklin, Aaron Sele (1).
Saves: Eddie Guardado (36).
Innings pitched: Jamie Moyer (200.0).
Strikeouts: Joel Pineiro (107).

GAMES BY POSITION

Catcher: Miguel Olivo 54, Yorvit Torrealba 41, Pat Borders 39, Miguel Ojeda 16, Rene Rivera 15, Wiki Gonzalez 14, Dan Wilson 11.

First base: Richie Sexson 151, Dave Hansen 9, Greg Dobbs 5, Raul Ibanez 4, Scott Spiezio 4, Willie Bloomquist 1.

Second base: Bret Boone 74, Jose Lopez 51, Willie Bloomquist 32, Yuniesky Betancourt 9, Ramon Santiago 2, Scott Spiezio 1.

Third base: Adrian Beltre 155, Dave Hansen 7, Willie Bloomquist 6, Scott Spiezio 6, Greg Dobbs 2, Jose Lopez 1.

Shortstop: Mike Morse 55, Yuniesky Betancourt 53, Wilson Valdez 42, Willie Bloomquist 24, Ramon Santiago 2.

Outfield: Ichiro Suzuki 158, Jeremy Reed 137, Randy Winn 96, Raul Ibanez 58, Willie Bloomquist 15, Jamal Strong 11, Chris Snelling 10, Mike Morse 8, Jaime Bubela 7, Shin-Soo Choo 5, Greg Dobbs 4.

Designated hitter: Raul Ibanez 101, Greg Dobbs 24, Mike Morse 9, Dave Hansen 5, Richie Sexson 5, Scott Spiezio 5, Jamal Strong 3, Ichiro Suzuki 3, Randy Winn 2, Adrian Beltre 1, Willie Bloomquist 1, Jaime Bubela 1.

TOP DRAFT CHOICES

1. **Jeff Clement,** C, USC.
4. **Justin Thomas,** LHP, Youngstown State.
5. **Stephen Kahn,** RHP, Loyola Marymount.
6. **Lance Lynn,** RHP, Brownsburg (Ind.) H.S.
7. **Robert Rohrbaugh,** LHP, Clemson.
8. **David Asher,** LHP, Florida International.
9. **Bryan Sabatella,** 3B, Quinnipiac.
10. **Ronnie Prettyman,** 3B, Cal State Fullerton.

TAMPA BAY DEVIL RAYS
AMERICAN LEAGUE EAST DIVISION

2006 SEASON

Devil Rays Schedule
Home games shaded.
All-Star Game July 11 at Pittsburgh. Schedule subject to change.

APRIL

SUN	MON	TUE	WED	THU	FRI	SAT
2	3 BAL	4	5 BAL	6 BAL	7 TOR	8 TOR
9 TOR	10 BAL	11 BAL	12 BAL	13 BAL	14 KC	15 KC
16 KC	17	18 BOS	19 BOS	20 BOS	21 TEX	22 TEX
23 TEX	24	25 NYY	26 NYY	27 NYY	28 BOS	29 BOS
30 BOS						

MAY

SUN	MON	TUE	WED	THU	FRI	SAT
	1 TEX	2 TEX	3 NYY	4 NYY	5 OAK	6 OAK
7 OAK	8 SEA	9 SEA	10 SEA	11	12 TOR	13 TOR
14 TOR	15	16 CHW	17 CHW	18 CHW	19 FLA	20 FLA
21 FLA	22 TOR	23 TOR	24 TOR	25 BOS	26 BOS	27 BOS
28 BOS	29	30 BAL	31 BAL			

JUNE

SUN	MON	TUE	WED	THU	FRI	SAT
				1 BAL	2 TOR	3 TOR
4 TOR	5 LAA	6 LAA	7 LAA	8	9 KC	10 KC
11 KC	12 DET	13 DET	14 DET	15 DET	16 PHI	17 PHI
18 PHI	19	20 ARI	21 ARI	22 ARI	23 ATL	24 ATL
25 ATL	26 FLA	27 FLA	28 FLA	29	30 WAS	

JULY

SUN	MON	TUE	WED	THU	FRI	SAT
						1 WAS
2 WAS	3 BOS	4 BOS	5 BOS	6 BOS	7 NYY	8 NYY
9 NYY	10	11 ALL-STAR	12	13	14 LAA	15 LAA
16 LAA	17 MIN	18 MIN	19 MIN	20 MIN	21 BAL	22 BAL
23 BAL	24 LAA	25 LAA	26 LAA	27	28 NYY	29 NYY
30 NYY	31 DET					

AUGUST

SUN	MON	TUE	WED	THU	FRI	SAT
		1 DET	2 DET	3 DET	4 BOS	5 BOS
6 BOS	7 SEA	8 SEA	9 SEA	10	11 OAK	12 OAK
13 OAK	14	15 TOR	16 TOR	17 TOR	18 CLE	19 CLE
20 CLE	21 TEX	22 TEX	23 TEX	24 TEX	25 BAL	26 BAL
27 BAL	28	29 CHW	30 CHW	31 CHW		

SEPTEMBER

SUN	MON	TUE	WED	THU	FRI	SAT
					1 SEA	2 SEA
3 SEA	4 MIN	5 MIN	6 MIN	7	8 OAK	9 OAK
10 OAK	11	12 NYY	13 NYY	14 NYY	15 TOR	16 TOR
17 TOR	18 BAL	19 BAL	20 BAL	21	22 NYY	23 NYY
24 NYY	25 NYY	26 BOS	27 BOS	28 CLE	29 CLE	30 CLE

OCTOBER

SUN	MON	TUE	WED	THU	FRI	SAT
1 CLE	2	3	4	5	6	7

Home games are shaded. All-Star
Game is July 11 at Pittsburgh.
Schedule is subject to change.

Crawford

CLUB DIRECTORY

Principal owner
Stuart Sternberg
President
Matthew P. Silverman
Executive v.p. of baseball operations
Andrew Friedman
Senior v.p. of baseball operations
Gerry Hunsicker
Sr. v.p. of administration/general counsel
John P. Higgins
Assistant general manager
Bart Braun
Special assistant to the general manager
Rick Williams
Director of minor league operations
Mitch Lukevics
Vice president/public relations
Rick Vaughn

Vice president/stadium operations
Rick Nafe
Vice president/guest relations
Jose Tavarez
Vice president/community relations
Veronica Costello
V.p./corporate sales and broadcasting
Mark Fernandez
Vice president/sales and marketing
Kevin L. Terry
Sr. dir. of creative services/entertainment
John Franzone
Director of media relations
Chris Costello
Director of Major League administration
Sandy Dengler
Traveling secretary
Jeff Ziegler

MINOR LEAGUE AFFILIATES

Class	Team	League	Manager
AAA	Durham	International	John Tamargo
AA	Montgomery	Southern	To be announced
Advanced A	Visalia	California	Mako Oliveras
A	Southwest Michigan	Midwest	Steve Livesey
Short-Season A	Hudson Valley	New York-Penn	Dave Howard
Advanced Rookie	Princeton	Appalachian	Jamie Nelson

BROADCAST INFORMATION

Radio: WHNZ-AM (1250).
Television: PAX TV.
Cable TV: Fox Sports Net Florida.

SPRING TRAINING

Ballpark (city): Progress Energy Park
Home of Al Lang Field (St. Petersburg, Fla.).
Ticket information: 727-825-3250.

For more on the Devil Rays, go to www.sportingnews.com/baseball/teams/devilrays/

SPRING TRAINING ROSTER

Manager—Joe Maddon.
Coaches—Mike Butcher, Bill Evers, Tom Foley (6), Steve Henderson, George Hendrick, Bobby Ramos.

No.	PITCHERS	B/T	Ht./Wt.	Age*
28	Danys Baez	R/R	6-3/225	28
38	Lance Carter	R/R	6-1/190	31
49	Jesus Colome	R/R	6-2/205	28
56	Tim Corcoran	R/R	6-2/205	27
15	Casey Fossum	L/L	6-1/160	28
	Jason Hammel	R/R	6-6/200	23
58	Travis Harper	L/R	6-4/192	29
	Chad Harville	R/R	5-9/185	29
30	Mark Hendrickson	L/L	6-9/230	31
	Carlos Hines	R/R	6-3/190	25
26	Scott Kazmir	L/L	6-0/170	22
37	Seth McClung	L/R	6-6/235	25
	Dan Miceli	R/R	6-0/215	35
	Shinji Mori	L/R	6-4/195	31
	Jeff Niemann	R/R	6-9/260	23
54	Chad Orvella	R/R	5-11/190	25
	Chris Seddon	L/L	6-3/190	22
	Jamie Shields	R/R	6-3/215	24
	Brian Stokes	R/R	6-1/203	26
	Jon Switzer	L/L	6-3/191	26
40	Doug Waechter	R/R	6-4/210	25

No.	CATCHERS	B/T	Ht./Wt.	Age*
17	Kevin Cash	R/R	6-0/185	28
44	Toby Hall	R/R	6-3/240	30
	Josh Paul	R/R	6-1/200	30
	Shawn Riggans	R/R	6-2/190	25

No.	INFIELDERS	B/T	Ht./Wt.	Age*
	Wes Bankston	R/R	6-4/210	22
	Sean Burroughs	L/R	6-2/200	25
3	Jorge Cantu	R/R	6-1/184	24
18	Nick Green	R/R	6-0/178	27
16	Travis Lee	L/L	6-3/225	30
23	Julio Lugo	R/R	6-1/170	30
9	B.J. Upton	R/R	6-3/180	21
	Ty Wigginton	R/R	6-0/225	28

No.	OUTFIELDERS	B/T	Ht./Wt.	Age*
5	Rocco Baldelli	R/R	6-4/200	24
13	Carl Crawford	L/L	6-2/219	24
1	Joey Gathright	L/R	5-10/170	24
31	Jonny Gomes	R/R	6-1/205	25
27	Damon Hollins	R/L	5-11/180	31
19	Aubrey Huff	L/R	6-4/231	29
	Delmon Young	R/R	6-3/205	20

*Age as of April 1, 2006.

BALLPARK INFORMATION

Ballpark (capacity, surface)
Tropicana Field (44,445, artificial)
Address
One Tropicana Drive
St. Petersburg, FL 33705
Official website
www.devilrays.com
Business phone
727-825-3137
Ticket information
727-825-3250
Field dimensions (from home plate)
To left field at foul line, 315 feet
To center field, 404 feet
To right field at foul line, 322 feet
First game played
March 31, 1998 (Tigers 11, Devil Rays 6)

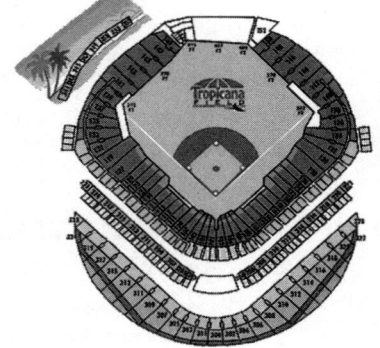

2006 SEASON *Tampa Bay Devil Rays*

Date	Opp.	Res.	Score	(inn.*)	Hits	Opp. hits	Winning pitcher	Losing pitcher	Save	Record	Pos.	GB
4-4	Tor.	L	2-5		10	7	Halladay	Brazelton	Batista	0-1	T4th	1.0
4-5	Tor.	L	3-6		7	10	Chacin	McClung	Batista	0-2	T4th	2.0
4-6	Tor.	W	8-5		11	9	Baez	Schoeneweis		1-2	T4th	1.0
4-8	Oak.	W	3-2	(10)	9	11	Baez	Cruz		2-2	T1st	...
4-9	Oak.	W	11-2		12	3	Nomo	Zito		3-2	T1st	...
4-10	Oak.	L	1-6		8	9	Harden	Brazelton		3-3	T2nd	1.0
4-12	Bal.	L	6-7		10	10	Williams	Fossum	Ryan	3-4	T3rd	2.5
4-13	Bal.	L	1-5		10	11	Kline	Hendrickson		3-5	T3rd	2.5
4-14	Bal.	W	12-7		14	12	Bell	Ponson		4-5	T3rd	2.5
4-15	At Bos.	L	0-10		7	10	Wells	Nomo		4-6	T4th	2.5
4-16	At Bos.	L	2-6		10	7	Clement	Brazelton		4-7	T4th	3.5
4-17	At Bos.	L	1-3		4	7	Wakefield	Kazmir	Foulke	4-8	T4th	4.0
4-18	At N.Y.	L	8-19		14	20	Wright	Bell		4-9	5th	4.0
4-19	At N.Y.	W	6-2		8	9	Nomo	Johnson		5-9	T4th	4.0
4-20	Tex.	L	10-12		15	11	Drese	Webb	Cordero	5-10	5th	4.0
4-21	Tex.	W	3-2		10	6	Brazelton	Rogers	Baez	6-10	5th	4.0
4-22	Bos.	W	5-4		10	8	Baez	Embree		7-10	T4th	3.0
4-23	Bos.	W	6-5		10	11	Fossum	Schilling	Carter	8-10	4th	3.0
4-24	Bos.	L	3-11		11	13	Arroyo	Nomo		8-11	T4th	4.0
4-26	At Tor.	L	5-7		11	10	Lilly	Brazelton	Batista	8-12	5th	5.5
4-27	At Tor.	L	2-8		8	12	Chacin	Kazmir		8-13	5th	6.0
4-28	At Tor.	L	4-7		9	12	Towers	Waechter	Batista	8-14	5th	6.5
4-29	At Bal.	L	0-5		6	8	Bedard	Nomo		8-15	5th	7.5
4-30	At Bal.	L	5-7		12	11	Williams	Harper	Ryan	8-16	5th	8.5
5-1	At Bal.	L	4-7		8	12	Chen	Brazelton	Ryan	8-17	5th	9.5
5-2	N.Y.	L	2-6		6	13	Mussina	Kazmir		8-18	5th	9.5
5-3	N.Y.	W	11-4		16	6	Waechter	Brown		9-18	5th	8.5
5-4	N.Y.	W	11-8		15	10	Fossum	Henn	Baez	10-18	5th	8.5
5-5	N.Y.	W	6-2		9	7	Hendrickson	Wang		11-18	T4th	8.0
5-6	Min.	L	1-7		6	14	Santana	Brazelton		11-19	T4th	9.0
5-7	Min.	L	1-8		7	11	Lohse	Kazmir		11-20	5th	10.0
5-8	Min.	L	6-9		9	11	Mays	Waechter	Nathan	11-21	5th	10.0
5-9	Chi.	W	4-2		10	8	Carter	Garcia	Baez	12-21	5th	10.0
5-10	Chi.	W	7-6		9	9	Colome	Takatsu		13-21	5th	9.0
5-11	Chi.	L	2-5		5	8	Hernandez	Brazelton	Hermanson	13-22	5th	10.0
5-12	At K.C.	L	5-7	(7)	7	7	Wood	Carter		13-23	5th	10.0
5-13	At K.C.	W	3-2		8	4	Baez	Burgos		14-23	5th	9.0
5-14	At K.C.	L	5-6		9	6	Hernandez	Colome	Wood	14-24	5th	10.0
5-15	At K.C.	L	3-4		9	9	MacDougal	Hendrickson	Wood	14-25	5th	11.0
5-17	At Det.	L	3-4	(11)	8	10	German	Harper		14-26	5th	12.0
5-18	At Det.	L	4-6		6	11	Ledezma	Waechter	Urbina	14-27	5th	13.0
5-19	At Det.	W	6-2		13	6	Kazmir	Maroth	Baez	15-27	5th	12.0
5-20	At Fla.	L	6-7		13	12	Leiter	Nomo	Jones	15-28	5th	12.0
5-21	At Fla.	L	3-4		7	8	Perisho	Colome	Jones	15-29	5th	13.0
5-22	At Fla.	L	5-8		13	9	Riedling	Fossum	Jones	15-30	5th	13.0
5-24	Oak.	W	5-4		9	9	Harper	Saarloos	Baez	16-30	5th	13.0
5-25	Oak.	W	14-6		15	9	Kazmir	Blanton		17-30	5th	13.0
5-26	Oak.	W	2-1		4	5	Nomo	Haren	Baez	18-30	5th	13.0
5-27	Sea.	W	5-4		11	8	Hendrickson	Meche	Baez	19-30	5th	12.0
5-28	Sea.	L	2-3		4	5	Sele	Fossum	Guardado	19-31	5th	12.0
5-29	Sea.	L	9-10		11	14	Villone	McClung	Guardado	19-32	5th	12.0
5-30	At Oak.	L	4-5	(11)	10	11	Street	Harper		19-33	5th	13.0
5-31	At Oak.	L	1-10		5	10	Haren	Nomo		19-34	5th	13.0
6-1	At Oak.	L	2-11		9	15	Zito	Hendrickson		19-35	5th	14.0
6-3	At Sea.	W	6-1		14	5	Waechter	Sele		20-35	5th	12.5
6-4	At Sea.	L	5-6		10	6	Mateo	Baez	Guardado	20-36	5th	13.5
6-5	At Sea.	L	5-6		11	14	Villone	Orvella		20-37	5th	14.5
6-7	At Cin.	L	7-9		10	10	Keisler	Harper	Weathers	20-38	5th	15.0
6-8	At Cin.	L	9-11		12	14	Weathers	Baez		20-39	5th	15.0
6-9	At Cin.	L	5-14		6	14	Hudson	Fossum		20-40	5th	15.5
6-10	At Pit.	L	2-7		9	7	Redman	Nomo		20-41	5th	16.5
6-11	At Pit.	L	2-18		7	20	Perez	Kazmir		20-42	5th	16.5
6-12	At Pit.	W	7-5	(13)	15	12	Nunez	Meadows	Orvella	21-42	5th	15.5
6-13	Mil.	W	5-3		13	9	Waechter	Capuano	Baez	22-42	5th	15.5
6-14	Mil.	L	0-4		9	10	Ohka	Fossum		22-43	5th	16.5
6-15	Mil.	W	5-3		9	6	Nomo	Santos	Baez	23-43	5th	16.5
6-17	StL.	L	4-6		8	12	Mulder	Harper	Isringhausen	23-44	5th	16.5

Date	Opp.	Res.	Score	(inn.*)	Hits	Opp. hits	Winning pitcher	Losing pitcher	Save	Record	Pos.	GB
6-18	StL.	L	2-5		7	10	Morris	Hendrickson	Isringhausen	23-45	5th	17.5
6-19	StL.	L	5-8		9	11	Suppan	Waechter	Isringhausen	23-46	5th	18.5
6-20	At N.Y.	W	5-4		10	6	Fossum	Henn	Baez	24-46	5th	17.5
6-21	At N.Y.	L	11-20		18	23	Groom	Harper		24-47	5th	18.5
6-22	At N.Y.	W	5-3		6	6	Kazmir	Pavano	Baez	25-47	5th	17.5
6-23	At N.Y.	W	9-4		11	11	Hendrickson	Wang	Baez	26-47	5th	16.5
6-24	Fla.	L	4-7		5	11	Mota	Waechter	Jones	26-48	5th	17.0
6-25	Fla.	L	2-6		6	14	Olsen	Fossum		26-49	5th	18.0
6-26	Fla.	L	0-1		2	3	Burnett	McClung		26-50	5th	19.0
6-27	Tor.	W	4-3		7	10	Nomo	Walker	Baez	27-50	5th	18.0
6-28	Tor.	L	1-3	(11)	8	11	Batista	Waechter		27-51	5th	18.0
6-29	Tor.	L	3-12		4	13	Towers	Hendrickson		27-52	5th	19.0
7-1	At Min.	L	4-7		10	6	Crain	Brazelton	Nathan	27-53	5th	19.0
7-2	At Min.	L	1-4		4	8	Lohse	McClung	Nathan	27-54	5th	20.0
7-3	At Min.	L	2-3		7	4	Mays	Kazmir	Nathan	27-55	5th	20.0
7-4	At Chi.	L	8-10		14	11	Vizcaino	Nomo	Hermanson	27-56	5th	20.0
7-5	At Chi.	L	4-6		8	12	Politte	Carter	Hermanson	27-57	5th	21.0
7-6	At Chi.	L	2-7		7	12	Contreras	Fossum		27-58	5th	22.0
7-7	Det.	L	4-6		7	9	Douglass	McClung	Percival	27-59	5th	22.0
7-8	Det.	L	3-7		8	10	German	Kazmir		27-60	5th	23.0
7-9	Det.	W	5-4		10	13	Baez	Percival		28-60	5th	22.0
7-10	Det.	L	4-9		10	15	Maroth	Hendrickson		28-61	5th	22.0
7-14	At Tor.	W	3-0		7	6	Fossum	Lilly	Baez	29-61	5th	21.0
7-15	At Tor.	L	6-11		11	15	Chacin	Nomo		29-62	5th	22.0
7-16	At Tor.	W	6-5		12	9	Hendrickson	Towers	Baez	30-62	5th	21.0
7-17	At Tor.	W	5-4		12	8	Orvella	Batista	Baez	31-62	5th	20.0
7-18	At Bos.	W	3-1		8	3	Kazmir	Miller	Baez	32-62	5th	19.5
7-19	At Bos.	L	2-5		8	9	Arroyo	Fossum	Schilling	32-63	5th	20.0
7-20	At Bos.	L	4-9		9	11	Wells	Hendrickson		32-64	5th	21.0
7-22	Bal.	W	7-5		10	8	McClung	Chen	Baez	33-64	5th	20.5
7-23	Bal.	W	3-2		9	5	Kazmir	Ponson	Baez	34-64	5th	20.5
7-24	Bal.	W	6-2		13	4	Fossum	Bedard		35-64	5th	19.5
7-25	Bos.	W	4-3	(10)	14	11	Colome	Schilling		36-64	5th	18.5
7-26	Bos.	L	9-10	(10)	15	16	Schilling	Baez		36-65	5th	19.5
7-27	Bos.	L	1-4		7	6	Wakefield	McClung	Schilling	36-66	5th	20.5
7-28	K.C.	W	10-5		14	7	Kazmir	Snyder		37-66	5th	20.0
7-29	K.C.	W	6-3		11	9	Fossum	Carrasco	Baez	38-66	5th	20.0
7-30	K.C.	W	7-3		11	7	Waechter	Greinke		39-66	5th	20.0
7-31	K.C.	W	6-2		13	5	Hendrickson	Lima		40-66	5th	20.0
8-2	At Tex.	W	10-8		14	8	McClung	Young	Baez	41-66	5th	20.0
8-3	At Tex.	W	8-5		15	11	Harper	Rodriguez	Baez	42-66	5th	20.0
8-4	At Tex.	L	5-13		12	15	Gryboski	Orvella		42-67	5th	21.0
8-5	At L.A.	L	4-5		5	9	Shields	Waechter	Rodriguez	42-68	5th	21.0
8-6	At L.A.	W	6-4		11	12	Hendrickson	Bootcheck	Baez	43-68	5th	20.0
8-7	At L.A.	L	4-10		10	10	Colon	McClung		43-69	5th	21.0
8-9	At Bal.	L	2-5		6	12	Bedard	Kazmir	Ryan	43-70	5th	22.5
8-10	At Bal.	L	5-9		9	9	Lopez	Fossum		43-71	5th	23.5
8-11	At Bal.	L	2-4		4	9	Chen	Waechter	Ryan	43-72	5th	24.0
8-12	At Cle.	W	8-6		12	17	Hendrickson	Westbrook	Baez	44-72	5th	24.0
8-13	At Cle.	W	8-2		14	10	McClung	Elarton		45-72	5th	24.0
8-14	At Cle.	W	1-0		8	7	Borowski	Wickman	Baez	46-72	5th	23.5
8-15	N.Y.	L	2-5		5	7	Wright	Fossum	Rivera	46-73	5th	23.5
8-16	N.Y.	W	4-3	(11)	8	9	Orvella	Embree		47-73	5th	23.5
8-17	N.Y.	W	7-6		7	7	Miller	Sturtze	Baez	48-73	5th	22.5
8-19	Tex.	W	2-1		9	3	McClung	Dominguez	Baez	49-73	5th	22.0
8-20	Tex.	W	4-2		8	6	Kazmir	Benoit	Baez	50-73	5th	21.0
8-21	Tex.	W	6-3		7	8	Fossum	Rogers	Baez	51-73	5th	21.0
8-22	Cle.	L	4-11		5	15	Millwood	Miller		51-74	5th	21.5
8-23	Cle.	L	4-5		14	9	Westbrook	Miller	Wickman	51-75	5th	22.5
8-24	Cle.	W	13-3		16	10	McClung	Elarton		52-75	5th	21.5
8-25	Cle.	L	4-12		6	19	Lee	Kazmir		52-76	5th	21.5
8-26	L.A.	W	12-8		18	14	Fossum	Santana		53-76	5th	21.5
8-27	L.A.	W	6-3		14	8	Waechter	Byrd	Baez	54-76	5th	20.5
8-28	L.A.	W	2-1		5	6	Hendrickson	Washburn	Baez	55-76	5th	20.5
8-29	At Bos.	L	6-10		11	13	Clement	McClung		55-77	5th	21.5
8-30	At Bos.	L	6-7		13	11	Timlin	Borowski		55-78	5th	22.5
8-31	At Bos.	L	6-7		7	8	Wakefield	Fossum	Timlin	55-79	5th	23.5
9-1	At Bos.	L	4-7		11	10	Arroyo	Waechter	Timlin	55-80	5th	24.5
9-2	At Tor.	L	3-4		8	10	Schoeneweis	Borowski	Batista	55-81	5th	24.5
9-3	At Tor.	W	3-2		6	2	McClung	Batista	Baez	56-81	5th	24.5

Date	Opp.	Res.	Score	(inn.*)	Hits	Opp. hits	Winning pitcher	Losing pitcher	Save	Record	Pos.	GB
9-4	At Tor.	W	1-0		7	4	Kazmir	Bush	Baez	57-81	5th	24.5
9-6	At N.Y.	W	4-3		9	11	Orvella	Rivera	Baez	58-81	5th	24.0
9-7	At N.Y.	L	4-5		8	8	Sturtze	Borowski	Rivera	58-82	5th	25.0
9-8	At N.Y.	W	7-4		13	6	Hendrickson	Wang	Baez	59-82	5th	24.0
9-9	Tor.	L	2-7		10	11	Towers	McClung		59-83	5th	24.0
9-10	Tor.	L	2-3		4	9	Bush	Baez	Batista	59-84	5th	25.0
9-11	Tor.	W	6-5	(11)	9	8	Harper	Schoeneweis		60-84	5th	24.0
9-13	N.Y.	L	3-17		5	20	Wright	Waechter		60-85	5th	24.5
9-14	N.Y.	L	5-6		9	11	Wang	Orvella	Rivera	60-86	5th	25.5
9-15	N.Y.	L	5-9		8	15	Small	McClung	Rivera	60-87	5th	25.5
9-16	At Bal.	W	6-1		11	5	Kazmir	Lopez	Baez	61-87	5th	25.5
9-17	At Bal.	L	1-2		2	9	Williams	Borowski	Ryan	61-88	5th	26.5
9-18	At Bal.	W	6-5		11	10	Harper	Williams	Baez	62-88	5th	25.5
9-19	Bos.	W	8-7		18	11	Hendrickson	Harville	Baez	63-88	5th	24.5
9-20	Bos.	L	2-15		6	21	Schilling	McClung		63-89	5th	25.5
9-21	Bos.	W	7-4		11	9	Miller	Timlin	Baez	64-89	5th	25.0
9-23	At L.A.	L	5-7		11	8	Shields	Borowski	Rodriguez	64-90	5th	26.5
9-24	At L.A.	L	3-7		6	10	Washburn	Waechter		64-91	5th	26.5
9-25	At L.A.	W	8-4		13	9	Hendrickson	Colon		65-91	5th	26.5
9-27	At Cle.	W	5-4		11	9	Kazmir	Elarton	Baez	66-91	5th	26.0
9-28	At Cle.	W	1-0		6	5	McClung	Lee	Baez	67-91	5th	26.0
9-29	At Cle.	L	0-6		5	10	Sabathia	Fossum		67-92	5th	27.0
9-30	Bal.	L	6-7		9	10	DuBose	Waechter	Ryan	67-93	5th	27.0
10-1	Bal.	L	3-4		7	8	Lopez	Hendrickson	Ryan	67-94	5th	28.0
10-2	Bal.	L	2-6		10	8	Chen	Colome		67-95	5th	28.0

Monthly records: April (8-16), May (11-18), June (8-18), July (13-14), August (15-13), September (12-14), October (0-2).
*Innings, if other than nine. ! First game of a doubleheader. & Second game of a doubleheader.

RECORDS

2005 regular-season record: 67-95
Position: 5th in A.L. East
Home: 40-41 **Road:** 27-54
A.L. East: 31-44 **A.L. Central:** 15-22
A.L. West: 18-14 **N.L.** 3-15
Vs. LH starters: 20-32
Vs. RH starters: 47-63
Grass: 22-46 **Artificial:** 45-49
Day: 17-23 **Night:** 50-72
1-Run: 29-25 **X-inn.:** 5-4
Doubleheaders: 0-0-0
Team record past five years: 317-491 (.392, ranks 13th in league in that span)

TEAM LEADERS

Batting average: Carl Crawford (.301).
At-bats: Carl Crawford (644).
Runs: Carl Crawford (101).
Hits: Carl Crawford (194).
Total Bases: Carl Crawford (302).
Doubles: Jorge Cantu (40).
Triples: Carl Crawford (15).
Home runs: Jorge Cantu (28).
Runs batted in: Jorge Cantu (117).
Stolen bases: Carl Crawford (46).
Slugging percentage: Jonny Gomes (.534).
On-base percentage: Jonny Gomes (.372).
Wins: Mark Hendrickson (11).
Earned-run average: Scott Kazmir (3.77).
Complete games: Mark Hendrickson (1).
Shutouts: None.
Saves: Danys Baez (41).

Innings pitched: Scott Kazmir (186.0).
Strikeouts: Scott Kazmir (174).

GAMES BY POSITION

Catcher: Toby Hall 135, Pete LaForest 21, Charles Johnson 19, Kevin Cash 13, Tim Laker 1.
First base: Travis Lee 124, Eduardo Perez 49, Aubrey Huff 25, Toby Hall 2, Pete LaForest 1, Eric Munson 1, Josh Phelps 1.
Second base: Nick Green 91, Jorge Cantu 80, Fernando Cortez 3.
Third base: Alex S. Gonzalez 98, Jorge Cantu 62, Nick Green 13, Aubrey Huff 4, Eduardo Perez 3, Eric Munson 2, Fernando Cortez 1.
Shortstop: Julio Lugo 156, Alex S. Gonzalez 12, Fernando Cortez 2.
Outfield: Carl Crawford 154, Damon Hollins 116, Aubrey Huff 97, Joey Gathright 70, Jonny Gomes 50, Alex Sanchez 31, Chris Singleton 19, Reggie Taylor 10, Eduardo Perez 4, Nick Green 1, Eric Munson 1.
Designated hitter: Jonny Gomes 49, Josh Phelps 42, Aubrey Huff 33, Jorge Cantu 13, Eduardo Perez 7, Alex Sanchez 7, Chris Singleton 4, Eric Munson 3, Nick Green 2, Pete LaForest 2, Carl Crawford 1, Joey Gathright 1.

TOP DRAFT CHOICES

1. **Wade Townsend,** RHP, Dripping Springs, Texas.
2. **Chris Mason,** RHP, UNC Greensboro.
3. **Bryan Morris,** RHP, Tullahoma (Tenn.) H.S.
4. **Jeremy Hellickson,** RHP, Hoover H.S., Des Moines, Iowa.
5. **Mike McCormick,** 3B, Marist H.S., Eugene, Ore.
6. **Greg Reinhard,** RHP, Wisconsin-Whitewater.
7. **Mike Wlodarczyk,** LHP, Boston College.
8. **Andrew Lopez,** OF, Elk Groove (Calif.) H.S.
9. **Derek Feldkamp,** RHP, Michigan.
10. **John Matulia,** OF, Eustis (Fla.) H.S.

TEXAS RANGERS
AMERICAN LEAGUE WEST DIVISION

2006 SEASON

Rangers Schedule
Home games shaded.
All-Star Game July 11 at Pittsburgh. Schedule subject to change.

APRIL

SUN	MON	TUE	WED	THU	FRI	SAT
2	3 BOS	4 BOS	5 BOS	6 DET	7 DET	8 DET
9 DET	10 LAA	11 LAA	12 LAA	13	14 OAK	15 OAK
16 OAK	17	18 SEA	19 SEA	20 SEA	21 TB	22 TB
23 TB	24 OAK	25 OAK	26 OAK	27	28 CLE	29 CLE
30 CLE						

MAY

SUN	MON	TUE	WED	THU	FRI	SAT
	1 TB	2 TB	3 BAL	4 BAL	5 NYY	6 NYY
7 NYY	8 MIN	9 MIN	10 MIN	11	12 BOS	13 BOS
14 BOS	15 NYY	16 NYY	17 NYY	18 NYY	19 HOU	20 HOU
21 HOU	22 LAA	23 LAA	24 LAA	25 OAK	26 OAK	27 OAK
28 OAK	29 SEA	30 SEA	31 SEA			

JUNE

SUN	MON	TUE	WED	THU	FRI	SAT
				1	2 CHW	3 CHW
4 CHW	5	6 KC	7 KC	8 KC	9 BOS	10 BOS
11 BOS	12 CHW	13 CHW	14 CHW	15 CHW	16 ARI	17 ARI
18 ARI	19	20 SD	21 SD	22 SD	23 COL	24 COL
25 COL	26	27 SF	28 SF	29 SF	30 HOU	

JULY

SUN	MON	TUE	WED	THU	FRI	SAT
						1 HOU
2 HOU	3 TOR	4 TOR	5 TOR	6	7 MIN	8 MIN
9 MIN	10	11 ALL-STAR	12	13 BAL	14 BAL	15 BAL
16 BAL	17 TOR	18 TOR	19 TOR	20	21 CHW	22 CHW
23 CHW	24 NYY	25 NYY	26 NYY	27	28 KC	29 KC
30 KC	31 MIN					

AUGUST

SUN	MON	TUE	WED	THU	FRI	SAT
		1 MIN	2 MIN	3 LAA	4 LAA	5 LAA
6 LAA	7 OAK	8 OAK	9 OAK	10 SEA	11 SEA	12 SEA
13 SEA	14	15 LAA	16 LAA	17 DET	18 DET	19 DET
20 DET	21 TB	22 TB	23 TB	24 TB	25 OAK	26 OAK
27 OAK	28	29 BAL	30 BAL	31 BAL		

SEPTEMBER

SUN	MON	TUE	WED	THU	FRI	SAT
					1 CLE	2 CLE
3 CLE	4 OAK	5 OAK	6 OAK	7	8 SEA	9 SEA
10 SEA	11	12 DET	13 DET	14 LAA	15 LAA	16 LAA
17 LAA	18 SEA	19 SEA	20 SEA	21	22 CLE	23 CLE
24 CLE	25 LAA	26 LAA	27 LAA	28	29 SEA	30 SEA

OCTOBER

SUN	MON	TUE	WED	THU	FRI	SAT
1 SEA	2	3	4	5	6	7

Home games are shaded. All-Star Game is July 11 at Pittsburgh. Schedule is subject to change.

Teixeira

CLUB DIRECTORY

Chairman of the board and owner
Thomas O. Hicks
President
Jeff Cogen
General manager
Jon Daniels
Senior adviser/baseball operations
John Hart
Executive vice president, Hicks Holdings
Casey Shilts
Executive v.p., business operations
Rick McLaughlin

Vice president, finance
Kellie Fischer
Executive directors to the president
Jim Sundberg, Orel Hershiser
Director of scouting
Ron Hopkins
Director of minor league operations
John Lombardo
Manager, pro and international scouting
A.J. Preller
Senior director, baseball media relations
Gregg Elkin

MINOR LEAGUE AFFILIATES

Class	Team	League	Manager
AAA	Oklahoma	Pacific Coast	Tim Ireland
AA	Frisco	Texas	Darryl Kennedy
Advanced A	Bakersfield	California	Carlos Subero
A	Clinton	Midwest	Andy Fox
Short-Season A	Spokane	Northwest	Mike Micucci
Rookie	Rangers	Arizona	To be announced

BROADCAST INFORMATION

Radio: KRLD-AM (1080); KESS (1270), Spanish.
TV: KDFW (Channel 4); KDFI (Channel 27).
Cable TV: Fox Sports Southwest.

SPRING TRAINING

Ballpark (city): Surprise Stadium (Surprise, Ariz.).
Ticket information: 623-594-5600.

For more on the Rangers, go to **www.sportingnews.com/baseball/teams/rangers/**

Manager—Buck Showalter (11).
Coaches—Dom Chiti (56), Mark Connor (52), Rudy Jaramillo (8), Bobby Jones (46), Steve Smith (1), Don Wakamatsu (18).

No.	PITCHERS	B/T	Ht./Wt.	Age*
	Omar Beltre	R/R	6-3/190	24
53	Joaquin Benoit	R/R	6-3/220	28
	Fabio Castro	L/L	5-8/150	21
31	Francisco Cordero	R/R	6-2/235	30
45	R.A. Dickey	R/R	6-3/220	31
41	Juan Dominguez	R/R	6-2/195	25
	Adam Eaton	R/R	6-2/196	28
39	Scott Feldman	L/R	6-5/210	23
50	Frank Francisco	R/R	6-2/180	26
	Armando Galarraga	R/R	6-4/170	24
	Jon Leicester	R/R	6-2/220	27
	Wes Littleton	R/R	6-3/200	23
43	Kameron Loe	R/R	6-8/225	24
33	Kevin Millwood	R/R	6-4/235	31
	Akinori Otsuka	R/R	6-0/200	34
	Vicente Padilla	R/R	6-2/219	28
54	Erasmo Ramirez	L/L	6-0/190	29
59	Josh Rupe	R/R	6-2/200	23
58	Brian Shouse	L/L	5-11/190	37
40	Edison Volquez	R/R	6-1/190	22
47	John Wasdin	R/R	6-2/190	33
36	C.J. Wilson	L/L	6-2/200	25

No.	CATCHERS	B/T	Ht./Wt.	Age*
27	Rod Barajas	R/R	6-2/220	30
6	Gerald Laird	R/R	6-2/220	26

No.	INFIELDERS	B/T	Ht./Wt.	Age*
	Joaquin Arias	R/R	6-1/160	21
9	Hank Blalock	L/R	6-1/200	25
7	Mark DeRosa	R/R	6-1/205	31
4	Ian Kinsler	R/R	6-0/175	23
20	Marshall McDougall	R/R	6-1/200	27
25	Phil Nevin	R/R	6-2/231	35
23	Mark Teixeira	B/R	6-3/220	25
10	Michael Young	R/R	6-1/190	29

No.	OUTFIELDERS	B/T	Ht./Wt.	Age*
44	Jason Botts	B/R	6-5/250	25
25	David Dellucci	L/L	5-11/190	32
14	Gary Matthews	B/R	6-3/225	31
28	Kevin Mench	R/R	6-0/225	28
17	Laynce Nix	L/L	6-0/200	25
	Brad Wilkerson	L/L	6-0/206	28

*Age as of April 1, 2006.

BALLPARK INFORMATION

Ballpark (capacity, surface)
Ameriquest Field in Arlington (48,911, grass)
Address
1000 Ballpark Way
Arlington, TX 76011
Official website
www.texasrangers.com
Business phone
817-273-5222
Ticket information
817-273-5100
Field dimensions (from home plate)
To left field at foul line, 332 feet
To center field, 400 feet
To right field at foul line, 325 feet
First game played
April 11, 1994 (Brewers 4, Rangers 3)

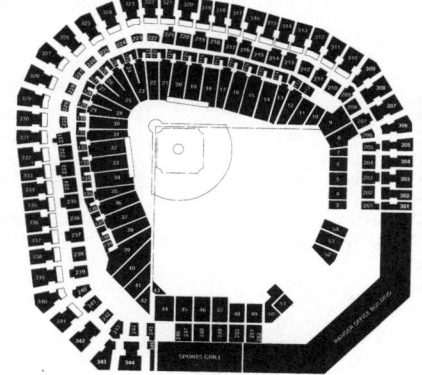

2006 SEASON *Texas Rangers*

Date	Opp.	Res.	Score	(inn.*)	Hits	Opp. hits	Winning pitcher	Losing pitcher	Save	Record	Pos.	GB
4-5	At L.A.	L	2-3		7	6	Colon	Drese	Rodriguez	0-1	T3rd	1.0
4-6	At L.A.	W	3-2	(12)	13	7	Shouse	Prinz		1-1	T1st	...
4-7	At L.A.	L	6-7		6	12	Shields	Shouse		1-2	T3rd	1.0
4-8	At Sea.	L	6-9		9	11	Putz	Regilio	Guardado	1-3	4th	1.0
4-9	At Sea.	W	7-6		10	11	Brocail	Guardado	Cordero	2-3	T2nd	1.0
4-10	At Sea.	W	7-6		11	8	Riley	Thornton	Cordero	3-3	T1st	...
4-11	L.A.	L	6-7	(10)	14	13	Shields	Dickey	Rodriguez	3-4	T2nd	1.0
4-12	L.A.	L	8-13		13	14	Lackey	Young	Shields	3-5	T3rd	2.0
4-13	L.A.	W	7-5		11	9	Park	Byrd	Cordero	4-5	T3rd	1.0
4-14	Tor.	L	1-2		5	5	Halladay	Astacio		4-6	4th	1.5
4-15	Tor.	W	4-2		7	6	Drese	Lilly	Cordero	5-6	3rd	1.5
4-16	Tor.	L	0-8		4	12	Chacin	Rogers		5-7	4th	1.5
4-17	Tor.	W	6-5		12	10	Young	Towers	Cordero	6-7	4th	0.5
4-18	Oak.	L	5-8		7	13	Haren	Park	Dotel	6-8	4th	1.5
4-19	Oak.	W	3-0		7	6	Astacio	Blanton	Cordero	7-8	4th	0.5
4-20	At T.B.	W	12-10		11	15	Drese	Webb	Cordero	8-8	3rd	0.5
4-21	At T.B.	L	2-3		6	10	Brazelton	Rogers	Baez	8-9	4th	1.5
4-22	At N.Y.	W	5-3		12	7	Young	Brown	Cordero	9-9	3rd	0.5
4-23	At N.Y.	W	10-2		19	5	Park	Wright		10-9	2nd	0.5
4-24	At N.Y.	L	1-11		3	14	Johnson	Astacio		10-10	2nd	1.5
4-26	Sea.	L	4-7		8	15	Pineiro	Drese	Guardado	10-11	T3rd	1.5
4-27	Sea.	W	8-2		11	6	Rogers	Franklin		11-11	T2nd	1.5
4-28	Sea.	L	1-4		5	7	Meche	Young	Guardado	11-12	4th	2.5
4-29	Bos.	W	7-2		10	3	Park	Wakefield	Mahay	12-12	3rd	1.5
4-30	Bos.	L	2-9		6	14	Arroyo	Astacio		12-13	4th	1.5
5-1	Bos.	L	5-6		6	13	Clement	Drese	Foulke	12-14	4th	2.5
5-2	At Oak.	W	3-2		6	5	Rogers	Harden	Cordero	13-14	3rd	2.5
5-3	At Oak.	W	6-1		7	9	Young	Saarloos		14-14	2nd	2.5
5-4	At Oak.	W	16-7		18	10	Shouse	Haren		15-14	2nd	2.5
5-6	Cle.	L	6-8		11	14	Lee	Astacio	Wickman	15-15	2nd	3.5
5-7	Cle.	W	6-1		9	6	Drese	Elarton		16-15	2nd	2.5
5-8	Cle.	W	7-2		12	10	Rogers	Westbrook	Cordero	17-15	2nd	1.5
5-9	Det.	L	0-2		7	8	Robertson	Cordero	Urbina	17-16	2nd	1.5
5-10	Det.	W	5-4		8	13	Brocail	Johnson	Cordero	18-16	2nd	1.5
5-11	Det.	L	5-6		7	11	Walker	Mahay	Urbina	18-17	2nd	1.5
5-13	At Min.	W	9-6	(11)	13	12	Brocail	Nathan	Cordero	19-17	2nd	1.0
5-14	At Min.	W	5-0		11	6	Rogers	Silva		20-17	2nd	0.5
5-15	At Min.	L	2-5		7	11	Radke	Mahay	Nathan	20-18	2nd	1.5
5-16	At Chi.	W	7-6		11	7	Regilio	Marte	Cordero	21-18	2nd	1.5
5-17	At Chi.	L	2-5		6	9	Garland	Astacio	Hermanson	21-19	2nd	1.5
5-18	At Chi.	L	0-7		9	11	Buehrle	Drese		21-20	2nd	2.5
5-20	Hou.	W	7-3		9	10	Rogers	Backe		22-20	2nd	2.5
5-21	Hou.	W	18-3		17	9	Young	Astacio		23-20	2nd	2.5
5-22	Hou.	W	2-0		8	6	Park	Oswalt	Cordero	24-20	2nd	1.5
5-24	K.C.	W	4-3		7	10	Drese	Hernandez	Cordero	25-20	2nd	1.0
5-25	K.C.	W	7-3		14	7	Astacio	Greinke		26-20	T1st	...
5-26	K.C.	W	8-1		7	6	Rogers	Lima		27-20	T1st	...
5-27	Chi.	W	6-2		9	9	Young	McCarthy	Cordero	28-20	T1st	...
5-29	Chi.	W	12-4		16	9	Park	Garland		29-20	2nd	0.5
5-31	At Det.	W	8-2		15	5	Rogers	Maroth		30-20	1st	+1.0
6-1	At Det.	L	4-6		10	11	Bonderman	Drese	Urbina	30-21	1st	...
6-2	At Det.	L	5-6	(10)	12	10	Urbina	Regilio		30-22	2nd	0.5
6-3	At K.C.	L	1-2		4	7	Sisco	Astacio	MacDougal	30-23	2nd	0.5
6-4	At K.C.	W	14-9		19	17	Park	Lima		31-23	2nd	0.5
6-5	At K.C.	W	8-1		13	5	Rogers	Greinke		32-23	1st	+0.5
6-7	At Phi.	L	5-8		7	12	Lieber	Drese	Wagner	32-24	1st	...
6-8	At Phi.	L	0-2		5	7	Fultz	Young	Wagner	32-25	2nd	1.0
6-9	At Phi.	L	8-10		8	14	Padilla	Astacio	Wagner	32-26	2nd	1.5
6-10	At Fla.	L	5-12		11	17	Jones	Brocail		32-27	2nd	2.5
6-11	At Fla.	L	5-6		9	9	Riedling	Dominguez	Jones	32-28	2nd	2.5
6-12	At Fla.	W	6-2		9	7	Rodriguez	Moehler	Wasdin	33-28	2nd	2.5
6-13	Atl.	W	7-3		11	6	Young	Hudson		34-28	2nd	2.5
6-14	Atl.	L	2-7		9	11	Sosa	Astacio		34-29	2nd	2.5
6-15	Atl.	W	9-5		14	13	Park	Davies	Cordero	35-29	2nd	1.5
6-17	Was.	W	8-1		15	8	Rogers	Patterson		36-29	2nd	1.5
6-18	Was.	W	7-4		9	7	Rodriguez	Armas		37-29	2nd	1.5
6-19	Was.	L	2-8		7	15	Hughes	Wilson		37-30	2nd	1.5

Date	Opp.	Res.	Score	(inn.*)	Hits	Opp. hits	Winning pitcher	Losing pitcher	Save	Record	Pos.	GB
6-20	At L.A.	L	1-5		6	15	Byrd	Young		37-31	2nd	2.5
6-21	At L.A.	L	6-8		11	15	Colon	Park		37-32	2nd	3.5
6-22	At L.A.	L	0-6		6	13	Washburn	Rogers		37-33	2nd	4.5
6-24	At Hou.	L	2-5		7	11	Oswalt	Rodriguez	Lidge	37-34	2nd	5.5
6-25	At Hou.	W	6-5		8	6	Young	Backe	Cordero	38-34	2nd	5.5
6-26	At Hou.	L	2-3	(10)	7	8	Qualls	Dominguez		38-35	2nd	6.5
6-27	L.A.	L	3-13		8	20	Colon	Wilson		38-36	2nd	7.5
6-28	L.A.	L	1-5	(11)	9	9	Donnelly	Loe		38-37	2nd	8.5
6-29	L.A.	W	7-6	(11)	13	9	Loe	Shields		39-37	2nd	7.5
6-30	L.A.	W	18-5		15	10	Young	Santana		40-37	2nd	6.5
7-1	At Sea.	W	6-2		10	5	Park	Sele		41-37	2nd	6.5
7-2	At Sea.	W	6-5		12	6	Loe	Putz	Cordero	42-37	2nd	6.5
7-3	At Sea.	L	1-2		4	6	Moyer	Rogers	Guardado	42-38	2nd	7.5
7-4	Bos.	W	6-5		10	8	Benoit	Foulke		43-38	2nd	6.5
7-5	Bos.	L	4-7		8	7	Wakefield	Young	Timlin	43-39	2nd	7.5
7-6	Bos.	L	4-7		9	10	Clement	Park	Embree	43-40	2nd	8.5
7-8	Tor.	W	7-6		14	6	Cordero	Batista		44-40	2nd	7.0
7-9	Tor.	W	12-10		15	15	Rogers	Downs	Cordero	45-40	2nd	6.0
7-10	Tor.	W	9-8		12	13	Loe	Frasor		46-40	2nd	5.0
7-14	At Oak.	L	0-6		2	8	Harden	Park		46-41	2nd	6.0
7-15	At Oak.	L	2-7		4	8	Zito	Wasdin		46-42	2nd	7.0
7-16	At Oak.	W	10-8		12	12	Rogers	Blanton	Cordero	47-42	2nd	6.0
7-17	At Oak.	L	4-5	(14)	13	13	Kennedy	Loe		47-43	2nd	7.0
7-18	N.Y.	L	10-11		12	13	Sturtze	Brocail	Rivera	47-44	2nd	8.0
7-19	N.Y.	W	2-1		7	7	Loe	Franklin	Cordero	48-44	2nd	7.0
7-20	N.Y.	L	4-8		8	10	Small	Benoit		48-45	3rd	7.0
7-21	Oak.	L	4-6		9	11	Witasick	Loe	Street	48-46	3rd	8.0
7-22	Oak.	L	10-11		11	15	Haren	Young	Duchscherer	48-47	3rd	9.0
7-23	Oak.	L	4-5		9	6	Saarloos	Rodriguez	Street	48-48	3rd	10.0
7-24	Oak.	L	3-8		7	13	Harden	Park		48-49	3rd	10.0
7-25	At Bal.	W	4-2		6	8	Benoit	Cabrera	Cordero	49-49	3rd	9.5
7-26	At Bal.	L	4-5		9	9	Grimsley	Baldwin	Ryan	49-50	3rd	9.5
7-27	At Bal.	W	11-8	(11)	20	13	Cordero	Julio	Baldwin	50-50	3rd	8.5
7-28	At Bal.	W	2-1		10	7	Loe	Ray	Cordero	51-50	3rd	7.5
7-29	At Tor.	W	4-1		9	6	Brocail	Downs	Cordero	52-50	3rd	7.5
7-30	At Tor.	W	3-2		7	6	Benoit	Frasor	Cordero	53-50	3rd	6.5
7-31	At Tor.	L	1-5		5	13	Chacin	Wilson		53-51	3rd	6.5
8-2	T.B.	L	8-10		8	14	McClung	Young	Baez	53-52	3rd	7.5
8-3	T.B.	L	5-8		11	15	Harper	Rodriguez	Baez	53-53	3rd	8.5
8-4	T.B.	W	13-5		15	12	Gryboski	Orvella		54-53	3rd	7.5
8-5	Bal.	L	5-10		7	15	Chen	Wilson		54-54	3rd	8.5
8-6	Bal.	W	10-3		10	8	Wasdin	Cabrera	Loe	55-54	3rd	7.5
8-7	Bal.	W	9-3		14	10	Young	Ponson		56-54	3rd	7.5
8-8	At Bos.	L	6-11		16	12	Gonzalez	Karsay		56-55	3rd	8.0
8-9	At Bos.	L	7-8	(10)	11	11	Schilling	Gryboski		56-56	3rd	9.0
8-10	At Bos.	L	5-16		10	15	Arroyo	Rogers		56-57	3rd	9.0
8-11	At N.Y.	L	8-9		10	13	Sturtze	Baldwin	Rivera	56-58	3rd	10.0
8-12	At N.Y.	L	5-6		9	12	Leiter	Wilson	Sturtze	56-59	3rd	10.0
8-13	At N.Y.	L	5-7	(11)	13	12	Small	Loe		56-60	3rd	11.0
8-14	At N.Y.	L	3-10		11	11	Chacon	Benoit		56-61	3rd	12.0
8-16	At Cle.	L	2-8		8	9	Sabathia	Rogers		56-62	3rd	12.5
8-17	At Cle.	W	3-0		4	2	Young	Millwood	Cordero	57-62	3rd	11.5
8-18	At Cle.	L	4-9		10	13	Westbrook	Wilson		57-63	3rd	12.5
8-19	At T.B.	L	1-2		3	9	McClung	Dominguez	Baez	57-64	3rd	12.5
8-20	At T.B.	L	2-4		6	8	Kazmir	Benoit	Baez	57-65	3rd	13.5
8-21	At T.B.	L	3-6		8	7	Fossum	Rogers	Baez	57-66	3rd	13.5
8-23	Sea.	W	6-4		12	9	Young	Moyer	Cordero	58-66	3rd	13.5
8-24	Sea.	W	8-1		15	4	Dominguez	Franklin	Wasdin	59-66	3rd	13.5
8-25	Sea.	L	2-8		6	6	Harris	Benoit		59-67	3rd	13.5
8-26	Min.	W	6-0		10	6	Loe	Lohse	Wilson	60-67	3rd	12.5
8-27	Min.	L	2-7	(11)	11	15	Nathan	Shouse		60-68	3rd	12.5
8-28	Min.	W	2-1		6	5	Brocail	Crain		61-68	3rd	12.0
8-29	Chi.	W	7-5		10	11	Dominguez	Buehrle	Brocail	62-68	3rd	12.0
8-30!	Chi.	W	8-6		7	12	Wilson	Garland	Cordero	63-68		
8-30&	Chi.	L	0-8		3	14	McCarthy	Volquez		63-69	3rd	12.5
8-31	Chi.	W	9-2		10	6	Loe	Hernandez		64-69	3rd	11.5
9-1	At K.C.	W	5-4		7	12	Rogers	Howell	Cordero	65-69	3rd	10.5
9-2	At K.C.	W	8-7	(10)	13	14	Cordero	MacDougal	Wasdin	66-69	3rd	10.5
9-3	At K.C.	W	5-3		10	5	Dominguez	Carrasco		67-69	3rd	9.5
9-4	At K.C.	L	8-17		12	18	Nunez	Volquez		67-70	3rd	10.5

Date	Opp.	Res.	Score	(inn.*)	Hits	Opp. hits	Winning pitcher	Losing pitcher	Save	Record	Pos.	GB
9-5	At Min.	W	7-0		9	5	Loe	Silva		68-70	3rd	10.0
9-6	At Min.	W	10-7		11	10	Wasdin	Nathan	Cordero	69-70	3rd	9.0
9-7	At Min.	L	6-8		14	9	Romero	Brocail	Nathan	69-71	3rd	9.0
9-9	Oak.	L	8-9		8	13	Zito	Dominguez	Street	69-72	3rd	10.5
9-10	Oak.	L	4-5		8	8	Blanton	Loe	Street	69-73	3rd	11.5
9-11	Oak.	W	7-4		9	10	Rogers	Kennedy	Wasdin	70-73	3rd	11.5
9-12	Bal.	L	2-4		7	7	Cabrera	Volquez	Ryan	70-74	3rd	11.5
9-13	Bal.	L	3-4		4	7	Ray	Wilson	Ryan	70-75	3rd	11.5
9-14	Bal.	W	7-6	(10)	12	13	Benoit	Grimsley		71-75	3rd	10.5
9-15	Sea.	W	4-3		5	9	Loe	Harris	Cordero	72-75	3rd	9.5
9-16	Sea.	W	5-3		9	11	Rupe	Hernandez	Cordero	73-75	3rd	9.5
9-17	Sea.	W	7-6		16	11	Shouse	Guardado		74-75	3rd	9.5
9-18	Sea.	W	8-6		9	8	Dickey	Franklin	Cordero	75-75	3rd	9.5
9-20	At L.A.	L	1-2		5	7	Colon	Dominguez	Rodriguez	75-76	3rd	10.5
9-21	At L.A.	L	5-6		8	10	Yan	Feldman	Rodriguez	75-77	3rd	11.5
9-22	At L.A.	L	4-7		7	9	Santana	Volquez	Escobar	75-78	3rd	12.5
9-23	At Oak.	W	3-1		9	5	Rogers	Haren	Cordero	76-78	3rd	12.5
9-24	At Oak.	L	6-7		9	10	Duchscherer	Wasdin	Street	76-79	3rd	13.5
9-25	At Oak.	W	6-2		12	10	Dominguez	Saarloos		77-79	3rd	12.5
9-27	At Sea.	W	3-2	(11)	7	9	Wasdin	Mateo	Cordero	78-79	3rd	13.0
9-28	At Sea.	W	7-3		11	7	Young	Pineiro	Cordero	79-79	3rd	12.0
9-29	At Sea.	L	3-4		6	9	Franklin	Rogers	Guardado	79-80	3rd	13.0
9-30	L.A.	L	1-7		5	12	Lackey	Dickey		79-81	3rd	14.0
10-1	L.A.	L	6-7		11	15	Shields	Dominguez	Rodriguez	79-82	3rd	15.0
10-2	L.A.	L	4-7		8	9	Santana	Loe	Rodriguez	79-83	3rd	16.0

Monthly records: April (12-13), May (18-7), June (10-17), July (13-14), August (11-18), September (15-12), October (0-2).
*Innings, if other than nine. ! First game of a doubleheader. & Second game of a doubleheader.

RECORDS

2005 regular-season record: 79-83
Position: 3rd in A.L. West
Home: 44-37   **Road:** 35-46
A.L. East: 20-27   **A.L. Central:** 25-15
A.L. West: 25-32   **N.L.** 9-9
Vs. LH starters: 14-25
Vs. RH starters: 65-58
Grass: 72-76   **Artificial:** 7-7
Day: 27-24   **Night:** 52-59
1-Run: 24-29   **X-inn.:** 7-8
Doubleheaders: 0-0-1
Team record past five years: 384-426 (.474, ranks 10th in league in that span)

TEAM LEADERS

Batting average: Michael Young (.331).
At-bats: Michael Young (668).
Runs: Michael Young (114).
Hits: Michael Young (221).
Total Bases: Mark Teixeira (370).
Doubles: Alfonso Soriano (43).
Triples: David Dellucci, Gary Matthews Jr., Michael Young (5).
Home runs: Mark Teixeira (43).
Runs batted in: Mark Teixeira (144).
Stolen bases: Alfonso Soriano (30).
Slugging percentage: Mark Teixeira (.575).
On-base percentage: Michael Young (.385).
Wins: Kenny Rogers (14).
Earned-run average: Kenny Rogers (3.46).

Complete games: Ryan Drese, Kenny Rogers (1).
Shutouts: Kenny Rogers (1).
Saves: Francisco Cordero (37).
Innings pitched: Kenny Rogers (195.1).
Strikeouts: Chris Young (137).

GAMES BY POSITION

Catcher: Rod Barajas 119, Sandy Alomar Jr. 46, Gerald Laird 13.

First base: Mark Teixeira 155, Adrian Gonzalez 10, Phil Nevin 3, Rod Barajas 1, Mark DeRosa 1.

Second base: Alfonso Soriano 153, Mark DeRosa 17, Marshall McDougall 2, Esteban German 1.

Third base: Hank Blalock 158, Mark DeRosa 5, Marshall McDougall 5, Esteban German 1, Phil Nevin 1.

Shortstop: Michael Young 155, Mark DeRosa 16, Marshall McDougall 1.

Outfield: Kevin Mench 148, Gary Matthews Jr. 123, Richard Hidalgo 85, Laynce Nix 61, David Dellucci 52, Mark DeRosa 25, Jason Botts 7, Andres Torres 5, Marshall McDougall 3, Chad Allen 2, Adrian Gonzalez 1, Gerald Laird 1.

Designated hitter: David Dellucci 67, Adrian Gonzalez 32, Phil Nevin 25, Chad Allen 18, Mark Teixeira 8, Mark DeRosa 4, Michael Young 4, Jason Botts 3, Hank Blalock 2, Marshall McDougall 2, Alfonso Soriano 2, Esteban German 1, Richard Hidalgo 1, Gary Matthews Jr. 1, Kevin Mench 1.

TOP DRAFT CHOICES

1. **John Mayberry,** OF, Stanford.
2. **Johnny Whittleman,** 3B, Kingwood (Texas) H.S.
3. **Taylor Teagarden,** C, Texas.
4. **Shane Funk,** RHP, Arnold H.S., Panama City Beach, Fla.
5. **Michael Kirkman,** LHP, Columbia H.S., Lake City, Fla.
6. **German Duran,** 2B, Weatherford (Texas) College.
7. **Jacob Rasner,** RHP, Earl Wooster H.S., Reno, Nev.
8. **Brad Barragar,** RHP, Golden West JC (Calif).
9. **R.J. Anderson,** OF, Armwood H.S., Seffner, Fla.
10. **Matt Nevarez,** RHP, San Fernando (Calif.) H.S.

TORONTO BLUE JAYS
AMERICAN LEAGUE EAST DIVISION

2006 SEASON

Blue Jays Schedule
Home games shaded.
All-Star Game July 11 at Pittsburgh. Schedule subject to change.

APRIL

SUN	MON	TUE	WED	THU	FRI	SAT
2	3	4 MIN	5 MIN	6 MIN	7 TB	8 TB
9 TB	10	11 BOS	12 BOS	13 BOS	14 CHW	15 CHW
16 CHW	17	18 NYY	19 NYY	20	21 BOS	22 BOS
23 BOS	24	25 BAL	26 BAL	27 BAL	28 NYY	29 NYY
30 NYY						

MAY

SUN	MON	TUE	WED	THU	FRI	SAT
	1 BAL	2 BAL	3 BOS	4 BOS	5 LAA	6 LAA
7 LAA	8 LAA	9 OAK	10 OAK	11 OAK	12 TB	13 TB
14 TB	15	16 LAA	17 LAA	18 LAA	19 COL	20 COL
21 COL	22 TB	23 TB	24 TB	25	26 CHW	27 CHW
28 CHW	29 BOS	30 BOS	31 BOS			

JUNE

SUN	MON	TUE	WED	THU	FRI	SAT
				1	2 TB	3 TB
4 TB	5 BAL	6 BAL	7 BAL	8 BAL	9 DET	10 DET
11 DET	12 BAL	13 BAL	14 BAL	15 BAL	16 FLA	17 FLA
18 FLA	19	20 ATL	21 ATL	22 ATL	23 NYM	24 NYM
25 NYM	26 WAS	27 WAS	28 WAS	29 WAS	30 PHI	

JULY

SUN	MON	TUE	WED	THU	FRI	SAT
						1 PHI
2 PHI	3 TEX	4 TEX	5 TEX	6 KC	7 KC	8 KC
9 KC	10	11 ALL-STAR	12	13	14 SEA	15 SEA
16 SEA	17 TEX	18 TEX	19 TEX	20 NYY	21 NYY	22 NYY
23 NYY	24 SEA	25 SEA	26 SEA	27 OAK	28 OAK	29 OAK
30 OAK	31					

AUGUST

SUN	MON	TUE	WED	THU	FRI	SAT
		1 NYY	2 NYY	3 NYY	4 CHW	5 CHW
6 CHW	7 BAL	8 BAL	9 BAL	10 MIN	11 MIN	12 MIN
13 MIN	14	15 TB	16 TB	17 TB	18 BAL	19 BAL
20 BAL	21 OAK	22 OAK	23 OAK	24	25 KC	26 KC
27 KC	28 CLE	29 CLE	30 CLE	31 BOS		

SEPTEMBER

SUN	MON	TUE	WED	THU	FRI	SAT
					1 BOS	2 BOS
3 BOS	4 CLE	5 CLE	6 CLE	7	8 LAA	9 LAA
10 LAA	11 SEA	12 SEA	13 SEA	14	15 TB	16 TB
17 TB	18 NYY	19 NYY	20 NYY	21	22 BOS	23 BOS
24 BOS	25 BOS	26 DET	27 DET	28 DET	29 NYY	30 NYY

OCTOBER

SUN	MON	TUE	WED	THU	FRI	SAT
1 NYY	2	3	4	5	6	7

Home games are shaded. All-Star Game is July 11 at Pittsburgh. Schedule is subject to change.

Wells

CLUB DIRECTORY

President and CEO
Paul Godfrey

Senior v.p., baseball operations & g.m.
J.P. Ricciardi

Sr. v.p., communications/external affairs
Rob Godfrey

Sr. v.p., operations & corp. development
Lisa Power

Assistant, baseball operations
Bart Given

Manager, team travel
Mike Shaw

Director, player personnel
Tony LaCava

Director, scouting
Jon Lalonde

Director, player development
Dick Scott

Manager, minor league operations
Charlie Wilson

Vice president, special projects
Howard Starkman

Vice president, communications
Jay Stenhouse

Director, public relations
Will Hill

MINOR LEAGUE AFFILIATES

Class	Team	League	Manager
AAA	Syracuse	International	Mike Basso
AA	New Hampshire	Eastern	Doug Davis
Advanced A	Dunedin	Florida State	Omar Malave
A	Lansing	Midwest	Ken Joyce
Short-Season A	Auburn	New York-Penn	Dennis Holmberg
Advanced Rookie	Pulaski	Appalachian	Dave Pano

BROADCAST INFORMATION

Radio: The Fan (590).
Cable TV: Rogers SportsNet (RSN), TSN.

SPRING TRAINING

Ballpark (city): Knology Park (Dunedin, Fla.).
Ticket information: 800-707-8269;
727-733-0429.

For more on the Blue Jays, go to www.sportingnews.com/baseball/teams/bluejays/

2006 SEASON *Toronto Blue Jays*

Manager—John Gibbons (5).
Coaches—Brad Arnsberg (38), Mickey Brantley (14), Brian Butterfield (55), Marty Pevey (58), Bruce Walton (52), Ernie Whitt (12).

No.	PITCHERS	B/T	Ht./Wt.	Age*
	Josh Banks	R/R	6-3/195	23
34	A.J. Burnett	R/R	6-4/230	29
39	Gustavo Chacin	L/L	5-11/193	25
50	Vinnie Chulk	R/R	6-2/195	27
37	Scott Downs	L/L	6-2/190	30
54	Jason Frasor	R/R	5-10/170	28
32	Roy Halladay	R/R	6-6/225	28
	Ryan Houston	R/R	6-4/205	26
22	Brandon League	R/R	6-3/192	23
31	Ted Lilly	L/L	6-1/190	30
28	Shawn Marcum	R/R	6-0/180	24
40	Dustin McGowan	R/R	6-3/220	24
33	Vince Perkins	L/R	6-5/220	24
26	Ismael Ramirez	R/R	6-3/200	25
36	Francisco Rosario	R/R	6-0/195	25
52	B.J. Ryan	L/L	6-6/260	30
60	Scott Schoeneweis	L/L	6-0/190	32
30	Justin Speier	R/R	6-4/205	32
7	Josh Towers	R/R	6-1/188	29
41	Pete Walker	R/R	6-2/195	36

No.	CATCHERS	B/T	Ht./Wt.	Age*
16	Guillermo Quiroz	R/R	6-1/202	24
9	Gregg Zaun	B/R	5-10/190	34

No.	INFIELDERS	B/T	Ht./Wt.	Age*
8	Russ Adams	L/R	6-1/180	25
	Rob Cosby	R/R	6-1/215	24
25	Troy Glaus	R/R	6-5/240	29
25	John Hattig	B/R	6-2/215	26
2	Aaron Hill	R/R	5-11/195	24
29	Shea Hillenbrand	R/R	6-1/211	30
11	Eric Hinske	L/R	6-2/235	28
	John McDonald	R/R	5-11/175	31
35	Lyle Overbay	L/L	6-2/225	29
	Ryan Roberts	R/R	5-11/190	25
	Sergio Santos	R/R	6-2/240	22

No.	OUTFIELDERS	B/T	Ht./Wt.	Age*
27	Frank Catalanotto	L/R	5-11/195	31
24	John-Ford Griffin	L/L	6-2/215	26
3	Reed Johnson	R/R	5-10/180	29
19	Miguel Negron	L/L	6-2/170	23
15	Alex Rios	R/R	6-5/195	25
10	Vernon Wells	R/R	6-1/225	27

*Age as of April 1, 2006.

BALLPARK INFORMATION

Ballpark (capacity, surface)
Rogers Centre (50,516, artificial)
Address
One Blue Jays Way
Suite 3200, Rogers Centre
Toronto, Ontario M5V 1J1
Official website
www.bluejays.com
Business phone
416-341-1000
Ticket information
416-341-1234 and 1-888-OK GO JAY
Field dimensions (from home plate)
To left field at foul line, 330 feet
To center field, 400 feet
To right field at foul line, 330 feet
First game played
June 5, 1989 (Brewers 5, Blue Jays 3)

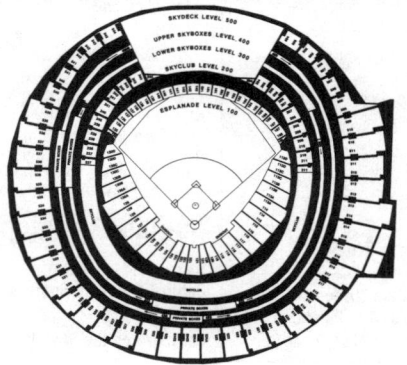

2006 SEASON *Toronto Blue Jays*

Date	Opp.	Res.	Score	(inn.*)	Hits	Opp. hits	Winning pitcher	Losing pitcher	Save	Record	Pos.	GB
4-4	At T.B.	W	5-2		7	10	Halladay	Brazelton	Batista	1-0	T1st	...
4-5	At T.B.	W	6-3		10	7	Chacin	McClung	Batista	2-0	T1st	...
4-6	At T.B.	L	5-8		9	11	Baez	Schoeneweis		2-1	T1st	...
4-8	Bos.	L	5-6		8	9	Arroyo	Bush	Foulke	2-2	T1st	...
4-9	Bos.	W	12-5		16	8	Frasor	Wells		3-2	T1st	...
4-10	Bos.	W	4-3		9	10	Batista	Timlin		4-2	1st	+1.0
4-11	At Oak.	W	10-3		12	9	Chacin	Saarloos		5-2	1st	+1.5
4-12	At Oak.	W	5-2		6	7	Towers	Haren	Batista	6-2	1st	+1.5
4-13	At Oak.	L	3-6		7	8	Calero	Frasor		6-3	1st	+0.5
4-14	At Tex.	W	2-1		5	5	Halladay	Astacio		7-3	1st	+1.5
4-15	At Tex.	L	2-4		6	7	Drese	Lilly	Cordero	7-4	1st	+0.5
4-16	At Tex.	W	8-0		12	4	Chacin	Rogers		8-4	1st	+0.5
4-17	At Tex.	L	5-6		10	12	Young	Towers	Cordero	8-5	2nd	0.5
4-18	At Bos.	L	7-12		18	15	Schilling	Bush		8-6	3rd	0.5
4-19	At Bos.	W	4-3		13	6	Halladay	Foulke	Batista	9-6	3rd	0.5
4-20	N.Y.	L	2-11		7	14	Pavano	Lilly		9-7	3rd	0.5
4-21	N.Y.	L	3-4		13	9	Mussina	Chacin	Rivera	9-8	3rd	1.5
4-22	Bal.	L	5-13		5	17	Williams	Speier		9-9	3rd	1.5
4-23	Bal.	L	1-4		9	8	Bedard	Bush		9-10	3rd	2.5
4-24	Bal.	L	1-7		5	14	Ponson	Halladay		9-11	3rd	3.5
4-26	T.B.	W	7-5		10	11	Lilly	Brazelton	Batista	10-11	3rd	4.0
4-27	T.B.	W	8-2		12	8	Chacin	Kazmir		11-11	3rd	3.5
4-28	T.B.	W	7-4		12	9	Towers	Waechter	Batista	12-11	3rd	3.0
4-29	At N.Y.	W	2-0		7	3	Halladay	Johnson		13-11	2nd	3.0
4-30	At N.Y.	L	3-4		8	10	Rivera	Chulk		13-12	3rd	4.0
5-1	At N.Y.	W	8-6		16	8	Walker	Stanton	Batista	14-12	3rd	4.0
5-2	At Bal.	W	6-2	(12)	14	7	Schoeneweis	Williams		15-12	2nd	3.0
5-3	At Bal.	W	1-0		5	3	Towers	Cabrera	Batista	16-12	2nd	2.0
5-4	At Bal.	L	1-5		5	12	Bedard	Halladay		16-13	3rd	3.0
5-6	Chi.	L	3-5		7	9	Hernandez	Frasor	Hermanson	16-14	3rd	4.0
5-7	Chi.	L	7-10		10	11	Garland	Lilly		16-15	3rd	5.0
5-8	Chi.	L	4-5		10	10	Buehrle	Chacin	Marte	16-16	3rd	5.0
5-9	K.C.	W	6-1		9	7	Towers	Hernandez		17-16	3rd	5.0
5-10	K.C.	W	3-1		6	8	Halladay	Greinke		18-16	3rd	4.0
5-11	K.C.	W	12-9		12	16	Batista	Burgos		19-16	3rd	4.0
5-13	At Cle.	L	4-6		5	8	Davis	Lilly	Wickman	19-17	3rd	3.5
5-14	At Cle.	L	2-3		7	5	Rhodes	Frasor	Wickman	19-18	3rd	4.5
5-15	At Cle.	W	5-2		8	6	Halladay	Sabathia		20-18	3rd	4.5
5-17	At Min.	W	10-3		14	9	Towers	Santana		21-18	3rd	4.5
5-18	At Min.	L	2-3		7	7	Lohse	Bush	Nathan	21-19	3rd	5.5
5-19	At Min.	L	0-4		7	10	Mays	Chacin		21-20	T3rd	5.5
5-20	Was.	W	6-1		11	6	Lilly	Vargas	Walker	22-20	T3rd	4.5
5-21	Was.	W	7-0		11	4	Halladay	Armas		23-20	3rd	4.5
5-22	Was.	L	2-9		7	13	Ohka	Towers		23-21	T3rd	4.5
5-24	Bos.	W	9-6		11	10	Batista	Embree		24-21	T3rd	4.5
5-25	Bos.	W	6-1		8	4	Lilly	Arroyo		25-21	T3rd	4.5
5-26	Bos.	W	8-1		9	9	Chacin	Miller	Walker	26-21	T2nd	4.5
5-27	Min.	L	2-7		5	16	Santana	Towers		26-22	3rd	4.5
5-28	Min.	L	3-4		9	6	Lohse	Bush	Nathan	26-23	4th	4.5
5-29	Min.	W	4-0		13	2	Halladay	Mays		27-23	T3rd	3.5
5-30	At Sea.	L	3-4		8	7	Moyer	Lilly	Guardado	27-24	4th	4.5
5-31	At Sea.	W	9-7		13	16	Gaudin	Franklin	Batista	28-24	3rd	3.5
6-1	At Sea.	L	0-3		6	10	Meche	Chacin	Guardado	28-25	3rd	4.5
6-2	At Oak.	L	3-5		9	8	Saarloos	Towers	Street	28-26	3rd	4.5
6-3	At Oak.	W	6-2		9	8	Halladay	Glynn		29-26	3rd	3.5
6-4	At Oak.	L	2-5		5	7	Blanton	Lilly	Street	29-27	3rd	4.5
6-5	At Oak.	L	4-12		6	16	Haren	Gaudin		29-28	3rd	5.5
6-6	At Chi.	W	4-1		7	8	Chacin	Koronka	Batista	30-28	3rd	5.5
6-7	At Chi.	W	6-4		10	10	Schoeneweis	Wellemeyer	Batista	31-28	3rd	4.5
6-8	At Chi.	L	0-2		3	7	Mitre	Halladay	Dempster	31-29	3rd	4.5
6-10	At Hou.	L	2-4		6	9	Rodriguez	Lilly	Lidge	31-30	3rd	5.5
6-11	At Hou.	L	3-6		7	13	Lidge	Schoeneweis		31-31	3rd	5.5
6-12	At Hou.	L	0-3		2	9	Oswalt	Towers		31-32	3rd	5.5
6-13	StL.	W	4-1		10	5	Halladay	Suppan		32-32	3rd	5.5
6-14	StL.	L	0-7		1	15	Carpenter	Gaudin		32-33	3rd	6.5
6-15	StL.	W	5-2		9	9	Lilly	Marquis	Batista	33-33	T3rd	6.5
6-17	Mil.	W	9-5		13	7	Walker	Davis		34-33	4th	5.5

Date	Opp.	Res.	Score	(inn.*)	Hits	Opp. hits	Winning pitcher	Losing pitcher	Save	Record	Pos.	GB
6-18	Mil.	L	2-5		8	10	Sheets	Halladay	Phelps	34-34	4th	6.5
6-19	Mil.	L	2-5		7	11	Capuano	Towers	Turnbow	34-35	4th	7.5
6-20	Bal.	W	11-2		16	3	Lilly	Chen		35-35	4th	6.5
6-21	Bal.	L	5-9		7	11	Lopez	Chacin		35-36	4th	7.5
6-22	Bal.	W	3-2		7	7	Walker	Cabrera	Batista	36-36	4th	6.5
6-23	Bal.	W	6-2		14	7	Halladay	Ponson		37-36	4th	5.5
6-24	At Was.	L	0-3		8	9	Loaiza	Towers	Cordero	37-37	4th	6.0
6-25	At Was.	L	2-5		7	6	Hernandez	Lilly	Cordero	37-38	4th	7.0
6-26	At Was.	W	9-5		9	6	Speier	Ayala	Batista	38-38	4th	7.0
6-27	At T.B.	L	3-4		10	7	Nomo	Walker	Baez	38-39	4th	7.0
6-28	At T.B.	W	3-1	(11)	11	8	Batista	Waechter		39-39	4th	6.0
6-29	At T.B.	W	12-3		13	4	Towers	Hendrickson		40-39	4th	6.0
7-1	At Bos.	W	15-2		13	9	Lilly	Clement		41-39	3rd	5.0
7-2	At Bos.	L	4-6		12	13	Timlin	Walker	Foulke	41-40	4th	6.0
7-3	At Bos.	W	5-2		10	8	Halladay	Arroyo	Schoeneweis	42-40	4th	5.0
7-5	Oak.	L	7-10	(11)	15	18	Duchscherer	Batista		42-41	4th	5.5
7-6	Oak.	W	8-0		12	7	Lilly	Blanton		43-41	4th	5.5
7-7	Oak.	W	4-2		6	7	Chacin	Harden	Batista	44-41	4th	4.5
7-8	At Tex.	L	6-7		6	14	Cordero	Batista		44-42	4th	5.5
7-9	At Tex.	L	10-12		15	15	Rogers	Downs	Cordero	44-43	4th	5.5
7-10	At Tex.	L	8-9		13	12	Loe	Frasor		44-44	4th	5.5
7-14	T.B.	L	0-3		6	7	Fossum	Lilly	Baez	44-45	4th	5.5
7-15	T.B.	W	11-6		15	11	Chacin	Nomo		45-45	4th	5.5
7-16	T.B.	L	5-6		9	12	Hendrickson	Towers	Baez	45-46	4th	5.5
7-17	T.B.	L	4-5		8	12	Orvella	Batista	Baez	45-47	4th	5.5
7-19	Sea.	W	12-10		17	16	Lilly	Sele	Batista	46-47	4th	5.0
7-20	Sea.	W	9-4		14	10	Chacin	Franklin		47-47	4th	5.0
7-21	Sea.	W	6-3		11	7	Towers	Pineiro	Batista	48-47	4th	5.0
7-22	At K.C.	L	3-5		9	6	Hernandez	Walker	MacDougal	48-48	4th	5.0
7-23	At K.C.	W	9-4		10	10	Bush	Snyder		49-48	4th	5.0
7-24	At K.C.	L	5-6		10	9	Carrasco	Gaudin	MacDougal	49-49	4th	5.0
7-26	L.A.	W	8-0		14	8	Chacin	Byrd		50-49	4th	4.5
7-27	L.A.	W	3-2	(10)	10	10	Batista	Donnelly		51-49	T3rd	4.5
7-28	L.A.	W	2-1	(18)	9	9	Walker	Shields		52-49	3rd	4.0
7-29	Tex.	L	1-4		6	9	Brocail	Downs	Cordero	52-50	3rd	5.0
7-30	Tex.	L	2-3		6	7	Benoit	Frasor	Cordero	52-51	3rd	6.0
7-31	Tex.	W	5-1		13	5	Chacin	Wilson		53-51	3rd	6.0
8-2	At Chi.	W	7-3		13	8	Towers	Garland		54-51	3rd	6.0
8-3	At Chi.	W	4-3		5	9	Bush	Hernandez	Batista	55-51	3rd	6.0
8-4	At Chi.	L	4-5		8	7	Vizcaino	Speier	Hermanson	55-52	3rd	7.0
8-5	N.Y.	L	2-6		9	11	Small	Chacin	Rivera	55-53	3rd	7.0
8-6	N.Y.	W	8-5		14	10	Walker	Johnson		56-53	3rd	6.0
8-7	N.Y.	L	2-6		7	12	Leiter	Towers	Rivera	56-54	3rd	7.0
8-8	Det.	L	8-9	(12)	20	15	Darensbourg	Schoeneweis	Dingman	56-55	3rd	8.0
8-9	Det.	W	6-4		7	11	McGowan	Douglass	Batista	57-55	3rd	8.0
8-10	Det.	W	4-3		9	5	Speier	Dingman		58-55	3rd	8.0
8-11	Det.	W	2-1		4	2	Downs	Bonderman	Batista	59-55	3rd	7.5
8-12	At Bal.	W	12-0		12	9	Towers	Cabrera		60-55	3rd	7.5
8-13	At Bal.	L	0-1		5	4	Maine	Bush	Ryan	60-56	3rd	8.5
8-14	At Bal.	W	7-6		14	11	Frasor	Byrdak	Batista	61-56	3rd	8.0
8-15	At L.A.	L	4-5	(11)	9	13	Shields	Walker		61-57	3rd	8.0
8-16	At L.A.	W	4-3		7	6	League	Rodriguez	Batista	62-57	3rd	8.0
8-17	At L.A.	W	4-1		11	8	Towers	Washburn	Batista	63-57	3rd	7.0
8-19	At Det.	L	5-9		12	12	Maroth	Bush	Dingman	63-58	3rd	7.5
8-20	At Det.	L	2-3	(13)	5	11	German	Batista		63-59	3rd	7.5
8-21	At Det.	L	6-17		11	15	Douglass	McGowan		63-60	3rd	8.5
8-22	At N.Y.	L	0-7		5	12	Wright	Downs		63-61	3rd	9.0
8-23	At N.Y.	L	4-5		10	9	Rivera	Batista		63-62	3rd	10.0
8-24	At N.Y.	W	9-5		12	13	Bush	Mussina		64-62	3rd	9.0
8-25	At N.Y.	L	2-6		6	11	Chacon	Chacin		64-63	3rd	9.0
8-26	Cle.	L	3-9		8	15	Sabathia	McGowan		64-64	3rd	10.0
8-27	Cle.	W	2-1		6	5	Downs	Millwood	Batista	65-64	3rd	9.0
8-28	Cle.	L	1-4		8	6	Westbrook	Towers	Wickman	65-65	3rd	10.0
8-30	Bal.	W	7-2		12	8	Bush	Lopez		66-65	3rd	10.5
8-31	Bal.	L	0-7		2	10	Chen	Chacin		66-66	3rd	11.5
9-1	Bal.	L	3-5		9	11	Penn	McGowan	Ryan	66-67	3rd	12.5
9-2	T.B.	W	4-3		10	8	Schoeneweis	Borowski	Batista	67-67	3rd	11.5
9-3	T.B.	L	2-3		2	6	McClung	Batista	Baez	67-68	3rd	12.5
9-4	T.B.	L	0-1		4	7	Kazmir	Bush	Baez	67-69	3rd	13.5
9-5	At Bal.	W	6-2		11	7	Chacin	Chen		68-69	3rd	12.5

Date	Opp.	Res.	Score	(inn.*)	Hits	Opp. hits	Winning pitcher	Losing pitcher	Save	Record	Pos.	GB
9-6	At Bal.	L	0-5		5	7	Cabrera	Lilly		68-70	3rd	13.5
9-7	At Bal.	W	7-4		10	9	Walker	Julio	Batista	69-70	3rd	13.5
9-9	At T.B.	W	7-2		11	10	Towers	McClung		70-70	3rd	12.0
9-10	At T.B.	W	3-2		9	4	Bush	Baez	Batista	71-70	3rd	12.0
9-11	At T.B.	L	5-6	(11)	8	9	Harper	Schoeneweis		71-71	3rd	12.0
9-12	Bos.	L	5-6	(11)	8	12	Papelbon	Walker		71-72	3rd	13.0
9-13	Bos.	W	9-3		9	9	Downs	Clement		72-72	3rd	12.0
9-14	Bos.	L	3-5		7	7	Wells	Towers	Timlin	72-73	3rd	13.0
9-16	N.Y.	L	10-11		14	12	Proctor	Bush	Rivera	72-74	3rd	13.5
9-17	N.Y.	L	0-1		6	10	Chacon	Chacin	Gordon	72-75	3rd	14.5
9-18	N.Y.	W	6-5		11	8	Lilly	Wright	Batista	73-75	3rd	13.5
9-19	Sea.	L	5-7		8	13	Sherrill	Batista	Guardado	73-76	3rd	13.5
9-20	Sea.	W	6-4		7	10	Towers	Harris	Frasor	74-76	3rd	13.5
9-21	Sea.	L	2-3		4	5	Hernandez	Bush	Guardado	74-77	3rd	14.0
9-22	Sea.	W	7-5		10	10	Speier	Pineiro	Batista	75-77	3rd	14.0
9-23	At N.Y.	L	0-5		4	8	Chacon	Lilly		75-78	3rd	15.0
9-24	At N.Y.	W	7-4		10	8	Downs	Wright	Batista	76-78	3rd	14.0
9-25	At N.Y.	L	4-8		9	12	Wang	Towers	Rivera	76-79	3rd	15.0
9-27#	At Bos.	L	1-3		5	6	Wakefield	Bush	Timlin	76-80		
9-27$	At Bos.	W	7-5		13	12	Frasor	Bradford	Batista	77-80	3rd	15.0
9-28	At Bos.	W	7-2		8	8	Lilly	Arroyo		78-80	3rd	15.0
9-29	At Bos.	L	4-5		10	10	Papelbon	Batista		78-81	3rd	16.0
9-30	K.C.	W	10-1		15	9	Towers	Greinke		79-81	3rd	15.0
10-1	K.C.	L	6-7		6	12	Burgos	Walker	MacDougal	79-82	3rd	16.0
10-2	K.C.	W	7-2		14	7	Chacin	Hernandez		80-82	3rd	15.0

Monthly records: April (13-12), May (15-12), June (12-15), July (13-12), August (13-15), September (13-15), October (1-1).
*Innings, if other than nine. ! First game of a doubleheader. & Second game of a doubleheader. # Day separate admission. $ Night separate admission.

RECORDS

2005 regular-season record: 80-82
Position: 3rd in A.L. East
Home: 43-38   **Road:** 37-44
A.L. East: 38-36   **A.L. Central:** 15-19
A.L. West: 19-17   **N.L.** 8-10
Vs. LH starters: 23-24
Vs. RH starters: 57-58
Grass: 30-39   **Artificial:** 50-43
Day: 22-35   **Night:** 58-47
1-Run: 16-31   **X-inn.:** 4-6
Doubleheaders: 0-0-0
Team record past five years: 391-418
(.483, ranks 9th in league in that span)

TEAM LEADERS

Batting average: Frank Catalanotto (.301).
At-bats: Vernon Wells (620).
Runs: Shea Hillenbrand (91).
Hits: Shea Hillenbrand (173).
Total Bases: Vernon Wells (287).
Doubles: Shea Hillenbrand (36).
Triples: Reed Johnson, Alex Rios (6).
Home runs: Vernon Wells (28).
Runs batted in: Vernon Wells (97).
Stolen bases: Alex Rios (14).
Slugging percentage: Vernon Wells (.463).
On-base percentage: Frank Catalanotto (.367).
Wins: Gustavo Chacin, Josh Towers (13).
Earned-run average: Roy Halladay (2.41).
Complete games: Roy Halladay (5).
Shutouts: Roy Halladay (2).

Saves: Miguel Batista (31).
Innings pitched: Josh Towers (208.2).
Strikeouts: Gustavo Chacin (121).

GAMES BY POSITION

Catcher: Gregg Zaun 132, Ken Huckaby 35, Guillermo Quiroz 10, Greg Myers 4, Andy Dominique 1.
First base: Eric Hinske 100, Shea Hillenbrand 67.
Second base: Orlando Hudson 130, Frank Menechino 26, Aaron Hill 22, John McDonald 5.
Third base: Corey Koskie 76, Shea Hillenbrand 54, Aaron Hill 35, Frank Menechino 9.
Shortstop: Russ Adams 132, John McDonald 32, Aaron Hill 16, Frank Menechino 1.
Outfield: Vernon Wells 155, Alex Rios 142, Reed Johnson 139, Frank Catalanotto 111, Gabe Gross 37.
Designated hitter: Eric Hinske 43, Aaron Hill 34, Shea Hillenbrand 33, Frank Menechino 25, Corey Koskie 19, Frank Catalanotto 15, John-Ford Griffin 4, Gabe Gross 2, Guillermo Quiroz 2, Vernon Wells 2, Alex Rios 1. .

TOP DRAFT CHOICES

1. **Ricky Romero,** LHP, Cal State Fullerton.
3. **Brian Pettway ,** OF, Mississippi.
4. **Ryan Patterson,** OF, LSU.
5. **Eric Fowler,** LHP, Mississippi.
6. **Josh Bell,** C, Auburn.
7. **Robert Ray,** RHP, Texas A&M.
8. **Jacob Butler,** OF, Nevada.
9. **Paul Phillips,** RHP, Oakland.
10. **Josh Sowers,** RHP, Yale.

ARIZONA DIAMONDBACKS
NATIONAL LEAGUE WEST DIVISION

2006 SEASON

Diamondbacks Schedule
Home games shaded.
All-Star Game July 11 at Pittsburgh. Schedule subject to change.

APRIL

SUN	MON	TUE	WED	THU	FRI	SAT
2	3 COL	4	5 COL	6 COL	7 MIL	8 MIL
9 MIL	10	11 COL	12 COL	13 COL	14 HOU	15 HOU
16 HOU	17 SF	18 SF	19 SF	20 SF	21 LAD	22 LAD
23 LAD	24 SD	25 SD	26 SD	27	28 SF	29 SF
30 SF						

MAY

SUN	MON	TUE	WED	THU	FRI	SAT
	1 LAD	2 LAD	3 CHC	4 CHC	5 CIN	6 CIN
7 CIN	8	9 PIT	10 PIT	11 PIT	12 STL	13 STL
14 STL	15 SD	16 SD	17 SD	18	19 ATL	20 ATL
21 ATL	22 PIT	23 PIT	24 PIT	25	26 CIN	27 CIN
28 CIN	29 NYM	30 NYM	31 NYM			

JUNE

SUN	MON	TUE	WED	THU	FRI	SAT
				1 ATL	2 ATL	3 ATL
4 ATL	5 PHI	6 PHI	7 PHI	8 NYM	9 NYM	10 NYM
11 NYM	12	13 SF	14 SF	15 SF	16 TEX	17 TEX
18 TEX	19	20 TB	21 TB	22 TB	23 LAA	24 LAA
25 LAA	26	27 SEA	28 SEA	29 SEA	30 OAK	

JULY

SUN	MON	TUE	WED	THU	FRI	SAT
						1 OAK
2 OAK	3 LAD	4 LAD	5 LAD	6	7 COL	8 COL
9 COL	10	11 ALL-STAR	12	13	14 MIL	15 MIL
16 MIL	17 LAD	18 LAD	19 LAD	20 COL	21 COL	22 COL
23 COL	24	25 PHI	26 PHI	27 PHI	28 HOU	29 HOU
30 HOU	31 CHC					

AUGUST

SUN	MON	TUE	WED	THU	FRI	SAT
		1 CHC	2 CHC	3 CHC	4 HOU	5 HOU
6 HOU	7 SF	8 SF	9 SF	10	11 FLA	12 FLA
13 FLA	14 COL	15 COL	16 COL	17 COL	18 SD	19 SD
20 SD	21 SF	22 SF	23 SF	24	25 LAD	26 LAD
27 LAD	28 SD	29 SD	30 SD	31		

SEPTEMBER

SUN	MON	TUE	WED	THU	FRI	SAT
					1 WAS	2 WAS
3 WAS	4 FLA	5 FLA	6 FLA	7 STL	8 STL	9 STL
10 STL	11 WAS	12 WAS	13 WAS	14	15 COL	16 COL
17 COL	18	19 SD	20 SD	21 SD	22 LAD	23 LAD
24 LAD	25 SF	26 SF	27 SF	28 SD	29 SD	30 SD

OCTOBER

SUN	MON	TUE	WED	THU	FRI	SAT
1 SD	2	3	4	5	6	7

Home games are shaded. All-Star Game is July 11 at Pittsburgh. Schedule is subject to change.

Tracy

CLUB DIRECTORY

Managing general partner
Ken Kendrick
General partner
Jeff Moorad
President
Richard Dozer
Sr. vice president and general manager
Josh Byrnes
Senior vice president, finance
Thomas Harris
Senior v.p., communications
Derrick Hall
Senior v.p., tickets & special services
Dianne Aguilar
Vice president, event services
Russ Amaral
V.p., sales/group and season tickets
Rob Kiese
Vice president, special asst. to the g.m.
Bob Gebhard
Assistant general manager
Peter Woodfork
Vice president, scouting operations
Mike Rizzo
Director, professional scouting
Jerry Dipoto
Assistant director, scouting
Chad MacDonald
Manager, minor league operations
A.J. Hinch
Director of public relations
Mike Swanson
Senior director, marketing
Mike Malo

MINOR LEAGUE AFFILIATES

Class	Team	League	Manager
AAA	Tucson	Pacific Coast	Chip Hale
AA	Tennessee	Southern	Bill Plummer
Advanced A	Lancaster	California	Brett Butler
A	South Bend	Midwest	Mark Haley
Short-Season A	Yakima	Northwest	Jay Gainer
Advanced Rookie	Missoula	Pioneer	Hector de la Cruz

BROADCAST INFORMATION

Radio: KTAR-AM (620).
TV: KTVK (Channel 3)
Cable TV: Fox Sports Net Arizona.

SPRING TRAINING

Ballpark (city): Tucson Electric Park (Tucson, Ariz.).
Ticket information: 866-672-1343.

For more on the D-backs, go to www.sportingnews.com/baseball/teams/diamondbacks/

Manager—Bob Melvin (3).
Coaches—Mike Aldrete (25), Jay Bell (33), Bryan Price, Glenn Sherlock (53), Lee Tinsley, Carlos Tosca (14).

No.	PITCHERS	B/T	Ht./Wt.	Age*
41	Greg Aquino	R/R	6-1/188	28
	Miguel Batista	R/R	6-1/197	35
30	Brian Bruney	R/R	6-2/245	24
50	Jason Bulger	R/R	6-4/215	27
49	Edgar Gonzalez	R/R	6-0/225	23
	Enrique Gonzalez	R/R	5-10/195	23
44	Mike Gosling	L/L	6-2/195	25
	Jason Grimsley	R/R	6-3/205	38
37	Brad Halsey	L/L	6-1/180	25
	Orlando Hernandez	R/R	6-2/220	36
38	Brandon Lyon	R/R	6-1/185	26
52	Brandon Medders	R/R	6-1/191	26
57	Dustin Nippert	R/R	6-7/217	24
48	Russ Ortiz	R/R	6-1/220	31
68	Tony Pena	R/R	6-2/220	24
	Michael Schultz	R/R	6-7/220	26
	Doug Slaten	L/L	6-5/200	26
47	Jose Valverde	R/R	6-4/254	26
29	Claudio Vargas	R/R	6-3/228	27
	Luis Vizcaino	R/R	5-11/185	31
17	Brandon Webb	R/R	6-2/228	26

No.	CATCHERS	B/T	Ht./Wt.	Age*
	Johnny Estrada	B/R	5-11/210	29
5	Koyie Hill	B/R	6-0/220	27
	Miguel Montero	L/R	5-11/195	22
19	Chris Snyder	R/R	6-3/230	25

No.	INFIELDERS	B/T	Ht./Wt.	Age*
12	Alex Cintron	B/R	6-2/199	27
34	Tony Clark	B/R	6-7/245	33
4	Craig Counsell	L/R	6-0/184	35
	Stephen Drew	L/R	6-1/195	23
	Damion Easley	R/R	5-11/190	36
1	Andy Green	R/R	5-9/180	28
	Orlando Hudson	B/R	6-0/185	28
16	Conor Jackson	R/R	6-2/225	23
18	Chad Tracy	L/R	6-2/200	25

No.	OUTFIELDERS	B/T	Ht./Wt.	Age*
	Eric Byrnes	R/R	6-2/210	30
20	Luis Gonzalez	L/R	6-2/200	38
5	Scott Hairston	R/R	6-0/200	25
15	Shawn Green	L/L	6-4/210	33
43	Josh Kroeger	L/L	6-2/220	23
27	Luis Terrero	R/R	6-2/225	25
	Chris Young	R/R	6-2/180	22

*Age as of April 1, 2006.

BALLPARK INFORMATION

Ballpark (capacity, surface)
Chase Field (49,033, grass)
Address
401 East Jefferson
Phoenix, AZ 85004
Official website
www.diamondbacks.com
Business phone
602-462-6500
Ticket information
602-514-8400
Field dimensions (from home plate)
To left field at foul line, 330 feet
To center field, 407 feet
To right field at foul line, 334 feet
First game played
March 31, 1998 (Rockies 9, Diamondbacks 2)

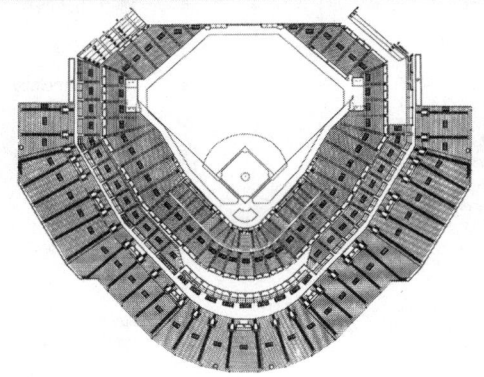

2006 SEASON *Arizona Diamondbacks*

2006 SEASON *Arizona Diamondbacks*

Date	Opp.	Res.	Score	(inn.*)	Hits	Opp. hits	Winning pitcher	Losing pitcher	Save	Record	Pos.	GB
4-4	Chi.	L	6-16		12	23	Rusch	Vazquez		0-1	T4th	1.0
4-5	Chi.	W	5-4		7	8	Ortiz	Maddux	Lyon	1-1	3rd	1.0
4-6	Chi.	W	8-3		13	9	Webb	Dempster		2-1	1st	+0.5
4-8	L.A.	L	7-8		7	11	Schmoll	Lyon	Brazoban	2-2	T2nd	1.0
4-9	L.A.	L	10-12	(11)	19	12	Brazoban	Gosling	Schmoll	2-3	4th	2.0
4-10	L.A.	W	5-4		8	12	Koplove	Sanchez	Lyon	3-3	T3rd	1.0
4-11	Col.	W	2-0		4	7	Halsey	Jennings	Lyon	4-3	T3rd	0.5
4-12	Col.	W	4-2		9	9	Webb	Fuentes	Lyon	5-3	2nd	0.5
4-13	Col.	W	5-2		7	6	Estes	Kim	Bruney	6-3	2nd	0.5
4-14	At Was.	L	3-5		4	9	Hernandez	Vazquez	Cordero	6-4	2nd	1.0
4-16	At Was.	L	3-9		8	9	Patterson	Ortiz		6-5	2nd	2.5
4-17	At Was.	L	3-7		8	11	Tucker	Koplove		6-6	3rd	3.5
4-18	At Col.	W	5-3		11	7	Webb	Speier	Lyon	7-6	2nd	3.5
4-19	At Col.	L	1-8		5	12	Francis	Estes		7-7	T2nd	4.5
4-20	At S.F.	W	2-1		3	11	Vazquez	Lowry	Lyon	8-7	2nd	4.5
4-21	At S.F.	L	3-4	(13)	11	6	Walker	Gosling		8-8	T2nd	4.5
4-22	S.D.	W	5-3		14	7	Halsey	Redding	Lyon	9-8	2nd	3.5
4-23	S.D.	W	2-1		7	5	Koplove	Otsuka		10-8	2nd	2.5
4-24	S.D.	W	8-6		14	7	Estes	Lawrence	Lyon	11-8	2nd	2.5
4-25	At L.A.	W	4-2		11	5	Vazquez	Lowe	Lyon	12-8	2nd	1.5
4-26	At L.A.	W	3-2		5	10	Ortiz	Erickson	Lyon	13-8	2nd	0.5
4-27	At L.A.	W	6-3		8	9	Cormier	Weaver	Lopez	14-8	1st	+0.5
4-29	At S.D.	L	4-5	(15)	8	20	Hammond	Lyon		14-9	2nd	0.5
4-30	At S.D.	L	0-2		2	4	Lawrence	Estes	Hoffman	14-10	2nd	1.5
5-1	At S.D.	W	5-2		9	6	Vazquez	Williams		15-10	2nd	1.5
5-2	S.F.	L	8-9	(10)	14	16	Brower	Bruney	Walker	15-11	2nd	1.5
5-3	S.F.	W	3-2		8	6	Lopez	Herges	Lyon	16-11	2nd	1.5
5-4	S.F.	W	6-2		10	6	Webb	Tomko		17-11	2nd	0.5
5-5	Pit.	L	2-6		6	11	Williams	Estes		17-12	2nd	1.0
5-6	Pit.	W	8-4		11	10	Vazquez	Perez		18-12	2nd	1.0
5-7	Pit.	L	2-3		2	14	Fogg	Ortiz	Mesa	18-13	2nd	1.0
5-8	Pit.	L	2-16		6	17	Wells	Halsey		18-14	2nd	2.0
5-9	Was.	L	3-4		11	12	Hernandez	Valverde	Cordero	18-15	T2nd	2.0
5-10	Was.	W	3-2		3	10	Estes	Armas	Lyon	19-15	2nd	2.0
5-11	Was.	W	3-2		10	6	Cormier	Rauch	Lyon	20-15	2nd	1.0
5-12	At Col.	W	6-3		9	11	Ortiz	Chacon		21-15	2nd	...
5-13	At Col.	L	3-18		9	19	Francis	Halsey		21-16	2nd	...
5-14	At Col.	W	10-4		12	9	Webb	Wright		22-16	2nd	...
5-15	At Col.	W	5-4		8	9	Estes	Jennings	Bruney	23-16	1st	+0.5
5-17	At Hou.	L	0-3		6	8	Oswalt	Vazquez	Lidge	23-17	2nd	1.0
5-18	At Hou.	W	7-6		14	13	Ortiz	Pettitte	Bruney	24-17	2nd	1.0
5-19	At Hou.	W	6-1		9	7	Halsey	Clemens	Valverde	25-17	2nd	0.5
5-20	At Det.	W	6-2		13	6	Webb	Walker	Bruney	26-17	2nd	0.5
5-21	At Det.	L	2-3	(11)	7	11	German	Bruney		26-18	2nd	0.5
5-22	At Det.	W	1-0		5	5	Vazquez	Johnson		27-18	1st	+0.5
5-24	S.D.	L	5-9		15	15	Eaton	Ortiz	Hoffman	27-19	2nd	0.5
5-25	S.D.	W	12-11		15	15	Valverde	Otsuka	Bruney	28-19	1st	+0.5
5-26	S.D.	L	0-10		2	13	Peavy	Webb		28-20	2nd	0.5
5-27	L.A.	L	4-7		8	10	Wunsch	Valverde	Gagne	28-21	2nd	1.5
5-28	L.A.	W	5-4		5	12	Cormier	Carrara		29-21	2nd	1.5
5-29	L.A.	L	3-6		9	12	Weaver	Ortiz	Gagne	29-22	2nd	2.5
5-31	At N.Y.	W	7-0		14	6	Halsey	Benson		30-22	2nd	3.0
6-1	At N.Y.	L	1-2		8	10	Zambrano	Webb	Looper	30-23	2nd	3.0
6-2	At N.Y.	L	1-6		7	9	Martinez	Estes		30-24	2nd	3.0
6-4!	At Phi.	L	6-10		9	14	Padilla	Vazquez		30-25		
6-4&	At Phi.	L	3-5		10	5	Myers	Ortiz	Wagner	30-26	2nd	4.0
6-5	At Phi.	L	6-7		10	10	Wolf	Halsey	Wagner	30-27	2nd	4.0
6-6	At Phi.	W	10-8		13	12	Webb	Lidle	Lopez	31-27	2nd	3.5
6-7	Min.	L	8-9		13	13	Rincon	Valverde	Nathan	31-28	2nd	3.5
6-8	Min.	L	0-10		4	15	Santana	Vargas		31-29	3rd	3.5
6-9	Min.	W	4-3		7	5	Vazquez	Lohse	Bruney	32-29	3rd	3.5
6-10	K.C.	W	12-11	(10)	20	13	Bruney	MacDougal		33-29	3rd	2.5
6-11	K.C.	L	5-8		11	18	Howell	Halsey		33-30	3rd	3.5
6-12	K.C.	L	4-9	(12)	12	15	Jensen	Lopez		33-31	3rd	3.5
6-13	At Chi.	W	8-1		11	8	Estes	Contreras		34-31	3rd	3.0
6-14	At Chi.	W	10-4		13	8	Vazquez	Hernandez		35-31	2nd	2.0
6-15	At Chi.	L	6-12		7	10	Garland	Ortiz		35-32	2nd	2.0

Date	Opp.	Res.	Score	(inn.*)	Hits	Opp. hits	Winning pitcher	Losing pitcher	Save	Record	Pos.	GB
6-17	At Cle.	L	6-13		11	13	Lee	Halsey		35-33	2nd	1.5
6-18	At Cle.	L	1-3		8	5	Elarton	Webb	Wickman	35-34	2nd	2.5
6-19	At Cle.	L	2-3		5	9	Westbrook	Estes	Wickman	35-35	2nd	3.5
6-20	At S.F.	L	3-8		10	14	Lowry	Vazquez		35-36	2nd	4.5
6-21	At S.F.	W	6-4		9	10	Vargas	Tomko	Bruney	36-36	2nd	4.5
6-22	At S.F.	L	0-4		5	9	Schmidt	Halsey		36-37	2nd	4.5
6-23	At S.F.	W	7-2		12	7	Webb	Rueter		37-37	2nd	3.5
6-24	Det.	W	2-1		9	8	Estes	Maroth	Bruney	38-37	2nd	2.5
6-25	Det.	L	1-5		6	11	Douglass	Vazquez		38-38	2nd	3.5
6-26	Det.	W	13-7		14	10	Vargas	Bonderman		39-38	2nd	3.5
6-28	S.F.	L	3-11		10	14	Schmidt	Halsey		39-39	2nd	4.0
6-29	S.F.	L	2-4		5	13	Christiansen	Webb	Walker	39-40	2nd	4.0
6-30	S.F.	L	2-9		4	7	Lowry	Estes	Tomko	39-41	2nd	4.5
7-1	At L.A.	L	0-7		3	10	Penny	Vazquez		39-42	2nd	4.5
7-2	At L.A.	W	7-5		12	7	Vargas	Lowe	Bruney	40-42	2nd	4.5
7-3	At L.A.	W	10-3		12	8	Halsey	Houlton		41-42	2nd	4.5
7-4	StL.	L	3-10		9	13	Morris	Webb		41-43	2nd	4.5
7-5	StL.	L	1-7		8	10	Suppan	Estes		41-44	2nd	4.5
7-6	StL.	L	1-2		4	3	Carpenter	Vazquez	Isringhausen	41-45	2nd	4.5
7-7	StL.	W	2-1		5	6	Cormier	King		42-45	2nd	4.5
7-8	Cin.	L	3-4		7	12	Weathers	Cormier	Mercker	42-46	2nd	5.5
7-9	Cin.	L	2-6		8	9	Coffey	Webb		42-47	2nd	5.5
7-10	Cin.	W	2-0		5	5	Cormier	Milton	Bruney	43-47	2nd	5.5
7-14	At S.D.	W	6-0		11	5	Vazquez	Lawrence		44-47	2nd	4.5
7-15	At S.D.	L	7-10		13	13	Linebrink	Aquino	Hoffman	44-48	2nd	5.5
7-16	At S.D.	L	1-4		6	5	Peavy	Vargas	Hoffman	44-49	2nd	6.5
7-17	At S.D.	W	6-1		12	7	Halsey	Stauffer	Valverde	45-49	2nd	5.5
7-18	Fla.	W	8-7	(11)	14	14	Medders	Jones		46-49	2nd	5.0
7-19	Fla.	L	3-6		8	11	Burnett	Vazquez	Jones	46-50	2nd	5.0
7-20	Fla.	L	2-9		13	14	Moehler	Webb		46-51	2nd	5.0
7-22	Atl.	W	6-5	(10)	12	12	Cormier	Brower		47-51	2nd	3.5
7-23	Atl.	L	2-3		5	6	Reitsma	Valverde		47-52	2nd	3.5
7-24	Atl.	W	3-2		9	4	Vazquez	Ramirez	Bruney	48-52	2nd	2.5
7-25	At Mil.	L	2-4		8	8	Sheets	Worrell	Turnbow	48-53	2nd	3.0
7-26	At Mil.	L	2-7		6	11	Eveland	Webb		48-54	2nd	3.0
7-27	At Mil.	W	3-0		5	8	Vargas	Ohka	Bruney	49-54	2nd	3.0
7-28	At Chi.	W	6-0		13	5	Halsey	Williams		50-54	2nd	2.0
7-29	At Chi.	L	3-4		7	8	Novoa	Bruney		50-55	2nd	2.0
7-30	At Chi.	W	3-2		9	6	Cormier	Novoa	Aquino	51-55	2nd	1.0
7-31	At Chi.	W	13-6		14	10	Webb	Maddux		52-55	1st	...
8-2	Hou.	L	1-3		6	9	Clemens	Vargas	Lidge	52-56	2nd	1.0
8-3	Hou.	L	0-7		7	13	Astacio	Vazquez		52-57	2nd	1.0
8-4	Hou.	W	7-3		8	10	Halsey	Rodriguez	Valverde	53-57	2nd	1.0
8-5	Col.	L	4-6		7	6	DeJean	Cormier	Fuentes	53-58	2nd	2.0
8-6	Col.	L	7-14		12	16	Francis	Gosling		53-59	2nd	3.0
8-7	Col.	W	9-4		14	5	Vargas	Wright		54-59	2nd	3.0
8-9	At Fla.	L	0-5		3	9	Burnett	Vazquez		54-60	2nd	4.0
8-10	At Fla.	L	5-10		8	12	Vargas	Halsey	Jones	54-61	2nd	4.0
8-11	At Fla.	W	3-1		10	4	Webb	de los Santos	Valverde	55-61	2nd	4.0
8-12	At Atl.	W	8-0		11	4	Vargas	Sosa		56-61	2nd	3.0
8-13	At Atl.	L	5-9		8	14	Foster	Cormier		56-62	2nd	3.0
8-14	At Atl.	L	8-13		15	13	Hampton	Vazquez		56-63	2nd	3.0
8-16	At StL.	L	2-8		5	15	Suppan	Halsey		56-64	2nd	4.0
8-17	At StL.	L	0-5		5	11	Mulder	Webb		56-65	2nd	4.0
8-18	At StL.	W	9-2		14	6	Vargas	Marquis		57-65	2nd	3.0
8-19	At Cin.	L	3-17		5	15	Claussen	Ortiz		57-66	2nd	4.0
8-20	At Cin.	W	6-2		11	7	Vazquez	Standridge		58-66	2nd	4.0
8-21	At Cin.	L	6-13		9	17	Milton	Halsey		58-67	2nd	4.0
8-22	N.Y.	L	1-4		5	7	Glavine	Webb	Looper	58-68	2nd	4.0
8-23	N.Y.	L	1-14		6	17	Zambrano	Vargas		58-69	2nd	5.0
8-24	N.Y.	L	4-18		8	20	Seo	Ortiz		58-70	2nd	6.0
8-25	N.Y.	L	1-3		4	5	Martinez	Vazquez	Looper	58-71	2nd	6.5
8-26	Phi.	L	3-11		5	11	Fultz	Halsey		58-72	2nd	6.5
8-27	Phi.	W	2-0		5	5	Webb	Lieber	Valverde	59-72	2nd	5.5
8-28	Phi.	W	10-5		9	9	Vargas	Padilla		60-72	2nd	5.5
8-29	At S.D.	W	7-5		8	8	Ortiz	Williams		61-72	2nd	4.5
8-30	At S.D.	L	3-5		10	9	Peavy	Halsey	Hoffman	61-73	2nd	5.5
8-31	At S.D.	L	5-9		9	14	Park	Vazquez		61-74	3rd	6.5
9-2	S.F.	L	3-6		4	9	Schmidt	Webb	Benitez	61-75	4th	7.0
9-3	S.F.	L	4-9		8	12	Lowry	Vargas		61-76	4th	8.0

Date	Opp.	Res.	Score	(inn.*)	Hits	Opp. hits	Winning pitcher	Losing pitcher	Save	Record	Pos.	GB
9-4	S.F.	L	2-3		5	6	Cain	Ortiz	Benitez	61-77	4th	8.0
9-6	At Pit.	W	4-2	(12)	7	15	Valverde	Grabow	Groom	62-77	4th	7.0
9-7	At Pit.	W	4-2		9	9	Webb	Redman	Valverde	63-77	4th	7.0
9-8	At Pit.	L	7-8	(12)	13	11	White	Groom		63-78	4th	8.0
9-9	At Col.	W	7-1		15	7	Estes	Kim		64-78	3rd	8.0
9-10	At Col.	W	8-5		12	11	Vargas	Day	Valverde	65-78	2nd	7.0
9-11	At Col.	L	2-7		8	10	Cook	Ortiz		65-79	3rd	7.0
9-13	Mil.	L	1-3		6	8	Capuano	Vazquez	Turnbow	65-80	4th	6.5
9-14	Mil.	W	2-1	(12)	8	8	Medders	Lehr		66-80	4th	6.5
9-15	Mil.	L	2-14		8	19	Ohka	Estes		66-81	4th	7.0
9-16	Col.	L	5-6		11	7	Williams	Medders	Fuentes	66-82	4th	7.0
9-17	Col.	W	6-5		11	9	Villarreal	Williams	Valverde	67-82	4th	7.0
9-18	Col.	L	1-7		6	11	Francis	Ortiz		67-83	4th	8.0
9-20	L.A.	W	4-1		9	5	Vazquez	Lowe	Valverde	68-83	3rd	7.5
9-21	L.A.	W	3-2		6	9	Webb	Osoria	Valverde	69-83	3rd	7.5
9-22	L.A.	W	7-4	(12)	13	12	Bulger	Sanchez		70-83	3rd	6.5
9-23	S.D.	L	3-5		7	11	Astacio	Vargas	Hoffman	70-84	3rd	7.5
9-24	S.D.	W	8-5		12	10	Worrell	Otsuka	Valverde	71-84	3rd	6.5
9-25	S.D.	W	4-3	(10)	13	2	Valverde	Otsuka		72-84	3rd	5.5
9-27	At L.A.	W	2-0		6	2	Webb	Weaver	Valverde	73-84	3rd	5.0
9-28	At L.A.	W	4-3		7	4	Medders	Brazoban	Valverde	74-84	T2nd	5.0
9-29	At L.A.	W	3-2		6	4	Nippert	Kuo	Lyon	75-84	2nd	5.0
9-30	At S.F.	W	7-3		12	13	Villarreal	Hawkins	Valverde	76-84	2nd	5.0
10-1	At S.F.	W	2-1	(11)	8	7	Medders	Benitez	Valverde	77-84	2nd	4.0
10-2	At S.F.	L	1-3		6	9	Tomko	Webb		77-85	2nd	5.0

Monthly records: April (14-10), May (16-12), June (9-19), July (13-14), August (9-19), September (15-10), October (1-1).
*Innings, if other than nine. ! First game of a doubleheader. & Second game of a doubleheader.

RECORDS

2005 regular-season record: 77-85
Position: 2nd in N.L. West
Home: 36-45   **Road:** 41-40
N.L. East: 11-21   **N.L. Central:** 17-22
N.L. West: 41-32   **A.L.** 8-10
Vs. LH starters: 18-23
Vs. RH starters: 59-62
Grass: 77-85   **Artificial:** 0-0
Day: 24-20   **Night:** 53-65
1-Run: 28-18   **X-inn.:** 8-7
Doubleheaders: 0-1-0
Team record past five years: 402-408
(.496, ranks 9th in league in that span)

TEAM LEADERS

Batting average: Chad Tracy (.308).
At-bats: Shawn Green (581).
Runs: Luis Gonzalez (90).
Hits: Shawn Green (166).
Total Bases: Troy Glaus (281).
Doubles: Luis Gonzalez, Shawn Green (37).
Triples: Royce Clayton, Craig Counsell, Shawn Green, Chad Tracy (4).
Home runs: Troy Glaus (37).
Runs batted in: Troy Glaus (97).
Stolen bases: Craig Counsell (26).
Slugging percentage: Tony Clark (.636).
On-base percentage: Tony Clark (.366).
Wins: Brandon Webb (14).
Earned-run average: Brandon Webb (3.54).
Complete games: Javier Vazquez (3).

Shutouts: Javier Vazquez (1).
Saves: Jose Valverde (15).
Innings pitched: Brandon Webb (229.0).
Strikeouts: Javier Vazquez (192).

GAMES BY POSITION

Catcher: Chris Snyder 113, Kelly Stinnett 56, Koyie Hill 32.
First base: Tony Clark 83, Chad Tracy 80, Conor Jackson 20.
Second base: Craig Counsell 143, Alex Cintron 23, Matt Kata 7, Andy Green 5.
Third base: Troy Glaus 145, Alex Cintron 32.
Shortstop: Royce Clayton 141, Alex Cintron 39, Andy Green 2, Craig Counsell 1.
Outfield: Shawn Green 155, Luis Gonzalez 152, Luis Terrero 77, Quinton McCracken 59, Jose Cruz Jr. 58, Chad Tracy 51, Scott Hairston 4, Andy Green 2, Conor Jackson 1.
Designated hitter: Tony Clark 7, Scott Hairston 2, Troy Glaus 1, Matt Kata 1, Chad Tracy 1.

TOP DRAFT CHOICES

1a. **Justin Upton,** SS, Great Bridge H.S., Chesapeake, Va.
1b. **Matt Torra,** RHP, Massachusetts.
2. **Matt Green,** RHP, Louisiana-Monroe.
3a. **Jason Neighborgall,** RHP, Georgia Tech.
3b. **Micah Owings,** RHP, Tulane.
4. **Mark Romanczuk,** LHP, Stanford.
5. **Chris Rahl,** OF, William & Mary.
6. **Greg Smith,** LHP, LSU.
7. **Anthony Cupps,** RHP, Mississippi.
8. **Ryan Schreppel,** LHP, Cal State Fullerton.
9. **Josh Ford,** C, Baylor.
10. **Cody Evans,** RHP, Long Beach State.

ATLANTA BRAVES
NATIONAL LEAGUE EAST DIVISION

2006 SEASON

A. Jones

Braves Schedule
Home games shaded.
All-Star Game July 11 at Pittsburgh. Schedule subject to change.

APRIL

SUN	MON	TUE	WED	THU	FRI	SAT
2	3 LAD	4 LAD	5 LAD	6 SF	7 SF	8 SF
9 SF	10 PHI	11	12 PHI	13 PHI	14 SD	15 SD
16 SD	17 NYM	18 NYM	19 NYM	20	21 WAS	22 WAS
23 WAS	24 MIL	25 MIL	26 MIL	27	28 NYM	29 NYM
30 NYM						

MAY

SUN	MON	TUE	WED	THU	FRI	SAT
	1 COL	2 COL	3 PHI	4 PHI	5 NYM	6 NYM
7 NYM	8	9 FLA	10 FLA	11 FLA	12 WAS	13 WAS
14 WAS	15 FLA	16 FLA	17 FLA	18 FLA	19 ARI	20 ARI
21 ARI	22 SD	23 SD	24 SD	25	26 CHC	27 CHC
28 CHC	29 LAD	30 LAD	31 LAD			

JUNE

SUN	MON	TUE	WED	THU	FRI	SAT
				1 ARI	2 ARI	3 ARI
4 ARI	5 WAS	6 WAS	7 WAS	8 HOU	9 HOU	10 HOU
11 HOU	12 FLA	13 FLA	14 FLA	15 FLA	16 BOS	17 BOS
18 BOS	19	20 TOR	21 TOR	22 TOR	23 TB	24 TB
25 TB	26 NYY	27 NYY	28 NYY	29	30 BAL	

JULY

SUN	MON	TUE	WED	THU	FRI	SAT
						1 BAL
2 BAL	3 STL	4 STL	5 STL	6 CIN	7 CIN	8 CIN
9 CIN	10	11 ALL-STAR	12	13	14 SD	15 SD
16 SD	17 STL	18 STL	19 STL	20	21 PHI	22 PHI
23 PHI	24 PHI	25 FLA	26 FLA	27 FLA	28 NYM	29 NYM
30 NYM	31					

AUGUST

SUN	MON	TUE	WED	THU	FRI	SAT
		1 PIT	2 PIT	3 PIT	4 CIN	5 CIN
6 CIN	7 PHI	8 PHI	9 PHI	10	11 MIL	12 MIL
13 MIL	14 WAS	15 WAS	16 WAS	17 WAS	18 FLA	19 FLA
20 FLA	21 PIT	22 PIT	23 PIT	24	25 WAS	26 WAS
27 WAS	28	29 SF	30 SF	31 SF		

SEPTEMBER

SUN	MON	TUE	WED	THU	FRI	SAT
					1 PHI	2 PHI
3 PHI	4 NYM	5 NYM	6 NYM	7	8 CHC	9 CHC
10 CHC	11 CHC	12 PHI	13 PHI	14 PHI	15 FLA	16 FLA
17 FLA	18	19 WAS	20 WAS	21 COL	22 COL	23 COL
24 COL	25	26 NYM	27 NYM	28 NYM	29 HOU	30 HOU

OCTOBER

SUN	MON	TUE	WED	THU	FRI	SAT
1 HOU	2	3	4	5	6	7

Home games are shaded. All-Star Game is July 11 at Pittsburgh. Schedule is subject to change.

CLUB DIRECTORY

Chairman and president
Terence McGuirk
Chairman emeritus
Bill Bartholomay
Senior vice president
Hank Aaron
Executive v.p. and general manager
John Schuerholz
Vice president/assistant general manager
Frank Wren
Assistant g.m./baseball operations
Dayton Moore
Executive v.p./business operations

Mike Plant
Sr. vice president, sales and marketing
Derek Schiller
Sr. v.p., public relations/communications
Greg Hughes
Vice president/team counsel
John Cooper
Vice president/controller
Chip Moore
Director of scouting
Roy Clark
Director of baseball operations
Tyrone Brooks

MINOR LEAGUE AFFILIATES

Class	Team	League	Manager
AAA	Richmond	International	Brian Snitker
AA	Mississippi	Southern	Jeff Blauser
Advanced A	Myrtle Beach	Carolina	Rocket Wheeler
A	Rome	South Atlantic	Randy Ingle
Advanced Rookie	Danville	Appalachian	Paul Runge
Rookie	Braves	Gulf Coast	Luis Ortiz

BROADCAST INFORMATION

Radio: WGST-AM (640).
TV: TBS-TV (Channel 17).
Cable TV: Fox Sports Net South, Turner South.

SPRING TRAINING

Ballpark (city): Cracker Jack Stadium - Walt Disney's Wide World of Sports (Kissimmee, Fla.).
Ticket information: 407-839-3900, 407-939-4263.

For more on the Braves, go to www.sportingnews.com/baseball/teams/braves/

2006 SEASON *Atlanta Braves*

Manager—Bobby Cox (6).
Coaches—Pat Corrales (39), Bobby Dews (53), Frank Fultz (59), Fredi Gonzalez (45), Glenn Hubbard (17), Roger McDowell, Terry Pendleton (9).

No.	PITCHERS	B/T	Ht./Wt.	Age*
	Jose Ascanio	R/R	6-0/150	20
	Brad Baker	R/R	6-2/180	25
48	Blaine Boyer	R/R	6-3/215	24
	Lance Cormier	R/R	5-11/200	25
26	Kyle Davies	R/R	6-2/205	22
28	Joey Devine	R/R	6-0/210	22
46	John Foster	L/L	6-0/200	27
32	Mike Hampton	R/L	5-10/195	33
15	Tim Hudson	R/R	6-1/170	30
36	Chuck James	L/L	6-0/170	24
50	Anthony Lerew	L/R	6-3/220	23
49	Macay McBride	L/L	5-11/210	23
30	Horacio Ramirez	L/L	6-1/210	26
37	Chris Reitsma	R/R	6-5/235	28
29	John Smoltz	R/R	6-3/220	38
34	Jorge Sosa	B/R	6-2/175	28
50	John Thomson	R/R	6-3/220	32
	Oscar Villarreal	L/R	6-0/215	24

No.	CATCHERS	B/T	Ht./Wt.	Age*
16	Brian McCann	L/R	6-3/210	22
8	Brayan Pena	B/R	5-11/220	24
	Todd Pratt	R/R	6-3/236	39

No.	INFIELDERS	B/T	Ht./Wt.	Age*
24	Wilson Betemit	B/R	6-3/200	25
22	Marcus Giles	R/R	5-8/175	27
75	Luis Hernandez	B/R	5-10/165	21
10	Chipper Jones	B/R	6-4/210	33
	James Jurries	R/R	6-0/195	26
19	Adam LaRoche	L/L	6-3/185	26
4	Pete Orr	L/R	6-1/185	26
2	Tony Pena	R/R	6-1/180	25
	Martin Prado	R/R	6-1/170	22
3	Edgar Renteria	R/R	6-1/200	30
60	Scott Thorman	L/R	6-3/225	24

No.	OUTFIELDERS	B/T	Ht./Wt.	Age*
	Josh Burrus	R/R	5-11/180	22
	Matt Diaz	R/R	6-1/206	28
7	Jeff Francoeur	R/R	6-4/220	22
27	Kelly Johnson	L/R	6-1/205	24
25	Andruw Jones	R/R	6-1/210	28
18	Ryan Langerhans	L/L	6-3/205	26

*Age as of April 1, 2006.

BALLPARK INFORMATION

Ballpark (capacity, surface)
Turner Field (49,583, grass)
Address
P.O. Box 4064
Atlanta, GA 30302
Official website
www.atlantabraves.com
Business phone
404-522-7630
Ticket information
404-249-6400 or 800-326-4000
Field dimensions (from home plate)
To left field at foul line, 335 feet
To center field, 401 feet
To right field at foul line, 330 feet
First game played
April 4, 1997 (Braves 5, Cubs 4)

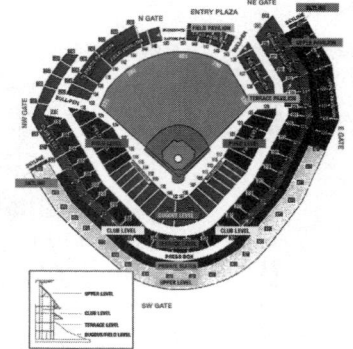

Date	Opp.	Res.	Score	(inn.*)	Hits	Opp. hits	Winning pitcher	Losing pitcher	Save	Record	Pos.	GB
4-5	At Fla.	L	0-9		5	13	Beckett	Smoltz		0-1	T3rd	1.0
4-6	At Fla.	W	2-1	(13)	10	10	Bernero	Bump	Kolb	1-1	T1st	...
4-7	At Fla.	W	4-2		8	9	Hudson	Burnett	Kolb	2-1	T1st	...
4-8	N.Y.	W	3-1		7	9	Thomson	Zambrano	Kolb	3-1	1st	+1.0
4-9	N.Y.	W	6-3		12	7	Bernero	Heilman		4-1	1st	+1.0
4-10	N.Y.	L	1-6		2	13	Martinez	Smoltz		4-2	1st	+1.0
4-11	Was.	W	11-2		15	8	Hampton	Day		5-2	1st	+1.0
4-12	Was.	L	3-4		9	8	Ayala	Kolb	Cordero	5-3	1st	+1.0
4-13	Was.	L	4-11		9	12	Ohka	Thomson		5-4	T1st	...
4-15	At Phi.	W	11-4		9	10	Ramirez	Floyd		6-4	T1st	...
4-16	At Phi.	L	1-2		9	6	Lieber	Smoltz	Wagner	6-5	T2nd	1.0
4-17	At Phi.	L	1-2	(10)	7	6	Madson	Kolb		6-6	T2nd	2.0
4-18	At Hou.	W	1-0	(12)	9	6	Sosa	Wheeler	Kolb	7-6	T2nd	1.0
4-19	At Hou.	L	3-5		9	10	Backe	Thomson	Lidge	7-7	T3rd	1.0
4-20	At Was.	L	0-2		5	6	Day	Ramirez	Cordero	7-8	T3rd	2.0
4-21	At Was.	W	2-1		4	5	Reitsma	Cordero	Kolb	8-8	T3rd	1.0
4-22	Phi.	W	6-2		7	7	Hampton	Myers	Kolb	9-8	T2nd	1.0
4-23	Phi.	W	11-1		13	6	Hudson	Wolf		10-8	T2nd	1.0
4-24	Phi.	W	4-0		6	6	Thomson	Padilla		11-8	T1st	...
4-25	At N.Y.	L	4-5		6	9	Heilman	Ramirez	Looper	11-9	T2nd	0.5
4-26	At N.Y.	W	4-3		7	12	Smoltz	Martinez	Foster	12-9	2nd	0.5
4-27	At N.Y.	W	8-4		13	9	Hampton	Glavine		13-9	2nd	...
4-29	StL.	L	5-6		10	11	Mulder	Hudson	Reyes	13-10	2nd	1.0
4-30	StL.	W	3-2		8	11	Kolb	Journell		14-10	2nd	1.0
5-1	StL.	W	2-1		4	10	Smoltz	Suppan	Kolb	15-10	2nd	...
5-3	Fla.	L	6-11		6	13	Leiter	Hampton		15-11	2nd	1.0
5-4	Fla.	W	5-2		13	6	Hudson	Burnett	Kolb	16-11	2nd	...
5-5	Hou.	W	9-3		11	3	Thomson	Backe		17-11	1st	+0.5
5-6	Hou.	W	9-4		11	7	Smoltz	Oswalt		18-11	1st	+0.5
5-7	Hou.	W	4-1		10	6	Ramirez	Pettitte	Kolb	19-11	1st	+0.5
5-8	Hou.	W	16-0		17	2	Hampton	Astacio		20-11	1st	+1.5
5-9	At Col.	L	6-7		12	12	Wright	Hudson	Tsao	20-12	1st	+1.5
5-10	At Col.	W	9-5		14	10	Sosa	Jennings		21-12	1st	+1.5
5-11	At Col.	L	5-6		8	12	Tsao	Kolb		21-13	1st	+0.5
5-13	At L.A.	L	4-7		7	14	Carrara	Reitsma	Brazoban	21-14	1st	+0.5
5-14	At L.A.	W	5-1		9	5	Bernero	Perez		22-14	1st	+1.5
5-15	At L.A.	W	5-2		6	9	Hudson	Alvarez	Kolb	23-14	1st	+2.5
5-16	At S.D.	L	3-5		7	10	Linebrink	Reitsma	Hoffman	23-15	1st	+1.5
5-17	At S.D.	L	2-3		6	7	Reyes	Kolb		23-16	1st	+1.5
5-18	At S.D.	L	4-8		10	11	Eaton	Ramirez	Hoffman	23-17	1st	+0.5
5-20	At Bos.	L	3-4		6	8	Miller	Hudson	Foulke	23-18	2nd	0.5
5-21	At Bos.	W	7-5		9	11	Davies	Wakefield		24-18	2nd	0.5
5-22	At Bos.	L	2-5		4	14	Clement	Colon		24-19	2nd	1.5
5-23	N.Y.	W	8-6		8	11	Ramirez	Ishii	Kolb	25-19	2nd	1.5
5-24	N.Y.	W	4-0		8	6	Hudson	Glavine		26-19	2nd	1.5
5-25	N.Y.	W	3-0		6	8	Davies	Zambrano	Reitsma	27-19	2nd	0.5
5-27	Phi.	L	1-5		8	12	Lidle	Smoltz		27-20	2nd	...
5-28	Phi.	L	5-12		11	16	Lieber	Ramirez		27-21	2nd	...
5-29	Phi.	W	7-2		6	6	Hudson	Myers		28-21	2nd	...
5-30	At Was.	L	2-3		4	9	Ohka	Davies	Cordero	28-22	2nd	...
5-31	At Was.	L	4-5		6	13	Ayala	Colon	Cordero	28-23	2nd	...
6-1	At Was.	W	5-4		9	8	Smoltz	Carrasco	Reitsma	29-23	1st	+1.0
6-2	At Was.	L	6-8		9	12	Carrasco	Kolb	Cordero	29-24	2nd	...
6-3	At Pit.	L	1-3		9	6	Wells	Hudson	Mesa	29-25	2nd	...
6-4	At Pit.	W	1-0		5	6	Foster	Gonzalez	Reitsma	30-25	1st	+0.5
6-5	At Pit.	L	2-5		5	11	Perez	Bernero	Mesa	30-26	2nd	0.5
6-6	L.A.	L	2-4		8	13	Donnelly	Smoltz	Rodriguez	30-27	T2nd	1.0
6-7	L.A.	W	3-2		9	5	Ramirez	Byrd	Reitsma	31-27	T2nd	1.0
6-8	L.A.	L	4-8		4	12	Donnelly	Foster		31-28	2nd	2.0
6-10	Oak.	L	4-6		9	10	Haren	Colon	Street	31-29	4th	3.5
6-11	Oak.	W	5-3		9	5	Smoltz	Duchscherer		32-29	4th	3.5
6-12	Oak.	L	5-11		7	13	Zito	Boyer		32-30	4th	4.5
6-13	At Tex.	L	3-7		6	11	Young	Hudson		32-31	T4th	4.5
6-14	At Tex.	W	7-2		11	9	Sosa	Astacio		33-31	4th	4.5
6-15	At Tex.	L	5-9		13	14	Park	Davies	Cordero	33-32	4th	5.5
6-16	At Cin.	W	5-2		13	5	Smoltz	Claussen	Reitsma	34-32	4th	5.0
6-17	At Cin.	W	10-5		16	11	Ramirez	Ortiz		35-32	3rd	4.0

Date	Opp.	Res.	Score	(inn.*)	Hits	Opp. hits	Winning pitcher	Losing pitcher	Save	Record	Pos.	GB
6-18	At Cin.	W	6-1		11	10	Bernero	Milton		36-32	3rd	3.0
6-19	At Cin.	L	8-11		13	17	Weathers	Bernero		36-33	3rd	4.0
6-21	Fla.	W	5-0		9	5	Smoltz	Burnett		37-33	3rd	3.5
6-22	Fla.	W	8-0		11	4	Ramirez	Moehler		38-33	3rd	3.5
6-23	Fla.	L	0-8		5	13	Willis	Sosa		38-34	3rd	4.0
6-24	Bal.	W	7-5		11	10	Davies	Penn	Reitsma	39-34	2nd	4.0
6-25	Bal.	W	5-4		11	12	Vasquez	Williams		40-34	2nd	4.0
6-26	Bal.	W	8-1		13	5	Smoltz	Lopez		41-34	2nd	3.0
6-27	At Fla.	W	7-2	(8)	12	6	Ramirez	Moehler		42-34	2nd	2.5
6-28	At Fla.	W	9-1		16	6	Sosa	Willis		43-34	2nd	2.5
6-29	At Fla.	L	5-6	(13)	12	17	Riedling	Bernero		43-35	2nd	3.5
6-30	At Fla.	L	2-6		4	10	Beckett	Colon		43-36	2nd	4.5
7-1	At Phi.	W	9-1		13	6	Smoltz	Padilla		44-36	2nd	4.5
7-2	At Phi.	L	3-6		4	11	Myers	Ramirez	Wagner	44-37	2nd	5.5
7-3	At Phi.	W	4-3		6	3	Brower	Wagner	Reitsma	45-37	2nd	5.5
7-4	Chi.	W	4-0		8	6	Davies	Wood		46-37	2nd	4.5
7-5	Chi.	W	5-1		9	8	Colon	Maddux		47-37	2nd	4.5
7-7#	Chi.	W	6-0		11	3	Ramirez	Prior		48-37		
7-7$	Chi.	W	9-4		14	6	Foster	Novoa		49-37	2nd	2.5
7-8	Mil.	W	2-1		8	10	Kolb	Santana		50-37	2nd	2.5
7-9	Mil.	L	6-9		11	12	Sheets	Davies		50-38	2nd	2.5
7-10	Mil.	L	4-8		10	11	Capuano	Colon		50-39	2nd	2.5
7-14	At N.Y.	L	3-6		6	8	Hernandez	Brower	Looper	50-40	2nd	2.5
7-15	At N.Y.	W	2-1		9	6	Smoltz	Hernandez	Reitsma	51-40	2nd	1.5
7-16	At N.Y.	W	3-0		10	6	Hudson	Zambrano	Reitsma	52-40	2nd	1.5
7-17	At N.Y.	L	1-8		6	13	Martinez	Hampton		52-41	2nd	1.5
7-18	At S.F.	W	6-1		7	7	Sosa	Correia		53-41	2nd	0.5
7-19	At S.F.	L	4-5		8	12	Walker	Kolb		53-42	2nd	1.5
7-20	At S.F.	W	4-1		6	7	Smoltz	Lowry	Reitsma	54-42	2nd	0.5
7-22	At Ari.	L	5-6	(10)	12	12	Cormier	Brower		54-43	T1st	...
7-23	At Ari.	W	3-2		6	5	Reitsma	Valverde		55-43	T1st	...
7-24	At Ari.	L	2-3		4	9	Vazquez	Ramirez	Bruney	55-44	T1st	...
7-26	Was.	W	3-2	(10)	8	8	Reitsma	Stanton		56-44	1st	+1.0
7-27	Was.	W	4-3		9	7	Kolb	Majewski	Reitsma	57-44	1st	+2.0
7-28	Was.	W	5-4		10	10	Sosa	Drese	Reitsma	58-44	1st	+3.0
7-29	Pit.	W	2-1		8	7	Ramirez	Williams	McBride	59-44	1st	+4.0
7-30	Pit.	W	9-6		13	5	Davies	Redman	Reitsma	60-44	1st	+5.0
7-31	Pit.	W	5-4		16	10	Smoltz	Grabow	Reitsma	61-44	1st	+5.0
8-1	Pit.	L	1-4		8	8	Duke	Hudson	Mesa	61-45	1st	+4.5
8-2	At Cin.	W	12-2		14	10	Sosa	Ortiz		62-45	1st	+5.5
8-3	At Cin.	L	5-8		11	9	Claussen	Ramirez	Mercker	62-46	1st	+4.5
8-4	At Cin.	W	7-4		13	6	Davies	Harang	Reitsma	63-46	1st	+4.5
8-5	At StL.	L	3-11		10	11	Mulder	Smoltz		63-47	1st	+4.5
8-6	At StL.	W	8-1		11	8	Hudson	Marquis		64-47	1st	+5.5
8-7	At StL.	L	3-5		6	9	King	Reitsma		64-48	1st	+5.5
8-9	S.F.	W	7-1		16	8	Ramirez	Hennessey		65-48	1st	+5.5
8-10	S.F.	W	5-4	(12)	8	11	Boyer	Cooper	Walker	66-48	1st	+6.0
8-11	S.F.	L	3-5		10	10	Schmidt	Hudson	Walker	66-49	1st	+6.0
8-12	Ari.	L	0-8		4	11	Vargas	Sosa		66-50	1st	+5.0
8-13	Ari.	W	9-5		14	8	Foster	Cormier		67-50	1st	+5.0
8-14	Ari.	W	13-8		13	15	Hampton	Vazquez		68-50	1st	+5.0
8-16	L.A.	L	4-6		6	12	Carrara	Reitsma	Sanchez	68-51	1st	+4.5
8-17	L.A.	W	10-2		16	8	Hudson	Perez		69-51	1st	+5.0
8-18	L.A.	L	4-7		10	11	Weaver	Thomson	Sanchez	69-52	1st	+4.5
8-19	S.D.	L	7-12		13	20	Park	Hampton		69-53	1st	+4.5
8-20	S.D.	L	2-7	(13)	12	11	Seanez	Devine		69-54	1st	+3.5
8-21	S.D.	W	6-2		9	10	Sosa	Otsuka		70-54	1st	+4.5
8-22	At Chi.	W	4-2		5	7	Hudson	Wood		71-54	1st	+4.5
8-23	At Chi.	L	1-10		3	15	Williams	Thomson	*	71-55	1st	+3.5
8-24	At Chi.	W	3-1		5	5	Sosa	Prior	Farnsworth	72-55	1st	+3.5
8-26	At Mil.	L	1-3		8	6	Sheets	Ramirez	Turnbow	72-56	1st	+2.5
8-27	At Mil.	W	8-4		17	4	Smoltz	Santos		73-56	1st	+3.5
8-28	At Mil.	W	5-2		4	7	Hudson	Capuano		74-56	1st	+4.5
8-30	Was.	L	2-3		9	11	Bergmann	Sosa	Cordero	74-57	1st	+4.5
8-31!	Was.	W	5-3		8	9	Ramirez	Loaiza	Farnsworth	75-57		
8-31&	Was.	L	3-4		11	11	Stanton	Reitsma	Cordero	75-58	1st	+4.0
9-1	Was.	W	8-7	(10)	8	12	Davies	Ayala		76-58	1st	+4.0
9-2	Cin.	W	7-4		10	14	Hudson	Milton	Farnsworth	77-58	1st	+4.0
9-3	Cin.	W	9-3		10	5	Sosa	Hudson		78-58	1st	+5.0
9-4	Cin.	L	3-8	(12)	5	13	Belisle	Kolb		78-59	1st	+5.0

Date	Opp.	Res.	Score	(inn.*)	Hits	Opp. hits	Winning pitcher	Losing pitcher	Save	Record	Pos.	GB
9-5	N.Y.	W	4-2		7	9	Boyer	Trachsel	Farnsworth	79-59	1st	+6.0
9-6	N.Y.	W	3-1		7	8	Smoltz	Martinez	Farnsworth	80-59	1st	+6.5
9-7	N.Y.	W	4-3	(10)	9	12	Foster	Looper		81-59	1st	+6.5
9-9	At Was.	L	6-8		10	11	Majewski	Foster	Cordero	81-60	1st	+6.0
9-10	At Was.	W	4-0		8	6	Sosa	Hernandez		82-60	1st	+6.0
9-11	At Was.	W	9-7		9	6	McBride	Cordero	Farnsworth	83-60	1st	+7.0
9-12	At Phi.	L	1-4		5	8	Brito	Hudson	Wagner	83-61	1st	+6.0
9-13	At Phi.	L	4-5		8	13	Fultz	Boyer	Wagner	83-62	1st	+5.0
9-14	At Phi.	L	4-12		11	15	Lidle	Ramirez		83-63	1st	+5.0
9-15	At Phi.	W	6-4		8	12	Sosa	Myers	Farnsworth	84-63	1st	+6.0
9-16	At N.Y.	L	0-4		6	8	Martinez	Smoltz		84-64	1st	+5.0
9-17	At N.Y.	W	7-4		14	7	Hudson	Trachsel	Farnsworth	85-64	1st	+5.0
9-18	At N.Y.	L	1-4		6	7	Glavine	Thomson		85-65	1st	+5.0
9-20	Phi.	W	4-1		9	3	Sosa	Lidle		86-65	1st	+6.0
9-21	Phi.	L	6-10	(10)	7	14	Geary	Davies		86-66	1st	+5.0
9-22	Phi.	L	0-4		6	6	Lieber	Hudson		86-67	1st	+4.0
9-23	Fla.	W	4-3		10	10	Boyer	Jones	Farnsworth	87-67	1st	+4.0
9-24	Fla.	W	6-1		10	5	Thomson	Moehler		88-67	1st	+5.0
9-25	Fla.	W	5-3		7	8	Boyer	Burnett	Farnsworth	89-67	1st	+5.0
9-26	Col.	L	5-6		11	15	Speier	Reitsma	Fuentes	89-68	1st	+5.0
9-27	Col.	W	12-3		13	6	Hudson	Cook		90-68	1st	+6.0
9-28	Col.	L	5-10		11	15	Francis	Davies		90-69	1st	+5.0
9-30	At Fla.	L	2-5		5	10	Villone	Thomson	Jones	90-70	1st	+4.0
10-1	At Fla.	L	4-6		7	10	Resop	Kolb	Jones	90-71	1st	+3.0
10-2	At Fla.	L	6-7	(10)	14	14	Villone	Davies		90-72	1st	+2.0

Monthly records: April (14-10), May (14-13), June (15-13), July (18-8), August (14-14), September (15-12), October (0-2).
*Innings, if other than nine. ! First game of a doubleheader. & Second game of a doubleheader. # Day separate admission. $ Night separate admission.

RECORDS

2005 regular-season record: 90-72
Position: 1st in N.L. East
Home: 53-28 **Road:** 37-44
N.L. East: 42-33 **N.L. Central:** 28-14
N.L. West: 13-17 **A.L.** 7-8
Vs. LH starters: 22-16
Vs. RH starters: 68-56
Grass: 90-72 **Artificial:** 0-0
Day: 25-23 **Night:** 65-49
1-Run: 23-20 **X-inn.:** 6-7
Doubleheaders: 0-0-1
Team record past five years: 476-332 (.589, ranks 2nd in league in that span)

TEAM LEADERS

Batting average: Chipper Jones (.296).
At-bats: Rafael Furcal (616).
Runs: Marcus Giles (104).
Hits: Rafael Furcal (175).
Total Bases: Andruw Jones (337).
Doubles: Marcus Giles (45).
Triples: Rafael Furcal (11).
Home runs: Andruw Jones (51).
Runs batted in: Andruw Jones (128).
Stolen bases: Rafael Furcal (46).
Slugging percentage: Andruw Jones(.575).
On-base percentage: Chipper Jones (.412).
Wins: Tim Hudson, John Smoltz (14).
Earned-run average: Jorge Sosa (2.55).
Complete games: John Smoltz (3).
Shutouts: Mike Hampton, Horacio Ramirez, John Smoltz (1).

Saves: Chris Reitsma (15).
Innings pitched: John Smoltz (229.2).
Strikeouts: John Smoltz (169).

GAMES BY POSITION

Catcher: Johnny Estrada 104, Brian McCann 57, Brayan Pena 15, Eddie Perez 13.
First base: Adam LaRoche 125, Julio Franco 62, Todd Hollandsworth 1.
Second base: Marcus Giles 149, Pete Orr 25, Wilson Betemit 1.
Third base: Chipper Jones 101, Wilson Betemit 63, Andy Marte 17, Pete Orr 12, Marcus Giles 1.
Shortstop: Rafael Furcal 152, Wilson Betemit 25, Pete Orr 1.
Outfield: Andruw Jones 159, Ryan Langerhans 114, Kelly Johnson 79, Jeff Francoeur 67, Brian Jordan 62, Raul Mondesi 40, Todd Hollandsworth 9, Pete Orr 3.
Designated hitter: Julio Franco 4, Kelly Johnson 1, Pete Orr 1.

TOP DRAFT CHOICES

1a.**Joey Devine,** RHP, North Carolina State.
1b.**Beau Jones,** LHP, Destrehan (La.) H.S.
2a.**Yuniel Escobar,** SS, Miami.
2b.**Jeff Lyman,** RHP, Monte Vista H.S., Alamo, Calif.
3. **Jordan Schafer,** OF, Winter Haven (Fla.) H.S.
4. **Mike Broadway,** RHP, Pope County H.S., Golconda, Ill.
5. **Will Startup,** LHP, Georgia.
6. **Tyler Bullock,** RHP, Baylor
7. **Brandon Monk,** 2B, a Grange (Ga). H.S.
8 **Kyle Cofield,** RHP, Southside H.S., Rainbow City, Ala.
9. **Stephen Garcia,** C, Temecula Valley H.S., Temecula, Calif.
10. **Colin Carter,** LHP, Grayson County College (Texas).

CHICAGO CUBS
NATIONAL LEAGUE CENTRAL DIVISION

2006 SEASON

Cubs Schedule
Home games shaded.
All-Star Game July 11 at Pittsburgh. Schedule subject to change.

APRIL

SUN	MON	TUE	WED	THU	FRI	SAT
2	3 CIN	4	5 CIN	6	7 STL	8 STL
9 STL	10	11 CIN	12 CIN	13 CIN	14 PIT	15 PIT
16 PIT	17 LAD	18 LAD	19 LAD	20	21 STL	22 STL
23 STL	24 FLA	25 FLA	26 FLA	27	28 MIL	29 MIL
30 MIL						

MAY

SUN	MON	TUE	WED	THU	FRI	SAT
	1 PIT	2 PIT	3 ARI	4 ARI	5 SD	6 SD
7 SD	8 SD	9 SF	10 SF	11 SF	12 SD	13 SD
14 SD	15	16 WAS	17 WAS	18 WAS	19 CHW	20 CHW
21 CHW	22 FLA	23 FLA	24 FLA	25	26 ATL	27 ATL
28 ATL	29 CIN	30 CIN	31 CIN			

JUNE

SUN	MON	TUE	WED	THU	FRI	SAT
				1	2 STL	3 STL
4 STL	5 HOU	6 HOU	7 HOU	8 CIN	9 CIN	10 CIN
11 CIN	12	13 HOU	14 HOU	15 HOU	16 DET	17 DET
18 DET	19 CLE	20 CLE	21 CLE	22	23 MIN	24 MIN
25 MIN	26 MIL	27 MIL	28 MIL	29 CHW	30 CHW	

JULY

SUN	MON	TUE	WED	THU	FRI	SAT
						1 CHW
2 CHW	3 HOU	4 HOU	5 HOU	6 MIL	7 MIL	8 MIL
9 MIL	10	11 ALL-STAR	12	13	14 NYM	15 NYM
16 NYM	17	18 HOU	19 HOU	20 HOU	21 WAS	22 WAS
23 WAS	24 NYM	25 NYM	26 NYM	27 STL	28 STL	29 STL
30 STL	31 ARI					

AUGUST

SUN	MON	TUE	WED	THU	FRI	SAT
		1 ARI	2 ARI	3 ARI	4 PIT	5 PIT
6 PIT	7	8 MIL	9 MIL	10 MIL	11 COL	12 COL
13 COL	14 HOU	15 HOU	16 HOU	17	18 STL	19 STL
20 STL	21 PHI	22 PHI	23 PHI	24 PHI	25 STL	26 STL
27 STL	28 PIT	29 PIT	30 PIT	31		

SEPTEMBER

SUN	MON	TUE	WED	THU	FRI	SAT
					1 SF	2 SF
3 SF	4 PIT	5 PIT	6 PIT	7 PIT	8 ATL	9 ATL
10 ATL	11 LAD	12 LAD	13 LAD	14 LAD	15 CIN	16 CIN
17 CIN	18 PHI	19 PHI	20 PHI	21	22 CIN	23 CIN
24 CIN	25 CIN	26 MIL	27 MIL	28	29 COL	30 COL

OCTOBER

SUN	MON	TUE	WED	THU	FRI	SAT
1 COL	2	3	4	5	6	7

Home games are shaded. All-Star Game is July 11 at Pittsburgh. Schedule is subject to change.

Lee

CLUB DIRECTORY

President and chief executive officer
Andrew B. MacPhail
Vice president, general manager
Jim Hendry
Director, baseball operations
Scott Nelson
Special assistants to the general manager
Keith Champion, Ken Kravec, Ed Lynch,

Billy Williams
Special assistant, scouting consultant
Randy Bush
Director of scouting
Tim Wilken
Dir. of player dev./Latin American ops.
Oneri Fleita
Director of media relations
Sharon Pannozzo

MINOR LEAGUE AFFILIATES

Class	Team	League	Manager
AAA	Iowa	Pacific Coast	Mike Quade
AA	West Tenn	Southern	Bobby Dickerson
Advanced A	Daytona	Florida State	Pat Listach
A	Peoria	Midwest	Jody Davis
Short-Season A	Boise	Northwest	Steve McFarland
Rookie	Cubs	Arizona	Don Buford

BROADCAST INFORMATION

Radio: WGN-AM (720).
TV: WGN-TV (Channel 9); WCIU-TV. (Channel 26).
Cable TV: Comcast Sports Net Chicago.

SPRING TRAINING

Ballpark (city): HoHoKam Park (Mesa, Ariz.).
Ticket information: 800-638-4253.

For more on the Cubs, go to www.sportingnews.com/baseball/teams/cubs/

SPRING TRAINING ROSTER

Manager—Dusty Baker (12).

Coaches—Gene Clines (2), Sonny Jackson (6), Juan Lopez (59), Gary Matthews (36), Dick Pole (39), Larry Rothschild (41), Chris Speier (35).

No.	PITCHERS	B/T	Ht./Wt.	Age*
	David Aardsma	R/R	6-5/200	24
46	Ryan Dempster	R/R	6-2/215	28
47	Scott Eyre	L/L	6-1/215	33
67	Angel Guzman	R/R	6-3/190	24
53	Rich Hill	L/L	6-5/205	26
	Bob Howry	L/R	6-5/220	32
49	John Koronka	L/L	6-1/180	25
31	Greg Maddux	R/R	6-0/180	39
	Carlos Marmol	R/R	6-2/180	23
	Sean Marshall	L/L	6-6/195	23
44	Roberto Novoa	R/R	6-5/200	26
45	Will Ohman	L/L	6-2/195	28
22	Mark Prior	R/R	6-5/230	25
33	Glendon Rusch	L/L	6-1/225	31
	Jae-kuk Ryu	R/R	6-3/220	22
40	Todd Wellemeyer	R/R	6-3/205	27
32	Jerome Williams	R/R	6-3/246	24
48	Scott Williamson	R/R	6-0/185	30
34	Kerry Wood	R/R	6-5/225	28
43	Michael Wuertz	R/R	6-3/205	27
38	Carlos Zambrano	B/R	6-5/255	24

No.	CATCHERS	B/T	Ht./Wt.	Age*
5	Michael Barrett	R/R	6-3/210	29
24	Henry Blanco	R/R	5-11/220	34
	Jose Reyes	B/R	5-11/180	22
58	Geovany Soto	R/R	6-1/230	23

No.	INFIELDERS	B/T	Ht./Wt.	Age*
11	Ronny Cedeno	R/R	6-0/180	23
	Brian Dopirak	R/R	6-4/235	22
25	Derrek Lee	R/R	6-5/245	30
	John Mabry	L/R	6-4/210	35
	Scott Moore	L/R	6-4/210	22
13	Neifi Perez	B/R	6-0/197	32
16	Aramis Ramirez	R/R	6-1/215	27
55	Ryan Theriot	R/R	5-11/175	26
7	Todd Walker	L/R	6-0/185	32

No.	OUTFIELDERS	B/T	Ht./Wt.	Age*
15	Jerry Hairston	R/R	5-10/183	29
	Jacque Jones	L/L	5-10/205	30
19	Matt Murton	R/R	6-1/215	24
	Felix Pie	L/L	6-2/175	21
9	Juan Pierre	L/L	6-0/180	28

*Age as of April 1, 2006

BALLPARK INFORMATION

Ballpark (capacity, surface)
Wrigley Field (41,118, grass)
Address
1060 W. Addison St.
Chicago, IL 60613-4397
Official website
www.cubs.com
Business phone
773-404-2827
Ticket information
773-404-2827
Field dimensions (from home plate)
To left field at foul line, 355 feet
To center field, 400 feet
To right field at foul line, 353 feet
First game played
April 20, 1916 (Cubs 7, Reds 6)

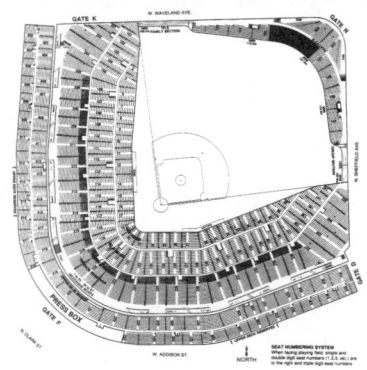

2006 SEASON *Chicago Cubs*

Date	Opp.	Res.	Score	(inn.*)	Hits	Opp. hits	Winning pitcher	Losing pitcher	Save	Record	Pos.	GB
4-4	At Ari.	W	16-6		23	12	Rusch	Vazquez		1-0	T1st	...
4-5	At Ari.	L	4-5		8	7	Ortiz	Maddux	Lyon	1-1	4th	0.5
4-6	At Ari.	L	3-8		9	13	Webb	Dempster		1-2	5th	1.5
4-8	Mil.	L	3-6	(12)	7	12	de la Rosa	Leicester	Adams	1-3	T5th	2.5
4-9	Mil.	W	4-0		8	1	Zambrano	Sheets		2-3	5th	1.5
4-10	Mil.	W	6-5	(12)	11	16	Rusch	Turnbow		3-3	T3rd	1.5
4-11	S.D.	L	0-1		6	4	Eaton	Dempster	Hoffman	3-4	4th	1.5
4-13!	S.D.	L	3-8		8	12	Peavy	Wood		3-5		
4-13&	S.D.	W	8-3		11	7	Prior	Lawrence		4-5	4th	1.5
4-15	At Pit.	L	5-8		7	13	Torres	Remlinger	Mesa	4-6	T5th	1.5
4-16	At Pit.	W	4-3		7	8	Dempster	Wells	Hawkins	5-6	5th	1.0
4-17	At Pit.	W	4-2		7	6	Wuertz	Redman	Hawkins	6-6	3rd	1.0
4-18	At Cin.	L	6-7		12	9	Mercker	Leicester	Graves	6-7	3rd	2.0
4-19	At Cin.	W	7-1		11	4	Prior	Claussen		7-7	3rd	2.0
4-20	At StL.	W	3-1		12	5	Zambrano	Suppan	Hawkins	8-7	3rd	1.0
4-21	At StL.	L	0-4		7	7	Carpenter	Dempster		8-8	4th	2.0
4-23	Pit.	L	3-4		9	6	Grabow	Hawkins	Mesa	8-9	T2nd	3.5
4-24	Pit.	W	5-2		7	6	Wood	Williams	Fox	9-9	T2nd	3.5
4-25	Cin.	W	10-6		12	10	Prior	Wilson		10-9	2nd	3.0
4-26	Cin.	L	9-11		13	15	Weathers	Wuertz	Graves	10-10	T2nd	4.0
4-27	Cin.	W	8-7		14	10	Hawkins	Belisle		11-10	2nd	4.0
4-29	At Hou.	W	3-2		10	7	Maddux	Clemens	Hawkins	12-10	2nd	3.5
4-30	At Hou.	L	5-7		8	10	Backe	Bartosh		12-11	2nd	3.5
5-1	At Hou.	L	3-9		12	11	Oswalt	Prior		12-12	2nd	3.5
5-3	At Mil.	L	1-4		5	9	Capuano	Zambrano	Turnbow	12-13	T2nd	5.0
5-4	At Mil.	L	3-4		8	9	Turnbow	Novoa		12-14	3rd	6.0
5-5	At Mil.	L	5-6		10	11	Turnbow	Hawkins		12-15	3rd	6.0
5-6	Phi.	L	2-3		5	6	Wagner	Hawkins		12-16	3rd	6.0
5-7	Phi.	L	1-4		5	10	Lieber	Rusch	Wagner	12-17	T3rd	6.0
5-8	Phi.	W	2-1		5	5	Zambrano	Myers		13-17	T3rd	6.0
5-9	N.Y.	L	4-7		10	13	DeJean	Hawkins	Looper	13-18	T3rd	7.0
5-10	N.Y.	W	7-0		13	3	Maddux	Benson		14-18	T3rd	6.0
5-11	N.Y.	W	4-3	(10)	5	6	Dempster	Bell		15-18	T3rd	6.0
5-13	At Was.	W	6-3		9	9	Ohman	Ayala	Wellemeyer	16-18	3rd	5.5
5-14	At Was.	L	3-4		10	6	Hernandez	Zambrano	Cordero	16-19	T3rd	6.5
5-15	At Was.	L	4-5		8	7	Carrasco	Bartosh	Cordero	16-20	4th	7.5
5-17	At Pit.	W	4-3		13	7	Ohman	Mesa	Dempster	17-20	3rd	6.5
5-18	At Pit.	W	3-2		6	7	Wuertz	Mesa	Dempster	18-20	3rd	6.5
5-20	Chi.	L	1-5		6	10	Garcia	Maddux		18-21	T3rd	7.0
5-21	Chi.	L	3-5		8	9	Contreras	Wuertz	Hermanson	18-22	4th	8.0
5-22	Chi.	W	4-3		8	6	Prior	Vizcaino		19-22	T3rd	7.0
5-23	Hou.	W	4-1		8	5	Rusch	Rodriguez	Dempster	20-22	3rd	7.0
5-24	Hou.	W	4-2		5	6	Wuertz	Lidge	Dempster	21-22	3rd	7.0
5-25	Hou.	L	1-5		7	9	Backe	Maddux		21-23	3rd	8.0
5-26	Col.	L	2-5		8	7	Jennings	Zambrano		21-24	3rd	8.5
5-27	Col.	W	10-3		11	6	Wellemeyer	Kennedy		22-24	3rd	8.5
5-28	Col.	W	5-1		10	6	Rusch	Kim		23-24	3rd	8.5
5-29	Col.	W	11-6		15	11	Novoa	Carvajal		24-24	2nd	7.5
5-30	At L.A.	W	5-3		10	6	Maddux	Alvarez	Dempster	25-24	2nd	7.5
5-31	At L.A.	W	2-1	(10)	10	1	Wuertz	Brazoban	Dempster	26-24	2nd	6.5
6-1	At L.A.	W	9-5		16	9	Koronka	Lowe		27-24	2nd	6.5
6-2	At S.D.	W	5-0		12	4	Rusch	Stauffer		28-24	2nd	5.5
6-3	At S.D.	L	2-6		8	10	Eaton	Mitre	Otsuka	28-25	2nd	6.5
6-4	At S.D.	W	11-5		17	12	Maddux	May		29-25	2nd	6.5
6-5	At S.D.	W	4-0		11	5	Zambrano	Williams		30-25	2nd	5.5
6-6	Tor.	L	1-4		8	7	Chacin	Koronka	Batista	30-26	2nd	6.5
6-7	Tor.	L	4-6		10	10	Schoeneweis	Wellemeyer	Batista	30-27	2nd	7.5
6-8	Tor.	W	2-0		7	3	Mitre	Halladay	Dempster	31-27	2nd	6.5
6-10	Bos.	W	14-6		20	10	Maddux	Arroyo		32-27	2nd	6.5
6-11	Bos.	W	7-6		12	9	Wellemeyer	Miller	Dempster	33-27	2nd	5.5
6-12	Bos.	L	1-8		5	17	Wakefield	Rusch		33-28	2nd	6.5
6-13	Fla.	L	1-9		8	11	Willis	Koronka		33-29	2nd	6.5
6-14	Fla.	W	14-0		18	5	Mitre	Beckett		34-29	2nd	6.5
6-15	Fla.	L	5-15		12	20	Burnett	Maddux		34-30	2nd	6.5
6-17	At N.Y.	L	6-9		12	15	Stanton	Ohman	Rivera	34-31	2nd	7.5
6-18	At N.Y.	L	1-8		5	13	Wang	Rusch		34-32	2nd	8.5
6-19	At N.Y.	L	3-6		8	9	Mussina	Mitre	Rivera	34-33	2nd	9.5

Date	Opp.	Res.	Score	(inn.*)	Hits	Opp. hits	Winning pitcher	Losing pitcher	Save	Record	Pos.	GB
6-20	At Mil.	W	5-4		11	9	Maddux	Ohka	Dempster	35-33	2nd	9.5
6-21	At Mil.	W	4-2		5	3	Williams	Santos	Dempster	36-33	2nd	8.5
6-22	At Mil.	L	4-9		8	8	Davis	Zambrano		36-34	2nd	8.5
6-23	At Mil.	L	7-8		11	12	Bottalico	Remlinger	Turnbow	36-35	2nd	8.5
6-24	At Chi.	L	2-12		5	13	Garcia	Mitre		36-36	2nd	9.5
6-25	At Chi.	W	6-2		10	5	Maddux	Contreras		37-36	2nd	9.5
6-26	At Chi.	W	2-0		5	1	Prior	Garland	Dempster	38-36	2nd	8.5
6-28	Mil.	W	2-0		4	3	Zambrano	Davis	Dempster	39-36	2nd	8.5
6-29	Mil.	W	3-2		8	5	Novoa	Santana		40-36	2nd	8.5
6-30	Mil.	L	6-10		9	16	Capuano	Maddux		40-37	2nd	8.5
7-1	Was.	L	3-4		10	12	Hernandez	Prior	Carrasco	40-38	2nd	9.5
7-2	Was.	L	2-4		8	5	Armas	Williams	Cordero	40-39	2nd	9.5
7-3	Was.	L	4-5	(12)	11	10	Eischen	Mitre		40-40	2nd	10.5
7-4	At Atl.	L	0-4		6	8	Davies	Wood		40-41	2nd	11.5
7-5	At Atl.	L	1-5		8	9	Colon	Maddux		40-42	T2nd	12.5
7-7#	At Atl.	L	0-6		3	11	Ramirez	Prior		40-43		
7-7$	At Atl.	L	4-9		6	14	Foster	Novoa		40-44	3rd	13.5
7-8	At Fla.	W	9-6		13	8	Zambrano	Willis	Dempster	41-44	3rd	13.5
7-9	At Fla.	W	8-2		10	6	Wood	Mota		42-44	3rd	12.5
7-10	At Fla.	W	9-2		13	6	Maddux	Leiter		43-44	3rd	12.5
7-14	Pit.	W	5-1		10	2	Prior	Redman		44-44	3rd	12.0
7-15	Pit.	W	11-1		16	4	Wood	Fogg		45-44	2nd	12.0
7-16	Pit.	L	0-3		8	5	Duke	Maddux	Mesa	45-45	2nd	13.0
7-17	Pit.	W	8-2		15	8	Zambrano	Wells		46-45	2nd	13.0
7-18	At Cin.	W	9-4		18	6	Williams	Claussen		47-45	2nd	13.0
7-19	At Cin.	W	7-3		11	7	Prior	Hudson		48-45	2nd	12.0
7-20	At Cin.	L	3-9		7	11	Harang	Wood		48-46	T2nd	13.0
7-21	At Cin.	L	6-9		14	14	Shackelford	Novoa		48-47	3rd	13.0
7-22	At StL.	L	1-2	(11)	9	6	Reyes	Mitre		48-48	3rd	14.0
7-23	At StL.	W	6-5		8	9	Williams	Morris	Dempster	49-48	3rd	13.0
7-24	At StL.	W	8-4	(10)	10	8	Dempster	Reyes		50-48	3rd	12.0
7-25	S.F.	W	3-2		12	8	Dempster	Walker		51-48	3rd	11.5
7-26	S.F.	L	2-3	(11)	10	13	Christiansen	Rusch	Walker	51-49	3rd	12.5
7-27	S.F.	W	4-3		8	13	Dempster	Correia		52-49	3rd	11.5
7-28	Ari.	L	0-6		5	13	Halsey	Williams		52-50	3rd	12.5
7-29	Ari.	W	4-3		8	7	Novoa	Bruney		53-50	3rd	11.5
7-30	Ari.	L	2-3		6	9	Cormier	Novoa	Aquino	53-51	3rd	12.5
7-31	Ari.	L	6-13		10	14	Webb	Maddux		53-52	3rd	13.5
8-2	At Phi.	W	2-1		9	4	Zambrano	Padilla	Dempster	54-52	3rd	13.0
8-3	At Phi.	L	3-4		6	11	Wagner	Remlinger		54-53	3rd	14.0
8-4	At Phi.	L	4-6		11	8	Myers	Prior	Wagner	54-54	3rd	14.0
8-5	At N.Y.	L	5-9		10	14	Glavine	Hill		54-55	4th	15.0
8-6	At N.Y.	L	0-2		4	4	Seo	Maddux	Looper	54-56	4th	15.0
8-7	At N.Y.	L	1-6		6	10	Zambrano	Zambrano		54-57	4th	16.0
8-8	Cin.	L	4-9		9	9	Claussen	Williams		54-58	4th	17.0
8-9	Cin.	L	3-8		8	13	Harang	Ohman		54-59	4th	18.0
8-10	Cin.	L	2-8		7	6	Milton	Hill		54-60	4th	19.0
8-11	StL.	W	11-4		16	12	Maddux	Mulder		55-60	4th	18.0
8-12	StL.	W	4-1		12	10	Zambrano	Marquis		56-60	T3rd	17.0
8-13	StL.	L	2-5		8	7	Carpenter	Williams		56-61	T3rd	18.0
8-14	StL.	W	5-4		14	8	Prior	Morris	Dempster	57-61	T3rd	17.0
8-15	At Hou.	L	4-12		7	16	Rodriguez	Rusch		57-62	T3rd	17.5
8-16	At Hou.	W	4-1		9	4	Maddux	Pettitte	Dempster	58-62	T3rd	17.5
8-17	At Hou.	W	4-2		9	3	Zambrano	Oswalt	Dempster	59-62	T3rd	17.5
8-19	At Col.	W	5-3		10	6	Prior	Kim	Dempster	60-62	3rd	17.0
8-20	At Col.	L	2-4		11	9	Cook	Rusch	Fuentes	60-63	4th	18.0
8-21	At Col.	L	7-9		14	10	Kim	Maddux		60-64	4th	18.0
8-22	Atl.	L	2-4		7	5	Hudson	Wood		60-65	4th	19.0
8-23	Atl.	W	10-1		15	3	Williams	Thomson		61-65	4th	18.0
8-24	Atl.	L	1-3		5	5	Sosa	Prior	Farnsworth	61-66	4th	19.0
8-26	Fla.	L	5-7		11	10	Vargas	Rusch	Jones	61-67	4th	19.5
8-27	Fla.	L	1-2		7	5	Willis	Maddux	Jones	61-68	T4th	20.5
8-28	Fla.	W	14-3		15	6	Zambrano	Beckett		62-68	T4th	20.5
8-29	L.A.	L	6-9		11	10	Houlton	Williams	Sanchez	62-69	5th	21.5
8-30	L.A.	W	6-3		11	10	Prior	Penny	Dempster	63-69	4th	20.5
8-31	L.A.	L	0-7		1	11	Lowe	Rusch		63-70	4th	21.5
9-2	At Pit.	W	7-3		12	12	Maddux	Fogg	Dempster	64-70	4th	20.5
9-3	At Pit.	W	9-5		13	6	Zambrano	Williams		65-70	4th	20.5
9-4	At Pit.	W	2-0		7	4	Williams	Wells	Dempster	66-70	4th	20.5
9-5	At StL.	L	4-6		7	9	King	Novoa	Tavarez	66-71	4th	21.5

Date	Opp.	Res.	Score	(inn.*)	Hits	Opp. hits	Winning pitcher	Losing pitcher	Save	Record	Pos.	GB
9-6	At StL.	W	5-2		13	6	Rusch	Morris	Dempster	67-71	4th	20.5
9-7	At StL.	W	2-1		10	9	Maddux	Mulder	Dempster	68-71	4th	19.5
9-8	At S.F.	W	5-3		11	7	Zambrano	Lowry	Dempster	69-71	T3rd	19.5
9-9	At S.F.	L	1-2		2	7	Cain	Williams		69-72	4th	20.5
9-10	At S.F.	W	5-2		11	6	Prior	Hennessey	Dempster	70-72	T3rd	20.5
9-11	At S.F.	W	3-2		6	7	Wuertz	Hawkins	Dempster	71-72	T3rd	19.5
9-12	Cin.	L	2-5		8	6	Harang	Maddux	Weathers	71-73	4th	20.5
9-13	Cin.	W	4-3	(10)	10	7	Wuertz	Weathers		72-73	4th	20.5
9-14	Cin.	L	4-7	(11)	8	13	Coffey	Van Buren		72-74	4th	20.5
9-15	StL.	L	1-6		8	9	Suppan	Prior		72-75	4th	21.5
9-16	StL.	W	5-3		9	8	Rusch	Morris	Dempster	73-75	4th	20.5
9-17	StL.	L	1-5		8	11	Mulder	Maddux		73-76	4th	21.5
9-18	StL.	W	7-4		9	10	Zambrano	Reyes		74-76	3rd	20.5
9-20	At Mil.	L	3-5		9	11	Davis	Williams	Turnbow	74-77	4th	20.5
9-21	At Mil.	L	6-7		12	11	Turnbow	Van Buren		74-78	4th	21.5
9-22	At Mil.	W	3-0		7	4	Maddux	Helling	Dempster	75-78	4th	20.5
9-23	Hou.	W	5-4		10	11	Rusch	Rodriguez	Dempster	76-78	4th	19.5
9-24	Hou.	L	3-8		4	12	Astacio	Zambrano		76-79	4th	19.5
9-25	Hou.	W	3-2		5	5	Williams	Gallo	Dempster	77-79	4th	19.5
9-27	Pit.	L	3-5		7	8	Duke	Maddux	Torres	77-80	4th	19.5
9-28	Pit.	L	2-3		7	7	Maholm	Prior	Gonzalez	77-81	4th	19.5
9-29	At Hou.	W	3-2		6	8	Rusch	Rodriguez	Dempster	78-81	4th	19.0
9-30	At Hou.	W	4-3		11	6	Novoa	Lidge	Dempster	79-81	4th	19.0
10-1	At Hou.	L	1-3		8	6	Clemens	Williams	Lidge	79-82	4th	20.0
10-2	At Hou.	L	4-6		10	11	Oswalt	Maddux	Lidge	79-83	4th	21.0

Monthly records: April (12-11), May (14-13), June (14-13), July (13-15), August (10-18), September (16-11), October (0-2).
*Innings, if other than nine. ! First game of a doubleheader. & Second game of a doubleheader. # Day separate admission. $ Night separate admission.

RECORDS

2005 regular-season record: 79-83
Position: 4th in N.L. Central
Home: 38-43   **Road:** 41-40
N.L. East: 11-23   **N.L. Central:** 43-36
N.L. West: 19-15   **A.L.** 6-9
Vs. LH starters: 24-27
Vs. RH starters: 55-56
Grass: 79-83   **Artificial:** 0-0
Day: 41-44   **Night:** 38-39
1-Run: 26-20   **X-inn.:** 5-5
Doubleheaders: 0-0-1
Team record past five years: 411-399
(.507, ranks 8th in league in that span)

TEAM LEADERS

Batting average: Derrek Lee (.335).
At-bats: Jeromy Burnitz (605).
Runs: Derrek Lee (120).
Hits: Derrek Lee (199).
Total Bases: Derrek Lee (393).
Doubles: Derrek Lee (50).
Triples: Michael Barrett, Derrek Lee, Corey Patterson, Todd Walker (3).
Home runs: Derrek Lee (46).
Runs batted in: Derrek Lee (107).
Stolen bases: Derrek Lee, Corey Patterson (15).
Slugging percentage: Derrek Lee (.662).
On-base percentage: Derrek Lee (.418).
Wins: Carlos Zambrano (14).
Earned-run average: Carlos Zambrano (3.26).
Complete games: Greg Maddux (3).

Shutouts: Sergio Mitre, Glendon Rusch (1).
Saves: Ryan Dempster (33).
Innings pitched: Greg Maddux (225.0).
Strikeouts: Carlos Zambrano (202).

GAMES BY POSITION

Catcher: Michael Barrett 122, Henry Blanco 54.

First base: Derrek Lee 158, Scott McClain 4, Todd Walker 4, Enrique Wilson 3, Todd Hollandsworth 1.

Second base: Todd Walker 97, Jerry Hairston Jr. 44, Neifi Perez 26, Jose Macias 20, Enrique Wilson 5, Ryan Theriot 3, Ronny Cedeno 1.

Third base: Aramis Ramirez 119, Nomar Garciaparra 34, Jose Macias 23, Neifi Perez 4, Scott McClain 3, Enrique Wilson 1.

Shortstop: Neifi Perez 130, Ronny Cedeno 29, Nomar Garciaparra 26, Enrique Wilson 3, Jerry Hairston Jr. 1.

Outfield: Jeromy Burnitz 160, Corey Patterson 122, Todd Hollandsworth 95, Jerry Hairston Jr. 62, Matt Murton 43, Jason Dubois 38, Jose Macias 20, Matt Lawton 19, Jody Gerut 5, Ben Grieve 1.

Designated hitter: Jason Dubois 3, Todd Walker 2, Michael Barrett 1.

TOP DRAFT CHOICES

1. **Mark Pawelek,** LHP, Springville (Utah) H.S.
2. **Donald Veal,** LHP, Pima CC (Ariz.).
3a. **Mark Holliman,** RHP, Mississippi.
3b. **Mike Billek.,** RHP, Central Florida.
4. **Dylan Johnston,** SS, Hamilton H.S., Chandler, Ariz.
5. **Scott Taylor,** RHP, Hermitage H.S., Richmond, Va.
6. **Kyle Reynolds,** SS, Baylor.
7. **Trey Taylor,** LHP, Baylor.
8. **Jake Muyco,** C, North Carolina State.
9. **Matt Avery,** RHP, Virginia.
10. **Joe Simokatis,** SS, Nebraska.

REDS CINCINNATI REDS
NATIONAL LEAGUE CENTRAL DIVISION

2006 SEASON

Reds Schedule
Home games shaded.
All-Star Game July 11 at Pittsburgh. Schedule subject to change.

APRIL

SUN	MON	TUE	WED	THU	FRI	SAT
2	3 CHC	4	5 CHC	6 PIT	7 PIT	8 PIT
9 PIT	10	11 CHC	12 CHC	13 CHC	14 STL	15 STL
16 STL	17 FLA	18 FLA	19 FLA	20 MIL	21 MIL	22 MIL
23 MIL	24 WAS	25 WAS	26 WAS	27	28 HOU	29 HOU
30 HOU						

MAY

SUN	MON	TUE	WED	THU	FRI	SAT
	1 STL	2 STL	3 COL	4 COL	5 ARI	6 ARI
7 ARI	8	9 WAS	10 WAS	11 WAS	12 PHI	13 PHI
14 PHI	15	16 PIT	17 PIT	18 PIT	19 DET	20 DET
21 DET	22 MIL	23 MIL	24 MIL	25	26 ARI	27 ARI
28 ARI	29 CHC	30 CHC	31 CHC			

JUNE

SUN	MON	TUE	WED	THU	FRI	SAT
				1	2 HOU	3 HOU
4 HOU	5 STL	6 STL	7 STL	8 CHC	9 CHC	10 CHC
11 CHC	12 MIL	13 MIL	14 MIL	15	16 CHW	17 CHW
18 CHW	19 NYM	20 NYM	21 NYM	22 NYM	23 CLE	24 CLE
25 CLE	26	27 KC	28 KC	29 KC	30 CLE	

JULY

SUN	MON	TUE	WED	THU	FRI	SAT
						1 CLE
2 CLE	3 MIL	4 MIL	5 MIL	6 ATL	7 ATL	8 ATL
9 ATL	10	11 ALL-STAR	12	13 COL	14 COL	15 COL
16 COL	17	18 NYM	19 NYM	20 NYM	21 MIL	22 MIL
23 MIL	24	25 HOU	26 HOU	27 HOU	28 MIL	29 MIL
30 MIL	31					

AUGUST

SUN	MON	TUE	WED	THU	FRI	SAT
		1 LAD	2 LAD	3 LAD	4 ATL	5 ATL
6 ATL	7 STL	8 STL	9 STL	10 STL	11 PHI	12 PHI
13 PHI	14	15 STL	16 STL	17 STL	18 PIT	19 PIT
20 PIT	21 HOU	22 HOU	23 HOU	24 SF	25 SF	26 SF
27 SF	28 LAD	29 LAD	30 LAD	31		

SEPTEMBER

SUN	MON	TUE	WED	THU	FRI	SAT
					1 SD	2 SD
3 SD	4 SF	5 SF	6 SF	7	8 PIT	9 PIT
10 PIT	11	12 SD	13 SD	14 SD	15 CHC	16 CHC
17 CHC	18 HOU	19 HOU	20 HOU	21	22 CHC	23 CHC
24 CHC	25 CHC	26 FLA	27 FLA	28 FLA	29 PIT	30 PIT

OCTOBER

SUN	MON	TUE	WED	THU	FRI	SAT
1 PIT	2	3	4	5	6	7

Home games are shaded. All-Star Game is July 11 at Pittsburgh. Schedule is subject to change.

Encarnacion

CLUB DIRECTORY

Chief operating officer
Robert Castellini

General manager
Dan O'Brien

Assistant general manager
Dean Taylor

Director of major league operations
Brad Kullman

Director of player development
Tim Naehring

Director of amateur scouting
Terry Reynolds

Director of international scouting
Johnny Almaraz

Manager of Florida operations
Jeff Maultsby

Director of media relations
Rob Butcher

Traveling secretary
Gary Wahoff

Medical director
Dr. Timothy Kremchek

MINOR LEAGUE AFFILIATES

Class	Team	League	Manager
AAA	Louisville	International	Rick Sweet
AA	Chattanooga	Southern	Jayhawk Owens
Advanced A	Sarasota	Florida State	Donnie Scott
A	Dayton	Midwest	Billy Gardner Jr.
Advanced Rookie	Billings	Pioneer	Rick Burleson
Rookie	Reds	Gulf Coast	Luis Aguayo

BROADCAST INFORMATION

Radio: WLW-AM (700).
Cable TV: Fox Sports Net.

SPRING TRAINING

Ballpark (city): Ed Smith Stadium (Sarasota, Fla.).
Ticket information: 941-954-4101.

For more on the Reds, go to www.sportingnews.com/baseball/teams/reds/

– 93 –

Manager—Jerry Narron (41)
Coaches—Mark Berry (55), Chris Chambliss (49), Bucky Dent, Tom Hume (47), John Moses (32), Vern Ruhle (58), Mike Stefanski (72).

No.	PITCHERS	B/T	Ht./Wt.	Age*
	Grant Balfour	R/R	6-2/195	28
31	Matt Belisle	R/R	6-3/195	25
31	Jung Bong	L/L	6-3/215	25
53	Mike Burns	R/R	6-1/205	27
65	Travis Chick	R/R	6-3/225	21
34	Brandon Claussen	R/L	6-1/200	26
56	Todd Coffey	R/R	6-5/230	25
66	Phillip Dumatrait	R/L	6-2/170	24
57	Justin Germano	R/R	6-1/190	23
45	Chris Hammond	L/L	6-1/210	40
39	Aaron Harang	R/R	6-7/270	27
54	Luke Hudson	R/R	6-3/195	28
50	Kent Mercker	L/L	6-2/205	38
22	Eric Milton	L/L	6-3/208	30
61	Bubba Nelson	R/R	6-1/195	24
45	Elizardo Ramirez	L/R	6-0/180	23
37	Brian Shackelford	L/L	6-1/195	29
46	Allan Simpson	R/R	6-4/200	28
35	Jason Standridge	R/R	6-4/230	27
38	Ryan Wagner	R/R	6-4/225	23
25	David Weathers	R/R	6-3/230	36
52	Dave Williams	L/L	6-3/230	27
40	Paul Wilson	R/R	6-5/215	33

No.	CATCHERS	B/T	Ht./Wt.	Age*
23	Jason LaRue	R/R	5-11/200	32
29	Miguel Perez	R/R	6-3/190	22
59	Dane Sardinha	R/R	6-0/215	26
17	Javier Valentin	B/R	5-10/210	30

No.	INFIELDERS	B/T	Ht./Wt.	Age*
33	Rich Aurilia	R/R	6-1/189	34
27	William Bergolla	R/R	6-0/175	23
12	Edwin Encarnacion	R/R	6-1/195	23
6	Ryan Freel	R/R	5-10/180	30
2	Felipe Lopez	B/R	6-1/185	25
4	Ranier Olmedo	B/R	5-11/155	24
64	Joseph Votto	L/R	6-2/220	22
15	Tony Womack	L/R	5-9/170	36

No.	OUTFIELDERS	B/T	Ht./Wt.	Age*
19	Chris Denorfia	R/R	6-0/195	25
44	Adam Dunn	L/R	6-6/275	26
30	Ken Griffey	L/L	6-3/220	36
28	Austin Kearns	R/R	6-3/245	25
26	Wily Mo Pena	R/R	6-3/245	24

*Age as of April 1, 2006.

BALLPARK INFORMATION

Ballpark (capacity, surface)
Great American Ball Park (42,271, grass)
Address
100 Main St.
Cincinnati, OH 45202
Official website
www.reds.com
Business phone
513-765-7000
Ticket information
513-765-7400
Field dimensions (from home plate)
To left field at foul line, 328 feet
To center field, 404 feet
To right field at foul line, 325 feet
First game played
March 31, 2003 (Pirates 10, Reds 1)

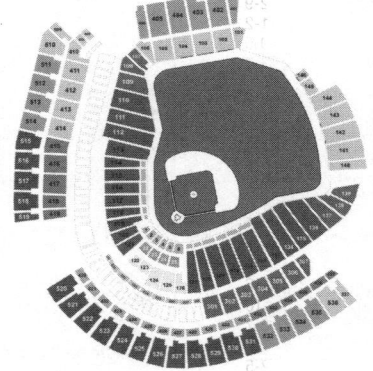

Date	Opp.	Res.	Score	(inn.*)	Hits	Opp. hits	Winning pitcher	Losing pitcher	Save	Record	Pos.	GB
4-4	N.Y.	W	7-6		8	14	Graves	Looper		1-0	T1st	...
4-6	N.Y.	W	9-5		14	12	Milton	Glavine		2-0	T1st	...
4-7	N.Y.	W	6-1		3	4	Harang	Ishii	Graves	3-0	1st	+0.5
4-8	At Hou.	L	2-3		8	8	Clemens	Belisle	Lidge	3-1	2nd	0.5
4-9	At Hou.	L	3-4		11	10	Lidge	Wagner		3-2	3rd	0.5
4-10	At Hou.	L	2-5		6	11	Oswalt	Milton	Lidge	3-3	T3rd	1.5
4-12	At StL.	L	1-5		6	5	Marquis	Harang		3-4	T4th	1.5
4-13	At StL.	W	6-5		15	9	Belisle	Mulder	Graves	4-4	3rd	1.0
4-15	Hou.	L	2-11		5	14	Oswalt	Wilson		4-5	4th	1.0
4-16	Hou.	W	3-2		8	5	Milton	Pettitte	Graves	5-5	T2nd	0.5
4-17	Hou.	W	6-5		7	9	Wagner	Qualls	Graves	6-5	2nd	0.5
4-18	Chi.	W	7-6		9	12	Mercker	Leicester	Graves	7-5	2nd	0.5
4-19	Chi.	L	1-7		4	11	Prior	Claussen		7-6	2nd	1.5
4-20	Pit.	W	6-4		11	12	Wilson	Torres	Graves	8-6	2nd	0.5
4-21	Pit.	L	2-4		6	6	Wells	Milton	Mesa	8-7	T2nd	1.5
4-22	At Fla.	L	2-4		5	12	Perisho	Mercker	Mota	8-8	T2nd	2.5
4-23	At Fla.	L	2-4		9	8	Willis	Belisle	Mota	8-9	T2nd	3.5
4-24	At Fla.	W	2-1		9	4	Claussen	Moehler	Graves	9-9	T2nd	3.5
4-25	At Chi.	L	6-10		10	12	Prior	Wilson		9-10	3rd	4.0
4-26	At Chi.	W	11-9		15	13	Weathers	Wuertz	Graves	10-10	T2nd	4.0
4-27	At Chi.	L	7-8		10	14	Hawkins	Belisle		10-11	3rd	5.0
4-29	At Mil.	L	3-4		6	6	Glover	Claussen	Turnbow	10-12	3rd	5.5
4-30	At Mil.	L	5-6		8	9	Turnbow	Valentine		10-13	T3rd	5.5
5-1	At Mil.	L	3-13		5	19	Davis	Ortiz		10-14	5th	5.5
5-2	StL.	L	9-10		14	15	Flores	Graves	Tavarez	10-15	5th	6.5
5-3	StL.	L	2-4		4	9	Marquis	Harang	Reyes	10-16	5th	7.5
5-4	StL.	L	3-7		6	12	Mulder	Claussen		10-17	6th	8.5
5-6	L.A.	L	6-13		8	12	Penny	Wilson		10-18	6th	8.0
5-7	L.A.	W	11-3		11	10	Weathers	Lowe		11-18	T5th	7.0
5-8	L.A.	L	3-9		9	14	Weaver	Milton		11-19	T5th	8.0
5-9	S.D.	L	5-6	(13)	13	14	Hammond	Belisle	Hoffman	11-20	6th	9.0
5-10	S.D.	W	5-1		7	12	Coffey	Lawrence		12-20	T5th	8.0
5-11	S.D.	L	2-7		5	16	Stauffer	Wilson		12-21	T5th	9.0
5-12	At Phi.	W	7-5		8	12	Ortiz	Lieber	Graves	13-21	5th	9.0
5-13	At Phi.	L	2-12		6	16	Myers	Milton		13-22	5th	9.0
5-14	At Phi.	W	12-4		17	9	Harang	Madson		14-22	5th	9.0
5-15	At Phi.	L	3-4		8	12	Padilla	Ramirez	Wagner	14-23	T5th	10.0
5-16	At N.Y.	L	2-9		4	13	Benson	Wilson		14-24	6th	10.5
5-17	At N.Y.	L	1-2		5	7	DeJean	Ortiz	Looper	14-25	6th	10.5
5-18	At N.Y.	L	6-10		13	13	Glavine	Milton		14-26	6th	11.5
5-20	Cle.	W	2-1		7	6	Harang	Millwood	Graves	15-26	T5th	11.0
5-21	Cle.	L	3-5		9	8	Sabathia	Ramirez	Wickman	15-27	T5th	12.0
5-22	Cle.	L	2-9		8	16	Lee	Ortiz		15-28	T5th	12.0
5-23	Was.	W	5-3		12	6	Milton	Loaiza	Weathers	16-28	5th	12.0
5-24	Was.	W	4-3	(14)	11	15	Keisler	Ayala		17-28	5th	12.0
5-25	Was.	W	12-3		14	8	Belisle	Vargas		18-28	5th	12.0
5-26	Pit.	L	4-8		6	13	Perez	Ramirez		18-29	5th	12.5
5-27	Pit.	W	6-5		11	13	Wagner	Gonzalez		19-29	5th	12.5
5-28	Pit.	L	2-9		5	15	Williams	Milton		19-30	5th	13.5
5-29	Pit.	W	11-2		11	7	Claussen	Wells		20-30	5th	12.5
5-30	At Hou.	W	9-0		10	5	Harang	Clemens		21-30	5th	12.5
5-31	At Hou.	L	3-4		10	8	Backe	Belisle	Lidge	21-31	5th	12.5
6-1	At Hou.	L	1-4		4	7	Oswalt	Ortiz	Lidge	21-32	5th	13.5
6-3	At Col.	L	4-12		7	19	Francis	Milton		21-33	5th	14.0
6-4	At Col.	L	5-7		12	11	Wright	Harang	Fuentes	21-34	5th	15.0
6-5	At Col.	L	6-8		13	14	Neal	Wagner	Fuentes	21-35	6th	15.0
6-7	T.B.	W	9-7		10	10	Keisler	Harper	Weathers	22-35	5th	15.5
6-8	T.B.	W	11-9		14	12	Weathers	Baez		23-35	5th	14.5
6-9	T.B.	W	14-5		14	6	Hudson	Fossum		24-35	5th	14.0
6-10	Bal.	L	3-4		6	7	Lopez	Harang	Ryan	24-36	6th	15.0
6-11	Bal.	W	10-1		9	4	Claussen	Cabrera		25-36	6th	14.0
6-12	Bal.	W	10-6		16	9	Ortiz	Ponson		26-36	6th	14.0
6-13	At Bos.	L	3-10		6	16	Clement	Milton		26-37	6th	14.0
6-14	At Bos.	L	0-7		1	10	Wells	Hudson		26-38	6th	15.0
6-15	At Bos.	L	1-6		8	10	Arroyo	Harang		26-39	6th	15.0
6-16	Atl.	L	2-5		5	13	Smoltz	Claussen	Reitsma	26-40	6th	15.5

Date	Opp.	Res.	Score	(inn.*)	Hits	Opp. hits	Winning pitcher	Losing pitcher	Save	Record	Pos.	GB
6-17	Atl.	L	5-10		11	16	Ramirez	Ortiz		26-41	6th	16.5
6-18	Atl.	L	1-6		10	11	Bernero	Milton		26-42	6th	17.5
6-19	Atl.	W	11-8		17	13	Weathers	Bernero		27-42	6th	17.5
6-20	StL.	L	1-6		4	12	Carpenter	Harang		27-43	6th	18.5
6-21	StL.	W	11-4		12	10	Claussen	Marquis		28-43	6th	17.5
6-22	StL.	W	7-6		13	8	Ortiz	Mulder	Mercker	29-43	6th	16.5
6-24	At Cle.	W	5-4		10	8	Mercker	Howry	Weathers	30-43	6th	16.0
6-25	At Cle.	L	7-12		13	21	Westbrook	Hudson		30-44	6th	17.0
6-26	At Cle.	L	3-4		8	9	Howry	Weathers	Wickman	30-45	6th	17.0
6-28	At StL.	L	1-2		8	4	Mulder	Claussen	Isringhausen	30-46	6th	18.0
6-29	At StL.	L	3-11		7	12	Morris	Ortiz		30-47	6th	19.0
6-30	Hou.	T	2-2	(7)	8	5				30-47	6th	18.5
7-1	Hou.	L	7-10		13	14	Pettitte	Hudson	Wheeler	30-48	6th	19.5
7-2!	Hou.	L	3-4		7	8	Rodriguez	Harang	Wheeler	30-49		
7-2&	Hou.	W	11-6		14	10	Ortiz	Astacio		31-49	6th	19.0
7-3	Hou.	L	0-9		4	12	Clemens	Claussen		31-50	6th	20.0
7-4	At S.F.	W	11-10		12	13	Wagner	Accardo	Belisle	32-50	6th	20.0
7-5	At S.F.	W	7-4		13	8	Milton	Lowry		33-50	6th	20.0
7-6	At S.F.	L	2-7		8	11	Correia	Hudson		33-51	6th	21.0
7-7	At S.F.	L	1-5		8	7	Tomko	Harang		33-52	6th	21.0
7-8	At Ari.	W	4-3		12	7	Weathers	Cormier	Mercker	34-52	6th	21.0
7-9	At Ari.	W	6-2		9	8	Coffey	Webb		35-52	6th	20.0
7-10	At Ari.	L	0-2		5	5	Cormier	Milton	Bruney	35-53	6th	21.0
7-15	Col.	W	4-3		7	6	Harang	Jennings	Weathers	36-53	6th	21.0
7-16	Col.	W	7-6		9	12	Standridge	Miceli	Weathers	37-53	6th	21.0
7-17	Col.	W	9-4		6	11	Ortiz	Wright		38-53	6th	21.0
7-18	Chi.	L	4-9		6	18	Williams	Claussen		38-54	6th	22.0
7-19	Chi.	L	3-7		7	11	Prior	Hudson		38-55	6th	22.0
7-20	Chi.	W	9-3		11	7	Harang	Wood		39-55	6th	22.0
7-21	Chi.	W	9-6		14	14	Shackelford	Novoa		40-55	6th	21.0
7-22	Mil.	W	11-6		15	11	Ortiz	Ohka		41-55	5th	21.0
7-23	Mil.	L	7-11		11	11	Santos	Claussen		41-56	6th	21.0
7-24	Mil.	W	3-2		7	7	Weathers	Santana		42-56	6th	20.0
7-25	At L.A.	L	0-4		1	9	Lowe	Harang		42-57	6th	20.5
7-26	At L.A.	L	4-7		11	11	Perez	Milton	Brazoban	42-58	6th	21.5
7-27	At L.A.	W	7-6		13	9	Standridge	Brazoban	Weathers	43-58	6th	20.5
7-28	At L.A.	W	6-1		7	6	Claussen	Houlton		44-58	T5th	20.5
7-29	At S.D.	W	8-3		10	6	Hudson	Lawrence		45-58	5th	19.5
7-30	At S.D.	W	9-1		14	7	Harang	Astacio		46-58	5th	19.5
7-31	At S.D.	W	7-1		9	5	Milton	Williams		47-58	5th	19.5
8-2	Atl.	L	2-12		10	14	Sosa	Ortiz		47-59	5th	20.0
8-3	Atl.	W	8-5		9	11	Claussen	Ramirez	Mercker	48-59	5th	20.0
8-4	Atl.	L	4-7		6	13	Davies	Harang	Reitsma	48-60	5th	20.0
8-5	Fla.	L	1-5		4	10	Vargas	Milton		48-61	5th	21.0
8-6	Fla.	W	4-3		8	5	Hudson	Moehler	Weathers	49-61	5th	20.0
8-7	Fla.	L	0-2		4	12	Willis	Ortiz	Jones	49-62	5th	21.0
8-8	At Chi.	W	9-4		9	9	Claussen	Williams		50-62	5th	21.0
8-9	At Chi.	W	8-3		13	8	Harang	Ohman		51-62	5th	21.0
8-10	At Chi.	W	8-2		6	7	Milton	Hill		52-62	5th	21.0
8-12	At Mil.	W	5-3		11	7	Hudson	Capuano	Weathers	53-62	5th	19.5
8-13	At Mil.	W	4-1		13	2	Ortiz	Ohka	Weathers	54-62	5th	19.5
8-14	At Mil.	L	3-8		5	9	Davis	Belisle		54-63	5th	19.5
8-15	S.F.	L	3-7		10	12	Correia	Harang		54-64	5th	20.0
8-16	S.F.	L	8-10		11	19	Fassero	Standridge	Walker	54-65	5th	21.0
8-17	S.F.	L	2-3		7	11	Lowry	Hudson	Hawkins	54-66	5th	22.0
8-18	S.F.	W	4-2		5	10	Ortiz	Tomko	Weathers	55-66	5th	21.0
8-19	Ari.	W	17-3		15	5	Claussen	Ortiz		56-66	5th	21.0
8-20	Ari.	L	2-6		7	11	Vazquez	Standridge		56-67	5th	22.0
8-21	Ari.	W	13-6		17	9	Milton	Halsey		57-67	5th	21.0
8-23	At Was.	W	6-2		11	4	Hudson	Armas		58-67	5th	20.5
8-24	At Was.	L	3-5		10	9	Patterson	Ortiz	Cordero	58-68	5th	21.5
8-25	At Was.	W	5-3		13	9	Claussen	Hernandez	Weathers	59-68	5th	21.5
8-26	At Pit.	W	6-1		11	8	Harang	Redman		60-68	5th	20.5
8-27	At Pit.	W	4-2	(10)	9	9	Weathers	Mesa	Mercker	61-68	T4th	20.5
8-28	At Pit.	W	7-2		7	8	Hudson	Wells	Coffey	62-68	T4th	20.5
8-30	At Hou.	L	2-5		5	9	Rodriguez	Ortiz		62-69	5th	21.0
8-31	At Hou.	L	0-10		4	15	Pettitte	Claussen		62-70	5th	22.0
9-1	At Hou.	L	1-3		6	5	Oswalt	Harang	Lidge	62-71	5th	22.5
9-2	At Atl.	L	4-7		14	10	Hudson	Milton	Farnsworth	62-72	5th	22.5
9-3	At Atl.	L	3-9		5	10	Sosa	Hudson		62-73	5th	23.5

Date	Opp.	Res.	Score	(inn.*)	Hits	Opp. hits	Winning pitcher	Losing pitcher	Save	Record	Pos.	GB
9-4	At Atl.	W	8-3	(12)	13	5	Belisle	Kolb		63-73	5th	23.5
9-5	Mil.	L	1-6		4	14	Ohka	Belisle	Eveland	63-74	5th	24.5
9-6	Mil.	W	2-1	(10)	10	8	Mercker	de la Rosa		64-74	5th	23.5
9-7	Mil.	L	5-14		10	17	Capuano	Milton		64-75	5th	23.5
9-9	Pit.	L	4-8		8	8	Vogelsong	Hudson		64-76	5th	25.0
9-10	Pit.	W	6-2		8	8	Ortiz	Wells		65-76	5th	25.0
9-11	Pit.	W	5-3		9	9	Belisle	Grabow	Weathers	66-76	5th	24.0
9-12	At Chi.	W	5-2		6	8	Harang	Maddux	Weathers	67-76	5th	24.0
9-13	At Chi.	L	3-4	(10)	7	10	Wuertz	Weathers		67-77	5th	25.0
9-14	At Chi.	W	7-4	(11)	13	8	Coffey	Van Buren		68-77	5th	24.0
9-16!	At Pit.	W	8-2		12	8	Claussen	Duke		69-77		
9-16&	At Pit.	L	4-5		7	13	Torres	Weathers		69-78	5th	24.0
9-17	At Pit.	L	0-4		4	7	Maholm	Harang		69-79	5th	25.0
9-18	At Pit.	L	7-9		10	12	Gonzalez	Belisle		69-80	5th	25.0
9-20	StL.	W	6-5		8	7	Hancock	King	Weathers	70-80	5th	24.0
9-21	StL.	L	1-5		9	12	Marquis	Ortiz		70-81	5th	25.0
9-22	StL.	W	6-2		5	8	Coffey	King		71-81	5th	24.0
9-23	Phi.	L	10-11		13	17	Cormier	Weathers	Wagner	71-82	5th	24.0
9-24	Phi.	W	3-2		4	7	Milton	Brito	Weathers	72-82	5th	23.0
9-25	Phi.	L	3-6		9	12	Lidle	Keisler	Wagner	72-83	5th	24.0
9-26	At Mil.	L	9-12		9	15	Capellan	Coffey	Turnbow	72-84	5th	24.5
9-27	At Mil.	L	2-6		6	8	Helling	Claussen	Turnbow	72-85	5th	24.5
9-28	At Mil.	W	11-4		14	15	Harang	Capuano		73-85	5th	23.5
9-29	At Mil.	L	0-2		3	5	Glover	Milton	Turnbow	73-86	5th	24.0
9-30	At StL.	L	6-12		9	17	Reyes	Hudson		73-87	5th	25.0
10-1	At StL.	L	6-9		9	7	Flores	Simpson	Isringhausen	73-88	5th	26.0
10-2	At StL.	L	5-7		10	16	Thompson	Claussen	Isringhausen	73-89	5th	27.0

Monthly records: April (10-13), May (11-18), June (9-16), July (17-11), August (15-12), September (11-17), October (0-2).
*Innings, if other than nine. ! First game of a doubleheader. & Second game of a doubleheader.

RECORDS

2005 regular-season record: 73-89
Position: 5th in N.L. Central
Home: 42-39   **Road:** 31-50
N.L. East: 16-19   **N.L. Central:** 33-46
N.L. West: 17-16   **A.L.** 7-8
Vs. LH starters: 24-29
Vs. RH starters: 49-60
Grass: 73-89   **Artificial:** 0-0
Day: 27-22   **Night:** 46-67
1-Run: 21-18   **X-inn.:** 5-2
Doubleheaders: 0-0-2
Team record past five years: 362-448 (.447, ranks 13th in league in that span)

TEAM LEADERS

Batting average: Sean Casey (.312).
At-bats: Felipe Lopez (580).
Runs: Adam Dunn (107).
Hits: Felipe Lopez (169).
Total Bases: Adam Dunn (293).
Doubles: Adam Dunn (35).
Triples: Felipe Lopez (5).
Home runs: Adam Dunn (40).
Runs batted in: Adam Dunn (101).
Stolen bases: Ryan Freel (36).
Slugging percentage: Ken Griffey Jr. (.576).
On-base percentage: Adam Dunn (.387).
Wins: Aaron Harang (11).
Earned-run average: Aaron Harang (3.83).
Complete games: Aaron Harang, Ramon Ortiz (1).

Shutouts: None.
Saves: David Weathers (15).
Innings pitched: Aaron Harang (211.2).
Strikeouts: Aaron Harang (163).

GAMES BY POSITION

Catcher: Jason LaRue 109, Javier Valentin 62, Miguel Perez 1, Dane Sardinha 1.
First base: Sean Casey 134, Adam Dunn 33, Jacob Cruz 5, Aaron Holbert 2, Javier Valentin 2.
Second base: Rich Aurilia 68, Ryan Freel 48, Ray Olmedo 31, D'Angelo Jimenez 27, William Bergolla 9, Felipe Lopez 7, Aaron Holbert 4, Luis Lopez 4.
Third base: Joe Randa 84, Edwin Encarnacion 56, Rich Aurilia 18, Ryan Freel 10, Luis Lopez 6, Aaron Holbert 2, Felipe Lopez 1.
Shortstop: Felipe Lopez 140, Rich Aurilia 30, Ray Olmedo 5, William Bergolla 1.
Outfield: Adam Dunn 133, Ken Griffey Jr. 124, Austin Kearns 107, Wily Mo Pena 83, Ryan Freel 51, Jacob Cruz 20, Jason Romano 14, Chris Denorfia 12, Kenny Kelly 4, Jason LaRue 1.
Designated hitter: Ken Griffey Jr. 2, Joe Randa 2, Sean Casey 1, Jacob Cruz 1, Kenny Kelly 1.

TOP DRAFT CHOICES

1. **Jay Bruce,** OF, West Brook H.S., Beaumont, Texas.
2. **Travis Wood,** LHP, Bryant H.S., Alexander, Ark.
3. **Zach Ward,** RHP, Gardner-Webb.
4. **Sam LeCure,** RHP, Texas.
5. **James Avery,** RHP, Niagara.
6. **Jeff Stevens,** RHP, Loyola Marymount.
7. **Brandon Roberts,** OF, Cal Poly San Luis Obispo.
8. **Michael Jones,** SS, Wayne County H.S., Jesup, Ga.
9. **Milton Loo,** 3B, Yavapai College (Ariz.).
10. **Bo Lanier,** RHP, Georgia.

COLORADO ROCKIES
NATIONAL LEAGUE WEST DIVISION

2006 SEASON

Rockies Schedule
Home games shaded.
All-Star Game July 11 at Pittsburgh. Schedule subject to change.

APRIL

SUN	MON	TUE	WED	THU	FRI	SAT
2	3 ARI	4	5 ARI	6 ARI	7 SD	8 SD
9 SD	10	11 ARI	12 ARI	13 ARI	14 PHI	15 PHI
16 PHI	17 SD	18 SD	19 SD	20	21 SF	22 SF
23 SF	24 PHI	25 PHI	26 PHI	27 PHI	28 FLA	29 FLA
30 FLA						

MAY

SUN	MON	TUE	WED	THU	FRI	SAT
	1 ATL	2 ATL	3 CIN	4 CIN	5 HOU	6 HOU
7 HOU	8 STL	9 STL	10 STL	11	12 HOU	13 HOU
14 HOU	15 LAD	16 LAD	17 LAD	18	19 TOR	20 TOR
21 TOR	22 LAD	23 LAD	24 LAD	25	26 SF	27 SF
28 SF	29 SD	30 SD	31 SD			

JUNE

SUN	MON	TUE	WED	THU	FRI	SAT
				1 FLA	2 FLA	3 FLA
4 FLA	5 PIT	6 PIT	7 PIT	8	9 LAD	10 LAD
11 LAD	12 WAS	13 WAS	14 WAS	15 WAS	16 STL	17 STL
18 STL	19 OAK	20 OAK	21 OAK	22	23 TEX	24 TEX
25 TEX	26 LAA	27 LAA	28 LAA	29	30 SEA	

JULY

SUN	MON	TUE	WED	THU	FRI	SAT
						1 SEA
2 SEA	3 SF	4 SF	5 SF	6	7 ARI	8 ARI
9 ARI	10	11 ALL-STAR	12	13 CIN	14 CIN	15 CIN
16 CIN	17 PIT	18 PIT	19 PIT	20	21 ARI	22 ARI
23 ARI	24 STL	25 STL	26 STL	27 SD	28 SD	29 SD
30 SD	31 MIL					

AUGUST

SUN	MON	TUE	WED	THU	FRI	SAT
		1 MIL	2 MIL	3	4 SF	5 SF
6 SF	7 LAD	8 LAD	9 LAD	10 LAD	11 CHC	12 CHC
13 CHC	14 ARI	15 ARI	16 ARI	17 ARI	18 NYM	19 NYM
20 NYM	21	22 MIL	23 MIL	24 MIL	25 SD	26 SD
27 SD	28	29 NYM	30 NYM	31 NYM		

SEPTEMBER

SUN	MON	TUE	WED	THU	FRI	SAT
					1 LAD	2 LAD
3 LAD	4 SD	5 SD	6 SD	7 WAS	8 WAS	9 WAS
10 WAS	11	12 SF	13 SF	14 SF	15 ARI	16 ARI
17 ARI	18 SF	19 SF	20 SF	21 ATL	22 ATL	23 ATL
24 ATL	25	26 LAD	27 LAD	28 LAD	29 CHC	30 CHC

OCTOBER

SUN	MON	TUE	WED	THU	FRI	SAT
1 CHC	2	3	4	5	6	7

Home games are shaded. All-Star
Game is July 11 at Pittsburgh.
Schedule is subject to change.

Helton

CLUB DIRECTORY

Chairman & chief executive officer
Charles K. Monfort
Vice chairman
Richard L. Monfort
President
Keli S. McGregor
Exec. vice president, general manager
Daniel J. O'Dowd
Sr. vice president, business operations
Gregory D. Feasel

Sr. vice president, chief financial officer
Harold R. Roth
V.p., public relations/communications
Jay E. Alves
Vice president, ballpark operations
Kevin Kahn
Vice president, finance
Michael J. Kent
Vice president, ticket operations & sales
Sue Ann McClaren

MINOR LEAGUE AFFILIATES

Class	Team	League	Manager
AAA	Colorado Springs	Pacific Coast	Tom Runnells
AA	Tulsa	Texas	Stu Cole
Advanced A	Modesto	California	To be announced
A	Asheville	South Atlantic	Joe Mikulik
Short-Season A	Tri-City	Northwest	Darron Cox
Advanced Rookie	Casper	Pioneer	P.J. Carey

BROADCAST INFORMATION

Radio: KOA-AM (850).
TV: UPN (Channel 20).
Cable TV: Fox Sports Rocky Mountain.

SPRING TRAINING

Ballpark (city): Hi Corbett Field
(Tucson, Ariz.).
Ticket information: 1-800-388-ROCK.

For more on the Rockies, go to www.sportingnews.com/baseball/teams/rockies/

Manager—Clint Hurdle (13).
Coaches—Bob Apodaca (36), Dave Collins (29), Duane Espy (52), Mike Gallego (2), Rick Mathews (53), Jamie Quirk (9), Mark Strittmatter (56).

No.	PITCHERS	B/T	Ht./Wt.	Age*
	Jaime Cerda	L/L	6-0/200	27
28	Aaron Cook	R/R	6-3/205	27
	Manuel Corpas	R/R	6-3/170	23
50	David Cortes	R/R	5-11/220	32
45	Zach Day	R/R	6-4/216	27
18	Mike DeJean	R/R	6-2/219	35
47	Scott Dohmann	R/R	6-1/190	28
35	Mike Esposito	R/R	6-0/190	24
26	Jeff Francis	L/L	6-5/200	25
40	Brian Fuentes	L/L	6-4/220	30
32	Jason Jennings	L/R	6-2/245	27
41	Ubaldo Jimenez	R/R	6-4/200	22
49	Byung-Hyun Kim	R/R	5-9/180	27
51	Sunny Kim	R/R	6-1/185	28
	Ray King	L/L	6-1/242	32
	Jose Mesa	R/R	6-3/232	39
65	Juan Morillo	R/R	6-3/190	22
	Ramon Ramirez	R/R	5-11/190	24
	Eduardo Sierra	R/R	6-3/185	23
23	Ryan Speier	R/R	6-7/200	26
71	Chin-hui Tsao	R/R	6-2/190	24

No.	CATCHERS	B/T	Ht./Wt.	Age*
55	Danny Ardoin	R/R	6-0/218	31
7	JD Closser	B/R	5-10/195	26
	Yorvit Torrealba	R/R	5-11/190	27

No.	INFIELDERS	B/T	Ht./Wt.	Age*
27	Garrett Atkins	R/R	6-3/210	26
10	Jeff Baker	R/R	6-2/210	24
12	Clint Barmes	R/R	6-0/190	27
4	Luis A. Gonzalez	R/R	5-11/200	26
17	Todd Helton	L/L	6-2/210	32
66	Jayson Nix	R/R	5-11/185	23
8	Omar Quintanilla	L/R	5-9/190	24
38	Ryan Shealy	R/R	6-5/240	26
	Josh Wilson	R/R	6-1/180	25

No.	OUTFIELDERS	B/T	Ht./Wt.	Age*
21	Choo Freeman	R/R	6-2/200	26
11	Brad Hawpe	L/L	6-3/205	26
5	Matt Holliday	R/R	6-4/235	26
3	Jorge Piedra	L/L	6-0/200	26
64	Jeff Salazar	L/L	6-0/190	25
31	Cory Sullivan	L/L	6-0/180	26

*Age as of April 1, 2006.

Ballpark (capacity, surface)
Coors Field (50,449, grass)
Address
2001 Blake St.
Denver, CO 80205-2000
Official website
www.coloradorockies.com
Business phone
303-292-0200
Ticket information
800-388-7625
Field dimensions (from home plate)
To left field at foul line, 347 feet
To center field, 415 feet
To right field at foul line, 350
First game played
April 26, 1995 (Rockies 11, Mets 9, 14 innings)

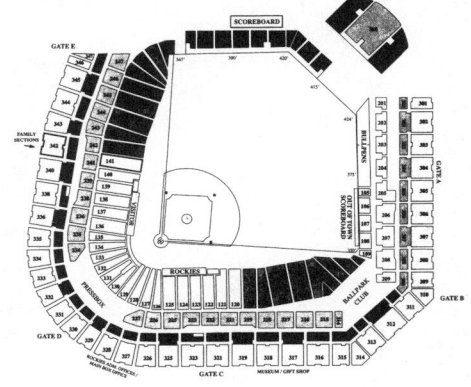

2006 SEASON *Colorado Rockies*

2005 REVIEW
DAY BY DAY

Date	Opp.	Res.	Score	(inn.*)	Hits	Opp. hits	Winning pitcher	Losing pitcher	Save	Record	Pos.	GB
4-4	S.D.	W	12-10		18	12	Speier	Hoffman		1-0	1st	+0.5
4-6	S.D.	L	6-14		11	13	Hammond	Jennings		1-1	T2nd	0.5
4-8	At S.F.	L	8-10		9	14	Christiansen	Fuentes		1-2	5th	1.5
4-9	At S.F.	L	2-4		6	5	Eyre	Dohmann	Benitez	1-3	5th	2.5
4-10	At S.F.	L	4-11		10	15	Schmidt	Kennedy		1-4	5th	2.5
4-11	At Ari.	L	0-2		7	4	Halsey	Jennings	Lyon	1-5	5th	3.0
4-12	At Ari.	L	2-4		9	9	Webb	Fuentes	Lyon	1-6	5th	4.0
4-13	At Ari.	L	2-5		6	7	Estes	Kim	Bruney	1-7	5th	5.0
4-15	S.F.	L	6-13		14	17	Lowry	Wright		1-8	5th	6.0
4-16	S.F.	W	5-4		10	11	Kennedy	Schmidt	Tsao	2-8	5th	6.0
4-17	S.F.	L	6-8		13	9	Herges	Kim	Benitez	2-9	5th	7.0
4-18	Ari.	L	3-5		7	11	Webb	Speier	Lyon	2-10	5th	8.0
4-19	Ari.	W	8-1		12	5	Francis	Estes		3-10	5th	8.0
4-20	At Phi.	W	7-4		16	9	Wright	Lidle		4-10	5th	8.0
4-21	At Phi.	L	3-6		9	10	Lieber	Kennedy	Wagner	4-11	5th	8.0
4-22	L.A.	W	9-1		16	10	Jennings	Weaver		5-11	5th	7.0
4-23	L.A.	W	8-6		11	12	Chacon	Perez	Tsao	6-11	5th	6.0
4-24	L.A.	L	6-8		11	11	Carrara	Kim	Brazoban	6-12	5th	7.0
4-26	Fla.	L	3-9		9	15	Beckett	Wright		6-13	5th	6.5
4-29	At L.A.	L	3-6		7	5	Perez	Jennings	Brazoban	6-14	5th	7.0
4-30	At L.A.	L	2-6		7	6	Penny	Kennedy	Brazoban	6-15	5th	8.0
5-1	At L.A.	L	1-2		6	4	Lowe	Chacon	Brazoban	6-16	5th	9.0
5-2	At S.D.	L	4-5		9	8	Eaton	Francis	Hoffman	6-17	5th	9.0
5-3	At S.D.	L	1-2		6	9	Otsuka	Witasick	Hoffman	6-18	5th	10.0
5-4	At S.D.	L	7-8	(12)	9	10	Reyes	Carvajal		6-19	5th	10.0
5-6	At Fla.	L	0-7		5	12	Willis	Kennedy		6-20	5th	11.0
5-7	At Fla.	L	1-4		7	8	Beckett	Chacon	Jones	6-21	5th	11.0
5-8	At Fla.	W	8-3		8	9	Francis	Leiter		7-21	5th	11.0
5-9	Atl.	W	7-6		12	12	Wright	Hudson	Tsao	8-21	5th	10.0
5-10	Atl.	L	5-9		10	14	Sosa	Jennings		8-22	5th	11.0
5-11	Atl.	W	6-5		12	8	Tsao	Kolb		9-22	5th	10.0
5-12	Ari.	L	3-6		11	9	Ortiz	Chacon		9-23	5th	10.0
5-13	Ari.	W	18-3		19	9	Francis	Halsey		10-23	5th	10.0
5-14	Ari.	L	4-10		9	12	Webb	Wright		10-24	5th	10.0
5-15	Ari.	L	4-5		9	8	Estes	Jennings	Bruney	10-25	5th	11.0
5-17	S.F.	W	9-4		13	14	Kennedy	Lowry		11-25	5th	11.0
5-18	S.F.	L	2-3		9	8	Brower	Fuentes	Walker	11-26	5th	12.0
5-19	S.F.	W	3-1		8	10	Francis	Tomko	Fuentes	12-26	5th	11.5
5-20	At Pit.	L	4-9		10	12	Redman	Wright		12-27	5th	12.5
5-21	At Pit.	L	3-8		3	11	Perez	Jennings	Gonzalez	12-28	5th	12.5
5-22	At Pit.	W	4-3		7	6	Kennedy	Fogg	Fuentes	13-28	5th	12.0
5-23	At Mil.	L	1-2		3	5	Capuano	Chacon	Bottalico	13-29	5th	12.5
5-24	At Mil.	L	1-6		7	11	Santos	Francis		13-30	5th	13.0
5-25	At Mil.	L	1-11		4	14	Glover	Wright		13-31	5th	13.5
5-26	At Chi.	W	5-2		7	8	Jennings	Zambrano		14-31	5th	13.0
5-27	At Chi.	L	3-10		6	11	Wellemeyer	Kennedy		14-32	5th	14.0
5-28	At Chi.	L	1-5		6	10	Rusch	Kim		14-33	5th	15.0
5-29	At Chi.	L	6-11		11	15	Novoa	Carvajal		14-34	5th	16.0
5-30	StL.	L	4-5		7	9	Marquis	Witasick	Isringhausen	14-35	5th	17.0
5-31	StL.	W	2-1		9	7	Jennings	Mulder	Fuentes	15-35	5th	17.0
6-1	StL.	L	6-8		12	17	Morris	Neal	Isringhausen	15-36	5th	17.0
6-2	StL.	W	8-7		12	11	Fuentes	Isringhausen		16-36	5th	16.0
6-3	Cin.	W	12-4		19	7	Francis	Milton		17-36	5th	16.0
6-4	Cin.	W	7-5		11	12	Wright	Harang	Fuentes	18-36	5th	15.0
6-5	Cin.	W	8-6		14	13	Neal	Wagner	Fuentes	19-36	5th	14.0
6-6	Chi.	L	3-9		2	15	Garcia	Kennedy		19-37	5th	14.5
6-7	Chi.	L	1-2		5	5	Contreras	Kim	Hermanson	19-38	5th	14.5
6-8	Chi.	L	5-15		8	22	Hernandez	Francis		19-39	5th	14.5
6-10	Det.	W	2-0		7	7	Wright	Maroth	Fuentes	20-39	5th	14.0
6-11	Det.	L	4-6		9	12	Bonderman	Jennings	Percival	20-40	5th	15.0
6-12	Det.	W	7-3		11	6	Kim	Robertson		21-40	5th	14.0
6-14	At Cle.	L	2-11		9	15	Westbrook	Francis		21-41	5th	14.0
6-15	At Cle.	L	6-7	(11)	11	11	Howry	Neal		21-42	5th	14.0
6-16	At Cle.	L	1-2		7	6	Millwood	Wright	Wickman	21-43	5th	14.0
6-17	At Bal.	W	2-1		8	7	Jennings	Cabrera	Fuentes	22-43	5th	13.0
6-18	At Bal.	L	2-7		9	13	Ponson	Kim		22-44	5th	14.0
6-19	At Bal.	L	2-4		5	11	Penn	Francis	Ryan	22-45	5th	15.0

Date	Opp.	Res.	Score	(inn.*)	Hits	Opp. hits	Winning pitcher	Losing pitcher	Save	Record	Pos.	GB
6-20	At Hou.	L	0-7		5	10	Pettitte	Kennedy		22-46	5th	16.0
6-21	At Hou.	L	5-6		8	9	Qualls	Wright	Lidge	22-47	5th	17.0
6-22	At Hou.	L	2-6		6	6	Clemens	Jennings		22-48	5th	17.0
6-24	K.C.	W	12-4		13	9	Kim	Carrasco		23-48	5th	15.5
6-25	K.C.	W	4-2		7	6	Francis	Hernandez	Fuentes	24-48	5th	15.5
6-26	K.C.	W	9-4		12	10	Kennedy	Lima		25-48	5th	15.5
6-27	Hou.	L	5-11		11	18	Rodriguez	Wright		25-49	5th	15.5
6-28	Hou.	W	6-5		8	9	Cortes	Springer	Fuentes	26-49	5th	15.5
6-29	Hou.	L	1-7		8	12	Oswalt	Kim		26-50	5th	15.5
6-30	At StL.	W	7-0		13	6	Francis	Suppan		27-50	5th	15.0
7-1	At StL.	L	0-6		5	11	Carpenter	Kennedy		27-51	5th	15.0
7-2	At StL.	W	3-1		8	8	Wright	Marquis	Fuentes	28-51	5th	15.0
7-3	At StL.	L	4-5		7	9	King	Witasick		28-52	5th	16.0
7-4	L.A.	L	3-4	(11)	7	12	Carrara	Witasick	Brazoban	28-53	5th	16.0
7-5	L.A.	W	6-1		12	12	Francis	Perez		29-53	5th	15.0
7-6	L.A.	L	5-9		13	11	Penny	Chacon		29-54	5th	15.0
7-7	L.A.	W	8-5		7	11	DeJean	Carrara	Fuentes	30-54	5th	15.0
7-8	S.D.	L	2-12		7	14	Stauffer	Wright		30-55	5th	16.0
7-9	S.D.	W	1-0		7	7	Jennings	Lawrence	Fuentes	31-55	5th	15.0
7-10	S.D.	L	5-8		14	9	Quantrill	Francis	Hoffman	31-56	5th	16.0
7-15	At Cin.	L	3-4		6	7	Harang	Jennings	Weathers	31-57	5th	16.5
7-16	At Cin.	L	6-7		12	9	Standridge	Miceli	Weathers	31-58	5th	17.5
7-17	At Cin.	L	4-9		11	6	Ortiz	Wright		31-59	5th	17.5
7-18	At Was.	W	5-4		9	9	Acevedo	Cordero	Fuentes	32-59	5th	17.0
7-19	At Was.	L	0-4		4	10	Patterson	Chacon	Cordero	32-60	5th	17.0
7-20	At Was.	W	3-2		9	8	Jennings	Hernandez	Fuentes	33-60	5th	16.0
7-21	At Pit.	L	1-8		10	13	Duke	Francis		33-61	5th	16.0
7-22	At Pit.	W	5-3	(10)	9	13	Fuentes	Mesa	Cortes	34-61	5th	15.0
7-23	At Pit.	L	3-5		3	7	Williams	Kim	Mesa	34-62	5th	15.0
7-24	At Pit.	L	0-3		7	8	Redman	Chacon	Mesa	34-63	5th	15.0
7-25	N.Y.	W	5-3		11	6	Acevedo	Glavine	Fuentes	35-63	5th	14.5
7-26	N.Y.	W	4-3		8	9	Francis	Ishii	Fuentes	36-63	5th	13.5
7-27	N.Y.	L	3-9		9	13	Zambrano	Wright		36-64	5th	14.5
7-28	Phi.	L	5-8		9	12	Urbina	DeJean	Wagner	36-65	5th	14.5
7-29	Phi.	L	3-5		7	9	Myers	Acevedo	Wagner	36-66	5th	14.5
7-30	Phi.	L	7-8		11	15	Lidle	Cook	Wagner	36-67	5th	14.5
7-31	Phi.	W	9-2		10	8	Francis	Lieber		37-67	5th	13.5
8-2	At S.F.	W	4-3		9	4	Wright	Tomko	Fuentes	38-67	5th	13.5
8-3	At S.F.	W	3-2		7	6	Miceli	Walker	Fuentes	39-67	5th	12.5
8-4	At S.F.	L	4-6		10	10	Munter	Miceli	Walker	39-68	5th	13.5
8-5	At Ari.	W	6-4		6	7	DeJean	Cormier	Fuentes	40-68	5th	13.5
8-6	At Ari.	W	14-7		16	12	Francis	Gosling		41-68	5th	13.5
8-7	At Ari.	L	4-9		5	14	Vargas	Wright		41-69	5th	14.5
8-8!	Fla.	W	4-3	(11)	10	8	Dohmann	de los Santos		42-69		
8-8&	Fla.	W	5-3		12	5	Kim	Valdez	Fuentes	43-69	5th	13.5
8-9	Pit.	L	4-12		11	19	Williams	Acevedo		43-70	5th	14.5
8-10	Pit.	W	6-5	(10)	8	7	Cortes	White		44-70	5th	13.5
8-11	Pit.	L	3-11		7	17	Fogg	Francis		44-71	5th	14.5
8-12	Was.	L	2-4		7	7	Loaiza	Wright	Cordero	44-72	5th	14.5
8-13	Was.	L	0-8		13	13	Armas	Kim		44-73	5th	14.5
8-14	Was.	L	2-9		11	10	Patterson	Acevedo		44-74	5th	14.5
8-15	Mil.	W	11-2		17	9	Cook	Sheets		45-74	5th	14.0
8-16	Mil.	L	4-6		9	9	Santos	Francis	Turnbow	45-75	5th	15.0
8-17	Mil.	L	0-2		8	5	Capuano	Wright	Turnbow	45-76	5th	15.0
8-19	Chi.	L	3-5		6	10	Prior	Kim	Dempster	45-77	5th	15.5
8-20	Chi.	W	4-2		9	11	Cook	Rusch	Fuentes	46-77	5th	15.5
8-21	Chi.	W	9-7		10	14	Kim	Maddux		47-77	5th	14.5
8-23	At L.A.	L	3-8		7	10	Weaver	Wright		47-78	5th	15.0
8-24	At L.A.	W	2-1		6	7	Williams	Schmoll	Fuentes	48-78	5th	15.0
8-25	At L.A.	W	5-4		5	10	Cook	Penny	Fuentes	49-78	5th	14.5
8-26	At S.D.	W	4-3		7	7	Francis	Eaton	Fuentes	50-78	5th	13.5
8-27	At S.D.	W	4-2		7	8	Kim	Lawrence	Cortes	51-78	5th	12.5
8-28	At S.D.	L	3-4		6	7	Astacio	Wright	Hoffman	51-79	5th	13.5
8-29	At S.F.	W	2-1		7	5	Kim	Cain	Fuentes	52-79	5th	12.5
8-30	At S.F.	L	3-4		8	11	Taschner	DeJean	Benitez	52-80	5th	13.5
8-31	At S.F.	L	3-5		11	8	Fassero	Francis	Benitez	52-81	5th	14.5
9-2	L.A.	W	11-3		13	9	Kim	Weaver	Acevedo	53-81	5th	14.0
9-3	L.A.	W	11-1		14	6	Kim	Houlton		54-81	5th	14.0
9-4	L.A.	W	7-6	(10)	11	13	Dohmann	Sanchez		55-81	5th	13.0
9-6	At S.D.	W	6-5		6	11	Cook	Park	Fuentes	56-81	5th	12.0

Date	Opp.	Res.	Score	(inn.*)	Hits	Opp. hits	Winning pitcher	Losing pitcher	Save	Record	Pos.	GB
9-7	At S.D.	L	2-4		6	8	Eaton	Francis	Hoffman	56-82	5th	13.0
9-8	At S.D.	L	2-3	(10)	5	8	Linebrink	Acevedo		56-83	5th	14.0
9-9	Ari.	L	1-7		7	15	Estes	Kim		56-84	5th	15.0
9-10	Ari.	L	5-8		11	12	Vargas	Day	Valverde	56-85	5th	15.0
9-11	Ari.	W	7-2		10	8	Cook	Ortiz		57-85	5th	14.0
9-12	At L.A.	L	0-7		3	12	Weaver	Francis		57-86	5th	14.0
9-13	At L.A.	W	6-4		6	7	Kim	Jackson	Fuentes	58-86	5th	13.0
9-14	At L.A.	W	8-7		12	8	Wright	Brazoban	Fuentes	59-86	5th	13.0
9-16	At Ari.	W	6-5		7	11	Williams	Medders	Fuentes	60-86	5th	12.0
9-17	At Ari.	L	5-6		9	11	Villarreal	Williams	Valverde	60-87	5th	13.0
9-18	At Ari.	W	7-1		11	6	Francis	Ortiz		61-87	5th	13.0
9-19	S.D.	L	7-8		15	14	Linebrink	Fuentes	Hoffman	61-88	5th	14.0
9-20	S.D.	W	20-1		23	6	Wright	Williams		62-88	5th	13.0
9-21	S.D.	L	2-5		8	11	Peavy	Esposito	Hoffman	62-89	5th	13.0
9-22	S.D.	W	4-2		8	11	Cook	Eaton	Fuentes	63-89	5th	13.0
9-23	S.F.	L	6-7		14	11	Accardo	DeJean	Walker	63-90	5th	14.0
9-24	S.F.	W	6-0		9	3	Kim	Lowry		64-90	5th	13.0
9-25	S.F.	L	2-6		5	12	Walker	Fuentes		64-91	5th	13.0
9-26	At Atl.	W	6-5		15	11	Speier	Reitsma	Fuentes	65-91	5th	12.0
9-27	At Atl.	L	3-12		6	13	Hudson	Cook		65-92	5th	13.0
9-28	At Atl.	W	10-5		15	11	Francis	Davies		66-92	5th	13.0
9-29	At N.Y.	L	0-11		2	15	Glavine	Kim		66-93	5th	14.0
9-30	At N.Y.	L	2-3		6	7	Benson	Kim	Heilman	66-94	5th	15.0
10-1	At N.Y.	L	1-3		7	6	Seo	Esposito	Hernandez	66-95	5th	15.0
10-2	At N.Y.	W	11-3		16	10	Cook	Zambrano		67-95	5th	15.0

Monthly records: April (6-15), May (9-20), June (12-15), July (10-17), August (15-14), September (14-13), October (1-1).
*Innings, if other than nine. ! First game of a doubleheader. & Second game of a doubleheader.

RECORDS

2005 regular-season record: 67-95
Position: 5th in N.L. West
Home: 40-41   **Road:** 27-54
N.L. East: 14-17   **N.L. Central:** 15-28
N.L. West: 32-41   **A.L.** 6-9
Vs. LH starters: 18-25
Vs. RH starters: 49-70
Grass: 67-95   **Artificial:** 0-0
Day: 22-30   **Night:** 45-65
1-Run: 25-24   **X-inn.:** 4-4
Doubleheaders: 1-0-0
Team record past five years: 355-455
(.438, ranks 14th in league in that span)

TEAM LEADERS

Batting average: Todd Helton (.320).
At-bats: Garrett Atkins (519).
Runs: Todd Helton (92).
Hits: Todd Helton (163).
Total Bases: Todd Helton (272).
Doubles: Todd Helton (45).
Triples: Matt Holliday (7).
Home runs: Todd Helton (20).
Runs batted in: Garrett Atkins (89).
Stolen bases: Matt Holliday (14).
Slugging percentage: Todd Helton (.534).
On-base percentage: Todd Helton (.445).
Wins: Jeff Francis (14).
Earned-run average: Byung-Hyun Kim (4.86).

Complete games: Aaron Cook (2).
Shutouts: Sunny Kim (1).
Saves: Brian Fuentes (31).
Innings pitched: Jeff Francis (183.2).
Strikeouts: Jeff Francis (128).

GAMES BY POSITION

Catcher: Danny Ardoin 80, JD Closser 80, Todd Greene 33.

First base: Todd Helton 144, Ryan Shealy 19, Luis A. Gonzalez 10.

Second base: Luis A. Gonzalez 83, Aaron Miles 79, Eddy Garabito 18, Desi Relaford 11, Omar Quintanilla 6.

Third base: Garrett Atkins 136, Desi Relaford 21, Luis A. Gonzalez 12, Jeff Baker 10, Alfredo Amezaga 1.

Shortstop: Clint Barmes 80, Desi Relaford 37, Omar Quintanilla 31, Luis A. Gonzalez 17, Anderson Machado 4, Eddy Garabito 2, Aaron Miles 1.

Outfield: Matt Holliday 123, Cory Sullivan 114, Brad Hawpe 89, Dustan Mohr 76, Preston Wilson 69, Jorge Piedra 26, Larry Bigbie 15, Eric Byrnes 14, Luis A. Gonzalez 8, Michael Restovich 8, Choo Freeman 6, Desi Relaford 4, Ryan Spilborghs 1.

Designated hitter: Ryan Shealy 5, Tim Olson 1, Jorge Piedra 1.

TOP DRAFT CHOICES

1a. **Troy Tulowitzki,** SS, Long Beach State.
1b. **Chaz Roe,** RHP, Lafayette H.S., Lexington, Ky.
2a. **Daniel Carte,** OF, Winthrop..
2b. **Zach Simons,** RHP, Everett (Wash.) CC.
3. **Kyle Hancock,** RHP, Rowlett (Texas) H.S.
4. **Brandon Durden,** LHP, Georgia College.
5. **Josh Sullivan,** RHP, Auburn.
6. **Corey Wimberly,** 2B, Alcorn State.
7. **Geoff Strickland,** SS, Florida Southern.
8. **James Burok,** RHP, Old Dominion.
9. **Andrew Johnston,** RHP, Missouri.
10. **Garner Wetzel,** SS, Millsaps.

FLORIDA MARLINS
NATIONAL LEAGUE EAST DIVISION

2006 SEASON

Marlins Schedule
Home games shaded.
All-Star Game July 11 at Pittsburgh. Schedule subject to change.

APRIL

SUN	MON	TUE	WED	THU	FRI	SAT
2	3 HOU	4 HOU	5 HOU	6	7 NYM	8 NYM
9 NYM	10	11 SD	12 SD	13 SD	14 WAS	15 WAS
16 WAS	17 CIN	18 CIN	19 CIN	20	21 PHI	22 PHI
23 PHI	24 CHC	25 CHC	26 CHC	27	28 COL	29 COL
30 COL						

MAY

SUN	MON	TUE	WED	THU	FRI	SAT
	1 PHI	2 PHI	3 WAS	4 WAS	5 STL	6 STL
7 STL	8	9 ATL	10 ATL	11 PIT	12 PIT	13 PIT
14 PIT	15 ATL	16 ATL	17 ATL	18 ATL	19 TB	20 TB
21 TB	22 CHC	23 CHC	24 CHC	25	26 NYM	27 NYM
28 NYM	29 SF	30 SF	31 SF			

JUNE

SUN	MON	TUE	WED	THU	FRI	SAT
				1	2 COL	3 COL
4 COL	5 SF	6 SF	7 SF	8	9 SD	10 SD
11 SD	12	13 ATL	14 ATL	15 ATL	16 TOR	17 TOR
18 TOR	19	20 BAL	21 BAL	22 BAL	23 NYY	24 NYY
25 NYY	26 TB	27 TB	28 TB	29	30 BOS	

JULY

SUN	MON	TUE	WED	THU	FRI	SAT
						1 BOS
2 BOS	3 WAS	4 WAS	5 WAS	6 WAS	7 NYM	8 NYM
9 NYM	10	11 ALL-STAR	12	13 HOU	14 HOU	15 HOU
16 HOU	17 WAS	18 WAS	19 WAS	20 PIT	21 PIT	22 PIT
23 PIT	24	25 ATL	26 ATL	27 ATL	28 PHI	29 PHI
30 PHI	31 PHI					

AUGUST

SUN	MON	TUE	WED	THU	FRI	SAT
		1 NYM	2 NYM	3 NYM	4 LAD	5 LAD
6 LAD	7	8 WAS	9 WAS	10 WAS	11 ARI	12 ARI
13 ARI	14 LAD	15 LAD	16 LAD	17	18 ATL	19 ATL
20 ATL	21 WAS	22 WAS	23 WAS	24	25 MIL	26 MIL
27 MIL	28 MIL	29 STL	30 STL	31 STL		

SEPTEMBER

SUN	MON	TUE	WED	THU	FRI	SAT
					1 MIL	2 MIL
3 MIL	4 ARI	5 ARI	6 ARI	7 PHI	8 PHI	9 PHI
10 PHI	11 NYM	12 NYM	13 NYM	14	15 ATL	16 ATL
17 ATL	18 NYM	19 NYM	20 NYM	21 NYM	22 PHI	23 PHI
24 PHI	25	26 CIN	27 CIN	28 CIN	29 PHI	30 PHI

OCTOBER

SUN	MON	TUE	WED	THU	FRI	SAT
1 PHI	2	3	4	5	6	7

Home games are shaded. All-Star Game is July 11 at Pittsburgh. Schedule is subject to change.

Willis

CLUB DIRECTORY

Owner/chief executive officer
Jeffrey H. Loria
President
David P. Samson
Vice chairman
Joel A. Mael
Executive v.p., chief financial officer
Michel Bussiere
Senior vice president, stadium development
Claude Delorme
Special assistants to the president
Andre Dawson, Tony Perez
Executive v.p. and general manager
Larry Beinfest
Sr. v.p., communications and broadcasting
P.J. Loyello
Vice president, player personnel
Dan Jennings

Vice president/assistant general manager
Michael Hill
V.p., player dev. and scouting/assistant g.m.
Jim Fleming
Vice president, new business development
Dale Hendricks
Vice president, marketing
Sean Flynn
Senior director, team travel
Bill Beck
Special assistant to the g.m./pro scout
Orrin Freeman
Director of player development
Brian Chattin
Director, media relations
Matt Roebuck

MINOR LEAGUE AFFILIATES

Class	Team	League	Manager
AAA	Albuquerque	Pacific Coast	Dean Treanor
AA	Carolina	Southern	Luis Dorante
Advanced A	Jupiter	Florida State	Tim Cossins
A	Greensboro	South Atlantic	Brandon Hyde
Short-Season A	Jamestown	New York-Pennsylvania	Bo Porter
Rookie	Marlins	Gulf Coast	Edwin Rodriguez

BROADCAST INFORMATION

Radio: WQAM 560-AM, WQBA 1140-AM (Spanish).
TV: PAX-TV.
Cable TV: Fox Sports Net Florida.

SPRING TRAINING

Ballpark (city): Roger Dean Stadium (Jupiter, Fla.).
Ticket information: 561-775-1818.

For more on the Marlins, go to **www.sportingnews.com/baseball/teams/marlins/**

Manager—Joe Girardi (25).
Coaches—Pierre Arsenault (67), Mike Harkey, Perry Hill (7), Rick Kranitz, Bobby Meacham, Jim Presley, Gary Tuck.

No.	PITCHERS	B/T	Ht./Wt.	Age*
	Allen Baxter	R/R	6-4/215	22
	Joe Borowski	R/R	6-2/225	34
	Adam Bostick	L/L	6-1/220	23
	Travis Bowyer	R/R	6-3/210	24
40	Nate Bump	L/R	6-2/196	29
	Jesus Delgado	R/R	6-1/200	21
	Harvey Garcia	R/R	6-2/170	22
	Jose Garcia	R/R	5-11/165	21
55	Josh Johnson	L/R	6-7/240	22
54	Logan Kensing	R/R	6-1/185	23
	Carlos Martinez	R/R	6-1/170	20
	Michael Megrew	L/L	6-6/210	22
23	Randy Messenger	R/R	6-6/247	24
	Sergio Mitre	R/R	6-4/210	25
36	Brian Moehler	R/R	6-3/235	34
	Ricky Nolasco	R/R	6-2/220	23
48	Scott Olsen	L/L	6-4/198	22
	Yusmeiro Petit	R/R	6-0/230	21
	Renyel Pinto	L/L	6-4/195	23
51	Chris Resop	R/R	6-3/222	23
	Anibal Sanchez	R/R	6-0/180	22
	Scott Tyler	R/R	6-5/265	23
56	Jason Vargas	L/L	6-0/215	23
35	Dontrelle Willis	L/L	6-4/239	24

No.	CATCHERS	B/T	Ht./Wt.	Age*
	Miguel Olivo	R/R	6-0/215	27
6	Matt Treanor	R/R	6-2/220	30
14	Josh Willingham	R/R	6-1/200	27

No.	INFIELDERS	B/T	Ht./Wt.	Age*
	Alfredo Amezaga	B/R	5-10/165	28
4	Robert Andino	R/R	6-0/170	21
24	Miguel Cabrera	R/R	6-2/210	22
	Wes Helms	R/R	6-4/231	29
	Mike Jacobs	L/R	6-2/200	25
	Hanley Ramirez	R/R	6-3/195	22
	Pokey Reese	R/R	5-11/190	32
60	Jason Stokes	R/R	6-4/225	24
	Daniel Uggla	R/R	5-10/200	26

No.	OUTFIELDERS	B/T	Ht./Wt.	Age*
	Reggie Abercrombie	R/R	6-3/225	25
3	Chris Aguila	R/R	5-11/180	27
27	Jeremy Hermida	L/R	6-4/200	22
	Eric Reed	L/L	5-11/170	25

*Age as of April 1, 2006.

BALLPARK INFORMATION

Ballpark (capacity, surface)
Dolphins Stadium (36,331, grass)
Address
2267 Dan Marino Blvd.
Miami, Fla. 33056
Official website
www.floridamarlins.com
Business phone
305-626-7400
Ticket information
1-877-MARLINS
Field dimensions (from home plate)
To left field at foul line, 330 feet
To center field, 434 feet
To right field at foul line, 345 feet
First game played
April 5, 1993 (Marlins 6, Dodgers 3)

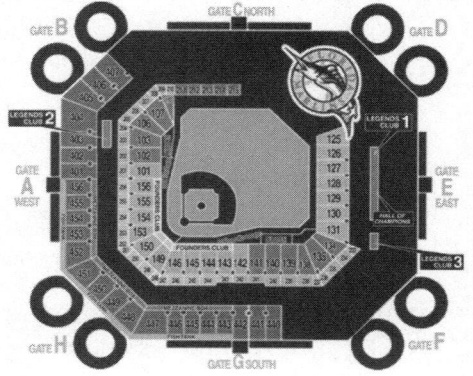

2006 SEASON Florida Marlins

Date	Opp.	Res.	Score	(inn.*)	Hits	Opp. hits	Winning pitcher	Losing pitcher	Save	Record	Pos.	GB
4-5	Atl.	W	9-0		13	5	Beckett	Smoltz		1-0	T1st	...
4-6	Atl.	L	1-2	(13)	10	10	Bernero	Bump	Kolb	1-1	T1st	...
4-7	Atl.	L	2-4		9	8	Hudson	Burnett	Kolb	1-2	T3rd	1.0
4-8	Was.	W	9-0		10	5	Willis	Ohka		2-2	T2nd	1.0
4-9	Was.	L	2-3	(10)	8	7	Cordero	Alfonseca		2-3	T3rd	2.0
4-10	Was.	W	8-0		12	5	Beckett	Patterson		3-3	T2nd	1.0
4-11	Phi.	L	1-4		5	7	Myers	Leiter	Wagner	3-4	T3rd	2.0
4-12	Phi.	W	8-2		11	8	Burnett	Wolf		4-4	T2nd	1.0
4-13	Phi.	W	4-0		8	3	Willis	Lidle		5-4	T1st	...
4-15	At N.Y.	L	0-4		1	5	Heilman	Beckett		5-5	T3rd	1.0
4-16	At N.Y.	L	3-4		6	8	Looper	Mota		5-6	T4th	2.0
4-17	At N.Y.	W	5-2		9	4	Burnett	Glavine		6-6	T2nd	2.0
4-18	At Was.	W	9-4		12	8	Willis	Ohka		7-6	T2nd	1.0
4-19	At Was.	W	6-3		10	10	Moehler	Hernandez		8-6	T1st	...
4-20	N.Y.	W	9-2		15	4	Beckett	Heilman		9-6	T1st	...
4-21	N.Y.	L	1-10		6	10	Martinez	Leiter		9-7	T1st	...
4-22	Cin.	W	4-2		12	5	Perisho	Mercker	Mota	10-7	1st	+1.0
4-23	Cin.	W	4-2		8	9	Willis	Belisle	Mota	11-7	1st	+1.0
4-24	Cin.	L	1-2		4	9	Claussen	Moehler	Graves	11-8	T1st	...
4-26	At Col.	W	9-3		15	9	Beckett	Wright		12-8	1st	+0.5
4-29	At Phi.	W	6-4		14	10	Burnett	Wolf	Jones	13-8	1st	+1.0
4-30	At Phi.	W	2-1	(6)	2	3	Willis	Padilla		14-8	1st	+1.0
5-1	At Phi.	L	6-8		12	13	Lidle	Beckett	Wagner	14-9	1st	...
5-3	At Atl.	W	11-6		13	6	Leiter	Hampton		15-9	1st	+1.0
5-4	At Atl.	L	2-5		6	13	Hudson	Burnett	Kolb	15-10	1st	...
5-6	Col.	W	7-0		12	5	Willis	Kennedy		16-10	2nd	0.5
5-7	Col.	W	4-1		8	7	Beckett	Chacon	Jones	17-10	2nd	0.5
5-8	Col.	L	3-8		9	8	Francis	Leiter		17-11	2nd	1.5
5-9	Hou.	L	1-2		5	6	Clemens	Burnett	Lidge	17-12	2nd	1.5
5-10	Hou.	W	6-2		10	7	Mecir	Springer		18-12	2nd	1.5
5-11	Hou.	W	2-1		5	7	Willis	Oswalt	Jones	19-12	2nd	0.5
5-13	At S.D.	L	2-3		7	9	Eaton	Beckett	Hoffman	19-13	2nd	0.5
5-14	At S.D.	L	1-2		5	3	Peavy	Leiter	Hoffman	19-14	2nd	1.5
5-15	At S.D.	L	4-12		10	15	Seanez	Burnett		19-15	2nd	2.5
5-16	At L.A.	W	6-2		16	10	Moehler	Penny		20-15	2nd	1.5
5-17	At L.A.	L	5-14		7	19	Lowe	Willis		20-16	2nd	1.5
5-18	At L.A.	W	8-3		13	7	Beckett	Weaver		21-16	2nd	0.5
5-20	T.B.	W	7-6		12	13	Leiter	Nomo	Jones	22-16	1st	+0.5
5-21	T.B.	W	4-3		8	7	Perisho	Colome	Jones	23-16	1st	+0.5
5-22	T.B.	W	8-5		9	13	Riedling	Fossum	Jones	24-16	1st	+1.5
5-23	Phi.	W	5-2		10	8	Willis	Lieber	Jones	25-16	1st	+1.5
5-24	Phi.	W	4-3	(10)	6	8	Riedling	Telemaco		26-16	1st	+1.5
5-25	Phi.	L	5-8		10	17	Wolf	Leiter	Wagner	26-17	1st	+0.5
5-26	N.Y.	L	4-12		9	14	Benson	Castillo		26-18	1st	...
5-27	N.Y.	L	0-1		5	5	Martinez	Moehler	Looper	26-19	1st	...
5-28	N.Y.	L	1-6		9	14	Ishii	Willis		26-20	1st	...
5-29	N.Y.	W	6-3		15	6	Beckett	Bell	Jones	27-20	1st	...
5-30	At Pit.	L	2-3	(10)	7	8	White	Jones		27-21	1st	...
5-31	At Pit.	L	4-5		8	7	Meadows	Bump	Mesa	27-22	1st	...
6-1	At Pit.	L	1-9		7	15	Fogg	Moehler	Torres	27-23	2nd	1.0
6-2	At Pit.	W	6-3		13	9	Willis	Williams	Jones	28-23	1st	...
6-3	At Was.	L	2-3	(11)	8	4	Ayala	Bump		28-24	1st	...
6-4	At Was.	L	3-7		12	11	Kim	Leiter		28-25	3rd	1.0
6-5	At Was.	L	3-6		13	9	Ayala	Riedling	Cordero	28-26	5th	1.5
6-7	Sea.	L	3-4		6	9	Hasegawa	Mecir	Guardado	28-27	5th	2.5
6-8	Sea.	W	5-4		8	11	Willis	Meche	Jones	29-27	5th	2.5
6-9	Sea.	L	0-8		5	11	Sele	Beckett		29-28	5th	3.5
6-10	Tex.	W	12-5		17	11	Jones	Brocail		30-28	3rd	3.5
6-11	Tex.	W	6-5		9	9	Riedling	Dominguez	Jones	31-28	3rd	3.5
6-12	Tex.	L	2-6		7	9	Rodriguez	Moehler	Wasdin	31-29	3rd	4.5
6-13	At Chi.	W	9-1		11	8	Willis	Koronka		32-29	3rd	3.5
6-14	At Chi.	L	0-14		5	18	Mitre	Beckett		32-30	3rd	4.5
6-15	At Chi.	W	15-5		20	12	Burnett	Maddux		33-30	3rd	4.5
6-17	At L.A.	L	2-3	(11)	11	9	Shields	Mecir		33-31	4th	4.5
6-18	At L.A.	L	1-2	(10)	6	14	Rodriguez	Jones		33-32	4th	4.5
6-19	At L.A.	W	7-5		12	11	Leiter	Santana	Jones	34-32	4th	4.5
6-21	At Atl.	L	0-5		5	9	Smoltz	Burnett		34-33	4th	5.0

Date	Opp.	Res.	Score	(inn.*)	Hits	Opp. hits	Winning pitcher	Losing pitcher	Save	Record	Pos.	GB
6-22	At Atl.	L	0-8		4	11	Ramirez	Moehler		34-34	4th	6.0
6-23	At Atl.	W	8-0		13	5	Willis	Sosa		35-34	4th	5.5
6-24	At T.B.	W	7-4		11	5	Mota	Waechter	Jones	36-34	4th	5.5
6-25	At T.B.	W	6-2		14	6	Olsen	Fossum		37-34	3rd	5.5
6-26	At T.B.	W	1-0		3	2	Burnett	McClung		38-34	3rd	4.5
6-27	Atl.	L	2-7	(8)	6	12	Ramirez	Moehler		38-35	3rd	5.0
6-28	Atl.	L	1-9		6	16	Sosa	Willis		38-36	3rd	6.0
6-29	Atl.	W	6-5	(13)	17	12	Riedling	Bernero		39-36	3rd	6.0
6-30	Atl.	W	6-2		10	4	Beckett	Colon		40-36	3rd	6.0
7-1	At N.Y.	L	6-7		13	9	Hernandez	Mecir	Looper	40-37	3rd	7.0
7-2	At N.Y.	W	7-3		11	9	Moehler	Benson		41-37	3rd	7.0
7-3	At N.Y.	W	3-0		8	3	Willis	Zambrano		42-37	3rd	7.0
7-4	Mil.	L	2-3		5	7	Sheets	Jones	Turnbow	42-38	3rd	7.0
7-5	Mil.	L	4-6		10	16	Capuano	Beckett	Turnbow	42-39	3rd	8.0
7-6	Mil.	W	5-4	(12)	13	4	de los Santos	Obermueller		43-39	3rd	7.0
7-7	Mil.	W	11-3		12	5	Moehler	Santos		44-39	3rd	6.0
7-8	Chi.	L	6-9		8	13	Zambrano	Willis	Dempster	44-40	3rd	7.0
7-9	Chi.	L	2-8		6	10	Wood	Mota		44-41	3rd	7.0
7-10	Chi.	L	2-9		6	13	Maddux	Leiter		44-42	3rd	7.0
7-14	At Phi.	L	7-13		12	13	Myers	Burnett		44-43	4th	7.0
7-15	At Phi.	W	9-7		17	14	Moehler	Lidle	Jones	45-43	3rd	6.0
7-16	At Phi.	L	5-10		11	14	Lieber	Olsen		45-44	4th	7.0
7-17	At Phi.	L	4-8		7	11	Padilla	Willis		45-45	T4th	7.0
7-18	At Ari.	L	7-8	(11)	14	14	Medders	Jones		45-46	5th	7.0
7-19	At Ari.	W	6-3		11	8	Burnett	Vazquez	Jones	46-46	5th	7.0
7-20	At Ari.	W	9-2		14	13	Moehler	Webb		47-46	5th	6.0
7-22	At S.F.	L	5-8		12	8	Tomko	Willis	Walker	47-47	5th	5.5
7-23	At S.F.	W	16-4		20	7	Beckett	Hennessey		48-47	5th	5.5
7-24	At S.F.	W	4-1		7	8	Burnett	Correia	Jones	49-47	5th	4.5
7-26	Pit.	L	3-6		12	16	Fogg	Moehler	Mesa	49-48	5th	5.5
7-27	Pit.	W	3-1		6	7	Vargas	Vogelsong	Jones	50-48	4th	5.5
7-28	Pit.	W	3-0		6	4	Willis	Wells	Jones	51-48	3rd	5.5
7-29	Was.	W	4-3		9	7	Beckett	Armas	Jones	52-48	3rd	5.5
7-30	Was.	W	3-0		7	4	Burnett	Patterson	Jones	53-48	3rd	5.5
7-31	Was.	L	2-4		11	11	Hernandez	Moehler	Cordero	53-49	3rd	6.5
8-1	At StL.	W	6-5		13	11	Valdez	Marquis	Jones	54-49	3rd	5.5
8-2	At StL.	L	1-3		3	5	Carpenter	Willis		54-50	3rd	6.5
8-3	At StL.	L	6-9		10	11	Morris	Villone		54-51	4th	6.5
8-4	At StL.	W	4-3		10	8	Burnett	Suppan	Jones	55-51	4th	6.5
8-5	At Cin.	W	5-1		10	4	Vargas	Milton		56-51	3rd	5.5
8-6	At Cin.	L	3-4		5	8	Hudson	Moehler	Weathers	56-52	4th	6.5
8-7	At Cin.	W	2-0		12	4	Willis	Ortiz	Jones	57-52	2nd	5.5
8-8!	At Col.	L	3-4	(11)	8	10	Dohmann	de los Santos		57-53		
8-8&	At Col.	L	3-5		5	12	Kim	Valdez	Fuentes	57-54	T4th	6.5
8-9	Ari.	W	5-0		9	3	Burnett	Vazquez		58-54	4th	6.5
8-10	Ari.	W	10-5		12	8	Vargas	Halsey	Jones	59-54	T3rd	6.5
8-11	Ari.	L	1-3		4	10	Webb	de los Santos	Valverde	59-55	T3rd	6.5
8-12	S.F.	L	0-1		4	5	Lowry	Willis	Walker	59-56	4th	6.5
8-13	S.F.	W	2-1		9	4	Beckett	Tomko		60-56	4th	6.5
8-14	S.F.	W	4-1		7	8	Burnett	Hennessey	Jones	61-56	4th	6.5
8-16	S.D.	L	2-4		10	7	Lawrence	Vargas	Hoffman	61-57	4th	6.5
8-17	S.D.	W	6-0		6	5	Willis	Williams		62-57	4th	6.5
8-18	S.D.	W	2-0		6	6	Beckett	Peavy	Jones	63-57	4th	5.5
8-19	L.A.	W	3-0		4	6	Burnett	Houlton	Jones	64-57	2nd	4.5
8-20	L.A.	L	6-11		9	12	Dessens	Villone	Sanchez	64-58	3rd	4.5
8-21	L.A.	W	7-1		11	6	Vargas	Lowe		65-58	3rd	4.5
8-22	L.A.	W	5-2		9	6	Willis	Jackson	Jones	66-58	2nd	4.5
8-23	At Mil.	L	2-11		9	13	Capuano	Beckett		66-59	3rd	4.5
8-24	At Mil.	L	4-6		10	8	Ohka	Burnett	Turnbow	66-60	T3rd	5.5
8-25	At Mil.	W	3-1	(10)	8	11	Alfonseca	Capellan	Jones	67-60	T3rd	5.0
8-26	At Chi.	W	7-5		10	11	Vargas	Rusch	Jones	68-60	T3rd	4.0
8-27	At Chi.	W	2-1		5	7	Willis	Maddux	Jones	69-60	3rd	4.0
8-28	At Chi.	L	3-14		6	15	Zambrano	Beckett		69-61	3rd	5.0
8-29	StL.	L	1-6		8	10	Carpenter	Burnett		69-62	3rd	5.5
8-30	StL.	W	7-6		10	7	Mota	Morris	Jones	70-62	T2nd	4.5
8-31	StL.	L	5-10		8	15	Suppan	Vargas		70-63	3rd	5.0
9-2	N.Y.	W	4-2		12	8	Willis	Zambrano	Jones	71-63	3rd	5.5
9-3	N.Y.	W	5-4		7	9	Villone	Padilla	Jones	72-63	3rd	5.5
9-4	N.Y.	L	1-7		5	12	Seo	Burnett		72-64	3rd	5.5
9-5	At Was.	L	2-5		6	11	Hernandez	Vargas		72-65	3rd	6.5

Date	Opp.	Res.	Score	(inn.*)	Hits	Opp. hits	Winning pitcher	Losing pitcher	Save	Record	Pos.	GB
9-6	At Was.	W	4-2		10	5	Valdez	Rasner	Jones	73-65	2nd	6.5
9-7	At Was.	W	12-1		17	5	Willis	Halama		74-65	2nd	6.5
9-8	At Was.	W	8-4		14	10	Beckett	Patterson		75-65	2nd	6.0
9-9	At Phi.	L	5-12		15	12	Lidle	Burnett		75-66	2nd	6.0
9-10	At Phi.	W	7-6		14	11	Resop	Madson	Jones	76-66	2nd	6.0
9-11	At Phi.	L	1-11		5	14	Lieber	Valdez		76-67	2nd	7.0
9-12	At Hou.	W	8-2		11	8	Willis	Backe		77-67	2nd	6.0
9-13	At Hou.	W	4-2		6	9	Beckett	Rodriguez	Jones	78-67	2nd	5.0
9-14	At Hou.	L	2-10		6	12	Clemens	Burnett		78-68	T2nd	5.0
9-15	At Hou.	L	1-4		5	8	Pettitte	Vargas	Lidge	78-69	T2nd	6.0
9-16	Phi.	L	3-13		7	17	Lieber	Mecir		78-70	3rd	6.0
9-17	Phi.	L	2-10		7	11	Urbina	Willis		78-71	3rd	7.0
9-18	Phi.	W	14-6		16	10	Beckett	Brito		79-71	3rd	6.0
9-20	At N.Y.	L	2-3	(12)	8	4	Heilman	Moehler		79-72	3rd	7.0
9-21	At N.Y.	L	4-5		14	11	Hernandez	Quantrill		79-73	3rd	7.0
9-22	At N.Y.	W	2-1		8	6	Willis	Martinez	Jones	80-73	3rd	6.0
9-23	At Atl.	L	3-4		10	10	Boyer	Jones	Farnsworth	80-74	3rd	7.0
9-24	At Atl.	L	1-6		5	10	Thomson	Moehler		80-75	3rd	8.0
9-25	At Atl.	L	3-5		8	7	Boyer	Burnett	Farnsworth	80-76	3rd	9.0
9-26	Was.	L	0-4		5	10	Carrasco	Vargas		80-77	3rd	9.0
9-27	Was.	L	1-11		9	15	Stanton	Willis		80-78	T4th	10.0
9-28	Was.	L	7-11		12	15	Loaiza	Moehler		80-79	5th	10.0
9-30	Atl.	W	5-2		10	5	Villone	Thomson	Jones	81-79	T4th	9.0
10-1	Atl.	W	6-4		10	7	Resop	Kolb	Jones	82-79	4th	8.0
10-2	Atl.	W	7-6	(10)	14	14	Villone	Davies		83-79	T3rd	7.0

Monthly records: April (14-8), May (13-14), June (13-14), July (13-13), August (17-14), September (11-16), October (2-0).
*Innings, if other than nine. ! First game of a doubleheader. & Second game of a doubleheader.

RECORDS

2005 regular-season record: 83-79
Position: 3rd in N.L. East
Home: 45-36   **Road:** 38-43
N.L. East: 34-39   **N.L. Central:** 21-22
N.L. West: 18-13   **A.L.** 10-5
Vs. LH starters: 21-16
Vs. RH starters: 62-63
Grass: 80-79   **Artificial:** 3-0
Day: 24-21   **Night:** 59-58
1-Run: 20-23   **X-inn.:** 5-9
Doubleheaders: 0-1-0
Team record past five years: 412-398 (.509, ranks 7th in league in that span)

TEAM LEADERS

Batting average: Miguel Cabrera (.323).
At-bats: Juan Pierre (656).
Runs: Miguel Cabrera (106).
Hits: Miguel Cabrera (198).
Total Bases: Miguel Cabrera (344).
Doubles: Miguel Cabrera (43).
Triples: Juan Pierre (13).
Home runs: Miguel Cabrera, Carlos Delgado (33).
Runs batted in: Miguel Cabrera (116).
Stolen bases: Juan Pierre (57).
Slugging percentage: Carlos Delgado (.582).
On-base percentage: Carlos Delgado (.399).
Wins: Dontrelle Willis (22).
Earned-run average: Dontrelle Willis (2.63).
Complete games: Dontrelle Willis (7).

Shutouts: Dontrelle Willis (5).
Saves: Todd Jones (40).
Innings pitched: Dontrelle Willis (236.1).
Strikeouts: A.J. Burnett (198).

GAMES BY POSITION

Catcher: Paul Lo Duca 128, Matt Treanor 55, Josh Willingham 8, Ryan Jorgensen 3.
First base: Carlos Delgado 141, Jeff Conine 45, Joe Dillon 1, Lenny Harris 1.
Second base: Luis Castillo 120, Damion Easley 46, Mike Lowell 9, Joe Dillon 4, Josh Wilson 4, Mike Mordecai 1.
Third base: Mike Lowell 135, Miguel Cabrera 29, Damion Easley 10, Joe Dillon 2, Lenny Harris 2.
Shortstop: Alex Gonzalez 124, Damion Easley 30, Robert Andino 17, Josh Wilson 6, Mike Mordecai 1.
Outfield: Juan Pierre 160, Juan Encarnacion 139, Miguel Cabrera 134, Jeff Conine 61, Chris Aguila 42, Jeremy Hermida 14, Joe Dillon 3, Lenny Harris 2, Josh Willingham 1.
Designated hitter: Jeff Conine 3, Lenny Harris 2, Carlos Delgado 1, Josh Willingham 1.

TOP DRAFT CHOICES

1a. **Chris Volstad,** RHP, Palm Beach Gardens (Fla.) H.S.
1b. **Aaron Thompson,** LHP, Second Baptist H.S., Houston.
1c. **Jacob Marceaux,** RHP, McNeese State.
1d. **Ryan Tucker,** RHP, Temple City (Calif.) H.S.
1e. **Sean West,** LHP, Captain Shreve H.S., Shreveport, La.
2a. **Kris Harvey,** OF, Clemson.
2b. **Brett Hayes,** C, Nevada.
3. **Matt Goyen,** LHP, Georgia College.
4. **Gaby Sanchez,** C, Miami.
5. **Kyle Winters,** RHP, Pomona H.S., Arvada, Colo.
6. **James Guerrero,** 2B, San Diego State.
7. **Chris Leroux,** RHP, Winthrop.
8. **Aaron Bates,** 1B, North Carolina State.
9. **Jim Brauer,** RHP, Michigan.
10. **Cody Allen,** 3B, Elk Grove (Calif.) H.S.

HOUSTON ASTROS
NATIONAL LEAGUE CENTRAL DIVISION

2006 SEASON

Astros Schedule
Home games shaded.
All-Star Game July 11 at Pittsburgh. Schedule subject to change.

APRIL

SUN	MON	TUE	WED	THU	FRI	SAT
2	3 FLA	4 FLA	5 FLA	6	7 WAS	8 WAS
9 WAS	10 WAS	11 SF	12 SF	13 SF	14 ARI	15 ARI
16 ARI	17 MIL	18 MIL	19 MIL	20	21 PIT	22 PIT
23 PIT	24 LAD	25 LAD	26 LAD	27	28 CIN	29 CIN
30 CIN						

MAY

SUN	MON	TUE	WED	THU	FRI	SAT
	1 MIL	2 MIL	3 STL	4 STL	5 COL	6 COL
7 COL	8	9 LAD	10 LAD	11 LAD	12 COL	13 COL
14 COL	15 SF	16 SF	17 SF	18	19 TEX	20 TEX
21 TEX	22 WAS	23 WAS	24 WAS	25 WAS	26 PIT	27 PIT
28 PIT	29 STL	30 STL	31 STL			

JUNE

SUN	MON	TUE	WED	THU	FRI	SAT
				1	2 CIN	3 CIN
4 CIN	5 CHC	6 CHC	7 CHC	8 ATL	9 ATL	10 ATL
11 ATL	12	13 CHC	14 CHC	15 CHC	16 KC	17 KC
18 KC	19	20 MIN	21 MIN	22 MIN	23 CHW	24 CHW
25 CHW	26 DET	27 DET	28 DET	29	30 TEX	

JULY

SUN	MON	TUE	WED	THU	FRI	SAT
						1 TEX
2 TEX	3 CHC	4 CHC	5 CHC	6 STL	7 STL	8 STL
9 STL	10	11 ALL-STAR	12	13 FLA	14 FLA	15 FLA
16 FLA	17	18 CHC	19 CHC	20 CHC	21 NYM	22 NYM
23 NYM	24	25 CIN	26 CIN	27 CIN	28 ARI	29 ARI
30 ARI	31					

AUGUST

SUN	MON	TUE	WED	THU	FRI	SAT
		1 SD	2 SD	3 SD	4 ARI	5 ARI
6 ARI	7	8 PIT	9 PIT	10 PIT	11 SD	12 SD
13 SD	14 CHC	15 CHC	16 CHC	17 MIL	18 MIL	19 MIL
20 MIL	21 CIN	22 CIN	23 CIN	24 PIT	25 PIT	26 PIT
27 PIT	28	29 MIL	30 MIL	31 MIL		

SEPTEMBER

SUN	MON	TUE	WED	THU	FRI	SAT
					1 NYM	2 NYM
3 NYM	4 PHI	5 PHI	6 PHI	7	8 MIL	9 MIL
10 MIL	11 STL	12 STL	13 STL	14	15 PHI	16 PHI
17 PHI	18 CIN	19 CIN	20 CIN	21 STL	22 STL	23 STL
24 STL	25	26 PIT	27 PIT	28 PIT	29 ATL	30 ATL

OCTOBER

SUN	MON	TUE	WED	THU	FRI	SAT
1 ATL	2	3	4	5	6	7

Home games are shaded. All-Star Game is July 11 at Pittsburgh. Schedule is subject to change.

Oswalt

CLUB DIRECTORY

Chairman and chief executive officer
Drayton McLane Jr.
President, baseball operations
Tal Smith
President, business operations
Pam Gardner
General manager
Tim Purpura
Assistant g.m./dir. of player development
Ricky Bennett
Senior director of player personnel
Paul Ricciarini
Senior director of baseball operations
David Gottfried

Special assistants to the general manager
Enos Cabell, Al Pedrique, Nolan Ryan
Coordinator of professional scouting
J.D. Elliby
Consultant
Matt Galante
Senior vice president, communications
Jay Lucas
Senior vice president, operations
Rob Matwick
Senior v.p., finance and administration
Jackie Traywick
Director of media relations
Jimmy Stanton

MINOR LEAGUE AFFILIATES

Class	Team	League	Manager
AAA	Round Rock	Pacific Coast	Jackie Moore
AA	Corpus Christi	Texas	Dave Clark
Advanced A	Salem	Carolina	Jim Pankovits
A	Lexington	South Atlantic	Jack Lind
Short-Season A	Tri-City	New York-Pennsylvania	Gregg Langbehn
Advanced Rookie	Greeneville	Appalachian	Ivan DeJesus

BROADCAST INFORMATION

Radio: KTRH-AM (740); KLAT-AM (1010), Spanish language.
TV: KNWS-TV 51.
Cable TV: Fox Sports Net.

SPRING TRAINING

Ballpark (city): Osceola County Stadium (Kissimmee, Fla.).
Ticket information: 321-697-3200.

For more on the Astros, go to www.sportingnews.com/baseball/teams/astros/

SPRING TRAINING ROSTER

Manager—Phil Garner (3).
Coaches—Mark Bailey (6), Cecil Cooper (15), Jose Cruz (25), Gary Gaetti (8), Jim Hickey (48), Doug Mansolino (29).

No.	PITCHERS	B/T	Ht./Wt.	Age*
	Matthew Albers	L/R	6-0/205	23
38	Ezequiel Astacio	R/R	6-3/160	26
41	Brandon Backe	R/R	6-0/180	27
	James Barthmaier	R/R	6-4/210	22
	Taylor Buchholz	R/R	6-4/220	24
45	Mike Gallo	L/L	6-0/175	28
	Juan Gutierrez	R/R	6-3/200	22
	Jason Hirsh	R/R	6-8/250	24
54	Brad Lidge	R/R	6-5/210	29
	Mark McLemore	L/L	6-2/220	25
	Trever Miller	R/L	6-3/200	32
	Fernando Nieve	R/R	6-0/195	23
44	Roy Oswalt	R/R	6-0/185	28
	Felipe Paulino	R/R	6-2/180	22
20	Andy Pettitte	L/L	6-5/225	33
50	Chad Qualls	R/R	6-5/220	27
51	Wandy Rodriguez	B/L	5-11/160	27
36	Russ Springer	R/R	6-4/211	37
35	Dan Wheeler	R/R	6-3/222	28

No.	CATCHERS	B/T	Ht./Wt.	Age*
11	Brad Ausmus	R/R	5-11/190	36
46	Raul Chavez	R/R	5-11/215	33
	Hector Gimenez	B/R	5-10/180	23
9	Humberto Quintero	R/R	5-9/215	26

No.	INFIELDERS	B/T	Ht./Wt.	Age*
5	Jeff Bagwell	R/R	6-0/215	37
7	Craig Biggio	R/R	5-11/185	40
4	Eric Bruntlett	R/R	6-0/190	28
2	Chris Burke	R/R	5-11/180	26
14	Morgan Ensberg	R/R	6-2/210	30
28	Adam Everett	R/R	6-0/170	29
26	Mike Lamb	L/R	6-1/190	30

No.	OUTFIELDERS	B/T	Ht./Wt.	Age*
	Joshua Anderson	L/R	6-2/195	23
17	Lance Berkman	B/L	6-1/220	30
52	Charlton Jimerson	R/R	6-3/210	26
24	Jason Lane	R/L	6-2/220	29
19	Orlando Palmeiro	L/L	5-11/180	37
30	Luke Scott	L/R	6-0/210	27
1	Willy Taveras	R/R	6-0/160	24
23	Preston Wilson	R/R	6-2/215	31

*Age as of April 1, 2006.

BALLPARK INFORMATION

Ballpark (capacity, surface)
Minute Maid Park (40,950, grass)
Address
P.O. Box 288
Houston, TX 77001-0288
Official website
www.astros.com
Business phone
713-259-8000
Ticket information
713-259-8500, 1-800-ASTROS-2
Field dimensions (from home plate)
To left field at foul line, 315 feet
To center field, 435 feet
To right field at foul line, 326 feet
First game played
April 7, 2000 (Phillies 4, Astros 1)

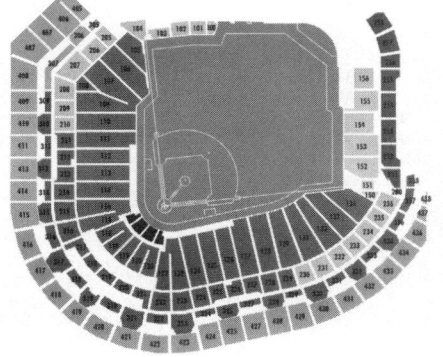

2006 SEASON *Houston Astros*

Date	Opp.	Res.	Score	(inn.*)	Hits	Opp. hits	Winning pitcher	Losing pitcher	Save	Record	Pos.	GB
44-5	StL.	L	3-7		7	11	Carpenter	Oswalt	Isringhausen	0-1	T5th	1.0
4-6	StL.	W	4-1		15	4	Qualls	Tavarez	Lidge	1-1	T3rd	1.0
4-8	Cin.	W	3-2		8	8	Clemens	Belisle	Lidge	2-1	T3rd	1.0
4-9	Cin.	W	4-3		10	11	Lidge	Wagner		3-1	T1st	...
4-10	Cin.	W	5-2		11	6	Oswalt	Milton	Lidge	4-1	1st	+1.0
4-11	At N.Y.	L	4-8		9	13	Hernandez	Springer		4-2	T1st	...
4-13	At N.Y.	L	0-1	(11)	4	4	DeJean	Wheeler		4-3	2nd	0.5
4-14	At N.Y.	L	3-4		10	7	Matthews	Franco	Looper	4-4	T2nd	1.0
4-15	At Cin.	W	11-2		14	5	Oswalt	Wilson		5-4	T1st	...
4-16	At Cin.	L	2-3		5	8	Milton	Pettitte	Graves	5-5	T2nd	0.5
4-17	At Cin.	L	5-6		9	7	Wagner	Qualls	Graves	5-6	T4th	1.5
4-18	Atl.	L	0-1	(12)	6	9	Sosa	Wheeler	Kolb	5-7	4th	2.5
4-19	Atl.	W	5-3		10	9	Backe	Thomson	Lidge	6-7	4th	2.5
4-20	Mil.	W	6-1		9	4	Oswalt	Sheets		7-7	4th	1.5
4-21	Mil.	W	8-7		8	9	Pettitte	Davis	Lidge	8-7	T2nd	1.5
4-22	At StL.	L	7-8		11	9	Marquis	Duckworth	Isringhausen	8-8	T2nd	2.5
4-23	At StL.	L	0-1	(10)	5	6	Mulder	Qualls		8-9	T2nd	3.5
4-24	At StL.	L	5-8		8	13	Morris	Backe	Isringhausen	8-10	4th	4.5
4-25	At Pit.	L	0-2		5	6	Perez	Oswalt	Mesa	8-11	4th	5.0
4-27	At Pit.	L	0-2		4	9	Wells	Pettitte	Mesa	8-12	T4th	6.5
4-29	Chi.	L	2-3		7	10	Maddux	Clemens	Hawkins	8-13	T5th	7.0
4-30	Chi.	W	7-5		10	8	Backe	Bartosh		9-13	5th	6.0
5-1	Chi.	W	9-3		11	12	Oswalt	Prior		10-13	4th	5.0
5-2	Pit.	W	11-4		12	5	Pettitte	Fogg		11-13	T3rd	5.0
5-3	Pit.	L	4-7		11	14	White	Qualls	Mesa	11-14	4th	6.0
5-4	Pit.	L	4-6		9	9	Torres	Lidge	Mesa	11-15	4th	7.0
5-5	At Atl.	L	3-9		3	11	Thomson	Backe		11-16	T4th	7.0
5-6	At Atl.	L	4-9		7	11	Smoltz	Oswalt		11-17	T4th	7.0
5-7	At Atl.	L	1-4		6	10	Ramirez	Pettitte	Kolb	11-18	T5th	7.0
5-8	At Atl.	L	0-16		2	17	Hampton	Astacio		11-19	T5th	8.0
5-9	At Fla.	W	2-1		6	5	Clemens	Burnett	Lidge	12-19	5th	8.0
5-10	At Fla.	L	2-6		7	10	Mecir	Springer		12-20	T5th	8.0
5-11	At Fla.	L	1-2		7	5	Willis	Oswalt	Jones	12-21	T5th	9.0
5-12	S.F.	L	3-6		8	9	Hennessey	Pettitte	Walker	12-22	6th	10.0
5-13	S.F.	L	2-4		8	9	Rueter	Astacio	Walker	12-23	6th	10.0
5-14	S.F.	W	4-1		7	5	Clemens	Tomko	Lidge	13-23	6th	10.0
5-15	S.F.	W	9-0		11	4	Backe	Fassero		14-23	T5th	10.0
5-17	Ari.	W	3-0		8	6	Oswalt	Vazquez	Lidge	15-23	5th	9.0
5-18	Ari.	L	6-7		13	14	Ortiz	Pettitte	Bruney	15-24	5th	10.0
5-19	Ari.	L	1-6		7	9	Halsey	Clemens	Valverde	15-25	5th	10.0
5-20	At Tex.	L	3-7		10	9	Rogers	Backe		15-26	T5th	11.0
5-21	At Tex.	L	3-18		9	17	Young	Astacio		15-27	T5th	12.0
5-22	At Tex.	L	0-2		6	8	Park	Oswalt	Cordero	15-28	T5th	12.0
5-23	At Chi.	L	1-4		5	8	Rusch	Rodriguez	Dempster	15-29	6th	13.0
5-24	At Chi.	L	2-4		6	5	Wuertz	Lidge	Dempster	15-30	6th	14.0
5-25	At Chi.	W	5-1		9	7	Backe	Maddux		16-30	6th	14.0
5-27	At Mil.	L	0-3		3	6	Davis	Oswalt	Turnbow	16-31	6th	15.0
5-28	At Mil.	W	9-6		6	13	Rodriguez	Sheets	Lidge	17-31	6th	15.0
5-29	At Mil.	W	2-1		5	6	Pettitte	Capuano	Lidge	18-31	6th	14.0
5-30	Cin.	L	0-9		5	10	Harang	Clemens		18-32	6th	15.0
5-31	Cin.	W	4-3		8	10	Backe	Belisle	Lidge	19-32	6th	14.0
6-1	Cin.	W	4-1		7	4	Oswalt	Ortiz	Lidge	20-32	6th	14.0
6-3	StL.	L	0-2		9	7	Carpenter	Pettitte	Tavarez	20-33	6th	14.5
6-4	StL.	L	9-11		12	14	Marquis	Rodriguez	Isringhausen	20-34	6th	15.5
6-5	StL.	W	6-4		11	11	Clemens	Mulder	Lidge	21-34	5th	14.5
6-7	At N.Y.	L	1-3		2	12	Martinez	Oswalt		21-35	6th	16.0
6-8	At N.Y.	W	4-1		8	6	Backe	Zambrano	Lidge	22-35	6th	15.0
6-9	At N.Y.	W	6-3	(11)	14	6	Springer	Bell	Lidge	23-35	6th	14.5
6-10	Tor.	W	4-2		9	6	Rodriguez	Lilly	Lidge	24-35	5th	14.5
6-11	Tor.	W	6-3		13	7	Lidge	Schoeneweis		25-35	5th	13.5
6-12	Tor.	W	3-0		9	2	Oswalt	Towers		26-35	5th	13.5
6-13	At Bal.	L	5-8		9	14	Penn	Backe	Ryan	26-36	5th	13.5
6-14	At Bal.	L	1-6		4	10	Chen	Pettitte		26-37	5th	14.5
6-15	At Bal.	L	1-5		4	10	Lopez	Rodriguez		26-38	5th	14.5
6-17	At K.C.	W	7-0		9	9	Clemens	Howell		27-38	5th	14.5
6-18	At K.C.	W	6-2		10	9	Oswalt	Carrasco		28-38	5th	14.5
6-19	At K.C.	L	1-7		2	11	Hernandez	Backe		28-39	5th	15.5

Date	Opp.	Res.	Score	(inn.*)	Hits	Opp. hits	Winning pitcher	Losing pitcher	Save	Record	Pos.	GB
6-20	Col.	W	7-0		10	5	Pettitte	Kennedy		29-39	5th	15.5
6-21	Col.	W	6-5		9	8	Qualls	Wright	Lidge	30-39	5th	14.5
6-22	Col.	W	6-2		6	6	Clemens	Jennings		31-39	5th	13.5
6-24	Tex.	W	5-2		11	7	Oswalt	Rodriguez	Lidge	32-39	5th	13.0
6-25	Tex.	L	5-6		6	8	Young	Backe	Cordero	32-40	5th	14.0
6-26	Tex.	W	3-2	(10)	8	7	Qualls	Dominguez		33-40	5th	13.0
6-27	At Col.	W	11-5		18	11	Rodriguez	Wright		34-40	T4th	12.5
6-28	At Col.	L	5-6		9	8	Cortes	Springer	Fuentes	34-41	T4th	12.5
6-29	At Col.	W	7-1		12	8	Oswalt	Kim		35-41	3rd	13.5
6-30	At Cin.	T	2-2	(7)	5	8				35-41	4th	13.0
7-1	At Cin.	W	10-7		14	13	Pettitte	Hudson	Wheeler	36-41	4th	13.0
7-2!	At Cin.	W	4-3		8	7	Rodriguez	Harang	Wheeler	37-41		
7-2&	At Cin.	L	6-11		10	14	Ortiz	Astacio		37-42	4th	12.5
7-3	At Cin.	W	9-0		12	4	Clemens	Claussen		38-42	3rd	12.5
7-4	S.D.	W	4-1		10	5	Oswalt	Lawrence		39-42	3rd	12.5
7-5	S.D.	W	6-2		11	6	Backe	Reyes		40-42	T2nd	12.5
7-6	S.D.	W	5-4		12	9	Pettitte	Peavy	Wheeler	41-42	2nd	12.5
7-7	S.D.	L	5-7		8	7	Williams	Rodriguez	Hoffman	41-43	2nd	12.5
7-8	L.A.	W	3-2		10	8	Lidge	Brazoban		42-43	2nd	12.5
7-9	L.A.	W	4-2		7	9	Oswalt	Weaver	Lidge	43-43	2nd	11.5
7-10	L.A.	W	6-5		9	9	Springer	Sanchez	Lidge	44-43	2nd	11.5
7-15	At StL.	L	3-4	(13)	12	8	Thompson	Harville		44-44	3rd	12.5
7-16	At StL.	L	2-4		6	9	Marquis	Oswalt	Isringhausen	44-45	3rd	13.5
7-17	At StL.	L	0-3		3	5	Carpenter	Clemens		44-46	4th	14.5
7-18	At Pit.	W	11-1		17	6	Backe	Williams		45-46	3rd	14.5
7-19!	At Pit.	W	9-3		14	8	Astacio	Snell		46-46		
7-19&	At Pit.	W	6-4		10	8	Rodriguez	Redman	Lidge	47-46	3rd	13.0
7-20	At Pit.	W	8-0		13	9	Pettitte	Fogg		48-46	T2nd	13.0
7-21	At Was.	W	3-2		11	8	Oswalt	Loaiza	Lidge	49-46	2nd	12.0
7-22	At Was.	W	14-1		19	6	Clemens	Drese		50-46	2nd	12.0
7-23	At Was.	L	2-4		4	7	Armas	Backe	Cordero	50-47	2nd	12.0
7-24	At Was.	W	4-1	(14)	10	4	Springer	Carrasco	Lidge	51-47	2nd	11.0
7-25	Phi.	W	7-1		9	7	Pettitte	Lidle		52-47	2nd	10.5
7-26	Phi.	W	2-1		7	8	Oswalt	Madson		53-47	2nd	10.5
7-27	Phi.	W	3-2		8	6	Clemens	Padilla	Lidge	54-47	2nd	9.5
7-28	N.Y.	W	3-2		6	7	Wheeler	Hernandez		55-47	2nd	9.5
7-29	N.Y.	W	5-2		8	5	Rodriguez	Benson	Lidge	56-47	2nd	8.5
7-30	N.Y.	W	2-0		7	3	Pettitte	Glavine	Lidge	57-47	2nd	8.5
7-31	N.Y.	L	4-9		10	17	Heilman	Wheeler		57-48	2nd	9.5
8-2	At Ari.	W	3-1		9	6	Clemens	Vargas	Lidge	58-48	2nd	9.0
8-3	At Ari.	W	7-0		13	7	Astacio	Vazquez		59-48	2nd	9.0
8-4	At Ari.	L	3-7		10	8	Halsey	Rodriguez	Valverde	59-49	2nd	9.0
8-5	At S.F.	L	0-4		3	8	Schmidt	Pettitte		59-50	2nd	10.0
8-6	At S.F.	L	2-5		4	10	Lowry	Oswalt		59-51	2nd	10.0
8-7	At S.F.	W	8-1		11	6	Clemens	Eyre		60-51	2nd	10.0
8-9	Was.	L	5-6		9	8	Patterson	Astacio	Cordero	60-52	2nd	11.5
8-10	Was.	W	7-6		13	11	Rodriguez	Hernandez	Lidge	61-52	2nd	11.5
8-11	Was.	W	6-3		11	5	Pettitte	Drese		62-52	2nd	10.5
8-12	Pit.	W	6-5		13	11	Wheeler	White	Lidge	63-52	2nd	9.5
8-13	Pit.	L	0-1		6	4	Torres	Lidge	Mesa	63-53	2nd	10.5
8-14	Pit.	L	0-8		5	10	Williams	Astacio		63-54	2nd	10.5
8-15	Chi.	W	12-4		16	7	Rodriguez	Rusch		64-54	2nd	10.0
8-16	Chi.	L	1-4		4	9	Maddux	Pettitte	Dempster	64-55	2nd	11.0
8-17	Chi.	L	2-4		3	9	Zambrano	Oswalt	Dempster	64-56	2nd	12.0
8-18	Mil.	L	2-5		8	7	Ohka	Clemens	Turnbow	64-57	2nd	12.0
8-19	Mil.	W	5-3		9	8	Springer	Davis	Lidge	65-57	2nd	12.0
8-20	Mil.	L	2-3		8	7	Sheets	Harville		65-58	2nd	13.0
8-21	Mil.	W	8-3		11	7	Pettitte	Santos		66-58	2nd	12.0
8-22	At S.D.	W	6-2		12	5	Oswalt	Williams		67-58	2nd	12.0
8-23	At S.D.	L	0-2		4	5	Peavy	Clemens		67-59	2nd	12.0
8-24	At S.D.	L	4-7		8	13	Park	Rodriguez	Hoffman	67-60	2nd	13.0
8-26	At L.A.	W	2-1		8	7	Pettitte	Lowe	Lidge	68-60	2nd	12.5
8-27	At L.A.	L	3-8		8	11	Jackson	Oswalt		68-61	2nd	13.5
8-28	At L.A.	L	0-1		8	4	Weaver	Qualls	Sanchez	68-62	2nd	14.5
8-30	Cin.	W	5-2		9	5	Rodriguez	Ortiz		69-62	2nd	14.0
8-31	Cin.	W	10-0		15	4	Pettitte	Claussen		70-62	2nd	14.0
9-1	Cin.	W	3-1		5	6	Oswalt	Harang	Lidge	71-62	2nd	13.5
9-2	StL.	W	6-5	(13)	8	13	Qualls	Tavarez		72-62	2nd	12.5
9-3	StL.	L	2-4		8	11	Carpenter	Springer		72-63	2nd	13.5
9-4	StL.	L	1-4		5	9	Marquis	Rodriguez		72-64	2nd	14.5

Date	Opp.	Res.	Score	(inn.*)	Hits	Opp. hits	Winning pitcher	Losing pitcher	Save	Record	Pos.	GB
9-5	At Phi.	W	4-3		6	9	Pettitte	Myers	Lidge	73-64	2nd	14.5
9-6	At Phi.	W	2-1		7	7	Oswalt	Wagner	Lidge	74-64	2nd	13.5
9-7	At Phi.	W	8-6		9	8	Qualls	Wagner	Lidge	75-64	2nd	12.5
9-9	At Mil.	L	4-7		9	11	Davis	Clemens	Turnbow	75-65	2nd	14.0
9-10	At Mil.	W	7-5		12	8	Pettitte	Ohka	Lidge	76-65	2nd	14.0
9-11	At Mil.	L	2-4		7	10	Helling	Oswalt	Turnbow	76-66	2nd	14.0
9-12	Fla.	L	2-8		8	11	Willis	Backe		76-67	2nd	15.0
9-13	Fla.	L	2-4		9	6	Beckett	Rodriguez	Jones	76-68	2nd	16.0
9-14	Fla.	W	10-2		12	6	Clemens	Burnett		77-68	2nd	15.0
9-15	Fla.	W	4-1		8	5	Pettitte	Vargas	Lidge	78-68	2nd	15.0
9-16	Mil.	W	2-1		7	8	Lidge	Eveland		79-68	2nd	14.0
9-17	Mil.	W	7-0		10	7	Backe	Obermueller		80-68	2nd	14.0
9-18	Mil.	W	6-1		6	5	Rodriguez	Capuano		81-68	2nd	13.0
9-19	At Pit.	L	0-7		4	15	Snell	Clemens		81-69	2nd	13.5
9-20	At Pit.	W	7-4		12	11	Pettitte	Gorzelanny		82-69	2nd	12.5
9-21	At Pit.	W	12-8		15	15	Oswalt	Wells		83-69	2nd	12.5
9-22	At Pit.	W	2-1		5	5	Backe	Duke	Lidge	84-69	2nd	11.5
9-23	At Chi.	L	4-5		11	10	Rusch	Rodriguez	Dempster	84-70	2nd	11.5
9-24	At Chi.	W	8-3		12	4	Astacio	Zambrano		85-70	2nd	10.5
9-25	At Chi.	L	2-3		5	5	Williams	Gallo	Dempster	85-71	2nd	11.5
9-27	At StL.	W	3-1		8	8	Oswalt	Morris	Lidge	86-71	2nd	10.5
9-28	At StL.	W	7-6		12	10	Qualls	Isringhausen	Lidge	87-71	2nd	9.5
9-29	Chi.	L	2-3		8	6	Rusch	Rodriguez	Dempster	87-72	2nd	10.0
9-30	Chi.	L	3-4		6	11	Novoa	Lidge	Dempster	87-73	2nd	11.0
10-1	Chi.	W	3-1		6	8	Clemens	Williams	Lidge	88-73	2nd	11.0
10-2	Chi.	W	6-4		11	10	Oswalt	Maddux	Lidge	89-73	2nd	11.0

Monthly records: April (9-13), May (10-19), June (16-9), July (22-7), August (13-14), September (17-11), October (2-0).
*Innings, if other than nine. ! First game of a doubleheader. & Second game of a doubleheader.

RECORDS

2005 regular-season record: 89-73
Position: 2nd in N.L. Central
Home: 53-28   **Road:** 36-45
N.L. East: 20-16   **N.L. Central:** 43-36
N.L. West: 19-13   **A.L.** 7-8
Vs. LH starters: 25-24
Vs. RH starters: 64-49
Grass: 89-73   **Artificial:** 0-0
Day: 22-23   **Night:** 67-50
1-Run: 25-21   **X-inn.:** 4-4
Doubleheaders: 1-0-1
Team record past five years: 445-365
(.549, ranks 4th in league in that span)

TEAM LEADERS

Batting average: Lance Berkman (.293).
At-bats: Willy Taveras (592).
Runs: Craig Biggio (94).
Hits: Willy Taveras (172).
Total Bases: Morgan Ensberg (293).
Doubles: Craig Biggio (40).
Triples: Mike Lamb (5).
Home runs: Morgan Ensberg (36).
Runs batted in: Morgan Ensberg (101).
Stolen bases: Willy Taveras (34).
Slugging percentage: Morgan Ensberg (.557).
On-base percentage: Lance Berkman (.411).
Wins: Roy Oswalt (20).
Earned-run average: Roger Clemens (1.87).
Complete games: Roy Oswalt (4).

Shutouts: Brandon Backe, Roy Oswalt (1).
Saves: Brad Lidge (42).
Innings pitched: Roy Oswalt (241.2).
Strikeouts: Roger Clemens (185).

GAMES BY POSITION

Catcher: Brad Ausmus 134, Raul Chavez 36, Humberto Quintero 16.
First base: Lance Berkman 96, Mike Lamb 68, Jeff Bagwell 24, Jose Vizcaino 13, Eric Bruntlett 1, Humberto Quintero 1.
Second base: Craig Biggio 141, Eric Bruntlett 28, Jose Vizcaino 23, Chris Burke 18, Brad Ausmus 1.
Third base: Morgan Ensberg 148, Mike Lamb 15, Eric Bruntlett 8, Jose Vizcaino 8.
Shortstop: Adam Everett 150, Jose Vizcaino 17, Eric Bruntlett 10, Brad Ausmus 1.
Outfield: Willy Taveras 148, Jason Lane 141, Chris Burke 84, Orlando Palmeiro 71, Lance Berkman 49, Eric Bruntlett 26, Luke Scott 24, Todd Self 15, Charles Gipson 13, Mike Lamb 13, Charlton Jimerson 1.
Designated hitter: Craig Biggio 5, Lance Berkman 3, Mike Lamb 1, Todd Self 1.

TOP DRAFT CHOICES

1a. **Brian Bogusevic**, LHP, Tulane.
1b. **Eli Iorg**, OF, Tennessee.
2. **Ralph Henriquez**, C, Key West (Fla.) H.S.
3a. **Tommy Manzella**, SS, Tulane.
3b. **Josh Lindblom**, RHP, Harrison H.S., West Lafayette, Ind.
4. **Josh Flores,** OF, Triton College (Ill.).
5. **Billy Hart**, 3B, USC.
6. **Brandon Barnes**, OF, Cypress College (Calif.).
7. **Timothy Johnson**, SS, Wissahickon H.S., Penllyn, Pa.
8. **Koby Clemens**, 3B, Memorial H.S., Houston.
9. **Jordan Meaker**, RHP, Flower Mound (Texas), H.S.
10. **Allen Langdon**, OF, Eagle H.S., Boise, Idaho.

LOS ANGELES DODGERS
NATIONAL LEAGUE WEST DIVISION

2006 SEASON

Dodgers Schedule
Home games shaded.
All-Star Game July 11 at Pittsburgh. Schedule subject to change.

APRIL

SUN	MON	TUE	WED	THU	FRI	SAT
2	3 ATL	4 ATL	5 ATL	6	7 PHI	8 PHI
9 PHI	10 PIT	11 PIT	12 PIT	13 PIT	14 SF	15 SF
16 SF	17 CHC	18 CHC	19 CHC	20	21 ARI	22 ARI
23 ARI	24 HOU	25 HOU	26 HOU	27	28 SD	29 SD
30 SD						

MAY

SUN	MON	TUE	WED	THU	FRI	SAT
	1 ARI	2 ARI	3 SD	4 SD	5 MIL	6 MIL
7 MIL	8	9 HOU	10 HOU	11 HOU	12 SF	13 SF
14 SF	15 COL	16 COL	17 COL	18	19 LAA	20 LAA
21 LAA	22 COL	23 COL	24 COL	25	26 WAS	27 WAS
28 WAS	29 ATL	30 ATL	31 ATL			

JUNE

SUN	MON	TUE	WED	THU	FRI	SAT
				1 PHI	2 PHI	3 PHI
4 PHI	5 NYM	6 NYM	7 NYM	8	9 COL	10 COL
11 COL	12	13 SD	14 SD	15 SD	16 OAK	17 OAK
18 OAK	19	20 SEA	21 SEA	22 SEA	23 PIT	24 PIT
25 PIT	26 MIN	27 MIN	28 MIN	29	30 LAA	

JULY

SUN	MON	TUE	WED	THU	FRI	SAT
						1 LAA
2 LAA	3 ARI	4 ARI	5 ARI	6 SF	7 SF	8 SF
9 SF	10	11 ALL-STAR	12	13 STL	14 STL	15 STL
16 STL	17 ARI	18 ARI	19 ARI	20 ARI	21 STL	22 STL
23 STL	24 SD	25 SD	26 SD	27	28 WAS	29 WAS
30 WAS	31					

AUGUST

SUN	MON	TUE	WED	THU	FRI	SAT
		1 CIN	2 CIN	3 CIN	4 FLA	5 FLA
6 FLA	7 COL	8 COL	9 COL	10 COL	11 SF	12 SF
13 SF	14 FLA	15 FLA	16 FLA	17	18 SF	19 SF
20 SF	21 SD	22 SD	23 SD	24	25 ARI	26 ARI
27 ARI	28 CIN	29 CIN	30 CIN	31		

SEPTEMBER

SUN	MON	TUE	WED	THU	FRI	SAT
					1 COL	2 COL
3 COL	4 MIL	5 MIL	6 MIL	7 NYM	8 NYM	9 NYM
10 NYM	11	12 CHC	13 CHC	14 CHC	15 SD	16 SD
17 SD	18 PIT	19 PIT	20 PIT	21 ARI	22 ARI	23 ARI
24 ARI	25	26 COL	27 COL	28 COL	29 SF	30 SF

OCTOBER

SUN	MON	TUE	WED	THU	FRI	SAT
1 SF	2	3	4	5	6	7

Home games are shaded. All-Star Game is July 11 at Pittsburgh. Schedule is subject to change.

Kent

CLUB DIRECTORY

Owner and chairman
Frank H. McCourt Jr.
Vice chairman
Jamie McCourt
Special adviser to the chairman
Tommy Lasorda
Executive vice president, COO
Marty Greenspun
Executive v.p., business development
Jeffrey Ingram
General manager
Ned Colletti
Senior vice president, communications
Camille Johnston
Senior vice president, chief financial officer
Cris Hurley
Senior vice president, public affairs
Howard Sunkin
Senior vice president, general counsel
Sam Fernandez

Chief marketing officer
Tagg Romney
Chief sales officer
Greg McElroy
Vice president, assistant general manager
Kim Ng
V.p., player development and scouting
Roy Smith
Vice president, finance
Amanda Shearer
V.p., spring training/minor league facilities
Craig Callan
Vice president, sales
Sergio del Prado
Vice president, ticket sales
Steve Shiffman
Vice president, stadium operations
Lon Rosenberg
Director, public relations
Josh Rawitch

MINOR LEAGUE AFFILIATES

Class	Team	League	Manager
AAA	Las Vegas	Pacific Coast	Jerry Royster
AA	Jacksonville	Southern	John Shoemaker
Advanced A	Vero Beach	Florida State	To be announced
A	Columbus	South Atlantic	To be announced
Advanced Rookie	Ogden	Pioneer	To be announced
Rookie	Dodgers	Gulf Coast	To be announced

BROADCAST INFORMATION

Radio: KFWB-AM (980); KWKW-AM (1330, Spanish language).
TV: KCOP-TV (Channel 13)
Cable TV: Fox Sports Net 2.

SPRING TRAINING

Ballpark (city): Holman Stadium (Vero Beach, Fla.).
Ticket information: 866-DODGERS.
General number: 772-569-4900.

For more on the Dodgers, go to **www.sportingnews.com/baseball/teams/dodgers/**

SPRING TRAINING ROSTER

Manager—Grady Little.
Coaches—Rich Donnelly, Mariano Duncan, Rick Honeycutt, Dave Jauss, Manny Mota, Eddie Murray, Dan Warthen.

No.	PITCHERS	B/T	Ht./Wt.	Age*
43	Yhency Brazoban	R/R	6-1/170	25
51	Jonathan Broxton	R/R	6-4/240	21
	Jose Diaz	R/R	6-4/230	22
38	Eric Gagne	R/R	6-2/235	30
	Tim Hamulack	L/L	6-4/220	29
	Joel Hanrahan	R/R	6-3/215	24
27	D.J. Houlton	R/R	6-4/220	26
58	Edwin Jackson	R/R	6-3/190	22
56	Hong-Chih Kuo	L/L	6-0/200	24
23	Derek Lowe	R/R	6-6/210	32
	Greg Miller	L/L	6-5/220	21
57	Franquelis Osoria	R/R	6-0/165	24
31	Brad Penny	R/R	6-4/250	27
45	Odalis Perez	L/L	6-0/220	28
	Jae Seo	R/R	6-1/215	28
	Brett Tomko	R/R	6-4/225	32

No.	CATCHERS	B/T	Ht./Wt.	Age*
	Sandy Alomar	R/R	6-5/235	39
	Russell Martin	R/R	5-11/200	23
41	Dioner Navarro	B/R	5-10/190	22

No.	INFIELDERS	B/T	Ht./Wt.	Age*
49	Willy Aybar	B/R	6-0/175	23
	Hee-Seop Choi	L/L	6-5/240	27
15	Rafael Furcal	B/R	5-10/175	27
	Nomar Garciaparra	R/R	6-0/190	32
	Joel Guzman	R/R	6-6/225	21
3	Cesar Izturis	B/R	5-9/175	26
12	Jeff Kent	R/R	6-1/210	38
	Andy LaRoche	R/R	6-1/200	22
	James Loney	L/L	6-3/200	21
	Bill Mueller	B/R	5-10/180	35
13	Oscar Robles	L/R	5-11/155	29
8	Olmedo Saenz	R/R	5-11/221	35
	Delwyn Young	B/R	5-10/180	23

No.	OUTFIELDERS	B/T	Ht./Wt.	Age*
22	Jose Cruz	B/R	6-0/210	31
7	J.D. Drew	L/R	6-1/200	30
	Andre Ethier	L/R	6-3/195	23
33	Ricky Ledee	L/L	6-1/216	32
	Kenny Lofton	L/L	6-0/190	38
17	Jason Repko	R/R	5-11/175	25
	Cody Ross	R/L	5-11/180	25
28	Jayson Werth	R/R	6-5/215	26

*Age as of April 1, 2006.

BALLPARK INFORMATION

Ballpark (capacity, surface)
Dodger Stadium (56,000, grass)
Address
1000 Elysian Park Ave.
Los Angeles, CA 90012
Official website
www.dodgers.com
Business phone
323-224-1500
Ticket information
866-DODGERS
Field dimensions (from home plate)
To left field at foul line, 330 feet
To center field, 395 feet
To right field at foul line, 330 feet
First game played
April 10, 1962 (Reds 6, Dodgers 3)

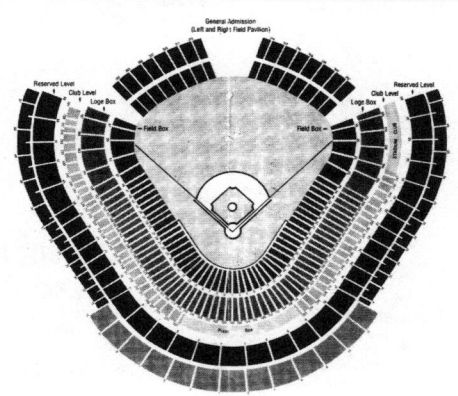

Date	Opp.	Res.	Score	(inn.*)	Hits	Opp. hits	Winning pitcher	Losing pitcher	Save	Record	Pos.	GB
4-5	At S.F.	L	2-4		5	10	Schmidt	Lowe	Benitez	0-1	T4th	1.0
4-6	At S.F.	W	10-4		14	9	Perez	Rueter		1-1	T2nd	0.5
4-7	At S.F.	W	6-0		8	5	Weaver	Tomko		2-1	T1st	...
4-8	At Ari.	W	8-7		11	7	Schmoll	Lyon	Brazoban	3-1	1st	+1.0
4-9	At Ari.	W	12-10	(11)	12	19	Brazoban	Gosling	Schmoll	4-1	1st	+1.0
4-10	At Ari.	L	4-5		12	8	Koplove	Sanchez	Lyon	4-2	T1st	...
4-12	S.F.	W	9-8		10	16	Carrara	Benitez		5-2	1st	+0.5
4-13	S.F.	W	4-1		10	5	Perez	Tomko	Brazoban	6-2	1st	+0.5
4-15	S.D.	W	4-0		8	3	Lowe	Williams		7-2	1st	+1.5
4-16	S.D.	W	8-3		11	6	Erickson	Eaton		8-2	1st	+2.5
4-17	S.D.	W	6-0		11	5	Weaver	Redding		9-2	1st	+3.0
4-18	At Mil.	W	7-3		11	3	Perez	Capuano		10-2	1st	+3.5
4-19	At Mil.	W	8-6	(10)	11	8	Carrara	Phelps	Brazoban	11-2	1st	+4.5
4-20	At S.D.	W	3-1	(10)	9	7	Sanchez	Linebrink	Brazoban	12-2	1st	+4.5
4-21	At S.D.	L	1-6		6	15	Eaton	Erickson		12-3	1st	+4.5
4-22	At Col.	L	1-9		10	16	Jennings	Weaver		12-4	1st	+3.5
4-23	At Col.	L	6-8		12	11	Chacon	Perez	Tsao	12-5	1st	+2.5
4-24	At Col.	W	8-6		11	11	Carrara	Kim	Brazoban	13-5	1st	+2.5
4-25	Ari.	L	2-4		5	11	Vazquez	Lowe	Lyon	13-6	1st	+1.5
4-26	Ari.	L	2-3		10	5	Ortiz	Erickson	Lyon	13-7	1st	+0.5
4-27	Ari.	L	3-6		9	8	Cormier	Weaver	Lopez	13-8	2nd	0.5
4-29	Col.	W	6-3		5	7	Perez	Jennings	Brazoban	14-8	1st	+0.5
4-30	Col.	W	6-2		6	7	Penny	Kennedy	Brazoban	15-8	1st	+1.5
5-1	Col.	W	2-1		4	6	Lowe	Chacon	Brazoban	16-8	1st	+1.5
5-2	Was.	L	2-6		4	13	Loaiza	Erickson		16-9	1st	+1.5
5-3	Was.	W	4-2		9	11	Weaver	Rauch	Brazoban	17-9	1st	+1.5
5-4	Was.	L	2-5		7	10	Hernandez	Perez		17-10	1st	+0.5
5-6	At Cin.	W	13-6		12	8	Penny	Wilson		18-10	1st	+1.0
5-7	At Cin.	L	3-11		10	11	Weathers	Lowe		18-11	1st	+1.0
5-8	At Cin.	W	9-3		14	9	Weaver	Milton		19-11	1st	+2.0
5-9	At StL.	L	2-4		8	8	Mulder	Perez	Reyes	19-12	1st	+2.0
5-10	At StL.	W	9-8		12	14	Alvarez	Jarvis	Brazoban	20-12	1st	+2.0
5-11	At StL.	L	3-9		9	19	Suppan	Penny		20-13	1st	+1.0
5-12	At StL.	L	3-10		8	13	Carpenter	Lowe		20-14	1st	...
5-13	Atl.	W	7-4		14	7	Carrara	Reitsma	Brazoban	21-14	1st	+1.0
5-14	Atl.	L	1-5		5	9	Bernero	Perez		21-15	1st	...
5-15	Atl.	L	2-5		9	6	Hudson	Alvarez	Kolb	21-16	3rd	1.0
5-16	Fla.	L	2-6		10	16	Moehler	Penny		21-17	3rd	1.5
5-17	Fla.	W	14-5		19	7	Lowe	Willis		22-17	3rd	1.5
5-18	Fla.	L	3-8		7	13	Beckett	Weaver		22-18	3rd	2.5
5-20	L.A.	L	0-9		6	9	Washburn	Erickson		22-19	3rd	3.5
5-21	L.A.	L	1-3		7	8	Donnelly	Carrara	Shields	22-20	3rd	3.5
5-22	L.A.	W	6-2		11	9	Lowe	Byrd		23-20	3rd	3.0
5-24	At S.F.	L	3-5		6	11	Schmidt	Weaver	Walker	23-21	3rd	3.5
5-25	At S.F.	L	2-10		6	12	Tomko	Alvarez		23-22	T3rd	4.0
5-26	At S.F.	W	6-4		8	10	Brazoban	Christiansen	Gagne	24-22	3rd	3.5
5-27	At Ari.	W	7-4		10	8	Wunsch	Valverde	Gagne	25-22	3rd	3.5
5-28	At Ari.	L	4-5		12	5	Cormier	Carrara		25-23	3rd	4.5
5-29	At Ari.	W	6-3		12	9	Weaver	Ortiz	Gagne	26-23	3rd	4.5
5-30	Chi.	L	3-5		6	10	Maddux	Alvarez	Dempster	26-24	3rd	5.5
5-31	Chi.	L	1-2	(10)	1	10	Wuertz	Brazoban	Dempster	26-25	3rd	6.5
6-1	Chi.	L	5-9		9	16	Koronka	Lowe		26-26	3rd	6.5
6-2	Mil.	W	6-4		9	9	Carrara	Sheets	Gagne	27-26	3rd	5.5
6-3	Mil.	L	5-7		9	6	Capuano	Weaver	Turnbow	27-27	3rd	6.5
6-4	Mil.	W	2-1		7	6	Houlton	Santos	Gagne	28-27	3rd	5.5
6-5	Mil.	W	10-6		15	14	Penny	Obermueller		29-27	3rd	4.5
6-6	Det.	W	5-3		8	5	Lowe	Bonderman	Gagne	30-27	3rd	4.0
6-7	Det.	L	4-8		5	13	Spurling	Sanchez		30-28	3rd	4.0
6-8	Det.	W	3-1		9	2	Weaver	Johnson	Gagne	31-28	2nd	3.0
6-10	Min.	W	6-5		9	9	Gagne	Mulholland		32-28	2nd	2.5
6-11	Min.	L	3-5		7	10	Silva	Lowe	Nathan	32-29	2nd	3.5
6-12	Min.	W	4-3		9	7	Houlton	Radke	Gagne	33-29	2nd	2.5
6-14	At K.C.	L	2-3		9	7	Hernandez	Weaver	MacDougal	33-30	3rd	2.5
6-15	At K.C.	L	1-3		5	8	Lima	Penny	MacDougal	33-31	3rd	2.5
6-16	At K.C.	L	6-9		11	15	Wood	Lowe		33-32	3rd	2.5
6-17	At Chi.	L	0-6		8	6	Buehrle	Houlton		33-33	3rd	2.5
6-18	At Chi.	L	3-5		7	6	Politte	Brazoban		33-34	3rd	3.5

Date	Opp.	Res.	Score	(inn.*)	Hits	Opp. hits	Winning pitcher	Losing pitcher	Save	Record	Pos.	GB
6-19	At Chi.	L	3-4		7	6	Politte	Sanchez	Hermanson	33-35	3rd	4.5
6-20	At S.D.	L	0-1		3	7	Peavy	Penny	Hoffman	33-36	3rd	5.5
6-21	At S.D.	L	1-2		6	9	Williams	Lowe	Hoffman	33-37	3rd	6.5
6-22	At S.D.	W	6-4		12	8	Houlton	Stauffer	Brazoban	34-37	3rd	5.5
6-23	At S.D.	W	4-3	(10)	7	7	Sanchez	Hoffman	Brazoban	35-37	3rd	4.5
6-24	At L.A.	L	0-7		5	8	Lackey	Weaver		35-38	3rd	4.5
6-25	At L.A.	L	1-3		9	4	Santana	Penny	Rodriguez	35-39	3rd	5.5
6-26	At L.A.	L	3-5		5	10	Donnelly	Wunsch	Rodriguez	35-40	3rd	6.5
6-27	S.D.	W	5-4		10	6	Houlton	Stauffer	Brazoban	36-40	3rd	5.5
6-28	S.D.	L	3-8		7	12	Lawrence	Dessens		36-41	3rd	6.5
6-29	S.D.	W	4-2		10	8	Weaver	May	Brazoban	37-41	3rd	5.5
7-1	Ari.	W	7-0		10	3	Penny	Vazquez		38-41	3rd	4.5
7-2	Ari.	L	5-7		7	12	Vargas	Lowe	Bruney	38-42	3rd	5.5
7-3	Ari.	L	3-10		8	12	Halsey	Houlton		38-43	3rd	6.5
7-4	At Col.	W	4-3	(11)	12	7	Carrara	Witasick	Brazoban	39-43	3rd	5.5
7-5	At Col.	L	1-6		12	12	Francis	Perez		39-44	3rd	5.5
7-6	At Col.	W	9-5		11	13	Penny	Chacon		40-44	3rd	4.5
7-7	At Col.	L	5-8		11	7	DeJean	Carrara	Fuentes	40-45	3rd	5.5
7-8	At Hou.	L	2-3		8	10	Lidge	Brazoban		40-46	3rd	6.5
7-9	At Hou.	L	2-4		9	7	Oswalt	Weaver	Lidge	40-47	3rd	6.5
7-10	At Hou.	L	5-6		9	9	Springer	Sanchez	Lidge	40-48	3rd	7.5
7-14	S.F.	L	3-4		7	7	Schmidt	Houlton	Walker	40-49	3rd	7.5
7-15	S.F.	L	0-6		2	15	Lowry	Lowe		40-50	3rd	8.5
7-16	S.F.	W	5-4		10	9	Schmoll	Walker		41-50	3rd	8.5
7-17	S.F.	L	1-4		7	9	Eyre	Brazoban	Hawkins	41-51	3rd	8.5
7-19	At Phi.	L	4-5	(10)	9	11	Wagner	Brazoban		41-52	T3rd	8.5
7-20	At Phi.	W	10-2		14	7	Lowe	Lidle		42-52	3rd	7.5
7-21	At Phi.	W	1-0		5	4	Perez	Lieber	Brazoban	43-52	3rd	6.5
7-22	At N.Y.	W	6-5		15	8	Weaver	Zambrano	Brazoban	44-52	3rd	5.5
7-23	At N.Y.	L	5-7		8	12	Martinez	Carrara	Looper	44-53	3rd	5.5
7-24	At N.Y.	L	0-6		4	12	Benson	Penny		44-54	3rd	5.5
7-25	Cin.	W	4-0		9	1	Lowe	Harang		45-54	3rd	5.0
7-26	Cin.	W	7-4		11	11	Perez	Milton	Brazoban	46-54	3rd	4.0
7-27	Cin.	L	6-7		9	13	Standridge	Brazoban	Weathers	46-55	3rd	5.0
7-28	Cin.	L	1-6		6	7	Claussen	Houlton		46-56	3rd	5.0
7-29	StL.	W	7-5		11	13	Sanchez	Morris	Brazoban	47-56	3rd	4.0
7-30	StL.	L	4-9		9	14	Suppan	Lowe		47-57	3rd	4.0
7-31	StL.	L	5-7	(11)	8	9	Eldred	Alvarez	Isringhausen	47-58	3rd	4.0
8-2	At Was.	W	5-4		6	9	Weaver	Loaiza	Brazoban	48-58	3rd	4.0
8-3	At Was.	L	1-3		6	8	Armas	Houlton	Cordero	48-59	3rd	4.0
8-4	At Was.	L	0-7		4	11	Patterson	Penny		48-60	3rd	5.0
8-5	At Pit.	W	12-6		15	9	Lowe	Fogg	Schmoll	49-60	3rd	5.0
8-6	At Pit.	L	4-9		12	15	Duke	Perez		49-61	3rd	6.0
8-7	At Pit.	W	6-4		8	9	Weaver	Snell	Schmoll	50-61	3rd	6.0
8-9	Phi.	L	4-8		7	12	Madson	Schmoll		50-62	3rd	7.0
8-10	Phi.	L	5-9		5	9	Urbina	Brazoban		50-63	3rd	7.0
8-11	Phi.	W	5-1		7	5	Perez	Lidle		51-63	3rd	7.0
8-12	N.Y.	W	7-6	(10)	11	10	Sanchez	Looper		52-63	3rd	6.0
8-13	N.Y.	L	1-5		5	8	Seo	Houlton		52-64	3rd	6.0
8-14	N.Y.	W	2-1		2	10	Penny	Martinez		53-64	3rd	5.0
8-16	At Atl.	W	6-4		12	6	Carrara	Reitsma	Sanchez	54-64	3rd	5.0
8-17	At Atl.	L	2-10		8	16	Hudson	Perez		54-65	3rd	5.0
8-18	At Atl.	W	7-4		11	10	Weaver	Thomson	Sanchez	55-65	3rd	4.0
8-19	At Fla.	L	0-3		6	4	Burnett	Houlton	Jones	55-66	3rd	5.0
8-20	At Fla.	W	11-6		12	9	Dessens	Villone	Sanchez	56-66	3rd	5.0
8-21	At Fla.	L	1-7		6	11	Vargas	Lowe		56-67	3rd	5.0
8-22	At Fla.	L	2-5		6	9	Willis	Jackson	Jones	56-68	3rd	5.0
8-23	Col.	W	8-3		10	7	Weaver	Wright		57-68	3rd	5.0
8-24	Col.	L	1-2		7	6	Williams	Schmoll	Fuentes	57-69	3rd	6.0
8-25	Col.	L	4-5		10	5	Cook	Penny	Fuentes	57-70	3rd	6.5
8-26	Hou.	L	1-2		7	8	Pettitte	Lowe	Lidge	57-71	3rd	6.5
8-27	Hou.	W	8-3		11	8	Jackson	Oswalt		58-71	3rd	5.5
8-28	Hou.	W	1-0		4	8	Weaver	Qualls	Sanchez	59-71	3rd	5.5
8-29	At Chi.	W	9-6		10	11	Houlton	Williams	Sanchez	60-71	3rd	4.5
8-30	At Chi.	L	3-6		10	11	Prior	Penny	Dempster	60-72	3rd	5.5
8-31	At Chi.	W	7-0		11	1	Lowe	Rusch		61-72	2nd	5.5
9-2	At Col.	L	3-11		9	13	Kim	Weaver	Acevedo	61-73	2nd	6.0
9-3	At Col.	L	1-11		6	14	Kim	Houlton		61-74	3rd	7.0
9-4	At Col.	L	6-7	(10)	13	11	Dohmann	Sanchez		61-75	3rd	7.0
9-5	S.F.	L	1-3		7	7	Hawkins	Brazoban	Benitez	61-76	3rd	7.5

Date	Opp.	Res.	Score	(inn.*)	Hits	Opp. hits	Winning pitcher	Losing pitcher	Save	Record	Pos.	GB
9-6	S.F.	W	4-2	(10)	8	9	Brazoban	Accardo		62-76	3rd	6.5
9-7	S.F.	W	9-8		9	10	Brazoban	Benitez		63-76	3rd	6.5
9-9	S.D.	L	1-3		5	7	Williams	Houlton	Hoffman	63-77	4th	8.0
9-10	S.D.	W	3-1		5	7	Lowe	Hensley	Sanchez	64-77	T3rd	7.0
9-11	S.D.	W	7-3		12	6	Penny	Cassidy		65-77	2nd	6.0
9-12	Col.	W	7-0		12	3	Weaver	Francis		66-77	2nd	5.0
9-13	Col.	L	4-6		7	6	Kim	Jackson	Fuentes	66-78	T2nd	5.0
9-14	Col.	L	7-8		8	12	Wright	Brazoban	Fuentes	66-79	T2nd	6.0
9-15	At S.F.	W	7-1		11	4	Lowe	Hennessey		67-79	2nd	5.5
9-16	At S.F.	L	4-5		12	8	Benitez	Sanchez		67-80	T2nd	5.5
9-17	At S.F.	L	1-2		3	5	Walker	Weaver	Benitez	67-81	3rd	6.5
9-18	At S.F.	L	3-5		10	10	Kinney	Osoria	Benitez	67-82	3rd	7.5
9-20	At Ari.	L	1-4		5	9	Vazquez	Lowe	Valverde	67-83	4th	8.0
9-21	At Ari.	L	2-3		9	6	Webb	Osoria	Valverde	67-84	4th	9.0
9-22	At Ari.	L	4-7	(12)	12	13	Bulger	Sanchez		67-85	4th	9.0
9-23	Pit.	W	4-3		9	5	Houlton	Maholm	Sanchez	68-85	4th	9.0
9-24	Pit.	L	3-8		6	13	Perez	Perez		68-86	4th	9.0
9-25	Pit.	W	9-2		11	7	Lowe	Fogg		69-86	4th	8.0
9-26	Pit.	W	9-4		11	7	Jackson	Wells		70-86	4th	7.0
9-27	Ari.	L	0-2		2	6	Webb	Weaver	Valverde	70-87	4th	8.0
9-28	Ari.	L	3-4		4	7	Medders	Brazoban	Valverde	70-88	4th	9.0
9-29	Ari.	L	2-3		4	6	Nippert	Kuo	Lyon	70-89	4th	10.0
9-30	At S.D.	L	1-3		4	5	Williams	Lowe	Linebrink	70-90	4th	11.0
10-1	At S.D.	W	2-1		6	3	Broxton	Park	Sanchez	71-90	4th	10.0
10-2	At S.D.	L	1-3		4	9	Eaton	Dessens	Hoffman	71-91	4th	11.0

Monthly records: April (15-8), May (11-17), June (11-16), July (10-17), August (14-14), September (9-18), October (1-1).
*Innings, if other than nine. ! First game of a doubleheader. & Second game of a doubleheader.

RECORDS

2005 regular-season record: 71-91
Position: 4th in N.L. West
Home: 40-41   **Road:** 31-50
N.L. East: 13-18   **N.L. Central:** 20-19
N.L. West: 33-41   **A.L.** 5-13
Vs. LH starters: 16-22
Vs. RH starters: 55-69
Grass: 71-91   **Artificial:** 0-0
Day: 20-25   **Night:** 51-66
1-Run: 20-23   **X-inn.:** 7-5
Doubleheaders: 0-0-0
Team record past five years: 427-383
(.527, ranks 5th in league in that span)

TEAM LEADERS

Batting average: Milton Bradley (.290).
At-bats: Jeff Kent (553).
Runs: Jeff Kent (100).
Hits: Jeff Kent (160).
Total Bases: Jeff Kent (283).
Doubles: Jeff Kent (36).
Triples: Jason Repko (3).
Home runs: Jeff Kent (29).
Runs batted in: Jeff Kent (105).
Stolen bases: Antonio Perez, Jayson Werth (11).
Slugging percentage: J.D. Drew (.520).
On-base percentage: J.D. Drew (.412).
Wins: Jeff Weaver (14).
Earned-run average: Derek Lowe (3.61).
Complete games: Jeff Weaver (3).
Shutouts: Derek Lowe, Jeff Weaver (2).
Saves: Yhency Brazoban (21).

Innings pitched: Jeff Weaver (224.0).
Strikeouts: Jeff Weaver (157).

GAMES BY POSITION

Catcher: Jason Phillips 93, Dioner Navarro 50, Paul Bako 13, Mike Rose 13.
First base: Hee-Seop Choi 83, Olmedo Saenz 66, Jason Phillips 21, Jeff Kent 14, Brian Myrow 5, Norihiro Nakamura 4, Jason Grabowski 3.
Second base: Jeff Kent 140, Antonio Perez 29, Willy Aybar 6, Norihiro Nakamura 1, Oscar Robles 1.
Third base: Oscar Robles 40, Mike Edwards 39, Antonio Perez 35, Jose Valentin 29, Willy Aybar 20, Olmedo Saenz 17, Norihiro Nakamura 10.
Shortstop: Cesar Izturis 106, Oscar Robles 54, Antonio Perez 9, Norihiro Nakamura 2, Mike Edwards 1, Jose Valentin 1.
Outfield: Jason Repko 118, Jayson Werth 101, Milton Bradley 72, J.D. Drew 72, Ricky Ledee 69, Jose Cruz Jr. 45, Mike Edwards 34, Jason Grabowski 32, Jose Valentin 22, Cody Ross 9, Chin-Feng Chen 3, Antonio Perez 1.
Designated hitter: Olmedo Saenz 8, Mike Edwards 2, Antonio Perez 1, Jason Repko 1, Oscar Robles 1, Jayson Werth 1.

TOP DRAFT CHOICES

1. **Luke Hochevar,** RHP, Tennessee.
2a. **Ivan De Jesus,** SS, Puerto Rico Baseball Academy, Guaynabo, P.R.
2b. **Josh Wall,** RHP, Central Private H.S., Walker, La.
3. **Sergio Pedroza,** OF, Cal State Fullerton.
4. **Josh Bell,** 3B, Santaluces H.S., Lantana, Fla.
5. **John Meloan,** RHP, Arizona.
6. **Brent Leach,** LHP, Delta State.
7. **Chris Hobdy,** RHP, Monterey H.S., Lubbock, Texas.
8. **David Horlacher,** RHP, BYU.
9. **Michael Davitt,** RHP, Davidson H.S., Mobile, Ala.
10. **Trayvon Robinson,** OF, Crenshaw H.S., Los Angeles.

MILWAUKEE BREWERS
NATIONAL LEAGUE CENTRAL DIVISION

2006 SEASON

Brewers Schedule
Home games shaded.
All-Star Game July 11 at Pittsburgh. Schedule subject to change.

Home games are shaded. All-Star Game is July 11 at Pittsburgh. Schedule is subject to change.

Fielder

CLUB DIRECTORY

Executive vice president/general manager
Doug Melvin
Executive v.p., business operations
Rick Schlesinger
Sr. vice president, chief financial officer
Robert J. Quinn
Assistant general manager
Gord Ash
Director, community relations
Leonard Peace
Director, media relations
To be announced
Special asst. to the g.m./dir. of scouting
Jack Zduriencik

Special asst. to g.m./player dev. director
Reid Nichols
Special assistant to the g.m./scouting
Dick Groch
Vice president/communications
Tyler Barnes
Sr. director/entertainment & broadcasting
Aleta Mercer
Vice president/corporate marketing
Tom Hecht
Vice president/Miller Park operations
Steve Ethier
Director/team travel
Dan Larrea

MINOR LEAGUE AFFILIATES

Class	Team	League	Manager
AAA	Nashville	Pacific Coast	Frank Kremblas
AA	Huntsville	Southern	Don Money
Advanced A	Brevard County	Florida State	To be announced
A	West Virginia	South Atlantic	Ramon Aviles
Advanced Rookie	Helena	Pioneer	Ed Sedar
Rookie	Brewers	Arizona	Mike Guerrero

BROADCAST INFORMATION

Radio: WTMJ-AM (620).
Cable TV: Fox Sports North.

SPRING TRAINING

Ballpark (city): Maryvale Baseball Park (Phoenix, Ariz.).
Ticket information: 1-800-933-7890.

For more on the Brewers, go to www.sportingnews.com/baseball/teams/brewers/

2006 SEASON *Milwaukee Brewers*

Manager—Ned Yost (3).
Coaches—Bill Castro (35), Mike Maddux (36), Dave Nelson (14), Dale Sveum (29), Butch Wynegar (16), Robin Yount (19).

No.	PITCHERS	B/T	Ht./Wt.	Age*
46	Mike Adams	R/R	6-5/190	27
	David Bush	R/R	6-2/212	26
52	Jose Capellan	R/R	6-4/235	25
39	Chris Capuano	L/L	6-3/220	27
49	Doug Davis	R/L	6-4/213	30
51	Kane Davis	R/R	6-3/194	30
47	Jorge de la Rosa	L/L	6-1/190	24
	Chris Demaria	B/R	6-3/210	25
37	Dana Eveland	L/L	6-1/220	22
30	Rick Helling	R/R	6-3/241	35
	Ben Hendrickson	R/R	6-4/190	25
	Mike Jones	R/R	6-4/200	22
	Dan Kolb	R/R	6-4/230	31
43	Justin Lehr	R/R	6-1/200	28
55	Tomo Ohka	R/R	6-1/200	30
	Manuel Parra	L/L	6-3/200	23
	Dennis Sarfate	R/R	6-4/210	24
15	Ben Sheets	R/R	6-1/220	27
59	Derrick Turnbow	R/R	6-3/210	28
	Carlos Villanueva	B/R	6-2/190	22
38	Matt Wise	R/R	6-4/200	30

No.	CATCHERS	B/T	Ht./Wt.	Age*
26	Damian Miller	R/R	6-3/220	36
21	Chad Moeller	R/R	6-3/210	31

No.	INFIELDERS	B/T	Ht./Wt.	Age*
6	Jeff Cirillo	R/R	6-1/200	36
28	Prince Fielder	L/R	6-0/260	21
2	Bill Hall	R/R	6-0/195	26
7	J.J. Hardy	R/R	6-2/181	23
	Hernan Iribarren	L/R	6-1/160	21
	Corey Koskie	L/R	6-3/219	32
	Zach Sorensen	B/R	6-0/190	29
23	Rickie Weeks	R/R	6-0/195	23

No.	OUTFIELDERS	B/T	Ht./Wt.	Age*
27	Brady Clark	R/R	6-2/202	32
8	Nelson Cruz	R/R	6-3/175	25
	Gabe Gross	L/R	6-3/209	26
	Tony Gwynn Jr.	L/R	6-0/185	23
1	Corey Hart	R/R	6-6/200	24
5	Geoff Jenkins	L/R	6-1/212	31
10	Dave Krynzel	L/L	6-1/180	24
45	Carlos Lee	R/R	6-2/240	29
	Brad Nelson	L/R	6-2/220	23

*Age as of April 1, 2006.

BALLPARK INFORMATION

Ballpark (capacity, surface)
Miller Park (41,900, grass)
Address
One Brewers Way
Milwaukee, WI 53214-3652
Official website
milwaukeebrewers.com
Business phone
414-902-4400
Ticket information
414-902-4000, 800-933-7890
Field dimensions (from home plate)
To left field at foul line, 342 feet
To center field, 400 feet
To right field at foul line, to be announced
First game played
April 6, 2001 (Brewers 5, Reds 4)

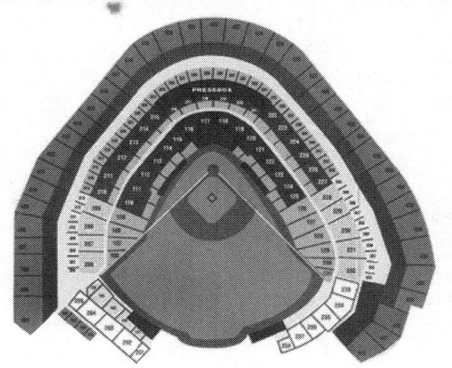

2006 SEASON *Milwaukee Brewers*

Date	Opp.	Res.	Score	(inn.*)	Hits	Opp. hits	Winning pitcher	Losing pitcher	Save	Record	Pos.	GB
4-4	At Pit.	W	9-2		9	9	Sheets	Perez		1-0	T1st	...
4-6	At Pit.	W	10-2		13	7	Davis	Wells		2-0	T1st	...
4-8	At Chi.	W	6-3	(12)	12	7	de la Rosa	Leicester	Adams	3-0	1st	+0.5
4-9	At Chi.	L	0-4		1	8	Zambrano	Sheets		3-1	T1st	...
4-10	At Chi.	L	5-6	(12)	16	11	Rusch	Turnbow		3-2	2nd	1.0
4-11	Pit.	W	6-2		8	8	Davis	Wells		4-2	T1st	...
4-12	Pit.	L	2-4		6	10	Redman	Glover	Mesa	4-3	2nd	0.5
4-13	Pit.	W	6-2		9	12	de la Rosa	White		5-3	1st	+0.5
4-15	StL.	L	0-3		5	5	Suppan	Sheets	Isringhausen	5-4	T1st	...
4-16	StL.	L	3-5		6	10	Carpenter	Davis	Isringhausen	5-5	T2nd	0.5
4-17	StL.	L	2-3		3	5	Marquis	Adams	Isringhausen	5-6	T4th	1.5
4-18	L.A.	L	3-7		3	11	Perez	Capuano		5-7	T4th	2.5
4-19	L.A.	L	6-8	(10)	8	11	Carrara	Phelps	Brazoban	5-8	5th	3.5
4-20	At Hou.	L	1-6		4	9	Oswalt	Sheets		5-9	5th	3.5
4-21	At Hou.	L	7-8		9	8	Pettitte	Davis	Lidge	5-10	5th	4.5
4-22	At S.F.	W	6-1		9	5	Santos	Rueter		6-10	5th	4.5
4-23	At S.F.	L	2-6		8	11	Tomko	Capuano	Benitez	6-11	T5th	5.5
4-24	At S.F.	W	8-5		13	11	Glover	Williams	Turnbow	7-11	5th	5.5
4-26	At StL.	L	3-5		8	8	Suppan	Davis	Flores	7-12	T5th	6.5
4-27	At StL.	L	3-6		9	11	Carpenter	Santos	Tavarez	7-13	6th	7.5
4-28	At StL.	W	4-3		6	8	Capuano	Marquis	Turnbow	8-13	6th	6.5
4-29	Cin.	W	4-3		6	6	Glover	Claussen	Turnbow	9-13	4th	6.5
4-30	Cin.	W	6-5		9	8	Turnbow	Valentine		10-13	T3rd	5.5
5-1	Cin.	W	13-3		19	5	Davis	Ortiz		11-13	3rd	4.5
5-3	Chi.	W	4-1		9	5	Capuano	Zambrano	Turnbow	12-13	T2nd	5.0
5-4	Chi.	W	4-3		9	8	Turnbow	Novoa		13-13	2nd	5.0
5-5	Chi.	W	6-5		11	10	Turnbow	Hawkins		14-13	2nd	4.0
5-6	N.Y.	L	4-7		9	8	Zambrano	Davis	Looper	14-14	2nd	4.0
5-7	N.Y.	L	5-7		3	9	Martinez	Santana	Hernandez	14-15	2nd	4.0
5-8	N.Y.	W	5-4		17	5	Turnbow	DeJean		15-15	2nd	4.0
5-9	Phi.	L	2-4		7	6	Wolf	Santos	Wagner	15-16	2nd	5.0
5-10	Phi.	W	8-5		12	10	Santana	Adams	Bottalico	16-16	2nd	4.0
5-11	Phi.	W	5-2		7	7	Davis	Lidle	Turnbow	17-16	2nd	4.0
5-13	At Pit.	W	4-3		7	8	Capuano	Mesa	Turnbow	18-16	2nd	3.5
5-14	At Pit.	L	0-2		4	9	Redman	Santos		18-17	2nd	4.5
5-15	At Pit.	L	2-4		12	6	Williams	Glover	Mesa	18-18	2nd	5.5
5-16	At Was.	L	2-5		6	10	Armas	Davis	Ayala	18-19	2nd	6.0
5-17	At Was.	W	8-2		12	3	Obermueller	Vargas		19-19	2nd	5.0
5-18	At Was.	L	0-1		6	7	Majewski	Capuano		19-20	2nd	6.0
5-19	At Was.	L	2-3		8	6	Hernandez	Santos	Cordero	19-21	2nd	6.0
5-20	At Min.	L	1-7		5	16	Silva	Glover		19-22	2nd	7.0
5-21	At Min.	W	6-0		10	7	Davis	Radke		20-22	2nd	7.0
5-22	At Min.	L	5-6	(11)	12	10	Crain	Wise		20-23	2nd	7.0
5-23	Col.	W	2-1		5	3	Capuano	Chacon	Bottalico	21-23	2nd	7.0
5-24	Col.	W	6-1		11	7	Santos	Francis		22-23	2nd	7.0
5-25	Col.	W	11-1		14	4	Glover	Wright		23-23	2nd	7.0
5-27	Hou.	W	3-0		6	3	Davis	Oswalt	Turnbow	24-23	2nd	7.0
5-28	Hou.	L	6-9		13	6	Rodriguez	Sheets	Lidge	24-24	2nd	8.0
5-29	Hou.	L	1-2		6	5	Pettitte	Capuano	Lidge	24-25	3rd	8.0
5-30	At S.D.	L	1-2		6	8	Linebrink	de la Rosa		24-26	3rd	9.0
5-31	At S.D.	L	4-8		10	11	Reyes	Glover		24-27	3rd	9.0
6-1	At S.D.	W	5-2		15	8	Davis	Lawrence	Santana	25-27	3rd	9.0
6-2	At L.A.	L	4-6		9	9	Carrara	Sheets	Gagne	25-28	3rd	9.0
6-3	At L.A.	W	7-5		6	9	Capuano	Weaver	Turnbow	26-28	3rd	9.0
6-4	At L.A.	L	1-2		6	7	Houlton	Santos	Gagne	26-29	3rd	10.0
6-5	At L.A.	L	6-10		14	15	Penny	Obermueller		26-30	4th	10.0
6-6	N.Y.	W	4-3		9	4	Davis	Johnson	Turnbow	27-30	3rd	10.0
6-7	N.Y.	W	2-1		6	4	Sheets	Pavano	Turnbow	28-30	3rd	10.0
6-8	N.Y.	L	3-12		6	16	Mussina	Capuano		28-31	4th	10.0
6-10	At Phi.	L	2-5		7	4	Madson	Wise		28-32	4th	11.0
6-11	At Phi.	L	5-7		8	11	Cormier	Bottalico	Urbina	28-33	4th	11.0
6-12	At Phi.	L	2-6		5	9	Lidle	Sheets		28-34	4th	12.0
6-13	At T.B.	L	3-5		9	13	Waechter	Capuano	Baez	28-35	4th	12.0
6-14	At T.B.	W	4-0		10	9	Ohka	Fossum		29-35	4th	12.0
6-15	At T.B.	L	3-5		6	9	Nomo	Santos	Baez	29-36	4th	12.0
6-17	At Tor.	L	5-9		7	13	Walker	Davis		29-37	4th	13.0
6-18	At Tor.	W	5-2		10	8	Sheets	Halladay	Phelps	30-37	4th	13.0

Date	Opp.	Res.	Score	(inn.*)	Hits	Opp. hits	Winning pitcher	Losing pitcher	Save	Record	Pos.	GB
6-19	At Tor.	W	5-2		11	7	Capuano	Towers	Turnbow	31-37	4th	13.0
6-20	Chi.	L	4-5		9	11	Maddux	Ohka	Dempster	31-38	4th	14.0
6-21	Chi.	L	2-4		3	5	Williams	Santos	Dempster	31-39	4th	14.0
6-22	Chi.	W	9-4		8	8	Davis	Zambrano		32-39	4th	13.0
6-23	Chi.	W	8-7		12	11	Bottalico	Remlinger	Turnbow	33-39	4th	12.0
6-24	Min.	W	3-1		7	7	Capuano	Radke	Turnbow	34-39	3rd	12.0
6-25	Min.	W	7-6		9	9	Wise	Santana	Turnbow	35-39	3rd	12.0
6-26	Min.	L	2-5		13	12	Lohse	Santos		35-40	3rd	12.0
6-28	At Chi.	L	0-2		3	4	Zambrano	Davis	Dempster	35-41	3rd	13.0
6-29	At Chi.	L	2-3		5	8	Novoa	Santos		35-42	4th	14.0
6-30	At Chi.	W	10-6		16	9	Capuano	Maddux		36-42	3rd	13.0
7-1	Pit.	W	8-4		10	10	Wise	Redman		37-42	3rd	13.0
7-2	Pit.	W	5-3		7	6	Bottalico	Torres	Turnbow	38-42	3rd	12.0
7-3	Pit.	L	10-11		9	16	Meadows	Phelps	Mesa	38-43	4th	13.0
7-4	At Fla.	W	3-2		7	5	Sheets	Jones	Turnbow	39-43	4th	13.0
7-5	At Fla.	W	6-4		16	10	Capuano	Beckett	Turnbow	40-43	4th	13.0
7-6	At Fla.	L	4-5	(12)	4	13	de los Santos	Obermueller		40-44	4th	14.0
7-7	At Fla.	L	3-11		5	12	Moehler	Santos		40-45	4th	14.0
7-8	At Atl.	L	1-2		10	8	Kolb	Santana		40-46	4th	15.0
7-9	At Atl.	W	9-6		12	11	Sheets	Davies		41-46	4th	14.0
7-10	At Atl.	W	8-4		11	10	Capuano	Colon		42-46	4th	14.0
7-14	Was.	W	4-2		11	4	Wise	Majewski	Turnbow	43-46	4th	13.5
7-15	Was.	W	4-3	(10)	10	11	Santana	Ayala		44-46	4th	13.5
7-16	Was.	L	3-5		8	8	Loaiza	Bottalico	Cordero	44-47	4th	14.5
7-17	Was.	W	5-3		8	5	Ohka	Drese	Turnbow	45-47	3rd	14.5
7-18	At StL.	L	4-11		10	14	Morris	Santos		45-48	4th	15.5
7-19	At StL.	W	5-4		13	11	Wise	Tavarez	Turnbow	46-48	4th	14.5
7-20	At StL.	L	2-4		8	7	Mulder	Sheets	Isringhausen	46-49	4th	15.5
7-21	At StL.	W	12-7		14	10	Capuano	Marquis		47-49	4th	14.5
7-22	At Cin.	L	6-11		11	15	Ortiz	Ohka		47-50	4th	15.5
7-23	At Cin.	W	11-7		11	11	Santos	Claussen		48-50	4th	14.5
7-24	At Cin.	L	2-3		7	7	Weathers	Santana		48-51	4th	14.5
7-25	Ari.	W	4-2		8	8	Sheets	Worrell	Turnbow	49-51	4th	14.0
7-26	Ari.	W	7-2		11	6	Eveland	Webb		50-51	4th	14.0
7-27	Ari.	L	0-3		8	5	Vargas	Ohka	Bruney	50-52	4th	14.0
7-28	S.F.	L	0-3		3	4	Hennessey	Santos	Walker	50-53	4th	15.0
7-29	S.F.	L	6-7		12	8	Fassero	Wise	Walker	50-54	4th	15.0
7-30	S.F.	W	7-1		6	6	Sheets	Schmidt		51-54	4th	15.0
7-31	S.F.	W	5-1		6	3	Capuano	Lowry		52-54	4th	15.0
8-2	At N.Y.	L	8-9	(11)	17	18	Looper	Santana		52-55	4th	15.5
8-3	At N.Y.	W	6-4		12	9	Helling	Looper	Turnbow	53-55	4th	15.5
8-4	At N.Y.	W	12-9		21	15	Santana	Hernandez	Turnbow	54-55	4th	14.5
8-5	At Phi.	W	3-1	(10)	7	5	Sheets	Geary	Wise	55-55	3rd	14.5
8-6	At Phi.	L	2-8		7	12	Lieber	Capuano		55-56	4th	14.5
8-7	At Phi.	W	2-0		4	5	Ohka	Padilla	Turnbow	56-56	3rd	14.5
8-8	StL.	L	4-8		7	10	Flores	Wise		56-57	4th	15.5
8-9	StL.	L	2-5		3	10	Reyes	Davis	Isringhausen	56-58	3rd	16.5
8-10	StL.	L	0-3		5	5	Suppan	Sheets	Isringhausen	56-59	3rd	17.5
8-12	Cin.	L	3-5		7	11	Hudson	Capuano	Weathers	56-60	T3rd	17.0
8-13	Cin.	L	1-4		2	13	Ortiz	Ohka	Weathers	56-61	T3rd	18.0
8-14	Cin.	W	8-3		9	5	Davis	Belisle		57-61	3rd	17.0
8-15	At Col.	L	2-11		9	17	Cook	Sheets		57-62	T3rd	17.5
8-16	At Col.	W	6-4		9	9	Santos	Francis	Turnbow	58-62	T3rd	17.5
8-17	At Col.	W	2-0		5	8	Capuano	Wright	Turnbow	59-62	T3rd	17.5
8-18	At Hou.	W	5-2		7	8	Ohka	Clemens	Turnbow	60-62	3rd	16.5
8-19	At Hou.	L	3-5		8	9	Springer	Davis	Lidge	60-63	4th	17.5
8-20	At Hou.	W	3-2		7	8	Sheets	Harville		61-63	3rd	17.5
8-21	At Hou.	L	3-8		7	11	Pettitte	Santos		61-64	3rd	17.5
8-23	Fla.	W	11-2		13	9	Capuano	Beckett		62-64	3rd	17.0
8-24	Fla.	W	6-4		8	10	Ohka	Burnett	Turnbow	63-64	3rd	17.0
8-25	Fla.	L	1-3	(10)	11	8	Alfonseca	Capellan	Jones	63-65	3rd	18.0
8-26	Atl.	W	3-1		6	8	Sheets	Ramirez	Turnbow	64-65	3rd	17.0
8-27	Atl.	L	4-8		4	17	Smoltz	Santos		64-66	3rd	18.0
8-28	Atl.	L	2-5		7	4	Hudson	Capuano		64-67	3rd	19.0
8-30	Pit.	L	0-6		4	8	Maholm	Davis		64-68	3rd	19.5
8-31	Pit.	W	6-5		12	11	Turnbow	Mesa		65-68	3rd	19.5
9-1	S.D.	L	5-6		6	9	Seanez	Davis	Hoffman	65-69	3rd	20.0
9-2	S.D.	W	12-2		11	6	Capuano	Lawrence		66-69	3rd	19.0
9-3	S.D.	L	1-6		6	9	Williams	Obermueller		66-70	3rd	20.0
9-4	S.D.	W	3-2		7	8	Turnbow	Otsuka		67-70	3rd	20.0

2006 SEASON Milwaukee Brewers

Date	Opp.	Res.	Score	(inn.*)	Hits	Opp. hits	Winning pitcher	Losing pitcher	Save	Record	Pos.	GB
9-5	At Cin.	W	6-1		14	4	Ohka	Belisle	Eveland	68-70	3rd	20.0
9-6	At Cin.	L	1-2	(10)	8	10	Mercker	de la Rosa		68-71	3rd	20.0
9-7	At Cin.	W	14-5		17	10	Capuano	Milton		69-71	3rd	19.0
9-9	Hou.	W	7-4		11	9	Davis	Clemens	Turnbow	70-71	3rd	19.5
9-10	Hou.	L	5-7		8	12	Pettitte	Ohka	Lidge	70-72	T3rd	20.5
9-11	Hou.	W	4-2		10	7	Helling	Oswalt	Turnbow	71-72	T3rd	19.5
9-13	At Ari.	W	3-1		8	6	Capuano	Vazquez	Turnbow	72-72	3rd	20.0
9-14	At Ari.	L	1-2	(12)	8	8	Medders	Lehr		72-73	3rd	20.0
9-15	At Ari.	W	14-2		19	8	Ohka	Estes		73-73	3rd	20.0
9-16	At Hou.	L	1-2		8	7	Lidge	Eveland		73-74	3rd	20.0
9-17	At Hou.	L	0-7		7	10	Backe	Obermueller		73-75	3rd	21.0
9-18	At Hou.	L	1-6		5	6	Rodriguez	Capuano		73-76	4th	21.0
9-20	Chi.	W	5-3		11	9	Davis	Williams	Turnbow	74-76	3rd	20.0
9-21	Chi.	W	7-6		11	12	Turnbow	Van Buren		75-76	3rd	20.0
9-22	Chi.	L	0-3		4	7	Maddux	Helling	Dempster	75-77	3rd	20.0
9-23	StL.	W	9-6		14	6	Capuano	Carpenter	Turnbow	76-77	3rd	19.0
9-24	StL.	W	8-7		10	10	Glover	Mulder	Turnbow	77-77	3rd	18.0
9-25	StL.	L	0-2		6	5	Suppan	Davis	Isringhausen	77-78	3rd	19.0
9-26	Cin.	W	12-9		15	9	Capellan	Coffey	Turnbow	78-78	3rd	18.5
9-27	Cin.	W	6-2		8	6	Helling	Claussen	Turnbow	79-78	3rd	17.5
9-28	Cin.	L	4-11		15	14	Harang	Capuano		79-79	3rd	17.5
9-29	Cin.	W	2-0		5	3	Glover	Milton	Turnbow	80-79	3rd	17.0
9-30	At Pit.	W	6-5		7	7	Lehr	Vogelsong	Turnbow	81-79	3rd	17.0
10-1	At Pit.	L	1-5		6	9	Wells	Ohka		81-80	3rd	18.0
10-2	At Pit.	L	1-3		9	9	Duke	Capuano	Torres	81-81	3rd	19.0

Monthly records: April (10-13), May (14-14), June (12-15), July (16-12), August (13-14), September (16-11), October (0-2).
*Innings, if other than nine. ! First game of a doubleheader. & Second game of a doubleheader.

RECORDS

2005 regular-season record: 81-81
Position: 3rd in N.L. Central
Home: 46-35   **Road:** 35-46
N.L. East: 18-18   **N.L. Central:** 38-41
N.L. West: 17-15   **A.L.** 8-7
Vs. LH starters: 27-20
Vs. RH starters: 54-61
Grass: 77-76   **Artificial:** 4-5
Day: 30-27   **Night:** 51-54
1-Run: 21-21   **X-inn.:** 3-8
Doubleheaders: 0-0-0
Team record past five years: 340-469 (.420, ranks 16th in league in that span)

TEAM LEADERS

Batting average: Brady Clark (.306).
At-bats: Carlos Lee (618).
Runs: Brady Clark (94).
Hits: Brady Clark (183).
Total Bases: Carlos Lee (301).
Doubles: Geoff Jenkins (42).
Triples: Bill Hall (6).
Home runs: Carlos Lee (32).
Runs batted in: Carlos Lee (114).
Stolen bases: Bill Hall (18).
Slugging percentage: Geoff Jenkins (.513).
On-base percentage: Geoff Jenkins (.375).
Wins: Chris Capuano (18).
Earned-run average: Ben Sheets (3.33).
Complete games: Ben Sheets (3).
Shutouts: Doug Davis, Tomo Ohka (1).

Saves: Derrick Turnbow (39).
Innings pitched: Doug Davis (222.2).
Strikeouts: Doug Davis (208).

GAMES BY POSITION

Catcher: Damian Miller 111, Chad Moeller 65.
First base: Lyle Overbay 154, Wes Helms 16, Prince Fielder 7, Russell Branyan 5, Jeff Cirillo 1.
Second base: Rickie Weeks 95, Junior Spivey 48, Bill Hall 23, Jeff Cirillo 3.
Third base: Russell Branyan 59, Bill Hall 59, Jeff Cirillo 53, Wes Helms 35, Trent Durrington 1.
Shortstop: J.J. Hardy 119, Bill Hall 66.
Outfield: Carlos Lee 162, Brady Clark 145, Geoff Jenkins 144, Chris Magruder 45, Corey Hart 16, Nelson Cruz 8, Russell Branyan 3, Dave Krynzel 1.
Designated hitter: Prince Fielder 5, Wes Helms 3, Geoff Jenkins 2, Russell Branyan 1.

TOP DRAFT CHOICES

1. **Ryan Braun,** 3B, Miami.
3. **Will Inman,** RHP, Tunstall H.S., Dry Fork, Va.
4. **Matthew Gamel,** 3B, Chipola JC (Fla.).
5. **Kevin Roberts,** RHP, Houston.
6. **Steve Hammond,** LHP, Long Beach State.
7. **Michael Brantley,** OF, Fort Pierce Central H.S., Port St. Lucie, Fla.
8. **Jemile Weeks,** SS, Lake Brantley H.S., Altamonte Springs, Fla.
9. **Carlos Hereaud,** 3B, Elkins H.S., Missouri City Texas.
10. **Steve Garrison,** LHP, The Hun School, Ewing, N.J.

NEW YORK METS
NATIONAL LEAGUE EAST DIVISION

2006 SEASON

Mets Schedule
Home games shaded.
All-Star Game July 11 at Pittsburgh. Schedule subject to change.

APRIL

SUN	MON	TUE	WED	THU	FRI	SAT
2	3 WAS	4	5 WAS	6 WAS	7 FLA	8 FLA
9 FLA	10	11 WAS	12 WAS	13 WAS	14 MIL	15 MIL
16 MIL	17 ATL	18 ATL	19 ATL	20 SD	21 SD	22 SD
23 SD	24 SF	25 SF	26 SF	27	28 ATL	29 ATL
30 ATL						

MAY

SUN	MON	TUE	WED	THU	FRI	SAT
	1 WAS	2 WAS	3 PIT	4 PIT	5 ATL	6 ATL
7 ATL	8	9 PHI	10 PHI	11 PHI	12 MIL	13 MIL
14 MIL	15	16 STL	17 STL	18 STL	19 NYY	20 NYY
21 NYY	22	23 PHI	24 PHI	25 PHI	26 FLA	27 FLA
28 FLA	29 ARI	30 ARI	31 ARI			

JUNE

SUN	MON	TUE	WED	THU	FRI	SAT
				1 SF	2 SF	3 SF
4 SF	5 LAD	6 LAD	7 LAD	8 ARI	9 ARI	10 ARI
11 ARI	12	13 PHI	14 PHI	15 PHI	16 BAL	17 BAL
18 BAL	19 CIN	20 CIN	21 CIN	22 TOR	23 TOR	24 TOR
25 TOR	26	27 BOS	28 BOS	29 BOS	30 NYY	

JULY

SUN	MON	TUE	WED	THU	FRI	SAT
						1 NYY
2 NYY	3 PIT	4 PIT	5 PIT	6 PIT	7 FLA	8 FLA
9 FLA	10	11 ALL-STAR	12	13	14 CHC	15 CHC
16 CHC	17	18 CIN	19 CIN	20 CIN	21 HOU	22 HOU
23 HOU	24 CHC	25 CHC	26 CHC	27	28 ATL	29 ATL
30 ATL	31					

AUGUST

SUN	MON	TUE	WED	THU	FRI	SAT
		1 FLA	2 FLA	3 FLA	4 PHI	5 PHI
6 PHI	7	8 SD	9 SD	10 SD	11 WAS	12 WAS
13 WAS	14 PHI	15 PHI	16 PHI	17 PHI	18 COL	19 COL
20 COL	21	22 STL	23 STL	24 STL	25 PHI	26 PHI
27 PHI	28	29 COL	30 COL	31 COL		

SEPTEMBER

SUN	MON	TUE	WED	THU	FRI	SAT
					1 HOU	2 HOU
3 HOU	4 ATL	5 ATL	6 ATL	7	8 LAD	9 LAD
10 LAD	11 FLA	12 FLA	13 FLA	14	15 PIT	16 PIT
17 PIT	18 FLA	19 FLA	20 FLA	21 FLA	22 WAS	23 WAS
24 WAS	25 ATL	26 ATL	27 ATL	28 ATL	29 WAS	30 WAS

OCTOBER

SUN	MON	TUE	WED	THU	FRI	SAT
1 WAS	2	3	4	5	6	7

Home games are shaded. All-Star Game is July 11 at Pittsburgh. Schedule is subject to change.

Beltran

CLUB DIRECTORY

Chairman and chief executive officer
Fred Wilpon
President
Saul Katz
Sr. executive v.p./chief operating officer
Jeffrey S. Wilpon
Executive v.p. and general manager
Omar Minaya
Assistant general manager
John Ricco
Special assistants to the general manager
Tony Bernazard, Al Goldis, Sandy Johnson, Bryan Lambe, Bill Livesey, Scott Nethery
Vice president, professional scouting
Gary LaRocque

Executive v.p., business operations
Dave Howard
Executive v.p. and general counsel
David Cohen
Senior vice president, corporate sales
Paul Danforth
Senior v.p., marketing communications
David Newman
Chief financial officer
Mark Peskin
Vice president, media relations
Jay Horwitz
Vice president, ticket sales and services
Bill Ianniciello
Director, minor league operations
Kevin Morgan

MINOR LEAGUE AFFILIATES

Class	Team	League	Manager
AAA	Norfolk	International	Ken Oberkfell
AA	Binghamton	Eastern	To be announced
Advanced A	St. Lucie	Florida State	Gary Carter
A	Hagerstown	South Atlantic	Frank Cacciatore
Short-Season A	Brooklyn	New York-Penn	George Greer
Advanced Rookie	Kingsport	Appalachian	Donovan Mitchell
Rookie	Mets	Gulf Coast	To be announced

BROADCAST INFORMATION

Radio: WFAN-AM (660).
TV: WPIX-TV (Channel 11).
Cable TV: Sports Net New York.

SPRING TRAINING

Ballpark (city): Tradition Field (Port St. Lucie, Fla.).
Ticket information: 772-871-2115.

For more on the Mets, go to www.sportingnews.com/baseball/teams/mets/

– 123 –

SPRING TRAINING ROSTER

Manager—Willie Randolph (12).
Coaches—Manny Acta (50), Sandy Alomar Sr. (2), Guy Conti (56), Rick Down (54), Jerry Manuel (53), Tom Nieto (55), Rick Peterson (51).

No.	PITCHERS	B/T	Ht./Wt.	Age*
	Brian Bannister	R/R	6-2/200	25
19	Heath Bell	R/R	6-2/220	28
34	Kris Benson	R/R	6-4/205	31
	Chad Bradford	R/R	6-5/203	31
43	Bartolome Fortunato	R/R	6-1/195	31
	Anderson Garcia	R/R	6-2/170	25
47	Tom Glavine	L/L	6-0/185	40
48	Aaron Heilman	R/R	6-5/220	27
	Philip Humber	R/R	6-4/210	23
67	Matt Lindstrom	R/R	6-4/210	26
45	Pedro Martinez	R/R	5-11/180	34
	Henry Owens	R/R	6-3/230	26
28	Juan Padilla	R/R	6-0/200	29
	Mike Pelfrey	R/R	6-7/210	22
	Juan Perez	R/L	6-1/170	27
22	Royce Ring	L/L	6-0/220	25
	Duaner Sanchez	R/R	6-0/190	26
	Steve Schmoll	R/R	6-2/200	26
29	Steve Trachsel	R/R	6-4/205	35
13	Billy Wagner	L/L	5-11/195	34
	Mitch Wylie	R/R	6-3/190	29
38	Victor Zambrano	B/R	6-0/203	30

No.	CATCHERS	B/T	Ht./Wt.	Age*
11	Ramon Castro	R/R	6-3/235	30
	Paul Lo Duca	R/R	5-10/185	33

No.	INFIELDERS	B/T	Ht./Wt.	Age*
	Aarom Baldiris	R/R	6-2/195	23
21	Carlos Delgado	L/R	6-3/240	33
	Julio Franco	R/R	6-1/210	47
1	Anderson Hernandez	B/R	5-9/168	23
6	Jeff Keppinger	R/R	6-0/180	25
25	Kazuo Matsui	B/R	5-10/185	30
7	Jose Reyes	B/R	6-0/175	22
	Jose Valentin	L/R	5-10/195	36
4	Chris Woodward	R/R	6-0/185	29
5	David Wright	R/R	6-0/200	23

No.	OUTFIELDERS	B/T	Ht./Wt.	Age*
15	Carlos Beltran	B/R	6-1/190	28
	Endy Chavez	L/L	5-10/155	28
20	Victor Diaz	R/R	6-0/200	24
30	Cliff Floyd	L/R	6-4/230	33
	Xavier Nady	R/R	6-2/205	27
	Angel Pagan	B/R	6-1/180	24
	Tike Redman	L/L	5-11/172	29

*Age as of April 1, 2006.

BALLPARK INFORMATION

Ballpark (capacity, surface)
Shea Stadium (57,333, grass)
Address
123-01 Roosevelt Ave.
Flushing, NY 11368
Official website
www.mets.com
Business phone
718-507-METS
Ticket information
718-507-TIXX
Field dimensions (from home plate)
To left field at foul line, 338 feet
To center field, 410 feet
To right field at foul line, 338 feet
First game played
April 17, 1964 (Pirates 4, Mets 3)

Date	Opp.	Res.	Score	(inn.*)	Hits	Opp. hits	Winning pitcher	Losing pitcher	Save	Record	Pos.	GB
4-4	At Cin.	L	6-7		14	8	Graves	Looper		0-1	T4th	1.0
4-6	At Cin.	L	5-9		12	14	Milton	Glavine		0-2	5th	1.0
4-7	At Cin.	L	1-6		4	3	Harang	Ishii	Graves	0-3	5th	2.0
4-8	At Atl.	L	1-3		9	7	Thomson	Zambrano	Kolb	0-4	5th	3.0
4-9	At Atl.	L	3-6		7	12	Bernero	Heilman		0-5	5th	4.0
4-10	At Atl.	W	6-1		13	2	Martinez	Smoltz		1-5	5th	3.0
4-11	Hou.	W	8-4		13	9	Hernandez	Springer		2-5	5th	3.0
4-13	Hou.	W	1-0	(11)	4	4	DeJean	Wheeler		3-5	5th	1.5
4-14	Hou.	W	4-3		7	10	Matthews	Franco	Looper	4-5	T4th	1.5
4-15	Fla.	W	4-0		5	1	Heilman	Beckett		5-5	T3rd	1.0
4-16	Fla.	W	4-3		8	6	Looper	Mota		6-5	T2nd	1.0
4-17	Fla.	L	2-5		4	9	Burnett	Glavine		6-6	T2nd	2.0
4-18	At Phi.	L	4-5		10	7	Wolf	Ishii	Worrell	6-7	5th	2.0
4-19	At Phi.	W	16-4		15	8	Zambrano	Padilla		7-7	T3rd	1.0
4-20	At Fla.	L	2-9		4	15	Beckett	Heilman		7-8	T3rd	2.0
4-21	At Fla.	W	10-1		10	6	Martinez	Leiter		8-8	T3rd	1.0
4-22	Was.	W	3-1		7	4	Glavine	Loaiza	Looper	9-8	T2nd	1.0
4-23	Was.	W	10-5		16	12	Seo	Ohka		10-8	T2nd	1.0
4-24	Was.	L	4-11		10	17	Hernandez	Zambrano		10-9	T3rd	1.0
4-25	Atl.	W	5-4		9	6	Heilman	Ramirez	Looper	11-9	T2nd	0.5
4-26	Atl.	L	3-4		12	7	Smoltz	Martinez	Foster	11-10	T3rd	1.5
4-27	Atl.	L	4-8		9	13	Hampton	Glavine		11-11	T3rd	2.0
4-29	At Was.	L	1-5		10	5	Hernandez	Seo	Cordero	11-12	4th	3.0
4-30	At Was.	L	3-5	(8)	3	10	Ohka	Zambrano	Carrasco	11-13	4th	4.0
5-1	At Was.	W	6-3		12	7	Hernandez	Ayala	Looper	12-13	4th	3.0
5-2	Phi.	W	5-1		9	4	Martinez	Adams		13-13	4th	2.5
5-3	Phi.	L	3-10		7	10	Myers	Glavine		13-14	4th	3.5
5-4	Phi.	W	3-2		5	3	Seo	Wolf	Looper	14-14	4th	2.5
5-5	Phi.	W	7-5		12	10	Heilman	Padilla	Looper	15-14	4th	2.5
5-6	At Mil.	W	7-4		8	9	Zambrano	Davis	Looper	16-14	4th	2.5
5-7	At Mil.	W	7-5		9	3	Martinez	Santana	Hernandez	17-14	4th	2.5
5-8	At Mil.	L	4-5		5	17	Turnbow	DeJean		17-15	4th	3.5
5-9	At Chi.	W	7-4		13	10	DeJean	Hawkins	Looper	18-15	4th	2.5
5-10	At Chi.	L	0-7		3	13	Maddux	Benson		18-16	4th	3.5
5-11	At Chi.	L	3-4	(10)	6	5	Dempster	Bell		18-17	4th	3.5
5-13	StL.	W	2-0		3	5	Glavine	Marquis	Looper	19-17	3rd	2.5
5-14	StL.	L	6-7		13	9	Tavarez	Hernandez	Isringhausen	19-18	4th	3.5
5-15	StL.	L	2-4		6	7	Morris	Heilman	Isringhausen	19-19	4th	4.5
5-16	Cin.	W	9-2		13	4	Benson	Wilson		20-19	4th	3.5
5-17	Cin.	W	2-1		7	5	DeJean	Ortiz	Looper	21-19	4th	2.5
5-18	Cin.	W	10-6		13	13	Glavine	Milton		22-19	4th	1.5
5-20	N.Y.	L	2-5		5	8	Brown	Zambrano	Rivera	22-20	4th	2.0
5-21	N.Y.	W	7-1		15	5	Benson	Johnson		23-20	T3rd	2.0
5-22	N.Y.	L	3-5		8	8	Pavano	Hernandez	Rivera	23-21	4th	3.0
5-23	At Atl.	L	6-8		11	8	Ramirez	Ishii	Kolb	23-22	4th	4.0
5-24	At Atl.	L	0-4		6	8	Hudson	Glavine		23-23	4th	5.0
5-25	At Atl.	L	0-3		8	6	Davies	Zambrano	Reitsma	23-24	4th	5.0
5-26	At Fla.	W	12-4		14	9	Benson	Castillo		24-24	4th	4.0
5-27	At Fla.	W	1-0		5	5	Martinez	Moehler	Looper	25-24	3rd	3.0
5-28	At Fla.	W	6-1		14	9	Ishii	Willis		26-24	3rd	2.0
5-29	At Fla.	L	3-6		6	15	Beckett	Bell	Jones	26-25	3rd	3.0
5-31	Ari.	L	0-7		6	14	Halsey	Benson		26-26	4th	2.5
6-1	Ari.	W	2-1		10	8	Zambrano	Webb	Looper	27-26	T3rd	2.5
6-2	Ari.	W	6-1		9	7	Martinez	Estes		28-26	T3rd	1.5
6-4	S.F.	W	5-1		12	11	Glavine	Lowry		29-26	4th	1.0
6-5!	S.F.	L	3-6		10	12	Tomko	Ishii	Walker	29-27		
6-5&	S.F.	W	12-1		13	6	Benson	Schmidt		30-27	T3rd	1.0
6-7	Hou.	W	3-1		12	2	Martinez	Oswalt		31-27	T2nd	1.0
6-8	Hou.	L	1-4		6	8	Backe	Zambrano	Lidge	31-28	T3rd	2.0
6-9	Hou.	L	3-6	(11)	6	14	Springer	Bell	Lidge	31-29	4th	3.0
6-10	L.A.	L	2-12		7	13	Colon	Ishii		31-30	5th	4.0
6-11	L.A.	W	5-3	(10)	9	8	Looper	Donnelly		32-30	5th	4.0
6-12	L.A.	L	3-4		7	8	Shields	Looper	Rodriguez	32-31	5th	5.0
6-14	At Oak.	L	0-5		4	12	Blanton	Glavine	Street	32-32	5th	5.5
6-15	At Oak.	L	2-3		5	6	Duchscherer	Ring		32-33	5th	6.5
6-16	At Oak.	W	9-6		9	11	Benson	Glynn	Looper	33-33	5th	6.0
6-17	At Sea.	L	0-5		6	9	Moyer	Ishii	Nelson	33-34	5th	6.0

Date	Opp.	Res.	Score	(inn.*)	Hits	Opp. hits	Winning pitcher	Losing pitcher	Save	Record	Pos.	GB
6-18	At Sea.	L	1-4		6	10	Franklin	Martinez	Guardado	33-35	5th	6.0
6-19	At Sea.	L	5-11		10	17	Meche	Glavine		33-36	5th	7.0
6-21	At Phi.	W	8-5		14	10	Benson	Myers	Looper	34-36	5th	6.5
6-22	At Phi.	L	4-8		5	10	Madson	Ring		34-37	5th	7.5
6-23	At Phi.	W	4-3		8	9	Ishii	Lidle	Looper	35-37	5th	7.0
6-24	At N.Y.	W	6-4		8	8	Martinez	Mussina		36-37	5th	7.0
6-25	At N.Y.	W	10-3		14	11	Glavine	Henn		37-37	5th	7.0
6-26	At N.Y.	L	4-5		7	8	Rivera	Looper		37-38	5th	7.0
6-28	Phi.	W	8-3		10	7	Zambrano	Tejeda		38-38	5th	7.0
6-29	Phi.	L	3-6		5	5	Lidle	Ishii	Wagner	38-39	5th	8.0
6-30	Phi.	W	5-3		7	8	Martinez	Lieber	Looper	39-39	5th	8.0
7-1	Fla.	W	7-6		9	13	Hernandez	Mecir	Looper	40-39	4th	8.0
7-2	Fla.	L	3-7		9	11	Moehler	Benson		40-40	5th	9.0
7-3	Fla.	L	0-3		3	8	Willis	Zambrano		40-41	5th	10.0
7-4	At Was.	W	5-2		10	5	Hernandez	Kim	Looper	41-41	4th	9.0
7-5	At Was.	L	2-3		8	8	Loaiza	Martinez	Cordero	41-42	5th	10.0
7-6	At Was.	W	5-3		10	9	Glavine	Hernandez	Looper	42-42	4th	9.0
7-7	At Was.	W	3-2	(11)	7	8	Bell	Ayala	Looper	43-42	4th	8.0
7-8	At Pit.	L	5-6	(10)	9	10	Mesa	Looper		43-43	4th	9.0
7-9	At Pit.	L	4-11		9	12	Williams	Ishii		43-44	5th	9.0
7-10	At Pit.	W	6-1		13	6	Martinez	Wells		44-44	5th	8.0
7-14	Atl.	W	6-3		8	6	Hernandez	Brower	Looper	45-44	5th	7.0
7-15	Atl.	L	1-2		6	9	Smoltz	Hernandez	Reitsma	45-45	5th	7.0
7-16	Atl.	L	0-3		6	10	Hudson	Zambrano	Reitsma	45-46	5th	8.0
7-17	Atl.	W	8-1		13	6	Martinez	Hampton		46-46	T4th	7.0
7-19	S.D.	W	3-1	(11)	9	6	Looper	Hammond		47-46	4th	6.5
7-20	S.D.	W	7-3		10	9	Glavine	Williams	Padilla	48-46	4th	5.5
7-21	S.D.	W	12-0		12	6	Ishii	Peavy		49-46	3rd	4.5
7-22	L.A.	L	5-6		8	15	Weaver	Zambrano	Brazoban	49-47	4th	4.5
7-23	L.A.	W	7-5		12	8	Martinez	Carrara	Looper	50-47	4th	4.5
7-24	L.A.	W	6-0		12	4	Benson	Penny		51-47	4th	3.5
7-25	At Col.	L	3-5		6	11	Acevedo	Glavine	Fuentes	51-48	4th	4.0
7-26	At Col.	L	3-4		9	8	Francis	Ishii	Fuentes	51-49	4th	5.0
7-27	At Col.	W	9-3		13	9	Zambrano	Wright		52-49	3rd	5.0
7-28	At Hou.	L	2-3		7	6	Wheeler	Hernandez		52-50	5th	6.0
7-29	At Hou.	L	2-5		5	8	Rodriguez	Benson	Lidge	52-51	5th	7.0
7-30	At Hou.	L	0-2		3	7	Pettitte	Glavine	Lidge	52-52	5th	8.0
7-31	At Hou.	W	9-4		17	10	Heilman	Wheeler		53-52	5th	8.0
8-2	Mil.	W	9-8	(11)	18	17	Looper	Santana		54-52	5th	7.5
8-3	Mil.	L	4-6		9	12	Helling	Looper	Turnbow	54-53	5th	7.5
8-4	Mil.	L	9-12		15	21	Santana	Hernandez	Turnbow	54-54	5th	8.5
8-5	Chi.	W	9-5		14	10	Glavine	Hill		55-54	5th	7.5
8-6	Chi.	W	2-0		4	4	Seo	Maddux	Looper	56-54	5th	7.5
8-7	Chi.	W	6-1		10	6	Zambrano	Zambrano		57-54	5th	6.5
8-9	At S.D.	L	3-8		9	15	Park	Martinez		57-55	5th	7.5
8-10	At S.D.	W	9-1		12	4	Benson	Lawrence		58-55	5th	7.5
8-11	At S.D.	L	1-2		6	10	Williams	Glavine	Hoffman	58-56	5th	7.5
8-12	At L.A.	L	6-7	(10)	10	11	Sanchez	Looper		58-57	5th	7.5
8-13	At L.A.	W	5-1		8	5	Seo	Houlton		59-57	5th	7.5
8-14	At L.A.	L	1-2		10	2	Penny	Martinez		59-58	5th	8.5
8-16	Pit.	W	6-2		6	8	Benson	Redman		60-58	5th	7.5
8-17	Pit.	W	5-1		6	9	Glavine	Fogg	Heilman	61-58	5th	7.5
8-18	Pit.	L	0-5		3	11	Duke	Zambrano		61-59	5th	7.5
8-19	Was.	W	1-0		8	5	Seo	Patterson	Looper	62-59	5th	6.5
8-20	Was.	W	9-8	(10)	11	14	Hernandez	Majewski		63-59	5th	5.5
8-21	Was.	L	4-7		8	13	Loaiza	Benson		63-60	5th	6.5
8-22	At Ari.	W	4-1		7	5	Glavine	Webb	Looper	64-60	5th	6.5
8-23	At Ari.	W	14-1		17	6	Zambrano	Vargas		65-60	T4th	5.5
8-24	At Ari.	W	18-4		20	8	Seo	Ortiz		66-60	T3rd	5.5
8-25	At Ari.	W	3-1		5	4	Martinez	Vazquez	Looper	67-60	T3rd	5.0
8-26	At S.F.	W	1-0		7	3	Trachsel	Correia	Looper	68-60	T3rd	4.0
8-27	At S.F.	L	1-2		4	5	Schmidt	Glavine	Benitez	68-61	4th	5.0
8-28	At S.F.	L	1-4		6	9	Lowry	Benson	Benitez	68-62	4th	6.0
8-30	Phi.	W	6-4		10	11	Padilla	Urbina	Looper	69-62	4th	5.0
8-31	Phi.	L	2-8		6	11	Myers	Martinez		69-63	4th	5.5
9-1	Phi.	L	1-3		4	7	Lieber	Glavine	Wagner	69-64	4th	6.5
9-2	At Fla.	L	2-4		8	12	Willis	Zambrano	Jones	69-65	4th	7.5
9-3	At Fla.	L	4-5		9	7	Villone	Padilla	Jones	69-66	5th	8.5
9-4	At Fla.	W	7-1		12	5	Seo	Burnett		70-66	5th	7.5
9-5	At Atl.	L	2-4		9	7	Boyer	Trachsel	Farnsworth	70-67	5th	8.5

Date	Opp.	Res.	Score	(inn.*)	Hits	Opp. hits	Winning pitcher	Losing pitcher	Save	Record	Pos.	GB
9-6	At Atl.	L	1-3		8	7	Smoltz	Martinez	Farnsworth	70-68	5th	9.5
9-7	At Atl.	L	3-4	(10)	12	9	Foster	Looper		70-69	5th	10.5
9-8	At StL.	L	0-5		4	10	Carpenter	Benson		70-70	5th	11.0
9-9	At StL.	L	2-3		8	8	Marquis	Seo	Isringhausen	70-71	5th	11.0
9-10	At StL.	L	2-4		10	6	Suppan	Trachsel	Isringhausen	70-72	5th	12.0
9-11	At StL.	W	7-2		13	10	Martinez	Morris		71-72	5th	12.0
9-13	Was.	L	2-4		5	9	Majewski	Glavine	Cordero	71-73	5th	11.5
9-14	Was.	L	3-6		8	10	Loaiza	Benson	Cordero	71-74	5th	11.5
9-15	Was.	L	5-6	(10)	12	13	Bergmann	Hernandez	Majewski	71-75	5th	12.5
9-16	Atl.	W	4-0		8	6	Martinez	Smoltz		72-75	5th	11.5
9-17	Atl.	L	4-7		7	14	Hudson	Trachsel	Farnsworth	72-76	5th	12.5
9-18	Atl.	W	4-1		7	6	Glavine	Thomson		73-76	5th	11.5
9-20	Fla.	W	3-2	(12)	4	8	Heilman	Moehler		74-76	5th	11.5
9-21	Fla.	W	5-4		11	14	Hernandez	Quantrill		75-76	5th	10.5
9-22	Fla.	L	1-2		6	8	Willis	Martinez	Jones	75-77	5th	10.5
9-23	At Was.	W	5-2	(10)	10	7	Hernandez	Majewski	Heilman	76-77	5th	10.5
9-24	At Was.	W	5-2		6	5	Glavine	Hernandez	Hernandez	77-77	5th	10.5
9-25	At Was.	W	6-5		8	9	Padilla	Hughes	Heilman	78-77	4th	10.5
9-26	At Phi.	W	6-5		7	9	Takatsu	Urbina	Hernandez	79-77	4th	9.5
9-27	At Phi.	W	3-2		9	4	Padilla	Lieber	Heilman	80-77	3rd	9.5
9-28	At Phi.	L	6-16		10	20	Padilla	Trachsel		80-78	4th	9.5
9-29	Col.	W	11-0		15	2	Glavine	Kim		81-78	3rd	9.0
9-30	Col.	W	3-2		7	6	Benson	Kim	Heilman	82-78	3rd	8.0
10-1	Col.	W	3-1		6	7	Seo	Esposito	Hernandez	83-78	3rd	7.0
10-2	Col.	L	3-11		10	16	Cook	Zambrano		83-79	T3rd	7.0

Monthly records: April (11-13), May (15-13), June (13-13), July (14-13), August (16-11), September (13-15), October (1-1).
*Innings, if other than nine. ! First game of a doubleheader. & Second game of a doubleheader.

RECORDS

2005 regular-season record: 83-79
Position: 3rd in N.L. East
Home: 48-33   Road: 35-46
N.L. East: 38-36   N.L. Central: 20-21
N.L. West: 20-12   A.L. 5-10
Vs. LH starters: 18-21
Vs. RH starters: 65-58
Grass: 83-79   Artificial: 0-0
Day: 26-26   Night: 57-53
1-Run: 21-24   X-inn.: 8-6
Doubleheaders: 0-0-1
Team record past five years: 377-431
(.467, ranks 12th in league in that span)

TEAM LEADERS

Batting average: David Wright (.306).
At-bats: Jose Reyes (696).
Runs: Jose Reyes, David Wright (99).
Hits: Jose Reyes (190).
Total Bases: David Wright (301).
Doubles: David Wright (42).
Triples: Jose Reyes (17).
Home runs: Cliff Floyd (34).
Runs batted in: David Wright (102).
Stolen bases: Jose Reyes (60).
Slugging percentage: David Wright (.523).
On-base percentage: David Wright (.388).
Wins: Pedro Martinez (15).
Earned-run average: Pedro Martinez (2.82).
Complete games: Pedro Martinez (4).
Shutouts: Tom Glavine, Aaron Heilman, Pedro Martinez (1).
Saves: Braden Looper (28).

Innings pitched: Pedro Martinez (217.0).
Strikeouts: Pedro Martinez (208).

GAMES BY POSITION

Catcher: Mike Piazza 101, Ramon Castro 99, Mike DiFelice 11.

First base: Doug Mientkiewicz 83, Chris Woodward 34, Mike Jacobs 28, Marlon Anderson 23, Jose Offerman 11, Miguel Cairo 8, Brian Daubach 6.

Second base: Miguel Cairo 82, Kazuo Matsui 71, Marlon Anderson 20, Anderson Hernandez 5, Chris Woodward 5, Jose Offerman 1.

Third base: David Wright 160, Chris Woodward 6, Miguel Cairo 3.

Shortstop: Jose Reyes 161, Chris Woodward 7, Anderson Hernandez 2.

Outfield: Carlos Beltran 150, Cliff Floyd 150, Victor Diaz 81, Mike Cameron 76, Gerald Williams 27, Marlon Anderson 23, Chris Woodward 23, Eric Valent 12, Miguel Cairo 3.

Designated hitter: Mike Piazza 5, Marlon Anderson 2, Brian Daubach 2, Chris Woodward 1.

TOP DRAFT CHOICES

1. **Mike Pelfrey,** RHP, Wichita State.
4. **Hector Pellot,** 2B, Puerto Rico Baseball Academy, Cidra, P.R.
5. **Drew Butera,** C, Central Florida.
6. **Greg Cain,** OF, Gahr H.S., Cerritos, Calif.
7. **Jon Niese,** LHP, Defiance (Ohio) H.S.
8. **Sean McCraw,** C, San Jacinto College (Houston).
9. **Bobby Parnell,** RHP, Charleston Southern.
10. **Courtney Billingslea,** OF, Sinclair CC (Ohio).

PHILADELPHIA PHILLIES
NATIONAL LEAGUE EAST DIVISION

2006 SEASON

Phillies Schedule
Home games shaded.
All-Star Game July 11 at Pittsburgh. Schedule subject to change.

APRIL

SUN	MON	TUE	WED	THU	FRI	SAT
2	3 STL	4	5 STL	6 STL	7 LAD	8 LAD
9 LAD	10 ATL	11	12 ATL	13 ATL	14 COL	15 COL
16 COL	17	18 WAS	19 WAS	20 WAS	21 FLA	22 FLA
23 FLA	24 COL	25 COL	26 COL	27 COL	28 PIT	29 PIT
30 PIT						

MAY

SUN	MON	TUE	WED	THU	FRI	SAT
	1 FLA	2 FLA	3 ATL	4 ATL	5 SF	6 SF
7 SF	8	9 NYM	10 NYM	11 NYM	12 CIN	13 CIN
14 CIN	15	16 MIL	17 MIL	18 MIL	19 BOS	20 BOS
21 BOS	22	23 NYM	24 NYM	25 NYM	26 MIL	27 MIL
28 MIL	29 WAS	30 WAS	31 WAS			

JUNE

SUN	MON	TUE	WED	THU	FRI	SAT
				1 LAD	2 LAD	3 LAD
4 LAD	5 ARI	6 ARI	7 ARI	8 WAS	9 WAS	10 WAS
11 WAS	12	13 NYM	14 NYM	15 NYM	16 TB	17 TB
18 TB	19 NYY	20 NYY	21 NYY	22	23 BOS	24 BOS
25 BOS	26	27 BAL	28 BAL	29 BAL	30 TOR	

JULY

SUN	MON	TUE	WED	THU	FRI	SAT
						1 TOR
2 TOR	3	4 SD	5 SD	6 SD	7 PIT	8 PIT
9 PIT	10	11 ALL-STAR	12	13	14 SF	15 SF
16 SF	17 SD	18 SD	19 SD	20	21 ATL	22 ATL
23 ATL	24 ATL	25 ARI	26 ARI	27 ARI	28 FLA	29 FLA
30 FLA	31 FLA					

AUGUST

SUN	MON	TUE	WED	THU	FRI	SAT
		1 STL	2 STL	3 STL	4 NYM	5 NYM
6 NYM	7 ATL	8 ATL	9 ATL	10	11 CIN	12 CIN
13 CIN	14 NYM	15 NYM	16 NYM	17 NYM	18 WAS	19 WAS
20 WAS	21 CHC	22 CHC	23 CHC	24 CHC	25 NYM	26 NYM
27 NYM	28	29 WAS	30 WAS	31 WAS		

SEPTEMBER

SUN	MON	TUE	WED	THU	FRI	SAT
					1 ATL	2 ATL
3 ATL	4 HOU	5 HOU	6 HOU	7	8 FLA	9 FLA
10 FLA	11	12 ATL	13 ATL	14 ATL	15 HOU	16 HOU
17 HOU	18 CHC	19 CHC	20 CHC	21	22 FLA	23 FLA
24 FLA	25	26 WAS	27 WAS	28 WAS	29 FLA	30 FLA

OCTOBER

SUN	MON	TUE	WED	THU	FRI	SAT
1 FLA	2	3	4	5	6	7

Home games are shaded. All-Star Game is July 11 at Pittsburgh. Schedule is subject to change.

Abreu

CLUB DIRECTORY

General partner, president and CEO
David Montgomery
Chairman
Bill Giles
Senior v.p., chief financial officer
Jerry Clothier
V.p., operations and administration
Michael Stiles
Vice president and general manager
Pat Gillick
Assistant general manager
Ruben Amaro Jr.
Assistant g.m., scouting and player dev.
Mike Arbuckle
Director, scouting
Marti Wolever
Director, minor league operations
Steve Noworyta
Director, Latin American operations

Sal Artiaga
Manager, equipment and team travel
Frank Coppenbarger
Vice president, public relations
Larry Shenk
Director, media relations
Leigh Tobin
Director, community relations
Gene Dias
Vice president, advertising sales
David Buck
Director, marketing programs and events
Kurt Funk
Director, entertainment
Chris Long
Manager, video production
Dan Stephenson
Vice president, ticket operations
Richard Deats

MINOR LEAGUE AFFILIATES

Class	Team	League	Manager
AAA	Scranton/Wilkes-Barre	International	John Russell
AA	Reading	Eastern	P.J. Forbes
Advanced A	Clearwater	Florida State	Greg Legg
A	Lakewood	South Atlantic	Dave Huppert
Short-Season A	Batavia	New York-Penn	Steve Roadcap
Rookie	Phillies	Gulf Coast	Jim Morrison

BROADCAST INFORMATION

Radio: WPHT-AM (950); WIP-AM (610) on Fridays.
TV: UPN (Channel 57).
Cable TV: Comcast SportsNet.

SPRING TRAINING

Ballpark (city): Bright House Networks Field (Clearwater, Fla.).
Ticket information: 215-463-1000, 727-442-8496.

For more on the Phillies, go to www.sportingnews.com/baseball/teams/phillies/

Manager—Charlie Manuel (41).
Coaches—Mick Billmeyer (17), Marc Bombard (23), Bill Dancy (16), Rich Dubee (28), Ramon Henderson (31), Milt Thompson (15), Gary Varsho (19).

No.	PITCHERS	B/T	Ht./Wt.	Age*
38	Chris Booker	R/R	6-3/230	29
58	Eude Brito	L/L	5-11/160	27
37	Rheal Cormier	L/L	5-10/195	38
34	Gavin Floyd	R/R	6-4/225	23
	Ryan Franklin	R/R	6-3/180	32
46	Aaron Fultz	L/L	6-0/205	32
56	Geoff Geary	R/R	6-0/180	29
45	Tom Gordon	R/R	5-10/190	38
79	Daniel Haigwood	R/L	6-2/200	22
77	Yoel Hernandez	R/R	6-2/170	25
30	Cory Lidle	R/R	5-11/192	34
21	Jon Lieber	L/R	6-2/230	35
63	Ryan Madson	L/R	6-6/190	25
78	Scott Mathieson	R/R	6-3/190	22
39	Brett Myers	R/R	6-4/223	25
47	Ricardo Rodriguez	L/R	6-3/190	27
48	Julio Santana	R/R	6-0/210	32
75	Zach Segovia	R/R	6-2/220	22
50	Robinson Tejeda	R/R	6-3/188	24
43	Randy Wolf	L/L	6-0/200	29

No.	CATCHERS	B/T	Ht./Wt.	Age*
13	Sal Fasano	R/R	6-2/245	34
24	Mike Lieberthal	R/R	6-0/190	34
51	Carlos Ruiz	R/R	5-10/180	27

No.	INFIELDERS	B/T	Ht./Wt.	Age*
25	David Bell	R/R	5-10/190	33
6	Ryan Howard	L/L	6-4/260	26
27	Matt Kata	B/R	6-1/195	28
3	Abraham Nunez	B/R	5-11/190	30
9	Tomas Perez	B/R	5-11/192	32
11	Jimmy Rollins	B/R	5-8/175	27
29	Danny Sandoval	B/R	5-11/192	26
26	Chase Utley	L/R	6-1/183	27

No.	OUTFIELDERS	B/T	Ht./Wt.	Age*
53	Bobby Abreu	L/R	6-0/211	32
76	Michael Bourn	L/R	5-11/180	23
5	Pat Burrell	R/R	6-4/230	29
	Josh Kroeger	L/L	6-2/220	23
22	Jason Michaels	R/R	6-0/204	29
80	Christopher Roberson	B/R	6-2/175	26
33	Aaron Rowand	R/R	6-0/205	28
8	Shane Victorino	B/R	5-9/160	25

*Age as of April 1, 2006.

Ballpark (capacity, surface)
Citizens Bank Park (43,647, grass)
Address
One Citizens Bank Way
Philadelphia, PA 19148
Official website
www.phillies.com
Business phone
215-463-6000
Ticket information
215-463-1000
Field dimensions (from home plate)
To left field at foul line, 329 feet
To center field, 401 feet
To right field at foul line, 330 feet
First game played
April 12, 2004 (Reds 4, Phillies 1)

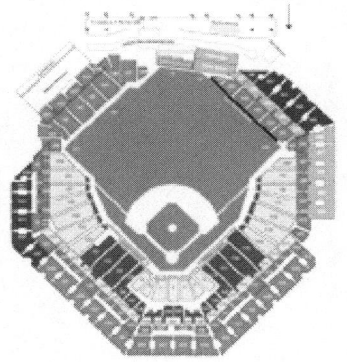

2006 SEASON Philadelphia Phillies

2006 SEASON *Philadelphia Phillies*

Date	Opp.	Res.	Score	(inn.*)	Hits	Opp. hits	Winning pitcher	Losing pitcher	Save	Record	Pos.	GB
4-4	Was.	W	8-4		14	13	Lieber	Hernandez		1-0	1st	+0.5
4-6	Was.	L	3-7		6	16	Eischen	Worrell		1-1	T1st	...
4-7	Was.	L	4-5	(10)	6	11	Cordero	Cormier		1-2	T3rd	...
4-8	At StL.	L	5-6		12	10	Reyes	Madson	Isringhausen	1-3	4th	2.0
4-9	At StL.	W	10-4		14	7	Floyd	Suppan		2-3	T2nd	2.0
4-10	At StL.	W	13-4		17	6	Lieber	Carpenter		3-3	T2nd	1.0
4-11	At Fla.	W	4-1		7	5	Myers	Leiter	Wagner	4-3	2nd	1.0
4-12	At Fla.	L	2-8		8	11	Burnett	Wolf		4-4	T2nd	1.0
4-13	At Fla.	L	0-4		3	8	Willis	Lidle		4-5	4th	1.0
4-15	Atl.	L	4-11		10	9	Ramirez	Floyd		4-6	5th	2.0
4-16	Atl.	W	2-1		6	9	Lieber	Smoltz	Wagner	5-6	T4th	2.0
4-17	Atl.	W	2-1	(10)	6	7	Madson	Kolb		6-6	T2nd	2.0
4-18	N.Y.	W	5-4		7	10	Wolf	Ishii	Worrell	7-6	T2nd	1.0
4-19	N.Y.	L	4-16		8	15	Zambrano	Padilla		7-7	T3rd	1.0
4-20	Col.	L	4-7		9	16	Wright	Lidle		7-8	T3rd	2.0
4-21	Col.	W	6-3		10	9	Lieber	Kennedy	Wagner	8-8	T3rd	1.0
4-22	At Atl.	L	2-6		7	7	Hampton	Myers	Kolb	8-9	5th	2.0
4-23	At Atl.	L	1-11		6	13	Hudson	Wolf		8-10	5th	3.0
4-24	At Atl.	L	0-4		6	6	Thomson	Padilla		8-11	5th	3.0
4-25	At Was.	W	5-4		7	12	Lidle	Day	Wagner	9-11	5th	2.5
4-26	At Was.	L	1-3		8	6	Patterson	Lieber	Cordero	9-12	5th	3.5
4-27	At Was.	W	3-0		7	4	Cormier	Loaiza	Wagner	10-12	5th	3.0
4-29	Fla.	L	4-6		10	14	Burnett	Wolf	Jones	10-13	5th	4.0
4-30	Fla.	L	1-2	(6)	3	2	Willis	Padilla		10-14	5th	5.0
5-1	Fla.	W	8-6		13	12	Lidle	Beckett	Wagner	11-14	5th	4.0
5-2	At N.Y.	L	1-5		4	9	Martinez	Adams		11-15	5th	4.5
5-3	At N.Y.	W	10-3		10	7	Myers	Glavine		12-15	5th	4.5
5-4	At N.Y.	L	2-3		3	5	Seo	Wolf	Looper	12-16	5th	4.5
5-5	At N.Y.	L	5-7		10	12	Heilman	Padilla	Looper	12-17	5th	5.5
5-6	At Chi.	W	3-2		6	5	Wagner	Hawkins		13-17	5th	5.5
5-7	At Chi.	W	4-1		10	5	Lieber	Rusch	Wagner	14-17	5th	5.5
5-8	At Chi.	L	1-2		5	5	Zambrano	Myers		14-18	5th	6.5
5-9	At Mil.	W	4-2		6	7	Wolf	Santos	Wagner	15-18	5th	5.5
5-10	At Mil.	L	5-8		10	12	Santana	Adams	Bottalico	15-19	5th	6.5
5-11	At Mil.	L	2-5		7	7	Davis	Lidle	Turnbow	15-20	5th	6.5
5-12	Cin.	L	5-7		12	8	Ortiz	Lieber	Graves	15-21	5th	7.0
5-13	Cin.	W	12-2		16	6	Myers	Milton		16-21	5th	6.0
5-14	Cin.	L	4-12		9	17	Harang	Madson		16-22	5th	7.0
5-15	Cin.	W	4-3		12	8	Padilla	Ramirez	Wagner	17-22	5th	7.0
5-17	StL.	W	7-5		10	8	Lidle	Suppan	Wagner	18-22	5th	5.5
5-18	StL.	L	4-8		9	9	Carpenter	Lieber		18-23	5th	5.5
5-19	StL.	W	7-4		12	7	Myers	Marquis		19-23	5th	5.0
5-20	At Bal.	W	9-3		12	8	Wolf	Cabrera		20-23	5th	4.5
5-21	At Bal.	L	0-7		5	13	Bedard	Padilla		20-24	5th	5.5
5-22	At Bal.	W	7-2		11	6	Lidle	Ponson		21-24	5th	5.5
5-23	At Fla.	L	2-5		8	10	Willis	Lieber	Jones	21-25	5th	6.5
5-24	At Fla.	L	3-4	(10)	8	6	Riedling	Telemaco		21-26	5th	7.5
5-25	At Fla.	W	8-5		17	10	Wolf	Leiter	Wagner	22-26	5th	6.5
5-27	At Atl.	W	5-1		12	8	Lidle	Smoltz		23-26	5th	5.0
5-28	At Atl.	W	12-5		16	11	Lieber	Ramirez		24-26	5th	4.0
5-29	At Atl.	L	2-7		6	6	Hudson	Myers		24-27	5th	5.0
5-31	S.F.	W	5-2		7	8	Wolf	Tomko		25-27	5th	3.5
6-1	S.F.	W	10-6		19	11	Madson	Hawkins		26-27	5th	3.5
6-2	S.F.	W	6-5		9	11	Lieber	Hennessey	Wagner	27-27	5th	2.5
6-4!	Ari.	W	10-6		14	9	Padilla	Vazquez		28-27		
6-4&	Ari.	W	5-3		5	10	Myers	Ortiz	Wagner	29-27	5th	1.5
6-5	Ari.	W	7-6		10	10	Wolf	Halsey	Wagner	30-27	T3rd	1.0
6-6	Ari.	L	8-10		12	13	Webb	Lidle	Lopez	30-28	5th	1.5
6-7	Tex.	W	8-5		12	7	Lieber	Drese	Wagner	31-28	4th	1.5
6-8	Tex.	W	2-0		7	5	Fultz	Young	Wagner	32-28	2nd	1.5
6-9	Tex.	W	10-8		14	8	Padilla	Astacio	Wagner	33-28	2nd	1.5
6-10	Mil.	W	5-2		4	7	Madson	Wise		34-28	2nd	1.5
6-11	Mil.	W	7-5		11	8	Cormier	Bottalico	Urbina	35-28	2nd	1.5
6-12	Mil.	W	6-2		9	5	Lidle	Sheets		36-28	2nd	1.5
6-14	At Sea.	L	1-3		3	10	Meche	Lieber	Guardado	36-29	2nd	2.0
6-15	At Sea.	L	1-5		8	10	Sele	Padilla		36-30	2nd	3.0
6-16	At Sea.	W	3-2	(13)	12	9	Geary	Mateo	Wagner	37-30	2nd	2.5

Date	Opp.	Res.	Score	(inn.*)	Hits	Opp. hits	Winning pitcher	Losing pitcher	Save	Record	Pos.	GB
6-17	At Oak.	W	6-1		11	5	Tejeda	Zito		38-30	2nd	1.5
6-18	At Oak.	L	1-2		9	5	Saarloos	Lidle	Duchscherer	38-31	2nd	1.5
6-19	At Oak.	L	2-5		6	11	Blanton	Lieber	Duchscherer	38-32	2nd	2.5
6-21	N.Y.	L	5-8		10	14	Benson	Myers	Looper	38-33	2nd	3.0
6-22	N.Y.	W	8-4		10	5	Madson	Ring		39-33	2nd	3.0
6-23	N.Y.	L	3-4		9	8	Ishii	Lidle	Looper	39-34	2nd	3.5
6-24	Bos.	L	0-8		3	12	Wakefield	Lieber		39-35	3rd	4.5
6-25	Bos.	L	1-7		8	12	Clement	Padilla		39-36	4th	5.5
6-26	Bos.	L	8-12		14	15	Timlin	Cormier		39-37	4th	5.5
6-28	At N.Y.	L	3-8		7	10	Zambrano	Tejeda		39-38	4th	6.5
6-29	At N.Y.	W	6-3		5	5	Lidle	Ishii	Wagner	40-38	4th	6.5
6-30	At N.Y.	L	3-5		8	7	Martinez	Lieber	Looper	40-39	4th	7.5
7-1	Atl.	L	1-9		6	13	Smoltz	Padilla		40-40	5th	8.5
7-2	Atl.	W	6-3		11	4	Myers	Ramirez	Wagner	41-40	4th	8.5
7-3	Atl.	L	3-4		3	6	Brower	Wagner	Reitsma	41-41	4th	9.5
7-4	At Pit.	W	12-1		18	7	Lidle	Williams		42-41	4th	8.5
7-5	At Pit.	L	0-3		4	9	Wells	Madson		42-42	4th	9.5
7-6	At Pit.	W	5-0		6	5	Padilla	Redman		43-42	4th	8.5
7-7	At Pit.	L	1-2		9	4	Duke	Myers	Mesa	43-43	5th	8.5
7-8	Was.	L	7-8		12	11	Drese	Tejeda	Cordero	43-44	5th	9.5
7-9	Was.	W	1-0		5	6	Wagner	Carrasco		44-44	4th	8.5
7-10	Was.	W	5-4	(12)	12	12	Cormier	Kim		45-44	4th	7.5
7-14	Fla.	W	13-7		13	12	Myers	Burnett		46-44	3rd	6.5
7-15	Fla.	L	7-9		14	17	Moehler	Lidle	Jones	46-45	4th	6.5
7-16	Fla.	W	10-5		14	11	Lieber	Olsen		47-45	3rd	6.5
7-17	Fla.	W	8-4		11	7	Padilla	Willis		48-45	3rd	5.5
7-19	L.A.	W	5-4	(10)	11	9	Wagner	Brazoban		49-45	3rd	5.0
7-20	L.A.	L	2-10		7	14	Lowe	Lidle		49-46	3rd	5.0
7-21	L.A.	L	0-1		4	5	Perez	Lieber	Brazoban	49-47	3rd	5.0
7-22	S.D.	W	8-6	(11)	11	11	Fultz	Quantrill		50-47	3rd	4.0
7-23	S.D.	W	2-0		7	4	Tejeda	Astacio	Wagner	51-47	3rd	4.0
7-24	S.D.	W	5-1		10	7	Myers	Lawrence		52-47	3rd	3.0
7-25	At Hou.	L	1-7		7	9	Pettitte	Lidle		52-48	3rd	3.5
7-26	At Hou.	L	1-2		8	7	Oswalt	Madson		52-49	3rd	4.5
7-27	At Hou.	L	2-3		6	8	Clemens	Padilla	Lidge	52-50	5th	5.5
7-28	At Col.	W	8-5		12	9	Urbina	DeJean	Wagner	53-50	4th	5.5
7-29	At Col.	W	5-3		9	7	Myers	Acevedo	Wagner	54-50	4th	5.5
7-30	At Col.	W	8-7		15	11	Lidle	Cook	Wagner	55-50	4th	5.5
7-31	At Col.	L	2-9		8	10	Francis	Lieber		55-51	4th	6.5
8-2	Chi.	L	1-2		4	9	Zambrano	Padilla	Dempster	55-52	4th	7.0
8-3	Chi.	W	4-3		11	6	Wagner	Remlinger		56-52	3rd	6.0
8-4	Chi.	W	6-4		8	11	Myers	Prior	Wagner	57-52	3rd	6.0
8-5	Mil.	L	1-3	(10)	5	7	Sheets	Geary	Wise	57-53	4th	6.0
8-6	Mil.	W	8-2		12	7	Lieber	Capuano		58-53	3rd	6.0
8-7	Mil.	L	0-2		5	4	Ohka	Padilla	Turnbow	58-54	4th	6.0
8-9	At L.A.	W	8-4		12	7	Madson	Schmoll		59-54	3rd	6.0
8-10	At L.A.	W	9-5		9	5	Urbina	Brazoban		60-54	2nd	6.0
8-11	At L.A.	L	1-5		5	7	Perez	Lidle		60-55	2nd	6.0
8-12	At S.D.	W	3-2		7	8	Lieber	Peavy	Wagner	61-55	2nd	5.0
8-13	At S.D.	W	5-2		8	6	Urbina	Hoffman	Wagner	62-55	2nd	5.0
8-14	At S.D.	W	8-3		9	5	Tejeda	Park		63-55	2nd	5.0
8-15	Was.	L	3-6		7	10	Hernandez	Myers		63-56	3rd	5.5
8-17	Was.	W	4-3		10	6	Lieber	Loaiza	Wagner	64-56	2nd	5.0
8-18#	Was.	W	2-1		7	7	Padilla	Armas	Wagner	65-56		
8-18$	Was.	L	4-5		8	10	Ayala	Urbina	Cordero	65-57	2nd	4.5
8-19	Pit.	L	2-11		4	13	Wells	Tejeda		65-58	3rd	4.5
8-20	Pit.	W	6-1		7	6	Myers	Williams		66-58	2nd	3.5
8-21	Pit.	W	4-3		8	9	Madson	White	Wagner	67-58	2nd	3.5
8-22	At S.F.	L	0-5		5	9	Lowry	Lieber		67-59	3rd	4.5
8-23	At S.F.	W	10-2		16	3	Padilla	Tomko		68-59	2nd	3.5
8-24	At S.F.	W	7-4		14	9	Tejeda	Hennessey	Wagner	69-59	2nd	3.5
8-26	At Ari.	W	11-3		11	5	Fultz	Halsey		70-59	2nd	2.5
8-27	At Ari.	L	0-2		5	5	Webb	Lieber	Valverde	70-60	2nd	3.5
8-28	At Ari.	L	5-10		9	9	Vargas	Padilla		70-61	2nd	4.5
8-30	At N.Y.	L	4-6		11	10	Padilla	Urbina	Looper	70-62	T2nd	4.5
8-31	At N.Y.	W	8-2		11	6	Myers	Martinez		71-62	2nd	4.0
9-1	At N.Y.	W	3-1		7	4	Lieber	Glavine	Wagner	72-62	2nd	4.0
9-2	At Was.	W	7-1		12	5	Padilla	Halama		73-62	2nd	4.0
9-3	At Was.	L	4-5	(12)	9	10	Carrasco	Lopez		73-63	2nd	5.0
9-4	At Was.	L	1-6		4	8	Loaiza	Floyd		73-64	2nd	5.0

Date	Opp.	Res.	Score	(inn.*)	Hits	Opp. hits	Winning pitcher	Losing pitcher	Save	Record	Pos.	GB
9-5	Hou.	L	3-4		9	6	Pettitte	Myers	Lidge	73-65	2nd	6.0
9-6	Hou.	L	1-2		7	7	Oswalt	Wagner	Lidge	73-66	3rd	7.0
9-7	Hou.	L	6-8		8	9	Qualls	Wagner	Lidge	73-67	3rd	8.0
9-9	Fla.	W	12-5		12	15	Lidle	Burnett		74-67	3rd	7.0
9-10	Fla.	L	6-7		11	14	Resop	Madson	Jones	74-68	3rd	8.0
9-11	Fla.	W	11-1		14	5	Lieber	Valdez		75-68	3rd	8.0
9-12	Atl.	W	4-1		8	5	Brito	Hudson	Wagner	76-68	3rd	7.0
9-13	Atl.	W	5-4		13	8	Fultz	Boyer	Wagner	77-68	3rd	6.0
9-14	Atl.	W	12-4		15	11	Lidle	Ramirez		78-68	T2nd	5.0
9-15	Atl.	L	4-6		12	8	Sosa	Myers	Farnsworth	78-69	T2nd	6.0
9-16	At Fla.	W	13-3		17	7	Lieber	Mecir		79-69	2nd	5.0
9-17	At Fla.	W	10-2		11	7	Urbina	Willis		80-69	2nd	5.0
9-18	At Fla.	L	6-14		10	16	Beckett	Brito		80-70	2nd	5.0
9-20	At Atl.	L	1-4		3	9	Sosa	Lidle		80-71	2nd	6.0
9-21	At Atl.	W	10-6	(10)	14	7	Geary	Davies		81-71	2nd	5.0
9-22	At Atl.	W	4-0		6	6	Lieber	Hudson		82-71	2nd	4.0
9-23	At Cin.	W	11-10		17	13	Cormier	Weathers	Wagner	83-71	2nd	4.0
9-24	At Cin.	L	2-3		7	4	Milton	Brito	Weathers	83-72	2nd	5.0
9-25	At Cin.	W	6-3		12	9	Lidle	Keisler	Wagner	84-72	2nd	5.0
9-26	N.Y.	L	5-6		9	7	Takatsu	Urbina	Hernandez	84-73	2nd	5.0
9-27	N.Y.	L	2-3		4	9	Padilla	Lieber	Heilman	84-74	2nd	6.0
9-28	N.Y.	W	16-6		20	10	Padilla	Trachsel		85-74	2nd	5.0
9-30	At Was.	W	4-3		11	8	Lidle	Hernandez	Wagner	86-74	2nd	4.0
10-1	At Was.	W	8-4		9	8	Myers	Patterson		87-74	2nd	3.0
10-2	At Was.	W	9-3		10	7	Lieber	Carrasco	Wagner	88-74	2nd	2.0

Monthly records: April (10-14), May (15-13), June (15-12), July (15-12), August (16-11), September (15-12), October (2-0).
*Innings, if other than nine. ! First game of a doubleheader. & Second game of a doubleheader # Day separate admission. $ Night separate admission.

RECORDS

2005 regular-season record: 88-74
Position: 2nd in N.L. East
Home: 46-35   **Road:** 42-39
N.L. East: 38-37   **N.L. Central:** 21-20
N.L. West: 22-9   **A.L.** 7-8
Vs. LH starters: 29-19
Vs. RH starters: 59-55
Grass: 88-74   **Artificial:** 0-0
Day: 34-20   **Night:** 54-54
1-Run: 21-23   **X-inn.:** 6-4
Doubleheaders: 1-0-0
Team record past five years: 426-383
(.527, ranks 6th in league in that span)

TEAM LEADERS

Batting average: Kenny Lofton (.335).
At-bats: Jimmy Rollins (677).
Runs: Jimmy Rollins (115).
Hits: Jimmy Rollins (196).
Total Bases: Chase Utley (293).
Doubles: Chase Utley (39).
Triples: Jimmy Rollins (11).
Home runs: Pat Burrell (32).
Runs batted in: Pat Burrell (117).
Stolen bases: Jimmy Rollins (41).
Slugging percentage: Ryan Howard (.567).
On-base percentage: Bobby Abreu (.405).
Wins: Jon Lieber (17).
Earned-run average: Brett Myers (3.72).
Complete games: Brett Myers (2).
Shutouts: None.

Saves: Billy Wagner (38).
Innings pitched: Jon Lieber (218.1).
Strikeouts: Brett Myers (208).

GAMES BY POSITION

Catcher: Mike Lieberthal 117, Todd Pratt 57.
First base: Ryan Howard 84, Jim Thome 52, Tomas Perez 24, Ramon Martinez 10, Chase Utley 8, Jose Offerman 4.
Second base: Chase Utley 135, Placido Polanco 29, Matt Kata 3, Ramon Martinez 1.
Third base: David Bell 150, Tomas Perez 15, Placido Polanco 8, Ramon Martinez 3.
Shortstop: Jimmy Rollins 157, Tomas Perez 14, Ramon Martinez 3, Matt Kata 1, Placido Polanco 1, Danny Sandoval 1.
Outfield: Bobby Abreu 158, Pat Burrell 153, Kenny Lofton 97, Jason Michaels 91, Endy Chavez 51, Shane Victorino 12, Marlon Byrd 5, Placido Polanco 5, Matt Kata 1, Michael Tucker 1.
Designated hitter: Jim Thome 5, Bobby Abreu 3, Kenny Lofton 1.

TOP DRAFT CHOICES

2. **Mike Costanzo,** 3B, Coastal Carolina.

3. **Matt Maloney,** LHP, Mississippi.
4. **Mike Durant,** 3B, Berkeley (Calif.) H.S.
5. **Brett Harker,** RHP, College of Charleston.
6. **Justin Blaine,** LHP, San Diego.
7. **Jermaine Williams,** OF, Los Angeles H.S.
8. **Jeremy Slayden,** OF, Georgia Tech.
9. **Clay Harris,** 2B, LSU.
10. **Josh Outman,** LHP, Central Missouri State.

PITTSBURGH PIRATES
NATIONAL LEAGUE CENTRAL DIVISION

2006 SEASON

Pirates Schedule
Home games shaded.
All-Star Game July 11 at Pittsburgh. Schedule subject to change.

APRIL

SUN	MON	TUE	WED	THU	FRI	SAT
2	3 MIL	4 MIL	5 MIL	6 CIN	7 CIN	8 CIN
9 CIN	10 LAD	11 LAD	12 LAD	13 LAD	14 CHC	15 CHC
16 CHC	17 STL	18 STL	19 STL	20	21 HOU	22 HOU
23 HOU	24 STL	25 STL	26 STL	27	28 PHI	29 PHI
30 PHI						

MAY

SUN	MON	TUE	WED	THU	FRI	SAT
	1 CHC	2 CHC	3 NYM	4 NYM	5 WAS	6 WAS
7 WAS	8	9 ARI	10 ARI	11 ARI	12 FLA	13 FLA
14 FLA	15	16 CIN	17 CIN	18 CIN	19 CLE	20 CLE
21 CLE	22 ARI	23 ARI	24 CIN	25	26 HOU	27 HOU
28 HOU	29 MIL	30 MIL	31 MIL			

JUNE

SUN	MON	TUE	WED	THU	FRI	SAT
				1 MIL	2 SD	3 SD
4 SD	5 COL	6 COL	7 COL	8 SF	9 SF	10 SF
11 SF	12	13 STL	14 STL	15 STL	16 MIN	17 MIN
18 MIN	19	20 KC	21 KC	22 KC	23 LAD	24 LAD
25 LAD	26	27 CHW	28 CHW	29 CHW	30 DET	

JULY

SUN	MON	TUE	WED	THU	FRI	SAT
						1 DET
2 DET	3	4 NYM	5 NYM	6 NYM	7 PHI	8 PHI
9 PHI	10	11 ALL-STAR	12	13	14 WAS	15 WAS
16 WAS	17 COL	18 COL	19 COL	20 FLA	21 FLA	22 FLA
23 FLA	24 MIL	25 MIL	26 MIL	27	28 SF	29 SF
30 SF	31					

AUGUST

SUN	MON	TUE	WED	THU	FRI	SAT
		1 ATL	2 ATL	3 ATL	4 CHC	5 CHC
6 CHC	7	8 HOU	9 HOU	10 HOU	11 STL	12 STL
13 STL	14 MIL	15 MIL	16 MIL	17	18 CIN	19 CIN
20 CIN	21 ATL	22 ATL	23 ATL	24 HOU	25 HOU	26 HOU
27 CHC	28 CHC	29 CHC	30 CHC	31		

SEPTEMBER

SUN	MON	TUE	WED	THU	FRI	SAT
					1 STL	2 STL
3 STL	4 CHC	5 CHC	6 CHC	7 CHC	8 CIN	9 CIN
10 CIN	11 MIL	12 MIL	13 MIL	14	15 NYM	16 NYM
17 NYM	18	19 LAD	20 LAD	21 LAD	22 SD	23 SD
24 SD	25	26 HOU	27 HOU	28 HOU	29 CIN	30 CIN

OCTOBER

SUN	MON	TUE	WED	THU	FRI	SAT
1 CIN	2	3	4	5	6	7

Home games are shaded. All-Star Game is July 11 at Pittsburgh. Schedule is subject to change.

Bay

CLUB DIRECTORY

Chairman of the board
Robert Nutting
General partner
Kevin S. McClatchy
Chief financial officer
Jim Plake
Senior vice president and general manager
Dave Littlefield
Vice president and general counsel
Larry Silverman
Assistant general manager
Doug Strange
Special assistants to the general manager
Jack Bowen, Louie Eljaua, Jesse Flores, Jax Robertson, Pete Vuckovich
Vice president, PNC Park operations
Dennis DaPra
Vice president, sales/marketing/broadcasting
Tim Schuldt
Vice president, communications
Patty Paytas
Senior director of marketing
Brian Chiera
Sr. director of ticket sales & fan development
Jim Alexander
Senior director of corporate development
Bob Derda
Director of media relations
Jim Trdinich
Director of player development
Brian Graham

MINOR LEAGUE AFFILIATES

Class	Team	League	Manager
AAA	Indianapolis	International	Trent Jewett
AA	Altoona	Eastern	Tim Leiper
Advanced A	Lynchburg	Carolina	Gary Green
A	Hickory	South Atlantic	Jeff Branson
Short-Season A	Williamsport	New York-Penn	Tom Prince
Rookie	Pirates	Gulf Coast	Pete Mackanin

BROADCAST INFORMATION

Radio: KDKA-AM (1020).
Cable TV: Fox Sports Pittsburgh.

SPRING TRAINING

Ballpark (city): McKechnie Field (Bradenton, Fla.).
Ticket information: 941-748-4610.

For more on the Pirates, go to www.sportingnews.com/baseball/teams/pirates/

2006 SEASON *Pittsburgh Pirates*

Manager—Jim Tracy (23).
Coaches—Jim Colborn (49), Jeff Cox (45), Bobby Cuellar (58), Jim Lett (15), Jeff Manto (30), John Shelby (31).

No.	PITCHERS	B/T	Ht./Wt.	Age*
54	Jonah Bayliss	R/R	6-2/210	25
46	Bryan Bullington	R/R	6-4/222	25
18	Sean Burnett	L/L	5-11/190	23
55	Matt Capps	R/R	6-3/238	22
57	Zach Duke	L/L	6-2/212	22
51	Mike Gonzalez	R/L	6-2/205	27
61	Tom Gorzelanny	L/L	6-2/207	23
39	John Grabow	L/L	6-2/210	27
34	Roberto Hernandez	R/R	6-4/250	41
37	Mike Johnston	L/L	6-2/225	27
28	Paul Maholm	L/L	6-2/225	23
43	Damaso Marte	L/L	6-2/200	31
48	Oliver Perez	L/L	6-2/200	24
52	Victor Santos	R/R	6-3/190	29
44	Joshua Sharpless	R/R	6-5/235	25
53	Ian Snell	R/R	5-11/180	24
16	Salomon Torres	R/R	5-11/210	34
47	John Van Benschoten	R/R	6-4/217	25
22	Ryan Vogelsong	R/R	6-3/213	28
32	Kip Wells	R/R	6-3/200	28

No.	CATCHERS	B/T	Ht./Wt.	Age*
11	Humberto Cota	R/R	6-0/195	27
41	Ryan Doumit	B/R	6-0/200	24
56	Ronny Paulino	R/R	6-3/235	24

No.	INFIELDERS	B/T	Ht./Wt.	Age*
7	Jose Bautista	R/R	6-0/192	25
25	Sean Casey	L/R	6-4/235	31
14	Jose Castillo	R/R	6-1/200	25
19	Yurendell DeCaster	R/R	6-1/205	26
35	Brad Eldred	R/R	6-5/270	25
6	Javier Guzman	B/R	5-11/165	21
5	Joe Randa	R/R	5-/190	36
12	Freddy Sanchez	R/R	5-10/192	28
3	Craig Stansberry	R/R	6-0/180	24
2	Jack Wilson	R/R	6-0/180	28

No.	OUTFIELDERS	B/T	Ht./Wt.	Age*
38	Jason Bay	R/R	6-2/200	27
	Jeromy Burnitz	L/R	6-0/210	36
10	Rajai Davis	R/R	5-11/190	25
26	Chris Duffy	L/L	5-10/180	25
29	Jody Gerut	L/L	6-0/190	28
	Nate McLouth	L/R	5-11/185	24
36	Craig Wilson	R/R	6-2/220	29

*Age as of April 1, 2006.

Ballpark (capacity, surface)
PNC Park (38,496, grass)
Address
PNC Park at North Shore
115 Federal Street
Pittsburgh, PA 15212
Official website
www.pirates.com
Business phone
412-323-5000
Ticket information
800-BUY-BUCS
Field dimensions (from home plate)
To left field at foul line, 325 feet
To center field, 399 feet
To right field at foul line, 320 feet
First game played
April 9, 2001 (Reds 8, Pirates 2)

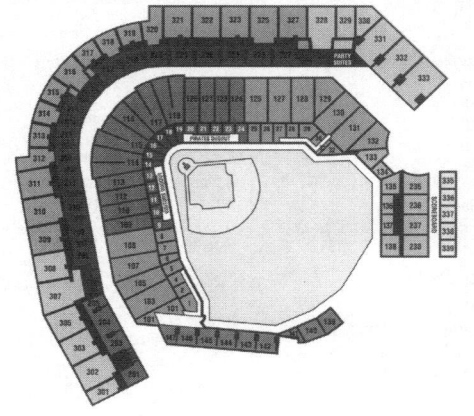

Date	Opp.	Res.	Score	(inn.*)	Hits	Opp. hits	Winning pitcher	Losing pitcher	Save	Record	Pos.	GB
4-4	Mil.	L	2-9		9	9	Sheets	Perez		0-1	6th	1.0
4-6	Mil.	L	2-10		7	13	Davis	Wells		0-2	6th	2.0
4-7	At S.D.	L	0-1	(12)	10	9	Seanez	White		0-3	6th	3.0
4-8	At S.D.	W	3-2		8	6	Fogg	Lawrence	Mesa	1-3	T5th	2.5
4-9	At S.D.	L	3-11		6	13	Williams	Perez		1-4	6th	2.5
4-10	At S.D.	W	6-3		7	7	Williams	Redding	Mesa	2-4	6th	2.5
4-11	At Mil.	L	2-6		8	8	Davis	Wells		2-5	6th	2.5
4-12	At Mil.	W	4-2		10	6	Redman	Glover	Mesa	3-5	6th	2.0
4-13	At Mil.	L	2-6		12	9	de la Rosa	White		3-6	6th	2.5
4-15	Chi.	W	8-5		13	7	Torres	Remlinger	Mesa	4-6	T5th	1.5
4-16	Chi.	L	3-4		8	7	Dempster	Wells	Hawkins	4-7	6th	2.0
4-17	Chi.	L	2-4		6	7	Wuertz	Redman	Hawkins	4-8	6th	3.0
4-18	StL.	L	1-11		2	13	Mulder	Williams		4-9	6th	4.0
4-19	StL.	L	1-7		5	14	Morris	Fogg		4-10	6th	5.0
4-20	At Cin.	L	4-6		12	11	Wilson	Torres	Graves	4-11	6th	5.0
4-21	At Cin.	W	4-2		6	6	Wells	Milton	Mesa	5-11	6th	5.0
4-23	At Chi.	W	4-3		6	9	Grabow	Hawkins	Mesa	6-11	T5th	5.5
4-24	At Chi.	L	2-5		6	7	Wood	Williams	Fox	6-12	6th	6.5
4-25	Hou.	W	2-0		6	5	Perez	Oswalt	Mesa	7-12	6th	6.0
4-27	Hou.	W	2-0		9	4	Wells	Pettitte	Mesa	8-12	T4th	6.5
4-29	S.F.	L	2-3		4	8	Tomko	Redman		8-13	T5th	7.0
4-30	S.F.	L	6-7		9	11	Walker	Williams	Brower	8-14	6th	7.0
5-1	S.F.	L	3-8		6	13	Hennessey	Perez		8-15	6th	7.0
5-2	At Hou.	L	4-11		5	12	Pettitte	Fogg		8-16	6th	8.0
5-3	At Hou.	W	7-4		14	11	White	Qualls	Mesa	9-16	6th	8.0
5-4	At Hou.	W	6-4		9	9	Torres	Lidge	Mesa	10-16	5th	8.0
5-5	At Ari.	W	6-2		11	6	Williams	Estes		11-16	T4th	7.0
5-6	At Ari.	L	4-8		10	11	Vazquez	Perez		11-17	T4th	7.0
5-7	At Ari.	W	3-2		14	2	Fogg	Ortiz	Mesa	12-17	T3rd	6.0
5-8	At Ari.	W	16-2		17	6	Wells	Halsey		13-17	T3rd	6.0
5-9	At S.F.	L	1-2		6	6	Tomko	Redman		13-18	T3rd	7.0
5-10	At S.F.	W	5-2		7	6	Williams	Brower	Mesa	14-18	T3rd	6.0
5-11	At S.F.	W	7-2		9	7	Fogg	Lowry	White	15-18	T3rd	6.0
5-13	Mil.	L	3-4		8	7	Capuano	Mesa	Turnbow	15-19	4th	6.5
5-14	Mil.	W	2-0		9	4	Redman	Santos		16-19	T3rd	6.5
5-15	Mil.	W	4-2		6	12	Williams	Glover	Mesa	17-19	3rd	6.5
5-17	Chi.	L	3-4		7	13	Ohman	Mesa	Dempster	17-20	T3rd	6.5
5-18	Chi.	L	2-3		7	6	Wuertz	Mesa	Dempster	17-21	4th	7.5
5-20	Col.	W	9-4		12	10	Redman	Wright		18-21	T3rd	7.0
5-21	Col.	W	8-3		11	3	Perez	Jennings	Gonzalez	19-21	3rd	7.0
5-22	Col.	L	3-4		6	7	Kennedy	Fogg	Fuentes	19-22	T3rd	7.0
5-23	At StL.	L	2-4		7	7	Carpenter	Williams	Isringhausen	19-23	4th	8.0
5-24	At StL.	L	1-2	(12)	11	6	Reyes	Mesa		19-24	4th	9.0
5-25	At StL.	L	5-11		9	14	Mulder	Redman		19-25	4th	10.0
5-26	At Cin.	W	8-4		13	6	Perez	Ramirez		20-25	4th	9.5
5-27	At Cin.	L	5-6		13	11	Wagner	Gonzalez		20-26	4th	10.5
5-28	At Cin.	W	9-2		15	5	Williams	Milton		21-26	4th	10.5
5-29	At Cin.	L	2-11		7	11	Claussen	Wells		21-27	4th	10.5
5-30	Fla.	W	3-2	(10)	8	7	White	Jones		22-27	4th	10.5
5-31	Fla.	W	5-4		7	8	Meadows	Bump	Mesa	23-27	4th	9.5
6-1	Fla.	W	9-1		15	7	Fogg	Moehler	Torres	24-27	4th	9.5
6-2	Fla.	L	3-6		9	13	Willis	Williams	Jones	24-28	4th	9.5
6-3	Atl.	W	3-1		6	9	Wells	Hudson	Mesa	25-28	4th	9.5
6-4	Atl.	L	0-1		6	5	Foster	Gonzalez	Reitsma	25-29	4th	10.5
6-5	Atl.	W	5-2		11	5	Perez	Bernero	Mesa	26-29	3rd	9.5
6-6	Bal.	L	3-4		9	9	Julio	Torres	Ryan	26-30	4th	10.5
6-7	Bal.	W	6-5		7	11	Meadows	Julio	Mesa	27-30	4th	10.5
6-8	Bal.	W	6-1		10	9	Wells	Chen		28-30	3rd	9.5
6-10	T.B.	W	7-2		7	9	Redman	Nomo		29-30	3rd	9.5
6-11	T.B.	W	18-2		20	7	Perez	Kazmir		30-30	3rd	8.5
6-12	T.B.	L	5-7	(13)	12	15	Nunez	Meadows	Orvella	30-31	3rd	9.5
6-14	At N.Y.	L	0-9		5	12	Mussina	Wells		30-32	3rd	10.0
6-15	At N.Y.	L	5-7	(10)	9	15	Rivera	Mesa		30-33	3rd	10.0
6-16	At N.Y.	L	1-6		5	9	Johnson	Perez		30-34	3rd	10.5
6-17	At Bos.	L	5-6		8	11	Foulke	White		30-35	3rd	11.5
6-18	At Bos.	W	2-0		10	6	White	Embree	Mesa	31-35	3rd	11.5
6-19	At Bos.	L	0-8		4	10	Clement	Wells		31-36	3rd	12.5

Date	Opp.	Res.	Score	(inn.*)	Hits	Opp. hits	Winning pitcher	Losing pitcher	Save	Record	Pos.	GB
6-20	Was.	L	4-7		10	12	Hernandez	Redman	Cordero	31-37	3rd	13.5
6-21	Was.	W	11-4		14	10	Perez	Drese		32-37	3rd	12.5
6-22	Was.	L	4-5		7	10	Carrasco	Gonzalez	Cordero	32-38	3rd	12.5
6-23	At StL.	W	11-7		12	9	Williams	Morris	White	33-38	3rd	11.5
6-24	At StL.	L	1-8		5	10	Suppan	Wells		33-39	4th	12.5
6-25	At StL.	L	0-8		4	11	Carpenter	Redman		33-40	4th	13.5
6-26	At StL.	W	5-4	(10)	7	11	Grabow	Reyes	Mesa	34-40	4th	12.5
6-28	At Was.	L	1-2		5	5	Drese	Fogg	Cordero	34-41	T4th	13.5
6-29	At Was.	L	2-3		8	8	Ayala	Torres	Cordero	34-42	5th	14.5
6-30	At Was.	L	5-7		12	8	Loaiza	Wells	Cordero	34-43	5th	14.5
7-1	At Mil.	L	4-8		10	10	Wise	Redman		34-44	5th	15.5
7-2	At Mil.	L	3-5		6	7	Bottalico	Torres	Turnbow	34-45	5th	15.5
7-3	At Mil.	W	11-10		16	9	Meadows	Phelps	Mesa	35-45	5th	15.5
7-4	Phi.	L	1-12		7	18	Lidle	Williams		35-46	5th	16.5
7-5	Phi.	W	3-0		9	4	Wells	Madson		36-46	5th	16.5
7-6	Phi.	L	0-5		5	6	Padilla	Redman		36-47	5th	17.5
7-7	Phi.	W	2-1		4	9	Duke	Myers	Mesa	37-47	5th	16.5
7-8	N.Y.	W	6-5	(10)	10	9	Mesa	Looper		38-47	5th	16.5
7-9	N.Y.	W	11-4		12	9	Williams	Ishii		39-47	5th	15.5
7-10	N.Y.	L	1-6		6	13	Martinez	Wells		39-48	5th	16.5
7-14	At Chi.	L	1-5		2	10	Prior	Redman		39-49	5th	17.0
7-15	At Chi.	L	1-11		4	16	Wood	Fogg		39-50	5th	18.0
7-16	At Chi.	W	3-0		5	8	Duke	Maddux	Mesa	40-50	5th	18.0
7-17	At Chi.	L	2-8		8	15	Zambrano	Wells		40-51	5th	19.0
7-18	Hou.	L	1-11		6	17	Backe	Williams		40-52	5th	20.0
7-19!	Hou.	L	3-9		8	14	Astacio	Snell		40-53		
7-19&	Hou.	L	4-6		8	10	Rodriguez	Redman	Lidge	40-54	5th	20.5
7-20	Hou.	L	0-8		9	13	Pettitte	Fogg		40-55	5th	21.5
7-21	Col.	W	8-1		13	10	Duke	Francis		41-55	5th	20.5
7-22	Col.	L	3-5	(10)	13	9	Fuentes	Mesa	Cortes	41-56	6th	21.5
7-23	Col.	W	5-3		7	3	Williams	Kim	Mesa	42-56	5th	20.5
7-24	Col.	W	3-0		8	7	Redman	Chacon	Mesa	43-56	5th	19.5
7-26	At Fla.	W	6-3		16	12	Fogg	Moehler	Mesa	44-56	5th	19.5
7-27	At Fla.	L	1-3		7	6	Vargas	Vogelsong	Jones	44-57	5th	19.5
7-28	At Fla.	L	0-3		4	6	Willis	Wells	Jones	44-58	T5th	20.5
7-29	At Atl.	L	1-2		7	8	Ramirez	Williams	McBride	44-59	6th	20.5
7-30	At Atl.	L	6-9		5	13	Davies	Redman	Reitsma	44-60	6th	21.5
7-31	At Atl.	L	4-5		10	16	Smoltz	Grabow	Reitsma	44-61	6th	22.5
8-1	At Atl.	W	4-1		8	8	Duke	Hudson	Mesa	45-61	6th	21.5
8-2	S.D.	L	3-11		9	15	Peavy	Wells		45-62	6th	22.5
8-3	S.D.	W	9-8		10	10	Mesa	Otsuka		46-62	6th	22.5
8-4	S.D.	L	7-12		13	14	Lawrence	Redman		46-63	6th	22.5
8-5	L.A.	L	6-12		9	15	Lowe	Fogg	Schmoll	46-64	6th	23.5
8-6	L.A.	W	9-4		15	12	Duke	Perez		47-64	6th	22.5
8-7	L.A.	L	4-6		9	8	Weaver	Snell	Schmoll	47-65	6th	23.5
8-9	At Col.	W	12-4		19	11	Williams	Acevedo		48-65	6th	24.0
8-10	At Col.	L	5-6	(10)	7	8	Cortes	White		48-66	6th	25.0
8-11	At Col.	W	11-3		17	7	Fogg	Francis		49-66	6th	24.0
8-12	At Hou.	L	5-6		11	13	Wheeler	White	Lidge	49-67	6th	24.0
8-13	At Hou.	W	1-0		4	6	Torres	Lidge	Mesa	50-67	6th	24.0
8-14	At Hou.	W	8-0		10	5	Williams	Astacio		51-67	6th	23.0
8-16	At N.Y.	L	2-6		8	6	Benson	Redman		51-68	6th	24.0
8-17	At N.Y.	L	1-5		9	6	Glavine	Fogg	Heilman	51-69	6th	25.0
8-18	At N.Y.	W	5-0		11	3	Duke	Zambrano		52-69	6th	24.0
8-19	At Phi.	W	11-2		13	4	Wells	Tejeda		53-69	6th	24.0
8-20	At Phi.	L	1-6		6	7	Myers	Williams		53-70	6th	25.0
8-21	At Phi.	L	3-4		9	8	Madson	White	Wagner	53-71	6th	25.0
8-22	StL.	L	1-3		3	12	Mulder	Fogg	Isringhausen	53-72	6th	26.0
8-23	StL.	W	10-0		16	5	Torres	Marquis		54-72	6th	25.0
8-24	StL.	L	3-8		4	12	Carpenter	Wells		54-73	6th	26.0
8-25	StL.	L	3-6		12	13	Morris	Williams	Isringhausen	54-74	6th	27.0
8-26	Cin.	L	1-6		8	11	Harang	Redman		54-75	6th	27.0
8-27	Cin.	L	2-4	(10)	9	9	Weathers	Mesa	Mercker	54-76	6th	28.0
8-28	Cin.	L	2-7		8	7	Hudson	Wells	Coffey	54-77	6th	29.0
8-30	At Mil.	W	6-0		8	4	Maholm	Davis		55-77	6th	28.5
8-31	At Mil.	L	5-6		11	12	Turnbow	Mesa		55-78	6th	29.5
9-2	Chi.	L	3-7		12	12	Maddux	Fogg	Dempster	55-79	6th	29.5
9-3	Chi.	L	5-9		6	13	Zambrano	Williams		55-80	6th	30.5
9-4	Chi.	L	0-2		4	7	Williams	Wells	Dempster	55-81	6th	31.5
9-6	Ari.	L	2-4	(12)	15	7	Valverde	Grabow	Groom	55-82	6th	32.0

Date	Opp.	Res.	Score	(inn.*)	Hits	Opp. hits	Winning pitcher	Losing pitcher	Save	Record	Pos.	GB
9-7	Ari.	L	2-4		9	9	Webb	Redman	Valverde	55-83	6th	32.0
9-8	Ari.	W	8-7	(12)	11	13	White	Groom		56-83	6th	32.0
9-9	At Cin.	W	8-4		8	8	Vogelsong	Hudson		57-83	6th	32.0
9-10	At Cin.	L	2-6		8	8	Ortiz	Wells		57-84	6th	33.0
9-11	At Cin.	L	3-5		9	9	Belisle	Grabow	Weathers	57-85	6th	33.0
9-12	At StL.	L	3-4		11	6	Isringhausen	Torres		57-86	6th	34.0
9-13	At StL.	L	4-5		13	7	Thompson	White		57-87	6th	35.0
9-14	At StL.	W	5-3		10	6	Vogelsong	Marquis	Gonzalez	58-87	6th	34.0
9-16!	Cin.	L	2-8		8	12	Claussen	Duke		58-88		
9-16&	Cin.	W	5-4		13	7	Torres	Weathers		59-88	6th	34.0
9-17	Cin.	W	4-0		7	4	Maholm	Harang		60-88	6th	34.0
9-18	Cin.	W	9-7		12	10	Gonzalez	Belisle		61-88	6th	33.0
9-19	Hou.	W	7-0		15	4	Snell	Clemens		62-88	6th	32.5
9-20	Hou.	L	4-7		11	12	Pettitte	Gorzelanny		62-89	6th	32.5
9-21	Hou.	L	8-12		15	15	Oswalt	Wells		62-90	6th	33.5
9-22	Hou.	L	1-2		5	5	Backe	Duke	Lidge	62-91	6th	33.5
9-23	At L.A.	L	3-4		5	9	Houlton	Maholm	Sanchez	62-92	6th	33.5
9-24	At L.A.	W	8-3		13	6	Perez	Perez		63-92	6th	32.5
9-25	At L.A.	L	2-9		7	11	Lowe	Fogg		63-93	6th	33.5
9-26	At L.A.	L	4-9		7	11	Jackson	Wells		63-94	6th	34.0
9-27	At Chi.	W	5-3		8	7	Duke	Maddux	Torres	64-94	6th	33.0
9-28	At Chi.	W	3-2		7	7	Maholm	Prior	Gonzalez	65-94	6th	32.0
9-30	Mil.	L	5-6		7	7	Lehr	Vogelsong	Turnbow	65-95	6th	33.0
10-1	Mil.	W	5-1		9	6	Wells	Ohka		66-95	6th	33.0
10-2	Mil.	W	3-1		9	9	Duke	Capuano	Torres	67-95	6th	33.0

Monthly records: April (8-14), May (15-13), June (11-16), July (10-18), August (11-17), September (10-17), October (2-0).
*Innings, if other than nine. ! First game of a doubleheader. & Second game of a doubleheader.

RECORDS

2005 regular-season record: 67-95
Position: 6th in N.L. Central
Home: 34-47 **Road:** 33-48
N.L. East: 14-19 **N.L. Central:** 30-50
N.L. West: 18-19 **A.L.** 5-7
Vs. LH starters: 19-27
Vs. RH starters: 48-68
Grass: 67-95 **Artificial:** 0-0
Day: 21-31 **Night:** 46-64
1-Run: 15-28 **X-inn.:** 4-8
Doubleheaders: 0-1-1
Team record past five years: 348-460 (.431, ranks 15th in league in that span)

TEAM LEADERS

Batting average: Jason Bay (.306).
At-bats: Jason Bay (599).
Runs: Jason Bay (110).
Hits: Jason Bay (183).
Total Bases: Jason Bay (335).
Doubles: Jason Bay (44).
Triples: Jack Wilson (7).
Home runs: Jason Bay (32).
Runs batted in: Jason Bay (101).
Stolen bases: Jason Bay (21).
Slugging percentage: Jason Bay (.559).
On-base percentage: Jason Bay (.402).
Wins: Dave Williams (10).
Earned-run average: Dave Williams (4.41).
Complete games: Mark Redman (2).
Shutouts: Mark Redman, Kip Wells, Dave Williams (1).
Saves: Jose Mesa (27).
Innings pitched: Kip Wells (182.0).
Strikeouts: Kip Wells (132).

GAMES BY POSITION

Catcher: Humberto Cota 87, Ryan Doumit 50, David Ross 35, Benito Santiago 6, Ronny Paulino 2.
First base: Daryle Ward 109, Brad Eldred 50, Craig Wilson 15, Rob Mackowiak 3, Ty Wigginton 3.
Second base: Jose Castillo 100, Freddy Sanchez 58, Rob Mackowiak 20, J.J. Furmaniak 9, Bobby Hill 1, Ty Wigginton 1.
Third base: Rob Mackowiak 65, Freddy Sanchez 65, Ty Wigginton 40, Bobby Hill 24, Jose Bautista 8.
Shortstop: Jack Wilson 157, Freddy Sanchez 11, J.J. Furmaniak 2, Alfredo Amezaga 1.
Outfield: Jason Bay 162, Matt Lawton 98, Tike Redman 85, Rob Mackowiak 63, Craig Wilson 47, Chris Duffy 34, Michael Restovich 31, Nate McLouth 29, Jody Gerut 4, Ryan Doumit 3, Ray Sadler 3.
Designated hitter: Ryan Doumit 6.

TOP DRAFT CHOICES

1. **Andrew McCutchen,** OF, Fort Meade (Fla.) H.S.
2. **Brad Corley,** OF, Mississippi State.
3. **James Boone,** OF, Missouri.
4. **Brent Lillibridge,** SS, Washington.
5. **Jeff Sues,** RHP, Vanderbilt.
6. **Cameron Blair,** 2B, Texas Tech.
7. **Justin Vaclavik,** RHP, Houston.
8. **Steve Pearce,** 1B, South Carolina.
9. **Derrik Moeves,** RHP, Northern Kentucky.
10. **Derek Antelo,** RHP, Nova Southeastern.

ST. LOUIS CARDINALS
NATIONAL LEAGUE CENTRAL DIVISION

2006 SEASON

Cardinals Schedule
Home games shaded.
All-Star Game July 11 at Pittsburgh. Schedule subject to change.

APRIL

SUN	MON	TUE	WED	THU	FRI	SAT
2	3 PHI	4	5 PHI	6 PHI	7 CHC	8 CHC
9 CHC	10 MIL	11	12 MIL	13 MIL	14 CIN	15 CIN
16 CIN	17 PIT	18 PIT	19 PIT	20	21 CHC	22 CHC
23 CHC	24 PIT	25 PIT	26 PIT	27 WAS	28 WAS	29 WAS
30 WAS						

MAY

SUN	MON	TUE	WED	THU	FRI	SAT
	1 CIN	2 CIN	3 HOU	4 HOU	5 FLA	6 FLA
7 FLA	8 COL	9 COL	10 COL	11	12 ARI	13 ARI
14 ARI	15	16 NYM	17 NYM	18 NYM	19 KC	20 KC
21 KC	22 SF	23 SF	24 SF	25	26 SD	27 SD
28 SD	29 HOU	30 HOU	31 HOU			

JUNE

SUN	MON	TUE	WED	THU	FRI	SAT
				1	2 CHC	3 CHC
4 CHC	5 CIN	6 CIN	7 CIN	8	9 MIL	10 MIL
11 MIL	12	13 PIT	14 PIT	15 PIT	16 COL	17 COL
18 COL	19	20 CHW	21 CHW	22 CHW	23 DET	24 DET
25 DET	26 CLE	27 CLE	28 CLE	29	30 KC	

JULY

SUN	MON	TUE	WED	THU	FRI	SAT
						1 KC
2 KC	3 ATL	4 ATL	5 ATL	6 HOU	7 HOU	8 HOU
9 HOU	10	11 ALL-STAR	12	13 LAD	14 LAD	15 LAD
16 LAD	17 ATL	18 ATL	19 ATL	20	21 LAD	22 LAD
23 LAD	24 COL	25 COL	26 COL	27 CHC	28 CHC	29 CHC
30 CHC	31					

AUGUST

SUN	MON	TUE	WED	THU	FRI	SAT
		1 PHI	2 PHI	3 PHI	4 MIL	5 MIL
6 MIL	7 CIN	8 CIN	9 CIN	10 CIN	11 PIT	12 PIT
13 PIT	14	15 CIN	16 CIN	17 CIN	18 CHC	19 CHC
20 CHC	21	22 NYM	23 NYM	24 NYM	25 CHC	26 CHC
27 CHC	28	29 FLA	30 FLA	31 FLA		

SEPTEMBER

SUN	MON	TUE	WED	THU	FRI	SAT
					1 PIT	2 PIT
3 PIT	4 WAS	5 WAS	6 WAS	7 ARI	8 ARI	9 ARI
10 ARI	11 HOU	12 HOU	13 HOU	14	15 SF	16 SF
17 SF	18 MIL	19 MIL	20 MIL	21 HOU	22 HOU	23 HOU
24 HOU	25 SD	26 SD	27 SD	28 MIL	29 MIL	30 MIL

OCTOBER

SUN	MON	TUE	WED	THU	FRI	SAT
1 MIL	2	3	4	5	6	7

Home games are shaded. All-Star Game is July 11 at Pittsburgh. Schedule is subject to change.

Pujols

CLUB DIRECTORY

Chairman of the board/general partner
William O. DeWitt Jr.
Vice chairman
Frederick O. Hanser
Secretary-treasurer
Andrew Baur
President
Mark C. Lamping
Senior vice president/general manager
Walt Jocketty
Vice president/player personnel
Jerry Walker
Special assistant to the general manager
Mike Jorgensen

Assistant general manager
John Mozeliak
Director, player development
Bruce Manno
Vice president/baseball development
Jeff Luhnow
Director, professional scouting
Marteese Robinson
Director, media relations
Brian Bartow
Sr. vice president, sales and marketing
Dan Farrell
Senior v.p., business development
Bill DeWitt III

MINOR LEAGUE AFFILIATES

Class	Team	League	Manager
AAA	Memphis	Pacific Coast	Danny Sheaffer
AA	Springfield	Texas	Chris Maloney
Advanced A	Palm Beach	Florida State	Ron Warner
A	Quad Cities	Midwest	Keith Mitchell
Short-Season A	State College	New York-Pennsylvania	Mark DeJohn
Advanced Rookie	Johnson City	Appalachian	Dan Radison

BROADCAST INFORMATION

Radio: KTRS-AM (550).
TV: KPLR-TV (Channel 11).
Cable TV: Fox Sports Midwest.

SPRING TRAINING

Ballpark (city): Roger Dean Stadium (Jupiter, Fla.).
Ticket information: 561-966-3309.

For more on the Cardinals, go to www.sportingnews.com/baseball/teams/cardinals/

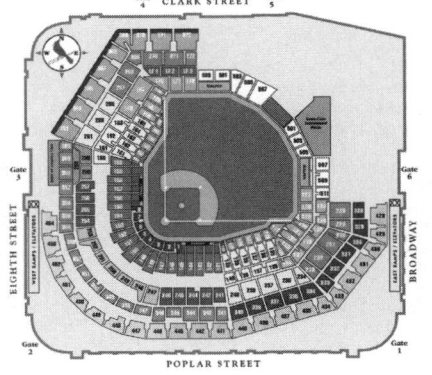

Manager—Tony La Russa (10).
Coaches—Dave Duncan (18), Marty Mason (38), Dave McKay (39), Hal McRae (8), Jose Oquendo (11), Joe Pettini (24).

No.	PITCHERS	B/T	Ht./Wt.	Age*
54	Carmen Cali	L/L	5-10/185	27
29	Chris Carpenter	R/R	6-6/230	30
34	Randy Flores	L/L	6-0/180	30
44	Jason Isringhausen	R/R	6-3/230	33
61	Tyler Johnson	B/L	6-2/180	24
	Braden Looper	R/R	6-3/220	31
21	Jason Marquis	L/R	6-1/210	27
	Juan Mateo	R/R	6-2/180	23
30	Mark Mulder	L/L	6-6/25	28
	Christopher Narveson	L/L	6-3/205	24
	Sidney Ponson	R/R	6-1/255	29
26	Anthony Reyes	R/R	6-2/215	24
	Ricardo Rincon	L/L	5-9/190	35
37	Jeff Suppan	R/R	6-2/220	31
48	Brad Thompson	R/R	6-1/190	24
60	Adam Wainwright	R/R	6-7/205	24

No.	CATCHERS	B/T	Ht./Wt.	Age*
	Gary Bennett	R/R	6-0/208	33
	Michel Hernandez	R/R	6-0/208	27
4	Yadier Molina	R/R	5-11/225	23

No.	INFIELDERS	B/T	Ht./Wt.	Age*
	Deivi Cruz	R/R	6-0/207	33
62	Chris Duncan	L/R	6-5/210	24
22	David Eckstein	R/R	5-7/165	31
	Travis Hanson	L/R	6-2/195	25
7	Hector Luna	R/R	6-1/170	26
	Aaron Miles	B/R	5-7/180	29
5	Albert Pujols	R/R	6-3/225	26
27	Scott Rolen	R/R	6-4/240	30
	Brendan Ryan	R/R	6-2/195	24
	Junior Spivey	R/R	6-0/200	31

No.	OUTFIELDERS	B/T	Ht./Wt.	Age*
49	Rick Ankiel	L/L	6-1/215	26
	Larry Bigbie	L/R	6-4/207	28
15	Jim Edmonds	L/L	6-1/212	35
	Juan Encarnacion	R/R	6-3/215	30
	John Gall	R/R	6-0/195	27
	Reid Gorecki	R/R	6-1/180	25
53	John Rodriguez	L/L	6-0/205	28
55	Skip Schumaker	L/R	5-10/175	26
99	So Taguchi	R/R	5-10/163	36

*Age as of April 1, 2006.

Ballpark (capacity, surface)
Busch Stadium (46,700, grass)
Address
424 South 7th Street
St. Louis, MO 63102
Official website
www.stlcardinals.com
Business phone
314-345-9600
Ticket information
314-345-9600
Field dimensions (from home plate)
To left field at foul line, 336 feet
To center field, 398 feet
To right field at foul line, 335 feet
First game played
Scheduled for April 10, 2006, vs. Milwaukee

St. Louis Cardinals

2006 SEASON

Date	Opp.	Res.	Score	(inn.*)	Hits	Opp. hits	Winning pitcher	Losing pitcher	Save	Record	Pos.	GB
4-5	At Hou.	W	7-3		11	7	Carpenter	Oswalt	Isringhausen	1-0	T1st	...
4-6	At Hou.	L	1-4		4	15	Qualls	Tavarez	Lidge	1-1	T3rd	1.0
4-8	Phi.	W	6-5		10	12	Reyes	Madson	Isringhausen	2-1	T3rd	1.0
4-9	Phi.	L	4-10		7	14	Floyd	Suppan		2-2	4th	1.0
4-10	Phi.	L	4-13		6	17	Lieber	Carpenter		2-3	5th	2.0
4-12	Cin.	W	5-1		5	6	Marquis	Harang		3-3	3rd	1.0
4-13	Cin.	L	5-6		9	15	Belisle	Mulder	Graves	3-4	5th	1.5
4-15	At Mil.	W	3-0		5	5	Suppan	Sheets	Isringhausen	4-4	3rd	0.5
4-16	At Mil.	W	5-3		10	6	Carpenter	Davis	Isringhausen	5-4	1st	+0.5
4-17	At Mil.	W	3-2		5	3	Marquis	Adams	Isringhausen	6-4	1st	+0.5
4-18	At Pit.	W	11-1		13	2	Mulder	Williams		7-4	1st	+0.5
4-19	At Pit.	W	7-1		14	5	Morris	Fogg		8-4	1st	+1.5
4-20	Chi.	L	1-3		5	12	Zambrano	Suppan	Hawkins	8-5	1st	+0.5
4-21	Chi.	W	4-0		7	7	Carpenter	Dempster		9-5	1st	+1.5
4-22	Hou.	W	8-7		9	11	Marquis	Duckworth	Isringhausen	10-5	1st	+2.5
4-23	Hou.	W	1-0	(10)	6	5	Mulder	Qualls		11-5	1st	+3.5
4-24	Hou.	W	8-5		13	8	Morris	Backe	Isringhausen	12-5	1st	+3.5
4-26	Mil.	W	5-3		8	8	Suppan	Davis	Flores	13-5	1st	+4.0
4-27	Mil.	W	6-3		11	9	Carpenter	Santos	Tavarez	14-5	1st	+4.0
4-28	Mil.	L	3-4		8	6	Capuano	Marquis	Turnbow	14-6	1st	+3.5
4-29	At Atl.	W	6-5		11	10	Mulder	Hudson	Reyes	15-6	1st	+3.5
4-30	At Atl.	L	2-3		11	8	Kolb	Journell		15-7	1st	+3.5
5-1	At Atl.	L	1-2		10	4	Smoltz	Suppan	Kolb	15-8	1st	+3.5
5-2	At Cin.	W	10-9		15	14	Flores	Graves	Tavarez	16-8	1st	+4.0
5-3	At Cin.	W	4-2		9	4	Marquis	Harang	Reyes	17-8	1st	+5.0
5-4	At Cin.	W	7-3		12	6	Mulder	Claussen		18-8	1st	+5.0
5-5	S.D.	L	3-8		7	12	Hammond	King		18-9	1st	+4.0
5-6	S.D.	L	5-6		8	11	Williams	Flores	Hoffman	18-10	1st	+4.0
5-7	S.D.	L	4-5		9	8	Eaton	Carpenter	Hoffman	18-11	1st	+4.0
5-8	S.D.	W	15-5		17	8	Marquis	Redding	Thompson	19-11	1st	+4.0
5-9	L.A.	W	4-2		8	8	Mulder	Perez	Reyes	20-11	1st	+5.0
5-10	L.A.	L	8-9		14	12	Alvarez	Jarvis	Brazoban	20-12	1st	+4.0
5-11	L.A.	W	9-3		19	9	Suppan	Penny		21-12	1st	+4.0
5-12	L.A.	W	10-3		13	8	Carpenter	Lowe		22-12	1st	+4.5
5-13	At N.Y.	L	0-2		5	3	Glavine	Marquis	Looper	22-13	1st	+3.5
5-14	At N.Y.	W	7-6		9	13	Tavarez	Hernandez	Isringhausen	23-13	1st	+4.5
5-15	At N.Y.	W	4-2		7	6	Morris	Heilman	Isringhausen	24-13	1st	+5.5
5-17	At Phi.	L	5-7		8	10	Lidle	Suppan	Wagner	24-14	1st	+5.0
5-18	At Phi.	W	8-4		9	9	Carpenter	Lieber		25-14	1st	+6.0
5-19	At Phi.	L	4-7		7	12	Myers	Marquis		25-15	1st	+6.0
5-20	At K.C.	W	7-6		13	10	Mulder	Greinke	Isringhausen	26-15	1st	+7.0
5-21	At K.C.	W	6-5		7	9	Morris	Cerda	Isringhausen	27-15	1st	+7.0
5-22	At K.C.	L	2-9		4	12	Jensen	Suppan		27-16	1st	+7.0
5-23	Pit.	W	4-2		7	7	Carpenter	Williams	Isringhausen	28-16	1st	+7.0
5-24	Pit.	W	2-1	(12)	6	11	Reyes	Mesa		29-16	1st	+7.0
5-25	Pit.	W	11-5		14	9	Mulder	Redman		30-16	1st	+7.0
5-27	Was.	W	6-3		9	6	Morris	Armas	Isringhausen	31-16	1st	+7.0
5-28	Was.	W	3-1		8	4	Suppan	Loaiza	Isringhausen	32-16	1st	+8.0
5-29	Was.	L	2-3		8	9	Hernandez	Carpenter	Cordero	32-17	1st	+7.5
5-30	At Col.	W	5-4		9	7	Marquis	Witasick	Isringhausen	33-17	1st	+7.5
5-31	At Col.	L	1-2		7	9	Jennings	Mulder	Fuentes	33-18	1st	+6.5
6-1	At Col.	W	8-6		17	12	Morris	Neal	Isringhausen	34-18	1st	+6.5
6-2	At Col.	L	7-8		11	12	Fuentes	Isringhausen		34-19	1st	+5.5
6-3	At Hou.	W	2-0		7	9	Carpenter	Pettitte	Tavarez	35-19	1st	+6.5
6-4	At Hou.	W	11-9		14	12	Marquis	Rodriguez	Isringhausen	36-19	1st	+6.5
6-5	At Hou.	L	4-6		11	11	Clemens	Mulder	Lidge	36-20	T1st	+5.5
6-6	Bos.	W	7-1		9	4	Morris	Wakefield		37-20	1st	+6.5
6-7	Bos.	W	9-2		9	9	Suppan	Clement		38-20	1st	+7.5
6-8	Bos.	L	0-4		6	9	Wells	Carpenter		38-21	1st	+6.5
6-10	N.Y.	W	8-1		10	6	Marquis	Wang		39-21	1st	+6.5
6-11	N.Y.	L	0-5		5	10	Johnson	Mulder	Rivera	39-22	1st	+5.5
6-12	N.Y.	W	5-3		10	9	King	Sturtze	Isringhausen	40-22	1st	+6.5
6-13	At Tor.	L	1-4		5	10	Halladay	Suppan		40-23	1st	+6.5
6-14	At Tor.	W	7-0		15	1	Carpenter	Gaudin		41-23	1st	+6.5
6-15	At Tor.	L	2-5		9	9	Lilly	Marquis	Batista	41-24	1st	+6.5
6-17	At T.B.	W	6-4		12	8	Mulder	Harper	Isringhausen	42-24	1st	+7.5
6-18	At T.B.	W	5-2		10	7	Morris	Hendrickson	Isringhausen	43-24	1st	+8.5

Date	Opp.	Res.	Score	(inn.*)	Hits	Opp. hits	Winning pitcher	Losing pitcher	Save	Record	Pos.	GB
6-19	At T.B.	W	8-5		11	9	Suppan	Waechter	Isringhausen	44-24	1st	+9.5
6-20	At Cin.	W	6-1		12	4	Carpenter	Harang		45-24	1st	+9.5
6-21	At Cin.	L	4-11		10	12	Claussen	Marquis		45-25	1st	+8.5
6-22	At Cin.	L	6-7		8	13	Ortiz	Mulder	Mercker	45-26	1st	+8.5
6-23	Pit.	L	7-11		9	12	Williams	Morris	White	45-27	1st	+8.5
6-24	Pit.	W	8-1		10	5	Suppan	Wells		46-27	1st	+9.5
6-25	Pit.	W	8-0		11	4	Carpenter	Redman		47-27	1st	+9.5
6-26	Pit.	L	4-5	(10)	11	7	Grabow	Reyes	Mesa	47-28	1st	+8.5
6-28	Cin.	W	2-1		4	8	Mulder	Claussen	Isringhausen	48-28	1st	+8.5
6-29	Cin.	W	11-3		12	7	Morris	Ortiz		49-28	1st	+8.5
6-30	Col.	L	0-7		6	13	Francis	Suppan		49-29	1st	+8.5
7-1	Col.	W	6-0		11	5	Carpenter	Kennedy		50-29	1st	+9.5
7-2	Col.	L	1-3		8	8	Wright	Marquis	Fuentes	50-30	1st	+9.5
7-3	Col.	W	5-4		9	7	King	Witasick		51-30	1st	+10.5
7-4	At Ari.	W	10-3		13	9	Morris	Webb		52-30	1st	+11.5
7-5	At Ari.	W	7-1		10	8	Suppan	Estes		53-30	1st	+12.5
7-6	At Ari.	W	2-1		3	4	Carpenter	Vazquez	Isringhausen	54-30	1st	+12.5
7-7	At Ari.	L	1-2		6	5	Cormier	King		54-31	1st	+12.5
7-8	At S.F.	W	3-1		8	8	Mulder	Schmidt	Isringhausen	55-31	1st	+12.5
7-9	At S.F.	L	0-2		3	6	Hennessey	Morris	Walker	55-32	1st	+11.5
7-10	At S.F.	W	4-3		10	13	Suppan	Lowry	Isringhausen	56-32	1st	+11.5
7-15	Hou.	W	4-3	(13)	8	12	Thompson	Harville		57-32	1st	+12.0
7-16	Hou.	W	4-2		9	6	Marquis	Oswalt	Isringhausen	58-32	1st	+13.0
7-17	Hou.	W	3-0		5	3	Carpenter	Clemens		59-32	1st	+13.0
7-18	Mil.	W	11-4		14	10	Morris	Santos		60-32	1st	+13.0
7-19	Mil.	L	4-5		11	13	Wise	Tavarez	Turnbow	60-33	1st	+12.0
7-20	Mil.	W	4-2		7	8	Mulder	Sheets	Isringhausen	61-33	1st	+13.0
7-21	Mil.	L	7-12		10	14	Capuano	Marquis		61-34	1st	+12.0
7-22	Chi.	W	2-1	(11)	6	9	Reyes	Mitre		62-34	1st	+12.0
7-23	Chi.	L	5-6		9	8	Williams	Morris	Dempster	62-35	1st	+12.0
7-24	Chi.	L	4-8	(10)	8	10	Dempster	Reyes		62-36	1st	+11.0
7-26	At S.D.	W	4-2		10	10	Mulder	Williams	Isringhausen	63-36	1st	+10.5
7-27	At S.D.	L	1-2		3	6	Hoffman	Marquis		63-37	1st	+9.5
7-28	At S.D.	W	11-3		17	10	Carpenter	Stauffer		64-37	1st	+9.5
7-29	At L.A.	L	5-7		13	11	Sanchez	Morris	Brazoban	64-38	1st	+8.5
7-30	At L.A.	W	9-4		14	9	Suppan	Lowe		65-38	1st	+8.5
7-31	At L.A.	W	7-5	(11)	9	8	Eldred	Alvarez	Isringhausen	66-38	1st	+9.5
8-1	Fla.	L	5-6		11	13	Valdez	Marquis	Jones	66-39	1st	+9.0
8-2	Fla.	W	3-1		5	3	Carpenter	Willis		67-39	1st	+9.0
8-3	Fla.	W	9-6		11	10	Morris	Villone		68-39	1st	+9.0
8-4	Fla.	L	3-4		8	10	Burnett	Suppan	Jones	68-40	1st	+9.0
8-5	Atl.	W	11-3		11	10	Mulder	Smoltz		69-40	1st	+10.0
8-6	Atl.	L	1-8		8	11	Hudson	Marquis		69-41	1st	+10.0
8-7	Atl.	W	5-3		9	6	King	Reitsma		70-41	1st	+10.0
8-8	At Mil.	W	8-4		10	7	Flores	Wise		71-41	1st	+10.5
8-9	At Mil.	W	5-2		10	3	Reyes	Davis	Isringhausen	72-41	1st	+11.5
8-10	At Mil.	W	3-0		5	5	Suppan	Sheets	Isringhausen	73-41	1st	+11.5
8-11	At Chi.	L	4-11		12	16	Maddux	Mulder		73-42	1st	+10.5
8-12	At Chi.	L	1-4		10	12	Zambrano	Marquis		73-43	1st	+9.5
8-13	At Chi.	W	5-2		7	8	Carpenter	Williams		74-43	1st	+10.5
8-14	At Chi.	L	4-5		8	14	Prior	Morris	Dempster	74-44	1st	+10.5
8-16	Ari.	W	8-2		15	5	Suppan	Halsey		75-44	1st	+11.0
8-17	Ari.	W	5-0		11	5	Mulder	Webb		76-44	1st	+12.0
8-18	Ari.	L	2-9		6	14	Vargas	Marquis		76-45	1st	+12.0
8-19	S.F.	W	5-4		12	9	Tavarez	Accardo		77-45	1st	+12.0
8-20	S.F.	W	4-2		6	9	Morris	Correia	Isringhausen	78-45	1st	+13.0
8-21	S.F.	L	2-4		8	7	Schmidt	Suppan	Benitez	78-46	1st	+12.0
8-22	At Pit.	W	3-1		12	3	Mulder	Fogg	Isringhausen	79-46	1st	+12.0
8-23	At Pit.	L	0-10		5	16	Torres	Marquis		79-47	1st	+12.0
8-24	At Pit.	W	8-3		12	4	Carpenter	Wells		80-47	1st	+13.0
8-25	At Pit.	W	6-3		13	12	Morris	Williams	Isringhausen	81-47	1st	+13.5
8-26	At Was.	L	1-4		3	8	Loaiza	Suppan	Cordero	81-48	1st	+12.5
8-27	At Was.	W	6-0		8	2	Marquis	White		82-48	1st	+13.5
8-28	At Was.	W	6-0		8	4	Thompson	Halama		83-48	1st	+14.5
8-29	At Fla.	W	6-1		10	8	Carpenter	Burnett		84-48	1st	+15.0
8-30	At Fla.	L	6-7		7	10	Mota	Morris	Jones	84-49	1st	+14.0
8-31	At Fla.	W	10-5		15	8	Suppan	Vargas		85-49	1st	+14.0
9-2	At Hou.	L	5-6	(13)	13	8	Qualls	Tavarez		85-50	1st	+12.5
9-3	At Hou.	W	4-2		11	8	Carpenter	Springer		86-50	1st	+13.5
9-4	At Hou.	W	4-1		9	5	Marquis	Rodriguez		87-50	1st	+14.5

Date	Opp.	Res.	Score	(inn.*)	Hits	Opp. hits	Winning pitcher	Losing pitcher	Save	Record	Pos.	GB
9-5	Chi.	W	6-4		9	7	King	Novoa	Tavarez	88-50	1st	+14.5
9-6	Chi.	L	2-5		6	13	Rusch	Morris	Dempster	88-51	1st	+13.5
9-7	Chi.	L	1-2		9	10	Maddux	Mulder	Dempster	88-52	1st	+12.5
9-8	N.Y.	W	5-0		10	4	Carpenter	Benson		89-52	1st	+13.0
9-9	N.Y.	W	3-2		8	8	Marquis	Seo	Isringhausen	90-52	1st	+14.0
9-10	N.Y.	W	4-2		6	10	Suppan	Trachsel	Isringhausen	91-52	1st	+14.0
9-11	N.Y.	L	2-7		10	13	Martinez	Morris		91-53	1st	+14.0
9-12	Pit.	W	4-3		6	11	Isringhausen	Torres		92-53	1st	+15.0
9-13	Pit.	W	5-4		7	13	Thompson	White		93-53	1st	+16.0
9-14	Pit.	L	3-5		6	10	Vogelsong	Marquis	Gonzalez	93-54	1st	+15.0
9-15	At Chi.	W	6-1		9	8	Suppan	Prior		94-54	1st	+15.0
9-16	At Chi.	L	3-5		8	9	Rusch	Morris	Dempster	94-55	1st	+14.0
9-17	At Chi.	W	5-1		11	8	Mulder	Maddux		95-55	1st	+14.0
9-18	At Chi.	L	4-7		10	9	Zambrano	Reyes		95-56	1st	+13.0
9-20	At Cin.	L	5-6		7	8	Hancock	King	Weathers	95-57	1st	+12.5
9-21	At Cin.	W	5-1		12	9	Marquis	Ortiz		96-57	1st	+12.5
9-22	At Cin.	L	2-6		8	5	Coffey	King		96-58	1st	+11.5
9-23	At Mil.	L	6-9		6	14	Capuano	Carpenter	Turnbow	96-59	1st	+11.5
9-24	At Mil.	L	7-8		10	10	Glover	Mulder	Turnbow	96-60	1st	+10.5
9-25	At Mil.	W	2-0		5	6	Suppan	Davis	Isringhausen	97-60	1st	+11.5
9-27	Hou.	L	1-3		8	8	Oswalt	Morris	Lidge	97-61	1st	+10.5
9-28	Hou.	L	6-7		10	12	Qualls	Isringhausen	Lidge	97-62	1st	+9.5
9-30	Cin.	W	12-6		17	9	Reyes	Hudson		98-62	1st	+11.0
10-1	Cin.	W	9-6		7	9	Flores	Simpson	Isringhausen	99-62	1st	+11.0
10-2	Cin.	W	7-5		16	10	Thompson	Claussen	Isringhausen	100-62	1st	+11.0

Monthly records: April (15-7), May (18-11), June (16-11), July (17-9), August (19-11), September (13-13), October (2-0).
*Innings, if other than nine. ! First game of a doubleheader. & Second game of a doubleheader.

RECORDS

2005 regular-season record: 100-62
Position: 1st in N.L. Central
Home: 50-31   **Road:** 50-31
N.L. East: 18-14   **N.L. Central:** 51-29
N.L. West: 21-14   **A.L.** 10-5
Vs. LH starters: 32-20
Vs. RH starters: 68-42
Grass: 96-60   **Artificial:** 4-2
Day: 33-26   **Night:** 67-36
1-Run: 21-25   **X-inn.:** 5-3
Doubleheaders: 0-0-0
Team record past five years: 480-330
(.593, ranks 1st in league in that span)

TEAM LEADERS

Batting average: Albert Pujols (.330).
At-bats: David Eckstein (630).
Runs: Albert Pujols (129).
Hits: Albert Pujols (195).
Total Bases: Albert Pujols (360).
Doubles: Albert Pujols (38).
Triples: David Eckstein (7).
Home runs: Albert Pujols (41).
Runs batted in: Albert Pujols (117).
Stolen bases: Albert Pujols (16).
Slugging percentage: Albert Pujols (.609).
On-base percentage: Albert Pujols (.430).
Wins: Chris Carpenter (21).
Earned-run average: Chris Carpenter (2.83).
Complete games: Chris Carpenter (7).
Shutouts: Chris Carpenter (4).
Saves: Jason Isringhausen (39).
Innings pitched: Chris Carpenter (241.2).
Strikeouts: Chris Carpenter (213).

GAMES BY POSITION

Catcher: Yadier Molina 114, Einar Diaz 50, Mike Mahoney 25.
First base: Albert Pujols 157, John Mabry 14, Scott Seabol 5, Einar Diaz 3, Chris Duncan 2, Yadier Molina 1.
Second base: Mark Grudzielanek 137, Hector Luna 22, Abraham O. Nunez 22, Scott Seabol 8.
Third base: Abraham O. Nunez 98, Scott Rolen 56, Scott Seabol 20, John Mabry 18, Hector Luna 7.
Shortstop: David Eckstein 156, Abraham O. Nunez 21, Hector Luna 6.
Outfield: Jim Edmonds 139, So Taguchi 131, Larry Walker 83, Reggie Sanders 81, John Mabry 70, John Rodriguez 45, Hector Luna 25, Skip Schumaker 21, Roger Cedeno 16, John Gall 10, Scott Seabol 4, Chris Duncan 1.
Designated hitter: Larry Walker 6, Scott Seabol 3, Reggie Sanders 1.

TOP DRAFT CHOICES

1a. **Colby Rasmus,** OF, Russell County H.S., Phenix City, Ala.
1b. **Tyler Greene,** SS, Georgia Tech.
1c. **Mark McCormick,** RHP, Baylor.
1d. **Tyler Herron,** RHP, Wellington (Fla.) Community H.S.
2a. **Josh Wilson,** RHP, Whitehouse H.S., Tyler, Texas.
2b. **Nick Webber,** RHP, Central Missouri State.
3. **Daryl Jones,** OF, Spring (Texas) H.S.
4. **Bryan Anderson,** C, Simi Valley (Calif.) H.S.
5. **Mitch Boggs,** RHP, Georgia.
6. **Wilfrido Pujols,** OF, Fort Osage H.S., Independence, Mo.
7. **Nick Stavinoha,** OF, LSU.
8. **Jason Cairns,** RHP, Central Michigan.
9. **Zach Zuercher,** LHP, Rhode Island.
10. **Randy Roth,** C, Southeastern Louisiana.

SAN DIEGO PADRES
NATIONAL LEAGUE WEST DIVISION

2006 SEASON

Padres Schedule
Home games shaded.
All-Star Game July 11 at Pittsburgh. Schedule subject to change.

APRIL

SUN	MON	TUE	WED	THU	FRI	SAT
2	3 SF	4 SF	5 SF	6	7 COL	8 COL
9 COL	10	11 FLA	12 FLA	13 FLA	14 ATL	15 ATL
16 ATL	17 COL	18 COL	19 COL	20 NYM	21 NYM	22 NYM
23 NYM	24 ARI	25 ARI	26 ARI	27	28 LAD	29 LAD
30 LAD						

MAY

SUN	MON	TUE	WED	THU	FRI	SAT
	1 SF	2 SF	3 LAD	4 LAD	5 CHC	6 CHC
7 CHC	8 CHC	9 MIL	10 MIL	11 MIL	12 CHC	13 CHC
14 CHC	15 ARI	16 ARI	17 ARI	18	19 SEA	20 SEA
21 SEA	22 ATL	23 ATL	24 ATL	25	26 STL	27 STL
28 STL	29 COL	30 COL	31 COL			

JUNE

SUN	MON	TUE	WED	THU	FRI	SAT
				1	2 PIT	3 PIT
4 PIT	5 MIL	6 MIL	7 MIL	8 MIL	9 FLA	10 FLA
11 FLA	12	13 LAD	14 LAD	15 LAD	16 LAA	17 LAA
18 LAA	19	20 TEX	21 TEX	22 TEX	23 SEA	24 SEA
25 SEA	26	27 OAK	28 OAK	29 OAK	30 SF	

JULY

SUN	MON	TUE	WED	THU	FRI	SAT
						1 SF
2 SF	3	4 PHI	5 PHI	6 PHI	7 WAS	8 WAS
9 WAS	10	11 ALL-STAR	12	13	14 ATL	15 ATL
16 ATL	17 PHI	18 PHI	19 PHI	20 SF	21 SF	22 SF
23 SF	24 LAD	25 LAD	26 LAD	27 COL	28 COL	29 COL
30 COL	31					

AUGUST

SUN	MON	TUE	WED	THU	FRI	SAT
		1 HOU	2 HOU	3 HOU	4 WAS	5 WAS
6 WAS	7	8 NYM	9 NYM	10 NYM	11 HOU	12 HOU
13 HOU	14 SF	15 SF	16 SF	17 SF	18 ARI	19 ARI
20 ARI	21 LAD	22 LAD	23 LAD	24	25 COL	26 COL
27 COL	28 ARI	29 ARI	30 ARI	31		

SEPTEMBER

SUN	MON	TUE	WED	THU	FRI	SAT
					1 CIN	2 CIN
3 CIN	4 COL	5 COL	6 COL	7	8 SF	9 SF
10 SF	11	12 CIN	13 CIN	14 CIN	15 LAD	16 LAD
17 LAD	18 LAD	19 ARI	20 ARI	21 ARI	22 PIT	23 PIT
24 PIT	25 STL	26 STL	27 STL	28 ARI	29 ARI	30 ARI

OCTOBER

SUN	MON	TUE	WED	THU	FRI	SAT
1 ARI	2	3	4	5	6	7

Home games are shaded. All-Star Game is July 11 at Pittsburgh. Schedule is subject to change.

Klesko

CLUB DIRECTORY

Chairman
John Moores
Chief operating officer
Sandy Alderson
President
Dick Freeman
Exec. v.p., baseball operations and g.m.
Kevin Towers
Exec. v.p. & managing dir. of ballpark op.
Richard Anderson
Executive v.p., chief financial officer
Fred Gerson
Executive v.p., communications
Jeff Overton
Executive v.p., general counsel
Katie Pothier

V.p./scouting and player development
Grady Fuson
Assistant general manager
Fred Uhlman Jr.
Vice president, community relations
Michele Anderson
Vice president/controller
Dan Fumai
Vice president/senior adviser
David Winfield
Director, scouting
Bill "Chief" Gayton
Director, minor league operations
Priscilla Oppenheimer
Director, baseball operations
Jeff Kingston

MINOR LEAGUE AFFILIATES

Class	Team	League	Manager
AAA	Portland	Pacific Coast	Craig Colbert
AA	Mobile	Southern	Gary Jones
Advanced A	Lake Elsinore	California	Rick Renteria
A	Fort Wayne	Midwest	Randy Ready
Short-Season A	Eugene	Northwest	Doug Dascenzo
Rookie	Padres	Arizona	Carlos Lezcano

BROADCAST INFORMATION

Radio: MIGHTY 1090, XEMO-AM (860, Spanish).
Cable TV: Channel 4 Padres.

SPRING TRAINING

Ballpark (city): Peoria Stadium (Peoria, Ariz.).
Ticket information: 623-878-4337, 800-409-1511.

For more on the Padres, go to www.sportingnews.com/baseball/teams/padres/

2006 SEASON San Diego Padres

Manager—Bruce Bochy (15).
Coaches—Darrel Akerfelds (48), Darren Balsley (36), Glenn Hoffman, Dave Magadan (12), Tony Muser (40), Tye Waller.

No.	PITCHERS	B/T	Ht./Wt.	Age*
	Stephen Andrade	R/R	6-1/220	28
	Kenny Baugh	R/R	6-4/195	27
	Dewon Brazelton	R/R	6-4/215	25
	Doug Brocail	L/R	6-5/250	38
56	Scott Cassidy	R/R	6-2/175	30
55	Shawn Estes	R/L	6-2/200	33
	Seth Etherton	R/R	6-1/200	29
52	Clay Hensley	R/R	5-11/190	26
51	Trevor Hoffman	R/R	6-0/215	38
38	Scott Linebrink	R/R	6-3/200	29
61	Chan Ho Park	R/R	6-2/210	32
44	Jake Peavy	R/R	6-1/180	24
	Brian Sikorski	R/R	6-1/200	31
47	Tim Stauffer	R/R	6-1/214	23
73	Sean Thompson	L/L	6-0/210	23
59	Rusty Tucker	L/L	6-0/190	25
	Jared Wells	R/R	6-4/200	24
17	Woody Williams	R/R	6-0/200	39
	Chris Young	R/R	6-10/260	26

No.	CATCHERS	B/T	Ht./Wt.	Age*
76	George Kottaras	L/R	6-0/190	22
	Pete LaForest	L/R	6-2/208	28
	Doug Mirabelli	R/R	6-1/220	35
9	David Ross	R/R	6-2/215	29

No.	INFIELDERS	B/T	Ht./Wt.	Age*
63	Josh Barfield	R/R	6-0/185	23
	Mark Bellhorn	B/R	6-1/205	31
	Geoff Blum	B/R	6-3/200	32
	Vinny Castilla	R/R	6-1/205	38
	Adrian Gonzalez	L/L	6-2/220	23
3	Khalil Greene	R/R	5-11/210	26
	Bobby Hill	B/R	5-9/180	27

No.	OUTFIELDERS	B/T	Ht./Wt.	Age*
	Mike Cameron	R/R	6-2/200	33
24	Brian Giles	L/L	5-10/205	35
	Freddy Guzman	B/R	5-10/165	25
	Ben Johnson	R/R	6-1/200	24
30	Ryan Klesko	L/L	6-3/220	34
18	Paul McAnulty	L/R	5-10/220	25
10	Dave Roberts	L/L	5-10/180	33
	Terrmel Sledge	L/L	6-0/185	29
7	Eric Young	R/R	5-8/186	38

*Age as of April 1, 2006.

BALLPARK INFORMATION

Ballpark (capacity, surface)
Petco Park (42,500, grass)
Address
100 Park Blvd.
San Diego, CA 92101
Official website
www.padres.com
Business phone
619-795-5000
Ticket information
1-877-FRIAR-TIX
Field dimensions (from home plate)
To left field at foul line, 334 feet
To center field, 396 feet
To right field at foul line, 322 feet
First game played
April 8, 2004 (Padres 4, Giants 3, 10 innings)

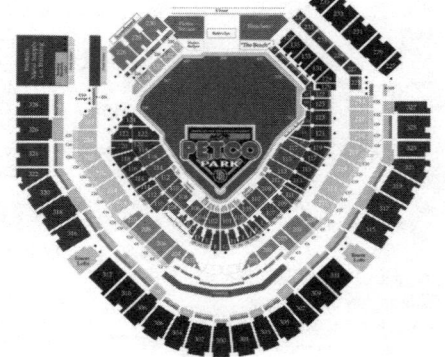

Date	Opp.	Res.	Score	(inn.*)	Hits	Opp. hits	Winning pitcher	Losing pitcher	Save	Record	Pos.	GB
4-4	At Col.	L	10-12		12	18	Speier	Hoffman		0-1	T4th	1.0
4-6	At Col.	W	14-6		13	11	Hammond	Jennings		1-1	T2nd	0.5
4-7	Pit.	W	1-0	(12)	9	10	Seanez	White		2-1	T1st	...
4-8	Pit.	L	2-3		6	8	Fogg	Lawrence	Mesa	2-2	T2nd	1.0
4-9	Pit.	W	11-3		13	6	Williams	Perez		3-2	T2nd	1.0
4-10	Pit.	L	3-6		7	7	Williams	Redding	Mesa	3-3	T3rd	1.0
4-11	At Chi.	W	1-0		4	6	Eaton	Dempster	Hoffman	4-3	T3rd	0.5
4-13!	At Chi.	W	8-3		12	8	Peavy	Wood		5-3		
4-13&	At Chi.	L	3-8		7	11	Prior	Lawrence		5-4	3rd	1.5
4-15	At L.A.	L	0-4		3	8	Lowe	Williams		5-5	4th	2.5
4-16	At L.A.	L	3-8		6	11	Erickson	Eaton		5-6	4th	3.5
4-17	At L.A.	L	0-6		5	11	Weaver	Redding		5-7	4th	4.5
4-18	S.F.	W	7-2		10	8	Peavy	Tomko		6-7	4th	4.5
4-19	S.F.	W	5-2		7	6	Lawrence	Williams	Hoffman	7-7	T2nd	4.5
4-20	L.A.	L	1-3	(10)	7	9	Sanchez	Linebrink	Brazoban	7-8	3rd	5.5
4-21	L.A.	W	6-1		15	6	Eaton	Erickson		8-8	T2nd	4.5
4-22	At Ari.	L	3-5		7	14	Halsey	Redding	Lyon	8-9	3rd	4.5
4-23	At Ari.	L	1-2		5	7	Koplove	Otsuka		8-10	4th	4.5
4-24	At Ari.	L	6-8		7	14	Estes	Lawrence	Lyon	8-11	4th	5.5
4-25	At S.F.	W	5-3		9	10	Williams	Lowry	Hoffman	9-11	3rd	4.5
4-26	At S.F.	L	5-6		10	8	Benitez	Otsuka		9-12	4th	4.5
4-27	At S.F.	L	3-10		7	11	Rueter	Redding		9-13	4th	5.0
4-29	Ari.	W	5-4	(15)	20	8	Hammond	Lyon		10-13	4th	4.5
4-30	Ari.	W	2-0		4	2	Lawrence	Estes	Hoffman	11-13	4th	4.5
5-1	Ari.	L	2-5		6	9	Vazquez	Williams		11-14	4th	5.5
5-2	Col.	W	5-4		8	9	Eaton	Francis	Hoffman	12-14	4th	4.5
5-3	Col.	W	2-1		9	6	Otsuka	Witasick	Hoffman	13-14	4th	4.5
5-4	Col.	W	8-7	(12)	10	9	Reyes	Carvajal		14-14	4th	3.5
5-5	At StL.	W	8-3		12	7	Hammond	King		15-14	4th	3.0
5-6	At StL.	W	6-5		11	8	Williams	Flores	Hoffman	16-14	3rd	3.0
5-7	At StL.	W	5-4		8	9	Eaton	Carpenter	Hoffman	17-14	3rd	2.0
5-8	At StL.	L	5-15		8	17	Marquis	Redding	Thompson	17-15	3rd	3.0
5-9	At Cin.	W	6-5	(13)	14	13	Hammond	Belisle	Hoffman	18-15	T2nd	2.0
5-10	At Cin.	L	1-5		12	7	Coffey	Lawrence		18-16	3rd	3.0
5-11	At Cin.	W	7-2		16	5	Stauffer	Wilson		19-16	3rd	2.0
5-13	Fla.	W	3-2		9	7	Eaton	Beckett	Hoffman	20-16	3rd	1.5
5-14	Fla.	W	2-1		3	5	Peavy	Leiter	Hoffman	21-16	3rd	0.5
5-15	Fla.	W	12-4		15	10	Seanez	Burnett		22-16	2nd	0.5
5-16	Atl.	W	5-3		10	7	Linebrink	Reitsma	Hoffman	23-16	T1st	...
5-17	Atl.	W	3-2		7	6	Reyes	Kolb		24-16	1st	+1.0
5-18	Atl.	W	8-4		11	10	Eaton	Ramirez	Hoffman	25-16	1st	+1.0
5-20	At Sea.	W	6-1		4	5	Peavy	Franklin		26-16	1st	+0.5
5-21	At Sea.	L	3-5		5	8	Meche	Lawrence	Guardado	26-17	1st	+0.5
5-22	At Sea.	L	0-5		4	10	Sele	Stauffer		26-18	2nd	0.5
5-24	At Ari.	W	9-5		15	15	Eaton	Ortiz	Hoffman	27-18	1st	+0.5
5-25	At Ari.	L	11-12		15	15	Valverde	Otsuka	Bruney	27-19	2nd	0.5
5-26	At Ari.	W	10-0		13	2	Peavy	Webb		28-19	1st	+0.5
5-27	At S.F.	W	9-3		15	6	Lawrence	Hennessey		29-19	1st	+1.5
5-28	At S.F.	W	5-3		9	8	Seanez	Fassero	Hoffman	30-19	1st	+1.5
5-29	At S.F.	W	9-6		16	10	Hammond	Walker	Hoffman	31-19	1st	+2.5
5-30	Mil.	W	2-1		8	6	Linebrink	de la Rosa		32-19	1st	+3.0
5-31	Mil.	W	8-4		11	10	Reyes	Glover		33-19	1st	+3.0
6-1	Mil.	L	2-5		8	15	Davis	Lawrence	Santana	33-20	1st	+3.0
6-2	Chi.	L	0-5		4	12	Rusch	Stauffer		33-21	1st	+3.0
6-3	Chi.	W	6-2		10	8	Eaton	Mitre	Otsuka	34-21	1st	+3.5
6-4	Chi.	L	5-11		12	17	Maddux	May		34-22	1st	+4.0
6-5	Chi.	L	0-4		5	11	Zambrano	Williams		34-23	1st	+4.0
6-7	Cle.	L	0-2	(11)	8	9	Betancourt	Hoffman	Wickman	34-24	1st	+3.5
6-8	Cle.	L	1-6		7	7	Elarton	Peavy	Howry	34-25	1st	+3.0
6-9	Cle.	W	3-2		3	9	Eaton	Westbrook	Hoffman	35-25	1st	+3.5
6-10	Chi.	L	2-4		7	9	Garland	Williams	Hermanson	35-26	1st	+2.5
6-11	Chi.	W	2-1		11	6	Linebrink	Hermanson		36-26	1st	+3.5
6-12	Chi.	L	5-8	(10)	10	13	Politte	Hoffman		36-27	1st	+2.5
6-14	At Det.	L	4-8		8	9	Rodney	Peavy		36-28	1st	+2.0
6-15	At Det.	L	2-8		7	11	Maroth	Eaton		36-29	1st	+2.0
6-16	At Det.	L	1-3		4	6	Bonderman	Williams	Percival	36-30	1st	+1.5
6-17	At Min.	L	4-5	(11)	14	12	Rincon	Reyes		36-31	1st	+1.5

Date	Opp.	Res.	Score	(inn.*)	Hits	Opp. hits	Winning pitcher	Losing pitcher	Save	Record	Pos.	GB
6-18	At Min.	W	7-2		16	7	Lawrence	Radke		37-31	1st	+2.5
6-19	At Min.	W	5-1		7	4	May	Santana		38-31	1st	+3.5
6-20	L.A.	W	1-0		7	3	Peavy	Penny	Hoffman	39-31	1st	+4.5
6-21	L.A.	W	2-1		9	6	Williams	Lowe	Hoffman	40-31	1st	+4.5
6-22	L.A.	L	4-6		8	12	Houlton	Stauffer	Brazoban	40-32	1st	+4.5
6-23	L.A.	L	3-4	(10)	7	7	Sanchez	Hoffman	Brazoban	40-33	1st	+3.5
6-24	Sea.	L	5-14		9	17	Meche	May		40-34	1st	+2.5
6-25	Sea.	W	8-5		9	9	Peavy	Sele	Hoffman	41-34	1st	+3.5
6-26	Sea.	W	5-4		8	8	Seanez	Mateo	Hoffman	42-34	1st	+3.5
6-27	At L.A.	L	4-5		6	10	Houlton	Stauffer	Brazoban	42-35	1st	+3.0
6-28	At L.A.	W	8-3		12	7	Lawrence	Dessens		43-35	1st	+4.0
6-29	At L.A.	L	2-4		8	10	Weaver	May	Brazoban	43-36	1st	+4.0
7-1	S.F.	L	2-3		9	6	Christiansen	Seanez	Walker	43-37	1st	+4.5
7-2	S.F.	W	5-3		12	6	Williams	Fassero	Hoffman	44-37	1st	+4.5
7-3	S.F.	W	9-6		10	11	Stauffer	Schmidt	Hoffman	45-37	1st	+4.5
7-4	At Hou.	L	1-4		5	10	Oswalt	Lawrence		45-38	1st	+4.5
7-5	At Hou.	L	2-6		6	11	Backe	Reyes		45-39	1st	+4.5
7-6	At Hou.	L	4-5		9	12	Pettitte	Peavy	Wheeler	45-40	1st	+4.5
7-7	At Hou.	W	7-5		7	8	Williams	Rodriguez	Hoffman	46-40	1st	+4.5
7-8	At Col.	W	12-2		14	7	Stauffer	Wright		47-40	1st	+5.5
7-9	At Col.	L	0-1		7	7	Jennings	Lawrence	Fuentes	47-41	1st	+5.5
7-10	At Col.	W	8-5		9	14	Quantrill	Francis	Hoffman	48-41	1st	+5.5
7-14	Ari.	L	0-6		5	11	Vazquez	Lawrence		48-42	1st	+4.5
7-15	Ari.	W	10-7		13	13	Linebrink	Aquino	Hoffman	49-42	1st	+5.5
7-16	Ari.	W	4-1		5	6	Peavy	Vargas	Hoffman	50-42	1st	+6.5
7-17	Ari.	L	1-6		7	12	Halsey	Stauffer	Valverde	50-43	1st	+5.5
7-19	At N.Y.	L	1-3	(11)	6	9	Looper	Hammond		50-44	1st	+5.0
7-20	At N.Y.	L	3-7		9	10	Glavine	Williams	Padilla	50-45	1st	+5.0
7-21	At N.Y.	L	0-12		6	12	Ishii	Peavy		50-46	1st	+4.5
7-22	At Phi.	L	6-8	(11)	11	11	Fultz	Quantrill		50-47	1st	+3.5
7-23	At Phi.	L	0-2		4	7	Tejeda	Astacio	Wagner	50-48	1st	+3.5
7-24	At Phi.	L	1-5		7	10	Myers	Lawrence		50-49	1st	+2.5
7-26	StL.	L	2-4		10	10	Mulder	Williams	Isringhausen	50-50	1st	+3.0
7-27	StL.	W	2-1		6	3	Hoffman	Marquis		51-50	1st	+3.0
7-28	StL.	L	3-11		10	17	Carpenter	Stauffer		51-51	1st	+2.0
7-29	Cin.	L	3-8		6	10	Hudson	Lawrence		51-52	1st	+2.0
7-30	Cin.	L	1-9		7	14	Harang	Astacio		51-53	1st	+1.0
7-31	Cin.	L	1-7		5	9	Milton	Williams		51-54	2nd	...
8-2	At Pit.	W	11-3		15	9	Peavy	Wells		52-54	1st	+1.0
8-3	At Pit.	L	8-9		10	10	Mesa	Otsuka		52-55	1st	+1.0
8-4	At Pit.	W	12-7		14	13	Lawrence	Redman		53-55	1st	+1.0
8-5	At Was.	W	6-5		16	5	Linebrink	Cordero	Hoffman	54-55	1st	+2.0
8-6	At Was.	W	3-2		11	5	Astacio	Drese	Hoffman	55-55	1st	+3.0
8-7	At Was.	W	3-0		6	5	Peavy	Loaiza		56-55	1st	+3.0
8-9	N.Y.	W	8-3		15	9	Park	Martinez		57-55	1st	+4.0
8-10	N.Y.	L	1-9		4	12	Benson	Lawrence		57-56	1st	+4.0
8-11	N.Y.	W	2-1		10	6	Williams	Glavine	Hoffman	58-56	1st	+4.0
8-12	Phi.	L	2-3		8	7	Lieber	Peavy	Wagner	58-57	1st	+3.0
8-13	Phi.	L	2-5		6	8	Urbina	Hoffman	Wagner	58-58	1st	+3.0
8-14	Phi.	L	3-8		5	9	Tejeda	Park		58-59	1st	+3.0
8-16	At Fla.	W	4-2		7	10	Lawrence	Vargas	Hoffman	59-59	1st	+4.0
8-17	At Fla.	L	0-6		5	6	Willis	Williams		59-60	1st	+4.0
8-18	At Fla.	L	0-2		6	6	Beckett	Peavy	Jones	59-61	1st	+3.0
8-19	At Atl.	W	12-7		20	13	Park	Hampton		60-61	1st	+4.0
8-20	At Atl.	W	7-2	(13)	11	12	Seanez	Devine		61-61	1st	+4.0
8-21	At Atl.	L	2-6		10	9	Sosa	Otsuka		61-62	1st	+4.0
8-22	Hou.	L	2-6		5	12	Oswalt	Williams		61-63	1st	+4.0
8-23	Hou.	W	2-0		5	4	Peavy	Clemens		62-63	1st	+5.0
8-24	Hou.	W	7-4		13	8	Park	Rodriguez	Hoffman	63-63	1st	+6.0
8-26	Col.	L	3-4		7	7	Francis	Eaton	Fuentes	63-64	1st	+6.5
8-27	Col.	L	2-4		8	7	Kim	Lawrence	Cortes	63-65	1st	+5.5
8-28	Col.	W	4-3		7	6	Astacio	Wright	Hoffman	64-65	1st	+5.5
8-29	Ari.	L	5-7		8	8	Ortiz	Williams		64-66	1st	+4.5
8-30	Ari.	W	5-3		9	10	Peavy	Halsey	Hoffman	65-66	1st	+5.5
8-31	Ari.	W	9-5		14	9	Park	Vazquez		66-66	1st	+5.5
9-1	At Mil.	W	6-5		9	6	Seanez	Davis	Hoffman	67-66	1st	+6.0
9-2	At Mil.	L	2-12		6	11	Capuano	Lawrence		67-67	1st	+6.0
9-3	At Mil.	W	6-1		9	6	Williams	Obermueller		68-67	1st	+6.5
9-4	At Mil.	L	2-3		8	7	Turnbow	Otsuka		68-68	1st	+5.5
9-6	Col.	L	5-6		11	6	Cook	Park	Fuentes	68-69	1st	+5.0

Date	Opp.	Res.	Score	(inn.*)	Hits	Opp. hits	Winning pitcher	Losing pitcher	Save	Record	Pos.	GB
9-7	Col.	W	4-2		8	6	Eaton	Francis	Hoffman	69-69	1st	+6.0
9-8	Col.	W	3-2	(10)	8	5	Linebrink	Acevedo		70-69	1st	+7.0
9-9	At L.A.	W	3-1		7	5	Williams	Houlton	Hoffman	71-69	1st	+7.0
9-10	At L.A.	L	1-3		7	5	Lowe	Hensley	Sanchez	71-70	1st	+7.0
9-11	At L.A.	L	3-7		6	12	Penny	Cassidy		71-71	1st	+6.0
9-12	At S.F.	L	3-4		5	12	Kinney	Eaton	Benitez	71-72	1st	+5.0
9-13	At S.F.	L	4-5		11	14	Lowry	Lawrence	Benitez	71-73	1st	+5.0
9-14	At S.F.	W	5-4	(10)	8	7	Seanez	Hawkins	Hoffman	72-73	1st	+6.0
9-16	Was.	L	1-5		3	9	Patterson	Peavy		72-74	1st	+5.5
9-17	Was.	W	8-5	(12)	11	12	Linebrink	Rauch		73-74	1st	+5.5
9-18	Was.	W	2-1		9	5	Otsuka	Eischen		74-74	1st	+5.5
9-19	At Col.	W	8-7		14	15	Linebrink	Fuentes	Hoffman	75-74	1st	+6.0
9-20	At Col.	L	1-20		6	23	Wright	Williams		75-75	1st	+5.0
9-21	At Col.	W	5-2		11	8	Peavy	Esposito	Hoffman	76-75	1st	+5.0
9-22	At Col.	L	2-4		11	8	Cook	Eaton	Fuentes	76-76	1st	+5.0
9-23	At Ari.	W	5-3		11	7	Astacio	Vargas	Hoffman	77-76	1st	+5.0
9-24	At Ari.	L	5-8		10	12	Worrell	Otsuka	Valverde	77-77	1st	+5.0
9-25	At Ari.	L	3-4	(10)	2	13	Valverde	Otsuka		77-78	1st	+4.0
9-26	S.F.	L	2-3		3	9	Walker	Hoffman	Benitez	77-79	1st	+3.0
9-27	S.F.	W	9-6		8	11	Hensley	Fassero	Hoffman	78-79	1st	+4.0
9-28	S.F.	W	9-1		15	9	Astacio	Schmidt		79-79	1st	+5.0
9-29	S.F.	W	1-0	(11)	9	3	Cassidy	Accardo		80-79	1st	+5.0
9-30	L.A.	W	3-1		5	4	Williams	Lowe	Linebrink	81-79	1st	+5.0
10-1	L.A.	L	1-2		3	6	Broxton	Park	Sanchez	81-80	1st	+4.0
10-2	L.A.	W	3-1		9	4	Eaton	Dessens	Hoffman	82-80	1st	+5.0

Monthly records: April (11-13), May (22-6), June (10-17), July (8-18), August (15-12), September (15-13), October (1-1).
*Innings, if other than nine. ! First game of a doubleheader. & Second game of a doubleheader.

RECORDS

2005 regular-season record: 82-80
Position: 1st in N.L. West
Home: 46-35   **Road:** 36-45
N.L. East: 16-14   **N.L. Central:** 20-21
N.L. West: 39-34   **A.L.** 7-11
Vs. LH starters: 21-23
Vs. RH starters: 61-57
Grass: 80-79   **Artificial:** 2-1
Day: 24-27   **Night:** 58-53
1-Run: 29-20   **X-inn.:** 9-8
Doubleheaders: 0-0-1
Team record past five years: 378-432
(.467, ranks 11th in league in that span)

TEAM LEADERS

Batting average: Brian Giles (.301).
At-bats: Brian Giles (545).
Runs: Brian Giles (92). `
Hits: Brian Giles (164).
Total Bases: Brian Giles (263).
Doubles: Brian Giles (38).
Triples: Dave Roberts (10).
Home runs: Ryan Klesko (18).
Runs batted in: Brian Giles (83).
Stolen bases: Dave Roberts (23).
Slugging percentage: Brian Giles (.483).
On-base percentage: Brian Giles (.423).
Wins: Jake Peavy (13).
Earned-run average: Jake Peavy (2.88).
Complete games: Jake Peavy (3).
Shutouts: Jake Peavy (3).
Saves: Trevor Hoffman (43).
Innings pitched: Jake Peavy (203.0).
Strikeouts: Jake Peavy (216).

GAMES BY POSITION

Catcher: Ramon Hernandez 97, Miguel Olivo 37, Robert Fick 28, Miguel Ojeda 25, David Ross 7, Phil Nevin 2.
First base: Phil Nevin 71, Mark Sweeney 53, Xavier Nady 44, Robert Fick 29, Geoff Blum 2, Manny Alexander 1, Ryan Klesko 1, Paul McAnulty 1.
Second base: Mark Loretta 105, Damian Jackson 35, Geoff Blum 19, Eric Young 14, Manny Alexander 5, Jesse Garcia 2.
Third base: Sean Burroughs 78, Joe Randa 58, Geoff Blum 34, Damian Jackson 8, Xavier Nady 3, Manny Alexander 1, Robert Fick 1, Mark Loretta 1.
Shortstop: Khalil Greene 121, Damian Jackson 26, Geoff Blum 14, Jesse Garcia 13, Wilson Valdez 8, Manny Alexander 4, Sean Burroughs 1.
Outfield: Brian Giles 155, Ryan Klesko 121, Dave Roberts 109, Xavier Nady 68, Damian Jackson 52, Ben Johnson 29, Eric Young 25, Robert Fick 13, Adam Hyzdu 12, Paul McAnulty 6, Mark Sweeney 6, Miguel Ojeda 5.
Designated hitter: Mark Sweeney 5, Ryan Klesko 3, Robert Fick 2, Xavier Nady 1, Miguel Ojeda 1.

TOP DRAFT CHOICES

1a. **Cesar Carrillo,** RHP, Miami.
1b. **Cesar Ramos,** LHP, Long Beach State.
2a. **Chase Headley,** 3B, Tennessee.
2b. **Nick Hundley,** C, Arizona.
3. **Josh Geer,** RHP, Rice.
4. **Mike Baxter,** OF, Vanderbilt.
5. **Seth Johnston,** SS, Texas.
6. **Neil Jamison,** RHP, Long Beach State.
7. **Will Venable,** OF, Princeton.
8. **John Madden,** RHP, Auburn.
9. **Casey Smith,** 1B, Erskine College.
10. **Josh Alley,** OF, Tennessee.

SAN FRANCISCO GIANTS
NATIONAL LEAGUE WEST DIVISION

2006 SEASON

Giants Schedule
Home games shaded.
All-Star Game July 11 at Pittsburgh. Schedule subject to change.

APRIL

SUN	MON	TUE	WED	THU	FRI	SAT
2	3 SD	4 SD	5 SD	6 ATL	7 ATL	1 ATL
9 ATL	10	11 HOU	12 HOU	13 HOU	14 LAD	15 LAD
16 LAD	17 ARI	18 ARI	19 ARI	20 ARI	21 COL	22 COL
23 COL	24 NYM	25 NYM	26 NYM	27	28 ARI	29 ARI
30 ARI						

MAY

SUN	MON	TUE	WED	THU	FRI	SAT
	1 SD	2 SD	3 MIL	4 MIL	5 PHI	6 PHI
7 PHI	8	9 CHC	10 CHC	11 CHC	12 LAD	13 LAD
14 LAD	15 HOU	16 HOU	17 HOU	18	19 OAK	20 OAK
21 OAK	22 STL	23 STL	24 STL	25	26 COL	27 COL
28 COL	29 FLA	30 FLA	31 FLA			

JUNE

SUN	MON	TUE	WED	THU	FRI	SAT
				1	2 NYM	3 NYM
4 NYM	5 FLA	6 FLA	7 FLA	8 PIT	9 PIT	10 PIT
11 PIT	12	13 ARI	14 ARI	15 ARI	16 SEA	17 SEA
18 SEA	19 LAA	20 LAA	21 LAA	22	23 OAK	24 OAK
25 OAK	26	27 TEX	28 TEX	29 TEX	30 SD	

JULY

SUN	MON	TUE	WED	THU	FRI	SAT
						1 SD
2 SD	3 COL	4 COL	5 COL	6 LAD	7 LAD	8 LAD
9 LAD	10	11 ALL-STAR	12	13	14 PHI	15 PHI
16 PHI	17 MIL	18 MIL	19 MIL	20 SD	21 SD	22 SD
23 SD	24	25 WAS	26 WAS	27 WAS	28 PIT	29 PIT
30 PIT	31 WAS					

AUGUST

SUN	MON	TUE	WED	THU	FRI	SAT
		1 WAS	2 WAS	3	4 COL	5 COL
6 COL	7 ARI	8 ARI	9 ARI	10	11 LAD	12 LAD
13 LAD	14 SD	15 SD	16 SD	17 SD	18 LAD	19 LAD
20 LAD	21 ARI	22 ARI	23 ARI	24 CIN	25 CIN	26 CIN
27 CIN	28	29 ATL	30 ATL	31 ATL		

SEPTEMBER

SUN	MON	TUE	WED	THU	FRI	SAT
					1 CHC	2 CHC
3 CHC	4 CIN	5 CIN	6 CIN	7	8 SD	9 SD
10 SD	11	12 COL	13 COL	14 COL	15 STL	16 STL
17 STL	18 COL	19 COL	20 COL	21 MIL	22 MIL	23 MIL
24 MIL	25 ARI	26 ARI	27 ARI	28	29 LAD	30 LAD

OCTOBER

SUN	MON	TUE	WED	THU	FRI	SAT
1 LAD	2	3	4	5	6	7

Home games are shaded. All-Star
Game is July 11 at Pittsburgh.
Schedule is subject to change.

Bonds

CLUB DIRECTORY

President and managing general partner
Peter A. Magowan
Executive vice president and COO
Larry Baer
Sr. vice president and general manager
Brian Sabean
Vice president, player personnel
Dick Tidrow
Special assistant to the general manager
Ron Perranoski
Director of player development
Jack Hiatt
Director of minor league operations
Bobby Evans

Coordinator of scouting
Matt Nerland
Coordinator of international operations
Rick Ragazzo
Coordinator, baseball operations
Jeremy Shelley
Vice president, communications
Staci Slaughter
Director of broadcasting & media services
Maria Jacinto
Director of media relations
Blake Rhodes
Media relations manager
Jim Moorehead

MINOR LEAGUE AFFILIATES

Class	Team	League	Manager
AAA	Fresno	Pacific Coast	Shane Turner
AA	Connecticut	Eastern	Dave Machemer
Advanced A	San Jose	California	Lenn Sakata
A	Augusta	South Atlantic	Robert Kelly
Short-Season A	Salem-Keizer	Northwest	Steve Decker
Rookie	Giants	Arizona	Bert Hunter

BROADCAST INFORMATION

Radio: KNBR-AM (680).
TV: KTVU-TV (Channel 2).
Cable TV: Fox Sports Net.
For more on the Giants, go to www.sportingnews.com/baseball/teams/giants/

SPRING TRAINING

Ballpark (city): Scottsdale Stadium
(Scottsdale, Ariz.).
Ticket information: 480-990-7972.

SPRING TRAINING ROSTER

Manager—Felipe Alou (23).
Coaches—Carlos Alfonso (17), Mark Gardner (26), Gene Glynn (15), Joe Lefebvre (16), Luis Pujols (55), Dave Righetti (19), Ron Wotus (10).

No.	PITCHERS	B/T	Ht./Wt.	Age*
59	Jeremy Accardo	R/R	6-2/190	24
60	Kelyn Acosta	R/R	6-2/195	20
49	Armando Benitez	R/R	6-4/245	33
48	Brian Burres	L/L	6-1/175	24
43	Matt Cain	R/R	6-3/231	21
53	Kevin Correia	R/R	6-3/210	25
61	Jon Coutlangus	L/L	6-1/180	25
14	Jeff Fassero	L/L	6-1/200	43
41	Brad Hennessey	R/R	6-2/195	26
34	Steve Kline	R/L	6-1/240	33
51	Noah Lowry	R/L	6-2/210	25
35	Matt Morris	R/R	6-5/220	31
54	Scott Munter	R/R	6-6/240	26
63	Jesus Reina	L/L	6-2/175	21
29	Jason Schmidt	R/R	6-5/215	33
56	Alfredo Simon	R/R	6-4/230	24
37	Jack Taschner	L/L	6-3/205	27
57	Erick Threets	L/L	6-5/240	24
65	Merkin Valdez	R/R	6-3/220	24
47	Tyler Walker	R/R	6-3/240	29
45	Tim Worrell	R/R	6-4/240	38

No.	CATCHERS	B/T	Ht./Wt.	Age*
52	Eliezer Alfonzo	R/R	6-0/225	27
33	Justin Knoedler	R/R	6-2/210	25
22	Mike Matheny	R/R	6-3/220	35

No.	INFIELDERS	B/T	Ht./Wt.	Age*
1	Angel Chavez	R/R	6-1/195	24
5	Ray Durham	B/R	5-8/196	34
7	Pedro Feliz	R/R	6-1/205	30
64	Travis Ishikawa	L/L	6-3/200	22
28	Lance Niekro	R/R	6-3/210	27
9	Mark Sweeney	L/L	6-1/215	36
	Jose Vizcaino	B/R	6-1/190	38
13	Omar Vizquel	B/R	5-9/185	38

No.	OUTFIELDERS	B/T	Ht./Wt.	Age*
18	Moises Alou	R/R	6-3/220	39
25	Barry Bonds	L/L	6-2/228	41
21	Jason Ellison	R/R	5-10/180	27
	Steve Finley	L/L	6-2/195	41
20	Frederick Lewis	L/R	6-2/190	25
39	Todd Linden	B/R	6-3/230	25
40	Dan Ortmeier	B/L	6-4/220	24
38	Nathan Schierholtz	L/R	6-2/215	22
2	Randy Winn	B/R	6-2/197	31

*Age as of April 1, 2006.

BALLPARK INFORMATION

Ballpark (capacity, surface)
SBC Park (41,584, grass)
Address
24 Willie Mays Plaza
San Francisco, CA 94107
Official website
www.sfgiants.com
Business phone
415-972-2000
Ticket information
415-972-2000
Field dimensions (from home plate)
To left field at foul line, 339 feet
To center field, 399 feet
To right field at foul line, 309 feet
First game played
April 11, 2000 (Dodgers 6, Giants 5)

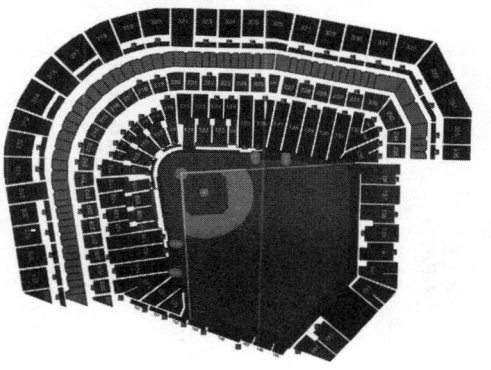

San Francisco Giants — 2006 SEASON

Date	Opp.	Res.	Score	(inn.*)	Hits	Opp. hits	Winning pitcher	Losing pitcher	Save	Record	Pos.	GB
4-5	L.A.	W	4-2		10	5	Schmidt	Lowe	Benitez	1-0	T1st	...
4-6	L.A.	L	4-10		9	14	Perez	Rueter		1-1	T2nd	0.5
4-7	L.A.	L	0-6		5	8	Weaver	Tomko		1-2	5th	1.0
4-8	Col.	W	10-8		14	9	Christiansen	Fuentes		2-2	T2nd	1.0
4-9	Col.	W	4-2		5	6	Eyre	Dohmann	Benitez	3-2	T2nd	1.0
4-10	Col.	W	11-4		15	10	Schmidt	Kennedy		4-2	T1st	...
4-12	At L.A.	L	8-9		16	10	Carrara	Benitez		4-3	T3rd	1.0
4-13	At L.A.	L	1-4		5	10	Perez	Tomko	Brazoban	4-4	4th	2.0
4-15	At Col.	W	13-6		17	14	Lowry	Wright		5-4	3rd	2.0
4-16	At Col.	L	4-5		11	10	Kennedy	Schmidt	Tsao	5-5	3rd	3.0
4-17	At Col.	W	8-6		9	13	Herges	Kim	Benitez	6-5	2nd	3.0
4-18	At S.D.	L	2-7		8	10	Peavy	Tomko		6-6	3rd	4.0
4-19	At S.D.	L	2-5		6	7	Lawrence	Williams	Hoffman	6-7	4th	5.0
4-20	Ari.	L	1-2		11	3	Vazquez	Lowry	Lyon	6-8	4th	6.0
4-21	Ari.	W	4-3	(13)	6	11	Walker	Gosling		7-8	4th	5.0
4-22	Mil.	L	1-6		5	9	Santos	Rueter		7-9	4th	5.0
4-23	Mil.	W	6-2		11	8	Tomko	Capuano	Benitez	8-9	3rd	4.0
4-24	Mil.	L	5-8		11	13	Glover	Williams	Turnbow	8-10	3rd	5.0
4-25	S.D.	L	3-5		10	9	Williams	Lowry	Hoffman	8-11	4th	5.0
4-26	S.D.	W	6-5		8	10	Benitez	Otsuka		9-11	3rd	4.0
4-27	S.D.	W	10-3		11	7	Rueter	Redding		10-11	3rd	3.5
4-29	At Pit.	W	3-2		8	4	Tomko	Redman		11-11	3rd	3.0
4-30	At Pit.	W	7-6		11	9	Walker	Williams	Brower	12-11	3rd	3.0
5-1	At Pit.	W	8-3		13	6	Hennessey	Perez		13-11	3rd	3.0
5-2	At Ari.	W	9-8	(10)	16	14	Brower	Bruney	Walker	14-11	3rd	2.0
5-3	At Ari.	L	2-3		6	8	Lopez	Herges	Lyon	14-12	3rd	3.0
5-4	At Ari.	L	2-6		6	10	Webb	Tomko		14-13	3rd	3.0
5-6	Was.	L	3-9		7	11	Rauch	Lowry		14-14	4th	4.0
5-7	Was.	L	8-11		10	14	Ayala	Accardo	Cordero	14-15	4th	4.0
5-8	Was.	W	4-3	(13)	12	11	Christiansen	Rauch		15-15	4th	4.0
5-9	Pit.	W	2-1		6	6	Tomko	Redman		16-15	4th	3.0
5-10	Pit.	L	2-5		6	7	Williams	Brower	Mesa	16-16	4th	4.0
5-11	Pit.	L	2-7		7	9	Fogg	Lowry	White	16-17	4th	4.0
5-12	At Hou.	W	6-3		9	8	Hennessey	Pettitte	Walker	17-17	4th	3.0
5-13	At Hou.	W	4-2		9	8	Rueter	Astacio	Walker	18-17	4th	3.0
5-14	At Hou.	L	1-4		5	7	Clemens	Tomko	Lidge	18-18	4th	3.0
5-15	At Hou.	L	0-9		4	11	Backe	Fassero		18-19	4th	4.0
5-17	At Col.	L	4-9		14	13	Kennedy	Lowry		18-20	4th	5.0
5-18	At Col.	W	3-2		8	9	Brower	Fuentes	Walker	19-20	4th	5.0
5-19	At Col.	L	1-3		10	8	Francis	Tomko	Fuentes	19-21	4th	5.5
5-20	Oak.	L	4-8		9	12	Yabu	Rueter		19-22	4th	6.5
5-21	Oak.	W	3-2		10	5	Fassero	Haren	Walker	20-22	4th	5.5
5-22	Oak.	W	3-1		6	8	Lowry	Zito	Walker	21-22	4th	5.0
5-24	L.A.	W	5-3		11	6	Schmidt	Weaver	Walker	22-22	4th	4.5
5-25	L.A.	W	10-2		12	6	Tomko	Alvarez		23-22	T3rd	4.0
5-26	L.A.	L	4-6		10	8	Brazoban	Christiansen	Gagne	23-23	4th	4.5
5-27	S.D.	L	3-9		6	15	Lawrence	Hennessey		23-24	4th	5.5
5-28	S.D.	L	3-5		8	9	Seanez	Fassero	Hoffman	23-25	4th	6.5
5-29	S.D.	L	6-9		10	16	Hammond	Walker	Hoffman	23-26	4th	7.5
5-31	At Phi.	L	2-5		8	7	Wolf	Tomko		23-27	4th	9.0
6-1	At Phi.	L	6-10		11	19	Madson	Hawkins		23-28	4th	9.0
6-2	At Phi.	L	5-6		11	9	Lieber	Hennessey	Wagner	23-29	4th	9.0
6-4	At N.Y.	L	1-5		11	12	Glavine	Lowry		23-30	4th	9.5
6-5!	At N.Y.	W	6-3		12	10	Tomko	Ishii	Walker	24-30		
6-5&	At N.Y.	L	1-12		6	13	Benson	Schmidt		24-31	4th	9.0
6-7	K.C.	L	1-8		5	13	Carrasco	Rueter		24-32	4th	9.0
6-8	K.C.	L	1-4		6	9	Hernandez	Fassero	MacDougal	24-33	4th	9.0
6-9	K.C.	W	9-7		14	13	Munter	Nunez	Walker	25-33	4th	9.0
6-10	Cle.	L	2-10		5	14	Sabathia	Tomko		25-34	4th	9.0
6-11	Cle.	L	6-7		12	10	Davis	Schmidt	Wickman	25-35	4th	10.0
6-12	Cle.	L	3-5		6	7	Lee	Rueter	Wickman	25-36	4th	10.0
6-14	At Min.	L	3-4	(11)	7	8	Crain	Fassero		25-37	4th	10.0
6-15	At Min.	W	8-4		14	8	Lowry	Lohse		26-37	4th	9.0
6-16	At Min.	W	14-7		18	12	Christiansen	Nathan		27-37	4th	8.0
6-17	At Det.	W	4-0		9	7	Schmidt	Robertson	Walker	28-37	4th	7.0
6-18	At Det.	L	2-8		12	14	Johnson	Rueter		28-38	4th	8.0
6-19	At Det.	L	8-10	(10)	12	11	Walker	Eyre		28-39	4th	9.0

Date	Opp.	Res.	Score	(inn.*)	Hits	Opp. hits	Winning pitcher	Losing pitcher	Save	Record	Pos.	GB
6-20	Ari.	W	8-3		14	10	Lowry	Vazquez		29-39	4th	9.0
6-21	Ari.	L	4-6		10	9	Vargas	Tomko	Bruney	29-40	4th	10.0
6-22	Ari.	W	4-0		9	5	Schmidt	Halsey		30-40	4th	9.0
6-23	Ari.	L	2-7		7	12	Webb	Rueter		30-41	4th	9.0
6-24	At Oak.	L	3-4		6	11	Blanton	Fassero	Duchscherer	30-42	4th	9.0
6-25	At Oak.	L	3-6		7	6	Haren	Lowry		30-43	4th	10.0
6-26	At Oak.	L	0-16		1	24	Harden	Tomko		30-44	4th	11.0
6-28	At Ari.	W	11-3		14	10	Schmidt	Halsey		31-44	4th	10.5
6-29	At Ari.	W	4-2		13	5	Christiansen	Webb	Walker	32-44	4th	9.5
6-30	At Ari.	W	9-2		7	4	Lowry	Estes	Tomko	33-44	4th	9.0
7-1	At S.D.	W	3-2		6	9	Christiansen	Seanez	Walker	34-44	4th	8.0
7-2	At S.D.	L	3-5		6	12	Williams	Fassero	Hoffman	34-45	4th	9.0
7-3	At S.D.	L	6-9		11	10	Stauffer	Schmidt	Hoffman	34-46	4th	10.0
7-4	Cin.	L	10-11		13	12	Wagner	Accardo	Belisle	34-47	4th	10.0
7-5	Cin.	L	4-7		8	13	Milton	Lowry		34-48	4th	10.0
7-6	Cin.	W	7-2		11	8	Correia	Hudson		35-48	4th	9.0
7-7	Cin.	W	5-1		7	8	Tomko	Harang		36-48	4th	9.0
7-8	StL.	L	1-3		8	8	Mulder	Schmidt	Isringhausen	36-49	4th	10.0
7-9	StL.	W	2-0		6	3	Hennessey	Morris	Walker	37-49	4th	9.0
7-10	StL.	L	3-4		13	10	Suppan	Lowry	Isringhausen	37-50	4th	10.0
7-14	At L.A.	W	4-3		7	7	Schmidt	Houlton	Walker	38-50	4th	9.0
7-15	At L.A.	W	6-0		15	2	Lowry	Lowe		39-50	4th	9.0
7-16	At L.A.	L	4-5		9	10	Schmoll	Walker		39-51	4th	10.0
7-17	At L.A.	W	4-1		9	7	Eyre	Brazoban	Hawkins	40-51	4th	9.0
7-18	Atl.	L	1-6		7	7	Sosa	Correia		40-52	4th	9.5
7-19	Atl.	W	5-4		12	8	Walker	Kolb		41-52	T3rd	8.5
7-20	Atl.	L	1-4		7	6	Smoltz	Lowry	Reitsma	41-53	4th	8.5
7-22	Fla.	W	8-5		8	12	Tomko	Willis	Walker	42-53	4th	7.0
7-23	Fla.	L	4-16		7	20	Beckett	Hennessey		42-54	4th	7.0
7-24	Fla.	L	1-4		8	7	Burnett	Correia	Jones	42-55	4th	7.0
7-25	At Chi.	L	2-3		8	12	Dempster	Walker		42-56	4th	7.5
7-26	At Chi.	W	3-2	(11)	13	10	Christiansen	Rusch	Walker	43-56	4th	6.5
7-27	At Chi.	L	3-4		13	8	Dempster	Correia		43-57	4th	7.5
7-28	At Mil.	W	3-0		4	3	Hennessey	Santos	Walker	44-57	4th	6.5
7-29	At Mil.	W	7-6		8	12	Fassero	Wise	Walker	45-57	4th	5.5
7-30	At Mil.	L	1-7		6	6	Sheets	Schmidt		45-58	4th	5.5
7-31	At Mil.	L	1-5		3	6	Capuano	Lowry		45-59	4th	5.5
8-2	Col.	L	3-4		4	9	Wright	Tomko	Fuentes	45-60	4th	6.5
8-3	Col.	L	2-3		6	7	Miceli	Walker	Fuentes	45-61	4th	6.5
8-4	Col.	W	6-4		10	10	Munter	Miceli	Walker	46-61	4th	6.5
8-5	Hou.	W	4-0		8	3	Schmidt	Pettitte		47-61	4th	6.5
8-6	Hou.	W	5-2		10	4	Lowry	Oswalt		48-61	4th	6.5
8-7	Hou.	L	1-8		6	11	Clemens	Eyre		48-62	4th	7.5
8-9	At Atl.	L	1-7		8	16	Ramirez	Hennessey		48-63	4th	8.5
8-10	At Atl.	L	4-5	(12)	11	8	Boyer	Cooper		48-64	4th	8.5
8-11	At Atl.	W	5-3		10	10	Schmidt	Hudson	Walker	49-64	4th	8.5
8-12	At Fla.	W	1-0		5	4	Lowry	Willis	Walker	50-64	4th	7.5
8-13	At Fla.	L	1-2		4	9	Beckett	Tomko		50-65	4th	7.5
8-14	At Fla.	L	1-4		8	7	Burnett	Hennessey	Jones	50-66	4th	7.5
8-15	At Cin.	W	7-3		12	10	Correia	Harang		51-66	4th	7.0
8-16	At Cin.	W	10-8		19	11	Fassero	Standridge	Walker	52-66	4th	7.0
8-17	At Cin.	W	3-2		11	7	Lowry	Hudson	Hawkins	53-66	4th	6.0
8-18	At Cin.	L	2-4		10	5	Ortiz	Tomko	Weathers	53-67	4th	6.0
8-19	At StL.	L	4-5		9	12	Tavarez	Accardo		53-68	4th	7.0
8-20	At StL.	L	2-4		9	6	Morris	Correia	Isringhausen	53-69	4th	8.0
8-21	At StL.	W	4-2		7	8	Schmidt	Suppan	Benitez	54-69	4th	7.0
8-22	Phi.	W	5-0		9	5	Lowry	Lieber		55-69	4th	6.0
8-23	Phi.	L	2-10		3	16	Padilla	Tomko		55-70	4th	7.0
8-24	Phi.	L	4-7		9	14	Tejeda	Hennessey	Wagner	55-71	4th	8.0
8-26	N.Y.	L	0-1		3	7	Trachsel	Correia	Looper	55-72	4th	8.0
8-27	N.Y.	W	2-1		5	4	Schmidt	Glavine	Benitez	56-72	4th	7.0
8-28	N.Y.	W	4-1		9	6	Lowry	Benson	Benitez	57-72	4th	7.0
8-29	Col.	L	1-2		5	7	Kim	Cain	Fuentes	57-73	4th	7.0
8-30	Col.	W	4-3		11	8	Taschner	DeJean	Benitez	58-73	4th	7.0
8-31	Col.	W	5-3		8	11	Fassero	Francis	Benitez	59-73	4th	7.0
9-2	At Ari.	W	6-3		9	4	Schmidt	Webb	Benitez	60-73	3rd	6.5
9-3	At Ari.	W	9-4		12	8	Lowry	Vargas		61-73	2nd	6.5
9-4	At Ari.	W	3-2		6	5	Cain	Ortiz	Benitez	62-73	2nd	5.5
9-5	At L.A.	W	3-1		7	7	Hawkins	Brazoban	Benitez	63-73	2nd	5.0
9-6	At L.A.	L	2-4	(10)	9	8	Brazoban	Accardo		63-74	2nd	5.0

Date	Opp.	Res.	Score	(inn.*)	Hits	Opp. hits	Winning pitcher	Losing pitcher	Save	Record	Pos.	GB
9-7	At L.A.	L	8-9		10	9	Brazoban	Benitez		63-75	2nd	6.0
9-8	Chi.	L	3-5		7	11	Zambrano	Lowry	Dempster	63-76	T2nd	7.0
9-9	Chi.	W	2-1		7	2	Cain	Williams		64-76	2nd	7.0
9-10	Chi.	L	2-5		6	11	Prior	Hennessey	Dempster	64-77	T3rd	7.0
9-11	Chi.	L	2-3		7	6	Wuertz	Hawkins	Dempster	64-78	4th	7.0
9-12	S.D.	W	4-3		12	5	Kinney	Eaton	Benitez	65-78	3rd	6.0
9-13	S.D.	W	5-4		14	11	Lowry	Lawrence	Benitez	66-78	T2nd	5.0
9-14	S.D.	L	4-5	(10)	7	8	Seanez	Hawkins	Hoffman	66-79	T2nd	6.0
9-15	L.A.	L	1-7		4	11	Lowe	Hennessey		66-80	3rd	6.5
9-16	L.A.	W	5-4		8	12	Benitez	Sanchez		67-80	T2nd	5.5
9-17	L.A.	W	2-1		5	3	Walker	Weaver	Benitez	68-80	2nd	5.5
9-18	L.A.	W	5-3		10	10	Kinney	Osoria	Benitez	69-80	2nd	5.5
9-20	At Was.	W	4-3		4	6	Taschner	Hernandez	Benitez	70-80	2nd	5.0
9-21	At Was.	W	5-1		11	5	Hennessey	Patterson	Benitez	71-80	2nd	5.0
9-22	At Was.	L	0-2		4	8	Rauch	Tomko	Cordero	71-81	2nd	5.0
9-23	At Col.	W	7-6		11	14	Accardo	DeJean	Walker	72-81	2nd	5.0
9-24	At Col.	L	0-6		3	9	Kim	Lowry		72-82	2nd	5.0
9-25	At Col.	W	6-2		12	5	Walker	Fuentes		73-82	2nd	4.0
9-26	At S.D.	W	3-2		9	3	Walker	Hoffman	Benitez	74-82	2nd	3.0
9-27	At S.D.	L	6-9		11	8	Hensley	Fassero	Hoffman	74-83	2nd	4.0
9-28	At S.D.	L	1-9		9	15	Astacio	Schmidt		74-84	T2nd	5.0
9-29	At S.D.	L	0-1	(11)	3	9	Cassidy	Accardo		74-85	3rd	6.0
9-30	Ari.	L	3-7		13	12	Villarreal	Hawkins	Valverde	74-86	3rd	7.0
10-1	Ari.	L	1-2	(11)	7	8	Medders	Benitez	Valverde	74-87	3rd	7.0
10-2	Ari.	W	3-1		9	6	Tomko	Webb		75-87	3rd	7.0

Monthly records: April (12-11), May (11-16), June (10-17), July (12-15), August (14-14), September (15-13), October (1-1).
*Innings, if other than nine. ! First game of a doubleheader. & Second game of a doubleheader.

RECORDS

2005 regular-season record: 75-87
Position: 3rd in N.L. West
Home: 37-44   **Road:** 38-43
N.L. East: 11-19   **N.L. Central:** 20-21
N.L. West: 38-35   **A.L.** 6-12
Vs. LH starters: 24-20
Vs. RH starters: 51-67
Grass: 73-86   **Artificial:** 2-1
Day: 22-30   **Night:** 53-57
1-Run: 27-25   **X-inn.:** 4-7
Doubleheaders: 0-0-1
Team record past five years: 451-357
(.558, ranks 3rd in league in that span)

TEAM LEADERS

Batting average: Moises Alou (.321).
At-bats: Pedro Feliz (569).
Runs: Pedro Feliz (69).
Hits: Omar Vizquel (154).
Total Bases: Pedro Feliz (240).
Doubles: Mike Matheny (34).
Triples: Randy Winn (5).
Home runs: Pedro Feliz (20).
Runs batted in: Pedro Feliz (81).
Stolen bases: Omar Vizquel (24).
Slugging percentage: Randy Winn (.680).
On-base percentage: Moises Alou (.400).
Wins: Noah Lowry (13).
Earned-run average: Noah Lowry (3.78).
Complete games: Brett Tomko (3).
Shutouts: None.

Saves: Tyler Walker (23).
Innings pitched: Noah Lowry (204.2).
Strikeouts: Noah Lowry (172).

GAMES BY POSITION

Catcher: Mike Matheny 132, Yorvit Torrealba 27, Yamid Haad 16, Justin Knoedler 4.

First base: J.T. Snow 108, Lance Niekro 74, Pedro Feliz 15.

Second base: Ray Durham 133, Deivi Cruz 33, Angel Chavez 5, Edgardo Alfonzo 2, Brian Dallimore 2.

Third base: Edgardo Alfonzo 97, Pedro Feliz 79, Deivi Cruz 5, Angel Chavez 1.

Shortstop: Omar Vizquel 150, Deivi Cruz 16, Angel Chavez 4, Brian Dallimore 1.

Outfield: Jason Ellison 122, Moises Alou 117, Pedro Feliz 75, Michael Tucker 72, Randy Winn 55, Todd Linden 52, Marquis Grissom 36, Barry Bonds 13, Alex Sanchez 10, Dan Ortmeier 7, Julio Ramirez 6, Adam Shabala 5, Ray Durham 1, Tony Torcato 1

Designated hitter: Michael Tucker 4, Moises Alou 3, Lance Niekro 1, Alex Sanchez 1, Yorvit Torrealba 1.

TOP DRAFT CHOICES

4. **Ben Copeland,** OF, Pittsburgh.
5. **Daniel Griffin,** RHP, Niagara.
6. **Brad Cuthbertson,** RHP, Lethbridge (Alberta) CC.
7. **Joey Dyche,** OF, Lewis-Clark State.
8. **Scotty Bridges,** 2B, Arkansas.
9. **Anthony Contreras,** SS, San Jose State.
10. **Nick Pereira,** RHP, San Francisco.

WASHINGTON NATIONALS
NATIONAL LEAGUE EAST DIVISION

2006 SEASON

Nationals Schedule
Home games shaded.
All-Star Game July 11 at Pittsburgh. Schedule subject to change.

APRIL

SUN	MON	TUE	WED	THU	FRI	SAT
2	3 NYM	4	5 NYM	6 NYM	7 HOU	8 HOU
9 HOU	10 HOU	11 NYM	12 NYM	13 NYM	14 FLA	15 FLA
16 FLA	17	18 PHI	19 PHI	20 PHI	21 ATL	22 ATL
23 ATL	24 CIN	25 CIN	26 CIN	27 STL	28 STL	29 STL
30 STL						

MAY

SUN	MON	TUE	WED	THU	FRI	SAT
	1 NYM	2 NYM	3 FLA	4 FLA	5 PIT	6 PIT
7 PIT	8	9 CIN	10 CIN	11 CIN	12 ATL	13 ATL
14 ATL	15	16 CHC	17 CHC	18 CHC	19 BAL	20 BAL
21 BAL	22 HOU	23 HOU	24 HOU	25 HOU	26 LAD	27 LAD
28 LAD	29 PHI	30 PHI	31 PHI			

JUNE

SUN	MON	TUE	WED	THU	FRI	SAT
				1	2 MIL	3 MIL
4 MIL	5 ATL	6 ATL	7 ATL	8 PHI	9 PHI	10 PHI
11 PHI	12 COL	13 COL	14 COL	15 COL	16 NYY	17 NYY
18 NYY	19 BOS	20 BOS	21 BOS	22	23 BAL	24 BAL
25 BAL	26	27 TOR	28 TOR	29 TOR	30 TB	

JULY

SUN	MON	TUE	WED	THU	FRI	SAT
						1 TB
2 TB	3 FLA	4 FLA	5 FLA	6 FLA	7 SD	8 SD
9 SD	10	11 ALL-STAR	12	13	14 PIT	15 PIT
16 PIT	17 FLA	18 FLA	19 FLA	20	21 CHC	22 CHC
23 CHC	24	25 SF	26 SF	27 SF	28 LAD	29 LAD
30 LAD	31 SF					

AUGUST

SUN	MON	TUE	WED	THU	FRI	SAT
		1 SF	2 SF	3	4 SD	5 SD
6 SD	7	8 FLA	9 FLA	10 FLA	11 NYM	12 NYM
13 NYM	14 ATL	15 ATL	16 ATL	17 ATL	18 PHI	19 PHI
20 PHI	21 FLA	22 FLA	23 FLA	24	25 ATL	26 ATL
27 ATL	28	29 PHI	30 PHI	31 PHI		

SEPTEMBER

SUN	MON	TUE	WED	THU	FRI	SAT
					1 ARI	2 ARI
3 ARI	4 STL	5 STL	6 STL	7 COL	8 COL	9 COL
10 COL	11 ARI	12 ARI	13 ARI	14	15 MIL	16 MIL
17 MIL	18	19 ATL	20 ATL	21	22 NYM	23 NYM
24 NYM	25 NYM	26 PHI	27 PHI	28 PHI	29 NYM	30 NYM

OCTOBER

SUN	MON	TUE	WED	THU	FRI	SAT
1 NYM	2	3	4	5	6	7

Home games are shaded. All-Star Game is July 11 at Pittsburgh. Schedule is subject to change.

Hernandez

CLUB DIRECTORY

President
Tony Tavares

Vice president and general manager
Jim Bowden

Assistant general manager
Tony Siegle

Director, baseball administration
Lee MacPhail IV

Director, player development
Andy Dunn

Director of amateur scouting
Dana Brown

Vice president, communications
Chartese Berry

Director, baseball information
John Dever

MINOR LEAGUE AFFILIATES

Class	Team	League	Manager
AAA	New Orleans	Pacific Coast	Tim Foli
AA	Harrisburg	Eastern	John Stearns
Advanced A	Potomac	Carolina	Randy Knorr
A	Savannah	South Atlantic	Bobby Williams
Short-Season A	Vermont	New York-Pennsylvania	Edgar Caceres
Rookie	Nationals	Gulf Coast	Bobby Henley

BROADCAST INFORMATION

Radio: To be announced.
TV: To be announced.
Cable TV: Mid-Atlantic Sports Network.

SPRING TRAINING

Ballpark (city): Space Coast Stadium (Melbourne, Fla.).
Ticket information: 321-633-8119.

For more on the Nationals, go to www.sportingnews.com/baseball/teams/nationals/

SPRING TRAINING ROSTER

Manager—Frank Robinson (20).
Coaches—Tony Beasley, Davey Lopes, Mitchell Page, Eddie Rodriguez (14), Randy St. Claire (46).

No.	PITCHERS	B/T	Ht./Wt.	Age*
36	Tony Armas	R/R	6-3/225	27
56	Luis Ayala	R/R	6-2/186	28
	Francis Beltran	R/R	6-6/230	26
57	Jay Bergmann	R/R	6-4/205	24
32	Chad Cordero	R/R	6-0/198	24
45	Ryan Drese	R/R	6-3/235	29
58	Joey Eischen	L/L	6-0/214	35
61	Livan Hernandez	R/R	6-2/245	31
	Michael Hinckley	R/L	6-3/170	23
34	Travis Hughes	R/R	6-5/240	27
	Josh Karp	R/R	6-5/210	26
	Brian Lawrence	R/R	6-0/197	29
38	Gary Majewski	R/R	6-1/215	26
	Ramon Ortiz	R/R	6-0/175	32
22	John Patterson	R/R	6-5/208	28
31	Darrell Rasner	R/R	6-3/210	25
51	Jon Rauch	R/R	6-11/260	27
	Mike Stanton	L/L	6-1/215	38

No.	CATCHERS	B/T	Ht./Wt.	Age*
39	Brian Schneider	L/R	6-1/196	29

No.	INFIELDERS	B/T	Ht./Wt.	Age*
	Marlon Anderson	L/R	5-11/200	32
	Larry Broadway	L/L	6-4/230	25
2	Jamey Carroll	R/R	5-9/170	32
	Kory Casto	L/R	6-1/190	24
	Bernie Castro	B/R	5-10/160	26
	Robert Fick	L/R	6-1/205	32
15	Cristian Guzman	B/R	6-0/205	28
	Brendan Harris	R/R	6-1/200	25
	Damian Jackson	R/R	5-11/185	32
24	Nick Johnson	L/L	6-3/224	27
	Alfonso Soriano	R/R	6-1/180	30
3	Jose Vidro	B/R	5-11/193	31
25	Ryan Zimmerman	R/R	6-3/220	21

No.	OUTFIELDERS	B/T	Ht./Wt.	Age*
	Tony Blanco	R/R	6-1/175	24
26	Marlon Byrd	R/R	6-0/235	28
19	Ryan Church	L/L	6-1/190	27
	Frank Diaz	R/R	6-2/180	22
1	Tyrell Godwin	L/R	6-0/200	26
6	Jose Guillen	R/R	5-11/190	29
	Michael Tucker	L/R	6-2/195	34
0	Brandon Watson	L/R	6-1/170	24

*Age as of April 1, 2006.

BALLPARK INFORMATION

Ballpark (capacity, surface)
RFK Stadium (46,382, grass)
Address
2400 East Capitol Street SE
Washington, DC 20003
Official website
www.nationals.com
Business phone
202-675-6287
Ticket information
202-675-6287
Field dimensions (from home plate)
To left field at foul line, 336 feet
To center field, 410 feet
To right field at foul line, 336 feet
First game played
April 14, 2005 (Nationals 5, Diamondbacks 3)

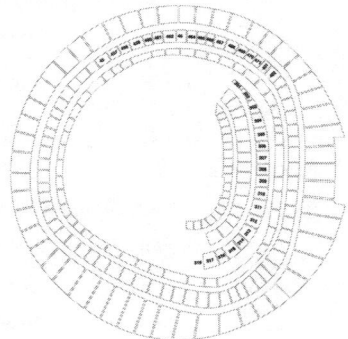

2006 SEASON *Washington Nationals*

Date	Opp.	Res.	Score	(inn.*)	Hits	Opp. hits	Winning pitcher	Losing pitcher	Save	Record	Pos.	GB
4-4	At Phi.	L	4-8		13	14	Lieber	Hernandez		0-1	T4th	1.0
4-6	At Phi.	W	7-3		16	6	Eischen	Worrell		1-1	T1st	...
4-7	At Phi.	W	5-4	(10)	11	6	Cordero	Cormier		2-1	T1st	...
4-8	At Fla.	L	0-9		5	10	Willis	Ohka		2-2	T2nd	1.0
4-9	At Fla.	W	3-2	(10)	7	8	Cordero	Alfonseca		3-2	2nd	1.0
4-10	At Fla.	L	0-8		5	12	Beckett	Patterson		3-3	T2nd	1.0
4-11	At Atl.	L	2-11		8	15	Hampton	Day		3-4	T3rd	2.0
4-12	At Atl.	W	4-3		8	9	Ayala	Kolb	Cordero	4-4	T2nd	1.0
4-13	At Atl.	W	11-4		12	9	Ohka	Thomson		5-4	T1st	...
4-14	Ari.	W	5-3		9	4	Hernandez	Vazquez	Cordero	6-4	1st	+0.5
4-16	Ari.	W	9-3		9	8	Patterson	Ortiz		7-4	1st	+1.0
4-17	Ari.	W	7-3		11	8	Tucker	Koplove		8-4	1st	+2.0
4-18	Fla.	L	4-9		8	12	Willis	Ohka		8-5	1st	+1.0
4-19	Fla.	L	3-6		10	10	Moehler	Hernandez		8-6	T1st	...
4-20	Atl.	W	2-0		6	5	Day	Ramirez	Cordero	9-6	T1st	...
4-21	Atl.	L	1-2		5	4	Reitsma	Cordero	Kolb	9-7	T1st	...
4-22	At N.Y.	L	1-3		4	7	Glavine	Loaiza	Looper	9-8	T2nd	1.0
4-23	At N.Y.	L	5-10		12	16	Seo	Ohka		9-9	4th	2.0
4-24	At N.Y.	W	11-4		17	10	Hernandez	Zambrano		10-9	T3rd	1.0
4-25	Phi.	L	4-5		12	7	Lidle	Day	Wagner	10-10	4th	1.5
4-26	Phi.	W	3-1		6	8	Patterson	Lieber	Cordero	11-10	T3rd	1.5
4-27	Phi.	L	0-3		4	7	Cormier	Loaiza	Wagner	11-11	T3rd	2.0
4-29	N.Y.	W	5-1		5	10	Hernandez	Seo	Cordero	12-11	3rd	2.0
4-30	N.Y.	W	5-3	(8)	10	3	Ohka	Zambrano	Carrasco	13-11	3rd	2.0
5-1	N.Y.	L	3-6		7	12	Hernandez	Ayala	Looper	13-12	3rd	2.0
5-2	At L.A.	W	6-2		13	4	Loaiza	Erickson		14-12	3rd	1.5
5-3	At L.A.	L	2-4		11	9	Weaver	Rauch	Brazoban	14-13	3rd	2.5
5-4	At L.A.	W	5-2		10	7	Hernandez	Perez		15-13	3rd	1.5
5-6	At S.F.	W	9-3		11	7	Rauch	Lowry		16-13	3rd	2.0
5-7	At S.F.	W	11-8		14	10	Ayala	Accardo	Cordero	17-13	3rd	2.0
5-8	At S.F.	L	3-4	(13)	11	12	Christiansen	Rauch		17-14	3rd	3.0
5-9	At Ari.	W	4-3		12	11	Hernandez	Valverde	Cordero	18-14	3rd	2.0
5-10	At Ari.	L	2-3		10	3	Estes	Armas	Lyon	18-15	3rd	3.0
5-11	At Ari.	L	2-3		6	10	Cormier	Rauch	Lyon	18-16	3rd	3.0
5-13	Chi.	L	3-6		9	9	Ohman	Ayala	Wellemeyer	18-17	4th	3.0
5-14	Chi.	W	4-3		6	10	Hernandez	Zambrano	Cordero	19-17	3rd	3.0
5-15	Chi.	W	5-4		7	8	Carrasco	Bartosh	Cordero	20-17	3rd	3.0
5-16	Mil.	W	5-2		10	6	Armas	Davis	Ayala	21-17	3rd	2.0
5-17	Mil.	L	2-8		3	12	Obermueller	Vargas		21-18	3rd	2.0
5-18	Mil.	W	1-0		7	6	Majewski	Capuano		22-18	3rd	1.0
5-19	Mil.	W	3-2		6	8	Hernandez	Santos	Cordero	23-18	3rd	0.5
5-20	At Tor.	L	1-6		6	11	Lilly	Vargas	Walker	23-19	3rd	1.0
5-21	At Tor.	L	0-7		4	11	Halladay	Armas		23-20	T3rd	2.0
5-22	At Tor.	W	9-2		13	7	Ohka	Towers		24-20	3rd	2.0
5-23	At Cin.	L	3-5		6	12	Milton	Loaiza	Weathers	24-21	3rd	3.0
5-24	At Cin.	L	3-4	(14)	15	11	Keisler	Ayala		24-22	3rd	4.0
5-25	At Cin.	L	3-12		8	14	Belisle	Vargas		24-23	3rd	4.0
5-27	At StL.	L	3-6		6	9	Morris	Armas	Isringhausen	24-24	4th	3.5
5-28	At StL.	L	1-3		4	8	Suppan	Loaiza	Isringhausen	24-25	4th	3.5
5-29	At StL.	W	3-2		9	8	Hernandez	Carpenter	Cordero	25-25	4th	3.5
5-30	Atl.	W	3-2		9	4	Ohka	Davies	Cordero	26-25	T3rd	2.5
5-31	Atl.	W	5-4		13	6	Ayala	Colon	Cordero	27-25	3rd	1.5
6-1	Atl.	L	4-5		8	9	Smoltz	Carrasco	Reitsma	27-26	T3rd	2.5
6-2	Atl.	W	8-6		12	9	Carrasco	Kolb	Cordero	28-26	T3rd	1.5
6-3	Fla.	W	3-2	(11)	4	8	Ayala	Bump		29-26	3rd	0.5
6-4	Fla.	W	7-3		11	12	Kim	Leiter		30-26	2nd	0.5
6-5	Fla.	W	6-3		9	13	Ayala	Riedling	Cordero	31-26	1st	+0.5
6-7	Oak.	W	2-1		5	8	Armas	Zito	Cordero	32-26	1st	+1.0
6-8	Oak.	W	7-2		12	5	Loaiza	Glynn		33-26	1st	+1.5
6-9	Oak.	W	4-3		8	10	Hernandez	Blanton	Cordero	34-26	1st	+1.5
6-10	Sea.	W	9-3		10	10	Ayala	Hasegawa		35-26	1st	+1.5
6-11	Sea.	W	2-1		7	6	Patterson	Putz	Cordero	36-26	1st	+1.5
6-12	Sea.	W	3-2		6	10	Armas	Franklin	Cordero	37-26	1st	+1.5
6-13	At L.A.	L	1-11		5	20	Byrd	Loaiza		37-27	1st	+1.0
6-14	At L.A.	W	6-3		7	11	Majewski	Shields	Cordero	38-27	1st	+2.0
6-15	At L.A.	W	1-0		8	4	Drese	Colon	Cordero	39-27	1st	+3.0
6-17	At Tex.	L	1-8		8	15	Rogers	Patterson		39-28	1st	+1.5

Date	Opp.	Res.	Score	(inn.*)	Hits	Opp. hits	Winning pitcher	Losing pitcher	Save	Record	Pos.	GB
6-18	At Tex.	L	4-7		7	9	Rodriguez	Armas		39-29	1st	+1.5
6-19	At Tex.	W	8-2		15	7	Hughes	Wilson		40-29	1st	+2.5
6-20	At Pit.	W	7-4		12	10	Hernandez	Redman	Cordero	41-29	1st	+3.0
6-21	At Pit.	L	4-11		10	14	Perez	Drese		41-30	1st	+3.0
6-22	At Pit.	W	5-4		10	7	Carrasco	Gonzalez	Cordero	42-30	1st	+3.0
6-24	Tor.	W	3-0		9	8	Loaiza	Towers	Cordero	43-30	1st	+4.0
6-25	Tor.	W	5-2		6	7	Hernandez	Lilly	Cordero	44-30	1st	+4.0
6-26	Tor.	L	5-9		6	9	Speier	Ayala	Batista	44-31	1st	+3.0
6-28	Pit.	W	2-1		5	5	Drese	Fogg	Cordero	45-31	1st	+2.5
6-29	Pit.	W	3-2		8	8	Ayala	Torres	Cordero	46-31	1st	+3.5
6-30	Pit.	W	7-5		8	12	Loaiza	Wells	Cordero	47-31	1st	+4.5
7-1	At Chi.	W	4-3		12	10	Hernandez	Prior	Carrasco	48-31	1st	+4.5
7-2	At Chi.	W	4-2		5	8	Armas	Williams	Cordero	49-31	1st	+5.5
7-3	At Chi.	W	5-4	(12)	10	11	Eischen	Mitre		50-31	1st	+5.5
7-4	N.Y.	L	2-5		5	10	Hernandez	Kim	Looper	50-32	1st	+4.5
7-5	N.Y.	W	3-2		8	8	Loaiza	Martinez	Cordero	51-32	1st	+4.5
7-6	N.Y.	L	3-5		9	10	Glavine	Hernandez	Looper	51-33	1st	+4.0
7-7	N.Y.	L	2-3	(11)	8	7	Bell	Ayala	Looper	51-34	1st	+2.5
7-8	At Phi.	W	8-7		11	12	Drese	Tejeda	Cordero	52-34	1st	+2.5
7-9	At Phi.	L	0-1		6	5	Wagner	Carrasco		52-35	1st	+2.5
7-10	At Phi.	L	4-5	(12)	12	12	Cormier	Kim		52-36	1st	+2.5
7-14	At Mil.	L	2-4		4	11	Wise	Majewski	Turnbow	52-37	1st	+2.5
7-15	At Mil.	L	3-4	(10)	11	10	Santana	Ayala		52-38	1st	+1.5
7-16	At Mil.	W	5-3		8	8	Loaiza	Bottalico	Cordero	53-38	1st	+1.5
7-17	At Mil.	L	3-5		5	8	Ohka	Drese	Turnbow	53-39	1st	+1.5
7-18	Col.	L	4-5		9	9	Acevedo	Cordero	Fuentes	53-40	1st	+0.5
7-19	Col.	W	4-0		10	4	Patterson	Chacon	Cordero	54-40	1st	+1.5
7-20	Col.	L	2-3		8	9	Jennings	Hernandez	Fuentes	54-41	1st	+0.5
7-21	Hou.	L	2-3		8	11	Oswalt	Loaiza	Lidge	54-42	T1st	...
7-22	Hou.	L	1-14		6	19	Clemens	Drese		54-43	T1st	...
7-23	Hou.	W	4-2		7	4	Armas	Backe	Cordero	55-43	T1st	...
7-24	Hou.	L	1-4	(14)	4	10	Springer	Carrasco	Lidge	55-44	T1st	...
7-26	At Atl.	L	2-3	(10)	8	8	Reitsma	Stanton		55-45	2nd	1.0
7-27	At Atl.	L	3-4		7	9	Kolb	Majewski	Reitsma	55-46	2nd	2.0
7-28	At Atl.	L	4-5		10	10	Sosa	Drese	Reitsma	55-47	2nd	3.0
7-29	At Fla.	L	3-4		7	9	Beckett	Armas	Jones	55-48	2nd	4.0
7-30	At Fla.	L	0-3		4	7	Burnett	Patterson	Jones	55-49	2nd	5.0
7-31	At Fla.	W	4-2		11	11	Hernandez	Moehler	Cordero	56-49	2nd	5.0
8-2	L.A.	L	4-5		9	6	Weaver	Loaiza	Brazoban	56-50	2nd	5.5
8-3	L.A.	W	3-1		8	6	Armas	Houlton	Cordero	57-50	2nd	4.5
8-4	L.A.	W	7-0		11	4	Patterson	Penny		58-50	2nd	4.5
8-5	S.D.	L	5-6		5	16	Linebrink	Cordero	Hoffman	58-51	2nd	4.5
8-6	S.D.	L	2-3		5	11	Astacio	Drese	Hoffman	58-52	2nd	5.5
8-7	S.D.	L	0-3		5	6	Peavy	Loaiza		58-53	3rd	5.5
8-9	At Hou.	W	6-5		8	9	Patterson	Astacio	Cordero	59-53	2nd	5.5
8-10	At Hou.	L	6-7		11	13	Rodriguez	Hernandez	Lidge	59-54	T3rd	6.5
8-11	At Hou.	L	3-6		5	11	Pettitte	Drese		59-55	T3rd	6.5
8-12	At Col.	W	4-2		7	7	Loaiza	Wright	Cordero	60-55	3rd	5.5
8-13	At Col.	W	8-0		13	13	Armas	Kim		61-55	3rd	5.5
8-14	At Col.	W	9-2		10	11	Patterson	Acevedo		62-55	3rd	5.5
8-15	At Phi.	W	6-3		10	7	Hernandez	Myers		63-55	2nd	5.0
8-17	At Phi.	L	3-4		6	10	Lieber	Loaiza	Wagner	63-56	3rd	5.5
8-18#	At Phi.	L	1-2		7	7	Padilla	Armas	Wagner	63-57		
8-18$	At Phi.	W	5-4		10	8	Ayala	Urbina	Cordero	64-57	3rd	5.0
8-19	At N.Y.	L	0-1		5	8	Seo	Patterson	Looper	64-58	4th	5.0
8-20	At N.Y.	L	8-9	(10)	14	11	Hernandez	Majewski		64-59	4th	5.0
8-21	At N.Y.	W	7-4		13	8	Loaiza	Benson		65-59	4th	5.0
8-23	Cin.	L	2-6		4	11	Hudson	Armas		65-60	T4th	5.5
8-24	Cin.	W	5-3		9	10	Patterson	Ortiz	Cordero	66-60	T3rd	5.5
8-25	Cin.	L	3-5		9	13	Claussen	Hernandez	Weathers	66-61	5th	6.0
8-26	StL.	W	4-1		8	3	Loaiza	Suppan	Cordero	67-61	5th	5.0
8-27	StL.	L	0-6		2	8	Marquis	White		67-62	5th	6.0
8-28	StL.	L	0-6		4	8	Thompson	Halama		67-63	5th	7.0
8-30	At Atl.	W	3-2		11	8	Bergmann	Sosa	Cordero	68-63	5th	6.0
8-31!	At Atl.	L	3-5		9	8	Ramirez	Loaiza	Farnsworth	68-64		
8-31&	At Atl.	W	4-3		11	11	Stanton	Reitsma	Cordero	69-64	5th	6.0
9-1	At Atl.	L	7-8	(10)	12	8	Davies	Ayala		69-65	5th	7.0
9-2	Phi.	L	1-7		5	12	Padilla	Halama		69-66	5th	8.0
9-3	Phi.	W	5-4	(12)	10	9	Carrasco	Lopez		70-66	4th	8.0
9-4	Phi.	W	6-1		8	4	Loaiza	Floyd		71-66	4th	7.0

Date	Opp.	Res.	Score	(inn.*)	Hits	Opp. hits	Winning pitcher	Losing pitcher	Save	Record	Pos.	GB
9-5	Fla.	W	5-2		11	6	Hernandez	Vargas		72-66	4th	7.0
9-6	Fla.	L	2-4		5	10	Valdez	Rasner	Jones	72-67	4th	8.0
9-7	Fla.	L	1-12		5	17	Willis	Halama		72-68	4th	9.0
9-8	Fla.	L	4-8		10	14	Beckett	Patterson		72-69	4th	9.5
9-9	Atl.	W	8-6		11	10	Majewski	Foster	Cordero	73-69	4th	8.5
9-10	Atl.	L	0-4		6	8	Sosa	Hernandez		73-70	4th	9.5
9-11	Atl.	L	7-9		6	9	McBride	Cordero	Farnsworth	73-71	4th	10.5
9-13	At N.Y.	W	4-2		9	5	Majewski	Glavine	Cordero	74-71	4th	9.0
9-14	At N.Y.	W	6-3		10	8	Loaiza	Benson	Cordero	75-71	4th	8.0
9-15	At N.Y.	W	6-5	(10)	13	12	Bergmann	Hernandez	Majewski	76-71	4th	8.0
9-16	At S.D.	W	5-1		9	3	Patterson	Peavy		77-71	4th	7.0
9-17	At S.D.	L	5-8	(12)	12	11	Linebrink	Rauch		77-72	4th	8.0
9-18	At S.D.	L	1-2		5	9	Otsuka	Eischen		77-73	4th	8.0
9-20	S.F.	L	3-4		6	4	Taschner	Hernandez	Benitez	77-74	4th	9.0
9-21	S.F.	L	1-5		5	11	Hennessey	Patterson	Benitez	77-75	4th	9.0
9-22	S.F.	W	2-0		8	4	Rauch	Tomko	Cordero	78-75	4th	8.0
9-23	N.Y.	L	2-5	(10)	7	10	Hernandez	Majewski	Heilman	78-76	4th	9.0
9-24	N.Y.	L	2-5		5	6	Glavine	Hernandez	Hernandez	78-77	4th	10.0
9-25	N.Y.	L	5-6		9	8	Padilla	Hughes	Heilman	78-78	5th	11.0
9-26	At Fla.	W	4-0		10	5	Carrasco	Vargas		79-78	5th	10.0
9-27	At Fla.	W	11-1		15	9	Stanton	Willis		80-78	T4th	10.0
9-28	At Fla.	W	11-7		15	12	Loaiza	Moehler		81-78	3rd	9.0
9-30	Phi.	L	3-4		8	11	Lidle	Hernandez	Wagner	81-79	T4th	9.0
10-1	Phi.	L	4-8		8	9	Myers	Patterson		81-80	5th	9.0
10-2	Phi.	L	3-9		7	10	Lieber	Carrasco	Wagner	81-81	5th	9.0

Monthly records: April (13-11), May (14-14), June (20-6), July (9-18), August (13-15), September (12-15), October (0-2).
*Innings, if other than nine. ! First game of a doubleheader. & Second game of a doubleheader. # Day separate admission. $ Night separate admission.

RECORDS

2005 regular-season record: 81-81
Position: 5th in N.L. East
Home: 41-40   **Road:** 40-41
N.L. East: 34-41   **N.L. Central:** 19-20
N.L. West: 16-14   **A.L.** 12-6
Vs. LH starters: 23-23
Vs. RH starters: 58-58
Grass: 80-79   **Artificial:** 1-2
Day: 25-30   **Night:** 56-51
1-Run: 30-31   **X-inn.:** 6-11
Doubleheaders: 0-0-1
Team record past five years: 382-428
(.472, ranks 10th in league in that span)

TEAM LEADERS

Batting average: Nick Johnson (.289).
At-bats: Brad Wilkerson (565).
Runs: Jose Guillen (81).
Hits: Jose Guillen (156).
Total Bases: Jose Guillen (264).
Doubles: Brad Wilkerson (42).
Triples: Brad Wilkerson (7).
Home runs: Jose Guillen (24).
Runs batted in: Jose Guillen (76).
Stolen bases: Brad Wilkerson (8).
Slugging percentage: Jose Guillen (.479).
On-base percentage: Nick Johnson (.408).
Wins: Livan Hernandez (15).
Earned-run average: John Patterson (3.13).

Complete games: Livan Hernandez, John Patterson (2).
Shutouts: John Patterson (1).
Saves: Chad Cordero (47).
Innings pitched: Livan Hernandez (246.1).
Strikeouts: John Patterson (185).

GAMES BY POSITION

Catcher: Brian Schneider 113, Gary Bennett 64, Keith Osik 5.
First base: Nick Johnson 129, Brad Wilkerson 25, Wil Cordero 12, Carlos Baerga 11, Tony Blanco 3, Rick Short 1.
Second base: Jose Vidro 79, Jamey Carroll 63, Junior Spivey 22, Deivi Cruz 16, Carlos Baerga 7, Rick Short 6, Brendan Harris 2, Henry Mateo 1.
Third base: Vinny Castilla 138, Carlos Baerga 20, Ryan Zimmerman 14, Jamey Carroll 12, Tony Blanco 5, Brendan Harris 1.
Shortstop: Cristian Guzman 142, Jamey Carroll 41, Deivi Cruz 8, Ryan Zimmerman 1.
Outfield: Jose Guillen 142, Brad Wilkerson 129, Ryan Church 85, Preston Wilson 68, Marlon Byrd 65, Terrmel Sledge 13, Brandon Watson 13, Tony Blanco 11, Jeffrey Hammonds 11, J.J. Davis 10, Matt Cepicky 6, Endy Chavez 6, Kenny Kelly 2.
Designated hitter: Wil Cordero 3, Marlon Byrd 2, Jose Guillen 2, Carlos Baerga 1, Tony Blanco 1, Jeffrey Hammonds 1.

TOP DRAFT CHOICES

1. **Ryan Zimmerman,** 3B, Virginia.
4. **Justin Maxwell,** OF, Maryland.
5. **Ryan Delaughter,** OF, Ryan H.S., Denton, Texas.
6. **Marco Estrada,** RHP, Long Beach State.
7. **Mike Daniel,** OF, North Carolina.
8. **Jack Spradlin,** LHP, USC.
9. **John-Michael Howell,** OF, Central Florida.
10. **Dee Brown,** OF, Central Florida.

2005 Season

YEAR IN REVIEW
THE TOP STORIES OF THE PAST YEAR

By STEVE GIETSCHIER
TSN Senior Managing Editor

Hard on the heels of the astounding 2004 postseason when the Boston Red Sox ended decades of futility by winning the World Series for the first time since 1918, the Chicago White Sox, similarly burdened by the curse of persistent mediocrity, did their own star turn. The Red Sox had amazed the baseball world by overcoming a three-games-to-none deficit in the American League Championship Series against the New York Yankees and then sweeping the St. Louis Cardinals in the Series. The White Sox varied this tune just a bit, sweeping Boston in the American League Division Series, eliminating the Los Angeles Angels of Anaheim in the ALCS and then sweeping the Houston Astros to win their first Series since 1917.

If a team playing baseball in the present can truly be encumbered by its franchise's past, then the White Sox certainly had a lot to overcome. During the first two decades of American League history, they won four pennants and two World Series, and the 1917 edition of the Sox is still considered one of the best teams ever. Misfortune struck in 1919 when Chicago lost the Series to the Cincinnati Reds, five games to three, amid rumors that the outcome had been fixed by a conspiracy of players and gamblers. In September 1920, a Cook County (Ill.) grand jury handed out indictments of eight team members who, although they were eventually acquitted, were banned from baseball for life. The Black Sox scandal, as it quickly came to be known, besmirched the team's reputation for decades, and whether coincidentally or not, the Sox did not win another pennant for 40 years. In fact, from 1921 through 1951, the White Sox finished as high as third place only three times. They broke this jinx in 1959, only to lose the Series in six games to the Los Angeles Dodgers, and in the era of division play, they qualified for the postseason three times prior to 2005 but never advanced to the Series. Much of the credit for the Sox's '05 triumph went to manager Ozzie Guillen, the SPORTING NEWS A.L. Manager of the Year, but in truth, the Sox have been a competitive team for more than a decade, finishing first or second in the A.L.'s Central Division every season but two since 1994.

Chicago's opponent in the Series had suffered through its own angst-ridden decades. Born in 1962 when the National League expanded from eight teams to 10, the Astros did not reach the .500 mark until 1969 and did not qualify for postseason play until 1980. In the eight seasons prior to 2005, they made the postseason five times but advanced to the NLCS only once, losing to the Cardinals in 2004. This time, it was different. Houston qualified as the wild-card team, defeated the Atlanta Braves in a four-game Division Series and ousted St. Louis in six games in the NLCS. But then they ran into destiny.

The excellence of the White Sox throughout the season, save for a late-summer swoon, and the competitive nature of the other divisional races boosted major league attendance to an all-time high. Nevertheless, a cloud hovered over the sport throughout the year, bringing with it the threat of federal legislation and leading ultimately to two significant revisions in the existing collective bargaining agreement (CBA). The extent to which players, past and present, have used performance-enhancing drugs, especially anabolic steroids, illegal without a prescription, has long been a subject for debate. But until ratification of the 2002 CBA, baseball had no testing procedure or penalties in place. Leaks from a grand jury investigation in northern California implicating several prominent players, including Barry Bonds, forced baseball to act. As the year unfolded, baseball confronted not only an alleged drug problem but also a public relations problem. Critics questioned the achievements of individual players, suggested that competition between players who used steroids and those who didn't was inherently unfair and argued that record books should be annotated to indicate suspicious behavior.

STEROIDS REMAIN IN FOREFRONT

Following months of adverse publicity and innuendo stemming in part from the federal case involving the Bay Area Laboratory Co-Operative (BALCO) and the many athletes, not just ballplayers, linked to it in newspaper stories and leaked grand jury testimony, Major League Baseball and the Major League Baseball Players Association announced a new drug-testing policy in January. Superseding the program of random testing for anabolic steroids implemented as part of the collective bargaining agreement of September 2002, the revisions included random, year-round testing and harsher penalties starting with the first offense: a suspension of up to 10 days for the first positive test, 30 days for the second, 60 days for the third, one year for the fourth and discipline determined by the commissioner for the fifth positive test. Commissioner Allan H. "Bud" Selig and Donald M. Fehr, executive director of the players' union, praised the agreement as a huge step forward, but some outside observers criticized it for not going far enough.

Despite this new policy, steroids remained prominent in the news, and baseball's testing program, along with that of the other major sports, attracted the attention of several Congressional committees. The subject got an additional jolt of publicity in February when former outfielder Jose Canseco published a book, *Juiced: Wild Times, Rampant 'Roids, Smash Hits, and How Baseball Got Big*, in which he admitted having taken steroids and implicated several former teammates as well. In March, the House Committee on Government Reform (with jurisdiction over the nation's drug policy) subpoenaed 11 baseball executives and current and former players, including Selig, Canseco, Jason Giambi, Mark McGwire, Rafael Palmeiro, Curt Schilling, Sammy Sosa and Frank Thomas. Conspicuously absent from the list was Bonds, who previously had testified to using BALCO products identified as steroids and masking agents. At the hearing held on March 17, Congressman Henry Waxman, D-Calif., ranking minority member, berated baseball for 30 years of inaction. Selig defended baseball's new policy, but other members of Congress criticized it as inadequate. Canseco expounded on sections of his book, McGwire dodged questions by saying "I didn't come here to talk about the past" and Palmeiro pointed his finger and asserted, "I never used steroids. Period. I don't know how to say it more clearly than that."

A subcommittee of the House Committee on Energy and Commerce and the House Committee on the Judiciary began their own investigations, and some in Congress introduced bills dealing with steroids in sports. Sen. John McCain, R-Ariz., joined with four House members to introduce the Clean Sports Act of 2005 with much more severe penalties applicable, if passed and signed into law, to the entire spectrum of sports across the United States.

Starting in April, 12 major league players were suspended 10 days each for testing positive once. They were: Alex Sanchez, Jorge Piedra, Agustin Montero, Jamal Strong, Juan Rincon, Rafael Betancourt, Palmeiro, Ryan Franklin, Mike Morse, Carlos Almanzar, Felix Heredia and Matt Lawton. Several dozen minor league players also were suspended under the minor leagues' stricter program.

Palmeiro's suspension, announced on August 1, nearly five months after his strident Congressional testimony, had ramifications not only for him but also for his sport. Since his denial of steroid use had been so unequivocal, the fact that he had tested positive on May 4 (for stanozolol, it was later revealed) branded him as a hypocrite in some eyes. Despite his 569 home runs and 3,020 hits (at season's end), his candidacy for the Hall of Fame was widely tarnished. Palmeiro denied that he had used steroids intentionally, but he did not explain publicly how he tested positive. He agreed to turn over the results of his drug tests to the Government Reform Committee, and the union filed a grievance on his behalf. He returned from his suspension to play a few more games before the Baltimore Orioles excused him for the rest of the season. In November, he seemed to implicate teammate Miguel Tejada for giving him vitamin B-12 that might have contributed to the positive test. He repeated this suggestion in December.

Even before Palmeiro's suspension, Selig had responded to the continuing controversy by proposing even tougher penalties. In an April letter to Fehr, he argued for a 50-game suspension for first-time offenders, a 100-game suspension for a second violation and a lifetime ban for a third offense. He also asked the union to help ban the use of amphetamines, ignored in all previous testing programs, and to turn over responsibility for the testing program to an outside party. The union answered cautiously, suggesting that further changes in the existing program might be beneficial but that a 50-game suspension for a first offense might be excessive. Fehr suggested a more moderate scale, 20 games for the first offense, 75 games for the second and a penalty set by the commissioner for the third. Five members of the Hall of Fame testified before the Senate Commerce Committee in September in favor of Selig's plan. In November, MLB and the union agreed to accept Selig's proposal, including testing for amphetamine usage.

BASEBALL RETURNS TO WASHINGTON

For the first time since the end of the 1971 season, when the second edition of the Senators left Washington, D.C., to become the Texas Rangers, a major league baseball team called the nation's capital home. After playing their first nine games on the road, the Washington Nationals, formerly the Montreal Expos, opened at a refurbished Robert F. Kennedy Stadium on April 14 against the Arizona Diamondbacks, winning, 5-3.

Throughout the year, MLB, which has owned the franchise since 2002, tried to resolve two key components of the Nationals' future: deciding which potential ownership group would be permitted to buy the club and reaching an agreement with District of Columbia officials on the terms of a lease to allow the club to use the new ballpark to be constructed along the Anacostia waterfront in the southeast section of the city. In March, MLB put a side issue to rest, reaching agreement with Baltimore owner Peter G. Angelos to form a joint regional sports network controlled by the Orioles that would allow Nationals games to be televised while addressing Baltimore's concern that a team in Washington would adversely affect the Orioles' financial interests.

MLB hoped to select an owner for the team by April, but protracted negotiations on the ballpark lease, which MLB decided had to be solved first, delayed this process time and again. When MLB solicited bids for the franchise in June, eight groups emerged, and three appeared to be front-runners. They were Washington developer Theodore Lerner; investors Frederic Malek and Jeffrey Zients, whose group included former Secretary of State Colin Powell; and Jeffrey Smulyan, CEO of Emmis Communications and former principal owner of the Seattle Mariners. The commissioner at one time proposed that MLB owners select an ownership group in November, but as terms of the ballpark lease remained unsettled, this vote was put off until 2006 when the price of the franchise is expected to be about $450 million.

The dispute over the terms of the lease was an extension of an earlier debate about how much public money should be used to construct the ballpark, including responsibility for cost overruns that might prove to be substantial. After Washington mayor Anthony Williams signed the Baseball Stadium Agreement in September 2004, several members of the D.C. Council delayed final approval and urged that construction be supported with a higher percentage of private financing. Later, three members of the council favorable to the agreement were replaced by three who were opposed. These officials transferred their objections to the terms of the lease, and in December Williams was forced to admit that the council would not vote on a lease until at least January 2006.

NEW UMPIRES CONTRACT

In February, major league umpires ratified a five-year contract agreed to in December 2004 by MLB and the umpires' union, the World Umpires Association. The contract called for annual pay increases of 5 percent with a salary scale for 2005 from $87,859 to $357,530. It also included resolution of a grievance filed by the WUA over MLB's use of QuesTec Inc.'s Umpire Information System that uses computers and cameras to evaluate the performance of home plate umpires calling balls and strikes.

The contract also provided for the rehiring of three umpires who lost their jobs during the 1999 labor dispute and providing severance pay for six others. The umpires to be rehired as vacancies occurred were Bob Davidson, Tom Hallion and Ed Hickox. Getting severance pay and health benefits were Jim Evans, Dale Ford, Eric Gregg, Mark Johnson, Ken Kaiser and Larry McCoy.

NINTH YEAR OF INTERLEAGUE PLAY

Regular-season games between A.L. and N.L. clubs continued for the ninth consecutive year. Teams in the A.L. East played most of their games against the N.L. Central, A.L. Central teams played the N.L. West and A.L. West teams played the N.L. East. There was one period of interleague play, June 6-19, surrounded by two weekends, May 20-22 and June 24-26, during which teams played their so-called traditional rivals. The schedule had all A.L. teams and four N.L. West teams playing 18 interleague games and most other N.L. teams playing 15 games.

Overall, A.L. teams won 136 games and lost 116, cutting the N.L.'s lead in total interleague play to 1,104-1,096.

ATLANTA EXTENDS TITLE STREAK

The Braves won the N.L. East crown for the 11th year in a row. Leaving aside the incomplete 1994 season, Atlanta has now won an unprecedented 14 straight division crowns. Although some preseason prognosticators had suggested that this would be the year the Braves' run would end, such was not the case. Led by Bobby Cox, TSN's N.L. Manager of the Year for the fourth consecutive year, the Braves ran neck-and-neck with the Florida Marlins through April and May and then trailed surprising Washington through most of July. Spurred by the performance of several rookies and young players, Atlanta took over first place on July 26. Thereafter, the Nationals faded, and the Braves held off the Philadelphia Phillies. Atlanta clinched the division title on September 27 when Philadelphia lost to the New York Mets.

Andruw Jones, TSN's Major League Player of the Year, led Atlanta's offense. Even though he batted only .263, he led the N.L. with 51 home runs and 128 RBIs. His 50th home run was the 300th of his career, making him the 12th player to reach 300 before his 30th birthday. No other Brave had more than 21 homers or 78 runs batted in. Wilson Betemit hit .305 in 115 games, and Pete Orr hit .300 in 112 games. The Braves ranked sixth in the league in batting and fourth in runs scored.

Atlanta's pitching staff ranked sixth in ERA. John Smoltz, returning to the starting rotation after three full seasons as a closer, and Tim Hudson won 14 games each, and Smoltz was fifth in innings pitched (229⅔). Jorge Sosa went 13-3 and led the league in winning percentage (.813), and Horacio Ramirez won 11 games. Chris Reitsma had 15 saves.

CARDINALS RULE CENTRAL AGAIN

St. Louis won 100 games to capture its second straight division title and qualify for postseason play for the sixth time in Tony La Russa's 10 years as Cardinals manager. With these victories, La Russa passed Joe McCarthy, Bucky Harris and Sparky Anderson on the all-time managerial wins list. He stands in third place with 2,214 wins, behind only Connie Mack (3,731) and John McGraw (2,763). The Cardinals moved into first place on April 16 and stayed there the rest of the season. They led the division by 6½ games over the Chicago Cubs at the end of May, 8½ games over the Cubs at the end of June, 9½ games over the Astros at the end of July and 14 games over the Astros at the end of August. They clinched a tie for the division title by beating the Cubs on September 15 and won the division outright on September 17 by beating the Cubs

again. The final regular-season game at Busch Stadium, played on October 2, saw the Cardinals defeat the Reds, 7-5.

St. Louis finished tied for second in the league in batting (.270), deadlocked for third in hits (1,494) and wound up third in runs (805). The Cardinals' Albert Pujols, who won the N.L. Most Valuable Player Award, batted .330 (second in the league) with 41 home runs (third) and 117 RBIs (tied for second). He led the league in multi-hit games and runs, finished second in slugging percentage, on-base percentage and total bases and fourth in hits. David Eckstein hit .294, and Jim Edmonds added 29 homers and 89 RBIs.

Cardinals pitchers led the league in earned-run average (3.49) and complete games (15) and were second in saves (48). Chris Carpenter (21-5, 2.83) won the N.L. Cy Young Award and was named TSN's N.L. Pitcher of the Year. He finished second in wins, shutouts (four) and strikeouts (213) and won 13 decisions in a row. Mark Mulder and Jeff Suppan added 16 victories each, and Jason Isringhausen saved 39 games (tied for fifth in the league).

ASTROS REPEAT AS WILD CARD

Houston finished second in the N.L. Central for the fourth straight year and qualified for postseason play for the second year in a row. After starting out 15-30, the team played at a .632 pace the rest of the way and won the wild-card spot over the Phillies on the season's last day. Lance Berkman led the Astros in batting (.293) and Morgan Ensberg was tops in home runs (36) and RBIs (101), but the team ranked 13th in the league in batting average and 11th in runs. Roy Oswalt won 20 games, and Andy Pettitte added 17 wins. Brad Lidge recorded 42 saves.

SAN DIEGO TAKES N.L. WEST

The Padres won the N.L. West title for the first time since 1998 when they lost the World Series to the Yankees. San Diego finished with 82 wins and 80 losses, just barely avoiding becoming the first team to win a division with a sub-.500 record. The Padres led the division by three games at the end of May and 4½ games at the end of June. Arizona pulled into a tie for first at the end of July, but then San Diego regained the lead for good. The Padres clinched the division title on September 28 by defeating the San Francisco Giants, 9-1.

Brian Giles led the San Diego offense by hitting .301 with 15 home runs and 83 runs batted in. Ryan Klesko added 18 home runs and 58 RBIs. The team finished 12th in the league in batting average and 13th in runs.

Jake Peavy won 13 games and led the league in strike-outs with 216. Adam Eaton won 11 games, and 16 other pitchers won at least one game. The team was seventh in ERA. Trevor Hoffman saved 43 games, second in the league.

YANKEES WIN EIGHTH STRAIGHT

New York won its eighth consecutive A.L. East title and its ninth in 10 seasons. In marked contrast to the team's many front-running performances, the Yankees did not move into first place for good until September 21. They trailed Baltimore by four games at the end of May and six games at the end of June, and Boston by 2½ games at the end of July and August. New York clinched the division title on October 1, the last Saturday of the season, by beating the Red Sox, 8-4.

The Yankees' offense finished second in the league in batting average, runs, hits and home runs. The offensive leader was Alex Rodriguez, who led the league in home runs with 48, finished second in batting average (.321) and fourth in RBIs (130). He also led the league in runs (124) and slugging percentage (.610). Derek Jeter and Hideki Matsui also hit over .300, and Matsui drove in 116 runs. Gary Sheffield hit 34 homers with 123 RBIs.

New York's pitching was unstable. The team used 28 pitchers, with 18 earning at least one win and 17 garnering at least one loss. Randy Johnson won 17 games and finished second in the league in strikeouts (211). Mike Mussina added 13 victories. Aaron Small, who was called up from the minors on July 17, finished 10-0. Mariano Rivera saved 43 games, tied for third in the league.

BOSTON TAKES WILD CARD AGAIN

The Red Sox finished second in the A.L. East for the eighth season in a row and were the wild card in the postseason for the third consecutive year. Boston's offense finished first in the league in batting average, runs and hits and ranked fifth in home runs. David Ortiz led the league in RBIs with 148 and finished second in home runs (47). Johnny Damon hit .316, fourth-best in the league, and had the league's longest hitting streak, 29 games. Red Sox pitching was not nearly as effective, finishing 11th in ERA. Tim Wakefield won 16 games, David Wells added 15 and Bronson Arroyo 14. Keith Foulke saved 15 games before being injured.

WHITE SOX SPRINT TO CENTRAL CROWN

Chicago won the A.L. Central title for the first time since 2000 by racing to a substantial lead over its rivals and then holding on through a late-season slump. The White Sox led the division by five games at the end of May, 10½ at the end of June and 14½ at the end of July. They pushed the lead to 15 games on August 1 before watching it dwindle steadily to 1½ on September 22. Thereafter, the Sox rebounded, and the Cleveland Indians, their nearest pursuers, slumped, giving the title to Chicago on September 29 with a win over the Detroit Tigers.

The White Sox played aggressive baseball all season long. No regular in their lineup hit over .290, with Scott Podsednik finishing exactly at that mark. Podsednik was second in the league in stolen bases with 59 (but was caught stealing a league-high 23 times). Paul Konerko hit 40 homers with 100 RBIs. Jermaine Dye hit 31 home runs, and Carl Everett drove in 87 runs.

Chicago's pitching staff finished tied for first in the league in complete games (nine) and ERA (3.61). Jon Garland won 18 games, and Mark Buehrle led the league in innings pitched (236⅔) and won 16 games, including nine in a row. Jose Contreras added 15 wins and Freddy Garcia 14. Dustin Hermanson saved 34 games.

ANGELS REPEAT IN A.L. WEST

The Angels won the A.L. West title for the second season in a row. The team was in first place for 171 of the season's 183 days, but the Angels had to contend with threats from Texas in the first half of the season and from the Oakland Athletics near the end. Los Angeles clinched the title on September 28 with a 4-3 win at Oakland.

The Angels' offense was powered by Vladimir Guerrero, who hit .317 (third in the league) with 32 homers and 108 RBIs. Adam Kennedy hit .300, and Garret Anderson drove in 96 runs. Chone Figgins led the league in stolen bases with 62.

The Los Angeles pitching staff finished third in the league in ERA and first in strikeouts. Three Angels pitchers finished in the top 10 in ERA: Jarrod Washburn (fourth), John Lackey (tied for fifth) and Bartolo Colon (eighth). Colon led the league in wins with 21 and was named TSN's A.L. Pitcher of the Year. Lackey won 14 games and finished third in the league in strikeouts (199). Francisco Rodriguez tied for the league lead in saves with 45.

OTHER FEATS AND EVENTS

Palmeiro became the 26th member of the 3,000-hit club when he doubled off the Mariners' Joel Pineiro in the fifth inning on July 15. Palmeiro joined Henry Aaron, Willie Mays and Eddie Murray as the only players with 3,000 hits and 500 home runs. The Cubs' Greg Maddux became the 13th pitcher in major league history to strike out 3,000 batters when he fanned Omar Vizquel of the Giants in a game played on July 26. Maddux finished the season with 3,052 career strikeouts and 318 wins.

Ichiro Suzuki of Seattle got 206 hits, becoming the first player to record 200 or more hits in each of his first five major league seasons. He led the A.L. with 679 at-bats and hit .303. Florida's Jeremy Hermida became the second player to hit a grand slam in his first major league at-bat when he homered as a pinch hitter against Al Reyes of the Cardinals on August 31. The first player to hit a grand slam in his first at-bat was William Duggleby of the Phillies on April 21, 1898. Johan Santana of the Minnesota Twins won his first four decisions of the season to extend his consecutive-game winning streak to 17. The streak ended on May 1 when he lost to the Angels. No pitcher threw a no-hitter in 2005.

Three players hit for the cycle: Brad Wilkerson of Washington on April 6, Mark Grudzielanek of St. Louis on April 27 and Randy Winn of San Francisco on August 15. Six players hit three homers in a game: Dmitri Young (Detroit) on opening day, Alex Rodriguez, Kevin Mench (Texas) and Jonny Gomes (Tampa Bay) in the A.L., and Ensberg and Hee Seop Choi (Los Angeles) in the N.L. Alfonso Soriano of the Rangers made the 30/30 club (30 stolen bases and 30 home runs) for the third time in four years.

Derrek Lee of the Cubs led the N.L. in batting with a .335 average. He also led the league in hits (199), total bases (393), extra-base hits (99) and slugging percentage (.662). Jose Reyes of the Mets led the league in triples (17) and stolen bases (60). Jimmy Rollins of Philadelphia had the longest hitting streak, 36 games, a streak that was intact at the end of the season. The Marlins' Dontrelle Willis led the league with 22 wins, and Houston's Roger Clemens won the ERA crown (1.87). In the A.L., Michael Young of the Rangers won the batting title (.331) and led the league in hits (221) and multi-hit games (66). Cleveland's Kevin Millwood topped the A.L. in ERA (2.86).

DIVISION SERIES WINNERS

Two division series were three-game sweeps, one went four games and one went the maximum five games. The

Cardinals won the first two games at home and then eliminated the Padres in Game 3 in San Diego. The White Sox did likewise against the Red Sox, winning the first two games in Chicago and Game 3 in Boston. The Astros and Braves split the first two games in Atlanta. Houston won Game 3 at home and then eliminated the Braves by winning Game 4, 7-6, in 18 innings. With one out, Chris Burke homered off Joey Devine to end the longest game in postseason history. The Angels and Yankees split the first four games, and Los Angeles won the deciding game, 5-3.

ASTROS DEFEAT CARDS IN SIX

The N.L. Championship Series opened in St. Louis, with the Cardinals winning the first game and the Astros the second. Carpenter held Houston to five hits over eight innings in Game 1, and Reggie Sanders hit a two-run homer in the first inning to power St. Louis to a 5-3 triumph. In Game 2, Oswalt outpitched Mulder to win, 4-1, despite giving up a Pujols home run in the sixth.

When the series shifted to Minute Maid Park, Clemens won Game 3, 4-3, as the Astros scored two runs in the fourth on a Mike Lamb home run and another two in the sixth, one on a Jason Lane single and the second on a throwing error by Hector Luna. Brandon Backe and four other pitchers held St. Louis to five hits in Game 4, winning, 2-1. In Game 5, the Cardinals were losing 4-2 with two outs in the ninth and Lidge on the mound. David Eckstein singled, Edmonds walked and Pujols hit a three-run homer to give St. Louis the lead. Isringhausen then pitched a perfect ninth to secure the win and stave off elimination.

Back in St. Louis for what turned out to be the final game in Busch Stadium, Houston closed out the series with a 5-1 victory in Game 6. Oswalt pitched three-hit ball over seven innings, and the Astros advanced to the World Series for the first time.

WHITE SOX DEFEAT ANGELS IN FIVE

The A.L. Championship Series featured outstanding pitching by the White Sox, who got an 8⅓-innings stint by Jose Contreras in Game 1 and then four complete games from Buehrle, Jon Garland, Freddy Garcia and Contreras. The Angels took Game 1, 3-2, as Paul Byrd and two relievers surrendered only seven hits. Anderson hit a home run in the second inning, and Los Angeles scored two more in the third. The White Sox bounced back in Game 2, winning 2-1. Joe Crede drove in the winning run in the ninth after a controversial play. With two outs, A.J. Pierzynski struck out swinging at a low pitch. Catcher Josh Paul thought he caught the ball cleanly and rolled it back to the mound. After hesitating, Pierzynski ran toward first and arrived safely. Home plate umpire Doug Eddings ruled that the ball had hit the dirt before Paul grabbed it, and his partners agreed. Pablo Ozuna ran for Pierzynski, stole second and scored the winning run on Crede's double.

In Anaheim, the White Sox closed out the series with three sterling wins. They took Game 3, 5-2, with Konerko hitting a two-run homer in the first inning. In Game 4, Konerko hit a three-run homer in the first. The Angels saw a rally snuffed out in the second by another controversial call. They scored a run and had two men on base when Steve Finley grounded into a double play to end the inning. Finley argued that Pierzynski's mitt had tipped his bat, a

play that should have resulted in a call of catcher's interference, but the umpires disagreed. Chicago scored single runs in the next three innings and won, 8-2. The Angels held a 3-2 lead in Game 6, but the White Sox scored once in the seventh on a Crede home run to tie the score, once in the eighth on a Crede single to take the lead and twice in the ninth to put the game away, 6-3, and win the Series. The White Sox thus advanced to the World Series for the first time since 1959.

CHICAGO WINS FIRST SERIES SINCE 1917

With all the media attention surrounding the alleged "Curse of the Bambino" that supposedly explained the failure of the Red Sox to win any World Series after 1918 until they did so in 2004, and the alleged "Curse of the Billy Goat" that supposedly explains the continuing failure of the Cubs to win any World Series since 1908, the White Sox's failure to win the World Series since 1917 had traditionally grabbed fewer headlines. Sox fans felt this pain, of course, but their agony seldom aroused much commiseration from others. Nevertheless, just one season after the Red Sox finally won it all again, the White Sox exorcised their own demons.

Since the A.L. squad had won the All-Star Game, 7-5, the World Series opened at U.S. Cellular Field. Chicago won Game 1, 5-3, behind Contreras, who, like every White Sox starter in the Series, pitched seven innings. (Buehrle started Game 2 and also relieved in Game 3.) Dye hit a home run in the first inning of Game 1 to open the scoring, and the Sox added two runs in the second on a groundout and a double. Houston countered with a Lamb homer in the second and a pair of runs in the third on a double by Berkman. The Sox took the lead in the fourth on a Crede home run and added an insurance run in the eighth on a triple by Podsednik. In Game 2, Houston took a 4-2 lead into the bottom of the seventh when the White Sox rallied for four runs on a two-out grand slam by Konerko. The White Sox had loaded the bases on a double, a walk and a hit-by-pitch call that replays suggested could have been called a foul ball. The Astros came back to tie the score in the ninth on a pinch single by Jose Vizcaino, but Podsednik won the game with a walkoff homer with one out in the ninth.

Game 3 in Minute Maid Park tied a World Series record for the longest game by innings (14) and set a Series record for longest game by time, 5 hours and 41 minutes, surpassing Game 1 of the 2000 Series between the Mets and the Yankees. Houston led, 4-0, after four innings, but Chicago scored five runs in the fifth. Crede homered, Tadahito Iguchi and Dye each drove in a run and Pierzynski doubled home two more. The Astros tied the score in the eighth on a Jason Lane double. Neither team scored until the 14th when Geoff Blum, a substitute acquired from San Diego on July 31, homered off Ezequiel Astacio. The Sox added another run and won, 7-5. Game 4 was scoreless until the eighth when Dye singled home pinch hitter Willie Harris with the game's only run.

Chicago awarded 42 full World Series shares, each worth $324,532.72 (up from $223,619.79 in 2004), six partial shares and 22 cash awards. The Astros voted 39 full shares, worth $191,985.45 each, plus 28 partial shares and eight cash awards. Television ratings for the Series hit an all-time low, falling below the 2000 Series.

HIGHEST ATTENDANCE EVER

According to figures released in November, major league baseball games drew 74,926,174 fans in 2005, the highest total ever. The 2004 total was 73,022,969. Average attendance was 30,987, up from 30,401 in 2004. N.L. teams drew 41,643,985 to their home games while A.L. teams attracted 33,282,189 to theirs.

The Yankees became the third franchise to exceed the four-million mark (4,090,692), setting an all-time A.L. record, and five other clubs drew more than three million: Los Angeles in the A.L., and Los Angeles, St. Louis, San Francisco and Chicago in the N.L. Eighteen other teams exceeded the two-million mark, and four clubs (the Yankees, Angels, Cardinals and Red Sox) set all-time franchise marks.

The Nationals, who drew 748,550 in the final season in Montreal, drew 2,731,993, an average of 33,728 per game.

MERRY-GO-ROUND OF MANAGERS

On the managerial front, Oakland rehired Ken Macha on October 14 after having announced on October 5 that he and the club had failed to reach an agreement on a new contract. Tony Pena resigned as manager of the Kansas City Royals on May 10 with the team mired in last place in the A.L. Central. Bob Schaeffer took over on an interim basis, and Buddy Bell was named manager on May 31. The Royals remained in last place, finishing with a record of 56-106, worst in the game. The Reds fired Dave Miley on June 21 when the team was in last place in the N.L. Central with a record of 27-43. The club named bench coach Jerry Narron interim manager, and the Reds finished in fifth place (73-89). Narron had the interim tag removed on September 29. Baltimore fired Lee Mazzilli on August 4 after an eight-game losing streak dropped the team to fourth place in the A.L. East. Bench coach Sam Perlozzo replaced him on an interim basis and was named permanent manager on October 12. The Orioles stayed in fourth place with a record of 74-88. The Pittsburgh Pirates fired Lloyd McClendon on September 6 with the team in last place in the N.L. Central at 55-81. Bench coach Pete Mackanin was named interim manager. The team finished sixth (67-95), and Mackanin was not retained.

As the season concluded, Marlins manager Jack McKeon announced his retirement, and Tampa Bay said that Lou Piniella would not return to fulfill the last year of his contract. The Marlins, who finished third in the N.L. East (83-79), named Yankees bench coach Joe Girardi to replace McKeon on October 19. The Devils Rays finished last in the A.L. East (67-95), and they named Angels bench coach Joe Maddon their new manager on November 15. The Tigers fired Alan Trammell the day after the season when the team finished fourth in the A.L. Central at 71-91. The club named Jim Leyland, former Pirates and Marlins manager, to replace him on October 4. The day before, the Dodgers discharged Jim Tracy, who had guided the team to fourth place in the N.L. West with a record of 71-91. Tracy became the Pirates' new manager on October 11, and the Dodgers hired Grady Little, former manager of the Red Sox, on December 6.

ANGELS CHANGE NAME

On January 3, the Anaheim Angels changed their name to the Los Angeles Angels of Anaheim, a switch that would, the team said, "strengthen the Angels' long-term economic health by enhancing (the team's) marketability

through this metropolitan area and beyond." The city of Anaheim filed a lawsuit in the Superior Court of Orange County along with motions seeking a temporary restraining order and an injunction against this change, arguing that it would violate terms of the club's stadium lease and hurt the city's ability to market itself as a tourist destination. Judges denied the city's motions and in June, the Court of Appeals for the Fourth Appellate District denied a request by the city to order the Superior Court to vacate its denial. The lawsuit was scheduled to go to trial in January 2006.

OWNERSHIP CHANGES

On January 13, owners approved the sale of the Milwaukee Brewers from the Selig family to Los Angeles investor Mark Attanasio for a reported $223 million. Attanasio, a group managing director of the Trust Company of the West, will keep the team in Milwaukee, thanks to a 30-year lease to play in Miller Park. In March, owners approved the sale of the A's from Steve Schott and Ken Hofmann, co-owners since 1995, to Los Angeles real estate developer Lewis Wolff for an estimated price of $180 million.

In October, New York investor Stuart Sternberg became managing general partner of the Devil Rays, replacing founding owner Vincent Naimoli. Sternberg headed a group that purchased 48 percent of the team in May 2004 for $65 million. He was scheduled to take control of the club after the 2006 season but paid Naimoli, who retains a 15 percent interest, to relinquish control earlier.

Carl Linder, CEO of the Reds, announced on November 2 that Cincinnati Reds LLC, the entity that owns the team, would sell a controlling interest to a group of Cincinnati residents headed by Robert H. Castellini, whose company, Castellini Company, wholesales fruits and vegetables. Several members of the existing ownership group will retain minority stakes. The purchase price of the interests to be sold was estimated to be about $270 million, with final approval pending at year's end.

LUXURY TAX

In the third year of the competitive balance tax, the so-called luxury tax, two teams exceeded the threshold on payrolls, $128 million. The Yankees, whose payroll was $213.1 million, were assessed $34,053,787, and Boston's bill, based on its payroll of $141.9 million, was $4,156,476. New York was taxed at the 40 percent rate for being over the threshold for the third year. The Red Sox were taxed at the 30 percent rate for being over the threshold for the second time.

NEW TELEVISION CONTRACT

In June, MLB and ESPN signed a new television contract worth $2.368 billion, covering the seasons from 2006 through 2013. The preceding contract ran for six years through 2005 and paid MLB $815 million. Under the new deal, ESPN will televise up to 80 games a year, including an exclusive game on Sunday nights and non-exclusive games on Mondays and Wednesdays. The package also includes 10 spring training games each year and the annual All-Star Home Run Derby.

THREE ARBITRATION CASES

Eighty-nine players filed for salary arbitration by the January 15 deadline, but only three cases, the lowest total since arbitration began in 1974, proceeded through the hearing and decision stage. Before teams and players exchanged figures on January 18, 49 players agreed to contracts, including Alfonso Soriano (one year, $7.5 million) with the Rangers and Rafael Furcal (one year, $5.6 million) with the Braves. Clemens headed the list of those exchanging figures. He sought $22 million from the Astros, who offered $13.5 million. They settled at $18 million, the highest salary ever for a pitcher. Johan Santana signed a four-year contract with the Twins for $40 million, and Eric Gagne signed a two-year contract with the Dodgers for $19 million.

Minnesota pitcher Kyle Lohse was the only player to win his hearing, getting $2.4 million instead of the team's offer, $2.15 million. Pitchers Jeremy Affeldt of Kansas City and Juan Cruz of Oakland lost their hearings. Owners now lead players in winning arbitration cases, 265-198.

The 89 players who filed earned an average salary increase of 123 percent, according to the Associated Press, down from 126 percent in 2004. They received an average salary of $2.8 million, down from $3.26 million in 2004. The largest percentage increase went to Cincinnati's Adam Dunn, who got a 934 percent raise from $445,000 to $4.6 million. The only player not to earn a raise was Arizona's Brandon Lyon, who did not pitch in 2004.

FINAL STANDINGS

AMERICAN LEAGUE

EAST DIVISION

Team	Bos	N.Y.	Tor	Bal	TB	Chi	Cle	Min	Det	K.C.	L.A.	Oak	Tex	Sea	N.L.	W	L	Pct.	GB	LD1st	DIF	Lead
New York	10	...	12	11	8	3	4	3	5	3	4	7	7	7	11-7	95	67	.586	.....	10/2	20	1.0
Boston	9	7	10	13	4	4	4	6	4	6	6	7		3	12-6	95	67	.586	.....	10/2	98	5.5
Toronto	11	6	...	10	11	2	2	2	3	6	5	5	3	6	8-10	80	82	.494	15.0	4/16	13	1.5
Baltimore	8	7	9	...	12	2	1	3	3	4	2	4	4	7	8-10	74	88	.457	21.0	6/23	69	4.5
Tampa Bay	6	11	8	6	...	2	6	0	2	5	5	5	6	2	3-15	67	95	.414	28.0	4/9	2	0.0

CENTRAL DIVISION

Team	Chi	Cle	Min	Det	K.C.	Bos	N.Y.	Tor	Bal	TB	L.A.	Oak	Tex	Sea	N.L.	W	L	Pct.	GB	LD1st	DIF	Lead
Chicago	...	14	11	14	13	3	3	4	6	4	4	2	3	6	12-6	99	63	.611	.....	10/2	182	15.0
Cleveland	5	...	10	12	13	2	3	4	6	4	3	6	3	7	15-3	93	69	.574	6.0	—	—	—
Minnesota	7	9	...	11	13	2	3	4	3	6	4	4	3	6	8-10	83	79	.512	16.0	4/17	5	0.0
Detroit	5	6	8	...	10	4	1	4	5	5	4	1	4	5	9-9	71	91	.438	28.0	4/7	3	0.0
Kansas City	5	6	6	9	...	2	3	3	2	3	2	2	2	2	9-9	56	106	.346	43.0	—	—	—

WEST DIVISION

Team	L.A.	Oak	Tex	Sea	Bos	N.Y.	Tor	Bal	TB	Chi	Cle	Min	Det	K.C.	N.L.	W	L	Pct.	GB	LD1st	DIF	Lead
Los Angeles	...	10	15	9	4	6	1	4	4	6	5	6	6	7	12-6	95	67	.586	.....	10/2	170	8.5
Oakland	9	...	11	12	4	2	5	6	4	7	3	6	5	4	10-8	88	74	.543	7.0	9/15	23	2.0
Texas	4	8	...	13	2	3	7	6	2	6	3	6	2	8	9-9	79	83	.488	16.0	6/7	11	1.0
Seattle	9	6	6	...	3	3	4	3	4	3	3	4	4	7	10-8	69	93	.426	26.0	4/20	6	0.5

NOTE: Read across for wins, down for losses; final standings are shaded.

Abbreviations: LD1st denotes last date in 1st place; DIF denotes days in first place; Lead denotes largest lead.

NATIONAL LEAGUE

EAST DIVISION

Team	Atl.	Phi.	N.Y.	Fla.	Was.	St.L.	Hou.	Mil.	Chi.	Cin.	Pit.	S.D.	Ari.	S.F.	L.A.	Col.	A.L.	W	L	Pct.	GB	LD1st	DIF	Lead
Atlanta	...	9	13	10	10	3	5	3	6	7	4	1	3	4	3	2	7-8	90	72	.556	.....	10/2	101	7.0
Philadelphia	10	...	7	10	11	4	0	5	4	4	6	4	5	3	4		7-8	88	74	.543	2.0	4/6	3	0.5
New York	6	11	...	10	11	2	5	3	4	3	3	4	6	3	4		5-10	83	79	.512	7.0			
Florida	8	9	8	...	9	3	4	3	4	4	3	2	4	4	5		10-5	83	79	.512	7.0	6/3	33	1.5
Washington	9	8	8	9	...	2	2	4	5	1	5	1	4	3	4		12-6	81	81	.500	9.0	7/25	62	5.5

CENTRAL DIVISION

Team	St.L.	Hou.	Mil.	Chi.	Cin.	Pit.	Atl.	Phi.	N.Y.	Fla.	Was.	S.D.	Ari.	S.F.	L.A.	Col.	A.L.	W	L	Pct.	GB	LD1st	DIF	Lead
St. Louis	...	11	11	6	11	12	3	2	5	4	4	3	5	4	5	4	10-5	100	62	.617	.....	10/2	171	16.0
Houston	5	...	10	7	12	9	1	6	5	3	5	4	3	3	4	5	7-8	89	73	.549	11.0	4/15	5	1.0
Milwaukee	5	5	...	9	10	9	3	4	3	4	4	3	4	1	5		8-7	81	81	.500	19.0	4/15	9	1.0
Chicago	10	9	7	...	6	11	1	2	2	5	1	4	2	5	4		6-9	79	83	.488	21.0	4/4	1	0.0
Cincinnati	5	4	6	9	...	9	3	3	3	2	5	4	4	3	3		7-8	73	89	.451	27.0	4/7	4	0.5
Pittsburgh	4	7	7	5	7	...	3	3	3	4	1	3	4	2	2	7	5-7	67	95	.414	33.0	—	—	—

WEST DIVISION

Team	S.D.	Ari.	S.F.	L.A.	Col.	Atl.	Phi.	N.Y.	Fla.	Was.	St.L.	Hou.	Mil.	Chi.	Cin.	Pit.	A.L.	W	L	Pct.	GB	LD1st	DIF	Lead
San Diego	...	9	12	7	11	5	0	2	4	5	4	3	4	3	2	4	7-11	82	80	.506	.....	10/2	136	7.0
Arizona	10	...	7	13	11	3	3	1	2	2	3	2	5	3			8-10	77	85	.475	5.0	8/1	11	0.5
San Francisco	6	11	...	10	11	2	1	3	2	3	2	4	3	2	5		6-12	75	87	.463	7.0	4/11	3	0.0
Los Angeles	11	5	9	...	8	3	3	2	2	2	5	2	4	5			5-13	71	91	.438	11.0	5/14	36	4.5
Colorado	7	7	7	11	...	4	2	3	2	4	1	1	3	3			6-9	67	95	.414	15.0	4/5	2	0.5

NOTE: Read across for wins, down for losses; final standings are shaded.

Abbreviations: LD1st denotes last date in 1st place; DIF denotes days in first place; Lead denotes largest lead.

SALARIES RISE

According to figures compiled by the Players Association and released by the Associated Press in December, the average major league salary rose 7.2 percent to $2,479,125, a reversal of the previous year's 2.5 percent decline. The Yankees had the highest average salary for the seventh consecutive year, a record $7,391,168 (up from $6,382,187), and the Pirates had the lowest, $963,674.

CONCLUSION

When major league players and owners announced a second revision in baseball's drug-testing program in mid-November, commissioner Selig said, "This is an important step to reaching our goal of ridding our sport of performance-enhancing substances and should restore the integrity of and public confidence in our great game." Union chief Fehr responded, "This agreement reaffirms that major league players are committed to the elimination of performance-enhancing substances and that the system of collective bargaining is responsive and effective in dealing with issues of this type." Whether these predictions and analyses prove accurate or not, here (beginning on page 166) is how the game on the field ended up in 2005:

INTERLEAGUE RECORDS

AMERICAN LEAGUE

EAST DIVISION

A.L. team vs.	Ari.	Atl.	Chi.	Cin.	Col.	Fla.	Hou.	L.A.	Mil.	N.Y.	Phi.	Pit.	St.L.	S.D.	S.F.	Was.	W	L	Pct.
New York........	0-0	0-0	3-0	0-0	0-0	0-0	0-0	0-0	1-2	3-3	0-0	3-0	1-2	0-0	0-0	0-0	11	7	.611
Boston...........	0-0	2-1	1-2	3-0	0-0	0-0	0-0	0-0	0-0	0-0	3-0	2-1	1-2	0-0	0-0	0-0	12	6	.667
Toronto	0-0	0-0	2-1	0-0	0-0	0-0	0-3	0-0	1-2	0-0	0-0	0-0	2-1	0-0	0-0	3-3	8	10	.444
Baltimore........	0-0	0-3	0-0	1-2	2-1	0-0	3-0	0-0	0-0	0-0	1-2	1-2	0-0	0-0	0-0	0-0	8	10	.444
Tampa Bay	0-0	0-0	0-0	0-3	0-0	0-6	0-0	0-0	2-1	0-0	0-0	1-2	0-3	0-0	0-0	0-0	3	15	.167

CENTRAL DIVISION

A.L. team vs.	Ari.	Atl.	Chi.	Cin.	Col.	Fla.	Hou.	L.A.	Mil.	N.Y.	Phi.	Pit.	St.L.	S.D.	S.F.	Was.	W	L	Pct.
Chicago..........	1-2	0-0	3-3	0-0	3-0	0-0	0-0	3-0	0-0	0-0	0-0	0-0	2-1	0-0	0-0		12	6	.667
Cleveland........	3-0	0-0	0-0	4-2	3-0	0-0	0-0	0-0	0-0	0-0	0-0	0-0	2-1	3-0	0-0		15	3	.833
Minnesota	2-1	0-0	0-0	0-0	0-0	0-0	0-0	1-2	3-3	0-0	0-0	0-0	0-0	1-2	1-2		8	10	.444
Detroit............	2-4	0-0	0-0	0-0	1-2	0-0	0-0	1-2	0-0	0-0	0-0	0-0	0-0	3-0	2-1		9	9	.500
Kansas City	2-1	0-0	0-0	0-0	0-3	0-0	1-2	3-0	0-0	0-0	0-0	0-0	1-2	0-0	2-1		9	9	.500

WEST DIVISION

A.L. team vs.	Ari.	Atl.	Chi.	Cin.	Col.	Fla.	Hou.	L.A.	Mil.	N.Y.	Phi.	Pit.	St.L.	S.D.	S.F.	Was.	W	L	Pct.
Los Angeles ..	0-0	2-1	0-0	0-0	0-0	2-1	0-0	5-1	0-0	2-1	0-0	0-0	0-0	0-0	0-0	1-2	12	6	.667
Oakland..........	0-0	2-1	0-0	0-0	0-0	0-0	0-0	0-0	0-0	2-1	2-1	0-0	0-0	0-0	4-2	0-3	10	8	.556
Texas..............	0-0	2-1	0-0	0-0	0-0	1-2	4-2	0-0	0-0	0-0	0-3	0-0	0-0	0-0	0-0	2-1	9	9	.500
Seattle............	0-0	0-0	0-0	0-0	0-0	2-1	0-0	0-0	0-0	3-0	2-1	0-0	0-0	3-3	0-0	0-3	10	8	.556

NATIONAL LEAGUE

EAST DIVISION

N.L. team vs.	Bal.	Bos.	Chi.	Cle.	Det.	K.C.	L.A.	Min.	N.Y.	Oak.	Sea.	TB.	Tex.	Tor.	W	L	Pct.
Atlanta...........	3-0	1-2	0-0	0-0	0-0	0-0	1-2	0-0	0-0	1-2	0-0	0-0	1-2	0-0	7	8	.467
Philadelphia....	2-1	0-3	0-0	0-0	0-0	0-0	0-0	0-0	0-0	1-2	1-2	0-0	3-0	0-0	7	8	.467
New York........	0-0	0-0	0-0	0-0	0-0	0-0	1-2	0-0	3-3	1-2	0-3	0-0	0-0	0-0	5	10	.333
Florida............	0-0	0-0	0-0	0-0	0-0	0-0	1-2	0-0	0-0	0-0	1-2	6-0	2-1	0-0	10	5	.667
Washington....	0-0	0-0	0-0	0-0	0-0	0-0	2-1	0-0	0-0	3-0	3-0	0-0	1-2	3-3	12	6	.667

CENTRAL DIVISION

N.L. team vs.	Bal.	Bos.	Chi.	Cle.	Det.	K.C.	L.A.	Min.	N.Y.	Oak.	Sea.	TB.	Tex.	Tor.	W	L	Pct.
St. Louis	0-0	2-1	0-0	0-0	0-0	2-1	0-0	0-0	2-1	0-0	0-0	3-0	0-0	1-2	10	5	.667
Houston	0-3	0-0	0-0	0-0	0-0	2-1	0-0	0-0	0-0	0-0	0-0	0-0	2-4	3-0	7	8	.467
Milwaukee......	0-0	0-0	0-0	0-0	0-0	0-0	0-0	3-3	2-1	0-0	0-0	1-2	0-0	2-1	8	7	.533
Chicago..........	0-0	2-1	3-3	0-0	0-0	0-0	0-0	0-0	0-3	0-0	0-0	0-0	0-0	1-2	6	9	.400
Cincinnati	2-1	0-3	0-0	2-4	0-0	0-0	0-0	0-0	0-0	0-0	0-0	3-0	0-0	0-0	7	8	.467
Pittsburgh	2-1	1-2	0-0	0-0	0-0	0-0	0-0	0-0	0-3	0-0	0-0	2-1	0-0	0-0	5	7	.417

WEST DIVISION

N.L. team vs.	Bal.	Bos.	Chi.	Cle.	Det.	K.C.	L.A.	Min.	N.Y.	Oak.	Sea.	TB.	Tex.	Tor.	W	L	Pct.
San Diego	0-0	0-0	1-2	1-2	0-3	0-0	0-0	2-1	0-0	0-0	3-3	0-0	0-0	0-0	7	11	.389
Arizona	0-0	0-0	2-1	0-3	4-2	1-2	0-0	1-2	0-0	0-0	0-0	0-0	0-0	0-0	8	10	.444
San Francisco	0-0	0-0	0-0	0-3	1-2	1-2	0-0	2-1	0-0	2-4	0-0	0-0	0-0	0-0	6	12	.333
Los Angeles ..	0-0	0-0	0-3	0-0	2-1	0-3	1-5	2-1	0-0	0-0	0-0	0-0	0-0	0-0	5	13	.278
Colorado	1-2	0-0	0-3	0-3	2-1	3-0	0-0	0-0	0-0	0-0	0-0	0-0	0-0	0-0	6	9	.400

BOSTON VS. CHICAGO

RESULTS

DAY	DATE	PLACE	SCORE
TUE.	OCT. 4	CHICAGO	CHICAGO 14, BOSTON 2
WED.	OCT. 5	CHICAGO	CHICAGO 5, BOSTON 4
FRI.	OCT. 7	BOSTON	CHICAGO 5, BOSTON 3

BOX SCORES

GAME 1

CHICAGO 14, BOSTON 2

TUESDAY, OCTOBER 4, AT CHICAGO

Boston	AB	R	H	BI	BB	SO	PO	A
Damon, cf	4	0	0	0	0	2	1	0
Cora, ss	0	0	0	0	0	0	0	0
Renteria, ss	4	0	1	0	0	0	0	2
Hyzdu, cf	0	0	0	0	0	0	1	0
D.Ortiz, dh	4	0	2	0	0	1	0	0
M.Ramirez, lf	4	0	0	0	0	0	2	0
Nixon, rf	4	1	2	0	0	0	1	0
Varitek, c	4	1	1	0	0	1	4	2
Millar, 1b	3	0	1	1	0	1	9	0
Olerud, ph	1	0	1	0	0	0	0	0
Mueller, 3b	4	0	0	0	0	1	0	1
Graffanino, 2b	4	0	1	0	0	0	6	2
Clement, p	0	0	0	0	0	0	0	1
Bradford, p	0	0	0	0	0	0	0	0
Gonzalez, p	0	0	0	0	0	0	0	1
Arroyo, p	0	0	0	0	0	0	0	0
TOTALS	36	2	9	1	0	6	24	11

Chi White Sox	AB	R	H	BI	BB	SO	PO	A
Podsednik, lf	3	2	2	3	1	0	3	0
Iguchi, 2b	3	0	0	0	0	1	3	4
W.Harris, ph-2b	1	0	1	1	0	0	1	0
Dye, rf	3	0	0	0	0	2	0	0
Ti.Perez, ph-rf	1	0	0	0	0	0	1	0
Konerko, 1b	4	2	1	2	0	0	9	0
Blum, ph-1b	1	0	0	0	0	0	0	0
C.Everett, dh	4	1	1	0	0	0	0	0
Rowand, cf	3	2	1	1	1	0	1	0
Pierzynski, c	3	4	3	4	0	0	6	0
Crede, 3b	3	1	0	0	1	0	1	3
Uribe, ss	4	2	2	3	0	1	0	4
Contreras, p	0	0	0	0	0	0	0	0
Cotts, p	0	0	0	0	0	0	0	0
Politte, p	0	0	0	0	0	0	0	0
TOTALS	33	14	11	14	3	2	27	11

				R	H	E	LOB
Boston	0 0 0	2 0 0	0 0 0—	2	9	0	7
Chi White Sox	5 0 1	2 0 4	0 2 x—	14	11	1	2

Boston	IP	H	R	ER	HR	BB	SO
Clement (L)	3.1	7	8	8	3	0	0
Bradford	1.1	0	0	0	0	0	1
Gonzalez	2.1	2	4	4	1	1	0
Arroyo	1.0	2	2	2	1	2	1

Chi White Sox	IP	H	R	ER	HR	BB	SO
Contreras (W)	7.2	8	2	2	0	0	6
Cotts	0.1	0	0	0	0	0	0
Politte	1.0	1	0	0	0	0	0

E—Crede. LOB—Boston 7, Chi White Sox 2. Scoring Position—Boston 2 for 12, Chi White Sox 6 for 11. 2B—Renteria, D.Ortiz, Millar, Graffanino, Olerud, Pierzynski. HR—Pierzynski (1st inning, 2 out, 2 on) off Clement, Konerko (3rd inning, 1 out, 0 on) off Clement, Uribe (4th inning, 1 out, 1 on) off Clement, Podsednik (6th inning, 1 out, 2 on) off Gonzalez, Pierzynski (8th inning, 0 out, 0 on) off Arroyo. SB—Podsednik. CS—Podsednik. SH—Iguchi. WP—Contreras. HBP—Dye by Clement, Pierzynski by Gonzalez, Podsednik by Clement. T—2:56. A—40,717. U—HP-Hirschbeck, 1B-Miller, 2B-Wegner, 3B-Carlson, LF-Everitt, RF-Iassogna.

HOW THEY SCORED

BOTTOM OF 1

White Sox first. Podsednik was hit by a pitch. Iguchi sacrificed, catcher Varitek to first baseman Millar, Podsednik to second. Dye was hit by a pitch. Podsednik stole third. Konerko grounded into fielder's choice, third baseman Mueller to second baseman Graffanino, Podsednik scored, Dye out. Everett singled to right, Konerko to second. Rowand singled to center, Konerko scored, Everett to third. Pierzynski homered to left on a 0-1 count, Everett scored, Rowand scored. Crede fouled out to catcher Varitek. Runs: 5, Hits: 3, Errors: 0

BOTTOM OF 3

White Sox third. Dye flied out to left fielder M.Ramirez. Konerko homered to left on a 2-1 count. Everett grounded out, pitcher Clement to first baseman Millar. Rowand lined out to left fielder M.Ramirez. Runs: 1, Hits: 1, Errors: 0

TOP OF 4

Red Sox fourth. Nixon singled to right. Varitek bunt single to third, Nixon to second. On Crede's error, Nixon to third, Varitek to second. On Contreras' wild pitch, Nixon scored, Varitek to third. Millar doubled to right, Varitek scored. Mueller grounded into fielder's choice, second baseman Iguchi to third baseman Crede, Millar out. Graffanino grounded into fielder's choice, shortstop Uribe to second baseman Iguchi, Mueller out. Damon struck out. Runs: 2, Hits: 3, Errors: 1

BOTTOM OF 4

White Sox fourth. Pierzynski doubled to right. Crede flied out to right fielder Nixon. Uribe homered to left on a 0-2 count, Pierzynski scored. Bradford pitching. Podsednik grounded out, pitcher Bradford to first baseman Millar. Iguchi struck out. Runs: 2, Hits: 2, Errors: 0

BOTTOM OF 6

White Sox sixth. Rowand walked on a full count. Pierzynski was hit by a pitch, Rowand to second. Crede popped out to second baseman Graffanino. Podsednik singled to left, Rowand scored, Pierzynski to second. Podsednik homered to right on a 1-1 count, Pierzynski scored, Uribe scored. Iguchi popped out to second baseman Graffanino. Dye grounded out, shortstop Renteria to first baseman Millar. Runs: 4, Hits: 2, Errors: 0

BOTTOM OF 8

White Sox eighth. Cora in as shortstop. Hyzdu in as center fielder. Arroyo pitching. Pierzynski homered to right on a 1-1 count. Crede walked on a full count. Uribe struck out. Podsednik walked on a full count, Crede to second. Harris pinch-hitting for Iguchi. Harris singled to right, Crede scored, Podsednik to second. Perez pinch-hitting for Dye. Perez flied out to center fielder Hyzdu. Blum pinch-hitting for Konerko. Blum popped out to second baseman Graffanino. Runs: 2, Hits: 2, Errors: 0

GAME 2

CHICAGO 5, BOSTON 4

WEDNESDAY, OCTOBER 5, AT CHICAGO

Boston	AB	R	H	BI	BB	SO	PO	A
Damon, cf	5	2	2	0	0	0	7	0
Renteria, ss	5	1	2	0	0	1	1	3
D.Ortiz, dh	4	1	1	0	1	0	0	0
M.Ramirez, lf	3	0	1	2	1	0	0	0
Varitek, c	4	0	2	1	0	0	3	0

Boston	AB	R	H	BI	BB	SO	PO	A
Nixon, rf	3	0	0	1	1	0	1	0
Mueller, 3b	4	0	0	0	0	1	2	1
Olerud, 1b	4	0	0	0	0	0	8	1
Graffanino, 2b	4	0	1	0	0	0	1	4
D.Wells, p	0	0	0	0	0	0	1	1
Papelbon, p	0	0	0	0	0	0	0	0
TOTALS	36	4	9	4	2	2	24	10

Chi White Sox	AB	R	H	BI	BB	SO	PO	A
Podsednik, lf	4	0	0	0	0	0	0	0
Iguchi, 2b	4	1	2	3	0	0	1	5
Dye, rf	4	0	1	0	0	1	2	0
Konerko, 1b	4	0	1	0	0	0	13	2
C.Everett, dh	4	1	2	0	0	0	0	0
Rowand, cf	3	1	1	1	0	0	6	0
Pierzynski, c	3	0	0	0	0	0	3	0
Crede, 3b	3	1	1	1	0	1	0	4
Uribe, ss	3	1	1	0	0	0	1	1
Buehrle, p	0	0	0	0	0	0	0	2
Jenks, p	0	0	0	0	0	0	1	1
TOTALS	32	5	9	5	0	2	27	15

				R	H	E	LOB
Boston	2 0 2	0 0 0	0 0 0—	4	9	1	7
Chi White Sox	0 0 0	0 5 0	0 0 x—	5	9	0	3

Boston	IP	H	R	ER	HR	BB	SO
D.Wells (L)	6.2	7	5	2	1	0	2
Papelbon	1.1	2	0	0	0	0	0

Chi White Sox	IP	H	R	ER	HR	BB	SO
Buehrle (W)	7.0	8	4	4	0	1	2
Jenks (S)	2.0	1	0	0	0	1	0

E—Graffanino. DP—Boston 2. LOB—Boston 7, Chi White Sox 3. Scoring Position—Boston 2 for 7, Chi White Sox 2 for 4. 2B—Renteria, D.Ortiz, Graffanino, Rowand. HR—Iguchi (5th inning, 2 out, 2 on) off D.Wells.T—2:29. A—40,799. U—HP-Miller, 1B-Wegner, 2B-Scott, 3B-Everitt,LF-Iassogna, RF-Hirschbeck.

HOW THEY SCORED

TOP OF 1
Red Sox first. Damon singled to left. Renteria doubled to left, Damon to third. Ortiz struck out. M.Ramirez singled to left, Damon scored, Renteria scored. Varitek grounded into fielder's choice, third baseman Crede to second baseman Iguchi, M.Ramirez out. Nixon grounded out, pitcher Buehrle to first baseman Konerko. Runs: 2, Hits: 3, Errors: 0

TOP OF 3
Red Sox third. Damon singled to left. Renteria flied out to center fielder Rowand. Ortiz doubled to left, Damon to third. M.Ramirez was intentionally walked. Varitek singled to right, Damon scored, Ortiz to third, M.Ramirez to second. Nixon grounded into fielder's choice, first baseman Konerko to shortstop Uribe, Ortiz scored, M.Ramirez to third, Varitek out. Mueller struck out. Runs: 2, Hits: 3, Errors: 0

BOTTOM OF 5
White Sox fifth. Everett singled to right. Rowand doubled to left, Everett scored. Pierzynski grounded out, second baseman Graffanino to first baseman Olerud, Rowand to third. Crede singled to center, Rowand scored. Uribe safe on Graffanino's error, Crede to third. Podsednik fouled out to third baseman Mueller. Iguchi homered to left on a 1-1 count, Crede scored, Uribe scored. Dye struck out. Runs: 5, Hits: 4, Errors: 1

GAME 3

CHICAGO 5, BOSTON 3
FRIDAY, OCTOBER 7, AT BOSTON

Chi White Sox	AB	R	H	BI	BB	SO	PO	A
Podsednik, lf	4	1	1	1	0	1	1	0
Iguchi, 2b	5	0	1	1	0	2	2	1
Dye, rf	3	1	1	0	1	1	1	0
Konerko, 1b	4	1	1	2	0	1	8	1
C.Everett, dh	3	0	0	0	0	0	0	0
Rowand, cf	4	0	2	0	0	1	1	0
Pierzynski, c	3	1	1	0	1	0	6	0
Crede, 3b	3	0	0	0	0	0	3	4
Uribe, ss	3	1	1	0	0	1	4	2
F.Garcia, p	0	0	0	0	0	0	0	1
D.Marte, p	0	0	0	0	0	0	0	0
O.Hernandez, p	0	0	0	0	0	0	1	0
Jenks, p	0	0	0	0	0	0	0	0
TOTALS	32	5	8	5	2	7	27	9

Boston	AB	R	H	BI	BB	SO	PO	A
Damon, cf	4	0	1	0	1	2	2	0
Renteria, ss	4	0	0	0	1	1	1	4
D.Ortiz, dh	4	1	1	1	0	1	0	0
M.Ramirez, lf	3	2	2	2	1	0	0	0
Nixon, rf	4	0	1	0	0	1	4	0
Mueller, 3b	3	0	0	0	1	0	0	2
Olerud, 1b	2	0	1	0	2	0	8	1
Al.Machado, pr	0	0	0	0	0	0	0	0
Millar, 1b	0	0	0	0	0	0	1	1
Mirabelli, c	2	0	0	0	0	0	5	1
Varitek, ph-c	2	0	0	0	0	1	2	0
Graffanino, 2b	4	0	1	0	0	0	3	3
Wakefield, p	0	0	0	0	0	0	1	1
Bradford, p	0	0	0	0	0	0	0	0
M.Myers, p	0	0	0	0	0	0	0	0
Papelbon, p	0	0	0	0	0	0	0	0
Timlin, p	0	0	0	0	0	0	0	0
TOTALS	32	3	7	3	6	6	27	13

				R	H	E	LOB
Chi White Sox	0 0 2	0 0 2	0 0 1—	5	8	0	6
Boston	0 0 0	2 0 1	0 0 0—	3	7	1	8

Chi White Sox	IP	H	R	ER	HR	BB	SO
F.Garcia (W)	5.0	5	3	3	3	4	1
D.Marte	0.0	1	0	0	0	2	0
O.Hernandez (HOLD)	3.0	1	0	0	0	0	4
Jenks (S)	1.0	0	0	0	0	0	1

Boston	IP	H	R	ER	HR	BB	SO
Wakefield (L)	5.1	6	4	4	1	1	4
Bradford	0.0	1	0	0	0	0	0
M.Myers	0.0	0	0	0	0	1	0
Papelbon	2.2	0	0	0	0	0	2
Timlin	1.0	1	1	1	0	0	1

F.Garcia pitched to 1 batter in the 6th. D.Marte pitched to 3 batters in the 6th. Bradford pitched to 1 batter in the 6th. M.Myers pitched to 1 batter in the 6th.

E—Timlin. DP—Chi White Sox 2, Boston 1. LOB—Chi White Sox 6, Boston 8. Scoring Position—Chi White Sox 2 for 9, Boston 0 for 5.2B—Podsednik, Rowand, Pierzynski, Uribe, Damon. HR—D.Ortiz (4th inning, 0 out, 0 on) off F.Garcia, M.Ramirez (4th inning, 0 out, 0 on) off F.Garcia, Konerko (6th inning, 0 out, 1 on) off Wakefield, M.Ramirez (6th inning, 0 out, 0 on) off F.Garcia. SB—Rowand, Pierzynski. CS—Podsednik. SH—Crede, Uribe. HBP—C.Everett by Wakefield, Podsednik by Wakefield. T—3:28. A—35,496. U—HP-Wegner, 1B-Scott, 2B-Everitt, 3B-Iassogna, LF-Hirschbeck, RF-Miller.

HOW THEY SCORED

TOP OF 3
White Sox third. Pierzynski lined out to right fielder Nixon. Crede

grounded out, shortstop Renteria to first baseman Olerud. Uribe doubled to center. Podsednik doubled to left, Uribe scored. Iguchi singled to center, Podsednik scored. Dye singled to right, Iguchi to third. Konerko flied out to right fielder Nixon. Runs: 2, Hits: 4, Errors: 0

BOTTOM OF 4

Red Sox fourth. Ortiz homered to center on a 1-1 count. M.Ramirez homered to right on a 2-2 count. Nixon flied out to right fielder Dye. Mueller popped out to shortstop Uribe. Olerud grounded out, shortstop Uribe to first baseman Konerko. Runs: 2, Hits: 2, Errors: 0

TOP OF 6

White Sox sixth. Dye walked. Konerko homered to left on a 1-1 count, Dye scored. Everett grounded out, first baseman Olerud to pitcher Wakefield. Bradford grounded. Rowand singled to center. Myers pitching.Rowand stole second. Pierzynski walked on a full count. Papelbon pitching. Crede fouled out to right fielder Nixon, Rowand to third. Pierzynski stole second. Uribe struck out. Runs:

2, Hits: 2, Errors: 0

BOTTOM OF 6

Red Sox sixth. M.Ramirez homered to left on a 0-1 count. Marte pitching. Nixon singled to right. Mueller walked on a full count, Nixon to second. Olerud walked, Nixon to third, Mueller to second. Varitek pinch-hitting for Mirabelli. Hernandez pitching. Varitek fouled out to first baseman Konerko. Graffanino popped out to shortstop Uribe. Damon struck out. Runs: 1, Hits: 2, Errors: 0

TOP OF 9

White Sox ninth. Millar in as first baseman. Timlin pitching. Pierzynski doubled to center. Crede sacrificed, first baseman Millar to second baseman Graffanino, Pierzynski to third. Uribe safe on sacrifice plus fielder's choice, Pierzynski scored. On Timlin's error on a pickoff attempt, Uribe to second. Podsednik grounded out, second baseman Graffanino to first baseman Millar, Uribe to third. Iguchi struck out. Runs: 1, Hits: 1, Errors: 1

STATISTICS

CHICAGO WHITE SOX'S BATTING AND FIELDING AVERAGES

Player, position	G	AB	R	H	TB	2B	3B	HR	RBI	BB	IBB	SO	Avg.	OBP	Slg.	PO	A	E	Avg.
Harris,2b-ph	1	1	0	1	1	0	0	0	1	0	0	0	1.000	1.000	1.000	1	0	0	1.000
Pierzynski,c	3	9	5	4	12	2	0	2	4	1	0	0	.444	.545	1.333	15	0	0	1.000
Rowand,cf	3	10	3	4	6	2	0	0	2	1	0	1	.400	.455	.600	8	0	0	1.000
Uribe,ss	3	10	4	4	8	1	0	1	4	0	0	2	.400	.400	.800	5	7	0	1.000
Everett,dh	3	11	2	3	3	0	0	0	0	0	0	0	.273	.333	.273	0	0	0	.000
Podsednik,lf	3	11	3	3	7	1	0	1	4	1	0	1	.273	.429	.636	4	0	0	1.000
Iguchi,2b	3	12	1	3	6	0	0	1	4	0	0	3	.250	.250	.500	6	10	0	1.000
Konerko,1b	3	12	3	3	9	0	0	2	4	0	0	1	.250	.250	.750	30	3	0	1.000
Dye,rf	3	10	1	2	2	0	0	0	0	1	0	2	.200	.333	.200	5	0	0	1.000
Crede,3b	3	9	2	1	1	0	0	0	1	1	0	1	.111	.200	.111	4	11	1	.938
Buehrle,p	1	0	0	0	0	0	0	0	0	0	0	0	.000	.000	.000	0	2	0	1.000
Contreras,p	1	0	0	0	0	0	0	0	0	0	0	0	.000	.000	.000	0	0	0	.000
Cotts,p	1	0	0	0	0	0	0	0	0	0	0	0	.000	.000	.000	0	0	0	.000
Garcia,p	1	0	0	0	0	0	0	0	0	0	0	0	.000	.000	.000	0	1	0	1.000
Hernandez,p	1	0	0	0	0	0	0	0	0	0	0	0	.000	.000	.000	1	0	0	1.000
Jenks,p	2	0	0	0	0	0	0	0	0	0	0	0	.000	.000	.000	1	1	0	1.000
Marte,p	1	0	0	0	0	0	0	0	0	0	0	0	.000	.000	.000	0	0	0	.000
Politte,p	1	0	0	0	0	0	0	0	0	0	0	0	.000	.000	.000	0	0	0	.000
Blum,1b-ph	1	1	0	0	0	0	0	0	0	0	0	0	.000	.000	.000	0	0	0	.000
Perez,rf-ph	1	1	0	0	0	0	0	0	0	0	0	0	.000	.000	.000	1	0	0	1.000
Totals	3	97	24	28	55	6	0	7	24	5	0	11	.289	.355	.567	81	35	1	.991

BOSTON RED SOX'S BATTING AND FIELDING AVERAGES

Player, position	G	AB	R	H	TB	2B	3B	HR	RBI	BB	IBB	SO	Avg.	OBP	Slg.	PO	A	E	Avg.
Ortiz,dh	3	12	2	4	9	2	0	1	1	0	0	3	.333	.333	.750	0	0	0	.000
Millar,1b	2	3	0	1	2	1	0	0	1	0	0	1	.333	.333	.667	10	1	0	1.000
Ramirez,lf	3	10	2	3	9	0	0	2	4	2	1	0	.300	.417	.900	2	0	0	1.000
Varitek,c-ph	3	10	1	3	3	0	0	0	1	0	0	2	.300	.300	.300	9	2	0	1.000
Olerud,ph-1b	3	7	0	2	3	1	0	0	0	2	0	0	.286	.444	.429	16	2	0	1.000
Nixon,rf	3	11	1	3	3	0	0	0	1	1	0	1	.273	.333	.273	6	0	0	1.000
Graffanino,2b	3	12	0	3	5	2	0	0	0	0	0	0	.250	.250	.417	10	9	1	.950
Damon,cf	3	13	2	3	4	1	0	0	0	1	0	4	.231	.286	.308	10	0	0	1.000
Renteria,ss	3	13	1	3	5	2	0	0	0	1	0	1	.231	.286	.385	2	9	0	1.000
Arroyo,p	1	0	0	0	0	0	0	0	0	0	0	0	.000	.000	.000	0	0	0	.000
Bradford,p	2	0	0	0	0	0	0	0	0	0	0	0	.000	.000	.000	0	2	0	1.000
Clement,p	1	0	0	0	0	0	0	0	0	0	0	0	.000	.000	.000	0	1	0	1.000
Cora,ss	1	0	0	0	0	0	0	0	0	0	0	0	.000	.000	.000	0	0	0	.000
Gonzalez,p	1	0	0	0	0	0	0	0	0	0	0	0	.000	.000	.000	0	1	0	1.000
Hyzdu,cf	1	0	0	0	0	0	0	0	0	0	0	0	.000	.000	.000	1	0	0	1.000
Machado,pr	1	0	0	0	0	0	0	0	0	0	0	0	.000	.000	.000	0	0	0	.000
Myers,p	1	0	0	0	0	0	0	0	0	0	0	0	.000	.000	.000	0	0	0	.000
Papelbon,p	2	0	0	0	0	0	0	0	0	0	0	0	.000	.000	.000	0	0	0	.000
Timlin,p	1	0	0	0	0	0	0	0	0	0	0	0	.000	.000	.000	0	0	1	.000
Wakefield,p	1	0	0	0	0	0	0	0	0	0	0	0	.000	.000	.000	1	1	0	1.000
Wells,p	1	0	0	0	0	0	0	0	0	0	0	0	.000	.000	.000	1	1	0	1.000

Player, position	G	AB	R	H	TB	2B	3B	HR	RBI	BB	IBB	SO	Avg.	OBP	Slg.	PO	A	E	Avg.
									BATTING								FIELDING		
Mirabelli,c 1	2	0	0	0	0	0	0	0	0	0	0	0	.000	.000	.000	5	1	0	1.000
Mueller,3b 3	11	0	0	0	0	0	0	0	0	1	0	2	.000	.083	.000	2	4	0	1.000
Totals 3	104	9	25	43	9	0	3	8	8	1	14	.240	.295	.413	75	34	2	.982

CHICAGO WHITE SOX'S PITCHING RECORDS

Pitcher	G	GS	CG	IP	H	R	ER	HR	BB	IBB	SO	HB	WP	W	L	Pct.	ERA
Hernandez 1	0	0	3.0	1	0	0	0	0	0	4	0	0	0	0	.000	0.00
Jenks 2	0	0	3.0	1	0	0	0	1	0	1	0	0	0	0	.000	0.00
Politte...............................1	0	0	1.0	1	0	0	0	0	0	0	0	0	0	0	.000	0.00
Cotts 1	0	0	0.1	0	0	0	0	0	0	0	0	0	0	0	.000	0.00
Contreras 1	1	0	7.2	8	2	2	0	0	0	6	0	1	1	0	1.000	2.35
Buehrle.............................1	1	0	7.0	8	4	4	0	1	1	2	0	0	1	0	1.000	5.14
Garcia...............................1	1	0	5.0	5	3	3	3	4	0	1	0	0	1	0	1.000	5.40
Marte 1	0	0	0.0	1	0	0	0	2	0	0	0	0	0	0	.000	-
Totals...............................3	3	0	27.0	25	9	9	3	8	1	14	0	1	3	0	1.000	3.00

No shutouts. Saves—Jenks 2.

BOSTON RED SOX'S PITCHING RECORDS

Pitcher	G	GS	CG	IP	H	R	ER	HR	BB	IBB	SO	HB	WP	W	L	Pct.	ERA
Papelbon 2	0	0	4.0	2	0	0	0	0	0	2	0	0	0	0	.000	0.00
Bradford 2	0	0	1.1	1	0	0	0	0	0	1	0	0	0	0	.000	0.00
Wells 1	1	0	6.2	7	5	2	1	0	0	2	0	0	0	1	.000	2.70
Wakefield 1	1	0	5.1	6	4	4	1	1	0	4	2	0	0	1	.000	6.75
Timlin 1	0	0	1.0	1	1	1	0	0	0	1	0	0	0	0	.000	9.00
Gonzalez...........................1	0	0	2.1	2	4	4	1	1	0	0	1	0	0	0	.000	15.43
Arroyo 1	0	0	1.0	2	2	2	1	2	0	1	0	0	0	0	.000	18.00
Clement 1	1	0	3.1	7	8	8	3	0	0	0	2	0	0	1	.000	21.60
Myers...............................1	0	0	0.0	0	0	0	0	1	0	0	0	0	0	0	.000	-
Totals...............................3	3	0	25.0	28	24	21	7	5	0	11	5	0	0	3	.000	7.56

No shutouts or saves.

SCORE BY INNINGS

Chicago...5	0	3		2	5	6		0	2	1— 24
Boston...2	0	2		4	0	1		0	0	0— 9

MISCELLANEOUS STATISTICS

Sacrifice hits —Crede, Iguchi, Uribe.
Sacrifice flies —None.
Stolen bases —Pierzynski, Podsednik, Rowand.
Caught stealing —Podsednik 2.
Double plays —Crede (unassisted); Garcia, Uribe and Konerko; Mueller, Graffanino and Olerud; Renteria and Olerud; Renteria,
    Graffanino and Olerud.
Left on bases —Chicago 2, 3, 6—11; Boston 7, 7, 8—22.
Scoring position —Chicago 6 for 11, 2 for 4, 2 for 9—10 for 24; Boston 2 for 12, 2 for 7, 0 for 5—4 for 24.
Hit by pitcher —by Wakefield 2 (Everett, Podsednik), by Clement 2 (Dye, Podsednik), by Gonzalez (Pierzynski).
Passed balls —None.
Balks —None.
Time of games —2:56, 3:28, 2:29—Avg.: 2:57.
Attendance —40,717, 35,496, 40,799—117,012.
Umpires —Hirschbeck, John; Miller, Bill; Wegner, Mark; Carlson, Mark; Scott, Dale; Everitt, Mike; and Iassogna, Dan.

LOS ANGELES VS. NEW YORK

RESULTS

Day	Date	Place	Score
TUE.	OCT. 4	ANAHEIM	NEW YORK 4, LOS ANGELES 2
WED.	OCT. 5	ANAHEIM	LOS ANGELES 5, NEW YORK 3
FRI.	OCT. 7	NEW YORK	LOS ANGELES 11, NEW YORK 7
SUN.	OCT. 9	NEW YORK	NEW YORK 3, LOS ANGELES 2
MON.	OCT. 10	ANAHEIM	LOS ANGELES 5, NEW YORK 3

BOX SCORES

GAME 1

NEW YORK 4, LOS ANGELES 2

TUESDAY, OCTOBER 4, AT ANAHEIM

NY Yankees	AB	R	H	BI	BB	SO	PO	A
Jeter, ss 3	1	2	0	1	0	1	2
A.Rodriguez, 3b 3	0	0	0	0	2	3	1

NY Yankees	AB	R	H	BI	BB	SO	PO	A
Ja.Giambi, 1b 4	1	2	1	0	1	7	0
T.Martinez, 1b 0	0	0	0	0	0	1	0
Sheffield, rf 4	1	2	0	0	1	2	0
H.Matsui, lf 4	1	1	0	0	1	3	0
Cano, 2b 4	0	1	3	0	0	1	4
Posada, c 4	0	0	0	0	0	6	1
B.Williams, dh 4	0	1	0	0	1	0	0
Bu.Crosby, cf 4	0	0	0	0	1	3	0
Mussina, p 0	0	0	0	0	0	0	1
Leiter, p 0	0	0	0	0	0	0	0
Sturtze, p 0	0	0	0	0	0	0	0
Gordon, p 0	0	0	0	0	0	0	0
M.Rivera, p 0	0	0	0	0	0	0	0
TOTALS.....................................34	4	9	4	1	7	27	9

Los Angeles	AB	R	H	BI	BB	SO	PO	A
Figgins, 3b 4	0	0	0	0	2	0	2
O.Cabrera, ss 4	0	1	0	0	0	2	1

Los Angeles	AB	R	H	BI	BB	SO	PO	A
G.Anderson, lf	4	0	0	0	0	0	6	0
V.Guerrero, rf	3	1	1	0	1	0	1	0
Erstad, 1b	4	0	1	1	0	3	6	0
B.Molina, c	4	1	1	1	0	0	7	0
Paul, pr	0	0	0	0	0	0	0	0
J.Rivera, dh	3	0	2	0	0	0	0	0
Kotchman, ph	1	0	0	0	0	0	0	0
Finley, cf	3	0	1	0	0	1	3	0
A.Kennedy, 2b	3	0	0	0	0	0	2	4
B.Colon, p	0	0	0	0	0	0	0	0
Shields, p	0	0	0	0	0	0	0	0
TOTALS	33	2	7	2	1	6	27	7

NY Yankees	AB	R	H	BI	BB	SO	PO	A
A.Rodriguez, 3b	2	1	0	0	3	0	1	3
Ja.Giambi, dh	3	0	1	0	1	1	0	0
Sheffield, rf	4	0	0	1	0	0	2	0
H.Matsui, lf	4	1	1	0	0	0	1	0
Cano, 2b	4	0	1	1	0	0	0	8
B.Williams, cf	4	0	1	0	0	1	2	0
Posada, c	3	1	2	1	1	0	1	2
T.Martinez, 1b	3	0	0	0	1	1	14	0
Wang, p	0	0	0	0	0	0	0	1
Leiter, p	0	0	0	0	0	0	0	0
Proctor, p	0	0	0	0	0	0	0	0
TOTALS	32	3	6	3	6	5	24	16

					R	H	E	LOB
NY Yankees	3 1 0	0 0 0	0 0 0—		4	9	0	5
Los Angeles	0 0 0	0 0 0	1 0 1—		2	7	0	5

NY Yankees	IP	H	R	ER	HR	BB	SO
Mussina (W)	5.2	5	0	0	0	0	4
Leiter	0.2	0	0	0	0	0	0
Sturtze	0.1	1	1	1	1	0	0
Gordon (HOLD)	1.1	0	0	0	0	0	1
M.Rivera (S)	1.0	1	1	1	0	1	0

Los Angeles	IP	H	R	ER	HR	BB	SO
B.Colon (L)	7.0	8	4	4	0	1	6
Shields	2.0	1	0	0	0	0	1

DP—Los Angeles 2. LOB—NY Yankees 5, Los Angeles 5. Scoring Position—NY Yankees 3 for 7, Los Angeles 1 for 3. 2B—Ja.Giambi, Cano, B.Williams, Finley. HR—B.Molina (7th inning, 1 out, 0 on) off Sturtze. SB—Jeter, V.Guerrero. CS—V.Guerrero. HBP—A.Rodriguez by B.Colon. T—2:59. A—45,142. U—HP-Darling, 1B-Meals, 2B-Cousins, 3B-Marquez, LF-West, RF-Reynolds.

HOW THEY SCORED

TOP OF 1

Yankees first. Jeter grounded out, third baseman Figgins to first baseman Erstad. A.Rodriguez struck out. Giambi singled to right. Sheffield singled to right, Giambi to second. Matsui singled to right, Giambi to third, Sheffield to second. Cano doubled to left, Giambi scored, Sheffield scored, Matsui scored. Posada grounded out, second baseman Kennedy to first baseman Erstad. Runs: 3, Hits: 4, Errors: 0

TOP OF 2

Yankees second. Williams struck out. Crosby struck out. Jeter singled to right. A.Rodriguez was hit by a pitch, Jeter to second. Giambi doubled to right, Jeter scored, A.Rodriguez to third. Sheffield struck out. Runs: 1, Hits: 2, Errors: 0

BOTTOM OF 7

Angels seventh. Erstad struck out. Sturtze pitching. B.Molina homered to center on a 1-1 count. Rivera grounded out, third baseman A.Rodriguez to first baseman Giambi. Gordon pitching. Finley flied out to right fielder Sheffield. Runs: 1, Hits: 1, Errors: 0

BOTTOM OF 9

Angels ninth. M.Rivera pitching. Anderson flied out to center fielder Crosby. Guerrero walked on a full count. Guerrero stole second. Erstad infield single to second, Guerrero scored. B.Molina grounded into fielder's choice, shortstop Jeter to second baseman Cano, Erstad out. Paul pinch-running for B.Molina. Kotchman pinch-hitting for Rivera. Kotchman popped out to third baseman A.Rodriguez. Runs: 1, Hits: 1, Errors: 0

GAME 2

LOS ANGELES 5, NEW YORK 3
WEDNESDAY, OCTOBER 5, AT ANAHEIM

NY Yankees	AB	R	H	BI	BB	SO	PO	A
Jeter, ss	5	0	0	0	0	2	3	2

Los Angeles	AB	R	H	BI	BB	SO	PO	A
Figgins, 3b	4	0	0	0	0	1	0	5
O.Cabrera, ss	4	1	1	2	0	0	5	1
G.Anderson, lf	4	0	0	0	0	0	2	0
V.Guerrero, rf	3	0	0	0	0	0	0	0
B.Molina, c	4	1	2	2	0	0	5	1
Erstad, 1b	4	0	1	0	0	0	10	1
J.Rivera, dh	3	1	2	1	0	0	0	0
DaVanon, pr-dh	0	1	0	0	0	0	0	0
Quinlan, ph	0	0	0	0	0	0	0	0
Kotchman, ph-dh	1	0	0	0	0	0	0	0
Finley, cf	2	1	0	0	0	0	2	0
A.Kennedy, 2b	2	0	1	0	0	0	1	6
Lackey, p	0	0	0	0	0	0	2	2
Shields, p	0	0	0	0	0	0	0	0
K.Escobar, p	0	0	0	0	0	0	0	0
F.Rodriguez, p	0	0	0	0	0	0	0	0
TOTALS	31	5	7	5	0	1	27	16

					R	H	E	LOB
NY Yankees	0 1 0	0 1 0	0 0 1—		3	6	3	8
Los Angeles	0 0 0	0 1 1	2 1 x—		5	7	0	5

NY Yankees	IP	H	R	ER	HR	BB	SO
Wang (L)	6.2	6	4	1	1	0	1
Leiter	1.0	1	1	1	1	0	0
Proctor	0.1	0	0	0	0	0	0

Los Angeles	IP	H	R	ER	HR	BB	SO
Lackey	5.2	5	2	2	0	5	3
Shields	0.1	0	0	0	0	0	0
K.Escobar (W)	2.0	0	0	0	0	1	1
F.Rodriguez (S)	1.0	1	1	1	1	0	1

E—Wang, Cano, A.Rodriguez. LOB—NY Yankees 8, Los Angeles 5. Scoring Position—NY Yankees 1 for 9, Los Angeles 2 for 5. 2B—Ja.Giambi, H.Matsui, Cano, B.Williams. HR—J.Rivera (5th inning, 0 out, 0 on) off Wang, B.Molina (8th inning, 1 out, 0 on) off Leiter, Posada (9th inning, 0 out, 0 on) off F.Rodriguez. SB—A.Rodriguez. CS—A.Rodriguez, A.Kennedy. SH—Finley, A.Kennedy. WP—Lackey. HBP—V.Guerrero by Wang. T—3:05. A—45,150. U—HP-Meals, 1B-Cousins, 2B-Marquez, 3B-West, LF-Reynolds, RF-Darling.

HOW THEY SCORED

TOP OF 2

Yankees second. Sheffield flied out to center fielder Finley. Matsui doubled to center. Cano doubled to left, Matsui scored. Williams struck out. Posada walked on a full count. Martinez grounded out, pitcher Lackey to first baseman Erstad. Runs: 1, Hits: 2, Errors: 0

TOP OF 5

Yankees fifth. Jeter struck out. A.Rodriguez walked on a full count. Giambi doubled to center, A.Rodriguez to third. Sheffield grounded out, third baseman Figgins to first baseman Erstad, A.Rodriguez scored. On Lackey's wild pitch, Giambi to third. Matsui grounded out, third baseman Figgins to first baseman Erstad. Runs: 1, Hits: 1, Errors: 0

BOTTOM OF 5

Angels fifth. Rivera homered to center on a full count. Finley grounded out, first baseman Martinez unassisted. Kennedy grounded out, third baseman A.Rodriguez to first baseman Martinez. Figgins grounded out, second baseman Cano to first baseman Martinez. Runs: 1, Hits: 1, Errors: 0

BOTTOM OF 6

Angels sixth. Cabrera safe on A.Rodriguez's error. Anderson popped out to shortstop Jeter. Guerrero grounded out, third baseman A.Rodriguez to first baseman Martinez, Cabrera to second. B.Molina singled to center, Cabrera scored. Erstad grounded out, second baseman Cano to first baseman Martinez. Runs: 1, Hits: 1, Errors: 1

BOTTOM OF 7

Angels seventh. Rivera infield single to short. DaVanon pinch-running for Rivera. Finley safe on a sacrifice plus pitcher Wang's throwing error. DaVanon to second. Kennedy sacrificed, pitcher Wang to first baseman Martinez, DaVanon to third, Finley to second. Figgins popped out to center fielder Williams. Cabrera singled to center, DaVanon scored, Finley scored. Leiter pitching. Anderson popped out to right fielder Sheffield. Runs: 2, Hits: 2, Errors: 1

BOTTOM OF 8

Angels eighth. Guerrero flied out to left fielder Matsui. B.Molina homered to left on a 2-2 count. Erstad popped out to third baseman A.Rodriguez. Quinlan pinch-hitting for DaVanon. Proctor pitching. Kotchman pinch-hitting for Quinlan. Kotchman grounded out, second baseman Cano to first baseman Martinez. Runs: 1, Hits: 1, Errors: 0

TOP OF 9

Yankees ninth. Kotchman in as designated hitter. Rodriguez pitching. Posada homered to center on a 1-0 count. Martinez struck out. Jeter grounded out, shortstop Cabrera to first baseman Erstad. A.Rodriguez grounded out, third baseman Figgins to first baseman Erstad. Runs: 1, Hits: 1, Errors: 0

GAME 3

LOS ANGELES 11, NEW YORK 7

FRIDAY, OCTOBER 7, AT NEW YORK

Los Angeles	AB	R	H	BI	BB	SO	PO	A
Figgins, cf-3b	6	1	2	1	0	1	2	0
O.Cabrera, ss	5	1	1	0	0	0	1	1
V.Guerrero, rf	4	3	2	0	1	0	0	0
B.Molina, c	3	2	2	2	0	0	6	0
J.Molina, pr-c	1	1	1	1	0	0	3	0
G.Anderson, lf	5	1	4	5	0	0	4	0
J.Rivera, dh	5	1	1	0	0	2	0	0
Erstad, 1b	5	1	3	1	0	1	8	0
Quinlan, 3b	2	0	1	0	0	0	0	1
Finley, ph-cf	2	0	0	1	0	1	2	0
A.Kennedy, 2b	5	0	2	0	0	1	1	4
P.Byrd, p	0	0	0	0	0	0	0	0
Donnelly, p	0	0	0	0	0	0	0	0
Shields, p	0	0	0	0	0	0	0	0
K.Escobar, p	0	0	0	0	0	0	0	0
F.Rodriguez, p	0	0	0	0	0	0	0	0
TOTALS	43	11	19	11	1	6	27	6

NY Yankees	AB	R	H	BI	BB	SO	PO	A
Jeter, ss	5	2	2	2	0	2	1	3
A.Rodriguez, 3b	4	0	2	0	1	1	0	3
Ja.Giambi, dh	5	0	2	1	0	1	0	0
Sheffield, rf	4	0	0	0	1	1	3	0
H.Matsui, lf	3	2	2	1	2	0	3	0
Cano, 2b	5	2	2	1	0	0	4	2
B.Williams, cf	4	1	2	1	0	0	3	0
T.Martinez, 1b	4	0	0	0	0	1	7	0

NY Yankees	AB	R	H	BI	BB	SO	PO	A
Sierra, ph	1	0	0	0	0	1	0	0
Flaherty, c	0	0	0	0	1	0	3	1
Posada, ph-c	3	0	0	1	0	2	3	0
R.Johnson, p	0	0	0	0	0	0	0	0
Small, p	0	0	0	0	0	0	0	0
Sturtze, p	0	0	0	0	0	0	0	0
Gordon, p	0	0	0	0	0	0	0	0
Leiter, p	0	0	0	0	0	0	0	0
Proctor, p	0	0	0	0	0	0	0	0
TOTALS	38	7	12	7	5	9	27	9

						R	H	E	LOB
Los Angeles	3 0 2	0 0 2	2 2 0	—		11	19	1	8
NY Yankees	0 0 0	4 2 0	0 1 0	—		7	12	2	10

Los Angeles	IP	H	R	ER	HR	BB	SO
P.Byrd	3.2	7	4	4	1	2	2
Donnelly	0.1	2	2	1	0	1	0
Shields (W)	2.0	1	0	0	0	2	4
K.Escobar (HOLD)	2.0	1	1	1	1	0	2
F.Rodriguez	1.0	1	0	0	0	0	1

NY Yankees	IP	H	R	ER	HR	BB	SO
R.Johnson	3.0	9	5	5	2	0	2
Small (L)	2.2	4	2	2	0	0	2
Sturtze	0.1	0	0	0	0	0	0
Gordon	0.0	2	2	1	0	0	0
Leiter	1.1	1	2	2	0	1	1
Proctor	1.2	3	0	0	0	0	1

Donnelly pitched to 2 batters in the 5th. R.Johnson pitched to 2 batters in the 4th. Gordon pitched to 4 batters in the 7th.

E—O.Cabrera, Cano, Sheffield. DP—NY Yankees 2. LOB—Los Angeles 8, NY Yankees 10. Scoring Position—Los Angeles 8 for 21, NY Yankees 2 for 10. 2B—O.Cabrera, J.Rivera, Erstad, A.Rodriguez, Cano. 3B—Figgins, G.Anderson. HR—G.Anderson (1st inning, 2 out, 2 on) off R.Johnson, B.Molina (3rd inning, 2 out, 1 on) off R.Johnson, H.Matsui (4th inning, 0 out, 0 on) off P.Byrd, Jeter (8th inning, 0 out, 0 on) off K.Escobar. CS—A.Kennedy. S—B.Williams. SH—Finley. WP—Proctor. HBP—B.Molina by Gordon. T—4:00. A—56,277. U—HP-Cousins, 1B-Marquez, 2B-West, 3B-Reynolds, LF-Darling, RF-Meals.

HOW THEY SCORED

TOP OF 1

Angels first. Figgins flied out to right fielder Sheffield. Cabrera flied out to center fielder Williams. Guerrero singled to right. B.Molina singled to center, Guerrero to third. Anderson homered to center on a 1-1 count, Guerrero scored, B.Molina scored. Rivera struck out. Runs: 3, Hits: 3, Errors: 0

TOP OF 3

Angels third. Figgins flied out to left fielder Matsui. Cabrera doubled to right. Guerrero grounded out, shortstop Jeter to first baseman Martinez. B.Molina homered to left on the first pitch, Cabrera scored. Anderson tripled to right. Rivera struck out. Runs: 2, Hits: 3, Errors: 0

BOTTOM OF 4

Yankees fourth. Matsui homered to left on a 2-1 count. Cano infield single to second. Williams singled to right, Cano to second. Martinez grounded out, first baseman Erstad unassisted, Cano to third, Williams to second. Posada pinch-hitting for Flaherty. Posada grounded out, first baseman Erstad unassisted, Cano scored, Williams to third. Jeter singled to right, Williams scored. A.Rodriguez walked on a full count, Jeter to second. Donnelly pitching. Giambi singled to center, Jeter scored, A.Rodriguez to third. Sheffield lined out to center fielder Figgins. Runs: 4, Hits: 5, Errors: 0

BOTTOM OF 5

Yankees fifth. Matsui walked on a full count. Cano doubled to center, Matsui scored. On Cabrera's error, Cano to third. Shields pitching. Williams hit a sacrifice fly to left fielder Anderson, Cano scored. Martinez struck out. Posada struck out. Runs: 2, Hits: 1, Errors: 1

TOP OF 6
Angels sixth. Anderson flied out to right fielder Sheffield. Rivera doubled to left. Erstad singled to right, Rivera scored. Finley pinch-hitting for Quinlan. Finley struck out. Kennedy singled to center, Erstad to third. Figgins singled to center, Erstad scored, Kennedy to third. Sturtze pitching. Cabrera flied out to right fielder Sheffield. Runs: 2, Hits: 4, Errors: 0

TOP OF 7
Angels seventh. Gordon pitching. Guerrero singled to left. B.Molina was hit by a pitch, Guerrero to second. J.Molina pinch-running for B.Molina. Anderson singled to right, Guerrero scored, J.Molina to second. On Sheffield's error, J.Molina to third. Rivera safe on fielder's choice and Cano's error, Anderson to second. Leiter pitching. Erstad struck out. Finley sacrificed, first baseman Martinez unassisted, J.Molina scored, Anderson to third, Rivera to second. Kennedy flied out to left fielder Matsui. Runs: 2, Hits: 2, Errors: 2

TOP OF 8
Angels eighth. Figgins tripled to left. Cabrera popped out to center fielder Williams. Guerrero was intentionally walked. Proctor pitching. J.Molina singled to center, Figgins scored, Guerrero to third. Anderson singled to right, Guerrero scored, J.Molina to second. Rivera lined into a double play, second baseman Cano unassisted, J.Molina out. Runs: 2, Hits: 3, Errors: 0

BOTTOM OF 8
Yankees eighth. Jeter homered to right on a 0-2 count. A.Rodriguez grounded out, shortstop Cabrera to first baseman Erstad. Giambi grounded out, first baseman Erstad unassisted. Sheffield struck out. Runs: 1, Hits: 1, Errors: 0

GAME 4

NEW YORK 3, LOS ANGELES 2

SUNDAY, OCTOBER 9, AT NEW YORK

Los Angeles	AB	R	H	BI	BB	SO	PO	A
Figgins, 3b	4	1	1	1	0	1	0	0
O.Cabrera, ss	4	0	1	1	0	1	2	1
V.Guerrero, rf	4	0	1	0	0	2	0	0
G.Anderson, lf	3	0	0	0	0	0	2	0
B.Molina, c	3	0	1	0	0	0	7	1
Erstad, 1b	3	0	0	0	0	1	9	1
J.Rivera, dh	2	1	0	0	1	0	0	0
Finley, cf	2	0	0	0	0	1	3	0
A.Kennedy, 2b	3	0	0	0	0	1	1	1
Lackey, p	0	0	0	0	0	0	0	3
Shields, p	0	0	0	0	0	0	0	0
K.Escobar, p	0	0	0	0	0	0	0	0
TOTALS	28	2	4	2	1	7	24	7

NY Yankees	AB	R	H	BI	BB	SO	PO	A
Jeter, ss	4	0	0	1	0	1	2	2
A.Rodriguez, 3b	2	1	0	0	2	1	0	2
Ja.Giambi, 1b	2	0	0	0	2	1	6	1
M.Rivera, p	0	0	0	0	0	0	0	1
Sheffield, rf	4	0	1	1	0	1	1	0
H.Matsui, lf	4	0	0	0	0	1	1	0
Cano, 2b	3	1	1	0	1	2	3	5
B.Williams, dh-cf	4	0	0	0	0	1	0	0
Posada, c	1	1	1	0	3	0	7	2
Bu.Crosby, cf	1	0	0	0	0	0	3	0
Sierra, ph	1	0	1	1	0	0	0	0
Womack, pr	0	0	0	0	0	0	0	0
T.Martinez, 1b	1	0	0	0	0	0	4	0

NY Yankees	AB	R	H	BI	BB	SO	PO	A
Chacon, p	0	0	0	0	0	0	0	0
Leiter, p	0	0	0	0	0	0	0	0
TOTALS	27	3	4	3	8	7	27	13

			R	H	E	LOB
Los Angeles	0 0 0	0 0 2	0 0 0—	2	4	0	1
NY Yankees	0 0 0	0 0 1	2 0 x—	3	4	1	9

Los Angeles	IP	H	R	ER	HR	BB	SO
Lackey	5.2	2	1	1	0	4	6
Shields (BS, L)	0.2	2	2	2	0	1	0
K.Escobar	1.2	0	0	0	0	3	1

NY Yankees	IP	H	R	ER	HR	BB	SO
Chacon	6.1	4	2	2	0	1	5
Leiter (W)	0.2	0	0	0	0	0	0
M.Rivera (S)	2.0	0	0	0	0	0	2

E—H.Matsui. DP—Los Angeles 1, NY Yankees 1. LOB—Los Angeles 1, NY Yankees 9. Scoring Position—Los Angeles 2 for 4, NY Yankees 2 for 9. 2B—Figgins, O.Cabrera, Posada. CS—Figgins. SH—Finley, Bu.Crosby. WP—Lackey, K.Escobar 2. T—3:13. A—56,226. U—HP-Marquez, 1B-West, 2B-Reynolds, 3B-Darling, LF-Meals, RF-Cousins.

HOW THEY SCORED

TOP OF 6
Angels sixth. Rivera walked on four pitches. Finley sacrificed, first baseman Giambi to second baseman Cano, Rivera to second. Kennedy grounded out, second baseman Cano to first baseman Giambi, Rivera to third. Figgins doubled to right, Rivera scored. Cabrera doubled to right, Figgins scored. Guerrero struck out. Runs: 2, Hits: 2, Errors: 0

BOTTOM OF 6
Yankees sixth. Jeter grounded out, shortstop Cabrera to first baseman Erstad. A.Rodriguez walked on a full count. Giambi grounded out, second baseman Kennedy to first baseman Erstad, A.Rodriguez to second. Sheffield singled to left, A.Rodriguez scored. Shields pitching. Matsui grounded out, first baseman Erstad unassisted. Runs: 1, Hits: 1, Errors: 0

BOTTOM OF 7
Yankees seventh. Cano infield single to short. Williams flied out to center fielder Finley. Posada walked on a full count, Cano to second. Sierra pinch-hitting for Crosby. Sierra singled to right, Cano scored, Posada to third. Jeter safe on failed fielder's choice, Posada scored, Sierra to second. Escobar pitching. Womack pinch-running for Sierra. A.Rodriguez walked on a full count, Womack to third, Jeter to second. Giambi struck out. Sheffield flied out to center fielder Finley. Runs: 2, Hits: 2, Errors: 0

GAME 5

LOS ANGELES 5, NEW YORK 3

MONDAY, OCTOBER 10, AT ANAHEIM

NY Yankees	AB	R	H	BI	BB	SO	PO	A
Jeter, ss	4	1	3	2	0	0	1	4
A.Rodriguez, 3b	4	0	0	0	1	0	0	1
Ja.Giambi, 1b	5	0	3	0	0	0	8	1
Bellhorn, pr	0	0	0	0	0	0	0	0
Sheffield, rf	5	0	3	0	0	0	1	0
Womack, pr	0	0	0	0	0	0	0	0
H.Matsui, lf-cf	5	0	0	0	1	2	0	0
Cano, 2b	3	0	0	0	1	2	3	2
B.Williams, dh	3	1	0	0	1	0	0	0
Posada, c	2	1	0	0	2	0	6	0
Bu.Crosby, cf	3	0	2	1	0	0	3	0

NY Yankees	AB	R	H	BI	BB	SO	PO	A
Sierra, ph-lf	1	0	0	0	0	0	0	0
Mussina, p	0	0	0	0	0	0	0	0
R.Johnson, p	0	0	0	0	0	0	0	0
Gordon, p	0	0	0	0	0	0	0	0
TOTALS	35	3	11	3	4	4	24	8

Los Angeles	AB	R	H	BI	BB	SO	PO	A
Figgins, 3b	3	0	0	0	1	3	0	1
O.Cabrera, ss	4	1	1	0	0	0	1	4
V.Guerrero, rf	4	1	2	0	0	0	3	0
G.Anderson, lf	3	1	1	2	0	0	4	0
B.Molina, c	4	1	2	0	0	0	3	3
Erstad, 1b	4	0	1	1	0	1	10	1
J.Rivera, dh	4	0	1	0	0	0	0	0
Finley, cf	2	1	0	0	1	1	2	0
A.Kennedy, 2b	4	0	1	2	0	1	3	3
B.Colon, p	0	0	0	0	0	0	0	0
E.Santana, p	0	0	0	0	0	0	0	0
K.Escobar, p	0	0	0	0	0	0	0	0
F.Rodriguez, p	0	0	0	0	0	0	1	0
TOTALS	32	5	9	5	2	6	27	12

					R	H	E	LOB
NY Yankees	0 2 0	0 0 0	1 0 0—		3	1	10	11
Los Angeles	0 3 2	0 0 0	0 0 x—		5	9	0	7

NY Yankees	IP	H	R	ER	HR	BB	SO
Mussina (L)	2.2	6	5	5	1	1	3
R.Johnson	4.1	3	0	0	0	1	2
Gordon	1.0	0	0	0	0	0	1

Los Angeles	IP	H	R	ER	HR	BB	SO
B.Colon	1.0	2	0	0	0	1	1
E.Santana (W)	5.1	5	3	3	1	2	2
K.Escobar (HOLD)	1.1	1	0	0	0	1	1
F.Rodriguez (S)	1.1	3	0	0	0	0	0

B.Colon pitched to 1 batter in the 2nd.

DP—Los Angeles 1. LOB—NY Yankees 11, Los Angeles 7. Scoring Position—NY Yankees 2 for 10, Los Angeles 2 for 8. 2B—Ja.Giambi, Erstad. 3B—A.Kennedy. HR—G.Anderson (2nd inning, 0 out, 0 on) off Mussina, Jeter (7th inning, 0 out, 0 on) off E.Santana. SB—Bu.Crosby. CS—Cano. S—Jeter, G.Anderson. SH—Finley. HBP—A.Rodriguez by E.Santana. T—3:29. A—45,133. U—HP-West, 1B-Reynolds, 2B-Darling, 3B-Meals, LF-Cousins, RF-Marquez.

HOW THEY SCORED

TOP OF 2
Yankees second. Santana pitching. Cano walked on a full count. Cano was caught stealing, catcher B.Molina to shortstop Cabrera, Cano out. Williams walked on a full count. Posada walked on four pitches, Williams to second. Crosby singled to right, Williams scored, Posada to third. Jeter hit a sacrifice fly to right fielder Guerrero, Posada scored. Crosby stole second. A.Rodriguez struck out. Runs: 2, Hits: 1, Errors: 0

BOTTOM OF 2
Angels second. Anderson homered to right on a 3-1 count. B.Molina singled to center. Rivera struck out. Rivera popped out to second baseman Cano. Finley walked on a full count, B.Molina to second. Kennedy tripled to center, B.Molina scored, Finley scored. Figgins struck out. Runs: 3, Hits: 3, Errors: 0

BOTTOM OF 3
Angels third. Cabrera singled to left. Guerrero singled to center, Cabrera to third. Anderson hit a sacrifice fly to center fielder Crosby, Cabrera scored. B.Molina singled to right, Guerrero to third. Erstad safe on failed fielder's choice, Guerrero scored, B.Molina to second. Rivera fouled out to left fielder Matsui. Ra.Johnson pitching. Finley grounded out, second baseman Cano to first baseman Giambi. Runs: 2, Hits: 3, Errors: 0

TOP OF 7
Yankees seventh. Jeter homered to center on a 0-1 count. A.Rodriguez grounded out, shortstop Cabrera to first baseman Erstad. Escobar pitching. Giambi doubled to center. Sheffield flied out to right fielder Guerrero. Matsui fouled out to catcher B.Molina. Runs: 1, Hits: 2, Errors: 0

STATISTICS

LOS ANGELES ANGELS' BATTING AND FIELDING AVERAGES

Player, position	G	AB	R	H	TB	2B	3B	HR	RBI	BB	IBB	SO	Avg.	OBP	Slg.	PO	A	E	Avg.
Molina,c-pr	1	1	1	1	1	0	0	0	1	0	0	0	1.000	1.000	1.000	3	0	0	1.000
Quinlan,3b	2	2	0	1	1	0	0	0	0	0	0	0	.500	.500	.500	0	1	0	1.000
Molina,c	5	18	5	8	17	0	0	3	5	0	0	0	.444	.474	.944	28	5	0	1.000
Rivera,dh	5	17	3	6	10	1	0	1	1	1	0	2	.353	.389	.588	0	0	0	.000
Guerrero,rf	5	18	5	6	6	0	0	0	0	2	1	2	.333	.429	.333	4	0	0	1.000
Erstad,1b	5	20	1	6	8	2	0	0	3	0	0	6	.300	.300	.400	43	3	0	1.000
Anderson,lf	5	19	2	5	13	0	1	2	7	0	0	0	.263	.250	.684	18	0	0	1.000
Cabrera,ss	5	21	3	5	7	2	0	0	3	0	0	1	.238	.238	.333	11	8	1	.950
Kennedy,2b	5	17	0	4	6	0	1	0	2	0	0	3	.235	.235	.353	8	18	0	1.000
Figgins,3b-cf	5	21	2	3	6	1	1	0	2	1	0	8	.143	.182	.286	2	8	0	1.000
Finley,cf-ph	5	11	2	1	2	1	0	0	1	1	0	4	.091	.167	.182	12	0	0	1.000
Byrd,p	1	0	0	0	0	0	0	0	0	0	0	0	.000	.000	.000	0	0	0	.000
Colon,p	2	0	0	0	0	0	0	0	0	0	0	0	.000	.000	.000	0	0	0	.000
DaVanon,dh-pr	1	0	1	0	0	0	0	0	0	0	0	0	.000	.000	.000	0	0	0	.000
Donnelly,p	1	0	0	0	0	0	0	0	0	0	0	0	.000	.000	.000	0	0	0	.000
Escobar,p	4	0	0	0	0	0	0	0	0	0	0	0	.000	.000	.000	0	0	0	.000
Lackey,p	2	0	0	0	0	0	0	0	0	0	0	0	.000	.000	.000	2	5	0	1.000
Paul,pr	1	0	0	0	0	0	0	0	0	0	0	0	.000	.000	.000	0	0	0	.000
Rodriguez,p	3	0	0	0	0	0	0	0	0	0	0	0	.000	.000	.000	1	0	0	1.000
Santana,p	1	0	0	0	0	0	0	0	0	0	0	0	.000	.000	.000	0	0	0	.000
Shields,p	4	0	0	0	0	0	0	0	0	0	0	0	.000	.000	.000	0	0	0	.000
Kotchman,dh	2	2	0	0	0	0	0	0	0	0	0	0	.000	.000	.000	0	0	0	.000
Totals	5	167	25	46	77	7	3	6	25	5	1	26	.275	.303	.461	132	48	1	.994

NEW YORK YANKEES' BATTING AND FIELDING AVERAGES

Player, position	G	AB	R	H	TB	2B	3B	HR	RBI	BB	IBB	SO	Avg.	OBP	Slg.	PO	A	E	Avg.
Giambi,1b-dh	5	19	1	8	11	3	0	0	2	3	0	4	.421	.500	.579	21	2	0	1.000
Jeter,ss	5	21	4	7	13	0	0	2	5	1	0	5	.333	.348	.619	8	13	0	1.000
Sierra,ph-lf	3	3	0	1	1	0	0	0	1	0	0	1	.333	.333	.333	0	0	0	.000
Sheffield,rf	5	21	1	6	6	0	0	0	2	1	0	2	.286	.318	.286	9	0	1	.900
Cano,2b	5	19	3	5	8	3	0	0	5	2	0	4	.263	.333	.421	11	21	2	.941
Crosby,cf	3	8	0	2	2	0	0	0	1	0	0	1	.250	.250	.250	9	0	0	1.000
Posada,c-ph	5	13	3	3	7	1	0	1	2	6	0	2	.231	.474	.538	23	5	0	1.000
Williams,dh-cf	5	19	2	4	6	2	0	0	1	1	0	3	.211	.238	.316	5	0	0	1.000
Matsui,lf-c	5	20	4	4	8	1	0	1	1	2	0	3	.200	.273	.400	10	0	1	.909
Rodriguez,3b	5	15	2	2	3	1	0	0	0	6	0	5	.133	.435	.200	4	10	1	.933
Bellhorn,pr	1	0	0	0	0	0	0	0	0	0	0	0	.000	.000	.000	0	0	0	.000
Chacon,p	1	0	0	0	0	0	0	0	0	0	0	0	.000	.000	.000	0	0	0	.000
Flaherty,c	1	0	0	0	0	0	0	0	0	1	0	0	.000	1.000	.000	3	1	0	1.000
Gordon,p	3	0	0	0	0	0	0	0	0	0	0	0	.000	.000	.000	0	0	0	.000
Johnson,p	2	0	0	0	0	0	0	0	0	0	0	0	.000	.000	.000	0	0	0	.000
Leiter,p	4	0	0	0	0	0	0	0	0	0	0	0	.000	.000	.000	0	0	0	.000
Mussina,p	2	0	0	0	0	0	0	0	0	0	0	0	.000	.000	.000	0	1	0	1.000
Proctor,p	2	0	0	0	0	0	0	0	0	0	0	0	.000	.000	.000	0	0	0	.000
Rivera,p	2	0	0	0	0	0	0	0	0	0	0	0	.000	.000	.000	0	1	0	1.000
Small,p	1	0	0	0	0	0	0	0	0	0	0	0	.000	.000	.000	0	0	0	.000
Sturtze,p	2	0	0	0	0	0	0	0	0	0	0	0	.000	.000	.000	0	0	0	.000
Wang,p	1	0	0	0	0	0	0	0	0	0	0	0	.000	.000	.000	0	1	1	.500
Womack,pr	2	0	0	0	0	0	0	0	0	0	0	0	.000	.000	.000	0	0	0	.000
Martinez,1b	4	8	0	0	0	0	0	0	0	0	1	0	2	.000	.111	.000	26	0	0	1.000
Totals	5	166	20	42	65	11	0	4	20	24	0	32	.253	.351	.392	129	55	6	.968

LOS ANGELES ANGELS' PITCHING RECORDS

Pitcher	G	GS	CG	IP	H	R	ER	HR	BB	IBB	SO	HB	WP	W	L	Pct.	ERA
Escobar	4	0	0	7.0	2	1	1	1	5	0	5	0	2	1	0	1.000	1.29
Lackey	2	2	0	11.1	7	3	3	0	9	0	9	0	2	0	0	.000	2.38
Rodriguez	3	0	0	3.1	5	1	1	1	0	0	2	0	0	0	0	.000	2.70
Shields	4	0	0	5.0	4	2	2	0	3	0	5	0	0	1	1	.500	3.60
Colon	2	2	0	8.0	10	4	4	0	2	0	7	1	0	0	1	.000	4.50
Santana	1	0	0	5.1	5	3	3	1	2	1	2	1	0	1	0	1.000	5.06
Byrd	1	1	0	3.2	7	4	4	1	2	0	2	0	0	0	0	.000	9.82
Donnelly	1	0	0	0.1	2	2	1	0	1	0	0	0	0	0	0	·000	27.00
Totals	5	5	0	44.0	42	20	19	4	24	0	32	2	4	3	2	.600	3.89

No shutouts. Saves_Rodriguez 2.

NEW YORK YANKEES' PITCHING RECORDS

Pitcher	G	GS	CG	IP	H	R	ER	HR	BB	IBB	SO	HB	WP	W	L	Pct.	ERA
Proctor	2	0	0	2.0	3	0	0	0	0	0	1	0	1	0	0	.000	0.00
Wang	1	1	0	6.2	6	4	1	1	0	0	1	1	0	0	1	.000	1.35
Chacon	1	1	0	6.1	4	2	2	0	1	0	5	0	0	0	0	.000	2.84
Rivera	2	0	0	3.0	1	1	1	0	1	0	2	0	0	0	0	.000	3.00
Gordon	3	0	0	2.1	2	2	1	0	0	0	2	1	0	0	0	.000	3.86
Mussina	2	2	0	8.1	11	5	5	1	1	0	7	0	0	1	1	.500	5.40
Johnson	2	1	0	7.1	12	5	5	2	1	0	4	0	0	0	0	.000	6.14
Small	1	0	0	2.2	4	2	2	0	0	0	2	0	0	0	1	.000	6.75
Leiter	4	0	0	3.2	2	3	3	1	1	1	2	0	0	1	0	1.000	7.36
Sturtze	2	0	0	0.2	1	1	1	1	0	0	0	0	0	0	0	.000	13.50
Totals	5	5	0	43.0	46	25	21	6	5	1	26	2	1	2	3	.400	4.40

No shutouts. Saves_Rivera 2.

SCORE BY INNINGS

Los Angeles	3	3	4	0	1	5	5	3	1	—25
New York	3	4	0	4	3	1	3	1	1	—20

MISCELLANEOUS STATISTICS

Sacrifice hits—Finley 4, Crosby, Kennedy.
Sacrifice flies—Anderson, Jeter, Williams.
Stolen bases—Crosby, Guerrero, Jeter, Rodriguez.
Caught stealing—Kennedy 2, Cano, Figgins, Guerrero, Rodriguez.
Double plays—Figgins, Kennedy and Erstad 2; Cano (unassisted); Cano, Jeter and Martinez; Erstad and Cabrera; Jeter, Cano and Giambi; Kennedy, Cabrera and Erstad.
Left on bases—Los Angeles 5, 5, 8, 1, 7—26; New York 5, 8, 10, 9, 11—43.
Scoring position—Los Angeles 1 for 3, 2 for 5, 8 for 21, 2 for 4, 2 for 8—15 for 41; New York 3 for 7, 1 for 9, 2 for 10, 2 for 9, 2 for 10—10 for 45.
Hit by pitcher—by Gordon (Molina), by Colon (Rodriguez), by Wang (Guerrero), by Santana (Rodriguez).
Passed balls—None.
Balks—None.
Time of games—2:59, 3:05, 4:00, 3:29, 3:13—Avg.: 3:21.
Attendance—45,142, 45,150, 56,277, 45,133, 56,226—247,928.
Umpires—Darling, Gary; Meals, Jerry; Cousins, Derryl; Marquez, Alfonso; West, Joe; and Reynolds, Jim.

ST. LOUIS VS. SAN DIEGO

RESULTS

Day	Date	Place	Score
TUE.	OCT. 4	ST. LOUIS	ST. LOUIS 8, SAN DIEGO 5
THU.	OCT. 6	ST. LOUIS	ST. LOUIS 6, SAN DIEGO 2
SAT.	OCT. 8	SAN DIEGO	ST. LOUIS 7, SAN DIEGO 4

BOX SCORES
GAME 1

ST. LOUIS 8, SAN DIEGO 5
TUESDAY, OCTOBER 4, AT ST. LOUIS

San Diego	AB	R	H	BI	BB	SO	PO	A
D.Roberts, cf	3	0	1	0	0	0	4	0
E.Young, ph—cf	2	1	1	2	0	0	0	0
Klesko, lf	4	1	2	0	1	1	1	0
Loretta, 2b	5	0	1	1	0	0	0	2
B.Giles, rf	5	0	2	1	0	1	1	0
Ma.Sweeney, 1b	2	1	2	0	1	0	10	0
B.Johnson, ph	0	0	0	0	0	0	0	0
Fick, ph—1b	1	0	1	0	1	0	1	0
Ra.Hernandez, c	5	0	1	0	0	1	5	0
K.Greene, ss	3	1	1	1	0	0	2	5
Randa, 3b	3	0	0	0	1	0	0	1
Peavy, p	2	0	0	0	0	2	0	2
C.Hensley, p	0	0	0	0	0	0	0	0
Lawrence, p	0	0	0	0	0	0	0	0
Burroughs, ph	0	0	0	0	0	0	0	0
Nady, ph	1	0	0	0	0	1	0	0
Otsuka, p	0	0	0	0	0	0	0	0
Linebrink, p	0	0	0	0	0	0	0	0
D.Jackson, ph	1	1	1	0	0	0	0	0
TOTALS	37	5	13	5	4	6	24	10

St. Louis	AB	R	H	BI	BB	SO	PO	A
Eckstein, ss	5	1	1	0	0	0	1	5
Edmonds, cf	4	3	3	1	0	0	6	0
Pujols, 1b	3	2	1	0	1	0	8	0
L.Walker, rf	2	1	0	0	2	1	3	0
Sanders, lf	4	1	2	6	0	1	1	0
Taguchi, lf	0	0	0	0	0	0	0	0
C.Eldred, p	0	0	0	0	0	0	0	0
Isringhausen, p	0	0	0	0	0	0	0	0
Grudzielanek, 2b	4	0	0	0	0	1	1	2
A.Nunez, 3b	3	0	1	0	1	1	1	2
Y.Molina, c	4	0	1	0	0	1	6	0
Carpenter, p	3	0	0	0	0	1	0	0
B.Thompson, p	0	0	0	0	0	0	0	0
Ra.Flores, p	0	0	0	0	0	0	0	0
Mabry, lf	1	0	1	0	0	0	0	0
TOTALS	33	8	10	7	4	5	27	9

						R	H	E	LOB
San Diego	0 0 0	0 0 0	1 1 3—			5	13	1	10
St. Louis	1 0 3	0 4 0	0 0 x—			8	10	1	5

San Diego	IP	H	R	ER	HR	BB	SO
Peavy (L)	4.1	8	8	8	2	3	3
C.Hensley	0.2	0	0	0	0	1	0
Lawrence	1.0	0	0	0	0	0	1
Otsuka	1.0	0	0	0	0	0	0
Linebrink	1.0	2	0	0	0	0	1

St. Louis	IP	H	R	ER	HR	BB	SO
Carpenter (W)	6.0	3	0	0	0	3	3
B.Thompson	0.2	2	1	1	0	0	0
Ra.Flores	1.0	2	1	1	1	0	2
C.Eldred	0.2	2	2	2	0	1	0
Isringhausen	0.2	4	1	1	0	0	1

E—K.Greene, Eckstein. DP—San Diego 2, St. Louis 3. LOB—San Diego 10, St. Louis 5. Scoring Position—San Diego 6 for 13, St. Louis 2 for 4. 2B—Ma.Sweeney, K.Greene, Edmonds. HR—Edmonds (1st inning, 1 out, 0 on) off Peavy, Sanders (5th inning, 1 out, 3 on) off Peavy, E.Young (8th inning, 0 out, 0 on) off Ra.Flores. SB—B.Giles, D.Jackson. S—K.Greene. WP—Peavy. T—2:57. A—52,349. U_HP—Montague, 1B—Hohn, 2B—Dreckman, 3B—Layne, LF—Hernandez, RF—Timmons.

HOW THEY SCORED

BOTTOM OF 1
Cardinals first. Eckstein flied out to left fielder Klesko. Edmonds homered to left on a 0-2 count. Pujols grounded out, shortstop Greene to first baseman M.Sweeney. Walker struck out. Runs: 1, Hits: 1, Errors:0

BOTTOM OF 3
Cardinals third. Carpenter grounded out, pitcher Peavy to first baseman M.Sweeney. Eckstein singled to center. Edmonds doubled to left, Eckstein to third. Pujols was intentionally walked. On Peavy's wild pitch, Eckstein scored, Edmonds to third, Pujols to second. Walker was intentionally walked. Sanders infield single to first, Edmonds scored, Pujols scored, Walker to third. Grudzielanek grounded into a double play, second baseman Loretta to shortstop Greene to first baseman M.Sweeney, Sanders out. Runs: 3, Hits: 3, Errors: 0

BOTTOM OF 5
Cardinals fifth. Eckstein grounded out, third baseman Randa to first baseman M.Sweeney. Edmonds infield single to short. Pujols singled to left, Edmonds to second. Walker walked, Edmonds to third, Pujols to second. Sanders homered to left on a 3-0 count, Edmonds scored, Pujols scored, Walker scored. Hensley pitching. Grudzielanek flied out to center fielder Roberts. Nunez walked on four pitches. Molina grounded out, shortstop Greene to first baseman M.Sweeney. Runs: 4, Hits: 3, Errors: 0

TOP OF 7
Padres seventh. Thompson pitching. M.Sweeney doubled to right. R.Hernandez singled to left, M.Sweeney to third. Greene hit a sacrifice fly to center fielder Edmonds, M.Sweeney scored. Randa flied out to center fielder Edmonds. Burroughs pinch-hitting for Lawrence. Flores pitching. Nady pinch-hitting for Burroughs. Nady struck out. Runs: 1, Hits: 2, Errors: 0

TOP OF 8
Padres eighth. Taguchi in as left fielder. Young pinch-hitting for Roberts. Young homered to left on a 1-2 count. Klesko struck out. Loretta flied out to right fielder Walker. Giles singled to center. Johnson pinch-hitting for M.Sweeney. Eldred pitching. Mabry in as left fielder. Fick pinch-hitting for Johnson.Giles stole second. Fick walked. R.Hernandez grounded out, shortstop Eckstein to first baseman Pujols. Runs: 1, Hits: 2, Errors: 0

TOP OF 9
Padres ninth. Greene doubled to left. Randa flied out to right fielder Walker. Jackson pinch-hitting for Linebrink. Jackson singled to left, Greene to third. Isringhausen pitching.Jackson stole second. Young grounded out, third baseman Nunez to first baseman Pujols, Greene scored. Klesko singled to right, Jackson to third. Loretta singled to center, Jackson scored, Klesko to second. Giles singled to center, Klesko scored, Loretta to second. Fick singled to right, Loretta to third, Giles to second. R.Hernandez struck out. Runs: 3, Hits: 6, Errors: 0

GAME 2

ST. LOUIS 6, SAN DIEGO 2

THURSDAY, OCTOBER 6, AT ST. LOUIS

San Diego	AB	R	H	BI	BB	SO	PO	A
E.Young, lf	3	0	0	0	0	0	0	0
Klesko, ph-lf	2	0	0	0	0	1	1	0
Loretta, 2b	5	0	1	0	0	0	3	2
Ra.Hernandez, c	4	1	2	0	0	0	6	0
B.Giles, cf-rf	3	0	0	0	1	0	2	0
K.Greene, ss	3	1	2	0	1	0	4	4
Randa, 3b	4	0	3	0	0	0	0	1
Nady, 1b	2	0	1	2	0	0	6	2
B.Johnson, rf	2	0	0	0	1	0	2	0
C.Hensley, p	0	0	0	0	0	0	0	0
Olivo, ph	1	0	0	0	0	0	0	0
Seanez, p	0	0	0	0	0	0	0	0
Ma.Sweeney, ph	1	0	0	0	0	1	0	0
Otsuka, p	0	0	0	0	0	0	1	0
P.Astacio, p	1	0	0	0	0	0	0	1
D.Jackson, ph-cf	1	0	1	0	0	0	1	0
D.Roberts, ph	1	0	0	0	0	0	0	0
TOTALS	33	2	10	2	2	4	24	10

St. Louis	AB	R	H	BI	BB	SO	PO	A
Eckstein, ss	4	0	1	2	0	0	3	6
Edmonds, cf	2	1	0	0	2	0	2	0
Pujols, 1b	3	1	2	1	1	0	14	1
L.Walker, rf	4	0	0	0	0	3	0	0
Sanders, lf	4	0	1	2	0	1	1	0
Taguchi, lf	0	0	0	0	0	0	0	0
Grudzielanek, 2b	4	1	1	0	0	1	2	5
A.Nunez, 3b	3	2	1	0	1	0	1	2
Y.Molina, c	4	1	0	1	0	0	4	0
Mulder, p	1	0	0	0	1	1	0	3
Tavarez, p	0	0	0	0	0	0	0	0
Ra.Flores, p	0	0	0	0	0	0	0	0
Gall, ph	1	0	0	0	0	0	0	0
Isringhausen, p	0	0	0	0	0	0	0	0
TOTALS	30	6	6	6	5	6	27	17

						R	H	E	LOB
San Diego	0 0 0	0 0 0	1 1 0—	2	10	1	9		
St. Louis	0 0 2	2 0 0	2 0 x—	6	6	0	7		

San Diego	IP	H	R	ER	HR	BB	SO
P.Astacio (L)	4.0	3	4	2	0	3	4
C.Hensley	2.0	1	0	0	0	1	0
Seanez	1.0	2	2	2	0	1	2
Otsuka	1.0	0	0	0	0	0	0

St. Louis	IP	H	R	ER	HR	BB	SO
Mulder (W)	6.2	8	1	1	0	1	2
Tavarez (HOLD)	1.0	2	1	1	0	1	0
Ra.Flores (HOLD)	0.1	0	0	0	0	0	1
Isringhausen	1.0	0	0	0	0	0	1

E—K.Greene. DP—San Diego 1, St. Louis 4. LOB—San Diego 9, St. Louis 7. Scoring Position—San Diego 3 for 9, St. Louis 1 for 10. 2B—K.Greene, Sanders, A.Nunez. SH—Eckstein, Mulder. HBP—D.Jackson by Mulder, Nady by Mulder; by Tavarez. T—2:54. A—52,599. U—HP-Hohn, 1B-Dreckman, 2B-Layne, 3B-Hernandez, LF-Timmons, RF-Montague.

HOW THEY SCORED

BOTTOM OF 3

Cardinals third. Nunez walked on a full count. Molina safe on Greene's error, Nunez to second. Mulder sacrificed, first baseman Nady to second baseman Loretta, Nunez to third, Molina to second. Eckstein safe on failed fielder's choice, Nunez scored, Molina to third. Edmonds walked on a full count, Eckstein to second. Pujols walked, Molina scored, Eckstein to third, Edmonds to

second. Walker struck out. Sanders struck out, safe on Astacio fielder's choice, Eckstein out, Edmonds to third, Pujols to second. Runs: 2, Hits: 0, Errors: 1

BOTTOM OF 4

Cardinals fourth. Grudzielanek singled to right. Nunez doubled to right, Grudzielanek to third. Molina safe on failed fielder's choice, Grudzielanek scored, Nunez to third. Mulder struck out. Eckstein sacrificed, pitcher Astacio to first baseman Nady, Nunez scored, Molina to second. Edmonds grounded out, second baseman Loretta to first baseman Nady. Runs: 2, Hits: 2, Errors: 0

TOP OF 7

Padres seventh. Greene doubled to center. Randa singled to center, Greene to third. Nady singled to left, Greene scored, Randa to second. Olivo pinch-hitting for Hensley. Olivo grounded into a double play, second baseman Grudzielanek to shortstop Eckstein to first baseman Pujols, Randa to third, Nady out. Jackson was hit by a pitch. Tavarez pitching. Klesko pinch-hitting for Young. Klesko flied out to left fielder Sanders. Runs: 1, Hits: 3, Errors: 0

BOTTOM OF 7

Cardinals seventh. Klesko in as left fielder. Seanez pitching. Edmonds walked on a full count. Pujols singled to right, Edmonds to third. Walker struck out. Sanders doubled to left, Edmonds scored, Pujols scored. Sanders to third. Grudzielanek struck out. Nunez flied out to right fielder Giles. Runs: 2, Hits: 2, Errors: 0

TOP OF 8

Padres eighth. Taguchi in as left fielder. Loretta grounded out, shortstop Eckstein to first baseman Pujols. R.Hernandez singled to left. Giles walked on a full count, R.Hernandez to second. Greene lined out to third baseman Nunez. Randa singled to center, R.Hernandez to third, Giles to second. Nady was hit by a pitch, R.Hernandez scored, Giles to third, Randa to second. M.Sweeney pinch-hitting for Seanez. Flores pitching. M.Sweeney struck out. Runs: 1, Hits: 2, Errors: 0

GAME 3

ST. LOUIS 7, SAN DIEGO 4

SATURDAY, OCTOBER 8, AT SAN DIEGO

St. Louis	AB	R	H	BI	BB	SO	PO	A
Eckstein, ss	4	2	3	2	1	1	2	0
Edmonds, cf	5	1	1	0	0	2	3	0
Pujols, 1b	3	1	2	1	2	0	9	0
L.Walker, rf	3	0	0	0	0	1	2	0
Taguchi, rf-lf	1	0	0	0	0	0	0	0
Sanders, lf	4	0	1	2	1	0	2	0
Isringhausen, p	0	0	0	0	0	0	0	1
Grudzielanek, 2b	5	1	1	0	0	0	0	5
A.Nunez, 3b	5	1	2	0	0	2	0	2
Y.Molina, c	5	0	2	2	0	0	8	0
M.Morris, p	2	1	1	0	0	0	0	1
J.Rodriguez, ph	1	0	0	0	0	0	0	0
B.Thompson, p	0	0	0	0	0	0	0	0
Ra.Flores, p	0	0	0	0	0	0	0	1
Tavarez, p	0	0	0	0	0	0	0	0
Mabry, rf	1	0	0	0	0	0	1	0
TOTALS	39	7	13	7	4	6	27	10

San Diego	AB	R	H	BI	BB	SO	PO	A
D.Roberts, cf	5	1	1	1	0	1	2	0
Loretta, 2b	5	0	2	1	0	0	2	2
B.Giles, rf	5	0	1	0	0	1	4	0
Klesko, lf	4	0	0	0	1	2	0	0
Ra.Hernandez, c	2	1	2	1	2	0	6	0
Fick, 1b	4	0	0	0	0	0	9	1
K.Greene, ss	4	0	1	0	0	2	1	3
Randa, 3b	4	1	1	0	0	0	0	2
W.Williams, p	0	0	0	0	0	0	0	2
Lawrence, p	0	0	0	0	0	0	0	0
Burroughs, ph	1	0	0	0	0	0	0	0
C.Hensley, p	0	0	0	0	0	0	0	1
E.Young, ph	1	1	1	1	0	0	0	0
Seanez, p	0	0	0	0	0	0	1	0

San Diego	AB	R	H	BI	BB	SO	PO	A
D.Jackson, ph	1	0	0	0	0	1	0	0
Otsuka, p	0	0	0	0	0	0	0	0
Hoffman, p	0	0	0	0	0	0	0	0
Ma.Sweeney, ph	0	0	0	0	1	0	0	0
TOTALS	36	4	9	4	4	7	27	11

							R	H	E	LOB
St. Louis	1 4 0		0 2 0		0 0 0	—	7	13	1	11
San Diego	0 0 0		0 2 0		1 1 0	—	4	9	0	9

St. Louis	IP	H	R	ER	HR	BB	SO
M.Morris (W)	6.0	5	2	2	0	3	4
B.Thompson	0.2	1	1	1	1	0	1
Ra.Flores	0.2	0	0	0	0	0	0
Tavarez	0.1	2	1	1	1	0	0
Isringhausen (S)	1.1	1	0	0	0	1	2

San Diego	IP	H	R	ER	HR	BB	SO
W.Williams (L)	1.2	6	5	5	1	2	2
Lawrence	1.1	1	0	0	0	0	1
C.Hensley	2.0	3	2	2	0	1	1
Seanez	2.0	1	0	0	0	0	2
Otsuka	1.0	1	0	0	0	1	0
Hoffman	1.0	1	0	0	0	0	0

E—Eckstein. LOB—St. Louis 11, San Diego 9. Scoring Position—St. Louis 2 for 11, San Diego 2 for 10. 2B—Edmonds, Pujols 2, Sanders, Randa. HR—Eckstein (2nd inning, 2 out, 1 on) off W.Williams, D.Roberts (7th inning, 1 out, 0 on) off B.Thompson, Ra.Hernandez (8th inning, 1 out, 0 on) off Tavarez. SB—A.Nunez. SH—M.Morris. HBP—L.Walker by W.Williams. T—3:07. A—45,093. U—HP-Dreckman, 1B-Layne, 2B-Hernandez, 3B-Timmons, LF-Hohn, RF-Montague.

HOW THEY SCORED

TOP OF 1
Cardinals first. Eckstein singled to center. Edmonds struck out. Pujols doubled to right, Eckstein scored. Walker grounded out, pitcher Williams to first baseman Fick, Pujols to third. Sanders walked on a full count. Grudzielanek flied out to right fielder Giles. Runs: 1, Hits: 2, Errors: 0

TOP OF 2
Cardinals second. Nunez struck out. Molina singled to right. Morris grounded into fielder's choice, pitcher Williams to shortstop Greene, Molina out. Eckstein homered to left on a 2-0 count, Morris scored. Edmonds doubled to right. Pujols was intentionally walked. Walker was hit by a pitch, Edmonds to third, Pujols to second. Sanders doubled to left, Edmonds scored, Pujols scored, Walker to third. Lawrence pitching. Grudzielanek flied out to center fielder Roberts. Runs: 4, Hits: 4, Errors: 0

TOP OF 5
Cardinals fifth. Sanders flied out to right fielder Giles. Grudzielanek singled to right. Nunez singled to right, Grudzielanek to third. Nunez stole second. Molina singled to right, Grudzielanek scored, Nunez scored. Morris sacrificed, pitcher Hensley to second baseman Loretta, Molina to second. Eckstein walked on four pitches. Edmonds grounded out, first baseman Fick unassisted. Runs: 2, Hits: 3, Errors: 0

BOTTOM OF 5
Padres fifth. Greene flied out to center fielder Edmonds. Randa doubled to left. Young pinch-hitting for Hensley. Young singled to right, Randa scored. Roberts grounded out, second baseman Grudzielanek to first baseman Pujols, Young to second. Loretta singled to left, Young scored. Giles singled to left, Loretta to third. Klesko struck out. Runs: 2, Hits: 4, Errors: 0

BOTTOM OF 7
Padres seventh. Taguchi in as right fielder. Thompson pitching. Jackson pinch-hitting for Seanez. Jackson struck out. Roberts homered to right on a 1-1 count. Loretta grounded out, third baseman Nunez to first baseman Pujols. Flores pitching. Giles grounded out, pitcher Flores to first baseman Pujols. Runs: 1, Hits: 1, Errors: 0

BOTTOM OF 8
Padres eighth. Klesko popped out to shortstop Eckstein. Tavarez pitching. R.Hernandez homered to center on the first pitch. Fick flied out to left fielder Sanders. Greene singled to right. Taguchi in as left fielder. Isringhausen pitching. Mabry in as right fielder. Randa flied out to right fielder Mabry. Runs: 1, Hits: 2, Errors: 0

STATISTICS

ST. LOUIS CARDINALS' BATTING AND FIELDING AVERAGES

Player, position	G	AB	R	H	TB	2B	3B	HR	RBI	BB	IBB	SO	Avg.	OBP	Slg.	PO	A	E	Avg.
Pujols,1b	3	9	4	5	7	2	0	0	2	4	3	0	.556	.692	.778	31	1	0	1.000
Mabry,lf-rf	2	2	0	1	1	0	0	0	0	0	0	0	.500	.500	.500	1	0	0	1.000
Morris,p	1	2	1	1	1	0	0	0	0	0	0	0	.500	.500	.500	0	1	0	1.000
Eckstein,ss	3	13	3	5	8	0	0	1	4	1	0	1	.385	.429	.615	6	11	2	.895
Edmonds,cf	3	11	5	4	9	2	0	1	1	2	0	2	.364	.462	.818	11	0	0	1.000
Nunez,3b	3	11	3	4	5	1	0	0	0	2	0	3	.364	.462	.455	2	6	0	1.000
Sanders,lf	3	12	1	4	9	2	0	1	10	1	0	2	.333	.385	.750	4	0	0	1.000
Molina,c	3	13	1	3	3	0	0	0	3	0	0	1	.231	.231	.231	18	0	0	1.000
Grudzielanek,2b	3	13	2	2	2	0	0	0	0	0	0	1	.154	.154	.154	3	12	0	1.000
Eldred,p	1	0	0	0	0	0	0	0	0	0	0	0	.000	.000	.000	0	0	0	.000
Flores,p	3	0	0	0	0	0	0	0	0	0	0	0	.000	.000	.000	0	1	0	1.000
Isringhausen,p	3	0	0	0	0	0	0	0	0	0	0	0	.000	.000	.000	0	1	0	1.000
Tavarez,p	2	0	0	0	0	0	0	0	0	0	0	0	.000	.000	.000	0	0	0	.000
Thompson,p	2	0	0	0	0	0	0	0	0	0	0	0	.000	.000	.000	0	0	0	.000
Gall,ph	1	1	0	0	0	0	0	0	0	0	0	0	.000	.000	.000	0	0	0	.000
Mulder,p	1	1	0	0	0	0	0	0	0	1	0	1	.000	.500	.000	0	3	0	1.000
Rodriguez,ph	1	1	0	0	0	0	0	0	0	0	0	0	.000	.000	.000	0	0	0	.000
Taguchi,lf-rf	3	1	0	0	0	0	0	0	0	0	0	0	.000	.000	.000	0	0	0	.000
Carpenter,p	1	3	0	0	0	0	0	0	0	0	0	1	.000	.000	.000	0	0	0	.000
Walker,rf	3	9	1	0	0	0	0	0	0	2	1	5	.000	.250	.000	5	0	0	1.000
Totals	3	102	21	29	45	7	0	3	20	13	4	17	.284	.371	.441	81	36	2	.983

SAN DIEGO PADRES' BATTING AND FIELDING AVERAGES

Player, position	G	AB	R	H	TB	2B	3B	HR	RBI	BB	IBB	SO	Avg.	OBP	Slg.	PO	A	E	Avg.
Jackson,ph-cf	3	3	1	2	2	0	0	0	0	0	0	1	.667	.750	.667	1	0	0	1.000
Sweeney,1b-ph	3	3	1	2	3	1	0	0	0	2	0	1	.667	.800	1.000	10	0	0	1.000

Player, position	G	AB	R	H	TB	2B	3B	HR	RBI	BB	IBB	SO	Avg.	OBP	Slg.	PO	A	E	Avg.
Hernandez,c	3	11	2	5	8	0	0	1	1	2	0	1	.455	.538	.727	17	0	0	1.000
Greene,ss	3	10	2	4	6	2	0	0	1	1	0	2	.400	.417	.600	7	12	2	.905
Randa,3b	3	11	1	4	5	1	0	0	0	1	0	0	.364	.417	.455	0	4	0	1.000
Young,cf-ph-lf	3	6	2	2	5	0	0	1	3	0	0	0	.333	.333	.833	0	0	0	.000
Nady,ph-1b	2	3	0	1	1	0	0	0	2	0	0	1	.333	.600	.333	6	2	0	1.000
Loretta,2b	3	15	0	4	4	0	0	0	2	0	0	0	.267	.267	.267	5	6	0	1.000
Giles,rf-cf	3	13	0	3	3	0	0	0	1	1	0	2	.231	.286	.231	7	0	0	1.000
Roberts,cf-ph	3	9	1	2	5	0	0	1	1	0	0	1	.222	.222	.556	6	0	0	1.000
Klesko,lf-ph	3	10	1	2	2	0	0	0	0	2	0	4	.200	.333	.200	4	0	0	1.000
Fick,1b-ph	2	5	0	1	1	0	0	0	0	1	0	0	.200	.333	.200	10	1	0	1.000
Hensley,p	3	0	0	0	0	0	0	0	0	0	0	0	.000	.000	.000	0	1	0	1.000
Hoffman,p	1	0	0	0	0	0	0	0	0	0	0	0	.000	.000	.000	0	0	0	.000
Lawrence,p	2	0	0	0	0	0	0	0	0	0	0	0	.000	.000	.000	0	0	0	.000
Linebrink,p	1	0	0	0	0	0	0	0	0	0	0	0	.000	.000	.000	0	0	0	.000
Otsuka,p	3	0	0	0	0	0	0	0	0	0	0	0	.000	.000	.000	1	0	0	1.000
Seanez,p	2	0	0	0	0	0	0	0	0	0	0	0	.000	.000	.000	1	0	0	1.000
Williams,p	1	0	0	0	0	0	0	0	0	0	0	0	.000	.000	.000	0	2	0	1.000
Astacio,p	1	1	0	0	0	0	0	0	0	0	0	0	.000	.000	.000	0	1	0	1.000
Burroughs,ph	2	1	0	0	0	0	0	0	0	0	0	0	.000	.000	.000	0	0	0	.000
Olivo,ph	1	1	0	0	0	0	0	0	0	0	0	0	.000	.000	.000	0	0	0	.000
Johnson,ph-rf	2	2	0	0	0	0	0	0	0	0	0	2	.000	.000	.000	0	0	0	.000
Peavy,p	1	2	0	0	0	0	0	0	0	0	0	2	.000	.000	.000	0	2	0	1.000
Totals	3	106	11	32	45	4	0	3	11	10	0	17	.302	.375	.425	75	31	2	.981

ST. LOUIS CARDINALS' PITCHING RECORDS

Pitcher	G	GS	CG	IP	H	R	ER	HR	BB	IBB	SO	HB	WP	W	L	Pct.	ERA
Carpenter	1	1	0	6.0	3	0	0	0	3	0	3	0	0	1	0	1.000	0.00
Mulder	1	1	0	6.2	8	1	1	0	1	0	2	2	0	1	0	1.000	1.35
Morris	1	1	0	6.0	5	2	2	0	3	0	4	0	0	1	0	1.000	3.00
Isringhausen	3	0	0	3.0	5	1	1	0	1	0	4	0	0	0	0	.000	3.00
Flores	3	0	0	2.0	2	1	1	1	0	0	3	0	0	0	0	.000	4.50
Tavarez	2	0	0	1.1	4	2	2	1	1	0	0	1	0	0	0	.000	13.50
Thompson	2	0	0	1.1	3	2	2	1	0	0	1	0	0	0	0	.000	13.50
Eldred	1	0	0	0.2	2	2	2	0	1	0	0	0	0	0	0	.000	27.00
Totals	3	3	0	27.0	32	11	11	3	10	0	17	3	0	3	0	1.000	3.67

No shutouts. Saves—Isringhausen.

SAN DIEGO PADRES' PITCHING RECORDS

Pitcher	G	GS	CG	IP	H	R	ER	HR	BB	IBB	SO	HB	WP	W	L	Pct.	ERA
LOtsuka	3	0	0	3.0	1	0	0	0	1	1	0	0	0	0	0	.000	0.00
Lawrence	2	0	0	2.1	1	0	0	0	2	0	0	0	0	0	0	.000	0.00
Hoffman	1	0	0	1.0	1	0	0	0	0	0	0	0	0	0	0	.000	0.00
Linebrink	1	0	0	1.0	2	0	0	0	0	0	1	0	0	0	0	.000	0.00
Hensley	3	0	0	4.2	4	2	2	0	3	0	1	0	0	0	0	.000	3.86
Astacio	1	1	0	4.0	3	4	2	0	3	0	4	0	0	0	1	.000	4.50
Seanez	2	0	0	3.0	3	2	2	0	1	0	4	0	0	0	0	.000	6.00
Peavy	1	1	0	4.1	8	8	8	2	3	2	3	0	1	0	1	.000	16.62
Williams	1	1	0	1.2	6	5	5	1	2	1	2	1	0	0	1	.000	27.00
Totals	3	3	0	25.0	29	21	19	3	13	4	17	1	1	0	3	.000	6.84

No shutouts or saves.

SCORE BY INNINGS

St. Louis	2	4	5		2	6	0		2	0	0—21
San Diego	0	0	0		0	2	0		3	3	3—11

MISCELLANEOUS STATISTICS

Sacrifice hits—Eckstein, Morris, Mulder.
Sacrifice flies—Greene.
Stolen bases—Giles, Jackson, Nunez.
Caught stealing—None.
Double plays—Eckstein, Grudzielanek and Pujols 3; Eckstein and Pujols; Greene and Sweeney; Greene, Loretta and Nady; Grudzielanek, Eckstein and Pujols; Loretta, Greene and Sweeney; Nunez and Pujols; Pujols, Eckstein and Pujols.
Left on bases—St. Louis 5, 7, 11—23; San Diego 10, 9, 9—28.
Scoring position—St. Louis 2 for 4, 1 for 10, 2 for 11—5 for 25; San Diego 6 for 13, 3 for 9, 2 for 10—11 for 32.
Hit by pitcher—by Mulder 2 (Jackson, Nady), by Williams (Walker), by Tavarez (Nady).
Passed balls—None.
Balks—None.
Time of games—2:57, 2:54, 3:07—Avg.: 2:59.
Attendance—52,349, 52,599, 45,093—150,041.
Umpires—Montague, Ed; Hohn, Bill; Dreckman, Bruce; Layne, Jerry; Hernandez, Angel; and Timmons, Tim.

HOUSTON VS. ATLANTA

RESULTS

DAY	DATE	PLACE	SCORE
WED.	OCT. 5	ATLANTA	HOUSTON 10, ATLANTA 5
THU.	OCT. 6	ATLANTA	ATLANTA 7, HOUSTON 1
SAT.	OCT. 8	HOUSTON	HOUSTON 7, ATLANTA 3
SUN.	OCT. 9	HOUSTON	HOUSTON 7, ATLANTA 6

BOX SCORES

GAME 1

HOUSTON 10, ATLANTA 5

WEDNESDAY, OCTOBER 5, AT ATLANTA

Houston	AB	R	H	BI	BB	SO	PO	A
Biggio, 2b	3	3	2	1	1	0	1	2
Springer, p	0	0	0	0	0	0	0	0
Gallo, p	0	0	0	0	0	0	0	0
Taveras, cf	2	1	0	0	1	0	0	0
Bagwell, ph	1	1	1	1	0	0	0	0
Bruntlett, cf	1	0	0	0	0	1	0	0
Berkman, 1b	2	0	0	0	3	1	10	0
Ensberg, 3b	4	1	3	5	1	1	0	3
Lane, rf	3	0	0	0	1	1	3	0
O.Palmeiro, lf	3	0	1	2	1	0	3	0
A.Everett, ss	4	1	1	0	1	0	1	3
Ausmus, c	5	2	2	0	0	1	9	0
Pettitte, p	2	1	1	0	0	1	0	2
Wheeler, p	0	0	0	0	0	0	0	0
J.Vizcaino, ph-2b	1	0	0	0	0	0	0	1
TOTALS	31	10	11	9	9	6	27	11

Atlanta	AB	R	H	BI	BB	SO	PO	A
Furcal, ss	5	1	1	0	0	1	0	4
M.Giles, 2b	3	1	1	0	0	0	6	3
C.Jones, 3b	4	1	2	2	0	1	0	5
A.Jones, cf	3	1	1	2	1	1	2	0
Franco, 1b	3	0	0	0	0	2	9	2
Francoeur, rf	4	1	2	0	0	0	1	0
Jordan, lf	3	0	0	0	0	0	2	0
Langerhans, ph	1	0	0	0	0	1	0	0
Estrada, c	4	0	1	1	0	2	6	0
T.Hudson, p	2	0	0	0	0	0	1	1
Devine, p	0	0	0	0	0	0	0	0
Reitsma, p	0	0	0	0	0	0	0	0
Foster, p	0	0	0	0	0	0	0	0
Brower, p	0	0	0	0	0	0	0	0
Orr, ph	1	0	0	0	0	0	0	0
McBride, p	0	0	0	0	0	0	0	1
K.Johnson, ph	0	0	0	0	0	0	0	0
Betemit, ph	1	0	1	0	0	0	0	0
TOTALS	34	5	9	5	2	8	27	16

							R	H	E	LOB
Houston	1 0 2	1 0 0	1 5 0	—	10	11	1	10
Atlanta	1 0 0	2 0 0	0 1 1	—	5	9	0	5

Houston	IP	H	R	ER	HR	BB	SO
Pettitte (W)	7.0	4	3	3	2	2	6
Wheeler	1.0	2	1	1	0	0	1
Springer	0.1	2	1	1	0	0	1
Gallo	0.2	1	0	0	0	0	0

Atlanta	IP	H	R	ER	HR	BB	SO
T.Hudson (L)	6.2	7	5	5	0	5	3
Devine	0.1	0	0	0	0	0	0
Reitsma	0.1	3	4	4	0	1	0
Foster	0.1	1	1	1	0	2	1
Brower	0.1	0	0	0	0	1	1
McBride	1.0	0	0	0	0	0	0

E—Ensberg. DP—Houston 1, Atlanta 2. LOB—Houston 10, Atlanta 5. Scoring Position—Houston 5 for 12, Atlanta 3 for 9. 2B—Biggio, Ausmus, Pettitte, M.Giles, C.Jones. 3B—Francoeur.

HR—C.Jones (1st inning, 2 out, 0 on) off Pettitte, A.Jones (4th inning, 1 out, 1 on) off Pettitte. S—Biggio. SH—Biggio, Taveras, Pettitte 2. WP—Foster. HBP—O.Palmeiro by T.Hudson, M.Giles by Wheeler, Lane by Devine. T—3:11. A—40,590. U—HP-Brinkman, 1B-Hudson, 2B-Nelson, 3B-Cederstrom, LF-Cooper, RF-Holbrook.

HOW THEY SCORED

TOP OF 1

Astros first. Biggio singled to center. Taveras sacrificed, third baseman C.Jones to first baseman Franco, Biggio to second. Berkman walked on four pitches. Ensberg singled to center, Biggio scored, Berkman to second. Lane grounded into a double play, third baseman C.Jones to second baseman Giles to first baseman Franco, Ensberg out. Runs: 1, Hits: 2, Errors: 0

BOTTOM OF 1

Braves first. Furcal grounded out, pitcher Pettitte to first baseman Berkman. Giles flied out to left fielder Palmeiro. C.Jones homered to right on a 1-0 count. A.Jones flied out to right fielder Lane. Runs: 1, Hits: 1, Errors: 0

TOP OF 3

Astros third. Pettitte struck out. Biggio doubled to center. Taveras walked on a full count. Berkman walked on four pitches, Biggio to third, Taveras to second. Ensberg singled to left, Biggio scored, Taveras scored, Berkman to second. Lane grounded into fielder's choice, third baseman C.Jones to second baseman Giles, Berkman to third, Ensberg out. Palmeiro was hit by a pitch, Lane to second. Everett grounded out, shortstop Furcal to first baseman Franco. Runs: 2, Hits: 2, Errors: 0

TOP OF 4

Astros fourth. Ausmus doubled to center. Pettitte sacrificed, pitcher Hudson to second baseman Giles, Ausmus to third. Biggio hit a sacrifice fly to center fielder A.Jones, Ausmus scored. Taveras grounded out, third baseman C.Jones to first baseman Franco. Runs: 1, Hits: 1, Errors: 0

BOTTOM OF 4

Braves fourth. Giles doubled to center. C.Jones grounded out, pitcher Pettitte to first baseman Berkman. A.Jones homered to center on a 0-1 count, Giles scored. Franco walked on a full count. Francoeur bunt single to third, Franco to second. Jordan grounded into a double play, shortstop Everett to second baseman Biggio to first baseman Berkman, Francoeur out. Runs: 2, Hits: 3, Errors: 0

TOP OF 7

Astros seventh. Pettitte doubled to left. Biggio sacrificed, first baseman Franco to second baseman Giles, Pettitte to third. Taveras grounded out, shortstop Furcal to first baseman Franco. Berkman was intentionally walked. Ensberg singled to left, Pettitte scored, Berkman to second. Devine pitching. Lane was hit by a pitch, Berkman to third, Ensberg to second. Palmeiro flied out to right fielder Francoeur. Runs: 1, Hits: 2, Errors: 0

TOP OF 8

Astros eighth. Reitsma pitching. Ausmus singled to center. Ausmus infield single to first, Everett to second. Pettitte sacrificed, third baseman C.Jones to second baseman Giles, Everett to third, Ausmus to second. Biggio was intentionally walked. Bagwell pinch-hitting for Taveras. Bagwell singled to left, Everett scored, Ausmus to third, Biggio to second. Foster pitching. Berkman struck out. Ensberg walked on a full count, Ausmus scored, Biggio to third, Bagwell to second. On Foster's wild pitch, Biggio scored, Bagwell to third, Ensberg to second. Lane was intentionally walked. Palmeiro singled to left, Bagwell scored, Ensberg scored, Lane to second. Brower pitching. Everett walked, Lane to third, Palmeiro to second. Ausmus struck out. Runs: 5, Hits: 4, Errors: 0

BOTTOM OF 8

Braves eighth. Bruntlett in as center fielder. Wheeler pitching. Orr pinch-hitting for Brower. Orr flied out to left fielder Palmeiro. Furcal singled to left. Giles was hit by a pitch, Furcal to second. C.Jones doubled to center, Furcal scored, Giles to third. A.Jones struck out. Franco grounded out, second baseman Biggio to first baseman Berkman. Runs: 1, Hits: 2, Errors: 0

BOTTOM OF 9
Braves ninth. Springer pitching. Vizcaino in as second baseman. Francoeur tripled to center. Langerhans pinch-hitting for Jordan. Langerhans struck out. Estrada singled to center, Francoeur scored. Johnson pinch-hitting for McBride. Gallo pitching. Betemit pinch-hitting for Johnson. Betemit infield single to third, Estrada to second. On Ensberg's error, Estrada to third. Furcal grounded into a double play, second baseman Vizcaino to shortstop Everett to first baseman Berkman, Betemit out. Runs: 1, Hits: 3, Errors: 1

GAME 2
ATLANTA 7, HOUSTON 1
THURSDAY, OCTOBER 6, AT ATLANTA

Houston	AB	R	H	BI	BB	SO	PO	A
Biggio, 2b	4	0	1	0	0	2	4	5
Taveras, cf	4	0	3	0	0	0	1	0
Berkman, 1b	4	1	2	0	0	0	10	2
Ensberg, 3b	4	0	0	0	0	0	2	4
Lane, rf	4	0	1	1	0	0	1	2
Lidge, p	0	0	0	0	0	0	0	0
O.Palmeiro, lf	3	0	0	0	1	0	1	0
A.Everett, ss	4	0	0	0	0	1	2	5
Ausmus, c	4	0	0	0	0	2	3	0
Clemens, p	2	0	0	0	0	1	0	0
Backe, p	0	0	0	0	0	0	0	1
Burke, ph	1	0	1	0	0	0	0	0
Qualls, p	0	0	0	0	0	0	0	0
Scott, rf	0	0	0	0	0	0	0	0
TOTALS	34	1	8	1	1	6	24	19

Atlanta	AB	R	H	BI	BB	SO	PO	A
Furcal, ss	4	0	2	0	1	0	3	2
M.Giles, 2b	5	1	1	0	0	0	2	1
C.Jones, 3b	3	1	0	0	1	0	1	2
A.Jones, cf	4	3	3	1	0	0	3	0
LaRoche, 1b	1	0	1	2	2	0	8	0
Francoeur, rf	3	1	1	1	1	1	3	0
Langerhans, lf	4	0	2	0	0	1	1	0
McCann, c	4	1	1	3	0	1	6	0
Smoltz, p	2	0	0	0	0	0	0	1
Reitsma, p	0	0	0	0	0	0	0	0
K.Johnson, ph	0	0	0	0	1	0	0	0
K.Farnsworth, p	0	0	0	0	0	0	0	0
TOTALS	30	7	11	7	6	3	27	6

						R	H	E	LOB
Houston	1 0 0	0 0 0	0 0 0—	1	8	1	7		
Atlanta	0 3 2	0 0 0	2 0 x—	7	11	0	7		

Houston	IP	H	R	ER	HR	BB	SO
Clemens (L)	5.0	6	5	5	1	3	2
Backe	1.0	1	0	0	0	0	1
Qualls	1.0	4	2	2	0	1	0
Lidge	1.0	0	0	0	0	2	0

Atlanta	IP	H	R	ER	HR	BB	SO
Smoltz (W)	7.0	7	1	1	0	1	5
Reitsma	1.0	1	0	0	0	0	0
K.Farnsworth	1.0	0	0	0	0	0	1

E—Qualls. DP—Houston 1, Atlanta 1. LOB—Houston 7, Atlanta 7. Scoring Position—Houston 1 for 4, Atlanta 5 for 9. 2B—Burke, LaRoche. HR—McCann (2nd inning, 2 out, on 2 on) off Clemens. SB—Furcal. SH—LaRoche, Smoltz. T—2:52. A—46,181. U—HP-Hudson, 1B-Nelson, 2B-Cederstrom, 3B-Cooper, LF-Holbrook, RF-Brinkman.

HOW THEY SCORED

TOP OF 1
Astros first. Biggio struck out. Taveras singled to center. Berkman singled to center, Taveras to second. Ensberg grounded into fielder's choice, third baseman C.Jones to second, Taveras out, Berkman to second. Lane singled to left, Berkman scored, Ensberg to third. Lane to second. Palmeiro was intentionally walked. Everett struck out. Runs: 1, Hits: 3, Errors: 0

BOTTOM OF 2
Braves second. A.Jones singled to left. LaRoche sacrificed, third baseman Ensberg to first baseman Berkman, A.Jones to second. Francoeur walked on a full count. Langerhans struck out. McCann homered to center on a 2-0 count, A.Jones scored, Francoeur scored. Smoltz grounded out, second baseman Biggio to first baseman Berkman. Runs: 3, Hits: 2, Errors: 0

BOTTOM OF 3
Braves third. Furcal grounded out, third baseman Ensberg to first baseman Berkman. Giles flied out to right fielder Lane. C.Jones walked. A.Jones singled to center, C.Jones to third. LaRoche doubled to center, C.Jones scored, A.Jones scored. Francoeur struck out. Runs: 2, Hits: 2, Errors: 0

BOTTOM OF 7
Braves seventh. Qualls pitching. Furcal infield single to third. On Qualls' error, Furcal was out advancing, right fielder Lane to third baseman Ensberg, Furcal out. Giles singled to left. C.Jones grounded out, second baseman Biggio to first baseman Berkman, Giles to second. A.Jones singled to center, Giles scored. A.Jones to second. LaRoche was intentionally walked. Francoeur singled to right, A.Jones scored, LaRoche to third. Francoeur was out advancing, right fielder Lane to shortstop Everett to second baseman Biggio to first baseman Berkman to second baseman Biggio, Francoeur out. Runs: 2, Hits: 4, Errors: 1

GAME 3
HOUSTON 7, ATLANTA 3
SATURDAY, OCTOBER 8, AT HOUSTON

Atlanta	AB	R	H	BI	BB	SO	PO	A
Furcal, ss	5	0	0	0	0	0	2	2
M.Giles, 2b	5	1	1	0	0	3	0	0
C.Jones, 3b	4	0	0	0	0	1	0	1
A.Jones, cf	4	0	3	1	0	1	8	0
LaRoche, 1b	3	1	1	0	1	0	6	1
Francoeur, rf	3	0	0	0	0	1	1	0
Langerhans, lf	2	1	0	0	1	1	2	0
Jordan, ph-lf	1	0	0	0	0	0	0	0
McCann, c	4	0	1	0	0	1	4	0
J.Sosa, p	2	0	1	1	0	1	0	2
K.Johnson, ph	1	0	0	0	0	0	0	0
Reitsma, p	0	0	0	0	0	0	0	0
Foster, p	0	0	0	0	0	0	0	0
Devine, p	0	0	0	0	0	0	0	0
Brower, p	0	0	0	0	0	0	1	0
Franco, ph	1	0	1	0	0	0	0	0
Orr, pr	0	0	0	0	0	0	0	0
TOTALS	35	3	8	3	2	9	24	7

Houston	AB	R	H	BI	BB	SO	PO	A
Biggio, 2b	5	2	3	0	0	1	1	3
Lidge, p	0	0	0	0	0	0	0	0
Taveras, cf	5	1	2	0	0	1	3	0
Berkman, lf-1b	3	2	1	1	0	2	3	0
Ensberg, 3b	4	1	2	2	0	0	1	2
Lamb, 1b	2	1	1	1	2	0	7	1
Burke, lf	0	0	0	0	0	0	0	0
Lane, rf	3	0	2	2	0	0	2	0
A.Everett, ss	3	0	1	1	0	0	0	0
Ausmus, c	3	0	0	0	1	0	9	1
Oswalt, p	3	0	0	0	0	0	1	0
Wheeler, p	0	0	0	0	0	0	0	0

Houston	AB	R	H	BI	BB	SO	PO	A
Gallo, p	0	0	0	0	0	0	0	0
O.Palmeiro, ph	1	0	0	0	0	0	0	0
Bruntlett, 2b	0	0	0	0	0	0	0	0
TOTALS	32	7	12	7	3	4	27	7

							R	H	E	LOB
Atlanta	0 2 0	0 0 0	0 1 0	—	3	8	0	8
Houston	2 0 1	0 0 0	4 0 x	—	7	12	1	7

Atlanta	IP	H	R	ER	HR	BB	SO
J.Sosa (L)	6.0	7	3	3	1	2	3
Reitsma	0.0	2	2	2	0	0	0
Foster	0.0	1	1	1	0	0	0
Devine	0.0	2	1	1	0	1	0
Brower	2.0	0	0	0	0	0	1

Houston	IP	H	R	ER	HR	BB	SO
Oswalt (W)	7.1	6	3	3	0	2	7
Wheeler	0.1	1	0	0	0	0	0
Gallo (HOLD)	0.1	0	0	0	0	0	0
Lidge	1.0	1	0	0	0	0	2

Reitsma pitched to 2 batters in the 7th. Foster pitched to 1 batter in the 7th. Devine pitched to 3 batters in the 7th.

E—A.Everett. DP—Atlanta 2, Houston 1. LOB—Atlanta 8, Houston 7. Scoring Position—Atlanta 2 for 9, Houston 5 for 13. 2B—A.Jones 2, Biggio 3, Taveras, Ensberg 2, Lane. HR—Lamb (3rd inning, 2 out, 0 on) off J.Sosa. S—Lane, A.Everett. HBP—Berkman by J.Sosa, Francoeur by Oswalt. T—2:50. A—43,759. U—HP-Nelson, 1B-Cederstrom, 2B-Cooper, 3B-Holbrook, LF-Brinkman, RF-Hudson.

HOW THEY SCORED

BOTTOM OF 1

Astros first. Biggio doubled to left. Taveras struck out. Berkman was hit by a pitch. Ensberg doubled to left, Biggio scored, Berkman to third. Lamb was intentionally walked. Lane hit a sacrifice fly to center fielder A.Jones, Berkman scored, Ensberg to third. Everett flied out to left fielder Langerhans. Runs: 2, Hits: 2, Errors: 0

TOP OF 2

Braves second. A.Jones singled to left. LaRoche walked, A.Jones to second. Francoeur grounded into a double play, third baseman Ensberg to first baseman Lamb, A.Jones out, LaRoche to second. Langerhans walked on four pitches. McCann singled to left, LaRoche scored, Langerhans to third. Sosa singled to left, Langerhans scored, McCann to second. Furcal grounded out, third baseman Ensberg to first baseman Lamb. Runs: 2, Hits: 3, Errors: 0

BOTTOM OF 3

Astros third. Berkman struck out. Ensberg flied out to center fielder A.Jones. Lamb homered to right on a 2-1 count. Lane grounded out, third baseman C.Jones to first baseman LaRoche. Runs: 1, Hits: 1, Errors: 0

BOTTOM OF 7

Astros seventh. Reitsma pitching. Biggio doubled to left. Taveras infield single to second, Biggio to third. Foster pitching. Berkman singled to left, Biggio scored, Taveras to second. Devine pitching. Ensberg doubled to left, Taveras scored, Berkman to third. Lamb was intentionally walked. Lane singled to left, Berkman scored, Ensberg to third, Lamb to second. Brower pitching. Everett hit a sacrifice fly to center fielder A.Jones, Ensberg scored, Lamb to third. Ausmus grounded into a double play, first baseman LaRoche to shortstop Furcal to pitcher Brower, Lane out. Runs: 4, Hits: 5, Errors: 0

TOP OF 8

Braves eighth. Giles singled to center. C.Jones flied out to center fielder Taveras. Wheeler pitching. A.Jones doubled to left, Giles scored. LaRoche flied out to center fielder Taveras. Francoeur safe on Everett's error, A.Jones to third. Gallo pitching. Jordan pinch-hitting for Langerhans. Jordan grounded into fielder's choice, second baseman Biggio unassisted, Francoeur out. Runs: 1, Hits: 2, Errors: 1

HOUSTON 7, ATLANTA 6
SUNDAY, OCTOBER 9, AT HOUSTON

Atlanta	AB	R	H	BI	BB	SO	PO	A
Furcal, ss	6	0	0	0	2	1	1	7
M.Giles, 2b	7	2	1	0	2	2	4	4
C.Jones, 3b	6	1	1	0	3	2	2	2
A.Jones, cf	6	1	1	1	1	1	6	0
LaRoche, 1b	4	1	2	4	0	1	6	0
Franco, 1b	5	0	1	0	0	1	8	0
Francoeur, rf	7	0	1	0	1	2	4	0
Langerhans, lf	5	0	2	0	2	0	7	0
McCann, c	8	1	1	1	0	4	14	1
T.Hudson, p	4	0	2	0	0	1	0	1
K.Farnsworth, p	0	0	0	0	0	0	0	0
K.Johnson, ph	1	0	0	0	0	1	0	0
Reitsma, p	0	0	0	0	0	0	0	1
Betemit, ph	1	0	0	0	0	1	0	0
Thomson, p	0	0	0	0	0	0	0	0
Orr, ph	1	0	0	0	0	0	0	0
Brower, p	0	0	0	0	0	0	0	0
Jordan, ph	1	0	1	0	0	0	0	0
Devine, p	0	0	0	0	0	0	0	0
TOTALS	62	6	13	6	11	16	52	16

Houston	AB	R	H	BI	BB	SO	PO	A
Biggio, 2b	7	1	0	0	1	2	3	6
Taveras, cf	3	0	0	0	0	0	3	0
Scott, ph-lf	2	1	0	0	0	1	0	0
Wheeler, p	0	0	0	0	0	0	0	1
Clemens, ph-p	1	0	0	0	0	1	1	0
Berkman, lf-1b	5	1	2	4	0	1	6	1
Burke, pr-cf-lf	2	1	1	1	1	0	1	0
Ensberg, 3b	6	0	0	0	1	2	1	3
Lamb, 1b	4	0	2	0	0	0	6	1
Qualls, p	0	0	0	0	0	0	1	0
Bagwell, ph	1	0	0	0	0	0	0	0
Lidge, p	0	0	0	0	0	0	1	0
R.Chavez, c-1b	1	0	0	0	1	0	6	1
Lane, rf	7	1	1	0	0	2	5	0
A.Everett, ss	3	0	1	0	0	0	2	4
W.Rodriguez, p	0	0	0	0	0	0	0	0
J.Vizcaino, ss-1b-ss	4	0	0	0	0	1	2	3
Ausmus, c-1b-c	6	1	2	1	1	1	15	0
Backe, p	1	0	0	0	0	0	1	0
Gallo, p	0	0	0	0	0	0	0	0
O.Palmeiro, ph	1	0	0	0	1	0	0	0
Springer, p	0	0	0	0	0	0	0	0
Bruntlett, ss-cf-ss-cf	5	1	1	0	0	3	1	0
TOTALS	58	7	10	7	6	14	54	20

							R	H	E	LOB
Atlanta	0 0 4	0 1 0	0 1 0	0 0 0	0 0 0	0 0 0	—	6	13	0	18
Houston	0 0 0	0 1 0	0 4 1	0 0 0	0 0 0	0 0 1	—	7	10	1	7

Atlanta	IP	H	R	ER	HR	BB	SO
T.Hudson	7.0	6	3	3	0	1	5
K.Farnsworth	2.0	2	3	3	2	1	3
Reitsma	2.0	1	0	0	0	1	0
Thomson	2.0	0	0	0	0	1	3
Brower	3.0	0	0	0	0	2	0
Devine (L)	1.1	1	1	1	1	0	3

Houston	IP	H	R	ER	HR	BB	SO
Backe	4.1	5	5	5	1	3	2
Gallo	0.2	0	0	0	0	1	0
Springer	2.0	3	0	0	0	1	0
W.Rodriguez	1.0	1	1	1	1	0	2
Qualls	2.0	1	0	0	0	1	1
Lidge	2.0	1	0	0	0	2	3
Wheeler	3.0	1	0	0	0	3	4
Clemens (W)	3.0	1	0	0	0	0	4

T.Hudson pitched to 2 batters in the 8th.

E—J.Vizcaino. DP—Atlanta 2, Houston 2. LOB—Atlanta 18, Houston 7. Scoring Position—Atlanta 1 for 18, Houston 2 for 6. 2B—C.Jones, A.Jones, Francoeur, Langerhans, T.Hudson, Jordan, Berkman. HR—LaRoche (3rd inning, 2 out, 3 on) off Backe, McCann (8th inning, 0 out, 0 on) off W.Rodriguez, Berkman (8th inning, 1 out, 3 on) off K.Farnsworth, Ausmus (9th inning, 2 out, 0 on) off K.Farnsworth, Burke (18th inning, 1 out, 0 on) off Devine. SB—Furcal 2, Langerhans, Biggio, Bruntlett. S—A.Jones, O.Palmeiro. SH—Furcal, Francoeur, Clemens. WP—Backe. HBP—A.Jones by Backe, Langerhans by Gallo. T—5:50.

A—43,413. U—HP-Cederstrom, 1B-Cooper, 2B-Holbrook, 3B-Brinkman, LF-Hudson, RF-Nelson.

HOW THEY SCORED

TOP OF 3

Braves third. Hudson grounded out, shortstop Everett to first baseman Lamb. Furcal walked on a full count. Giles grounded into fielder's choice, third baseman Ensberg to second baseman Biggio, Furcal out. C.Jones walked, Giles to second. A.Jones was hit by a pitch, Giles to third, C.Jones to second. LaRoche homered to center on a 2-2 count, Giles scored, C.Jones scored, A.Jones scored. Francoeur flied out to center fielder Taveras. Runs: 4, Hits: 1, Errors: 0

TOP OF 5

Braves fifth. Giles singled to right. C.Jones doubled to left, Giles to third. A.Jones hit a sacrifice fly to left fielder Berkman, Giles scored, C.Jones to third. Gallo pitching. LaRoche grounded out, first baseman Lamb unassisted. Francoeur was intentionally walked. Langerhans was hit by a pitch, Francoeur to second. McCann grounded out, second baseman Biggio to first baseman Lamb. Runs: 1, Hits: 2, Errors: 0

BOTTOM OF 5

Astros fifth. Lamb singled to center. Lane grounded into fielder's choice, shortstop Furcal to second baseman Giles, Lamb out. Everett singled to left, Lane to second. Ausmus singled to center, Lane to

third, Everett to second. Palmeiro pinch-hitting for Gallo. Palmeiro hit a sacrifice fly to center fielder A.Jones, Lane scored, Everett to third. Biggio flied out to left fielder Langerhans. Runs: 1, Hits: 3, Errors: 0

TOP OF 8

Braves eighth. Rodriguez pitching. Bruntlett in as shortstop. McCann homered to right on a 1-0 count. Hudson struck out. Furcal flied out to left fielder Berkman. Giles struck out. Runs: 1, Hits: 1, Errors: 0

BOTTOM OF 8

Astros eighth. Franco in as first baseman. Ausmus walked on a full count. Bruntlett infield single to short, Ausmus to second. Farnsworth pitching. Biggio grounded into fielder's choice, third baseman C.Jones unassisted, Ausmus out, Bruntlett to second. Scott pinch-hitting for Taveras.Bruntlett stole third.Biggio stole second. Scott walked on a full count. Berkman homered to left on a 2-1 count, Bruntlett scored, Biggio scored, Scott scored. Ensberg struck out. Lamb flied out to right fielder Francoeur. Runs: 4, Hits: 2, Errors: 0

BOTTOM OF 9

Astros ninth. Lane grounded out, third baseman C.Jones to first baseman Franco. Vizcaino struck out. Ausmus homered to center on a 2-0 count. Bruntlett struck out. Runs: 1, Hits: 1, Errors: 0

BOTTOM OF 18

Astros eighteenth. Clemens struck out. Burke homered to left on a 2-0 count. Runs: 1, Hits: 1, Errors: 0

STATISTICS

HOUSTON ASTROS' BATTING AND FIELDING AVERAGES

Player, position	G	AB	R	H	TB	2B	3B	HR	RBI	BB	IBB	SO	Avg.	OBP	Slg.	PO	A	E	Avg.
Burke,ph-lf-cf-pr	3	3	1	2	6	1	0	1	1	1	0	0	.667	.750	2.000	1	0	0	1.000
Lamb,1b	2	6	1	3	6	0	0	1	1	2	2	0	.500	.625	1.000	13	2	0	1.000
Bagwell,ph	2	2	1	1	1	0	0	0	1	0	0	0	.500	.500	.500	0	0	0	.000
Pettitte,p	1	2	1	1	2	1	0	0	0	0	0	1	.500	.500	1.000	0	2	0	1.000
Berkman,1b-lf	4	14	4	5	9	1	0	1	5	3	1	4	.357	.500	.643	29	3	0	1.000
Taveras,cf	4	14	2	5	6	1	0	0	0	1	0	1	.357	.400	.429	7	0	0	1.000
Biggio,2b	4	19	6	6	10	4	0	0	1	2	1	5	.316	.364	.526	9	16	0	1.000
Ensberg,3b	4	18	2	5	7	2	0	0	7	2	1	3	.278	.350	.389	4	12	1	.941
Lane,rf	4	17	1	4	5	1	0	0	3	1	1	3	.235	.300	.294	11	2	0	1.000
Ausmus,c-1b	4	18	3	4	8	1	0	1	1	2	1	4	.222	.300	.444	36	1	0	1.000
Everett,ss	4	14	1	3	3	0	0	0	1	1	0	1	.214	.250	.214	5	12	1	.944
Bruntlett,cf-2b-ss	3	6	1	1	1	0	0	0	0	0	0	4	.167	.167	.167	1	0	0	1.000
Palmeiro,lf-ph	4	7	0	1	1	0	0	0	3	2	1	0	.143	.364	.143	4	0	0	1.000
Gallo,p	3	0	0	0	0	0	0	0	0	0	0	0	.000	.000	.000	0	0	0	.000
Lidge,p	3	0	0	0	0	0	0	0	0	0	0	0	.000	.000	.000	1	0	0	1.000
Qualls,p	2	0	0	0	0	0	0	0	0	0	0	0	.000	.000	.000	0	0	1	.000
Rodriguez,p	1	0	0	0	0	0	0	0	0	0	0	0	.000	.000	.000	0	0	0	.000
Springer,p	2	0	0	0	0	0	0	0	0	0	0	0	.000	.000	.000	0	0	0	.000
Wheeler,p	3	0	0	0	0	0	0	0	0	0	0	0	.000	.000	.000	0	1	0	1.000
Backe,p	2	1	0	0	0	0	0	0	0	0	0	0	.000	.000	.000	1	1	0	1.000
Chavez,c-1b	1	1	0	0	0	0	0	0	0	1	0	0	.000	.500	.000	6	1	0	1.000
Scott,rf-lf-ph	2	2	1	0	0	0	0	0	0	1	0	1	.000	.333	.000	0	0	0	.000
Clemens,p-ph	2	3	0	0	0	0	0	0	0	0	0	2	.000	.000	.000	1	0	0	1.000
Oswalt,p	1	3	0	0	0	0	0	0	0	0	0	0	.000	.000	.000	1	0	0	1.000
Vizcaino,2b-ph-1b-ss	2	5	0	0	0	0	0	0	0	0	0	1	.000	.000	.000	2	4	1	.857
Totals	4	155	25	41	65	12	0	4	24	19	8	30	.265	.348	.419	132	57	4	.979

ATLANTA BRAVES' BATTING AND FIELDING AVERAGES

Player, position	G	AB	R	H	TB	2B	3B	HR	RBI	BB	IBB	SO	Avg.	OBP	Slg.	PO	A	E	Avg.
LaRoche,1b	3	8	2	4	8	1	0	1	6	3	1	1	.500	.636	1.000	20	1	0	1.000
Betemit,ph	2	2	0	1	1	0	0	0	0	0	0	1	.500	.500	.500	0	0	0	.000
Sosa,p	1	2	0	1	1	0	0	0	1	0	0	1	.500	.500	.500	0	2	0	1.000
Jones,cf	4	17	5	8	14	3	0	1	5	2	0	3	.471	.524	.824	19	0	0	1.000
Langerhans,ph-lf	4	12	1	4	5	1	0	0	0	3	1	3	.333	.500	.417	10	0	0	1.000
Hudson,p	2	6	0	2	3	1	0	0	0	0	0	1	.333	.333	.500	1	2	0	1.000
Estrada,c	1	4	0	1	1	0	0	0	1	0	0	2	.250	.250	.250	6	0	0	1.000
Francoeur,rf	4	17	2	4	7	1	1	0	1	2	1	4	.235	.350	.412	9	0	0	1.000
Franco,1b-ph	3	9	0	2	2	0	0	0	0	1	0	3	.222	.300	.222	17	2	0	1.000

Player, position	G	AB	R	H	TB	2B	3B	HR	RBI	BB	IBB	SO	Avg.	OBP	Slg.	PO	A	E	Avg.
							BATTING										FIELDING		
Giles,2b	4	20	5	4	5	1	0	0	0	2	0	5	.200	.304	.250	12	8	0	1.000
Jordan,lf-ph	3	5	0	1	2	1	0	0	0	0	0	0	.200	.200	.400	2	0	0	1.000
McCann,c	3	16	2	3	9	0	0	2	5	0	0	6	.188	.188	.563	24	1	0	1.000
Jones,3b	4	17	3	3	8	2	0	1	2	4	0	4	.176	.333	.471	3	10	0	1.000
Furcal,ss	4	20	1	3	3	0	0	0	0	3	0	2	.150	.261	.150	6	15	0	1.000
Brower,p	3	0	0	0	0	0	0	0	0	0	0	0	.000	.000	.000	1	1	0	1.000
Devine,p	3	0	0	0	0	0	0	0	0	0	0	0	.000	.000	.000	0	0	0	.000
Farnsworth,p	2	0	0	0	0	0	0	0	0	0	0	0	.000	.000	.000	0	0	0	.000
Foster,p	2	0	0	0	0	0	0	0	0	0	0	0	.000	.000	.000	0	0	0	.000
McBride,p	1	0	0	0	0	0	0	0	0	0	0	0	.000	.000	.000	0	1	0	1.000
Reitsma,p	4	0	0	0	0	0	0	0	0	0	0	0	.000	.000	.000	0	1	0	1.000
Thomson,p	1	0	0	0	0	0	0	0	0	0	0	0	.000	.000	.000	0	0	0	.000
Johnson,ph	4	2	0	0	0	0	0	0	0	1	0	0	.000	.333	.000	0	0	0	.000
Orr,ph-pr	3	2	0	0	0	0	0	0	0	0	0	0	.000	.000	.000	0	0	0	.000
Smoltz,p	1	2	0	0	0	0	0	0	0	0	0	0	.000	.000	.000	0	1	0	1.000
Totals	4	161	21	41	69	11	1	5	21	21	3	36	.255	.353	.429	130	45	0	1.000

HOUSTON ASTROS' PITCHING RECORDS

Pitcher	G	GS	CG	IP	H	R	ER	HR	BB	IBB	SO	HB	WP	W	L	Pct.	ERA
Lidge	3	0	0	4.0	2	0	0	0	4	0	5	0	0	0	0	.000	0.00
Gallo	3	0	0	1.2	1	0	0	0	1	1	0	1	0	0	0	.000	0.00
Wheeler	3	0	0	4.1	4	1	1	0	3	1	5	1	0	0	0	.000	2.08
Oswalt	1	1	0	7.1	6	3	3	0	2	0	7	1	0	1	0	1.000	3.68
Pettitte	1	1	0	7.0	4	3	3	2	2	0	6	0	0	1	0	1.000	3.86
Springer	2	0	0	2.1	5	1	1	0	1	0	1	0	0	0	0	.000	3.86
Clemens	2	1	0	8.0	7	5	5	1	3	0	6	0	0	1	1	.500	5.63
Qualls	2	0	0	3.0	5	2	2	0	2	1	1	0	0	0	0	.000	6.00
Backe	2	1	0	5.1	6	5	5	1	3	0	3	1	1	0	0	.000	8.44
Rodriguez	1	0	0	1.0	1	1	1	1	0	0	2	0	0	0	0	.000	9.00
Totals	4	4	0	44.0	41	21	21	5	21	3	36	4	1	3	1	.750	4.30

No shutouts or saves.

ATLANTA BRAVES' PITCHING RECORDS

Pitcher	G	GS	CG	IP	H	R	ER	HR	BB	IBB	SO	HB	WP	W	L	Pct.	ERA
Brower	3	0	0	5.1	0	0	0	0	3	0	2	0	0	0	0	.000	0.00
Thomson	1	0	0	2.0	0	0	0	0	1	0	3	0	0	0	0	.000	0.00
McBride	1	0	0	1.0	0	0	0	0	0	1	1	0	0	0	0	.000	0.00
Smoltz	1	1	0	7.0	7	1	1	0	1	1	5	0	0	1	0	1.000	1.29
Sosa	1	1	0	6.0	7	3	3	1	2	2	3	1	0	0	1	.000	4.50
Hudson	2	2	0	13.2	13	8	8	0	6	1	8	1	0	0	1	.000	5.27
Farnsworth	2	0	0	3.0	2	3	3	2	1	0	4	0	0	0	0	.000	9.00
Devine	3	0	0	1.2	3	2	2	1	1	1	3	1	0	0	1	.000	10.80
Reitsma	4	0	0	3.1	7	6	6	0	2	2	0	0	0	0	0	.000	16.20
Foster	2	0	0	0.1	2	2	2	0	2	1	1	0	1	0	0	.000	54.00
Totals	4	4	0	43.1	41	25	25	4	19	8	30	3	1	1	3	.250	5.19

No shutouts or saves.

SCORE BY INNINGS

Houston	4	0	3	1	1	0	5	9	1	0	0	0	0	0	0	0	0	1—25
Atlanta	1	5	6	2	1	0	2	3	1	0	0	0	0	0	0	0	0	0—21

MISCELLANEOUS STATISTICS

Sacrifice hits —Pettitte 2, Biggio, Clemens, Francoeur, Furcal, LaRoche, Smoltz, Taveras.

Sacrifice flies —Biggio, Everett, Jones, Lane, Palmeiro.

Stolen bases —Furcal 3, Biggio, Bruntlett, Langerhans.

Caught stealing —None.

Double plays —Furcal, Giles and Franco 2; Backe, Everett and Biggio; Biggio, Everett and Lamb; Ensberg and Lamb; Ensberg, Biggio and Berkman; Everett, Biggio and Berkman; Furcal, Giles and LaRoche; Giles, Furcal and LaRoche; Jones, Giles and Franco; LaRoche, Furcal and Brower; Sosa, Furcal and LaRoche; Vizcaino, Everett and Berkman.

Left on bases —Houston 10, 7, 7, 7—31; Atlanta 5, 7, 8, 18—38.

Scoring position —Houston 5 for 12, 1 for 4, 5 for 13, 2 for 6—13 for 35; Atlanta 3 for 9, 5 for 9, 2 for 9, 1 for 18—11 for 45.

Hit by pitcher —by Hudson (Palmeiro), by Wheeler (Giles), by Oswalt (Francoeur), by Sosa (Berkman), by Backe (Jones), by Gallo (Langerhans), by Devine (Lane).

Passed balls —None.

Balks —None.

Time of games —3:11, 2:52, 2:50, 5:50—Avg.: 3:40.

Attendance —40,590, 46,181, 43,759, 43,413—173,943.

Umpires —Brinkman, Joe; Hudson, Marvin; Nelson, Jeff; Cederstrom, Gary; Cooper, Eric; and Holbrook, Sam.

2005 REVIEW N.L. Division Series

A.L. CHAMPIONSHIP SERIES

LOS ANGELES VS. CHICAGO

RESULTS

DAY	DATE	PLACE	SCORE
TUE.	OCT. 11	CHICAGO	LOS ANGELES 3, CHICAGO 2
WED.	OCT. 12	CHICAGO	CHICAGO 2, LOS ANGELES 1
FRI.	OCT. 14	ANAHEIM	CHICAGO 5, LOS ANGELES 2
SAT.	OCT. 15	ANAHEIM	CHICAGO 8, LOS ANGELES 2
SUN.	OCT. 16	ANAHEIM	CHICAGO 6, LOS ANGELES 3

BOX SCORES

GAME 1

LOS ANGELES 3, CHICAGO 2

TUESDAY, OCTOBER 11, AT CHICAGO

Los Angeles	AB	R	H	BI	BB	SO	PO	A
Figgins, 3b	3	0	1	0	0	1	0	2
O.Cabrera, ss	4	0	1	1	0	0	5	1
V.Guerrero, dh	4	0	0	1	0	0	0	0
G.Anderson, lf	4	1	1	1	0	1	4	0
B.Molina, c	4	1	0	0	0	0	3	2
Erstad, 1b	4	0	1	0	0	0	7	0
J.Rivera, rf	4	0	0	0	0	0	3	0
Finley, cf	3	1	1	0	0	2	3	0
A.Kennedy, 2b	3	1	1	0	0	0	1	3
P.Byrd, p	0	0	0	0	0	0	1	0
Shields, p	0	0	0	0	0	0	0	0
F.Rodriguez, p	0	0	0	0	0	0	0	0
TOTALS	33	3	7	3	0	4	27	8

Chi White Sox	AB	R	H	BI	BB	SO	PO	A
Podsednik, lf	3	0	1	0	1	1	1	0
Iguchi, 2b	4	0	1	0	0	0	4	2
Dye, rf	4	0	1	0	0	0	0	0
Konerko, 1b	4	0	0	0	0	0	14	0
C.Everett, dh	4	1	1	0	0	0	0	0
Ozuna, pr	0	0	0	0	0	0	0	0
Rowand, cf	3	0	0	0	0	0	2	0
Pierzynski, c	4	0	1	1	0	0	4	0
Crede, 3b	4	1	1	1	0	2	1	2
Uribe, ss	3	0	1	0	0	0	1	6
Contreras, p	0	0	0	0	0	0	0	3
Cotts, p	0	0	0	0	0	0	0	0
TOTALS	33	2	7	2	1	3	27	13

					R	H	E	LOB
Los Angeles	0 1 2	0 0 0	0 0 0—		3	7	1	4
Chi White Sox	0 0 1	1 0 0	0 0 0—		2	7	0	6

Los Angeles	IP	H	R	ER	HR	BB	SO
P.Byrd (W)	6.0	5	2	2	1	1	1
Shields (HOLD)	2.0	2	0	0	0	0	1
F.Rodriguez (S)	1.0	0	0	0	0	0	1

Chi White Sox	IP	H	R	ER	HR	BB	SO
Contreras (L)	8.1	7	3	3	1	0	4
Cotts	0.2	0	0	0	0	0	0

P.Byrd pitched to 1 batter in the 7th.

E—Figgins. LOB—Los Angeles 4, Chi White Sox 6. Scoring Position—Los Angeles 1 for 6, Chi White Sox 1 for 3. HR—G.Anderson (2nd inning, 0 out, 0 on) off Contreras, Crede (3rd inning, 1 out, 0 on) off P.Byrd. SB—Figgins, Erstad. CS—Podsednik, Pierzynski. SH—Figgins. HBP—Rowand by P.Byrd. T—2:47. A—40,659. U—HP-Crawford, 1B-Eddings, 2B-Barrett, 3B-Kulpa, LF-Rapuano, RF-Marsh.

HOW THEY SCORED

TOP OF 2

Angels second. Anderson homered to right on a 2-0 count. B.Molina grounded out, shortstop Uribe to first baseman Konerko. Erstad grounded out, first baseman Konerko unassisted. Rivera grounded out, pitcher Contreras to first baseman Konerko. Runs: 1, Hits: 1, Errors: 0

TOP OF 3

Angels third. Finley singled to right. Kennedy singled to left, Finley to second. Figgins sacrificed, third baseman Crede to second baseman Iguchi, Finley to third, Kennedy to second. Cabrera infield single to third, Finley scored, Kennedy to third. Guerrero grounded into fielder's choice, pitcher Contreras to second baseman Iguchi, Kennedy scored, Cabrera out. Anderson grounded out, second baseman Iguchi to first baseman Konerko. Runs: 2, Hits: 3, Errors: 0

BOTTOM OF 3

White Sox third. Pierzynski grounded out, shortstop Cabrera to first baseman Erstad. Crede homered to left on a 0-1 count. Uribe lined out to left fielder Anderson. Podsednik singled to center. Iguchi singled to center, Podsednik to second. Dye fouled out to first baseman Erstad. Runs: 1, Hits: 3, Errors: 0

BOTTOM OF 4

White Sox fourth. Konerko grounded out, second baseman Kennedy to first baseman Erstad. Everett singled to center. Rowand grounded out, first baseman Erstad unassisted, Everett to second. Pierzynski singled to right, Everett scored. Crede struck out. Runs: 1, Hits: 2, Errors: 0

GAME 2

CHICAGO 2, LOS ANGELES 1

WEDNESDAY, OCTOBER 12, AT CHICAGO

Los Angeles	AB	R	H	BI	BB	SO	PO	A
Figgins, cf	4	0	0	0	0	0	0	0
O.Cabrera, ss	4	0	2	0	0	0	0	4
V.Guerrero, rf	4	0	0	0	0	0	2	0
B.Molina, dh	3	0	0	0	0	1	0	0
G.Anderson, lf	4	0	0	0	0	1	1	1
Quinlan, 3b	3	1	1	1	0	2	1	2
Erstad, 1b	3	0	1	0	0	0	10	0
J.Molina, c	3	0	1	0	0	0	5	0
DaVanon, pr	0	0	0	0	0	0	0	0
Paul, c	0	0	0	0	0	0	4	0
A.Kennedy, 2b	2	0	0	0	0	0	3	0
Washburn, p	0	0	0	0	0	0	0	3
Donnelly, p	0	0	0	0	0	0	0	0
Shields, p	0	0	0	0	0	0	0	0
K.Escobar, p	0	0	0	0	0	0	0	0
TOTALS	30	1	5	1	0	4	26	10

Chi White Sox	AB	R	H	BI	BB	SO	PO	A
Podsednik, lf	4	1	1	0	0	1	1	0
Iguchi, 2b	2	0	0	0	0	1	4	4
Dye, rf	4	0	1	1	0	1	2	0
Konerko, 1b	4	0	1	0	0	2	10	0
C.Everett, dh	4	0	0	0	0	1	0	0
Rowand, cf	4	0	1	0	0	1	2	0
Pierzynski, c	3	0	0	0	1	2	4	1
Ozuna, pr	0	1	0	0	0	0	0	0

Chi White Sox	AB	R	H	BI	BB	SO	PO	A
Crede, 3b	4	0	2	1	0	0	0	2
Uribe, ss	3	0	1	0	0	0	3	5
Buehrle, p	0	0	0	0	0	0	1	3
TOTALS	32	2	7	2	1	9	27	16

						R	H	E	LOB
Los Angeles	0 0 0	0 1 0	0 0 0—	1	5	3	4
Chi White Sox	1 0 0	0 0 0	0 0 1—	2	7	1	7

Los Angeles	IP	H	R	ER	HR	BB	SO
Washburn	4.2	4	1	0	0	1	1
Donnelly	0.1	0	0	0	0	0	1
Shields	1.0	0	0	0	0	0	2
K.Escobar (L)	2.2	3	1	0	0	0	5

Chi White Sox	IP	H	R	ER	HR	BB	SO
Buehrle (W)	9.0	5	1	1	1	0	4

E—Washburn, Paul, V.Guerrero, Uribe. DP—Los Angeles 1, Chi White Sox 2. LOB—Los Angeles 4, Chi White Sox 7. Scoring Position—Los Angeles 0 for 5, Chi White Sox 1 for 5. 2B—O.Cabrera, Rowand, Crede 2. HR—Quinlan (5th inning, 0 out, 0 on) off Buehrle. SB—Ozuna. SH—A.Kennedy, Iguchi. PB—Pierzynski. HBP—B.Molina by Buehrle, Iguchi by Washburn. T—2:34. A—41,013. U—HP-Eddings, 1B-Barrett, 2B-Kulpa, 3B-Rapuano, LF-Marsh, RF-Crawford.

HOW THEY SCORED

BOTTOM OF 1
White Sox first. Podsednik safe at second on Washburn's error. Iguchi sacrificed, pitcher Washburn to first baseman Erstad, Podsednik to third. Dye grounded out, shortstop Cabrera to first baseman Erstad, Podsednik scored. Konerko singled to left. Everett grounded out, shortstop Cabrera to first baseman Erstad. Runs: 1, Hits: 1, Errors: 1

TOP OF 5
Angels fifth. Quinlan homered to left on a 1-0 count. Erstad singled to center. J.Molina grounded into fielder's choice, catcher Pierzynski to shortstop Uribe, Erstad out. Kennedy grounded into fielder's choice, second baseman Iguchi to shortstop Uribe, J.Molina out. On Pierzynski's passed ball, Kennedy to second. Figgins flied out to right fielder Dye. Runs: 1, Hits: 2, Errors: 0

BOTTOM OF 9
White Sox ninth. Everett grounded out, first baseman Erstad unassisted. Rowand struck out. Pierzynski struck out, safe on Paul's fielding error. Ozuna pinch-running for Pierzynski. Ozuna stole second. Crede doubled to left, Ozuna scored. Runs: 1, Hits: 1, Errors: 1

GAME 3

CHICAGO 5, LOS ANGELES 2

FRIDAY, OCTOBER 14, AT ANAHEIM

Chi White Sox	AB	R	H	BI	BB	SO	PO	A
Podsednik, lf	5	1	2	0	0	1	2	0
Iguchi, 2b	4	2	2	0	2	2	2	3
Dye, rf	2	1	1	1	2	1	2	1
Konerko, 1b	4	1	3	3	0	1	9	0
C.Everett, dh	4	0	1	1	0	1	0	0
Rowand, cf	4	0	0	0	0	0	2	0
Pierzynski, c	4	0	1	0	0	1	7	0
Crede, 3b	4	0	0	0	0	0	2	2
Uribe, ss	4	0	1	0	0	2	1	2
Garland, p	0	0	0	0	0	0	0	3
TOTALS	35	5	11	5	2	9	27	11

Los Angeles	AB	R	H	BI	BB	SO	PO	A
Figgins, 3b	3	0	0	0	1	0	0	4

Los Angeles	AB	R	H	BI	BB	SO	PO	A
O.Cabrera, ss	4	1	1	2	0	2	2	3
V.Guerrero, rf	4	0	1	0	0	1	3	0
G.Anderson, lf	3	0	0	0	0	1	2	0
B.Molina, c	3	0	0	0	0	1	9	0
Erstad, 1b	3	0	1	0	0	1	9	0
J.Rivera, dh	2	0	0	0	0	1	0	0
DaVanon, ph-dh	1	0	0	0	0	0	0	0
Finley, cf	3	0	0	0	0	0	0	0
A.Kennedy, 2b	3	1	1	0	0	0	2	1
Lackey, p	0	0	0	0	0	0	0	1
Gregg, p	0	0	0	0	0	0	0	0
Donnelly, p	0	0	0	0	0	0	0	0
TOTALS	29	2	4	2	1	7	27	9

						R	H	E	LOB
Chi White Sox	3 0 1	0 1 0	0 0 0—	5	11	0	6
Los Angeles	0 0 0	0 0 2	0 0 0—	2	4	0	1

Chi White Sox	IP	H	R	ER	HR	BB	SO
Garland (W)	9.0	4	2	2	1	1	7

Los Angeles	IP	H	R	ER	HR	BB	SO
Lackey (L)	5.0	8	5	5	1	1	3
Gregg	2.0	0	0	0	0	1	3
Donnelly	2.0	2	0	0	0	0	3

Gregg pitched to 2 batters in the 8th.

DP—Chi White Sox 1, Los Angeles 2. LOB—Chi White Sox 6, Los Angeles 1. Scoring Position—Chi White Sox 4 for 11, Los Angeles 0 for 2. 2B—Iguchi, Dye, Erstad. HR—Konerko (1st inning, 1 out, 1 on) off Lackey, O.Cabrera (6th inning, 2 out, 1 on) off Garland. SH—Iguchi. T—2:42. A—44,725. U—HP-Barrett, 1B-Kulpa, 2B-Rapuano, 3B-Marsh, LF-Crawford, RF-Eddings.

HOW THEY SCORED

TOP OF 1
White Sox first. Podsednik singled to right. Iguchi sacrificed, third baseman Figgins to first baseman Erstad, Podsednik to second. Dye doubled to center, Podsednik scored. Konerko homered to left on a full count, Dye scored. Everett grounded out, second baseman Kennedy to first baseman Erstad. Rowand flied out to right fielder Guerrero. Runs: 3, Hits: 3, Errors: 0

TOP OF 3
White Sox third. Iguchi singled to left. Dye walked on a full count, Iguchi to second. Konerko struck out. Everett singled to left, Iguchi scored, Dye to second. Rowand lined into a double play, shortstop Cabrera to second baseman Kennedy, Dye out. Runs: 1, Hits: 2, Errors: 0

TOP OF 5
White Sox fifth. Podsednik grounded out, third baseman Figgins to first baseman Erstad. Iguchi doubled to center. Dye struck out. Konerko singled to center, Iguchi scored. Konerko to second. Everett flied out to left fielder Anderson. Runs: 1, Hits: 2, Errors: 0

BOTTOM OF 6
Angels sixth. Finley popped out to third baseman Crede. Kennedy singled to left. Figgins flied out to left fielder Podsednik. Cabrera homered to left on a 2-2 count, Kennedy scored. Guerrero struck out. Runs: 2, Hits: 2, Errors: 0

GAME 4

CHICAGO 8, LOS ANGELES 2

SATURDAY, OCTOBER 15, AT ANAHEIM

Chi White Sox	AB	R	H	BI	BB	SO	PO	A
Podsednik, lf	2	2	1	0	3	0	4	0
Iguchi, 2b	4	1	0	0	0	2	1	3
Dye, rf	5	1	0	0	0	0	1	0

Chi White Sox	AB	R	H	BI	BB	SO	PO	A
Konerko, 1b	4	1	1	3	1	0	12	0
C.Everett, dh	3	1	2	2	1	0	0	0
Rowand, cf	4	1	1	0	0	1	2	0
Pierzynski, c	4	1	1	1	0	2	4	1
Crede, 3b	4	0	2	2	0	1	1	4
Uribe, ss	3	0	0	0	1	0	2	6
F.Garcia, p	0	0	0	0	0	0	0	0
TOTALS	33	8	8	8	6	6	27	14

Los Angeles	AB	R	H	BI	BB	SO	PO	A
Figgins, 3b	4	0	0	0	0	2	0	1
O.Cabrera, ss	4	0	0	0	0	0	1	4
M.Izturis, ss	0	0	0	0	0	0	0	0
V.Guerrero, rf	4	0	0	0	0	0	4	0
G.Anderson, lf	4	1	1	0	0	2	1	0
Erstad, 1b	3	1	1	0	1	0	6	1
DaVanon, pr	0	0	0	0	0	0	0	0
Kotchman, dh	4	0	2	1	0	0	0	0
B.Molina, c	3	0	1	1	0	0	6	1
Finley, cf	3	0	1	0	0	0	4	1
A.Kennedy, 2b	3	0	0	0	0	1	5	2
E.Santana, p	0	0	0	0	0	0	0	0
Shields, p	0	0	0	0	0	0	0	0
Donnelly, p	0	0	0	0	0	0	0	0
Yan, p	0	0	0	0	0	0	0	0
TOTALS	32	2	6	2	1	5	27	10

						R	H	E	LOB
Chi White Sox	3 0 1		1 1 0		0 2 0 —		8	8	1	5
Los Angeles	0 1 0		1 0 0		0 0 0 —		2	6	1	4

Chi White Sox	IP	H	R	ER	HR	BB	SO
F.Garcia (W)	9.0	6	2	2	0	1	5

Los Angeles	IP	H	R	ER	HR	BB	SO
E.Santana (L)	4.1	3	6	5	2	3	2
Shields	1.2	2	0	0	0	1	1
Donnelly	1.0	0	0	0	0	1	1
Yan	2.0	3	2	2	0	1	2

E—F.Garcia, O.Cabrera. DP—Chi White Sox 1, Los Angeles 1. LOB—Chi White Sox 5, Los Angeles 4. Scoring Position—Chi White Sox 4 for 13, Los Angeles 1 for 5. 2B—Rowand, Kotchman. 3B—Podsednik. HR—Konerko (1st inning, 1 out, 2 on) off E.Santana, Pierzynski (4th inning, 1 out, 0 on) off E.Santana. SB—Podsednik 2, Dye. CS—Crede. HBP—Iguchi by E.Santana. T—2:46. A—44,857. U—HP-Kulpa, 1B-Rapuano, 2B-Marsh, 3B-Crawford, LF-Eddings, RF-Barrett.

HOW THEY SCORED

TOP OF 1
White Sox first. Podsednik walked on a full count. Iguchi was hit by a pitch, Podsednik to second. Dye flied out to center fielder Finley, Podsednik to third, Iguchi to second. Konerko homered to center on a full count, Podsednik scored, Iguchi scored. Everett flied out to right fielder Guerrero. Rowand struck out. Runs: 3, Hits: 1, Errors: 0

BOTTOM OF 2
Angels second. Anderson flied out to right fielder Dye. Erstad walked on four pitches. Kotchman infield single to third, Erstad to second. On Garcia's error, Erstad to third, Kotchman to second. B.Molina singled to center, Erstad scored, Kotchman to third. Finley grounded into a double play, second baseman Iguchi to shortstop Uribe to first baseman Konerko, B.Molina out. Runs: 1, Hits: 2, Errors: 1

TOP OF 3
White Sox third. Iguchi popped out to second baseman Kennedy. Dye safe on Cabrera's error. Konerko flied out to center fielder Finley. Dye stole second. Everett singled to center, Dye scored. Everett was out advancing, center fielder Finley to first baseman

Erstad to second baseman Kennedy, Everett out. Runs: 1, Hits: 1, Errors: 1

TOP OF 4
White Sox fourth. Rowand grounded out, shortstop Cabrera to first baseman Erstad. Pierzynski homered to center on a 0-1 count. Crede struck out. Uribe popped out to first baseman Erstad. Runs: 1, Hits: 1, Errors: 0

BOTTOM OF 4
Angels fourth. Guerrero grounded out, shortstop Uribe to first baseman Konerko. Anderson singled to center. Erstad popped out to shortstop Uribe. Kotchman doubled to center, Anderson scored. B.Molina grounded out, shortstop Uribe to first baseman Konerko. Runs: 1, Hits: 2, Errors: 0

TOP OF 5
White Sox fifth. Podsednik walked on a full count. Iguchi flied out to center fielder Finley. Shields pitching. Podsednik stole second. Dye grounded out, second baseman Kennedy to first baseman Erstad. Konerko was intentionally walked. Everett singled to left, Podsednik scored, Konerko to second. Rowand grounded into fielder's choice, shortstop Cabrera to second baseman Kennedy, Everett out. Runs: 1, Hits: 1, Errors: 0

TOP OF 8
White Sox eighth. Yan pitching. Everett walked on a full count. Rowand doubled to left, Everett to third. Pierzynski struck out. Crede singled to left, Everett scored, Rowand scored. Uribe grounded into a double play, third baseman Figgins to second baseman Kennedy to first baseman Erstad, Crede out. Runs: 2, Hits: 2, Errors: 0

GAME 5

CHICAGO 6, LOS ANGELES 3

SUNDAY, OCTOBER 16, AT ANAHEIM

Chi White Sox	AB	R	H	BI	BB	SO	PO	A
Podsednik, lf	3	0	0	0	2	2	2	0
Iguchi, 2b	3	1	0	0	1	1	4	3
Dye, rf	4	1	2	1	1	1	2	0
Konerko, 1b	5	0	1	1	0	1	12	0
C.Everett, dh	5	0	1	0	0	2	0	0
Rowand, cf	3	2	1	1	1	0	3	0
Pierzynski, c	3	0	0	0	0	1	2	0
Crede, 3b	3	1	2	3	0	0	1	1
Uribe, ss	3	1	1	0	1	1	0	7
Contreras, p	0	0	0	0	0	0	1	1
TOTALS	32	6	8	6	6	9	27	12

Los Angeles	AB	R	H	BI	BB	SO	PO	A
Figgins, 3b	3	1	1	1	0	0	1	3
O.Cabrera, ss	4	0	0	0	0	0	1	0
G.Anderson, cf	2	0	1	1	1	0	2	0
V.Guerrero, rf	4	0	0	0	0	0	2	1
Erstad, 1b	4	0	0	0	0	1	8	0
B.Molina, c	4	0	0	0	0	0	8	4
Kotchman, dh	3	0	0	0	1	1	0	0
J.Rivera, lf	3	1	1	0	0	0	4	0
A.Kennedy, 2b	3	1	2	1	0	1	1	2
P.Byrd, p	0	0	0	0	0	0	0	0
Shields, p	0	0	0	0	0	0	0	0
K.Escobar, p	0	0	0	0	0	0	0	0
F.Rodriguez, p	0	0	0	0	0	0	0	0
TOTALS	30	3	5	3	2	2	27	10

						R	H	E	LOB
Chi White Sox	0 1 0		0 1 0		1 1 2 —		6	8	1	9
Los Angeles	0 0 1		0 2 0		0 0 0 —		3	5	2	4

Chi White Sox	IP	H	R	ER	HR	BB	SO
Contreras (W)	9.0	5	3	3	0	2	2

Los Angeles	IP	H	R	ER	HR	BB	SO
P.Byrd	4.2	5	2	2	0	1	1
Shields	1.1	0	0	0	0	0	1
K.Escobar (BS, L)	1.2	1	2	1	1	2	5
F.Rodriguez	1.1	2	2	0	0	3	2

E—Contreras, K.Escobar, A.Kennedy. DP—Los Angeles 1. LOB—Chi White Sox 9, Los Angeles 4. Scoring Position—Chi White Sox 3 for 11, Los Angeles 1 for 4. 2B—Dye, Konerko, Rowand, Uribe, Figgins, J.Kennedy. HR—Crede (7th inning, 0 out, 0 on) off K.Escobar. SB—Podsednik. CS—Iguchi. S—Rowand, Crede, G.Anderson. SH—Pierzynski, Figgins. PB—Pierzynski. HBP—Iguchi by P.Byrd. T—3:11. A—44,712. U—HP-Rapuano, 1B-Marsh, 2B-Crawford, 3B-Eddings, LF-Barrett, RF-Kulpa.

HOW THEY SCORED

TOP OF 2

White Sox second. Rowand doubled to right. Pierzynski sacrificed, catcher B.Molina to first baseman Erstad, Rowand to third. Crede hit a sacrifice fly to center fielder Anderson, Rowand scored. Uribe grounded out, third baseman Figgins to first baseman Erstad. Runs: 1, Hits: 1, Errors: 0

BOTTOM OF 3

Angels third. Rivera doubled to left. On Contreras' error on a pick-off attempt, Rivera to third. Kennedy singled to center, Rivera scored. Figgins sacrificed, third baseman Crede to second baseman Iguchi, Kennedy to second. Cabrera grounded out, shortstop Uribe to first baseman Konerko. On Pierzynski's passed ball, Kennedy to third. Anderson walked on four pitches. Guerrero grounded into fielder's choice, shortstop Uribe to second baseman Iguchi, Anderson out. Runs: 1, Hits: 2, Errors: 1

TOP OF 5

White Sox fifth. Crede grounded out, third baseman Figgins to first baseman Erstad. Uribe doubled to left. Podsednik walked on a full count. Iguchi flied out to left fielder Rivera. Dye doubled to center, Uribe scored, Podsednik to third. Shields pitching. Konerko flied out to left fielder Rivera. Runs: 1, Hits: 2, Errors: 0

BOTTOM OF 5

Angels fifth. Kennedy infield single to third. Figgins doubled to right, Kennedy scored. Cabrera grounded out, second baseman Iguchi to first baseman Konerko, Figgins to third. Anderson hit a sacrifice fly to right fielder Dye, Figgins scored. Guerrero grounded out, second baseman Iguchi to first baseman Konerko. Runs: 2, Hits: 2, Errors: 0

TOP OF 7

White Sox seventh. Escobar pitching. Crede homered to left on a 0-1 count. Uribe struck out. Podsednik walked. Podsednik stole second. Iguchi struck out. Dye struck out. Runs: 1, Hits: 1, Errors: 0

TOP OF 8

White Sox eighth. Konerko struck out. Everett struck out. Rowand walked on a full count. Pierzynski safe on Escobar's error, Rowand to second. Rodriguez pitching. Crede infield single to short, Rowand scored, Pierzynski to second. Uribe walked on four pitches, Pierzynski to third, Crede to second. Podsednik struck out. Runs: 1, Hits: 1, Errors: 1

TOP OF 9

White Sox ninth. Iguchi walked on a full count. Iguchi safe, though caught stealing, on second baseman Kennedy's error, Iguchi to second. Dye walked on a full count. Konerko doubled to right, Iguchi scored, Dye to third. Everett struck out. Rowand hit a sacrifice fly to right fielder Guerrero, Dye scored. Konerko was out advancing, right fielder Guerrero to catcher B.Molina to third baseman Figgins, Konerko out. Runs: 2, Hits: 1, Errors: 1

STATISTICS

CHICAGO WHITE SOX'S BATTING AND FIELDING AVERAGES

Player, position	G	AB	R	H	TB	2B	3B	HR	RBI	BB	IBB	SO	Avg.	OBP	Slg.	PO	A	E	Avg.
Crede,3b	5	19	2	7	15	2	0	2	7	0	0	3	.368	.350	.789	5	11	0	1.000
Podsednik,lf	5	17	4	5	7	0	1	0	0	6	0	5	.294	.478	.412	10	0	0	1.000
Konerko,1b	5	21	2	6	13	1	0	2	7	1	1	4	.286	.318	.619	57	1	0	1.000
Dye,rf	5	19	3	5	7	2	0	0	3	3	0	3	.263	.364	.368	7	1	0	1.000
Everett,dh	5	20	2	5	5	0	0	0	3	1	0	4	.250	.286	.250	0	0	0	.000
Uribe,ss	5	16	1	4	5	1	0	0	0	2	0	3	.250	.333	.313	7	26	1	.971
Iguchi,2b	5	17	4	3	4	1	0	0	0	1	0	6	.176	.333	.235	15	15	0	1.000
Pierzynski,c	5	18	1	3	6	0	0	1	2	1	0	6	.167	.211	.333	21	2	0	1.000
Rowand,cf	5	18	3	3	6	3	0	0	1	1	0	2	.167	.238	.333	11	0	0	1.000
Buehrle,lf	1	0	0	0	0	0	0	0	0	0	0	0	.000	.000	.000	1	3	0	1.000
Contreras,p	2	0	0	0	0	0	0	0	0	0	0	0	.000	.000	.000	1	4	1	.833
Cotts,p	1	0	0	0	0	0	0	0	0	0	0	0	.000	.000	.000	0	0	0	.000
Garcia,p	1	0	0	0	0	0	0	0	0	0	0	0	.000	.000	.000	0	0	1	.000
Garland,p	1	0	0	0	0	0	0	0	0	0	0	0	.000	.000	.000	0	3	0	1.000
Ozuna,pr	2	0	1	0	0	0	0	0	0	0	0	0	.000	.000	.000	0	0	0	.000
Totals	5	165	23	41	68	10	1	5	23	16	1	36	.248	.326	.412	135	66	3	.985

LOS ANGELES ANGELS' BATTING AND FIELDING AVERAGES

Player, position	G	AB	R	H	TB	2B	3B	HR	RBI	BB	IBB	SO	Avg.	OBP	Slg.	PO	A	E	Avg.
Molina,c	1	3	0	1	1	0	0	0	0	0	0	0	.333	.333	.333	5	0	0	1.000
Quinlan,3b	1	3	1	1	4	0	0	1	1	0	0	2	.333	.333	1.333	1	2	0	1.000
Kennedy,2b	5	14	3	4	4	0	0	0	1	0	0	1	.286	.286	.286	12	8	1	.952
Kotchman,dh	2	7	0	2	3	1	0	0	1	1	0	2	.286	.375	.429	0	0	0	.000
Erstad,1b	5	17	1	4	5	1	0	0	0	1	0	2	.235	.278	.294	40	1	0	1.000
Finley,cf	3	9	1	2	2	0	0	0	0	0	0	2	.222	.222	.222	7	1	0	1.000
Cabrera,ss	5	20	1	4	8	1	0	1	3	0	0	2	.200	.200	.400	9	12	1	.955
Anderson,lf-cf	5	17	2	3	6	0	0	1	2	1	0	5	.176	.211	.353	10	1	0	1.000
Figgins,3b-cf	5	17	1	2	3	1	0	0	1	1	0	3	.118	.167	.176	1	10	1	.917

Player, position	G	AB	R	H	TB	2B	3B	HR	RBI	BB	IBB	SO	Avg.	OBP	Slg.	PO	A	E	Avg.
Molina,c-dh	5	17	0	2	2	0	0	0	1	0	0	2	.118	.167	.118	26	7	0	1.000
Rivera,rf-dh-lf	3	9	1	1	2	1	0	0	0	0	0	1	.111	.111	.222	7	0	0	1.000
Guerrero,dh-rf	5	20	0	1	1	0	0	0	1	0	0	1	.050	.050	.050	11	1	1	.923
Byrd,p	2	0	0	0	0	0	0	0	0	0	0	0	.000	.000	.000	1	0	0	1.000
Donnelly,p	3	0	0	0	0	0	0	0	0	0	0	0	.000	.000	.000	0	0	0	.000
Escobar,p	2	0	0	0	0	0	0	0	0	0	0	0	.000	.000	.000	0	0	1	.000
Gregg,p	1	0	0	0	0	0	0	0	0	0	0	0	.000	.000	.000	0	0	0	.000
Izturis,ss	1	0	0	0	0	0	0	0	0	0	0	0	.000	.000	.000	0	0	0	.000
Lackey,p	1	0	0	0	0	0	0	0	0	0	0	0	.000	.000	.000	0	1	0	1.000
Paul,c	1	0	0	0	0	0	0	0	0	0	0	0	.000	.000	.000	4	0	1	.800
Rodriguez,p	2	0	0	0	0	0	0	0	0	0	0	0	.000	.000	.000	0	0	0	.000
Santana,p	1	0	0	0	0	0	0	0	0	0	0	0	.000	.000	.000	0	0	0	.000
Shields,p	4	0	0	0	0	0	0	0	0	0	0	0	.000	.000	.000	0	0	0	.000
Washburn,p	1	0	0	0	0	0	0	0	0	0	0	0	.000	.000	.000	0	3	1	.750
Yan,p	1	0	0	0	0	0	0	0	0	0	0	0	.000	.000	.000	0	0	0	.000
DaVanon,pr-dh	3	1	0	0	0	0	0	0	0	0	0	0	.000	.000	.000	0	0	0	.000
Totals	5	154	11	27	41	5	0	3	11	4	0	22	.175	.200	.266	134	47	7	.963

CHICAGO WHITE SOX'S PITCHING RECORDS

Pitcher	G	GS	CG	IP	H	R	ER	HR	BB	IBB	SO	HB	WP	W	L	Pct.	ERA
Cotts	1	0	0	0.2	0	0	0	0	0	0	0	0	0	0	0	.000	0.00
Buehrle	1	1	1	9.0	5	1	1	1	0	0	4	1	0	1	0	1.000	1.00
Garcia	1	1	1	9.0	6	2	2	0	1	0	5	0	0	1	0	1.000	2.00
Garland	1	1	1	9.0	4	2	2	1	1	0	7	0	0	1	0	1.000	2.00
Contreras	2	2	1	17.1	12	6	6	1	2	0	6	0	0	1	1	.500	3.12
Totals	5	5	4	45.0	27	11	11	3	4	0	22	1	0	4	1	.800	2.20

No shutouts or saves.

LOS ANGELES ANGELS' PITCHING RECORDS

Pitcher	G	GS	CG	IP	H	R	ER	HR	BB	IBB	SO	HB	WP	W	L	Pct.	ERA
Shields	4	0	0	6.0	4	0	0	0	1	1	5	0	0	0	0	.000	0.00
Washburn	1	1	0	4.2	4	1	0	0	1	0	1	1	0	0	0	.000	0.00
Donnelly	3	0	0	3.1	2	0	0	0	1	0	5	0	0	0	0	.000	0.00
Rodriguez	2	0	0	2.1	2	2	0	0	3	0	3	0	0	0	0	.000	0.00
Gregg	1	0	0	2.0	1	0	0	0	1	0	3	0	0	0	0	.000	0.00
Escobar	2	0	0	4.1	4	3	1	1	2	0	10	0	0	0	2	.000	2.08
Byrd	2	2	0	10.2	10	4	4	1	2	0	2	2	0	1	0	1.000	3.38
Lackey	1	1	0	5.0	8	5	5	1	1	0	3	0	0	0	1	.000	9.00
Yan	1	0	0	2.0	3	2	2	0	1	0	2	0	0	0	0	.000	9.00
Santana	1	1	0	4.1	3	6	5	2	3	0	2	1	0	0	1	.000	10.38
Totals	5	5	0	44.2	41	23	17	5	16	1	36	4	0	1	4	.200	3.43

No shutouts. Saves—Rodriguez.

SCORE BY INNINGS

Chicago	7	1	3	2	3	0	1	3	3—23
Los Angeles	0	2	3	1	3	2	0	0	0—11

MISCELLANEOUS STATISTICS

Sacrifice hits —Figgins 2, Iguchi 2, Kennedy, Pierzynski.

Sacrifice flies —Anderson, Crede, Rowand.

Stolen bases —Podsednik 3, Dye, Erstad, Figgins, Ozuna.

Caught stealing —Crede, Iguchi, Pierzynski, Podsednik.

Double plays —Anderson and Kennedy; Buehrle, Uribe and Konerko; Cabrera and Erstad; Cabrera and Kennedy; Figgins, Kennedy and Erstad; Iguchi and Konerko; Iguchi, Uribe and Konerko; Uribe, Iguchi and Konerko.

Left on bases —Chicago 6, 7, 6, 5, 9—33; Los Angeles 4, 4, 1, 4, 4—17.

Scoring position —Chicago 1 for 3, 1 for 5, 4 for 11, 4 for 13, 3 for 11—13 for 43; Los Angeles 1 for 6, 0 for 5, 0 for 0, 1 for 5, 1 for 4—3 for 20.

Hit by pitcher —by Byrd 2 (Iguchi, Rowand), by Washburn (Iguchi), by Buehrle (Molina), by Santana (Iguchi).

Passed balls —Pierzynski 2.

Balks—None.

Time of games —2:47, 2:34, 2:42, 2:46, 3:11—Avg.: 2:48.

Attendance —40,659, 41,013, 44,725, 44,857, 44,712—215,966.

Umpires —Crawford, Jerry; Eddings, Doug; Barrett, Ted; Kulpa, Ron; Rapuano, Ed; and Marsh, Randy.

N.L. CHAMPIONSHIP SERIES

ST. LOUIS VS. HOUSTON

RESULTS

DAY	DATE	PLACE	SCORE
WED.	OCT. 12	ST. LOUIS	ST. LOUIS 5, HOUSTON 3
THU.	OCT. 13	ST. LOUIS	HOUSTON 4, ST. LOUIS 1
SAT.	OCT. 15	HOUSTON	HOUSTON 4, ST. LOUIS 3
SUN.	OCT. 16	HOUSTON	HOUSTON 2, ST. LOUIS 1
MON.	OCT. 17	HOUSTON	ST. LOUIS 5, HOUSTON 4
WED.	OCT. 19	ST. LOUIS	HOUSTON 5, ST. LOUIS 1

BOX SCORES

GAME 1

ST. LOUIS 5, HOUSTON 3

WEDNESDAY, OCTOBER 12, AT ST. LOUIS

Houston	AB	R	H	BI	BB	SO	PO	A
Biggio, 2b	3	0	0	0	1	1	5	3
Taveras, cf	3	0	0	0	1	1	3	0
Berkman, lf	4	0	1	0	0	0	2	0
Ensberg, 3b	4	0	1	0	0	0	0	1
Lamb, 1b	4	1	1	0	0	0	6	1
Lane, rf	3	0	0	0	1	1	2	0
A.Everett, ss	4	1	2	0	0	1	1	2
Ausmus, c	3	0	1	1	0	0	5	0
Pettitte, p	1	0	0	0	0	0	0	2
Burke, ph	1	1	1	2	0	0	0	0
Springer, p	0	0	0	0	0	0	0	0
E.Astacio, p	0	0	0	0	0	0	0	0
J.Vizcaino, ph	1	0	0	0	0	0	0	0
TOTALS	31	3	7	3	3	4	24	9

St. Louis	AB	R	H	BI	BB	SO	PO	A
Eckstein, ss	4	2	2	1	0	0	1	1
Edmonds, cf	3	0	0	0	1	0	2	0
Pujols, 1b	3	0	1	1	1	0	17	0
Sanders, lf	3	1	1	2	1	0	1	0
L.Walker, rf	4	0	1	0	0	2	1	0
Isringhausen, p	0	0	0	0	0	0	0	0
Grudzielanek, 2b	4 1	1	0	0	2	0	8	
Y.Molina, c	3	0	0	0	0	0	5	0
A.Nunez, 3b	3	1	2	0	0	0	0	4
Carpenter, p	1	0	0	1	0	1	0	4
Taguchi, rf	0	0	0	0	0	0	0	0
TOTALS	28	5	8	5	3	5	27	17

				R	H	E	LOB
Houston	0 0 0	0 0 0	2 0 1—	3	7	0	6
St. Louis	2 1 0	0 2 0	0 0 x—	5	8	1	4

Houston	IP	H	R	ER	HR	BB	SO
Pettitte (L)	6.0	8	5	5	1	2	2
Springer	1.0	0	0	0	0	1	1
E.Astacio	1.0	0	0	0	0	0	2

St. Louis	IP	H	R	ER	HR	BB	SO
Carpenter (W)	8.0	5	2	2	1	3	3
Isringhausen (S)	1.0	2	1	0	0	0	1

E—Eckstein. DP—Houston 2, St. Louis 1. LOB—Houston 6, St. Louis 4. Scoring Position—Houston 0 for 6, St. Louis 2 for 5. 2B—Berkman, Ensberg. HR—Sanders (1st inning, 2 out, 1 on) off Pettitte, Burke (7th inning, 2 out, 1 on) off Carpenter. SH—Pettitte, Carpenter 2. T—2:29. A—52,332. U—HP-McClelland, 1B-Gibson, 2B-Bell, 3B-Cuzzi, LF-Poncino, RF-Davis.

HOW THEY SCORED

BOTTOM OF 1

Cardinals first. Eckstein singled to right. Edmonds popped out to second baseman Biggio. Pujols flied out to left fielder Berkman. Sanders homered to left on a 1-2 count, Eckstein scored. Walker struck out. Runs: 2, Hits: 2, Errors: 0

BOTTOM OF 2

Cardinals second. Grudzielanek singled to center. Molina flied out to left fielder Berkman. Nunez singled to right, Grudzielanek to third. Carpenter sacrificed, pitcher Pettitte to second baseman Biggio, Grudzielanek scored, Nunez to second. Eckstein lined out to first baseman Lamb. Runs: 1, Hits: 2, Errors: 0

BOTTOM OF 5

Cardinals fifth. Nunez singled to center. Carpenter sacrificed, pitcher Pettitte to second baseman Biggio, Nunez to second. Eckstein singled to right, Nunez scored. Eckstein to second. Edmonds flied out to center fielder Taveras. Pujols singled to center, Eckstein scored. Sanders walked on four pitches, Pujols to second. Walker grounded out, second baseman Biggio to first baseman Lamb. Runs: 2, Hits: 3, Errors: 0

TOP OF 7

Astros seventh. Lane fouled out to first baseman Pujols. Everett singled to left. Ausmus lined out to right fielder Walker. Burke pinch-hitting for Pettitte. Burke homered to left on a 2-0 count, Everett scored. Biggio struck out. Runs: 2, Hits: 2, Errors: 0

TOP OF 9

Astros ninth. Isringhausen pitching. Taguchi in as right fielder. Lamb singled to left. Lane struck out. Everett infield single to third, Lamb to second. On Eckstein's error, Lamb to third, Everett to second. Ausmus hit a sacrifice fly to center fielder Edmonds, Lamb scored. Vizcaino pinch-hitting for Astacio. Vizcaino grounded out, first baseman Pujols unassisted. Runs: 1, Hits: 2, Errors: 1

GAME 2

HOUSTON 4, ST. LOUIS 1

THURSDAY, OCTOBER 13, AT ST. LOUIS

Houston	AB	R	H	BI	BB	SO	PO	A
Biggio, 2b	5	0	2	1	0	2	1	1
Taveras, cf	5	0	2	0	0	0	2	0
Berkman, 1b	4	1	2	0	0	1	11	2
Ensberg, 3b	4	0	0	0	0	0	0	2
Lane, rf	4	0	0	0	0	2	2	0
Burke, lf	4	2	2	1	0	0	1	0
A.Everett, ss	4	0	1	1	0	1	0	2
Lidge, p	0	0	0	0	0	0	0	0
Ausmus, c	3	1	1	0	1	1	8	2
Oswalt, p	1	0	1	0	1	0	2	3
Bruntlett, ss	1	0	0	0	0	1	0	1
TOTALS	35	4	11	3	2	8	27	13

St. Louis	AB	R	H	BI	BB	SO	PO	A
Eckstein, ss	3	0	0	0	1	0	0	4
Edmonds, cf	4	0	1	0	0	2	2	0
Pujols, 1b	4	1	1	1	0	0	10	0
L.Walker, rf	3	0	0	0	1	1	2	0
Marquis, p	0	0	0	0	0	0	0	0

St. Louis	AB	R	H	BI	BB	SO	PO	A
/sabnSanders, lf	3	0	1	0	0	1	0	0
Taguchi, lf	1	0	0	0	0	1	0	0
Grudzielanek, 2b	4	0	0	0	0	0	5	2
A.Nunez, 3b	4	0	1	0	0	1	0	2
Y.Molina, c	4	0	2	0	0	1	8	1
Mulder, p	2	0	0	0	0	0	0	3
J.Rodriguez, ph	0	0	0	0	1	0	0	0
Tavarez, p	0	0	0	0	0	0	0	0
Mabry, rf	1	0	0	0	0	0	0	0
TOTALS	33	1	6	1	3	9	27	12

					R	H	E	LOB
Houston	0 1 0	0 1 0	0 2 0 —		4	11	1	7
St. Louis	0 0 0	0 0 1	0 0 0 —		1	6	0	8

Houston	IP	H	R	ER	HR	BB	SO
Oswalt (W)	7.0	5	1	1	1	3	6
Lidge (S)	2.0	1	0	0	0	0	3

St. Louis	IP	H	R	ER	HR	BB	SO
Mulder (L)	7.0	8	2	1	0	2	6
Tavarez	1.0	3	2	2	0	0	0
Marquis	1.0	0	0	0	0	0	2

E—Ensberg. DP—St. Louis 1. LOB—Houston 7, St. Louis 8. Scoring Position—Houston 1 for 10, St. Louis 0 for 8. 2B—Berkman, Ausmus, Y.Molina 2. 3B—Burke, A.Everett. HR—Pujols (6th inning, 0 out, 0 on) off Oswalt. SB—Ausmus. CS—Taveras. SH—Oswalt. WP—Tavarez. PB—Y.Molina. T—3:03. A—52,358. U—HP-Gibson, 1B-Bell, 2B-Cuzzi, 3B-Poncino, LF-Davis, RF-McClelland.

HOW THEY SCORED

TOP OF 2

Astros second. Lane struck out. Burke tripled to center. Everett grounded out, pitcher Mulder to first baseman Pujols. Ausmus was intentionally walked. Ausmus stole second. On Molina's passed ball, Burke scored. Oswalt walked on four pitches. Biggio struck out. Runs: 1, Hits: 1, Errors: 0

TOP OF 5

Astros fifth. Ausmus doubled to center. Oswalt sacrificed, third baseman Nunez to second baseman Grudzielanek, Ausmus to third. Biggio grounded out, shortstop Eckstein to first baseman Pujols, Ausmus scored. Taveras grounded out, pitcher Mulder to first baseman Pujols. Runs: 1, Hits: 1, Errors: 0

BOTTOM OF 6

Cardinals sixth. Pujols homered to left on a 0-1 count. Walker grounded out, first baseman Berkman unassisted. Sanders struck out. Grudzielanek grounded out, pitcher Oswalt to first baseman Berkman. Runs: 1, Hits: 1, Errors: 0

TOP OF 8

Astros eighth. Tavarez pitching. Berkman doubled to right. Ensberg grounded out, shortstop Eckstein to first baseman Pujols. Lane grounded out, shortstop Eckstein to first baseman Pujols. On Tavarez's wild pitch, Berkman to third. Burke singled to left, Berkman scored. Everett tripled to left, Burke scored. Taguchi in as left fielder. Ausmus lined out to second baseman Grudzielanek. Runs: 2, Hits: 3, Errors: 0

GAME 3

HOUSTON 4, ST. LOUIS 3

SATURDAY, OCTOBER 15, AT HOUSTON

St. Louis	AB	R	H	BI	BB	SO	PO	A
Eckstein, ss	4	0	0	1	0	0	1	3
Taguchi, lf	4	0	0	0	0	2	3	0

St. Louis	AB	R	H	BI	BB	SO	PO	A
Pujols, 1b	4	1	2	0	0	0	8	0
Edmonds, cf	3	0	1	0	1	1	2	0
L.Walker, rf	2	0	0	1	1	0	3	0
Grudzielanek, 2b	4	0	0	0	0	1	2	1
Y.Molina, c	4	1	2	0	0	0	4	1
A.Nunez, 3b	3	0	1	0	0	0	1	2
B.Thompson, p	0	0	0	0	0	0	0	0
Ra.Flores, p	0	0	0	0	0	0	0	0
Tavarez, p	0	0	0	0	0	0	0	1
J.Rodriguez, ph	0	1	0	0	1	0	0	0
M.Morris, p	1	0	0	0	0	0	0	1
Luna, 3b	1	0	0	0	0	1	0	1
Mabry, ph	1	0	1	1	0	0	0	0
TOTALS	31	3	7	3	3	5	24	10

Houston	AB	R	H	BI	BB	SO	PO	A
Biggio, 2b	4	0	2	0	0	0	1	4
Bruntlett, 2b	0	0	0	0	0	0	0	0
Burke, cf-lf	4	0	1	0	0	0	4	0
Berkman, lf-1b	4	0	1	0	0	1	1	0
Ensberg, 3b	2	1	0	0	2	0	0	1
Lamb, 1b	4	2	2	2	0	0	11	0
Taveras, cf	0	0	0	0	0	0	1	0
Lane, rf	4	1	1	1	0	0	3	0
Ausmus, c	4	0	1	0	0	2	5	1
A.Everett, ss	4	0	1	0	0	0	1	4
Clemens, p	2	0	1	0	0	1	0	1
O.Palmeiro, ph	1	0	1	0	0	0	0	0
Qualls, p	0	0	0	0	0	0	0	0
Bagwell, ph	1	0	0	0	0	0	0	0
Lidge, p	0	0	0	0	0	0	0	0
TOTALS	34	4	11	3	2	4	27	11

					R	H	E	LOB
St. Louis	0 0 0	0 1 1	0 0 1—		3	7	1	7
Houston	0 0 0	2 0 2	0 0 x—		4	11	0	8

St. Louis	IP	H	R	ER	HR	BB	SO
M.Morris (L)	5.1	8	4	3	1	1	3
B.Thompson	0.2	2	0	0	0	0	0
Ra.Flores	1.0	0	0	0	0	1	0
Tavarez	1.0	1	0	0	0	0	1

Houston	IP	H	R	ER	HR	BB	SO
Clemens (W)	6.0	6	2	2	0	2	1
Qualls (HOLD)	2.0	0	0	0	0	0	3
Lidge (S)	1.0	1	1	1	0	1	1

B.Thompson pitched to 1 batter in the 7th.

E—Luna. DP—St. Louis 1. LOB—St. Louis 7, Houston 8. Scoring Position—St. Louis 1 for 5, Houston 1 for 7. 2B—Mabry, Lamb, A.Everett. HR—Lamb (4th inning, 0 out, 1 on) off M.Morris. SB—Edmonds. S—Eckstein, L.Walker. SH—M.Morris. T—3:00. A—42,823. U—HP-Bell, 1B-Cuzzi, 2B-Poncino, 3B-Davis, LF-McClelland, RF-Gibson.

HOW THEY SCORED

BOTTOM OF 4

Astros fourth. Ensberg walked. Lamb homered to left on a 2-1 count, Ensberg scored. Lane flied out to center fielder Edmonds. Ausmus flied out to left fielder Taguchi. A.Everett grounded out, shortstop Eckstein to first baseman Pujols. Runs: 2, Hits: 1, Errors: 0

TOP OF 5

Cardinals fifth. Y.Molina singled to left. Abraham O.Nunez infield single to first, Y.Molina to second. M.Morris sacrificed, pitcher Clemens to second baseman Biggio, Y.Molina to third, Abraham O.Nunez to second. Eckstein hit a sacrifice fly to right fielder Lane, Y.Molina scored, Abraham O.Nunez to third. Taguchi flied out to right fielder Lane. Runs: 1, Hits: 2, Errors: 0

TOP OF 6

Cardinals sixth. Pujols singled to center. Edmonds singled to center, Pujols to third. L.Walker hit a sacrifice fly to center fielder C.Burke, Pujols scored. Grudzielanek flied out to center fielder C.Burke. Y.Molina singled to center, Edmonds to third. Abraham O.Nunez grounded out, catcher Ausmus to first baseman Lamb. Runs: 1, Hits: 3, Errors: 0

BOTTOM OF 6

Astros sixth. Ensberg flied out to right fielder L.Walker. Lamb doubled to center. Lane singled to right, Lamb scored. Ausmus singled to right, Lane to third. Luna in as third baseman. B.Thompson pitching. A.Everett safe on fielder's choice and throwing error by third baseman Luna, Lane scored, Ausmus to second, A.Everett to first. Ausmus was out advancing, catcher Y.Molina to shortstop Eckstein, Ausmus out. O.Palmeiro pinch-hitting for Clemens. O.Palmeiro singled to center, A.Everett to second. Biggio grounded out, third baseman Luna to first baseman Pujols. Runs: 2, Hits: 4, Errors: 1

TOP OF 9

Cardinals ninth. Bruntlett in as second baseman. C.Burke in as left fielder. Berkman in as first baseman. Taveras in as center fielder. Lidge pitching. Grudzielanek struck out. Y.Molina fouled out to first baseman Berkman. Joh.Rodriguez walked on four pitches for Tavarez. Mabry pinch-hitting for Luna. On defensive indifference, Joh.Rodriguez to second. Mabry doubled to left, Joh.Rodriguez scored. Eckstein flied out to center fielder Taveras. Runs: 1, Hits: 1, Errors: 0

GAME 4

HOUSTON 2, ST. LOUIS 1

SUNDAY, OCTOBER 16, AT HOUSTON

St. Louis	AB	R	H	BI	BB	SO	PO	A
Eckstein, ss	2	1	0	0	2	1	1	6
Edmonds, cf	3	0	1	0	0	1	3	0
J.Rodriguez, ph	1	0	0	0	0	0	0	0
Taguchi, cf	0	0	0	0	0	0	0	0
Pujols, 1b	3	0	2	1	0	1	8	0
L.Walker, rf	3	0	1	0	1	0	0	0
Sanders, lf	4	0	0	0	0	2	3	0
Mabry, 3b	4	0	0	0	0	1	1	2
Y.Molina, c	3	0	0	0	0	0	6	0
Grudzielanek, 2b	3	0	1	0	0	0	2	1
Suppan, p	2	0	0	0	0	1	0	1
Marquis, p	1	0	0	0	0	0	0	0
TOTALS	29	1	5	1	3	7	24	10

Houston	AB	R	H	BI	BB	SO	PO	A
Biggio, 2b	3	0	0	0	1	0	1	6
Lidge, p	0	0	0	0	0	0	0	0
Burke, cf-lf	3	0	0	0	1	0	3	0
Berkman, lf-1b	2	0	0	0	2	0	1	0
Ensberg, 3b	3	0	2	1	0	0	0	1
Lamb, 1b	4	0	0	0	0	2	10	0
Wheeler, p	0	0	0	0	0	0	0	0
Bruntlett, 2b	0	0	0	0	0	0	0	1
Lane, rf	3	1	2	1	1	0	1	0
Ausmus, c	4	0	0	0	0	3	8	1
A.Everett, ss	4	0	1	0	0	0	2	5
Backe, p	2	0	0	0	0	1	0	0
Gallo, p	0	0	0	0	0	0	0	0
Qualls, p	0	0	0	0	0	0	0	0
O.Palmeiro, ph	0	0	0	0	1	0	0	0
Taveras, pr-cf	1	1	1	0	0	0	1	0
TOTALS	29	2	6	2	6	6	27	14

					R	H	E	LOB
St. Louis	0 0 0	1 0 0	0 0 0 —	1	5	1	5
Houston	0 0 0	1 0 0	1 0 x —	2	6	0	11

St. Louis	IP	H	R	ER	HR	BB	SO
Suppan	5.0	3	1	1	1	3	5
Marquis (L)	3.0	3	1	0	0	3	1

Houston	IP	H	R	ER	HR	BB	SO
Backe	5.2	2	1	1	0	3	7
Gallo	0.1	0	0	0	0	0	0
Qualls (W)	1.0	0	0	0	0	0	0
Wheeler (HOLD)	1.0	1	0	0	0	0	0
Lidge (S)	1.0	2	0	0	0	0	0

E—Marquis. DP—Houston 1. LOB—St. Louis 5, Houston 11. Scoring Position—St. Louis 0 for 4, Houston 0 for 8. 2B—Edmonds. HR—Lane (4th inning, 1 out, 0 on) off Suppan. S—Pujols, Ensberg. SH—Biggio. T—3:11. A—43,010. U—HP-Cuzzi, 1B-Poncino, 2B-Davis, 3B-McClelland, LF-Gibson, RF-Bell.

HOW THEY SCORED

TOP OF 4

Cardinals fourth. Eckstein walked on four pitches. Edmonds doubled to left, Eckstein to third. Pujols hit a sacrifice fly to right fielder Lane, Eckstein scored. Walker walked on a full count. Sanders struck out. Mabry flied out to center fielder Burke. Runs: 1, Hits: 1, Errors: 0

BOTTOM OF 4

Astros fourth. Lamb struck out. Lane homered to left on a 1-2 count. Ausmus struck out. Everett grounded out, shortstop Eckstein to first baseman Pujols. Runs: 1, Hits: 1, Errors: 0

BOTTOM OF 7

Astros seventh. Palmeiro pinch-hitting for Qualls. Palmeiro walked. Biggio safe on a sacrifice plus pitcher Marquis' fielding error. Palmeiro to second. Burke flied out to left fielder Sanders. Berkman walked on four pitches, Palmeiro to third, Biggio to second. Taveras pinch-running for Palmeiro. Ensberg hit a sacrifice fly to center fielder Edmonds, Taveras scored. Lamb popped out to left fielder Sanders. Runs: 1, Hits: 0, Errors: 1

GAME 5

ST. LOUIS 5, HOUSTON 4

MONDAY, OCTOBER 17, AT HOUSTON

St. Louis	AB	R	H	BI	BB	SO	PO	A
Eckstein, ss	4	2	2	0	0	0	0	3
Edmonds, cf	3	2	1	0	2	0	3	0
Pujols, 1b	5	1	1	3	0	1	12	1
Sanders, lf	5	0	1	0	0	2	2	1
L.Walker, rf	3	0	0	0	1	0	1	0
Isringhausen, p	0	0	0	0	0	0	0	0
Grudzielanek, 2b	4	0	2	2	0	0	2	0
Y.Molina, c	4	0	2	0	0	1	6	1
Luna, 3b	3	0	0	0	0	1	0	2
J.Rodriguez, ph	1	0	0	0	0	1	0	0
Taguchi, rf	0	0	0	0	0	0	1	0
Carpenter, p	3	0	0	0	0	0	0	4
Mabry, rf-3b	1	0	0	0	0	1	0	0
TOTALS	36	5	9	5	3	7	27	12

Houston	AB	R	H	BI	BB	SO	PO	A
Biggio, 2b	4	1	2	1	0	0	1	2
Bruntlett, 2b	0	0	0	0	0	0	0	0
J.Vizcaino, ph	1	0	0	0	0	0	0	0
Burke, cf-lf	4	1	1	0	0	2	0	0
Berkman, lf-1b	3	1	2	3	1	0	4	1
Ensberg, 3b	4	0	1	0	0	2	2	6
Lamb, 1b	4	0	0	0	0	1	10	1
Gallo, p	0	0	0	0	0	0	0	1
Wheeler, p	0	0	0	0	0	0	0	0
Lidge, p	0	0	0	0	0	0	0	0

Houston	AB	R	H	BI	BB	SO	PO	A
Lane, rf	3	0	1	0	0	0	2	0
Ausmus, c	4	1	1	0	0	0	6	3
A.Everett, ss	4	0	1	0	0	1	1	1
Pettitte, p	1	0	0	0	0	0	0	2
Qualls, p	0	0	0	0	0	0	0	0
O.Palmeiro, ph	1	0	0	0	0	0	0	0
Taveras, cf	1	0	0	0	0	0	1	0
TOTALS	34	4	9	4	1	6	27	17

						R	H	E	LOB
St. Louis	0 0 2	0 0 0	0 0 3—			5	9	1	8
Houston	0 1 0	0 0 0	3 0 0—			4	9	2	7

St. Louis	IP	H	R	ER	HR	BB	SO
Carpenter	7.0	9	4	3	1	1	6
Isringhausen (W)	2.0	0	0	0	0	0	0

Houston	IP	H	R	ER	HR	BB	SO
Pettitte	6.1	7	2	2	0	2	4
Qualls	0.2	0	0	0	0	0	0
Gallo (HOLD)	0.1	0	0	0	0	0	0
Wheeler (HOLD)	0.2	0	0	0	0	0	0
Lidge (BS, L)	1.0	2	3	3	1	1	3

Pettitte pitched to 2 batters in the 7th.

E—Luna, Lamb, A.Everett. LOB—St. Louis 8, Houston 7. Scoring Position—St. Louis 3 for 13, Houston 2 for 8. 2B—Y.Molina, Ausmus. HR—Berkman (7th inning, 1 out, 2 on) off Carpenter, Pujols (9th inning, 2 out, 2 on) off Lidge. SB—Eckstein, Sanders. CS—Eckstein. SH—Burke, Pettitte. HBP—Eckstein by Pettitte, Lane by Carpenter. T—3:19. A—43,470. U—HP-Poncino, 1B-Davis, 2B-McClelland, 3B-Gibson, LF-Bell, RF-Cuzzi.

HOW THEY SCORED

BOTTOM OF 2

Astros second. Lane singled to left. Ausmus doubled to left, Lane to third. Everett struck out. Pettitte grounded into fielder's choice, first baseman Pujols to catcher Molina, Lane out, Ausmus to third. Biggio singled to left, Ausmus scored, Pettitte to second. Burke struck out. Runs: 1, Hits: 3, Errors: 0

TOP OF 3

Cardinals third. Eckstein singled to center. Eckstein stole second. Edmonds singled to right, Eckstein to third. Pujols struck out. Sanders struck out. Walker walked on a full count, Edmonds to second. Grudzielanek singled to right, Eckstein scored, Edmonds scored, Walker to third. Molina struck out. Runs: 2, Hits: 3, Errors: 0

BOTTOM OF 7

Astros seventh. Palmeiro pinch-hitting for Qualls. Palmeiro grounded out, shortstop Eckstein to first baseman Pujols. Biggio safe on Luna's error. Burke singled to right, Biggio to third. Berkman homered to left on the first pitch, Biggio scored, Burke scored. Ensberg singled to left. Ensberg was out advancing, left fielder Sanders to second baseman Grudzielanek, Ensberg out. Lamb flied out to center fielder Edmonds. Runs: 3, Hits: 3, Errors: 1

TOP OF 9

Cardinals ninth. Lidge pitching. Rodriguez pinch-hitting for Luna. Rodriguez struck out. Mabry struck out. Eckstein singled to left. On defensive indifference, Eckstein to second. Edmonds walked. Pujols homered to left on a 0-1 count, Eckstein scored, Edmonds scored. Sanders struck out. Runs: 3, Hits: 2, Errors: 0

GAME 6

HOUSTON 5, ST. LOUIS 1

WEDNESDAY, OCTOBER 19, AT ST. LOUIS

Houston	AB	R	H	BI	BB	SO	PO	A
Biggio, 2b	5	1	2	1	0	0	0	3
Wheeler, p	0	0	0	0	0	0	0	0

Houston	AB	R	H	BI	BB	SO	PO	A
Taveras, cf	4	0	2	0	0	0	1	0
Berkman, 1b	4	0	0	1	1	1	11	1
Ensberg, 3b	4	0	1	1	0	0	0	3
Lane, rf	4	1	1	1	0	1	1	0
Burke, lf	4	1	1	0	0	1	0	0
Ausmus, c	4	1	3	0	0	0	9	0
A.Everett, ss	3	1	1	1	0	1	3	4
Oswalt, p	2	0	0	0	0	1	2	2
Qualls, p	0	0	0	0	0	0	0	0
O.Palmeiro, ph	1	0	0	0	0	0	0	0
Bruntlett, 2b	0	0	0	0	0	0	0	0
TOTALS	35	5	11	4	1	5	27	13

St. Louis	AB	R	H	BI	BB	SO	PO	A
Eckstein, ss	3	0	0	0	0	1	1	6
Edmonds, cf	3	0	0	0	1	1	0	0
Pujols, 1b	4	0	0	0	0	1	10	0
L.Walker, rf	4	0	1	0	0	1	5	0
Sanders, lf	3	0	0	0	0	3	3	0
Tavarez, p	0	0	0	0	0	0	0	0
Mabry, lf	1	0	0	0	0	1	0	0
Grudzielanek, 2b	3	1	1	0	0	0	3	0
Y.Molina, c	4	0	1	0	0	0	5	0
A.Nunez, 3b	3	0	1	0	0	0	0	4
Mulder, p	1	0	0	0	0	1	0	2
B.Thompson, p	0	0	0	0	0	0	0	0
J.Rodriguez, ph	0	0	0	1	0	0	0	0
Marquis, p	0	0	0	0	0	0	0	0
Ra.Flores, p	0	0	0	0	0	0	0	0
Taguchi, lf	1	0	0	0	0	1	0	0
Isringhausen, p	0	0	0	0	0	0	0	0
TOTALS	30	1	4	1	1	9	27	12

						R	H	E	LOB
Houston	0 0 2	1 0 1	1 1 0—			5	11	0	7
St. Louis	0 0 0	0 1 0	0 0 0—			1	4	1	6

Houston	IP	H	R	ER	HR	BB	SO
Oswalt (W)	7.0	3	1	1	0	1	6
Qualls	1.0	0	0	0	0	0	1
Wheeler	1.0	1	0	0	0	0	2

St. Louis	IP	H	R	ER	HR	BB	SO
Mulder (L)	4.2	6	3	3	1	1	2
B.Thompson	0.1	0	0	0	0	0	0
Marquis	1.1	3	2	2	0	0	1
Ra.Flores	0.1	0	0	0	0	0	0
Tavarez	1.1	1	0	0	0	0	1
Isringhausen	1.0	1	0	0	0	0	1

E—Edmonds. LOB—Houston 7, St. Louis 6. Scoring Position—Houston 2 for 6, St. Louis 0 for 2. 2B—L.Walker. HR—Lane (4th inning, 1 out, 0 on) off Mulder. S—J.Rodriguez. SH—Taveras, A.Everett, Oswalt. WP—Mulder 2, Tavarez. HBP—Grudzielanek by Oswalt, Eckstein by Oswalt. T—2:53. A—52,438. U—HP-Davis, 1B-McClelland, 2B-Gibson, 3B-Bell, LF-Cuzzi, RF-Poncino.

HOW THEY SCORED

TOP OF 3

Astros third. Ausmus singled to left. Everett infield single to first, Ausmus to second. Oswalt sacrificed, pitcher Mulder to second baseman Grudzielanek, Ausmus to third, Everett to second. On Mulder's wild pitch, Ausmus scored, Everett to third. Biggio singled to left, Everett scored. Taveras lined out to right fielder Walker. Berkman grounded into fielder's choice, shortstop Eckstein to second baseman Grudzielanek, Biggio out. Runs: 2, Hits: 3, Errors: 0

TOP OF 4

Astros fourth. Ensberg flied out to right fielder Walker. Lane homered to left on a 1-1 count. Burke flied out to left fielder Sanders. Ausmus singled to right. Everett flied out to left fielder Sanders. Runs: 1, Hits: 2, Errors: 0

BOTTOM OF 5

Cardinals fifth. Grudzielanek was hit by a pitch. Molina singled to right, Grudzielanek to second. Nunez grounded into fielder's choice, pitcher Oswalt to shortstop Everett, Grudzielanek to third, Molina out. Rodriguez pinch-hitting for Thompson. Rodriguez hit a sacrifice fly to center fielder Taveras, Grudzielanek scored. Eckstein struck out. Runs: 1, Hits: 1, Errors: 0

TOP OF 6

Astros sixth. Marquis pitching. Lane grounded out, shortstop Eckstein to first baseman Pujols. Burke singled to left. Ausmus singled to right, Burke to third. Everett sacrificed, third baseman Nunez to first baseman Pujols, Burke scored, Ausmus to second. Oswalt struck out. Runs: 1, Hits: 2, Errors: 0

TOP OF 7

Astros seventh. Biggio singled to left. Taveras sacrificed, third baseman Nunez to first baseman Pujols, Biggio to second. Flores pitching. Berkman flied out to right fielder Walker. Tavarez pitching. Ensberg singled to center, Biggio scored. On Edmonds' error, Ensberg to second. On Tavarez's wild pitch, Ensberg to third. Lane grounded out, shortstop Eckstein to first baseman Pujols. Runs: 1, Hits: 2, Errors: 1

STATISTICS

ST. LOUIS CARDINALS' BATTING AND FIELDING AVERAGES

Player, position	G	AB	R	H	TB	2B	3B	HR	RBI	BB	IBB	SO	Avg.	OBP	Slg.	PO	A	E	Avg.
Nunez,3b	4	13	1	5	5	0	0	0	0	0	0	1	.385	.385	.385	1	12	0	1.000
Molina,c	6	22	1	7	10	3	0	0	0	0	0	2	.318	.318	.455	34	3	0	1.000
Pujols,1b	6	23	3	7	13	0	0	2	6	1	0	3	.304	.320	.565	65	1	0	1.000
Grudzielanek,2b	6	22	2	5	5	0	0	0	2	0	0	3	.227	.261	.227	14	12	0	1.000
Edmonds,cf	6	19	2	4	5	1	0	0	0	5	0	5	.211	.375	.263	12	0	1	.923
Eckstein,ss	6	20	5	4	4	0	0	0	2	3	0	2	.200	.346	.200	4	23	1	.964
Sanders,lf	5	18	1	3	6	0	0	1	2	1	0	8	.167	.211	.333	9	1	0	1.000
Walker,rf	6	19	0	3	4	1	0	0	1	4	0	4	.158	.292	.211	12	0	0	1.000
Mabry,rf-ph-3b-lf	5	8	0	1	2	1	0	0	1	0	0	3	.125	.125	.250	1	2	0	1.000
Flores,p	2	0	0	0	0	0	0	0	0	0	0	0	.000	.000	.000	0	0	0	.000
Isringhausen,p	3	0	0	0	0	0	0	0	0	0	0	0	.000	.000	.000	0	0	0	.000
Tavarez,p	3	0	0	0	0	0	0	0	0	0	0	0	.000	.000	.000	0	1	0	1.000
Thompson,p	2	0	0	0	0	0	0	0	0	0	0	0	.000	.000	.000	0	0	0	.000
Marquis,p	3	1	0	0	0	0	0	0	0	0	0	0	.000	.000	.000	0	0	1	.000
Morris,p	1	1	0	0	0	0	0	0	0	0	0	0	.000	.000	.000	0	1	0	1.000
Rodriguez,ph	5	2	1	0	0	0	0	0	1	2	0	1	.000	.400	.000	0	0	0	.000
Suppan,p	1	2	0	0	0	0	0	0	0	0	0	1	.000	.000	.000	0	1	0	1.000
Mulder,p	2	3	0	0	0	0	0	0	0	0	0	3	.000	.000	.000	0	5	0	1.000
Carpenter,p	2	4	0	0	0	0	0	0	1	0	0	1	.000	.000	.000	0	8	0	1.000
Luna,3b	4	4	0	0	0	0	0	0	0	0	0	2	.000	.000	.000	0	3	2	.600
Taguchi,rf-lf-cf	6	6	0	0	0	0	0	0	0	0	0	3	.000	.000	.000	4	0	0	1.000
Totals	6	187	16	39	54	6	0	3	16	16	0	42	.209	.276	.289	156	73	5	.979

HOUSTON ASTROS' BATTING AND FIELDING AVERAGES

Player, position	G	AB	R	H	TB	2B	3B	HR	RBI	BB	IBB	SO	Avg.	OBP	Slg.	PO	A	E	Avg.
Clemens,p	1	2	0	1	1	0	0	0	0	0	0	1	.500	.500	.500	0	1	0	1.000
Taveras,cf-pr	6	14	1	5	5	0	0	0	0	1	0	1	.357	.400	.357	9	0	0	1.000
Biggio,2b	6	24	2	8	8	0	0	0	3	2	0	3	.333	.385	.333	9	19	0	1.000
Oswalt,p	2	3	0	1	1	0	0	0	0	1	0	1	.333	.500	.333	4	5	0	1.000
Palmeiro,ph	4	3	0	1	1	0	0	0	0	1	0	0	.333	.500	.333	0	0	0	.000
Ausmus,c	6	22	3	7	9	2	0	0	1	1	1	6	.318	.333	.409	41	7	0	1.000
Everett,ss	6	23	2	7	10	1	1	0	2	0	0	4	.304	.304	.435	8	18	1	.963
Burke,ph-lf-cf	6	20	5	6	11	0	1	1	3	1	0	3	.300	.333	.550	8	0	0	1.000
Berkman,lf-1b	6	21	2	6	11	2	0	1	3	4	0	3	.286	.400	.524	30	4	0	1.000
Ensberg,3b	6	21	1	5	6	1	0	0	2	2	0	2	.238	.292	.286	2	14	1	.941
Lane,rf	6	21	3	5	11	0	0	2	3	2	0	4	.238	.333	.524	11	0	0	1.000
Lamb,1b	4	16	3	3	7	1	0	1	2	0	0	3	.188	.188	.438	37	2	1	.975
Astacio,p	1	0	0	0	0	0	0	0	0	0	0	0	.000	.000	.000	0	0	0	.000
Gallo,p	2	0	0	0	0	0	0	0	0	0	0	0	.000	.000	.000	0	1	0	1.000
Lidge,p	4	0	0	0	0	0	0	0	0	0	0	0	.000	.000	.000	0	0	0	.000
Qualls,p	4	0	0	0	0	0	0	0	0	0	0	0	.000	.000	.000	0	0	0	.000
Springer,p	1	0	0	0	0	0	0	0	0	0	0	0	.000	.000	.000	0	0	0	.000
Wheeler,p	3	0	0	0	0	0	0	0	0	0	0	0	.000	.000	.000	0	0	0	.000
Bagwell,ph	1	1	0	0	0	0	0	0	0	0	0	0	.000	.000	.000	0	0	0	.000
Bruntlett,ss-2b	5	1	0	0	0	0	0	0	0	0	0	1	.000	.000	.000	0	2	0	1.000
Backe,p	1	2	0	0	0	0	0	0	0	0	0	3	.000	.000	.000	0	0	0	.000
Pettitte,p	2	2	0	0	0	0	0	0	0	0	0	0	.000	.000	.000	0	4	0	1.000
Vizcaino,ph	2	2	0	0	0	0	0	0	0	0	0	0	.000	.000	.000	0	0	0	.000
Totals	6	198	22	55	81	7	2	5	19	15	1	33	.278	.329	.409	159	77	3	.987

ST. LOUIS CARDINALS' PITCHING RECORDS

Pitcher	G	GS	CG	IP	H	R	ER	HR	BB	IBB	SO	HB	WP	W	L	Pct.	ERA
Isringhausen	3	0	0	4.0	3	1	0	0	0	0	2	0	0	1	0	1.000	0.00
Flores	2	0	0	1.1	0	0	0	0	1	0	0	0	0	0	0	.000	0.00
Thompson	2	0	0	1.0	2	0	0	0	0	0	0	0	0	0	0	.000	0.00
Suppan	1	1	0	5.0	3	1	1	1	3	0	5	0	0	0	0	.000	1.80
Carpenter	2	2	0	15.0	14	6	5	2	4	0	9	1	0	1	0	1.000	3.00
Mulder	2	2	0	11.2	14	5	4	1	3	1	8	0	2	0	2	.000	3.09
Marquis	3	0	0	5.1	6	3	2	0	3	0	4	0	0	0	1	.000	3.38
Morris	1	1	0	5.1	8	4	3	1	1	0	3	0	0	0	1	.000	5.06
Tavarez	3	0	0	3.1	5	2	2	0	0	0	2	0	2	0	0	.000	5.40
Totals	6	6	0	52.0	55	22	17	5	15	1	33	1	4	2	4	.333	2.94

No shutouts. Saves—Isringhausen.

HOUSTON ASTROS' PITCHING RECORDS

Pitcher	G	GS	CG	IP	H	R	ER	HR	BB	IBB	SO	HB	WP	W	L	Pct.	ERA
Qualls	4	0	0	4.2	0	0	0	0	0	0	4	0	0	1	0	1.000	0.00
Wheeler	3	0	0	2.2	2	0	0	0	0	0	2	0	0	0	0	.000	0.00
Astacio	1	0	0	1.0	0	0	0	0	0	0	2	0	0	0	0	.000	0.00
Springer	1	0	0	1.0	0	0	0	0	1	0	1	0	0	0	0	.000	0.00
Gallo	2	0	0	0.2	0	0	0	0	0	0	0	0	0	0	0	.000	0.00
Oswalt	2	2	0	14.0	8	2	2	1	4	0	12	2	0	2	0	1.000	1.29
Backe	1	1	0	5.2	2	1	1	0	3	0	7	0	0	0	0	.000	1.59
Clemens	1	1	0	6.0	6	2	2	0	2	0	1	0	0	1	0	1.000	3.00
Pettitte	2	2	0	12.1	15	7	7	1	4	0	6	1	0	0	1	.000	5.11
Lidge	4	0	0	5.0	6	4	4	1	2	0	7	0	0	0	1	.000	7.20
Totals	6	6	0	53.0	39	16	16	3	16	0	42	3	0	4	2	.667	2.72

No shutouts. Saves—Lidge 3.

SCORE BY INNINGS

Houston	0	2	2	4	1	3	7	2	1	—	22
St. Louis	2	1	2	1	4	2	0	0	4	—	6

MISCELLANEOUS STATISTICS

Sacrifice hits —Carpenter 2, Oswalt 2, Pettitte 2, Biggio, Burke, Everett, Morris, Taveras.
Sacrifice flies —Ausmus, Eckstein, Ensberg, Pujols, Rodriguez, Walker.
Stolen bases —Ausmus, Eckstein, Edmonds, Sanders.
Caught stealing —Eckstein, Taveras.
Double plays —Biggio, Everett and Lamb; Bruntlett, Everett and Berkman; Ensberg, Biggio and Lamb; Grudzielanek and Pujols; Grudzielanek, Eckstein and Pujols; Lamb, Everett and Lamb; Mulder, Grudzielanek and Pujols.
Left on bases —Houston 6, 7, 8, 11, 7, 7—46; St. Louis 4, 8, 7, 5, 8, 6—38.
Scoring position—Houston 0 for 6, 1 for 10, 1 for 7, 0 for 8, 2 for 8, 2 for 6—6 for 45; St. Louis 2 for 5, 0 for 8, 1 for 5, 0 for 4, 3 for 13, 0 for 2—6 for 37.
Hit by pitcher —by Oswalt 2 (Eckstein, Grudzielanek), by Pettitte (Eckstein), by Carpenter (Lane).
Passed balls —Molina.
Balks —None.
Time of games —2:29, 3:03, 3:00, 3:11, 3:19, 2:53—Avg.: 2:59.
Attendance —52,332, 52,358, 42,823, 43,010, 43,470, 52,438—286,431.
Umpires —McClelland, Tim; Gibson, Greg; Bell, Wally; Cuzzi, Phil; Poncino, Larry; and Davis, Gerry.

WORLD SERIES
HOUSTON VS. CHICAGO

RESULTS

DAY	DATE	PLACE	SCORE
SAT.	OCT. 22	CHICAGO	CHICAGO 5, HOUSTON 3
SUN.	OCT. 23	CHICAGO	CHICAGO 7, HOUSTON 6
TUE.	OCT. 25	HOUSTON	CHICAGO 7, HOUSTON 5
WED.	OCT. 26	HOUSTON	CHICAGO 1, HOUSTON 0

BOX SCORES
GAME 1

CHICAGO 5, HOUSTON 3
SATURDAY, OCTOBER 22, AT CHICAGO

Houston	AB	R	H	BI	BB	SO	PO	A
Biggio, 2b	4	1	1	0	0	0	2	3
Taveras, cf	3	0	2	0	0	0	0	0
Berkman, lf	4	0	2	2	0	1	1	0
Burke, pr-lf	0	0	0	0	0	0	1	0
Ensberg, 3b	4	0	0	0	0	1	0	4
Lamb, 1b	4	1	1	1	0	2	7	3
Bagwell, dh	2	0	0	0	0	1	0	0
Lane, rf	4	0	0	0	0	1	3	0
Ausmus, c	3	0	1	0	0	0	4	0
A.Everett, ss	4	1	0	0	0	1	4	4
Clemens, p	0	0	0	0	0	0	0	0
W.Rodriguez, p	0	0	0	0	0	0	2	0
Qualls, p	0	0	0	0	0	0	0	0
Springer, p	0	0	0	0	0	0	0	0
TOTALS	32	3	7	3	0	7	24	14

Chi White Sox	AB	R	H	BI	BB	SO	PO	A
Podsednik, lf	5	0	2	1	0	1	1	0
Iguchi, 2b	5	0	0	0	0	1	2	2
Dye, rf	2	1	1	1	2	0	3	0
Konerko, 1b	4	0	2	0	0	0	12	0
C.Everett, dh	3	1	1	0	0	1	0	0
Rowand, cf	3	0	1	0	1	1	0	0
Pierzynski, c	4	2	1	1	0	0	7	0
Crede, 3b	4	1	1	1	0	0	0	5
Uribe, ss	2	0	1	1	2	0	2	4
Contreras, p	0	0	0	0	0	0	0	2
Cotts, p	0	0	0	0	0	0	0	0
Jenks, p	0	0	0	0	0	0	0	0
TOTALS	32	5	10	5	5	4	27	13

							R	H	E	LOB
Houston	0 1 2	0 0 0	0 0 0—				3	7	1	6
Chi White Sox	1 2 0	1 0 0	0 1 x—				5	10	0	9

Houston	IP	H	R	ER	HR	BB	SO
Clemens	2.0	4	3	3	1	0	1
W.Rodriguez (L)	3.1	4	1	1	1	5	1
Qualls	1.2	0	0	0	0	0	2
Springer	1.0	2	1	1	0	0	0

Chi White Sox	IP	H	R	ER	HR	BB	SO
Contreras (W)	7.0	6	3	3	1	0	2
Cotts (HOLD)	0.2	1	0	0	0	0	2
Jenks (S)	1.1	0	0	0	0	0	3

Contreras pitched to 1 batter in the 8th.

Bases on balls—Off W.Rodriguez 5 (Dye 2, Uribe 2, Rowand).

Strikeouts—By Clemens 1 (Podsednik), by W.Rodriguez 1 (C.Everett), by Qualls 2 (Rowand, Iguchi), by Contreras 2 (Berkman, Lamb), by Cotts 2 (Lamb, Ensberg), by Jenks 3 (Bagwell, A.Everett, Lane). E—A.Everett. DP—Houston 2, Chi White Sox 1. LOB—Houston 6, Chi White Sox 9. Scoring Position—Houston 2 for 11, Chi White Sox 2 for 10. 2B—Taveras 2, Berkman, Uribe. 3B—Podsednik. HR—Dye (1st inning, 2 out, 0 on) off Clemens, Lamb (2nd inning, 1 out, 0 on) off Contreras, Crede (4th inning, 1 out, 0 on) off W.Rodriguez. SB—Burke, Podsednik, Pierzynski. SH—Taveras, C.Everett. HBP—Bagwell by Contreras; by Contreras, Ausmus by Contreras. T—3:13. A—41,206. U—HP-West, 1B-Nelson, 2B-Layne, 3B-Cousins, LF-Cederstrom, RF-Hernandez.

PLAY BY PLAY

Top of 1
Astros first. Biggio grounded out, third baseman Crede to first baseman Konerko. Taveras popped out to shortstop Uribe. Berkman struck out. Runs: 0, Hits: 0, Errors: 0

Bottom of 1
White Sox first. Podsednik grounded out, shortstop Everett to first baseman Lamb. Iguchi grounded out, third baseman Ensberg to first baseman Lamb. Dye homered to right on a full count. Konerko grounded out, shortstop Everett to first baseman Lamb. Runs: 1, Hits: 1, Errors: 0

Top of 2
Astros second. Ensberg flied out to right fielder Dye. Lamb homered to center on a 1-0 count. Bagwell was hit by a pitch. Lane grounded into a double play, shortstop Uribe to second baseman Iguchi to first baseman Konerko, Bagwell out. Runs: 1, Hits: 1, Errors: 0

Bottom of 2
White Sox second. Everett singled to center. Rowand singled to right, Everett to third. Pierzynski grounded into fielder's choice, first baseman Lamb to shortstop Everett, Everett scored, Rowand out. Crede grounded out, third baseman Ensberg to first baseman Lamb, Pierzynski to second. Uribe doubled to center, Pierzynski scored. Podsednik struck out. Runs: 2, Hits: 3, Errors: 0

Top of 3
Astros third. Ausmus singled to right. Everett grounded into fielder's choice, pitcher Contreras to shortstop Uribe, Ausmus out. Biggio singled to center, Everett to second. Taveras sacrificed, pitcher Contreras to first baseman Konerko, Everett to third, Biggio to second. Berkman doubled to right, Everett scored, Biggio scored. Ensberg grounded out, shortstop Uribe to first baseman Konerko. Runs: 2, Hits: 3, Errors: 0

Bottom of 3
White Sox third. Rodriguez pitching. Iguchi grounded out, second baseman Biggio to first baseman Lamb. Dye walked. Konerko singled to right, Dye to second. Everett struck out. Rowand grounded into fielder's choice, third baseman Ensberg to second baseman Biggio, Konerko out. Runs: 0, Hits: 1, Errors: 0

Top of 4
Astros fourth. Lamb struck out. Bagwell flied out to left fielder Podsednik. Lane flied out to right fielder Dye. Runs: 0, Hits: 0, Errors: 0

Bottom of 4
White Sox fourth. Pierzynski grounded out, first baseman Lamb to pitcher Rodriguez. Crede homered to left on a 0-2 count. Uribe walked on a full count. Podsednik singled to center, Uribe to second. Iguchi grounded into a double play, second baseman Biggio to shortstop Everett to first baseman Lamb, Podsednik out. Runs: 1, Hits: 2, Errors: 0

Top of 5
Astros fifth. Ausmus flied out to right fielder Dye. Everett grounded out, third baseman Crede to first baseman Konerko. Biggio grounded out, third baseman Crede to first baseman Konerko. Runs: 0, Hits: 0, Errors: 0

Bottom of 5

White Sox fifth. Dye walked on four pitches. Konerko singled to center, Dye to second. Everett sacrificed, third baseman Ensberg to first baseman Lamb, Dye to third, Konerko to second. Rowand was intentionally walked. Pierzynski grounded into a double play, first baseman Lamb to shortstop Everett to pitcher Rodriguez, Rowand out. Runs: 0, Hits: 1, Errors: 0

Top of 6

Astros sixth. Taveras doubled to center. Berkman grounded out, first baseman Konerko unassisted, Taveras to third. Ensberg grounded out, third baseman Crede to first baseman Konerko. Lamb grounded out, second baseman Iguchi to first baseman Konerko. Runs: 0, Hits: 1, Errors: 0

Bottom of 6

White Sox sixth. Crede popped out to second baseman Biggio. Uribe walked on a full count. Qualls pitching. Podsednik grounded into fielder's choice, second baseman Biggio to shortstop Everett, Uribe out. Podsednik stole second. Iguchi struck out. Runs: 0, Hits: 0, Errors: 0

Top of 7

Astros seventh. Bagwell was hit by a pitch. Lane fouled out to first baseman Konerko. Ausmus was hit by a pitch, Bagwell to second. Everett grounded into fielder's choice, shortstop Uribe to second baseman Iguchi, Bagwell to third, Ausmus out. Biggio grounded out, third baseman Crede to first baseman Konerko. Runs: 0, Hits: 0, Errors: 0

Bottom of 7

White Sox seventh. Dye safe on Everett's error. Konerko flied out to right fielder Lane. Everett flied out to left fielder Berkman. Rowand struck out. Runs: 0, Hits: 0, Errors: 1

Top of 8

Astros eighth. Taveras doubled to center. Cotts pitching. Berkman singled to left, Taveras to third. Ensberg struck out. Lamb struck out. Jenks pitching. Burke pinch-running for Berkman. Burke stole second. Bagwell struck out. Runs: 0, Hits: 2, Errors: 0

Bottom of 8

White Sox eighth. Burke in as left fielder. Springer pitching. Pierzynski singled to right. Crede flied out to right fielder Lane. Uribe popped out to left fielder Burke. Pierzynski stole second. Podsednik tripled to center, Pierzynski scored. Iguchi flied out to right fielder Lane. Runs: 1, Hits: 2, Errors: 0

Top of 9

Astros ninth. Lane struck out. Ausmus grounded out, shortstop Uribe to first baseman Konerko. Everett struck out. Runs: 0, Hits: 0, Errors: 0

GAME 2

CHICAGO 7, HOUSTON 6

SUNDAY, OCTOBER 23, AT CHICAGO

Houston	AB	R	H	BI	BB	SO	PO	A
Biggio, 2b	4	0	0	0	0	1	0	1
Bruntlett, 2b	0	0	0	0	0	0	1	1
Lamb, ph-1b	1	0	0	0	0	0	0	0
Taveras, cf	4	2	2	0	0	0	2	0
Berkman, 1b-lf	3	0	1	3	0	2	9	0
Ensberg, 3b	4	1	1	1	0	1	1	3
Bagwell, dh	4	1	1	0	0	0	0	0
Lane, rf	4	0	1	0	0	2	4	1
Burke, lf-2b	3	1	0	0	1	0	0	0
Ausmus, c	4	1	2	0	0	0	5	1
A.Everett, ss	3	0	0	0	0	2	3	1
J.Vizcaino, ph-ss	1	0	1	2	0	0	0	0
Pettitte, p	0	0	0	0	0	0	0	2
Wheeler, p	0	0	0	0	0	0	0	0
Qualls, p	0	0	0	0	0	0	0	0
Gallo, p	0	0	0	0	0	0	0	0
Lidge, p	0	0	0	0	0	0	0	0
TOTALS	35	6	9	6	1	8	25	10

Chi White Sox	AB	R	H	BI	BB	SO	PO	A
Podsednik, lf	5	1	1	1	0	1	2	0
Iguchi, 2b	3	1	1	0	1	1	0	2
Dye, rf	3	1	1	0	0	0	2	0
Konerko, 1b	4	1	1	4	0	1	9	0
C.Everett, dh	4	0	2	0	0	1	0	0
Rowand, cf	4	1	2	0	0	0	3	0
Pierzynski, c	4	1	1	0	0	1	8	0
Crede, 3b	4	0	1	1	0	0	2	2
Uribe, ss	4	1	2	1	0	0	1	1
Buehrle, p	0	0	0	0	0	0	0	1
Politte, p	0	0	0	0	0	0	0	0
Jenks, p	0	0	0	0	0	0	0	0
Cotts, p	0	0	0	0	0	0	0	0
TOTALS	35	7	12	7	1	5	27	6

						R	H	E	LOB
Houston	0 1 1	0 2 0	0 0 2—			6	9	0	4
Chi White Sox	0 2 0	0 0 0	4 0 1—			7	12	0	5

Houston	IP	H	R	ER	HR	BB	SO
Pettitte	6.0	8	2	2	0	0	4
Wheeler (HOLD)	0.2	1	3	3	0	1	1
Qualls (BS)	0.2	2	1	1	1	0	0
Gallo	0.2	0	0	0	0	0	0
Lidge (L)	0.1	1	1	1	1	0	0

Chi White Sox	IP	H	R	ER	HR	BB	SO
Buehrle	7.0	7	4	4	1	0	6
Politte (HOLD)	1.0	0	0	0	0	0	1
Jenks (BS)	0.2	2	2	2	0	1	1
Cotts (W)	0.1	0	0	0	0	0	0

Qualls pitched to 2 batters in the 7th.

Bases on balls—Off Wheeler 1 (Iguchi), off Jenks 1 (Burke).

Strikeouts—By Pettitte 4 (C.Everett, Konerko, Pierzynski, Iguchi), by Wheeler 1 (Podsednik), by Buehrle 6 (Biggio, Berkman, A.Everett 2, Ensberg, Lane), by Politte 1 (Berkman), by Jenks 1 (Lane). LOB—Houston 4, Chi White Sox 5. Scoring Position—Houston 4 for 10, Chi White Sox 2 for 10. 2B—Berkman, Ausmus, Rowand, Uribe 2. 3B—Taveras. HR—Ensberg (2nd inning, 0 out, 0 on) off Buehrle, Konerko (7th inning, 2 out, 3 on) off Qualls, Podsednik (9th inning, 1 out, 0 on) off Lidge. SB—Lane, Uribe. CS—C.Everett. S—Berkman. HBP—Dye by Wheeler. T—3:11. A—41,432. U—HP-Nelson, 1B-Layne, 2B-Cousins, 3B-Cederstrom, LF-Hernandez, RF-West.

PLAY BY PLAY

Top of 1

Astros first. Biggio flied out to center fielder Rowand. Taveras was out bunting, pitcher Buehrle to first baseman Konerko. Berkman struck out. Runs: 0, Hits: 0, Errors: 0

Bottom of 1

White Sox first. Podsednik lined out to right fielder Lane. Iguchi struck out. Dye singled to center. Konerko struck out. Runs: 0, Hits: 1, Errors: 0

Top of 2

Astros second. Ensberg homered to left on the first pitch. Bagwell grounded out, third baseman Crede to first baseman Konerko. Lane singled to center. Burke flied out to right fielder Dye. Lane stole second. Ausmus infield single to third, Lane to third. Everett struck out. Runs: 1, Hits: 3, Errors: 0

Bottom of 2

White Sox second. Everett struck out. Rowand singled to left. Pierzynski singled to left, Rowand to second. Crede singled to right, Rowand scored, Pierzynski to third. Uribe grounded into fielder's choice, right fielder Lane to shortstop Everett, Pierzynski scored, Crede out. Uribe stole second. Podsednik grounded out, first baseman Berkman unassisted. Runs: 2, Hits: 3, Errors: 0

Top of 3

Astros third. Biggio grounded out, third baseman Crede to first baseman Konerko. Taveras tripled to right. Berkman hit a sacrifice fly to center fielder Rowand, Taveras scored. Ensberg struck out. Runs: 1, Hits: 1, Errors: 0

Bottom of 3
White Sox third. Iguchi singled to left. Dye grounded out, first baseman Berkman unassisted, Iguchi to second. Konerko grounded out, second baseman Biggio to first baseman Berkman, Iguchi to third. Everett grounded out, third baseman Ensberg to first baseman Berkman. Runs: 0, Hits: 1, Errors: 0

Top of 4
Astros fourth. Bagwell grounded out, second baseman Iguchi to first baseman Konerko. Lane grounded out, first baseman Konerko unassisted. Burke grounded out, first baseman Konerko unassisted. Runs: 0, Hits: 0, Errors: 0

Bottom of 4
White Sox fourth. Rowand flied out to right fielder Lane. Pierzynski struck out. Crede grounded out, shortstop Everett to first baseman Berkman. Runs: 0, Hits: 0, Errors: 0

Top of 5
Astros fifth. Ausmus infield double to third. Everett struck out. Biggio grounded out, second baseman Iguchi to first baseman Konerko. Taveras infield single to third, Ausmus to third. Berkman doubled to left, Ausmus scored, Taveras scored. Ensberg lined out to shortstop Uribe. Runs: 2, Hits: 3, Errors: 0

Bottom of 5
White Sox fifth. Uribe doubled to left. Podsednik flied out to center fielder Taveras. Iguchi grounded into fielder's choice, pitcher Pettitte to shortstop Everett, Uribe out. Iguchi was picked off, pitcher Pettitte to first baseman Berkman, Iguchi out. Runs: 0, Hits: 1, Errors: 0

Top of 6
Astros sixth. Bagwell lined out to third baseman Crede. Lane struck out. Burke flied out to left fielder Podsednik. Runs: 0, Hits: 0, Errors: 0

Bottom of 6
White Sox sixth. Dye lined out to right fielder Lane. Konerko flied out to right fielder Lane. Everett singled to center. Rowand doubled to left, Everett to third. Pierzynski popped out to shortstop Everett. Runs: 0, Hits: 2, Errors: 0

Top of 7
Astros seventh. Ausmus flied out to center fielder Rowand. Everett lined out to third baseman Crede. Biggio struck out. Runs: 0, Hits: 0, Errors: 0

Bottom of 7
White Sox seventh. Bruntlett in as second baseman. Wheeler pitching. Crede fouled out to third baseman Ensberg. Uribe doubled to center. Podsednik struck out. Iguchi walked on a full count. Dye was hit by a pitch, Uribe to third, Iguchi to second. Qualls pitching. Konerko homered to left on a full count, Uribe scored, Iguchi scored, Dye scored. Everett singled to right. Everett was caught stealing, catcher Ausmus to second baseman Bruntlett, Everett out. Runs: 4, Hits: 3, Errors: 0

Top of 8
Astros eighth. Politte pitching. Taveras flied out to right fielder Dye. Berkman struck out. Ensberg grounded out, shortstop Uribe to first baseman Konerko. Runs: 0, Hits: 0, Errors: 0

Bottom of 8
White Sox eighth. Rowand grounded out, third baseman Ensberg to first baseman Berkman. Gallo pitching. Pierzynski grounded out, second baseman Bruntlett to first baseman Berkman. Crede grounded out, third baseman Ensberg to first baseman Berkman. Runs: 0, Hits: 0, Errors: 0

Top of 9
Astros ninth. Jenks pitching. Bagwell singled to center. Lane struck out. Burke walked on four pitches, Bagwell to second. Ausmus grounded out, first baseman Konerko unassisted, Bagwell to third, Burke to second. Vizcaino pinch-hitting for Everett. Vizcaino singled to left, Bagwell scored, Burke scored, Vizcaino to second. Lamb pinch-hitting for Bruntlett. Cotts pitching. Lamb flied out to left fielder Podsednik. Runs: 2, Hits: 2, Errors: 0

Bottom of 9
White Sox ninth. Lamb in as first baseman. Berkman in as left fielder. Burke in as second baseman. Vizcaino in as shortstop. Lidge pitching. Uribe flied out to center fielder Taveras. Podsednik homered to center on a 2-1 count. Runs: 1, Hits: 1, Errors: 0

GAME 3

CHICAGO 7, HOUSTON 5

TUESDAY, OCTOBER 25, AT HOUSTON

Chi White Sox	AB	R	H	BI	BB	SO	PO	A
Podsednik, lf	8	1	2	0	0	2	2	0
Iguchi, 2b	7	1	2	1	0	1	4	1
D.Marte, p	0	0	0	0	0	0	0	0
Buehrle, p	0	0	0	0	0	0	0	0
Dye, rf	7	1	2	1	0	1	0	0
Konerko, 1b	4	0	1	0	2	0	10	0
Pierzynski, c	3	0	1	2	2	0	6	3
O.Hernandez, p	0	0	0	0	0	0	0	0
L.Vizcaino, p	0	0	0	0	0	0	0	1
Ti.Perez, ph	1	0	0	0	0	0	0	0
Jenks, p	0	0	0	0	0	0	0	1
Blum, 2b	1	1	1	1	0	0	2	0
Rowand, cf	6	1	1	0	1	3	3	0
Crede, 3b	5	1	2	1	1	0	1	1
Uribe, ss	6	1	1	0	1	1	5	5
Garland, p	3	0	0	0	0	2	0	2
C.Everett, ph	1	0	1	0	0	0	0	0
W.Harris, pr	0	0	0	0	0	0	0	0
Politte, p	0	0	0	0	0	0	0	0
Cotts, p	0	0	0	0	0	0	0	0
Hermanson, p	0	0	0	0	0	0	0	0
Widger, c	1	0	0	1	2	1	9	0
TOTALS	53	7	14	7	9	11	42	14

Houston	AB	R	H	BI	BB	SO	PO	A
Biggio, 2b	6	2	2	1	1	3	1	4
E.Astacio, p	0	0	0	0	0	0	0	0
W.Rodriguez, p	0	0	0	0	0	0	0	0
Taveras, cf	6	0	0	0	0	3	4	0
Berkman, lf-1b	5	0	2	1	2	1	8	0
Ensberg, 3b	6	1	1	1	1	3	0	4
Lamb, 1b	3	0	0	0	1	1	9	0
Bruntlett, pr-lf	0	0	0	0	0	0	0	0
Lidge, p	0	0	0	0	0	0	0	0
O.Palmeiro, ph-lf	1	0	0	0	2	0	0	0
Lane, rf	6	1	2	2	1	0	3	0
Ausmus, c	6	0	0	0	1	2	11	1
A.Everett, ss	5	1	1	0	1	1	4	6
Oswalt, p	1	0	0	0	0	0	0	1
Springer, p	0	0	0	0	0	0	1	0
Bagwell, ph	1	0	0	0	0	0	0	0
Wheeler, p	0	0	0	0	0	0	0	0
Gallo, p	0	0	0	0	0	0	0	0
Burke, lf	1	0	0	1	0	0	0	0
Qualls, p	0	0	0	0	0	0	0	0
J.Vizcaino, ph-2b	0	0	0	0	1	0	1	1
TOTALS	47	5	8	5	12	14	42	17

				R	H	E	LOB
Chi White Sox	000	050	000	000	0 2—7	14	3	15
Houston	102	100	010	000	0 0—5	8	1	15

Chi White Sox	IP	H	R	ER	HR	BB	SO
Garland	7.0	7	4	2	1	2	4
Politte (HOLD)	0.2	0	1	1	0	1	1
Cotts	0.0	0	0	0	0	1	0
Hermanson (BS)	0.1	1	0	0	0	0	1
O.Hernandez	1.0	0	0	0	0	4	2
L.Vizcaino	1.0	0	0	0	0	1	0
Jenks	2.0	0	0	0	0	1	3
D.Marte (W)	1.2	0	0	0	0	2	3
Buehrle (S)	0.1	0	0	0	0	0	0

Houston	IP	H	R	ER	HR	BB	SO
Oswalt	6.0	8	5	5	1	5	3
Springer	1.0	0	0	0	0	1	1
Wheeler	1.1	1	0	0	0	0	0
Gallo	0.1	0	0	0	0	0	0

Houston	IP	H	R	ER	HR	BB	SO
Lidge	1.1	0	0	0	0	0	3
Qualls	3.0	1	0	0	0	2	3
E.Astacio (L)	0.2	4	2	2	1	2	0
W.Rodriguez	0.1	0	0	0	0	0	1

Cotts pitched to 1 batter in the 8th. O.Hernandez pitched to 1 batter in the 10th. Oswalt pitched to 1 batter in the 7th.

Bases on balls—Off Garland 2 (Ausmus, Lane), off Politte 1 (Ensberg), off Cotts 1 (Lamb), off O.Hernandez 4 (Biggio, O.Palmeiro, Berkman, Burke), off L.Vizcaino 1 (A.Everett), off Jenks 1 (Berkman), off D.Marte 2 (J.Vizcaino, O.Palmeiro), off Oswalt 5 (Konerko, Pierzynski, 2, Crede, Rowand), off Qualls 2 (Widger, Konerko), off E.Astacio 2 (Widger, Uribe).

Strikeouts—By Garland 4 (Biggio, Lamb, Ensberg, Taveras), by Politte 1 (Berkman), by Hermanson 1 (Ausmus), by O.Hernandez 2 (Ensberg, Taveras), by Jenks 3 (Biggio, Ausmus, A.Everett), by D.Marte 3 (Biggio, Ensberg, Taveras), by Oswalt 3 (Garland 2, Podsednik), by Springer 1 (Rowand), by Lidge 3 (Widger, Uribe, Rowand), by Qualls 3 (Dye, Rowand, Iguchi), by W.Rodriguez 1 (Podsednik). E—O.Hernandez, Uribe 2, Ensberg. DP—Chi White Sox 2, Houston 4. LOB—Chi White Sox 15, Houston 15. Scoring Position—Chi White Sox 3 for 14, Houston 4 for 16. 2B—Konerko, Pierzynski, Biggio, Lane. HR—Lane (4th inning, 0 out, 0 on) off Garland, Crede (5th inning, 0 out, 0 on) off Oswalt, Blum (14th inning, 2 out, 0 on) off E.Astacio. SB—Podsednik, W.Harris, Burke. CS—A.Everett. SH—A.Everett, Oswalt. HBP—Konerko by Wheeler, Crede by Oswalt, Taveras by Jenks. T—5:41. A—42,848. U—HP-Layne, 1B-Cousins, 2B-Cederstrom, 3B-Hernandez, LF-West, RF-Nelson.

PLAY BY PLAY

Top of 1
White Sox first. Podsednik struck out. Iguchi singled to right. Dye grounded into a double play, shortstop Everett to first baseman Lamb, Iguchi out. Runs: 0, Hits: 1, Errors: 0

Bottom of 1
Astros first. Biggio doubled to left. Taveras flied out on a bunt to third baseman Crede. Berkman singled to left, Biggio scored. Ensberg grounded into a double play, shortstop Uribe to second baseman Iguchi to first baseman Konerko, Berkman out. Runs: 1, Hits: 2, Errors: 0

Top of 2
White Sox second. Konerko doubled to left. Pierzynski walked. Rowand lined into a double play, shortstop Everett to second baseman Biggio, Konerko out. Crede walked on a full count, Pierzynski to second. Uribe fouled out to first baseman Lamb. Runs: 0, Hits: 1, Errors: 0

Bottom of 2
Astros second. Lamb flied out to center fielder Rowand. Lane walked on a full count. Ausmus grounded into a double play, shortstop Uribe to first baseman Konerko, Lane out. Runs: 0, Hits: 0, Errors: 0

Top of 3
White Sox third. Garland struck out. Podsednik grounded out, third baseman Ensberg to first baseman Lamb. Iguchi grounded out, pitcher Oswalt to first baseman Lamb. Runs: 0, Hits: 0, Errors: 0

Bottom of 3
Astros third. Everett infield single to short. Everett safe, though caught stealing, on shortstop Uribe's error. Oswalt sacrificed, catcher Pierzynski to second baseman Iguchi, Everett to second. Biggio singled to right, Everett scored. Taveras struck out. Berkman singled to right, Biggio to third. Ensberg singled to left, Biggio scored, Berkman to second. Lamb struck out. Runs: 2, Hits: 4, Errors: 1

Top of 4
White Sox fourth. Dye flied out to center fielder Taveras. Konerko flied out to center fielder Taveras. Pierzynski walked on a full count. Rowand grounded out, third baseman Ensberg to first baseman Lamb. Runs: 0, Hits: 0, Errors: 0

Bottom of 4
Astros fourth. Lane homered to center on a 0-1 count. Ausmus

grounded out, pitcher Garland to first baseman Konerko. Everett grounded out, shortstop Uribe to first baseman Konerko. Oswalt grounded out, pitcher Garland to first baseman Konerko. Runs: 1, Hits: 1, Errors: 0

Top of 5
White Sox fifth. Crede homered to right on a 0-1 count. Uribe singled to left. Garland struck out. Podsednik singled to right, Uribe to second. Iguchi singled to center, Uribe scored, Podsednik to second. Dye singled to center, Podsednik scored, Iguchi to second. Konerko flied out to center fielder Taveras. Pierzynski doubled to center, Iguchi scored, Dye scored. Rowand walked on a full count. Crede was hit by a pitch, Pierzynski to third, Rowand to second. Uribe flied out to right fielder Lane. Runs: 5, Hits: 6, Errors: 0

Bottom of 5
Astros fifth. Biggio grounded out, third baseman Crede to first baseman Konerko. Taveras popped out to second baseman Iguchi. Berkman flied out to center fielder Rowand. Runs: 0, Hits: 0, Errors: 0

Top of 6
White Sox sixth. Garland grounded out, shortstop Everett to first baseman Lamb. Podsednik grounded out, second baseman Biggio to first baseman Lamb. Iguchi safe on Ensberg's error. Dye flied out to center fielder Taveras. Runs: 0, Hits: 0, Errors: 1

Bottom of 6
Astros sixth. Ensberg struck out. Lamb popped out to shortstop Uribe. Lane grounded out, shortstop Uribe to first baseman Konerko. Runs: 0, Hits: 0, Errors: 0

Top of 7
White Sox seventh. Konerko walked on four pitches. Springer pitching. Pierzynski popped out to pitcher Springer. Rowand struck out. Crede grounded out, second baseman Biggio to first baseman Lamb. Runs: 0, Hits: 0, Errors: 0

Bottom of 7
Astros seventh. Ausmus walked. Everett sacrificed, catcher Pierzynski to second baseman Iguchi, Ausmus to second. Bagwell pinch-hitting for Springer. Bagwell popped out to first baseman Konerko. Biggio struck out. Runs: 0, Hits: 0, Errors: 0

Top of 8
White Sox eighth. Wheeler pitching. Uribe flied out to right fielder Lane. Everett pinch-hitting for Garland. Everett singled to right. Harris pinch-running for Everett.Harris stole second. Podsednik flied out to left fielder Berkman. Iguchi grounded out, third baseman Ensberg to first baseman Lamb. Runs: 0, Hits: 1, Errors: 0

Bottom of 8
Astros eighth. Politte pitching. Taveras flied out to left fielder Podsednik. Berkman struck out. Ensberg walked on a full count. Cotts pitching. Lamb walked, Ensberg to second. Hermanson pitching. Bruntlett pinch-running for Lamb. Lane doubled to left, Ensberg scored, Bruntlett to third. Ausmus struck out. Runs: 1, Hits: 1, Errors: 0

Top of 9
White Sox ninth. Berkman in as first baseman. Bruntlett in as left fielder. Dye grounded out, shortstop Everett to first baseman Berkman. Konerko was hit by a pitch. Gallo pitching. Pierzynski grounded out, second baseman Biggio to first baseman Berkman, Konerko to second. Lidge pitching. Burke in as left fielder. Rowand struck out. Runs: 0, Hits: 0, Errors: 0

Bottom of 9
Astros ninth. Hernandez pitching. Widger in as catcher. Everett popped out to shortstop Uribe. Burke walked on four pitches. On Hernandez's error on a pickoff attempt, Burke to second. Burke stole third. Biggio walked on four pitches. Taveras struck out. Berkman was intentionally walked, Biggio to second. Ensberg struck out. Runs: 0, Hits: 0, Errors: 1

Top of 10
White Sox tenth. Crede grounded out, second baseman Biggio to first baseman Berkman. Uribe struck out. Widger struck out. Runs: 0, Hits: 0, Errors: 0

Bottom of 10
Astros tenth. Palmeiro pinch-hitting for Lidge. Palmeiro walked on

four pitches. Vizcaino pitching. Lane fouled out to catcher Widger. Ausmus flied out to center fielder Rowand. Everett walked on a full count, Palmeiro to second. Burke grounded out, pitcher Vizcaino to first baseman Konerko. Runs: 0, Hits: 0, Errors: 0

Top of 11
White Sox eleventh. Palmeiro in as left fielder. Qualls pitching. Podsednik singled to right. Podsednik stole second. Iguchi flied out to right fielder Lane. Dye struck out. Konerko was intentionally walked. Perez pinch-hitting for Vizcaino. Perez grounded out, first baseman Berkman unassisted. Runs: 0, Hits: 1, Errors: 0

Bottom of 11
Astros eleventh. Jenks pitching. Biggio struck out. Taveras was hit by a pitch. Berkman walked on a full count, Taveras to second. Ensberg popped out to shortstop Uribe. Palmeiro grounded out, pitcher Jenks to first baseman Konerko. Runs: 0, Hits: 0, Errors: 0

Top of 12
White Sox twelfth. Rowand struck out. Crede grounded out, shortstop Everett to first baseman Berkman. Uribe popped out to shortstop Everett. Runs: 0, Hits: 0, Errors: 0

Bottom of 12
Astros twelfth. Lane flied out to left fielder Podsednik. Ausmus struck out. Everett struck out. Runs: 0, Hits: 0, Errors: 0

Top of 13
White Sox thirteenth. Widger walked on a full count. Podsednik bunted into a double play, catcher Ausmus to shortstop Everett to first baseman Berkman, Widger out. Iguchi struck out. Runs: 0, Hits: 0, Errors: 0

Bottom of 13
Astros thirteenth. Marte pitching. Blum in as second baseman. Vizcaino pinch-hitting for Qualls. Vizcaino walked on a full count. Biggio struck out. Taveras struck out. Berkman grounded into fielder's choice, shortstop Uribe to second baseman Blum, Vizcaino out. Runs: 0, Hits: 0, Errors: 0

Top of 14
White Sox fourteenth. Astacio pitching. Vizcaino in as second baseman. Dye singled to right. Konerko grounded into a double play, third baseman Ensberg to second baseman Vizcaino to first baseman Berkman, Dye out. Blum homered to right on a 2-0 count. Rowand infield single to third. Crede infield single to third, Rowand to second. Uribe walked on a full count, Rowand to third, Crede to second. Widger walked, Rowand scored, Crede to third, Uribe to second. Rodriguez pitching. Podsednik struck out. Runs: 2, Hits: 4, Errors: 0

Bottom of 14
Astros fourteenth. Ensberg struck out. Palmeiro walked. Lane popped out to second baseman Blum. On defensive indifference, Palmeiro to second. Ausmus safe on Uribe's error, Palmeiro to third. Buehrle pitching. Everett popped out to shortstop Uribe. Runs: 0, Hits: 0, Errors: 1

GAME 4

CHICAGO 1, HOUSTON 0

WEDNESDAY, OCTOBER 26, AT HOUSTON

Chi White Sox	AB	R	H	BI	BB	SO	PO	A
Podsednik, lf	3	0	1	0	0	0	1	0
Iguchi, 2b	3	0	0	0	0	2	3	
C.Everett, ph	1	0	0	0	0	0	0	0
Politte, p	0	0	0	0	0	0	0	0
Cotts, p	0	0	0	0	0	0	0	0
Jenks, p	0	0	0	0	0	0	0	0
Dye, rf	4	0	3	1	0	1	1	0
Konerko, 1b	4	0	0	0	0	2	12	1
Pierzynski, c	4	0	1	0	0	1	7	1
Rowand, cf	4	0	1	0	0	2	1	0
Crede, 3b	4	0	1	0	0	2	0	6
Uribe, ss	4	0	0	0	0	2	2	4
F.Garcia, p	2	0	0	0	0	0	0	1
W.Harris, ph-2b	1	1	1	0	0	0	1	0
TOTALS	34	1	8	1	0	10	27	16

Houston	AB	R	H	BI	BB	SO	PO	A
Biggio, 2b	4	0	1	0	0	0	1	1
Taveras, cf	2	0	1	0	0	0	2	0
Berkman, lf	1	0	0	0	3	1	2	0
Ensberg, 3b	4	0	0	0	0	2	0	3
Lamb, 1b	2	0	1	0	1	0	8	1
J.Vizcaino, ph-1b	1	0	0	0	0	0	2	0
Lane, rf	4	0	1	0	0	2	2	0
Ausmus, c	3	0	1	0	0	1	9	1
A.Everett, ss	3	0	0	0	0	0	0	3
Burke, ph	1	0	0	0	0	0	0	0
Backe, p	2	0	0	0	0	1	1	2
Bagwell, ph	1	0	0	0	0	0	0	0
Lidge, p	0	0	0	0	0	0	0	1
O.Palmeiro, ph	1	0	0	0	0	0	0	0
TOTALS	29	0	5	0	4	7	27	12

					R	H	E	LOB
Chi White Sox	0 0 0	0 0 0	0 1 0—	1	8	0	7
Houston	0 0 0	0 0 0	0 0 0—	0	5	0	9

Chi White Sox	IP	H	R	ER	HR	BB	SO
F.Garcia (W)	7.0	4	0	0	0	3	7
Politte (HOLD)	0.2	0	0	0	0	1	0
Cotts (HOLD)	0.1	0	0	0	0	0	0
Jenks (S)	1.0	1	0	0	0	0	0

Houston	IP	H	R	ER	HR	BB	SO
Backe	7.0	5	0	0	0	0	7
Lidge (L)	2.0	3	1	1	0	0	3

Bases on balls—Off F.Garcia 3 (Berkman 2, Lamb), off Politte 1 (Berkman).

Strikeouts—By F.Garcia 7 (Ausmus, Berkman, Ensberg 2, Lane 2, Backe), by Backe 7 (Dye, Konerko, Pierzynski, Crede, Uribe 2, Rowand), by Lidge 3 (Konerko, Crede, Rowand).

DP—Chi White Sox 1. LOB—Chi White Sox 7, Houston 9. Scoring Position—Chi White Sox 1 for 8, Houston 0 for 11. 2B—Dye, Pierzynski, Crede, Lamb. 3B—Podsednik. SB—Taveras, Berkman. SH—Podsednik, Taveras, Ausmus. WP—Politte. HBP—Taveras by Politte. T—3:20. A—42,936. U—HP-Cousins, 1B-Cederstrom, 2B-Hernandez, 3B-West, LF-Nelson, RF-Layne.

PLAY BY PLAY

Top of 1
White Sox first. Podsednik flied out to left fielder Berkman. Iguchi flied out to right fielder Lane. Dye doubled to center. Konerko grounded out, pitcher Backe to first baseman Lamb. Runs: 0, Hits: 1, Errors: 0

Bottom of 1
Astros first. Biggio singled to left. Taveras sacrificed, third baseman Crede to first baseman Konerko, Biggio to second. Berkman struck out. Ensberg grounded out, pitcher Garcia to first baseman Konerko. Runs: 0, Hits: 1, Errors: 0

Top of 2
White Sox second. Pierzynski grounded out, pitcher Backe to first baseman Lamb. Rowand grounded out, third baseman Ensberg to first baseman Lamb. Crede flied out to right fielder Lane. Runs: 0, Hits: 0, Errors: 0

Bottom of 2
Astros second. Lamb doubled to right. Lane struck out. Ausmus struck out. Everett grounded out, third baseman Crede to first baseman Konerko. Runs: 0, Hits: 1, Errors: 0

Top of 3
White Sox third. Uribe flied out to center fielder Taveras. Garcia flied out to center fielder Taveras. Podsednik tripled to center. Iguchi grounded out, shortstop Everett to first baseman Lamb. Runs: 0, Hits: 1, Errors: 0

Bottom of 3
Astros third. Backe struck out. Biggio grounded out, third baseman

Crede to first baseman Konerko. Taveras grounded out, third baseman Crede to first baseman Konerko. Runs: 0, Hits: 0, Errors: 0

Top of 4
White Sox fourth. Dye singled to left. Konerko struck out. Pierzynski struck out. Rowand struck out. Runs: 0, Hits: 1, Errors: 0

Bottom of 4
Astros fourth. Berkman walked. Ensberg struck out. Lamb grounded into fielder's choice, second baseman Iguchi to shortstop Uribe, Berkman out. Lane grounded into fielder's choice, shortstop Uribe to second baseman Iguchi, Lamb out. Runs: 0, Hits: 0, Errors: 0

Top of 5
White Sox fifth. Crede struck out. Uribe struck out. Garcia grounded out, third baseman Ensberg to first baseman Lamb. Runs: 0, Hits: 0, Errors: 0

Bottom of 5
Astros fifth. Ausmus singled to center. Everett grounded into a double play, third baseman Crede to second baseman Iguchi to first baseman Konerko, Ausmus out. Backe grounded out, third baseman Crede to first baseman Konerko. Runs: 0, Hits: 1, Errors: 0

Top of 6
White Sox sixth. Podsednik grounded out, shortstop Everett to first baseman Lamb. Iguchi grounded out, shortstop Everett to first baseman Lamb. Dye struck out. Runs: 0, Hits: 0, Errors: 0

Bottom of 6
Astros sixth. Biggio was out bunting, catcher Pierzynski to first baseman Konerko. Taveras singled to right. Berkman walked on four pitches, Taveras to second. Ensberg struck out. Taveras stole third.Berkman stole second. Lamb was intentionally walked. Lane struck out. Runs: 0, Hits: 1, Errors: 0

Top of 7
White Sox seventh. Konerko flied out to left fielder Berkman. Pierzynski grounded out, first baseman Lamb to pitcher Backe.

Rowand singled to center. Crede doubled to left, Rowand to third. Uribe struck out. Runs: 0, Hits: 2, Errors: 0

Bottom of 7
Astros seventh. Ausmus flied out to right fielder Dye. Everett flied out to left fielder Podsednik. Bagwell pinch-hitting for Backe. Bagwell grounded out, second baseman Iguchi to first baseman Konerko. Runs: 0, Hits: 0, Errors: 0

Top of 8
White Sox eighth. Lidge pitching. Harris pinch-hitting for Garcia. Harris singled to left. Podsednik sacrificed, pitcher Lidge to second baseman Biggio, Harris to second. Everett pinch-hitting for Iguchi. Everett grounded out, second baseman Biggio to first baseman Lamb, Harris to third. Dye singled to center, Harris scored. Konerko struck out. Runs: 1, Hits: 2, Errors: 0

Bottom of 8
Astros eighth. Politte pitching. Harris in as second baseman. Biggio grounded out, shortstop Uribe to first baseman Konerko. Taveras was hit by a pitch. On Politte's wild pitch, Taveras to second. Berkman was intentionally walked. Ensberg flied out to center fielder Rowand, Taveras to third. Cotts pitching. Vizcaino pinch-hitting for Lamb. Vizcaino grounded out, shortstop Uribe to first baseman Konerko. Runs: 0, Hits: 0, Errors: 0

Top of 9
White Sox ninth. Vizcaino in as first baseman. Pierzynski doubled to right. Rowand struck out. Crede struck out. Uribe grounded out, third baseman Ensberg to first baseman Vizcaino. Runs: 0, Hits: 1, Errors: 0

Bottom of 9
Astros ninth. Jenks pitching. Lane singled to center. Ausmus sacrificed, first baseman Konerko to second baseman Harris, Lane to second. Burke pinch-hitting for Everett. Burke fouled out to shortstop Uribe. Palmeiro pinch-hitting for Lidge. Palmeiro grounded out, shortstop Uribe to first baseman Konerko. Runs: 0, Hits: 1, Errors: 0

STATISTICS

CHICAGO WHITE SOX'S BATTING AND FIELDING AVERAGES

Player, position	G	AB	R	H	TB	2B	3B	HR	RBI	BB	IBB	SO	Avg.	OBP	Slg.	PO	A	E	Avg.
Blum,2b	1	1	1	1	4	0	0	1	1	0	0	0	1.000	1.000	4.000	2	0	0	1.000
Harris,pr-2b-ph	2	1	1	1	1	0	0	0	0	0	0	0	1.000	1.000	1.000	1	0	0	1.000
Everett,dh-ph	4	9	1	4	4	0	0	0	0	0	0	2	.444	.444	.444	0	0	0	.000
Dye,rf	4	16	3	7	11	1	0	1	3	2	0	2	.438	.526	.688	6	0	0	1.000
Crede,3b	4	17	2	5	12	1	0	2	3	1	0	2	.294	.368	.706	3	14	0	1.000
Rowand,cf	4	17	2	5	6	1	0	0	0	2	1	6	.294	.368	.353	7	0	0	1.000
Podsednik,lf	4	21	6	6	13	0	2	1	2	0	0	4	.286	.286	.619	6	0	0	1.000
Pierzynski,c	4	15	3	4	6	2	0	0	3	2	0	2	.267	.353	.400	28	4	0	1.000
Konerko,1b	4	16	1	4	8	1	0	1	4	2	1	3	.250	.368	.500	43	1	0	1.000
Uribe,ss	4	16	2	4	7	3	0	0	2	3	0	3	.250	.368	.438	10	14	2	.923
Iguchi,2b	4	18	2	3	3	0	0	0	1	1	0	3	.167	.211	.167	8	8	0	1.000
Buehrle,p	2	0	0	0	0	0	0	0	0	0	0	0	.000	.000	.000	0	1	0	1.000
Contreras,p	1	0	0	0	0	0	0	0	0	0	0	0	.000	.000	.000	0	2	0	1.000
Cotts,p	4	0	0	0	0	0	0	0	0	0	0	0	.000	.000	.000	0	0	0	.000
Hermanson,p	1	0	0	0	0	0	0	0	0	0	0	0	.000	.000	.000	0	0	0	.000
Hernandez,p	1	0	0	0	0	0	0	0	0	0	0	0	.000	.000	.000	0	0	1	.000
Jenks,p	4	0	0	0	0	0	0	0	0	0	0	0	.000	.000	.000	0	1	0	1.000
Marte,p	1	0	0	0	0	0	0	0	0	0	0	0	.000	.000	.000	0	0	0	.000
Politte,p	3	0	0	0	0	0	0	0	0	0	0	0	.000	.000	.000	0	0	0	.000
Vizcaino,p	1	0	0	0	0	0	0	0	0	0	0	0	.000	.000	.000	0	1	0	1.000
Perez,ph	1	1	0	0	0	0	0	0	0	0	0	0	.000	.000	.000	0	0	0	.000
Widger,c	1	1	0	0	0	0	0	0	1	2	0	1	.000	.667	.000	9	0	0	1.000
Garcia,p	1	2	0	0	0	0	0	0	0	0	0	0	.000	.000	.000	0	1	0	1.000
Garland,p	1	3	0	0	0	0	0	0	0	0	0	2	.000	.000	.000	0	2	0	1.000
Totals	4	154	20	44	75	9	2	6	20	15	2	30	.286	.360	.487	123	49	3	.983

HOUSTON ASTROS' BATTING AND FIELDING AVERAGES

Player, position	G	AB	R	H	TB	2B	3B	HR	RBI	BB	IBB	SO	Avg.	OBP	Slg.	PO	A	E	Avg.
Vizcaino,ss-ph-2b-1b	3	2	0	1	1	0	0	0	2	1	0	0	.500	.667	.500	3	1	0	1.000
Berkman,lf-1b	4	13	0	5	7	2	0	0	6	5	2	5	.385	.526	.538	20	0	0	1.000
Taveras,cf	4	15	2	5	9	2	1	0	0	0	0	3	.333	.412	.600	8	0	0	1.000
Ausmus,c	4	16	1	4	5	1	0	0	0	1	0	3	.250	.333	.313	29	3	0	1.000
Biggio,2b	4	18	3	4	5	1	0	0	1	1	0	4	.222	.263	.278	4	9	0	1.000

Player, position	G	AB	R	H	TB	2B	3B	HR	RBI	BB	IBB	SO	Avg.	OBP	Slg.	PO	A	E	Avg.
Lane,rf	4	18	1	4	8	1	0	1	2	1	0	5	.222	.263	.444	12	1	0	1.000
Lamb,1b-ph	4	10	1	2	6	1	0	1	1	2	1	3	.200	.333	.600	24	4	0	1.000
Bagwell,dh-ph	4	8	1	1	1	0	0	0	0	0	0	1	.125	.300	.125	0	0	0	.000
Ensberg,3b	4	18	2	2	5	0	0	1	2	1	0	7	.111	.158	.278	1	14	1	.938
Everett,ss	4	15	2	1	1	0	0	0	0	1	0	4	.067	.125	.067	11	14	1	.962
Astacio,p	1	0	0	0	0	0	0	0	0	0	0	0	.000	.000	.000	0	0	0	.000
Bruntlett,2b-lf-pr	2	0	0	0	0	0	0	0	0	0	0	0	.000	.000	.000	1	1	0	1.000
Clemens,p	1	0	0	0	0	0	0	0	0	0	0	0	.000	.000	.000	0	0	0	.000
Gallo,p	2	0	0	0	0	0	0	0	0	0	0	0	.000	.000	.000	0	0	0	.000
Lidge,p	3	0	0	0	0	0	0	0	0	0	0	0	.000	.000	.000	0	1	0	1.000
Pettitte,p	1	0	0	0	0	0	0	0	0	0	0	0	.000	.000	.000	0	2	0	1.000
Qualls,p	3	0	0	0	0	0	0	0	0	0	0	0	.000	.000	.000	0	0	0	.000
Rodriguez,p	2	0	0	0	0	0	0	0	0	0	0	0	.000	.000	.000	2	0	0	1.000
Springer,p	2	0	0	0	0	0	0	0	0	0	0	0	.000	.000	.000	1	0	0	1.000
Wheeler,p	2	0	0	0	0	0	0	0	0	0	0	0	.000	.000	.000	0	0	0	.000
Oswalt,p	1	1	0	0	0	0	0	0	0	0	0	0	.000	.000	.000	0	1	0	1.000
Backe,p	1	2	0	0	0	0	0	0	0	0	0	1	.000	.000	.000	1	2	0	1.000
Palmeiro,lf-ph	2	2	0	0	0	0	0	0	0	2	0	0	.000	.500	.000	0	0	0	.000
Burke,lf-pr-2b-ph	4	5	1	0	0	0	0	0	0	2	0	0	.000	.286	.000	1	0	0	1.000
Totals	4	143	14	29	48	8	1	3	14	17	3	36	.203	.307	.336	118	53	2	.988

CHICAGO WHITE SOX'S PITCHING RECORDS

Pitcher	G	GS	CG	IP	H	R	ER	HR	BB	IBB	SO	HB	WP	W	L	Pct.	ERA
Garcia	1	1	0	7.0	4	0	0	0	3	1	7	0	0	1	0	1.000	0.00
Marte	1	0	0	1.2	0	0	0	0	2	0	3	0	0	1	0	1.000	0.00
Cotts	4	0	0	1.1	1	0	0	0	1	0	2	0	0	1	0	1.000	0.00
Hernandez	1	0	0	1.0	0	0	0	0	4	1	2	0	0	0	0	.000	0.00
Vizcaino	1	0	0	1.0	0	0	0	0	1	0	0	0	0	0	0	.000	0.00
Hermanson	1	0	0	0.1	1	0	0	0	0	0	1	0	0	0	0	.000	0.00
Garland	1	1	0	7.0	7	4	2	1	2	0	4	0	0	0	0	.000	2.57
Jenks	4	0	0	5.0	3	2	2	0	2	0	7	1	0	0	0	.000	3.60
Contreras	1	1	0	7.0	6	3	3	1	0	0	2	3	0	1	0	1.000	3.86
Politte	3	0	0	2.1	0	1	1	0	2	1	2	1	1	0	0	.000	3.86
Buehrle	2	1	0	7.1	7	4	4	1	0	0	6	0	0	0	0	.000	4.91
Totals	4	4	0	41.0	29	14	12	3	17	3	36	5	1	4	0	1.000	2.63

No shutouts. Saves—Jenks 2, Buehrle.

HOUSTON ASTROS' PITCHING RECORDS

Pitcher	G	GS	CG	IP	H	R	ER	HR	BB	IBB	SO	HB	WP	W	L	Pct.	ERA
Backe	1	1	0	7.0	5	0	0	0	0	0	7	0	0	0	0	.000	0.00
Gallo	2	0	0	1.0	0	0	0	0	0	0	0	0	0	0	0	.000	0.00
Qualls	3	0	0	5.1	3	1	1	1	2	1	5	0	0	0	0	.000	1.69
Rodriguez	2	0	0	3.2	4	1	1	1	5	1	2	0	0	0	1	.000	2.45
Pettitte	1	1	0	6.0	8	2	2	0	0	0	4	0	0	0	0	.000	3.00
Springer	2	0	0	2.0	2	1	1	0	0	0	1	0	0	0	0	.000	4.50
Lidge	3	0	0	3.2	4	2	2	1	0	0	6	0	0	0	2	.000	4.91
Oswalt	1	1	0	6.0	8	5	5	1	5	0	3	1	0	0	0	.000	7.50
Clemens	1	1	0	2.0	4	3	3	1	0	0	1	0	0	0	0	.000	13.50
Wheeler	2	0	0	2.0	2	3	3	0	1	0	1	2	0	0	0	.000	13.50
Astacio	1	0	0	0.2	4	2	2	1	2	0	0	0	0	0	1	.000	27.00
Totals	4	4	0	39.1	44	20	20	6	15	2	30	3	0	0	4	.000	4.58

No shutouts or saves.

SCORE BY INNINGS

Chicago	1	4	0		1	5	0		4	2	1		0	0	0	0	2—20
Houston	1	2	5		1	2	0		0	1	2		0	0	0	0	0—14

MISCELLANEOUS STATISTICS

Sacrifice hits —Taveras 2, Ausmus, Everett, Everett, Oswalt, Podsednik.

Sacrifice flies —Berkman.

Stolen bases —Burke 2, Podsednik 2, Berkman, Harris, Lane, Pierzynski, Taveras, Uribe.

Caught stealing —Everett, Everett.

Double plays —Uribe, Iguchi and Konerko 2; Ausmus, Everett and Berkman; Biggio, Everett and Lamb; Crede, Iguchi and Konerko; Ensberg, Vizcaino and Berkman; Everett and Biggio; Everett and Lamb; Lamb, Everett and Rodriguez; Uribe and Konerko.

Left on bases —Chicago 9, 5, 15, 7—36; Houston 6, 4, 15, 9—34.

Scoring position—Chicago 2 for 10, 2 for 10, 3 for 14, 1 for 8—8 for 42; Houston 2 for 11, 4 for 10, 4 for 16, 0 for 11—10 for 48.

Hit by pitcher —by Contreras 3 (Bagwell 2, Ausmus), by Wheeler 2 (Dye, Konerko), by Politte (Taveras), by Oswalt (Crede), by Jenks (Taveras).

Passed balls —None.

Balks —None.

Time of games —3:13, 3:11, 5:41, 3:20—Avg.: 3:51.

Attendance —41,206, 41,432, 42,848, 42,936—168,422.

Umpires —West, Joe; Nelson, Jeff; Layne, Jerry; Cousins, Derryl; Cederstrom, Gary; and Hernandez, Angel.

ALL-STAR GAME

BOX SCORE

AMERICAN 7, NATIONAL 5

TUESDAY, JULY 12, AT COMERICA PARK, DETROIT

American League	AB	R	H	RBI	BB	SO	PO	A
Damon, cf (Red Sox)	2	1	1	0	0	0	1	0
Suzuki, cf-rf (Mariners)	2	0	1	2	0	0	3	0
A.Rodriguez, 3b (Yankees)	2	1	1	0	1	0	0	1
Hillenbrand, 3b (Blue Jays)	0	0	0	0	0	0	0	2
D.Ortiz, dh (Red Sox)	3	0	2	1	0	0	0	0
Mi.Sweeney, ph-dh (Royals)	1	0	0	0	0	1	0	0
M.Ramirez, lf (Red Sox)	2	0	0	0	0	1	0	0
G.Anderson, lf (Angels)	2	0	0	0	0	1	0	0
Tejada, ss (Orioles)	3	1	1	2	0	1	2	
M.Young, ss (Rangers)	1	0	1	0	0	0	2	
V.Guerrero, rf (Angels)	3	0	1	0	0	0	1	0
A.Soriano, pr-2b (Rangers)	1	1	0	0	0	3	1	
Teixeira, 1b (Rangers)	3	1	1	2	0	4	0	
Konerko, 1b (White Sox)	1	0	0	0	1	4	0	
Varitek, c (Red Sox)	1	1	1	1	0	4	0	
I.Rodriguez, c (Tigers)	1	0	0	0	1	1	2	0
B.Roberts, 2b (Orioles)	2	1	1	0	0	4	4	
Sheffield, ph-rf (Yankees)	1	0	0	0	0	0	0	0
Podsednik, cf (White Sox)	0	0	0	0	0	0	0	0
Buehrle, p (White Sox)	0	0	0	0	0	0	0	0
B.Colon, p (Angels)	0	0	0	0	0	0	0	0
J.Santana, p (Twins)	0	0	0	0	0	0	0	0
Clement, p (Red Sox)	0	0	0	0	0	0	0	0
Garland, p (White Sox)	0	0	0	0	0	0	0	0
Rogers, p (Rangers)	0	0	0	0	0	0	0	0
Nathan, p (Twins)	0	0	0	0	0	0	0	0
Wickman, p (Indians)	0	0	0	0	0	0	0	0
B.Ryan, p (Orioles)	0	0	0	0	0	0	0	1
M.Rivera, p (Yankees)	0	0	0	0	0	0	0	0
TOTALS	32	7	11	7	3	6	27	13

National League	AB	R	H	BI	BB	SO	PO	A
Abreu, rf (Phillies)	2	0	1	0	1	0	0	0
Rollins, ss (Phillies)	1	0	1	0	0	0	1	1
L.Gonzalez, ph (Diamondbacks)	1	1	1	1	0	0	0	0
C.Beltran, lf (Mets)	3	0	1	0	0	1	1	0
Lo Duca, c (Marlins)	2	0	0	0	0	0	4	1
Pujols, dh (Cardinals)	2	0	1	0	0	0	0	0
C.Lee, ph-dh (Brewers)	3	0	0	1	0	1	0	0
D.Lee, 1b (Cubs)	3	0	1	0	0	1	8	1
Ensberg, 1b (Astros)	0	0	0	0	0	1	1	0
Edmonds, cf-rf (Cardinals)	1	0	0	0	1	0	1	0
Alou, ph-rf (Giants)	1	1	1	0	1	0	0	0
A.Ramirez, 3b (Cubs)	2	0	1	0	0	0	0	1
F.Lopez, 3b (Reds)	1	0	1	0	0	0	0	0
Piazza, c (Mets)	2	0	0	0	0	1	1	0
M.Cabrera, lf (Marlins)	2	0	0	1	0	0	1	0
Kent, 2b (Dodgers)	1	0	0	0	0	1	1	1
L.Castillo, 2b (Marlins)	3	1	1	0	0	0	2	3
Eckstein, ss (Cardinals)	2	0	0	0	0	0	1	3
A.Jones, cf (Braves)	1	2	1	2	1	0	1	0
Carpenter, p (Cardinals)	0	0	0	0	0	0	0	0
Smoltz, p (Braves)	0	0	0	0	0	0	1	0
Oswalt, p (Astros)	0	0	0	0	0	0	0	0
L.Hernandez, p (Nationals)	0	0	0	0	0	0	0	1
Clemens, p (Astros)	0	0	0	0	0	0	0	0
Willis, p (Marlins)	0	0	0	0	0	0	0	0
Lidge, p (Astros)	0	0	0	0	0	0	0	0
Peavy, p (Padres)	0	0	0	0	0	0	0	0
C.Cordero, p (Nationals)	0	0	0	0	0	0	0	0
TOTALS	35	5	11	5	5	6	24	12

							R	H	E	LOB
National League	0 0 0	0 0 0	2 1 2	—	5	11	0	8
American League	0 1 2	2 0 2	0 0 x	—	7	11	1	4

American League	IP	H	R	ER	HR	BB	SO
Buehrle (White Sox) (W)	2.0	3	0	0	0	0	3
B.Colon (Angels)	1.0	1	0	0	0	0	0
J.Santana (Twins)	1.0	1	0	0	0	1	0
Clement (Red Sox)	1.0	0	0	0	0	1	1
Garland (White Sox)	1.0	0	0	0	0	2	0
Rogers (Rangers)	1.0	3	2	2	1	0	1
Nathan (Twins)	1.0	2	1	1	0	0	0
Wickman (Indians)	0.0	0	1	1	0	1	0
B.Ryan (Orioles)	0.2	1	1	1	0	0	0
M.Rivera (Yankees) (S)	0.1	0	0	0	0	0	1

Wickman pitched to 1 batter in the 9th.

National League	IP	H	R	ER	HR	BB	SO
Carpenter (Cardinals)	1.0	2	0	0	0	0	0
Smoltz (Braves) (L)	1.0	2	1	1	1	0	0
Oswalt (Astros)	1.0	2	2	2	0	1	1
L.Hernandez (Nationals)	1.0	2	2	2	0	1	0
Clemens (Astros)	1.0	0	0	0	0	0	0
Willis (Marlins)	1.0	2	2	2	1	1	0
Lidge (Astros)	1.0	0	0	0	0	0	3
Peavy (Padres)	0.2	1	0	0	0	0	1
C.Cordero (Nationals)	0.1	0	0	0	0	0	1

E—B.Colon. DP—National League 2, American League 3. LOB—National League 8, American League 4. Scoring Position—National League 1 for 8, American League 2 for 9. 2B—D.Lee, Alou, L.Gonzalez, B.Roberts, M.Young. HR—Tejada (2nd inning, 0 out, 0 on) off Smoltz, Teixeira (6th inning, 0 out, 0 on) off Willis, A.Jones (7th inning, 0 out, 1 on) off Rogers. WP—Garland. T—2:41. A—41,617. U—HP-West, 1B-Welke, 2B-Cooper, 3B-DiMuro, LF-Bucknor, RF-Fletcher.

PLAY BY PLAY

FIRST INNING

N.L.—Abreu singled to left. C.Beltran grounded into a double play, shortstop Tejada to second baseman B.Roberts to first baseman Teixeira, Abreu out. Pujols singled to center. D.Lee struck out.
Runs: 0, Hits: 2, Errors: 0

A.L.—Damon grounded out, shortstop Eckstein to first baseman D.Lee. A.Rodriguez singled to left. D.Ortiz singled to right, A.Rodriguez to third. M.Ramirez grounded into a double play, shortstop Eckstein to second baseman Kent to first baseman D.Lee, D.Ortiz out.
Runs: 0, Hits: 2, Errors: 0

SECOND INNING

N.L.—Edmonds lined out to second baseman B.Roberts. A.Ramirez singled to right. Piazza struck out. Kent struck out.
Runs: 0, Hits: 1, Errors: 0

A.L.—L.Castillo in as second baseman. Smoltz pitching. Tejada homered to center on a 0-1 count. V.Guerrero popped out to shortstop Eckstein. Teixeira grounded out, first baseman D.Lee to pitcher Smoltz. Varitek infield single to short. B.Roberts flied out to left fielder C.Beltran.
Runs: 1, Hits: 2, Errors: 0

THIRD INNING

N.L.—B.Colon pitching. Eckstein flied out to right fielder V.Guerrero. Abreu grounded out, second baseman B.Roberts to first baseman Teixeira. C.Beltran singled to center. On pickoff attempt, error by pitcher B.Colon, C.Beltran to third. Pujols flied out to center fielder Damon.
Runs: 0, Hits: 1, Errors: 1

A.L.—Oswalt pitching. Damon infield single to short. A.Rodriguez

walked on a full count, Damon to second. D.Ortiz singled to right, Damon scored, A.Rodriguez to third. M.Ramirez struck out. Tejada grounded out, shortstop Eckstein to first baseman D.Lee, A.Rodriguez scored, D.Ortiz to second. V.Guerrero grounded out, third baseman A.Ramirez to first baseman D.Lee.
Runs: 2, Hits: 2, Errors: 0

FOURTH INNING

N.L.—Suzuki in as center fielder. G.Anderson in as left fielder. Jo.Santana pitching. D.Lee doubled to left. Edmonds walked on four pitches. A.Ramirez grounded into a double play, second baseman B.Roberts to shortstop Tejada to first baseman Teixeira, D.Lee to third, Edmonds out. Piazza grounded out, second baseman B.Roberts to first baseman Teixeira.
Runs: 0, Hits: 1, Errors: 0

A.L.—L.Hernandez pitching. Teixeira popped out to second baseman L.Castillo. Varitek walked. B.Roberts doubled to right, Varitek to third. Suzuki singled to right, Varitek scored, B.Roberts scored. A.Rodriguez flied out to center fielder Edmonds. Suzuki was picked off, pitcher L.Hernandez to first baseman D.Lee, Suzuki out.
Runs: 2, Hits: 2, Errors: 0

FIFTH INNING

N.L.—Mora in as third baseman. Clement pitching. L.Castillo flied out to center fielder Suzuki. Eckstein flied out to center fielder Suzuki. Abreu walked on a full count. C.Beltran struck out.
Runs: 0, Hits: 0, Errors: 0

A.L.—Rollins in as shortstop. Lo Duca in as catcher. Edmonds in as right fielder. M.Cabrera in as left fielder. A.Jones in as center fielder. Clemens pitching. D.Ortiz flied out to left fielder M.Cabrera. G.Anderson grounded out, second baseman L.Castillo to first baseman D.Lee. Tejada grounded out, second baseman L.Castillo to first baseman D.Lee.
Runs: 0, Hits: 0, Errors: 0

SIXTH INNING

N.L.—M.Young in as shortstop. I.Rodriguez in as catcher. Garland pitching. C.Lee pinch-hitting for Pujols. C.Lee flied out to center fielder Suzuki. D.Lee popped out to second baseman B.Roberts. Alou pinch-hitting for Edmonds. Alou walked. On wild pitch by Garland, Alou to second. A.Ramirez walked on four pitches. M.Cabrera grounded into fielder's choice, shortstop M.Young to second baseman B.Roberts, M.Cabrera to first, A.Ramirez out.
Runs: 0, Hits: 0, Errors: 0

A.L.—C.Lee in as designated hitter. Alou in as right fielder. Willis

pitching. V.Guerrero singled to center. A.Soriano pinch-running for V.Guerrero. Teixeira homered to center on a full count, A.Soriano scored. I.Rodriguez walked on a full count. Sheffield pinch-hitting for B.Roberts. Sheffield grounded into a double play, shortstop Rollins to second baseman L.Castillo to first baseman D.Lee, I.Rodriguez out. Suzuki flied out to center fielder A.Jones.
Runs: 2, Hits: 2, Errors: 0

SEVENTH INNING

N.L.—A.Soriano in as second baseman. Konerko in as first baseman. Sheffield in as right fielder. K.Rogers pitching. L.Castillo singled to left. A.Jones homered to left on a 1-1 count, L.Castillo scored. Rollins infield single to third. Lo Duca grounded into a double play, third baseman Mora to second baseman A.Soriano to first baseman Konerko, Rollins out. C.Lee struck out.
Runs: 2, Hits: 3, Errors: 0

A.L.—Ensberg in as first baseman. F.Lopez in as third baseman. Lidge pitching. Mora struck out, catcher Lo Duca to first baseman Ensberg. Mi.Sweeney pinch-hitting for D.Ortiz. Mi.Sweeney struck out. G.Anderson struck out.
Runs: 0, Hits: 0, Errors: 0

EIGHTH INNING

N.L.—Hillenbrand in as third baseman. Mi.Sweeney in as designated hitter. Nathan pitching. Ensberg fouled out to first baseman Konerko. Alou doubled to left. F.Lopez singled to center, Alou to third. M.Cabrera grounded into fielder's choice, third baseman Hillenbrand to second baseman A.Soriano, Alou scored, M.Cabrera to first. L.Castillo grounded into fielder's choice, third baseman Hillenbrand to second baseman A.Soriano, L.Castillo to first, M.Cabrera out.
Runs: 1, Hits: 2, Errors: 0

A.L.—Peavy pitching. M.Young doubled to left. A.Soriano popped out to shortstop Rollins. Konerko struck out. C.Cordero pitching. I.Rodriguez struck out.
Runs: 0, Hits: 1, Errors: 0

NINTH INNING

N.L.—Suzuki in as right fielder. Podsednik in as center fielder. Wickman pitching. A.Jones walked. L.Gonzalez pinch-hitting for Rollins. B.Ryan pitching. L.Gonzalez doubled to center, A.Jones scored. Lo Duca grounded out, pitcher B.Ryan to first baseman Konerko, L.Gonzalez to third. C.Lee grounded out, shortstop M.Young to first baseman Konerko, L.Gonzalez scored. M.Rivera pitching. Ensberg struck out.
Runs: 2, Hits: 1, Errors: 0

NOTABLE PERFORMANCES

LOW-HIT GAMES

AMERICAN LEAGUE

ONE-HIT GAMES

Date   **Pitcher(s), Team, Opponent, Result—Player with hit**
6-14   David Wells (7 inn.), Mike Timlin (1 inn.) and Keith Foulke (1 inn.), Boston vs. Cincinnati, W 7-0—Ryan Freel (single in sixth)
6-26   Rich Harden (7 inn.), Ron Flores (1 inn.) and Kiko Calero (1 inn.), Oakland vs. San Francisco, W 16-0—Deivi Cruz (single in fifth)
8-23   Freddy Garcia, Chicago at Minnesota, L 0-1—Jacque Jones (home run in eighth)

TWO-HIT GAMES

Date   **Pitcher(s), Team, Opponent, Result—Player(s) with hit(s)**
4-4   Mark Buehrle (8 inn.) and Shingo Takatsu (1 inn.), Chicago vs. Cleveland, W 1-0—Victor Martinez (single in fifth), Coco Crisp (single in seventh)
4-15   Bartolo Colon (7 inn.), Scot Shields (1 inn.) and Francisco Rodriguez (1 inn.), Los Angeles at Oakland, W 6-1—Mark Kotsay (double in fourth), Scott Hatteberg (single in fourth)
5-1   Johan Santana (8 inn.) and Juan Rincon (1 inn.), Minnesota vs. Los Angeles, L 1-2—Vladimir Guerrero (home run in fourth), Jose Molina (home run in sixth)
5-5   Zack Greinke (7.1 inn.), Andrew Sisco (.1 inn.) and Ambiorix Burgos (.1 inn.), Kansas City at Chicago, L 1-2—A.J. Pierzynski (single in third), Scott Podsednik (single in fourth)
5-9   Kevin Millwood (8 inn.) and Bob Wickman (1 inn.), Cleveland at Los Angeles, W 3-0—Jose Molina (double in third), Chone Figgins (single in ninth)
5-29   Roy Halladay, Toronto vs. Minnesota, W 4-0—Nick Punto (single in first), Shannon Stewart (single in sixth)
6-6   Freddy Garcia (8 inn.) and Shingo Takatsu (1 inn.), Chicago at Colorado, W 9-3—Eddy Garabito (single in first), Brad Hawpe (home run in first)
6-19   Runelvys Hernandez (7 inn.), Ambiorix Burgos (0 inn.), Mike Wood (1 inn.) and Mike MacDougal (1 inn.), Kansas City vs. Houston, W 7-1—Brad Ausmus (single in fifth), Willy Taveras (single in eighth)
7-1   Paul Byrd, Los Angeles at Kansas City, W 5-0—Matt Stairs (single in fifth), Mike Sweeney (double in seventh)
7-14   Daniel Cabrera (8 inn.) and B.J. Ryan (1 inn.), Baltimore at Seattle, W 5-3—Adrian Beltre (single in second), Willie Bloomquist (single in second)
7-14   Rich Harden, Oakland vs. Texas, W 6-0—Alfonso Soriano (single in eighth), David Dellucci (single in ninth)
7-26   Randy Johnson (8 inn.) and Tom Gordon (1 inn.), New York vs. Minnesota, W 4-0—Juan Castro (single in sixth), Lew Ford (double in eighth)
8-1   Joe Blanton (7 inn.), Kiko Calero (1 inn.) and Huston Street (1 inn.), Oakland at Minnesota, W 2-1—Justin Morneau (home run in second), Lew Ford (single in fifth)
8-11   Scott Downs (7 inn.), Jason Frasor (.2 inn.) and Miguel Batista (1.1 inn.), Toronto vs. Detroit, W 2-1—Vance Wilson (single in third), Rondell White (home run in eighth)
8-17   Chris Young (8 inn.) and Francisco Cordero (1 inn.), Texas at Cleveland, W 3-0—Coco Crisp (single in third), Travis Hafner (single in seventh)
8-23   Nate Robertson (8 inn.) and Fernando Rodney (1 inn.), Detroit vs. Oakland, W 4-1—Jay Payton (single in second), Bobby Crosby (double in seventh)
8-31   Bruce Chen (8 inn.) and Chris Ray (1 inn.), Baltimore at Toronto, W 7-0—Aaron Hill (single in second), Corey Koskie (single in eighth)
9-3   Seth McClung (8 inn.) and Danys Baez (1 inn.), Tampa Bay at Toronto, W 3-2—Orlando Hudson (triple in sixth), Alex Rios (single in seventh)
9-8   J.P. Howell (6 inn.), Andrew Sisco (1 inn.), Ambiorix Burgos (1 inn.) and Mike MacDougal (1 inn.), Kansas City at Chicago, W 4-2—Chris Widger (double in fifth), Scott Podsednik (single in fifth)
9-17   Bruce Chen (7 inn.), Todd Williams (1 inn.) and B.J. Ryan (1 inn.), Baltimore vs. Tampa Bay, W 2-1—Carl Crawford (home run in fourth), Julio Lugo (single in sixth)

NATIONAL LEAGUE

ONE-HIT GAMES

Date   **Pitcher(s), Team, Opponent, Result—Player with hit**
4-9   Carlos Zambrano (7.1 inn.), Chad Fox (.2 inn.) and LaTroy Hawkins (1 inn.), Chicago vs. Milwaukee, W 4-0—Russell Branyan (single in second)
4-15   Aaron Heilman, New York vs. Florida, W 4-0—Luis Castillo (single in fourth)
5-31   Carlos Zambrano (8 inn.), Michael Wuertz (1 inn.) and Ryan Dempster (1 inn.), Chicago at Los Angeles, W 2-1—Cesar Izturis (double in third)
6-14   Chris Carpenter, St. Louis at Toronto, W 7-0—Russ Adams (double in sixth)
6-26   Mark Prior (6 inn.), Jerome Williams (2 inn.) and Ryan Dempster (1 inn.), Chicago at Chicago, W 2-0—Pablo Ozuna (single in third)
7-25   Derek Lowe (8 inn.) and Steve Schmoll (1 inn.), Los Angeles vs. Cincinnati, W 4-0—Rich Aurilia (single in fifth)
8-31   Derek Lowe, Los Angeles at Chicago, W 7-0—Jerry Hairston Jr. (single in first)

TWO-HIT GAMES

Date   **Pitcher(s), Team, Opponent, Result—Player(s) with hit(s)**
4-10   Pedro Martinez, New York at Atlanta, W 6-1—Andruw Jones (triple in second), Johnny Estrada (double in fourth)
4-18   Mark Mulder (8 inn.) and Jimmy Journell (1 inn.), St. Louis at Pittsburgh, W 11-1—Freddy Sanchez (single in fifth), Craig Wilson (double in sixth)
4-30   Brian Lawrence (8 inn.) and Trevor Hoffman (1 inn.), San Diego vs. Arizona, W 2-0—Craig Counsell (double in first), Troy Glaus

(single in seventh)
4-30   Vicente Padilla (5 inn.) and Ryan Madson (1 inn.), Philadelphia vs. Florida, L 1-2—Mike Lowell (double in second), Alex Gonzalez (single in second)
5-7   Josh Fogg (7 inn.), Mike Gonzalez (1 inn.) and Jose Mesa (1 inn.), Pittsburgh at Arizona, W 3-2—Chad Tracy (home run in fifth), Craig Counsell (single in sixth)
5-8   Mike Hampton, Atlanta vs. Houston, W 16-0—Mike Lamb (single in second), Orlando Palmeiro (single in ninth)
5-26   Jake Peavy, San Diego at Arizona, W 10-0—Troy Glaus (single in second), Shawn Green (double in eighth)
6-7   Pedro Martinez, New York vs. Houston, W 3-1—Chris Burke (home run in seventh), Lance Berkman (single in seventh)
6-8   Jeff Weaver (7 inn.), Yhency Brazoban (1 inn.) and Eric Gagne (1 inn.), Los Angeles vs. Detroit, W 3-1—Brandon Inge (double in first), Jason Johnson (home run in third)
6-12   Roy Oswalt, Houston vs. Toronto, W 3-0—Shea Hillenbrand (single in second), Alex Rios (double in ninth)
6-26   A.J. Burnett, Florida at Tampa Bay, W 1-0—Jonny Gomes (single in third), Nick Green (triple in sixth)
7-14   Mark Prior (8 inn.) and Ryan Dempster (1 inn.), Chicago vs. Pittsburgh, W 5-1—Matt Lawton (single in third), Tike Redman (single in eighth)
7-15   Noah Lowry (7.1 inn.) and Scott Eyre (1.2 inn.), San Francisco at Los Angeles, W 6-0—Jason Phillips (double in fourth), Jason Repko (single in fifth)
8-13   Ramon Ortiz (6 inn.), Matt Belisle (1 inn.), Jason Standridge (1 inn.) and David Weathers (1 inn.), Cincinnati at Milwaukee, W 4-1—Geoff Jenkins (single in fifth), Bill Hall (double in fifth)
8-14   Pedro Martinez, New York at Los Angeles, L 1-2—Antonio Perez (triple in eighth), Jayson Werth (home run in eighth)
8-27   Jason Marquis, St. Louis at Washington, W 6-0—Cristian Guzman (single in third), Marlon Byrd (single in sixth)
9-9   Matt Cain, San Francisco vs. Chicago, W 2-1—Derrek Lee (home run in fourth), Jerry Hairston Jr. (single in ninth)
9-25   Javier Vazquez (7 inn.), Tim Worrell (2 inn.) and Jose Valverde (1 inn.), Arizona vs. San Diego, W 4-3—Brian Giles (double in first), Joe Randa (home run in fourth)
9-27   Brandon Webb (7 inn.), Tim Worrell (1 inn.) and Jose Valverde (1 inn.), Arizona at Los Angeles, W 2-0—Hee-Seop Choi (single in first and single in seventh)
9-29   Tom Glavine, New York vs. Colorado, W 11-0—Choo Freeman (single in third), Matt Holliday (single in seventh)

15-STRIKEOUT GAMES

AMERICAN LEAGUE

No occurrences

NATIONAL LEAGUE

Date	Pitcher, Team, Opponent	IP	H	R	ER	BB	SO	Result
4-10	John Smoltz, Atlanta vs. New York	7.1	8	2	2	2	15	L 1-6

10-STRIKEOUT GAMES

AMERICAN LEAGUE

Team	No.	Pitchers
Minnesota	8	Johan Santana 8.
Tampa Bay	4	Scott Kazmir 3, Casey Fossum 1.
Baltimore	3	Daniel Cabrera 2, Erik Bedard 1.
Boston	3	Tim Wakefield 2, Curt Schilling 1.
Los Angeles	3	John Lackey 2, Bartolo Colon 1.
New York	3	Randy Johnson 3.
Toronto	3	Roy Halladay 1, Ted Lilly 1, Scott Downs 1.
Chicago	2	Freddy Garcia 1, Mark Buehrle 1.
Cleveland	1	C.C. Sabathia 1.
Oakland	1	Joe Blanton 1.
Seattle	1	Felix Hernandez 1.
Texas	1	Juan Dominguez 1.
Detroit	0	None.
Kansas City	0	None.

NATIONAL LEAGUE

Team	No.	Pitchers
Chicago	11	Mark Prior 6, Carlos Zambrano 4, Greg Maddux 1.
San Diego	7	Jake Peavy 6, Adam Eaton 1.
New York	6	Pedro Martinez 5, Tom Glavine 1.
Florida	6	A.J. Burnett 3, Dontrelle Willis 2, Josh Beckett 1.
Arizona	6	Javier Vazquez 4, Brandon Webb 2.
St. Louis	5	Chris Carpenter 4, Mark Mulder 1.
Milwaukee	4	Doug Davis 2, Gary Glover 1, Ben Sheets 1.
Washington	4	Esteban Loaiza 2, John Patterson 2.
Philadelphia	4	Brett Myers 3, Cory Lidle 1.
Houston	3	Roger Clemens 2, Roy Oswalt 1.
San Francisco	3	Jason Schmidt 3.
Atlanta	2	John Smoltz 1, Tim Hudson 1.
Cincinnati	2	Aaron Harang 2.
Pittsburgh	2	Kip Wells 1, Oliver Perez 1.
Los Angeles	1	Jeff Weaver 1.
Colorado	0	None.

1-0 GAMES

AMERICAN LEAGUE

Date	Winner	Loser	Inn.*	Site
4-4	~Mark Buehrle, Chicago	Jake Westbrook, Cleveland	7	Chicago
4-16	~Kiko Calero, Oakland	~Scot Shields, Los Angeles	10	Oakland
4-21	~Matt Clement, Boston	~Rodrigo Lopez, Baltimore	2	Baltimore
4-24	~Scot Shields, Los Angeles	Joe Blanton, Oakland	7	Los Angeles
5-3	~Josh Towers, Toronto	~Daniel Cabrera, Baltimore	8	Baltimore
7-3	~Chien-Ming Wang, New York	Nate Robertson, Detroit	4	Detroit
7-14	~Jose Contreras, Chicago	~Kevin Millwood, Cleveland	1	Cleveland
8-9	~Felix Hernandez, Seattle	~Kyle Lohse, Minnesota	7	Seattle

Date	Winner	Loser	Inn.*	Site
8-12	Johan Santana, Minnesota	Danny Haren, Oakland	5	Oakland
8-13	~John Maine, Baltimore	Dave Bush, Toronto	3	Baltimore
8-14	~Joe Borowski, Tampa Bay	~Bob Wickman, Cleveland	9	Cleveland
8-14	+~Mike Maroth, Detroit	Jose Lima, Kansas City	5	Kansas City
8-23	~Johan Santana, Minnesota	Freddy Garcia, Chicago	8	Minnesota
8-31	~Mike MacDougal, Kansas City	~Matt Guerrier, Minnesota	9	Kansas City
9-4	~Scott Kazmir, Tampa Bay	~Dave Bush, Toronto	2	Toronto
9-7	~Jose Contreras, Chicago	~Mike Wood, Kansas City	3	Chicago
9-11	~Randy Johnson, New York	Tim Wakefield, Boston	1	New York
9-17	~Shawn Chacon, New York	~Gustavo Chacin, Toronto	2	Toronto
9-28	~Seth McClung, Tampa Bay	~Cliff Lee, Cleveland	8	Cleveland

PLAYERS HITTING HOME RUNS IN 1-0 GAMES: 4-24, Steve Finley, Los Angeles; 8-14, Travis Lee, Tampa Bay; 8-23, Jacque Jones, Minnesota; 9-7, Paul Konerko, Chicago; 9-11, Jason Giambi, New York.
*Inning in which run scored. ~Did not pitch complete game. + Second game of doubleheader

NATIONAL LEAGUE

Date	Winner	Loser	Inn.*	Site
4-7	~Rudy Seanez, San Diego	~Rick White, Pittsburgh	12	San Diego
4-11	~Adam Eaton, San Diego	~Ryan Dempster, Chicago	6	Chicago
4-13	~Mike DeJean, New York	~Dan Wheeler, Houston	11	New York
4-18	~Jorge Sosa, Atlanta	~Dan Wheeler, Houston	12	Houston
4-23	Mark Mulder, St. Louis	~Chad Qualls, Houston	10	St. Louis
5-18	~Gary Majewski, Washington	~Chris Capuano, Milwaukee	9	Washington
5-22	Javier Vazquez, Arizona	~Jason Johnson, Detroit	8	Detroit
5-27	~Pedro Martinez, New York	~Brian Moehler, Florida	4	Florida
6-4	~John Foster, Atlanta	~Mike Gonzalez, Pittsburgh	9	Pittsburgh
6-15	~Ryan Drese, Washington	Bartolo Colon, Los Angeles	6	Los Angeles
6-20	~Jake Peavy, San Diego	~Brad Penny, Los Angeles	4	San Diego
6-26	A.J. Burnett, Florida	~Seth McClung, Tampa Bay	3	Tampa Bay
7-9	~Billy Wagner, Philadelphia	~Hector Carrasco, Washington	9	Philadelphia
7-9	~Jason Jennings, Colorado	~Brian Lawrence, San Diego	6	Colorado
7-21	~Odalis Perez, Los Angeles	~Jon Lieber, Philadelphia	1	Philadelphia
8-12	~Noah Lowry, San Francisco	~Dontrelle Willis, Florida	6	Florida
8-13	~Salomon Torres, Pittsburgh	~Brad Lidge, Houston	9	Houston
8-19	~Jae Seo, New York	~John Patterson, Washington	7	New York
8-26	~Steve Trachsel, New York	~Kevin Correia, San Francisco	2	San Francisco
8-28	~Jeff Weaver, Los Angeles	~Chad Qualls, Houston	8	Los Angeles
9-29	~Scott Cassidy, San Diego	~Jeremy Accardo, San Francisco	11	San Diego

PLAYERS HITTING HOME RUNS IN 1-0 GAMES: 4-18, Ryan Langerhans, Atlanta; 6-15, Brian Schneider, Washington; 8-12, Randy Winn, San Francisco; 8-13, Jack Wilson, Pittsburgh; 8-26, David Wright, New York.
*Inning in which run scored. ~Did not pitch complete game.

FOUR OR MORE HITS IN ONE GAME
AMERICAN LEAGUE

Team	No.	Hitters
Minnesota	15	Joe Mauer 3, Shannon Stewart 2, Torii Hunter 2, Nick Punto 2, Justin Morneau 2, Mike Redmond 1, Michael Cuddyer 1, Lew Ford 1, Jason Bartlett 1.
Boston	14	Johnny Damon 4, Manny Ramirez 3, David Ortiz 3, Trot Nixon 2, Edgar Renteria 1, Jason Varitek 1.
New York	14	Alex Rodriguez 5, Derek Jeter 3, Hideki Matsui 3, Gary Sheffield 1, Bernie Williams 1, Robinson Cano 1.
Texas	13	Michael Young 3, Mark Teixeira 3, Hank Blalock 2, David Dellucci 1, Alfonso Soriano 1, Gary Matthews Jr. 1, Kevin Mench 1, Laynce Nix 1.
Oakland	12	Mark Kotsay 2, Eric Chavez 2, Bobby Crosby 2, Scott Hatteberg 1, Jay Payton 1, Eric Byrnes 1, Bobby Kielty 1, Mark Ellis 1, Dan Johnson 1.
Detroit	11	Placido Polanco 3, Ivan Rodriguez 2, Dmitri Young 1, Carlos Guillen 1, Brandon Inge 1, Craig Monroe 1, Chris Shelton 1, Curtis Granderson 1.
Cleveland	9	Coco Crisp 3, Victor Martinez 2, Grady Sizemore 2, Aaron Boone 1, Travis Hafner 1.
Kansas City	9	Tony Graffanino 2, Mike Sweeney 1, Emil Brown 1, Angel Berroa 1, John Buck 1, David DeJesus 1, Mark Teahen 1, Ruben Gotay 1.
Baltimore	8	Miguel Tejada 5, Rafael Palmeiro 1, Melvin Mora 1, Luis Matos 1.
Los Angeles	8	Juan Rivera 3, Adam Kennedy 2, Garret Anderson 1, Vladimir Guerrero 1, Bengie Molina 1.
Tampa Bay	8	Julio Lugo 3, Carl Crawford 2, Alex S. Gonzalez 1, Toby Hall 1.
Chicago	7	Tadahito Iguchi 2, Jermaine Dye 1, Paul Konerko 1, Pablo Ozuna 1, Scott Podsednik 1, Aaron Rowand 1.
Seattle	7	Raul Ibanez 2, Randy Winn 2, Ichiro Suzuki 2, Jose Lopez 1.
Toronto	7	Frank Catalanotto 2, Shea Hillenbrand 2, Corey Koskie 1, Alex Rios 1, Aaron Hill 1.

NATIONAL LEAGUE

Team	No.	Hitters
San Diego	17	Mark Loretta 3, Brian Giles 3, Dave Roberts 3, Damian Jackson 2, Xavier Nady 2, Khalil Greene 2, Ryan Klesko 1, Ramon Hernandez 1.

Team	No.	Hitters
Colorado	15	Aaron Miles 3, Clint Barmes 3, Matt Holliday 3, Cory Sullivan 2, Todd Helton 1, Preston Wilson 1, Garrett Atkins 1, Luis A. Gonzalez 1.
Milwaukee	14	Brady Clark 5, Bill Hall 3, Geoff Jenkins 2, Carlos Lee 2, Lyle Overbay 1, J.J. Hardy 1.
San Francisco	14	Randy Winn 4, Moises Alou 2, J.T. Snow 2, Omar Vizquel 1, Michael Tucker 1, Ray Durham 1, Edgardo Alfonzo 1, Deivi Cruz 1, Pedro Feliz 1.
Washington	13	Brad Wilkerson 3, Ryan Church 3, Vinny Castilla 2, Jose Guillen 1, Preston Wilson 1, Brian Schneider 1, Marlon Byrd 1, Jamey Carroll 1.
New York	13	Jose Reyes 5, Mike Piazza 2, David Wright 2, Mike Cameron 1, Carlos Beltran 1, Victor Diaz 1, Mike Jacobs 1.
Philadelphia	13	Pat Burrell 3, Jimmy Rollins 3, Kenny Lofton 2, Todd Pratt 1, David Bell 1, Bobby Abreu 1, Placido Polanco 1, Ryan Howard 1.
Pittsburgh	12	Matt Lawton 3, Chris Duffy 2, Tike Redman 2, Craig Wilson 1, Jack Wilson 1, Rob Mackowiak 1, Jose Castillo 1, Ryan Doumit 1, Brad Eldred 1.
Florida	12	Miguel Cabrera 4, Juan Pierre 3, Luis Castillo 2, Carlos Delgado 1, Juan Encarnacion 1, Paul Lo Duca 1.
Los Angeles	11	Jeff Kent 1, J.D. Drew 1, Milton Bradley 1, Jayson Werth 1, Hee-Seop Choi 1, Cesar Izturis 1, Jason Phillips 1, Antonio Perez 1, Jason Repko 1, Oscar Robles 1, Willy Aybar 1.
St. Louis	11	David Eckstein 3, Mark Grudzielanek 2, Abraham O. Nunez 2, Reggie Sanders 1, John Mabry 1, So Taguchi 1, Yadier Molina 1.
Arizona	11	Royce Clayton 3, Craig Counsell 2, Chad Tracy 2, Shawn Green 1, Quinton McCracken 1, Alex Cintron 1, Chris Snyder 1.
Atlanta	10	Marcus Giles 3, Rafael Furcal 2, Adam LaRoche 2, Chipper Jones 1, Wilson Betemit 1, Jeff Francoeur 1.
Chicago	9	Derrek Lee 5, Neifi Perez 1, Henry Blanco 1, Jerry Hairston Jr. 1, Matt Murton 1.
Houston	9	Willy Taveras 4, Morgan Ensberg 3, Craig Biggio 1, Jason Lane 1.
Cincinnati	8	Sean Casey 4, Felipe Lopez 3, Ryan Freel 1.

FIVE OR MORE HITS IN ONE GAME

AMERICAN LEAGUE

Date	Player, Team, Opponent	AB	R	H	2B	3B	HR	RBI	Result
4-18	Alex Rodriguez, New York vs. Tampa Bay	6	5	5	2	0	2	6	W 19-8
4-30	Mark Kotsay, Oakland vs. Seattle	6	2	5	1	0	0	1	W 6-5
5-29	Tony Graffanino, Kansas City at Los Angeles	5	1	5	1	0	0	3	L 6-7
6-1	Torii Hunter, Minnesota vs. Cleveland	5	1	5	2	0	1	6	W 6-2
6-12	Eric Chavez, Oakland at Atlanta	5	2	5	1	0	2	4	W 11-5
6-21	Derek Jeter, New York vs. Tampa Bay	6	5	5	1	0	1	1	W 20-11
7-9	Miguel Tejada, Baltimore vs. Boston	5	2	5	2	1	0	1	W 9-1
7-9	Mike Sweeney, Kansas City vs. Minnesota	6	1	5	2	0	0	3	W 12-8
7-10	Paul Konerko, Chicago vs. Oakland	6	3	5	0	0	1	1	L 8-9
7-22	Craig Monroe, Detroit vs. Minnesota	5	1	5	3	0	0	6	W 12-6
8-8	Alex Rios, Toronto vs. Detroit	5	2	5	0	0	1	2	L 8-9
9-18	Curtis Granderson, Detroit at Los Angeles	5	0	5	1	0	0	0	L 3-5
9-22	Grady Sizemore, Cleveland at Kansas City	6	2	5	2	0	0	2	W 11-6

NATIONAL LEAGUE

Date	Player, Team, Opponent	AB	R	H	2B	3B	HR	RBI	Result
4-4	Aaron Miles, Colorado vs. San Diego	6	3	5	3	0	0	1	W 12-10
4-29	Mark Loretta, San Diego vs. Arizona	8	0	5	1	0	0	1	W 5-4
5-1	Lyle Overbay, Milwaukee vs. Cincinnati	5	2	5	1	0	1	3	W 13-3
5-8	Juan Pierre, Florida vs. Colorado	5	1	5	0	0	0	1	L 3-8
5-11	Mark Loretta, San Diego at Cincinnati	6	2	5	1	0	0	1	W 7-2
5-17	Cesar Izturis, Los Angeles vs. Florida	6	2	5	2	0	0	2	W 14-5
5-18	Sean Casey, Cincinnati at New York	5	2	5	1	0	1	4	L 6-10
6-1	Derrek Lee, Chicago at Los Angeles	5	2	5	0	0	1	4	W 9-5
6-5	Carlos Lee, Milwaukee at Los Angeles	5	0	5	1	0	0	2	L 6-10
6-16	Omar Vizquel, San Francisco at Minnesota	6	3	5	1	1	0	4	W 14-7
6-16	Jimmy Rollins, Philadelphia at Seattle	6	2	5	1	1	0	0	W 3-2
7-4	Oscar Robles, Los Angeles at Colorado	6	0	5	1	0	0	2	W 4-3
7-10	Rafael Furcal, Atlanta vs. Milwaukee	5	1	5	1	0	1	1	L 4-8
8-4	Geoff Jenkins, Milwaukee at New York	5	2	5	2	0	0	1	W 12-9
8-7	Craig Counsell, Arizona vs. Colorado	5	3	5	0	0	0	0	W 9-4
8-16	Pedro Feliz, San Francisco at Cincinnati	5	4	5	2	1	0	0	W 10-8
8-16	Deivi Cruz, San Francisco at Cincinnati	5	2	5	1	0	1	5	W 10-8
9-5	Geoff Jenkins, Milwaukee at Cincinnati	5	1	5	2	0	0	2	W 6-1
9-15	Bill Hall, Milwaukee at Arizona	6	3	5	1	1	0	0	W 14-2
9-16	Kenny Lofton, Philadelphia at Florida	6	2	5	0	0	0	1	W 13-3
9-16	#Felipe Lopez, Cincinnati at Pittsburgh	5	0	5	1	0	0	2	W 8-2
10-2	Juan Pierre, Florida vs. Atlanta	6	0	5	0	0	0	3	W 7-6

First game of doubleheader.

HITTING STREAKS OF 15 OR MORE GAMES

AMERICAN LEAGUE

G	Player, Team	Span of streak
29	Johnny Damon, Boston	June 10-July 17
25	Michael Young, Texas	Sept. 2-Sept. 29
21	Darin Erstad, Los Angeles	May 28-June 21
20	Rondell White, Detroit	May 8-June 4
	Brian Roberts, Baltimore	May 9-May 31
	Magglio Ordonez, Detroit	July 5-July 27
18	Johnny Damon, Boston	Apr. 22-May 13
17	Victor Martinez, Cleveland	June 17-July 6
16	Michael Young, Texas	May 18-June 7
	Emil Brown, Kansas City	June 11-June 29
15	Alfonso Soriano, Texas	May 24-June 13
	Chris Shelton, Detroit	July 6-July 23
	Johnny Damon, Boston	July 25-Aug. 12
	Alfonso Soriano, Texas	July 31-Aug. 16

NATIONAL LEAGUE

G	Player, Team	Span of streak
36	Jimmy Rollins, Philadelphia	Aug. 23-Oct. 2
20	Cliff Floyd, New York	Apr. 8-May 4
	Jose Reyes, New York	July 17-Aug. 7
18	Derrek Lee, Chicago	Apr. 17-May 7
17	Alex Gonzalez, Florida	June 9-June 27
	Albert Pujols, St. Louis	June 18-July 5
	Freddy Sanchez, Pittsburgh	Sept. 16-Oct. 2
16	Nick Johnson, Washington	Apr. 10-Apr. 26
	Albert Pujols, St. Louis	Apr. 19-May 5
	Geoff Jenkins, Milwaukee	July 5-July 23
	Garrett Atkins, Colorado	Aug. 25-Sept. 11
15	Carlos Delgado, Florida	June 4-June 21
	David Wright, New York	July 10-July 28
	Marcus Giles, Atlanta	July 27-Aug. 11
	Ken Griffey Jr., Cincinnati	Aug. 14-Aug. 30

MULTI-HOMER GAMES

AMERICAN LEAGUE

Team	No.	Hitters
Texas	22	Mark Teixeira 7, Alfonso Soriano 4, David Dellucci 3, Rod Barajas 2, Kevin Mench 2, Richard Hidalgo 1, Gary Matthews Jr. 1, Michael Young 1, Hank Blalock 1.
New York	20	Jason Giambi 7, Alex Rodriguez 4, Gary Sheffield 2, Tino Martinez 2, Jorge Posada 2, Bernie Williams 1, Derek Jeter 1, Robinson Cano 1.
Boston	17	David Ortiz 9, Manny Ramirez 4, Kevin Millar 2, John Olerud 1, Jason Varitek 1.
Cleveland	10	Travis Hafner 3, Jose Hernandez 2, Ben Broussard 2, Aaron Boone 1, Casey Blake 1, Jhonny Peralta 1.
Baltimore	8	Melvin Mora 3, Sammy Sosa 2, Sal Fasano 1, Miguel Tejada 1, Geronimo Gil 1.
Toronto	8	Vernon Wells 2, Russ Adams 2, Frank Menechino 1, Eric Hinske 1, Orlando Hudson 1, Reed Johnson 1.
Tampa Bay	7	Jorge Cantu 4, Eduardo Perez 2, Jonny Gomes 1.
Los Angeles	6	Vladimir Guerrero 4, Juan Rivera 1, Casey Kotchman 1.
Chicago	6	Paul Konerko 2, Carl Everett 1, Jermaine Dye 1, Joe Crede 1, Brian N. Anderson 1.
Kansas City	6	Mike Sweeney 4, Matt Stairs 1, Eli Marrero 1.
Detroit	5	Carlos Pena 3, Dmitri Young 1, Brandon Inge 1.
Oakland	5	Eric Chavez 3, Nick Swisher 2.
Seattle	5	Richie Sexson 3, Adrian Beltre 1, Ichiro Suzuki 1.
Minnesota	4	Torii Hunter 2, Matthew LeCroy 1, Michael Cuddyer 1.

NATIONAL LEAGUE

Team	No.	Hitters
Atlanta	22	Andruw Jones 9, Chipper Jones 2, Rafael Furcal 2, Marcus Giles 2, Ryan Langerhans 2, Julio Franco 1, Raul Mondesi 1, Adam LaRoche 1, Kelly Johnson 1, Jeff Francoeur 1.
Cincinnati	19	Adam Dunn 6, Wily Mo Pena 4, Ken Griffey Jr. 2, Rich Aurilia 2, Javier Valentin 2, Sean Casey 1, Jason LaRue 1, Austin Kearns 1.
Chicago	15	Derrek Lee 8, Jeromy Burnitz 2, Aramis Ramirez 2, Todd Walker 1, Michael Barrett 1, Corey Patterson 1.
New York	15	Cliff Floyd 3, David Wright 3, Mike Piazza 2, Marlon Anderson 2, Victor Diaz 2, Carlos Beltran 1, Jose Reyes 1, Mike Jacobs 1.
Arizona	15	Luis Gonzalez 4, Tony Clark 4, Shawn Green 2, Jose Cruz Jr. 1, Troy Glaus 1, Chad Tracy 1, Chris Snyder 1, Conor Jackson 1.
Philadelphia	12	Chase Utley 5, Pat Burrell 3, Mike Lieberthal 2, Bobby Abreu 1, Placido Polanco 1.
St. Louis	10	Larry Walker 3, Reggie Sanders 2, Jim Edmonds 2, Albert Pujols 2, So Taguchi 1.
Milwaukee	9	Carlos Lee 3, Lyle Overbay 2, Geoff Jenkins 2, Russell Branyan 1, Bill Hall 1, Rickie Weeks 1.
Los Angeles	9	Hee-Seop Choi 3, J.D. Drew 2, Milton Bradley 2, Jose Cruz Jr. 1, Jayson Werth 1.
Colorado	9	Matt Holliday 3, Todd Helton 2, Preston Wilson 2, Clint Barmes 2.
Pittsburgh	7	Jason Bay 2, Daryle Ward 1, Ty Wigginton 1, David Ross 1, Ryan Doumit 1, Brad Eldred 1.
Houston	6	Craig Biggio 2, Morgan Ensberg 2, Lance Berkman 1, Jason Lane 1.
Washington	6	Jose Guillen 4, Preston Wilson 1, Ryan Church 1.
San Diego	6	Khalil Greene 2, Ryan Klesko 1, Damian Jackson 1, Geoff Blum 1, Xavier Nady 1.
San Francisco	4	Randy Winn 2, Moises Alou 1, Pedro Feliz 1.
Florida	3	Miguel Cabrera 3.

THREE-HOMER GAMES

Date	Player, Team, Opponent	AB	R	H	2B	3B	HR	RBI	Result
4-4	Dmitri Young, Detroit vs. Kansas City	4	4	4	0	0	3	5	W 11-2
4-26	Alex Rodriguez, New York vs. Los Angeles	5	3	4	0	0	3	10	W 12-4
5-15	Morgan Ensberg, Houston vs. San Francisco	4	3	4	0	0	3	5	W 9-0
6-12	Hee-Seop Choi, Los Angeles vs. Minnesota	4	3	3	0	0	3	3	W 4-3

Date	Player, Team, Opponent	AB	R	H	2B	3B	HR	RBI	Result
6-30	Kevin Mench, Texas vs. Los Angeles	4	3	3	0	0	3	5	W 18-5
7-30	Jonny Gomes, Tampa Bay vs. Kansas City	4	3	3	0	0	3	3	W 7-3

GRAND SLAMS
AMERICAN LEAGUE

Date	Batter, Team	Pitcher, Team	Inn.*	Site
4-9	Marcus Thames, Detroit	Jake Westbrook, Cleveland	3	Detroit
4-9	Gregg Zaun, Toronto	Blaine Neal, Boston	8	Toronto
4-15	David Ortiz, Boston	Hideo Nomo, Tampa Bay	2	Boston
4-16	Manny Ramirez, Boston	Dewon Brazelton, Tampa Bay	4	Boston
4-17	Miguel Tejada, Baltimore	Kevin Brown, New York	2	Baltimore
4-18	Tino Martinez, New York	Lance Carter, Tampa Bay	2	New York
4-20	Bret Boone, Seattle	Barry Zito, Oakland	1	Seattle
4-20	Rod Barajas, Texas	John Webb, Tampa Bay	4	Tampa Bay
4-24	Jay Payton, Boston	Rob Bell, Tampa Bay	8	Tampa Bay
4-26	Alex Rodriguez, New York	Bartolo Colon, Los Angeles	4	New York
4-30	Ken Harvey, Kansas City	Cliff Lee, Cleveland	3	Cleveland
5-3	Doug Mirabelli, Boston	Mike Maroth, Detroit	5	Detroit
5-8	+Richie Sexson, Seattle	Cla Meredith, Boston	7	Boston
5-14	Trot Nixon, Boston	J.J. Putz, Seattle	7	Seattle
5-16	A.J. Pierzynski, Chicago	Chan Ho Park, Texas	1	Chicago
5-16	Bernie Williams, New York	J.J. Putz, Seattle	7	Seattle
5-20	Juan Rivera, Los Angeles	Yhency Brazoban, Los Angeles	9	Los Angeles
5-28	Edgar Renteria, Boston	Paul Quantrill, New York	5	New York
5-30	David Newhan, Baltimore	Bronson Arroyo, Boston	3	Boston
6-1	Torii Hunter, Minnesota	Cliff Lee, Cleveland	3	Minnesota
6-2	Eric Chavez, Oakland	Josh Towers, Toronto	5	Oakland
6-4	Melvin Mora, Baltimore	Doug Creek, Detroit	9	Detroit
6-4	Rafael Palmeiro, Baltimore	Wilfredo Ledezma, Detroit	5	Detroit
6-8	Eduardo Perez, Tampa Bay	Eric Milton, Cincinnati	5	Cincinnati
6-11	Kevin Mench, Texas	Al Leiter, Florida	2	Florida
6-18	Derek Jeter, New York	Joe Borowski, Chicago	6	New York
6-26	Manny Ramirez, Boston	Brett Myers, Philadelphia	4	Philadelphia
6-28	Travis Hafner, Cleveland	Keith Foulke, Boston	9	Boston
6-28	Garret Anderson, Los Angeles	Brian Shouse, Texas	11	Texas
7-1	Reed Johnson, Toronto	Mike Myers, Boston	6	Boston
7-4	Jermaine Dye, Chicago	Hideo Nomo, Tampa Bay	1	Chicago
7-5	Manny Ramirez, Boston	Chris Young, Texas	3	Texas
7-8	Randy Winn, Seattle	Joel Peralta, Los Angeles	6	Los Angeles
7-14	Matt Stairs, Kansas City	Franklyn German, Detroit	8	Detroit
7-15	David Ortiz, Boston	Buddy Groom, New York	6	Boston
7-21	Vladimir Guerrero, Los Angeles	Tom Gordon, New York	7	Los Angeles
7-22	Aubrey Huff, Tampa Bay	Bruce Chen, Baltimore	2	Tampa Bay
7-26	Aubrey Huff, Tampa Bay	Chad Bradford, Boston	3	Tampa Bay
7-29	John Olerud, Boston	J.C. Romero, Minnesota	8	Boston
7-30	Jay Payton, Oakland	Nate Robertson, Detroit	4	Oakland
8-4	Jason Varitek, Boston	Leo Nunez, Kansas City	4	Boston
8-6	David Dellucci, Texas	Daniel Cabrera, Baltimore	2	Texas
8-7	Casey Kotchman, Los Angeles	Seth McClung, Tampa Bay	3	Los Angeles
8-9	Vladimir Guerrero, Los Angeles	Rich Harden, Oakland	2	Oakland
8-10	Jay Gibbons, Baltimore	Casey Fossum, Tampa Bay	1	Baltimore
8-10	Grady Sizemore, Cleveland	Zack Greinke, Kansas City	2	Kansas City
8-11	Jeff Liefer, Cleveland	D.J. Carrasco, Kansas City	7	Kansas City
8-16	Craig Monroe, Detroit	Mike Remlinger, Boston	10	Detroit
8-17	Paul Phillips, Kansas City	Matt Thornton, Seattle	9	Seattle
8-17	Adrian Beltre, Seattle	D.J. Carrasco, Kansas City	1	Seattle
8-20	Richie Sexson, Seattle	Matt Guerrier, Minnesota	10	Minnesota
8-23	Miguel Tejada, Baltimore	Francisco Rodriguez, Los Angeles	9	Baltimore
8-25	Ichiro Suzuki, Seattle	Justin Thompson, Texas	9	Texas
8-25	Ronnie Belliard, Cleveland	Travis Harper, Tampa Bay	3	Tampa Bay
8-27	Dmitri Young, Detroit	Bronson Arroyo, Boston	4	Boston
8-29	Dmitri Young, Detroit	Scott Elarton, Cleveland	1	Cleveland
9-6	David Dellucci, Texas	Kyle Lohse, Minnesota	2	Minnesota
9-10	Dan Johnson, Oakland	Kameron Loe, Texas	2	Texas
9-15	Robinson Cano, New York	Seth McClung, Tampa Bay	6	Tampa Bay
9-19	Richie Sexson, Seattle	Miguel Batista, Toronto	9	Toronto
9-20	Gary Sheffield, New York	James Baldwin, Baltimore	2	New York
9-22	Mark Teahen, Kansas City	Cliff Lee, Cleveland	4	Kansas City
9-27	Gary Sheffield, New York	Bruce Chen, Baltimore	4	Baltimore
9-30	Justin Morneau, Minnesota	Jamie Walker, Detroit	8	Minnesota

+Night separate admission.*Inning in which grand slam was hit.

Date	Batter, Team	Pitcher, Team	Inn.*	Site
4-5	Juan Encarnacion, Florida	John Smoltz, Atlanta	1	Florida
4-6	Joe Randa, Cincinnati	Mike DeJean, New York	8	Cincinnati
4-9	Brian Jordan, Atlanta	Aaron Heilman, New York	2	Atlanta
4-9	Michael Tucker, San Francisco	Scott Dohmann, Colorado	8	San Francisco
4-10	Juan Encarnacion, Florida	Antonio Osuna, Washington	8	Florida
4-15	Pedro Feliz, San Francisco	Jamey Wright, Colorado	4	Colorado
4-17	Michael Tucker, San Francisco	Byung-Hyun Kim, Colorado	7	Colorado
4-19	David Wright, New York	Gavin Floyd, Philadelphia	6	Philadelphia
4-21	Doug Mientkiewicz, New York	Al Leiter, Florida	2	Florida
4-27	Felipe Lopez, Cincinnati	Ryan Dempster, Chicago	3	Chicago
4-29	Hee-Seop Choi, Los Angeles	Jason Jennings, Colorado	5	Los Angeles
5-1	Mike Lamb, Houston	Mark Prior, Chicago	5	Houston
5-2	Mike Matheny, San Francisco	Russ Ortiz, Arizona	3	Arizona
5-7	Moises Alou, San Francisco	John Patterson, Washington	3	San Francisco
5-8	Jason Phillips, Los Angeles	Eric Milton, Cincinnati	6	Cincinnati
5-8	Aaron Miles, Colorado	Al Leiter, Florida	4	Florida
5-8	Matt Lawton, Pittsburgh	Javier Lopez, Arizona	8	Arizona
5-13	Adam LaRoche, Atlanta	Jeff Weaver, Los Angeles	8	Los Angeles
5-13	Milton Bradley, Los Angeles	Chris Reitsma, Atlanta	8	Los Angeles
5-20	John Mabry, St. Louis	Zack Greinke, Kansas City	1	Kansas City
5-27	Jeff Kent, Los Angeles	Shawn Estes, Arizona	3	Arizona
6-1	Chase Utley, Philadelphia	LaTroy Hawkins, San Francisco	8	Philadelphia
6-1	Rob Mackowiak, Pittsburgh	Guillermo Mota, Florida	7	Pittsburgh
6-3	Carlos Lee, Milwaukee	Jeff Weaver, Los Angeles	1	Los Angeles
6-4	Reggie Sanders, St. Louis	Wandy Rodriguez, Houston	3	Houston
6-10	Mike Lowell, Florida	Brian Shouse, Texas	8	Florida
6-11	Felipe Lopez, Cincinnati	Daniel Cabrera, Baltimore	2	Cincinnati
6-17	Kelly Johnson, Atlanta	Randy Keisler, Cincinnati	6	Cincinnati
6-25	Aramis Ramirez, Chicago	Jose Contreras, Chicago	1	Chicago
6-27	Julio Franco, Atlanta	Valerio de los Santos, Florida	8	Florida
6-28	Morgan Ensberg, Houston	Jason Jennings, Colorado	5	Colorado
6-28	Garrett Atkins, Colorado	Russ Springer, Houston	8	Colorado
7-4	Bobby Abreu, Philadelphia	Dave Williams, Pittsburgh	3	Pittsburgh
7-7	Carlos Delgado, Florida	Ricky Bottalico, Milwaukee	5	Florida
7-8	Ryan Klesko, San Diego	Byung-Hyun Kim, Colorado	6	Colorado
7-9	Jack Wilson, Pittsburgh	Danny Graves, New York	7	Pittsburgh
7-9	Adam Dunn, Cincinnati	Brandon Webb, Arizona	8	Arizona
7-15	Jerry Hairston Jr., Chicago	Brian Meadows, Pittsburgh	6	Chicago
7-17	Javier Valentin, Cincinnati	Jamey Wright, Colorado	6	Cincinnati
7-23	Lyle Overbay, Milwaukee	Brandon Claussen, Cincinnati	4	Cincinnati
7-24	Neifi Perez, Chicago	Al Reyes, St. Louis	10	St. Louis
7-31	Chris Snyder, Arizona	Mike Remlinger, Chicago	5	Chicago
7-31	Adam Dunn, Cincinnati	Woody Williams, San Diego	5	San Diego
8-4	Brad Wilkerson, Washington	Duaner Sanchez, Los Angeles	8	Washington
8-4	Bobby Abreu, Philadelphia	Mark Prior, Chicago	1	Philadelphia
8-6	Andruw Jones, Atlanta	Jason Marquis, St. Louis	6	St. Louis
8-7	David Eckstein, St. Louis	Chris Reitsma, Atlanta	9	St. Louis
8-10	Ryan Howard, Philadelphia	Yhency Brazoban, Los Angeles	9	Los Angeles
8-14	Jack Wilson, Pittsburgh	Mike Burns, Houston	8	Houston
8-20	Xavier Nady, San Diego	Joey Devine, Atlanta	13	Atlanta
8-23	Jeromy Burnitz, Chicago	Joey Devine, Atlanta	4	Chicago
8-26	Bobby Abreu, Philadelphia	Tim Worrell, Arizona	7	Arizona
8-27	Todd Helton, Colorado	Brian Lawrence, San Diego	5	San Diego
8-28	Shawn Green, Arizona	Vicente Padilla, Philadelphia	3	Arizona
8-31	Jeremy Hermida, Florida	Al Reyes, St. Louis	7	Florida
9-2	Geoff Jenkins, Milwaukee	Chris Oxspring, San Diego	2	Milwaukee
9-2	David Bell, Philadelphia	John Halama, Washington	3	Washington
9-4	Jason LaRue, Cincinnati	Dan Kolb, Atlanta	12	Atlanta
9-4	Jeff Kent, Los Angeles	David Cortes, Colorado	7	Colorado
9-7	J.J. Hardy, Milwaukee	Chris Booker, Cincinnati	6	Cincinnati
9-14	Garrett Atkins, Colorado	D.J. Houlton, Los Angeles	5	Los Angeles
9-14	Ramon Martinez, Philadelphia	Horacio Ramirez, Atlanta	3	Philadelphia
9-15	Cliff Floyd, New York	Livan Hernandez, Washington	5	New York
9-17	Khalil Greene, San Diego	Chad Cordero, Washington	9	San Diego
9-21	Ryan Howard, Philadelphia	John Foster, Atlanta	10	Atlanta
9-24	David Wright, New York	Livan Hernandez, Washington	1	Washington
9-27	Ramon Hernandez, San Diego	Jeff Fassero, San Francisco	4	San Diego
9-30	Albert Pujols, St. Louis	Matt Belisle, Cincinnati	7	St. Louis

*Inning in which grand slam was hit.

TRANSACTIONS

JANUARY 4
Tigers agreed to contract terms with IF Ramon Martinez.

JANUARY 6
White Sox signed C A.J. Pierzynski.
Rockies signed OF Dustan Mohr and IF Desi Relaford.
Tigers acquired C Vance Wilson from the **Mets** for minor league IF Anderson Hernandez.
Royals signed RHP Ryan Jensen and OF Emil Brown to minor league contracts.
Cardinals signed 2B Mark Grudzielanek.

JANUARY 8
Indians signed RHP Kevin Millwood.

JANUARY 10
White Sox acquired 1B Travis Hinton from the **Brewers** as the player to be named in the Carlos Lee trade.
Mets signed IF Miguel Cairo.

JANUARY 11
Diamondbacks traded LHP Randy Johnson to the **Yankees** for RHP Javier Vazquez, LHP Brad Halsey, C Dioner Navarro and cash. Acquired OF Shawn Green from the **Dodgers** for Navarro and RHPs Danny Muegge, Beltran Perez and William Juarez.
Orioles signed RHP James Baldwin to a minor league contract.
Indians signed OF Juan Gonzalez to a minor league contract.
Dodgers signed RHP Derek Lowe.
Mets signed OF Carlos Beltran.
Padres signed LHP Chris Hammond.
Blue Jays signed LHP Scott Schoeneweis.

JANUARY 12
Diamondbacks traded IF Shea Hillenbrand to the **Blue Jays** for RHP Adam Peterson. Signed LHP Shawn Estes.
Athletics signed RHP Keiichi Yabu.
Devil Rays signed IF Alex S. Gonzalez.

JANUARY 13
Dodgers signed C Paul Bako.

JANUARY 14
Braves signed OF Raul Mondesi.
Cubs agreed to terms with RHP Chad Fox on a minor league contract.

JANUARY 18
Cubs agreed to terms with RHP Scott Williamson on a minor league contract.
Indians signed IF Alex Cora.
Royals signed RHP Denny Hocking to a minor league contract.
Mets signed RHP Roberto Hernandez to a minor league contract.

JANUARY 19
Braves signed OF Brian Jordan.
Brewers signed RHP Ricky Bottalico.
Phillies signed IF/OF Jose Offerman to a minor league contract.
Rangers signed IF Mark DeRosa to a minor league contract.
Nationals signed RHPs Antonio Osuna and Esteban Loaiza.

JANUARY 20
Devil Rays signed 2B Roberto Alomar to a one-year contract.

JANUARY 21
Orioles signed RHP Steve Reed.
Angels agreed to terms with IF Lou Merloni on a minor league contract.

JANUARY 23
Astros signed LHP John Franco.

JANUARY 24
Diamondbacks signed 1B Tony Clark.

JANUARY 25
Mariners signed RHP Aaron Sele to a minor league contract.

JANUARY 26
Marlins signed 1B Carlos Delgado.

JANUARY 27
White Sox signed IF Tadahito Iguchi from the Japan League.
Angels signed C Josh Paul.
Mets acquired 1B Doug Mientkiewicz and conditional cash from the **Red Sox** for minor league 1B Ian Bladergroen.
Pirates signed RHP Rick White to a minor league contract.
Devil Rays signed RHP Hideo Nomo to a minor league contract.

FEBRUARY 1
Red Sox signed RHPs Jack Cressend and Jeremi Gonzalez, C Shawn Wooten and IFs Dave Berg, Tim Hummel and Kenny Perez to minor league contracts.

FEBRUARY 2
Cubs traded OF Sammy Sosa to the **Orioles** for OF Jerry Hairston, IF Mike Fontenot and RHP Dave Crouthers. Signed OF Jeromy Burnitz.
Marlins signed RHP Jim Mecir.

FEBRUARY 3
Dodgers agreed to terms with 3B Norihiro Nakamura on a minor league contract.

FEBRUARY 5
Brewers signed IF Jeff Cirillo to a minor league contract.
Rangers signed RHP Pedro Astacio and claimed RHP Ryan Bukvich off waivers from the **Padres**.

FEBRUARY 6
Diamondbacks obtained OF Jose Cruz Jr. and cash from the **Devil Rays** for LHP Casey Fossum.

FEBRUARY 7
Tigers signed OF Magglio Ordonez.
Yankees signed LHP Buddy Groom to a minor league contract.

FEBRUARY 8
Red Sox agreed to terms with 1B Roberto Petagine on a minor league contract.

FEBRUARY 9
Cubs traded RHP Kyle Farnsworth and a player to be named to the **Tigers** for RHP Roberto Novoa, IF Scott Moore and non-roster OF Bo Flowers.

FEBRUARY 18
Reds agreed to contract terms with RHP Ramon Ortiz.
Yankees signed IF Rey Sanchez.

FEBRUARY 21
Nationals agreed to terms with IF Carlos Baerga on a minor league contract.

MARCH 15
Tigers released OF Alex Sanchez.

MARCH 17
Mets released IF Joe McEwing.
Astros released RHP Pete Munro.

MARCH 18
Devil Rays released LHP Mark Guthrie.

MARCH 19
Devil Rays signed OF Alex Sanchez. Announced the retirements of 2B and OF Danny Bautista.

MARCH 20
Dodgers traded LHP Kazuhisa Ishii to the **Mets** for C Jason Phillips.

MARCH 22
Padres traded RHP Blaine Neal to the **Red Sox** for OF Adam Hyzdu.

MARCH 28
Astros traded RHP Tim Redding and cash to the **Padres** for C Humberto Quintero.

MARCH 29
Red Sox obtained LHP Mike Myers from the **Cardinals** for minor league OF Carlos de la Cruz and LHP Kevin Ool.
Cubs traded RHP Ronald Bay to the **Indians** for LHP Cliff Bartosh.
Angels traded C Wil Nieves to the **Yankees** for RHP Bret Prinz.
Mets acquired IF Benji Gil from the **Mariners** for cash considerations and signed C Kelly Stinnett to a minor league contract.

MARCH 30
Orioles traded LHP Matt Riley and C Keith McDonald to the **Rangers** for OF Ramon Nivar.
Red Sox traded RHP Byung-Hyun Kim to the **Rockies** for LHP Chris Narveson and C Charles Johnson.
Cubs traded IF Cody Ransom to the **Rangers** for a player to be named.
Pirates acquired C David Ross from the **Dodgers** for cash.

MARCH 31
Braves accquired RHP Jorge Sosa from the **Devil Rays** for IF Nick Green.

APRIL 2
Tigers traded LHP Steve Colyer to the **Mets** for RHP Matt Ginter.

APRIL 4
Devil Rays signed 3B Eric Munson to a minor league contract.

APRIL 8
Devil Rays acquired OF Reggie Taylor from the **Rockies** for LHP Bobby Seay.

APRIL 9
Rockies acquired RHP Jose Acevedo from the **Reds** for RHP Allan Simpson.

APRIL 14
Diamondbacks claimed LHP Javier Lopez off waivers from the **Rockies**.
Braves claimed LHP Frank Brooks off waivers from the **Dodgers**.

APRIL 28
Mariners signed IF Dave Hansen to a minor league contract.

MAY 8
Pirates released C Benito Santiago.

MAY 11
Rockies claimed RHP Blaine Neal off waivers from the **Red Sox** and LHP Randy Williams off waivers from the **Padres**. Traded OF Michael Restovich to the **Pirates** for a player to be named or cash considerations.

MAY 12
Yankees released RHP Steve Karsay.

MAY 14
Phillies traded OF Marlon Byrd to the **Nationals** for OF Endy Chavez.

MAY 17
Cubs signed IF Enrique Wilson.

MAY 26
Nationals signed LHP C.J. Nitkowski.

MAY 28
Cubs traded RHP LaTroy Hawkins and cash to the **Giants** for RHPs Jerome Williams and David Aardsma.

JUNE 2
Reds released RHP Danny Graves.

JUNE 3
Diamondbacks claimed RHP Claudio Vargas off waivers from the **Nationals**.
Giants traded RHP Matt Herges and cash considerations to the **Diamondbacks** for OF Doug DeVore.

JUNE 8
Orioles accquired OF Eli Marrero from the **Royals** for nonroster IF Pete Maestrales.
Phillies traded IF Placido Polanco to the **Tigers** for RHP Ugueth Urbina and IF Ramon Martinez.
Mets signed IF Jose Offerman to a minor league contract.

JUNE 9
Phillies designated RHP Amaury Telemaco for assignment.

JUNE 10
Brewers traded IF Junior Spivey to the **Nationals** for RHP Tomo Ohka.
Nationals claimed RHP Ryan Drese off waivers from the **Rangers** and RHP Jacobo Sequea off waivers from the **Orioles**.

JUNE 20
Mets released RHP Mike DeJean.

JUNE 21
Rangers released RHP Pedro Astacio.

JUNE 23
Giants claimed OF Alex Sanchez off waivers from the **Devil Rays**.

JUNE 29
Cubs designated RHP Joe Borowski for assignment.

JULY 1
Astros designated LHP John Franco for assignment.
Yankees acquired LHP Darrell May, RHP Tim Redding and cash considerations from the **Padres** for RHP Paul Quantrill.

JULY 7
Red Sox traded IF Ramon Vazquez to the **Indians** for IF Alex Cora.
Rockies signed RHP Mike DeJean.

JULY 11
Twins obtained 2B Bret Boone and cash from the **Mariners** for a player to be named.
Yankees released LHP Mike Stanton.
Devil Rays signed RHP Joe Borowski.

JULY 13
Red Sox traded OF Jay Payton to the **Athletics** for RHP Chad Bradford.
Rockies acquired RHP Zach Day, OF J.J. Davis and a minor league player to be named and cash considerations from the **Nationals** for OF Preston Wilson and cash considerations. Acquired OF Eric Byrnes and IF Omar Quintanilla from the **Athletics** for LHP Joe Kennedy and RHP Jay Witasick.
Nationals signed LHP Mike Stanton.

JULY 15
Red Sox signed OF Gabe Kapler.

JULY 16
Marlins traded LHP Al Leiter and cash considerations to the **Yankees** for a player to be named.
Devil Rays designated RHP Hideo Nomo for assignment.

JULY 18
Orioles designated RHP James Baldwin for assignment.
Cubs traded OF Jason Dubois to the **Indians** for OF Jody Gerut.

JULY 19
Red Sox acquired OF Adam Hyzdu from the **Padres** for nonroster RHP Scott Cassidy. Obtained IF Tony Graffanino from the **Royals** for nonroster OF Chip Ambres and LHP Juan Cedeno.

JULY 21

Diamondbacks traded IF Matt Kata to the **Phillies** for RHP Tim Worrell and cash considerations.

Braves acquired minor league RHP Matt Lorenzo from the **Rangers** for RHP Kevin Gryboski.

Rangers claimed RHP James Baldwin off waivers from the **Orioles**.

JULY 22

Tigers acquired IF John McDonald from the **Blue Jays** for a player to be named.

JULY 23

Reds traded 3B Joe Randa to the **Padres** for minor league RHPs Jason Germano and RHP Travis Chick.

JULY 25

Devil Rays released RHP Hideo Nomo.

JULY 28

Rockies traded RHP Shawn Chacon to the **Yankees** for minor league RHPs Ramon Ramirez and Eduardo Sierra.

Padres traded minor league IF J.J. Furmaniak to the **Pirates** for C David Ross.

Yankees signed RHP Hideo Nomo to a minor league contract.

JULY 29

Red Sox released LHP Alan Embree.

JULY 30

Red Sox obtained OF Jose Cruz Jr. and cash considerations from the **Diamondbacks** for minor league IF Kenny Perez and minor league RHP Kyle Bono.

Rockies traded OF Eric Byrnes to the **Orioles** for OF Larry Bigbie.

Yankees signed LHP Alan Embree.

Padres traded IF Phil Nevin to the **Rangers** for RHP Chan Ho Park and cash.

JULY 31

Diamondbacks obtained LHP Buddy Groom from the **Yankees** for a player to be named.

Braves traded RHPs Zach Miner and Roman Colon to the **Tigers** for RHP Kyle Farnsworth.

Cubs traded OF Jody Gerut to the **Pirates** for OF Matt Lawton and cash.

White Sox acquired IF Geoff Blum from the **Padres** for LHP Ryan Meaux.

Mariners traded LHP Ron Villone to the **Marlins** for RHPs Yorman Bazardo and Michael Flannery. Traded OF Randy Winn to the **Giants** for RHP Jesse Foppert and C Yorvit Torrealba.

Padres acquired C Miguel Olivo from the **Mariners** for C Miguel Ojeda and RHP Nathanel Mateo.

AUGUST 1

White Sox requested waivers on RHP Shingo Takatsu.

Twins released 2B Bret Boone.

AUGUST 2

Yankees signed LHP Dennys Reyes to a minor league contract.

AUGUST 5

Rockies claimed RHP Sunny Kim off waivers from the **Nationals**.

Royals released C Alberto Castillo.

AUGUST 8

Mariners released C Pat Borders.

AUGUST 9

Red Sox traded OF Jose Cruz Jr. to the **Dodgers** for a player to be named. Acquired LHP Mike Remlinger and cash considerations from the **Cubs** for minor league RHP Olivo Astacio.

AUGUST 10

Giants released OF Marquis Grissom.

AUGUST 19

Red Sox designated IF Mark Bellhorn for assignment.

Giants released LHP Kirk Rueter.

AUGUST 22

Orioles claimed RHP James Baldwin off waivers from the **Rangers**.

AUGUST 23

Mets designated RHP Danny Graves for assignment.

AUGUST 27

Cubs traded OF Matt Lawton to the **Yankees** for minor League RHP Justin Berg.

AUGUST 28

Phillies acquired OF Michael Tucker from the **Giants** for non-roster RHP Kelvin Pichardo.

AUGUST 29

Braves acquired OF Todd Hollandsworth from the **Cubs** for non-roster LHP Todd Blackford and nonroster RHP Angelo Burrows.

Red Sox claimed RHP Chad Harville off waivers from the **Astros**.

AUGUST 30

Angels traded LHP Dusty Bergman and RHP Ronnie Ray to the **Giants** for LHP Jason Christiansen.

Yankees signed IF Mark Bellhorn.

Giants acquired RHP Benjamin Cox from the **Nationals** for IF Deivi Cruz.

AUGUST 31

Padres designated RHP Paul Quantrill for assignment.

SEPTEMBER 9

Marlins signed RHP Paul Quantrill. Designated C Ryan Jorgensen for assignment.

SEPTEMBER 12

Marlins signed IF Mike Mordecai.

SEPTEMBER 29

Red Sox obtained LHP Mike Stanton from the **Nationals** for RHPs Rhys Taylor and Yader Peralta.

OCTOBER 15

Red Sox released OF Adam Hyzdu.

OCTOBER 21

Royals claimed LHP Bobby Madritsch off waivers from the **Mariners**.

OCTOBER 27

Nationals signed IF Damian Jackson and 2B Bernie Castro.

NOVEMBER 3

Reds signed OF Dewayne Wise to a minor league contract.

Tigers sent cash considerations to the **Blue Jays** to complete an earlier trade in which John McDonald was acquired.

Padres traded RHP Brian Lawrence and cash to the **Nationals** for 3B Vinny Castilla.

Rangers signed C/3B Jamie Burke, OF Adam Hyzdu, C Nick Trzesniak and RHPs Chris Baker and Shane Bazzell to minor league contracts.

NOVEMBER 8

Rockies signed RHP Nate Field and IF Jason Smith to minor league contracts.

NOVEMBER 9

Rangers signed RHP Rick Bauer and OF Adrian Brown to minor league contracts.

NOVEMBER 10

Blue Jays reacquired IF John McDonald from the **Tigers** for cash considerations.

NOVEMBER 14
Cardinals signed C Michel Hernandez.

NOVEMBER 15
Astros released OF Charles Gipson.
Nationals released OF Kenny Kelly.

NOVEMBER 16
Reds claimed RHP Mike Burns off waivers from the **Astros**.
Padres signed IF Geoff Blum.
Cubs traded RHP Jon Leicester to the **Rangers** for a player to be named.

NOVEMBER 17
Cubs signed LHP Scott Eyre.

NOVEMBER 18
Royals signed IF Mike Coolbaugh, RHPs Victor Santos and Joe Nelson, 1B Chris Richard, OF Kerry Robinson and SS Wilson Valdez to minor league contracts.
Brewers claimed IF Zach Sorensen off waivers from the **Angels**.
Red Sox released OF Gabe Kapler.
Mets traded OF Mike Cameron to the **Padres** for IF/OF Xavier Nady.
Athletics signed RHP Matt Roney.
Nationals agreed to contract terms with IF/OF Marlon Anderson.

NOVEMBER 21
Pirates traded IF Bobby Hill to the **Padres** for a player to be named.

NOVEMBER 22
Royals signed RHPs Adam Bernero and Seth Etherton to minor league contracts.
Brewers signed IFs Brian Dallimore and Brent Abernathy, Cs Mark Johnson and Mike Rivera and RHPs Jerome Gamble and Jared Fernandez to minor league contracts.
Mariners signed C Kenji Johjima.
Devil Rays signed RHP Chad Harville and designated LHP Joe Beimel for assignment.

NOVEMBER 24
Red Sox obtained RHP Josh Beckett, 3B Mike Lowell and RHP Guillermo Mota from the **Marlins** for SS Hanley Ramirez and RHPs Anibal Sanchez, Jesus Delgado and Harvey Garcia.
Marlins traded 1B Carlos Delgado and cash to the **Mets** for 1B Mike Jacobs, RHP Yusmeiro Petit and IF Grant Psomas.

NOVEMBER 25
White Sox traded OF Aaron Rowand, LHP Daniel Haigwood and a player to be named to the **Phillies** for 1B Jim Thome.
Tigers signed RHP Tim Crabtree to a minor league contract.

NOVEMBER 28
Mets acquired OF Tike Redman from the **Pirates** for cash.
Athletics agreed to contract terms with RHP Esteban Loaiza.
Pirates unconditionally released OF Michael Restovich.
Giants claimed RHP Jeff Miller off waivers from the **Pirates**.
Blue Jays signed LHP B.J. Ryan.

NOVEMBER 29
Cubs signed RHP Bob Howry.
Mets signed LHP Billy Wagner.
Phillies signed IF Abraham Nunez.
Pirates signed RHPs Britt Reames, Joe Roa, Jason Roach and Matt Whiteside and IF Jason Alfaro to minor league contracts.

NOVEMBER 30
Phillies signed RHP Julio Santana.
Reds signed IFs Anderson Machado and Aaron Herr and RHP Jake Robbins to minor league contracts.
Yankees signed C Kelly Stinnett.

DECEMBER 1
Red Sox acquired RHP Jermaine Van Buren from the **Cubs** for a player to be named or cash considerations.
Brewers signed LHP Jason Kershner to a minor league contract.
Phillies signed C Sal Fasano.
Giants signed RHP Tim Worrell.

DECEMBER 2
Marlins traded 2B Luis Castillo to the **Twins** for RHPs Travis Bowyer and Scott Tyler.
Angels signed RHP Hector Carrasco.
Yankees signed RHP Kyle Farnsworth.
Phillies released RHPs Franklin Perez and Pedro Liriano.

DECEMBER 3
Phillies signed RHP Tom Gordon.

DECEMBER 5
Indians signed RHP Paul Byrd.
Mets acquired C Paul Lo Duca from the **Marlins** for two players to be named.
Athletics acquired RHP Chad Gaudin from the **Blue Jays** for a player to be named.
Cardinals signed C Gary Bennett and IF Deivi Cruz.

DECEMBER 6
Orioles traded LHP Steve Kline to the **Giants** for RHP LaTroy Hawkins.
Blue Jays signed RHP A.J. Burnett.

DECEMBER 7
Diamondbacks traded RHPs Lance Cormier and Oscar Villarreal to the **Braves** for C Johnny Estrada.
Braves acquired RHP Wes Obermueller from the **Brewers** for RHP Dan Kolb.
Red Sox traded C Doug Mirabelli to the **Padres** for IF Mark Loretta.
Cubs obtained OF Juan Pierre from the **Marlins** for RHPs Sergio Mitre and Ricky Nolasco and LHP Renyel Pinto. Agreed to contract terms with IF/OF John Mabry.
Reds released LHP Randy Keisler and signed 1B Jacob Cruz to a minor league contract.
Rockies traded OF Larry Bigbie and 2B Aaron Miles to the **Cardinals** for LHP Ray King. Acquired C Yorvit Torrealba from the **Mariners** for RHP Marcos Carvajal.
Royals released RHP D.J. Carrasco. Obtained LHP Mark Redman from the **Pirates** for RHP Jonah Bayliss and a player to be named.
Dodgers signed SS Rafael Furcal.
Brewers traded 1B Lyle Overbay to the **Blue Jays** for RHP Dave Bush, OF Gabe Gross and nonroster LHP Zach Jackson.
Padres traded 3B Sean Burroughs to the **Devil Rays** for RHP Dewon Brazelton.

DECEMBER 8
Braves traded IF Andy Marte to the **Red Sox** for SS Edgar Renteria and cash considerations.
Reds traded minor league IF Kevin Howard and OF Ben Himes to the **Yankees** for IF/OF Tony Womack and cash.
Pirates traded LHP Dave Williams to the **Reds** for 1B Sean Casey and cash. Acquired RHP Chad Blackwell from the **Royals**, completing the Mark Redman/Jonah Bayliss trade. Released 3B Ty Wigginton.
Rockies signed RHP Jose Mesa.
Tigers agreed to contract terms with RHP Todd Jones. Traded RHP Chris Booker, a Rule 5 draft choice, to the **Phillies** for cash considerations.
Royals signed RHP Elmer Dessens. Traded LHP Fabio Castro, a Rule 5 draft choice, to the **Rangers** for IF Esteban German.
Mets signed IF Jose Valentin to a minor league contract.
Yankees signed OF Chris Prieto to a minor league contract.
Athletics sent minor league OF Dustin Majewski to the **Blue Jays** as the player to be named in the December 5 trade for Chad Gaudin.
Phillies obtained LHP Gio Gonzalez from the **White Sox** as the player to be named in the teams' November 25 trade.
Padres acquired RHP Steven Andrade, a Rule 5 draft selection of the **Devil Rays**, for cash considerations. Sent RHP Clayton Hamilton to the **Pirates** as the player to be named in the November 21 trade for Bobby Hill.

DECEMBER 9
Braves signed C Todd Pratt.
Indians signed IF Lou Merloni to a minor league contract.
Mets sent RHP Gabriel Hernandez and OF Dante Brinkley to the **Marlins** as the players to be named in the December 5 trade for Paul Lo Duca.

Angels traded minor league IF Alexi Casilla to the **Twins** for LHP J.C. Romero.
Mets signed 1B Julio Franco.
Rangers signed RHPs Jayson Durocher and Jose Silva to minor league contracts.

DECEMBER 12
Tigers agreed to contract terms with LHP Kenny Rogers. Acquired RHP Ricky Steik from the **Padres** for RHP Kenny Baugh.
Giants signed RHP Matt Morris.
Diamondbacks signed IF Damion Easley.
Rangers acquire RHP Vicente Padilla from the **Phillies** for a player to be named.

DECEMBER 13
Orioles signed C Ramon Hernandez.
White Sox traded LHP Damaso Marte to the **Pirates** for IF/OF Rob Mackowiak.
Dodgers traded OF Milton Bradley and IF Antonio Perez to the **Athletics** for OF Andre Ethier.
Cardinals signed LHP Ricardo Rincon.
Rangers traded 2B Alfonso Soriano to the **Nationals** for OFs Brad Wilkerson and Terrmel Sledge and RHP Armando Galarraga.
Nationals signed 1B/OF/C Robert Fick. Signed Cs Alberto Castillo, Wiki Gonzalez, Mike DiFelice and Brandon Harper to minor league contracts.
Diamondbacks signed RHP Jason Grimsley.

DECEMBER 14
Indians signed OF Todd Donovan and IFs Jose Flores and Andy Tracy to minor league contracts.
Dodgers signed 3B Bill Mueller and C Sandy Alomar Jr.
Brewers signed LHP Wilfredo Rodriguez to a minor league contract.
Mets signed LHP Matt Perisho, IF Juan Tejada, C Sandy Martinez and OF Julio Ramirez to minor league contracts.
Mariners signed DH/OF Carl Everett.

DECEMBER 15
Marlins agreed to minor league contract terms with OFs Matt Cepicky and Mark Little, IFs Lenny Harris, Mickey Lopez and Michael Kinkade, RHPs Buddy Carlyle and Ryan Rupe and LHP Joshua Stewart. Claimed C John Baker off waivers from the **Athletics**.
Angels requested unconditional release waivers on OF Jeff DaVanon.
Twins signed 3B Tony Batista.
Yankees signed LHP Mike Myers.
Pirates signed RHP Roberto Hernandez.
Giants signed RHP Brian Cooper, Cs Yamid Haad and Guillermo Rodriguez and IF Chad Santos to minor league contracts.
Cardinals signed RHP Braden Looper.

DECEMBER 16
Rockies traded LHP Luis Enrique Gonzalez, a Rule 5 draft choice, to the **Mariners** for cash considerations. Acquired minor league 1B Aaron Rifkin from the **Cubs** for a player to be named or cash considerations.
Marlins traded LHP Ron Villone to the **Yankees** for minor league LHP Ben Julianel.
Royals signed RHP Scott Elarton, 2B Mark Grudzielanek, 1B Doug Mientkiewicz and C Paul Bako.
Dodgers released OF Jason Grabowski.
Padres signed RHP Doug Brocail.
Rangers signed IF D'Angelo Jimenez and RHP Kasey Ueno to minor league contracts.
Nationals sent minor league OF Cedrick "Doc" Brooks to the **Rockies** as the player to be named in the July 13 trade for Preston Wilson.

DECEMBER 19
Reds signed IF Aaron Holbert and OF Andy Abad to minor league contracts.
Indians signed RHPs Danny Graves and Steve Karsay to minor league contracts.
Rockies signed RHP Bret Prinz and LHP Steve Colyer to minor league contracts.
Dodgers signed IF Nomar Garciaparra.

Mets signed LHPs Darren Oliver and Pedro Feliciano and RHP Jose Parra to minor league contracts.
Rangers sent RHP Ricardo A. Rodriguez to the **Phillies** as the player to be named in the December 12 trade for Vicente Padilla.
Devil Rays traded nonroster 3B Travis Schlichting to the **Angels** for C Josh Paul.

DECEMBER 20
Diamondbacks traded RHP Javier Vazquez and cash considerations to the **White Sox** for RHPs Orlando Hernandez and Luis Vizcaino and OF Chris Young.
Braves acquired OF Matt Diaz from the **Royals** for nonroster RHP Ricardo F. Rodriquez.
Orioles signed 1B Alejandro Freire, 3B Napoleon Calzado, IF Eddy Garabito, OFs Keith Reed and Howie Clark, C Brandon Marsters and RHPs John Stephens, Winston Abreu and Orber Moreno to minor league contracts.
Red Sox signed RHP Rudy Seanez.
Cubs signed OF Jacque Jones.
Reds signed LHP Chris Hammond.
Dodgers signed OF Kenny Lofton. Signed 3B Chris Truby to a minor league contract.
Brewers signed LHP Justin Thompson to a minor league contract.
Mariners signed LHP Jarrod Washburn and claimed LHP Jake Woods off waivers from the **Angels**.

DECEMBER 21
Royals traded RHP Chris Demaria to the **Brewers** for RHP Justin Barnes.
Giants traded 3B Edgardo Alfonzo to the **Angels** for OF Steve Finley.
Cardinals signed RHP Sidney Ponson. Signed 1B/OF Brian Daubach and RHP John Riedling to minor league contracts.

DECEMBER 22
Twins signed OF/DH Rondell White.
Dodgers signed RHP Brett Tomko.
Padres agreed to contract terms with IF Mark Bellhorn and RHP Brian Sikorski.
Astros signed RHPs Dave Borkowski and Steve Sparks and IFs Danny Klassen, Eric Munson and Kevin Orie to minor league contracts.

DECEMBER 23
Red Sox signed C John Flaherty.
Royals signed OF Reggie Sanders and RHP Joe Mays.
Mets signed OF Endy Chavez.
Yankees signed OF Johnny Damon.
Giants signed IF Jose Vizcaino.
Cardinals signed OF Juan Encarnacion and 2B Junior Spivey.

DECEMBER 24
Nationals signed LHP Mike Stanton.

DECEMBER 26
Indians signed RHP Jason Johnson.

DECEMBER 27
Diamondbacks traded 3B Troy Glaus and SS Sergio Santos to the **Blue Jays** for RHP Miguel Batista and 2B Orlando Hudson.

DECEMBER 28
Mets signed RHP Chad Bradford.

DECEMBER 29
Marlins signed IF Pokey Reese and RHP Joe Borowski.
Yankees signed RHP Octavio Dotel.
Rangers signed RHP Kevin Millwood.
Nationals signed RHP Ramon Ortiz.

DECEMBER 30
Diamondbacks signed OF Eric Byrnes.
Marlins signed C Miguel Olivo and IF Wes Helms.

DECEMBER 31
Pirates signed 3B Joe Randa.

AWARD WINNERS

THE SPORTING NEWS

AMERICAN LEAGUE

Pitcher of the Year: Bartolo Colon, Los Angeles
Rookie Player of the Year: Huston Street, P, Oakland
Relievers of the Year: Mariano Rivera, New York; Joe Nathan, Minnesota
Comeback Player of the Year: Jason Giambi, 1B, New York
Manager of the Year: Ozzie Guillen, White Sox

MAJOR LEAGUE

Player of the Year: Andruw Jones, Atlanta
Executive of the Year: Mark Shapiro, Cleveland

NATIONAL LEAGUE

Pitcher of the Year: Chris Carpenter, St. Louis
Rookie Player of the Year: Willy Taveras, OF, Houston
Reliever of the Year: Chad Cordero, Washington
Comeback Player of the Year: Ken Griffey Jr., OF, Cincinnati
Manager of the Year: Bobby Cox, Atlanta

MINOR LEAGUE

Player of the Year: Brandon Wood, SS, Rancho Cucamonga, California, and Salt Lake, Pacific Coast
Manager of the Year: Larry Parrish, Toledo, International
Executive of the Year: Robert Murphy, president, Dayton, Midwest

BASEBALL WRITERS' ASSOCIATION OF AMERICA

AMERICAN LEAGUE

MOST VALUABLE PLAYER

Player, Team	1	2	3	4	5	6	7	8	9	10	Pts.
Alex Rodriguez, New York	16	11	1	-	-	-	-	-	-	-	331
David Ortiz, Boston	11	17	-	-	-	-	-	-	-	-	307
Vladimir Guerrero, Los Angeles	1	-	9	8	7	1	1	1	-	-	196
Manny Ramirez, Boston	-	-	9	1	6	2	6	2	-	1	156
Travis Hafner, Cleveland	-	-	5	6	4	4	3	3	2	-	151
Paul Konerko, Chicago	-	-	2	4	6	5	1	3	5	-	128
Mark Teixeira, Texas	-	-	1	5	-	3	7	4	2	4	106
Gary Sheffield, New York	-	-	-	3	2	6	2	2	3	1	84
Mariano Rivera, New York	-	-	1	1	1	3	3	1	3	2	59
Derek Jeter, New York	-	-	-	-	1	-	3	1	1	-	23
Michael Young, Texas	-	-	-	-	-	2	-	2	1	2	20
Scott Podsednik, Chicago	-	-	-	1	1	-	1	-	-	1	15
Johnny Damon, Boston	-	-	-	-	-	-	1	1	2	1	12
Hideki Matsui, New York	-	-	-	-	-	-	-	2	1	-	8
Richie Sexson, Seattle	-	-	-	-	-	-	-	2	-	1	7
Miguel Tejada, Baltimore	-	-	-	-	-	-	-	2	3	7
Chone Figgins, Los Angeles	-	-	-	-	-	-	-	1	4	6
Victor Martinez, Cleveland	-	-	-	-	-	1	-	-	-	-	5
Jason Giambi, New York	-	-	-	-	-	-	-	1	1	-	5
Brian Roberts, Baltimore	-	-	-	-	-	-	-	1	-	2	5
Jason Varitek, Boston	-	-	-	-	-	-	1	-	-	-	4
Eric Chavez, Oakland	-	-	-	-	-	-	-	-	1	2	4
Huston Street, Oakland	-	-	-	-	-	-	-	1	-	-	3
Bartolo Colon, Los Angeles	-	-	-	-	-	-	-	-	1	1	3
Grady Sizemore, Cleveland	-	-	-	-	-	-	-	-	1	1	3
Bob Wickman, Cleveland	-	-	-	-	-	-	-	-	1	-	2
Jorge Cantu, Tampa Bay	-	-	-	-	-	-	-	-	-	1	1
Jose Contreras, Chicago	-	-	-	-	-	-	-	-	-	1	1

Fourteen points awarded for a first-place vote, nine for second and down to one for 10th.

CY YOUNG AWARD

Pitcher, Team	1	2	3	Pts.
Bartolo Colon, Los Angeles	17	11	-	118
Mariano Rivera, New York	8	7	7	68
Johan Santana, Minnesota	3	8	12	51
Cliff Lee, Cleveland	-	2	2	8
Mark Buehrle, Chicago	-	-	5	5
Jon Garland, Chicago	-	-	1	1
Kevin Millwood, Cleveland	-	-	1	1

Five points awarded for a first-place vote, three for second and one for third.

MANAGER OF THE YEAR

Manager, Team	1	2	3	Pts.
Ozzie Guillen, Chicago	17	5	5	105
Eric Wedge, Cleveland	6	11	8	71
Joe Torre, New York	4	7	2	43
Ken Macha, Oakland	1	3	7	21
Mike Scioscia, Los Angeles	-	1	4	7
Terry Francona, Boston	-	1	1	4

Manager, Team	1	2	3	Pts.
John Gibbons, Toronto	-	-	1	1

Five points awarded for a first-place vote, three for second and one for third.

ROOKIE OF THE YEAR

Player, Team	1	2	3	Pts.
Huston Street, Oakland	15	6	4	97
Robinson Cano, New York	4	10	7	57
Jonny Gomes, Tampa Bay	2	8	5	39
Tadahito Iguchi, Chicago	5	1	2	30
Gustavo Chacin, Toronto	2	-	4	14
Nick Swisher, Oakland	-	2	-	6
Joe Blanton, Oakland	-	1	3	6
Jesse Crain, Minnesota	-	-	2	2
Scott Kazmir, Tampa Bay	-	-	1	1

Five points awarded for a first-place vote, three for second and one for third.

2005 REVIEW Award winners

MOST VALUABLE PLAYER

Player, Team	1	2	3	4	5	6	7	8	9	10	Pts.
Albert Pujols, St. Louis	18	14	-	-	-	-	-	-	-	-	378
Andruw Jones, Atlanta	13	17	2	-	-	-	-	-	-	-	351
Derek Lee, Chicago..	1	1	30	-	-	-	-	-	-	-	263
Morgan Ensberg, Houston	-	-	-	10	7	7	2	1	1	-	160
Miguel Cabrera, Florida	-	-	-	13	4	1	2	3	4	1	146
Carlos Delgado, Florida	-	-	-	2	6	2	4	2	1	-	84
Pat Burrell, Philadelphia	-	-	-	-	4	6	1	-	3	1	65
Chris Carpenter, St. Louis	-	-	-	1	3	3	1	2	1	-	52
Brian Giles, San Diego	-	-	-	1	2	2	2	1	2	4	48
Jimmy Rollins, Philadelphia	-	-	-	2	1	-	2	4	1	3	45
Dontrelle Willis, Florida	-	-	-	-	2	3	2	1	2	-	42
Jason Bay, Pittsburgh	-	-	-	1	-	1	4	1	5	-	41
Chase Utley, Philadelphia	-	-	-	-	-	2	2	-	1	2	22
Lance Berkman, Houston	-	-	-	1	-	1	1	1	3	1	21
Bobby Abreu, Philadelphia	-	-	-	-	1	1	1	2	-	-	21
Chad Cordero, Washington	-	-	-	-	-	1	2	-	2	4	21
Trevor Hoffman, San Diego	-	-	-	1	-	-	2	1	-	1	19
Carlos Lee, Milwaukee	-	-	-	-	-	1	1	2	1	2	19
Jeff Kent, Los Angeles	-	-	-	-	1	1	-	2	-	1	18
David Wright, New York	-	-	-	-	1	-	1	2	-	2	18
David Eckstein, St. Louis	-	-	-	-	-	1	2	-	-	2	15
Roger Clemens, Houston	-	-	-	-	-	-	-	2	1	-	8
Roy Oswalt, Houston	-	-	-	-	-	-	-	1	1	1	6
Ken Griffey Jr., Cincinnati	-	-	-	-	-	-	-	1	1	-	5
Andy Pettitte, Houston	-	-	-	-	-	-	-	-	2	1	5
Jim Edmonds, St. Louis	-	-	-	-	-	-	-	1	-	-	3
Cliff Floyd, New York	-	-	-	-	-	-	-	1	-	-	3
Marcus Giles, Atlanta	-	-	-	-	-	-	-	1	-	-	3
Adam Dunn, Cincinnati	-	-	-	-	-	-	-	-	-	3	3
Scott Eyre, San Francisco	-	-	-	-	-	-	-	-	-	1	1
Brad Lidge, Houston	-	-	-	-	-	-	-	-	-	1	1
Jose Reyes, New York	-	-	-	-	-	-	-	-	-	1	1

Fourteen points awarded for a first-place vote, nine for second and down to one for 10th.

CY YOUNG AWARD

Pitcher, Team	1	2	3	Pts.
Chris Carpenter, St. Louis	19	12	1	132
Dontrelle Willis, Florida	11	18	3	112
Roger Clemens, Houston	2	2	24	40
Roy Oswalt, Houston	-	-	2	2
Chad Cordero, Washington	-	-	1	1
Andy Pettitte, Houston	-	-	1	1

Five points awarded for a first-place vote, three for second and one for third.

Player, Team	1	2	3	Pts.
Zach Duke, Pittsburgh	3	-	1	16
Jeff Francis, Colorado	-	1	-	3
Ricky Weeks, Milwaukee	-	1	-	3
Clint Barmes, Colorado	-	-	1	1
Jason Vargas, Florida	-	-	1	1

Five points awarded for a first-place vote, three for second and one for third.

MANAGER OF THE YEAR

Manager, Team	1	2	3	Pts.
Bobby Cox, Atlanta	28	4	-	152
Tony La Russa, St. Louis	2	13	3	52
Phil Garner, Houston	-	9	11	38
Frank Robinson, Washington	2	4	7	29
Ned Yost, Milwaukee	-	-	7	7
Charlie Manuel, Philadelphia	-	1	2	5
Bruch Bochy, San Diego	-	1	1	4
Willie Randolph, New York	-	-	1	1

Five points awarded for a first-place vote, three for second and one for third.

ROOKIE OF THE YEAR

Player, Team	1	2	3	Pts.
Ryan Howard, Philadelphia	19	3	5	109
Willy Taveras, Houston	7	11	10	78
Jeff Francouer, Atlanta	2	14	8	60
Garrett Atkins, Colorado	1	2	6	17

MISCELLANEOUS

ATTENDANCE

AMERICAN LEAGUE

	2005				2004			*Pct.
	Home	Dates	Average	Road	Home	Dates	Average	Change
New York	4,090,692	81	50,502	2,997,599	3,775,292	79	47,789	+5.7
Los Angeles	3,404,686	81	42,033	2,462,630	3,375,677	81	41,675	+0.8
Boston	2,847,898	81	35,159	3,054,438	2,837,304	81	35,028	+0.4
Seattle	2,725,549	81	33,649	2,235,895	2,940,731	81	36,305	-7.3
Baltimore	2,624,740	81	32,404	2,463,427	2,747,573	80	34,345	-5.7
Texas	2,525,231	80	31,565	2,197,296	2,513,685	79	31,819	-0.8
Chicago	2,342,833	81	28,924	2,253,661	1,930,537	79	24,437	+18.4
Oakland	2,109,118	81	26,038	2,420,446	2,201,516	81	27,179	-4.2
Minnesota	2,034,243	81	25,114	2,217,442	1,911,418	81	23,598	+6.4
Detroit	2,024,485	80	25,306	2,081,809	1,917,004	80	23,963	+5.6
Toronto	2,014,987	81	24,876	2,421,950	1,900,041	81	23,457	+6.0
Cleveland	2,013,763	81	24,861	2,222,000	1,814,401	81	22,400	+11.0
Kansas City	1,371,181	79	17,357	2,109,805	1,661,478	79	21,031	-17.5
Tampa Bay	1,152,793	81	14,232	2,367,929	1,275,011	79	16,139	-11.8
Totals	33,282,189	1,130	29,453	33,506,327	32,801,668	1,122	29,235	+0.7

*Percentage refers to the change in average home attendance from 2004 to 2005.

NATIONAL LEAGUE

	2005				2004			*Pct.
	Home	Dates	Average	Road	Home	Dates	Average	Change
Los Angeles	3,603,646	81	44,489	2,638,150	3,488,283	81	43,065	+3.3
St. Louis	3,538,948	81	43,691	2,479,591	3,048,427	81	37,635	+16.1
San Francisco	3,181,023	81	39,272	2,536,294	3,256,858	81	40,208	-2.3
Chicago	3,099,992	80	38,750	2,953,637	3,170,184	81	39,138	-1.0
San Diego	2,869,787	81	35,429	2,531,411	3,016,752	81	37,244	-4.9
New York	2,829,931	80	35,374	2,836,264	2,318,321	80	28,979	+22.0
Houston	2,804,760	81	34,627	2,451,857	3,087,872	81	38,122	-9.2
Washington	2,731,993	81	33,728	2,564,538	**748,550	**80	**9,357	+260.5
Philadelphia	2,665,304	80	33,316	2,372,051	3,250,092	80	40,626	-18.0
Atlanta	2,521,527	80	31,519	2,653,372	2,322,565	79	29,400	+7.2
Milwaukee	2,211,023	81	27,297	2,376,626	2,062,382	81	25,462	+7.2
Arizona	2,058,741	81	25,417	2,585,874	2,519,560	81	31,106	-18.3
Cincinnati	1,943,068	80	24,288	2,596,780	2,287,250	81	28,238	-14.0
Colorado	1,914,389	80	23,930	2,540,969	2,338,069	79	29,596	-19.1
Florida	1,852,608	81	22,872	2,628,299	1,723,105	78	22,091	+3.5
Pittsburgh	1,817,245	79	23,003	2,674,134	1,583,031	75	21,107	+9.0
Totals	41,643,985	1,288	32,332	41,419,847	40,221,301	1,280	31,423	+2.9
Major League totals	74,926,174	2,418	30,987	74,926,174	73,022,969	2,402	30,401	+1.9

*Percentage refers to the change in average home attendance from 2004 to 2005.

**Montreal figures.

DEBUTS

Player	Pos.	Team	Birth date	Birthplace	Debut	*Age
Burgos, Ambiorix	P	Kansas City	4-19-84	Nagua, Dominican Republic	4-23	21
Burns, Michael John	P	Houston	7-14-78	Westminster, California	5-13	26
Bynum, Freddie Lee Jr.	PR	Oakland	3-15-80	Wilson, North Carolina	8-30	25
Cabrera, Melky	CF	New York A.L.	8-11-84	Santo Domingo, Dominican Republic	7-7	20
Cain, Matthew T.	P	San Francisco	10- 1-84	Dothan, Alabama	8-29	20
Calzado, Napoleon	PH	Baltimore	2- 9-77	Santo Domingo, Dominican Republic	5-29	28
Campillo, Jorge Hidalgo	P	Seattle	8-10-78	Tijuana, Mexico	5-20	26
Cano, Robinson Jose	2B	New York A.L.	10-22-82	San Pedro de Macoris, Dominican Republic	5-3	22
Capps, Matthew Dicus	P	Pittsburgh	9- 3-83	Douglasville, Georgia	9-16	22
Carvajal, Marcos Jose	P	Colorado	8-19-84	Bolivar, Venezuela	4-6	20
Castro, Bernabel	DH	Baltimore	7-14-79	Santo Domingo, Dominican Republic	9-1	26
Cedeno, Ronny Alexander	PR	Chicago N.L.	2- 2-83	Carabobo, Venezuela	4-23	22
Chavez, Angel Aristedes	SS	San Francisco	7-22-81	Panama City, Panama	8-30	24
Choo, Shin-Soo	PH	Seattle	7-13-82	Pusan, South Korea	4-21	22
Clark, Douglas	PH	San Francisco	3- 5-76	Springfield, Massachusetts	9-14	29

Player	Pos.	Team	Birth date	Birthplace	Debut	*Age
Coffey, Justin Todd	P	Cincinnati	9- 9-80	Shelby, North Carolina	4-19	24
Corcoran, Timothy Hugh	P	Tampa Bay	4-15-78	Baton Rouge, Louisiana	6-14	27
Cortez, Fernando	PH	Tampa Bay	8-10-81	Stockton, California	7-5	23
Costa, Shane Jeremy	LF	Kansas City	12-12-81	Visalia, California	6-2	23
Cruz, Nelson Ramon	RF	Milwaukee	7- 1-80	Monte Cristi, Dominican Republic	9-17	25
Davies, Hiram Kyle	P	Atlanta	9- 9-83	Decatur, Georgia	5-21	21
Delcarmen, Manuel	P	Boston	2-16-82	Boston, Massachusetts	7-26	23
Demaria, Christopher Neil	P	Kansas City	9-28-80	Torrance, California	9-9	24
Denorfia, Christopher Anthony	PH	Cincinnati	7-15-80	Bristol, Connecticut	9-7	25
Devine, Joseph	P	Atlanta	9-19-83	Junction City, Kansas	8-20	21
Dillon, Joseph William	3B	Florida	8- 2-75	Modesto, California	5-18	29
Doumit, Ryan Matthew	PH	Pittsburgh	4- 3-81	Moses Lake, Washington	6-5	24
Duffy, Christopher Ellis	PH	Pittsburgh	4-20-80	Brattleboro, Vermont	4-7	24
Duke, Zachary Thomas	P	Pittsburgh	4-19-83	Clifton, Texas	7-2	22
Duncan, Christopher E.	PH	St. Louis	5- 5-81	Tucson, Arizona	9-10	24
Eldred, Bradley Ross	1B	Pittsburgh	7-12-80	Fort Lauderdale, Florida	7-22	25
Encarnacion, Edwin	3B	Cincinnati	1- 7-83	La Romana, Dominican Republic	6-24	22
Esposito, Michael Anthony	P	Colorado	9-27-81	Los Angeles, California	9-21	23
Eveland, Dana J.	P	Milwaukee	10-29-83	Olympia, Washington	7-16	21
Feldman, Scott Wayne	P	Texas	2- 7-83	Kailua, Hawaii	8-31	22
Fielder, Prince Semien	DH	Milwaukee	5-18-84	Ontario, California	6-13	21
Fiorentino, Jeffrey Philip	CF	Baltimore	4-14-83	Pembroke Pines, Florida	5-12	22
Flores, Ronald Joel	P	Oakland	8- 9-79	Whittier, California	6-17	25
Fontenot, Michael Eugene	PR	Chicago N.L.	6- 9-80	New Iberia, Louisiana	4-13	24
Francoeur, Jeffrey Braden	RF	Atlanta	1- 8-84	Atlanta, Georgia	7-7	21
Freire, Alejandro	DH	Baltimore	8-23-74	Caracas, Venezuela	8-9	30
Furmaniak, Jason Joseph	2B	Pittsburgh	7-31-79	Naperville, Illinois	9-13	26
Gall, John Christopher	LF	St. Louis	4- 2-78	Stanford, California	7-26	27
Garabito, Eddy Jorge	PH	Colorado	12- 2-76	Manrreza, Dominican Republic	5-27	28
Garko, Ryan F.	PH	Cleveland	1- 2-81	Pittsburgh, Pennsylvania	9-18	24
Gassner, David K.	P	Minnesota	12-14-78	Hortonville, Wisconsin	4-16	26
Giarratano, Anthony J.	SS	Detroit	11-29-82	Queens, New York	6-1	22
Godwin, Carlton Tyrell	PH	Washington	7-10-79	Wilmington, North Carolina	5-27	25
Gorzelanny, Thomas Stephen	P	Pittsburgh	7-12-82	Evergreen Park, Illinois	9-20	23
Greenberg, Adam Daniel	PH	Chicago N.L.	2-21-81	New Haven, Connecticut	7-9	24
Griffin, John-Ford David	PH	Toronto	11-19-79	Sarasota, Florida	9-6	25
Gutierrez, Franklin Rafael	PR	Cleveland	2-21-83	Caricuao, Venezuela	8-31	22
Hamulack, Timothy William Alexander	P	New York N.L.	11-14-76	Ithaca, New York	9-2	28
Hansen, Craig R.	P	Boston	11-15-83	Glen Cove, New York	9-19	21
Hardy, James Jerry	SS	Milwaukee	8-19-82	Tucson, Arizona	4-4	22
Harris, Jeffrey Austin	P	Seattle	7- 4-74	Alameda, California	8-2	31
Heintz, Christopher John	C	Minnesota	8- 6-74	Syosset, New York	9-10	31
Henn, Sean Michael	P	New York A.L.	4-23-81	Fort Worth, Texas	5-4	24
Hensley, Clayton Allen	P	San Diego	8-31-79	Tomball, Texas	7-20	25
Hermida, Jeremy Ryan	PH	Florida	1-30-84	Marietta, Georgia	8-31	21
Hernandez, Anderson	2B	New York N.L.	10-30-82	Santo Domingo, Dominican Republic	9-18	22
Hernandez, Felix Abraham	P	Seattle	4- 8-86	Valencia, Venezuela	8-4	19
Hill, Aaron Walter	DH	Toronto	3-21-82	Visalia, California	5-20	23
Hill, Richard Joseph	P	Chicago N.L.	3-11-80	Boston, Massachusetts	6-15	25
Hooper, Kevin J.	LF	Detroit	12- 7-76	Lawrence, Kansas	7-9	28
Houlton, Dennis Sean	P	Los Angeles N.L.	8-12-79	Fullerton, California	4-9	25
Howell, James Phillip	P	Kansas City	4-25-83	Modesto, California	6-11	22
Huber, Justin Patrick	PH	Kansas City	7- 1-82	Melbourne, Australia	6-21	22
Iguchi, Tadahito	2B	Chicago A.L.	12- 4-74	Tokyo, Japan	4-4	30
Jackson, Conor S.	PH	Arizona	5- 7-82	Austin, Texas	7-28	23
Jacobs, Michael James	PH	New York N.L.	10-30-80	Chula Vista, California	8-21	24
James, Charles H.	P	Atlanta	11- 9-81	Atlanta, Georgia	9-28	23
Jenks, Robert Scott	P	Chicago A.L.	3-14-81	Mission Hills, California	7-6	24
Jimerson, Charlton Maxwell	CF	Houston	9-22-79	San Leandro, California	9-14	25
Johnson, Benjamin Joseph	LF	San Diego	6-18-81	Memphis, Tennessee	6-26	24
Johnson, Daniel Ryan	1B	Oakland	8-10-79	Coon Rapids, Minnesota	5-27	25
Johnson, Joshua Michael	P	Florida	1-31-84	Minneapolis, Minnesota	9-10	21
Johnson, Kelly Andrew	LF	Atlanta	2-22-82	Austin, Texas	5-29	23
Johnson, Tyler James	P	St. Louis	6- 7-81	Columbia, Missouri	9-6	24

Player	Pos.	Team	Birth date	Birthplace	Debut	*Age
Jorgensen, Ryan Wayne	C	Florida	5- 4-79	Jacksonville, Florida	8-8	26
Koo, Dae-Sung	P	New York N.L.	8- 2-68	Daejeon, South Korea	4-4	36
Koronka, John Vincent	P	Chicago N.L.	7- 3-80	Clearwater, Florida	6-1	24
Kuo, Hong-Chih	P	Los Angeles N.L.	7-23-81	Tainan City, Taiwan	9-2	24
Lerew, Anthony Allen	P	Atlanta	10-28-82	Carlisle, Pennsylvania	9-4	22
Liriano, Francisco Casillas	P	Minnesota	10-26-83	San Cristobal, Dominican Republic	9-5	21
Lopez, Pedro Michel	SS	Chicago A.L.	4-28-84	Moca, Dominican Republic	5-1	21
Machado, Alejandro Jose	2B	Boston	4-26-82	Caracas, Venezuela	9-2	23
Maholm, Paul G.	P	Pittsburgh	6-25-82	Greenwood, Mississippi	8-30	23
Marcum, Shaun M.	P	Toronto	12-14-81	Kansas City, Missouri	9-6	23
Marte, Andy M.	3B	Atlanta	10-21-83	Villa Tapia, Dominican Republic	6-7	21
Mathis, Jeffery Stephen	PH	Los Angeles A.L.	3-31-83	Marianna, Florida	8-12	22
McAnulty, Paul Michael	PH	San Diego	2-24-81	Oxnard, California	6-22	24
McBride, Joseph Macay	P	Atlanta	10-24-82	Augusta, Georgia	7-22	22
McCann, Brian Michael	C	Atlanta	2-20-84	Athens, Georgia	6-10	21
McCarthy, Brandon Patrick	P	Chicago A.L.	7- 7-83	Glendale, California	5-22	21
McDougall, Marshall James	PH	Texas	12-19-78	Jacksonville, Florida	6-7	26
McGowan, Dustin Michael	P	Toronto	3-24-82	Savannah, Georgia	7-30	23
McLouth, Nathan Richard	PH	Pittsburgh	10-28-81	Muskegon, Michigan	6-29	23
Medders, Brandon Edward	P	Arizona	1-26-80	Tuscaloosa, Alabama	6-20	25
Meredith, Olise C.	P	Boston	6- 4-83	Richmond, Virginia	5-8	21
Messenger, Randall Jerome	P	Florida	8-13-81	Reno, Nevada	6-22	23
Morse, Michael John	PH	Seattle	3-22-82	Fort Lauderdale, Florida	5-31	23
Munter, Scott	P	San Francisco	3- 7-80	Norfolk, Nebraska	5-11	25
Murton, Matthew Henry	LF	Chicago N.L.	10- 3-81	Fort Lauderdale, Florida	7-8	23
Myrow, Brian Shawn	PH	Los Angeles N.L.	9- 4-76	Fort Worth, Texas	9-6	29
Nakamura, Norihiro	PH	Los Angeles N.L.	7-24-73	Osaka, Japan	4-10	31
Nippert, Dustin David	P	Arizona	5- 6-81	Wheeling, West Virginia	9-8	24
Nunez, Leonel	P	Kansas City	8-14-83	Jamoa Norte, Dominican Republic	5-9	21
Olsen, Scott M.	P	Florida	1-12-84	Kalamazoo, Michigan	6-25	21
Orr, Peterson T.	2B	Atlanta	6- 8-79	Richmond Hill, Ontario	4-5	25
Ortmeier, Daniel D.	PH	San Francisco	5-11-81	Chattanooga, Tennessee	9-5	24
Orvella, Chad Robert	P	Tampa Bay	10- 1-80	Renton, Washington	5-31	24
Osoria, Franquelis Antonio	P	Los Angeles N.L.	9-12-81	Santiago, Dominican Republic	6-7	23
Oxspring, Chris Andrew	P	San Diego	5-13-77	Ipswich, Australia	9-2	28
Papelbon, Jonathan R.	P	Boston	11-23-80	Baton Rouge, Louisiana	7-31	24
Paulino, Ronny Leonel	C	Pittsburgh	4-21-81	Santo Domingo, Dominican Republic	9-25	24
Pena, Brayan Eduardo	C	Atlanta	1- 7-82	Havana, Cuba	5-23	23
Penn, Hayden	P	Baltimore	10-13-84	La Jolla, California	5-28	20
Peralta, Joel	P	Los Angeles A.L.	3-23-76	Bonao, Dominican Republic	5-25	29
Perez, Miguel A.	PH	Cincinnati	9-25-83	Caracas, Venezuela	9-7	21
Prieto, Christian Michael	CF	Los Angeles A.L.	8-24-72	Carmel, California	5-14	32
Quintanilla, Omar	SS	Colorado	10-24-81	El Paso, Texas	7-31	23
Ramirez, Hanley	SS	Boston	12-23-83	Samana, Dominican Republic	9-20	21
Rasner, Darrell W.	P	Washington	1-13-81	Carson City, Nevada	9-6	24
Ray, Christopher T.	P	Baltimore	1-12-82	Tampa, Florida	6-14	23
Reed, Keith A.	RF	Baltimore	10- 8-78	Yarmouth Port, Massachusetts	5-11	26
Reese, Kevin Patrick	LF	New York A.L.	3-11-78	San Diego, California	6-26	27
Repko, Jason Edward	LF	Los Angeles N.L.	12-27-80	East Chicago, Indiana	4-6	24
Resop, Christopher Paul	P	Florida	11- 4-82	Naples, Florida	6-28	22
Reyes, Anthony L.	P	St. Louis	10-16-81	Downey, California	8-9	23
Ring, Roger Royce	P	New York N.L.	12-21-80	La Mesa, California	4-29	24
Robles, Oscar M.	3B	Los Angeles N.L.	4- 9-76	Tijuana, Mexico	5-10	29
Rodriguez, John Joseph	LF	St. Louis	1-20-78	New York, New York	7-18	27
Rodriguez, Luis Orlando	SS	Minnesota	6-27-80	San Carlos, Venezuela	5-21	24
Rodriguez, Wandy E.	P	Houston	1-18-79	Santiago, Dominican Republic	5-23	26
Rupe, Joshua Matthew	P	Texas	8-18-82	Portsmouth, Virginia	9-16	23
Sadler, Raymond Lee	LF	Pittsburgh	9-19-80	Clifton, Texas	5-8	24
Sandoval, Danny E.	PH	Philadelphia	4- 7-79	Lara, Venezuela	7-17	26
Santana, Ervin Ramon	P	Los Angeles A.L.	1-10-83	La Romana, Dominican Republic	5-17	22
Saunders, Joseph Francis	P	Los Angeles A.L.	6-16-81	Falls Church, Virginia	8-16	24
Schmoll, Stephen John	P	Los Angeles N.L.	2- 4-80	Silver Spring, Maryland	4-6	25
Schumaker, Jared Michael	PH	St. Louis	2- 3-80	Torrance, California	6-8	25
Scott, Luke Brandon	LF	Houston	6-25-78	Deleon Springs, Florida	4-5	26
Self, Todd Douglas	PH	Houston	11- 9-78	Shreveport, Louisiana	5-12	26
Shabala, Adam Jason	LF	San Francisco	2- 6-78	Streator, Illinois	6-16	27
Shackelford, Brian Wesley	P	Cincinnati	8-30-76	McAlester, Oklahoma	6-26	28
Shealy, Ryan Nelson	DH	Colorado	8-29-79	Fort Lauderdale, Florida	6-14	25
Shoppach, Kelly Brian	C	Boston	4-29-80	Fort Worth, Texas	5-28	25
Short, Richard Ryan	PH	Washington	12- 6-72	Elgin, Illinois	6-10	32
Sisco, Andrew Frank	P	Kansas City	1-13-83	Steamboat Springs, Colorado	4-4	22

Player	Pos.	Team	Birth date	Birthplace	Debut	*Age
Soto, Geovany	PH	Chicago N.L.	1-20-83	San Juan, Puerto Rico	9-23	22
Speier, Ryan Andrew	P	Colorado	7-24-79	Frankfort, Kentucky	4-4	25
Spilborghs, Ryan A.	RF	Colorado	9- 5-79	Santa Barbara, California	7-16	25
Stauffer, Timothy James	P	San Diego	6- 2-82	Portland, Maine	5-11	22
Stemle, Stephen J.	P	Kansas City	5-20-77	Louisville, Kentucky	5-26	28
Stern, Adam James	CF	Boston	2-12-80	London, Ontario	7-7	25
Street, Huston Lowell	P	Oakland	8- 2-83	Austin, Texas	4-6	21
Sullivan, Cory	LF	Colorado	8-20-79	Tulsa, Oklahoma	4-4	25
Taschner, Jack Girard	P	San Francisco	4-21-78	Milwaukee, Wisconsin	6-11	27
Teahen, Mark Thomas	3B	Kansas City	9- 6-81	Redlands, California	4-4	23
Tejeda, Robinson Garcia	P	Philadelphia	3-24-82	Bani, Dominican Republic	5-10	23
Theriot, Ryan Stewart	PH	Chicago N.L.	12- 7-79	Baton Rouge, Louisiana	9-13	25
Thompson, Bradley Joseph	P	St. Louis	1-31-82	Las Vegas, Nevada	5-8	23
Thompson, Derek R.	P	Los Angeles N.L.	1- 8-81	Tampa, Florida	5-28	24
Van Buren, Jermaine Russell	P	Chicago N.L.	7- 2-80	Laurel, Mississippi	8-31	25
Vargas, Jason M.	P	Florida	2- 2-83	Seattle, Washington	7-14	22
Vento, Michael	PR	New York A.L.	5-25-78	Albuquerque, New Mexico	9-13	27
Verlander, Justin B.	P	Detroit	2-20-83	Manakin-Sabot, Virginia	7-4	22
Volquez, Edison	P	Texas	7- 3-83	La Segunda, Dominican Republic	8-30	22
Wainwright, Adam P.	P	St. Louis	8-30-81	Brunswick, Georgia	9-11	24
Wang, Chien-Ming	P	New York A.L.	3-31-80	Tainan, Taiwan	4-30	25
Watson, Brandon	LF	Washington	9-30-81	Los Angeles, California	8-9	23
Whiteside, Dustin Eli	C	Baltimore	10-22-79	New Albany, Mississippi	7-5	25
Williams, Glenn David	PH	Minnesota	7-18-77	Gosford, Australia	6-7	27
Wilson, Christopher John	P	Texas	11-18-80	Newport Beach, California	6-10	24
Wilson, Joshua Aaron	PH	Florida	3-26-81	Pittsburgh, Pennsylvania	9-7	24
Woods, Jacob Thomas	P	Los Angeles A.L.	9- 3-81	Fresno, California	4-8	23
Woodyard, Mark Anthony	P	Detroit	12-19-78	Mobile, Alabama	9-17	26
Yabu, Keiichi	P	Oakland	9-28-68	Mie, Japan	4-9	36
Young, Walter Earnest	PH	Baltimore	2-18-80	Hattiesburg, Mississippi	9-6	25
Zimmerman, Ryan	PH	Washington	9-28-84	Washington, North Carolina	9-1	20

2005 FREE-AGENT FILINGS

AMERICAN LEAGUE

Baltimore: James Baldwin, Jason Grimsley, Eli Marrero, Rafael Palmeiro, B.J. Ryan, Sammy Sosa, B.J. Surhoff.

Boston: Johnny Damon, Tony Graffanino, Matt Mantei, Kevin Millar, Bill Mueller, Mike Myers, John Olerud.

Chicago: Geoff Blum, Raul Casanova, Carl Everett, Paul Konerko, Frank Thomas.

Cleveland: Scott Elarton, Juan Gonzalez, Jose Hernandez, Bobby Howry, Kevin Millwood, Bob Wickman.

Detroit: Jason Johnson, Bobby Higginson, Fernando Vina, Rondell White.

Kansas City: Brian Anderson, Denny Hocking, Jose Lima, Joe McEwing, Scott Sullivan.

Los Angeles: Paul Byrd, Jason Christiansen, Lou Merloni, Bengie Molina, Tim Salmon, Jarrod Washburn.

Minnesota: Jacque Jones, Joe Mays, Terry Mulholland.

New York: Kevin Brown, Alan Embree, John Flaherty, Tom Gordon, Matt Lawton, Al Leiter, Tino Martinez, Ramiro Mendoza, Felix Rodriguez, Rey Sanchez, Ruben Sierra, Tanyon Sturtze, Bernie Williams.

Oakland: Alberto Castillo, Octavio Dotel, Erubiel Durazo, Scott Hatteberg, Ricardo Rincon.

Seattle: Shigetoshi Hasegawa, Dave Hansen, Jamie Moyer, Jeff Nelson, Pokey Reese, Dan Wilson.

Tampa Bay: Roberto Alomar, Danny Bautista, Alex S. Gonzalez, Travis Lee, Eduardo A. Perez.

Texas: Sandy Alomar Jr., Doug Brocail, Greg Colbrunn, Richard Hidalgo, Steve Karsay, Kenny Rogers, John Wasdin.

Toronto: None.

NATIONAL LEAGUE

Arizona: Royce Clayton, Shawn Estes, Buddy Groom, Tim Worrell.

Atlanta: Kyle Farnsworth, Julio Franco, Rafael Furcal, Todd Hollandsworth, Brian Jordan, Eduardo Perez, Jay Powell.

Chicago: Jeromy Burnitz, Chad Fox, Nomar Garciaparra.

Cincinnati: Rich Aurilia, Jacob Cruz, Luis Lopez.

Colorado: Todd Greene, Byung-Hyun Kim, Dan Miceli, Jamey Wright.

Florida: Antonio Alfonseca, A.J. Burnett, Jeff Conine, Damion Easley, Juan Encarnacion, Alex Gonzalez, Lenny Harris, Todd Jones, Jim Mecir, Brian Moehler, Mike Mordecai, Paul Quantrill, Ismael Valdez.

Houston: Brad Ausmus, Roger Clemens, Orlando Palmeiro, Russ Springer, Jose Vizcaino.

Los Angeles: Wilson Alvarez, Paul Bako, Elmer Dessens, Darren Dreifort, Olmedo Saenz, Jose Valentin, Jeff Weaver.

Milwaukee: Jeff Cirillo, Rick Helling, Wes Helms.

New York: Marlon Anderson, Miguel Cairo, Mike DeFelice, Danny Graves, Roberto Hernandez, Braden Looper, Doug Mientkiewicz, Jose Offerman, Mike Piazza, Felix Heredia, Shingo Takatsu, Gerald Williams.

Philadelphia: Terry Adams, Kenny Lofton, Ramon E. Martinez, Todd Pratt, Michael Tucker, Ugueth Urbina, Billy Wagner.

Pittsburgh: Brian Meadows, Jose Mesa, Daryle Ward, Rick White.

St. Louis: Einar Diaz, Cal Eldred, Mark Grudzielanek, John Mabry, Matt Morris, Abraham Nunez, Al Reyes, Reggie Sanders, Julian Tavarez, Larry Walker.

San Diego: Pedro Astacio, Robert Fick, Brian Giles, Chris Hammond, Ramon J. Hernandez, Trevor Hoffman, Joe Randa, Rudy Seanez, Mark Sweeney, Eric Young.

San Francisco: Scott Eyre, J.T. Snow, Brett Tomko.

Washington: Tony Armas Jr., Carlos Baerga, Gary Bennett, Hector Carrasco, Deivi Cruz, Joey Eischen, Jeffrey Hammonds, Esteban Loaiza, Preston Wilson.

(Listed in order of selection)

Player	Pos.	Drafted by	Drafted from (major league organization)
Fabio Castro	LHP	Kansas City	Charlotte, International League (White Sox)
Luis Enrique Gonzalez	LHP	Colorado	Las Vegas, Pacific Coast League (Dodgers)
Stephen Andrade	RHP	Tampa Bay	Syracuse, International League (Blue Jays)
Victor Santos	RHP	Pittsburgh	Omaha, Pacific Coast League (Royals)
Christopher Booker	RHP	Detroit	New Orleans, Pacific Coast League (Nationals)
Seth Etherton	RHP	San Diego	Omaha, Pacific Coast League (Royals)
Mitchell Wylie	RHP	New York N.L.	Fresno, Pacific Coast League (Giants)
Daniel Uggla	IF	Florida	Tucson, Pacific Coast League (Diamondbacks)
Jason Pridie	OF	Minnesota	Durham, International League (Devil Rays)
James Vermilyea	RHP	Boston	Syracuse, International League (Blue Jays)
Juan Mateo	RHP	St. Louis	Iowa, Pacific Coast League (Cubs)
Michael Megrew	LHP	Florida	Las Vegas, Pacific Coast League (Dodgers)

2004 REVIEW *Miscellaneous*

Bob Allen, 91, at Chesapeake, Va., on October 30. Allen, a righthanded pitcher, lost his only decision while appearing in three games for the 1937 Phillies.

Monty Basgall, 83, at Tucson, Ariz., on September 22. Second baseman Basgall played for the Pirates in 1948, 1949 and 1951. He appeared in 107 games in '49, hitting .218. Basgall also was a longtime Dodgers coach.

Joe Bauman, 83, at Roswell, N.M., on September 20. Bauman held the single-season homer record in professional baseball for 47 years. Playing for Roswell of the Class C Longhorn League in 1954, Bauman hit 72 home runs (and batted .400, with 224 RBIs in 138 games). His mark fell in 2001 when the Giants' Barry Bonds smashed 73 homers.

Mike Bishop, 46, at Bakersfield, Calif., on February 8. Bishop, a catcher, appeared in three games for the 1983 Mets.

Bill "Bud" Black, 73, at St. Louis, Mo., on October 2. Righthander Black appeared in 10 games overall while pitching for the Tigers in 1952, 1955 and 1956.

Don Blasingame, 73, at Fountain Hills, Ariz., on April 13. Blasingame was two months into his first full season in the majors in 1956 when he took over at second base for St. Louis after longtime Cardinals star Red Schoendienst was traded to the New York Giants. He played four full years with the Cards—he scored 108 runs in 1957—and then was with San Francisco, Cincinnati, Washington and the Kansas City A's. An All-Star Game participant in 1958 and a regular with the Reds' 1961 National League champions, Blasingame batted .258 over 12 big-league seasons. He went on to play and manage in Japan.

Ted Bonda, 88, at Chagrin Falls, Ohio, on October 22. Bonda was owner of the Indians when Cleveland broke the managerial racial barrier in the majors by naming Frank Robinson to manage the club in 1975.

Harry Boyles, 93, at McAllen, Texas, on January 7. Righthander Boyles was 0-4 in nine games with the 1938 White Sox and 0-0 in two appearances with the Sox in '39.

Nelson Briles, 61, at Orlando on February 13. Briles, mostly a bullpen operative in 1966 while posting a 4-15 record for the Cardinals, was thrust into St. Louis' rotation in 1967 when Bob Gibson was injured and won his last nine starts in a 14-5 season that helped the Cards win the pennant. In the Cardinals' World Series triumph over the Red Sox, Briles won Game 3. A 19-game winner for St. Louis in 1968, Briles was a member of another Series championship team in 1971 when he compiled an 8-4 record for Pittsburgh and tossed a two-hit shutout against Baltimore in Game 5 of the fall classic. In 14 major league seasons, the righthander was 129-112.

Bob Broeg, 87, at Creve Coeur, Mo., on October 28. Broeg, a member of the writers' wing of the Baseball Hall of Fame, was a longtime sports editor of the *St. Louis Post-Dispatch* who covered the Cardinals and also the Browns in a journalism career that spanned six decades.

Bob Carpenter, 87, at Evergreen Park, Ill., on October 19. A righthanded pitcher, Carpenter broke into the majors late in the 1940 season and went 2-0 that September for the Giants. He won 11 games for the New York club in both 1941 and 1942 but pitched only briefly in the majors thereafter.

Chico Carrasquel, 79, at Caracas, Venezuela, on May 26. The first standout player from Venezuela in the big leagues, shortstop Carrasquel was the All-Star Game starter for the American League in 1951, 1953 and 1954 while a member of the White Sox. Carrasquel batted .282 for the Sox in 1950, his first season in the majors, and spent six years with the club before being traded to Cleveland and later to the Kansas City A's and Baltimore. He hit .258 in 10 big-league seasons.

Tom Cheek, 66, at Oldsmar, Fla., on October 9. Cheek broadcast every Blue Jays game from the team's inception in 1977 to June 2004.

Donn Clendenon, 70, at Sioux Falls, S.D., on September 17. First baseman Clendenon batted .274 with 159 home runs over a 12-year major league career. His best overall season was 1966, when he hit .299 for the Pirates with 28 homers and 98 RBIs. Selected by the Expos in the expansion draft after the 1968 season, Clendenon was traded to the Mets in June 1969 and helped New York win the World Series that fall. He was named Series MVP in '69, contributing three homers and a .357 average in the Mets' upset of the Orioles.

Nick Colosi, 77, at New York on February 25. Colosi was a National League umpire from late in the 1968 season through 1982.

Sandy Consuegra, 85, at Miami on November 16. Consuegra led the A.L. in winning percentage (.842) in 1954, going 16-3 for the White Sox. In four consecutive big-league seasons beginning in 1952 (a year in which he was 6-0 for Washington), the righthander posted ERAs of 3.05, 2.86, 2.69 and 2.64. In his eight-season career in the majors, Consuegra was 51-32 with a 3.37 ERA. He also pitched for the Orioles and Giants.

Ray Cunningham, 100, at Pearland, Texas, on July 30. Infielder Cunningham appeared in a total of 14 games for the Cardinals in 1931 and 1932.

Harry Dalton, 77, at Carefree, Ariz., on October 23. An executive with the Orioles, Angels and Brewers, Dalton helped put together Baltimore teams that won four pennants and two World Series (1966, 1970) and the Milwaukee club that captured the 1982 A.L. championship.

Brandy Davis, 76, at Newark, Del., on June 12. Davis, an outfielder, played a total of 67 games for the Pirates in 1952 and 1953. He batted .187.

Dick Dietz, 63, at Clayton, Ga., on June 28. Catcher Dietz hit 22 home runs and drove in 107 runs for the 1970 Giants. After a 19-homer, 72-RBI season for San Francisco in 1971, he wound up his eight-year career in the majors as a reserve with the Dodgers in 1972 and as a part-time player with the Braves in 1973.

Mario Encarnacion, 30, at Danshuei, Taiwan, on October 3. Outfielder Encarnacion appeared in 20 games for the 2001 Rockies and in three games for the 2002 Cubs.

Tommy Fine, 90, at Little Elm, Texas, on January 10. Righthander Fine was 1-2 for the 1947 Red Sox and 0-1 for the 1950 St. Louis Browns.

Danny Gardella, 85, at Yonkers, N.Y., on March 6. Outfielder Gardella hit 18 home runs for the New York Giants in 1945, his second season in the majors, before jumping to the Mexican League in 1946, a move for which he and 17 other major leaguers received a five-year ban from Organized Baseball. The ban was lifted in June 1949, but Gardella appeared in only one big-league game after the '45 season—as a pinch hitter for the Cardinals in 1950.

Pete Gebrian, at Stuart, Fla., on May 6. Righthander Gebrian pitched in 27 games for the 1947 White Sox and was 2-3 with a 4.48 ERA.

Al Gettel, 88, at Norfolk, Va., on April 8. Gettel, a righthander, was 38-45 in a seven-year major league career. He went 9-8 for the Yankees in his rookie season of 1945 and won a career-best 11 games for the Indians in 1947. He also pitched for the White Sox, Senators, Giants and Cardinals. In 1954, he pitched all 21 innings for Oakland in a Pacifc Coast League game, not allowing a run after the first inning and emerging with a 5-1 victory.

Milt Graff, 74, at Bryan, Texas, on August 2. Second baseman Graff appeared in a total of 61 games for the Kansas City A's in 1957 and 1958.

Hal Griggs, 76, at Tucson, Ariz., on May 10. Griggs, a righthander, posted a 6-26 record from 1956 through 1959 for Washington teams that finished last three times and next-to-last the other season. In a 1957 game against the Red Sox, Griggs got Ted Williams to ground out, ending Williams' streak of reaching base 16 consecutive times (a major league record).

Marv Grissom, 87, at Red Bluff, Calif., on September 19. Grissom was the bullpen ace for the 1954 World Series champion New York Giants. In 56 games overall (53 relief appearances) that year, Grissom went 10-7 with a 2.35 ERA and saved 19 games. The righthander was the winning pitching in Game 1 of the 1954 World Series against Cleveland, entering the game immediately after Willie Mays' historic catch and working 2⅔ scoreless innings. In 1956, Grissom fashioned a 1.56 ERA in 43 games for the Giants. He also pitched for the Tigers, White Sox, Red Sox and Cardinals in his 10-year major league career, during which he compiled a 47-45 record.

Harley Grossman, 75, at Evansville, Ind., on July 13. Righthander Grossman's major league career consisted of one relief appearance for the 1952 Senators.

Cesar Gutierrez, 61, at Maracaibo, Venezuela, on January 22. Shortstop Gutierrez played in only 223 games over four seasons in the majors and batted just .235, but on June 21, 1970, he became the first player in modern big-league history to go 7-for-7 in a game. Playing for the Tigers in the nightcap of a double-header at Cleveland, Gutierrez collected six singles and a double in a 12-inning Detroit triumph.

Kent Hadley, 70, at Pocatello, Idaho, on March 10. The Yankees acquired first baseman Hadley from Kansas City in the December 11, 1959, trade in which the Yanks also obtained Roger Maris from the Athletics. Hadley played sparingly for New York in 1960 after batting .253 with 10 home runs in 288 at-bats for the '59 A's.

Elrod Hendricks, 64, at Glen Burnie, Md., on December 21. Catcher Hendricks was a key player on Orioles teams that won three consecutive A.L. pennants (1969, 1970, 1971) and one World Series title ('70). He spent most of his 12-year major league playing career with Baltimore and, starting in 1978, was the club's bullpen coach for 28 seasons. A .220 hitter in 711 big-league games, Hendricks batted .364 with a home run and four RBIs in the '70 Series against Cincinnati.

Francisco "Pancho" Herrera, 70, at Miami on April 28. Herrera was the Phillies' No. 1 first baseman in 1960 and 1961. In '60, he batted .281 with 17 homers and 71 RBIs.

Eli Hodkey, 87, at Lorain, Ohio, on August 30. The lefthander pitched in two games for the 1946 Phillies.

Cal Hogue, 77, at Kettering, Ohio, on August 5. Righthander Hogue compiled a 2-10 record while pitching for the Pirates in 1952, 1953 and 1954.

Frank House, 75, at Birmingham, Ala., on March 13. One of baseball's early bonus signees, catcher House wound up playing 653 games over 10 big-league seasons. Signed by the Tigers in 1948, he broke into the majors in 1950 and had his best season in 1955 (.259 average for Detroit, with 15 homers and 53 RBIs in 328 at-bats). He also played for the Kansas City A's and Cincinnati.

Bennie Huffman, 90, at Richmond, Va., on February 22. Huffman was a reserve catcher for the 1937 St. Louis Browns, hitting .273 in 76 games.

Vic Johnson, 85, at Eau Claire, Wis., on May 10. Lefthander Johnson pitched in 26 of his 42 major league games in 1945, going 6-4 that season for the Red Sox. One of his victories was a shutout of the Yankees at Yankee Stadium.

Pat Kelly, 61, at Baltimore on October 2. Outfielder Kelly played for the Twins, Royals, White Sox, Orioles and Indians in a 15-year major league career. His best seasons were with the Sox, for whom he batted .280 as the club's everyday right fielder in 1973 and .281 as a designater hitter/outfielder in 1974. Kelly was an original member of the Royals, playing for the expansion team in 1969 and again in 1970. In 1979, he was a part-time player for the pennant-winning Orioles. Kelly hit .264 and stole 250 bases (40 for the '69 Royals) in 1,385 big-league games.

Bob Kennedy, 85, at Mesa, Ariz., on April 7. Outfielder/third baseman Kennedy batted .254 over 16 major league seasons, played for the Indians in the 1948 World Series and managed the Cubs (1963-65) and Oakland A's (1968, the Athletics' first season on the West Coast). In 1940, a year in which he turned 20 late in the season, he played all 154 games at third base for the White Sox, a team for which he had three stints as a player. Kennedy, who also played for the Orioles, Tigers and Brooklyn Dodgers, had his best season in 1950 when he hit .291 for Cleveland with nine home runs, 79 runs scored and 54 runs batted in. In 1963, he guided the Cubs to their first winning season (82-80) in 17 years; in '68, he managed the A's franchise to its first winning record (also 82-80) in 16 seasons.

Bill King, 78, at San Leandro, Calif., on October 18. Longtime radio play-by-play man for the Athletics, King for a time balanced play-by-play duties simultaneously with the A's, NFL Raiders and NBA Warriors.

Hal Lebovitz, 89, at Cleveland on October 18. A fixture on the Cleveland sports scene for more than six decades and former *Plain Dealer* columnist and sports editor, Lebovitz was inducted into the writers' wing of the Baseball Hall of Fame in 1999.

Don LeJohn, 70, at California, Pa., on February 25. LeJohn, a third baseman, batted .256 in 34 games for the Dodgers in 1965 and made one pinch-hitting appearance in the '65 World Series against Minnesota.

Bob Lennon, 76, at Dix Hills, N.Y., on June 14. Lennon hit 64 home runs for the New York Giants' Class AA Nashville affiliate in 1954, but the outfielder homered only once in the majors (in 79 at-bats), connecting for the Cubs in a game in 1957.

Al Lopez, 97, at Tampa on October 30. From 1949 through 1964, only two teams other than the Yankees won A.L. pennants—the 1954 Indians and the 1959 White Sox, both of whom were managed by Lopez. In his 15 full seasons as a big-league manager (he managed parts of two other years), Lopez's teams won 90 or more games 10 times and never finished worse than eight games above .500. The Hall of Famer's '54 Cleveland club set an A.L. record (since broken) with 111 victories. As a player, he was the longtime record holder for career games played by a catcher.

Bob Mabe, 75, at Danville, Va., on January 9. Mabe, who lost the vision in one eye in a boyhood accident, pitched for the Cardinals in 1958, the Reds in 1959 and briefly for the Orioles in 1960. The righthander compiled a 7-11 record in 51 big-league games.

Rick Mahler, 51, at Jupiter, Fla., on March 2. Righthander Mahler won 17 games for the Braves in 1985 and was 96-111 over 13 big-league seasons. He also was a double-figure winner for Atlanta in 1984 and 1986. In 1990, he was 7-6 for the World Series champion Reds.

Mal Mallette, 83, at Durham, N.C., on November 25. Mallette, a lefthander, pitched in two games for Brooklyn in 1950.

Gene Mauch, 79, at Rancho Mirage, Calif., on August 8. Mauch managed four teams in the majors—the Phillies, Expos, Twins and Angels—and was considered one of the game's great minds. He managed two division champions—the 1982 and 1986 Angels, teams that blew sizable leads in the American League Championship Series—and was the first manager of the expansion Montreal franchise in 1969. In 1964, Mauch's Phils had a 6½-game lead in the National League pennant race with 12 games to play, but then lost 10 straight and finished tied for second, one game behind St. Louis. In addition to his 26 years as a big-league manager, Mauch was a reserve infielder over nine seasons for the Dodgers, Pirates, Cubs, Braves, Cardinals and Red Sox.

Bobby Mavis, 86, at Little Rock, Ark., on March 1. Mavis appeared in one major league game—as a pinch runner for the Tigers in 1949.

John McMullen, 87, at Montclair, N.J., on September 16. McMullen owned the Astros franchise from 1979 to 1992 and also was longtime owner of the NHL's New Jersey Devils.

Eddie Miksis, 78, at Huntingdon Valley, Pa., on April 8. Handyman Miksis played more than 100 games at four spots—second base, the outfield, third base and shortstop—during a 14-year major league career in which he played mostly for the Dodgers and Cubs but also for the Cardinals, Orioles and Reds. His most extensive duty came in 1953 when he played in 142 games and had 577 at-bats for the Cubs. A .251 hitter in '53, he had a career .236 batting mark. In 1947, Miksis scored the winning run in one of the most storied games in World Series history, crossing the plate for Brooklyn in the ninth inning of Game 4 on Cookie Lavagetto's two-run, two-out double that ruined a no-hit bid by the Yankees' Bill Bevens.

Al Milnar, 91, at Cleveland on June 30. Lefthander Milnar was an 18-game winner for the 1940 Indians and was 57-58 overall in eight major league seasons with Cleveland, the St. Louis Browns and the Phillies.

Herb Moford, 77, at Cincinnati on December 3. The righthander saw his most use in the majors in 1958, appearing in 25 games for the Tigers and compiling a 4-9 record. He also pitched for the Cardinals, Red Sox and Mets in his four seasons in the big leagues. Working in relief, Moford appeared in the first game in Mets history in 1962.

Ron Mrozinski, 75, at Washington, N.J., on October 19. Lefthander Mrozinski pitched in 37 games overall for the 1954 and 1955 Phillies, compiling a 1-3 record.

Mickey Owen, 89, at Mount Vernon, Mo., on July 13. Owen was a major league catcher for 13 seasons with the Cardinals, Dodgers, Cubs and Red Sox and was a member of the starting lineup for the N.L. in the 1941 All-Star Game. Playing for Brooklyn in the '41 World Series, he let strike three get past him with two out in the ninth inning of Game 4—a misplay that ignited a come-from-behind, four-run outburst by the Yankees just when it appeared the Series would be deadlocked at two victories apiece. After that stunning triumph, the Yanks won the Series the next day. In 1946, Owen was banned from Organized Baseball after jumping to the Mexican League, but he was reinstated in 1949. In 1,209 big-league games, he batted .255.

Jim Pearce, 80, at Raleigh, N.C., on July 17. Righthander Pearce appeared in 30 major league games—20 of them for the 1950

Senators. Mainly a reliever, he also pitched for Washngton in 1949 and 1953 and for Cincinnati in 1954 and 1955. His overall record: 3-4.

Vic Power, 74, at Bayamon, Puerto Rico, on November 29. Beginning in 1958, the flashy Power won seven consecutive A.L. Gold Gloves at first base. A solid hitter—he topped the .300 mark three times in a four-year stretch, with a high of .319—Power batted .284 over 12 seasons while playing for the Philadelphia and Kansas City A's, Indians, Twins, Angels and Phillies. A heads-up baserunner, the Puerto Rican standout stole home twice for Cleveland in a 1958 game against Detroit—the second theft proving decisive in the 10th inning. He played in five All-Star Games.

Dick Radatz, 67, at Easton, Mass., on March 16. The 6-6, 230-pound Radatz, one of the game's most intimidating pitchers, was a standout reliever for the Red Sox in his first three big-league seasons, saving 78 games and compiling a 40-21 record. In his second year, 1963, Radatz was 15-6 with a 1.97 ERA and struck out 162 batters in 132⅓ innings. Over seven seasons in the majors—the hard-throwing righthander also pitched for the Indians, Cubs, Tigers and Expos—he was 52-43 with a 3.13 ERA.

Ted "Double Duty" Radcliffe, 103, at Chicago on August 11. Negro leagues standout Radcliffe was given his nickname by writer Damon Runyon, who was inspired by Radcliffe's dual skills as a catcher and a pitcher.

Don Rowe, 69, at Newport Beach, Calif., on October 15. Lefthander Rowe pitched in 26 games for the 1963 Mets and later was a pitching coach for the White Sox and Brewers.

Marius Russo, 90, at Fort Myers, Fla., on March 26. Russo posted an 8-3 record for the Yankees in his rookie season of 1939 and was a 14-game winner for New York in 1940 and 1941. The lefthander was 2-0 in World Series competition, stopping the Dodgers on a four-hitter in Game 3 of the '41 Series and beating the Cardinals with a seven-hitter in Game 4 in '43.

Luis Sanchez, 51, at La Guaira, Venezuela, on February 4. Sanchez made 150 relief appearances for the Angels from 1982 through 1984 and compiled a 28-21 record and 3.75 ERA in five seasons with the A.L. club.

Jack Sanford, 87, at Greensboro, N.C., on January 4. First baseman Sanford played in a total of 47 games for the Senators in 1940, 1941 and 1946.

Carroll Sembera, 63, at Shiner, Texas, on June 14. The righthanded reliever was 3-11 with a 4.69 ERA over five big-league seasons, pitching for the Astros (1965-67) and the Expos (1969-70).

Dick Sipek, 82, at Quincy, Ill., on July 17. Outfielder Sipek overcame deafness to reach the major leagues, appearing in 82 games for the 1945 Reds. He batted .244 in 156 at-bats.

Frank Smith, 77, at Malone, Fla., on September 24. Reliever Smith, a righthander, pitched in 50 or more games for the Reds for four consecutive seasons in the early 1950s. He saved 20 games in 1954, a year in which he finished 5-8 with a 2.67 ERA.

Lee Stine, 91, at Hemet, Calif., on May 6. Righthander Stine posted only three major league victories, but one of them was a complete-game 1-0 triumph over the Giants and Carl Hubbell in 1936. Stine finished 3-8 for Cincinnati that year and pitched briefly for the White Sox in 1934 and 1935 and for the Yankees in 1938.

Chuck Thompson, 83, at Towson, Md., on March 6. Thompson, voted into the broadcasters wing of the Baseball Hall of Fame in 1993, called Orioles games for more than 30 seasons. He also did network television work in baseball and football, calling the NFL's landmark 1958 Colts-Giants overtime title game.

Mike Ulisney, 87, at New Smyrna Beach, Fla., on September 22. In an 11-game stint in the majors, catcher Ulisney went 7-for-18 (.389) at the plate for the 1945 Braves. Among his hits was a home run.

Corky Valentine, 76, at Canton, Ga., on January 21. Righthander Valentine went 12-11 for the Reds in 1954, tossing three shutouts. He was 2-1 for Cincinnati in 1955 and then bowed out of the majors.

Bill Voiselle, 86, at Greenwood, S.C., on January 31. Voiselle was the Sporting News' N.L. Pitcher of the Year in 1944 when he compiled a 21-16 record for the New York Giants. He notched 14 victories for the Giants in 1945 and was a 13-game winner for the 1948 N.L. champion Boston Braves. The righthander started and lost decisive Game 6 of the '48 Series against Cleveland, allowing three runs and seven hits in seven innings. Honoring his hometown of Ninety Six, S.C., Voiselle wore uniform No. 96 after joining the Braves.

Ken Weafer, 91, at Guilderland, N.Y., on June 4. Righthander Weafer pitched in one game for the 1936 Boston Bees (nee Braves).

Al Widmar, 80, at Tulsa, Okla., on October 15. Widmar was pitching coach for the Blue Jays for 10 years beginning in 1980. Previously, he had been a coach for the Phillies and Brewers. A pitcher for the Red Sox, Browns and White Sox, the righthander was 13-30 in his five-season major league career (1947-48 and 1950-52).

Charlie Williams, 61, at Oak Lawn, Ill., on September 10. Williams became a National League umpire in 1978 and wound up his career in 2001. He worked two All-Star Games, two N.L. Championship Series and the 1993 World Series.

Earl Wilson, 70, at Detroit on April 23. Wilson was the first black pitcher in American League history to throw a no-hitter, won 121 games over 11 years in the majors and swung a powerful bat. The righthander, pitching for the Red Sox in his first full big-league season, held the Angels hitless on June 26, 1962. He won 22 games for the Tigers in 1967 and was 13-12 with a career-low 2.85 ERA for Detroit's 1968 World Series championship team. Although batting only .195 in 740 career at-bats, Wilson hit 35 home runs—33 as a pitcher, which ranks fifth on the majors' all-time list.

Frank Zupo, 65, at Burlingame, Calif., on March 25. Signed to a bonus contract by Baltimore in 1957, catcher Zupo wound up with only 18 at-bats for the Orioles over three seasons and was just 21 years old when he played his last big-league game.

2005 American League Statistics

Batting

Designated hitting

Pinch-hitting

Pitching

Fielding

Miscellaneous

BATTING

TEAM

Team	G	TPA	AB	R	H	TB	2B	3B	HR	RBI	SH	SF	HP	BB	IBB	SO	SB	CS	GDP	LOB	ShO	Avg.	OBP	Slg.
Boston	162	6403	5626	910	1579	2557	339	21	199	863	14	63	47	653	34	1044	45	12	135	1249	5	.281	.357	.454
New York	162	6406	5624	886	1552	2530	259	16	229	847	28	43	73	637	41	989	84	27	125	1264	2	.276	.355	.450
Tampa Bay	162	6120	5552	750	1519	2359	289	40	157	717	34	51	69	412	25	990	151	49	133	1065	5	.274	.329	.425
Detroit	162	6136	5602	723	1521	2398	283	45	168	678	44	52	53	384	24	1038	66	28	137	1077	10	.272	.321	.428
Cleveland	162	6255	5609	790	1522	2540	337	30	207	760	39	50	54	503	33	1093	62	36	128	1148	11	.271	.334	.453
Los Angeles	162	6186	5624	761	1520	2299	278	30	147	726	43	39	29	447	51	848	161	57	125	1086	6	.270	.325	.409
Baltimore	162	6134	5551	729	1492	2409	296	27	189	700	40	42	54	447	31	902	83	37	145	1103	5	.269	.327	.434
Texas	162	6301	5716	865	1528	2677	311	29	260	834	32	48	49	495	20	1112	67	15	123	1104	7	.267	.329	.468
Toronto	162	6233	5581	775	1480	2273	307	39	136	735	21	56	89	486	18	955	72	35	126	1118	14	.265	.331	.407
Kansas City	162	6086	5503	701	1445	2180	289	34	126	653	46	50	63	424	23	1008	53	33	139	1062	10	.263	.320	.396
Oakland	162	6275	5627	772	1476	2291	310	20	155	739	19	40	52	537	22	819	31	22	148	1170	12	.262	.330	.407
Chicago	162	6146	5529	741	1450	2349	253	23	200	713	53	49	79	435	27	1002	137	67	122	1098	7	.262	.322	.425
Minnesota	162	6192	5564	688	1441	2176	269	32	134	644	42	42	59	485	49	978	102	44	155	1109	10	.259	.323	.391
Seattle	162	6095	5507	699	1408	2155	289	34	130	657	37	37	48	466	50	986	102	47	115	1076	5	.256	.317	.391
Totals	1134	86968	78215	10790	20933	33193	4109	420	2437	10266	469	646	817	6811	448	13764	1216	509	1856	15663	109	.268	.330	.424

INDIVIDUAL

TOP QUALIFIERS FOR BATTING CHAMPIONSHIP

Minimum 502 plate appearances. *Lefthanded batter. †Switch-hitter.

Player, Team	G	TPA	AB	R	H	TB	2B	3B	HR	RBI	SH	SF	HP	BB	IBB	SO	SB	CS	GDP	Avg.	OBP	Slg.
Young, Michael, Tex.	159	732	668	114	221	343	40	5	24	91	0	3	3	58	0	91	5	2	20	.331	.385	.513
Rodriguez, Alex, N.Y.	162	715	605	124	194	369	29	1	48	130	0	3	16	91	8	139	21	6	8	.321	.421	.610
Guerrero, Vladimir, L.A.	141	594	520	95	165	294	29	2	32	108	0	5	8	61	26	48	13	1	16	.317	.394	.565
Damon, Johnny, Bos.*	148	688	624	117	197	274	35	6	10	75	0	9	2	53	3	69	18	1	5	.316	.366	.439
Roberts, Brian, Bal.†	143	640	561	92	176	289	45	7	18	73	5	4	3	67	5	83	27	10	6	.314	.387	.515
Jeter, Derek, N.Y.	159	752	654	122	202	294	25	5	19	70	7	3	11	77	3	117	14	5	15	.309	.389	.450
Martinez, Victor, Cle.†	147	622	547	73	167	260	33	0	20	80	0	7	5	63	9	78	0	1	16	.305	.378	.475
Matsui, Hideki, N.Y.*	162	704	629	108	192	312	45	3	23	116	0	8	3	63	7	78	2	2	16	.305	.367	.496
Hafner, Travis, Cle.*	137	578	486	94	148	289	42	0	33	108	0	4	9	79	7	123	0	0	9	.305	.408	.595
Tejada, Miguel, Bal.	162	704	654	89	199	337	50	5	26	98	0	3	7	40	9	83	5	1	26	.304	.349	.515
Suzuki, Ichiro, Sea.*	162	739	679	111	206	296	21	12	15	68	2	6	4	48	23	66	33	8	5	.303	.350	.436
Teixeira, Mark, Tex.†	162	730	644	112	194	370	41	3	43	144	0	3	11	72	5	124	4	0	18	.301	.379	.575
Crawford, Carl, TB.*	156	687	644	101	194	302	33	15	15	81	5	6	5	27	1	84	46	8	11	.301	.331	.469
Sweeney, Mike, K.C.	122	514	470	63	141	243	39	0	21	83	1	6	4	33	7	61	3	0	16	.300	.347	.517
Crisp, Coco, Cle.†	145	656	594	86	178	276	42	4	16	69	13	5	0	44	1	81	15	6	7	.300	.345	.465

DEPARTMENTAL LEADERS: G_Ibanez, Sea., Matsui, N.Y., A. Rodriguez, N.Y., Suzuki, Sea., Teixeira, Tex., Tejada, Bal., 162; AB_Suzuki, Sea., 679; R_A. Rodriguez, N.Y., 124; H_M. Young, Tex., 221; TB_Teixeira, Tex., 370; 1B_Suzuki, Sea., 158; 2B_Tejada, Bal., 50; 3B_Crawford, TB., 15; HR_A. Rodriguez, N.Y., 48; RBI_Ortiz, Bos., 148; SH_Crisp, Cle., 13; SF_Monroe, Det., 12; HP_Hillenbrand, Tor., 22; BB_Giambi, N.Y., 108; IBB_Guerrero, L.A., 26; SO_Sexson, Sea., 167; SB_Figgins, L.A., 62; CS_Podsednik, Chi., 23; GDP_Kendall, Oak., Tejada, Bal., 26; Slg._A. Rodriguez, N.Y., .610; OBP_Giambi, N.Y., .440.

ALL PLAYERS

*Lefthanded batter. †Switch-hitter.

Player, Team	G	TPA	AB	R	H	TB	2B	3B	HR	RBI	SH	SF	HP	BB	IBB	SO	SB	CS	GDP	Avg.	OBP	Slg.
Abernathy, Brent, Min.	24	79	67	5	16	20	1	0	1	6	3	1	1	7	0	9	2	0	2	.239	.316	.299
Adams, Russ, Tor.*	139	545	481	68	123	184	27	5	8	63	3	8	3	50	1	57	11	2	5	.256	.325	.383
Allen, Chad, Tex.	21	56	53	5	15	18	1	1	0	5	1	0	0	2	0	13	0	1	2	.283	.309	.340
Alomar Jr., Sandy, Tex.	46	137	128	11	35	42	7	0	0	14	3	0	1	5	0	12	0	0	3	.273	.306	.328
Ambres, Chip, K.C.	53	167	145	25	35	55	8	0	4	9	3	1	2	16	1	32	3	2	5	.241	.323	.379
Anderson, Brian N., Chi.	13	35	34	3	6	13	1	0	2	3	1	0	0	0	0	12	1	0	2	.176	.176	.382
Anderson, Garret, L.A.*	142	603	575	68	163	250	34	1	17	96	0	5	0	23	8	84	1	1	13	.283	.308	.435
Arroyo, Bronson, Bos.	35	1	1	0	0	0	0	0	0	0	0	0	0	0	0	1	0	0	0	.000	.000	.000
Astacio, Pedro, Tex.	12	1	1	0	0	0	0	0	0	0	0	0	0	0	0	0	0	0	0	.000	.000	.000
Baldwin, James, Bal.-Tex.	28	1	1	0	0	0	0	0	0	0	0	0	0	0	0	0	0	0	0	.000	.000	.000
Barajas, Rod, Tex.	120	450	410	53	104	191	24	0	21	60	4	3	6	26	0	70	0	0	6	.254	.306	.466
Bard, Josh, Cle.†	34	95	83	6	16	23	4	0	1	9	1	2	0	9	0	11	0	0	2	.193	.266	.277
Bartlett, Jason, Min.	74	252	224	33	54	75	10	1	3	16	2	1	4	21	0	37	4	6	4	.241	.316	.335
Bellhorn, Mark, Bos.-N.Y.†	94	355	300	43	63	107	20	0	8	30	0	3	0	52	1	112	3	0	4	.210	.324	.357
Belliard, Ronnie, Cle.	145	587	536	71	152	241	36	1	17	78	8	7	1	35	0	72	2	2	17	.284	.325	.450
Beltre, Adrian, Sea.	156	650	603	69	154	249	36	1	19	87	0	4	5	38	6	108	3	1	15	.255	.303	.413
Benoit, Joaquin, Tex.	33	1	1	0	0	0	0	0	0	0	0	0	0	0	0	0	0	0	0	.000	.000	.000
Berroa, Angel, K.C.	159	652	608	68	164	228	21	5	11	55	10	2	14	18	3	108	7	5	13	.270	.305	.375
Betancourt, Yuniesky, Sea.	60	228	211	24	54	78	11	5	1	15	2	2	2	11	0	24	1	3	2	.256	.296	.370
Bigbie, Larry, Bal.*	67	234	206	22	51	77	9	1	5	21	5	2	0	21	1	49	3	3	2	.248	.314	.374
Blake, Casey, Cle.	147	583	523	72	126	229	32	1	23	58	2	5	10	43	3	116	4	5	9	.241	.308	.438
Blalock, Hank, Tex.*	161	705	647	80	170	279	34	0	25	92	0	4	3	51	1	132	1	0	16	.263	.318	.431
Blanco, Andres, K.C.†	26	86	79	6	17	19	0	1	0	5	4	2	1	0	0	5	0	1	3	.215	.220	.241
Blanton, Joe, Oak.	33	4	3	0	1	1	0	0	0	0	1	0	0	0	0	0	0	0	0	.333	.333	.333
Bloomquist, Willie, Sea.	82	267	249	27	64	83	5	2	0	22	4	2	1	11	0	38	14	1	5	.257	.289	.333
Blum, Geoff, Chi.†	31	99	95	6	19	26	2	1	1	3	0	0	4	1	0	15	0	1	1	.200	.232	.274
Bocachica, Hiram, Oak.	9	19	19	2	2	2	0	0	0	0	0	0	0	0	0	7	0	0	0	.105	.105	.105
Bonderman, Jeremy, Det.	29	6	6	0	0	0	0	0	0	0	0	0	0	0	0	3	0	0	0	.000	.000	.000

Player, Team	G	TPA	AB	R	H	TB	2B	3B	HR	RBI	SH	SF	HP	BB	IBB	SO	SB	CS	GDP	Avg.	OBP	Slg.
Boone, Aaron, Cle.	143	565	511	61	124	193	19	1	16	60	4	6	9	35	3	92	9	3	16	.243	.299	.378
Boone, Bret, Sea.-Min.	88	360	326	33	72	114	15	3	7	37	1	1	4	28	2	65	4	2	12	.221	.290	.350
Borchard, Joe, Chi.†	7	12	12	0	5	7	2	0	0	0	0	0	0	0	0	4	0	1	0	.417	.417	.583
Borders, Pat, Sea.	39	125	117	12	23	31	5	0	1	7	2	1	1	4	1	22	0	0	4	.197	.228	.265
Botts, Jason, Tex.†	10	30	27	4	8	8	0	0	0	3	0	0	0	3	0	13	0	0	1	.296	.367	.296
Broussard, Ben, Cle.*	142	505	466	59	119	216	30	5	19	68	0	3	4	32	5	98	2	2	4	.255	.307	.464
Brown, Emil, K.C.	150	609	545	75	156	248	31	5	17	86	1	7	8	48	1	108	10	1	14	.286	.349	.455
Brown, Kevin, N.Y.	13	2	2	0	1	2	1	0	0	0	0	0	0	0	0	1	0	0	0	.500	.500	1.000
Bubela, Jaime, Sea.*	11	20	19	3	2	2	0	0	0	0	0	0	0	1	0	4	1	0	1	.105	.150	.105
Buck, John, K.C.	118	430	401	40	97	156	21	1	12	47	1	2	3	23	2	94	2	2	9	.242	.287	.389
Buehrle, Mark, Chi.*	33	3	3	0	0	0	0	0	0	0	0	0	0	0	0	1	0	0	0	.000	.000	.000
Burke, Jamie, Chi.	1	1	1	0	0	0	0	0	0	0	0	0	0	0	0	0	0	0	0	.000	.000	.000
Bynum, Freddie, Oak.*	7	7	7	0	2	3	1	0	0	1	0	0	0	0	0	3	0	0	0	.286	.286	.429
Byrd, Paul, L.A.	31	4	4	0	1	1	0	0	0	0	0	0	0	0	0	0	0	0	0	.250	.250	.250
Byrnes, Eric, Oak.-Bal.	111	396	359	47	83	141	22	3	10	35	3	1	8	25	0	60	5	2	6	.231	.295	.393
Cabrera, Daniel, Bal.	29	1	1	0	0	0	0	0	0	0	0	0	0	0	0	1	0	0	0	.000	.000	.000
Cabrera, Melky, N.Y.†	6	19	19	1	4	4	0	0	0	0	0	0	0	0	0	2	0	0	0	.211	.211	.211
Cabrera, Orlando, L.A.	141	587	540	70	139	197	28	3	8	57	4	2	3	38	4	50	21	4	10	.257	.309	.365
Calero, Kiko, Oak.	58	1	1	0	0	0	0	0	0	0	0	0	0	0	0	1	0	0	0	.000	.000	.000
Calzado, Napoleon, Bal.	4	5	5	0	1	1	0	0	0	0	0	0	0	0	0	1	0	0	0	.200	.200	.200
Cano, Robinson, N.Y.*	132	551	522	78	155	239	34	4	14	62	7	3	3	16	1	68	1	3	16	.297	.320	.458
Cantu, Jorge, TB.	150	631	598	73	171	297	40	1	28	117	0	7	6	19	1	83	1	0	24	.286	.311	.497
Carrasco, D.J., K.C.	21	8	7	0	0	0	0	0	0	0	0	0	0	0	0	1	0	0	0	.000	.000	.000
Casanova, Raul, Chi.†	6	5	5	0	1	1	0	0	0	0	0	0	0	0	0	1	0	0	0	.200	.200	.200
Cash, Kevin, TB.	13	33	31	4	5	12	1	0	2	2	0	0	1	1	0	13	0	0	3	.161	.212	.387
Castillo, Alberto, K.C.-Oak.	35	115	101	13	21	31	5	1	1	14	1	1	0	12	0	22	1	0	2	.208	.289	.307
Castro, Bernie, Bal.†	24	89	80	14	23	28	3	1	0	7	0	0	0	9	0	10	6	2	0	.288	.360	.350
Castro, Juan, Min.	97	292	272	27	70	105	18	1	5	33	9	2	0	9	1	39	0	1	8	.257	.279	.386
Catalanotto, Frank, Tor.*	130	475	419	56	126	189	29	5	8	59	4	5	10	37	0	53	0	2	9	.301	.367	.451
Chacin, Gustavo, Tor.*	34	8	7	1	0	0	0	0	0	0	1	0	0	0	0	2	0	0	0	.000	.000	.000
Chavez, Eric, Oak.*	160	694	625	92	168	291	40	1	27	101	0	9	2	58	4	129	6	0	9	.269	.329	.466
Chen, Bruce, Bal.*	34	4	3	0	1	1	0	0	0	0	0	0	0	1	0	0	0	0	0	.333	.500	.333
Choo, Shin-Soo, Sea.*	10	21	18	1	1	1	0	0	0	1	0	0	0	3	0	4	0	0	0	.056	.190	.056
Clark, Jermaine, Oak.*	4	1	0	2	0	0	0	0	0	0	0	0	0	1	0	0	0	0	0	.000	1.000	.000
Clement, Matt, Bos.	32	4	3	0	0	0	0	0	0	0	0	0	0	1	0	2	0	0	0	.000	.250	.000
Colon, Bartolo, L.A.	33	3	3	0	1	1	0	0	0	1	0	0	0	0	0	2	0	0	0	.333	.333	.333
Contreras, Jose, Chi.	32	4	3	0	0	0	0	0	0	0	0	0	0	1	0	2	0	0	0	.000	.250	.000
Cora, Alex, Cle.-Bos.*	96	273	250	25	58	83	8	4	3	24	4	3	5	11	0	30	7	2	6	.232	.275	.332
Cortez, Fernando, TB.*	8	14	13	0	1	1	0	0	0	1	0	0	0	1	0	3	0	0	0	.077	.143	.077
Costa, Shane, K.C.*	27	88	81	13	19	27	2	0	2	7	1	0	1	5	0	11	0	0	3	.235	.287	.333
Crawford, Carl, TB.*	156	687	644	101	194	302	33	15	15	81	5	6	5	27	1	84	46	8	11	.301	.331	.469
Crede, Joe, Chi.	132	471	432	54	109	196	21	0	22	62	2	4	8	25	3	66	1	1	7	.252	.303	.454
Crisp, Coco, Cle.†	145	656	594	86	178	276	42	4	16	69	13	5	0	44	1	81	15	6	7	.300	.345	.465
Crosby, Bobby, Oak.	84	371	333	66	92	152	25	4	9	38	1	1	1	35	0	54	0	0	10	.276	.346	.456
Crosby, Bubba, N.Y.*	76	103	98	15	27	32	0	1	1	6	1	0	0	4	0	14	4	1	1	.276	.304	.327
Cruz Jr., Jose, Bos.†	4	13	12	0	3	4	1	0	0	0	0	0	0	1	0	4	0	0	0	.250	.308	.333
Cuddyer, Michael, Min.	126	470	422	55	111	178	25	3	12	42	1	3	4	41	5	93	3	4	19	.263	.330	.422
Cummings, Midre, Bal.*	2	2	2	0	0	0	0	0	0	0	0	0	0	0	0	1	0	0	0	.000	.000	.000
Damon, Johnny, Bos.*	148	688	624	117	197	274	35	6	10	75	0	9	2	53	3	69	18	1	5	.316	.366	.439
DaVanon, Jeff, L.A.†	108	271	225	42	52	70	10	1	2	15	3	2	2	39	1	44	11	6	6	.231	.347	.311
Davis, Jason, Cle.	11	3	2	0	0	0	0	0	0	0	1	0	0	0	0	2	0	0	0	.000	.000	.000
DeJesus, David, K.C.*	122	523	461	69	135	205	31	6	9	56	5	6	9	42	1	76	5	5	6	.293	.359	.445
Dellucci, David, Tex.*	128	518	435	97	109	223	17	5	29	65	0	2	5	76	0	121	5	3	7	.251	.367	.513
DeRosa, Mark, Tex.	66	166	148	26	36	65	5	0	8	20	0	0	2	16	0	35	1	0	5	.243	.325	.439
Diaz, Matt, K.C.	34	97	89	7	25	36	4	2	1	9	1	1	2	4	0	15	0	1	3	.281	.323	.404
Dobbs, Greg, Sea.*	59	154	142	8	35	47	7	1	1	20	1	2	0	9	3	25	1	0	4	.246	.288	.331
Dominique, Andy, Tor.	2	3	3	0	0	0	0	0	0	0	0	0	0	0	0	0	0	0	0	.000	.333	.000
Donnelly, Brendan, L.A.	66	1	1	0	0	0	0	0	0	0	0	0	0	0	0	0	0	0	0	.000	.000	.000
Douglass, Sean, Det.	18	2	2	0	0	0	0	0	0	0	0	0	0	0	0	1	0	0	0	.000	.000	.000
Drese, Ryan, Tex.	12	1	1	0	0	0	0	0	0	0	0	0	0	0	0	1	0	0	0	.000	.000	.000
Dubois, Jason, Cle.	14	50	45	6	10	16	0	0	2	2	0	0	0	5	0	25	0	0	0	.222	.300	.356
Durazo, Erubiel, Oak.*	41	167	152	15	36	56	6	1	4	16	0	0	1	14	0	24	1	0	6	.237	.305	.368
Dye, Jermaine, Chi.	145	579	529	74	145	271	29	2	31	86	0	2	9	39	3	99	11	4	15	.274	.333	.512
Elarton, Scott, Cle.	31	2	2	0	0	0	0	0	0	0	0	0	0	0	0	0	0	0	0	.000	.000	.000
Ellis, Mark, Oak.	122	486	434	76	137	207	21	5	13	52	4	0	4	44	1	51	1	3	10	.316	.384	.477
Erstad, Darin, L.A.*	153	667	609	86	166	226	33	3	7	66	4	2	1	47	3	109	10	3	8	.273	.325	.371
Escalona, Felix, N.Y.	10	17	14	0	4	5	1	0	0	2	1	0	1	1	0	4	0	0	1	.286	.375	.357
Escobar, Kelvim, L.A.	16	2	1	0	0	0	0	0	0	0	1	0	0	0	0	0	0	0	0	.000	.000	.000
Everett, Carl, Chi.†	135	547	490	58	123	213	17	2	23	87	0	10	5	42	2	99	4	5	11	.251	.311	.435
Fasano, Sal, Bal.	64	174	160	25	40	76	3	0	11	20	0	0	5	9	0	41	0	0	5	.250	.310	.475
Figgins, Chone, L.A.†	158	720	642	113	186	255	25	10	8	57	9	5	0	64	1	101	62	17	9	.290	.352	.397
Finley, Steve, L.A.*	112	440	406	41	90	152	20	3	12	54	1	4	3	26	3	71	8	4	6	.222	.271	.374
Fiorentino, Jeff, Bal.*	13	47	44	7	11	16	2	0	1	5	0	1	0	2	0	10	1	0	0	.250	.277	.364
Flaherty, John, N.Y.	47	138	127	10	21	32	5	0	2	11	2	2	1	6	0	26	0	0	4	.165	.206	.252
Ford, Lew, Min.	147	590	522	70	138	197	30	4	7	53	2	5	16	45	2	85	13	6	9	.264	.338	.377
Fossum, Casey, TB.*	36	3	2	0	0	0	0	0	0	0	0	0	0	0	0	2	0	0	0	.000	.000	.000
Franklin, Ryan, Sea.	32	5	4	0	0	0	0	0	0	0	1	0	0	0	0	0	0	0	0	.000	.200	.000
Freire, Alejandro, Bal.	25	72	65	7	16	22	3	0	1	6	0	0	1	6	0	17	0	0	4	.246	.319	.338
Garcia, Freddy, Chi.	33	9	7	0	0	0	0	0	0	0	2	0	0	0	0	1	0	0	0	.000	.000	.000
Garko, Ryan, Cle.	1	1	1	0	0	0	0	0	0	0	0	0	0	0	0	0	0	0	0	.000	.000	.000
Garland, Jon, Chi.	32	2	2	0	1	1	0	0	0	0	0	0	0	0	0	0	0	0	0	.500	.500	.500
Gathright, Joey, TB.*	76	218	203	29	56	69	7	3	0	13	3	0	2	10	0	39	20	5	5	.276	.316	.340

Player, Team	G	TPA	AB	R	H	TB	2B	3B	HR	RBI	SH	SF	HP	BB	IBB	SO	SB	CS	GDP	Avg.	OBP	Slg.
German, Esteban, Tex.	5	4	4	3	3	4	1	0	0	1	0	0	0	0	0	1	2	0	0	.750	.750	1.000
Gerut, Jody, Cle.*	44	157	138	12	38	52	9	1	1	12	0	1	0	18	1	14	1	1	3	.275	.357	.377
Giambi, Jason, N.Y.*	139	545	417	74	113	223	14	0	32	87	0	1	19	108	5	109	0	0	7	.271	.440	.535
Giarratano, Tony, Det.†	15	47	42	4	6	9	0	0	1	4	0	0	0	5	0	7	1	0	1	.143	.234	.214
Gibbons, Jay, Bal.*	139	518	488	72	135	252	33	3	26	79	0	1	1	28	3	56	0	0	15	.277	.317	.516
Gil, Geronimo, Bal.	64	134	125	7	24	39	3	0	4	17	2	2	0	5	0	23	0	0	10	.192	.220	.312
Ginter, Keith, Oak.	51	156	137	12	22	36	5	0	3	25	2	3	1	13	0	25	0	0	5	.161	.234	.263
Gload, Ross, Chi.*	28	44	42	2	7	9	2	0	0	5	0	0	0	2	0	9	0	0	1	.167	.205	.214
Glynn, Ryan, Oak.	5	1	1	0	0	0	0	0	0	0	0	0	0	0	0	1	0	0	0	.000	.000	.000
Gomes, Jonny, TB.	101	407	348	61	98	186	13	6	21	54	1	5	14	39	1	113	9	5	6	.282	.372	.534
Gomez, Alexis, Det.*	9	18	16	2	3	3	0	0	0	1	0	0	0	2	0	2	0	0	0	.188	.278	.188
Gomez, Chris, Bal.	89	254	219	27	61	75	11	0	1	18	6	1	1	27	1	17	2	1	14	.279	.359	.342
Gonzalez, Adrian, Tex.*	43	162	150	17	34	61	7	1	6	17	0	2	0	10	2	37	0	0	3	.227	.272	.407
Gonzalez, Alex S., TB.	109	383	349	47	94	143	20	1	9	38	2	3	3	26	1	74	2	1	13	.269	.323	.410
Gonzalez, Juan, Cle.	1	1	1	0	0	0	0	0	0	0	0	0	0	0	0	0	0	0	0	.000	.000	.000
Gonzalez, Wiki, Sea.	14	47	45	7	12	17	5	0	0	2	0	0	0	2	0	3	0	0	1	.267	.298	.378
Gotay, Ruben, K.C.†	86	317	282	32	64	97	14	2	5	29	4	5	4	22	0	51	2	2	3	.227	.288	.344
Graffanino, Tony, K.C.-Bos.	110	417	379	68	117	161	17	3	7	38	2	1	4	31	2	51	7	2	14	.309	.366	.425
Granderson, Curtis, Det.*	47	174	162	18	44	80	6	3	8	20	2	0	0	10	0	43	1	1	2	.272	.314	.494
Green, Nick, TB.	111	375	318	53	76	110	15	2	5	29	10	3	11	33	0	86	3	1	5	.239	.329	.346
Greinke, Zack, K.C.	33	2	2	1	1	4	0	0	1	1	0	0	0	0	0	0	0	0	0	.500	.500	2.000
Griffin, John-Ford, Tor.*	7	13	13	3	4	9	2	0	1	6	0	0	0	0	0	4	0	0	0	.308	.308	.692
Gross, Gabe, Tor.*	40	102	92	11	23	32	4	1	1	7	0	0	0	10	0	21	1	1	0	.250	.324	.348
Guerrero, Vladimir, L.A.	141	594	520	95	165	294	29	2	32	108	0	5	8	61	26	48	13	1	16	.317	.394	.565
Guerrier, Matt, Min.	43	1	1	0	0	0	0	0	0	0	0	0	0	0	0	0	0	0	0	.000	.000	.000
Guiel, Aaron, K.C.*	33	121	109	18	32	49	5	0	4	7	0	1	5	6	1	21	1	0	3	.294	.355	.450
Guillen, Carlos, Det.*	87	361	334	48	107	145	15	4	5	23	0	1	2	24	3	45	2	3	9	.320	.368	.434
Gutierrez, Franklin, Cle.	7	2	1	2	0	0	0	0	0	0	0	0	0	1	0	0	0	0	0	.000	.500	.000
Hafner, Travis, Cle.*	137	578	486	94	148	289	42	0	33	108	0	4	9	79	7	123	0	0	9	.305	.408	.595
Hall, Toby, TB.	135	463	432	28	124	159	20	0	5	48	3	7	5	16	1	39	0	0	15	.287	.315	.368
Halladay, Roy, Tor.	19	2	2	0	0	0	0	0	0	0	0	0	0	0	0	1	0	0	0	.000	.000	.000
Hansen, Dave, Sea.*	60	88	75	5	13	19	0	0	2	11	2	2	0	9	1	19	1	0	1	.173	.256	.253
Haren, Danny, Oak.	34	5	5	0	2	3	1	0	0	2	0	0	0	0	0	4	0	0	0	.400	.400	.600
Harper, Travis, TB.*	52	1	1	0	0	0	0	0	0	0	0	0	0	0	0	1	0	0	0	.000	.000	.000
Harris, Willie, Chi.*	56	139	121	17	31	38	2	1	1	8	4	0	1	13	0	25	10	3	1	.256	.333	.314
Harvey, Ken, K.C.	12	48	45	4	10	16	3	0	1	5	0	0	0	3	0	13	0	0	0	.222	.271	.356
Hatteberg, Scott, Oak.*	134	523	464	52	119	159	19	0	7	59	2	2	4	51	4	54	0	1	22	.256	.334	.343
Heintz, Chris, Min.	8	26	25	1	5	8	3	0	0	2	0	0	0	1	0	6	0	0	1	.200	.231	.320
Hendrickson, Mark, TB.*	31	7	7	1	1	1	0	0	0	0	0	0	0	0	0	3	0	0	0	.143	.143	.143
Hernandez, Jose, Cle.	84	256	234	28	54	79	7	0	6	31	3	3	2	14	0	60	1	3	11	.231	.277	.338
Hernandez, Orlando, Chi.	24	3	3	0	1	1	0	0	0	0	0	0	0	0	0	1	0	0	0	.333	.333	.333
Hernandez, Runelvys, K.C.	29	5	5	0	0	0	0	0	0	0	0	0	0	0	0	1	0	0	0	.000	.000	.000
Hidalgo, Richard, Tex.	88	339	308	43	68	128	12	0	16	43	0	1	4	26	1	74	1	2	8	.221	.289	.416
Higginson, Bobby, Det.*	10	27	26	1	2	2	0	0	0	1	0	0	0	1	0	5	0	0	0	.077	.111	.077
Hill, Aaron, Tor.	105	407	361	49	99	139	25	3	3	40	3	4	5	34	0	41	2	1	5	.274	.342	.385
Hillenbrand, Shea, Tor.	152	645	594	91	173	267	36	2	18	82	0	3	22	26	2	79	5	1	21	.291	.343	.449
Hinske, Eric, Tor.*	147	537	477	79	125	205	31	2	15	68	0	6	8	46	4	121	8	4	8	.262	.333	.430
Hocking, Denny, K.C.†	23	71	60	14	16	17	1	0	0	7	1	0	0	10	0	10	0	1	1	.267	.371	.283
Hollins, Damon, TB.	120	369	342	44	85	143	17	1	13	46	1	2	1	23	0	63	8	1	8	.249	.296	.418
Hooper, Kevin, Det.	6	7	5	0	1	1	0	0	0	0	0	0	2	0	0	0	0	0	0	.200	.200	.200
Howell, J.P., K.C.*	15	3	3	0	0	0	0	0	0	0	0	0	0	0	0	1	0	0	0	.000	.000	.000
Howry, Bob, Cle.*	79	1	1	0	0	0	0	0	0	0	0	0	0	0	0	0	0	0	0	.000	.000	.000
Huber, Justin, K.C.	25	85	78	6	17	20	3	0	0	6	0	1	1	5	0	20	0	0	1	.218	.271	.256
Huckaby, Ken, Tor.	35	96	87	8	18	22	4	0	0	6	4	0	0	5	0	19	0	0	4	.207	.250	.253
Hudson, Orlando, Tor.†	131	501	461	62	125	190	25	5	10	63	0	7	3	30	1	65	7	1	10	.271	.315	.412
Huff, Aubrey, TB.*	154	636	575	70	150	246	26	2	22	92	0	7	5	49	13	88	8	7	12	.261	.321	.428
Hunter, Torii, Min.	98	416	372	63	100	168	24	1	14	56	0	4	6	34	3	65	23	7	8	.269	.337	.452
Hyzdu, Adam, Bos.	12	18	16	1	4	5	1	0	0	0	0	0	0	2	0	3	0	0	0	.250	.333	.313
Ibanez, Raul, Sea.*	162	690	614	92	172	268	32	2	20	89	0	3	2	71	6	99	9	4	12	.280	.355	.436
Iguchi, Tadahito, Chi.	135	582	511	74	142	224	25	6	15	71	11	6	6	47	0	114	15	5	16	.278	.342	.438
Infante, Omar, Det.	121	434	406	36	90	149	28	2	9	43	8	2	2	16	0	73	8	0	5	.222	.254	.367
Inge, Brandon, Det.	160	694	616	75	161	258	31	9	16	72	6	3	6	63	1	140	7	6	14	.261	.330	.419
Izturis, Maicer, L.A.†	77	210	191	18	47	66	8	4	1	15	1	1	0	17	2	21	9	3	5	.246	.306	.346
Jensen, Ryan, K.C.	9	1	1	0	0	0	0	0	0	0	0	0	0	0	0	0	0	0	0	.000	.000	.000
Jeter, Derek, N.Y.	159	752	654	122	202	294	25	5	19	70	7	3	11	77	3	117	14	5	15	.309	.389	.450
Johnson, Charles, TB.	19	55	46	5	9	13	4	0	0	5	0	0	0	9	0	11	0	0	2	.196	.327	.283
Johnson, Dan, Oak.*	109	434	375	54	103	169	21	0	15	58	0	8	1	50	1	52	0	1	11	.275	.355	.451
Johnson, Jason, Det.	33	2	2	1	1	4	0	0	1	1	0	0	0	0	0	1	0	0	0	.500	.500	2.000
Johnson, Randy, N.Y.	34	8	8	0	0	0	0	0	0	0	0	0	0	0	0	2	0	0	0	.000	.000	.000
Johnson, Reed, Tor.	142	439	398	55	107	164	21	6	8	58	2	1	16	22	1	82	5	6	8	.269	.332	.412
Johnson, Russ, N.Y.	22	20	18	5	4	6	2	0	0	0	0	0	0	1	0	4	0	0	0	.222	.300	.333
Jones, Jacque, Min.*	142	585	523	74	130	229	22	4	23	73	2	4	5	51	12	120	13	4	17	.249	.319	.438
Kapler, Gabe, Bos.	36	104	97	15	24	34	7	0	1	9	1	1	2	3	0	15	1	0	1	.247	.282	.351
Kazmir, Scott, TB.*	32	1	1	0	0	0	0	0	0	0	0	0	0	0	0	0	0	0	0	.000	.000	.000
Kendall, Jason, Oak.	150	676	601	70	163	193	28	1	0	53	0	5	20	50	0	39	8	3	26	.271	.345	.321
Kennedy, Adam, L.A.*	129	460	416	49	125	154	23	0	2	37	5	3	7	29	1	64	19	4	5	.300	.354	.370
Kielty, Bobby, Oak.†	116	433	377	55	99	149	20	1	10	57	2	2		50	3	67	3	2	14	.263	.350	.395
Konerko, Paul, Chi.	158	664	575	98	163	307	24	0	40	100	0	3	5	81	10	109	0	0	9	.283	.375	.534
Koskie, Corey, Tor.*	97	404	354	49	88	141	20	0	11	36	0	2	4	44	3	90	4	1	10	.249	.337	.398
Kotchman, Casey, L.A.*	47	143	126	16	35	61	5	0	7	22	1	1	0	15	0	18	1	1	3	.278	.352	.484
Kotsay, Mark, Oak.*	139	629	582	75	163	245	35	1	15	82	2	4	1	40	5	51	5	5	13	.280	.325	.421
Lackey, John, L.A.	33	6	6	0	0	0	0	0	0	0	0	0	0	0	0	1	0	0	0	.000	.000	.000

Player, Team	G	TPA	AB	R	H	TB	2B	3B	HR	RBI	SH	SF	HP	BB	IBB	SO	SB	CS	GDP	Avg.	OBP	Slg.
LaForest, Pete, TB.*	25	70	64	5	11	17	3	0	1	4	0	0	0	6	1	23	0	1	2	.172	.243	.266
Laird, Gerald, Tex.	13	42	40	7	9	14	2	0	1	4	0	0	0	2	0	7	0	0	1	.225	.262	.350
Laker, Tim, TB.	1	1	1	0	0	0	0	0	0	0	0	0	0	0	0	1	0	0	0	.000	.000	.000
Lawton, Matt, N.Y.*	21	57	48	6	6	12	0	0	2	4	0	0	2	7	0	8	1	0	0	.125	.263	.250
LeCroy, Matthew, Min.	101	350	304	33	79	135	5	0	17	50	0	1	4	41	2	85	0	0	7	.260	.354	.444
Lee, Cliff, Cle.*	32	8	8	0	0	0	0	0	0	0	0	0	0	0	0	2	0	0	0	.000	.000	.000
Lee, Travis, TB.*	129	441	404	54	110	172	22	2	12	49	0	1	1	35	4	66	7	4	7	.272	.331	.426
Liefer, Jeff, Cle.*	19	57	56	5	11	16	2	0	1	8	0	0	0	1	0	15	0	0	1	.196	.211	.286
Lilly, Ted, Tor.*	25	3	3	0	0	0	0	0	0	0	0	0	0	0	0	2	0	0	0	.000	.000	.000
Lima, Jose, K.C.	32	4	3	0	1	1	0	0	0	0	1	0	0	0	0	2	0	0	0	.333	.333	.333
Logan, Nook, Det.†	129	356	322	47	83	108	12	5	1	17	12	0	1	21	3	52	23	6	5	.258	.305	.335
Lohse, Kyle, Min.	31	5	5	0	0	0	0	0	0	0	0	0	0	0	0	1	0	0	1	.000	.000	.000
Long, Terrence, K.C.*	137	489	455	62	127	172	21	3	6	53	0	4	0	30	0	56	3	3	15	.279	.321	.378
Lopez, Javy, Bal.	103	423	395	47	110	181	24	1	15	49	0	2	7	19	2	68	0	1	10	.278	.322	.458
Lopez, Jose, Sea.	54	203	190	18	47	72	19	0	2	25	1	2	4	6	0	25	4	2	5	.247	.282	.379
Lopez, Pedro, Chi.	2	8	7	1	2	2	0	0	0	2	1	0	0	0	0	1	0	0	0	.286	.286	.286
Lopez, Rodrigo, Bal.	35	4	4	0	0	0	0	0	0	0	0	0	0	0	0	2	0	0	0	.000	.000	.000
Ludwick, Ryan, Cle.	19	48	41	8	9	21	0	0	4	5	0	0	0	7	0	13	0	1	1	.220	.333	.512
Lugo, Julio, TB.	158	690	616	89	182	248	36	6	6	57	3	4	6	61	0	72	39	11	5	.295	.362	.403
Machado, Alejandro, Bos.† ..	10	6	5	4	1	2	1	0	0	0	0	0	0	1	0	1	0	0	0	.200	.333	.400
Maroth, Mike, Det.*	35	6	4	0	2	2	0	0	0	1	1	0	0	1	0	2	0	0	0	.500	.600	.500
Marrero, Eli, K.C.-Bal.	54	156	138	15	25	57	7	2	7	19	1	5	1	11	0	38	1	0	3	.181	.239	.413
Martinez, Ramon, Det.	19	62	56	4	15	16	1	0	0	5	2	1	0	3	0	4	0	0	1	.268	.300	.286
Martinez, Tino, N.Y.*	131	348	303	43	73	133	9	0	17	49	0	4	3	38	3	54	2	0	10	.241	.328	.439
Martinez, Victor, Cle.†	147	622	547	73	167	260	33	0	20	80	0	7	5	63	9	78	0	1	16	.305	.378	.475
Mathis, Jeff, L.A.	5	3	3	1	1	1	0	0	0	0	0	0	0	0	0	1	0	0	0	.333	.333	.333
Matos, Luis, Bal.	121	433	389	53	109	145	20	2	4	32	3	4	10	27	0	58	17	9	4	.280	.340	.373
Matranga, Dave, L.A.	1	1	1	0	0	0	0	0	0	0	0	0	0	0	0	0	0	0	0	.000	.000	.000
Matsui, Hideki, N.Y.*	162	704	629	108	192	312	45	3	23	116	0	8	3	63	7	78	2	2	16	.305	.367	.496
Matthews Jr., Gary, Tex.† ...	131	526	475	72	121	207	25	5	17	55	1	3	0	47	1	90	9	2	11	.255	.320	.436
Mauer, Joe, Min.*	131	554	489	61	144	201	26	2	9	55	0	3	1	61	12	64	13	1	9	.294	.372	.411
Mays, Joe, Min.†	31	3	3	0	1	1	0	0	0	0	0	0	0	0	0	0	0	0	0	.333	.333	.333
McCarthy, Brandon, Chi.	12	2	2	0	0	0	0	0	0	0	0	0	0	0	0	2	0	0	0	.000	.000	.000
McCarty, Dave, Bos.	13	6	4	2	2	2	0	0	0	2	0	0	0	2	0	0	0	0	0	.500	.667	.500
McDonald, John, Tor.-Det. ...	68	184	166	18	46	54	6	1	0	16	3	2	2	11	0	24	6	1	6	.277	.326	.325
McDougall, Marshall, Tex.....	18	18	18	3	3	4	1	0	0	0	0	0	0	0	0	10	0	0	1	.167	.167	.222
McEwing, Joe, K.C.	83	191	180	16	43	53	7	0	1	6	5	0	0	6	0	35	4	4	5	.239	.263	.294
McPherson, Dallas, L.A.*	61	220	205	29	50	92	14	2	8	26	0	0	1	14	0	64	3	3	5	.244	.295	.449
Meche, Gil, Sea.	29	4	4	0	1	1	0	0	0	1	0	0	0	0	0	1	0	0	0	.250	.250	.250
Melhuse, Adam, Oak.†	39	102	97	11	24	37	7	0	2	12	0	0	0	5	0	28	0	0	0	.247	.284	.381
Mench, Kevin, Tex.	150	615	557	71	147	261	33	3	25	73	0	3	5	50	4	68	4	3	6	.264	.328	.469
Menechino, Frank, Tor.	70	180	148	22	32	51	7	0	4	13	1	0	6	25	0	33	0	1	3	.216	.352	.345
Merloni, Lou, L.A.	5	7	5	1	0	0	0	0	0	1	0	1	0	1	0	2	0	0	0	.000	.143	.000
Millar, Kevin, Bos.	134	519	449	57	122	179	28	1	9	50	0	8	8	54	0	74	0	1	12	.272	.355	.399
Miller, Corky, Min.	5	12	12	0	0	0	0	0	0	0	0	0	0	0	0	2	0	0	0	.000	.000	.000
Miller, Wade, Bos.	16	3	3	0	2	2	0	0	0	0	0	0	0	0	0	1	0	0	0	.667	.667	.667
Millwood, Kevin, Cle.	30	2	2	0	0	0	0	0	0	0	0	0	0	0	0	1	0	0	0	.000	.000	.000
Mirabelli, Doug, Bos.	50	152	136	16	31	56	7	0	6	18	0	0	2	14	0	48	2	0	2	.228	.309	.412
Molina, Bengie, L.A.	119	449	410	45	121	183	17	0	15	69	5	6	1	27	2	41	0	2	14	.295	.336	.446
Molina, Jose, L.A.	75	203	184	14	42	64	4	0	6	25	4	0	2	13	0	41	2	0	5	.228	.286	.348
Monroe, Craig, Det.	157	623	567	69	157	253	30	3	20	89	1	12	3	40	4	95	8	3	16	.277	.322	.446
Mora, Melvin, Bal.	149	664	593	86	168	281	30	1	27	88	8	3	10	50	0	112	7	4	9	.283	.348	.474
Morneau, Justin, Min.*	141	543	490	62	117	214	23	4	22	79	0	5	4	44	8	94	0	2	12	.239	.304	.437
Morse, Mike, Sea.	72	258	230	27	64	85	10	1	3	23	0	2	8	18	0	50	3	1	9	.278	.349	.370
Moyer, Jamie, Sea.*	32	2	1	0	0	0	0	0	0	0	0	1	0	0	0	0	0	0	0	.000	.000	.000
Mueller, Bill, Bos.†	150	590	519	69	153	223	34	3	10	62	0	6	6	59	3	74	0	0	22	.295	.369	.430
Munson, Eric, TB.*	11	24	18	2	3	4	1	0	0	2	0	1	1	4	0	3	0	0	2	.167	.333	.222
Murphy, Donnie, K.C.	32	88	77	4	12	20	5	0	1	8	1	1	0	9	0	23	0	1	3	.156	.241	.260
Mussina, Mike, N.Y.*	30	3	3	0	0	0	0	0	0	0	0	0	0	0	0	2	0	0	0	.000	.000	.000
Myers, Greg, Tor.*	6	13	12	0	1	1	0	0	0	1	0	0	0	1	0	1	0	0	2	.083	.154	.083
Nevin, Phil, Tex.	29	108	99	15	18	32	5	0	3	8	0	0	1	8	0	30	2	0	6	.182	.250	.323
Newhan, David, Bal.*	96	249	218	31	44	68	9	0	5	21	5	2	2	22	1	45	9	2	2	.202	.279	.312
Nieves, Wil, N.Y.	3	4	4	0	0	0	0	0	0	0	0	0	0	0	0	1	0	0	0	.000	.000	.000
Nivar, Ramon, Bal.	7	15	13	1	4	4	0	0	0	1	1	0	1	0	0	2	0	1	0	.308	.353	.308
Nix, Laynce, Tex.*	63	240	229	28	55	91	12	3	6	32	0	2	0	9	3	45	2	0	3	.240	.267	.397
Nixon, Trot, Bos.*	124	470	408	64	112	182	29	1	13	67	0	6	3	53	1	59	2	1	7	.275	.357	.446
Nomo, Hideo, TB.	19	4	4	0	0	0	0	0	0	0	0	0	0	0	0	1	0	0	0	.000	.000	.000
Ojeda, Miguel, Sea.	16	37	29	2	5	8	0	0	1	3	2	0	0	6	0	3	0	1	0	.172	.314	.276
Olerud, John, Bos.*	87	192	173	18	50	78	7	0	7	37	0	3	0	16	2	20	0	0	6	.289	.344	.451
Olivo, Miguel, Sea.	54	157	152	14	23	42	4	0	5	18	0	1	0	4	0	49	1	1	3	.151	.172	.276
Ordonez, Magglio, Det.	82	343	305	38	92	133	17	0	8	46	0	7	1	30	1	35	0	0	8	.302	.359	.436
Ortiz, David, Bos.*	159	713	601	119	180	363	40	1	47	148	0	9	1	102	9	124	1	0	13	.300	.397	.604
Ozuna, Pablo, Chi.	70	217	203	27	56	67	7	2	0	11	3	0	4	7	0	26	14	7	5	.276	.313	.330
Palmeiro, Rafael, Bal.*	110	422	369	47	98	165	13	0	18	60	0	8	2	43	4	43	2	0	9	.266	.339	.447
Park, Chan Ho, Tex.	20	5	5	0	2	2	0	0	0	1	0	0	0	0	0	2	0	0	0	.400	.400	.400
Paul, Josh, L.A.	34	40	37	4	7	14	1	0	2	4	1	0	0	2	0	9	0	0	1	.189	.231	.378
Pavano, Carl, N.Y.	17	7	7	0	0	0	0	0	0	0	0	0	0	0	0	4	0	0	0	.000	.000	.000
Payton, Jay, Bos.-Oak.	124	435	408	62	109	181	16	1	18	63	0	3	0	24	2	47	0	1	8	.267	.306	.444
Pena, Carlos, Det.*	79	295	260	37	61	124	9	0	18	44	0	0	4	31	2	95	0	1	3	.235	.325	.477
Penn, Hayden, Bal.	8	3	1	0	0	0	0	0	0	0	1	0	0	1	0	0	0	0	0	.000	.500	.000
Peralta, Jhonny, Cle.	141	570	504	82	147	262	35	4	24	78	1	4	3	58	3	128	0	2	12	.292	.366	.520
Perez, Eduardo, TB.	77	190	161	23	41	80	6	0	11	28	0	0	3	26	0	30	0	2	6	.255	.368	.497

Player, Team	G	TPA	AB	R	H	TB	2B	3B	HR	RBI	SH	SF	HP	BB	IBB	SO	SB	CS	GDP	Avg.	OBP	Slg.
Perez, Timo, Chi.*	76	196	179	13	39	53	8	0	2	15	4	1	0	12	1	25	2	2	3	.218	.266	.296
Petagine, Roberto, Bos.*	18	36	32	4	9	14	2	0	1	9	0	0	0	4	0	5	0	0	3	.281	.361	.438
Phelps, Josh, TB.	47	177	158	21	42	67	10	0	5	26	0	3	4	12	1	48	0	0	3	.266	.328	.424
Phillips, Andy, N.Y.	27	41	40	7	6	13	4	0	1	4	0	0	0	1	0	13	0	0	1	.150	.171	.325
Phillips, Brandon, Cle.	6	9	9	1	0	0	0	0	0	0	0	0	0	0	0	4	0	0	0	.000	.000	.000
Phillips, Paul, K.C.	23	67	67	6	18	27	4	1	1	9	0	0	0	0	0	5	0	0	4	.269	.269	.403
Pickering, Calvin, K.C.*	7	31	27	4	4	7	0	0	1	3	0	1	0	3	0	14	0	0	0	.148	.226	.259
Pierzynski, A.J., Chi.*	128	497	460	61	118	193	21	0	18	56	1	1	12	23	5	68	0	2	13	.257	.308	.420
Pineiro, Joel, Sea.	30	5	4	0	0	0	0	0	0	0	1	0	0	0	0	1	0	0	0	.000	.000	.000
Podsednik, Scott, Chi.*	129	568	507	80	147	177	28	1	0	25	6	5	3	47	0	75	59	23	7	.290	.351	.349
Polanco, Placido, Det.	86	378	343	58	116	158	20	2	6	36	2	4	8	21	0	16	4	3	9	.338	.386	.461
Politte, Cliff, Chi.	68	1	1	1	1	1	0	0	0	1	0	0	0	0	0	0	0	0	0	1.000	1.000	1.000
Ponson, Sidney, Bal.	23	4	4	0	1	2	1	0	0	0	0	0	0	0	0	0	0	0	0	.250	.250	.500
Posada, Jorge, N.Y.†	142	546	474	67	124	204	23	0	19	71	0	4	2	66	5	94	1	0	8	.262	.352	.430
Pride, Curtis, L.A.*	11	11	11	2	1	2	1	0	0	0	0	0	0	0	0	4	0	0	0	.091	.091	.182
Prieto, Chris, L.A.*	2	3	2	0	0	0	0	0	0	0	0	0	0	0	0	0	0	0	0	.000	.000	.000
Punto, Nick, Min.†	112	439	394	45	94	132	18	4	4	26	7	2	0	36	0	86	13	8	9	.239	.301	.335
Quinlan, Robb, L.A.	54	143	134	17	31	54	8	0	5	14	0	1	1	7	0	26	0	1	4	.231	.273	.403
Quiroz, Guillermo, Tor.	12	39	36	3	7	9	2	0	0	4	0	0	1	2	0	13	0	0	0	.194	.256	.250
Radke, Brad, Min.	31	7	5	0	0	0	0	0	0	0	2	0	0	0	0	2	0	0	0	.000	.000	.000
Ramirez, Hanley, Bos.	2	2	2	0	0	0	0	0	0	0	0	0	0	0	0	2	0	0	0	.000	.000	.000
Ramirez, Manny, Bos.	152	650	554	112	162	329	30	1	45	144	0	6	10	80	9	119	1	0	20	.292	.388	.594
Redmond, Mike, Min.	45	159	148	17	46	58	9	0	1	26	2	0	3	6	0	14	0	0	9	.311	.350	.392
Reed, Jeremy, Sea.*	141	544	488	61	124	172	33	3	3	45	4	2	2	48	1	74	12	11	10	.254	.322	.352
Reed, Keith, Bal.	6	6	5	1	1	1	0	0	0	1	0	0	0	1	0	2	0	0	0	.200	.333	.200
Reese, Kevin, N.Y.*	2	2	1	0	0	0	0	0	0	0	0	0	0	1	0	1	0	0	0	.000	.500	.000
Renteria, Edgar, Bos.	153	692	623	100	172	240	36	4	8	70	6	5	3	55	0	100	9	4	15	.276	.335	.385
Rios, Alex, Tor.	146	519	481	71	126	191	23	6	10	59	0	5	5	28	1	101	14	9	14	.262	.306	.397
Rivas, Luis, Min.	59	148	136	21	35	43	3	1	1	12	0	1	2	9	0	17	4	0	2	.257	.311	.316
Rivera, Juan, L.A.	106	376	350	46	95	159	17	1	15	59	2	1	0	23	0	44	1	9	15	.271	.316	.454
Rivera, Rene, Sea.	16	50	48	3	19	25	3	0	1	6	1	0	0	1	0	11	0	0	0	.396	.408	.521
Roberts, Brian, Bal.†	143	640	561	92	176	289	45	7	18	73	5	4	3	67	5	83	27	10	6	.314	.387	.515
Robertson, Nate, Det.	32	4	3	0	0	0	0	0	0	0	1	0	0	0	0	1	0	0	0	.000	.000	.000
Rodriguez, Alex, N.Y.	162	715	605	124	194	369	29	1	48	130	0	3	16	91	8	139	21	6	8	.321	.421	.610
Rodriguez, Ivan, Det.	129	525	504	71	139	224	33	5	14	50	1	7	2	11	2	93	7	3	19	.276	.290	.444
Rodriguez, Luis, Min.*	79	203	175	21	47	67	10	2	2	20	6	3	1	18	0	23	2	2	4	.269	.335	.383
Rodriguez, Ricardo, Tex.*	12	3	3	0	1	1	0	0	0	1	0	0	0	0	0	1	0	0	0	.333	.333	.333
Rogers, Ed, Bal.	8	1	1	4	1	4	0	0	1	2	0	0	0	0	0	0	0	0	2	1.000	1.000	4.000
Rogers, Kenny, Tex.*	30	3	3	0	1	3	0	1	0	1	0	0	0	0	0	0	0	0	0	.333	.333	1.000
Rowand, Aaron, Chi.	157	640	578	77	156	235	30	5	13	69	5	4	21	32	3	116	16	5	17	.270	.329	.407
Ryan, Michael, Min.*	57	131	117	7	27	38	5	0	2	13	4	1	0	9	1	22	1	2	5	.231	.283	.325
Saarloos, Kirk, Oak.	29	1	1	0	0	0	0	0	0	0	0	0	0	0	0	0	0	0	0	.000	.000	.000
Sabathia, C.C., Cle.*	31	6	6	1	2	6	1	0	1	4	0	0	0	0	0	1	0	0	0	.333	.333	1.000
Sanchez, Alex, TB.*	43	145	133	28	46	62	8	1	2	13	3	2	0	7	1	25	6	3	3	.346	.373	.466
Sanchez, Rey, N.Y.	23	48	43	7	12	13	1	0	0	2	2	0	1	2	0	3	0	1	2	.279	.326	.302
Santana, Johan, Min.*	33	6	6	1	1	1	0	0	0	0	0	0	0	0	0	0	0	0	0	.167	.167	.167
Santiago, Ramon, Sea.†	8	13	8	2	1	1	0	0	0	0	1	0	3	1	0	2	0	0	0	.125	.417	.125
Scutaro, Marco, Oak.	118	423	381	48	94	149	22	3	9	37	4	2	0	36	1	48	5	2	6	.247	.310	.391
Sele, Aaron, Sea.	21	4	3	1	0	0	0	0	0	0	1	0	0	0	0	0	0	0	0	.000	.000	.000
Sexson, Richie, Sea.	156	656	558	99	147	302	36	1	39	121	0	3	6	89	4	167	1	1	14	.263	.369	.541
Sheffield, Gary, N.Y.	154	675	584	104	170	299	27	0	34	123	0	5	8	78	7	76	10	2	11	.291	.379	.512
Shelton, Chris, Det.	107	431	388	61	116	198	22	3	18	59	0	4	5	34	0	87	0	0	11	.299	.360	.510
Shields, Scot, L.A.	78	1	1	0	0	0	0	0	0	0	0	0	0	0	0	1	0	0	0	.000	.000	.000
Shoppach, Kelly, Bos.	9	16	15	1	0	0	0	0	0	0	0	0	1	0	0	7	0	0	0	.000	.063	.000
Sierra, Ruben, N.Y.†	61	181	170	14	39	63	12	0	4	29	0	2	0	9	1	41	0	0	2	.229	.265	.371
Silva, Carlos, Min.	27	2	2	0	0	0	0	0	0	0	0	0	0	0	0	2	0	0	0	.000	.000	.000
Singleton, Chris, TB.*	28	68	59	9	16	21	5	0	0	11	1	0	1	6	0	14	0	0	1	.271	.348	.356
Sisco, Andrew, K.C.*	67	1	1	0	0	0	0	0	0	0	0	0	0	0	0	1	0	0	0	.000	.000	.000
Sizemore, Grady, Cle.*	158	706	640	111	185	310	37	11	22	81	5	2	7	52	1	132	22	10	17	.289	.348	.484
Smith, Jason, Det.*	27	63	58	4	11	16	1	2	0	2	4	0	1	0	0	16	2	1	0	.190	.203	.276
Snelling, Chris, Sea.*	15	35	29	4	8	13	2	0	1	1	1	0	0	5	0	2	0	2	0	.276	.382	.448
Sorensen, Zach, L.A.†	12	13	12	3	2	3	1	0	0	1	0	0	0	0	0	2	0	0	0	.167	.167	.250
Soriano, Alfonso, Tex.	156	682	637	102	171	326	43	2	36	104	0	5	7	33	3	125	30	2	6	.268	.309	.512
Sosa, Sammy, Bal.	102	424	380	39	84	143	15	1	14	45	0	3	2	39	3	84	1	1	15	.221	.295	.376
Spiezio, Scott, Sea.†	29	51	47	2	3	7	1	0	1	1	0	0	0	4	0	18	0	0	1	.064	.137	.149
Stairs, Matt, K.C.*	127	466	396	55	109	176	26	1	13	66	0	5	5	60	4	69	1	2	9	.275	.373	.444
Stern, Adam, Bos.*	36	16	15	4	2	5	0	0	1	2	0	0	1	0	0	4	1	1	0	.133	.188	.333
Stewart, Shannon, Min.	132	599	551	69	151	214	27	3	10	56	1	5	8	34	2	73	7	5	11	.274	.323	.388
Strong, Jamal, Sea.	16	24	20	6	5	7	0	1	0	2	0	1	1	2	0	6	0	0	0	.250	.333	.350
Surhoff, B.J., Bal.*	91	321	303	30	78	108	11	2	5	34	2	4	1	11	1	32	0	0	6	.257	.282	.356
Suzuki, Ichiro, Sea.*	162	739	679	111	206	296	21	12	15	68	2	6	4	48	23	66	33	8	5	.303	.350	.436
Sweeney, Mike, K.C.	122	514	470	63	141	243	39	0	21	83	1	6	4	33	7	61	3	0	16	.300	.347	.517
Swisher, Nick, Oak.†	131	522	462	66	109	206	32	1	21	74	0	1	4	55	3	110	0	1	9	.236	.322	.446
Taylor, Reggie, TB.*	11	24	22	2	4	6	2	0	0	1	0	0	0	2	0	7	2	0	0	.182	.250	.273
Teahen, Mark, K.C.*	130	491	447	60	110	168	29	4	7	55	2	1	1	40	2	107	7	2	13	.246	.309	.376
Teixeira, Mark, Tex.†	162	730	644	112	194	370	41	3	43	144	0	3	11	72	5	124	4	0	18	.301	.379	.575
Tejada, Miguel, Bal.	162	704	654	89	199	337	50	5	26	98	0	3	7	40	9	83	5	1	26	.304	.349	.515
Thames, Marcus, Det.	38	118	107	11	21	44	2	0	7	16	0	1	1	9	1	38	0	0	1	.196	.263	.411
Thomas, Charles, Oak.*	30	55	46	4	5	5	0	0	0	1	0	0	4	5	0	8	0	0	0	.109	.255	.109
Thomas, Frank, Chi.	34	124	105	19	23	62	3	0	12	26	0	3	0	16	0	31	0	0	2	.219	.315	.590
Tiffee, Terry, Min.†	54	159	150	9	31	44	8	1	1	15	0	1	0	8	1	15	1	0	10	.207	.245	.293
Torrealba, Yorvit, Sea.	42	119	108	14	26	36	4	0	2	8	3	0	1	7	0	25	0	0	5	.241	.293	.333

Player, Team	G	TPA	AB	R	H	TB	2B	3B	HR	RBI	SH	SF	HP	BB	IBB	SO	SB	CS	GDP	Avg.	OBP	Slg.
Torres, Andres, Tex.†	8	21	19	2	3	4	1	0	0	1	0	1	0	1	0	6	1	0	0	.158	.190	.211
Towers, Josh, Tor.	33	6	6	0	0	0	0	0	0	0	0	0	0	0	0	2	0	0	0	.000	.000	.000
Tyner, Jason, Min.*	18	60	56	8	18	21	1	1	0	5	0	0	0	4	0	4	2	0	2	.321	.367	.375
Uribe, Juan, Chi.	146	540	481	58	121	198	23	3	16	71	11	10	4	34	0	77	4	6	7	.252	.301	.412
Valdez, Wilson, Sea.	42	133	126	9	25	32	5	1	0	8	1	0	0	6	0	25	2	2	1	.198	.235	.254
Varitek, Jason, Bos.†	133	539	470	70	132	230	30	1	22	70	1	3	3	62	3	117	2	0	10	.281	.366	.489
Vazquez, Ramon, Bos.-Cle.*	39	92	85	7	18	23	5	0	0	5	2	0	0	5	0	17	0	0	0	.212	.256	.271
Vento, Mike, N.Y.	2	2	2	0	0	0	0	0	0	0	0	0	0	0	0	1	0	0	0	.000	.000	.000
Waechter, Doug, T.B.	29	3	2	1	0	0	0	0	0	0	1	0	0	0	0	0	0	0	0	.000	.000	.000
Wakefield, Tim, Bos.	33	9	8	1	2	2	0	0	0	1	1	0	0	0	0	2	0	0	0	.250	.250	.250
Wang, Chien-Ming, N.Y.	18	1	1	0	0	0	0	0	0	0	0	0	0	0	0	0	0	0	0	.000	.000	.000
Wasdin, John, Tex.	31	1	1	0	0	0	0	0	0	0	0	0	0	0	0	0	0	0	0	.000	.000	.000
Washburn, Jarrod, L.A.*	29	5	4	1	0	0	0	0	0	0	0	0	0	1	0	0	0	0	0	.000	.200	.000
Watson, Matt, Oak.*	19	50	48	4	9	12	3	0	0	5	0	0	0	2	0	4	0	0	1	.188	.220	.250
Wells, David, Bos.*	30	7	7	1	1	1	0	0	0	1	0	0	0	0	0	2	0	0	0	.143	.143	.143
Wells, Vernon, Tor.	156	678	620	78	167	287	30	3	28	97	0	8	3	47	3	86	8	3	13	.269	.320	.463
Westbrook, Jake, Cle.	34	2	2	0	0	0	0	0	0	0	0	0	0	0	0	2	0	0	0	.000	.000	.000
White, Rondell, Det.	97	400	374	49	117	183	24	3	12	53	0	4	5	17	0	48	1	0	8	.313	.348	.489
Whiteside, Eli, Bal.	9	12	12	1	3	3	0	0	0	1	0	0	0	0	0	2	0	0	1	.250	.250	.250
Widger, Chris, Chi.	45	154	141	18	34	54	8	0	4	11	2	0	1	10	0	22	0	2	5	.241	.296	.383
Williams, Bernie, N.Y.†	141	546	485	53	121	178	19	1	12	64	1	6	1	53	1	75	1	2	16	.249	.321	.367
Williams, Glenn, Min.†	13	43	40	3	17	18	1	0	0	3	1	0	0	2	0	7	1	2	0	.425	.452	.450
Wilson, Dan, Sea.	11	28	27	2	5	5	0	0	0	2	0	0	1	0	0	10	0	1	1	.185	.214	.185
Wilson, Vance, Det.	61	173	152	18	30	43	4	0	3	19	2	2	6	11	0	26	0	0	6	.197	.275	.283
Winn, Randy, Sea.†	102	436	386	46	106	151	25	1	6	37	6	3	4	37	3	53	12	6	7	.275	.342	.391
Womack, Tony, N.Y.*	108	351	329	46	82	92	8	1	0	15	7	2	1	12	0	49	27	5	7	.249	.276	.280
Wooten, Shawn, Bos.	1	1	1	0	0	0	0	0	0	0	0	0	0	0	0	0	0	0	0	.000	.000	.000
Yabu, Keiichi, Oak.	40	1	1	0	0	0	0	0	0	0	0	0	0	0	0	0	0	0	0	.000	.000	.000
Youkilis, Kevin, Bos.	44	95	79	11	22	32	7	0	1	9	0	0	2	14	0	19	0	1	0	.278	.400	.405
Young, Chris, Tex.	31	5	5	0	0	0	0	0	0	0	0	0	0	0	0	3	0	0	0	.000	.000	.000
Young, Dmitri, Det.†	126	509	469	61	127	221	25	3	21	72	0	1	9	29	7	100	1	0	16	.271	.325	.471
Young, Michael, Tex.	159	732	668	114	221	343	40	5	24	91	0	3	3	58	0	91	5	2	20	.331	.385	.513
Young, Walter, Bal.*	14	37	33	2	10	14	1	0	1	3	0	0	0	4	1	7	0	0	1	.303	.378	.424
Zaun, Gregg, Tor.†	133	512	434	61	109	162	18	1	11	61	0	5	0	73	2	70	2	3	11	.251	.355	.373
Zito, Barry, Oak.*	35	7	7	0	1	1	0	0	0	0	0	0	0	0	0	2	0	0	0	.143	.143	.143

AWARDED FIRST BASE ON OBSTRUCTION OR CATCHER'S INTERFERENCE _ Erstad, Los Angeles 4 (Posada, Laird, Olivo, Olivo); Barajas, Texas (Mauer); Cantu, Tampa Bay (Zaun); Iguchi, Chicago (Buck); Matsui, New York (Hall); Singleton, Tampa Bay (Widger); Young, Detroit (Martinez).

PLAYERS WITH TWO OR MORE TEAMS

Player, Team	G	TPA	AB	R	H	TB	2B	3B	HR	RBI	SH	SF	HP	BB	IBB	SO	SB	CS	GDP	Avg.	OBP	Slg.
Bellhorn, Mark, Bos.†	85	335	283	41	61	102	20	0	7	28	0	3	0	49	1	109	3	0	4	.216	.328	.360
Bellhorn, Mark, N.Y.†	9	20	17	2	2	5	0	0	1	2	0	0	0	3	0	3	0	0	0	.118	.250	.294
Boone, Bret, Sea.	74	302	273	30	63	105	15	3	7	34	1	1	3	24	2	52	4	2	9	.231	.299	.385
Boone, Bret, Min.	14	58	53	3	9	9	0	0	0	3	0	0	1	4	0	13	0	0	3	.170	.241	.170
Byrnes, Eric, Oak.	59	215	192	30	51	91	15	2	7	24	1	1	7	14	0	27	2	2	1	.266	.336	.474
Byrnes, Eric, Bal.	52	181	167	17	32	50	7	1	3	11	2	0	1	11	0	33	3	0	5	.192	.246	.299
Castillo, Alberto, K.C.	34	114	100	13	21	31	5	1	1	14	1	1	0	12	0	21	1	0	2	.210	.292	.310
Castillo, Alberto, Oak.	1	1	1	0	0	0	0	0	0	0	0	0	0	0	0	1	0	0	0	.000	.000	.000
Cora, Alex, Cle.*	49	157	146	11	30	42	5	2	1	8	1	1	4	5	0	18	6	0	3	.205	.250	.288
Cora, Alex, Bos.*	47	116	104	14	28	41	3	2	2	16	3	2	1	6	0	12	1	2	3	.269	.310	.394
Graffanino, Tony, K.C.	59	217	191	29	57	75	5	2	3	18	2	0	2	22	1	28	3	1	6	.298	.377	.393
Graffanino, Tony, Bos.	51	200	188	39	60	86	12	1	4	20	0	1	2	9	1	23	4	1	8	.319	.355	.457
Marrero, Eli, K.C.	32	100	88	11	14	30	4	0	4	9	1	3	1	7	0	18	1	0	2	.159	.222	.341
Marrero, Eli, Bal.	22	56	50	8	11	27	3	2	3	10	0	2	0	4	0	20	0	0	1	.220	.268	.540
McDonald, John, Tor.	37	106	93	8	27	30	3	0	0	12	3	2	2	6	0	12	5	0	3	.290	.340	.323
McDonald, John, Det.	31	78	73	10	19	24	3	1	0	4	0	0	0	5	0	12	1	1	3	.260	.308	.329
Payton, Jay, Bos.	55	144	133	24	35	57	7	0	5	21	0	1	0	10	0	14	0	0	4	.263	.313	.429
Payton, Jay, Oak.	69	291	275	38	74	124	9	1	13	42	0	2	0	14	2	33	0	1	4	.269	.302	.451
Vazquez, Ramon, Bos.*	27	66	61	6	12	14	2	0	0	4	2	0	0	3	0	14	0	0	0	.197	.234	.230
Vazquez, Ramon, Cle.*	12	26	24	1	6	9	3	0	0	1	0	0	0	2	0	3	0	0	0	.250	.308	.375

DESIGNATED HITTING

TEAM

Team	G	TPA	AB	R	H	TB	2B	3B	HR	RBI	SH	SF	HP	BB	IBB	SO	SB	CS	GDP	Avg.	OBP	Slg.
Boston	153	702	588	115	171	345	40	1	44	146	0	9	1	104	9	124	1	0	13	.291	.393	.587
Cleveland	153	674	578	105	168	324	45	0	37	115	0	4	9	83	5	150	0	0	9	.291	.386	.561
Detroit	153	649	600	83	164	288	37	3	27	84	0	2	7	40	2	140	1	1	12	.273	.325	.480
Toronto	153	646	570	86	154	246	45	4	13	69	3	4	17	52	1	113	2	4	16	.270	.347	.432
Seattle	153	638	575	73	154	224	22	3	14	79	2	3	2	56	5	96	8	1	14	.268	.333	.390
Tampa Bay	153	648	564	81	151	261	38	3	22	96	1	10	15	58	5	138	11	4	17	.268	.346	.463
Kansas City	153	648	564	83	148	251	36	2	21	82	1	8	4	71	8	104	2	2	15	.262	.345	.445
New York	153	658	556	87	143	251	21	0	29	108	0	4	11	87	4	117	3	1	16	.257	.366	.451
Los Angeles	153	650	584	78	149	221	26	2	14	69	4	7	1	54	5	102	15	5	20	.255	.316	.378
Minnesota	153	658	586	71	146	225	18	5	17	73	1	3	8	60	8	123	6	1	10	.249	.326	.384
Texas	153	673	591	99	144	250	20	4	26	70	1	3	5	73	2	157	4	3	17	.244	.330	.423
Chicago	153	665	592	76	144	273	26	2	33	108	0	12	5	56	2	126	5	6	13	.243	.308	.461
Oakland	153	656	582	69	140	200	23	2	11	72	3	1	3	67	2	87	1	0	23	.241	.322	.344
Baltimore	153	631	569	66	119	207	27	2	19	71	1	6	0	55	7	105	3	4	22	.209	.276	.364
Totals	2402	9196	8099	1172	2095	3566	424	33	327	1242	17	76	88	916	65	1682	62	32	217	.259	.338	.440

TOP DESIGNATED HITTERS

Minimum 100 at-bats. *Lefthanded batter. †Switch-hitter.

Player, Team	G	TPA	AB	R	H	TB	2B	3B	HR	RBI	SH	SF	HP	BB	IBB	SO	SB	CS	GDP	Avg.	OBP	Slg.
Hillenbrand, Shea, Tor.	33	141	128	21	41	56	9	0	2	12	0	0	7	6	1	15	2	1	5	.320	.383	.438
Hinske, Eric, Tor.*	43	133	114	22	36	54	10	1	2	8	0	1	4	14	0	23	0	3	2	.316	.406	.474
Sweeney, Mike, K.C.	73	304	275	40	84	144	21	0	13	47	0	4	3	22	6	38	1	0	11	.305	.359	.524
Hafner, Travis, Cle.*	130	568	479	91	146	284	42	0	32	106	0	4	9	76	5	120	0	0	9	.305	.407	.593
Ortiz, David, Bos.*	148	666	558	111	166	336	39	1	43	141	0	9	1	98	9	118	1	0	13	.297	.398	.602
Huff, Aubrey, TB.*	33	138	124	22	36	69	9	0	8	29	0	2	1	11	1	15	0	1	4	.290	.348	.556
Gomes, Jonny, TB.	49	207	170	27	49	89	10	3	8	28	0	4	9	24	1	54	8	3	4	.288	.396	.524
Ibanez, Raul, Sea.*	101	425	378	54	107	164	19	1	12	54	0	2	2	43	2	60	6	1	9	.283	.358	.434
White, Rondell, Det.	30	127	121	12	33	49	10	0	2	10	0	0	1	5	0	17	0	0	2	.273	.307	.405
Phelps, Josh, TB.	42	171	153	20	41	66	10	0	5	26	0	3	4	11	1	46	0	0	3	.268	.327	.431
Dellucci, David, Tex.*	67	288	237	53	63	114	5	2	14	27	0	1	4	46	0	69	2	2	3	.266	.392	.481
Ford, Lew, Min.	44	193	170	24	45	68	13	2	2	17	1	2	6	14	1	31	3	1	3	.265	.339	.400
Young, Dmitri, Det.†	71	301	277	39	73	129	14	3	12	39	0	1	5	18	1	65	1	0	7	.264	.319	.466
LeCroy, Matthew, Min.	63	244	216	23	55	99	2	0	14	37	0	0	2	26	2	61	0	0	5	.255	.340	.458
Hill, Aaron, Tor.	34	129	118	16	30	49	9	2	2	12	1	0	2	8	0	18	0	0	2	.254	.313	.415

ALL DESIGNATED HITTERS

*Lefthanded batter. †Switch-hitter.

Player, Team	G	TPA	AB	R	H	TB	2B	3B	HR	RBI	SH	SF	HP	BB	IBB	SO	SB	CS	GDP	Avg.	OBP	Slg.
Abernathy, Brent, Min.	2	4	4	0	0	0	0	0	0	0	0	0	0	0	0	1	0	0	0	.000	.000	.000
Allen, Chad, Tex.	18	51	48	5	14	17	1	1	0	5	1	0	0	2	0	11	0	1	2	.292	.320	.354
Ambres, Chip, K.C.	2	3	1	1	0	0	0	0	0	0	1	0	1	0	1	0	0	0	0	.000	.333	.000
Anderson, Garret, L.A.*	36	158	151	13	30	41	8	0	1	15	0	1	0	6	2	27	0	0	5	.199	.228	.272
Bartlett, Jason, Min.	5	2	2	1	1	1	0	0	0	0	0	0	0	0	0	0	0	0	0	.500	.500	.500
Beltre, Adrian, Sea.	1	5	5	1	3	3	0	0	0	1	0	0	0	0	0	2	0	0	0	.600	.600	.600
Blalock, Hank, Tex.*	3	8	8	0	1	1	0	0	0	0	0	0	0	0	0	2	0	0	0	.125	.125	.125
Bloomquist, Willie, Sea.	1	1	1	1	1	1	0	0	0	0	0	0	0	0	0	0	0	0	0	1.000	1.000	1.000
Bocachica, Hiram, Oak.	1	1	1	0	0	0	0	0	0	0	0	0	0	0	0	1	0	0	0	.000	.000	.000
Boone, Aaron, Cle.	1	4	4	1	1	4	0	0	1	1	0	0	0	0	0	0	0	0	0	.250	.250	1.000
Borchard, Joe, Chi.†	3	9	9	0	3	5	2	0	0	0	0	0	0	0	0	4	0	0	0	.333	.333	.556
Botts, Jason, Tex.†	3	11	10	1	4	4	0	0	0	0	0	0	0	1	0	5	0	0	0	.400	.455	.400
Broussard, Ben, Cle.*	2	8	8	1	2	2	0	0	0	0	0	0	0	0	0	1	0	0	0	.250	.250	.250
Brown, Emil, K.C.	10	36	33	2	9	15	2	2	0	1	0	0	0	3	1	9	0	0	0	.273	.333	.455
Bubela, Jaime, Sea.*	1	0	0	0	0	0	0	0	0	0	0	0	0	0	0	1	0	0	0	.000	.000	.000
Byrnes, Eric, Oak.	4	14	11	0	0	0	0	0	0	0	0	0	1	2	0	3	0	0	0	.000	.214	.000
Cantu, Jorge, TB.	13	56	53	5	9	16	4	0	1	5	0	1	0	2	1	9	1	0	4	.170	.196	.302
Castro, Bernie, Bal.†	9	32	29	2	8	12	2	1	0	3	0	0	0	3	0	5	3	2	0	.276	.344	.414
Catalanotto, Frank, Tor.*	15	58	53	11	17	33	5	1	3	14	1	0	0	4	0	8	0	0	3	.321	.368	.623
Chavez, Eric, Oak.*	6	25	25	3	7	13	1	1	1	3	0	0	0	0	0	5	0	0	0	.280	.280	.520
Costa, Shane, K.C.*	4	15	14	3	3	3	0	0	0	1	0	0	0	1	0	1	0	0	1	.214	.267	.214
Crawford, Carl, TB.*	1	5	4	0	0	0	0	0	0	0	0	0	0	1	0	0	0	0	0	.000	.200	.000
Crede, Joe, Chi.	1	3	3	0	0	0	0	0	0	0	0	0	0	0	0	0	0	0	0	.000	.000	.000
Crosby, Bubba, N.Y.*	4	0	0	1	0	0	0	0	0	0	0	0	0	0	0	0	0	0	0	.000	.000	.000
Damon, Johnny, Bos.*	1	4	3	0	0	0	0	0	0	0	0	0	0	1	0	1	0	0	0	.000	.250	.000
DaVanon, Jeff, L.A.†	30	102	86	21	23	26	3	0	0	7	2	1	0	13	0	18	7	2	1	.267	.360	.302
Dellucci, David, Tex.*	67	288	237	53	63	114	5	2	14	27	0	1	4	46	0	69	2	2	3	.266	.392	.481
DeRosa, Mark, Tex.	4	6	3	0	0	0	0	0	0	0	0	0	0	0	0	0	0	0	0	.000	.500	.000
Diaz, Matt, K.C.	7	22	19	1	6	7	1	0	0	2	1	0	0	2	0	4	0	0	2	.316	.381	.368
Dobbs, Greg, Sea.*	24	94	85	5	22	28	3	0	1	12	1	1	0	7	3	7	1	0	3	.259	.312	.329
Dubois, Jason, Cle.	7	25	22	2	3	6	0	0	1	1	0	0	0	3	0	11	0	0	0	.136	.240	.273
Durazo, Erubiel, Oak.*	39	162	147	15	35	55	6	1	4	15	0	0	1	14	0	24	1	0	5	.238	.309	.374

Player, Team	G	TPA	AB	R	H	TB	2B	3B	HR	RBI	SH	SF	HP	BB	IBB	SO	SB	CS	GDP	Avg.	OBP	Slg.
Dye, Jermaine, Chi.	1	5	5	0	1	1	0	0	0	1	0	0	0	0	0	2	0	0	0	.200	.200	.200
Ellis, Mark, Oak.	1	1	0	0	0	0	0	0	0	0	0	0	0	1	0	0	0	0	0	.000	1.000	.000
Erstad, Darin, L.A.*	5	21	20	3	6	11	2	0	1	3	0	0	0	1	0	6	0	1	0	.300	.333	.550
Everett, Carl, Chi.†	107	448	397	47	98	173	14	2	19	70	0	9	5	37	2	78	3	5	10	.247	.313	.436
Fasano, Sal, Bal.	3	6	6	2	2	8	0	0	2	2	0	0	0	0	0	2	0	0	0	.333	.333	1.333
Figgins, Chone, L.A.†	7	30	26	5	8	11	1	1	0	2	0	0	0	4	0	6	4	1	1	.308	.400	.423
Finley, Steve, L.A.*	5	19	18	2	4	6	0	1	0	4	0	0	0	1	0	6	0	0	0	.222	.263	.333
Ford, Lew, Min.	44	193	170	24	45	68	13	2	2	17	1	2	6	14	1	31	3	1	3	.265	.339	.400
Freire, Alejandro, Bal.	9	28	26	3	5	9	1	0	1	2	0	0	0	2	0	8	0	0	3	.192	.250	.346
Garko, Ryan, Cle.	1	1	1	0	0	0	0	0	0	0	0	0	0	0	0	0	0	0	0	.000	.000	.000
Gathright, Joey, TB.*	1	1	1	0	0	0	0	0	0	0	0	0	0	0	0	0	0	0	0	.000	.000	.000
Gerut, Jody, Cle.*	3	10	10	0	3	4	1	0	0	1	0	0	0	0	0	0	0	0	0	.300	.300	.400
Giambi, Jason, N.Y.*	60	235	177	26	37	65	4	0	8	22	0	0	10	48	2	52	0	0	1	.209	.404	.367
Gibbons, Jay, Bal.*	42	163	151	23	33	65	12	1	6	22	0	1	0	11	3	14	0	0	5	.219	.270	.430
Ginter, Keith, Oak.	9	25	24	2	3	4	1	0	0	4	0	0	0	1	0	4	0	0	0	.125	.160	.167
Gomes, Jonny, TB.	49	207	170	27	49	89	10	3	8	28	0	4	9	24	1	54	8	3	4	.288	.396	.524
Gomez, Chris, Bal.	6	22	18	2	5	7	2	0	0	5	0	0	0	4	1	1	0	0	3	.278	.409	.389
Gonzalez, Adrian, Tex.*	32	127	118	14	27	51	7	1	5	14	0	2	0	7	2	32	0	0	3	.229	.268	.432
Gotay, Ruben, K.C.†	2	8	7	1	1	1	0	0	0	0	0	0	0	1	0	0	0	0	0	.143	.250	.143
Graffanino, Tony, K.C.	1	1	1	1	1	1	0	0	0	0	0	0	0	0	0	0	0	0	0	1.000	1.000	1.000
Griffin, John-Ford, Tor.*	4	10	10	3	3	7	1	0	1	6	0	0	0	0	0	3	0	0	0	.300	.300	.700
Gross, Gabe, Tor.*	2	3	3	0	0	0	0	0	0	0	0	0	0	0	0	3	0	0	0	.000	.000	.000
Guerrero, Vladimir, L.A.	19	82	71	11	20	36	1	0	5	13	0	2	1	8	2	10	2	1	3	.282	.354	.507
Guillen, Carlos, Det.†	10	37	36	4	15	17	2	0	0	3	0	0	0	1	0	8	0	1	1	.417	.432	.472
Gutierrez, Franklin, Cle.	3	1	0	2	0	0	0	0	0	0	0	0	0	1	0	0	0	0	0	.000	1.000	.000
Hafner, Travis, Cle.*	130	568	479	91	146	284	42	0	32	106	0	4	9	76	5	120	0	0	9	.305	.407	.593
Hansen, Dave, Sea.*	5	20	19	0	3	3	0	0	0	2	1	0	0	0	0	0	0	0	0	.158	.158	.158
Harris, Willie, Chi.*	9	9	8	1	1	1	0	0	0	1	0	0	0	1	0	3	2	1	0	.125	.222	.125
Harvey, Ken, K.C.	7	30	28	3	6	12	3	0	1	4	0	0	0	2	0	9	0	0	0	.214	.267	.429
Hatteberg, Scott, Oak.*	79	305	267	32	64	87	11	0	4	35	2	1	1	34	2	28	0	0	16	.240	.327	.326
Hernandez, Jose, Cle.	1	1	1	0	0	0	0	0	0	0	0	0	0	0	0	1	0	0	0	.000	.000	.000
Hidalgo, Richard, Tex.	1	5	4	0	0	0	0	0	0	0	0	0	0	1	0	1	0	0	0	.000	.200	.000
Higginson, Bobby, Det.*	1	1	1	0	0	0	0	0	0	0	0	0	0	0	0	0	0	0	0	.000	.000	.000
Hill, Aaron, Tor.	34	129	118	16	30	49	9	2	2	12	1	0	2	8	0	18	0	0	2	.254	.313	.415
Hillenbrand, Shea, Tor.	33	141	128	21	41	56	9	0	2	12	0	0	7	6	1	15	2	1	5	.320	.383	.438
Hinske, Eric, Tor.*	43	133	114	22	36	54	10	1	2	8	0	1	4	14	0	23	0	3	2	.316	.406	.474
Huber, Justin, K.C.	4	15	12	1	2	3	1	0	0	1	0	1	0	2	0	2	0	0	0	.167	.267	.250
Huff, Aubrey, TB.*	33	138	124	22	36	69	9	0	8	29	0	2	1	11	1	15	0	1	4	.290	.348	.556
Hunter, Torii, Min.	5	24	20	2	2	3	1	0	0	2	0	1	0	3	1	5	1	0	0	.100	.208	.150
Ibanez, Raul, Sea.*	101	425	378	54	107	164	19	1	12	54	0	2	2	43	2	60	6	1	9	.283	.358	.434
Jeter, Derek, N.Y.	1	5	5	1	1	1	0	0	0	0	0	0	0	0	0	0	0	0	0	.200	.200	.200
Johnson, Dan, Oak.*	5	24	19	5	7	11	1	0	1	3	0	0	0	5	0	4	0	0	1	.368	.500	.579
Johnson, Russ, N.Y.	3	0	0	1	0	0	0	0	0	0	0	0	0	0	0	0	0	0	0	.000	.000	.000
Jones, Jacque, Min.*	9	35	34	3	9	11	0	1	0	3	0	0	0	1	0	7	1	0	0	.265	.286	.324
Kendall, Jason, Oak.	3	14	13	2	3	4	1	0	0	1	0	0	0	1	0	1	0	0	0	.231	.286	.308
Kielty, Bobby, Oak.†	17	55	46	8	13	14	1	0	0	10	0	0	0	9	0	11	0	0	1	.283	.400	.304
Konerko, Paul, Chi.	11	46	43	8	14	28	5	0	3	10	0	0	0	3	0	4	0	0	1	.326	.370	.651
Koskie, Corey, Tor.*	19	77	69	3	11	20	6	0	1	9	0	2	0	6	0	24	0	0	2	.159	.221	.290
Kotchman, Casey, L.A.*	20	75	67	7	16	28	3	0	3	6	1	0	0	7	0	12	1	0	2	.239	.311	.418
Kotsay, Mark, Oak.*	2	9	8	0	3	4	1	0	0	0	1	0	0	0	0	0	0	0	0	.375	.375	.500
LaForest, Pete, TB.*	2	6	4	0	0	0	0	0	0	0	0	0	0	2	1	3	0	0	0	.000	.333	.000
LeCroy, Matthew, Min.	63	244	216	23	55	99	2	0	14	37	0	0	2	26	2	61	0	0	5	.255	.340	.458
Liefer, Jeff, Cle.*	9	34	33	2	8	10	2	0	0	3	0	0	0	1	0	9	0	0	0	.242	.265	.303
Logan, Nook, Det.†	3	1	1	2	0	0	0	0	0	0	0	0	0	0	0	0	0	0	0	.000	.000	.000
Long, Terrence, K.C.*	4	14	13	2	3	4	1	0	0	1	0	0	0	1	0	1	0	0	0	.231	.286	.308
Lopez, Javy, Bal.	28	111	104	12	25	39	5	0	3	9	0	0	0	7	0	18	0	0	1	.240	.288	.375
Ludwick, Ryan, Cle.	3	11	9	4	3	9	0	0	2	2	0	0	0	2	0	3	0	0	0	.333	.455	1.000
Marrero, Eli, K.C.	2	1	1	1	0	0	0	0	0	0	0	0	0	0	0	0	0	0	0	.000	.000	.000
Martinez, Tino, N.Y.*	1	1	0	0	0	0	0	0	0	0	0	0	0	1	0	0	0	0	0	.000	1.000	.000
Martinez, Victor, Cle.†	2	10	10	1	2	5	0	0	1	1	0	0	0	0	0	3	0	0	0	.200	.200	.500
Mathis, Jeff, L.A.	2	2	2	1	1	1	0	0	0	0	0	0	0	0	0	1	0	0	0	.500	.500	.500
Matsui, Hideki, N.Y.*	19	82	71	15	24	48	6	0	6	21	0	1	0	10	2	7	0	0	4	.338	.415	.676
Matthews Jr., Gary, Tex.†	1	5	5	1	2	2	0	0	0	1	0	0	0	0	0	0	0	0	1	.400	.400	.400
Mauer, Joe, Min.*	13	59	51	5	15	18	1	1	0	3	0	0	0	8	3	6	0	0	0	.294	.390	.353
McDougall, Marshall, Tex.	2	4	4	1	1	1	0	0	0	0	0	0	0	0	0	1	0	0	0	.250	.250	.250
McEwing, Joe, K.C.	6	7	6	3	1	1	0	0	0	0	0	0	0	1	0	1	0	1	0	.167	.286	.167
Melhuse, Adam, Oak.†	8	21	21	2	5	8	0	0	1	1	0	0	0	0	0	7	0	0	0	.238	.238	.381
Mench, Kevin, Tex.	1	4	3	0	0	0	0	0	0	0	0	0	0	1	0	1	0	0	0	.000	.250	.000
Menechino, Frank, Tor.	25	77	60	8	12	21	3	0	2	4	1	0	4	12	0	18	0	0	2	.200	.368	.350
Miller, Corky, Min.	1	1	1	0	0	0	0	0	0	0	0	0	0	0	0	0	0	0	0	.000	.000	.000
Mirabelli, Doug, Bos.	5	14	12	2	4	7	0	0	1	5	0	0	0	2	0	3	0	0	0	.333	.429	.583
Molina, Bengie, L.A.	11	38	30	3	13	19	3	0	1	7	0	3	0	5	1	2	0	0	1	.433	.474	.633
Molina, Jose, L.A.	5	9	8	0	3	3	0	0	0	2	0	0	0	1	0	0	0	0	1	.375	.444	.375
Monroe, Craig, Det.	1	1	0	0	0	0	0	0	0	0	0	0	0	1	0	0	0	0	0	.000	1.000	.000
Mora, Melvin, Bal.	1	1	1	0	0	0	0	0	0	0	0	0	0	0	0	0	0	0	0	.000	.000	.000
Morneau, Justin, Min.*	1	2	1	0	0	0	0	0	0	0	0	0	1	1	0	0	0	0	1	.000	.500	.000
Morse, Mike, Sea.	9	30	28	3	5	5	0	0	0	2	0	0	1	0	0	11	0	0	1	.179	.233	.179
Munson, Eric, TB.*	3	12	9	2	3	4	1	0	0	1	0	0	1	2	0	3	0	0	0	.333	.500	.444
Murphy, Donnie, K.C.	1	3	2	0	0	0	0	0	0	0	0	0	0	1	0	0	0	0	0	.000	.333	.000
Nevin, Phil, Tex.	25	100	91	15	16	30	5	0	3	8	0	0	1	8	0	27	2	0	6	.176	.250	.330
Newhan, David, Bal.*	7	15	13	1	0	0	0	0	0	0	0	1	0	1	0	3	0	0	0	.000	.071	.000
Nixon, Trot, Bos.*	2	2	1	0	0	0	0	0	0	0	0	0	0	1	0	0	0	0	0	.000	.500	.000

Player, Team	G	TPA	AB	R	H	TB	2B	3B	HR	RBI	SH	SF	HP	BB	IBB	SO	SB	CS	GDP	Avg.	OBP	Slg.
Ordonez, Magglio, Det.	1	4	4	0	0	0	0	0	0	0	0	0	0	0	0	0	0	0	0	.000	.000	.000
Ortiz, David, Bos.*...............	148	666	558	111	166	336	39	1	43	141	0	9	1	98	9	118	1	0	13	.297	.398	.602
Ozuna, Pablo, Chi.	4	4	4	0	1	2	1	0	0	0	0	0	0	0	0	3	0	0	0	.250	.250	.500
Palmeiro, Rafael, Bal.*	15	63	56	4	9	16	1	0	2	4	0	1	0	6	2	10	0	0	6	.161	.238	.286
Pena, Carlos, Det.*	24	94	86	13	23	58	5	0	10	21	0	0	1	7	1	34	0	0	1	.267	.330	.674
Perez, Eduardo, T.B.	7	20	17	1	5	8	3	0	0	4	0	0	0	3	0	2	0	0	1	.294	.400	.471
Perez, Timo, Chi.*	11	22	21	2	4	5	1	0	0	2	0	0	0	1	0	4	0	0	0	.190	.227	.238
Petagine, Roberto, Bos.*.......	3	3	2	0	0	0	0	0	0	0	0	0	0	1	0	1	0	0	0	.000	.333	.000
Phelps, Josh, T.B.	42	171	153	20	41	66	10	0	5	26	0	3	4	11	1	46	0	0	3	.268	.327	.431
Phillips, Andy, N.Y.	6	12	12	2	1	2	1	0	0	0	0	0	0	0	0	3	0	0	1	.083	.083	.167
Phillips, Brandon, Cle.	1	1	1	1	0	0	0	0	0	0	0	0	0	0	0	1	0	0	0	.000	.000	.000
Phillips, Paul, K.C.	2	3	3	0	0	0	0	0	0	0	0	0	0	0	0	0	0	0	0	.000	.000	.000
Pickering, Calvin, K.C.*	7	31	27	4	4	7	0	0	1	3	0	1	0	3	0	14	0	0	0	.148	.226	.259
Posada, Jorge, N.Y.†	3	12	10	2	3	3	0	0	0	1	0	1	0	1	0	3	0	0	0	.300	.333	.300
Pride, Curtis, L.A.*	3	6	6	2	1	2	1	0	0	0	0	0	0	0	0	2	0	0	0	.167	.167	.333
Punto, Nick, Min.†	5	1	1	2	0	0	0	0	0	0	0	0	0	0	0	1	0	0	0	.000	.000	.000
Quiroz, Guillermo, Tor............	2	7	6	0	1	2	1	0	0	2	0	0	0	1	0	1	0	0	0	.167	.286	.333
Ramirez, Manny, Bos.	2	9	8	1	1	2	1	0	0	0	0	0	0	1	0	0	0	0	0	.125	.222	.250
Rios, Alex, Tor.	1	1	0	0	0	0	0	0	0	0	0	0	0	1	0	0	0	0	0	.000	1.000	.000
Rivera, Juan, L.A.	28	108	99	10	24	37	4	0	3	10	1	0	0	8	0	12	1	0	6	.242	.299	.374
Rodriguez, Alex, N.Y.	1	5	2	2	1	4	0	0	1	1	0	0	0	3	0	0	0	0	0	.500	.800	2.000
Rodriguez, Ivan, Det.	3	14	14	2	5	8	3	0	0	0	0	0	0	0	0	1	0	0	0	.357	.357	.571
Rodriguez, Luis, Min.†	3	1	1	0	0	0	0	0	0	0	0	0	0	0	0	0	0	0	0	.000	.000	.000
Rogers, Ed, Bal.	2	0	0	1	0	0	0	0	0	0	0	0	0	0	0	0	1	0	0	.000	.000	.000
Ryan, Michael, Min.*	13	32	30	3	5	8	0	0	1	4	0	0	0	2	0	4	0	0	1	.167	.219	.267
Sanchez, Alex, T.B.*	7	23	21	2	6	7	1	0	0	1	1	0	0	1	0	4	2	0	0	.286	.318	.333
Sanchez, Rey, N.Y.	2	0	0	1	0	0	0	0	0	0	0	0	0	0	0	0	0	0	0	.000	.000	.000
Sexson, Richie, Sea.	5	22	19	4	4	7	0	0	1	5	0	0	0	3	0	8	0	0	0	.211	.318	.368
Sheffield, Gary, N.Y.	23	104	93	15	29	53	3	0	7	24	0	0	1	10	0	9	0	0	2	.312	.385	.570
Shelton, Chris, Det.	15	57	51	8	13	22	3	0	2	10	0	1	0	5	0	12	0	0	1	.255	.316	.431
Shoppach, Kelly, Bos.	2	3	3	1	0	0	0	0	0	0	0	0	0	0	0	1	0	0	0	.000	.000	.000
Sierra, Ruben, N.Y.†	30	104	98	8	22	36	5	0	3	19	0	1	0	5	0	29	0	0	0	.224	.260	.367
Singleton, Chris, T.B.*	4	9	8	2	2	2	0	0	0	2	0	0	0	1	0	2	0	0	1	.250	.333	.250
Smith, Jason, Det.*	1	1	1	0	1	1	0	0	0	0	0	0	0	0	0	0	0	0	0	1.000	1.000	1.000
Soriano, Alfonso, Tex.	2	8	8	1	1	4	0	0	1	3	0	0	0	0	0	1	0	0	0	.125	.125	.500
Sosa, Sammy, Bal.	35	146	123	14	25	40	3	0	4	19	0	3	0	20	1	35	0	1	3	.203	.308	.325
Spiezio, Scott, Sea.†	5	17	16	0	0	0	0	0	0	0	0	0	0	1	0	5	0	0	0	.000	.059	.000
Stairs, Matt, K.C.*	40	155	122	20	28	53	7	0	6	21	0	1	1	31	1	23	1	1	0	.230	.387	.434
Stewart, Shannon, Min.	5	25	23	3	7	7	0	0	0	1	0	0	0	2	0	3	0	0	0	.304	.360	.304
Strong, Jamal, Sea.	3	2	2	1	1	3	0	1	0	0	0	0	0	0	0	0	0	0	0	.500	.500	1.500
Surhoff, B.J., Bal.*	7	28	26	1	4	5	1	0	0	3	0	1	0	1	0	4	0	0	1	.154	.179	.192
Suzuki, Ichiro, Sea.*	3	14	14	2	6	8	0	1	0	3	0	0	0	0	0	2	0	0	0	.429	.429	.571
Sweeney, Mike, K.C.	73	304	275	40	84	144	21	0	13	47	0	4	3	22	6	38	1	0	11	.305	.359	.524
Teixeira, Mark, Tex.†	8	35	34	5	10	21	2	0	3	11	0	0	0	1	0	3	0	0	2	.294	.314	.618
Tejada, Miguel, Bal.	2	9	9	0	1	1	0	0	0	1	0	0	0	0	0	2	0	0	0	.111	.111	.111
Thames, Marcus, Det.	4	11	8	3	1	4	0	0	1	1	0	0	0	3	0	3	0	0	0	.125	.364	.500
Thomas, Frank, Chi.	28	118	101	18	22	58	3	0	11	24	0	3	0	14	0	28	0	0	2	.218	.305	.574
Tiffee, Terry, Min.†	10	27	25	3	6	9	1	1	0	6	0	0	0	2	0	4	1	0	0	.240	.296	.360
Tyner, Jason, Min.*	3	8	7	2	1	1	0	0	0	0	0	0	0	1	0	0	0	0	0	.143	.250	.143
Vazquez, Ramon, Bos.*..........	1	1	1	0	0	0	0	0	0	0	0	0	0	0	0	0	0	0	0	.000	.000	.000
Wells, Vernon, Tor.	2	10	9	2	3	4	1	0	0	2	0	1	0	0	0	0	0	0	0	.333	.300	.444
White, Rondell, Det.	30	127	121	12	33	49	10	0	2	10	0	0	1	5	0	17	0	0	2	.273	.307	.405
Widger, Chris, Chi.................	1	1	1	0	0	0	0	0	0	0	0	0	0	0	0	0	0	0	0	.000	.000	.000
Williams, Bernie, N.Y.†	23	94	85	10	25	39	2	0	4	19	0	0	0	9	0	13	0	1	6	.294	.362	.459
Winn, Randy, Sea.†	2	8	8	2	2	2	0	0	0	0	0	0	0	0	0	1	0	0	0	.250	.250	.250
Womack, Tony, N.Y.*.............	11	4	3	3	0	0	0	0	0	1	0	1	0	0	0	1	3	0	1	.000	.000	.000
Young, Dmitri, Det.†	71	301	277	39	73	129	14	3	12	39	0	1	5	18	1	65	1	0	7	.264	.319	.466
Young, Michael, Tex.	4	21	18	3	5	5	0	0	0	0	0	0	0	3	0	4	0	0	0	.278	.381	.278
Young, Walter, Bal.*	3	7	7	1	2	5	0	0	1	1	0	0	0	0	0	3	0	0	0	.286	.286	.714

The following designated hitters, each of whom appeared in at least one game, had no plate appearances, runs scored or stolen base attempts:
Green, Nick, Tampa Bay (2); German, Esteban, Texas; Guiel, Aaron, Kansas City; Paul, Josh, Los Angeles; Rivas, Luis, Minnesota; Sorensen, Zach, Los Angeles.

PINCH-HITTING

TEAM

Team	G	TPA	AB	R	H	TB	2B	3B	HR	RBI	SH	SF	HP	BB	IBB	SO	SB	CS	GDP	Avg.	OBP	Slg.
Tampa Bay	83	118	97	11	30	43	1	0	4	16	1	3	2	15	2	22	1	0	5	.309	.402	.443
Toronto	89	144	121	15	37	54	8	0	3	22	0	2	2	19	1	23	3	1	4	.306	.403	.446
Detroit	57	74	64	5	17	21	2	1	0	14	0	4	1	5	0	22	1	0	3	.266	.311	.328
Minnesota	77	104	81	7	21	31	4	0	2	13	1	1	1	20	3	17	1	0	5	.259	.408	.383
New York	71	94	78	9	19	29	4	0	2	12	0	1	0	15	1	13	1	0	2	.244	.362	.372
Texas	45	57	54	5	13	23	1	0	3	7	0	0	0	3	0	23	0	0	0	.241	.281	.426
Los Angeles	65	90	77	10	18	27	6	0	1	12	2	1	0	10	2	16	1	1	1	.234	.318	.351
Seattle	84	121	103	9	22	33	6	1	1	13	2	3	1	12	0	34	0	0	1	.214	.294	.320
Cleveland	64	87	75	6	16	20	4	0	0	10	0	4	0	8	4	17	1	0	1	.213	.276	.267
Chicago	68	100	88	4	18	30	6	0	2	12	2	0	0	10	3	24	1	0	3	.205	.286	.341
Boston	79	108	94	6	19	24	2	0	1	13	0	1	0	13	0	22	0	0	4	.202	.296	.255
Oakland	63	82	70	4	11	14	3	0	0	8	0	0	0	12	2	15	0	0	3	.157	.280	.200
Kansas City	80	130	115	12	18	24	3	0	1	10	0	4	1	11	0	31	0	0	2	.157	.254	.209
Baltimore	59	85	71	4	9	16	2	1	0	6	2	1	2	9	2	22	1	0	2	.127	.241	.225
Totals	984	1394	1188	107	268	389	52	3	21	168	10	21	13	162	20	301	11	2	36	.226	.320	.327

TOP PINCH-HITTERS

Minimum 20 at-bats. *Lefthanded batter. †Switch-hitter.

Player, Team	G	TPA	AB	R	H	TB	2B	3B	HR	RBI	SH	SF	HP	BB	IBB	SO	SB	CS	GDP	Avg.	OBP	Slg.
Lee, Travis, TB.*	23	21	21	2	10	16	0	0	2	7	0	0	0	0	0	3	0	0	0	.476	.476	.762
Dobbs, Greg, Sea.*	26	26	24	1	6	9	3	0	0	5	0	1	0	1	0	9	0	0	1	.250	.269	.375
Ryan, Michael, Min.*	25	25	21	1	4	5	1	0	0	5	0	1	0	3	1	5	0	0	1	.190	.280	.238
Sierra, Ruben, N.Y.†	24	24	23	0	4	6	2	0	0	3	0	0	0	1	0	7	0	0	0	.174	.208	.261
Perez, Timo, Chi.*	25	25	24	0	4	6	2	0	0	1	0	0	0	1	0	5	0	0	0	.167	.200	.250
Hansen, Dave, Sea.*	41	39	31	0	2	2	0	0	0	4	1	2	0	5	0	13	0	0	0	.065	.184	.065

NOTE: Only 6 batters (rather than the usual 15) are listed above since they are the only players to have the minimum 20 pinch-hit at-bats during the 2005 American League season.

ALL PINCH-HITTERS

*Lefthanded batter. †Switch-hitter.

Player, Team	G	TPA	AB	R	H	TB	2B	3B	HR	RBI	SH	SF	HP	BB	IBB	SO	SB	CS	GDP	Avg.	OBP	Slg.
Abernathy, Brent, Min.	3	3	2	0	0	0	0	0	0	0	1	0	0	0	0	1	0	0	0	.000	.000	.000
Adams, Russ, Tor.*	14	14	14	1	5	6	1	0	0	2	0	0	0	0	0	3	0	0	1	.357	.357	.429
Allen, Chad, Tex.	7	7	7	0	2	2	0	0	0	1	0	0	0	0	0	4	0	0	0	.286	.286	.286
Alomar Jr., Sandy, Tex.	2	2	2	0	0	0	0	0	0	0	0	0	0	0	0	0	0	0	0	.000	.000	.000
Ambres, Chip, K.C.	10	10	5	2	1	1	0	0	0	0	0	0	1	4	0	1	0	0	0	.200	.600	.200
Anderson, Brian N., Chi.	3	3	3	0	0	0	0	0	0	0	0	0	0	0	0	1	0	1	0	.000	.000	.000
Bard, Josh, Cle.†	5	5	4	0	1	1	0	0	0	1	0	1	0	0	0	0	0	0	0	.250	.200	.250
Bellhorn, Mark, Bos.-N.Y.†	2	2	1	0	0	0	0	0	0	0	0	0	0	1	0	0	0	0	0	.000	.500	.000
Belliard, Ronnie, Cle.	5	5	3	0	0	0	0	0	0	1	0	1	0	1	0	1	0	0	0	.000	.200	.000
Bigbie, Larry, Bal.*	4	4	3	0	0	0	0	0	0	0	1	0	0	0	0	1	0	0	0	.000	.000	.000
Blake, Casey, Cle.	4	4	3	0	0	0	0	0	0	1	0	1	0	0	0	1	0	0	0	.000	.000	.000
Blalock, Hank, Tex.*	4	3	3	1	2	3	1	0	0	2	0	0	0	0	0	0	0	0	0	.667	.667	1.000
Bloomquist, Willie, Sea.	4	4	4	0	1	1	0	0	0	0	0	0	0	0	0	1	0	0	0	.250	.250	.250
Blum, Geoff, Chi.†	4	4	4	0	0	0	0	0	0	0	0	0	0	0	0	1	0	0	1	.000	.000	.000
Bocachica, Hiram, Oak.	2	2	2	0	0	0	0	0	0	0	0	0	0	0	0	1	0	0	0	.000	.000	.000
Borchard, Joe, Chi.†	4	4	4	0	3	3	0	0	0	0	0	0	0	0	0	1	0	0	0	.750	.750	.750
Broussard, Ben, Cle.*	16	16	14	2	4	6	2	0	0	1	0	0	0	2	2	5	0	0	0	.286	.375	.429
Brown, Emil, K.C.	3	3	2	1	0	0	0	0	0	1	0	0	0	1	0	1	0	0	0	.000	.333	.000
Bubela, Jaime, Sea.*	1	1	1	0	0	0	0	0	0	0	0	0	0	0	0	0	0	0	0	.000	.000	.000
Buck, John, K.C.	1	1	1	0	0	0	0	0	0	0	0	0	0	0	0	0	0	0	1	.000	.000	.000
Burke, Jamie, Chi.	1	1	1	0	0	0	0	0	0	0	0	0	0	0	0	0	0	0	0	.000	.000	.000
Bynum, Freddie, Oak.*	2	2	2	0	0	0	0	0	0	0	0	0	0	0	0	1	0	0	0	.000	.000	.000
Byrnes, Eric, Oak.-Bal.	4	4	2	0	0	0	0	0	0	0	0	0	0	2	0	1	0	0	0	.000	.500	.000
Calzado, Napoleon, Bal.	2	2	2	0	1	1	0	0	0	0	0	0	0	0	0	1	0	0	0	.500	.500	.500
Cano, Robinson, N.Y.*	2	2	2	1	1	4	0	0	1	2	0	0	0	0	0	0	0	0	0	.500	.500	2.000
Cantu, Jorge, TB.	2	2	2	0	0	0	0	0	0	0	0	0	0	0	0	0	0	0	0	.000	.000	.000
Casanova, Raul, Chi.†	1	1	1	0	0	0	0	0	0	0	0	0	0	0	0	1	0	0	0	.000	.000	.000
Cash, Kevin, TB.	1	1	1	0	0	0	0	0	0	0	0	0	0	0	0	1	0	0	0	.000	.000	.000
Castro, Bernie, Bal.†	3	3	3	1	1	1	0	0	0	0	0	0	0	0	0	0	0	1	0	.333	.333	.333
Catalanotto, Frank, Tor.*	17	17	11	4	4	5	1	0	0	3	0	1	0	5	0	0	0	0	0	.364	.529	.455
Chavez, Eric, Oak.*	1	1	1	0	0	0	0	0	0	0	0	0	0	0	0	0	0	0	0	.000	.000	.000
Choo, Shin-Soo, Sea.*	4	4	4	0	1	1	0	0	0	1	0	0	0	0	0	1	0	0	0	.250	.250	.250
Clark, Jermaine, Oak.*	1	1	0	1	0	0	0	0	0	0	0	0	0	1	0	0	0	0	0	.000	1.000	.000
Cora, Alex, Cle.-Bos.*	11	11	11	2	2	3	1	0	0	0	0	0	0	0	0	1	1	0	0	.182	.182	.273
Cortez, Fernando, TB.*	4	3	2	0	0	0	0	0	0	0	0	0	0	1	0	0	0	0	0	.000	.333	.000
Costa, Shane, K.C.*	4	4	3	1	1	1	0	0	0	0	0	0	0	1	0	1	0	0	0	.333	.500	.333
Crawford, Carl, TB.*	1	1	0	1	0	0	0	0	0	0	0	0	0	1	0	0	0	0	0	.000	1.000	.000
Crede, Joe, Chi.	2	2	1	0	0	0	0	0	0	0	0	0	0	1	0	0	0	0	0	.000	.500	.000
Crosby, Bubba, N.Y.*	2	2	2	1	1	1	0	0	0	0	0	0	0	0	0	0	0	0	0	.500	.500	.500
Cuddyer, Michael, Min.	3	3	2	0	2	3	1	0	0	0	0	0	0	1	1	0	0	0	0	1.000	1.000	1.500

Player, Team	G	TPA	AB	R	H	TB	2B	3B	HR	RBI	SH	SF	HP	BB	IBB	SO	SB	CS	GDP	Avg.	OBP	Slg.
Cummings, Midre, Bal.*	1	1	1	0	0	0	0	0	0	0	0	0	0	0	0	1	0	0	0	.000	.000	.000
Damon, Johnny, Bos.*	2	2	1	1	0	0	0	0	0	0	0	0	0	1	0	0	0	0	0	.000	.500	.000
DaVanon, Jeff, L.A.†	20	19	15	3	3	3	0	0	0	1	0	0	0	4	0	2	0	1	0	.200	.368	.200
DeJesus, David, K.C.*	2	2	1	0	0	0	0	0	0	0	0	0	1	0	0	1	0	0	0	.000	.500	.000
Dellucci, David, Tex.*	16	16	14	2	4	10	0	0	2	3	0	0	0	2	0	7	0	0	0	.286	.375	.714
DeRosa, Mark, Tex.	5	5	4	1	1	4	0	0	1	1	0	0	0	1	0	2	0	0	0	.250	.400	1.000
Diaz, Matt, K.C.	9	9	9	0	1	1	0	0	0	0	0	0	0	0	0	2	0	0	0	.111	.111	.111
Dobbs, Greg, Sea.*	26	26	24	1	6	9	3	0	0	5	0	1	0	1	0	9	0	0	1	.250	.269	.375
Dominique, Andy, Tor.	1	1	1	0	0	0	0	0	0	0	0	0	0	0	0	0	0	0	0	.000	.000	.000
Durazo, Erubiel, Oak.*	2	2	2	0	2	2	0	0	0	1	0	0	0	0	0	0	0	0	0	1.000	1.000	1.000
Dye, Jermaine, Chi.	3	3	3	0	0	0	0	0	0	0	0	0	0	0	0	2	0	0	0	.000	.000	.000
Ellis, Mark, Oak.	2	2	1	0	0	0	0	0	0	0	0	0	0	1	0	0	0	0	0	.000	.500	.000
Everett, Carl, Chi.†	8	8	8	0	1	1	0	0	0	1	0	0	0	0	0	3	0	0	1	.125	.125	.125
Fasano, Sal, Bal.	3	3	2	1	1	4	0	0	1	1	0	0	1	0	0	1	0	0	0	.500	.667	2.000
Figgins, Chone, L.A.†	1	1	1	0	0	0	0	0	0	0	0	0	0	0	0	0	0	0	0	.000	.000	.000
Finley, Steve, L.A.*	7	7	7	0	0	0	0	0	0	0	0	0	0	0	0	4	0	0	0	.000	.000	.000
Fiorentino, Jeff, Bal.*	1	1	1	0	0	0	0	0	0	0	0	0	0	0	0	1	0	0	0	.000	.000	.000
Flaherty, John, N.Y.	1	1	1	0	0	0	0	0	0	0	0	0	0	0	0	0	0	0	0	.000	.000	.000
Ford, Lew, Min.	12	12	7	0	4	4	0	0	0	1	0	0	1	4	0	1	1	0	0	.571	.750	.571
Freire, Alejandro, Bal.	1	1	1	0	0	0	0	0	0	0	0	0	0	0	0	0	0	0	0	.000	.000	.000
Garko, Ryan, Cle.	1	1	1	0	0	0	0	0	0	0	0	0	0	0	0	1	0	0	0	.000	.000	.000
Gathright, Joey, TB.*	3	3	2	0	0	0	0	0	0	1	0	0	0	1	0	0	0	0	0	.000	.333	.000
Gerut, Jody, Cle.*	6	6	6	0	2	2	0	0	0	1	0	0	0	0	0	0	0	0	0	.333	.333	.333
Giambi, Jason, N.Y.*	4	4	4	0	0	0	0	0	0	0	0	0	0	0	0	0	0	0	0	.000	.000	.000
Giarratano, Tony, Det.†	2	2	1	0	0	0	0	0	0	0	0	0	0	1	0	0	0	0	0	.000	.500	.000
Gibbons, Jay, Bal.*	10	10	10	0	0	0	0	0	0	0	0	0	0	0	0	1	0	0	0	.000	.000	.000
Gil, Geronimo, Bal.	3	3	3	0	0	0	0	0	0	0	0	0	0	0	0	0	0	0	2	.000	.000	.000
Ginter, Keith, Oak.	11	11	11	0	2	3	1	0	0	2	0	0	0	0	0	1	0	0	0	.182	.182	.273
Gload, Ross, Chi.*	4	4	4	0	1	1	0	0	0	1	0	0	0	0	0	0	0	0	0	.250	.250	.250
Gomes, Jonny, TB.	4	4	4	2	2	5	0	0	1	1	0	0	0	0	0	2	0	0	0	.500	.500	1.250
Gomez, Alexis, Det.*	2	2	2	0	0	0	0	0	0	0	0	0	0	0	0	0	0	0	0	.000	.000	.000
Gomez, Chris, Bal.	7	7	5	0	1	1	0	0	0	1	0	0	0	2	0	2	0	0	0	.200	.429	.200
Gonzalez, Adrian, Tex.*	2	2	2	0	0	0	0	0	0	0	0	0	0	0	0	1	0	0	0	.000	.000	.000
Gonzalez, Alex S., TB.	4	4	3	0	1	2	1	0	0	0	0	0	0	1	0	1	0	0	1	.333	.500	.667
Gotay, Ruben, K.C.†	8	8	8	0	1	2	1	0	0	2	0	0	0	0	0	2	0	0	0	.125	.125	.250
Graffanino, Tony, K.C.-Bos.	8	8	6	1	1	1	0	0	0	0	0	0	0	2	0	1	0	0	0	.167	.375	.167
Granderson, Curtis, Det.*	3	3	3	0	1	1	0	0	0	0	0	0	0	0	0	2	0	0	0	.333	.333	.333
Green, Nick, TB.	6	6	3	1	1	1	0	0	0	0	1	0	1	1	0	1	0	0	0	.333	.600	.333
Griffin, John-Ford, Tor.*	4	4	4	0	1	2	1	0	0	1	0	0	0	0	0	1	0	0	0	.250	.250	.500
Gross, Gabe, Tor.*	6	6	6	0	1	1	0	0	0	0	0	0	0	0	0	3	1	0	0	.167	.167	.167
Guerrero, Vladimir, L.A.	2	2	1	0	0	0	0	0	0	0	0	0	0	1	1	0	0	0	0	.000	.500	.000
Guiel, Aaron, K.C.*	6	5	5	1	1	1	0	0	0	0	0	0	0	0	0	1	0	0	0	.200	.200	.200
Guillen, Carlos, Det.†	5	5	4	0	1	1	0	0	0	1	0	1	0	0	0	2	0	0	0	.250	.200	.250
Gutierrez, Franklin, Cle.	1	1	1	0	0	0	0	0	0	0	0	0	0	0	0	0	0	0	0	.000	.000	.000
Hafner, Travis, Cle.*	7	7	4	2	1	1	0	0	0	1	0	0	0	3	2	1	0	0	0	.250	.571	.250
Hall, Toby, TB.	3	3	3	0	2	2	0	0	0	1	0	0	0	0	0	0	0	0	1	.667	.667	.667
Hansen, Dave, Sea.*	41	39	31	0	2	2	0	0	0	4	1	2	0	5	0	13	0	0	0	.065	.184	.065
Harris, Willie, Chi.*	12	12	10	1	1	1	0	0	0	0	1	0	0	1	0	4	1	0	0	.100	.182	.100
Hatteberg, Scott, Oak.*	11	11	7	0	0	0	0	0	0	1	0	0	0	4	2	1	0	0	2	.000	.364	.000
Hernandez, Jose, Cle.	14	13	12	0	3	4	1	0	0	2	0	1	0	0	0	4	0	0	0	.250	.231	.333
Hidalgo, Richard, Tex.	4	4	4	0	0	0	0	0	0	0	0	0	0	0	0	3	0	0	0	.000	.000	.000
Higginson, Bobby, Det.*	3	3	3	0	0	0	0	0	0	0	0	0	0	0	0	1	0	0	0	.000	.000	.000
Hill, Aaron, Tor.	4	4	4	0	2	3	1	0	0	0	0	0	0	0	0	0	0	1	0	.500	.500	.750
Hillenbrand, Shea, Tor.	2	2	1	0	0	0	0	0	0	0	0	0	0	1	0	1	0	0	0	.000	.500	.000
Hinske, Eric, Tor.*	18	18	13	6	4	8	1	0	1	4	0	1	0	4	0	2	1	1	0	.308	.444	.615
Hocking, Denny, K.C.†	9	9	8	0	2	2	0	0	0	2	0	0	0	1	0	3	0	0	0	.250	.333	.250
Hollins, Damon, TB.	7	7	7	1	1	1	0	0	0	0	0	0	0	0	0	3	0	0	0	.143	.143	.143
Huber, Justin, K.C.	3	3	3	0	1	2	1	0	0	1	0	0	0	0	0	1	0	0	0	.333	.333	.667
Huckaby, Ken, Tor.	1	1	1	0	1	1	0	0	0	0	0	0	0	0	0	0	0	0	0	1.000	1.000	1.000
Hudson, Orlando, Tor.†	8	8	7	2	5	9	1	0	1	1	0	0	0	1	0	1	0	0	0	.714	.750	1.286
Huff, Aubrey, TB.*	6	5	4	0	1	1	0	0	0	0	0	0	0	1	1	1	0	0	0	.250	.400	.250
Hunter, Torii, Min.	1	1	1	0	0	0	0	0	0	0	0	0	0	0	0	0	0	0	0	.000	.000	.000
Hyzdu, Adam, Bos.	1	1	1	0	0	0	0	0	0	0	0	0	0	0	0	1	0	0	0	.000	.000	.000
Iguchi, Tadahito, Chi.	5	5	4	2	3	7	1	0	1	6	0	0	0	1	0	0	0	0	0	.750	.800	1.750
Infante, Omar, Det.	4	4	4	0	1	2	1	0	0	1	0	0	0	0	0	3	0	0	0	.250	.250	.500
Izturis, Maicer, L.A.†	2	2	2	1	1	1	0	0	0	0	0	0	0	0	0	0	1	0	1	.500	.500	.500
Johnson, Dan, Oak.*	6	6	5	0	0	0	0	0	0	0	0	0	0	1	0	0	0	0	0	.000	.167	.000
Johnson, Reed, Tor.	22	21	19	1	4	9	2	0	1	5	0	0	0	2	1	4	0	0	0	.211	.286	.474
Johnson, Russ, N.Y.	3	3	3	0	0	0	0	0	0	0	0	0	0	0	0	2	0	0	0	.000	.000	.000
Jones, Jacque, Min.*	2	2	2	2	2	6	1	0	1	1	0	0	0	0	0	0	0	0	0	1.000	1.000	3.000
Kapler, Gabe, Bos.	4	4	4	0	1	1	0	0	0	0	0	0	0	0	0	0	0	1	0	.250	.250	.250
Kennedy, Adam, L.A.*	2	2	2	0	1	1	0	0	0	0	0	0	0	0	0	0	0	0	0	.500	.500	.500
Kielty, Bobby, Oak.†	14	14	11	2	2	2	0	0	0	1	0	0	0	3	0	3	0	0	0	.182	.357	.182
Konerko, Paul, Chi.	2	2	0	0	0	0	0	0	0	0	0	0	0	2	2	0	0	0	0	.000	1.000	.000
Koskie, Corey, Tor.*	3	3	3	0	1	1	0	0	0	0	0	0	0	0	0	1	0	0	0	.333	.333	.333
Kotchman, Casey, L.A.*	11	11	9	1	2	3	1	0	0	3	0	0	0	2	0	3	0	0	0	.222	.364	.333
LaForest, Pete, TB.*	2	2	1	0	1	1	0	0	0	0	0	0	0	1	1	0	0	0	0	1.000	1.000	1.000
Laker, Tim, TB.	1	1	1	0	0	0	0	0	0	0	0	0	0	0	0	0	0	0	0	.000	.000	.000
LeCroy, Matthew, Min.	17	17	12	0	1	1	0	0	0	1	0	0	0	5	0	4	0	0	2	.083	.353	.083
Lee, Travis, TB.*	23	21	21	2	10	16	0	0	2	7	0	0	0	0	0	3	0	0	0	.476	.476	.762
Liefer, Jeff, Cle.*	7	7	7	1	1	1	0	0	0	1	0	0	0	0	0	2	0	0	0	.143	.143	.143
Logan, Nook, Det.†	3	3	3	2	3	5	0	1	0	3	0	0	0	0	0	0	1	0	0	1.000	1.000	1.667

Player, Team	G	TPA	AB	R	H	TB	2B	3B	HR	RBI	SH	SF	HP	BB	IBB	SO	SB	CS	GDP	Avg.	OBP	Slg.
Long, Terrence, K.C.*	19	18	17	3	4	4	0	0	0	1	0	0	0	1	0	3	0	0	1	.235	.278	.235
Lopez, Javy, Bal.	1	1	1	0	0	0	0	0	0	0	0	0	0	0	0	1	0	0	0	.000	.000	.000
Lopez, Jose, Sea.	2	2	2	0	0	0	0	0	0	0	0	0	0	0	0	0	0	0	0	.000	.000	.000
Lugo, Julio, TB.	3	3	1	0	0	0	0	0	0	1	0	1	0	1	0	0	0	0	0	.000	.333	.000
Maroth, Mike, Det.*	1	1	1	0	0	0	0	0	0	0	0	0	0	0	0	1	0	0	0	.000	.000	.000
Marrero, Eli, K.C.-Bal.	14	14	12	1	1	3	0	1	0	1	0	1	0	1	0	5	0	0	0	.083	.143	.250
Martinez, Ramon, Det.......	2	1	1	0	1	1	0	0	0	1	0	0	0	0	0	0	0	0	0	1.000	1.000	1.000
Martinez, Tino, N.Y.*	11	11	7	1	1	1	0	0	0	1	0	0	0	4	0	1	0	0	0	.143	.455	.143
Martinez, Victor, Cle.†	5	5	3	0	1	1	0	0	0	1	0	0	0	2	0	0	0	0	0	.333	.600	.333
Mathis, Jeff, L.A.	1	1	1	0	0	0	0	0	0	0	0	0	0	0	0	1	0	0	0	.000	.000	.000
Matos, Luis, Bal.	3	3	3	0	0	0	0	0	0	0	0	0	0	0	0	1	0	0	0	.000	.000	.000
Matsui, Hideki, N.Y.*	1	1	1	0	1	1	0	0	0	0	0	0	0	0	0	0	0	0	0	1.000	1.000	1.000
Matthews Jr., Gary, Tex.†	4	4	4	1	1	1	0	0	0	0	0	0	0	0	0	0	0	0	0	.250	.250	.250
Mauer, Joe, Min.*	7	7	4	1	0	0	0	0	0	0	0	0	0	3	1	1	0	0	0	.000	.429	.000
McCarty, Dave, Bos.	2	2	2	0	1	1	0	0	0	2	0	0	0	0	0	0	0	0	0	.500	.500	.500
McDonald, John, Tor.-Det.......	9	9	7	0	2	2	0	0	0	1	0	0	0	2	0	1	0	0	0	.286	.444	.286
McDougall, Marshall, Tex.	3	3	3	0	1	1	0	0	0	0	0	0	0	0	0	1	0	0	0	.333	.333	.333
McEwing, Joe, K.C.	17	16	15	1	3	3	0	0	0	0	0	0	0	1	0	3	0	0	0	.200	.250	.200
McPherson, Dallas, L.A.*	1	1	1	1	1	4	0	0	1	2	0	0	0	0	0	0	0	0	0	1.000	1.000	4.000
Melhuse, Adam, Oak.†	14	14	14	1	4	6	2	0	0	2	0	0	0	0	0	6	0	0	0	.286	.286	.429
Mench, Kevin, Tex.	3	3	3	0	0	0	0	0	0	0	0	0	0	0	0	1	0	0	0	.000	.000	.000
Menechino, Frank, Tor.	17	14	11	0	0	0	0	0	0	1	0	2	1	0	0	4	0	0	0	.000	.214	.000
Millar, Kevin, Bos.	7	7	6	0	2	2	0	0	0	0	0	0	0	1	0	1	0	0	0	.333	.429	.333
Miller, Corky, Min.	1	1	1	0	0	0	0	0	0	0	0	0	0	0	0	0	0	0	0	.000	.000	.000
Mirabelli, Doug, Bos.	7	7	6	1	1	4	0	0	1	3	0	0	0	1	0	1	0	0	0	.167	.286	.667
Molina, Bengie, L.A.	7	7	5	0	2	3	1	0	0	2	0	1	0	1	1	0	0	0	0	.400	.429	.600
Molina, Jose, L.A.	6	5	5	0	2	2	0	0	0	2	0	0	0	0	0	1	0	0	0	.400	.400	.400
Monroe, Craig, Det.	1	1	0	0	0	0	0	0	0	0	0	0	0	1	0	0	0	0	0	.000	1.000	.000
Mora, Melvin, Bal.	1	1	1	0	0	0	0	0	0	0	0	0	0	0	0	0	0	0	0	.000	.000	.000
Morneau, Justin, Min.*	4	4	3	2	1	4	0	0	1	3	0	0	0	1	0	0	0	0	1	.333	.500	1.333
Morse, Mike, Sea.	4	4	3	0	1	1	0	0	0	0	0	0	0	1	0	2	0	0	0	.333	.500	.333
Mueller, Bill, Bos.†	5	5	5	0	1	1	0	0	0	1	0	0	0	0	0	1	0	0	0	.200	.200	.200
Munson, Eric, TB.*	7	6	3	0	0	0	0	0	0	1	0	1	0	2	0	0	0	0	1	.000	.333	.000
Murphy, Donnie, K.C.	6	6	5	1	1	2	1	0	0	0	0	0	0	1	0	4	0	0	0	.200	.333	.400
Myers, Greg, Tor.*	3	3	3	0	1	1	0	0	0	0	0	0	0	0	0	0	0	0	1	.333	.333	.333
Nevin, Phil, Tex.	3	3	3	0	1	1	0	0	0	0	0	0	0	0	0	2	0	0	0	.333	.333	.333
Newhan, David, Bal.*	11	11	8	1	1	2	1	0	0	0	1	0	0	2	1	4	0	0	0	.125	.300	.250
Nivar, Ramon, Bal.	3	3	2	0	0	0	0	0	0	0	0	0	1	0	0	1	0	0	0	.000	.333	.000
Nix, Laynce, Tex.*	1	1	1	0	0	0	0	0	0	0	0	0	0	0	0	0	0	0	0	.000	.000	.000
Nixon, Trot, Bos.*	13	13	10	1	1	1	0	0	0	1	0	1	0	2	0	3	0	0	0	.100	.231	.100
Olerud, John, Bos.*	14	14	12	2	2	3	1	0	0	1	0	0	0	2	0	3	0	0	0	.167	.286	.250
Ordonez, Magglio, Det.	2	2	1	0	0	0	0	0	0	0	0	1	0	0	0	0	0	0	0	.000	.000	.000
Ortiz, David, Bos.*	3	3	2	0	0	0	0	0	0	0	0	0	0	1	0	0	0	0	0	.000	.333	.000
Ozuna, Pablo, Chi.	10	10	8	0	3	6	3	0	0	1	1	0	0	1	0	1	0	0	0	.375	.444	.750
Palmeiro, Rafael, Bal.*	3	3	2	0	0	0	0	0	0	0	0	0	0	1	0	1	0	0	0	.000	.333	.000
Paul, Josh, L.A.	3	3	2	0	0	0	0	0	0	0	1	0	0	0	0	1	0	0	0	.000	.000	.000
Payton, Jay, Bos.-Oak.	11	11	10	0	3	4	1	0	0	2	0	0	0	1	0	0	0	0	2	.300	.364	.400
Pena, Carlos, Det.*	5	5	5	0	0	0	0	0	0	0	0	0	0	0	0	3	0	0	0	.000	.000	.000
Peralta, Jhonny, Cle.	1	1	1	0	0	0	0	0	0	0	0	0	0	0	0	0	0	0	0	.000	.000	.000
Perez, Eduardo, TB................	22	20	16	1	4	7	0	0	1	3	0	1	3	0	2	0	0	1	.250	.400	.438
Perez, Timo, Chi.*	25	25	24	0	4	6	2	0	0	1	0	0	1	0	5	0	0	0	.167	.200	.250
Petagine, Roberto, Bos.*........	7	7	6	0	0	0	0	0	0	0	0	0	0	1	0	3	0	0	0	.000	.143	.000
Phelps, Josh, TB.	5	5	4	1	1	1	0	0	0	0	0	0	0	1	0	1	0	0	0	.250	.400	.250
Phillips, Andy, N.Y.	3	3	3	1	1	2	1	0	0	0	0	0	0	0	0	0	0	0	0	.333	.333	.667
Phillips, Paul, K.C.	2	2	2	0	0	0	0	0	0	0	0	0	0	0	0	0	0	0	0	.000	.000	.000
Pierzynski, A.J., Chi.*	2	2	1	0	0	0	0	0	0	0	0	0	1	1	0	0	0	0	0	.000	.500	.000
Podsednik, Scott, Chi.*	3	3	3	0	0	0	0	0	0	0	0	0	0	0	0	1	0	0	0	.000	.000	.000
Polanco, Placido, Det.	1	1	1	0	0	0	0	0	0	0	0	0	0	0	0	0	0	0	0	.000	.000	.000
Posada, Jorge, N.Y.†	16	16	12	0	3	4	1	0	0	2	0	0	0	4	1	3	1	0	0	.250	.438	.333
Pride, Curtis, L.A.*	3	3	3	0	0	0	0	0	0	0	0	0	0	0	0	1	0	0	0	.000	.000	.000
Punto, Nick, Min.†.................	2	2	1	0	0	0	0	0	0	0	0	0	0	1	0	0	0	0	0	.000	.500	.000
Quinlan, Robb, L.A.	12	12	11	3	4	6	2	0	0	1	0	0	0	1	0	0	0	0	0	.364	.417	.545
Ramirez, Hanley, Bos.	1	1	1	0	0	0	0	0	0	0	0	0	0	0	0	1	0	0	0	.000	.000	.000
Ramirez, Manny, Bos.	3	3	2	0	1	1	0	0	0	1	0	0	0	1	0	1	0	0	0	.500	.667	.500
Reed, Jeremy, Sea.*	9	8	8	3	3	4	1	0	0	0	0	0	0	0	0	2	0	0	0	.375	.375	.500
Renteria, Edgar, Bos.	3	3	3	0	2	2	0	0	0	0	0	0	0	0	0	1	0	0	0	.667	.667	.667
Rios, Alex, Tor.	10	10	9	1	3	3	0	0	0	1	0	0	0	1	0	1	0	0	1	.333	.400	.333
Rivas, Luis, Min.	1	1	0	0	0	0	0	0	0	0	0	0	0	1	0	0	0	0	0	.000	1.000	.000
Rivera, Juan, L.A.	13	13	12	0	2	4	2	0	0	1	0	0	0	1	0	3	0	0	0	.167	.231	.333
Rivera, Rene, Sea.	2	2	2	0	0	0	0	0	0	0	0	0	0	0	0	0	0	0	0	.000	.000	.000
Roberts, Brian, Bal.†	3	3	3	0	1	2	1	0	0	0	0	0	0	0	0	0	0	0	0	.333	.333	.667
Rodriguez, Ivan, Det.	5	5	5	0	1	1	0	0	0	0	0	0	0	0	0	1	0	1	0	.200	.200	.200
Rodriguez, Luis, Min.†	6	6	6	1	2	2	0	0	0	1	0	0	0	0	0	0	0	0	0	.333	.333	.333
Rowand, Aaron, Chi.	4	4	4	0	1	1	0	0	0	0	0	0	0	0	0	2	0	0	0	.250	.250	.250
Ryan, Michael, Min.*	25	25	21	1	4	5	1	0	0	5	0	1	0	3	1	5	0	0	1	.190	.280	.238
Sanchez, Alex, TB.*	8	6	5	1	3	3	0	0	0	1	0	1	0	0	0	1	0	0	0	.600	.500	.600
Sanchez, Rey, N.Y.	5	5	5	2	3	3	0	0	0	0	0	0	0	0	0	0	0	0	1	.600	.600	.600
Santiago, Ramon, Sea.†	4	4	2	0	0	0	0	0	0	0	1	0	1	0	0	0	0	0	0	.000	.333	.000
Scutaro, Marco, Oak.	3	3	3	0	1	1	0	0	0	1	0	0	0	0	0	0	0	0	0	.333	.333	.333
Sheffield, Gary, N.Y...............	1	1	1	0	0	0	0	0	0	0	0	0	0	0	0	0	0	0	0	.000	.000	.000
Shelton, Chris, Det.	10	10	6	2	2	2	0	0	0	3	0	1	1	2	0	1	0	0	1	.333	.500	.333
Shoppach, Kelly, Bos.	2	2	2	0	0	0	0	0	0	0	0	0	0	0	0	1	0	0	0	.000	.000	.000

Player, Team	G	TPA	AB	R	H	TB	2B	3B	HR	RBI	SH	SF	HP	BB	IBB	SO	SB	CS	GDP	Avg.	OBP	Slg.
Sierra, Ruben, N.Y.†	24	24	23	0	4	6	2	0	0	3	0	0	0	1	0	7	0	0	0	.174	.208	.261
Singleton, Chris, TB.*	12	12	11	1	2	2	0	0	0	0	0	0	0	1	0	3	0	0	1	.182	.250	.182
Sizemore, Grady, Cle.*	5	5	5	0	2	2	0	0	0	0	0	0	0	0	0	0	0	0	0	.400	.400	.400
Smith, Jason, Det.*	5	5	5	0	1	1	0	0	0	0	0	0	0	0	0	1	0	0	0	.200	.200	.200
Snelling, Chris, Sea.*	5	4	3	1	2	3	1	0	0	0	0	0	0	1	0	0	0	0	0	.667	.750	1.000
Sorensen, Zach, L.A.†	1	1	0	1	0	0	0	0	0	0	1	0	0	0	0	0	0	0	0	.000	.000	.000
Soriano, Alfonso, Tex.	1	1	1	0	1	1	0	0	0	0	0	0	0	0	0	0	0	0	0	1.000	1.000	1.000
Sosa, Sammy, Bal.	1	1	1	0	1	1	0	0	0	0	0	0	0	0	0	0	0	0	0	1.000	1.000	1.000
Spiezio, Scott, Sea.†	15	15	14	1	3	7	1	0	1	1	0	0	0	1	0	6	0	0	0	.214	.267	.500
Stairs, Matt, K.C.*	14	14	13	1	1	4	0	0	1	2	0	0	1	0	0	4	0	0	0	.077	.143	.308
Stern, Adam, Bos.*	1	1	1	0	0	0	0	0	0	0	0	0	0	0	0	0	0	0	0	.000	.000	.000
Stewart, Shannon, Min.	2	2	2	0	0	0	0	0	0	0	0	0	0	0	0	1	0	0	0	.000	.000	.000
Strong, Jamal, Sea.	3	3	2	3	2	4	0	1	0	1	0	0	0	1	0	0	0	0	0	1.000	1.000	2.000
Surhoff, B.J., Bal.*	12	12	10	0	0	0	0	0	0	2	0	0	0	2	1	1	0	0	0	.000	.167	.000
Suzuki, Ichiro, Sea.*	1	1	1	0	0	0	0	0	0	0	0	0	0	0	0	0	0	0	0	.000	.000	.000
Swisher, Nick, Oak.†	3	3	3	0	0	0	0	0	0	0	0	0	0	0	0	1	0	0	0	.000	.000	.000
Taylor, Reggie, TB.*	3	3	3	0	1	1	0	0	0	0	0	0	0	0	0	2	1	0	0	.333	.333	.333
Teahen, Mark, K.C.*	5	5	5	0	0	0	0	0	0	0	0	0	0	0	0	2	0	0	0	.000	.000	.000
Thames, Marcus, Det.	4	4	4	0	0	0	0	0	0	0	0	0	0	0	0	4	0	0	0	.000	.000	.000
Thomas, Charles, Oak.*	2	2	2	0	0	0	0	0	0	0	0	0	0	0	0	0	0	0	0	.000	.000	.000
Thomas, Frank, Chi.	6	6	4	1	1	4	0	0	1	2	0	0	0	2	0	3	0	0	0	.250	.500	1.000
Tiffee, Terry, Min.†	16	16	15	0	3	4	1	0	0	1	0	0	0	1	0	4	0	0	0	.200	.250	.267
Torres, Andres, Tex.†	3	3	3	0	0	0	0	0	0	0	0	0	0	0	0	2	0	0	0	.000	.000	.000
Varitek, Jason, Bos.†	6	6	5	0	2	2	0	0	0	1	1	0	0	0	0	1	0	0	1	.400	.400	.400
Vazquez, Ramon, Bos.-Cle.*	7	7	7	0	1	1	0	0	0	1	0	0	0	0	0	1	0	0	0	.143	.143	.143
Watson, Matt, Oak.*	6	5	5	0	0	0	0	0	0	0	0	0	0	0	0	1	0	0	1	.000	.000	.000
White, Rondell, Det.	2	2	1	0	0	0	0	0	0	1	0	1	0	0	0	0	0	0	0	.000	.000	.000
Widger, Chris, Chi.	1	1	1	0	0	0	0	0	0	0	0	0	0	0	0	0	0	0	0	.000	.000	.000
Williams, Bernie, N.Y.†	16	16	11	2	3	6	0	0	1	4	0	1	0	4	0	0	0	0	0	.273	.438	.545
Williams, Glenn, Min.†	2	2	2	0	2	2	0	0	0	0	0	0	0	0	0	0	0	0	0	1.000	1.000	1.000
Wilson, Vance, Det.	6	6	6	1	2	3	1	0	0	1	0	0	0	0	0	2	0	0	0	.333	.333	.500
Winn, Randy, Sea.†	4	4	2	0	1	1	0	0	0	0	0	0	0	2	0	0	0	0	0	.500	.750	.500
Womack, Tony, N.Y.*	4	4	3	1	1	1	0	0	0	0	0	0	0	1	0	0	0	0	1	.333	.500	.333
Youkilis, Kevin, Bos.	10	8	7	0	0	0	0	0	0	0	0	0	0	1	0	4	0	0	0	.000	.125	.000
Young, Dmitri, Det.†	7	7	6	0	4	4	0	0	0	2	0	0	0	1	0	1	0	0	0	.667	.714	.667
Young, Walter, Bal.*	4	4	3	0	1	1	0	0	0	1	0	0	0	1	0	1	0	0	0	.333	.500	.333
Zaun, Gregg, Tor.†	11	11	9	0	3	3	0	0	0	3	0	0	0	2	0	2	0	0	1	.333	.455	.333

PINCH-HITTERS WITH TWO OR MORE TEAMS

Player, Team	G	TPA	AB	R	H	TB	2B	3B	HR	RBI	SH	SF	HP	BB	IBB	SO	SB	CS	GDP	Avg.	OBP	Slg.
Bellhorn, Mark, Bos.†	1	1	1	0	0	0	0	0	0	0	0	0	0	0	0	0	0	0	0	.000	.000	.000
Bellhorn, Mark, N.Y.†	1	1	0	0	0	0	0	0	0	0	0	0	0	1	0	0	0	0	0	.000	1.000	.000
Byrnes, Eric, Oak.	3	3	1	0	0	0	0	0	0	0	0	0	0	2	0	0	0	0	0	.000	.667	.000
Byrnes, Eric, Bal.	1	1	1	0	0	0	0	0	0	0	0	0	0	0	0	1	0	0	0	.000	.000	.000
Cora, Alex, Cle.*	9	9	9	1	1	2	1	0	0	0	0	0	0	0	0	1	1	0	0	.111	.111	.222
Cora, Alex, Bos.*	2	2	2	1	1	1	0	0	0	0	0	0	0	0	0	0	0	0	0	.500	.500	.500
Marrero, Eli, K.C.	7	7	7	0	0	0	0	0	0	0	0	0	0	2	0	0	0	0	0	.000	.000	.000
Marrero, Eli, Bal.	7	7	5	1	1	3	0	1	0	1	0	1	0	1	0	3	0	0	0	.200	.286	.600
McDonald, John, Tor.	7	7	5	0	2	2	0	0	0	1	0	0	0	2	0	1	0	0	0	.400	.571	.400
McDonald, John, Det.	2	2	2	0	0	0	0	0	0	0	0	0	0	0	0	0	0	0	0	.000	.000	.000
Vazquez, Ramon, Bos.*	5	5	5	0	1	1	0	0	0	1	0	0	0	0	0	1	0	0	0	.200	.200	.200
Vazquez, Ramon, Cle.*	2	2	2	0	0	0	0	0	0	0	0	0	0	0	0	0	0	0	0	.000	.000	.000

PITCHING

TEAM

Team	W	L	Pct.	ERA	G	CG	ShO	Rel.	Sv.-Op.	IP	H	TBF	R	ER	HR	SH	SF	HB	BB	IBB	SO	WP	Bk.
Cleveland	93	69	.574	3.61	162	6	10	409	51-66	1452.2	1363	6048	642	582	157	36	41	41	413	20	1050	26	4
Chicago	99	63	.611	3.61	162	9	10	412	54-73	1475.2	1392	6176	645	592	167	45	35	52	459	42	1040	65	9
Los Angeles	95	67	.586	3.68	162	7	11	378	54-71	1464.1	1419	6158	643	598	158	39	35	48	443	24	1126	70	1
Oakland	88	74	.543	3.69	162	9	12	410	38-56	1450.1	1315	6080	658	594	154	32	38	60	504	42	1075	41	3
Minnesota	83	79	.512	3.71	162	9	8	396	44-60	1464.1	1458	6072	662	604	169	50	40	43	348	38	965	35	4
Toronto	80	82	.494	4.06	162	9	8	432	35-56	1447.0	1475	6166	705	653	185	31	43	68	444	29	958	39	5
Seattle	69	93	.426	4.49	162	6	7	433	39-59	1427.2	1483	6172	751	712	179	37	51	57	496	32	892	36	4
Detroit	71	91	.438	4.51	162	7	2	425	37-57	1435.2	1504	6139	787	719	193	39	60	51	461	33	907	53	5
New York	95	67	.586	4.52	162	8	14	418	46-67	1430.2	1495	6182	789	718	164	27	49	84	463	25	985	37	6
Baltimore	74	88	.457	4.56	162	2	9	474	38-57	1427.2	1458	6242	800	724	180	25	46	52	580	32	1052	70	11
Boston	95	67	.586	4.74	162	6	8	442	38-57	1429.0	1550	6227	805	752	164	27	50	89	440	28	959	56	4
Texas	79	83	.488	4.96	162	2	6	454	46-68	1440.0	1589	6371	858	794	159	45	44	60	522	31	932	44	4
Tampa Bay	67	95	.414	5.39	162	1	4	401	43-69	1421.2	1570	6384	936	851	194	47	59	64	615	41	949	53	5
Kansas City	56	106	.346	5.49	162	4	4	443	25-43	1413.1	1640	6370	935	862	178	34	49	74	580	33	924	69	9
Totals	1144	1124	.504	4.35	1134	85	113	5927	588-859	20180.0	20711	86787	10616	9755	2401	514	640	843	6768	450	13814	694	74

NOTE_Totals for earned runs for several clubs do not agree with composite total for all pitchers of each respective club due to instances in which provisions of Section 10.18(i) of the Scoring Rules were applied. The following differences are to be noted: Oakland pitchers add to 596; Minnesota pitchers add to 606; Detroit pitchers add to 721; New York pitchers add to 721; Boston pitchers add to 753; Texas pitchers add to 795; Tampa Bay pitchers add to 853; Kansas City pitchers add to 873.

TOP QUALIFIERS FOR EARNED-RUN AVERAGE TITLE

Minimum 162 innings. *Throws lefthanded.

Pitcher, Team	W	L	Pct.	ERA	G	GS	CG	ShO	GF	Sv.-Op.	IP	H	TBF	R	ER	HR	SH	SF	HB	BB	IBB	SO	WP	Bk.
Millwood, Kevin, Cle.	9	11	.450	2.86	30	30	1	0		0-0	192.0	182	799	72	61	20	6	4	4	52	0	146	2	0
Santana, Johan, Min.*	16	7	.696	2.87	33	33	3	2	0	0-0	231.2	180	910	77	74	22	6	2	1	45	1	238	8	0
Buehrle, Mark, Chi.*	16	8	.667	3.12	33	33	3	1	0	0-0	236.2	240	971	99	82	20	7	4	4	40	4	149	2	2
Washburn, Jarrod, L.A.*	8	8	.500	3.20	29	29	1	1	0	0-0	177.1	184	740	66	63	19	4	6	8	51	0	94	2	0
Silva, Carlos, Min.	9	8	.529	3.44	27	27	2	0	0	0-0	188.1	212	749	83	72	25	2	5	3	9	2	71	0	0
Lackey, John, L.A.	14	5	.737	3.44	33	33	1	0	0	0-0	209.0	208	892	85	80	13	1	2	11	71	3	199	18	0
Rogers, Kenny, Tex.*	14	8	.636	3.46	30	30	1	1	0	0-0	195.1	205	828	86	75	15	5	6	8	53	1	87	0	0
Colon, Bartolo, L.A.	21	8	.724	3.48	33	33	2	0	0	0-0	222.2	215	906	93	86	26	9	4	3	43	0	157	2	1
Garland, Jon, Chi.	18	10	.643	3.50	32	32	3	2	0	0-0	221.0	212	901	93	86	26	9	8	7	47	3	115	2	0
Blanton, Joe, Oak.	12	12	.500	3.53	33	33	2	0	0	0-0	201.1	178	835	86	79	23	2	7	5	67	3	116	4	2
Contreras, Jose, Chi.	15	7	.682	3.61	32	32	1	1	0	0-0	204.2	177	857	91	82	23	7	2	9	75	2	154	20	2
Towers, Josh, Tor.	13	12	.520	3.71	33	33	2	1	0	0-0	208.2	237	876	101	86	24	3	7	6	29	2	112	1	1
Chacin, Gustavo, Tor.*	13	9	.591	3.72	34	34	0	0	0	0-0	203.0	213	872	93	84	20	8	10	8	70	3	121	3	0
Haren, Danny, Oak.	14	12	.538	3.73	34	34	3	0	0	0-0	217.0	212	897	101	90	26	3	5	6	53	5	163	6	0
Byrd, Paul, L.A.	12	11	.522	3.74	31	31	2	1	0	0-0	204.1	216	842	95	85	22	7	7	7	28	1	102	1	0

DEPARTMENTAL LEADERS: W_Colon, L.A., 21; L_Greinke, K.C., 17; G_Timlin, Bos., 81; GS_Lopez, Bal., Zito, Oak., 35; CG_Halladay, Tor., 5; ShO_Garland, Chi., 3; GF_Rivera, N.Y., 67; Sv._Rodriguez, L.A., Wickman, Cle., 45; IP_Buehrle, Chi., 236; H_Buehrle, Chi., 240; TBF_Buehrle, Chi., 971; R_Lima, K.C., 140; ER_Lima, K.C., 131; HR_Wakefield, Bos., 35; SH_Colon, L.A., Crain, Min., Garland, Chi., Johnson, Det., 9; SF_Maroth, Det., Robertson, Det., 11; HB_Fossum, TB., 18; TBB_Kazmir, TB., 100; IBB_Harper, TB., 9; SO_Santana, Min., 238; WP_Contreras, Chi., Garcia, Chi., 20; Blk._Carrasco, K.C., Kline, Bal., 3.

ALL PITCHERS

*Throws lefthanded.

Pitcher, Team	W	L	Pct.	ERA	G	GS	CG	ShO	GF	Sv.-Op.	IP	H	TBF	R	ER	HR	SH	SF	HB	BB	IBB	SO	WP	Bk.
Adkins, Jon, Chi.	0	1	.000	8.64	5	0	0	0	4	0-0	8.1	13	42	8	8	0	0	0	1	4	2	1	0	0
Affeldt, Jeremy, K.C.*	2	2	.000	5.26	49	0	0	0	13	0-0	49.2	56	232	35	29	3	0	1	0	29	2	39	5	0
Almanzar, Carlos, Tex.	0	0	.000	14.40	6	0	0	0	2	0-0	5.0	10	33	8	8	2	0	2	1	7	0	3	4	0
Alvarez, Abe, Bos.*	0	0	.000	15.43	2	0	0	0	1	0-0	2.1	6	13	4	4	1	0	0	0	0	1	1	0	0
Anderson, Brian, K.C.*	1	2	.333	6.75	6	6	0	0	0	0-0	30.2	39	133	24	23	7	0	1	0	4	1	17	0	1
Anderson, Jason, N.Y.	1	0	1.000	7.94	3	0	0	0	1	0-0	5.2	4	27	5	5	0	0	0	0	7	1	2	0	0
Arroyo, Bronson, Bos.	14	10	.583	4.51	35	32	0	0	1	0-0	205.1	213	878	116	103	22	4	4	14	54	3	100	5	1
Astacio, Pedro, Tex.	2	8	.200	6.04	12	12	0	0	0	0-0	67.0	79	288	45	45	13	3	2	1	11	1	45	3	1
Atchison, Scott, Sea.	0	0	.000	6.75	6	0	0	0	2	0-0	6.2	7	27	5	5	1	0	0	0	1	0	9	0	0
Baez, Danys, TB.	5	4	.556	2.86	67	0	0	0	64	41-49	72.1	66	308	27	23	7	4	2	2	30	0	51	0	0
Bajenaru, Jeff, Chi.	0	0	.000	6.23	4	0	0	0	3	0-0	4.1	4	18	3	3	2	0	0	0	0	0	3	1	0
Baker, Scott, Min.	3	3	.500	3.35	10	9	0	0	0	0-0	53.2	48	217	21	20	5	2	2	0	14	0	32	0	0
Baldwin, James, Bal.-Tex.	0	2	.000	3.81	28	0	0	0	13	1-1	56.2	54	238	28	24	8	1	5	3	16	1	29	2	1
Batista, Miguel, Tor.	5	8	.385	4.10	71	0	0	0	62	31-39	74.2	80	331	39	34	9	2	2	2	27	5	54	3	0
Bauer, Rick, Bal.	0	0	.000	9.72	5	0	0	0	2	0-0	8.1	13	40	9	9	2	0	0	0	4	0	5	0	0
Bautista, Denny, K.C.	2	2	.500	5.08	7	7	0	0	0	0-0	35.2	36	160	23	23	2	1	1	2	17	0	23	3	0
Bayliss, Jonah, K.C.	0	0	.000	4.63	11	0	0	0	7	0-0	11.2	7	48	6	6	2	0	0	2	4	0	10	0	0
Bean, Colter, N.Y.	0	0	.000	4.50	1	0	0	0	1	0-0	2.0	1	9	1	1	0	0	0	0	2	0	2	0	0
Bedard, Erik, Bal.*	6	8	.429	4.00	24	24	0	0	0	0-0	141.2	139	606	66	63	10	3	6	5	57	1	125	4	1
Beimel, Joe, TB.*	0	0	.000	3.27	7	0	0	0	3	0-0	11.0	15	51	4	4	1	0	0	0	4	1	3	1	0
Bell, Rob, TB.	1	1	.500	8.28	3	3	0	0	4	0-0	25.0	41	129	25	23	7	0	1	2	12	0	13	3	0

Pitcher, Team	W	L	Pct.	ERA	G	GS	CG	ShO	GF	Sv.-Op.	IP	H	TBF	R	ER	HR	SH	SF	HB	BB	IBB	SO	WP	Bk.
Benoit, Joaquin, Tex.	4	4	.500	3.72	32	9	0	0	6	0-0	87.0	69	369	39	36	9	2	1	2	38	0	78	1	0
Betancourt, Rafael, Cle.	4	3	.571	2.79	54	0	0	0	12	1-3	67.2	57	272	23	21	5	1	0	0	17	2	73	0	0
Blanton, Joe, Oak.	12	12	.500	3.53	33	33	2	0	0	0-0	201.1	178	835	86	79	23	2	7	5	67	3	116	4	2
Bonderman, Jeremy, Det.	14	13	.519	4.57	29	29	4	0	0	0-0	189.0	199	801	101	96	21	3	3	4	57	0	145	5	1
Bootcheck, Chris, L.A.	0	1	.000	3.38	5	2	0	0	1	1-1	18.2	19	79	7	7	1	0	1	0	4	1	8	1	0
Borowski, Joe, TB.	1	5	.167	3.82	32	0	0	0	4	0-4	35.1	26	137	15	15	3	1	0	0	11	1	16	1	0
Bowyer, Travis, Min.	0	1	.000	5.59	8	0	0	0	5	0-1	9.2	10	42	6	6	3	0	1	1	3	0	12	1	0
Bradford, Chad, Bos.	2	1	.667	3.86	31	0	0	0	2	0-1	23.1	29	104	10	10	1	3	1	3	4	1	10	2	0
Brazelton, Dewon, TB.	1	8	.111	7.61	20	8	0	0	2	0-1	71.0	87	354	65	60	12	4	3	4	60	3	43	5	0
Brocail, Doug, Tex.	5	3	.625	5.52	61	0	0	0	13	1-4	73.1	90	344	48	45	2	3	4	4	34	3	61	4	0
Brown, Kevin, N.Y.	4	7	.364	6.50	13	13	0	0	0	0-0	73.1	107	346	57	53	5	3	3	7	19	1	50	6	0
Buehrle, Mark, Chi.*	16	8	.667	3.12	33	33	3	1	0	0-0	236.2	240	971	99	82	20	7	4	4	40	4	149	2	2
Bukvich, Ryan, Tex.	0	0	.000	11.25	4	0	0	0	0	0-0	4.0	2	19	5	5	0	1	0	0	6	0	4	0	0
Burgos, Ambiorix, K.C.	3	5	.375	3.98	59	0	0	0	17	2-6	63.1	60	278	29	28	6	2	1	5	31	1	65	8	2
Bush, Dave, Tor.	5	11	.313	4.49	25	24	2	0	1	0-0	136.1	142	575	73	68	20	3	2	13	29	3	75	2	0
Byrd, Paul, L.A.	12	11	.522	3.74	31	31	2	1	0	0-0	204.1	216	842	95	85	22	7	7	7	28	1	102	1	0
Byrdak, Tim, Bal.*	0	1	.000	4.05	41	0	0	0	3	1-1	26.2	27	131	14	12	1	2	1	1	21	1	31	5	0
Cabrera, Daniel, Bal.	10	13	.435	4.52	29	29	0	0	0	0-0	161.1	144	716	92	81	14	2	3	11	87	2	157	9	1
Cabrera, Fernando, Cle.	2	1	.667	1.47	15	0	0	0	6	0-0	30.2	24	124	7	5	1	0	0	0	11	1	29	1	1
Calero, Kiko, Oak.	4	1	.800	3.23	58	0	0	0	15	1-2	55.2	45	229	20	20	6	1	1	1	18	2	52	2	0
Camp, Shawn, K.C.	1	4	.200	6.43	29	0	0	0	7	0-2	49.0	69	228	40	35	4	0	3	4	13	3	28	3	0
Campillo, Jorge, Sea.	0	0	.000	0.00	2	1	0	0	1	0-0	2.0	1	9	0	0	0	0	0	0	1	0	1	0	0
Carrasco, D.J., K.C.	6	8	.429	4.79	21	20	1	0	0	0-0	114.2	129	511	67	61	11	3	5	6	51	2	49	7	3
Carter, Lance, TB.	1	2	.333	4.89	39	0	0	0	18	1-4	57.0	61	239	31	31	9	1	3	1	15	1	22	0	0
Cassidy, Scott, Bos.	0	0	.000	40.50	1	0	0	0	0	0-0	0.2	4	6	3	3	0	0	0	0	0	0	0	0	0
Cerda, Jaime, K.C.*	1	4	.200	6.63	20	0	0	0	1	0-1	19.0	21	89	14	14	3	3	1	0	11	2	18	2	0
Chacin, Gustavo, Tor.*	13	9	.591	3.72	34	34	0	0	0	0-0	203.0	213	872	93	84	20	8	10	8	70	3	121	3	0
Chacon, Shawn, N.Y.	7	3	.700	2.85	14	12	0	0	0	0-0	79.0	66	330	26	25	7	0	1	6	30	0	40	3	1
Chen, Bruce, Bal.*	13	10	.565	3.83	34	32	1	0	0	0-0	197.1	187	832	94	84	33	3	3	9	63	0	133	2	1
Christiansen, Jason, L.A.*	0	0	.000	2.45	12	0	0	0	1	0-0	3.2	7	20	1	1	0	0	0	0	2	0	4	0	0
Chulk, Vinnie, Tor.	1	0	1.000	3.88	62	0	0	0	10	0-1	72.0	68	301	33	31	9	3	4	1	26	3	39	5	0
Clement, Matt, Bos.	13	6	.684	4.57	32	32	1	0	0	0-0	191.0	192	830	102	97	18	2	6	16	68	1	146	13	0
Colome, Jesus, TB.	2	3	.400	4.57	36	0	0	0	18	0-1	45.1	54	212	29	23	7	1	0	2	18	3	28	5	0
Colon, Bartolo, L.A.	21	8	.724	3.48	33	33	2	0	0	0-0	222.2	215	906	93	86	26	9	4	3	43	0	157	2	1
Colon, Roman, Det.	1	1	.500	6.12	12	3	0	0	1	0-1	25.0	35	115	17	17	7	0	1	0	7	0	17	2	0
Contreras, Jose, Chi.	15	7	.682	3.61	32	32	1	0	0	0-0	204.2	177	857	91	82	23	7	2	9	75	2	154	20	2
Corcoran, Tim, TB.	0	0	.000	5.96	10	1	0	0	4	0-0	22.2	19	97	15	15	1	0	0	1	12	0	13	2	0
Cordero, Francisco, Tex.	3	1	.750	3.39	69	0	0	0	60	37-45	69.0	61	302	28	26	5	4	3	4	30	2	79	0	0
Cotts, Neal, Chi.*	4	0	1.000	1.94	69	0	0	0	10	0-2	60.1	38	248	15	13	1	0	3	4	29	5	58	3	0
Crain, Jesse, Min.	12	5	.706	2.71	75	0	0	0	17	1-4	79.2	61	326	28	24	6	9	3	5	29	7	25	2	0
Creek, Doug, Det.*	0	0	.000	6.85	20	0	0	0	8	0-0	22.1	27	101	18	17	7	1	1	0	7	0	18	0	0
Cruz, Juan, Oak.	0	3	.000	7.44	28	0	0	0	14	0-0	32.2	38	159	33	27	5	0	2	4	22	4	34	3	0
Darensbourg, Vic, Det.*	1	1	.500	2.82	22	0	0	0	4	0-0	22.1	24	96	7	7	2	2	2	0	7	2	9	0	0
Davis, Jason, Cle.	4	2	.667	4.69	11	4	0	0	2	0-0	40.1	44	182	22	21	4	0	3	3	20	0	32	2	0
Delcarmen, Manny, Bos.	0	0	.000	3.00	10	0	0	0	2	0-0	9.0	8	41	3	3	0	0	0	1	7	0	9	0	0
Demaria, Chris, K.C.	1	0	1.000	9.00	8	0	0	0	5	0-0	9.0	14	44	10	9	3	0	0	0	5	0	11	1	0
DePaula, Jorge, N.Y.	0	0	.000	8.10	3	0	0	0	2	0-0	6.2	8	30	6	6	2	0	0	0	3	0	3	0	0
Dickey, R.A., Tex.	1	2	.333	6.67	9	4	0	0	2	0-0	29.2	29	134	23	22	4	0	1	2	17	0	15	2	0
DiNardo, Lenny, Bos.*	0	1	.000	1.84	8	1	0	0	3	0-0	14.2	13	62	6	3	1	1	0	5	1	15	1	0
Dingman, Craig, Det.	2	3	.400	3.66	34	0	0	0	18	4-5	32.0	30	128	14	13	5	2	0	1	9	0	24	0	0
Dominguez, Juan, Tex.	4	6	.400	4.22	22	10	0	0	3	0-1	70.1	78	312	37	33	11	1	2	2	25	0	45	2	0
Donnelly, Brendan, L.A.	9	3	.750	3.72	65	0	0	0	14	0-5	65.1	60	271	30	27	9	3	1	2	19	3	53	3	0
Dotel, Octavio, Oak.	1	2	.333	3.52	15	0	0	0	13	7-11	15.1	10	65	6	6	2	0	0	0	11	2	16	1	0
Douglass, Sean, Det.	5	5	.500	5.56	18	16	0	0	1	0-0	87.1	92	374	57	54	13	1	5	2	33	2	55	2	0
Downs, Scott, Tor.*	4	3	.571	4.31	26	13	0	0	0	0-0	94.0	93	407	49	45	12	0	1	5	34	0	75	3	0
Drese, Ryan, Tex.	4	6	.400	6.46	12	12	1	0	0	0-0	69.2	96	317	52	50	5	2	1	3	24	1	20	1	0
DuBose, Eric, Bal.*	2	3	.400	5.52	15	3	0	0	2	0-0	29.1	28	135	21	18	4	0	1	1	19	0	17	1	0
Duchscherer, Justin, Oak.	7	4	.636	2.21	65	0	0	0	24	5-7	85.2	67	338	25	21	7	4	2	2	19	3	85	2	0
Elarton, Scott, Cle.	11	9	.550	4.61	31	31	1	0	0	0-0	181.2	189	774	100	93	32	3	10	6	48	1	103	4	1
Embree, Alan, Bos.-N.Y.*	2	5	.286	7.62	67	0	0	0	15	1-3	52.0	62	231	47	44	10	3	3	2	14	3	38	1	1
Escobar, Kelvim, L.A.	3	2	.600	3.02	16	7	0	0	2	1-1	59.2	45	242	21	20	4	2	0	2	21	1	63	4	0
Etherton, Seth, Oak.	1	1	.500	6.62	3	3	0	0	0	0-0	17.2	16	74	13	13	4	0	1	0	5	0	10	1	1
Farnsworth, Kyle, Det.	1	1	.500	2.32	46	0	0	0	16	6-8	42.2	29	174	12	11	1	1	1	1	20	0	55	2	0
Feldman, Scott, Tex.	0	1	.000	0.96	8	0	0	0	3	0-0	9.1	9	37	1	1	0	0	0	2	1	4	0	0
Field, Nate, K.C.	0	0	.000	9.45	7	0	0	0	2	0-0	6.2	13	35	7	7	1	0	0	5	2	4	1	0
Flores, Ron, Oak.*	0	0	.000	1.04	11	0	0	0	4	0-0	8.2	8	34	1	1	1	0	0	0	6	1	0	0
Fossum, Casey, TB.*	8	12	.400	4.92	36	25	0	0	1	0-1	162.2	170	725	100	89	21	3	5	18	60	3	128	8	1
Foulke, Keith, Bos.	5	5	.500	5.91	43	0	0	0	37	15-19	45.2	53	210	30	30	8	2	1	5	18	1	34	0	0
Franklin, Ryan, Sea.	8	15	.348	5.10	32	30	2	1	0	0-0	190.2	212	832	110	108	28	3	3	7	62	4	93	3	1
Franklin, Wayne, N.Y.*	1	1	.000	6.39	13	0	0	0	2	0-0	12.2	11	57	12	9	1	1	1	1	8	0	10	0	0
Frasor, Jason, Tor.	3	5	.375	3.25	67	0	0	0	12	1-3	74.2	67	305	31	27	8	2	1	3	28	2	62	1	0
Garcia, Freddy, Chi.	14	8	.636	3.87	33	33	0	0	0	0-0	228.0	225	943	102	98	26	5	5	3	60	2	146	20	1
Garcia, Jairo, Oak.	0	0	.000	3.00	3	0	0	0	3	0-0	3.0	2	12	1	1	0	0	0	0	1	0	4	0	0
Gardner, Lee, TB.	0	0	.000	4.91	5	0	0	0	2	0-0	7.1	12	37	9	4	2	0	1	0	2	0	4	0	0
Garland, Jon, Chi.	18	10	.643	3.50	32	32	3	0	0	0-0	221.0	212	901	93	86	26	9	8	7	47	3	115	2	0
Gassner, Dave, Min.*	1	0	1.000	5.87	2	2	0	0	0	0-0	7.2	9	34	7	5	1	0	1	0	2	0	2	0	0
Gaudin, Chad, Tor.	1	3	.250	13.15	5	3	0	0	0	0-0	13.0	31	74	19	19	6	0	1	1	6	0	12	0	0
German, Franklyn, Det.	4	0	1.000	3.66	58	0	0	0	19	1-3	59.0	63	270	26	24	7	2	5	7	34	4	38	4	1
Ginter, Matt, Det.	0	1	.000	6.17	14	1	0	0	4	0-0	35.0	49	157	25	24	6	1	1	2	9	1	15	0	0
Glynn, Ryan, Oak.	0	4	.000	6.88	5	3	0	0	2	0-0	17.0	24	82	16	13	5	0	0	7	10	0	9	1	0
Gobble, Jimmy, K.C.*	1	1	.500	5.70	28	4	0	0	11	0-0	53.2	64	249	34	34	9	3	1	1	30	4	38	2	0
Gonzalez, Jeremi, Bos.	2	1	.667	6.11	28	3	0	0	7	0-0	56.0	64	244	39	38	7	0	4	2	16	2	28	1	0

Pitcher, Team	W	L	Pct.	ERA	G	GS	CG	ShO	GF	Sv.-Op.	IP	H	TBF	R	ER	HR	SH	SF	HB	BB	IBB	SO	WP	Bk.
Good, Andrew, Det.	0	0	.000	5.40	2	0	0	0	2	0-0	5.0	4	20	3	3	1	0	0	0	1	0	7	0	0
Gordon, Tom, N.Y.	5	4	.556	2.57	79	0	0	0	17	2-9	80.2	59	324	25	23	8	1	3	0	29	4	69	1	1
Graman, Alex, N.Y.*	0	0	.000	13.50	2	0	0	0	1	0-0	1.1	3	9	2	2	1	0	0	0	2	1	0	0	0
Gregg, Kevin, L.A.	1	2	.333	5.04	33	2	0	0	9	0-1	64.1	70	290	37	36	8	1	1	3	29	2	52	5	0
Greinke, Zack, K.C.	5	17	.227	5.80	33	33	2	0	0	0-0	183.0	233	829	125	118	23	4	4	13	53	0	114	4	2
Grilli, Jason, Det.	1	1	.500	3.38	3	2	0	0	0	0-0	16.0	14	63	6	6	1	1	1	0	6	0	5	0	0
Grimsley, Jason, Bal.	1	2	.333	5.73	22	0	0	0	9	0-3	22.0	24	93	15	14	5	0	1	0	9	2	10	1	0
Groom, Buddy, N.Y.*	1	0	1.000	4.91	24	0	0	0	8	0-0	25.2	32	116	14	14	3	0	1	3	7	2	13	0	0
Gryboski, Kevin, Tex.	1	1	.500	11.17	11	0	0	0	2	0-0	9.2	17	55	15	12	1	1	0	1	8	2	2	1	0
Guardado, Eddie, Sea.*	2	3	.400	2.72	58	0	0	0	55	36-41	56.1	52	238	23	17	7	3	2	0	15	3	48	1	0
Guerrier, Matt, Min.	0	3	.000	3.39	43	0	0	0	14	0-0	71.2	71	306	29	27	6	4	1	3	24	5	46	3	0
Guthrie, Jeremy, Cle.	0	0	.000	6.00	1	0	0	0	1	0-0	6.0	9	29	4	4	2	1	1	0	2	0	3	0	0
Halama, John, Bos.*	1	1	.500	6.18	30	1	0	0	13	0-0	43.2	56	205	33	30	5	1	1	7	9	3	26	2	0
Halladay, Roy, Tor.	12	4	.750	2.41	19	19	5	2	0	0-0	141.2	118	553	39	38	11	2	1	7	18	2	108	2	1
Hansen, Craig, Bos.	0	0	.000	6.00	4	0	0	0	1	0-1	3.0	6	16	2	2	1	0	1	0	1	0	3	0	0
Harden, Rich, Oak.	10	5	.667	2.53	22	19	2	1	0	0-0	128.0	93	514	42	36	7	4	2	2	43	0	121	6	0
Haren, Danny, Oak.	14	12	.538	3.73	34	34	3	0	0	0-0	217.0	212	897	101	90	26	3	5	6	53	5	163	6	0
Harikkala, Tim, Oak.	0	0	.000	6.39	8	0	0	0	5	0-0	12.2	16	56	9	9	3	0	0	0	4	0	7	0	0
Harper, Travis, TB.	4	6	.400	6.75	52	0	0	0	13	0-3	73.1	88	321	57	55	14	5	2	1	24	9	40	2	0
Harris, Jeff, Sea.	2	5	.286	4.19	11	8	0	0	1	0-0	53.2	48	227	27	25	9	0	2	3	20	2	25	0	0
Harville, Chad, Bos.	0	1	.000	6.43	8	0	0	0	4	0-0	7.0	7	30	5	5	1	0	0	1	3	0	3	0	0
Hasegawa, Shigetoshi, Sea.	1	3	.250	4.19	46	0	0	0	17	0-1	66.2	66	279	31	31	4	2	3	3	16	1	30	0	0
Hendrickson, Mark, TB.*	11	8	.579	5.90	31	31	1	0	0	0-0	178.1	227	796	126	117	24	8	7	2	49	1	89	4	1
Henn, Sean, N.Y.*	0	3	.000	11.12	3	3	0	0	0	0-0	11.1	18	61	16	14	3	0	0	0	11	0	3	0	0
Hermanson, Dustin, Chi.	2	4	.333	2.04	57	0	0	0	45	34-39	57.1	46	228	17	13	4	3	0	1	17	4	33	3	0
Hernandez, Felix, Sea.	4	4	.500	2.67	12	12	0	0	0	0-0	84.1	61	328	26	25	5	1	2	2	23	0	77	3	0
Hernandez, Orlando, Chi.	9	9	.500	5.12	24	22	0	0	1	1-1	128.1	137	568	77	73	18	3	5	12	50	1	91	3	2
Hernandez, Runelvys, K.C.	8	14	.364	5.52	29	29	0	0	0	0-0	159.2	172	706	101	98	18	1	6	7	70	0	88	4	0
Howell, J.P., K.C.*	3	5	.375	6.19	15	15	0	0	0	0-0	72.2	73	328	55	50	9	3	3	6	39	0	54	7	0
Howry, Bob, Cle.	7	4	.636	2.47	79	0	0	0	24	3-5	73.0	49	277	23	20	4	3	2	0	16	1	48	0	0
Jenks, Bobby, Chi.	1	1	.500	2.75	32	0	0	0	18	6-8	39.1	34	168	15	12	3	1	0	1	15	3	50	4	0
Jensen, Ryan, K.C.	3	2	.600	7.11	9	3	0	0	3	0-1	25.1	31	115	20	20	4	0	2	2	7	1	18	0	0
Johnson, Jason, Det.	8	13	.381	4.54	33	33	1	0	0	0-0	210.0	233	888	117	106	23	9	7	6	49	4	93	17	0
Johnson, Randy, N.Y.*	17	8	.680	3.79	34	34	4	0	0	0-0	225.2	207	920	102	95	32	5	5	12	47	2	211	3	1
Jones, Greg, L.A.	0	0	.000	6.75	6	0	0	0	6	0-0	5.1	7	24	4	4	2	0	0	0	2	0	6	0	0
Julio, Jorge, Bal.	3	5	.375	5.90	67	0	0	0	19	0-2	71.2	76	313	50	47	14	1	3	2	24	4	58	10	0
Karnuth, Jason, Det.	0	0	.000	5.40	3	0	0	0	2	0-0	1.2	2	7	1	1	0	0	0	0	0	0	0	0	0
Karsay, Steve, N.Y.-Tex.	0	1	.000	7.06	20	0	0	0	10	0-0	21.2	36	106	19	17	2	0	2	0	7	1	14	1	0
Kazmir, Scott, TB.*	10	9	.526	3.77	32	32	0	0	0	0-0	186.0	172	818	90	78	12	6	9	10	100	3	174	7	1
Kennedy, Joe, Oak.*	4	5	.444	4.45	19	8	0	0	3	0-2	60.2	64	262	33	30	8	0	1	1	20	2	45	1	0
Kida, Masao, Sea.	0	0	.000	4.50	1	0	0	0	1	0-0	2.0	2	8	1	1	1	0	0	0	0	0	0	0	0
Kline, Steve, Bal.*	2	4	.333	4.28	67	0	0	0	23	0-3	61.0	59	264	34	29	11	2	2	0	30	5	36	4	3
Lackey, John, L.A.	14	5	.737	3.44	33	33	1	0	0	0-0	209.0	208	892	85	80	13	1	2	11	71	3	199	18	0
League, Brandon, Tor.	1	0	1.000	6.56	20	0	0	0	4	0-0	35.2	42	162	27	26	8	0	1	2	20	1	17	5	0
Ledezma, Wilfredo, Det.*	2	4	.333	7.07	10	10	0	0	0	0-0	49.2	61	234	46	39	10	3	4	2	24	0	30	2	2
Lee, Cliff, Cle.*	18	5	.783	3.79	32	32	1	0	0	0-0	202.0	194	838	91	85	22	5	7	0	52	1	143	4	0
Leiter, Al, N.Y.*	4	5	.444	5.49	16	10	0	0	2	0-0	62.1	66	293	42	38	4	0	3	6	38	0	45	2	0
Lilly, Ted, Tor.*	10	11	.476	5.56	25	25	0	0	0	0-0	126.1	135	566	79	78	23	3	5	3	58	1	96	2	2
Lima, Jose, K.C.	5	16	.238	6.99	32	32	1	0	0	0-0	168.2	219	780	140	131	31	5	7	9	61	1	80	5	0
Liriano, Francisco, Min.*	1	2	.333	5.70	6	4	0	0	2	0-0	23.2	19	93	15	15	4	0	0	0	7	0	33	0	0
Loe, Kameron, Tex.	9	6	.600	3.42	48	8	0	0	13	1-4	92.0	89	392	43	35	7	5	1	2	31	6	45	2	0
Lohse, Kyle, Min.	9	13	.409	4.18	31	30	0	0	1	0-0	178.2	211	769	85	83	22	3	7	9	44	5	86	4	1
Lopez, Rodrigo, Bal.	15	12	.556	4.90	35	35	0	0	0	0-0	209.1	232	918	126	114	28	3	5	7	63	1	118	5	1
MacDougal, Mike, K.C.	5	6	.455	3.33	68	0	0	0	53	21-25	70.1	69	298	32	26	6	1	1	3	24	2	72	6	1
Madritsch, Bobby, Sea.*	0	1	.000	6.23	1	1	0	0	0	0-0	4.1	4	18	3	3	1	0	0	0	1	0	1	0	0
Mahay, Ron, Tex.*	0	2	.000	6.81	30	0	0	0	9	1-1	35.2	47	167	28	27	8	0	1	0	16	1	30	2	0
Maine, John, Bal.	2	3	.400	6.30	10	8	0	0	1	0-0	40.0	39	184	30	28	8	0	2	1	24	0	24	0	1
Mantei, Matt, Bos.	1	0	1.000	6.49	34	0	0	0	5	0-0	26.1	23	125	20	19	1	0	0	5	24	1	22	5	0
Marcum, Shaun, Tor.	0	0	.000	0.00	5	0	0	0	3	0-0	8.0	6	32	0	0	0	0	0	0	4	0	4	0	0
Maroth, Mike, Det.*	14	14	.500	4.74	34	34	0	0	0	0-0	209.0	235	889	123	110	30	3	11	9	51	1	115	5	0
Marte, Damaso, Chi.*	3	4	.429	3.77	66	0	0	0	15	4-8	45.1	45	213	21	19	5	1	0	3	33	4	54	1	1
Mateo, Julio, Sea.	3	6	.333	3.06	55	1	0	0	7	0-2	88.1	79	364	32	30	12	5	2	7	17	6	52	1	0
May, Darrell, N.Y.*	0	1	.000	16.71	2	1	0	0	0	0-0	7.0	14	38	13	13	4	0	0	0	3	0	3	0	0
Mays, Joe, Min.	6	10	.375	5.65	31	26	1	1	1	0-0	156.0	203	690	109	98	23	5	3	3	41	1	59	4	0
McCarthy, Brandon, Chi.	3	2	.600	4.03	12	10	0	0	0	0-0	67.0	62	277	30	30	13	1	1	2	17	0	48	1	1
McClung, Seth, TB.	7	11	.389	6.59	34	17	0	0	3	0-1	109.1	106	500	85	80	20	0	5	7	62	1	92	6	0
McGowan, Dustin, Tor.	1	3	.250	6.35	13	7	0	0	2	0-0	45.1	49	205	34	32	7	0	4	7	17	0	34	7	0
Meche, Gil, Sea.	10	8	.556	5.09	29	26	0	0	2	0-0	143.1	153	638	92	81	18	1	5	2	72	1	83	4	0
Mendoza, Ramiro, N.Y.	0	0	.000	18.00	1	0	0	0	1	0-0	1.0	2	5	2	2	1	0	0	0	0	0	1	0	0
Meredith, Cla, Bos.	0	0	.000	27.00	3	0	0	0	0	0-0	2.1	6	18	7	7	1	0	0	1	4	0	0	1	0
Miller, Justin, Tor.	0	0	.000	15.43	1	0	0	0	0	0-0	2.1	5	12	4	4	3	0	0	0	0	0	2	0	0
Miller, Matt, Cle.	1	0	1.000	1.82	23	0	0	0	4	1-2	29.2	22	118	6	6	1	0	1	3	10	3	23	1	1
Miller, Trever, TB.*	2	2	.500	4.06	61	0	0	0	13	0-3	44.1	45	206	23	20	4	3	5	7	29	6	35	2	0
Miller, Wade, Bos.	4	4	.500	4.95	16	16	0	0	0	0-0	91.0	96	414	53	50	8	1	4	3	47	0	64	6	0
Millwood, Kevin, Cle.	9	11	.450	2.86	30	30	1	0	0	0-0	192.0	182	799	72	61	20	6	4	4	52	0	146	2	0
Moyer, Jamie, Sea.*	13	7	.650	4.28	32	32	1	0	0	0-0	200.0	225	868	99	95	23	6	6	8	52	2	102	3	0
Mulholland, Terry, Min.*	0	2	.000	4.27	49	0	0	0	26	0-1	59.0	61	246	30	28	6	5	1	2	17	4	18	3	1
Mussina, Mike, N.Y.	13	8	.619	4.41	30	30	2	2	0	0-0	179.2	199	766	93	88	23	6	4	7	47	0	142	2	0
Myers, Mike, Bos.*	3	1	.750	3.13	65	0	0	0	11	0-1	37.1	30	151	14	13	3	1	1	2	13	2	21	0	0
Nageotte, Clint, Sea.	0	0	.000	6.75	3	0	0	0	0	0-0	4.0	6	19	3	3	0	0	0	1	1	0	1	0	0
Nathan, Joe, Min.	7	4	.636	2.70	69	0	0	0	58	43-48	70.0	46	276	22	21	5	1	2	0	22	1	94	2	0
Neal, Blaine, Bos.	0	1	.000	9.00	8	0	0	0	4	0-0	8.0	15	41	9	8	2	2	1	0	3	0	3	0	0

Pitcher, Team	W	L	Pct.	ERA	G	GS	CG	ShO	GF	Sv.-Op.	IP	H	TBF	R	ER	HR	SH	SF	HB	BB	IBB	SO	WP	Bk.
Nelson, Jeff, Sea.	1	3	.250	3.93	49	0	0	0	15	1-4	36.2	32	166	17	16	3	4	1	4	22	0	34	1	1
Nomo, Hideo, TB.	5	8	.385	7.24	19	19	0	0	0	0-0	100.2	127	472	82	81	16	6	8	2	51	2	59	3	0
Nunez, Franklin, TB.	1	0	1.000	10.80	5	0	0	0	0	0-0	5.0	5	22	6	6	0	0	0	0	4	0	2	0	0
Nunez, Leo, K.C.	3	2	.600	7.55	41	0	0	0	10	0-1	53.2	73	246	45	45	9	1	2	3	18	2	32	1	0
Orvella, Chad, TB.	3	3	.500	3.60	37	0	0	0	9	1-2	50.0	47	220	26	20	4	1	4	1	23	2	43	0	0
Papelbon, Jonathan, Bos.	3	1	.750	2.65	17	3	0	0	4	0-1	34.0	33	148	11	10	4	1	0	3	17	2	34	1	0
Park, Chan Ho, Tex.	8	5	.615	5.66	20	20	0	0	0	0-0	109.2	130	502	70	69	8	5	2	6	54	1	80	3	0
Parrish, John, Bal.*	1	0	1.000	3.12	14	0	0	0	2	0-0	17.1	19	86	6	6	1	1	0	0	17	1	25	6	0
Pavano, Carl, N.Y.	4	6	.400	4.77	17	17	1	1	0	0-0	100.0	129	442	66	53	17	4	3	8	18	1	56	2	1
Penn, Hayden, Bal.	3	2	.600	6.34	8	8	0	0	0	0-0	38.1	46	178	30	27	6	1	0	0	21	3	18	3	1
Peralta, Joel, L.A.	1	0	1.000	3.89	28	0	0	0	10	0-0	34.2	28	145	15	15	6	2	1	0	14	2	30	2	0
Percival, Troy, Det.	1	3	.250	5.76	26	0	0	0	23	8-11	25.0	19	107	16	16	7	1	1	2	11	3	20	0	0
Perisho, Matt, Bos.*	0	0	.000	0.00	1	0	0	0	0	0-0	0.0	1	1	1	1	0	0	0	0	0	0	0	0	0
Pineiro, Joel, Sea.	7	11	.389	5.62	30	30	2	0	0	0-0	189.0	224	822	118	118	23	5	7	6	56	4	107	7	1
Politte, Cliff, Chi.	7	1	.875	2.00	68	0	0	0	14	1-2	67.1	42	262	15	15	7	2	4	3	21	4	57	1	0
Ponson, Sidney, Bal.	7	11	.389	6.21	23	23	1	0	0	0-0	130.1	177	595	97	90	16	2	8	3	48	1	68	10	0
Prinz, Bret, L.A.	0	1	.000	3.00	3	0	0	0	2	0-0	3.0	4	14	1	1	1	0	0	0	1	0	1	0	0
Proctor, Scott, N.Y.	1	0	1.000	6.04	29	1	0	0	11	0-0	44.2	46	199	32	30	10	0	1	2	17	4	36	4	1
Putz, J.J., Sea.	6	5	.545	3.60	64	0	0	0	20	1-4	60.0	58	259	27	24	8	3	3	2	23	2	45	2	0
Quantrill, Paul, N.Y.	1	0	1.000	6.75	22	0	0	0	6	0-1	32.0	48	149	24	24	5	0	7	2	7	2	11	0	1
Radke, Brad, Min.	9	12	.429	4.04	31	31	3	1	0	0-0	200.2	214	831	98	90	33	4	10	7	23	1	117	2	0
Rakers, Aaron, Bal.	1	0	1.000	3.29	10	0	0	0	1	0-0	13.2	11	55	5	5	3	0	2	0	3	0	11	0	0
Ramirez, Erasmo, Tex.*	0	0	.000	3.91	16	0	0	0	4	0-1	23.0	24	96	10	10	3	3	0	2	3	0	6	0	0
Ray, Chris, Bal.	1	3	.250	2.66	41	0	0	0	8	0-4	40.2	34	174	15	12	5	1	1	1	18	3	43	0	1
Reames, Britt, Oak.	0	0	.000	9.53	2	0	0	0	0	0-0	5.2	10	29	6	6	2	0	1	1	2	0	4	1	0
Redding, Tim, N.Y.	0	1	.000	54.00	1	1	0	0	0	0-0	1.0	4	11	6	6	0	0	0	0	4	0	2	0	0
Reed, Steve, Bal.	1	2	.333	6.61	30	0	0	0	6	0-0	32.2	41	149	24	24	5	0	1	4	11	2	15	0	0
Regilio, Nick, Tex.	1	2	.333	4.58	18	0	0	0	5	0-2	17.2	22	83	10	9	2	0	1	1	7	1	14	0	0
Remlinger, Mike, Bos.*	0	0	.000	14.85	8	0	0	0	2	0-0	6.2	15	41	14	11	2	0	0	0	5	0	5	2	0
Rhodes, Arthur, Cle.*	3	1	.750	2.08	47	0	0	0	8	0-3	43.1	33	175	13	10	2	0	2	1	12	2	43	0	0
Riley, Matt, Tex.*	1	0	1.000	9.95	7	0	0	0	0	0-0	12.2	16	62	14	14	2	0	1	1	10	0	4	1	1
Rincon, Juan, Min.	6	6	.500	2.45	75	0	0	0	18	0-5	77.0	63	319	26	21	2	4	1	3	30	3	84	5	1
Rincon, Ricardo, Oak.*	1	1	.500	4.34	67	0	0	0	4	0-2	37.1	34	162	19	18	7	2	1	1	20	4	27	1	0
Riske, David, Cle.	3	4	.429	3.10	58	0	0	0	33	1-1	72.2	55	288	28	25	11	3	1	4	15	0	48	0	0
Rivera, Mariano, N.Y.	7	4	.636	1.38	71	0	0	0	67	43-47	78.1	50	306	18	12	2	0	1	4	18	0	80	0	0
Robertson, Nate, Det.*	7	16	.304	4.48	32	32	2	0	0	0-0	196.2	202	846	113	98	28	3	11	7	65	2	122	6	1
Rodney, Fernando, Det.	2	3	.400	2.86	39	0	0	0	26	9-15	44.0	39	185	14	14	5	2	0	2	17	3	42	2	0
Rodriguez, Felix, N.Y.	0	0	.000	5.01	34	0	0	0	10	0-0	32.1	33	147	18	18	2	0	0	2	20	0	18	3	0
Rodriguez, Francisco, L.A.	2	5	.286	2.67	66	0	0	0	58	45-50	67.1	45	279	20	20	7	1	1	0	32	3	91	8	0
Rodriguez, Ricardo, Tex.	2	3	.400	5.53	12	10	0	0	0	0-0	57.0	67	254	39	35	11	3	1	1	17	0	24	2	0
Rogers, Kenny, Tex.*	14	8	.636	3.46	30	30	1	1	0	0-0	195.1	205	828	86	75	15	5	6	8	53	1	87	0	0
Romero, J.C., Min.*	4	3	.571	3.47	68	0	0	0	11	0-1	57.0	50	264	26	22	6	5	1	6	39	8	48	1	1
Rupe, Josh, Tex.	1	0	1.000	2.79	4	1	0	0	1	0-0	9.2	7	39	4	3	0	1	0	2	4	0	6	1	0
Ryan, B.J., Bal.*	1	4	.200	2.43	69	0	0	0	61	36-41	70.1	54	290	20	19	4	1	1	2	26	2	100	5	0
Saarloos, Kirk, Oak.	10	9	.526	4.17	29	27	2	1	0	0-0	159.2	170	682	75	74	11	3	3	11	54	8	53	1	0
Sabathia, C.C., Cle.*	15	10	.600	4.03	31	31	1	0	0	0-0	196.2	185	823	92	88	19	6	3	7	62	1	161	7	0
Sanders, David, Chi.*	0	0	.000	13.50	2	0	0	0	0	0-0	2.0	3	10	3	3	1	0	1	0	1	0	1	0	0
Santana, Ervin, L.A.	12	8	.600	4.65	23	23	1	1	0	0-0	133.2	139	583	73	69	17	1	4	8	47	2	99	4	0
Santana, Johan, Min.*	16	7	.696	2.87	33	33	3	2	0	0-0	231.2	180	910	77	74	22	6	2	1	45	1	238	8	0
Sauerbeck, Scott, Cle.*	1	0	1.000	4.04	58	0	0	0	10	0-2	35.2	35	157	18	16	4	1	1	4	16	2	35	2	0
Saunders, Joe, L.A.*	0	0	.000	7.71	2	2	0	0	0	0-0	9.1	10	41	8	8	3	0	0	0	4	0	4	1	0
Schilling, Curt, Bos.	8	8	.500	5.69	32	11	0	0	21	9-11	93.1	121	418	59	59	12	3	5	3	22	0	87	1	1
Schoeneweis, Scott, Tor.*	3	4	.429	3.32	80	0	0	0	15	1-4	57.0	54	250	23	21	2	1	0	4	25	5	43	2	0
Sele, Aaron, Sea.	6	12	.333	5.66	21	21	1	1	0	0-0	116.0	147	523	76	73	18	1	9	5	41	2	53	2	0
Sherrill, George, Sea.*	4	3	.571	5.21	29	0	0	0	2	0-0	19.0	13	77	12	11	3	1	1	1	7	2	24	0	0
Shields, Scot, L.A.	10	11	.476	2.75	78	0	0	0	21	7-13	91.2	66	375	33	28	5	4	3	2	37	2	98	12	0
Shouse, Brian, Tex.*	3	2	.600	5.23	64	0	0	0	12	0-2	53.1	55	233	37	31	7	2	3	3	18	4	35	2	0
Silva, Carlos, Min.	9	8	.529	3.44	27	27	2	0	0	0-0	188.1	212	749	83	72	25	2	5	3	9	2	71	0	0
Sisco, Andrew, K.C.*	2	5	.286	3.11	67	0	0	0	13	0-5	75.1	68	329	27	26	6	2	3	2	42	4	76	2	0
Small, Aaron, N.Y.	10	0	1.000	3.20	15	9	1	1	1	0-1	76.0	71	316	27	27	4	1	2	5	24	0	37	0	0
Snyder, Kyle, K.C.	1	3	.250	6.75	13	3	0	0	4	0-0	36.0	55	169	29	27	3	0	2	1	10	1	19	1	0
Soriano, Rafael, Sea.	0	0	.000	2.45	7	0	0	0	4	0-0	7.1	6	30	2	2	0	0	1	1	1	0	9	0	0
Speier, Justin, Tor.	3	2	.600	2.57	65	0	0	0	36	0-4	66.2	48	264	20	19	10	4	0	3	15	2	56	1	1
Spurling, Chris, Det.	3	4	.429	3.44	56	0	0	0	8	0-1	70.2	58	284	30	27	8	3	5	2	22	6	26	4	0
Standridge, Jason, Tex.	0	0	.000	11.57	2	0	0	0	0	0-0	2.1	7	16	3	3	0	0	0	0	1	1	2	1	0
Stanton, Mike, N.Y.-Bos.*	1	2	.333	6.60	29	0	0	0	6	0-0	15.0	18	67	11	11	1	0	1	0	6	0	13	1	0
Stemle, Steve, K.C.	0	0	.000	5.06	6	0	0	0	1	0-0	10.2	10	43	6	6	0	0	0	0	4	0	9	0	0
Street, Huston, Oak.	5	1	.833	1.72	67	0	0	0	47	23-27	78.1	53	306	17	15	3	3	2	2	26	4	72	1	0
Sturtze, Tanyon, N.Y.	5	3	.625	4.73	64	1	0	0	12	1-6	78.0	76	332	43	41	10	1	2	6	27	1	45	3	0
Switzer, Jon, TB.*	0	0	.000	6.75	2	0	0	0	0	0-0	4.0	5	25	4	3	0	0	0	0	7	0	5	0	0
Tadano, Kazuhito, Cle.	0	0	.000	2.25	1	0	0	0	1	0-0	4.0	4	16	1	1	0	0	0	0	0	0	1	0	0
Takatsu, Shingo, Chi.	1	2	.333	5.97	31	0	0	0	20	8-9	28.2	30	130	19	19	9	2	1	0	16	1	32	1	0
Tallet, Brian, Cle.*	0	0	.000	7.71	2	0	0	0	0	0-0	4.2	6	24	4	4	2	0	0	1	3	0	2	0	0
Tejera, Michael, Tex.*	0	0	.000	13.50	3	0	0	0	1	0-0	2.0	5	13	3	3	1	0	0	1	1	0	2	1	0
Thompson, Justin, Tex.*	0	0	.000	21.60	2	0	0	0	2	0-0	1.2	4	9	4	4	2	0	0	0	0	0	1	0	0
Thornton, Matt, Sea.*	0	4	.000	5.21	55	0	0	0	15	0-1	57.0	54	262	33	33	13	1	1	0	42	2	57	7	0
Timlin, Mike, Bos.	7	3	.700	2.24	81	0	0	0	27	13-20	80.1	86	342	23	20	2	3	6	2	20	5	59	3	0
Towers, Josh, Tor.	13	12	.520	3.71	33	33	2	1	0	0-0	208.2	237	876	101	86	24	3	7	6	29	2	112	1	1
Urbina, Ugueth, Det.	1	3	.250	2.63	25	0	0	0	14	9-11	27.1	21	116	9	8	4	0	0	1	14	2	31	1	0
Verlander, Justin, Det.	0	2	.000	7.15	2	2	0	0	0	0-0	11.1	15	54	9	9	1	0	0	1	5	0	7	1	0
Villone, Ron, Sea.*	2	3	.400	2.45	52	0	0	0	14	1-6	40.1	33	178	14	11	2	1	3	5	23	1	41	2	1
Vizcaino, Luis, Chi.	6	5	.545	3.73	65	0	0	0	20	0-3	70.0	74	305	30	29	8	4	1	2	29	6	43	3	0

Pitcher, Team	W	L	Pct.	ERA	G	GS	CG	ShO	GF	Sv.-Op.	IP	H	TBF	R	ER	HR	SH	SF	HB	BB	IBB	SO	WP	Bk.
Volquez, Edison, Tex.	0	4	.000	14.21	6	3	0	0	0	0-0	12.2	25	75	22	20	3	0	1	2	10	0	11	0	0
Waechter, Doug, TB.	5	12	.294	5.62	29	25	0	0	3	0-0	157.0	191	692	109	98	29	4	4	3	38	5	87	4	2
Wakefield, Tim, Bos.	16	12	.571	4.15	33	33	3	0	0	0-0	225.1	210	943	113	104	35	1	6	11	68	4	151	8	0
Walker, Jamie, Det.*	4	3	.571	3.70	66	0	0	0	11	0-2	48.2	49	208	22	20	5	1	1	2	13	3	30	0	0
Walker, Kevin, Chi.*	0	1	.000	9.00	9	0	0	0	3	0-1	7.0	10	35	7	7	1	0	0	0	5	1	5	0	0
Walker, Pete, Tor.	6	6	.500	3.54	41	4	0	0	8	2-5	84.0	81	358	33	33	10	0	4	2	33	0	43	2	0
Wang, Chien-Ming, N.Y......	8	5	.615	4.02	18	17	0	0	0	0-0	116.1	113	486	58	52	9	3	4	6	32	3	47	3	0
Wasdin, John, Tex.	3	2	.600	4.28	31	6	0	0	7	4-6	75.2	77	319	37	36	9	1	2	1	20	2	44	2	0
Washburn, Jarrod, L.A.*	8	8	.500	3.20	29	29	1	1	0	0-0	177.1	184	740	66	63	19	4	6	8	51	0	94	2	0
Webb, John, TB.	0	1	.000	18.00	1	1	0	0	0	0-0	4.0	6	23	8	8	1	0	0	1	4	0	2	0	0
Wells, David, Bos.*	15	7	.682	4.45	30	30	2	0	0	0-0	184.0	220	780	95	91	21	1	6	9	21	0	107	4	1
Westbrook, Jake, Cle.	15	15	.500	4.49	34	34	2	0	0	0-0	210.2	218	895	121	105	19	5	4	7	56	3	119	3	0
Whiteside, Matt, Tor.	0	0	.000	19.64	2	0	0	0	0	0-0	3.2	6	23	8	8	3	0	0	1	5	0	5	0	0
Wickman, Bob, Cle.	0	4	.000	2.47	64	0	0	0	55	45-50	62.0	57	257	17	17	9	2	2	1	21	3	41	0	1
Williams, Todd, Bal.	5	5	.500	3.30	72	0	0	0	12	1-3	76.1	72	321	34	28	5	2	4	3	26	4	38	4	1
Wilson, C.J., Tex.*	1	7	.125	6.94	24	6	0	0	5	1-1	48.0	63	220	39	37	5	1	2	2	18	1	30	4	1
Witasick, Jay, Oak.	1	1	.500	3.25	28	0	0	0	4	1-3	27.2	26	129	15	10	2	0	0	3	17	2	33	3	0
Wood, Mike, K.C.	5	8	.385	4.46	47	10	0	0	10	2-2	115.0	129	520	66	57	18	5	5	8	52	5	60	7	0
Woods, Jake, L.A.*	1	1	.500	4.55	28	0	0	0	10	0-0	27.2	30	122	18	14	7	1	0	2	8	0	20	2	0
Woodyard, Mark, Det.	0	0	.000	1.50	3	0	0	0	0	0-0	6.0	4	22	1	1	1	0	0	0	3	0	3	0	0
Wright, Jaret, N.Y.	5	5	.500	6.08	13	13	0	0	0	0-0	63.2	81	302	51	43	8	0	5	6	32	1	34	4	0
Yabu, Keiichi, Oak.	4	0	1.000	4.50	40	0	0	0	15	1-2	58.0	64	262	34	29	6	2	3	8	26	3	44	2	0
Yan, Esteban, L.A.	1	1	.500	4.59	49	0	0	0	21	0-0	66.2	66	293	36	34	8	3	4	0	30	4	45	5	0
Young, Chris, Tex.	12	7	.632	4.26	31	31	0	0	0	0-0	164.2	162	700	84	78	19	2	4	7	45	2	137	3	0
Zito, Barry, Oak.*	14	13	.519	3.86	35	35	0	0	0	0-0	228.1	185	953	106	98	26	8	7	13	89	0	171	4	0

PITCHERS WITH TWO OR MORE TEAMS

Pitcher, Team	W	L	Pct.	ERA	G	GS	CG	ShO	GF	Sv.-Op.	IP	H	TBF	R	ER	HR	SH	SF	HB	BB	IBB	SO	WP	Bk.
Baldwin, James, Bal.	0	0	.000	3.20	20	0	0	0	11	0-0	39.1	36	162	18	14	5	1	3	2	9	0	20	1	0
Baldwin, James, Tex.	0	2	.000	5.19	8	0	0	0	2	1-1	17.1	18	76	10	10	3	0	2	1	7	1	9	1	1
Embree, Alan, Bos.*	1	4	.200	7.65	43	0	0	0	11	1-3	37.2	42	163	33	32	8	1	2	1	11	2	30	1	1
Embree, Alan, N.Y.*	1	1	.500	7.53	24	0	0	0	4	0-0	14.1	20	68	14	12	2	2	1	1	3	1	8	0	0
Karsay, Steve, N.Y.	0	0	.000	6.00	6	0	0	0	2	0-0	6.0	10	29	5	4	0	0	1	0	2	1	5	0	0
Karsay, Steve, Tex.	0	1	.000	7.47	14	0	0	0	8	0-0	15.2	26	77	14	13	2	0	1	0	5	0	9	1	0
Stanton, Mike, N.Y.*	1	2	.333	7.07	28	0	0	0	6	0-0	14.0	17	64	11	11	1	0	1	0	6	0	12	1	0
Stanton, Mike, Bos.*	0	0	.000	0.00	1	0	0	0	0	0-0	1.0	1	3	0	0	0	0	0	0	0	0	1	0	0

NOTE—The following pitchers combined to pitch shutout games: Baltimore (9)—Cabrera and Ryan; Bedard, Julio and Kline; Lopez, Kline, Julio and Ryan; Bedard and Julio; Cabrera, Byrdak and Ryan; Maine, Byrdak, Williams and Ryan; Lopez, Byrdak, Williams and Ryan; Chen and Ray; Cabrera, Byrdak and Rakers; Boston (8)—Wells and Foulke; Wells, Mantei and Halama; Clement and Foulke; Wells and Neal; Wells, Timlin and Foulke; Wakefield and Embree; Clement and Embree; Miller, Myers, Timlin and Schilling; Chicago (6)—Buehrle, Politte and Cotts; Buehrle and Takatsu; Contreras, Politte, Marte and Hermanson; Garland, Cotts and Politte; McCarthy and Jenks; Contreras, Jenks, Marte and Hermanson; Cleveland (10)—Millwood and Wickman; Sabathia, Riske and Betancourt; Lee, Rhodes, Howry, Sauerbeck, Betancourt and Wickman; Millwood, Howry and Sauerbeck; Davis, Miller, Howry and Riske; Westbrook, Howry and Wickman; Elarton, Howry and Wickman; Sabathia and Cabrera; Elarton and Howry; Sabathia and Betancourt; Detroit (2)—Robertson, Walker and Urbina; Maroth and Rodney; Kansas City (4)—Hernandez, Nunez, Affeldt and MacDougal; Greinke, Burgos and MacDougal; Wood, Sisco and MacDougal; Howell, Sisco, Burgos and Affeldt; Los Angeles (8)—Washburn and Donnelly; Washburn, Donnelly and Yan; Escobar, Shields and Rodriguez; Colon and Rodriguez; Washburn, Peralta and Yan; Lackey, Shields and Donnelly; Santana and Rodriguez; Byrd, Shields and Rodriguez; Minnesota (4)—Radke, Mulholland and Guerrier; Santana and Nathan; Santana and Nathan; Baker, Guerrier and Nathan; New York (10)—Brown, Gordon and Sturtze; Johnson, Gordon and Rivera; Wang, Gordon and Rivera; Johnson and Gordon; Chacon and Rodriguez; Wright, Embree, Sturtze and Proctor; Johnson, Gordon and Rivera; Johnson, Gordon and Rivera; Chacon and Gordon; Chacon and Proctor; Oakland (10)—Saarloos, Rincon, Street and Dotel; Harden and Calero; Harden, Rincon, Duchscherer and Dotel; Blanton, Calero and Street; Harden, Flores and Calero; Zito, Duchscherer and Street; Haren, Calero and Duchscherer; Harden, Calero, Witasick, Kennedy and Street; Haren, Yabu, Rincon and Cruz; Haren, Calero, Rincon, Duchscherer and Street; Seattle (5)—Meche, Villone, Nelson, Thornton and Guardado; Moyer and Nelson; Sele, Putz and Villone; Hernandez and Guardado; Hernandez, Putz, Sherrill and Guardado; Tampa Bay (4)—Fossum and Baez; Kazmir, Borowski and Baez; Kazmir, Borowski and Baez; McClung and Baez; Texas (5)—Park, Shouse and Cordero; Astacio and Cordero; Young and Cordero; Loe and Wilson; Loe and Wilson; Toronto (5)—Towers and Batista; Halladay, Schoeneweis and Speier; Chacin and Batista; Lilly, Frasor and Speier; Chacin and Batista.

FIELDING

TEAM

Team	G	PO	A	E	TC	DP	TP	PB	Pct.
Oakland	162	4351	1649	88	6088	166	0	5	.986
Seattle	162	4283	1575	86	5944	144	0	14	.986
Los Angeles	162	4393	1521	87	6001	139	0	13	.986
Chicago	162	4427	1670	94	6191	167	0	9	.985
Toronto	162	4341	1757	95	6193	154	0	6	.985
New York	162	4292	1688	95	6075	151	0	11	.984
Minnesota	162	4393	1764	102	6259	171	0	9	.984
Cleveland	162	4358	1646	106	6110	156	0	6	.983
Baltimore	162	4283	1679	107	6069	154	0	13	.982
Texas	162	4320	1678	108	6108	149	0	11	.982
Detroit	162	4307	1791	110	6208	171	0	4	.982
Boston	162	4287	1623	109	6019	135	0	13	.982
Kansas City	162	4240	1646	125	6011	162	0	5	.979
Tampa Bay	162	4265	1446	124	5835	139	0	13	.979
Totals	1134	60540	23133	1436	85109	2158	0	132	.983

INDIVIDUAL

FIRST BASEMEN

NOTE: All caps denotes fielding-percentage leader based on 81 games for catchers, 108 for all other non-pitchers and 162 innings for pitchers. *Throws Lefthanded.

Player, Team	G	GS	PO	A	E	TC	DP	Pct.
Barajas, Rod, Tex.	1	0	1	0	0	1	0	1.000
Blake, Casey, Cle.	4	4	28	5	1	34	4	.971
Bloomquist, Willie, Sea.	1	0	0	1	0	1	0	1.000
Blum, Geoff, Chi.	12	9	91	6	0	97	7	1.000
Broussard, Ben, Cle.*	138	112	1082	60	9	1151	112	.992
Burke, Jamie, Chi.	1	0	0	0	0	0	0	.000
Cuddyer, Michael, Min.	8	3	37	1	0	38	8	1.000
DeRosa, Mark, Tex.	1	0	2	0	0	2	1	1.000
Dobbs, Greg, Sea.	5	4	32	8	0	40	0	1.000
Durazo, Erubiel, Oak.*	1	1	8	0	0	8	2	1.000
Dye, Jermaine, Chi.	1	1	7	1	0	8	0	1.000
Ellis, Mark, Oak.	2	0	3	0	0	3	0	1.000
Erstad, Darin, L.A.*	147	144	1218	79	4	1301	109	.997
Escalona, Felix, N.Y.	1	0	2	0	0	2	0	1.000
Fasano, Sal, Bal.	1	0	0	0	0	0	0	.000
Flaherty, John, N.Y.	1	0	1	0	0	1	0	1.000
Freire, Alejandro, Bal.	16	13	101	5	1	107	10	.991
Giambi, Jason, N.Y.	78	77	581	19	7	607	50	.988
Gibbons, Jay, Bal.*	22	19	171	8	1	180	10	.994
Gload, Ross, Chi.*	24	6	72	4	1	77	9	.987
Gomez, Chris, Bal.	42	27	252	15	2	269	29	.993
Gonzalez, Adrian, Tex.*	10	7	85	6	2	93	7	.978
Graffanino, Tony, K.C.	22	14	137	8	1	146	19	.993
Hafner, Travis, Cle.	1	1	6	2	0	8	0	1.000
Hall, Toby, TB.	2	0	5	2	0	7	0	1.000
Hansen, Dave, Sea.	9	0	18	2	0	20	3	1.000
Harvey, Ken, K.C.	5	5	41	0	0	41	2	1.000
Hatteberg, Scott, Oak.	53	50	423	38	7	468	47	.985
Hernandez, Jose, Cle.	45	41	339	27	2	368	28	.995
Hillenbrand, Shea, Tor.	67	65	627	48	6	681	69	.991
Hinske, Eric, Tor.	100	97	868	69	7	944	77	.993
Huber, Justin, K.C.	19	17	123	8	3	134	16	.978
Huff, Aubrey, TB.	25	18	134	5	0	139	15	1.000
Ibanez, Raul, Sea.	4	4	26	3	0	29	0	1.000
Johnson, Dan, Oak.	101	98	897	57	6	960	94	.994
Johnson, Russ, N.Y.	7	2	30	0	0	30	5	1.000
Konerko, Paul, Chi.	146	145	1321	82	5	1408	135	.996
Kotchman, Casey, L.A.*	20	13	112	7	0	119	10	1.000
LaForest, Pete, TB.	1	1	4	0	0	4	0	1.000
LeCroy, Matthew, Min.	23	21	204	8	3	215	18	.986
Lee, Travis, TB.*	124	101	875	67	4	946	87	.996
Liefer, Jeff, Cle.	5	4	17	2	1	20	2	.950
Lopez, Javy, Bal.	1	0	1	0	1	2	1	.000
Marrero, Eli, K.C.	9	8	72	3	1	76	7	.987
Martinez, Ramon, Det.	2	0	3	0	0	3	0	1.000
Martinez, Tino, N.Y.	122	78	797	49	8	854	73	.991
McCarty, Dave, Bos.*	12	0	19	3	0	22	3	1.000
McEwing, Joe, K.C.	20	8	101	11	0	112	16	1.000
Merloni, Lou, L.A.	1	0	0	0	0	0	0	.000
Millar, Kevin, Bos.	110	102	798	85	7	890	67	.992
Molina, Jose, L.A.	4	1	10	0	0	10	2	1.000
Morneau, Justin, Min.	138	128	1191	91	8	1290	123	.994
Munson, Eric, TB.	1	0	3	0	0	3	1	1.000
Nevin, Phil, Tex.	3	1	13	1	0	14	1	1.000
Olerud, John, Bos.*	80	38	416	40	1	457	41	.998
Ortiz, David, Bos.*	10	10	69	11	2	82	8	.976
Ozuna, Pablo, Chi.	2	0	2	1	0	3	0	1.000
Palmeiro, Rafael, Bal.*	93	82	747	58	4	809	68	.995
Pena, Carlos, Det.*	51	49	418	35	3	456	46	.993
Perez, Eduardo, TB.	49	42	264	18	2	284	22	.993
Perez, Timo, Chi.*	2	1	13	1	1	15	1	.933
Petagine, Roberto, Bos.*	10	7	51	6	1	58	4	.983
Phelps, Josh, TB.	1	0	5	0	0	5	2	1.000
Phillips, Andy, N.Y.	19	5	75	2	1	78	7	.987
Quinlan, Robb, L.A.	9	4	38	1	0	39	5	1.000
Sexson, Richie, Sea.	151	151	1148	120	7	1275	121	.995
Shelton, Chris, Det.	84	83	778	60	6	844	87	.993
Smith, Jason, Det.	1	0	10	1	0	11	0	1.000
Spiezio, Scott, Sea.	4	3	31	0	0	31	1	1.000
Stairs, Matt, K.C.	64	61	499	37	4	540	60	.993
Surhoff, B.J., Bal.	18	14	116	8	1	125	14	.992
Sweeney, Mike, K.C.	49	49	441	29	1	471	29	.998
Swisher, Nick, Oak.*	21	13	109	10	0	119	10	1.000
TEIXEIRA, Mark, Tex.	155	154	1377	101	3	1481	127	.998
Tiffee, Terry, Min.	13	10	92	7	1	100	6	.990
Widger, Chris, Chi.	1	0	0	0	0	0	0	.000
Youkilis, Kevin, Bos.	9	5	48	0	0	48	4	1.000
Young, Dmitri, Det.	30	30	265	22	3	290	25	.990
Young, Walter, Bal.	10	7	55	6	0	61	9	1.000

SECOND BASEMEN

Player, Team	G	GS	PO	A	E	TC	DP	Pct.
Abernathy, Brent, Min.	17	14	24	37	2	63	9	.968
Bellhorn, Mark, Bos.-N.Y.	85	84	152	264	7	423	56	.983
Belliard, Ronnie, Cle.	141	139	257	413	13	683	95	.981
Betancourt, Yuniesky, Sea.	9	6	23	21	0	44	5	1.000
Blanco, Andres, K.C.	24	22	57	68	3	128	23	.977
Bloomquist, Willie, Sea.	32	29	58	81	2	141	21	.986
Blum, Geoff, Chi.	2	2	3	4	0	7	2	1.000
Boone, Bret, Sea.-Min.	88	88	169	229	9	407	54	.978
Bynum, Freddie, Oak.	3	0	0	0	0	0	0	.000
Cano, Robinson, N.Y.	131	130	258	391	17	666	77	.974
Cantu, Jorge, TB.	80	76	119	181	9	309	40	.971
Castro, Bernie, Bal.	11	11	17	31	3	51	7	.941
Castro, Juan, Min.	5	3	4	9	0	13	3	1.000
Clark, Jermaine, Oak.	2	0	0	0	0	0	0	.000
Cora, Alex, Cle.-Bos.	50	35	76	110	2	188	29	.989
Cortez, Fernando, TB.	3	3	0	3	0	3	0	1.000
Cuddyer, Michael, Min.	11	6	12	18	0	30	7	1.000
DeRosa, Mark, Tex.	17	8	14	20	1	35	4	.971
Ellis, Mark, Oak.	115	109	203	333	6	542	82	.989
Escalona, Felix, N.Y.	1	1	1	4	0	5	1	1.000
Figgins, Chone, L.A.	42	36	67	101	5	173	20	.971
German, Esteban, Tex.	1	1	3	8	1	12	2	.917
Ginter, Keith, Oak.	25	24	49	69	3	121	17	.975
Gomez, Chris, Bal.	18	13	31	40	1	72	12	.986
Gotay, Ruben, K.C.	81	74	155	232	8	395	50	.980
Graffanino, Tony, K.C.-Bos.	73	71	121	186	4	311	37	.987
Green, Nick, TB.	91	83	141	195	4	340	44	.988
Harris, Willie, Chi.	32	28	58	78	2	138	20	.986
Hernandez, Jose, Cle.	4	3	6	9	0	15	6	1.000
Hill, Aaron, Tor.	22	19	33	77	1	111	15	.991
Hocking, Denny, K.C.	13	12	33	48	2	83	13	.976
Hooper, Kevin, Det.	1	1	2	1	0	3	0	1.000
HUDSON, Orlando, Tor.	130	120	302	391	6	699	80	.991
Iguchi, Tadahito, Chi.	133	129	235	375	14	624	85	.978
Infante, Omar, Det.	69	65	153	186	4	343	52	.988
Izturis, Maicer, L.A.	1	1	4	4	0	8	0	1.000
Johnson, Russ, N.Y.	1	0	0	0	0	0	0	.000
Kennedy, Adam, L.A.	127	123	212	352	5	569	71	.991
Lopez, Jose, Sea.	51	50	123	159	6	288	32	.979

Player, Team	G	GS	PO	A	E	TC	DP	Pct.
Lopez, Pedro, Chi.	1	1	3	5	0	8	2	1.000
Machado, Alejandro, Bos.	3	0	0	0	0	0	0	.000
Martinez, Ramon, Det.	4	4	10	12	2	24	3	.917
Matranga, Dave, L.A.	1	0	2	1	0	3	1	1.000
McDonald, John, Tor.-Det.	13	5	14	16	0	30	6	1.000
McDougall, Marshall, Tex.	2	0	0	0	0	0	0	.000
McEwing, Joe, K.C.	11	10	15	25	0	40	6	1.000
Menechino, Frank, Tor.	26	21	37	70	1	108	18	.991
Mueller, Bill, Bos.	5	5	10	13	1	24	1	.958
Murphy, Donnie, K.C.	29	23	42	61	3	106	14	.972
Ozuna, Pablo, Chi.	6	2	6	6	1	13	0	.923
Phillips, Brandon, Cle.	2	2	5	4	0	9	2	1.000
Polanco, Placido, Det.	84	83	187	248	3	438	69	.993
Punto, Nick, Min.	73	63	131	193	7	331	44	.979
Rivas, Luis, Min.	53	40	77	112	1	190	26	.995
Roberts, Brian, Bal.	141	138	238	413	8	659	93	.988
Rodriguez, Luis, Min.	40	22	53	73	0	126	22	1.000
Sanchez, Rey, N.Y.	9	7	18	24	1	43	5	.977
Santiago, Ramon, Sea.	2	2	0	4	0	4	1	1.000
Scutaro, Marco, Oak.	30	29	56	92	1	149	19	.993
Smith, Jason, Det.	6	6	8	16	1	25	4	.960
Sorensen, Zach, L.A.	5	2	3	5	0	8	1	1.000
Soriano, Alfonso, Tex.	153	153	284	448	21	753	101	.972
Spiezio, Scott, Sea.	1	1	1	1	0	2	0	1.000
Vazquez, Ramon, Bos.-Cle.	12	7	20	16	2	38	6	.947
Womack, Tony, N.Y.	24	22	42	89	1	132	22	.992
Youkilis, Kevin, Bos.	2	1	0	2	0	2	0	1.000

SECOND BASEMEN WITH TWO OR MORE TEAMS

Player, Team	G	GS	PO	A	E	TC	DP	Pct.
Bellhorn, Mark, Bos.	83	82	148	253	6	407	54	.985
Bellhorn, Mark, N.Y.	2	2	4	11	1	16	2	.938
Boone, Bret, Sea.	74	74	130	192	7	329	43	.979
Boone, Bret, Min.	4	14	39	37	2	78	11	.974
Cora, Alex, Cle.	15	14	24	47	0	71	11	1.000
Cora, Alex, Bos.	35	21	52	63	2	117	18	.98
Graffanino, Tony, K.C.	22	21	30	46	1	77	8	.987
Graffanino, Tony, Bos.	51	50	91	140	3	234	29	.987
McDonald, John, Tor.	5	2	9	7	0	16	3	1.000
McDonald, John, Det.	8	3	5	9	0	14	3	1.000
Vazquez, Ramon, Cle.	4	3	3	6	2	11	1	.818
Vazquez, Ramon, Cle.	8	4	17	10	0	27	5	1.000

THIRD BASEMEN

Player, Team	G	GS	PO	A	E	TC	DP	Pct.
Bellhorn, Mark, N.Y.	4	1	1	3	0	4	0	1.000
Beltre, Adrian, Sea.	155	155	140	271	14	425	27	.967
Blake, Casey, Cle.	6	6	4	9	1	14	1	.929
BLALOCK, Hank, Tex.	158	156	96	304	11	411	23	.973
Bloomquist, Willie, Sea.	6	1	1	4	0	5	0	1.000
Blum, Geoff, Chi.	12	9	4	29	3	36	2	.917
Bocachica, Hiram, Oak.	2	2	2	3	0	5	1	1.000
Boone, Aaron, Cle.	142	139	81	299	18	398	20	.955
Cantu, Jorge, T.B.	62	58	31	93	12	136	7	.912
Castro, Juan, Min.	22	13	14	22	4	40	1	.900
Chavez, Eric, Oak.	153	153	121	302	15	438	28	.966
Cora, Alex, Bos.	5	2	2	7	3	12	0	.750
Cortez, Fernando, T.B.	1	0	0	0	0	0	0	.000
Crede, Joe, Chi.	130	122	95	243	10	348	28	.971
Cuddyer, Michael, Min.	95	92	56	189	15	260	14	.942
DeRosa, Mark, Tex.	5	4	2	5	1	8	1	.875
Dobbs, Greg, Sea.	2	1	4	5	0	9	1	1.000
Escalona, Felix, N.Y.	3	0	0	1	0	1	0	1.000
Figgins, Chone, L.A.	56	48	34	95	3	132	8	.977
German, Esteban, Tex.	1	0	0	0	0	0	0	.000
Ginter, Keith, Oak.	12	5	12	11	3	26	0	.885
Gomez, Chris, Bal.	17	13	11	23	1	35	1	.971
Gonzalez, Alex S., T.B.	98	90	66	173	14	253	10	.945
Graffanino, Tony, K.C.	17	14	7	31	5	43	3	.884
Green, Nick, T.B.	13	11	4	21	3	28	2	.893
Hansen, Dave, Sea.	7	4	5	7	0	12	0	1.000
Hernandez, Jose, Cle.	21	17	15	36	0	51	2	1.000
Hill, Aaron, Tor.	35	32	21	73	5	99	8	.949
Hillenbrand, Shea, Tor.	54	52	31	94	6	131	8	.954
Hocking, Denny, K.C.	1	0	0	0	0	0	0	.000
Huff, Aubrey, T.B.	8	2	2	2	0	4	1	1.000
Inge, Brandon, Det.	160	159	129	378	23	530	42	.957
Izturis, Maicer, L.A.	45	26	20	62	8	90	5	.911
Johnson, Russ, N.Y.	8	0	1	2	0	3	0	1.000
Koskie, Corey, Tor.	76	74	52	158	7	217	19	.968
Lopez, Jose, Sea.	1	1	2	2	1	5	0	.800
Martinez, Ramon, Det.	1	0	0	0	0	0	0	.000
McDonald, John, Det.	1	1	2	0	0	2	0	1.000
McDougall, Marshall, Tex.	5	2	3	4	0	7	0	1.000
McEwing, Joe, K.C.	29	26	18	57	3	78	2	.962
McPherson, Dallas, L.A.	60	55	32	86	7	125	14	.944
Menechino, Frank, Tor.	9	4	2	9	0	11	2	1.000
Merloni, Lou, L.A.	4	2	1	8	0	9	0	1.000
Mora, Melvin, Bal.	148	148	96	302	18	416	23	.957
Mueller, Bill, Bos.	142	140	87	265	10	362	20	.972
Munson, Eric, T.B.	2	1	1	1	0	2	0	1.000
Nevin, Phil, Tex.	1	0	0	1	0	1	0	1.000
Newhan, David, Bal.	8	1	1	3	0	4	1	1.000
Ozuna, Pablo, Chi.	32	30	29	67	6	102	4	.941
Perez, Eduardo, T.B.	3	0	2	0	0	2	0	1.000
Phillips, Andy, N.Y.	1	0	0	0	0	0	0	.000
Polanco, Placido, Det.	1	1	1	3	0	4	0	1.000
Punto, Nick, Min.	12	7	6	22	0	28	4	1.000
Quinlan, Robb, L.A.	33	30	22	51	7	80	4	.913
Rodriguez, Alex, N.Y.	161	161	115	288	12	415	26	.971
Rodriguez, Luis, Min.	27	21	14	43	3	60	4	.950
Ryan, Michael, Min.	1	0	0	0	0	0	0	.000
Sanchez, Rey, N.Y.	1	0	0	0	0	0	0	.000
Scutaro, Marco, Oak.	5	2	4	6	0	10	1	1.000
Smith, Jason, Det.	3	1	5	6	0	11	2	1.000
Sorensen, Zach, L.A.	1	1	2	3	1	6	0	.833
Spiezio, Scott, Sea.	6	0	1	1	0	2	1	1.000
Teahen, Mark, K.C.	128	122	113	245	20	378	24	.947
Tiffee, Terry, Min.	24	20	18	34	5	57	6	.912
Vazquez, Ramon, Bos.	8	6	6	11	0	17	3	1.000
Widger, Chris, Chi.	1	1	1	1	0	2	1	1.000
Williams, Glenn, Min.	12	9	7	19	2	28	2	.929
Youkilis, Kevin, Bos.	24	14	10	29	0	39	3	1.000

SHORTSTOPS

Player, Team	G	GS	PO	A	E	TC	DP	Pct.
Adams, Russ, Tor.	132	122	194	326	26	546	68	.952
Bartlett, Jason, Min.	68	65	95	227	7	329	45	.979
Bellhorn, Mark, Bos.-N.Y.	3	1	3	5	1	9	0	.889
Berroa, Angel, K.C.	159	159	254	441	25	720	108	.965
Betancourt, Yuniesky, Sea.	53	52	83	138	5	226	35	.978
Blanco, Andres, K.C.	7	2	7	7	0	14	2	1.000
Bloomquist, Willie, Sea.	24	21	34	49	3	86	6	.965
Blum, Geoff, Chi.	6	4	6	10	0	16	2	1.000
CABRERA, Orlando, L.A.	140	139	229	347	7	583	81	.988
Castro, Juan, Min.	73	66	97	232	5	334	50	.985
Cora, Alex, Cle.-Bos.	35	27	38	107	3	148	16	.980
Cortez, Fernando, T.B.	2	0	1	2	0	3	0	1.000
Crede, Joe, Chi.	1	1	1	3	0	4	2	1.000
Crosby, Bobby, Oak.	84	84	117	251	7	375	60	.981
DeRosa, Mark, Tex.	16	7	17	38	1	56	5	.982
Dye, Jermaine, Chi.	1	0	0	0	0	0	0	.000
Ellis, Mark, Oak.	7	5	6	15	0	21	4	1.000
Escalona, Felix, N.Y.	5	2	8	8	0	16	3	1.000
Figgins, Chone, L.A.	4	1	2	4	0	6	1	1.000
Giarratano, Tony, Det.	13	12	16	40	3	59	5	.949
Gomez, Chris, Bal.	10	2	5	8	1	14	3	.929
Gonzalez, Alex S., T.B.	12	7	12	18	2	32	1	.938
Graffanino, Tony, K.C.	1	0	1	0	0	1	0	1.000
Guillen, Carlos, Det.	75	74	85	228	7	320	44	.978
Harris, Willie, Chi.	5	2	1	9	0	10	1	1.000
Hernandez, Jose, Cle.	1	0	1	1	0	2	0	1.000
Hill, Aaron, Tor.	16	15	18	48	0	66	9	1.000
Hocking, Denny, K.C.	1	0	1	1	0	2	1	1.000
Hooper, Kevin, Det.	2	0	2	3	1	6	0	.833
Infante, Omar, Det.	50	43	82	149	6	237	35	.975
Izturis, Maicer, L.A.	29	21	44	55	2	101	8	.980
Jeter, Derek, N.Y.	157	157	262	454	15	731	96	.979
Lopez, Pedro, Chi.	1	1	0	2	0	2	0	1.000
Lugo, Julio, T.B.	156	155	310	424	24	758	94	.968
Machado, Alejandro, Bos.	1	0	1	1	0	2	0	1.000
Martinez, Ramon, Det.	12	11	13	29	2	44	4	.955
McDonald, John, Tor.-Det.	54	42	67	157	8	232	35	.966
McDougall, Marshall, Tex.	1	0	1	1	0	2	1	1.000
McEwing, Joe, K.C.	6	1	7	10	1	18	4	.944
Menechino, Frank, Tor.	1	0	1	1	0	2	1	1.000
Morse, Mike, Sea.	55	50	91	120	12	223	34	.946
Murphy, Donnie, K.C.	2	0	0	1	1	2	0	.000
Ozuna, Pablo, Chi.	15	11	19	35	2	56	12	.964
Peralta, Jhonny, Cle.	141	138	207	413	19	639	104	.970
Phillips, Brandon, Cle.	1	0	1	2	1	4	1	.750
Punto, Nick, Min.	34	26	47	76	2	125	16	.984

Player, Team	G	GS	PO	A	E	TC	DP	Pct.
Ramirez, Hanley, Bos.	2	0	0	1	0	1	0	1.000
Renteria, Edgar, Bos.	153	150	227	398	30	655	90	.954
Rivas, Luis, Min.	6	2	3	5	1	9	1	.889
Rodriguez, Alex, N.Y.	3	0	1	2	0	3	0	1.000
Rodriguez, Luis, Min.	10	3	8	14	0	22	4	1.000
Rogers, Ed, Bal.	1	0	0	0	0	0	0	.000
Sanchez, Rey, N.Y.	10	3	7	14	1	22	4	.955
Santiago, Ramon, Sea.	2	0	0	1	1	2	0	.500
Scutaro, Marco, Oak.	81	73	115	213	8	336	50	.976
Smith, Jason, Det.	15	5	14	27	0	41	6	1.000
Tejada, Miguel, Bal.	160	160	252	479	22	753	105	.971
Uribe, Juan, Chi.	146	143	249	422	16	687	99	.977
Valdez, Wilson, Sea.	42	39	66	111	5	182	22	.973
Vazquez, Ramon, Bos.-Cle.	14	8	18	20	1	39	4	.974
Young, Michael, Tex.	155	155	238	427	18	683	95	.974

SHORTSTOPS WITH TWO OR MORE TEAMS

Player, Team	G	GS	PO	A	E	TC	DP	Pct.
Bellhorn, Mark, Bos.	1	1	1	3	1	5	0	.800
Bellhorn, Mark, N.Y.	2	0	2	2	0	4	0	1.000
Cora, Alex, Cle.	24	22	29	83	3	115	11	.974
Cora, Alex, Bos.	11	5	9	24	0	33	5	1.000
McDonald, John, Tor.	32	25	38	88	3	129	19	.977
McDonald, John, Det.	22	17	29	69	5	103	16	.951
Vazquez, Ramon, Bos.	12	6	16	15	1	32	3	.969
Vazquez, Ramon, Cle.	2	2	2	5	0	7	1	1.000

OUTFIELDERS

Player, Team	G	GS	PO	A	E	TC	DP	Pct.
Abernathy, Brent, Min.	5	3	5	0	0	5	0	1.000
Allen, Chad, Tex.	2	1	1	0	0	1	0	1.000
Ambres, Chip, K.C.	47	34	83	2	1	86	0	.988
Anderson, Brian N., Chi.	12	7	19	1	0	20	1	1.000
Anderson, Garret, L.A.*	106	106	201	4	5	210	1	.976
Bigbie, Larry, Bal.	62	60	108	3	0	111	0	1.000
Blake, Casey, Cle.	138	132	287	3	8	298	0	.973
Bloomquist, Willie, Sea.	15	13	25	1	1	27	1	.963
Bocachica, Hiram, Oak.	6	3	6	0	0	6	0	1.000
Borchard, Joe, Chi.	2	0	3	0	0	3	0	1.000
Botts, Jason, Tex.	7	5	8	1	1	10	1	.900
Brown, Emil, K.C.	139	135	264	9	12	285	0	.958
Bubela, Jaime, Sea.	7	5	17	0	0	17	0	1.000
Bynum, Freddie, Oak.	2	1	5	0	0	5	0	1.000
Byrnes, Eric, Oak.-Bal.	105	90	208	6	5	219	2	.977
Cabrera, Melky, N.Y.*	6	6	9	0	0	9	0	1.000
Calzado, Napoleon, Bal.	2	1	2	0	0	2	0	1.000
Castro, Bernie, Bal.	1	1	1	0	1	2	0	.500
CATALANOTTO, Frank, Tor.	111	99	163	4	0	167	0	1.000
Choo, Shin-Soo, Sea.*	5	5	16	0	0	16	0	1.000
Clark, Jermaine, Oak.	1	0	0	0	0	0	0	.000
Cora, Alex, Cle.	1	0	0	0	0	0	0	.000
Costa, Shane, K.C.	20	18	30	1	0	31	0	1.000
Crawford, Carl, TB.*	154	150	361	3	2	366	1	.995
Crisp, Coco, Cle.	145	143	315	3	5	323	0	.985
Crosby, Bubba, N.Y.*	67	23	83	2	0	85	1	1.000
Cruz Jr., Jose, Bos.	4	4	2	0	0	2	0	1.000
Cuddyer, Michael, Min.	20	18	35	0	0	35	0	1.000
Cummings, Midre, Bal.	1	0	0	0	0	0	0	.000
Damon, Johnny, Bos.*	147	144	394	5	6	405	0	.985
DaVanon, Jeff, L.A.	63	33	105	1	1	107	0	.991
DeJesus, David, K.C.*	119	118	306	7	4	317	3	.987
Dellucci, David, Tex.*	52	49	93	4	3	100	1	.970
DeRosa, Mark, Tex.	25	21	46	1	0	47	0	1.000
Diaz, Matt, K.C.	21	17	38	0	2	40	0	.950
Dobbs, Greg, Sea.	4	2	4	0	0	4	0	1.000
Dubois, Jason, Cle.	7	7	14	0	0	14	0	1.000
Dye, Jermaine, Chi.	140	140	259	9	8	276	2	.971
Everett, Carl, Chi.	22	22	34	1	0	35	1	1.000
Figgins, Chone, L.A.	72	65	170	3	2	175	1	.989
Finley, Steve, L.A.*	104	100	266	5	4	275	2	.985
Fiorentino, Jeff, Bal.	12	10	29	0	0	29	0	1.000
Ford, Lew, Min.	95	88	198	9	6	213	1	.972
Freire, Alejandro, Bal.	1	0	0	0	0	0	0	.000
Gathright, Joey, TB.	70	56	180	3	3	186	2	.984
Gerut, Jody, Cle.*	38	35	58	1	0	59	0	1.000
Gibbons, Jay, Bal.*	71	69	133	6	2	141	1	.986
Ginter, Keith, Oak.	2	0	0	0	0	0	0	.000
Gload, Ross, Chi.*	3	2	5	0	0	5	0	1.000
Gomes, Jonny, TB.	50	48	98	7	4	109	1	.963
Gomez, Alexis, Det.*	9	4	9	0	0	9	0	1.000

Player, Team	G	GS	PO	A	E	TC	DP	Pct.
Gonzalez, Adrian, Tex.*	1	1	3	0	1	4	0	.750
Granderson, Curtis, Det.	45	42	129	2	0	131	0	1.000
Green, Nick, TB.	1	0	0	0	0	0	0	.000
Gross, Gabe, Tor.	37	24	51	2	1	54	1	.981
Guerrero, Vladimir, L.A.	120	120	242	8	3	253	2	.988
Guiel, Aaron, K.C.	30	26	64	1	1	66	0	.985
Gutierrez, Franklin, Cle.	2	0	1	0	0	1	0	1.000
Hernandez, Jose, Cle.	6	4	4	0	0	4	0	1.000
Hidalgo, Richard, Tex.	85	80	179	3	2	184	0	.989
Higginson, Bobby, Det.	7	6	8	1	0	9	0	1.000
Hollins, Damon, TB.*	116	90	250	8	6	264	4	.977
Hooper, Kevin, Det.	3	0	1	0	0	1	0	1.000
Huff, Aubrey, TB.	97	95	204	6	3	213	2	.986
Hunter, Torii, Min.	93	92	218	9	3	230	4	.987
Hyzdu, Adam, Bos.	12	3	10	0	1	11	0	.909
Ibanez, Raul, Sea.	58	57	106	6	2	114	3	.982
Inge, Brandon, Det.	2	0	2	0	0	2	0	1.000
Izturis, Maicer, L.A.	1	0	1	1	0	2	1	1.000
Johnson, Reed, Tor.	139	90	196	5	2	203	0	.990
Johnson, Russ, N.Y.	3	0	1	0	0	1	0	1.000
Jones, Jacque, Min.*	132	130	278	10	4	292	2	.986
Kapler, Gabe, Bos.	36	25	65	0	0	65	0	1.000
Kielty, Bobby, Oak.	96	89	166	5	3	174	1	.983
Kotsay, Mark, Oak.*	137	137	299	7	4	310	3	.987
Laird, Gerald, Tex.	1	0	0	0	0	0	0	.000
Lawton, Matt, N.Y.	19	15	31	0	1	32	0	.969
Liefer, Jeff, Cle.	3	1	4	0	0	4	0	1.000
Logan, Nook, Det.	123	93	282	3	6	291	2	.979
Long, Terrence, K.C.*	121	113	203	12	3	218	0	.986
Ludwick, Ryan, Cle.*	15	11	22	0	1	23	0	.957
Machado, Alejandro, Bos.	6	0	3	0	0	3	0	1.000
Marrero, Eli, K.C.-Bal.	36	28	55	2	2	59	0	.966
Matos, Luis, Bal.	120	110	298	5	7	310	2	.984
Matsui, Hideki, N.Y.	142	143	279	7	3	289	1	.990
Matthews Jr., Gary, Tex.	123	121	317	7	6	330	4	.982
McCarty, Dave, Bos.*	1	0	0	0	0	0	0	.000
McDougall, Marshall, Tex.	3	1	0	0	0	0	0	.000
McEwing, Joe, K.C.	5	0	1	0	0	1	0	1.000
Mench, Kevin, Tex.	148	144	290	8	4	302	3	.987
Millar, Kevin, Bos.	34	24	41	1	0	42	0	1.000
Monroe, Craig, Det.	156	154	294	10	6	310	4	.981
Morse, Mike, Sea.	8	7	10	1	0	11	1	1.000
Munson, Eric, TB.	1	0	1	0	0	1	0	1.000
Newhan, David, Bal.	73	54	99	1	1	101	0	.990
Nivar, Ramon, Bal.	4	3	10	0	0	10	0	1.000
Nix, Laynce, Tex.*	61	60	160	3	2	165	1	.988
Nixon, Trot, Bos.*	118	107	240	8	1	249	3	.996
Ordonez, Magglio, Det.	81	79	139	5	1	145	0	.993
Ozuna, Pablo, Chi.	10	8	10	0	0	10	0	1.000
Paul, Josh, L.A.	2	0	0	0	0	0	0	.000
PAYTON, Jay, Bos.-Oak.	122	98	235	5	0	240	0	1.000
Perez, Eduardo, TB.	4	2	5	0	0	5	0	1.000
Perez, Timo, Chi.*	50	35	75	5	3	83	1	.964
Petagine, Roberto, Bos.*	2	0	0	0	0	0	0	.000
Phillips, Andy, N.Y.	1	0	0	0	0	0	0	.000
Podsednik, Scott, Chi.*	127	124	274	3	3	280	1	.989
Pride, Curtis, L.A.	4	0	2	0	0	2	0	1.000
Prieto, Chris, L.A.*	2	1	5	0	0	5	0	1.000
Punto, Nick, Min.	3	1	1	0	0	1	0	1.000
Quinlan, Robb, L.A.	6	2	3	0	0	3	0	1.000
Ramirez, Manny, Bos.	149	147	243	17	7	267	0	.974
Reed, Jeremy, Sea.*	137	129	383	7	3	393	1	.992
Reed, Keith, Bal.	6	1	3	0	0	3	0	1.000
Reese, Kevin, N.Y.*	2	1	2	0	0	2	0	1.000
Rios, Alex, Tor.	142	120	257	7	2	266	1	.992
Rivera, Juan, L.A.	74	59	127	5	1	133	1	.992
Rowand, Aaron, Chi.	157	151	388	3	3	394	1	.992
Ryan, Michael, Min.	25	16	30	2	0	32	1	1.000
Sanchez, Alex, TB.*	31	29	65	1	3	69	0	.957
Scutaro, Marco, Oak.	2	1	5	0	0	5	0	1.000
Sheffield, Gary, N.Y.	131	130	239	5	3	247	0	.988
Shelton, Chris, Det.	1	0	0	0	0	0	0	.000
Sierra, Ruben, N.Y.	18	13	23	0	1	24	0	.958
Singleton, Chris, TB.*	19	11	35	1	1	37	0	.973
Sizemore, Grady, Cle.*	155	152	373	3	3	379	1	.992
Snelling, Chris, Sea.*	10	8	20	2	0	22	1	1.000
Sosa, Sammy, Bal.	66	66	121	3	3	127	1	.976
Stairs, Matt, K.C.	15	12	18	0	0	18	0	1.000
Stern, Adam, Bos.	21	2	10	0	0	10	0	1.000
Stewart, Shannon, Min.	125	125	249	7	4	260	2	.985
Strong, Jamal, Sea.	11	6	12	1	0	13	0	1.000
Surhoff, B.J., Bal.	60	54	109	3	1	113	0	.991

Player, Team	G	GS	PO	A	E	TC	DP	Pct.
Suzuki, Ichiro, Sea.	158	158	381	10	2	393	2	.995
Swisher, Nick, Oak.*	121	115	196	6	2	204	2	.990
Taylor, Reggie, TB.	10	5	17	0	0	17	0	1.000
Thames, Marcus, Det.	31	25	45	0	1	46	0	.978
Thomas, Charles, Oak.*	27	12	38	1	2	41	0	.951
Torres, Andres, Tex.	5	3	12	0	0	12	0	1.000
Tyner, Jason, Min.*	15	13	30	0	0	30	0	1.000
Vento, Mike, N.Y.	2	0	2	1	0	3	1	1.000
Watson, Matt, Oak.	17	12	30	0	0	30	0	1.000
WELLS, Vernon, Tor.	155	153	351	12	0	363	4	1.000
White, Rondell, Det.	65	65	119	0	0	119	0	1.000
Williams, Bernie, N.Y.	112	100	226	6	2	234	1	.991
Winn, Randy, Sea.	96	96	245	3	0	248	0	1.000
Womack, Tony, N.Y.	66	58	113	2	2	117	0	.983
Young, Dmitri, Det.	20	18	35	1	0	36	0	1.000

OUTFIELDERS WITH TWO OR MORE TEAMS

Player, Team	G	GS	PO	A	E	TC	DP	Pct.
Byrnes, Eric, Oak.	54	48	117	4	2	123	2	.984
Byrnes, Eric, Bal.	51	42	91	2	3	96	0	.969
Marrero, Eli, K.C.	20	13	27	2	1	30	0	.967
Marrero, Eli, Oak.	16	15	28	0	1	29	0	.966
Payton, Jay, Bos.	53	30	82	3	0	85	0	1.000
Payton, Jay, Oak.	69	68	153	2	0	155	0	1.000

CATCHERS

Player, Team	G	GS	PO	A	E	TC	DP	PB	Pct.
Alomar Jr., Sandy, Tex.	46	34	231	6	2	239	0	3	.992
Barajas, Rod, Tex.	119	117	689	41	9	739	5	7	.988
Bard, Josh, Cle.	31	23	164	10	3	177	2	3	.983
Borders, Pat, Sea.	39	37	174	16	2	192	2	3	.990
Buck, John, K.C.	117	112	640	56	3	699	5	3	.996
Casanova, Raul, Chi.	6	0	9	0	0	9	0	0	1.000
Cash, Kevin, TB.	13	10	56	8	0	64	1	4	1.000
Castillo, Alberto, K.C.-Oak.	35	32	237	10	2	249	3	0	.992
Dominique, Andy, Tor.	1	1	4	0	0	4	0	1	1.000
Fasano, Sal, Bal.	60	47	284	26	4	314	1	6	.987
Flaherty, John, N.Y.	45	39	291	19	2	312	3	3	.994
Gil, Geronimo, Bal.	62	37	265	25	2	292	5	3	.993
Gonzalez, Wiki, Sea.	14	13	78	8	0	86	2	1	1.000
Hall, Toby, TB.	135	122	759	51	9	819	5	8	.989
Heintz, Chris, Min.	8	6	48	1	0	49	0	0	1.000
Huckaby, Ken, Tor.	35	27	144	11	2	157	1	1	.987
Johnson, Charles, The.	19	16	90	3	4	97	0	1	.959
Kendall, Jason, Oak.	147	146	986	51	7	1044	6	4	.993
LaForest, Pete, TB.	21	14	74	3	0	77	1	0	1.000
Laird, Gerald, Tex.	13	11	61	5	3	69	2	1	.957
Laker, Tim, TB.	1	0	1	0	0	1	0	0	1.000
LeCroy, Matthew, Min.	1	0	0	0	0	0	0	0	.000
Lopez, Javy, Bal.	75	75	500	26	3	529	4	4	.994
Martinez, Victor, Cle.	142	139	904	58	5	967	6	3	.995
Mathis, Jeff, L.A.	3	0	4	0	0	4	0	0	1.000
Mauer, Joe, Min.	116	110	693	44	5	742	6	5	.993
Melhuse, Adam, Oak.	24	16	115	7	0	122	0	1	1.000
Miller, Corky, Min.	4	3	24	2	0	26	0	2	1.000
Mirabelli, Doug, Bos.	43	33	224	17	3	244	0	6	.988
Molina, Bengie, L.A.	105	100	641	47	3	691	5	10	.996
Molina, Jose, L.A.	65	53	408	41	3	452	6	3	.993
Myers, Greg, Tor.	4	3	20	1	0	21	0	0	1.000
Nieves, Wil, N.Y.	3	0	11	0	0	11	0	0	1.000
Ojeda, Miguel, Sea.	16	10	69	3	1	73	2	2	.986
Olivo, Miguel, Sea.	54	45	281	15	4	300	1	5	.987
Paul, Josh, L.A.	29	9	84	4	1	89	0	0	.989
Phillips, Paul, K.C.	20	18	91	10	1	102	2	2	.990
PIERZYNSKI, A.J., Chi.	128	124	803	48	1	852	8	7	.999
Posada, Jorge, N.Y.	133	123	718	76	3	797	6	8	.996
Quiroz, Guillermo, Tor.	10	10	56	5	0	61	1	0	1.000
Redmond, Mike, Min.	45	43	230	12	0	242	2	1	1.000
Rivera, Rene, Sea.	15	12	69	4	3	76	2	3	.961
Rodriguez, Ivan, Det.	123	121	702	60	4	766	4	4	.995
Shoppach, Kelly, Bos.	7	2	14	0	0	14	0	0	1.000
Torrealba, Yorvit, Sea.	41	36	225	18	0	243	2	0	1.000
Varitek, Jason, Bos.	130	127	784	32	8	824	4	7	.990
Whiteside, Eli, Bal.	9	3	21	4	2	27	1	0	.926
Widger, Chris, Chi.	42	38	252	12	5	269	2	2	.981
Wilson, Dan, Sea.	11	9	36	3	1	40	1	0	.975
Wilson, Vance, Det.	60	41	234	29	3	266	4	0	.989
Wooten, Shawn, Bos.	1	0	0	0	0	0	0	0	.000
Zaun, Gregg, Tor.	132	121	761	49	8	818	3	5	.990

CATCHERS WITH TWO OR MORE TEAMS

Player, Team	G	GS	PO	A	E	TC	DP	PB	Pct.
Castillo, Alberto, K.C.	34	32	235	10	2	247	3	0	.992
Castillo, Alberto, Oak.	1	0	2	0	0	2	0	0	1.000

CATCHERS—SPECIAL STATS*

Player, Team	G	Inn.	SBA	CCS	PCS	CS%	ER	CERA
Alomar Jr., Sandy, Tex.	46	315.2	17	0	0	0	173	4.9
Barajas, Rod, Tex.	119	1025.1	67	21	2	.32	566	4.97
Bard, Josh, Cle.	31	219.2	11	2	2	.22	78	3.20
Borders, Pat, Sea.	39	313.0	35	9	1	.26	142	4.08
Buck, John, K.C.	117	976.2	91	27	4	.31	609	5.61
Casanova, Raul, CWS	6	14.0	0	0	0	0	2	1.29
Cash, Kevin, TB	13	89.0	6	3	0	.50	69	6.98
Castillo, Alberto, TOT	35	280.0	12	6	0	.50	153	4.92
Castillo, Alberto, K.C.	34	277.0	12	6	0	.50	153	4.97
Castillo, Alberto, Oak	1	3.0	0	0	0	0	0	0.00
Dominique, Andy, Tor	1	6.0	2	0	0	0	3	4.50
Fasano, Sal, Bal	60	417.0	44	5	2	.12	236	5.09
Flaherty, John, NYY	45	345.0	46	9	2	.20	158	4.12
Gil, Geronimo, Bal	62	349.1	33	9	1	.28	145	3.74
Gonzalez, Wiki, Sea	14	115.0	6	3	0	.50	70	5.48
Hall, Toby, TB	135	1061.2	79	28	5	.38	606	5.14
Heintz, Chris, Min	8	60.0	4	1	0	.25	26	3.90
Huckaby, Ken, Tor	35	243.0	22	8	2	.40	131	4.85
Johnson, Charles, TB	19	136.0	18	2	3	.13	95	6.29
Kendall, Jason, Oak	147	1286.0	123	18	4	.15	540	3.78
LaForest, Pete, TB	21	133.0	10	2	2	.25	80	5.41
Laird, Gerald, Tex	13	99.0	11	3	0	.27	55	5.00
Laker, Tim, TB	1	2.0	0	0	0	0	1	4.50
LeCroy, Matthew, Min	1	1.0	0	0	0	0	0	0.00
Lopez, Javy, Bal	75	628.2	68	11	5	.17	329	4.71
Martinez, Victor, Cle	142	1233.0	125	25	4	.21	504	3.68
Mathis, Jeff, LAA	3	5.0	0	0	0	0	0	0.00
Mauer, Joe, Min	116	999.2	54	17	6	.35	410	3.69
Melhuse, Adam, Oak	24	161.1	11	3	0	.27	54	3.01
Miller, Corky, Min	4	27.1	3	2	0	.67	8	2.63
Mirabelli, Doug, Bos	43	309.0	28	5	3	.20	128	3.73
Molina, Bengie, LAA	105	873.1	64	17	3	.28	344	3.55
Molina, Jose, LAA	65	480.1	39	18	2	.49	195	3.65
Myers, Greg, Tor	4	25.0	4	1	0	.25	14	5.04
Nieves, Wil, NYY	3	9.0	0	0	0	0	4	4.00
Ojeda, Miguel, Sea	16	94.2	11	3	2	.33	49	4.66
Olivo, Miguel, Sea	54	402.2	31	9	1	.30	210	4.69
Paul, Josh, LAA	29	105.2	7	2	0	.29	59	5.03
Phillips, Paul, KC	20	159.2	11	6	1	.60	100	5.64
Pierzynski, A.J., CWS	128	1117.2	102	20	3	.20	464	3.74
Posada, Jorge, NYY	133	1076.2	129	35	4	.28	556	4.65
Quiroz, Guillermo, Tor	10	85.0	14	2	1	.15	47	4.98
Redmond, Mike, Min	45	376.1	19	8	2	.47	160	3.83
Rivera, Rene, Sea	15	111.0	6	1	1	.20	54	4.38
Rodriguez, Ivan, Det	123	1032.2	68	26	9	.44	509	4.44
Shoppach, Kelly, Bos	7	29.0	2	0	0	0	16	4.97
Torrealba, Yorvit, Sea	41	319.1	36	8	2	.24	157	4.42
Varitek, Jason, Bos	130	1089.0	86	16	5	.20	608	5.02
Whiteside, Eli, Bal	9	32.2	4	1	0	.25	14	3.86
Widger, Chris, CWS	42	344.0	26	2	0	.08	126	3.30
Wilson, Dan, Sea	11	72.0	7	2	1	.33	30	3.75
Wilson, Vance, Det	60	403.0	41	9	5	.25	210	4.69
Wooten, Shawn, Bos	1	2.0	0	0	0	0	0	0.00
Zaun, Gregg, Tor	132	1088.0	93	17	4	.19	458	3.79
Average	49	388.0	33	8	2	.30	188	4.36

*Inn. denotes the number of innings the catcher was behind the plate. SBA denotes stolen bases attempted. CCS denotes number of runners caught stealing by the catcher. PCS denotes number of runners caught stealing by the pitcher. CS% denotes the catcher's caught stealing percentage, figured by subtracting PCS from SBA and dividing this number into CCS. ER denotes number of earned runs scored when catcher was behind the plate. CERA denotes catcher's ERA when he was behind the plate, figured the same way a pitcher's ERA is completed (ER*9/IP).

PITCHERS

Player, Team	G	GS	PO	A	E	TC	DP	Pct.
Adkins, Jon, Chi.	5	0	0	2	0	2	0	1.000
Affeldt, Jeremy, K.C.*	49	0	1	6	1	8	0	.875
Almanzar, Carlos, Tex.	6	0	0	0	0	0	0	.000
Alvarez, Abe, Bos.*	2	0	0	1	0	1	0	1.000
Anderson, Brian, K.C.*	6	6	2	4	0	6	1	1.000
Anderson, Jason, N.Y.	3	0	0	0	0	0	0	.000
Arroyo, Bronson, Bos.	35	32	21	21	2	44	1	.955
Astacio, Pedro, Tex.	12	12	2	13	0	15	0	1.000
Atchison, Scott, Sea.	6	0	1	0	0	1	0	1.000
Baez, Danys, TB.	67	0	11	11	0	22	1	1.000

Player, Team	G	GS	PO	A	E	TC	DP	Pct.
Bajenaru, Jeff, Chi.	4	0	0	0	0	0	0	.000
Baker, Scott, Min.	10	9	8	3	0	11	1	1.000
Baldwin, James, Bal.-Tex.	28	0	4	4	0	8	1	1.000
Batista, Miguel, Tor.	71	0	2	6	1	9	0	.889
Bauer, Rick, Bal.	5	0	0	0	0	0	0	.000
Bautista, Denny, K.C.	7	7	3	9	0	12	0	1.000
Bayliss, Jonah, K.C.	11	0	0	0	0	0	0	.000
Bean, Colter, N.Y.	1	0	0	1	0	1	0	1.000
Bedard, Erik, Bal.*	24	24	6	22	1	29	3	.966
Beimel, Joe, TB.*	7	0	1	2	0	3	0	1.000
Bell, Rob, TB.	8	3	5	1	1	7	0	.857
Benoit, Joaquin, Tex.	32	9	2	7	0	9	0	1.000
Betancourt, Rafael, Cle.	54	0	3	3	0	6	0	1.000
Blanton, Joe, Oak.	33	33	13	20	1	34	1	.971
Bonderman, Jeremy, Det.	29	29	18	11	5	34	2	.853
Bootcheck, Chris, L.A.	5	2	1	3	1	5	0	.800
Borowski, Joe, TB.	32	0	3	3	0	6	0	1.000
Bowyer, Travis, Min.	8	0	1	1	0	2	0	1.000
Bradford, Chad, Bos.	31	0	1	6	0	7	0	1.000
Brazelton, Dewon, TB.	20	8	3	14	2	19	1	.895
Brocail, Doug, Tex.	61	0	9	13	2	24	1	.917
Brown, Kevin, N.Y.	13	13	4	8	1	13	1	.923
Buehrle, Mark, Chi.*	33	33	13	45	2	60	2	.967
Bukvich, Ryan, Tex.	4	0	0	1	0	1	0	1.000
Burgos, Ambiorix, K.C.	59	0	1	1	0	2	0	1.000
Bush, Dave, Tor.	25	24	18	20	0	38	1	1.000
Byrd, Paul, L.A.	31	31	16	20	2	38	0	.947
Byrdak, Tim, Bal.*	41	0	0	4	0	4	0	1.000
Cabrera, Daniel, Bal.	29	29	11	12	1	24	0	.958
Cabrera, Fernando, Cle.	15	0	1	1	0	2	0	1.000
Calero, Kiko, Oak.	58	0	2	5	0	7	0	1.000
Camp, Shawn, K.C.	29	0	3	7	0	10	0	1.000
Campillo, Jorge, Sea.	2	1	0	0	0	0	0	.000
Carrasco, D.J., K.C.	21	20	16	16	0	32	0	1.000
Carter, Lance, TB.	39	0	1	7	0	8	2	1.000
Cassidy, Scott, Bos.	1	0	0	0	0	0	0	.000
Cerda, Jaime, K.C.*	20	0	0	1	0	1	0	1.000
Chacin, Gustavo, Tor.*	34	34	10	26	2	38	0	.947
Chacon, Shawn, N.Y.	14	12	6	8	0	14	0	1.000
Chen, Bruce, N.Y.*	34	32	10	25	2	37	1	.946
Christiansen, Jason, L.A.*	12	0	0	0	0	0	0	.000
Chulk, Vinnie, Tor.	62	0	4	13	2	19	2	.895
Clement, Matt, Bos.	32	32	22	20	1	43	4	.977
Colome, Jesus, TB.	36	0	5	5	1	11	0	.909
Colon, Bartolo, L.A.	33	33	8	16	0	24	0	1.000
Colon, Roman, Det.	12	3	3	2	0	5	0	1.000
Contreras, Jose, Chi.	32	32	11	24	2	37	1	.946
Corcoran, Tim, TB.	10	1	1	1	0	2	0	1.000
Cordero, Francisco, Tex.	69	0	2	10	0	12	0	1.000
Cotts, Neal, Chi.*	69	0	2	14	0	16	2	1.000
Crain, Jesse, Min.	75	0	11	17	1	29	3	.966
Creek, Doug, Det.*	20	0	2	2	1	5	0	.800
Cruz, Juan, Oak.	28	0	2	1	0	3	0	1.000
Darensbourg, Vic, Det.*	22	0	4	4	1	9	1	.889
Davis, Jason, Cle.	11	4	3	1	0	4	1	1.000
Delcarmen, Manny, Bos.	10	0	1	1	0	2	0	1.000
Demaria, Chris, K.C.	8	0	0	1	0	1	1	1.000
DePaula, Jorge, N.Y.	3	0	0	1	0	1	0	1.000
Dickey, R.A., Tex.	9	4	1	9	0	10	1	1.000
DiNardo, Lenny, Bos.*	8	1	0	2	0	2	0	1.000
Dingman, Craig, Det.	34	0	1	1	1	3	0	.667
Dominguez, Juan, Tex.	22	10	4	3	0	7	0	1.000
Donnelly, Brendan, L.A.	65	0	3	4	1	8	0	.875
Dotel, Octavio, Oak.	15	0	0	1	1	2	0	.500
Douglass, Sean, Det.	18	16	8	7	0	15	2	1.000
Downs, Scott, Tor.*	26	13	9	14	1	24	0	.958
Drese, Ryan, Tex.	12	12	9	9	1	19	1	.947
DuBose, Eric, Bal.*	15	3	1	4	0	5	0	1.000
Duchscherer, Justin, Oak.	65	0	1	14	3	18	3	.833
Elarton, Scott, Cle.	31	31	7	11	2	20	2	.900
Embree, Alan, Bos.-N.Y.*	67	0	2	8	1	11	0	.909
Escobar, Kelvim, L.A.	16	7	5	4	1	10	0	.900
Etherton, Seth, Oak.	3	3	1	0	0	1	0	1.000
Farnsworth, Kyle, Det.	46	0	3	3	0	6	1	1.000
Feldman, Scott, Tex.	8	0	0	2	0	2	0	1.000
Field, Nate, K.C.	7	0	2	1	0	3	0	1.000
Flores, Ron, Oak.*	11	0	1	0	0	1	0	1.000
Fossum, Casey, TB.*	36	25	11	16	1	28	2	.964
Foulke, Keith, Bos.	43	0	0	3	0	3	0	1.000
Franklin, Ryan, Sea.	32	30	14	13	0	27	0	1.000
Franklin, Wayne, N.Y.*	13	0	0	1	0	1	0	1.000
Frasor, Jason, Tor.	67	0	6	7	1	14	1	.929
Garcia, Freddy, Chi.	33	33	18	29	0	47	4	1.000
Garcia, Jairo, Oak.	3	0	0	0	0	0	0	.000
ardner, Lee, TB.	5	0	0	1	0	1	0	1.000
Garland, Jon, Chi.	32	32	12	35	1	48	1	.979
Gassner, Dave, Min.*	2	2	0	1	1	2	0	.500
Gaudin, Chad, Tor.	5	3	0	4	0	4	0	1.000
German, Franklyn, Det.	58	0	4	3	0	7	0	1.000
Ginter, Matt, Det.	14	1	4	4	0	8	1	1.000
Glynn, Ryan, Oak.	5	3	0	4	0	4	0	1.000
Gobble, Jimmy, K.C.*	28	4	2	4	2	8	1	.750
Gonzalez, Jeremi, Bos.	28	3	2	6	0	8	0	1.000
Good, Andrew, Det.	2	0	0	0	0	0	0	.000
Gordon, Tom, N.Y.	79	0	7	13	1	21	0	.952
Graman, Alex, N.Y.*	2	0	0	0	0	0	0	.000
Gregg, Kevin, L.A.	33	2	4	6	0	10	0	1.000
Greinke, Zack, K.C.	33	33	19	25	1	45	2	.978
Grilli, Jason, Det.	3	2	2	3	0	5	0	1.000
Grimsley, Jason, Bal.	22	0	0	2	0	2	1	1.000
Groom, Buddy, N.Y.*	24	0	0	2	1	3	0	.667
Gryboski, Kevin, Tex.	11	0	2	1	0	3	0	1.000
Guardado, Eddie, Sea.*	58	0	2	4	1	7	0	.857
Guerrier, Matt, Min.	43	0	9	15	0	24	0	1.000
Guthrie, Jeremy, Cle.	1	0	2	1	0	3	1	1.000
Halama, John, Bos.*	30	1	2	7	1	10	1	.900
Halladay, Roy, Tor.	19	19	9	24	1	34	1	.971
Hansen, Craig, Bos.	4	0	0	0	0	0	0	.000
Harden, Rich, Oak.	22	19	12	8	1	21	2	.952
Haren, Danny, Oak.	34	34	22	18	2	42	4	.952
Harikkala, Tim, Oak.	8	0	1	1	0	2	0	1.000
Harper, Travis, TB.	52	0	1	6	1	8	0	.875
Harris, Jeff, Sea.	11	8	3	6	1	10	1	.900
Harville, Chad, Bos.	8	0	0	3	0	3	0	1.000
Hasegawa, Shigetoshi, Sea.	46	0	7	12	0	19	1	1.000
Hendrickson, Mark, TB.*	31	31	16	23	1	40	1	.975
Henn, Sean, N.Y.*	3	3	0	3	0	3	0	1.000
Hermanson, Dustin, Chi.	57	0	0	6	1	7	1	.857
Hernandez, Felix, Sea.	12	12	11	16	0	27	1	1.000
Hernandez, Orlando, Chi.	24	22	7	21	2	30	4	.933
Hernandez, Runelvys, K.C.	29	29	9	17	4	30	3	.867
Howell, J.P., K.C.*	15	15	2	8	0	10	0	1.000
Howry, Bob, Cle.	79	0	6	6	1	13	2	.923
Jenks, Bobby, Chi.	32	0	2	3	1	6	0	.833
Jensen, Ryan, K.C.	9	3	0	2	2	4	0	.500
Johnson, Jason, Det.	33	33	10	32	4	46	2	.913
Johnson, Randy, N.Y.*	34	34	2	26	2	30	1	.933
Jones, Greg, L.A.	6	0	1	1	0	2	0	1.000
Julio, Jorge, Bal.	67	0	2	2	1	5	0	.800
Karnuth, Jason, Det.	3	0	0	0	0	0	0	.000
Karsay, Steve, N.Y.-Tex.	20	0	2	3	0	5	0	1.000
Kazmir, Scott, TB.*	32	32	7	17	3	27	0	.889
Kennedy, Joe, Oak.*	19	8	2	6	0	8	0	1.000
Kida, Masao, Sea.	1	0	0	0	0	0	0	.000
Kline, Steve, Bal.*	67	0	2	14	1	17	1	.941
Lackey, John, L.A.	33	33	5	25	3	33	0	.909
League, Brandon, Tor.	20	0	3	4	1	8	0	.875
Ledezma, Wilfredo, Det.*	10	10	2	7	2	11	0	.818
Lee, Cliff, Cle.*	32	32	5	10	3	18	0	.833
Leiter, Al, N.Y.*	16	10	2	5	1	8	1	.875
Lilly, Ted, Tor.*	25	25	2	13	0	15	0	1.000
Lima, Jose, K.C.	32	32	6	22	0	28	2	1.000
Liriano, Francisco, Min.*	6	4	2	3	0	5	1	1.000
Loe, Kameron, Tex.	48	8	9	17	4	30	0	.867
Lohse, Kyle, Min.	31	30	13	27	0	40	0	1.000
Lopez, Rodrigo, Bal.	35	35	19	31	3	53	2	.943
MacDougal, Mike, K.C.	68	0	2	11	2	15	0	.867
Madritsch, Bobby, Sea.*	1	1	0	2	0	2	0	1.000
Mahay, Ron, Tex.*	30	0	2	3	1	6	0	.833
Maine, John, Bal.	10	8	3	4	1	8	1	.875
Mantei, Matt, Bos.	34	0	1	3	0	4	0	1.000
Marcum, Shaun, Tor.	5	0	0	0	0	0	0	.000
Maroth, Mike, Det.*	34	34	6	30	0	36	0	1.000
Marte, Damaso, Chi.*	66	0	2	5	0	7	0	1.000
Mateo, Julio, Sea.	55	1	1	10	0	11	1	1.000
May, Darrell, N.Y.*	2	1	0	0	0	0	0	.000
Mays, Joe, Min.	31	26	19	17	1	37	2	.973
McCarthy, Brandon, Chi.	12	10	3	4	0	7	1	1.000
McClung, Seth, TB.	34	17	4	9	0	13	2	1.000
McGowan, Dustin, Tor.	13	7	2	5	1	8	0	.875
Meche, Gil, Sea.	29	26	8	22	1	31	1	.968
Mendoza, Ramiro, N.Y.	1	0	0	0	0	0	0	.000
Meredith, Cla, Bos.	3	0	0	1	0	1	0	1.000
Miller, Justin, Tor.	1	0	0	0	0	0	0	.000

Player, Team	G	GS	PO	A	E	TC	DP	Pct.
Miller, Matt, Cle.	23	0	5	6	0	11	0	1.000
Miller, Trever, TB.*	61	0	2	5	1	8	2	.875
Miller, Wade, Bos.	16	16	8	10	1	19	0	.947
Millwood, Kevin, Cle.	30	30	8	17	0	25	2	1.000
Moyer, Jamie, Sea.*	32	32	18	28	0	46	2	1.000
Mulholland, Terry, Min.*	49	0	3	9	0	12	1	1.000
Mussina, Mike, N.Y.	30	30	9	24	4	37	5	.892
Myers, Mike, Bos.*	65	0	3	10	0	13	2	1.000
Nageotte, Clint, Sea.	3	0	0	2	0	2	0	1.000
Nathan, Joe, Min.	69	0	2	6	1	9	0	.889
Neal, Blaine, Bos.	8	0	0	2	0	2	0	1.000
Nelson, Jeff, Sea.	49	0	1	7	0	8	1	1.000
Nomo, Hideo, TB.	19	19	2	16	0	18	0	1.000
Nunez, Franklin, TB.	5	0	0	0	0	0	0	.000
Nunez, Leo, K.C.	41	0	5	6	0	11	2	1.000
Orvella, Chad, TB.	37	0	6	2	1	9	0	.889
Papelbon, Jonathan, Bos.	17	3	3	2	0	5	0	1.000
Park, Chan Ho, Tex.	20	20	7	31	1	39	2	.974
Parrish, John, Bal.*	14	0	0	4	0	4	0	1.000
Pavano, Carl, N.Y.	17	17	4	9	0	13	1	1.000
Penn, Hayden, Bal.	8	8	9	9	0	18	1	1.000
Peralta, Joel, L.A.	28	0	1	6	0	7	0	1.000
Percival, Troy, Det.	26	0	2	1	0	3	0	1.000
Perisho, Matt, Bos.*	1	0	0	0	0	0	0	.000
Pineiro, Joel, Sea.	30	30	23	18	1	42	5	.976
Politte, Cliff, Chi.	68	0	1	6	1	8	0	.875
Ponson, Sidney, Bal.	23	23	10	18	2	30	1	.933
Prinz, Bret, L.A.	3	0	0	0	0	0	0	.000
Proctor, Scott, N.Y.	29	1	3	5	0	8	0	1.000
Putz, J.J., Sea.	64	0	4	13	0	17	2	1.000
Quantrill, Paul, N.Y.	22	0	2	2	0	4	0	1.000
Radke, Brad, Min.	31	31	20	26	2	48	1	.958
Rakers, Aaron, Bal.	10	0	0	1	0	1	0	1.000
Ramirez, Erasmo, Tex.*	16	0	1	4	0	5	0	1.000
Ray, Chris, Bal.	41	0	4	3	1	8	0	.875
Reames, Britt, Oak.	2	0	0	1	0	1	0	1.000
Redding, Tim, N.Y.	1	1	0	0	0	0	0	.000
Reed, Steve, Bal.	30	0	2	5	0	7	1	1.000
Regilio, Nick, Tex.	18	0	0	4	1	5	1	.800
Remlinger, Mike, Bos.*	8	0	0	1	0	1	0	1.000
Rhodes, Arthur, Cle.*	47	0	3	4	1	8	1	.875
Riley, Matt, Tex.*	7	0	1	1	0	2	0	1.000
Rincon, Juan, Min.	75	0	5	12	1	18	0	.944
Rincon, Ricardo, Oak.*	67	0	3	3	2	8	0	.750
Riske, David, Cle.	58	0	2	7	0	9	1	1.000
Rivera, Mariano, N.Y.	71	0	7	22	0	29	1	1.000
Robertson, Nate, Det.*	32	32	8	25	3	36	3	.917
Rodney, Fernando, Det.	39	0	3	3	1	7	0	.857
Rodriguez, Felix, N.Y.	34	0	2	2	0	4	0	1.000
Rodriguez, Francisco, L.A.	66	0	7	4	1	12	0	.917
Rodriguez, Ricardo, Tex.	12	10	4	8	1	13	2	.923
Rogers, Kenny, Tex.*	30	30	18	47	1	66	7	.985
Romero, J.C., Min.*	68	0	7	10	3	20	0	.850
Rupe, Josh, Tex.	4	1	2	1	1	4	0	.750
Ryan, B.J., Bal.*	69	0	1	4	2	7	1	.714
Saarloos, Kirk, Oak.	29	27	22	33	2	57	3	.965
Sabathia, C.C., Cle.*	31	31	2	17	2	21	0	.905
Sanders, David, Chi.*	2	0	0	0	0	0	0	.000
Santana, Ervin, L.A.	23	23	10	10	0	20	2	1.000
Santana, Johan, Min.*	33	33	12	26	2	40	0	.950
Sauerbeck, Scott, Cle.*	58	0	6	3	0	9	0	1.000
Saunders, Joe, L.A.*	2	2	0	0	0	0	0	.000
Schilling, Curt, Bos.	32	11	7	7	2	16	1	.875
Schoeneweis, Scott, Tor.*	80	0	5	18	1	24	2	.958
Sele, Aaron, Sea.	21	21	14	6	0	20	1	1.000
Sherrill, George, Sea.*	29	0	1	3	0	4	0	1.000
Shields, Scot, L.A.	78	0	8	14	2	24	2	.917
Shouse, Brian, Tex.*	64	0	6	18	3	27	2	.889
Silva, Carlos, Min.	27	27	14	26	0	40	3	1.000
Sisco, Andrew, K.C.*	67	0	1	3	1	5	0	.800
Small, Aaron, N.Y.	15	9	1	7	0	8	0	1.000
Snyder, Kyle, K.C.	13	3	2	4	0	6	0	1.000
Soriano, Rafael, Sea.	7	0	0	0	0	0	0	.000
Speier, Justin, Tor.	65	0	0	7	0	7	0	1.000
Spurling, Chris, Det.	56	0	4	8	0	12	2	1.000
Standridge, Jason, Tex.	2	0	0	0	0	0	0	.000
Stanton, Mike, N.Y.-Bos.*	29	0	0	4	0	4	0	1.000
Stemle, Steve, K.C.	6	0	0	2	0	2	0	1.000
Street, Huston, Oak.	67	0	7	12	0	19	2	1.000
Sturtze, Tanyon, N.Y.	64	1	2	16	0	18	1	1.000
Switzer, Jon, TB.*	2	0	0	0	0	0	0	.000
Tadano, Kazuhito, Cle.	1	0	0	0	0	0	0	.000
Takatsu, Shingo, Chi.	31	0	3	2	0	5	0	1.000
Tallet, Brian, Cle.*	2	0	0	0	0	0	0	.000
Tejera, Michael, Tex.*	3	0	0	0	0	0	0	.000
Thompson, Justin, Tex.*	2	0	0	0	0	0	0	.000
Thornton, Matt, Sea.*	55	0	0	6	0	6	1	1.000
Timlin, Mike, Bos.	81	0	6	12	1	19	0	.947
TOWERS, Josh, Tor.	33	33	29	31	0	60	3	1.000
Urbina, Ugueth, Det.	25	0	2	1	0	3	0	1.000
Verlander, Justin, Det.	2	2	2	2	1	5	0	.800
Villone, Ron, Sea.*	52	0	6	8	0	14	0	1.000
Vizcaino, Luis, Chi.	65	0	6	7	0	13	1	1.000
Volquez, Edison, Tex.	6	3	0	1	0	1	0	1.000
Waechter, Doug, TB.	29	25	11	8	3	22	1	.864
Wakefield, Tim, Bos.	33	33	30	20	2	52	2	.962
Walker, Jamie, Det.*	66	0	2	7	1	10	0	.900
Walker, Kevin, Chi.*	9	0	0	1	0	1	0	1.000
Walker, Pete, Tor.	41	4	6	10	1	17	0	.941
Wang, Chien-Ming, N.Y.	18	17	4	38	1	43	3	.977
Wasdin, John, Tex.	31	6	0	5	0	5	0	1.000
Washburn, Jarrod, L.A.*	29	29	6	16	4	26	3	.846
Webb, John, TB.	1	1	0	0	0	0	0	.000
Wells, David, Bos.*	30	30	3	19	3	25	2	.880
Westbrook, Jake, Cle.	34	34	31	49	2	82	2	.976
Whiteside, Matt, Tor.	2	0	0	0	0	0	0	.000
Wickman, Bob, Cle.	64	0	7	5	2	14	1	.857
Williams, Todd, Bal.	72	0	5	7	1	13	0	.923
Wilson, C.J., Tex.*	24	6	2	10	0	12	1	1.000
Witasick, Jay, Oak.	28	0	1	1	0	2	1	1.000
Wood, Mike, K.C.	47	10	9	16	0	25	2	1.000
Woods, Jake, L.A.*	28	0	0	2	0	2	0	1.000
Woodyard, Mark, Det.	3	0	1	2	0	3	0	1.000
Wright, Jaret, N.Y.	13	13	2	9	2	13	1	.846
Yabu, Keiichi, Oak.	40	0	5	5	0	10	0	1.000
Yan, Esteban, L.A.	49	0	7	10	0	17	0	1.000
Young, Chris, Tex.	31	31	8	13	0	21	0	1.000
Zito, Barry, Oak.*	35	35	12	34	0	46	1	1.000

PITCHERS WITH TWO OR MORE TEAMS

Player, Team	G	GS	PO	A	E	TC	DP	Pct.
Baldwin, James, Bal.	20	0	2	3	0	5	1	1.000
Baldwin, James, Tex.	8	0	2	1	0	3	0	1.000
Embree, Alan, Bos.*	43	0	2	6	0	8	0	1.000
Embree, Alan, N.Y.*	24	0	0	2	1	3	0	.667
Karsay, Steve, N.Y.	6	0	1	0	0	1	0	1.000
Karsay, Steve, Tex.	14	0	1	3	0	4	0	1.000
Stanton, Mike, N.Y.*	28	0	0	3	0	3	0	1.000
Stanton, Mike, Bos.*	1	0	0	1	0	1	0	1.000

SHUTOUT GAMES

Read across for wins, down for losses.

Team	N.Y.	L.A.	Bal.	Bos.	Chi.	Sea.	Oak.	Cle.	Tex.	Min.	TB.	Tor.	K.C.	Det.	N.L.	W	L	Pct.
New York	..	0	0	1	1	2	3	0	0	1	0	3	0	1	2	14	2	.875
Los Angeles	0	..	0	1	1	1	2	1	1	0	0	0	2	0	2	11	6	.647
Baltimore	0	1	..	0	0	0	1'	1	0	1	1	3	0	0	1	9	5	.643
Boston	0	0	2	..	1	0	0	0	0	0	1	0	0	0	4	8	5	.615
Chicago	0	0	0	0	..	0	1	3	2	0	0	0	1	2	1	10	7	.588
Seattle	0	0	0	0	0	..	1	0	0	1	0	1	1	0	3	7	5	.583
Oakland	1	2	1	0	0	2	..	1	1	0	0	0	2	0	2	12	12	.500
Cleveland	0	1	0	1	1	0	1	..	0	0	1	0	2	1	1	10	11	.476
Texas	0	0	0	0	0	0	1	1	..	3	0	0	0	0	1	6	7	.462
Minnesota	0	0	0	1	2	0	1	1	0	..	0	1	0	1	1	8	10	.444
Tampa Bay	0	0	0	0	0	0	0	2	0	0	..	2	0	0	1	4	5	.444
Toronto	1	1	2	0	0	0	1	0	1	1	0	..	0	0	1	8	14	.364
Kansas City	0	0	0	0	0	0	0	1	0	2	0	0	..	1	0	4	10	.286
Detroit	0	0	0	0	0	0	0	0	0	0	0	0	1	..	0	2	10	.167
N.L. Clubs	0	1	0	1	1	0	0	0	1	1	2	4	1	3	..	19	..	..
Lost	2	6	5	5	7	5	12	11	7	10	5	14	10	10	19	113	109	.509

A.L. shutouts vs N.L. clubs (19): Baltimore vs Philadelphia, Boston vs Cincinnati, Boston vs Philadelphia, Boston vs Pittsburgh, Boston vs St. Louis, Los Angeles vs Los Angeles 2, Chicago vs Los Angeles, Cleveland vs San Diego, Minnesota vs Arizona, New York vs Pittsburgh, New York vs St. Louis, Oakland vs New York, Oakland vs San Francisco, Seattle vs New York, Seattle vs San Diego, Seattle vs Florida, Texas vs Houston, Toronto vs Washington.

HOME RECORD

Read across for wins, down for losses.

Team	Bos.	N.Y.	L.A.	Chi.	Min.	Oak.	Tex.	Cle.	Tor.	TB.	Det.	Sea.	Bal.	K.C.	N.L.	W	L	Pct.
Boston	..	5	4	2	3	5	3	1	4	9	2	2	4	3	7	54	27	.667
New York	5	..	3	1	2	2	5	3	6	3	3	3	7	3	7	53	28	.654
Los Angeles	2	3	..	2	2	5	8	3	1	4	4	3	2	4	6	49	32	.605
Chicago	2	1	2	..	5	0	2	5	1	3	7	4	2	8	5	47	34	.580
Minnesota	2	2	3	3	..	1	2	5	2	3	7	3	2	6	7	45	36	.556
Oakland	2	1	5	4	3	..	4	2	4	3	3	6	0	1	7	45	36	.556
Texas	2	1	3	5	2	2	..	2	5	1	1	7	3	3	7	44	37	.543
Cleveland	0	2	1	1	6	5	2	..	2	1	4	2	3	6	8	43	38	.531
Toronto	6	2	3	0	1	2	1	1	..	5	3	5	4	5	5	43	38	.531
Tampa Bay	5	5	3	2	0	5	4	1	3	..	1	1	4	4	2	40	41	.494
Detroit	3	1	1	2	6	1	2	1	3	2	..	4	1	6	6	39	42	.481
Seattle	2	3	3	1	3	3	3	2	2	2	2	..	3	3	7	39	42	.481
Baltimore	3	5	1	0	2	1	1	1	3	7	1	3	..	2	6	36	45	.444
Kansas City	2	3	0	4	3	0	2	2	2	3	5	2	1	..	5	34	47	.420
N.L. Clubs	4	5	3	2	5	6	7	2	6	8	6	6	7	5	..	..	..	..
Lost on Road	40	39	35	29	43	38	46	31	44	54	49	51	43	59	82	611	523	.539

HOME RECORDS IN INTERLEAGUE GAMES

Team				Total	Team				Total
Baltimore	3-0 vs. Hou.	1-2 vs. Phi.	2-1 vs. Col.	6-3	Minnesota	2-1 vs. Mil.	1-2 vs. S.D.	1-2 vs. S.F.	4-5
Boston	2-1 vs. Atl.	3-0 vs. Cin.	2-1 vs. Pit.	7-2	New York	3-0 vs. Chi.	1-2 vs. N.Y.	3-0 vs. Pit.	7-2
Chicago	1-2 vs. Chi.	3-0 vs. L.A.	1-2 vs. Ari.	5-4	Oakland	2-1 vs. N.Y.	2-1 vs. Phi.	3-0 vs. S.F.	7-2
Cleveland	2-1 vs. Cin.	3-0 vs. Col.	3-0 vs. Ari.	8-1	Seattle	3-0 vs. N.Y.	2-1 vs. Phi.	2-1 vs. S.D.	7-2
Detroit	3-0 vs. S.D.	2-1 vs. S.F.	1-2 vs. Ari.	6-3	Tampa Bay	2-1 vs. Mil.	0-3 vs. St.L.	0-3 vs. Fla.	2-7
Kansas City	1-2 vs. Hou.	3-0 vs. L.A.	1-2 vs. St.L.	5-4	Texas	2-1 vs. Atl.	3-0 vs. Hou.	2-1 vs. Was.	7-2
Los Angeles	3-0 vs. L.A.	1-2 vs. Was.	2-1 vs. Fla.	6-3	Toronto	1-2 vs. Mil.	2-1 vs. Was.	2-1 vs. St.L.	5-4

ROAD RECORD

Read across for wins, down for losses.

Team	Chi.	Cle.	L.A.	Oak.	N.Y.	Bos.	Bal.	Min.	Tor.	Tex.	Det.	Sea.	TB.	K.C.	N.L.	W	L	Pct.
Chicago	..	9	2	2	2	1	4	6	3	1	7	2	1	5	7	52	29	.642
Cleveland	4	..	2	1	1	2	3	4	2	1	8	5	3	7	7	50	31	.617
Los Angeles	4	2	..	5	3	2	2	4	0	7	2	6	0	3	6	46	35	.568
Oakland	3	1	4	..	1	2	6	3	1	7	2	6	1	3	3	43	38	.531
New York	2	1	1	5	..	5	4	1	6	2	2	4	5	0	4	42	39	.519
Boston	2	3	2	1	4	..	6	1	3	4	4	1	4	1	5	41	40	.506
Baltimore	2	0	1	3	2	5	..	1	6	3	2	4	5	2	2	38	43	.469
Minnesota	4	4	1	3	1	0	1	..	2	1	4	3	3	7	4	38	43	.469
Toronto	2	1	2	3	4	5	6	1	..	2	0	1	6	1	3	37	44	.457
Texas	1	1	1	6	2	0	3	4	2	..	1	6	1	2	2	35	46	.432
Detroit	3	5	3	0	0	1	4	2	1	2	..	1	3	4	3	32	49	.395
Seattle	2	1	6	3	0	1	1	2	3	2	2	..	2	4	3	30	51	.370
Tampa Bay	0	5	2	0	6	1	2	0	5	2	1	1	..	1	1	27	54	.333
Kansas City	1	4	2	2	0	0	1	3	1	0	4	0	0	..	4	22	59	.272
N.L. Clubs	4	1	3	2	2	2	3	5	4	2	3	2	7	4	..	..	..	..
Lost at home	34	38	32	36	28	27	45	36	38	37	42	42	41	47	54	533	601	.470

BALTIMORE—74-88

Pitcher	Bos. W-L	Chi. W-L	Cle. W-L	Det. W-L	K.C. W-L	L.A. W-L	Min. W-L	N.Y. W-L	Oak. W-L	Sea. W-L	TB. W-L	Tex. W-L	Tor. W-L	N.L. W-L	Totals W-L
Bedard, Erik	0-1	1-1	0-0	0-1	0-0	0-2	0-0	0-1	0-0	0-1	2-1	0-0	2-0	1-0	6-8
Byrdak, Tim	0-0	0-0	0-0	0-0	0-0	0-0	0-0	0-0	0-0	0-0	0-0	0-0	0-1	0-0	0-1
Cabrera, Daniel	1-2	1-1	1-0	1-0	0-0	0-0	1-0	1-1	0-1	2-0	0-0	1-2	1-3	0-3	10-13
Chen, Bruce	2-1	0-1	0-1	0-1	2-0	0-0	0-0	1-1	1-1	1-0	3-1	1-0	1-2	1-1	13-10
DuBose, Eric	0-0	0-0	0-0	0-0	0-0	0-1	0-0	0-1	1-1	0-0	1-0	0-0	0-0	0-0	2-3
Grimsley, Jason	0-0	0-0	0-0	0-0	0-0	0-1	0-0	0-0	0-0	0-0	0-0	1-1	0-0	0-0	1-2
Julio, Jorge	1-0	0-0	0-0	0-1	0-0	0-0	1-0	0-0	0-0	0-0	0-0	0-1	0-1	1-1	3-5
Kline, Steve	0-0	0-0	0-1	0-0	0-0	0-0	0-1	1-1	0-1	0-0	1-0	0-0	0-0	0-0	2-4
Lopez, Rodrigo	2-2	0-1	0-2	0-0	0-1	2-0	0-0	1-3	2-0	3-0	2-1	0-0	1-1	2-1	15-12
Maine, John	1-1	0-0	0-0	0-0	0-0	0-0	0-0	0-1	0-1	0-0	0-0	0-0	1-0	0-0	2-3
Parrish, John	0-0	0-0	0-0	0-0	1-0	0-0	0-0	0-0	0-0	0-0	0-0	0-0	0-0	0-0	1-0
Penn, Hayden	0-0	0-0	0-1	0-0	0-0	0-0	0-0	0-0	0-0	0-0	0-0	0-0	1-0	2-1	3-2
Ponson, Sidney	1-1	0-0	0-1	1-1	1-0	0-1	1-0	1-0	0-0	0-1	0-2	0-1	1-1	1-2	7-11
Rakers, Aaron	0-0	0-0	0-0	0-0	0-0	0-0	1-0	0-0	0-0	0-0	0-0	0-0	0-0	0-0	1-0
Ray, Chris	0-0	0-1	0-0	0-0	0-0	0-0	0-0	0-0	0-0	0-1	0-0	1-1	0-0	0-0	1-3
Reed, Steve	0-0	0-0	0-0	1-1	0-0	0-0	0-0	0-1	0-0	0-0	0-0	0-0	0-0	0-0	1-2
Ryan, B.J.	0-2	0-0	0-0	0-0	0-0	0-0	0-1	1-1	0-0	0-0	0-0	0-0	0-0	0-0	1-4
Williams, Todd	0-0	0-1	0-0	0-0	0-1	0-0	0-0	0-0	0-0	1-0	3-1	0-0	1-1	0-1	5-5
Totals	8-10	2-6	1-6	3-5	4-2	2-4	3-3	7-11	4-6	7-3	12-6	4-6	9-10	8-10	74-88

No-decisions-- James Baldwin, Rick Bauer.
INTERLEAGUE: Hayden Penn 0-1, Todd Williams 0-1, Rodrigo Lopez 0-1 vs. Braves; Rodrigo Lopez 1-0, Daniel Cabrera 0-1, Sidney Ponson 0-1 vs. Reds; Daniel Cabrera 0-1, Sidney Ponson 1-0, Hayden Penn 1-0 vs. Rockies; Hayden Penn 1-0, Bruce Chen 1-0, Rodrigo Lopez 1-0 vs. Astros; Daniel Cabrera 0-1, Erik Bedard 1-0, Sidney Ponson 0-1 vs. Phillies; Jorge Julio 1-1, Bruce Chen 0-1 vs. Pirates. Total: 8-10.

BOSTON—95-67

Pitcher	Bal. W-L	Chi. W-L	Cle. W-L	Det. W-L	K.C. W-L	L.A. W-L	Min. W-L	N.Y. W-L	Oak. W-L	Sea. W-L	TB. W-L	Tex. W-L	Tor. W-L	N.L. W-L	Totals W-L
Arroyo, Bronson	2-1	0-1	1-1	1-0	0-1	1-1	1-1	0-0	1-0	0-0	3-0	2-0	1-3	1-1	14-10
Bradford, Chad	0-0	1-0	0-0	1-0	0-0	0-0	0-0	0-0	0-0	0-0	0-0	0-0	0-1	0-0	2-1
Clement, Matt	2-0	0-0	0-0	0-0	1-0	0-1	0-0	1-1	0-1	1-0	2-0	2-0	0-2	4-1	13-6
DiNardo, Lenny	0-1	0-0	0-0	0-0	0-0	0-0	0-0	0-0	0-0	0-0	0-0	0-0	0-0	0-0	0-1
Embree, Alan	0-0	0-0	0-0	0-0	0-0	0-0	0-0	0-0	1-0	0-0	0-1	0-0	0-1	0-1	1-4
Foulke, Keith	1-1	0-0	1-1	0-0	0-0	0-0	0-0	1-1	1-0	0-0	0-0	0-1	0-1	1-0	5-5
Gonzalez, Jeremi	0-0	0-0	0-0	0-0	0-0	0-0	0-0	0-0	0-0	1-1	0-0	1-0	0-0	0-0	2-1
Halama, John	0-0	0-0	0-0	1-0	0-0	0-0	0-0	0-0	0-1	0-0	0-0	0-0	0-0	0-0	1-1
Harville, Chad	0-0	0-0	0-0	0-0	0-0	0-0	0-0	0-0	0-0	0-0	0-1	0-0	0-0	0-0	0-1
Mantei, Matt	0-0	0-0	0-0	0-0	0-0	0-0	0-0	0-0	1-0	0-0	0-0	0-0	0-0	0-0	1-0
Miller, Wade	1-1	1-0	0-0	0-0	1-0	0-0	0-0	0-0	0-0	0-0	0-1	0-0	0-1	1-1	4-4
Myers, Mike	0-0	0-0	0-0	0-0	0-0	2-0	0-0	0-1	1-0	0-0	0-0	0-0	0-0	0-0	3-1
Neal, Blaine	0-0	0-0	0-0	0-1	0-0	0-0	0-0	0-0	0-0	0-0	0-0	0-0	0-0	0-0	0-1
Papelbon, Jonathan	1-0	0-0	0-0	0-1	0-0	0-0	0-0	0-0	0-0	0-0	0-0	0-0	2-0	0-0	3-1
Schilling, Curt	0-0	1-1	0-0	0-1	0-1	0-1	0-0	2-2	0-1	0-0	2-2	1-0	1-0	0-0	8-8
Timlin, Mike	0-0	0-0	0-0	0-0	0-0	1-0	1-1	1-0	1-0	0-0	1-1	0-0	1-1	1-0	7-3
Wakefield, Tim	0-2	1-1	1-0	2-0	1-0	1-1	1-1	1-4	1-0	0-1	3-0	1-1	1-0	2-2	16-12
Wells, David	3-2	0-0	1-0	1-1	1-0	0-0	1-0	3-2	0-1	0-0	2-0	0-0	1-1	2-0	15-7
Totals	10-8	4-3	4-2	6-4	4-2	6-4	4-2	9-10	6-4	3-3	13-6	7-2	7-11	12-6	95-67

No-decisions-- Abe Alvarez, Scott Cassidy, Manny Delcarmen, Craig Hansen, Cla Meredith, Matt Perisho, Mike Remlinger, Mike Stanton.
INTERLEAGUE: Wade Miller 1-0, Tim Wakefield 0-1, Matt Clement 1-0 vs. Braves; Bronson Arroyo 0-1, Wade Miller 0-1, Tim Wakefield 1-0 vs. Cubs; Matt Clement 1-0, David Wells 1-0, Bronson Arroyo 1-0 vs. Reds; Tim Wakefield 1-0, Matt Clement 1-0, Mike Timlin 1-0 vs. Phillies; Keith Foulke 1-0, Alan Embree 0-1, Matt Clement 1-0 vs. Pirates; Tim Wakefield 0-1, Matt Clement 0-1, David Wells 1-0 vs. Cardinals. Total: 12-6.

CHICAGO—99-63

Pitcher	Bal. W-L	Bos. W-L	Cle. W-L	Det. W-L	K.C. W-L	L.A. W-L	Min. W-L	N.Y. W-L	Oak. W-L	Sea. W-L	TB. W-L	Tex. W-L	Tor. W-L	N.L. W-L	Totals W-L
Adkins, Jon	0-0	0-0	0-0	0-0	0-0	0-0	0-1	0-0	0-0	0-0	0-0	0-0	0-0	0-0	0-1
Buehrle, Mark	2-0	0-1	2-0	3-0	2-2	0-0	2-2	0-0	0-0	2-0	0-0	1-1	1-0	1-0	16-8
Contreras, Jose	0-1	1-0	1-0	2-1	3-0	0-1	2-1	2-0	0-1	1-0	1-0	0-0	0-0	2-2	15-7
Cotts, Neal	1-0	0-0	0-0	0-0	2-0	0-0	0-0	1-0	0-0	0-0	0-0	0-0	0-0	0-0	4-0
Garcia, Freddy	1-1	0-0	2-0	3-1	3-1	1-0	1-1	0-0	0-0	0-3	0-1	0-0	0-0	3-0	14-8
Garland, Jon	1-0	1-1	3-1	3-0	1-0	0-2	1-0	0-1	2-1	2-0	0-0	1-2	1-1	2-1	18-10
Hermanson, Dustin	0-0	0-0	1-1	0-0	0-0	0-1	0-0	0-0	0-0	0-0	0-0	0-0	0-0	0-1	2-4
Hernandez, Orlando	1-0	0-1	1-1	1-0	1-0	0-1	2-1	0-2	0-0	0-0	1-0	0-1	1-1	1-1	9-9
Jenks, Bobby	0-0	0-0	0-0	0-0	0-0	1-1	0-0	0-0	0-0	0-0	0-0	0-0	0-0	0-0	1-1
Marte, Damaso	0-0	0-0	1-1	1-0	1-0	0-0	0-0	0-2	0-0	0-0	0-1	0-0	0-0	0-0	3-4
McCarthy, Brandon	0-0	1-0	1-0	0-1	0-0	0-0	0-0	0-0	0-0	0-0	1-0	0-0	0-0	0-0	3-2
Politte, Cliff	0-0	0-0	0-0	0-0	0-0	2-0	0-0	0-0	0-0	1-0	0-0	0-0	3-0	1-0	7-1
Takatsu, Shingo	0-0	0-0	0-0	1-1	0-0	0-0	0-0	0-0	0-0	0-1	0-0	0-0	0-0	0-0	1-2
Vizcaino, Luis	0-0	0-1	1-1	1-0	0-1	0-0	1-0	0-0	0-1	0-0	1-0	0-0	1-0	0-1	6-5
Walker, Kevin	0-0	0-0	0-0	0-0	0-0	0-0	0-0	0-0	0-0	0-0	0-0	0-0	0-0	0-1	0-1
Totals	6-2	3-4	14-5	14-5	13-5	4-6	11-7	3-3	2-7	6-3	4-2	3-6	4-2	12-6	99-63

No-decisions-- Jeff Bajenaru, David Sanders.
INTERLEAGUE: Jose Contreras 0-1, Orlando Hernandez 0-1, Jon Garland 1-0 vs. Diamondbacks; Freddy Garcia 2-0, Luis Vizcaino 0-1, Jose Contreras 1-1, Jon Garland 0-1 vs. Cubs; Freddy Garcia 1-0, Jose Contreras 1-0, Orlando Hernandez 1-0 vs. Rockies; Mark Buehrle 1-0, Cliff Politte 2-0 vs. Dodgers; Jon Garland 1-0, Dustin Hermanson 0-1, Cliff Politte 1-0 vs. Padres. Total: 12-6.

2005 A.L. STATISTICS *Miscellaneous*

CLEVELAND—93-69

Pitcher	Bal. W-L	Bos. W-L	Chi. W-L	Det. W-L	K.C. W-L	L.A. W-L	Min. W-L	N.Y. W-L	Oak. W-L	Sea. W-L	TB. W-L	Tex. W-L	Tor. W-L	N.L. W-L	Totals W-L
Betancourt, Rafael	0-0	0-0	2-0	1-1	0-1	0-0	0-1	0-0	0-0	0-0	0-0	0-0	0-0	1-0	4-3
Cabrera, Fernando	1-0	0-0	0-1	1-0	0-0	0-0	0-0	0-0	0-0	0-0	0-0	0-0	0-0	0-0	2-1
Davis, Jason	0-0	0-0	0-1	2-0	0-0	0-1	0-0	0-0	0-0	0-0	0-0	0-0	1-0	1-0	4-2
Elarton, Scott	0-0	0-1	1-2	2-0	1-0	1-0	1-0	2-0	1-0	0-2	0-3	0-1	0-0	2-0	11-9
Howry, Bob	0-0	0-0	0-1	0-0	1-1	0-0	3-1	0-0	0-0	1-0	0-0	0-0	0-0	2-1	7-4
Lee, Cliff	2-0	0-0	0-0	1-0	4-1	1-1	1-1	1-1	1-0	2-0	1-1	1-0	0-0	3-0	18-5
Miller, Matt	0-0	1-0	0-0	0-0	0-0	0-0	0-0	0-0	0-0	0-0	0-0	0-0	0-0	0-0	1-0
Millwood, Kevin	0-1	1-1	0-2	0-1	2-1	1-0	0-1	0-1	1-0	2-0	1-0	0-1	0-1	1-1	9-11
Rhodes, Arthur	0-0	0-0	1-0	0-0	0-1	0-0	1-0	0-0	0-0	0-0	0-0	0-0	1-0	0-0	3-1
Riske, David	0-0	0-0	1-1	2-0	0-0	0-0	0-2	0-0	0-1	0-0	0-0	0-0	0-0	0-0	3-4
Sabathia, C.C.	2-0	0-1	0-1	2-1	3-1	0-1	2-1	0-0	0-2	1-1	1-0	1-0	1-1	2-0	15-10
Sauerbeck, Scott	0-0	0-0	0-0	0-0	1-0	0-0	0-0	0-0	0-0	0-0	0-0	0-0	0-0	0-0	1-0
Westbrook, Jake	1-0	0-0	0-4	1-3	1-0	0-2	2-2	0-1	3-0	1-0	1-1	1-1	1-0	3-1	15-15
Wickman, Bob	0-0	0-1	0-1	0-0	0-0	0-0	0-0	0-0	0-1	0-0	0-1	0-0	0-0	0-0	0-4
Totals	6-1	2-4	5-14	12-6	13-6	3-5	10-9	3-4	6-3	7-3	4-6	3-3	4-2	15-3	93-69

No-decisions-- Jeremy Guthrie, Kazuhito Tadano, Brian Tallet.
INTERLEAGUE: Cliff Lee 1-0, Scott Elarton 1-0, Jake Westbrook 1-0 vs. Diamondbacks; Kevin Millwood 0-1, C.C. Sabathia 1-0, Bob Howry 1-1, Cliff Lee 1-0, Jake Westbrook 1-0 vs. Reds; Jake Westbrook 1-0, Bob Howry 1-0, Kevin Millwood 1-0 vs. Rockies; Rafael Betancourt 1-0, Scott Elarton 1-0, Jake Westbrook 0-1 vs. Padres; C.C. Sabathia 1-0, Jason Davis 1-0, Cliff Lee 1-0 vs. Giants. Total: 15-3.

DETROIT—71-91

Pitcher	Bal. W-L	Bos. W-L	Chi. W-L	Cle. W-L	K.C. W-L	L.A. W-L	Min. W-L	N.Y. W-L	Oak. W-L	Sea. W-L	TB. W-L	Tex. W-L	Tor. W-L	N.L. W-L	Totals W-L
Bonderman, Jeremy	0-0	2-0	1-2	2-3	2-2	1-0	2-0	1-1	0-2	0-0	0-0	1-0	0-1	2-2	14-13
Colon, Roman	0-0	1-0	0-0	0-1	0-0	0-0	0-0	0-0	0-0	0-0	0-0	0-0	0-0	0-0	1-1
Darensbourg, Vic	0-0	0-0	0-0	0-0	0-0	0-1	0-0	0-0	0-0	0-0	0-0	0-0	1-0	0-0	1-1
Dingman, Craig	0-0	0-1	0-0	0-0	1-1	0-0	1-0	0-0	0-0	0-0	0-0	0-0	0-1	0-0	2-3
Douglass, Sean	0-0	0-0	0-2	0-0	0-1	0-0	1-0	0-0	0-1	1-0	1-0	0-0	0-0	1-1	5-5
Farnsworth, Kyle	0-0	0-1	0-0	0-0	0-0	0-0	1-0	0-0	0-0	0-0	0-0	0-0	0-0	0-0	1-1
German, Franklyn	0-0	0-0	0-0	0-0	0-0	0-0	0-0	0-0	0-0	0-0	2-0	0-0	1-0	1-0	4-0
Ginter, Matt	0-0	0-0	0-0	0-0	0-0	0-1	0-0	0-0	0-0	0-0	0-0	0-0	0-0	0-0	0-1
Grilli, Jason	0-0	0-0	0-1	0-0	0-0	0-0	0-0	0-0	0-0	1-0	0-0	0-0	0-0	0-0	0-4
Johnson, Jason	3-0	0-1	0-2	0-2	3-0	0-0	0-4	0-0	1-1	0-0	0-1	0-0	0-1	1-2	8-13
Ledezma, Wilfredo	0-0	0-0	0-2	1-0	0-0	0-1	0-0	0-0	0-0	1-0	0-0	0-0	0-0	0-0	2-4
Maroth, Mike	0-1	0-1	0-1	3-1	2-2	3-0	1-1	0-1	0-1	2-1	1-1	0-1	1-0	1-2	14-14
Percival, Troy	0-0	0-0	0-0	0-0	0-0	0-0	1-1	0-1	0-0	0-1	0-0	0-0	0-0	0-0	1-3
Robertson, Nate	1-1	0-1	2-2	0-2	1-1	0-1	1-3	0-1	1-1	0-1	0-0	1-0	0-0	0-2	7-16
Rodney, Fernando	0-0	0-0	1-1	0-1	0-1	0-0	0-0	0-0	0-0	0-0	0-0	0-0	0-0	1-0	2-3
Spurling, Chris	1-0	0-0	0-1	0-0	1-0	0-1	0-1	0-0	0-0	0-0	0-0	0-0	0-0	1-0	3-4
Urbina, Ugueth	0-0	0-1	0-0	0-1	0-1	0-1	0-0	0-0	0-0	0-0	0-0	0-0	1-0	0-0	1-3
Verlander, Justin	0-0	0-0	0-1	0-1	0-0	0-0	0-1	0-0	0-0	0-0	0-0	0-0	0-0	0-0	0-2
Walker, Jamie	0-1	1-0	1-0	0-0	0-0	0-1	0-0	0-0	0-0	0-0	0-0	1-0	0-0	1-1	4-3
Totals	5-3	4-6	5-14	6-12	9-10	4-6	8-11	1-5	1-5	5-4	5-2	4-2	4-3	9-9	71-91

No-decisions-- Doug Creek, Andrew Good, Jason Karnuth, Mark Woodyard.
INTERLEAGUE: Jeremy Bonderman 0-1, Jamie Walker 0-1, Franklyn German 1-0, Jason Johnson 0-1, Mike Maroth 0-1, Sean Douglass 1-0 vs. Diamondbacks; Mike Maroth 0-1, Jeremy Bonderman 1-0, Nate Robertson 0-1 vs. Rockies; Jeremy Bonderman 0-1, Chris Spurling 1-0, Jason Johnson 0-1 vs. Dodgers; Fernando Rodney 1-0, Mike Maroth 1-0, Jeremy Bonderman 1-0 vs. Padres; Nate Robertson 0-1, Jason Johnson 1-0, Jamie Walker 1-0 vs. Giants. Total: 9-9.

KANSAS CITY—56-106

Pitcher	Bal. W-L	Bos. W-L	Chi. W-L	Cle. W-L	Det. W-L	L.A. W-L	Min. W-L	N.Y. W-L	Oak. W-L	Sea. W-L	TB. W-L	Tex. W-L	Tor. W-L	N.L. W-L	Totals W-L
Affeldt, Jeremy	0-0	0-0	0-0	0-0	0-0	0-0	0-0	0-0	0-1	0-1	0-0	0-0	0-0	0-0	0-2
Anderson, Brian	0-0	0-0	0-0	0-0	0-1	1-0	0-1	0-0	0-0	0-0	0-0	0-0	0-0	0-0	1-2
Bautista, Denny	0-1	0-0	0-0	1-0	0-0	1-0	0-0	0-0	0-0	0-1	0-0	0-0	0-0	0-0	2-2
Burgos, Ambiorix	1-0	0-1	1-0	0-0	0-1	0-0	0-1	0-0	0-0	0-0	0-1	0-0	1-1	0-0	3-5
Camp, Shawn	0-0	0-0	1-1	0-0	0-0	0-0	0-2	0-1	0-0	0-0	0-0	0-0	0-0	0-0	1-4
Carrasco, D.J.	0-1	0-0	0-0	0-2	0-0	0-0	2-0	1-0	0-0	1-1	0-1	0-1	1-0	1-2	6-8
Cerda, Jaime	0-1	0-0	0-0	0-0	1-0	0-0	0-0	0-0	0-1	0-0	0-0	0-0	0-1	0-0	1-4
Demaria, Chris	0-0	0-0	1-0	0-0	0-0	0-0	0-0	0-0	0-0	0-0	0-0	0-0	0-0	0-0	1-0
Gobble, Jimmy	0-0	0-0	0-0	0-1	0-0	0-0	0-0	0-0	1-0	0-0	0-0	0-0	0-0	0-0	1-1
Greinke, Zack	0-0	0-1	0-3	1-3	3-0	0-1	0-2	1-1	0-0	0-0	0-1	0-2	0-2	0-1	5-17
Hernandez, Runelvys	0-0	0-0	0-2	0-1	2-1	0-2	0-1	0-0	0-1	1-2	1-0	0-1	1-2	3-1	8-14
Howell, J.P.	0-0	0-0	1-1	0-1	0-0	0-0	0-0	0-0	0-1	0-0	0-0	0-1	0-0	1-1	3-5
Jensen, Ryan	0-0	0-0	0-1	0-1	0-0	0-1	0-0	1-0	0-0	0-0	0-0	0-0	0-0	2-0	3-2
Lima, Jose	0-1	1-0	1-1	1-1	0-4	0-2	1-1	0-0	0-2	0-0	0-1	0-2	0-0	1-1	5-16
MacDougal, Mike	0-0	0-0	0-1	2-2	1-0	0-1	0-0	0-0	0-0	0-0	0-0	0-0	0-1	0-1	5-6
Nunez, Leo	1-0	0-1	0-0	0-0	0-0	0-0	0-0	1-0	0-0	0-0	0-0	1-0	0-0	0-1	3-2
Sisco, Andrew	0-0	1-0	0-1	0-1	0-1	0-0	0-2	0-0	0-0	0-0	0-0	0-0	0-0	0-0	2-5
Snyder, Kyle	0-0	0-0	0-2	0-0	1-0	0-0	0-0	0-0	0-0	0-0	0-0	0-1	0-0	0-1	1-3
Wood, Mike	0-0	0-0	0-2	1-1	1-2	0-0	0-2	0-1	1-0	0-0	1-0	0-0	0-0	1-0	5-8
Totals	2-4	2-4	5-13	6-13	9-10	2-7	6-13	3-3	2-4	2-7	3-5	2-8	3-6	9-9	56-106

No-decisions-- Jonah Bayliss, Nate Field, Steve Stemle.
INTERLEAGUE: Mike MacDougal 0-1, J.P. Howell 1-0, Ryan Jensen 1-0 vs. Diamondbacks; D.J. Carrasco 0-1, Runelvys Hernandez 0-1, Jose Lima 0-1 vs. Rockies; J.P. Howell 0-1, D.J. Carrasco 0-1, Runelvys Hernandez 1-0 vs. Astros; Runelvys Hernandez 1-0, Jose Lima 1-0, Mike Wood 1-0 vs. Dodgers; D.J. Carrasco 1-0, Runelvys Hernandez 1-0, Leo Nunez 0-1 vs. Giants; Zack Greinke 0-1, Jaime Cerda 0-1, Ryan Jensen 1-0 vs. Cardinals. Total: 9-9.

LOS ANGELES—95-67

Pitcher	Bal. W-L	Bos. W-L	Chi. W-L	Cle. W-L	Det. W-L	K.C. W-L	Min. W-L	N.Y. W-L	Oak. W-L	Sea. W-L	TB. W-L	Tex. W-L	Tor. W-L	N.L. W-L	Totals W-L
Bootcheck, Chris	0-0	0-0	0-0	0-0	0-0	0-0	0-0	0-0	0-0	0-0	0-1	0-0	0-0	0-0	0-1
Byrd, Paul	0-0	1-1	1-0	2-0	1-0	1-1	1-1	0-0	0-2	3-1	0-1	1-1	0-1	1-2	12-11
Colon, Bartolo	2-0	2-0	1-0	2-0	0-2	2-1	1-1	1-1	2-0	2-1	1-1	4-0	0-0	1-1	21-8
Donnelly, Brendan	0-0	0-0	1-1	0-0	1-0	0-0	0-0	0-0	0-0	2-0	0-0	1-0	0-1	4-1	9-3
Escobar, Kelvim	0-0	0-0	0-0	0-1	2-0	1-0	0-1	0-0	0-0	0-0	0-0	0-0	0-0	0-0	3-2
Gregg, Kevin	0-0	0-0	0-0	0-0	0-0	1-0	0-0	0-1	0-0	0-1	0-0	0-0	0-0	0-0	1-2
Lackey, John	1-1	0-0	2-0	0-1	1-0	0-0	1-1	2-0	3-1	1-1	0-0	2-0	0-0	0-0	14-5
Peralta, Joel	0-0	0-0	0-0	0-0	0-0	0-0	0-0	0-0	0-0	0-0	0-0	0-0	0-0	0-0	1-0
Prinz, Bret	0-0	0-0	0-0	0-0	0-0	0-0	0-0	0-0	0-0	0-0	0-0	0-1	0-0	0-0	0-1
Rodriguez, Francisco	0-0	0-0	0-0	1-0	0-0	0-0	0-0	0-1	0-2	0-0	0-0	0-0	0-1	1-0	2-5
Santana, Ervin	0-1	1-1	1-0	0-1	1-0	0-0	1-0	2-0	3-0	0-2	0-1	2-1	0-0	1-1	12-8
Shields, Scot	0-0	0-3	0-1	0-0	0-0	1-0	0-0	0-0	1-3	0-1	2-0	3-1	1-1	2-1	10-11
Washburn, Jarrod	1-0	0-0	0-1	0-0	0-2	1-0	1-0	1-1	0-1	1-1	1-1	1-0	0-1	1-0	8-8
Woods, Jake	0-0	0-1	0-0	0-0	0-0	0-0	0-0	0-0	1-0	0-0	0-0	0-0	0-0	0-0	1-1
Yan, Esteban	0-0	0-0	0-1	0-0	0-0	0-0	0-0	0-0	0-0	0-0	0-0	1-0	0-0	0-0	1-1
Totals	4-2	4-6	6-4	5-3	6-4	7-2	6-4	6-4	10-9	9-9	4-5	15-4	1-5	12-6	95-67

No-decisions-- Jason Christiansen, Greg Jones, Joe Saunders.
INTERLEAGUE: Brendan Donnelly 2-0, Paul Byrd 0-1 vs. Braves; Francisco Rodriguez 1-0, Scot Shields 1-0, Ervin Santana 0-1 vs. Marlins; Jarrod Washburn 1-0, Brendan Donnelly 2-0, John Lackey 1-0, Paul Byrd 0-1, Ervin Santana 0-1 vs. Dodgers; Bartolo Colon 1-0, Scot Shields 0-1, Brendan Donnelly 0-1 vs. Mets; Paul Byrd 1-0, Scot Shields 0-1, Bartolo Colon 0-1 vs. Nationals. Total: 12-6.

MINNESOTA—83-79

Pitcher	Bal. W-L	Bos. W-L	Chi. W-L	Cle. W-L	Det. W-L	K.C. W-L	L.A. W-L	N.Y. W-L	Oak. W-L	Sea. W-L	TB. W-L	Tex. W-L	Tor. W-L	N.L. W-L	Totals W-L
Baker, Scott	0-0	0-0	0-0	0-1	2-0	0-1	0-1	0-0	1-0	0-0	0-0	0-0	0-0	0-0	3-3
Bowyer, Travis	0-0	0-0	0-0	0-0	0-0	0-1	0-0	0-0	0-0	0-0	0-0	0-0	0-0	0-0	0-1
Crain, Jesse	2-0	0-0	1-2	3-0	0-0	3-1	0-0	0-0	0-1	0-0	1-0	0-1	0-0	2-0	12-5
Gassner, Dave	0-0	0-0	0-0	1-0	0-0	0-0	0-0	0-0	0-0	0-0	0-0	0-0	0-0	0-0	1-0
Guerrier, Matt	0-1	0-0	0-0	0-0	0-0	0-1	0-0	0-0	0-0	0-1	0-0	0-0	0-0	0-0	0-3
Liriano, Francisco	0-0	0-0	0-1	0-0	1-0	0-0	0-0	0-0	0-1	0-0	0-0	0-0	0-0	0-0	1-2
Lohse, Kyle	0-0	0-1	1-3	0-1	2-2	0-1	0-1	1-0	0-0	0-1	2-0	0-1	2-0	1-2	9-13
Mays, Joe	0-0	0-1	0-2	0-1	0-2	2-0	0-1	0-1	0-1	1-0	2-0	0-0	1-1	0-0	6-10
Mulholland, Terry	0-0	0-0	0-0	0-0	0-1	0-0	0-0	0-0	0-0	0-0	0-0	0-0	0-0	0-1	0-2
Nathan, Joe	1-0	1-0	0-0	1-0	2-0	1-1	1-1	0-1	1-0	1-0	0-0	1-2	0-0	0-1	7-4
Radke, Brad	0-0	1-0	0-2	2-1	2-0	1-1	1-1	0-1	0-1	1-1	0-0	1-0	0-0	0-2	9-12
Rincon, Juan	0-1	0-1	0-1	0-1	1-2	2-0	0-0	0-0	1-0	0-0	0-0	0-0	2-0	0-0	6-6
Romero, J.C.	0-0	0-0	1-0	1-2	0-0	0-0	0-0	0-1	0-0	0-0	1-0	0-0	0-0	0-0	4-3
Santana, Johan	0-0	0-0	4-0	1-1	2-0	2-0	1-2	1-0	1-1	1-0	1-0	0-0	1-1	1-2	16-7
Silva, Carlos	0-1	0-1	0-0	0-2	1-1	1-0	2-0	1-0	0-0	2-1	0-0	0-2	0-0	2-0	9-8
Totals	3-3	2-4	7-11	9-10	11-8	13-6	4-6	3-3	4-6	6-4	6-0	3-6	4-2	8-10	83-79

INTERLEAGUE: Juan Rincon 1-0, Johan Santana 1-0, Kyle Lohse 0-1 vs. Diamondbacks; Terry Mulholland 0-1, Carlos Silva 1-0, Brad Radke 0-1 vs. Dodgers; Carlos Silva 1-0, Brad Radke 0-2, Jesse Crain 1-0, Johan Santana 0-1, Kyle Lohse 1-0 vs. Brewers; Juan Rincon 1-0, Brad Radke 0-1, Johan Santana 0-1 vs. Padres; Joe Nathan 0-1, Jesse Crain 1-0, Kyle Lohse 0-1 vs. Giants. Total: 8-10.

NEW YORK—95-67

Pitcher	Bal. W-L	Bos. W-L	Chi. W-L	Cle. W-L	Det. W-L	K.C. W-L	L.A. W-L	Min. W-L	Oak. W-L	Sea. W-L	TB. W-L	Tex. W-L	Tor. W-L	N.L. W-L	Totals W-L
Anderson, Jason	1-0	0-0	0-0	0-0	0-0	0-0	0-0	0-0	0-0	0-0	0-0	0-0	0-0	0-0	1-0
Brown, Kevin	0-1	0-0	0-0	0-0	1-0	0-1	0-2	0-1	2-0	0-0	0-1	0-1	0-0	1-0	4-7
Chacon, Shawn	1-0	0-1	1-1	0-0	0-0	0-0	0-0	0-0	1-0	0-1	0-0	1-0	3-0	0-0	7-3
Embree, Alan	0-0	0-0	0-0	0-0	0-0	1-0	0-0	0-0	0-0	0-1	0-0	0-0	0-0	0-0	1-1
Franklin, Wayne	0-0	0-0	0-0	0-0	0-0	0-0	0-0	0-0	0-0	0-0	0-0	0-1	0-0	0-0	0-1
Gordon, Tom	0-1	1-1	0-0	1-0	1-0	0-0	1-1	1-0	0-0	0-1	0-0	0-0	0-0	0-0	5-4
Groom, Buddy	0-0	0-0	0-0	0-0	0-0	0-0	0-0	0-0	0-0	1-0	0-0	0-0	0-0	0-1	1-0
Henn, Sean	0-0	0-0	0-0	0-0	0-0	0-0	0-0	0-0	0-0	0-2	0-0	0-0	0-0	0-1	0-3
Johnson, Randy	3-0	5-0	0-1	1-0	0-1	1-1	0-0	1-0	1-0	2-0	0-1	1-0	0-2	2-2	17-8
Leiter, Al	0-1	1-0	0-0	0-1	0-0	0-0	0-1	0-1	0-1	0-0	0-0	1-0	0-0	0-0	4-5
May, Darrell	0-0	0-0	0-0	0-1	0-0	0-0	0-0	0-0	0-0	0-0	0-0	0-0	0-0	0-0	0-1
Mussina, Mike	1-0	0-2	2-0	1-1	1-0	0-0	1-2	0-1	2-0	0-0	1-0	0-0	1-1	3-1	13-8
Pavano, Carl	0-2	0-1	0-0	0-0	0-0	0-1	1-0	0-0	0-0	1-0	0-1	0-0	1-1	0-0	4-6
Proctor, Scott	0-0	0-0	0-0	0-0	0-0	0-0	0-0	0-0	0-0	0-0	0-0	0-0	1-0	0-0	1-0
Quantrill, Paul	0-0	0-0	0-0	0-0	0-0	0-0	0-0	0-0	0-0	1-0	0-0	0-0	0-0	0-0	1-0
Redding, Tim	0-0	0-1	0-0	0-0	0-0	0-0	0-0	0-0	0-0	0-0	0-0	0-0	0-0	0-0	0-1
Rivera, Mariano	1-0	1-1	0-1	0-1	0-0	0-0	1-0	0-0	0-1	0-0	0-0	0-0	2-0	2-0	7-4
Small, Aaron	2-0	1-0	0-0	0-0	0-0	0-0	0-0	1-0	1-0	1-0	2-0	1-0	0-0	0-0	10-0
Stanton, Mike	0-1	0-0	0-0	0-0	0-0	0-0	0-0	0-0	0-0	0-0	0-0	0-0	0-1	1-0	1-2
Sturtze, Tanyon	2-0	0-0	0-0	0-0	0-0	0-0	0-0	0-0	0-1	1-1	2-0	0-0	0-1	0-1	5-3
Wang, Chien-Ming	0-0	0-1	0-0	1-0	2-0	0-0	0-0	0-0	0-0	1-3	0-0	0-1	1-1	1-1	8-5
Wright, Jaret	0-1	1-1	0-0	0-0	0-0	0-0	0-0	0-0	0-0	0-0	3-0	0-1	1-2	0-0	5-5
Totals	11-7	10-9	3-3	4-3	5-1	3-3	4-6	3-3	7-2	7-3	8-11	7-3	12-6	11-7	95-67

No-decisions-- Colter Bean, Jorge DePaula, Alex Graman, Steve Karsay, Ramiro Mendoza, Felix Rodriguez.
INTERLEAGUE: Mike Stanton 1-0, Chien-Ming Wang 1-0, Mike Mussina 1-0 vs. Cubs; Randy Johnson 0-1, Carl Pavano 0-1, Mike Mussina 1-0 vs. Brewers; Kevin Brown 1-0, Mariano Rivera 1-0, Randy Johnson 0-1, Carl Pavano 1-0, Mike Mussina 0-1, Sean Henn 0-1 vs. Mets; Mike Mussina 1-0, Mariano Rivera 1-0, Randy Johnson 1-0 vs. Pirates; Chien-Ming Wang 0-1, Randy Johnson 1-0, Tanyon Sturtze 0-1 vs. Cardinals. Total: 11-7.

OAKLAND—88-74

Pitcher	Bal. W-L	Bos. W-L	Chi. W-L	Cle. W-L	Det. W-L	K.C. W-L	L.A. W-L	Min. W-L	N.Y. W-L	Sea. W-L	TB. W-L	Tex. W-L	Tor. W-L	N.L. W-L	Totals W-L
Blanton, Joe	1-0	1-0	0-0	0-1	0-0	1-0	0-3	2-0	0-2	2-1	0-1	1-2	1-1	3-1	12-12
Calero, Kiko	1-0	0-0	0-0	0-0	0-0	0-1	2-0	0-0	0-0	0-0	0-0	0-0	1-0	0-0	4-1
Cruz, Juan	0-0	0-2	0-0	0-0	0-0	0-0	0-0	0-0	0-0	0-0	0-1	0-0	0-0	0-0	0-3
Dotel, Octavio	0-0	0-2	0-0	0-0	0-0	0-0	0-0	0-1	0-0	0-0	0-0	0-0	0-0	0-0	1-2
Duchscherer, Justin	0-0	0-0	2-0	0-1	0-0	0-0	2-0	0-2	0-0	0-0	0-0	1-0	1-0	1-1	7-4
Etherton, Seth	0-0	1-0	0-0	0-1	0-0	0-0	0-0	0-0	0-0	0-0	0-0	0-0	0-0	0-0	1-1
Glynn, Ryan	0-0	0-0	0-0	0-0	0-0	0-0	0-0	0-0	0-1	0-0	0-0	0-0	0-1	0-2	0-4
Harden, Rich	0-0	0-0	1-0	0-0	1-0	1-0	1-1	0-0	0-2	2-0	1-0	2-1	0-1	1-0	10-5
Haren, Danny	1-1	0-2	0-0	1-0	0-1	1-0	1-1	1-1	1-0	2-1	1-1	2-2	1-1	2-1	14-12
Kennedy, Joe	1-0	0-0	0-0	0-0	0-0	1-0	0-2	0-1	0-0	1-1	0-0	1-1	0-0	0-0	4-5
Rincon, Ricardo	1-0	0-0	0-0	0-0	0-0	0-0	0-0	0-0	0-1	0-0	0-0	0-0	0-0	0-0	1-1
Saarloos, Kirk	1-0	1-0	1-1	0-1	2-0	0-0	0-1	1-0	0-1	1-1	0-1	1-2	1-1	1-0	10-9
Street, Huston	0-0	0-0	1-0	1-0	0-0	0-0	1-0	0-0	0-0	1-1	1-0	0-0	0-0	0-0	5-1
Witasick, Jay	0-1	0-0	0-0	0-0	0-0	0-0	0-0	0-0	0-0	0-0	0-0	1-0	0-0	0-0	1-1
Yabu, Keiichi	0-0	1-0	0-0	0-0	0-0	0-0	1-0	0-0	0-0	1-0	0-0	0-0	0-0	1-0	4-0
Zito, Barry	0-2	0-0	2-1	1-2	2-0	0-1	1-2	2-0	0-1	2-0	1-1	2-0	0-0	1-3	14-13
Totals	**6-4**	**4-6**	**7-2**	**3-6**	**5-1**	**4-2**	**9-10**	**6-4**	**2-7**	**12-6**	**4-5**	**11-8**	**5-5**	**10-8**	**88-74**

No-decisions-- Ron Flores, Jairo Garcia, Tim Harikkala, Britt Reames.
INTERLEAGUE: Danny Haren 1-0, Justin Duchscherer 0-1, Barry Zito 1-0 vs. Braves; Joe Blanton 1-0, Justin Duchscherer 1-0, Ryan Glynn 0-1 vs. Mets; Barry Zito 0-1, Kirk Saarloos 1-0, Joe Blanton 1-0 vs. Phillies; Joe Blanton 1-0, Keiichi Yabu 1-0, Danny Haren 1-1, Barry Zito 0-1, Rich Harden 1-0 vs. Giants; Barry Zito 0-1, Ryan Glynn 0-1, Joe Blanton 0-1 vs. Nationals. Total: 10-8.

SEATTLE—69-93

Pitcher	Bal. W-L	Bos. W-L	Chi. W-L	Cle. W-L	Det. W-L	K.C. W-L	L.A. W-L	Min. W-L	N.Y. W-L	Oak. W-L	TB. W-L	Tex. W-L	Tor. W-L	N.L. W-L	Totals W-L
Franklin, Ryan	0-1	1-0	0-1	1-0	1-0	2-0	1-2	0-1	0-0	0-3	0-0	1-3	0-2	1-2	8-15
Guardado, Eddie	0-0	0-0	0-0	0-0	0-0	0-0	1-0	0-0	0-0	1-1	0-0	0-2	0-0	0-0	2-3
Harris, Jeff	0-1	0-0	0-1	0-0	0-0	0-0	0-1	0-0	1-0	0-0	0-0	1-1	0-1	0-0	2-5
Hasegawa, Shigetoshi	0-0	0-0	0-0	0-0	0-1	0-0	0-0	0-0	0-1	0-0	0-0	0-0	0-0	1-1	1-3
Hernandez, Felix	0-1	0-0	0-0	0-0	0-1	1-0	0-0	1-0	0-0	1-0	0-0	0-1	1-0	0-0	4-4
Madritsch, Bobby	0-0	0-0	0-0	0-0	0-0	0-0	0-0	0-1	0-0	0-0	0-0	0-0	0-0	0-0	0-1
Mateo, Julio	0-0	1-0	0-0	0-0	1-1	0-0	0-0	0-0	0-1	0-1	1-0	0-1	0-0	0-2	3-6
Meche, Gil	1-0	1-0	1-0	0-2	0-1	0-1	1-1	1-0	0-0	0-1	1-0	1-0	1-0	4-1	10-8
Moyer, Jamie	1-1	0-1	1-1	1-0	1-1	2-0	2-1	1-0	0-0	1-1	0-0	1-1	1-0	1-0	13-7
Nelson, Jeff	0-0	0-0	0-1	0-0	0-0	0-0	0-0	1-1	0-0	0-0	0-0	0-0	0-0	0-0	1-3
Pineiro, Joel	0-1	0-1	1-2	0-1	0-0	1-0	2-0	0-1	0-0	2-2	0-0	1-1	0-2	0-0	7-11
Putz, J.J.	1-1	0-0	0-0	1-1	1-0	0-0	2-1	0-0	0-0	0-0	0-0	1-1	0-0	0-1	6-5
Sele, Aaron	0-1	0-0	0-0	0-3	0-0	1-1	0-2	0-0	0-1	1-0	1-1	0-1	0-1	3-1	6-12
Sherrill, George	0-0	0-0	0-0	0-0	0-0	0-0	0-1	2-1	1-0	0-1	0-0	0-0	1-0	0-0	4-3
Thornton, Matt	0-0	0-0	0-0	0-0	0-0	0-0	0-0	0-1	0-2	0-1	0-0	0-1	0-0	0-0	0-6
Villone, Ron	0-0	0-1	0-0	0-0	0-0	0-0	0-0	0-0	0-1	0-2	2-0	0-0	0-0	0-0	2-3
Totals	**3-7**	**3-3**	**3-6**	**3-7**	**4-5**	**7-2**	**9-9**	**4-6**	**3-7**	**6-12**	**4-2**	**6-13**	**4-6**	**10-8**	**69-93**

No-decisions-- Scott Atchison, Jorge Campillo, Masao Kida, Clint Nageotte, Rafael Soriano.
INTERLEAGUE: Shigetoshi Hasegawa 1-0, Gil Meche 0-1, Aaron Sele 1-0 vs. Marlins; Jamie Moyer 1-0, Ryan Franklin 1-0, Gil Meche 1-0 vs. Mets; Gil Meche 1-0, Aaron Sele 1-0, Julio Mateo 0-1 vs. Phillies; Ryan Franklin 0-1, Gil Meche 2-0, Julio Mateo 0-1, Aaron Sele 1-1 vs. Padres; Shigetoshi Hasegawa 0-1, J.J. Putz 0-1, Ryan Franklin 0-1 vs. Nationals. Total: 10-8.

TAMPA BAY—67-95

Pitcher	Bal. W-L	Bos. W-L	Chi. W-L	Cle. W-L	Det. W-L	K.C. W-L	L.A. W-L	Min. W-L	N.Y. W-L	Oak. W-L	Sea. W-L	Tex. W-L	Tor. W-L	N.L. W-L	Totals W-L
Baez, Danys	0-0	1-1	0-0	0-0	1-0	1-0	0-0	0-0	0-0	1-0	0-1	0-0	1-1	0-1	5-4
Bell, Rob	1-0	0-0	0-0	0-0	0-0	0-0	0-0	0-0	0-1	0-0	0-0	0-0	0-0	0-0	1-1
Borowski, Joe	0-1	0-1	0-0	1-0	0-0	0-0	0-1	0-0	0-1	0-0	0-0	0-0	0-1	0-0	1-5
Brazelton, Dewon	0-1	0-1	0-1	0-0	0-0	0-0	0-0	0-2	0-0	0-1	0-0	1-0	0-2	0-0	1-8
Carter, Lance	0-0	0-0	1-1	0-0	0-0	0-0	0-1	0-0	0-0	0-0	0-0	0-0	0-0	0-0	1-2
Colome, Jesus	0-1	1-0	1-0	0-0	0-1	0-0	0-0	0-0	0-0	0-0	0-0	0-0	0-0	0-1	2-3
Fossum, Casey	1-2	1-2	0-1	0-1	0-0	0-1	0-0	0-0	2-1	0-0	0-1	1-0	1-0	0-4	8-12
Harper, Travis	1-1	0-0	0-0	0-0	0-1	0-0	0-0	0-0	0-1	1-1	0-0	1-0	1-0	0-2	4-6
Hendrickson, Mark	0-2	1-1	0-0	1-0	0-1	1-1	3-0	0-0	3-0	0-1	1-0	0-0	1-1	0-1	11-8
Kazmir, Scott	2-1	1-1	0-0	1-1	1-1	1-0	0-0	0-2	1-1	1-0	0-0	1-0	1-1	0-1	10-9
McClung, Seth	1-0	0-3	0-0	3-0	0-1	0-0	0-1	0-1	0-1	0-0	0-0	2-0	1-2	0-1	7-11
Miller, Trever	0-0	1-0	0-0	0-2	0-0	0-0	0-0	0-0	0-0	1-0	0-0	0-0	0-0	0-0	2-2
Nomo, Hideo	0-0	0-2	0-1	0-0	0-0	0-0	0-0	0-0	0-0	1-0	2-1	0-0	1-1	1-2	5-8
Nunez, Franklin	0-0	0-0	0-0	0-0	0-0	0-0	0-0	0-0	0-0	0-0	0-0	0-0	0-0	1-0	1-0
Orvella, Chad	0-0	0-0	0-0	0-0	0-0	0-0	0-0	0-0	2-1	0-0	0-1	0-1	1-0	0-0	3-3
Waechter, Doug	0-2	0-1	0-0	0-0	0-1	1-0	1-2	0-1	1-1	0-0	1-0	0-0	0-2	1-2	5-12
Webb, John	0-0	0-0	0-0	0-0	0-0	0-0	0-0	0-0	0-0	0-0	0-0	0-1	0-0	0-0	0-1
Totals	**6-12**	**6-13**	**2-4**	**6-4**	**2-5**	**5-3**	**5-4**	**0-6**	**11-8**	**5-4**	**2-4**	**6-2**	**8-11**	**3-15**	**67-95**

No-decisions-- Joe Beimel, Tim Corcoran, Lee Gardner, Jon Switzer.
INTERLEAGUE: Travis Harper 0-1, Danys Baez 0-1, Casey Fossum 0-1 vs. Reds; Hideo Nomo 0-1, Jesus Colome 0-1, Casey Fossum 0-2, Seth McClung 0-1, Doug Waechter 0-1 vs. Marlins; Doug Waechter 1-0, Casey Fossum 0-1, Hideo Nomo 1-0 vs. Brewers; Hideo Nomo 0-1, Scott Kazmir 0-1, Franklin Nunez 1-0 vs. Pirates; Travis Harper 0-1, Mark Hendrickson 0-1, Doug Waechter 0-1 vs. Cardinals. Total: 3-15.

TEXAS—79-83

Pitcher	Bal. W-L	Bos. W-L	Chi. W-L	Cle. W-L	Det. W-L	K.C. W-L	L.A. W-L	Min. W-L	N.Y. W-L	Oak. W-L	Sea. W-L	TB. W-L	Tor. W-L	N.L. W-L	Totals W-L
Astacio, Pedro	0-0	0-1	0-1	0-1	0-0	1-1	0-0	0-0	0-1	1-0	0-0	0-0	0-1	0-2	2-8
Baldwin, James	0-1	0-0	0-0	0-0	0-0	0-0	0-0	0-0	0-1	0-0	0-0	0-0	0-0	0-0	0-2
Benoit, Joaquin	2-0	1-0	0-0	0-0	0-0	0-0	0-0	0-0	0-2	0-0	0-1	0-1	1-0	0-0	4-4
Brocail, Doug	0-0	0-0	0-0	0-0	1-0	0-0	0-0	2-1	0-1	0-0	1-0	0-0	1-0	0-1	5-3
Cordero, Francisco	1-0	0-0	0-0	0-0	0-1	1-0	0-0	0-0	0-0	0-0	0-0	0-0	1-0	0-0	3-1
Dickey, R.A.	0-0	0-0	0-0	0-0	0-0	0-0	0-2	0-0	0-0	0-0	1-0	0-0	0-0	0-0	1-2
Dominguez, Juan	0-0	0-0	1-0	0-0	0-0	1-0	0-2	0-0	0-0	1-1	1-0	0-1	0-0	0-2	4-6
Drese, Ryan	0-0	0-1	0-1	1-0	0-1	1-0	0-1	0-0	0-0	0-0	0-1	1-0	1-0	0-1	4-6
Feldman, Scott	0-0	0-0	0-0	0-0	0-0	0-0	0-1	0-0	0-0	0-0	0-0	0-0	0-0	0-0	0-1
Gryboski, Kevin	0-0	0-1	0-0	0-0	0-0	0-0	0-0	0-0	0-0	0-0	0-0	0-0	0-0	0-0	0-1
Karsay, Steve	0-0	0-1	0-0	0-0	0-0	0-0	0-0	0-0	0-0	0-0	0-0	0-0	0-0	0-0	0-1
Loe, Kameron	1-0	0-0	1-0	0-0	0-0	0-0	1-2	2-0	1-1	0-3	2-0	0-0	1-0	0-0	9-6
Mahay, Ron	0-0	0-0	0-0	0-0	0-1	0-0	0-0	0-1	0-0	0-0	0-0	0-0	0-0	0-0	0-2
Park, Chan Ho	0-0	1-1	1-0	0-0	0-0	1-0	1-1	0-0	1-0	0-3	1-0	0-0	0-0	2-0	8-5
Regilio, Nick	0-0	0-0	1-0	0-0	0-1	0-0	0-0	0-0	0-0	0-0	0-1	0-0	0-0	0-0	1-2
Riley, Matt	0-0	0-0	0-0	0-0	0-0	0-0	0-0	0-0	0-0	0-0	1-0	0-0	0-0	0-0	1-0
Rodriguez, Ricardo	0-0	0-0	0-0	0-0	0-0	0-0	0-0	0-0	0-1	0-0	0-0	0-1	0-0	2-1	2-3
Rogers, Kenny	0-0	0-1	0-0	1-1	1-0	3-0	0-1	1-0	0-0	4-0	1-2	0-2	1-1	2-0	14-8
Rupe, Josh	0-0	0-0	0-0	0-0	0-0	0-0	0-0	0-0	0-0	0-0	1-0	0-0	0-0	0-0	1-0
Shouse, Brian	0-0	0-0	0-0	0-0	0-0	0-0	1-1	0-1	0-0	1-0	1-0	0-0	0-0	0-0	3-2
Volquez, Edison	0-1	0-0	0-1	0-0	0-0	0-1	0-1	0-0	0-0	0-0	0-0	0-0	0-0	0-0	0-4
Wasdin, John	1-0	0-0	0-0	0-0	0-0	0-0	0-0	1-0	0-0	0-2	1-0	0-0	0-0	0-0	3-2
Wilson, C.J.	0-2	0-0	1-0	0-1	0-0	0-0	0-1	0-0	0-1	0-0	0-0	0-0	0-1	0-1	1-7
Young, Chris	1-0	0-1	1-0	1-0	0-0	0-0	1-2	0-0	1-0	1-1	2-1	0-1	1-0	3-1	12-7
Totals	6-4	2-7	6-3	3-3	2-4	8-2	4-15	6-3	3-7	8-11	13-6	2-6	7-3	9-9	79-83

No-decisions-- Carlos Almanzar, Ryan Bukvich, Erasmo Ramirez, Jason Standridge, Michael Tejera, Justin Thompson.
INTERLEAGUE: Chris Young 1-0, Pedro Astacio 0-1, Chan Ho Park 1-0 vs. Braves; Juan Dominguez 0-1, Doug Brocail 0-1, Ricardo Rodriguez 1-0 vs. Marlins; Kenny Rogers 1-0, Chris Young 2-0, Chan Ho Park 1-0, Ricardo Rodriguez 0-1, Juan Dominguez 0-1 vs. Astros; Ryan Drese 0-1, Chris Young 0-1, Pedro Astacio 0-1 vs. Phillies; Kenny Rogers 1-0, Ricardo Rodriguez 1-0, C.J. Wilson 0-1 vs. Nationals. Total: 9-9.

TORONTO—80-82

Pitcher	Bal. W-L	Bos. W-L	Chi. W-L	Cle. W-L	Det. W-L	K.C. W-L	L.A. W-L	Min. W-L	N.Y. W-L	Oak. W-L	Sea. W-L	TB. W-L	Tex. W-L	N.L. W-L	Totals W-L
Batista, Miguel	0-0	2-1	0-0	0-0	0-1	1-0	1-0	0-0	0-1	0-1	0-1	1-2	0-1	0-0	5-8
Bush, Dave	1-2	0-3	1-0	0-0	0-1	1-0	0-0	0-2	1-1	0-0	0-1	1-1	0-0	0-0	5-11
Chacin, Gustavo	1-2	1-0	0-1	0-0	0-0	1-0	1-0	0-1	0-4	2-0	1-1	3-0	2-0	1-0	13-9
Chulk, Vinnie	0-0	0-0	0-0	0-0	0-0	0-0	0-0	0-0	0-1	0-0	0-0	0-0	0-0	0-0	0-1
Downs, Scott	0-0	1-0	0-0	1-0	1-0	0-0	0-0	0-0	1-1	0-0	0-0	0-0	0-2	0-0	4-3
Frasor, Jason	1-0	2-0	0-1	0-1	0-0	0-0	0-0	0-0	0-1	0-0	0-0	0-0	0-2	0-0	3-5
Gaudin, Chad	0-0	0-0	0-0	0-1	0-0	0-0	0-0	0-0	0-0	0-0	1-0	0-0	0-1	0-1	1-3
Halladay, Roy	1-2	2-0	0-0	1-0	1-0	0-0	1-0	1-0	1-0	0-0	0-0	1-0	1-0	2-2	12-4
League, Brandon	0-0	0-0	0-0	0-0	0-0	1-0	0-0	0-0	0-0	0-0	0-0	1-0	0-0	0-0	2-0
Lilly, Ted	1-1	3-0	0-1	0-1	0-0	1-0	0-0	0-0	1-2	1-1	1-1	1-1	0-1	2-2	10-11
McGowan, Dustin	0-1	0-0	0-0	0-1	1-1	0-0	0-0	0-0	0-0	0-0	0-0	0-0	0-0	0-0	1-3
Schoeneweis, Scott	1-0	0-0	0-0	0-0	0-1	0-0	0-0	0-0	0-0	0-0	0-0	1-2	0-0	1-1	3-4
Speier, Justin	0-1	0-0	0-1	0-0	1-0	0-0	0-0	0-0	0-0	0-0	1-0	0-0	0-0	1-0	3-2
Towers, Josh	2-0	0-1	1-0	0-0	0-1	2-0	1-0	1-1	0-2	1-1	2-0	3-1	0-1	0-4	13-12
Walker, Pete	2-0	0-2	0-0	0-0	0-0	0-2	1-1	0-0	2-0	0-0	0-0	0-1	0-0	1-0	6-6
Totals	10-9	11-7	2-4	2-4	3-4	6-3	5-1	2-4	6-12	5-5	6-4	11-8	3-7	8-10	80-82

No-decisions-- Shaun Marcum, Justin Miller, Matt Whiteside.
INTERLEAGUE: Gustavo Chacin 1-0, Scott Schoeneweis 1-0, Roy Halladay 0-1 vs. Cubs; Ted Lilly 0-1, Scott Schoeneweis 0-1, Josh Towers 0-1 vs. Astros; Pete Walker 1-0, Roy Halladay 0-1, Josh Towers 0-1 vs. Brewers; Roy Halladay 1-0, Chad Gaudin 0-1, Ted Lilly 1-0 vs. Cardinals; Ted Lilly 1-1, Roy Halladay 1-0, Justin Speier 1-0, Josh Towers 0-2 vs. Nationals. Total: 8-10.

HOME RUNS BY PARKS

	At Bal.	At Bos.	At CWS.	At Cle.	At Det.	At KC.	At LAA.	At Min.	At NYY.	At Oak.	At Sea.	At TB.	At Tex.	At Tor.	At N.L. Parks	Totals 2005	Totals 2004	HR Allow.
Baltimore	93	10	5	0	3	7	1	3	7	1	7	15	4	19	14	189	169	180
Boston	5	92	7	8	7	2	3	2	11	2	6	17	8	10	19	199	222	164
Chicago	6	8	115	5	12	8	3	6	2	4	5	0	5	8	13	200	242	167
Cleveland	2	6	16	91	15	13	8	14	5	3	8	9	2	6	9	207	184	157
Detroit	8	5	10	6	89	9	9	9	1	3	1	7	1	4	6	168	201	193
Kansas City	4	5	10	14	12	51	5	10	1	0	1	2	1	5	5	126	150	178
Los Angeles	0	5	11	0	1	0	71	4	7	10	12	3	15	1	7	147	162	158
Minnesota	2	4	6	6	8	4	2	67	2	6	2	5	1	4	15	134	191	169
New York	12	14	0	7	2	2	8	2	126	10	11	11	9	10	5	229	242	164
Oakland	16	4	5	2	7	5	5	3	2	71	7	5	11	5	7	155	189	154
Seattle	1	1	3	3	3	4	6	7	5	7	63	3	7	10	7	130	136	179
Tampa Bay	9	8	6	10	5	2	8	3	10	1	1	71	3	10	10	157	145	194
Texas	8	0	2	3	3	15	8	9	11	15	10	7	153	2	14	260	227	159
Toronto	5	8	3	3	4	2	1	2	6	7	5	6	4	76	4	136	145	185
N.L. clubs	9	1	14	11	4	7	7	7	10	6	2	4	9	9		100	129	...
2005 Totals	180	171	213	169	175	131	145	148	206	146	141	165	233	179	135	2437	....	2401
2004 Totals	168	188	272	164	182	146	171	172	215	184	179	168	213	173	....	....	2605	....

2005 A.L. STATISTICS Miscellaneous

AT BALTIMORE (180):

Baltimore (93)—Tejada 16, Gibbons 13, Mora 13, J. Lopez 12, Palmeiro 11, Roberts 9, Sosa 4, Bigbie 3, Matos 3, Byrnes 2, Fasano 1, Fiorentino 1, Gil 1, Marrero 1, Newhan 1, Rogers 1, Surhoff 1. Boston (5)—M. Ramirez 2, Damon 1, Nixon 1, Varitek 1. Chicago (6)—Pierzynski 2, Crede 1, Dye 1, Everett 1, Konerko 1. Cleveland (2)—Broussard 1, Hafner 1. Colorado (3)—Garabito 1, Helton 1, Wilson 1. Detroit (8)—Monroe 3, Young 3, Infante 2. Houston (3)—Lane 2, Ensberg 1. Kansas City (4)—Sweeney 2, Berroa 1, Stairs 1. Minnesota (2)—Jones 1, Stewart 1. New York (12)—Sheffield 3, Giambi 2, Matsui 2, A. Rodriguez 2, Cano 1, Jeter 1, Sierra 1. Oakland (16)—Ellis 3, Swisher 3, Chavez 2, Crosby 2, Byrnes 1, Ginter 1, Hatteberg 1, Johnson 1, Payton 1, Scutaro 1. Philadelphia (3)—Burrell 1, Lieberthal 1, Utley 1. Seattle (1)—Reed 1. Tampa Bay (9)—Cantu 2, Crawford 2, Gomes 2, Hall 1, Huff 1, Perez 1. Texas (8)—Matthews Jr. 3, Soriano 2, Barajas 1, Dellucci 1, Teixeira 1. Toronto (5)—Zaun 2, Hillenbrand 1, Koskie 1, Rios 1.

AT BOSTON (171):

Baltimore (10)—Gibbons 2, Tejada 2, Freire 1, Gil 1, J. Lopez 1, Newhan 1, Sosa 1, Surhoff 1. Boston (92)—M. Ramirez 22, Ortiz 20, Millar 8, Varitek 7, Mueller 6, Nixon 5, Olerud 5, Mirabelli 4, Bellhorn 3, Damon 3, Graffanino 3, Renteria 3, Payton 2, Petagine 1. Chicago (8)—Konerko 3, Dye 1, Everett 1, Iguchi 1, Rowand 1, Uribe 1. Cincinnati (1)—Valentin 1. Cleveland (6)—Hafner 2, Blake 1, Boone 1, Martinez 1, Sizemore 1. Detroit (5)—Granderson 1, Inge 1, Ordonez 1, Rodriguez 1, Young 1. Kansas City (5)—Sweeney 2, Ambres 1, Brown 1, Stairs 1. Los Angeles (5)—Figgins 2, Anderson 1, Cabrera 1, B. Molina 1. Minnesota (4)—Jones 2, Mauer 1, Morneau 1. New York (14)—A. Rodriguez 4, Sheffield 3, Giambi 2, Williams 2, Jeter 1, Matsui 1, Posada 1. Oakland (4)—Chavez 2, Byrnes 1, Scutaro 1. Seattle (1)—Sexson 1. Tampa Bay (8)—Lee 2, Perez 2, Crawford 1, Gomes 1, Huff 1, Lugo 1. Toronto (8)—Catalanotto 2, Wells 2, Hinske 1, Johnson 1, Koskie 1, Zaun 1.

AT CHICAGO (213):

Arizona (9)—Glaus 2, S. Green 2, Clark 1, L. Gonzalez 1, Snyder 1, Stinnett 1, Tracy 1. Baltimore (5)—Fasano 1, Gibbons 1, Newhan 1, Palmeiro 1, Surhoff 1. Boston (7)—M. Ramirez 2, Varitek 2, Damon 1, Ortiz 1, Stern 1. Chicago (4)—Dubois 1, Hollandsworth 1, Patterson 1, Ramirez 1. Chicago (115)—Konerko 23, Dye 15, Everett 15, Crede 12, Pierzynski 10, Uribe 10, Thomas 9, Rowand 8, Iguchi 7, Widger 2, Harris 1, Perez 1. Cleveland (16)—Hafner 6, Blake 3, Crisp 3, Boone 2, Belliard 1, Martinez 1, Sizemore 1. Detroit (10)—Infante 2, Inge 2, Monroe 2, Polanco 1, Rodriguez 1, Shelton 1, White 1. Kansas City (10)—Buck 2, Sweeney 2, Berroa 1, Brown 1, Gotay 1, Graffanino 1, Long 1, Marrero 1. Los Angeles (11)—Anderson 3, Figgins 2, Finley 2, Erstad 1, Guerrero 1, McPherson 1, Quinlan 1. Los Angeles (1)—Kent 1. Minnesota (6)—LeCroy 2, Cuddyer 1, Jones 1, Mauer 1, Morneau 1. Oakland (5)—Kotsay 2, Chavez 1, Johnson 1, Swisher 1. Seattle (3)—Ibanez 1, Sexson 1, Suzuki 1. Tampa Bay (6)—Crawford 2, Huff 2, Cantu 1, Green 1. Texas (2)—Mench 2. Toronto (3)—Adams 2, Hudson 1.

AT CLEVELAND (169):

Arizona (3)—Clayton 1, Counsell 1, Cruz Jr. 1. Boston (8)—Ortiz 2, M. Ramirez 2, Damon 1, Olerud 1, Renteria 1, Varitek 1. Chicago (5)—Iguchi 1, Dye 1, Konerko 1, Pierzynski 1. Cincinnati (7)—Griffey Jr. 2, LaRue 1, F. Lopez 1, Randa 1, Romano 1, Valentin 1. Cleveland (91)—Hafner 14, Peralta 14, Broussard 11, Martinez 10, Sizemore 10, Belliard 7, Blake 7, Boone 5, Crisp 4, Hernandez 2, Ludwick 2, Cora 1, Dubois 1, Gerut 1. Colorado (1)—Shealy 1. Detroit (6)—Monroe 1, Ordonez 1, Pena 1, Rodriguez 1, White 1, Young 1. Kansas City (14)—Brown 2, Buck 2, Marrero 2, Sweeney 2, Berroa 1, DeJesus 1, Harvey 1, Long 1, Murphy 1, Teahen 1. Minnesota (6)—Hunter 2, Ford 1, Jones 1, Morneau 1, Stewart 1. New York (7)—Giambi 2, A. Rodriguez 2, Flaherty 1, Martinez 1, Posada 1. Oakland (2)—Kotsay 1, Swisher 1. Seattle (3)—Beltre 1, Sexson 1, Suzuki 1. Tampa Bay (10)—Cantu 3, Lee 2, Lugo 2, Gomes 1, Gonzalez 1, Huff 1. Texas (3)—Barajas 1, Nevin 1, M. Young 1. Toronto (3)—Rios 2, Wells 1.

AT DETROIT (175):

Baltimore (3)—Mora 1, Palmeiro 1, Tejada 1. Boston (7)—Ortiz 3, Varitek 2, Cora 1, Mirabelli 1. Chicago (12)—Crede 3, Konerko 3, Dye 2, Everett 1, Rowand 1, Thomas 1, Uribe 1. Cleveland (15)—Blake 4, Boone 3, Crisp 2, Sizemore 2, Belliard 1, Hafner 1, Hernandez 1, Peralta 1. Detroit (89)—Pena 14, Inge 10, Shelton 10, Young 10, Monroe 9, Rodriguez 8, White 7, Granderson 5, Polanco 4, Guillen 3, Infante 3, Thames 3, Ordonez 2, Wilson 1. Kansas City (12)—Stairs 2, Sweeney 2, Berroa 1, Brown 1, Buck 1, DeJesus 1, Guiel 1, McEwing 1, Pickering 1, Teahen 1. Los Angeles (1)—Rivera 1. Minnesota (8)—Morneau 2, Bartlett 1, Castro 1, Jones 1, LeCroy 1, Mauer 1, Rivas 1. New York (2)—Matsui 1, Williams 1. Oakland (7)—Ellis 2, Chavez 1, Crosby 1, Johnson 1, Kotsay 1, Payton 1. San Diego (2)—Roberts 1, Sweeney 1. San Francisco (2)—Linden 1, Niekro 1. Seattle (3)—Beltre 2, Ibanez 1. Tampa Bay (5)—Green 1, Hall 1, Hollins 1, Lugo 1, Phelps 1. Texas (3)—Mench 2, Hidalgo 1. Toronto (4)—Hinske 2, Koskie 1, Wells 1.

AT KANSAS CITY (131):

Baltimore (7)—Mora 2, Fasano 1, Gibbons 1, Newhan 1, Palmeiro 1, Roberts 1. Boston (2)—Millar 1, Varitek 1. Chicago (8)—Crede 2, Dye 2, Uribe 2, Iguchi 1, Pierzynski 1. Cleveland (13)—Crisp 2, Hafner 2, Peralta 2, Sizemore 2, Belliard 1, Blake 1, Broussard 1, Liefer 1, Martinez 1. Detroit (9)—Monroe 2, Shelton 2, Granderson 1, Pena 1, Rodriguez 1, White 1, Wilson 1. Houston (2)—Bruntlett 1, Ensberg 1. Kansas City (51)—Brown 8, Sweeney 7, Berroa 6, DeJesus 6, Stairs 5, Buck 3, Guiel 3, Teahen 3, Ambres 2, Gotay 2, Long 2, Castillo 1, Costa 1, Graffanino 1, Marrero 1. Los Angeles (3)—Choi 1, Drew 1, Grabowski 1. Minnesota (4)—LeCroy 1, Morneau 1, Punto 1. New York (2)—Matsui 1, Williams 1. Oakland (5)—Johnson 2, Melhuse 1, Payton 1, Swisher 1. St. Louis (2)—Mabry 1, Walker 1. Seattle (4)—Beltre 2, Ibanez 1, Sexson 1. Tampa Bay (2)—Gonzalez 1, Lugo 1. Texas (15)—Barajas 5, Dellucci 2, Teixeira 2, Gonzalez 1, Laird 1, Mench 1, Nix 1, Soriano 1, M. Young 1. Toronto (2)—Hinske 1, Wells 1.

AT LOS ANGELES (145):

Baltimore (1)—Sosa 1. Boston (3)—Mueller 1, M. Ramirez 1, Renteria 1. Chicago (3)—Everett 1, Konerko 1, Widger 1. Cleveland (8)—Belliard 2, Crisp 2, Peralta 2, Blake 1, Broussard 1. Detroit (9)—Thames 2, Granderson 1, Inge 1, Monroe 1, Ordonez 1, Pena 1, Polanco 1, Shelton 1. Florida (2)—Cabrera 1, Conine 1. Kansas City (5)—Brown 1, Buck 1, Gotay 1, Stairs 1, Teahen 1. Los Angeles (71)—Guerrero 19, B. Molina 8, Rivera 8, McPherson 6, Anderson 5, Kotchman 5, Erstad 4, Finley 3, Quinlan 3, Cabrera 2, Figgins 2, J. Molina 2, Paul 2, DaVanon 1, Kennedy 1. Los Angeles (3)—Werth 3. Minnesota (3)—Jones 1, Redmond 1. New York (3)—Giambi 3, Matsui 2, Cano 1, Jeter 1, A. Rodriguez 1. Oakland (3)—Kielty 2, Ellis 1, Johnson 1, Kotsay 1. Seattle (6)—Sexson 2, Winn 2, Ibanez 1, Olivo 1. Tampa Bay (8)—Huff 3, Gomes 2, Cantu 1, Gonzalez 1, Lee 1. Texas (8)—Dellucci 2, Soriano 2, Blalock 1, Hidalgo 1, Teixeira 1, M. Young 1. Toronto (1)—Hillenbrand 1. Washington (2)—Guillen 1, Schneider 1.

AT MINNESOTA (148):

Baltimore (3)—Palmeiro 1, Sosa 1, Tejada 1. Boston (3)—Kapler 1, M. Ramirez 1. Chicago (6)—Everett 2, Konerko 2, Perez 1, Rowand 1. Cleveland (14)—Broussard 4, Hafner 3, Blake 2, Martinez 2, Bard 1, Crisp 1, Sizemore 1. Detroit (9)—Inge 2, Shelton 2, Infante 1, Monroe 1, Pena 1, White 1, Young 1. Kansas City (10)—Buck 2, Sweeney 2, Berroa 1, Brown 1, Costa 1, DeJesus 1, Diaz 1, Teahen 1. Los Angeles (4)—Cabrera 1, DaVanon 1, Guerrero 1, J. Molina 1. Milwaukee (3)—Clark 1, Lee 1, Miller 1. Minnesota (67)—LeCroy 10, Jones 9, Morneau 9, Cuddyer 8, Ford 6, Hunter 6, Mauer 4, Stewart 4, Punto 3, Bartlett 2, Castro 2, Abernathy 1, Rodriguez 1, Ryan 1, Tiffee 1. New York (2)—Cano 1, Sheffield 1. Oakland (3)—Johnson 2, Chavez 1. San Diego (2)—Klesko 1, Roberts 1. San Francisco (2)—Durham 1, Vizquel 1. Seattle (7)—Beltre 2, Sexson 2, Dobbs 1, Ibanez 1, Reed 1. Tampa Bay (3)—Cantu 1, Huff 1, Lee 1. Texas (9)—M. Young 2, Dellucci 1, Gonzalez 1, Hidalgo 1, Matthews Jr. 1, Mench 1, Soriano 1, Teixeira 1. Toronto (2)—Hudson 1, Wells 1.

AT NEW YORK (206):

Baltimore (7)—Roberts 3, Gibbons 2, Gomez 1, Mora 1. Boston (11)—Ortiz 3, Renteria 2, Varitek 2, Nixon 1, Olerud 1, Payton 1, M. Ramirez 1. Chicago (2)—Burnitz 1, Dubois 1. Chicago (2)—Iguchi 1, Konerko 1. Cleveland (5)—Hernandez 2, Peralta 2, Sizemore 1. Detroit (1)—Thames 1. Kansas City (1)—Sweeney 1. Los Angeles (7)—Anderson 2, B. Molina 2, Finley 1, J. Molina 1, Rivera 1. Minnesota (2)—Jones 1, Morneau 1. New York (5)—Floyd 3, Beltran 1, Wright 1. New York (126)—A. Rodriguez 26, Sheffield 19, Giambi 16, Matsui 15, Jeter 12, Posada 11, Martinez 9, Williams 7, Cano 5, Sierra 3, Crosby 1, Lawton 1, Phillips 1. Oakland (2)—Byrnes 1, Kielty 1. Pittsburgh (2)—Bay 1, Restovich 1, J. Wilson 1. Seattle (5)—Beltre 1, Boone 1, Ibanez 1, Sexson 1, Suzuki 1. Tampa Bay (10)—Cantu 2, Gomes 2, Perez 2, Cash 1, Green 1, Hollins 1, Huff 1. Texas (11)—Dellucci 3, Mench 2, Soriano 2, Teixeira 2, Barajas 1, M. Young 1. Toronto (6)—Hinske 2, Koskie 2, Wells 2.

AT OAKLAND (146):

Baltimore (1)—Matos 1. Boston (2)—Bellhorn 1, Varitek 1. Chicago (4)—Crede 1, Dye 1, Thomas 1, Widger 1. Cleveland (3)—Boone 1, Peralta 1, Sizemore 1. Detroit (3)—Guillen 1, Ordonez 1, Wilson 1. Los Angeles (10)—Finley 3, Guerrero 3, Anderson 1, B. Molina 1, J. Molina 1, Quinlan 1. Minnesota (6)—Cuddyer 2, Morneau 2, Jones 1, Ryan 1. New York (2)—Beltran 1, Piazza 1. New York (10)—Martinez 3, Jeter 2, Bellhorn 1, Giambi 1, Posada 1, A. Rodriguez 1, Sheffield 1. Oakland (71)—Chavez 15, Swisher 11, Payton 9, Kielty 6, Ellis 5, Scutaro 5, Hatteberg 4, Kotsay 4, Byrnes 3, Crosby 3, Durazo 3, Johnson 2, Melhuse 1. Philadelphia (1)—Rollins 1. San Francisco (3)—Alou 1, Feliz 1, Matheny 1. Seattle (7)—Boone 2, Sexson 2, Beltre 1, Ibanez 1, Suzuki 1. Tampa Bay (1)—Hollins 1. Texas (15)—Teixeira 3, Blalock 2, Hidalgo 2, Mench 2, Soriano 1, M. Young 2, Barajas 1, Dellucci 1. Toronto (7)—Wells 2, Catalanotto 1, Hinske 1, Johnson 1, Rios 1, Zaun 1.

AT SEATTLE (141):

Baltimore (7)—Fasano 2, Gibbons 2, Mora 2, Palmeiro 1. Boston (6)—Nixon 2, M. Ramirez 2, Bellhorn 1, Ortiz 1. Chicago (5)—Anderson 2, Dye 1, Everett 1, Iguchi 1. Cleveland (8)—Belliard 2, Martinez 2, Blake 1, Boone 1, Dubois 1, Sizemore 1. Detroit (1)—Young 1. Kansas City (1)—Phillips 1. Los Angeles (12)—Guerrero 4, Finley 2, B. Molina 2, Anderson 1, Figgins 1, Kotchman 1, Rivera 1. Minnesota (2)—Jones 1, LeCroy 1. New York (1)—Floyd 1. New York (11)—A. Rodriguez 4, Giambi 3, Cano 1, Lawton 1, Sheffield 1, Williams 1. Oakland (7)—Kotsay 2, Durazo 1, Ellis 1, Johnson 1, Kielty 1, Swisher 1. San Diego (1)—Hernandez 1. Seattle (63)—Sexson 21, Ibanez 9, Suzuki 8, Beltre 7, Olivo 4, Morse 3, Boone 2, Hansen 2, Winn 2, Betancourt 1, Lopez 1, Ojeda 1, Snelling 1, Torrealba 1. Tampa Bay (1)—Huff 1. Texas (10)—Dellucci 4, Matthews Jr. 2, Blalock 1, Hidalgo 1, Nix 1, M. Young 1. Toronto (5)—Wells 2, Hillenbrand 1, Hudson 1, Johnson 1.

AT TAMPA BAY (165):

Baltimore (15)—Mora 4, Fasano 3, Sosa 2, Tejada 2, Bigbie 1, Gibbons 1, J. Lopez 1, Roberts 1. Boston (17)—Ortiz 6, M. Ramirez 5, Damon 2, Cora 1, Nixon 1, Payton 1, Varitek 1. Cleveland (9)—Martinez 2, Belliard 1, Blake 1, Broussard 1, Crisp 1, Hafner 1, Peralta 1, Sizemore 1. Detroit (7)—Shelton 2, Young 2, Monroe 1, Ordonez 1, Rodriguez 1. Kansas City (2)—Ambres 1, Long 1. Los Angeles (3)—Cabrera 1, Izturis 1, Kotchman 1. Milwaukee (3)—Clark 1, Moeller 1, Overbay 1. Minnesota (5)—Mauer 2, Morneau 2, LeCroy 1. New York (11)—A. Rodriguez 3, Sheffield 3, Martinez 2, Cano 1, Giambi 1, Posada 1. Oakland (5)—Hatteberg 2, Ginter 1, Kotsay 1, Scutaro 1. St. Louis (1)—Pujols 1. Seattle (3)—Boone 1, Borders 1, Reed 1. Tampa Bay (71)—Cantu 16, Gomes 11, Huff 9, Crawford 5, Hollins 5, Lee 5, Perez 5, Gonzalez 4, Phelps 4, Green 2, Sanchez 2, Cash 1, Hall 1, LaForest 1. Texas (7)—Barajas 2, Matthews Jr. 2, Mench 1, Soriano 1, Teixeira 1. Toronto (6)—Wells 2, Adams 1, Hinske 1, Hudson 1, Koskie 1.

AT TEXAS (233):

Atlanta (3)—Franco 1, Johnson 1, A. Jones 1. Baltimore (4)—Gibbons 1, Newhan 1, Roberts 1, Young 1. Boston (8)—Ortiz 2, M. Ramirez 2, Damon 1, Mueller 1, Nixon 1, Varitek 1. Chicago (5)—Dye 2, Blum 1, Konerko 1, Pierzynski 1. Cleveland (2)—Hafner 1, Peralta 1. Detroit (1)—Thames 1. Houston (2)—Ensberg 1, Everett 1. Kansas City (1)—Stairs 1. Los Angeles (15)—Anderson 4, Guerrero 3, Cabrera 2, Rivera 2, Erstad 1, Figgins 1, Kennedy 1, McPherson 1. Minnesota (1)—Jones 1. New York (9)—Giambi 2, Martinez 2, Posada 2, Cano 1, Matsui 1, Sheffield 1. Oakland (11)—Johnson 3, Chavez 2, Swisher 2, Ellis 1, Kotsay 1, Payton 1, Scutaro 1. Seattle (7)—Suzuki 3, Sexson 2, Beltre 1, Ibanez 1. Tampa Bay (3)—Gonzalez 1, Hollins 1, Huff 1. Texas (153)—Teixeira 30, Soriano 25, Blalock 20, Dellucci 14, Mench 10, M. Young 12, Hidalgo 9, Matthews Jr. 8, Barajas 7, DeRosa 7, Gonzalez 3, Nix 3, Nevin 2. Toronto (4)—Catalanotto 2, Hillenbrand 2. Washington (2)—Church 2, Guzman 2.

AT TORONTO (179):

Baltimore (19)—Gibbons 3, Gil 2, Marrero 2, Mora 2, Roberts 2, Sosa 2, Tejada 2, Byrnes 1, J. Lopez 1, Palmeiro 1, Surhoff 1. Boston (10)—Ortiz 5, Graffanino 1, Mueller 1, Nixon 1, M. Ramirez 1, Varitek 1. Chicago (8)—Dye 2, Konerko 2, Uribe 2, Iguchi 1, Rowand 1. Cleveland (6)—Hafner 2, Belliard 1, Blake 1, Boone 1, Martinez 1. Detroit (4)—Guillen 1, Ordonez 1, White 1, Young 1. Kansas City (5)—Brown 2, Long 1, Stairs 1, Sweeney 1. Los Angeles (1)—Guerrero 1. Milwaukee (3)—Hall 1, Jenkins 1, Lee 1. Minnesota (4)—Castro 2, Stewart 2. New York (10)—A. Rodriguez 3, Cano 2, Sheffield 2, Flaherty 1, Jeter 1, Posada 1. Oakland (5)—Byrnes 1, Crosby 1, Johnson 1, Kotsay 1, Swisher 1. St. Louis (5)—Walker 2, Mabry 1, Pujols 1, Sanders 1. Seattle (10)—Sexson 3, Beltre 2, Ibanez 1, Lopez 1, Spiezio 1, Torrealba 1, Winn 1. Tampa Bay (10)—Crawford 2, Gomes 2, Hollins 2, Cantu 1, Huff 1, Lee 1, Lugo 1. Texas (2)—Gonzalez 1, Matthews Jr. 1. Toronto (76)—Wells 14, Hillenbrand 13, Hinske 7, Zaun 7, Adams 5, Koskie 5, Rios 5, Hudson 4, Johnson 4, Menechino 4, Catalanotto 3, Hill 3, Griffin 1, Gross 1. Washington (1)—Blanco 1.

This section contains selected batting statistics for all American League parks for 2005. A key component of this section is an index number for each category, which is used to determine how a given park influences a particular statistic. For example, Chicago's U.S. Cellular Field has had a reputation as being pitcher-friendly, but last year's park index of 131 for home runs was the highest in the A.L. for a second straight year. The park has boosted homers, especially for righthanded batters, since the outfield fences were moved in in 2001.

For each A.L. park, we show how the home team and its opponents performed, both at home and on the road, with the exception being that we do not include data from interleague games. The differences in interleague opponents and ballparks would skew the data.

By comparing the per-game averages at the home park and on the road, we can evaluate the park's impact. This is done by simply dividing the home average by the road average and multiplying the result by 100, generating a park index. If the home and road per-game averages are equal, the index equals 100, and it can be concluded that the park had no impact. An index above 100 means that the park favors that particular statistic. The indexes for at-bats, runs, hits, errors and infield errors are determined on a per-game basis; all other stats are calculated on a per-at-bat basis. "E-infield" denotes infield *fielding* errors. "Alt." is the approximate elevation of the ballpark.

For most parks, data is presented both for 2005 and for the last three years overall. If the park's dimensions have changed over that time, however, the data from the old and new configurations will not be combined. Following all the teams' charts is a ranking section that shows which parks most inflate runs, home runs and batting average.

BALTIMORE

Home park: Oriole Park at Camden Yards   **Alt.:** 20 feet   **Surface:** Grass

| | 2005 Season | | | | | | | 2003-05 Seasons | | | | | | |
| | Home Games | | | Road Games | | | | Home Games | | | Road Games | | | |
Category	Bal.	Opp.	Total	Bal.	Opp.	Total	Index	Bal.	Opp.	Total	Bal.	Opp.	Total	Index
G	72	72	144	72	72	144		216	216	432	217	217	434	
Avg	.258	.261	.259	.277	.266	.271	96	.272	.265	.268	.274	.270	.272	99
AB	2395	2512	4907	2552	2423	4975	99	7291	7626	14917	7731	7328	15059	100
R	287	356	643	368	357	725	89	987	1097	2084	1097	1059	2156	97
H	618	655	1273	706	644	1350	94	1984	2021	4005	2119	1976	4095	98
2B	110	108	218	149	123	272	81	383	345	728	414	372	786	94
3B	12	5	17	11	14	25	69	22	25	47	34	43	77	62
HR	83	78	161	82	80	162	101	225	247	472	223	230	453	105
BB	233	273	506	165	251	416	123	649	824	1473	607	770	1377	108
SO	350	473	823	443	465	908	92	1089	1384	2473	1313	1381	2694	93
E	48	35	83	55	53	108	77	143	143	286	143	159	302	95
E-Infield	35	32	67	51	47	98	68	120	118	238	130	140	270	89
LHB-Avg	.239	.271	.257	.300	.288	.294	87	.257	.277	.268	.288	.272	.280	96
LHB-HR	31	34	65	34	35	69	93	82	116	198	93	105	198	100
RHB-Avg	.269	.252	.261	.262	.250	.256	102	.283	.255	.269	.264	.268	.266	101
RHB-HR	52	44	96	48	45	93	107	143	131	274	130	125	255	110

BOSTON

Home park: Fenway Park   **Alt.:** 21 feet   **Surface:** Grass

| | 2005 Season | | | | | | | 2003-05 Seasons | | | | | | |
| | Home Games | | | Road Games | | | | Home Games | | | Road Games | | | |
Category	Bos.	Opp.	Total	Bos.	Opp.	Total	Index	Bos.	Opp.	Total	Bos.	Opp.	Total	Index
G	72	72	144	72	72	144		216	216	432	216	216	432	
Avg	.277	.278	.277	.279	.282	.280	99	.297	.264	.280	.265	.267	.266	105
AB	2411	2584	4995	2577	2448	5025	99	7425	7667	15092	7721	7385	15106	100
R	429	366	795	376	369	745	107	1343	1059	2402	1122	1060	2182	110
H	667	718	1385	719	690	1409	98	2208	2024	4232	2048	1972	4020	105
2B	166	188	354	128	135	263	135	537	498	1035	404	408	812	128
3B	5	16	21	9	20	29	73	30	45	75	31	56	87	86
HR	85	78	163	88	77	165	99	282	208	490	294	212	506	97
BB	301	206	507	286	195	481	106	880	593	1473	813	628	1441	102
SO	457	422	879	470	416	886	100	1331	1421	2752	1484	1432	2916	94
E	49	50	99	52	48	100	99	157	147	304	144	125	269	113
E-Infield	42	45	87	44	37	81	107	135	128	263	120	102	222	118
LHB-Avg	.277	.284	.281	.285	.268	.277	101	.296	.265	.280	.262	.259	.261	108
LHB-HR	42	33	75	53	35	88	84	127	89	216	153	102	255	83
RHB-Avg	.276	.272	.274	.273	.294	.284	97	.299	.263	.280	.268	.275	.271	103
RHB-HR	43	45	88	35	42	77	118	155	119	274	141	110	251	112

CHICAGO

Home park: U.S. Cellular Field   **Alt.:** 595 feet   **Surface:** Grass

Category	2005 Season — Home Games Chi.	Opp.	Total	Road Games Chi.	Opp.	Total	Index	2003-05 Seasons — Home Games Chi.	Opp.	Total	Road Games Chi.	Opp.	Total	Index
G	72	72	144	72	72	144		216	216	432	216	216	432	
Avg	.261	.256	.258	.264	.247	.256	101	.265	.261	.263	.263	.255	.259	102
AB	2375	2531	4906	2548	2456	5004	98	7154	7527	14681	7575	7164	14739	100
R	321	303	624	322	276	598	104	1074	974	2048	1027	963	1990	103
H	620	647	1267	672	607	1279	99	1898	1966	3864	1994	1827	3821	101
2B	113	120	233	114	134	248	96	359	366	725	383	379	762	96
3B	10	10	20	12	13	25	82	28	31	59	30	34	64	93
HR	99	84	183	72	62	134	139	335	273	608	244	209	453	135
BB	201	211	412	189	199	388	108	651	649	1300	617	696	1313	99
SO	427	471	898	447	446	893	103	1227	1461	2688	1337	1302	2639	102
E	35	33	68	51	42	93	73	107	124	231	150	136	286	81
E-Infield	29	29	58	42	34	76	76	86	109	195	129	114	243	80
LHB-Avg	.257	.277	.269	.257	.239	.247	109	.250	.273	.265	.257	.257	.257	103
LHB-HR	23	44	67	11	29	40	163	73	132	205	61	97	158	131
RHB-Avg	.263	.237	.251	.267	.254	.261	96	.271	.251	.262	.266	.253	.261	101
RHB-HR	76	40	116	61	33	94	129	262	141	403	183	112	295	137

CLEVELAND

Home park: Jacobs Field   **Alt.:** 660 feet   **Surface:** Grass

Category	2005 Season — Home Games Cle.	Opp.	Total	Road Games Cle.	Opp.	Total	Index	2003-05 Seasons — Home Games Cle.	Opp.	Total	Road Games Cle.	Opp.	Total	Index
G	72	72	144	72	72	144		216	216	432	216	216	432	
Avg	.260	.238	.249	.276	.258	.268	93	.259	.255	.257	.273	.269	.271	95
AB	2389	2447	4836	2595	2455	5050	96	7209	7551	14760	7746	7382	15128	98
R	308	268	576	376	319	695	83	962	963	1925	1110	1089	2199	88
H	622	582	1204	717	634	1351	89	1869	1922	3791	2111	1984	4095	93
2B	146	119	265	146	122	268	103	434	399	833	415	405	820	104
3B	7	5	12	18	9	27	46	26	28	54	49	37	86	64
HR	76	67	143	107	72	179	83	201	214	415	298	264	562	76
BB	237	169	406	216	205	421	101	731	647	1378	666	684	1350	105
SO	464	459	923	512	447	959	101	1358	1427	2785	1445	1287	2732	104
E	50	51	101	47	43	90	112	145	179	324	154	123	277	117
E-Infield	39	41	80	42	36	78	103	118	147	265	136	103	239	111
LHB-Avg	.268	.244	.258	.296	.270	.285	90	.266	.254	.261	.281	.272	.277	94
LHB-HR	41	21	62	52	28	80	82	121	85	206	157	107	264	79
RHB-Avg	.253	.234	.243	.257	.251	.254	95	.252	.255	.253	.264	.267	.265	96
RHB-HR	35	46	81	55	44	99	84	80	129	209	141	157	298	72

DETROIT

Home park: Comerica Park   **Alt.:** 585 feet   **Surface:** Grass

Category	2005 Season — Home Games Det.	Opp.	Total	Road Games Det.	Opp.	Total	Index	2004-05 Seasons — Home Games Det.	Opp.	Total	Road Games Det.	Opp.	Total	Index
G	72	72	144	72	72	144		144	144	288	144	144	288	
Avg	.279	.273	.276	.269	.274	.272	102	.275	.275	.275	.270	.276	.273	101
AB	2461	2552	5013	2529	2376	4905	102	4905	5130	10035	5080	4801	9881	102
R	321	346	667	326	370	696	96	656	728	1384	725	739	1464	95
H	687	697	1384	680	652	1332	104	1350	1412	2762	1371	1323	2694	103
2B	107	112	219	142	118	260	82	206	242	448	288	246	534	83
3B	26	19	45	12	13	25	176	59	40	99	24	24	48	203
HR	81	82	163	73	95	168	95	157	170	327	178	180	358	90
BB	171	209	380	172	197	369	101	401	443	844	401	426	827	100
SO	424	426	850	485	374	859	97	886	876	1762	1036	795	1831	95
E	49	49	98	50	35	85	115	107	81	188	122	83	205	92
E-Infield	42	44	86	45	24	69	125	86	71	157	102	63	165	95
LHB-Avg	.277	.293	.287	.257	.273	.267	108	.268	.276	.272	.258	.267	.263	104
LHB-HR	32	29	61	14	38	52	118	66	63	129	63	67	130	98
RHB-Avg	.280	.260	.271	.273	.275	.274	99	.279	.274	.277	.276	.281	.279	99
RHB-HR	49	53	102	59	57	116	85	91	107	198	115	113	228	85

KANSAS CITY

Home park: Ewing M. Kauffman Stadium   **Alt.:** 750 feet   **Surface:** Grass

| Category | 2005 Season | | | | | | | 2004-05 Seasons | | | | | | |
| | Home Games | | | Road Games | | | | Home Games | | | Road Games | | | |
	K.C.	Opp.	Total	K.C.	Opp.	Total	Index	K.C.	Opp.	Total	K.C.	Opp.	Total	Index
G	72	72	144	72	72	144		143	143	286	145	145	290	
Avg	.266	.292	.279	.249	.296	.272	103	.265	.288	.277	.253	.296	.274	101
AB	2403	2601	5004	2450	2404	4854	103	4759	5131	9890	5022	4908	9930	101
R	313	412	725	287	428	715	101	626	790	1416	623	861	1484	97
H	639	759	1398	610	711	1321	106	1263	1476	2739	1272	1452	2724	102
2B	137	172	309	119	140	259	116	242	335	577	250	299	549	106
3B	15	20	35	11	19	30	113	28	38	66	21	32	53	125
HR	45	73	118	70	87	157	73	96	157	253	153	193	346	73
BB	199	251	450	173	258	431	101	414	460	874	374	493	867	101
SO	397	420	817	498	391	889	89	810	838	1648	1030	761	1791	92
E	49	44	93	62	47	109	85	95	84	179	131	105	236	77
E-Infield	40	36	76	52	39	91	84	81	71	152	107	89	196	79
LHB-Avg	.260	.301	.282	.260	.296	.278	101	.259	.296	.279	.255	.309	.281	99
LHB-HR	18	30	48	23	39	62	72	39	58	97	53	79	132	73
RHB-Avg	.270	.284	.277	.241	.295	.268	103	.269	.282	.276	.252	.287	.270	102
RHB-HR	27	43	70	47	48	95	74	57	99	156	100	114	214	74

LOS ANGELES

Home park: Angel Stadium of Anaheim   **Alt.:** 160 feet   **Surface:** Grass

| Category | 2005 Season | | | | | | | 2003-05 Seasons | | | | | | |
| | Home Games | | | Road Games | | | | Home Games | | | Road Games | | | |
	L.A.	Opp.	Total	L.A.	Opp.	Total	Index	L.A.	Opp.	Total	L.A.	Opp.	Total	Index
G	72	72	144	72	72	144		217	217	434	215	215	430	
Avg	.265	.250	.257	.273	.264	.269	96	.274	.261	.267	.274	.265	.269	99
AB	2408	2540	4948	2589	2448	5037	98	7235	7661	14896	7628	7211	14839	99
R	322	289	611	353	306	659	93	999	932	1931	1080	985	2065	93
H	638	636	1274	706	647	1353	94	1979	1999	3978	2088	1911	3999	99
2B	117	138	255	134	118	252	103	350	398	748	396	369	765	97
3B	14	13	27	11	16	27	102	37	29	66	46	46	92	71
HR	63	67	130	69	78	147	90	195	226	421	206	235	441	95
BB	201	189	390	190	209	399	100	591	634	1225	628	651	1279	95
SO	375	501	876	393	493	886	101	1128	1497	2625	1206	1398	2604	100
E	44	54	98	33	55	88	111	133	127	260	114	154	268	96
E-Infield	34	46	80	28	45	73	110	103	107	210	96	129	225	92
LHB-Avg	.254	.263	.258	.277	.268	.273	95	.269	.263	.266	.284	.267	.275	97
LHB-HR	22	32	54	32	35	67	85	69	114	183	86	108	194	93
RHB-Avg	.277	.240	.257	.268	.261	.264	97	.277	.259	.268	.265	.263	.264	101
RHB-HR	41	35	76	37	43	80	93	126	112	238	120	127	247	97

MINNESOTA

Home park: Hubert H. Humphrey Metrodome   **Alt.:** 815 feet   **Surface:** Turf

| Category | 2005 Season | | | | | | | 2004-05 Seasons | | | | | | |
| | Home Games | | | Road Games | | | | Home Games | | | Road Games | | | |
	Min.	Opp.	Total	Min.	Opp.	Total	Index	Min.	Opp.	Total	Min.	Opp.	Total	Index
G	72	72	144	72	72	144		144	144	288	144	144	288	
Avg	.264	.246	.255	.251	.270	.260	98	.267	.257	.262	.258	.269	.263	100
AB	2388	2482	4870	2546	2470	5016	97	4837	5082	9919	5087	4931	10018	99
R	312	281	593	293	291	584	102	685	601	1286	620	611	1231	104
H	631	611	1242	639	666	1305	95	1291	1307	2598	1310	1327	2637	99
2B	113	106	219	120	122	242	93	250	212	462	257	238	495	94
3B	16	8	24	13	16	29	85	25	17	42	24	25	49	87
HR	59	74	133	52	72	124	110	142	148	290	141	146	287	102
BB	213	129	342	220	175	395	89	453	303	756	444	394	838	91
SO	431	451	882	428	396	824	110	851	988	1839	860	841	1701	109
E	43	59	102	48	49	97	105	89	100	189	92	100	192	98
E-Infield	38	52	90	39	43	82	110	79	88	167	77	85	162	103
LHB-Avg	.257	.250	.253	.260	.258	.259	98	.266	.254	.259	.256	.269	.262	100
LHB-HR	27	31	58	29	33	62	100	66	65	131	70	74	144	93
RHB-Avg	.269	.243	.257	.244	.278	.261	98	.268	.260	.264	.259	.269	.264	100
RHB-HR	32	43	75	23	39	62	121	76	83	159	71	72	143	111

2005 A.L. STATISTICS *Miscellaneous*

NEW YORK

Home park: Yankee Stadium   **Alt.:** 55 feet   **Surface:** Grass

Category	2005 Season Home Games N.Y.	Opp.	Total	Road Games N.Y.	Opp.	Total	Index	2003-05 Seasons Home Games N.Y.	Opp.	Total	Road Games N.Y.	Opp.	Total	Index
G	72	72	144	72	72	144		217	217	434	214	214	428	
Avg	.287	.276	.281	.267	.268	.267	105	.274	.268	.271	.270	.271	.271	100
AB	2446	2567	5013	2552	2389	4941	101	7242	7710	14952	7595	7285	14880	99
R	420	345	765	373	374	747	102	1163	1010	2173	1192	1058	2250	95
H	701	708	1409	681	640	1321	107	1981	2066	4047	2052	1976	4028	99
2B	109	119	228	119	141	260	86	343	388	731	404	434	838	87
3B	8	16	24	8	13	21	113	20	35	55	26	44	70	78
HR	116	70	186	98	76	174	105	321	215	536	304	209	513	104
BB	264	186	450	281	234	515	86	825	558	1383	903	607	1510	91
SO	444	467	911	437	405	842	107	1308	1481	2789	1354	1296	2650	105
E	43	56	99	40	49	89	111	138	158	296	129	134	263	111
E-Infield	38	52	90	35	41	76	118	119	130	249	113	116	229	107
LHB-Avg	.275	.276	.275	.266	.265	.266	104	.263	.272	.268	.267	.270	.269	100
LHB-HR	53	30	83	53	25	78	106	151	104	255	155	89	244	108
RHB-Avg	.301	.276	.287	.268	.270	.269	107	.284	.264	.274	.273	.272	.273	100
RHB-HR	63	40	103	45	51	96	104	170	111	281	149	120	269	100

OAKLAND

Home park: McAfee Coliseum   **Alt.:** 25 feet   **Surface:** Grass

Category	2005 Season Home Games Oak.	Opp.	Total	Road Games Oak.	Opp.	Total	Index	2003-05 Seasons Home Games Oak.	Opp.	Total	Road Games Oak.	Opp.	Total	Index
G	72	72	144	72	72	144		216	216	432	216	216	432	
Avg	.264	.243	.254	.257	.242	.249	102	.260	.241	.251	.260	.254	.257	97
AB	2454	2495	4949	2570	2380	4950	100	7278	7480	14758	7719	7197	14916	99
R	343	319	662	344	276	620	107	996	871	1867	1051	920	1971	95
H	649	607	1256	660	575	1235	102	1892	1805	3697	2004	1830	3834	96
2B	147	116	263	124	114	238	111	412	369	781	430	336	766	103
3B	10	8	18	8	13	21	86	23	23	46	26	34	60	77
HR	62	69	131	77	68	145	90	221	196	417	243	196	439	96
BB	229	240	469	249	208	457	103	733	691	1424	781	676	1457	99
SO	337	485	822	419	485	904	91	1155	1421	2576	1334	1375	2709	96
E	39	41	80	36	53	89	90	114	146	260	136	129	265	98
E-Infield	30	35	65	33	48	81	80	94	120	214	116	112	228	94
LHB-Avg	.268	.252	.261	.250	.245	.248	105	.268	.248	.259	.262	.260	.261	99
LHB-HR	37	26	63	49	29	78	81	116	59	175	141	79	220	82
RHB-Avg	.260	.236	.247	.264	.239	.251	99	.251	.237	.243	.257	.251	.254	96
RHB-HR	25	43	68	28	39	67	101	105	137	242	102	117	219	109

SEATTLE

Home park: Safeco Field   **Alt.:** -2 feet   **Surface:** Grass

Category	2005 Season Home Games Sea.	Opp.	Total	Road Games Sea.	Opp.	Total	Index	2003-05 Seasons Home Games Sea.	Opp.	Total	Road Games Sea.	Opp.	Total	Index
G	72	72	144	72	72	144		217	217	434	215	215	430	
Avg	.257	.270	.263	.248	.278	.263	100	.260	.254	.257	.272	.276	.274	94
AB	2420	2571	4991	2455	2388	4843	103	7280	7631	14911	7698	7255	14953	99
R	313	341	654	300	350	650	101	969	984	1953	1014	1060	2074	93
H	621	693	1314	608	664	1272	103	1893	1938	3831	2097	2000	4097	93
2B	124	126	250	125	126	251	97	352	377	729	410	368	778	94
3B	11	5	16	17	11	28	55	33	20	53	44	30	74	72
HR	53	76	129	60	91	151	83	182	262	444	185	261	446	100
BB	205	230	435	216	196	412	102	710	699	1409	669	655	1324	107
SO	458	431	889	409	365	774	111	1373	1395	2768	1313	1206	2519	110
E	39	46	85	41	53	94	90	120	142	262	118	135	253	103
E-Infield	34	36	70	39	43	82	85	103	122	225	106	107	213	105
LHB-Avg	.276	.277	.277	.266	.270	.268	103	.277	.256	.266	.289	.275	.282	94
LHB-HR	17	36	53	23	34	57	91	67	136	203	60	112	172	119
RHB-Avg	.242	.263	.253	.233	.285	.258	98	.247	.253	.250	.260	.276	.268	93
RHB-HR	36	40	76	37	57	94	78	115	126	241	125	149	274	88

2005 A.L. STATISTICS   Miscellaneous

TAMPA BAY

Home park: Tropicana Field   **Alt.:** 15 feet   **Surface:** Turf

Category	2005 Season Home Games T.B.	Opp.	Total	Road Games T.B.	Opp.	Total	Index	2003-05 Seasons Home Games T.B.	Opp.	Total	Road Games T.B.	Opp.	Total	Index
G	72	72	144	72	72	144		213	213	426	216	216	432	
Avg	.285	.272	.278	.266	.284	.275	101	.269	.260	.265	.264	.280	.272	97
AB	2429	2570	4999	2504	2390	4894	102	7214	7519	14733	7575	7184	14759	101
R	366	400	766	311	410	721	106	987	1093	2080	950	1239	2189	96
H	692	699	1391	667	679	1346	103	1942	1956	3898	1999	2013	4012	99
2B	126	130	256	126	149	275	91	369	395	764	383	452	835	92
3B	23	18	41	13	18	31	129	62	41	103	41	42	83	124
HR	64	90	154	76	84	160	94	181	260	441	216	268	484	91
BB	200	261	461	169	285	454	99	598	767	1365	531	852	1383	99
SO	424	471	895	461	372	833	105	1262	1313	2575	1359	1124	2483	104
E	61	43	104	50	39	89	117	161	144	305	152	123	275	112
E-Infield	50	37	87	42	33	75	116	135	131	266	120	109	229	118
LHB-Avg	.289	.268	.278	.275	.278	.277	100	.275	.260	.268	.265	.275	.270	99
LHB-HR	21	39	60	27	35	62	96	97	120	217	104	117	221	98
RHB-Avg	.283	.274	.278	.261	.288	.274	102	.264	.261	.262	.263	.284	.274	96
RHB-HR	43	51	94	49	49	98	93	84	140	224	112	151	263	86

TEXAS

Home park: The Ballpark in Arlington   **Alt.:** 551 feet   **Surface:** Grass

Category	2005 Season Home Games Tex.	Opp.	Total	Road Games Tex.	Opp.	Total	Index	2003-05 Seasons Home Games Tex.	Opp.	Total	Road Games Tex.	Opp.	Total	Index
G	72	72	144	72	72	144		216	216	432	216	216	432	
Avg	.273	.278	.276	.261	.278	.269	102	.282	.279	.281	.250	.279	.264	106
AB	2477	2608	5085	2618	2473	5091	100	7412	7784	15196	7682	7317	14999	101
R	407	390	797	357	381	738	108	1289	1190	2479	966	1123	2089	119
H	675	726	1401	683	687	1370	102	2090	2175	4265	1919	2045	3964	108
2B	131	152	283	143	139	282	100	410	456	866	406	399	805	106
3B	15	18	33	11	6	17	194	57	52	109	33	32	65	166
HR	130	71	201	93	67	160	126	361	250	611	271	235	506	119
BB	222	230	452	214	247	461	98	683	736	1419	627	776	1403	100
SO	447	414	861	520	402	922	93	1342	1341	2683	1523	1253	2776	95
E	51	40	91	49	42	91	100	142	128	270	147	125	272	99
E-Infield	42	36	78	41	38	79	99	121	108	229	127	107	234	98
LHB-Avg	.266	.281	.274	.268	.259	.263	104	.278	.274	.276	.246	.271	.259	106
LHB-HR	57	45	102	34	23	57	170	170	129	299	110	100	210	136
RHB-Avg	.277	.276	.277	.256	.293	.273	101	.284	.284	.284	.253	.286	.268	106
RHB-HR	73	26	99	59	44	103	100	191	121	312	161	135	296	107

TORONTO

Home park: Rogers Centre   **Alt.:** 300 feet   **Surface:** Turf

Category	2005 Season Home Games Tor.	Opp.	Total	Road Games Tor.	Opp.	Total	Index	2003-04 Seasons Home Games Tor.	Opp.	Total	Road Games Tor.	Opp.	Total	Index
G	72	72	144	72	72	144		144	144	288	143	143	286	
Avg	.276	.264	.270	.262	.266	.264	102	.273	.283	.278	.265	.266	.265	105
AB	2468	2556	5024	2531	2424	4955	101	4877	5165	10042	5082	4786	9868	101
R	364	318	682	348	319	667	102	749	800	1549	689	678	1367	113
H	680	674	1354	664	644	1308	104	1331	1460	2791	1346	1272	2618	106
2B	149	114	263	131	114	245	106	311	298	609	278	234	512	117
3B	20	8	28	15	11	26	106	34	29	63	24	29	53	117
HR	65	94	159	56	72	128	123	147	183	330	142	153	295	110
BB	204	178	382	222	221	443	85	504	503	1007	452	473	925	107
SO	415	462	877	431	393	824	105	924	940	1864	1030	778	1808	101
E	51	48	99	35	43	78	127	88	102	190	92	92	184	103
E-Infield	47	47	94	35	32	67	140	80	86	166	78	76	154	107
LHB-Avg	.275	.244	.260	.265	.268	.266	98	.271	.282	.277	.265	.263	.264	105
LHB-HR	25	33	58	29	28	57	104	78	86	164	71	74	145	111
RHB-Avg	.276	.277	.277	.260	.264	.262	106	.274	.284	.279	.264	.268	.266	105
RHB-HR	40	61	101	27	44	71	137	69	97	166	71	79	150	109

RUNS PER GAME

Team	Games	Home Games Team	Opp.	Total	Games	Road Games Team	Opp.	Total	Index
Tex	216	1289	1190	2479	216	966	1123	2089	119
Bos..............	216	1343	1059	2402	216	1122	1060	2182	110
Min*..............	144	685	601	1286	144	620	611	1231	104
CWS..............	216	1074	974	2048	216	1027	963	1990	103
Tor**	72	364	318	682	72	348	319	667	102
Bal	216	987	1097	2084	217	1097	1059	2156	97
KC*	143	626	790	1416	145	623	861	1484	97
TB	213	987	1093	2080	216	950	1239	2189	96
Det*	144	656	728	1384	144	725	739	1464	95
NYY	217	1163	1010	2173	214	1192	1058	2250	95
Oak..............	216	996	871	1867	216	1051	920	1971	95
LAA	217	999	932	1931	215	1080	985	2065	93
Sea..............	217	969	984	1953	215	1014	1060	2074	93
Cle	216	962	963	1925	216	1110	1089	2199	88

*Current dimensions began 2004; **Current dimensions began 2005

HOME RUNS PER AT-BAT

Team	Games	Home Games Team	Opp.	Total	Games	Road Games Team	Opp.	Total	Index
CWS..............	216	335	273	608	216	244	209	453	135
Tor**	72	65	94	159	72	56	72	128	123
Tex	216	361	250	611	216	271	235	506	119
Bal	216	225	247	472	217	223	230	453	105
NYY	217	321	215	536	214	304	209	513	104
Min*..............	144	142	148	290	144	141	146	287	102
Sea..............	217	182	262	444	215	185	261	446	100
Bos..............	216	282	208	490	216	294	212	506	97
Oak..............	216	221	196	417	216	243	196	439	96
LAA	217	195	226	421	215	206	235	441	95
TB	213	181	260	441	216	216	268	484	91
Det*	144	157	170	327	144	178	180	358	90
Cle	216	201	214	415	216	298	264	562	76
KC*	143	96	157	253	145	153	193	346	73

*Current dimensions began 2004; **Current dimensions began 2005

BATTING AVERAGE

Team	Games	Home Games Team	Opp.	Total	Games	Road Games Team	Opp.	Total	Index
Tex	216	.282	.279	.281	216	.250	.279	.264	106
Bos..............	216	.297	.264	.280	216	.265	.267	.266	105
Tor**	72	.276	.264	.270	72	.262	.266	.264	102
CWS..............	216	.265	.261	.263	216	.263	.255	.259	102
KC*	143	.265	.288	.277	145	.253	.296	.274	101
Det*	144	.275	.275	.275	144	.270	.276	.273	101
NYY	217	.274	.268	.271	214	.270	.271	.271	100
Min*..............	144	.267	.257	.262	144	.258	.269	.263	100
LAA	217	.274	.261	.267	215	.274	.265	.269	99
Bal	216	.272	.265	.268	217	.274	.270	.272	99
Oak..............	216	.260	.241	.251	216	.260	.254	.257	97
TB	213	.269	.260	.265	216	.264	.280	.272	97
Cle	216	.259	.255	.257	216	.273	.269	.271	95
Sea..............	217	.260	.254	.257	215	.272	.276	.274	94

*Current dimensions began 2004; **Current dimensions began 2005

2005 A.L. STATISTICS *Miscellaneous*

2005 National League Statistics

Batting

Designated hitting

Pinch-hitting

Pitching

Fielding

Miscellaneous

BATTING

TEAM

Team	G	TPA	AB	R	H	TB	2B	3B	HR	RBI	SH	SF	HP	BB	IBB	SO	SB	CS	GDP	LOB	ShO	Avg.	OBP	Slg.
SFlorida	162	6214	5502	717	1499	2253	306	32	128	678	82	50	67	512	61	918	96	38	144	1181	8	.272	.339	.409
St. Louis	162	6246	5538	805	1494	2343	287	26	170	757	77	35	62	534	60	947	83	36	127	1152	6	.270	.339	.423
Chicago	162	6161	5584	703	1506	2457	323	23	194	674	69	37	50	419	49	920	65	39	131	1133	8	.270	.324	.440
Philadelphia	162	6345	5542	807	1494	2347	282	35	167	760	62	46	56	639	76	1083	116	27	107	1251	9	.270	.348	.423
Colorado	162	6238	5542	740	1477	2275	280	34	150	704	88	34	64	509	36	1103	65	32	125	1197	10	.267	.333	.411
Atlanta	162	6186	5486	769	1453	2387	308	37	184	733	75	46	45	534	56	1084	92	32	146	1114	6	.265	.333	.435
San Francisco	162	6077	5462	649	1427	2162	299	26	128	617	91	44	49	431	26	901	71	35	147	1093	7	.261	.319	.396
Cincinnati	163	6321	5565	820	1453	2484	335	15	222	784	43	39	62	611	42	1303	72	23	116	1176	8	.261	.339	.446
Milwaukee	162	6156	5448	726	1413	2303	327	19	175	689	66	38	73	531	55	1162	79	34	137	1120	12	.259	.331	.423
Pittsburgh	162	6221	5573	680	1445	2230	292	38	139	656	56	49	72	471	38	1092	73	30	130	1193	9	.259	.322	.400
New York	162	6146	5505	722	1421	2289	279	32	175	683	69	38	48	486	49	1075	153	40	103	1122	11	.258	.322	.416
San Diego	162	6271	5502	684	1416	2153	269	39	130	655	72	48	49	600	41	977	99	44	122	1220	12	.257	.333	.391
Houston	163	6139	5462	693	1400	2228	281	32	161	654	82	42	72	481	43	1037	115	44	116	1136	17	.256	.322	.408
Arizona	162	6327	5550	696	1419	2337	291	27	191	670	71	45	55	606	51	1094	67	26	132	1247	9	.256	.332	.421
Los Angeles	162	6134	5433	685	1374	2147	284	21	149	653	57	33	67	541	30	1094	58	35	139	1135	9	.253	.326	.395
Washington	162	6142	5426	639	1367	2093	311	32	117	615	91	45	89	491	55	1090	45	45	130	1137	11	.252	.322	.386
Totals	1297	99324	88120	11535	23058	36488	4754	468	2580	10982	1151	669	980	8396	768	16880	1349	560	2052	18607	152	.262	.330	.414

INDIVIDUAL

TOP QUALIFIERS FOR BATTING CHAMPIONSHIP

Minimum 502 plate appearances. *Lefthanded batter. †Switch-hitter.

Player, Team	G	TPA	AB	R	H	TB	2B	3B	HR	RBI	SH	SF	HP	BB	IBB	SO	SB	CS	GDP	Avg.	OBP	Slg.
Lee, Derrek, Chi.	158	691	594	120	199	393	50	3	46	107	0	7	5	85	23	109	15	3	12	.335	.418	.662
Pujols, Albert, St.L.	161	700	591	129	195	360	38	2	41	117	0	3	9	97	27	65	16	2	19	.330	.430	.609
Cabrera, Miguel, Fla.	158	685	613	106	198	344	43	2	33	116	0	6	2	64	12	125	1	0	20	.323	.385	.561
Helton, Todd, Col.*	144	626	509	92	163	272	45	2	20	79	1	1	9	106	22	80	3	0	14	.320	.445	.534
Casey, Sean, Cin.*	137	587	529	75	165	224	32	0	9	58	0	5	5	48	3	48	2	0	27	.312	.371	.423
Tracy, Chad, Ari.*	145	553	503	73	155	278	34	4	27	72	1	6	8	35	4	78	3	1	10	.308	.359	.553
Holliday, Matt, Col.	125	526	479	68	147	242	24	7	19	87	0	4	7	36	1	79	14	3	11	.307	.361	.505
Wright, David, N.Y.	160	657	575	99	176	301	42	1	27	102	0	3	7	72	2	113	17	7	16	.306	.388	.523
Clark, Brady, Mil.	145	674	599	94	183	255	31	1	13	53	8	2	18	47	1	55	10	13	13	.306	.372	.426
Bay, Jason, Pit.	162	707	599	110	183	335	44	6	32	101	0	7	6	95	9	142	21	1	12	.306	.402	.559
Ramirez, Aramis, Chi.	123	506	463	72	140	263	30	0	31	92	0	2	6	35	4	60	0	1	15	.302	.358	.568
Griffey Jr., Ken, Cin.*	128	555	491	85	148	283	30	0	35	92	0	7	3	54	3	93	0	1	9	.301	.369	.576
Delgado, Carlos, Fla.*	144	616	521	81	157	303	41	3	33	115	0	6	17	72	20	121	0	0	16	.301	.399	.582
Giles, Brian, S.D.*	158	674	545	92	164	263	38	8	15	83	0	8	2	119	9	64	13	5	14	.301	.423	.483
Castillo, Luis, Fla.†	122	524	439	72	132	164	12	4	4	30	7	1	1	65	1	32	10	7	11	.301	.391	.374

DEPARTMENTAL LEADERS: G_Abreu, Phi., Bay, Pit., Lee, Mil., Pierre, Fla., 162; AB_Reyes, N.Y., 696; R_Pujols, St.L., 129; H_Lee, Chi., 199; TB_Lee, Chi., 393; 1B_Taveras, Hou., 152; 2B_Lee, Chi., 50; 3B_Reyes, N.Y., 17; HR_A. Jones, Atl., 51; RBI_A. Jones, Atl., 128; SH_Vizquel, S.F., 20; SF_Lee, Mil., 11; HP_Guillen, Was., Jenkins, Mil., 19; BB_Giles, S.D., 119; IBB_Pujols, St.L., 27; SO_Dunn, Cin., 168; SB_Reyes, N.Y., 60; CS_Pierre, Fla., 17; GDP_Casey, Cin., 27; Slg._Lee, Chi., .662; OBP_Helton, Col., .445.

ALL PLAYERS

*Lefthanded batter. †Switch-hitter.

Player, Team	G	TPA	AB	R	H	TB	2B	3B	HR	RBI	SH	SF	HP	BB	IBB	SO	SB	CS	GDP	Avg.	OBP	Slg.
AAbreu, Bobby, Phi.*	162	719	588	104	168	279	37	1	24	102	0	8	6	117	15	134	31	9	7	.286	.405	.474
Accardo, Jeremy, S.F.	28	2	2	0	1	1	0	0	0	0	0	0	0	0	0	0	0	0	0	.500	.500	.500
Acevedo, Jose, Col.	36	11	8	0	1	1	0	0	0	0	1	0	1	1	0	6	0	0	0	.125	.300	.125
Aguila, Chris, Fla.	65	81	78	11	19	22	3	0	0	4	0	0	0	3	0	19	0	1	0	.244	.272	.282
Alexander, Manny, S.D.	10	21	18	0	2	3	1	0	0	0	0	0	0	2	1	5	0	0	0	.111	.238	.167
Alfonzo, Edgardo, S.F.	109	402	368	36	102	127	17	1	2	43	1	4	2	27	1	34	2	0	11	.277	.327	.345
Alou, Moises, S.F.	123	490	427	67	137	221	21	3	19	63	0	4	3	56	1	43	5	1	11	.321	.400	.518
Alvarez, Wilson, L.A.*	21	3	2	0	0	0	0	0	0	0	0	1	0	0	0	1	0	0	0	.000	.000	.000
Amezaga, Alfredo, Col.-Pit.†	5	7	6	2	1	1	0	0	0	0	0	0	0	1	0	1	0	0	0	.167	.286	.167
Anderson, Marlon, N.Y.*	123	260	235	31	62	92	9	0	7	19	4	2	1	18	0	45	6	1	2	.264	.316	.391
Andino, Robert, Fla.	17	50	44	4	7	11	4	0	0	1	1	0	0	5	1	8	1	0	2	.159	.245	.250
Ardoin, Danny, Col.	80	248	210	28	48	76	10	0	6	22	7	2	9	20	2	69	1	1	8	.229	.320	.362
Armas, Tony, Was.	19	34	32	1	4	4	0	0	0	0	1	0	0	1	0	13	0	0	0	.125	.152	.125
Astacio, Ezequiel, Hou.	22	23	21	0	3	3	0	0	0	1	0	0	2	0	0	12	0	0	0	.143	.143	.143
Astacio, Pedro, S.D.	12	22	16	1	1	1	0	0	0	1	5	0	0	1	0	5	0	0	2	.063	.118	.063
Atkins, Garrett, Col.	138	573	519	62	149	221	31	1	13	89	0	4	5	45	1	72	0	2	18	.287	.347	.426
Aurilia, Rich, Cin.	114	468	426	61	120	189	23	2	14	68	1	3	1	37	2	67	2	0	8	.282	.338	.444
Ausmus, Brad, Hou.	134	451	387	35	100	128	19	0	3	47	7	1	5	51	8	48	5	3	17	.258	.351	.331
Ayala, Luis, Was.	68	4	3	0	1	1	0	0	0	0	1	0	0	0	0	0	0	0	0	.333	.333	.333
Aybar, Willy, L.A.†	26	105	86	12	28	39	8	0	1	10	0	0	1	18	0	11	3	1	0	.326	.448	.453
Backe, Brandon, Hou.	28	53	45	5	10	16	2	2	0	6	5	0	0	3	0	12	1	0	0	.222	.271	.356
Baerga, Carlos, Was.†	93	174	158	18	40	53	7	0	2	19	1	0	8	7	0	17	0	0	4	.253	.318	.335
Bagwell, Jeff, Hou.	39	123	100	11	25	38	4	0	3	19	0	4	1	18	1	21	0	0	2	.250	.358	.380
Baker, Jeff, Col.	12	43	38	6	8	15	4	0	1	4	0	0	0	5	0	12	0	0	1	.211	.302	.395
Bako, Paul, L.A.*	13	47	40	1	10	12	2	0	0	4	0	0	3	7	1	12	0	0	0	.250	.362	.300

Player, Team	G	TPA	AB	R	H	TB	2B	3B	HR	RBI	SH	SF	HP	BB	IBB	SO	SB	CS	GDP	Avg.	OBP	Slg.
Barmes, Clint, Col.	81	377	350	55	101	152	19	1	10	46	4	1	6	16	1	36	6	4	4	.289	.330	.434
Barrett, Michael, Chi.	133	477	424	48	117	203	32	3	16	61	2	4	7	40	3	61	0	3	7	.276	.345	.479
Bartosh, Cliff, Chi.*	19	1	1	0	1	1	0	0	0	0	0	0	0	0	0	0	0	0	0	1.000	1.000	1.000
Bautista, Jose, Pit.	11	31	28	3	4	5	1	0	0	1	0	0	0	3	0	7	1	0	2	.143	.226	.179
Bay, Jason, Pit.	162	707	599	110	183	335	44	6	32	101	0	7	6	95	9	142	21	1	12	.306	.402	.559
Bazardo, Yorman, Fla.	1	1	1	0	0	0	0	0	0	0	0	0	0	0	0	1	0	0	0	.000	.000	.000
Beckett, Josh, Fla.	29	71	59	5	9	15	3	0	1	6	4	1	0	7	0	17	0	0	1	.153	.239	.254
Belisle, Matt, Cin.†	61	8	7	0	1	1	0	0	0	0	1	0	0	0	0	3	0	0	0	.143	.143	.143
Bell, David, Phi.	150	617	557	53	138	201	31	1	10	61	4	4	5	47	6	69	0	1	24	.248	.310	.361
Bell, Heath, N.Y.	42	3	3	0	0	0	0	0	0	0	0	0	0	0	0	1	0	0	0	.000	.000	.000
Beltran, Carlos, N.Y.†	151	650	582	83	155	241	34	2	16	78	4	6	2	56	5	96	17	6	9	.266	.330	.414
Bennett, Gary, Was.	68	228	199	11	44	54	7	0	1	21	3	3	2	21	3	37	0	1	7	.221	.298	.271
Benson, Kris, N.Y.	28	61	49	4	9	10	1	0	0	6	6	0	1	5	0	22	0	0	0	.184	.273	.204
Bergmann, Jay, Was.	15	4	3	2	1	1	0	0	0	0	0	0	0	1	0	0	0	0	0	.333	.500	.333
Bergolla, William, Cin.	17	38	38	3	5	5	0	0	0	1	0	0	0	0	0	10	0	0	1	.132	.132	.132
Berkman, Lance, Hou.†	132	565	468	76	137	245	34	1	24	82	0	2	4	91	12	72	4	1	18	.293	.411	.524
Bernero, Adam, Atl.	36	2	1	0	1	1	0	0	0	0	1	0	0	0	0	0	0	0	0	.000	1.000	1.000
Betemit, Wilson, Atl.†	115	274	246	36	75	107	12	4	4	20	4	2	0	22	4	55	1	3	5	.305	.359	.435
Bigbie, Larry, Col.*	23	70	66	5	14	17	1	1	0	2	0	0	1	3	0	18	2	0	0	.212	.257	.258
Biggio, Craig, Hou.	155	651	590	94	156	276	40	1	26	69	4	3	17	37	2	90	11	1	10	.264	.325	.468
Blanco, Henry, Chi.	54	178	161	16	39	63	6	0	6	25	4	2	0	11	1	24	0	0	6	.242	.287	.391
Blanco, Tony, Was.	56	65	62	7	11	17	3	0	1	7	0	0	1	2	0	19	1	0	0	.177	.215	.274
Blum, Geoff, S.D.†	78	252	224	26	54	84	13	1	5	22	0	1	3	24	0	28	3	2	5	.241	.321	.375
Bonds, Barry, S.F.*	14	52	42	8	12	28	1	0	5	10	0	1	0	9	3	6	0	0	0	.286	.404	.667
Bradley, Milton, L.A.†	75	316	283	49	82	137	14	1	13	38	4	1	2	25	1	47	6	1	6	.290	.350	.484
Branyan, Russell, Mil.*	85	242	202	23	52	99	11	0	12	31	1	0	0	39	10	80	1	0	3	.257	.378	.490
Brazoban, Yhency, L.A.	74	2	2	0	0	0	0	0	0	0	0	0	0	0	0	1	0	0	0	.000	.000	.000
Breslow, Craig, S.D.*	14	1	1	0	0	0	0	0	0	0	0	0	0	0	0	0	0	0	0	.000	.000	.000
Brito, Eude, Phi.*	6	7	7	1	1	1	0	0	0	0	0	0	0	0	0	2	0	0	0	.143	.143	.143
Brower, Jim, S.F.-Atl.	69	2	2	0	0	0	0	0	0	0	0	0	0	0	0	1	0	0	0	.000	.000	.000
Bruney, Brian, Ari.	47	1	1	0	0	0	0	0	0	0	0	0	0	0	0	0	0	0	0	.000	.000	.000
Bruntlett, Eric, Hou.	91	121	109	19	24	45	5	2	4	14	1	0	1	10	0	25	7	2	4	.220	.292	.413
Bump, Nate, Fla.*	31	6	5	1	1	1	0	0	0	1	0	0	0	0	0	4	0	0	0	.200	.200	.200
Burke, Chris, Hou.	108	359	318	49	79	117	19	2	5	26	9	3	6	23	0	62	11	6	7	.248	.309	.368
Burnett, A.J., Fla.	32	79	68	3	10	19	2	2	1	2	9	0	1	1	0	34	0	0	1	.147	.171	.279
Burnitz, Jeromy, Chi.*	160	671	605	84	156	263	31	2	24	87	1	5	3	57	3	109	5	4	12	.258	.322	.435
Burrell, Pat, Phi.	154	669	562	78	158	283	27	1	32	117	0	5	3	99	6	160	0	0	12	.281	.389	.504
Burroughs, Sean, S.D.*	93	317	284	20	71	85	7	2	1	17	3	1	5	24	4	41	4	0	7	.250	.318	.299
Byrd, Marlon, Phi.-Was.	79	259	229	20	61	86	15	2	2	26	5	4	2	19	1	50	5	1	5	.266	.323	.376
Byrnes, Eric, Col.	15	60	53	2	10	12	2	0	0	5	0	0	0	7	0	11	2	0	1	.189	.283	.226
Cabrera, Miguel, Fla.	158	685	613	106	198	344	43	2	33	116	0	6	2	64	12	125	1	0	20	.323	.385	.561
Cain, Matt, S.F.	7	16	15	1	1	2	1	0	0	1	0	0	0	0	0	6	0	0	0	.067	.067	.133
Cairo, Miguel, N.Y.	100	367	327	31	82	106	18	0	2	19	12	5	4	19	2	31	13	3	5	.251	.296	.324
Cameron, Mike, N.Y.	76	343	308	47	84	147	23	2	12	39	1	1	4	29	0	85	13	1	5	.273	.342	.477
Capuano, Chris, Mil.*	35	79	71	5	12	15	3	0	0	9	5	1	0	2	0	33	0	0	1	.169	.189	.211
Carpenter, Chris, St.L.	33	93	77	7	5	7	2	0	0	2	10	1	0	5	0	23	0	1	2	.065	.120	.091
Carrara, Giovanni, L.A.	72	2	1	0	0	0	0	0	0	0	1	0	0	0	0	1	0	0	0	.000	.000	.000
Carrasco, Hector, Was.	64	10	8	1	0	0	0	0	0	0	2	0	0	0	0	7	0	0	0	.000	.000	.000
Carroll, Jamey, Was.	113	358	303	44	76	86	8	1	0	22	13	3	5	34	1	55	3	4	2	.251	.333	.284
Carvajal, Marcos, Col.	39	4	4	0	1	1	0	0	0	2	0	0	0	0	0	3	0	0	0	.250	.250	.250
Casey, Sean, Cin.*	137	587	529	75	165	224	32	0	9	58	0	5	5	48	3	48	2	0	27	.312	.371	.423
Cassidy, Scott, S.D.	10	2	1	0	0	0	0	0	0	0	0	0	0	1	0	1	0	0	0	.000	.500	.000
Castilla, Vinny, Was.	142	549	494	53	125	199	36	1	12	66	1	4	7	43	7	82	4	2	16	.253	.319	.403
Castillo, Frank, Fla.	1	1	1	0	0	0	0	0	0	0	0	0	0	0	0	0	0	0	0	.000	.000	.000
Castillo, Jose, Pit.	101	398	370	49	99	154	16	3	11	53	1	4	0	23	3	59	2	3	11	.268	.307	.416
Castillo, Luis, Fla.†	122	524	439	72	132	164	12	4	4	30	18	1	1	65	1	32	10	7	11	.301	.391	.374
Castro, Ramon, N.Y.	99	240	209	26	51	91	16	0	8	41	3	3	0	25	2	58	1	0	7	.244	.321	.435
Cedeno, Roger, St.L.†	37	61	57	4	9	10	1	0	0	8	1	1	2	0	6	0	2	2	.158	.197	.175
Cedeno, Ronny, Chi.	41	89	80	13	24	30	3	0	1	6	2	0	2	5	1	11	1	0	4	.300	.356	.375
Cepicky, Matt, Was.*	11	26	25	1	6	9	3	0	0	3	0	0	0	1	0	8	0	1	1	.240	.269	.360
Chacon, Shawn, Col.	13	25	20	0	3	3	0	0	0	1	3	0	0	2	0	8	0	0	1	.150	.227	.150
Chavez, Angel, S.F.	10	20	19	1	5	6	1	0	0	1	1	0	0	0	0	3	0	0	0	.263	.263	.316
Chavez, Endy, Was.-Phi.*	98	130	116	19	25	35	4	3	0	11	7	0	0	7	0	14	2	3	0	.216	.260	.302
Chavez, Raul, Hou.	37	105	99	6	17	26	3	0	2	6	0	1	1	4	0	18	1	0	5	.172	.210	.263
Chen, Chin-Feng, L.A.	7	8	8	1	2	2	0	0	0	2	0	0	0	0	0	4	0	0	0	.250	.250	.250
Choi, Hee-Seop, L.A.*	133	368	320	40	81	145	15	2	15	42	2	4	8	34	1	80	1	3	10	.253	.336	.453
Church, Ryan, Was.*	102	301	268	41	77	125	15	3	9	42	1	3	5	24	0	70	3	2	6	.287	.353	.466
Cintron, Alex, Ari.†	122	348	330	36	90	137	19	2	8	48	2	3	1	12	3	33	1	2	8	.273	.298	.415
Cirillo, Jeff, Mil.	77	219	185	29	52	79	15	0	4	23	7	0	4	23	0	22	4	2	3	.281	.373	.427
Clark, Brady, Mil.	145	674	599	94	183	255	31	1	13	53	8	2	18	47	1	55	10	13	13	.306	.372	.426
Clark, Doug, S.F.*	8	6	5	2	0	0	0	0	0	0	0	0	0	1	0	2	0	0	0	.000	.167	.000
Clark, Tony, Ari.†	130	393	349	47	106	222	22	2	30	87	0	6	1	37	6	88	0	0	10	.304	.366	.636
Claussen, Brandon, Cin.	29	64	55	3	5	5	0	0	0	0	6	0	0	3	0	22	0	0	0	.091	.138	.091
Clayton, Royce, Ari.	143	573	522	59	141	183	28	4	2	44	10	2	1	38	0	105	13	3	19	.270	.320	.351
Clemens, Roger, Hou.	32	69	58	2	12	14	2	0	0	4	5	0	1	5	0	18	0	0	1	.207	.281	.241
Closser, JD, Col.†	92	272	237	31	52	89	12	2	7	27	1	1	1	32	1	48	1	0	9	.219	.314	.376
Coffey, Todd, Cin.	57	3	3	0	0	0	0	0	0	0	0	0	0	0	0	1	0	0	0	.000	.000	.000
Colon, Roman, Atl.	23	8	7	0	0	0	0	0	0	0	0	0	0	0	0	5	0	0	0	.000	.000	.000
Conine, Jeff, Fla.	131	384	335	42	102	135	20	2	3	33	2	6	3	38	2	58	2	0	12	.304	.374	.403
Cook, Aaron, Col.	13	36	30	3	5	7	0	1	0	0	5	0	0	1	0	12	0	0	0	.167	.194	.233
Cooper, Brian, S.F.	8	2	2	0	1	1	0	0	0	0	0	0	0	0	0	1	0	0	0	.500	.500	.500
Cordero, Wil, Was.	29	56	51	2	6	8	2	0	0	2	0	2	0	3	1	14	0	0	0	.118	.161	.157

Player, Team	G	TPA	AB	R	H	TB	2B	3B	HR	RBI	SH	SF	HP	BB	IBB	SO	SB	CS	GDP	Avg.	OBP	Slg.
Cormier, Lance, Ari.	67	7	6	0	2	2	0	0	0	1	1	0	0	0	0	1	0	0	1	.333	.333	.333
Cormier, Rheal, Phi.*	57	3	1	0	0	0	0	0	0	0	2	0	0	0	0	1	0	0	0	.000	.000	.000
Correia, Kevin, S.F.	16	18	14	0	1	1	0	0	0	0	1	0	0	3	0	5	0	0	0	.071	.235	.071
Cortes, David, Col.	50	2	2	0	0	0	0	0	0	0	0	0	0	0	0	0	0	0	0	.000	.000	.000
Cota, Humberto, Pit.	93	320	297	29	72	115	20	1	7	43	1	3	2	17	2	80	0	0	8	.242	.285	.387
Counsell, Craig, Ari.*	150	670	578	85	148	217	34	4	9	42	2	4	8	78	4	69	26	7	8	.256	.350	.375
Cruz Jr., Jose, Ari.-L.A.†	111	424	358	46	90	171	23	2	18	50	0	1	0	65	3	97	0	2	10	.251	.366	.478
Cruz, Deivi, S.F.-Was.	101	275	260	28	69	97	11	1	5	20	3	0	1	11	1	34	0	1	5	.265	.298	.373
Cruz, Jacob, Cin.*	110	145	127	12	30	52	10	0	4	18	0	1	1	16	1	46	0	0	0	.236	.324	.409
Cruz, Nelson, Mil.	8	7	5	1	1	2	1	0	0	0	0	0	0	2	0	0	0	0	0	.200	.429	.400
Dallimore, Brian, S.F.	7	7	7	1	1	2	1	0	0	0	0	0	0	0	0	0	0	0	1	.143	.143	.286
Daubach, Brian, N.Y.*	15	34	25	4	3	8	2	0	1	3	0	1	1	7	1	5	0	0	2	.120	.324	.320
Davies, Kyle, Atl.	21	28	15	0	3	3	0	0	0	4	10	1	0	2	0	3	0	0	0	.200	.278	.200
Davis, Doug, Mil.	35	76	73	2	10	15	3	1	0	3	2	0	0	1	0	34	0	0	1	.137	.149	.205
Davis, J.J., Was.	14	28	26	0	6	6	0	0	0	2	0	0	0	2	0	7	1	1	2	.231	.286	.231
Day, Zach, Was.-Col.	17	12	11	1	2	2	0	0	0	0	1	0	0	0	0	3	0	0	0	.182	.182	.182
Delgado, Carlos, Fla.*	144	616	521	81	157	303	41	3	33	115	0	6	17	72	20	121	0	1	16	.301	.399	.582
Dempster, Ryan, Chi.	63	14	14	0	1	1	0	0	0	0	0	0	0	0	0	5	0	0	0	.071	.071	.071
Denorfia, Chris, Cin.	18	44	38	8	10	16	3	0	1	2	0	0	0	6	0	9	1	0	1	.263	.364	.421
Dessens, Elmer, L.A.	28	10	10	0	0	0	0	0	0	0	0	0	0	0	0	6	0	0	0	.000	.000	.000
Devine, Joey, Atl.	5	1	1	0	0	0	0	0	0	0	0	0	0	0	0	1	0	0	0	.000	.000	.000
Diaz, Einar, St.L.	58	139	130	14	27	36	6	0	1	17	2	0	2	5	0	12	0	0	8	.208	.248	.277
Diaz, Victor, N.Y.	89	313	280	41	72	131	17	3	12	38	0	2	1	30	7	82	6	2	13	.257	.329	.468
DiFelice, Mike, N.Y.	11	19	17	0	2	2	0	0	0	0	0	0	0	2	0	5	0	0	1	.118	.211	.118
Dillon, Joe, Fla.	27	39	36	6	6	10	1	0	1	1	1	0	1	1	0	8	0	0	3	.167	.211	.278
Dohmann, Scott, Col.	32	1	1	0	0	0	0	0	0	0	0	0	0	0	0	0	0	0	0	.000	.000	.000
Doumit, Ryan, Pit.†	75	257	231	25	59	92	13	1	6	35	1	1	13	11	1	48	2	1	5	.255	.324	.398
Drese, Ryan, Was.	12	19	14	0	1	1	0	0	0	0	5	0	0	0	0	6	0	0	0	.071	.071	.071
Drew, J.D., L.A.*	72	311	252	48	72	131	12	1	15	36	0	3	5	51	3	50	1	1	3	.286	.412	.520
Dubois, Jason, Chi.	52	152	142	15	34	67	12	0	7	22	0	0	3	7	1	49	0	1	3	.239	.289	.472
Duckworth, Brandon, Hou.	7	3	3	1	2	3	1	0	0	0	0	0	0	0	0	0	0	0	0	.667	.667	1.000
Duffy, Chris, Pit.*	39	136	126	22	43	54	4	2	1	9	1	0	2	7	0	22	2	2	1	.341	.385	.429
Duke, Zach, Pit.*	14	31	28	1	4	4	0	0	0	1	0	1	0	2	0	10	0	0	2	.143	.194	.143
Duncan, Chris, St.L.*	9	10	10	2	2	6	1	0	1	3	0	0	0	0	0	5	0	0	1	.200	.200	.600
Dunn, Adam, Cin.*	160	671	543	107	134	293	35	2	40	101	0	2	12	114	14	168	4	2	6	.247	.387	.540
Durham, Ray, S.F.†	142	560	497	67	144	213	33	0	12	62	1	7	7	48	2	59	6	3	19	.290	.356	.429
Durrington, Trent, Mil.	28	18	14	3	3	4	1	0	0	2	3	0	0	1	0	3	5	2	0	.214	.267	.286
Easley, Damion, Fla.	102	304	267	37	64	112	19	1	9	30	3	4	4	26	3	47	4	1	6	.240	.312	.419
Eaton, Adam, S.D.	26	52	46	2	8	10	1	0	0	2	3	0	0	3	0	18	0	1	0	.174	.224	.217
Eckstein, David, St.L.	158	713	630	90	185	249	26	7	8	61	8	4	13	58	0	44	11	8	13	.294	.363	.395
Edmonds, Jim, St.L.*	142	567	467	88	123	249	37	1	29	89	1	4	4	91	10	139	5	5	6	.263	.385	.533
Edwards, Mike, L.A.	88	258	239	23	59	81	9	2	3	15	1	0	2	16	0	34	1	1	6	.247	.300	.339
Eischen, Joey, Was.*	58	4	3	0	1	1	0	0	0	0	0	0	0	0	0	2	0	0	0	.333	.333	.333
Eldred, Brad, Pit.	55	208	190	23	42	87	9	0	12	27	0	2	3	13	0	77	1	1	5	.221	.279	.458
Eldred, Cal, St.L.	31	2	2	0	0	0	0	0	0	0	0	0	0	0	0	2	0	0	0	.000	.000	.000
Ellison, Jason, S.F.	131	386	352	49	93	127	18	2	4	24	6	1	3	24	1	44	14	6	7	.264	.316	.361
Encarnacion, Edwin, Cin.	69	234	211	25	49	92	16	0	9	31	0	3	2	20	2	60	3	0	8	.232	.308	.436
Encarnacion, Juan, Fla.	141	563	506	59	145	226	27	3	16	76	4	3	9	41	2	104	6	5	9	.287	.349	.447
Ensberg, Morgan, Hou.	150	624	526	86	149	293	30	3	36	101	0	5	8	85	9	119	6	7	12	.283	.388	.557
Erickson, Scott, L.A.	19	14	13	0	2	2	0	0	0	0	1	0	0	0	0	5	0	0	0	.154	.154	.154
Esposito, Mike, Col.	3	6	5	0	1	1	0	0	0	0	1	0	0	0	0	0	0	0	0	.200	.200	.200
Estes, Shawn, Ari.	21	31	29	2	2	4	0	1	0	0	2	0	0	0	0	7	1	0	1	.069	.069	.138
Estrada, Johnny, Atl.†	105	383	357	31	93	131	26	0	4	39	0	3	3	20	6	38	0	0	13	.261	.303	.367
Eveland, Dana, Mil.*	27	2	1	0	0	0	0	0	0	0	1	0	0	0	0	0	0	0	0	.000	.000	.000
Everett, Adam, Hou.	152	595	549	58	136	200	27	2	11	54	8	4	8	26	1	103	21	7	5	.248	.290	.364
Eyre, Scott, S.F.*	86	3	2	0	0	0	0	0	0	0	0	0	0	1	0	2	0	0	0	.000	.333	.000
Fassero, Jeff, S.F.*	48	14	13	0	0	0	0	0	0	0	1	0	0	0	0	6	0	0	0	.000	.000	.000
Feliz, Pedro, S.F.	156	615	569	69	142	240	30	4	20	81	1	6	1	38	1	102	0	2	20	.250	.295	.422
Fick, Robert, S.D.*	93	260	230	25	61	84	10	2	3	30	1	2	1	26	2	33	0	2	4	.265	.340	.365
Fielder, Prince, Mil.*	39	62	59	2	17	27	4	0	2	10	0	1	0	2	0	17	0	0	0	.288	.306	.458
Flores, Randy, St.L.*	50	1	1	0	0	0	0	0	0	0	0	0	0	0	0	0	0	0	0	.000	.000	.000
Floyd, Cliff, N.Y.*	150	626	550	85	150	278	22	2	34	98	0	2	11	63	13	98	12	2	5	.273	.358	.505
Floyd, Gavin, Phi.	7	9	9	0	1	1	0	0	0	0	0	0	0	0	0	5	0	0	0	.111	.111	.111
Fogg, Josh, Pit.	34	56	47	3	5	6	1	0	0	3	6	0	0	3	0	14	0	0	0	.106	.160	.128
Fontenot, Mike, Chi.*	7	5	2	4	0	0	0	0	0	0	0	0	1	2	0	0	0	0	0	.000	.600	.000
Francis, Jeff, Col.*	33	71	58	7	6	8	2	0	0	4	6	0	0	7	0	27	0	0	1	.103	.200	.138
Franco, Julio, Atl.	108	265	233	30	64	105	12	1	9	42	1	3	1	27	1	57	4	0	10	.275	.348	.451
Francoeur, Jeff, Atl.	70	274	257	41	77	141	20	1	14	45	0	2	4	11	3	58	3	2	4	.300	.336	.549
Freel, Ryan, Cin.	103	432	369	69	100	137	19	3	4	21	3	0	8	51	0	59	36	10	9	.271	.371	.371
Freeman, Choo, Col.	18	22	22	6	6	9	1	0	0	0	0	0	0	0	0	5	0	0	0	.273	.273	.409
Fultz, Aaron, Phi.*	62	3	3	1	1	1	0	0	0	0	0	0	0	0	0	2	0	0	0	.333	.333	.333
Furcal, Rafael, Atl.†	154	689	616	100	175	264	31	11	12	58	5	5	1	62	3	78	46	10	11	.284	.348	.429
Furmaniak, J.J., Pit.	13	30	26	3	5	8	1	0	1	1	0	0	4	0	0	4	0	0	0	.192	.300	.308
Gall, John, St.L.	22	39	37	5	10	19	3	0	2	10	0	1	0	1	0	8	0	0	0	.270	.282	.514
Garabito, Eddy, Col.†	42	102	88	15	27	35	5	0	1	8	3	0	3	8	0	12	3	2	2	.307	.384	.398
Garcia, Jesse, S.D.	16	39	36	4	6	12	0	0	2	4	0	0	3	1	1	0	0	0	0	.167	.231	.333
Garciaparra, Nomar, Chi.	62	247	230	28	65	104	12	0	9	30	0	3	2	12	0	24	0	0	6	.283	.320	.452
Geary, Geoff, Phi.	40	6	6	0	1	1	0	0	0	0	0	0	0	0	0	4	0	0	0	.167	.167	.167
Gerut, Jody, Chi.-Pit.*	15	34	32	3	5	7	2	0	0	2	0	0	0	2	0	6	0	0	1	.156	.206	.219
Giles, Brian, S.D.*	158	674	545	92	164	263	38	8	15	83	0	8	2	119	9	64	13	5	14	.301	.423	.483
Giles, Marcus, Atl.	152	654	577	104	168	266	45	4	15	63	4	5	4	64	1	108	16	3	13	.291	.365	.461
Gipson, Charles, Hou.	19	14	11	2	2	3	1	0	0	1	2	0	0	1	0	3	1	1	0	.182	.250	.273

Player, Team	G	TPA	AB	R	H	TB	2B	3B	HR	RBI	SH	SF	HP	BB	IBB	SO	SB	CS	GDP	Avg.	OBP	Slg.
Glaus, Troy, Ari.	149	634	538	78	139	281	29	1	37	97	0	5	7	84	2	145	4	2	7	.258	.363	.522
Glavine, Tom, N.Y.*	33	71	64	2	13	13	0	0	0	3	5	0	2	0	0	13	0	0	0	.203	.227	.203
Glover, Gary, Mil.	15	26	20	3	2	2	0	0	0	1	3	0	1	2	0	9	0	0	0	.100	.217	.100
Godwin, Tyrell, Was.*	3	3	3	0	0	0	0	0	0	0	0	0	0	0	0	1	0	0	0	.000	.000	.000
Gonzalez, Alex, Fla.	130	478	435	45	115	160	30	0	5	45	4	3	5	31	10	81	5	3	11	.264	.319	.368
Gonzalez, Luis, Ari.*	155	672	579	90	157	266	37	0	24	79	0	4	11	78	12	90	4	1	14	.271	.366	.459
Gonzalez, Luis A., Col.	128	442	404	51	118	170	25	0	9	44	8	3	6	20	0	63	3	4	7	.292	.333	.421
Gorzelanny, Tom, Pit.*	3	2	1	0	0	0	0	0	0	0	1	0	0	0	0	1	0	0	0	.000	.000	.000
Gosling, Mike, Ari.*	13	7	6	0	0	0	0	0	0	0	1	0	0	0	0	4	0	0	0	.000	.000	.000
Grabowski, Jason, L.A.*	65	124	112	14	18	30	0	0	4	12	0	1	0	10	1	29	1	0	4	.161	.228	.268
Green, Andy, Ari.	17	39	31	5	7	8	1	0	0	2	0	1	0	7	0	3	0	0	1	.226	.359	.258
Green, Shawn, Ari.*	158	656	581	87	166	277	37	4	22	73	0	8	5	62	6	95	8	4	18	.286	.355	.477
Greenberg, Adam, Chi.*	1	1	0	0	0	0	0	0	0	0	0	0	1	0	0	0	0	0	0	.000	1.000	.000
Greene, Khalil, S.D.	121	476	436	51	109	188	30	2	15	70	3	6	6	25	3	93	5	0	8	.250	.296	.431
Greene, Todd, Col.	38	134	126	10	32	57	4	0	7	23	0	0	1	7	0	21	0	0	5	.254	.299	.452
Greisinger, Seth, Atl.	1	2	2	0	0	0	0	0	0	0	0	0	0	0	0	0	0	0	0	.000	.000	.000
Grieve, Ben, Chi.*	23	25	20	1	5	5	0	0	0	1	0	0	0	5	1	7	0	0	0	.250	.400	.250
Griffey Jr., Ken, Cin.*	128	555	491	85	148	283	30	0	35	92	0	7	3	54	3	93	0	1	9	.301	.369	.576
Grissom, Marquis, S.F.	44	147	137	8	29	39	4	0	2	15	2	1	0	7	0	18	1	1	9	.212	.248	.285
Grudzielanek, Mark, St.L.	137	563	528	64	155	215	30	3	8	59	0	2	7	26	3	81	8	6	14	.294	.334	.407
Guillen, Jose, Was.	148	611	551	81	156	264	32	2	24	76	1	9	19	31	6	102	1	1	14	.283	.338	.479
Guzman, Cristian, Was.†	142	492	456	39	100	143	19	6	4	31	8	2	1	25	6	76	7	4	12	.219	.260	.314
Haad, Yamid, S.F.	17	32	28	0	2	3	1	0	0	1	0	1	0	3	0	7	0	0	2	.071	.156	.107
Hairston Jr., Jerry, Chi.	114	430	380	51	99	140	25	2	4	30	7	0	12	31	0	46	8	9	5	.261	.336	.368
Hairston, Scott, Ari.	15	20	20	0	2	3	1	0	0	0	0	0	0	0	0	6	0	0	1	.100	.100	.150
Halama, John, Was.*	10	5	5	0	1	1	0	0	0	0	0	0	0	0	0	1	0	0	0	.200	.200	.200
Hall, Bill, Mil.	146	546	501	69	146	248	39	6	17	62	2	3	1	39	2	103	18	6	11	.291	.342	.495
Halsey, Brad, Ari.*	28	60	48	2	3	3	0	0	0	2	6	0	0	6	0	18	0	0	0	.063	.167	.063
Hammond, Chris, S.D.*	55	3	3	0	0	0	0	0	0	0	0	0	0	0	0	1	0	0	0	.000	.000	.000
Hammonds, Jeffrey, Was.	13	37	32	3	7	8	1	0	0	1	2	0	1	2	1	4	0	0	0	.219	.286	.250
Hampton, Mike, Atl.	12	29	25	4	8	12	1	0	1	1	3	0	1	0	0	9	0	0	2	.320	.346	.480
Harang, Aaron, Cin.	32	78	74	1	2	2	0	0	0	3	4	0	0	0	0	39	0	0	0	.027	.027	.027
Hardy, J.J., Mil.	124	427	372	46	92	143	22	1	9	50	8	2	1	44	7	48	0	0	10	.247	.327	.384
Harris, Brendan, Was.	4	10	9	1	3	7	1	0	1	3	0	0	1	0	0	0	0	0	2	.333	.400	.778
Harris, Lenny, Fla.*	83	78	70	5	22	29	4	0	1	13	0	1	0	7	1	11	0	1	3	.314	.385	.414
Hart, Corey, Mil.	21	63	57	9	11	21	2	1	2	7	0	0	0	6	0	11	2	0	6	.193	.270	.368
Harville, Chad, Hou.	37	1	1	0	0	0	0	0	0	0	0	0	0	0	0	1	0	0	0	.000	.000	.000
Hawpe, Brad, Col.*	101	351	305	38	80	123	10	3	9	47	0	3	0	43	3	70	2	2	5	.262	.350	.403
Heilman, Aaron, N.Y.	53	17	14	0	0	0	0	0	0	0	2	0	0	1	0	7	0	0	0	.000	.067	.000
Helling, Rick, Mil.	15	14	13	0	0	0	0	0	0	0	1	0	0	0	0	9	0	0	1	.000	.000	.000
Helms, Wes, Mil.	95	188	168	18	50	77	13	1	4	24	0	3	3	14	0	30	0	1	7	.298	.356	.458
Helton, Todd, Col.*	144	626	509	92	163	272	45	2	20	79	1	1	9	106	22	80	3	0	14	.320	.445	.534
Hennessey, Brad, S.F.	21	41	39	3	9	16	1	0	2	5	2	0	0	0	0	12	0	0	0	.231	.231	.410
Hensley, Clay, S.D.	24	6	6	0	1	2	1	0	0	0	0	0	0	0	0	3	0	0	0	.167	.167	.333
Hermida, Jeremy, Fla.*	23	47	41	9	12	26	2	0	4	11	0	0	0	6	1	12	2	0	1	.293	.383	.634
Hernandez, Anderson, N.Y.† ...	6	19	18	1	1	1	0	0	0	0	0	0	0	1	0	4	0	1	0	.056	.105	.056
Hernandez, Livan, Was.*	35	97	82	7	20	30	2	1	2	7	14	0	1	0	0	8	0	0	4	.244	.253	.366
Hernandez, Ramon, S.D.	99	392	369	36	107	166	19	2	12	58	1	3	1	18	0	40	1	0	14	.290	.322	.450
Hill, Bobby, Pit.†	58	105	93	12	25	31	6	0	0	11	0	1	2	9	0	17	0	0	3	.269	.343	.333
Hill, Koyie, Ari.†	34	91	78	6	17	22	5	0	0	6	0	2	0	11	0	27	0	1	0	.218	.308	.282
Hill, Rich, Chi.*	10	6	6	1	2	2	0	0	0	0	0	0	0	0	0	2	0	0	0	.333	.333	.333
Holbert, Aaron, Cin.	22	32	27	3	6	9	3	0	0	2	1	1	0	3	1	8	1	0	1	.222	.290	.333
Hollandsworth, Todd, Chi.-Atl.*	131	330	303	26	74	113	17	2	6	36	1	2	1	23	1	66	4	5	5	.244	.298	.373
Holliday, Matt, Col.	125	526	479	68	147	242	24	7	19	87	0	4	7	36	1	79	14	3	11	.307	.361	.505
Houlton, D.J., L.A.	35	35	30	1	3	4	1	0	0	1	2	0	0	3	0	18	0	0	0	.100	.182	.133
Howard, Ryan, Phi.*	88	348	312	52	90	177	17	2	22	63	0	2	1	33	8	100	0	1	6	.288	.356	.567
Hudson, Luke, Cin.	21	29	25	7	8	10	2	0	0	3	2	0	0	2	0	9	0	0	0	.320	.370	.400
Hudson, Tim, Atl.	29	72	65	2	9	13	2	1	0	6	4	0	0	3	0	26	0	0	4	.138	.176	.200
Hyzdu, Adam, S.D.	17	25	20	1	3	4	1	0	0	4	1	1	0	3	0	4	1	0	1	.150	.250	.200
Ishii, Kazuhisa, N.Y.*	19	30	25	1	5	5	0	0	0	2	4	0	0	1	0	12	0	0	0	.200	.231	.200
Izturis, Cesar, L.A.†	106	478	444	48	114	143	19	2	2	31	4	1	4	25	1	51	8	8	11	.257	.302	.322
Jackson, Conor, Ari.	40	99	85	8	17	26	3	0	2	8	0	1	1	12	0	11	0	0	6	.200	.303	.306
Jackson, Damian, S.D.	118	313	275	44	70	94	9	0	5	23	3	1	4	30	1	45	15	2	4	.255	.335	.342
Jackson, Edwin, L.A.	10	11	10	0	2	2	0	0	0	1	0	0	0	1	0	2	0	0	0	.200	.273	.200
Jacobs, Mike, N.Y.*	30	112	100	19	31	71	7	0	11	23	0	1	1	10	0	22	0	0	5	.310	.375	.710
James, Chuck, Atl.*	2	1	1	0	1	1	0	0	0	1	0	0	0	0	0	0	0	0	0	1.000	1.000	1.000
Jenkins, Geoff, Mil.*	148	618	538	87	157	276	42	1	25	86	0	5	19	56	9	138	0	0	13	.292	.375	.513
Jennings, Jason, Col.*	22	44	38	0	6	7	1	0	0	1	4	0	0	2	0	12	0	0	0	.158	.200	.184
Jimenez, D'Angelo, Cin.†	35	119	105	14	24	31	7	0	0	5	0	0	0	14	0	23	2	1	1	.229	.319	.295
Johnson, Ben, S.D.	31	88	75	10	16	35	8	1	3	13	1	1	0	11	1	23	0	2	4	.213	.310	.467
Johnson, Josh, Fla.*	4	4	4	1	1	1	0	0	0	0	0	0	0	0	0	2	0	0	0	.250	.250	.250
Johnson, Kelly, Atl.*	87	334	290	46	70	115	12	3	9	40	2	1	1	40	1	75	2	1	11	.241	.334	.397
Johnson, Nick, Was.*	131	547	453	66	131	217	35	3	15	74	0	2	12	80	8	87	3	8	15	.289	.408	.479
Jones, Andruw, Atl.	160	672	586	95	154	337	24	3	51	128	0	7	15	64	13	112	5	3	19	.263	.347	.575
Jones, Chipper, Atl.†	109	432	358	66	106	199	30	0	21	72	0	2	0	72	5	56	5	1	9	.296	.412	.556
Jones, Todd, Fla.*	68	3	3	0	1	1	0	0	0	0	0	0	0	0	0	2	0	0	0	.333	.333	.333
Jordan, Brian, Atl.	76	251	231	25	57	78	8	2	3	24	0	3	3	14	0	46	2	0	5	.247	.295	.338
Jorgensen, Ryan, Fla.	4	4	4	0	0	0	0	0	0	0	0	0	0	0	0	1	0	0	0	.000	.000	.000
Kata, Matt, Ari.-Phi.†	40	44	37	7	7	11	2	1	0	2	1	0	0	5	0	6	0	1	0	.189	.286	.297
Kearns, Austin, Cin.	112	448	387	62	93	175	26	1	18	67	0	5	8	48	2	107	0	0	8	.240	.333	.452
Keisler, Randy, Cin.*	24	15	15	3	4	9	2	0	1	2	0	0	0	0	0	8	0	0	1	.267	.267	.600
Kelly, Kenny, Cin.-Was.	24	14	13	5	4	5	1	0	0	2	0	0	0	1	0	6	1	2	0	.308	.357	.385

Player, Team	G	TPA	AB	R	H	TB	2B	3B	HR	RBI	SH	SF	HP	BB	IBB	SO	SB	CS	GDP	Avg.	OBP	Slg.
Kennedy, Joe, Col.	16	35	29	1	5	5	0	0	0	1	5	0	0	1	0	8	0	0	1	.172	.200	.172
Kent, Jeff, L.A.	149	637	553	100	160	283	36	0	29	105	0	4	8	72	8	85	6	2	19	.289	.377	.512
Kim, Byung-Hyun, Col.	40	45	38	0	3	3	0	0	0	2	4	1	0	2	0	6	0	0	0	.079	.122	.079
Kim, Sunny, Was.-Col.	24	26	19	2	2	2	0	0	0	3	6	1	0	0	0	5	0	0	1	.105	.100	.105
Kinney, Matt, S.F.	5	3	3	0	1	1	0	0	0	0	0	0	0	0	0	1	0	0	0	.333	.333	.333
Klesko, Ryan, S.D.*	137	520	443	61	110	185	19	1	18	58	0	1	1	75	2	80	3	4	6	.248	.358	.418
Knoedler, Justin, S.F.	8	11	10	0	1	1	0	0	0	0	0	0	1	0	0	1	0	0	0	.100	.182	.100
Kolb, Dan, Atl.	65	1	1	0	0	0	0	0	0	0	0	0	0	0	0	1	0	0	0	.000	.000	.000
Koo, Dae-Sung, N.Y.*	33	2	2	1	1	2	1	0	0	0	0	0	0	0	0	1	0	0	0	.500	.500	1.000
Koplove, Mike, Ari.	44	2	2	0	0	0	0	0	0	0	0	0	0	0	0	1	0	0	0	.000	.000	.000
Koronka, John, Chi.*	4	5	4	0	0	0	0	0	0	0	0	0	0	1	0	3	0	0	0	.000	.200	.000
Krynzel, Dave, Mil.*	5	7	7	0	0	0	0	0	0	0	0	0	0	0	0	3	0	0	0	.000	.000	.000
Lamb, Mike, Hou.*	125	349	322	41	76	135	13	5	12	53	0	4	1	22	1	65	1	1	10	.236	.284	.419
Lane, Jason, Hou.	145	561	517	65	138	258	34	4	26	78	0	5	7	32	1	105	6	2	10	.267	.316	.499
Langerhans, Ryan, Atl.*	128	373	326	48	87	139	22	3	8	42	2	3	5	37	3	75	0	2	2	.267	.348	.426
LaRoche, Adam, Atl.*	141	502	451	53	117	205	28	0	20	78	2	6	4	39	7	87	0	2	15	.259	.320	.455
LaRue, Jason, Cin.	110	422	361	38	94	163	27	0	14	60	5	2	13	41	7	101	0	1	8	.260	.355	.452
Lawrence, Brian, S.D.	33	69	59	2	5	5	0	0	0	1	7	1	0	2	0	29	0	0	2	.085	.113	.085
Lawton, Matt, Pit.-Chi.*	120	528	452	61	121	186	30	1	11	49	0	4	10	62	0	69	17	9	10	.268	.366	.412
Ledee, Ricky, L.A.*	102	266	237	31	66	105	16	1	7	39	0	6	3	20	1	55	0	0	5	.278	.335	.443
Lee, Carlos, Mil.	162	688	618	85	164	301	41	0	32	114	0	11	2	57	7	87	13	4	8	.265	.324	.487
Lee, Derrek, Chi.	158	691	594	120	199	393	50	3	46	107	0	7	5	85	23	109	15	3	12	.335	.418	.662
Lehr, Justin, Mil.	23	3	3	0	0	0	0	0	0	0	0	0	0	0	0	2	0	0	1	.000	.000	.000
Leicester, Jon, Chi.	6	1	0	0	0	0	0	0	0	0	1	0	0	0	0	0	0	0	0	.000	.000	.000
Leiter, Al, Fla.*	17	22	18	0	0	0	0	0	0	0	4	0	0	0	0	12	0	0	0	.000	.000	.000
Levine, Al, S.F.*	9	2	2	0	0	0	0	0	0	0	0	0	0	0	0	0	0	0	0	.000	.000	.000
Lidle, Cory, Phi.	31	67	58	2	8	8	0	0	0	2	8	0	0	1	0	30	0	0	0	.138	.153	.138
Lieber, Jon, Phi.*	36	78	73	7	7	9	2	0	0	4	3	1	0	1	0	29	0	0	3	.096	.107	.123
Lieberthal, Mike, Phi.	118	443	392	48	103	164	25	0	12	47	0	5	11	35	14	35	0	0	6	.263	.336	.418
Ligtenberg, Kerry, Ari.	7	1	0	0	0	0	0	0	0	0	0	0	0	0	0	1	0	0	0	.000	.000	.000
Linden, Todd, S.F.†	60	187	171	20	37	57	8	0	4	13	1	0	5	10	0	54	3	0	5	.216	.280	.333
Linebrink, Scott, S.D.	73	1	1	0	0	0	0	0	0	0	0	0	0	0	0	0	0	0	0	.000	.000	.000
Liriano, Pedro, Phi.	5	1	0	0	0	0	0	0	0	0	1	0	0	0	0	0	0	0	0	.000	.000	.000
Lo Duca, Paul, Fla.	132	496	445	45	126	169	23	1	6	57	5	8	4	34	5	31	4	3	16	.283	.334	.380
Loaiza, Esteban, Was.	34	80	74	3	12	14	2	0	0	4	6	0	0	0	0	23	0	1	1	.162	.162	.189
Lofton, Kenny, Phi.*	110	406	367	67	123	154	15	5	2	36	5	0	2	32	2	41	22	3	3	.335	.392	.420
Lopez, Aquilino, Col.-Phi.	11	1	1	0	0	0	0	0	0	0	0	0	0	0	0	0	0	0	0	.000	.000	.000
Lopez, Felipe, Cin.†	148	648	580	97	169	282	34	5	23	85	3	7	1	57	2	111	15	7	8	.291	.352	.486
Lopez, Luis, Cin.†	17	28	27	0	6	9	3	0	0	2	0	0	1	0	0	6	0	0	1	.222	.250	.333
Loretta, Mark, S.D.	105	463	404	54	113	140	16	1	3	38	2	4	8	45	4	34	8	4	11	.280	.360	.347
Lowe, Derek, L.A.	35	76	65	3	10	12	2	0	0	4	9	0	0	2	0	17	1	0	2	.154	.179	.185
Lowell, Mike, Fla.	150	558	500	56	118	180	36	1	8	58	1	9	2	46	1	58	4	0	14	.236	.298	.360
Lowry, Noah, S.F.	34	75	59	6	16	22	6	0	0	7	12	1	0	3	0	12	0	0	0	.271	.302	.373
Luna, Hector, St.L.	64	153	137	26	39	56	10	2	1	18	2	1	4	9	0	25	10	2	4	.285	.344	.409
Mabry, John, St.L.*	112	274	246	26	59	100	15	1	8	32	6	2	0	20	1	63	0	0	6	.240	.295	.407
Machado, Anderson, Cin.-Col.†	6	15	12	1	0	0	0	0	0	0	2	0	1	0	2	6	0	0	0	.000	.133	.000
Macias, Jose, Chi.†	112	190	177	15	45	56	8	0	1	13	4	3	0	6	0	24	4	3	6	.254	.274	.316
Mackowiak, Rob, Pit.*	142	512	463	57	126	180	21	3	9	58	2	1	3	43	4	100	8	4	7	.272	.337	.389
Maddux, Greg, Chi.	35	83	76	4	13	16	0	0	1	5	7	0	0	0	0	15	1	0	4	.171	.171	.211
Madson, Ryan, Phi.*	78	8	6	0	0	0	0	0	0	0	1	0	0	1	0	0	0	0	1	.000	.143	.000
Magruder, Chris, Mil.†	101	155	138	16	28	43	9	0	2	13	4	1	5	7	1	33	3	0	3	.203	.265	.312
Maholm, Paul, Pit.*	6	17	15	1	2	2	0	0	0	0	1	0	0	1	0	6	0	0	0	.133	.188	.133
Mahoney, Mike, St.L.	26	75	64	5	10	14	1	0	1	6	6	0	1	4	1	10	0	0	3	.156	.217	.219
Majewski, Gary, Was.	79	7	6	0	0	0	0	0	0	0	1	0	0	0	0	3	0	0	0	.000	.000	.000
Marquis, Jason, St.L.*	44	91	87	10	27	40	8	1	1	10	2	0	0	2	0	11	0	0	3	.310	.326	.460
Marte, Andy, Atl.	24	66	57	3	8	12	2	1	0	4	0	2	0	7	0	13	0	1	2	.140	.227	.211
Martinez, Pedro, N.Y.	31	76	69	2	6	6	0	0	0	1	6	0	0	1	0	26	0	0	1	.087	.100	.087
Martinez, Ramon, Phi.	33	65	56	7	16	21	2	0	1	9	2	3	1	3	0	7	0	1	1	.286	.317	.375
Mateo, Henry, Was.†	1	2	1	0	0	0	0	0	0	0	0	0	0	1	0	0	0	0	0	.000	.500	.000
Matheny, Mike, St.L.	134	485	443	42	107	180	34	0	13	59	3	4	6	29	10	91	0	2	11	.242	.295	.406
Matsui, Kazuo, N.Y.†	87	295	267	31	68	94	9	4	3	24	5	4	5	14	1	43	6	1	2	.255	.300	.352
May, Darrell, S.D.*	22	10	9	0	1	1	0	0	0	0	1	0	0	0	0	5	0	0	1	.111	.111	.111
McAnulty, Paul, S.D.*	22	29	24	4	5	5	0	0	0	0	1	0	1	3	1	7	1	0	0	.208	.321	.208
McCann, Brian, Atl.	59	204	180	20	50	72	7	0	5	23	4	1	1	18	5	26	1	1	5	.278	.345	.400
McClain, Scott, Chi.	13	16	14	1	2	3	1	0	0	1	0	0	0	2	0	2	0	0	1	.143	.250	.214
McCracken, Quinton, Ari.†	134	246	215	23	51	64	4	3	1	13	6	1	1	23	4	35	4	0	4	.237	.313	.298
McLouth, Nate, Pit.*	41	120	109	20	28	49	6	0	5	12	2	1	5	3	0	20	2	0	3	.257	.305	.450
Meadows, Brian, Pit.	65	1	1	0	0	0	0	0	0	0	0	0	0	0	0	0	0	0	0	.000	.000	.000
Medders, Brandon, Ari.	27	1	1	0	0	0	0	0	0	0	0	0	0	0	0	0	0	0	0	.000	.000	.000
Mesa, Jose, Pit.	55	2	1	0	0	0	0	0	0	0	1	0	0	0	0	1	0	0	0	.000	.000	.000
Messenger, Randy, Fla.	29	4	3	0	1	1	0	0	0	0	0	0	0	1	0	1	0	0	0	.333	.500	.333
Michaels, Jason, Phi.	105	343	289	54	88	120	16	2	4	31	2	4	4	44	1	45	3	3	3	.304	.399	.415
Mientkiewicz, Doug, N.Y.*	87	313	275	36	66	112	13	0	11	29	2	2	2	32	7	39	0	1	11	.240	.322	.407
Miles, Aaron, Col.†	99	347	324	37	91	115	12	3	2	28	10	1	4	8	1	38	4	2	6	.281	.306	.355
Miller, Damian, Mil.	114	431	385	50	105	159	25	1	9	43	2	3	4	37	6	94	0	1	16	.273	.340	.413
Milton, Eric, Cin.*	34	64	56	7	8	15	1	0	2	4	5	0	0	3	0	25	0	0	0	.143	.186	.268
Mitre, Sergio, Chi.	21	12	11	2	4	5	1	0	0	1	1	0	0	0	0	6	0	0	0	.364	.364	.455
Moehler, Brian, Fla.	37	47	40	1	3	4	1	0	0	3	5	0	1	1	0	15	0	0	0	.075	.119	.100
Moeller, Chad, Mil.	66	216	199	23	41	73	9	1	7	23	2	1	1	13	1	48	0	0	9	.206	.257	.367
Mohr, Dustan, Col.	98	293	266	34	57	124	10	3	17	38	0	2	2	23	2	94	1	2	3	.214	.280	.466
Molina, Yadier, St.L.	114	421	385	36	97	138	15	1	8	49	8	3	2	23	3	30	2	3	10	.252	.295	.358
Mondesi, Raul, Atl.	41	155	142	17	30	51	7	1	4	17	0	1	0	12	3	35	0	1	5	.211	.271	.359

Player, Team	G	TPA	AB	R	H	TB	2B	3B	HR	RBI	SH	SF	HP	BB	IBB	SO	SB	CS	GDP	Avg.	OBP	Slg.
Mordecai, Mike, Fla.	2	2	2	0	0	0	0	0	0	0	0	0	0	0	0	1	0	0	0	.000	.000	.000
Morris, Matt, St.L.	31	69	57	4	5	5	0	0	0	2	8	0	0	4	0	23	0	0	0	.088	.148	.088
Mosquera, Julio, Mil.	1	1	1	0	0	0	0	0	0	0	0	0	0	0	0	0	0	0	0	.000	.000	.000
Mota, Guillermo, Fla.	56	3	3	0	0	0	0	0	0	0	0	0	0	0	0	3	0	0	0	.000	.000	.000
Mulder, Mark, St.L.*	32	67	62	3	9	9	0	0	0	3	1	1	0	3	0	25	0	0	1	.145	.182	.145
Munter, Scott, S.F.	45	1	0	0	0	0	0	0	0	0	1	0	0	0	0	0	0	0	0	.000	.000	.000
Murton, Matt, Chi.	51	160	140	19	45	73	3	2	7	14	2	2	0	16	4	22	2	1	4	.321	.386	.521
Myers, Brett, Phi.	34	80	65	1	10	11	1	0	0	5	11	0	0	4	0	19	0	0	1	.154	.203	.169
Myrow, Brian, L.A.*	19	25	20	2	4	5	1	0	0	0	0	0	0	5	0	8	0	0	0	.200	.360	.250
Nady, Xavier, S.D.	124	356	326	40	85	143	15	2	13	43	1	0	7	22	1	67	2	1	5	.261	.321	.439
Nakamura, Norihiro, L.A.	17	41	39	1	5	7	2	0	0	3	0	0	0	2	0	7	0	0	3	.128	.171	.179
Navarro, Dioner, L.A.†	50	199	176	21	48	66	9	0	3	14	1	0	2	20	1	21	0	0	3	.273	.354	.375
Neal, Blaine, Col.*	11	1	1	0	0	0	0	0	0	0	0	0	0	0	0	1	0	0	0	.000	.000	.000
Nevin, Phil, S.D.	73	306	281	31	72	112	11	1	9	47	0	5	1	19	0	67	1	0	2	.256	.301	.399
Niekro, Lance, S.F.	113	302	278	32	70	128	16	3	12	46	0	5	2	17	0	53	0	2	11	.252	.295	.460
Nippert, Dustin, Ari.	3	5	4	0	1	1	0	0	0	0	0	0	0	1	0	3	0	0	0	.250	.400	.250
Novoa, Roberto, Chi.	49	1	1	0	0	0	0	0	0	0	0	0	0	0	0	0	0	0	0	.000	.000	.000
Nunez, Abraham O., St.L.†	139	467	421	64	120	152	13	2	5	44	9	0	0	37	4	63	0	1	6	.285	.343	.361
Obermueller, Wes, Mil.	24	16	15	1	3	6	1	1	0	0	1	0	0	0	0	2	0	0	0	.200	.200	.400
Offerman, Jose, Phi.-N.Y.†	86	118	105	11	24	35	3	1	2	13	1	0	1	11	0	17	0	0	4	.229	.308	.333
Ohka, Tomo, Was.-Mil.	33	59	54	2	6	6	0	0	0	3	3	0	0	2	0	25	0	0	0	.111	.143	.111
Ojeda, Miguel, S.D.	43	83	73	6	10	15	3	1	0	6	1	0	0	9	2	21	1	1	2	.137	.232	.205
Olivo, Miguel, S.D.	37	124	115	16	35	56	7	1	4	16	1	1	3	4	2	31	6	1	4	.304	.341	.487
Olmedo, Ray, Cin.†	54	88	77	10	17	26	4	1	1	4	3	1	1	6	0	22	4	0	1	.221	.282	.338
Olsen, Scott, Fla.*	5	4	3	0	0	0	0	0	0	0	1	0	0	0	0	1	0	0	0	.000	.000	.000
Olson, Tim, Col.	3	3	2	0	0	0	0	0	0	0	0	0	0	1	0	2	0	0	0	.000	.333	.000
Orr, Pete, Atl.*	112	162	150	32	45	58	8	1	1	8	5	0	1	6	0	23	7	1	2	.300	.331	.387
Ortiz, Ramon, Cin.	30	61	54	1	4	6	2	0	0	6	0	0	1	0	0	23	0	0	0	.074	.091	.111
Ortiz, Russ, Ari.	24	43	34	1	7	8	1	0	0	1	6	0	0	3	0	9	0	0	1	.206	.270	.235
Ortmeier, Dan, S.F.†	15	26	22	1	3	3	0	0	0	1	0	0	1	3	0	5	1	0	2	.136	.269	.136
Osik, Keith, Was.	6	4	4	0	0	0	0	0	0	0	0	0	0	0	0	0	0	0	0	.000	.000	.000
Osoria, Franquelis, L.A.	24	3	3	0	0	0	0	0	0	0	0	0	0	0	0	2	0	0	0	.000	.000	.000
Oswalt, Roy, Hou.	35	83	73	1	13	13	0	0	0	2	7	0	1	2	0	19	0	0	0	.178	.211	.178
Otsuka, Akinori, S.D.	66	1	1	0	0	0	0	0	0	0	0	0	0	0	0	0	0	0	0	.000	.000	.000
Overbay, Lyle, Mil.*	158	622	537	80	148	241	34	1	19	72	1	4	2	78	8	98	1	0	17	.276	.367	.449
Oxspring, Chris, S.D.*	5	2	2	0	0	0	0	0	0	0	0	0	0	0	0	0	0	0	0	.000	.000	.000
Padilla, Juan, N.Y.	24	2	2	0	1	1	0	0	0	0	0	0	0	0	0	1	0	0	0	.500	.500	.500
Padilla, Vicente, Phi.†	27	51	41	2	6	9	1	1	0	4	5	0	0	5	0	24	0	0	1	.146	.239	.220
Palmeiro, Orlando, Hou.*	114	231	204	22	58	88	17	2	3	20	5	3	4	15	1	23	3	1	4	.284	.341	.431
Park, Chan Ho, S.D.	10	18	14	2	3	3	0	0	0	0	2	4	0	0	0	6	0	0	0	.214	.214	.214
Patterson, Corey, Chi.*	126	483	451	47	97	157	15	3	13	34	5	1	1	23	3	118	15	5	5	.215	.254	.348
Patterson, John, Was.	31	68	59	2	6	9	3	0	0	8	0	1	0	0	0	23	0	0	0	.102	.117	.153
Paulino, Ronny, Pit.	2	5	4	1	2	2	0	0	0	0	0	0	1	0	0	0	0	0	0	.500	.600	.500
Peavy, Jake, S.D.	30	63	53	5	10	11	1	0	0	2	5	0	1	4	0	16	0	0	1	.189	.259	.208
Pena, Brayan, Atl.†	18	40	39	2	7	9	2	0	0	4	0	0	0	1	1	7	0	0	1	.179	.200	.231
Pena, Wily Mo, Cin.	99	335	311	42	79	153	17	0	19	51	0	1	3	20	0	116	2	1	7	.254	.304	.492
Penny, Brad, L.A.	29	61	50	1	8	11	3	0	0	3	9	0	1	1	0	17	0	0	0	.160	.192	.220
Perez, Antonio, L.A.	98	287	259	28	77	103	13	2	3	23	1	1	5	21	1	61	11	4	4	.297	.360	.398
Perez, Eddie, Atl.	16	39	38	3	8	16	2	0	2	6	0	0	0	1	0	5	0	0	1	.211	.231	.421
Perez, Miguel, Cin.	2	3	3	0	0	0	0	0	0	0	0	0	0	0	0	1	0	0	0	.000	.000	.000
Perez, Neifi, Chi.†	154	609	572	59	157	219	33	1	9	54	12	4	3	18	3	47	8	4	22	.274	.298	.383
Perez, Odalis, L.A.*	19	42	33	2	4	4	0	0	0	0	8	0	0	1	0	10	0	0	0	.121	.147	.121
Perez, Oliver, Pit.*	20	42	33	1	6	6	0	0	0	3	7	1	0	1	0	11	1	0	0	.182	.200	.182
Perez, Tomas, Phi.†	94	176	159	17	37	44	7	0	0	22	3	1	2	11	2	27	1	0	6	.233	.289	.277
Pettitte, Andy, Hou.*	33	79	62	1	5	5	0	0	0	3	15	1	0	1	0	19	0	0	0	.081	.094	.081
Phillips, Jason, L.A.	121	434	399	38	95	145	20	0	10	55	2	4	4	25	4	50	0	1	16	.238	.287	.363
Piazza, Mike, N.Y.	113	442	398	41	100	180	23	0	19	62	0	3	4	41	6	67	0	0	7	.251	.326	.452
Piedra, Jorge, Col.*	61	124	112	19	35	63	8	1	6	16	0	1	1	10	0	15	2	1	2	.313	.371	.563
Pierre, Juan, Fla.*	162	719	656	96	181	232	19	13	2	47	10	2	9	41	1	45	57	17	10	.276	.326	.354
Polanco, Placido, Phi.	43	173	158	26	50	66	7	0	3	20	0	0	3	12	0	9	0	0	3	.316	.376	.418
Pratt, Todd, Phi.	60	196	175	17	44	69	4	0	7	23	0	0	2	19	5	50	0	0	3	.251	.332	.394
Prior, Mark, Chi.	27	56	48	5	11	13	2	0	0	3	6	0	0	2	0	14	0	0	0	.229	.260	.271
Pujols, Albert, St.L.	161	700	591	129	195	360	38	2	41	117	0	3	9	97	27	65	16	2	19	.330	.430	.609
Qualls, Chad, Hou.	77	1	1	0	0	0	0	0	0	0	0	0	0	0	0	1	0	0	0	.000	.000	.000
Quantrill, Paul, S.D.-Fla.*	28	1	1	0	0	0	0	0	0	0	0	0	0	0	0	0	0	0	0	.000	.000	.000
Quintanilla, Omar, Col.*	39	143	128	16	28	31	1	1	0	7	6	0	0	9	0	15	2	1	3	.219	.270	.242
Quintero, Humberto, Hou.	18	57	54	6	10	14	1	0	1	8	2	0	0	1	1	10	0	0	3	.185	.200	.259
Ramirez, Aramis, Chi.	123	506	463	72	140	263	30	0	31	92	0	2	6	35	4	60	0	1	15	.302	.358	.568
Ramirez, Elizardo, Cin.*	6	8	8	0	0	0	0	0	0	0	0	0	0	0	0	3	0	0	1	.000	.000	.000
Ramirez, Horacio, Atl.*	34	77	73	4	16	19	3	0	0	2	3	0	0	1	0	17	0	0	2	.219	.230	.260
Ramirez, Julio, S.F.	12	4	4	3	1	1	0	0	0	1	0	0	0	0	0	1	0	0	0	.250	.250	.250
Randa, Joe, Cin.-S.D.	150	609	555	71	153	251	43	2	17	68	0	3	4	47	3	81	0	1	11	.276	.335	.452
Rauch, Jon, Was.	15	8	7	1	1	1	0	0	0	1	1	0	0	0	0	5	0	0	0	.143	.143	.143
Redding, Tim, S.D.	9	9	8	0	0	0	0	0	0	0	1	0	0	0	0	5	0	0	0	.000	.000	.000
Redman, Mark, Pit.*	30	60	53	1	6	6	0	0	0	2	4	0	0	3	0	21	0	0	4	.113	.161	.113
Redman, Tike, Pit.*	135	344	319	33	80	106	12	4	2	26	2	3	1	19	0	27	4	1	8	.251	.292	.332
Reitsma, Chris, Atl.	76	1	1	0	0	0	0	0	0	0	0	0	0	0	0	0	0	0	0	.000	.000	.000
Relaford, Desi, Col.†	73	238	210	24	47	67	13	2	1	16	1	1	4	22	2	42	3	3	1	.224	.308	.319
Repko, Jason, L.A.	129	301	276	43	61	106	15	3	8	30	2	0	7	16	1	80	5	0	7	.221	.281	.384
Resop, Chris, Fla.	15	1	1	0	0	0	0	0	0	0	0	0	0	0	0	1	0	0	0	.000	.000	.000
Restovich, Michael, Col.-Pit.	66	126	115	15	27	43	5	1	3	8	0	0	0	11	0	29	0	0	5	.235	.302	.374
Reyes, Al, St.L.	65	3	1	0	0	0	0	0	0	0	1	0	0	1	0	1	0	0	0	.000	.500	.000

Player, Team	G	TPA	AB	R	H	TB	2B	3B	HR	RBI	SH	SF	HP	BB	IBB	SO	SB	CS	GDP	Avg.	OBP	Slg.
Reyes, Anthony, St.L.	4	4	4	0	0	0	0	0	0	0	0	0	0	0	0	1	0	0	0	.000	.000	.000
Reyes, Dennys, S.D.	36	5	5	0	1	1	0	0	0	0	0	0	0	0	0	2	0	0	0	.200	.200	.200
Reyes, Jose, N.Y.†	161	733	696	99	190	269	24	17	7	58	4	4	2	27	0	78	60	15	7	.273	.300	.386
Riedling, John, Fla.	29	2	2	0	0	0	0	0	0	0	0	0	0	0	0	1	0	0	0	.000	.000	.000
Roberts, Dave, S.D.*	115	480	411	65	113	176	19	10	8	38	11	4	1	53	3	59	23	12	9	.275	.356	.428
Robles, Oscar, L.A.*	110	399	364	44	99	134	18	1	5	34	1	1	2	31	0	33	0	8	8	.272	.332	.368
Rodriguez, John, St.L.*	56	176	149	15	44	65	6	0	5	24	3	2	3	19	4	45	2	0	0	.295	.382	.436
Rodriguez, Wandy, Hou.†	25	43	40	3	6	6	0	0	0	1	1	0	0	2	0	16	0	0	0	.150	.190	.150
Rolen, Scott, St.L.	56	223	196	28	46	75	12	1	5	28	0	1	1	25	1	28	1	2	3	.235	.323	.383
Rollins, Jimmy, Phi.†	158	732	677	115	196	292	38	11	12	54	2	2	4	47	8	71	41	6	9	.290	.338	.431
Romano, Jason, Cin.	19	34	30	3	8	13	2	0	1	3	0	0	1	3	0	9	0	0	0	.267	.353	.433
Rose, Mike, L.A.†	15	46	43	2	9	14	2	0	1	1	0	0	0	3	0	6	0	0	3	.209	.261	.326
Ross, Cody, L.A.	14	26	25	1	4	5	1	0	0	1	0	0	0	1	0	10	0	0	1	.160	.192	.200
Ross, David, Pit.-S.D.	51	138	125	11	30	49	8	1	3	15	2	3	2	6	0	28	0	0	3	.240	.279	.392
Rueter, Kirk, S.F.*	21	37	30	1	5	6	1	0	0	1	6	0	0	1	0	2	0	0	1	.167	.194	.200
Rusch, Glendon, Chi.*	46	43	41	2	6	8	2	0	0	0	0	0	1	1	0	9	0	0	2	.146	.186	.195
Sadler, Ray, Pit.	3	8	8	1	2	5	0	0	1	1	0	0	0	0	0	1	0	0	0	.250	.250	.625
Saenz, Olmedo, L.A.	109	352	319	39	84	153	24	0	15	63	0	2	3	27	1	63	0	0	12	.263	.325	.480
Sanchez, Alex, S.F.*	19	47	43	4	11	14	3	0	0	3	2	0	1	1	0	9	2	2	0	.256	.289	.326
Sanchez, Duaner, L.A.	79	4	4	0	0	0	0	0	0	0	0	0	0	0	0	0	0	0	0	.000	.000	.000
Sanchez, Freddy, Pit.	132	492	453	54	132	181	26	4	5	35	4	3	5	27	1	36	2	2	6	.291	.336	.400
Sanders, Reggie, St.L.	93	329	295	49	80	161	14	2	21	54	0	2	4	28	1	75	14	1	8	.271	.340	.546
Sandoval, Danny, Phi.†	3	2	2	1	0	0	0	0	0	0	0	0	0	0	0	1	0	0	0	.000	.000	.000
Santana, Julio, Mil.	41	1	1	0	0	0	0	0	0	0	0	0	0	0	0	0	0	0	0	.000	.000	.000
Santiago, Benito, Pit.	6	23	23	1	6	9	1	1	0	0	0	0	0	0	0	3	0	0	1	.261	.261	.391
Santos, Victor, Mil.	29	43	40	1	3	3	0	0	0	0	3	0	0	0	0	13	0	0	0	.075	.075	.075
Sardinha, Dane, Cin.	1	3	3	0	0	0	0	0	0	0	0	0	0	0	0	1	0	0	0	.000	.000	.000
Schmidt, Jason, S.F.	29	60	53	2	5	8	0	0	1	2	6	0	1	0	0	32	0	0	0	.094	.111	.151
Schmoll, Steve, L.A.	48	1	1	0	0	0	0	0	0	0	0	0	0	0	0	0	0	0	0	.000	.000	.000
Schneider, Brian, Was.*	116	408	369	38	99	151	20	1	10	44	2	2	6	29	7	48	1	0	10	.268	.330	.409
Schumaker, Skip, St.L.*	27	26	24	9	6	7	1	0	0	1	0	0	0	2	0	2	1	0	0	.250	.308	.292
Scott, Luke, Hou.*	34	89	80	6	15	23	4	2	0	4	0	0	0	9	1	23	1	1	0	.188	.270	.288
Seabol, Scott, St.L.	59	114	105	11	23	31	5	0	1	10	0	1	0	8	0	23	0	0	1	.219	.272	.295
Self, Todd, Hou.*	21	49	45	7	9	14	2	0	1	4	1	0	0	3	0	9	0	0	2	.200	.250	.311
Seo, Jae, N.Y.	14	34	29	2	3	4	1	0	0	4	2	0	0	3	0	11	0	0	0	.103	.188	.138
Shabala, Adam, S.F.*	6	18	15	1	3	3	0	0	0	4	1	1	0	1	0	5	0	0	1	.200	.235	.200
Shackelford, Brian, Cin.*	37	1	1	0	0	0	0	0	0	0	0	0	0	0	0	0	0	0	0	.000	.000	.000
Shealy, Ryan, Col.	36	104	91	14	30	43	7	0	2	16	0	0	0	13	0	22	1	0	6	.330	.413	.473
Sheets, Ben, Mil.	22	53	45	0	1	1	0	0	0	0	7	0	1	0	0	17	0	0	0	.022	.043	.022
Short, Rick, Was.	11	17	15	4	6	14	2	0	2	4	0	0	1	1	0	1	0	0	0	.400	.471	.933
Sledge, Terrmel, Was.*	20	46	37	7	9	14	0	1	1	8	0	2	0	7	1	8	2	1	3	.243	.348	.378
Smoltz, John, Atl.	33	83	68	1	10	14	2	1	0	3	12	0	0	3	0	26	0	0	3	.147	.183	.206
Snell, Ian, Pit.	15	8	8	0	0	0	0	0	0	0	0	0	0	0	0	3	0	0	0	.000	.000	.000
Snow, J.T., S.F.*	117	410	367	40	101	134	17	2	4	40	2	2	7	32	1	61	1	0	6	.275	.343	.365
Snyder, Chris, Ari.	115	373	326	24	66	98	14	0	6	28	3	0	4	40	5	87	0	1	6	.202	.297	.301
Sosa, Jorge, Atl.	45	35	31	1	3	3	0	0	0	0	3	0	0	1	0	15	0	0	1	.097	.125	.097
Soto, Geovany, Chi.	1	1	1	0	0	0	0	0	0	0	0	0	0	0	0	0	0	0	0	.000	.000	.000
Speier, Ryan, Col.	22	2	2	0	0	0	0	0	0	0	0	0	0	0	0	0	0	0	0	.000	.000	.000
Spilborghs, Ryan, Col.	1	4	4	0	2	2	0	0	0	1	0	0	0	0	0	1	0	0	0	.500	.500	.500
Spivey, Junior, Mil.-Was.	77	293	259	37	60	98	15	1	7	24	1	1	3	29	2	83	9	3	3	.232	.315	.378
Stanton, Mike, Was.*	30	1	1	1	0	0	0	0	0	0	0	0	0	0	0	0	0	0	0	.000	.000	.000
Stauffer, Tim, S.D.	15	27	24	1	3	4	1	0	0	1	3	0	0	0	0	10	0	0	0	.125	.125	.167
Stinnett, Kelly, Ari.	59	143	129	15	32	54	4	0	6	12	1	0	1	12	3	32	0	0	4	.248	.317	.419
Stone, Ricky, Cin.	23	2	2	0	0	0	0	0	0	0	0	0	0	0	0	1	0	0	0	.000	.000	.000
Sullivan, Cory, Col.*	139	424	378	64	111	146	15	4	4	30	10	5	3	28	0	83	12	3	6	.294	.343	.386
Suppan, Jeff, St.L.	32	67	58	5	12	17	2	0	1	5	6	0	3	0	9	0	0	0	2	.207	.246	.293
Sweeney, Mark, S.D.*	135	267	221	31	65	103	12	1	8	40	1	5	0	40	3	58	4	0	6	.294	.395	.466
Taguchi, So, St.L.	143	424	396	45	114	163	21	2	8	53	2	4	2	20	2	62	11	2	11	.288	.322	.412
Tavarez, Julian, St.L.*	74	1	0	0	0	0	0	0	0	0	1	0	0	0	0	0	0	0	0	.000	.000	.000
Taveras, Willy, Hou.	152	635	592	82	172	202	13	4	3	29	7	4	7	25	1	103	34	11	4	.291	.325	.341
Tejeda, Robinson, Phi.	26	25	20	1	2	4	0	1	0	0	5	0	0	0	0	9	0	0	0	.100	.100	.200
Terrero, Luis, Ari.	88	184	161	23	37	57	6	1	4	20	2	1	6	14	0	40	3	2	5	.230	.313	.354
Theriot, Ryan, Chi.	9	14	13	3	2	3	1	0	0	0	0	0	0	1	0	2	0	0	0	.154	.214	.231
Thome, Jim, Phi.*	59	242	193	26	40	68	7	0	7	30	0	2	2	45	4	59	0	0	5	.207	.360	.352
Thompson, Brad, St.L.	41	7	6	0	1	1	0	0	0	0	1	0	0	0	0	2	0	0	0	.167	.167	.167
Thompson, Derek, L.A.*	4	5	4	0	0	0	0	0	0	0	1	0	0	0	0	2	0	0	0	.000	.000	.000
Thomson, John, Atl.	17	36	25	2	5	7	2	0	0	2	9	0	0	2	0	12	0	0	0	.200	.259	.280
Tomko, Brett, S.F.	33	67	55	3	9	10	1	0	0	5	10	0	0	2	0	16	0	0	0	.164	.193	.182
Torcato, Tony, S.F.*	11	12	11	1	3	3	0	0	0	1	0	0	0	1	0	2	0	0	2	.273	.333	.273
Torrealba, Yorvit, S.F.	34	105	93	18	21	32	8	0	1	7	2	0	1	9	1	25	1	0	3	.226	.301	.344
Torres, Salomon, Pit.	78	4	4	0	2	2	0	0	0	0	0	0	0	0	0	0	0	0	0	.500	.500	.500
Trachsel, Steve, N.Y.	6	15	15	0	1	1	0	0	0	0	0	0	0	0	0	7	0	0	0	.067	.067	.067
Tracy, Chad, Ari.*	145	553	503	73	155	278	34	4	27	72	1	6	8	35	4	78	3	1	10	.308	.359	.553
Treanor, Matt, Fla.	58	154	134	10	27	35	8	0	0	13	1	0	3	16	1	28	0	0	5	.201	.301	.261
Tucker, Michael, S.F.-Phi.*	126	307	268	35	64	97	16	1	5	36	2	4	2	31	3	52	4	0	7	.239	.318	.362
Utley, Chase, Phi.*	147	628	543	93	158	293	39	6	28	105	0	7	9	69	5	109	16	3	10	.291	.376	.540
Valdez, Ismael, Fla.	14	16	13	0	2	2	0	0	0	0	3	0	0	0	0	7	0	0	0	.154	.154	.154
Valdez, Wilson, S.D.	9	15	13	0	3	5	2	0	0	1	0	0	0	2	0	1	0	0	1	.231	.333	.385
Valent, Eric, N.Y.*	28	50	43	4	8	11	3	0	0	1	0	0	0	7	3	17	0	0	0	.186	.300	.256
Valentin, Javier, Cin.†	76	254	221	36	62	115	11	0	14	50	0	3	0	30	3	37	0	0	5	.281	.362	.520
Valentin, Jose, L.A.*	56	184	147	17	25	39	4	2	2	14	0	2	4	31	2	38	3	1	2	.170	.326	.265
Vargas, Claudio, Was.-Ari.	25	45	36	1	4	4	0	0	0	3	7	0	0	2	0	7	0	0	2	.111	.158	.111

Player, Team	G	TPA	AB	R	H	TB	2B	3B	HR	RBI	SH	SF	HP	BB	IBB	SO	SB	CS	GDP	Avg.	OBP	Slg.
Vargas, Jason, Fla.*	18	27	26	3	8	10	2	0	0	2	0	0	0	1	0	7	0	0	0	.308	.333	.385
Vasquez, Jorge, Atl.	7	1	1	0	0	0	0	0	0	0	0	0	0	0	0	1	0	0	0	.000	.000	.000
Vazquez, Javier, Ari.	33	72	63	2	15	19	1	0	1	2	6	0	0	3	0	10	0	0	0	.238	.273	.302
Victorino, Shane, Phi.†	21	19	17	5	5	11	0	0	2	8	0	2	0	0	0	3	0	0	0	.294	.263	.647
Vidro, Jose, Was.†	87	347	309	38	85	131	21	2	7	32	2	4	1	31	3	30	0	0	8	.275	.339	.424
Villone, Ron, Fla.*	27	1	1	0	0	0	0	0	0	0	0	0	0	0	0	1	0	0	0	.000	.000	.000
Vizcaino, Jose, Hou.†	98	205	187	15	46	63	10	2	1	23	1	2	0	15	4	40	2	0	2	.246	.299	.337
Vizquel, Omar, S.F.†	152	651	568	66	154	199	28	4	3	45	20	2	5	56	0	58	24	10	10	.271	.341	.350
Vogelsong, Ryan, Pit.	44	10	9	0	1	2	1	0	0	0	0	0	1	0	0	4	0	0	0	.111	.200	.222
Wagner, Billy, Phi.*	75	3	3	0	1	1	0	0	0	0	0	0	0	0	0	2	0	0	0	.333	.333	.333
Wagner, Ryan, Cin.	42	2	1	1	0	0	0	0	0	0	1	0	0	0	0	1	0	0	0	.000	.000	.000
Walker, Larry, St.L.*	100	367	315	66	91	158	20	1	15	52	0	2	9	41	3	64	2	1	9	.289	.384	.502
Walker, Todd, Chi.*	110	433	397	50	121	188	25	3	12	40	2	2	1	31	1	40	1	1	8	.305	.355	.474
Walker, Tyler, S.F.	67	1	1	0	0	0	0	0	0	0	0	0	0	0	0	0	0	0	0	.000	.000	.000
Ward, Daryle, Pit.*	133	453	407	46	106	165	21	1	12	63	0	8	1	37	10	60	0	2	18	.260	.318	.405
Watson, Brandon, Was.*	25	48	40	8	7	13	1	1	1	5	4	0	0	4	0	8	0	2	0	.175	.250	.325
Weaver, Jeff, L.A.	39	78	70	6	16	18	2	0	0	7	6	0	0	2	0	19	0	0	0	.229	.250	.257
Webb, Brandon, Ari.	33	76	62	0	6	6	0	0	0	2	13	0	0	1	0	30	0	0	0	.097	.111	.097
Weeks, Rickie, Mil.	96	414	360	56	86	142	13	2	13	42	2	1	11	40	2	96	15	2	11	.239	.333	.394
Wellemeyer, Todd, Chi.	22	4	4	1	1	1	0	0	0	0	0	0	0	0	0	2	0	0	0	.250	.250	.250
Wells, Kip, Pit.	34	61	57	4	9	13	1	0	1	2	3	0	1	0	0	26	0	0	0	.158	.172	.228
Werth, Jayson, L.A.	102	395	337	46	79	126	22	2	7	43	1	3	6	48	2	114	11	2	10	.234	.338	.374
White, Matt, Was.	1	1	1	0	0	0	0	0	0	0	0	0	0	0	0	0	0	0	0	.000	.000	.000
White, Rick, Pit.	71	2	2	0	0	0	0	0	0	0	0	0	0	0	0	0	0	0	0	.000	.000	.000
Wigginton, Ty, Pit.	57	171	155	20	40	72	9	1	7	25	1	0	1	14	0	30	0	1	3	.258	.324	.465
Wilkerson, Brad, Was.*	148	661	565	76	140	229	42	7	11	57	3	2	7	84	9	147	8	10	6	.248	.351	.405
Williams, Dave, Pit.*	25	50	42	2	5	6	1	0	0	4	6	1	0	1	0	21	0	0	0	.119	.136	.143
Williams, Gerald, N.Y.	39	32	30	9	7	12	2	0	1	3	1	0	0	1	0	7	2	0	0	.233	.258	.400
Williams, Jerome, S.F.-Chi.	22	40	34	1	3	4	1	0	0	0	6	0	0	0	0	16	0	0	0	.088	.088	.118
Williams, Randy, S.D.-Col.*	32	1	1	0	0	0	0	0	0	0	0	0	0	0	0	0	0	0	0	.000	.000	.000
Williams, Woody, S.D.	30	55	46	3	7	7	0	0	0	3	8	1	0	0	0	19	1	0	1	.152	.149	.152
Willingham, Josh, Fla.	16	28	23	3	7	8	1	0	0	4	1	0	2	2	0	5	0	0	1	.304	.407	.348
Willis, Dontrelle, Fla.*	40	101	92	14	24	31	4	0	1	11	4	1	1	3	0	13	0	0	2	.261	.289	.337
Wilson, Craig, Pit.	59	238	197	23	52	83	14	1	5	22	0	1	10	30	2	69	3	0	6	.264	.387	.421
Wilson, Enrique, Chi.†	15	25	22	1	3	5	2	0	0	0	0	0	0	3	0	1	0	0	0	.136	.240	.227
Wilson, Jack, Pit.	158	639	587	60	151	213	24	7	8	52	11	4	6	31	6	58	7	3	11	.257	.299	.363
Wilson, Josh, Fla.	11	11	10	2	1	2	1	0	0	0	0	0	1	0	0	4	0	0	0	.100	.182	.200
Wilson, Paul, Cin.	9	19	17	1	3	3	0	0	0	1	2	0	0	0	0	11	0	0	0	.176	.176	.176
Wilson, Preston, Col.-Was.	139	576	520	73	135	243	29	2	25	90	1	3	7	45	0	148	6	5	18	.260	.325	.467
Winn, Randy, S.F.†	58	247	231	39	83	157	22	5	14	26	4	0	1	11	1	38	7	5	4	.359	.391	.680
Wise, Matt, Mil.	49	1	1	0	1	1	0	0	0	1	0	0	0	0	0	0	0	0	0	1.000	1.000	1.000
Wolf, Randy, Phi.*	15	28	26	2	4	6	2	0	0	1	1	0	0	1	0	8	0	0	0	.154	.185	.231
Wood, Kerry, Chi.	21	21	18	0	2	4	2	0	0	2	2	0	0	1	0	6	0	0	0	.111	.158	.222
Woodward, Chris, N.Y.	81	192	173	16	49	68	10	0	3	18	2	2	2	13	0	46	0	0	2	.283	.337	.393
Worrell, Tim, Phi.-Ari.	51	1	1	0	0	0	0	0	0	0	0	0	0	0	0	1	0	0	0	.000	.000	.000
Wright, David, N.Y.	160	657	575	99	176	301	42	1	27	102	0	3	7	72	2	113	17	7	16	.306	.388	.523
Wright, Jamey, Col.	35	59	55	2	8	9	1	0	0	3	3	0	0	1	0	21	0	0	0	.145	.161	.164
Wuertz, Michael, Chi.	75	2	2	0	0	0	0	0	0	0	0	0	0	0	0	2	0	0	0	.000	.000	.000
Wunsch, Kelly, L.A.*	46	1	1	0	0	0	0	0	0	0	0	0	0	0	0	0	0	0	0	.000	.000	.000
Young, Eric, S.D.	56	163	142	22	39	54	9	0	2	12	3	0	0	18	0	12	7	6	4	.275	.356	.380
Zambrano, Carlos, Chi.†	34	84	80	8	24	37	6	2	1	6	4	0	0	0	0	25	0	2	3	.300	.300	.463
Zambrano, Victor, N.Y.†	31	58	53	2	7	9	0	1	0	2	5	0	0	0	0	22	0	0	0	.132	.132	.170
Zimmerman, Ryan, Was.	20	62	58	6	23	33	10	0	0	6	0	1	0	3	0	12	0	0	1	.397	.419	.569

AWARDED FIRST BASE ON OBSTRUCTION OR CATCHER'S INTERFERENCE _ Patterson, Chicago 2 (Molina, Closser); Bradley, Los Angeles (Mahoney); Freel, Cincinnati (Pratt); Gonzalez, Colorado (Haad); Grabowski, Los Angeles (Stinnett); Pierre, Florida (LaRue); Saenz, Los Angeles (Fick).

PLAYERS WITH TWO OR MORE TEAMS

Player, Team	G	TPA	AB	R	H	TB	2B	3B	HR	RBI	SH	SF	HP	BB	IBB	SO	SB	CS	GDP	Avg.	OBP	Slg.
Amezaga, Alfredo, Col.†	2	3	3	1	1	1	0	0	0	0	0	0	0	0	0	0	0	0	0	.333	.333	.333
Amezaga, Alfredo, Pit.†	3	4	3	1	0	0	0	0	0	0	0	0	1	0	0	1	0	0	0	.000	.250	.000
Byrd, Marlon, Phi.	5	15	13	0	4	4	0	0	0	0	0	0	1	1	0	3	0	0	0	.308	.400	.308
Byrd, Marlon, Was.	74	244	216	20	57	82	15	2	2	26	5	4	1	18	1	47	5	1	5	.264	.318	.380
Chavez, Endy, Was.*	7	12	9	2	2	3	1	0	0	1	0	0	0	3	0	1	0	1	1	.222	.417	.333
Chavez, Endy, Phi.*	91	118	107	17	23	32	3	3	0	10	7	0	0	4	0	13	2	1	2	.215	.243	.299
Cruz Jr., Jose, Ari.†	64	245	202	23	43	88	9	0	12	28	0	1	0	42	2	54	0	1	6	.213	.347	.436
Cruz Jr., Jose, L.A.†	47	179	156	23	47	83	14	2	6	22	0	0	0	23	1	43	0	1	4	.301	.391	.532
Cruz, Deivi, S.F.	81	221	209	26	56	83	10	1	5	19	2	0	0	10	1	31	0	1	5	.268	.301	.397
Cruz, Deivi, Was.	20	54	51	2	13	14	1	0	0	1	1	0	1	1	0	3	0	0	0	.255	.283	.275
Day, Zach, Was.	11	9	8	0	1	1	0	0	0	0	1	0	0	0	0	3	0	0	0	.125	.125	.125
Day, Zach, Col.	5	3	3	1	1	1	0	0	0	0	0	0	0	0	0	0	0	0	0	.333	.333	.333
Gerut, Jody, Chi.*	11	16	14	1	1	2	1	0	0	0	0	0	0	2	0	3	0	0	0	.071	.188	.143
Gerut, Jody, Pit.*	4	18	18	2	4	5	1	0	0	2	0	0	0	0	0	3	0	0	1	.222	.222	.278
Hollandsworth, Todd, Chi.*	107	290	268	23	68	104	17	2	5	35	1	2	1	18	1	53	4	4	4	.254	.301	.388
Hollandsworth, Todd, Atl.*	24	40	35	3	6	9	0	0	1	1	0	0	0	5	0	13	0	1	1	.171	.275	.257
Kata, Matt, Ari.†	30	38	31	6	6	10	2	1	0	0	2	0	0	5	0	4	0	1	0	.194	.306	.323
Kata, Matt, Phi.†	10	6	6	1	1	1	0	0	0	0	0	0	0	0	0	2	0	0	0	.167	.167	.167
Kelly, Kenny, Cin.	7	9	9	2	3	3	0	0	0	2	0	0	0	0	0	3	0	0	0	.333	.333	.333
Kelly, Kenny, Was.	17	5	4	3	1	2	1	0	0	0	0	0	0	1	0	3	1	1	0	.250	.400	.500
Kim, Sunny, Was.	10	6	4	0	0	0	0	0	0	0	0	0	0	1	0	1	0	0	0	.000	.000	.000

Player, Team	G	TPA	AB	R	H	TB	2B	3B	HR	RBI	SH	SF	HP	BB	IBB	SO	SB	CS	GDP	Avg.	OBP	Slg.
Kim, Sunny, Col.	12	20	15	2	2	2	0	0	0	3	4	1	0	0	0	4	0	0	0	.133	.125	.133
Lawton, Matt, Pit.*	101	445	374	53	102	162	28	1	10	44	0	4	9	58	0	61	16	9	7	.273	.380	.433
Lawton, Matt, Chi.*	19	83	78	8	19	24	2	0	1	5	0	0	1	4	0	8	1	0	3	.244	.289	.308
Machado, Anderson, Cin.†	2	2	2	0	0	0	0	0	0	0	0	0	0	0	0	1	0	0	0	.000	.000	.000
Machado, Anderson, Col.†	4	13	10	1	0	0	0	0	0	2	0	1	0	2	0	5	0	0	0	.000	.154	.000
Offerman, Jose, Phi.†	33	38	33	6	6	12	1	1	1	3	0	0	0	5	0	6	0	0	1	.182	.289	.364
Offerman, Jose, N.Y.†	53	80	72	5	18	23	2	0	1	10	1	0	1	6	0	11	0	0	3	.250	.316	.319
Ohka, Tomo, Was.	10	17	16	1	4	4	0	0	0	0	1	0	0	0	0	5	0	0	0	.250	.250	.250
Ohka, Tomo, Mil.	21	42	38	1	2	2	0	0	0	3	2	0	0	2	0	20	0	0	0	.053	.100	.053
Randa, Joe, Cin.	92	368	332	44	96	163	26	1	13	48	0	1	2	33	2	52	0	0	6	.289	.356	.491
Randa, Joe, S.D.	58	241	223	27	57	88	17	1	4	20	0	2	2	14	1	29	0	1	5	.256	.303	.395
Restovich, Michael, Col.	14	34	31	5	9	14	2	0	1	3	0	0	0	3	0	5	0	0	2	.290	.353	.452
Restovich, Michael, Pit.	52	92	84	10	18	29	3	1	2	5	0	0	0	8	0	24	0	0	3	.214	.283	.345
Ross, David, Pit.	40	119	108	9	24	41	8	0	3	15	1	3	1	6	0	24	0	0	3	.222	.263	.380
Ross, David, S.D.	11	19	17	2	6	8	0	1	0	0	1	0	1	0	0	4	0	0	0	.353	.389	.471
Spivey, Junior, Mil.	49	202	182	22	43	68	8	1	5	17	1	0	1	18	1	57	7	3	3	.236	.308	.374
Spivey, Junior, Was.	28	91	77	15	17	30	7	0	2	7	0	1	2	11	1	26	2	0	0	.221	.330	.390
Tucker, Michael, S.F.*	104	286	250	32	60	93	16	1	5	33	2	4	2	28	3	48	4	0	6	.240	.317	.372
Tucker, Michael, Phi.*	22	21	18	3	4	4	0	0	0	3	0	0	0	3	0	4	0	0	1	.222	.333	.222
Vargas, Claudio, Was.	3	2	2	0	1	1	0	0	0	0	0	0	0	0	0	0	0	0	0	.500	.500	.500
Vargas, Claudio, Ari.	19	43	34	1	3	3	0	0	0	3	7	0	0	2	0	7	0	0	2	.088	.139	.088
Williams, Jerome, S.F.	4	4	4	0	0	0	0	0	0	0	0	0	0	0	0	0	0	0	0	.000	.000	.000
Williams, Jerome, Chi.	17	36	30	1	3	4	1	0	0	0	6	0	0	0	0	16	0	0	0	.100	.100	.133
Wilson, Preston, Col.	71	296	267	39	69	131	15	1	15	47	1	2	1	25	0	77	3	2	8	.258	.322	.491
Wilson, Preston, Was.	68	280	253	34	66	112	14	1	10	43	0	1	6	20	0	71	3	4	10	.261	.329	.443

DESIGNATED HITTING

TEAM

Team	G	TPA	AB	R	H	TB	2B	3B	HR	RBI	SH	SF	HP	BB	IBB	SO	SB	CS	GDP	Avg.	OBP	Slg.
St. Louis	9	38	29	10	12	25	4	0	3	10	0	0	1	8	0	4	0	0	0	.414	.553	.862
Colorado	6	25	23	2	9	14	2	0	1	3	0	0	2	0	0	7	1	0	1	.391	.440	.609
San Francisco	9	37	29	7	11	16	2	0	1	6	1	2	1	4	0	6	0	0	0	.379	.444	.552
Atlanta	6	25	24	3	8	12	1	0	1	4	0	0	0	1	0	5	0	0	1	.333	.360	.500
Milwaukee	9	38	33	2	10	13	3	0	0	5	0	1	0	4	0	7	0	0	0	.303	.368	.394
Philadelphia	9	40	32	5	9	10	1	0	0	1	0	0	0	8	2	6	0	0	1	.281	.425	.313
Chicago	6	22	19	2	5	11	0	0	2	4	0	0	1	2	0	5	0	0	1	.263	.364	.579
Los Angeles	9	38	35	3	9	12	3	0	0	3	0	0	1	2	0	12	0	0	0	.257	.316	.343
New York	9	38	35	3	8	13	2	0	1	1	0	0	0	3	0	3	0	0	1	.229	.289	.371
Washington	9	38	37	1	8	10	2	0	0	4	0	0	1	0	0	3	0	0	1	.216	.237	.270
San Diego	9	39	35	6	7	13	3	0	1	4	0	0	4	0	0	6	0	0	0	.200	.282	.371
Pittsburgh	6	26	23	2	4	5	1	0	0	4	0	0	2	1	0	10	2	0	0	.174	.269	.217
Arizona	9	40	38	3	6	11	2	0	1	6	0	1	0	1	0	14	0	0	0	.158	.175	.289
Florida	6	27	20	1	3	3	0	0	0	1	0	0	2	5	0	6	0	1	0	.150	.370	.150
Houston	9	39	35	4	5	6	1	0	0	1	0	0	1	3	0	5	1	0	0	.143	.231	.171
Cincinnati	6	24	22	1	3	6	0	0	1	1	0	0	1	1	0	11	0	0	0	.136	.208	.273
Totals	147	534	469	55	117	180	27	0	12	58	1	4	11	49	2	110	4	1	6	.249	.332	.384

TOP DESIGNATED HITTERS

Minimum 15 at-bats. *Lefthanded batter. †Switch-hitter.

Player, Team	G	TPA	AB	R	H	TB	2B	3B	HR	RBI	SH	SF	HP	BB	IBB	SO	SB	CS	GDP	Avg.	OBP	Slg.
Walker, Larry, St.L.*	6	26	19	7	7	18	2	0	3	9	0	0	1	6	0	3	0	0	0	.368	.538	.947
Shealy, Ryan, Col.	5	20	18	2	6	10	1	0	1	3	0	0	2	0	0	6	0	0	1	.333	.400	.556
Fielder, Prince, Mil.*	5	17	17	0	5	8	3	0	0	1	0	0	0	0	0	3	0	0	0	.294	.294	.471
Saenz, Olmedo, L.A.	8	31	29	1	7	9	2	0	1	1	0	0	1	1	0	10	0	0	0	.241	.290	.310
Piazza, Mike, N.Y.	5	22	21	2	5	10	2	0	1	1	0	0	0	1	0	1	0	0	0	.238	.273	.476
Sweeney, Mark, S.D.*	5	19	17	2	4	9	2	0	1	2	0	0	0	2	0	4	0	0	0	.235	.316	.529
Clark, Tony, Ari.†	7	30	28	2	6	11	2	0	1	6	0	1	0	1	0	8	0	0	0	.214	.233	.393
Doumit, Ryan, Pit.†	6	26	23	2	4	5	1	0	0	4	0	0	2	1	0	10	2	0	0	.174	.269	.217
Thome, Jim, Phi.*	5	21	19	2	3	3	0	0	0	1	0	0	0	2	0	5	0	0	0	.158	.238	.158
Biggio, Craig, Hou.	5	22	20	3	2	2	0	0	0	0	0	0	1	1	0	4	1	0	0	.100	.182	.100

ALL DESIGNATED HITTERS

*Lefthanded batter. †Switch-hitter.

Player, Team	G	TPA	AB	R	H	TB	2B	3B	HR	RBI	SH	SF	HP	BB	IBB	SO	SB	CS	GDP	Avg.	OBP	Slg.
Abreu, Bobby, Phi.*	3	14	9	1	3	4	1	0	0	0	0	0	0	5	2	0	0	0	1	.333	.571	.444
Alou, Moises, S.F.	3	15	13	4	7	11	1	0	1	1	0	0	0	2	0	2	0	0	0	.538	.600	.846
Anderson, Marlon, N.Y.*	2	7	6	0	2	2	0	0	0	0	0	0	0	1	0	0	0	0	0	.333	.429	.333
Baerga, Carlos, Was.†	1	4	4	0	1	1	0	0	0	0	0	0	0	0	0	0	0	0	0	.250	.250	.250
Barrett, Michael, Chi.	1	3	2	0	0	0	0	0	0	0	0	0	0	1	0	0	0	0	0	.000	.333	.000
Berkman, Lance, Hou.†	3	12	11	1	2	3	1	0	0	0	0	0	0	1	0	0	0	0	0	.182	.250	.273
Biggio, Craig, Hou.	5	22	20	3	2	2	0	0	0	0	0	0	1	1	0	4	1	0	0	.100	.182	.100
Branyan, Russell, Mil.*	1	3	3	0	0	0	0	0	0	0	0	0	0	0	0	0	0	0	0	.000	.000	.000
Byrd, Marlon, Was.	2	9	9	0	2	2	0	0	0	1	0	0	0	0	0	2	0	0	1	.222	.222	.222
Casey, Sean, Cin.*	1	4	3	0	0	0	0	0	0	0	0	0	1	0	0	1	0	0	0	.000	.250	.000
Clark, Tony, Ari.†	7	30	28	2	6	11	2	0	1	6	0	1	0	1	0	8	0	0	0	.214	.233	.393
Conine, Jeff, Fla.	3	13	10	1	1	1	0	0	0	0	0	0	0	3	0	2	0	0	0	.100	.308	.100
Cordero, Wil, Was.	3	12	12	1	1	1	0	0	0	0	0	0	0	0	0	1	0	0	0	.083	.083	.083
Cruz, Jacob, Cin.*	1	4	4	0	0	0	0	0	0	0	0	0	0	0	0	3	0	0	0	.000	.000	.000
Daubach, Brian, N.Y.*	2	8	7	1	0	0	0	0	0	0	0	0	0	1	0	2	0	0	1	.000	.125	.000
Delgado, Carlos, Fla.*	1	4	3	0	1	1	0	0	0	1	0	0	0	0	0	2	0	0	0	.333	.500	.333
Doumit, Ryan, Pit.†	6	26	23	2	4	5	1	0	0	4	0	0	2	1	0	10	2	0	0	.174	.269	.217
Dubois, Jason, Chi.	3	10	9	2	2	8	0	0	2	2	0	0	1	0	0	4	0	0	0	.222	.300	.889
Edwards, Mike, L.A.	2	1	1	0	0	0	0	0	0	0	0	0	0	0	0	0	0	0	0	.000	.000	.000
Fick, Robert, S.D.*	2	6	6	1	1	2	1	0	0	0	0	0	0	0	0	1	0	0	0	.167	.167	.333
Fielder, Prince, Mil.*	5	17	17	0	5	8	3	0	0	1	0	0	0	0	0	3	0	0	0	.294	.294	.471
Franco, Julio, Atl.	4	15	14	2	4	8	1	0	1	4	0	0	0	1	0	1	0	0	1	.286	.333	.571
Glaus, Troy, Ari.	1	5	5	0	0	0	0	0	0	0	0	0	0	0	0	3	0	0	0	.000	.000	.000
Griffey Jr., Ken, Cin.*	2	7	6	0	0	0	0	0	0	0	0	0	0	1	0	3	0	0	0	.000	.143	.000
Guillen, Jose, Was.	2	9	9	0	3	5	2	0	0	3	0	0	0	0	0	2	0	0	0	.333	.333	.556
Hairston, Scott, Ari.	2	4	4	0	0	0	0	0	0	0	0	0	0	0	0	2	0	0	0	.000	.000	.000
Hammonds, Jeffrey, Was.	1	4	3	0	1	1	0	0	0	0	0	0	1	0	0	0	0	0	0	.333	.500	.333
Harris, Lenny, Fla.*	2	7	6	0	1	1	0	0	0	0	0	0	0	1	0	1	0	0	1	.167	.286	.167
Helms, Wes, Mil.	3	8	6	0	1	1	0	0	0	3	0	1	0	1	0	1	0	0	0	.167	.250	.167
Jenkins, Geoff, Mil.*	2	10	7	2	4	4	0	0	0	1	0	0	0	3	0	1	0	0	0	.571	.700	.571
Johnson, Kelly, Atl.*	1	4	4	0	1	1	0	0	0	0	0	0	0	0	0	1	0	0	0	.250	.250	.250
Kata, Matt, Ari.†	1	0	0	1	0	0	0	0	0	0	0	0	0	0	0	0	0	0	0	.000	.000	.000
Kelly, Kenny, Cin.	1	1	1	0	0	0	0	0	0	0	0	0	0	0	0	1	0	0	0	.000	.000	.000
Klesko, Ryan, S.D.*	3	12	10	2	2	2	0	0	0	0	0	0	0	2	0	1	0	0	0	.200	.333	.200
Lamb, Mike, Hou.*	1	5	4	0	1	1	0	0	0	1	0	0	0	1	0	1	0	0	0	.250	.400	.250

Player, Team	G	TPA	AB	R	H	TB	2B	3B	HR	RBI	SH	SF	HP	BB	IBB	SO	SB	CS	GDP	Avg.	OBP	Slg.
Lofton, Kenny, Phi.*	1	5	4	2	3	3	0	0	0	0	0	0	0	1	0	1	0	0	0	.750	.800	.750
Nady, Xavier, S.D.	1	1	1	0	0	0	0	0	0	0	0	0	0	0	0	0	0	0	0	.000	.000	.000
Niekro, Lance, S.F.	1	4	4	1	1	1	0	0	0	0	0	0	0	0	0	1	0	0	0	.250	.250	.250
Ojeda, Miguel, S.D.	1	1	1	1	0	0	0	0	0	1	0	0	0	0	0	0	0	0	0	.000	.000	.000
Olson, Tim, Col.	1	1	1	0	0	0	0	0	0	0	0	0	0	0	0	1	0	0	0	.000	.000	.000
Orr, Pete, Atl.*	1	6	6	1	3	3	0	0	0	0	0	0	0	0	0	1	0	0	0	.500	.500	.500
Perez, Antonio, L.A.	1	5	4	1	1	1	0	0	0	0	0	0	0	1	0	1	0	0	0	.250	.400	.250
Piazza, Mike, N.Y.	5	22	21	2	5	10	2	0	1	1	0	0	0	1	0	1	0	0	0	.238	.273	.476
Piedra, Jorge, Col.*	1	4	4	0	3	4	1	0	0	0	0	0	0	0	0	0	1	0	0	.750	.750	1.000
Randa, Joe, Cin.	2	8	8	1	3	6	0	0	1	1	0	0	0	0	0	3	0	0	0	.375	.375	.750
Saenz, Olmedo, L.A.	8	31	29	1	7	9	2	0	0	1	0	0	1	1	0	10	0	0	0	.241	.290	.310
Sanchez, Alex, S.F.*	1	2	1	0	0	0	0	0	0	0	0	0	0	1	0	0	0	0	0	.000	.500	.000
Sanders, Reggie, St.L.	1	1	1	0	0	0	0	0	0	0	0	0	0	0	0	0	0	0	0	.000	.000	.000
Seabol, Scott, St.L.	3	11	9	3	5	7	2	0	0	1	0	0	0	2	0	1	0	0	0	.556	.636	.778
Shealy, Ryan, Col.	5	20	18	2	6	10	1	0	1	3	0	0	0	2	0	6	0	0	1	.333	.400	.556
Sweeney, Mark, S.D.*	5	19	17	2	4	9	2	0	1	2	0	0	0	2	0	4	0	0	0	.235	.316	.529
Thome, Jim, Phi.*	5	21	19	2	3	3	0	0	0	1	0	0	0	2	0	5	0	0	0	.158	.238	.158
Torrealba, Yorvit, S.F.	1	4	3	0	0	0	0	0	0	0	0	0	1	0	0	2	0	0	0	.000	.250	.000
Tracy, Chad, Ari.*	1	1	1	0	0	0	0	0	0	0	0	0	0	0	0	1	0	0	0	.000	.000	.000
Tucker, Michael, S.F.*	4	12	8	2	3	4	1	0	0	5	1	2	0	1	0	1	0	0	0	.375	.364	.500
Walker, Larry, St.L.*	6	26	19	7	7	18	2	0	3	9	0	0	1	6	0	3	0	0	0	.368	.538	.947
Walker, Todd, Chi.*	2	9	8	0	3	3	0	0	0	2	0	0	0	1	0	1	0	0	1	.375	.444	.375
Werth, Jayson, L.A.	1	1	1	1	1	2	1	0	0	2	0	0	0	0	0	0	0	0	0	1.000	1.000	2.000
Willingham, Josh, Fla.	1	3	1	0	0	0	0	0	0	0	0	0	2	0	0	1	0	0	0	.000	.667	.000
Woodward, Chris, N.Y.	1	1	1	0	1	1	0	0	0	0	0	0	0	0	0	0	0	0	0	1.000	1.000	1.000

The following designated hitters, each of whom appeared in at least one game, had no plate appearances, runs scored or stolen base attempts:
Blanco, Tony, Washington; Repko, Jason, Los Angeles; Robles, Oscar, Los Angeles; Self, Todd, Houston.

PINCH-HITTING

TEAM

Team	G	TPA	AB	R	H	TB	2B	3B	HR	RBI	SH	SF	HP	BB	IBB	SO	SB	CS	GDP	Avg.	OBP	Slg.
New York	133	220	196	22	57	75	3	0	5	27	2	1	2	19	0	42	3	0	3	.291	.358	.383
Florida	128	236	216	20	59	85	14	0	4	42	0	2	3	15	2	41	0	0	4	.273	.326	.394
San Francisco	127	238	214	20	54	83	14	3	3	26	2	2	4	16	1	51	0	0	5	.252	.314	.388
Houston	138	250	218	24	55	86	16	3	3	35	3	5	3	21	3	49	3	1	8	.252	.320	.394
Milwaukee	139	255	216	22	53	79	8	0	6	32	5	3	6	25	1	64	1	0	5	.245	.336	.366
Cincinnati	143	260	229	24	54	95	17	0	8	34	4	2	1	24	1	72	1	1	6	.236	.309	.415
Philadelphia	137	262	227	30	53	77	4	4	4	37	5	5	1	24	2	50	0	0	4	.233	.304	.339
Los Angeles	143	298	260	27	60	82	10	0	4	34	0	4	5	29	1	82	1	2	3	.231	.315	.315
Arizona	151	310	273	27	63	107	15	1	9	38	4	1	3	29	2	57	1	0	6	.231	.310	.392
Atlanta	134	245	212	18	48	64	7	0	3	27	5	1	1	26	1	63	2	0	4	.226	.313	.302
St. Louis	125	265	243	25	55	86	9	2	6	37	1	6	1	14	2	57	2	0	5	.226	.265	.354
Colorado	142	272	237	29	53	81	14	1	4	34	7	3	4	21	1	77	1	2	1	.224	.294	.342
San Diego	140	274	230	27	48	75	13	1	4	28	3	1	2	38	5	62	3	1	5	.209	.325	.326
Washington	131	266	226	24	45	59	6	1	2	25	4	3	5	28	4	66	3	1	8	.199	.298	.261
Pittsburgh	133	268	238	19	47	58	6	1	1	24	2	0	2	26	0	57	1	2	4	.197	.282	.244
Chicago	132	240	215	13	42	59	9	1	2	22	1	2	5	17	0	57	1	0	7	.195	.268	.274
Totals	2176	4159	3650	371	846	1251	165	18	68	502	48	41	48	372	26	947	23	10	78	.232	.308	.343

TOP PINCH-HITTERS

Minimum 20 at-bats. *Lefthanded batter. †Switch-hitter.

Player, Team	G	TPA	AB	R	H	TB	2B	3B	HR	RBI	SH	SF	HP	BB	IBB	SO	SB	CS	GDP	Avg.	OBP	Slg.
Piedra, Jorge, Col.*	37	37	33	7	15	24	6	0	1	8	0	1	0	3	0	4	1	0	0	.455	.486	.727
Helms, Wes, Mil.	50	50	42	6	16	26	4	0	2	6	0	1	1	6	0	7	0	0	0	.381	.460	.619
Fick, Robert, S.D.*	34	34	27	4	10	15	2	0	1	7	1	0	0	6	1	9	0	1	0	.370	.485	.556
Anderson, Marlon, N.Y.*	64	64	56	9	18	21	0	0	1	6	0	0	0	8	0	11	2	0	1	.321	.406	.375
Clark, Tony, Ari.†	48	48	44	4	14	27	4	0	3	15	0	0	0	4	1	14	0	0	0	.318	.375	.614
Ledee, Ricky, L.A.*	43	43	35	7	11	15	1	0	1	9	0	1	1	6	0	8	0	0	0	.314	.419	.429
Harris, Lenny, Fla.*	77	67	61	5	19	26	4	0	1	13	0	1	1	5	1	10	0	0	2	.311	.373	.426
Franco, Julio, Atl.	52	52	45	3	14	20	3	0	1	12	1	0	1	5	0	14	0	0	1	.311	.392	.444
Cintron, Alex, Ari.†	49	49	46	4	14	26	3	0	3	12	0	0	0	3	1	5	0	0	1	.304	.347	.565
Tucker, Michael, S.F.-Phi.*	57	54	47	6	14	16	2	0	0	5	0	0	0	7	1	10	0	0	2	.298	.389	.340
Sweeney, Mark, S.D.*	82	76	62	8	18	29	5	0	2	12	0	1	0	13	2	15	2	0	1	.290	.408	.468
Hill, Bobby, Pit.†	35	35	31	2	9	10	1	0	0	4	0	0	1	3	0	4	0	0	2	.290	.371	.323
Palmeiro, Orlando, Hou.*	64	63	52	10	15	27	7	1	1	8	2	2	1	6	1	7	1	0	1	.288	.361	.519
Fielder, Prince, Mil.*	30	30	28	2	8	14	0	0	2	9	0	1	0	1	0	11	0	0	0	.286	.300	.500
Vizcaino, Jose, Hou.†	56	56	50	2	14	19	5	0	0	9	0	1	0	5	1	18	1	0	0	.280	.339	.380

ALL PINCH-HITTERS

*Lefthanded batter. †Switch-hitter.

Player, Team	G	TPA	AB	R	H	TB	2B	3B	HR	RBI	SH	SF	HP	BB	IBB	SO	SB	CS	GDP	Avg.	OBP	Slg.
Abreu, Bobby, Phi.*	1	1	0	0	0	0	0	0	0	0	0	0	0	1	0	0	0	0	0	.000	1.000	.000
Aguila, Chris, Fla.	22	22	21	1	2	2	0	0	0	0	0	0	0	1	0	8	0	0	0	.095	.136	.095
Alexander, Manny, S.D.	1	1	0	0	0	0	0	0	0	0	0	0	0	1	0	0	0	0	0	.000	1.000	.000
Alfonzo, Edgardo, S.F.	11	11	8	0	0	0	0	0	0	1	0	1	0	2	0	3	0	0	0	.000	.182	.000
Alou, Moises, S.F.	3	3	2	0	0	0	0	0	0	0	0	0	0	1	0	0	0	0	0	.000	.333	.000
Amezaga, Alfredo, Col.-Pit.†	2	2	2	0	0	0	0	0	0	0	0	0	0	0	0	0	0	0	0	.000	.000	.000
Anderson, Marlon, N.Y.*	64	64	56	9	18	21	0	0	1	6	0	0	0	8	0	11	2	0	1	.321	.406	.375
Andino, Robert, Fla.	1	1	1	0	0	0	0	0	0	0	0	0	0	0	0	0	0	0	0	.000	.000	.000
Ardoin, Danny, Col.	3	3	2	0	0	0	0	0	0	1	1	0	0	0	0	2	0	0	0	.000	.000	.000
Atkins, Garrett, Col.	2	2	2	0	1	1	0	0	0	1	0	0	0	0	0	0	0	0	0	.500	.500	.500
Aurilia, Rich, Cin.	6	6	6	0	1	1	0	0	0	0	0	0	0	0	0	1	0	0	0	.167	.167	.167
Ausmus, Brad, Hou.	1	1	1	0	0	0	0	0	0	0	0	0	0	0	0	0	0	0	0	.000	.000	.000
Ayala, Luis, Was.	1	1	1	0	1	1	0	0	0	0	0	0	0	0	0	0	0	0	0	1.000	1.000	1.000
Aybar, Willy, L.A.†	2	2	2	0	0	0	0	0	0	0	0	0	0	0	0	1	0	0	0	.000	.000	.000
Backe, Brandon, Hou.	2	2	2	0	0	0	0	0	0	0	0	0	0	0	0	0	0	0	0	.000	.000	.000
Baerga, Carlos, Was.†	61	61	54	6	13	17	1	0	1	7	0	0	3	4	0	7	0	0	3	.241	.328	.315
Bagwell, Jeff, Hou.	15	15	12	0	3	3	0	0	0	0	0	0	1	1	1	3	0	0	0	.250	.333	.250
Baker, Jeff, Col.	2	2	2	0	0	0	0	0	0	0	0	0	0	0	0	0	0	0	0	.000	.000	.000
Barmes, Clint, Col.	1	1	1	0	0	0	0	0	0	0	0	0	0	0	0	0	0	0	0	.000	.000	.000
Barrett, Michael, Chi.	15	15	13	1	3	3	0	0	0	0	0	0	1	1	1	5	0	0	0	.231	.333	.231
Bautista, Jose, Pit.	3	3	2	0	0	0	0	0	0	0	0	0	0	1	0	1	0	0	0	.000	.333	.000
Bell, David, Phi.	1	1	1	0	1	1	0	0	0	1	0	0	0	0	0	0	0	0	0	1.000	1.000	1.000
Beltran, Carlos, N.Y.†	2	2	2	0	0	0	0	0	0	0	0	0	0	0	0	0	0	0	0	.000	.000	.000
Bennett, Gary, Was.	7	7	7	0	0	0	0	0	0	0	0	0	0	0	0	1	0	0	0	.000	.000	.000
Bergolla, William, Cin.	7	7	7	1	1	1	0	0	0	0	0	0	0	0	0	3	0	0	1	.143	.143	.143
Betemit, Wilson, Atl.†	26	26	20	1	2	2	0	0	0	0	0	1	0	5	0	5	0	0	1	.100	.280	.100
Bigbie, Larry, Col.*	8	8	7	0	0	0	0	0	0	0	0	0	0	1	0	5	0	0	0	.000	.125	.000
Biggio, Craig, Hou.	9	9	9	0	2	2	0	0	0	1	0	0	0	0	0	1	0	0	1	.222	.222	.222
Blanco, Tony, Was.	29	29	27	1	4	5	1	0	0	2	0	0	2	0	0	12	0	0	1	.148	.207	.185
Blum, Geoff, S.D.†	16	15	13	1	2	3	1	0	0	0	0	0	0	2	0	3	0	0	0	.154	.267	.231
Bonds, Barry, S.F.*	1	1	1	0	0	0	0	0	0	0	0	0	0	0	0	1	0	0	0	.000	.000	.000
Bradley, Milton, L.A.†	2	2	1	0	0	0	0	0	0	0	0	0	0	1	1	0	0	0	1	.000	.500	.000

Player, Team	G	TPA	AB	R	H	TB	2B	3B	HR	RBI	SH	SF	HP	BB	IBB	SO	SB	CS	GDP	Avg.	OBP	Slg.
Branyan, Russell, Mil.*	22	19	16	1	1	1	0	0	0	0	0	0	0	3	0	10	0	0	0	.063	.211	.063
Bruntlett, Eric, Hou.	17	17	15	3	4	5	1	0	0	0	0	0	0	2	0	1	0	1	2	.267	.353	.333
Burke, Chris, Hou.	15	15	13	1	1	1	0	0	0	1	0	1	0	1	0	2	0	0	0	.077	.143	.077
Burnitz, Jeromy, Chi.*	2	2	2	0	0	0	0	0	0	0	0	0	0	0	0	1	0	0	0	.000	.000	.000
Burrell, Pat, Phi.	1	1	1	0	1	1	0	0	0	0	0	0	0	0	0	0	0	0	0	1.000	1.000	1.000
Burroughs, Sean, S.D.*	16	16	15	0	3	4	1	0	0	2	0	0	0	1	0	1	0	0	0	.200	.250	.267
Byrd, Marlon, Phi.-Was.	13	13	10	2	4	6	2	0	0	2	1	1	0	1	0	3	1	0	0	.400	.417	.600
Byrnes, Eric, Col.	1	1	1	0	0	0	0	0	0	0	0	0	0	0	0	0	0	0	0	.000	.000	.000
Cabrera, Miguel, Fla.	1	1	1	0	1	1	0	0	0	1	0	0	0	0	0	0	0	0	0	1.000	1.000	1.000
Cairo, Miguel, N.Y.	12	12	11	0	6	6	0	0	0	1	1	0	0	0	0	0	1	0	1	.545	.545	.545
Carroll, Jamey, Was.	13	13	10	2	4	4	0	0	0	1	2	0	0	1	0	3	0	0	1	.400	.455	.400
Casey, Sean, Cin.*	3	3	2	1	1	1	0	0	0	0	0	0	0	1	0	0	0	0	0	.500	.667	.500
Castilla, Vinny, Was.	4	4	4	0	0	0	0	0	0	0	0	0	0	0	0	0	0	0	0	.000	.000	.000
Castillo, Luis, Fla.†	2	2	2	0	0	0	0	0	0	0	0	0	0	0	0	0	0	0	0	.000	.000	.000
Castro, Ramon, N.Y.	1	1	1	0	1	2	1	0	0	1	0	0	0	0	0	0	0	0	0	1.000	1.000	2.000
Cedeno, Roger, St.L.†	26	26	24	1	4	5	1	0	0	5	0	1	0	1	0	5	0	0	0	.167	.192	.208
Cedeno, Ronny, Chi.	12	12	11	1	3	3	0	0	0	0	0	0	0	1	0	2	0	0	0	.273	.333	.273
Cepicky, Matt, Was.*	5	5	5	0	0	0	0	0	0	0	0	0	0	0	0	3	0	0	1	.000	.000	.000
Chavez, Angel, S.F.	1	1	1	0	1	1	0	0	0	0	0	0	0	0	0	0	0	0	0	1.000	1.000	1.000
Chavez, Endy, Was.-Phi.*	49	48	44	4	11	16	1	2	0	5	2	0	0	2	0	6	0	0	2	.250	.283	.364
Chavez, Raul, Hou.	2	2	2	1	0	0	0	0	0	0	0	0	0	0	0	0	0	0	0	.000	.000	.000
Chen, Chin-Feng, L.A.	4	4	4	0	1	1	0	0	0	2	0	0	0	0	0	0	0	0	0	.250	.250	.250
Choi, Hee-Seop, L.A.*	50	48	42	5	8	13	2	0	1	3	0	1	2	3	0	17	0	0	1	.190	.271	.310
Church, Ryan, Was.*	29	29	24	3	3	3	0	0	0	2	0	0	0	5	0	11	0	0	1	.125	.276	.125
Cintron, Alex, Ari.†	49	49	46	4	14	26	3	0	3	12	0	0	0	3	1	5	0	0	1	.304	.347	.565
Cirillo, Jeff, Mil.	31	31	23	4	5	5	0	0	0	5	1	0	2	5	0	2	1	0	1	.217	.400	.217
Clark, Doug, S.F.*	6	6	5	0	0	0	0	0	0	0	0	0	0	1	0	2	0	0	0	.000	.167	.000
Clark, Tony, Ari.†	48	48	44	4	14	27	4	0	3	15	0	0	0	4	1	14	0	0	0	.318	.375	.614
Clayton, Royce, Ari.	3	3	2	1	0	0	0	0	0	0	0	0	0	0	0	1	0	0	0	.000	.333	.000
Closser, JD, Col.†	21	20	18	1	2	5	0	0	1	2	1	0	0	1	0	9	0	0	0	.111	.158	.278
Conine, Jeff, Fla.	40	40	36	3	10	14	4	0	0	5	0	1	0	3	1	6	0	0	0	.278	.325	.389
Cordero, Wil, Was.	15	15	14	0	0	0	0	0	0	0	0	0	0	1	1	4	0	0	0	.000	.067	.000
Cota, Humberto, Pit.	6	6	6	1	1	4	0	0	1	1	0	0	0	0	0	3	0	0	0	.167	.167	.667
Counsell, Craig, Ari.*	8	8	6	2	0	0	0	0	0	0	0	0	0	2	0	1	1	0	0	.000	.250	.000
Cruz Jr., Jose, Ari.-L.A.†	10	10	8	0	0	0	0	0	0	0	0	0	0	2	0	1	0	0	1	.000	.200	.000
Cruz, Deivi, S.F.-Was.	26	25	24	1	5	11	1	1	1	4	0	0	1	0	0	6	0	0	0	.208	.240	.458
Cruz, Jacob, Cin.*	88	88	76	7	20	35	6	0	3	11	0	1	0	11	1	29	0	0	4	.263	.352	.461
Dallimore, Brian, S.F.	4	4	4	1	1	2	1	0	0	0	0	0	0	0	0	0	0	0	0	.250	.250	.500
Daubach, Brian, N.Y.*	8	7	6	1	2	6	1	0	1	2	0	1	0	0	0	2	0	0	0	.333	.286	1.000
Davis, J.J., Was.	5	5	5	0	2	2	0	0	0	0	0	0	0	0	0	2	0	0	0	.400	.400	.400
Delgado, Carlos, Fla.*	3	3	2	2	2	5	0	0	1	6	0	0	1	0	0	0	0	0	0	1.000	1.000	2.500
Denorfia, Chris, Cin.	8	8	7	1	1	4	0	0	1	1	0	0	0	1	0	3	0	0	0	.143	.250	.571
Diaz, Einar, St.L.	9	9	9	1	2	3	1	0	0	2	0	0	0	0	0	1	0	0	1	.222	.222	.333
Diaz, Victor, N.Y.	11	11	10	0	1	1	0	0	0	1	0	0	0	1	0	3	0	0	0	.100	.182	.100
Dillon, Joe, Fla.	18	18	18	4	4	8	1	0	1	1	0	0	0	0	0	3	0	0	1	.222	.222	.444
Doumit, Ryan, Pit.†	17	17	16	1	3	3	0	0	0	2	0	0	1	0	0	5	0	1	0	.188	.235	.188
Dubois, Jason, Chi.	12	12	12	1	2	6	1	0	1	2	0	0	0	0	0	4	0	0	0	.167	.167	.500
Duffy, Chris, Pit.*	9	9	8	0	1	2	1	0	0	2	1	0	0	0	0	4	0	0	0	.125	.125	.250
Duncan, Chris, St.L.*	9	9	9	1	1	4	0	0	1	1	0	0	0	0	0	5	0	0	1	.111	.111	.444
Dunn, Adam, Cin.*	5	5	5	0	1	2	1	0	0	0	0	0	0	0	0	2	0	0	0	.200	.200	.400
Durham, Ray, S.F.†	9	9	8	2	3	7	1	0	1	4	0	0	0	1	0	0	0	0	1	.375	.444	.875
Durrington, Trent, Mil.	17	17	13	1	3	4	1	0	0	2	3	0	0	1	0	2	0	0	0	.231	.286	.308
Easley, Damion, Fla.	23	23	21	1	4	7	3	0	0	1	0	0	1	1	0	4	0	0	0	.190	.261	.333
Eaton, Adam, S.D.	2	2	2	0	2	2	0	0	0	0	0	0	0	0	0	0	0	0	0	1.000	1.000	1.000
Eckstein, David, St.L.	2	2	2	0	0	0	0	0	0	0	0	0	0	0	0	0	0	0	0	.000	.000	.000
Edmonds, Jim, St.L.*	9	9	6	0	2	3	1	0	0	2	0	1	0	2	0	2	1	0	0	.333	.444	.500
Edwards, Mike, L.A.	18	18	16	1	6	8	2	0	0	4	0	0	1	1	0	3	0	0	0	.375	.444	.500
Eischen, Joey, Was.*	1	1	1	0	0	0	0	0	0	0	0	0	0	0	0	1	0	0	0	.000	.000	.000
Eldred, Brad, Pit.	6	6	6	0	1	2	1	0	0	0	0	0	0	0	0	4	0	0	1	.167	.167	.333
Ellison, Jason, S.F.	13	13	12	2	4	9	0	1	1	1	1	0	0	0	0	1	0	0	0	.333	.333	.750
Encarnacion, Edwin, Cin.	13	13	11	0	3	5	2	0	0	1	0	0	0	2	0	5	0	0	1	.273	.385	.455
Encarnacion, Juan, Fla.	4	4	3	0	0	0	0	0	0	0	0	0	0	1	0	1	0	0	0	.000	.250	.000
Ensberg, Morgan, Hou.	2	2	1	0	1	1	0	0	0	0	0	0	0	1	0	0	0	0	0	1.000	1.000	1.000
Estrada, Johnny, Atl.†	3	3	3	0	3	3	0	0	0	2	0	0	0	0	0	0	0	0	0	1.000	1.000	1.000
Everett, Adam, Hou.	2	2	1	0	1	1	0	0	0	0	0	0	0	1	0	0	0	0	0	1.000	1.000	1.000
Feliz, Pedro, S.F.	8	8	8	2	3	6	3	0	0	2	0	0	0	0	0	2	0	0	0	.375	.375	.750
Fick, Robert, S.D.*	34	34	27	4	10	15	2	0	1	7	1	0	0	6	1	9	0	1	0	.370	.485	.556
Fielder, Prince, Mil.*	30	30	28	2	8	14	0	0	2	9	0	1	0	1	0	11	0	0	0	.286	.300	.500
Floyd, Cliff, N.Y.*	2	2	2	0	0	0	0	0	0	0	0	0	0	0	0	1	0	0	0	.000	.000	.000
Fontenot, Mike, Chi.*	5	5	2	2	0	0	0	0	0	0	0	0	0	2	0	0	0	0	0	.000	.600	.000
Franco, Julio, Atl.	52	52	45	3	14	20	3	0	1	12	1	0	1	5	0	14	0	0	1	.311	.392	.444
Francoeur, Jeff, Atl.	2	2	1	0	0	0	0	0	0	0	0	0	0	1	0	0	0	0	0	.000	.500	.000
Freel, Ryan, Cin.	9	9	8	2	3	5	2	0	0	1	0	0	0	1	0	2	0	1	2	.375	.375	.625
Freeman, Choo, Col.	4	4	4	0	0	0	0	0	0	0	0	0	0	0	0	1	0	0	0	.000	.000	.000
Furcal, Rafael, Atl.†	1	1	1	0	0	0	0	0	0	0	0	0	0	0	0	0	0	0	0	.000	.000	.000
Furmaniak, J.J., Pit.	3	3	2	1	1	1	0	0	0	0	0	0	0	1	0	1	0	0	0	.500	.667	.500
Gall, John, St.L.	14	14	14	1	5	9	1	0	1	3	0	0	0	0	0	4	0	0	0	.357	.357	.643
Garabito, Eddy, Col.†	23	23	19	5	7	8	1	0	0	2	1	0	1	2	0	4	0	0	2	.368	.455	.421
Garcia, Jesse, S.D.	3	2	2	0	1	1	0	0	0	0	1	0	0	0	0	1	0	0	0	.500	.500	.500
Garciaparra, Nomar, Chi.	2	2	1	0	0	0	0	0	0	0	0	0	0	1	0	0	0	0	0	.000	.500	.000
Gerut, Jody, Chi.-Pit.*	7	7	6	1	0	0	0	0	0	0	0	0	0	1	0	2	0	0	0	.000	.143	.000
Giles, Brian, S.D.*	3	3	3	0	1	1	0	0	0	0	0	0	0	0	0	0	0	0	0	.333	.333	.333

Player, Team	G	TPA	AB	R	H	TB	2B	3B	HR	RBI	SH	SF	HP	BB	IBB	SO	SB	CS	GDP	Avg.	OBP	Slg.
Giles, Marcus, Atl.	3	3	3	1	1	1	0	0	0	0	0	0	0	0	0	1	0	0	0	.333	.333	.333
Gipson, Charles, Hou.	1	1	1	0	0	0	0	0	0	0	0	0	0	0	0	0	0	0	0	.000	.000	.000
Glaus, Troy, Ari.	4	4	4	1	1	4	0	0	1	3	0	0	0	0	0	2	0	0	0	.250	.250	1.000
Godwin, Tyrell, Was.*	3	3	3	0	0	0	0	0	0	0	0	0	0	0	0	1	0	0	0	.000	.000	.000
Gonzalez, Alex, Fla.	1	1	1	0	0	0	0	0	0	0	0	0	0	0	0	1	0	0	0	.000	.000	.000
Gonzalez, Luis, Ari.*	5	5	3	0	1	2	1	0	0	0	0	0	0	2	0	1	0	0	0	.333	.600	.667
Gonzalez, Luis A., Col.	22	22	19	2	3	5	2	0	0	3	1	1	0	0	0	5	0	0	0	.158	.190	.263
Grabowski, Jason, L.A.*	32	32	27	3	4	7	0	0	1	3	0	1	0	4	0	10	0	0	1	.148	.250	.259
Green, Andy, Ari.	9	9	8	1	1	1	0	0	0	0	0	0	0	1	0	2	0	0	0	.125	.222	.125
Green, Shawn, Ari.*	5	5	4	1	3	8	2	0	1	1	0	0	0	1	0	0	0	0	0	.750	.800	2.000
Greenberg, Adam, Chi.*	1	1	0	0	0	0	0	0	0	0	0	0	1	0	0	0	0	0	0	.000	1.000	.000
Greene, Todd, Col.	5	5	5	0	2	3	1	0	0	1	0	0	0	0	0	0	0	0	0	.400	.400	.600
Grieve, Ben, Chi.*	22	22	18	1	5	5	0	0	0	1	0	0	0	4	0	6	0	0	0	.278	.409	.278
Griffey Jr., Ken, Cin.*	2	2	2	0	0	0	0	0	0	0	0	0	0	0	0	0	0	0	0	1.000	.000	.000
Grissom, Marquis, S.F.	7	7	7	0	2	2	0	0	0	0	0	0	0	0	0	1	0	0	0	.286	.286	.286
Grudzielanek, Mark, St.L.	1	1	1	0	1	1	0	0	0	0	0	0	0	0	0	0	0	0	0	1.000	1.000	1.000
Guillen, Jose, Was.	8	8	7	1	2	2	0	0	0	2	0	0	1	0	0	1	0	0	0	.286	.375	.286
Guzman, Cristian, Was.†	3	3	3	0	0	0	0	0	0	0	0	0	0	0	0	0	0	0	0	.000	.000	.000
Haad, Yamid, S.F.	1	1	1	0	0	0	0	0	0	0	0	0	0	0	0	0	0	0	0	.000	.000	.000
Hairston Jr., Jerry, Chi.	15	15	15	2	3	6	1	1	0	1	0	0	0	0	0	0	0	0	1	.200	.200	.400
Hairston, Scott, Ari.	10	10	10	0	1	1	0	0	0	0	0	0	0	0	0	3	0	0	1	.100	.100	.100
Hall, Bill, Mil.	16	16	15	0	1	1	0	0	0	2	0	0	0	1	0	6	0	0	0	.067	.125	.067
Hammonds, Jeffrey, Was.	3	3	1	1	0	0	0	0	0	0	0	0	0	2	1	0	0	0	0	.000	.667	.000
Hardy, J.J., Mil.	6	6	6	0	2	2	0	0	0	1	0	0	0	0	0	1	0	0	0	.333	.333	.333
Harris, Brendan, Was.	1	1	1	1	1	4	0	0	1	2	0	0	0	0	0	0	0	0	0	1.000	1.000	4.000
Harris, Lenny, Fla.*	77	67	61	5	19	26	4	0	1	13	0	1	5	1	0	10	0	0	2	.311	.373	.426
Hart, Corey, Mil.	3	3	3	1	1	4	0	0	1	2	0	0	0	0	0	1	0	0	1	.333	.333	1.333
Hawpe, Brad, Col.*	20	20	17	2	6	8	2	0	0	6	0	1	0	2	0	7	0	0	0	.353	.400	.471
Helms, Wes, Mil.	50	50	42	6	16	26	4	0	2	6	0	1	1	6	0	7	0	0	3	.381	.460	.619
Helton, Todd, Col.*	1	1	0	1	0	0	0	0	0	0	0	0	0	1	1	0	0	0	0	.000	1.000	.000
Hermida, Jeremy, Fla.*	10	10	9	1	2	5	0	0	1	4	0	0	0	1	0	2	0	0	0	.222	.300	.556
Hernandez, Ramon, S.D.	3	3	3	0	0	0	0	0	0	0	0	0	0	0	0	1	0	0	1	.000	.000	.000
Hill, Bobby, Pit.†	35	35	31	2	9	10	1	0	0	4	0	0	1	3	0	4	0	0	2	.290	.371	.323
Hill, Koyie, Ari.†	3	3	2	0	0	0	0	0	0	0	0	0	0	1	0	1	0	0	0	.000	.333	.000
Holbert, Aaron, Cin.	14	14	12	2	2	3	1	0	0	0	1	0	0	1	0	4	1	0	0	.167	.231	.250
Hollandsworth, Todd, Chi.-Atl.*	46	46	43	1	10	15	2	0	1	7	0	0	1	2	0	15	0	0	1	.233	.283	.349
Holliday, Matt, Col.	2	2	2	0	0	0	0	0	0	0	0	0	0	0	0	0	0	0	0	.000	.000	.000
Howard, Ryan, Phi.*	8	8	7	2	2	3	1	0	0	0	0	0	0	1	0	4	0	0	0	.286	.375	.429
Hyzdu, Adam, S.D.	7	7	5	1	0	0	0	0	0	0	0	0	0	2	0	2	0	0	0	.000	.286	.000
Jackson, Conor, Ari.	19	19	13	1	0	0	0	0	0	1	0	1	0	5	0	1	0	0	0	.000	.263	.000
Jackson, Damian, S.D.	8	7	6	0	0	0	0	0	0	0	0	0	0	1	0	2	0	0	0	.000	.143	.000
Jacobs, Mike, N.Y.*	2	2	2	2	2	5	0	0	1	3	0	0	0	0	0	0	0	0	0	1.000	1.000	2.500
Jenkins, Geoff, Mil.*	2	2	2	0	1	1	0	0	0	0	0	0	0	0	0	1	0	0	0	.500	.500	.500
Jennings, Jason, Col.*	2	2	2	0	0	0	0	0	0	0	0	0	0	0	0	0	0	0	0	.000	.000	.000
Jimenez, D'Angelo, Cin.†	9	9	7	2	2	3	1	0	0	2	0	0	0	2	0	0	0	0	0	.286	.444	.429
Johnson, Ben, S.D.	5	5	5	0	0	0	0	0	0	0	0	0	0	0	0	3	0	0	0	.000	.000	.000
Johnson, Kelly, Atl.*	5	5	4	4	2	2	0	0	0	0	0	0	0	1	0	0	0	0	0	.500	.600	.500
Johnson, Nick, Was.*	3	3	2	0	0	0	0	0	0	0	0	0	0	1	0	0	0	0	0	.000	.333	.000
Jones, Andruw, Atl.	1	1	1	0	0	0	0	0	0	0	0	0	0	0	0	0	0	0	0	.000	.000	.000
Jones, Chipper, Atl.†	9	9	7	0	0	0	0	0	0	2	0	0	0	2	0	3	0	0	0	.000	.222	.000
Jordan, Brian, Atl.	17	17	14	0	2	2	0	0	0	1	0	1	0	2	0	7	0	0	0	.143	.235	.143
Jorgensen, Ryan, Fla.	1	1	1	0	0	0	0	0	0	0	0	0	0	0	0	1	0	0	0	.000	.000	.000
Kata, Matt, Ari.-Phi.†	26	26	23	1	4	7	1	1	0	1	0	1	0	2	0	4	0	0	0	.174	.240	.304
Kearns, Austin, Cin.	7	7	6	2	2	5	0	0	1	4	0	0	0	1	0	2	0	0	0	.333	.429	.833
Kelly, Kenny, Cin.-Was.	9	9	8	1	2	3	1	0	0	0	0	0	0	1	0	4	0	0	0	.250	.333	.375
Kent, Jeff, L.A.	1	1	1	0	0	0	0	0	0	0	0	0	0	0	0	0	0	0	0	.000	.000	.000
Klesko, Ryan, S.D.*	13	13	9	0	0	0	0	0	0	0	0	0	0	4	1	2	0	0	0	.000	.308	.000
Knoedler, Justin, S.F.	4	4	3	0	1	1	0	0	0	0	0	0	1	0	0	0	0	0	0	.333	.500	.333
Krynzel, Dave, Mil.*	3	3	3	0	0	0	0	0	0	0	0	0	0	0	0	2	0	0	0	.000	.000	.000
Lamb, Mike, Hou.*	40	40	37	4	8	13	0	1	1	9	0	1	0	2	1	10	0	0	1	.216	.250	.351
Lane, Jason, Hou.	5	5	4	0	2	5	1	1	0	2	0	0	1	0	0	0	0	0	1	.500	.600	1.250
Langerhans, Ryan, Atl.*	16	16	14	2	3	4	1	0	0	1	0	0	0	2	0	3	0	0	0	.214	.313	.286
LaRoche, Adam, Atl.*	19	19	18	0	4	5	1	0	0	2	0	0	0	1	0	6	0	0	1	.222	.263	.278
LaRue, Jason, Cin.	3	3	3	2	2	8	0	0	2	6	0	0	0	0	0	0	0	0	0	.667	.667	2.667
Lawton, Matt, Pit.-Chi.*	3	3	3	0	0	0	0	0	0	0	0	0	0	0	0	0	0	0	0	.000	.000	.000
Ledee, Ricky, L.A.*	43	43	35	7	11	15	1	0	1	9	0	1	1	6	0	8	0	0	0	.314	.419	.429
Lieberthal, Mike, Phi.	1	1	1	0	0	0	0	0	0	0	0	0	0	0	0	1	0	0	0	.000	.000	.000
Linden, Todd, S.F.†	11	11	10	2	2	3	1	0	0	0	0	0	1	0	0	4	0	0	0	.200	.273	.300
Lo Duca, Paul, Fla.	12	12	12	0	4	5	1	0	0	6	0	0	0	0	0	2	0	0	0	.333	.333	.417
Lofton, Kenny, Phi.*	15	15	13	1	3	3	0	0	0	0	0	0	0	2	1	7	0	0	0	.231	.333	.231
Lopez, Felipe, Cin.†	5	5	4	1	1	1	0	0	0	1	0	0	0	1	0	1	0	0	0	.250	.400	.250
Lopez, Luis, Cin.†	9	9	9	0	1	2	1	0	0	1	0	0	0	0	0	2	0	0	0	.111	.111	.222
Lowell, Mike, Fla.	10	10	8	1	4	5	1	0	0	1	0	1	0	1	0	0	0	0	0	.500	.500	.625
Lowry, Noah, S.F.	1	1	1	0	0	0	0	0	0	0	0	0	0	0	0	0	0	0	0	.000	.000	.000
Luna, Hector, St.L.	19	19	16	3	5	7	0	1	0	1	0	0	1	2	0	2	1	0	1	.313	.421	.438
Mabry, John, St.L.*	39	37	34	3	9	16	2	1	1	4	0	2	0	1	0	5	0	0	1	.265	.270	.471
Machado, Anderson, Cin.-Col.†	2	2	2	0	0	0	0	0	0	0	0	0	0	0	0	1	0	0	0	.000	.000	.000
Macias, Jose, Chi.†	59	59	54	2	10	13	3	0	0	5	1	2	0	2	0	10	1	0	3	.185	.207	.241
Mackowiak, Rob, Pit.*	21	21	16	2	3	3	0	0	0	0	0	0	0	5	0	6	0	0	0	.188	.381	.188
Magruder, Chris, Mil.†	61	61	53	5	13	19	3	0	1	4	1	1	3	3	1	14	0	0	0	.245	.317	.358
Mahoney, Mike, St.L.	1	1	1	0	0	0	0	0	0	0	0	0	0	0	0	0	0	0	0	.000	.000	.000
Majewski, Gary, Was.	1	1	1	0	0	0	0	0	0	0	0	0	0	0	0	1	0	0	0	.000	.000	.000

Player, Team	G	TPA	AB	R	H	TB	2B	3B	HR	RBI	SH	SF	HP	BB	IBB	SO	SB	CS	GDP	Avg.	OBP	Slg.
Marquis, Jason, St.L.*	9	9	9	2	3	3	0	0	0	0	0	0	0	0	0	2	0	0	0	.333	.333	.333
Marte, Andy, Atl.	7	6	4	1	0	0	0	0	0	0	0	0	0	2	0	3	0	0	0	.000	.333	.000
Martinez, Ramon, Phi.	17	17	14	0	6	6	0	0	0	2	1	1	0	1	0	1	0	0	0	.429	.438	.429
Matheny, Mike, S.F.	3	3	3	0	0	0	0	0	0	0	0	0	0	0	0	0	0	0	0	.000	.000	.000
Matsui, Kazuo, N.Y.†	19	19	18	1	4	4	0	0	0	0	1	0	0	0	0	4	0	0	0	.222	.222	.222
McAnulty, Paul, S.D.*	16	16	13	1	0	0	0	0	0	0	1	0	0	2	1	5	0	0	0	.000	.133	.000
McCann, Brian, Atl.*	2	2	1	0	0	0	0	0	0	0	0	0	0	1	0	0	0	0	0	.000	.500	.000
McClain, Scott, Chi.	6	6	5	0	1	2	1	0	0	1	0	0	0	1	0	0	0	0	1	.200	.333	.400
McCracken, Quinton, Ari.†	80	80	72	7	19	21	2	0	0	1	2	0	1	5	0	13	0	0	1	.264	.321	.292
McLouth, Nate, Pit.*	14	14	14	2	2	3	1	0	0	2	0	0	0	0	0	4	0	0	0	.143	.143	.214
Michaels, Jason, Phi.	32	32	26	6	5	8	1	1	0	3	0	2	0	4	0	5	0	0	0	.192	.281	.308
Mientkiewicz, Doug, N.Y.*	7	6	6	0	0	0	0	0	0	0	0	0	0	0	0	3	0	0	0	.000	.000	.000
Miles, Aaron, Col.†	24	24	22	2	4	7	1	1	0	3	0	0	1	1	0	4	0	0	0	.182	.250	.318
Miller, Damian, Mil.	5	5	5	1	2	2	0	0	0	1	0	0	0	0	0	3	0	0	0	.400	.400	.400
Moeller, Chad, Mil.	1	1	1	0	0	0	0	0	0	0	0	0	0	0	0	0	0	0	0	.000	.000	.000
Mohr, Dustan, Col.	26	26	23	1	1	4	0	0	1	1	0	0	0	3	0	14	0	0	0	.043	.154	.174
Mondesi, Raul, Atl.	2	2	2	0	1	1	0	0	0	1	0	0	0	0	0	1	0	0	0	.500	.500	.500
Mosquera, Julio, Mil.	1	1	1	0	0	0	0	0	0	0	0	0	0	0	0	0	0	0	0	.000	.000	.000
Murton, Matt, Chi.	12	12	10	1	2	2	0	0	0	1	0	0	0	2	0	5	0	0	1	.200	.333	.200
Myrow, Brian, L.A.*	15	14	11	1	3	4	1	0	0	0	0	0	0	3	0	3	0	0	0	.273	.429	.364
Nady, Xavier, S.D.	17	16	13	1	2	2	0	0	0	0	0	0	2	1	0	4	0	0	1	.154	.313	.154
Nakamura, Norihiro, L.A.	7	7	7	0	1	1	0	0	0	0	0	0	0	0	0	4	0	0	0	.143	.143	.143
Nevin, Phil, S.D.	1	1	1	1	1	4	0	0	1	2	0	0	0	0	0	0	0	0	0	1.000	1.000	4.000
Niekro, Lance, S.F.	45	45	41	2	10	16	4	1	0	9	0	1	1	2	0	13	0	0	1	.244	.289	.390
Nunez, Abraham O., St.L.†	25	25	24	5	6	10	1	0	1	5	1	0	0	0	0	3	0	0	0	.250	.250	.417
Obermueller, Wes, Mil.	1	1	1	0	0	0	0	0	0	0	0	0	0	0	0	0	0	0	0	.000	.000	.000
Offerman, Jose, Phi.-N.Y.†	74	74	65	9	17	26	1	1	2	9	0	0	1	8	0	10	0	0	2	.262	.351	.400
Ojeda, Miguel, S.D.	17	17	15	3	2	3	1	0	0	2	0	0	0	2	0	5	0	0	0	.133	.235	.200
Olivo, Miguel, S.D.	2	2	2	0	0	0	0	0	0	0	0	0	0	0	0	0	0	0	0	.000	.000	.000
Olmedo, Ray, Cin.†	21	21	18	0	5	7	2	0	0	1	2	0	0	1	0	2	0	0	0	.278	.316	.389
Olson, Tim, Col.	2	2	1	0	0	0	0	0	0	0	0	0	0	1	0	1	0	0	0	.000	.500	.000
Orr, Pete, Atl.*	54	53	48	5	10	14	1	0	1	2	3	0	0	2	0	10	2	0	0	.208	.240	.292
Ortiz, Russ, Ari.	2	2	1	0	0	0	0	0	0	0	1	0	0	0	0	0	0	0	0	.000	.000	.000
Ortmeier, Dan, S.F.†	8	8	8	0	1	1	0	0	0	0	0	0	0	0	0	3	0	0	0	.125	.125	.125
Osik, Keith, Was.	1	1	1	0	0	0	0	0	0	0	0	0	0	0	0	1	0	0	0	.000	.000	.000
Overbay, Lyle, Mil.*	6	5	1	1	0	0	0	0	0	0	0	0	0	4	0	1	0	0	0	.000	.800	.000
Palmeiro, Orlando, Hou.*	64	63	52	10	15	27	7	1	1	8	2	2	1	6	1	7	1	0	1	.288	.361	.519
Patterson, Corey, Chi.*	9	9	9	0	0	0	0	0	0	0	0	0	0	0	0	6	0	0	1	.000	.000	.000
Pena, Brayan, Atl.†	6	6	6	0	3	4	1	0	0	3	0	0	0	0	0	2	0	0	0	.500	.500	.667
Pena, Wily Mo, Cin.	18	18	17	1	3	6	0	0	1	2	0	0	0	1	0	7	0	0	0	.176	.222	.353
Perez, Antonio, L.A.	27	26	22	0	3	3	0	0	0	1	0	0	0	4	0	11	1	1	0	.136	.269	.136
Perez, Eddie, Atl.	3	3	2	0	0	0	0	0	0	0	0	0	0	1	0	0	0	0	0	.000	.333	.000
Perez, Miguel, Cin.	2	2	2	0	0	0	0	0	0	0	0	0	0	0	0	1	0	0	0	.000	.000	.000
Perez, Neifi, Chi.†	8	8	8	0	0	0	0	0	0	1	0	0	0	0	0	0	0	0	0	.000	.000	.000
Perez, Tomas, Phi.†	52	52	43	5	6	6	0	0	0	6	2	0	1	6	1	10	0	0	1	.140	.260	.140
Phillips, Jason, L.A.	13	12	12	2	4	4	0	0	0	3	0	0	0	0	0	2	0	0	0	.333	.333	.333
Piazza, Mike, N.Y.	7	7	6	0	1	1	0	0	0	2	0	0	0	1	0	3	0	0	0	.167	.286	.167
Piedra, Jorge, Col.*	37	37	33	7	15	24	6	0	1	8	0	1	0	3	0	4	1	0	0	.455	.486	.727
Pierre, Juan, Fla.*	2	2	2	0	2	2	0	0	0	2	0	0	0	0	0	0	0	0	0	1.000	1.000	1.000
Polanco, Placido, Phi.	4	4	3	0	1	1	0	0	0	2	0	0	0	1	0	0	0	0	0	.333	.500	.333
Pratt, Todd, Phi.	4	4	4	0	0	0	0	0	0	0	0	0	0	0	0	3	0	0	0	.000	.000	.000
Pujols, Albert, St.L.	6	6	5	0	2	2	0	0	0	2	0	0	0	1	1	2	0	0	0	.400	.500	.400
Quintero, Humberto, Hou.	3	3	3	0	0	0	0	0	0	0	0	0	0	0	0	2	0	0	0	.000	.000	.000
Ramirez, Aramis, Chi.	4	4	4	0	1	1	0	0	0	1	0	0	0	0	0	2	0	0	0	.250	.250	.250
Ramirez, Horacio, Atl.*	1	1	1	0	0	0	0	0	0	0	0	0	0	0	0	0	0	0	0	.000	.000	.000
Ramirez, Julio, S.F.	2	2	2	1	1	1	0	0	0	1	0	0	0	0	0	1	0	0	0	.500	.500	.500
Randa, Joe, Cin.-S.D.	7	7	5	1	2	3	1	0	0	2	0	1	1	0	0	1	0	0	0	.400	.429	.600
Redman, Tike, Pit.*	59	58	51	5	11	12	1	0	0	5	0	0	0	7	0	5	1	0	0	.216	.310	.235
Relaford, Desi, Col.†	8	8	6	0	0	0	0	0	0	0	0	0	0	2	0	2	0	0	0	.000	.250	.000
Repko, Jason, L.A.	12	12	11	1	2	2	0	0	0	0	0	0	0	1	0	4	0	0	0	.182	.250	.182
Restovich, Michael, Col.-Pit.	28	28	27	0	4	4	0	0	0	2	0	0	0	1	0	14	0	0	0	.148	.179	.148
Reyes, Dennys, S.D.	1	1	1	0	0	0	0	0	0	0	0	0	0	0	0	1	0	0	0	.000	.000	.000
Reyes, Jose, N.Y.†	1	1	0	0	0	0	0	0	0	0	0	0	0	1	0	0	0	0	0	.000	1.000	.000
Roberts, Dave, S.D.*	5	5	4	1	1	1	0	0	0	0	0	0	0	1	0	2	0	0	0	.250	.400	.250
Robles, Oscar, L.A.*	21	21	19	3	8	10	2	0	0	0	0	0	1	1	0	2	0	1	0	.421	.476	.526
Rodriguez, John, St.L.*	14	12	8	0	2	2	0	0	0	1	0	0	0	4	1	4	0	0	0	.250	.500	.250
Rolen, Scott, St.L.	1	1	1	0	0	0	0	0	0	0	0	0	0	0	0	0	0	0	0	.000	.000	.000
Romano, Jason, Cin.	6	6	6	0	1	1	0	0	0	0	0	0	0	0	0	4	0	0	0	.167	.167	.167
Rose, Mike, L.A.†	2	2	2	0	1	1	0	0	0	0	0	0	0	0	0	0	0	0	0	.500	.500	.500
Ross, Cody, L.A.	5	5	5	0	0	0	0	0	0	0	0	0	0	0	0	3	0	0	0	.000	.000	.000
Ross, David, Pit.-S.D.	11	10	9	0	1	3	0	1	0	0	0	0	0	1	0	3	0	0	0	.111	.200	.333
Rueter, Kirk, S.F.*	1	1	0	0	0	0	0	0	0	0	1	0	0	0	0	0	0	0	0	.000	.000	.000
Saenz, Olmedo, L.A.	32	32	28	1	5	6	1	0	0	5	0	1	0	3	0	7	0	0	0	.179	.250	.214
Sanchez, Alex, S.F.*	8	8	7	2	2	3	1	0	0	1	0	0	0	1	0	1	0	0	0	.286	.375	.429
Sanchez, Freddy, Pit.	20	20	18	3	6	9	1	1	0	3	0	0	0	2	0	1	0	1	0	.333	.400	.500
Sanders, Reggie, St.L.	13	13	11	2	2	2	0	0	0	0	0	0	0	2	0	5	0	0	0	.182	.308	.182
Sandoval, Danny, Phi.†	2	2	2	0	0	0	0	0	0	0	0	0	0	0	0	1	0	0	0	.000	.000	.000
Schneider, Brian, Was.*	8	8	5	3	2	2	0	0	0	0	0	0	1	2	0	0	0	0	2	.400	.625	.400
Schumaker, Skip, St.L.*	8	8	8	2	1	1	0	0	0	1	0	0	0	0	0	2	0	0	0	.125	.125	.125
Scott, Luke, Hou.*	11	11	9	2	3	5	2	0	0	0	0	0	0	2	0	4	0	0	0	.333	.455	.556
Seabol, Scott, St.L.	29	29	27	2	5	8	0	0	1	3	0	1	0	1	0	7	0	0	0	.185	.207	.296
Self, Todd, Hou.*	5	5	5	1	1	4	0	0	1	2	0	0	0	0	0	2	0	0	0	.200	.200	.800
Shabala, Adam, S.F.*	2	2	2	1	1	1	0	0	0	0	0	0	0	0	0	1	0	0	0	.500	.500	.500

Player, Team	G	TPA	AB	R	H	TB	2B	3B	HR	RBI	SH	SF	HP	BB	IBB	SO	SB	CS	GDP	Avg.	OBP	Slg.
Shealy, Ryan, Col.	14	14	12	2	3	3	0	0	0	2	0	0	0	2	0	4	0	0	0	.250	.357	.250
Short, Rick, Was.	5	5	4	0	2	2	0	0	0	1	0	0	0	1	0	0	0	0	0	.500	.600	.500
Sledge, Terrmel, Was.*	10	10	5	3	1	3	0	1	0	4	0	1	0	4	0	2	2	0	0	.200	.500	.600
Snow, J.T., S.F.*	12	11	10	1	4	4	0	0	0	2	0	0	0	1	0	3	0	0	0	.400	.455	.400
Snyder, Chris, Ari.	2	2	2	1	1	4	0	0	1	2	0	0	0	0	0	0	0	0	0	.500	.500	2.000
Soto, Geovany, Chi.	1	1	1	0	0	0	0	0	0	0	0	0	0	0	0	0	0	0	0	.000	.000	.000
Spivey, Junior, Mil.-Was.	4	4	4	0	0	0	0	0	0	0	0	0	0	0	0	4	0	0	0	.000	.000	.000
Stinnett, Kelly, Ari.	6	6	6	0	0	0	0	0	0	0	0	0	0	0	0	3	0	0	1	.000	.000	.000
Sullivan, Cory, Col.*	35	35	29	5	7	11	1	0	1	3	3	0	0	3	0	9	0	0	1	.241	.313	.379
Sweeney, Mark, S.D.*	82	76	62	8	18	29	5	0	2	12	0	1	0	13	2	15	2	0	1	.290	.408	.468
Taguchi, So, St.L.	23	23	23	1	3	7	1	0	1	5	0	0	0	0	0	6	0	0	0	.130	.130	.304
Taveras, Willy, Hou.	1	1	1	0	0	0	0	0	0	0	0	0	0	0	0	1	0	0	0	.000	.000	.000
Terrero, Luis, Ari.	7	7	6	0	2	3	1	0	0	1	0	0	1	0	0	1	0	0	0	.333	.429	.500
Theriot, Ryan, Chi.	5	5	4	0	1	1	0	0	0	0	0	0	0	1	0	2	0	0	0	.250	.400	.250
Thome, Jim, Phi.*	2	2	2	0	0	0	0	0	0	0	0	0	0	0	0	1	0	0	0	.000	.000	.000
Torcato, Tony, S.F.†	10	10	9	0	3	3	0	0	0	0	0	0	0	1	0	2	0	0	2	.333	.400	.333
Torrealba, Yorvit, S.F.	4	4	3	0	0	0	0	0	0	0	0	0	0	1	0	1	0	0	0	.000	.250	.000
Tracy, Chad, Ari.*	20	20	19	3	3	4	1	0	0	2	0	0	1	0	0	4	0	0	1	.158	.200	.211
Treanor, Matt, Fla.	3	3	3	0	1	1	0	0	0	0	0	0	0	0	0	0	0	0	0	.333	.333	.333
Tucker, Michael, S.F.-Phi.*	57	54	47	6	14	16	2	0	0	5	0	0	0	7	1	10	0	0	2	.298	.389	.340
Utley, Chase, Phi.*	6	6	4	1	1	4	0	0	1	5	0	1	0	1	0	1	0	0	0	.250	.333	1.000
Valdez, Wilson, S.D.	1	1	1	0	0	0	0	0	0	0	0	0	0	0	0	0	0	0	0	.000	.000	.000
Valent, Eric, N.Y.*	18	18	16	2	3	4	1	0	0	1	0	0	0	2	0	7	0	0	0	.188	.278	.250
Valentin, Javier, Cin.†	13	13	11	0	2	2	0	0	0	2	0	0	0	2	0	1	0	0	0	.182	.308	.182
Valentin, Jose, L.A.*	11	11	9	2	2	5	0	0	1	2	0	0	0	2	0	3	0	0	0	.222	.364	.556
Victorino, Shane, Phi.†	14	14	13	3	5	11	0	0	2	7	0	1	0	0	0	1	0	0	0	.385	.357	.846
Vidro, Jose, Was.†	8	8	7	0	2	2	0	0	0	0	0	0	0	1	0	1	0	0	0	.286	.375	.286
Vizcaino, Jose, Hou.†	56	56	50	2	14	19	5	0	0	9	0	1	0	5	1	18	1	0	0	.280	.339	.380
Vizquel, Omar, S.F.†	3	3	3	0	0	0	0	0	0	0	0	0	0	0	0	1	0	0	0	.000	.000	.000
Walker, Larry, St.L.*	13	12	11	1	2	3	1	0	0	2	0	1	0	0	0	5	0	0	1	.182	.167	.273
Walker, Todd, Chi.*	9	9	9	1	3	6	0	0	1	2	0	0	0	0	0	1	0	0	0	.333	.333	.667
Ward, Daryle, Pit.*	26	24	22	1	4	4	0	0	0	2	0	0	0	2	0	2	0	0	1	.182	.250	.182
Watson, Brandon, Was.*	12	12	10	1	2	2	0	0	0	0	1	0	0	1	0	4	0	0	1	.200	.273	.200
Weaver, Jeff, L.A.	1	1	1	0	0	0	0	0	0	0	0	0	0	0	0	1	0	0	0	.000	.000	.000
Weeks, Rickie, Mil.	1	1	0	0	0	0	0	0	0	0	0	0	0	1	0	0	0	0	0	.000	1.000	.000
Wells, Kip, Pit.	1	1	1	0	0	0	0	0	0	0	0	0	0	0	0	0	0	0	0	.000	.000	.000
Werth, Jayson, L.A.*	2	2	2	1	1	2	1	0	0	2	0	0	0	0	0	1	0	0	0	.500	.500	1.000
Wigginton, Ty, Pit.	16	16	13	1	1	1	0	0	0	1	0	0	0	3	0	5	0	0	0	.077	.250	.077
Wilkerson, Brad, Was.*	3	3	3	0	0	0	0	0	0	0	0	0	0	0	0	3	0	0	0	.000	.000	.000
Williams, Gerald, N.Y.	7	7	7	2	2	2	0	0	0	0	0	0	0	0	0	0	0	0	0	.286	.286	.286
Williams, Woody, S.D.	2	2	1	0	0	0	0	0	0	0	1	0	0	0	0	1	0	0	0	.000	.000	.000
Willingham, Josh, Fla.	9	9	7	1	3	3	0	0	0	2	0	0	0	2	0	2	0	0	0	.429	.556	.429
Willis, Dontrelle, Fla.*	6	6	6	1	1	1	0	0	0	0	0	0	0	0	0	1	0	0	1	.167	.167	.167
Wilson, Craig, Pit.	3	3	3	0	0	0	0	0	0	0	0	0	0	0	0	1	0	0	0	.000	.000	.000
Wilson, Enrique, Chi.†	6	6	5	0	1	2	1	0	0	0	0	0	0	1	0	1	0	0	0	.200	.333	.400
Wilson, Jack, Pit.	2	2	1	0	1	1	0	0	0	1	1	0	0	0	0	0	0	0	0	1.000	1.000	1.000
Wilson, Josh, Fla.	1	1	1	0	0	0	0	0	0	0	0	0	0	0	0	0	0	0	0	.000	.000	.000
Wilson, Preston, Col.-Was.	4	4	4	1	1	1	0	0	0	1	0	0	0	0	0	0	0	0	0	.250	.250	.250
Winn, Randy, S.F.†	3	3	2	0	0	0	0	0	0	0	0	0	0	1	0	0	0	0	0	.000	.333	.000
Wolf, Randy, Phi.*	1	1	1	0	0	0	0	0	0	0	0	0	0	0	0	1	0	0	0	.000	.000	.000
Woodward, Chris, N.Y.	18	18	16	1	6	9	0	0	1	4	0	0	1	1	0	3	0	0	0	.375	.444	.563
Young, Eric, S.D.	23	22	20	6	3	6	3	0	0	2	0	0	2	0	0	2	1	0	2	.150	.227	.300
Zimmerman, Ryan, Was.	5	5	4	0	1	2	1	0	0	2	0	1	0	0	0	1	0	0	0	.250	.200	.500

PINCH-HITTERS WITH TWO OR MORE TEAMS

Player, Team	G	TPA	AB	R	H	TB	2B	3B	HR	RBI	SH	SF	HP	BB	IBB	SO	SB	CS	GDP	Avg.	OBP	Slg.
Amezaga, Alfredo, Col.†	1	1	1	0	0	0	0	0	0	0	0	0	0	0	0	0	0	0	0	.000	.000	.000
Amezaga, Alfredo, Pit.†	1	1	1	0	0	0	0	0	0	0	0	0	0	0	0	0	0	0	0	.000	.000	.000
Chavez, Endy, Was.*	2	2	1	0	0	0	0	0	0	0	0	0	0	1	0	0	0	0	1	.000	.500	.000
Chavez, Endy, Phi.*	47	46	43	4	11	16	1	2	0	5	2	0	0	1	0	6	0	0	1	.256	.273	.372
Cruz Jr., Jose, Ari.†	7	7	5	0	0	0	0	0	0	0	0	0	0	2	0	1	0	0	1	.000	.286	.000
Cruz Jr., Jose, L.A.†	3	3	3	0	0	0	0	0	0	0	0	0	0	0	0	0	0	0	0	.000	.000	.000
Hollandsworth, Todd, Chi.*	28	28	26	0	7	9	2	0	0	6	0	0	1	1	0	8	0	0	0	.269	.321	.346
Hollandsworth, Todd, Atl.*	18	18	17	1	3	6	0	0	1	1	0	0	0	1	0	7	0	0	1	.176	.222	.353
Kata, Matt, Ari.†	23	23	20	1	3	6	1	1	0	0	1	0	0	2	0	4	0	0	0	.150	.227	.300
Kata, Matt, Phi.†	3	3	3	0	1	1	0	0	0	0	0	0	0	0	0	0	0	0	0	.333	.333	.333
Kelly, Kenny, Cin.	4	4	4	1	1	1	0	0	0	0	0	0	0	0	0	1	0	0	0	.250	.250	.250
Kelly, Kenny, Was.	5	5	4	0	1	2	1	0	0	0	0	0	0	1	0	3	0	0	0	.250	.400	.500
Offerman, Jose, Phi.†	31	31	28	5	6	12	1	1	1	3	0	0	0	3	0	5	0	0	1	.214	.290	.429
Offerman, Jose, N.Y.†	43	43	37	4	11	14	0	0	1	6	0	0	1	5	0	5	0	0	1	.297	.395	.378
Randa, Joe, Cin.	6	6	4	1	1	2	1	0	0	2	0	1	1	0	0	1	0	0	0	.250	.333	.500
Randa, Joe, S.D.	1	1	1	0	1	1	0	0	0	0	0	0	0	0	0	0	0	0	0	1.000	1.000	1.00
Restovich, Michael, Col.	6	6	6	0	1	1	0	0	0	1	0	0	0	0	0	3	0	0	0	.167	.167	.167
Restovich, Michael, Pit.	22	22	21	0	3	3	0	0	0	1	0	0	0	1	0	11	0	0	0	.143	.182	.143
Ross, David, Pit.	5	4	3	0	0	0	0	0	0	0	0	0	0	1	0	0	0	0	0	.000	.250	.000
Ross, David, S.D.	6	6	6	0	1	3	0	0	0	0	0	0	0	0	0	3	0	0	0	.167	.167	.500
Spivey, Junior, Mil.	3	3	3	0	0	0	0	0	0	0	0	0	0	0	0	3	0	0	0	.000	.000	.000
Spivey, Junior, Was.	1	1	1	0	0	0	0	0	0	0	0	0	0	0	0	1	0	0	0	.000	.000	.000
Tucker, Michael, S.F.*	35	33	29	3	10	12	2	0	0	2	0	0	0	4	1	6	0	0	1	.345	.424	.414
Tucker, Michael, Phi.*	22	21	18	3	4	4	0	0	0	3	0	0	0	3	0	4	0	0	1	.222	.333	.222
Wilson, Preston, Col.	3	3	3	1	1	1	0	0	0	0	0	0	0	0	0	1	0	0	0	.333	.333	.333
Wilson, Preston, Was.	1	1	1	0	0	0	0	0	0	0	0	0	0	0	0	0	0	0	0	.000	.000	.000

PITCHING

TEAM

Team	W	L	Pct.	ERA	G	CG	ShO	Rel.	Sv.-Op.	IP	H	TBF	R	ER	HR	SH	SF	HB	BB	IBB	SO	WP	Bk.
St. Louis	100	62	.617	3.49	162	15	14	436	48-65	1445.2	1399	6047	634	560	153	61	37	60	443	27	974	41	5
Houston	89	73	.549	3.51	163	6	11	434	45-58	1443.0	1336	6023	609	563	155	61	33	59	440	29	1164	38	8
New York	83	79	.512	3.76	162	8	11	392	38-59	1453.2	1390	6121	648	599	135	83	34	56	491	43	1012	32	4
Washington	81	81	.500	3.87	162	4	9	470	51-69	1458.0	1456	6286	673	627	140	79	46	72	539	77	997	49	8
Milwaukee	81	81	.500	3.97	162	7	6	395	46-67	1438.0	1382	6208	697	635	169	54	33	45	569	52	1173	66	8
Atlanta	90	72	.556	3.98	162	8	12	484	38-62	1443.2	1487	6186	674	639	145	61	28	32	520	52	929	42	5
San Diego	82	80	.506	4.13	162	4	8	456	48-55	1455.1	1452	6253	726	668	146	46	45	46	503	45	1133	36	3
Florida	83	79	.512	4.16	162	14	15	449	42-60	1442.1	1459	6236	732	666	116	80	42	65	563	57	1125	45	3
Chicago	79	83	.488	4.19	162	8	10	457	39-58	1440.0	1357	6185	714	671	186	84	40	50	576	48	1256	57	7
Philadelphia	88	74	.543	4.21	162	4	6	442	40-63	1435.0	1379	6119	726	672	189	65	41	72	487	51	1159	36	9
San Francisco	75	87	.463	4.33	162	4	8	511	46-74	1444.1	1456	6280	745	695	151	67	50	42	592	42	972	38	3
Los Angeles	71	91	.438	4.38	162	6	9	458	40-59	1427.1	1434	6113	755	695	182	90	39	64	471	34	1004	36	6
Pittsburgh	67	95	.414	4.42	162	4	14	451	35-47	1436.0	1456	6264	769	706	162	68	57	65	612	65	958	53	4
Arizona	77	85	.475	4.84	162	6	10	458	45-62	1456.1	1580	6402	856	783	193	78	45	62	537	43	1038	58	5
Colorado	67	95	.414	5.13	162	4	4	459	37-63	1418.2	1600	6385	862	808	175	66	55	84	604	54	981	65	5
Cincinnati	73	89	.451	5.15	163	2	1	491	31-47	1433.0	1657	6397	889	820	219	63	50	80	642	47	955	53	3
Totals	1286	1306	.496	4.22	1297	104	148	7243	666-978	23052.1	23280	99505	11709	10807	2616	1106	675	954	8439	766	16830	745	87

NOTE_Totals for earned runs for several clubs do not agree with composite total for all pitchers of each respective club due to instances in which provisions of Section 10.18(i) of the Scoring Rules were applied. The following differences are to be noted: Houston pitchers add to 564; New York pitchers add to 602; Milwaukee pitchers add to 636; Florida pitchers add to 671; San Francisco pitchers add to 698; Pittsburgh pitchers add to 708; Arizona pitchers add to 788; Colorado pitchers add to 810; Cincinnati pitchers add to 824.

INDIVIDUAL

TOP QUALIFIERS FOR EARNED-RUN AVERAGE TITLE

Minimum 162 innings. *Throws lefthanded.

Pitcher, Team	W	L	Pct.	ERA	G	GS	CG	ShO	GF	Sv.-Op.	IP	H	TBF	R	ER	HR	SH	SF	HB	BB	IBB	SO	WP	Bk.
Clemens, Roger, Hou.	13	8	.619	1.87	32	32	1	0	0	0-0	211.1	151	838	51	44	11	9	3	3	62	5	185	3	1
Pettitte, Andy, Hou.*	17	9	.654	2.39	33	33	0	0	0	0-0	222.1	188	875	66	59	17	10	4	3	41	0	171	2	0
Willis, Dontrelle, Fla.*	22	10	.688	2.63	34	34	7	5	0	0-0	236.1	213	960	79	69	11	14	5	8	55	3	170	2	1
Martinez, Pedro, N.Y.	15	8	.652	2.82	31	31	4	1	0	0-0	217.0	159	843	69	68	19	9	2	4	47	3	208	4	0
Carpenter, Chris, St.L.	21	5	.808	2.83	33	33	7	4	0	0-0	241.2	204	953	82	76	18	7	7	3	51	0	213	5	0
Peavy, Jake, S.D.	13	7	.650	2.88	30	30	3	3	0	0-0	203.0	162	812	70	65	18	4	5	7	50	3	216	3	1
Oswalt, Roy, Hou.	20	12	.625	2.94	35	35	4	1	0	0-0	241.2	243	1002	85	79	18	12	7	8	48	3	184	5	1
Smoltz, John, Atl.	14	7	.667	3.06	33	33	3	1	0	0-0	229.2	210	931	83	78	18	10	3	1	53	7	169	2	1
Patterson, John, Was.	9	7	.563	3.13	31	31	2	1	0	0-0	198.1	172	817	71	69	19	5	4	5	65	11	185	9	1
Zambrano, Carlos, Chi.	14	6	.700	3.26	33	33	2	0	0	0-0	223.1	170	909	88	81	21	9	5	8	86	3	202	7	0
Beckett, Josh, Fla.	15	8	.652	3.38	29	29	2	1	0	0-0	178.2	153	728	75	67	14	8	2	7	58	2	166	5	0
Burnett, A.J., Fla.	12	12	.500	3.44	32	32	4	2	0	0-0	209.0	184	873	97	80	12	7	5	7	79	1	198	12	0
Hudson, Tim, Atl.	14	9	.609	3.52	29	29	2	0	0	0-0	192.0	194	817	79	75	20	9	1	9	65	5	115	4	0
Glavine, Tom, N.Y.*	13	13	.500	3.53	33	33	2	1	0	0-0	211.1	227	901	88	83	12	19	3	3	61	5	105	1	1
Webb, Brandon, Ari.	14	12	.538	3.54	33	33	1	0	0	0-0	229.0	229	943	98	90	21	10	7	2	59	4	172	14	1

DEPARTMENTAL LEADERS: W_Willis, Fla., 22; L_Wells, Pit., 18; G_Eyre, S.F., 86; GS_Capuano, Mil., D. Davis, Mil., Hernandez, Was., Lieber, Phi., Lowe, L.A., Maddux, Chi., Oswalt, Hou., 35; CG_Carpenter, St.L., Willis, Fla., 7; ShO_Willis, Fla., 5; GF_Wagner, Phi., 70; Sv._Cordero, Was., 47; IP_Hernandez, Was., 246; H_Hernandez, Was., 268; TBF_Hernandez, Was., 1065; R_Milton, Cin., 141; ER_Milton, Cin., 134; HR_Milton, Cin., 40; SH_Glavine, N.Y., Maddux, Chi., 19; SF_Francis, Col., Wells, Pit., 10; HB_Weaver, L.A., 18; TBB_Wells, Pit., 99; IBB_Hernandez, Was., 14; SO_Peavy, S.D., 216; WP_Webb, Ari., 14; Blk._Capuano, Mil., Myers, Phi., 4.

ALL PITCHERS

*Throws lefthanded.

Pitcher, Team	W	L	Pct.	ERA	G	GS	CG	ShO	GF	Sv.-Op.	IP	H	TBF	R	ER	HR	SH	SF	HB	BB	IBB	SO	WP	Bk.
Accardo, Jeremy, S.F.	1	5	.167	3.94	28	0	0	0	7	0-1	29.2	26	124	13	13	2	1	1	1	9	1	16	1	0
Acevedo, Jose, Col.	2	4	.333	6.47	36	5	0	0	1	1-2	64.0	86	292	48	46	13	2	5	1	16	3	31	0	1
Adams, Mike, Mil.	0	1	.000	2.70	13	0	0	0	7	1-2	13.1	12	61	4	4	2	0	0	0	10	1	14	1	0
Adams, Terry, Phi.	0	2	.000	12.83	16	0	0	0	5	0-1	13.1	25	77	19	19	3	1	0	4	10	2	4	0	0
Alfonseca, Antonio, Fla.	1	1	.500	4.94	33	0	0	0	0	0-2	27.1	29	118	15	15	2	3	2	2	14	4	16	1	0
Almanza, Armando, Ari.*	0	0	.000	2.25	6	0	0	0	1	0-1	4.0	5	19	1	1	1	0	0	0	3	0	2	1	0
Alvarez, Wilson, L.A.*	1	4	.200	5.63	21	2	0	0	6	0-0	24.0	31	109	15	15	7	2	2	0	7	0	16	0	0
Anderson, Matt, Col.	0	0	.000	12.60	12	0	0	0	6	0-0	10.0	19	62	17	14	3	1	1	2	11	0	4	0	0
Aquino, Greg, Ari.	0	0	.000	7.76	35	0	0	0	11	1-3	31.1	42	155	29	27	7	1	1	4	17	1	34	2	1
Armas, Tony, Was.	7	7	.500	4.97	19	19	0	0	0	0-0	101.1	100	452	57	56	16	4	1	5	54	4	59	6	2
Astacio, Ezequiel, Hou.	3	6	.333	5.67	22	14	0	0	5	0-0	81.0	100	366	56	51	23	2	6	1	25	2	66	4	1
Astacio, Pedro, S.D.	4	2	.667	3.17	12	10	0	0	1	0-0	54.0	54	252	21	21	4	4	2	1	26	3	33	3	0
Ayala, Luis, Was.	8	7	.533	2.66	68	0	0	0	18	1-3	71.0	75	293	23	21	7	8	3	6	14	4	40	0	0
Aybar, Manny, N.Y.	0	0	.000	6.04	22	0	0	0	4	0-1	25.1	31	114	17	17	4	1	2	1	7	1	27	0	0
Backe, Brandon, Hou.	10	8	.556	4.76	26	25	1	1	0	0-0	149.1	161	653	82	79	19	7	1	4	67	1	97	5	2
Bartosh, Cliff, Chi.*	0	2	.000	5.49	19	0	0	0	7	0-0	19.2	23	91	13	12	7	2	1	2	11	0	15	0	0
Bazardo, Yorman, Fla.	0	0	.000	21.60	1	0	0	0	0	0-0	1.2	5	12	5	4	0	0	0	0	2	0	2	1	0
Beckett, Josh, Fla.	15	8	.652	3.38	29	29	2	1	0	0-0	178.2	153	728	75	67	14	8	2	7	58	2	166	5	0
Belisle, Matt, Cin.	4	8	.333	4.41	60	5	0	0	17	1-4	85.2	101	382	49	42	11	4	2	6	26	6	59	3	0
Bell, Heath, N.Y.	1	3	.250	5.59	42	0	0	0	12	0-0	46.2	56	206	30	29	3	4	0	1	13	3	43	0	1

Pitcher, Team	W	L	Pct.	ERA	G	GS	CG	ShO	GF	Sv.-Op.	IP	H	TBF	R	ER	HR	SH	SF	HB	BB	IBB	SO	WP	Bk.
Benitez, Armando, S.F.	2	3	.400	4.50	30	0	0	0	27	19-23	30.0	25	127	17	15	5	0	2	0	16	0	23	0	0
Benson, Kris, N.Y.	10	8	.556	4.13	28	28	0	0	0	0-0	174.1	171	737	86	80	24	5	3	4	49	5	95	4	0
Bentz, Chad, Fla.*	0	0	.000	31.50	4	0	0	0	0	0-0	2.0	8	14	7	7	2	0	0	0	0	0	0	0	0
Bergmann, Jay, Was.	2	0	1.000	2.75	15	1	0	0	4	0-0	19.2	14	85	6	6	1	1	1	2	11	1	21	0	0
Bernero, Adam, Atl.	4	3	.571	6.51	36	0	0	0	12	0-1	47.0	61	216	35	34	5	2	3	4	12	3	37	1	0
Booker, Chris, Cin.	0	0	.000	31.50	3	0	0	0	1	0-0	2.0	6	15	8	7	2	0	0	0	4	0	2	0	0
Borowski, Joe, Chi.	0	0	.000	6.55	11	0	0	0	3	0-0	11.0	12	47	8	8	5	0	0	0	1	0	11	0	0
Bottalico, Ricky, Mil.	2	2	.500	4.54	40	0	0	0	11	2-6	41.2	43	187	24	21	7	1	2	3	19	0	29	7	0
Boyer, Blaine, Atl.	4	2	.667	3.11	43	0	0	0	5	0-2	37.2	32	158	13	13	1	1	1	2	17	0	33	2	0
Brazoban, Yhency, L.A.	4	10	.286	5.33	74	0	0	0	44	21-27	72.2	70	317	46	43	11	7	2	5	32	4	61	1	0
Breslow, Craig, S.D.*	0	0	.000	2.20	14	0	0	0	3	0-0	16.1	15	78	6	4	1	0	1	1	13	0	14	1	0
Brito, Eude, Phi.*	1	2	.333	3.68	6	5	0	0	0	0-0	22.0	20	94	9	9	2	0	1	2	11	1	15	0	1
Brooks, Frank, Atl.*	0	0	.000	0.00	1	0	0	0	1	0-0	0.1	1	1	0	0	0	0	0	0	0	0	0	0	0
Brower, Jim, S.F.-Atl.	3	3	.500	5.37	69	0	0	0	12	1-3	60.1	73	282	36	36	11	2	1	5	32	3	53	4	0
Broxton, Jonathan, L.A.	1	0	1.000	5.93	14	0	0	0	5	0-1	13.2	13	68	11	9	0	0	2	1	12	2	22	2	0
Bruney, Brian, Ari.	1	3	.250	7.43	47	0	0	0	21	12-16	46.0	56	230	39	38	6	2	1	5	35	2	51	2	0
Bulger, Jason, Ari.	1	0	1.000	5.40	9	0	0	0	5	0-0	10.0	14	48	6	6	1	1	0	0	5	1	9	0	0
Bullington, Bryan, Pit.	0	0	.000	13.50	1	0	0	0	0	0-0	1.1	1	7	2	2	0	0	1	1	1	0	1	0	0
Bump, Nate, Fla.	0	3	.000	4.03	31	0	0	0	2	0-1	38.0	43	165	18	17	5	2	0	2	12	1	18	0	0
Burnett, A.J., Fla.	12	12	.500	3.44	32	32	4	2	0	0-0	209.0	184	873	97	80	12	7	5	7	79	1	198	12	0
Burns, Mike, Hou.	0	0	.000	4.94	27	0	0	0	10	0-0	31.0	29	136	18	17	6	1	0	5	8	1	20	1	0
Burroughs, Sean, S.D.	0	0	.000	27.00	1	0	0	0	1	0-0	1.0	4	7	3	3	1	0	0	0	0	0	0	0	0
Cain, Matt, S.F.	2	1	.667	2.33	7	7	1	0	0	0-0	46.1	24	181	12	12	4	2	1	0	19	1	30	1	0
Cali, Carmen, St.L.*	0	0	.000	10.50	6	0	0	0	3	0-0	6.0	10	33	8	7	3	0	1	0	6	1	5	1	0
Capellan, Jose, Mil.	1	1	.500	2.87	17	0	0	0	7	0-0	15.2	17	67	6	5	1	2	2	0	5	0	14	0	0
Capps, Matt, Pit.	0	0	.000	4.50	4	0	0	0	0	0-0	4.0	5	16	2	2	0	0	0	1	0	0	3	0	0
Capuano, Chris, Mil.*	18	12	.600	3.99	35	35	0	0	0	0-0	219.0	212	949	105	97	31	14	5	12	91	6	176	3	4
Carlyle, Buddy, L.A.	0	0	.000	8.36	10	0	0	0	2	0-1	14.0	16	62	13	13	4	2	0	1	4	0	13	0	0
Carpenter, Chris, St.L.	21	5	.808	2.83	33	33	7	4	0	0-0	241.2	204	953	82	76	18	7	7	3	51	0	213	5	0
Carrara, Giovanni, L.A.	7	4	.636	3.93	72	0	0	0	18	0-2	75.2	65	326	35	33	6	9	5	6	38	5	56	4	0
Carrasco, Hector, Was.	5	4	.556	2.04	64	5	0	0	13	2-4	88.1	59	358	23	20	6	4	4	6	38	7	75	6	1
Carvajal, Marcos, Col.	0	2	.000	5.09	39	0	0	0	11	0-1	53.0	52	229	30	30	8	2	2	3	21	0	47	4	0
Cassidy, Scott, S.D.	1	1	.500	6.57	10	0	0	0	4	0-0	12.1	15	54	10	9	3	2	0	0	3	0	12	0	0
Castillo, Frank, Fla.	0	1	.000	10.38	1	1	0	0	0	0-0	4.1	4	22	5	5	0	0	0	0	5	0	4	0	0
Chacon, Shawn, Col.	1	7	.125	4.09	13	12	0	0	0	0-0	72.2	69	322	33	33	7	9	4	8	36	4	39	3	0
Childers, Matt, Atl.	0	0	.000	4.50	3	0	0	0	1	0-0	4.0	5	21	2	2	1	0	0	1	3	0	2	0	0
Choate, Randy, Ari.*	0	0	.000	9.00	8	0	0	0	0	0-0	7.0	8	35	7	7	0	0	0	1	5	1	4	1	0
Christiansen, Jason, S.F.*	6	1	.857	5.36	56	0	0	0	10	0-2	42.0	48	188	27	25	4	1	4	0	15	2	17	0	0
Claussen, Brandon, Cin.*	10	11	.476	4.21	29	29	0	0	0	0-0	166.2	178	731	89	78	24	8	6	7	57	5	121	2	1
Clemens, Roger, Hou.	13	8	.619	1.87	32	32	1	0	0	0-0	211.1	151	838	51	44	11	9	3	3	62	5	185	3	1
Coffey, Todd, Cin.	4	1	.800	4.50	57	0	0	0	14	1-2	58.0	84	265	33	29	5	3	2	5	11	2	26	1	0
Colon, Roman, Atl.	1	5	.167	5.28	23	4	0	0	6	0-0	44.1	47	191	28	26	10	2	2	0	14	1	30	2	1
Cook, Aaron, Col.	7	2	.778	3.67	13	13	2	0	0	0-0	83.1	101	357	38	34	8	1	3	2	16	2	24	3	0
Cooper, Brian, S.F.	0	1	.000	3.06	8	1	0	0	3	0-0	17.2	15	73	6	6	0	1	0	0	8	0	7	0	0
Cordero, Chad, Was.	2	4	.333	1.82	74	0	0	0	62	47-54	74.1	55	300	24	15	9	2	1	2	17	2	61	0	0
Cormier, Lance, Ari.	7	3	.700	5.11	67	0	0	0	13	0-1	79.1	86	356	50	45	7	4	1	5	43	5	63	6	0
Cormier, Rheal, Phi.*	4	2	.667	5.89	57	0	0	0	10	0-2	47.1	56	211	33	31	9	2	2	2	16	1	34	3	0
Correia, Kevin, S.F.	2	5	.286	4.63	16	11	0	0	1	0-0	58.1	61	264	31	30	12	5	1	4	31	2	44	2	0
Cortes, David, Col.	2	0	1.000	4.10	50	0	0	0	14	2-3	52.2	50	213	24	24	9	1	2	1	10	2	36	3	0
Crowell, Jim, Fla.*	0	0	.000	21.60	4	0	0	0	2	0-0	3.1	10	22	8	8	1	0	1	2	0	0	2	0	0
Davies, Kyle, Atl.	7	6	.538	4.93	21	14	0	0	2	0-1	87.2	98	403	51	48	8	3	0	1	49	5	62	4	0
Davis, Doug, Mil.*	11	11	.500	3.84	35	35	2	1	0	0-0	222.2	196	946	103	95	26	12	2	4	93	5	208	3	2
Davis, Kane, Mil.	1	1	.500	2.70	15	0	0	0	3	0-2	16.2	10	70	6	5	2	0	0	0	10	0	11	1	0
Day, Zach, Was.-Col.	1	3	.250	6.85	17	8	0	0	4	0-1	47.1	61	229	40	36	6	1	1	1	32	4	23	2	0
de la Rosa, Jorge, Mil.*	2	2	.500	4.46	38	0	0	0	13	0-2	42.1	48	208	23	21	1	2	2	0	38	4	42	6	0
de los Santos, Valerio, Fla.*	1	2	.333	6.14	27	0	0	0	5	0-1	22.0	25	103	15	15	4	0	0	2	12	3	16	4	0
DeJean, Mike, N.Y.-Col.	5	4	.556	4.48	66	0	0	0	19	0-3	62.1	62	282	33	31	3	3	3	3	30	3	52	5	0
Dempster, Ryan, Chi.	5	3	.625	3.13	63	6	0	0	53	33-35	92.0	83	401	35	32	4	5	0	4	49	7	89	4	0
Dessens, Elmer, L.A.	1	2	.333	3.56	28	7	0	0	4	0-0	65.2	63	277	30	26	6	1	3	1	19	2	37	1	0
Devine, Joey, Atl.	0	1	.000	12.60	5	0	0	0	1	0-0	5.0	6	26	7	7	2	0	0	0	5	1	3	0	0
Dohmann, Scott, Col.	2	1	.667	6.10	32	0	0	0	10	0-3	31.0	33	143	21	21	6	0	0	0	19	1	35	0	0
Drese, Ryan, Was.	3	6	.333	4.98	11	11	0	0	0	0-0	59.2	66	266	38	33	3	2	4	5	22	1	26	3	0
Driskill, Travis, Hou.	0	0	.000	0.00	1	0	0	0	1	0-0	1.0	1	4	0	0	0	0	0	0	0	0	2	0	0
Duckworth, Brandon, Hou.	0	1	.000	11.02	7	2	0	0	1	0-0	16.1	24	82	20	20	4	0	1	5	7	1	10	0	0
Duke, Zach, Pit.*	8	2	.800	1.81	14	14	0	0	0	0-0	84.2	79	341	20	17	3	3	1	2	23	2	58	1	0
Eaton, Adam, S.D.	11	5	.688	4.27	24	22	0	0	2	0-0	128.2	140	568	70	61	14	4	6	5	44	6	100	5	0
Eischen, Joey, Was.*	2	1	.667	3.22	57	0	0	0	14	0-1	36.1	34	168	14	13	1	6	2	6	19	7	30	5	1
Eldred, Cal, St.L.	1	0	1.000	2.19	31	1	0	0	15	0-1	37.0	35	160	9	9	3	4	1	2	18	3	29	0	0
Erickson, Scott, L.A.	1	4	.200	6.02	19	8	0	0	6	0-0	55.1	62	249	37	37	12	3	2	4	25	0	15	1	0
Esposito, Mike, Col.	0	2	.000	6.75	3	3	0	0	0	0-0	14.2	21	73	11	11	3	1	0	0	9	1	5	0	0
Estes, Shawn, Ari.*	7	8	.467	4.80	21	21	2	0	0	0-0	123.2	132	535	70	66	15	10	4	4	45	0	63	4	0
Eveland, Dana, Mil.*	1	1	.500	5.97	27	0	0	0	3	1-2	31.2	40	146	21	21	2	0	1	1	18	3	23	1	0
Eyre, Scott, S.F.*	2	2	.500	2.63	86	0	0	0	15	0-2	68.1	48	277	21	20	3	4	3	4	26	0	65	3	0
Falkenborg, Brian, S.D.	0	0	.000	8.18	10	0	0	0	3	0-0	11.0	17	54	11	10	2	0	0	0	5	1	10	2	0
Farnsworth, Kyle, Atl.	0	0	.000	1.98	26	0	0	0	18	10-10	27.1	15	103	6	6	4	1	0	2	7	0	32	1	1
Fassero, Jeff, S.F.*	4	7	.364	4.05	48	6	0	0	11	0-2	91.0	92	384	48	41	7	7	3	0	31	1	60	3	0
Flores, Randy, St.L.*	3	1	.750	3.46	50	0	0	0	6	1-3	41.2	37	174	22	16	5	1	3	3	13	0	43	2	0
Floyd, Gavin, Phi.	1	2	.333	10.04	7	4	0	0	0	0-0	26.0	30	127	31	29	5	1	1	3	16	2	17	2	0
Fogg, Josh, Pit.	6	11	.353	5.05	34	28	0	0	1	0-0	169.1	196	742	106	95	27	4	6	6	53	11	85	2	1
Foppert, Jesse, S.F.	0	0	.000	5.23	3	2	0	0	0	0-0	10.1	11	53	7	6	2	0	2	1	13	0	6	0	1
Foster, John, Atl.*	4	2	.667	4.15	62	0	0	0	9	1-2	34.2	27	150	17	16	3	2	0	2	19	0	32	1	0
Fox, Chad, Chi.	0	0	.000	6.75	11	0	0	0	4	1-1	8.0	8	38	6	6	2	0	1	0	8	0	11	0	0

Pitcher, Team	W	L	Pct.	ERA	G	GS	CG	ShO	GF	Sv.-Op.	IP	H	TBF	R	ER	HR	SH	SF	HB	BB	IBB	SO	WP	Bk.
Francis, Jeff, Col.*	14	12	.538	5.68	33	33	0	0	0	0-0	183.2	228	828	119	116	26	6	10	8	70	5	128	2	0
Franco, John, Hou.*	0	1	.000	7.20	31	0	0	0	4	0-1	15.0	23	77	13	12	0	0	1	9	2	16	0	0
Fuentes, Brian, Col.*	2	5	.286	2.91	78	0	0	0	55	31-34	74.1	59	321	25	24	6	5	1	10	34	4	91	8	0
Fultz, Aaron, Phi.*	4	0	1.000	2.24	62	0	0	0	16	0-1	72.1	47	286	21	18	6	4	1	5	23	2	54	0	0
Gagne, Eric, L.A.	1	0	1.000	2.70	14	0	0	0	13	8-8	13.1	10	53	4	4	2	0	0	3	0	22	3	0	
Gallo, Mike, Hou.*	0	1	.000	2.66	36	0	0	0	5	0-2	20.1	18	87	6	6	1	2	1	2	10	2	12	0	0
Geary, Geoff, Phi.	2	1	.667	3.72	40	0	0	0	12	0-1	58.0	54	247	29	24	5	2	4	1	21	4	42	3	0
Glavine, Tom, N.Y.*	13	13	.500	3.53	33	33	2	1	0	0-0	211.1	227	901	88	83	12	19	3	3	61	5	105	1	0
Glover, Gary, Mil.	5	4	.556	5.57	15	11	0	0	1	0-0	64.2	74	284	41	40	10	3	2	2	20	0	58	3	0
Gonzalez, Edgar, Ari.	0	0	.000	108.00	1	0	0	0	0	0-0	0.1	2	5	4	4	1	0	0	0	2	0	1	1	0
Gonzalez, Mike, Pit.*	1	3	.250	2.70	51	0	0	0	15	3-3	50.0	35	212	15	15	2	0	2	1	31	2	58	3	0
Gorzelanny, Tom, Pit.*	0	1	.000	12.00	3	1	0	0	0	0-0	6.0	10	32	8	8	1	1	0	0	3	0	3	0	0
Gosling, Mike, Ari.*	0	3	.000	4.45	13	5	0	0	5	0-0	32.1	40	154	20	16	2	2	0	0	19	2	14	0	0
Grabow, John, Pit.*	2	3	.400	4.85	63	0	0	0	8	0-1	52.0	46	222	31	28	6	2	0	2	25	2	42	1	0
Graves, Danny, Cin.-N.Y.	1	1	.500	6.52	40	0	0	0	29	10-12	38.2	59	197	35	28	9	3	1	3	20	4	20	3	0
Greisinger, Seth, Atl.	0	0	.000	3.60	1	1	0	0	0	0-0	5.0	7	21	2	2	1	0	0	1	2	0	1	0	0
Groom, Buddy, Ari.*	0	1	.000	4.70	23	0	0	0	5	1-1	15.1	19	70	8	8	2	1	1	0	5	1	7	0	0
Gryboski, Kevin, Atl.	0	0	.000	2.95	31	0	0	0	7	0-2	21.1	24	99	10	7	0	3	2	2	13	3	8	1	0
Halama, John, Was.*	0	3	.000	4.64	10	3	0	0	3	0-0	21.1	23	93	11	11	1	1	1	0	8	0	11	0	0
Halsey, Brad, Ari.*	8	12	.400	4.61	28	26	0	0	1	0-0	160.0	191	700	101	82	20	11	5	9	39	3	82	2	1
Hammond, Chris, S.D.*	5	1	.833	3.84	55	0	0	0	17	0-3	58.2	51	242	25	25	9	1	2	2	14	0	34	0	0
Hampton, Mike, Atl.*	5	3	.625	3.50	12	12	1	1	0	0-0	69.1	74	284	28	27	5	2	1	0	18	0	27	1	0
Hamulack, Tim, N.Y.*	0	0	.000	23.14	6	0	0	0	2	0-0	2.1	7	14	6	6	3	0	0	1	1	0	2	0	0
Hancock, Josh, Cin.	1	0	1.000	1.93	11	0	0	0	5	0-0	14.0	11	54	4	3	1	0	0	0	1	0	5	0	0
Harang, Aaron, Cin.	11	13	.458	3.83	32	32	1	0	0	0-0	211.2	217	887	93	90	22	11	5	8	51	3	163	6	0
Harville, Chad, Hou.	0	2	.000	4.46	37	0	0	0	16	0-1	38.1	36	173	21	19	7	1	2	4	24	1	33	4	0
Hawkins, LaTroy, Chi.-S.F.	2	8	.200	3.83	66	0	0	0	21	6-15	56.1	58	247	27	24	7	3	1	0	24	3	43	1	0
Heilman, Aaron, N.Y.	5	3	.625	3.17	53	7	1	1	20	5-6	108.0	87	439	40	38	6	4	1	6	37	4	106	1	1
Helling, Rick, Mil.	3	1	.750	2.39	15	7	0	0	2	0-0	49.0	39	199	13	13	2	0	1	2	18	1	42	1	0
Hennessey, Brad, S.F.	5	8	.385	4.64	21	21	0	0	1	0-0	118.1	127	521	63	61	15	2	3	4	52	3	64	3	1
Hensley, Clay, S.D.	1	1	.500	1.70	24	1	0	0	5	0-0	47.2	33	189	12	9	0	1	2	0	17	2	28	2	0
Heredia, Felix, N.Y.*	0	0	.000	0.00	3	0	0	0	1	0-0	2.2	1	10	0	0	0	1	1	0	2	0	0		
Herges, Matt, S.F.-Ari.	1	1	.500	7.14	28	0	0	0	7	0-0	29.0	35	132	23	23	6	2	2	1	12	1	9	0	0
Hernandez, Livan, Was.	15	10	.600	3.98	35	35	2	0	0	0-0	246.1	268	1065	116	109	25	15	9	13	84	14	147	3	2
Hernandez, Roberto, N.Y.	8	6	.571	2.58	67	0	0	0	20	4-10	69.2	57	291	20	20	5	9	2	2	28	4	61	4	0
Hill, Rich, Chi.*	0	2	.000	9.13	10	4	0	0	1	0-0	23.2	25	115	24	24	3	1	1	1	17	1	21	0	0
Hoffman, Trevor, S.D.	1	6	.143	2.97	60	0	0	0	54	43-46	57.2	52	240	23	19	3	2	3	1	12	1	54	1	0
Horgan, Joe, Was.*	0	0	.000	21.00	8	0	0	0	1	0-0	6.0	19	44	15	14	0	1	1	4	0	5	1	0	
Houlton, D.J., L.A.	6	9	.400	5.16	35	19	0	0	4	0-0	129.0	145	578	79	74	21	11	5	8	52	3	90	2	0
Hudson, Luke, Cin.	6	9	.400	6.38	19	16	0	0	1	0-0	84.2	83	380	62	60	14	5	4	11	50	2	53	5	0
Hudson, Tim, Atl.	14	9	.609	3.52	29	29	2	0	0	0-0	192.0	194	817	79	75	20	9	1	9	65	5	115	4	0
Hughes, Travis, Was.	1	1	.500	5.54	14	0	0	0	1	0-1	13.0	18	64	8	8	4	1	0	1	8	1	8	4	0
Ishii, Kazuhisa, N.Y.*	3	9	.250	5.14	19	16	0	0	0	0-0	91.0	87	399	59	52	13	6	3	3	49	3	53	2	0
Isringhausen, Jason, St.L.	1	2	.333	2.14	63	0	0	0	52	39-43	59.0	43	245	14	14	4	3	1	1	27	5	51	2	0
Jackson, Edwin, L.A.	2	2	.500	6.28	7	6	0	0	0	0-0	28.2	31	134	22	20	2	2	1	2	17	0	13	2	1
James, Chuck, Atl.*	0	0	.000	1.59	2	0	0	0	0	0-0	5.2	4	23	1	1	0	0	0	0	3	0	5	1	0
Jarvis, Kevin, St.L.	0	1	.000	13.50	4	0	0	0	1	0-1	3.1	3	17	5	5	1	0	0	2	3	0	2	0	0
Jennings, Jason, Col.	6	9	.400	5.02	20	20	0	0	0	0-0	122.0	130	551	73	68	11	6	3	5	62	4	75	8	0
Johnson, Josh, Fla.	0	0	.000	3.65	4	1	0	0	0	0-0	12.1	11	55	5	5	0	1	0	1	10	0	10	0	0
Johnson, Tyler, St.L.*	0	0	.000	0.00	9	0	0	0	4	0-1	2.2	3	13	0	0	0	0	0	0	3	0	4	0	0
Johnston, Mike, Pit.*	0	0	.000	36.00	1	0	0	0	1	0-0	1.0	4	7	4	4	2	0	0	0	0	0	2	0	0
Jones, Todd, Fla.	1	5	.167	2.10	68	0	0	0	55	40-45	73.0	61	289	19	17	2	6	1	3	14	2	62	2	0
Journell, Jimmy, St.L.	0	1	.000	10.38	5	0	0	0	3	0-0	4.1	6	23	6	5	1	0	0	0	5	0	5	0	0
Keisler, Randy, Cin.*	2	1	.667	6.27	24	4	0	0	7	0-0	56.0	64	262	45	39	10	1	1	1	28	2	43	2	0
Kennedy, Joe, Col.*	4	8	.333	7.04	16	16	0	0	0	0-0	92.0	128	442	81	72	12	4	5	6	44	4	52	7	1
Kensing, Logan, Fla.	0	0	.000	11.12	3	0	0	0	0	0-0	5.2	11	31	7	7	2	0	1	0	3	0	4	0	0
Kim, Byung-Hyun, Col.	5	12	.294	4.86	40	22	0	0	3	0-2	148.0	156	667	82	80	17	8	7	14	71	8	115	11	1
Kim, Sunny, Was.-Col.	6	3	.667	4.90	24	10	1	1	3	0-0	82.2	97	363	46	45	10	5	3	3	21	2	55	4	0
King, Ray, St.L.*	4	4	.500	3.38	77	0	0	0	18	0-6	40.0	46	177	17	15	4	0	1	3	16	0	23	1	0
Kinney, Matt, S.F.	2	0	1.000	6.00	5	1	0	0	1	0-1	12.0	18	55	8	8	2	1	0	1	6	0	3	0	0
Kolb, Dan, Atl.	3	8	.273	5.93	65	0	0	0	34	11-18	57.2	78	270	39	38	5	2	1	1	29	5	39	5	0
Koo, Dae-Sung, N.Y.*	0	0	.000	3.91	33	0	0	0	4	0-2	23.0	22	106	12	10	2	0	3	2	13	1	23	0	0
Koplove, Mike, Ari.	2	1	.667	5.07	44	0	0	0	11	0-2	49.2	48	217	31	28	6	1	3	6	20	3	28	1	1
Koronka, John, Chi.*	1	2	.333	7.47	4	3	0	0	1	0-0	15.2	19	76	13	13	2	1	0	0	8	0	10	1	2
Kuo, Hong-Chih, L.A.*	0	1	.000	6.75	9	0	0	0	4	0-0	5.1	5	26	4	4	1	0	0	0	5	1	10	0	1
Lawrence, Brian, S.D.	7	15	.318	4.83	33	33	1	0	0	0-0	195.2	211	852	106	105	18	3	7	11	57	7	109	3	1
Lehr, Justin, Mil.	1	1	.500	3.89	23	0	0	0	9	0-1	34.2	32	154	19	15	4	2	1	1	18	2	23	1	1
Leicester, Jon, Chi.	0	2	.000	9.00	6	1	0	0	4	0-0	9.0	11	46	10	9	2	0	1	2	9	0	7	1	0
Leiter, Al, Fla.*	3	7	.300	6.64	17	16	0	0	0	0-0	80.0	88	377	61	59	9	7	3	6	60	2	52	0	0
Lerew, Anthony, Atl.	0	0	.000	5.63	7	0	0	0	4	0-1	8.0	9	37	5	5	1	1	0	0	4	1	4	0	0
Levine, Al, S.F.	0	0	.000	9.58	9	0	0	0	3	0-0	10.1	16	51	11	11	2	0	0	0	4	1	4	0	0
Lidge, Brad, Hou.	4	4	.500	2.29	70	0	0	0	65	42-46	70.2	58	291	21	18	5	4	1	3	23	1	103	6	0
Lidle, Cory, Phi.	13	11	.542	4.53	31	31	0	0	0	0-0	184.2	210	792	105	93	18	11	8	6	40	5	121	6	0
Lieber, Jon, Phi.	17	13	.567	4.20	35	35	1	0	0	0-0	218.1	223	912	107	102	33	13	5	5	41	6	149	3	0
Ligtenberg, Kerry, Ari.	0	0	.000	13.97	7	0	0	0	2	0-0	9.2	16	48	15	15	4	0	0	4	5	0	7	0	0
Linebrink, Scott, S.D.	8	1	.889	1.83	73	0	0	0	17	1-6	73.2	55	288	17	15	4	0	0	2	23	4	70	3	0
Liriano, Pedro, Phi.	0	0	.000	10.57	9	0	0	0	1	0-0	7.2	10	40	11	9	3	1	1	1	6	1	6	1	0
Loaiza, Esteban, Was.	12	10	.545	3.77	34	34	0	0	0	0-0	217.0	227	912	93	91	18	9	3	5	55	3	173	6	0
Looper, Braden, N.Y.	4	7	.364	3.94	60	0	0	0	54	28-36	59.1	65	271	31	26	7	4	0	5	22	3	27	1	0
Lopez, Aquilino, Col.-Phi.	0	2	.000	6.26	11	0	0	0	5	0-0	16	16	72	5	4	2	1	0	0	7	1	22	1	0
Lopez, Javier, Col.-Ari.*	1	1	.500	11.02	32	0	0	0	6	2-4	16.1	26	87	20	20	2	1	0	1	11	3	12	0	0
Lowe, Derek, L.A.	12	15	.444	3.61	35	35	2	2	0	0-0	222.0	223	934	113	89	28	12	5	5	55	1	146	3	2

Pitcher, Team	W	L	Pct.	ERA	G	GS	CG	ShO	GF	Sv.-Op.	IP	H	TBF	R	ER	HR	SH	SF	HB	BB	IBB	SO	WP	Bk.
Lowry, Noah, S.F.*	13	13	.500	3.78	33	33	0	0	0	0-0	204.2	193	875	92	86	21	13	3	7	76	1	172	2	0
Lyon, Brandon, Ari.	0	2	.000	6.44	32	0	0	0	22	14-15	29.1	44	144	25	21	6	2	1	2	10	2	17	1	1
Maddux, Greg, Chi.	13	15	.464	4.24	35	35	3	0	0	0-0	225.0	239	936	112	106	29	19	6	7	36	4	136	8	0
Madson, Ryan, Phi.	6	5	.545	4.14	78	0	0	0	10	0-7	87.0	84	365	44	40	11	5	5	6	25	6	79	6	1
Maholm, Paul, Pit.*	3	1	.750	2.18	6	6	0	0	0	0-0	41.1	31	168	10	10	2	0	0	3	17	0	26	0	0
Majewski, Gary, Was.	4	4	.500	2.93	79	0	0	0	24	1-5	86.0	80	376	32	28	2	5	4	7	37	6	50	1	0
Marquis, Jason, St.L.	13	14	.481	4.13	33	32	3	1	0	0-0	207.0	206	868	110	95	29	4	3	5	69	2	100	10	3
Martin, Tom, Atl.*	0	0	.000	19.29	4	0	0	0	1	0-0	2.1	6	14	5	5	1	0	0	0	2	0	0	0	0
Martinez, Pedro, N.Y.	15	8	.652	2.82	31	31	4	1	0	0-0	217.0	159	843	69	68	19	9	2	4	47	3	208	4	0
Matthews, Mike, N.Y.*	1	0	1.000	10.80	6	0	0	0	0	0-0	5.0	9	28	6	6	0	1	2	0	4	1	2	2	0
May, Darrell, S.D.*	1	3	.250	5.61	22	8	0	0	9	0-0	59.1	73	264	38	37	10	1	2	0	20	1	32	0	0
McBride, Macay, Atl.*	1	0	1.000	5.79	23	0	0	0	4	1-1	14.0	18	68	11	9	0	1	1	0	7	0	22	2	0
Meadows, Brian, Pit.	3	1	.750	4.58	65	0	0	0	9	0-2	74.2	84	326	42	38	8	3	9	0	21	7	44	3	0
Mecir, Jim, Fla.	1	4	.200	3.12	52	0	0	0	13	0-0	43.1	39	184	17	15	2	3	2	5	17	2	34	0	0
Medders, Brandon, Ari.	4	1	.800	1.78	27	0	0	0	10	0-0	30.1	21	122	6	6	2	0	2	1	11	0	31	1	0
Mercker, Kent, Cin.*	3	1	.750	3.65	78	0	0	0	23	4-7	61.2	64	265	27	25	8	4	2	3	19	4	45	1	0
Mesa, Jose, Pit.	2	8	.200	4.76	55	0	0	0	48	27-34	56.2	61	257	30	30	7	8	6	3	26	3	37	2	0
Messenger, Randy, Fla.	0	0	.000	5.35	29	0	0	0	8	0-0	37.0	39	178	22	22	5	2	3	0	30	7	29	1	0
Miceli, Dan, Col.	1	2	.333	5.89	19	0	0	0	3	0-2	18.1	19	86	12	12	1	2	0	1	13	0	19	0	0
Milton, Eric, Cin.*	8	15	.348	6.47	34	34	0	0	0	0-0	186.1	237	855	141	134	40	6	6	7	52	2	123	8	0
Mitre, Sergio, Chi.	2	5	.286	5.37	21	7	1	1	7	0-0	60.1	62	268	37	36	11	1	3	3	23	2	37	5	0
Moehler, Brian, Fla.	6	12	.333	4.55	37	25	0	0	4	0-0	158.1	198	696	82	80	16	13	4	5	42	9	95	1	0
Morris, Matt, St.L.	14	10	.583	4.11	31	31	2	0	0	0-0	192.2	209	818	101	88	22	10	5	8	37	3	117	1	1
Mota, Guillermo, Fla.	2	2	.500	4.70	56	0	0	0	24	2-4	67.0	65	293	38	35	5	1	3	1	32	7	60	4	0
Mulder, Mark, St.L.*	16	8	.667	3.64	32	32	3	2	0	0-0	205.0	212	868	90	83	19	9	4	9	70	1	111	9	0
Munter, Scott, S.F.	2	0	1.000	2.56	45	0	0	0	7	0-3	38.2	40	159	15	11	1	2	1	1	12	1	11	1	0
Myers, Brett, Phi.	13	8	.619	3.72	34	34	2	0	0	0-0	215.1	193	905	94	89	31	9	3	11	68	2	208	4	4
Neal, Blaine, Col.	1	2	.333	6.14	11	0	0	0	3	0-2	14.2	20	70	10	10	2	0	2	0	9	2	8	1	0
Nippert, Dustin, Ari.	1	0	1.000	5.52	3	3	0	0	0	0-0	14.2	10	68	9	9	1	0	0	1	13	0	11	1	0
Nitkowski, C.J., Was.*	0	0	.000	8.10	7	0	0	0	0	0-0	3.1	5	17	3	3	0	1	0	0	2	0	2	0	0
Novoa, Roberto, Chi.	4	5	.444	4.43	49	0	0	0	11	0-5	44.2	47	205	22	22	4	2	0	0	25	6	47	4	1
Obermueller, Wes, Mil.	1	4	.200	5.26	23	8	0	0	4	0-0	65.0	74	305	41	38	7	4	4	5	36	2	33	3	0
Ohka, Tomo, Was.-Mil.	11	9	.550	4.04	32	29	1	1	0	0-0	180.1	189	774	88	81	22	7	4	3	55	5	98	8	0
Ohman, Will, Chi.*	2	2	.500	2.91	69	0	0	0	13	0-3	43.1	32	187	14	14	6	1	0	3	24	3	45	4	1
Olsen, Scott, Fla.*	1	1	.500	3.98	5	4	0	0	0	0-0	20.1	21	91	13	9	5	0	0	0	10	0	21	1	0
Ortiz, Ramon, Cin.	9	11	.450	5.36	30	30	1	0	0	0-0	171.1	206	755	110	102	34	7	8	7	51	1	96	4	1
Ortiz, Russ, Ari.	5	11	.313	6.89	22	22	0	0	0	0-0	115.0	147	551	92	88	18	5	8	4	65	3	46	5	0
Osoria, Franquelis, L.A.	0	2	.000	3.94	24	0	0	0	6	0-2	29.2	28	122	14	13	3	3	0	3	8	0	15	0	0
Osuna, Antonio, Was.	0	0	.000	42.43	4	0	0	0	1	0-0	2.1	9	23	11	11	2	0	1	0	7	1	0	0	0
Oswalt, Roy, Hou.	20	12	.625	2.94	35	35	4	1	0	0-0	241.2	243	1002	85	79	18	12	7	8	48	3	184	5	1
Otsuka, Akinori, S.D.	2	8	.200	3.59	66	0	0	0	17	1-7	62.2	55	276	28	25	3	5	0	2	34	8	60	1	0
Oxspring, Chris, S.D.	0	0	.000	3.75	5	0	0	0	0	0-0	12.0	9	49	8	5	2	1	2	0	6	0	11	0	0
Padilla, Juan, N.Y.	3	1	.750	1.49	24	0	0	0	5	1-2	36.1	24	149	7	6	0	1	0	2	13	2	17	0	0
Padilla, Vicente, Phi.	9	12	.429	4.71	27	27	0	0	0	0-0	147.0	146	654	79	77	22	7	3	8	74	9	103	1	0
Park, Chan Ho, S.D.	4	3	.571	5.91	10	9	0	0	0	0-0	45.2	50	213	33	30	3	2	1	4	26	0	33	3	0
Patterson, John, Was.	9	7	.563	3.13	31	31	2	1	0	0-0	198.1	172	817	71	69	19	5	4	5	65	11	185	9	1
Peavy, Jake, S.D.	13	7	.650	2.88	30	30	3	0	0	0-0	203.0	162	812	70	65	18	4	5	7	50	3	216	3	1
Penny, Brad, L.A.	7	9	.438	3.90	29	29	1	0	0	0-0	175.1	185	738	78	76	17	7	1	3	41	2	122	3	0
Perez, Odalis, L.A.*	7	8	.467	4.56	19	19	0	0	0	0-0	108.2	109	453	59	55	13	8	1	0	28	2	74	3	0
Perez, Oliver, Pit.*	7	5	.583	5.85	20	20	0	0	0	0-0	103.0	102	471	68	67	23	5	4	6	70	1	97	3	0
Perisho, Matt, Fla.*	2	0	1.000	1.93	24	0	0	0	4	0-0	14.0	12	64	4	3	1	2	1	1	11	0	10	0	0
Pettitte, Andy, Hou.*	17	9	.654	2.39	33	33	0	0	0	0-0	222.1	188	875	66	59	17	10	4	3	41	0	171	2	0
Phelps, Tommy, Mil.*	0	2	.000	4.63	29	0	0	0	8	1-2	23.1	25	106	12	12	2	0	2	12	4	14	2	0
Powell, Jay, Atl.	0	0	.000	0.00	5	0	0	0	1	0-0	3.1	1	15	0	0	0	0	0	0	4	0	1	0	0
Prior, Mark, Chi.	11	7	.611	3.67	27	27	1	0	0	0-0	166.2	143	701	73	68	25	5	3	4	59	2	188	4	1
Puffer, Brandon, S.F.	0	0	.000	10.29	4	0	0	0	2	0-0	7.0	9	31	8	8	2	0	0	0	2	0	1	0	0
Pulsipher, Bill, St.L.*	0	0	.000	6.75	5	0	0	0	2	0-0	4.0	5	19	3	3	0	2	1	0	2	1	1	0	0
Qualls, Chad, Hou.	6	4	.600	3.28	77	0	0	0	19	0-6	79.2	73	329	33	29	7	4	3	6	23	2	60	1	0
Quantrill, Paul, S.D.-Fla.	1	2	.333	4.14	28	0	0	0	9	0-0	37.0	45	160	20	17	3	0	3	1	7	1	25	0	0
Ramirez, Elizardo, Cin.	0	3	.000	8.46	6	4	0	0	1	0-0	22.1	33	110	22	21	5	2	0	2	10	2	9	2	0
Ramirez, Horacio, Atl.*	11	9	.550	4.63	33	32	1	1	0	0-0	202.1	214	847	108	104	31	13	5	2	67	4	80	4	1
Rasner, Darrell, Was.	0	1	.000	3.68	5	1	0	0	1	0-0	7.1	5	31	3	3	0	1	0	2	2	1	4	0	0
Rauch, Jon, Was.	2	4	.333	3.60	15	1	0	0	3	0-0	30.0	24	124	12	12	3	1	1	1	11	2	23	0	0
Redding, Tim, S.D.	0	5	.000	9.10	9	6	0	0	0	0-0	29.2	40	143	35	30	7	3	3	2	13	1	17	1	0
Redman, Mark, Pit.*	5	15	.250	4.90	30	30	2	1	0	0-0	178.1	188	751	100	97	18	11	5	2	56	3	101	7	3
Reitsma, Chris, Atl.	3	6	.333	3.93	76	0	0	0	37	15-24	73.1	79	307	32	32	3	1	2	0	14	3	42	2	0
Remlinger, Mike, Chi.*	0	0	.000	4.91	35	0	0	0	7	0-1	33.0	31	141	19	18	5	3	0	2	12	2	30	0	0
Resop, Chris, Fla.	2	0	1.000	8.47	15	0	0	0	6	0-0	17.0	22	80	16	16	1	0	2	1	9	0	15	3	0
Reyes, Al, St.L.	4	2	.667	2.15	65	0	0	0	18	3-3	62.2	38	244	15	15	5	3	1	5	20	2	67	1	0
Reyes, Anthony, St.L.	1	1	.500	2.70	4	1	0	0	0	0-0	13.1	6	51	4	4	2	1	1	0	4	1	12	2	0
Reyes, Dennys, S.D.*	3	2	.600	5.15	36	1	0	0	9	0-1	43.2	57	215	30	25	3	1	0	1	32	2	35	3	1
Riedling, John, Fla.	4	1	.800	7.16	19	0	0	0	7	0-0	27.2	34	130	23	22	3	1	1	1	13	2	16	6	0
Ring, Royce, N.Y.*	0	0	.000	5.06	15	0	0	0	2	0-0	10.2	10	51	6	6	0	1	0	1	8	0	6	0	0
Rodriguez, Wandy, Hou.*	10	10	.500	5.53	25	22	0	0	0	0-0	128.2	135	560	82	79	19	3	3	8	53	2	80	5	1
Rueter, Kirk, S.F.*	2	7	.222	5.95	20	18	0	0	1	0-0	107.1	131	489	78	71	12	3	8	1	47	3	25	3	0
Rusch, Glendon, Chi.*	9	8	.529	4.52	46	19	1	1	6	0-1	145.1	175	655	79	73	14	13	9	1	53	8	111	1	1
Sanchez, Duaner, L.A.	4	7	.364	3.73	79	0	0	0	31	8-12	82.0	75	353	36	34	8	10	1	3	36	6	71	1	0
Santana, Julio, Mil.	3	5	.375	4.50	41	0	0	0	12	1-4	42.0	34	177	21	21	6	1	3	0	19	4	49	5	0
Santiago, Jose, N.Y.	0	0	.000	3.18	4	0	0	0	1	0-0	5.2	10	27	2	2	0	0	0	1	2	0	3	0	0
Santos, Victor, Mil.	4	13	.235	4.57	29	24	0	0	2	0-0	141.2	153	640	87	72	20	5	1	5	60	8	89	7	0
Schmidt, Jason, S.F.	12	7	.632	4.40	29	29	0	0	0	0-0	172.0	160	757	90	84	16	8	8	5	85	4	165	7	1
Schmoll, Steve, L.A.	2	2	.500	5.01	48	0	0	0	14	3-4	46.2	47	205	29	26	4	5	4	3	22	2	29	0	1

Pitcher, Team	W	L	Pct.	ERA	G	GS	CG	ShO	GF	Sv.-Op.	IP	H	TBF	R	ER	HR	SH	SF	HB	BB	IBB	SO	WP	Bk.
Seanez, Rudy, S.D.	7	1	.875	2.69	57	0	0	0	9	0-2	60.1	49	248	19	18	4	2	1	2	22	4	84	4	0
Seay, Bobby, Col.*	0	0	.000	8.49	17	0	0	0	5	0-1	11.2	18	58	11	11	3	1	0	0	8	1	11	0	1
Seo, Jae, N.Y.	8	2	.800	2.59	14	14	1	0	0	0-0	90.1	84	363	26	26	9	9	3	4	16	0	59	2	0
Shackelford, Brian, Cin.*	1	0	1.000	2.43	37	0	0	0	5	0-0	29.2	21	119	9	8	2	0	1	6	9	1	17	3	1
Sheets, Ben, Mil.	10	9	.526	3.33	22	22	3	0	0	0-0	156.2	142	633	66	58	19	6	2	2	25	1	141	7	0
Simpson, Allan, Col.-Cin.	0	1	.000	12.27	11	0	0	0	2	0-1	7.1	6	36	10	10	1	0	1	1	8	0	6	2	0
Smith, Travis, Fla.	0	0	.000	6.75	12	0	0	0	4	0-0	10.2	17	52	8	8	1	0	1	0	5	1	9	0	0
Smoltz, John, Atl.	14	7	.667	3.06	33	33	3	1	0	0-0	229.2	210	931	83	78	18	10	3	1	53	7	169	1	0
Snell, Ian, Pit.	1	2	.333	5.14	15	5	0	0	2	0-0	42.0	43	189	25	24	5	2	1	1	24	3	34	4	0
Sosa, Jorge, Atl.	13	3	.813	2.55	44	20	0	0	5	0-0	134.0	122	577	42	38	12	5	2	0	64	8	85	3	0
Speier, Ryan, Col.	2	1	.667	3.65	22	0	0	0	10	0-1	24.2	26	111	12	10	0	2	1	1	13	0	10	2	0
Springer, Russ, Hou.	4	4	.500	4.73	62	0	0	0	11	0-3	59.0	49	246	34	31	9	1	0	3	21	3	54	2	0
Standridge, Jason, Cin.	2	2	.500	4.06	32	0	0	0	6	0-0	31.0	38	140	14	14	3	2	0	1	16	7	17	1	0
Stanton, Mike, Was.*	2	1	.667	3.58	30	0	0	0	6	0-1	27.2	31	118	13	11	2	3	0	0	9	4	14	0	1
Stauffer, Tim, S.D.	3	6	.333	5.33	15	14	0	0	0	0-0	81.0	92	355	50	48	10	2	0	2	29	0	49	0	0
Stone, Ricky, Cin.	0	0	.000	6.75	23	0	0	0	4	0-0	30.2	48	143	24	23	8	0	2	7	2	15	2	0
Strickland, Scott, Hou.	0	0	.000	6.75	5	0	0	0	1	0-0	4.0	4	16	3	3	2	0	0	0	0	0	2	0	0
Suppan, Jeff, St.L.	16	10	.615	3.57	32	32	0	0	0	0-0	194.1	206	834	93	77	24	11	5	7	63	1	114	6	1
Takatsu, Shingo, N.Y.	1	1	.000	2.35	9	0	0	0	4	0-0	7.2	11	38	2	2	2	0	0	0	3	1	6	0	0
Taschner, Jack, S.F.*	2	0	1.000	1.59	24	0	0	0	7	0-1	22.2	15	95	5	4	0	0	1	0	13	0	19	0	0
Tavarez, Julian, St.L.	2	3	.400	3.43	74	0	0	0	16	4-6	65.2	68	278	28	25	6	3	3	8	19	4	47	1	0
Tejeda, Robinson, Phi.	4	3	.571	3.57	26	13	0	0	5	0-0	85.2	67	371	36	34	5	3	2	8	51	4	72	3	1
Telemaco, Amaury, Phi.	0	1	.000	4.22	7	0	0	0	4	0-0	10.2	5	41	5	5	2	0	1	0	4	0	8	0	0
Thompson, Brad, St.L.	4	0	1.000	2.95	40	0	0	0	8	1-1	55.0	46	225	22	18	5	3	0	4	15	2	29	0	0
Thompson, Derek, L.A.*	0	0	.000	3.50	4	3	0	0	0	0-0	18.0	16	74	7	7	0	1	1	0	10	1	13	0	0
Thomson, John, Atl.	4	6	.400	4.47	17	17	1	0	0	0-0	98.2	111	427	52	49	6	4	2	4	28	2	61	3	0
Tomko, Brett, S.F.	8	15	.348	4.48	33	30	3	0	1	1-1	190.2	205	823	99	95	20	6	5	7	57	11	114	5	0
Torres, Salomon, Pit.	5	5	.500	2.76	78	0	0	0	32	3-3	94.2	76	388	34	29	7	3	2	5	36	7	55	5	0
Trachsel, Steve, N.Y.	1	4	.200	4.14	6	6	0	0	0	0-0	37.0	37	157	20	17	6	2	2	1	12	0	24	1	0
Tsao, Chin-hui, Col.	1	0	1.000	6.55	10	0	0	0	9	3-4	11.0	16	56	8	8	3	1	1	1	5	1	4	1	0
Tucker, T.J., Was.	1	0	1.000	6.39	13	0	0	0	1	0-0	12.2	20	58	9	9	4	1	1	0	2	0	5	1	0
Turnbow, Derrick, Mil.	7	1	.875	1.74	69	0	0	0	62	39-43	67.1	49	271	15	13	5	0	0	1	24	2	64	9	0
Urbina, Ugueth, Phi.	4	3	.571	4.13	56	0	0	0	8	1-7	52.1	35	214	25	24	8	0	1	0	25	2	66	0	0
Valdez, Ismael, Fla.	2	2	.500	5.33	14	7	0	0	1	0-0	50.2	64	237	32	30	6	4	2	5	22	6	27	1	2
Valentine, Joe, Cin.	0	1	.000	8.16	16	0	0	0	5	0-1	14.1	18	76	15	13	4	1	1	2	11	0	9	1	0
Valverde, Jose, Ari.	3	4	.429	2.44	61	0	0	0	34	15-17	66.1	51	268	19	18	5	3	1	2	20	1	75	3	0
Van Buren, Jermaine, Chi.	0	2	.000	3.00	6	0	0	0	1	0-0	6.0	2	27	2	2	0	1	0	0	9	2	3	0	0
Vargas, Claudio, Was.-Ari.	9	9	.500	5.24	25	23	0	0	0	0-0	132.1	146	586	81	77	25	6	1	7	47	5	95	6	0
Vargas, Jason, Fla.*	5	5	.500	4.03	17	13	1	0	0	0-0	73.2	71	325	34	33	4	4	1	4	31	4	59	0	0
Vasquez, Jorge, Atl.	1	0	1.000	3.00	7	0	0	0	2	0-0	9.0	11	42	4	3	2	0	0	0	5	0	9	1	1
Vazquez, Javier, Ari.	11	15	.423	4.42	33	33	3	1	0	0-0	215.2	223	904	112	106	35	13	3	5	46	4	192	7	0
Villarreal, Oscar, Ari.	2	0	1.000	5.27	11	0	0	0	0	0-2	13.2	11	57	8	8	2	2	1	1	6	2	5	0	0
Villone, Ron, Fla.*	3	2	.600	6.85	27	0	0	0	10	0-3	23.2	24	109	20	18	2	2	2	2	12	1	29	1	0
Vogelsong, Ryan, Pit.	2	2	.500	4.43	44	0	0	0	19	0-1	81.1	82	369	43	40	5	1	4	8	40	1	52	7	0
Wagner, Billy, Phi.*	4	3	.571	1.51	75	0	0	0	70	38-41	77.2	45	297	17	13	6	0	2	3	20	2	87	3	1
Wagner, Ryan, Cin.	3	2	.600	6.11	42	0	0	0	8	0-1	45.2	56	210	33	31	4	1	3	4	17	1	39	2	0
Wainwright, Adam, St.L.	0	0	.000	13.50	2	0	0	0	1	0-0	2.0	2	9	3	3	1	0	0	0	1	0	0	0	0
Walker, Tyler, S.F.	6	4	.600	4.23	67	0	0	0	39	23-28	61.2	68	279	31	29	9	5	1	3	27	6	54	4	0
Weathers, David, Cin.	7	4	.636	3.94	73	0	0	0	41	15-19	77.2	71	331	36	34	7	4	2	2	29	2	61	4	0
Weaver, Jeff, L.A.	14	11	.560	4.22	34	34	3	2	0	0-0	224.0	220	930	111	105	35	8	3	18	43	1	157	2	0
Webb, Brandon, Ari.	14	12	.538	3.54	33	33	1	0	0	0-0	229.0	229	943	98	90	21	10	7	2	59	4	172	14	1
Weber, Ben, Cin.	0	0	.000	8.03	10	0	0	0	3	0-0	12.1	20	66	11	11	0	0	1	9	1	8	0	0
Wellemeyer, Todd, Chi.	2	1	.667	6.12	22	0	0	0	6	1-1	32.1	32	146	23	22	7	2	1	0	22	1	32	3	0
Wells, Kip, Pit.	8	18	.308	5.09	33	33	1	1	0	0-0	182.0	186	828	116	103	23	9	10	12	99	8	132	6	0
Wheeler, Dan, Hou.	2	3	.400	2.21	71	0	0	0	20	3-5	73.1	53	288	18	18	7	5	1	3	19	3	69	0	0
White, Gabe, St.L.*	0	0	.000	2.16	6	0	0	0	3	0-0	8.1	14	38	2	2	1	0	0	0	1	1	1	0	0
White, Matt, Was.*	0	1	.000	9.00	1	1	0	0	0	0-0	4.0	4	20	4	4	0	0	1	3	0	3	1	0
White, Rick, Pit.	4	7	.364	3.72	71	0	0	0	23	2-3	75.0	90	338	39	31	3	9	4	4	29	10	40	4	0
Williams, Dave, Pit.*	10	11	.476	4.41	25	25	1	1	0	0-0	138.2	137	600	74	68	20	7	2	8	58	5	88	3	0
Williams, Jerome, S.F.-Chi.	6	10	.375	4.26	22	20	0	0	0	0-0	122.2	119	532	62	58	14	11	8	10	49	1	70	2	0
Williams, Randy, S.D.-Col.*	3	1	.750	6.84	32	0	0	0	6	0-2	26.1	33	125	21	20	5	0	1	1	13	3	21	0	0
Williams, Woody, S.D.	9	12	.429	4.85	28	28	0	0	0	0-0	159.2	174	697	92	86	24	6	5	3	51	1	106	1	0
Williamson, Scott, Chi.	0	0	.000	5.65	17	0	0	0	4	0-0	14.1	15	65	9	9	3	2	0	2	6	0	23	4	1
Willis, Dontrelle, Fla.*	22	10	.688	2.63	34	34	7	5	0	0-0	236.1	213	960	79	69	11	14	5	8	55	3	170	2	1
Wilson, Paul, Cin.	1	5	.167	7.77	9	9	0	0	0	0-0	46.1	68	224	41	40	10	2	3	4	17	1	30	2	0
Wise, Matt, Mil.	4	4	.500	3.36	49	0	0	0	11	1-3	64.1	37	262	25	24	6	1	2	3	25	5	62	1	1
Witasick, Jay, Col.	0	0	.000	2.52	32	0	0	0	6	0-1	35.2	27	148	11	10	2	4	0	3	12	3	40	2	0
Wolf, Randy, Phi.*	6	4	.600	4.39	13	13	0	0	0	0-0	80.0	87	346	40	39	14	4	1	6	26	2	61	1	0
Wood, Kerry, Chi.	3	4	.429	4.23	21	10	0	0	4	0-0	66.0	52	273	32	31	14	2	1	2	26	0	77	0	0
Worrell, Tim, Phi.-Ari.	1	2	.333	4.07	51	0	0	0	17	1-4	48.2	59	220	30	22	8	4	5	2	12	2	39	0	1
Wright, Jamey, Col.	8	16	.333	5.46	34	27	0	0	1	0-0	171.1	201	782	119	104	22	4	3	15	81	4	101	2	2
Wuertz, Michael, Chi.	6	2	.750	3.81	75	0	0	0	12	0-3	75.2	60	319	36	32	6	3	2	0	40	7	89	7	0
Wunsch, Kelly, L.A.*	1	1	.500	4.56	45	0	0	0	6	0-1	23.2	20	105	12	12	2	1	0	2	14	2	22	2	0
Zambrano, Carlos, Chi.	14	6	.700	3.26	33	33	2	0	0	0-0	223.1	170	909	88	81	21	9	5	8	86	3	202	7	0
Zambrano, Victor, N.Y.	7	12	.368	4.17	31	27	0	0	2	0-0	166.1	170	784	85	77	12	6	6	15	77	2	112	8	2

PITCHERS WITH TWO OR MORE TEAMS

Pitcher, Team	W	L	Pct.	ERA	G	GS	CG	ShO	GF	Sv.-Op.	IP	H	TBF	R	ER	HR	SH	SF	HB	BB	IBB	SO	WP	Bk.
Brower, Jim, S.F.	2	1	.667	6.53	32	0	0	0	8	1-3	30.1	40	144	22	22	5	1	1	2	15	0	25	2	0
Brower, Jim, Atl.	1	2	.333	4.20	37	0	0	0	4	0-0	30.0	33	138	14	14	6	1	0	3	17	3	28	2	0
Day, Zach, Was.	1	2	.333	6.75	12	5	0	0	4	0-0	36.0	41	170	29	27	4	1	1	1	25	3	16	1	0

Pitcher, Team	W	L	Pct.	ERA	G	GS	CG	ShO	GF	Sv.-Op.	IP	H	TBF	R	ER	HR	SH	SF	HB	BB	IBB	SO	WP	Bk.
Day, Zach, Col.	0	1	.000	7.15	5	3	0	0	0	0-1	11.1	20	59	11	9	2	0	0	0	7	1	7	1	0
DeJean, Mike, N.Y.	3	1	.750	6.31	28	0	0	0	12	0-0	25.2	36	131	19	18	3	1	1	1	18	2	17	2	0
DeJean, Mike, Col.	2	3	.400	3.19	38	0	0	0	7	0-3	36.2	26	151	14	13	0	2	2	2	12	1	35	3	0
Graves, Danny, Cin.	1	1	.500	7.36	20	0	0	0	18	10-12	18.1	30	99	18	15	4	2	1	0	12	3	8	3	0
Graves, Danny, N.Y.	0	0	.000	5.75	20	0	0	0	11	0-0	20.1	29	98	17	13	5	1	0	3	8	1	12	0	0
Hawkins, LaTroy, Chi.	1	4	.200	3.32	21	0	0	0	12	4-8	19.0	18	80	9	7	4	1	0	0	7	0	13	0	0
Hawkins, LaTroy, S.F.	1	4	.200	4.10	45	0	0	0	9	2-7	37.1	40	167	18	17	3	2	1	0	17	3	30	1	0
Herges, Matt, S.F.	1	1	.500	4.71	21	0	0	0	5	0-0	21.0	23	90	11	11	2	2	1	0	7	1	6	0	0
Herges, Matt, Ari.	0	0	.000	13.50	7	0	0	0	2	0-0	8.0	12	42	12	12	4	0	1	1	5	0	3	0	0
Kim, Sunny, Was.	1	2	.333	6.14	12	2	0	0	3	0-0	29.1	41	135	20	20	3	1	2	2	8	2	17	1	0
Kim, Sunny, Col.	5	1	.833	4.22	12	8	1	1	0	0-0	53.1	56	228	26	25	7	4	1	1	13	0	38	3	0
Lopez, Aquilino, Col.	0	0	.000	2.25	1	0	0	0	0	0-0	4.0	3	15	1	1	0	0	0	0	0	0	6	0	0
Lopez, Aquilino, Phi.	0	1	.000	2.13	10	0	0	0	5	0-0	12.2	13	57	4	3	2	1	0	0	7	1	16	1	0
Lopez, Javier, Col.*	0	0	.000	22.50	3	0	0	0	1	0-1	2.0	7	13	5	5	0	0	0	0	0	1	0	0	
Lopez, Javier, Ari.*	1	1	.500	9.42	29	0	0	0	5	2-3	14.1	19	74	15	15	2	1	0	1	11	3	11	0	0
Ohka, Tomo, Was.	4	3	.571	3.33	10	9	0	0	0	0-0	54.0	44	231	23	20	6	6	1	1	27	1	17	3	0
Ohka, Tomo, Mil.	7	6	.538	4.35	22	20	1	1	0	0-0	126.1	145	543	65	61	16	1	3	2	28	4	81	5	0
Quantrill, Paul, S.D.	1	1	.500	3.41	22	0	0	0	7	0-0	31.2	37	132	13	12	2	0	3	1	2	1	24	0	0
Quantrill, Paul, Fla.	0	1	.000	8.44	6	0	0	0	2	0-0	5.1	8	28	7	5	1	0	0	0	5	0	1	0	0
Simpson, Allan, Col.	0	0	.000	67.50	2	0	0	0	0	0-0	0.2	3	8	5	5	0	0	1	0	3	0	0	1	0
Simpson, Allan, Cin.	0	0	.000	6.75	9	0	0	0	2	0-1	6.2	3	28	5	5	1	0	0	1	5	0	6	1	0
Vargas, Claudio, Was.	0	3	.000	9.24	4	4	0	0	0	0-0	12.2	22	66	15	13	4	0	0	0	7	2	5	0	0
Vargas, Claudio, Ari.	9	6	.600	4.81	21	19	0	0	2	0-0	119.2	124	520	66	64	21	6	1	7	40	3	90	6	0
Williams, Jerome, S.F.	0	2	.000	6.48	4	3	0	0	0	0-0	16.2	21	73	12	12	2	1	0	1	4	1	11	0	0
Williams, Jerome, Chi.	6	8	.429	3.91	18	17	0	0	0	0-0	106.0	98	459	50	46	12	10	8	9	45	0	59	2	0
Williams, Randy, S.D.*	1	0	1.000	12.46	2	0	0	0	0	0-0	4.1	7	25	6	6	1	0	0	1	4	0	2	0	0
Williams, Randy, Col.*	2	1	.667	5.73	30	0	0	0	6	0-2	22.0	26	100	15	14	4	0	1	0	9	3	19	0	0
Worrell, Tim, Phi.	0	0	.000	7.41	19	0	0	0	9	1-3	17.0	29	83	17	14	4	1	1	1	3	0	17	0	1
Worrell, Tim, Ari.	1	1	.500	2.27	32	0	0	0	8	0-1	31.2	30	137	13	8	4	3	4	1	9	2	22	0	0

NOTE—The following pitchers combined to pitch shutout games: Arizona (9)—Halsey, Koplove and Valverde; Halsey, Bruney, Koplove and Lyon; Gosling, Cormier, Almanza, Valverde and Bruney; Vazquez and Almanza; Vargas, Valverde and Almanza; Halsey, Worrell, Valverde and Aquino; Vargas, Aquino and Groom; Webb, Groom and Valverde; Webb, Worrell and Valverde; Atlanta (9)—Thomson, Reitsma and Kolb; Hudson and Reitsma; Davies, Foster, Bernero and Reitsma; Davies, Foster and Reitsma; Hudson, Reitsma, Sosa and Kolb; Ramirez, Gryboski, Boyer, Brower and Kolb; Davies, Foster, Boyer and Reitsma; Hudson, Brower, Kolb and Reitsma; Sosa and Farnsworth; Chicago (8)—Maddux, Wuertz and Remlinger; Zambrano, Ohman and Dempster; Zambrano, Fox and Hawkins; Mitre, Wuertz and Dempster; Prior, Williams and Dempster; Zambrano and Dempster; Williams, Ohman, Novoa and Dempster; Maddux and Dempster; Cincinnati (1)—Harang, Weathers and Coffey; Colorado (3)—Wright, Witasick and Fuentes; Francis, Miceli, Witasick and Cortes; Jennings, Witasick and Fuentes; Florida (7)—Willis, Bump and Moehler; Beckett, Mecir, Jones and Mota; Willis, Mota and Jones; Burnett, Mota and Jones; Willis and Jones; Beckett, Villone and Jones; Burnett and Jones; Houston (9)—Oswalt and Lidge; Pettitte, Franco and Qualls; Clemens, Qualls, Franco and Harville; Clemens, Gallo and Burns; Pettitte, Springer and Harville; Pettitte and Lidge; Astacio, Springer, Burns, Wheeler and Harville; Pettitte, Qualls and Gallo; Backe, Gallo, Springer and Astacio; Los Angeles (5)—Weaver and Wunsch; Penny and Osoria; Perez, Schmoll, Alvarez and Brazoban; Lowe and Schmoll; Weaver and Sanchez; Milwaukee (4)—D. Davis, de la Rosa and Turnbow; Ohka and Turnbow; Capuano, Eveland, Capellan and Turnbow; Glover, Capellan, Santana and Turnbow; New York (8)—Glavine, Hernandez and Looper; Martinez and Looper; Ishii, Hernandez, Looper and DeJean; Ishii, Koo, Bell and Graves; Benson and Heilman; Seo, Koo, Hernandez and Looper; Seo and Looper; Trachsel and Looper; Philadelphia (6)—Tejeda, Fultz, Madson and Wagner; Myers, Cormier and Wagner; Lidle and Wagner; Padilla, Madson, Urbina and Wagner; Tejeda, Madson, Cormier and Wagner; Lieber and Wagner; Pittsburgh (11)—Perez, White and Mesa; Wells, White and Mesa; Williams, White and Mesa; Duke and Mesa; Redman and Mesa; Wells, Torres and Mesa; Duke, White and Mesa; Duke, Torres, White, Grabow and Vogelsong; Maholm and Torres; Maholm and Torres; Snell and Mesa; San Diego (5)—Peavy, Linebrink, Hoffman, Otsuka and Seanez; Eaton, Linebrink, Otsuka and Hoffman; Lawrence and Hoffman; Peavy and Hoffman; Lawrence and Cassidy; San Francisco (8)—Schmidt and Walker; Schmidt, Eyre and Walker; Hennessey, Hawkins and Walker; Lowry and Eyre; Hennessey, Munter and Walker; Schmidt and Hawkins; Lowry, Accardo and Walker; Lowry and Hawkins; St. Louis (7)—Carpenter, King and Tavarez; Suppan and Isringhausen; Carpenter, King and Tavarez; Suppan, A. Reyes, King and Isringhausen; Eldred, Thompson, Tavarez, A. Reyes and King; Carpenter, A. Reyes, Tavarez and King; Suppan and Isringhausen; Washington (8)—Loaiza and Majewski; Day, Ayala and Cordero; Drese and Cordero; Loaiza, Majewski, Ayala and Cordero; Patterson, Stanton and Cordero; Armas, Stanton, Carrasco and Eischen; Carrasco, Ayala, Rauch, Majewski and Cordero; Carrasco, Bergmann, Eischen and Majewski.

FIELDING

TEAM

Team	G	PO	A	E	TC	DP	TP	PB	Pct.	Team	G	PO	A	E	TC	DP	TP	PB	Pct.
Atlanta	162	4331	1802	86	6219	170	0	8	.986	Los Angeles	162	4282	1727	106	6115	141	0	9	.983
Houston	163	4329	1700	89	6118	146	0	6	.985	Cincinnati	163	4299	1587	104	5990	133	0	9	.983
San Francisco	162	4333	1630	90	6053	146	0	5	.985	New York	162	4307	1657	106	6070	146	0	5	.983
Philadelphia	162	4305	1608	90	6003	132	0	12	.985	San Diego	162	4366	1529	109	6004	136	0	12	.982
Arizona	162	4369	1794	94	6257	159	0	11	.985	Pittsburgh	162	4308	1803	117	6228	193	0	16	.981
Washington	162	4374	1548	92	6014	156	0	7	.985	Colorado	162	4256	1706	118	6080	158	0	14	.981
St. Louis	162	4337	1951	100	6388	196	1	12	.984	Milwaukee	162	4314	1482	119	5915	139	0	8	.980
Chicago	162	4320	1658	101	6079	136	0	6	.983	Totals	1297	69157	26841	1624	97622	2464	1	149	.983
Florida	162	4327	1659	103	6089	177	0	9	.983										

INDIVIDUAL

FIRST BASEMEN

NOTE: All caps denotes fielding-percentage leader based on 81 games for catchers, 108 for all other non-pitchers and 162 innings for pitchers. *Throws Lefthanded.

Player, Team	G	GS	PO	A	E	TC	DP	Pct.
Alexander, Manny, S.D.	1	0	0	0	0	0	0	.000
Anderson, Marlon, N.Y.	23	16	173	16	2	191	18	.990
Baerga, Carlos, Was.	11	9	65	2	1	68	2	.985
Bagwell, Jeff, Hou.	24	24	211	14	0	225	13	1.000
Berkman, Lance, Hou.*	96	84	772	49	5	826	77	.994
Blanco, Tony, Was.	3	1	11	1	2	14	2	.857
Blum, Geoff, S.D.	2	0	1	0	0	1	0	1.000
Branyan, Russell, Mil.	5	2	28	2	0	30	0	1.000
Bruntlett, Eric, Hou.	1	0	1	0	0	1	0	1.000
Cairo, Miguel, N.Y.	8	6	48	2	1	51	6	.980
CASEY, Sean, Cin.	134	132	1153	55	2	1210	91	.998
Choi, Hee-Seop, L.A.*	83	78	698	62	2	762	59	.997
Cirillo, Jeff, Mil.	1	0	0	0	0	0	0	.000
Clark, Tony, Ari.	83	70	663	44	2	709	59	.997
Conine, Jeff, Fla.	45	22	247	17	4	268	27	.985
Cordero, Wil, Was.	12	7	66	2	0	68	5	1.000
Cruz, Jacob, Cin.*	5	2	15	1	0	16	2	1.000
Daubach, Brian, N.Y.	6	4	39	3	1	43	3	.977
Delgado, Carlos, Fla.	141	140	1147	83	14	1244	133	.989
Diaz, Einar, St.L.	3	0	9	0	0	9	2	1.000
Dillon, Joe, Fla.	1	0	2	0	0	2	0	1.000
Duncan, Chris, St.L.	2	0	1	0	0	1	0	1.000
Dunn, Adam, Cin.	33	27	244	11	4	259	31	.985
Eldred, Brad, Pit.	50	46	435	15	7	457	46	.985
Feliz, Pedro, S.F.	15	9	76	7	1	84	7	.988
Fick, Robert, S.D.	29	22	224	12	2	238	23	.992
Fielder, Prince, Mil.	7	3	26	4	0	30	2	1.000
Franco, Julio, Atl.	62	45	450	37	5	492	47	.990
Gonzalez, Luis A., Col.	10	3	37	3	0	40	4	1.000
Grabowski, Jason, L.A.	3	1	11	0	0	11	1	1.000
Harris, Lenny, Fla.	1	0	3	0	0	3	2	1.000
Helms, Wes, Mil.	16	14	103	9	1	113	9	.991
Helton, Todd, Col.*	144	142	1237	120	5	1362	136	.996
Holbert, Aaron, Cin.	2	0	4	0	0	4	0	1.000
Hollandsworth, Todd, Chi.-Atl.*	2	0	3	0	0	3	0	1.000
Howard, Ryan, Phi.*	84	79	707	40	5	752	53	.993
Jackson, Conor, Ari.	20	20	171	12	5	188	19	.973
Jacobs, Mike, N.Y.	28	28	237	10	4	251	24	.984
Johnson, Nick, Was.*	129	126	1018	96	5	1119	109	.996
Kent, Jeff, L.A.	14	10	92	6	2	100	9	.980
Klesko, Ryan, S.D.*	1	0	2	0	0	2	0	1.000
Lamb, Mike, Hou.	68	47	428	28	5	461	39	.989
LaRoche, Adam, Atl.*	125	117	1070	77	7	1154	105	.994
Lee, Derrek, Chi.	158	158	1322	122	6	1450	118	.996
Mabry, John, St.L.	14	5	55	8	0	63	8	1.000
Mackowiak, Rob, Pit.	3	1	18	1	0	19	4	1.000
Martinez, Ramon, Phi.	10	9	75	6	0	81	8	1.000
McAnulty, Paul, S.D.	1	0	4	0	0	4	1	1.000
McClain, Scott, Chi.	4	1	16	0	0	16	1	1.000
Mientkiewicz, Doug, N.Y.	83	79	691	42	4	737	59	.995
Molina, Yadier, St.L.	1	0	0	0	0	0	0	.000
Myrow, Brian, L.A.	5	2	20	0	0	20	2	1.000
Nady, Xavier, S.D.	44	34	261	27	4	292	26	.986
Nakamura, Norihiro, L.A.	4	1	18	0	1	19	2	.947
Nevin, Phil, S.D.	71	70	590	38	4	621	51	.994
Niekro, Lance, S.F.	74	57	544	38	5	587	56	.991
Offerman, Jose, Phi.-N.Y.	15	9	96	4	2	102	10	.980
Overbay, Lyle, Mil.*	154	143	1134	96	10	1240	104	.992

Player, Team	G	GS	PO	A	E	TC	DP	Pct.
Perez, Tomas, Phi.	24	15	148	10	0	158	17	1.000
Phillips, Jason, L.A.	21	18	143	12	0	155	16	1.000
Pujols, Albert, St.L.	157	154	1597	97	14	1708	175	.992
Quintero, Humberto, Hou.	1	0	0	1	0	1	0	1.000
Saenz, Olmedo, L.A.	66	52	460	19	1	480	36	.998
Seabol, Scott, St.L.	5	2	33	3	0	36	4	1.000
Shealy, Ryan, Col.	19	17	155	8	0	163	8	1.000
Short, Rick, Was.	1	0	4	1	0	5	0	1.000
Snow, J.T., S.F.*	108	96	814	57	3	874	62	.997
Sweeney, Mark, S.D.*	53	36	314	21	4	339	26	.988
Thome, Jim, Phi.	52	52	405	30	0	435	36	1.000
Tracy, Chad, Ari.	80	72	705	47	3	755	75	.996
Utley, Chase, Phi.	8	6	45	9	1	55	7	.982
Valentin, Javier, Cin.	2	2	21	0	0	21	2	1.000
Vizcaino, Jose, Hou.	13	8	63	4	2	69	7	.971
Walker, Todd, Chi.	4	3	26	4	0	30	4	1.000
Ward, Daryle, Pit.*	109	101	863	77	6	946	114	.994
Wigginton, Ty, Pit.	3	3	22	2	0	24	1	1.000
Wilkerson, Brad, Was.*	25	19	172	14	1	187	20	.995
Wilson, Craig, Pit.	15	11	86	7	1	94	10	.989
Wilson, Enrique, Chi.	3	0	7	0	0	7	1	1.000
Woodward, Chris, N.Y.	34	21	206	10	2	218	16	.991

FIRST BASEMEN WITH TWO OR MORE TEAMS

Player, Team	G	GS	PO	A	E	TC	DP	Pct.
Hollandsworth, Todd, Chi.*	1	0	3	0	0	3	0	1.000
Hollandsworth, Todd, Atl.*	1	0	0	0	0	0	0	.000
Offerman, Jose, Phi.	4	1	15	0	1	16	1	.938
Offerman, Jose, N.Y.	11	8	81	4	1	86	9	.988

SECOND BASEMEN

Player, Team	G	GS	PO	A	E	TC	DP	Pct.
Alexander, Manny, S.D.	5	1	1	4	0	5	0	1.000
Alfonzo, Edgardo, S.F.	2	2	4	4	0	8	2	1.000
Anderson, Marlon, N.Y.	20	16	35	47	1	83	9	.988
Aurilia, Rich, Cin.	68	64	128	175	6	309	38	.981
Ausmus, Brad, Hou.	1	0	0	0	0	0	0	.000
Aybar, Willy, L.A.	6	2	2	6	0	8	1	1.000
Baerga, Carlos, Was.	7	5	15	19	3	37	3	.919
Bergolla, William, Cin.	9	6	11	29	0	40	6	1.000
Betemit, Wilson, Atl.	1	1	1	3	0	4	0	1.000
Biggio, Craig, Hou.	141	141	250	396	16	662	81	.976
Blum, Geoff, S.D.	19	18	28	48	0	76	9	1.000
Bruntlett, Eric, Hou.	28	5	10	16	2	28	3	.929
Burke, Chris, Hou.	18	7	15	24	0	39	5	1.000
Cairo, Miguel, N.Y.	82	74	150	212	6	368	58	.984
Carroll, Jamey, Was.	63	44	96	145	5	246	33	.980
Castillo, Jose, Pit.	100	99	237	279	12	528	93	.977
Castillo, Luis, Fla.	120	116	245	352	7	604	87	.988
Cedeno, Ronny, Chi.	1	0	0	1	0	1	0	1.000
Chavez, Angel, S.F.	5	1	3	4	0	7	0	1.000
Cintron, Alex, Ari.	23	15	31	39	1	71	12	.986
Cirillo, Jeff, Mil.	3	1	4	2	0	6	1	1.000
Counsell, Craig, Ari.	143	140	305	459	8	772	97	.990
Cruz, Deivi, S.F.-Was.	49	35	81	101	2	184	32	.989
Dallimore, Brian, S.F.	2	1	0	6	0	6	3	1.000
Dillon, Joe, Fla.	4	2	5	7	1	13	2	.923
Durham, Ray, S.F.	133	131	249	341	11	601	82	.982
Easley, Damion, Fla.	46	34	80	98	4	182	26	.978
Freel, Ryan, Cin.	48	48	91	127	6	224	24	.973
Furmaniak, J.J., Pit.	9	6	14	10	1	25	1	.960

Player, Team	G	GS	PO	A	E	TC	DP	Pct.
Garabito, Eddy, Col.	18	16	33	37	1	71	12	.986
Garcia, Jesse, S.D.	2	0	2	3	0	5	1	1.000
Giles, Marcus, Atl.	149	147	266	469	12	747	97	.984
Gonzalez, Luis A., Col.	83	66	121	196	0	317	40	1.000
Green, Andy, Ari.	5	4	10	12	0	22	4	1.000
GRUDZIELANEK, Mark, St.L.	137	132	245	442	7	694	108	.990
Hairston Jr., Jerry, Chi.	44	36	69	111	5	185	23	.973
Hall, Bill, Mil.	23	21	44	53	4	101	5	.960
Harris, Brendan, Was.	2	1	2	5	0	7	1	1.000
Hernandez, Anderson, N.Y.	5	5	9	18	0	27	1	1.000
Hill, Bobby, Pit.	1	0	0	0	1	1	0	.000
Holbert, Aaron, Cin.	4	3	11	8	1	20	3	.950
Jackson, Damian, S.D.	35	28	53	93	1	147	21	.993
Jimenez, D'Angelo, Cin.	27	23	56	63	2	121	17	.983
Kata, Matt, Ari.-Phi.	10	3	8	12	0	20	6	1.000
Kent, Jeff, L.A.	140	138	284	424	16	724	87	.978
Lopez, Felipe, Cin.	7	5	15	11	0	26	4	1.000
Lopez, Luis, Cin.	4	2	3	5	0	8	0	1.000
Loretta, Mark, S.D.	105	105	201	262	6	469	61	.987
Lowell, Mike, Fla.	9	9	18	13	1	32	3	.969
Luna, Hector, St.L.	22	15	41	52	2	95	15	.979
Macias, Jose, Chi.	20	11	27	34	0	61	8	1.000
Mackowiak, Rob, Pit.	20	17	37	43	2	82	10	.976
Martinez, Ramon, Phi.	1	1	1	2	1	4	0	.750
Mateo, Henry, Was.	1	1	1	2	0	3	0	1.000
Matsui, Kazuo, N.Y.	71	64	107	187	9	303	32	.970
Miles, Aaron, Col.	79	69	154	208	6	368	48	.984
Mordecai, Mike, Fla.	1	1	2	2	0	4	0	1.000
Nakamura, Norihiro, L.A.	1	0	1	0	0	1	0	1.000
Nunez, Abraham O., St.L.	22	15	26	38	2	66	15	.970
Offerman, Jose, N.Y.	1	0	0	0	0	0	0	.000
Olmedo, Ray, Cin.	31	12	38	40	2	80	9	.975
Orr, Pete, Atl.	25	14	35	57	5	97	11	.948
Perez, Antonio, L.A.	29	21	40	58	3	101	10	.970
Perez, Neifi, Chi.	26	18	32	47	2	81	10	.975
Polanco, Placido, Phi.	29	26	57	74	0	131	26	1.000
Quintanilla, Omar, Col.	6	3	10	10	0	20	5	1.000
Relaford, Desi, Col.	11	8	10	31	2	43	4	.953
Robles, Oscar, L.A.	1	1	0	1	1	2	1	.500
Sanchez, Freddy, Pit.	58	39	108	115	2	225	40	.991
Seabol, Scott, St.L.	8	0	1	5	0	6	0	1.000
Short, Rick, Was.	6	3	7	8	1	16	2	.938
Spivey, Junior, Mil.-Was.	70	67	127	179	7	313	41	.978
Theriot, Ryan, Chi.	3	2	3	9	0	12	0	1.000
Utley, Chase, Phi.	135	135	296	376	15	687	72	.978
Vidro, Jose, Was.	79	79	134	192	5	331	39	.985
Vizcaino, Jose, Hou.	23	10	30	39	0	69	14	1.000
Walker, Todd, Chi.	97	93	164	243	6	413	44	.985
Weeks, Rickie, Mil.	95	94	178	233	21	432	60	.951
Wigginton, Ty, Pit.	1	1	3	2	0	5	0	1.000
Wilson, Enrique, Chi.	5	2	4	9	1	14	5	.929
Wilson, Josh, Fla.	4	0	1	1	0	2	0	1.000
Woodward, Chris, N.Y.	5	3	4	7	2	13	1	.846
Young, Eric, S.D.	14	10	25	26	3	54	8	.944

SECOND BASEMEN WITH TWO OR MORE TEAMS

Player, Team	G	GS	PO	A	E	TC	DP	Pct.
Cruz, Deivi, S.F.	33	27	54	76	2	132	22	.985
Cruz, Deivi, Was.	16	8	27	25	0	52	10	1.000
Kata, Matt, Ari.	7	3	8	12	0	20	6	1.000
Kata, Matt, Phi.	3	0	0	0	0	0	0	.000
Spivey, Junior, Mil.	48	46	93	117	7	217	27	.968
Spivey, Junior, Was.	22	21	34	62	0	96	14	1.000

THIRD BASEMEN

Player, Team	G	GS	PO	A	E	TC	DP	Pct.
Alexander, Manny, S.D.	1	0	0	0	0	0	0	.000
Alfonzo, Edgardo, S.F.	97	92	76	158	8	242	10	.967
Amezaga, Alfredo, Col.	1	0	0	0	0	0	0	.000
Atkins, Garrett, Col.	136	136	78	262	18	358	23	.950
Aurilia, Rich, Cin.	18	14	12	33	1	46	4	.978
Aybar, Willy, L.A.	20	20	16	35	2	53	3	.962
Baerga, Carlos, Was.	20	10	7	16	2	25	1	.920
Baker, Jeff, Col.	10	10	3	20	1	24	1	.958
Bautista, Jose, Pit.	8	7	6	14	1	21	2	.952
Bell, David, Phi.	150	148	105	304	21	430	22	.951
Betemit, Wilson, Atl.	63	46	26	94	6	126	6	.952
Blanco, Tony, Was.	5	0	0	3	0	3	0	1.000
Blum, Geoff, S.D.	34	26	20	62	3	85	7	.965
Branyan, Russell, Mil.	59	56	40	82	7	129	10	.946

Player, Team	G	GS	PO	A	E	TC	DP	Pct.
Bruntlett, Eric, Hou.	8	0	1	1	0	2	0	1.000
Burroughs, Sean, S.D.	78	70	59	145	8	212	16	.962
Cabrera, Miguel, Fla.	29	28	22	46	2	70	5	.971
Cairo, Miguel, N.Y.	3	0	0	2	0	2	0	1.000
Carroll, Jamey, Was.	12	5	1	8	0	9	0	1.000
Castilla, Vinny, Was.	138	135	142	209	11	362	23	.970
Chavez, Angel, S.F.	1	0	0	0	0	0	0	.000
Cintron, Alex, Ari.	32	18	15	41	2	58	9	.966
Cirillo, Jeff, Mil.	53	40	28	70	5	103	8	.951
Cruz, Deivi, S.F.	5	3	1	11	0	12	0	1.000
Dillon, Joe, Fla.	2	0	2	1	0	3	0	1.000
Durrington, Trent, Mil.	1	0	0	0	3	3	0	.000
Easley, Damion, Fla.	10	7	9	16	1	26	1	.962
Edwards, Mike, L.A.	39	33	22	56	7	85	5	.918
Encarnacion, Edwin, Cin.	56	55	54	116	10	180	10	.944
Ensberg, Morgan, Hou.	148	147	100	296	15	411	31	.964
Feliz, Pedro, S.F.	79	67	47	143	6	196	17	.969
Fick, Robert, S.D.	1	0	0	0	0	0	0	.000
Freel, Ryan, Cin.	10	8	5	25	2	32	1	.938
Garciaparra, Nomar, Chi.	34	34	20	65	6	91	1	.934
Giles, Marcus, Atl.	1	0	0	6	0	6	0	1.000
Glaus, Troy, Ari.	145	144	113	310	24	447	26	.946
Gonzalez, Luis A., Col.	12	4	6	7	0	13	1	1.000
Hall, Bill, Mil.	59	49	39	84	6	129	11	.953
Harris, Brendan, Was.	1	1	1	4	0	5	0	1.000
Harris, Lenny, Fla.	2	0	0	0	0	0	0	.000
Helms, Wes, Mil.	35	17	12	41	2	55	4	.964
Hill, Bobby, Pit.	24	14	10	32	1	43	4	.977
Holbert, Aaron, Cin.	2	1	0	5	0	5	0	1.000
Jackson, Damian, S.D.	8	7	2	6	1	9	1	.889
Jones, Chipper, Atl.	101	100	80	169	5	254	18	.980
Lamb, Mike, Hou.	15	12	16	34	1	51	0	.980
Lopez, Felipe, Cin.	1	0	0	1	0	1	0	1.000
Lopez, Luis, Cin.	6	2	5	4	1	10	0	.900
Loretta, Mark, S.D.	1	0	0	0	0	0	0	.000
LOWELL, Mike, Fla.	135	126	107	243	6	356	34	.983
Luna, Hector, St.L.	7	4	4	7	0	11	2	1.000
Mabry, John, St.L.	18	12	12	19	1	32	2	.969
Macias, Jose, Chi.	23	7	6	15	2	23	1	.913
Mackowiak, Rob, Pit.	65	50	38	122	8	168	15	.952
Marte, Andy, Atl.	17	13	4	14	3	21	1	.857
Martinez, Ramon, Phi.	3	2	1	3	0	4	0	1.000
McClain, Scott, Chi.	3	1	1	1	0	2	0	1.000
Nady, Xavier, S.D.	3	2	0	6	0	6	0	1.000
Nakamura, Norihiro, L.A.	10	6	3	16	0	19	2	1.000
Nunez, Abraham O., St.L.	98	77	54	203	10	267	19	.963
Orr, Pete, Atl.	12	3	2	14	1	17	3	.941
Perez, Antonio, L.A.	35	33	18	70	5	93	5	.946
Perez, Neifi, Chi.	4	0	0	1	0	1	0	1.000
Perez, Tomas, Phi.	15	7	11	17	0	28	2	1.000
Polanco, Placido, Phi.	8	5	6	17	0	23	2	1.000
Ramirez, Aramis, Chi.	119	119	70	218	16	304	14	.947
Randa, Joe, Cin.-S.D.	142	140	126	225	12	363	21	.967
Relaford, Desi, Col.	21	12	9	22	2	33	2	.939
Robles, Oscar, L.A.	40	31	24	70	2	96	5	.979
Rolen, Scott, St.L.	56	55	22	150	6	178	17	.966
Saenz, Olmedo, L.A.	17	15	17	22	2	41	3	.951
Sanchez, Freddy, Pit.	65	55	39	130	4	173	19	.977
Seabol, Scott, St.L.	20	14	9	30	3	42	5	.929
Valentin, Jose, L.A.	29	24	19	54	7	80	4	.913
Vizcaino, Jose, Hou.	8	4	2	9	3	14	2	.786
Wigginton, Ty, Pit.	40	36	19	57	9	85	5	.894
Wilson, Enrique, Chi.	1	1	0	0	0	0	0	.000
Woodward, Chris, N.Y.	6	2	1	11	0	12	0	1.000
Wright, David, N.Y.	160	160	101	336	24	461	23	.948
Zimmerman, Ryan, Was.	14	11	6	26	0	32	5	1.000

THIRD BASEMEN WITH TWO OR MORE TEAMS

Player, Team	G	GS	PO	A	E	TC	DP	Pct.
Randa, Joe, Cin.	84	83	76	148	6	230	13	.974
Randa, Joe, S.D.	58	57	50	77	6	133	8	.955

SHORTSTOPS

Player, Team	G	GS	PO	A	E	TC	DP	Pct.
AAlexander, Manny, S.D.	4	3	4	10	1	15	1	.933
Amezaga, Alfredo, Pit.	1	0	1	2	0	3	1	1.000
Andino, Robert, Fla.	17	13	18	25	2	45	7	.956
Aurilia, Rich, Cin.	30	29	29	86	3	118	14	.975
Ausmus, Brad, Hou.	1	0	1	1	0	2	1	1.000

Player, Team	G	GS	PO	A	E	TC	DP	Pct.
Barmes, Clint, Col.	80	78	138	247	17	402	62	.958
Bergolla, William, Cin.	1	0	0	1	0	1	0	1.000
Betemit, Wilson, Atl.	25	10	24	40	1	65	10	.985
Blum, Geoff, S.D.	14	9	12	25	0	37	6	1.000
Bruntlett, Eric, Hou.	10	4	9	21	0	30	4	1.000
Burroughs, Sean, S.D.	1	0	0	0	0	0	0	.000
Carroll, Jamey, Was.	41	23	53	65	0	118	19	1.000
Cedeno, Ronny, Chi.	29	18	30	39	1	70	8	.986
Chavez, Angel, S.F.	4	3	6	5	1	12	2	.917
Cintron, Alex, Ari.	39	31	43	99	5	147	19	.966
Clayton, Royce, Ari.	141	131	180	404	11	595	91	.982
Counsell, Craig, Ari.	1	0	0	0	0	0	0	.000
Cruz, Deivi, S.F.-Was.	24	20	26	61	2	89	15	.978
Dallimore, Brian, S.F.	1	0	0	0	0	0	0	.000
Easley, Damion, Fla.	30	24	43	77	4	124	14	.968
Eckstein, David, St.L.	156	154	243	517	15	775	123	.981
Edwards, Mike, L.A.	1	0	0	2	0	2	0	1.000
Everett, Adam, Hou.	150	147	209	421	14	644	96	.978
Furcal, Rafael, Atl.	152	152	255	504	15	774	119	.981
Furmaniak, J.J., Pit.	2	1	1	4	0	5	0	1.000
Garabito, Eddy, Col.	2	2	3	5	0	8	0	1.000
Garcia, Jesse, S.D.	13	8	15	19	0	34	4	1.000
Garciaparra, Nomar, Chi.	26	25	41	51	6	98	16	.939
Gonzalez, Alex, Fla.	124	124	221	367	16	604	102	.974
Gonzalez, Luis A., Col.	17	16	28	34	4	66	13	.939
Green, Andy, Ari.	2	0	1	4	0	5	0	1.000
Greene, Khalil, S.D.	121	120	161	312	14	487	64	.971
Guzman, Cristian, Was.	142	133	216	327	15	558	85	.973
Hairston Jr., Jerry, Chi.	1	0	1	1	0	2	1	1.000
Hall, Bill, Mil.	66	58	87	158	6	251	31	.976
Hardy, J.J., Mil.	119	104	133	259	10	402	52	.975
Hernandez, Anderson, N.Y.	2	0	0	1	1	1	0	.000
Izturis, Cesar, L.A.	106	105	145	327	11	483	61	.977
Jackson, Damian, S.D.	26	18	34	54	7	95	14	.926
Kata, Matt, Phi.	1	0	0	0	0	0	0	.000
Lopez, Felipe, Cin.	140	133	186	358	17	561	71	.970
Luna, Hector, St.L.	6	0	3	3	1	7	0	.857
Machado, Anderson, Col.	4	4	7	6	1	14	1	.929
Martinez, Ramon, Phi.	3	0	2	0	0	2	0	1.000
Miles, Aaron, Col.	1	0	0	1	0	1	0	.000
Mordecai, Mike, Fla.	1	0	0	0	0	0	0	.000
Nakamura, Norihiro, L.A.	2	0	0	1	0	1	1	1.000
Nunez, Abraham O., St.L.	21	8	14	30	2	46	9	.957
Olmedo, Ray, Cin.	5	1	4	6	0	10	2	1.000
Orr, Pete, Atl.	1	0	0	0	0	0	0	.000
Perez, Antonio, L.A.	9	8	10	25	1	36	6	.972
Perez, Neifi, Chi.	130	118	175	385	10	570	81	.982
Perez, Tomas, Phi.	14	5	8	12	0	20	2	1.000
Polanco, Placido, Phi.	1	1	3	2	0	5	1	1.000
Quintanilla, Omar, Col.	31	30	41	89	1	131	16	.992
Relaford, Desi, Col.	37	32	45	100	6	151	16	.960
Reyes, Jose, N.Y.	161	159	236	428	18	682	105	.974
Robles, Oscar, L.A.	54	49	75	132	4	211	28	.981
Rollins, Jimmy, Phi.	157	156	207	411	12	630	80	.981
Sanchez, Freddy, Pit.	11	6	11	25	0	36	3	1.000
Sandoval, Danny, Phi.	1	0	0	1	0	1	0	1.000
Valdez, Wilson, S.D.	8	5	9	8	1	18	2	.944
Valentin, Jose, L.A.	1	0	0	2	0	2	1	1.000
Vizcaino, Jose, Hou.	17	12	9	34	0	43	1	1.000
VIZQUEL, Omar, S.F.	150	144	234	426	8	668	81	.988
Wilson, Enrique, Chi.	3	1	2	6	0	8	1	1.000
Wilson, Jack, Pit.	157	155	246	523	14	783	126	.982
Wilson, Josh, Fla.	6	1	3	6	0	9	2	1.000
Woodward, Chris, N.Y.	7	3	5	7	1	13	1	.923
Zimmerman, Ryan, Was.	1	1	3	4	2	9	0	.778

SHORTSTOPS WITH TWO OR MORE TEAMS

Player, Team	G	GS	PO	A	E	TC	DP	Pct.
Cruz, Deivi, S.F.	16	15	22	48	1	71	13	.986
Cruz, Deivi, Was.	8	5	4	13	1	18	2	.944

OUTFIELDERS

Player, Team	G	GS	PO	A	E	TC	DP	Pct.
Abreu, Bobby, Phi.	158	158	266	7	4	277	0	.986
Aguila, Chris, Fla.	42	12	40	1	0	41	0	1.000
Alou, Moises, S.F.	117	117	222	5	8	235	3	.966
Anderson, Marlon, N.Y.	23	13	22	2	0	24	1	1.000
Bay, Jason, Pit.	162	162	322	4	4	330	1	.988
Beltran, Carlos, N.Y.	150	149	378	6	3	387	1	.990

Player, Team	G	GS	PO	A	E	TC	DP	Pct.
Berkman, Lance, Hou.*	49	45	66	2	3	71	1	.958
Bigbie, Larry, Col.	15	15	36	1	0	37	1	1.000
Blanco, Tony, Was.	11	5	10	1	0	11	1	1.000
Bonds, Barry, S.F.*	13	13	18	0	0	18	0	1.000
Bradley, Milton, L.A.	72	72	181	6	2	189	0	.989
Branyan, Russell, Mil.	3	0	1	0	0	1	0	1.000
Bruntlett, Eric, Hou.	26	12	46	3	0	49	2	1.000
Burke, Chris, Hou.	84	75	121	3	1	125	1	.992
Burnitz, Jeromy, Chi.	160	155	311	6	5	322	1	.984
Burrell, Pat, Phi.	153	153	236	10	7	253	2	.972
Byrd, Marlon, Phi.-Was.	70	54	130	5	2	137	2	.985
Byrnes, Eric, Col.	14	14	39	1	1	41	1	.976
Cabrera, Miguel, Fla.	134	128	188	12	5	205	3	.976
Cairo, Miguel, N.Y.	3	1	1	0	0	1	0	1.000
Cameron, Mike, N.Y.	76	76	151	3	6	160	1	.963
Cedeno, Roger, St.L.	16	9	9	0	2	11	0	.818
Cepicky, Matt, Was.	6	6	18	0	0	18	0	1.000
Chavez, Endy, Was.-Phi.*	57	13	49	4	1	54	1	.981
Chen, Chin-Feng, L.A.	3	1	2	0	0	2	0	1.000
Church, Ryan, Was.*	85	63	169	2	0	171	0	1.000
Clark, Brady, Mil.	145	145	399	5	2	406	4	.995
Conine, Jeff, Fla.	61	51	105	2	3	110	0	.973
Cruz, Jacob, Cin.*	20	10	12	1	0	13	1	1.000
Cruz, Nelson, Mil.	8	1	4	0	0	4	0	1.000
Cruz Jr., Jose, Ari.-L.A.	103	99	198	5	7	210	0	.967
Davis, J.J., Was.	10	7	16	1	0	17	0	1.000
Denorfia, Chris, Cin.	12	7	25	0	1	26	0	.962
Diaz, Victor, N.Y.	81	77	156	3	3	162	1	.981
Dillon, Joe, Fla.	3	0	2	0	0	2	0	1.000
Doumit, Ryan, Pit.	3	3	0	0	0	0	0	.000
Drew, J.D., L.A.	72	72	147	3	2	152	0	.987
Dubois, Jason, Chi.	38	35	47	2	1	50	0	.980
Duffy, Chris, Pit.*	34	27	80	1	1	82	0	.988
Duncan, Chris, St.L.	1	0	0	0	0	0	0	.000
Dunn, Adam, Cin.	133	126	246	6	5	257	0	.981
Durham, Ray, S.F.	1	0	0	0	0	0	0	.000
Edmonds, Jim, St.L.*	139	132	318	6	2	326	1	.994
Edwards, Mike, L.A.	34	28	53	0	0	53	0	1.000
Ellison, Jason, S.F.	122	82	235	5	8	248	1	.968
Encarnacion, Juan, Fla.	139	132	226	4	4	234	0	.983
Feliz, Pedro, S.F.	75	70	138	0	3	141	0	.979
Fick, Robert, S.D.	13	8	17	1	0	18	0	1.000
Floyd, Cliff, N.Y.	150	147	283	15	2	300	0	.993
Francoeur, Jeff, Atl.	67	65	131	13	5	149	3	.966
Freel, Ryan, Cin.	51	33	109	7	0	116	0	1.000
Freeman, Choo, Col.	6	5	12	2	0	14	1	1.000
Gall, John, St.L.	10	6	7	1	0	8	0	1.000
Gerut, Jody, Chi.-Pit.*	9	6	12	0	0	12	0	1.000
Giles, Brian, S.D.*	155	155	329	6	4	339	1	.988
Gipson, Charles, Hou.	13	2	6	0	0	6	0	1.000
Gonzalez, Luis, Ari.	152	149	270	7	3	280	1	.989
Gonzalez, Luis A., Col.	8	6	16	0	0	16	0	1.000
Grabowski, Jason, L.A.	32	22	36	1	1	38	0	.974
Green, Andy, Ari.	2	2	3	0	0	3	0	1.000
GREEN, Shawn, Ari.*	155	149	313	4	0	317	1	1.000
Grieve, Ben, Chi.	1	1	0	0	0	0	0	.000
Griffey Jr., Ken, Cin.*	124	124	285	6	3	294	1	.990
Grissom, Marquis, S.F.	36	36	69	0	1	70	0	.986
Guillen, Jose, Was.	142	137	301	10	7	318	5	.978
Hairston, Scott, Ari.	4	1	3	0	0	3	1	1.000
Hairston Jr., Jerry, Chi.	62	55	114	3	2	119	0	.983
Hammonds, Jeffrey, Was.	11	9	18	0	0	18	0	1.000
Harris, Lenny, Fla.	2	0	0	0	0	0	0	.000
Hart, Corey, Mil.	16	14	27	1	1	29	0	.966
Hawpe, Brad, Col.*	89	79	148	10	3	161	2	.981
Hermida, Jeremy, Fla.	14	8	20	0	0	20	0	1.000
Hollandsworth, Todd, Chi.-Atl.*	104	67	106	2	2	110	0	.982
Holliday, Matt, Col.	123	121	236	5	7	248	2	.972
Hyzdu, Adam, S.D.	12	2	14	1	0	15	1	1.000
Jackson, Conor, Ari.	1	1	0	0	0	0	0	.000
Jackson, Damian, S.D.	52	10	48	2	0	50	0	1.000
Jenkins, Geoff, Mil.	144	144	307	10	5	322	7	.984
Jimerson, Charlton, Hou.	1	0	0	0	0	0	0	.000
Johnson, Ben, S.D.	29	20	51	0	2	53	0	.962
Johnson, Kelly, Atl.	79	73	166	6	0	172	1	1.000
Jones, Andruw, Atl.	159	158	365	11	2	378	1	.995
Jordan, Brian, Atl.	62	59	112	6	0	118	1	1.000
Kata, Matt, Phi.	1	0	0	0	0	0	0	.000
Kearns, Austin, Cin.	107	103	238	8	3	249	3	.988
Kelly, Kenny, Cin.-Was.	6	1	4	0	0	4	1	1.000
Klesko, Ryan, S.D.*	121	120	204	7	4	215	1	.981
Krynzel, Dave, Mil.*	1	1	2	0	0	2	0	1.000

Player, Team	G	GS	PO	A	E	TC	DP	Pct.
Lamb, Mike, Hou.	13	12	12	0	0	12	0	1.000
Lane, Jason, Hou.*	141	133	239	4	6	249	0	.976
Langerhans, Ryan, Atl.*	114	84	194	3	1	198	1	.995
LaRue, Jason, Cin.	1	0	1	0	0	1	0	1.000
Lawton, Matt, Pit.-Chi.	117	117	239	4	2	245	2	.992
Ledee, Ricky, L.A.*	69	55	76	2	2	80	1	.975
Lee, Carlos, Mil.	162	161	308	8	6	322	3	.981
Linden, Todd, S.F.	52	43	114	0	2	116	0	.983
Lofton, Kenny, Phi.*	97	88	201	7	4	212	1	.981
Luna, Hector, St.L.	25	13	33	3	2	38	0	.947
Mabry, John, St.L.	70	37	54	1	2	57	0	.965
Macias, Jose, Chi.	20	8	26	2	2	30	0	.933
Mackowiak, Rob, Pit.	63	44	102	4	2	108	2	.981
Magruder, Chris, Mil.	45	20	54	0	2	56	0	.964
McAnulty, Paul, S.D.	6	2	5	0	0	5	0	1.000
McCracken, Quinton, Ari.	59	33	75	2	2	79	0	.975
McLouth, Nate, Pit.	29	24	46	0	2	48	0	.958
Michaels, Jason, Phi.	91	68	185	8	2	195	2	.990
Mohr, Dustan, Col.	76	64	147	4	2	153	1	.987
Mondesi, Raul, Atl.	40	39	67	2	1	70	0	.986
Murton, Matt, Chi.	43	38	62	1	2	65	1	.969
Nady, Xavier, S.D.	68	41	83	0	2	85	0	.976
Ojeda, Miguel, S.D.	5	4	10	0	0	10	0	1.000
Orr, Pete, Atl.	3	3	5	0	0	5	0	1.000
Ortmeier, Dan, S.F.*	7	5	13	0	0	13	0	1.000
Palmeiro, Orlando, Hou.*	71	35	68	2	1	71	2	.986
Patterson, Corey, Chi.	122	111	239	6	5	250	2	.980
Pena, Wily Mo, Cin.	83	78	161	2	4	167	0	.976
Perez, Antonio, L.A.	1	0	0	0	0	0	0	.000
Piedra, Jorge, Col.*	26	22	27	1	0	28	0	1.000
Pierre, Juan, Fla.*	160	155	332	7	4	343	3	.988
Polanco, Placido, Phi.	5	4	10	0	0	10	0	1.000
Ramirez, Julio, S.F.	6	0	3	0	0	3	0	1.000
Redman, Tike, Pit.*	85	59	170	5	7	182	0	.962
Relaford, Desi, Col.	4	0	0	1	0	1	0	1.000
Repko, Jason, L.A.	118	73	173	7	6	186	3	.968
Restovich, Michael, Col.-Pit.	39	25	57	1	1	59	0	.983
Roberts, Dave, S.D.*	109	101	235	4	2	241	0	.992
Rodriguez, John, St.L.*	45	36	69	3	2	74	0	.973
Romano, Jason, Cin.	14	7	15	1	1	17	0	.941
Ross, Cody, L.A.*	9	5	12	2	1	15	1	.933
Sadler, Ray, Pit.	3	3	4	0	0	4	0	1.000
Sanchez, Alex, S.F.*	10	9	19	1	3	23	0	.870
Sanders, Reggie, St.L.	81	79	108	6	2	116	0	.983
Schumaker, Skip, St.L.	21	1	13	0	0	13	0	1.000
Scott, Luke, Hou.	24	20	24	2	1	27	0	.963
Seabol, Scott, St.L.	4	4	6	0	0	6	0	1.000
Self, Todd, Hou.	15	11	23	0	0	23	0	1.000
Shabala, Adam, S.F.	5	3	7	0	1	8	0	.875
Sledge, Terrmel, Was.*	13	9	21	1	0	22	0	1.000
Spilborghs, Ryan, Col.	1	1	6	1	0	7	1	1.000
Sullivan, Cory, Col.*	114	83	211	7	3	221	2	.986
Sweeney, Mark, S.D.*	6	1	5	0	1	6	0	.833
Taguchi, So, St.L.	131	91	183	5	2	190	1	.989
Taveras, Willy, Hou.	148	144	332	10	3	345	2	.991
Terrero, Luis, Ari.	77	43	124	1	2	127	0	.984
Torcato, Tony, S.F.	1	0	1	0	0	1	0	1.000
Tracy, Chad, Ari.	51	51	93	2	2	97	0	.979
Tucker, Michael, S.F.-Phi.	73	53	109	6	2	117	1	.983
Valent, Eric, N.Y.*	12	8	21	0	1	22	0	.955
Valentin, Jose, L.A.	22	19	35	0	1	36	0	.972
Victorino, Shane, Phi.	12	0	0	0	0	0	0	.000
Walker, Larry, St.L.	83	80	108	5	2	115	0	.983
Watson, Brandon, Was.	13	7	13	1	1	15	0	.933
Werth, Jayson, L.A.	101	96	218	6	3	227	2	.987
Wilkerson, Brad, Was.*	129	124	312	6	5	323	1	.985
Williams, Gerald, N.Y.	27	4	16	1	0	17	0	1.000
Willingham, Josh, Fla.	1	0	0	0	0	0	0	.000
Wilson, Craig, Pit.	47	45	77	4	1	82	1	.988
Wilson, Preston, Col.-Was.	137	135	289	5	3	297	0	.990
Winn, Randy, S.F.	55	55	165	1	1	167	1	.994
Woodward, Chris, N.Y.	23	11	28	3	1	32	1	.969
Young, Eric, S.D.	25	22	53	0	0	53	0	1.000

Player, Team	G	GS	PO	A	E	TC	DP	Pct.
Gerut, Jody, Chi.*	5	2	9	0	0	9	0	1.000
Gerut, Jody, Pit.*	4	4	3	0	0	3	0	1.000
Hollandsworth, Todd, Chi.*	95	62	96	2	2	100	0	.980
Hollandsworth, Todd, Atl.*	9	5	10	0	0	10	0	1.000
Kelly, Kenny, Cin.	4	1	4	0	0	4	0	1.000
Kelly, Kenny, Was.	2	0	0	0	0	0	0	.000
Lawton, Matt, Pit.	98	98	206	4	1	211	2	.995
Lawton, Matt, Chi.	19	19	33	0	1	34	0	.971
Restovich, Michael, Col.	8	8	18	0	0	18	0	1.000
Restovich, Michael, Pit.	31	17	39	1	1	41	0	.976
Tucker, Michael, S.F.	72	53	109	6	2	117	1	.983
Tucker, Michael, Phi.	1	0	0	0	0	0	0	.000
Wilson, Preston, Col.	69	68	140	2	3	145	0	.979
Wilson, Preston, Was.	68	67	149	3	0	152	0	1.000

CATCHERS

Player, Team	G	GS	PO	A	E	TC	DP	PB	Pct.
Ardoin, Danny, Col.	80	66	452	48	6	506	5	6	.988
AUSMUS, Brad, Hou.	134	118	884	65	1	950	6	5	.999
Bako, Paul, L.A.	13	13	61	6	1	68	0	1	.985
Barrett, Michael, Chi.	122	114	870	51	6	927	8	4	.994
Bennett, Gary, Was.	64	57	384	24	6	414	1	4	.986
Blanco, Henry, Chi.	54	48	407	31	1	439	2	2	.998
Castro, Ramon, N.Y.	99	57	402	22	3	427	3	2	.993
Chavez, Raul, Hou.	36	30	213	19	2	234	2	1	.991
Closser, JD, Col.	80	64	410	25	8	443	1	5	.982
Cota, Humberto, Pit.	87	77	475	38	4	517	4	8	.992
Diaz, Einar, St.L.	50	30	189	21	1	211	1	4	.995
DiFelice, Mike, N.Y.	11	5	39	2	1	42	1	0	.976
Doumit, Ryan, Pit.	50	48	286	30	8	324	1	4	.975
Estrada, Johnny, Atl.	104	97	574	51	2	627	6	2	.997
Fick, Robert, S.D.	28	20	167	10	4	181	0	2	.978
Greene, Todd, Col.	33	32	151	7	4	162	0	3	.975
Haad, Yamid, S.F.	16	10	61	6	3	70	1	0	.957
Hernandez, Ramon, S.D.	97	94	640	36	8	684	4	6	.988
Hill, Koyie, Ari.	32	23	144	13	0	157	1	3	1.000
Jorgensen, Ryan, Fla.	3	1	7	0	0	7	0	1	1.000
Knoedler, Justin, S.F.	4	1	8	1	0	9	0	0	1.000
LaRue, Jason, Cin.	109	104	646	52	5	703	2	6	.993
Lieberthal, Mike, Phi.	117	113	808	44	6	858	5	7	.993
Lo Duca, Paul, Fla.	128	118	817	61	8	886	8	4	.991
Mahoney, Mike, St.L.	25	21	110	11	2	123	2	0	.984
Matheny, Mike, S.F.	132	127	784	77	1	862	13	4	.999
McCann, Brian, Atl.	57	49	310	21	3	334	1	5	.991
Miller, Damian, Mil.	111	104	723	50	3	776	10	4	.996
Moeller, Chad, Mil.	65	58	454	32	3	489	6	4	.994
Molina, Yadier, St.L.	114	111	684	66	7	757	4	8	.991
Navarro, Dioner, L.A.	50	49	336	29	2	367	1	3	.995
Nevin, Phil, S.D.	2	2	11	1	0	12	0	1	1.000
Ojeda, Miguel, S.D.	25	12	100	7	0	107	1	2	1.000
Olivo, Miguel, S.D.	37	32	224	14	5	243	2	2	.979
Osik, Keith, Was.	5	0	8	0	0	8	0	1	1.000
Paulino, Ronny, Pit.	2	1	10	0	0	10	0	1	1.000
Pena, Brayan, Atl.	15	7	46	5	0	51	0	1	1.000
Perez, Eddie, Atl.	13	9	38	4	0	42	1	1	1.000
Perez, Michael, Cin.	1	0	2	0	0	2	0	0	1.000
Phillips, Jason, L.A.	93	88	564	34	5	603	6	4	.992
Piazza, Mike, N.Y.	101	100	618	39	2	659	5	3	.997
Pratt, Todd, Phi.	57	49	377	18	1	396	4	5	.997
Quintero, Humberto, Hou.	16	15	86	5	1	92	0	0	.989
Rose, Mike, L.A.	13	12	83	5	2	90	2	1	.978
Ross, David, Pit.-S.D.	42	33	211	23	3	237	5	4	.987
Santiago, Benito, Pit.	6	5	43	0	0	43	0	0	1.000
Sardinha, Dane, Cin.	1	1	7	0	0	7	0	0	1.000
Schneider, Brian, Was.	113	105	654	52	5	711	11	3	.993
Snyder, Chris, Ari.	113	105	679	44	2	725	0	7	.997
Stinnett, Kelly, Ari.	56	34	237	15	6	258	2	1	.977
Torrealba, Yorvit, S.F.	27	24	147	16	0	163	1	1	1.000
Treanor, Matt, Fla.	55	41	309	14	5	328	4	4	.985
Valentin, Javier, Cin.	62	58	341	28	3	372	2	3	.992
Willingham, Josh, Fla.	8	2	22	0	0	22	0	1	1.000

OUTFIELDERS WITH TWO OR MORE TEAMS

Player, Team	G	GS	PO	A	E	TC	DP	Pct.
Byrd, Marlon, Phi.	5	4	6	0	0	6	0	1.000
Byrd, Marlon, Was.	65	50	124	5	2	131	2	.985
Chavez, Endy, Was.*	6	2	4	0	0	4	0	1.000
Chavez, Endy, Phi.*	51	11	45	4	1	50	1	.980
Cruz Jr., Jose, Ari.	58	57	98	2	2	102	0	.980
Cruz Jr., Jose, L.A.	45	42	100	3	5	108	0	.954

CATCHERS WITH TWO OR MORE TEAMS

Player, Team	G	GS	PO	A	E	TC	DP	PB	Pct.
Ross, David, Pit.	35	31	183	23	3	209	4	4	.986
Ross, David, S.D.	7	2	28	0	0	28	1	0	1.000

CATCHERS—SPECIAL STATS*

Player, Team	G	Inn.	SBA	CCS	PCS	CS%	ER	CERA
Ardoin, Danny, Col.	80	591.0	45	18	4	.44	320	4.87
Ausmus, Brad, Hou.	134	1065.2	57	13	5	.25	373	3.15

Player, Team	G	Inn.	SBA	CCS	PCS	CS%	ER	CERA
Bako,Paul LAD	13	107.0	4	2	1	.67	64	5.38
Barrett,Michael ChC	122	1017.2	91	20	1	.22	503	4.45
Bennett,Gary Was	64	523.1	34	6	3	.19	225	3.87
Blanco,Henry ChC	54	422.1	39	19	0	.49	168	3.58
Castro,Ramon NYM	99	576.1	35	9	2	.27	228	3.56
Chavez,Raul Hou	36	253.1	18	11	0	.61	136	4.83
Closser,JD Col	80	565.2	64	7	4	.12	336	5.35
Cota,Humberto Pit	87	681.2	47	11	2	.24	330	4.36
Diaz,Einar StL	50	299.0	19	6	2	.35	125	3.76
DiFelice,Mike NYM	11	50.0	2	1	0	.50	22	3.96
Doumit,Ryan Pit	50	422.0	35	10	4	.32	215	4.59
Estrada,Johnny Atl	104	826.1	84	21	5	.27	360	3.92
Fick,Robert SD	28	189.2	24	2	1	.09	97	4.60
Greene,Todd Col	33	262.0	30	1	3	.04	152	5.22
Haad,Yamid SF	16	89.2	10	5	0	.50	25	2.51
Hernandez,Ramon SD	97	806.0	70	18	0	.26	362	4.04
Hill,Koyie Ari	32	211.1	16	2	2	.14	128	5.45
Jorgensen,Ryan Fla	3	10.2	2	0	0	0	6	5.06
Knoedler,Justin SF	4	15.1	0	0	0	0	2	1.17
LaRue,Jason Cin	109	914.2	76	22	3	.30	535	5.26
Lieberthal,Mike Phi	117	998.2	80	15	2	.19	501	4.52
Lo Duca,Paul Fla	128	1033.1	118	24	5	.21	435	3.79
Mahoney,Mike StL	25	187.1	7	0	0	0	74	3.56
Matheny,Mike SF	132	1122.0	102	30	9	.32	555	4.45
McCann,Brian Atl	57	449.1	27	5	0	.19	201	4.03
Miller,Damian Mil	111	917.1	76	15	9	.22	410	4.02
Moeller,Chad Mil	65	520.2	44	6	4	.15	225	3.89
Molina,Yadier StL	114	959.1	39	17	8	.55	361	3.39
Navarro,Dioner LAD	50	435.2	42	8	1	.20	210	4.34
Nevin,Phil SD	2	17.1	0	0	0	0	15	7.79
Ojeda,Miguel SD	25	124.0	9	0	0	0	60	4.35
Olivo,Miguel SD	37	287.1	15	3	1	.21	116	3.63
Osik,Keith Was	5	8.0	3	0	0	0	2	2.25
Paulino,Ronny Pit	2	11.0	1	0	0	0	2	1.64
Pena,Brayan Atl	15	81.0	10	1	1	.11	57	6.33
Perez,Eddie Atl	13	87.0	4	3	0	.75	21	2.17
Perez,Miguel Cin	1	2.0	0	0	0	0	0	0.00
Phillips,Jason LAD	93	774.0	97	15	4	.16	373	4.34
Piazza,Mike NYM	101	809.1	95	10	3	.11	349	3.88
Pratt,Todd Phi	57	436.1	28	9	0	.32	171	3.53
Quintero,Humberto Hou	16	124.0	9	1	1	.13	54	3.92
Rose,Mike LAD	13	110.2	21	3	0	.14	48	3.90
Ross,David TOT	42	304.0	15	7	2	.54	140	4.14
Ross,David Pit	35	273.0	14	7	2	.58	122	4.02
Ross,David SD	7	31.0	1	0	0	0	18	5.23
Santiago,Benito Pit	6	48.1	3	0	0	0	37	6.89
Sardinha,Dane Cin	1	8.0	0	0	0	0	7	7.88
Schneider,Brian Was	113	926.2	80	29	3	.38	400	3.88
Snyder,Chris Ari	113	915.2	63	12	5	.21	460	4.52
Stinnett,Kelly Ari	56	329.1	27	4	3	.17	195	5.33
Torrealba,Yorvit SF	27	217.1	20	7	3	.41	113	4.68
Treanor,Matt Fla	55	366.2	33	9	0	.27	191	4.69
Valentin,Javier Cin	62	508.1	35	9	1	.26	278	4.92
Willingham,Josh Fla	8	31.2	3	0	0	0	34	9.66
Average	55	427.0	35	8	2	.29	200	4.22

Inn. denotes the number of innings the catcher was behind the plate. **SBA** denotes stolen bases attempted. **CCS** denotes number of runners caught stealing by the catcher. **PCS** denotes number of runners caught stealing by the pitcher. **CS%** denotes the catcher's caught stealing percentage, figured by subtracting PCS from SBA and dividing this number into CCS. **ER** denotes number of earned runs scored when catcher was behind the plate. **CERA** denotes catcher's ERA when he was behind the plate, figured the same way a pitcher's ERA is completed (ER*9/IP).

PITCHERS

Player, Team	G	GS	PO	A	E	TC	DP	Pct.
Accardo, Jeremy, S.F.	28	0	1	4	1	6	1	.833
Acevedo, Jose, Col.	36	5	8	7	0	15	1	1.000
Adams, Mike, Mil.	13	0	1	0	0	1	0	1.000
Adams, Terry, Phi.	16	0	0	2	0	2	0	1.000
Alfonseca, Antonio, Fla.	33	0	3	4	0	7	2	1.000
Almanza, Armando, Ari.*	6	0	1	1	0	2	1	1.000
Alvarez, Wilson, L.A.*	21	2	0	2	0	2	0	1.000
Anderson, Matt, Col.	12	0	1	0	0	1	0	1.000
Aquino, Greg, Ari.	35	0	4	7	0	11	0	1.000
Armas, Tony, Was.	19	19	7	14	2	23	1	.913
Astacio, Ezequiel, Hou.	22	14	5	6	1	12	1	.917
Astacio, Pedro, S.D.	12	10	4	7	0	11	0	1.000
Ayala, Luis, Was.	68	0	7	15	0	22	1	1.000
Aybar, Manny, N.Y.	22	0	1	1	0	2	0	1.000
Backe, Brandon, Hou.	26	25	8	19	0	27	1	1.000
Bartosh, Cliff, Chi.*	19	0	1	0	0	1	1	1.000
Bazardo, Yorman, Fla.	1	0	0	0	0	0	0	.000
Beckett, Josh, Fla.	29	29	6	30	1	37	1	.973
Belisle, Matt, Cin.	60	5	6	10	2	18	1	.889
Bell, Heath, N.Y.	42	0	2	8	0	10	2	1.000
Benitez, Armando, S.F.	30	0	2	2	1	5	0	.800
Benson, Kris, N.Y.	28	28	7	29	0	36	2	1.000
Bentz, Chad, Fla.*	4	0	0	0	0	0	0	.000
Bergmann, Jay, Was.	15	1	1	2	0	3	0	1.000
Bernero, Adam, Atl.	36	0	3	4	1	8	0	.875
Booker, Chris, Cin.	3	0	0	0	0	0	0	.000
Borowski, Joe, Chi.	11	0	0	2	0	2	0	1.000
Bottalico, Ricky, Mil.	40	0	2	6	1	9	1	.889
Boyer, Blaine, Atl.	43	0	1	3	0	4	0	1.000
Brazoban, Yhency, L.A.	74	0	4	10	0	14	0	1.000
Breslow, Craig, S.D.*	14	0	0	1	1	1	0	.000
Brito, Eude, Phi.*	6	5	1	7	0	8	0	1.000
Brooks, Frank, Atl.*	1	0	0	0	0	0	0	.000
Brower, Jim, S.F.-Atl.	69	0	4	8	0	12	0	1.000
Broxton, Jonathan, L.A.	14	0	0	0	0	0	0	.000
Bruney, Brian, Ari.	47	0	1	7	0	8	1	1.000
Bulger, Jason, Ari.	9	0	1	2	0	3	0	1.000
Bullington, Bryan, Pit.	1	0	0	0	0	0	0	.000
Bump, Nate, Fla.	31	0	3	8	1	12	1	.917
Burnett, A.J., Fla.	32	32	11	18	2	31	1	.935
Burns, Mike, Hou.	27	0	7	3	0	10	0	1.000
Burroughs, Sean, S.D.	1	0	0	0	0	0	0	.000
Cain, Matt, S.F.	7	7	1	2	1	4	0	.750
Cali, Carmen, St.L.*	6	0	0	0	0	0	0	.000
Capellan, Jose, Mil.	17	0	1	0	0	1	0	1.000
Capps, Matt, Pit.	4	0	0	2	0	2	0	1.000
Capuano, Chris, Mil.*	35	35	7	37	4	48	1	.917
Carlyle, Buddy, L.A.	10	0	1	1	0	2	0	1.000
Carpenter, Chris, St.L.	33	33	15	40	1	56	2	.982
Carrara, Giovanni, L.A.	72	0	4	20	2	26	3	.923
Carrasco, Hector, Was.	64	5	5	10	0	15	0	1.000
Carvajal, Marcos, Col.	39	0	5	8	0	13	0	1.000
Cassidy, Scott, S.D.	10	0	1	5	0	6	1	1.000
Castillo, Frank, Fla.	1	1	0	0	0	0	0	.000
Chacon, Shawn, Col.	13	12	3	12	1	16	2	.938
Childers, Matt, Atl.	3	0	1	0	0	1	0	1.000
Choate, Randy, Ari.*	8	0	1	2	1	4	0	.750
Christiansen, Jason, S.F.*	56	0	3	5	2	10	0	.800
Claussen, Brandon, Cin.*	29	29	5	19	1	25	1	.960
Clemens, Roger, Hou.	32	32	8	36	1	45	1	.978
Coffey, Todd, Cin.	57	0	1	7	0	8	0	1.000
Colon, Roman, Atl.	23	4	2	1	0	3	0	1.000
Cook, Aaron, Col.	13	13	6	13	2	21	1	.905
Cooper, Brian, S.F.	8	1	0	0	0	0	0	.000
Cordero, Chad, Was.	74	0	2	4	2	8	0	.750
Cormier, Lance, Ari.	67	0	3	10	1	14	1	.929
Cormier, Rheal, Phi.*	57	0	4	10	0	14	1	1.000
Correia, Kevin, S.F.	16	11	1	3	0	4	0	1.000
Cortes, David, Col.	50	0	8	6	0	14	1	1.000
Crowell, Jim, Fla.*	4	0	0	0	0	0	0	.000
Davies, Kyle, Atl.	21	14	7	9	1	17	2	.941
Davis, Doug, Mil.*	35	35	14	29	2	45	0	.956
Davis, Kane, Mil.	15	0	0	4	1	5	0	.800
Day, Zach, Was.-Col.	17	8	6	8	0	14	1	1.000
de la Rosa, Jorge, Mil.*	38	0	1	6	1	8	0	.875
de los Santos, Valerio, Fla.*	27	0	0	2	0	2	0	1.000
DeJean, Mike, N.Y.-Col.	66	0	5	11	1	17	0	.941
Dempster, Ryan, Chi.	63	6	3	17	0	20	1	1.000
Dessens, Elmer, L.A.	28	7	5	12	0	17	2	1.000
Devine, Joey, Atl.	5	0	0	1	0	1	0	1.000
Dohmann, Scott, Col.	32	0	3	0	1	4	0	.750
Drese, Ryan, Was.	11	11	4	6	2	12	0	.833
Driskill, Travis, Hou.	1	0	0	0	0	0	0	.000
Duckworth, Brandon, Hou.	7	2	0	0	1	1	0	.000
Duke, Zach, Pit.*	14	14	4	15	0	19	2	1.000
Eaton, Adam, S.D.	24	22	7	16	1	24	1	.958
Eischen, Joey, Was.*	57	0	2	6	1	9	0	.889
Eldred, Cal, St.L.	31	1	2	6	0	8	0	1.000
Erickson, Scott, L.A.	19	8	4	15	0	19	1	1.000
Esposito, Mike, Col.	3	3	1	2	0	3	0	1.000
Estes, Shawn, Ari.*	21	21	15	25	2	42	1	.952
Eveland, Dana, Mil.*	27	0	3	2	0	5	1	1.000
Eyre, Scott, S.F.*	86	0	0	6	1	7	1	.857
Falkenborg, Brian, S.D.	10	0	0	0	0	0	0	.000
Farnsworth, Kyle, Atl.	26	0	1	4	1	6	1	.833
Fassero, Jeff, S.F.*	48	6	7	24	0	31	2	1.000
Flores, Randy, St.L.*	50	0	2	2	1	5	0	.800
Floyd, Gavin, Phi.	7	4	3	2	0	5	0	1.000
Fogg, Josh, Pit.	34	28	11	26	3	40	1	.925

Player, Team	G	GS	PO	A	E	TC	DP	Pct.
Foppert, Jesse, S.F.	3	2	1	1	0	2	0	1.000
Foster, John, Atl.*	62	0	1	7	0	8	0	1.000
Fox, Chad, Chi.	11	0	1	0	0	1	0	1.000
Francis, Jeff, Col.*	33	33	5	20	0	25	0	1.000
Franco, John, Hou.*	31	0	0	0	0	0	0	.000
Fuentes, Brian, Col.*	78	0	0	8	0	8	0	1.000
Fultz, Aaron, Phi.*	62	0	7	12	0	19	2	1.000
Gagne, Eric, L.A.	14	0	2	4	0	6	0	1.000
Gallo, Mike, Hou.*	36	0	0	4	0	4	1	1.000
Geary, Geoff, Phi.	40	0	3	9	1	13	0	.923
GLAVINE, Tom, N.Y.*	33	33	12	43	0	55	5	1.000
Glover, Gary, Mil.	15	11	3	4	1	8	0	.875
Gonzalez, Edgar, Ari.	1	0	0	0	0	0	0	.000
Gonzalez, Mike, Pit.*	51	0	1	6	0	7	1	1.000
Gorzelanny, Tom, Pit.*	3	1	2	1	0	3	0	1.000
Gosling, Mike, Ari.*	13	5	1	4	2	7	2	.714
Grabow, John, Pit.*	63	0	0	8	1	9	1	.889
Graves, Danny, Cin.-N.Y.	40	0	1	7	2	10	0	.800
Greisinger, Seth, Atl.	1	1	0	0	0	0	0	.000
Groom, Buddy, Ari.*	23	0	1	1	0	2	0	1.000
Gryboski, Kevin, Atl.	31	0	3	1	0	4	0	1.000
Halama, John, Was.*	10	3	1	4	0	5	0	1.000
Halsey, Brad, Ari.*	28	26	5	25	3	33	2	.909
Hammond, Chris, S.D.*	55	0	1	8	0	9	0	1.000
Hampton, Mike, Atl.*	12	12	2	11	2	15	1	.867
Hamulack, Tim, N.Y.*	6	0	0	0	0	0	0	.000
Hancock, Josh, Cin.	11	0	0	2	0	2	0	1.000
Harang, Aaron, Cin.	32	32	6	24	0	30	2	1.000
Harville, Chad, Hou.	37	0	0	4	0	4	1	1.000
Hawkins, LaTroy, Chi.-S.F.	66	0	3	8	2	13	1	.846
Heilman, Aaron, N.Y.	53	7	5	19	0	24	3	1.000
Helling, Rick, Mil.	15	7	4	3	0	7	0	1.000
Hennessey, Brad, S.F.	21	21	14	14	0	28	2	1.000
Hensley, Clay, S.D.	24	1	0	11	1	12	0	.917
Heredia, Felix, N.Y.*	3	0	0	0	0	0	0	.000
Herges, Matt, S.F.-Ari.	28	0	0	3	0	3	0	1.000
Hernandez, Livan, Was.	35	35	16	45	1	62	7	.984
Hernandez, Roberto, N.Y.	67	0	1	16	0	17	1	1.000
Hill, Rich, Chi.*	10	4	1	1	0	2	0	1.000
Hoffman, Trevor, S.D.	60	0	3	5	1	9	0	.889
Horgan, Joe, Was.*	8	0	1	0	0	1	0	1.000
Houlton, D.J., L.A.	35	19	3	18	0	21	1	1.000
Hudson, Luke, Cin.	19	16	2	8	0	10	1	1.000
Hudson, Tim, Atl.	29	29	27	36	1	64	4	.984
Hughes, Travis, Was.	14	0	1	1	0	2	0	1.000
Ishii, Kazuhisa, N.Y.*	19	16	4	9	0	13	1	1.000
Isringhausen, Jason, St.L.	63	0	4	10	1	15	1	.933
Jackson, Edwin, L.A.	7	6	0	2	0	2	0	1.000
James, Chuck, Atl.*	2	0	0	0	0	0	0	.000
Jarvis, Kevin, St.L.	4	0	1	0	0	1	0	1.000
Jennings, Jason, Col.	20	20	14	17	2	33	2	.939
Johnson, Josh, Fla.	4	1	3	2	0	5	1	1.000
Johnson, Tyler, St.L.*	5	0	0	0	0	0	0	.000
Johnston, Mike, Pit.*	1	0	0	0	0	0	0	.000
Jones, Todd, Fla.	68	0	5	13	1	19	0	.947
Journell, Jimmy, St.L.	5	0	0	0	0	0	0	.000
Keisler, Randy, Cin.*	24	4	1	9	0	10	0	1.000
Kennedy, Joe, Col.*	16	16	3	11	2	16	0	.875
Kensing, Logan, Fla.	3	0	0	0	0	0	0	.000
Kim, Byung-Hyun, Col.	40	22	9	22	2	33	2	.939
Kim, Sunny, Was.-Col.	24	10	3	8	2	13	0	.846
King, Ray, St.L.*	77	0	2	3	2	7	1	.714
Kinney, Matt, S.F.	5	1	0	2	0	2	0	1.000
Kolb, Dan, Atl.	65	0	2	4	1	7	0	.857
Koo, Dae-Sung, N.Y.*	33	0	1	6	0	7	0	1.000
Koplove, Mike, Ari.	44	0	2	7	0	9	0	1.000
Koronka, John, Chi.*	4	3	1	2	0	3	0	1.000
Kuo, Hong-Chih, L.A.*	9	0	0	0	0	0	0	.000
Lawrence, Brian, S.D.	33	33	12	31	2	45	4	.956
Lehr, Justin, Mil.	23	0	4	10	0	14	0	1.000
Leicester, Jon, Chi.	6	1	0	1	0	1	0	1.000
Leiter, Al, Fla.*	17	16	1	12	0	13	1	1.000
Lerew, Anthony, Atl.	7	0	0	3	0	3	0	1.000
Levine, Al, S.F.	9	0	1	3	0	4	0	1.000
Lidge, Brad, Hou.	70	0	2	4	1	7	0	.857
Lidle, Cory, Phi.	31	31	16	29	1	46	1	.978
Lieber, Jon, Phi.	35	35	12	27	4	43	0	.907
Ligtenberg, Kerry, Ari.	7	0	1	1	0	2	0	1.000
Linebrink, Scott, S.D.	73	0	1	3	1	5	2	.800
Liriano, Pedro, Phi.	5	0	0	2	0	2	0	1.000
Loaiza, Esteban, Was.	34	34	13	30	1	44	3	.977
Looper, Braden, N.Y.	60	0	0	8	1	9	0	.889
Lopez, Aquilino, Col.-Phi.	11	0	0	2	0	2	0	1.000
Lopez, Javier, Col.-Ari.*	32	0	2	2	0	4	0	1.000
Lowe, Derek, L.A.	35	35	21	48	1	70	5	.986
Lowry, Noah, S.F.*	33	33	10	25	0	35	0	1.000
Lyon, Brandon, Ari.	32	0	2	4	0	6	0	1.000
Maddux, Greg, Chi.	35	35	19	49	3	71	6	.958
Madson, Ryan, Phi.	78	0	2	10	0	12	0	1.000
Maholm, Paul, Pit.*	6	6	1	6	0	7	0	1.000
Majewski, Gary, Was.	79	0	3	8	0	11	0	1.000
Marquis, Jason, St.L.	33	32	18	23	2	43	3	.953
Martin, Tom, Atl.*	4	0	1	1	0	2	1	1.000
Martinez, Pedro, N.Y.	31	31	6	19	0	25	0	1.000
Matthews, Mike, N.Y.*	6	0	0	2	0	2	0	1.000
May, Darrell, S.D.*	22	8	5	7	1	13	0	.923
McBride, Macay, Atl.*	23	0	0	2	0	2	0	1.000
Meadows, Brian, Pit.	65	0	3	13	1	17	2	.941
Mecir, Jim, Fla.	52	0	4	5	1	10	1	.900
Medders, Brandon, Ari.	27	0	1	1	0	2	0	1.000
Mercker, Kent, Cin.*	78	0	0	11	2	13	0	.846
Mesa, Jose, Pit.	55	0	2	13	1	16	1	.938
Messenger, Randy, Fla.	29	0	2	5	0	7	0	1.000
Miceli, Dan, Col.	19	0	1	2	0	3	0	1.000
Milton, Eric, Cin.*	34	34	3	16	0	19	0	1.000
Mitre, Sergio, Chi.	21	7	7	12	0	19	1	1.000
Moehler, Brian, Fla.	37	25	21	26	1	48	2	.979
Morris, Matt, St.L.	31	31	6	27	1	34	2	.971
Mota, Guillermo, Fla.	56	0	1	6	0	7	0	1.000
Mulder, Mark, St.L.*	32	32	5	52	2	59	3	.966
Munter, Scott, S.F.	45	0	3	12	0	15	2	1.000
Myers, Brett, Phi.	34	34	12	36	2	50	0	.960
Neal, Blaine, Col.	11	0	1	2	0	3	0	1.000
Nippert, Dustin, Ari.	3	3	1	4	0	5	0	1.000
Nitkowski, C.J., Was.*	7	0	0	2	0	2	0	1.000
Novoa, Roberto, Chi.	49	0	1	2	0	3	0	1.000
Obermueller, Wes, Mil.	23	8	4	10	1	15	0	.933
Ohka, Tomo, Was.-Mil.	32	29	8	27	1	36	2	.972
Ohman, Will, Chi.*	69	0	3	3	0	6	0	1.000
Olsen, Scott, Fla.*	5	4	0	3	1	4	0	.750
Ortiz, Ramon, Cin.	30	30	10	28	7	45	2	.844
Ortiz, Russ, Ari.	22	22	7	17	0	24	2	1.000
Osoria, Franquelis, L.A.	24	0	6	4	0	10	0	1.000
Osuna, Antonio, Was.	4	0	0	1	0	1	0	1.000
Oswalt, Roy, Hou.	35	35	19	31	0	50	2	1.000
Otsuka, Akinori, S.D.	66	0	5	7	1	13	1	.923
Oxspring, Chris, S.D.	5	0	0	1	0	1	0	1.000
Padilla, Juan, N.Y.	24	0	1	6	0	7	1	1.000
Padilla, Vicente, Phi.	27	27	4	23	1	28	2	.964
Park, Chan Ho, S.D.	10	9	4	6	0	10	0	1.000
Patterson, John, Was.	31	31	12	16	1	29	2	.966
Peavy, Jake, S.D.	30	30	10	24	1	35	1	.971
Penny, Brad, L.A.	29	29	11	25	0	36	3	1.000
Perez, Odalis, L.A.*	19	19	4	13	0	17	1	1.000
Perez, Oliver, Pit.*	20	20	2	10	1	13	0	.923
Perisho, Matt, Fla.*	24	0	2	2	0	4	0	1.000
Pettitte, Andy, Hou.*	33	33	12	40	1	53	3	.981
Phelps, Tommy, Mil.*	29	0	2	3	0	5	1	1.000
Powell, Jay, Atl.	5	0	0	0	0	0	0	.000
Prior, Mark, Chi.	27	27	9	9	1	19	0	.947
Puffer, Brandon, S.F.	3	0	1	2	0	3	0	1.000
Pulsipher, Bill, St.L.*	5	0	0	2	0	2	0	1.000
Qualls, Chad, Hou.	77	0	7	12	0	19	0	1.000
Quantrill, Paul, S.D.-Fla.	28	0	3	3	0	6	0	1.000
Ramirez, Elizardo, Cin.	6	4	1	1	1	3	0	.667
Ramirez, Horacio, Atl.*	33	32	7	43	2	52	8	.962
Rasner, Darrell, Was.	5	1	0	0	0	0	0	.000
Rauch, Jon, Was.	15	1	4	1	0	5	0	1.000
Redding, Tim, S.D.	9	6	3	5	1	9	1	.889
Redman, Mark, Pit.*	30	30	15	35	1	51	5	.980
Reitsma, Chris, Atl.	76	0	5	12	0	17	1	1.000
Remlinger, Mike, Chi.*	35	0	1	5	0	6	0	1.000
Resop, Chris, Fla.	15	0	1	1	0	2	0	1.000
Reyes, Al, St.L.	65	0	3	6	0	9	2	1.000
Reyes, Anthony, St.L.	4	1	1	0	0	1	0	1.000
Reyes, Dennys, S.D.*	36	1	2	8	1	11	1	.909
Riedling, John, Fla.	29	0	2	6	0	8	0	1.000
Ring, Royce, N.Y.*	15	0	0	3	0	3	0	1.000
Rodriguez, Wandy, Hou.*	25	22	10	19	2	31	4	.935
Rueter, Kirk, S.F.*	20	18	13	32	1	46	5	.978
Rusch, Glendon, Chi.*	46	19	4	17	2	23	2	.913
Sanchez, Duaner, L.A.	79	0	4	9	0	13	0	1.000
Santana, Julio, Mil.	41	0	2	3	1	6	0	.833
Santiago, Jose, N.Y.	4	0	0	2	0	2	1	1.000

Player, Team	G	GS	PO	A	E	TC	DP	Pct.
Santos, Victor, Mil.	29	24	15	17	0	32	0	1.000
Schmidt, Jason, S.F.	29	29	11	9	1	21	0	.952
Schmoll, Steve, L.A.	48	0	4	4	1	9	1	.889
Seanez, Rudy, S.D.	57	0	4	5	0	9	0	1.000
Seay, Bobby, Col.*	17	0	0	2	1	3	0	.667
Seo, Jae, N.Y.	14	14	5	11	0	16	1	1.000
Shackelford, Brian, Cin.*	37	0	0	2	0	2	0	1.000
Sheets, Ben, Mil.	22	22	7	6	3	16	0	.813
Simpson, Allan, Col.-Cin.	11	0	0	1	0	1	0	1.000
Smith, Travis, Fla.	12	0	1	0	0	1	0	1.000
Smoltz, John, Atl.	33	33	22	31	0	53	4	1.000
Snell, Ian, Pit.	15	5	2	2	0	4	0	1.000
Sosa, Jorge, Atl.	44	20	6	5	3	14	0	.786
Speier, Ryan, Col.	22	0	1	7	0	8	0	1.000
Springer, Russ, Hou.	62	0	1	7	0	8	0	1.000
Standridge, Jason, Cin.	32	0	0	4	0	4	1	1.000
Stanton, Mike, Was.*	30	0	2	9	0	11	1	1.000
Stauffer, Tim, S.D.	15	14	5	12	0	17	1	1.000
Stone, Ricky, Cin.	23	0	2	2	0	4	0	1.000
Strickland, Scott, Hou.	5	0	0	1	0	1	0	1.000
Suppan, Jeff, St.L.	32	32	12	28	1	41	3	.976
Takatsu, Shingo, N.Y.	9	0	0	2	0	2	1	1.000
Taschner, Jack, S.F.*	24	0	1	3	0	4	0	1.000
Tavarez, Julian, St.L.	74	0	3	7	0	10	0	1.000
Tejeda, Robinson, Phi.	26	13	5	6	0	11	0	1.000
Telemaco, Amaury, Phi.	7	0	2	1	0	3	0	1.000
Thompson, Brad, St.L.	40	0	3	12	0	15	1	1.000
Thompson, Derek, L.A.*	4	3	1	4	0	5	1	1.000
Thomson, John, Atl.	17	17	6	14	0	20	2	1.000
Tomko, Brett, S.F.	33	30	13	19	1	33	3	.970
Torres, Salomon, Pit.	78	0	4	14	1	19	1	.947
Trachsel, Steve, N.Y.	6	6	2	8	1	11	1	.909
Tsao, Chin-hui, Col.	10	0	0	2	1	3	0	.667
Tucker, T.J., Was.	13	0	1	2	0	3	0	1.000
Turnbow, Derrick, Mil.	69	0	6	4	0	10	0	1.000
Urbina, Ugueth, Phi.	56	0	0	3	0	3	0	1.000
Valdez, Ismael, Fla.	14	7	5	7	0	12	1	1.000
Valentine, Joe, Cin.	16	0	0	2	1	3	0	.667
Valverde, Jose, Ari.	61	0	3	7	0	10	0	1.000
Van Buren, Jermaine, Chi.	6	0	0	0	1	1	0	.000
Vargas, Claudio, Was.-Ari.	25	23	7	10	0	17	1	1.000
Vargas, Jason, Fla.*	17	13	2	13	0	15	1	1.000
Vasquez, Jorge, Atl.	7	0	0	1	0	1	0	1.000
Vazquez, Javier, Ari.	33	33	8	35	3	46	2	.935
Villarreal, Oscar, Ari.	11	0	1	1	0	2	0	1.000
Villone, Ron, Fla.*	27	0	2	2	1	5	0	.800
Vogelsong, Ryan, Pit.	44	0	7	6	0	13	0	1.000
Wagner, Billy, Phi.*	75	0	4	6	0	10	1	1.000
Wagner, Ryan, Cin.	42	0	2	6	0	8	0	1.000
Wainwright, Adam, St.L.	2	0	0	0	0	0	0	.000
Walker, Tyler, S.F.	67	0	2	7	1	10	1	.900
Weathers, David, Cin.	73	0	2	4	0	6	0	1.000
Weaver, Jeff, L.A.	34	34	11	26	2	39	1	.949
Webb, Brandon, Ari.	33	33	18	44	2	64	7	.969
Weber, Ben, Cin.	10	0	3	3	0	6	0	1.000
Wellemeyer, Todd, Chi.	22	0	1	2	0	3	0	1.000
Wells, Kip, Pit.	33	33	6	33	2	41	4	.951
Wheeler, Dan, Hou.	71	0	3	11	0	14	0	1.000
White, Gabe, St.L.*	6	0	0	1	0	1	0	1.000
White, Matt, Was.*	1	1	0	0	0	0	0	.000
White, Rick, Pit.	71	0	2	16	1	19	0	.947
Williams, Dave, Pit.*	25	25	6	23	2	31	5	.935
Williams, Jerome, S.F.-Chi.	22	20	8	25	1	34	3	.971
Williams, Randy, S.D.-Col.*	32	0	3	3	0	6	1	1.000
Williams, Woody, S.D.	28	28	11	18	0	29	1	1.000
Williamson, Scott, Chi.	17	0	0	1	0	1	0	1.000
Willis, Dontrelle, Fla.*	34	34	9	37	3	49	3	.939
Wilson, Paul, Cin.	9	9	1	6	1	8	0	.875
Wise, Matt, Mil.	49	0	3	4	0	7	0	1.000
Witasick, Jay, Col.	32	0	1	4	0	5	1	1.000
Wolf, Randy, Phi.*	13	13	3	8	0	11	2	1.000
Wood, Kerry, Chi.	21	10	3	3	2	8	0	.750
Worrell, Tim, Phi.-Ari.	51	0	2	4	0	6	0	1.000
Wright, Jamey, Col.	34	27	11	24	2	37	1	.946
Wuertz, Michael, Chi.	75	0	2	7	0	9	2	1.000
Wunsch, Kelly, L.A.*	45	0	2	6	0	8	1	1.000
Zambrano, Carlos, Chi.	33	33	21	34	2	57	4	.965
Zambrano, Victor, N.Y.	31	27	20	20	3	43	2	.930

PITCHERS WITH TWO OR MORE TEAMS

Player, Team	G	GS	PO	A	E	TC	DP	Pct.
Brower, Jim, S.F.	32	0	1	5	0	6	0	1.000
Brower, Jim, Atl.	37	0	3	3	0	6	0	1.000
Day, Zach, Was.	12	5	4	5	0	9	1	1.000
Day, Zach, Col.	5	3	2	3	0	5	0	1.000
DeJean, Mike, N.Y.	28	0	2	5	0	7	0	1.000
DeJean, Mike, Col.	38	0	3	6	1	10	0	.900
Graves, Danny, Cin.	20	0	1	4	1	6	0	.833
Graves, Danny, N.Y.	20	0	3	1	0	4	0	.750
Hawkins, LaTroy, Chi.	21	0	1	4	1	6	1	.833
Hawkins, LaTroy, S.F.	45	0	2	4	1	7	0	.857
Herges, Matt, S.F.	21	0	0	2	0	2	0	1.000
Herges, Matt, Ari.	7	0	0	1	0	1	0	1.000
Kim, Sunny, Was.	12	2	1	2	1	4	0	.750
Kim, Sunny, Col.	12	8	2	6	1	9	0	.889
Lopez, Aquilino, Col.	1	0	0	0	0	0	0	.000
Lopez, Aquilino, Phi.	10	0	0	2	0	2	0	1.000
Lopez, Javier, Col.*	3	0	1	0	0	1	0	1.000
Lopez, Javier, Ari.*	29	0	1	2	0	3	0	1.000
Ohka, Tomo, Was.	10	9	1	9	1	11	0	.909
Ohka, Tomo, Mil.	22	20	7	18	0	25	2	1.000
Quantrill, Paul, S.D.	22	0	3	1	0	4	0	1.000
Quantrill, Paul, Fla.	6	0	0	2	0	2	0	1.000
Simpson, Allan, Col.	2	0	0	1	0	1	0	1.000
Simpson, Allan, Cin.	9	0	0	0	0	0	0	.000
Vargas, Claudio, Was.	4	4	1	0	0	1	0	1.000
Vargas, Claudio, Ari.	21	19	6	10	0	16	1	1.000
Williams, Jerome, S.F.	4	3	2	2	0	4	0	1.000
Williams, Jerome, Chi.	18	17	6	23	1	30	3	.967
Williams, Randy, S.D.*	2	0	0	2	0	2	0	1.000
Williams, Randy, Col.*	30	0	3	1	0	4	1	1.000
Worrell, Tim, Phi.	19	0	1	1	0	2	0	1.000
Worrell, Tim, Ari.	32	0	1	3	0	4	0	1.000
Wheeler, Dan, Hou.	14	0	0	0	0	0	0	.000

SHUTOUT GAMES

Read across for wins, down for losses.

Team	St.L.	Atl.	Fla.	Pit.	Chi.	S.F.	Ari.	N.Y.	L.A.	Was.	S.D.	Phi.	Hou.	Mil.	Col.	Cin.	A.L.	W	L	Pct.
St. Louis	..	0	0	1	1	0	1	1	0	2	0	0	3	3	1	0	1	14	6	.700
Atlanta	0	..	2	1	2	0	0	3	0	1	0	1	2	0	0	0	0	12	6	.667
Florida	0	2	..	1	0	0	1	1	1	3	2	1	0	0	1	1	1	15	8	.652
Pittsburgh	1	0	0	..	1	0	0	1	0	0	0	1	5	2	1	1	1	14	9	.609
Chicago	0	0	1	1	..	0	0	1	0	0	2	0	0	3	0	0	2	10	8	.556
San Francisco	1	0	1	0	0	..	1	0	1	0	0	1	1	1	0	0	1	8	7	.533
Arizona	0	1	0	0	1	0	..	1	1	0	1	1	0	1	1	1	1	10	9	.526
New York	1	1	2	0	1	1	0	..	1	1	1	0	1	0	1	0	0	11	11	.500
Los Angeles	0	0	0	0	1	1	1	0	..	0	2	1	1	0	1	1	0	9	9	.500
Washington	0	1	1	0	0	1	0	0	1	..	0	0	1	2	0	0	2	9	11	.450
San Diego	0	0	0	1	1	1	2	0	1	1	..	0	1	0	0	0	0	8	12	.400
Philadelphia	0	1	0	0	1	0	0	0	0	2	1	..	0	0	0	0	1	6	9	.400
Houston	0	0	0	1	0	1	2	1	0	0	0	0	..	1	1	2	2	11	17	.393
Milwaukee	0	0	0	0	0	0	0	0	0	0	0	1	1	..	1	1	2	6	12	.333
Colorado	1	0	0	0	0	1	0	0	0	0	0	1	0	0	..	0	1	4	10	.286
Cincinnati	0	0	0	0	0	0	0	0	0	0	0	0	1	0	0	..	0	1	8	.111
A.L. Clubs	2	0	1	2	0	1	1	2	3	1	2	2	1	0	0	1	..			..
Lost	6	6	8	9	8	7	9	11	9	11	12	9	17	12	10	8	15	148	152	.493

N.L. shutouts vs A.L. clubs (15): Milwaukee vs Minnesota, Milwaukee vs Tampa Bay, Chicago vs Chicago, Chicago vs Toronto, Houston vs Kansas City, Houston vs Toronto, Washington vs Los Angeles, Washington vs Toronto, Philadelphia vs Texas, Pittsburgh vs Boston, St. Louis vs Toronto, San Francisco vs Detroit, Colorado vs Detroit, Florida vs Tampa Bay, Arizona vs Detroit.

HOME RECORD

Read across for wins, down for losses.

Team	Atl.	Hou.	St.L.	N.Y.	Mil.	Phi.	S.D.	Fla.	Cin.	Was.	L.A.	Col.	Chi.	S.F.	Ari.	Pit.	A.L.	W	L	Pct.
Atlanta	..	4	2	8	1	5	1	6	2	6	1	1	4	2	2	3	5	53	28	.654
Houston	1	..	3	3	7	3	3	2	8	2	3	3	5	2	1	2	5	53	28	.654
St. Louis	2	6	..	3	4	1	1	2	6	2	3	2	3	2	2	7	4	50	31	.617
New York	5	4	1	..	1	6	3	5	3	4	2	3	3	2	2	2	4	48	33	.593
Milwaukee	1	3	2	1	..	2	2	2	7	3	0	3	7	2	2	5	4	46	35	.568
Philadelphia	6	0	2	3	4	..	3	6	2	5	1	1	2	3	3	2	3	46	35	.568
San Diego	3	2	1	2	2	0	..	3	0	2	5	6	1	7	6	2	4	46	35	.568
Florida	6	2	1	4	2	5	2	..	2	4	3	2	0	2	2	6	45	36	.556
Cincinnati	2	3	4	3	3	1	1	1	..	3	1	3	3	1	2	5	6	42	39	.519
Washington	5	1	1	3	3	3	0	4	1	..	2	1	2	1	3	3	8	41	40	.506
Los Angeles	1	2	1	2	3	1	7	1	2	1	..	5	0	5	1	3	5	40	41	.494
Colorado	2	1	2	2	1	1	4	2	3	0	7	..	2	4	3	1	5	40	41	.494
Chicago	1	4	5	2	4	1	1	2	3	0	1	3	..	2	1	4	4	38	43	.469
San Francisco	1	2	1	2	1	1	4	1	2	1	6	6	1	..	4	1	3	37	44	.457
Arizona	2	1	1	0	1	2	6	1	1	2	5	5	2	2	..	1	4	36	45	.444
Pittsburgh	2	3	1	2	4	2	1	3	3	1	1	5	1	0	1	..	4	34	47	.420
A.L. Clubs	4	7	3	6	5	5	6	2	5	5	9	5	4	6	5	5	..			
Lost on Road	44	45	31	46	46	39	45	43	50	41	50	54	40	43	40	48	72	695	601	.536

HOME RECORDS IN INTERLEAGUE GAMES

Team				Total	Team				Total
Arizona	2-1 vs. Det.	1-2 vs. K.C.	1-2 vs. Min.	4-5	Milwaukee	2-1 vs. Min.	2-1 vs. N.Y.		4-2
Atlanta	3-0 vs. Bal.	1-2 vs. L.A.	1-2 vs. Oak.	5-4	New York	1-2 vs. L.A.	1-2 vs. N.Y.		2-4
Chicago	2-1 vs. Bos.	1-2 vs. Chi.	1-2 vs. Tor.	4-5	Philadelphia	0-3 vs. Bos.	3-0 vs. Tex.		3-3
Cincinnati	2-1 vs. Bal.	1-2 vs. Cle.	3-0 vs. TB.	6-3	Pittsburgh	2-1 vs. Bal.	2-1 vs. TB.		4-2
Colorado	0-3 vs. Chi.	2-1 vs. Det.	3-0 vs. K.C.	5-4	St. Louis	2-1 vs. Bos.	2-1 vs. N.Y.		4-2
Florida	1-2 vs. Sea.	2-1 vs. Tex.	3-0 vs. TB.	6-3	San Diego	1-2 vs. Chi.	1-2 vs. Cle.	2-1 vs. Sea.	4-5
Houston	2-1 vs. Tex.	3-0 vs. Tor.		5-1	San Francisco	0-3 vs. Cle.	1-2 vs. K.C.	2-1 vs. Oak.	3-6
Los Angeles	1-2 vs. L.A.	2-1 vs. Det.	2-1 vs. Min.	5-4	Washington	3-0 vs. Oak.	3-0 vs. Sea.	2-1 vs. Tor.	8-1

ROAD RECORD

Read across for wins, down for losses.

Team	St.L.	Phi.	Chi.	Ari.	Was.	S.F.	Fla.	Atl.	Hou.	S.D.	Mil.	N.Y.	Pit.	Cin.	L.A.	Col.	A.L.	W	L	Pct.
St. Louis	..	1	3	3	2	2	2	1	5	2	7	2	5	5	2	2	6	50	31	.617
Philadelphia	2	..	2	1	6	2	4	4	0	3	1	4	2	2	2	3	4	42	39	.519
Chicago	5	1	..	1	1	3	3	0	5	3	3	0	7	3	3	1	2	41	40	.506
Arizona	1	1	3	..	0	5	1	1	2	4	1	1	2	1	8	6	4	41	40	.506
Washington	1	5	3	1	..	2	5	4	1	1	1	5	2	0	2	3	4	40	41	.494
San Francisco	1	0	1	7	2	..	1	1	2	2	2	1	3	3	4	5	3	38	43	.469
Florida	2	4	4	2	5	2	..	2	2	0	1	4	1	2	2	1	4	38	43	.469
Atlanta	1	4	2	1	4	2	4	..	1	0	2	5	1	5	2	1	2	37	44	.457
Houston	2	3	2	2	3	1	1	0	..	1	3	2	7	4	1	2	2	36	45	.444
San Diego	3	0	2	3	3	5	1	2		..	2	0	2	2	2	5	3	36	45	.444

Team	St.L.	Phi.	Chi.	Ari.	Was.	S.F.	Fla.	Atl.	Hou.	S.D.	Mil.	N.Y.	Pit.	Cin.	L.A.	Col.	A.L.	W	L	Pct.
Milwaukee	3	2	2	2	1	2	2	2	2	1	..	2	4	3	1	2	4	35	46	.432
New York	1	5	1	4	7	1	5	1	1	1	2	..	1	0	1	1	3	35	46	.432
Pittsburgh	3	1	4	3	0	2	1	1	4	2	3	1	..	4	1	2	1	33	48	.407
Cincinnati	1	2	6	2	2	2	1	1	1	3	3	0	4	..	2	0	1	31	50	.383
Los Angeles	1	2	2	4	1	4	1	2	0	4	2	1	2	2	..	3	0	31	50	.383
Colorado	2	1	1	4	2	3	1	2	0	3	0	1	2	0	4	..	1	27	54	.333
A.L. Clubs	2	3	5	5	1	6	3	4	1	5	2	4	2	3	4	4	..			
Lost at home	31	35	43	45	40	44	36	28	28	35	35	33	47	39	41	41	44	591	705	.456

PITCHING AGAINST EACH CLUB

ARIZONA—77-85

Pitcher	Atl. W-L	Chi. W-L	Cin. W-L	Col. W-L	Fla. W-L	Hou. W-L	L.A. W-L	Mil. W-L	N.Y. W-L	Phi. W-L	Pit. W-L	S.D. W-L	S.F. W-L	St.L. W-L	Was. W-L	A.L. W-L	Totals W-L
Aquino, Greg	0-0	0-0	0-0	0-0	0-0	0-0	0-0	0-0	0-0	0-0	0-0	0-1	0-0	0-0	0-0	0-0	0-1
Bruney, Brian	0-0	0-1	0-0	0-0	0-0	0-0	0-0	0-0	0-0	0-0	0-0	0-1	0-0	0-0	0-0	1-1	1-3
Bulger, Jason	0-0	0-0	0-0	0-0	0-0	0-0	1-0	0-0	0-0	0-0	0-0	0-0	0-0	0-0	0-0	0-0	1-0
Cormier, Lance	1-1	1-0	1-1	0-1	0-0	0-0	0-0	0-0	0-0	0-0	0-0	0-0	0-0	1-0	1-0	0-0	7-3
Estes, Shawn	0-0	0-0	0-0	3-1	0-0	0-0	0-0	0-1	0-1	0-1	0-1	1-1	0-1	0-1	1-0	2-1	7-8
Gosling, Mike	0-0	0-0	0-0	0-1	0-0	0-0	0-1	0-0	0-0	0-0	0-0	0-0	0-0	0-0	0-0	0-0	0-3
Groom, Buddy	0-0	0-0	0-0	0-0	0-0	0-0	0-0	0-0	0-0	0-1	0-0	0-0	0-0	0-0	0-0	0-0	0-1
Halsey, Brad	0-0	1-0	0-1	1-1	0-0	1-0	2-0	1-0	0-0	1-0	0-2	0-1	2-1	0-2	0-1	0-0	0-2	8-12
Koplove, Mike	0-0	0-0	0-0	0-0	0-0	0-0	0-0	0-0	0-0	0-0	0-0	1-0	0-0	0-0	0-1	0-0	2-1
Lopez, Javier	0-0	0-0	0-0	0-0	0-0	0-0	0-0	0-0	0-0	0-0	0-0	0-0	1-0	0-0	0-0	0-1	1-1
Lyon, Brandon	0-0	0-0	0-0	0-0	0-0	0-0	0-1	0-0	0-0	0-0	0-0	0-0	0-0	0-0	0-0	0-1	0-2
Medders, Brandon	0-0	0-0	0-1	1-0	0-0	1-0	1-0	0-0	0-0	0-0	0-0	1-0	0-0	0-0	0-0	0-0	4-1
Nippert, Dustin	0-0	0-0	0-0	0-0	0-0	0-0	1-0	0-0	0-0	0-0	0-0	0-0	0-0	0-0	0-0	0-0	1-0
Ortiz, Russ	0-0	1-0	0-1	1-2	0-0	1-0	1-1	0-0	0-1	0-1	0-1	1-1	0-1	0-0	0-1	0-1	5-11
Valverde, Jose	0-1	0-0	0-0	0-0	0-0	0-0	0-0	0-0	0-0	0-0	1-0	2-0	0-0	0-0	0-1	0-1	3-4
Vargas, Claudio	1-0	0-0	0-0	2-0	0-0	0-1	1-0	1-0	0-1	1-0	0-0	0-2	1-1	1-0	0-0	1-1	9-6
Vazquez, Javier	1-1	0-1	1-0	0-0	0-2	0-2	2-1	0-1	0-1	0-1	1-0	2-1	1-1	0-1	0-1	3-1	11-15
Villarreal, Oscar	0-0	0-0	1-0	0-0	0-0	0-0	0-0	0-0	0-1	0-0	0-0	0-0	0-0	0-0	0-0	0-0	0-1
Webb, Brandon	0-0	2-0	0-1	3-0	1-1	0-0	2-0	0-1	0-2	2-0	1-0	0-1	2-3	0-2	0-0	1-1	14-12
Worrell, Tim	0-0	0-0	0-0	0-0	0-0	0-0	0-0	0-0	0-0	0-0	0-0	1-0	0-0	0-0	0-0	0-0	1-1
Totals	3-3	5-2	2-4	11-7	2-4	3-3	13-5	2-4	1-6	3-4	3-4	10-9	7-11	2-5	2-4	8-10	77-85

No-decisions-- Armando Almanza, Randy Choate, Edgar Gonzalez, Matt Herges, Kerry Ligtenberg.
INTERLEAGUE: Shawn Estes 1-0, Javier Vazquez 1-0, Russ Ortiz 0-1 vs. White Sox; Brad Halsey 0-1, Brandon Webb 0-1, Shawn Estes 0-1 vs. Indians; Brandon Webb 1-0, Brian Bruney 0-1, Shawn Estes 1-0, Javier Vazquez 1-1, Claudio Vargas 1-0 vs. Tigers; Javier Lopez 0-1, Brian Bruney 1-0, Brad Halsey 0-1 vs. Royals; Jose Valverde 0-1, Claudio Vargas 0-1, Javier Vazquez 1-0 vs. Twins. Total: 8-10.

ATLANTA—90-72

Pitcher	Ari. W-L	Chi. W-L	Cin. W-L	Col. W-L	Fla. W-L	Hou. W-L	L.A. W-L	Mil. W-L	N.Y. W-L	Phi. W-L	Pit. W-L	S.D. W-L	S.F. W-L	St.L. W-L	Was. W-L	A.L. W-L	Totals W-L
Bernero, Adam	0-0	0-0	1-1	0-0	1-1	0-0	1-0	0-0	1-0	0-0	0-1	0-0	0-0	0-0	0-0	0-0	4-3
Boyer, Blaine	0-0	0-0	0-0	0-0	2-0	0-0	0-0	1-0	0-1	0-0	0-0	1-0	0-0	0-0	0-0	0-1	4-2
Brower, Jim	0-1	0-0	0-0	0-0	0-0	0-0	0-0	0-0	0-1	1-0	0-0	0-0	0-0	0-0	0-0	0-0	1-2
Colon, Roman	0-0	1-0	0-0	0-0	0-0	0-0	0-0	0-1	0-0	0-0	0-0	0-0	0-0	0-0	0-1	0-2	1-5
Davies, Kyle	0-0	1-0	1-0	0-1	0-1	0-0	0-0	0-1	1-0	0-1	1-0	0-0	0-0	0-0	1-1	2-1	7-6
Devine, Joey	0-0	0-0	0-0	0-0	0-0	0-0	0-0	0-0	0-0	0-0	0-1	0-0	0-0	0-0	0-0	0-0	0-1
Foster, John	1-0	0-0	0-0	0-0	0-0	0-0	0-0	0-0	0-0	0-0	1-0	0-0	0-0	0-1	0-1	0-1	4-2
Hampton, Mike	0-0	0-0	0-0	0-0	0-1	1-0	0-0	0-0	1-1	1-0	0-0	0-1	0-0	0-0	1-0	0-0	5-3
Hudson, Tim	0-0	1-0	1-0	1-1	2-0	0-0	2-0	1-0	3-0	2-2	0-2	0-0	0-1	1-1	0-0	0-2	14-9
Kolb, Dan	0-0	0-0	0-1	0-1	0-1	0-0	0-0	0-1	0-0	0-1	0-0	0-1	0-1	1-0	1-2	0-0	3-8
McBride, Macay	0-0	0-0	0-0	0-0	0-0	0-0	0-0	0-0	0-0	0-0	0-0	0-0	1-0	0-0	0-0	0-0	1-0
Ramirez, Horacio	0-1	1-0	1-1	0-0	2-0	1-0	0-0	0-1	1-1	1-3	1-0	0-1	1-0	0-0	1-1	1-0	11-9
Reitsma, Chris	1-0	0-0	0-1	0-0	0-0	0-0	0-2	0-0	0-0	0-0	0-1	0-0	0-0	2-1	0-0	3-0	3-6
Smoltz, John	0-0	0-0	1-0	0-0	1-1	1-0	0-0	1-0	3-2	1-2	1-0	0-0	1-1	1-0	2-1	14-7
Sosa, Jorge	0-1	1-0	2-0	1-0	1-1	1-0	0-0	0-0	0-0	2-0	1-0	1-0	0-0	2-1	1-0	13-3
Thomson, John	0-0	0-1	0-0	0-0	1-1	1-1	0-1	0-0	0-0	1-1	1-0	0-0	0-0	0-1	0-0	4-6
Vasquez, Jorge	0-0	0-0	0-0	0-0	0-0	0-0	0-0	0-0	0-0	0-0	0-0	0-0	0-0	0-0	1-0	1-0
Totals	3-3	6-1	7-3	2-4	10-8	5-1	3-3	3-3	13-6	9-10	4-3	1-5	4-2	3-3	10-9	7-8	90-72

No-decisions-- Frank Brooks, Matt Childers, Kyle Farnsworth, Seth Greisinger, Kevin Gryboski, Chuck James, Anthony Lerew, Tom Martin, Jay Powell.
INTERLEAGUE: Kyle Davies 1-0, Jorge Vasquez 1-0, John Smoltz 1-0 vs. Orioles; Tim Hudson 0-1, Kyle Davies 1-0, Roman Colon 0-1 vs. Red Sox; John Smoltz 0-1, John Foster 0-1, Horacio Ramirez 1-0 vs. Angels; Roman Colon 0-1, John Smoltz 1-0, Blaine Boyer 0-1 vs. Athletics; Tim Hudson 0-1, Jorge Sosa 1-0, Kyle Davies 0-1 vs. Rangers. Total: 7-8.

CHICAGO—79-83

Pitcher	Ari. W-L	Atl. W-L	Cin. W-L	Col. W-L	Fla. W-L	Hou. W-L	L.A. W-L	Mil. W-L	N.Y. W-L	Phi. W-L	Pit. W-L	S.D. W-L	S.F. W-L	St.L. W-L	Was. W-L	A.L. W-L	Totals W-L
Bartosh, Cliff	0-0	0-0	0-0	0-0	0-0	0-1	0-0	0-0	0-0	0-0	0-0	0-0	0-0	0-0	0-1	0-0	0-2
Dempster, Ryan	0-1	0-0	0-0	0-0	0-0	0-0	0-0	1-0	0-0	1-0	0-1	2-0	1-1	0-0	0-0	5-3
Hawkins, LaTroy	0-0	0-0	1-0	0-0	0-0	0-0	0-0	0-1	0-1	0-1	0-1	0-0	0-0	0-0	0-0	1-4
Hill, Rich	0-0	0-0	0-1	0-0	0-0	0-0	0-0	0-0	0-0	0-0	0-0	0-0	0-0	0-0	0-1	0-2
Koronka, John	0-0	0-0	0-0	0-0	0-1	0-0	1-0	0-0	0-0	0-0	0-0	0-0	0-0	0-0	0-1	1-2
Leicester, Jon	0-0	0-0	0-1	0-0	0-0	0-0	0-0	0-1	0-0	0-0	0-0	0-0	0-0	0-0	0-0	0-2
Maddux, Greg	0-2	0-1	0-1	0-1	1-2	2-2	1-0	2-1	1-1	0-0	1-2	1-0	0-0	2-1	0-0	2-1	13-15
Mitre, Sergio	0-0	0-0	0-0	0-0	0-0	0-0	0-0	0-0	0-0	0-0	0-1	0-0	0-0	0-1	0-1	1-2	2-5
Novoa, Roberto	1-1	0-1	0-1	1-0	0-0	1-0	0-0	1-1	0-0	0-0	0-0	0-0	0-0	0-0	0-0	4-5
Ohman, Will	0-0	0-0	0-1	0-0	0-0	0-0	0-0	0-0	0-0	1-0	0-0	0-0	0-0	1-0	0-1	2-2

Pitcher	Ari. W-L	Atl. W-L	Cin. W-L	Col. W-L	Fla. W-L	Hou. W-L	L.A. W-L	Mil. W-L	N.Y. W-L	Phi. W-L	Pit. W-L	S.D. W-L	S.F. W-L	St.L. W-L	Was. W-L	A.L. W-L	Totals W-L
Prior, Mark	0-0	0-2	3-0	1-0	0-0	0-1	1-0	0-0	0-0	0-1	1-1	1-0	1-0	1-1	0-1	2-0	11-7
Remlinger, Mike	0-0	0-0	0-0	0-0	0-0	0-0	0-0	0-1	0-0	0-1	0-1	0-0	0-0	0-0	0-0	0-0	0-3
Rusch, Glendon	1-0	0-0	0-0	1-1	0-1	3-1	0-1	1-0	0-0	0-1	0-0	1-0	0-1	2-0	0-0	0-2	9-8
VanBuren, Jermaine	0-0	0-0	0-1	0-0	0-0	0-0	0-0	0-1	0-0	0-0	0-0	0-0	0-0	0-0	0-0	0-0	0-2
Wellemeyer, Todd	0-0	0-0	0-0	1-0	0-0	0-0	0-0	0-0	0-0	0-0	0-0	0-0	0-0	0-0	0-0	1-1	2-1
Williams, Jerome	0-1	1-0	1-1	0-0	0-0	1-1	0-1	1-1	0-0	0-0	1-0	0-0	0-0	0-1	1-1	0-1	6-8
Wood, Kerry	0-0	0-2	0-1	0-0	1-0	0-0	0-0	0-0	0-0	0-0	2-0	1-0	0-0	0-0	0-0	0-0	3-4
Wuertz, Michael	0-0	0-0	1-1	0-0	0-0	1-0	1-0	0-0	0-0	0-0	2-0	0-0	1-0	0-0	0-0	0-1	6-2
Zambrano, Carlos	0-0	0-0	0-0	0-1	2-0	1-1	0-0	2-2	0-1	0-0	2-0	1-0	1-0	3-0	0-1	0-0	14-6
Totals	2-5	1-6	6-9	4-3	5-4	9-7	4-2	7-9	2-4	2-4	11-5	4-3	5-2	10-6	1-5	6-9	79-83

No-decisions-- Joe Borowski, Chad Fox, Scott Williamson.
INTERLEAGUE: Greg Maddux 1-0, Todd Wellemeyer 1-0, Glendon Rusch 0-1 vs. Red Sox; Greg Maddux 1-1, Michael Wuertz 0-1, Mark Prior 2-0, Sergio Mitre 0-1 vs. White Sox; Will Ohman 0-1, Glendon Rusch 0-1, Sergio Mitre 0-1 vs. Yankees; John Koronka 0-1, Todd Wellemeyer 0-1, Sergio Mitre 1-0 vs. Blue Jays. Total: 6-9.

CINCINNATI—73-89

Pitcher	Ari. W-L	Atl. W-L	Chi. W-L	Col. W-L	Fla. W-L	Hou. W-L	L.A. W-L	Mil. W-L	N.Y. W-L	Phi. W-L	Pit. W-L	S.D. W-L	S.F. W-L	St.L. W-L	Was. W-L	A.L. W-L	Totals W-L
Belisle, Matt	0-0	0-0	0-1	0-0	0-1	0-2	0-0	0-2	0-0	0-0	1-1	0-1	0-0	1-0	1-0	0-0	4-8
Claussen, Brandon	1-0	1-1	1-2	0-0	1-0	0-2	1-0	0-3	0-0	0-0	2-0	0-0	1-3	1-0	1-0		10-11
Coffey, Todd	1-0	0-0	1-0	0-0	0-0	0-0	0-0	0-1	0-0	0-0	0-0	1-0	0-0	1-0	0-0	0-0	4-1
Graves, Danny	0-0	0-0	0-0	0-0	0-0	0-0	0-0	1-0	0-0	0-0	0-0	0-0	0-1	0-0	0-0	0-0	1-1
Hancock, Josh	0-0	0-0	0-0	0-0	0-0	0-0	0-0	0-0	0-0	0-0	0-0	0-0	0-0	1-0	0-0	0-0	1-0
Harang, Aaron	0-0	0-1	3-0	1-1	0-0	1-2	0-1	1-0	1-0	1-1	1-0	0-2	0-3	0-0	1-2	11-13
Hudson, Luke	0-0	0-1	0-1	0-0	1-0	0-1	0-0	1-0	0-0	0-0	1-1	1-0	0-2	0-1	1-2	6-9
Keisler, Randy	0-0	0-0	0-0	0-0	0-0	0-0	0-0	0-0	0-1	0-0	0-0	0-0	0-0	1-0	2-1
Mercker, Kent	0-0	0-0	1-0	0-0	0-1	0-0	1-0	0-0	0-0	0-0	0-0	0-0	0-0	1-0	3-1
Milton, Eric	1-1	0-2	1-0	0-1	0-1	1-1	0-2	1-1	1-1	0-2	1-0	1-0	0-0	1-0	0-1	8-15
Ortiz, Ramon	0-0	0-2	0-0	1-0	0-1	1-2	0-0	2-1	0-1	1-0	0-0	1-0	1-2	0-1	1-1	9-11
Ramirez, Elizardo	0-0	0-0	0-0	0-0	0-0	0-0	0-0	0-0	0-1	0-1	0-0	0-0	0-0	0-0	0-1	0-3
Shackelford, Brian	0-0	0-0	1-0	0-0	0-0	0-0	0-0	0-0	0-0	0-0	0-0	0-0	0-0	0-0	0-0	1-0
Simpson, Allan	0-0	0-0	0-0	0-0	0-0	0-0	0-0	0-0	0-0	0-0	0-0	0-0	0-0	0-0	0-1	0-1
Standridge, Jason	0-1	0-0	0-0	0-0	0-0	0-0	0-0	0-0	0-0	0-0	0-0	0-1	0-0	0-0	0-0	2-2
Valentine, Joe	0-0	0-0	0-0	0-0	0-0	0-0	0-0	0-1	0-0	0-0	0-0	0-0	0-0	0-0	0-0	0-1
Wagner, Ryan	0-0	0-0	0-0	0-1	0-0	1-1	0-0	0-0	0-0	0-0	0-0	1-0	0-0	0-0	0-0	3-2
Weathers, David	1-0	1-0	1-1	0-0	0-0	0-0	0-0	1-0	1-0	0-0	0-1	1-1	0-0	0-0	1-1	7-4
Wilson, Paul	0-0	0-0	0-0	0-0	0-0	0-1	0-1	0-0	0-1	0-0	1-0	0-1	0-0	0-0	0-0	1-5
Totals	4-2	3-7	9-6	3-3	2-4	4-12	3-4	6-10	3-3	3-4	9-7	4-2	3-5	5-11	5-1	7-8	73-89

No-decisions-- Chris Booker, Ricky Stone, Ben Weber.
INTERLEAGUE: Aaron Harang 0-1, Brandon Claussen 1-0, Ramon Ortiz 1-0 vs. Orioles; Eric Milton 0-1, Luke Hudson 0-1, Aaron Harang 0-1 vs. Red Sox; Aaron Harang 1-0, Kent Mercker 1-0, Elizardo Ramirez 0-1, Ramon Ortiz 0-1, David Weathers 0-1, Luke Hudson 0-1 vs. Indians; Randy Keisler 1-0, David Weathers 1-0, Luke Hudson 1-0 vs. Devil Rays. Total: 7-8.

COLORADO—67-96

Pitcher	Ari. W-L	Atl. W-L	Chi. W-L	Cin. W-L	Fla. W-L	Hou. W-L	L.A. W-L	Mil. W-L	N.Y. W-L	Phi. W-L	Pit. W-L	S.D. W-L	S.F. W-L	St.L. W-L	Was. W-L	A.L. W-L	Totals W-L
Acevedo, Jose	0-0	0-0	0-0	0-0	0-0	0-0	0-0	0-0	1-0	0-1	0-1	0-1	0-0	0-0	1-1	0-0	2-4
Carvajal, Marcos	0-0	0-0	0-1	0-0	0-0	0-0	0-0	0-0	0-0	0-0	0-0	0-1	0-0	0-0	0-0	0-0	0-2
Chacon, Shawn	0-0	0-0	0-0	0-0	0-1	0-0	1-2	0-1	0-0	0-0	0-1	0-0	0-0	0-1	0-0	1-7
Cook, Aaron	1-0	0-1	1-0	0-0	0-0	1-0	1-0	1-0	0-1	0-0	0-0	2-0	0-0	0-0	0-0	7-2
Cortes, David	0-0	0-0	0-0	0-0	0-0	1-0	0-0	0-0	0-0	0-0	1-0	0-0	0-0	0-0	0-0	2-0
Day, Zach	0-1	0-0	0-0	0-0	0-0	0-0	0-0	0-0	0-0	0-0	0-0	0-0	0-0	0-0	0-0	0-1
DeJean, Mike	1-0	0-0	0-0	0-0	0-0	0-0	1-0	0-0	0-1	0-0	0-2	0-0	0-0	0-0	0-0	2-3
Dohmann, Scott	0-0	0-0	0-0	0-0	1-0	0-0	1-0	0-0	0-0	0-0	0-1	0-0	0-0	0-0	0-0	2-1
Esposito, Mike	0-0	0-0	0-0	0-0	0-0	0-0	0-0	0-0	0-0	0-1	0-0	0-0	0-0	0-0	0-0	0-1
Francis, Jeff	4-0	1-0	0-0	1-0	1-0	0-0	1-1	0-2	1-0	1-0	0-2	1-3	1-1	1-0	1-3	14-12
Fuentes, Brian	0-1	0-0	0-0	0-0	0-0	0-0	0-0	0-0	0-0	1-0	0-1	0-3	1-0	0-0	0-0	2-5
Jennings, Jason	0-2	0-1	1-0	0-0	0-0	0-1	1-1	1-1	0-0	0-0	1-1	0-0	1-0	1-0	1-1	6-9
Kennedy, Joe	0-0	0-0	0-1	0-0	0-1	0-0	0-1	0-0	0-0	0-1	1-0	2-1	0-1	0-1	1-1	4-8
Kim, Byung-Hyun	0-2	0-0	0-2	0-0	1-1	0-0	0-1	0-0	0-1	0-0	1-1	0-0	0-1	2-2	5-12
Kim, Sunny	0-0	0-0	0-0	0-0	0-0	2-0	0-0	0-1	0-0	0-0	1-0	0-0	0-0	0-0	0-0	5-1
Miceli, Dan	0-0	0-0	0-0	0-1	0-0	0-0	0-0	0-0	0-0	0-0	0-0	1-1	0-0	0-0	0-0	1-2
Neal, Blaine	0-0	0-0	1-0	0-0	0-0	0-0	0-0	0-0	0-0	0-0	0-0	0-0	0-1	0-0	0-1	1-2
Speier, Ryan	0-1	1-0	0-0	0-0	0-0	0-0	0-0	0-0	0-0	0-0	0-0	1-0	0-0	0-0	0-0	2-1
Tsao, Chin-hui	0-0	1-0	0-0	0-0	0-0	0-0	0-0	0-0	0-0	0-0	0-0	0-0	0-0	0-0	0-0	1-0
Williams, Randy	1-1	0-0	0-0	0-0	0-0	0-0	0-0	1-0	0-0	0-0	0-0	0-0	0-0	0-0	0-0	2-1
Witasick, Jay	0-0	0-0	0-0	0-0	0-0	0-0	0-0	0-0	0-0	0-0	0-0	0-1	0-0	0-2	0-0	0-4
Wright, Jamey	0-2	1-0	0-0	0-1	1-0	0-2	1-0	0-2	0-1	1-0	0-1	1-2	1-1	1-0	0-1	1-1	8-16
Totals	7-11	4-2	3-4	3-3	3-3	1-5	11-8	1-5	3-4	2-4	3-7	7-11	7-11	4-4	2-4	6-9	67-95

No-decisions-- Matt Anderson, Aquilino Lopez, Javier Lopez, Bobby Seay, Allan Simpson.
INTERLEAGUE: Jason Jennings 1-0, Byung-Hyun Kim 0-1, Jeff Francis 0-1 vs. Orioles; Joe Kennedy 0-1, Byung-Hyun Kim 0-1, Jeff Francis 0-1 vs. White Sox; Jeff Francis 0-1, Blaine Neal 0-1, Jamey Wright 0-1 vs. Indians; Jamey Wright 1-0, Jason Jennings 0-1, Byung-Hyun Kim 1-0 vs. Tigers; Byung-Hyun Kim 1-0, Jeff Francis 1-0, Joe Kennedy 1-0 vs. Royals. Total: 6-9.

FLORIDA—83-79

Pitcher	Ari. W-L	Atl. W-L	Chi. W-L	Cin. W-L	Col. W-L	Hou. W-L	L.A. W-L	Mil. W-L	N.Y. W-L	Phi. W-L	Pit. W-L	S.D. W-L	S.F. W-L	St.L. W-L	Was. W-L	A.L. W-L	Totals W-L
Alfonseca, Antonio	0-0	0-0	0-0	0-0	0-0	0-0	0-0	1-0	0-0	0-0	0-0	0-0	0-0	0-0	0-1	0-0	1-1
Beckett, Josh	0-0	2-0	0-2	0-0	2-0	1-0	1-0	0-2	2-1	1-1	0-0	1-1	2-0	0-0	3-0	0-1	15-8
Bump, Nate	0-0	0-1	0-0	0-0	0-0	0-0	0-0	0-0	0-0	0-1	0-0	0-0	0-0	0-1	0-0	0-3
Burnett, A.J.	2-0	0-4	1-0	0-0	0-0	0-2	1-0	0-1	1-1	2-2	0-0	0-1	2-0	1-1	1-0	1-0	12-12

Pitcher	Ari. W-L	Atl. W-L	Chi. W-L	Cin. W-L	Col. W-L	Hou. W-L	L.A. W-L	Mil. W-L	N.Y. W-L	Phi. W-L	Pit. W-L	S.D. W-L	S.F. W-L	St.L. W-L	Was. W-L	A.L. W-L	Totals W-L
Castillo, Frank	0-0	0-0	0-0	0-0	0-0	0-0	0-0	0-0	0-1	0-0	0-0	0-0	0-0	0-0	0-0	0-0	0-1
delos Santos, Valerio	0-0	0-0	0-0	0-0	0-1	0-0	0-0	1-0	0-0	0-0	0-0	0-0	0-0	0-0	0-0	0-0	1-2
Jones, Todd	0-1	0-1	0-0	0-0	0-0	0-0	0-0	0-1	0-0	0-0	0-1	0-0	0-0	0-0	0-0	1-1	1-5
Leiter, Al	0-0	1-0	0-1	0-0	0-1	0-0	0-0	0-0	0-1	0-2	0-0	0-1	0-0	0-0	0-0	2-0	3-7
Mecir, Jim	0-0	0-0	0-0	0-0	0-0	0-0	1-0	0-0	0-1	0-1	0-0	0-0	0-0	0-0	0-0	0-2	1-4
Moehler, Brian	1-0	0-3	0-0	0-2	0-0	0-0	1-0	1-0	1-2	1-0	0-2	0-0	0-0	0-0	1-2	0-1	6-12
Mota, Guillermo	0-0	0-0	0-1	0-0	0-0	0-0	0-0	0-0	0-1	0-0	0-0	0-0	1-0	0-0	0-0	1-0	2-2
Olsen, Scott	0-0	0-0	0-0	0-0	0-0	0-0	0-0	0-0	0-0	0-0	0-0	0-0	0-0	0-0	1-0	1-0	2-0
Perisho, Matt	0-0	0-0	0-0	1-0	0-0	0-0	0-0	0-0	0-0	0-0	0-0	0-0	0-0	0-0	0-0	1-0	2-0
Quantrill, Paul	0-0	0-0	0-0	0-0	0-0	0-0	0-0	0-1	0-0	0-0	0-0	0-0	0-0	0-0	0-0	0-0	0-1
Resop, Chris	0-0	1-0	0-0	0-0	0-0	0-0	0-0	0-0	1-0	0-0	0-0	0-0	0-0	0-0	0-0	0-0	2-0
Riedling, John	0-0	1-0	0-0	0-0	0-0	0-0	0-0	0-0	0-0	1-0	0-0	0-0	0-0	0-0	0-1	2-0	4-1
Valdez, Ismael	0-0	0-0	0-0	0-0	0-1	0-0	0-0	0-0	0-1	0-0	0-0	1-0	1-0	0-0	0-0	0-0	2-2
Vargas, Jason	1-0	0-0	1-0	1-0	0-0	0-1	1-0	0-0	0-0	0-0	1-0	0-1	0-0	0-1	0-0	0-2	5-5
Villone, Ron	0-0	2-0	0-0	0-0	0-0	0-0	0-1	0-0	1-0	0-0	0-0	0-0	0-1	0-0	0-0	0-0	3-2
Willis, Dontrelle	0-0	1-1	2-1	2-0	1-0	2-0	1-1	0-0	3-1	3-2	2-0	1-0	0-2	0-1	3-1	1-0	22-10
Totals	4-2	8-10	4-5	4-2	3-3	4-3	5-2	3-4	8-10	9-10	3-4	2-4	4-2	3-4	9-9	10-5	83-79

No-decisions-- Yorman Bazardo, Chad Bentz, Jim Crowell, Josh Johnson, Logan Kensing, Randy Messenger, Travis Smith.

INTERLEAGUE: Todd Jones 0-1, Jim Mecir 0-1, Al Leiter 1-0 vs. Angels; Jim Mecir 0-1, Dontrelle Willis 1-0, Josh Beckett 0-1 vs. Mariners; Al Leiter 1-0, A.J. Burnett 1-0, Matt Perisho 1-0, John Riedling 1-0, Guillermo Mota 1-0, Scott Olsen 1-0 vs. Devil Rays; Todd Jones 0-1, John Riedling 1-0, Brian Moehler 0-1 vs. Rangers. Total: 10-5.

HOUSTON—89-73

Pitcher	Ari. W-L	Atl. W-L	Chi. W-L	Cin. W-L	Col. W-L	Fla. W-L	L.A. W-L	Mil. W-L	N.Y. W-L	Phi. W-L	Pit. W-L	S.D. W-L	S.F. W-L	St.L. W-L	Was. W-L	A.L. W-L	Totals W-L
Astacio, Ezequiel	1-0	0-1	1-0	0-1	0-0	0-0	0-0	0-0	0-0	0-0	1-1	0-0	0-1	0-0	0-1	0-1	3-6
Backe, Brandon	0-0	1-1	2-0	1-0	0-0	0-1	0-0	1-0	1-0	0-0	2-0	1-0	1-0	0-1	0-1	0-4	10-8
Clemens, Roger	1-1	0-0	1-1	2-1	1-0	2-0	0-0	0-2	0-0	1-0	0-1	0-1	2-0	1-1	1-0	0-1	13-8
Duckworth, Brandon	0-0	0-0	0-0	0-0	0-0	0-0	0-0	0-0	0-0	0-0	0-0	0-0	0-0	0-1	0-0	0-0	0-1
Franco, John	0-0	0-0	0-0	0-0	0-0	0-0	0-0	0-1	0-0	0-0	0-0	0-0	0-0	0-0	0-0	0-0	0-1
Gallo, Mike	0-0	0-0	0-1	0-0	0-0	0-0	0-0	0-0	0-0	0-0	0-0	0-0	0-0	0-1	0-0	0-0	0-2
Harville, Chad	0-0	0-0	0-0	0-0	0-0	0-0	0-0	0-1	0-0	0-0	0-0	0-0	0-1	0-0	0-0	0-0	0-2
Lidge, Brad	0-0	0-0	0-2	1-0	0-0	0-0	1-0	1-0	0-0	0-0	0-2	0-0	0-0	0-0	0-0	0-0	4-4
Oswalt, Roy	1-0	0-1	2-1	4-0	1-0	0-1	1-1	1-2	0-1	2-0	1-1	2-0	0-1	1-2	1-0	3-1	20-12
Pettitte, Andy	0-1	0-1	0-1	2-1	1-0	1-0	1-0	4-0	1-0	2-0	3-1	1-0	0-2	0-1	1-0	1-1	17-9
Qualls, Chad	0-0	0-0	0-0	0-1	1-0	0-0	0-1	0-0	0-0	1-0	0-1	0-0	3-1	0-0	1-0	0-0	6-4
Rodriguez, Wandy	0-1	0-0	1-3	2-0	1-0	0-0	0-0	2-0	1-0	0-0	1-0	0-2	0-0	0-2	1-1	1-1	10-10
Springer, Russ	0-0	0-1	0-0	0-0	0-0	0-1	0-1	1-0	1-0	1-1	0-0	0-0	0-0	0-1	1-0	0-0	4-4
Wheeler, Dan	0-0	0-1	0-0	0-0	0-0	0-0	0-0	0-0	1-2	0-0	1-0	0-0	0-0	0-0	0-0	0-0	2-3
Totals	3-3	1-5	7-9	12-4	5-1	3-4	4-2	10-5	5-5	6-0	9-7	4-3	3-4	5-11	5-2	7-8	89-73

No-decisions-- Mike Burns, Travis Driskill, Scott Strickland.

INTERLEAGUE: Brandon Backe 0-1, Andy Pettitte 0-1, Wandy Rodriguez 0-1 vs. Orioles; Roger Clemens 1-0, Roy Oswalt 1-0, Brandon Backe 0-1 vs. Royals; Brandon Backe 0-2, Ezequiel Astacio 0-1, Roy Oswalt 1-1, Chad Qualls 1-0 vs. Rangers; Wandy Rodriguez 1-0, Brad Lidge 1-0, Roy Oswalt 1-0 vs. Blue Jays. Total: 7-8.

LOS ANGELES—71-91

Pitcher	Ari. W-L	Atl. W-L	Chi. W-L	Cin. W-L	Col. W-L	Fla. W-L	Hou. W-L	Mil. W-L	N.Y. W-L	Phi. W-L	Pit. W-L	S.D. W-L	S.F. W-L	St.L. W-L	Was. W-L	A.L. W-L	Totals W-L
Alvarez, Wilson	0-0	0-1	0-1	0-0	0-0	0-0	0-0	0-0	0-0	0-0	0-0	0-0	0-1	1-1	0-0	0-0	1-4
Brazoban, Yhency	1-1	0-0	0-1	0-1	0-1	0-0	0-1	0-0	0-0	0-2	0-0	0-0	3-2	0-0	0-0	0-1	4-10
Broxton, Jonathan	0-0	0-0	0-0	0-0	0-0	0-0	0-0	0-0	0-0	0-0	0-0	1-0	0-0	0-0	0-0	0-0	1-0
Carrara, Giovanni	0-1	2-0	0-0	0-0	2-1	0-0	0-0	2-0	0-1	0-0	0-0	1-0	0-0	0-0	0-0	0-1	7-4
Dessens, Elmer	0-0	0-0	0-0	0-0	0-0	1-0	0-0	0-0	0-0	0-0	0-0	0-2	0-0	0-0	0-0	0-0	1-2
Erickson, Scott	0-0	0-0	0-0	0-0	0-0	0-0	0-0	0-0	0-0	0-0	0-0	1-1	0-0	0-1	0-1	0-1	1-4
Gagne, Eric	0-0	0-0	0-0	0-0	0-0	0-0	0-0	0-0	0-0	0-0	0-0	0-0	0-0	0-0	0-0	1-0	1-0
Houlton, D.J.	0-1	1-0	0-1	0-1	0-1	0-1	1-0	0-1	0-0	1-0	2-1	0-1	0-0	0-0	0-1	1-1	6-9
Jackson, Edwin	0-0	0-0	0-0	0-0	0-1	0-1	1-0	0-0	0-0	1-0	0-0	0-0	0-0	0-0	0-0	0-0	2-2
Kuo, Hong-Chih	0-1	0-0	0-0	0-0	0-0	0-0	0-0	0-0	0-0	0-0	0-0	0-0	0-0	0-0	0-0	0-0	0-1
Lowe, Derek	0-3	0-0	1-1	1-1	1-0	1-1	0-1	0-0	0-0	1-0	2-0	2-2	1-2	0-2	0-0	2-2	12-15
Osoria, Franquelis	0-1	0-0	0-0	0-0	0-0	0-0	0-0	0-0	0-0	0-0	0-1	0-0	0-0	0-0	0-0	0-0	0-2
Penny, Brad	1-0	0-0	0-1	1-0	2-1	0-1	0-1	1-1	0-0	0-0	1-1	0-0	0-1	0-1	0-1	0-1	7-9
Perez, Odalis	0-0	0-2	0-0	1-2	0-0	1-0	0-0	1-0	0-0	2-0	0-2	2-0	0-1	0-1	0-0	0-0	7-8
Sanchez, Duaner	0-2	0-0	0-0	0-0	0-1	0-0	0-1	0-0	0-0	0-0	0-0	2-0	0-1	1-0	0-0	0-2	4-7
Schmoll, Steve	1-0	0-0	0-0	0-0	0-1	0-0	0-0	0-0	0-0	0-1	0-0	0-0	1-0	0-0	0-0	0-0	2-2
Weaver, Jeff	1-2	1-0	0-0	0-0	2-2	0-1	1-1	0-1	0-0	0-0	1-0	2-0	1-2	2-0	0-1	1-2	14-11
Wunsch, Kelly	1-0	0-0	0-0	0-0	0-0	0-0	0-0	0-0	0-0	0-0	0-0	0-0	0-0	0-0	0-0	0-1	1-1
Totals	5-13	3-3	2-4	4-3	8-11	2-5	2-4	5-1	3-3	3-3	5-2	11-7	9-10	2-5	2-4	5-13	71-91

No-decisions-- Buddy Carlyle, Derek Thompson.

INTERLEAGUE: D.J. Houlton 0-1, Duaner Sanchez 0-1, Yhency Brazoban 0-1 vs. White Sox; Derek Lowe 1-0, Duaner Sanchez 0-1, Jeff Weaver 1-0 vs. Tigers; Jeff Weaver 0-1, Brad Penny 0-1, Derek Lowe 0-1 vs. Royals; Scott Erickson 0-1, Kelly Wunsch 0-1, Brad Penny 0-1, Giovanni Carrara 0-1, Derek Lowe 1-0, Jeff Weaver 0-1 vs. Angels; Eric Gagne 1-0, Derek Lowe 0-1, D.J. Houlton 1-0 vs. Twins. Total: 5-13.

MILWAUKEE—81-81

Pitcher	Ari. W-L	Atl. W-L	Chi. W-L	Cin. W-L	Col. W-L	Fla. W-L	Hou. W-L	L.A. W-L	N.Y. W-L	Phi. W-L	Pit. W-L	S.D. W-L	S.F. W-L	St.L. W-L	Was. W-L	A.L. W-L	Totals W-L
Adams, Mike	0-0	0-0	0-0	0-0	0-0	0-0	0-0	0-0	0-0	0-0	0-0	0-0	0-0	0-1	0-0	0-0	0-1
Bottalico, Ricky	0-0	0-0	1-0	0-0	0-0	0-0	0-0	0-0	0-0	0-0	1-0	0-0	0-0	0-0	0-1	0-0	2-2
Capellan, Jose	0-0	0-0	0-0	1-0	0-0	0-1	0-0	0-0	0-0	0-0	0-0	0-0	0-0	0-0	0-0	0-0	1-1
Capuano, Chris	1-0	1-1	2-0	1-2	2-0	2-0	0-2	1-1	0-0	0-1	1-1	1-0	1-1	3-0	0-1	2-2	18-12
Davis, Doug	0-0	0-0	2-1	1-0	0-0	2-2	0-0	0-1	1-0	2-1	1-0	0-0	0-4	0-1	2-1	0-0	11-11
Davis, Kane	0-0	0-0	0-0	1-0	0-0	0-0	0-0	0-0	0-0	0-0	0-1	0-0	0-0	0-0	0-0	0-0	1-1

Pitcher	Ari. W-L	Atl. W-L	Chi. W-L	Cin. W-L	Col. W-L	Fla. W-L	Hou. W-L	L.A. W-L	N.Y. W-L	Phi. W-L	Pit. W-L	S.D. W-L	S.F. W-L	St.L. W-L	Was. W-L	A.L. W-L	Totals W-L
de la Rosa, Jorge	0-0	0-0	1-0	0-1	0-0	0-0	0-0	0-0	0-0	0-0	1-0	0-1	0-0	0-0	0-0	0-0	2-2
Eveland, Dana	1-0	0-0	0-0	0-0	0-0	0-0	0-1	0-0	0-0	0-0	0-0	0-0	0-0	0-0	0-0	0-0	1-1
Glover, Gary	0-0	0-0	0-0	2-0	1-0	0-0	0-0	0-0	0-0	0-0	0-2	0-1	1-0	1-0	0-0	0-1	5-4
Helling, Rick	0-0	0-0	0-1	1-0	0-0	0-0	1-0	0-0	1-0	0-0	0-0	0-0	0-0	0-0	0-0	0-0	3-1
Lehr, Justin	0-1	0-0	0-0	0-0	0-0	0-0	0-0	0-0	0-0	0-0	1-0	0-0	0-0	0-0	0-0	0-0	1-1
Obermueller, Wes	0-0	0-0	0-0	0-0	0-0	0-1	0-1	0-1	0-0	0-0	0-0	0-1	0-0	0-0	1-0	0-0	1-4
Ohka, Tomo	1-1	0-0	0-1	1-2	0-0	1-0	1-1	0-0	0-0	1-0	0-1	0-0	0-0	0-0	1-0	1-0	7-6
Phelps, Tommy	0-0	0-0	0-0	0-0	0-0	0-0	0-0	0-1	0-0	0-0	0-1	0-0	0-0	0-0	0-0	0-0	0-2
Santana, Julio	0-0	0-1	0-1	0-1	0-0	0-0	0-0	0-0	1-2	1-0	0-0	0-0	0-0	1-0	0-0	0-0	3-5
Santos, Victor	0-0	0-1	0-1	1-0	2-0	0-1	0-1	0-1	0-0	0-1	0-1	0-0	1-1	0-2	0-1	0-2	4-13
Sheets, Ben	1-0	2-0	0-1	0-0	0-1	1-0	1-2	0-0	0-0	1-1	1-0	0-0	1-0	0-3	0-0	2-0	10-9
Turnbow, Derrick	0-0	0-0	3-1	1-0	0-0	0-0	0-0	0-0	1-0	0-0	1-0	0-0	0-0	0-0	0-0	0-0	7-1
Wise, Matt	0-0	0-0	0-0	0-0	0-0	0-0	0-0	0-0	0-1	1-0	0-0	0-1	1-1	1-0	1-1	0-0	4-4
Totals	4-2	3-3	9-7	10-6	5-1	4-3	5-10	1-5	3-3	4-5	9-7	3-4	4-3	5-11	4-4	8-7	81-81

INTERLEAGUE: Gary Glover 0-1, Doug Davis 1-0, Matt Wise 1-1, Chris Capuano 1-0, Victor Santos 0-1 vs. Twins; Doug Davis 1-0, Ben Sheets 1-0, Chris Capuano 0-1 vs. Yankees; Chris Capuano 0-1, Tomo Ohka 1-0, Victor Santos 0-1 vs. Devil Rays; Doug Davis 0-1, Ben Sheets 1-0, Chris Capuano 1-0 vs. Blue Jays. Total: 8-7.

NEW YORK—83-79

Pitcher	Ari. W-L	Atl. W-L	Chi. W-L	Cin. W-L	Col. W-L	Fla. W-L	Hou. W-L	L.A. W-L	Mil. W-L	Phi. W-L	Pit. W-L	S.D. W-L	S.F. W-L	St.L. W-L	Was. W-L	A.L. W-L	Totals W-L
Bell, Heath	0-0	0-0	0-1	0-0	0-0	0-1	0-1	0-0	0-0	0-0	0-0	0-0	0-0	0-0	1-0	0-0	1-3
Benson, Kris	0-1	0-0	0-1	1-0	1-0	1-1	0-1	1-0	0-0	1-0	0-0	1-0	1-1	0-1	0-2	2-0	10-8
DeJean, Mike	0-0	0-0	1-0	1-0	0-0	0-0	1-0	0-0	0-1	0-0	0-0	0-0	0-0	0-0	0-0	0-0	3-1
Glavine, Tom	1-0	1-2	1-0	1-1	1-1	0-1	0-1	0-0	0-2	1-0	1-1	1-1	1-1	3-1	1-2	0-0	13-13
Heilman, Aaron	0-0	1-1	0-0	0-0	0-0	2-1	1-0	0-0	0-0	1-0	0-0	0-0	0-1	0-0	0-0	0-0	5-3
Hernandez, Roberto	0-0	1-1	0-0	0-0	0-0	2-0	1-1	0-0	0-1	0-0	0-0	0-0	0-1	4-1	0-1	0-0	8-6
Ishii, Kazuhisa	0-0	0-1	0-0	0-1	0-1	1-0	0-0	0-1	1-2	0-1	0-1	0-0	0-1	0-0	0-2	0-0	3-9
Looper, Braden	0-0	0-1	0-0	0-1	0-0	1-0	0-0	0-1	1-1	0-0	0-1	1-0	0-0	0-0	1-2	0-0	4-7
Martinez, Pedro	2-0	3-2	0-0	0-0	0-0	2-1	1-0	1-1	1-1	2-1	1-0	0-1	0-0	1-1	1-1	0-0	15-8
Matthews, Mike	0-0	0-0	0-0	0-0	0-0	0-0	0-0	0-0	0-0	0-0	0-0	0-0	0-0	0-0	1-0	0-0	1-0
Padilla, Juan	0-0	0-0	0-0	0-0	0-0	0-1	0-0	0-0	0-0	2-0	0-0	0-0	0-0	1-0	0-0	0-0	3-1
Ring, Royce	0-0	0-0	0-0	0-0	0-0	0-0	0-0	0-0	0-0	0-1	0-0	0-0	0-0	0-0	0-1	0-0	0-2
Seo, Jae	1-0	0-0	1-0	0-0	1-0	0-0	1-0	0-0	1-0	0-0	0-0	0-0	0-1	2-1	0-0	0-0	8-2
Takatsu, Shingo	0-0	0-0	0-0	0-0	0-0	0-0	0-0	0-0	1-0	0-0	0-0	0-0	0-0	0-0	0-0	0-0	1-0
Trachsel, Steve	0-0	0-2	0-0	0-0	0-0	0-0	0-0	0-0	0-1	0-0	0-0	1-0	0-1	0-0	0-0	0-0	1-4
Zambrano, Victor	2-0	0-3	0-0	0-0	1-1	0-2	0-1	1-0	0-0	0-1	0-0	0-0	0-0	0-2	0-1	0-0	7-12
Totals	6-1	6-13	4-2	3-3	4-3	10-8	5-5	3-3	3-3	11-7	3-3	4-2	3-3	2-5	11-8	5-10	83-79

No-decisions-- Manny Aybar, Danny Graves, Tim Hamulack, Felix Heredia, Dae-Sung Koo, Jose Santiago.
INTERLEAGUE: Kazuhisa Ishii 0-1, Braden Looper 1-1 vs. Angels; Victor Zambrano 0-1, Roberto Hernandez 0-1, Kris Benson 1-0, Braden Looper 0-1, Pedro Martinez 1-0, Tom Glavine 1-0 vs. Yankees; Tom Glavine 0-1, Royce Ring 0-1, Kris Benson 1-0 vs. Athletics; Kazuhisa Ishii 0-1, Pedro Martinez 1-0, Tom Glavine 0-1 vs. Mariners. Total: 5-10.

PHILIDELPHIA—88-74

Pitcher	Ari. W-L	Atl. W-L	Chi. W-L	Cin. W-L	Col. W-L	Fla. W-L	Hou. W-L	L.A. W-L	Mil. W-L	N.Y. W-L	Pit. W-L	S.D. W-L	S.F. W-L	St.L. W-L	Was. W-L	A.L. W-L	Totals W-L
Adams, Terry	0-0	0-0	0-0	0-0	0-0	0-0	0-0	0-0	0-1	0-1	0-0	0-0	0-0	0-0	0-0	0-0	0-2
Brito, Eude	0-0	1-0	0-0	0-1	0-0	0-1	0-0	0-0	0-0	0-0	0-0	0-0	0-0	0-0	0-0	0-0	1-2
Cormier, Rheal	0-0	0-0	0-0	1-0	0-0	0-0	0-0	0-0	1-0	0-0	0-0	0-0	0-0	0-0	2-1	0-1	4-2
Floyd, Gavin	0-0	0-1	0-0	0-0	0-0	0-0	0-0	0-0	0-0	0-0	0-0	0-0	1-0	0-0	0-0	0-0	1-2
Fultz, Aaron	1-0	1-0	0-0	0-0	0-0	0-0	0-0	0-0	0-0	0-0	1-0	0-0	0-0	0-0	1-0	0-0	4-0
Geary, Geoff	0-0	1-0	0-0	0-0	0-0	0-0	0-0	0-1	0-0	0-0	0-0	0-0	0-0	0-0	1-0	0-0	2-1
Lidle, Cory	0-1	2-1	0-0	1-0	1-1	2-2	0-1	0-2	1-1	1-1	1-0	0-0	0-0	1-0	2-0	1-1	13-11
Lieber, Jon	0-1	3-0	0-0	0-1	1-1	3-1	0-0	0-1	1-0	1-2	0-0	1-0	1-1	1-1	3-1	1-3	17-13
Lopez, Aquilino	0-0	0-0	0-0	0-0	0-0	0-0	0-0	0-1	0-0	0-0	0-0	0-0	0-0	0-0	0-0	0-0	0-1
Madson, Ryan	0-0	1-0	0-0	0-1	0-0	0-0	0-1	1-0	1-0	1-0	1-1	0-0	1-0	0-1	0-0	0-0	6-5
Myers, Brett	1-0	1-3	1-1	1-0	1-0	2-0	0-1	0-0	0-0	2-1	1-1	0-0	1-0	1-0	0-0	0-0	13-8
Padilla, Vicente	1-1	0-2	0-1	1-0	0-0	0-0	0-1	0-0	0-1	1-2	1-0	0-0	1-0	0-0	2-0	1-3	9-12
Tejeda, Robinson	0-0	0-0	0-0	0-0	0-0	0-0	0-0	0-0	0-1	0-1	0-1	2-0	1-0	0-0	0-1	1-0	4-3
Telemaco, Amaury	0-0	0-0	0-0	0-0	0-0	0-0	0-0	0-0	0-0	0-0	0-0	0-0	0-0	0-0	0-0	0-1	0-1
Urbina, Ugueth	0-0	0-0	0-0	0-0	1-0	1-0	0-0	1-0	0-0	0-2	0-0	1-0	0-0	0-0	0-0	0-0	4-3
Wagner, Billy	0-0	0-1	2-0	0-0	0-0	0-0	0-2	1-0	0-0	0-0	0-0	0-0	0-0	1-0	0-0	0-0	4-3
Wolf, Randy	1-0	0-1	0-0	0-0	0-0	1-2	0-0	0-0	1-0	1-1	0-0	0-0	1-0	0-0	0-0	1-0	6-4
Worrell, Tim	0-0	0-0	0-0	0-0	0-0	0-0	0-0	0-0	0-0	0-0	0-0	0-0	0-0	0-0	0-1	0-0	0-1
Totals	4-3	10-9	4-2	4-3	4-2	10-9	0-6	3-3	5-4	7-11	4-3	6-0	5-1	4-2	11-8	7-8	88-74

No-decisions-- Pedro Liriano.
INTERLEAGUE: Randy Wolf 1-0, Vicente Padilla 0-1, Cory Lidle 1-0 vs. Orioles; Jon Lieber 0-1, Vicente Padilla 0-1, Rheal Cormier 0-1 vs. Red Sox; Robinson Tejeda 1-0, Cory Lidle 0-1, Jon Lieber 0-1 vs. Athletics; Jon Lieber 0-1, Vicente Padilla 0-1, Geoff Geary 1-0 vs. Mariners; Jon Lieber 1-0, Aaron Fultz 1-0, Vicente Padilla 1-0 vs. Rangers. Total: 7-8.

PITTSBURGH—67-95

Pitcher	Ari. W-L	Atl. W-L	Chi. W-L	Cin. W-L	Col. W-L	Fla. W-L	Hou. W-L	L.A. W-L	Mil. W-L	N.Y. W-L	Phi. W-L	S.D. W-L	S.F. W-L	St.L. W-L	Was. W-L	A.L. W-L	Totals W-L
Duke, Zach	0-0	1-0	2-0	0-1	1-0	0-0	0-1	1-0	1-0	1-0	1-0	0-0	0-0	0-0	0-0	0-0	8-2
Fogg, Josh	1-0	0-0	0-2	0-0	1-1	2-0	0-2	0-2	0-0	0-1	0-0	1-0	1-0	0-2	0-1	0-0	6-11
Gonzalez, Mike	0-0	0-1	0-0	1-1	0-0	0-0	0-0	0-0	0-0	0-0	0-0	0-0	0-0	0-0	0-0	0-0	1-3
Gorzelanny, Tom	0-0	0-0	0-0	0-0	0-0	0-0	0-1	0-0	0-0	0-0	0-0	0-0	0-0	0-0	0-0	0-0	0-1
Grabow, John	0-1	0-1	1-0	0-1	0-0	0-0	0-0	0-0	0-0	0-0	0-0	0-0	1-0	0-0	0-0	0-0	2-3
Maholm, Paul	0-0	0-0	1-0	1-0	0-0	0-0	0-0	1-0	0-0	0-0	0-0	0-0	0-0	0-0	0-0	0-0	3-1
Meadows, Brian	0-0	0-0	0-0	0-0	0-0	1-0	0-0	0-0	1-0	0-0	0-0	0-0	0-0	0-0	1-1		3-1
Mesa, Jose	0-0	0-0	0-2	0-1	0-1	0-0	0-0	0-2	1-0	0-0	1-0	0-0	0-1	0-0	0-1		2-8

Pitcher	Ari. W-L	Atl. W-L	Chi. W-L	Cin. W-L	Col. W-L	Fla. W-L	Hou. W-L	L.A. W-L	Mil. W-L	N.Y. W-L	Phi. W-L	S.D. W-L	S.F. W-L	St.L. W-L	Was. W-L	A.L. W-L	Totals W-L
Perez, Oliver	0-1	1-0	0-0	1-0	1-0	0-0	1-0	1-0	0-1	0-0	0-0	0-1	0-1	0-0	1-0	1-1	7-5
Redman, Mark	0-1	0-1	0-2	0-1	2-0	0-0	0-1	0-0	2-1	0-1	0-1	0-1	0-2	0-2	0-1	1-0	5-15
Snell, Ian	0-0	0-0	0-0	0-0	0-0	0-0	1-1	0-1	0-0	0-0	0-0	0-0	0-0	0-0	0-0	0-0	1-2
Torres, Salomon	0-0	0-0	1-0	1-1	0-0	0-0	2-0	0-0	0-1	0-0	0-0	0-0	0-0	1-1	0-1	0-1	5-5
Vogelsong, Ryan	0-0	0-0	0-0	1-0	0-0	0-1	0-0	0-0	0-1	0-0	0-0	0-0	1-0	0-0	0-0	0-0	2-2
Wells, Kip	1-0	1-0	0-3	1-3	0-0	0-1	1-1	0-1	1-2	0-1	2-0	0-1	0-0	0-2	0-1	1-2	8-18
White, Rick	1-0	0-0	0-0	0-0	0-1	1-0	1-1	0-0	0-1	0-0	0-1	0-1	0-0	0-1	0-0	1-1	4-7
Williams, Dave	1-0	0-1	0-2	1-0	2-0	0-1	1-1	0-0	1-0	1-0	0-2	1-0	1-1	1-3	0-0	0-0	10-11
Totals	4-3	3-4	5-11	7-9	7-3	4-3	7-9	2-5	7-9	3-3	3-4	3-4	2-4	4-12	1-5	5-7	67-95

No-decisions-- Bryan Bullington, Matt Capps, Mike Johnston.
INTERLEAGUE: Salomon Torres 0-1, Brian Meadows 1-0, Kip Wells 1-0 vs. Orioles; Rick White 1-1, Kip Wells 0-1 vs. Red Sox; Kip Wells 0-1, Jose Mesa 0-1, Oliver Perez 0-1 vs. Yankees; Mark Redman 1-0, Oliver Perez 1-0, Brian Meadows 0-1 vs. Devil Rays. Total: 5-7.

SAN DIEGO—82-80

Pitcher	Ari. W-L	Atl. W-L	Chi. W-L	Cin. W-L	Col. W-L	Fla. W-L	Hou. W-L	L.A. W-L	Mil. W-L	N.Y. W-L	Phi. W-L	Pit. W-L	S.F. W-L	St.L. W-L	Was. W-L	A.L. W-L	Totals W-L
Astacio, Pedro	1-0	0-0	0-0	0-1	1-0	0-0	0-0	0-0	0-0	0-0	0-1	0-0	1-0	0-0	1-0	0-0	4-2
Cassidy, Scott	0-0	0-0	0-0	0-0	0-0	0-0	0-0	0-1	0-0	0-0	0-0	0-0	1-0	0-0	0-0	0-0	1-1
Eaton, Adam	1-0	1-0	2-0	0-0	2-2	1-0	0-0	2-1	0-0	0-0	0-0	0-1	1-0	0-0	0-0	1-1	11-5
Hammond, Chris	1-0	0-0	0-0	1-0	1-0	0-0	0-0	0-0	0-0	0-1	0-0	0-0	1-0	0-0	0-0	0-0	5-1
Hensley, Clay	0-0	0-0	0-0	0-0	0-0	0-0	0-0	0-1	0-0	0-0	0-0	0-0	1-0	0-0	0-0	0-0	1-1
Hoffman, Trevor	0-0	0-0	0-0	0-0	0-1	0-0	0-0	0-0	0-0	0-1	0-0	0-1	1-0	0-0	0-2	0-1	1-6
Lawrence, Brian	1-2	0-0	0-1	0-2	2-1	0-0	1-1	1-0	0-2	0-1	0-1	1-1	2-1	0-0	0-1	1-1	7-15
Linebrink, Scott	1-0	0-0	0-0	0-0	2-0	0-0	0-0	0-1	1-0	0-0	0-0	0-0	0-0	2-0	1-0	0-1	8-1
May, Darrell	0-0	0-0	0-1	0-0	1-0	0-0	0-0	0-1	0-0	0-0	0-0	0-0	0-0	0-0	1-1		1-3
Otsuka, Akinori	0-4	0-1	0-0	0-0	1-0	0-0	0-0	0-1	0-0	0-0	0-1	0-0	1-0	0-0	0-0		2-8
Park, Chan Ho	1-0	1-0	0-0	0-0	0-1	0-0	1-0	0-0	1-0	0-0	1-0	0-0	0-0	0-0	0-0		4-3
Peavy, Jake	3-0	0-0	1-0	0-0	1-1	1-1	1-1	0-0	0-1	0-1	1-0	0-0	1-0	0-0	1-1	2-2	13-7
Quantrill, Paul	0-0	0-0	0-0	0-0	0-1	0-0	0-0	0-0	0-1	0-0	0-0	0-0	0-0	0-0	0-0		1-1
Redding, Tim	0-1	0-0	0-0	0-0	0-0	0-0	0-0	0-0	0-0	0-0	0-1	0-0	0-1	0-0	0-1		0-5
Reyes, Dennys	0-0	1-0	0-0	0-0	1-0	0-0	0-1	0-0	1-0	0-0	0-0	0-0	0-0	0-0	0-0	0-1	3-2
Seanez, Rudy	0-0	1-0	0-0	0-0	0-0	0-1	1-0	0-0	0-0	0-0	1-0	2-1	0-0	0-0	1-0		7-1
Stauffer, Tim	0-1	0-0	0-1	1-0	0-0	0-0	0-0	0-2	0-0	0-0	0-0	1-0	0-1	0-0	0-1		3-6
Williams, Randy	0-0	0-0	0-0	0-0	0-0	0-0	0-0	0-0	0-0	0-0	0-0	1-0	0-0	0-0	0-0		1-0
Williams, Woody	0-2	0-0	0-1	0-1	0-1	0-1	1-1	3-1	1-0	1-1	0-0	1-0	2-0	0-1	0-0	0-2	9-12
Totals	9-10	5-1	3-4	2-4	11-7	4-2	3-4	7-11	4-3	2-4	0-6	4-3	12-6	4-3	5-1	7-11	82-80

No-decisions-- Craig Breslow, Sean Burroughs, Brian Falkenborg, Chris Oxspring.
INTERLEAGUE: Woody Williams 0-1, Scott Linebrink 1-0, Trevor Hoffman 0-1 vs. White Sox; Trevor Hoffman 0-1, Jake Peavy 0-1, Adam Eaton 1-0 vs. Indians; Jake Peavy 0-1, Adam Eaton 0-1, Woody Williams 0-1 vs. Tigers; Dennys Reyes 0-1, Brian Lawrence 1-0, Darrell May 1-0 vs. Twins; Jake Peavy 2-0, Brian Lawrence 0-1, Rudy Seanez 1-0, Tim Stauffer 0-1, Darrell May 0-1 vs. Mariners. Total: 7-11.

SAN FRANCISCO—75-87

Pitcher	Ari. W-L	Atl. W-L	Chi. W-L	Cin. W-L	Col. W-L	Fla. W-L	Hou. W-L	L.A. W-L	Mil. W-L	N.Y. W-L	Phi. W-L	Pit. W-L	S.D. W-L	St.L. W-L	Was. W-L	A.L. W-L	Totals W-L
Accardo, Jeremy	0-0	0-0	0-0	0-1	1-0	0-0	0-0	0-1	0-0	0-0	0-0	0-0	0-1	0-1	0-1	0-0	1-5
Benitez, Armando	0-1	0-0	0-0	0-0	0-0	0-0	0-0	1-2	0-0	0-0	0-0	0-0	1-0	0-0	0-0	0-0	2-3
Brower, Jim	1-0	0-0	0-0	0-0	1-0	0-0	0-0	0-0	0-0	0-0	0-0	0-1	0-0	0-0	0-0	0-0	2-1
Cain, Matt	1-0	0-0	1-0	0-0	0-1	0-0	0-0	0-0	0-0	0-0	0-0	0-0	0-0	0-0	0-0	0-0	2-1
Christiansen, Jason	1-0	0-0	1-0	0-0	1-0	0-0	0-0	0-1	0-0	0-0	0-0	0-0	1-0	0-0	1-0	1-0	6-1
Cooper, Brian	0-0	0-1	0-0	0-0	0-0	0-0	0-0	0-0	0-0	0-0	0-0	0-0	0-0	0-0	0-0	0-0	0-1
Correia, Kevin	0-0	0-1	0-1	2-0	0-0	0-1	0-0	0-0	0-0	0-1	0-0	0-0	0-1	0-0	0-0	0-0	2-5
Eyre, Scott	0-0	0-0	0-0	0-0	1-0	0-0	0-1	1-0	0-0	0-0	0-0	0-0	0-0	0-0	0-0	0-1	2-2
Fassero, Jeff	0-0	0-0	0-0	1-0	0-0	0-0	0-1	0-0	0-0	0-0	0-0	0-3	0-0	0-0	1-3		4-7
Hawkins, LaTroy	0-1	0-0	0-1	0-0	0-0	0-0	1-0	0-1	0-0	0-1	0-0	0-1	0-0	0-0	0-0		1-4
Hennessey, Brad	0-0	0-1	0-1	0-0	0-0	0-2	1-0	0-1	1-0	0-0	0-2	1-0	1-0	1-0	0-0		5-8
Herges, Matt	0-1	0-0	0-1	0-0	1-0	0-0	0-0	1-0	0-0	0-0	0-0	0-0	0-0	0-0	0-0		1-1
Kinney, Matt	0-0	0-0	0-0	0-0	0-0	0-0	0-0	0-0	0-0	0-0	0-0	0-0	1-0	0-0	0-0	0-0	2-0
Lowry, Noah	3-1	0-1	0-0	1-1	1-2	1-0	1-0	1-0	0-1	1-1	0-0	0-1	1-1	0-1	0-1	2-1	13-13
Munter, Scott	0-0	0-0	0-0	0-0	0-0	1-0	0-0	0-0	0-0	0-0	0-0	0-0	0-0	0-0	1-0		2-0
Rueter, Kirk	0-1	0-0	0-0	0-0	0-0	0-0	1-0	0-1	0-0	0-0	0-0	0-0	1-0	0-0	0-0	0-4	2-7
Schmidt, Jason	3-0	1-0	0-0	0-0	1-1	0-0	0-0	3-0	0-1	1-1	0-0	0-0	0-2	1-1	0-0	1-1	12-7
Taschner, Jack	0-0	0-0	0-0	0-0	1-0	0-0	0-0	0-0	0-0	0-0	0-0	0-0	0-0	1-0	0-0	0-0	2-0
Tomko, Brett	1-2	0-0	0-0	0-1	0-2	1-1	0-1	1-2	1-0	1-0	0-2	2-0	0-1	0-1	0-2		8-15
Walker, Tyler	1-0	1-0	0-1	0-0	1-1	0-0	0-1	1-0	0-0	1-0	0-0	1-0	1-1	0-0	0-0		6-4
Williams, Jerome	0-0	0-0	0-0	0-0	0-0	0-0	0-0	0-0	0-0	0-1	0-0	0-0	0-1	0-0	0-0	0-0	0-2
Totals	11-7	2-4	2-5	5-3	11-7	2-4	4-3	10-9	3-4	3-3	1-5	4-2	6-12	2-4	3-3	6-12	75-87

No-decisions-- Jesse Foppert, Al Levine, Brandon Puffer.
INTERLEAGUE: Brett Tomko 0-1, Jason Schmidt 0-1, Kirk Rueter 0-1 vs. Indians; Jason Schmidt 1-0, Kirk Rueter 0-1, Scott Eyre 0-1 vs. Tigers; Kirk Rueter 0-1, Jeff Fassero 0-1, Scott Munter 1-0 vs. Royals; Jason Christiansen 1-0, Jeff Fassero 0-1, Noah Lowry 1-0 vs. Twins; Kirk Rueter 0-1, Jeff Fassero 1-1, Noah Lowry 1-1, Brett Tomko 0-1 vs. Athletics. Total: 6-12.

ST. LOUIS—100-62

Pitcher	Ari. W-L	Atl. W-L	Chi. W-L	Cin. W-L	Col. W-L	Fla. W-L	Hou. W-L	L.A. W-L	Mil. W-L	N.Y. W-L	Phi. W-L	Pit. W-L	S.D. W-L	S.F. W-L	Was. W-L	A.L. W-L	Totals W-L
Carpenter, Chris	1-0	0-0	2-0	1-0	1-0	2-0	4-0	1-0	2-1	1-0	1-1	3-0	1-1	0-0	0-1	1-1	21-5
Eldred, Cal	0-0	0-0	0-0	0-0	0-0	0-0	1-0	0-0	0-0	0-0	0-0	0-0	0-0	0-0	0-0	0-0	1-0
Flores, Randy	0-0	0-0	2-0	0-0	0-0	0-0	0-0	0-0	1-0	0-0	0-0	0-1	0-0	0-0	0-0	0-0	3-1
Isringhausen, Jason	0-0	0-0	0-0	0-0	0-1	0-0	0-1	0-0	0-0	0-0	0-0	1-0	0-0	0-0	0-0	0-0	1-2
Jarvis, Kevin	0-0	0-0	0-0	0-0	0-0	0-0	0-1	0-0	0-0	0-0	0-0	0-0	0-0	0-0	0-0	0-0	0-1

Pitcher	Ari. W-L	Atl. W-L	Chi. W-L	Cin. W-L	Col. W-L	Fla. W-L	Hou. W-L	L.A. W-L	Mil. W-L	N.Y. W-L	Phi. W-L	Pit. W-L	S.D. W-L	S.F. W-L	Was. W-L	A.L. W-L	Totals W-L
Journell, Jimmy	0-0	0-1	0-0	0-0	0-0	0-0	0-0	0-0	0-0	0-0	0-0	0-0	0-0	0-0	0-0	0-0	0-1
King, Ray	0-1	1-0	1-0	0-2	1-0	0-0	0-0	0-0	0-0	0-0	0-0	0-0	0-1	0-0	0-0	1-0	4-4
Marquis, Jason	0-1	0-1	0-1	3-1	1-1	0-1	4-0	0-0	0-1	1-1	0-1	0-2	1-1	0-0	1-0	1-1	13-14
Morris, Matt	1-0	0-0	0-4	1-0	1-0	1-1	1-1	0-1	1-0	1-1	0-0	2-1	0-0	1-1	1-0	3-0	14-10
Mulder, Mark	1-0	2-0	1-2	2-2	0-1	0-0	1-1	1-0	1-1	0-0	0-0	3-0	1-0	1-0	0-0	2-1	16-8
Reyes, Al	0-0	0-0	1-1	1-0	0-0	0-0	0-0	0-0	0-0	1-0	1-1	0-0	0-0	0-0	0-0	0-0	4-2
Reyes, Anthony	0-0	0-0	0-1	0-0	0-0	0-0	0-0	1-0	0-0	0-0	0-0	0-0	0-0	0-0	0-0	0-0	1-1
Suppan, Jeff	2-0	0-1	1-1	0-0	0-1	1-1	0-0	2-0	4-0	1-0	0-2	1-0	0-0	1-1	1-1	2-2	16-10
Tavarez, Julian	0-0	0-0	0-0	0-0	0-0	0-0	0-2	0-0	0-1	1-0	0-0	0-0	0-0	0-0	1-0	0-0	2-3
Thompson, Brad	0-0	0-0	0-0	1-0	0-0	0-0	0-0	0-0	0-0	0-0	0-0	1-0	0-0	0-0	1-0	0-0	4-0
Totals	**5-2**	**3-3**	**6-10**	**11-5**	**4-4**	**4-3**	**11-5**	**5-2**	**11-5**	**5-2**	**2-4**	**12-4**	**3-4**	**4-2**	**4-2**	**10-5**	**100-62**

No-decisions-- Carmen Cali, Tyler Johnson, Bill Pulsipher, Adam Wainwright, Gabe White.
INTERLEAGUE: Matt Morris 1-0, Jeff Suppan 1-0, Chris Carpenter 0-1 vs. Red Sox; Mark Mulder 1-0, Matt Morris 1-0, Jeff Suppan 0-1 vs. Royals; Jason Marquis 1-0, Mark Mulder 0-1, Ray King 1-0 vs. Yankees; Mark Mulder 1-0, Matt Morris 1-0, Jeff Suppan 1-0 vs. Devil Rays; Jeff Suppan 0-1, Chris Carpenter 1-0, Jason Marquis 0-1 vs. Blue Jays. Total: 10-5.

WASHINGTON—81-81

Pitcher	Ari. W-L	Atl. W-L	Chi. W-L	Cin. W-L	Col. W-L	Fla. W-L	Hou. W-L	L.A. W-L	Mil. W-L	N.Y. W-L	Phi. W-L	Pit. W-L	S.D. W-L	S.F. W-L	St.L. W-L	A.L. W-L	Totals W-L
Armas, Tony	0-1	0-0	1-0	0-1	1-0	0-1	0-1	1-0	1-0	0-0	0-1	0-0	0-0	0-0	0-1	2-2	7-7
Ayala, Luis	0-0	2-1	0-1	0-1	0-0	2-0	0-0	0-0	0-1	2-1	1-0	1-0	0-0	1-0	0-0	1-1	8-7
Bergmann, Jay	1-0	0-0	0-0	0-0	0-0	0-0	0-0	0-0	1-0	0-0	0-0	0-0	0-0	0-0	0-0	0-0	2-0
Carrasco, Hector	0-0	1-1	1-0	0-0	0-0	1-0	0-1	0-0	0-0	0-0	1-2	1-0	0-0	0-0	0-0	0-0	5-4
Cordero, Chad	0-0	0-2	0-0	0-0	0-1	1-0	0-0	0-0	0-0	0-0	1-0	0-0	0-1	0-0	0-0	0-0	2-4
Day, Zach	0-0	1-1	0-0	0-0	0-0	0-0	0-0	0-0	0-0	0-1	0-0	0-0	0-0	0-0	0-0	0-0	1-2
Drese, Ryan	0-0	0-1	0-0	0-0	0-0	0-0	0-0	0-0	0-1	1-0	1-1	0-1	0-0	0-0	0-0	1-0	3-6
Eischen, Joey	0-0	0-0	1-0	0-0	0-0	0-0	0-0	0-0	0-0	1-0	0-0	0-0	0-0	0-0	0-0	0-0	2-1
Halama, John	0-0	0-0	0-0	0-0	0-0	0-0	0-0	0-0	0-0	0-1	0-0	0-0	0-0	0-0	0-1	0-0	0-3
Hernandez, Livan	2-0	0-1	2-0	0-1	0-1	2-1	0-1	1-0	1-0	2-2	1-2	1-0	0-0	0-1	1-0	2-0	15-10
Hughes, Travis	0-0	0-0	0-0	0-0	0-0	0-0	0-0	0-0	0-1	0-0	0-0	0-0	0-0	0-0	0-0	1-0	1-1
Kim, Sunny	0-0	0-0	0-0	0-0	0-0	1-0	0-0	0-0	0-0	0-1	0-1	0-0	0-0	0-0	0-0	0-0	1-2
Loaiza, Esteban	0-0	0-1	0-0	0-1	1-0	1-0	0-0	0-1	1-1	3-1	1-2	1-0	0-1	0-0	0-1	2-1	12-10
Majewski, Gary	0-0	1-1	0-0	0-0	0-0	0-0	0-0	0-0	0-1	1-2	0-0	0-0	0-0	0-0	0-0	2-0	4-4
Ohka, Tomo	0-0	2-0	0-0	0-0	0-0	0-2	0-0	0-0	0-1	0-0	0-0	0-0	0-0	0-0	0-0	1-0	4-3
Patterson, John	1-0	0-0	0-0	1-0	2-0	0-3	1-0	1-0	0-0	0-1	1-1	0-0	0-1	0-0	0-0	1-1	9-7
Rasner, Darrell	0-0	0-0	0-0	0-0	0-0	0-0	0-0	0-0	0-0	0-0	0-0	0-0	0-0	0-0	0-1	0-0	0-1
Rauch, Jon	0-1	0-0	0-0	0-0	0-0	0-0	0-0	0-1	0-0	0-0	0-0	0-0	0-0	2-1	0-0	0-0	2-4
Stanton, Mike	0-0	1-1	0-0	0-0	0-0	0-0	0-0	0-0	0-0	0-0	0-1	0-0	0-0	0-0	0-0	0-0	2-1
Tucker, T.J.	1-0	0-0	0-0	0-0	0-0	0-0	0-0	0-0	0-0	0-0	0-0	0-0	0-0	0-0	0-0	0-0	1-0
Vargas, Claudio	0-0	0-0	0-0	0-1	0-0	0-0	0-0	0-0	0-1	0-0	0-0	0-0	0-0	0-0	0-0	0-1	0-3
White, Matt	0-0	0-0	0-0	0-0	0-0	0-0	0-0	0-0	0-0	0-0	0-0	0-0	0-0	0-0	0-1	0-0	0-1
Totals	**4-2**	**9-10**	**5-1**	**1-5**	**4-2**	**9-9**	**2-5**	**4-2**	**4-4**	**8-11**	**8-11**	**5-1**	**1-5**	**3-3**	**2-4**	**12-6**	**81-81**

No-decisions-- Joe Horgan, C.J. Nitkowski, Antonio Osuna.
INTERLEAGUE: Esteban Loaiza 0-1, Gary Majewski 1-0, Ryan Drese 1-0 vs. Angels; Tony Armas 1-0, Esteban Loaiza 1-0, Livan Hernandez 1-0 vs. Athletics; Luis Ayala 1-0, John Patterson 1-0, Tony Armas 1-0 vs. Mariners; John Patterson 0-1, Tony Armas 0-1, Travis Hughes 1-0 vs. Rangers; Claudio Vargas 0-1, Tony Armas 0-1, Tomo Ohka 1-0, Esteban Loaiza 1-0, Luis Ayala 0-1, Livan Hernandez 1-0 vs. Blue Jays. Total: 12-6.

HOME RUNS BY PARKS

	At Ari.	At Atl.	At ChC.	At Cin.	At Col.	At Fla.	At Hou.	At LAD.	At Mil.	At NYM.	At Phi.	At Pit.	At StL.	At SD.	At SF.	At Was.	At A.L. Parks	Totals 2005	Totals 2004	HR Allow.
Arizona	97	7	8	2	16	2	2	11	1	2	6	3	3	13	4	2	12	191	135	193
Atlanta	4	89	3	17	4	9	2	8	2	8	13	1	4	2	5	10	3	184	178	145
Chicago	4	2	99	18	5	4	11	5	12	2	0	10	8	3	4	1	6	194	235	186
Cincinnati	2	5	16	126	5	1	5	6	10	2	6	7	8	8	4	3	8	222	194	219
Colorado	8	1	6	3	86	2	1	7	1	3	2	5	6	6	8	1	4	150	202	175
Florida	5	5	6	2	2	57	7	6	1	3	8	5	4	1	7	7	2	128	148	116
Houston	2	2	5	8	7	1	93	4	6	2	5	7	6	1	2	5	7	161	187	155
Los Angeles	10	1	4	6	5	1	1	80	5	2	3	4	3	5	7	5	7	149	203	182
Milwaukee	4	3	8	9	2	2	6	3	91	7	7	6	8	3	4	3	9	175	135	169
New York	9	8	3	5	4	5	2	4	9	83	18	4	1	1	7		8	175	185	135
Philadelphia	7	6	2	6	1	2	1	4	9	15	94	1	4	1	1	9	4	167	215	189
Pittsburgh	7	3	6	10	2	0	13	5	7	2	3	59	12	0	6	1	3	139	142	162
St. Louis	3	1	5	11	1	5	11	6	6	4	5	6	92	3	2	1	8	170	214	153
San Diego	12	4	4	3	14	0	1	3	1	3	3	5	6	54	9	3	5	130	139	146
San Francisco	10	1	1	5	9	2	1	8	3	2	3	4	2	2	64	4	7	128	183	151
Washington	2	7	3	4	2	8	8	2	4	5	11	5	0	2	1	46		117	151	140
A.L. clubs	11	9	16	11	5	8	6	10	9	3	14	8	4	13	4	4		135	139	
2005 Totals	**197**	**154**	**195**	**246**	**170**	**109**	**171**	**170**	**179**	**146**	**201**	**140**	**174**	**118**	**133**	**112**	**100**	**2580**	....	**2616**
2004 Totals	**187**	**176**	**233**	**220**	**221**	**154**	**187**	**192**	**149**	**152**	**228**	**135**	**170**	**132**	**165**	**155**	....	....	**2846**	....

AT ARIZONA (197):

Arizona (97)--Glaus 20, Clark 19, S. Green 12, L. Gonzalez 10, Tracy 9, Cruz Jr. 6, Cintron 5, Counsell 5, Jackson 2, Snyder 2, Stinnett 2, Terrero 2, Clayton 1, McCracken 1, Vazquez 1. Atlanta (4)--A. Jones 3, Johnson 1. Chicago (4)--Barrett 1, Hollandsworth 1, Lee 1, Ramirez 1. Cincinnati (2)--Dunn 1, Griffey Jr. 1. Colorado (8)--Ardoin 2, Atkins 1, Barmes 1, Gonzalez 1, Holliday 1, Mohr 1, Piedra 1. Detroit (1)--Infante 1. Florida (5)--Cabrera 2, Delgado 2, Encarnacion 1. Houston (2)--Ensberg 1, Lamb 1. Kansas City (3)--Buck 1, Gotay 1, Greinke 1. Los Angeles (10)--Kent 4, Saenz 2, Choi 1, Drew 1, Repko 1, Valentin 1. Milwaukee (4)--Lee 2, Cirillo 1, Jenkins 1. Minnesota (7)--Hunter 2, Jones 2, Cuddyer 1, Morneau 1, Stewart 1. New York (9)--Jacobs 3, Diaz 2, Reyes 2, Wright 2. Philadelphia (7)--Burrell 2, Utley 2, Abreu 1, Howard 1, Lieberthal 1. Pittsburgh (7)--Lawton 2, Bay 1, Castillo 1, Ward 1, Wigginton 1, J. Wilson 1. St. Louis (3)--Edmonds 1, Pujols 1, Taguchi 1. San Diego (12)--Hernandez 2, Klesko 2, Nevin 2, Fick 1, Garcia 1, Giles 1, Greene 1, Nady 1, Randa 1. San Francisco (10)--Durham 2, Niekro 2, Winn 2, Alou 1, Feliz 1, Matheny 1, Snow 1. Washington (2)--Church 1, Johnson 1.

AT ATLANTA (154):

Arizona (7)--Clark 2, S. Green 2, Glaus 1, Snyder 1, Stinnett 1. Atlanta (89)--A. Jones 21, Francoeur 11, Giles 11, LaRoche 11, Furcal 9, C. Jones 9, Franco 3, Langerhans 3, Estrada 2, Johnson 2, Jordan 2, McCann 2, Hampton 1, Mondesi 1, Perez 1. Baltimore (3)--Bigbie 1, Palmeiro 1, Roberts 1. Chicago (2)--Hollandsworth 1, Ramirez 1. Cincinnati (5)--Griffey Jr. 2, Kearns 1, LaRue 1, Valentin 1. Colorado (1)--Greene 1. Florida (5)--Cabrera 3, Delgado 2. Houston (2)--Ensberg 1, Lane 1. Los Angeles (1)--B. Molina 1. Los Angeles (1)--Bradley 1. Milwaukee (3)--Branyan 1, Jenkins 1, Overbay 1. New York (8)--Wright 2, Beltran 1, Cameron 1, Floyd 1, Piazza 1, Reyes 1, Woodward 1. Oakland (5)--Chavez 3, Crosby 1, Kotsay 1. Philadelphia (6)--Bell 1, Howard 1, Lieberthal 1, Michaels 1, Thome 1, Victorino 1. Pittsburgh (3)--Bay 1, Castillo 1, Duffy 1. St. Louis (1)--Pujols 1. San Diego (4)--Nady 1, Olivo 1, Randa 1, Sweeney 1. San Francisco (1)--Winn 1. Washington (7)--Guillen 4, Vidro 2, Byrd 1.

AT CHICAGO (195):

Arizona (8)--L. Gonzalez 3, Snyder 2, Clark 1, Glaus 1, Tracy 1. Atlanta (3)--C. Jones 2, A. Jones 1. Boston (9)--Ortiz 2, Bellhorn 1, Damon 1, Mueller 1, Nixon 1, Payton 1, M. Ramirez 1, Youkilis 1. Chicago (99)--Lee 24, Burnitz 17, Ramirez 11, Barrett 9, Patterson 9, Garciaparra 5, Walker 5, Perez 4, Dubois 3, Hairston Jr. 3, Blanco 2, Hollandsworth 2, Murton 2, Lawton 1, Macias 1, Maddux 1. Chicago (6)--Dye 3, Crede 1, Iguchi 1, Konerko 1. Cincinnati (16)--Dunn 3, Encarnacion 2, Griffey Jr. 2, Kearns 2, F. Lopez 2, Pena 2, Freel 1, LaRue 1, Valentin 1. Colorado (6)--Wilson 3, Closser 1, Gonzalez 1, Greene 1. Florida (6)--L. Castillo 2, Delgado 2, Cabrera 1, Encarnacion 1. Houston (5)--Biggio 2, Ausmus 1, Berkman 1, Ensberg 1. Los Angeles (4)--Edwards 1, Kent 1, Saenz 1, Werth 1. Milwaukee (8)--Lee 2, Miller 2, Overbay 2, Hall 1, Spivey 1. New York (3)--Matsui 1, Mientkiewicz 1, Piazza 1. Philadelphia (2)--Abreu 1, Burrell 1. Pittsburgh (6)--Bay 3, McLouth 2, Castillo 1. St. Louis (5)--Pujols 2, Edmonds 1, Mahoney 1, Rodriguez 1. San Diego (4)--Blum 2, Giles 1, Klesko 1. San Francisco (1)--Feliz 1. Toronto (1)--Johnson 1. Washington (3)--Guillen 2, Schneider 1.

AT CINCINNATI (246):

Arizona (2)--Cintron 1, Clark 1. Atlanta (17)--A. Jones 4, Franco 3, Betemit 2, Johnson 2, Estrada 1, Francoeur 1, Furcal 1, Giles 1, C. Jones 1, McCann 1. Baltimore (4)--Sosa 2, Fasano 1, Mora 1. Chicago (18)--Lee 5, Ramirez 5, Walker 3, Burnitz 2, Patterson 2, Barrett 1. Cincinnati (126)--Dunn 26, F. Lopez 16, Griffey Jr. 15, Aurilia 11, Pena 11, Kearns 9, Randa 9, Valentin 7, LaRue 6, Casey 4, Cruz 3, Encarnacion 3, Freel 2, Denorfia 1, Keisler 1, Milton 1, Olmedo 1. Cleveland (2)--Ludwick 1, Sabathia 1. Colorado (3)--Closser 1, Piedra 1, Sullivan 1. Florida (2)--Cabrera 1, Gonzalez 1. Houston (8)--Lane 3, Ensberg 2, Everett 2, Palmeiro 1. Los Angeles (6)--Choi 2, Bradley 1, Drew 1, Kent 1, Phillips 1. Milwaukee (9)--Overbay 3, Clark 1, Hardy 1, Jenkins 1, Lee 1, Moeller 1, Weeks 1. New York (5)--Beltran 1, Floyd 1, Matsui 1, Mientkiewicz 1, Wright 1. Philadelphia (6)--Utley 3, Bell 1, Howard 1, Rollins 1. Pittsburgh (10)--Bay 4, Cota 1, Lawton 1, Mackowiak 1, Restovich 1, Ward 1, Wigginton 1. St. Louis (11)--Taguchi 2, Eckstein 1, Edmonds 1, Gall 1, Grudzielanek 1, Mabry 1, Nunez 1, Pujols 1, Rolen 1, Sanders 1. San Diego (3)--Klesko 2, Jackson 1. San Francisco (5)--Cruz 1, Durham 1, Linden 1, Snow 1, Winn 1. Tampa Bay (5)--Crawford 2, Cantu 1, Hall 1, Perez 1. Washington (4)--Guillen 2, Harris 1, Johnson 1.

AT COLORADO (170):

Arizona (16)--Glaus 6, Tracy 3, Counsell 2, Cruz Jr. 2, Clark 1, S. Green 1, Stinnett 1. Atlanta (4)--Langerhans 2, A. Jones 1, LaRoche 1. Chicago (5)--Burnitz 1, Lee 1, Perez 1, Ramirez 1, Walker 1. Chicago (3)--Crede 1, Konerko 1, Thomas 1. Cincinnati (5)--Aurilia 2, Casey 1, Kearns 1, Randa 1. Colorado (86)--Helton 13, Mohr 13, Holliday 12, Wilson 10, Atkins 9, Barmes 7, Hawpe 5, Ardoin 3, Gonzalez 3, Greene 3, Piedra 3, Closser 2, Baker 1, Restovich 1, Sullivan 1. Detroit (1)--Logan 1. Florida (2)--Gonzalez 1, Pierre 1. Houston (7)--Ensberg 2, Lane 2, Berkman 1, Biggio 1, Chavez 1. Kansas City (1)--Stairs 1. Los Angeles (5)--Kent 2, Edwards 1, A. Perez 1, Phillips 1. Milwaukee (2)--Helms 1, Weeks 1. New York (4)--Anderson 2, Castro 1, Wright 1. Philadelphia (1)--Utley 1. Pittsburgh (2)--Bay 1, Eldred 1. St. Louis (1)--Pujols 1. San Diego (14)--Giles 3, Greene 3, Nady 2, Hernandez 1, Klesko 1, Loretta 1, Nevin 1, Sweeney 1. San Francisco (9)--Feliz 3, Tucker 2, Grissom 1, Matheny 1, Niekro 1, Winn 1. Washington (2)--Guillen 1, Johnson 1.

AT FLORIDA (109):

Arizona (2)--Glaus 1, Tracy 1. Atlanta (9)--C. Jones 2, Franco 1, Giles 1, Johnson 1, A. Jones 1, Jordan 1, Langerhans 1, McCann 1. Chicago (4)--Lee 2, Burnitz 1, Walker 1. Cincinnati (1)--F. Lopez 1. Colorado (2)--Barmes 1, Miles 1. Florida (57)--Delgado 16, Cabrera 11, Encarnacion 8, Easley 5, Lowell 5, Hermida 4, Gonzalez 2, Lo Duca 2, Conine 1, Dillon 1, Harris 1, Pierre 1. Houston (1)--Taveras 1. Los Angeles (1)--Ledee 1. Milwaukee (2)--Branyan 1, Weeks 1. New York (5)--Floyd 2, Mientkiewicz 2, Beltran 1. Philadelphia (2)--Burrell 1, Rollins 1. St. Louis (5)--Eckstein 1, Grudzielanek 1, Luna 1, Mabry 1, Walker 1. San Francisco (2)--Feliz 1, Winn 1. Seattle (2)--Ibanez 1, Winn 1. Tampa Bay (4)--Hollins 2, Crawford 1, Hall 1. Texas (2)--Hidalgo 1, Mench 1. Washington (8)--Johnson 2, Byrd 1, Castilla 1, Church 1, Guillen 1, Schneider 1, Wilson 1.

AT HOUSTON (171):

Arizona (2)--Glaus 1, L. Gonzalez 1. Atlanta (2)--C. Jones 1, Langerhans 1. Chicago (11)--Lee 2, Murton 2, Barrett 1, Burnitz 1, Dubois 1, Garciaparra 1, Ramirez 1, Walker 1, Zambrano 1. Cincinnati (5)--Randa 2, Freel 1, Griffey Jr. 1, Pena 1. Colorado (1)--Hawpe 1. Florida (7)--Cabrera 2, Delgado 2, Conine 1, Lo Duca 1, Willis 1. Houston (93)--Ensberg 20, Biggio 19, Lane 14, Berkman 13, Everett 7, Lamb 4, Bagwell 3, Ausmus 2, Bruntlett 2, Burke 2, Taveras 2, Chavez 1, Palmeiro 1, Quintero 1, Self 1, Vizcaino 1. Los Angeles (1)--Phillips 1. Milwaukee (6)--Jenkins 2, Clark 1, Miller 1, Overbay 1, Weeks 1. New York (2)--Cairo 1, Floyd 1. Philadelphia (1)--Rollins 1. Pittsburgh (13)--Bay 3, J. Wilson 3, Castillo 2, Doumit 1, Eldred 1, T. Redman 1, Ward 1, C. Wilson 1. St. Louis (11)--Edmonds 3, Sanders 3, Pujols 2, Marquis 1, Molina 1, Walker 1. San Diego (1)--Nady 1. San Francisco (1)--Ellison 1. Texas (5)--Barajas 2, M. Young 2, Nix 1. Toronto (1)--Rios 1. Washington (8)--Castilla 1, Guillen 1, Hernandez 1, Schneider 1, Vidro 1, Watson 1, Wilkerson 1, Wilson 1.

AT LOS ANGELES (170):

Arizona (11)--Tracy 4, S. Green 3, Cintron 1, Cruz Jr. 1, L. Gonzalez 1, Terrero 1. Atlanta (8)--A. Jones 3, C. Jones 2, LaRoche 2, Mondesi 1. Chicago (5)--Barrett 1, Hairston Jr. 1, Lee 1, Perez 1, Ramirez 1. Cincinnati (6)--Griffey Jr. 2, LaRue 2, Cruz 1, Milton 1. Colorado (7)--Atkins 1, Hawpe 1, Holliday 1, Miles 1, Mohr 1, Piedra 1, Sullivan 1. Detroit (4)--Giarratano 1, Johnson 1, Rodriguez 1, Young 1. Florida (6)--Cabrera 2, Delgado 2, Easley 1, Encarnacion 1. Houston (2)--Biggio 1, Burke 1. Los Angeles (3)--Rivera 2, J. Molina 1. Los Angeles (80)--Kent 15, Drew 10, Choi 9, Saenz 9, Bradley 6, Phillips 6, Cruz Jr. 5, Ledee 5, Repko 4, Navarro 3, Grabowski 2, Robles 2, Edwards 1, Izturis 1, A. Perez 1, Werth 1. Milwaukee (3)--Hall 1, Jenkins 1, Lee 1. Minnesota (3)--Hunter 1, Jones 1, Morneau 1. New York (4)--Diaz 2, Castro 1, Williams 1. Philadelphia (4)--Howard 2, Abreu 1, Burrell 1. Pittsburgh (5)--Bay 1, Eldred 1, McLouth 1, Sanchez 1, C. Wilson 1. St. Louis (5)--Edmonds 2, Eckstein 1, Grudzielanek 1, Mabry 1, Pujols 1. San Diego (3)--Hernandez 1, Jackson 1, Nady 1. San Francisco (8)--Feliz 2, Tucker 2, Durham 1, Matheny 1, Vizquel 1, Winn 1. Washington (2)--Guillen 1, Johnson 1.

AT MILWAUKEE (179):

Arizona (1)--Clark 1. Atlanta (2)--A. Jones 2. Chicago (12)--Lee 4, Ramirez 3, Barrett 1, Blanco 1, Cedeno 1, Garciaparra 1, Murton 1. Cincinnati (10)--Griffey Jr. 2, Pena 2, Casey 1, Dunn 1, Encarnacion 1, Kearns 1, F. Lopez 1, Valentin 1. Colorado (2)--Hawpe 1, Helton 1. Florida (1)--Delgado 1. Houston (6)--Berkman 1, Burke 1, Ensberg 1, Everett 1, Lamb 1, Lane 1. Los Angeles (5)--Bradley 3, Grabowski 1, Repko 1. Milwaukee (91)--Lee 15, Hall 12, Jenkins 10, Overbay 10, Clark 8, Weeks 8, Hardy 6, Moeller 5, Branyan 3, Miller 3, Fielder 2, Hart 2, Helms 2, Magruder 2, Spivey 2, Cirillo 1. Minnesota (5)--Hunter 3, Rodriguez 1, Stewart 1. New York (9)--Beltran 2, Cameron 2, Piazza 2, Wright 2, Mientkiewicz 1. New York (4)--A. Rodriguez 2, Cano 1, Jeter 1. Philadelphia (9)--Abreu 3, Lieberthal 2, Utley 2, Michaels 1, Polanco 1. Pittsburgh (7)--Bay 1, Castillo 1, Lawton 1, Ross 1, Sanchez 1, Ward 1, Wigginton 1. St. Louis (6)--Pujols 2, Rolen 2, Edmonds 1, Grudzielanek 1. San Diego (3)--Johnson 2, Greene 1. San Francisco (3)--Alou 1, Feliz 1, Hennessey 1. Washington (4)--Guillen 1, Vidro 1, Wilkerson 1, Wilson 1.

AT NEW YORK (146):

Arizona (2)--Clark 1, Cruz Jr. 1. Atlanta (8)--Giles 2, LaRoche 2, Betemit 1, A. Jones 1, Orr 1, Perez 1. Chicago (2)--Lee 1, Ramirez 1. Cincinnati (2)--Casey 1, Griffey Jr. 1. Colorado (3)--Barmes 1, Helton 1, Holliday 1. Florida (3)--Delgado 1, Lo Duca 1, Lowell 1. Houston (2)--Burke 1, Palmeiro 1. Los Angeles (3)--Cabrera 1, Erstad 1, Finley 1. Los Angeles (2)--Kent 1, Saenz 1. Milwaukee (7)--Jenkins 2, Lee 2, Branyan 1, Hall 1, Miller 1. New York (83)--Floyd 21, Wright 12, Piazza 9, Cameron 7, Beltran 6, Jacobs 6, Castro 5, Diaz 4, Anderson 3, Mientkiewicz 3, Reyes 2, Woodward 2, Cairo 1, Matsui 1, Offerman 1. Philadelphia (15)--Utley 4, Burrell 2, Howard 2, Rollins 2, Abreu 1, Bell 1, Lieberthal 1, Lofton 1, Michaels 1. Pittsburgh (2)--Bay 1, Eldred 1. St. Louis (4)--Grudzielanek 1, Mabry 1, Nunez 1, Sanders 1. San Diego (1)--Greene 1. San Francisco (2)--Alou 1, Niekro 1. Washington (5)--Guzman 2, Castilla 1, Wilkerson 1, Wilson 1.

AT PHILADELPHIA (201):

Arizona (6)--L. Gonzalez 2, Cintron 1, Clark 1, Counsell 1, Cruz Jr. 1. Atlanta (13)--LaRoche 3, Furcal 2, A. Jones 2, C. Jones 2, Mondesi 2, Hollandsworth 1, Johnson 1. Boston (7)--M. Ramirez 3, Bellhorn 1, Mirabelli 1, Ortiz 1, Varitek 1. Cincinnati (6)--Dunn 3, Griffey Jr. 2, LaRue 1. Colorado (2)--Hawpe 1, Relaford 1. Florida (8)--Cabrera 2, Encarnacion 2, Lo Duca 2, Easley 1, Gonzalez 1. Houston (5)--Berkman 2, Biggio 2, Lamb 1. Los Angeles (3)--Kent 1, Robles 1, Werth 1. Milwaukee (7)--Branyan 1, Cirillo 1, Hall 1, Hardy 1, Helms 1, Jenkins 1, Lee 1. New York (18)--Floyd 3, Mientkiewicz 3, Anderson 2, Diaz 2, Piazza 2, Reyes 2, Wright 2, Daubach 1, Jacobs 1. Philadelphia (94)--Burrell 20, Abreu 15, Utley 12, Howard 11, Pratt 7, Lieberthal 6, Thome 6, Bell 5, Rollins 5, Polanco 2, Lofton 1, Martinez 1, Michaels 1, Offerman 1, Victorino 1. Pittsburgh (3)--Eldred 2, Wells 1. St. Louis (5)--Pujols 2, Eckstein 1, Edmonds 1, Molina 1. San Diego (3)--Blum 1, Giles 1, Loretta 1. San Francisco (3)--Alou 1, Ellison 1, Snow 1. Texas (7)--Teixeira 2, Barajas 1, Blalock 1, Dellucci 1, DeRosa 1, M. Young 1. Washington (11)--Guillen 2, Wilson 2, Baerga 1, Castilla 1, Johnson 1, Schneider 1, Sledge 1, Vidro 1, Wilkerson 1.

AT PITTSBURGH (140):

Arizona (3)--Clark 2, Terrero 1. Atlanta (1)--Langerhans 1. Baltimore (7)--Fasano 2, Tejada 2, Mora 1, Sosa 1, Surhoff 1. Chicago (10)--Garciaparra 2, Lee 2, Barrett 1, Blanco 1, Dubois 1, Murton 1, Perez 1, Ramirez 1. Cincinnati (7)--Griffey Jr. 3, Casey 1, Dunn 1, Kearns 1, LaRue 1. Colorado (5)--Holliday 2, Atkins 1, Helton 1, Sullivan 1. Florida (5)--Delgado 2, Cabrera 1, Easley 1, Encarnacion 1. Houston (7)--Berkman 3, Lamb 2, Ensberg 1, Lane 1. Los Angeles (4)--Saenz 2, Kent 1, Ledee 1. Milwaukee (6)--Jenkins 2, Cirillo 1, Lee 1, Miller 1, Spivey 1. New York (4)--Beltran 1, Cameron 1, Castro 1, Floyd 1. Philadelphia (1)--Abreu 1. Pittsburgh (59)--Bay 9, Mackowiak 7, Ward 7, Lawton 6, Cota 5, Doumit 4, Eldred 4, Sanchez 3, C. Wilson 3, J. Wilson 3, Castillo 2, McLouth 2, Ross 2, T. Redman 1, Wigginton 1. St. Louis (6)--Edmonds 3, Pujols 2, Rodriguez 1. San Diego (5)--Greene 2, Olivo 2, Young 1. San Francisco (4)--Alou 1, Cruz 1, Matheny 1, Niekro 1. Tampa Bay (1)--Gonzalez 1. Washington (5)--Guillen 4, Wilkerson 1.

AT SAN DIEGO (118):

Arizona (13)--Glaus 4, Tracy 4, L. Gonzalez 2, S. Green 2, Stinnett 1. Atlanta (2)--A. Jones 2. Chicago (3)--Perez 1, Ramirez 1, Walker 1. Chicago (4)--Crede 1, Everett 1, Pierzynski 1, Rowand 1. Cincinnati (8)--Dunn 3, Aurilia 1, Casey 1, Encarnacion 1, Pena 1, Valentin 1. Cleveland (5)--Boone 2, Crisp 1, Hafner 1, Sizemore 1. Colorado (6)--Helton 3, Gonzalez 1, Greene 1, Mohr 1. Florida (1)--Cabrera 1. Houston (1)--Berkman 1. Los Angeles (5)--Drew 1, Repko 1, Robles 1, Rose 1, Werth 1. Milwaukee (3)--Branyan 1, Jenkins 1, Lee 1. New York (1)--Wright 1. Philadelphia (1)--Burrell 1. St. Louis (3)--Edmonds 1, Pujols 1, Rodriguez 1. San Diego (54)--Klesko 10, Giles 6, Greene 6, Hernandez 5, Nady 5, Roberts 5, Nevin 4, Jackson 3, Sweeney 3, Randa 2, Blum 1, Burroughs 1, Johnson 1, Loretta 1, Olivo 1. San Francisco (2)--Bonds 1, Niekro 1. Seattle (4)--Boone 1, Ibanez 1, Rivera 1, Sexson 1. Washington (2)--Johnson 1, Wilson 1.

AT SAN FRANCISCO (133):

Arizona (4)--Tracy 3, Glaus 1. Atlanta (5)--A. Jones 2, Francoeur 1, C. Jones 1, LaRoche 1. Chicago (4)--Barrett 1, Blanco 1, Lee 1, Murton 1. Cincinnati (4)--Dunn 1, Griffey Jr. 1, LaRue 1, Pena 1. Cleveland (2)--Belliard 1, Blake 1. Colorado (8)--Gonzalez 2, Holliday 2, Closser 1, Greene 1, Helton 1, Shealy 1. Florida (7)--Cabrera 3, Burnett 1, Delgado 1, Encarnacion 1, Lowell 1. Houston (2)--Ensberg 1, Lane 1. Kansas City (1)--Graffanino 1. Los Angeles (7)--Aybar 1, Cruz Jr. 1, Drew 1, Izturis 1, A. Perez 1, Robles 1, Valentin 1. Milwaukee (4)--Lee 2, Branyan 1, Spivey 1. New York (1)--Wright 1. Oakland (1)--Ginter 1. Philadelphia (1)--Howard 1. Pittsburgh (6)--Bay 1, Castillo 1, Cota 1, Sadler 1, Ward 1, Wigginton 1. St. Louis (2)--Sanders 1, Walker 1. San Diego (9)--Hernandez 2, Nevin 2, Blum 1, Fick 1, Giles 1, Greene 1, Sweeney 1. San Francisco (64)--Alou 12, Feliz 10, Matheny 8, Winn 7, Durham 6, Niekro 5, Cruz 3, Alfonzo 2, Bonds 2, Ellison 2, Linden 2, Grissom 1, Schmidt 1, Snow 1, Torrealba 1, Tucker 1. Washington (1)--Guillen 1.

AT ST. LOUIS (174):

Arizona (3)--L. Gonzalez 3. Atlanta (4)--A. Jones 2, Francoeur 1, Johnson 1. Boston (3)--Ortiz 1, Renteria 1, Varitek 1. Chicago (8)--Lee 2, Ramirez 2, Blanco 1, Burnitz 1, Patterson 1, Perez 1. Cincinnati (8)--Kearns 3, F. Lopez 2, Dunn 1, Encarnacion 1, Pena 1. Colorado (6)--Ardoin 1, Atkins 1, Closser 1, Gonzalez 1, Mohr 1, Wilson 1. Florida (4)--Cabrera 1, L. Castillo 1, Easley 1, Lowell 1. Houston (6)--Ensberg 2, Berkman 1, Biggio 1, Lamb 1, Lane 1. Los Angeles (3)--Bradley 1, Choi 1, Kent 1. Milwaukee (8)--Branyan 3, Jenkins 2, Hardy 1, Overbay 1, Weeks 1. New York (4)--Diaz 2, Beltran 1, Piazza 1. New York (1)--Posada 1. Philadelphia (4)--Burrell 2, Abreu 1, Utley 1. Pittsburgh (12)--Bay 5, Castillo 2, Eldred 2, Wigginton 2, Doumit 1. St. Louis (92)--Pujols 23, Edmonds 15, Sanders 14, Walker 9, Molina 6, Taguchi 5, Eckstein 3, Grudzielanek 3, Nunez 3, Mabry 2, Rodriguez 2, Rolen 2, Diaz 1, Duncan 1, Gall 1, Seabol 1, Suppan 1. San Diego (6)--Giles 2, Fick 1, Garcia 1, Klesko 1, Sweeney 1. San Francisco (2)--Durham 1, Vizquel 1.

AT WASHINGTON (112):

Arizona (2)--L. Gonzalez 1, Tracy 1. Atlanta (10)--A. Jones 5, Betemit 1, Estrada 1, Franco 1, C. Jones 1, McCann 1. Chicago (1)--Ramirez 1. Cincinnati (3)--Encarnacion 1, Griffey Jr. 1, Valentin 1. Colorado (1)--Closser 1. Florida (7)--Cabrera 2, Delgado 2, Beckett 1, L. Castillo 1, Encarnacion 1. Houston (5)--Lamb 2, Berkman 1, Ensberg 1. Los Angeles (5)--Bradley 1, Choi 1, Kent 1, Phillips 1, Repko 1. Milwaukee (3)--Lee 2, Clark 1. New York (7)--Piazza 2, Wright 2, Beltran 1, Cameron 1, Jacobs 1. Oakland (1)--Crosby 1. Philadelphia (9)--Howard 3, Bell 2, Utley 2, Burrell 1, Rollins 1. Pittsburgh (1)--Mackowiak 1. St. Louis (1)--Eckstein 1. San Diego (3)--Nady 1, Roberts 1, Young 1. San Francisco (4)--Bonds 2, Alou 1, Hennessey 1. Seattle (1)--Sexson 1. Toronto (2)--Hudson 2. Washington (46)--Castilla 8, Johnson 7, Wilkerson 6, Church 5, Schneider 5, Guillen 3, Wilson 3, Short 2, Spivey 2, Vidro 2, Baerga 1, Bennett 1, Hernandez 1.

This section contains selected batting statistics for all National League parks for 2005. A key component of this section is an index number for each category, which is used to determine how a given park influences a particular statistic. To illustrate, see the indexes for runs and extra-base hits at Arizona's Bank One Ballpark, where the elevation ranks second only to Colorado's Coors Field and aids N.L. hitters. While Arizona and Milwaukee tied for the league's lowest home-run total in 2004, only five N.L. parks allowed more homers than BOB.

For each N.L. park, we show how the home team and its opponents performed, both at home and on the road, with the exception being that we do not include data from interleague games. The differences in interleague opponents and ballparks would skew the data.

By comparing the per-game averages at the home park and on the road, we can evaluate the park's impact. This is done by simply dividing the home average by the road average and multiplying the result by 100, generating a park index. If the home and road per-game averages are equal, the index equals 100, and it can be concluded that the park had no impact. An index above 100 means that the park favors that particular statistic. The indexes for at-bats, runs, hits, errors and infield errors are determined on a per-game basis; all other stats are calculated on a per-at-bat basis. "E-infield" denotes infield *fielding* errors. "Alt." is the approximate elevation of the ballpark.

For most parks, data is presented both for 2005 and for the last three years overall. If the park's dimensions have changed over that time, however, the data from the old and new configurations will not be combined. Following all the teams' charts is a ranking section that shows which parks most inflate runs, home runs and batting average.

ARIZONA — Home park: Bank One Ballpark/Chase Field — Alt.: 1,090 feet — Surface: Grass

Category	2005 Season — Home Games — Ari.	Opp.	Total	— Road Games — Ari.	Opp.	Total	Index	2003-05 Seasons — Home Games — Ari.	Opp.	Total	— Road Games — Ari.	Opp.	Total	Index
G	72	72	144	72	72	144		219	219	438	216	216	432	
Avg	.252	.281	.267	.254	.275	.264	101	.264	.265	.264	.247	.264	.255	104
AB	2398	2582	4980	2509	2448	4957	100	7355	7727	15082	7515	7236	14751	101
R	286	410	696	319	342	661	105	954	1155	2109	824	1029	1853	112
H	605	725	1330	638	672	1310	102	1939	2047	3986	1859	1907	3766	104
2B	115	178	293	141	127	268	109	405	461	866	375	349	724	117
3B	16	19	35	7	15	22	158	59	51	110	38	38	76	142
HR	81	89	170	82	81	163	104	226	266	492	203	223	426	113
BB	268	259	527	280	226	506	104	750	802	1552	692	768	1460	104
SO	462	467	929	508	452	960	96	1330	1623	2953	1483	1519	3002	96
E	33	33	66	47	47	94	70	133	113	246	163	120	283	86
E-Infield	28	28	56	43	37	80	70	109	98	207	141	94	235	87
LHB-Avg	.258	.290	.272	.269	.263	.267	102	.274	.281	.277	.257	.271	.263	105
LHB-HR	46	36	82	57	34	91	89	119	113	232	117	91	208	109
RHB-Avg	.245	.274	.262	.234	.282	.262	100	.252	.254	.253	.237	.259	.249	102
RHB-HR	35	53	88	25	47	72	122	107	153	260	86	132	218	117

ATLANTA — Home park: Turner Field — Alt.: 1,050 feet — Surface: Grass

Category	2005 Season — Home Games — Atl.	Opp.	Total	— Road Games — Atl.	Opp.	Total	Index	2003-05 Seasons — Home Games — Atl.	Opp.	Total	— Road Games — Atl.	Opp.	Total	Index
G	72	72	144	69	69	138		219	219	438	209	209	418	
Avg	.268	.258	.263	.273	.264	.269	98	.272	.250	.261	.270	.260	.265	98
AB	2418	2507	4925	2426	2299	4725	100	7309	7573	14882	7439	7006	14445	98
R	361	291	652	340	277	617	101	1074	888	1962	1044	871	1915	98
H	648	647	1295	663	607	1270	98	1988	1893	3881	2011	1819	3830	97
2B	125	106	231	131	98	229	97	381	347	728	406	343	749	94
3B	17	5	22	18	11	29	73	45	28	73	41	37	78	91
HR	81	75	156	72	59	131	114	256	197	453	244	186	430	102
BB	273	236	509	253	223	476	103	770	736	1506	729	722	1451	101
SO	529	498	1027	480	395	875	113	1375	1391	2766	1397	1296	2693	100
E	52	39	91	46	44	90	97	162	145	307	149	135	284	103
E-Infield	49	29	78	44	38	82	91	141	116	257	135	110	245	100
LHB-Avg	.270	.272	.271	.292	.270	.282	96	.276	.257	.266	.276	.252	.265	100
LHB-HR	40	34	74	37	22	59	118	87	69	156	69	63	132	113
RHB-Avg	.267	.247	.257	.258	.260	.259	99	.270	.246	.258	.267	.264	.265	97
RHB-HR	41	41	82	35	37	72	111	169	128	297	175	123	298	98

CHICAGO

Home park: Wrigley Field **Alt.:** 595 feet **Surface:** Grass

Category	2005 Season Home Games Chi.	Opp.	Total	Road Games Chi.	Opp.	Total	Index	2003-05 Seasons Home Games Chi.	Opp.	Total	Road Games Chi.	Opp.	Total	Index
G	72	72	144	75	75	150		220	220	440	218	218	436	
Avg	.270	.245	.258	.271	.251	.261	99	.266	.244	.255	.265	.244	.255	100
AB	2441	2494	4935	2647	2425	5072	101	7455	7629	15084	7649	7126	14775	101
R	317	316	633	329	318	647	102	1027	960	1987	993	884	1877	105
H	659	612	1271	718	608	1326	100	1984	1861	3845	2027	1739	3766	101
2B	136	126	262	158	109	267	101	400	353	753	445	320	765	96
3B	12	7	19	9	10	19	103	32	30	62	33	32	65	93
HR	90	80	170	89	82	171	102	300	234	534	256	210	466	112
BB	189	263	452	203	264	467	99	664	801	1465	625	762	1387	103
SO	401	583	984	436	563	999	101	1430	1879	3309	1451	1744	3195	101
E	51	39	90	40	59	99	95	145	154	299	125	151	276	107
E-Infield	40	34	74	35	49	84	92	120	122	242	105	125	230	104
LHB-Avg	.264	.245	.255	.256	.259	.257	99	.260	.244	.251	.257	.258	.257	98
LHB-HR	33	32	65	21	37	58	119	74	104	178	65	105	170	104
RHB-Avg	.274	.246	.259	.284	.246	.265	98	.269	.244	.257	.270	.235	.253	101
RHB-HR	57	48	105	68	45	113	93	226	130	356	191	105	296	117

CINCINNATI

Home park: Great American Ball Park **Alt.:** 550 feet **Surface:** Grass

Category	2005 Season Home Games Cin.	Opp.	Total	Road Games Cin.	Opp.	Total	Index	2003-05 Seasons Home Games Cin.	Opp.	Total	Road Games Cin.	Opp.	Total	Index
G	73	73	146	75	75	150		223	223	446	222	222	444	
Avg	.264	.299	.282	.256	.281	.268	105	.250	.278	.265	.252	.287	.269	98
AB	2433	2674	5107	2620	2514	5134	102	7386	8007	15393	7770	7585	15355	100
R	386	413	799	351	386	737	111	1016	1211	2227	1041	1207	2248	99
H	643	799	1442	671	706	1377	108	1847	2226	4073	1959	2176	4135	98
2B	157	191	348	155	135	290	121	393	505	898	402	460	862	104
3B	5	12	17	9	25	34	50	21	27	48	41	74	115	42
HR	106	109	215	88	90	178	121	282	335	617	251	271	522	118
BB	273	220	493	298	223	521	95	773	721	1494	821	766	1587	94
SO	537	454	991	636	407	1043	96	1709	1394	3103	1904	1224	3128	99
E	44	36	80	56	41	97	85	165	124	289	168	131	299	96
E-Infield	37	32	69	47	29	76	93	134	110	244	139	104	243	100
LHB-Avg	.281	.313	.296	.272	.260	.267	111	.265	.277	.271	.266	.279	.272	99
LHB-HR	56	44	100	48	30	78	127	153	130	283	137	106	243	117
RHB-Avg	.251	.291	.273	.243	.291	.269	102	.239	.279	.261	.241	.292	.267	97
RHB-HR	50	65	115	40	60	100	117	129	205	334	114	165	279	119

COLORADO

Home park: Coors Field **Alt.:** 5,280 feet **Surface:** Grass

Category	2005 Season Home Games Col.	Opp.	Total	Road Games Col.	Opp.	Total	Index	2003-05 Seasons Home Games Col.	Opp.	Total	Road Games Col.	Opp.	Total	Index
G	72	72	144	75	75	150		216	216	432	222	222	444	
Avg	.305	.295	.300	.232	.276	.254	118	.300	.297	.298	.237	.277	.257	116
AB	2536	2602	5138	2509	2453	4962	108	7476	7813	15289	7527	7305	14832	106
R	404	402	806	274	383	657	128	1297	1276	2573	874	1122	1996	132
H	773	768	1541	581	677	1258	128	2245	2318	4563	1786	2022	3808	123
2B	142	171	313	112	155	267	113	477	476	953	376	432	808	114
3B	19	19	38	14	11	25	147	60	60	120	31	38	69	169
HR	79	79	158	60	84	144	106	283	283	566	216	238	454	121
BB	236	271	507	221	292	513	95	799	818	1617	727	865	1592	99
SO	426	438	864	554	427	981	85	1332	1279	2611	1738	1208	2946	86
E	49	60	109	58	56	114	100	141	180	321	148	140	288	115
E-Infield	42	48	90	47	47	94	100	111	142	253	121	118	239	109
LHB-Avg	.302	.308	.305	.242	.282	.262	116	.317	.305	.311	.250	.288	.269	115
LHB-HR	21	29	50	22	36	58	85	107	112	219	80	91	171	126
RHB-Avg	.307	.286	.297	.224	.272	.247	120	.290	.291	.291	.229	.269	.249	117
RHB-HR	58	50	108	38	48	86	120	176	171	347	136	147	283	118

2005 N.L. STATISTICS Miscellaneous

FLORIDA

Home park: Dolphins Stadium **Alt.:** 10 feet **Surface:** Grass

| | 2005 Season | | | | | | | 2003-05 Seasons | | | | | | |
| | Home Games | | | Road Games | | | | Home Games | | | Road Games | | | |
Category	Fla.	Opp.	Total	Fla.	Opp.	Total	Index	Fla.	Opp.	Total	Fla.	Opp.	Total	Index
G	72	72	144	75	75	150		213	213	426	219	219	438	
Avg	.266	.253	.259	.278	.278	.278	93	.268	.246	.257	.268	.272	.270	95
AB	2382	2448	4830	2619	2516	5135	98	7038	7313	14351	7605	7271	14876	99
R	297	292	589	349	378	727	84	930	835	1765	996	1043	2039	89
H	634	619	1253	727	700	1427	91	1884	1800	3684	2037	1979	4016	94
2B	115	125	240	159	153	312	82	350	355	705	425	435	860	85
3B	18	20	38	11	23	34	119	54	56	110	41	50	91	125
HR	50	44	94	69	59	128	78	172	161	333	207	201	408	85
BB	246	255	501	203	264	467	114	700	731	1431	642	713	1355	109
SO	434	561	995	403	470	873	121	1267	1654	2921	1301	1355	2656	114
E	35	46	81	61	51	112	75	96	145	241	150	162	312	79
E-Infield	30	39	69	53	38	91	79	81	119	200	127	128	255	81
LHB-Avg	.272	.256	.263	.281	.276	.278	95	.285	.247	.263	.278	.271	.274	96
LHB-HR	20	21	41	19	19	38	115	33	72	105	28	72	100	104
RHB-Avg	.263	.251	.257	.276	.280	.278	93	.260	.246	.253	.264	.273	.268	95
RHB-HR	30	23	53	50	40	90	63	139	89	228	179	129	308	79

HOUSTON

Home park: Minute Maid Park **Alt.:** 22 feet **Surface:** Grass

| | 2005 Season | | | | | | | 2003-05 Seasons | | | | | | |
| | Home Games | | | Road Games | | | | Home Games | | | Road Games | | | |
Category	Hou.	Opp.	Total	Hou.	Opp.	Total	Index	Hou.	Opp.	Total	Hou.	Opp.	Total	Index
G	75	75	150	73	73	146		222	222	444	220	220	440	
Avg	.270	.237	.253	.246	.251	.249	102	.271	.242	.257	.254	.258	.256	100
AB	2451	2532	4983	2514	2399	4913	99	7313	7528	14841	7676	7309	14985	98
R	334	256	590	306	283	589	97	1072	866	1938	1022	917	1939	99
H	662	600	1262	619	602	1221	101	1984	1824	3808	1947	1883	3830	99
2B	116	111	227	142	124	266	84	375	337	712	425	387	812	89
3B	17	10	27	14	15	29	92	56	47	103	34	34	68	153
HR	84	72	156	61	62	123	125	256	229	485	232	207	439	112
BB	238	184	422	198	210	408	102	761	620	1381	720	754	1474	95
SO	451	551	1002	507	516	1023	97	1298	1701	2999	1498	1566	3064	99
E	51	46	97	34	47	81	117	138	141	279	120	143	263	105
E-Infield	41	40	81	30	43	73	108	117	118	235	98	127	225	104
LHB-Avg	.232	.242	.238	.252	.247	.249	96	.258	.251	.253	.262	.269	.266	95
LHB-HR	16	26	42	20	23	43	97	51	76	127	79	87	166	77
RHB-Avg	.281	.234	.260	.245	.254	.248	105	.275	.236	.258	.251	.250	.251	103
RHB-HR	68	46	114	41	39	80	140	205	153	358	153	120	273	133

LOS ANGELES

Home park: Dodger Stadium **Alt.:** 340 feet **Surface:** Grass

| | 2005 Season | | | | | | | 2003-05 Seasons | | | | | | |
| | Home Games | | | Road Games | | | | Home Games | | | Road Games | | | |
Category	L.A.	Opp.	Total	L.A.	Opp.	Total	Index	L.A.	Opp.	Total	L.A.	Opp.	Total	Index
G	72	72	144	72	72	144		216	216	432	216	216	432	
Avg	.248	.250	.249	.262	.280	.271	92	.249	.240	.244	.260	.264	.262	93
AB	2326	2464	4790	2525	2411	4936	97	7035	7304	14339	7627	7180	14807	97
R	311	303	614	323	368	691	89	874	805	1679	960	971	1931	87
H	576	617	1193	661	675	1336	89	1752	1750	3502	1981	1892	3873	90
2B	130	129	259	136	134	270	99	332	298	630	368	377	745	87
3B	6	5	11	13	24	37	31	24	17	41	46	59	105	40
HR	65	80	145	62	85	147	102	214	221	435	207	215	422	106
BB	277	200	477	219	228	447	110	673	643	1316	680	732	1412	96
SO	466	497	963	511	403	914	109	1358	1602	2960	1474	1398	2872	106
E	42	44	86	51	44	95	91	134	135	269	136	149	285	94
E-Infield	33	33	66	39	36	75	88	104	113	217	101	121	222	88
LHB-Avg	.254	.263	.259	.258	.309	.284	91	.250	.254	.252	.251	.277	.262	96
LHB-HR	28	39	67	23	40	63	112	96	91	187	89	87	176	108
RHB-Avg	.242	.240	.241	.265	.253	.259	93	.248	.230	.238	.268	.255	.261	91
RHB-HR	37	41	78	39	45	84	94	118	130	248	118	128	246	106

MILWAUKEE

Home park: Miller Park **Alt.:** 635 feet **Surface:** Grass

Category	2005 Season Home Games Mil.	Opp.	Total	Road Games Mil.	Opp.	Total	Index	2003-05 Seasons Home Games Mil.	Opp.	Total	Road Games Mil.	Opp.	Total	Index
G	75	75	150	72	72	144		225	225	450	218	218	436	
Avg	.259	.233	.246	.260	.263	.262	94	.254	.253	.253	.252	.273	.263	97
AB	2416	2536	4952	2523	2452	4975	96	7488	7949	15437	7517	7378	14895	100
R	355	307	662	313	326	639	99	988	1091	2079	893	1068	1961	103
H	626	592	1218	657	646	1303	90	1899	2014	3913	1893	2017	3910	97
2B	141	130	271	157	137	294	93	413	437	850	400	415	815	101
3B	13	10	23	5	18	23	100	38	47	85	31	52	83	99
HR	83	79	162	75	71	146	111	242	265	507	220	236	456	107
BB	256	256	512	236	250	486	106	800	761	1561	702	719	1421	106
SO	516	588	1104	537	486	1023	108	1688	1642	3330	1675	1400	3075	104
E	58	40	98	52	36	88	107	167	141	308	159	142	301	99
E-Infield	49	34	83	45	29	74	108	147	124	271	133	119	252	104
LHB-Avg	.245	.239	.242	.289	.253	.269	90	.263	.257	.260	.266	.264	.265	98
LHB-HR	25	24	49	31	27	58	86	87	92	179	93	78	171	100
RHB-Avg	.264	.230	.248	.248	.270	.258	96	.248	.251	.250	.243	.279	.261	96
RHB-HR	58	55	113	44	44	88	128	155	173	328	127	158	285	112

NEW YORK

Home park: Shea Stadium **Alt.:** 20 feet **Surface:** Grass

Category	2005 Season Home Games N.Y.	Opp.	Total	Road Games Mon.	Opp.	Total	Index	2003-05 Seasons Home Games N.Y.	Opp.	Total	Road Games Mon.	Opp.	Total	Index
G	75	75	150	72	72	144		221	221	442	209	209	418	
Avg	.262	.254	.258	.259	.251	.255	101	.256	.260	.258	.248	.264	.256	101
AB	2497	2590	5087	2501	2347	4848	101	7335	7704	15039	7165	6893	14058	101
R	341	282	623	322	290	612	98	920	939	1859	898	924	1822	96
H	653	659	1312	648	589	1237	102	1879	2004	3883	1780	1820	3600	102
2B	120	132	252	129	123	252	95	376	412	788	361	372	733	100
3B	12	8	20	18	11	29	66	28	27	55	43	53	96	54
HR	79	60	139	84	64	148	90	198	193	391	230	211	441	83
BB	238	212	450	204	223	427	100	690	744	1434	638	716	1354	99
SO	467	483	950	520	449	969	93	1408	1394	2802	1498	1189	2687	97
E	54	59	113	39	45	84	129	177	153	330	129	128	257	121
E-Infield	42	51	93	36	41	77	116	145	136	281	110	107	217	122
LHB-Avg	.262	.266	.264	.259	.244	.253	104	.265	.263	.264	.253	.253	.253	104
LHB-HR	38	27	65	41	28	69	93	80	77	157	87	72	159	93
RHB-Avg	.261	.246	.253	.259	.256	.257	98	.251	.258	.255	.245	.271	.258	99
RHB-HR	41	33	74	43	36	79	86	118	116	234	143	139	282	77

PHILADELPHIA

Home park: Citizens Bank Park **Alt.:** 20 feet **Surface:** Grass

Category	2005 Season Home Games Phil.	Opp.	Total	Road Games Phil.	Opp.	Total	Index	2004-05 Seasons Home Games Phil.	Opp.	Total	Road Games Phil.	Opp.	Total	Index
G	75	75	150	72	72	144		147	147	294	144	144	288	
Avg	.281	.264	.272	.260	.238	.250	109	.275	.262	.268	.262	.249	.256	105
AB	2516	2625	5141	2508	2312	4820	102	4954	5165	10119	5069	4725	9794	101
R	398	355	753	350	301	651	111	775	705	1480	707	614	1321	110
H	706	693	1399	653	550	1203	112	1362	1351	2713	1328	1175	2503	106
2B	137	158	295	125	131	256	108	266	286	552	267	274	541	99
3B	20	15	35	13	11	24	137	33	30	63	23	25	48	127
HR	87	93	180	69	73	142	119	187	195	382	154	152	306	121
BB	309	196	505	286	242	528	90	584	412	996	573	468	1041	93
SO	430	551	981	550	513	1063	87	892	1046	1938	1074	961	2035	92
E	38	49	87	42	43	85	98	73	89	162	80	89	169	94
E-Infield	26	44	70	37	29	66	102	55	78	133	67	71	138	94
LHB-Avg	.278	.270	.274	.268	.260	.265	104	.276	.276	.276	.270	.264	.267	103
LHB-HR	47	46	93	42	31	73	117	93	83	176	88	53	141	121
RHB-Avg	.284	.259	.270	.252	.222	.236	114	.274	.252	.262	.255	.238	.247	106
RHB-HR	40	47	87	27	42	69	120	94	112	206	66	99	165	120

2005 N.L. STATISTICS Miscellaneous

PITTSBURGH — Home park: PNC Park — Alt.: 730 feet — Surface: Grass

| | 2005 Season | | | | | | | 2003-05 Seasons (Veterans Stadium) | | | | | | |
| | Home Games | | | Road Games | | | | Home Games | | | Road Games | | | |
Category	Pit.	Opp.	Total	Pit.	Opp.	Total	Index	Pit.	Opp.	Total	Pit.	Opp.	Total	Index
G	75	75	150	75	75	150		224	224	448	221	221	442	
Avg	.262	.268	.265	.258	.260	.259	102	.268	.267	.267	.258	.265	.261	102
AB	2526	2627	5153	2631	2414	5045	102	7510	7833	15343	7722	7244	14966	101
R	299	369	668	323	343	666	100	950	1049	1999	972	1032	2004	98
H	661	705	1366	678	628	1306	105	2015	2089	4104	1995	1918	3913	103
2B	146	150	296	124	143	267	109	406	437	843	360	399	759	108
3B	21	11	32	12	11	23	136	58	33	91	52	43	95	93
HR	54	73	127	77	75	152	82	195	202	397	209	240	449	86
BB	230	280	510	206	292	498	100	646	762	1408	653	790	1443	95
SO	498	482	980	513	412	925	104	1399	1407	2806	1556	1318	2874	95
E	64	50	114	43	57	100	114	171	139	310	141	148	289	106
E-Infield	54	41	95	35	45	80	119	145	114	259	117	123	240	106
LHB-Avg	.264	.295	.279	.247	.261	.253	110	.272	.293	.283	.256	.270	.262	108
LHB-HR	24	27	51	18	28	46	107	79	76	155	67	82	149	102
RHB-Avg	.260	.255	.257	.265	.260	.262	98	.266	.251	.258	.260	.262	.261	99
RHB-HR	30	46	76	59	47	106	71	116	126	242	142	158	300	78

SAN DIEGO — Home park: Petco Park — Alt.: 20 feet — Surface: Grass

| | 2005 Season | | | | | | | 2004-05 Seasons | | | | | | |
| | Home Games | | | Road Games | | | | Home Games | | | Road Games | | | |
Category	S.D.	Opp.	Total	S.D.	Opp.	Total	Index	S.D.	Opp.	Total	S.D.	Opp.	Total	Index
G	72	72	144	72	72	144		144	144	288	144	144	288	
Avg	.257	.237	.247	.263	.281	.272	91	.256	.250	.253	.278	.275	.277	91
AB	2357	2504	4861	2541	2488	5029	97	4710	5003	9713	5139	4926	10065	97
R	277	272	549	344	370	714	77	573	578	1151	744	701	1445	80
H	606	594	1200	669	699	1368	88	1204	1250	2454	1429	1354	2783	88
2B	106	132	238	140	152	292	84	223	274	497	294	293	587	88
3B	21	19	40	14	15	29	143	40	34	74	25	30	55	139
HR	41	51	92	71	74	145	66	89	116	205	148	174	322	66
BB	265	235	500	292	233	525	99	544	420	964	526	430	956	104
SO	435	546	981	438	455	893	114	827	1038	1865	847	927	1774	109
E	54	36	90	49	50	99	91	90	80	170	108	104	212	80
E-Infield	49	29	78	40	47	87	90	79	62	141	88	92	180	78
LHB-Avg	.258	.245	.251	.289	.278	.284	88	.267	.253	.259	.288	.275	.281	92
LHB-HR	21	27	48	25	29	54	90	34	58	92	48	74	122	78
RHB-Avg	.256	.231	.244	.246	.283	.263	93	.248	.247	.248	.271	.275	.273	91
RHB-HR	20	24	44	46	45	91	51	55	58	113	100	100	200	59

SAN FRANCISCO — Home park: SBC Park — Alt.: 0 feet — Surface: Grass

| | 2005 Season | | | | | | | 2004-05 Seasons (Qualcomm Stadium) | | | | | | |
| | Home Games | | | Road Games | | | | Home Games | | | Road Games | | | |
Category	S.F.	Opp.	Total	S.F.	Opp.	Total	Index	S.F.	Opp.	Total	S.F.	Opp.	Total	Index
G	72	72	144	72	72	144		145	145	290	141	141	282	
Avg	.261	.255	.258	.262	.262	.262	99	.274	.264	.269	.260	.259	.260	104
AB	2347	2495	4842	2504	2397	4901	99	4788	5051	9839	4912	4718	9630	99
R	281	319	600	291	315	606	99	664	681	1345	639	630	1269	103
H	613	636	1249	655	628	1283	97	1312	1333	2645	1279	1220	2499	103
2B	127	117	244	140	125	265	93	279	265	544	270	251	521	102
3B	11	15	26	14	16	30	88	34	33	67	18	37	55	119
HR	59	65	124	57	68	125	100	135	134	269	139	142	281	94
BB	188	257	445	195	275	470	96	502	491	993	488	516	1004	97
SO	354	454	808	454	425	879	93	721	920	1641	856	832	1688	95
E	38	39	77	41	34	75	103	85	88	173	82	69	151	111
E-Infield	24	33	57	30	26	56	102	61	71	132	68	56	124	104
LHB-Avg	.258	.264	.262	.281	.260	.270	97	.276	.272	.274	.280	.265	.272	101
LHB-HR	16	20	36	23	26	49	73	55	51	106	67	58	125	83
RHB-Avg	.263	.248	.256	.251	.263	.257	100	.273	.258	.266	.248	.254	.251	106
RHB-HR	43	45	88	34	42	76	119	80	83	163	72	84	156	102

ST. LOUIS

Home park: Busch Stadium **Alt.:** 536 feet **Surface:** Grass

| | 2005 Season | | | | | | | 2003-05 Seasons | | | | | | |
| | Home Games | | | Road Games | | | | Home Games | | | Road Games | | | |
Category	St.L.	Opp.	Total	S.F.	Opp.	Total	Index	St.L.	Opp.	Total	S.F.	Opp.	Total	Index
G	75	75	150	72	72	144		222	222	444	219	219	438	
Avg	.272	.260	.266	.268	.256	.262	102	.279	.254	.266	.268	.265	.267	100
AB	2518	2612	5130	2517	2332	4849	102	7452	7720	15172	7718	7316	15034	100
R	379	307	686	353	271	624	106	1121	925	2046	1136	946	2082	97
H	685	680	1365	674	597	1271	103	2077	1964	4041	2071	1940	4011	99
2B	143	125	268	126	111	237	107	454	395	849	408	395	803	105
3B	10	7	17	15	13	28	57	29	30	59	45	33	78	75
HR	88	78	166	70	64	134	117	252	228	480	277	252	529	90
BB	252	204	456	239	204	443	97	760	641	1401	753	638	1391	100
SO	399	488	887	463	401	864	97	1253	1452	2705	1448	1277	2725	98
E	54	66	120	36	58	94	123	126	161	287	119	168	287	99
E-Infield	43	57	100	32	50	82	117	102	134	236	98	143	241	97
LHB-Avg	.265	.246	.254	.261	.254	.257	99	.273	.246	.258	.267	.265	.266	97
LHB-HR	30	32	62	27	28	55	103	100	92	192	101	104	205	92
RHB-Avg	.275	.270	.273	.271	.257	.265	103	.282	.261	.271	.269	.265	.267	101
RHB-HR	58	46	104	43	36	79	127	152	136	288	176	148	324	88

WASHINGTON

Home park: RFK Stadium **Alt.:** 25 feet **Surface:** Grass

| | 2005 Season | | | | | | | 2003-04 (Olympic Stadium) | | | | | | |
| | Home Games | | | Road Games | | | | Home Games | | | Road Games | | | |
Category	Wash.	Opp.	Total	Wash.	Opp.	Total	Index	Wash.	Opp.	Total	Wash.	Opp.	Total	Index
G	72	72	144	72	72	144		109	109	218	145	145	290	
Avg	.234	.248	.241	.270	.274	.272	89	.265	.260	.262	.245	.269	.257	102
AB	2299	2495	4794	2548	2442	4990	96	3589	3800	7389	4997	4858	9855	100
R	249	297	546	319	307	626	87	518	478	996	549	655	1204	110
H	538	618	1156	687	670	1357	85	950	988	1938	1226	1309	2535	102
2B	128	124	252	155	130	285	92	243	219	462	218	251	469	131
3B	16	6	22	12	10	22	104	24	14	38	20	26	46	110
HR	39	62	101	64	59	123	85	106	118	224	132	153	285	105
BB	210	229	439	222	259	481	95	355	345	700	448	479	927	101
SO	465	495	960	518	407	925	108	572	713	1285	927	900	1827	94
E	45	39	84	40	38	78	108	59	65	124	94	94	188	88
E-Infield	36	36	72	34	31	65	111	49	58	107	80	74	154	92
LHB-Avg	.248	.256	.252	.276	.272	.274	92	.262	.259	.261	.247	.285	.264	99
LHB-HR	20	28	48	24	27	51	99	51	40	91	64	63	127	100
RHB-Avg	.223	.240	.231	.264	.276	.270	86	.267	.261	.263	.243	.258	.251	105
RHB-HR	19	34	53	40	32	72	76	55	78	133	68	90	158	108

2003-2005 N.L. BALLPARK INDEX RANKINGS

RUNS PER GAME

Team	Home Games				Road Games				Index
	Games	Team	Opp.	Total	Games	Team	Opp.	Total	
Col	216	1297	1276	2573	222	874	1122	1996	132
Ari	219	954	1155	2109	216	824	1029	1853	112
Phi*	147	775	705	1480	144	707	614	1321	110
ChC	220	1027	960	1987	218	993	884	1877	105
Mil	225	988	1091	2079	218	893	1068	1961	103
SF*	145	664	681	1345	141	639	630	1269	103
Atl	219	1132	917	2049	213	1078	925	2003	99
Cin	223	1016	1211	2227	222	1041	1207	2248	99
Hou	222	1072	866	1938	220	1022	917	1939	99
Pit	224	950	1049	1999	221	972	1032	2004	98
StL................	222	1121	925	2046	219	1136	946	2082	97
NYM	221	920	939	1859	209	898	924	1822	96
Fla	213	930	835	1765	219	996	1043	2039	89
LAD	216	874	805	1679	216	960	971	1931	87
Was**	72	249	297	546	72	319	307	626	87
SD*	144	573	578	1151	144	744	701	1445	80

*Current dimensions began 2004; **Current dimensions began 2005

HOME RUNS PER AT-BAT

Team	Home Games				Road Games				Index
	Games	Team	Opp.	Total	Games	Team	Opp.	Total	
Col	216	283	283	566	222	216	238	454	121
Phi*	147	187	195	382	144	154	152	306	121
Cin	223	282	335	617	222	251	271	522	118
Ari.................	219	226	266	492	216	203	223	426	113
ChC................	220	300	234	534	218	256	210	466	112
Hou	222	256	229	485	220	232	207	439	112
Mil	225	242	265	507	218	220	236	456	107
LAD	216	214	221	435	216	207	215	422	106
Atl	219	260	195	455	213	268	203	471	95
SF*	145	135	134	269	141	139	142	281	94
StL.................	222	252	228	480	219	277	252	529	90
Pit..................	224	195	202	397	221	209	240	449	86
Was**	72	39	62	101	72	64	59	123	85
Fla.................	213	172	161	333	219	207	201	408	85
NYM	221	198	193	391	209	230	211	441	83
SD*	144	89	116	205	144	148	174	322	66

*Current dimensions began 2004; **Current dimensions began 2005

BATTING AVERAGE

Team	Home Games				Road Games				Index
	Games	Team	Opp.	Total	Games	Team	Opp.	Total	
Col	216	.300	.297	.298	222	.237	.277	.257	116
Phi*	147	.275	.262	.268	144	.262	.249	.256	105
SF*	145	.274	.264	.269	141	.260	.259	.260	104
Ari.................	219	.264	.265	.264	216	.247	.264	.255	104
Pit..................	224	.268	.267	.267	221	.258	.265	.261	102
NYM	221	.256	.260	.258	209	.248	.264	.256	101
Hou	222	.271	.242	.257	220	.254	.258	.256	100
ChC................	220	.266	.244	.255	218	.265	.244	.255	100
StL.................	222	.279	.254	.266	219	.268	.265	.267	100
Atl	219	.279	.256	.267	213	.269	.269	.269	100
Cin	223	.250	.278	.265	222	.252	.287	.269	98
Mil	225	.254	.253	.253	218	.252	.273	.263	97
Fla.................	213	.268	.246	.257	219	.268	.272	.270	95
LAD	216	.249	.240	.244	216	.260	.264	.262	93
SD*	144	.256	.250	.253	144	.278	.275	.277	91
Was**	72	.234	.248	.241	72	.270	.274	.272	89

*Current dimensions began 2004; **Current dimensions began 2005

2005 Statistical Leaders

2005 AMERICAN LEAGUE LEADERS

Batting Average
(minimum 502 PA)

Player, Team	AB	H	Avg.
M Young, Tex	668	221	.331
A Rodriguez, NYY	605	194	.321
V Guerrero, LAA	520	165	.317
J Damon, Bos	624	197	.316
B Roberts, Bal	561	176	.314
D Jeter, NYY	654	202	.309
V Martinez, Cle	547	167	.305
H Matsui, NYY	629	192	.305
T Hafner, Cle	486	148	.305
M Tejada, Bal	654	199	.304

On-Base Percentage
(minimum 502 PA; *AB+BB+HBP+SF)

Player, Team	AB	H	Avg.
J Giambi, NYY	545	240	.440
A Rodriguez, NYY	715	301	.421
T Hafner, Cle	578	236	.408
D Ortiz, Bos	713	283	.397
V Guerrero, LAA	594	234	.394
D Jeter, NYY	745	290	.389
M Ramirez, Bos	650	252	.388
B Roberts, Bal	635	246	.387
M Young, Tex	732	282	.385
M Teixeira, Tex	730	277	.379

Slugging Percentage
(minimum 502 PA)

Player, Team	AB	H	Avg.
A Rodriguez, NYY	605	369	.610
D Ortiz, Bos	601	363	.604
T Hafner, Cle	486	289	.595
M Ramirez, Bos	554	329	.594
M Teixeira, Tex	644	370	.575
V Guerrero, LAA	520	294	.565
R Sexson, Sea	558	302	.541
J Giambi, NYY	417	223	.535
P Konerko, CWS	575	307	.534
J Peralta, Cle	504	262	.520

Games
R Ibanez, Sea	162
H Matsui, NYY	162
A Rodriguez, NYY	162
I Suzuki, Sea	162
M Teixeira, Tex	162
M Tejada, Bal	162

Singles
I Suzuki, Sea	158
D Jeter, NYY	153
M Young, Tex	152
J Damon, Bos	146
C Figgins, LAA	143

Total Bases
M Teixeira, Tex	370
A Rodriguez, NYY	369
D Ortiz, Bos	363
M Young, Tex	343
M Tejada, Bal	337

Sacrifice Hits
C Crisp, Cle	13
N Logan, Det	12
T Iguchi, CWS	11
J Uribe, CWS	11
2 tied with	10

Walks
J Giambi, NYY	108
D Ortiz, Bos	102
A Rodriguez, NYY	91
R Sexson, Sea	89
P Konerko, CWS	81

Plate Appearances
D Jeter, NYY	752
I Suzuki, Sea	739
M Young, Tex	732
M Teixeira, Tex	730
C Figgins, LAA	720

Doubles
M Tejada, Bal	50
H Matsui, NYY	45
B Roberts, Bal	45
A Soriano, Tex	43
2 tied with	42

Runs Scored
A Rodriguez, NYY	124
D Jeter, NYY	122
D Ortiz, Bos	119
J Damon, Bos	117
M Young, Tex	114

Sacrifice Flies
C Monroe, Det	12
C Everett, CWS	10
J Uribe, CWS	10
3 tied with	9

Intentional Walks
V Guerrero, LAA	26
I Suzuki, Sea	23
A Huff, TB	13
J Jones, Min	12
J Mauer, Min	12

At-Bats
I Suzuki, Sea	679
M Young, Tex	668
D Jeter, NYY	654
M Tejada, Bal	654
H Blalock, Tex	647

Triples
C Crawford, TB	15
I Suzuki, Sea	12
G Sizemore, Cle	11
C Figgins, LAA	10
B Inge, Det	9

Runs Batted In
D Ortiz, Bos	148
M Ramirez, Bos	144
M Teixeira, Tex	144
A Rodriguez, NYY	130
G Sheffield, NYY	123

Stolen Bases
C Figgins, LAA	62
S Podsednik, CWS	59
C Crawford, TB	46
J Lugo, TB	39
I Suzuki, Sea	33

Hit by Pitch
S Hillenbrand, Tor	22
A Rowand, CWS	21
J Kendall, Oak	20
J Giambi, NYY	19
3 tied with	16

Hits
M Young, Tex	221
I Suzuki, Sea	206
D Jeter, NYY	202
M Tejada, Bal	199
J Damon, Bos	197

Home Runs
A Rodriguez, NYY	48
D Ortiz, Bos	47
M Ramirez, Bos	45
M Teixeira, Tex	43
P Konerko, CWS	40

GDP
J Kendall, Oak	26
M Tejada, Bal	26
J Cantu, TB	24
S Hatteberg, Oak	22
B Mueller, Bos	22

Caught Stealing
S Podsednik, CWS	23
C Figgins, LAA	17
J Lugo, TB	11
J Reed, Sea	11
2 tied with	10

Strikeouts
R Sexson, Sea	167
B Inge, Det	140
A Rodriguez, NYY	139
H Blalock, Tex	132
G Sizemore, Cle	132

SCORING POSITION AVG
minimum 100 PA

Player,Team	AB	H	AVG.
F Catalanotto, Tor	88	36	.409
M Young, Tex	136	50	.368
M Teixeira, Tex	161	59	.366
G Sheffield, NYY	162	59	.364
R White, Det	99	36	.364
M Ramirez, Bos	159	57	.358
D Ortiz, Bos	162	57	.352
M Kotsay, Oak	127	44	.346
J Kendall, Oak	128	44	.344
V Guerrero, LAA	130	44	.338

LEADOFF OBP
minimum 150 PA; * AB + BB + HBP + SF

Player,Team	PA*	OB	OBP
D Jeter, NYY	726	284	.391
B Roberts, Bal	632	243	.384
P Polanco, Det	230	88	.383
B Inge, Det	345	128	.371
J Damon, Bos	684	251	.367
J Lugo, TB	246	90	.366
R Johnson, Tor	227	83	.366
C Figgins, LAA	585	208	.356
G Sizemore, Cle	589	208	.353
D DeJesus, KC	352	124	.352

CLEANUP SLG
minimum 150 PA

Player,Team	AB	TB	SLG
M Ramirez, Bos	438	268	.612
V Guerrero, LAA	191	114	.597
T Hafner, Cle	321	189	.589
P Konerko, CWS	549	304	.554
A Rodriguez, NYY	329	182	.553
R Sexson, Sea	554	300	.542
E Chavez, Oak	409	217	.531
V Martinez, Cle	183	92	.503
M Tejada, Bal	259	124	.479
R White, Det	193	91	.472

AVG VS. LHP
minimum 125 PA

B Molina, LAA	393
G Sheffield, NYY	359
H Matsui, NYY	354
I Suzuki, Sea	352
V Wells, Tor	347

AVG VS. RHP
minimum 377 PA

B Roberts, Bal	332
M Young, Tex	328
A Rodriguez, NYY	327
C Crawford, TB	326
C Crisp, Cle	324

AVG AT HOME
minimum 251 PA

D Jeter, NYY	354
A Rodriguez, NYY	351
J Damon, Bos	334
M Teixeira, Tex	334
M Young, Tex	331

AVG ON THE ROAD
minimum 251 PA

M Ellis, Oak	335
R Cano, NYY	335
M Young, Tex	330
B Roberts, Bal	325
G Sizemore, Cle	324

OBP VS. LHP
minimum 125 PA

R Sexson, Sea	458
G Sheffield, NYY	436
B Molina, LAA	430
J Giambi, NYY	418
J Varitek, Bos	418

OBP VS. RHP
minimum 377 PA

A Rodriguez, NYY	423
T Hafner, Cle	423
D Ortiz, Bos	413
J Mauer, Min	411
B Roberts, Bal	404

LATE & CLOSE
minimum 50 PA

V Guerrero, LAA	408
V Martinez, Cle	372
M Kotsay, Oak	360
A Kennedy, LAA	351
2 tied with	346

BASES LOADED
minimum 10 PA

R Johnson, Tor	625
R Adams, Tor	600
B Mueller, Bos	526
R Sexson, Sea	500
H Matsui, NYY	474

SLG VS. LHP
minimum 125 PA

V Wells, Tor	673
G Sheffield, NYY	673
R Sexson, Sea	659
B Molina, LAA	648
M LeCroy, Min	621

SLG VS. RHP
minimum 377 PA

D Ortiz, Bos	641
T Hafner, Cle	639
M Ramirez, Bos	622
A Rodriguez, NYY	622
M Teixeira, Tex	603

AB PER HR
minimum 502 PA

M Ramirez, Bos	12.3
A Rodriguez, NYY	12.6
D Ortiz, Bos	12.8
J Giambi, NYY	13.0
R Sexson, Sea	14.3

TIMES ON BASE

A Rodriguez, NYY	301
D Jeter, NYY	290
D Ortiz, Bos	283
M Young, Tex	282
M Teixeira, Tex	277

PITCHES SEEN

D Jeter, NYY	2875
D Ortiz, Bos	2848
C Figgins, LAA	2813
A Rodriguez, NYY	2794
B Inge, Det	2774

PITCHES PER PA
minimum 502 PA

C Blake, Cle	4.28
G Zaun, Tor	4.25
D Dellucci, Tex	4.22
J Giambi, NYY	4.20
T Hafner, Cle	4.16

% PITCHES TAKEN
minimum 1500 pitches

J Giambi, NYY	64.9
S Hatteberg, Oak	62.8
J Kendall, Oak	62.7
S Podsednik, CWS	62.0
D Johnson, Oak	61.5

GROUND/FLY RATIO
minimum 502 PA

D Jeter, NYY	2.69
J Jones, Min	2.53
J Mauer, Min	2.11
S Podsednik, CWS	2.08
I Suzuki, Sea	2.06

GDP/GDP OPP
minimum 50 PA

B Broussard, Cle	0.04
J Damon, Bos	0.05
M Bellhorn, Bos-NYY	0.05
R Adams, Tor	0.05
I Suzuki, Sea	0.05

SB SUCCESS %
minimum 20 SB attempts

A Soriano, Tex	93.8
O Cabrera, LAA	91.3
C Crawford, TB	85.2
T Womack, NYY	84.4
A Kennedy, LAA	82.6

STEALS OF THIRD

S Podsednik, CWS	17
J Lugo, TB	12
D Jeter, NYY	9
B Roberts, Bal	9
C Crawford, TB	7

% CS BY CATCHERS
minimum 70 SB attempts

T Hall, TB	37.8
J Buck, KC	31.0
J Posada, NYY	28.0
V Martinez, Cle	20.7
A Pierzynski, CWS	20.2

†**Scoring-Position Average** denotes batting average when a runner is at second and/or third base. **Leadoff OBP** denotes OBP for a player batting in the first position of the batting order. **Cleanup Slugging** denotes slugging percentage for a player batting in the fourth position of the batting order. **Late & Close Avg.** refers to batting average when the game is in the seventh inning or later and the batting team is either leading by one run, tied, or has the potential tying run on base, at bat or on deck (a batting situation coming close to a pitcher's save situation). **Ground/Fly Ratio** denotes ground balls hit divided by fly balls hit. All batted balls except line drives and bunts are included. **GDP/GDP Opp.** denotes the ratio of times grounding into double plays per opportunities to do so (any situation with a runner on first and less than two out).

2005 STATISTICAL LEADERS A.L.

Earned Run Average
(minimum 162 IP)

Pitcher, Team	IP	ER	ERA
K Millwood, Cle	192.0	61	2.86
J Santana, Min	231.2	74	2.87
M Buehrle, CWS	236.2	82	3.12
J Washburn, LAA	177.1	63	3.20
C Silva, Min	188.1	72	3.44
J Lackey, LAA	209.0	80	3.44
K Rogers, Tex	195.1	75	3.46
B Colon, LAA	222.2	86	3.48
J Garland, CWS	221.0	86	3.50
J Blanton, Oak	201.1	79	3.53

Won-Lost Percentage
(minimum 15 decisions)

Pitcher, Team	W	L	Pct.
C Lee, Cle	18	5	.783
R Halladay, Tor	12	4	.750
J Lackey, LAA	14	5	.737
B Colon, LAA	21	8	.724
J Crain, Min	12	5	.706
J Santana, Min	16	7	.696
M Clement, Bos	13	6	.684
J Contreras, CWS	15	7	.682
D Wells, Bos	15	7	.682
R Johnson, NYY	17	8	.680

Opponents' Batting Average
(minimum 162 IP)

Pitcher, Team	AB	H	Avg.
J Santana, Min	856	180	.210
B Zito, Oak	836	185	.221
J Contreras, CWS	763	177	.232
J Blanton, Oak	754	178	.236
R Johnson, NYY	851	207	.243
T Wakefield, Bos	857	210	.245
B Chen, Bal	754	187	.248
S Kazmir, TB	693	172	.248
K Millwood, Cle	733	182	.248
C Sabathia, Cle	745	185	.248

GAMES

M Timlin, Bos	81
S Schoeneweis, Tor	80
T Gordon, NYY	79
B Howry, Cle	79
S Shields, LAA	78

WINS

B Colon, LAA	21
J Garland, CWS	18
C Lee, Cle	18
R Johnson, NYY	17
3 tied with	16

HITS ALLOWED

M Buehrle, CWS	240
J Towers, Tor	237
M Maroth, Det	235
Z Greinke, KC	233
J Johnson, Det	233

BATTERS FACED

M Buehrle, CWS	971
B Zito, Oak	953
F Garcia, CWS	943
T Wakefield, Bos	943
R Johnson, NYY	920

WALKS ALLOWED

S Kazmir, TB	100
B Zito, Oak	89
D Cabrera, Bal	87
J Contreras, CWS	75
G Meche, Sea	72

GAMES STARTED

R Lopez, Bal	35
B Zito, Oak	35
5 tied with	34

LOSSES

Z Greinke, KC	17
J Lima, KC	16
N Robertson, Det	16
R Franklin, Sea	15
J Westbrook, Cle	15

DOUBLES ALLOWED

J Lima, KC	58
B Arroyo, Bos	56
M Hendrickson, TB	56
R Lopez, Bal	52
Z Greinke, KC	48

INNINGS PITCHED

M Buehrle, CWS	236.2
J Santana, Min	231.2
B Zito, Oak	228.1
F Garcia, CWS	228.0
R Johnson, NYY	225.2

HIT BATSMEN

C Fossum, TB	18
M Clement, Bos	16
B Arroyo, Bos	14
3 tied with	13

COMPLETE GAMES

R Halladay, Tor	5
J Bonderman, Det	4
R Johnson, NYY	4
6 tied with	3

SAVES

F Rodriguez, LAA	45
B Wickman, Cle	45
J Nathan, Min	43
M Rivera, NYY	43
D Baez, TB	41

TRIPLES ALLOWED

B Arroyo, Bos	8
J Bonderman, Det	7
Z Greinke, KC	7
N Robertson, Det	7
5 tied with	6

RUNS ALLOWED

J Lima, KC	140
M Hendrickson, TB	126
R Lopez, Bal	126
Z Greinke, KC	125
M Maroth, Det	123

WILD PITCHES

JJ Contreras, CWS	20
F Garcia, CWS	20
J Lackey, LAA	18
J Johnson, Det	17
M Clement, Bos	13

GAMES FINISHED

M Rivera, NYY	67
D Baez, TB	64
M Batista, Tor	62
B Ryan, Bal	61
F Cordero, Tex	60

SHUTOUTS

J Garland, CWS	3
R Halladay, Tor	2
M Mussina, NYY	2
J Santana, Min	2
14 tied with	1

HOME RUNS ALLOWED

T Wakefield, Bos	35
B Chen, Bal	33
B Radke, Min	33
S Elarton, Cle	32
R Johnson, NYY	32

STRIKEOUTS

J Santana, Min	238
R Johnson, NYY	211
J Lackey, LAA	199
S Kazmir, TB	174
B Zito, Oak	171

BALKS

D Carrasco, KC	3
S Kline, Bal	3
9 tied with	2

SAVES

Player,Team	Saves
F Rodriguez, LAA	45
B Wickman, Cle	45
J Nathan, Min	43
M Rivera, NYY	43
D Baez, TB	41
F Cordero, Tex	37
E Guardado, Sea	36
B Ryan, Bal	36
D Hermanson, CWS	34
M Batista, Tor	31

SAVE PERCENTAGE
minimum 20 SvOp

Pitcher, Team	W	L	Pct.
Player,Team............OPP.		SV.	PCT.
M Rivera, NYY 47		43	91.5
B Wickman, Cle 50		45	90.0
F Rodriguez, LAA 50		45	90.0
J Nathan, Min 48		43	89.6
E Guardado, Sea 41		36	87.8
B Ryan, Bal 41		36	87.8
D Hermanson, CWS 39		34	87.2
H Street, Oak 27		23	85.2
M MacDougal, KC 25		21	84.0
D Baez, TB 49		41	83.7

RELIEF ERA
minimum 50 relief IP

Player,Team	IP	ER	ERA
M Rivera, NYY 78.1		12	1.38
H Street, Oak 78.1		15	1.72
N Cotts, CWS 60.1		13	1.94
C Politte, CWS..........67.1		15	2.00
D Hermanson, CWS..57.1		13	2.04
J Duchscherer, Oak..85.2		21	2.21
M Timlin, Bos 80.1		20	2.24
B Ryan, Bal 70.1		19	2.43
J Rincon, Min 77.0		21	2.45
B Howry, Cle 73.0		20	2.47

RELIEF WINS

J Crain, Min 12
S Shields, LAA 10
B Donnelly, LAA 9
6 tied with 7

RELIEF GAMES

M Timlin, Bos 81
S Schoeneweis, Tor.............80
T Gordon, NYY.........79
B Howry, Cle 79
S Shields, LAA 78

OPPOSITION AVG
minimum 50 relief IP

M Rivera, NYY 177
N Cotts, CWS 179
C Politte, CWS 181
J Nathan, Min 183
F Rodriguez, LAA 184

AVG VS. LHB
minimum 50 relief IP

J Nathan, Min 158
J Speier, Tor.........167
M Rivera, NYY 177
B Howry, Cle 180
C Politte, CWS 182

RELIEF LOSSES

S Shields, LAA 11
M Batista, Tor 8
T Harper, TB 6
M MacDougal, KC 6
J Rincon, Min 6

GAMES FINISHED

M Rivera, NYY 67
D Baez, TB 64
M Batista, Tor 62
B Ryan, Bal 61
F Cordero, Tex.........60

OPPOSITION OBP
minimum 50 relief IP

M Rivera, NYY 235
B Howry, Cle 237
J Nathan, Min 247
C Politte, CWS 254
J Speier, Tor.........254

AVG VS. RHB
minimum 50 relief IP

F Rodriguez, LAA 153
N Cotts, CWS 155
K Calero, Oak.........162
H Street, Oak 172
M Rivera, NYY 176

HOLDS

T Gordon, NYY.........33
S Shields, LAA 33
B Howry, Cle 29
J Rincon, Min 25
M Timlin, Bos 24

RELIEF INNINGS

S Shields, LAA 91.2
J Duchscherer, Oak 85.2
J Mateo, Sea 83.1
T Gordon, NYY 80.2
M Timlin, Bos.........80.1

OPPOSITION SLG
minimum 50 relief IP

M Rivera, NYY 230
N Cotts, CWS 241
H Street, Oak 267
J Rincon, Min.........274
B Howry, Cle 277

AVG RUNNERS ON
minimum 50 relief IP

B Wickman, Cle 149
C Politte, CWS 165
F Rodriguez, LAA 173
B Ryan, Bal 181
D Hermanson, CWS 183

BLOWN SAVES

D Baez, TB 8
M Batista, Tor 8
F Cordero, Tex.........8
T Gordon, NYY.........7
M Timlin, Bos 7

% INH RUNNERS SCORED
minimum 30 inherited runners

V Chulk, Tor 10.8
R Rincon, Oak 13.9
J Frasor, Tor.........15.0
S Sauerbeck, Cle 15.6
2 tied with 18.2

1ST BATTER AVG
minimum 40 first BFP

M Rivera, NYY 092
N Cotts, CWS 119
K Farnsworth, Det 146
D Riske, Cle.........151
S Sauerbeck, Cle 163

AVG ALLOWED SCPOS
minimum 50 relief IP

B Wickman, Cle 094
C Politte, CWS 154
J Nathan, Min 158
F Rodriguez, LAA 161
B Ryan, Bal 167

BATTER
minimum 50 relief IP

T Mulholland, Min 3.30
J Crain, Min 3.33
M Timlin, Bos.........3.42
S Schoeneweis, Tor 3.48
K Yabu, Oak 3.49

2005 STATISTICAL LEADERS *A.L.*

†**Holds** denote the number of times a relief pitcher enters the game in a save situation, records at least one out and leaves the game never having relinquished the lead. A pitcher cannot finish the game and receive credit for a hold, nor can he earn a hold and a save in the same game. **Blown Saves** denote the number of times a relief pitcher enters a game in a save situation and allows the tying or go-ahead run to score. **Pct. Inherited Scored** denotes the percent of inherited runners (those on base when a reliever enters the game) that score. **Avg., Runners On** denotes batting average allowed when runners are on base. **Avg., Scoring Pos.** denotes batting average allowed when a runner is at second and/or third base. **Easy Saves** denote saves in which the first batter faced doesn't represent the tying run and the reliever pitches one inning or less. **Regular Saves** denote those saves that are not Easy Saves or Tough Saves. **Tough Saves** denote saves which occur after the reliever enters with the tying run anywhere on base.

BASERUNNERS PER 9 IP
minimum 162 IP

Player,Team	IP	BR	BR/9
J Santana, Min	231.2	226	8.78
B Colon, LAA	222.2	261	10.55
R Johnson, NYY	225.2	266	10.61
C Silva, Min	188.1	224	10.70
M Buehrle, CWS	236.2	284	10.80
J Garland, CWS	221.0	266	10.83
B Radke, Min	200.2	244	10.94
C Lee, Cle	202.0	246	10.96
P Byrd, LAA	204.1	251	11.06
K Millwood, Cle	192.0	238	11.16

STRIKEOUTS PER 9 IP
minimum 162 IP

Player,Team	IP	SO	SO/9
J Santana, Min	231.2	238	9.25
J Lackey, LAA	209.0	199	8.57
S Kazmir, TB	186.0	174	8.42
R Johnson, NYY	225.2	211	8.42
C Young, Tex	164.2	137	7.49
C Sabathia, Cle	196.2	161	7.37
M Mussina, NYY	179.2	142	7.11
C Fossum, TB	162.2	128	7.08
J Bonderman, Det	189.0	145	6.90
M Clement, Bos	191.0	146	6.88

RUN SUPPORT PER 9 IP
minimum 162 IP

Player,Team	IP	R	R/9
D Wells, Bos	184.0	163	7.97
C Young, Tex	164.2	134	7.32
M Clement, Bos	191.0	146	6.88
C Lee, Cle	202.0	145	6.46
G Chacin, Tor	203.0	140	6.21
K Rogers, Tex	195.1	134	6.17
B Colon, LAA	222.2	149	6.02
F Garcia, CWS	228.0	151	5.96
M Hendrickson, TB	178.1	118	5.96
D Haren, Oak	217.0	143	5.93

OPPOSITION OBP
minimum 162 IP

J Santana, Min	.250
R Johnson, NYY	.291
B Colon, LAA	.291
M Buehrle, CWS	.295
B Radke, Min	.295

OPPOSITION SLG
minimum 162 IP

J Santana, Min	.346
B Zito, Oak	.361
J Lackey, LAA	.362
J Contreras, CWS	.372
C Sabathia, Cle	.373

HITS PER 9 IP
minimum 162 IP

J Santana, Min	6.99
B Zito, Oak	7.29
J Contreras, CWS	7.78
J Blanton, Oak	7.96
R Johnson, NYY	8.26

HOME RUNS PER 9 IP
minimum 162 IP

J Lackey, LAA	0.56
S Kazmir, TB	0.58
K Rogers, Tex	0.69
M Buehrle, CWS	0.76
J Westbrook, Cle	0.81

AVG VS. LHB
minimum 125 BFP

J Nathan, Min	.158
S Kazmir, TB	.174
M Rivera, NYY	.177
R Harden, Oak	.179
F Hernandez, Sea	.182

AVG VS. RHB
minimum 225 BFP

D Cabrera, Bal	.174
S McClung, TB	.197
J Santana, Min	.200
C Young, Tex	.220
R Harden, Oak	.221

AVG ALLOWED SCPOS
minimum 125 BFP

K Millwood, Cle	.194
F Garcia, CWS	.197
M Wood, KC	.214
J Contreras, CWS	.221
B Zito, Oak	.222

OBP LEAD OFF INNING
minimum 150 BFP

J Santana, Min	.237
J Blanton, Oak	.246
T Wakefield, Bos	.252
C Sabathia, Cle	.270
J Lackey, LAA	.278

K/BB RATIO
minimum 162 IP

C Silva, Min	7.89
J Santana, Min	5.29
D Wells, Bos	5.10
B Radke, Min	5.09
R Johnson, NYY	4.49

GRD/FLY RATIO OFF
minimum 162 IP

J Westbrook, Cle	3.13
J Johnson, Det	1.74
F Garcia, CWS	1.60
N Robertson, Det	1.59
C Silva, Min	1.55

PITCHES PER START
minimum 30 games started

B Zito, Oak	108.7
J Lackey, LAA	105.7
M Buehrle, CWS	105.4
J Garland, CWS	103.6
S Kazmir, TB	103.1

PITCHES PER BATTER
minimum 162 IP

C Silva, Min	3.06
J Towers, Tor	3.37
J Johnson, Det	3.38
N Robertson, Det	3.46
P Byrd, LAA	3.47

STEALS ALLOWED

K Millwood, Cle	33
J Contreras, CWS	28
J Moyer, Sea	27
R Johnson, NYY	23
2 tied with	22

CAUGHT STEALING OFF

R Johnson, NYY	14
M Maroth, Det	12
G Chacin, Tor	10
S Kazmir, TB	9
4 tied with	8

SB% ALLOWED
minimum 162 IP

J Washburn, LAA	0.0
M Maroth, Det	25.0
4 tied with	33.3

PICKOFFS

M Maroth, Det	11
M Buehrle, CWS	5
G Chacin, Tor	5
M Hendrickson, TB	5
5 tied with	4

PKOF THROW/RUNNER
minimum 162 IP

B Chen, Bal	0.93
J Garland, CWS	0.76
M Maroth, Det	0.75
R Lopez, Bal	0.69
N Robertson, Det	0.61

GDP INDUCED

C Silva, Min	34
M Buehrle, CWS	29
D Haren, Oak	26
5 tied with	25

GDP PER 9 IP
minimum 162 IP

C Silva, Min	1.6
J Washburn, LAA	1.2
J Pineiro, Sea	1.2
K Lohse, Min	1.2
K Rogers, Tex	1.2

QUALITY STARTS

J Santana, Min	24
6 tied with	22

†**Run Support per 9 IP** denotes the number of runs scored by a pitcher's team while he was still in the game times nine divided by his innings pitched. **Avg. Allowed Sc. Pos.** denotes batting average when a runner is at second and/or third base. **Grd/Fly Ratio Off** denotes ground balls allowed divided by fly balls allowed. All batted balls except line drives and bunts are included. **PkOf Throw/Runner** denotes the number of pickoff throws made by a pitcher divided by the number of runners on first base. **Quality Starts** denote the number of outings in which a starting pitcher works at least six innings and allows three or fewer earned runs.

NATIONAL LEAGUE BATTING LEADERS

BATTING AVERAGE
minimum 502 PA

Player,Team	AB	H	AVG
D Lee, ChC	594	199	.335
A Pujols, StL	591	195	.330
M Cabrera, Fla	613	198	.323
T Helton, Col	509	163	.320
S Casey, Cin	529	165	.312
C Tracy, Ari	503	155	.308
M Holliday, Col	479	147	.307
D Wright, NYM	575	176	.306
J Bay, Pit	599	183	.306
B Clark, Mil	599	183	.306

ON-BASE PERCENTAGE
minimum 502 PA; * AB + BB + HBP + SF

Player,Team	PA*	OB	OBP
T Helton, Col	625	278	.445
A Pujols, StL	700	301	.430
B Giles, SD	674	285	.423
D Lee, ChC	691	289	.418
L Berkman, Hou	565	232	.411
N Johnson, Was	547	223	.408
B Abreu, Phi	719	291	.405
J Bay, Pit	707	284	.402
C Delgado, Fla	616	246	.399
L Castillo, Fla	506	198	.391

SLUGGING PERCENTAGE
minimum 502 PA

Player,Team	AB	TB	SLG
D Lee, ChC	594	393	.662
A Pujols, StL	591	360	.609
C Delgado, Fla	521	303	.582
K Griffey Jr., Cin	491	283	.576
A Jones, Atl	586	337	.575
A Ramirez, ChC	463	263	.568
M Cabrera, Fla	613	344	.561
J Bay, Pit	599	335	.559
M Ensberg, Hou	526	293	.557
C Tracy, Ari	503	278	.553

GAMES

B Abreu, Phi	162
J Bay, Pit	162
C Lee, Mil	162
J Pierre, Fla	162
2 tied with	161

PLATE APPEARANCES

J Reyes, NYM	733
J Rollins, Phi	732
B Abreu, Phi	719
J Pierre, Fla	719
D Eckstein, StL	713

AT-BATS

J Reyes, NYM	696
J Rollins, Phi	677
J Pierre, Fla	656
D Eckstein, StL	630
C Lee, Mil	618

HITS

D Lee, ChC	199
M Cabrera, Fla	198
J Rollins, Phi	196
A Pujols, StL	195
J Reyes, NYM	190

SINGLES

W Taveras, Hou	152
J Pierre, Fla	147
D Eckstein, StL	144
J Reyes, NYM	142
B Clark, Mil	138

DOUBLES

D Lee, ChC	50
M Giles, Atl	45
T Helton, Col	45
J Bay, Pit	44
2 tied with	43

TRIPLES

J Reyes, NYM	17
J Pierre, Fla	13
R Furcal, Atl	11
J Rollins, Phi	11
D Roberts, SD	10

HOME RUNS

A Jones, Atl	51
D Lee, ChC	46
A Pujols, StL	41
A Dunn, Cin	40
T Glaus, Ari	37

TOTAL BASES

D Lee, ChC	393
A Pujols, StL	360
M Cabrera, Fla	344
A Jones, Atl	337
J Bay, Pit	335

RUNS SCORED

A Pujols, StL	129
D Lee, ChC	120
J Rollins, Phi	115
J Bay, Pit	110
A Dunn, Cin	107

RUNS BATTED IN

A Jones, Atl	128
P Burrell, Phi	117
A Pujols, StL	117
M Cabrera, Fla	116
C Delgado, Fla	115

GDP

S Casey, Cin	27
D Bell, Phi	24
N Perez, ChC	22
M Cabrera, Fla	20
P Feliz, SF	20

SACRIFICE HITS

O Vizquel, SF	20
L Castillo, Fla	18
A Pettitte, Hou	15
L Hernandez, Was	14
2 tied with	13

SACRIFICE FLIES

C Lee, Mil	11
J Guillen, Was	9
M Lowell, Fla	9
5 tied with	8

STOLEN BASES

J Reyes, NYM	60
J Pierre, Fla	57
R Furcal, Atl	46
J Rollins, Phi	41
R Freel, Cin	36

CAUGHT STEALING

J Pierre, Fla	17
J Reyes, NYM	15
B Clark, Mil	13
D Roberts, SD	12
W Taveras, Hou	11

WALKS

B Giles, SD	119
B Abreu, Phi	117
A Dunn, Cin	114
T Helton, Col	106
P Burrell, Phi	99

INTENTIONAL WALKS

A Pujols, StL	27
D Lee, ChC	23
T Helton, Col	22
C Delgado, Fla	20
B Abreu, Phi	15

HIT BY PITCH

J Guillen, Was	19
G Jenkins, Mil	19
B Clark, Mil	18
C Biggio, Hou	17
C Delgado, Fla	17

STRIKEOUTS

A Dunn, Cin	168
P Burrell, Phi	160
P Wilson, Col-Was	148
B Wilkerson, Was	147
T Glaus, Ari	145

2005 STATISTICAL LEADERS N.L.

2005 STATISTICAL LEADERS *N.L.*

SCORING POSITION AVG
minimum 100 PA

Player,Team	AB	H	AVG.
S Taguchi, StL	91	37	.407
D Eckstein, StL	126	47	.373
J Kent, LAD	134	49	.366
B Giles, SD	136	49	.360
J Bay, Pit	153	53	.346
R Aurilia, Cin	108	37	.343
O Saenz, LAD	93	31	.333
J Encarnacion, Fla	151	50	.331
D Lee, ChC	124	41	.331
O Vizquel, SF	124	41	.331

LEADOFF OBP
minimum 150 PA; * AB + BB + HBP + SF

Player,Team	PA*	OB	OBP
F Sanchez, Pit	164	64	.390
R Winn, SF	212	81	.382
B Clark, Mil	666	248	.372
R Freel, Cin	407	151	.371
M Lawton, Pit-ChC	451	165	.366
D Eckstein, StL	703	256	.364
B Wilkerson, Was	626	221	.353
D Roberts, SD	460	162	.352
C Counsell, Ari	659	231	.351
R Furcal, Atl	683	238	.348

CLEANUP SLG
minimum 150 PA

Player,Team	AB	TB	SLG
T Clark, Ari	140	97	.693
M Cabrera, Fla	291	189	.649
M Ensberg, Hou	265	159	.600
K Griffey Jr., Cin	227	135	.595
A Jones, Atl	407	238	.585
C Delgado, Fla	288	165	.573
A Ramirez, ChC	253	144	.569
J Guillen, Was	250	140	.560
M Holliday, Col	242	129	.533
N Johnson, Was	168	87	.518

AVG VS. LHP
minimum 125 PA

D Bell, Phi	.400
L Gonzalez, Col	.380
A Ramirez, ChC	.355
J Bay, Pit	.347
B Hall, Mil	.336

AVG VS. RHP
minimum 377 PA

T Helton, Col	.353
A Pujols, StL	.340
D Lee, ChC	.336
M Cabrera, Fla	.329
C Delgado, Fla	.326

AVG AT HOME
minimum 251 PA

M Holliday, Col	.357
T Helton, Col	.353
G Atkins, Col	.339
W Taveras, Hou	.330
D Lee, ChC	.328

AVG ON THE ROAD
minimum 251 PA

A Pujols, StL	.349
D Lee, ChC	.342
M Cabrera, Fla	.341
J Bay, Pit	.337
B Giles, SD	.333

OBP VS. LHP
minimum 125 PA

D Bell, Phi	.461
J Bay, Pit	.444
N Johnson, Was	.444
P Burrell, Phi	.442
D Lee, ChC	.439

OBP VS. RHP
minimum 377 PA

T Helton, Col	.480
A Pujols, StL	.432
B Giles, SD	.431
C Delgado, Fla	.431
B Abreu, Phi	.430

LATE & CLOSE
minimum 50 PA

R Hernandez, SD	.448
D Lee, ChC	.414
T Clark, Ari	.397
C Jones, Atl	.397
O Robles, LAD	.384

BASES LOADED
minimum 10 PA

J Pierre, Fla	.625
F Lopez, Cin	.600
A Nunez, StL	.600
R Church, Was	.571
J Guillen, Was	.556

SLG VS. LHP
minimum 125 PA

A Ramirez, ChC	.694
D Lee, ChC	.673
M Barrett, ChC	.624
J Bay, Pit	.620
D Wright, NYM	.602

SLG VS. RHP
minimum 377 PA

D Lee, ChC	.658
A Pujols, StL	.633
T Helton, Col	.630
C Delgado, Fla	.626
A Jones, Atl	.588

AB PER HR
minimum 502 PA

A Jones, Atl	11.5
D Lee, ChC	12.9
A Dunn, Cin	13.6
K Griffey Jr., Cin	14.0
A Pujols, StL	14.4

TIMES ON BASE

A Pujols, StL	301
B Abreu, Phi	291
D Lee, ChC	289
B Giles, SD	285
J Bay, Pit	284

PITCHES SEEN

B Abreu, Phi	3159
D Eckstein, StL	2859
P Burrell, Phi	2855
A Dunn, Cin	2848
D Lee, ChC	2786

PITCHES PER PA
minimum 502 PA

B Abreu, Phi	4.39
P Burrell, Phi	4.27
A Dunn, Cin	4.24
B Wilkerson, Was	4.21
J Edmonds, StL	4.17

% PITCHES TAKEN
minimum 1500 pitches

B Abreu, Phi	66.5
B Giles, SD	66.0
O Robles, LAD	64.9
D Roberts, SD	64.4
C Counsell, Ari	63.8

GROUND/FLY RATIO
minimum 502 PA

L Castillo, Fla	3.42
R Clayton, Ari	2.69
J Pierre, Fla	2.46
W Taveras, Hou	1.85
M Lawton, Pit-ChC	1.84

GDP/GDP OPP
minimum 50 PA

P Nevin, SD	0.03
R Langerhans, Atl	0.04
K Lofton, Phi	0.04
A Dunn, Cin	0.04
D Mohr, Col	0.04

SB SUCCESS %
minimum 20 SB attempts

J Bay, Pit	95.5
K Lofton, Phi	88.0
J Rollins, Phi	87.2
R Furcal, Atl	82.1
J Reyes, NYM	80.0

STEALS OF THIRD

J Rollins, Phi	13
J Reyes, NYM	11
R Freel, Cin	8
J Pierre, Fla	8
3 tied with	6

% CS BY CATCHERS
minimum 70 SB attempts

B Schneider, Was	37.7
M Matheny, SF	32.3
J LaRue, Cin	30.1
J Estrada, Atl	26.6
R Hernandez, SD	25.7

†**Scoring-Position Average** denotes batting average when a runner is at second and/or third base. **Leadoff OBP** denotes OBP for a player batting in the first position of the batting order. **Cleanup Slugging** denotes slugging percentage for a player batting in the fourth position of the batting order. **Late & Close Avg.** refers to batting average when the game is in the seventh inning or later and the batting team is either leading by one run, tied, or has the potential tying run on base, at bat or on deck (a batting situation coming close to a pitcher's save situation). **Ground/Fly Ratio** denotes ground balls hit divided by fly balls hit. All batted balls except line drives and bunts are included. **GDP/GDP Opp.** denotes the ratio of times grounding into double plays per opportunities to do so (any situation with a runner on first and less than two out).

EARNED RUN AVERAGE
minimum 162 IP

Player,Team	IP	ER	ERA
R Clemens, Hou	211.1	44	1.87
A Pettitte, Hou	222.1	59	2.39
D Willis, Fla	236.1	69	2.63
P Martinez, NYM	217.0	68	2.82
C Carpenter, StL	241.2	76	2.83
J Peavy, SD	203.0	65	2.88
R Oswalt, Hou	241.2	79	2.94
J Smoltz, Atl	229.2	78	3.06
J Patterson, Was	198.1	69	3.13
C Zambrano, ChC	223.1	81	3.26

WON-LOST PERCENTAGE
minimum 15 decisions

Pitcher,Team	W	L	Pct
J Sosa, Atl	13	3	.813
C Carpenter, StL	21	5	.808
C Zambrano, ChC	14	6	.700
D Willis, Fla	22	10	.688
A Eaton, SD	11	5	.688
M Mulder, StL	16	8	.667
J Smoltz, Atl	14	7	.667
A Pettitte, Hou	17	9	.654
J Beckett, Fla	15	8	.652
P Martinez, NYM	15	8	.652

OPPOSITION AVG
minimum 162 IP

Pitcher,Team	AB	H	AVG
R Clemens, Hou	761	151	.198
P Martinez, NYM	781	159	.204
C Zambrano, ChC	801	170	.212
J Peavy, SD	746	162	.217
M Prior, ChC	630	143	.227
A Pettitte, Hou	817	188	.230
C Carpenter, StL	884	204	.231
J Patterson, Was	738	172	.233
J Beckett, Fla	653	153	.234
D Davis, Mil	835	196	.235

GAMES
S Eyre, SF	86
G Majewski, Was	79
D Sanchez, LAD	79
4 tied with	78

WINS
D Willis, Fla	22
C Carpenter, StL	21
R Oswalt, Hou	20
C Capuano, Mil	18
2 tied with	17

HITS ALLOWED
L Hernandez, Was	268
R Oswalt, Hou	243
G Maddux, ChC	239
E Milton, Cin	237
B Webb, Ari	229

BATTERS FACED
L Hernandez, Was	1065
R Oswalt, Hou	1002
D Willis, Fla	960
C Carpenter, StL	953
C Capuano, Mil	949

WALKS ALLOWED
K Wells, Pit	99
D Davis, Mil	93
C Capuano, Mil	91
C Zambrano, ChC	86
J Schmidt, SF	85

GAMES STARTED
C Capuano, Mil	35
D Davis, Mil	35
L Hernandez, Was	35
J Lieber, Phi	35
D Lowe, LAD	35
G Maddux, ChC	35
R Oswalt, Hou	35

LOSSES
K Wells, Pit	18
J Wright, Col	16
7 tied with	15

DOUBLES ALLOWED
E Milton, Cin	55
A Harang, Cin	52
J Wright, Col	51
3 tied with	50

INNINGS PITCHED
L Hernandez, Was	246.1
C Carpenter, StL	241.2
R Oswalt, Hou	241.2
D Willis, Fla	236.1
J Smoltz, Atl	229.2

HIT BATSMEN
J Weaver, LAD	18
J Wright, Col	15
V Zambrano, NYM	15
B Kim, Col	14
L Hernandez, Was	13

COMPLETE GAMES
C Carpenter, StL	7
D Willis, Fla	7
A Burnett, Fla	4
P Martinez, NYM	4
R Oswalt, Hou	4

SAVES
C Cordero, Was	47
T Hoffman, SD	43
B Lidge, Hou	42
T Jones, Fla	40
2 tied with	39

TRIPLES ALLOWED
B Tomko, SF	10
D Willis, Fla	9
A Harang, Cin	8
R Ortiz, Ari	8
R Oswalt, Hou	8

RUNS ALLOWED
E Milton, Cin	141
J Francis, Col	119
J Wright, Col	119
L Hernandez, Was	116
K Wells, Pit	116

WILD PITCHES
B Webb, Ari	14
A Burnett, Fla	12
B Kim, Col	11
J Marquis, StL	10
3 tied with	9

GAMES FINISHED
B Wagner, Phi	70
B Lidge, Hou	65
C Cordero, Was	62
D Turnbow, Mil	62
2 tied with	55

SHUTOUTS
D Willis, Fla	5
C Carpenter, StL	4
J Peavy, SD	3
4 tied with	2

HOME RUNS ALLOWED
E Milton, Cin	40
J Vazquez, Ari	35
J Weaver, LAD	35
R Ortiz, Cin	34
J Lieber, Phi	33

STRIKEOUTS
J Peavy, SD	216
C Carpenter, StL	213
D Davis, Mil	208
P Martinez, NYM	208
B Myers, Phi	208

BALKS
C Capuano, Mil	4
B Myers, Phi	4
J Marquis, StL	3
M Redman, Pit	3
W Rodriguez, Hou	3

SAVES

Player,Team	Saves
C Cordero, Was	47
T Hoffman, SD	43
B Lidge, Hou	42
T Jones, Fla	40
J Isringhausen, StL	39
D Turnbow, Mil	39
B Wagner, Phi	38
R Dempster, ChC	33
B Fuentes, Col	31
B Looper, NYM	28

SAVE PERCENTAGE
minimum 20 SvOp

Player,Team	OPP.	SV.	PCT.
R Dempster, ChC	35	33	94.3
T Hoffman, SD	46	43	93.5
B Wagner, Phi	41	38	92.7
B Lidge, Hou	46	42	91.3
B Fuentes, Col	34	31	91.2
J Isringhausen, StL	43	39	90.7
D Turnbow, Mil	43	39	90.7
T Jones, Fla	45	40	88.9
C Cordero, Was	54	47	87.0
A Benitez, SF	23	19	82.6

RELIEF ERA
minimum 50 relief IP

Player,Team	IP	ER	ERA
B Wagner, Phi	77.2	13	1.51
D Turnbow, Mil	67.1	13	1.74
C Cordero, Was	74.1	15	1.82
S Linebrink, SD	73.2	15	1.83
R Dempster, ChC	58.1	12	1.85
H Carrasco, Was	61.2	14	2.04
T Jones, Fla	73.0	17	2.10
J Isringhausen, StL	59.0	14	2.14
A Reyes, StL	62.2	15	2.15
A Heilman, NYM	66.0	16	2.18

RELIEF WINS

L Ayala, Was	8
R Hernandez, NYM	8
S Linebrink, SD	8
5 tied with	7

RELIEF GAMES

S Eyre, SF	86
G Majewski, Was	79
D Sanchez, LAD	79
4 tied with	78

OPPOSITION AVG
minimum 50 relief IP

M Wise, Mil	160
B Wagner, Phi	165
A Reyes, StL	177
A Fultz, Phi	186
U Urbina, Phi	186

AVG VS. LHB
minimum 50 relief IP

B Wagner, Phi	128
M Wise, Mil	130
J Fassero, SF	149
M Gonzalez, Pit	152
C Hammond, SD	164

RELIEF LOSSES

Y Brazoban, LAD	10
L Hawkins, ChC-SF	8
D Kolb, Atl	8
J Mesa, Pit	8
A Otsuka, SD	8

GAMES FINISHED

B Wagner, Phi	70
B Lidge, Hou	65
C Cordero, Was	62
D Turnbow, Mil	62
2 tied with	55

OPPOSITION OBP
minimum 50 relief IP

B Wagner, Phi	229
C Cordero, Was	248
M Wise, Mil	249
A Reyes, StL	261
D Wheeler, Hou	265

AVG VS. RHB
minimum 50 relief IP

D Turnbow, Mil	167
A Fultz, Phi	170
A Reyes, StL	172
B Wagner, Phi	173
T Hoffman, SD	179

HOLDS

S Eyre, SF	32
R Madson, Phi	32
J Tavarez, StL	32
S Linebrink, SD	26
G Majewski, Was	24

RELIEF INNINGS

S Torres, Pit	94.2
R Madson, Phi	87.0
G Majewski, Was	86.0
D Sanchez, LAD	82.0
R Vogelsong, Pit	81.1

OPPOSITION SLG
minimum 50 relief IP

A Heilman, NYM	249
B Wagner, Phi	265
R Dempster, ChC	265
M Wise, Mil	281
T Jones, Fla	283

AVG RUNNERS ON
minimum 50 relief IP

B Wagner, Phi	147
A Reyes, StL	155
D Turnbow, Mil	165
S Eyre, SF	167
M Gonzalez, Pit	169

BLOWN SAVES

L Hawkins, ChC-SF	9
C Reitsma, Atl	9
B Looper, NYM	8
4 tied with	7

% INH RUNNERS SCORED
minimum 30 inherited runners

J Grabow, Pit	10.3
S Eyre, SF	15.4
R Cormier, Phi	15.6
K Wunsch, LAD	16.2
J Eischen, Was	16.7

1ST BATTER AVG
minimum 40 first BFP

S Eyre, SF	107
J Santana, Mil	121
A Heilman, NYM	140
U Urbina, Phi	151
B Wagner, Phi	153

AVG ALLOWED SCPOS
minimum 50 relief IP

B Fuentes, Col	128
B Wagner, Phi	130
D Turnbow, Mil	130
B Thompson, StL	139
J Isringhausen, StL	140

PITCHES PER BATTER
minimum 50 relief IP

C Qualls, Hou	3.40
B Thompson, StL	3.44
B Meadows, Pit	3.46
T Coffey, Cin	3.48
L Ayala, Was	3.48

†**Holds** denote the number of times a relief pitcher enters the game in a save situation, records at least one out and leaves the game never having relinquished the lead. A pitcher cannot finish the game and receive credit for a hold, nor can he earn a hold and a save in the same game. **Blown Saves** denote the number of times a relief pitcher enters a game in a save situation and allows the tying or go-ahead run to score. **Pct. Inherited Scored** denotes the percent of inherited runners (those on base when a reliever enters the game) that score. **Avg., Runners On** denotes batting average allowed when runners are on base. **Avg., Scoring Pos.** denotes batting average allowed when a runner is at second and/or third base. **Easy Saves** denote saves in which the first batter faced doesn't represent the tying run and the reliever pitches one inning or less. **Regular Saves** denote those saves that are not Easy Saves or Tough Saves. **Tough Saves** denote saves which occur after the reliever enters with the tying run anywhere on base.

BASERUNNERS PER 9 IP
minimum 162 IP

Player,Team	IP	BR	BR/9
P Martinez, NYM	217.0	210	8.71
R Clemens, Hou	211.1	216	9.20
A Pettitte, Hou	222.1	232	9.39
C Carpenter, StL	241.2	258	9.61
J Peavy, SD	203.0	219	9.71
J Smoltz, Atl	229.2	264	10.35
D Willis, Fla	236.1	276	10.51
C Zambrano, ChC	223.1	264	10.64
J Beckett, Fla	178.2	218	10.98
J Patterson, Was	198.1	242	10.98

STRIKEOUTS PER 9 IP
minimum 162 IP

Player,Team	IP	SO	SO/9
M Prior, ChC	166.2	188	10.15
J Peavy, SD	203.0	216	9.58
B Myers, Phi	215.1	208	8.69
J Schmidt, SF	172.0	165	8.63
P Martinez, NYM	217.0	208	8.63
A Burnett, Fla	209.0	198	8.53
D Davis, Mil	222.2	208	8.41
J Patterson, Was	198.1	185	8.39
J Beckett, Fla	178.2	166	8.36
C Zambrano, ChC	223.1	202	8.14

RUN SUPPORT PER 9 IP
minimum 162 IP

Player,Team	IP	R	R/9
J Francis, Col	183.2	130	6.37
M Morris, StL	192.2	134	6.26
J Beckett, Fla	178.2	117	5.89
B Claussen, Cin	166.2	104	5.62
K Benson, NYM	174.1	108	5.58
J Suppan, StL	194.1	120	5.56
C Lidle, Phi	184.2	114	5.56
B Myers, Phi	215.1	132	5.52
C Carpenter, StL	241.2	148	5.51
C Capuano, Mil	219.0	133	5.47

OPPOSITION OBP
minimum 162 IP

P Martinez, NYM	.252
R Clemens, Hou	.261
A Pettitte, Hou	.268
J Peavy, SD	.271
C Carpenter, StL	.273

OPPOSITION SLG
minimum 162 IP

R Clemens, Hou	.284
P Martinez, NYM	.334
A Burnett, Fla	.334
C Zambrano, ChC	.338
A Pettitte, Hou	.348

HITS PER 9 IP
minimum 162 IP

R Clemens, Hou	6.43
P Martinez, NYM	6.59
C Zambrano, ChC	6.85
J Peavy, SD	7.18
C Carpenter, StL	7.60

HOME RUNS PER 9 IP
minimum 162 IP

D Willis, Fla	0.42
R Clemens, Hou	0.47
T Glavine, NYM	0.51
A Burnett, Fla	0.52
V Zambrano, NYM	0.65

AVG VS. LHB
minimum 125 BFP

C Cordero, Was	.192
R Clemens, Hou	.195
S Linebrink, SD	.195
A Pettitte, Hou	.200
M Mulder, StL	.201

AVG VS. RHB
minimum 225 BFP

B Wagner, Phi	.173
S Torres, Pit	.189
P Martinez, NYM	.192
C Carpenter, StL	.199
R Clemens, Hou	.202

AVG ALLOWED SCPOS
minimum 125 BFP

R Clemens, Hou	.138
J Sosa, Atl	.194
A Pettitte, Hou	.203
V Padilla, Phi	.205
P Martinez, NYM	.209

OBP LEAD OFF INNING
minimum 150 BFP

C Carpenter, StL	.239
R Clemens, Hou	.242
P Martinez, NYM	.253
K Benson, NYM	.254
A Pettitte, Hou	.258

K/BB RATIO
minimum 162 IP

P Martinez, NYM	4.43
J Peavy, SD	4.32
C Carpenter, StL	4.18
J Vazquez, Ari	4.17
A Pettitte, Hou	4.17

GRD/FLY RATIO OFF
minimum 162 IP

B Webb, Ari	4.34
D Lowe, LAD	2.92
M Mulder, StL	2.74
T Hudson, Atl	2.50
A Burnett, Fla	2.42

PITCHES PER START
minimum 30 games started

L Hernandez, Was	114.6
C Zambrano, ChC	107.9
N Lowry, SF	107.5
A Harang, Cin	106.7
D Davis, Mil	106.5

PITCHES PER BATTER
minimum 162 IP

G Maddux, ChC	3.31
J Lieber, Phi	3.43
B Lawrence, SD	3.46
M Mulder, StL	3.47
J Wright, Col	3.49

STEALS ALLOWED

G Maddux, ChC	32
J Patterson, Was	26
B Webb, Ari	26
J Wright, Col	25
V Zambrano, NYM	25

CAUGHT STEALING OFF

J Francis, Col	11
L Hernandez, Was	11
J Patterson, Was	11
3 tied with	9

SB% ALLOWED
minimum 162 IP

C Zambrano, ChC	10.0
C Carpenter, StL	16.7
D Willis, Fla	16.7
C Capuano, Mil	18.2
M Mulder, StL	20.0

PICKOFFS

C Capuano, Mil	12
J Wright, Col	6
4 tied with	5

PKOF THROW/RUNNER
minimum 162 IP

C Capuano, Mil	1.17
R Clemens, Hou	0.78
D Davis, Mil	0.75
B Halsey, Ari	0.70
K Benson, NYM	0.67

GDP INDUCED

M Mulder, StL	32
H Ramirez, Atl	32
B Webb, Ari	30
J Marquis, StL	29
J Suppan, StL	29

GDP PER 9 IP
minimum 162 IP

H Ramirez, Atl	1.4
M Mulder, StL	1.4
J Suppan, StL	1.3
J Marquis, StL	1.3
M Redman, Pit	1.2

QUALITY STARTS

C Carpenter, StL	27
A Pettitte, Hou	27
R Clemens, Hou	26
R Oswalt, Hou	25
D Willis, Fla	25

†**Run Support per 9 IP** denotes the number of runs scored by a pitcher's team while he was still in the game times nine divided by his innings pitched. **Avg. Allowed Sc. Pos.** denotes batting average allowed when a runner is at second and/or third base. **Grd/Fly Ratio Off** denotes ground balls allowed divided by fly balls allowed. All batted balls except line drives and bunts are included. **PkOf Throw/Runner** denotes the number of pickoff throws made by a pitcher divided by the number of runners on first base. **Quality Starts** denote the number of outings in which a starting pitcher works at least six innings and allows three or fewer earned runs.

2005 STATISTICAL LEADERS N.L.

BATTING

2005 STATISTICAL LEADERS *Active career*

BATTING AVERAGE
minimum 1000 PA

Rk.	Player	AB	H	AVG
1	Todd Helton	4560	1535	.337
2	Albert Pujols	2954	982	.332
3	Ichiro Suzuki	3401	1130	.332
4	Vladimir Guerrero	4895	1586	.324
5	Nomar Garciaparra	4363	1395	.320
6	Derek Jeter	6167	1936	.314
7	Manny Ramirez	6126	1922	.314
8	Larry Walker	6907	2160	.313
9	Mike Piazza	6203	1929	.311
10	Frank Thomas	6956	2136	.307
11	Alex Rodriguez	6195	1901	.307
12	Magglio Ordonez	4112	1259	.306
13	Sean Casey	4017	1225	.305
14	Juan Pierre	3411	1040	.305
15	Ivan Rodriguez	7198	2190	.304
16	Mike Sweeney	4187	1273	.304
17	Chipper Jones	5974	1811	.303
18	Bobby Abreu	4728	1432	.303
19	Jose Vidro	3794	1146	.302
20	Jason Kendall	5207	1572	.302
21	Lance Berkman	3151	951	.302
22	Moises Alou	6315	1901	.301
23	Mark Loretta	4275	1285	.301
24	Placido Polanco	3265	981	.300
25	2 tied with			.300

ON-BASE PERCENTAGE
minimum 1000 PA; * AB + BB + HBP + SF

Rk.	Player	*PA	OB	OBP
1	Barry Bonds	11632	5146	.442
2	Todd Helton	5421	2348	.433
3	Frank Thomas	8602	3673	.427
4	Albert Pujols	3427	1427	.416
5	Lance Berkman	3812	1584	.416
6	Jason Giambi	6327	2616	.413
7	Brian Giles	5656	2334	.413
8	Bobby Abreu	5677	2333	.411
9	Manny Ramirez	7223	2953	.409
10	Jim Thome	7280	2972	.408
11	Jeff Bagwell	9428	3843	.408
12	Chipper Jones	7063	2834	.401
13	Larry Walker	8023	3211	.400
14	Gary Sheffield	9385	3743	.399
15	John Olerud	9051	3602	.398
16	Carlos Delgado	6634	2608	.393
17	J.D. Drew	3163	1242	.393
18	Vladimir Guerrero	5494	2146	.391
19	Travis Hafner	1545	600	.388
20	Jason Bay	1281	496	.387
21	Derek Jeter	6939	2675	.386
22	Alex Rodriguez	7084	2729	.385
23	Jim Edmonds	6481	2490	.384
24	Bernie Williams	8580	3291	.384
25	Nick Johnson	1761	675	.383

SLUGGING PERCENTAGE
minimum 1000 PA

Rk.	Player	AB	TB	SLG.
1	Albert Pujols	2954	1834	.621
2	Barry Bonds	9140	5584	.611
3	Todd Helton	4560	2769	.607
4	Manny Ramirez	6126	3668	.599
5	Vladimir Guerrero	4895	2871	.587
6	Alex Rodriguez	6195	3576	.577
7	Frank Thomas	6956	3949	.568
8	Larry Walker	6907	3904	.565
9	Jim Thome	5919	3327	.562
10	Ken Griffey Jr.	7870	4414	.561
11	Juan Gonzalez	6556	3676	.561
12	Carlos Delgado	5529	3089	.559
13	Lance Berkman	3151	1756	.557
14	Travis Hafner	1321	735	.556
15	Mike Piazza	6203	3440	.555
16	Jason Bay	1097	607	.553
17	Nomar Garciaparra	4363	2373	.544
18	Jim Edmonds	5557	3016	.543
19	Brian Giles	4656	2522	.542
20	Mark Teixeira	1718	929	.541
21	Jeff Bagwell	7797	4213	.540
22	Jason Giambi	5174	2791	.539
23	Chipper Jones	5974	3213	.538
24	Sammy Sosa	8401	4511	.537
25	David Ortiz	3108	1660	.534

HITS

Rafael Palmeiro	3020
Craig Biggio	2795
Barry Bonds	2742
Julio Franco	2521
Steve Finley	2426
Gary Sheffield	2345
B.J. Surhoff	2326
Jeff Bagwell	2314
Ken Griffey Jr.	2304
Sammy Sosa	2304
Omar Vizquel	2301
Marquis Grissom	2251
John Olerud	2239
Bernie Williams	2218
Luis Gonzalez	2214
Ivan Rodriguez	2190
Larry Walker	2160
Ruben Sierra	2147
Kenny Lofton	2142
Frank Thomas	2136

HOME RUNS

Barry Bonds	708
Sammy Sosa	588
Rafael Palmeiro	569
Ken Griffey Jr.	536
Jeff Bagwell	449
Gary Sheffield	449
Frank Thomas	448
Manny Ramirez	435
Juan Gonzalez	434
Jim Thome	430
Alex Rodriguez	429
Mike Piazza	397
Larry Walker	383
Carlos Delgado	369
Tino Martinez	339
Jim Edmonds	331
Chipper Jones	331
Jeff Kent	331
Luis Gonzalez	316
Vinny Castilla	315

RUNS BATTED IN

Barry Bonds	1853
Rafael Palmeiro	1835
Sammy Sosa	1575
Ken Griffey Jr.	1536
Jeff Bagwell	1529
Gary Sheffield	1476
Frank Thomas	1465
Manny Ramirez	1414
Juan Gonzalez	1404
Ruben Sierra	1318
Jeff Kent	1312
Larry Walker	1311
Tino Martinez	1271
Luis Gonzalez	1251
John Olerud	1230
Alex Rodriguez	1226
Mike Piazza	1223
Bernie Williams	1196
Jim Thome	1193
Carlos Delgado	1173

STOLEN BASES

Kenny Lofton	567
Barry Bonds	506
Eric Young	457
Marquis Grissom	429
Craig Biggio	407
Tony Womack	362
Omar Vizquel	342
Steve Finley	313
Reggie Sanders	297
Luis Castillo	281
Johnny Damon	281
Julio Franco	273
Juan Pierre	267
Ray Durham	248
Edgar Renteria	246
Bobby Abreu	241
Sammy Sosa	234
Larry Walker	230
Mike Cameron	229
Raul Mondesi	229

SEASONS PLAYED

Roger Clemens	22
Julio Franco	21
John Franco	21
Rafael Palmeiro	20
Barry Bonds	20
Benito Santiago	20
Greg Maddux	20
Ruben Sierra	19
Jamie Moyer	19
Terry Mulholland	19
B.J. Surhoff	19
Kevin Brown	19
David Wells	19
Tom Glavine	19
Al Leiter	19

DOUBLES

Craig Biggio	604
Rafael Palmeiro	585
Barry Bonds	564
John Olerud	500
Luis Gonzalez	495
Jeff Bagwell	488
Jeff Kent	474
Larry Walker	471
Frank Thomas	447
Ivan Rodriguez	445

TOTAL BASES

Barry Bonds	5584
Rafael Palmeiro	5388
Sammy Sosa	4511
Ken Griffey Jr.	4414
Craig Biggio	4283
Jeff Bagwell	4213
Gary Sheffield	4153
Steve Finley	3966
Frank Thomas	3949
Larry Walker	3904

STRIKEOUTS

Sammy Sosa	2194
Jim Thome	1762
Jeff Bagwell	1558
Craig Biggio	1557
Reggie Sanders	1513
Barry Bonds	1434
Ken Griffey Jr.	1416
Jim Edmonds	1411
Carlos Delgado	1363
Jose Hernandez	1351

SB SUCCESS %
minimum 100 SB attempts

Carlos Beltran	87.8
Tony Womack	83.2
Jose Reyes	82.1
Carl Crawford	81.6
Alex Rodriguez	80.1
Aaron Boone	80.0

Alfonso Soriano	79.7
Kenny Lofton	79.3
Mike Cameron	79.2
Derek Jeter	79.0

GAMES

Rafael Palmeiro	2831
Barry Bonds	2730
Craig Biggio	2564
Steve Finley	2401
Julio Franco	2377
B.J. Surhoff	2313
Omar Vizquel	2290
Sammy Sosa	2240
John Olerud	2234
Gary Sheffield	2190

TRIPLES

Steve Finley	112
Kenny Lofton	98
Johnny Damon	80
Barry Bonds	77
Jose Offerman	72
Ray Durham	70
Cristian Guzman	67
Luis Gonzalez	63
Larry Walker	62
Neifi Perez	60

WALKS

Barry Bonds	2311
Frank Thomas	1466
Jeff Bagwell	1401
Rafael Palmeiro	1353
Gary Sheffield	1280
John Olerud	1275
Jim Thome	1257
Craig Biggio	1097
Ken Griffey Jr.	1038
Bernie Williams	1036

K/BB RATIO
minimum 1000 AB

Barry Bonds	.621
Eric Young	.689
Brian Giles	.700
Gary Sheffield	.746
Frank Thomas	.795
John Olerud	.797
Todd Helton	.805
Orlando Palmeiro	.844
Albert Pujols	.858
Jason Kendall	.877

CAUGHT STEALING

Eric Young	166
Kenny Lofton	148
Barry Bonds	141
Omar Vizquel	139
Craig Biggio	119
Steve Finley	118
Marquis Grissom	116
Luis Castillo	114

Reggie Sanders	107
Sammy Sosa	107

AT-BATS

Rafael Palmeiro	10472
Craig Biggio	9811
Barry Bonds	9140
Steve Finley	8877
Julio Franco	8422
Sammy Sosa	8401
Omar Vizquel	8387
Marquis Grissom	8275
B.J. Surhoff	8258
Ruben Sierra	8016

AB PER HR
minimum 1000 AB

Barry Bonds	12.9
Jim Thome	13.8
Manny Ramirez	14.1
Sammy Sosa	14.3
Adam Dunn	14.4
Alex Rodriguez	14.4
Ken Griffey Jr.	14.7
Albert Pujols	14.7
Carlos Delgado	15.0
Juan Gonzalez	15.1

INTENTIONAL WALKS

Barry Bonds	607
Ken Griffey Jr.	210
Rafael Palmeiro	172
Vladimir Guerrero	170
Frank Thomas	162
John Olerud	157
Jeff Bagwell	155
Sammy Sosa	151
Carlos Delgado	148
Mike Piazza	144

SACRIFICE HITS

Omar Vizquel	205
Tom Glavine	191
Greg Maddux	159
Jose Vizcaino	105
John Smoltz	104
Royce Clayton	103
Curt Schilling	102
Rey Sanchez	93
Neifi Perez	92
Craig Biggio	89

GDP

Julio Franco	299
Ivan Rodriguez	239
John Olerud	232
Rafael Palmeiro	232
Jeff Bagwell	221
Vinny Castilla	217
Bernie Williams	209
Mike Piazza	207
Benito Santiago	204
Royce Clayton	197

RUNS SCORED

Barry Bonds	2078
Craig Biggio	1697
Rafael Palmeiro	1663
Jeff Bagwell	1517
Sammy Sosa	1422
Gary Sheffield	1411
Ken Griffey Jr.	1405
Steve Finley	1368
Kenny Lofton	1363
Larry Walker	1355

AB PER RBI
minimum 1000 AB

Manny Ramirez	4.3
Juan Gonzalez	4.7
Carlos Delgado	4.7
Frank Thomas	4.7
Albert Pujols	4.8
Richie Sexson	4.9
Barry Bonds	4.9
Jim Thome	5.0
David Ortiz	5.0
Todd Helton	5.0

HIT BY PITCH

Craig Biggio	273
Jason Kendall	197
Carlos Delgado	139
Larry Walker	138
Jeff Bagwell	128
Gary Sheffield	118
Damion Easley	115
Jason Giambi	111
Jeff Kent	105
Derek Jeter	103

SACRIFICE FLIES

Rafael Palmeiro	119
Ruben Sierra	119
Frank Thomas	109
B.J. Surhoff	104
Jeff Bagwell	102
Gary Sheffield	101
John Olerud	96
Jeff Kent	92
Jeff Conine	91
Barry Bonds	88

AB PER GDP
minimum 1000 AB

Ichiro Suzuki	136.0
Jose Reyes	132.2
Rob Mackowiak	123.4
Dave Roberts	121.8
Omar Infante	120.2
Carl Crawford	119.9
Greg Maddux	117.2
Russell Branyan	104.6
Johnny Damon	99.6
Tom Glavine	99.6

2005 STATISTICAL LEADERS *Active career*

WINS

Roger Clemens	341
Greg Maddux	318
Tom Glavine	275
Randy Johnson	263
David Wells	227
Mike Mussina	224
Kevin Brown	211
Jamie Moyer	205
Pedro Martinez	197
Curt Schilling	192

GAMES

John Franco	1119
Mike Stanton	1027
Mike Timlin	893
Roberto Hernandez	892
Jose Mesa	887
Paul Quantrill	841
Steve Reed	833
Todd Jones	812
Jeff Nelson	792
Buddy Groom	786

COMPLETE GAMES

Roger Clemens	118
Greg Maddux	108
Randy Johnson	96
Curt Schilling	82
Kevin Brown	72
Mike Mussina	56
Tom Glavine	55
David Wells	54
Scott Erickson	51
John Smoltz	50

STRIKEOUTS

Roger Clemens	4502
Randy Johnson	4372
Greg Maddux	3052
Pedro Martinez	2861
Curt Schilling	2832
John Smoltz	2567
Mike Mussina	2400
Kevin Brown	2397
Tom Glavine	2350
David Wells	2081

LOSSES

Greg Maddux	189
Tom Glavine	184
Roger Clemens	172
Jamie Moyer	152
Kevin Brown	144
David Wells	143
Terry Mulholland	142
Scott Erickson	136
Randy Johnson	136
Steve Trachsel	135

GAMES STARTED

Roger Clemens	671
Greg Maddux	639
Tom Glavine	603
Randy Johnson	513
Jamie Moyer	485
Kevin Brown	476
David Wells	447
Mike Mussina	443
Kenny Rogers	400
John Smoltz	394

COMPLETE GAME %
minimum 100 GS

Curt Schilling	0.22
Randy Johnson	0.19
Roger Clemens	0.18
Greg Maddux	0.17
Kevin Brown	0.15
Livan Hernandez	0.15
Scott Erickson	0.14
Terry Mulholland	0.14
Mark Mulder	0.14
Pedro Martinez	0.13

WALKS ALLOWED

Roger Clemens	1520
Randy Johnson	1349
Tom Glavine	1337
Al Leiter	1163
Kenny Rogers	1017
Tom Gordon	922
Greg Maddux	907
Hideo Nomo	904
Kevin Brown	901
Tim Wakefield	897

WINNING PERCENTAGE
minimum 100 decisions

Pedro Martinez	701
Tim Hudson	688
Roy Oswalt	680
Roger Clemens	665
Mark Mulder	660
Randy Johnson	659
Andy Pettitte	654
Roy Halladay	648
Mike Mussina	638
Bartolo Colon	629

INNINGS PITCHED

Roger Clemens	4704.1
Greg Maddux	4406.1
Tom Glavine	3951.2
Randy Johnson	3593.2
Kevin Brown	3256.1
David Wells	3206.1
Jamie Moyer	3139.2
Mike Mussina	3013.0
John Smoltz	2929.1
Curt Schilling	2906.0

SHUTOUTS

Roger Clemens	46
Randy Johnson	37
Greg Maddux	35
Tom Glavine	24
Mike Mussina	23
Curt Schilling	19
Kevin Brown	17
Scott Erickson	17
Pedro Martinez	17
John Smoltz	15

STRIKEOUTS/9 IP
minimum 750 IP

Randy Johnson	10.95
Kerry Wood	10.44
Pedro Martinez	10.25
Trevor Hoffman	10.01
Jeff Nelson	9.52
Johan Santana	9.47
Arthur Rhodes	8.81
Mike Remlinger	8.77
Curt Schilling	8.77
Hideo Nomo	8.74

ERA
minimum 750 IP

Mariano Rivera	2.33
Pedro Martinez	2.72
Trevor Hoffman	2.76
John Franco	2.89
Greg Maddux	3.01
Roy Oswalt	3.07
Randy Johnson	3.11
Roger Clemens	3.12
Carlos Zambrano	3.26
John Smoltz	3.26

BATTERS FACED

Roger Clemens	19369
Greg Maddux	17925
Tom Glavine	16626
Randy Johnson	14784
Kevin Brown	13542
David Wells	13395
Jamie Moyer	13341
Kenny Rogers	12374
Mike Mussina	12314
John Smoltz	11997

QUALITY START %
minimum 100 GS

Pedro Martinez	70.7
Randy Johnson	70.0
Roy Oswalt	69.0
Greg Maddux	67.0
Curt Schilling	66.9
Carlos Zambrano	66.4
Roger Clemens	66.0
Kevin Brown	66.0
Tim Hudson	65.6
Barry Zito	64.9

WALKS PER 9 INNINGS
minimum 750 IP

Brad Radke	1.62
Jon Lieber	1.75
Greg Maddux	1.85
David Wells	1.87
Brian Anderson	1.96
Ben Sheets	2.00
Mike Mussina	2.04
Ramiro Mendoza	2.04
Curt Schilling	2.04
Mark Buehrle	2.06

K/BB RATIO
minimum 750 IP

Pedro Martinez	4.32
Curt Schilling	4.29
Trevor Hoffman	3.86
Ben Sheets	3.79
Roy Oswalt	3.78
Jon Lieber	3.71
Mike Mussina	3.51
Johan Santana	3.40
Mariano Rivera	3.39
Greg Maddux	3.36

OPPOSITION AVG
minimum 750 IP

Trevor Hoffman	208
Pedro Martinez	208
Mariano Rivera	212
Kerry Wood	214
Randy Johnson	215
Johan Santana	221
Jeff Nelson	223
Barry Zito	228
Carlos Zambrano	228
Roger Clemens	229

HIT BATSMEN

Randy Johnson	168
Roger Clemens	150
Kevin Brown	139
Tim Wakefield	136
Greg Maddux	125
Pedro Martinez	119
Al Leiter	117
Chan Ho Park	116
Pedro Astacio	110
2 tied with	108

SAVES

Trevor Hoffman	436
John Franco	424
Mariano Rivera	379
Roberto Hernandez	324
Troy Percival	324
Jose Mesa	319
Billy Wagner	284
Armando Benitez	263
Ugueth Urbina	237
Todd Jones	226

†**Quality Starts** denote the number of outings in which a starting pitcher works at least six innings and allows three or fewer earned runs.

HITS PER 9 INNINGS
minimum 750 IP

Pedro Martinez	6.82
Trevor Hoffman	6.86
Kerry Wood	6.95
Mariano Rivera	7.03
Randy Johnson	7.06
Jeff Nelson	7.25
Johan Santana	7.35
Carlos Zambrano	7.51
Barry Zito	7.57
A.J. Burnett	7.58

OPPOSITION OBP
minimum 750 IP

Trevor Hoffman	265
Mariano Rivera	269
Pedro Martinez	269
Curt Schilling	284
Johan Santana	284
Greg Maddux	289
John Smoltz	291
Roger Clemens	294
Mike Mussina	294
Randy Johnson	295

WILD PITCHES

Roger Clemens	133
John Smoltz	130
Kevin Brown	108
Hideo Nomo	108
Tom Gordon	102
David Wells	100
Matt Clement	98
Randy Johnson	98
Jason Grimsley	95
Jeff Fassero	84

SAVE %
minimum 50 SvOp

Eric Gagne	96.4
John Smoltz	91.7
Trevor Hoffman	89.5
Joe Nathan	88.0
Mariano Rivera	87.9
Billy Wagner	86.3
Jason Isringhausen	86.1
Armando Benitez	85.9
Troy Percival	85.9
Jose Mesa	85.3

BASERUNNERS PER 9 INNINGS
minimum 750 IP

Trevor Hoffman	9.53
Pedro Martinez	9.62
Mariano Rivera	9.70
Curt Schilling	10.28
Johan Santana	10.34
Greg Maddux	10.45
John Smoltz	10.63
Mike Mussina	10.76
Roger Clemens	10.84
Randy Johnson	10.86

OPPOSITION SLG
minimum 750 IP

Mariano Rivera	290
Pedro Martinez	324
Jeff Nelson	330
Trevor Hoffman	337
Roger Clemens	341
Randy Johnson	341
Carlos Zambrano	341
John Franco	343
Kevin Brown	349
A.J. Burnett	350

GDP INDUCED

Greg Maddux	375
Tom Glavine	374
Kevin Brown	328
Roger Clemens	310
Scott Erickson	308
Kenny Rogers	292
Terry Mulholland	266
Mike Hampton	262
Jamie Moyer	252
David Wells	244

GAMES FINISHED

John Franco	774
Trevor Hoffman	632
Roberto Hernandez	628
Jose Mesa	586
Mariano Rivera	541
Troy Percival	489
Billy Wagner	487
Todd Jones	472
Armando Benitez	468
Bob Wickman	416

HOME RUNS/9 IP
minimum 750 IP

Mariano Rivera	0.47
Kevin Brown	0.57
John Franco	0.59
Greg Maddux	0.61
Jeff Nelson	0.62
Carlos Zambrano	0.65
Terry Adams	0.65
Roger Clemens	0.66
Tom Glavine	0.68
Julian Tavarez	0.69

HOME RUNS ALLOWED

Jamie Moyer	381
David Wells	374
Roger Clemens	347
Randy Johnson	333
Mike Mussina	323
Brad Radke	302
Tom Glavine	300
Greg Maddux	298
Curt Schilling	298
2 tied with	296

GDP/9 IP
minimum 750 IP

Shawn Estes	1.29
Julian Tavarez	1.22
Bob Wickman	1.19
Scott Erickson	1.18
Jamey Wright	1.16
Mike Hampton	1.14
Scott Schoeneweis	1.13
Jon Garland	1.09
Mark Mulder	1.09
Danny Graves	1.09

SB % ALLOWED
minimum 750 IP

Kirk Rueter	34.3
Chris Carpenter	39.3
Terry Mulholland	41.2
Mark Buehrle	42.4
Kenny Rogers	43.1
Carlos Zambrano	45.2
Johan Santana	48.6
Brian Anderson	49.1
Tomo Ohka	50.0
Roy Oswalt	50.0

History

All-time results

Award winners

Hall of Fame

AMERICAN LEAGUE CHAMPIONS

Year	Team	Manager
1901—Chicago		Clark Griffith
1902—Philadelphia		Connie Mack
1903—Boston		Jimmy Collins
1904—Boston		Jimmy Collins
1905—Philadelphia		Connie Mack
1906—Chicago		Fielder Jones
1907—Detroit		Hugh Jennings
1908—Detroit		Hugh Jennings
1909—Detroit		Hugh Jennings
1910—Philadelphia		Connie Mack
1911—Philadelphia		Connie Mack
1912—Boston		Jake Stahl
1913—Philadelphia		Connie Mack
1914—Philadelphia		Connie Mack
1915—Boston		Bill Carrigan
1916—Boston		Bill Carrigan
1917—Chicago		Pants Rowland
1918—Boston		Ed Barrow
1919—Chicago		Kid Gleason
1920—Cleveland		Tris Speaker
1921—New York		Miller Huggins
1922—New York		Miller Huggins
1923—New York		Miller Huggins
1924—Washington		Bucky Harris
1925—Washington		Bucky Harris
1926—New York		Miller Huggins
1927—New York		Miller Huggins
1928—New York		Miller Huggins
1929—Philadelphia		Connie Mack
1930—Philadelphia		Connie Mack
1931—Philadelphia		Connie Mack
1932—New York		Joe McCarthy
1933—Washington		Joe Cronin
1934—Detroit		Mickey Cochrane
1935—Detroit		Mickey Cochrane
1936—New York		Joe McCarthy
1937—New York		Joe McCarthy
1938—New York		Joe McCarthy
1939—New York		Joe McCarthy
1940—Detroit		Del Baker
1941—New York		Joe McCarthy
1942—New York		Joe McCarthy
1943—New York		Joe McCarthy
1944—St. Louis		Luke Sewell
1945—Detroit		Steve O'Neill
1946—Boston		Joe Cronin
1947—New York		Bucky Harris
1948—Cleveland*		Lou Boudreau
1949—New York		Casey Stengel
1950—New York		Casey Stengel
1951—New York		Casey Stengel
1952—New York		Casey Stengel
1953—New York		Casey Stengel
1954—Cleveland		Al Lopez
1955—New York		Casey Stengel
1956—New York		Casey Stengel
1957—New York		Casey Stengel
1958—New York		Casey Stengel
1959—Chicago		Al Lopez
1960—New York		Casey Stengel
1961—New York		Ralph Houk
1962—New York		Ralph Houk
1963—New York		Ralph Houk
1964—New York		Yogi Berra
1965—Minnesota		Sam Mele
1966—Baltimore		Hank Bauer
1967—Boston		Dick Williams
1968—Detroit		Mayo Smith
1969—Baltimore (East Division)		Earl Weaver
1970—Baltimore (East Division)		Earl Weaver
1971—Baltimore (East Division)		Earl Weaver
1972—Oakland (West Division)		Dick Williams
1973—Oakland (West Division)		Dick Williams
1974—Oakland (West Division)		Al Dark
1975—Boston (East Division)		Darrell Johnson
1976—New York (East Division)		Billy Martin
1977—New York (East Division)		Billy Martin
1978—New York (East Division)		Billy Martin, Bob Lemon
1979—Baltimore (East Division)		Earl Weaver
1980—Kansas City (West Division)		Jim Frey
1981—New York (East Division)		Gene Michael, Bob Lemon
1982—Milwaukee (East Division)		Buck Rodgers, Harvey Kuenn
1983—Baltimore (East Division)		Joe Altobelli
1984—Detroit (East Division)		Sparky Anderson
1985—Kansas City (West Division)		Dick Howser
1986—Boston (East Division)		John McNamara
1987—Minnesota (West Division)		Tom Kelly
1988—Oakland (West Division)		Tony La Russa
1989—Oakland (West Division)		Tony La Russa
1990—Oakland (West Division)		Tony La Russa
1991—Minnesota (West Division)		Tom Kelly
1992—Toronto (East Division)		Cito Gaston
1993—Toronto (East Division)		Cito Gaston
1994—None†		
1995—Cleveland (Central Division)		Mike Hargrove
1996—New York (East Division)		Joe Torre
1997—Cleveland (Central Division)		Mike Hargrove
1998—New York (East Division)		Joe Torre
1999—New York (East Division)		Joe Torre
2000—New York (East Division)		Joe Torre
2001—New York (East Division)		Joe Torre
2002—Anaheim (West Division)		Mike Scioscia
2003—New York (East Division)		Joe Torre
2004—Boston (East Division)		Terry Francona
2005—Chicago (Central Division)		Ozzie Guillen

*Defeated Boston in one-game playoff. †New York finished the strike-shortened season with the league's best record.

NATIONAL LEAGUE CHAMPIONS

Year	Team	Manager
1876—Chicago		Albert Spalding
1877—Boston		Harry Wright
1878—Boston		Harry Wright
1879—Providence		George Wright
1880—Chicago		Cap Anson
1881—Chicago		Cap Anson
1882—Chicago		Cap Anson
1883—Boston		Jack Burdock, John Morrill
1884—Providence		Frank Bancroft
1885—Chicago		Cap Anson
1886—Chicago		Cap Anson
1887—Detroit		William Watkins
1888—New York		James Mutrie
1889—New York		James Mutrie
1890—Brooklyn		William McGunnigle
1891—Boston		Frank Selee
1892—Boston		Frank Selee
1893—Boston		Frank Selee
1894—Baltimore		Ned Hanlon
1895—Baltimore		Ned Hanlon
1896—Baltimore		Ned Hanlon
1897—Boston		Frank Selee
1898—Boston		Frank Selee
1899—Brooklyn		Ned Hanlon

Year	Team	Manager	Year	Team	Manager
1900—Brooklyn	Ned Hanlon		1957—Milwaukee	Fred Haney	
1901—Pittsburgh	Fred Clarke		1958—Milwaukee	Fred Haney	
1902—Pittsburgh	Fred Clarke		1959—Los Angeles‡	Walter Alston	
1903—Pittsburgh	Fred Clarke		1960—Pittsburgh	Danny Murtaugh	
1904—New York	John McGraw		1961—Cincinnati	Fred Hutchinson	
1905—New York	John McGraw		1962—San Francisco§	Al Dark	
1906—Chicago	Frank Chance		1963—Los Angeles	Walter Alston	
1907—Chicago	Frank Chance		1964—St. Louis	Johnny Keane	
1908—Chicago	Frank Chance		1965—Los Angeles	Walter Alston	
1909—Pittsburgh	Fred Clarke		1966—Los Angeles	Walter Alston	
1910—Chicago	Frank Chance		1967—St. Louis	Red Schoendienst	
1911—New York	John McGraw		1968—St. Louis	Red Schoendienst	
1912—New York	John McGraw		1969—New York (East Division)	Gil Hodges	
1913—New York	John McGraw		1970—Cincinnati (West Division)	Sparky Anderson	
1914—Boston	George Stallings		1971—Pittsburgh (East Division)	Danny Murtaugh	
1915—Philadelphia	Pat Moran		1972—Cincinnati (West Division)	Sparky Anderson	
1916—Brooklyn	Wilbert Robinson		1973—New York (East Division)	Yogi Berra	
1917—New York	John McGraw		1974—Los Angeles (West Division)	Walter Alston	
1918—Chicago	Fred Mitchell		1975—Cincinnati (West Division)	Sparky Anderson	
1919—Cincinnati	Pat Moran		1976—Cincinnati (West Division)	Sparky Anderson	
1920—Brooklyn	Wilbert Robinson		1977—Los Angeles (West Division)	Tommy Lasorda	
1921—New York	John McGraw		1978—Los Angeles (West Division)	Tommy Lasorda	
1922—New York	John McGraw		1979—Pittsburgh (East Division)	Chuck Tanner	
1923—New York	John McGraw		1980—Philadelphia (East Division)	Dallas Green	
1924—New York	John McGraw		1981—Los Angeles (West Division)	Tommy Lasorda	
1925—Pittsburgh	Bill McKechnie		1982—St. Louis (East Division)	Whitey Herzog	
1926—St. Louis	Rogers Hornsby		1983—Philadelphia (East Division)	Pat Corrales, Paul Owens	
1927—Pittsburgh	Donie Bush		1984—San Diego (West Division)	Dick Williams	
1928—St. Louis	Bill McKechnie		1985—St. Louis (East Division)	Whitey Herzog	
1929—Chicago	Joe McCarthy		1986—New York (East Division)	Dave Johnson	
1930—St. Louis	Gabby Street		1987—St. Louis (East Division)	Whitey Herzog	
1931—St. Louis	Gabby Street		1988—Los Angeles (West Division)	Tommy Lasorda	
1932—Chicago	Rogers Hornsby, Charlie Grimm		1989—San Francisco (West Division)	Roger Craig	
1933—New York	Bill Terry		1990—Cincinnati (West Division)	Lou Piniella	
1934—St. Louis	Frank Frisch		1991—Atlanta (West Division)	Bobby Cox	
1935—Chicago	Charlie Grimm		1992—Atlanta (West Division)	Bobby Cox	
1936—New York	Bill Terry		1993—Philadelphia (East Division)	Jim Fregosi	
1937—New York	Bill Terry		1994—None∞		
1938—Chicago	Charlie Grimm, Gabby Hartnett		1995—Atlanta (East Division)	Bobby Cox	
1939—Cincinnati	Bill McKechnie		1996—Atlanta (East Division)	Bobby Cox	
1940—Cincinnati	Bill McKechnie		1997—Florida (East Division)	Jim Leyland	
1941—Brooklyn	Leo Durocher		1998—San Diego (West Division)	Bruce Bochy	
1942—St. Louis	Billy Southworth		1999—Atlanta (East Division)	Bobby Cox	
1943—St. Louis	Billy Southworth		2000—New York (East Division)	Bobby Valentine	
1944—St. Louis	Billy Southworth		2001—Arizona (West Division)	Bob Brenly	
1945—Chicago	Charlie Grimm		2002—San Francisco (West Division)	Dusty Baker	
1946—St. Louis*	Eddie Dyer		2003—Florida (East Division)	Jeff Torborg, Jack McKeon	
1947—Brooklyn	Clyde Sukeforth, Burt Shotton		2004—St. Louis (Central Division)	Tony La Russa	
1948—Boston	Billy Southworth		2005—Houston (Central Division)	Phil Garner	
1949—Brooklyn	Burt Shotton				
1950—Philadelphia	Eddie Sawyer				
1951—New York†	Leo Durocher				
1952—Brooklyn	Charlie Dressen				
1953—Brooklyn	Charlie Dressen				
1954—New York	Leo Durocher				
1955—Brooklyn	Walter Alston				
1956—Brooklyn	Walter Alston				

*Defeated Brooklyn, two games to none, in playoff for pennant.
†Defeated Brooklyn, two games to one, in playoff for pennant.
‡Defeated Milwaukee, two games to none, in playoff for pennant.
§Defeated Los Angeles, two games to one, in playoff for pennant.
∞Montreal finished the strike-shortened season with the league's best record.

WORLD SERIES

Year	Winner	Loser	Games	Year	Winner	Loser	Games
1903—Boston A.L.	Pittsburgh N.L.	5-3		1915—Boston A.L.	Philadelphia N.L.	4-1
1904—No Series				1916—Boston A.L.	Brooklyn N.L.	4-1
1905—New York N.L.	Philadelphia A.L.	4-1		1917—Chicago A.L.	New York N.L.	4-2
1906—Chicago A.L.	Chicago N.L.	4-2		1918—Boston A.L.	Chicago N.L.	4-2
1907—Chicago N.L.	Detroit A.L.	*4-0		1919—Cincinnati N.L.	Chicago A.L.	5-3
1908—Chicago N.L.	Detroit A.L.	4-1		1920—Cleveland A.L.	Brooklyn N.L.	5-2
1909—Pittsburgh N.L.	Detroit A.L.	4-3		1921—New York N.L.	New York A.L.	5-3
1910—Philadelphia A.L.	Chicago N.L.	4-1		1922—New York N.L.	New York A.L.	*4-0
1911—Philadelphia A.L.	New York N.L.	4-2		1923—New York A.L.	New York N.L.	4-2
1912—Boston A.L.	New York N.L.	*4-3		1924—Washington A.L.	New York N.L.	4-3
1913—Philadelphia A.L.	New York N.L.	4-1		1925—Pittsburgh N.L.	Washington A.L.	4-3
1914—Boston N.L.	Philadelphia A.L.	4-0		1926—St. Louis N.L.	New York A.L.	4-3

Year	Winner	Loser	Games
1927—New York A.L.	Pittsburgh, N.L.	4-0
1928—New York A.L.	St. Louis N.L.	4-0
1929—Philadelphia A.L.	Chicago N.L.	4-1
1930—Philadelphia A.L.	St. Louis N.L.	4-2
1931—St. Louis N.L.	Philadelphia A.L.	4-3
1932—New York A.L.	Chicago N.L.	4-0
1933—New York N.L.	Washington A.L.	4-1
1934—St. Louis N.L.	Detroit A.L.	4-3
1935—Detroit A.L.	Chicago N.L.	4-2
1936—New York A.L.	New York N.L.	4-2
1937—New York A.L.	New York N.L.	4-1
1938—New York A.L.	Chicago N.L.	4-0
1939—New York A.L.	Cincinnati N.L.	4-0
1940—Cincinnati N.L.	Detroit A.L.	4-3
1941—New York A.L.	Brooklyn N.L.	4-1
1942—St. Louis N.L.	New York A.L.	4-1
1943—New York A.L.	St. Louis N.L.	4-1
1944—St. Louis N.L.	St. Louis A.L.	4-2
1945—Detroit A.L.	Chicago N.L.	4-3
1946—St. Louis N.L.	Boston A.L.	4-3
1947—New York A.L.	Brooklyn, N.L.	4-3
1948—Cleveland A.L.	Boston N.L.	4-2
1949—New York A.L.	Brooklyn N.L.	4-1
1950—New York A.L.	Philadelphia N.L.	4-0
1951—New York A.L.	New York N.L.	4-2
1952—New York A.L.	Brooklyn N.L.	4-3
1953—New York A.L.	Brooklyn N.L.	4-2
1954—New York N.L.	Cleveland A.L.	4-0
1955—Brooklyn N.L.	New York A.L.	4-3
1956—New York A.L.	Brooklyn N.L.	4-3
1957—Milwaukee N.L.	New York A.L.	4-3
1958—New York A.L.	Milwaukee N.L.	4-3
1959—Los Angeles N.L.	Chicago A.L.	4-2
1960—Pittsburgh N.L.	New York A.L.	4-3
1961—New York A.L.	Cincinnati N.L.	4-1
1962—New York A.L.	San Francisco N.L.	4-3
1963—Los Angeles N.L.	New York A.L.	4-0
1964—St. Louis N.L.	New York A.L.	4-3
1965—Los Angeles N.L.	Minnesota A.L.	4-3
1966—Baltimore A.L.	Los Angeles N.L.	4-0
1967—St. Louis N.L.	Boston A.L.	4-3
1968—Detroit A.L.	St. Louis N.L.	4-3
1969—New York N.L.	Baltimore A.L.	4-1
1970—Baltimore A.L.	Cincinnati N.L.	4-1
1971—Pittsburgh N.L.	Baltimore A.L.	4-3
1972—Oakland A.L.	Cincinnati N.L.	4-3
1973—Oakland A.L.	New York N.L.	4-3
1974—Oakland A.L.	Los Angeles N.L.	4-1
1975—Cincinnati N.L.	Boston A.L.	4-3
1976—Cincinnati N.L.	New York A.L.	4-0
1977—New York A.L.	Los Angeles N.L.	4-2
1978—New York A.L.	Los Angeles N.L.	4-2
1979—Pittsburgh N.L.	Baltimore A.L.	4-3
1980—Philadelphia N.L.	Kansas City A.L.	4-2
1981—Los Angeles N.L.	New York A.L.	4-2
1982—St. Louis N.L.	Milwaukee A.L.	4-3
1983—Baltimore A.L.	Philadelphia N.L.	4-1
1984—Detroit A.L.	San Diego N.L.	4-1
1985—Kansas City A.L.	St. Louis N.L.	4-3
1986—New York N.L.	Boston A.L.	4-3
1987—Minnesota A.L.	St. Louis N.L.	4-3
1988—Los Angeles N.L.	Oakland A.L.	4-1
1989—Oakland A.L.	San Francisco N.L.	4-0
1990—Cincinnati N.L.	Oakland A.L.	4-0
1991—Minnesota A.L.	Atlanta N.L.	4-3
1992—Toronto A.L.	Atlanta N.L.	4-2
1993—Toronto A.L.	Philadelphia N.L.	4-2
1994—No Series		
1995—Atlanta N.L.	Cleveland A.L.	4-2
1996—New York A.L.	Atlanta N.L.	4-2
1997—Florida N.L.	Cleveland A.L.	4-3
1998—New York A.L.	San Diego N.L.	4-0
1999—New York A.L.	Atlanta N.L.	4-0
2000—New York A.L.	New York N.L.	4-1
2001—Arizona N.L.	New York A.L.	4-3
2002—Anaheim A.L.	San Francisco N.L.	4-3
2003—Florida N.L.	New York A.L.	4-2
2004—Boston A.L.	St. Louis N.L.	4-0
2005—Chicago A.L.	Houston N.L.	4-0

*Includes tie game.

DIVISION SERIES

AMERICAN LEAGUE

Year	Winner (Division)	Loser (Division)	Games
1981—New York (East)	Milwaukee (East)	3-2
Oakland (West)	Kansas City (West)	3-0
1995—Cleveland (Central)	Boston (East)	3-0
Seattle (West)	New York* (East)	3-2
1996—New York (East)	Texas (West)	3-1
Baltimore (East)*	Cleveland (Central)	3-1
1997—Baltimore (East)	Seattle (West)	3-1
Cleveland (Central)	New York (East)*	3-2
1998—New York (East)	Texas (West)	3-0
Cleveland (Central)	Boston (East)*	3-1
1999—New York (East)	Texas (West)	3-0
Boston (East)*	Cleveland (Central)	3-2
2000—New York (East)	Oakland (West)	3-2
Seattle (West)*	Chicago (Central)	3-0
2001—New York (East)	Oakland (West)*	3-2
Seattle (West)	Cleveland (Central)	3-2
2002—Anaheim (West)*	New York (East)	3-1
Minnesota (Central)	Oakland (West)	3-2
2003—Boston (East)*	Oakland (West)	3-2
New York (East)	Minnesota (Central)	3-1
2004—Boston (East)*	Anaheim (West)	3-0
New York (East)	Minnesota (Central)	3-1
2005—Chicago (Central)	Boston (East)*	3-0
Los Angeles (West)	New York (East)	3-2

NATIONAL LEAGUE

Year	Winner (Division)	Loser (Division)	Games
1981—Montreal (East)	Philadelphia (East)	3-2
Los Angeles (West)	Houston (West)	3-2
1995—Atlanta (East)	Colorado* (West)	3-1
Cincinnati (Central)	Los Angeles (West)	3-0
1996—Atlanta (East)	Los Angeles (West)*	3-0
St. Louis (Central)	San Diego (West)	3-0
1997—Atlanta (East)	Houston (Central)	3-0
Florida (East)*	San Francisco (West)	3-0
1998—Atlanta (East)	Chicago (Central)*	3-0
San Diego (West)	Houston (Central)	3-1
1999—Atlanta (East)	Houston (Central)	3-1
New York (East)*	Arizona (West)	3-1
2000—St. Louis (Central)	Atlanta (East)	3-0
New York (East)*	San Francisco (West)	3-1
2001—Arizona (West)	St. Louis (Central)*	3-2
Atlanta (East)	Houston (Central)	3-0
2002—St. Louis (Central)	Arizona (West)	3-0
San Francisco (West)*	Atlanta (East)	3-2
2003—Chicago (Central)	Atlanta (East)	3-2
Florida (East)*	San Francisco (West)	3-1
2004—St. Louis (Central)	Los Angeles (West)	3-1
Houston (Central)*	Atlanta (East)	3-2
2005—St. Louis (Central)	San Diego (West)	3-0
Houston (Central)*	Atlanta (East)	3-1

*Wild-card team.

CHAMPIONSHIP SERIES

AMERICAN LEAGUE

Year	Winner (Division)	Loser (Division)	Games
1969	Baltimore (East)	Minnesota (West)	3-0
1970	Baltimore (East)	Minnesota (West)	3-0
1971	Baltimore (East)	Oakland (West)	3-0
1972	Oakland (West)	Detroit (East)	3-2
1973	Oakland (West)	Baltimore (East)	3-2
1974	Oakland (West)	Baltimore (East)	3-1
1975	Boston (East)	Oakland (West)	3-0
1976	New York (East)	Kansas City (West)	3-2
1977	New York (East)	Kansas City (West)	3-2
1978	New York (East)	Kansas City (West)	3-1
1979	Baltimore (East)	California (West)	3-1
1980	Kansas City (West)	New York (East)	3-0
1981	New York (East)	Oakland (West)	3-0
1982	Milwaukee (East)	California (West)	3-2
1983	Baltimore (East)	Chicago (West)	3-1
1984	Detroit (East)	Kansas City (West)	3-0
1985	Kansas City (West)	Toronto (East)	4-3
1986	Boston (East)	California (West)	4-3
1987	Minnesota (West)	Detroit (East)	4-1
1988	Oakland (West)	Boston (East)	4-0
1989	Oakland (West)	Toronto (East)	4-1
1990	Oakland (West)	Boston (East)	4-0
1991	Minnesota (West)	Toronto (East)	4-1
1992	Toronto (East)	Oakland (West)	4-2
1993	Toronto (East)	Chicago (West)	4-2
1994	No series		
1995	Cleveland (Central)	Seattle (West)	4-2
1996	New York (East)	Baltimore (East)*	4-1
1997	Cleveland (Central)	Baltimore (East)	4-2
1998	New York (East)	Cleveland (Central)	4-2
1999	New York (East)	Boston (East)*	4-1
2000	New York (East)	Seattle (West)	4-2
2001	New York (East)	Seattle (West)	4-1
2002	Anaheim (West)*	Minnesota (Central)	4-1
2003	New York (East)	Boston (East)*	4-3
2004	Boston (East)*	New York (East)	4-3
2005	Chicago (Central)	Los Angeles (West)	4-1

NATIONAL LEAGUE

Year	Winner (Division)	Loser (Division)	Games
1969	New York (East)	Atlanta (West)	3-0
1970	Cincinnati (West)	Pittsburgh (East)	3-0
1971	Pittsburgh (East)	San Francisco (West)	3-1
1972	Cincinnati (West)	Pittsburgh (East)	3-2
1973	New York (East)	Cincinnati (West)	3-2
1974	Los Angeles (West)	Pittsburgh (East)	3-1
1975	Cincinnati (West)	Pittsburgh (East)	3-0
1976	Cincinnati (West)	Philadelphia (East)	3-0
1977	Los Angeles (West)	Philadelphia (East)	3-1
1978	Los Angeles (West)	Philadelphia (East)	3-1
1979	Pittsburgh (East)	Cincinnati (West)	3-0
1980	Philadelphia (East)	Houston (West)	3-2
1981	Los Angeles (West)	Montreal (East)	3-2
1982	St. Louis (East)	Atlanta (West)	3-0
1983	Philadelphia (East)	Los Angeles (West)	3-1
1984	San Diego (West)	Chicago (East)	3-2
1985	St. Louis (East)	Los Angeles (West)	4-2
1986	New York (East)	Houston (West)	4-2
1987	St. Louis (East)	San Francisco (West)	4-3
1988	Los Angeles (West)	New York (East)	4-3
1989	San Francisco (West)	Chicago (East)	4-1
1990	Cincinnati (West)	Pittsburgh (East)	4-2
1991	Atlanta (West)	Pittsburgh (East)	4-3
1992	Atlanta (West)	Pittsburgh (East)	4-3
1993	Philadelphia (East)	Atlanta (West)	4-2
1994	No series		
1995	Atlanta (East)	Cincinnati (Central)	4-0
1996	Atlanta (East)	St. Louis (Central)	4-3
1997	Florida (East)*	Atlanta (East)	4-2
1998	San Diego (West)	Atlanta (East)	4-2
1999	Atlanta (East)	New York (East)*	4-2
2000	New York (East)*	St. Louis (Central)	4-1
2001	Arizona (West)	Atlanta (East)	4-1
2002	San Francisco (West)*	St. Louis (Central)	4-1
2003	Florida (East)*	Chicago (Central)	4-3
2004	St. Louis (Central)	Houston (Central)*	4-3
2005	Houston (Central)*	St. Louis (Central)	4-2

*Wild-card team.

ALL-STAR GAME

Date	Site	Score (Winner)	Winning pitcher (Losing pitcher)	Winning manager (Losing manager)	Att.
7-6-33	Comiskey Park Chicago	4-2 (A.L.)	Lefty Gomez, Yankees (Bill Hallahan, Cardinals)	Connie Mack, Athletics (John McGraw, Giants)	47,595
7-10-34	Polo Grounds New York	9-7 (A.L.)	Mel Harder, Indians (Van Mungo, Dodgers)	Joe Cronin, Senators (Bill Terry, Giants)	48,363
7-8-35	Municipal Stadium Cleveland	4-1 (A.L.)	Lefty Gomez, Yankees (Bill Walker, Cardinals)	Mickey Cochrane, Tigers (Frankie Frisch, Cardinals)	69,831
7-7-36	Braves Field Boston	4-3 (N.L.)	Dizzy Dean, Cardinals (Lefty Grove, Red Sox)	Charlie Grimm, Cubs (Joe McCarthy, Yankees)	25,556
7-7-37	Griffith Stadium Washington	8-3 (A.L.)	Lefty Gomez, Yankees (Dizzy Dean, Cardinals)	Joe McCarthy, Yankees (Bill Terry, Giants)	31,391
7-6-38	Crosley Field Cincinnati	4-1 (N.L.)	Johnny Vander Meer, Reds (Lefty Gomez, Yankees)	Bill Terry, Giants (Joe McCarthy, Yankees)	27,067
7-11-39	Yankee Stadium New York	3-1 (A.L.)	Tommy Bridges, Tigers (Bill Lee, Cubs)	Joe McCarthy, Yankees (Gabby Hartnett, Cubs)	62,892
7-9-40	Sportsman's Park St. Louis	4-0 (N.L.)	Paul Derringer, Reds (Red Ruffing, Yankees)	Bill McKechnie, Reds (Joe Cronin, Red Sox)	32,373

Date	Site	Score (Winner)	Winning pitcher (Losing pitcher)	Winning manager (Losing manager)	Att.
7-8-41	Briggs Stadium	7-5	Ed Smith, White Sox	Del Baker, Tigers	54,674
	Detroit	(A.L.)	(Claude Passeau, Cubs)	(Bill McKechnie, Reds)	
7-6-42	Polo Grounds	3-1	Spud Chandler, Yankees	Joe McCarthy, Yankees	33,694
	New York	(A.L.)	(Mort Cooper, Cardinals)	(Leo Durocher, Dodgers)	
7-13-43	Shibe Park	5-3	Dutch Leonard, Senators	Joe McCarthy, Yankees	31,938
	Philadelphia	(A.L.)	(Mort Cooper, Cardinals)	(Billy Southworth, Cardinals)	
7-11-44	Forbes Field	7-1	Ken Raffensberger, Phillies	Billy Southworth, Cardinals	29,589
	Pittsburgh	(N.L.)	(Tex Hughson, Red Sox)	(Joe McCarthy, Yankees)	
1945	No game played.				
7-9-46	Fenway Park	12-0	Bob Feller, Indians	Steve O'Neill, Tigers	34,906
	Boston	(A.L.)	(Claude Passeau, Cubs)	(Charlie Grimm, Cubs)	
7-8-47	Wrigley Field	2-1	Frank Shea, Yankees	Joe Cronin, Red Sox	41,123
	Chicago	(A.L.)	(Johnny Sain, Braves)	(Eddie Dyer, Cardinals)	
7-13-48	Sportsman's Park	5-2	Vic Raschi, Yankees	Bucky Harris, Yankees	34,009
	St. Louis	(A.L.)	(Johnny Schmitz, Cubs)	(Leo Durocher, Dodgers)	
7-12-49	Ebbets Field	11-7	Virgil Trucks, Tigers	Lou Boudreau, Indians	32,577
	Brooklyn	(A.L.)	(Don Newcombe, Dodgers)	(Billy Southworth, Braves)	
7-11-50	Comiskey Park	4-3*	Ewell Blackwell, Reds	Burt Shotton, Dodgers	46,127
	Chicago	(N.L.)	(Ted Gray, Tigers)	(Casey Stengel, Yankees)	
7-10-51	Briggs Stadium	8-3	Sal Maglie, Giants	Eddie Sawyer, Phillies	52,075
	Detroit	(N.L.)	(Ed Lopat, Yankees)	(Casey Stengel, Yankees)	
7-8-52	Shibe Park	3-2†	Bob Rush, Cubs	Leo Durocher, Giants	32,785
	Philadelphia	(N.L.)	(Bob Lemon, Indians)	(Casey Stengel, Yankees)	
7-14-53	Crosley Field	5-1	Warren Spahn, Braves	Chuck Dressen, Dodgers	30,846
	Cincinnati	(N.L.)	(Allie Reynolds, Yankees)	(Casey Stengel, Yankees)	
7-13-54	Municipal Stadium	11-9	Dean Stone, Senators	Casey Stengel, Yankees	68,751
	Cleveland	(A.L.)	(Gene Conley, Braves)	(Walter Alston, Dodgers)	
7-12-55	Milwaukee Co. Stadium	6-5‡	Gene Conley, Braves	Leo Durocher, Giants	45,314
	Milwaukee	(N.L.)	(Frank Sullivan, Red Sox)	(Al Lopez, Indians)	
7-10-56	Griffith Stadium	7-3	Bob Friend, Pirates	Walter Alston, Dodgers	28,843
	Washington	(N.L.)	(Billy Pierce, White Sox)	(Casey Stengel, Yankees)	
7-9-57	Busch Stadium	6-5	Jim Bunning, Tigers	Casey Stengel, Yankees	30,693
	St. Louis	(A.L.)	(Curt Simmons, Phillies)	(Walter Alston, Dodgers)	
7-8-58	Memorial Stadium	4-3	Early Wynn, White Sox	Casey Stengel, Yankees	48,829
	Baltimore	(A.L.)	(Bob Friend, Pirates)	(Fred Haney, Braves)	
7-7-59	Forbes Field	5-4	Johnny Antonelli, Giants	Fred Haney, Braves	35,277
	Pittsburgh	(N.L.)	(Whitey Ford, Yankees)	(Casey Stengel, Yankees)	
8-3-59	Memorial Coliseum	5-3	Jerry Walker, Orioles	Casey Stengel, Yankees	55,105
	Los Angeles	(A.L.)	(Don Drysdale, Dodgers)	(Fred Haney, Braves)	
7-11-60	Municipal Stadium	5-3	Bob Friend, Pirates	Walter Alston, Dodgers	30,619
	Kansas City	(N.L.)	(Bill Monbouquette, Red Sox)	(Al Lopez, White Sox)	
7-13-60	Yankee Stadium	6-0	Vernon Law, Pirates	Walter Alston, Dodgers	38,362
	New York	(N.L.)	(Whitey Ford, Yankees)	(Al Lopez, White Sox)	
7-11-61	Candlestick Park	5-4§	Stu Miller, Giants	Danny Murtaugh, Pirates	44,115
	San Francisco	(N.L.)	(Hoyt Wilhelm, Orioles)	(Paul Richards, Orioles)	
7-31-61	Fenway Park	1-1		Paul Richards, Orioles (A.L.)	31,851
	Boston	(tie)		Danny Murtaugh, Pirates (N.L.)	
7-10-62	District of Col. Stad.	3-1	Juan Marichal, Giants	Fred Hutchinson, Reds	45,480
	Washington	(N.L.)	(Camilo Pascual, Twins)	(Ralph Houk, Yankees)	
7-30-62	Wrigley Field	9-4	Ray Herbert, White Sox	Ralph Houk, Yankees	38,359
	Chicago	(A.L.)	(Art Mahaffey, Phillies)	(Fred Hutchinson, Reds)	
7-9-63	Municipal Stadium	5-3	Larry Jackson, Cubs	Alvin Dark, Giants	44,160
	Cleveland	(N.L.)	(Jim Bunning, Tigers)	(Ralph Houk, Yankees)	
7-7-64	Shea Stadium	7-4	Juan Marichal, Giants	Walter Alston, Dodgers	50,850
	New York	(N.L.)	(Dick Radatz, Red Sox)	(Al Lopez, White Sox)	
7-13-65	Metropolitan Stadium	6-5	Sandy Koufax, Dodgers	Gene Mauch, Phillies	46,706
	Bloomington, Minn.	(N.L.)	(Sam McDowell, Indians)	(Al Lopez, White Sox)	
7-12-66	Busch Stadium	2-1§	Gaylord Perry, Giants	Walter Alston, Dodgers	49,936
	St. Louis	(N.L.)	(Pete Richert, Senators)	(Sam Mele, Twins)	
7-11-67	Anaheim Stadium	2-1∞	Don Drysdale, Dodgers	Walter Alston, Dodgers	46,309
	Anaheim, Calif.	(N.L.)	(Jim Hunter, Athletics)	(Hank Bauer, Orioles)	
7-9-68	Astrodome	1-0	Don Drysdale, Dodgers	Red Schoendienst, Cardinals	48,321
	Houston	(N.L.)	(Luis Tiant, Indians)	(Dick Williams, Red Sox)	
7-23-69	R.F.K. Stadium	9-3	Steve Carlton, Cardinals	Red Schoendienst, Cardinals	45,259
	Washington	(N.L.)	(Mel Stottlemyre, Yankees)	(Mayo Smith, Tigers)	
7-14-70	Riverfront Stadium	5-4‡	Claude Osteen, Dodgers	Gil Hodges, Mets	51,838
	Cincinnati	(N.L.)	(Clyde Wright, Angels)	(Earl Weaver, Orioles)	
7-13-71	Tiger Stadium	6-4	Vida Blue, Athletics	Earl Weaver, Orioles	53,559
	Detroit	(A.L.)	(Dock Ellis, Pirates)	(Sparky Anderson, Reds)	

Date	Site	Score (Winner)	Winning pitcher (Losing pitcher)	Winning manager (Losing manager)	Att.
7-25-72	Atlanta Stadium Atlanta	4-3§ (N.L.)	Tug McGraw, Mets (Dave McNally, Orioles)	Danny Murtaugh, Pirates (Earl Weaver, Orioles)	53,107
7-24-73	Royals Stadium Kansas City	7-1 (N.L.)	Rick Wise, Cardinals (Bert Blyleven, Twins)	Sparky Anderson, Reds (Dick Williams, Athletics)	40,849
7-23-74	Three Rivers Stadium Pittsburgh	7-2 (N.L.)	Ken Brett, Pirates (Luis Tiant, Red Sox)	Yogi Berra, Mets (Dick Williams, Athletics)	50,706
7-15-75	Milwaukee Co. Stadium Milwaukee	6-3 (N.L.)	Jon Matlack, Mets (Jim Hunter, Yankees)	Walter Alston, Dodgers (Alvin Dark, Athletics)	51,480
7-13-76	Veterans Stadium Philadelphia	7-1 (N.L)	Randy Jones, Padres (Mark Fidrych, Tigers)	Sparky Anderson, Reds (Darrell Johnson, Red Sox)	63,974
7-19-77	Yankee Stadium New York	7-5 (N.L.)	Don Sutton, Dodgers (Jim Palmer, Orioles)	Sparky Anderson, Reds (Billy Martin, Yankees)	56,683
7-11-78	San Diego Stadium San Diego	7-3 (N.L.)	Bruce Sutter, Cubs (Rich Gossage, Yankees)	Tommy Lasorda, Dodgers (Billy Martin, Yankees)	51,549
7-17-79	Kingdome Seattle	7-6 (N.L.)	Bruce Sutter, Cubs (Jim Kern, Rangers)	Tommy Lasorda, Dodgers (Bob Lemon, Yankees)	58,905
7-8-80	Dodger Stadium Los Angeles	4-2 (N.L.)	Jerry Reuss, Dodgers (Tommy John, Yankees)	Chuck Tanner, Pirates (Earl Weaver, Orioles)	56,088
8-9-81	Municipal Stadium Cleveland	5-4 (N.L.)	Vida Blue, Giants (Rollie Fingers, Brewers)	Dallas Green, Phillies (Jim Frey, Royals)	72,086
7-13-82	Olympic Stadium Montreal	4-1 (N.L.)	Steve Rogers, Expos (Dennis Eckersley, Red Sox)	Tommy Lasorda, Dodgers (Billy Martin, Athletics)	59,057
7-6-83	Comiskey Park Chicago	13-3 (A.L.)	Dave Stieb, Blue Jays (Mario Soto, Reds)	Harvey Kuenn, Brewers (Whitey Herzog, Cardinals)	43,801
7-10-84	Candlestick Park San Francisco	3-1 (N.L.)	Charlie Lea, Expos (Dave Stieb, Blue Jays)	Paul Owens, Phillies (Joe Altobelli, Orioles)	57,756
7-16-85	Metrodome Minneapolis	6-1 (N.L.)	LaMarr Hoyt, Padres (Jack Morris, Tigers)	Dick Williams, Padres (Sparky Anderson, Tigers)	54,960
7-15-86	Astrodome Houston	3-2 (A.L.)	Roger Clemens, Red Sox (Dwight Gooden, Mets)	Dick Howser, Royals (Whitey Herzog, Cardinals)	45,774
7-14-87	Oak.-Alameda Co. Col. Oakland	2-0▲ (N.L.)	Lee Smith, Cubs (Jay Howell, Athletics)	Dave Johnson, Mets (John McNamara, Red Sox)	49,671
7-12-88	Riverfront Stadium Cincinnati	2-1 (A.L.)	Frank Viola, Twins (Dwight Gooden, Mets)	Tom Kelly, Twins (Whitey Herzog, Cardinals)	55,837
7-11-89	Anaheim Stadium Anaheim, Calif.	5-3 (A.L.)	Nolan Ryan, Rangers (John Smoltz, Braves)	Tony La Russa, Athletics (Tommy Lasorda, Dodgers)	64,036
7-10-90	Wrigley Field Chicago	2-0 (A.L.)	Bret Saberhagen, Royals (Jeff Brantley, Giants)	Tony La Russa, Athletics (Roger Craig, Giants)	39,071
7-9-91	SkyDome Toronto	4-2 (A.L.)	Jimmy Key, Blue Jays (Dennis Martinez, Expos)	Tony La Russa, Athletics (Lou Piniella, Reds)	52,383
7-14-92	Jack Murphy Stadium San Diego	13-6 (A.L.)	Kevin Brown, Rangers (Tom Glavine, Braves)	Tom Kelly, Twins (Bobby Cox, Braves)	59,372
7-13-93	Oriole Park at Camden Yards, Baltimore	9-3 (A.L.)	Jack McDowell, White Sox (John Burkett, Giants)	Cito Gaston, Blue Jays (Bobby Cox, Braves)	48,147
7-12-94	Three Rivers Stadium Pittsburgh	8-7§ (N.L.)	Doug Jones, Phillies (Jason Bere, White Sox)	Jim Fregosi, Phillies (Cito Gaston, Blue Jays)	59,568
7-11-95	Ballpark in Arlington Arlington, Texas	3-2 (N.L.)	Heathcliff Slocumb, Phillies (Steve Ontiveros, A's)	Felipe Alou, Expos (Buck Showalter, Yankees)	50,920
7-9-96	Veterans Stadium Philadelphia	6-0 (N.L.)	John Smoltz, Braves (Charles Nagy, Indians)	Bobby Cox, Braves (Mike Hargrove, Indians)	62,670
7-8-97	Jacobs Field Cleveland	3-1 (A.L.)	Jose Rosado, Royals (Shawn Estes, Giants)	Joe Torre, Yankees (Bobby Cox, Braves)	44,916
7-7-98	Coors Field Colorado	13-8 (A.L.)	Bartolo Colon, Indians (Ugueth Urbina, Expos)	Mike Hargrove, Indians (Jim Leyland, Marlins)	51,267
7-13-99	Fenway Park Boston	4-1 (A.L.)	Pedro Martinez, Red Sox (Curt Schilling, Phillies)	Joe Torre, Yankees (Bruce Bochy, Padres)	34,187
7-11-00	Turner Field Atlanta	6-3 (A.L.)	James Baldwin, White Sox (Al Leiter, Mets)	Joe Torre, Yankees (Bobby Cox, Braves)	51,323
7-10-01	Safeco Field Seattle	4-1 (A.L.)	Freddy Garcia, Mariners (Chan Ho Park, Dodgers)	Joe Torre, Yankees (Bobby Valentine, Mets)	47,364
7-9-02	Miller Park Milwaukee	7-7■ (tie)		Joe Torre, Yankees Bob Brenly, Diamondbacks	41,871
7-15-03	U.S. Cellular Field Chicago	7-6 (A.L.)	Brendan Donnelly, Angels (Eric Gagne, Dodgers)	Mike Scioscia, Angels (Dusty Baker, Cubs)	47,609
7-13-04	Minute Maid Park Houston	9-4 (A.L.)	Mark Mulder, Athletics (Roger Clemens, Astros)	Joe Torre, Yankees (Jack McKeon, Marlins)	41,886
7-12-05	Comerica Park Detroit	7-5 (A.L.)	Mark Buehrle, White Sox (John Smoltz, Braves)	Terry Francona, Red Sox (Tony La Russa, Cardinals)	41,617

*14 innings. †5 innings (rain). ‡12 innings. §10 innings. ∞15 innings. ▲13 innings. ■11 innings.

THE SPORTING NEWS
MOST VALUABLE PLAYER

AMERICAN LEAGUE

Year	Player	Team	Pos.	Points
1929—Al Simmons	Philadelphia	OF	40
1930—Joe Cronin	Washington	SS	52
1931—Lou Gehrig	New York	1B	40
1932—Jimmie Foxx	Philadelphia	1B	46
1933—Jimmie Foxx	Philadelphia	1B	49
1934—Lou Gehrig	New York	1B	51
1935—Hank Greenberg	Detroit	1B	64
1936—Lou Gehrig	New York	1B	55
1937—Charlie Gehringer	Detroit	2B	78
1938—Jimmie Foxx	Boston	1B	304
1939—Joe DiMaggio	New York	OF	280
1940—Hank Greenberg	Detroit	OF	292
1941—Joe DiMaggio	New York	OF	291
1942—Joe Gordon	New York	2B	270
1943—Spud Chandler	New York	P	246
1944—Bobby Doerr	Boston	2B	
1945—Eddie Mayo	Detroit	2B	

NATIONAL LEAGUE

Year	Player	Team	Pos.	Points
1929—No selection			
1930—Bill Terry	New York	1B	47
1931—Chuck Klein	Philadelphia	OF	40
1932—Chuck Klein	Philadelphia	OF	46
1933—Carl Hubbell	New York	P	64
1934—Dizzy Dean	St. Louis	P	57
1935—Arky Vaughan	Pittsburgh	SS	42
1936—Carl Hubbell	New York	P	61
1937—Joe Medwick	St. Louis	OF	70
1938—Ernie Lombardi	Cincinnati	C	229
1939—Bucky Walters	Cincinnati	P	303
1940—Frank McCormick	Cincinnati	1B	274
1941—Dolf Camilli	Brooklyn	1B	300
1942—Mort Cooper	St. Louis	P	263
1943—Stan Musial	St. Louis	OF	267
1944—Marty Marion	St. Louis	SS	
1945—Tommy Holmes	Boston	OF	

PLAYER AND PITCHER OF THE YEAR

AMERICAN LEAGUE

Year	Player	Team	Pos.
1944—Bobby Doerr	Boston	2B
Hal Newhouser	Detroit	P
1945—Eddie Mayo	Detroit	2B
Hal Newhouser	Detroit	P
1946—No selections		
1947—No selections		
1948—Lou Boudreau	Cleveland	SS
Bob Lemon	Cleveland	P
1949—Ted Williams	Boston	OF
Ellis Kinder	Boston	P
1950—Phil Rizzuto	New York	SS
Bob Lemon	Cleveland	P
1951—Ferris Fain	Philadelphia	1B
Bob Feller	Cleveland	P
1952—Luke Easter	Cleveland	1B
Bobby Shantz	Philadelphia	P
1953—Al Rosen	Cleveland	3B
Bob Porterfield	Washington	P
1954—Bobby Avila	Cleveland	2B
Bob Lemon	Cleveland	P
1955—Al Kaline	Detroit	OF
Whitey Ford	New York	P
1956—Mickey Mantle	New York	OF
Billy Pierce	Chicago	P
1957—Ted Williams	Boston	OF
Billy Pierce	Chicago	P
1958—Jackie Jensen	Boston	OF
Bob Turley	New York	P
1959—Nellie Fox	Chicago	2B
Early Wynn	Chicago	P
1960—Roger Maris	New York	OF
Chuck Estrada	Baltimore	P
1961—Roger Maris	New York	OF
Whitey Ford	New York	P
1962—Mickey Mantle	New York	OF
Dick Donovan	Cleveland	P
1963—Al Kaline	Detroit	OF
Whitey Ford	New York	P
1964—Brooks Robinson	Baltimore	3B
Dean Chance	Los Angeles	P
1965—Tony Oliva	Minnesota	OF
Jim Grant	Minnesota	P
1966—Frank Robinson	Baltimore	OF
Jim Kaat	Minnesota	P

NATIONAL LEAGUE

Year	Player	Team	Pos.
1944—Marty Marion	St. Louis	SS
Bill Voiselle	New York	P
1945—Tommy Holmes	Boston	OF
Hank Borowy	Chicago	P
1946—No selections		
1947—No selections		
1948—Stan Musial	St. Louis	OF-1B
Johnny Sain	Boston	P
1949—Enos Slaughter	St. Louis	OF
Howard Pollet	St. Louis	P
1950—Ralph Kiner	Pittsburgh	OF
Jim Konstanty	Philadelphia	P
1951—Stan Musial	St. Louis	OF
Preacher Roe	Brooklyn	P
1952—Hank Sauer	Chicago	OF
Robin Roberts	Philadelphia	P
1953—Roy Campanella	Brooklyn	C
Warren Spahn	Milwaukee	P
1954—Willie Mays	New York	OF
Johnny Antonelli	New York	P
1955—Duke Snider	Brooklyn	OF
Robin Roberts	Philadelphia	P
1956—Hank Aaron	Milwaukee	OF
Don Newcombe	Brooklyn	P
1957—Stan Musial	St. Louis	1B
Warren Spahn	Milwaukee	P
1958—Ernie Banks	Chicago	SS
Warren Spahn	Milwaukee	P
1959—Ernie Banks	Chicago	SS
Sam Jones	San Francisco	P
1960—Dick Groat	Pittsburgh	SS
Vern Law	Pittsburgh	P
1961—Frank Robinson	Cincinnati	OF
Warren Spahn	Milwaukee	P
1962—Maury Wills	Los Angeles	SS
Don Drysdale	Los Angeles	P
1963—Hank Aaron	Milwaukee	OF
Sandy Koufax	Los Angeles	P
1964—Ken Boyer	St. Louis	3B
Sandy Koufax	Los Angeles	P
1965—Willie Mays	San Francisco	OF
Sandy Koufax	Los Angeles	P
1966—Roberto Clemente	Pittsburgh	OF
Sandy Koufax	Los Angeles	P

HISTORY *Award winners*

Year	Player	Team	Pos.	Year	Player	Team	Pos.
1967—	Carl Yastrzemski	Boston	OF	1967—	Orlando Cepeda	St. Louis	1B
	Jim Lonborg	Boston	P		Mike McCormick	San Francisco	P
1968—	Ken Harrelson	Boston	OF	1968—	Pete Rose	Cincinnati	OF
	Denny McLain	Detroit	P		Bob Gibson	St. Louis	P
1969—	Harmon Killebrew	Minnesota	1B-3B	1969—	Willie McCovey	San Francisco	1B
	Denny McLain	Detroit	P		Tom Seaver	New York	P
1970—	Harmon Killebrew	Minnesota	3B	1970—	Johnny Bench	Cincinnati	C
	Sam McDowell	Cleveland	P		Bob Gibson	St. Louis	P
1971—	Tony Oliva	Minnesota	OF	1971—	Joe Torre	St. Louis	3B
	Vida Blue	Oakland	P		Ferguson Jenkins	Chicago	P
1972—	Dick Allen	Chicago	1B	1972—	Billy Williams	Chicago	OF
	Wilbur Wood	Chicago	P		Steve Carlton	Philadelphia	P
1973—	Reggie Jackson	Oakland	OF	1973—	Bobby Bonds	San Francisco	OF
	Jim Palmer	Baltimore	P		Ron Bryant	San Francisco	P
1974—	Jeff Burroughs	Texas	OF	1974—	Lou Brock	St. Louis	OF
	Jim Hunter	Oakland	P		Mike Marshall	Los Angeles	P
1975—	Fred Lynn	Boston	OF	1975—	Joe Morgan	Cincinnati	2B
	Jim Palmer	Baltimore	P		Tom Seaver	New York	P
1976—	Thurman Munson	New York	C	1976—	George Foster	Cincinnati	OF
	Jim Palmer	Baltimore	P		Randy Jones	San Diego	P
1977—	Rod Carew	Minnesota	1B	1977—	George Foster	Cincinnati	OF
	Nolan Ryan	California	P		Steve Carlton	Philadelphia	P
1978—	Jim Rice	Boston	OF	1978—	Dave Parker	Pittsburgh	OF
	Ron Guidry	New York	P		Vida Blue	San Francisco	P
1979—	Don Baylor	California	OF	1979—	Keith Hernandez	St. Louis	1B
	Mike Flanagan	Baltimore	P		Joe Niekro	Houston	P
1980—	George Brett	Kansas City	3B	1980—	Mike Schmidt	Philadelphia	3B
	Steve Stone	Baltimore	P		Steve Carlton	Philadelphia	P
1981—	Tony Armas	Oakland	OF	1981—	Andre Dawson	Montreal	OF
	Jack Morris	Detroit	P		Fernando Valenzuela	Los Angeles	P
1982—	Robin Yount	Milwaukee	SS	1982—	Dale Murphy	Atlanta	OF
	Dave Stieb	Toronto	P		Steve Carlton	Philadelphia	P
1983—	Cal Ripken Jr.	Baltimore	SS	1983—	Dale Murphy	Atlanta	OF
	LaMarr Hoyt	Chicago	P		John Denny	Philadelphia	P
1984—	Don Mattingly	New York	1B	1984—	Ryne Sandberg	Chicago	2B
	Willie Hernandez	Detroit	P		Rick Sutcliffe	Chicago	P
1985—	Don Mattingly	New York	1B	1985—	Willie McGee	St. Louis	OF
	Bret Saberhagen	Kansas City	P		Dwight Gooden	New York	P
1986—	Don Mattingly	New York	1B	1986—	Mike Schmidt	Philadelphia	3B
	Roger Clemens	Boston	P		Mike Scott	Houston	P
1987—	George Bell	Toronto	OF	1987—	Andre Dawson	Chicago	OF
	Jimmy Key	Toronto	P		Rick Sutcliffe	Chicago	P
1988—	Jose Canseco	Oakland	OF	1988—	Andy Van Slyke	Pittsburgh	OF
	Frank Viola	Minnesota	P		Orel Hershiser	Los Angeles	P
1989—	Ruben Sierra	Texas	OF	1989—	Kevin Mitchell	San Francisco	OF
	Bret Saberhagen	Kansas City	P		Mark Davis	San Diego	P
1990—	Cecil Fielder	Detroit	1B	1990—	Barry Bonds	Pittsburgh	OF
	Bob Welch	Oakland	P		Doug Drabek	Pittsburgh	P
1991—	Cal Ripken Jr.	Baltimore	SS	1991—	Barry Bonds	Pittsburgh	OF
	Roger Clemens	Boston	P		Tom Glavine	Atlanta	P

PITCHER OF THE YEAR

AMERICAN LEAGUE

Year	Pitcher	Team
1992—	Dennis Eckersley	Oakland
1993—	Jack McDowell	Chicago
1994—	Jimmy Key	New York
1995—	Randy Johnson	Seattle
1996—	Pat Hentgen	Toronto
1997—	Roger Clemens	Toronto
1998—	Roger Clemens	Toronto
1999—	Pedro Martinez	Boston
2000—	Pedro Martinez	Boston
2001—	Roger Clemens	New York
2002—	Barry Zito	Oakland
2003—	Roy Halladay	Toronto
2004—	Johan Santana	Minnesota
2005—	Bartolo Colon	Los Angeles

NATIONAL LEAGUE

Year	Pitcher	Team
1992—	Greg Maddux	Chicago
1993—	Greg Maddux	Atlanta
1994—	Greg Maddux	Atlanta
1995—	Greg Maddux	Atlanta
1996—	John Smoltz	Atlanta
1997—	Pedro Martinez	Montreal
1998—	Kevin Brown	San Diego
1999—	Mike Hampton	Houston
2000—	Tom Glavine	Atlanta
2001—	Curt Schilling	Arizona
2002—	Curt Schilling	Arizona
2003—	Eric Gagne	Los Angeles
2004—	Jason Schmidt	San Francisco
2005—	Chris Carpenter	St. Louis

1946—Combined selection—Del Ennis, Philadelphia N.L., OF
1947—Combined selection—Jackie Robinson, Brooklyn N.L., 1B
1948—Combined selection—Richie Ashburn, Philadelphia N.L., OF

AMERICAN LEAGUE

Year	Player	Team	Pos.
1949—Roy Sievers	St. Louis	OF
1950—Whitey Ford	New York	P
1951—Minnie Minoso	Chicago	OF
1952—Clint Courtney	St. Louis	C
1953—Harvey Kuenn	Detroit	SS
1954—Bob Grim	New York	P
1955—Herb Score	Cleveland	P
1956—Luis Aparicio	Chicago	SS
1957—Tony Kubek	New York	IF-OF
(No pitcher named)		
1958—Albie Pearson	Washington	OF
Ryne Duren	New York	P
1959—Bob Allison	Washington	OF
1960—Ron Hansen	Baltimore	SS
1961—Dick Howser	Kansas City	SS
Don Schwall	Boston	P
1962—Tom Tresh	New York	OF-SS
1963—Pete Ward	Chicago	3B
Gary Peters	Chicago	P
1964—Tony Oliva	Minnesota	OF
Wally Bunker	Baltimore	P
1965—Curt Blefary	Baltimore	OF
Marcelino Lopez	California	P
1966—Tommie Agee	Chicago	OF
Jim Nash	Kansas City	P
1967—Rod Carew	Minnesota	2B
Tom Phoebus	Baltimore	P
1968—Del Unser	Washington	OF
Stan Bahnsen	New York	P
1969—Carlos May	Chicago	OF
Mike Nagy	Boston	P
1970—Roy Foster	Cleveland	OF
Bert Blyleven	Minnesota	P
1971—Chris Chambliss	Cleveland	1B
Bill Parsons	Milwaukee	P
1972—Carlton Fisk	Boston	C
Dick Tidrow	Cleveland	P
1973—Al Bumbry	Baltimore	OF
Steve Busby	Kansas City	P
1974—Mike Hargrove	Texas	1B
Frank Tanana	California	P
1975—Fred Lynn	Boston	OF
Dennis Eckersley	Cleveland	P
1976—Butch Wynegar	Minnesota	C
Mark Fidrych	Detroit	P
1977—Mitchell Page	Oakland	OF
Dave Rozema	Detroit	P
1978—Paul Molitor	Milwaukee	2B
Rich Gale	Kansas City	P
1979—Pat Putnam	Texas	1B
Mark Clear	California	P
1980—Joe Charboneau	Cleveland	OF
Britt Burns	Chicago	P
1981—Rich Gedman	Boston	C
Dave Righetti	New York	P
1982—Cal Ripken Jr.	Baltimore	SS-3B
Ed Vande Berg	Seattle	P
1983—Ron Kittle	Chicago	OF
Mike Boddicker	Baltimore	P
1984—Alvin Davis	Seattle	1B
Mark Langston	Seattle	P
1985 Ozzie Guillen	Chicago	SS
Teddy Higuera	Milwaukee	P
1986—Jose Canseco	Oakland	OF
Mark Eichhorn	Toronto	P
1987—Mark McGwire	Oakland	1B
Mike Henneman	Detroit	P
1988—Walt Weiss	Oakland	SS
Bryan Harvey	California	P

NATIONAL LEAGUE

Year	Player	Team	Pos.
1949—Don Newcombe	Brooklyn	P
1950—Combined A.L.-N.L. selection		
1951—Willie Mays	New York	OF
1952—Joe Black	Brooklyn	P
1953—Jim Gilliam	Brooklyn	2B
1954—Wally Moon	St. Louis	OF
1955—Bill Virdon	St. Louis	OF
1956—Frank Robinson	Cincinnati	OF
1957—Ed Bouchee	Philadelphia	1B
Jack Sanford	Philadelphia	P
1958—Orlando Cepeda	San Francisco	1B
Carlton Willey	Milwaukee	P
1959—Willie McCovey	San Francisco	1B
1960—Frank Howard	Los Angeles	OF
1961—Billy Williams	Chicago	OF
Ken Hunt	Cincinnati	P
1962—Ken Hubbs	Chicago	2B
1963—Pete Rose	Cincinnati	2B
Ray Culp	Philadelphia	P
1964—Dick Allen	Philadelphia	3B
Billy McCool	Cincinnati	P
1965—Joe Morgan	Houston	2B
Frank Linzy	San Francisco	P
1966—Tommy Helms	Cincinnati	3B
Don Sutton	Los Angeles	P
1967—Lee May	Cincinnati	1B
Dick Hughes	St. Louis	P
1968—Johnny Bench	Cincinnati	C
Jerry Koosman	New York	P
1969—Coco Laboy	Montreal	3B
Tom Griffin	Houston	P
1970—Bernie Carbo	Cincinnati	OF
Carl Morton	Montreal	P
1971—Earl Williams	Atlanta	C
Reggie Cleveland	St. Louis	P
1972—Dave Rader	San Francisco	C
Jon Matlack	New York	P
1973—Gary Matthews	San Francisco	OF
Steve Rogers	Montreal	P
1974—Greg Gross	Houston	OF
John D'Acquisto	San Francisco	P
1975—Gary Carter	Montreal	OF-C
John Montefusco	San Francisco	P
1976—Larry Herndon	San Francisco	OF
Butch Metzger	San Diego	P
1977—Andre Dawson	Montreal	OF
Bob Owchinko	San Diego	P
1978—Bob Horner	Atlanta	3B
Don Robinson	Pittsburgh	P
1979—Jeff Leonard	Houston	OF
Rick Sutcliffe	Los Angeles	P
1980—Lonnie Smith	Philadelphia	OF
Bill Gullickson	Montreal	P
1981—Tim Raines	Montreal	OF
Fernando Valenzuela	Los Angeles	P
1982—Johnny Ray	Pittsburgh	2B
Steve Bedrosian	Atlanta	P
1983—Darryl Strawberry	New York	OF
Craig McMurtry	Atlanta	P
1984—Juan Samuel	Philadelphia	2B
Dwight Gooden	New York	P
1985—Vince Coleman	St. Louis	OF
Tom Browning	Cincinnati	P
1986—Robby Thompson	San Francisco	2B
Todd Worrell	St. Louis	P
1987—Benito Santiago	San Diego	C
Mike Dunne	Pittsburgh	P
1988—Mark Grace	Chicago	1B
Tim Belcher	Los Angeles	P

HISTORY *Award winners*

Year	Player	Team	Pos.		Year	Player	Team	Pos.
1989	Craig Worthington	Baltimore	3B		1989	Jerome Walton	Chicago	OF
	Tom Gordon	Kansas City	P			Andy Benes	San Diego	P
1990	Sandy Alomar Jr.	Cleveland	C		1990	David Justice	Atlanta	OF
	Kevin Appier	Kansas City	P			Mike Harkey	Chicago	P
1991	Chuck Knoblauch	Minnesota	2B		1991	Jeff Bagwell	Houston	1B
	Juan Guzman	Toronto	P			Al Osuna	Houston	P
1992	Pat Listach	Milwaukee	SS		1992	Eric Karros	Los Angeles	1B
	Cal Eldred	Milwaukee	P			Tim Wakefield	Pittsburgh	P
1993	Tim Salmon	California	OF		1993	Mike Piazza	Los Angeles	C
	Aaron Sele	Boston	P			Kirk Rueter	Montreal	P
1994	Bob Hamelin	Kansas City	DH		1994	Raul Mondesi	Los Angeles	OF
	Brian Anderson	California	P			Steve Trachsel	Chicago	P
1995	Garret Anderson	California	OF		1995	Chipper Jones	Atlanta	3B
	Julian Tavarez	Cleveland	P			Hideo Nomo	Los Angeles	P
1996	Derek Jeter	New York	SS		1996	Jason Kendall	Pittsburgh	C
	James Baldwin	Chicago	P			Alan Benes	St. Louis	P
1997	Nomar Garciaparra	Boston	SS		1997	Scott Rolen	Philadelphia	3B
	Jason Dickson	Anaheim	P			Matt Morris	St. Louis	P
1998	Ben Grieve	Oakland	OF		1998	Todd Helton	Colorado	1B
	Rolando Arrojo	Tampa Bay	P			Kerry Wood	Chicago	P
1999	Carlos Beltran	Kansas City	OF		1999	Preston Wilson	Florida	OF
	Tim Hudson	Oakland	P			Scott Williamson	Cincinnati	P
2000	Mark Quinn	Kansas City	OF-DH		2000	Rafael Furcal	Atlanta	2B-SS
	Kazuhiro Sasaki	Seattle	P			Rick Ankiel	St. Louis	P
2001	Ichiro Suzuki	Seattle	OF		2001	Albert Pujols	St. Louis	O-3-1B
	C.C. Sabathia	Cleveland	P			Roy Oswalt	Houston	P
2002	Eric Hinske	Toronto	3B		2002	Brad Wilkerson	Montreal	OF-1B
	Rodrigo Lopez	Baltimore	P			Jason Jennings	Colorado	P
2003	Jody Gerut	Cleveland	OF		2003	Scott Podsednik	Milwaukee	OF
	Rafael Soriano	Seattle	P			Dontrelle Willis	Florida	P
2004	Bobby Crosby	Oakland	SS		2004	Jason Bay	Pittsburgh	OF
2005	Huston Street	Oakland	P		2005	Willy Taveras	Houston	OF

RELIEVER OF THE YEAR

AMERICAN LEAGUE

NATIONAL LEAGUE

Year	Pitcher	Team		Year	Pitcher	Team
1960	Mike Fornieles	Boston		1960	Lindy McDaniel	St. Louis
1961	Luis Arroyo	New York		1961	Stu Miller	San Francisco
1962	Dick Radatz	Boston		1962	Roy Face	Pittsburgh
1963	Stu Miller	Baltimore		1963	Lindy McDaniel	Chicago
1964	Dick Radatz	Boston		1964	Al McBean	Pittsburgh
1965	Eddie Fisher	Chicago		1965	Ted Abernathy	Chicago
1966	Jack Aker	Kansas City		1966	Phil Regan	Los Angeles
1967	Minnie Rojas	California		1967	Ted Abernathy	Cincinnati
1968	Wilbur Wood	Chicago		1968	Phil Regan	L.A.-Chicago
1969	Ron Perranoski	Minnesota		1969	Wayne Granger	Cincinnati
1970	Ron Perranoski	Minnesota		1970	Wayne Granger	Cincinnati
1971	Ken Sanders	Milwaukee		1971	Dave Giusti	Pittsburgh
1972	Sparky Lyle	New York		1972	Clay Carroll	Cincinnati
1973	John Hiller	Detroit		1973	Mike Marshall	Montreal
1974	Terry Forster	Chicago		1974	Mike Marshall	Los Angeles
1975	Rich Gossage	Chicago		1975	Al Hrabosky	St. Louis
1976	Bill Campbell	Minnesota		1976	Rawly Eastwick	Cincinnati
1977	Bill Campbell	Boston		1977	Rollie Fingers	San Diego
1978	Rich Gossage	New York		1978	Rollie Fingers	San Diego
1979	Mike Marshall	Minnesota		1979	Bruce Sutter	Chicago
	Jim Kern	Texas				
1980	Dan Quisenberry	Kansas City		1980	Rollie Fingers	San Diego
					Tom Hume	Cincinnati
1981	Rollie Fingers	Milwaukee		1981	Bruce Sutter	St. Louis
1982	Dan Quisenberry	Kansas City		1982	Bruce Sutter	St. Louis
1983	Dan Quisenberry	Kansas City		1983	Al Holland	Philadelphia
					Lee Smith	Chicago
1984	Dan Quisenberry	Kansas City		1984	Bruce Sutter	St. Louis
1985	Dan Quisenberry	Kansas City		1985	Jeff Reardon	Montreal
1986	Dave Righetti	New York		1986	Todd Worrell	St. Louis
1987	Dave Righetti	New York		1987	Steve Bedrosian	Philadelphia
	Jeff Reardon	Minnesota				
1988	Dennis Eckersley	Oakland		1988	John Franco	Cincinnati
1989	Jeff Russell	Texas		1989	Mark Davis	San Diego
1990	Bobby Thigpen	Chicago		1990	John Franco	New York
1991	Dennis Eckersley	Oakland		1991	Lee Smith	St. Louis
	Bryan Harvey	California				
1992	Dennis Eckersley	Oakland		1992	Doug Jones	Houston
					Lee Smith	St. Louis
1993	Jeff Montgomery	Kansas City		1993	Randy Myers	Chicago

AMERICAN LEAGUE

Year	Pitcher	Team
1994—Lee Smith		Baltimore
1995—Jose Mesa		Cleveland
1996—John Wetteland		New York
1997—Mariano Rivera		New York
1998—Tom Gordon		Boston
1999—Mariano Rivera		New York
2000—Todd Jones		Detroit
2001—Mariano Rivera		New York
2002—Billy Koch		Oakland
2003—Keith Foulke		Oakland
2004—Mariano Rivera		New York
2005—Mariano Rivera		New York
Joe Nathan		Minnesota

NATIONAL LEAGUE

Year	Pitcher	Team
1994—John Franco		New York
1995—Randy Myers		Chicago
1996—Trevor Hoffman		San Diego
1997—Jeff Shaw		Cincinnati
1998—Trevor Hoffman		San Diego
1999—Ugueth Urbina		Montreal
2000—Antonio Alfonseca		Florida
2001—Armando Benitez		New York
Robb Nen		San Francisco
2002—John Smoltz		Atlanta
2003—Eric Gagne		Los Angeles
2004—Eric Gagne		Los Angeles
2005—Chad Cordero		Washington

COMEBACK PLAYER OF THE YEAR

AMERICAN LEAGUE

Year	Pitcher	Team
1965—Norm Cash		Detroit
1966—Boog Powell		Baltimore
1967—Dean Chance		Minnesota
1968—Ken Harrelson		Boston
1969—Tony Conigliaro		Boston
1970—Clyde Wright		California
1971—Norm Cash		Detroit
1972—Luis Tiant		Boston
1973—John Hiller		Detroit
1974—Ferguson Jenkins		Texas
1975—Boog Powell		Cleveland
1976—Dock Ellis		New York
1977—Eric Soderholm		Chicago
1978—Mike Caldwell		Milwaukee
1979—Willie Horton		Seattle
1980—Matt Keough		Oakland
1981—Richie Zisk		Seattle
1982—Andre Thornton		Cleveland
1983—Alan Trammell		Detroit
1984—Dave Kingman		Oakland
1985—Gorman Thomas		Seattle
1986—John Candelaria		California
1987—Bret Saberhagen		Kansas City
1988—Storm Davis		Oakland
1989—Bert Blyleven		California
1990—Dave Winfield		California
1991—Jose Guzman		Texas
1992—Rick Sutcliffe		Baltimore
1993—Bo Jackson		Chicago
1994—Jose Canseco		Texas
1995—Tim Wakefield		Boston
1996—Kevin Elster		Texas
1997—David Justice		Cleveland
1998—Bret Saberhagen		Boston
1999—John Jaha		Oakland
2000—Frank Thomas		Chicago
2001—Ruben Sierra		Texas
2002—Tim Salmon		Anaheim
2003—Gil Meche		Seattle
2004—Paul Konerko		Chicago
2005—Jason Giambi		New York

NATIONAL LEAGUE

Year	Pitcher	Team
1965—Vernon Law		Pittsburgh
1966—Phil Regan		Los Angeles
1967—Mike McCormick		San Francisco
1968—Alex Johnson		Cincinnati
1969—Tommie Agee		New York
1970—Jim Hickman		Chicago
1971—Al Downing		Los Angeles
1972—Bobby Tolan		Cincinnati
1973—Dave Johnson		Atlanta
1974—Jim Wynn		Los Angeles
1975—Randy Jones		San Diego
1976—Tommy John		Los Angeles
1977—Willie McCovey		San Francisco
1978—Willie Stargell		Pittsburgh
1979—Lou Brock		St. Louis
1980—Jerry Reuss		Los Angeles
1981—Bob Knepper		Houston
1982—Joe Morgan		San Francisco
1983—John Denny		Philadelphia
1984—Joaquin Andujar		St. Louis
1985—Rick Reuschel		Pittsburgh
1986—Ray Knight		New York
1987—Rick Sutcliffe		Chicago
1988—Tim Leary		Los Angeles
1989—Lonnie Smith		Atlanta
1990—John Tudor		St. Louis
1991—Terry Pendleton		Atlanta
1992—Gary Sheffield		San Diego
1993—Andres Galarraga		Colorado
1994—Tim Wallach		Los Angeles
1995—Ron Gant		Cincinnati
1996—Eric Davis		Cincinnati
1997—Darren Daulton		Phi.-Fla.
1998—Greg Vaughn		San Diego
1999—Rickey Henderson		New York
2000—Andres Galarraga		Atlanta
2001—Matt Morris		St. Louis
2002—Mike Lieberthal		Philadelphia
2003—Javy Lopez		Atlanta
2004—Chris Carpenter		St. Louis
2005—Ken Griffey Jr.		Cincinnati

MAJOR LEAGUE PLAYER OF THE YEAR

Year	Player	Team	Year	Player	Team	Year	Player	Team
1936—Carl Hubbell		New York N.L.	1948—Lou Boudreau		Cleveland A.L.	1960—Bill Mazeroski		Pittsburgh N.L.
1937—Johnny Allen		Cleveland A.L.	1949—Ted Williams		Boston A.L.	1961—Roger Maris		New York A.L.
1938—Johnny Vander Meer		Cincinnati N.L.	1950—Phil Rizzuto		New York A.L.	1962—Maury Wills		Los Angeles N.L.
1939—Joe DiMaggio		New York A.L.	1951—Stan Musial		St. Louis N.L.	Don Drysdale		Los Angeles N.L.
1940—Bob Feller		Cleveland A.L.	1952—Robin Roberts		Philadelphia N.L.	1963—Sandy Koufax		Los Angeles N.L.
1941—Ted Williams		Boston A.L.	1953—Al Rosen		Cleveland A.L.	1964—Ken Boyer		St. Louis N.L.
1942—Ted Williams		Boston A.L.	1954—Willie Mays		New York N.L.	1965—Sandy Koufax		Los Angeles N.L.
1943—Spud Chandler		New York A.L.	1955—Duke Snider		Brooklyn N.L.	1966—Frank Robinson		Baltimore A.L.
1944—Marty Marion		St. Louis N.L.	1956—Mickey Mantle		New York A.L.	1967—Carl Yastrzemski		Boston A.L.
1945—Hal Newhouser		Detroit A.L.	1957—Ted Williams		Boston A.L.	1968—Denny McLain		Detroit A.L.
1946—Stan Musial		St. Louis N.L.	1958—Bob Turley		New York A.L.	1969—Willie McCovey		San Francisco N.L.
1947—Ted Williams		Boston A.L.	1959—Early Wynn		Chicago A.L.	1970—Johnny Bench		Cincinnati N.L.

Year	Player	Team	Year	Player	Team	Year	Player	Team
1971—Joe Torre	St. Louis N.L.		1983—Cal Ripken Jr.	Baltimore A.L.		1995—Albert Belle	Cleveland A.L.	
1972—Billy Williams	Chicago N.L.		1984—Ryne Sandberg	Chicago N.L.		1996—Alex Rodriguez	Seattle A.L.	
1973—Reggie Jackson	Oakland A.L.		1985—Don Mattingly	New York A.L.		1997—Ken Griffey Jr.	Seattle A.L.	
1974—Lou Brock	St. Louis N.L.		1986—Roger Clemens	Boston A.L.		1998—Sammy Sosa	Chicago N.L.	
1975—Joe Morgan	Cincinnati N.L.		1987—George Bell	Toronto A.L.		1999—Rafael Palmeiro	Texas A.L.	
1976—Joe Morgan	Cincinnati N.L.		1988—Orel Hershiser	Los Angeles N.L.		2000—Carlos Delgado	Toronto A.L.	
1977—Rod Carew	Minnesota A.L.		1989—Kevin Mitchell	San Francisco N.L.		2001—Barry Bonds	San Francisco N.L.	
1978—Ron Guidry	New York A.L.		1990—Barry Bonds	Pittsburgh N.L.		2002—Alex Rodriguez	Texas A.L	
1979—Willie Stargell	Pittsburgh N.L.		1991—Cal Ripken Jr.	Baltimore A.L.		2003—Albert Pujols	St. Louis N.L.	
1980—George Brett	Kansas City A.L.		1992—Gary Sheffield	San Diego N.L.		2004—Barry Bonds	San Francisco N.L.	
1981—Fernando Valenzuela	Los Angeles N.L.		1993—Frank Thomas	Chicago A.L.		2005—Andruw Jones	Atlanta N.L.	
1982—Robin Yount	Milwaukee A.L.		1994—Jeff Bagwell	Houston N.L.				

MAJOR LEAGUE MANAGER OF THE YEAR

Year	Manager	Team	Year	Manager	Team	Year	Manager	Team
1936—Joe McCarthy	New York A.L.		1967—Dick Williams	Boston A.L.			Bobby Cox	Atlanta N.L.	
1937—Bill McKechnie	Boston N.L.		1968—Mayo Smith	Detroit A.L.		1992—Tony La Russa	Oakland A.L.	
1938—Joe McCarthy	New York A.L.		1969—Gil Hodges	New York N.L.			Jim Leyland	Pittsburgh N.L.	
1939—Leo Durocher	Brooklyn N.L.		1970—Danny Murtaugh	Pittsburgh N.L.		1993—Johnny Oates	Baltimore A.L.	
1940—Bill McKechnie	Cincinnati N.L.		1971—Charlie Fox	San Francisco N.L.			Bobby Cox	Atlanta N.L.	
1941—Billy Southworth	St. Louis N.L.		1972—Chuck Tanner	Chicago A.L.		1994—Buck Showalter	New York A.L.	
1942—Billy Southworth	St. Louis N.L.		1973—Gene Mauch	Montreal N.L.			Felipe Alou	Montreal N.L.	
1943—Joe McCarthy	New York A.L.		1974—Bill Virdon	New York A.L.		1995—Mike Hargrove	Cleveland A.L.	
1944—Luke Sewell	St. Louis A.L.		1975—Darrell Johnson	Boston A.L.			Don Baylor	Colorado N.L.	
1945—Ossie Bluege	Washington A.L.		1976—Danny Ozark	Philadelphia N.L.		1996—Johnny Oates	Texas A.L.	
1946—Eddie Dyer	St. Louis N.L.		1977—Earl Weaver	Baltimore A.L.			Bruce Bochy	San Diego N.L.	
1947—Bucky Harris	New York A.L.		1978—George Bamberger	Milwaukee A.L.		1997—Dave Johnson	Baltimore A.L.	
1948—Bill Meyer	Pittsburgh N.L.		1979—Earl Weaver	Baltimore A.L.			Dusty Baker	San Fran. N.L.	
1949—Casey Stengel	New York A.L.		1980—Bill Virdon	Houston N.L.		1998—Joe Torre	New York A.L.	
1950—Red Rolfe	Detroit A.L.		1981—Billy Martin	Oakland A.L.			Bruce Bochy	San Diego N.L.	
1951—Leo Durocher	New York N.L.		1982—Whitey Herzog	St. Louis N.L.		1999—Jimy Williams	Boston A.L.	
1952—Eddie Stanky	St. Louis N.L.		1983—Tony La Russa	Chicago A.L.			Bobby Cox	Atlanta N.L.	
1953—Casey Stengel	New York A.L.		1984—Jim Frey	Chicago N.L.		2000—Jerry Manuel	Chicago A.L.	
1954—Leo Durocher	New York N.L.		1985—Bobby Cox	Toronto A.L.			Dusty Baker	San Fran. N.L.	
1955—Walter Alston	Brooklyn N.L.		1986—John McNamara	Boston A.L.		2001—Lou Piniella	Seattle A.L.	
1956—Birdie Tebbetts	Cincinnati N.L.			Hal Lanier	Houston N.L.			Larry Bowa	Philadelphia N.L.	
1957—Fred Hutchinson	St. Louis N.L.		1987—Sparky Anderson	Detroit A.L.		2002—Mike Scioscia	Anaheim A.L.	
1958—Casey Stengel	New York A.L.			Buck Rodgers	Montreal A.L.			Bobby Cox	Atlanta N.L.	
1959—Walter Alston	Los Angeles N.L.		1988—Tony La Russa	Oakland A.L.		2003—Tony Pena	Kansas City A.L.	
1960—Danny Murtaugh	Pittsburgh N.L.			Tommy Lasorda	L.A. N.L. (tie)			Bobby Cox	Atlanta N.L.	
1961—Ralph Houk	New York A.L.			Jim Leyland	Pit. N.L. (tie)		2004—Buck Showalter	Texas A.L.	
1962—Bill Rigney	Los Angeles A.L.		1989—Frank Robinson	Baltimore A.L.			Ron Gardenhire	Minnesota A.L.	
1963—Walter Alston	Los Angeles N.L.			Don Zimmer	Chicago N.L.			Bobby Cox	Atlanta N.L.	
1964—Johnny Keane	St. Louis N.L.		1990—Jeff Torborg	Chicago A.L.		2005—Ozzie Guillen	Chicago A.L.	
1965—Sam Mele	Minnesota A.L.			Jim Leyland	Pittsburgh N.L.			Bobby Cox	Atlanta N.L.	
1966—Hank Bauer	Baltimore A.L.		1991—Tom Kelly	Minnesota A.L.					

MAJOR LEAGUE EXECUTIVE OF THE YEAR

Year	Executive	Team	Year	Executive	Team	Year	Executive	Team
1936—Branch Rickey	St. Louis N.L.		1960—George Weiss	New York A.L.		1984—Dallas Green	Chicago N.L.	
1937—Ed Barrow	New York A.L.		1961—Dan Topping	New York A.L.		1985—John Schuerholz	Kansas City A.L.	
1938—Warren Giles	Cincinnati N.L.		1962—Fred Haney	Los Angeles A.L.		1986—Frank Cashen	New York N.L.	
1939—Larry MacPhail	Brooklyn N.L.		1963—Bing Devine	St. Louis N.L.		1987—Al Rosen	San Francisco N.L.	
1940—Walter Briggs Sr.	Detroit A.L.		1964—Bing Devine	St. Louis N.L.		1988—Fred Claire	Los Angeles N.L.	
1941—Ed Barrow	New York A.L.		1965—Cal Griffith	Minnesota A.L.		1989—Roland Hemond	Baltimore A.L.	
1942—Branch Rickey	St. Louis N.L.		1966—Lee MacPhail	Commissioner's Off.		1990—Bob Quinn	Cincinnati N.L.	
1943—Clark Griffith	Washington A.L.		1967—Dick O'Connell	Boston A.L.		1991—Andy MacPhail	Minnesota A.L.	
1944—Bill DeWitt	St. Louis A.L.		1968—Jim Campbell	Detroit A.L.		1992—Dan Duquette	Montreal N.L.	
1945—Phil Wrigley	Chicago N.L.		1969—John Murphy	New York N.L.		1993—Lee Thomas	Philadelphia N.L.	
1946—Tom Yawkey	Boston A.L.		1970—Harry Dalton	Baltimore A.L.		1994—John Hart	Cleveland A.L.	
1947—Branch Rickey	Brooklyn N.L.		1971—Cedric Tallis	Kansas City A.L.		1995—John Hart	Cleveland A.L.	
1948—Bill Veeck	Cleveland A.L.		1972—Roland Hemond	Chicago A.L.		1996—Doug Melvin	Texas A.L.	
1949—Bob Carpenter	Philadelphia N.L.		1973—Bob Howsam	Cincinnati N.L.		1997—Cam Bonifay	Pittsburgh N.L.	
1950—George Weiss	New York A.L.		1974—Gabe Paul	New York A.L.		1998—Gerry Hunsicker	Houston N.L.	
1951—George Weiss	New York A.L.		1975—Dick O'Connell	Boston A.L.		1999—Billy Beane	Oakland A.L.	
1952—George Weiss	New York A.L.		1976—Joe Burke	Kansas City A.L.		2000—Walt Jocketty	St. Louis N.L.	
1953—Lou Perini	Milwaukee N.L.		1977—Bill Veeck	Chicago A.L.		2001—Pat Gillick	Seattle A.L.	
1954—Horace Stoneham	New York N.L.		1978—Spec Richardson	San Francisco N.L.		2002—Terry Ryan	Minnesota A.L.	
1955—Walter O'Malley	Brooklyn N.L.		1979—Hank Peters	Baltimore A.L.		2003—Brian Sabean	San Francisco N.L.	
1956—Gabe Paul	Cincinnati N.L.		1980—Tal Smith	Houston N.L.		2004—Walt Jocketty	St. Louis N.L.	
1957—Frank Lane	St. Louis N.L.		1981—John McHale	Montreal N.L.		2005—Mark Shapiro	Cleveland A.L.	
1958—Joe Brown	Pittsburgh N.L.		1982—Harry Dalton	Milwaukee A.L.					
1959—Buzzie Bavasi	Los Angeles N.L.		1983—Hank Peters	Baltimore A.L.					

HISTORY *Award winners*

1925
1B— Jim Bottomley, St. Louis N.L.
2B— Rogers Hornsby, St. Louis N.L.
SS— Glenn Wright, Pittsburgh N.L.
3B— Pie Traynor, Pittsburgh N.L.
OF— Kiki Cuyler, Pittsburgh N.L.
OF— Max Carey, Pittsburgh N.L.
OF— Goose Goslin, Washington A.L.
C— Mickey Cochrane, Phil. A.L.
P— Walter Johnson, Washington A.L.
P— Ed Rommel, Philadelphia A.L.
P— Dazzy Vance, Brooklyn N.L.

1926
1B— George Burns, Cleveland A.L.
2B— Rogers Hornsby, St. Louis N.L.
SS— Joe Sewell, Cleveland A.L.
3B— Pie Traynor, Pittsburgh N.L.
OF— Goose Goslin, Washington A.L.
OF— John Mostil, Chicago A.L.
OF— Babe Ruth, New York A.L.
C— Bob O'Farrell, St. Louis N.L.
P— Herb Pennock, New York A.L.
P— George Uhle, Cleveland A.L.
P— Grover Alexander, St. Louis N.L.

1927
1B— Lou Gehrig, New York A.L.
2B— Rogers Hornsby, New York N.L.
SS— Travis Jackson, New York N.L.
3B— Pie Traynor, Pittsburgh N.L.
OF— Babe Ruth, New York A.L.
OF— Al Simmons, Philadelphia A.L.
OF— Paul Waner, Pittsburgh N.L.
C— Gabby Hartnett, Chicago N.L.
P— Charley Root, Chicago N.L.
P— Ted Lyons, Chicago A.L.

1928
1B— Lou Gehrig, New York A.L.
2B— Rogers Hornsby, Boston N.L.
SS— Travis Jackson, New York N.L.
3B— Fred Lindstrom, New York N.L.
OF— Babe Ruth, New York A.L.
OF— Heinie Manush, St. Louis A.L.
OF— Paul Waner, Pittsburgh N.L.
C— Mickey Cochrane, Phil. A.L.
P— Lefty Grove, Philadelphia A.L.
P— Waite Hoyt, New York A.L.

1929
1B— Jimmie Foxx, Philadelphia A.L.
2B— Rogers Hornsby, Chicago N.L.
SS— Travis Jackson, New York N.L.
3B— Pie Traynor, Pittsburgh, N.L.
OF— Al Simmons, Philadelphia A.L.
OF— Hack Wilson, Chicago N.L.
OF— Babe Ruth, New York A.L.
C— Mickey Cochrane, Phil. A.L.
P— Lefty Grove, Philadelphia A.L.
P— Burleigh Grimes, Pittsburgh N.L.

1930
1B— Bill Terry, New York N.L.
2B— Frank Frisch, St. Louis N.L.
SS— Joe Cronin, Washington A.L.
3B— Fred Lindstrom, New York N.L.
OF— Al Simmons, Philadelphia A.L.
OF— Hack Wilson, Chicago N.L.
OF— Babe Ruth, New York A.L.
C— Mickey Cochrane, Phil. A.L.
P— Lefty Grove, Philadelphia A.L.
P— Wes Ferrell, Cleveland A.L.

1931
1B— Lou Gehrig, New York A.L.
2B— Frank Frisch, St. Louis N.L.
SS— Joe Cronin, Washington A.L.
3B— Pie Traynor, Pittsburgh N.L.
OF— Al Simmons, Philadelphia A.L.
OF— Earl Averill, Cleveland A.L.
OF— Babe Ruth, New York A.L.
C— Mickey Cochrane, Phil. A.L.
P— Lefty Grove, Philadelphia A.L.
P— George Earnshaw, Phil. A.L.

1932
1B— Jimmie Foxx, Philadelphia A.L.
2B— Tony Lazzeri, New York A.L.
SS— Joe Cronin, Washington A.L.
3B— Pie Traynor, Pittsburgh N.L.
OF— Lefty O'Doul, Brooklyn N.L.
OF— Earl Averill, Cleveland A.L.
OF— Chuck Klein, Philadelphia N.L.
C— Bill Dickey, New York A.L.
P— Lefty Grove, Philadelphia A.L.
P— Lon Warneke, Chicago N.L.

1933
1B— Jimmie Foxx, Philadelphia A.L.
2B— Charley Gehringer, Detroit A.L.
SS— Joe Cronin, Washington A.L.
3B— Pie Traynor, Pittsburgh N.L.
OF— Al Simmons, Chicago A.L.
OF— Wally Berger, Boston N.L.
OF— Chuck Klein, Philadelphia N.L.
C— Bill Dickey, New York A.L.
P— Alvin Crowder, Washington A.L.
P— Carl Hubbell, New York N.L.

1934
1B— Lou Gehrig, New York A.L.
2B— Charley Gehringer, Detroit A.L.
SS— Joe Cronin, Washington A.L.
3B— Mike Higgins, Philadelphia A.L.
OF— Al Simmons, Chicago A.L.
OF— Earl Averill, Cleveland A.L.
OF— Mel Ott, New York N.L.
C— Mickey Cochrane, Detroit A.L.
P— Lefty Gomez, New York A.L.
P— Schoolboy Rowe, Detroit A.L.
P— Dizzy Dean, St. Louis N.L.

1935
1B— Hank Greenberg, Detroit A.L.
2B— Charley Gehringer, Detroit A.L.
SS— Arky Vaughan, Pittsburgh N.L.
3B— Pepper Martin, St. Louis N.L.
OF— Joe Medwick, St. Louis N.L.
OF— Doc Cramer, Philadelphia A.L.
OF— Mel Ott, New York N.L.
C— Mickey Cochrane, Detroit A.L.
P— Carl Hubbell, New York N.L.
P— Dizzy Dean, St. Louis N.L.

1936
1B— Lou Gehrig, New York A.L.
2B— Charley Gehringer, Detroit A.L.
SS— Luke Appling, Chicago A.L.
3B— Mike Higgins, Philadelphia A.L.
OF— Joe Medwick, St. Louis N.L.
OF— Earl Averill, Cleveland A.L.
OF— Mel Ott, New York N.L.
C— Bill Dickey, New York A.L.
P— Carl Hubbell, New York N.L.
P— Dizzy Dean, St. Louis N.L.

1937
1B— Lou Gehrig, New York A.L.
2B— Charley Gehringer, Detroit A.L.
SS— Dick Bartell, New York N.L.
3B— Red Rolfe, New York A.L.
OF— Joe Medwick, St. Louis N.L.
OF— Joe DiMaggio, New York A.L.
OF— Paul Waner, Pittsburgh N.L.
C— Gabby Hartnett, Chicago N.L.
P— Carl Hubbell, New York N.L.
P— Red Ruffing, New York A.L.

1938
1B— Jimmie Foxx, Boston A.L.
2B— Charley Gehringer, Detroit A.L.
SS— Joe Cronin, Boston A.L.
3B— Red Rolfe, New York A.L.
OF— Joe Medwick, St. Louis N.L.
OF— Joe DiMaggio, New York A.L.
OF— Mel Ott, New York N.L.
C— Bill Dickey, New York A.L.
P— Red Ruffing, New York A.L.
P— Lefty Gomez, New York A.L.
P— Johnny Vander Meer, Cin. N.L.

1939
1B— Jimmie Foxx, Boston A.L.
2B— Joe Gordon, New York A.L.
SS— Joe Cronin, Boston A.L.
3B— Red Rolfe, New York A.L.
OF— Joe Medwick, St. Louis N.L.
OF— Joe DiMaggio, New York A.L.
OF— Ted Williams, Boston A.L.
C— Bill Dickey, New York A.L.
P— Red Ruffing, New York A.L.
P— Bob Feller, Cleveland A.L.
P— Bucky Walters, Cincinnati N.L.

1940
1B— Frank McCormick, Cincinnati N.L.
2B— Joe Gordon, New York A.L.
SS— Luke Appling, Chicago A.L.
3B— Stan Hack, Chicago N.L.
OF— Hank Greenberg, Detroit A.L.
OF— Joe DiMaggio, New York A.L.
OF— Ted Williams, Boston A.L.
C— Harry Danning, New York N.L.
P— Bob Feller, Cleveland A.L.
P— Bucky Walters, Cincinnati N.L.
P— Paul Derringer, Cincinnati N.L.

1941
1B— Dolf Camilli, Brooklyn N.L.
2B— Joe Gordon, New York A.L.
SS— Cecil Travis, Washington A.L.
3B— Stan Hack, Chicago N.L.
OF— Ted Williams, Boston A.L.
OF— Joe DiMaggio, New York A.L.
OF— Pete Reiser, Brooklyn N.L.
C— Bill Dickey, New York A.L.
P— Bob Feller, Cleveland A.L.
P— Whitlow Wyatt, Brooklyn N.L.
P— Thornton Lee, Chicago A.L.

1942
1B— Johnny Mize, New York N.L.
2B— Joe Gordon, New York A.L.
SS— Johnny Pesky, Boston A.L.
3B— Stan Hack, Chicago N.L.
OF— Ted Williams, Boston A.L.
OF— Joe DiMaggio, New York A.L.
OF— Enos Slaughter, St. Louis N.L.
C— Mickey Owen, Brooklyn N.L.
P— Mort Cooper, St. Louis N.L.
P— Tiny Bonham, New York A.L.
P— Tex Hughson, Boston A.L.

1943
1B— Rudy York, Detroit A.L.
2B— Billy Herman, Brooklyn N.L.
SS— Luke Appling, Chicago A.L.
3B— Billy Johnson, New York A.L.
OF— Dick Wakefield, Detroit A.L.
OF— Stan Musial, St. Louis N.L.
OF— Bill Nicholson, Chicago N.L.
C— Walker Cooper, St. Louis N.L.
P— Spud Chandler, New York A.L.
P— Mort Cooper, St. Louis N.L.
P— Rip Sewell, Pittsburgh N.L.

1944
1B— Ray Sanders, St. Louis N.L.
2B— Bobby Doerr, Boston A.L.
SS— Marty Marion, St. Louis N.L.
3B— Bob Elliott, Pittsburgh N.L.
OF— Stan Musial, St. Louis N.L.
OF— Dick Wakefield, Detroit A.L.
OF— Dixie Walker, Brooklyn, N.L.
C— Walker Cooper, St. Louis N.L.
P— Hal Newhouser, Detroit A.L.
P— Mort Cooper, St. Louis N.L.
P— Dizzy Trout, Detroit A.L.

1945
1B— Phil Cavarretta, Chicago N.L.
2B— George Stirnweiss, N.Y. A.L.
SS— Marty Marion, St. Louis N.L.
3B— Whitey Kurowski, St. Louis N.L.
OF— Tommy Holmes, Boston N.L.
OF— Andy Pafko, Chicago N.L.
OF— Goody Rosen, Brooklyn N.L.
C— Paul Richards, Detroit A.L.
P— Hal Newhouser, Detroit A.L.
P— Boo Ferriss, Boston A.L.
P— Hank Borowy, Chicago N.L.

1946
1B— Stan Musial, St. Louis N.L.
2B— Bobby Doerr, Boston A.L.
SS— Johnny Pesky, Boston A.L.
3B— George Kell, Detroit A.L.
OF— Ted Williams, Boston A.L.
OF— Dom DiMaggio, Boston A.L.
OF— Enos Slaughter, St. Louis N.L.
C— Aaron Robinson, New York A.L.
P— Hal Newhouser, Detroit A.L.
P— Bob Feller, Cleveland A.L.
P— Boo Ferriss, Boston A.L.

1947
1B— Johnny Mize, New York N.L.
2B— Joe Gordon, Cleveland A.L.
SS— Lou Boudreau, Cleveland A.L.
3B— George Kell, Detroit A.L.
OF— Ted Williams, Boston A.L.
OF— Joe DiMaggio, New York A.L.
OF— Ralph Kiner, Pittsburgh N.L.
C— Walker Cooper, New York N.L.
P— Ewell Blackwell, Cincinnati N.L.
P— Bob Feller, Cleveland A.L.
P— Ralph Branca, Brooklyn N.L.

1948
1B— Johnny Mize, New York N.L.
2B— Joe Gordon, Cleveland A.L.
SS— Lou Boudreau, Cleveland A.L.
3B— Bob Elliott, Boston N.L.
OF— Ted Williams, Boston A.L.
OF— Joe DiMaggio, New York A.L.
OF— Stan Musial, St. Louis N.L.
C— Birdie Tebbetts, Boston A.L.
P— Johnny Sain, Boston N.L.
P— Bob Lemon, Cleveland A.L.
P— Harry Brecheen, St. Louis N.L.

1949
1B— Tommy Henrich, New York A.L.
2B— Jackie Robinson, Brooklyn N.L.
SS— Phil Rizzuto, New York A.L.
3B— George Kell, Detroit A.L.
OF— Ted Williams, Boston A.L.
OF— Stan Musial, St. Louis N.L.
OF— Ralph Kiner, Pittsburgh N.L.
C— Roy Campanella, Brooklyn N.L.
P— Mel Parnell, Boston A.L.
P— Ellis Kinder, Boston A.L.
P— Joe Page, New York A.L.

1950
1B— Walt Dropo, Boston A.L.
2B— Jackie Robinson, Brooklyn N.L.
SS— Phil Rizzuto, New York A.L.
3B— George Kell, Detroit A.L.
OF— Stan Musial, St. Louis N.L.
OF— Ralph Kiner, Pittsburgh N.L.
OF— Larry Doby, Cleveland A.L.
C— Yogi Berra, New York A.L.
P— Vic Raschi, New York A.L.
P— Bob Lemon, Cleveland A.L.
P— Jim Konstanty, Phil. N.L.

1951
1B— Ferris Fain, Philadelphia A.L.
2B— Jackie Robinson, Brooklyn N.L.
SS— Phil Rizzuto, New York A.L.
3B— George Kell, Detroit A.L.
OF— Stan Musial, St. Louis N.L.
OF— Ted Williams, Boston A.L.
OF— Ralph Kiner, Pittsburgh N.L.
C— Roy Campanella, Brooklyn N.L.
P— Sal Maglie, New York N.L.
P— Preacher Roe, Brooklyn N.L.
P— Allie Reynolds, New York A.L.

1952
1B— Ferris Fain, Philadelphia A.L.
2B— Jackie Robinson, Brooklyn N.L.
SS— Phil Rizzuto, New York A.L.
3B— George Kell, Boston A.L.
OF— Stan Musial, St. Louis N.L.
OF— Hank Sauer, Chicago N.L.
OF— Mickey Mantle, New York A.L.
C— Yogi Berra, New York A.L.
P— Robin Roberts, Philadelphia N.L.
P— Bobby Shantz, Philadelphia A.L.
P— Allie Reynolds, New York A.L.

1953
1B— Mickey Vernon, Washington A.L.
2B— Red Schoendienst, St. Louis N.L.
SS— Pee Wee Reese, Brooklyn N.L.
3B— Al Rosen, Cleveland A.L.
OF— Stan Musial, St. Louis N.L.
OF— Duke Snider, Brooklyn N.L.
OF— Carl Furillo, Brooklyn N.L.
C— Roy Campanella, Brooklyn N.L.
P— Robin Roberts, Philadelphia N.L.
P— Warren Spahn, Milwaukee N.L.
P— Bob Porterfield, Washington A.L.

1954
1B— Ted Kluszewski, Cincinnati N.L.
2B— Bobby Avila, Cleveland A.L.
SS— Alvin Dark, New York N.L.
3B— Al Rosen, Cleveland A.L.
OF— Willie Mays, New York N.L.
OF— Stan Musial, St. Louis N.L.
OF— Duke Snider, Brooklyn N.L.
C— Yogi Berra, New York A.L.
P— Bob Lemon, Cleveland A.L.
P— Johnny Antonelli, New York N.L.
P— Robin Roberts, Philadelphia N.L.

1955
1B— Ted Kluszewski, Cincinnati N.L.
2B— Nellie Fox, Chicago A.L.
SS— Ernie Banks, Chicago N.L.
3B— Ed Mathews, Milwaukee N.L.
OF— Duke Snider, Brooklyn N.L.
OF— Ted Williams, Boston A.L.
OF— Al Kaline, Detroit A.L.
C— Roy Campanella, Brooklyn N.L.
P— Robin Roberts, Philadelphia N.L.
P— Don Newcombe, Brooklyn N.L.
P— Whitey Ford, New York A.L.

1956
1B— Ted Kluszewski, Cincinnati N.L.
2B— Nellie Fox, Chicago A.L.
SS— Harvey Kuenn, Detroit A.L.
3B— Ken Boyer, St. Louis N.L.
OF— Mickey Mantle, New York A.L.
OF— Hank Aaron, Milwaukee N.L.
OF— Ted Williams, Boston A.L.
C— Yogi Berra, New York A.L.
P— Don Newcombe, Brooklyn N.L.
P— Whitey Ford, New York A.L.
P— Billy Pierce, Chicago A.L.

1957
1B— Stan Musial, St. Louis N.L.
2B— Red Schoendienst, N.Y.-Mil. N.L.
SS— Gil McDougald, New York A.L.
3B— Ed Mathews, Milwaukee N.L.
OF— Mickey Mantle, New York A.L.
OF— Ted Williams, Boston A.L.
OF— Willie Mays, New York N.L.
C— Yogi Berra, New York A.L.
P— Warren Spahn, Milwaukee N.L.
P— Billy Pierce, Chicago A.L.
P— Jim Bunning, Detroit A.L.

1958
1B— Stan Musial, St. Louis N.L.
2B— Nellie Fox, Chicago A.L.
SS— Ernie Banks, Chicago N.L.
3B— Frank Thomas, Pittsburgh N.L.
OF— Ted Williams, Boston A.L.
OF— Willie Mays, San Francisco N.L.
OF— Hank Aaron, Milwaukee N.L.
C— Del Crandall, Milwaukee N.L.
P— Bob Turley, New York A.L.
P— Warren Spahn, Milwaukee N.L.
P— Bob Friend, Pittsburgh N.L.

1959
1B— Orlando Cepeda, S.F. N.L.
2B— Nellie Fox, Chicago A.L.
SS— Ernie Banks, Chicago N.L.
3B— Ed Mathews, Milwaukee N.L.
OF— Minnie Minoso, Cleveland A.L.
OF— Willie Mays, San Francisco N.L.
OF— Hank Aaron, Milwaukee N.L.
C— Sherm Lollar, Chicago A.L.
P— Early Wynn, Chicago A.L.
P— Sam Jones, San Francisco N.L.
P— Johnny Antonelli, S.F. N.L.

1960
1B— Bill Skowron, New York A.L.
2B— Bill Mazeroski, Pittsburgh N.L.
SS— Ernie Banks, Chicago N.L.
3B— Ed Mathews, Milwaukee N.L.
OF— Minnie Minoso, Chicago A.L.
OF— Willie Mays, San Francisco N.L.
OF— Roger Maris, New York A.L.
C— Del Crandall, Milwaukee N.L.
P— Vernon Law, Pittsburgh N.L.
P— Warren Spahn, Milwaukee N.L.
P— Ernie Broglio, St. Louis N.L.

1961

AMERICAN LEAGUE
1B— Norm Cash, Detroit
2B— Bobby Richardson, New York
SS— Tony Kubek, New York
3B— Brooks Robinson, Baltimore
OF— Mickey Mantle, New York
OF— Roger Maris, New York
OF— Rocky Colavito, Detroit
C— Elston Howard, New York
P— Whitey Ford, New York
P— Frank Lary, Detroit

NATIONAL LEAGUE
1B— Orlando Cepeda, San Francisco
2B— Frank Bolling, Milwaukee
SS— Maury Wills, Los Angeles
3B— Ken Boyer, St. Louis
OF— Willie Mays, San Francisco
OF— Frank Robinson, Cincinnati
OF— Roberto Clemente, Pittsburgh
C— Smoky Burgess, Pittsburgh
P— Joey Jay, Cincinnati
P— Warren Spahn, Milwaukee

1962

AMERICAN LEAGUE
1B— Norm Siebern, Kansas City
2B— Bobby Richardson, New York
SS— Tom Tresh, New York
3B— Brooks Robinson, Baltimore
OF— Leon Wagner, Los Angeles
OF— Mickey Mantle, New York
OF— Al Kaline, Detroit
C— Earl Battey, Minnesota
P— Ralph Terry, New York
P— Dick Donovan, Cleveland

NATIONAL LEAGUE
1B— Orlando Cepeda, San Francisco
2B— Bill Mazeroski, Pittsburgh
SS— Maury Wills, Los Angeles
3B— Ken Boyer, St. Louis
OF— Tommy Davis, Los Angeles
OF— Willie Mays, San Francisco
OF— Frank Robinson, Cincinnati
C— Del Crandall, Milwaukee
P— Don Drysdale, Los Angeles
P— Bob Purkey, Cincinnati

1963

AMERICAN LEAGUE
1B— Joe Pepitone, New York
2B— Bobby Richardson, New York
SS— Luis Aparicio, Baltimore
3B— Frank Malzone, Boston
OF— Carl Yastrzemski, Boston
OF— Albie Pearson, Los Angeles
OF— Al Kaline, Detroit
C— Elston Howard, New York
P— Whitey Ford, New York
P— Gary Peters, Chicago

NATIONAL LEAGUE
1B— Bill White, St. Louis
2B— Jim Gilliam, Los Angeles
SS— Dick Groat, St. Louis
3B— Ken Boyer, St. Louis
OF— Tommy Davis, Los Angeles
OF— Willie Mays, San Francisco
OF— Hank Aaron, Milwaukee
C— John Edwards, Cincinnati
P— Sandy Koufax, Los Angeles
P— Juan Marichal, San Francisco

1964

AMERICAN LEAGUE
1B— Dick Stuart, Boston
2B— Bobby Richardson, New York
SS— Jim Fregosi, Los Angeles
3B— Brooks Robinson, Baltimore
OF— Harmon Killebrew, Minnesota
OF— Mickey Mantle, New York
OF— Tony Oliva, Minnesota
C— Elston Howard, New York
P— Dean Chance, Los Angeles
P— Gary Peters, Chicago

NATIONAL LEAGUE
1B— Bill White, St. Louis
2B— Ron Hunt, New York
SS— Dick Groat, St. Louis
3B— Ken Boyer, St. Louis
OF— Billy Williams, Chicago
OF— Willie Mays, San Francisco
OF— Roberto Clemente, Pittsburgh
C— Joe Torre, Milwaukee
P— Sandy Koufax, Los Angeles
P— Jim Bunning, Philadelphia

1965

AMERICAN LEAGUE
1B— Fred Whitfield, Cleveland
2B— Bobby Richardson, New York
SS— Zoilo Versalles, Minnesota
3B— Brooks Robinson, Baltimore
OF— Carl Yastrzemski, Boston
OF— Jimmie Hall, Minnesota
OF— Tony Oliva, Minnesota
C— Earl Battey, Minnesota
P— Jim Grant, Minnesota
P— Mel Stottlemyre, New York

NATIONAL LEAGUE
1B— Willie McCovey, San Francisco
2B— Pete Rose, Cincinnati
SS— Maury Wills, Los Angeles
3B— Deron Johnson, Cincinnati
OF— Willie Stargell, Pittsburgh
OF— Willie Mays, San Francisco
OF— Hank Aaron, Milwaukee
C— Joe Torre, Milwaukee
P— Sandy Koufax, Los Angeles
P— Juan Marichal, San Francisco

1966

AMERICAN LEAGUE
1B— Boog Powell, Baltimore
2B— Bobby Richardson, New York
SS— Luis Aparicio, Baltimore
3B— Brooks Robinson, Baltimore
OF— Frank Robinson, Baltimore
OF— Al Kaline, Detroit
OF— Tony Oliva, Minnesota
C— Paul Casanova, Washington
P— Jim Kaat, Minnesota
P— Earl Wilson, Detroit

NATIONAL LEAGUE
1B— Felipe Alou, Atlanta
2B— Pete Rose, Cincinnati
SS— Gene Alley, Pittsburgh
3B— Ron Santo, Chicago
OF— Willie Stargell, Pittsburgh
OF— Willie Mays, San Francisco
OF— Roberto Clemente, Pittsburgh
C— Joe Torre, Atlanta
P— Sandy Koufax, Los Angeles
P— Juan Marichal, San Francisco

1967

AMERICAN LEAGUE
1B— Harmon Killebrew, Minnesota
2B— Rod Carew, Minnesota
SS— Jim Fregosi, California
3B— Brooks Robinson, Baltimore
OF— Carl Yastrzemski, Boston
OF— Al Kaline, Detroit
OF— Frank Robinson, Baltimore
C— Bill Freehan, Detroit
P— Jim Lonborg, Boston
P— Earl Wilson, Detroit

NATIONAL LEAGUE
1B— Orlando Cepeda, St. Louis
2B— Bill Mazeroski, Pittsburgh
SS— Gene Alley, Pittsburgh
3B— Ron Santo, Chicago
OF— Hank Aaron, Atlanta
OF— Jim Wynn, Houston
OF— Roberto Clemente, Pittsburgh
C— Tim McCarver, St. Louis
P— Mike McCormick, San Francisco
P— Ferguson Jenkins, Chicago

1968

AMERICAN LEAGUE
1B— Boog Powell, Baltimore
2B— Rod Carew, Minnesota
SS— Luis Aparicio, Chicago
3B— Brooks Robinson, Baltimore
OF— Ken Harrelson, Boston
OF— Willie Horton, Detroit
OF— Frank Howard, Washington
C— Bill Freehan, Detroit
P— Dave McNally, Baltimore
P— Denny McLain, Detroit

NATIONAL LEAGUE
1B— Willie McCovey, San Francisco
2B— Tommy Helms, Cincinnati
SS— Don Kessinger, Chicago
3B— Ron Santo, Chicago
OF— Billy Williams, Chicago
OF— Curt Flood, St. Louis
OF— Pete Rose, Cincinnati
C— Johnny Bench, Cincinnati
P— Bob Gibson, St. Louis
P— Juan Marichal, San Francisco

1969

AMERICAN LEAGUE
1B— Boog Powell, Baltimore
2B— Rod Carew, Minnesota
SS— Rico Petrocelli, Boston
3B— Harmon Killebrew, Minnesota
OF— Frank Howard, Washington
OF— Paul Blair, Baltimore
OF— Reggie Jackson, Oakland
C— Bill Freehan, Detroit
RHP— Denny McLain, Detroit
LHP— Mike Cuellar, Baltimore

NATIONAL LEAGUE
1B— Willie McCovey, San Francisco
2B— Glenn Beckert, Chicago
SS— Don Kessinger, Chicago
3B— Ron Santo, Chicago
OF— Cleon Jones, New York
OF— Matty Alou, Pittsburgh
OF— Hank Aaron, Atlanta
C— Johnny Bench, Cincinnati
RHP— Tom Seaver, New York
LHP— Steve Carlton, St. Louis

1970

AMERICAN LEAGUE
1B— Boog Powell, Baltimore
2B— Dave Johnson, Baltimore
SS— Luis Aparicio, Chicago
3B— Harmon Killebrew, Minnesota
OF— Frank Howard, Washington
OF— Reggie Smith, Boston
OF— Tony Oliva, Minnesota
C— Ray Fosse, Cleveland
RHP— Jim Perry, Minnesota
LHP— Sam McDowell, Cleveland

NATIONAL LEAGUE
1B— Willie McCovey, San Francisco
2B— Glenn Beckert, Chicago
SS— Don Kessinger, Chicago
3B— Tony Perez, Cincinnati
OF— Billy Williams, Chicago
OF— Bobby Tolan, Cincinnati
OF— Hank Aaron, Atlanta
C— Johnny Bench, Cincinnati
RHP— Bob Gibson, St. Louis
LHP— Jim Merritt, Cincinnati

1971

AMERICAN LEAGUE
1B— Norm Cash, Detroit
2B— Cookie Rojas, Kansas City
SS— Leo Cardenas, Minnesota
3B— Brooks Robinson, Baltimore
OF— Merv Rettenmund, Baltimore
OF— Bobby Murcer, New York
OF— Tony Oliva, Minnesota
C— Bill Freehan, Detroit
RHP— Jim Palmer, Baltimore
LHP— Vida Blue, Oakland

NATIONAL LEAGUE
1B— Lee May, Cincinnati
2B— Glenn Beckett, Chicago
SS— Bud Harrelson, New York
3B— Joe Torre, St. Louis
OF— Willie Stargell, Pittsburgh
OF— Willie Davis, Los Angeles
OF— Hank Aaron, Atlanta
C— Manny Sanguillen, Pittsburgh
RHP—Ferguson Jenkins, Chicago
LHP— Steve Carlton, St. Louis

1972

AMERICAN LEAGUE
1B— Dick Allen, Chicago
2B— Rod Carew, Minnesota
SS— Luis Aparicio, Boston
3B— Brooks Robinson, Baltimore
OF— Joe Rudi, Oakland
OF— Bobby Murcer, New York
OF— Richie Scheinblum, Kansas City
C— Carlton Fisk, Boston
RHP— Gaylord Perry, Cleveland
LHP— Wilbur Wood, Chicago

NATIONAL LEAGUE
1B— Willie Stargell, Pittsburgh
2B— Joe Morgan, Cincinnati
SS— Chris Speier, San Francisco
3B— Ron Santo, Chicago
OF— Billy Williams, Chicago
OF— Cesar Cedeno, Houston
OF— Roberto Clemente, Pittsburgh
C— Johnny Bench, Cincinnati
RHP— Ferguson Jenkins, Chicago
LHP— Steve Carlton, Philadelphia

1973

AMERICAN LEAGUE
1B— John Mayberry, Kansas City
2B— Rod Carew, Minnesota
SS— Bert Campaneris, Oakland
3B— Sal Bando, Oakland
OF— Reggie Jackson, Oakland
OF— Amos Otis, Kansas City
OF— Bobby Murcer, New York
C— Thurman Munson, New York
RHP— Jim Palmer, Baltimore
LHP— Ken Holtzman, Oakland

NATIONAL LEAGUE
1B— Tony Perez, Cincinnati
2B— Dave Johnson, Atlanta
SS— Bill Russell, Los Angeles
3B— Darrell Evans, Atlanta
OF— Bobby Bonds, San Francisco
OF— Cesar Cedeno, Houston
OF— Pete Rose, Cincinnati
C— Johnny Bench, Cincinnati
RHP— Tom Seaver, New York
LHP— Ron Bryant, San Francisco

1974

AMERICAN LEAGUE
1B— Dick Allen, Chicago
2B— Rod Carew, Minnesota
SS— Bert Campaneris, Oakland
3B— Sal Bando, Oakland
OF— Joe Rudi, Oakland
OF— Paul Blair, Baltimore
OF— Jeff Burroughs, Texas
C— Thurman Munson, New York
DH— Tommy Davis, Baltimore
RHP— Jim Hunter, Oakland
LHP— Mike Cuellar, Baltimore

NATIONAL LEAGUE
1B— Steve Garvey, Los Angeles
2B— Joe Morgan, Cincinnati
SS— Dave Concepcion, Cincinnati
3B— Mike Schmidt, Philadelphia
OF— Lou Brock, St. Louis
OF— Jim Wynn, Los Angeles
OF— Richie Zisk, Pittsburgh
C— Johnny Bench, Cincinnati
RHP— Andy Messersmith, Los Angeles
LHP— Don Gullett, Cincinnati

1975

AMERICAN LEAGUE
1B— John Mayberry, Kansas City
2B— Rod Carew, Minnesota
SS— Toby Harrah, Texas
3B— Graig Nettles, New York
OF— Jim Rice, Boston
OF— Fred Lynn, Boston
OF— Reggie Jackson, Oakland
C— Thurman Munson, New York
DH— Willie Horton, Detroit
RHP— Jim Palmer, Baltimore
LHP— Jim Kaat, Chicago

NATIONAL LEAGUE
1B— Steve Garvey, Los Angeles
2B— Joe Morgan, Cincinnati
SS— Larry Bowa, Philadelphia
3B— Bill Madlock, Chicago
OF— Greg Luzinski, Philadelphia
OF— Al Oliver, Pittsburgh
OF— Dave Parker, Pittsburgh
C— Johnny Bench, Cincinnati
RHP— Tom Seaver, New York
LHP— Randy Jones, San Diego

1976

AMERICAN LEAGUE
1B— Chris Chambliss, New York
2B— Bobby Grich, Baltimore
3B— George Brett, Kansas City
SS— Mark Belanger, Baltimore
OF— Joe Rudi, Oakland
OF— Mickey Rivers, New York
OF— Reggie Jackson, Baltimore
C— Thurman Munson, New York
DH— Hal McRae, Kansas City
RHP— Jim Palmer, Baltimore
LHP— Frank Tanana, California

NATIONAL LEAGUE
1B— Willie Montanez, S.F.-Atl.
2B— Joe Morgan, Cincinnati
3B— Mike Schmidt, Philadelphia
SS— Dave Concepcion, Cincinnati
OF— George Foster, Cincinnati
OF— Cesar Cedeno, Houston
OF— Ken Griffey, Cincinnati
C— Bob Boone, Philadelphia
RHP— Don Sutton, Los Angeles
LHP— Randy Jones, San Diego

1977

AMERICAN LEAGUE
1B— Rod Carew, Minnesota
2B— Willie Randolph, New York
3B— Graig Nettles, New York
SS— Rick Burleson, Boston
OF— Jim Rice, Boston
OF— Larry Hisle, Minnesota
OF— Bobby Bonds, California
C— Carlton Fisk, Boston
DH— Hal McRae, Kansas City
RHP— Nolan Ryan, California
LHP— Frank Tanana, California

NATIONAL LEAGUE
1B— Steve Garvey, Los Angeles
2B— Joe Morgan, Cincinnati
3B— Mike Schmidt, Philadelphia
SS— Garry Templeton, St. Louis
OF— George Foster, Cincinnati
OF— Dave Parker, Pittsburgh
OF— Greg Luzinski, Philadelphia
C— Ted Simmons, St. Louis
RHP— Rick Reuschel, Chicago
LHP— Steve Carlton, Philadelphia

1978

AMERICAN LEAGUE
1B— Rod Carew, Minnesota
2B— Frank White, Kansas City
3B— Graig Nettles, New York
SS— Robin Yount, Milwaukee
OF— Jim Rice, Boston
OF— Larry Hisle, Milwaukee
OF— Fred Lynn, Boston
C— Jim Sundberg, Texas
DH— Rusty Staub, Detroit
RHP— Jim Palmer, Baltimore
LHP— Ron Guidry, New York

NATIONAL LEAGUE
1B— Steve Garvey, Los Angeles
2B— Dave Lopes, Los Angeles
3B— Pete Rose, Cincinnati
SS— Larry Bowa, Philadelphia
OF— George Foster, Cincinnati
OF— Dave Parker, Pittsburgh
OF— Jack Clark, San Francisco
C— Ted Simmons, St. Louis
RHP— Gaylord Perry, San Diego
LHP— Vida Blue, San Francisco

1979

AMERICAN LEAGUE
1B— Cecil Cooper, Milwaukee
2B— Bobby Grich, California
3B— George Brett, Kansas City
SS— Roy Smalley, Minnesota
OF— Jim Rice, Boston
OF— Fred Lynn, Boston
OF— Ken Singleton, Baltimore
C— Darrell Porter, Kansas City
DH— Don Baylor, California
RHP— Jim Kern, Texas
LHP— Mike Flanagan, Baltimore

NATIONAL LEAGUE
1B— Keith Hernandez, St. Louis
2B— Dave Lopes, Los Angeles
3B— Mike Schmidt, Philadelphia
SS— Garry Templeton, St. Louis
OF— Dave Kingman, Chicago
OF— Omar Moreno, Pittsburgh
OF— Dave Winfield, San Diego
C— Ted Simmons, St. Louis
RHP— Joe Niekro, Houston
LHP— Steve Carlton, Philadelphia

1980

AMERICAN LEAGUE
1B— Cecil Cooper, Milwaukee
2B— Willie Randolph, New York
3B— George Brett, Kansas City
SS— Robin Yount, Milwaukee
OF— Ben Oglivie, Milwaukee
OF— Al Bumbry, Baltimore
OF— Reggie Jackson, New York
DH— Reggie Jackson, New York
C— Rick Cerone, New York
RHP— Steve Stone, Baltimore
LHP— Tommy John, New York

NATIONAL LEAGUE
1B— Keith Hernandez, St. Louis
2B— Manny Trillo, Philadelphia
3B— Mike Schmidt, Philadelphia
SS— Garry Templeton, St. Louis
OF— Dusty Baker, Los Angeles
OF— Cesar Cedeno, Houston
OF— George Hendrick, St. Louis
C— Gary Carter, Montreal
RHP— Jim Bibby, Pittsburgh
LHP— Steve Carlton, Philadelphia

1981

AMERICAN LEAGUE
1B— Cecil Cooper, Milwaukee
2B— Bobby Grich, California
3B— Buddy Bell, Texas
SS— Rick Burleson, California
OF— Rickey Henderson, Oakland
OF— Dwayne Murphy, Oakland
OF— Tony Armas, Oakland
C— Jim Sundberg, Texas
DH— Richie Zisk, Seattle
RHP— Jack Morris, Detroit
LHP— Ron Guidry, New York

NATIONAL LEAGUE
1B— Pete Rose, Philadelphia
2B— Manny Trillo, Philadelphia
3B— Mike Schmidt, Philadelphia
SS— Dave Concepcion, Cincinnati
OF— George Foster, Cincinnati
OF— Andre Dawson, Montreal
OF— Pedro Guerrero, Los Angeles
C— Gary Carter, Montreal
RHP— Tom Seaver, Cincinnati
LHP— Fernando Valenzuela, Los Angeles

1982

AMERICAN LEAGUE
1B— Cecil Cooper, Milwaukee
2B— Damaso Garcia, Toronto
3B— Doug DeCinces, California
SS— Robin Yount, Milwaukee
OF— Dave Winfield, New York
OF— Gorman Thomas, Milwaukee
OF— Dwight Evans, Boston
C— Lance Parrish, Detroit
DH— Hal McRae, Kansas City
RHP— Dave Stieb, Toronto
LHP— Geoff Zahn, California

NATIONAL LEAGUE
1B— Al Oliver, Montreal
2B— Manny Trillo, Philadelphia
3B— Mike Schmidt, Philadelphia
SS— Ozzie Smith, St. Louis
OF— Lonnie Smith, St. Louis
OF— Dale Murphy, Atlanta
OF— Pedro Guerrero, Los Angeles
C— Gary Carter, Montreal
RHP— Steve Rogers, Montreal
LHP— Steve Carlton, Philadelphia

1983

AMERICAN LEAGUE
1B— Eddie Murray, Baltimore
2B— Lou Whitaker, Detroit
3B— Wade Boggs, Boston
SS— Cal Ripken, Baltimore
OF— Jim Rice, Boston
OF— Dave Winfield, New York
OF— Lloyd Moseby, Toronto
C— Carlton Fisk, Chicago
DH— Greg Luzinski, Chicago
RHP— LaMarr Hoyt, Chicago
LHP— Ron Guidry, New York

NATIONAL LEAGUE
1B— George Hendrick, St. Louis
2B— Glenn Hubbard, Atlanta
3B— Mike Schmidt, Philadelphia
SS— Dickie Thon, Houston
OF— Dale Murphy, Atlanta
OF— Andre Dawson, Montreal
OF— Tim Raines, Montreal
C— Tony Pena, Pittsburgh
RHP— John Denny, Philadelphia
LHP— Larry McWilliams, Pittsburgh

1984

AMERICAN LEAGUE
1B— Don Mattingly, New York
2B— Lou Whitaker, Detroit
3B— Buddy Bell, Texas
SS— Cal Ripken, Baltimore
OF— Tony Armas, Boston
OF— Dwight Evans, Boston
OF— Dave Winfield, New York
C— Lance Parrish, Detroit
DH— Dave Kingman, Oakland
RHP— Mike Boddicker, Baltimore
LHP— Willie Hernandez, Detroit

NATIONAL LEAGUE
1B— Keith Hernandez, New York
2B— Ryne Sandberg, Chicago
3B— Mike Schmidt, Philadelphia
SS— Ozzie Smith, St. Louis
OF— Dale Murphy, Atlanta
OF— Jose Cruz, Houston
OF— Tony Gwynn, San Diego
C— Gary Carter, Montreal
RHP— Rick Sutcliffe, Chicago
LHP— Mark Thurmond, San Diego

1985

AMERICAN LEAGUE
1B— Don Mattingly, New York
2B— Damaso Garcia, Toronto
3B— Wade Boggs, Boston
SS— Cal Ripken, Baltimore
OF— Rickey Henderson, New York
OF— Harold Baines, Chicago
OF— Phil Bradley, Seattle
C— Carlton Fisk, Chicago
DH— Don Baylor, New York
RHP— Bret Saberhagen, Kansas City
LHP— Ron Guidry, New York

NATIONAL LEAGUE
1B— Keith Hernandez, New York
2B— Tom Herr, St. Louis
3B— Tim Wallach, Montreal
SS— Ozzie Smith, St. Louis
OF— Dave Parker, Cincinnati
OF— Willie McGee, St. Louis
OF— Dale Murphy, Atlanta
C— Gary Carter, New York
RHP— Dwight Gooden, New York
LHP— John Tudor, St. Louis

1986

AMERICAN LEAGUE
1B— Don Mattingly, New York
2B— Tony Bernazard, Cleveland
3B— Wade Boggs, Boston
SS— Tony Fernandez, Toronto
OF— Jim Rice, Boston
OF— George Bell, Toronto
OF— Kirby Puckett, Minnesota
C— Rich Gedman, Boston
DH— Don Baylor, Boston
RHP— Roger Clemens, Boston
LHP— Teddy Higuera, Milwaukee

NATIONAL LEAGUE
1B— Keith Hernandez, New York
2B— Steve Sax, Los Angeles
3B— Mike Schmidt, Philadelphia
SS— Ozzie Smith, St. Louis
OF— Tim Raines, Montreal
OF— Tony Gwynn, San Diego
OF— Dave Parker, Cincinnati
C— Gary Carter, New York
RHP— Mike Scott, Houston
LHP— Fernando Valenzuela, Los Angeles

1987

AMERICAN LEAGUE
1B— Don Mattingly, New York
2B— Willie Randolph, New York
3B— Wade Boggs, Boston
SS— Alan Trammell, Detroit
OF— George Bell, Toronto
OF— Kirby Puckett, Minnesota
OF— Dwight Evans, Boston
C— Matt Nokes, Detroit
DH— Paul Molitor, Milwaukee
RHP— Roger Clemens, Boston
LHP— Jimmy Key, Toronto

NATIONAL LEAGUE
1B— Jack Clark, St. Louis
2B— Juan Samuel, Philadelphia
3B— Tim Wallach, Montreal
SS— Ozzie Smith, St. Louis
OF— Andre Dawson, Chicago
OF— Tony Gwynn, San Diego
OF— Eric Davis, Cincinnati
C— Benito Santiago, San Diego
RHP— Rick Sutcliffe, Chicago
LHP— Zane Smith, Atlanta

1988

AMERICAN LEAGUE
1B— George Brett, Kansas City
2B— Johnny Ray, California
3B— Wade Boggs, Boston
SS— Alan Trammell, Detroit
OF— Kirby Puckett, Minnesota
OF— Mike Greenwell, Boston
OF— Jose Canseco, Oakland
C— Ernie Whitt, Toronto
DH— Harold Baines, Chicago
RHP— Dave Stewart, Oakland
LHP— Frank Viola, Minnesota

NATIONAL LEAGUE
1B— Will Clark, San Francisco
2B— Ryne Sandberg, Chicago
3B— Bobby Bonilla, Pittsburgh
SS— Barry Larkin, Cincinnati
OF— Darryl Strawberry, New York
OF— Andy Van Slyke, Pittsburgh
OF— Kevin McReynolds, New York
C— Mike LaValliere, Pittsburgh
RHP— Orel Hershiser, Los Angeles
LHP— Danny Jackson, Cincinnati

1989

AMERICAN LEAGUE
1B— Fred McGriff, Toronto
2B— Julio Franco, Texas
3B— Carney Lansford, Oakland
SS— Cal Ripken, Baltimore
OF— Ruben Sierra, Texas
OF— Kirby Puckett, Minnesota
OF— Robin Yount, Milwaukee
C— Mickey Tettleton, Baltimore
DH— Harold Baines, Chi.-Tex.
RHP— Bret Saberhagen, Kansas City
LHP— Chuck Finley, California

NATIONAL LEAGUE
1B— Will Clark, San Francisco
2B— Ryne Sandberg, Chicago
3B— Howard Johnson, New York
SS— Shawon Dunston, Chicago
OF— Tony Gwynn, San Diego
OF— Kevin Mitchell, San Francisco
OF— Eric Davis, Cincinnati
C— Benito Santiago, San Diego
RHP— Mike Scott, Houston
LHP— Mark Davis, San Diego

1990

AMERICAN LEAGUE
1B— Cecil Fielder, Detroit
2B— Julio Franco, Texas
3B— Kelly Gruber, Toronto
SS— Alan Trammell, Detroit
OF— Rickey Henderson, Oakland
OF— Jose Canseco, Oakland
OF— Ellis Burks, Boston
C— Carlton Fisk, Chicago
DH— Dave Parker, Milwaukee
RHP— Bob Welch, Oakland
LHP— Chuck Finley, California

NATIONAL LEAGUE
1B— Eddie Murray, Los Angeles
2B— Ryne Sandberg, Chicago
3B— Matt Williams, San Francisco
SS— Barry Larkin, Cincinnati
OF— Barry Bonds, Pittsburgh
OF— Bobby Bonilla, Pittsburgh
OF— Darryl Strawberry, New York
C— Mike Scioscia, Los Angeles
RHP— Doug Drabek, Pittsburgh
LHP— Frank Viola, New York

1991

AMERICAN LEAGUE
1B— Cecil Fielder, Detroit
2B— Julio Franco, Texas
3B— Wade Boggs, Boston
SS— Cal Ripken, Baltimore
OF— Jose Canseco, Oakland
OF— Joe Carter, Toronto
OF— Ken Griffey Jr., Seattle
C— Mickey Tettleton, Detroit
RHP— Roger Clemens, Boston
LHP— Jim Abbott, California

NATIONAL LEAGUE
1B— Will Clark, San Francisco
2B— Ryne Sandberg, Chicago
3B— Terry Pendleton, Atlanta
SS— Barry Larkin, Cincinnati
OF— Barry Bonds, Pittsburgh
OF— Bobby Bonilla, Pittsburgh
OF— Ron Gant, Atlanta
C— Benito Santiago, San Diego
RHP— Jose Rijo, Cincinnati
LHP— Tom Glavine, Atlanta

1992

AMERICAN LEAGUE
1B— Mark McGwire, Oakland
2B— Roberto Alomar, Toronto
3B— Edgar Martinez, Seattle
SS— Travis Fryman, Detroit
OF— Joe Carter, Toronto
OF— Mike Devereaux, Baltimore
OF— Kirby Puckett, Minnesota
C— Mickey Tettleton, Detroit
RHP— Jack McDowell, Chicago
LHP— Dave Fleming, Seattle

NATIONAL LEAGUE
1B— Fred McGriff, San Diego
2B— Ryne Sandberg, Chicago
3B— Gary Sheffield, San Diego
SS— Barry Larkin, Cincinnati
OF— Barry Bonds, Pittsburgh
OF— Andy Van Slyke, Pittsburgh
OF— Larry Walker, Montreal
C— Darren Daulton, Philadelphia
RHP— Greg Maddux, Chicago
LHP— Tom Glavine, Atlanta

1993

AMERICAN LEAGUE
1B— Frank Thomas, Chicago
2B— Carlos Baerga, Cleveland
3B— Travis Fryman, Detroit
SS— Cal Ripken Jr., Baltimore
OF— Albert Belle, Cleveland
OF— Juan Gonzalez, Texas
OF— Ken Griffey Jr., Seattle
C— Mike Stanley, New York
DH— Paul Molitor, Toronto
RHP— Jack McDowell, Chicago
LHP— Jimmy Key, New York

NATIONAL LEAGUE
1B— Fred McGriff, S.D.-Atl.
2B— Robby Thompson, San Francisco
3B— Matt Williams, San Francisco
SS— Jay Bell, Pittsburgh
OF— Barry Bonds, San Francisco
OF— Lenny Dykstra, Philadelphia
OF— David Justice, Atlanta
C— Mike Piazza, Los Angeles
RHP— Greg Maddux, Atlanta
LHP— Steve Avery, Atlanta

1994

AMERICAN LEAGUE
1B— Frank Thomas, Chicago
2B— Chuck Knoblauch, Minnesota
3B— Wade Boggs, New York
SS— Cal Ripken Jr., Baltimore
OF— Albert Belle, Cleveland
OF— Ken Griffey Jr., Seattle
OF— Kirby Puckett, Minnesota
C— Ivan Rodriguez, Texas
DH— Paul Molitor, Toronto
RHP— David Cone, Kansas City
LHP— Jimmy Key, New York

NATIONAL LEAGUE
1B— Jeff Bagwell, Houston
2B— Craig Biggio, Houston
3B— Matt Williams, San Francisco
SS— Barry Larkin, Cincinnati
OF— Moises Alou, Montreal
OF— Barry Bonds, San Francisco
OF— Tony Gwynn, San Diego
C— Mike Piazza, Los Angeles
RHP— Greg Maddux, Atlanta
LHP— Danny Jackson, Philadelphia

1995

AMERICAN LEAGUE
1B— Mo Vaughn, Boston
2B— Carlos Baerga, Cleveland
3B— Jim Thome, Cleveland
SS— Cal Ripken Jr., Baltimore
OF— Albert Belle, Cleveland
OF— Tim Salmon, California
OF— Jim Edmonds, California
Manny Ramirez, Cleveland
C— Ivan Rodriguez, Texas
DH— Edgar Martinez, Seattle
RHP— Mike Mussina, Baltimore
LHP— Randy Johnson, Seattle

NATIONAL LEAGUE
1B— Eric Karros, Los Angeles
2B— Craig Biggio, Houston
3B— Vinny Castilla, Colorado
SS— Barry Larkin, Cincinnati
OF— Reggie Sanders, Cincinnati
OF— Dante Bichette, Colorado
OF— Sammy Sosa, Chicago
C— Mike Piazza, Los Angeles
RHP— Greg Maddux, Atlanta
LHP— Pete Schourek, Cincinnati

1996

AMERICAN LEAGUE
1B— Mark McGwire, Oakland
2B— Roberto Alomar, Baltimore
3B— Jim Thome, Cleveland
SS— Alex Rodriguez, Seattle
OF— Albert Belle, Cleveland
OF— Juan Gonzalez, Texas
OF— Ken Griffey Jr., Seattle
C— Ivan Rodriguez, Texas
DH— Paul Molitor, Minnesota
RHP— Pat Hentgen, Toronto
LHP— Andy Pettitte, New York

NATIONAL LEAGUE
1B— Jeff Bagwell, Houston
2B— Eric Young, Colorado
3B— Ken Caminiti, San Diego
SS— Barry Larkin, Cincinnati
OF— Barry Bonds, San Francisco
OF— Ellis Burks, Colorado
OF— Gary Sheffield, Florida
C— Mike Piazza, Los Angeles
RHP— John Smoltz, Atlanta
LHP— Al Leiter, Florida

1997

AMERICAN LEAGUE
1B— Tino Martinez, New York
2B— Chuck Knoblauch, Minnesota
3B— Matt Williams, Cleveland
SS— Nomar Garciaparra, Boston
OF— Ken Griffey Jr., Seattle
OF— David Justice, Cleveland
OF— Tim Salmon, Anaheim
C— Ivan Rodriguez, Texas
DH— Edgar Martinez, Seattle
RHP— Roger Clemens, Toronto
LHP— Randy Johnson, Seattle

NATIONAL LEAGUE
1B— Jeff Bagwell, Houston
2B— Craig Biggio, Houston
3B— Vinny Castillo, Colorado
SS— Jeff Blauser, Atlanta
OF— Barry Bonds, San Francisco
OF— Tony Gwynn, San Diego
OF— Larry Walker, Colorado
C— Mike Piazza, Los Angeles
RHP— Pedro Martinez, Montreal
LHP— Denny Neagle, Atlanta

1998

AMERICAN LEAGUE
1B— Rafael Palmeiro, Baltimore
2B— Roberto Alomar, Baltimore
3B— Scott Brosius, New York
SS— Alex Rodriguez, Seattle
OF— Ken Griffey Jr., Seattle
OF— Juan Gonzalez, Texas
OF— Albert Belle, Chicago
C— Ivan Rodriguez, Texas
DH— Jose Canseco, Toronto
RHP— Pedro Martinez, Boston
LHP— David Wells, New York

NATIONAL LEAGUE
1B— Mark McGwire, St. Louis
2B— Craig Biggio, Houston
3B— Vinny Castillo, Colorado
SS— Barry Larkin, Cincinnati
OF— Sammy Sosa, Chicago
OF— Moises Alou, Houston
OF— Greg Vaughn, San Diego
C— Mike Piazza, L.A.-Fla.-N.Y.
RHP— Kevin Brown, San Diego
LHP— Tom Glavine, Atlanta

1999

AMERICAN LEAGUE
1B— Rafael Palmeiro, Texas
2B— Roberto Alomar, Cleveland
3B— Dean Palmer, Detroit
SS— Nomar Garciaparra, Boston
OF— Shawn Green, Toronto
OF— Ken Griffey Jr., Seattle
OF— Manny Ramirez, Cleveland
C— Ivan Rodriguez, Texas
RHP— Pedro Martinez, Boston
LHP— Jamie Moyer, Seattle

NATIONAL LEAGUE
1B— Jeff Bagwell, Houston
2B— Edgardo Alfonzo, New York
3B— Chipper Jones, Atlanta
SS— Barry Larkin, Cincinnati
OF— Sammy Sosa, Chicago
OF— Vladimir Guerrero, Montreal
OF— Larry Walker, Colorado
C— Mike Piazza, New York
RHP— Jose Lima, Houston
LHP— Mike Hampton, Houston

2000

AMERICAN LEAGUE
1B— Carlos Delgado, Toronto
2B— Roberto Alomar, Cleveland
3B— Travis Fryman, Cleveland
SS— Alex Rodriguez, Seattle
OF— Darin Erstad, Anaheim
OF— Magglio Ordonez, Chicago
OF— Bernie Williams, New York
C— Jorge Posada, New York
RHP— Pedro Martinez, Boston
LHP— David Wells, Toronto

NATIONAL LEAGUE
1B— Todd Helton, Colorado
2B— Jeff Kent, San Francisco
3B— Chipper Jones, Atlanta
SS— Edgar Renteria, St. Louis
OF— Barry Bonds, San Francisco
OF— Vladimir Guerrero, Montreal
OF— Sammy Sosa, Chicago
C— Mike Piazza, New York
RHP— Greg Maddux, Atlanta
LHP— Tom Glavine, Atlanta

2001

AMERICAN LEAGUE
1B— Jim Thome, Cleveland
2B— Bret Boone, Seattle
3B— Troy Glaus, Anaheim
SS— Alex Rodriguez, Texas
OF— Juan Gonzalez, Cleveland
OF— Manny Ramirez, Boston
OF— Ichiro Suzuki, Seattle
C— Jorge Posada, New York
RHP— Roger Clemens, New York
LHP— Mark Mulder, Oakland
DH— Edgar Martinez, Seattle

NATIONAL LEAGUE
1B— Todd Helton, Colorado
2B— Craig Biggio, Houston
3B— Chipper Jones, Atlanta
SS— Rich Aurilia, San Francisco
OF— Barry Bonds, San Francisco
OF— Luis Gonzalez, Arizona
OF— Sammy Sosa, Chicago
C— Mike Piazza, New York
RHP— Curt Schilling, Arizona
LHP— Randy Johnson, Arizona

2002

AMERICAN LEAGUE
1B— Jason Giambi, New York
2B— Alfonso Soriano, New York
3B— Eric Chavez, Oakland
SS— Alex Rodriguez, Texas
OF— Garret Anderson, Anaheim
OF— Torii Hunter, Minnesota
OF— Bernie Williams, New York
C— Jorge Posada, New York
RHP— Derek Lowe, Boston
LHP— Barry Zito, Oakland
DH— Manny Ramirez, Boston

NATIONAL LEAGUE
1B— Todd Helton, Colorado
2B— Jeff Kent, San Francisco
3B— Scott Rolen, Phil.-St.L.
SS— Edgar Renteria, St. Louis
OF— Barry Bonds, San Francisco
OF— Vladimir Guerrero, Montreal
OF— Sammy Sosa, Chicago
C— Mike Piazza, New York
RHP— Curt Schilling, Arizona
LHP— Randy Johnson, Arizona

2003

AMERICAN LEAGUE
1B— Carlos Delgado, Toronto
2B— Bret Boone, Seattle
3B— Bill Mueller, Boston
SS— Alex Rodriguez, Texas
OF— Garret Anderson, Anaheim
OF— Vernon Wells, Toronto
OF— Magglio Ordonez, White Sox
C— Jorge Posada, New York
RHP— Roy Halladay, Toronto
LHP— Andy Pettitte, New York
DH— Frank Thomas, Chicago

NATIONAL LEAGUE
1B— Todd Helton, Colorado
2B— Marcus Giles, Atlanta
3B— Scott Rolen, St. Louis
SS— Edgar Renteria, St. Louis
OF— Barry Bonds, San Francisco
OF— Albert Pujols, St. Louis
OF— Gary Sheffield, Atlanta
C— Javy Lopez, Atlanta
RHP— Eric Gagne, Los Angeles
LHP— Randy Wolf, Philadelphia

2004

AMERICAN LEAGUE
1B— Paul Konerko, Chicago
2B— Alfonso Soriano, Texas
3B— Melvin Mora, Baltimore
SS— Miguel Tejada, Baltimore
OF— Ichiro Suzuki, Seattle
OF— Manny Ramirez, Boston
OF— Vladimir Guerrero, Anaheim
C— Ivan Rodriguez, Detroit
P— Johan Santana, Minnesota
DH— David Ortiz, Boston

NATIONAL LEAGUE
1B— Albert Pujols, St. Louis
2B— Mark Loretta, San Diego
3B— Scott Rolen, St. Louis
SS— Edgar Renteria, St. Louis
OF— Barry Bonds, San Francisco
OF— Jim Edmonds, St. Louis
OF— J.D. Drew, Atlanta
C— Johnny Estrada, Atlanta
P— Jason Schmidt, San Francisco

2005

AMERICAN LEAGUE
1B— Mark Teixeira, Texas
2B— Brian Roberts, Baltimore
3B— Alex Rodriguez, New York
SS— Michael Young, Texas
OF— Johnny Damon, Boston
OF— Vladimir Guerrero, Los Angeles
OF— Manny Ramirez, Boston
C— Jason Varitek, Boston
P— Bartolo Colon, Los Angeles
DH— David Ortiz, Boston

NATIONAL LEAGUE
1B— Albert Pujols, St. Louis
2B— Jeff Kent, Los Angeles
3B— Morgan Ensberg, Houston
SS— Felipe Lopez, Cincinnati
OF— Andruw Jones, Atlanta
OF— Miguel Cabrera, Florida
OF— Ken Griffey Jr., Cincinnati
C— Paul Lo Duca, Florida
P— Chris Carpenter, St. Louis

Year	Player, Team, League
1936	John Vander Meer, Durham, Piedmont
1937	Charlie Keller, Newark, International
1938	Fred Hutchinson, Seattle, Pacific Coast
1939	Lou Novikoff, Tulsa, Texas; Los Angeles, Pacific Coast
1940	Phil Rizzuto, Kansas City, American Association
1941	John Lindell, Newark, International
1942	Dick Barrett, Seattle, Pacific Coast
1943	Chet Covington, Scranton, Eastern
1944	Rip Collins, Albany, Eastern
1945	Gil Coan, Chattanooga, Southern
1946	Sibby Sisti, Indianapolis, American Association
1947	Hank Sauer, Syracuse, International
1948	Gene Woodling, San Francisco, Pacific Coast
1949	Orie Arntzen, Albany, Eastern
1950	Frank Saucier, San Antonio, Texas
1951	Gene Conley, Hartford, Eastern
1952	Bill Skowron, Kansas City, American Association
1953	Gene Conley, Toledo, American Association
1954	Herb Score, Indianapolis, American Association
1955	John Murff, Dallas, Texas
1956	Steve Bilko, Los Angeles, Pacific Coast
1957	Norm Siebern, Denver, American Association
1958	Jim O'Toole, Nashville, Southern
1959	Frank Howard, Victoria-Spokane
1960	Willie Davis, Spokane, Pacific Coast
1961	Howie Koplitz, Birmingham, Southern
1962	Bob Bailey, Columbus, International
1963	Don Buford, Indianapolis, International
1964	Mel Stottlemyre, Richmond, International
1965	Joe Foy, Toronto, International
1966	Mike Epstein, Rochester, International
1967	Johnny Bench, Buffalo, International
1968	Merv Rettenmund, Rochester, International
1969	Danny Walton, Oklahoma City, American Association
1970	Don Baylor, Rochester, International
1971	Bobby Grich, Rochester, International
1972	Tom Paciorek, Albuquerque, Pacific Coast
1973	Steve Ontiveros, Phoenix, Pacific Coast
1974	Jim Rice, Pawtucket, International
1975	Hector Cruz, Tulsa, American Association
1976	Pat Putnam, Asheville, Western Carolina
1977	Ken Landreaux, Salt Lake, Pacific Coast; El Paso, Texas
1978	Champ Summers, Indianapolis, American Association
1979	Mark Bomback, Vancouver, Pacific Coast
1980	Tim Raines, Denver, American Association
1981	Mike Marshall, Albuquerque, Pacific Coast
1982	Ron Kittle, Edmonton, Pacific Coast
1983	Kevin McReynolds, Las Vegas, Pacific Coast
1984	Alan Knicely, Wichita, American Association
1985	Jose Canseco, Huntsville, Southern; Tacoma., Pacific Coast
1986	Tim Pyznarski, Las Vegas, Pacific Coast
1987	Randy Milligan, Tidewater, International
1988	Sandy Alomar Jr., Las Vegas, Pacific Coast / Gary Sheffield, Denver, American Association (tie)
1989	Sandy Alomar Jr., Las Vegas, Pacific Coast
1990	Jose Offerman, Albuquerque, Pacific Coast
1991	Pedro Martinez, Albuquerque, Pacific Coast
1992	Tim Salmon, Edmonton, Pacific Coast
1993	Cliff Floyd, Harrisburg, Eastern
1994	Derek Jeter, Tampa, Florida State; Albany, Eastern; Columbus, International
1995	Karim Garcia, Albuquerque, Pacific Coast
1996	Vladimir Guerrero, West Palm Beach, Florida State; Harrisburg, Eastern
1997	Ben Grieve, Huntsville, Southern; Edmonton, Pacific Coast
1998	Gabe Kapler, Jacksonville, Southern
1999	Rick Ankiel, Arkansas, Texas; Memphis, Pacific Coast
2000	Jon Rauch, Win.-Salem, Carolina; Birmingham, Southern
2001	Josh Beckett, Brevard County, Fla. State; Portland, Eastern
2002	Jason Stokes, Kane County, Midwest
2003	Zack Greinke, Wilmington, Carolina; Wichita, Texas
2004	Dallas McPherson, Arkansas, Texas; Salt Lake, Pacific Coast
2005	Brandon Wood, Rancho Cucamonga, California; Salt Lake, Pacific Coast

MINOR LEAGUE MANAGER OF THE YEAR

Year	Manager, Team, League
1936	Al Sothoron, Milwaukee, American Association
1937	Jake Flowers, Salisbury, Eastern Shore
1938	Paul Richards, Atlanta, Southern
1939	Bill Meyer, Kansas City, American Association
1940	Larry Gilbert, Nashville, Southern
1941	Burt Shotton, Columbus, American Association
1942	Eddie Dyer, Columbus, American Association
1943	Nick Cullop, Columbus, American Association
1944	Al Thomas, Baltimore, International
1945	Lefty O'Doul, San Francisco, Pacific Coast
1946	Clay Hopper, Montreal, International
1947	Nick Cullop, Milwaukee, American Association
1948	Casey Stengel, Oakland, Pacific Coast
1949	Fred Haney, Hollywood, Pacific Coast
1950	Rollie Hemsley, Columbus, American Association
1951	Charlie Grimm, Milwaukee, American Association
1952	Luke Appling, Memphis, Southern
1953	Bobby Bragan, Hollywood, Pacific Coast
1954	Kerby Farrell, Indianapolis, American Association
1955	Bill Rigney, Minneapolis, American Association
1956	Kerby Farrell, Indianapolis, American Association
1957	Ben Geraghty, Wichita, American Association
1958	Cal Ermer, Birmingham, Southern
1959	Pete Reiser, Victoria, Texas
1960	Mel McGaha, Toronto, International
1961	Kerby Farrell, Buffalo, International
1962	Ben Geraghty, Jacksonville, International
1963	Rollie Hemsley, Indianapolis, International
1964	Harry Walker, Jacksonville, International
1965	Grady Hatton, Oklahoma City, Pacific Coast
1966	Bob Lemon, Seattle, Pacific Coast
1967	Bob Skinner, San Diego, Pacific Coast
1968	Jack Tighe, Toledo, International
1969	Clyde McCullough, Tidewater, International
1970	Tommy Lasorda, Spokane, Pacific Coast
1971	Del Rice, Salt Lake City, Pacific Coast
1972	Hank Bauer, Tidewater, International
1973	Joe Morgan, Charleston, International
1974	Joe Altobelli, Rochester, International
1975	Joe Frazier, Tidewater, International
1976	Vern Rapp, Denver, American Association
1977	Tommy Thompson, Arkansas, Texas
1978	Les Moss, Evansville, American Association
1979	Vern Benson, Syracuse, International
1980	Hal Lanier, Springfield, American Association
1981	Del Crandall, Albuquerque, Pacific Coast
1982	George Scherger, Indianapolis, American Association
1983	Bill Dancy, Reading, Eastern
1984	Bob Rodgers, Indianapolis, American Association
1985	Jim Fregosi, Louisville, American Association
1986	Joe Sparks, Indianapolis, American Association
1987	Terry Collins, Albuquerque, Pacific Coast
1988	Joe Sparks, Indianapolis, American Association
1989	Bob Bailor, Syracuse, International
1990	Sal Rende, Omaha, American Association
1991	Chris Chambliss, Greenville, Southern
1992	Grady Little, Greenville, Southern
1993	Jim Tracy, Harrisburg, Eastern
1994	Mike Jirschele, Wilmington, Carolina
1995	Pete Mackanin, Ottawa, International
1996	John Mizerock, Wilmington, Carolina
1997	Marv Foley, Rochester, International
1998	Doug Davis, Columbia, South Atlantic
1999	DeMarlo Hale, Trenton, Eastern

HISTORY *Award winners*

Year	Manager, Team, League
2000	Joel Skinner, Buffalo, International
2001	Tony Pena, New Orleans, Pacific Coast
2002	Eric Wedge, Buffalo, International

Year	Manager, Team, League
2003	Tony DeFrancesco, Sacramento, Pacific Coast
2004	Wally Backman, Lancaster, California
2005	Larry Parrish, Toledo, International

MINOR LEAGUE EXECUTIVE OF THE YEAR (HIGHER CLASSIFICATIONS, 1936-1992)

(Restricted to Class AAA starting in 1963)

Year	Executive, Team, League
1936	Earl Mann, Atlanta, Southern
1937	Robert LaMotte, Savannah, Sally
1938	Louis McKenna, St. Paul, American Association
1939	Bruce Dudley, Louisville, American Association
1940	Roy Hamey, Kansas City, American Association
1941	Emil Sick, Seattle, Pacific Coast
1942	Bill Veeck, Milwaukee, American Association
1943	Clarence Rowland, Los Angeles, Pacific Coast
1944	William Mulligan, Seattle, Pacific Coast
1945	Bruce Dudley, Louisville, American Association
1946	Earl Mann, Atlanta, Southern
1947	William Purnhage, Waterloo, I.I.I.
1948	Edward Glennon, Birmingham, Southern
1949	Ted Sullivan, Indianapolis, American Association
1950	Clearnce (Brick) Laws, Oakland, Pacific Coast
1951	Robert Howsam, Denver, West
1952	Jack Cooke, Toronto, International
1953	Richard Burnett, Dallas, Texas
1954	Edward Stumpf, Indianapolis, American Association
1955	Dewey Soriano, Seattle, Pacific Coast
1956	Robert Howsam, Denver American Association
1957	John Stiglmeier, Buffalo, International
1958	Edward Glennon, Birmingham, Southern
1959	Edward Leishman, Salt Lake City, Pacific Coast
1960	Ray Winder, Little Rock, Southern
1961	Elten Schiller, Omaha, American Association
1962	George Sisler Jr., Rochester, International
1963	Lewis Matlin, Hawaii, Pacific Coast

Year	Executive, Team, League
1964	Edward Leishman, San Diego, Pacific Coast
1965	Harold Cooper, Columbus, International
1966	John Quinn Jr., Hawaii, Pacific Coast
1967	Hillman Lyons, Richmond, International
1968	Gabe Paul Jr., Tulsa, Pacific Coast
1969	Bill Gardner, Louisville, International
1970	Dick King, Wichita, American Association
1971	Carl Steinfeldt Jr., Rochester, International
1972	Don Labbruzzo, Evansville, American Association
1973	Merle Miller, Tucson, Pacific Coast
1974	John Carbray, Sacramento, Pacific Coast
1975	Stan Naccarato, Tacoma, Pacific Coast
1976	Art Teece, Salt Lake City, Pacific Coast
1977	George Sisler Jr., Columbus, International
1978	Willie Sanchez, Albuquerque, Pacific Coast
1979	George Sisler Jr., Columbus, International
1980	Jim Burris, Denver, American Association
1981	Pat McKernan, Albuquerque, Pacific Coast
1982	A. Ray Smith, Louisville, American Association
1983	A. Ray Smith, Louisville, American Association
1984	Mike Tamburro, Pawtucket, International
1985	Patty Cox Hampton, Oklahoma City, American Association
1986	Bob Goughan, Rochester, International
1987	Stu Kehoe, Vancouver, Pacific Coast
1988	Bob Rich, Buffalo, American Association
1989	Larry Schmittou, Nashville, American Association
1990	Greg Corns, Phoenix, Pacific Coast
1991	Tom Maloney, Denver, American Association
1992	Lou Schwechheimer, Pawtucket, International

MINOR LEAGUE EXECUTIVE OF THE YEAR (LOWER CLASSIFICATIONS, 1950-1990)

(Separate awards for Class AA and Class A started in 1963; for Short Class A in 1988)

Year	Executive, Team, League
1950	H. Cooper, Hutchinson, Western Association
1951	O. W. (Bill) Hayes, Triple, B.S.
1952	Hillman Lyons, Danville, MOV
1953	Carl Roth, Peoria, I.I.I.
1954	James Meagham, Cedar Rapids, I.I.I.
1955	John Petrakis, Dubuque, MOV
1956	Marvin Milkes, Fresno, California
1957	Richard Wagner, Lincoln, West.
1958	Gerald Waring, Macon, Sally
1959	Clay Dennis, Des Moines, I.I.I.
1960	Hubert Kittle, Yakima, Northwest
1961	David Steele, Fresno, California
1962	John Quinn Jr., San Jose, California
1963	Hugh Finnerty, Tulsa, Texas
	Ben Jewell, M. Valley, Pioneer
1964	Glynn West, Birmingham, Southern
	James Bayens, Rock Hill, W. Carolina
1965	Dick Butler, Dallas-Ft. Worth, Texas
	Ken. Blackman, Quad Cities, Midwest
1966	Tom Fleming, Evansville, Southern
	Cappy Harada, Lodi, California
1967	Robert Quinn, Reading, Eastern
	Pat Williams, Spar'burg, W.C.
1968	Phil Howser, Charlotte, Southern
	Merle Miller, Burlington, Midwest
1969	Charlie Blaney, Albuquerque, Texas
	Bill Gorman, Visalia, California
1970	Carl Sawatski, Arkansas, Texas
	Bob Williams, Bakersfield, California
1971	Miles Wolff, Savannah, Dixie Association
	Ed Holtz, Appleton, Midwest
1972	John Begzos, S. Antonio, Texas
	Bob Piccinini, Modesto, California
1973	Dick Kravitz, Jacksonville, Southern
	Fritz Colschen, Clinton, Midwest
1974	Jim Paul, El Paso, Texas

Year	Executive, Team, League
	Bing Russell, Portland, Northwest
1975	Jim Paul, El Paso, Texas
	Cordy Jensen, Eugene, Northwest
1976	Woodrow Reid, Chattanooga, Southern
	Don Buchheister, Cedar Rapids, Midwest
1977	Jim Paul, El Paso, Texas
	Harry Pells, Quad Cities, Midwest
1978	Larry Schmittou, Nashville, Southern
	Dave Hersh, Appleton, Midwest
1979	Bill Rigney Jr., Midland, Texas
	Tom Romenesko, Greensboro, W.C.
1980	Frances Crockett, Charlotte, Southern
	Tom Romenesko, Greensboro, W.C.
1981	Allie Prescott, Memphis, Southern
	Dan Overstreet, Hagerstown, Caro.
1982	Art Clarkson, Birmingham, Southern
	Bob Carruesco, Stockton, California
1983	Edward Kenney, New Britain, Eastern
	Terry Reynolds, Vero Beach, Florida State
1984	Bruce Baldwin, Greenville, Southern
	Dave Tarrolly, Beloit, Midwest
1985	Ben Bernard, Albany-Colonie, Eastern
	Pete Vonachen, Peoria, Midwest
1986	Bill Davidson, Midland, Texas
	Rob Dlugozima, Durham, Carolina
1987	Joe Preseren, Tulsa, Texas
	Skip Weisman, Greensboro, South Atlantic
1988	Bill Valentine, Arkansas, Texas
	Dennis Bastien, Charleston (W.Va.), South Atlantic
	Bob Beban, Eugene, Northwest
1989	Chuck Domino, Reading, Eastern
	John Baxter, South Bend, Midwest
	Bill Pereira, Boise, Northwest
1990	Joe Preseren, Tulsa, Texas
	Dan Chapman, Stockton, California
	Dave Baggott, Salt Lake City, Pioneer

Year Executive, Team, League
1993—Todd Vander Woude, Harrisburg, Eastern (AA)
1994—Scott Lane, West Michigan, Midwest (A)
1995—Jack and Mary Cain, Portland, Northwest (A)
1996—Wayne Hodes, Trenton, Eastern (AA)

Year Executive, Team, League
1997—Andy Milovich, Erie, New York-Pennsylvania (A)
1998—Chuck Domino, Reading, Eastern (AA)
1999—Ben Mondor, Pawtucket, International (AAA)
2000—Art Savage, Sacramento, Pacific Coast (AAA)

Year Executive, Team, League
2001—Jay Miller, Round Rock, Texas (AA)
2002—Gary Arthur, Sacramento, Pacific Coast (AAA)
2003—Jay Miller, Round Rock, Texas (AA)
2004—Peter Bragan and Peter Bragan Jr., Jacksonville, Southern (AA)
2005—Robert Murphy, Dayton, Midwest (A)

RAWLINGS GOLD GLOVE TEAMS

1957
MAJORS
P— Bobby Shantz, New York A.L.
C— Sherm Lollar, Chicago A.L.
1B— Gil Hodges, Brooklyn N.L.
2B— Nellie Fox, Chicago A.L.
3B— Frank Malzone, Boston A.L.
SS— Roy McMillan, Cincinnati N.L.
OF— Minnie Minoso, Chicago A.L.
OF— Willie Mays, New York N.L.
OF— Al Kaline, Detroit A.L.

1958
AMERICAN LEAGUE
P— Bobby Shantz, New York
C— Sherm Lollar, Chicago
1B— Vic Power, K.C.-Cle.
2B— Frank Bolling, Detroit
3B— Frank Malzone, Boston
SS— Luis Aparicio, Chicago
OF— Norm Siebern, New York
OF— Jimmy Piersall, Boston
OF— Al Kaline, Detroit

NATIONAL LEAGUE
P— Harvey Haddix, Cincinnati
C— Del Crandall, Milwaukee
1B— Gil Hodges, Los Angeles
2B— Bill Mazeroski, Pittsburgh
3B— Ken Boyer, St. Louis
SS— Roy McMillan, Cincinnati
OF— Frank Robinson, Cincinnati
OF— Willie Mays, San Francisco
OF— Hank Aaron, Milwaukee

1959
AMERICAN LEAGUE
P— Bobby Shantz, New York
C— Sherm Lollar, Chicago
1B— Vic Power, Cleveland
2B— Nellie Fox, Chicago
3B— Frank Malzone, Boston
SS— Luis Aparicio, Chicago
OF— Minnie Minoso, Cleveland
OF— Al Kaline, Detroit
OF— Jackie Jensen, Boston

NATIONAL LEAGUE
P— Harvey Haddix, Pittsburgh
C— Del Crandall, Milwaukee
1B— Gil Hodges, Los Angeles
2B— Charley Neal, Los Angeles
3B— Ken Boyer, St. Louis
SS— Roy McMillan, Cincinnati
OF— Jackie Brandt, San Francisco
OF— Willie Mays, San Francisco
OF— Hank Aaron, Milwaukee

1960
AMERICAN LEAGUE
P— Bobby Shantz, New York
C— Earl Battey, Washington
1B— Vic Power, Cleveland

2B— Nellie Fox, Chicago
3B— Brooks Robinson, Baltimore
SS— Luis Aparicio, Chicago
OF— Minnie Minoso, Chicago
OF— Jim Landis, Chicago
OF— Roger Maris, New York

NATIONAL LEAGUE
P— Harvey Haddix, Pittsburgh
C— Del Crandall, Milwaukee
1B— Bill White, St. Louis
2B— Bill Mazeroski, Pittsburgh
3B— Ken Boyer, St. Louis
SS— Ernie Banks, Chicago
OF— Wally Moon, Los Angeles
OF— Willie Mays, San Francisco
OF— Hank Aaron, Milwaukee

1961
AMERICAN LEAGUE
P— Frank Lary, Detroit
C— Earl Battey, Minnesota
1B— Vic Power, Cleveland
2B— Bobby Richardson, New York
3B— Brooks Robinson, Baltimore
SS— Luis Aparicio, Chicago
OF— Al Kaline, Detroit
OF— Jimmy Piersall, Cleveland
OF— Jim Landis, Chicago

NATIONAL LEAGUE
P— Bobby Shantz, Pittsburgh
C— John Roseboro, Los Angeles
1B— Bill White, St. Louis
2B— Bill Mazeroski, Pittsburgh
3B— Ken Boyer, St. Louis
SS— Maury Wills, Los Angeles
OF— Willie Mays, San Francisco
OF— Roberto Clemente, Pittsburgh
OF— Vada Pinson, Cincinnati

1962
AMERICAN LEAGUE
P— Jim Kaat, Minnesota
C— Earl Battey, Minnesota
1B— Vic Power, Minnesota
2B— Bobby Richardson, New York
3B— Brooks Robinson, Baltimore
SS— Luis Aparicio, Chicago
OF— Jim Landis, Chicago
OF— Mickey Mantle, New York
OF— Al Kaline, Detroit

NATIONAL LEAGUE
P— Bobby Shantz, Hou.-St.L.
C— Del Crandall, Milwaukee
1B— Bill White, St. Louis
2B— Ken Hubbs, Chicago
3B— Jim Davenport, San Francisco
SS— Maury Wills, Los Angeles
OF— Willie Mays, San Francisco
OF— Roberto Clemente, Pittsburgh

OF— Bill Virdon, Pittsburgh

1963
AMERICAN LEAGUE
P— Jim Kaat, Minnesota
C— Elston Howard, New York
1B— Vic Power, Minnesota
2B— Bobby Richardson, New York
3B— Brooks Robinson, Baltimore
SS— Zoilo Versalles, Minnesota
OF— Al Kaline, Detroit
OF— Carl Yastrzemski, Boston
OF— Jim Landis, Chicago

NATIONAL LEAGUE
P— Bobby Shantz, St. Louis
C— Johnny Edwards, Cincinnati
1B— Bill White, St. Louis
2B— Bill Mazeroski, Pittsburgh
3B— Ken Boyer, St. Louis
SS— Bobby Wine, Philadelphia
OF— Willie Mays, San Francisco
OF— Roberto Clemente, Pittsburgh
OF— Curt Flood, St. Louis

1964
AMERICAN LEAGUE
P— Jim Kaat, Minnesota
C— Elston Howard, New York
1B— Vic Power, Min.-L.A.
2B— Bobby Richardson, New York
3B— Brooks Robinson, Baltimore
SS— Luis Aparicio, Baltimore
OF— Al Kaline, Detroit
OF— Jim Landis, Chicago
OF— Vic Davalillo, Cleveland

NATIONAL LEAGUE
P— Bobby Shantz, St.L.-Chi.-Phi.
C— Johnny Edwards, Cincinnati
1B— Bill White, St. Louis
2B— Bill Mazeroski, Pittsburgh
3B— Ron Santo, Chicago
SS— Ruben Amaro, Philadelphia
OF— Willie Mays, San Francisco
OF— Roberto Clemente, Pittsburgh
OF— Curt Flood, St. Louis

1965
AMERICAN LEAGUE
P— Jim Kaat, Minnesota
C— Bill Freehan, Detroit
1B— Joe Pepitone, New York
2B— Bobby Richardson, New York
3B— Brooks Robinson, Baltimore
SS— Zoilo Versalles, Minnesota
OF— Al Kaline, Detroit
OF— Tom Tresh, New York
OF— Carl Yastrzemski, Boston

NATIONAL LEAGUE
P— Bob Gibson, St. Louis
C— Joe Torre, Milwaukee

HISTORY *Award winners*

1B— Bill White, St. Louis
2B— Bill Mazeroski, Pittsburgh
3B— Ron Santo, Chicago
SS— Leo Cardenas, Cincinnati
OF— Willie Mays, San Francisco
OF— Roberto Clemente, Pittsburgh
OF— Curt Flood, St. Louis

1966
AMERICAN LEAGUE
P— Jim Kaat, Minnesota
C— Bill Freehan, Detroit
1B— Joe Pepitone, New York
2B— Bobby Knoop, California
3B— Brooks Robinson, Baltimore
SS— Luis Aparicio, Baltimore
OF— Al Kaline, Detroit
OF— Tommie Agee, Chicago
OF— Tony Oliva, Minnesota

NATIONAL LEAGUE
P— Bob Gibson, St. Louis
C— John Roseboro, Los Angeles
1B— Bill White, Philadelphia
2B— Bill Mazeroski, Pittsburgh
3B— Ron Santo, Chicago
SS— Gene Alley, Pittsburgh
OF— Willie Mays, San Francisco
OF— Curt Flood, St. Louis
OF— Roberto Clemente, Pittsburgh

1967
AMERICAN LEAGUE
P— Jim Kaat, Minnesota
C— Bill Freehan, Detroit
1B— George Scott, Boston
2B— Bobby Knoop, California
3B— Brooks Robinson, Baltimore
SS— Jim Fregosi, California
OF— Carl Yastrzemski, Boston
OF— Paul Blair, Baltimore
OF— Al Kaline, Detroit

NATIONAL LEAGUE
P— Bob Gibson, St. Louis
C— Randy Hundley, Chicago
1B— Wes Parker, Los Angeles
2B— Bill Mazeroski, Pittsburgh
3B— Ron Santo, Chicago
SS— Gene Alley, Pittsburgh
OF— Roberto Clemente, Pittsburgh
OF— Curt Flood, St. Louis
OF— Willie Mays, San Francisco

1968
AMERICAN LEAGUE
P— Jim Kaat, Minnesota
C— Bill Freehan, Detroit
1B— George Scott, Boston
2B— Bobby Knoop, California
3B— Brooks Robinson, Baltimore
SS— Luis Aparicio, Chicago
OF— Mickey Stanley, Detroit
OF— Carl Yastrzemski, Boston
OF— Reggie Smith, Boston

NATIONAL LEAGUE
P— Bob Gibson, St. Louis
C— Johnny Bench, Cincinnati
1B— Wes Parker, Los Angeles
2B— Glenn Beckert, Chicago
3B— Ron Santo, Chicago
SS— Dal Maxvill, St. Louis
OF— Willie Mays, San Francisco
OF— Roberto Clemente, Pittsburgh
OF— Curt Flood, St. Louis

1969
AMERICAN LEAGUE
P— Jim Kaat, Minnesota
C— Bill Freehan, Detroit
1B— Joe Pepitone, New York
2B— Dave Johnson, Baltimore
3B— Brooks Robinson, Baltimore
SS— Mark Belanger, Baltimore
OF— Paul Blair, Baltimore
OF— Mickey Stanley, Detroit
OF— Carl Yastrzemski, Boston

NATIONAL LEAGUE
P— Bob Gibson, St. Louis
C— Johnny Bench, Cincinnati
1B— Wes Parker, Los Angeles
2B— Felix Millan, Atlanta
3B— Clete Boyer, Atlanta
SS— Don Kessinger, Chicago
OF— Roberto Clemente, Pittsburgh
OF— Curt Flood, St. Louis
OF— Pete Rose, Cincinnati

1970
AMERICAN LEAGUE
P— Jim Kaat, Minnesota
C— Ray Fosse, Cleveland
1B— Jim Spencer, California
2B— Dave Johnson, Baltimore
3B— Brooks Robinson, Baltimore
SS— Luis Aparicio, Chicago
OF— Mickey Stanley, Detroit
OF— Paul Blair, Baltimore
OF— Ken Berry, Chicago

NATIONAL LEAGUE
P— Bob Gibson, St. Louis
C— Johnny Bench, Cincinnati
1B— Wes Parker, Los Angeles
2B— Tommy Helms, Cincinnati
3B— Doug Rader, Houston
SS— Don Kessinger, Chicago
OF— Roberto Clemente, Pittsburgh
OF— Tommie Agee, New York
OF— Pete Rose, Cincinnati

1971
AMERICAN LEAGUE
P— Jim Kaat, Minnesota
C— Ray Fosse, Cleveland
1B— George Scott, Boston
2B— Dave Johnson, Baltimore
3B— Brooks Robinson, Baltimore
SS— Mark Belanger, Baltimore
OF— Paul Blair, Baltimore
OF— Amos Otis, Kansas City
OF— Carl Yastrzemski, Boston

NATIONAL LEAGUE
P— Bob Gibson, St. Louis
C— Johnny Bench, Cincinnati
1B— Wes Parker, Los Angeles
2B— Tommy Helms, Cincinnati
3B— Doug Rader, Houston
SS— Bud Harrelson, New York
OF— Roberto Clemente, Pittsburgh
OF— Bobby Bonds, San Francisco
OF— Willie Davis, Los Angeles

1972
AMERICAN LEAGUE
P— Jim Kaat, Minnesota
C— Carlton Fisk, Boston
1B— George Scott, Milwaukee
2B— Doug Griffin, Boston
3B— Brooks Robinson, Baltimore

SS— Ed Brinkman, Detroit
OF— Paul Blair, Baltimore
OF— Bobby Murcer, New York
OF— Ken Berry, California

NATIONAL LEAGUE
P— Bob Gibson, St. Louis
C— Johnny Bench, Cincinnati
1B— Wes Parker, Los Angeles
2B— Felix Millan, Atlanta
3B— Doug Rader, Houston
SS— Larry Bowa, Philadelphia
OF— Roberto Clemente, Pittsburgh
OF— Cesar Cedeno, Houston
OF— Willie Davis, Los Angeles

1973
AMERICAN LEAGUE
P— Jim Kaat, Chicago
C— Thurman Munson, New York
1B— George Scott, Milwaukee
2B— Bobby Grich, Baltimore
3B— Brooks Robinson, Baltimore
SS— Mark Belanger, Baltimore
OF— Paul Blair, Baltimore
OF— Amos Otis, Kansas City
OF— Mickey Stanley, Detroit

NATIONAL LEAGUE
P— Bob Gibson, St. Louis
C— Johnny Bench, Cincinnati
1B— Mike Jorgensen, Montreal
2B— Joe Morgan, Cincinnati
3B— Doug Rader, Houston
SS— Roger Metzger, Houston
OF— Bobby Bonds, San Francisco
OF— Cesar Cedeno, Houston
OF— Willie Davis, Los Angeles

1974
AMERICAN LEAGUE
P— Jim Kaat, Chicago
C— Thurman Munson, New York
1B— George Scott, Milwaukee
2B— Bobby Grich, Baltimore
3B— Brooks Robinson, Baltimore
SS— Mark Belanger, Baltimore
OF— Paul Blair, Baltimore
OF— Amos Otis, Kansas City
OF— Joe Rudi, Oakland

NATIONAL LEAGUE
P— Andy Messersmith, Los Angeles
C— Johnny Bench, Cincinnati
1B— Steve Garvey, Los Angeles
2B— Joe Morgan, Cincinnati
3B— Doug Rader, Houston
SS— Dave Concepcion, Cincinnati
OF— Cesar Cedeno, Houston
OF— Cesar Geronimo, Cincinnati
OF— Bobby Bonds, San Francisco

1975
AMERICAN LEAGUE
P— Jim Kaat, Chicago
C— Thurman Munson, New York
1B— George Scott, Milwaukee
2B— Bobby Grich, Baltimore
3B— Brooks Robinson, Baltimore
SS— Mark Belanger, Baltimore
OF— Paul Blair, Baltimore
OF— Joe Rudi, Oakland
OF— Fred Lynn, Boston

NATIONAL LEAGUE
P— Andy Messersmith, Los Angeles
C— Johnny Bench, Cincinnati
1B— Steve Garvey, Los Angeles

2B— Joe Morgan, Cincinnati
3B— Ken Reitz, St. Louis
SS— Dave Concepcion, Cincinnati
OF— Cesar Cedeno, Houston
OF— Cesar Geronimo, Cincinnati
OF— Garry Maddox, S.F.-Phi.

1976
AMERICAN LEAGUE
P— Jim Palmer, Baltimore
C— Jim Sundberg, Texas
1B— George Scott, Milwaukee
2B— Bobby Grich, Baltimore
3B— Aurelio Rodriguez, Detroit
SS— Mark Belanger, Baltimore
OF— Joe Rudi, Oakland
OF— Dwight Evans, Boston
OF— Rick Manning, Cleveland

NATIONAL LEAGUE
P— Jim Kaat, Philadelphia
C— Johnny Bench, Cincinnati
1B— Steve Garvey, Los Angeles
2B— Joe Morgan, Cincinnati
3B— Mike Schmidt, Philadelphia
SS— Dave Concepcion, Cincinnati
OF— Cesar Cedeno, Houston
OF— Cesar Geronimo, Cincinnati
OF— Garry Maddox, Philadelphia

1977
AMERICAN LEAGUE
P— Jim Palmer, Baltimore
C— Jim Sundberg, Texas
1B— Jim Spencer, Chicago
2B— Frank White, Kansas City
3B— Graig Nettles, New York
SS— Mark Belanger, Baltimore
OF— Juan Beniquez, Texas
OF— Carl Yastrzemski, Boston
OF— Al Cowens, Kansas City

NATIONAL LEAGUE
P— Jim Kaat, Philadelphia
C— Johnny Bench, Cincinnati
1B— Steve Garvey, Los Angeles
2B— Joe Morgan, Cincinnati
3B— Mike Schmidt, Philadelphia
SS— Dave Concepcion, Cincinnati
OF— Cesar Geronimo, Cincinnati
OF— Garry Maddox, Philadelphia
OF— Dave Parker, Pittsburgh

1978
AMERICAN LEAGUE
P— Jim Palmer, Baltimore
C— Jim Sundberg, Texas
1B— Chris Chambliss, New York
2B— Frank White, Kansas City
3B— Graig Nettles, New York
SS— Mark Belanger, Baltimore
OF— Fred Lynn, Boston
OF— Dwight Evans, Boston
OF— Rick Miller, California

NATIONAL LEAGUE
P— Phil Niekro, Atlanta
C— Bob Boone, Philadelphia
1B— Keith Hernandez, St. Louis
2B— Dave Lopes, Los Angeles
3B— Mike Schmidt, Philadelphia
SS— Larry Bowa, Philadelphia
OF— Garry Maddox, Philadelphia
OF— Dave Parker, Pittsburgh
OF— Ellis Valentine, Montreal

1979
AMERICAN LEAGUE
P— Jim Palmer, Baltimore
C— Jim Sundberg, Texas

1B— Cecil Cooper, Milwaukee
2B— Frank White, Kansas City
3B— Buddy Bell, Texas
SS— Rick Burleson, Boston
OF— Dwight Evans, Boston
OF— Sixto Lezcano, Milwaukee
OF— Fred Lynn, Boston

NATIONAL LEAGUE
P— Phil Niekro, Atlanta
C— Bob Boone, Philadelphia
1B— Keith Hernandez, St. Louis
2B— Manny Trillo, Philadelphia
3B— Mike Schmidt, Philadelphia
SS— Dave Concepcion, Cincinnati
OF— Garry Maddox, Philadelphia
OF— Dave Parker, Pittsburgh
OF— Dave Winfield, San Diego

1980
AMERICAN LEAGUE
P— Mike Norris, Oakland
C— Jim Sundberg, Texas
1B— Cecil Cooper, Milwaukee
2B— Frank White, Kansas City
3B— Buddy Bell, Texas
SS— Alan Trammell, Detroit
OF— Fred Lynn, Boston
OF— Dwayne Murphy, Oakland
OF— Willie Wilson, Kansas City

NATIONAL LEAGUE
P— Phil Niekro, Atlanta
C— Gary Carter, Montreal
1B— Keith Hernandez, St. Louis
2B— Doug Flynn, New York
3B— Mike Schmidt, Philadelphia
SS— Ozzie Smith, San Diego
OF— Andre Dawson, Montreal
OF— Garry Maddox, Philadelphia
OF— Dave Winfield, San Diego

1981
AMERICAN LEAGUE
P— Mike Norris, Oakland
C— Jim Sundberg, Texas
1B— Mike Squires, Chicago
2B— Frank White, Kansas City
3B— Buddy Bell, Texas
SS— Alan Trammell, Detroit
OF— Dwayne Murphy, Oakland
OF— Dwight Evans, Boston
OF— Rickey Henderson, Oakland

NATIONAL LEAGUE
P— Steve Carlton, Philadelphia
C— Gary Carter, Montreal
1B— Keith Hernandez, St. Louis
2B— Manny Trillo, Philadelphia
3B— Mike Schmidt, Philadelphia
SS— Ozzie Smith, San Diego
OF— Andre Dawson, Montreal
OF— Garry Maddox, Philadelphia
OF— Dusty Baker, Los Angeles

1982
AMERICAN LEAGUE
P— Ron Guidry, New York
C— Bob Boone, California
1B— Eddie Murray, Baltimore
2B— Frank White, Kansas City
3B— Buddy Bell, Texas
SS— Robin Yount, Milwaukee
OF— Dwight Evans, Boston
OF— Dave Winfield, New York
OF— Dwayne Murphy, Oakland

NATIONAL LEAGUE
P— Phil Niekro, Atlanta
C— Gary Carter, Montreal

1B— Keith Hernandez, St. Louis
2B— Manny Trillo, Philadelphia
3B— Mike Schmidt, Philadelphia
SS— Ozzie Smith, St. Louis
OF— Andre Dawson, Montreal
OF— Dale Murphy, Atlanta
OF— Garry Maddox, Philadelphia

1983
AMERICAN LEAGUE
P— Ron Guidry, New York
C— Lance Parrish, Detroit
1B— Eddie Murray, Baltimore
2B— Lou Whitaker, Detroit
3B— Buddy Bell, Texas
SS— Alan Trammell, Detroit
OF— Dwight Evans, Boston
OF— Dave Winfield, New York
OF— Dwayne Murphy, Oakland

NATIONAL LEAGUE
P— Phil Niekro, Atlanta
C— Tony Pena, Pittsburgh
1B— Keith Hernandez, St.L.-N.Y.
2B— Ryne Sandberg, Chicago
3B— Mike Schmidt, Philadelphia
SS— Ozzie Smith, St. Louis
OF— Andre Dawson, Montreal
OF— Dale Murphy, Atlanta
OF— Willie McGee, St. Louis

1984
AMERICAN LEAGUE
P— Ron Guidry, New York
C— Lance Parrish, Detroit
1B— Eddie Murray, Baltimore
2B— Lou Whitaker, Detroit
3B— Buddy Bell, Texas
SS— Alan Trammell, Detroit
OF— Dwight Evans, Boston
OF— Dave Winfield, New York
OF— Dwayne Murphy, Oakland

NATIONAL LEAGUE
P— Joaquin Andujar, St. Louis
C— Tony Pena, Pittsburgh
1B— Keith Hernandez, New York
2B— Ryne Sandberg, Chicago
3B— Mike Schmidt, Philadelphia
SS— Ozzie Smith, St. Louis
OF— Dale Murphy, Atlanta
OF— Bob Dernier, Chicago
OF— Andre Dawson, Montreal

1985
AMERICAN LEAGUE
P— Ron Guidry, New York
C— Lance Parrish, Detroit
1B— Don Mattingly, New York
2B— Lou Whitaker, Detroit
3B— George Brett, Kansas City
SS— Alfredo Griffin, Oakland
OF— Gary Pettis, California
OF— Dave Winfield, New York
OF— Dwight Evans, Boston (tie)
        Dwayne Murphy, Oakland (tie)

NATIONAL LEAGUE
P— Rick Reuschel, Pittsburgh
C— Tony Pena, Pittsburgh
1B— Keith Hernandez, New York
2B— Ryne Sandberg, Chicago
3B— Tim Wallach, Montreal
SS— Ozzie Smith, St. Louis
OF— Willie McGee, St. Louis
OF— Dale Murphy, Atlanta
OF— Andre Dawson, Montreal

1986
AMERICAN LEAGUE
P— Ron Guidry, New York
C— Bob Boone, California
1B— Don Mattingly, New York
2B— Frank White, Kansas City
3B— Gary Gaetti, Minnesota
SS— Tony Fernandez, Toronto
OF— Gary Pettis, California
OF— Jesse Barfield, Toronto
OF— Kirby Puckett, Minnesota

NATIONAL LEAGUE
P— Fernando Valenzuela, Los Angeles
C— Jody Davis, Chicago
1B— Keith Hernandez, New York
2B— Ryne Sandberg, Chicago
3B— Mike Schmidt, Philadelphia
SS— Ozzie Smith, St. Louis
OF— Tony Gwynn, San Diego
OF— Dale Murphy, Atlanta
OF— Willie McGee, St. Louis

1987
AMERICAN LEAGUE
P— Mark Langston, Seattle
C— Bob Boone, California
1B— Don Mattingly, New York
2B— Frank White, Kansas City
3B— Gary Gaetti, Minnesota
SS— Tony Fernandez, Toronto
OF— Jesse Barfield, Toronto
OF— Kirby Puckett, Minnesota
OF— Dave Winfield, New York

NATIONAL LEAGUE
P— Rick Reuschel, Pit.-S.F.
C— Mike LaValliere, Pittsburgh
1B— Keith Hernandez, New York
2B— Ryne Sandberg, Chicago
3B— Terry Pendleton, St. Louis
SS— Ozzie Smith, St. Louis
OF— Eric Davis, Cincinnati
OF— Tony Gwynn, San Diego
OF— Andre Dawson, Chicago

1988
AMERICAN LEAGUE
P— Mark Langston, Seattle
C— Bob Boone, California
1B— Don Mattingly, New York
2B— Harold Reynolds, Seattle
3B— Gary Gaetti, Minnesota
SS— Tony Fernandez, Toronto
OF— Kirby Puckett, Minnesota
OF— Devon White, California
OF— Gary Pettis, Detroit

NATIONAL LEAGUE
P— Orel Hershiser, Los Angeles
C— Benito Santiago, San Diego
1B— Keith Hernandez, New York
2B— Ryne Sandberg, Chicago
3B— Tim Wallach, Montreal
SS— Ozzie Smith, St. Louis
OF— Andy Van Slyke, Pittsburgh
OF— Eric Davis, Cincinnati
OF— Andre Dawson, Chicago

1989
AMERICAN LEAGUE
P— Bret Saberhagen, Kansas City
C— Bob Boone, Kansas City
1B— Don Mattingly, New York
2B— Harold Reynolds, Seattle
3B— Gary Gaetti, Minnesota
SS— Tony Fernandez, Toronto
OF— Kirby Puckett, Minnesota
OF— Devon White, California
OF— Gary Pettis, Detroit

NATIONAL LEAGUE
P— Ron Darling, New York
C— Benito Santiago, San Diego
1B— Andres Galarraga, Montreal
2B— Ryne Sandberg, Chicago
3B— Terry Pendleton, St. Louis
SS— Ozzie Smith, St. Louis
OF— Andy Van Slyke, Pittsburgh
OF— Tony Gwynn, San Diego
OF— Eric Davis, Cincinnati

1990
AMERICAN LEAGUE
P— Mike Boddicker, Boston
C— Sandy Alomar Jr., Cleveland
1B— Mark McGwire, Oakland
2B— Harold Reynolds, Seattle
3B— Kelly Gruber, Toronto
SS— Ozzie Guillen, Chicago
OF— Ken Griffey Jr., Seattle
OF— Ellis Burks, Boston
OF— Gary Pettis, Texas

NATIONAL LEAGUE
P— Greg Maddux, Chicago
C— Benito Santiago, San Diego
1B— Andres Galarraga, Montreal
2B— Ryne Sandberg, Chicago
3B— Tim Wallach, Montreal
SS— Ozzie Smith, St. Louis
OF— Barry Bonds, Pittsburgh
OF— Andy Van Slyke, Pittsburgh
OF— Tony Gwynn, San Diego

1991
AMERICAN LEAGUE
P— Mark Langston, California
C— Tony Pena, Boston
1B— Don Mattingly, New York
2B— Roberto Alomar, Toronto
3B— Robin Ventura, Chicago
SS— Cal Ripken, Baltimore
OF— Ken Griffey Jr., Seattle
OF— Kirby Puckett, Minnesota
OF— Devon White, Toronto

NATIONAL LEAGUE
P— Greg Maddux, Chicago
C— Tom Pagnozzi, St. Louis
1B— Will Clark, San Francisco
2B— Ryne Sandberg, Chicago
3B— Matt Williams, San Francisco
SS— Ozzie Smith, St. Louis
OF— Barry Bonds, Pittsburgh
OF— Andy Van Slyke, Pittsburgh
OF— Tony Gwynn, San Diego

1992
AMERICAN LEAGUE
P— Mark Langston, California
C— Ivan Rodriguez, Texas
1B— Don Mattingly, New York
2B— Roberto Alomar, Toronto
3B— Robin Ventura, Chicago
SS— Cal Ripken, Baltimore
OF— Ken Griffey Jr., Seattle
OF— Kirby Puckett, Minnesota
OF— Devon White, Toronto

NATIONAL LEAGUE
P— Greg Maddux, Chicago
C— Tom Pagnozzi, St. Louis
1B— Mark Grace, Chicago
2B— Jose Lind, Pittsburgh
3B— Terry Pendleton, Atlanta
SS— Ozzie Smith, St. Louis
OF— Barry Bonds, Pittsburgh
OF— Andy Van Slyke, Pittsburgh
OF— Larry Walker, Montreal

1993
AMERICAN LEAGUE
P— Mark Langston, California
C— Ivan Rodriguez, Texas
1B— Don Mattingly, New York
2B— Roberto Alomar, Toronto
3B— Robin Ventura, Chicago
SS— Omar Vizquel, Seattle
OF— Ken Griffey Jr., Seattle
OF— Kenny Lofton, Cleveland
OF— Devon White, Toronto

NATIONAL LEAGUE
P— Greg Maddux, Atlanta
C— Kirt Manwaring, San Francisco
1B— Mark Grace, Chicago
2B— Robby Thompson, San Fran.
3B— Matt Williams, San Francisco
SS— Jay Bell, Pittsburgh
OF— Barry Bonds, San Francisco
OF— Marquis Grissom, Montreal
OF— Larry Walker, Montreal

1994
AMERICAN LEAGUE
P— Mark Langston, California
C— Ivan Rodriguez, Texas
1B— Don Mattingly, New York
2B— Roberto Alomar, Toronto
3B— Wade Boggs, New York
SS— Omar Vizquel, Cleveland
OF— Ken Griffey Jr., Seattle
OF— Kenny Lofton, Cleveland
OF— Devon White, Toronto

NATIONAL LEAGUE
P— Greg Maddux, Atlanta
C— Tom Pagnozzi, St. Louis
1B— Jeff Bagwell, Houston
2B— Craig Biggio, Houston
3B— Matt Williams, San Francisco
SS— Barry Larkin, Cincinnati
OF— Barry Bonds, San Francisco
OF— Marquis Grissom, Montreal
OF— Darren Lewis, San Francisco

1995
AMERICAN LEAGUE
P— Mark Langston, California
C— Ivan Rodriguez, Texas
1B— J.T. Snow, California
2B— Roberto Alomar, Toronto
3B— Wade Boggs, New York
SS— Omar Vizquel, Cleveland
OF— Ken Griffey Jr., Seattle
OF— Kenny Lofton, Cleveland
OF— Devon White, Toronto

NATIONAL LEAGUE
P— Greg Maddux, Atlanta
C— Charles Johnson, Florida
1B— Mark Grace, Chicago
2B— Craig Biggio, Houston
3B— Ken Caminiti, San Diego
SS— Barry Larkin, Cincinnati
OF— Raul Mondesi, Los Angeles
OF— Marquis Grissom, Atlanta
OF— Steve Finley, San Diego

1996
AMERICAN LEAGUE
P— Mike Mussina, Baltimore
C— Ivan Rodriguez, Texas
1B— J.T. Snow, California
2B— Roberto Alomar, Baltimore
3B— Robin Ventura, Chicago
SS— Omar Vizquel, Cleveland
OF— Jay Buhner, Seattle
OF— Ken Griffey Jr., Seattle
OF— Kenny Lofton, Cleveland

NATIONAL LEAGUE
P— Greg Maddux, Atlanta
C— Charles Johnson, Florida
1B— Mark Grace, Chicago
2B— Craig Biggio, Houston
3B— Ken Caminiti, San Diego
SS— Barry Larkin, Cincinnati
OF— Barry Bonds, San Francisco
OF— Marquis Grissom, Atlanta
OF— Steve Finley, San Diego

1997
AMERICAN LEAGUE
P— Mike Mussina, Baltimore
C— Ivan Rodriguez, Texas
1B— Rafael Palmeiro, Baltimore
2B— Chuck Knoblauch, Minnesota
3B— Matt Williams, Cleveland
SS— Omar Vizquel, Cleveland
OF— Jim Edmonds, Anaheim
OF— Ken Griffey Jr., Seattle
OF— Bernie Williams, New York

NATIONAL LEAGUE
P— Greg Maddux, Atlanta
C— Charles Johnson, Florida
1B— J.T. Snow, San Francisco
2B— Craig Biggio, Houston
3B— Ken Caminiti, San Diego
SS— Rey Ordonez, New York
OF— Barry Bonds, San Francisco
OF— Raul Mondesi, Los Angeles
OF— Larry Walker, Colorado

1998
AMERICAN LEAGUE
P— Mike Mussina, Baltimore
C— Ivan Rodriguez, Texas
1B— Rafael Palmeiro, Baltimore
2B— Roberto Alomar, Baltimore
3B— Robin Ventura, White Sox
SS— Omar Vizquel, Cleveland
OF— Jim Edmonds, Anaheim
OF— Ken Griffey Jr., Seattle
OF— Bernie Williams, New York

NATIONAL LEAGUE
P— Greg Maddux, Atlanta
C— Charles Johnson, Fla.-L.A.
1B— J.T. Snow, San Francisco
2B— Bret Boone, Cincinnati
3B— Scott Rolen, Philadelphia
SS— Rey Ordonez, New York
OF— Barry Bonds, San Francisco
OF— Andruw Jones, Atlanta
OF— Larry Walker, Colorado

1999
AMERICAN LEAGUE
P— Mike Mussina, Baltimore
C— Ivan Rodriguez, Texas
1B— Rafael Palmeiro, Texas
2B— Roberto Alomar, Cleveland
3B— Scott Brosius, New York
SS— Omar Vizquel, Cleveland
OF— Shawn Green, Toronto
OF— Ken Griffey Jr., Seattle
OF— Bernie Williams, New York

NATIONAL LEAGUE
P— Greg Maddux, Atlanta
C— Mike Lieberthal, Philadelphia
1B— J.T. Snow, San Francisco
2B— Pokey Reese, Cincinnati

3B— Robin Ventura, New York
SS— Rey Ordonez, New York
OF— Steve Finley, Arizona
OF— Andruw Jones, Atlanta
OF— Larry Walker, Colorado

2000
AMERICAN LEAGUE
P— Kenny Rogers, Texas
C— Ivan Rodriguez, Texas
1B— John Olerud, Seattle
2B— Roberto Alomar, Cleveland
3B— Travis Fryman, Cleveland
SS— Omar Vizquel, Cleveland
OF— Jermaine Dye, Kansas City
OF— Darin Erstad, Anaheim
OF— Bernie Williams, New York

NATIONAL LEAGUE
P— Greg Maddux, Atlanta
C— Mike Matheny, St. Louis
1B— J.T. Snow, San Francisco
2B— Pokey Reese, Cincinnati
3B— Scott Rolen, Philadelphia
SS— Neifi Perez, Colorado
OF— Jim Edmonds, St. Louis
OF— Steve Finley, Arizona
OF— Andruw Jones, Atlanta

2001
AMERICAN LEAGUE
P— Mike Mussina, New York
C— Ivan Rodriguez, Texas
1B— Doug Mientkiewicz, Minnesota
2B— Roberto Alomar, Cleveland
3B— Eric Chavez, Oakland
SS— Omar Vizquel, Cleveland
OF— Mike Cameron, Seattle
OF— Torii Hunter, Minnesota
OF— Ichiro Suzuki, Seattle

NATIONAL LEAGUE
P— Greg Maddux, Atlanta
C— Brad Ausmus, Houston
1B— Todd Helton, Colorado
2B— Fernando Vina, St. Louis
3B— Scott Rolen, Philadelphia
SS— Orlando Cabrera, Montreal
OF— Jim Edmonds, St. Louis
OF— Andruw Jones, Atlanta
OF— Larry Walker, Colorado

2002
AMERICAN LEAGUE
P— Kenny Rogers, Texas
C— Bengie Molina, Anaheim
1B— John Olerud, Seattle
2B— Bret Boone, Seattle
3B— Eric Chavez, Oakland
SS— Alex Rodriguez, Texas
OF— Darin Erstad, Anaheim
OF— Torii Hunter, Minnesota
OF— Ichiro Suzuki, Seattle

NATIONAL LEAGUE
P— Greg Maddux, Atlanta
C— Brad Ausmus, Houston
1B— Todd Helton, Colorado
2B— Fernando Vina, St. Louis
3B— Scott Rolen, Phil.-St.L.
SS— Edgar Renteria, St. Louis
OF— Jim Edmonds, St. Louis
OF— Andruw Jones, Atlanta
OF— Larry Walker, Colorado

2003
AMERICAN LEAGUE
P— Mike Mussina, New York
C— Bengie Molina, Anaheim
1B— John Olerud, Seattle
2B— Bret Boone, Seattle
3B— Eric Chavez, Oakland
SS— Alex Rodriguez, Texas
OF— Mike Cameron, Seattle
OF— Torii Hunter, Minnesota
OF— Ichiro Suzuki, Seattle

NATIONAL LEAGUE
P— Mike Hampton, Atlanta
C— Mike Matheny, St. Louis
1B— Derrek Lee, Florida
2B— Luis Castillo, Florida
3B— Scott Rolen, St. Louis
SS— Edgar Renteria, St. Louis
OF— Jim Edmonds, St. Louis
OF— Andruw Jones, Atlanta
OF— Jose Cruz Jr., San Francisco

2004
AMERICAN LEAGUE
P— Kenny Rogers, Texas
C— Ivan Rodriguez, Detroit
1B—Darin Erstad, Anaheim
2B— Bret Boone, Seattle
3B— Eric Chavez, Oakland
SS—Derek Jeter, New York
OF— Vernon Wells, Toronto
OF—Ichiro Suzuki, Seattle
OF— Torii Hunter, Minnesota

NATIONAL LEAGUE
P— Greg Maddux, Chicago
C—Mike Matheny, St. Louis
1B— Todd Helton, Colorado
2B—Luis Castillo, Florida
3B— Scott Rolen, St. Louis
SS—Cesar Izturis, Los Angeles
OF—Jim Edmonds, St. Louis
OF—Andruw Jones, Atlanta
OF—Steve Finley, Ariz.-Los Angeles

2005
AMERICAN LEAGUE
P— Kenny Rogers, Texas
C— Jason Varitek, Boston
1B—Mark Teixeira, Texas
2B—Orlando Hudson, Toronto
3B—Eric Chavez, Oakland
SS—Derek Jeter, New York
OF— Vernon Wells, Toronto
OF—Ichiro Suzuki, Seattle
OF— Torii Hunter, Minnesota

NATIONAL LEAGUE
P— Greg Maddux, Chicago
C—Mike Matheny, San Francisco
1B—Derrek Lee, Chicago
2B—Luis Castillo, Florida
3B—Mike Lowell, Florida
SS—Omar Vizquel, San Francisco
OF—Jim Edmonds, St. Louis
OF—Andruw Jones, Atlanta
OF—Bobby Abreu, Philadelphia

HILLERICH & BRADSBY SILVER SLUGGER TEAMS

1980
AMERICAN LEAGUE
1B— Cecil Cooper, Milwaukee
2B— Willie Randolph, New York
3B— George Brett, Kansas City

SS— Robin Yount, Milwaukee
OF— Ben Oglivie, Milwaukee
OF— Al Oliver, Texas
OF— Willie Wilson, Kansas City
C— Lance Parrish, Detroit

DH— Reggie Jackson, New York

NATIONAL LEAGUE
1B— Keith Hernandez, St. Louis
2B— Manny Trillo, Philadelphia

3B— Mike Schmidt, Philadelphia
SS— Garry Templeton, St. Louis
OF— Dusty Baker, Los Angeles
OF— Andre Dawson, Montreal
OF— George Hendrick, St. Louis
C— Ted Simmons, St. Louis
P— Bob Forsch, St. Louis

1981
AMERICAN LEAGUE
1B— Cecil Cooper, Milwaukee
2B— Bobby Grich, California
3B— Carney Lansford, Boston
SS— Rick Burleson, California
OF— Rickey Henderson, Oakland
OF— Dwight Evans, Boston
OF— Dave Winfield, New York
C— Carlton Fisk, Chicago
DH— Al Oliver, Texas

NATIONAL LEAGUE
1B— Pete Rose, Philadelphia
2B— Manny Trillo, Philadelphia
3B— Mike Schmidt, Philadelphia
SS— Dave Concepcion, Cincinnati
OF— Andre Dawson, Montreal
OF— George Foster, Cincinnati
OF— Dusty Baker, Los Angeles
C— Gary Carter, Montreal
P— Fernando Valenzuela, Los Angeles

1982
AMERICAN LEAGUE
1B— Cecil Cooper, Milwaukee
2B— Damaso Garcia, Toronto
3B— Doug DeCinces, California
SS— Robin Yount, Milwaukee
OF— Dave Winfield, New York
OF— Willie Wilson, Kansas City
OF— Reggie Jackson, California
C— Lance Parrish, Detroit
DH— Hal McRae, Kansas City

NATIONAL LEAGUE
1B— Al Oliver, Montreal
2B— Joe Morgan, San Francisco
3B— Mike Schmidt, Philadelphia
SS— Dave Concepcion, Cincinnati
OF— Dale Murphy, Atlanta
OF— Pedro Guerrero, Los Angeles
OF— Leon Durham, Chicago
C— Gary Carter, Montreal
P— Don Robinson, Pittsburgh

1983
AMERICAN LEAGUE
1B— Eddie Murray, Baltimore
2B— Lou Whitaker, Detroit
3B— Wade Boggs, Boston
SS— Cal Ripken Jr., Baltimore
OF— Jim Rice, Boston
OF— Dave Winfield, New York
OF— Lloyd Moseby, Toronto
C— Lance Parrish, Detroit
DH— Don Baylor, New York

NATIONAL LEAGUE
1B— George Hendrick, St. Louis
2B— Johnny Ray, Pittsburgh
3B— Mike Schmidt, Philadelphia
SS— Dickie Thon, Houston
OF— Andre Dawson, Montreal
OF— Dale Murphy, Atlanta
OF— Jose Cruz, Houston
C— Terry Kennedy, San Diego
P— Fernando Valenzuela, Los Angeles

1984
AMERICAN LEAGUE
1B— Eddie Murray, Baltimore
2B— Lou Whitaker, Detroit
3B— Buddy Bell, Texas
SS— Cal Ripken Jr., Baltimore
OF— Tony Armas, Boston
OF— Jim Rice, Boston
OF— Dave Winfield, New York
C— Lance Parrish, Detroit
DH— Andre Thornton, Cleveland

NATIONAL LEAGUE
1B— Keith Hernandez, New York
2B— Ryne Sandberg, Chicago
3B— Mike Schmidt, Philadelphia
SS— Garry Templeton, San Diego
OF— Dale Murphy, Atlanta
OF— Jose Cruz, Houston
OF— Tony Gwynn, San Diego
C— Gary Carter, Montreal
P— Rick Rhoden, Pittsburgh

1985
AMERICAN LEAGUE
1B— Don Mattingly, New York
2B— Lou Whitaker, Detroit
3B— George Brett, Kansas City
SS— Cal Ripken Jr., Baltimore
OF— Rickey Henderson, New York
OF— Dave Winfield, New York
OF— George Bell, Toronto
C— Carlton Fisk, Chicago
DH— Don Baylor, New York

NATIONAL LEAGUE
1B— Jack Clark, St. Louis
2B— Ryne Sandberg, Chicago
3B— Tim Wallach, Montreal
SS— Hubie Brooks, Montreal
OF— Willie McGee, St. Louis
OF— Dale Murphy, Atlanta
OF— Dave Parker, Cincinnati
C— Gary Carter, New York
P— Rick Rhoden, Pittsburgh

1986
AMERICAN LEAGUE
1B— Don Mattingly, New York
2B— Frank White, Kansas City
3B— Wade Boggs, Boston
SS— Cal Ripken Jr., Baltimore
OF— George Bell, Toronto
OF— Kirby Puckett, Minnesota
OF— Jesse Barfield, Toronto
C— Lance Parrish, Detroit
DH— Don Baylor, Boston

NATIONAL LEAGUE
1B— Glenn Davis, Houston
2B— Steve Sax, Los Angeles
3B— Mike Schmidt, Philadelphia
SS— Hubie Brooks, Montreal
OF— Tony Gwynn, San Diego
OF— Tim Raines, Montreal
OF— Dave Parker, Cincinnati
C— Gary Carter, New York
P— Rick Rhoden, Pittsburgh

1987
AMERICAN LEAGUE
1B— Don Mattingly, New York
2B— Lou Whitaker, Detroit
3B— Wade Boggs, Boston
SS— Alan Trammell, Detroit
OF— George Bell, Toronto
OF— Dwight Evans, Boston
OF— Kirby Puckett, Minnesota
C— Matt Nokes, Detroit
DH— Paul Molitor, Milwaukee

NATIONAL LEAGUE
1B— Jack Clark, St. Louis

2B— Juan Samuel, Philadelphia
3B— Tim Wallach, Montreal
SS— Ozzie Smith, St. Louis
OF— Andre Dawson, Chicago
OF— Eric Davis, Cincinnati
OF— Tony Gwynn, San Diego
C— Benito Santiago, San Diego
P— Bob Forsch, St. Louis

1988
AMERICAN LEAGUE
1B— George Brett, Kansas City
2B— Julio Franco, Cleveland
3B— Wade Boggs, Boston
SS— Alan Trammell, Detroit
OF— Kirby Puckett, Minnesota
OF— Jose Canseco, Oakland
OF— Mike Greenwell, Boston
C— Carlton Fisk, Chicago
DH— Paul Molitor, Milwaukee

NATIONAL LEAGUE
1B— Andres Galarraga, Montreal
2B— Ryne Sandberg, Chicago
3B— Bobby Bonilla, Pittsburgh
SS— Barry Larkin, Cincinnati
OF— Darryl Strawberry, New York
OF— Andy Van Slyke, Pittsburgh
OF— Kirk Gibson, Los Angeles
C— Benito Santiago, San Diego
P— Tim Leary, Los Angeles

1989
AMERICAN LEAGUE
1B— Fred McGriff, Toronto
2B— Julio Franco, Texas
3B— Wade Boggs, Boston
SS— Cal Ripken Jr., Baltimore
OF— Kirby Puckett, Minnesota
OF— Ruben Sierra, Texas
OF— Robin Yount, Milwaukee
C— Mickey Tettleton, Baltimore
DH— Harold Baines, Chi.-Tex.

NATIONAL LEAGUE
1B— Will Clark, San Francisco
2B— Ryne Sandberg, Chicago
3B— Howard Johnson, New York
SS— Barry Larkin, Cincinnati
OF— Kevin Mitchell, San Francisco
OF— Tony Gwynn, San Diego
OF— Eric Davis, Cincinnati
C— Craig Biggio, Houston
P— Don Robinson, San Francisco

1990
AMERICAN LEAGUE
1B— Cecil Fielder, Detroit
2B— Julio Franco, Texas
3B— Kelly Gruber, Toronto
SS— Alan Trammell, Detroit
OF— Rickey Henderson, Oakland
OF— Jose Canseco, Oakland
OF— Ellis Burks, Boston
C— Lance Parrish, California
DH— Dave Parker, Milwaukee

NATIONAL LEAGUE
1B— Eddie Murray, Los Angeles
2B— Ryne Sandberg, Chicago
3B— Matt Williams, San Francisco
SS— Barry Larkin, Cincinnati
OF— Barry Bonds, Pittsburgh
OF— Bobby Bonilla, Pittsburgh
OF— Darryl Strawberry, New York
C— Benito Santiago, San Diego
P— Don Robinson, San Francisco

1991
AMERICAN LEAGUE
1B— Cecil Fielder, Detroit
2B— Julio Franco, Texas
3B— Wade Boggs, Boston

SS— Cal Ripken Jr., Baltimore
OF— Jose Canseco, Oakland
OF— Joe Carter, Toronto
OF— Ken Griffey Jr., Seattle
C— Mickey Tettleton, Detroit
DH— Frank Thomas, Chicago

NATIONAL LEAGUE
1B— Will Clark, San Francisco
2B— Ryne Sandberg, Chicago
3B— Howard Johnson, New York
SS— Barry Larkin, Cincinnati
OF— Barry Bonds, Pittsburgh
OF— Bobby Bonilla, Pittsburgh
OF— Ron Gant, Atlanta
C— Benito Santiago, San Diego
P— Tom Glavine, Atlanta

1992
AMERICAN LEAGUE
1B— Mark McGwire, Oakland
2B— Roberto Alomar, Toronto
3B— Edgar Martinez, Seattle
SS— Travis Fryman, Detroit
OF— Joe Carter, Toronto
OF— Juan Gonzalez, Texas
OF— Kirby Puckett, Minnesota
C— Mickey Tettleton, Detroit
DH— Dave Winfield, Toronto

NATIONAL LEAGUE
1B— Fred McGriff, San Diego
2B— Ryne Sandberg, Chicago
3B— Gary Sheffield, San Diego
SS— Barry Larkin, Cincinnati
OF— Barry Bonds, Pittsburgh
OF— Andy Van Slyke, Pittsburgh
OF— Larry Walker, Montreal
C— Darren Daulton, Philadelphia
P— Dwight Gooden, New York

1993
AMERICAN LEAGUE
1B— Frank Thomas, Chicago
2B— Carlos Baerga, Cleveland
3B— Wade Boggs, New York
SS— Cal Ripken Jr., Baltimore
OF— Albert Belle, Cleveland
OF— Juan Gonzalez, Texas
OF— Ken Griffey Jr., Seattle
C— Mike Stanley, New York
DH— Paul Molitor, Toronto

NATIONAL LEAGUE
1B— Fred McGriff, S.D.-Atl.
2B— Robby Thompson, San Fran.
3B— Matt Williams, San Francisco
SS— Jay Bell, Pittsburgh
OF— Barry Bonds, San Francisco
OF— Lenny Dykstra, Philadelphia
OF— David Justice, Atlanta
C— Mike Piazza, Los Angeles
P— Orel Hershiser, Los Angeles

1994
AMERICAN LEAGUE
1B— Frank Thomas, Chicago
2B— Carlos Baerga, Cleveland
3B— Wade Boggs, New York
SS— Cal Ripken Jr., Baltimore
OF— Albert Belle, Cleveland
OF— Ken Griffey Jr., Seattle
OF— Kirby Puckett, Minnesota
C— Ivan Rodriguez, Texas
DH— Julio Franco, Chicago

NATIONAL LEAGUE
1B— Jeff Bagwell, Houston
2B— Craig Biggio, Houston
3B— Matt Williams, San Francisco
SS— Wil Cordero, Montreal
OF— Moises Alou, Montreal
OF— Barry Bonds, San Francisco

OF— Tony Gwynn, San Diego
C— Mike Piazza, Los Angeles
P— Mark Portugal, San Francisco

1995
AMERICAN LEAGUE
1B— Mo Vaughn, Boston
2B— Chuck Knoblauch, Minnesota
3B— Gary Gaetti, Kansas City
SS— John Valentin, Boston
OF— Albert Belle, Cleveland
OF— Tim Salmon, California
OF— Manny Ramirez, Cleveland
C— Ivan Rodriguez, Texas
DH— Edgar Martinez, Seattle

NATIONAL LEAGUE
1B— Eric Karros, Los Angeles
2B— Craig Biggio, Houston
3B— Vinny Castilla, Colorado
SS— Barry Larkin, Cincinnati
OF— Dante Bichette, Colorado
OF— Tony Gwynn, San Diego
OF— Sammy Sosa, Chicago
C— Mike Piazza, Los Angeles
P— Tom Glavine, Atlanta

1996
AMERICAN LEAGUE
1B— Mark McGwire, Oakland
2B— Roberto Alomar, Baltimore
3B— Jim Thome, Cleveland
SS— Alex Rodriguez, Seattle
OF— Albert Belle, Cleveland
OF— Juan Gonzalez, Texas
OF— Ken Griffey Jr., Seattle
C— Ivan Rodriguez, Texas
DH— Paul Molitor, Minnesota

NATIONAL LEAGUE
1B— Andres Galarraga, Colorado
2B— Eric Young, Colorado
3B— Ken Caminiti, San Diego
SS— Barry Larkin, Cincinnati
OF— Barry Bonds, San Francisco
OF— Ellis Burks, Colorado
OF— Gary Sheffield, Florida
C— Mike Piazza, Los Angeles
P— Tom Glavine, Atlanta

1997
AMERICAN LEAGUE
1B— Tino Martinez, New York
2B— Chuck Knoblauch, Minnesota
3B— Matt Williams, Cleveland
SS— Nomar Garciaparra, Boston
OF— Juan Gonzalez, Texas
OF— Ken Griffey Jr., Seattle
OF— David Justice, Cleveland
C— Ivan Rodriguez, Texas
DH— Edgar Martinez, Seattle

NATIONAL LEAGUE
1B— Jeff Bagwell, Houston
2B— Craig Biggio, Houston
3B— Vinny Castilla, Colorado
SS— Jeff Blauser, Atlanta
OF— Barry Bonds, San Francisco
OF— Tony Gwynn, San Diego
OF— Larry Walker, Colorado
C— Mike Piazza, Los Angeles
P— John Smoltz, Atlanta

1998
AMERICAN LEAGUE
1B— Rafael Palmeiro, Baltimore
2B— Damion Easley, Detroit
3B— Dean Palmer, Kansas City
SS— Alex Rodriguez, Seattle

OF— Juan Gonzalez, Texas
OF— Ken Griffey Jr., Seattle
OF— Albert Belle, Chicago
C— Ivan Rodriguez, Texas
DH— Jose Canseco, Toronto

NATIONAL LEAGUE
1B— Mark McGwire, St. Louis
2B— Craig Biggio, Houston
3B— Vinny Castilla, Colorado
SS— Barry Larkin, Cincinnati
OF— Sammy Sosa, Chicago
OF— Moises Alou, Houston
OF— Greg Vaughn, San Diego
C— Mike Piazza, L.A.-Fla.-N.Y.
P— Tom Glavine, Atlanta

1999
AMERICAN LEAGUE
1B— Carlos Delgado, Toronto
2B— Roberto Alomar, Cleveland
3B— Dean Palmer, Detroit
SS— Alex Rodriguez, Seattle
OF— Shawn Green, Toronto
OF— Ken Griffey Jr., Seattle
OF— Manny Ramirez, Cleveland
C— Ivan Rodriguez, Texas
DH— Rafael Palmeiro, Texas

NATIONAL LEAGUE
1B— Jeff Bagwell, Houston
2B— Edgardo Alfonzo, New York
3B— Chipper Jones, Atlanta
SS— Barry Larkin, Cincinnati
OF— Sammy Sosa, Chicago
OF— Vladimir Guerrero, Montreal
OF— Larry Walker, Colorado
C— Mike Piazza, New York
P— Mike Hampton, Houston

2000
AMERICAN LEAGUE
1B— Carlos Delgado, Toronto
2B— Roberto Alomar, Cleveland
3B— Troy Glaus, Anaheim
SS— Alex Rodriguez, Seattle
OF— Darin Erstad, Anaheim
OF— Manny Ramirez, Cleveland
OF— Magglio Ordonez, Chicago
C— Jorge Posada, New York
DH— Frank Thomas, Chicago

NATIONAL LEAGUE
1B— Todd Helton, Colorado
2B— Jeff Kent, San Francisco
3B— Chipper Jones, Atlanta
SS— Edgar Renteria, St. Louis
OF— Sammy Sosa, Chicago
OF— Barry Bonds, San Francisco
OF— Vladimir Guerrero, Montreal
C— Mike Piazza, New York
P— Mike Hampton, New York

2001
AMERICAN LEAGUE
1B— Jason Giambi, Oakland
2B— Bret Boone, Seattle
3B— Troy Glaus, Anaheim
SS— Alex Rodriguez, Texas
OF— Juan Gonzalez, Cleveland
OF— Manny Ramirez, Boston
OF— Ichiro Suzuki, Seattle
C— Jorge Posada, New York
DH— Edgar Martinez, Seattle

NATIONAL LEAGUE
1B— Todd Helton, Colorado
2B— Jeff Kent, San Francisco
3B— Albert Pujols, St. Louis
SS— Rich Aurilia, San Francisco

OF— Barry Bonds, San Francisco
OF— Luis Gonzalez, Arizona
OF— Sammy Sosa, Chicago
C— Mike Piazza, New York
P— Mike Hampton, Colorado

2002
AMERICAN LEAGUE
1B— Jason Giambi, New York
2B— Alfonso Soriano, New York
3B— Eric Chavez, Oakland
SS— Alex Rodriguez, Texas
OF— Garret Anderson, Anaheim
OF— Magglio Ordonez, Chicago
OF— Bernie Williams, New York
C— Jorge Posada, New York
DH— Manny Ramirez, Boston

NATIONAL LEAGUE
1B— Todd Helton, Colorado
2B— Jeff Kent, San Francisco
3B— Scott Rolen, Phi.-St.L.
SS— Edgar Renteria, St. Louis
OF— Barry Bonds, San Francisco
OF— Vladimir Guerrero, Montreal
OF— Sammy Sosa, Chicago
C— Mike Piazza, New York
P— Mike Hampton, Colorado

2003
AMERICAN LEAGUE
1B— Carlos Delgado, Toronto
2B— Bret Boone, Seattle
3B— Bill Mueller, Boston

SS— Alex Rodriguez, Texas
OF— Garret Anderson, Anaheim
OF— Vernon Wells, Toronto
OF— Manny Ramirez, Boston
C— Jorge Posada, New York
DH— Edgar Martinez, Seattle

NATIONAL LEAGUE
1B— Todd Helton, Colorado
2B— Jose Vidro, Montreal
3B— Mike Lowell, Florida
SS— Edgar Renteria, St. Louis
OF— Barry Bonds, San Francisco
OF— Albert Pujols, St. Louis
OF— Gary Sheffield, Atlanta
C— Javy Lopez, Atlanta
P— Mike Hampton, Atlanta

2004
AMERICAN LEAGUE
1B— Mark Teixeira, Texas
2B— Alfonso Soriano, Texas
3B— Melvin Mora, Baltimore
SS— Miguel Tejada, Baltimore
OF— Manny Ramirez, Boston
OF— Gary Sheffield, New York
OF— Vladimir Guerrero, Anaheim
C— Ivan Rodriguez, Detroit
    Victor Martinez, Cleveland
DH— David Ortiz, Boston

NATIONAL LEAGUE
1B— Albert Pujols, St. Louis

2B— Mark Loretta, San Diego
3B— Adrian Beltre, Los Angeles
SS— Jack Wilson, Pittsburgh
OF— Barry Bonds, San Francisco
OF— Jim Edmonds, St. Louis
OF— Bobby Abreu, Philadelphia
C— Johnny Estrada, Atlanta
P— Livan Hernandez, Montreal

2005
AMERICAN LEAGUE
1B— Mark Teixeira, Texas
2B— Alfonso Soriano, Texas
3B— Alex Rodriguez, New York
SS— Miguel Tejada, Baltimore
OF— Manny Ramirez, Boston
OF— Gary Sheffield, New York
OF— Vladimir Guerrero, Los Angeles
C— Jason Varitek, Boston
DH— David Ortiz, Boston

NATIONAL LEAGUE
1B— Derrek Lee, Chicago
2B— Jeff Kent, Los Angeles
3B— Morgan Ensberg, Houston
SS— Felipe Lopez, Cincinnati
OF— Andruw Jones, Atlanta
OF— Miguel Cabrera, Florida
OF— Carlos Lee, Milwaukee
C— Michael Barrett, Chicago
P— Jason Marquis, St. Louis

BASEBALL WRITERS' ASSOCIATION OF AMERICA
MOST VALUABLE PLAYER

AMERICAN LEAGUE

Year	Player	Team	Pos.	Points
1931—Lefty Grove	Philadelphia	P	78
1932—Jimmie Foxx	Philadelphia	1B	75
1933—Jimmie Foxx	Philadelphia	1B	74
1934—Mickey Cochrane	Detroit	C	67
1935—Hank Greenberg	Detroit	1B	*80
1936—Lou Gehrig	New York	1B	73
1937—Charley Gehringer	Detroit	2B	78
1938—Jimmie Foxx	Boston	1B	305
1939—Joe DiMaggio	New York	OF	280
1940—Hank Greenberg	Detroit	OF	292
1941—Joe DiMaggio	New York	OF	291
1942—Joe Gordon	New York	2B	270
1943—Spud Chandler	New York	P	246
1944—Hal Newhouser	Detroit	P	236
1945—Hal Newhouser	Detroit	P	236
1946—Ted Williams	Boston	OF	224
1947—Joe DiMaggio	New York	OF	202
1948—Lou Boudreau	Cleveland	SS	324
1949—Ted Williams	Boston	OF	272
1950—Phil Rizzuto	New York	SS	284
1951—Yogi Berra	New York	C	184
1952—Bobby Shantz	Philadelphia	P	280
1953—Al Rosen	Cleveland	3B	*336
1954—Yogi Berra	New York	C	230
1955—Yogi Berra	New York	C	218
1956—Mickey Mantle	New York	OF	*336
1957—Mickey Mantle	New York	OF	233
1958—Jackie Jensen	Boston	OF	233
1959—Nellie Fox	Chicago	2B	295
1960—Roger Maris	New York	OF	225
1961—Roger Maris	New York	OF	202
1962—Mickey Mantle	New York	OF	234
1963—Elston Howard	New York	C	248
1964—Brooks Robinson	Baltimore	3B	269
1965—Zoilo Versalles	Minnesota	SS	275
1966—Frank Robinson	Baltimore	OF	*280
1967—Carl Yastrzemski	Boston	OF	275
1968—Denny McLain	Detroit	P	*280
1969—Harmon Killebrew	Minnesota	1B-3B	294

NATIONAL LEAGUE

Year	Player	Team	Pos.	Points
1931—Frank Frisch	St. Louis	2B	65
1932—Chuck Klein	Philadelphia	OF	78
1933—Carl Hubbell	New York	P	77
1934—Dizzy Dean	St. Louis	P	78
1935—Gabby Hartnett	Chicago	C	75
1936—Carl Hubbell	New York	P	60
1937—Joe Medwick	St. Louis	OF	70
1938—Ernie Lombardi	Cincinnati	C	229
1939—Bucky Walters	Cincinnati	P	303
1940—Frank McCormick	Cincinnati	1B	274
1941—Dolf Camilli	Brooklyn	1B	300
1942—Mort Cooper	St. Louis	P	263
1943—Stan Musial	St. Louis	OF	267
1944—Marty Marion	St. Louis	SS	190
1945—Phil Cavarretta	Chicago	1B	279
1946—Stan Musial	St. Louis	1B	319
1947—Bob Elliott	Boston	3B	205
1948—Stan Musial	St. Louis	OF	303
1949—Jackie Robinson	Brooklyn	2B	264
1950—Jim Konstanty	Philadelphia	P	286
1951—Roy Campanella	Brooklyn	C	243
1952—Hank Sauer	Chicago	OF	226
1953—Roy Campanella	Brooklyn	C	297
1954—Willie Mays	New York	OF	283
1955—Roy Campanella	Brooklyn	C	226
1956—Don Newcombe	Brooklyn	P	223
1957—Hank Aaron	Milwaukee	OF	239
1958—Ernie Banks	Chicago	SS	283
1959—Ernie Banks	Chicago	SS	232 1/2
1960—Dick Groat	Pittsburgh	SS	276
1961—Frank Robinson	Cincinnati	OF	219
1962—Maury Wills	Los Angeles	SS	209
1963—Sandy Koufax	Los Angeles	P	237
1964—Ken Boyer	St. Louis	3B	243
1965—Willie Mays	San Francisco	OF	224
1966—Roberto Clemente	Pittsburgh	OF	218
1967—Orlando Cepeda	St. Louis	1B	*280
1968—Bob Gibson	St. Louis	P	242
1969—Willie McCovey	San Francisco	1B	265

HISTORY *Award winners*

Year	Player	Team	Pos.	Points	Year	Player	Team	Pos.	Points
1970—Boog Powell	Baltimore	1B	234		1970—Johnny Bench	Cincinnati	C	326	
1971—Vida Blue	Oakland	P	268		1971—Joe Torre	St. Louis	3B	318	
1972—Dick Allen	Chicago	1B	321		1972—Johnny Bench	Cincinnati	C	263	
1973—Reggie Jackson	Oakland	OF	*336		1973—Pete Rose	Cincinnati	OF	274	
1974—Jeff Burroughs	Texas	OF	248		1974—Steve Garvey	Los Angeles	1B	270	
1975—Fred Lynn	Boston	OF	326		1975—Joe Morgan	Cincinnati	2B	321½	
1976—Thurman Munson	New York	C	304		1976—Joe Morgan	Cincinnati	2B	311	
1977—Rod Carew	Minnesota	1B	273		1977—George Foster	Cincinnati	OF	291	
1978—Jim Rice	Boston	OF	352		1978—Dave Parker	Pittsburgh	OF	320	
1979—Don Baylor	California	OF	347		1979—Willie Stargell	Pittsburgh	1B	216	
Keith Hernandez	St. Louis	1B	216						
1980—George Brett	Kansas City	3B	335		1980—Mike Schmidt	Philadelphia	3B	*336	
1981—Rollie Fingers	Milwaukee	P	319		1981—Mike Schmidt	Philadelphia	3B	321	
1982—Robin Yount	Milwaukee	SS	385		1982—Dale Murphy	Atlanta	OF	283	
1983—Cal Ripken Jr.	Baltimore	SS	322		1983—Dale Murphy	Atlanta	OF	318	
1984—Willie Hernandez	Detroit	P	306		1984—Ryne Sandberg	Chicago	2B	326	
1985—Don Mattingly	New York	1B	367		1985—Willie McGee	St. Louis	OF	280	
1986—Roger Clemens	Boston	P	339		1986—Mike Schmidt	Philadelphia	3B	287	
1987—George Bell	Toronto	OF	332		1987—Andre Dawson	Chicago	OF	269	
1988—Jose Canseco	Oakland	OF	*392		1988—Kirk Gibson	Los Angeles	OF	272	
1989—Robin Yount	Milwaukee	OF	256		1989—Kevin Mitchell	San Francisco	OF	314	
1990—Rickey Henderson	Oakland	OF	317		1990—Barry Bonds	Pittsburgh	OF	331	
1991—Cal Ripken Jr.	Baltimore	SS	318		1991—Terry Pendleton	Atlanta	3B	274	
1992—Dennis Eckersley	Oakland	P	306		1992—Barry Bonds	Pittsburgh	OF	304	
1993—Frank Thomas	Chicago	1B	*392		1993—Barry Bonds	San Francisco	OF	372	
1994—Frank Thomas	Chicago	1B	372		1994—Jeff Bagwell	Houston	1B	*392	
1995—Mo Vaughn	Boston	1B	308		1995—Barry Larkin	Cincinnati	SS	281	
1996—Juan Gonzalez	Texas	OF	290		1996—Ken Caminiti	San Diego	3B	*392	
1997—Ken Griffey Jr.	Seattle	OF	*392		1997—Larry Walker	Colorado	OF	359	
1998—Juan Gonzalez	Texas	OF	357		1998—Sammy Sosa	Chicago	OF	438	
1999—Ivan Rodriguez	Texas	C	252		1999—Chipper Jones	Atlanta	3B	432	
2000—Jason Giambi	Oakland	1B	317		2000—Jeff Kent	San Francisco	2B	392	
2001—Ichiro Suzuki	Seattle	OF	289		2001—Barry Bonds	San Francisco	OF	438	
2002—Miguel Tejada	Oakland	SS	356		2002—Barry Bonds	San Francisco	OF	*448	
2003—Alex Rodriguez	Texas	SS	242		2003—Barry Bonds	San Francisco	OF	426	
2004—Vladimir Guerrero	Anaheim	OF	354		2004—Barry Bonds	San Francisco	OF	407	
2005—Alex Rodriguez	New York	3B	331		2005—Albert Pujols	St. Louis	1B	378	

*Unanimous selection.

CY YOUNG MEMORIAL AWARD

Year	Pitcher	Team	Votes	Year	Pitcher	Team	Votes
1956—Don Newcombe	Brooklyn	10		1980—A.L.—Steve Stone	Baltimore	100	
1957—Warren Spahn	Milwaukee	15		N.L.—Steve Carlton	Philadelphia	118	
1958—Bob Turley	New York A.L.	5		1981—A.L.—Rollie Fingers	Milwaukee	126	
1959—Early Wynn	Chicago A.L.	13		N.L.—Fernando Valenzuela	Los Angeles	70	
1960—Vernon Law	Pittsburgh	8		1982—A.L.—Pete Vuckovich	Milwaukee	87	
1961—Whitey Ford	New York A.L.	9		N.L.—Steve Carlton	Philadelphia	112	
1962—Don Drysdale	Los Angeles N.L.	14		1983—A.L.—LaMarr Hoyt	Chicago	116	
1963—Sandy Koufax	Los Angeles N.L.	*20		N.L.—John Denny	Philadelphia	103	
1964—Dean Chance	Los Angeles A.L.	17		1984—A.L.—Willie Hernandez	Detroit	88	
1965—Sandy Koufax	Los Angeles N.L.	*20		N.L.—Rick Sutcliffe	Chicago	*120	
1966—Sandy Koufax	Los Angeles N.L.	*20		1985—A.L.—Bret Saberhagen	Kansas City	127	
1967—A.L.—Jim Lonborg	Boston	18		N.L.—Dwight Gooden	New York	*120	
N.L.—Mike McCormick	San Francisco	18		1986—A.L.—Roger Clemens	Boston	*140	
1968—A.L.—Denny McLain	Detroit	*20		N.L.—Mike Scott	Houston	98	
N.L.—Bob Gibson	St. Louis	*20		1987—A.L.—Roger Clemens	Boston	124	
1969—A.L.—Denny McLain	Detroit	10		N.L.—Steve Bedrosian	Philadelphia	57	
Mike Cuellar	Baltimore	10		1988—A.L.—Frank Viola	Minnesota	138	
N.L.—Tom Seaver	New York	23		N.L.—Orel Hershiser	Los Angeles	*120	
1970—A.L.—Jim Perry	Minnesota	55		1989—A.L.—Bret Saberhagen	Kansas City	138	
N.L.—Bob Gibson	St. Louis	118		N.L.—Mark Davis	San Diego	107	
1971—A.L.—Vida Blue	Oakland	98		1990—A.L.—Bob Welch	Oakland	107	
N.L.—Fergie Jenkins	Chicago	97		N.L.—Doug Drabek	Pittsburgh	118	
1972—A.L.—Gaylord Perry	Cleveland	64		1991—A.L.—Roger Clemens	Boston	119	
N.L.—Steve Carlton	Philadelphia	*120		N.L.—Tom Glavine	Atlanta	110	
1973—A.L.—Jim Palmer	Baltimore	88		1992—A.L.—Dennis Eckersley	Oakland	107	
N.L.—Tom Seaver	New York	71		N.L.—Greg Maddux	Chicago	112	
1974—A.L.—Jim Hunter	Oakland	90		1993—A.L.—Jack McDowell	Chicago	124	
N.L.—Mike Marshall	Los Angeles	96		N.L.—Greg Maddux	Atlanta	119	
1975—A.L.—Jim Palmer	Baltimore	98		1994—A.L.—David Cone	Kansas City	108	
N.L.—Tom Seaver	New York	98		N.L.—Greg Maddux	Atlanta	*140	
1976—A.L.—Jim Palmer	Baltimore	108		1995—A.L.—Randy Johnson	Seattle	136	
N.L.—Randy Jones	San Diego	96		N.L.—Greg Maddux	Atlanta	*140	
1977—A.L.—Sparky Lyle	New York	56½		1996—A.L.—Pat Hentgen	Toronto	110	
N.L.—Steve Carlton	Philadelphia	104		N.L.—John Smoltz	Atlanta	136	
1978—A.L.—Ron Guidry	New York	*140		1997—A.L.—Roger Clemens	Toronto	134	
N.L.—Gaylord Perry	San Diego	116		N.L.—Pedro Martinez	Montreal	134	
1979—A.L.—Mike Flanagan	Baltimore	136		1998—A.L.—Roger Clemens	Toronto	*140	
N.L.—Bruce Sutter	Chicago	72		N.L.—Tom Glavine	Atlanta	99	
				1999—A.L.—Pedro Martinez	Boston	*140	

Year	Pitcher	Team	Votes	Year	Pitcher	Team	Votes
	N.L.—Randy Johnson	Arizona	134	2003—A.L.—Roy Halladay	Toronto	136	
2000—A.L.—Pedro Martinez	Boston	*140		N.L.—Eric Gagne	Los Angeles	146	
	N.L.—Randy Johnson	Arizona	133	2004 A.L.—Johan Santana	Minnesota	*140	
2001—A.L.—Roger Clemens	New York	122		N.L.—Roger Clemens	Houston	140	
	N.L.—Randy Johnson	Arizona	156	2005 A.L.—Bartolo Colon	Los Angeles	118	
2002—A.L.—Barry Zito	Oakland	114		N.L.—Chris Carpenter	St. Louis	132	
	N.L.—Randy Johnson	Arizona	*160	*Unanimous selection.			

ROOKIE OF THE YEAR

1947—Combined selection—Jackie Robinson, Brooklyn N.L., 1B
1948—Combined selection—Alvin Dark, Boston N.L., SS

AMERICAN LEAGUE

Year	Player	Team	Pos.	Votes
1949—Roy Sievers	St. Louis	OF	10	
1950—Walt Dropo	Boston	1B	15	
1951—Gil McDougald	New York	3B	13	
1952—Harry Byrd	Philadelphia	P	9	
1953—Harvey Kuenn	Detroit	SS	23	
1954—Bob Grim	New York	P	15	
1955—Herb Score	Cleveland	P	18	
1956—Luis Aparicio	Chicago	SS	22	
1957—Tony Kubek	New York	IF-OF	23	
1958—Albie Pearson	Washington	OF	14	
1959—Bob Allison	Washington	OF	18	
1960—Ron Hansen	Baltimore	SS	22	
1961—Don Schwall	Boston	P	7	
1962—Tom Tresh	New York	OF-SS	13	
1963—Gary Peters	Chicago	P	10	
1964—Tony Oliva	Minnesota	OF	19	
1965—Curt Blefary	Baltimore	OF	12	
1966—Tommie Agee	Chicago	OF	16	
1967—Rod Carew	Minnesota	2B	19	
1968—Stan Bahnsen	New York	P	17	
1969—Lou Piniella	Kansas City	OF	9	
1970—Thurman Munson	New York	C	23	
1971—Chris Chambliss	Cleveland	1B	11	
1972—Carlton Fisk	Boston	C	*24	
1973—Al Bumbry	Baltimore	OF	13½	
1974—Mike Hargrove	Texas	1B	16½	
1975—Fred Lynn	Boston	OF	23½	
1976—Mark Fidrych	Detroit	P	22	
1977—Eddie Murray	Baltimore	DH-1B	12½	
1978—Lou Whitaker	Detroit	2B	21	
1979—John Castino	Minnesota	3B	7	
Alfredo Griffin	Toronto	SS	7	
1980—Joe Charboneau	Cleveland	OF	102	
1981—Dave Righetti	New York	P	127	
1982—Cal Ripken	Baltimore	SS-3B	132	
1983—Ron Kittle	Chicago	OF	104	
1984—Alvin Davis	Seattle	1B	134	
1985—Ozzie Guillen	Chicago	SS	101	
1986—Jose Canseco	Oakland	OF	110	
1987—Mark McGwire	Oakland	1B	*140	
1988—Walt Weiss	Oakland	SS	103	
1989—Gregg Olson	Baltimore	P	136	
1990—Sandy Alomar Jr.	Cleveland	C	*140	
1991—Chuck Knoblauch	Minnesota	2B	136	
1992—Pat Listach	Milwaukee	SS	122	
1993—Tim Salmon	California	OF	*140	
1994—Bob Hamelin	Kansas City	DH	134	
1995—Marty Cordova	Minnesota	3B	105	
1996—Derek Jeter	New York	SS	*140	
1997—Nomar Garciaparra	Boston	SS	*140	
1998—Ben Grieve	Oakland	OF	130	
1999—Carlos Beltran	Kansas City	OF	133	
2000—Kazuhiro Sasaki	Seattle	P	104	
2001—Ichiro Suzuki	Seattle	OF	138	
2002—Eric Hinske	Toronto	3B	122	
2003—Angel Berroa	Kansas City	SS	88	
2004—Bobby Crosby	Oakland	SS	138	
2005—Huston Street	Oakland	P	97	

NATIONAL LEAGUE

Year	Player	Team	Pos.	Votes
1949—Don Newcombe	Brooklyn	P	21	
1950—Sam Jethroe	Boston	OF	11	
1951—Willie Mays	New York	OF	18	
1952—Joe Black	Brooklyn	P	19	
1953—Jim Gilliam	Brooklyn	2B	11	
1954—Wally Moon	St. Louis	OF	17	
1955—Bill Virdon	St. Louis	OF	15	
1956—Frank Robinson	Cincinnati	OF	*24	
1957—Jack Sanford	Philadelphia	P	16	
1958—Orlando Cepeda	San Francisco	1B	*†21	
1959—Willie McCovey	San Francisco	1B	*24	
1960—Frank Howard	Los Angeles	OF	12	
1961—Billy Williams	Chicago	OF	10	
1962—Ken Hubbs	Chicago	2B	19	
1963—Pete Rose	Cincinnati	2B	17	
1964—Dick Allen	Philadelphia	3B	18	
1965—Jim Lefebvre	Los Angeles	2B	13	
1966—Tommy Helms	Cincinnati	3B	12	
1967—Tom Seaver	New York	P	11	
1968—Johnny Bench	Cincinnati	C	10½	
1969—Ted Sizemore	Los Angeles	2B	14	
1970—Carl Morton	Montreal	P	11	
1971—Earl Williams	Atlanta	C	18	
1972—Jon Matlack	New York	P	19	
1973—Gary Matthews	San Francisco	OF	11	
1974—Bake McBride	St. Louis	OF	16	
1975—John Montefusco	San Francisco	P	12	
1976—Butch Metzger	San Diego	P	11	
Pat Zachry	Cincinnati	P	11	
1977—Andre Dawson	Montreal	OF	10	
1978—Bob Horner	Atlanta	3B	12½	
1979—Rick Sutcliffe	Los Angeles	P	20	
1980—Steve Howe	Los Angeles	P	80	
1981—Fernando Valenzuela	Los Angeles	P	107	
1982—Steve Sax	Los Angeles	2B	63	
1983—Darryl Strawberry	New York	OF	106	
1984—Dwight Gooden	New York	P	118	
1985—Vince Coleman	St. Louis	OF	*120	
1986—Todd Worrell	St. Louis	P	118	
1987—Benito Santiago	San Diego	C	*120	
1988—Chris Sabo	Cincinnati	3B	79	
1989—Jerome Walton	Chicago	OF	116	
1990—Dave Justice	Atlanta	OF	118	
1991—Jeff Bagwell	Houston	1B	118	
1992—Eric Karros	Los Angeles	1B	116	
1993—Mike Piazza	Los Angeles	C	*140	
1994—Raul Mondesi	Los Angeles	OF	*140	
1995—Hideo Nomo	Los Angeles	P	118	
1996—Todd Hollandsworth	Los Angeles	OF	105	
1997—Scott Rolen	Philadelphia	3B	*140	
1998—Kerry Wood	Chicago	P	128	
1999—Scott Williamson	Cincinnati	P	118	
2000—Rafael Furcal	Atlanta	SS-2B	144	
2001—Albert Pujols	St. Louis	OF-3B-1B	*160	
2002—Jason Jennings	Colorado	P	150	
2003—Dontrelle Willis	Florida	P	118	
2004—Jason Bay	Pittsburgh	OF	146	
2005—Ryan Howard	Philadelphia	1B	109	

*Unanimous selection. †Three writers did not vote.

MANAGER OF THE YEAR

AMERICAN LEAGUE

Year	Manager	Team	Points
1983—Tony La Russa	Chicago	17
1984—Sparky Anderson	Detroit	96
1985—Bobby Cox	Toronto	104
1986—John McNamara	Boston	95
1987—Sparky Anderson	Detroit	90
1988—Tony La Russa	Oakland	103
1989—Frank Robinson	Baltimore	125
1990—Jeff Torborg	Chicago	128
1991—Tom Kelly	Minnesota	138
1992—Tony La Russa	Oakland	132
1993—Gene Lamont	Chicago	72
1994—Buck Showalter	New York	132
1995—Lou Piniella	Seattle	86
1996—Johnny Oates	Texas	89
Joe Torre	New York	89
1997—Dave Johnson	Baltimore	88
1998—Joe Torre	New York	128
1999—Jimy Williams	Boston	115
2000—Jerry Manuel	Chicago	134
2001—Lou Piniella	Seattle	128
2002—Mike Scioscia	Anaheim	116
2003—Tony Pena	Kansas City	130
2004—Buck Showalter	Texas	101
2005—Ozzie Guillen	Chicago	105

NATIONAL LEAGUE

Year	Manager	Team	Points
1983— Tommy Lasorda	Los Angeles	10
1984— Jim Frey	Chicago	101
1985— Whitey Herzog	St. Louis	86
1986— Hal Lanier	Houston	108
1987— Buck Rodgers	Montreal	92
1988— Tommy Lasorda	Los Angeles	101
1989— Don Zimmer	Chicago	118
1990— Jim Leyland	Pittsburgh	99
1991— Bobby Cox	Atlanta	96
1992— Jim Leyland	Pittsburgh	109
1993— Dusty Baker	San Francisco	105
1994— Felipe Alou	Montreal	138
1995— Don Baylor	Colorado	122
1996— Bruce Bochy	San Diego	76
1997— Dusty Baker	San Francisco	110
1998— Larry Dierker	Houston	102
1999— Jack McKeon	Cincinnati	115
2000— Dusty Baker	San Francisco	154
2001— Larry Bowa	Philadelphia	113
2002— Tony La Russa	St. Louis	129
2003— Jack McKeon	Florida	116
2004— Bobby Cox	Atlanta	140
2005— Bobby Cox	Atlanta	152

EARLY MOST VALUABLE PLAYER AWARDS
CHALMERS AWARD

AMERICAN LEAGUE

Year	Player	Team	Pos.	Points
1911—Ty Cobb	Detroit	OF	64
1912—Tris Speaker	Boston	OF	59
1913—Walter Johnson	Washington	P	54
1914—Eddie Collins	Philadelphia	2B	63

NATIONAL LEAGUE

Year	Player	Team	Pos.	Points
1911—Frank Schulte	Chicago	OF	29
1912—Larry Doyle	New York	2B	48
1913—Jake Daubert	Brooklyn	1B	50
1914—Johnny Evers	Boston	2B	50

LEAGUE AWARDS

AMERICAN LEAGUE

Year	Player	Team	Pos.	Points
1922—George Sisler	St. Louis	1B	59
1923—Babe Ruth	New York	OF	64
1924—Walter Johnson	Washington	P	55
1925—Roger Peckinpaugh	Washington	SS	45
1926—George Burns	Cleveland	1B	63
1927—Lou Gehrig	New York	1B	56
1928—Mickey Cochrane	Philadelphia	C	53
1929—No selection			

NATIONAL LEAGUE

Year	Player	Team	Pos.	Points
1922—No selection			
1923—No selection			
1924—Dazzy Vance	Brooklyn	P	74
1925—Rogers Hornsby	St. Louis	2B	73
1926—Bob O'Farrell	St. Louis	C	79
1927—Paul Waner	Pittsburgh	OF	72
1928—Jim Bottomley	St. Louis	1B	76
1929—Rogers Hornsby	Chicago	2B	60

HALL OF FAME

ROSTER OF MEMBERS

Name	Des.*	Elec. year	Votes rec.†	Votes cast‡	% of vote	Teams as player
Aaron, Hank	P	1982	406	415	97.8	Milwaukee NL, Atlanta NL, Milwaukee AL
Alexander, Grover C.	P	1938	212	262	80.9	Philadelphia NL, Chicago NL, St. Louis NL
Alston, Walter	M	1983	CV	—	—	St. Louis NL
Anderson, Sparky	M	2000	CV	—	—	Philadelphia NL
Anson, Cap	P	1939	C1	—	—	Chicago NL
Aparicio, Luis	P	1984	341	403	84.6	Chicago AL, Baltimore AL, Boston AL
Appling, Luke	P	1964	189	225	84.0	Chicago AL
Ashburn, Richie	P	1995	CV	—	—	Philadelphia NL, Chicago NL, New York NL
Averill, Earl	P	1975	CV	—	—	Cleveland AL, Detroit AL, Boston NL
Baker, Home Run	P	1955	CV	—	—	Philadelphia AL, New York AL
Bancroft, Dave	P	1971	CV	—	—	Philadelphia NL, New York NL, Boston NL, Brooklyn NL
Banks, Ernie	P	1977	321	383	83.8	Chicago NL
Barlick, Al	U	1989	CV	—	—	
Barrow, Ed	E	1953	CV	—	—	
Beckley, Jake	P	1971	CV	—	—	Pittsburgh NL, Pittsburgh PL, New York NL, Cincinnati NL, St. Louis NL

Name	Des.*	Elec. year	Votes rec.†	Votes cast‡	% of vote	Teams as player
Bell, Cool Papa	P	1974	SCNL	—	—	Negro Leagues
Bench, Johnny	P	1989	431	447	96.4	Cincinnati NL
Bender, Chief	P	1953	CV	—	—	Philadelphia AL, Philadelphia NL, Chicago AL
Berra, Yogi	P	1972	339	396	85.6	New York AL, New York NL
Boggs, Wade	P	2005	474	516	91.9	Boston AL, New York AL, Tampa Bay AL
Bottomley, Jim	P	1974	CV	—	—	St. Louis NL, Cincinnati NL, St. Louis AL
Boudreau, Lou	P	1970	232	300	77.3	Cleveland AL, Boston AL
Bresnahan, Roger	P	1945	C2	—	—	Washington NL, Chicago NL, Baltimore AL, New York NL, St. Louis NL
Brett, George	P	1999	488	497	98.2	Kansas City AL
Brock, Lou	P	1985	315	395	79.7	Chicago NL, St. Louis NL
Brouthers, Dan	P	1945	C2	—	—	Troy NL, Buffalo NL, Detroit NL, Boston NL, Boston PL, Boston AA,Brooklyn NL,Louisville NL, Philadelphia NL, New York NL
Brown, Three Finger	P	1949	C2	—	—	St. Louis NL, Chicago NL, Cincinnati NL
Bulkeley, Morgan	E	1937	CC	—	—	
Bunning, Jim	P	1996	CV	—	—	Detroit AL, Philadelphia NL, Pittsburgh NL, Los Angeles NL
Burkett, Jesse	P	1946	C2	—	—	New York NL, Cleveland NL, St. Louis NL, St. Louis AL, Boston AL
Campanella, Roy	P	1969	270	340	79.4	Brooklyn NL
Carew, Rod	P	1991	401	443	90.5	Minnesota AL, California AL
Carey, Max	P	1961	CV	—	—	Pittsburgh NL, Brooklyn NL
Carlton, Steve	P	1994	436	455	95.8	St. Louis NL, Philadelphia NL, San Francisco NL, Chicago AL, Cleveland AL, Minnesota AL
Carter, Gary	P	2003	387	496	78.0	Montreal NL, New York NL, San Francisco NL, Los Angeles NL
Cartwright, Alexander	O	1938	CC	—	—	
Cepeda, Orlando	P	1999	CV	—	—	San Francisco NL, St. Louis NL, Atlanta NL, Oakland AL, Boston AL, Kansas City AL
Chadwick, Henry	O	1938	CC	—	—	
Chance, Frank	P	1946	C2	—	—	Chicago NL, New York AL
Chandler, Happy	E	1982	CV	—	—	
Charleston, Oscar	P	1976	SCNL	—	—	Negro Leagues
Chesbro, Jack	P	1946	C2	—	—	Pittsburgh NL, New York AL, Boston AL
Chylak, Nestor	U	1999	CV	—	—	
Clarke, Fred	P	1945	C2	—	—	Louisville NL, Pittsburgh NL
Clarkson, John	P	1963	CV	—	—	Worcester NL, Chicago NL, Boston NL, Cleveland NL
Clemente, Roberto	P	1973	393	424	92.7	Pittsburgh NL
Cobb, Ty	P	1936	222	226	98.2	Detroit AL, Philadelphia AL
Cochrane, Mickey	P	1947	128	161	79.5	Philadelphia AL, Detroit AL
Collins, Eddie	P	1939	213	274	77.7	Philadelphia AL, Chicago AL
Collins, Jimmy	P	1945	C2	—	—	Boston NL, Louisville NL, Boston AL, Philadelphia AL
Combs, Earle	P	1970	CV	—	—	New York AL
Comiskey, Charley	F/P	1939	C1	—	—	St. Louis AA, Chicago PL, Cincinnati NL
Conlan, Jocko	U	1974	CV	—	—	Chicago AL
Connolly, Tommy	U	1953	CV	—	—	
Connor, Roger	P	1976	CV	—	—	Troy NL, New York NL, New York PL, Philadelphia NL, St. Louis NL
Coveleski, Stan	P	1969	CV	—	—	Philadelphia AL, Cleveland AL, Washington AL, New York AL
Crawford, Sam	P	1957	CV	—	—	Cincinnati NL, Detroit AL
Cronin, Joe	P	1956	152	193	78.8	Pittsburgh NL, Washington AL, Boston AL
Cummings, Candy	P	1939	C1	—	—	Hartford NL, Cincinnati NL
Cuyler, Kiki	P	1968	CV	—	—	Pittsburgh NL, Chicago NL, Cincinnati NL, Brooklyn NL
Dandridge, Ray	P	1987	CV	—	—	Negro Leagues
Davis, George S.	P	1998	CV	—	—	Cleveland NL, New York NL, Chicago AL
Day, Leon	P	1995	CV	—	—	Negro Leagues
Dean, Dizzy	P	1953	209	264	79.2	St. Louis NL, Chicago NL, St. Louis AL
Delahanty, Ed	P	1945	C2	—	—	Philadelphia NL, Cleveland PL, Washington AL
Dickey, Bill	P	1954	202	252	80.2	New York AL
Dihigo, Martin	P	1977	SCNL	—	—	Negro Leagues
DiMaggio, Joe	P	1955	223	251	88.8	New York AL
Doby, Larry	P	1998	CV	—	—	Cleveland AL, Chicago AL, Detroit AL
Doerr, Bobby	P	1986	CV	—	—	Boston AL
Drysdale, Don	P	1984	316	403	78.4	Brooklyn NL, Los Angeles NL
Duffy, Hugh	P	1945	C2	—	—	Chicago NL, Chicago PL, Boston AA, Boston NL, Milwaukee AL, Philadelphia NL
Durocher, Leo	M	1994	CV	—	—	New York NL, Cincinnati NL, St. Louis NL, Brooklyn NL
Eckersley, Dennis	P	2004	421	506	83.2	Cleveland AL, Boston AL, Chicago NL, Oakland AL, St. Louis NL
Evans, Billy	U	1973	CV	—	—	
Evers, Johnny	P	1946	C2	—	—	Chicago NL, Boston NL, Philadelphia NL, Chicago AL
Ewing, Buck	P	1939	C1	—	—	Troy NL, New York NL, New York PL, Cleveland NL, Cincinnati NL
Faber, Red	P	1964	CV	—	—	Chicago AL
Feller, Bob	P	1962	150	160	93.8	Cleveland AL
Ferrell, Rick	P	1984	CV	—	—	St. Louis AL, Boston AL, Washington AL
Fingers, Rollie	P	1992	349	430	81.2	Oakland AL, San Diego NL, Milwaukee AL

Name	Des.*	Elec. year	Votes rec.†	Votes cast‡	% of vote	Teams as player
Fisk, Carlton	P	2000	397	499	79.6	Boston AL, Chicago AL
Flick, Elmer	P	1963	CV	—	—	Philadelphia NL, Philadelphia AL, Cleveland AL
Ford, Whitey	P	1974	284	365	77.8	New York AL
Foster, Bill	P	1996	CV	—	—	Negro Leagues
Foster, Rube	P	1981	CV	—	—	Negro Leagues
Fox, Nellie	P	1997	CV	—	—	Philadelphia AL, Chicago AL, Houston NL
Foxx, Jimmie	P	1951	179	226	79.2	Philadelphia AL, Boston AL, Chicago NL, Philadelphia NL
Frick, Ford	E	1970	CV	—	—	
Frisch, Frankie	P	1947	136	161	84.5	New York NL, St. Louis NL
Galvin, Pud	P	1965	CV	—	—	Buffalo NL, Pittsburgh AA, Pittsburgh NL, Pittsburgh PL, St. Louis NL
Gehrig, Lou	P	1939	SE	—	—	New York AL
Gehringer, Charlie	P	1949	159	187	85.0	Detroit AL
Gibson, Bob	P	1981	337	401	84.0	St. Louis NL
Gibson, Josh	P	1972	SCNL	—	—	Negro Leagues
Giles, Warren	E	1979	CV	—	—	
Gomez, Lefty	P	1972	CV	—	—	New York AL, Washington AL
Goslin, Goose	P	1968	CV	—	—	Washington AL, St. Louis AL, Detroit AL
Greenberg, Hank	P	1956	164	193	85.0	Detroit AL, Pittsburgh NL
Griffith, Clark	E	1946	C2	—	—	St. Louis AA, Boston AA, Chicago NL, Chicago AL, New York AL, Cincinnati NL, Washington AL
Grimes, Burleigh	P	1964	CV	—	—	Pittsburgh NL, Brooklyn NL, New York NL, Boston NL, St. Louis NL, Chicago NL, New York AL
Grove, Lefty	P	1947	123	161	76.4	Philadelphia AL, Boston AL
Hafey, Chick	P	1971	CV	—	—	St. Louis NL, Cincinnati NL
Haines, Jesse	P	1970	CV	—	—	Cincinnati NL, St. Louis NL
Hamilton, Billy	P	1961	CV	—	—	Kansas City AA, Philadelphia NL, Boston NL
Hanlon, Ned	M	1996	CV	—	—	Cleveland NL, Detroit NL, Pittsburgh NL, Pittsburgh PL, Baltimore NL
Harridge, Will	E	1972	CV	—	—	
Harris, Bucky	M	1975	CV	—	—	Washington AL, Detroit AL
Hartnett, Gabby	P	1955	195	251	77.7	Chicago NL, New York NL
Heilmann, Harry	P	1952	203	234	86.8	Detroit AL, Cincinnati NL
Herman, Billy	P	1975	CV	—	—	Chicago NL, Brooklyn NL, Boston NL, Pittsburgh NL
Hooper, Harry	P	1971	CV	—	—	Boston AL, Chicago AL
Hornsby, Rogers	P	1942	182	233	78.1	St. Louis NL, New York NL, Boston NL, Chicago NL, St. Louis AL
Hoyt, Waite	P	1969	CV	—	—	New York NL, Boston AL, New York AL, Detroit AL, Philadelphia NL, Brooklyn NL, Pittsburgh NL
Hubbard, Cal	U	1976	CV	—	—	
Hubbell, Carl	P	1947	140	161	87.0	New York NL
Huggins, Miller	M	1964	CV	—	—	Cincinnati NL, St. Louis NL
Hulbert, William	F	1995	CV	—	—	
Hunter, Catfish	P	1987	315	413	76.3	Kansas City AL, Oakland AL, New York AL
Irvin, Monte	P	1973	SCNL	—	—	New York NL, Chicago NL, Negro Leagues
Jackson, Reggie	P	1993	396	423	93.6	Kansas City AL, Oakland AL, Baltimore AL, New York AL, California AL
Jackson, Travis	P	1982	CV	—	—	New York NL
Jenkins, Ferguson	P	1991	334	443	75.4	Philadelphia NL, Chicago NL, Texas AL, Boston AL
Jennings, Hugh	P	1945	C2	—	—	Louisville AA, Louisville NL, Baltimore NL, Brooklyn NL, Philadelphia NL, Detroit AL
Johnson, Ban	E	1937	CC	—	—	
Johnson, Judy	P	1975	SCNL	—	—	Negro Leagues
Johnson, Walter	P	1936	189	226	83.6	Washington AL
Joss, Addie	P	1978	CV	—	—	Cleveland AL
Kaline, Al	P	1980	340	385	88.3	Detroit AL
Keefe, Tim	P	1964	CV	—	—	Troy NL, New York AA, New York NL, New York PL, Philadelphia NL
Keeler, Willie	P	1939	207	274	75.5	New York NL, Brooklyn NL, Baltimore NL, New York AL
Kell, George	P	1983	CV	—	—	Philadelphia AL, Detroit AL, Boston AL, Chicago AL, Baltimore AL
Kelley, Joe	P	1971	CV	—	—	Boston NL, Pittsburgh NL, Baltimore NL, Brooklyn NL, Baltimore AL, Cincinnati NL
Kelly, George	P	1973	CV	—	—	New York NL, Pittsburgh NL, Cincinnati NL, Chicago NL, Brooklyn NL
Kelly, King	P	1945	C2	—	—	Cincinnati NL, Chicago NL, Boston NL, Boston PL, Cincinnati AA, Boston AA, New York NL
Killebrew, Harmon	P	1984	335	403	83.1	Washington AL, Minnesota AL, Kansas City AL
Kiner, Ralph	P	1975	273	362	75.4	Pittsburgh NL, Chicago NL, Cleveland AL
Klein, Chuck	P	1980	CV	—	—	Philadelphia NL, Chicago NL, Pittsburgh NL
Klem, Bill	U	1953	CV	—	—	
Koufax, Sandy	P	1972	344	396	86.9	Brooklyn NL, Los Angeles NL
Lajoie, Nap	P	1937	168	201	83.6	Philadelphia NL, Philadelphia AL, Cleveland AL
Landis, Kenesaw M.	E	1944	C2	—	—	
Lasorda, Tommy	M	1997	CV	—	—	Brooklyn NL, Kansas City AL
Lazzeri, Tony	P	1991	CV	—	—	New York AL, Chicago NL, Brooklyn NL, New York NL
Lemon, Bob	P	1976	305	388	78.6	Cleveland AL

Name	Des.*	Elec. year	Votes rec.†	Votes cast‡	% of vote	Teams as player
Leonard, Buck	P	1972	SCNL	—	—	Negro Leagues
Lindstrom, Fred	P	1976	CV	—	—	New York NL, Pittsburgh NL, Chicago NL, Brooklyn NL
Lloyd, John Henry	P	1977	SCNL	—	—	Negro Leagues
Lombardi, Ernie	P	1986	CV	—	—	Brooklyn NL, Cincinnati NL, Boston NL, New York NL
Lopez, Al	M	1977	CV	—	—	Brooklyn NL, Boston NL, Pittsburgh NL, Cleveland AL
Lyons, Ted	P	1955	217	251	86.5	Chicago AL
Mack, Connie	M	1937	CC	—	—	Washington NL, Buffalo PL, Pittsburgh NL
MacPhail, Larry	E	1978	CV	—	—	
MacPhail, Lee	E	1998	CV	—	—	
Mantle, Mickey	P	1974	322	365	88.2	New York AL
Manush, Heinie	P	1964	CV	—	—	Detroit AL, St. Louis AL, Washington AL, Boston AL, Brooklyn NL, Pittsburgh NL
Maranville, Rabbit	P	1954	209	252	82.9	Boston NL, Pittsburgh NL, Chicago NL, Brooklyn NL, St. Louis NL
Marichal, Juan	P	1983	313	374	83.7	San Francisco NL, Boston AL, Los Angeles NL
Marquard, Rube	P	1971	CV	—	—	New York NL, Brooklyn NL, Cincinnati NL, Boston NL
Mathews, Eddie	P	1978	301	379	79.4	Boston NL, Milwaukee NL, Atlanta NL, Houston NL, Detroit AL
Mathewson, Christy	P	1936	205	226	90.7	New York NL, Cincinnati NL
Mays, Willie	P	1979	409	432	94.7	New York (Giants) NL, San Francisco NL, New York (Mets) NL
Mazeroski, Bill	P	2001	CV	—	—	Pittsburgh NL
McCarthy, Joe	M	1957	CV	—	—	
McCarthy, Tommy	P	1946	C2	—	—	Boston UA, Boston NL, Philadelphia NL, St. Louis AA, Brooklyn NL
McCovey, Willie	P	1986	346	425	81.4	San Francisco NL, San Diego NL, Oakland AL
McGinnity, Joe	P	1946	C2	—	—	Baltimore NL, Brooklyn NL, Baltimore AL, New York NL
McGowan, Bill	U	1992	CV	—	—	
McGraw, John	M	1937	CC	—	—	Baltimore AA, Baltimore NL, St. Louis NL, Baltimore NL, New York NL
McKechnie, Bill	M	1962	CV	—	—	Pittsburgh NL, Boston NL, New York AL, New York NL, Cincinnati NL
McPhee, Bid	P	2000	CV	—	—	Cincinnati AA, Cincinnati NL
Medwick, Joe	P	1968	240	283	84.8	St. Louis NL, Brooklyn NL, New York NL, Boston NL
Mize, Johnny	P	1981	CV	—	—	St. Louis NL, New York NL, New York AL
Molitor, Paul	P	2004	431	506	85.2	Milwaukee AL, Toronto AL, Minnesota AL
Morgan, Joe	P	1990	363	444	81.8	Houston NL, Cincinnati NL, San Francisco NL, Philadelphia NL, Oakland AL
Murray, Eddie	P	2003	423	496	85.3	Baltimore AL, Los Angeles NL, New York NL, Cleveland AL, Anaheim AL
Musial, Stan	P	1969	317	340	93.2	St. Louis NL
Newhouser, Hal	P	1992	CV	—	—	Detroit AL, Cleveland AL
Nichols, Kid	P	1949	C2	—	—	Boston NL, St. Louis NL, Philadelphia NL
Niekro, Phil	P	1997	380	473	80.3	Milwaukee NL, Atlanta NL, New York AL, Cleveland AL, Toronto AL
O'Rourke, Jim	P	1945	C2	—	—	Boston NL, Providence NL, Buffalo NL, New York NL, New York PL, Washington NL
Ott, Mel	P	1951	197	226	87.2	New York NL
Paige, Satchel	P	1971	SCNL	—	—	Cleveland AL, St. Louis AL, Kansas City AL, Negro Leagues
Palmer, Jim	P	1990	411	444	92.6	Baltimore AL
Pennock, Herb	P	1948	94	121	77.7	Philadelphia AL, Boston AL, New York AL
Perez, Tony	P	2000	385	499	77.2	Cincinnati NL, Montreal NL, Boston AL, Philadelphia NL
Perry, Gaylord	P	1991	342	443	77.2	San Francisco NL, Cleveland AL, Texas AL, San Diego NL, New York AL, Atlanta NL, Seattle AL, Kansas City AL
Plank, Eddie	P	1946	C2	—	—	Philadelphia AL, St. Louis AL
Puckett, Kirby	P	2001	423	515	82.1	Minnesota AL
Radbourn, Old Hoss	P	1939	C1	—	—	Buffalo NL, Providence NL, Boston NL, Boston PL, Cincinnati NL
Reese, Pee Wee	P	1984	CV	—	—	Brooklyn NL, Los Angeles NL
Rice, Sam	P	1963	CV	—	—	Washington AL, Cleveland AL
Rickey, Branch	E	1967	CV	—	—	St. Louis AL, New York AL
Rixey, Eppa	P	1963	CV	—	—	Philadelphia NL, Cincinnati NL
Rizzuto, Phil	P	1994	CV	—	—	New York AL
Roberts, Robin	P	1976	337	388	86.9	Philadelphia NL, Baltimore AL, Houston NL, Chicago NL
Robinson, Brooks	P	1983	344	374	92.0	Baltimore AL
Robinson, Frank	P	1982	370	415	89.2	Cincinnati NL, Baltimore AL, Los Angeles NL, California NL, Cleveland AL
Robinson, Jackie	P	1962	124	160	77.5	Brooklyn NL
Robinson, Wilbert	M	1945	C2	—	—	Philadelphia AA, Baltimore AA, Baltimore NL, St. Louis NL, Baltimore AL
Rogan, Bullet Joe	P	1998	CV	—	—	Negro Leagues
Roush, Edd	P	1962	CV	—	—	Chicago AL, New York NL, Cincinnati NL
Ruffing, Red	P	1967	266	306	86.9	Boston AL, New York AL, Chicago AL
Rusie, Amos	P	1977	CV	—	—	Indianapolis NL, New York NL, Cincinnati NL
Ruth, Babe	P	1936	215	226	95.1	Boston AL, New York AL, Boston NL

Name	Des.*	Elec. year	Votes rec.†	Votes cast‡	% of vote	Teams as player
Ryan, Nolan	P	1999	491	497	98.8	New York NL, California AL, Houston NL, Texas AL
Sandberg, Ryne	P	2005	393	516	76.2	Philadelphia NL, Chicago NL
Schalk, Ray	P	1955	CV	—	—	Chicago AL, New York NL
Schmidt, Mike	P	1995	444	460	96.5	Philadelphia NL
Schoendienst, Red	P	1989	CV	—	—	St. Louis NL, New York (Giants) NL, Milwaukee NL
Seaver, Tom	P	1992	425	430	98.8	New York NL, Cincinnati NL, Chicago AL, Boston AL
Selee, Frank	M	1999	CV	—	—	
Sewell, Joe	P	1977	CV	—	—	Cleveland AL, New York AL
Simmons, Al	P	1953	199	264	75.4	Philadelphia AL, Chicago AL, Detroit AL, Washington AL, Boston NL, Cincinnati NL, Boston AL
Sisler, George	P	1939	235	274	85.8	St. Louis AL, Washington AL, Boston NL
Slaughter, Enos	P	1985	CV	—	—	St. Louis NL, New York AL, Kansas City AL, Milwaukee NL
Smith, Hilton	P	2001	CV	—	—	Negro Leagues
Smith, Ozzie	P	2002	433	472	91.7	San Diego NL, St. Louis NL
Snider, Duke	P	1980	333	385	86.5	Brooklyn NL, Los Angeles NL, New York NL, San Francisco NL
Spahn, Warren	P	1973	316	380	83.2	Boston NL, Milwaukee NL, New York NL, San Francisco NL
Spalding, Al	P	1939	C1	—	—	Chicago NL
Speaker, Tris	P	1937	165	201	82.1	Boston AL, Cleveland AL, Washington AL, Philadelphia AL
Stargell, Willie	P	1988	352	427	82.4	Pittsburgh NL
Stearnes, Turkey	P	2000	CV	—	—	Negro Leagues
Stengel, Casey	M	1966	CV	—	—	Brooklyn NL, Pittsburgh NL, Philadelphia NL, New York NL, Boston NL
Sutter, Bruce	P	2006	400	520	76.9	Chicago NL, St. Louis NL, Atlanta NL
Sutton, Don	P	1998	386	473	81.6	Los Angeles NL, Houston NL, Milwaukee AL, Oakland AL, California AL
Terry, Bill	P	1954	195	252	77.4	New York NL
Thompson, Sam	P	1974	CV	—	—	Detroit NL, Philadelphia NL, Detroit AL
Tinker, Joe	P	1946	C2	—	—	Chicago NL, Cincinnati NL
Traynor, Pie	P	1948	93	121	76.9	Pittsburgh NL
Vance, Dazzy	P	1955	205	251	81.7	Pittsburgh NL, New York AL, Brooklyn NL, St. Louis NL, Cincinnati NL
Vaughan, Arky	P	1985	CV	—	—	Pittsburgh NL, Brooklyn NL
Veeck, Bill	E	1991	CV	—	—	
Waddell, Rube	P	1946	C2	—	—	Louisville NL, Pittsburgh NL, Chicago NL, Philadelphia AL, St. Louis AL
Wagner, Honus	P	1936	215	226	95.1	Louisville NL, Pittsburgh NL
Wallace, Bobby	P	1953	CV	—	—	Cleveland NL, St. Louis NL, St. Louis AL
Walsh, Ed	P	1946	C2	—	—	Chicago AL, Boston NL
Waner, Lloyd	P	1967	CV	—	—	Pittsburgh NL, Boston NL, Cincinnati NL, Philadelphia NL, Brooklyn NL
Waner, Paul	P	1952	195	234	83.3	Pittsburgh NL, Brooklyn NL, Boston NL, New York AL
Ward, Monte	P	1964	CV	—	—	Providence NL, New York NL, Brooklyn PL, Brooklyn NL
Weaver, Earl	M	1996	CV	—	—	
Weiss, George	E	1971	CV	—	—	
Welch, Mickey	P	1973	CV	—	—	Troy NL, New York NL
Wells, Willie	P	1997	CV	—	—	Negro Leagues
Wheat, Zack	P	1959	CV	—	—	Brooklyn NL, Philadelphia AL
Wilhelm, Hoyt	P	1985	331	395	83.8	New York NL, St. Louis NL, Cleveland AL, Baltimore AL, Chicago AL, California AL, Atlanta NL, Chicago NL, Los Angeles NL
Williams, Billy	P	1987	354	413	85.7	Chicago NL, Oakland AL
Williams, Smokey Joe	P	1999	CV	—	—	Negro Leagues
Williams, Ted	P	1966	282	302	93.4	Boston AL
Willis, Vic	P	1995	CV	—	—	Boston NL, Pittsburgh NL, St. Louis NL
Wilson, Hack	P	1979	CV	—	—	New York NL, Chicago NL, Brooklyn NL, Philadelphia NL
Winfield, Dave	P	2001	435	515	84.5	San Diego NL, New York AL, California AL, Toronto AL, Minnesota AL, Cleveland AL
Wright, George	P	1937	CC	—	—	Boston NL, Providence NL
Wright, Harry	M	1953	CV	—	—	Boston NL
Wynn, Early	P	1972	301	396	76.0	Washington AL, Cleveland AL, Chicago AL
Yastrzemski, Carl	P	1989	423	447	94.6	Boston AL
Yawkey, Tom	E	1980	CV	—	—	
Young, Cy	P	1937	153	201	76.1	Cleveland NL, St. Louis NL, Boston AL, Cleveland AL, Boston NL
Youngs, Ross	P	1972	CV	—	—	New York NL
Yount, Robin	P	1999	385	497	77.5	Milwaukee AL

*Designation for which he was honored. Abbreviations: E—executive; F—founder; M—manager; O—organizer; P—player; U—umpire.
†Where an abbreviation is listed rather than a vote total, the enshrinee was selected by one of the following groups: Centennial Commission (CC), committee of old-time players and writers (C1), committee on old-timers (C2), Committee on Veterans (CV), special election by Baseball Writers' Association of America (SE) or Special Committee on Negro Leagues (SCNL).
‡Votes cast by eligible members of the Baseball Writers' Association of America.
League abbreviations: AA—American Association; AL—American League; NL—National League; PL—Players League; UA—Union Association.

Minor Leagues

2006 BASEBALL GUIDE

2006 FARM SYSTEMS

AMERICAN LEAGUE

BALTIMORE (7): AAA—Ottawa. AA—Bowie. A—Frederick, Delmarva, Aberdeen. Rookie—Bluefield, Gulf Coast Orioles.
BOSTON (6): AAA—Pawtucket. AA—Portland (Maine). A—Wilmington, Greenville, Lowell. Rookie—Gulf Coast Red Sox.
CHICAGO (6): AAA—Charlotte. AA—Birmingham. A—Winston-Salem, Kannapolis. Rookie—Bristol, Great Falls.
CLEVELAND (6): AAA—Buffalo. AA—Akron. A—Kinston, Lake County, Mahoning Valley. Rookie—Burlington (N.C.).
DETROIT (6): AAA—Toledo. AA—Erie. A—Lakeland, West Michigan, Oneonta. Rookie—Gulf Coast Tigers.
KANSAS CITY (6): AAA—Omaha. AA—Wichita. A—High Desert, Burlington (Iowa). Rookie—Idaho Falls, Arizona Royals.
LOS ANGELES (6): AAA—Salt Lake. AA—Arkansas. A—Rancho Cucamonga, Cedar Rapids. Rookie—Orem, Arizona Angels.
MINNESOTA (6): AAA—Rochester. AA—New Britain. A—Fort Myers, Beloit. Rookie—Elizabethton, Gulf Coast Twins.
NEW YORK (6): AAA—Columbus (Ohio). AA—Trenton. A—Tampa, Charleston (S.C.), Staten Island. Rookie—Gulf Coast Yankees.
OAKLAND (6): AAA—Sacramento. AA—Midland. A—Stockton, Kane County, Vancouver. Rookie—Arizona A's.
SEATTLE (6): AAA—Tacoma. AA—San Antonio. A—Inland Empire, Wisconsin, Everett. Rookie—Arizona Mariners.
TAMPA BAY (6): AAA—Durham. AA—Montgomery. A—Visalia, Southwest Michigan, Hudson Valley. Rookie—Princeton.
TEXAS (6): AAA—Oklahoma. AA—Frisco. A—Bakersfield, Clinton, Spokane. Rookie—Arizona Rangers.
TORONTO (6): AAA—Syracuse. AA—New Hampshire. A—Dunedin, Lansing, Auburn. Rookie—Pulaski.

NATIONAL LEAGUE

ARIZONA (6): AAA—Tucson. AA—Tennessee. A—Lancaster, South Bend, Yakima. Rookie—Missoula.
ATLANTA (6): AAA—Richmond. AA—Mississippi. A—Myrtle Beach, Rome. Rookie—Danville, Gulf Coast Braves.
CHICAGO (6): AAA—Iowa. AA—West Tenn. A—Daytona, Peoria (Ill.), Boise. Rookie—Mesa Cubs.
CINCINNATI (6): AAA—Louisville. AA—Chattanooga. A—Sarasota, Dayton. Rookie—Billings, Gulf Coast Reds.
COLORADO (6): AAA—Colorado Springs. AA—Tulsa. A—Modesto, Asheville, Tri-City (Wash.). Rookie—Casper.
FLORIDA (6): AAA—Albuquerque. AA—Carolina. A—Jupiter, Greensboro, Jamestown. Rookie—Gulf Coast Marlins.
HOUSTON (6): AAA—Round Rock. AA—Corpus Christi. A—Salem, Lexington, Tri-City (N.Y.). Rookie—Greeneville.
LOS ANGELES (6): AAA—Las Vegas. AA—Jacksonville. A—Vero Beach, Columbus (Ga.). Rookie—Ogden, Gulf Coast Dodgers.
MILWAUKEE (6): AAA—Nashville. AA—Huntsville. A—Brevard County, West Virginia. Rookie—Helena, Arizona Brewers.
NEW YORK (6): AAA—Norfolk. AA—Binghamton. A—St. Lucie, Hagerstown, Brooklyn. Rookie—Kingsport, Gulf Coast Mets.
PHILADELPHIA (6): AAA—Scranton/Wilkes-Barre. AA—Reading. A—Clearwater, Lakewood, Batavia. Rookie—Gulf Coast Phillies.
PITTSBURGH (6): AAA—Indianapolis. AA—Altoona. A—Lynchburg, Hickory, Williamsport. Rookie—Gulf Coast Pirates.
ST. LOUIS (6): AAA—Memphis. AA—Springfield. A—Palm Beach, Quad Cities, State College. Rookie—Johnson City.
SAN DIEGO (6): AAA—Portland (Ore.). AA—Mobile. A—Lake Elsinore, Fort Wayne, Eugene. Rookie—Arizona Padres.
SAN FRANCISCO (6): AAA—Fresno. AA—Connecticut. A—San Jose, Augusta, Salem-Keizer. Rookie—Arizona Giants.
WASHINGTON (6): AAA—New Orleans. AA—Harrisburg. A—Potomac, Savannah, Vermont. Rookie—Gulf Coast Nationals.

INTERNATIONAL LEAGUE

LEAGUE OFFICE

President
Randy Mobley

Address
55 S. High St., Suite 202
Dublin, OH 43017

Phone
614-791-9300

TEAMS

BUFFALO BISONS

General manager
Mike Buczkowski
Manager
Torey Lovullo
Ballpark (capacity, surface)
Dunn Tire Park (18,025, grass)
Affiliation
Indians
Address
275 Washington St.
Buffalo, NY 14203
Phone
716-846-2000

CHARLOTTE KNIGHTS

General manager
Dan Rajkowski
Manager
Razor Shines
Ballpark (capacity, surface)
Knights Stadium (10,002, grass)
Affiliation
White Sox
Address
2280 Deerfield Drive
Fort Mill, SC 29715
Phone
704-357-8071

COLUMBUS CLIPPERS

General manager/president
Ken Schnacke
Manager
Dave Miley
Ballpark (capacity, surface)
Cooper Stadium (15,000, grass)
Affiliation
Yankees
Address
1155 W. Mound St.
Columbus, OH 43223
Phone
614-462-5250

DURHAM BULLS

General manager
Mike Birling
Manager
John Tamargo
Ballpark (capacity, surface)
Durham Bulls Athletic Park
(10,000, grass)
Affiliation
Devil Rays
Address
409 Blackwell St.
Durham, NC 27701
Phone
919-687-6500

INDIANAPOLIS INDIANS

General manager
Cal Burleson
Manager
Trent Jewett
Ballpark (capacity, surface)
Victory Field (15,500, grass)
Affiliation
Pirates
Address
501 W. Maryland St.
Indianapolis, IN 46225
Phone
317-269-3542

LOUISVILLE BATS

President
Gary Ulmer
Manager
Rick Sweet
Ballpark (capacity, surface)
Louisville Slugger Field (13,131, grass)
Affiliation
Reds
Address
401 E. Main Street
Louisville, KY 40202
Phone
502-212-2287

NORFOLK TIDES

General manager
Dave Rosenfield
Manager
Ken Oberkfell
Ballpark (capacity, surface)
Harbor Park (12,067, grass)
Affiliation
Mets
Address
150 Park Ave.
Norfolk, VA 23510
Phone
757-622-2222

OTTAWA LYNX

General manager
Kyle Bostwick
Manager
Dave Trembley
Ballpark (capacity, surface)
Lynx Stadium (10,332, grass)
Affiliation
Orioles
Address
300 Coventry Rd.
Ottawa, Ontario K1K 4P5
Phone
613-747-5969

PAWTUCKET RED SOX

President
Mike Tamburro
Manager
Ron Johnson
Ballpark (capacity, surface)
McCoy Stadium (10,031, grass)
Affiliation
Red Sox
Address
P.O. Box 2365
Pawtucket, RI 02861
Phone
401-724-7303

RICHMOND BRAVES

General manager
Bruce Baldwin
Manager
Brian Snitker
Ballpark (capacity, surface)
The Diamond (12,134, grass)
Affiliation
Braves
Address
P.O. Box 6667
Richmond, VA 23230
Phone
804-359-4444

ROCHESTER RED WINGS

General manager
Dan Mason
Manager
Stan Cliburn
Ballpark (capacity, surface)
Frontier Field (10,840, grass)
Affiliation
Twins
Address
1 Morrie Silver Way
Rochester, NY 14608
Phone
585-454-1001

SCRANTON/WILKES-BARRE RED BARONS

General manager
Jeremy Ruby
Manager
John Russell
Ballpark (capacity, surface)
Lackawanna County Multi-Purpose
Stadium (10,982, artificial)
Affiliation
Phillies
Address
P.O. Box 3449
Scranton, PA 18505
Phone
570-969-2255

SYRACUSE SKYCHIEFS

General manager
John Simone
Manager
Mike Basso
Ballpark (capacity, surface)
Alliance Bank Stadium (11,071, artificial)
Affiliation
Blue Jays

Address
One Tex Simone Dr.
Syracuse, NY 13208
Phone
315-474-7833

TOLEDO MUD HENS

General manager
Joe Napoli
Manager
Larry Parrish

Ballpark (capacity, surface)
Fifth Third Field (8,943, grass)
Affiliation
Tigers
Address
406 Washington St.
Toledo, OH 43604
Phone
419-725-4367

2005 FINAL STANDINGS

NORTH DIVISION

Team	W	L	T	Pct.	GB
Buffalo Bisons	82	62	-	0.569	...
Pawtucket Red Sox	75	69	-	0.521	7
Rochester Red Wings	75	69	-	0.521	7
Syracuse SkyChiefs	71	73	-	0.493	11
Ottawa Lynx	69	75	-	0.479	13
Scranton-Wilkes Barre Red Barons	69	75	-	0.479	13

SOUTH DIVISION

Team	W	L	T	Pct.	GB
Norfolk Tides	79	65	-	0.549	...
Durham Bulls	65	79	-	0.451	14
Charlotte Knights	57	87	-	0.396	22
Richmond Braves	56	88	-	0.389	23

WEST DIVISION

Team	W	L	T	Pct.	GB
Toledo Mud Hens	89	55	-	0.618	...
Indianapolis Indians	78	66	-	0.542	11
Columbus Clippers	77	67	-	0.535	12
Louisville Bats	66	78	-	0.458	23

COMPOSITE

CLUB (AFFILIATE), ABBREV	TOL	BUF	NOR	IND	COL	PAW	ROC	SYR	OTT	SWB	LOU	DUR	CHA	RIC	W	L	PCT	GB
Toledo (Tigers), TOL	...	3	6	8	12	7	4	5	5	5	10	7	8	9	89	55	.618	-
Buffalo (Indians), BUF	5	...	7	3	4	7	7	9	10	9	7	5	5	4	82	62	.569	7.0
Norfolk (Mets), NOR	6	1	...	7	8	1	5	4	5	3	7	11	10	11	79	65	.549	10.0
Indianapolis (Pirates), IND	8	5	5	...	5	6	4	5	2	5	8	9	8	8	78	66	.542	11.0
Columbus (Yankees), COL	4	4	4	11	...	5	5	4	7	2	8	4	10	9	77	67	.535	12.0
Pawtucket (Red Sox), PAW	1	9	7	2	3	...	9	8	9	11	4	5	1	6	75	69	.521	14.0
Rochester (Twins), ROC	4	9	3	4	3	7	...	8	9	10	4	4	4	6	75	69	.521	14.0
Syracuse (Blue Jays), SYR	3	7	4	3	4	8	8	...	11	6	3	2	6	6	71	73	.493	18.0
Ottawa (Orioles), OTT	3	6	3	6	1	7	7	5	...	11	4	5	6	5	69	75	.479	20.0
Scranton/WB (Phillies), SWB	3	7	5	3	6	5	6	10	5	...	5	3	6	5	69	75	.479	20.0
Louisville (Reds), LOU	6	1	5	8	4	4	4	5	4	3	...	7	7	4	66	78	.458	23.0
Durham (Devil Rays), DUR	5	3	5	3	8	3	4	6	3	5	5	...	8	7	65	79	.451	24.0
Charlotte (White Sox), CHA	4	3	6	4	2	7	4	2	2	5	8	4	...	8	57	87	.396	32.0
Richmond (Braves), RIC	3	4	5	4	3	2	2	3	3	8	9	8	8	...	56	88	.389	33.0

Major league affiliations in parentheses.

PLAYOFFS: Semifinals: Toledo defeated Norfolk, three games to two, and Indianapolis defeated Buffalo, three games to two. Finals: Toledo defeated Indianapolis, three games to none.

REGULAR-SEASON ATTENDANCE: Durham, 520,371. Louisville, 643,466. Buffalo, 596,758. Richmond, 359,755. Columbus, 500,104. Indianapolis, 558,911. Charlotte, 289,495. Ottawa, 160,544. Toledo, 556,995. Scranton/Wilkes-Barre, 400,726. Pawtucket, 688,421. Rochester, 452,302. Syracuse, 382,492. Norfolk, 502,504. League total, 6,612,844. Postseason (13 games), 60,887.

MANAGERS: Durham, Bill Evers. Louisville, Rick Sweet. Buffalo, Marty Brown. Richmond, Pat Kelly. Columbus, Bucky Dent. Indianapolis, Trent Jewett. Charlotte, Nick Leyva (through July 16) and Manny Trillo, (July 17 through end of season). Ottawa, Dave Trembley. Toledo, Larry Parrish. Scranton/WB, Gene Lamont. Pawtucket, Ron Johnson. Rochester, Phil Roof (through April 19) and Rich Miller (April 20 through end of season). Syracuse, Marty Pevey. Norfolk, Ken Oberkfell.

ALL-STAR TEAM: 1B-Mitch Jones, Columbus. 2B-Bernie Castro, Ottawa. 3B-Edwin Encarnacion, Louisville. SS-B.J. Upton, Durham. OF-Curtis Granderson, Toledo. OF-John-Ford Griffin, Syracuse. OF-Shane Victorino, Scranton/WB. C-Kelly Shoppach, Pawtucket. DH-Brian Daubach, Norfolk. UTIL-Ryan Garko, Buffalo. SP-Zach Duke, Indianapolis. Relief Pitcher-Travis Bowyer, Rochester. Most Valuable Player-Shane Victorino, Scranton/WB. Most Valuable Pitcher-Zach Duke, Indianapolis. Rookie of the Year-Francisco Liriano, Rochester. Manager of the Year-Larry Parrish, Toledo.

2005 BATTING

TEAM

Team	G	TPA	AB	R	H	TB	2B	3B	HR	RBI	SH	SF	HP	BB	IBB	SO	SB	CS	GDP	LOB	ShO	Avg.	OBP	Slg.
Scranton/WB	144	5482	4874	677	1380	2032	265	45	99	634	71	59	68	410	25	824	70	55	135	2144	5	.283	.343	.417
Buffalo	144	5495	4845	805	1347	2239	293	31	179	746	29	48	125	446	20	988	63	44	123	2137	4	.278	.351	.462
Ottawa	144	5376	4880	638	1355	1987	276	28	100	584	52	35	55	349	22	835	132	52	116	2021	7	.278	.331	.407
Indianapolis	144	5543	4907	725	1350	2154	259	37	157	677	53	49	65	468	27	1045	163	65	108	2167	6	.275	.343	.439
Pawtucket	144	5702	4950	788	1352	2195	285	27	168	744	14	60	78	599	23	1011	80	29	126	2411	5	.273	.357	.443
Rochester	144	5419	4826	693	1315	2025	255	19	139	649	52	42	71	428	17	833	57	37	121	2049	5	.272	.338	.420
Durham	144	5625	5027	773	1346	2288	284	32	198	721	26	32	53	486	17	1105	145	49	119	2078	5	.268	.337	.455
Charlotte	144	5474	4896	649	1305	2088	271	16	160	613	57	41	50	430	18	965	40	35	140	2044	10	.267	.330	.426
Columbus	144	5609	4924	700	1313	2073	289	30	137	650	56	44	97	484	22	988	70	37	138	2203	8	.267	.341	.421
Louisville	144	5433	4926	615	1316	2012	297	36	109	576	48	30	60	365	27	1069	98	29	112	2042	7	.267	.323	.408
Norfolk	144	5472	4842	674	1293	2026	270	35	131	628	68	36	34	491	35	987	124	61	108	2124	5	.267	.336	.418
Toledo	144	5473	4853	697	1285	2107	266	44	156	660	35	42	60	483	26	1095	145	59	89	2076	6	.265	.336	.434
Syracuse	144	5478	4927	697	1283	2061	264	26	154	658	37	38	49	426	23	1019	58	25	104	2044	13	.260	.323	.418
Richmond	144	5386	4780	519	1225	1819	248	32	94	482	60	42	56	448	22	952	106	59	112	2108	15	.256	.325	.381

TOP QUALIFIERS FOR BATTING CHAMPIONSHIP

Minimum 389 plate appearances. *Lefthanded batter. †Switch-hitter.

Player, Team	G	TPA	AB	R	H	TB	2B	3B	HR	RBI	SH	SF	HP	BB	IBB	SO	SB	CS	GDP	Avg.	OBP	Slg.
Sandoval, Danny, Scranton/Wilkes-Barre †	104	438	390	53	129	170	20	0	7	48	11	4	2	31	6	49	11	11	16	.331	.379	.436
Daubach, Brian, Norfolk *	99	412	345	63	112	191	29	1	16	62	1	3	1	62	8	68	1	2	6	.325	.426	.554
Castro, Bernie, Ottawa †	126	559	502	81	158	192	21	5	1	36	9	6	0	42	3	50	41	6	5	.315	.364	.382
Rushford, Jim, Scranton/Wilkes-Barre *	117	467	414	61	129	190	29	1	10	63	2	6	11	34	1	40	5	1	11	.312	.374	.459
Darula, Robert, Ottawa *	109	443	402	66	125	168	25	6	2	40	2	0	11	28	4	36	17	5	5	.311	.372	.418
Victorino, Shane, Scranton/Wilkes-Barre †	126	559	494	93	153	264	25	16	18	70	5	4	5	51	2	74	17	9	4	.310	.377	.534
Gomez, Alexis, Toledo *	114	460	424	51	130	191	28	6	7	55	3	4	2	27	3	91	21	7	7	.307	.348	.450
Calzado, Napoleon, Ottawa	120	478	447	54	137	194	22	1	11	61	1	3	6	21	0	46	10	6	13	.306	.344	.434
Brown, Roosevelt, Charlotte *	103	445	389	62	119	190	31	2	12	53	2	7	5	42	2	59	3	2	14	.306	.375	.488
Berg, Dave, Pawtucket	112	502	425	73	130	169	28	1	3	60	0	9	4	63	4	67	1	0	13	.306	.393	.398
Barker, Kevin, Syracuse *	91	397	351	58	107	202	24	1	23	87	0	5	3	38	1	89	1	0	4	.305	.373	.575
Garko, Ryan, Buffalo	127	520	452	75	137	225	25	3	19	77	2	4	18	44	2	92	1	3	11	.303	.384	.498
Upton, B.J., Durham	139	632	545	98	165	267	36	6	18	74	1	3	4	78	1	127	44	13	15	.303	.392	.490
Toca, Jorge, Charlotte	115	487	454	56	137	235	24	1	24	77	0	3	6	24	2	87	0	1	11	.302	.343	.518
Machado, Alejandro, Pawtucket	117	427	383	60	115	145	17	2	3	43	4	3	5	32	0	47	21	4	10	.300	.359	.379
Freire, Alejandro, Charlotte	106	442	391	57	117	200	24	1	19	69	0	2	9	40	2	57	1	0	18	.299	.376	.512
McLouth, Nate, Indianapolis *	110	455	397	64	118	159	20	3	5	39	5	7	7	39	1	58	34	8	10	.297	.364	.401
Gross, Gabe, Syracuse *	102	449	390	64	116	171	29	4	6	46	2	3	2	52	3	83	14	2	5	.297	.380	.438
Anderson, Brian N., Charlotte	118	501	448	71	132	210	24	3	16	57	1	4	4	44	0	115	4	2	11	.295	.360	.469
Bergolla, William, Louisville	98	428	400	59	117	156	23	5	2	38	6	2	1	19	0	39	16	3	12	.293	.325	.390
Abad, Andy, Buffalo *	121	474	423	68	124	215	29	1	20	85	0	4	3	44	5	60	3	4	16	.293	.361	.508

DEPARTMENTAL LEADERS: G—Upton, 139. AB—Upton, 545. R—Upton, 98. H—Upton, 165. TB—Upton, 267. 2B—Reese, 38. 3B—Victorino, 16. HR—Griffin, 30. RBI—Griffin, 103. SH—Raines, 20. SF—Berg and Wooten, 9. HP—Kinkade, 30. BB—Upton, 78. IBB—Daubach, 8. SO—Jones, 174. SB—Snead, 46. CS—Pagan and Pena, 15. GIDP—Coste, 25. OBP—Daubach, .426. Slg.—Barker, .575.

ALL PLAYERS

*Lefthanded batter. †Switch-hitter.

Player, Team	G	TPA	AB	R	H	TB	2B	3B	HR	RBI	SH	SF	HP	BB	IBB	SO	SB	CS	GDP	Avg.	OBP	Slg.
Abad, Andy, Buffalo *	121	474	423	68	124	215	29	1	20	85	0	4	3	44	5	60	3	4	16	.293	.361	.508
Abernathy, Brent, Rochester	57	249	215	35	70	101	13	0	6	25	7	3	3	21	0	20	7	3	7	.326	.388	.470
Aceves, Jonathan, Charlotte	16	60	54	8	11	20	4	1	1	2	1	0	0	5	0	18	0	0	4	.204	.271	.370
Adams, Terry, Scranton/Wilkes-Barre	5	0	0	0	0	0	0	0	0	0	0	0	0	0	...	0	0	0	0	...	...	...
Alfaro, Jason, Syracuse	105	407	381	42	94	150	24	1	10	45	3	2	3	18	0	63	0	1	13	.247	.285	.394
Almonte, Hector, Richmond	10	2	2	0	0	0	0	0	0	0	0	0	0	0	0	2	0	0	0	.000	.000	.000
Alvarez, Tony, Charlotte	5	19	19	1	4	5	1	0	0	2	0	0	0	0	0	2	0	1	0	.211	.211	.263
Ambres, Chip, Pawtucket	84	332	279	47	82	138	20	3	10	50	0	2	4	47	2	64	19	5	8	.294	.401	.495
Amezaga, Alfredo, Indianapolis †	64	211	185	28	63	82	12	2	1	12	5	2	2	17	1	27	14	7	1	.341	.398	.443
Anderson, Brian N., Charlotte	118	501	448	71	132	210	24	3	16	57	1	4	4	44	0	115	4	2	11	.295	.360	.469
Anderson, Drew, Louisville †	13	40	39	4	6	10	2	1	0	1	1	0	0	0	0	13	0	0	0	.154	.154	.256
Arteaga, Joshua, Richmond	13	43	43	3	11	14	3	0	0	4	0	0	0	0	0	13	0	0	1	.256	.256	.326
Asadoorian, Eric, Louisville	33	116	109	10	23	35	5	2	1	7	2	0	1	4	1	29	6	0	2	.211	.246	.321
Aurilia, Rich, Louisville	1	5	3	2	1	2	1	0	0	1	0	0	0	2	0	1	0	0	0	.333	.600	.667
Aybar, Manny, Norfolk	10	1	1	0	0	0	0	0	0	0	0	0	0	0	0	1	0	0	0	.000	.000	.000
Bacani, David, Norfolk	9	28	24	1	3	4	1	0	0	5	0	0	2	2	0	2	1	1	1	.125	.250	.167
Bacsik, Mike, Scranton/Wilkes-Barre *	9	16	15	1	3	3	0	0	0	0	0	0	0	1	0	4	0	0	0	.200	.250	.200
Badeaux, Brooks, Durham †	63	250	229	28	54	78	13	1	3	20	5	3	1	12	0	41	1	0	2	.236	.273	.341
Bailey, Jeffrey, Pawtucket	31	104	95	15	24	47	5	0	6	12	0	0	1	8	0	26	1	0	3	.253	.317	.495
Bajenaru, Jeff, Charlotte	1	0	0	0	0	0	0	0	0	0	0	0	0	0	...	0	0	0	0	...	...	...
Bannister, Brian, Norfolk	1	2	2	0	0	0	0	0	0	0	0	0	0	0	0	1	0	0	0	.000	.000	.000
Bannon, Jeff, Louisville	41	180	174	20	49	77	14	1	4	18	1	1	2	2	1	41	2	0	2	.282	.296	.443
Barker, Kevin, Syracuse *	91	397	351	58	107	202	24	1	23	87	0	5	3	38	1	89	1	0	4	.305	.373	.575
Barkett, Andy, Richmond *	37	138	118	9	24	34	7	0	1	12	0	1	1	18	2	25	0	0	1	.203	.312	.288
Barnes, John, Richmond	90	348	318	30	88	115	18	0	3	29	1	2	6	21	2	25	1	1	11	.277	.331	.362
Barry, Kevin, Richmond	8	6	4	0	0	0	0	0	0	0	1	0	0	1	0	1	0	0	0	.000	.200	.000
Bartlett, Jason, Rochester	61	269	229	41	76	105	10	2	5	33	0	7	4	29	0	34	2	2	3	.332	.405	.459
Basak, Christopher, Norfolk	93	326	279	52	76	125	17	4	8	41	9	5	3	30	1	54	17	3	3	.272	.344	.448
Basner, Ryan, Richmond	2	0	0	0	0	0	0	0	0	0	0	0	0	0	0	0	0	0	0	...	...	...
Bautista, Jose, Indianapolis	13	55	51	6	13	19	3	0	1	4	0	0	0	4	0	10	1	1	2	.255	.309	.373
Becker, Brian, Charlotte	7	19	19	3	3	11	0	1	2	2	0	0	0	0	0	8	0	0	0	.158	.158	.579
Bell, Heath, Norfolk	6	1	1	0	1	1	0	0	0	0	0	0	0	0	0	0	0	0	0	1.000	1.000	1.000
Bell, Rick, Louisville	17	51	45	3	8	9	1	0	0	5	1	2	1	2	0	7	0	0	3	.178	.220	.200
Bellhorn, Mark, Pawtucket †	16	74	68	9	12	22	4	0	2	9	0	0	2	4	0	24	0	0	1	.176	.243	.324
Berg, Dave, Pawtucket	112	502	425	73	130	169	28	1	3	60	0	9	4	63	4	67	1	0	13	.306	.393	.398
Bergolla, William, Louisville	98	428	400	59	117	156	23	5	2	38	6	2	1	19	0	39	16	3	12	.293	.325	.390
Bernard, Miguel, Richmond	2	7	7	0	1	2	1	0	0	1	0	0	0	0	0	1	0	0	1	.143	.143	.286
Bernero, Adam, Richmond	3	6	4	1	2	3	1	0	0	0	2	0	0	0	0	2	0	0	0	.500	.500	.750
Bigbie, Larry, Ottawa *	4	17	17	3	5	10	2	0	1	2	0	0	0	0	0	6	0	0	1	.294	.294	.588
Bikowski, Scott, Charlotte *	94	333	296	36	70	98	18	2	2	26	4	1	2	30	0	67	3	5	5	.236	.310	.331
Booker, Chris, Louisville	22	0	0	0	0	0	0	0	0	0	0	0	0	0	0	0	0	0	0	...	...	...
Borchard, Joe, Charlotte †	134	550	494	69	130	237	20	0	29	67	1	1	4	50	4	143	6	4	19	.263	.335	.480
Boscan, Jean, Richmond	72	248	212	17	47	62	6	0	3	20	5	2	4	25	1	59	1	2	8	.222	.313	.292
Bourgeois, Jason, Richmond	119	428	388	33	93	123	20	2	2	16	3	2	4	31	1	57	8	5	3	.240	.301	.317
Bowen, Rob, Rochester †	87	303	262	38	70	105	13	2	6	25	0	0	4	37	2	68	0	2	7	.267	.366	.401
Bradley, Bobby, Indianapolis	4	1	1	0	0	0	0	0	0	0	0	0	0	0	0	1	0	0	0	.000	.000	.000

Player, Team	G	TPA	AB	R	H	TB	2B	3B	HR	RBI	SH	SF	HP	BB	IBB	SO	SB	CS	GDP	Avg.	OBP	Slg.
Brazell, Craig, Norfolk *	52	187	173	22	43	76	11	2	6	28	1	0	0	13	3	32	2	0	6	.249	.301	.439
Brito, Eude, Scranton/Wilkes-Barre *	7	3	3	0	0	0	0	0	0	0	0	0	0	0	0	1	0	0	0	.000	.000	.000
Brooks, Frank, Richmond *	16	1	1	0	0	0	0	0	0	0	0	0	0	0	0	1	0	0	0	.000	.000	.000
Brower, Jim, Richmond	2	0	0	0	0	0	0	0	0	0	0	...	0	0	0	0	0	0	0	...	...	...
Brown, Roosevelt, Charlotte *	103	445	389	62	119	190	31	2	12	53	2	7	5	42	2	59	3	2	14	.306	.375	.488
Buchanan, Brian, Rochester	29	121	114	17	36	55	7	0	4	16	0	0	0	7	0	31	0	1	2	.316	.355	.482
Buckley, James, Pawtucket	15	46	38	7	6	7	1	0	0	5	1	0	0	7	0	18	0	0	1	.158	.289	.184
Budzinski, Mark, Scranton/Wilkes-Barre *	124	519	467	72	126	183	26	8	5	42	6	1	3	42	2	108	9	4	4	.270	.333	.392
Bullinger, Kirk, Indianapolis	24	1	1	0	0	0	0	0	0	0	0	0	0	0	0	1	0	0	0	.000	.000	.000
Bullington, Bryan, Indianapolis	9	22	17	1	3	4	1	0	0	0	3	0	0	2	0	4	0	0	0	.176	.263	.235
Burke, Erick, Scranton/Wilkes-Barre *	3	0	0	0	0	0	0	0	0	0	0	0	0	0	0	0	0	0	0	...	...	...
Burke, Jamie, Charlotte	102	414	358	50	95	149	22	1	10	53	3	4	13	36	0	53	1	3	12	.265	.350	.416
Burrus, Josh, Richmond	5	22	19	1	6	8	2	0	0	0	0	0	1	2	0	5	2	0	0	.316	.409	.421
Byrd, Marlon, Scranton/Wilkes-Barre *	5	19	19	4	7	17	1	0	3	5	0	0	0	0	0	3	0	0	0	.368	.368	.895
Cabrera, Melky, Columbus †	26	112	101	15	25	37	3	0	3	17	2	0	0	9	0	15	2	0	3	.248	.309	.366
Calloway, Ron, Norfolk *	110	443	392	56	103	158	25	0	10	44	5	2	2	42	1	81	14	6	9	.263	.336	.403
Calzado, Napoleon, Ottawa	120	478	447	54	137	194	22	1	11	61	1	3	6	21	0	46	10	6	13	.306	.344	.434
Cameron, Mike, Norfolk	2	10	7	2	2	4	0	1	0	2	0	0	0	3	0	3	0	0	0	.286	.500	.571
Cannizaro, Andrew, Columbus	56	202	170	22	43	60	10	2	1	18	6	0	9	17	0	11	1	1	11	.253	.352	.353
Cano, Robinson, Columbus *	24	114	108	19	36	62	8	3	4	24	0	0	0	6	3	13	0	0	2	.333	.368	.574
Cardona, Javier, Buffalo	16	57	50	5	17	24	4	0	1	7	4	0	0	3	0	10	0	0	2	.340	.377	.480
Casanova, Raul, Charlotte †	70	255	233	25	62	114	13	0	13	42	0	1	1	20	2	29	0	0	13	.266	.325	.489
Cash, Kevin, Durham	42	165	147	25	43	80	10	0	9	27	1	2	3	12	0	42	0	0	3	.293	.354	.544
Castellano, John, Scranton/Wilkes-Barre *	90	335	299	44	81	115	16	0	6	45	0	6	3	27	1	41	3	2	14	.271	.331	.385
Castillo, Jose, Indianapolis *	4	15	13	2	5	12	1	0	2	2	0	0	0	2	0	1	0	0	0	.385	.467	.923
Castro, Bernie, Ottawa †	126	559	502	81	158	192	21	5	1	36	9	6	0	42	3	50	41	6	5	.315	.364	.382
Chantres, Carlos, Scranton/Wilkes-Barre	1	2	2	0	0	0	0	0	0	0	0	0	0	0	0	2	0	0	0	.000	.000	.000
Chiaffredo, Paul, Indianapolis	56	144	135	18	28	57	8	0	7	21	5	0	0	4	0	45	2	0	5	.207	.230	.422
Chiavacci, Ronald, Indianapolis *	4	0	0	0	0	0	0	0	0	0	0	0	...	0	0	0	0	0	0	...	...	...
Childers, Jason, Richmond	10	0	0	0	0	0	0	0	0	0	0	0	0	0	0	0	0	0	0	...	...	...
Childers, Matt, Richmond	16	1	1	0	0	0	0	0	0	0	0	0	0	0	0	1	0	0	0	.000	.000	.000
Childress, Daylan, Louisville	3	1	1	0	0	0	0	0	0	0	0	0	0	0	0	1	0	0	0	.000	.000	.000
Christian, Justin, Columbus	1	0	0	0	0	0	0	0	0	0	0	0	0	0	0	0	0	0	0	...	...	...
Cliffords, Benjamin, Ottawa *	9	28	21	3	4	7	1	1	0	2	1	0	0	6	0	5	0	0	0	.190	.370	.333
Coffey, Todd, Louisville	1	0	0	0	0	0	0	0	0	0	0	0	0	0	0	0	0	0	0	...	...	...
Colon, Roman, Richmond	1	2	2	0	0	0	0	0	0	0	0	0	0	0	0	0	0	0	0	.000	.000	.000
Colyer, Steve, Norfolk *	9	0	0	0	0	0	0	0	0	0	0	0	0	0	0	0	0	0	0	...	...	...
Condrey, Clay, Scranton/Wilkes-Barre	5	10	9	0	3	4	1	0	0	1	1	0	0	0	0	2	0	1	0	.333	.333	.444
Connolly, Michael, Indianapolis *	5	9	8	0	0	0	0	0	0	0	0	0	0	1	0	3	0	0	0	.000	.111	.000
Cooper, Jason, Buffalo *	73	285	253	43	65	125	12	3	14	58	1	6	2	23	2	76	1	4	5	.257	.317	.494
Coquillette, Trace, Charlotte	36	119	103	10	28	45	5	0	4	18	6	2	1	7	0	29	0	1	2	.272	.319	.437
Cordero, Wil, Norfolk	8	36	31	3	4	6	2	0	0	2	0	0	0	5	0	11	0	0	1	.129	.250	.194
Corey, Mark, Indianapolis	18	2	2	0	0	0	0	0	0	0	0	0	0	0	0	2	0	0	0	.000	.000	.000
Cortez, Fernando, Durham *	58	255	238	26	54	72	8	2	2	26	3	1	3	10	0	38	13	1	6	.227	.266	.303
Cosme, Caonabo, Columbus	62	244	211	26	56	89	13	1	6	24	2	1	3	23	0	41	5	1	9	.265	.345	.422
Coste, Christopher, Scranton/Wilkes-Barre	134	562	506	73	148	236	26	1	20	89	0	7	9	40	0	85	3	4	25	.292	.351	.466
Cota, Humberto, Indianapolis	3	11	11	0	3	3	0	0	0	1	0	0	0	0	0	3	0	0	2	.273	.273	.273
Cox, Steve, Durham *	19	73	62	7	13	27	5	0	3	9	0	0	0	11	0	18	0	0	0	.210	.329	.435
Crespo, Cesar, Indianapolis †	112	457	399	73	106	163	22	4	9	51	4	2	2	50	1	68	31	9	10	.266	.349	.409
Crosby, Bubba, Columbus *	42	183	160	18	37	58	7	1	4	22	3	2	6	12	0	28	2	1	2	.231	.306	.363
Crozier, Eric, Syracuse-Louisville *	64	248	221	25	50	94	22	2	6	24	0	2	1	24	0	77	4	2	2	.226	.302	.425
Cuddyer, Michael, Rochester	3	12	9	1	1	1	0	0	0	0	0	0	0	3	0	1	2	0	0	.111	.333	.111
Cummings, Midre, Ottawa *	74	309	264	39	75	125	14	0	12	40	0	5	4	36	5	69	0	1	3	.284	.372	.473
Curry, Michael, Durham *	12	60	54	5	12	13	1	0	0	6	1	0	0	5	0	10	3	1	1	.222	.288	.241
Curtis, Daniel, Richmond	8	15	12	0	1	1	0	0	0	1	1	1	0	1	0	3	0	0	0	.083	.143	.083
Daigle, Leo, Charlotte	25	94	91	8	20	31	5	0	2	8	1	0	0	2	0	27	0	0	1	.220	.237	.341
Darula, Robert, Ottawa *	109	443	402	66	125	168	25	6	2	40	2	0	11	28	4	36	17	5	5	.311	.372	.418
Daubach, Brian, Norfolk *	99	412	345	63	112	191	29	1	16	62	1	3	1	62	8	68	1	2	6	.325	.426	.554
Davies, Kyle, Richmond	6	13	12	0	3	3	0	0	0	0	1	0	0	0	0	4	0	0	0	.250	.250	.250
Davis, Ben, Charlotte †	10	35	33	1	8	11	0	0	1	3	0	1	0	1	0	4	0	0	3	.242	.257	.333
Dawkins, Gookie, Toledo	103	399	355	56	86	147	21	5	10	38	3	3	7	31	1	75	10	7	6	.242	.313	.414
Deardorff, Jeff, Durham	96	383	336	50	84	148	13	3	15	41	2	3	0	42	1	82	3	2	8	.250	.331	.440
De Caster, Yurendell, Indianapolis	122	462	415	60	116	188	31	4	11	61	2	2	6	37	1	103	7	5	9	.280	.346	.453
Dehart, James, Richmond *	1	1	1	0	0	0	0	0	0	0	0	0	0	0	0	0	0	0	0	.000	.000	.000
Denorfia, Chris, Louisville	91	374	323	50	100	163	12	6	13	61	3	3	4	41	1	54	8	3	7	.310	.391	.505
DePastino, Joe, Syracuse	55	194	175	22	48	68	11	0	3	22	2	2	0	15	0	36	0	0	7	.274	.328	.389
Diaz, Victor, Norfolk	42	184	170	30	51	92	11	0	10	34	0	0	0	14	1	47	6	2	6	.300	.353	.541
DiFelice, Mike, Norfolk	81	343	300	31	74	133	17	0	14	52	2	0	5	36	2	72	1	2	13	.247	.337	.443
Dominique, Andy, Syracuse	39	136	117	18	28	43	6	0	3	10	2	0	2	15	1	20	0	0	6	.239	.336	.368
Doumit, Ryan, Indianapolis †	51	188	165	41	57	104	11	0	12	35	0	2	5	16	3	36	1	3	3	.345	.415	.630
Dubois, Jason, Buffalo	13	57	53	7	15	30	3	0	4	10	0	0	1	3	0	14	1	1	2	.283	.333	.566
Duenas, Yobal, Columbus	2	7	6	0	0	0	0	0	0	0	1	0	0	0	0	2	0	0	0	.000	.000	.000
Duffy, Chris, Indianapolis *	78	340	308	55	95	143	13	7	7	31	2	4	10	16	1	57	17	9	4	.308	.358	.464
Duke, Zach, Indianapolis *	4	10	9	0	0	0	0	0	0	0	1	0	0	0	0	5	0	0	0	.000	.000	.000
Duncan, Jeff, Norfolk *	3	1	1	2	1	1	0	0	0	0	0	0	0	0	0	0	0	0	0	1.000	1.000	1.000
Dunwoody, Todd, Rochester *	96	323	300	30	74	111	18	2	5	40	2	2	2	17	4	69	6	6	8	.247	.290	.370
Duran, Carlos, Richmond *	6	24	22	3	6	13	1	0	2	4	2	0	0	0	0	6	0	0	0	.273	.273	.591
Eldred, Brad, Indianapolis	54	214	195	31	55	115	13	1	15	48	0	2	3	14	1	57	4	0	3	.282	.336	.590
Ellis, Robert, Scranton/Wilkes-Barre	2	3	3	0	1	1	0	0	0	0	0	0	0	0	0	0	0	1	0	.333	.333	.333
Encarnacion, Edwin, Louisville	78	330	290	44	91	159	23	0	15	54	0	3	4	33	1	53	7	2	8	.314	.388	.548

Player, Team	G	TPA	AB	R	H	TB	2B	3B	HR	RBI	SH	SF	HP	BB	IBB	SO	SB	CS	GDP	Avg.	OBP	Slg.
Enochs, Chris, Indianapolis	10	6	6	0	2	2	0	0	0	0	0	0	0	0	0	0	0	0	0	.333	.333	.333
Escalona, Felix, Columbus	91	368	307	42	84	121	14	1	7	45	10	5	18	28	3	58	5	0	5	.274	.363	.394
Espinosa, David, Toledo †	17	50	41	8	10	12	0	1	0	2	1	0	0	8	0	10	5	2	0	.244	.367	.293
Fasano, Sal, Ottawa	14	49	45	6	12	27	3	0	4	12	0	0	2	2	0	15	0	0	1	.267	.327	.600
Fernandez, Alexander, Louisville *	44	124	120	14	32	50	6	0	4	17	1	0	0	3	0	16	1	1	4	.267	.285	.417
Fernandez, Jared, Louisville-Scranton/Wilkes-Barre	5	12	10	1	1	2	1	0	0	0	1	0	0	1	0	5	0	0	0	.100	.182	.200
Fesh, Sean, Scranton/Wilkes-Barre *	10	0	0	0	0	0	0	0	0	0	0	0	...	0	0	0	0	0	0	...	...	...
Figueroa, Luis, Pawtucket †	109	439	402	58	116	161	22	1	7	48	2	5	1	29	0	28	2	6	10	.289	.334	.400
Finegan, Brian, Buffalo	4	13	12	1	4	4	0	0	0	0	0	0	0	0	0	2	0	0	0	.333	.333	.333
Fleming, Ryan, Scranton/Wilkes-Barre *	3	10	10	0	2	2	0	0	0	0	0	0	0	0	0	1	0	1	0	.200	.200	.200
Floyd, Gavin, Scranton/Wilkes-Barre	6	14	14	0	1	1	0	0	0	0	0	0	0	0	0	6	0	0	1	.071	.071	.071
Foster, John, Richmond *	2	0	0	0	0	0	0	0	0	0	0	0	...	0	0	0	0	0	0	...	...	...
Francisco, Louis, Buffalo	4	18	16	4	8	9	1	0	0	3	0	1	0	1	0	3	1	0	1	.500	.500	.563
Franco, Iker, Richmond	9	34	32	0	8	9	1	0	0	1	0	0	0	2	0	9	0	0	1	.250	.294	.281
Franco, Martire, Scranton/Wilkes-Barre	11	6	5	2	1	1	0	0	0	0	1	0	0	0	0	1	0	0	0	.200	.200	.200
Freire, Alejandro, Ottawa	106	442	391	57	117	200	24	1	19	69	0	2	9	40	2	57	1	0	18	.299	.376	.512
French, Anton, Syracuse *	96	387	350	54	92	152	13	10	9	39	5	5	2	24	3	84	15	3	3	.263	.310	.434
Furmaniak, J.J., Indianapolis	36	147	139	12	40	57	5	3	2	21	1	1	2	4	0	32	5	3	1	.288	.315	.410
Garcia, Danny, Buffalo	2	6	6	0	1	1	0	0	0	0	0	0	0	0	0	2	0	0	0	.167	.167	.167
Garcia, Luis, Norfolk	41	165	151	23	33	66	6	0	9	24	0	0	0	14	0	37	2	0	11	.219	.285	.437
Garko, Ryan, Buffalo	127	520	452	75	137	225	25	3	19	77	2	4	18	44	2	92	1	3	11	.303	.384	.498
Gathright, Joey, Durham *	58	260	226	46	69	92	10	5	1	18	2	1	2	29	0	47	31	8	0	.305	.388	.407
Gautreau, Jacob, Buffalo *	113	477	427	75	108	194	30	1	18	57	2	3	7	38	1	87	2	2	7	.253	.322	.454
Geary, Geoff, Scranton/Wilkes-Barre	3	0	0	0	0	0	0	0	0	0	0	0	...	0	0	0	0	0	0	...	...	...
Germano, Justin, Louisville	4	9	8	0	1	2	1	0	0	0	1	0	0	0	0	4	0	0	0	.125	.125	.250
Gerut, Jody, Buffalo *	12	56	48	12	21	35	5	0	3	8	0	0	2	6	0	7	0	0	2	.438	.518	.729
Gettis, Byron, Toledo	35	117	106	13	20	31	2	0	3	12	0	0	1	10	0	33	1	1	3	.189	.265	.292
Giambi, Jeremy, Charlotte *	4	10	8	0	0	0	0	0	0	0	0	0	0	2	1	4	0	0	0	.000	.200	.000
Gibson, Derrick, Richmond	27	75	70	7	14	22	2	0	2	7	0	0	3	2	0	13	0	0	3	.200	.253	.314
Giese, Daniel, Scranton/Wilkes-Barre	9	0	0	0	0	0	0	0	0	0	0	0	...	0	0	0	0	0	0	...	...	...
Gil, Benji, Norfolk	68	249	229	27	59	89	9	0	7	28	1	1	4	14	1	64	4	6	5	.258	.305	.389
Gload, Ross, Charlotte *	60	263	236	45	86	155	22	1	15	45	1	3	1	22	3	37	0	1	5	.364	.416	.657
Gomes, Jonny, Durham *	45	202	162	34	52	107	13	0	14	46	0	2	8	30	2	44	7	1	2	.321	.446	.660
Gomez, Alexis, Toledo *	114	460	424	51	130	191	28	6	7	55	3	4	2	27	3	91	21	7	7	.307	.348	.450
Gonzalez, Juan, Buffalo	5	21	21	1	6	6	0	0	0	1	0	0	0	0	0	3	0	0	1	.286	.286	.286
Gonzalez, Mike, Indianapolis	2	0	0	0	0	0	0	0	0	0	0	0	...	0	0	0	0	0	0	...	...	...
Gradoville, Timothy, Scranton/Wilkes-Barre	9	21	19	0	5	5	0	0	0	4	1	0	0	1	0	6	0	1	0	.263	.300	.263
Graman, Alex, Louisville *	1	1	1	0	0	0	0	0	0	0	0	0	0	0	0	1	0	0	0	.000	.000	.000
Granderson, Curtis, Toledo *	111	503	445	79	129	229	29	13	15	65	2	5	3	48	4	129	22	6	7	.290	.359	.515
Graves, Danny, Norfolk	1	0	0	0	0	0	0	0	0	0	0	0	0	0	0	0	0	0	0	...	...	...
Greisinger, Seth, Richmond	7	15	15	1	1	1	0	0	0	0	0	0	0	0	0	6	0	0	0	.067	.067	.067
Griffin, John-Ford, Syracuse *	135	582	512	80	130	243	21	1	30	103	0	5	3	62	4	140	1	2	10	.254	.335	.475
Grimm, Eric, Ottawa †	2	6	5	0	1	1	0	0	0	0	0	0	0	1	0	3	0	0	1	.200	.333	.200
Grindell, Nathan, Scranton/Wilkes-Barre	60	226	210	17	50	64	11	0	1	23	1	3	2	10	0	29	1	3	5	.238	.276	.305
Gross, Gabe, Syracuse *	102	449	390	64	116	171	29	4	6	46	2	3	2	52	3	83	14	2	5	.297	.380	.438
Guerrero, Wilton, Charlotte †	21	92	83	11	20	31	5	0	2	12	3	0	0	6	1	9	1	2	3	.241	.292	.373
Gutierrez, Franklin, Buffalo	19	75	67	10	17	27	6	2	0	7	0	1	1	6	1	13	2	2	1	.254	.320	.403
Gutierrez, Ricky, Charlotte	36	144	118	15	22	25	3	0	0	8	7	1	3	15	0	22	1	0	5	.186	.292	.212
Guzman, Edwards, Indianapolis *	21	69	65	2	17	23	3	0	1	5	1	0	1	2	2	4	0	1	0	.262	.294	.354
Hamulack, Tim, Norfolk *	6	0	0	0	0	0	0	0	0	0	0	0	...	0	0	0	0	0	0	...	...	...
Hancock, Josh, Louisville	3	5	5	0	0	0	0	0	0	0	0	0	0	0	0	3	0	0	0	.000	.000	.000
Hankins, Ryan, Columbus	79	311	275	31	71	108	18	2	5	27	3	1	5	27	1	56	1	0	8	.258	.334	.393
Hannahan, John, Toledo *	68	269	238	31	64	91	15	0	4	28	0	3	3	25	2	58	6	3	5	.269	.342	.382
Hannahan, Leonard, Scranton/Wilkes-Barre	95	344	295	38	71	94	12	4	1	22	9	3	9	28	1	81	4	4	2	.241	.322	.319
Hansen, Jed, Norfolk	17	63	54	8	10	15	5	0	0	3	0	0	3	6	2	19	1	0	0	.185	.302	.278
Harper, Brandon, Toledo	81	290	252	33	62	96	14	1	6	34	0	3	7	28	1	36	4	0	8	.246	.334	.381
Harris, Willie, Charlotte *	28	129	109	21	29	45	11	1	1	10	4	0	0	16	0	27	10	2	0	.266	.360	.413
Hattig, John, Syracuse †	26	106	95	15	30	40	7	0	1	10	0	0	1	10	0	16	0	0	5	.316	.387	.421
Heintz, Chris, Rochester	89	360	329	38	100	146	18	2	8	58	4	5	0	22	0	61	0	0	16	.304	.343	.444
Hernandez, Anderson, Norfolk †	66	293	261	34	79	99	6	4	2	30	5	4	1	22	1	46	24	9	2	.303	.354	.379
Hernandez, Buddy, Richmond	3	0	0	0	0	0	0	0	0	0	0	0	0	0	0	0	0	0	0	...	...	...
Hernandez, Yoel, Scranton/Wilkes-Barre *	9	1	1	0	0	0	0	0	0	0	0	0	0	0	0	0	0	0	0	.000	.000	.000
Herrera, Alex, Richmond *	9	0	0	0	0	0	0	0	0	0	0	0	0	0	0	0	0	0	0	...	...	...
Hessman, Mike, Toledo	134	547	473	69	101	206	19	1	28	74	3	2	11	58	3	154	5	4	11	.214	.313	.436
Hietpas, Joe, Norfolk	26	87	72	5	14	16	2	0	0	6	3	1	3	8	0	15	0	0	4	.194	.298	.222
Hill, Aaron, Syracuse	38	168	156	22	47	73	11	0	5	18	0	2	6	4	0	17	2	0	6	.301	.339	.468
Hill, Bobby, Indianapolis †	35	137	116	15	28	32	4	0	0	5	3	1	3	14	0	29	2	0	5	.241	.336	.276
Hinch, A.J., Scranton/Wilkes-Barre	85	306	269	30	75	103	15	2	3	44	2	4	9	22	2	45	0	0	8	.279	.349	.383
Hodges, Trey, Richmond	1	0	0	0	0	0	0	0	0	0	0	0	0	0	0	0	0	0	0	...	...	...
Holbert, Aaron, Louisville	68	252	230	33	70	106	14	2	6	23	4	1	6	11	1	31	12	5	5	.304	.351	.461
Hollins, Damon, Durham	22	99	81	11	24	35	5	0	2	17	0	1	2	15	0	17	3	2	3	.296	.414	.432
Hooper, Kevin, Toledo	85	350	313	41	75	95	13	2	1	27	10	3	2	22	1	37	16	4	4	.240	.291	.304
Hoover, Paul, Durham	79	291	257	32	60	94	17	1	5	26	4	0	5	25	1	56	5	1	7	.233	.314	.366
Howard, Ryan, Scranton/Wilkes-Barre *	61	257	210	38	78	145	19	0	16	54	0	1	6	39	6	66	0	0	3	.371	.467	.690
Hubbard, Trenidad, Durham	25	99	84	14	19	22	3	0	0	2	0	0	1	14	0	5	5	3	4	.226	.343	.262
Hubele, Ryan, Ottawa	13	45	40	4	7	13	1	1	1	8	1	2	2	0	0	10	0	0	3	.175	.205	.325
Huckaby, Ken, Syracuse	15	58	56	3	15	19	1	0	1	3	1	0	0	1	0	13	0	0	1	.268	.281	.339
Hummel, Tim, Pawtucket	64	260	224	35	56	88	18	1	4	27	2	2	6	26	1	35	1	1	7	.250	.341	.393
Hyzdu, Adam, Pawtucket	31	134	118	17	30	49	7	0	4	25	0	0	0	16	0	32	0	1	2	.254	.343	.415
Inglett, Joseph, Buffalo *	95	366	327	57	108	152	20	9	2	40	10	3	9	17	1	41	13	6	7	.330	.376	.465

CLASS AAA International League

Player, Team	G	TPA	AB	R	H	TB	2B	3B	HR	RBI	SH	SF	HP	BB	IBB	SO	SB	CS	GDP	Avg.	OBP	Slg.
Ishii, Kazuhisa, Norfolk *	1	2	2	0	1	1	0	0	0	0	0	0	0	0	0	0	0	0	0	.500	.500	.500
Izquierdo, Hansel, Indianapolis	1	3	2	1	0	0	0	0	0	0	1	0	0	0	0	1	0	0	0	.000	.000	.000
James, Chuck, Richmond *	2	3	3	0	0	0	0	0	0	0	0	0	0	0	0	0	0	0	0	.000	.000	.000
Jeroloman, Charles, Pawtucket	2	5	4	0	0	0	0	0	0	0	0	0	0	1	0	2	0	0	0	.000	.200	.000
Johnson, Kelly, Richmond *	44	192	155	35	48	90	12	3	8	22	0	1	2	34	7	22	7	1	3	.310	.438	.581
Johnson, Russ, Columbus	73	325	281	43	82	135	26	0	9	40	1	3	1	39	0	50	5	5	8	.292	.377	.480
Johnston, Mike, Indianapolis *	19	3	2	0	1	1	0	0	0	0	0	0	0	1	0	1	0	0	0	.500	.667	.500
Jones, Garrett, Richmond *	134	527	488	71	119	217	22	2	24	72	1	1	1	36	4	109	5	1	5	.244	.297	.445
Jones, Mitchell, Columbus	128	551	489	82	131	248	30	3	27	79	0	2	8	52	3	174	2	5	10	.268	.347	.507
Junge, Eric, Norfolk	7	13	11	1	2	2	0	0	0	0	1	0	0	1	0	7	0	0	0	.182	.250	.182
Jurries, James, Richmond	106	417	363	53	103	195	23	3	21	72	0	8	5	41	3	107	1	1	15	.284	.357	.537
Kapler, Gabriel, Pawtucket	6	22	22	7	14	25	3	1	2	6	0	0	0	0	0	3	0	0	0	.636	.636	1.136
Karnuth, Jason, Toledo	1	0	0	0	0	0	0	0	0	0	0	0	0	0	...	0	0	0	0	...	...	...
Kata, Matt, Scranton/Wilkes-Barre †	24	102	96	10	30	37	5	1	0	4	2	0	0	4	0	14	2	1	0	.313	.340	.385
Kearns, Austin, Louisville	28	123	111	24	38	76	15	1	7	21	0	0	1	11	2	30	0	0	9	.342	.407	.685
Keisler, Randy, Louisville *	5	8	7	0	2	3	1	0	0	0	1	0	0	0	0	2	0	0	0	.286	.286	.429
Kelly, Donald, Toledo *	43	176	160	22	40	51	8	0	1	13	3	0	0	13	0	15	8	2	2	.250	.306	.319
Kelly, Kenny, Louisville	61	260	233	43	76	102	9	4	3	17	6	0	1	20	0	49	18	4	7	.326	.382	.438
Kelly, Steven, Louisville	8	16	11	0	0	0	0	0	0	0	4	0	0	1	0	9	0	0	0	.000	.083	.000
Keppel, Robert, Norfolk	3	6	5	0	1	1	0	0	0	1	1	0	0	0	0	2	0	1	0	.200	.200	.200
Keppinger, Jeff, Norfolk	64	278	255	40	86	116	15	3	3	29	5	1	1	16	1	13	5	1	7	.337	.377	.455
Kingsale, Gene, Ottawa †	20	73	64	10	22	28	6	0	0	3	1	0	2	6	1	7	1	2	3	.344	.417	.438
Kinkade, Mike, Buffalo	128	548	473	84	134	223	35	3	16	74	0	7	30	38	2	82	8	5	16	.283	.369	.471
Koo, Dae-Sung, Norfolk *	1	1	1	0	0	0	0	0	0	0	0	0	0	0	0	0	0	0	0	.000	.000	.000
Koonce, Graham, Indianapolis *	120	494	422	60	113	206	22	1	23	77	0	8	7	57	4	109	0	1	12	.268	.358	.488
Koskie, Corey, Syracuse *	7	30	25	1	6	8	2	0	0	2	0	0	2	3	1	6	0	0	1	.240	.367	.320
Kozlowski, Ben, Louisville *	1	2	2	0	0	0	0	0	0	0	0	0	0	0	0	0	0	0	0	.000	.000	.000
Kroski, Christopher, Louisville *	1	1	0	0	0	0	0	0	0	0	0	0	0	1	0	0	0	0	0	...	1.000	...
Laforest, Pierre, Durham	70	292	270	41	73	156	18	1	21	52	...	2	3	17	...	98	2	0	1	.270	.318	.578
Laker, Tim, Durham	89	370	327	48	74	126	19	0	11	44	0	4	2	37	1	80	0	0	12	.226	.305	.385
Lambin, Chase, Norfolk †	61	236	211	35	61	111	16	2	10	34	2	2	1	20	5	47	2	3	2	.289	.350	.526
Lavigne, Tim, Norfolk	16	5	4	0	1	1	0	0	0	0	1	0	0	0	0	0	0	0	0	.250	.250	.250
Lee, Dave, Norfolk	7	1	1	0	0	0	0	0	0	0	0	0	0	0	0	0	0	0	0	.000	.000	.000
Leon, Carlos, Scranton/Wilkes-Barre	6	23	19	2	4	6	2	0	0	3	0	0	1	3	0	2	0	1	1	.211	.348	.316
Leon, Donny, Charlotte †	4	18	14	1	2	2	0	0	0	1	0	0	0	4	0	0	0	0	0	.143	.333	.143
Leon, Jose, Indianapolis-Louisville	91	333	305	31	78	127	15	2	10	52	0	3	1	24	3	83	0	0	7	.256	.309	.416
Lerew, Anthony, Richmond *	2	6	6	0	1	1	0	0	0	0	0	0	0	0	0	2	0	0	0	.167	.167	.167
Liefer, Jeff, Buffalo *	89	361	321	59	103	191	27	2	19	68	0	3	2	35	1	62	2	1	8	.321	.388	.595
Liriano, Pedro, Scranton/Wilkes-Barre	5	7	6	0	0	0	0	0	0	0	0	0	0	1	0	3	0	0	0	.000	.143	.000
Lockwood, Michael, Pawtucket *	97	357	327	40	75	126	13	4	10	50	0	4	1	25	2	43	5	1	11	.229	.283	.385
Lomasney, Steve, Louisville	50	159	144	11	23	30	4	0	1	9	1	1	1	11	1	62	0	0	6	.160	.223	.208
Lombard, George, Pawtucket *	131	579	496	90	130	234	28	8	20	65	2	5	9	67	3	159	23	5	2	.262	.357	.472
Lopez, Aquilino, Scranton/Wilkes-Barre	1	0	0	0	0	0	0	0	0	0	0	0	0	0	...	0	0	0	0	...	...	...
Lopez, Gabe, Columbus	44	194	163	24	37	50	4	0	3	15	7	3	5	16	0	20	2	2	9	.227	.310	.307
Lopez, Luis, Louisville †	29	98	87	10	23	34	8	0	1	9	0	0	3	8	0	18	0	2	0	.264	.347	.391
Lopez, Pedro, Charlotte	55	208	188	14	38	53	6	0	3	17	9	2	2	7	0	24	1	1	4	.202	.236	.282
Ludwick, Ryan, Buffalo	54	215	188	27	36	62	10	2	4	16	0	3	5	17	0	48	0	1	9	.191	.272	.330
Lunar, Fernando, Norfolk	28	91	88	5	15	20	2	0	1	8	1	0	0	2	0	15	0	0	1	.170	.189	.227
Machado, Alejandro, Pawtucket	117	427	383	60	115	145	17	2	3	43	4	3	5	32	0	47	21	4	10	.300	.359	.379
Machado, Anderson, Louisville †	21	93	80	9	11	15	2	1	0	6	0	1	0	12	0	23	1	2	0	.138	.247	.188
Maholm, Paul, Indianapolis *	1	2	2	0	1	1	0	0	0	0	0	0	0	0	0	0	0	0	0	.500	.500	.500
Mallette, Brian, Indianapolis	6	0	0	0	0	0	0	0	0	0	0	0	0	0	...	0	0	0	0	...	...	...
Marte, Andy, Richmond	109	460	389	51	107	197	26	2	20	74	0	7	0	64	2	83	0	3	8	.275	.372	.506
Martinez, Felix, Charlotte †	97	379	346	36	87	118	22	0	3	27	3	4	3	23	1	57	3	3	7	.251	.301	.341
Martinez, Octavio, Ottawa	39	125	116	8	27	32	1	2	0	12	3	0	1	5	0	16	0	1	11	.233	.270	.276
Martinez, Ramon, Toledo	3	16	15	4	11	11	0	0	0	1	0	0	0	1	0	1	0	0	0	.733	.750	.733
Martinez, Sandy, Toledo *	81	298	272	29	72	104	17	0	5	35	0	4	2	20	0	58	2	2	3	.265	.315	.382
Matos, Julius, Syracuse	113	455	421	49	110	153	23	1	6	37	8	1	7	18	2	58	3	4	10	.261	.302	.363
Matthews, Mike, Norfolk *	2	2	2	0	0	0	0	0	0	0	0	0	0	0	0	1	0	0	0	.000	.000	.000
Maza, Luis, Rochester	76	293	275	43	80	131	14	2	11	43	1	4	2	11	1	34	2	1	11	.291	.318	.476
McBride, Macay, Richmond *	9	7	7	0	1	2	1	0	0	0	0	0	0	0	0	4	0	0	0	.143	.143	.286
McCarthy, William, Richmond	66	265	239	26	54	81	10	1	5	23	1	1	7	17	0	58	1	4	7	.226	.295	.339
McConnell, Sam, Richmond *	7	15	14	1	1	1	0	0	0	0	1	0	0	0	0	5	0	0	1	.071	.071	.071
McCullough, Clayton, Buffalo *	1	3	3	0	1	2	1	0	0	1	0	0	0	0	0	0	0	0	0	.333	.333	.667
McCurdy, Joshua, Ottawa	5	20	19	1	8	8	0	0	0	7	0	0	0	1	0	5	1	0	0	.421	.450	.421
McDade, Neal, Indianapolis	5	0	0	0	0	0	0	0	0	0	0	0	0	0	...	0	0	0	0	...	...	...
McDonald, Darnell, Buffalo-Durham	99	389	359	56	101	164	20	2	13	38	0	0	3	27	0	81	7	1	5	.281	.337	.457
McGinley, Blake, Norfolk	17	6	5	0	0	0	0	0	0	0	1	0	0	0	0	3	0	0	0	.000	.000	.000
McLouth, Nate, Indianapolis *	110	455	397	64	118	159	20	3	5	39	5	7	7	39	1	58	34	6	10	.297	.364	.401
Mears, Chris, Richmond	14	1	0	0	0	0	0	0	0	0	1	0	0	0	0	0	0	0	0	...	...	...
Medrano, Anthony, Scranton/Wilkes-Barre	111	422	367	45	81	105	15	0	3	45	16	6	6	27	0	46	6	1	12	.221	.281	.286
Mendez, Carlos, Richmond	47	194	179	13	44	61	8	0	3	18	1	3	1	10	0	22	0	0	8	.246	.285	.341
Mendez, Deivi, Columbus	12	35	33	5	9	10	1	0	0	1	0	0	0	2	0	8	0	0	0	.273	.314	.303
Miller, Corky, Rochester	59	219	170	35	39	79	7	0	11	25	8	0	14	27	1	30	0	2	4	.229	.379	.465
Miller, Jeffrey, Indianapolis	19	6	4	0	0	0	0	0	0	0	1	0	0	1	0	2	0	0	0	.000	.200	.000
Miner, Zachary, Richmond	5	9	7	1	1	1	0	0	0	0	2	0	0	0	0	5	0	0	0	.143	.143	.143
Minix, Travis, Scranton/Wilkes-Barre	3	0	0	0	0	0	0	0	0	0	0	0	0	0	...	0	0	0	0	...	...	...
Morban, Jose, Buffalo	43	144	134	20	36	54	6	0	4	19	0	0	0	10	0	39	6	0	3	.269	.319	.403
Moriarty, Mike, Pawtucket-Ottawa	75	241	210	25	44	74	18	0	4	18	1	1	6	23	0	54	5	1	2	.210	.304	.352
Mottola, Chad, Syracuse	125	520	478	67	122	218	27	3	21	69	0	3	4	35	2	100	2	5	4	.255	.310	.456

Player, Team	G	TPA	AB	R	H	TB	2B	3B	HR	RBI	SH	SF	HP	BB	IBB	SO	SB	CS	GDP	Avg.	OBP	Slg.
Munoz, Arnie, Charlotte *	2	1	1	0	0	0	0	0	0	0	0	0	0	0	0	1	0	0	0	.000	.000	.000
Munson, Eric, Durham *	100	425	382	67	109	206	22	0	25	71	1	2	2	38	4	81	1	1	11	.285	.351	.539
Musser, Neal, Norfolk *	8	14	12	1	1	1	0	0	0	0	2	0	0	0	0	4	0	0	0	.083	.083	.083
Nelson, Bry, Syracuse †	138	600	540	68	134	176	19	1	7	60	6	3	3	48	3	50	8	4	14	.248	.311	.326
Neuberger, Scott, Durham	3	6	6	1	2	3	1	0	0	1	0	0	0	0	0	3	0	0	0	.333	.333	.500
Newhan, David, Ottawa *	11	45	41	11	15	22	4	0	1	8	0	1	1	2	0	6	2	0	0	.366	.400	.537
Nieves, Raul, Pawtucket †	2	8	8	0	1	1	0	0	0	0	0	0	0	0	0	1	0	0	0	.125	.125	.125
Nieves, Wil, Columbus	102	404	380	45	110	150	22	3	4	37	4	5	2	13	1	38	1	1	16	.289	.313	.395
Nitkowski, C.J., Indianapolis *	7	0	0	0	0	0	0	0	0	0	0	0	0	0	0	0	0	0	0	...	...	...
Nivar, Ramon, Ottawa	33	121	111	13	22	29	4	0	1	5	4	1	2	3	0	10	9	4	4	.198	.231	.261
Nixon, Trot, Pawtucket *	2	9	6	3	3	6	0	0	1	2	0	1	0	2	1	2	0	0	0	.500	.556	1.000
Norton, Greg, Charlotte †	90	381	330	57	94	166	19	1	17	56	1	2	1	47	2	67	0	2	12	.285	.374	.503
Nunez, Vladimir, Indianapolis	4	1	1	0	0	0	0	0	0	0	0	0	0	0	0	0	0	0	0	.000	.000	.000
Nunnally, Jon, Indianapolis *	80	241	213	30	48	81	6	3	7	30	0	0	1	27	3	55	6	1	2	.225	.315	.380
Nye, Rodney, Norfolk	108	422	375	47	108	159	19	4	8	54	5	3	3	36	2	63	5	5	11	.288	.353	.424
O'Connor, Brian, Richmond	1	2	2	0	0	0	0	0	0	0	0	0	0	0	...	1	0	0	0	.000	.000	.000
Offerman, Jose, Norfolk †	9	37	36	1	6	6	0	0	0	1	0	0	0	1	0	4	1	0	2	.167	.189	.167
Ojeda, Augie, Rochester *	105	370	313	42	70	95	16	0	3	33	7	3	14	33	0	33	3	2	7	.224	.322	.304
O'Keefe, Michael, Richmond *	5	16	13	1	2	5	0	0	1	1	0	0	0	3	0	3	0	0	0	.154	.313	.385
Olerud, John, Pawtucket *	3	12	10	2	3	6	0	0	1	2	0	0	0	2	0	1	0	0	2	.300	.417	.600
Olmedo, Ranier, Louisville	14	60	58	8	16	22	3	0	1	5	0	0	1	1	0	11	2	2	0	.276	.300	.379
Olszta, Edwin, Indianapolis	8	5	5	2	0	0	0	0	0	0	0	0	0	0	0	4	2	0	0	.000	.000	.000
Ordaz, Luis, Durham	39	136	125	17	36	47	8	0	1	19	2	3	0	6	0	13	0	0	4	.288	.313	.376
Ordonez, Magglio, Toledo	4	16	14	3	3	7	1	0	1	2	0	0	0	2	0	3	0	0	0	.214	.313	.500
Ortega, Jose, Buffalo	2	3	1	0	0	0	0	0	0	0	0	0	0	2	0	0	0	1	0	.000	.667	.000
Pachot, John, Norfolk	21	68	64	6	13	23	7	0	1	9	1	2	0	1	0	9	0	1	1	.203	.209	.359
Padilla, Jorge, Scranton/Wilkes-Barre	59	227	204	25	55	66	6	1	1	17	5	1	2	15	1	41	4	5	9	.270	.324	.324
Padilla, Juan, Norfolk	15	5	4	0	2	2	0	0	0	0	0	0	0	0	0	0	0	0	0	.500	.500	.500
Padilla, Vicente, Scranton/Wilkes-Barre	1	2	2	0	0	0	0	0	0	0	0	0	0	0	0	1	0	0	0	.000	.000	.000
Pagan, Angel, Norfolk †	129	579	516	69	140	204	20	10	8	40	9	4	1	49	2	111	27	15	7	.271	.333	.395
Paronto, Chad, Richmond	6	1	1	0	0	0	0	0	0	0	0	0	0	0	0	1	0	0	0	.000	.000	.000
Parrish, David, Columbus	79	317	283	35	70	104	10	0	8	35	5	1	4	24	0	79	0	0	8	.247	.314	.367
Patchett, Gary, Louisville	9	27	22	3	5	6	1	0	0	1	0	1	0	3	0	7	0	0	0	.227	.333	.273
Paulino, Ronny, Indianapolis	77	302	273	49	86	147	18	2	13	42	1	2	0	26	1	48	3	0	11	.315	.372	.538
Pedroia, Dustin, Pawtucket	51	240	204	39	52	78	9	1	5	24	1	2	9	24	0	17	1	0	6	.255	.356	.382
Pelaez, Alex, Louisville	89	332	316	23	76	105	18	1	3	26	1	2	0	13	5	32	0	0	10	.241	.269	.332
Pena, Brayan, Richmond †	81	319	282	27	92	117	21	2	0	25	6	3	0	28	2	19	3	1	15	.326	.383	.415
Pena, Carlos, Toledo *	71	309	257	43	80	135	17	1	12	45	0	1	6	45	5	65	3	4	4	.311	.424	.525
Pena, Tony, Richmond	138	526	490	49	122	170	25	4	5	40	6	4	5	21	0	113	17	15	7	.249	.285	.347
Pena, Wily Mo, Louisville	7	25	24	1	7	11	1	0	1	4	0	0	0	1	0	10	0	0	0	.292	.320	.458
Perez, Franklin, Scranton/Wilkes-Barre	14	0	0	0	0	0	0	0	0	0	0	0	0	0	0	0	0	0	0	...	...	...
Perez, Kenny, Pawtucket †	14	51	42	10	7	12	2	0	1	5	1	0	1	7	0	7	0	0	2	.167	.300	.286
Perez, Miguel, Louisville	21	80	72	5	15	21	3	0	1	5	0	1	2	5	1	19	0	0	2	.208	.275	.292
Perez, Oliver, Indianapolis *	1	1	1	0	0	0	0	0	0	0	0	0	0	0	0	0	0	0	0	.000	.000	.000
Perez, Tomas, Louisville †	64	264	233	40	72	106	22	3	2	17	4	3	2	22	1	58	10	2	3	.309	.369	.455
Petagine, Roberto, Pawtucket	74	336	266	54	87	169	18	2	20	69	...	5	2	63		46	0	1	9	.327	.452	.635
Phelps, Josh, Durham	59	243	222	35	60	122	14	3	14	33	0	1	5	15	1	53	0	1	6	.270	.329	.550
Phelps, Travis, Louisville	6	0	0	0	0	0	0	0	0	0	0	0	0	0	0	0	0	0	0	...	...	...
Phillips, Andy, Columbus	75	340	300	60	90	172	14	1	22	54	0	1	3	36	3	61	2	0	15	.300	.379	.573
Phillips, Brandon, Buffalo	112	518	465	79	119	190	24	1	15	46	2	2	10	39	0	90	7	5	11	.256	.326	.409
Piazza, Anthony, Norfolk	2	7	6	0	0	0	0	0	0	0	0	0	0	0	0	2	0	0	0	.000	.143	.000
Pinckney, Brandon, Buffalo	3	9	9	0	0	0	0	0	0	0	0	0	0	0	0	2	0	0	0	.000	.000	.000
Podsednik, Scott, Charlotte *	2	9	9	2	2	4	2	0	0	1	0	0	0	0	0	1	0	1	0	.222	.222	.444
Pond, Simon, Pawtucket *	1	5	4	1	2	2	0	0	0	1	0	0	0	1	0	2	0	0	0	.500	.600	.500
Porter, Colin, Columbus *	57	227	198	26	35	52	9	1	2	14	1	2	1	25	2	62	1	3	2	.177	.270	.263
Pratt, Scott, Richmond *	106	386	343	38	88	148	23	5	9	38	4	0	2	37	2	94	4	5	6	.257	.332	.431
Punto, Nick, Rochester †	4	17	15	2	3	4	1	0	0	1	0	0	0	2	0	2	0	0	0	.200	.294	.267
Pyzik, Steven, Richmond	6	15	15	1	1	1	0	0	0	1	0	0	0	0	0	1	0	0	2	.067	.067	.067
Quiroz, Guillermo, Syracuse	25	94	83	11	19	40	3	0	6	18	0	1	1	9	1	19	0	0	5	.229	.309	.482
Rabe, Joshua, Rochester	90	321	285	50	68	118	17	0	11	49	2	2	3	29	0	57	5	2	7	.239	.313	.414
Raburn, Ryan, Toledo	130	524	471	62	119	206	22	4	19	64	1	2	5	45	2	109	8	3	12	.253	.323	.437
Raines Jr., Tim, Ottawa	122	510	457	69	116	172	28	5	6	42	20	1	2	30	2	116	27	13	7	.254	.302	.376
Ramirez, Elizardo, Louisville †	5	12	11	2	4	7	1	1	0	2	0	0	0	1	0	4	0	0	0	.364	.417	.636
Ray, Ken, Richmond	6	6	6	1	3	4	1	0	0	1	0	0	0	0	0	1	0	0	0	.500	.500	.667
Raymundo, Gregg, Indianapolis	6	8	6	1	1	1	0	0	0	0	0	0	0	2	0	1	0	0	0	.167	.375	.167
Redman, Prentice, Norfolk	76	287	256	34	76	118	25	1	5	32	3	4	1	23	1	49	9	1	1	.297	.352	.461
Reed, Keith, Ottawa	80	286	271	39	79	124	19	1	8	37	1	3	1	10	0	55	1	3	5	.292	.316	.458
Reese, Kevin, Columbus *	133	620	540	92	149	243	38	7	14	69	2	5	10	63	4	86	16	5	10	.276	.359	.450
Reid, Justin, Indianapolis	9	7	4	0	0	0	0	0	0	0	3	0	0	0	0	1	0	0	0	.000	.000	.000
Reith, Brian, Indianapolis	7	1	1	0	0	0	0	0	0	0	0	0	0	0	0	1	0	0	0	.000	.000	.000
Relaford, Desi, Syracuse †	22	93	76	15	16	24	2	0	2	6	0	0	4	13	0	12	5	0	1	.211	.355	.316
Reyes, Guillermo, Charlotte †	59	225	205	24	51	66	8	2	1	12	4	3	1	12	0	32	2	2	5	.249	.290	.322
Ring, Royce, Norfolk *	14	1	1	0	0	0	0	0	0	0	0	0	0	0	0	1	0	0	0	.000	.000	.000
Rivas, Luis, Rochester	43	159	145	17	36	56	14	0	2	22	2	4	0	8	1	18	3	1	2	.248	.280	.386
Roa, Joe, Indianapolis	4	3	3	0	0	0	0	0	0	0	0	0	0	0	0	2	0	0	0	.000	.000	.000
Robertson, Jeriome, Louisville *	12	18	16	1	2	2	0	0	0	1	0	1	0	1	0	9	0	0	0	.125	.167	.125
Robinson, Kerry, Richmond *	58	227	204	29	67	81	9	1	1	12	8	1	1	13	0	23	13	6	2	.328	.370	.397
Rodriguez, John, Buffalo *	46	196	170	25	42	76	13	3	5	23	1	4	6	15	1	40	5	0	1	.247	.323	.447
Rodriguez, Luis, Rochester †	40	157	138	19	42	55	10	0	1	15	2	1	0	16	0	14	0	1	3	.304	.381	.399
Rogers, Eddie, Ottawa	125	455	431	52	113	161	21	3	7	48	5	1	1	17	0	66	14	6	9	.262	.291	.374
Rojas, Thomas, Columbus	1	1	1	0	0	0	0	0	0	0	0	0	0	0	0	0	0	0	0	.000	.000	.000

Player, Team	G	TPA	AB	R	H	TB	2B	3B	HR	RBI	SH	SF	HP	BB	IBB	SO	SB	CS	GDP	Avg.	OBP	Slg.
Rolls, Damian, Columbus	25	103	88	10	23	31	5	0	1	9	1	2	1	11	0	24	4	2	1	.261	.343	.352
Romano, Jason, Louisville	56	243	224	34	69	102	17	2	4	32	2	2	1	14	0	36	5	1	4	.308	.349	.455
Rosa, Wally, Charlotte	18	60	54	3	10	11	1	0	0	3	3	2	0	1	0	10	0	0	2	.185	.193	.204
Rosamond, George, Richmond	26	62	58	5	13	19	3	0	1	7	1	0	1	2	0	20	1	0	2	.224	.262	.328
Rose, Brian, Louisville	6	7	6	0	3	3	0	0	0	2	1	0	0	0	0	3	0	0	0	.500	.500	.500
Ross, David, Indianapolis	6	23	19	1	4	5	1	0	0	1	0	1	0	3	0	7	0	0	0	.211	.304	.263
Ruiz, Carlos, Scranton/Wilkes-Barre	100	388	347	50	104	159	25	9	4	40	1	7	3	30	2	48	4	5	14	.300	.354	.458
Rushford, Jim, Scranton/Wilkes-Barre *	117	467	414	61	129	190	29	1	10	63	2	6	11	34	1	40	5	1	11	.312	.374	.459
Ryan, Michael, Rochester *	46	170	152	16	43	70	7	1	6	26	1	2	0	15	0	34	0	3	4	.283	.343	.461
Sadler, Ray, Indianapolis	69	275	251	28	65	106	9	1	10	30	1	3	5	15	1	57	8	6	5	.259	.310	.422
Saladin, Miguel, Louisville	6	2	2	0	0	0	0	0	0	0	0	0	0	0	0	2	0	0	0	.000	.000	.000
Salmon, Bradley, Louisville *	6	3	3	0	1	1	0	0	0	0	0	0	0	0	0	2	0	0	0	.333	.333	.333
Sanches, Brian, Scranton/Wilkes-Barre	13	2	2	0	0	0	0	0	0	0	0	0	0	0	0	0	0	0	0	.000	.000	.000
Sanders, Anthony, Syracuse	2	5	3	1	1	1	0	0	0	1	1	0	0	1	0	1	0	0	0	.333	.500	.333
Sandoval, Danny, Scranton/Wilkes-Barre †	104	438	390	53	129	170	20	0	7	48	11	4	2	31	6	49	11	11	16	.331	.379	.436
Santiago, Benito, Norfolk	9	39	33	5	8	9	1	0	0	4	0	1	1	4	0	8	0	0	1	.242	.333	.273
Santiago, Jose, Norfolk	8	9	8	0	0	0	0	0	0	1	0	1	0	0	0	1	0	0	0	.000	.000	.000
Sardinha, Dane, Louisville	86	330	299	36	67	107	10	0	10	36	3	2	4	22	1	72	1	0	12	.224	.284	.358
Schneider, John, Syracuse	34	116	95	13	17	29	3	0	3	10	2	1	2	16	0	37	0	1	2	.179	.307	.305
Schrager, Anthony, Pawtucket	15	57	51	4	11	14	1	1	0	0	0	0	0	6	0	13	0	0	1	.216	.298	.275
Schuerholz, Jonathan, Richmond	44	162	143	10	25	29	2	1	0	12	1	2	0	16	0	29	1	2	1	.175	.265	.203
Scobie, Jason, Norfolk	8	18	15	2	2	2	0	0	0	0	2	0	0	1	0	6	0	0	0	.133	.188	.133
Seo, Jae Weong, Norfolk	7	17	14	1	2	3	1	0	0	0	3	0	0	0	0	9	0	0	1	.143	.143	.214
Serrano, Jimmy, Louisville	6	14	12	0	0	0	0	0	0	0	1	0	0	1	0	9	0	0	0	.000	.077	.000
Shackelford, Brian, Louisville *	11	1	1	0	0	0	0	0	0	0	0	0	0	0	0	0	0	0	0	.000	.000	.000
Shearn, Tom, Louisville	14	4	3	0	0	0	0	0	0	0	0	1	0	0	0	2	0	0	0	.000	.000	.000
Shelton, Chris, Toledo	48	211	181	34	60	103	19	0	8	39	0	2	3	25	0	33	0	2	3	.331	.417	.569
Sherrod, Justin, Pawtucket	120	490	433	65	112	191	29	1	16	65	0	7	5	45	0	141	2	2	10	.259	.331	.441
Shoppach, Kelly, Pawtucket	102	432	371	60	94	188	16	0	26	75	0	3	12	46	2	116	0	0	9	.253	.352	.507
Sierra, Ruben, Columbus †	3	13	11	2	2	5	0	0	1	1	0	0	0	2	1	3	0	0	0	.182	.308	.455
Simpson, Allan, Louisville	18	2	1	0	0	0	0	0	0	0	0	1	0	0	0	1	0	0	0	.000	.000	.000
Singleton, Chris, Durham *	1	3	3	0	1	1	0	0	0	0	0	0	0	0	0	0	0	0	0	.333	.333	.333
Singleton, Justin, Syracuse *	100	344	318	48	81	135	20	2	10	36	5	1	1	19	2	98	5	1	4	.255	.298	.425
Skrehot, Shaun, Indianapolis	34	84	78	5	18	20	2	0	0	8	4	1	0	1	0	14	2	1	2	.231	.238	.256
Smith, Jason, Toledo *	55	207	187	24	43	76	11	2	6	25	6	3	0	11	0	53	8	4	1	.230	.269	.406
Smitherman, Stephen, Louisville	40	147	141	12	35	47	9	0	1	11	0	1	0	5	0	34	1	0	2	.248	.272	.333
Snead, Esix, Richmond †	95	416	347	49	84	108	11	5	1	10	11	0	10	48	0	62	46	14	3	.242	.351	.311
Snell, Ian, Indianapolis	8	17	12	1	0	0	0	0	0	2	1	0	0	3	0	5	0	0	0	.000	.200	.000
Snyder, Earl, Durham	130	557	505	80	130	253	32	2	29	92	0	4	6	42	2	99	1	1	18	.257	.320	.501
Solano, Danny, Syracuse	57	193	173	26	42	59	6	1	3	22	0	3	2	15	0	37	1	2	2	.243	.306	.341
Sosa, Juan, Scranton/Wilkes-Barre	56	184	172	18	42	59	10	2	1	15	6	2	0	4	1	23	1	0	6	.244	.258	.343
Spidale, Michael, Charlotte	46	177	161	17	37	44	4	0	1	7	3	0	3	10	0	22	5	3	3	.230	.287	.273
Stachowsky, Mitchel, Pawtucket	4	5	4	0	0	0	0	0	0	0	0	0	0	0	0	3	0	0	0	.000	.200	.000
Standridge, Jason, Louisville	2	0	0	0	0	0	0	0	0	0	...	0	0	0	...	0	0	0	0	...	...	...
Stern, Adam, Pawtucket *	20	92	81	16	26	40	8	0	2	14	1	1	1	8	1	10	3	1	2	.321	.385	.494
Stewart, Cory, Indianapolis *	9	20	19	1	2	3	1	0	0	0	0	0	0	0	0	7	0	0	0	.105	.105	.158
Stewart, Josh, Charlotte *	1	1	1	0	0	0	0	0	0	0	0	0	0	0	0	0	0	0	0	.000	.000	.000
Stewart, Paul, Indianapolis	1	0	0	0	0	0	0	0	0	0	...	0	0	0	...	0	0	0	0	...	...	...
Stewart, Scott, Norfolk	10	1	1	0	0	0	0	0	0	0	0	0	0	0	0	1	0	0	0	.000	.000	.000
Stone, Ricky, Louisville	3	0	0	0	0	0	0	0	0	0	0	0	0	0	0	0	0	0	0	...	...	...
Stratton, Robert, Louisville	8	29	26	5	8	20	0	0	4	5	0	0	1	2	0	5	0	0	0	.308	.379	.769
Strickland, Scott, Norfolk	8	0	0	0	0	0	0	0	0	0	0	0	0	0	0	0	0	0	0	...	...	...
Swann, Pedro, Louisville *	127	511	456	67	130	223	29	5	18	85	0	4	15	36	5	101	5	0	8	.285	.354	.489
Taylor, Reggie, Durham *	67	283	253	30	66	103	10	3	7	35	3	0	3	24	1	55	12	10	5	.261	.332	.407
Tejeda, Robinson, Scranton/Wilkes-Barre	1	1	0	0	0	0	0	0	0	0	0	1	0	0	0	0	0	0	0	...	...	...
Telemaco, Amaury, Scranton/Wilkes-Barre	1	0	0	0	0	0	0	0	0	0	...	0	0	0	...	0	0	0	0	...	...	...
Thames, Marcus, Toledo	73	314	265	53	90	180	18	3	22	56	0	5	3	41	3	59	4	1	5	.340	.427	.679
Thomas, Frank, Charlotte	11	46	42	3	8	12	1	0	1	4	0	0	0	4	0	9	0	0	2	.190	.261	.286
Thompson, Kevin, Columbus	58	246	209	28	52	75	17	0	2	28	4	4	6	23	0	45	18	5	4	.249	.335	.359
Thompson, Rich, Indianapolis *	29	107	91	9	19	27	1	2	1	3	3	0	4	9	0	12	13	2	1	.209	.308	.297
Thorman, Scott, Richmond *	52	224	210	23	58	92	10	3	6	27	0	2	3	9	0	42	0	0	3	.276	.313	.438
Thrower, James, Buffalo †	35	126	119	12	31	40	9	0	0	9	1	2	1	3	0	16	2	2	2	.261	.280	.336
Thurston, Joe, Columbus *	29	118	107	13	25	40	3	3	2	7	3	0	1	7	0	19	2	1	1	.234	.287	.374
Tiffee, Terry, Rochester †	58	252	229	33	61	104	11	1	10	39	0	5	3	15	2	24	0	1	9	.266	.313	.454
Timmons, Wesley, Richmond	5	22	18	1	4	5	1	0	0	3	0	2	0	2	0	0	0	0	0	.222	.273	.278
Toca, Jorge, Charlotte	115	487	454	56	137	235	24	1	24	77	0	3	6	24	2	87	0	1	11	.302	.343	.518
Trachsel, Steve, Norfolk	1	3	2	0	1	1	0	0	0	0	0	0	0	0	0	1	0	0	0	.500	.500	.500
Tucker, Glenn, Richmond †	1	0	0	0	0	0	0	0	0	0	...	0	0	0	...	0	0	0	0	...	...	...
Tyner, Jason, Rochester *	133	591	524	81	150	175	18	2	1	36	13	1	5	48	0	57	18	6	9	.286	.351	.334
Upton, B.J., Durham	139	632	545	98	165	267	36	6	18	74	1	3	4	78	1	127	44	13	15	.303	.392	.490
Urick, John, Columbus *	1	3	2	0	0	0	0	0	0	0	0	0	1	0	0	0	0	0	0	.000	.333	.000
Valent, Eric, Norfolk *	79	334	275	44	70	112	13	1	9	38	1	1	1	55	4	58	1	1	6	.255	.380	.407
Valentine, Joe, Louisville	18	2	1	0	0	0	0	0	0	0	0	0	0	1	0	1	0	0	0	.000	.500	.000
Van Hekken, Andy, Richmond-Louisville	11	3	2	0	0	0	0	0	0	0	0	0	0	0	0	2	0	0	0	.000	.000	.000
Vasquez, Jorge, Richmond	5	1	1	0	0	1	0	0	0	0	0	0	0	0	0	0	0	0	0	1.000	1.000	1.000
Vazquez, Ramon, Buffalo *	21	92	84	13	18	23	3	1	0	4	1	0	0	7	0	16	1	1	2	.214	.275	.274
Velandia, Jorge, Indianapolis	105	376	328	47	91	126	22	2	3	39	5	6	4	33	1	48	2	3	8	.277	.345	.384
Velazquez, Gilbert, Rochester	17	34	34	3	9	12	1	1	0	3	0	0	0	0	0	8	0	0	1	.265	.265	.353
Vento, Mike, Columbus	130	571	501	62	146	223	37	2	12	84	1	7	13	49	1	96	1	4	13	.291	.365	.445
Victorino, Shane, Scranton/Wilkes-Barre †	126	559	494	93	153	264	25	16	18	70	5	4	5	51	2	74	17	9	4	.310	.377	.534
Ward, Jeremy, Richmond	10	0	0	0	0	0	0	0	0	0	...	0	0	0	...	0	0	0	0	...	...	...

Player, Team	G	TPA	AB	R	H	TB	2B	3B	HR	RBI	SH	SF	HP	BB	IBB	SO	SB	CS	GDP	Avg.	OBP	Slg.
Wathan, Dusty, Buffalo	83	300	256	41	67	118	9	0	14	51	4	2	14	24	0	51	2	2	9	.262	.355	.461
Weber, Ben, Louisville	2	1	1	0	0	0	0	0	0	0	0	0	0	0	0	0	0	0	0	.000	.000	.000
West, Kevin, Rochester	125	485	425	60	115	203	26	1	20	64	0	3	12	45	1	94	2	2	13	.271	.355	.478
Whiteside, Eli, Ottawa	95	348	317	28	74	110	22	1	4	27	1	3	2	21	1	65	1	3	7	.233	.283	.347
Whittaker, Timothy, Syracuse	6	9	8	0	0	0	0	0	0	0	0	0	0	1	0	1	0	0	0	.000	.111	.000
Wigginton, Ty, Indianapolis	72	328	280	53	82	142	18	0	14	52	0	2	1	45	4	56	8	5	4	.293	.390	.507
Wilken, Kristopher, Ottawa †	86	209	192	15	44	58	8	0	2	18	1	1	0	15	0	45	0	0	4	.229	.284	.302
Williams, Gerald, Norfolk	47	151	139	24	32	58	10	2	4	16	1	1	1	9	0	21	1	2	1	.230	.280	.417
Williams, Glenn, Rochester †	48	187	175	21	53	82	12	1	5	22	2	0	3	7	1	35	2	0	3	.303	.341	.469
Wilson, Andrew, Norfolk	3	8	7	0	0	0	0	0	0	0	0	0	0	1	0	0	0	0	0	.000	.125	.000
Wilson, Craig, Indianapolis	7	25	21	4	8	18	1	0	3	11	0	0	1	3	0	6	1	0	1	.381	.480	.857
Wilson, Enrique, Ottawa †	20	71	61	7	17	30	4	0	3	8	2	0	0	8	0	5	1	0	1	.279	.362	.492
Wise, Dewayne, Toledo *	108	417	384	42	90	136	12	5	8	45	3	2	5	23	1	76	22	7	8	.234	.285	.354
Woodyard, Mark, Toledo	1	0	0	0	0	0	0	0	0	0	0	...	0	0	0	0	0	0	0	...	...	...
Wooten, Shawn, Pawtucket	114	480	427	45	114	185	20	0	17	60	0	9	9	35	2	72	0	0	16	.267	.329	.433
Youkilis, Kevin, Pawtucket	43	194	152	30	49	90	15	1	8	27	0	2	5	35	0	29	1	2	0	.322	.459	.592
Young, Delmon, Durham	52	234	228	33	65	102	13	3	6	28	0	0	2	4	0	33	7	4	6	.285	.303	.447
Young, Ernie, Buffalo	114	472	393	76	109	183	14	0	20	78	0	3	12	64	2	115	6	3	7	.277	.392	.466
Young, Walter, Ottawa *	123	506	466	48	134	204	29	1	13	81	0	5	5	30	4	91	1	1	14	.288	.334	.438
Zapp, Andrew, Louisville *	125	446	399	31	97	143	28	0	6	40	2	1	6	38	5	113	0	0	5	.243	.318	.358

PLAYERS WITH TWO OR MORE TEAMS

Player, Team	G	TPA	AB	R	H	TB	2B	3B	HR	RBI	SH	SF	HP	BB	IBB	SO	SB	CS	GDP	Avg.	OBP	Slg.
Crozier, Eric, Syracuse *	37	135	124	20	28	57	12	1	5	14	0	1	1	9	0	39	1	0	1	.226	.281	.460
Crozier, Eric, Louisville *	27	113	97	5	22	37	10	1	1	10	0	1	0	15	0	38	3	2	1	.227	.327	.381
Fernandez, Jared, Louisville	3	6	5	0	0	0	0	0	0	0	0	0	0	0	0	3	0	0	0	.000	.167	.000
Fernandez, Jared, Scranton/Wilkes-Barre	2	6	5	1	1	2	1	0	0	0	0	1	0	0	0	2	0	0	0	.200	.200	.400
Leon, Jose, Indianapolis	71	255	231	25	62	107	11	2	10	45	0	3	1	20	2	65	0	0	7	.268	.325	.463
Leon, Jose, Louisville	20	78	74	6	16	20	4	0	0	7	0	0	0	4	1	18	0	0	0	.216	.256	.270
McDonald, Darnell, Buffalo	26	83	74	11	20	30	7	0	1	4	0	0	2	7	0	19	0	1	0	.270	.349	.405
McDonald, Darnell, Durham	73	306	285	45	81	134	13	2	12	34	0	1	1	20	0	62	7	0	5	.284	.333	.470
Moriarty, Mike, Pawtucket	6	10	10	1	1	2	1	0	0	0	0	0	0	0	0	3	0	0	1	.100	.100	.200
Moriarty, Mike, Ottawa	69	231	200	24	43	72	17	0	4	18	1	1	6	23	0	51	5	1	1	.215	.313	.360
Van Hekken, Andy, Richmond	2	3	2	0	0	0	0	0	0	0	0	0	1	0	0	2	0	0	0	.000	.000	.000
Van Hekken, Andy, Louisville	9	0	0	0	0	0	0	0	0	0	0	...	0	0	0	0	0	0	0	...	...	...

GRAND SLAMS—C. Ambres, J. Griffin, M. Jones, E. Munson, J. Rabe, 2 each; B. Abernathy, K. Barker, D. Berg, R. Bowen, R. Brown, J. Burke, M. Cabrera, J. Cooper, T. Coquillette, C. Coste, B. Daubach, Y. De Caster, V. Diaz, A. Fernandez, A. Freire, R. Garko, R. Gload, C. Heintz, A. Holbert, R. Howard, A. Hyzdu, G. Jones, G. Koonce, T. Laker, M. Lockwood, N. McLouth, A. Medrano, J. Padilla, R. Petagine, J. Sherrod, K. Shoppach, J. Singleton, E. Snyder, P. Swann, T. Tiffee, J. Toca, E. Valent, S. Victorino, D. Wathan, T. Wigginton, D. Wise, 1 each.

AWARDED FIRST BASE ON CATCHER'S INTERFERENCE—C. Cosme 4 (D. Sardinha, J. DePastino, R. Doumit, S. Lomasney); E. Whiteside 4 (C. Heintz, C. Ruiz, D. Parrish, S. Martinez); R. Ludwick 2 (D. Parrish, S. Martinez); D. Berg (R. Garko); A. French (K. Cash); S. Lomasney (C. Coste); I. Snell (B. Pena); B. Upton (S. Martinez); E. Valent (K. Cash).

2005 PITCHING

TEAM

Team	W	L	Pct.	ERA	G	CG	ShO	Sv.	IP	H	TBF	R	ER	HR	SH	SF	HB	BB	IBB	SO	WP	Bk.
Toledo	89	55	.618	3.70	144	5	15	43	1273	1224	5443	583	524	116	45	31	68	474	26	1036	42	3
Norfolk	79	65	.549	3.73	144	0	10	45	1270.1	1241	5393	585	526	121	54	34	63	426	12	974	44	4
Richmond	56	88	.389	4.07	144	1	11	28	1255.1	1247	5471	675	567	122	65	47	54	532	34	879	51	5
Rochester	75	69	.521	4.13	144	3	9	37	1251.1	1250	5406	638	574	128	35	41	47	494	19	1077	49	5
Indianapolis	78	66	.542	4.29	144	5	6	36	1271	1290	5508	691	607	146	58	43	63	477	37	912	52	4
Columbus	77	67	.535	4.32	144	1	6	37	1287	1330	5546	690	618	148	43	39	68	425	21	1073	32	4
Ottawa	69	75	.479	4.32	144	3	9	28	1251	1310	5415	668	601	132	45	45	78	406	32	866	44	8
Pawtucket	75	69	.521	4.40	144	1	8	24	1267.2	1297	5444	681	620	137	46	46	67	411	17	1057	44	11
Scranton/WB	69	75	.479	4.44	144	3	4	37	1257.1	1327	5473	691	620	137	46	45	72	465	23	936	43	5
Buffalo	82	62	.569	4.46	144	4	2	42	1247.2	1345	5457	716	618	160	53	50	71	395	17	986	56	8
Louisville	66	78	.458	4.54	144	0	9	35	1265.2	1356	5514	716	639	131	38	39	58	450	15	1012	61	6
Syracuse	71	73	.493	4.56	144	2	7	44	1271	1361	5489	703	644	157	42	50	76	362	16	976	47	8
Charlotte	57	87	.396	4.83	144	3	4	30	1267.2	1378	5581	748	680	192	46	42	66	490	40	1016	49	10
Durham	65	79	.451	5.03	144	1	2	27	1285	1509	5827	865	718	154	45	49	70	506	15	916	94	10

INDIVIDUAL

TOP QUALIFIERS FOR EARNED-RUN AVERAGE TITLE

Minimum 115 innings. *Lefthanded pitcher.

Pitcher, Team	W	L	Pct.	ERA	G	GS	CG	ShO	GF	Sv.	IP	H	TBF	R	ER	HR	SH	SF	HB	BB	IBB	SO	WP	Bk.
Baker, Scott, Rochester	5	8	.385	3.01	22	22	1	1	0	0	134.2	123	544	50	45	15	0	3	7	26	1	107	4	0
Graman, Alex, Columbus-Louisville *	7	7	.500	3.16	28	20	0	0	4	1	119.2	118	511	49	42	14	3	1	3	48	2	115	6	0
Scobie, Jason, Norfolk	15	7	.682	3.34	27	26	0	0	0	0	167.0	163	694	71	62	13	6	6	7	55	2	96	5	0
Gaudin, Chad, Syracuse *	9	8	.529	3.35	23	23	2	2	0	0	150.1	140	610	61	56	12	7	9	8	35	1	113	5	2
Baugh, Kenneth, Toledo	12	8	.600	3.38	28	28	1	1	0	0	165.1	159	699	72	62	13	7	4	7	60	0	107	9	0
Fiore, Tony, Ottawa	9	5	.643	3.63	30	28	0	0	0	0	166.1	168	703	79	67	14	3	6	11	49	1	97	4	0
Good, Andrew, Toledo	9	5	.643	3.68	23	23	0	0	0	0	134.1	129	562	61	55	18	3	5	6	42	3	89	4	0
Miner, Zachary, Richmond-Toledo	5	8	.385	3.71	23	23	0	0	0	0	123.2	125	546	57	51	10	3	2	4	65	1	83	3	0
Ramirez, Elizardo, Louisville	7	7	.500	3.77	21	21	0	0	0	0	131.1	150	546	60	55	14	3	2	3	18	1	82	5	0
Junge, Eric, Norfolk	10	7	.588	3.80	26	26	0	0	3	2	135.0	125	564	61	57	18	4	2	3	52	2	114	2	1
Fernandez, Jared, Louisville-Scranton/Wilkes-Barre	9	7	.563	3.82	20	20	0	0	0	0	125.0	126	524	63	53	12	5	5	3	40	0	81	8	0
McCarthy, Brandon, Charlotte	7	7	.500	3.92	20	19	1	1	1	0	119.2	104	482	52	52	16	3	1	2	32	0	130	5	1

Pitcher, Team	W	L	Pct.	ERA	G	GS	CG	ShO	GF	Sv.	IP	H	TBF	R	ER	HR	SH	SF	HB	BB	IBB	SO	WP	Bk.
Rosario, Francisco, Syracuse	2	7	.222	3.95	30	18	0	0	4	2	116.1	111	484	59	51	16	5	1	10	42	1	80	5	1
Bonser, Boof, Rochester	11	9	.550	3.99	28	28	0	0	0	0	160.1	153	677	80	71	22	7	8	2	57	0	168	3	0
Grilli, Jason, Toledo	12	9	.571	4.09	28	28	3	2	0	0	167.1	170	717	89	76	21	4	3	9	58	0	120	1	0
Condrey, Clay, Scranton/Wilkes-Barre	7	8	.467	4.15	25	24	2	0	0	0	132.1	159	565	66	61	13	6	3	3	29	1	74	2	0
Watkins, Steve, Buffalo	9	2	.818	4.16	31	17	0	0	2	0	129.2	142	559	72	60	13	6	10	10	34	1	86	4	0
Santiago, Jose, Norfolk	7	6	.538	4.26	29	17	0	0	1	0	122.2	138	528	62	58	10	4	1	7	40	1	61	2	0
Munoz, Arnie, Charlotte *	8	14	.364	4.27	40	18	0	0	7	1	132.2	150	593	79	63	16	3	5	5	60	2	109	10	3
Seo, Jae Weong, Norfolk	7	4	.636	4.29	19	19	0	0	0	0	121.2	126	507	64	58	13	7	6	1	30	0	111	2	1
Borkowski, Dave, Ottawa	10	10	.500	4.34	29	28	1	0	1	0	182.2	217	788	99	88	18	4	15	38	3	104	3	0

DEPARTMENTAL LEADERS: W—Scobie, 15. L—Munoz, 14. Pct.—Watkins, .818. G—Smith, 66. GS—six pitchers tied with 28. CG—Grilli, 3. ShO—Gaudin and Grilli, 2. GF—Corey, 55. Sv.—Corey, 28. IP—Borkowski, 182.2. H—Borkowski, 217. TBF—Borkowski, 792. R—Webb and Floyd, 103. ER—Floyd, 94. HR—Webb and Bacsik, 23. SAC—Davis and Bullington, 10. SF—Stewart, 11. HB—Floyd, 19. BB—Stewart, 67. IBB—Sanders, 8. SO—Bonser, 168. WP—Simpson, 12. BK—Seddon and Ramirez, 5.

ALL PITCHERS

*Lefthanded pitcher.

Pitcher, Team	W	L	Pct.	ERA	G	GS	CG	ShO	GF	Sv.	IP	H	TBF	R	ER	HR	SH	SF	HB	BB	IBB	SO	WP	Bk.
Abad, Andy, Buffalo *	0	0	.000	0.00	1	0	0	0	1	0	2.0	3	7	0	0	0	0	0	0	0	0	1	0	0
Abbott, James, Rochester	0	3	.000	9.00	6	0	0	0	3	0	13.0	14	62	15	13	5	0	0	1	8	2	10	0	0
Acevedo, Jose, Louisville	0	0	.000	0.00	1	1	0	0	0	0	4.0	2	12	0	0	0	0	0	0	0	0	3	0	0
Adams, Terry, Scranton/Wilkes-Barre	1	2	.333	4.41	14	0	0	0	9	0	16.1	22	84	8	8	1	0	1	1	8	1	14	2	1
Adkins, Jon, Charlotte	4	9	.308	5.37	23	21	0	0	1	0	127.1	148	549	81	76	20	3	2	3	43	1	92	0	0
Alfaro, Jason, Syracuse	0	0	.000	4.50	1	0	0	0	1	0	2.0	4	9	1	1	0	0	0	0	0	0	2	0	0
Almonte, Hector, Richmond	1	1	.500	2.70	18	0	0	0	5	0	26.2	30	123	12	8	2	2	1	0	16	2	25	2	1
Alvarez, Abe, Pawtucket *	11	6	.647	4.85	26	26	0	0	0	0	144.2	143	600	84	78	17	4	5	4	31	0	109	0	0
Amaya, Jose, Buffalo	0	1	.000	14.73	1	1	0	0	0	0	3.2	8	23	6	6	1	0	0	0	4	0	1	0	0
Anderson, Jason, Columbus	4	1	.800	2.66	55	0	0	0	24	10	67.2	44	254	21	20	4	3	3	1	18	1	60	3	0
Anderson, Jimmy, Rochester-Durham	6	8	.429	3.48	22	20	0	0	0	0	113.2	114	503	53	44	5	5	4	5	54	0	62	7	0
Arnold, Jason, Syracuse	0	4	.000	6.39	47	0	0	0	21	5	62.0	60	279	46	44	14	2	1	8	27	1	53	4	0
Artiles, Carlos, Columbus *	0	0	.000	4.50	2	0	0	0	2	1	2.0	4	10	1	1	0	0	0	0	1	0	0	0	0
Aybar, Manny, Norfolk	3	0	1.000	1.41	24	0	0	0	10	4	32.0	26	127	7	5	1	1	2	2	8	0	27	0	0
Bacsik, Mike, Scranton/Wilkes-Barre *	7	10	.412	4.55	30	27	0	0	1	0	160.1	184	689	90	81	23	5	3	5	41	2	112	3	0
Bajenaru, Jeff, Charlotte	4	6	.400	1.41	61	0	0	0	48	19	70.1	45	272	14	11	4	5	0	0	29	5	83	1	1
Baker, Chris, Syracuse	8	7	.533	5.30	31	21	0	0	3	0	130.2	165	573	80	77	13	6	3	6	30	0	87	5	1
Baker, Scott, Rochester	5	8	.385	3.01	22	22	1	1	0	0	134.2	123	544	50	45	15	0	3	7	26	1	107	4	0
Baldwin, James, Ottawa	3	2	.600	4.60	8	8	0	0	0	0	47.0	52	198	25	24	6	1	1	2	4	0	25	0	2
Bannister, Brian, Norfolk	4	1	.800	3.18	8	8	0	0	0	0	45.1	48	196	19	16	0	1	4	1	13	0	48	4	0
Barkett, Andy, Richmond *	0	0	.000	0.00	1	0	0	0	1	0	1.0	1	4	0	0	0	0	0	0	0	0	0	0	0
Barnes, John, Richmond	0	0	.000	18.00	1	0	0	0	1	0	1.0	1	8	3	2	0	0	1	0	3	0	0	0	0
Barrett, William, Rochester *	4	4	.500	6.71	40	5	0	0	12	0	63.0	70	300	48	47	10	2	3	5	48	4	64	2	1
Barry, Kevin, Richmond	5	3	.625	2.85	32	8	0	0	12	1	79.0	60	335	28	25	8	2	2	2	44	1	73	0	0
Basner, Ryan, Richmond	0	0	.000	0.00	2	0	0	0	0	0	1.2	1	9	0	0	0	0	0	0	3	1	0	0	0
Bauer, Rick, Ottawa	3	8	.273	4.00	30	10	0	0	3	1	74.1	84	325	38	33	12	6	2	2	35	3	43	4	0
Baugh, Kenneth, Toledo	12	8	.600	3.38	28	28	1	1	0	0	165.1	159	699	72	62	13	7	4	7	60	0	107	9	0
Bausher, Timothy, Pawtucket	3	2	.600	3.41	44	0	0	0	20	5	71.1	66	309	36	27	9	3	3	3	36	3	65	8	0
Bean, Colter, Columbus	4	7	.364	3.01	65	0	0	0	20	0	71.2	66	314	33	24	5	8	2	8	39	7	82	0	0
Beimel, Joe, Durham *	1	2	.333	3.93	48	0	0	0	14	0	52.2	58	233	28	23	3	2	1	1	21	1	36	4	0
Bell, Heath, Norfolk	1	0	1.000	1.69	13	2	0	0	8	6	26.2	15	96	5	5	1	1	1	0	5	0	29	1	0
Bell, Rob, Durham	1	3	.250	7.71	22	2	0	0	5	0	44.1	64	209	39	38	12	6	2	1	20	2	26	4	0
Bere, Jason, Buffalo	1	1	.500	13.15	3	3	0	0	0	0	13.0	26	68	20	19	5	0	1	0	5	0	5	1	0
Bernero, Adam, Richmond	5	5	.500	3.40	10	9	0	0	1	0	53.0	57	226	27	20	6	3	1	2	15	0	41	0	0
Bikowski, Scott, Charlotte *	0	0	.000	0.00	1	0	0	0	1	0	0.2	1	4	0	0	0	0	0	1	0	0	0	0	0
Blackburn, Robert, Rochester	0	0	.000	5.14	3	3	0	0	0	0	14.0	20	64	11	8	2	1	0	0	3	0	7	0	0
Boehringer, Brian, Columbus	0	1	.000	21.32	6	0	0	0	2	0	6.1	12	36	15	15	3	0	0	1	6	0	2	0	0
Bonilla, Vicente, Rochester	6	7	.462	5.11	35	16	0	0	3	2	118.0	138	516	75	67	14	4	3	8	44	3	63	2	1
Bonser, Boof, Rochester	11	9	.550	3.99	28	28	0	0	0	0	160.1	153	677	80	71	22	7	8	2	57	0	168	3	0
Booker, Chris, Louisville	8	4	.667	2.49	59	0	0	0	48	20	65.0	46	263	20	18	2	0	3	1	28	1	91	3	0
Borkowski, Dave, Ottawa	10	10	.500	4.34	29	28	1	0	1	0	182.2	217	788	99	88	18	4	15	38	3	104	3	0
Bottalico, Ricky, Pawtucket	0	0	.000	4.32	6	0	0	0	1	0	8.1	5	31	4	4	1	0	2	0	4	0	6	1	0
Bowyer, Travis, Rochester	4	2	.667	2.78	59	0	0	0	41	23	74.1	51	304	23	23	4	2	0	2	40	0	96	3	2
Bradley, Bobby, Indianapolis	0	1	.000	13.14	11	2	0	0	1	0	12.1	10	81	23	18	0	1	0	5	30	0	8	10	0
Brazelton, Dewon, Durham	2	2	.500	3.72	5	5	0	0	0	0	29.0	29	133	17	12	3	1	3	1	14	0	26	1	0
Brito, Eude, Scranton/Wilkes-Barre *	6	2	.750	4.85	28	15	0	0	3	0	98.1	97	417	59	53	13	2	5	8	39	0	76	3	3
Brock, Terrence, Durham	2	5	.286	5.65	15	5	0	0	2	1	36.2	53	174	31	23	6	1	2	1	12	0	27	2	0
Brooks, Frank, Richmond *	3	4	.429	2.73	54	0	0	0	15	0	56.0	46	237	27	17	4	2	6	0	24	2	49	3	1
Brower, Jim, Richmond	0	1	.000	2.25	4	0	0	0	3	1	4.0	1	14	1	1	0	0	1	0	2	0	1	0	0
Brown, Andrew, Buffalo	4	2	.667	3.36	49	0	0	0	21	4	69.2	52	279	28	26	7	0	2	3	19	0	81	4	0
Bruback, Matt, Ottawa	0	6	.000	5.37	9	9	0	0	0	0	52.0	64	233	36	31	7	2	6	2	14	0	28	3	0
Bruksch, Jeffrey, Louisville	1	0	1.000	1.80	1	1	0	0	0	0	5.0	4	18	1	1	1	1	0	0	2	0	1	0	0
Bullard, James, Charlotte *	3	2	.600	5.67	15	9	0	0	4	0	54.0	57	248	34	34	12	1	2	2	31	1	39	0	0
Bullinger, Jim, Charlotte	1	0	1.000	9.53	10	0	0	0	4	0	17.0	23	82	20	18	3	2	1	2	9	1	13	1	0
Bullinger, Kirk, Indianapolis	2	7	.222	3.39	55	0	0	0	19	4	69.0	72	280	29	26	7	8	0	1	15	6	40	1	0
Bullington, Bryan, Indianapolis	5	4	.643	3.38	18	18	1	0	0	0	109.1	104	446	48	41	11	10	2	4	26	1	82	0	0
Bumatay, Michael, Toledo *	0	0	.000	0.00	3	0	0	0	1	0	4.1	4	18	0	0	0	0	0	0	2	0	5	0	0
Burke, Erick, Scranton/Wilkes-Barre *	3	0	1.000	2.97	32	0	0	0	3	1	33.1	29	144	12	11	2	1	2	0	22	3	33	0	0
Burnside, Adrian, Syracuse *	4	4	.500	2.98	50	0	0	0	15	0	57.1	52	240	20	19	4	1	4	4	16	1	45	3	0
Bush, David, Syracuse	2	2	.500	4.42	9	9	0	0	0	0	55.0	65	230	28	27	6	2	1	2	9	0	41	0	1
Bynum, Mike, Toledo *	2	1	.667	6.97	8	2	0	0	0	0	20.2	29	99	21	16	5	1	0	3	13	0	12	1	0
Byrdak, Tim, Ottawa *	3	2	.600	2.09	37	0	0	0	25	11	38.2	23	153	12	9	4	0	3	0	15	1	44	0	0
Cabrera, Fernando, Buffalo	6	1	.857	1.23	30	0	0	0	18	3	51.1	36	196	8	7	3	3	1	0	11	2	68	1	0

Pitcher, Team	W	L	Pct.	ERA	G	GS	CG	ShO	GF	Sv.	IP	H	TBF	R	ER	HR	SH	SF	HB	BB	IBB	SO	WP	Bk.
Cahill, Casey, Ottawa	0	0	.000	18.00	1	0	0	0	0	0	2.0	4	12	4	4	2	0	0	0	2	0	1	0	0
Carlson, Jesse, Syracuse *	1	1	.500	4.82	22	0	0	0	6	0	18.2	26	92	10	10	4	1	0	5	7	1	17	0	0
Carmona, Fausto, Buffalo	7	4	.636	3.25	13	12	1	0	0	0	83.0	76	332	32	30	10	4	2	3	15	0	49	2	0
Carnes, Thomas, Durham	5	1	.833	4.45	37	0	0	0	13	0	54.2	54	227	30	27	4	2	6	1	15	1	39	3	0
Carter, Lance, Durham	1	5	.167	5.14	8	7	0	0	0	0	35.0	40	152	24	20	8	0	2	0	12	0	30	2	0
Cassidy, Scott, Pawtucket	6	3	.667	4.05	26	3	0	0	6	0	60.0	54	251	31	27	5	4	4	2	23	2	66	0	0
Cevette, Daniel, Buffalo *	0	1	.000	14.40	1	1	0	0	0	0	5.0	9	25	8	8	5	0	2	0	2	0	2	0	0
Chantres, Carlos, Scranton/Wilkes-Barre	0	0	.000	3.00	1	1	0	0	0	0	6.0	4	25	4	2	1	0	0	0	3	0	3	0	0
Chenard, Kenneth, Norfolk	1	0	1.000	1.35	1	1	0	0	0	0	6.2	3	27	1	1	0	0	0	4	0	4	0	0
Chiavacci, Ronald, Indianapolis	0	0	.000	1.50	10	0	0	0	3	0	12.0	6	45	2	2	1	0	1	2	0	14	0	0
Childers, Jason, Richmond	1	2	.333	2.09	38	0	0	0	29	16	38.2	32	158	14	9	2	4	0	0	20	1	31	2	0
Childers, Matt, Richmond	4	2	.667	3.93	51	1	0	0	12	2	73.1	69	307	37	32	4	5	3	4	21	1	62	6	0
Childress, Daylan, Louisville-Rochester	0	1	.000	8.10	16	0	0	0	6	0	23.1	28	109	22	21	3	1	2	1	12	0	16	3	0
Clippard, Tyler, Columbus	0	0	.000	0.00	1	0	0	0	0	0	1.0	0	3	0	0	0	0	0	0	0	0	2	0	0
Coffey, Todd, Louisville	0	0	.000	5.19	8	0	0	0	5	3	8.2	8	35	5	5	1	1	0	0	2	1	5	0	0
Colon, Roman, Richmond	1	1	.500	1.93	3	3	0	0	0	0	14.0	12	57	3	3	0	1	0	1	5	0	9	2	1
Colyer, Steve, Norfolk *	4	2	.667	5.67	28	0	0	0	5	1	27.0	25	121	17	17	2	3	0	2	19	0	31	2	0
Condrey, Clay, Scranton/Wilkes-Barre ..	7	8	.467	4.15	25	24	2	0	0	0	132.1	159	565	66	61	13	5	3	3	29	1	74	2	0
Connolly, Michael, Indianapolis *	2	4	.333	4.42	13	13	0	0	0	0	71.1	74	309	37	35	9	1	1	3	29	3	44	2	0
Cooper, Christopher, Buffalo *	0	0	.000	5.74	12	0	0	0	8	0	15.2	20	68	11	10	5	2	1	1	3	1	15	0	0
Corcoran, Tim, Durham	5	1	.833	2.89	29	0	0	0	3	0	56.0	49	238	22	18	3	0	1	2	22	0	49	4	0
Corey, Mark, Indianapolis	5	5	.500	4.02	61	0	0	0	55	28	65.0	62	281	30	29	6	1	1	2	23	4	60	4	0
Coste, Christopher, Scranton/Wilkes-Barre	0	0	.000	0.00	1	0	0	0	1	0	1.0	1	5	0	0	0	0	0	0	1	0	0	0	0
Creek, Doug, Toledo *	2	2	.500	4.61	28	1	0	0	4	0	27.1	28	123	14	14	2	0	2	2	14	4	32	2	0
Cressend, Jack, Pawtucket	5	5	.500	5.06	40	3	0	0	14	0	69.1	79	305	42	39	15	5	5	2	23	1	68	2	0
Cruceta, Francisco, Buffalo	6	4	.600	5.19	30	13	1	0	6	0	102.1	123	452	65	59	16	2	1	5	32	0	92	8	2
Cruz, Nelson, Toledo	5	4	.556	4.20	14	11	0	0	3	0	64.1	69	272	31	30	8	2	0	7	17	1	55	1	1
Curtis, Daniel, Richmond	3	8	.273	5.20	18	17	0	0	0	0	88.1	102	396	61	51	5	4	3	7	38	3	40	2	0
Darensbourg, Vic, Toledo *	2	0	1.000	0.29	44	0	0	0	15	7	30.2	17	113	3	1	0	1	1	2	11	1	30	0	0
Davies, Kyle, Richmond	5	2	.714	3.44	13	13	0	0	0	0	73.1	66	306	28	28	6	1	3	0	34	2	62	7	0
Davis, Allen, Scranton/Wilkes-Barre * ..	1	1	.500	2.03	3	3	0	0	0	0	13.1	11	50	3	3	0	1	2	0	1	0	6	0	0
Davis, Jason, Buffalo	8	5	.615	4.61	16	16	1	0	0	0	95.2	106	409	65	49	9	10	3	4	27	0	77	5	2
Deardorff, Jeff, Durham	0	0	.000	0.00	1	0	0	0	1	0	1.0	2	5	0	0	0	0	0	0	0	0	1	0	0
Dehart, James, Richmond *	0	1	.000	13.50	2	0	0	0	0	0	2.0	5	14	5	3	1	1	0	1	1	0	2	0	0
Delcarmen, Manny, Pawtucket	3	1	.750	1.29	15	0	0	0	10	2	21.0	17	92	3	3	0	0	0	1	13	1	23	1	1
Denham, Daniel, Buffalo	0	2	.000	10.80	3	2	0	0	0	0	10.0	16	51	13	12	3	1	0	1	8	0	6	0	0
Denney, Kyle, Buffalo	1	1	.500	5.12	9	9	0	0	0	0	38.2	52	178	22	22	9	0	4	0	10	0	22	0	1
De Paula, Jorge, Columbus	4	2	.667	4.58	21	20	0	0	0	0	116.0	109	491	63	59	22	4	3	8	41	0	90	1	0
Deschenes, Mark, Pawtucket	2	2	.500	2.94	11	4	0	0	3	0	33.2	22	129	12	11	5	0	0	1	5	1	28	1	0
Devine, Joey, Richmond	0	0	.000	18.00	1	0	0	0	0	0	1.0	3	6	2	2	0	0	0	0	1	0	1	0	0
Diaz, Felix, Charlotte	6	8	.429	5.00	21	21	1	0	0	0	122.1	149	532	72	68	15	4	8	7	33	1	108	4	1
Diaz, Jose, Buffalo	1	2	.333	3.89	20	0	0	0	7	0	34.2	27	155	19	15	4	1	3	4	26	3	44	4	0
DiNardo, Lenny, Pawtucket *	6	3	.667	3.15	23	22	0	0	0	0	108.2	109	460	51	38	7	7	4	10	35	0	93	1	3
Dingman, Craig, Toledo	2	1	.667	2.81	35	0	0	0	12	4	48.0	42	201	18	15	3	1	1	4	13	0	67	3	1
Douglass, Sean, Toledo	9	1	.900	2.87	14	14	0	0	0	0	81.2	61	331	26	26	5	2	3	3	27	1	76	2	0
Downs, Scott, Syracuse *	2	3	.400	4.81	7	7	0	0	0	0	39.1	45	161	21	21	5	0	0	0	3	0	35	0	0
DuBose, Eric, Ottawa *	0	1	.000	11.42	2	2	0	0	0	0	8.2	17	44	13	11	5	0	0	0	1	0	7	0	0
Duff, Matt, Syracuse	5	0	1.000	3.51	15	0	0	0	2	0	25.2	21	104	10	10	3	1	0	1	7	0	28	1	0
Duke, Zach, Indianapolis *	12	3	.800	2.92	16	16	1	0	0	0	108.0	108	431	39	35	8	5	1	2	23	1	66	1	2
Durbin, J.D., Rochester	5	5	.500	4.33	22	19	0	0	0	0	104.0	97	447	52	50	8	3	4	6	51	1	90	10	0
Ellis, Robert, Scranton/Wilkes-Barre	0	1	.000	6.38	4	4	0	0	0	0	18.1	24	82	14	13	2	0	0	0	7	0	13	0	0
Ennis, John, Toledo	3	5	.375	4.85	50	1	0	0	10	1	72.1	77	320	41	39	7	3	6	5	30	1	65	1	0
Enochs, Chris, Indianapolis	4	4	.500	5.17	33	14	0	0	6	0	102.2	116	452	62	59	8	4	7	7	42	3	58	7	0
Estrada, Horacio, Ottawa *	2	2	.500	7.56	5	4	0	0	0	0	16.2	23	77	14	14	2	0	3	3	4	0	5	1	0
Evans, Kyle, Buffalo	0	1	.000	3.00	1	0	0	0	1	0	3.0	2	14	3	1	0	2	0	2	2	0	3	0	0
Eyre, Willie, Rochester	10	3	.769	2.72	56	0	0	0	23	7	82.2	79	345	30	25	3	3	0	4	28	1	74	4	0
Fernandez, Jared, Louisville-Scranton/Wilkes-Barre..	9	7	.563	3.82	20	20	0	0	0	0	125.0	126	524	63	53	12	5	5	3	40	0	81	8	0
Fesh, Sean, Scranton/Wilkes-Barre * ...	2	0	1.000	5.89	27	0	0	0	4	0	18.1	21	87	13	12	3	1	0	2	15	1	11	1	0
Fields, Joshua, Charlotte	4	5	.444	2.75	55	0	0	0	8	0	68.2	61	279	23	21	6	2	3	21	5	51	1	2
Fiore, Tony, Ottawa	9	5	.643	3.63	30	28	0	0	0	0	166.1	168	703	79	67	14	3	6	11	49	1	97	4	0
Floyd, Gavin, Scranton/Wilkes-Barre	6	9	.400	6.16	24	23	0	0	0	0	137.1	155	626	103	94	11	6	7	19	66	1	97	10	0
Foster, John, Richmond *	0	0	.000	1.59	3	0	0	0	2	1	5.2	2	20	1	1	0	0	0	0	1	0	5	0	0
Franco, Martire, Scranton/Wilkes-Barre	5	6	.455	4.86	44	10	0	0	12	2	100.0	122	449	59	54	7	4	2	3	39	3	71	4	0
Franklin, Wayne, Columbus *	2	3	.400	3.61	46	0	0	0	11	1	42.1	36	171	18	17	4	1	0	4	11	1	50	0	0
Gardner, Lee, Durham	4	3	.571	3.29	48	0	0	0	44	15	52.0	56	219	25	19	8	4	2	0	15	0	35	1	0
Gassner, Dave, Rochester *	8	8	.500	4.95	22	20	2	0	0	0	116.1	138	498	65	64	18	4	5	3	33	0	64	1	0
Gaudin, Chad, Syracuse	9	8	.529	3.35	23	23	2	2	0	0	150.1	140	610	61	56	12	7	9	8	35	1	113	5	2
Geary, Geoff, Scranton/Wilkes-Barre	1	2	.333	2.70	10	0	0	0	3	1	16.2	15	65	5	5	0	0	0	0	2	0	14	1	0
Germano, Justin, Louisville	3	2	.600	4.01	8	8	0	0	0	0	49.1	62	209	27	22	7	1	1	5	5	0	38	2	0
Giese, Daniel, Scranton/Wilkes-Barre ...	3	4	.429	5.68	26	0	0	0	5	2	38.0	51	164	28	24	9	2	1	1	0	28	1	1
Gil, Benji, Norfolk	0	0	.000	0.00	1	0	0	0	1	0	1.0	1	3	0	0	0	0	0	0	0	0	0	0	0
Ginter, Matt, Toledo	4	3	.571	4.33	17	10	0	0	1	0	68.2	72	281	35	33	9	0	3	10	0	49	1	1
Glynn, Ryan, Syracuse	2	4	.333	6.27	9	6	0	0	0	0	37.1	41	162	27	26	6	1	4	2	11	0	23	2	0
Gonzalez, Jeremi, Pawtucket	5	2	.714	2.61	11	11	0	0	0	0	69.0	63	276	20	20	8	1	0	5	14	0	62	1	1
Gonzalez, Mike, Indianapolis *	0	0	.000	0.00	2	0	0	0	1	0	3.1	0	9	0	0	0	1	0	0	0	0	5	0	0
Good, Andrew, Toledo	9	5	.643	3.68	23	23	0	0	0	0	134.1	129	562	61	55	18	3	5	6	42	3	89	4	0
Graman, Alex, Columbus-Louisville	7	7	.500	3.16	28	20	0	0	0	0	119.2	118	511	49	42	14	3	1	3	48	2	115	6	0
Graves, Danny, Norfolk	0	1	.000	18.00	5	0	0	0	1	0	6.0	15	38	12	12	2	0	0	0	7	0	4	0	0
Green, Steve, Toledo	2	5	.529	5.29	24	0	0	0	10	2	32.1	42	153	20	19	2	3	0	0	20	3	41	5	0
Greisinger, Seth, Richmond	4	7	.364	3.01	16	16	1	0	0	0	98.2	75	392	36	33	4	5	2	9	28	2	56	1	0
Grilli, Jason, Toledo	12	9	.571	4.09	28	28	3	2	0	0	167.1	170	717	89	76	21	4	3	9	58	0	120	1	0

Pitcher, Team	W	L	Pct.	ERA	G	GS	CG	ShO	GF	Sv.	IP	H	TBF	R	ER	HR	SH	SF	HB	BB	IBB	SO	WP	Bk.
Gronkiewicz, Lee, Syracuse	0	1	.000	2.22	28	0	0	0	12	6	28.1	21	116	9	7	3	1	1	0	13	2	26	1	0
Groom, Buddy, Columbus *	0	0	.000	5.79	6	0	0	0	0	0	4.2	6	19	4	3	2	0	1	0	0	0	5	1	0
Guthrie, Jeremy, Buffalo	12	10	.545	5.08	25	25	1	0	0	0	136.1	152	599	88	77	15	7	6	12	49	0	100	4	2
Hammel, Jason, Durham	3	2	.600	4.12	10	10	0	0	0	0	54.2	57	246	31	25	8	1	0	3	27	0	48	4	0
Hampton, Mike, Richmond *	0	0	.000	2.25	1	1	0	0	0	0	4.0	4	16	1	1	0	0	0	0	0	0	3	0	0
Hamulack, Tim, Norfolk *	3	1	.750	1.02	28	0	0	0	16	6	35.1	20	130	5	4	1	3	0	1	9	1	34	2	0
Hancock, Josh, Louisville	1	2	.333	5.93	11	8	0	0	1	0	44.0	59	200	33	29	5	3	0	3	17	0	38	3	0
Hankins, Ryan, Columbus	0	1	.000	9.00	1	0	0	0	1	0	1.0	2	5	2	1	0	0	0	0	0	0	0	0	0
Haynes, Jimmy, Durham	1	2	.333	8.18	7	4	0	0	0	0	22.0	35	108	23	20	4	1	2	1	9	0	12	1	0
Henkel, Robert, Toledo *	1	1	.500	7.82	10	0	0	0	6	0	12.2	14	62	12	11	2	1	0	1	11	0	9	1	0
Henn, Sean, Columbus *	5	5	.500	3.23	16	16	1	1	0	0	86.1	79	345	37	31	5	3	3	4	27	1	64	0	0
Hernandez, Buddy, Richmond	0	2	.000	6.75	7	0	0	0	1	0	12.0	15	59	9	9	3	0	1	0	8	2	11	1	0
Hernandez, Orlando, Charlotte	0	1	.000	2.25	1	1	0	0	0	0	4.0	4	15	1	1	0	0	0	0	0	0	2	0	0
Hernandez, Yoel, Scranton/Wilkes-Barre	6	4	.600	3.40	40	0	0	0	19	3	55.2	53	238	21	21	5	3	3	4	24	2	52	1	0
Herrera, Alex, Richmond *	0	1	.000	7.27	13	0	0	0	4	0	17.1	15	84	15	14	3	1	2	3	18	0	14	0	0
Hessman, Mike, Toledo	0	0	.000	0.00	1	0	0	0	1	0	0.2	1	4	0	0	0	0	0	0	0	0	0	0	0
Hill, Jeremy, Norfolk	0	0	.000	0.00	2	0	0	0	1	0	1.2	1	5	0	0	0	0	0	0	0	0	0	0	0
Hines, Carlos, Durham	3	1	.750	3.28	26	0	0	0	6	0	35.2	39	160	16	13	1	3	0	2	17	0	22	3	0
Hodge, Kevin, Scranton/Wilkes-Barre	3	2	.600	5.40	20	0	0	0	6	3	28.1	27	114	17	17	5	2	1	1	8	1	28	3	0
Hodges, Trey, Rochester-Richmond	0	3	.000	6.89	15	4	0	0	5	0	32.2	43	161	32	25	4	1	3	1	19	0	21	2	0
Hooper, Kevin, Toledo	0	0	.000	0.00	1	0	0	0	1	1	1.0	0	3	0	0	0	0	0	0	0	0	1	0	0
Isaacson, Charlie, Columbus	0	0	.000	6.75	7	0	0	0	1	0	10.2	19	58	8	8	1	0	0	0	7	1	7	2	0
Ishii, Kazuhisa, Norfolk *	2	2	.500	1.76	5	2	0	0	1	0	15.1	16	71	4	3	0	0	3	8	0	18	2	0
Izquierdo, Hansel, Indianapolis	1	1	.500	6.14	7	5	0	0	0	0	29.1	45	146	27	20	3	1	1	4	10	1	23	2	0
Jackson, Zach, Syracuse *	4	4	.500	5.13	8	8	0	0	0	0	47.1	61	213	33	27	3	3	1	2	21	1	33	1	0
James, Chuck, Richmond *	1	3	.250	3.48	6	6	0	0	0	0	33.2	21	131	13	13	4	0	1	1	10	0	30	2	0
Johnson, Mark, Toledo	0	1	.000	8.05	7	2	0	0	2	0	19.0	24	87	19	17	2	1	2	1	8	2	14	0	0
Johnston, Mike, Indianapolis *	2	1	.667	2.97	52	0	0	0	7	0	57.2	43	242	21	19	5	3	1	4	30	2	52	6	0
Jones, Bobby M., Charlotte *	0	2	.000	8.39	16	2	0	0	4	0	24.2	37	127	25	23	3	0	3	2	14	0	25	4	0
Junge, Eric, Norfolk	10	7	.588	3.80	26	22	0	0	3	2	135.0	125	564	61	57	18	4	2	3	52	2	114	2	1
Karnuth, Jason, Toledo	7	2	.778	2.13	63	0	0	0	51	23	67.2	65	267	19	16	1	6	0	1	17	4	36	0	0
Keisler, Randy, Louisville *	5	2	.714	2.88	12	7	0	0	2	2	56.1	54	231	19	18	6	0	2	0	13	0	46	0	0
Kelly, Steven, Louisville	5	5	.500	4.82	19	19	0	0	0	0	104.2	108	446	62	56	10	7	4	4	41	0	67	2	1
Kemp, Beau, Rochester	4	5	.444	3.38	62	0	0	0	36	5	80.0	74	346	35	30	1	2	3	3	32	6	68	4	0
Keppel, Robert, Norfolk	2	1	.667	3.29	5	5	0	0	0	0	27.1	24	111	11	10	0	0	4	6	0	19	1	0
Kershner, Jason, Pawtucket *	0	2	.000	5.68	15	0	0	0	11	2	19.0	24	85	12	12	3	0	2	0	6	1	10	2	0
Kester, Timothy, Pawtucket	11	9	.550	4.95	30	28	1	0	0	0	165.1	199	704	101	91	17	3	7	7	29	1	105	2	1
King, Jeremy, Columbus	0	0	.000	0.00	1	1	0	0	0	0	6.0	3	22	1	0	0	0	0	0	0	0	3	1	0
Kleine, Victor, Buffalo *	0	0	.000	2.45	6	0	0	0	2	0	11.0	9	47	3	3	2	1	0	2	7	1	5	0	0
Koo, Dae-Sung, Norfolk *	0	0	.000	0.00	2	1	0	0	0	0	4.0	4	15	0	0	0	0	0	0	0	0	0	0	0
Koo, Dae-Sung, Norfolk	0	0	.000	0.00	2	1	0	0	0	0	4.0	4	15	0	0	0	...	0	0	0	0	0	0	...
Kozlowski, Ben, Louisville *	2	3	.400	4.63	8	8	0	0	0	0	44.2	52	200	29	23	3	1	2	3	18	1	30	1	0
Laker, Tim, Durham	0	1	.000	27.00	1	0	0	0	1	0	0.1	1	2	1	1	0	1	0	0	1	0	0	1	0
Lavigne, Tim, Norfolk	1	3	.250	3.65	45	0	0	0	16	1	69.0	66	295	29	28	5	4	1	2	35	2	41	3	0
League, Brandon, Syracuse	4	4	.500	5.71	19	10	0	0	1	0	63.0	78	280	44	40	7	2	3	4	18	0	35	5	0
Ledezma, Wilfredo, Toledo *	5	3	.625	5.29	11	10	0	0	0	0	51.0	52	229	30	30	3	2	1	1	27	0	44	2	0
Lee, Dave, Norfolk	2	2	.500	3.09	28	0	0	0	14	5	35.0	32	150	13	12	4	1	1	7	13	1	25	1	0
Lee, Seung Hak, Scranton/Wilkes-Barre	0	0	.000	23.62	1	0	0	0	0	0	2.2	5	16	7	7	2	0	0	0	3	0	1	0	0
Lerew, Anthony, Richmond	4	4	.500	3.48	13	13	0	0	0	0	72.1	63	300	34	28	9	2	3	3	23	0	53	1	0
Lilly, Ted, Syracuse *	0	1	.000	3.12	2	2	0	0	0	0	8.2	5	38	4	3	1	0	1	3	5	0	9	0	0
Liriano, Francisco, Rochester *	9	2	.818	1.78	14	14	0	0	0	0	91.0	56	343	25	18	4	0	2	0	24	0	112	2	1
Liriano, Pedro, Scranton/Wilkes-Barre	4	9	.308	3.90	22	17	1	0	3	0	99.1	90	427	49	43	11	4	3	8	48	1	79	2	0
Little, Jeffrey, Charlotte	2	1	.667	4.91	9	3	0	0	1	0	25.2	20	105	15	14	5	1	2	2	8	1	17	0	0
Lomasney, Steve, Louisville	0	0	.000	0.00	1	0	0	0	1	0	0.2	0	2	0	0	0	0	0	0	0	0	0	0	0
Lopez, Aquilino, Scranton/Wilkes-Barre	0	0	.000	1.00	4	0	0	0	0	1	9.0	5	33	1	1	0	0	0	0	1	0	11	0	0
Lundberg, David, Syracuse	8	6	.571	3.95	50	3	0	0	15	1	86.2	101	384	48	38	5	6	7	7	25	3	65	1	1
Maduro, Calvin, Columbus	0	0	.000	4.97	6	2	0	0	1	0	12.2	20	61	8	7	0	0	2	4	0	6	0	0
Magrane, James, Durham	1	5	.167	6.68	26	5	0	0	6	0	62.0	95	286	54	46	12	2	2	7	1	38	3	0
Maholm, Paul, Indianapolis *	1	1	.500	3.53	6	6	0	0	0	0	35.2	40	153	19	14	2	0	0	1	12	0	21	1	0
Maine, John, Ottawa	6	11	.353	4.56	23	23	1	1	0	0	128.1	128	549	72	65	13	5	3	6	42	0	111	3	2
Malaska, Mark, Pawtucket *	5	3	.625	4.14	39	5	0	0	8	1	87.0	74	367	44	40	2	4	6	6	39	2	86	5	1
Mallette, Brian, Indianapolis	2	1	.667	4.46	25	0	0	0	9	0	38.1	38	169	22	19	6	2	3	2	21	1	30	0	0
Manning, Charles, Columbus *	1	1	.500	5.59	7	0	0	0	0	0	9.2	8	46	6	6	0	0	0	9	1	6	0	0
Marcum, Shawn, Syracuse	6	4	.600	4.95	18	18	0	0	0	0	103.2	112	438	59	57	17	1	2	4	18	2	90	2	0
Marsonek, Sam, Columbus	3	7	.300	6.61	49	3	0	0	22	7	77.2	93	359	63	57	8	3	13	35	1	61	8	0
Marte, Damaso, Charlotte *	0	0	.000	5.40	1	0	0	0	0	0	1.2	4	11	1	1	0	0	0	1	0	2	1	0
Martinez, Anastacio, Pawtucket	3	4	.429	5.98	35	6	0	0	11	1	58.2	74	278	43	39	4	2	3	3	27	2	46	2	1
Matos, Josue, Syracuse	5	3	.625	6.63	14	10	0	0	2	0	55.2	73	248	44	41	16	1	3	2	10	1	32	1	1
Matos, Julius, Syracuse	0	0	.000	0.00	1	0	0	0	0	0	0.2	0	2	0	0	0	0	0	0	0	0	0	0	0
Matthews, Mike, Norfolk *	0	1	.000	12.10	5	3	0	0	0	0	9.2	14	50	13	13	1	0	1	0	8	0	6	0	0
Mattison, Kieran, Buffalo	0	0	.000	27.00	1	0	0	0	0	0	1.0	2	7	3	3	0	0	0	0	2	0	2	1	0
May, Darrell, Columbus *	6	2	.750	4.17	10	7	0	0	0	0	58.1	67	240	29	27	6	1	2	0	5	0	39	0	0
McBride, Macay, Richmond *	1	5	.167	4.33	25	1	0	0	6	2	43.2	49	194	27	21	5	7	1	2	22	2	47	0	0
McCarthy, Brandon, Charlotte	7	7	.500	3.92	20	19	1	1	1	0	119.1	104	482	53	52	16	3	1	2	32	0	130	5	1
McClung, Seth, Durham	2	0	1.000	3.93	6	3	0	0	1	0	18.1	23	83	12	8	1	0	0	1	6	1	19	5	0
McConnell, Sam, Richmond *	4	9	.308	5.48	20	17	0	0	1	0	92.0	130	419	63	56	18	3	3	22	1	44	2	1
McDade, Neal, Indianapolis	2	0	1.000	6.33	14	2	0	0	4	0	27.0	37	123	23	19	3	1	2	3	8	1	27	0	0
McGinley, Blake, Norfolk *	4	4	.500	3.43	44	5	0	0	11	2	84.0	77	345	39	32	16	6	5	21	1	69	2	1
McNichol, Brian, Ottawa *	6	7	.462	4.32	36	9	0	0	5	0	83.1	90	363	41	40	9	6	4	8	28	1	49	3	0
Mears, Chris, Richmond	3	5	.500	5.20	31	1	0	0	21	3	45.0	60	190	27	26	4	2	1	3	23	3	12	4	0
Mendoza, Ramiro, Columbus	1	0	1.000	0.75	8	0	0	0	3	1	12.0	4	42	2	1	0	0	0	1	0	15	1	1

Pitcher, Team	W	L	Pct.	ERA	G	GS	CG	ShO	GF	Sv.	IP	H	TBF	R	ER	HR	SH	SF	HB	BB	IBB	SO	WP	Bk.
Meredith, Cla, Pawtucket	2	5	.286	5.59	40	0	0	0	25	10	48.1	63	215	30	30	6	1	0	1	12	2	42	2	0
Miller, Corky, Rochester	0	0	.000	9.00	1	0	0	0	1	0	1.0	2	5	1	1	0	0	0	0	0	0	0	0	0
Miller, Jason, Rochester *	2	0	1.000	3.81	13	0	0	0	3	0	26.0	28	121	14	11	4	0	1	0	17	0	27	2	0
Miller, Jeffrey, Indianapolis	5	7	.417	3.53	58	0	0	0	15	0	81.2	79	345	37	32	13	3	4	5	27	6	62	2	1
Miller, Justin, Syracuse	3	1	.750	2.32	28	4	0	0	9	2	50.1	39	204	15	13	3	0	1	3	14	0	56	5	0
Miller, Matt, Buffalo	0	0	.000	0.87	9	0	0	0	6	3	10.1	3	36	1	1	0	1	0	0	2	0	15	0	0
Miller, Wade, Pawtucket	0	0	.000	2.53	2	2	0	0	0	0	10.2	10	46	4	3	1	0	0	0	6	0	10	0	0
Miner, Zachary, Richmond-Toledo	5	8	.385	3.71	23	23	0	0	0	0	123.2	125	546	57	51	10	3	2	4	65	1	83	3	0
Minix, Travis, Scranton/Wilkes-Barre	1	0	1.000	1.53	14	0	0	0	5	1	17.2	9	63	3	3	2	0	1	0	3	0	13	0	0
Mitchell, Andy, Ottawa	8	0	1.000	4.87	47	0	0	0	12	0	77.2	83	341	47	42	6	1	3	2	31	7	38	3	0
Munoz, Arnie, Charlotte *	8	14	.364	4.27	40	18	0	0	7	1	132.2	150	593	79	63	16	3	5	5	60	2	109	10	3
Munro, Pete, Columbus	10	7	.588	4.56	43	13	0	0	7	0	116.1	132	517	68	59	14	5	4	6	37	0	80	0	0
Musser, Neal, Norfolk *	6	11	.353	5.02	24	24	0	0	0	0	123.2	140	555	75	69	12	6	6	9	52	0	89	7	1
Nannini, Michael, Syracuse	2	3	.400	5.25	19	0	0	0	7	1	36.0	25	149	21	21	4	1	2	0	21	0	24	1	0
Narveson, Christopher, Pawtucket *	4	5	.444	4.77	21	20	0	0	1	0	111.1	109	473	62	59	15	4	1	10	46	0	66	4	1
Nelson, Joe, Durham	0	3	.000	4.11	35	0	0	0	14	6	46.0	41	203	25	21	9	0	2	1	21	1	62	6	0
Nitkowski, C.J., Indianapolis *	2	0	1.000	0.83	18	0	0	0	5	2	21.2	6	76	5	2	0	1	1	0	9	0	18	1	0
Nomo, Hideo, Columbus	2	3	.400	3.62	7	7	0	0	0	0	37.1	30	161	19	15	1	0	3	0	22	1	41	0	0
Nunez, Franklin, Durham	5	1	.833	6.34	27	0	0	0	11	3	32.2	32	151	27	23	1	2	2	2	21	0	34	5	0
Nunez, Vladimir, Indianapolis	1	0	1.000	0.90	7	0	0	0	2	0	10.0	5	37	1	1	0	0	1	0	3	0	11	1	0
O'Connor, Brian, Richmond	1	0	1.000	1.59	2	1	0	0	0	0	5.2	4	22	1	1	0	0	0	...	2	0	2	...	...
Olszta, Edwin, Indianapolis	0	1	.000	18.00	1	0	0	0	0	0	1.0	3	7	2	2	0	0	0	1	0	0	1	0	0
Ormond, William, Ottawa	4	1	.800	3.63	40	1	0	0	19	0	69.1	56	284	31	28	7	1	3	4	32	3	53	1	0
Oropesa, Eddie, Ottawa *	0	0	.000	0.00	5	0	0	0	4	0	6.0	3	24	0	0	0	0	2	0	5	2	5	2	0
Ortiz, Javier, Charlotte	1	1	.500	7.84	10	2	0	0	2	0	20.2	37	99	19	18	2	0	2	4	4	0	10	2	0
Padilla, Juan, Norfolk	3	2	.600	1.42	37	2	0	0	24	11	63.1	45	243	13	10	4	3	1	5	9	0	59	5	0
Padilla, Vicente, Scranton/Wilkes-Barre	1	0	1.000	3.60	1	1	0	0	0	0	5.0	6	21	2	2	0	0	0	0	2	0	4	0	0
Papelbon, Jonathan, Pawtucket	1	2	.333	2.93	7	4	0	0	3	1	27.2	21	105	9	9	2	2	0	1	3	0	27	0	0
Paronto, Chad, Richmond	3	1	.750	3.95	26	0	0	0	4	0	41.0	43	172	18	18	4	3	0	2	17	0	28	1	0
Pelaez, Alex, Louisville	0	0	.000	0.00	1	0	0	0	1	0	1.0	4	7	4	0	0	0	0	0	0	0	0	0	0
Perez, Franklin, Scranton/Wilkes-Barre	1	7	.125	4.96	58	0	0	0	52	23	65.1	60	283	40	36	11	5	1	5	35	5	42	8	0
Perez, Juan, Pawtucket *	4	5	.444	4.50	40	1	0	0	18	1	62.0	61	269	31	31	7	5	1	5	29	0	74	5	2
Perez, Oliver, Indianapolis *	0	1	.000	9.90	3	3	0	0	0	0	10.0	14	57	11	11	3	0	1	1	12	1	4	1	0
Perisho, Matt, Pawtucket *	2	0	1.000	2.08	13	0	0	0	3	0	13.0	6	49	3	3	0	0	0	0	6	0	7	0	0
Person, Robert, Charlotte	2	3	.400	7.00	7	7	0	0	0	0	36.0	34	163	28	28	11	1	1	1	25	3	24	1	0
Petit, Yusmeiro, Norfolk	0	3	.000	9.20	3	3	0	0	0	0	14.2	24	70	16	15	5	1	0	0	6	0	4	0	0
Phelps, Travis, Louisville	1	0	1.000	6.50	16	0	0	0	2	1	18.0	17	83	14	13	3	0	2	0	12	0	16	3	0
Phillips, Heath Michael, Charlotte *	0	3	.000	8.31	5	5	0	0	0	0	21.2	29	101	22	20	10	1	0	1	13	0	16	1	0
Phillips, Jason C., Durham	3	5	.375	5.70	30	13	0	0	5	1	101.0	133	453	77	64	8	4	4	5	28	3	73	4	2
Piersoll, Chris, Ottawa	1	0	1.000	3.46	9	0	0	0	3	1	13.0	8	47	6	5	2	2	0	0	3	0	11	1	0
Porzio, Mike, Richmond *	0	1	.000	6.75	2	1	0	0	1	0	5.1	5	23	4	4	1	0	0	0	4	0	2	0	0
Prochaska, Michael, Durham *	0	0	.000	1.80	2	0	0	0	2	1	5.0	3	21	1	1	0	0	0	0	3	0	3	0	0
Proctor, Scott, Columbus	6	1	.857	4.22	35	1	0	0	29	14	42.2	47	183	20	20	8	2	1	3	11	0	54	5	0
Rakers, Aaron, Ottawa	6	5	.545	2.57	57	0	0	0	34	7	77.0	69	316	26	22	9	6	0	1	21	4	92	2	0
Ramirez, Elizardo, Louisville	7	7	.500	3.77	21	21	0	0	0	0	131.1	150	546	63	55	14	3	2	3	18	1	82	3	5
Ramirez, Ramon, Columbus	1	3	.250	5.33	6	6	0	0	0	0	27.0	32	115	16	16	3	0	0	1	9	0	26	1	0
Ray, Ken, Richmond	2	4	.333	3.90	17	10	0	0	3	0	67.0	68	291	34	29	6	7	4	4	35	1	40	2	0
Rayborn, George, Buffalo	2	0	1.000	4.89	17	0	0	0	5	2	38.2	46	175	25	21	3	0	1	3	12	0	32	3	0
Raymundo, Gregg, Indianapolis	0	0	.000	9.00	1	0	0	0	1	0	2.0	2	9	2	2	1	0	0	0	1	0	0	0	0
Redding, Tim, Columbus	3	4	.429	5.08	10	10	0	0	0	0	51.1	62	226	29	29	5	1	1	2	13	0	47	0	0
Reid, Justin, Indianapolis	7	5	.583	5.82	25	18	0	0	1	0	99.0	122	450	74	64	20	3	3	6	44	4	61	1	0
Reimers, Cameron, Syracuse	0	0	.000	15.75	1	1	0	0	0	0	4.0	7	20	7	7	2	0	0	0	2	0	2	0	1
Reith, Brian, Indianapolis	2	2	.500	4.94	24	1	0	0	6	1	31.0	35	135	22	17	4	1	0	1	12	2	19	2	0
Ring, Royce, Norfolk *	3	0	1.000	3.26	33	0	0	0	11	2	38.2	34	158	16	14	2	4	0	3	13	1	26	2	0
Roa, Joe, Indianapolis	1	1	.500	6.05	6	4	0	0	1	0	19.1	27	87	13	13	4	2	1	0	7	0	13	0	0
Roach, Jason, Durham	5	5	.500	5.53	22	13	0	0	1	0	84.2	116	379	66	52	10	1	3	4	25	1	30	8	2
Robbins, Jake, Buffalo	3	5	.375	3.08	49	0	0	0	44	23	52.2	51	237	19	18	2	2	1	5	24	8	28	2	0
Robertson, Jeriome, Louisville *	5	11	.313	5.46	28	18	0	0	1	0	120.1	162	535	77	73	18	4	3	4	29	1	82	2	0
Rodney, Fernando, Toledo	0	0	.000	3.00	3	0	0	0	1	0	3.0	2	14	1	1	0	0	0	2	1	0	4	0	0
Rodney, Thomas, Toledo	0	0	.000	2.25	1	0	0	0	0	0	4.0	4	16	1	1	0	0	0	0	3	0	0	1	0
Rodriguez, Eddy, Scranton/Wilkes-Barre	2	3	.400	3.77	50	0	0	0	22	3	62.0	57	271	30	26	2	1	2	3	36	4	51	4	0
Rojas, Christopher, Scranton/Wilkes-Barre	0	1	.000	3.86	1	1	0	0	0	0	7.0	6	29	4	3	1	0	1	1	2	0	4	1	0
Roney, Matt, Toledo	1	1	.500	0.95	14	0	0	0	6	3	28.1	23	115	3	3	0	1	0	2	11	3	27	0	0
Rosario, Francisco, Syracuse	2	7	.222	3.95	30	18	0	0	4	2	116.1	111	484	59	51	16	5	1	10	42	1	80	5	1
Rose, Brian, Louisville	5	6	.455	6.82	18	13	0	0	4	0	68.2	90	320	60	52	11	6	4	7	23	1	34	0	0
Saladin, Miguel, Louisville	0	2	.000	7.79	22	1	0	0	8	0	32.1	47	156	34	28	2	1	1	6	11	0	29	2	0
Salmon, Bradley, Louisville	0	0	.000	3.31	9	0	0	0	3	0	16.1	14	67	6	6	0	2	0	0	7	0	8	0	0
Sanches, Brian, Scranton/Wilkes-Barre	5	3	.625	3.69	51	2	0	0	13	1	83.0	81	351	36	34	9	1	4	7	25	2	75	1	0
Sanders, David, Charlotte *	4	2	.667	3.02	57	0	0	0	18	1	65.2	68	291	28	22	10	4	0	5	32	8	47	2	0
Santiago, Jose, Norfolk	7	6	.538	4.26	29	17	0	0	1	0	122.2	138	528	62	58	10	4	1	7	40	1	61	2	0
Schilling, Curt, Pawtucket	0	2	.000	6.63	6	3	0	0	2	0	19.0	27	87	15	14	3	0	0	0	3	0	21	0	0
Schmitt, Eric, Columbus	4	2	.667	4.61	23	5	0	0	3	0	54.2	58	236	30	28	10	2	3	3	17	1	31	1	0
Schoening, Edward, Rochester	3	4	.333	6.05	35	4	0	0	10	0	64.0	78	288	45	43	9	4	1	1	29	1	50	4	0
Scobie, Jason, Norfolk	15	7	.682	3.34	27	26	0	0	0	0	167.0	163	694	71	62	13	5	6	7	55	2	96	5	0
Seddon, Christopher, Durham *	4	9	.308	5.46	19	19	0	0	0	0	95.2	114	452	74	58	11	1	9	13	43	1	70	7	5
Sedlacek, Shawn, Ottawa	0	2	.000	11.00	2	2	0	0	0	0	9.0	13	45	11	11	1	0	0	1	4	0	3	1	0
Seo, Jae Weong, Norfolk	7	4	.636	4.29	19	19	0	0	0	0	121.2	126	507	64	58	13	7	6	1	30	0	111	2	1
Sequea, Jacobo, Ottawa	0	1	.000	7.58	18	0	0	0	12	5	19.0	27	94	18	16	1	2	3	1	10	1	7	3	0
Serrano, Jimmy, Louisville	4	4	.500	3.75	12	12	0	0	0	0	69.2	69	294	34	29	10	1	0	0	29	2	70	0	0
Shackelford, Brian, Louisville *	1	6	.143	5.23	31	0	0	0	8	1	32.2	35	136	19	19	1	3	0	2	10	0	21	1	0
Shearn, Tom, Louisville	4	5	.444	4.26	44	9	0	0	9	1	93.0	83	400	50	44	11	1	1	3	44	1	93	6	0

Pitcher, Team	W	L	Pct.	ERA	G	GS	CG	ShO	GF	Sv.	IP	H	TBF	R	ER	HR	SH	SF	HB	BB	IBB	SO	WP	Bk.
Shields, James, Durham	1	0	1.000	6.00	1	1	0	0	0	0	6.0	9	29	4	4	0	0	0	0	3	0	6	1	0
Shoemaker, Scott, Pawtucket	0	1	.000	5.56	2	2	0	0	0	0	11.1	11	48	7	7	2	1	0	1	4	0	7	0	0
Simpson, Allan, Louisville	4	4	.500	4.06	50	0	0	0	14	1	64.1	51	289	30	29	5	1	3	8	38	1	89	12	0
Skrehot, Shaun, Indianapolis	0	0	.000	4.50	1	0	0	0	1	0	2.0	2	10	1	1	0	0	0	0	1	0	2	0	0
Small, Aaron, Columbus	1	4	.200	4.96	11	10	0	0	0	0	49.0	62	210	30	27	5	2	1	1	8	0	21	2	0
Smith, Bud, Rochester *	1	0	1.000	4.76	3	0	0	0	0	0	5.2	5	27	4	3	0	0	1	3	0	4	4	0	0
Smith, Cam, Durham	1	2	.333	4.54	26	0	0	0	12	0	35.2	28	162	24	18	5	0	0	3	24	0	40	10	0
Smith, Chuck, Ottawa	2	7	.222	5.37	11	11	1	0	0	0	67.0	72	294	41	40	6	3	3	6	27	4	46	4	4
Smith, Joshua, Columbus	1	0	1.000	0.00	2	0	0	0	1	0	1.1	1	7	0	0	0	0	1	0	2	0	0	0	0
Smith, Matthew, Columbus *	2	0	1.000	2.60	25	0	0	0	7	1	27.2	24	122	9	8	3	1	0	3	13	1	33	0	0
Smith, Matthew, Charlotte	1	6	.143	3.86	66	0	0	0	22	4	84.0	95	371	41	36	12	2	2	4	32	5	56	6	0
Smith, Mike, Scranton/Wilkes-Barre	0	0	.000	9.82	1	0	0	0	0	0	3.2	5	20	4	4	1	0	0	1	3	0	2	0	0
Snell, Ian, Indianapolis	11	3	.786	3.70	18	18	2	1	0	0	112.0	90	442	49	46	14	4	2	1	23	0	104	6	1
Sowers, Jeremy, Buffalo	1	0	1.000	1.59	1	1	0	0	0	...	5.2	7	25	1	1	0	...	...	...	1	0	4	...	...
Speigner, Jimmy, Rochester	0	1	.000	7.36	2	1	0	0	0	0	7.1	14	37	7	6	0	1	2	0	1	0	5	0	0
Spurling, Chris, Toledo	2	1	.667	4.12	12	0	0	0	4	1	19.2	18	77	10	9	2	1	0	0	3	0	15	0	0
Standridge, Jason, Louisville	0	0	.000	16.20	2	0	0	0	0	0	1.2	3	9	3	3	0	0	0	1	0	0	4	0	0
Stanford, Jason, Buffalo *	0	0	.000	1.29	4	1	0	0	0	0	7.0	7	30	2	1	0	0	0	0	1	0	7	1	0
Stark, Denny, Buffalo	0	1	.000	9.45	3	1	0	0	0	0	6.2	12	38	9	7	1	0	2	0	6	0	7	1	0
Stephens, John, Pawtucket-Charlotte-Ottawa	4	5	.444	4.48	23	13	0	0	3	0	84.1	92	357	45	42	9	4	3	10	17	1	59	4	0
Stewart, Cory, Indianapolis *	7	10	.412	5.52	24	23	1	0	0	0	132.0	144	589	91	81	18	6	11	7	67	1	77	4	0
Stewart, Josh, Charlotte *	4	4	.500	4.25	14	11	0	0	0	0	65.2	65	273	34	31	6	2	2	2	16	1	41	0	1
Stewart, Paul, Indianapolis	2	0	1.000	0.87	3	1	0	0	1	0	10.1	4	38	1	1	0	1	1	0	1	0	10	0	0
Stewart, Scott, Norfolk *	1	2	.333	5.25	20	1	0	0	8	0	24.0	29	103	16	14	2	0	0	1	5	0	16	1	0
Stone, Ricky, Louisville	2	1	.667	2.57	9	0	0	0	7	3	14.0	10	56	4	4	0	0	0	1	3	0	15	0	0
Strickland, Scott, Norfolk	0	3	.000	5.40	13	0	0	0	11	5	11.2	14	52	9	7	1	0	0	0	5	1	9	1	0
Sweeney, Brian, Durham	3	4	.429	4.06	10	10	0	0	0	0	51.0	70	236	30	23	5	1	4	2	20	1	39	3	0
Switzer, Jon, Durham *	0	5	.000	7.11	17	8	0	0	2	0	44.1	64	218	38	35	6	1	2	7	22	1	28	3	0
Tadano, Kazuhito, Buffalo	5	5	.500	4.39	32	8	0	0	11	5	96.1	105	408	54	47	16	3	6	1	22	3	86	3	0
Takatsu, Shingo, Norfolk	0	1	.000	3.38	7	1	0	0	2	0	8.0	6	31	3	3	3	0	0	0	1	0	10	0	0
Tallet, Brian, Buffalo *	6	5	.545	4.05	22	17	0	0	2	0	97.2	98	409	51	44	17	4	4	3	25	0	61	4	1
Tejeda, Robinson, Scranton/Wilkes-Barre	2	0	1.000	2.22	5	5	0	0	0	0	28.1	21	114	8	7	0	0	3	0	13	0	28	0	0
Telemaco, Amaury, Scranton/Wilkes-Barre	0	1	.000	4.09	9	3	0	0	1	0	22.0	24	96	11	10	1	0	2	0	8	0	14	0	0
Thomas, John, Rochester *	0	1	.000	15.00	1	1	0	0	0	0	3.0	11	20	5	5	0	0	0	0	1	0	1	0	0
Thomson, John, Richmond	0	0	.000	4.91	1	1	0	0	0	0	3.2	5	16	2	2	0	0	0	1	1	0	2	0	0
Tolar, Kevin, Syracuse *	1	2	.333	8.40	17	0	0	0	3	0	15.0	25	81	15	14	3	0	0	1	12	1	18	2	0
Tomori, Denney, Pawtucket	0	5	.000	5.03	15	2	0	0	7	1	34.0	37	147	21	19	6	0	3	4	8	1	27	6	0
Traber, Billy, Buffalo *	3	7	.300	5.75	19	12	0	0	0	0	76.2	96	354	59	49	7	2	3	2	30	1	55	5	0
Trachsel, Steve, Norfolk	0	1	.000	2.57	2	2	0	0	0	0	14.0	10	54	4	4	2	0	0	0	2	0	12	0	0
Tucker, Glenn, Richmond	0	0	.000	0.00	2	0	0	0	1	0	1.1	1	5	0	0	0	0	0	1	0	0	1	0	0
Ulacia, Dennis, Charlotte *	4	7	.364	6.54	21	17	1	0	1	0	96.1	116	438	73	70	21	5	5	9	40	1	58	6	1
Valdes, Marc, Columbus	0	0	.000	9.82	8	0	0	0	1	0	7.1	15	35	8	8	0	1	0	0	1	0	4	0	0
Valentine, Joe, Louisville	0	7	.000	5.70	49	0	0	0	22	3	53.2	56	248	36	34	4	2	1	2	39	4	44	5	0
Van Hekken, Andy, Richmond-Louisville	1	3	.250	5.66	31	5	0	0	3	0	55.2	61	236	36	35	8	1	3	1	19	0	35	6	1
Vasquez, Jorge, Richmond	0	1	.000	10.93	14	0	0	0	8	2	14.0	16	67	17	17	1	2	1	1	9	1	20	1	0
Vermilyea, James, Syracuse	3	0	1.000	5.60	16	4	0	0	4	0	35.1	49	164	27	22	6	1	2	3	11	0	24	0	1
Villacis, Eduardo, Charlotte	1	2	.333	9.47	9	5	0	0	1	0	25.2	37	123	28	27	9	0	0	2	13	1	24	1	0
Voyles, Brad, Columbus	6	5	.545	4.97	19	14	0	0	2	1	88.2	88	369	55	49	15	2	2	2	31	1	73	2	0
Waechter, Doug, Durham	2	0	1.000	9.22	3	3	0	0	0	0	13.2	17	62	14	14	3	0	0	1	5	0	16	0	1
Walker, Kevin, Charlotte *	1	2	.333	5.28	51	0	0	0	18	5	46.0	49	210	35	27	7	5	1	6	21	3	52	2	0
Wang, Chien-Ming, Columbus	2	1	.667	4.24	6	6	0	0	0	0	34.0	40	141	16	16	4	1	2	0	6	0	21	1	0
Ward, Jeremy, Richmond	3	4	.429	3.74	31	0	0	0	12	0	55.1	51	230	36	23	8	5	3	2	19	5	30	6	0
Watkins, Steve, Buffalo	9	2	.818	4.16	31	17	0	0	2	0	129.2	142	559	72	60	13	6	10	10	34	1	86	4	0
Webb, John, Durham	10	6	.625	4.85	28	27	1	0	1	0	163.1	175	715	103	88	23	7	2	13	61	2	86	7	0
Weber, Ben, Louisville	0	1	.000	6.43	7	0	0	0	2	0	7.0	8	36	5	5	0	0	1	2	6	0	5	0	0
Whiteside, Matt, Syracuse	0	4	.000	2.59	40	0	0	0	36	27	41.2	35	165	14	12	4	0	1	5	1	0	39	2	0
Wilson, Kris, Columbus	4	1	.800	4.28	29	7	0	0	3	0	67.1	78	294	39	32	8	1	4	2	17	1	52	0	3
Winkelsas, Joseph, Charlotte	0	0	.000	6.48	4	0	0	0	1	0	8.1	11	38	6	6	2	0	1	0	4	1	3	0	0
Wolfe, Brian, Rochester	0	2	.000	8.53	3	0	0	0	0	0	6.1	10	31	8	6	1	0	0	0	2	0	5	0	0
Woodyard, Mark, Toledo	5	2	.714	3.84	45	0	0	0	11	1	70.1	67	302	34	30	7	1	1	2	32	2	62	6	0
Young, Jason, Buffalo	2	0	1.000	5.87	4	4	0	0	0	0	23.0	26	103	17	15	4	0	1	1	9	0	21	0	0
Zerbe, Chad, Buffalo *	5	2	.714	3.62	16	0	0	0	7	0	27.1	33	119	12	11	3	2	0	2	6	1	11	2	0
Zink, Charles, Pawtucket	2	1	.667	10.45	4	1	0	0	0	0	10.1	17	53	12	12	1	0	0	1	8	0	5	1	0
Zumaya, Joel, Toledo	1	2	.333	2.66	8	8	1	0	0	0	44.0	30	185	13	13	2	1	1	5	24	1	56	2	0

PITCHERS WITH TWO OR MORE TEAMS

Pitcher, Team	W	L	Pct.	ERA	G	GS	CG	ShO	GF	Sv.	IP	H	TBF	R	ER	HR	SH	SF	HB	BB	IBB	SO	WP	Bk.
Anderson, Jimmy, Rochester *	4	4	.500	2.90	12	11	0	0	0	0	62.0	62	279	24	20	5	1	4	3	32	0	41	5	0
Anderson, Jimmy, Durham *	2	4	.333	4.18	10	9	0	0	0	0	51.2	52	224	29	24	0	4	0	2	22	0	21	2	0
Childress, Daylan, Louisville	0	0	.000	6.75	11	0	0	0	3	0	14.2	18	68	11	11	1	0	1	1	7	0	7	2	0
Childress, Daylan, Rochester	0	1	.000	10.38	5	0	0	0	3	0	8.2	10	41	11	10	2	1	1	0	5	0	9	1	0
Fernandez, Jared, Louisville	5	5	.500	4.38	13	13	0	0	0	0	84.1	86	352	45	41	8	3	5	2	26	0	51	8	0
Fernandez, Jared, Scranton/Wilkes-Barre	4	2	.667	2.66	7	7	0	0	0	0	40.2	40	172	18	12	4	2	0	1	14	0	30	0	0
Graman, Alex, Columbus *	5	6	.455	3.18	23	16	0	0	4	1	96.1	95	409	40	34	12	2	1	2	36	2	96	3	0
Graman, Alex, Louisville *	2	1	.667	3.09	5	4	0	0	0	0	23.1	23	102	9	8	2	1	0	1	12	0	19	3	0
Hodges, Trey, Rochester	0	0	.000	5.63	9	0	0	0	5	0	16.0	17	75	10	10	0	0	2	1	10	0	12	2	0
Hodges, Trey, Richmond	0	3	.000	8.10	6	4	0	0	0	0	16.2	26	86	22	15	4	1	1	0	9	0	9	0	0
Miner, Zachary, Richmond	2	7	.222	4.23	17	17	0	0	0	0	89.1	97	401	47	42	6	1	1	2	44	1	63	3	0
Miner, Zachary, Toledo	3	1	.750	2.36	6	6	0	0	0	0	34.1	28	145	10	9	4	2	1	2	20	0	20	0	0
Stephens, John, Pawtucket	0	1	.000	9.00	1	1	0	0	0	0	4.0	6	19	4	4	1	0	0	1	0	0	4	0	0

Pitcher, Team	W	L	Pct.	ERA	G	GS	CG	ShO	GF	Sv.	IP	H	TBF	R	ER	HR	SH	SF	HB	BB	IBB	SO	WP	Bk.
Stephens, John, Charlotte	0	2	.000	3.99	10	3	0	0	2	0	29.1	34	129	16	13	2	2	2	4	8	0	14	1	0
Stephens, John, Ottawa	4	2	.667	4.41	12	9	0	0	1	0	51.0	52	209	25	25	6	2	1	6	8	0	41	3	0
Van Hekken, Andy, Richmond *	0	3	.000	9.16	4	4	0	0	0	0	18.2	25	87	20	19	4	1	2	1	8	0	11	3	1
Van Hekken, Andy, Louisville	1	0	1.000	3.89	27	1	0	0	3	0	37.0	36	149	16	16	4	0	1	0	11	0	24	3	0

COMBINATION SHUTOUTS: Buffalo (2) -- Tallet-Cabrera, Guthrie-Watkins-Cabrera. Charlotte (3) -- McCarthy-Fields-Walker-Smith, Stewart-Fields-Bajenaru, McCarthy-Bajenaru. Columbus (5) -- Wang-Bean-Groom-Proctor, Voyles-Marsonek-Bean, Henn-Bean-Proctor, Wilson-Munro-Graman, Nomo-Smith-Bean. Durham (2) -- Anderson-Corcoran-Hines, Seddon-Phillips-Gardner. Indianapolis (5) -- Duke-Johnston-Reith, Reid-Nitkowski-Bradley, Duke-Bullinger-Nitkowski, Bullington-McDade, Bullington-Corey. Louisville (9) -- Ramirez-Keisler-Booker, Ramirez-Stone, Rose-Valentine-Shackelford-Booker, Fernandez-Valentine-Shackelford-Booker, Ramirez-Booker, Serrano-Keisler, Serrano-Phelps, Germano-Van Hekken-Valentine, Serrano-Simpson-Shearn-Booker. Norfolk (10) -- Seo-Strickland-Padilla, Seo-Padilla, Santiago-Colyer-Padilla, Musser-Hamulack-Lee, Junge-Aybar-Ring-Hamulack, Scobie-McGinley, Junge-McGinley, Musser-Bell, Musser-Lavigne-Hamulack, Koo-Scobie-Aybar. Ottawa (8) -- Baldwin-Rakers-Byrdak, Bauer-Rakers-Byrdak, Fiore-Mitchell, Fiore-Bauer-Rakers, Stephens-Rakers, Fiore-Rodriguez-Rakers, Stephens-Rodriguez-Rakers, Stephens-Rodriguez-Bauer-Rakers. Pawtucket (8) -- Alvarez-Kershner, DiNardo-Cassidy-Kershner, Miller-Kester-Cressend-Perez, DiNardo-Tomori-Meredith, Alvarez-Cassidy-Meredith, DiNardo-Delcarmen-Schilling-Meredith, Alvarez-Bausher, Malaska-Bottalico-Bausher. Richmond (11) -- Greisinger-Hernandez, Ray-Childers-Brooks-Childers, Greisinger-Childers, Bernero-McBride-Ward, Lerew-Bernero, Barry-Paronto-Brooks-Childers, Barry-Childers, James-Childers, Davies-McBride-Childers, Davies-Ray-Brooks, Bernero-Brower-McBride. Rochester (8) -- Baker-Bowyer-Barrett, Gassner-Bonilla-Kemp, Bonser-Schoening-Eyre-Bowyer, Anderson-Schoening-Kemp, Bonser-Kemp-Eyre, Baker-Bowyer-Kemp, Liriano-Kemp, Durbin-Gassner-Kemp-Barrett-Bowyer. Scranton/WB (4) -- Liriano-Giese-Sanches, Brito-Hernandez-Perez, Fernandez-Geary, Franco-Sanches-Burke-Perez. Syracuse (5) -- Baker-Nannini-Arnold, Rosario-Carlson-Lundberg-Arnold, Marcum-Arnold-Carlson-Whiteside, Baker-Arnold-Miller-Whiteside, Baker-Miller-League. Toledo (12) -- Douglass-Dingman, Grilli-Spurling-Darensbourg-Karnuth, Cruz-Roney-Woodyard, Baugh-Ennis-Darensbourg-Karnuth, Good-Dingman-Karnuth-Darensbourg, Good-Roney, Grilli-Darensbourg-Ennis-Karnuth, Baugh-Karnuth, Grilli-Karnuth, Zumaya-Woodyard-Creek, Miner-Ginter, Good-Karnuth.

NO-HIT GAMES: Snell, Indianapolis, defeated Norfolk, 4-0, May 15.

2005 FIELDING

TEAM

Team	G	PO	A	E	TC	DP	TP	PB	Pct.
Rochester	144	3754	1400	106	5260	148	1	12	.980
Syracuse	144	3813	1436	108	5357	128	0	8	.980
Indianapolis	144	3819	1502	114	5435	145	0	13	.979
Louisville	144	3797	1449	111	5357	135	1	26	.979
Pawtucket	144	3803	1354	110	5267	127	0	12	.979
Scranton/WB	144	3772	1610	116	5498	175	0	13	.979
Buffalo	144	3743	1462	118	5323	126	0	10	.978
Columbus	144	3860	1449	117	5426	138	0	15	.978
Charlotte	144	3803	1368	121	5292	146	0	12	.977
Norfolk	144	3811	1569	128	5508	130	0	8	.977
Ottawa	144	3753	1536	122	5411	137	0	13	.977
Richmond	144	3764	1436	130	5330	136	1	9	.976
Toledo	144	3819	1503	130	5452	143	0	11	.976
Durham	144	3854	1580	198	5632	155	1	18	.965

INDIVIDUAL

FIRST BASEMEN

NOTE: All caps denotes fielding-percentage leader based on 72 games for catchers, 96 for all other non-pitchers and 115 innings for pitchers. *Throws lefthanded.

Player, Team	Pct.	G	PO	A	E	TC	DP
Abad, Andy, Buffalo *	.992	30	237	11	2	250	21
Alfaro, Jason, Syracuse	1.000	8	48	2	0	50	4
Bailey, Jeffrey, Pawtucket	1.000	13	85	3	0	88	8
Barker, Kevin, Syracuse *	.998	89	747	54	2	803	76
Barkett, Andy, Richmond *	.989	34	245	21	3	269	33
Becker, Brian, Charlotte	1.000	3	24	1	0	25	2
Bell, Rick, Louisville	.987	10	69	5	1	75	5
Berg, Dave, Pawtucket	1.000	25	158	9	0	167	15
Brazell, Craig, Norfolk	.987	8	67	9	1	77	9
Buchanan, Brian, Rochester	.983	8	56	3	1	60	10
Burke, Jamie, Charlotte	1.000	3	21	2	0	23	2
Calzado, Napoleon, Ottawa	1.000	2	0	1	0	1	0
Casanova, Raul, Charlotte	1.000	1	3	0	0	3	0
Cash, Kevin, Durham	1.000	1	1	0	0	1	0
Castellano, John, Scranton/Wilkes-Barre	...	1	0	0	0	0	0
Chiaffredo, Paul, Indianapolis	1.000	1	1	0	0	1	0
Cordero, Wil, Norfolk	1.000	7	57	4	0	61	3
Coste, Christopher, Scranton/Wilkes-Barre	1.000	29	225	27	0	252	25
Cox, Steve, Durham *	.971	3	29	5	1	35	4
Crozier, Eric, Syracuse-Louisville	.977	38	326	16	8	350	23
Cuddyer, Michael, Rochester	1.000	1	8	1	0	9	2
Daigle, Leo, Charlotte	1.000	3	20	3	0	23	0
Daubach, Brian, Norfolk	.997	71	617	47	2	666	61
Deardorff, Jeff, Durham	1.000	12	82	5	0	87	7
De Caster, Yurendell, Indianapolis	.994	25	150	12	1	163	18
Diaz, Victor, Norfolk	.992	26	225	16	2	243	20
Dunwoody, Todd, Rochester *	1.000	7	44	3	0	47	8
Eldred, Brad, Indianapolis	.989	41	325	22	4	351	38
Fasano, Sal, Ottawa	1.000	1	8	0	0	8	2
Freire, Alejandro, Ottawa	.988	63	543	50	7	600	48
Garcia, Luis, Norfolk	.974	14	141	7	4	152	14

Player, Team	Pct.	G	PO	A	E	TC	DP
Garko, Ryan, Buffalo	.991	66	503	43	5	551	53
Gload, Ross, Charlotte *	1.000	36	314	12	0	326	41
Guzman, Edwards, Indianapolis	1.000	8	54	6	0	60	4
Hankins, Ryan, Columbus	1.000	2	16	1	0	17	4
Hannahan, John, Toledo	.974	5	36	2	1	39	4
Harper, Brandon, Toledo	1.000	1	11	1	0	12	2
Hessman, Mike, Toledo	1.000	31	278	21	0	299	26
Holbert, Aaron, Louisville	1.000	8	36	2	0	38	1
Hooper, Kevin, Toledo	...	1	0	0	0	0	0
Hoover, Paul, Durham	1.000	5	38	3	0	41	4
Howard, Ryan, Scranton/Wilkes-Barre *	.986	58	533	40	8	581	64
Huckaby, Ken, Syracuse	.800	1	4	0	1	5	0
Hummel, Tim, Pawtucket	1.000	6	44	2	0	46	5
Johnson, Russ, Columbus	1.000	6	42	3	0	45	6
Jones, Garrett, Rochester *	.990	124	947	81	11	1071	100
Jones, Mitchell, Columbus	.986	110	905	79	14	998	94
Jurries, James, Richmond	.991	29	204	9	2	215	19
Kinkade, Mike, Buffalo	.991	15	109	7	1	117	6
Koonce, Graham, Indianapolis *	.990	75	632	45	7	684	59
Leon, Jose, Indianapolis	1.000	2	10	0	0	10	1
Liefer, Jeff, Buffalo	.994	35	299	11	2	312	18
Lockwood, Michael, Pawtucket *	1.000	2	1	0	0	1	1
Lomasney, Steve, Louisville	.833	5	4	1	1	6	0
Martinez, Octavio, Ottawa	1.000	1	1	1	0	2	0
Martinez, Sandy, Toledo	.000	1	0	0	1	1	0
Matos, Julius, Syracuse	.975	4	38	1	1	40	4
Mendez, Carlos, Richmond	1.000	29	247	17	0	264	23
Miller, Corky, Rochester	1.000	2	11	0	0	11	1
Mottola, Chad, Syracuse	1.000	10	70	6	0	76	4
Munson, Eric, Durham	.983	93	808	58	15	881	85
Norton, Greg, Charlotte	.989	10	78	9	1	88	9
Nye, Rodney, Norfolk	1.000	3	11	3	0	14	1
Offerman, Jose, Norfolk	1.000	9	75	3	0	78	4
O'Keefe, Michael, Richmond *	1.000	2	16	0	0	16	1
Olerud, John, Pawtucket *	1.000	2	11	4	0	15	2
Olszta, Edwin, Indianapolis	1.000	1	1	0	0	1	0
Pelaez, Alex, Louisville	1.000	25	172	5	0	177	27
Pena, Brayan, Richmond	1.000	1	3	0	0	3	0
Pena, Carlos, Toledo *	.986	62	519	33	8	560	49
Perez, Tomas, Louisville	1.000	1	5	1	0	6	2
Phelps, Josh, Durham	.971	20	183	21	6	210	22
Phillips, Andy, Columbus	.984	27	224	16	4	244	24
Pratt, Scott, Richmond	1.000	2	9	0	0	9	2
Rolls, Damian, Columbus	1.000	1	13	0	0	13	0
Rosamond, George, Richmond	.982	7	55	1	1	57	3
Ruiz, Carlos, Scranton/Wilkes-Barre	1.000	2	14	0	0	14	0
Rushford, Jim, Scranton/Wilkes-Barre *	.986	65	506	49	8	563	68
Schneider, John, Syracuse	1.000	1	0	1	0	1	0
Shelton, Chris, Toledo	.989	31	252	22	3	277	34
Smith, Jason, Toledo	.986	17	134	8	2	144	15
Snyder, Earl, Durham	.989	11	83	6	1	90	7
Thorman, Scott, Richmond	.991	52	435	27	4	466	41
Tiffee, Terry, Rochester	1.000	10	76	5	0	81	9
Toca, Jorge, Charlotte	.991	91	690	52	7	749	76
Urick, John, Columbus *	1.000	1	9	0	0	9	0
Valent, Eric, Norfolk *	.991	13	101	6	1	108	8
Wathan, Dusty, Buffalo	1.000	8	53	9	0	62	7

Player, Team	Pct.	G	PO	A	E	TC	DP
Wigginton, Ty, Indianapolis	1.000	11	76	10	0	86	11
Wilken, Kristopher, Ottawa	.986	49	207	10	3	220	27
Williams, Glenn, Rochester	1.000	1	14	0	0	14	2
Wilson, Craig, Indianapolis	1.000	2	13	2	0	15	2
Wooten, Shawn, Pawtucket	.996	34	240	19	1	260	24
Youkilis, Kevin, Pawtucket	.993	16	126	10	1	137	16
Young, Ernie, Buffalo	.857	2	6	0	1	7	0
Young, Walter, Ottawa	.981	63	478	43	10	531	48
ZAPP, ANDREW, Louisville	.993	113	868	72	7	947	88

FIRST BASEMEN WITH TWO OR MORE TEAMS

Player, Team	Pct.	G	PO	A	E	TC	DP
Crozier, Eric, Syracuse *	.977	37	319	15	8	342	23
Crozier, Eric, Louisville *	1.000	1	7	1	0	8	0

SECOND BASEMEN

Player, Team	Pct.	G	PO	A	E	TC	DP
Abernathy, Brent, Rochester	.960	25	35	61	4	100	18
Alfaro, Jason, Syracuse	.974	40	76	113	5	194	29
Amezaga, Alfredo, Indianapolis	.961	18	26	47	3	76	15
Anderson, Drew, Louisville	1.000	5	5	4	0	9	0
Arteaga, Joshua, Richmond	.857	2	1	5	1	7	1
Badeaux, Brooks, Durham	.967	43	85	118	7	210	31
Basak, Christopher, Norfolk	.990	38	77	119	2	198	29
Bellhorn, Mark, Pawtucket	.914	9	16	16	3	35	3
Berg, Dave, Pawtucket	.945	11	24	28	3	55	8
Bergolla, William, Louisville	.979	80	162	204	8	374	62
Bourgeois, Jason, Richmond	.964	92	160	246	15	421	60
Burke, Jamie, Charlotte	1.000	5	7	11	0	18	0
Cannizaro, Andrew, Columbus	1.000	1	4	2	0	6	2
Cano, Robinson, Columbus	.966	22	48	65	4	117	18
Castillo, Jose, Indianapolis	1.000	4	5	5	0	10	2
Castro, Bernie, Ottawa	.972	120	238	357	17	612	72
Christian, Justin, Columbus	1.000	1	0	1	0	1	0
Coquillette, Trace, Charlotte	.963	25	43	60	4	107	20
Cortez, Fernando, Durham	.963	57	124	160	11	295	33
Cosme, Caonabo, Columbus	.986	33	53	91	2	146	24
Crespo, Cesar, Indianapolis	.976	68	114	165	7	286	43
De Caster, Yurendell, Indianapolis	.948	13	28	27	3	58	9
Escalona, Felix, Columbus	1.000	14	22	37	0	59	8
Figueroa, Luis, Pawtucket	.982	22	52	56	2	110	15
Finegan, Brian, Buffalo	1.000	1	4	3	0	7	0
Furmaniak, J.J., Indianapolis	1.000	2	3	4	0	7	0
Gautreau, Jacob, Buffalo	.968	56	114	162	9	285	40
Gil, Benji, Norfolk	1.000	2	2	6	0	8	1
Guerrero, Wilton, Charlotte	.957	21	39	50	4	93	14
Guzman, Edwards, Indianapolis	.933	5	5	9	1	15	1
Hannahan, John, Toledo	1.000	2	5	5	0	10	3
Hannahan, Leonard, Scranton/Wilkes-Barre	.990	20	43	59	1	103	16
Harris, Willie, Charlotte	.977	28	71	59	3	133	19
Hernandez, Anderson, Norfolk	.973	37	76	101	5	182	23
Hill, Bobby, Indianapolis	1.000	19	25	35	0	60	9
Holbert, Aaron, Louisville	.948	23	40	70	6	116	15
Hooper, Kevin, Toledo	.974	36	80	105	5	190	28
Hoover, Paul, Durham	.963	32	45	85	5	135	17
Hummel, Tim, Pawtucket	1.000	1	3	2	0	5	3
Inglett, Joseph, Buffalo	.970	56	103	155	8	266	26
Johnson, Russ, Columbus	1.000	3	7	3	0	10	1
Kata, Matt, Scranton/Wilkes-Barre	1.000	11	23	39	0	62	11
Keppinger, Jeff, Norfolk	.989	54	111	159	3	273	39
Lambin, Chase, Norfolk	.958	21	33	58	4	95	7
Leon, Carlos, Scranton/Wilkes-Barre	1.000	1	3	5	0	8	2
Lopez, Gabe, Columbus	.972	44	92	116	6	214	29
Lopez, Luis, Louisville	1.000	2	4	2	0	6	0
Lopez, Pedro, Charlotte	.956	10	15	28	2	45	5
Machado, Alejandro, Pawtucket	.989	69	121	156	3	280	37
Machado, Anderson, Louisville	1.000	1	1	4	0	5	0
Martinez, Felix, Charlotte	.985	52	117	153	4	274	40
Martinez, Ramon, Toledo	1.000	1	1	2	0	3	0
Matos, Julius, Syracuse	.938	3	7	8	1	16	2
Maza, Luis, Rochester	.991	30	43	64	1	108	17
MEDRANO, ANTHONY, Scranton/Wilkes-Barre	.978	108	179	315	11	505	82
Morban, Jose, Buffalo	.929	3	7	6	1	14	4
Moriarty, Mike, Pawtucket-Ottawa	.857	3	3	3	1	7	2
Nelson, Bry, Syracuse	.959	57	91	140	10	241	28
Nivar, Ramon, Ottawa	.750	1	1	2	1	4	0
Nye, Rodney, Norfolk	1.000	1	1	2	0	3	1
Ojeda, Augie, Rochester	1.000	27	42	66	0	108	15
Olmedo, Ranier, Louisville	1.000	14	28	39	0	67	10

Player, Team	Pct.	G	PO	A	E	TC	DP
Olszta, Edwin, Indianapolis	1.000	1	1	0	0	1	1
Ordaz, Luis, Durham	.959	21	44	50	4	98	14
Ortega, Jose, Buffalo	1.000	2	1	6	0	7	1
Patchett, Gary, Louisville	1.000	2	1	3	0	4	1
Pedroia, Dustin, Pawtucket	.990	39	83	110	2	195	27
Pelaez, Alex, Louisville	.991	26	41	69	1	111	19
Perez, Tomas, Louisville	.960	4	9	15	1	25	2
Phillips, Andy, Columbus	1.000	4	4	7	0	11	0
Pinckney, Brandon, Buffalo	1.000	3	7	6	0	13	3
Pratt, Scott, Richmond	.955	18	27	37	3	67	8
Punto, Nick, Rochester	.900	4	8	10	2	20	6
Raburn, Ryan, Toledo	.959	99	214	277	21	512	63
Raymundo, Gregg, Indianapolis	.818	2	5	4	2	11	1
Relaford, Desi, Syracuse	.979	20	44	50	2	96	12
Reyes, Guillermo, Charlotte	1.000	5	7	12	0	19	6
Rivas, Luis, Rochester	.973	38	49	96	4	149	25
Rodriguez, Luis, Rochester	.992	27	45	78	1	124	16
Rogers, Eddie, Ottawa	.979	25	63	74	3	140	26
Rolls, Damian, Columbus	1.000	1	0	2	0	2	0
Rosa, Wally, Charlotte	.778	2	2	5	2	9	1
Sandoval, Danny, Scranton/Wilkes-Barre	1.000	1	1	4	0	5	0
Schuerholz, Jonathan, Richmond	.972	43	71	101	5	177	19
Skrehot, Shaun, Indianapolis	.965	15	22	33	2	57	5
Smith, Jason, Toledo	.965	14	20	35	2	57	10
Snyder, Earl, Durham	...	1	0	0	0	0	0
Solano, Danny, Syracuse	.965	32	49	90	5	144	20
Sosa, Juan, Scranton/Wilkes-Barre	.980	12	21	27	1	49	7
Thrower, Jason, Buffalo	1.000	24	41	67	0	108	13
Thurston, Joe, Columbus	.969	28	61	65	4	130	12
Vazquez, Ramon, Buffalo	.929	3	4	9	1	14	3
Velandia, Jorge, Indianapolis	1.000	22	40	50	0	90	9
Velazquez, Gilbert, Rochester	1.000	6	9	15	0	24	5
Wigginton, Ty, Indianapolis	.968	5	12	18	1	31	7
Williams, Glenn, Rochester	1.000	3	3	6	0	9	0
Wilson, Enrique, Ottawa	1.000	1	1	1	0	2	1
Youkilis, Kevin, Pawtucket	.900	2	5	4	1	10	2

SECOND BASEMEN WITH TWO OR MORE TEAMS

Player, Team	Pct.	G	PO	A	E	TC	DP
Moriarty, Mike, Pawtucket	.800	1	2	2	1	5	1
Moriarty, Mike, Ottawa	1.000	2	1	1	0	2	1

THIRD BASEMEN

Player, Team	Pct.	G	PO	A	E	TC	DP
Abernathy, Brent, Rochester	.800	3	4	4	2	10	0
Alfaro, Jason, Syracuse	.976	51	33	90	3	126	5
Amezaga, Alfredo, Indianapolis	1.000	3	0	4	0	4	0
Bacani, David, Norfolk	1.000	6	4	5	0	9	1
Badeaux, Brooks, Durham	1.000	9	6	13	0	19	2
Bailey, Jeffrey, Pawtucket	...	1	0	0	0	0	0
Bannon, Jeff, Louisville	1.000	5	3	8	0	11	2
Basak, Christopher, Norfolk	1.000	2	1	2	0	3	0
Bautista, Jose, Indianapolis	1.000	13	6	26	0	32	2
Bell, Rick, Louisville	1.000	5	0	8	0	8	0
Berg, Dave, Pawtucket	.949	42	17	57	4	78	5
Burke, Jamie, Charlotte	.971	47	30	72	3	105	4
Calzado, Napoleon, Ottawa	.953	91	66	178	12	256	22
Cano, Robinson, Columbus	1.000	1	2	2	0	4	0
Coquillette, Trace, Charlotte	.857	8	4	14	3	21	1
Cosme, Caonabo, Columbus	1.000	4	2	3	0	5	0
Coste, Christopher, Scranton/Wilkes-Barre	.956	93	47	192	11	250	22
Crespo, Cesar, Indianapolis	.667	2	2	4	3	9	0
Cuddyer, Michael, Rochester	1.000	2	0	3	0	3	0
Daigle, Leo, Charlotte	.875	19	12	30	6	48	2
Deardorff, Jeff, Durham	1.000	10	6	13	0	19	1
De Caster, Yurendell, Indianapolis	.915	28	15	39	5	59	6
DePastino, Joe, Syracuse	1.000	1	1	1	0	2	0
Duenas, Yobal, Columbus	1.000	2	0	6	0	6	1
Encarnacion, Edwin, Louisville	.917	77	51	158	19	228	20
Escalona, Felix, Columbus	.886	12	9	22	4	35	2
Figueroa, Luis, Pawtucket	.980	44	26	73	2	101	7
Furmaniak, J.J., Indianapolis	1.000	4	2	4	0	6	0
Gautreau, Jacob, Buffalo	.967	53	43	103	5	151	10
Gil, Benji, Norfolk	.889	7	5	11	2	18	0
Grimm, Eric, Charlotte	1.000	2	0	3	0	3	1
Grindell, Nathan, Scranton/Wilkes-Barre	1.000	7	2	15	0	17	2
Gutierrez, Ricky, Charlotte	.887	18	13	34	6	53	5
Guzman, Edwards, Indianapolis	.947	6	6	12	1	19	2
Hankins, Ryan, Columbus	.956	37	27	59	4	90	2
Hannahan, John, Toledo	.946	52	39	102	8	149	7

- 386 -

Player, Team	Pct.	G	PO	A	E	TC	DP
Hannahan, Leonard, Scranton/Wilkes-Barre ..	.910	26	16	55	7	78	9
Hansen, Jed, Norfolk	.895	17	11	40	6	57	6
Hattig, John, Syracuse	1.000	24	13	37	0	50	2
Heintz, Chris, Rochester	.879	21	7	22	4	33	1
Hessman, Mike, Toledo	.987	75	52	169	3	224	16
Hill, Bobby, Indianapolis	.739	13	4	13	6	23	3
Holbert, Aaron, Louisville	.933	9	5	23	2	30	4
Hooper, Kevin, Toledo	1.000	4	0	6	0	6	2
Hoover, Paul, Durham	.927	16	9	29	3	41	6
Hummel, Tim, Pawtucket	.902	22	11	35	5	51	4
Jeroloman, Charles, Pawtucket	1.000	1	0	1	0	1	0
Johnson, Kelly, Richmond	1.000	4	6	4	0	10	0
Johnson, Russ, Columbus	.980	53	24	125	3	152	13
Kata, Matt, Scranton/Wilkes-Barre	.800	4	1	3	1	5	0
Kelly, Donald, Toledo	.917	7	1	10	1	12	0
Keppinger, Jeff, Norfolk	.938	5	2	13	1	16	2
Kinkade, Mike, Buffalo	.912	82	64	142	20	226	21
Koskie, Corey, Syracuse	1.000	5	1	4	0	5	0
Lambin, Chase, Norfolk	.828	11	8	16	5	29	1
Leon, Donny, Charlotte	.800	4	2	2	1	5	0
Leon, Jose, Indianapolis-Louisville	.951	60	27	90	6	123	7
Liefer, Jeff, Buffalo	1.000	2	2	3	0	5	1
Marte, Andy, Richmond	.950	109	68	220	15	303	21
Martinez, Felix, Charlotte	.958	16	7	16	1	24	0
Matos, Julius, Syracuse	1.000	7	2	13	0	15	2
Maza, Luis, Rochester	.914	32	22	42	6	70	2
Mendez, Carlos, Richmond	.875	8	6	8	2	16	2
Mendez, Deivi, Columbus	1.000	2	1	0	0	1	0
Morban, Jose, Buffalo	.913	11	3	18	2	23	1
Moriarty, Mike, Pawtucket	1.000	2	2	1	0	3	0
Munson, Eric, Durham	.500	1	1	0	1	2	0
Nelson, Bry, Syracuse	.904	53	34	79	12	125	8
Norton, Greg, Charlotte	.929	45	35	70	8	113	11
NYE, RODNEY, Norfolk	.953	101	62	223	14	299	19
Ojeda, Augie, Rochester	.955	10	4	17	1	22	1
Olszta, Edwin, Indianapolis	1.000	1	1	0	0	1	0
Ordaz, Luis, Durham	.971	11	5	28	1	34	1
Pelaez, Alex, Louisville	.977	41	23	62	2	87	7
Perez, Kenny, Pawtucket	1.000	3	0	5	0	5	1
Perez, Tomas, Louisville	.923	5	5	7	1	13	1
Phillips, Andy, Columbus	.960	29	14	58	3	75	8
Pratt, Scott, Richmond	1.000	22	14	32	0	46	0
Raymundo, Gregg, Indianapolis	1.000	1	0	1	0	1	0
Rodriguez, Luis, Rochester	1.000	7	1	9	0	10	0
Rogers, Eddie, Ottawa	.929	31	13	52	5	70	6
Rolls, Damian, Columbus	.857	11	7	11	3	21	2
Schrager, Anthony, Pawtucket	.833	6	1	9	2	12	2
Skrehot, Shaun, Indianapolis	.750	1	1	2	1	4	0
Smith, Jason, Toledo	.962	14	7	18	1	26	4
Snyder, Earl, Durham	.940	105	73	208	18	299	22
Solano, Danny, Syracuse	1.000	15	6	30	0	36	3
Sosa, Juan, Scranton/Wilkes-Barre	.947	23	15	57	4	76	12
Thrower, Jason, Buffalo	1.000	3	0	5	0	5	1
Tiffee, Terry, Rochester	.940	46	41	69	7	117	13
Timmons, Wesley, Richmond	1.000	5	5	11	0	16	2
Toca, Jorge, Charlotte	1.000	1	0	2	0	2	0
Vazquez, Ramon, Buffalo	1.000	1	1	2	0	3	0
Velazquez, Gilbert, Rochester	1.000	3	0	2	0	2	1
Whiteside, Eli, Ottawa	...	1	0	0	0	0	0
Wigginton, Ty, Buffalo	.963	55	32	125	6	163	11
Wilken, Kristopher, Ottawa	.961	31	13	60	3	76	5
Williams, Glenn, Rochester	.927	38	24	77	8	109	6
Wooten, Shawn, Pawtucket	.912	17	9	22	3	34	4
Youkilis, Kevin, Pawtucket	.946	24	15	38	3	56	4

THIRD BASEMEN WITH TWO OR MORE TEAMS

Player, Team	Pct.	G	PO	A	E	TC	DP
Leon, Jose, Indianapolis	.974	40	14	62	2	78	5
Leon, Jose, Louisville	.911	20	13	28	4	45	2

SHORTSTOPS

Player, Team	Pct.	G	PO	A	E	TC	DP
Alfaro, Jason, Syracuse	1.000	4	5	6	0	11	0
Amezaga, Alfredo, Indianapolis	.957	26	29	59	4	92	16
Arteaga, Joshua, Richmond	1.000	3	2	7	0	9	0
Aurilia, Rich, Louisville	1.000	1	1	6	0	7	1
Badeaux, Brooks, Durham	1.000	12	20	22	0	42	8
Bannon, Jeff, Louisville	.989	38	56	120	2	178	30
Bartlett, Jason, Rochester	.956	59	86	176	12	274	45
Basak, Christopher, Norfolk	.960	47	59	110	7	176	29

Player, Team	Pct.	G	PO	A	E	TC	DP
Berg, Dave, Pawtucket	1.000	1	1	6	0	7	1
Bergolla, William, Louisville	.912	20	11	41	5	57	4
Bourgeois, Jason, Richmond	.857	1	2	4	1	7	1
Cannizaro, Andrew, Columbus	.970	54	65	132	6	203	24
Cosme, Caonabo, Columbus	.958	23	37	55	4	96	8
Crespo, Cesar, Indianapolis	1.000	9	8	18	0	26	5
Dawkins, Gookie, Toledo	.946	79	122	213	19	354	52
Escalona, Felix, Columbus	.965	65	96	207	11	314	52
Figueroa, Luis, Pawtucket	.930	45	67	120	14	201	30
Finegan, Brian, Buffalo	1.000	2	5	1	0	6	1
Furmaniak, J.J., Indianapolis	.965	29	48	90	5	143	15
Gil, Benji, Norfolk	.969	53	71	146	7	224	34
Gutierrez, Ricky, Charlotte	1.000	17	24	46	0	70	10
Hannahan, Leonard, Scranton/Wilkes-Barre ..	.947	21	23	66	5	94	18
Hernandez, Anderson, Norfolk	.969	30	45	80	4	129	17
Hill, Aaron, Syracuse	.945	38	62	110	10	182	23
Hill, Bobby, Indianapolis	1.000	1	0	1	0	1	0
Holbert, Aaron, Louisville	.965	23	36	47	3	86	13
Hooper, Kevin, Toledo	.963	25	32	73	4	109	20
Hummel, Tim, Pawtucket	.977	33	44	81	3	128	17
Inglett, Joseph, Buffalo	1.000	3	6	8	0	14	1
Jeroloman, Charles, Pawtucket	.750	1	1	2	1	4	0
Johnson, Kelly, Richmond	.833	1	3	2	1	6	2
Kata, Matt, Scranton/Wilkes-Barre	.895	6	4	13	2	19	1
Kelly, Donald, Toledo	.951	34	38	98	7	143	25
Keppinger, Jeff, Norfolk	1.000	3	4	5	0	9	3
Lambin, Chase, Norfolk	.902	21	21	62	9	92	7
Leon, Carlos, Scranton/Wilkes-Barre	.923	5	6	18	2	26	3
Lopez, Luis, Louisville	.956	23	33	53	4	90	11
Lopez, Pedro, Charlotte	.943	45	59	122	11	192	35
Machado, Alejandro, Pawtucket	.977	39	60	109	4	173	25
Machado, Anderson, Louisville	.946	20	27	43	4	74	8
Martinez, Felix, Charlotte	.961	34	57	92	6	155	28
Martinez, Ramon, Toledo	1.000	2	3	2	0	5	0
Matos, Julius, Syracuse	.964	97	113	293	15	421	66
Medrano, Anthony, Scranton/Wilkes-Barre	1.000	1	2	2	0	4	0
Mendez, Deivi, Columbus	.973	10	10	26	1	37	3
Morban, Jose, Buffalo	.971	9	12	21	1	34	5
Moriarty, Mike, Pawtucket-Ottawa	.965	66	96	176	10	282	35
Nieves, Raul, Pawtucket	1.000	2	2	9	0	11	0
Ojeda, Augie, Rochester	.974	70	92	173	7	272	51
Olmedo, Ranier, Louisville	1.000	1	1	3	0	4	1
Olszta, Edwin, Indianapolis	...	1	0	0	0	0	0
Ordaz, Luis, Durham	.900	8	9	18	3	30	5
Patchett, Gary, Louisville	.952	7	4	16	1	21	4
Pedroia, Dustin, Pawtucket	1.000	10	12	27	0	39	3
Pena, Tony, Richmond	.953	136	222	420	32	674	94
Perez, Kenny, Pawtucket	1.000	10	19	35	0	54	11
Perez, Tomas, Louisville	.921	25	24	46	6	76	7
Phillips, Brandon, Buffalo	.958	111	151	331	21	503	55
Pratt, Scott, Richmond	1.000	7	9	6	0	15	1
Relaford, Desi, Syracuse	1.000	1	1	3	0	4	0
Reyes, Guillermo, Charlotte	.936	53	70	136	14	220	27
Rivas, Luis, Rochester	.955	5	8	13	1	22	5
Rodriguez, Luis, Rochester	1.000	11	21	26	0	47	9
Rogers, Eddie, Ottawa	.970	67	98	195	9	302	39
SANDOVAL, DANNY, Scranton/Wilkes-Barre ..	.976	102	162	321	12	495	79
Schrager, Anthony, Pawtucket	.971	7	9	24	1	34	3
Skrehot, Shaun, Indianapolis	1.000	13	18	33	0	51	7
Smith, Jason, Toledo	.968	8	16	14	1	31	3
Solano, Danny, Syracuse	.931	8	6	21	2	29	4
Sosa, Juan, Scranton/Wilkes-Barre	.984	18	25	37	1	63	11
Thrower, Jason, Buffalo	.938	7	11	19	2	32	1
Upton, B.J., Durham	.921	133	219	396	53	668	95
Vazquez, Ramon, Buffalo	.963	17	24	54	3	81	14
Velandia, Jorge, Louisville	.977	82	110	223	8	341	53
Velazquez, Gilbert, Rochester	.905	6	6	13	2	21	2
Williams, Glenn, Rochester	.875	4	3	4	1	8	1
Wilson, Enrique, Ottawa	.959	18	15	56	3	74	12

SHORTSTOPS WITH TWO OR MORE TEAMS

Player, Team	Pct.	G	PO	A	E	TC	DP
Moriarty, Mike, Pawtucket	1.000	1	1	2	0	3	0
Moriarty, Mike, Ottawa	.964	65	95	174	10	279	35

OUTFIELDERS

Player, Team	Pct.	G	PO	A	E	TC	DP
Abad, Andy, Buffalo *	.984	68	120	3	2	125	0
Abernathy, Brent, Rochester	1.000	19	24	0	0	24	0
Alvarez, Tony, Charlotte	1.000	3	2	0	0	2	0

Player, Team	Pct.	G	PO	A	E	TC	DP
Ambres, Chip, Pawtucket	.973	73	137	5	4	146	2
Amezaga, Alfredo, Indianapolis	.958	14	23	0	1	24	0
Anderson, Brian N., Charlotte	.986	115	278	14	4	296	4
Anderson, Drew, Louisville	.800	5	4	0	1	5	0
Arteaga, Joshua, Richmond	1.000	1	3	0	0	3	0
Asadoorian, Eric, Louisville	1.000	31	63	4	0	67	1
Badeaux, Brooks, Durham	1.000	3	1	1	0	2	0
Bailey, Jeffrey, Pawtucket	1.000	8	16	0	0	16	0
Barnes, John, Richmond	.976	52	118	5	3	126	1
Berg, Dave, Pawtucket	1.000	16	13	1	0	14	0
Bigbie, Larry, Ottawa	...	2	0	0	0	0	0
Bikowski, Scott, Charlotte *	1.000	80	132	10	0	142	2
Borchard, Joe, Charlotte	.989	123	261	1	3	265	1
Bourgeois, Jason, Richmond	.976	21	38	3	1	42	0
Brazell, Craig, Norfolk	.818	22	18	0	4	22	0
Brown, Roosevelt, Charlotte	.983	88	164	13	3	180	3
Buchanan, Brian, Rochester	1.000	6	7	1	0	8	0
Budzinski, Mark, Scranton/Wilkes-Barre *	.990	120	192	8	2	202	2
Burrus, Josh, Richmond	.909	5	10	0	1	11	0
Byrd, Marlon, Scranton/Wilkes-Barre	.824	5	14	0	3	17	0
Cabrera, Melky, Columbus *	1.000	23	63	2	0	65	0
Calloway, Ron, Norfolk	.961	101	168	6	7	181	1
Calzado, Napoleon, Ottawa	.953	34	60	1	3	64	1
Cameron, Mike, Norfolk	1.000	2	3	0	0	3	0
Cash, Kevin, Durham	...	1	0	0	0	0	0
Castellano, John, Scranton/Wilkes-Barre	.966	17	27	1	1	29	0
Cliffords, Benjamin, Ottawa	1.000	9	16	0	0	16	0
Cooper, Jason, Buffalo *	.992	70	118	4	1	123	0
Coquillette, Trace, Charlotte	...	1	0	0	0	0	0
Cosme, Caonabo, Columbus	1.000	4	5	1	0	6	0
Crespo, Cesar, Indianapolis	.988	37	78	1	1	80	0
Crosby, Bubba, Columbus *	.989	38	84	2	1	87	0
Crozier, Eric, Louisville *	.983	26	54	5	1	60	0
Cummings, Midre, Ottawa	.981	51	101	3	2	106	0
Curry, Michael, Durham	.964	12	26	1	1	28	0
Darula, Robert, Ottawa	.994	97	154	4	1	159	0
Daubach, Brian, Norfolk	.875	9	7	0	1	8	0
Dawkins, Gookie, Toledo	1.000	9	9	1	0	10	0
Deardorff, Jeff, Durham	1.000	77	120	5	0	125	0
De Caster, Yurendell, Indianapolis	.983	58	114	4	2	120	1
Denorfia, Chris, Louisville	1.000	89	205	6	0	211	0
Diaz, Victor, Norfolk	1.000	17	36	1	0	37	1
Doumit, Ryan, Indianapolis	1.000	4	6	0	0	6	0
Dubois, Jason, Buffalo	1.000	12	16	1	0	17	0
Duffy, Chris, Indianapolis *	.989	76	172	3	2	177	1
Duncan, Jeff, Norfolk *	1.000	1	1	0	0	1	0
Dunwoody, Todd, Rochester *	.989	86	183	2	2	187	0
Duran, Carlos, Richmond *	.944	6	16	1	1	18	0
Espinosa, David, Toledo	1.000	7	5	0	0	5	0
Fernandez, Alexander, Louisville *	.954	34	60	2	3	65	1
Fleming, Ryan, Scranton/Wilkes-Barre *	.800	2	3	1	1	5	0
Francisco, Louis, Buffalo	1.000	4	9	0	0	9	0
French, Anton, Syracuse	.987	93	218	2	3	223	0
Furmaniak, J.J., Indianapolis	1.000	1	1	0	0	1	0
Garcia, Luis, Norfolk	1.000	23	33	2	0	35	2
Gathright, Joey, Durham	.948	56	122	6	7	135	2
Gerut, Jody, Buffalo *	.947	8	17	1	1	19	0
Gettis, Byron, Toledo	.980	30	45	5	1	51	0
Giambi, Jeremy, Charlotte *	1.000	2	1	0	0	1	0
Gibson, Derrick, Richmond	.960	17	23	1	1	25	0
Gload, Ross, Charlotte *	.952	11	20	0	1	21	0
Gomes, Jonny, Durham	.948	45	67	6	4	77	1
Gomez, Alexis, Toledo *	.968	113	177	7	6	190	1
Gonzalez, Juan, Buffalo	1.000	4	7	0	0	7	0
Granderson, Curtis, Toledo	.985	107	256	15	4	275	3
Griffin, John-Ford, Syracuse *	.979	71	133	7	3	143	1
Grindell, Nathan, Scranton/Wilkes-Barre	.973	52	69	4	2	75	2
Gross, Gabe, Syracuse	.981	99	191	13	4	208	2
Gutierrez, Franklin, Buffalo	1.000	19	57	2	0	59	2
Hankins, Ryan, Columbus	1.000	6	8	0	0	8	0
Hannahan, Leonard, Scranton/Wilkes-Barre	.976	25	39	2	1	42	0
Harper, Brandon, Toledo	1.000	3	1	0	0	1	0
Hessman, Mike, Toledo	1.000	16	17	1	0	18	0
Hollins, Damon, Durham *	1.000	21	48	3	0	51	0
Hooper, Kevin, Toledo	1.000	21	29	3	0	32	1
Hoover, Paul, Durham	.971	17	31	2	1	34	0
Hubbard, Trenidad, Durham	.981	25	47	4	1	52	0
Hyzdu, Adam, Pawtucket	1.000	29	61	0	0	61	0
Inglett, Joseph, Buffalo	.987	33	73	1	1	75	1
Johnson, Kelly, Richmond	.978	40	87	1	2	90	0
Johnson, Russ, Columbus	1.000	11	20	0	0	20	0
Jones, Garrett, Rochester *	.750	7	3	0	1	4	0
Jones, Mitchell, Columbus	.933	7	14	0	1	15	0
Jurries, James, Richmond	1.000	43	62	1	0	63	0
Kapler, Gabriel, Pawtucket	1.000	6	15	0	0	15	0
Kata, Matt, Scranton/Wilkes-Barre	.923	6	11	1	1	13	0
Kearns, Austin, Louisville	1.000	26	50	2	0	52	0
Kelly, Donald, Toledo	...	1	0	0	0	0	0
Kelly, Kenny, Louisville	1.000	59	155	3	0	158	2
Kingsale, Gene, Ottawa	.926	19	24	1	2	27	0
Kinkade, Mike, Buffalo	.947	19	36	0	2	38	0
Koonce, Graham, Indianapolis *	1.000	15	20	1	0	21	1
Lambin, Chase, Norfolk	1.000	2	4	1	0	5	0
Liefer, Jeff, Buffalo	1.000	16	26	0	0	26	0
Lockwood, Michael, Pawtucket *	.982	75	160	4	3	167	0
Lombard, George, Pawtucket	.996	124	249	3	1	253	1
Ludwick, Ryan, Buffalo *	.983	54	115	2	2	119	2
Machado, Alejandro, Pawtucket	1.000	7	16	0	0	16	0
Matos, Julius, Syracuse	1.000	1	2	0	0	2	0
Maza, Luis, Rochester	.950	22	18	1	1	20	0
McCarthy, William, Richmond	1.000	58	113	5	0	118	2
McCurdy, Joshua, Ottawa	1.000	5	6	0	0	6	0
McDonald, Darnell, Buffalo-Durham	.992	97	236	9	2	247	4
McLouth, Nate, Indianapolis	.986	105	214	3	3	220	0
Morban, Jose, Buffalo	.971	20	29	4	1	34	1
Mottola, Chad, Syracuse	.973	73	142	3	4	149	1
Nelson, Bry, Syracuse	.981	19	48	4	1	53	2
Neuberger, Scott, Durham	1.000	2	1	1	0	2	0
Newhan, David, Ottawa	1.000	11	21	0	0	21	0
Nivar, Ramon, Ottawa	.968	31	83	8	3	94	2
Nixon, Trot, Pawtucket *	1.000	1	3	0	0	3	0
Nunnally, Jon, Indianapolis	.942	61	109	4	7	120	1
O'Keefe, Michael, Richmond *	1.000	2	2	0	0	2	0
Olszta, Edwin, Indianapolis	.667	3	2	0	1	3	0
Ordonez, Magglio, Toledo	1.000	3	3	0	0	3	0
Padilla, Jorge, Scranton/Wilkes-Barre	.983	59	113	5	2	120	1
Pagan, Angel, Norfolk	.972	110	306	8	9	323	3
Pena, Wily Mo, Louisville	.889	5	8	0	1	9	0
Perez, Tomas, Louisville	1.000	30	64	3	0	67	0
Podsednik, Scott, Charlotte *	1.000	2	6	1	0	7	0
Porter, Colin, Columbus *	.991	56	110	2	1	113	0
Pratt, Scott, Richmond	.973	53	105	2	3	110	0
Rabe, Joshua, Rochester	.972	75	103	3	3	109	0
Raburn, Ryan, Toledo	...	1	0	0	0	0	0
Raines Jr., Tim, Ottawa	.990	119	277	6	3	286	1
Redman, Prentice, Norfolk	.973	67	104	4	3	111	1
Reed, Keith, Ottawa	.983	76	164	5	3	172	0
Reese, Kevin, Columbus *	.984	122	235	7	4	246	3
Robinson, Kerry, Richmond *	.990	55	103	1	1	105	0
Rodriguez, John, Buffalo *	.989	45	90	2	1	93	0
Rogers, Eddie, Ottawa	...	1	0	0	0	0	0
Rolls, Damian, Columbus	.957	12	21	1	1	23	1
Romano, Jason, Louisville	.985	53	122	6	2	130	0
Rosa, Wally, Charlotte	1.000	1	1	0	0	1	0
Rosamond, George, Richmond	1.000	15	26	0	0	26	0
Rushford, Jim, Scranton/Wilkes-Barre *	.970	49	61	4	2	67	3
Ryan, Michael, Rochester	1.000	39	69	0	0	69	0
Sadler, Ray, Indianapolis	.980	68	137	9	3	149	0
Sherrod, Justin, Pawtucket	.974	99	218	8	6	232	3
Singleton, Chris, Durham *	1.000	1	2	0	0	2	0
Singleton, Justin, Syracuse	.991	92	222	10	2	234	1
Smith, Jason, Toledo	1.000	5	3	0	0	3	0
Smitherman, Stephen, Louisville	1.000	29	45	3	0	48	0
Snead, Esix, Richmond	.986	95	271	8	4	283	2
Spidale, Michael, Charlotte	1.000	27	56	0	0	56	0
Stern, Adam, Pawtucket	.980	20	47	1	1	49	0
Swann, Pedro, Louisville	.959	60	89	5	4	98	1
Taylor, Reggie, Durham	.960	66	138	5	6	149	0
Thames, Marcus, Toledo	.975	56	75	4	2	81	0
Thompson, Kevin, Columbus	.967	54	113	3	4	120	1
Thompson, Rich, Indianapolis	.985	26	65	2	1	68	1
TYNER, JASON, Rochester *	.996	126	247	9	1	257	2
Valent, Eric, Norfolk *	.983	58	109	6	2	117	0
Velandia, Jorge, Indianapolis	1.000	1	1	1	0	2	1
Vento, Mike, Columbus	.982	109	216	8	4	228	1
Victorino, Shane, Scranton/Wilkes-Barre	.991	126	307	14	3	324	4
West, Kevin, Rochester	.968	89	174	7	6	187	4
Wilken, Kristopher, Ottawa	1.000	6	8	1	0	9	0
Williams, Gerald, Norfolk	1.000	35	67	4	0	71	0
Wilson, Craig, Indianapolis	.800	4	4	0	1	5	0
Wise, Dewayne, Toledo *	.980	92	190	3	4	197	0
Young, Delmon, Durham	.943	51	94	5	6	105	1
Young, Ernie, Buffalo	.992	52	115	5	1	121	2
Zapp, Andrew, Louisville	1.000	5	5	0	0	5	0

OUTFIELDERS WITH TWO OR MORE TEAMS

Player, Team	Pct.	G	PO	A	E	TC	DP
McDonald, Darnell, Buffalo	1.000	25	48	2	0	50	2
McDonald, Darnell, Durham	.990	72	188	7	2	197	2

CATCHERS

Player, Team	Pct.	G	PO	A	E	TC	DP
Aceves, Jonathan, Charlotte	.992	16	118	8	1	127	1
Bailey, Jeffrey, Pawtucket	1.000	4	8	0	0	8	0
Bernard, Miguel, Richmond	1.000	2	11	1	0	12	0
Boscan, Jean, Richmond	.986	68	400	32	6	438	5
Bowen, Rob, Rochester	.992	69	467	38	4	509	4
Buckley, James, Pawtucket	.991	15	103	5	1	109	0
Burke, Jamie, Charlotte	.991	48	319	26	3	348	7
Calzado, Napoleon, Ottawa	1.000	1	7	0	0	7	0
Cardona, Javier, Buffalo	.992	16	114	9	1	124	1
Casanova, Raul, Charlotte	.990	62	460	27	5	492	2
Cash, Kevin, Durham	.990	38	259	26	3	288	5
Castellano, John, Scranton/Wilkes-Barre	...	1	0	0	0	0	0
Chiaffredo, Paul, Indianapolis	.997	54	264	21	1	286	2
Coste, Christopher, Scranton/Wilkes-Barre	.980	9	43	7	1	51	1
Cota, Humberto, Indianapolis	1.000	3	21	2	0	23	0
Davis, Ben, Charlotte	.989	10	80	6	1	87	0
DePastino, Joe, Syracuse	.992	50	339	25	3	367	2
DiFelice, Mike, Norfolk	.993	71	498	49	4	551	2
Dominique, Andy, Syracuse	1.000	31	193	13	0	206	3
Doumit, Ryan, Indianapolis	.983	39	221	12	4	237	1
Fasano, Sal, Ottawa	.984	12	54	9	1	64	3
Franco, Iker, Richmond	1.000	9	55	7	0	62	1
Garko, Ryan, Buffalo	.993	59	401	20	3	424	7
Gradoville, Timothy, Scranton/Wilkes-Barre	.929	6	24	2	2	28	1
Hankins, Ryan, Columbus	1.000	4	29	1	0	30	0
HARPER, BRANDON, Toledo	.997	74	536	34	2	572	2
Heintz, Chris, Rochester	.996	31	208	15	1	224	0
Hietpas, Joe, Norfolk	.984	25	170	14	3	187	0
Hinch, A.J., Scranton/Wilkes-Barre	.985	80	499	33	8	540	7
Hooper, Kevin, Toledo	1.000	1	1	0	0	1	0
Hoover, Paul, Durham	1.000	13	90	8	0	98	2
Hubele, Ryan, Ottawa	.986	13	66	6	1	73	2
Huckaby, Ken, Syracuse	1.000	14	97	5	0	102	2
Kinkade, Mike, Buffalo	1.000	2	10	2	0	12	0
Kroski, Christopher, Louisville	1.000	1	3	0	0	3	0
Laker, Tim, Durham	.987	64	411	42	6	459	6
Lomasney, Steve, Louisville	.987	43	275	32	4	311	2
Lunar, Fernando, Norfolk	.982	24	148	19	3	170	1
Martinez, Octavio, Ottawa	1.000	38	226	23	0	249	1
Martinez, Sandy, Toledo	.982	76	515	46	10	571	5
McCullough, Clayton, Buffalo	...	1	0	0	0	0	0
Mendez, Carlos, Richmond	1.000	4	12	0	0	12	1
Miller, Corky, Rochester	.993	53	425	22	3	450	4
Munson, Eric, Durham	1.000	1	1	0	0	1	0
Nieves, Wil, Columbus	.991	87	695	52	7	754	5
Pachot, John, Norfolk	.992	21	110	14	1	125	2
Parrish, David, Columbus	.979	56	361	20	8	389	0
Paulino, Ronny, Indianapolis	.989	69	410	33	5	448	3
Pena, Brayan, Richmond	.991	63	402	22	4	428	6
Perez, Miguel, Louisville	1.000	21	166	16	0	182	1
Piazza, Anthony, Norfolk	.800	1	4	0	1	5	0
Pyzik, Steven, Richmond	1.000	6	35	3	0	38	1
Quiroz, Guillermo, Syracuse	.988	23	160	11	2	173	4
Rojas, Thomas, Columbus	1.000	1	2	0	0	2	0
Rosa, Wally, Charlotte	.989	15	86	7	1	94	0
Ross, David, Indianapolis	.971	6	31	3	1	35	1
Ruiz, Carlos, Scranton/Wilkes-Barre	.991	56	402	30	4	436	6
Santiago, Benito, Norfolk	1.000	8	51	3	0	54	1
Sardinha, Dane, Louisville	.991	84	603	46	6	655	7
Schneider, John, Syracuse	.995	31	184	12	1	197	3
Shelton, Chris, Toledo	.958	3	21	2	1	24	1
Shoppach, Kelly, Pawtucket	.993	87	644	42	5	691	4
Stachowsky, Mitchel, Pawtucket	1.000	3	5	1	0	6	0
Wathan, Dusty, Buffalo	.990	76	460	52	5	517	9
Whiteside, Eli, Ottawa	.993	91	544	40	4	588	4
Whittaker, Timothy, Syracuse	1.000	6	23	0	0	23	0
Wilson, Andrew, Norfolk	1.000	1	1	0	0	1	0
Wooten, Shawn, Pawtucket	.986	50	326	15	5	346	4

PITCHERS

Player, Team	Pct.	G	PO	A	E	TC	DP
Abad, Andy, Buffalo *	1.000	1	0	1	0	1	1
Abbott, James, Rochester	1.000	6	1	1	0	2	0
Acevedo, Jose, Louisville	1.000	1	1	2	0	3	0

Player, Team	Pct.	G	PO	A	E	TC	DP
Adams, Terry, Scranton/Wilkes-Barre	1.000	14	0	1	0	1	0
Adkins, Jon, Charlotte	.944	23	6	11	1	18	0
Alfaro, Jason, Syracuse	...	1	0	0	0	0	0
Almonte, Hector, Richmond	1.000	18	0	3	0	3	0
Alvarez, Abe, Pawtucket *	.917	26	7	15	2	24	1
Amaya, Jose, Buffalo	...	1	0	0	0	0	0
Anderson, Jason, Columbus	.909	55	5	5	1	11	0
Anderson, Jimmy, Rochester-Durham	.923	22	6	18	2	26	1
Arnold, Jason, Syracuse	1.000	47	7	3	0	10	0
Artiles, Carlos, Columbus *	1.000	2	1	2	0	3	0
Aybar, Manny, Norfolk	1.000	24	2	3	0	5	1
BACSIK, MIKE, Scranton/Wilkes-Barre *	1.000	30	14	24	0	38	1
Bajenaru, Jeff, Charlotte	1.000	61	5	7	0	12	0
Baker, Chris, Syracuse	1.000	30	9	22	0	31	1
Baker, Scott, Rochester	.962	22	12	13	1	26	0
Baldwin, James, Ottawa	.933	8	6	8	1	15	0
Bannister, Brian, Norfolk	1.000	8	2	4	0	6	1
Barkett, Andy, Richmond *	...	1	0	0	0	0	0
Barnes, John, Richmond	...	1	0	0	0	0	0
Barrett, William, Rochester *	1.000	40	5	8	0	13	0
Barry, Kevin, Richmond	1.000	32	3	10	0	13	0
Basner, Ryan, Richmond	...	2	0	0	0	0	0
Bauer, Rick, Ottawa	.933	30	4	10	1	15	0
Baugh, Kenneth, Toledo	.917	28	11	22	3	36	0
Bausher, Timothy, Pawtucket	.714	44	2	8	4	14	0
Bean, Colter, Columbus	.938	65	3	12	1	16	0
Beimel, Joe, Durham *	1.000	48	4	11	0	15	1
Bell, Heath, Norfolk	.800	13	2	2	1	5	0
Bell, Rob, Durham	.833	22	0	5	1	6	0
Bere, Jason, Buffalo	1.000	3	1	0	0	1	0
Bernero, Adam, Richmond	.714	10	3	7	4	14	3
Bikowski, Scott, Charlotte *	...	1	0	0	0	0	0
Blackburn, Robert, Rochester	1.000	3	0	2	0	2	0
Boehringer, Brian, Columbus	1.000	6	0	1	0	1	0
Bonilla, Vincente, Rochester	1.000	35	9	23	0	32	2
Bonser, Boof, Rochester	.964	28	10	17	1	28	2
Booker, Chris, Louisville	1.000	59	2	4	0	6	0
Borkowski, Dave, Ottawa	.932	29	12	29	3	44	2
Bottalico, Ricky, Pawtucket	1.000	6	1	0	0	1	0
Bowyer, Travis, Rochester	1.000	59	5	10	0	15	1
Bradley, Bobby, Indianapolis	1.000	11	1	2	0	3	0
Brazelton, Dewon, Durham	.889	5	2	6	1	9	0
Brito, Eude, Scranton/Wilkes-Barre *	.964	28	14	13	1	28	5
Brock, Terrence, Durham	.833	15	1	4	1	6	0
Brooks, Frank, Richmond *	.667	54	2	2	2	6	0
Brower, Jim, Richmond	1.000	4	0	1	0	1	0
Brown, Andrew, Buffalo	1.000	49	5	4	0	9	1
Bruback, Matt, Ottawa	.800	9	7	5	3	15	0
Bruksch, Jeffrey, Louisville	1.000	1	0	1	0	1	0
Bullard, James, Charlotte *	1.000	15	1	3	0	4	0
Bullinger, Jim, Charlotte	1.000	10	1	3	0	4	0
Bullinger, Kirk, Indianapolis	1.000	55	7	25	0	32	2
Bullington, Bryan, indianapolis	.944	18	5	12	1	18	1
Bumatay, Michael, Toledo *	...	3	0	0	0	0	0
Burke, Erick, Scranton/Wilkes-Barre *	.750	32	0	3	1	4	0
Burnside, Adrian, Syracuse *	1.000	50	5	3	0	8	0
Bush, David, Syracuse	1.000	9	4	2	0	6	1
Bynum, Mike, Toledo *	1.000	8	3	7	0	10	1
Byrdak, Tim, Ottawa *	1.000	37	2	3	0	5	0
Cabrera, Fernando, Buffalo	1.000	30	2	5	0	7	0
Cahill, Casey, Ottawa	1.000	1	1	0	0	1	0
Carlson, Jesse, Syracuse *	1.000	22	2	4	0	6	0
Carmona, Fausto, Buffalo	.929	13	4	9	1	14	1
Carnes, Thomas, Durham	.833	37	1	4	1	6	0
Carter, Lance, Durham	1.000	8	1	4	0	5	1
Cassidy, Scott, Pawtucket	.875	26	2	5	1	8	0
Cevette, Daniel, Buffalo *	...	1	0	0	0	0	0
Chantres, Carlos, Scranton/Wilkes-Barre	.500	1	0	1	1	2	0
Chenard, Kenneth, Norfolk	1.000	1	1	0	0	1	0
Chiavacci, Ronald, Indianapolis	1.000	10	1	1	0	2	0
Childers, Jason, Richmond	1.000	38	1	5	0	6	0
Childers, Matt, Richmond	.900	51	3	6	1	10	2
Childress, Daylan, Louisville-Rochester	.667	16	1	3	2	6	0
Clippard, Tyler, Columbus	...	1	0	0	0	0	0
Coffey, Todd, Louisville	1.000	8	1	0	0	1	0
Colon, Roman, Richmond	1.000	3	0	2	0	2	0
Colyer, Steve, Norfolk *	1.000	28	1	4	0	5	0
Condrey, Clay, Scranton/Wilkes-Barre	.976	25	19	22	1	42	3
Connolly, Michael, Indianapolis *	1.000	13	5	10	0	15	1
Cooper, Christopher, Buffalo *	.000	12	0	0	1	1	0
Corcoran, Tim, Durham	.889	29	4	4	1	9	0

Player, Team	Pct.	G	PO	A	E	TC	DP
Corey, Mark, Indianapolis	.875	61	3	4	1	8	0
Coste, Christopher, Scranton/Wilkes-Barre	...	1	0	0	0	0	0
Creek, Doug, Toledo *	1.000	28	0	2	0	2	0
Cressend, Jack, Pawtucket	1.000	40	3	6	0	9	0
Cruceta, Francisco, Buffalo	1.000	30	5	7	0	12	0
Cruz, Nelson, Toledo	1.000	14	5	8	0	13	1
Curtis, Daniel, Richmond	1.000	18	8	18	0	26	1
Darensbourg, Vic, Toledo *	1.000	44	3	5	0	8	3
Davies, Kyle, Richmond	.875	13	2	5	1	8	0
Davis, Allen, Scranton/Wilkes-Barre *	1.000	3	0	1	0	1	0
Davis, Jason, Buffalo	.929	16	11	15	2	28	0
Deardorff, Jeff, Durham	1.000	1	0	1	0	1	0
Dehart, James, Richmond *	.500	2	0	1	1	2	0
Delcarmen, Manny, Pawtucket	1.000	15	2	0	0	2	0
Denham, Daniel, Buffalo	.333	3	1	0	2	3	0
Denney, Kyle, Buffalo	1.000	9	2	4	0	6	0
De Paula, Jorge, Columbus	1.000	21	10	15	0	25	2
Deschenes, Mark, Pawtucket	.857	11	3	3	1	7	0
Devine, Joey, Richmond	...	1	0	0	0	0	0
Diaz, Felix, Charlotte	.960	21	7	17	1	25	1
Diaz, Jose, Buffalo	1.000	20	1	4	0	5	0
DiNardo, Lenny, Pawtucket	.914	23	9	23	3	35	0
Dingman, Craig, Toledo	1.000	35	1	2	0	3	0
Douglass, Sean, Toledo	1.000	14	2	7	0	9	0
Downs, Scott, Syracuse *	1.000	7	4	6	0	10	1
DuBose, Eric, Ottawa *	1.000	2	2	0	0	2	0
Duff, Matt, Syracuse	1.000	15	1	5	0	6	0
Duke, Zach, Indianapolis *	.971	16	10	23	1	34	1
Durbin, J.D., Rochester	.947	22	9	9	1	19	0
Ellis, Robert, Scranton/Wilkes-Barre	1.000	4	1	3	0	4	0
Ennis, John, Toledo	1.000	50	6	9	0	15	0
Enochs, Chris, Indianapolis	.957	33	9	13	1	23	2
Estrada, Horacio, Ottawa *	1.000	5	3	3	0	6	0
Evans, Kyle, Buffalo	.500	1	0	1	1	2	0
Eyre, Willie, Rochester	.889	56	8	16	3	27	1
Fernandez, Jared, Louisville-Scranton/Wilkes-Barre	1.000	20	8	17	0	25	1
Fesh, Sean, Scranton/Wilkes-Barre *	1.000	27	1	3	0	4	0
Fields, Joshua, Charlotte	.923	55	2	10	1	13	1
Fiore, Tony, Ottawa	.961	30	21	28	2	51	2
Floyd, Gavin, Scranton/Wilkes-Barre	.931	24	9	18	2	29	0
Foster, John, Richmond *	1.000	3	0	1	0	1	0
Franco, Martire, Scranton/Wilkes-Barre	.900	44	9	9	2	20	1
Franklin, Wayne, Columbus *	1.000	46	2	2	0	4	0
Gardner, Lee, Indianapolis	1.000	48	8	8	0	16	1
Gassner, Dave, Rochester *	1.000	22	3	17	0	20	4
Gaudin, Chad, Syracuse	1.000	23	9	21	0	30	1
Geary, Geoff, Scranton/Wilkes-Barre	...	10	0	0	0	0	0
Germano, Justin, Louisville	1.000	8	2	6	0	8	1
Giese, Daniel, Scranton/Wilkes-Barre	.875	26	3	4	1	8	1
Gil, Benji, Norfolk	...	1	0	0	0	0	0
Ginter, Matt, Toledo	1.000	17	8	9	0	17	0
Glynn, Ryan, Syracuse	.750	9	0	3	1	4	0
Gonzalez, Jeremi, Pawtucket	.875	11	1	6	1	8	2
Gonzalez, Mike, Indianapolis *	...	2	0	0	0	0	0
Good, Andrew, Toledo	.862	23	10	15	4	29	1
Graman, Alex, Columbus-Louisville	.900	28	4	14	2	20	1
Graves, Danny, Norfolk	1.000	5	1	0	0	1	0
Green, Steve, Toledo	1.000	24	0	3	0	3	0
Greisinger, Seth, Richmond	.941	16	3	13	1	17	0
Grilli, Jason, Toledo	.943	28	5	28	2	35	1
Gronkiewicz, Lee, Syracuse	.800	28	1	3	1	5	1
Groom, Buddy, Columbus *	1.000	6	0	2	0	2	0
Guthrie, Jeremy, Buffalo	.955	25	2	19	1	22	2
Hammel, Jason, Durham	1.000	10	3	7	0	10	0
Hampton, Mike, Richmond *	1.000	1	0	1	0	1	0
Hamulack, Tim, Norfolk *	1.000	28	1	9	0	10	0
Hancock, Josh, Louisville	1.000	11	2	3	0	5	0
Hankins, Ryan, Columbus	...	1	0	0	0	0	0
Haynes, Jimmy, Durham	1.000	7	1	7	0	8	0
Henkel, Robert, Toledo *	1.000	10	0	1	0	1	0
Henn, Sean, Columbus *	.923	16	2	10	1	13	2
Hernandez, Buddy, Richmond	1.000	7	0	2	0	2	0
Hernandez, Orlando, Charlotte	...	1	0	0	0	0	0
Hernandez, Yoel, Scranton/Wilkes-Barre	1.000	40	4	8	0	12	1
Herrera, Alex, Richmond *	.000	13	0	0	1	1	0
Hessman, Mike, Toledo	...	1	0	0	0	0	0
Hill, Jeremy, Norfolk	...	2	0	0	0	0	0
Hines, Carlos, Durham	.727	26	2	6	3	11	1
Hodge, Kevin, Scranton/Wilkes-Barre	1.000	20	1	1	0	2	0
Hodges, Trey, Rochester-Richmond	1.000	15	2	5	0	7	0
Hooper, Kevin, Toledo	...	1	0	0	0	0	0
Isaacson, Charlie, Columbus	1.000	7	1	4	0	5	0
Ishii, Kazuhisa, Norfolk *	1.000	5	0	2	0	2	0
Izquierdo, Hansel, Indianapolis	.800	7	3	5	2	10	0
Jackson, Zach, Syracuse *	1.000	8	2	12	0	14	0
James, Chuck, Richmond *	1.000	6	1	1	0	2	0
Johnson, Mark, Toledo	1.000	7	3	1	0	4	1
Johnston, Mike, Indianapolis *	.929	52	1	12	1	14	1
Jones, Bobby M., Charlotte *	.667	16	0	2	1	3	0
Junge, Eric, Norfolk	1.000	26	11	16	0	27	0
Karnuth, Jason, Toledo	.938	63	5	10	1	16	0
Keisler, Randy, Louisville *	.929	12	3	10	1	14	0
Kelly, Steven, Louisville	.933	19	5	9	1	15	0
Kemp, Beau, Rochester	1.000	62	8	10	0	18	2
Keppel, Robert, Norfolk	.909	5	4	6	1	11	0
Kershner, Jason, Pawtucket *	1.000	15	0	4	0	4	0
Kester, Timothy, Pawtucket	.912	30	13	18	3	34	1
King, Jeremy, Columbus	1.000	1	0	1	0	1	0
Kleine, Victor, Buffalo *	1.000	6	1	7	0	8	1
Koo, Dae-Sung, Norfolk *	...	2	0	0	0	0	0
Kozlowski, Ben, Louisville	1.000	8	1	1	0	2	0
Laker, Tim, Durham	1.000	1	0	1	0	1	0
Lavigne, Tim, Norfolk	1.000	45	6	16	0	22	0
League, Brandon, Syracuse	.857	19	4	8	2	14	1
Ledezma, Wilfredo, Toledo *	1.000	11	1	5	0	6	0
Lee, Dave, Norfolk	1.000	28	1	1	0	2	0
Lee, Seung Hak, Scranton/Wilkes-Barre	...	1	0	0	0	0	0
Lerew, Anthony, Richmond	.917	13	2	9	1	12	0
Lilly, Ted, Syracuse *	1.000	2	0	2	0	2	0
Liriano, Francisco, Rochester *	1.000	14	8	9	0	17	0
Liriano, Pedro, Scranton/Wilkes-Barre	1.000	22	10	14	0	24	2
Little, Jeffrey, Charlotte	1.000	9	1	4	0	5	0
Lomasney, Steve, Louisville	...	1	0	0	0	0	0
Lopez, Aquilino, Scranton/Wilkes-Barre	...	4	0	0	0	0	0
Lundberg, David, Syracuse	.870	50	3	17	3	23	1
Maduro, Calvin, Columbus	1.000	6	0	2	0	2	0
Magrane, James, Durham	.833	26	2	13	3	18	1
Maholm, Paul, Indianapolis *	.889	6	3	5	1	9	0
Maine, John, Ottawa	1.000	23	9	6	0	15	2
Malaska, Mark, Pawtucket *	.833	39	3	12	3	18	1
Mallette, Brian, Indianapolis	1.000	25	3	3	0	6	0
Manning, Charles, Columbus *	.667	7	1	1	1	3	0
Marcum, Shawn, Syracuse	1.000	18	9	13	0	22	0
Marsonek, Sam, Columbus	1.000	49	9	7	0	16	2
Marte, Damaso, Charlotte *	...	1	0	0	0	0	0
Martinez, Anastacio, Pawtucket	1.000	35	1	6	0	7	0
Matos, Josue, Syracuse	1.000	14	5	7	0	12	1
Matos, Julius, Syracuse	...	1	0	0	0	0	0
Matthews, Mike, Norfolk *	...	5	0	0	0	0	0
Mattison, Kieran, Buffalo	...	1	0	0	0	0	0
May, Darrell, Columbus *	1.000	10	2	3	0	5	0
McBride, Macay, Richmond *	.800	25	1	3	1	5	0
McCarthy, Brandon, Charlotte	.789	20	3	12	4	19	0
McClung, Seth, Durham	.833	6	2	3	1	6	0
McConnell, Sam, Richmond	1.000	20	2	8	0	10	0
McDade, Neal, Indianapolis	1.000	14	0	2	0	2	1
McGinley, Blake, Norfolk *	.895	44	5	12	2	19	1
McNichol, Brian, Ottawa *	1.000	36	6	16	0	22	1
Mears, Chris, Richmond	1.000	31	6	10	0	16	3
Mendoza, Ramiro, Columbus	1.000	8	0	1	0	1	0
Meredith, Cla, Pawtucket	1.000	40	1	6	0	7	0
Miller, Corky, Rochester	1.000	1	0	1	0	1	0
Miller, Jason, Rochester *	1.000	13	0	2	0	2	1
Miller, Jeffrey, Indianapolis	1.000	58	5	16	0	21	3
Miller, Justin, Syracuse	1.000	28	0	5	0	5	1
Miller, Matt, Buffalo	.500	9	0	1	1	2	0
Miller, Wade, Pawtucket	1.000	2	0	3	0	3	0
Miner, Zachary, Richmond-Toledo	.975	23	10	29	1	40	3
Minix, Travis, Scranton/Wilkes-Barre	1.000	14	3	1	0	4	0
Mitchell, Andy, Ottawa	.920	47	7	16	2	25	0
Munoz, Arnie, Charlotte *	.912	40	4	27	3	34	0
Munro, Pete, Columbus	.949	43	15	22	2	39	2
Musser, Neal, Norfolk *	.895	24	5	12	2	19	0
Nannini, Michael, Syracuse	1.000	19	4	1	0	5	0
Narveson, Christopher, Pawtucket *	1.000	21	6	19	0	25	1
Nelson, Joe, Durham	.800	35	5	3	2	10	1
Nitkowski, C.J., Indianapolis *	1.000	18	0	6	0	6	0
Nomo, Hideo, Columbus	.750	7	0	3	1	4	0
Nunez, Franklin, Durham	.714	27	2	3	2	7	0
Nunez, Vladimir, Indianapolis	1.000	7	1	0	0	1	0
Olszta, Edwin, Indianapolis	...	1	0	0	0	0	0
Ormond, William, Ottawa	.933	40	3	11	1	15	2

Player, Team	Pct.	G	PO	A	E	TC	DP
Oropesa, Eddie, Ottawa *	...	5	0	0	0	0	0
Ortiz, Javier, Charlotte	1.000	10	1	2	0	3	1
Padilla, Juan, Norfolk	.952	37	8	12	1	21	0
Padilla, Vicente, Scranton/Wilkes-Barre	1.000	1	0	1	0	1	0
Papelbon, Jonathan, Pawtucket	1.000	7	2	5	0	7	1
Paronto, Chad, Richmond	.909	26	5	5	1	11	1
Pelaez, Alex, Louisville	...	1	0	0	0	0	0
Perez, Franklin, Scranton/Wilkes-Barre	1.000	58	11	8	0	19	2
Perez, Juan, Pawtucket *	1.000	40	3	4	0	7	0
Perez, Oliver, Indianapolis *	1.000	3	0	1	0	1	0
Perisho, Matt, Pawtucket *	.500	13	0	1	1	2	0
Person, Robert, Charlotte	1.000	7	1	4	0	5	0
Petit, Yusmeiro, Norfolk	1.000	3	1	1	0	2	0
Phelps, Travis, Louisville	1.000	16	1	3	0	4	0
Phillips, Heath Michael, Charlotte *	1.000	5	0	3	0	3	0
Phillips, Jason C., Durham	.966	30	6	22	1	29	2
Piersoll, Chris, Ottawa	1.000	9	2	2	0	4	0
Porzio, Mike, Richmond *	1.000	2	0	2	0	2	0
Prochaska, Michael, Durham *	...	2	0	0	0	0	0
Proctor, Scott, Columbus	1.000	35	2	1	0	3	1
Rakers, Aaron, Ottawa	.923	57	3	9	1	13	1
Ramirez, Elizardo, Louisville	.947	21	8	28	2	38	1
Ramirez, Ramon, Columbus	1.000	6	0	4	0	4	0
Ray, Ken, Richmond	.944	17	3	14	1	18	1
Rayborn, George, Buffalo	1.000	17	2	6	0	8	0
Raymundo, Gregg, Indianapolis	...	1	0	0	0	0	0
Redding, Tim, Columbus	.875	10	2	5	1	8	0
Reid, Justin, Indianapolis	1.000	25	6	13	0	19	0
Reimers, Cameron, Syracuse	1.000	1	0	1	0	1	0
Reith, Brian, Indianapolis	1.000	24	0	4	0	4	1
Ring, Royce, Norfolk *	1.000	33	3	3	0	6	0
Roa, Joe, Indianapolis	1.000	6	3	1	0	4	0
Roach, Jason, Durham	1.000	22	4	14	0	18	5
Robbins, Jake, Buffalo	1.000	49	5	6	0	11	0
Robertson, Jeriome, Louisville *	.963	28	6	20	1	27	2
Rodney, Fernando, Toledo	...	3	0	0	0	0	0
Rodney, Thomas, Toledo	1.000	1	0	1	0	1	0
Rodriguez, Eddy, Ottawa	1.000	50	3	6	0	9	3
Rojas, Christopher, Scranton/Wilkes-Barre	1.000	1	3	0	0	3	1
Roney, Matt, Toledo	1.000	14	2	3	0	5	0
Rosario, Francisco, Syracuse	1.000	30	10	19	0	29	2
Rose, Brian, Louisville	1.000	18	3	7	0	10	0
Saladin, Miguel, Louisville	1.000	22	2	4	0	6	1
Salmon, Bradley, Louisville	1.000	9	7	1	0	8	0
Sanches, Brian, Scranton/Wilkes-Barre	1.000	51	3	11	0	14	1
Sanders, David, Charlotte *	.917	57	3	8	1	12	1
Santiago, Jose, Norfolk	1.000	29	9	21	0	30	2
Schilling, Curt, Pawtucket	.667	6	0	2	1	3	0
Schmitt, Eric, Columbus	1.000	23	2	7	0	9	0
Schoening, Edward, Rochester	.950	35	5	14	1	20	3
Scobie, Jason, Norfolk	.915	27	13	30	4	47	1
Seddon, Christopher, Durham *	.727	19	0	8	3	11	0
Sedlacek, Shawn, Ottawa	1.000	2	1	2	0	3	0
Seo, Jae Weong, Norfolk	1.000	19	8	19	0	27	0
Sequea, Jacobo, Ottawa	.667	18	1	3	2	6	0
Serrano, Jimmy, Louisville	.923	12	7	5	1	13	0
Shackelford, Brian, Louisville *	1.000	31	3	5	0	8	0
Shearn, Tom, Louisville	.929	44	7	6	1	14	1
Shields, James, Durham	1.000	1	0	1	0	1	0
Shoemaker, Scott, Pawtucket	1.000	2	2	2	0	4	1
Simpson, Allan, Louisville	.600	50	2	4	4	10	0
Skrehot, Shaun, Indianapolis	...	1	0	0	0	0	0
Small, Aaron, Columbus	.909	11	6	4	1	11	1
Smith, Bud, Rochester *	...	3	0	0	0	0	0
Smith, Cam, Durham	1.000	26	1	4	0	5	1
Smith, Chuck, Ottawa	1.000	11	5	10	0	15	0
Smith, Joshua, Columbus	...	2	0	0	0	0	0
Smith, Matthew, Columbus *	1.000	25	1	4	0	5	0
Smith, Matthew, Charlotte	1.000	66	4	12	0	16	3
Smith, Mike, Scranton/Wilkes-Barre	1.000	1	1	2	0	3	0
Snell, Ian, Indianapolis	1.000	18	13	11	0	24	0

Player, Team	Pct.	G	PO	A	E	TC	DP
Speigner, Jimmy, Rochester	...	2	0	0	0	0	0
Spurling, Chris, Toledo	1.000	12	1	2	0	3	0
Standridge, Jason, Louisville	...	2	0	0	0	0	0
Stanford, Jason, Buffalo *	1.000	4	1	0	0	1	0
Stark, Denny, Buffalo	1.000	3	0	1	0	1	0
Stephens, John, Pawtucket-Charlotte-Ottawa	.947	23	8	10	1	19	2
Stewart, Cory, Indianapolis *	.963	24	3	23	1	27	1
Stewart, Josh, Charlotte *	1.000	14	1	10	0	11	0
Stewart, Paul, Indianapolis	1.000	3	0	1	0	1	0
Stewart, Scott, Norfolk *	1.000	20	2	5	0	7	0
Stone, Ricky, Louisville	1.000	9	1	1	0	2	0
Strickland, Scott, Norfolk	1.000	13	0	2	0	2	0
Sweeney, Brian, Durham	.941	16	6	10	1	17	0
Switzer, Jon, Durham *	.800	17	3	5	2	10	0
Tadano, Kazuhito, Buffalo	.929	32	4	9	1	14	0
Takatsu, Shingo, Norfolk	...	7	0	0	0	0	0
Tallet, Brian, Buffalo *	.875	22	2	12	2	16	0
Tejeda, Robinson, Scranton/Wilkes-Barre	1.000	5	2	1	0	3	0
Telemaco, Amaury, Scranton/Wilkes-Barre	1.000	9	6	2	0	8	0
Thomas, John, Rochester	...	1	0	0	0	0	0
Thomson, John, Richmond	1.000	1	0	1	0	1	0
Tolar, Kevin, Syracuse *	1.000	17	1	1	0	2	0
Tomori, Denney, Pawtucket	.875	15	4	3	1	8	0
Traber, Billy, Buffalo *	1.000	19	10	17	0	27	1
Trachsel, Steve, Norfolk	1.000	2	1	4	0	5	0
Tucker, Glenn, Richmond	1.000	2	2	1	0	3	1
Ulacia, Dennis, Charlotte *	1.000	21	5	11	0	16	3
Valdes, Marc, Columbus	1.000	8	2	0	0	2	0
Valentine, Joe, Louisville	1.000	49	4	6	0	10	0
Van Hekken, Andy, Richmond-Louisville	1.000	31	7	5	0	12	0
Vasquez, Jorge, Richmond	1.000	14	1	1	0	2	0
Vermilyea, James, Syracuse	.857	16	2	4	1	7	0
Villacis, Eduardo, Charlotte	1.000	9	2	5	0	7	0
Voyles, Brad, Columbus	1.000	19	8	8	0	16	0
Waechter, Doug, Durham	1.000	3	2	1	0	3	0
Walker, Kevin, Charlotte *	.900	51	3	6	1	10	0
Wang, Chien-Ming, Columbus	.846	6	6	5	2	13	0
Ward, Jeremy, Richmond	.846	31	4	7	2	13	0
Watkins, Steve, Buffalo	.962	31	9	16	1	26	0
Webb, John, Durham	.955	28	16	26	2	44	2
Weber, Ben, Louisville	1.000	7	0	2	0	2	0
Whiteside, Matt, Syracuse	1.000	40	9	2	0	11	1
Wilson, Kris, Columbus	1.000	29	7	13	0	20	1
Winkelsas, Joseph, Charlotte	1.000	4	1	0	0	1	0
Wolfe, Brian, Rochester	...	3	0	0	0	0	0
Woodyard, Mark, Toledo	.857	45	5	13	3	21	2
Young, Jason, Buffalo	1.000	4	2	1	0	3	0
Zerbe, Chad, Buffalo *	1.000	16	1	5	0	6	1
Zink, Charles, Pawtucket	1.000	4	1	2	0	3	0
Zumaya, Joel, Toledo	1.000	8	3	3	0	6	0

PITCHERS WITH TWO OR MORE TEAMS

Player, Team	Pct.	G	PO	A	E	TC	DP
Anderson, Jimmy, Rochester *	1.000	12	2	8	0	10	0
Anderson, Jimmy, Durham *	.875	10	4	10	2	16	1
Childress, Daylan, Louisville	1.000	11	1	2	0	3	0
Childress, Daylan, Rochester	.333	5	0	1	2	3	0
Fernandez, Jared, Louisville	1.000	13	5	14	0	19	1
Fernandez, Jared, Scranton/Wilkes-Barre	1.000	7	3	3	0	6	0
Graman, Alex, Columbus *	.882	23	3	12	2	17	1
Graman, Alex, Louisville *	1.000	5	1	2	0	3	0
Hodges, Trey, Rochester	1.000	9	1	2	0	3	0
Hodges, Trey, Richmond	1.000	6	1	3	0	4	0
Miner, Zachary, Richmond	.964	17	8	19	1	28	1
Miner, Zachary, Toledo	1.000	6	2	10	0	12	2
Stephens, John, Pawtucket	.667	1	1	1	1	3	0
Stephens, John, Charlotte	1.000	10	4	5	0	9	2
Stephens, John, Ottawa	1.000	12	3	4	0	7	0
Van Hekken, Andy, Richmond *	1.000	4	1	1	0	2	0
Van Hekken, Andy, Louisville	1.000	27	6	4	0	10	0

LEAGUE CHAMPIONS

Year	Team	Pct.	Year	Team	Pct.	Year	Team	Pct.
1884—	Trenton	.520	1890—	Detroit	.617	1894—	Providence	.696
1885—	Syracuse	.584	1891—	Buffalo (reg. season)	.727	1895—	Springfield	.687
1886—	Utica	.646		Buffalo (supplemental)	.680	1896—	Providence	.602
1887—	Toronto	.644	1892—	Providence	.615	1897—	Syracuse	.632
1888—	Syracuse	.723		Binghamton*	.667	1898—	Montreal	.586
1889—	Detroit	.649	1893—	Erie	.606	1899—	Rochester	.624

Year	Team	Pct.
1900—	Providence	.616
1901—	Rochester	.642
1902—	Toronto	.669
1903—	Jersey City	.742
1904—	Buffalo	.657
1905—	Providence	.638
1906—	Buffalo	.607
1907—	Toronto	.619
1908—	Baltimore	.593
1909—	Rochester	.596
1910—	Rochester	.601
1911—	Rochester	.645
1912—	Toronto	.595
1913—	Newark	.625
1914—	Providence	.617
1915—	Buffalo	.632
1916—	Buffalo	.586
1917—	Toronto	.604
1918—	Toronto	.693
1919—	Baltimore	.671
1920—	Baltimore	.719
1921—	Baltimore	.717
1922—	Baltimore	.689
1923—	Baltimore	.677
1924—	Baltimore	.709
1925—	Baltimore	.633
1926—	Toronto	.657
1927—	Buffalo	.667
1928—	Rochester	.549
1929—	Rochester	.613
1930—	Rochester	.629
1931—	Rochester	.601
1932—	Newark	.649
1933—	Newark	.622
	Buffalo (4th)†	.494
1934—	Newark	.608
	Toronto (3rd)†	.559
1935—	Montreal	.597
	Syracuse (2nd)†	.565
1936—	Buffalo‡	.610
1937—	Newark‡	.717
1938—	Newark‡	.684
1939—	Jersey City	.582
	Rochester (2nd)†	.556
1940—	Rochester	.611
	Newark (2nd)†	.594
1941—	Newark	.649
	Montreal (2nd)†	.584
1942—	Newark	.601
	Syracuse (3rd)†	.513
1943—	Toronto	.625
	Syracuse (3rd)†	.536
1944—	Baltimore‡	.553
1945—	Montreal	.621
	Newark (2nd)†	.582
1946—	Montreal‡	.649
1947—	Jersey City	.610
	Syracuse (3rd)†	.575
1948—	Montreal‡	.614
1949—	Buffalo	.584
	Montreal (3rd)†	.545
1950—	Rochester	.609
	Baltimore (3rd)†	.556
1951—	Montreal‡	.617
1952—	Montreal	.629
	Rochester (3rd)†	.619
1953—	Rochester	.630
	Montreal (2nd)†	.586
1954—	Toronto	.630
	Syracuse (4th)§	.510
1955—	Montreal	.617
	Rochester (4th)†	.497
1956—	Toronto	.566
	Rochester (2nd)†	.553
1957—	Toronto	.575
	Buffalo (2nd)†	.571
1958—	Montreal‡	.588
1959—	Buffalo	.582
	Havana (3rd)†	.523
1960—	Toronto‡	.649
1961—	Columbus	.597
	Buffalo (3rd)†	.559
1962—	Jacksonville	.610
	Atlanta (3rd)†	.539
1963—	Syracuse∞	.533
	Indianapolis‡	.562
1964—	Jacksonville	.589
	Rochester (4th)†	.532
1965—	Columbus	.582
	Toronto (3rd)†	.556
1966—	Rochester	.565
	Toronto (2nd-tied)†	.558
1967—	Richmond	.574
	Toledo (3rd)†	.525
1968—	Toledo	.565
	Jacksonville (4th)†	.514
1969—	Tidewater	.563
	Syracuse (3rd)†	.536
1970—	Syracuse‡	.600
1971—	Rochester‡	.614
1972—	Louisville	.563
	Tidewater (3rd)†	.545
1973—	Charleston	.586
	Pawtucket†	.534
1974—	Memphis	.613
	Rochester ∞‡	.611
1975—	Tidewater‡	.610
1976—	Rochester	.638
	Syracuse (2nd)†	.590
1977—	Pawtucket	.571
	Charleston (2nd)‡	.557
1978—	Charleston	.607
	Richmond (4th)†	.511
1979—	Columbus‡	.612
1980—	Columbus‡	.593
1981—	Columbus‡	.633
1982—	Richmond	.590
	Tidewater (3rd)†	.540
1983—	Columbus	.593
	Tidewater (4th)†	.511
1984—	Columbus	.590
	Pawtucket (4th)†	.536
1985—	Syracuse	.564
	Tidewater (4th)†	.540
1986—	Richmond‡	.571
1987—	Tidewater	.579
	Columbus†	.550
1988—	Rochester♦	.546
	Tidewater	.546
1989—	Syracuse	.572
	Richmond♦	.555
1990—	Rochester♦	.614
	Columbus	.596
1991—	Columbus♦	.590
	Pawtucket	.552
1992—	Columbus♦	.660
	Scr. W.B.	.592
1993—	Charlotte♦	.610
	Rochester	.525
1994—	Richmond♦	.567
	Pawtucket	.549
1995—	Norfolk	.606
	Ottawa♦	.507
1996—	Columbus♦	.599
	Rochester	.511
1997—	Rochester♦	.589
	Columbus	.556
1998—	Buffalo■	.566
1999—	Columbus	.589
	Charlotte▲	.569
2000—	Buffalo	.593
	Indianapolis▲	.563
2001—	Buffalo	.641
	Louisville▼	.583
2002—	Scranton/Wilkes-Barre	.632
	Durham▲	.556
2003—	Pawtucket	.576
	Durham▲	.521
2004—	Buffalo	.590
2005—	Toledo▲	.618

*Won split-season playoff. †Won four-team playoff. ‡Won championship and four-team playoff. §Defeated Havana in game to decide fourth place, then won four-team playoff. ∞League was divided into Northern, Southern divisions. ♦League divided into Eastern, Western divisions; won playoffs. ■League divided into Eastern, Northern and Southern divisions; won four-team playoff. ▲League divided into North, South and West divisions; won four-team playoff. ▼League divided into North, South and West divisions; was leading final series of four-team playoff and was declared champion when Professional Baseball declared a stoppage of play. (NOTE—Known as Eastern League in 1884, New York State League in 1885, International League in 1886-87, International Association in 1888, International League in 1889-90, Eastern Association in 1891 and Eastern League from 1892 until 1912.)

MEXICAN LEAGUE

CLASS AAA Mexican League

2005 FINAL STANDINGS

FIRST HALF

NORTHERN DIVISION

Team	W	L	T	Pct.	GB
Saltillo Sarape Makers	32	24	-	0.571	...
Monterrey Sultans	32	24	-	0.571	...
Tijuana Colts	29	27	-	0.518	3
Mexico Red Devils	29	27	-	0.518	3
Aguascalientes Railroadmen	28	28	-	0.5	4
Monclova Steelers	28	28	-	0.5	4
Laguna Cowboys	22	34	-	0.393	10
San Luis Potosi Cactus Pear Growers	20	36	-	0.357	12

SOUTHERN DIVISION

Team	W	L	T	Pct.	GB
Campeche Pirates	38	18	-	0.679	...
Angelopolis Tigers	34	22	-	0.607	4
Yucatan Lions	31	25	-	0.554	7
Veracruz Reds	28	28	-	0.5	10
Oaxaca Warriors	26	30	-	0.464	12
Puebla Parrots	25	31	-	0.446	13
Tabasco Olmecas	24	32	-	0.429	14
Cancun Lobstermen	22	34	-	0.393	16

SECOND HALF

NORTHERN DIVISION

Team	W	L	T	Pct.	GB
Tijuana Colts	35	19	-	0.648	...
Saltillo Sarape Makers	31	23	-	0.574	4
Mexico Red Devils	27	24	-	0.529	6.5
Aguascalientes Railroadmen	27	25	-	0.519	7
Monclova Steelers	25	27	-	0.481	9
Monterrey Sultans	24	26	-	0.48	9
San Luis Potosi Cactus Pear Growers	25	27	-	0.481	9
Laguna Cowboys	16	37	-	0.302	18.5

SOUTHERN DIVISION

Team	W	L	T	Pct.	GB
Angelopolis Tigers	32	19	-	0.627	...
Oaxaca Warriors	31	20	-	0.608	1
Tabasco Olmecas	29	23	-	0.558	3.5
Yucatan Lions	26	25	-	0.51	6
Puebla Parrots	26	27	-	0.491	7
Campeche Pirates	24	25	-	0.49	7
Veracruz Reds	23	30	-	0.434	10
Cancun Lobstermen	15	39	-	0.278	18.5

COMPOSITE

CLUB, ABBREV	TIG	CAM	TIJ	SLT	OAX	YUC	MTY	MXO	AGU	MVA	TAB	PUE	VRA	SLP	VAQ	CAN	W	L	PCT	GB
Angelopolis,TIG		6	2	1	8	8	2	2	1	2	4	9	7	2	3	9	66	41	.617	-
Campeche,CAM	5	...	3	3	4	7	1	2	0	2	7	8	6	2	3	9	62	43	.590	3.0
Tijuana,TIJ	1	0	...	8	2	2	8	5	9	5	2	2	3	8	7	2	64	46	.582	3.5
Saltillo,SLT	2	0	4	...	1	2	7	8	7	6	2	1	1	11	8	3	63	47	.573	4.5
Oaxaca,OAX	3	7	1	2	...	6	2	1	2	2	8	8	8	1	0	6	57	50	.533	9.0
Yucatan,YUC	3	4	1	1	6	...	1	0	2	3	9	4	9	3	2	9	57	50	.533	9.0
Monterrey,MTY	1	1	4	7	1	2	...	4	7	7	1	2	3	6	7	3	56	50	.528	9.5
Mexico,MXO	1	1	9	4	2	3	6	...	6	4	1	1	1	5	10	2	56	51	.523	10.0
Aguascalientes,AGU	2	3	3	5	1	1	5	6	...	6	0	3	1	8	9	2	55	53	.509	11.5
Monclova,MVA	1	1	7	6	1	0	5	8	4	...	2	1	2	4	9	2	53	55	.491	13.5
Tabasco,TAB	8	7	1	1	3	3	1	2	3	1	...	5	7	2	2	7	53	55	.491	13.5
Puebla,PUE	5	4	1	2	4	7	1	2	0	2	7	...	4	2	2	8	51	58	.468	16.0
Veracruz,VRA	5	0	2	6	3	0	2	2	1	5	8		...	2	2	8	51	58	.468	16.0
San Luis Potosi,SLP	1	1	4	1	2	0	6	6	6	8	1	1	1	...	6	1	45	63	.417	21.5
Laguna,VAQ	0	0	5	4	3	1	5	2	3	5	1	1	1	5	...	2	38	71	.349	29.0
Cancun,CAN	3	1	0	6	5	0	1	1	5	4	2	2	4	2	1	...	37	73	.336	30.5

PLAYOFFS: First Round: Monterrey defeated Mexico, four games to two; Saltillo defeated Aguascalientes, four games to two; Yucatan defeated Oaxaca, four games to three; Tabasco defeated Campeche, four games to three. Division Series: Tijuana defeated Mexico, four games to two; Saltillo defeated Monterrey, four games to two; Angelopolis defeated Oaxaca, four games to three; Yucatan defeated Tabasco, four games to three. Semifinals: Angelopolis defeated Yucatan, four games to two, and Saltillo defeated Tijuana, four games to three. Finals: Angelopolis defeated Saltillo, four games to two.

REGULAR-SEASON ATTENDANCE: Tijuana, 385,871. Tabasco, 135,637. Laguna, 178,500. Yucatan, 18,504. Cancun, 93,500. Saltillo, 175,877. Puebla, 20,002. Campeche, 116,934. Aguascalientes, 258,000. Mexico, 134,028. Veracruz, 107,731. Monclova, 128,700. Monterrey, 49,653. Angelopolis, 42,488. San Luis Potosi, 57,001. Oaxaca, 17,165. All-Star Game (at Angelopolis), 12,000. League total, 1,919,591. Postseason (77 games), 771,160.

MANAGERS: Tijuana, Raul Cano (through May 24) and Jose Juan Bellazetin (May 25 through end of season). Tabasco, Juan Francisco Rodriguez (through May 6), Julian Yan (May 7 through May 8) and Mario Mendoza (May 9 through end of season). Laguna, Gerardo Sanchez (through May 1), Antonio Aguilera (May 2 through June 13), Wes Clemens (June 14 through July 8) and Hector Estrada (July 9 through end of season). Yucatan, Bernie Tatis (through June 24), Roberto Perez (June 25) and Lino Rivera (June 26 through end of season). Cancun, Juan Jose Pacho (through June 27)and Carlos Paz (June 28 through end of season). Saltillo, Derek Bryant. Puebla, Armando Cabrera (through April 29), Bernardo Calvo (April 30 through May 2)and Mako Oliveras (May 3 through end of season). Campeche, Francisco Estrada. Aguascalientes, Alex Taveras. Mexico, Alfonso Jimenez. Veracruz, Fernando Elizondo (through April 18), Miguel Angel Ruiz (April 19 through April 24), Fernando Elizondo (April 25 through April 28), Miguel Angel Ruiz (April 29 through May 5), Fernando Elizondo (May 6 through June 27) and Juan Jose Pacho (June 28 through end of season). Monclova, Lino Rivera (through June 6) and Francisco Rodriguez (June 7 through end of season). Monterrey, Hector Torres (through April 25), Leo Rodriguez (April 26 through July 11) and Bernie Tatis (July 12 through end of season). Angelopolis, Enrique Reyes. San Luis Potosi, Dan Firova, Oaxaca, Homar Rojas.

ALL-STAR TEAM: 1B-Jorge Vazquez, Angelopolis. 2B-Carlos Gastelum, Angelopolis. 3B-Willis Otanez, Veracruz. SS-Javier Robles, Angelopolis. CF-Rontrez Johnson, Aguascalientes. LF-Ruben Rivera, Campeche. RF-Mario Valenzuela, Saltillo. C-Noe Munoz, Saltillo. DH-Robert Saucedo, Mexico. RHS-Francisco Campos, Campeche. LHS-Eric Knott, Puebla. C-Isidro Marquez, Campeche. Mexican League Finals Most Valuable Player-Javier Robles, Angelopolis.

2005 BATTING

TEAM

Team	G	TPA	AB	R	H	TB	2B	3B	HR	RBI	SH	SF	HP	BB	IBB	SO	SB	CS	GDP	LOB	ShO	Avg.	OBP	Slg.
Angelopolis	107	4292	3806	792	1289	2096	236	20	177	739	27	44	64	351	23	552	76	38	102	1599	3	.339	.400	.551
Saltillo	110	4524	3899	754	1244	1939	205	11	156	707	45	35	86	459	15	625	22	29	141	1920	5	.319	.399	.497
Tijuana	110	4559	4021	753	1271	2096	241	10	188	700	15	38	55	430	21	552	38	24	114	1849	6	.316	.386	.521

Team	G	TPA	AB	R	H	TB	2B	3B	HR	RBI	SH	SF	HP	BB	IBB	SO	SB	CS	GDP	LOB	ShO	Avg.	OBP	Slg.
Yucatan	107	4300	3799	616	1201	1775	188	37	104	577	42	39	40	380	22	483	110	49	116	1707	7	.316	.381	.467
Aguascalientes	108	4342	3872	688	1211	1853	227	14	129	643	22	28	61	359	24	561	69	40	108	1761	3	.313	.378	.479
Oaxaca	108	4298	3726	653	1159	1742	214	24	107	608	45	26	47	452	29	520	92	46	101	1773	1	.311	.390	.468
Veracruz	109	4226	3726	611	1157	1700	168	9	119	572	42	27	57	374	27	518	68	39	133	1726	2	.311	.380	.456
Laguna	109	4480	3922	653	1214	1847	237	15	122	619	29	39	48	442	22	585	50	31	140	1851	2	.310	.383	.471
Puebla	109	4209	3703	638	1149	1729	206	28	106	578	42	38	53	372	15	535	66	58	108	1719	3	.310	.378	.467
Mexico	107	4373	3784	721	1164	1916	227	21	161	680	31	27	50	480	14	585	43	28	115	1695	2	.308	.390	.506
Campeche	105	4120	3609	659	1108	1731	177	16	138	615	23	39	80	369	15	467	68	29	110	1663	4	.307	.380	.480
San Luis Potosi	108	4307	3773	664	1159	1838	270	17	125	625	38	38	40	417	14	647	94	67	97	1709	8	.307	.379	.487
Monterrey	106	4204	3678	580	1104	1636	207	14	99	531	31	34	47	414	27	528	93	44	96	1715	5	.300	.375	.445
Monclova	108	4384	3747	628	1114	1659	190	8	113	602	54	38	57	488	20	649	36	33	113	1802	0	.297	.383	.443
Tabasco	109	4274	3670	607	1061	1610	174	24	109	560	50	39	52	462	33	559	104	51	106	1762	6	.289	.373	.439
Cancun	110	4172	3664	493	1028	1483	188	15	79	459	46	27	70	365	13	517	48	32	136	1745	8	.281	.355	.405

INDIVIDUAL

TOP QUALIFIERS FOR BATTING CHAMPIONSHIP

Minimum 297 plate appearances. *Lefthanded batter. †Switch-hitter.

Player, Team	G	TPA	AB	R	H	TB	2B	3B	HR	RBI	SH	SF	HP	BB	IBB	SO	SB	CS	GDP	Avg.	OBP	Slg.
Robles, Javier, Angelopolis	96	431	375	101	147	256	21	2	28	101	0	3	7	46	3	39	13	3	21	.392	.464	.683
Vazquez, Jorge, Angelopolis	71	305	285	61	108	227	20	0	33	96	0	2	4	14	2	55	1	2	16	.379	.413	.796
Brinkley, Darryl, San Luis Potosi	99	438	380	76	143	218	32	2	13	79	0	5	0	53	3	43	23	16	10	.376	.447	.574
Otanez, Willis, Veracruz	108	473	402	76	151	262	19	1	30	123	0	7	2	62	9	68	2	1	17	.376	.455	.652
Jose, Felix, Oaxaca †	105	468	365	87	137	246	19	0	30	113	0	5	5	93	10	64	3	2	8	.375	.502	.674
Gastelum, Carlos Alberto, Angelopolis	101	478	444	97	165	217	26	4	6	44	8	0	9	21	0	30	21	9	8	.375	.415	.493
Bass, Jayson, Saltillo *	94	445	392	80	145	231	15	1	23	91	0	4	2	47	2	61	2	3	17	.370	.436	.589
Adriana, Sharnol, San Luis Potosi	108	509	437	105	161	277	35	3	25	77	2	2	9	59	3	67	32	21	7	.368	.452	.634
White, Derrick, Tijuana *	109	504	427	93	157	264	29	0	26	97	0	4	10	63	3	78	3	2	19	.368	.456	.618
Romero, Wilson, Yucatan	104	456	399	65	146	238	29	3	19	89	2	9	1	45	4	56	13	5	14	.366	.423	.596
Johnson, Rontrez, Aguascalientes	98	461	377	96	137	199	24	4	10	61	3	2	12	67	5	43	39	14	7	.363	.472	.528
Velasquez, Guillermo, Angelopolis *	92	364	304	54	110	180	19	0	17	76	0	3	0	57	3	62	0	4	5	.362	.459	.592
Carrillo, Matias, Angelopolis *	96	405	356	93	128	230	23	5	23	92	0	7	4	38	5	24	11	2	6	.360	.420	.646
Valenzuela, Mario, Saltillo	93	403	367	75	132	244	17	1	31	103	0	6	10	20	0	73	1	2	10	.360	.402	.665
Quintero, Christian, Oaxaca	104	466	423	90	152	229	23	9	12	76	7	1	5	30	0	34	22	6	9	.359	.407	.541
Sievers, Carlos, Tabasco *	107	460	378	81	135	215	25	2	17	96	1	6	9	66	6	53	13	9	9	.357	.458	.569
Villalobos, Carlos, Puebla-San Luis Potosi ..	104	470	409	85	145	243	39	1	19	97	0	8	3	50	2	78	6	7	11	.355	.421	.594
Garcia, Luis, Veracruz	90	387	363	64	128	195	16	0	17	63	1	0	1	22	2	32	5	4	13	.353	.391	.537
Espinosa, Ramon, Laguna	65	307	290	50	102	156	27	0	9	36	1	1	5	10	3	31	7	5	12	.352	.382	.538
Borges, Luis, Yucatan *	80	305	279	38	97	118	11	5	0	29	4	2	1	19	0	19	2	2	5	.348	.389	.423
Garcia, Cornelio, Laguna	94	453	394	71	137	214	33	4	12	63	2	1	0	56	0	64	2	4	13	.348	.428	.543

DEPARTMENTAL LEADERS: G—Valencia, 110. AB—Valencia, 489. R—Adriana, 105. H—Gastelum, 165. TB, Adriana, 277. 2B, Hernandez and Villalobos, 39. 3B, McDonald, 10. HR—Saucedo, 35. RBI—Otanez, 123. SH—Castro, 14. SF—Valencia, 10. HP—Burkhart, 22. BB—Jose, 93. IBB—Jose, 10. SO—Yan, 109. SB—McDonald, 53. CS—Adriana, 21. GIDP—Quinones, 26. OBP—Jose, .502. Slg.—Vazquez, .796.

ALL PLAYERS

*Lefthanded batter. †Switch-hitter.

Player, Team	G	TPA	AB	R	H	TB	2B	3B	HR	RBI	SH	SF	HP	BB	IBB	SO	SB	CS	GDP	Avg.	OBP	Slg.
Acuna, Jose, Cancun	77	298	239	60	72	91	10	0	3	12	5	0	4	50	0	36	11	1	3	.301	.430	.381
Adriana, Sharnol, San Luis Potosi	108	509	437	105	161	277	35	3	25	77	2	2	9	59	3	67	32	21	7	.368	.452	.634
Aganza, Ruben, Monclova	42	79	71	6	18	24	0	0	2	6	0	1	1	6	0	10	0	0	4	.254	.316	.338
Ahumada, Alejandro, San Luis Potosi	70	243	209	33	53	79	8	3	4	20	3	2	3	26	0	36	3	7	6	.254	.342	.378
Alcantara, Israel, Veracruz	27	107	89	13	25	45	5	0	5	15	0	1	2	15	2	17	0	1	3	.281	.393	.506
Alejos, Fernando, Cancun	25	75	66	5	10	20	3	2	1	4	2	0	0	7	0	13	0	1	1	.152	.233	.303
Alfonso, Manuel, Tabasco *	29	44	37	7	14	17	3	0	0	2	2	0	2	3	0	5	4	1	0	.378	.452	.459
Almeida, Shamar, Mexico *	53	93	64	12	15	26	2	0	3	13	0	0	3	26	1	20	0	1	3	.234	.473	.406
Alvarez, Hector, Monterrey-Oaxaca	64	226	205	27	75	97	13	0	3	22	2	3	5	11	1	32	0	2	4	.366	.406	.473
Alvarez, Rafael, Laguna-Cancun	56	237	204	38	63	120	16	1	13	38	0	0	2	31	1	38	5	2	8	.309	.405	.588
Amado, Jose, Cancun	87	378	329	45	112	157	21	0	8	68	0	4	6	39	2	18	6	1	11	.340	.415	.477
Amador, Jose, Laguna	109	509	433	77	133	212	35	1	14	68	5	4	5	62	0	46	7	5	14	.307	.397	.490
Amezcua, Adan, Monterrey	91	346	295	43	92	132	23	1	5	35	1	2	11	37	4	52	2	3	1	.312	.406	.447
Angulo, Gregorio, Yucatan †	55	55	51	16	14	16	0	1	0	3	1	0	0	3	0	13	0	1	0	.275	.315	.314
Arano, Eloy, Veracruz *	85	294	266	25	77	80	3	0	0	23	1	1	3	23	2	23	10	4	7	.289	.352	.301
Arano, Wilfredo, Tijuana *	83	309	269	54	87	138	16	1	11	43	1	1	5	33	0	14	2	1	7	.323	.406	.513
Araujo, Ivan, Laguna	1	0	0	0	1	0	0	0	0	0	0	0	0	0	0	0	0	0	0	...	...	...
Arauz, Ignacio, Saltillo	11	17	14	5	6	12	0	0	2	4	1	0	2	0	0	1	0	0	1	.429	.500	.857
Arauz, Leobardo, Monclova †	105	497	396	95	122	188	19	1	15	54	2	2	11	86	3	77	4	5	9	.308	.442	.475
Arias, Francisco, Saltillo	91	382	335	62	108	134	14	3	2	34	12	2	12	21	1	45	1	2	6	.322	.381	.400
Arias, George, Tijuana	89	401	346	63	105	196	20	1	23	81	0	6	1	48	7	51	2	0	6	.303	.384	.566
Armenta, Alejandro, Angelopolis *	1	0	0	0	0	0	0	0	0	0	0	0	0	0	...	0	0	0	0	...	...	...
Arredondo, Alan, Yucatan †	52	64	63	17	18	21	1	1	0	4	0	0	0	1	0	14	5	3	1	.286	.297	.333
Arredondo, Eduardo, Tabasco-Mexico	68	210	178	23	40	61	9	0	4	21	4	3	5	20	1	19	5	2	6	.225	.316	.343
Arredondo, Hernando, Tabasco	100	387	357	43	104	168	22	0	14	60	6	6	3	15	1	42	1	2	13	.291	.320	.471
Arredondo, Jesus, Puebla *	64	220	187	24	53	59	6	0	0	12	7	3	3	20	0	22	0	1	6	.283	.357	.316
Arredondo, Luis, Yucatan *	104	507	455	83	144	183	13	7	4	32	6	2	3	41	3	36	47	16	5	.316	.375	.402
Baez, Carlos, Tabasco	1	0	0	0	0	0	0	0	0	0	0	0	0	0	0	0	0	0	0	...	...	...
Bass, Jayson, Saltillo *	94	445	392	80	145	231	15	1	23	91	0	4	2	47	2	61	2	3	17	.370	.436	.589
Beltran, Juan, Campeche	52	120	104	23	31	46	9	0	2	16	1	1	3	11	0	23	0	1	2	.298	.378	.442
Bernal, Cosme, Mexico	17	24	22	5	6	10	1	0	1	3	0	0	0	2	0	3	0	1	0	.273	.333	.455

Player, Team	G	TPA	AB	R	H	TB	2B	3B	HR	RBI	SH	SF	HP	BB	IBB	SO	SB	CS	GDP	Avg.	OBP	Slg.
Bojorquez, Victor, Mexico	107	457	424	64	126	231	23	2	26	94	5	3	4	21	2	49	6	3	10	.297	.334	.545
Borges, Luis, Yucatan *	80	305	279	38	97	118	11	5	0	29	4	2	1	19	0	19	2	2	5	.348	.389	.423
Brena, Jaime, Oaxaca	100	444	366	73	121	160	29	2	2	55	12	3	6	57	1	36	10	7	4	.331	.426	.437
Brinkley, Darryl, San Luis Potosi	99	438	380	76	143	218	32	2	13	79	0	5	0	53	3	43	23	16	10	.376	.447	.574
Brito, Tilson, Veracruz	36	149	133	21	47	76	14	0	5	30	1	0	6	9	1	13	0	0	8	.353	.419	.571
Buelna, Lorenzo, Puebla	105	455	404	73	134	213	28	6	13	69	6	5	5	35	0	57	10	9	17	.332	.388	.527
Bueno, Geraldo, Cancun	5	15	12	1	0	0	0	0	0	0	0	0	1	2	0	4	0	0	0	.000	.200	.000
Bullett, Scott, Yucatan *	101	438	394	70	125	231	19	6	25	86	0	3	5	36	4	76	12	2	16	.317	.379	.586
Burkhart, Morgan, Saltillo †	98	453	345	91	105	201	18	0	26	72	0	2	22	84	3	71	0	2	8	.304	.466	.583
Bustillos, Luis, San Luis Potosi	29	105	96	12	30	47	8	0	3	8	3	0	0	6	0	29	0	2	3	.313	.353	.490
Camilo, Juan, Tabasco *	71	312	254	65	78	138	13	1	15	54	2	3	1	52	5	69	12	3	4	.307	.423	.543
Canizalez, Juan, Yucatan †	97	412	379	46	109	156	19	2	8	51	1	4	3	25	5	48	3	2	21	.288	.333	.412
Carrillo, Matias, Angelopolis *	96	405	356	93	128	230	23	5	23	92	0	7	4	38	5	24	11	2	6	.360	.420	.646
Carrillo, Oscar, Mexico	54	80	75	11	19	23	2	1	0	6	3	0	0	2	0	12	1	0	1	.253	.273	.307
Casillas, Hector, Monclova	21	35	32	2	5	5	0	0	0	1	1	0	0	2	1	6	0	0	1	.156	.206	.156
Castaneda, Hector, Yucatan *	72	219	180	21	55	69	9	1	1	35	1	2	1	35	0	31	0	0	5	.306	.417	.383
Castaneda, Jose, Saltillo	24	17	15	2	3	4	1	0	0	2	0	1	0	1	0	5	0	1	0	.200	.235	.267
Castaneda, Rafael, Laguna	70	196	172	22	52	75	8	0	5	32	0	2	2	20	1	20	1	0	6	.302	.378	.436
Castellano, Pedro, Yucatan	102	443	373	71	124	200	19	0	19	78	1	7	5	57	2	47	1	0	9	.332	.421	.536
Castillo, Jesus, Yucatan	22	46	39	6	10	16	1	1	1	6	3	0	1	3	0	8	0	0	0	.256	.326	.410
Castro, Arnoldo, Cancun-Tabasco	100	398	349	35	93	122	14	0	5	42	11	5	1	32	2	50	0	3	12	.266	.326	.350
Castro, Domingo, Monclova	102	480	419	61	118	150	21	1	3	44	14	5	5	37	0	43	14	10	10	.282	.343	.358
Cazarin, Manuel, Veracruz	58	195	171	16	41	65	3	0	7	22	4	3	0	17	0	18	0	2	14	.240	.304	.380
Cervantes, Ivan, Oaxaca	106	448	403	65	117	153	23	2	3	48	4	3	6	32	3	44	7	5	11	.290	.349	.380
Cervantes, Refugio, Aguascalientes	100	414	373	64	104	180	20	1	18	59	1	2	4	34	4	52	0	0	8	.279	.344	.483
Cervera, Francisco, Yucatan	54	116	103	17	34	49	7	1	2	14	3	1	4	5	1	18	0	1	3	.330	.381	.476
Cesar, Dionys, Monterrey †	104	471	426	71	128	198	32	1	12	65	2	2	5	36	2	55	31	7	12	.300	.360	.465
Cobos, Rogelio, Mexico	41	123	113	18	29	56	6	0	7	27	3	0	0	7	0	27	1	0	1	.257	.300	.496
Connell, Lino, Veracruz †	82	362	318	45	97	141	15	1	9	48	2	5	2	35	4	39	10	6	14	.305	.372	.443
Contreras, Albino, Puebla-Angelopolis	198	745	643	125	194	313	39	10	20	98	3	10	18	71	3	113	17	12	11	.302	.381	.487
Cota, Angel, San Luis Potosi	8	17	12	0	0	0	0	0	0	0	2	0	0	3	0	3	0	0	0	.000	.176	.000
Crespo, Jorge, Oaxaca	29	76	65	11	13	20	4	0	1	8	5	0	1	5	0	20	2	0	1	.200	.268	.308
Cruz, Fausto, Campeche	51	220	190	41	65	96	4	0	9	53	1	1	4	24	0	27	2	0	5	.342	.425	.505
Cruz, Luis, Mexico	61	239	226	29	64	97	15	3	4	23	1	1	1	10	0	26	4	1	3	.283	.315	.429
Cruz, Marco Antonio, Campeche	39	82	73	8	20	31	5	0	2	6	2	1	3	3	0	11	0	0	6	.274	.325	.425
De La Torre, Omar, Laguna	76	256	234	41	64	100	14	2	6	34	2	3	1	16	0	55	0	1	10	.274	.319	.427
Delgado, Alex, Aguascalientes	88	361	327	57	110	168	29	1	9	47	1	5	12	16	2	34	0	5	9	.336	.383	.514
Diaz, Eddy, Yucatan	105	446	391	54	128	193	21	1	14	66	2	5	1	47	2	35	4	3	15	.327	.396	.494
Diaz, Edwin, Puebla	30	133	120	19	31	52	6	0	5	25	0	1	3	9	2	22	0	2	4	.258	.323	.433
Diaz, Pedro, Monclova	93	382	350	48	109	139	16	1	4	48	4	4	5	19	0	58	3	2	6	.311	.352	.397
Diaz, Remigio, Tabasco	103	426	379	49	99	126	14	2	3	29	8	3	3	32	0	41	1	4	17	.261	.321	.332
Dominguez, Carlos, Angelopolis *	1	0	0	0	0	0	0	0	0	0	0	0	0	0	...	0	0	0	0	.---	.---	.---
Doster, Dave, San Luis Potosi	104	445	404	58	113	185	34	1	12	59	3	7	0	31	0	59	4	3	12	.280	.326	.458
Echevarria, Angel, Monclova	35	148	134	21	42	64	4	0	6	22	0	1	0	13	0	21	0	1	6	.313	.372	.478
Esparragoza, Francisco, Saltillo	16	15	15	1	3	6	0	0	1	1	0	0	0	0	0	1	1	0	0	.200	.200	.400
Espino, Daniel, Cancun-Veracruz	69	266	235	23	64	84	14	0	2	31	3	1	15	12	3	24	0	2	9	.272	.346	.357
Espinosa, Ramon, Laguna	65	307	290	50	102	156	27	0	9	36	1	1	5	10	3	31	7	5	12	.352	.382	.538
Espinoza, Efren, Mexico	63	218	194	40	61	105	16	5	6	24	0	3	6	15	0	42	3	5	4	.314	.381	.541
Espinoza, Jose, Tijuana *	80	293	256	46	79	112	13	1	6	30	3	0	2	32	1	46	4	1	3	.309	.390	.438
Esqueda, Jonathan, Campeche	16	32	28	2	8	11	0	0	1	2	0	0	1	3	0	8	2	0	1	.286	.375	.393
Estrada, Hector, Laguna	86	289	253	27	61	88	12	0	5	33	5	6	2	23	0	44	0	1	7	.241	.303	.348
Feliciano, Jesus, Oaxaca *	22	104	100	16	30	42	8	2	0	9	0	0	0	4	0	9	2	3	2	.300	.327	.420
Fentanes, Oscar, Veracruz	67	246	212	24	59	75	10	0	2	27	3	1	12	18	1	20	2	1	9	.278	.366	.354
Fernandez, Daniel, Mexico *	74	329	278	58	80	102	16	3	0	15	2	2	4	43	1	40	6	5	5	.288	.388	.367
Figueroa, Luis, Tijuana	106	467	411	66	135	191	27	1	9	51	5	0	4	47	0	33	6	3	15	.328	.403	.465
Flores, Kevin, Angelopolis	52	111	105	22	33	62	9	1	6	20	0	1	1	4	0	28	1	1	1	.314	.342	.590
Flores, Miguel, Monterrey	62	282	243	36	71	90	13	0	2	37	2	2	1	34	0	17	8	2	5	.292	.379	.370
Fornes, Daniel, Monterrey *	82	267	238	29	59	80	3	0	6	26	3	2	3	21	3	21	3	3	9	.248	.314	.336
Garanzuay, Hector, Monclova	104	383	321	47	97	139	23	2	5	48	10	3	4	45	1	38	4	5	8	.302	.391	.433
Garcia, Amaury, Veracruz	103	478	408	87	138	186	21	3	7	44	3	1	4	62	1	71	14	9	7	.338	.429	.456
Garcia, Cornelio, Mexico	94	453	394	71	137	214	33	4	12	63	2	1	0	56	0	64	2	4	13	.348	.428	.543
Garcia, Guillermo, Monclova	107	479	396	83	126	236	25	0	29	99	0	6	11	66	7	75	0	1	15	.318	.424	.596
Garcia, Hector, Tabasco	72	241	217	28	71	85	9	1	1	25	2	3	1	18	0	18	2	1	5	.327	.377	.392
Garcia, Luis, Veracruz	90	387	363	64	128	195	16	0	17	63	1	0	1	22	2	32	5	4	13	.353	.391	.537
Garcia, Luis, Monterrey	38	166	150	24	41	68	10	1	5	28	0	3	0	13	2	28	0	0	4	.273	.325	.453
Garcia, Nicolas, Saltillo	106	406	363	49	105	145	28	0	4	51	12	6	3	22	0	67	2	4	16	.289	.330	.399
Garzon, Eliseo, Oaxaca	41	132	119	14	34	44	4	0	2	14	1	0	0	12	0	22	0	0	5	.286	.351	.370
Gastelum, Carlos, Yucatan	33	49	44	1	8	9	1	0	0	2	3	0	1	1	0	7	0	0	3	.182	.217	.205
Gastelum, Carlos Alberto, Angelopolis	101	478	440	97	165	217	26	4	6	44	8	0	9	21	0	30	21	9	8	.375	.415	.493
Gastelum, Sergio, Angelopolis	99	453	379	82	120	169	28	0	7	53	5	6	13	50	1	37	3	3	10	.317	.408	.446
Gavia, Jesus, Aguascalientes	44	130	127	20	40	75	5	0	10	31	0	0	2	1	0	15	0	0	4	.315	.331	.591
Gomez, Heber, Monterrey	102	420	369	51	109	140	21	2	2	41	3	4	4	40	0	30	9	5	14	.295	.367	.379
Gonzalez, Fernando, Cancun	27	52	48	6	9	15	3	0	1	3	2	0	1	1	0	12	0	1	0	.188	.220	.313
Gonzalez, Julio, Puebla	27	45	40	8	8	15	1	0	2	7	...	1	1	3	0	11	1	0	1	.200	.267	.375
Gonzalez, Roman, Aguascalientes	78	226	204	35	63	74	9	1	0	23	2	3	3	15	0	33	3	1	7	.309	.363	.363
Gonzalez, Santiago, Veracruz	92	275	248	44	62	72	4	0	2	17	7	0	3	17	0	53	8	4	10	.250	.306	.290
Gonzalez, Vinicio, Mexico	1	2	2	0	0	0	0	0	0	0	0	0	0	0	0	1	0	0	0	.000	.000	.000
Gracia, Ernesto, Aguascalientes	31	72	66	9	20	27	4	0	1	10	0	0	2	4	0	25	0	0	1	.303	.361	.409
Guerrero, Sergio, Saltillo	58	236	207	34	60	74	14	0	0	24	2	3	12	12	0	15	0	0	13	.290	.359	.357
Guizar, Hector, Aguascalientes	71	306	284	34	73	97	15	0	3	37	3	1	2	16	0	31	0	3	12	.257	.300	.342
Gutierrez, Andres, Tabasco	59	139	121	22	32	46	7	2	1	15	4	4	3	7	0	12	0	3	6	.264	.311	.380

Player, Team	G	TPA	AB	R	H	TB	2B	3B	HR	RBI	SH	SF	HP	BB	IBB	SO	SB	CS	GDP	Avg.	OBP	Slg.
Gutierrez, Ricardo, Yucatan	67	209	188	23	44	74	7	1	7	32	5	0	5	11	1	30	1	1	10	.234	.294	.394
Guzman, Edwards, Puebla *	57	242	210	37	81	132	15	0	12	47	5	3	2	22	1	10	3	3	3	.386	.443	.629
Guzman, Jorge, Saltillo *	34	66	58	12	15	21	3	0	1	8	0	1	0	7	0	18	0	0	1	.259	.333	.362
Hermansen, Chad, Campeche	11	41	33	3	6	14	3	1	1	3	0	0	0	8	0	20	0	0	0	.182	.341	.424
Hernandez, Adrian, Laguna	1	0	0	0	1	0	0	0	0	0	0	0	0	0	0	0	0	0	0	...	...	...
Hernandez, Hector, Veracruz *	86	314	289	46	87	117	7	1	7	26	10	3	2	10	1	48	6	1	9	.301	.326	.405
Hernandez, Julio, Tijuana	109	513	430	101	138	230	39	1	17	69	1	2	16	64	1	46	1	1	8	.321	.426	.535
Herrera, Christian, Oaxaca	76	159	134	29	37	55	6	3	2	11	2	0	1	22	0	29	3	2	4	.276	.382	.410
Higuera, Ottoniel, Oaxaca	6	6	6	0	1	1	0	0	0	0	0	0	0	0	0	2	0	0	0	.167	.167	.167
Hinojosa, Daniel, Monterrey *	15	7	7	4	0	0	0	0	0	0	0	0	0	0	0	0	1	1	0	.000	.000	.000
Hurtado, Hector, Puebla	99	383	352	47	115	162	20	0	9	50	4	3	4	20	0	50	0	1	16	.327	.367	.460
Ibarra, Juvenal, Tijuana	30	83	75	13	29	45	7	0	3	10	0	2	0	6	0	14	0	0	2	.387	.422	.600
Inzunza, Miguel, Yucatan	1	0	0	0	0	0	0	0	0	0	0	...	0	0	0	0	0	0	0	...	...	...
Irazoqui, Rosario, Tijuana	3	2	2	1	0	0	0	0	0	0	0	0	0	0	0	1	0	0	0	.000	.000	.000
Iturbe, Pedro, Puebla *	92	389	363	48	109	147	22	2	4	50	0	4	5	17	2	60	3	4	14	.300	.337	.405
Jimenez, Eduardo, Saltillo *	4	13	11	1	4	4	0	0	0	1	0	0	0	2	0	3	0	0	1	.364	.462	.364
Johnson, Rontrez, Aguascalientes	98	461	377	96	137	199	24	4	10	61	3	2	12	67	5	43	39	14	7	.363	.472	.528
Jose, Felix, Oaxaca †	105	468	365	87	137	246	19	0	30	113	0	5	5	93	10	64	3	2	8	.375	.502	.674
Landaeta, Luis, Tijuana *	65	284	252	36	81	120	15	0	8	31	0	1	4	27	4	26	9	7	7	.321	.394	.476
Lara, Idelfonso, Aguascalientes-Laguna	98	409	364	50	107	158	12	3	11	51	1	1	2	41	2	95	2	0	7	.294	.368	.434
Leon, Donny, Puebla †	27	114	99	19	36	76	7	0	11	28	0	2	1	12	1	11	0	0	2	.364	.430	.768
Leyva, Octavio, Oaxaca *	27	50	47	6	11	14	0	0	1	4	0	0	1	2	1	5	0	0	1	.234	.280	.298
Lizarraga, Norberto, Laguna	18	27	24	2	2	2	0	0	0	0	0	0	0	3	0	9	0	1	1	.083	.185	.083
Llano, Paul, Tijuana	7	4	4	3	1	1	0	0	0	0	0	0	0	0	0	0	0	0	0	.250	.250	.250
Lopez, Fabian, Campeche *	45	114	102	21	36	63	4	1	7	27	1	0	1	10	2	9	1	0	2	.353	.416	.618
Lopez, Fausto, Tabasco	32	53	49	8	13	14	1	0	0	5	0	0	0	4	0	7	3	0	3	.265	.321	.286
Lopez, Jose Manuel, San Luis Potosi *	34	61	55	9	13	17	4	0	0	4	1	0	2	3	0	12	0	0	1	.236	.300	.309
Lopez, Raul, Veracruz-Laguna	93	411	359	57	119	190	26	3	13	72	3	5	2	42	2	41	1	3	12	.331	.400	.529
Lucca, Lou, Cancun-Laguna	36	152	136	10	37	53	4	0	4	20	0	0	5	11	1	22	1	0	9	.272	.349	.390
Lugo, Roberto, Monterrey	32	62	58	9	19	21	2	0	0	5	0	0	1	3	0	11	1	0	0	.328	.371	.362
Lujan, Enrique, Tijuana	20	39	37	3	7	15	2	0	2	5	0	0	0	2	0	14	0	0	1	.189	.231	.405
Macias, Roberto, Aguascalientes *	47	132	117	18	34	57	6	1	5	14	1	0	0	14	1	34	1	3	6	.291	.366	.487
Magallanes, Ever, Oaxaca *	27	98	88	11	23	38	3	0	4	14	0	1	0	9	0	7	1	2	2	.261	.327	.432
Manzano, Adrian, Angelopolis	1	0	0	0	0	0	0	0	0	0	0	...	0	0	0	0	0	0	0	...	...	...
Marmolejo, Ivan, Cancun	36	98	89	10	22	27	5	0	0	7	0	0	2	7	0	25	0	0	4	.247	.316	.303
Martinez, Abel, Laguna	95	415	360	56	122	174	17	1	11	62	2	4	7	37	4	41	16	7	17	.333	.401	.475
Martinez, Enrique, San Luis Potosi	61	172	154	22	39	59	9	1	3	17	0	1	0	17	1	25	0	2	6	.253	.326	.383
Martinez, Greg, Laguna †	6	28	26	6	6	8	2	0	0	0	0	0	0	2	0	3	2	0	1	.231	.286	.308
Martinez, Grimaldo, Aguascalientes	96	428	376	60	130	178	26	2	6	62	4	2	4	42	3	38	3	2	11	.346	.415	.473
Martinez, Luis Carlos, Puebla	95	364	334	48	101	132	17	1	4	35	9	2	2	17	0	40	4	11	9	.302	.338	.395
Martinez, Manny, Puebla	105	469	401	74	132	229	27	2	22	83	0	2	1	65	7	53	18	9	4	.329	.422	.571
Martinez, Ray, Mexico	106	475	406	87	132	227	22	2	23	84	1	2	13	52	0	79	6	3	15	.325	.416	.559
Mata, Noe, Aguascalientes-Cancun	100	396	354	65	108	167	22	2	11	46	2	1	7	32	0	68	18	4	12	.305	.373	.472
McDonald, Donzell, Tabasco †	107	514	431	86	128	216	20	10	16	67	5	2	12	64	3	91	53	12	5	.297	.401	.501
Medina, Jose Ramon, Monclova	42	88	73	13	22	32	5	1	1	12	1	2	2	10	0	19	0	0	3	.301	.391	.438
Mejia, Roberto, Campeche	33	138	124	16	33	47	6	1	2	15	0	0	3	11	1	11	4	1	5	.266	.341	.379
Mendez, Francisco, Monterrey *	63	153	130	24	40	64	6	0	6	26	0	0	1	22	2	18	0	0	5	.308	.412	.492
Mendez, Roberto, Mexico	103	449	366	81	123	207	21	3	19	66	2	1	2	78	3	65	3	4	11	.336	.454	.566
Mendoza, Omar, San Luis Potosi	99	442	377	75	105	163	35	1	7	46	12	1	2	50	0	63	4	3	9	.279	.365	.432
Mere, Carlos, Veracruz	5	11	10	0	2	3	1	0	0	1	0	0	0	1	0	2	0	1	1	.200	.273	.300
Mere, Pedro, Aguascalientes	54	221	202	35	53	77	12	0	4	33	1	0	1	17	1	31	1	1	6	.262	.323	.381
Meyers, Chad, Oaxaca	108	505	413	98	134	206	31	4	11	56	3	3	14	70	3	61	36	11	5	.324	.436	.499
Meza, Alfredo, San Luis Potosi †	70	214	195	21	49	64	9	0	2	18	6	1	2	10	1	23	0	1	6	.251	.293	.328
Meza, Gonzalo, Monclova *	86	286	251	47	84	132	13	1	11	39	7	2	2	24	2	35	2	2	5	.335	.394	.526
Meza, Jorge, Tijuana	1	0	0	0	0	0	0	0	0	0	0	...	0	0	0	0	0	0	0	...	...	...
Montano, Angel, Tijuana *	12	16	13	2	2	2	0	0	0	0	0	0	1	2	0	2	0	0	0	.154	.313	.154
Montenegro, Jose, Oaxaca	80	271	231	22	60	86	11	0	5	33	3	4	1	32	2	25	0	2	15	.260	.347	.372
Morales, Carlos, Tabasco	5	4	4	0	1	2	1	0	0	0	0	0	0	0	0	2	0	0	0	.250	.250	.500
Morales, Ramon, Tabasco	12	9	8	2	1	1	0	0	0	0	0	0	0	1	0	2	0	0	0	.125	.222	.125
Morejon, Oswaldo, Yucatan	102	477	410	78	131	184	29	6	4	48	9	4	8	46	0	36	22	12	6	.320	.395	.449
Munoz, Adan, Angelopolis	96	410	358	74	115	185	34	0	12	68	1	8	6	37	2	57	1	3	6	.321	.386	.517
Munoz, Jose, Saltillo *	86	336	285	64	96	141	16	1	9	39	2	1	1	47	1	52	7	6	7	.337	.431	.495
Munoz, Leonardo, Angelopolis *	1	0	0	0	0	0	0	0	0	0	0	0	0	0	0	0	0	0	0	...	...	...
Munoz, Noe, Saltillo	107	466	395	81	126	179	26	0	9	76	0	4	0	67	2	53	1	3	14	.319	.423	.453
Nava, Lipso, Cancun	14	62	50	7	12	15	0	0	1	8	0	1	0	11	0	6	0	0	2	.240	.371	.300
Navarro, Luis, Yucatan	1	0	0	0	0	0	0	0	0	0	0	0	0	0	0	0	0	0	0	...	...	...
Nieves, Jose, Veracruz-Aguascalientes	49	217	190	41	68	110	12	0	10	45	1	6	4	16	0	15	2	1	3	.358	.407	.579
Nieves, Melvin, Laguna †	36	166	124	43	42	86	8	0	12	35	0	1	1	40	4	38	2	0	5	.339	.500	.694
Nunez, Jose, Puebla	1	0	0	0	0	0	0	0	0	0	0	0	0	0	0	0	0	0	0	...	...	...
O'Leary, Troy, Cancun *	1	1	1	0	0	0	0	0	0	1	0	0	0	0	0	0	0	0	0	.000	.000	.000
Orantes, Ramon, Monterrey	65	264	233	28	74	99	13	0	4	31	5	3	3	20	0	29	1	2	13	.318	.375	.425
Orrantia, Carlos, Monterrey	71	167	149	23	44	59	8	2	1	22	6	1	1	10	0	22	2	2	3	.295	.342	.396
O'Sullivan, Patrick, San Luis Potosi	108	467	412	81	131	241	32	3	24	95	0	4	4	47	2	98	12	4	11	.318	.390	.585
Otanez, Willis, Veracruz	108	473	402	76	151	262	19	1	30	123	0	7	2	62	9	68	2	1	17	.376	.455	.652
Owens, Eric, Tijuana-Saltillo	24	124	111	16	30	39	3	0	2	15	1	2	0	10	1	14	2	2	2	.270	.325	.351
Pacho, Carlos, Laguna	53	142	130	24	35	50	6	0	3	11	0	1	2	9	0	25	2	0	5	.269	.324	.385
Paez, Hector, Campeche *	97	396	370	40	114	164	17	0	11	72	0	5	6	15	3	32	1	1	12	.308	.341	.443
Paez, Raul, Oaxaca *	41	61	51	2	14	17	3	0	0	9	2	2	0	6	1	2	0	0	3	.275	.339	.333
Palafox, Sergio, Saltillo-Cancun	83	285	252	35	62	91	15	1	4	22	5	3	4	21	0	30	2	3	7	.246	.311	.361
Parra, Orlando, Campeche	1	0	0	1	0	0	0	0	0	0	0	0	0	0	0	0	0	0	0	...	...	...
Pearson, Eddie, Tijuana †	27	116	109	13	29	45	4	0	4	12	0	0	1	6	1	16	0	0	2	.266	.310	.413

Player, Team	G	TPA	AB	R	H	TB	2B	3B	HR	RBI	SH	SF	HP	BB	IBB	SO	SB	CS	GDP	Avg.	OBP	Slg.
Pemberton, Rudy, Laguna-Cancun	74	322	270	50	91	138	14	0	11	43	1	3	10	38	5	30	0	0	13	.337	.433	.511
Pena, Angel, Oaxaca	93	393	351	60	117	209	15	1	25	97	0	4	3	35	4	75	2	2	18	.333	.394	.595
Pena, Cesar, Tijuana	19	39	37	6	10	20	5	1	1	6	0	1	0	1	0	9	0	0	1	.270	.282	.541
Perez, Alfredo, Veracruz	39	122	102	12	28	31	3	0	0	12	4	1	2	13	0	14	1	1	0	.275	.364	.304
Perez, Francisco, San Luis Potosi-Puebla ..	42	74	65	5	15	24	3	0	2	13	0	1	4	4	1	18	0	0	3	.231	.311	.369
Perez, Jose, San Luis Potosi	78	273	247	32	70	89	11	1	2	36	2	1	4	19	0	44	1	2	7	.283	.343	.360
Perez, Noel, Campeche	11	15	12	1	0	0	0	0	0	0	0	0	0	3	0	7	0	0	0	.000	.200	.000
Piste, Carlos, Yucatan †	26	58	51	10	14	18	2	1	0	2	1	0	1	5	0	9	0	1	3	.275	.351	.353
Ponce, Angel, Veracruz	5	4	4	2	1	3	0	1	0	2	0	0	0	0	0	2	0	0	0	.250	.250	.750
Presichi, Cristhian, Saltillo	85	333	292	53	93	159	15	3	15	61	3	2	1	35	0	42	7	0	9	.318	.391	.545
Quinones, Ruben, Cancun	85	302	287	25	78	106	13	0	5	26	4	4	2	5	0	48	0	2	26	.272	.285	.369
Quintero, Christian, Oaxaca	104	466	423	90	152	229	23	9	12	76	7	1	5	30	0	34	22	6	9	.359	.407	.541
Quintero, Edgar, Monterrey *	96	355	309	60	102	178	19	0	19	70	2	5	0	39	5	60	10	5	7	.330	.399	.576
Ramirez, Jesus, Cancun	43	115	96	15	22	31	4	1	1	12	2	1	2	14	0	14	2	1	7	.229	.336	.323
Ramirez, Omar, Veracruz	106	470	410	89	124	213	27	1	20	66	3	1	2	54	2	59	9	1	14	.302	.385	.520
Ramirez, Oscar, Campeche	91	381	336	51	79	130	11	2	12	44	1	2	8	34	2	61	3	3	13	.235	.318	.387
Ramos, Eddy, Monclova †	1	0	0	0	0	0	0	0	0	0	...	0	0	0	...	0	0	0	0	...	...	...
Resendez, Carlos, Monclova	35	97	79	13	19	36	2	0	5	15	2	0	3	13	0	30	0	1	2	.241	.368	.456
Reyes, Jesus, Oaxaca *	37	81	71	7	21	26	3	1	0	4	1	0	0	9	0	11	2	1	1	.296	.375	.366
Reyes, Julio, Laguna *	83	293	268	37	84	128	12	1	10	53	0	2	2	21	2	53	1	0	10	.313	.365	.478
Rincon, Isaias, Mexico-Oaxaca	42	94	81	12	22	24	2	0	0	10	3	0	1	9	0	24	0	0	2	.272	.352	.296
Rios, Eduardo, Aguascalientes	105	471	407	77	130	249	22	2	31	111	0	6	5	53	4	65	2	4	12	.319	.399	.612
Rios, Fernando, Monterrey-San Luis Potosi	64	258	227	34	78	110	12	1	6	46	4	3	5	18	1	17	8	0	3	.344	.399	.485
Rivera, Francisco, Veracruz-Cancun	87	271	244	21	64	90	9	1	5	33	1	3	3	20	1	39	1	0	7	.262	.322	.369
Rivera, Jesus, Tabasco *	63	184	156	19	42	59	9	1	2	14	4	1	2	21	5	14	1	1	6	.269	.361	.378
Rivera, Paul, Tabasco *	1	0	0	0	0	0	0	0	0	0	...	0	0	0	...	0	0	0	0	...	...	...
Rivera, Ruben, Campeche	80	354	298	70	102	185	16	2	21	71	0	5	7	44	0	66	14	3	8	.342	.432	.621
Robles, Javier, Angelopolis	96	431	375	101	147	256	21	2	28	101	0	3	7	46	3	39	13	3	21	.392	.464	.683
Robles, Juan, Tabasco	45	103	97	10	21	27	3	0	1	12	0	1	1	4	0	15	0	1	0	.216	.252	.278
Robles, Oscar, Mexico *	30	140	118	27	46	65	7	0	4	21	1	1	1	19	0	8	1	1	6	.390	.475	.551
Robles, Trinidad, Angelopolis	59	173	154	35	44	67	8	0	5	17	2	1	1	15	0	31	3	1	3	.286	.351	.435
Rodriguez, Armando, Tijuana	11	40	40	7	14	29	3	0	4	13	0	0	0	0	0	8	0	0	2	.350	.350	.725
Rodriguez, Carlos, San Luis Potosi	70	227	189	34	46	78	8	0	8	32	0	3	4	31	1	58	2	1	5	.243	.357	.413
Rodriguez, Erick, Oaxaca	73	256	241	30	64	97	18	0	5	28	2	0	1	12	0	24	2	0	6	.266	.303	.402
Rodriguez, Ferdinand, Monclova *	35	156	121	23	34	52	6	0	4	23	1	0	1	33	0	35	5	3	4	.281	.439	.430
Rodriguez, Fernando, Monclova	80	334	298	36	95	128	24	0	3	55	4	2	5	25	2	37	0	0	15	.319	.379	.430
Rodriguez, Henry, Tabasco *	4	13	13	1	2	5	0	0	1	1	0	0	0	0	0	4	0	0	1	.154	.154	.385
Rodriguez, Leonardo, Monterrey	20	32	29	5	6	6	0	0	0	1	0	0	0	3	0	5	0	0	1	.207	.281	.207
Rodriguez, Liu, Cancun †	91	381	317	52	105	161	17	3	11	53	6	3	18	37	1	24	8	4	10	.331	.427	.508
Rodriguez, Serafin, Angelopolis	64	197	180	24	59	78	5	1	4	22	2	0	3	12	0	23	7	2	7	.328	.379	.433
Romero, Flavio, Campeche *	99	457	378	96	126	203	20	0	19	51	6	5	6	62	1	60	27	12	2	.333	.430	.537
Romero, Marco, Saltillo	52	127	115	14	29	42	4	0	3	10	1	0	0	11	0	28	0	0	7	.252	.317	.365
Romero, Wilson, Yucatan	104	456	399	65	146	238	29	3	19	89	2	9	1	45	4	56	13	5	14	.366	.423	.596
Romo, Jesus, Angelopolis *	20	19	17	8	6	9	0	0	1	3	0	0	0	2	0	3	1	1	1	.353	.421	.529
Rosas, Ezequiel, Oaxaca	13	23	21	4	4	5	1	0	0	3	0	0	0	2	0	3	0	0	1	.190	.261	.238
Ruiz, Juan De Dios, Monclova-Tijuana	8	14	11	0	3	4	1	0	0	3	0	1	0	2	0	2	0	1	0	.273	.357	.364
Ruiz, Ricardo, Laguna	25	84	72	14	21	29	2	0	2	6	2	0	1	9	0	10	1	1	0	.292	.378	.403
Saenz, Ricardo, Monclova	99	412	354	61	113	197	21	0	21	85	0	6	2	50	4	74	1	1	7	.319	.400	.556
Salas, Heriberto, Laguna	107	441	389	53	112	143	20	1	3	57	5	6	7	34	0	30	4	4	10	.288	.351	.368
Salazar, Oscar, Cancun	71	302	264	39	72	106	12	2	6	32	3	1	2	32	3	32	2	2	10	.273	.355	.402
Salcedo, Eder, San Luis Potosi	25	58	53	4	10	14	1	0	1	6	1	0	1	3	0	10	0	0	1	.189	.246	.264
Salgado, Eduardo, Cancun	2	7	6	1	1	4	0	0	1	1	0	0	0	1	0	4	0	0	1	.167	.286	.667
Sanchez, Jose, Tijuana	19	14	13	7	2	2	0	0	0	0	0	0	0	1	0	1	0	1	1	.154	.214	.154
Sanchez, Orlando, Monclova	37	93	77	15	27	41	3	1	3	13	0	2	2	12	0	17	1	0	1	.351	.441	.532
Sanchez, Raul, Cancun-Aguascalientes	97	416	375	70	114	182	24	1	14	58	8	3	5	25	0	59	9	10	7	.304	.353	.485
Sanchez, Roque, Campeche	81	286	268	39	80	126	14	4	8	46	5	2	2	9	0	21	2	0	20	.299	.324	.470
Sandoval, Jose, Mexico	106	443	377	64	116	196	32	0	16	74	3	2	5	56	2	61	2	0	12	.308	.402	.520
Sandoval, Octavio, Angelopolis	56	151	143	23	43	63	11	0	3	17	1	1	2	4	1	30	1	2	4	.301	.327	.441
Santana, Mario, Tabasco	89	342	293	32	90	106	10	0	2	38	5	4	2	38	0	27	2	6	10	.307	.386	.362
Saucedo, Robert, Mexico	99	460	403	96	137	261	19	0	35	114	0	5	5	47	2	50	1	2	17	.340	.411	.648
Selby, Bill, Campeche *	101	457	387	92	123	229	27	2	25	93	0	6	7	57	5	43	3	1	6	.318	.409	.592
Sequea, Jorge, Tabasco †	16	66	56	8	15	16	1	0	0	7	0	0	1	9	2	9	2	0	2	.268	.379	.286
Serrano, Elio, Laguna	1	1	1	0	0	0	0	0	0	0	0	0	0	0	0	0	0	0	0	.000	.000	.000
Sherman, Darrell, Puebla *	76	354	288	70	97	128	13	6	2	30	2	0	4	60	1	32	13	3	9	.337	.457	.444
Sievers, Carlos, Tabasco *	107	460	378	81	135	215	25	2	17	96	1	6	9	66	6	53	13	9	9	.357	.458	.569
Simon, Randall, Tijuana *	64	292	273	52	99	173	17	0	19	71	0	3	3	13	3	32	2	0	7	.363	.394	.634
Smith, Charles, Monterrey	101	439	372	59	103	184	18	0	21	67	0	6	4	57	3	67	1	1	14	.277	.374	.495
Smith, Demond, Monterrey *	79	368	324	61	108	169	20	7	9	36	5	1	4	34	4	44	23	11	2	.333	.402	.522
Soriano, Ricardo, Aguascalientes *	79	321	286	56	90	120	16	1	4	33	2	0	6	27	2	27	1	2	3	.315	.386	.420
Soto, Saul, Mexico	87	348	291	48	85	138	24	1	9	59	3	7	2	45	0	40	1	1	15	.292	.383	.474
Sotomayor, Gilberto, Monclova *	73	70	63	21	18	21	3	0	0	2	1	0	1	5	0	9	1	1	2	.286	.348	.333
Suarez, Luis, Angelopolis	89	333	293	56	98	172	15	4	17	68	5	4	8	23	3	45	5	1	6	.334	.393	.587
Tapia, Cesar, Puebla	42	78	71	11	16	25	3	0	2	12	0	2	2	3	0	6	0	0	2	.225	.269	.352
Timmons, Ozzie, Campeche-Monclova	13	58	50	2	10	14	1	0	1	5	0	0	1	7	0	13	0	0	1	.200	.310	.280
Torrero, Miguel, Puebla	70	149	137	22	31	36	3	1	0	17	1	1	1	9	0	16	1	2	2	.226	.277	.263
Torres, Ivan, Monclova-Veracruz	7	6	6	0	0	0	0	0	0	0	0	0	0	0	0	1	0	0	0	.000	.000	.000
Trapaga, Julio, Puebla	39	107	95	15	29	48	1	3	4	20	1	2	0	9	0	22	3	0	3	.305	.358	.505
Valdes (Manzo), Pedro, Saltillo *	66	301	243	54	75	131	12	1	14	50	0	3	5	50	4	31	0	0	12	.309	.432	.539
Valdez, Emmanuel, Tijuana	94	383	331	62	100	171	14	0	19	65	2	4	4	42	0	90	2	1	8	.302	.383	.517
Valdez, Francisco, Veracruz	67	242	212	36	59	90	10	0	7	41	3	3	12	12	2	30	0	2	6	.278	.347	.425

Player, Team	G	TPA	AB	R	H	TB	2B	3B	HR	RBI	SH	SF	HP	BB	IBB	SO	SB	CS	GDP	Avg.	OBP	Slg.
Valdez, Mario, Monterrey *	65	259	216	32	63	94	13	0	6	25	0	0	3	40	2	43	0	1	3	.292	.409	.435
Valdez, Ramon, Campeche	70	270	239	41	67	80	9	2	0	17	3	2	9	17	0	22	5	3	10	.280	.348	.335
Valencia, Abraham, Tijuana-Oaxaca	40	145	129	17	37	58	9	0	4	17	0	1	3	12	2	29	1	1	7	.287	.359	.450
Valencia, Carlos, Tijuana	110	530	489	98	141	263	18	4	32	88	3	10	3	25	0	35	4	4	16	.288	.321	.538
Valencia, Christian, Monterrey	5	5	5	1	1	1	0	0	0	0	0	0	0	0	0	1	1	1	1	.200	.200	.200
Valenzuela, Irving, Puebla	26	76	62	5	11	13	2	0	0	3	1	0	3	10	0	17	0	1	5	.177	.320	.210
Valenzuela, Mario, Saltillo	93	403	367	75	132	244	17	1	31	103	0	6	10	20	0	73	1	2	10	.360	.402	.665
Valle, Cosme, San Luis Potosi	15	24	21	3	5	5	0	0	0	0	1	0	1	1	0	5	0	0	1	.238	.304	.238
Valle, Jorge Luis, Cancun-Saltillo	100	348	316	44	93	148	18	2	11	49	3	2	6	21	0	53	1	4	17	.294	.348	.468
Vazquez, Gregorio, Tabasco	72	258	221	34	66	86	13	2	1	20	5	0	6	26	1	16	5	3	7	.299	.387	.389
Vazquez, Jorge, Angelopolis	71	305	285	61	108	227	20	0	33	96	0	2	4	14	2	55	1	2	16	.379	.413	.796
Vega, Edgar, Monclova	93	334	282	35	59	69	7	0	1	35	7	2	2	41	0	57	1	0	14	.209	.312	.245
Vega, Jesus, Angelopolis	50	131	124	13	29	42	1	0	4	18	0	2	1	4	0	34	0	2	3	.234	.260	.339
Velasquez, Guillermo, Angelopolis *	92	364	304	54	110	180	19	0	17	76	0	3	0	57	3	62	0	4	5	.362	.459	.592
Velez, Manuel, Mexico	91	419	362	69	112	150	18	1	6	49	4	2	2	49	1	48	6	1	11	.309	.393	.414
Verdugo, Vicente, Campeche	72	246	226	39	69	88	5	1	4	28	1	3	2	14	0	17	0	1	6	.305	.347	.389
Villaescusa, Fernando, Campeche	11	15	14	1	5	5	0	0	0	0	0	0	0	1	0	3	1	1	1	.357	.400	.357
Villalobos, Carlos, Puebla-San Luis Potosi ..	104	470	409	85	145	243	39	1	19	97	0	8	3	50	2	78	6	7	11	.355	.421	.594
Villarreal, Alejandro, Tijuana	7	6	6	0	1	1	0	0	0	1	0	0	0	0	0	1	0	0	1	.167	.167	.167
Villegas, Felipe, Aguascalientes	6	5	4	0	0	0	0	0	0	0	0	0	1	0	0	1	0	0	0	.000	.200	.000
Villegas, Fernando, Saltillo	18	55	43	7	15	17	2	0	0	12	4	1	4	3	0	6	0	0	0	.349	.431	.395
Virgen, Constancio, Mexico	5	5	4	0	2	3	1	0	0	1	0	0	0	1	0	2	0	0	0	.500	.600	.750
Vizcarra, Roberto, Campeche	100	462	401	73	139	204	26	0	13	67	2	6	17	36	1	21	3	2	11	.347	.417	.509
White, Derrick, Tijuana	109	504	427	93	157	264	29	0	26	97	0	4	10	63	3	78	3	2	19	.368	.456	.618
Yan, Julian, Tabasco	109	481	396	94	102	218	14	3	32	87	0	2	2	81	9	109	2	2	7	.258	.385	.551
Yepez, Daniel, Puebla	12	26	26	4	9	14	2	0	1	6	0	0	0	0	0	7	0	0	0	.346	.346	.538
Zazueta, Christian, Cancun	30	97	96	11	25	35	7	0	1	5	0	0	0	1	0	21	3	0	1	.260	.268	.365
Zazueta, Juan, Saltillo †	58	140	130	17	39	51	4	1	2	17	1	1	0	8	2	15	0	1	6	.300	.338	.392
Zazueta, Mauricio, Oaxaca-Mexico	23	48	46	3	7	11	4	0	0	7	0	0	0	2	1	8	0	1	0	.152	.188	.239

PLAYERS WITH TWO OR MORE TEAMS

Player, Team	G	TPA	AB	R	H	TB	2B	3B	HR	RBI	SH	SF	HP	BB	IBB	SO	SB	CS	GDP	Avg.	OBP	Slg.
Alvarez, Hector, Monterrey	42	135	120	18	43	52	6	0	1	16	2	3	5	5	0	20	0	0	2	.358	.398	.433
Alvarez, Hector, Oaxaca	22	91	85	9	32	45	7	0	2	6	0	0	0	6	1	12	0	2	2	.376	.418	.529
Alvarez, Rafael, Laguna *	16	71	60	12	20	36	5	1	3	11	0	0	2	9	1	12	3	0	3	.333	.437	.600
Alvarez, Rafael, Cancun *	40	166	144	26	43	84	11	0	10	27	0	0	0	22	0	26	2	2	5	.299	.392	.583
Arredondo, Eduardo, Tabasco *	48	151	129	13	32	46	8	0	2	16	4	2	3	13	1	11	3	2	5	.248	.327	.357
Arredondo, Eduardo, Mexico *	20	59	49	10	8	15	1	0	2	5	0	1	2	7	0	8	2	0	1	.163	.288	.306
Castro, Arnoldo, Cancun	76	313	277	30	78	103	13	0	4	30	9	3	0	24	2	39	0	2	9	.282	.336	.372
Castro, Arnoldo, Tabasco	24	85	72	5	15	19	1	0	1	12	2	2	1	8	0	11	0	1	3	.208	.289	.264
Contreras, Albino, Puebla *	101	414	350	76	110	174	23	7	9	54	...	4	13	47	...	59	9	10	6	.314	.411	.497
Contreras, Albino, Angelopolis *	97	331	293	49	84	139	16	3	11	44	3	6	5	24	3	54	8	2	5	.287	.345	.474
Espino, Daniel, Cancun	60	240	212	22	57	75	12	0	2	30	3	1	12	12	3	22	0	2	8	.269	.342	.354
Espino, Daniel, Veracruz	9	26	23	1	7	9	2	0	0	1	0	0	3	0	0	2	0	0	1	.304	.385	.391
Lara, Idelfonso, Aguascalientes	50	217	197	25	55	79	7	1	5	26	0	1	0	19	2	49	2	0	7	.279	.341	.401
Lara, Idelfonso, Laguna	48	192	167	25	52	79	5	2	6	25	1	0	2	22	0	46	0	0	5	.311	.398	.473
Lopez, Raul, Veracruz *	7	25	25	3	10	16	4	1	0	6	0	0	0	0	0	1	1	0	0	.400	.400	.640
Lopez, Raul, Laguna *	86	386	334	54	109	174	22	2	13	66	3	5	2	42	2	40	1	2	12	.326	.399	.521
Lucca, Lou, Cancun	28	119	106	8	28	44	4	0	4	14	0	0	4	9	1	20	0	0	7	.264	.345	.415
Lucca, Lou, Laguna	8	33	30	2	9	9	0	0	0	6	0	0	1	2	0	2	1	0	2	.300	.364	.300
Mata, Noe, Aguascalientes	63	235	212	41	63	99	12	0	8	29	2	1	5	15	0	44	11	2	8	.297	.356	.467
Mata, Noe, Cancun	37	161	142	24	45	68	10	2	3	17	0	0	2	17	0	24	7	2	4	.317	.398	.479
Nieves, Jose, Veracruz	6	28	24	6	9	12	3	0	0	2	0	0	1	3	0	3	1	0	0	.375	.464	.500
Nieves, Jose, Aguascalientes	43	189	166	35	59	98	9	0	10	43	1	6	3	13	0	12	1	1	3	.355	.399	.590
Owens, Eric, Tijuana	20	106	96	16	26	35	3	0	2	12	0	2	0	8	1	12	2	2	2	.271	.321	.365
Owens, Eric, Saltillo	4	18	15	0	4	4	0	0	0	3	1	0	0	2	0	2	0	0	0	.267	.353	.267
Palafox, Sergio, Saltillo	40	110	95	23	25	41	4	0	4	12	3	1	2	9	0	12	1	1	4	.263	.336	.432
Palafox, Sergio, Cancun	43	175	157	12	37	50	11	1	0	10	2	2	2	12	0	18	1	2	3	.236	.295	.318
Pemberton, Rudy, Laguna	42	190	155	35	51	84	9	0	8	21	1	3	6	25	5	16	0	0	7	.329	.434	.542
Pemberton, Rudy, Cancun	32	132	115	15	40	54	5	0	3	22	0	0	4	13	0	14	0	0	6	.348	.432	.470
Perez, Francisco, San Luis Potosi *	7	7	6	0	0	0	0	0	0	0	0	0	1	0	0	2	0	0	1	.000	.143	.000
Perez, Francisco, Puebla *	35	67	59	5	15	24	3	0	2	13	0	1	3	4	1	16	0	0	2	.254	.328	.407
Rincon, Isaias, Mexico	9	5	5	1	2	2	0	0	0	1	0	0	0	0	0	2	0	0	0	.400	.400	.400
Rincon, Isaias, Oaxaca	33	89	76	11	20	22	2	0	0	9	3	0	1	9	0	22	0	0	2	.263	.349	.289
Rios, Fernando, Monterrey	3	6	5	1	1	1	0	0	0	0	0	0	1	0	0	1	0	0	0	.200	.333	.200
Rios, Fernando, San Luis Potosi	61	252	222	33	77	109	12	1	6	46	4	3	4	18	1	16	8	0	3	.347	.401	.491
Rivera, Francisco, Veracruz *	6	14	13	1	5	9	1	0	1	3	0	0	0	1	0	2	0	0	0	.385	.429	.692
Rivera, Francisco, Cancun *	81	257	231	20	59	81	5	1	4	30	1	3	3	19	1	37	1	0	7	.255	.316	.351
Ruiz, Juan De Dios, Monclova	2	5	4	0	1	1	0	0	0	0	0	0	0	0	0	0	0	0	0	.250	.400	.250
Ruiz, Juan De Dios, Tijuana..	6	9	7	0	2	3	1	0	0	3	0	1	0	1	0	2	0	0	0	.286	.333	.429
Sanchez, Raul, Cancun	60	263	228	44	64	106	13	1	9	34	7	3	5	20	0	32	4	8	3	.281	.348	.465
Sanchez, Raul, Aguascalientes	37	153	147	26	50	76	11	0	5	24	1	0	0	5	0	27	5	2	4	.340	.362	.517
Timmons, Ozzie, Campeche	8	34	26	1	5	9	1	0	1	4	0	0	1	7	0	5	0	0	0	.192	.382	.346
Timmons, Ozzie, Monclova	5	24	24	1	5	5	0	0	0	1	0	0	0	0	0	8	0	0	1	.208	.208	.208
Torres, Ivan, Monclova	1	2	2	0	0	0	0	0	0	0	0	0	0	0	0	0	0	0	0	.000	.000	.000
Torres, Ivan, Veracruz	6	4	4	0	0	0	0	0	0	0	0	0	0	0	0	1	0	0	0	.000	.000	.000
Valencia, Abraham, Tijuana	30	109	98	11	26	40	8	0	2	12	0	1	1	9	0	21	1	1	6	.265	.330	.408
Valencia, Abraham, Oaxaca..	10	36	31	6	11	18	1	0	2	5	0	0	2	3	2	8	0	0	1	.355	.444	.581
Valle, Jorge Luis, Cancun	52	163	152	15	37	50	6	2	1	13	0	1	0	10	0	28	1	1	9	.243	.288	.329
Valle, Jorge Luis, Saltillo	48	185	164	29	56	98	12	0	10	36	3	1	6	11	0	25	0	3	8	.341	.401	.598

Player, Team	G	TPA	AB	R	H	TB	2B	3B	HR	RBI	SH	SF	HP	BB	IBB	SO	SB	CS	GDP	Avg.	OBP	Slg.
Villalobos, Carlos, Puebla	26	117	105	19	31	50	7	0	4	17	0	2	0	10	0	24	1	2	3	.295	.350	.476
Villalobos, Carlos, San Luis Potosi ..	78	353	304	66	114	193	32	1	15	80	0	6	3	40	2	54	5	5	8	.375	.445	.635
Zazueta, Mauricio, Oaxaca	16	41	39	2	6	9	3	0	0	6	0	0	0	2	1	5	0	1	0	.154	.195	.231
Zazueta, Mauricio, Mexico	7	7	7	1	1	2	1	0	0	1	0	0	0	0	0	3	0	0	0	.143	.143	.286

GRAND SLAMS—B. Selby, 4; P. O'Sullivan, P. Valdes, M. Valenzuela, 3 each; J. Amado, R. Martinez, D. McDonald, A. Pena, O. Ramirez, R. Saenz, J. Sandoval, R. Saucedo, E. Valdez, 2 each; A. Amezcua, L. Arauz, J. Bass, D. Brinkley, T. Brito, M. Burkhart, J. Camilo, P. Castellano, F. Cervera, R. Cobos, O. De La Torre, E. Diaz, P. Diaz, A. Echevarria, D. Espino, G. Garcia, S. Gonzalez, H. Guizar, S. Gutierrez, F. Jose, E. Magallanes, G. Martinez, R. Mendez, N. Munoz, M. Nieves, C. Pacho, H. Paez, J. Perez, C. Presichi, E. Quintero, J. Reyes, F. Rios, J. Robles, A. Rodriguez, B. Rodriguez, E. Rodriguez, W. Romero, O. Sanchez, R. Sanchez, R. Simon, S. Soto, C. Tapia, F. Valdez, C. Valencia, C. Villalobos, R. Vizcarra, J. Yan, 1 each.

AWARDED FIRST BASE ON CATCHER'S INTERFERENCE—C. Meyers 2 (H. Estrada, J. Vega); A. Contreras (R. Quinones); R. Diaz (M. Antonio Cruz); R. Martinez (N. Munoz); F. Rios (R. Lugo).

2005 PITCHING

TEAM

Team	W	L	Pct.	ERA	G	CG	ShO	Sv.	IP	H	TBF	R	ER	HR	SH	SF	HB	BB	IBB	SO	WP	Bk.
Yucatan	57	50	.533	4.56	107	4	2	27	949	1073	4166	521	481	78	35	32	52	365	17	590	53	4
Tabasco	53	55	.491	4.90	109	3	6	22	943.2	1181	4263	553	514	92	54	35	75	337	27	459	51	2
Saltillo	63	47	.573	4.95	110	2	6	23	965.1	1109	4379	584	531	113	30	23	55	472	22	685	73	3
Campeche	62	43	.590	5.00	105	6	7	26	907.2	1066	4066	577	504	136	46	24	37	361	14	613	62	1
Tijuana	64	46	.582	5.36	110	2	5	25	983	1094	4434	641	585	132	38	30	63	455	32	669	71	6
Monterrey	56	50	.528	5.47	106	4	8	27	932.1	1018	4198	621	567	113	31	34	67	452	12	609	55	2
Monclova	53	55	.491	5.51	108	3	6	24	956.1	1157	4323	645	586	126	31	40	36	389	30	542	50	1
Oaxaca	57	50	.533	5.61	108	7	4	29	930	1188	4257	639	580	134	40	39	51	371	23	528	43	5
Veracruz	51	58	.468	5.66	109	5	3	22	932	1180	4294	654	586	121	47	41	69	368	27	533	44	3
Angelopolis	66	41	.617	5.89	107	2	3	25	922.2	1096	4196	653	604	110	29	32	41	468	19	467	58	5
Mexico	56	51	.523	5.89	107	3	4	27	942	1229	4325	655	616	126	36	38	46	393	14	563	62	1
Puebla	51	58	.468	6.07	107	1	2	21	921.2	1134	4231	693	622	133	33	39	67	440	25	483	63	8
San Luis Potosi ..	45	63	.417	6.13	108	1	2	18	942	1240	4418	738	642	130	30	37	51	418	22	519	58	1
Cancun	37	73	.336	6.20	108	3	3	22	936	1229	4368	713	645	148	35	35	60	406	14	464	73	1
Aguascalientes ..	55	53	.509	6.30	108	2	1	21	948	1293	4438	718	664	166	36	40	56	400	19	488	49	5
Laguna	38	71	.349	7.76	109	1	1	18	963.2	1346	4707	905	831	174	31	37	81	519	17	671	79	4

INDIVIDUAL

TOP QUALIFIERS FOR EARNED-RUN AVERAGE TITLE

Minimum 88 innings.*Lefthanded pitcher.

Pitcher, Team	W	L	Pct.	ERA	G	GS	CG	ShO	GF	Sv.	IP	H	TBF	R	ER	HR	SH	SF	HB	BB	IBB	SO	WP	Bk.
Campos, Francisco, Campeche	11	4	.733	2.84	22	22	3	0	0	0	152.0	137	632	54	48	18	4	2	5	50	1	170	11	0
Knott, Eric, Puebla *	14	4	.778	3.25	23	22	1	0	0	0	144.0	135	560	62	52	11	7	2	3	20	3	62	0	0
Beltran, Rigo, Saltillo *	13	4	.765	3.40	20	19	0	0	0	0	108.2	114	468	44	41	11	4	1	3	40	0	83	4	0
Rios, Jesus, Tabasco	8	3	.727	3.42	21	21	1	1	0	0	123.2	140	532	53	47	10	8	3	14	32	1	80	3	0
Beltran, Alonso, Tijuana	8	6	.571	3.45	21	21	1	0	0	0	125.1	110	528	52	48	13	0	3	5	56	2	117	5	0
Bourgeois, Steve, Saltillo	8	4	.667	3.58	19	18	0	0	0	0	100.2	93	427	44	40	9	2	4	4	48	2	78	13	1
Acosta, Aaron, Veracruz	9	9	.500	3.72	21	21	2	0	0	0	121.0	132	520	61	50	10	2	3	9	36	1	60	2	0
Giron, Isabel, Monterrey	6	2	.750	3.77	18	17	2	1	0	0	102.2	97	430	50	43	9	6	2	8	36	0	77	0	0
Lopez, Emigdio, Veracruz	8	3	.727	3.78	20	20	1	0	0	0	112.0	109	461	56	47	18	7	3	6	25	1	54	1	0
Vargas, Joel, Tabasco	9	5	.643	3.81	21	21	0	0	0	0	127.2	149	544	60	54	9	2	7	6	20	0	58	2	1
Rivera, Oscar, Yucatan	7	6	.538	3.92	20	20	0	0	0	0	114.2	126	483	55	50	7	2	3	4	31	0	92	5	3
Delgadillo, Juan, Tabasco	9	5	.643	4.09	23	22	0	0	0	0	125.1	137	554	60	57	9	4	2	9	61	4	52	9	1
Fernandez, Osvaldo, Tabasco	7	9	.438	4.14	23	21	2	1	1	1	130.1	166	567	63	60	12	6	4	6	32	1	65	2	0
Palafox, Juan Manuel, Yucatan	10	5	.667	4.30	19	18	1	0	0	0	102.2	110	447	51	49	6	4	2	4	52	0	45	4	0
Aceves, Alfredo, Yucatan	9	8	.529	4.32	22	21	3	0	0	0	145.2	155	609	77	70	12	8	4	10	44	3	101	7	0
Alvarez, Juan Jesus, Campeche	8	6	.571	4.39	22	17	0	0	2	0	106.2	146	473	61	52	12	3	2	5	31	0	53	5	0
Ortega, Pablo, Angelopolis	8	5	.615	4.45	23	21	0	0	0	0	115.1	136	497	61	57	13	0	2	5	38	0	51	3	0
Pulido, Carlos, Oaxaca *	7	7	.500	4.72	23	23	3	1	0	0	150.2	179	649	88	79	21	5	2	1	37	1	67	3	0
Rodriguez, Raul, Monclova-Yucatan	3	10	.231	4.72	21	19	0	0	0	0	108.2	132	471	66	57	12	2	6	8	26	0	46	5	0
Montano, Ignacio, Cancun-Aguascalientes	8	3	.727	4.76	19	18	1	0	0	0	115.1	136	499	65	61	16	2	4	6	38	1	72	5	1
Castellanos, Hugo, Tijuana	7	4	.636	4.82	28	18	0	0	0	0	112.0	93	483	63	60	10	2	4	11	65	0	69	3	0

DEPARTMENTAL LEADERS: W—Knott, 14. L—Mairena, 13. Pct.—Armenta, .813. G—Nunez, 58. GS—Ramirez, 24. CG—three pitchers tied with 3. ShO—Coco, 2. GF—Simas, 50. Sv.—Marquez and De La Rosa, 25. IP—Campos, 152. H—Ramirez, 206. TBF—Ramirez, 666. R—Gomez, 112. ER—Mairena, 101. HR—Moreno, 25. SAC—four pitchers tied with 8. SF—Perez and Gomez, 8. HB—Posadas and Rios, 14. BB—Castellanos, 65. IBB—Estrella and Garibay, 8. SO—Campos, 170. WP—Hurtado and Pina, 14. BK—three pitchers tied with 3.

ALL PITCHERS

*Lefthanded pitcher.

Pitcher, Team	W	L	Pct.	ERA	G	GS	CG	ShO	GF	Sv.	IP	H	TBF	R	ER	HR	SH	SF	HB	BB	IBB	SO	WP	Bk.
Abreu, Winston, Oaxaca	4	0	1.000	1.35	18	0	0	0	17	10	20.0	10	76	4	3	0	0	0	0	5	1	32	3	0
Acevedo, Juan, Monterrey	1	2	.333	4.50	29	0	0	0	2	0	32.0	43	145	19	16	2	2	1	1	8	1	26	0	0
Aceves, Alfredo, Yucatan	9	8	.529	4.32	22	21	3	0	0	0	145.2	155	609	77	70	12	8	4	10	44	3	101	7	0
Acosta, Aaron, Veracruz	9	9	.500	3.72	21	21	2	0	0	0	121.0	132	520	61	50	10	2	3	9	36	1	60	2	0
Acosta, Jasiel, Monclova *	3	6	.333	6.25	21	13	0	0	3	0	72.0	90	337	53	50	11	4	1	3	41	1	39	2	0
Aguilar, Gerardo, Aguascalientes *	0	0	.000	6.31	38	1	0	0	6	1	41.1	61	203	31	29	9	1	0	3	22	3	13	5	0
Aguilar, Hugo, Veracruz *	2	3	.400	6.90	30	0	0	0	3	1	44.1	65	218	40	34	3	4	2	2	27	1	33	2	0
Aguilar, Mario, Campeche *	1	0	1.000	12.27	16	0	0	0	2	0	7.1	12	38	10	10	1	0	0	2	5	0	4	0	0
Aguirre, Alejandro, Monclova	0	0	.000	7.71	4	0	0	0	3	0	4.2	6	21	4	4	1	0	0	0	1	0	2	0	0
Aguirre, Gaudencio, Monterrey	0	1	.000	2.23	35	0	0	0	8	0	48.1	35	190	15	12	2	1	0	6	18	2	29	6	1

Pitcher, Team	W	L	Pct.	ERA	G	GS	CG	ShO	GF	Sv.	IP	H	TBF	R	ER	HR	SH	SF	HB	BB	IBB	SO	WP	Bk.
Aguirre, Rodolfo, Puebla	3	1	.750	7.67	21	1	0	0	3	1	29.1	34	136	26	25	7	2	0	3	17	0	22	3	0
Ahumada, Edgar, Saltillo-Laguna	1	1	.500	10.50	24	0	0	0	2	0	12.0	19	73	14	14	2	0	0	3	17	0	3	1	0
Alberro, Jose, Monclova	2	1	.667	6.87	11	2	0	0	1	1	18.1	22	85	14	14	1	1	1	2	12	3	16	0	0
Almonte, Hector, Saltillo	2	0	1.000	1.54	10	0	0	0	5	1	11.2	7	51	2	2	0	0	0	1	8	0	7	1	0
Alvarez, Antonio, Aguascalientes	6	4	.600	7.69	32	7	0	0	2	0	57.1	98	294	52	49	13	1	2	4	30	2	27	4	1
Alvarez, Gabriel, Mexico-Monclova	0	1	.000	9.37	17	0	0	0	6	0	16.1	26	85	17	17	1	0	0	0	14	0	6	8	0
Alvarez, Juan, Puebla *	3	0	1.000	3.19	8	7	0	0	0	0	42.1	36	180	17	15	0	0	2	3	22	0	35	4	1
Alvarez, Juan Jesus, Campeche	8	6	.571	4.39	22	17	0	0	2	0	106.2	146	473	61	52	12	3	2	5	31	0	53	5	0
Alvarez, Victor, Mexico *	5	2	.714	4.73	18	16	0	0	1	0	85.2	114	377	49	45	7	4	2	2	21	1	49	1	0
Arellano, Salvador, Yucatan	1	1	.500	6.53	20	4	0	0	1	1	41.1	59	198	32	30	5	1	0	2	23	0	29	4	1
Armas, Noel, Puebla	1	0	1.000	3.52	9	0	0	0	1	0	15.1	19	69	6	6	4	0	1	1	9	0	4	1	0
Armenta, Alejandro, Angelopolis *	13	3	.813	5.50	23	20	2	1	1	0	103.0	112	450	66	63	17	4	4	3	59	0	51	8	0
Avalos, Jose, Oaxaca	5	2	.714	5.22	44	0	0	0	9	1	39.2	45	188	24	23	3	3	1	4	26	2	27	4	0
Baez, Sixto, Veracruz	2	4	.333	3.77	42	0	0	0	36	18	45.1	46	193	22	19	2	5	6	4	16	5	23	0	1
Barradas, Roberto, Campeche	1	2	.333	8.80	13	1	0	0	4	0	15.1	22	77	17	15	1	1	1	1	9	0	11	2	1
Barreras, Juan, Laguna	1	0	1.000	10.44	38	0	0	0	5	0	35.1	59	194	44	41	6	1	2	5	31	1	26	1	1
Beltran, Alonso, Tijuana	8	6	.571	3.45	21	21	1	0	0	0	125.1	110	528	52	48	13	0	3	5	56	2	117	5	0
Beltran, Rigo, Saltillo *	13	4	.765	3.40	20	19	0	0	0	0	108.2	114	468	44	41	11	4	1	3	40	0	83	4	0
Bernal, Christian, Laguna	0	1	.000	7.51	31	1	0	0	7	0	44.1	54	213	38	37	7	0	1	2	26	0	29	3	0
Bernal, Manuel, Laguna	1	3	.250	10.69	10	7	0	0	0	0	33.2	64	178	44	40	9	1	1	4	13	1	18	2	0
Blancas, Rigoberto, Cancun *	0	0	.000	5.50	14	0	0	0	4	1	18.0	22	77	11	11	5	0	0	0	4	0	5	1	0
Bland, Nate, Tijuana *	5	2	.714	4.62	29	11	1	0	15	5	85.2	91	351	45	44	7	6	2	3	23	0	66	7	3
Borbon, Sergio, Saltillo	0	0	.000	0.00	2	0	0	0	1	0	2.0	3	11	0	0	0	0	0	0	1	0	0	0	0
Bourgeois, Steve, Saltillo	8	4	.667	3.58	19	18	0	0	0	0	100.2	93	427	44	40	9	2	4	4	48	2	78	13	1
Bueno, Geraldo, Cancun	2	2	.500	10.21	30	0	0	0	17	6	27.1	42	138	33	31	10	2	2	3	18	0	17	1	1
Bustillos, Oscar, Angelopolis	0	3	.000	10.74	27	1	0	0	8	1	29.1	43	148	36	35	5	1	0	1	25	2	25	3	1
Camara, Pedro, Yucatan *	1	0	1.000	6.08	42	0	0	0	9	1	26.2	34	126	21	18	5	3	1	3	17	2	11	2	0
Campos, Francisco, Campeche	11	4	.733	2.84	22	22	3	0	0	0	152.0	137	632	54	48	18	4	2	5	50	1	170	11	0
Cantu, Jacobo, Tabasco	0	0	.000	9.53	4	1	0	0	1	0	5.2	9	29	7	6	0	1	0	2	5	1	1	3	0
Carbajal, Luis, Laguna *	0	0	.000	0.00	1	0	0	0	1	0	1.0	0	3	0	0	0	0	0	0	0	0	0	0	0
Carrasco, Alejandro, Yucatan	4	1	.800	4.06	33	8	0	0	13	6	77.2	80	333	38	35	8	2	6	2	37	0	26	1	0
Carrillo, Guillermo, Angelopolis	1	1	.500	4.02	27	1	0	0	4	1	40.1	43	172	24	18	3	2	1	1	17	2	17	3	0
Castaneda, Federico, Laguna-Aguascalientes	0	0	.000	4.13	18	2	0	0	4	0	28.1	36	131	15	13	3	0	0	1	14	0	20	0	0
Castellanos, Hugo, Tijuana	7	4	.636	4.82	28	18	0	0	0	0	112.0	93	483	63	60	10	2	4	11	65	0	69	3	0
Castillo, Jorge, Mexico *	0	0	.000	6.15	20	0	0	0	7	1	26.1	28	112	18	18	1	2	5	0	12	0	22	1	0
Cazares, Rosario, Saltillo-Cancun	2	4	.333	6.45	20	7	0	0	3	0	44.2	55	203	38	32	9	2	3	4	11	0	37	5	1
Cerros, Juan, San Luis Potosi	3	3	.500	5.29	31	0	0	0	26	9	34.0	32	153	20	20	3	1	2	3	18	1	21	3	0
Cervantes, Pedro, San Luis Potosi	0	3	.000	4.50	13	3	0	0	3	0	22.0	27	101	16	11	2	0	1	0	10	2	6	0	0
Chavarria, Hector, Cancun	0	9	.000	7.03	29	11	0	0	3	1	73.0	101	342	62	57	17	5	1	8	31	0	34	5	0
Chavez, Alejandro, Mexico	0	1	.000	8.44	4	1	0	0	0	0	5.1	11	34	7	5	1	0	0	0	7	0	4	2	0
Chavez, Jose, Monterrey	0	0	.000	13.50	1	0	0	0	0	0	0.2	1	2	1	1	0	0	0	0	0	0	0	0	0
Chouinard, Bobby, Yucatan	0	0	.000	4.15	4	0	0	0	2	0	4.1	8	23	2	2	0	0	0	0	2	0	2	0	0
Cobos, Jose, Monterrey-San Luis Potosi	0	1	.000	5.61	25	0	0	0	11	0	33.2	38	159	21	21	2	1	2	3	20	1	22	3	0
Coco, Pasqual, Saltillo-Veracruz	9	5	.643	4.86	29	16	2	2	11	2	103.2	103	464	62	56	15	5	3	8	56	2	97	8	0
Cordova, Alejandro, San Luis Potosi	0	0	.000	9.00	2	0	0	0	1	0	1.0	4	7	1	1	0	0	0	0	0	0	2	0	0
Cordova, Francisco, Mexico	5	9	.357	5.65	33	14	0	0	15	6	106.2	138	480	69	67	17	2	4	4	32	3	71	2	0
Cruz, Javier, Veracruz	0	0	.000	16.20	7	0	0	0	3	0	5.0	14	29	10	9	3	0	1	1	0	0	1	0	0
DeHart, Rick, Monterrey *	2	2	.500	9.50	5	5	0	0	0	0	18.0	23	95	28	19	3	0	2	1	15	0	14	0	0
De La Hoya, Javier, Campeche	1	4	.200	6.82	7	7	0	0	0	0	30.1	44	149	30	23	2	3	3	2	22	1	16	1	0
De La Rosa, Maximo, Monterrey	2	5	.286	2.41	51	0	0	0	46	25	52.1	41	208	16	14	5	4	1	1	14	2	44	4	0
Delfin, Adolfo, Tijuana	4	0	1.000	4.87	44	0	0	0	10	0	61.0	68	276	37	33	8	5	2	5	33	3	51	8	0
Delgadillo, Juan, Tabasco	9	5	.643	4.09	23	22	0	0	0	0	125.1	137	554	60	57	9	4	2	9	61	4	52	9	1
Desgue, Fernando, Tabasco	7	1	.875	2.02	32	0	0	0	26	7	35.2	36	149	10	8	1	2	0	5	9	1	11	3	0
Diaz, Marco, Aguascalientes	6	3	.667	3.94	44	0	0	0	19	4	48.0	48	203	23	21	5	2	2	2	16	2	28	1	0
Diaz, Rafael, Saltillo	8	2	.800	4.10	16	11	0	0	0	0	74.2	66	314	35	34	8	2	2	3	33	1	48	0	0
Dominguez, Carlos, Saltillo-Angelopolis-Puebla	0	1	.000	10.64	36	1	0	0	5	0	33.0	46	163	39	39	9	0	0	1	21	2	18	4	0
Dominguez, David, Mexico	3	3	.500	6.69	46	0	0	0	15	3	39.0	48	182	33	29	7	2	2	3	19	2	28	3	0
Dorame, Randey, Monclova *	0	1	.000	6.65	10	3	0	0	2	0	21.2	24	99	16	16	4	0	0	3	12	0	9	0	0
Duarte, Mauricio, Cancun	1	2	.333	7.11	6	1	0	0	3	0	12.2	21	62	10	10	1	0	0	1	6	1	2	1	0
Duarte, Miguel, Saltillo	2	3	.400	4.05	50	0	0	0	34	14	53.1	61	237	28	24	5	1	1	3	20	3	49	2	0
Elizalde, Carlos, Oaxaca	1	2	.333	6.85	7	3	0	0	2	0	23.2	32	110	19	18	2	1	1	0	11	2	10	0	0
Elvira, Abraham, Aguascalientes *	3	5	.375	5.63	19	17	0	0	0	0	94.1	121	431	66	59	9	5	2	2	48	0	58	2	0
Elvira, Joaquin, Tabasco	0	3	.000	11.00	13	1	0	0	4	0	9.0	16	50	11	11	2	1	2	1	10	1	4	1	0
Elvira, Narciso, Campeche *	0	1	.000	4.76	2	2	0	0	0	0	11.1	11	47	7	6	2	2	0	0	4	0	5	0	0
Escobedo, Edgar, Mexico-Oaxaca	0	1	.000	7.79	17	1	0	0	3	0	34.2	46	165	31	30	7	1	1	4	23	0	19	3	0
Espadas, Gary, Yucatan	2	2	.500	3.56	38	0	0	0	12	1	48.0	43	202	21	19	5	1	0	5	16	1	24	0	0
Esparza, Emerson, Laguna	2	1	.667	15.55	17	0	0	0	1	0	11.0	18	59	19	19	4	2	0	2	11	0	9	3	0
Espinoza, Omar, Puebla	1	4	.200	5.98	30	3	0	0	7	0	52.2	64	235	39	35	3	3	1	2	22	3	32	9	0
Esquer, Mercedes, San Luis Potosi *	3	7	.300	5.91	13	13	0	0	0	0	53.1	77	249	49	35	8	1	3	0	18	0	19	2	0
Estrada, Horacio, Oaxaca *	4	4	.500	4.04	13	12	1	0	1	0	82.1	108	370	46	37	12	6	3	6	27	0	54	3	0
Estrella, Leo, Laguna-Veracruz	3	8	.273	6.03	49	3	0	0	14	3	77.2	94	360	56	52	7	5	2	5	38	8	46	4	0
Federico, Gustavo, Puebla	3	4	.429	7.20	13	9	0	0	0	0	45.0	55	218	42	36	6	0	4	5	27	0	17	4	0
Felix, Francisco, Saltillo	0	2	.000	6.75	15	0	0	0	5	0	20.0	28	97	19	15	5	0	1	1	9	0	14	1	1
Fernandez, Osvaldo, Tabasco	7	9	.438	4.14	23	21	2	1	1	1	130.1	166	567	63	60	12	6	4	6	32	1	65	2	0
Flores, Ignacio, Saltillo-Angelopolis-Puebla	2	6	.250	10.66	15	10	0	0	2	0	38.0	65	201	53	45	9	0	1	3	22	2	25	3	0
Flores, Ignacio, Yucatan	1	6	.143	5.79	29	7	0	0	3	1	60.2	79	284	42	39	7	0	2	2	25	1	64	5	0
Flores, Jorge, Monclova *	3	0	1.000	4.99	49	0	0	0	6	0	52.1	75	238	31	29	3	2	3	3	11	3	27	2	0
Flores, Manuel, Yucatan	0	0	.000	0.00	2	0	0	0	1	0	2.0	3	8	0	0	0	0	0	0	0	0	0	1	0
Flores, Renato, Monclova	2	3	.400	7.14	38	0	0	0	9	1	46.2	52	226	38	37	10	0	4	2	37	4	34	0	0
Flores, Wilfrido, Tabasco	0	0	.000	8.22	18	0	0	0	3	1	23.0	35	110	21	21	6	0	2	5	9	2	6	1	0
Galvez, Randy, Oaxaca-Tabasco	0	3	.000	6.70	33	2	0	0	6	0	41.2	61	201	32	31	3	3	3	1	25	4	14	5	0

Pitcher, Team	W	L	Pct.	ERA	G	GS	CG	ShO	GF	Sv.	IP	H	TBF	R	ER	HR	SH	SF	HB	BB	IBB	SO	WP	Bk.
Garcia, Adolfo, Veracruz	2	1	.667	5.18	36	0	0	0	8	0	41.2	54	186	27	24	7	6	1	4	14	3	9	0	0
Garcia, Alfredo, Oaxaca	0	5	.000	8.35	6	5	0	0	0	0	18.1	29	98	20	17	3	0	0	0	14	1	11	1	0
Garcia, Carlos, Laguna	0	2	.000	15.09	5	4	0	0	0	0	11.1	30	70	19	19	1	0	1	0	7	0	6	0	1
Garcia, Gerardo, Angelopolis	2	0	1.000	2.45	8	3	0	0	0	0	22.0	22	96	8	6	1	0	1	4	6	0	14	3	0
Garcia, Humberto, San Luis Potosi *	2	2	.500	6.35	51	1	0	0	4	0	28.1	29	121	22	20	3	1	0	0	15	2	19	5	0
Garcia, Jonathan, Campeche	1	2	.333	7.44	22	0	0	0	6	0	32.2	41	158	32	27	11	1	1	1	21	1	16	3	0
Garcia, Jose Luis, Campeche *	4	3	.571	8.41	48	2	0	0	11	0	46.0	71	212	45	43	12	7	2	0	18	5	36	5	0
Garcia, Rafael, Aguascalientes-Cancun	0	4	.000	14.09	6	3	0	0	0	0	15.1	30	86	25	24	2	4	0	1	16	0	5	2	0
Garcia, Ramon Antonio, San Luis Potosi	1	3	.250	7.48	20	8	0	0	8	1	49.1	81	240	46	41	10	0	1	2	21	0	20	6	0
Garibaldi, Cecilio, Angelopolis	3	4	.429	5.11	35	0	0	0	7	1	49.1	57	221	31	28	5	2	2	0	27	1	29	4	0
Garibay, Roberto, Tijuana	7	2	.778	3.95	45	0	0	0	10	3	57.0	62	242	29	25	6	1	2	6	16	2	22	3	0
Garibay, Salvador, Tijuana	4	4	.500	5.61	46	0	0	0	7	1	61.0	68	258	42	38	8	6	3	0	19	8	20	3	0
Garza, Conrado, Cancun *	4	0	1.000	4.91	48	0	0	0	13	1	36.2	47	167	21	20	3	1	1	2	14	2	26	3	0
Garza, Luis, Cancun	1	1	.500	3.41	22	0	0	0	7	0	31.2	40	149	17	12	1	0	2	0	15	0	6	5	0
Giron, Isabel, Monterrey	6	2	.750	3.77	18	17	2	1	0	0	102.2	97	430	50	43	9	6	2	8	36	0	77	0	0
Gomes, Wayne, Yucatan-Saltillo	2	2	.500	4.97	13	0	0	0	12	5	12.2	15	53	8	7	0	1	1	1	6	2	9	1	0
Gomez, Martin, Laguna	4	8	.333	7.67	22	21	0	0	0	0	112.2	181	554	112	96	18	3	8	7	47	3	59	8	0
Gonzalez, Antonio, Tijuana	0	0	.000	9.00	2	0	0	0	1	0	1.0	2	7	0	0	0	0	0	0	1	0	0	0	0
Gonzalez, Gilberto, San Luis Potosi-Puebla	0	5	.000	8.68	19	5	0	0	2	0	28.0	53	147	31	27	6	0	1	2	12	0	19	5	1
Gonzalez, Leonardo, Tijuana	8	7	.533	7.79	23	23	0	0	0	0	106.1	146	527	102	92	18	1	4	9	60	0	84	10	0
Gonzalez, Mario, Monclova	1	0	1.000	2.16	3	1	0	0	0	0	8.1	5	33	2	2	2	0	0	0	3	0	3	0	0
Gonzalez, Miguel, Saltillo	5	7	.417	6.22	26	17	0	0	2	0	94.0	119	436	69	65	11	3	5	4	53	1	64	11	0
Gonzalez, Rudy, Mexico	8	7	.533	6.19	27	19	0	0	1	0	113.1	156	527	81	78	16	7	4	3	51	2	89	11	0
Gonzalez, Vinicio, Tabasco	6	8	.429	5.35	33	15	0	0	6	1	109.1	135	488	69	65	9	8	3	9	45	2	68	4	0
Gracia, Mario, Oaxaca	0	0	.000	16.20	1	0	0	0	0	0	1.2	3	9	3	3	2	0	0	1	1	0	0	0	0
Grajales, Norberto, Campeche	1	0	1.000	18.00	6	0	0	0	0	0	5.0	14	29	10	10	3	3	0	0	2	0	3	0	0
Guerrero, Fernando, Laguna	0	0	.000	5.84	9	0	0	0	3	0	12.1	18	59	9	8	1	0	0	1	6	0	5	3	0
Gutierrez, Carlos, Laguna	0	4	.000	7.06	21	0	0	0	9	0	29.1	38	141	31	23	2	0	1	4	16	1	17	3	0
Gutierrez, Jorge, Cancun-Laguna	2	4	.333	4.96	18	0	0	0	6	0	16.1	14	69	11	9	2	0	2	0	6	1	10	5	0
Gutierrez, Luis, Tijuana	0	1	.000	10.80	3	0	0	0	1	0	3.1	7	19	4	4	2	0	0	0	3	0	2	0	0
Guzman, Jesus, Angelopolis *	2	4	.333	6.43	28	17	0	0	3	0	77.0	102	347	59	55	9	2	0	4	27	3	34	7	0
Guzman, Ricardo, Monclova	1	4	.200	8.18	36	5	0	0	5	1	47.1	63	215	44	43	12	0	2	0	11	0	29	7	0
Hammond, Matthew, Tijuana	0	2	.000	7.36	7	1	0	0	2	0	11.0	15	54	9	9	1	1	0	0	9	3	13	1	0
Haro, Esteban, Angelopolis	0	0	.000	6.75	2	0	0	0	0	0	2.2	2	12	2	2	0	0	0	2	0	1	1	1	
Hermosillo, Victor, Laguna-Tabasco	0	0	.000	18.69	7	0	0	0	2	0	8.2	15	53	18	18	4	1	0	3	10	0	5	3	0
Hernandez, Adrian, Laguna	3	6	.333	5.34	18	15	1	0	1	0	94.1	113	426	59	56	12	0	0	7	43	1	74	4	0
Hernandez, Esteban, Oaxaca-Tijuana	2	3	.400	7.02	19	4	0	0	6	0	42.1	63	194	37	33	12	0	0	3	8	0	25	0	0
Hernandez, Fernando, Monterrey-Aguascalientes	4	3	.571	5.58	22	10	0	0	3	0	69.1	84	320	46	43	11	3	2	11	36	1	29	4	0
Hernandez, Jose Manuel, Veracruz-Puebla	0	1	.000	8.31	24	0	0	0	3	1	13.0	21	66	13	12	4	0	1	2	6	2	7	1	1
Hernandez, Santos, Tabasco-Puebla	1	6	.143	6.54	29	0	0	0	23	14	31.2	46	156	24	23	2	3	2	3	18	3	17	4	0
Herrera, Enrique, Tabasco	0	0	.000	6.00	11	0	0	0	2	0	9.0	13	45	8	6	2	0	1	3	3	0	1	1	0
Hildago, Romeo, Campeche	0	0	.000	7.97	16	0	0	0	2	0	20.1	25	93	22	18	5	0	0	5	6	0	9	3	0
Huerta, Armando, Laguna	0	0	.000	27.00	1	0	0	0	0	0	1.0	4	7	3	3	3	0	0	0	0	0	0	0	0
Huerta, Edgar, Angelopolis *	4	4	.500	5.55	25	0	0	0	5	1	24.1	37	114	15	15	1	0	0	1	6	0	20	3	0
Huerta, Martin, Laguna	2	0	1.000	10.23	20	0	0	0	4	0	22.0	36	121	25	25	4	0	1	3	23	1	13	6	1
Hurtado, Edwin, Monclova-Monterrey	8	10	.444	6.32	25	20	1	1	1	0	109.2	130	498	83	77	18	5	5	2	61	1	69	14	0
Jacome, Jason, Monclova-Puebla	6	6	.500	5.31	22	20	0	0	0	0	115.1	143	509	74	68	15	5	3	5	36	2	66	1	0
Jimenez, Jose De Jesus, Oaxaca	3	3	.500	5.28	48	3	0	0	8	1	44.1	47	190	31	26	5	5	0	3	23	4	38	3	1
Jimenez, Julio, Laguna *	2	5	.286	9.64	37	8	0	0	6	0	60.2	84	304	73	65	12	1	4	5	45	2	48	10	0
Johnson, Adam, Puebla	1	1	.500	9.00	5	5	0	0	0	0	21.0	37	102	25	21	7	1	0	2	7	0	16	0	0
Kamar, Emil, Angelopolis-Puebla	3	2	.600	8.35	34	3	0	0	15	5	46.1	64	224	47	43	6	3	1	3	29	0	19	2	0
Knott, Eric, Puebla *	14	4	.778	3.25	23	22	1	0	0	0	144.0	135	560	62	52	11	7	2	3	20	3	62	0	0
Lara, Jorge, Puebla-Tabasco	3	3	.500	8.72	29	1	0	0	5	0	32.0	55	157	31	31	9	1	1	2	10	1	16	1	0
Lara, Mauricio, Monterrey *	1	0	1.000	5.40	43	1	0	0	8	0	40.0	36	174	26	24	4	0	1	4	24	0	22	3	0
Larreal, Guillermo, Cancun	1	1	.500	3.97	10	0	0	0	8	4	11.1	15	48	5	5	1	2	0	1	4	2	4	0	0
Leon, Cupertino, Oaxaca	7	1	.875	4.53	45	0	0	0	11	0	51.2	59	224	28	26	6	2	4	3	19	2	20	0	0
Leon, Juan, Tabasco	0	1	.000	33.75	3	0	0	0	0	0	2.2	11	23	10	10	1	1	0	1	4	1	1	0	0
Leyva, Aldo, Yucatan *	0	0	.000	4.15	3	0	0	0	0	0	4.1	5	19	3	2	1	0	0	0	1	0	1	0	0
Leyva, Edgar, San Luis Potosi	3	5	.375	4.95	22	10	0	0	4	0	63.2	83	289	43	35	7	1	3	3	17	1	39	4	0
Lira, Felipe, Aguascalientes	0	1	.000	6.98	4	4	0	0	0	0	19.1	26	97	16	15	3	0	1	2	12	0	3	0	0
Lizarraga, Edgar, Mexico	2	1	.667	8.21	27	0	0	0	7	0	34.0	45	163	35	31	6	3	0	2	23	2	22	8	0
Lizarraga, Sergio, Monterrey	2	2	.500	4.50	8	5	1	1	1	0	34.0	40	153	21	17	3	1	3	4	15	0	27	2	0
Llamas, Eder, Angelopolis	1	0	1.000	7.50	7	0	0	0	2	1	12.0	20	61	10	10	3	0	0	0	6	1	5	1	0
Lomeli, Israel, Veracruz	1	4	.200	7.64	29	4	0	0	6	0	53.0	62	256	48	45	12	5	2	6	41	3	50	5	0
Lontayo, Alejandro, Oaxaca *	3	4	.429	6.79	12	12	0	0	0	0	58.1	71	273	46	44	10	3	3	3	37	1	36	9	2
Lopez, Daniel, Monclova	3	1	.750	3.21	9	6	0	0	1	0	42.0	36	172	15	15	6	0	0	2	12	0	18	3	0
Lopez, Emigdio, Veracruz	8	3	.727	3.78	20	20	1	0	0	0	112.0	109	461	56	47	18	7	3	6	25	1	54	1	0
Lopez, Jesus, Laguna	0	0	.000	10.67	12	0	0	0	6	0	14.1	22	78	19	17	7	0	2	2	10	0	23	3	0
Lopez, Jose, San Luis Potosi-Oaxaca	2	5	.286	5.63	39	0	0	0	18	8	40.0	55	180	26	25	6	3	1	13	4	25	1	0	
Lopez, Miguel, San Luis Potosi	3	0	1.000	5.31	49	0	0	0	10	0	40.2	46	186	27	24	4	4	5	3	23	3	21	2	0
Loya, Rigoberto, Monterrey	3	6	.333	6.84	21	15	0	0	2	0	77.2	102	365	65	59	10	1	3	38	0	25	3	1	
Luevano, Juan, Aguascalientes	2	2	.500	6.16	55	0	0	0	16	0	49.2	66	232	38	34	7	3	2	6	22	1	27	0	2
Lugo, Carlos, Tijuana *	0	0	.000	7.76	25	2	0	0	4	0	31.1	33	154	30	27	4	3	2	3	31	1	14	4	0
Lyons, Michael, Yucatan	0	0	.000	9.00	5	0	0	0	3	1	3.0	5	16	3	3	1	1	0	2	0	0	0	0	
Macias, Luis, Puebla	1	4	.200	7.90	42	3	0	0	9	0	49.0	61	247	46	43	9	0	1	6	5	42	1	25	0	
Madero, Francisco, Oaxaca	5	3	.625	4.70	19	12	0	0	2	0	82.1	95	354	50	43	8	4	3	3	28	1	52	4	1
Magee, Daniel, Campeche *	5	3	.625	3.99	18	13	1	0	0	0	76.2	78	332	39	34	11	6	1	0	47	0	46	3	0
Mairena, Oswaldo, Oaxaca-Laguna	3	13	.188	8.12	25	22	0	0	1	0	112.0	167	543	111	101	23	3	3	2	49	0	73	0	0
Manning, David, Campeche	6	1	.857	3.74	33	5	0	0	5	0	53.0	53	229	26	22	6	3	1	1	26	1	41	4	0
Manrique, Alberto, San Luis Potosi-Campeche	1	5	.167	9.47	26	7	0	0	3	0	57.0	89	293	69	60	11	0	4	6	31	0	31	4	0
Manzanillo, Josias, Puebla	2	5	.286	7.45	26	4	0	0	17	5	38.2	58	194	36	32	9	1	2	5	21	5	26	3	0

Pitcher, Team	W	L	Pct.	ERA	G	GS	CG	ShO	GF	Sv.	IP	H	TBF	R	ER	HR	SH	SF	HB	BB	IBB	SO	WP	Bk.
Manzanillo, Ravelo, Puebla *	2	1	.667	6.98	4	4	0	0	0	0	19.1	23	87	15	15	0	1	2	1	13	0	7	2	0
Manzano, Adrian, Angelopolis	1	2	.333	2.92	35	0	0	0	31	15	37.0	28	145	16	12	5	4	1	2	10	4	25	2	0
Mariscal, Jesus, Angelopolis	0	0	.000	1.00	10	0	0	0	5	0	18.0	12	71	2	2	1	0	0	1	6	0	11	2	0
Marquez, Isidro, Campeche	3	2	.600	1.85	38	0	0	0	38	25	39.0	35	154	12	8	2	1	1	2	7	0	32	0	0
Martinez, Cesar, Tijuana-Laguna	5	4	.556	9.51	25	12	0	0	1	0	58.2	106	311	67	62	14	2	1	9	37	1	33	3	0
Martinez, Gustavo, Cancun	1	1	.500	7.64	4	4	0	0	0	0	17.2	26	89	17	15	1	0	0	2	9	0	3	1	0
Martinez, Juan Jesus, Aguascalientes-Cancun	2	6	.250	7.23	26	8	0	0	3	0	69.2	104	339	64	56	15	3	5	3	39	1	19	9	0
Medina, Roberto, Puebla *	0	0	.000	4.50	4	0	0	0	1	0	2.0	1	8	1	1	0	0	0	0	1	0	1	0	0
Medrano, Leobardo, Monterrey	0	0	.000	22.50	2	0	0	0	0	0	2.0	5	15	5	5	0	0	1	1	2	0	1	2	0
Melgarejo, Thomas, Saltillo *	0	0	.000	3.97	31	1	0	0	5	0	22.2	22	100	11	10	3	1	0	0	19	0	14	3	0
Mendoza, Mario, Saltillo	3	3	.500	3.55	51	0	0	0	11	2	66.0	70	283	31	26	2	0	0	4	23	5	44	3	0
Mercedes, Jose, Saltillo	4	6	.400	6.67	15	13	2	1	2	0	86.1	121	410	66	64	14	2	3	7	37	0	57	3	0
Meyer, Jake, Oaxaca	0	0	.000	27.00	1	1	0	0	0	0	1.0	2	8	3	3	0	0	0	0	3	0	1	0	0
Meza, Jorge, Tijuana *	1	0	1.000	5.06	15	0	0	0	2	0	16.0	13	69	10	9	2	0	0	0	8	1	29	3	0
Molina, Gabe, San Luis Potosi	7	9	.438	5.86	34	15	0	0	16	6	110.2	127	513	78	72	8	2	5	7	55	4	80	8	0
Montano, Ignacio, Cancun-Aguascalientes	8	3	.727	4.76	19	18	1	0	0	0	115.1	136	499	65	61	16	2	4	6	38	1	72	5	1
Montemayor, Humberto, San Luis Potosi	7	7	.500	5.65	24	23	0	0	0	0	127.1	167	561	91	80	24	8	2	5	30	0	81	3	1
Montoya, Francisco, San Luis Potosi	2	3	.400	7.35	24	6	0	0	2	0	60.0	90	314	50	49	6	1	2	4	53	2	39	5	0
Mora, Eleazar, Oaxaca *	7	3	.700	5.83	32	14	2	1	1	1	92.2	149	440	71	60	16	4	5	6	23	0	44	3	0
Mora, Sergio, Monterrey	8	2	.800	5.18	40	2	0	0	7	0	57.1	57	246	33	33	10	0	3	2	24	1	42	4	0
Morales, Luis Fernando, Veracruz *	4	2	.667	7.94	13	8	0	0	0	0	39.2	61	192	37	35	6	1	1	1	18	1	26	1	0
Morales, Reynaldo, Oaxaca	0	0	.000	6.75	16	2	0	0	4	0	25.1	30	122	19	19	5	0	0	3	19	0	16	4	0
Moreno, Angel, Veracruz *	6	5	.545	5.95	21	20	0	0	0	0	98.1	150	462	77	65	12	6	1	2	30	1	50	3	0
Moreno, Claudio, Mexico	10	10	.500	5.76	25	22	1	0	0	0	140.2	170	625	97	90	25	4	4	4	56	0	62	4	0
Moreno, Leobardo, Veracruz *	2	2	.500	2.34	40	0	0	0	9	0	34.2	33	136	9	9	4	0	1	0	6	0	21	0	0
Munoz, Leonardo, Angelopolis *	1	2	.333	5.29	41	0	0	0	11	2	32.1	35	148	20	19	3	0	0	0	14	0	21	3	0
Munoz, Pablo, Aguascalientes-Cancun	0	4	.000	11.23	29	3	0	0	5	1	33.2	72	188	52	42	11	2	3	2	15	0	6	3	0
Murguia, Edgar, Laguna	0	0	.000	18.00	4	0	0	0	0	0	3.0	7	22	6	6	1	0	0	0	7	0	2	1	0
Navarro, Hector, Veracruz-Angelopolis	5	4	.556	7.83	40	0	0	0	5	1	46.0	67	215	44	40	5	6	4	3	18	2	21	1	0
Navarro, Joel, Oaxaca-Tijuana	4	4	.500	7.33	25	12	0	0	3	0	81.0	112	371	67	66	21	3	4	4	31	2	35	2	2
Navarro, Jose Felix, Monclova-Veracruz	2	0	1.000	6.82	22	1	0	0	3	0	33.0	49	160	26	25	9	1	0	4	13	1	22	5	0
Navarro, Luis, Yucatan	3	1	.750	3.34	39	0	0	0	9	2	35.0	32	143	13	13	1	2	4	2	15	1	22	1	0
Neri, Eduardo, Tijuana *	1	1	.500	6.28	22	0	0	0	7	0	14.1	14	62	10	10	1	3	0	0	11	2	9	1	0
Nieblas, Mauro, Monterrey *	2	0	1.000	5.84	28	1	0	0	2	0	37.0	43	169	26	24	5	1	1	1	21	0	27	1	0
Nieblas, Omar, Cancun *	1	4	.200	8.08	21	8	0	0	0	0	45.2	60	217	42	41	8	0	1	1	25	0	18	6	0
Nunez, Javier, Aguascalientes-Cancun	0	2	.000	7.85	30	1	0	0	6	1	55.0	85	268	52	48	6	2	2	4	31	1	23	8	0
Nunez, Jose, Puebla	4	3	.571	4.91	58	0	0	0	18	4	58.2	64	255	36	32	8	6	3	4	22	4	35	6	1
Nunez, Jose, Aguascalientes	2	5	.286	6.75	9	9	0	0	0	0	48.0	78	220	37	36	10	3	3	0	9	0	15	2	0
Ochoa, Pablo, Monterrey	9	8	.529	5.61	23	21	0	0	1	0	112.1	125	504	78	70	15	1	2	7	60	2	66	6	0
Olague, Jesus, Angelopolis	9	4	.692	6.36	22	21	0	0	0	0	99.0	116	445	75	70	17	4	4	3	59	0	60	2	0
Orea, Flavio, Aguascalientes	6	3	.667	7.49	45	0	0	0	12	4	45.2	55	200	39	38	13	2	3	3	13	3	24	0	0
Oropesa, Eddie, Tabasco *	0	2	.000	2.92	26	0	0	0	7	2	24.2	25	110	11	8	0	2	1	1	18	2	19	2	0
Orrantia, Carlos, Monterrey	0	0	.000	13.50	1	0	0	0	0	0	0.2	2	4	2	1	1	0	0	0	0	0	0	0	0
Ortega, Pablo, Angelopolis	8	5	.615	4.45	23	21	0	0	0	0	115.1	136	497	61	57	13	0	2	5	38	0	51	3	0
Ortega, Roberto, Puebla *	0	2	.000	4.79	37	0	0	0	7	0	20.2	25	92	11	11	1	3	1	1	16	2	5	0	1
Ortega, Wilbert, Yucatan *	1	0	1.000	5.89	37	0	0	0	6	1	18.1	25	81	13	12	3	0	0	0	4	2	14	2	0
Osuna, Adrian, Oaxaca	0	0	.000	18.00	1	0	0	0	1	0	1.0	1	5	2	2	1	0	0	0	1	0	0	1	0
Osuna, Ulises, San Luis Potosi	0	1	.000	6.75	5	1	0	0	1	0	6.2	10	34	5	5	1	0	0	0	6	1	4	1	0
Pablos, Rene, Saltillo *	0	2	.000	6.16	22	2	0	0	3	2	30.2	36	140	23	21	6	2	0	1	19	1	20	9	0
Palafox, Juan Manuel, Yucatan	10	5	.667	4.30	19	18	1	0	0	0	102.2	110	447	51	49	6	6	2	4	52	0	45	4	0
Palki, Jeromy, Yucatan	3	1	.750	2.70	12	0	0	0	6	1	13.1	12	52	4	4	1	1	0	1	3	1	5	1	0
Palma, Ricardo, Cancun-Aguascalientes	6	4	.600	5.97	16	16	0	0	0	0	98.0	125	442	70	65	10	5	5	4	37	1	63	7	0
Parra, Julio, Tijuana	4	1	.800	2.32	40	0	0	0	8	3	42.2	38	179	13	11	3	3	3	1	20	4	38	6	1
Parra, Orlando, Campeche *	0	0	.000	2.45	8	0	0	0	4	0	7.1	6	32	6	2	1	0	1	0	4	0	6	2	0
Patrick, Bronswell, Tabasco-Yucatan	3	3	.500	6.91	12	10	0	0	1	0	54.2	88	260	46	42	7	2	1	1	18	0	27	0	0
Pena, Joel, Tabasco	1	1	.500	6.14	20	0	0	0	9	0	14.2	15	63	10	10	3	3	0	1	8	1	5	0	0
Pena, Juan, Aguascalientes	2	2	.500	7.12	7	7	0	0	0	0	36.2	52	174	31	29	8	1	0	3	13	0	31	1	1
Perez, Edgar, Cancun-Aguascalientes	7	6	.538	5.28	20	20	1	0	0	0	119.1	150	542	74	70	18	1	8	7	49	0	64	6	0
Perez, Guadalupe, Veracruz-Cancun-Aguascalientes	5	6	.455	5.87	32	11	1	0	8	2	84.1	109	392	59	55	16	0	3	6	35	1	54	3	0
Perez, Manuel, San Luis Potosi *	0	0	.000	9.00	14	0	0	0	0	0	4.0	11	27	4	4	1	1	0	0	6	0	2	0	0
Perez, Miguel, Saltillo	5	3	.625	4.68	29	5	0	0	4	1	67.1	76	304	40	35	4	2	1	4	34	4	65	5	0
Pimentel, Roberto, Tabasco *	1	3	.250	6.35	40	1	0	0	4	0	34.0	44	147	25	24	6	5	2	1	11	1	19	1	0
Pina, Rafael, Veracruz	2	9	.182	8.80	21	14	0	0	1	0	75.2	112	371	78	74	12	3	7	11	41	0	36	14	0
Pinales, Aquiles, Cancun	0	3	.000	10.48	5	5	0	0	0	0	22.1	36	122	27	26	3	2	1	3	20	0	10	1	0
Pineda, Isauro, Monterrey	6	7	.462	5.63	20	20	0	0	0	0	96.0	98	441	61	60	12	2	4	9	64	0	66	8	0
Pizzaro, Melvin, Yucatan *	1	1	.500	2.57	12	0	0	0	3	0	14.0	10	61	5	4	0	1	0	1	10	1	7	4	0
Pons, Christian, Monclova	0	1	.000	27.00	1	0	0	0	...	0	0.2	2	6	2	2	0	...	...	...	2	1	0	...	...
Posadas, Obedt, Saltillo-Laguna	2	6	.250	7.94	22	14	0	0	1	0	79.1	125	403	73	70	14	1	5	14	36	0	31	11	1
Pulido, Carlos, Oaxaca *	7	7	.500	4.72	23	23	3	1	0	0	150.2	179	649	88	79	21	5	2	1	37	1	67	3	0
Pulido, Raymundo, Campeche-Laguna	1	0	1.000	6.43	16	0	0	0	5	0	21.0	22	95	16	15	4	1	4	1	16	1	7	2	1
Quinones, Enrique, San Luis Potosi	2	8	.200	7.92	25	9	0	0	4	0	75.0	116	354	74	66	11	5	4	8	22	0	25	2	0
Quintanilla, Juan, Oaxaca	4	3	.571	5.25	37	5	0	0	22	8	72.0	94	330	45	42	8	2	4	8	28	2	33	1	0
Quiroz, Aaron, Tijuana	4	5	.444	5.95	17	17	0	0	0	0	78.2	101	368	60	52	11	1	1	5	34	0	30	3	0
Raggio, Brady, Campeche	2	2	.500	6.00	8	5	1	0	0	0	30.0	36	128	23	20	8	1	0	0	3	0	18	1	0
Ramirez, Adrian, Monclova *	4	2	.667	4.55	43	0	0	0	7	0	29.2	44	139	21	15	2	4	1	0	11	3	26	2	0
Ramirez, Omar, Veracruz	0	0	.000	0.00	1	0	0	0	1	0	1.0	1	4	0	0	0	0	0	0	0	0	0	0	0
Ramirez, Roberto, Mexico *	10	8	.556	6.12	24	24	2	0	0	0	145.2	206	660	106	99	20	6	6	9	52	0	63	4	1
Ramon, Jose, Tabasco	1	1	.500	7.15	14	0	0	0	3	0	11.1	15	50	9	9	3	1	0	1	3	0	6	0	0
Ramos, Eddy, Monclova-Yucatan	3	5	.375	5.60	28	6	1	1	7	1	62.2	77	269	42	39	8	1	1	1	23	2	29	3	0
Renovato, Nestor, San Luis Potosi	6	2	.750	5.86	39	4	1	0	7	2	90.2	112	407	65	59	12	1	0	4	38	4	32	4	0
Reyes, Nathanael, Campeche *	4	4	.500	6.52	19	11	0	0	2	0	48.1	65	230	37	35	11	2	1	4	26	2	21	3	0

Pitcher, Team	W	L	Pct.	ERA	G	GS	CG	ShO	GF	Sv.	IP	H	TBF	R	ER	HR	SH	SF	HB	BB	IBB	SO	WP	Bk.
Rios, Alejandro, Saltillo	1	3	.250	6.33	34	0	0	0	9	0	42.2	53	188	31	30	6	3	0	1	16	1	25	4	0
Rios, Jesus, Tabasco	8	3	.727	3.42	21	21	1	1	0	0	123.2	140	532	53	47	10	8	3	14	32	1	80	3	0
Rivera, Bienvenido, Laguna-Aguascalientes	5	5	.500	3.78	44	0	0	0	38	14	51.1	43	202	23	22	8	5	0	2	13	1	55	4	0
Rivera, Francisco, Aguascalientes	5	11	.313	6.08	25	20	0	0	0	0	131.2	174	584	94	89	23	3	5	11	38	0	71	9	0
Rivera, Luis, Angelopolis	8	5	.615	5.42	23	19	0	0	1	0	89.2	102	427	60	54	4	2	6	11	64	0	39	6	1
Rivera, Oscar, Yucatan *	7	6	.538	3.92	20	20	0	0	0	0	114.2	126	483	55	50	7	2	3	4	31	0	92	5	3
Rivera, Oscar, Saltillo	2	3	.400	5.43	24	10	0	0	3	0	58.0	74	288	41	35	8	2	1	7	49	1	29	4	0
Rivera, Paul, Tabasco *	0	0	.000	4.31	40	0	0	0	8	0	31.1	34	136	19	15	1	0	2	11	0	9	3	0
Roberts, Willis, Campeche	1	3	.250	1.86	29	0	0	0	9	0	38.2	34	154	12	8	0	3	1	2	6	1	43	4	0
Rodriguez, Enoc, Aguascalientes *	3	0	1.000	5.84	30	7	0	0	8	1	49.1	59	234	34	32	11	1	3	1	34	1	19	6	0
Rodriguez, Francisco, Oaxaca *	0	0	.000	1.23	6	0	0	0	2	0	7.1	4	30	1	1	1	0	1	0	3	1	3	0	0
Rodriguez, Francisco, Puebla	4	4	.500	5.61	33	10	0	0	2	0	85.0	94	374	58	53	10	2	1	7	45	1	36	5	0
Rodriguez, Jesus, Monclova	6	4	.600	5.40	26	15	0	0	2	0	98.1	112	430	63	59	8	3	5	1	41	2	31	3	0
Rodriguez, Manuel, Campeche	0	0	.000	9.00	1	0	0	0	1	0	1.0	2	6	1	1	0	0	0	0	1	0	0	0	0
Rodriguez, Nerio, Monclova	4	1	.800	3.44	10	10	2	1	0	0	68.0	68	276	32	26	9	0	3	3	11	0	40	2	0
Rodriguez, Raul, Monclova-Yucatan	3	10	.231	4.72	21	19	0	0	0	0	108.2	132	471	66	57	12	2	6	8	26	0	46	5	0
Rodriguez, Rosario, Tijuana *	1	1	.500	6.30	18	0	0	0	1	0	10.0	13	50	9	7	1	1	1	1	7	1	6	2	0
Romero, Josmir, Oaxaca	4	2	.667	4.59	9	9	1	1	0	0	51.0	61	223	28	26	7	0	4	2	15	0	29	3	1
Romo, Noe, Puebla *	3	4	.429	6.03	28	11	0	0	0	0	71.2	79	324	50	48	6	0	4	3	43	1	39	6	3
Roque, Jorge, Cancun	0	0	.000	7.50	8	0	0	0	2	0	6.0	9	32	5	5	1	0	0	0	4	0	4	0	0
Roque, Rafael, Puebla-Monterrey	0	1	.000	32.40	2	2	0	0	0	0	1.2	6	15	6	6	2	0	0	0	5	0	2	1	0
Rubio, Carlos, Cancun	0	0	.000	9.20	9	1	0	0	4	0	14.2	16	79	16	15	4	0	2	4	16	0	3	5	0
Rubio, Miguel, Monterrey	6	1	.857	4.34	33	0	0	0	12	1	37.1	32	161	18	18	5	1	1	2	16	1	33	2	0
Ruelas, Heriberto, Mexico *	0	2	.000	11.25	35	0	0	0	4	0	16.0	26	84	21	20	2	0	0	3	8	0	16	3	0
Ruiz, Arturo, Saltillo *	0	0	.000	5.29	28	0	0	0	4	0	17.0	22	72	10	10	2	1	0	1	7	0	12	1	0
Ruiz, Cecilio, Tabasco *	0	0	.000	10.80	3	0	0	0	1	0	3.1	7	18	4	4	3	0	0	0	1	0	1	2	0
Ruiz, Miguel, Campeche	2	0	1.000	4.30	7	1	0	0	0	0	14.2	15	64	7	7	2	0	0	0	5	0	3	3	0
Sabido, Eduardo, Veracruz	0	0	.000	16.87	2	0	0	0	0	0	2.2	6	15	5	5	0	0	0	0	2	0	1	1	0
Saipe, Mike, Saltillo	1	1	.500	8.64	2	2	0	0	0	0	8.1	17	42	8	8	1	0	1	1	1	0	3	0	0
Salas, Noel, Saltillo	0	0	.000	2.08	14	1	0	0	4	0	17.1	21	80	8	4	1	0	1	0	10	0	12	3	0
Saldana, Jose, Cancun-Puebla	0	2	.000	10.70	8	2	0	0	1	0	17.2	43	96	24	21	7	1	3	1	4	0	7	0	0
Salgado, Eduardo, Cancun	6	11	.353	5.48	30	17	2	1	4	0	131.1	175	579	86	80	20	4	3	8	27	3	69	4	0
Sanchez, Alejandro, Cancun	4	2	.667	5.65	53	0	0	0	21	3	63.2	76	292	41	40	12	3	1	4	36	2	41	1	0
Sanchez, Claudio, Veracruz	2	1	.667	7.46	46	0	0	0	12	0	44.2	73	218	40	37	9	0	3	2	14	1	13	3	0
Sanchez, Efrain, Campeche	8	4	.667	5.23	24	16	1	0	2	0	105.0	121	465	67	61	17	6	4	5	44	1	42	5	0
Sanchez, Jose, Tijuana	1	0	1.000	11.05	7	0	0	0	2	0	7.1	14	43	9	9	1	0	0	1	9	0	2	1	0
Sangeado, Juan, Cancun	0	0	.000	4.91	6	0	0	0	0	0	11.0	15	51	6	6	3	2	0	0	5	0	8	1	0
Serrano, Elio, Tabasco-Laguna	3	5	.375	5.48	41	0	0	0	16	3	47.2	49	204	29	29	7	3	3	3	20	3	37	8	0
Serrano, Wascar, Campeche-Yucatan	1	2	.333	12.79	8	6	0	0	0	0	19.0	33	103	30	27	5	1	1	1	13	0	13	6	0
Shibilo, Andy, Tijuana	1	0	1.000	2.60	13	0	0	0	11	5	17.1	12	68	5	5	2	1	0	0	6	0	19	2	0
Silva, Jose, Mexico	4	6	.400	6.03	43	5	0	0	29	17	68.2	102	320	46	46	6	4	3	4	28	1	37	7	0
Silva, Walter, Monterrey	0	2	.000	13.08	12	0	0	0	3	0	21.1	39	115	31	31	3	1	0	3	14	1	17	0	0
Simas, Bill, Monclova	4	6	.400	2.82	55	0	0	0	50	21	70.1	64	292	28	22	6	5	2	1	24	7	59	0	1
Sinohui, David, Tijuana-Monclova	2	4	.333	8.54	30	0	0	0	21	8	26.1	37	133	28	25	6	1	2	3	11	3	15	8	0
Solis, Tomas, Angelopolis *	0	0	.000	12.27	6	0	0	0	1	0	3.2	7	19	5	5	2	0	0	1	0	0	1	0	0
Soria, Joakim, Mexico	5	0	1.000	4.48	30	5	0	0	4	0	66.1	75	299	34	33	7	0	4	4	31	0	60	4	0
Sotelo, Martin, Mexico	0	0	.000	0.00	2	0	0	0	2	0	3.1	2	14	0	0	0	0	0	1	1	0	1	0	0
Soto, Cruz Antonio, Puebla	1	4	.200	5.63	26	4	0	0	8	1	40.0	49	187	28	25	4	0	2	5	22	1	23	1	0
Sparks, Jeff, Yucatan	0	0	.000	6.75	3	0	0	0	1	0	2.2	2	14	2	2	0	0	0	1	4	0	4	0	0
Sulu, Mario, Tabasco	0	1	.000	7.53	14	0	0	0	5	0	14.1	22	71	12	12	2	1	2	3	4	0	8	2	0
Tejeda, Felix, Veracruz *	0	0	.000	18.00	7	0	0	0	2	0	3.0	8	18	6	6	1	0	0	0	1	0	0	0	0
Tequida, Mauricio, Mexico	4	1	.800	4.11	44	0	0	0	11	0	50.1	48	216	26	23	3	2	2	5	29	2	22	3	0
Torres, Jorge, Oaxaca *	0	0	.000	6.55	22	0	0	0	0	0	11.0	11	47	9	8	2	1	1	0	6	1	4	0	0
Trevino, Jesus, Laguna *	0	0	.000	7.62	17	0	0	0	3	0	13.0	13	54	11	11	4	2	0	1	6	0	13	1	0
Urdaneta, Lino, Aguascalientes-Cancun	4	3	.571	3.49	32	0	0	0	30	13	38.2	42	163	19	15	2	4	2	12	4	23	4	0
Valdez, Armando, Puebla	0	4	.000	5.01	7	7	0	0	0	0	23.1	36	110	19	13	2	1	1	3	8	0	8	1	0
Valdez, Joel, Oaxaca	0	0	.000	10.80	3	0	0	0	1	0	1.2	2	11	2	2	1	0	1	3	1	0	1	0	0
Valenzuela, Jose, Angelopolis	0	0	.000	18.69	9	0	0	0	3	0	8.2	17	50	18	18	3	1	2	1	8	0	3	0	0
Valerio, Julio, Mexico *	0	0	.000	4.20	32	0	0	0	1	0	15.0	24	69	7	7	3	0	2	0	3	1	6	1	0
Vargas, Joel, Tabasco	9	5	.643	3.81	21	21	0	0	0	0	127.2	149	544	60	54	9	2	7	6	20	0	58	2	1
Vargas, Jose, Laguna-Yucatan	3	4	.429	6.81	33	0	0	0	18	6	39.2	48	189	35	30	6	4	2	5	18	3	57	1	0
Vazquez, Adrian, Cancun-Veracruz	2	2	.500	8.35	21	1	0	0	2	0	36.2	55	178	34	34	6	1	2	5	18	0	15	1	1
Vega, Obed, Cancun-Veracruz	0	0	.000	3.44	6	6	0	0	0	0	18.1	16	79	7	7	1	0	1	3	6	0	6	2	0
Verdugo, Hugo, Laguna	3	7	.300	7.63	31	8	0	0	4	0	59.0	67	280	52	50	6	1	1	8	41	1	48	6	0
Verdugo, Oswaldo, Yucatan-Laguna	5	2	.714	4.28	37	2	0	0	12	2	69.1	80	306	35	33	6	4	2	1	35	1	51	7	0
Verdugo, Roberto, Angelopolis-San Luis Potosi	0	1	.000	6.37	33	0	0	0	4	0	35.1	53	174	28	25	5	3	3	6	14	1	13	3	1
Viera, Rolando, Tabasco *	0	0	.000	6.43	6	0	0	0	2	0	7.0	11	36	5	5	2	1	1	0	6	1	4	0	0
Villalobos, Fernando, Monterrey-San Luis Potosi	5	3	.625	5.94	17	7	0	0	0	1	53.0	57	238	41	35	8	1	2	2	23	0	39	5	0
Villarreal, Salvador, San Luis Potosi	1	2	.333	4.14	38	0	0	0	9	0	50.0	54	222	29	23	6	1	3	2	26	1	33	1	0
Vizcarra, Ernesto, Campeche	0	0	1.000	6.02	42	0	0	0	10	1	43.1	59	191	31	29	7	0	1	1	6	1	26	3	0
Vizcarra, William, Yucatan-Monclova	3	2	.600	7.40	36	5	0	0	6	0	62.0	98	289	54	51	6	1	3	18	0	23	2	0
Ward, Bryan, Monclova *	6	8	.429	4.84	21	20	0	0	0	0	115.1	140	510	71	62	14	6	7	6	41	1	77	5	0
Zambrano, Baudel, Angelopolis	8	0	1.000	4.06	36	0	0	0	12	2	62.0	56	260	29	28	5	1	4	0	35	3	17	3	1
Zavala, Marcos, Monterrey *	0	0	.000	12.32	24	0	0	0	2	0	19.0	35	101	30	26	6	2	0	0	11	0	11	1	0

PITCHERS WITH TWO OR MORE TEAMS

Pitcher, Team	W	L	Pct.	ERA	G	GS	CG	ShO	GF	Sv.	IP	H	TBF	R	ER	HR	SH	SF	HB	BB	IBB	SO	WP	Bk.
Ahumada, Edgar, Saltillo *	0	0	.000	6.00	5	0	0	0	0	0	3.0	5	22	2	2	0	0	0	2	6	0	0	0	0
Ahumada, Edgar, Laguna *	1	1	.500	12.00	19	0	0	0	2	0	9.0	14	51	12	12	2	0	0	1	11	0	3	1	0
Alvarez, Gabriel, Mexico	0	0	.000	9.00	7	0	0	0	4	0	6.0	12	33	6	6	0	0	0	0	5	0	3	5	0
Alvarez, Gabriel, Monclova	0	1	.000	9.58	10	0	0	0	2	0	10.1	14	52	11	11	1	0	0	0	9	0	3	3	0

Pitcher, Team	W	L	Pct.	ERA	G	GS	CG	ShO	GF	Sv.	IP	H	TBF	R	ER	HR	SH	SF	HB	BB	IBB	SO	WP	Bk.
Castaneda, Federico, Laguna	0	0	.000	4.40	11	0	0	0	1	0	14.1	20	69	7	7	2	0	0	1	6	0	10	0	0
Castaneda, Federico, Aguascalientes	0	0	.000	3.86	7	2	0	0	3	0	14.0	16	62	8	6	1	0	0	0	8	0	10	0	0
Cazares, Rosario, Saltillo	1	0	1.000	9.90	10	0	0	0	2	0	10.0	11	45	12	11	4	0	1	1	3	0	10	2	1
Cazares, Rosario, Cancun	1	4	.200	5.45	10	7	0	0	1	0	34.2	44	158	26	21	5	2	2	3	8	0	27	3	0
Cobos, Jose, Monterrey	0	1	.000	6.11	21	0	0	0	8	0	28.0	34	138	19	19	2	1	2	3	18	1	16	2	0
Cobos, Jose, San Luis Potosi	0	0	.000	3.18	4	0	0	0	3	0	5.2	4	21	2	2	0	0	0	0	2	0	6	1	0
Coco, Pasqual, Saltillo	5	0	1.000	5.89	18	5	0	0	11	2	44.1	48	202	31	29	10	5	0	4	25	2	35	1	0
Coco, Pasqual, Veracruz	4	5	.444	4.10	11	11	2	2	0	0	59.1	55	262	31	27	5	0	3	4	31	0	62	7	0
Dominguez, Carlos, Saltillo *	0	1	.000	16.20	6	0	0	0	0	0	1.2	3	10	3	3	0	0	0	0	2	0	1	2	0
Dominguez, Carlos, Angelopolis *	0	0	.000	13.14	10	0	0	0	3	0	12.1	22	64	18	18	2	0	0	0	8	2	6	1	0
Dominguez, Carlos, Puebla *	0	0	.000	8.53	20	1	0	0	2	0	19.0	21	89	18	18	7	0	0	1	11	0	11	1	0
Escobedo, Edgar, Mexico	0	1	.000	8.69	10	1	0	0	3	0	19.2	24	94	20	19	5	0	0	2	15	0	8	3	0
Escobedo, Edgar, Oaxaca	0	0	.000	6.60	7	0	0	0	0	0	15.0	22	71	11	11	2	1	1	2	8	0	11	0	0
Estrella, Leo, Laguna	0	2	.000	15.43	3	3	0	0	0	0	11.2	19	64	21	20	3	0	0	1	7	0	8	1	0
Estrella, Leo, Veracruz	3	6	.333	4.36	46	0	0	0	14	3	66.0	75	296	35	32	4	5	2	4	31	8	38	3	0
Flores, Ignacio, Saltillo	2	3	.400	7.77	6	6	0	0	0	0	22.0	33	106	22	19	3	0	0	2	8	1	15	1	0
Flores, Ignacio, Angelopolis	0	1	.000	18.00	4	1	0	0	1	0	6.0	11	37	12	12	1	0	0	0	7	0	2	1	0
Flores, Ignacio, Puebla	0	2	.000	12.60	5	3	0	0	1	0	10.0	21	58	19	14	5	0	1	1	7	1	8	1	0
Galvez, Randy, Oaxaca	0	2	.000	9.00	12	2	0	0	1	0	16.0	28	84	17	16	2	1	0	0	12	0	7	0	0
Galvez, Randy, Tabasco	0	1	.000	5.26	21	0	0	0	5	0	25.2	33	117	15	15	1	2	3	1	13	4	7	5	0
Garcia, Rafael, Aguascalientes	0	1	.000	31.50	3	0	0	0	1	0	2.0	7	17	8	7	0	0	0	0	5	0	2	0	0
Garcia, Rafael, Cancun	0	1	.000	11.48	3	3	0	0	0	0	13.1	23	69	17	17	2	4	0	1	11	0	3	2	0
Gomes, Wayne, Yucatan	1	2	.333	5.91	11	0	0	0	10	4	10.2	12	45	8	7	0	1	1	1	5	2	9	1	0
Gomes, Wayne, Saltillo	1	0	1.000	0.00	2	0	0	0	2	1	2.0	3	8	0	0	0	0	0	0	1	0	0	0	0
Gonzalez, Gilberto, San Luis Potosi	0	1	.000	6.00	11	1	0	0	2	0	9.0	12	45	8	6	1	0	0	1	5	0	9	1	0
Gonzalez, Gilberto, Puebla	0	4	.000	9.95	8	4	0	0	0	0	19.0	41	102	23	21	5	0	1	1	7	0	10	4	1
Gutierrez, Jorge, Cancun	1	4	.200	5.40	15	0	0	0	5	0	13.1	13	59	10	8	2	0	2	0	5	1	8	4	0
Gutierrez, Jorge, Laguna	1	0	1.000	3.00	3	0	0	0	1	0	3.0	1	10	1	1	0	0	0	0	1	0	2	1	0
Hermosillo, Victor, Laguna	0	0	.000	18.69	7	0	0	0	2	0	8.2	15	53	18	18	4	1	0	3	10	0	5	2	0
Hernandez, Esteban, Oaxaca	0	0	.000	10.80	8	0	0	0	3	0	10.0	18	52	12	12	3	0	0	2	4	0	3	0	0
Hernandez, Esteban, Tijuana	2	3	.400	5.85	11	4	0	0	3	0	32.1	45	142	25	21	9	0	0	1	4	0	22	0	0
Hernandez, Fernando, Monterrey	2	2	.500	5.28	6	6	0	0	0	0	30.2	33	135	18	18	2	1	1	8	16	0	10	3	0
Hernandez, Fernando, Aguascalientes	2	1	.667	5.82	16	4	0	0	3	0	38.2	51	185	28	25	9	2	1	3	20	1	19	1	0
Hernandez, Jose Manuel, Veracruz *	0	0	.000	6.35	9	0	0	0	2	0	5.2	8	28	5	4	1	0	1	0	3	1	6	1	1
Hernandez, Jose Manuel, Puebla *	0	1	.000	9.82	15	0	0	0	1	1	7.1	13	38	8	8	3	0	0	2	3	1	1	0	0
Hernandez, Santos, Tabasco	1	5	.167	6.63	18	0	0	0	13	10	19.0	30	94	14	14	0	2	1	2	10	2	10	3	0
Hernandez, Santos, Puebla	0	1	.000	6.39	11	0	0	0	10	4	12.2	16	62	10	9	2	1	1	1	8	1	7	1	0
Hurtado, Edwin, Monclova	3	5	.375	7.31	12	9	0	0	1	0	44.1	59	217	41	36	7	0	2	1	33	0	25	9	0
Hurtado, Edwin, Monterrey	5	5	.500	5.65	13	11	1	1	0	0	65.1	71	281	42	41	11	5	3	1	28	1	44	5	0
Jacome, Jason, Monclova *	5	4	.556	5.09	14	13	0	0	0	0	74.1	89	330	45	42	10	3	2	2	27	2	43	1	0
Jacome, Jason, Puebla *	1	2	.333	5.71	8	7	0	0	0	0	41.0	54	179	29	26	5	2	1	3	9	0	23	0	0
Kamar, Emil, Angelopolis	1	1	.500	9.68	17	3	0	0	2	0	30.2	44	153	34	33	3	1	0	1	22	0	12	1	0
Kamar, Emil, Puebla	2	1	.667	5.74	17	0	0	0	13	5	15.2	18	71	13	10	3	2	1	2	7	0	7	1	0
Lara, Jorge, Puebla	1	1	.500	11.42	8	1	0	0	1	0	8.2	19	46	11	11	5	0	0	0	3	0	8	1	0
Lara, Jorge, Tabasco	2	2	.500	7.71	21	0	0	0	4	0	23.1	36	111	20	20	4	1	1	2	7	1	11	1	0
Lopez, Jose, San Luis Potosi	0	0	.000	10.80	5	0	0	0	2	0	5.0	11	28	6	6	2	1	0	0	4	0	2	0	0
Lopez, Jose, Oaxaca	2	5	.286	4.89	34	0	0	0	16	8	35.0	44	152	20	19	4	1	3	1	9	4	23	1	0
Mairena, Oswaldo, Oaxaca *	0	2	.000	40.50	2	2	0	0	0	0	3.1	12	26	15	15	3	0	0	4	0	0	2	0	0
Mairena, Oswaldo, Laguna *	3	11	.214	7.12	23	20	0	0	1	0	108.2	155	517	96	86	20	3	3	2	45	0	71	0	0
Manrique, Alberto, San Luis Potosi	1	4	.200	10.52	17	7	0	0	1	0	45.1	74	236	61	53	11	0	3	5	23	0	25	4	0
Manrique, Alberto, Campeche	0	1	.000	5.40	9	0	0	0	2	0	11.2	15	57	8	7	0	0	1	1	8	0	6	0	0
Martinez, Cesar, Tijuana	1	1	.500	10.00	7	4	0	0	1	0	18.0	34	94	20	20	5	1	0	4	7	0	10	1	0
Martinez, Cesar, Laguna *	4	3	.571	9.30	18	8	0	0	0	0	40.2	72	217	47	42	9	1	1	5	30	1	23	2	0
Martinez, Juan Jesus, Aguascalientes	0	1	.000	7.23	15	0	0	0	3	0	18.2	29	93	18	15	1	2	1	3	15	1	2	2	0
Martinez, Juan Jesus, Cancun	2	5	.286	7.24	11	8	0	0	0	0	51.0	75	246	46	41	14	1	4	0	24	0	17	7	0
Montano, Ignacio, Cancun *	6	2	.750	4.27	14	13	0	0	0	0	84.1	100	361	44	40	9	1	2	6	25	1	50	4	0
Montano, Ignacio, Aguascalientes *	2	1	.667	6.10	5	5	1	0	0	0	31.0	36	138	21	21	7	1	2	0	13	0	22	1	1
Munoz, Pablo, Aguascalientes *	0	1	.000	8.59	10	0	0	0	2	0	7.1	18	40	9	7	0	0	1	0	1	0	0	0	0
Munoz, Pablo, Cancun *	0	3	.000	11.96	19	3	0	0	3	1	26.1	54	148	43	35	11	2	3	1	15	0	5	3	0
Navarro, Hector, Veracruz *	1	2	.333	11.25	9	0	0	0	0	0	8.0	16	43	10	10	0	2	0	2	3	1	6	0	0
Navarro, Hector, Angelopolis *	4	2	.667	7.11	31	0	0	0	5	1	38.0	51	172	34	30	5	4	4	1	15	1	15	1	0
Navarro, Joel, Oaxaca	1	2	.333	15.34	8	3	0	0	0	0	14.2	32	75	25	25	7	1	2	0	7	0	4	0	0
Navarro, Joel, Tijuana	3	2	.600	5.56	17	9	0	0	3	0	66.1	80	296	42	41	14	2	2	4	24	2	31	2	2
Navarro, Jose Felix, Monclova	1	0	1.000	7.71	14	1	0	0	0	0	21.0	37	107	19	18	6	1	0	1	10	1	10	3	0
Navarro, Jose Felix, Veracruz	1	0	1.000	5.25	8	0	0	0	0	0	12.0	12	53	7	7	3	0	0	3	3	0	12	2	0
Nunez, Javier, Aguascalientes	0	1	.000	9.09	22	0	0	0	4	0	32.2	56	165	37	33	5	1	1	3	20	1	18	7	0
Nunez, Javier, Cancun	0	1	.000	6.04	8	1	0	0	2	1	22.1	29	103	15	15	1	1	1	1	11	0	5	1	0
Palma, Ricardo, Cancun *	0	2	.000	7.07	5	5	0	0	0	0	28.0	39	133	22	22	2	2	1	2	16	1	23	5	0
Palma, Ricardo, Aguascalientes *	6	2	.750	5.53	11	11	0	0	0	0	70.0	86	309	48	43	8	3	4	2	21	0	40	2	0
Patrick, Bronswell, Tabasco	1	2	.333	9.10	6	6	0	0	0	0	28.2	53	141	33	29	6	1	0	0	11	0	11	0	0
Patrick, Bronswell, Yucatan	2	1	.667	4.50	6	4	0	0	1	0	26.0	35	119	13	13	1	1	1	1	7	0	16	0	0
Perez, Edgar, Cancun	4	6	.400	5.07	13	13	0	0	0	0	76.1	87	337	46	43	7	0	4	3	33	0	39	3	0
Perez, Edgar, Aguascalientes	3	0	1.000	5.65	7	7	1	0	0	0	43.0	63	205	28	27	11	1	4	4	16	0	25	3	0
Perez, Guadalupe, Veracruz	1	1	.500	8.56	16	0	0	0	5	0	13.2	25	72	15	13	4	0	1	0	6	0	13	0	0
Perez, Guadalupe, Cancun	1	2	.333	2.70	9	4	1	0	3	2	36.2	30	153	13	11	3	0	0	5	15	1	26	2	0
Perez, Guadalupe, Aguascalientes	3	3	.500	8.21	7	7	0	0	0	0	34.0	54	167	31	31	9	0	2	1	14	0	15	1	0
Posadas, Obedt, Saltillo	0	0	.000	27.00	1	0	0	0	0	0	1.0	3	7	3	3	0	0	0	1	0	0	0	0	0
Posadas, Obedt, Laguna	2	6	.250	7.70	21	14	0	0	0	0	78.1	122	396	70	67	14	1	4	13	36	0	31	11	1
Pulido, Raymundo, Campeche	0	0	.000	9.00	2	0	0	0	0	0	2.0	3	14	2	2	0	0	0	0	5	0	1	1	0
Pulido, Raymundo, Laguna	1	0	1.000	6.16	14	0	0	0	5	0	19.0	19	81	14	13	4	1	4	1	11	1	6	1	1

Pitcher, Team	W	L	Pct.	ERA	G	GS	CG	ShO	GF	Sv.	IP	H	TBF	R	ER	HR	SH	SF	HB	BB	IBB	SO	WP	Bk.
Ramos, Eddy, Monclova	3	5	.375	6.80	15	6	1	1	3	0	45.0	63	205	37	34	8	1	1	1	20	2	20	1	0
Ramos, Eddy, Yucatan	0	0	.000	2.55	13	0	0	0	4	1	17.2	14	64	5	5	0	0	0	0	3	0	9	2	0
Rivera, Bienvenido, Laguna	5	5	.500	3.80	40	0	0	0	35	14	47.1	41	189	21	20	6	5	0	2	13	1	54	4	0
Rivera, Bienvenido, Aguascalientes	0	0	.000	4.50	4	0	0	0	3	0	4.0	2	13	2	2	0	0	0	0	0	0	1	0	0
Rodriguez, Raul, Monclova	0	2	.000	3.09	6	4	0	0	0	0	23.1	22	96	14	8	0	0	2	2	6	0	17	1	0
Rodriguez, Raul, Yucatan	3	8	.273	5.17	15	15	0	0	0	0	85.1	110	375	52	49	12	2	4	6	20	0	29	4	0
Roque, Rafael, Monterrey *	0	1	.000	32.40	2	2	0	0	0	0	1.2	6	15	6	6	2	0	0	0	5	0	2	1	0
Saldana, Jose, Cancun	0	2	.000	7.71	2	2	0	0	0	0	9.1	18	46	8	8	0	1	2	1	3	0	2	0	0
Saldana, Jose, Puebla	0	0	.000	14.04	6	0	0	0	1	0	8.1	25	50	16	13	7	0	1	0	1	0	5	0	0
Serrano, Elio, Tabasco	0	1	.000	7.20	4	0	0	0	3	0	5.0	9	23	4	4	0	0	0	3	1	2	2	0	
Serrano, Elio, Laguna	3	4	.429	5.27	37	0	0	0	13	3	42.2	40	181	25	25	7	3	3	3	17	2	35	6	0
Serrano, Wascar, Campeche	0	1	.000	16.20	5	3	0	0	0	0	10.0	21	55	18	18	4	0	1	0	5	0	5	3	0
Serrano, Wascar, Yucatan	1	1	.500	9.00	3	3	0	0	0	0	9.0	12	48	12	9	1	1	0	1	8	0	8	3	0
Sinohui, David, Tijuana	2	4	.333	7.92	28	0	0	0	20	8	25.0	35	126	25	22	6	1	1	3	10	3	14	6	0
Sinohui, David, Monclova	0	0	.000	20.25	2	0	0	0	1	0	1.1	2	7	3	3	0	0	1	0	1	0	1	2	0
Urdaneta, Lino, Aguascalientes	4	3	.571	4.31	26	0	0	0	25	11	31.1	37	136	19	15	2	4	2	2	11	4	17	2	0
Urdaneta, Lino, Cancun	0	0	.000	0.00	6	0	0	0	5	2	7.1	5	27	0	0	0	0	0	0	1	0	6	2	0
Vargas, Jose, Laguna	0	1	.000	10.91	14	0	0	0	2	0	15.2	26	86	23	19	5	3	1	1	11	1	19	0	0
Vargas, Jose, Yucatan	3	3	.500	4.13	19	0	0	0	16	6	24.0	22	103	12	11	1	1	1	4	7	2	38	1	0
Vazquez, Adrian, Cancun	1	1	.500	19.29	2	0	0	0	0	0	2.1	5	15	5	5	2	0	0	0	3	0	0	0	0
Vazquez, Adrian, Veracruz	1	1	.500	7.60	19	1	0	0	2	0	34.1	50	163	29	29	4	1	2	5	15	0	15	1	1
Vega, Obed, Cancun	0	0	.000	1.23	2	2	0	0	0	0	7.1	3	28	1	1	0	0	0	0	1	0	2	2	0
Vega, Obed, Veracruz	0	0	.000	4.91	4	4	0	0	0	0	11.0	13	51	6	6	1	0	1	3	5	0	4	0	0
Verdugo, Oswaldo, Yucatan	3	1	.750	4.83	17	2	0	0	3	1	41.0	50	187	24	22	1	2	2	1	23	0	24	5	0
Verdugo, Oswaldo, Laguna	2	1	.667	3.49	20	0	0	0	9	1	28.1	30	119	11	11	5	2	0	0	12	1	27	2	0
Verdugo, Roberto, Angelopolis	0	0	.000	12.60	9	0	0	0	0	0	10.0	18	56	17	14	2	1	1	2	6	0	8	0	1
Verdugo, Roberto, San Luis Potosi	0	1	.000	3.91	24	0	0	0	4	0	25.1	35	118	11	11	3	2	2	4	8	1	5	3	0
Villalobos, Fernando, Monterrey	1	1	.500	5.50	8	0	0	0	1	0	18.0	20	79	12	11	1	1	1	2	6	0	10	2	0
Villalobos, Fernando, San Luis Potosi	4	2	.667	6.17	9	7	0	0	0	0	35.0	37	159	29	24	7	0	1	0	17	0	29	3	0
Vizcarra, William, Yucatan	1	2	.333	5.50	5	5	0	0	0	0	21.0	30	89	13	13	1	0	0	0	5	0	8	0	0
Vizcarra, William, Monclova	2	0	1.000	8.34	31	0	0	0	6	0	41.0	68	200	41	38	5	1	3	3	13	0	15	2	0

COMBINATION SHUTOUTS: Aguascalientes (1) -- Pena-Diaz-Urdaneta. Angelopolis (2) -- Rivera-Zambrano-Manzano, Armenta-Garcia-Bustillos-Manzano. Campeche (7) -- Reyes-Serrano-Barradas, Sanchez-Garcia-Barradas, Campos-Roberts, Manning-Garcia-Roberts, Miguel Ruiz-Vizcarra, Alvarez-Roberts, Magee-Garcia-Manrique-Garcia. Cancun (2) -- Nieblas-Gutierrez-Sanchez, Perez-Cazares-Urdaneta. Laguna (1) -- Hernandez-Jimenez-Esparza-Ahumada. Mexico (4) -- Moreno-Cordova, Moreno-Silva, Alvarez-Silva, Ramirez-Silva. Monclova (4) -- Rodriguez-Ramos, Ward-Rodriguez-Ramos-Simas, Lopez-Flores-Alberro-Simas, Acosta-Alberro. Monterrey (5) -- Loya-Mora-Cobos, Hernandez-Nieblas-Lara-De La Rosa, Pineda-Villalobos-Aguirre-De La Rosa, Ochoa-Lara-Rubio-De La Rosa, Pineda-Acevedo-Rubio-De La Rosa. Oaxaca (1) -- Madero-Abreu. Puebla (2) -- Manzanillo-Soto, Knott-Macias-Hernandez-Nunez. Saltillo (5) -- Rivera-Ruiz-Mendoza-Pablos-Coco, Beltran-Duarte-Salas-Rios, Bourgeois-Duarte-Almonte, Beltran-Almonte-Duarte, Gonzalez-Perez-Almonte-Duarte. San Luis Potosi (2) -- Leyva-Garcia-Cerros, Molina-Garcia-Cerros,

Tabasco (4) -- Vargas-Pimentel-Ramon, Vargas-Galvez-Pena, Gonzalez-Oropesa, Vargas-Oropesa-Desgue. Tijuana (5) -- Beltran-Parra-Sinohui, Beltran-Parra-Garibay, Beltran-Garibay, Beltran-Delfin-Sinohui-Bland, Beltran-Delfin-Parra-Shibulo. Veracruz (1) -- Aguilar-Moreno-Estrella-Baez. Yucatan (2) -- Patrick-Sparks, Carrasco-Ramos-Vargas.

NO-HIT GAMES: Beltran (6 innings), Delfin (1 inning), Parra (1 inning) and Shibilo (1 inning), Tijuana, defeated Saltillo, 5-0, July 26.

2005 FIELDING

TEAM

Team	G	PO	A	E	TC	DP	TP	PB	Pct.
Mexico	107	2826	1317	76	4219	133	0	3	.982
Yucatan	107	2847	1224	74	4145	139	0	10	.982
Tabasco	109	2831	1243	77	4151	140	0	7	.981
Aguascalientes	108	2843	1266	89	4198	145	0	6	.979
Monclova	108	2869	1297	89	4255	128	0	11	.979
Monterrey	106	2797	1158	85	4040	133	0	10	.979
Puebla	107	2765	1296	87	4148	148	0	6	.979
Saltillo	110	2896	1244	92	4232	143	0	4	.978
Angelopolis	107	2768	1267	94	4129	175	0	14	.977
Oaxaca	108	2790	1259	99	4148	155	1	10	.976
Tijuana	110	2949	1211	101	4261	134	0	7	.976
Laguna	109	2893	1154	104	4151	131	1	15	.975
Campeche	105	2723	1170	103	3996	118	0	9	.974
Cancun	108	2807	1136	107	4050	126	1	8	.974
San Luis Potosi	108	2826	1194	113	4133	148	0	10	.973
Veracruz	109	2796	1178	117	4091	119	0	8	.971

INDIVIDUAL

FIRST BASEMEN

NOTE: All caps denotes fielding-percentage leader based on 55 games for catchers, 73 for all other non-pitchers and 88 innings for pitchers. *Throws lefthanded.

Player, Team	Pct.	G	PO	A	E	TC	DP
Adriana, Sharnol, San Luis Potosi	.986	95	850	51	13	914	113
Aganza, Ruben, Monclova	.972	10	34	1	1	36	3
Almeida, Shamar, Mexico	1.000	23	120	5	0	125	11
Amado, Jose, Cancun	.998	55	431	25	1	457	61
Arias, George, Tijuana	.992	36	339	27	3	369	49
Burkhart, Morgan, Saltillo *	.997	98	839	55	3	897	111
Camilo, Juan, Tabasco	1.000	1	1	0	0	1	0
Castaneda, Hector, Yucatan	1.000	6	51	5	0	56	7

Player, Team	Pct.	G	PO	A	E	TC	DP
Castaneda, Jose, Saltillo	1.000	1	3	0	0	3	0
Castaneda, Rafael, Laguna	1.000	14	61	4	0	65	3
Castellano, Pedro, Yucatan	.997	98	891	62	3	956	116
Cervantes, Refugio, Aguascalientes	.977	40	323	16	8	347	44
Cervera, Francisco, Yucatan	1.000	1	1	0	0	1	0
Cobos, Rogelio, Mexico	.800	3	4	0	1	5	1
Connell, Lino, Veracruz	.988	65	605	32	8	645	76
Contreras, Albino, Angelopolis *	1.000	14	79	3	0	82	12
Diaz, Eddy, Yucatan	1.000	17	44	3	0	47	3
Echevarria, Angel, Monclova	1.000	2	5	0	0	5	0
Espino, Daniel, Cancun-Veracruz	1.000	21	110	7	0	117	14
Espinosa, Ramon, Laguna	1.000	8	60	3	0	63	6
Fornes, Daniel, Monterrey *	.909	4	10	0	1	11	1
Garcia, Cornelio, Laguna	1.000	1	2	0	0	2	1
GARCIA, GUILLERMO, Monclova	.999	101	938	41	1	980	111
Gastelum, Sergio, Angelopolis	1.000	4	3	1	0	4	1
Gavia, Jesus, Aguascalientes	1.000	1	3	0	0	3	1
Gonzalez, Fernando, Cancun	1.000	2	6	0	0	6	0
Gonzalez, Roman, Aguascalientes	...	1	0	0	0	0	0
Gracia, Ernesto, Aguascalientes	1.000	2	14	1	0	15	1
Guzman, Jorge, Saltillo	1.000	1	0	1	0	1	0
Ibarra, Juvenal, Tijuana	1.000	8	49	6	0	55	6
Iturbe, Pedro, Puebla *	.994	91	814	43	5	862	110
Landaeta, Luis, Tijuana *	1.000	1	10	0	0	10	0
Lara, Idelfonso, Aguascalientes-Laguna	.995	70	608	41	3	652	87
Leon, Donny, Puebla	1.000	2	24	2	0	26	4
Lopez, Raul, Veracruz-Laguna	.995	48	386	34	2	422	46
Lujan, Enrique, Tijuana	1.000	1	2	0	0	2	0
Macias, Roberto, Aguascalientes	.989	25	177	8	2	187	24
Marmolejo, Ivan, Cancun	.979	12	85	7	2	94	12
Martinez, Ray, Yucatan	.989	91	835	76	10	921	111
Mendez, Francisco, Monterrey	.994	31	159	12	1	172	18
Montano, Angel, Tijuana	1.000	3	8	1	0	9	1
Montenegro, Jose, Oaxaca	.991	16	107	8	1	116	20
Morales, Carlos, Tabasco	1.000	2	3	0	0	3	0
Morales, Ramon, Tabasco	1.000	2	3	0	0	3	1

Player, Team	Pct.	G	PO	A	E	TC	DP
Munoz, Adan, Angelopolis	.982	13	99	9	2	110	18
Nava, Lipso, Cancun	.993	14	130	6	1	137	7
Nieves, Jose, Aguascalientes	1.000	1	9	1	0	10	1
Nieves, Melvin, Laguna	.980	8	46	3	1	50	6
Orantes, Ramon, Monterrey	1.000	6	27	2	0	29	1
O'Sullivan, Patrick, San Luis Potosi	.978	17	130	6	3	139	14
Otanez, Willis, Veracruz	.993	34	274	25	2	301	28
Paez, Hector, Campeche	1.000	4	24	2	0	26	4
Paez, Raul, Oaxaca *	.991	29	107	8	1	116	13
Palafox, Sergio, Saltillo	1.000	4	11	5	0	16	2
Pearson, Eddie, Tijuana	.984	12	113	9	2	124	11
Pena, Angel, Oaxaca	.990	86	728	51	8	787	108
Pena, Cesar, Tijuana	1.000	5	11	1	0	12	1
Perez, Francisco, Puebla *	1.000	6	39	1	0	40	3
Quinones, Ruben, Cancun	1.000	1	2	0	0	2	0
Quintero, Edgar, Monterrey *	1.000	1	1	1	0	2	0
Reyes, Julio, Laguna	.997	43	290	21	1	312	32
Rincon, Isaias, Mexico	...	1	0	0	0	0	0
Rivera, Francisco, Cancun	1.000	16	105	8	0	113	10
Rivera, Jesus, Tabasco	1.000	4	12	0	0	12	0
Rodriguez, Carlos, San Luis Potosi	.926	2	24	1	2	27	2
Rodriguez, Ferdinand, Monclova	1.000	4	8	0	0	8	1
Rodriguez, Fernando, Monclova	1.000	4	24	3	0	27	2
Rodriguez, Liu, Cancun	1.000	12	88	4	0	92	13
Romero, Flavio, Campeche	1.000	1	5	0	0	5	0
Romero, Marco, Saltillo *	.975	25	116	1	3	120	18
Sanchez, Roque, Campeche	.995	23	174	18	1	193	15
Saucedo, Robert, Mexico	1.000	5	46	2	0	48	2
Selby, Bill, Campeche	1.000	3	20	2	0	22	3
Sievers, Carlos, Tabasco	.988	17	149	14	2	165	16
Simon, Randall, Tijuana *	.988	54	463	37	6	506	51
Smith, Charles, Monterrey	.994	56	487	37	3	527	61
Soto, Saul, Mexico	1.000	2	13	1	0	14	2
Sotomayor, Gilberto, Monclova *	...	1	0	0	0	0	0
Tapia, Cesar, Puebla	1.000	2	1	0	0	1	0
Trapaga, Julio, Puebla	1.000	1	1	0	0	1	0
Valdez, Mario, Monterrey	.992	29	231	14	2	247	31
Valencia, Abraham, Tijuana-Oaxaca	1.000	2	13	2	0	15	3
Valle, Cosme, San Luis Potosi	1.000	5	12	1	0	13	3
Valle, Jorge Luis, Cancun	...	1	0	0	0	0	0
Vazquez, Jorge, Angelopolis	.996	50	459	31	2	492	62
Vega, Edgar, Monclova	1.000	1	10	0	0	10	2
Vega, Jesus, Angelopolis	...	1	0	0	0	0	0
Velasquez, Guillermo, Angelopolis	.989	41	335	23	4	362	68
Villalobos, Carlos, Puebla	1.000	10	106	8	0	114	13
Villarreal, Alejandro, Tijuana	1.000	1	2	0	0	2	0
Virgen, Constancio, Mexico	1.000	2	4	0	0	4	0
Vizcarra, Roberto, Campeche	.987	79	682	62	10	754	84
Yan, Julian, Tabasco	.995	92	850	62	5	917	109
Yepez, Daniel, Puebla	1.000	5	20	1	0	21	4
Zazueta, Mauricio, Oaxaca	1.000	4	24	1	0	25	4

FIRST BASEMEN WITH TWO OR MORE TEAMS

Player, Team	Pct.	G	PO	A	E	TC	DP
Espino, Daniel, Cancun	1.000	16	69	2	0	71	8
Espino, Daniel, Veracruz	1.000	5	41	5	0	46	6
Lara, Idelfonso, Aguascalientes	.996	49	471	24	2	497	60
Lara, Idelfonso, Laguna	.994	21	137	17	1	155	27
Lopez, Raul, Veracruz	.982	7	45	11	1	57	2
Lopez, Raul, Laguna	.997	41	341	23	1	365	44
Valencia, Abraham, Tijuana	1.000	1	11	1	0	12	3
Valencia, Abraham, Oaxaca	1.000	1	2	1	0	3	0

SECOND BASEMEN

Player, Team	Pct.	G	PO	A	E	TC	DP
Alejos, Fernando, Cancun	1.000	2	2	4	0	6	2
Alfonso, Manuel, Tabasco	.966	10	10	18	1	29	2
Amador, Jose, Laguna	.975	107	237	303	14	554	86
Arano, Eloy, Veracruz	...	1	0	0	0	0	0
Arias, Francisco, Saltillo	.989	85	193	245	5	443	62
Arredondo, Alan, Yucatan	.750	2	1	2	1	4	0
Arredondo, Jesus, Puebla	.974	55	114	186	8	308	60
Beltran, Juan, Campeche	1.000	1	1	0	0	1	0
BRENA, JAIME, Oaxaca	.992	99	280	308	5	593	105
Bueno, Geraldo, Cancun	.967	5	12	17	1	30	9
Bustillos, Luis, San Luis Potosi	.667	2	1	1	1	3	1
Carrillo, Oscar, Mexico	1.000	29	20	38	0	58	9
Casillas, Hector, Monclova	1.000	6	10	17	0	27	4
Castaneda, Jose, Saltillo	...	2	0	0	0	0	0
Castaneda, Rafael, Laguna	1.000	1	3	3	0	6	2

Player, Team	Pct.	G	PO	A	E	TC	DP
Castillo, Jesus, Yucatan	1.000	4	2	8	0	10	1
Castro, Arnoldo, Cancun-Tabasco	.988	100	238	268	6	512	69
Cesar, Dionys, Monterrey	.961	20	43	55	4	102	14
Cota, Angel, San Luis Potosi	1.000	3	6	5	0	11	1
Cruz, Luis, Mexico	.995	39	90	128	1	219	27
Diaz, Edwin, Puebla	1.000	8	14	28	0	42	6
Espinoza, Efren, Mexico	.970	19	39	57	3	99	22
Flores, Kevin, Angelopolis	.984	29	50	70	2	122	25
Flores, Miguel, Monterrey	.989	61	133	145	3	281	43
Garanzuay, Hector, Monclova *	.981	102	232	281	10	523	79
Garcia, Amaury, Veracruz	.976	100	226	301	13	540	80
Gastelum, Carlos Alberto, Angelopolis	.988	83	237	278	6	521	108
Gastelum, Sergio, Angelopolis	1.000	2	3	3	0	6	2
Gracia, Ernesto, Aguascalientes	1.000	5	13	9	0	22	3
Guerrero, Sergio, Saltillo	1.000	11	25	32	0	57	11
Gutierrez, Andres, Tabasco	.957	47	108	90	9	207	29
Guzman, Edwards, Puebla	1.000	4	4	9	0	13	1
Hernandez, Hector, Veracruz	.889	4	10	6	2	18	1
Herrera, Christian, Oaxaca	.864	7	11	8	3	22	3
Hinojosa, Daniel, Monterrey *	.857	6	2	4	1	7	1
Leyva, Octavio, Oaxaca	1.000	10	13	25	0	38	9
Llano, Paul, Tijuana	...	1	0	0	0	0	0
Lopez, Fabian, Campeche	1.000	3	5	3	0	8	0
Lopez, Fausto, Tabasco	.980	11	27	23	1	51	8
Macias, Roberto, Aguascalientes	1.000	1	0	1	0	1	0
Martinez, Abel, Laguna	.952	7	9	11	1	21	0
Martinez, Enrique, San Luis Potosi	1.000	1	0	1	0	1	0
Martinez, Grimaldo, Aguascalientes	.984	82	200	237	7	444	84
Mendez, Francisco, Monterrey	1.000	2	1	1	0	2	0
Mendoza, Omar, San Luis Potosi	.979	61	149	179	7	335	54
Mere, Pedro, Aguascalientes	.992	26	64	64	1	129	18
Morejon, Oswaldo, Yucatan	.978	102	272	309	13	594	94
Orrantia, Carlos, Monterrey	.978	41	78	103	4	185	40
Palafox, Sergio, Saltillo-Cancun	.966	37	63	78	5	146	20
Perez, Alfredo, Veracruz	.961	11	23	26	2	51	6
Perez, Jose, San Luis Potosi	.982	53	106	165	5	276	34
Piste, Carlos, Yucatan	.972	10	17	18	1	36	6
Ramirez, Jesus, Cancun	1.000	2	6	5	0	11	3
Rios, Eduardo, Aguascalientes	1.000	2	4	4	0	8	2
Rivera, Jesus, Tabasco	.984	42	82	107	3	192	34
Robles, Juan, Tabasco	1.000	1	0	1	0	1	0
Robles, Oscar, Mexico	.989	30	74	107	2	183	29
Robles, Trinidad, Angelopolis	.952	18	24	36	3	63	11
Rodriguez, Liu, Cancun	.952	18	26	33	3	62	10
Romero, Flavio, Campeche	.969	49	109	137	8	254	38
Ruiz, Juan De Dios, Monclova	1.000	2	2	1	0	3	1
Ruiz, Ricardo, Laguna	.833	4	2	3	1	6	1
Sanchez, Jose, Tijuana	1.000	1	2	0	0	2	0
Sanchez, Orlando, Monclova	.946	22	45	43	5	93	13
Sequea, Jorge, Tabasco	.932	9	16	25	3	44	4
Suarez, Luis, Angelopolis	...	1	0	0	0	0	0
Torrero, Miguel, Puebla	.982	40	51	59	2	112	19
Trapaga, Julio, Puebla	.985	30	65	67	2	134	21
Valencia, Carlos, Tijuana	.976	110	262	309	14	585	88
Valenzuela, Irving, Puebla	1.000	11	14	27	0	41	6
Valle, Jorge Luis, Cancun-Saltillo	1.000	2	1	2	0	3	1
Velez, Manuel, Mexico	1.000	16	29	57	0	86	13
Verdugo, Vicente, Campeche	.982	65	139	190	6	335	50
Zazueta, Juan, Saltillo	.966	28	34	52	3	89	18
Zazueta, Mauricio, Oaxaca-Mexico	.800	5	1	3	1	5	0

SECOND BASEMEN WITH TWO OR MORE TEAMS

Player, Team	Pct.	G	PO	A	E	TC	DP
Castro, Arnoldo, Cancun	.985	76	178	204	6	388	46
Castro, Arnoldo, Tabasco	1.000	24	60	64	0	124	23
Palafox, Sergio, Saltillo	.984	21	25	36	1	62	12
Palafox, Sergio, Cancun	.952	16	38	42	4	84	8
Valle, Jorge Luis, Cancun	1.000	1	0	1	0	1	0
Valle, Jorge Luis, Saltillo	1.000	1	1	1	0	2	1
Zazueta, Mauricio, Oaxaca	.800	1	1	3	1	5	0
Zazueta, Mauricio, Mexico	...	4	0	0	0	0	0

THIRD BASEMEN

Player, Team	Pct.	G	PO	A	E	TC	DP
Aganza, Ruben, Monclova	.941	14	5	27	2	34	1
Ahumada, Alejandro, San Luis Potosi	...	1	0	0	0	0	0
Alejos, Fernando, Cancun	.946	13	13	22	2	37	1
Alfonso, Manuel, Tabasco	1.000	1	1	1	0	2	0
Amado, Jose, Cancun	.902	19	25	30	6	61	1
Arano, Eloy, Veracruz	.940	39	35	59	6	100	7

Player, Team	Pct.	G	PO	A	E	TC	DP
Arias, Francisco, Saltillo	1.000	1	0	1	0	1	0
Arias, George, Tijuana	.952	16	13	27	2	42	3
Arredondo, Alan, Yucatan	1.000	8	2	4	0	6	0
Arredondo, Eduardo, Tabasco *	...	1	0	0	0	0	0
Arredondo, Hernando, Tabasco	.951	99	85	205	15	305	22
Arredondo, Jesus, Puebla	...	1	0	0	0	0	0
Beltran, Juan, Campeche	1.000	6	7	9	0	16	1
Brena, Jaime, Oaxaca	1.000	1	1	0	0	1	0
Brito, Tilson, Veracruz	.938	17	8	37	3	48	2
Carrillo, Oscar, Mexico	.875	6	3	4	1	8	1
Casillas, Hector, Monclova	1.000	11	3	14	0	17	0
Castaneda, Jose, Saltillo	.889	13	1	7	1	9	2
Castaneda, Rafael, Laguna	.890	31	21	44	8	73	0
Cervantes, Ivan, Oaxaca	.962	55	25	75	4	104	14
Cervera, Francisco, Yucatan	1.000	28	13	19	0	32	0
Cesar, Dionys, Monterrey	.934	59	50	120	12	182	15
Cota, Angel, San Luis Potosi	1.000	2	0	2	0	2	1
Crespo, Jorge, Oaxaca	1.000	1	0	1	0	1	0
Cruz, Fausto, Campeche	.961	34	25	73	4	102	9
Cruz, Luis, Mexico	.978	24	9	35	1	45	2
Diaz, Eddy, Yucatan	.968	99	80	226	10	316	39
Diaz, Edwin, Puebla	.972	22	18	52	2	72	4
Diaz, Pedro, Monclova	.960	93	79	235	13	327	18
Doster, Dave, San Luis Potosi	.948	72	46	154	11	211	22
Figueroa, Luis, Tijuana	.951	92	78	212	15	305	24
Flores, Kevin, Angelopolis	1.000	5	2	5	0	7	1
Gastelum, Carlos Alberto, Angelopolis	.500	2	0	1	1	2	0
Gastelum, Sergio, Angelopolis	.936	97	84	194	19	297	30
Gomez, Heber, Monterrey	.964	6	8	19	1	28	3
Gracia, Ernesto, Aguascalientes	1.000	8	3	4	0	7	1
Guerrero, Sergio, Saltillo	.944	45	41	95	8	144	13
Gutierrez, Andres, Tabasco	.909	5	2	8	1	11	0
Guzman, Edwards, Puebla	.971	50	53	114	5	172	16
Hinojosa, Daniel, Monterrey *	...	1	0	0	0	0	0
Leon, Donny, Puebla	.889	3	5	3	1	9	0
Leyva, Octavio, Oaxaca	1.000	11	3	8	0	11	1
Lopez, Fabian, Campeche	.875	5	2	5	1	8	1
Lopez, Raul, Laguna	.625	5	3	2	3	8	1
Lucca, Lou, Cancun-Laguna	.889	8	5	19	3	27	2
Macias, Roberto, Aguascalientes	.667	2	0	2	1	3	1
Magallanes, Ever, Oaxaca	.892	26	24	42	8	74	5
Martinez, Abel, Laguna	.968	84	89	150	8	247	10
Martinez, Ray, Mexico	.895	17	9	25	4	38	3
Mejia, Roberto, Campeche	.930	33	29	77	8	114	6
Mendoza, Omar, San Luis Potosi	.936	43	30	73	7	110	7
Mere, Pedro, Aguascalientes	.800	2	0	4	1	5	0
Meza, Gonzalo, Monclova	.667	2	1	1	1	3	0
Montenegro, Jose, Oaxaca	.941	47	24	88	7	119	18
Morales, Carlos, Tabasco	1.000	2	0	1	0	1	0
Morales, Ramon, Tabasco	1.000	3	1	1	0	2	0
Nieves, Jose, Aguascalientes	1.000	1	0	4	0	4	0
Orantes, Ramon, Monterrey	.962	49	37	91	5	133	7
Orrantia, Carlos, Monterrey	.889	11	2	6	1	9	1
Otanez, Willis, Veracruz	.935	57	68	118	13	199	14
Palafox, Sergio, Saltillo	.850	10	5	12	3	20	0
Pena, Cesar, Tijuana	.667	2	0	4	2	6	0
Perez, Alfredo, Veracruz	1.000	2	1	0	0	1	0
Piste, Carlos, Yucatan	1.000	2	0	1	0	1	0
Quinones, Ruben, Cancun	1.000	9	7	19	0	26	2
Ramirez, Oscar, Campeche	.962	14	16	35	2	53	2
Rios, Eduardo, Aguascalientes	.972	103	97	278	11	386	35
Rivera, Jesus, Tabasco	.970	13	6	26	1	33	4
Robles, Javier, Angelopolis	1.000	1	0	2	0	2	0
Robles, Trinidad, Angelopolis	.939	17	7	24	2	33	4
Romero, Flavio, Campeche	.889	3	1	7	1	9	2
Rosas, Ezequiel, Oaxaca	.889	11	1	15	2	18	1
Ruiz, Juan De Dios, Tijuana	1.000	2	0	2	0	2	0
Salazar, Oscar, Cancun	.947	32	26	63	5	94	12
Sanchez, Orlando, Monclova	.867	3	3	10	2	15	3
Sanchez, Roque, Campeche	.957	26	17	28	2	47	2
Sequea, Jorge, Tabasco	1.000	6	2	7	0	9	1
Tapia, Cesar, Puebla	1.000	1	1	0	0	1	0
Torrero, Miguel, Puebla	.932	27	17	52	5	74	6
Valenzuela, Irving, Puebla	.857	4	1	5	1	7	0
Valle, Jorge Luis, Cancun-Saltillo	.973	89	64	184	7	255	23
Vazquez, Angelopolis	1.000	1	0	1	0	1	0
VELEZ, MANUEL, Mexico	.981	80	58	194	5	257	28
Villalobos, Carlos, Puebla-San Luis Potosi	.941	10	9	23	2	34	6
Villarreal, Alejandro, Tijuana	1.000	3	1	0	0	1	0
Zazueta, Juan, Saltillo	.974	22	11	27	1	39	2
Zazueta, Mauricio, Oaxaca	1.000	6	3	8	0	11	1

THIRD BASEMEN WITH TWO OR MORE TEAMS

Player, Team	Pct.	G	PO	A	E	TC	DP
Lucca, Lou, Cancun	.846	3	3	8	2	13	0
Lucca, Lou, Laguna	.929	5	2	11	1	14	2
Valle, Jorge Luis, Cancun	.967	43	31	88	4	123	10
Valle, Jorge Luis, Saltillo	.977	46	33	96	3	132	13
Villalobos, Carlos, Puebla	.941	8	9	23	2	34	6
Villalobos, Carlos, San Luis Potosi	...	2	0	0	0	0	0

SHORTSTOPS

Player, Team	Pct.	G	PO	A	E	TC	DP
Ahumada, Alejandro, San Luis Potosi	.944	68	120	217	20	357	60
Alejos, Fernando, Cancun	1.000	2	3	5	0	8	1
Alfonso, Manuel, Tabasco	.923	10	6	18	2	26	4
Amado, Jose, Cancun	1.000	1	1	0	0	1	0
Amador, Jose, Laguna	.941	8	4	12	1	17	3
Arias, Francisco, Saltillo	.964	19	9	18	1	28	5
Arredondo, Alan, Yucatan	.933	11	7	21	2	30	3
Arredondo, Jesus, Puebla	.962	7	5	20	1	26	4
Beltran, Juan, Campeche	.973	23	22	50	2	74	7
Borges, Luis, Yucatan	.968	80	127	270	13	410	50
Brito, Tilson, Veracruz	.966	7	5	23	1	29	1
Bustillos, Luis, San Luis Potosi	.971	26	44	90	4	138	19
Carrillo, Oscar, Mexico	1.000	11	3	3	0	6	1
Casillas, Hector, Monclova	.875	3	2	5	1	8	0
Castaneda, Jose, Saltillo	...	1	0	0	0	0	0
Castillo, Jesus, Yucatan	.932	16	16	25	3	44	6
Castro, Domingo, Monclova	.964	102	220	398	23	641	93
Cervantes, Ivan, Oaxaca	.953	78	117	267	19	403	60
Cervera, Francisco, Yucatan	.949	8	15	22	2	39	6
Connell, Lino, Veracruz	.813	2	4	9	3	16	1
Cota, Angel, San Luis Potosi	1.000	1	1	1	0	2	0
Cruz, Luis, Mexico	1.000	1	3	4	0	7	1
Diaz, Pedro, Monclova	...	1	0	0	0	0	0
DIAZ, REMIGIO, Tabasco	.990	103	179	323	5	507	73
Doster, Dave, San Luis Potosi	.972	23	38	67	3	108	20
Figueroa, Luis, Tijuana	1.000	1	0	1	0	1	0
Flores, Kevin, Angelopolis	1.000	10	15	16	0	31	5
Garanzuay, Hector, Monclova *	.500	2	2	1	3	6	0
Garcia, Nicolas, Saltillo	.969	106	147	357	16	520	86
Gomez, Heber, Monterrey	.971	97	163	309	14	486	79
Guizar, Hector, Aguascalientes	.952	71	126	272	20	418	55
Gutierrez, Andres, Tabasco	...	1	0	0	0	0	0
Hernandez, Hector, Veracruz	.949	75	133	222	19	374	55
Hernandez, Julio, Tijuana	.969	108	186	354	17	557	86
Herrera, Christian, Oaxaca	.950	62	62	146	11	219	38
Leyva, Octavio, Oaxaca	1.000	1	0	1	0	1	0
Lopez, Fausto, Tabasco	.895	14	4	13	2	19	4
Martinez, Grimaldo, Aguascalientes	1.000	8	14	20	0	34	4
Martinez, Luis Carlos, Puebla	.956	95	155	321	22	498	76
Mere, Carlos, Veracruz	.950	4	10	9	1	20	0
Nieves, Jose, Veracruz-Aguascalientes	.946	37	50	108	9	167	28
Orrantia, Carlos, Monterrey	.967	16	20	38	2	60	7
Palafox, Sergio, Cancun	.952	10	16	24	2	42	5
Perez, Alfredo, Veracruz	.929	25	28	64	7	99	16
Piste, Carlos, Yucatan	.903	9	10	18	3	31	2
Ramirez, Oscar, Campeche	.922	80	117	224	29	370	58
Robles, Javier, Angelopolis	.962	89	136	320	18	474	100
Robles, Trinidad, Angelopolis	.961	19	31	42	3	76	15
Rodriguez, Liu, Cancun	.982	60	97	173	5	275	36
Romero, Flavio, Campeche	.952	8	16	24	2	42	6
Salas, Heriberto, Laguna	.969	107	194	342	17	553	91
Salazar, Oscar, Cancun	.920	20	49	55	9	113	17
Sanchez, Jose, Tijuana	.714	6	5	5	4	14	0
Sanchez, Orlando, Monclova	1.000	9	9	18	0	27	5
Sandoval, Jose, Mexico	.967	106	177	352	18	547	76
Sequea, Jorge, Tabasco	1.000	1	1	2	0	3	1
Torrero, Miguel, Puebla	1.000	3	2	2	0	4	1
Valenzuela, Irving, Puebla	.976	11	14	27	1	42	6
Valle, Jorge Luis, Saltillo	1.000	8	6	10	0	16	4
Villaescusa, Fernando, Campeche	.800	6	1	7	2	10	3
Zazueta, Christian, Cancun	.927	25	58	69	10	137	20
Zazueta, Juan, Saltillo	...	1	0	0	0	0	0

SHORTSTOPS WITH TWO OR MORE TEAMS

Player, Team	Pct.	G	PO	A	E	TC	DP
Nieves, Jose, Veracruz	.931	6	9	18	2	29	5
Nieves, Jose, Aguascalientes	.949	31	41	90	7	138	23

OUTFIELDERS

Player, Team	Pct.	G	PO	A	E	TC	DP
Acuna, Jose, Cancun	.980	72	144	5	3	152	0
Adriana, Sharnol, San Luis Potosi	.941	19	15	1	1	17	0
Aganza, Ruben, Monclova	1.000	1	1	0	0	1	0
Alcantara, Israel, Veracruz	...	1	0	0	0	0	0
Alejos, Fernando, Cancun	1.000	5	5	0	0	5	0
Alvarez, Hector, Monterrey-Oaxaca	.972	61	102	2	3	107	1
Alvarez, Rafael, Laguna-Cancun	.981	46	95	6	2	103	0
Amado, Jose, Cancun	.938	10	15	0	1	16	0
Angulo, Gregorio, Yucatan	1.000	30	24	3	0	27	2
Arano, Eloy, Veracruz	1.000	39	55	3	0	58	1
Arano, Wilfredo, Tijuana	.986	74	141	2	2	145	0
Arauz, Leobardo, Monclova	.980	105	231	11	5	247	1
Arias, George, Tijuana	.727	11	8	0	3	11	0
Arredondo, Alan, Yucatan	1.000	21	29	0	0	29	0
Arredondo, Eduardo, Tabasco-Mexico	.992	61	115	3	1	119	0
Arredondo, Luis, Yucatan *	.977	103	201	8	5	214	3
Bass, Jayson, Saltillo *	.907	33	39	0	4	43	0
Beltran, Juan, Campeche	1.000	17	20	1	0	21	0
Bernal, Cosme, Mexico	1.000	13	11	1	0	12	0
Bojorquez, Victor, Mexico	.970	107	217	9	7	233	0
Brinkley, Darryl, San Luis Potosi	.984	59	119	8	2	129	0
Buelna, Lorenzo, Puebla	.981	105	183	19	4	206	3
Bullett, Scott, Yucatan *	.969	83	117	6	4	127	1
Burkhart, Morgan, Saltillo *	1.000	5	3	0	0	3	0
Camilo, Juan, Tabasco	.947	69	115	10	7	132	0
Canizalez, Juan, Yucatan	1.000	24	39	2	0	41	1
Carrillo, Matias, Angelopolis *	.992	69	117	6	1	124	2
Carrillo, Oscar, Mexico	...	1	0	0	0	0	0
Castaneda, Jose, Saltillo	1.000	5	2	0	0	2	0
Cesar, Dionys, Monterrey	.985	37	61	6	1	68	1
Connell, Lino, Veracruz	1.000	5	10	1	0	11	0
Contreras, Albino, Angelopolis *	.974	88	181	9	5	195	2
Crespo, Jorge, Oaxaca	.903	25	26	2	3	31	1
Cruz, Fausto, Campeche	.935	22	27	2	2	31	0
Cruz, Luis, Mexico	.938	10	14	1	1	16	0
De La Torre, Omar, Laguna	.970	71	156	6	5	167	1
Doster, Dave, San Luis Potosi	1.000	12	18	2	0	20	1
Echevarria, Angel, Monclova	1.000	15	24	0	0	24	0
Esparragoza, Francisco, Saltillo	...	1	0	0	0	0	0
Espino, Daniel, Cancun-Veracruz	.941	51	91	4	6	101	1
Espinoza, Ramon, Laguna	.957	57	107	4	5	116	1
Espinoza, Efren, Mexico	.984	43	56	5	1	62	2
Espinoza, Jose, Tijuana	.962	76	125	3	5	133	1
Esqueda, Jonathan, Campeche	1.000	11	9	0	0	9	0
Feliciano, Jesus, Oaxaca *	.982	22	54	1	1	56	0
Fentanes, Oscar, Veracruz	.930	34	38	2	3	43	0
FERNANDEZ, DANIEL, Mexico *	1.000	74	142	5	0	147	1
Flores, Kevin, Angelopolis	...	1	0	0	0	0	0
Fornes, Daniel, Monterrey *	.971	70	127	6	4	137	3
Garcia, Amaury, Veracruz	1.000	1	4	0	0	4	0
Garcia, Cornelio, Laguna	.857	8	12	0	2	14	1
Garcia, Hector, Tabasco	.981	63	94	9	2	105	4
Garcia, Luis, Veracruz	.968	89	141	10	5	156	0
Garcia, Luis, Monterrey	.963	38	101	4	4	109	2
Garcia, Nicolas, Saltillo	...	3	0	0	0	0	0
Gastelum, Carlos Alberto, Angelopolis	1.000	30	44	0	0	44	0
Gonzalez, Fernando, Cancun	1.000	2	3	0	0	3	0
Gonzalez, Roman, Aguascalientes	.978	73	125	11	3	139	1
Gonzalez, Santiago, Veracruz	.976	88	156	5	4	165	1
Gracia, Ernesto, Aguascalientes	1.000	2	1	0	0	1	0
Guerrero, Sergio, Saltillo	...	1	0	0	0	0	0
Gutierrez, Andres, Tabasco	1.000	2	4	0	0	4	0
Guzman, Jorge, Saltillo	.971	26	31	3	1	35	1
Hermansen, Chad, Campeche	1.000	2	3	0	0	3	0
Ibarra, Juvenal, Tijuana	1.000	15	17	0	0	17	0
Johnson, Rontrez, Aguascalientes	.978	98	256	6	6	268	1
Jose, Felix, Oaxaca	...	1	0	0	0	0	0
Landaeta, Luis, Tijuana *	.980	45	95	2	2	99	1
Lara, Ildefonso, Laguna	.935	30	28	1	2	31	0
Llano, Paul, Tijuana	...	3	0	0	0	0	0
Lopez, Jose Manuel, San Luis Potosi	.977	31	40	2	1	43	0
Lopez, Raul, Laguna	.956	49	81	6	4	91	1
Lucca, Lou, Laguna	1.000	2	4	0	0	4	0
Lujan, Enrique, Tijuana	...	1	0	0	0	0	0
Macias, Roberto, Aguascalientes	1.000	13	6	0	0	6	0
Marmolejo, Ivan, Cancun	.500	1	1	0	1	2	0
Martinez, Abel, Laguna	1.000	7	18	0	0	18	0
Martinez, Enrique, San Luis Potosi	.955	54	83	1	4	88	1
Martinez, Greg, Laguna	.941	6	16	0	1	17	0

Player, Team	Pct.	G	PO	A	E	TC	DP
Martinez, Manny, Puebla	.980	70	136	10	3	149	3
Mata, Noe, Aguascalientes-Cancun	.986	99	210	6	3	219	2
McDonald, Donzell, Tabasco	.993	107	267	10	2	279	2
Medina, Jose Ramon, Monclova	1.000	22	37	0	0	37	0
Mendez, Francisco, Monterrey	1.000	3	4	0	0	4	0
Mendez, Roberto, Mexico	.981	95	148	4	3	155	1
Meyers, Chad, Oaxaca	.991	108	218	4	2	224	0
Meza, Gonzalo, Monclova	1.000	65	96	0	0	96	0
Montenegro, Jose, Oaxaca	1.000	9	8	0	0	8	0
Munoz, Adan, Angelopolis	1.000	5	9	0	0	9	0
Munoz, Jose, Saltillo *	.942	97	151	11	10	172	0
Nieves, Melvin, Laguna	.967	32	58	1	2	61	0
O'Sullivan, Patrick, San Luis Potosi	1.000	41	77	3	0	80	1
Owens, Eric, Tijuana-Saltillo	.959	24	44	3	2	49	1
Pacho, Carlos, Laguna	...	2	0	0	0	0	0
Paez, Hector, Campeche	1.000	6	5	0	0	5	0
Palafox, Sergio, Saltillo-Cancun	.972	22	33	2	1	36	0
Pemberton, Rudy, Laguna-Cancun	.967	56	111	7	4	122	1
Pena, Cesar, Tijuana	1.000	10	10	0	0	10	0
Perez, Francisco, San Luis Potosi-Puebla	1.000	7	3	0	0	3	0
Perez, Jose, San Luis Potosi	1.000	15	13	0	0	13	0
Ponce, Angel, Veracruz	...	3	0	0	0	0	0
Presichi, Cristhian, Saltillo	.976	83	153	7	4	164	1
Quinones, Ruben, Cancun	1.000	2	1	0	0	1	0
Quintero, Christian, Oaxaca	.990	102	182	8	2	192	3
QUINTERO, EDGAR, Monterrey *	1.000	80	115	5	0	120	0
Ramirez, Jesus, Cancun	.981	29	50	3	1	54	0
Ramirez, Omar, Veracruz	.992	106	228	7	2	237	1
Reyes, Jesus, Oaxaca	1.000	32	37	2	0	39	0
Reyes, Julio, Laguna	.969	30	30	1	1	32	0
Rincon, Isaias, Mexico-Oaxaca	.981	38	52	0	1	53	0
Rios, Fernando, Monterrey-San Luis Potosi	.978	63	131	3	3	137	0
Rivera, Ruben, Campeche	.993	73	128	11	1	140	0
Robles, Oscar, Mexico	1.000	2	1	0	0	1	0
Rodriguez, Ferdinand, Monclova	.946	34	52	1	3	56	0
Rodriguez, Fernando, Monclova	.938	14	14	1	1	16	1
Rodriguez, Henry, Tabasco *	.750	3	3	0	1	4	0
Rodriguez, Serafin, Angelopolis	.956	60	84	2	4	90	0
Romero, Flavio, Campeche	.964	44	75	5	3	83	0
Romero, Wilson, Yucatan	.991	100	220	7	2	229	0
Romo, Jesus, Angelopolis *	1.000	10	8	0	0	8	0
Ruiz, Ricardo, Laguna	.929	22	25	1	2	28	0
Saenz, Ricardo, Monclova	.986	78	137	5	2	144	0
Salazar, Oscar, Cancun	1.000	28	41	1	0	42	0
Salcedo, Eder, San Luis Potosi	.959	23	44	3	2	49	2
Sanchez, Raul, Cancun-Aguascalientes	.986	96	206	12	3	221	4
Sanchez, Roque, Campeche	...	1	0	0	0	0	0
Sandoval, Octavio, Angelopolis	.980	55	91	9	2	102	0
Selby, Bill, Campeche	.994	98	154	12	1	167	4
Sequea, Jorge, Tabasco	1.000	3	1	0	0	1	0
Sherman, Darrell, Puebla *	.994	66	151	5	1	157	2
Sievers, Carlos, Tabasco	1.000	2	2	0	0	2	0
Smith, Demond, Monterrey	.982	79	161	7	3	171	3
Soriano, Ricardo, Aguascalientes *	.993	79	138	12	1	151	1
Sotomayor, Gilberto, Monclova *	1.000	42	23	0	0	23	0
Suarez, Luis, Angelopolis	.992	85	122	7	1	130	1
Tapia, Cesar, Puebla	.909	9	9	1	1	11	0
Timmons, Ozzie, Monclova	.833	5	5	0	1	6	0
Valdes (Manzo), Pedro, Saltillo *	1.000	36	44	2	0	46	0
Valdez, Ramon, Campeche	1.000	70	165	9	0	174	2
Valencia, Abraham, Tijuana-Oaxaca	1.000	17	20	3	0	23	1
Valencia, Christian, Monterrey	1.000	5	3	0	0	3	0
Valenzuela, Mario, Saltillo	.975	84	181	14	5	200	2
Vazquez, Gregorio, Tabasco	1.000	66	110	13	0	123	2
Vega, Jesus, Angelopolis	...	1	0	0	0	0	0
Villalobos, Carlos, Puebla-San Luis Potosi	.978	64	129	4	3	136	1
Villegas, Fernando, Saltillo	.941	16	15	1	1	17	0
White, Derrick, Tijuana	.989	106	179	9	2	190	1
Zazueta, Christian, Cancun	1.000	2	2	0	0	2	0
Zazueta, Juan, Saltillo	1.000	2	2	0	0	2	0

OUTFIELDERS WITH TWO OR MORE TEAMS

Player, Team	Pct.	G	PO	A	E	TC	DP
Alvarez, Hector, Monterrey	.962	39	48	2	2	52	1
Alvarez, Hector, Oaxaca	.982	22	54	0	1	55	0
Alvarez, Rafael, Laguna *	.971	16	31	2	1	34	0
Alvarez, Rafael, Cancun	.986	30	64	4	1	69	0
Arredondo, Eduardo, Tabasco *	.987	42	76	2	1	79	0
Arredondo, Eduardo, Mexico *	1.000	19	39	1	0	40	0
Espino, Daniel, Cancun	.941	50	91	4	6	101	1

Player, Team	Pct.	G	PO	A	E	TC	DP
Espino, Daniel, Veracruz	...	1	0	0	0	0	0
Mata, Noe, Aguascalientes	.984	62	116	4	2	122	1
Mata, Noe, Cancun	.990	37	94	2	1	97	1
Owens, Eric, Tijuana	.958	20	43	3	2	48	1
Owens, Eric, Saltillo	1.000	4	1	0	0	1	0
Palafox, Sergio, Saltillo	1.000	5	3	0	0	3	0
Palafox, Sergio, Cancun	.970	17	30	2	1	33	0
Pemberton, Rudy, Laguna	.974	37	71	5	2	78	1
Pemberton, Rudy, Cancun	.955	19	40	2	2	44	0
Perez, Francisco, San Luis Potosi *	...	3	0	0	0	0	0
Perez, Francisco, Puebla *	1.000	4	3	0	0	3	0
Rincon, Isaias, Mexico	1.000	7	2	0	0	2	0
Rincon, Isaias, Oaxaca	.980	31	50	0	1	51	0
Rios, Fernando, Monterrey	1.000	2	1	0	0	1	0
Rios, Fernando, San Luis Potosi	.978	61	130	3	3	136	0
Sanchez, Raul, Cancun	.981	59	145	10	3	158	3
Sanchez, Raul, Aguascalientes	1.000	37	61	2	0	63	1
Valencia, Abraham, Tijuana	1.000	9	5	2	0	7	0
Valencia, Abraham, Oaxaca	1.000	8	15	1	0	16	1
Villalobos, Carlos, Puebla	1.000	1	3	0	0	3	0
Villalobos, Carlos, San Luis Potosi	.977	63	126	4	3	133	1

CATCHERS

Player, Team	Pct.	G	PO	A	E	TC	DP
Amezcua, Adan, Monterrey	.988	89	526	41	7	574	13
Arauz, Ignacio, Saltillo	1.000	10	32	2	0	34	0
Baez, Carlos, Tabasco	...	1	0	0	0	0	0
Castaneda, Hector, Yucatan	.996	51	214	20	1	235	3
Castaneda, Rafael, Laguna	1.000	1	3	0	0	3	0
Cazarin, Manuel, Veracruz	.985	57	287	33	5	325	2
Cobos, Rogelio, Mexico	.986	33	128	17	2	147	0
Cruz, Marco Antonio, Campeche	.978	37	120	11	3	134	0
Delgado, Alex, Aguascalientes	.990	87	425	48	5	478	10
Esparragoza, Francisco, Saltillo	.977	15	36	7	1	44	1
Espino, Daniel, Cancun	...	1	0	0	0	0	0
Esqueda, Jonathan, Campeche	1.000	3	6	1	0	7	0
Estrada, Hector, Laguna	.988	84	447	42	6	495	6
Garzon, Eliseo, Oaxaca	.977	37	158	12	4	174	2
Gastelum, Carlos, Yucatan	1.000	33	78	12	0	90	2
Gavia, Jesus, Aguascalientes	.969	35	118	7	4	129	0
Gonzalez, Fernando, Cancun	1.000	22	52	2	0	54	2
Gonzalez, Roman, Aguascalientes	...	1	0	0	0	0	0
Gonzalez, Santiago, Veracruz	1.000	1	1	0	0	1	0
Gutierrez, Andres, Tabasco	...	1	0	0	0	0	0
Gutierrez, Ricardo, Yucatan	.981	66	330	40	7	377	7
Guzman, Edwards, Puebla	1.000	5	14	5	0	19	0
Higuera, Ottoniel, Oaxaca	1.000	4	2	0	0	2	0
Hurtado, Hector, Puebla	.990	98	451	52	5	508	9
Lizarraga, Norberto, Laguna	.979	15	44	2	1	47	1
Lugo, Roberto, Monterrey	.968	30	85	6	3	94	1
Lujan, Enrique, Tijuana	.969	15	56	6	2	64	1
Marmolejo, Ivan, Cancun	.926	12	24	1	2	27	0
Medina, Jose Ramon, Monclova	1.000	6	2	0	0	2	0
Meza, Alfredo, San Luis Potosi	.974	68	320	21	9	350	6
Meza, Gonzalo, Monclova	1.000	1	1	0	0	1	0
Montano, Angel, Tijuana	1.000	8	21	2	0	23	0
Montenegro, Jose, Oaxaca	1.000	22	50	3	0	53	2
Morales, Ramon, Tabasco	1.000	5	3	0	0	3	0
Munoz, Adan, Angelopolis	.982	86	341	48	7	396	5
Munoz, Noe, Saltillo	.988	106	643	42	8	693	11
Pacho, Carlos, Laguna	.983	48	214	18	4	236	1
Paez, Hector, Campeche	.984	85	520	47	9	576	7
Pena, Angel, Oaxaca	1.000	2	7	0	0	7	0
Perez, Noel, Campeche	1.000	4	7	1	0	8	0
Quinones, Ruben, Cancun	.977	75	336	50	9	395	10
Resendez, Carlos, Monclova	.976	34	115	6	3	124	0
Reyes, Julio, Laguna	...	1	0	0	0	0	0
Rivera, Francisco, Veracruz-Cancun	.977	27	115	12	3	130	1
Rivera, Jesus, Tabasco	...	1	0	0	0	0	0
Robles, Juan, Tabasco	.985	43	122	10	2	134	0
Rodriguez, Armando, Tijuana	1.000	11	66	3	0	69	1
Rodriguez, Carlos, San Luis Potosi	.981	63	230	25	5	260	7
Rodriguez, Erick, Oaxaca	.984	73	352	26	6	384	4
Rodriguez, Leonardo, Monterrey	1.000	16	52	7	0	59	1
Santana, Mario, Tabasco	.988	89	369	51	5	425	7
Soto, Saul, Mexico	.994	83	474	34	3	511	5
Sotomayor, Gilberto, Monclova *	1.000	1	1	0	0	1	0
Tapia, Cesar, Puebla	1.000	25	49	6	0	55	0
Torres, Ivan, Monclova-Veracruz	.800	6	3	1	1	5	0
Valdez, Emmanuel, Tijuana	.978	92	559	51	14	624	13
Valdez, Francisco, Veracruz	.984	64	287	24	5	316	1

Player, Team	Pct.	G	PO	A	E	TC	DP
Valencia, Abraham, Tijuana	...	1	0	0	0	0	0
Valle, Cosme, San Luis Potosi	1.000	4	9	0	0	9	0
Vazquez, Jorge, Angelopolis	...	1	0	0	0	0	0
VEGA, EDGAR, Veracruz	.994	92	466	51	3	520	7
Vega, Jesus, Angelopolis	.977	42	153	15	4	172	1
Villegas, Felipe, Aguascalientes	1.000	4	4	0	0	4	0
Zazueta, Mauricio, Oaxaca	...	1	0	0	0	0	0

CATCHERS WITH TWO OR MORE TEAMS

Player, Team	Pct.	G	PO	A	E	TC	DP
Rivera, Francisco, Veracruz	1.000	1	2	0	0	2	0
Rivera, Francisco, Cancun	.977	26	113	12	3	128	1
Torres, Ivan, Monclova	1.000	1	1	1	0	2	0
Torres, Ivan, Veracruz	.667	5	2	0	1	3	0

PITCHERS

Player, Team	Pct.	G	PO	A	E	TC	DP
Abreu, Winston, Oaxaca	1.000	18	1	1	0	2	0
Acevedo, Juan, Monterrey	1.000	29	0	5	0	5	0
Aceves, Alfredo, Yucatan	.944	22	5	12	1	18	1
Acosta, Aaron, Veracruz	.933	21	10	18	2	30	2
Acosta, Jasiel, Monclova *	.929	21	2	11	1	14	1
Aguilar, Gerardo, Aguascalientes *	.923	38	3	9	1	13	2
Aguilar, Hugo, Veracruz *	.667	30	0	4	2	6	0
Aguilar, Mario, Campeche *	1.000	16	1	1	0	2	0
Aguirre, Alejandro, Monclova	1.000	5	0	1	0	1	0
Aguirre, Gaudencio, Monterrey	1.000	35	3	8	0	11	1
Aguirre, Rodolfo, Puebla	.500	21	0	1	1	2	0
Ahumada, Edgar, Saltillo-Laguna	1.000	24	0	2	0	2	0
Alberro, Jose, Monclova	1.000	11	3	4	0	7	1
Almonte, Hector, Saltillo	...	10	0	0	0	0	0
Alvarez, Antonio, Aguascalientes	1.000	32	2	6	0	8	1
Alvarez, Gabriel, Mexico-Monclova	1.000	17	0	1	0	1	0
Alvarez, Juan, Puebla *	1.000	8	1	3	0	4	0
Alvarez, Juan Jesus, Campeche	.963	22	9	17	1	27	2
Alvarez, Victor, Mexico *	1.000	18	2	16	0	18	0
Amarillas, Asdrubal, Cancun	...	1	0	0	0	0	0
Arellano, Salvador, Yucatan	1.000	20	3	6	0	9	1
Armas, Noel, Puebla	...	9	0	0	0	0	0
Armenta, Alejandro, Angelopolis *	1.000	23	4	19	0	23	3
Avalos, Jose, Oaxaca	1.000	44	3	6	0	9	1
Baez, Sixto, Veracruz	1.000	42	4	11	0	15	4
Barradas, Roberto, Campeche	.750	13	2	1	1	4	0
Barreras, Juan, Laguna	1.000	38	0	4	0	4	0
Beltran, Alonso, Tijuana	1.000	21	10	14	0	24	3
Beltran, Rigo, Saltillo *	.952	20	7	13	1	21	4
Bernal, Christian, Laguna	1.000	31	2	4	0	6	0
Bernal, Manuel, Laguna	.875	10	3	4	1	8	0
Blancas, Rigoberto, Cancun *	1.000	14	0	1	0	1	1
Bland, Nate, Tijuana *	.905	29	6	13	2	21	2
Borbon, Sergio, Saltillo	...	2	0	0	0	0	0
Bourgeois, Steve, Saltillo	1.000	19	7	5	0	12	0
Bueno, Geraldo, Cancun	1.000	30	3	4	0	7	2
Bustillos, Oscar, Angelopolis	.667	27	2	2	2	6	2
Camara, Pedro, Yucatan *	1.000	42	2	5	0	7	0
Campos, Francisco, Campeche	.958	22	6	17	1	24	2
Cantu, Jacobo, Tabasco	1.000	4	1	0	0	1	1
Carbajal, Luis, Laguna *	...	1	0	0	0	0	0
Carrasco, Alejandro, Yucatan	1.000	33	6	8	0	14	1
Carrillo, Guillermo, Angelopolis	1.000	27	4	6	0	10	2
Castaneda, Federico, Laguna-Aguascalientes	1.000	18	1	4	0	5	2
Castellanos, Hugo, Tijuana	1.000	28	8	19	0	27	2
Castillo, Jorge, Mexico *	1.000	20	3	2	0	5	0
Cazares, Rosario, Saltillo-Cancun	.818	20	4	5	2	11	1
Cerros, Juan, San Luis Potosi	1.000	31	2	3	0	5	0
Cervantes, Pedro, San Luis Potosi	1.000	13	3	2	0	5	0
Chavarria, Hector, Veracruz	1.000	29	3	10	0	13	2
Chavez, Alejandro, Mexico	...	4	0	0	0	0	0
Chavez, Jose, Monterrey	...	1	0	0	0	0	0
Chouinard, Bobby, Yucatan	...	4	0	0	0	0	0
Cobos, Jose, Monterrey-San Luis Potosi	1.000	25	0	6	0	6	0
Coco, Pasqual, Saltillo-Veracruz	.923	29	4	8	1	13	2
Cordova, Alejandro, San Luis Potosi	...	2	0	0	0	0	0
Cordova, Francisco, Mexico	.947	33	4	14	1	19	0
Cruz, Javier, Veracruz	...	7	0	0	0	0	0
DeHart, Rick, Monterrey *	1.000	5	1	2	0	3	0
De La Hoya, Javier, Campeche	1.000	7	1	5	0	6	0
De La Rosa, Maximo, Monterrey	1.000	51	4	3	0	7	0
Delfin, Adolfo, Tijuana	1.000	44	5	12	0	17	0
Delgadillo, Juan, Tabasco	.913	23	5	16	2	23	2

Player, Team	Pct.	G	PO	A	E	TC	DP
Desgue, Fernando, Tabasco	1.000	32	3	3	0	6	1
Diaz, Marco, Aguascalientes	1.000	44	1	5	0	6	0
Diaz, Rafael, Saltillo	1.000	16	4	6	0	10	0
Dominguez, Carlos, Saltillo-Angelopolis-Puebla	.857	36	2	4	1	7	1
Dominguez, David, Mexico	1.000	46	1	4	0	5	0
Dorame, Randey, Monclova *	1.000	10	0	2	0	2	1
Duarte, Mauricio, Cancun	1.000	6	0	1	0	1	0
Duarte, Miguel, Saltillo	.875	50	3	4	1	8	1
Elizalde, Carlos, Oaxaca	1.000	7	2	0	0	2	0
Elvira, Abraham, Aguascalientes *	.929	19	1	12	1	14	0
Elvira, Joaquin, Tabasco	1.000	13	0	2	0	2	0
Elvira, Narciso, Campeche *	1.000	2	0	3	0	3	0
Escobedo, Edgar, Mexico-Oaxaca	1.000	17	2	5	0	7	0
Espadas, Gary, Yucatan	1.000	38	4	1	0	5	0
Esparza, Emerson, Laguna	1.000	17	2	3	0	5	1
Espinoza, Omar, Puebla	.833	30	2	3	1	6	1
Esquer, Mercedes, San Luis Potosi *	1.000	13	1	4	0	5	0
Estrada, Horacio, Oaxaca *	.882	13	2	13	2	17	2
Estrella, Leo, Laguna-Veracruz	1.000	49	4	12	0	16	1
Federico, Gustavo, Puebla	1.000	13	5	8	0	13	0
Felix, Francisco, Saltillo	1.000	15	1	3	0	4	0
Fernandez, Osvaldo, Tabasco	.943	23	12	21	2	35	0
Flores, Ignacio, Saltillo-Angelopolis-Puebla	1.000	15	6	5	0	11	0
Flores, Ignacio, Yucatan	.846	29	4	7	2	13	0
Flores, Jorge, Monclova *	1.000	49	1	13	0	14	2
Flores, Manuel, Yucatan	1.000	2	0	1	0	1	0
Flores, Renato, Monclova	1.000	38	0	8	0	8	1
Flores, Wilfrido, Tabasco	1.000	18	1	2	0	3	1
Galvez, Randy, Oaxaca-Tabasco	1.000	33	5	9	0	14	2
Garcia, Adolfo, Veracruz	1.000	36	5	9	0	14	1
Garcia, Alfredo, Oaxaca	1.000	6	0	3	0	3	0
Garcia, Carlos, Laguna	1.000	5	0	2	0	2	0
Garcia, Gerardo, Angelopolis	1.000	8	1	3	0	4	0
Garcia, Humberto, San Luis Potosi *	1.000	51	2	1	0	3	0
Garcia, Jonathan, Campeche	1.000	22	1	0	0	1	0
Garcia, Jose Luis, Campeche *	1.000	48	4	10	0	14	0
Garcia, Rafael, Aguascalientes-Cancun	1.000	6	2	5	0	7	0
Garcia, Ramon Antonio, San Luis Potosi	1.000	20	1	2	0	3	0
Garibaldi, Cecilio, Angelopolis	.846	35	4	7	2	13	1
Garibay, Javier, Angelopolis *	...	1	0	0	0	0	0
Garibay, Roberto, Tijuana	1.000	45	4	8	0	12	0
Garibay, Salvador, Tijuana	1.000	46	6	15	0	21	0
Garza, Conrado, Cancun *	1.000	48	0	7	0	7	0
Garza, Luis, Cancun	1.000	22	1	4	0	5	0
Giron, Isabel, Monterrey	.909	18	5	15	2	22	2
Gomes, Wayne, Yucatan-Saltillo	1.000	13	1	1	0	2	0
Gomez, Martin, Laguna	.933	22	5	9	1	15	1
Gonzalez, Antonio, Tijuana	...	2	0	0	0	0	0
Gonzalez, Gilberto, San Luis Potosi-Puebla	.833	19	0	5	1	6	0
Gonzalez, Leonardo, Tijuana	1.000	23	6	11	0	17	2
Gonzalez, Mario, Monclova	1.000	3	0	1	0	1	0
Gonzalez, Miguel, Saltillo	.833	26	7	8	3	18	1
GONZALEZ, RUDY, Mexico	1.000	27	10	24	0	34	2
Gonzalez, Vinicio, Tabasco	.963	33	7	19	1	27	1
Gracia, Mario, Oaxaca	1.000	1	0	1	0	1	0
Grajales, Norberto, Campeche	1.000	6	0	2	0	2	0
Guerrero, Fernando, Laguna	1.000	9	3	2	0	5	2
Gutierrez, Carlos, Laguna	1.000	21	5	1	0	6	2
Gutierrez, Jorge, Cancun-Laguna	1.000	18	2	2	0	4	0
Gutierrez, Luis, Tijuana	1.000	3	0	1	0	1	1
Guzman, Jesus, Angelopolis *	1.000	28	10	6	0	16	1
Guzman, Ricardo, Monclova	1.000	36	2	7	0	9	0
Hammond, Matthew, Tijuana	1.000	7	2	0	0	2	0
Haro, Esteban, Angelopolis	1.000	2	1	0	0	1	0
Hermosillo, Victor, Laguna-Tabasco	1.000	8	1	0	0	1	0
Hernandez, Adrian, Laguna	1.000	18	5	19	0	24	2
Hernandez, Esteban, Oaxaca-Tijuana	1.000	19	0	6	0	6	1
Hernandez, Fernando, Monterrey-Aguascalientes	.769	22	3	7	3	13	2
Hernandez, Jose Manuel, Veracruz-Puebla	1.000	24	1	0	0	1	0
Hernandez, Santos, Tabasco-Puebla	1.000	29	1	5	0	6	0
Herrera, Enrique, Tabasco	1.000	11	1	3	0	4	0
Hildago, Romeo, Campeche	1.000	16	1	0	0	1	1
Huerta, Armando, Laguna	...	1	0	0	0	0	0
Huerta, Edgar, Angelopolis *	1.000	25	0	2	0	2	0
Huerta, Martin, Puebla	1.000	20	2	1	0	3	2
Hurtado, Edwin, Monclova-Monterrey	.897	25	10	16	3	29	4
Jacome, Jason, Monclova-Puebla	.926	22	6	19	2	27	0
Jimenez, Jose De Jesus, Oaxaca	1.000	48	1	12	0	13	0
Jimenez, Julio, Laguna *	.857	37	1	5	1	7	0
Johnson, Adam, Puebla	1.000	5	1	2	0	3	0
Kamar, Emil, Angelopolis-Puebla	1.000	34	4	3	0	7	0
Knott, Eric, Puebla *	1.000	23	6	19	0	25	2
Lara, Jorge, Puebla-Tabasco	.750	29	2	1	1	4	0
Lara, Mauricio, Monterrey *	.933	43	3	11	1	15	2
Larreal, Guillermo, Cancun	1.000	10	0	3	0	3	1
Leon, Cupertino, Oaxaca	.882	45	4	11	2	17	2
Leon, Juan, Tabasco	...	3	0	0	0	0	0
Leyva, Aldo, Yucatan *	...	3	0	0	0	0	0
Leyva, Edgar, San Luis Potosi	1.000	22	4	9	0	13	1
Lira, Felipe, Aguascalientes	1.000	4	0	4	0	4	1
Lizarraga, Edgar, Mexico	1.000	27	2	3	0	5	0
Lizarraga, Sergio, Monterrey	1.000	8	0	7	0	7	1
Llamas, Eder, Angelopolis	1.000	7	1	0	0	1	0
Lomeli, Israel, Veracruz	1.000	29	1	3	0	4	0
Lontayo, Alejandro, Oaxaca *	.833	12	1	4	1	6	0
Lopez, Daniel, Monclova	1.000	9	0	4	0	4	0
Lopez, Emigdio, Veracruz	.967	20	9	20	1	30	1
Lopez, Jesus, Laguna	1.000	12	1	0	0	1	0
Lopez, Jose, San Luis Potosi-Oaxaca	1.000	39	2	7	0	9	1
Lopez, Miguel, San Luis Potosi	.923	49	2	10	1	13	2
Loya, Rigoberto, Monterrey	.923	21	9	3	1	13	0
Luevano, Juan, Aguascalientes	1.000	55	2	7	0	9	1
Lugo, Carlos, Tijuana *	1.000	25	2	2	0	4	0
Lyons, Michael, Yucatan	...	5	0	0	0	0	0
Macias, Luis, Puebla	.800	42	0	4	1	5	0
Madero, Francisco, Oaxaca	.917	19	1	10	1	12	2
Magee, Daniel, Campeche *	.952	13	6	14	1	21	3
Mairena, Oswaldo, Oaxaca-Laguna	.923	25	0	12	1	13	0
Manning, David, Campeche	1.000	33	10	2	0	12	0
Manrique, Alberto, San Luis Potosi-Campeche	.833	26	1	9	2	12	2
Manzanillo, Josias, Puebla	1.000	26	3	7	0	10	2
Manzanillo, Ravelo, Puebla *	1.000	4	0	6	0	6	0
Manzano, Adrian, Angelopolis	1.000	35	0	4	0	4	0
Mariscal, Jesus, Angelopolis	1.000	10	0	1	0	1	0
Marquez, Isidro, Campeche	1.000	38	4	6	0	10	3
Martinez, Cesar, Tijuana-Laguna	1.000	25	3	3	0	6	0
Martinez, Gustavo, Cancun	.500	4	0	3	3	6	0
Martinez, Juan Jesus, Aguascalientes-Cancun	1.000	26	6	13	0	19	4
Medina, Roberto, Puebla *	1.000	4	1	0	0	1	0
Medrano, Leobardo, Monterrey	1.000	2	1	0	0	1	0
Melendez, Nestor, San Luis Potosi	...	3	0	0	0	0	0
Melgarejo, Thomas, Saltillo *	1.000	31	0	1	0	1	0
Mendoza, Mario, Saltillo	1.000	51	6	15	0	21	1
Mercedes, Jose, Saltillo	.941	15	4	12	1	17	1
Meyer, Jake, Oaxaca	...	1	0	0	0	0	0
Meza, Jorge, Tijuana *	1.000	15	1	1	0	2	0
Molina, Gabe, San Luis Potosi	.870	34	12	8	3	23	2
Montano, Ignacio, Cancun-Aguascalientes	1.000	19	10	19	0	29	1
Montemayor, Humberto, San Luis Potosi	1.000	24	2	13	0	15	1
Montoya, Francisco, San Luis Potosi	1.000	24	2	13	0	15	1
Mora, Eleazar, Oaxaca *	1.000	32	7	18	0	25	3
Mora, Sergio, Monterrey	1.000	40	3	4	0	7	0
Morales, Luis Fernando, Veracruz *	1.000	13	0	2	0	2	0
Morales, Reynaldo, Oaxaca	1.000	16	3	0	0	3	0
Moreno, Angel, Veracruz *	1.000	21	4	20	0	24	1
Moreno, Claudio, Mexico	.875	25	12	16	4	32	1
Moreno, Leobardo, Veracruz	1.000	40	3	5	0	8	0
Munoz, Leonardo, Angelopolis *	.875	41	1	6	1	8	0
Munoz, Pablo, Aguascalientes-Cancun	...	29	0	0	0	0	0
Murguia, Edgar, Laguna	1.000	4	0	1	0	1	0
Navarro, Hector, Veracruz-Angelopolis	1.000	40	3	11	0	14	1
Navarro, Joel, Oaxaca-Tijuana	1.000	25	1	8	0	9	0
Navarro, Jose Felix, Monclova-Veracruz	1.000	22	3	4	0	7	0
Navarro, Luis, Yucatan	1.000	39	1	5	0	6	0
Neri, Eduardo, Tijuana *	1.000	22	1	4	0	5	1
Nieblas, Mauro, Monterrey *	1.000	28	3	6	0	9	0
Nieblas, Omar, Cancun *	.750	21	0	6	2	8	1
Nunez, Javier, Aguascalientes-Cancun	.947	30	6	12	1	19	2
Nunez, Jose, Puebla	.800	58	1	7	2	10	0
Nunez, Jose, Aguascalientes	.857	9	1	5	1	7	0
Ochoa, Pablo, Monterrey	1.000	23	8	4	0	12	0
Olague, Jesus, Aguascalientes	.923	22	2	10	1	13	1
Orea, Flavio, Aguascalientes	.833	45	1	4	1	6	1
Oropesa, Eddie, Tabasco *	1.000	26	2	2	0	4	1
Orrantia, Carlos, Monterrey	...	1	0	0	0	0	0
Ortega, Pablo, Angelopolis	1.000	23	7	9	0	16	0
Ortega, Roberto, Puebla *	1.000	37	2	6	0	8	1
Ortega, Wilbert, Veracruz *	1.000	37	0	2	0	2	0
Osuna, Adrian, Oaxaca	...	1	0	0	0	0	0
Osuna, Ulises, San Luis Potosi	1.000	5	1	1	0	2	0
Pablos, Rene, Saltillo *	.875	22	3	4	1	8	1
Palafox, Juan Manuel, Yucatan	1.000	19	4	15	0	19	2

Player, Team	Pct.	G	PO	A	E	TC	DP
Palki, Jeromy, Yucatan	1.000	12	2	2	0	4	0
Palma, Ricardo, Cancun-Aguascalientes	1.000	16	4	14	0	18	1
Parra, Julio, Tijuana	1.000	40	0	5	0	5	0
Parra, Orlando, Campeche *	.000	8	0	0	1	1	0
Patrick, Bronswell, Tabasco-Yucatan	1.000	12	4	8	0	12	0
Pena, Joel, Tabasco	1.000	20	1	2	0	3	0
Pena, Juan, Aguascalientes	1.000	7	2	5	0	7	0
Perez, Edgar, Cancun-Aguascalientes	1.000	20	3	13	0	16	2
Perez, Guadalupe, Veracruz-Cancun-Aguascalientes ..	.875	32	2	5	1	8	0
Perez, Manuel, San Luis Potosi *	...	14	0	0	0	0	0
Perez, Miguel, Saltillo	.933	29	4	10	1	15	0
Pimentel, Roberto, Tabasco *	1.000	40	0	12	0	12	0
Pina, Rafael, Veracruz	1.000	21	3	9	0	12	0
Pinales, Aquiles, Cancun	1.000	5	1	3	0	4	0
Pineda, Isauro, Monterrey	1.000	20	7	15	0	22	0
Pizzaro, Melvin, Yucatan *	1.000	12	0	2	0	2	1
Posadas, Obedt, Saltillo-Laguna	.941	22	6	10	1	17	1
Pulido, Carlos, Oaxaca *	1.000	23	6	22	0	28	4
Pulido, Raymundo, Campeche-Laguna	1.000	16	0	1	0	1	1
Quinones, Enrique, San Luis Potosi	1.000	25	4	10	0	14	1
Quintanilla, Juan, Oaxaca	1.000	37	3	7	0	10	2
Quiroz, Aaron, Tijuana	1.000	17	14	12	0	26	1
Raggio, Brady, Campeche	1.000	8	3	3	0	6	0
Ramirez, Adrian, Monclova *	1.000	43	1	7	0	8	0
Ramirez, Omar, Veracruz	...	1	0	0	0	0	0
Ramirez, Roberto, Mexico *	.909	24	10	40	5	55	4
Ramon, Jose, Tabasco	1.000	14	0	1	0	1	0
Ramos, Eddy, Monclova-Yucatan	.950	28	8	11	1	20	3
Renovato, Nestor, San Luis Potosi	1.000	39	3	12	0	15	2
Reyes, Nathanael, Campeche	.889	19	3	5	1	9	0
Rios, Alejandro, Saltillo	1.000	34	1	8	0	9	0
Rios, Jesus, Tabasco	1.000	21	4	10	0	14	1
Rivera, Bienvenido, Laguna-Aguascalientes	1.000	44	1	7	0	8	0
Rivera, Francisco, Aguascalientes	.974	25	7	30	1	38	4
Rivera, Luis, Angelopolis	.957	23	7	15	1	23	0
Rivera, Oscar, Yucatan *	1.000	20	3	13	0	16	0
Rivera, Oscar, Saltillo	.778	24	6	1	2	9	0
Rivera, Paul, Tabasco *	.857	40	1	5	1	7	0
Roberts, Willis, Campeche	1.000	29	6	3	0	9	0
Rodriguez, Enoc, Aguascalientes *	.833	30	2	3	1	6	0
Rodriguez, Francisco, Oaxaca *	1.000	6	1	2	0	3	0
Rodriguez, Francisco, Puebla	.889	33	8	16	3	27	2
Rodriguez, Jesus, Monclova	.938	26	5	10	1	16	1
Rodriguez, Manuel, Campeche	...	1	0	0	0	0	0
Rodriguez, Nerio, Monclova	.833	10	1	4	1	6	0
Rodriguez, Raul, Monclova-Yucatan	1.000	21	2	17	0	19	1
Rodriguez, Rosario, Tijuana *	.667	18	0	2	1	3	0
Romero, Josmir, Oaxaca	.769	9	4	6	3	13	0
Romo, Noe, Puebla *	1.000	28	3	10	0	13	2
Roque, Jorge, Cancun	...	8	0	0	0	0	0
Roque, Rafael, Puebla-Monterrey	...	3	0	0	0	0	0
Rubio, Carlos, Cancun	1.000	9	2	1	0	3	0
Rubio, Miguel, Monterrey	1.000	33	3	3	0	6	0
Ruelas, Heriberto, Mexico *	1.000	35	0	1	0	1	0
Ruiz, Arturo, Saltillo *	1.000	28	0	2	0	2	1
Ruiz, Cecilio, Tabasco *	1.000	3	1	0	0	1	0
Ruiz, Miguel, Campeche	1.000	7	4	2	0	6	0
Sabido, Eduardo, Veracruz	1.000	2	1	0	0	1	0
Saipe, Mike, Saltillo	1.000	2	0	1	0	1	0
Salas, Noel, Saltillo	1.000	14	0	1	0	1	0
Saldana, Jose, Cancun-Puebla	1.000	8	0	1	0	1	0
Salgado, Eduardo, Cancun	1.000	30	8	15	0	23	2
Sanchez, Alejandro, Cancun	.900	53	0	9	1	10	2
Sanchez, Claudio, Veracruz	.818	46	5	4	2	11	0
Sanchez, Efrain, Campeche	1.000	24	8	18	0	26	1
Sanchez, Jose, Tijuana	...	7	0	0	0	0	0
Sangeado, Juan, Cancun	1.000	6	0	3	0	3	0
Serrano, Elio, Tabasco-Laguna	1.000	41	1	9	0	10	0
Serrano, Wascar, Campeche-Yucatan	.750	8	0	3	1	4	0
Shibilo, Andy, Tijuana	.750	13	2	1	1	4	0
Silva, Jose, Mexico	.947	43	3	15	1	19	1
Silva, Walter, Monterrey	1.000	12	4	5	0	9	1
Simas, Bill, Monclova	.900	55	2	7	1	10	1
Sinohui, David, Tijuana-Monclova	1.000	30	1	2	0	3	0
Solis, Tomas, Angelopolis *	...	6	0	0	0	0	0
Soria, Joakim, Mexico	.909	30	7	3	1	11	2
Sotelo, Martin, Mexico	1.000	2	0	1	0	1	0
Soto, Cruz Antonio, Puebla	1.000	26	3	9	0	12	2
Sparks, Jeff, Yucatan	...	3	0	0	0	0	0
Sulu, Mario, Tabasco	1.000	14	2	5	0	7	0
Tejeda, Felix, Veracruz *	...	7	0	0	0	0	0
Tequida, Mauricio, Mexico	1.000	44	3	7	0	10	2
Torres, Jorge, Oaxaca *	1.000	22	1	3	0	4	0
Trevino, Jesus, Laguna *	1.000	17	0	1	0	1	1
Urdaneta, Lino, Aguascalientes-Cancun	1.000	32	1	6	0	7	1
Valdez, Armando, Puebla	1.000	7	0	3	0	3	1
Valdez, Joel, Oaxaca	1.000	3	0	1	0	1	0
Valenzuela, Jose, Angelopolis	1.000	9	0	1	0	1	0
Valerio, Julio, Mexico *	.750	32	0	3	1	4	0
Vargas, Joel, Tabasco	1.000	21	6	7	0	13	0
Vargas, Jose, Laguna-Yucatan	.600	33	0	3	2	5	0
Vazquez, Adrian, Cancun-Veracruz	.889	21	4	4	1	9	1
Vega, Obed, Cancun-Veracruz	1.000	6	2	1	0	3	1
Verdugo, Hugo, Laguna	.933	31	5	9	1	15	2
Verdugo, Oswaldo, Yucatan-Laguna	1.000	37	4	7	0	11	2
Verdugo, Roberto, Angelopolis-San Luis Potosi..	1.000	33	2	6	0	8	3
Viera, Rolando, Tabasco *	1.000	6	0	2	0	2	1
Villalobos, Fernando, Monterrey-San Luis Potosi	.857	17	1	5	1	7	0
Villarreal, Salvador, San Luis Potosi	1.000	38	3	4	0	7	1
Vizcarra, Ernesto, Campeche	1.000	42	2	5	0	7	0
Vizcarra, William, Yucatan-Monclova	1.000	36	3	11	0	14	1
Ward, Bryan, Monclova *	.938	21	1	14	1	16	0
Zambrano, Baudel, Angelopolis	1.000	36	3	7	0	10	2
Zavala, Marcos, Monterrey *	.750	24	0	3	1	4	0

PITCHERS WITH TWO OR MORE TEAMS

Player, Team	Pct.	G	PO	A	E	TC	DP
Ahumada, Edgar, Saltillo *	...	5	0	0	0	0	0
Ahumada, Edgar, Laguna *	1.000	19	0	2	0	2	0
Alvarez, Gabriel, Mexico	...	7	0	0	0	0	0
Alvarez, Gabriel, Monclova	1.000	10	0	1	0	1	0
Castaneda, Federico, Laguna	1.000	11	0	1	0	1	0
Castaneda, Federico, Aguascalientes	1.000	7	1	3	0	4	2
Cazares, Rosario, Saltillo	1.000	10	1	1	0	2	0
Cazares, Rosario, Cancun	.778	10	3	4	2	9	1
Cobos, Jose, Monterrey	1.000	21	0	5	0	5	0
Cobos, Jose, San Luis Potosi	1.000	4	0	1	0	1	0
Coco, Pasqual, Saltillo	1.000	18	2	6	0	8	0
Coco, Pasqual, Veracruz	.800	11	2	2	1	5	2
Dominguez, Carlos, Saltillo *	...	6	0	0	0	0	0
Dominguez, Carlos, Angelopolis *	.500	10	0	1	1	2	0
Dominguez, Carlos, Puebla	1.000	20	2	3	0	5	1
Escobedo, Edgar, Mexico	1.000	10	1	3	0	4	0
Escobedo, Edgar, Oaxaca	1.000	7	1	2	0	3	0
Estrella, Leo, Laguna	1.000	3	0	1	0	1	0
Estrella, Leo, Veracruz	1.000	46	4	11	0	15	1
Flores, Ignacio, Laguna	1.000	6	4	2	0	6	0
Flores, Ignacio, Angelopolis	1.000	4	2	1	0	3	0
Flores, Ignacio, Puebla	1.000	5	0	2	0	2	0
Galvez, Randy, Oaxaca	1.000	12	1	2	0	3	1
Galvez, Randy, Tabasco	1.000	21	4	7	0	11	1
Garcia, Rafael, Aguascalientes	...	3	0	0	0	0	0
Garcia, Rafael, Mexico	1.000	3	2	5	0	7	0
Gomes, Wayne, Yucatan	1.000	11	1	0	0	1	0
Gomes, Wayne, Saltillo	1.000	2	0	1	0	1	0
Gonzalez, Gilberto, San Luis Potosi	1.000	11	0	2	0	2	0
Gonzalez, Gilberto, Puebla	.750	8	0	3	1	4	0
Gutierrez, Jorge, Cancun	1.000	15	2	1	0	3	0
Gutierrez, Jorge, Laguna	1.000	3	0	1	0	1	0
Hermosillo, Victor, Laguna	1.000	7	1	0	0	1	0
Hermosillo, Victor, Monclova	...	1	0	0	0	0	0
Hernandez, Esteban, Oaxaca	1.000	8	1	0	0	2	0
Hernandez, Esteban, Tijuana	1.000	11	0	4	0	4	1
Hernandez, Fernando, Monterrey	.750	6	1	2	1	4	0
Hernandez, Fernando, Aguascalientes	.778	16	2	5	2	9	2
Hernandez, Jose Manuel, Veracruz *	1.000	9	1	0	0	1	0
Hernandez, Jose Manuel, Puebla *	...	15	0	0	0	0	0
Hernandez, Santos, Tabasco	1.000	18	1	4	0	5	0
Hernandez, Santos, Puebla	1.000	11	0	1	0	1	0
Hurtado, Edwin, Monclova	.800	12	4	4	2	10	1
Hurtado, Edwin, Monterrey	.947	13	6	12	1	19	3
Jacome, Jason, Monclova *	.917	14	3	8	1	12	0
Jacome, Jason, Monterrey *	.933	8	3	11	1	15	0
Kamar, Emil, Angelopolis	1.000	17	2	2	0	4	0
Kamar, Emil, Puebla	1.000	17	2	1	0	3	0
Lara, Jorge, Puebla	...	8	0	0	0	0	0
Lara, Jorge, Tabasco	.750	21	2	1	1	4	0
Lopez, Jose, San Luis Potosi	...	5	0	0	0	0	0
Lopez, Jose, Oaxaca	1.000	34	2	7	0	9	1
Mairena, Oswaldo, Oaxaca *	...	2	0	0	0	0	0
Mairena, Oswaldo, Laguna *	.923	23	0	12	1	13	0
Manrique, Alberto, San Luis Potosi	.778	17	0	7	2	9	2

CLASS AAA *Mexican League*

Player, Team	Pct.	G	PO	A	E	TC	DP
Manrique, Alberto, Campeche	1.000	9	1	2	0	3	0
Martinez, Cesar, Tijuana *	1.000	7	0	1	0	1	0
Martinez, Cesar, Laguna *	1.000	18	3	2	0	5	0
Martinez, Juan Jesus, Aguascalientes	1.000	15	0	5	0	5	1
Martinez, Juan Jesus, Cancun	1.000	11	6	8	0	14	3
Montano, Ignacio, Cancun *	1.000	14	10	15	0	25	1
Montano, Ignacio, Aguascalientes *	1.000	5	0	4	0	4	0
Munoz, Pablo, Aguascalientes *	...	10	0	0	0	0	0
Munoz, Pablo, Cancun *	...	19	0	0	0	0	0
Navarro, Hector, Veracruz *	1.000	9	0	3	0	3	0
Navarro, Hector, Angelopolis *	1.000	31	3	8	0	11	1
Navarro, Joel, Oaxaca	1.000	8	0	3	0	3	0
Navarro, Joel, Tijuana	1.000	17	1	5	0	6	0
Navarro, Jose Felix, Monclova	1.000	14	0	3	0	3	0
Navarro, Jose Felix, Veracruz	1.000	8	3	1	0	4	0
Nunez, Javier, Aguascalientes	1.000	22	4	6	0	10	1
Nunez, Javier, Cancun	.889	8	2	6	1	9	1
Palma, Ricardo, Cancun *	1.000	5	0	4	0	4	0
Palma, Ricardo, Aguascalientes *	1.000	11	4	10	0	14	1
Patrick, Bronswell, Tabasco	1.000	6	3	4	0	7	0
Patrick, Bronswell, Yucatan	1.000	6	1	4	0	5	0
Perez, Edgar, Cancun	1.000	13	3	7	0	10	2
Perez, Edgar, Aguascalientes *	1.000	7	0	6	0	6	0
Perez, Guadalupe, Veracruz	1.000	16	0	1	0	1	0
Perez, Guadalupe, Cancun	.800	9	2	2	1	5	0
Perez, Guadalupe, Aguascalientes	1.000	7	0	2	0	2	0
Posadas, Obedt, Saltillo	...	1	0	0	0	0	0
Posadas, Obedt, Laguna	.941	21	6	10	1	17	1
Pulido, Raymundo, Campeche	...	2	0	0	0	0	0
Pulido, Raymundo, Laguna	1.000	14	0	1	0	1	1
Ramos, Eddy, Monclova	.923	15	4	8	1	13	2
Ramos, Eddy, Yucatan	1.000	13	4	3	0	7	1
Rivera, Bienvenido, Laguna	1.000	40	1	6	0	7	0
Rivera, Bienvenido, Aguascalientes	1.000	4	0	1	0	1	0
Rodriguez, Raul, Monclova	1.000	6	1	3	0	4	0
Rodriguez, Raul, Yucatan	1.000	15	1	14	0	15	1
Roque, Rafael, Puebla *	...	1	0	0	0	0	0
Roque, Rafael, Monterrey *	...	2	0	0	0	0	0
Saldana, Jose, Cancun	1.000	2	0	1	0	1	0
Saldana, Jose, Puebla	...	6	0	0	0	0	0
Serrano, Elio, Tabasco	1.000	4	0	1	0	1	0
Serrano, Elio, Laguna	1.000	37	1	8	0	9	0
Serrano, Wascar, Campeche	1.000	5	0	1	0	1	0
Serrano, Wascar, Yucatan	.667	3	0	2	1	3	0
Sinohui, David, Tijuana	1.000	28	1	2	0	3	0
Sinohui, David, Monclova	...	2	0	0	0	0	0
Urdaneta, Lino, Aguascalientes	1.000	26	1	5	0	6	1
Urdaneta, Lino, Cancun	1.000	6	0	1	0	1	0
Vargas, Jose, Laguna	.500	14	0	2	2	4	0
Vargas, Jose, Yucatan	1.000	19	0	1	0	1	0
Vazquez, Adrian, Cancun	...	2	0	0	0	0	0
Vazquez, Adrian, Veracruz	.889	19	4	4	1	9	1
Vega, Obed, Cancun	1.000	2	1	0	0	1	0
Vega, Obed, Veracruz	1.000	4	1	1	0	2	1
Verdugo, Oswaldo, Yucatan	1.000	17	3	4	0	7	1
Verdugo, Oswaldo, Laguna	1.000	20	1	3	0	4	1
Verdugo, Roberto, Angelopolis	1.000	9	0	2	0	2	1
Verdugo, Roberto, San Luis Potosi	1.000	24	2	4	0	6	2
Villalobos, Fernando, Monterrey	1.000	8	0	4	0	4	0
Villalobos, Fernando, San Luis Potosi	.667	9	1	1	1	3	0
Vizcarra, William, Yucatan	1.000	5	2	6	0	8	1
Vizcarra, William, Monclova	1.000	31	1	5	0	6	0

LEAGUE CHAMPIONS

Year	Team	Pct.
1955—	Mexico City Tigers*	.539
1956—	Mexico City Reds	.692
1957—	Yucatan	.567
	Mex. C. Reds (2nd)†	.550
1958—	Nuevo Laredo	.625
1959—	Poza Rica	.575
	Mex. C. Reds (3rd)†	.507
1960—	Mexico City Tigers	.538
1961—	Veracruz	.575
1962—	Monterrey	.592
1963—	Puebla	.606
1964—	Mexico City Reds	.586
1965—	Mexico City Tigers	.590
1966—	Mexico City Tigers‡	.614
	Mexico City Reds	.571
1967—	Jalisco	.607
1968—	Mexico City Reds	.586
1969—	Reynosa	.591
1970—	Aguila§	.580
	Mexico City Reds	.607
1971—	Jalisco§	.558
	Saltillo	.593
1972—	Saltillo	.636
	Cordoba§	.541
1973—	Saltillo	.656
	Mexico City Reds∞	.590
1974—	Jalisco	.627
	Mexico City Reds∞	.551
1975—	Tampico∞	.541
	Cordoba	.649
1976—	Mexico City Reds∞	.543
	Union Laguna	.547
1977—	Mexico City Reds	.623
	Nuevo Laredo∞	.507
1978—	Aguascalientes∞	.589
	Union Laguna	.523
1979—	Saltillo	.704
	Puebla∞	.628
1980—	No champion▲	
1981—	Mexico City Reds	.615
	Reynosa	.492
1982—	Ciudad Juarez∞	.570
	Mexico City Tigers	.508
1983—	Campeche◆	.614
	Ciudad Juarez	.535
1984—	Yucatan◆	.560
	Ciudad Juarez	.509
1985—	Mexico City Reds◆	.606
	Nuevo Laredo	.5275
1986—	Puebla◆	.682
	Monclova	.598
1987—	Mexico City Reds◆	.605
	Monterrey	.536
1988—	Mexico City Reds◆	.646
	Nuevo Laredo	.602
1989—	Nuevo Laredo◆	.621
	Yucatan	.539
1990—	Nuevo Laredo	.618
	Leon◆	.565
1991—	Monterrey◆	.683
	Mexico City Reds	.627
1992—	Mexico City Tigers◆	.594
	Nuevo Laredo	.538
1993—	Nuevo Laredo	.589
	Tabasco◆	.528
1994—	Mexico City Red Devils◆	.646
	Monterrey Sultans	.608
1995—	Mexico City Red Devils	.708
	Monterrey Sultans◆	.570
1996—	Monterrey Sultans	.713
	Mexico City Reds◆	.619
1997—	Mexico City Red Devils	.686
	Mexico City Tigers■	.658
1998—	Monterrey	.672
	Oaxaca■	.576
1999—	Mexico City Tigers	.664
	Mexico City Reds■	.632
2000—	Saltillo	.647
	Mexico City Tigers■	.627
2001—	Mexico City Tigers■	.632
	Mexico City Reds	.575
2002—	Mexico City Reds▼	.673
2003—	Mexico▼	.630
2004—	Campeche▼▼	.567
2005—	Angelopolis▼▼	.613

*Defeated Nuevo Laredo, two games to none, in playoff for pennant. †Won four-team playoff. ‡Won split-season playoff. §League divided into Northern, Southern divisions; won two-team playoff. ∞League divided into Northern, Southern zones; sub-divided into Eastern, Western divisions, won eight-team playoff. ▲ A players strike on July 1 forced the cancellation of the regular season and playoff schedule. ◆ League divided into Northern, Southern zones; four clubs from each zone qualified for postseason play. Won final series for league championship. ■ League divided into Northern, Central and Southern zones; played split season, with top eight teams qualifying for playoffs. Won final series for league championship. ▼ League divided into Northern and Southern divisions; played split season, with top eight teams qualifying for playoffs. Won final series for league championship. ▼▼ League divided into Northern and Southern divisions; played split season, with 12 teams qualifying for playoffs. Won final series for league championship.

PACIFIC COAST LEAGUE

LEAGUE OFFICE

President
Branch Rickey

Address
1631 Mesa Ave., Suite A
Colorado Springs, CO 80906-2917

Phone
719-636-3399

Pacific Coast League

CLASS AAA

TEAMS

ALBUQUERQUE ISOTOPES

General manager
John Traub

Manager
Dean Treanor

Ballpark (capacity, surface)
Isotopes Park (11,124, grass)

Affiliation
Marlins

Address
1601 Avenida Cesar Chavez SE
Albuquerque, NM 87106

Phone
505-924-2255

COLORADO SPRINGS SKY SOX

General manager/president
Tony Ensor

Manager
Tom Runnells

Ballpark (capacity, surface)
Security Service Field (9,000, grass)

Affiliation
Rockies

Address
4385 Tutt Blvd.
Colorado Springs, CO 80922

Phone
719-597-1449

FRESNO GRIZZLIES

General manager
Pat Filippone

Manager
Shane Turner

Ballpark (capacity, surface)
Grizzlies Stadium (12,500, grass)

Affiliation
Giants

Address
1800 Tulari Street
Fresno, CA 93721

Phone
559-442-1994

IOWA CUBS

General manager
Sam Bernabe

Manager
Mike Quade

Ballpark (capacity, surface)
Principal Park (10,500, grass)

Affiliation
Cubs

Address
One Line Drive
Des Moines, IA 50309

Phone
515-243-6111

LAS VEGAS 51s

General manager/president
Don Logan

Manager
Jerry Royster

Ballpark (capacity, surface)
Cashman Field (9,334, grass)

Affiliation
Dodgers

Address
850 Las Vegas Blvd. N
Las Vegas, NV 89101

Phone
702-386-7200

MEMPHIS REDBIRDS

President/general manager
Dave Chase

Manager
Danny Sheaffer

Ballpark (capacity, surface)
AutoZone Park (14,200, grass)

Affiliation
Cardinals

Address
175 Toyota Plaza, Suite 300
Memphis, TN 38103

Phone
901-721-6050

NASHVILLE SOUNDS

General manager
Glenn Yaeger

Manager
Frank Kremblas

Ballpark (capacity, surface)
Greer Stadium (10,139, grass)

Affiliation
Brewers

Address
534 Chestnut Street
Nashville, TN 37203

Phone
615-242-4371

NEW ORLEANS ZEPHYRS

Vice president/general manager
Mike Schline

Manager
Tim Foli

Ballpark (capacity, surface)
Zephyr Field (11,000, grass)

Affiliation
Nationals

Address
6000 Airline Dr.
Metairie, LA 70003

Phone
504-734-5155

OKLAHOMA REDHAWKS

President/general manager
Scott Pruitt

Manager
Tim Ireland

Ballpark (capacity, surface)
SBC Bricktown Ballpark (13,066, grass)

Affiliation
Rangers

Address
2 South Mickey Mantle Dr.
Oklahoma City, OK 73104

Phone
405-218-1000

OMAHA ROYALS

Vice president/general manager
Doug Stewart

Manager
Mike Jirschele

Ballpark (capacity, surface)
Omaha's Rosenblatt Stadium (24,000, grass)

Affiliation
Royals

Address
1202 Bert Murphy Ave.
Omaha, NE 68107

Phone
402-734-2550

PORTLAND BEAVERS

General manager
John Cunningham

Manager
Craig Colbert

Ballpark (capacity, surface)
PGE Park (19,566, artificial)

Affiliation
Padres

Address
1844 SW Morrison
Portland, OR 97205

Phone
503-553-5400

ROUND ROCK EXPRESS

President
Jay Miller

Manager
Jackie Moore

Ballpark (capacity, surface)
The Dell Diamond (8,496, grass)

Affiliation
Astros

Address
3400 E. Palm Valley Blvd.
Round Rock, TX 78664

Phone
512-255-2255

SACRAMENTO RIVER CATS

President/General Manager
Alan Ledford

Manager
Tony DeFrancesco

Ballpark (capacity, surface)
Raley Field (14,414, grass)

Affiliation
Athletics

Address
400 Ballpark Drive
West Sacramento, CA 95691

Phone
916-376-4700

SALT LAKE BEES

Vice president/ general manager
Marc Amicone

Manager
Brian Harper

Ballpark (capacity, surface)
Franklin Covey Field (15,500, grass)

Affiliation
Angels

Address
77 West 1300 South
Salt Lake City, UT 84115

Phone
801-485-3800

TACOMA RAINIERS

General manager
Dave Lewis

Manager
Dave Brundage

Ballpark (capacity, surface)
Cheney Stadium (9,600, grass)

Affiliation
Mariners

Address
2502 S. Tyler Street
Tacoma, WA 98405

Phone
253-752-7707

TUCSON SIDEWINDERS

General manager
Rick Parr

Manager
Chip Hale

Ballpark (capacity, surface)
Tucson Electric Park (12,500, grass)

Affiliation
Diamondbacks

Address
P.O. Box 27045
Tucson, AZ 85726

Phone
520-434-1021

2005 FINAL STANDINGS

AMERICAN NORTH

Team	W	L	T	Pct.	GB
Nashville Sounds	75	69	-	0.521	...
Omaha Royals	72	72	-	0.5	3
Memphis Redbirds	71	72	-	0.497	3.5
Iowa Cubs	64	75	-	0.46	8.5

AMERICAN SOUTH

Team	W	L	T	Pct.	GB
Oklahoma RedHawks	80	63	-	0.559	...
Albuquerque Isotopes	78	66	-	0.542	2.5
Round Rock Express	74	70	-	0.514	6.5
New Orleans Zephyrs	64	76	-	0.457	14.5

PACIFIC NORTH

Team	W	L	T	Pct.	GB
Tacoma Rainiers	80	64	-	0.556	...
Salt Lake Stingers	79	65	-	0.549	1
Portland Beavers	70	73	-	0.49	9.5
Colorado Springs Sky Sox	65	78	-	0.455	14.5

PACIFIC SOUTH

Team	W	L	T	Pct.	GB
Sacramento River Cats	80	64	-	0.556	...
Fresno Grizzlies	68	76	-	0.472	12
Tucson Sidewinders	68	76	-	0.472	12
Las Vegas 51s	57	86	-	0.399	22.5

COMPOSITE

CLUB (AFFILIATE), ABBREV	OKL	SAC	TAC	SLC	ALB	NAS	ROU	OMA	MEM	POR	FRE	TUC	IOW	NOZ	CSP	LVG	W	L	PCT	GB
Oklahoma (Rangers), OKL		0	4	2	11	7	6	9	11	3	3	1	9	7	4	3	80	63	.559	-
Sacramento (Athletics), SAC	4	...	8	8	2	3	2	2	2	7	11	6	2	1	9	13	80	64	.556	0.5
Tacoma (Mariners), TAC	0	8	...	11	0	3	2	1	3	11	9	8	4	2	6	12	80	64	.556	0.5
Salt Lake (Angels), SLC	2	8	5	...	3	0	1	3	1	8	10	11	2	3	11	11	79	65	.549	1.5
Albuquerque (Marlins), ALB	5	2	4	1	...	8	9	12	10	2	2	2	10	7	1	3	78	66	.542	2.5
Nashville (Brewers), NAS	9	1	1	4	8	...	7	7	8	1	1	2	11	11	3	1	75	69	.521	5.5
Round Rock (Astros), ROU	10	2	2	3	7	9	...	6	9	3	3	2	6	10	2	0	74	70	.514	6.5
Omaha (Royals), OMA	7	2	3	1	4	9	10	...	4	3	2	3	8	11	2	3	72	72	.500	8.5
Memphis (Cardinals), MEM	5	2	1	3	6	8	7	12	...	2	1	2	11	8	1	2	71	72	.497	9.0
Portland (Padres), POR	9	5	8	2	3	1	1	2	...	9	9	1	2	10	8	70	73	.490	10.0	
Fresno (Giants), FRE	1	5	7	6	2	3	1	2	3	7	...	8	2	2	11	8	68	76	.472	12.5
Tucson (Diamondbacks), TUC	3	10	8	5	2	2	2	1	2	7	8	...	2	0	8	8	68	76	.472	12.5
Iowa (Cubs), IOW	7	2	0	2	6	5	10	8	5	3	2	2	...	7	2	3	64	75	.460	14.0
New Orleans (Nationals), NOZ	9	3	2	1	9	5	6	5	8	2	4	4	5	...	1	2	64	76	.457	14.5
Colorado Springs (Rockies), CSP	0	7	10	5	3	1	2	2	2	6	5	8	2	3	...	9	65	78	.455	15.0
Las Vegas (Dodgers), LVG	1	3	4	5	1	3	4	1	2	8	8	8	0	2	7	...	57	86	.399	23.0

Major league affiliations in parentheses.

PLAYOFFS: Semifinals: Tacoma defeated Sacramento, three games to two, and Nashville defeated Oklahoma, three games to two. Finals: Nashville defeated Tacoma, three games to none.

REGULAR-SEASON ATTENDANCE: Round Rock, 700,277. Sacramento, 755,750. Memphis, 696,083. Oklahoma, 542,095. Portland, 360,772. Fresno, 495,791. Albuquerque, 582,839. Las Vegas, 334,485. Iowa, 529,354. Tacoma, 335,031. Omaha, 303,749. Tucson, 287,116. Colorado Springs, 235,502. Nashville, 419,412. Salt Lake, 437,686. New Orleans, 330,466. All-Star Game (at Sacramento), 14,414. League total, 7,346,408. Postseason (13 games), 59,937.

MANAGERS: Round Rock, Jackie Moore. Sacramento, Tony DeFrancesco. Memphis, Danny Sheaffer. Oklahoma, Bobby Jones. Portland, Craig Colbert. Fresno, Shane Turner. Albuquerque, Dean Treanor. Las Vegas, Jerry Royster. Iowa, Mike Quade. Tacoma, Dan Rohn. Omaha, Mike Jirschele. Tucson, Chip Hale. Colorado Springs, Marv Foley. Nashville, Frank Kremblas. Salt Lake, Dino Ebel. New Orleans, Tim Foli.

ALL-STAR TEAM: 1B-Conor Jackson, Tucson. 2B-Andy Green, Tucson. 3B-Mike Coolbaugh, Round Rock. SS-Danny Klassen, Round Rock. OF-Aaron Guiel, Omaha. OF-Todd Linden, Fresno. OF-Brandon Watson, New Orleans. C-Jeff Mathis, Salt Lake. DH-Rick Short, New Orleans. RHP-Felix Hernandez, Tacoma. LHP-Matt White, New Orleans. Relief Pitcher-Jermaine Van Buren, Iowa. League Championship Most Valuable Player-Nelson Cruz, Nashville. Most Valuable Player-Andy Green, Tucson. Rookie of the Year-Felix Hernandez, Tacoma. Pitcher of the Year-Felix Hernandez, Tacoma. Manager of the Year-Dan Rohn, Tacoma.

2005 BATTING

TEAM

Team	G	TPA	AB	R	H	TB	2B	3B	HR	RBI	SH	SF	HP	BB	IBB	SO	SB	CS	GDP	LOB	ShO	Avg.	OBP	Slg.
Colorado Springs	143	5515	4858	816	1439	2294	326	47	145	762	75	42	51	488	13	973	89	43	138	2101	8	.296	.364	.472
Oklahoma	143	5705	5036	893	1490	2394	297	47	171	850	21	42	52	552	16	1037	144	40	143	2235	9	.296	.369	.475

Team	G	TPA	AB	R	H	TB	2B	3B	HR	RBI	SH	SF	HP	BB	IBB	SO	SB	CS	GDP	LOB	ShO	Avg.	OBP	Slg.
New Orleans ..	140	5391	4770	692	1385	2028	252	29	111	642	73	38	46	464	32	827	112	64	136	2055	3	.290	.356	.425
Salt Lake	144	5500	4831	820	1372	2223	275	69	146	762	56	47	34	532	22	919	132	74	100	2089	5	.284	.356	.460
Albuquerque ..	144	5638	4947	795	1396	2282	251	43	183	749	53	58	43	495	22	1074	104	46	126	2189	3	.282	.354	.461
Tucson	144	5633	4971	790	1402	2210	292	45	142	749	40	52	72	498	19	972	76	23	134	2274	6	.282	.353	.445
Fresno	144	5708	5113	774	1438	2341	297	39	176	738	72	42	87	394	22	993	122	52	97	2163	8	.281	.340	.458
Round Rock	144	5580	4977	703	1372	2201	291	26	162	677	43	43	61	456	22	1061	89	26	120	2262	7	.276	.341	.442
Tacoma	144	5570	4889	732	1348	2063	277	36	122	688	45	43	63	530	20	981	126	58	117	2336	4	.276	.351	.422
Las Vegas	143	5589	4847	770	1327	2150	262	36	163	720	57	53	49	582	11	965	57	45	111	2190	8	.274	.354	.444
Sacramento ...	144	5755	4991	780	1363	2130	303	37	130	734	57	52	47	608	11	1132	106	42	104	2313	9	.273	.354	.427
Nashville	144	5500	4813	738	1311	2148	275	36	164	697	71	40	71	504	23	1062	175	68	106	2082	8	.272	.347	.446
Iowa	139	5288	4653	642	1257	1890	241	34	108	606	49	32	49	504	25	915	91	32	147	2158	8	.270	.346	.406
Omaha...........	144	5467	4870	734	1307	2142	261	35	168	692	28	30	56	483	16	1097	86	29	143	2102	3	.268	.339	.440
Portland	143	5469	4767	681	1278	2018	251	24	147	649	56	43	61	542	9	991	100	36	122	2214	8	.268	.347	.423
Memphis	143	5424	4811	676	1248	2053	277	18	164	648	46	43	44	479	30	906	60	39	108	1986	9	.259	.329	.427

INDIVIDUAL

TOP QUALIFIERS FOR BATTING CHAMPIONSHIP

Minimum 389 plate appearances.   *Lefthanded batter.   †Switch-hitter.

Player, Team	G	TPA	AB	R	H	TB	2B	3B	HR	RBI	SH	SF	HP	BB	IBB	SO	SB	CS	GDP	Avg.	OBP	Slg.
Short, Rick, New Orleans	108	433	376	72	144	214	35	1	11	70	1	3	7	46	6	27	5	4	8	.383	.456	.569
Dillon, Joe, Albuquerque	98	425	350	80	126	221	21	1	24	72	0	6	12	57	4	59	11	1	7	.360	.459	.631
Watson, Brandon, New Orleans *	88	408	372	69	132	156	15	3	1	25	5	2	1	28	0	33	31	13	5	.355	.400	.419
Jackson, Conor, Tucson..........................	93	409	333	66	118	184	38	2	8	73	0	7	0	69	1	32	3	2	8	.354	.457	.553
Orie, Kevin, Nashville-New Orleans..........	113	413	349	67	123	220	35	1	20	89	0	3	4	57	5	43	4	1	13	.352	.446	.630
Green, Andy, Tucson...............................	135	609	530	125	182	311	46	13	19	80	2	3	6	68	2	82	9	6	9	.343	.422	.587
Flores, Jose, Las Vegas	96	397	327	64	110	145	11	6	4	42	6	4	6	54	1	33	1	6	6	.336	.435	.443
Pickler, Jeff, Colorado Springs *	128	475	423	72	140	193	26	6	5	50	6	4	1	41	1	46	16	6	8	.331	.388	.456
Shealy, Ryan, Colorado Springs...............	108	468	411	85	135	247	30	2	26	88	2	7	7	41	2	81	4	0	13	.328	.393	.601
Linden, Todd, Fresno †	95	415	340	81	109	232	25	4	30	80	1	2	10	62	5	97	6	2	11	.321	.437	.682
Godwin, Tyrell, New Orleans *	129	561	499	83	160	221	22	6	9	48	6	1	5	50	2	77	22	12	6	.321	.387	.443
Prieto, Chris, Salt Lake *	97	443	363	71	115	166	18	12	3	45	12	3	5	60	1	41	26	10	3	.317	.418	.457
Clark, Doug, Fresno *	127	518	472	81	149	228	30	5	13	59	3	3	5	35	1	87	29	12	6	.316	.367	.483
Watson, Matthew, Sacramento	113	498	419	82	132	216	27	3	17	81	...	10	2	67	...	57	12	1	7	.315	.404	.516
German, Esteban, Oklahoma....................	117	564	489	103	153	207	27	6	5	68	1	2	7	65	0	74	43	6	20	.313	.400	.423
Rivera, Carlos, Round Rock *	129	496	455	64	142	230	35	1	17	68	0	3	8	30	2	65	0	0	16	.312	.363	.505
Cervenak, Michael, Fresno	127	547	494	68	154	246	29	3	19	103	0	5	10	38	3	61	5	0	7	.312	.369	.498
Johnson, Ben, Portland............................	107	472	414	79	129	231	27	0	25	83	0	1	6	51	0	88	6	1	7	.312	.394	.558
Barfield, Joshua, Portland	137	578	516	74	160	232	25	1	15	72	2	7	1	52	1	108	20	5	10	.310	.370	.450
Hart, Corey, Nashville	113	489	429	85	132	230	29	9	17	69	3	6	3	48	1	88	31	7	11	.308	.377	.536
Alexander, Manny, Oklahoma-Portland	112	484	433	64	133	206	25	6	12	68	2	6	4	39	0	70	27	10	8	.307	.365	.476

DEPARTMENTAL LEADERS: G—Wilson, 143. AB—Brown, 553. R—Green, 125. H—Green, 182. TB—Green, 311. 2B—Green, 46. 3B—Green, 13. HR—Scott, 31. RBI—Gorneault, 108. SH—Rouse and Santiago, 17. SF—Wilson, 12. HP—Quentin, 29. BB—Cust, 115. IBB—Nunez, 7. SO—Cust, 153. SB—German, 43. CS—Watson, 13. GIDP—Wood, 24. OBP—Dillon, .459. Slg.—Linden, .682.

ALL PLAYERS

*Lefthanded batter. †Switch-hitter.

Player, Team	G	TPA	AB	R	H	TB	2B	3B	HR	RBI	SH	SF	HP	BB	IBB	SO	SB	CS	GDP	Avg.	OBP	Slg.
Abreu, Winston, Tucson............................	17	0	0	0	0	0	0	0	0	0	...	0	0	0	0	0	0	0	0	...	...	...
Accardo, Jeremy, Fresno	16	2	2	0	0	0	0	0	0	0	0	0	0	0	0	0	0	0	0	.000	.000	.000
Acevedo, Jose, Colorado Springs	1	3	3	0	1	1	0	0	0	1	0	0	0	0	0	2	0	0	0	.333	.333	.333
Adams, Mike, Nashville	21	2	2	0	0	0	0	0	0	0	0	0	0	0	0	2	0	0	0	.000	.000	.000
Aguila, Chris, Albuquerque	35	153	138	27	49	87	13	2	7	25	0	1	0	14	0	21	8	2	3	.355	.412	.630
Aldridge, Cory, Omaha *	24	88	82	8	16	29	4	0	3	7	0	0	0	6	0	28	4	0	0	.195	.250	.354
Alexander, Manny, Oklahoma-Portland	112	484	433	64	133	206	25	6	12	68	2	6	4	39	0	70	27	10	8	.307	.365	.476
Alfonzo, Edgardo, Fresno	4	15	15	2	7	9	2	0	0	1	0	0	0	0	0	0	0	0	0	.467	.467	.600
Alfonzo, Eliezer, Fresno	4	16	14	3	4	8	1	0	1	3	0	0	1	1	0	2	0	0	1	.286	.375	.571
Allen, Chad, Oklahoma-Memphis	70	306	286	45	94	145	18	0	11	46	0	3	0	17	2	45	10	4	9	.329	.363	.507
Allen, Luke, Salt Lake *	128	519	460	85	132	235	20	7	23	92	0	4	1	54	5	87	13	3	10	.287	.360	.511
Almanza, Armando, Fresno-Tucson-Memphis	18	2	1	0	0	0	0	0	0	0	1	0	0	0	0	1	0	0	0	.000	.000	.000
Alvarez, Wilson, Las Vegas *	4	1	1	0	0	0	0	0	0	0	0	0	0	0	0	1	0	0	0	.000	.000	.000
Anderson, Jimmy, Iowa-Round Rock	6	14	14	2	4	5	1	0	0	2	0	0	0	0	0	5	0	0	1	.286	.286	.357
Anderson, Luke, Fresno	4	0	0	0	0	0	0	0	0	0	0	0	0	0	0	0	0	0	0	...	...	...
Anderson, Matt, Colorado Springs	30	1	1	0	0	0	0	0	0	0	0	0	0	0	0	1	0	0	0	.000	.000	.000
Ansman, Craig, Tucson............................	11	41	36	4	6	9	0	0	1	3	0	0	2	3	0	9	0	0	0	.167	.268	.250
Apodaca, Juan, Las Vegas	2	7	7	0	1	1	0	0	0	0	0	0	0	0	0	1	0	0	0	.143	.143	.143
Appert, Luke, Sacramento *	1	1	1	0	0	0	0	0	0	0	0	0	0	0	0	1	0	0	0	.000	.000	.000
Aquino, Greg, Tucson..............................	5	0	0	0	0	0	0	0	0	0	0	0	0	0	0	0	0	0	0	...	...	...
Ardoin, Danny, Colorado Springs	44	170	142	27	48	82	12	2	6	24	1	1	6	20	2	38	3	1	7	.338	.438	.577
Armas, Tony, New Orleans	5	8	7	1	2	4	0	1	0	1	0	0	0	0	0	4	0	0	0	.286	.286	.571
Arteaga, Joshua, Iowa	4	6	4	1	1	1	0	0	0	0	0	0	0	1	0	1	0	0	0	.250	.400	.250
Asencio, Miguel, Portland	2	4	2	0	0	0	0	0	0	0	0	0	0	1	0	1	0	0	0	.000	.333	.000
Ashby, Andy, Portland	1	1	0	0	0	0	0	0	0	0	0	0	0	0	0	0	0	0	0	...	...	...
Ashby, Christopher, Albuquerque	67	197	174	20	43	49	6	0	0	14	2	1	2	18	0	26	0	2	5	.247	.323	.282
Astacio, Ezequiel, Round Rock	9	19	17	2	2	2	0	0	0	1	0	0	0	2	0	8	0	0	1	.118	.118	.118
Athas, Jamie, Fresno *	35	84	76	7	16	26	1	0	3	10	1	1	0	6	1	18	0	2	0	.211	.265	.342
Atkins, Garrett, Colorado Springs	5	23	21	4	7	11	1	0	1	3	0	0	0	2	0	0	0	0	0	.333	.391	.524
Auty, Timothy, Tacoma	3	11	10	1	1	1	1	0	0	0	0	0	0	1	0	1	0	0	0	.100	.182	.100

Player, Team	G	TPA	AB	R	H	TB	2B	3B	HR	RBI	SH	SF	HP	BB	IBB	SO	SB	CS	GDP	Avg.	OBP	Slg.
Aybar, Willy, Las Vegas †	108	450	401	47	119	168	26	4	5	60	1	7	1	40	0	56	1	6	8	.297	.356	.419
Bacon, Dwaine, Iowa †	18	61	52	8	9	12	1	1	0	3	1	0	1	7	0	15	7	0	1	.173	.283	.231
Baez, Federico, Iowa	3	1	1	0	0	0	0	0	0	0	0	0	0	0	0	1	0	0	0	.000	.000	.000
Baker, Bradley, Portland	32	2	0	0	0	0	0	0	0	0	0	2	0	0	0	0	0	0	0	...	...	...
Baker, Jeff, Colorado Springs	61	248	228	40	69	117	16	1	10	41	1	2	1	16	0	44	3	1	7	.303	.348	.513
Baker, John, Sacramento *	103	387	346	43	81	126	24	3	5	41	7	0	4	30	0	90	1	0	5	.234	.303	.364
Barden, Brian, Tucson	135	576	518	78	159	250	36	5	15	85	3	6	11	38	3	111	14	5	15	.307	.363	.483
Barfield, Joshua, Portland	137	578	516	74	160	232	25	1	15	72	2	7	1	52	1	108	20	5	10	.310	.370	.450
Barnes, Larry, Albuquerque *	71	234	219	30	55	90	9	1	8	26	1	2	1	11	0	45	2	2	9	.251	.288	.411
Barnwell, Christopher, Nashville	100	288	261	30	64	89	14	1	3	20	4	2	3	18	1	46	5	3	6	.245	.299	.341
Bartosh, Cliff, Iowa *	10	0	0	0	0	0	0	0	0	0	0	0	0	0	0	0	0	0	0	...	...	...
Barzilla, Philip, Round Rock *	1	0	0	0	0	0	0	0	0	0	0	0	0	0	0	0	0	0	0	...	...	...
Bauer, Peter, Albuquerque-Round Rock *	9	16	15	2	4	4	0	0	0	0	0	0	0	1	0	5	0	0	1	.267	.313	.267
Beattie, Andrew, Sacramento †	113	517	442	80	131	199	36	4	8	55	5	10	3	57	1	100	10	6	8	.296	.373	.450
Bell, Mike, Memphis	8	15	14	0	1	1	0	0	0	1	0	0	0	1	0	1	0	1	0	.071	.071	.071
Bell, Rick, Iowa	16	30	25	6	5	6	1	0	0	2	0	1	0	4	0	5	0	0	1	.200	.300	.240
Bennett, Jeff, Nashville	34	3	3	0	0	0	0	0	0	0	0	0	0	0	0	2	0	0	0	.000	.000	.000
Bentz, Chad, Albuquerque	21	1	0	0	0	0	0	0	0	0	0	0	1	0	0	0	0	0	0	...	...	...
Berger, Brandon, Memphis	109	339	300	48	70	140	13	0	19	57	1	3	4	30	1	58	3	2	4	.233	.309	.467
Bergman, Dusty, Fresno *	1	0	0	0	0	0	0	0	0	0	0	0	0	0	0	0	0	0	0	...	...	...
Bergmann, Jay, New Orleans	14	4	4	0	0	0	0	0	0	0	0	0	0	0	0	0	0	0	0	.000	.000	.000
Berkman, Lance, Round Rock †	4	17	14	2	4	5	1	0	0	1	0	0	0	3	1	4	0	0	0	.286	.412	.357
Betancourt, Yuniesky, Tacoma	49	194	183	13	54	81	9	6	2	30	2	1	2	6	0	14	7	5	3	.295	.323	.443
Bevis, P. J., Colorado Springs	10	6	5	0	1	2	1	0	0	1	0	1	0	0	0	3	0	0	0	.200	.167	.400
Bigbie, Larry, Colorado Springs *	3	10	8	4	3	7	2	1	0	2	0	0	0	2	0	3	0	0	0	.375	.500	.875
Blakeley, Eric, Tacoma	4	14	11	3	3	3	0	0	0	2	0	0	0	3	0	2	0	0	0	.273	.429	.273
Blanco, Andres, Omaha †	35	129	114	13	29	40	4	2	1	9	2	0	3	10	0	23	2	0	3	.254	.331	.351
Blanco, Tony, New Orleans	16	68	64	7	18	28	4	0	2	14	0	2	0	2	0	13	1	0	6	.281	.294	.438
Blank, Matt, Albuquerque *	6	3	3	0	0	0	0	0	0	0	0	0	0	0	0	1	0	0	0	.000	.000	.000
Bocachica, Hiram, Sacramento	4	18	17	2	7	15	2	0	2	6	0	0	0	1	0	4	0	0	0	.412	.444	.882
Bohn, Thomas, Tacoma	22	86	81	15	26	32	3	0	1	7	0	0	3	2	0	23	4	0	5	.321	.360	.395
Bonine, Eddie, Portland	1	0	0	0	0	0	0	0	0	0	0	0	0	0	0	0	0	0	0	...	...	...
Borders, Pat, Nashville	26	102	98	8	24	35	2	0	3	14	0	1	0	3	0	18	1	2	6	.245	.265	.357
Borland, Toby, Memphis	11	2	2	0	1	1	0	0	0	0	0	0	0	0	0	1	0	0	0	.500	.500	.500
Borowski, Joe, Iowa	5	0	0	0	0	0	0	0	0	0	0	0	0	0	0	0	0	0	0	...	...	...
Botts, Jason, Oklahoma †	133	590	510	93	146	266	31	7	25	102	0	4	8	67	2	152	2	4	13	.286	.375	.522
Bouknight, Kip, New Orleans	5	12	9	2	1	1	0	0	0	1	0	1	1	1	0	3	0	0	0	.111	.250	.111
Bowers, Timothy, New Orleans	118	398	333	29	79	101	12	2	2	38	15	4	7	39	3	55	9	3	7	.237	.326	.303
Bozied, Robert, Portland	14	62	54	6	14	24	4	0	2	10	0	2	3	3	0	6	0	0	2	.259	.323	.444
Bradford Jr., Samuel, Tacoma *	3	11	8	1	1	1	0	0	0	2	0	0	1	0	0	1	0	0	0	.125	.182	.125
Bradley, Milton, Las Vegas †	5	14	13	2	4	4	0	0	0	1	0	0	0	1	0	2	1	1	0	.308	.357	.308
Branyan, Russell, Nashville *	6	20	17	4	5	12	4	0	1	3	0	0	0	3	0	8	0	0	0	.294	.400	.706
Bray, Bill, New Orleans	15	0	0	0	0	0	0	0	0	0	0	0	0	0	0	0	0	0	0	...	...	...
Breslow, Craig, Portland *	5	0	0	0	0	0	0	0	0	0	0	0	0	0	0	0	0	0	0	...	...	...
Brewer, Jace, Oklahoma	23	82	74	11	20	26	6	0	0	10	1	1	0	6	0	10	2	2	5	.270	.321	.351
Bridges, Donnie, New Orleans	7	15	11	1	4	8	1	0	1	2	1	1	0	2	0	3	0	0	0	.364	.429	.727
Brito, Juan, Tucson	72	261	235	30	61	89	10	0	6	31	3	1	1	21	0	58	0	0	3	.260	.322	.379
Broadway, Larry, New Orleans *	18	64	57	4	11	14	3	0	0	5	0	0	0	7	0	17	2	0	2	.193	.281	.246
Brooks, Frank, Las Vegas *	1	0	0	0	0	0	0	0	0	0	0	0	0	0	0	0	0	0	0	...	...	...
Broshuis, Garrett, Fresno	1	3	3	0	1	1	0	0	0	0	0	0	0	0	0	1	0	0	0	.333	.333	.333
Brown, Adrian, Omaha †	140	640	553	104	151	222	28	8	9	49	6	3	4	74	0	73	33	7	17	.273	.361	.401
Brown, Andrew, Tacoma	100	380	337	53	98	151	30	1	7	53	0	2	8	33	1	71	8	4	7	.291	.366	.448
Brown, Dee, New Orleans *	30	83	77	4	22	35	4	0	3	16	0	2	1	3	1	13	0	2	4	.286	.313	.455
Brown, Nebasett, Tucson *	14	30	26	2	9	12	1	1	0	4	1	0	1	2	0	4	0	0	0	.346	.414	.462
Brownlie, Robert, Iowa	15	22	21	1	2	3	1	0	0	0	1	0	0	0	0	5	0	0	0	.095	.095	.143
Bruney, Brian, Tucson	2	0	0	0	0	0	0	0	0	0	0	0	0	0	0	0	0	0	0	...	...	...
Buchanan, Brian, Colorado Springs	72	294	259	50	77	128	17	2	10	41	0	1	7	27	0	55	4	1	10	.297	.378	.494
Buchholz, Taylor, Round Rock	17	18	17	0	5	5	0	0	0	2	1	0	0	0	0	4	0	0	0	.294	.294	.294
Budde, Ryan, Salt Lake	58	208	196	26	45	78	9	3	6	25	2	0	1	9	0	41	3	1	3	.230	.267	.398
Bulger, Jason, Tucson	34	1	1	0	0	0	0	0	0	0	0	0	0	0	0	0	0	0	0	.000	.000	.000
Bump, Nate, Albuquerque *	1	2	1	0	0	0	0	0	0	0	0	0	0	1	0	0	0	0	0	.000	.000	.000
Bumstead, Michael, Portland	9	4	3	0	1	2	1	0	0	2	1	0	0	0	0	1	0	0	0	.333	.333	.667
Burba, Dave, Round Rock	11	8	5	2	1	3	0	1	0	0	3	0	0	0	0	2	0	0	0	.200	.200	.600
Burke, Chris, Round Rock	22	101	90	15	28	44	6	2	2	11	1	0	2	8	0	13	9	0	2	.311	.380	.489
Burns, Mike, Round Rock	18	2	1	0	0	0	0	0	0	0	0	0	0	0	0	0	0	0	0	.000	.000	.000
Burroughs, Sean, Portland *	32	138	124	21	36	53	8	0	3	14	0	0	5	9	0	15	0	0	5	.290	.362	.427
Bynum, Freddie, Sacramento *	102	428	378	56	105	145	16	9	2	40	7	2	3	38	1	83	23	7	3	.278	.347	.384
Byrd, Marlon, New Orleans	21	92	81	19	33	54	6	0	5	11	0	0	2	9	0	7	4	1	6	.407	.478	.667
Cabrera, Asdrubal, Tacoma †	6	25	23	4	5	7	0	1	0	3	1	0	0	1	0	2	0	0	1	.217	.250	.304
Cabrera, Mayke, Las Vegas *	3	8	8	0	2	2	0	0	0	0	0	0	0	0	0	1	0	0	2	.250	.250	.250
Cain, Matt, Fresno	16	36	29	3	7	9	2	0	0	0	6	0	0	1	0	15	0	0	0	.241	.267	.310
Caldera, Jose, Salt Lake	6	14	13	3	3	3	0	0	0	1	0	0	0	1	0	2	0	0	1	.231	.286	.231
Cali, Carmen, Memphis	33	2	2	0	0	0	0	0	0	0	0	0	0	0	0	2	0	0	0	.000	.000	.000
Callaspo, Alberto, Salt Lake †	50	228	212	28	67	95	21	2	1	31	2	3	1	10	1	13	2	5	7	.316	.345	.448
Cameron, Troy, Portland †	10	15	14	1	1	1	0	0	0	0	0	0	0	0	0	7	0	0	0	.071	.133	.071
Camilo, Juan, Tucson *	8	23	20	3	4	8	1	0	1	3	0	1	0	2	0	6	0	0	0	.200	.261	.400
Cancel, Robinson, Memphis	29	105	95	12	24	38	3	1	3	13	0	1	1	8	0	18	0	0	0	.253	.314	.400
Cannon, Jonathan, Tucson	10	21	18	3	9	16	4	0	1	4	2	0	1	0	0	8	0	0	0	.500	.526	.889
Capellan, Jose, Nashville	25	18	16	3	4	4	0	0	0	1	0	0	0	1	0	4	0	0	0	.250	.294	.250
Cardona, Javier, Memphis	7	22	19	3	4	10	0	0	2	6	0	0	3	1	1	0	0	0	0	.211	.318	.526

Player, Team	G	TPA	AB	R	H	TB	2B	3B	HR	RBI	SH	SF	HP	BB	IBB	SO	SB	CS	GDP	Avg.	OBP	Slg.
Carlyle, Buddy, Las Vegas *	9	8	8	2	1	1	0	0	0	1	0	0	0	0	0	1	0	0	1	.125	.125	.125
Carrasco, Hector, New Orleans	6	0	0	0	0	0	0	0	0	0	0	...	0	0	0	1	0	0	0	...	...	...
Carroll, Wesley, New Orleans	70	141	132	10	32	44	6	0	2	10	3	1	0	5	0	23	2	1	8	.242	.268	.333
Casilla, Alexi, Salt Lake †	13	46	39	3	10	10	0	0	0	1	4	0	0	3	0	6	1	1	1	.256	.310	.256
Cassel, Joseph, Portland	9	2	2	0	0	0	0	0	0	0	0	0	0	0	0	2	0	0	0	.000	.000	.000
Cassidy, Scott, Portland	15	0	0	0	0	0	0	0	0	0	0	0	0	0	0	0	0	0	0	.000	.000	.000
Castillo, Alberto, Sacramento	4	14	13	2	1	1	0	0	0	0	0	0	0	1	0	4	0	0	0	.077	.143	.077
Castillo, Frank, Albuquerque	18	40	34	1	3	3	0	0	0	1	5	0	0	1	0	9	0	0	0	.088	.114	.088
Cedeno, Roger, Memphis †	8	26	23	3	4	5	1	0	0	2	0	0	0	3	1	5	0	0	0	.174	.269	.217
Cedeno, Ronny, Iowa	65	275	245	42	87	127	14	1	8	36	7	2	1	20	2	31	11	3	9	.355	.403	.518
Cepicky, Matt, New Orleans *	99	390	342	52	92	163	23	3	14	68	1	4	0	43	3	85	1	3	11	.269	.347	.477
Cervenak, Michael, Fresno	127	547	494	68	154	246	29	3	19	103	0	5	10	38	3	61	6	0	7	.312	.369	.498
Chacon, Shawn, Colorado Springs	1	2	2	0	0	0	0	0	0	0	0	0	0	0	0	1	0	0	0	.000	.000	.000
Chavez, Angel, Fresno	89	361	334	46	94	150	17	3	11	64	5	2	3	17	1	59	5	1	6	.281	.320	.449
Chavez, Endy, New Orleans *	23	101	87	11	22	29	4	0	1	4	4	0	0	10	1	7	6	1	2	.253	.330	.333
Chavez, Raul, Round Rock	34	128	119	9	30	38	8	0	0	14	1	0	3	5	1	24	0	0	4	.252	.299	.319
Chavez, Wilton, Colorado Springs	16	21	18	1	4	6	2	0	0	2	3	0	0	0	0	8	0	0	0	.222	.222	.333
Chen, Chin-Feng, Las Vegas	87	363	317	59	88	157	20	2	15	63	1	5	2	38	0	82	3	3	3	.278	.354	.495
Chiasson, Scott, Colorado Springs	9	2	2	0	1	1	0	0	0	0	0	0	0	0	0	0	0	0	0	.500	.500	.500
Cho, Hyung, Tacoma	2	5	5	0	0	0	0	0	0	0	0	0	0	0	0	1	0	0	0	.000	.000	.000
Choate, Randy, Tucson *	29	0	0	0	0	0	0	0	0	0	0	...	0	0	0	0	0	0	0	...	...	...
Choo, Shin-Soo, Tacoma *	115	502	429	73	121	185	21	5	11	54	2	1	1	69	0	97	20	10	8	.282	.382	.431
Christianson, Ryan, Tacoma	79	324	286	36	70	110	13	0	9	40	1	0	2	35	0	96	2	1	7	.245	.331	.385
Cirillo, Jeff, Nashville	9	33	29	2	7	8	1	0	0	6	1	2	1	0	0	5	0	1	1	.241	.250	.276
Clark, Doug, Fresno *	127	518	472	81	149	228	30	5	13	59	3	3	5	35	1	87	29	12	6	.316	.367	.483
Clark, Jermaine, Sacramento *	70	305	256	32	64	100	13	4	5	28	2	4	2	41	0	33	14	8	5	.250	.353	.391
Clontz, Brad, Albuquerque	11	1	1	0	0	0	0	0	0	0	0	0	0	0	0	1	0	0	0	.000	.000	.000
Colamarino, Brant, Sacramento *	74	307	280	37	68	122	15	3	11	47	1	3	4	19	1	76	0	0	9	.243	.297	.436
Colangelo, Mike, Albuquerque	98	383	334	58	98	168	18	2	16	55	2	6	10	31	3	73	2	2	5	.293	.365	.503
Colbrunn, Greg, Oklahoma	11	44	40	3	8	11	3	0	0	2	0	0	0	4	0	7	0	0	1	.200	.273	.275
Conrad, Brooks, Round Rock †	113	483	418	84	110	201	22	3	21	57	5	4	4	52	3	104	12	3	7	.263	.347	.481
Conti, Jason, Oklahoma *	117	517	462	80	119	196	26	3	15	73	7	2	5	40	2	116	4	1	8	.258	.322	.424
Conway, Daniel, Colorado Springs	46	153	134	14	29	42	6	2	1	18	1	0	7	11	0	39	1	0	5	.216	.309	.313
Cook, Aaron, Colorado Springs	1	2	2	0	0	0	0	0	0	0	0	0	0	0	0	1	0	0	0	.000	.000	.000
Coolbaugh, Mike, Round Rock	123	550	488	88	137	250	30	1	27	101	1	9	5	47	4	111	10	0	14	.281	.344	.512
Cooper, Brian, Fresno	20	32	24	1	3	3	0	0	0	1	7	0	0	1	0	8	0	0	1	.125	.160	.125
Corcoran, Roy, New Orleans	36	3	3	1	2	2	0	0	0	0	0	0	0	0	0	1	0	0	0	.667	.667	.667
Corey, Bryan, Albuquerque	36	6	6	0	0	0	0	0	0	0	0	0	0	0	0	4	0	0	0	.000	.000	.000
Correia, Kevin, Fresno	19	5	3	0	0	0	0	0	0	0	2	0	0	0	0	1	0	0	0	.000	.000	.000
Cortes, David, Colorado Springs	9	0	0	0	0	0	0	0	0	0	0	0	0	0	0	0	0	0	0	...	...	...
Costa, Shane, Omaha *	4	16	16	1	3	4	1	0	0	1	0	0	0	0	0	1	0	0	0	.188	.188	.250
Cota, Jesus, Tucson *	37	133	126	16	27	42	4	1	3	17	0	1	0	6	0	22	0	0	2	.214	.248	.333
Cresse, Bradley, Memphis	41	134	115	10	24	43	10	0	3	16	2	2	3	12	0	26	0	0	2	.209	.295	.374
Crockett, William, Colorado Springs	1	2	2	0	0	0	0	0	0	0	0	0	0	0	0	1	0	0	0	.000	.000	.000
Crosby, Bobby, Sacramento	3	12	12	0	1	1	0	0	0	1	0	0	0	0	0	3	0	0	0	.083	.083	.083
Crowell, Jim, Albuquerque	37	2	2	0	0	0	0	0	0	0	0	0	0	0	0	1	0	0	0	.000	.000	.000
Cruz , Jose, Tucson †	1	3	3	1	1	2	1	0	0	1	0	0	0	0	0	1	0	0	0	.333	.333	.667
Cruz, Nelson, Nashville	60	246	208	33	56	102	13	0	11	27	0	0	8	30	2	62	9	4	4	.269	.382	.490
Cummings, Jeremy, Memphis	8	12	9	2	2	2	0	0	0	0	0	0	0	3	0	2	0	0	0	.222	.417	.222
Cunnane, Will, Iowa-Round Rock	40	3	3	1	0	0	0	0	0	0	0	0	0	0	0	2	0	0	0	.000	.000	.000
Cust, Jack, Sacramento *	134	600	479	95	123	210	28	1	19	75	0	3	3	115	5	153	2	4	14	.257	.402	.438
Dallimore, Brian, Fresno	100	445	398	67	120	174	26	2	8	45	1	2	12	32	0	43	7	2	14	.302	.369	.437
Dannemiller, Beau, Las Vegas	21	0	0	0	0	0	0	0	0	0	0	...	0	0	0	0	0	0	0	...	...	...
Davis, J.J., New Orleans-Colorado Springs	72	273	241	46	64	122	13	0	15	46	0	3	4	25	2	73	4	5	6	.266	.341	.506
Davis, Kane, Nashville	28	1	1	0	0	0	0	0	0	0	0	0	0	0	0	0	0	0	0	.000	.000	.000
Dawley, Joe, Portland-Iowa	10	0	0	0	0	0	0	0	0	0	0	0	0	0	0	0	0	0	0	...	...	...
Day, Zach, Colorado Springs	5	8	7	0	0	0	0	0	0	0	1	0	0	0	0	0	0	0	0	.000	.000	.000
Deago, Roger, Portland	2	3	3	0	0	0	0	0	0	0	0	0	0	0	0	1	0	0	1	.000	.000	.000
Delarosa, Tomas, Colorado Springs	89	355	311	44	91	129	18	1	6	48	9	5	1	29	0	39	9	4	11	.293	.350	.415
Del Chiaro, Brenton, Salt Lake	2	3	3	1	1	4	0	0	1	1	0	0	0	0	0	2	0	0	0	.333	.333	1.333
Delgado, Wilson, Albuquerque †	98	387	351	52	100	150	22	5	6	37	3	3	1	29	1	55	3	4	12	.285	.339	.427
de los Santos, Valerio, Albuquerque *	6	0	0	0	0	0	0	0	0	0	0	0	0	0	0	0	0	0	0	...	...	...
Delucchi, Dustin, Tacoma-Portland	87	348	279	61	80	111	18	2	3	20	8	3	1	57	1	43	12	3	9	.287	.406	.398
Dement, Daniel, New Orleans	56	130	112	21	35	48	7	3	0	8	3	1	1	13	0	32	3	0	1	.313	.386	.429
De Renne, Keoni, Tucson †	72	265	232	43	68	92	11	2	3	26	6	3	2	22	0	23	5	0	6	.293	.355	.397
Dessens, Elmer, Las Vegas	2	1	1	0	0	0	0	0	0	0	0	0	0	0	0	1	0	0	0	.000	.000	.000
DeVore, Doug, Tucson-Fresno	109	390	350	59	103	183	22	2	18	67	0	5	2	33	4	85	4	2	11	.294	.354	.523
Diaz, Matt, Omaha	65	277	259	48	96	168	22	4	14	56	0	1	5	12	1	49	10	3	14	.371	.408	.649
DiFelice, Mark, New Orleans	11	8	6	0	1	1	0	0	0	1	0	0	1	0	0	3	0	0	0	.167	.286	.167
Dillon, Joe, Albuquerque	98	425	350	80	126	221	21	1	24	72	0	6	12	57	4	59	11	1	7	.360	.459	.631
Dobbs, Greg, Tacoma *	50	208	190	27	61	79	9	0	3	22	1	2	1	14	2	22	5	2	4	.321	.367	.416
Dohmann, Scott, Colorado Springs	16	2	2	0	0	0	0	0	0	0	0	0	0	0	0	1	0	0	0	.000	.000	.000
Dominguez, Jeffrey, Tacoma †	2	1	1	0	0	0	0	0	0	0	0	0	0	0	0	0	0	0	0	.000	.000	.000
Donovan, Todd, Las Vegas	13	52	45	7	17	20	1	1	0	6	0	1	1	5	0	8	3	3	0	.378	.442	.444
Doster, Dave, Tucson	24	86	74	12	25	29	4	0	0	10	2	1	2	7	1	10	0	0	2	.338	.405	.392
Drew, Tim, Colorado Springs	6	16	13	2	5	7	2	0	0	3	2	0	0	1	0	4	0	0	0	.385	.429	.538
Driskill, Travis, Round Rock	32	11	10	1	1	1	0	0	0	1	1	0	0	0	0	3	0	0	0	.100	.100	.100
Dubois, Jason, Iowa	18	17	4	9	13	1	0	1	5	0	0	0	0	3	0	0	0	5	.529	.556	.765
Duckworth, Brandon, Round Rock	16	36	32	3	9	14	2	0	1	4	1	0	0	3	0	6	0	0	1	.281	.343	.438
Duenas, Tomas, Omaha	4	13	12	1	3	3	0	0	0	0	0	0	0	1	0	6	0	0	1	.250	.308	.250

Player, Team	G	TPA	AB	R	H	TB	2B	3B	HR	RBI	SH	SF	HP	BB	IBB	SO	SB	CS	GDP	Avg.	OBP	Slg.
Duncan, Chris, Memphis *	128	500	431	57	114	202	21	2	21	73	0	4	2	63	3	104	1	3	14	.265	.358	.469
Duran, Enmanuel, Tucson	1	0	0	0	0	0	0	0	0	0	0	0	...	0	0	0	0	0	0	...	...	...
Durbin, Chad, New Orleans †	19	26	22	5	7	7	0	0	0	2	3	0	0	1	0	3	0	0	0	.318	.348	.318
Durrington, Trent, Nashville	92	371	313	61	94	128	15	2	5	31	11	1	5	41	1	63	30	12	5	.300	.389	.409
Eaton, Adam, Portland	2	4	4	0	0	0	0	0	0	0	0	0	0	0	0	3	0	0	0	.000	.000	.000
Echevarria, Angel, Iowa	18	54	51	4	7	10	0	0	1	7	0	0	1	2	0	13	0	0	1	.137	.185	.196
Eckelman, Thomas, Round Rock	61	180	168	16	42	55	7	0	2	15	0	1	4	7	0	21	3	2	6	.250	.294	.327
Eckert, Harold, Las Vegas	19	27	19	0	0	0	0	0	0	1	6	0	0	2	0	10	0	0	1	.000	.095	.000
Edwards, Mike, Las Vegas	32	133	118	18	33	51	6	0	4	21	0	1	3	11	0	21	3	1	4	.280	.353	.432
Eischen, Joey, New Orleans *	3	0	0	0	0	0	0	0	0	0	0	0	0	0	0	0	0	0	0	...	...	...
Eldridge, Rashad, Oklahoma †	91	364	303	61	89	139	27	4	5	34	4	2	1	54	0	76	4	2	8	.294	.400	.459
Ellison, Jason, Fresno	8	41	38	5	9	11	2	0	0	3	0	0	1	2	0	9	0	0	0	.237	.293	.289
Emanuel, Dennis, Portland	24	10	10	0	0	0	0	0	0	0	0	0	0	0	0	5	0	0	0	.000	.000	.000
Erickson, Matt, Nashville-Albuquerque	34	80	67	8	21	23	2	0	0	6	3	0	4	6	0	10	0	0	1	.313	.403	.343
Erickson, Scott, Las Vegas	3	8	8	0	0	0	0	0	0	0	0	0	0	0	0	3	0	0	1	.000	.000	.000
Espineli, Eugene, Fresno *	6	1	1	0	0	0	0	0	0	0	0	0	0	0	0	1	0	0	0	.000	.000	.000
Esposito, Brian, Oklahoma	8	29	27	6	11	12	1	0	0	4	0	0	1	1	0	6	0	0	1	.407	.448	.444
Esposito, Mike, Colorado Springs	16	38	28	4	5	6	1	0	0	1	7	0	0	3	0	6	0	0	0	.179	.258	.214
Estes, Shawn, Tucson	2	3	3	0	1	2	1	0	0	1	0	0	0	0	0	2	0	0	0	.333	.333	.667
Ethier, Andre, Sacramento *	4	17	15	0	4	5	1	0	0	2	0	0	0	2	0	3	0	0	0	.267	.353	.333
Evans, Lee, Portland †	12	42	37	1	1	2	1	0	0	0	0	0	0	5	0	14	0	0	0	.027	.143	.054
Evert, Brett, Nashville *	9	5	5	0	2	3	1	0	0	1	0	0	0	0	0	1	0	0	1	.400	.400	.600
Falkenborg, Brian, Portland-Memphis	23	1	1	0	0	0	0	0	0	0	0	0	0	0	0	1	0	0	0	.000	.000	.000
Farmer, Thomas, Las Vegas	11	1	1	0	0	0	0	0	0	0	0	0	0	0	0	0	0	0	0	.000	.000	.000
Fick, Robert, Portland *	10	44	32	5	12	22	1	0	3	11	0	1	1	10	1	3	1	0	1	.375	.523	.688
Fielder, Prince, Nashville	103	441	378	68	110	215	21	0	28	86	0	2	7	54	0	93	8	5	12	.291	.388	.569
Fikac, Jeremy, Fresno	34	11	9	1	1	2	1	0	0	0	2	0	0	0	0	3	0	0	0	.111	.111	.222
Fitzpatrick, Reginald, New Orleans *	4	16	16	2	3	4	1	0	0	1	0	0	0	0	0	6	1	0	0	.188	.188	.250
Flannery, Michael, Albuquerque	11	1	1	0	0	0	0	0	0	0	0	0	0	0	0	1	0	0	0	.000	.000	.000
Flores, Jose, Las Vegas	96	397	327	64	110	145	11	6	4	42	6	4	6	54	1	33	1	6	6	.336	.435	.443
Flores, Randy, Memphis *	4	0	0	0	0	0	0	0	0	0	0	0	0	0	0	0	0	0	0	...	...	...
Flury, Patrick, Albuquerque	16	0	0	0	0	0	0	0	0	0	0	0	0	0	0	0	0	0	0	...	...	...
Fontenot, Mike, Iowa *	111	449	379	60	103	163	22	10	6	39	3	2	6	59	3	77	3	2	4	.272	.377	.430
Foppert, Jesse, Fresno	5	6	5	2	1	2	1	0	0	0	1	0	0	0	0	2	0	0	0	.200	.200	.400
Fox, Andy, Salt Lake *	15	59	48	8	10	17	2	1	1	7	0	0	1	10	0	10	1	1	2	.208	.356	.354
Frandsen, Kevin, Fresno	20	98	94	18	33	51	10	1	2	16	0	0	2	2	0	5	1	1	6	.351	.378	.543
Freed, Mark, Tucson *	19	26	21	2	5	6	1	0	0	1	3	0	0	2	0	7	0	0	2	.238	.304	.286
Freeman, Choo, Colorado Springs	97	390	354	46	99	151	10	6	10	59	1	4	2	29	0	78	4	3	13	.280	.334	.427
Frese, Nate, Iowa	67	224	204	25	50	75	10	0	5	27	3	1	1	15	2	44	0	0	17	.245	.299	.368
Fuell, Jerrod, Albuquerque	8	0	0	0	0	0	0	0	0	0	0	0	0	0	0	0	0	0	0	...	...	...
Fulchino, Jeffrey, Albuquerque	20	43	36	4	11	16	2	0	1	2	6	0	0	1	0	13	0	1	0	.306	.324	.444
Furmaniak, J.J., Portland	99	428	387	54	103	169	16	4	14	47	5	2	6	28	0	86	9	5	8	.266	.324	.437
Fussell, Chris, Round Rock	14	8	6	1	0	0	0	0	0	0	1	0	0	1	0	1	0	0	0	.000	.143	.000
Gagne, Eric, Las Vegas	2	0	0	0	0	0	0	0	0	0	0	0	...	0	0	0	0	0	0	...	...	...
Gall, John, Memphis	114	426	374	61	101	162	22	0	13	64	0	6	1	45	2	42	9	2	12	.270	.345	.433
Gallo, Mike, Round Rock *	29	3	3	0	1	1	0	0	0	0	0	0	0	0	0	1	0	0	0	.333	.333	.333
Garabito, Eddy, Colorado Springs †	67	296	258	56	79	125	16	3	8	39	6	1	2	29	0	34	8	4	6	.306	.379	.484
Garcia, Jesse, Portland	63	221	210	18	42	62	7	2	3	26	3	2	0	6	0	34	6	1	6	.200	.220	.295
Garrett, Shawn, Sacramento †	131	558	508	69	150	230	27	1	17	82	6	10	5	29	0	111	13	4	9	.295	.333	.453
Gemoll, Justin, Omaha	121	496	448	58	117	164	21	1	8	50	4	1	5	38	2	101	7	1	16	.261	.325	.366
Gerber, Joseph, Portland *	28	51	46	2	5	6	1	0	0	4	0	1	0	4	0	16	0	0	1	.109	.176	.130
German, Esteban, Oklahoma	117	564	489	103	153	207	27	6	5	68	1	2	7	65	0	74	43	6	20	.313	.400	.423
Germano, Justin, Portland	11	23	16	0	0	0	0	0	0	0	5	0	0	2	0	3	0	0	0	.000	.111	.000
Gil, David, New Orleans	9	6	6	0	1	2	1	0	0	0	0	0	0	0	0	3	0	0	0	.167	.167	.333
Gil, Rotsen, Las Vegas †	7	15	15	3	5	9	1	0	1	3	0	0	0	0	0	4	0	0	0	.333	.333	.600
Ginter, Keith, Sacramento	14	63	57	9	19	36	8	0	3	12	1	0	1	4	0	11	0	0	0	.333	.387	.632
Gipson, Charles, Round Rock	110	431	393	58	119	155	24	3	2	25	4	1	8	25	0	75	19	9	3	.303	.356	.394
Giron, Roberto, Round Rock	16	12	11	0	1	1	0	0	0	1	1	0	0	0	0	3	0	0	0	.091	.091	.091
Gissell, Chris, Memphis	15	32	28	3	3	7	1	0	1	3	0	0	2	2	0	12	0	0	0	.107	.219	.250
Glover, Gary, Nashville	13	22	19	0	5	5	0	0	0	2	2	0	1	0	0	6	0	0	0	.263	.300	.263
Godwin, Tyrell, New Orleans *	129	561	499	83	160	221	22	6	9	48	6	1	5	50	0	77	22	12	6	.321	.387	.443
Gomez, Francis, Sacramento	3	14	12	5	6	8	2	0	0	1	1	0	0	1	0	4	0	1	1	.500	.538	.667
Gomez, Rodolfo, Omaha	13	53	49	5	11	11	0	0	0	2	1	0	0	3	0	7	0	0	2	.224	.269	.224
Gonzalez, Adrian, Oklahoma *	84	368	328	61	111	184	17	1	18	65	0	4	4	32	3	44	0	0	13	.338	.399	.561
Gonzalez, Alfredo, Las Vegas	30	5	5	1	1	4	0	0	1	2	0	0	0	0	0	1	0	0	0	.200	.200	.800
Gonzalez, Edgar, Tucson	16	42	37	2	8	8	0	0	0	2	5	0	0	0	0	7	0	0	3	.216	.216	.216
Gonzalez, Edgar, New Orleans	23	50	48	12	17	21	4	0	0	4	1	0	0	1	0	10	0	0	2	.354	.367	.438
Gonzalez, Luis, Las Vegas *	7	0	0	0	0	0	0	0	0	0	0	0	...	0	0	0	0	0	0	...	...	...
Gonzalez, Raul, Memphis	93	388	347	62	107	176	21	3	14	50	1	2	0	38	3	47	3	5	11	.308	.375	.507
Gonzalez, Wiki, Tacoma	47	196	176	25	55	82	10	1	5	28	1	1	2	16	0	13	0	0	7	.313	.374	.466
Gordon, Brian, Salt Lake *	101	378	343	50	94	178	25	4	17	55	3	5	1	26	5	103	7	5	4	.274	.323	.519
Gorneault, Nicolas, Salt Lake	130	555	488	106	143	268	25	11	26	108	1	6	2	58	1	119	7	6	11	.293	.366	.549
Gosling, Mike, Tucson *	14	26	24	1	1	1	0	0	0	1	0	0	0	1	0	14	0	0	0	.042	.080	.042
Gothreaux, Jared, Round Rock	12	21	21	0	2	3	1	0	0	0	0	0	0	0	0	8	0	0	0	.095	.095	.143
Grabowski, Jason, Las Vegas *	52	212	181	37	56	92	16	1	6	33	0	0	1	30	1	26	0	0	5	.309	.408	.508
Gracesqui, Franklyn, Albuquerque †	14	0	0	0	0	0	0	0	0	0	0	0	0	0	0	0	0	0	0	...	...	...
Green, Andy, Tucson	135	609	530	125	182	311	46	13	19	80	2	3	6	68	2	82	9	6	9	.343	.422	.587
Greene, Todd, Colorado Springs	11	34	33	4	13	22	0	0	3	8	0	0	0	1	0	3	0	0	2	.394	.412	.667
Gregorio, Tom, Sacramento	29	95	89	4	25	31	6	0	0	16	0	0	1	5	0	20	0	0	4	.281	.326	.348
Grieve, Ben, Iowa *	86	342	293	44	78	141	19	1	14	51	0	0	1	48	4	59	0	0	9	.266	.371	.481

Player, Team	G	TPA	AB	R	H	TB	2B	3B	HR	RBI	SH	SF	HP	BB	IBB	SO	SB	CS	GDP	Avg.	OBP	Slg.
Griffiths, Jeremy, Round Rock	3	1	1	0	0	0	0	0	0	0	0	0	0	0	0	0	0	0	0	.000	.000	.000
Grissom, Marquis, Fresno	4	15	15	4	3	6	0	0	1	2	0	0	0	0	0	3	0	0	0	.200	.200	.400
Guerrero, Cristian, New Orleans	4	18	16	4	4	7	0	0	1	2	0	0	0	2	0	5	0	2	0	.250	.333	.438
Guerrero, Wilton, Memphis †	36	74	68	7	21	32	6	1	1	6	0	0	1	5	0	8	1	1	1	.309	.365	.471
Guiel, Aaron, Omaha *	128	582	496	94	137	267	32	4	30	95	0	7	15	64	4	103	6	3	14	.276	.371	.538
Gutierrez, Gabriel, Las Vegas	4	15	13	1	6	6	0	0	0	3	0	0	0	2	0	2	0	0	0	.462	.533	.462
Haad, Yamid, Fresno	63	231	216	23	61	106	13	1	10	34	2	3	2	8	0	32	2	0	5	.282	.310	.491
Haines, Joseph, Iowa	11	1	1	0	0	0	0	0	0	0	0	0	0	0	0	1	0	0	0	.000	.000	.000
Hairston, Jerry, Iowa	5	25	22	3	7	9	0	1	0	2	0	1	0	2	0	3	3	0	0	.318	.360	.409
Hairston, Scott, Tucson	58	237	209	45	65	127	8	3	16	40	0	2	5	21	0	40	3	0	4	.311	.384	.608
Halama, John, New Orleans *	2	2	2	0	0	0	0	0	0	0	0	0	0	0	0	2	0	0	0	.000	.000	.000
Hall, David, Tacoma	1	0	0	0	0	0	0	0	0	0	0	0	0	0	...	0	0	0	0	...	...	...
Halter, Shane, Iowa	16	55	48	10	11	18	4	0	1	8	0	0	0	7	0	8	1	0	1	.229	.327	.375
Hammock, Robby, Tucson	3	12	11	0	4	4	0	0	0	3	0	1	0	0	0	1	0	0	0	.364	.333	.364
Hammonds, Jeffrey, New Orleans	19	70	60	10	15	28	5	1	2	9	0	1	2	7	1	5	1	0	2	.250	.343	.467
Hampson, Justin, Colorado Springs *	15	30	26	1	1	1	0	0	0	2	3	0	0	1	0	12	0	0	2	.038	.074	.038
Hansen, Dave, Tacoma *	6	23	20	2	6	6	0	0	0	3	0	1	0	2	0	4	0	0	1	.300	.348	.300
Hansen, Jed, Fresno	71	272	240	49	60	104	16	2	8	30	1	3	6	22	0	62	8	2	4	.250	.325	.433
Harris, Brendan, New Orleans	127	519	470	67	127	196	22	4	13	81	2	4	3	40	3	77	9	5	12	.270	.329	.417
Hart, Bo, Memphis	133	532	468	78	126	188	33	1	9	47	8	7	3	46	4	74	11	3	9	.269	.334	.402
Hart, Corey, Nashville †	54	113	95	9	17	25	5	0	1	5	1	0	0	17	2	20	1	1	2	.179	.304	.263
Hart, Corey, Nashville	113	489	429	85	132	230	29	9	17	69	3	6	3	48	1	88	31	7	11	.308	.377	.536
Harvey, Ken, Omaha	25	110	104	10	36	51	4	1	3	18	0	1	0	5	0	18	0	0	2	.346	.373	.490
Hawkins, LaTroy, Fresno	2	0	0	0	0	0	0	0	0	0	0	0	...	0	0	0	0	0	0	...	...	...
Hawpe, Brad, Colorado Springs *	7	34	28	7	13	25	3	0	3	11	0	0	0	6	0	7	0	0	2	.464	.559	.893
Haynes, Charles, Memphis-New Orleans	11	46	43	10	11	20	3	0	2	7	0	0	0	3	0	6	1	0	1	.256	.304	.465
Helling, Rick, Nashville	14	35	26	2	3	4	1	0	0	1	4	1	0	4	0	10	0	0	0	.115	.226	.154
Helton, Todd, Colorado Springs *	2	7	5	1	3	5	2	0	0	1	0	0	1	1	0	0	0	0	0	.600	.714	1.000
Hendrickson, Ben, Nashville	20	40	29	1	4	4	0	0	0	1	9	0	0	2	0	9	0	0	1	.138	.194	.138
Hennessey, Brad, Fresno	9	25	20	2	6	9	3	0	0	5	5	0	0	0	0	4	0	0	0	.300	.300	.450
Hensley, Clay, Portland	8	20	15	1	3	3	0	0	0	0	4	0	0	1	0	7	0	0	0	.200	.250	.200
Herges, Matt, Tucson *	14	2	2	0	0	0	0	0	0	0	0	0	0	0	0	1	0	0	0	.000	.000	.000
Hernandez, Carlos, Round Rock †	16	22	21	3	5	7	2	0	0	2	1	0	0	0	0	9	0	0	0	.238	.238	.333
Hernandez, Michel, Portland	82	309	264	19	76	96	9	1	3	31	2	6	0	37	3	34	0	0	13	.288	.368	.364
Herrera, Javier, Sacramento	5	15	12	5	5	9	1	0	1	3	0	0	2	1	0	1	1	0	0	.417	.533	.750
Hill, Jason, Albuquerque	2	4	3	0	1	1	0	0	0	1	0	1	0	0	0	2	0	0	0	.333	.250	.333
Hill, Koyie, Tucson †	50	193	168	22	41	67	9	1	5	26	0	1	1	23	0	37	3	0	9	.244	.337	.399
Hill, Rich, Iowa *	5	12	10	3	2	2	0	0	0	1	1	0	0	1	0	4	0	0	1	.200	.273	.200
Hocking, Denny, Omaha †	68	263	230	37	66	84	14	2	0	24	5	3	0	25	2	44	1	0	5	.287	.353	.365
Hodge, Kevin, Round Rock	6	0	0	0	0	0	0	0	0	0	0	0	0	0	0	0	0	0	0	...	...	...
Hodges, Scott, New Orleans *	9	15	14	0	2	3	1	0	0	1	0	0	0	1	0	5	0	0	0	.143	.200	.214
Hoffpauir, James, Iowa *	119	439	392	48	105	134	14	3	3	47	1	4	3	38	4	59	2	0	11	.268	.334	.342
Horgan, Joe, New Orleans *	29	7	7	1	2	2	0	0	0	0	0	0	0	0	0	3	0	0	0	.286	.286	.286
Housman, Jeff, Nashville *	18	31	28	1	4	7	0	0	1	3	0	0	0	3	0	15	1	0	0	.143	.226	.250
Howard, Ben, Albuquerque	37	8	8	1	1	2	1	0	0	0	0	0	0	0	0	3	0	0	0	.125	.125	.250
Hubbard, Trenidad, Round Rock-Iowa	79	343	302	42	91	124	19	1	4	32	2	1	5	33	0	36	19	10	7	.301	.378	.411
Huber, Justin, Omaha	32	131	113	19	31	60	6	1	7	23	0	0	2	16	1	33	3	0	3	.274	.374	.531
Huffman, Royce, Round Rock	124	455	391	57	111	168	32	2	7	45	0	5	4	55	0	54	8	3	9	.284	.374	.430
Hughes, Travis, New Orleans	33	5	4	1	1	1	0	0	0	0	0	0	0	1	0	2	0	0	0	.250	.400	.250
Hull, Eric, Las Vegas	1	2	2	0	1	1	0	0	0	0	0	0	0	0	0	0	0	0	0	.500	.500	.500
Hummel, Tim, Memphis	56	205	189	20	52	82	12	0	6	23	1	1	1	13	0	22	0	1	6	.275	.324	.434
Hyzdu, Adam, Portland	62	257	207	38	57	101	9	1	11	32	1	1	1	47	1	61	2	5	5	.275	.410	.488
Infante, Larry, Salt Lake †	7	7	7	0	2	2	0	0	0	2	0	0	0	0	0	2	0	0	0	.286	.286	.286
Izturis, Maicer, Salt Lake †	10	39	31	10	14	18	4	0	0	2	1	0	0	7	0	4	4	2	2	.452	.553	.581
Jackson, Conor, Tucson	93	409	333	66	118	184	38	2	8	73	0	7	0	69	1	32	3	2	8	.354	.457	.553
Jackson, Damian, Portland	14	65	51	14	18	33	4	1	3	10	0	1	0	13	0	9	1	1	0	.353	.477	.647
Jackson, Derry, Las Vegas	9	28	27	4	7	12	0	1	1	6	1	0	0	0	0	10	1	0	0	.259	.259	.444
Jackson, Edwin, Las Vegas	10	19	16	1	5	5	0	0	0	2	3	0	0	0	0	2	1	0	0	.313	.313	.313
Jackson, Steve, Sacramento	33	110	105	11	19	35	5	1	3	12	0	1	0	4	0	31	0	0	3	.181	.209	.333
Jacobs, Gregory, Tacoma *	16	63	59	6	12	22	1	0	3	8	0	1	0	3	0	11	0	0	2	.203	.238	.373
Jacobsen, Bucky, Tacoma	18	75	66	7	9	12	3	0	0	8	0	0	2	7	0	18	0	0	1	.136	.240	.182
Jaramillo, Milko, Memphis †	20	42	38	5	15	16	1	0	0	2	0	0	1	3	0	6	0	1	1	.395	.452	.421
Jarvis, Kevin, Memphis *	17	40	34	2	7	8	1	0	0	4	0	0	2	0	0	7	0	0	0	.206	.250	.235
Jimerson, Charlton, Round Rock	7	25	23	1	7	8	1	0	0	1	1	0	0	0	0	7	3	0	0	.304	.292	.348
Johnson, Ben, Portland	107	472	414	79	129	231	27	0	25	83	0	1	6	51	0	88	6	1	7	.312	.394	.558
Johnson, Dan, Sacramento *	47	217	182	36	59	100	17	0	8	41	0	2	1	32	2	24	0	1	1	.324	.424	.549
Johnson, Mark, Iowa *	60	216	177	19	47	68	10	1	3	26	2	1	2	34	3	25	0	1	7	.266	.388	.384
Johnson, Nick, New Orleans *	3	7	6	0	0	0	0	0	0	0	0	0	0	1	0	2	0	0	0	.000	.143	.000
Johnson, Tyler, Memphis †	37	1	1	0	0	0	0	0	0	0	0	0	0	0	0	0	0	0	0	.000	.000	.000
Jones, Jamie, Omaha *	58	216	195	37	52	77	8	1	5	21	0	2	2	17	0	48	0	2	5	.267	.329	.395
Jones, Kennard, Portland *	8	35	33	3	7	8	1	0	0	3	0	0	1	1	0	11	0	1	1	.212	.257	.242
Jorgensen, Ryan, Albuquerque	53	161	137	20	27	38	5	0	2	11	2	0	1	21	3	46	1	0	1	.197	.308	.277
Journell, Jimmy, Memphis	25	1	1	0	0	0	0	0	0	0	0	0	0	0	0	0	0	0	0	.000	.000	.000
Karp, Joshua, New Orleans	13	5	5	0	0	0	0	0	0	0	0	0	0	0	0	1	0	0	1	.000	.000	.000
Kata, Matt, Tucson	46	214	200	25	62	87	10	3	3	28	4	3	1	6	0	25	5	1	4	.310	.329	.435
Kelly, Kenny, New Orleans	20	91	82	11	19	24	3	1	0	6	0	0	0	9	0	15	3	2	2	.232	.308	.293
Kelton, David, Iowa	122	495	460	59	130	193	28	1	11	67	0	2	3	30	2	78	14	5	12	.283	.329	.420
Kennedy, Adam, Salt Lake *	4	20	17	4	7	8	1	0	0	4	0	1	0	2	0	2	2	0	0	.412	.450	.471
Kent, Steve, Colorado Springs †	5	0	0	0	0	0	0	0	0	0	0	0	...	0	0	0	0	0	0	...	...	...
Kershner, Jason, Portland *	28	3	3	0	2	3	1	0	0	1	0	0	0	0	0	0	0	0	0	.667	.667	1.000

CLASS AAA Pacific Coast League

Player, Team	G	TPA	AB	R	H	TB	2B	3B	HR	RBI	SH	SF	HP	BB	IBB	SO	SB	CS	GDP	Avg.	OBP	Slg.
Kieschnick, Brooks, Round Rock *	49	54	46	6	14	25	2	0	3	10	0	0	0	8	0	13	0	0	1	.304	.407	.543
Kim, Sun-Woo, New Orleans	7	14	12	0	3	4	1	0	0	0	2	0	0	0	0	2	0	0	0	.250	.250	.333
Kinney, Joshua, Memphis	20	0	0	0	0	0	0	0	0	0	...	0	0	0	...	0	0	0	0	...	...	...
Kinney, Matt, Fresno	12	28	22	2	4	6	2	0	0	1	4	0	0	2	0	10	0	0	0	.182	.250	.273
Kinsler, Ian, Oklahoma	131	597	530	102	145	246	28	2	23	94	2	3	9	53	0	89	19	5	21	.274	.348	.464
Kirby, Brian, Colorado Springs *	2	2	2	0	0	0	0	0	0	0	0	0	0	0	0	2	0	0	0	.000	.000	.000
Klassen, Danny, Round Rock	88	378	342	61	109	183	23	3	15	53	2	2	5	27	1	80	7	1	11	.319	.375	.535
Knoedler, Justin, Fresno	85	322	287	35	78	111	19	1	4	32	...	2	7	26	0	61	5	5	2	.272	.345	.387
Knott, Jon, Portland	134	577	503	81	126	243	34	4	25	78	0	8	11	55	0	112	1	0	17	.250	.333	.483
Knox, Ryan, Nashville	99	344	301	31	70	97	12	0	5	26	8	5	7	23	1	70	20	8	2	.233	.298	.322
Koplove, Mike, Tucson	4	0	0	0	0	0	0	0	0	0	...	0	0	0	0	0	0	0	0	...	...	...
Koronka, John, Iowa *	16	33	27	3	5	5	0	0	0	2	4	0	0	2	0	12	0	0	0	.185	.241	.185
Kotchman, Casey, Salt Lake *	94	417	363	62	105	160	23	1	10	58	0	4	7	43	2	40	0	2	15	.289	.372	.441
Kroeger, Josh, Tucson *	129	516	472	73	123	199	28	3	14	62	0	4	4	36	3	108	17	4	12	.261	.316	.422
Krynzel, Dave, Nashville *	115	511	450	71	115	187	25	7	11	51	8	5	5	43	2	138	24	8	3	.256	.324	.416
Kuzmic, Craig, New Orleans †	54	174	145	19	38	63	7	0	6	22	2	4	3	20	1	39	1	0	2	.262	.355	.434
Labandeira, Josh, New Orleans	11	32	30	3	9	10	1	0	0	3	0	0	1	1	0	10	1	1	0	.300	.344	.333
Laird, Gerald, Oklahoma	75	317	281	51	87	158	12	4	17	55	1	2	5	28	1	61	12	2	5	.310	.380	.562
Lee, Dave, Fresno-Memphis	8	0	0	0	0	0	0	0	0	0	0	0	0	0	0	0	0	0	0	...	...	...
Leek, Randy, Memphis *	1	2	1	0	0	0	0	0	0	0	0	0	0	1	0	0	0	0	0	.000	.500	.000
Lehr, Justin, Nashville	17	21	18	4	7	11	1	0	1	7	1	0	0	2	0	8	0	0	0	.389	.450	.611
Leicester, Jon, Iowa	14	14	10	0	2	2	0	0	0	1	4	0	0	0	0	1	0	0	0	.200	.200	.200
Leone, Justin, Tacoma	87	370	313	51	76	120	19	2	7	38	2	2	2	51	1	93	5	2	14	.243	.351	.383
Levine, Al, Fresno *	7	0	0	0	0	0	0	0	0	0	0	0	0	0	0	0	0	0	0	...	...	...
Lewis, Richard, Iowa	87	287	263	28	57	79	10	3	2	23	2	0	4	18	0	64	4	2	11	.217	.277	.300
Ligtenberg, Kerry, Tucson	18	6	6	0	1	1	0	0	0	1	0	0	0	0	0	2	0	0	0	.167	.167	.167
Linden, Todd, Fresno †	95	415	340	81	109	232	25	4	30	80	1	2	10	62	5	97	6	2	11	.321	.437	.682
Little, Mark, Albuquerque	83	364	312	62	86	163	13	5	18	52	1	3	14	32	1	84	16	7	6	.276	.366	.522
Lizarraga, Sergio, Tucson	1	2	2	0	0	0	0	0	0	0	0	0	0	0	0	0	0	0	0	.000	.000	.000
Lopez, Aquilino, Las Vegas-Colorado Springs	27	5	3	1	1	1	0	0	0	1	1	0	0	1	0	2	0	0	0	.333	.500	.333
Lopez, Javier, Tucson *	14	1	1	0	1	1	0	0	0	0	0	0	0	0	0	0	0	0	0	1.000	1.000	1.000
Lopez, Jose, Tacoma	44	194	182	29	58	92	19	0	5	31	2	0	2	8	1	25	2	3	6	.319	.354	.505
Lopez, Mickey, Fresno †	113	478	423	65	121	181	24	9	6	42	4	7	12	32	4	65	18	9	3	.286	.348	.428
Loretta, Mark, Portland	3	12	10	0	1	1	0	0	0	0	0	0	2	0	1	0	0	0	0	.100	.250	.100
Luna, Hector, Memphis	57	247	223	24	50	74	13	1	3	21	2	0	2	20	0	38	11	4	2	.224	.294	.332
Lyon, Brandon, Tucson	2	0	0	0	0	0	0	0	0	0	0	0	0	0	0	0	0	0	0	...	...	...
Machado, Anderson, Colorado Springs †	25	81	63	6	10	15	3	1	0	8	1	1	0	16	0	17	0	1	1	.159	.325	.238
MacRae, Scott, Round Rock	9	5	4	0	1	1	0	0	0	1	0	0	0	1	0	1	0	0	0	.250	.250	.250
Mahomes, Pat, Las Vegas	25	24	20	2	2	3	1	0	0	0	2	0	0	2	0	6	0	0	0	.100	.182	.150
Mahoney, Mike, Memphis	71	255	230	30	61	97	19	1	5	27	2	2	7	14	3	40	2	0	9	.265	.324	.422
Majewski, Gary, New Orleans	3	1	1	0	0	0	0	0	0	0	0	0	0	0	0	0	0	0	0	.000	.000	.000
Martin, Tom, Round Rock *	15	0	0	0	0	0	0	0	0	0	0	0	0	0	0	0	0	0	0	...	...	...
Martinez, Brett, Salt Lake	4	10	10	2	2	4	2	0	0	0	0	0	0	0	0	5	0	0	1	.200	.200	.400
Martinez, Carlos, Albuquerque	2	0	0	0	0	0	0	0	0	0	0	0	0	0	0	0	0	0	0	...	...	...
Mateo, Henry, New Orleans †	9	34	31	2	9	9	0	0	0	3	0	0	0	3	0	7	3	1	0	.290	.353	.290
Mathews, T.J., Round Rock	16	1	1	0	1	1	0	0	0	0	0	0	0	0	0	0	0	0	0	1.000	1.000	1.000
Mathis, Jeff, Salt Lake	112	479	427	78	118	213	26	3	21	73	5	4	1	42	1	85	4	3	7	.276	.340	.499
Matos, Pascual, Colorado Springs	56	188	178	24	49	74	13	0	4	24	2	1	1	6	0	43	1	1	5	.275	.301	.416
Matranga, Dave, Salt Lake	56	218	176	31	42	67	12	2	3	19	6	2	3	31	0	39	6	3	2	.239	.358	.381
McAnulty, Paul, Portland *	38	168	151	27	52	85	15	0	6	27	0	1	0	16	0	29	0	0	4	.344	.405	.563
McCauley, Seth, Portland †	3	3	3	0	0	0	0	0	0	0	0	0	0	0	0	2	0	0	0	.000	.000	.000
McClain, Scott, Iowa	121	481	423	75	123	244	27	2	30	93	0	9	4	45	2	84	1	1	17	.291	.358	.577
McClaskey, Timothy, Round Rock †	2	4	4	0	1	1	0	0	0	1	0	0	0	0	0	2	0	0	0	.250	.250	.250
McClellan, Zachary, Colorado Springs	27	11	8	0	1	1	0	0	0	2	0	0	1	0	5	0	0	0	.125	.222	.125
McDaniel, Denton, Round Rock *	13	0	0	0	0	0	0	0	0	0	0	0	0	0	0	0	0	0	0	...	...	...
McDonald, Keith, Oklahoma	66	264	233	28	56	79	15	1	2	33	0	5	1	25	0	54	0	0	7	.240	.311	.339
McDougall, Marshall, Oklahoma	57	256	223	40	76	129	16	2	11	64	1	2	0	30	1	45	5	0	4	.341	.416	.578
McEwing, Joe, Omaha	5	22	18	4	3	4	1	0	0	1	0	0	0	4	0	2	0	0	1	.167	.318	.222
McGlinchy, Kevin, Iowa	13	2	2	0	2	2	0	0	0	0	0	0	0	0	0	0	0	0	0	1.000	1.000	1.000
McKay, Cody, Memphis *	19	58	47	4	10	15	2	0	1	5	0	0	3	8	0	10	0	0	1	.213	.362	.319
McLeary, Marty, Portland	24	24	20	3	3	6	1	1	0	2	1	0	1	2	0	5	0	0	1	.150	.261	.300
McPherson, Dallas, Salt Lake *	14	63	54	8	15	38	1	2	6	19	0	2	0	7	0	20	1	2	1	.278	.349	.704
Medders, Brandon, Tucson	26	0	0	0	0	0	0	0	0	0	0	0	0	0	0	0	0	0	0	...	...	...
Melo, Juan, New Orleans †	84	339	311	44	99	152	17	3	10	56	2	2	4	20	1	38	2	4	16	.318	.365	.489
Mendez, Adalberto, Iowa	3	0	0	0	0	0	0	0	0	0	0	0	0	0	0	0	0	0	0	...	...	...
Mendez, Donaldo, Fresno	18	73	70	7	18	24	3	0	1	4	0	0	1	2	0	23	0	0	3	.257	.288	.343
Mercedes, Jose, Iowa	10	0	0	0	0	0	0	0	0	0	0	0	0	0	0	0	0	0	0	...	...	...
Merloni, Lou, Salt Lake	6	28	25	6	8	11	3	0	0	6	0	0	1	2	0	5	0	0	1	.320	.393	.440
Merrill, Ronald, Portland †	14	57	50	7	12	14	2	0	0	2	0	0	0	7	0	10	0	0	2	.240	.333	.280
Messenger, Randy, Albuquerque	22	5	5	0	0	0	0	0	0	0	0	0	0	0	0	3	0	0	0	.000	.000	.000
Meyer, Drew, Oklahoma *	42	195	178	25	44	63	11	4	0	19	2	1	0	14	0	43	5	2	6	.247	.301	.354
Meyers, Mike, Nashville	19	14	14	2	4	4	0	0	0	0	0	0	0	0	0	3	0	0	0	.286	.286	.286
Miadich, Bart, Albuquerque	17	2	1	2	1	2	0	0	0	2	0	0	0	0	0	0	0	0	0	1.000	1.000	1.000
Miceli, Dan, Colorado Springs	2	0	0	0	0	0	0	0	0	0	0	0	0	0	0	0	0	0	0	...	...	...
Michaelis, Derek, Las Vegas *	16	36	32	2	5	8	0	0	1	4	0	0	0	4	0	9	0	0	1	.156	.250	.250
Michalak, Chris, Tucson *	17	43	36	3	5	5	0	0	0	2	2	0	0	5	0	10	0	0	0	.139	.244	.139
Miles, Aaron, Colorado Springs †	8	34	32	6	7	9	0	1	0	1	1	0	1	0	0	3	1	0	0	.219	.242	.281
Misch, Patrick, Fresno	12	26	20	1	2	2	0	0	0	1	6	0	0	0	0	3	0	0	0	.100	.100	.100
Mitre, Sergio, Iowa	12	26	20	0	2	2	0	0	0	0	1	0	0	5	0	6	0	0	0	.100	.280	.100
Mohr, Dustan, Colorado Springs	3	12	12	2	3	8	2	0	1	4	0	0	0	0	0	4	0	0	1	.250	.250	.667

Player, Team	G	TPA	AB	R	H	TB	2B	3B	HR	RBI	SH	SF	HP	BB	IBB	SO	SB	CS	GDP	Avg.	OBP	Slg.
Molina, Gabe, Colorado Springs	8	1	1	0	1	1	0	0	0	0	0	0	0	0	0	0	0	0	0	1.000	1.000	1.000
Moriarty, Mike, Iowa	18	52	46	3	10	20	2	1	2	7	0	0	1	5	0	15	0	1	1	.217	.308	.435
Morris, Jed, Sacramento *	1	4	2	2	1	1	0	0	0	0	1	0	0	1	0	1	0	0	0	.500	.667	.500
Morris, Warren, Nashville *	64	256	230	39	61	93	7	2	7	27	2	2	0	22	1	32	9	2	4	.265	.327	.404
Morrissey, Adam, Sacramento	55	220	188	30	47	66	7	0	4	21	3	1	1	27	0	74	3	1	4	.250	.346	.351
Morse, Mike, Tacoma	49	203	182	20	46	74	12	2	4	23	1	2	2	16	1	36	1	0	6	.253	.317	.407
Mosquera, Julio, Nashville	64	254	240	32	62	92	18	0	4	30	1	1	1	10	0	34	4	1	11	.258	.290	.383
Moylan, Daniel, Memphis *	7	18	17	0	1	1	0	0	0	0	0	0	0	1	0	1	0	0	2	.059	.111	.059
Munhall, Brian, Fresno	19	61	53	8	14	21	4	0	1	6	3	0	1	4	0	12	0	0	3	.264	.328	.396
Munter, Scott, Fresno	9	0	0	0	0	0	0	0	0	0	...	0	0	0	0	0	0	0	0	...	...	...
Murphy, William, Tucson *	16	32	28	1	6	8	2	0	0	3	3	1	0	0	0	8	0	0	2	.214	.207	.286
Murray, Calvin, Iowa	135	579	499	77	148	203	26	7	5	50	5	5	12	58	2	72	18	7	10	.297	.380	.407
Murton, Matt, Iowa	9	38	34	4	12	17	2	0	1	3	0	0	0	4	0	8	0	0	2	.353	.421	.500
Myers, Corey, Tucson	82	287	260	30	62	88	10	2	4	36	0	2	0	25	3	55	0	1	10	.238	.303	.338
Myrow, Brian, Las Vegas *	121	481	393	83	111	215	28	5	22	73	0	5	9	74	3	83	4	2	4	.282	.403	.547
Nakamura, Norihiro, Las Vegas	101	408	357	54	89	174	17	1	22	67	0	5	1	45	0	70	0	0	19	.249	.331	.487
Nall, Thomas, Las Vegas	18	19	17	0	1	1	0	0	0	0	1	0	0	1	0	10	0	0	0	.059	.111	.059
Nance, Shane, Tucson *	17	0	0	0	0	0	0	0	0	0	...	0	0	0	0	0	0	0	0	...	...	...
Narveson, Christopher, Memphis *	1	1	1	0	0	0	0	0	0	0	0	0	0	0	0	0	0	0	0	.000	.000	.000
Navarro, Dioner, Las Vegas †	75	286	241	31	64	94	12	0	6	29	2	3	2	38	3	24	2	2	9	.266	.366	.390
Neal, Blaine, Colorado Springs *	1	0	0	0	0	0	0	0	0	0	...	0	0	0	0	0	0	0	0	...	...	...
Nelson, Brad, Nashville *	81	331	281	50	71	112	16	2	7	39	2	1	2	45	4	74	4	5	5	.253	.359	.399
Nelson, John, Memphis	128	485	427	56	103	174	27	1	14	49	1	2	4	51	4	141	2	3	4	.241	.326	.407
Neu, Michael, Las Vegas †	18	14	12	1	3	4	1	0	0	1	0	0	1	1	0	4	0	0	0	.250	.357	.333
Nevin, Phil, Portland	2	7	7	0	1	1	0	0	0	1	0	0	0	0	0	2	0	0	1	.143	.143	.143
Nicholson, Thomas, Colorado Springs *	32	93	85	9	25	28	3	0	0	6	2	0	0	6	0	18	1	0	2	.294	.341	.329
Niekro, Lance, Fresno	1	4	4	0	1	1	0	0	0	0	0	0	0	0	0	1	0	0	0	.250	.250	.250
Nieve, Fernando, Round Rock	8	21	17	2	3	3	0	0	0	1	3	0	0	1	0	7	0	0	1	.176	.222	.176
Nieves, Melvin, New Orleans †	25	97	75	17	17	34	2	0	5	17	0	2	2	18	0	28	0	1	0	.227	.381	.453
Niles, Frank, Albuquerque †	25	69	61	11	18	27	3	0	2	13	1	1	0	6	0	13	1	0	3	.295	.353	.443
Nina, Elvin, Tucson	7	1	1	0	0	0	0	0	0	0	0	0	0	0	0	1	0	0	0	.000	.000	.000
Nitkowski, C.J., New Orleans *	16	1	1	1	1	1	0	0	0	0	0	0	0	0	0	0	0	0	0	1.000	1.000	1.000
Nix, Laynce, Oklahoma *	10	45	36	8	12	24	1	1	3	6	0	0	0	9	2	6	0	1	0	.333	.467	.667
Nixon, Michael, Las Vegas	46	134	124	12	28	40	6	0	2	17	1	3	1	5	0	28	0	0	2	.226	.256	.323
Nolen, Walt, Iowa	2	0	0	0	0	0	0	0	0	0	0	0	0	0	0	0	0	0	0	...	...	...
Norton, Phil, Round Rock-Iowa	23	10	8	3	2	4	2	0	0	0	1	0	0	1	0	4	0	0	0	.250	.333	.500
Novoa, Roberto, Iowa	14	1	1	0	0	0	0	0	0	0	0	0	0	0	0	0	0	0	0	.000	.000	.000
Nunez, Abraham, Tacoma †	127	563	481	82	132	215	26	3	17	86	2	8	1	71	7	109	12	10	14	.274	.364	.447
Nunez, Vladimir, Memphis-Tucson	19	0	0	0	0	0	0	0	0	0	0	0	0	0	0	0	0	0	0	...	...	...
Nussbeck, Mark, Memphis	12	14	12	0	0	0	0	0	0	0	1	0	0	1	0	6	0	0	0	.000	.077	.000
Obermueller, Wes, Nashville	6	10	9	1	2	5	1	1	0	2	1	0	0	0	0	3	0	0	0	.222	.222	.556
Ohman, Will, Iowa *	8	0	0	0	0	0	0	0	0	0	...	0	0	0	0	0	0	0	0	...	...	...
Ojeda, Miguel, Portland-Tacoma	26	100	90	15	22	42	2	0	6	16	0	0	2	8	0	21	0	0	0	.244	.320	.467
Oliver, Darren, Tucson-Iowa	5	7	5	0	0	0	0	0	0	0	2	0	0	0	0	2	0	0	0	.000	.000	.000
Olivo, Miguel, Tacoma	24	99	90	13	21	36	4	1	3	21	0	1	1	7	0	19	8	1	1	.233	.293	.400
Olson, Tim, Colorado Springs	89	364	322	53	96	162	26	2	12	51	5	4	5	28	2	70	9	7	9	.298	.359	.503
O'Malley, Ryan, Iowa	5	8	6	1	1	1	0	0	0	0	1	0	0	1	0	3	0	0	0	.167	.286	.167
Orie, Kevin, Nashville-New Orleans	113	413	349	67	123	220	35	1	20	89	0	3	4	57	5	43	4	1	13	.352	.446	.630
Oropesa, Eddie, Iowa *	7	0	0	0	0	0	0	0	0	0	...	0	0	0	0	0	0	0	0	...	...	...
Ortiz, Hector, New Orleans	74	272	254	13	63	72	6	0	1	28	3	1	1	13	1	33	0	1	14	.248	.286	.283
Osborne, Donovan, Albuquerque *	10	23	19	0	4	4	0	0	0	2	2	0	0	2	0	9	0	0	2	.211	.286	.211
Osik, Keith, New Orleans	17	50	44	3	9	11	2	0	0	3	1	1	0	4	0	7	1	0	2	.205	.265	.250
Osoria, Franquelis, Las Vegas	29	1	1	0	0	0	0	0	0	0	0	0	0	0	0	1	0	0	0	.000	.000	.000
Osuna, Antonio, New Orleans	2	1	0	0	0	0	0	0	0	0	1	0	0	0	0	0	0	0	0	...	1.000	...
Oxspring, Chris, Portland *	18	44	36	3	5	6	1	0	0	3	5	0	0	3	0	14	0	0	1	.139	.205	.167
Pachot, John, Albuquerque	35	103	96	6	19	27	5	0	1	8	2	1	0	4	1	11	0	1	4	.198	.228	.281
Padgett, Matthew, Albuquerque *	123	515	460	71	136	221	28	3	17	72	0	5	3	47	1	131	3	1	11	.296	.360	.480
Parker, Christian, Colorado Springs	7	14	12	1	2	5	0	0	1	1	2	0	0	0	0	3	0	0	0	.167	.167	.417
Paronto, Chad, Nashville	20	1	1	0	0	0	0	0	0	0	0	0	0	0	0	1	0	0	0	.000	.000	.000
Patterson, Corey, Iowa *	24	102	91	16	27	46	4	0	5	12	1	0	2	8	1	19	6	1	0	.297	.366	.505
Patterson, Danny, Portland	4	0	0	0	0	0	0	0	0	0	0	0	0	0	0	0	0	0	0	...	...	...
Paul, Josh, Salt Lake	9	39	33	6	9	13	4	0	0	6	0	0	0	6	1	7	1	0	0	.273	.385	.394
Pavkovich, Adam, Salt Lake	106	384	342	50	92	143	19	4	8	51	7	5	3	27	1	65	5	6	9	.269	.324	.418
Pearce, Josh, Memphis	18	2	2	0	0	0	0	0	0	0	0	0	0	0	0	0	0	0	0	.000	.000	.000
Pellow, Kit, Tacoma	4	17	12	3	5	9	1	0	1	3	0	1	1	3	0	4	0	0	0	.417	.529	.750
Pena, Elvis, Colorado Springs †	92	294	255	34	74	94	16	2	0	27	5	0	2	32	1	44	4	5	13	.290	.374	.369
Penny, Brad, Las Vegas	1	2	2	0	0	0	0	0	0	0	0	0	0	0	0	0	0	0	0	.000	.000	.000
Perez, Antonio, Las Vegas	16	62	56	8	13	22	3	0	2	6	1	1	1	3	0	20	2	1	1	.232	.279	.393
Perez, Odalis, Las Vegas *	2	4	3	0	0	0	0	0	0	0	0	0	0	1	0	0	0	0	1	.000	.250	.000
Perisho, Matt, Albuquerque *	12	1	0	0	0	0	0	0	0	0	0	1	0	0	0	0	0	0	0	...	...	...
Petersen, Jeffrey, Fresno	2	0	0	0	0	0	0	0	0	0	0	0	0	0	0	0	0	0	0	...	...	...
Peterson, Adam, Tucson	1	0	0	0	0	0	0	0	0	0	0	0	0	0	0	0	0	0	0	...	...	...
Phelps, Tommy, Nashville *	4	4	3	0	0	0	0	0	0	0	0	0	0	1	0	0	0	0	1	.000	.250	.000
Phelps, Travis, Colorado Springs-Iowa	18	5	3	1	0	0	0	0	0	0	0	0	0	1	0	0	0	0	0	.000	.250	.000
Phillips, J.R., Round Rock *	9	20	17	3	4	5	1	0	0	0	0	0	0	3	0	8	0	0	0	.235	.350	.294
Phillips, Paul, Omaha	87	362	332	45	89	133	21	1	7	42	2	3	4	21	0	44	1	4	7	.268	.317	.401
Pickering, Calvin, Omaha *	92	396	335	56	92	177	16	0	23	67	0	1	4	56	2	130	1	0	4	.275	.384	.528
Pickler, Jeff, Colorado Springs *	128	475	423	72	140	193	26	6	5	50	6	4	1	41	1	46	16	6	8	.331	.388	.456
Piedra, Jorge, Colorado Springs *	47	208	186	35	58	98	20	1	6	45	0	2	1	18	0	23	4	2	4	.312	.372	.527
Pignatiello, Carmen, Iowa *	14	7	7	0	2	2	0	0	0	1	0	0	0	0	0	1	0	0	0	.286	.286	.286

Player, Team	G	TPA	AB	R	H	TB	2B	3B	HR	RBI	SH	SF	HP	BB	IBB	SO	SB	CS	GDP	Avg.	OBP	Slg.
Pinto, Renyel, Iowa *	5	10	9	0	0	0	0	0	0	0	0	0	0	1	0	5	0	0	1	.000	.100	.000
Polanco, Phillip, Portland	1	0	0	0	0	0	0	0	0	0	0	0	...	0	...	0	0	0	0	...	...	...
Porter, Colin, Tucson *	25	68	62	7	11	13	2	0	0	1	1	0	1	4	0	24	0	0	0	.177	.239	.210
Powell, Brian, New Orleans	21	38	28	1	7	7	0	0	0	0	7	0	0	3	0	8	0	0	1	.250	.323	.250
Pratt, Andy, Nashville *	18	13	12	0	4	4	0	0	0	0	1	0	0	0	0	2	0	0	1	.333	.333	.333
Price, Jared, Omaha	24	92	88	8	21	40	4	0	5	11	1	0	1	2	1	23	0	1	1	.239	.264	.455
Pride, Curtis, Salt Lake *	82	330	280	44	81	137	17	6	9	56	0	0	1	49	3	65	10	5	6	.289	.397	.489
Prieto, Alex, Omaha	46	176	160	17	45	64	11	1	2	23	3	1	0	12	0	34	4	2	5	.281	.329	.400
Prieto, Ariel, Albuquerque	17	32	30	1	4	5	1	0	0	1	1	0	0	1	0	8	0	0	1	.133	.161	.167
Prieto, Chris, Salt Lake *	97	443	363	71	115	166	18	12	3	45	12	3	5	60	1	41	26	10	3	.317	.418	.457
Puffer, Brandon, Fresno	34	7	5	0	0	0	0	0	0	0	1	0	0	1	0	5	0	0	0	.000	.167	.000
Pulsipher, Bill, Memphis *	19	31	26	1	4	7	0	0	1	4	3	0	0	2	0	13	0	0	0	.154	.214	.269
Quentin, Carlos, Tucson	136	561	452	98	136	235	28	4	21	89	0	8	29	72	0	71	9	1	14	.301	.422	.520
Quinlan, Robb, Salt Lake	15	62	60	13	23	32	6	0	1	4	0	0	0	2	0	8	0	0	4	.383	.403	.533
Quintanilla, Omar, Colorado Springs *	13	57	52	14	18	28	3	2	1	7	1	1	0	3	0	8	0	0	0	.346	.375	.538
Quintero, Humberto, Round Rock	52	205	191	23	55	92	13	0	8	31	0	2	2	10	1	30	2	1	3	.288	.327	.482
Ramirez, Julio, Fresno	113	416	386	57	93	177	13	1	23	60	3	2	3	22	0	113	22	8	10	.241	.286	.459
Randall, Scott, Colorado Springs	5	3	3	0	0	0	0	0	0	0	0	0	0	0	0	0	0	0	0	.000	.000	.000
Randolph, Stephen, New Orleans-Fresno	20	15	13	2	4	5	1	0	0	2	1	0	0	1	0	3	0	0	0	.308	.357	.385
Ransom, Cody, Oklahoma-Iowa	89	288	263	35	64	97	10	1	7	33	0	2	1	22	0	88	6	1	8	.243	.302	.369
Rauch, Jon, New Orleans	4	7	6	1	2	2	0	0	0	1	1	0	0	0	0	1	0	0	0	.333	.333	.333
Reames, Britt, Sacramento	1	0	0	0	0	0	0	0	0	0	0	0	...	0	0	0	0	0	0	...	...	...
Redding, Tim, Portland	1	2	2	0	0	0	0	0	0	0	0	0	0	0	0	2	0	0	0	.000	.000	.000
Reed, Eric, Albuquerque *	39	181	171	19	53	69	5	4	1	20	2	1	4	3	0	31	17	7	1	.310	.335	.404
Relaford, Desi, Colorado Springs †	3	16	12	4	4	5	1	0	0	0	0	0	1	3	0	3	1	0	0	.333	.500	.417
Repko, Jason, Las Vegas	8	32	31	6	12	21	0	0	3	6	1	0	0	0	0	4	1	0	0	.387	.387	.677
Reyes, Anthony, Memphis	15	37	27	3	5	9	1	0	1	2	5	0	2	3	0	13	0	0	0	.185	.313	.333
Reynolds, Wilton, Round Rock	5	11	10	1	2	5	0	0	1	2	0	0	0	1	0	3	0	0	1	.200	.273	.500
Richard, Chris, Oklahoma *	98	412	362	67	109	177	20	3	14	66	0	3	6	41	3	75	5	2	6	.301	.379	.489
Riedling, John, Albuquerque	11	2	2	0	0	0	0	0	0	0	0	0	0	0	0	1	0	0	0	.000	.000	.000
Rifkin, Aaron, Tacoma *	105	438	384	55	99	177	30	3	14	54	1	2	4	47	2	87	4	2	5	.258	.343	.461
Risinger, Benjamin, Portland	41	160	128	17	27	43	7	0	3	14	0	0	13	19	1	28	0	1	4	.211	.369	.336
Rivera, Carlos, Round Rock *	129	496	455	64	142	230	35	1	17	68	0	3	8	30	2	65	0	0	16	.312	.363	.505
Rivera, Michael, Nashville	60	228	214	34	61	123	12	1	16	43	0	2	3	9	1	37	3	1	9	.285	.320	.575
Rivera, Rene, Tacoma	14	51	49	3	10	16	3	0	1	6	0	0	0	2	0	12	0	1	2	.204	.235	.327
Robinson, Kerry, Portland *	61	269	253	40	73	88	5	2	2	17	3	2	1	10	1	26	26	7	4	.289	.316	.348
Rodriguez, John, Memphis *	34	137	120	24	41	97	5	0	17	47	1	0	3	13	3	28	1	1	2	.342	.419	.808
Rodriguez, Jose, Albuquerque *	9	0	0	0	0	0	0	0	0	0	0	0	...	0	0	0	0	0	0	...	...	...
Rodriguez, Nerio, Memphis	1	2	1	0	0	0	0	0	0	0	0	0	0	1	0	0	0	0	0	.000	.500	.000
Rodriguez, Orlando, Las Vegas *	2	0	0	0	0	0	0	0	0	0	0	0	...	0	0	0	0	0	0	...	...	...
Rodriguez, Wandy, Round Rock †	4	8	5	0	1	1	0	0	0	0	3	0	0	0	0	1	0	0	0	.200	.200	.200
Rohan, James, Las Vegas	10	22	20	1	5	5	0	0	0	1	0	0	0	2	0	4	0	1	1	.250	.318	.250
Rohlicek, Russel, Iowa	40	3	3	0	0	0	0	0	0	0	0	0	0	0	0	2	0	0	0	.000	.000	.000
Romano, Jason, Albuquerque	1	2	1	0	0	0	0	0	0	0	0	0	0	1	0	0	0	0	0	.000	.500	.000
Rose, Mike, Las Vegas †	69	236	205	31	53	90	20	1	5	36	0	3	3	25	1	51	2	0	3	.259	.343	.439
Ross, Cody, Las Vegas	115	448	393	79	105	200	21	4	22	63	0	4	2	49	1	103	4	2	8	.267	.348	.509
Ross, David, Portland	6	23	21	3	3	4	1	0	0	1	0	0	0	2	0	4	0	0	0	.143	.217	.190
Rottino, Vincent, Nashville	9	32	29	4	10	14	1	0	1	2	0	0	0	3	0	6	0	1	1	.345	.406	.483
Rouse, Michael, Sacramento *	130	554	469	69	126	183	30	3	7	72	17	2	7	59	0	115	2	4	6	.269	.358	.390
Rupe, Ryan, Las Vegas	13	17	15	2	3	4	1	0	0	3	2	0	0	0	0	5	0	0	0	.200	.200	.267
Rust, Evan, Memphis	6	1	1	0	0	0	0	0	0	0	0	0	0	0	0	0	0	0	0	.000	.000	.000
Sain, Gregory, Portland	56	194	176	22	48	85	13	0	8	38	0	3	1	14	0	29	1	0	8	.273	.325	.483
Salazar, Jeffrey, Colorado Springs *	59	272	236	42	62	103	17	3	6	26	3	1	0	32	0	58	5	2	1	.263	.349	.436
Sanchez, Alex, Fresno *	2	9	9	0	1	1	0	0	0	1	0	0	0	0	0	0	0	1	0	.111	.111	.111
Santana, Julio, Nashville	4	0	0	0	0	0	0	0	0	0	0	0	0	0	0	0	0	0	0	...	...	...
Santiago, Ramon, Tacoma †	129	517	441	68	111	169	22	3	10	50	17	6	15	38	0	62	18	7	11	.252	.328	.383
Santos, Chad, Omaha *	120	478	433	50	112	186	26	0	16	64	1	1	5	38	1	133	2	1	17	.259	.325	.430
Santos, Sergio, Tucson	132	532	490	55	117	180	21	3	12	68	0	6	2	34	3	108	2	2	16	.239	.288	.367
Sardinha, Duke, Colorado Springs	1	1	0	0	0	0	0	0	0	0	0	0	0	1	0	0	0	0	0	...	1.000	...
Sarfate, Dennis, Nashville	2	4	4	0	0	0	0	0	0	0	0	0	0	0	0	3	0	0	0	.000	.000	.000
Scales, Bobby, Portland †	120	436	376	50	103	168	19	2	14	61	0	1	6	53	0	98	9	4	9	.274	.372	.447
Scarborough, Stephen, Nashville	130	459	404	50	103	167	27	2	11	58	7	5	4	39	2	93	6	5	6	.255	.323	.413
Schmoll, Steve, Las Vegas	17	2	1	0	0	0	0	0	0	0	1	0	0	0	0	1	0	0	0	.000	.000	.000
Schrager, Anthony, Las Vegas	86	304	249	47	58	103	15	0	10	34	3	6	3	43	0	53	3	3	6	.233	.346	.414
Schroder, Christopher, New Orleans	13	2	1	0	0	0	0	0	0	0	1	0	0	0	0	1	0	0	0	.000	.000	.000
Schumaker, Skip, Memphis *	115	487	443	66	127	178	24	3	7	34	8	5	2	29	1	54	14	3	14	.287	.330	.402
Scott, Luke, Round Rock *	103	449	398	69	114	240	25	4	31	87	0	2	6	43	1	96	2	2	4	.286	.363	.603
Seabol, Scott, Memphis	54	224	203	34	54	103	18	2	9	33	0	1	0	20	0	40	0	0	5	.266	.330	.507
Sears, Todd, Albuquerque *	92	361	316	44	102	159	14	2	13	63	0	4	4	38	4	75	0	1	9	.323	.399	.503
Seay, Bobby, Colorado Springs *	13	1	1	0	0	0	0	0	0	0	0	0	0	0	0	1	0	0	0	.000	.000	.000
Sedlacek, Shawn, Colorado Springs-Memphis	4	5	3	0	0	0	0	0	0	0	2	0	0	0	0	1	0	0	0	.000	.000	.000
Self, Todd, Round Rock *	100	391	326	42	97	150	25	2	8	47	0	3	4	58	5	91	4	1	5	.298	.407	.460
Serrano, Alex, Colorado Springs	11	4	4	0	0	0	0	0	0	0	0	0	0	0	0	1	0	0	0	.000	.000	.000
Shabala, Adam, Fresno	95	416	373	58	102	170	24	1	14	42	3	1	4	35	0	73	10	2	4	.273	.341	.456
Shanks, James, Albuquerque	19	78	71	11	19	28	3	3	0	5	0	0	0	7	0	15	1	1	2	.268	.333	.394
Shealy, Ryan, Colorado Springs	108	468	411	85	135	247	30	2	26	88	2	7	7	41	2	81	4	0	13	.328	.393	.601
Short, Rick, New Orleans	108	433	376	72	144	214	35	1	11	70	1	3	7	46	6	27	5	4	8	.383	.456	.569
Smith, Bobby, Sacramento	102	453	409	64	117	179	19	2	13	64	1	2	4	37	1	74	9	0	18	.286	.350	.438
Smith, Casey, Salt Lake	83	303	272	37	60	70	6	2	0	18	2	2	3	24	1	40	6	3	3	.221	.289	.257
Smith, Dan, New Orleans	17	0	0	0	0	0	0	0	0	0	0	0	0	0	0	0	0	0	0	...	...	...

Player, Team	G	TPA	AB	R	H	TB	2B	3B	HR	RBI	SH	SF	HP	BB	IBB	SO	SB	CS	GDP	Avg.	OBP	Slg.
Smith, Travis, Albuquerque	14	31	28	1	7	10	3	0	0	1	2	0	0	1	0	8	0	0	0	.250	.276	.357
Smith, William, Oklahoma *	48	194	169	30	57	98	13	2	8	36	0	4	1	20	0	31	0	0	7	.337	.402	.580
Snare, Ryan, Portland *	6	11	8	0	2	2	0	0	0	0	3	0	0	0	0	3	0	0	1	.250	.250	.250
Snelling, Chris, Tacoma *	65	291	246	50	91	136	17	2	8	46	1	4	4	36	5	43	2	3	1	.370	.452	.553
Sodowsky, Clint, Albuquerque *	5	1	1	0	0	0	0	0	0	0	0	0	0	0	0	0	0	0	0	.000	.000	.000
Song, Seung, Fresno	5	8	5	0	0	0	0	0	0	0	3	0	0	0	0	3	0	0	0	.000	.000	.000
Sorensen, Zach, Salt Lake †	78	338	287	47	87	110	11	3	2	41	10	6	1	34	0	55	21	9	5	.303	.372	.383
Soto, Geovany, Iowa	91	345	292	30	74	100	14	0	4	39	3	2	0	48	0	77	0	1	15	.253	.357	.342
Sparks, Steve, Portland	1	3	2	1	2	3	1	0	0	0	1	0	0	0	0	0	0	0	0	1.000	1.000	1.500
Specht, Brian, Salt Lake †	73	291	263	40	81	133	18	5	8	36	1	0	2	25	0	47	12	7	2	.308	.372	.506
Speier, Ryan, Colorado Springs	27	3	3	0	0	0	0	0	0	0	0	0	0	0	0	1	0	0	0	.000	.000	.000
Spiehs, Randall, Portland-Fresno	12	1	1	0	0	0	0	0	0	0	0	0	0	0	0	0	0	0	0	.000	.000	.000
Spiezio, Scott, Tacoma †	14	63	58	11	19	30	3	1	2	9	0	3	1	1	0	9	0	0	2	.328	.333	.517
Spilborghs, Ryan, Colorado Springs	60	253	227	49	77	125	23	5	5	30	1	0	3	22	0	53	7	3	5	.339	.405	.551
Stamler, Keith, Sacramento *	1	0	0	0	0	0	0	0	0	0	...	0	0	0	0	0	0	0	0	...	...	...
Stanley, Henri, Las Vegas *	99	380	337	52	86	156	15	5	15	46	5	2	1	35	0	72	7	7	8	.255	.325	.463
Stark, Denny, Colorado Springs	8	14	11	0	3	3	0	0	0	1	0	0	2	0	2	0	0	0	.273	.385	.273
Stauffer, Tim, Portland	7	14	12	1	3	4	1	0	0	3	1	0	0	1	0	4	0	0	0	.250	.308	.333
Stetter, Mitchel, Nashville *	19	1	1	0	0	0	0	0	0	0	0	0	0	0	0	1	0	0	0	.000	.000	.000
Stewart, Scott, Portland	7	2	2	0	0	0	0	0	0	0	0	0	0	0	0	0	0	0	1	.000	.000	.000
Stinnett, Kelly, Tucson	11	40	35	4	8	13	2	0	1	2	0	0	2	3	0	12	0	0	0	.229	.325	.371
Stockman, Phillip, Tucson	13	4	3	1	1	1	0	0	0	0	0	0	0	1	0	1	0	0	0	.333	.500	.333
Stokes, Jason, Albuquerque	13	50	46	12	13	31	1	1	5	15	0	0	1	3	0	16	2	0	1	.283	.340	.674
Stone, Ricky, Memphis	10	0	0	0	0	0	0	0	0	0	...	0	0	0	0	0	0	0	0	...	...	...
Strickland, Scott, Round Rock	11	0	0	0	0	0	0	0	0	0	...	0	0	0	0	0	0	0	0	...	...	...
Strong, Jamal, Tacoma	93	437	382	57	112	150	16	5	4	36	6	1	5	43	0	67	25	6	4	.293	.371	.393
Stults, Eric, Las Vegas *	8	14	11	0	3	5	2	0	0	0	2	0	0	1	0	2	0	0	0	.273	.333	.455
Swanson, Brent, Fresno *	6	6	3	1	0	0	0	0	0	0	0	0	1	2	0	1	0	0	0	.000	.500	.000
Sweeney, Brian, Portland	15	32	25	1	5	7	2	0	0	5	3	0	0	4	0	7	0	0	0	.200	.310	.280
Swisher, Nicholas, Sacramento †	6	26	23	4	9	12	3	0	0	1	0	0	1	2	0	7	0	1	0	.391	.462	.522
Taschner, Jack, Fresno *	30	0	0	0	0	0	0	0	0	0	0	0	0	0	0	0	0	0	0	...	...	...
Tavares, Anderson, Iowa	2	1	1	0	0	0	0	0	0	0	0	0	0	0	0	0	0	0	0	.000	.000	.000
Taylor, Reggie, Colorado Springs-Memphis	35	120	111	18	26	39	6	2	1	12	2	1	1	5	1	21	1	5	1	.234	.271	.351
Teahen, Mark, Omaha *	8	34	27	4	7	9	2	0	0	4	0	0	0	7	0	9	0	0	1	.259	.412	.333
Tena, Hector, Colorado Springs	12	36	34	1	6	8	2	0	0	2	1	1	0	0	0	11	1	0	1	.176	.171	.235
Terrero, Luis, Tucson	7	33	30	4	8	9	1	0	0	1	1	0	1	1	0	9	1	0	2	.267	.313	.300
Terveen, Bryce, Tacoma *	19	68	61	5	15	22	4	0	1	8	0	1	3	3	0	15	0	1	0	.246	.309	.361
Teut, Nathan, Iowa	2	1	1	0	0	0	0	0	0	0	0	0	0	1	0	0	0	0	0	.000	.000	.000
Theodorou, Nicholas, Las Vegas †..........	97	298	262	40	66	85	10	3	1	23	3	0	3	30	0	43	6	1	10	.252	.336	.324
Thigpen, Judson, Colorado Springs	12	44	41	4	13	20	5	1	0	2	1	0	0	2	0	10	0	0	1	.317	.349	.488
Thomas, Charles, Sacramento *	75	320	277	43	63	100	16	3	5	33	3	2	3	35	0	56	16	4	7	.227	.319	.361
Thompson, Brad, Memphis	3	0	0	0	0	0	0	0	0	0	...	0	0	0	0	0	0	0	0	...	...	...
Thompson, Chris, Tucson	1	0	0	0	0	0	0	0	0	0	...	0	0	0	0	0	0	0	0	...	...	...
Thompson, Derek, Las Vegas *	4	7	7	0	0	0	0	0	0	0	0	0	0	0	0	3	0	0	1	.000	.000	.000
Thompson, Michael, Portland	7	19	12	1	1	1	0	0	0	1	5	1	0	1	0	4	0	0	0	.083	.143	.083
Thurston, Joe, Las Vegas *	84	286	257	32	74	106	10	2	6	35	10	3	3	13	0	36	4	5	3	.288	.326	.412
Tolar, Kevin, Tucson	18	0	0	0	0	0	0	0	0	0	0	0	0	0	0	0	0	0	0	...	...	...
Tollberg, Brian, Round Rock	8	14	11	2	2	2	0	0	0	0	2	0	0	1	0	4	0	0	1	.182	.250	.182
Torcato, Tony, Fresno *	105	407	376	41	101	156	15	5	10	57	1	5	4	21	4	43	3	4	7	.269	.310	.415
Torres, Andres, Oklahoma †	15	69	63	12	19	24	3	1	0	1	0	0	6	0	17	6	1	0	.302	.362	.381
Totten, Heath, Las Vegas	13	26	22	1	5	9	4	0	0	2	3	0	0	1	0	7	0	0	0	.227	.261	.409
Tovar, Angel, Portland	10	1	1	1	1	2	1	0	0	2	0	0	0	0	0	0	0	0	0	1.000	1.000	2.000
Tracy, Andy, Colorado Springs *	12	55	40	14	13	28	1	1	4	13	0	0	0	15	0	12	2	1	1	.325	.509	.700
Tremie, Chris, Round Rock	63	209	190	17	39	53	5	0	3	23	0	3	2	14	1	37	0	0	7	.205	.263	.279
Truby, Chris, Omaha	106	435	396	56	96	181	19	3	20	66	0	3	0	36	1	82	1	3	13	.242	.303	.457
Trzesniak, Nicholas, Portland	24	86	79	13	30	41	8	0	1	12	0	0	2	5	0	16	1	1	1	.380	.430	.519
Tsao, Chin-hui, Colorado Springs	1	0	0	0	0	0	0	0	0	0	...	0	0	0	0	0	0	0	0	...	...	...
Tucker, T.J., New Orleans	1	0	0	0	0	0	0	0	0	0	...	0	0	0	0	0	0	0	0	...	...	...
Ugueto, Luis, Omaha †	80	305	265	39	55	96	8	6	7	29	2	3	3	32	1	73	11	2	9	.208	.297	.362
Valbuena, Luis, Tacoma *	3	5	4	0	0	0	0	0	0	0	0	0	0	1	0	2	0	0	0	.000	.200	.000
Valdes, Raul, Iowa *	16	27	24	0	6	8	2	0	0	2	3	0	0	0	0	9	0	0	0	.250	.250	.333
Valdez, Ismael, Albuquerque	1	3	2	0	1	1	0	0	0	0	1	0	0	0	0	0	0	0	0	.500	.500	.500
Valdez, Wilson, Tacoma-Portland	51	179	159	14	38	52	5	3	1	16	4	1	0	15	0	28	8	0	4	.239	.303	.327
Valentin, Jose, Las Vegas *	12	43	35	8	14	23	3	0	2	5	0	0	1	7	1	6	1	0	0	.400	.512	.657
Van Buren, Jermaine, Iowa	40	0	0	0	0	0	0	0	0	0	0	0	0	0	0	0	0	0	0	...	...	...
Vargas, Claudio, New Orleans	5	11	8	0	0	0	0	0	0	0	3	0	0	0	0	3	0	0	0	.000	.000	.000
Venafro, Mike, Las Vegas *	28	0	0	0	0	0	0	0	0	0	0	0	0	0	0	0	0	0	0	...	...	...
Villafuerte, Brandon, Fresno	35	6	5	0	1	1	0	0	0	0	1	0	0	0	0	3	0	0	0	.200	.200	.200
Villarreal, Oscar, Tucson *	6	2	2	0	0	0	0	0	0	0	0	0	0	0	0	2	0	0	0	.000	.000	.000
Wainwright, Adam, Memphis	22	53	50	4	7	13	3	0	1	4	1	0	0	2	0	17	0	0	0	.140	.173	.260
Walker, Todd, Iowa *	9	38	37	3	8	11	3	0	0	3	0	0	0	1	0	4	0	0	4	.216	.237	.297
Walrond, Les, Albuquerque *	11	25	18	0	0	0	0	0	0	0	6	0	0	1	0	8	0	0	0	.000	.053	.000
Walter, Scott, Omaha	38	153	145	20	39	72	9	0	8	30	1	0	3	4	0	33	0	0	3	.269	.303	.497
Wathan, Derek, Albuquerque †	83	277	250	34	58	91	14	2	5	36	4	2	2	19	0	40	10	3	7	.232	.289	.364
Watson, Brandon, New Orleans *	88	408	372	69	132	156	15	3	1	25	5	2	1	28	0	33	31	13	5	.355	.400	.419
Watson, Matthew, Sacramento	113	498	419	82	132	216	27	3	17	81	...	10	2	67	...	57	12	1	7	.315	.404	.516
Wayne, Justin, Las Vegas	2	0	0	0	0	0	0	0	0	0	0	0	0	0	0	0	0	0	0	...	...	...
Weeks, Rickie, Nashville	55	249	203	43	65	133	14	9	12	48	3	1	14	28	0	51	10	1	3	.320	.435	.655
Weibl, Clint, Nashville	31	9	7	1	0	0	0	0	0	0	0	0	0	2	0	3	0	0	0	.000	.222	.000
Wellemeyer, Todd, Iowa	8	13	13	1	1	1	0	0	0	1	0	0	0	0	0	8	0	0	0	.077	.077	.077

Player, Team	G	TPA	AB	R	H	TB	2B	3B	HR	RBI	SH	SF	HP	BB	IBB	SO	SB	CS	GDP	Avg.	OBP	Slg.
Werth, Jayson, Las Vegas	15	64	49	9	18	27	0	0	3	10	0	0	2	13	0	17	6	1	0	.367	.516	.551
Wesson, Barry, Round Rock	126	430	402	39	109	161	19	3	9	43	4	3	2	19	0	84	6	2	10	.271	.305	.400
White, Gabe, Memphis *	5	0	0	0	0	0	0	0	0	0	...	0	0	0	...	0	0	0	0	...	...	...
White, Matt, New Orleans	24	24	21	0	1	1	0	0	0	0	2	0	0	1	0	8	0	0	1	.048	.091	.048
Whiteman, Tommy, Round Rock	80	270	237	23	48	68	5	0	5	27	2	3	1	27	2	69	0	0	10	.203	.284	.287
Williams, Jerome, Fresno-Iowa	7	15	13	1	1	2	1	0	0	0	2	0	0	0	0	6	0	0	0	.077	.077	.154
Williams, Randy, Portland-Colorado Springs	16	2	2	0	0	0	0	0	0	0	0	0	0	0	0	1	0	0	0	.000	.000	.000
Williamson, Scott, Iowa	3	0	0	0	0	0	0	0	0	0	...	0	0	0	...	0	0	0	0	...	...	...
Willingham, Josh, Albuquerque	66	279	219	56	71	148	14	3	19	54	0	4	9	47	1	54	5	1	5	.324	.455	.676
Wilson, Brian, Fresno	4	0	0	0	0	0	0	0	0	0	...	0	0	0	...	0	0	0	0	...	...	...
Wilson, John, New Orleans	25	78	66	8	14	20	6	0	0	4	1	1	1	9	2	9	0	3	1	.212	.312	.303
Wilson, Josh, Albuquerque	143	598	526	88	135	229	31	6	17	82	3	12	9	48	2	114	17	7	8	.257	.323	.435
Wilson, Tom, Colorado Springs	64	246	210	39	70	125	18	2	11	49	0	2	1	33	1	43	0	0	4	.333	.423	.595
Witasick, Jay, Colorado Springs	6	0	0	0	0	0	0	0	0	0	...	0	0	0	...	0	0	0	0	...	...	...
Wood, Jason, Albuquerque	129	516	452	75	136	223	18	3	21	77	2	6	8	48	1	81	5	3	24	.301	.374	.493
Wood, Kerry, Iowa	2	2	2	1	1	3	0	1	0	0	0	0	0	0	0	1	0	0	0	.500	.500	1.500
Wood, Richard, Salt Lake	4	19	19	1	6	10	2	1	0	1	0	0	0	0	0	6	0	0	0	.316	.316	.526
Wylie, Mitch, Fresno	13	15	14	2	3	4	1	0	0	0	1	0	0	0	0	6	0	0	0	.214	.214	.286
Yan, Ruddy, Oklahoma †	5	20	19	1	6	6	0	0	0	1	0	0	0	1	0	2	1	0	1	.316	.350	.316
Yarnall, Ed, New Orleans *	14	18	17	1	2	2	0	0	0	0	0	0	0	1	0	11	0	0	0	.118	.167	.118
Young, Delwyn, Las Vegas †	36	170	160	23	52	76	12	0	4	14	1	0	1	8	0	35	0	0	3	.325	.361	.475
Young, Eric, Portland	5	22	16	3	0	0	0	0	0	0	0	0	0	6	0	2	0	0	0	.000	.273	.000
Young, Jason, Colorado Springs	15	30	27	4	7	17	4	0	2	7	3	0	0	0	0	5	0	0	1	.259	.259	.630
Zinter, Alan, Tucson †	47	123	111	9	24	36	4	1	2	14	0	0	0	12	2	30	0	0	4	.216	.293	.324
Zoccolillo, Peter, Memphis *	79	252	222	27	58	94	9	0	9	34	0	4	1	25	2	30	0	2	7	.261	.333	.423
Zorn, Dean, Tacoma †	1	0	0	0	0	0	0	0	0	0	...	0	0	0	...	0	0	0	0	...	...	...
Zumwalt, Sean, Nashville	8	3	2	0	0	0	0	0	0	0	0	0	0	1	0	1	0	0	1	.000	.333	.000
Zuniga, Jose, Nashville	65	255	235	35	76	111	14	0	7	43	0	0	2	18	1	28	5	0	6	.323	.376	.472

PLAYERS WITH TWO OR MORE TEAMS

Player, Team	G	TPA	AB	R	H	TB	2B	3B	HR	RBI	SH	SF	HP	BB	IBB	SO	SB	CS	GDP	Avg.	OBP	Slg.
Alexander, Manny, Oklahoma	108	467	417	64	129	200	23	6	12	67	2	6	4	38	0	66	27	9	8	.309	.368	.480
Alexander, Manny, Portland	4	17	16	0	4	6	2	0	0	1	0	0	0	1	0	4	0	1	0	.250	.294	.375
Allen, Chad, Oklahoma	45	211	200	34	69	105	12	0	8	33	0	1	0	10	2	31	9	2	8	.345	.374	.525
Allen, Chad, Memphis	25	95	86	11	25	40	6	0	3	13	0	2	0	7	0	14	1	2	1	.291	.337	.465
Almanza, Armando, Fresno *	1	0	0	0	0	0	0	0	0	0	...	0	0	0	...	0	0	0	0	...	...	...
Almanza, Armando, Tucson *	11	2	1	0	0	0	0	0	0	0	0	0	0	1	0	1	0	0	0	.000	.500	.000
Almanza, Armando, Memphis *	6	0	0	0	0	0	0	0	0	0	...	0	0	0	...	0	0	0	0	...	...	...
Anderson, Jimmy, Iowa *	2	3	3	1	2	3	1	0	0	2	0	0	0	0	0	0	0	0	0	.667	.667	1.000
Anderson, Jimmy, Round Rock *	4	11	11	1	2	2	0	0	0	0	0	0	0	0	0	5	0	0	1	.182	.182	.182
Bauer, Peter, Albuquerque *	8	13	12	2	4	4	0	0	0	1	0	0	0	1	0	4	0	0	1	.333	.385	.333
Bauer, Peter, Round Rock *	1	3	3	0	0	0	0	0	0	0	0	0	0	0	0	1	0	0	0	.000	.000	.000
Cunnane, Will, Iowa	21	3	3	1	0	0	0	0	0	0	0	0	0	0	0	2	0	0	0	.000	.000	.000
Cunnane, Will, Round Rock	19	0	0	0	0	0	0	0	0	0	...	0	0	0	...	0	0	0	0	...	...	...
Davis, J.J., New Orleans	51	195	174	34	49	95	10	0	12	31	0	3	3	18	2	53	3	4	4	.282	.359	.546
Davis, J.J., Colorado Springs	21	78	67	12	15	27	3	0	3	15	0	3	1	7	0	20	1	1	2	.224	.295	.403
Dawley, Joe, Portland	8	0	0	0	0	0	0	0	0	0	...	0	0	0	...	0	0	0	0	...	...	...
Dawley, Joe, Iowa	2	0	0	0	0	0	0	0	0	0	...	0	0	0	...	0	0	0	0	...	...	...
Delucchi, Dustin, Tacoma *	23	97	82	12	20	24	1	0	1	5	5	1	0	9	0	14	3	0	3	.244	.315	.293
Delucchi, Dustin, Portland *	64	251	197	49	60	87	17	2	2	15	3	2	1	48	1	29	9	3	6	.305	.440	.442
DeVore, Doug, Tucson *	44	163	149	25	43	75	9	1	7	32	0	1	0	13	1	34	3	1	7	.289	.344	.503
DeVore, Doug, Fresno *	65	227	201	34	60	108	13	1	11	35	0	4	2	20	3	51	1	1	4	.299	.361	.537
Erickson, Matt, Nashville *	16	24	18	2	7	8	1	0	0	2	1	0	2	3	0	2	0	0	0	.389	.522	.444
Erickson, Matt, Albuquerque *	18	56	49	6	14	15	1	0	0	4	2	0	2	3	0	8	0	0	1	.286	.352	.306
Falkenborg, Brian, Portland	12	1	1	0	0	0	0	0	0	0	0	0	0	0	0	0	0	0	0	.000	.000	.000
Falkenborg, Brian, Memphis	11	0	0	0	0	0	0	0	0	0	...	0	0	0	...	0	0	0	0	...	...	...
Haynes, Charles, Memphis	2	5	5	1	1	1	0	0	0	0	0	0	0	0	0	2	0	0	0	.200	.200	.200
Haynes, Charles, New Orleans	9	41	38	9	10	19	3	0	2	7	0	0	0	3	0	4	1	0	1	.263	.317	.500
Hubbard, Trenidad, Round Rock	17	69	58	8	13	17	2	1	0	3	1	1	1	8	0	10	4	2	2	.224	.324	.293
Hubbard, Trenidad, Iowa	62	274	244	34	78	107	17	0	4	29	1	0	4	25	0	26	15	8	5	.320	.392	.439
Lee, Dave, Fresno	5	0	0	0	0	0	0	0	0	0	...	0	0	0	...	0	0	0	0	...	...	...
Lee, Dave, Memphis	3	0	0	0	0	0	0	0	0	0	...	0	0	0	...	0	0	0	0	...	...	...
Lopez, Aquilino, Las Vegas	22	3	2	0	1	1	0	0	0	1	1	0	0	0	0	1	0	0	0	.500	.500	.500
Lopez, Aquilino, Colorado Springs	5	2	1	1	0	0	0	0	0	0	0	0	0	1	0	1	0	0	0	.000	.500	.000
Norton, Phil, Round Rock	6	0	0	0	0	0	0	0	0	0	...	0	0	0	...	0	0	0	0	...	...	...
Norton, Phil, Iowa	17	10	8	3	2	4	2	0	0	0	1	0	0	1	0	4	0	0	0	.250	.333	.500
Nunez, Vladimir, Memphis	11	0	0	0	0	0	0	0	0	0	...	0	0	0	...	0	0	0	0	...	...	...
Nunez, Vladimir, Tucson	8	0	0	0	0	0	0	0	0	0	...	0	0	0	...	0	0	0	0	...	...	...
Ojeda, Miguel, Portland	17	65	57	8	11	21	1	0	3	5	0	0	1	7	0	16	0	0	0	.193	.292	.368
Ojeda, Miguel, Tacoma	9	35	33	7	11	21	1	0	3	11	0	0	1	1	0	5	0	0	0	.333	.371	.636
Oliver, Darren, Tucson	2	4	3	0	0	0	0	0	0	0	1	0	0	0	0	2	0	0	0	.000	.000	.000
Oliver, Darren, Iowa	3	3	2	0	0	0	0	0	0	0	1	0	0	0	0	0	0	0	0	.000	.000	.000
Orie, Kevin, Nashville	61	217	180	32	62	116	18	0	12	49	0	3	3	31	0	20	4	1	4	.344	.442	.644
Orie, Kevin, New Orleans	52	196	169	35	61	104	17	1	8	40	0	0	1	26	5	23	0	0	9	.361	.449	.615
Phelps, Travis, Colorado Springs	6	2	1	0	0	0	0	0	0	0	1	0	0	0	0	0	0	0	0	.000	.000	.000
Phelps, Travis, Iowa	12	3	2	1	0	0	0	0	0	0	1	0	0	0	0	1	0	0	0	.000	.333	.000
Randolph, Stephen, New Orleans *	10	10	8	2	3	4	1	0	0	1	1	0	0	1	0	0	0	0	0	.375	.444	.500
Randolph, Stephen, Fresno *	10	5	5	0	1	1	0	0	0	1	0	0	0	0	0	3	0	0	0	.200	.200	.200
Ransom, Cody, Oklahoma	24	100	92	13	24	44	5	0	5	17	0	0	0	8	0	32	0	1	1	.261	.320	.478
Ransom, Cody, Iowa	65	188	171	22	40	53	5	1	2	16	0	2	1	14	0	56	6	0	7	.234	.293	.310
Sedlacek, Shawn, Colorado Springs	1	1	1	0	0	0	0	0	0	0	0	0	0	0	0	0	0	0	0	.000	.000	.000

Player, Team	G	TPA	AB	R	H	TB	2B	3B	HR	RBI	SH	SF	HP	BB	IBB	SO	SB	CS	GDP	Avg.	OBP	Slg.
Sedlacek, Shawn, Memphis	3	4	2	0	0	0	0	0	0	0	2	0	0	0	0	1	0	0	0	.000	.000	.000
Spiehs, Randall, Portland	9	0	0	0	0	0	0	0	0	0	0	0	0	0	...	0	0	0	0	...	...	...
Spiehs, Randall, Fresno	3	1	1	0	0	0	0	0	0	0	0	0	0	0	0	0	0	0	0	.000	.000	.000
Taylor, Reggie, Colorado Springs *	1	4	4	0	1	2	1	0	0	1	0	0	0	0	0	0	0	0	0	.250	.250	.500
Taylor, Reggie, Memphis *	34	116	107	18	25	37	5	2	1	11	2	1	1	5	1	21	1	5	1	.234	.272	.346
Valdez, Wilson, Tacoma	1	4	4	0	0	0	0	0	0	1	0	0	0	0	0	1	0	0	0	.000	.000	.000
Valdez, Wilson, Portland	50	175	155	14	38	52	5	3	1	15	4	1	0	15	0	27	8	0	4	.245	.310	.335
Williams, Jerome, Fresno	4	9	9	0	0	0	0	0	0	0	0	0	0	0	0	5	0	0	0	.000	.000	.000
Williams, Jerome, Iowa	3	6	4	1	1	2	1	0	0	2	0	0	0	1	0	1	0	0	0	.250	.250	.500
Williams, Randy, Portland *	5	1	1	0	0	0	0	0	0	0	0	0	0	0	0	1	0	0	0	.000	.000	.000
Williams, Randy, Colorado Springs *	11	1	1	0	0	0	0	0	0	0	0	0	0	0	0	1	0	0	0	.000	.000	.000

GRAND SLAMS—J. Rodriguez 4; J. Conti, P. Fielder, N. Gorneault, D. Klassen, B. Myrow, C. Quentin, P. Zoccolillo, 2 each; C. Aguila, L. Allen, L. Barnes, B. Berger, J. Botts, H. Brown, S. Burroughs, F. Bynum, M. Cervenak, A. Chavez, S. Choo, R. Christianson, D. Clark, B. Colamarino, M. Colangelo, M. Coolbaugh, J. Davis, T. Delarosa, D. DeVore, M. Diaz, J. Dillon, C. Freeman, S. Garrett, E. German, T. Godwin, W. Gonzalez, B. Gordon, J. Grabowski, C. Hart, K. Hill, B. Johnson, D. Johnson, G. Laird, H. Luna, D. Matranga, S. McClain, K. McDonald, M. McDougall, D. McPherson, C. Myers, C. Ransom, A. Rifkin, G. Sain, S. Santos, W. Smith, C. Snelling, J. Stokes, C. Truby, M. Watson, T. Wilson, J. Wood, 1 each.

AWARDED FIRST BASE ON CATCHER'S INTERFERENCE—M. Little 2 (J. Mosquera, K. McDonald); B. Berger (K. McDonald); J. Botts (J. Willingham); J. Conti (C. Tremie); J. Grabowski (J. Mathis); J. Hoffpauir (S. Jackson); J. Mosquera (J. Willingham); J. Piedra (D. Navarro).

2005 PITCHING

TEAM

Team	W	L	Pct.	ERA	G	CG	ShO	Sv.	IP	H	TBF	R	ER	HR	SH	SF	HB	BB	IBB	SO	WP	Bk.
Sacramento	80	64	.556	4.21	144	0	8	40	1291.1	1311	5709	708	604	112	56	59	55	546	35	1139	69	2
Memphis	71	72	.497	4.22	143	5	8	37	1254.1	1320	5408	657	588	144	52	32	48	408	27	1090	61	2
Tacoma	80	64	.556	4.36	144	4	17	37	1268.1	1263	5524	676	614	113	46	45	53	560	4	999	61	3
Nashville	75	69	.521	4.43	144	2	3	33	1256.2	1289	5520	708	618	138	52	47	49	550	17	1117	63	3
Portland	70	73	.490	4.50	143	6	8	41	1243	1293	5350	697	621	136	49	39	43	413	17	967	45	9
Round Rock	74	70	.514	4.58	144	3	9	39	1274.1	1356	5543	708	649	169	48	46	56	497	43	904	34	3
Tucson	68	76	.472	4.68	144	3	6	26	1262.1	1383	5579	753	657	154	58	44	48	507	9	928	57	5
Albuquerque	78	66	.542	4.73	144	3	4	42	1273	1383	5597	768	669	165	60	32	72	491	17	940	55	4
Oklahoma	80	63	.559	4.81	143	6	6	46	1267.2	1407	5591	748	677	132	34	38	68	489	23	950	58	8
Iowa	64	75	.460	4.82	139	2	10	36	1206	1266	5302	706	646	145	64	35	52	511	24	1044	58	8
Fresno	68	76	.472	4.84	144	3	7	28	1293.1	1338	5722	773	695	162	68	49	52	569	8	1077	55	8
New Orleans	64	76	.457	4.87	140	1	4	36	1220.2	1272	5410	757	661	167	64	34	74	499	23	1006	62	6
Omaha	72	72	.500	4.88	144	1	8	36	1253.1	1397	5557	753	679	163	30	51	47	486	8	923	59	5
Salt Lake	79	65	.549	5.28	144	1	3	40	1237	1480	5557	797	726	152	46	53	52	481	7	884	62	2
Colorado Springs	65	78	.455	5.86	143	3	2	24	1221.2	1453	5576	875	795	154	58	44	75	503	12	960	72	8
Las Vegas	57	86	.399	6.21	143	3	3	29	1243	1522	5787	952	858	196	57	52	82	601	39	977	48	5

INDIVIDUAL

TOP QUALIFIERS FOR EARNED-RUN AVERAGE TITLE

Minimum 115 innings.*Lefthanded pitcher.

Pitcher, Team	W	L	Pct.	ERA	G	GS	CG	ShO	GF	Sv.	IP	H	TBF	R	ER	HR	SH	SF	HB	BB	IBB	SO	WP	Bk.
Elder, Dave, Omaha	2	0	1.000	0.00	11	0	0	0	5	0	16.0	8	64	2	0	0	1	0	0	7	0	16	2	0
Stemle, Steve, Omaha	1	1	.500	0.45	14	0	0	0	5	3	20.0	13	73	3	1	0	1	2	0	3	0	12	0	0
Clontz, Brad, Albuquerque	1	0	1.000	0.69	11	0	0	0	5	3	13.0	9	47	1	1	0	0	0	1	0	0	11	0	0
Phelps, Tommy, Nashville *	1	0	1.000	1.13	5	4	0	0	0	0	16.0	13	60	3	2	0	0	0	0	2	0	14	0	0
Harikkala, Tim, Sacramento	1	2	.333	1.27	11	0	0	0	6	3	21.1	13	79	5	3	1	4	0	0	7	3	14	0	0
Santana, Julio, Nashville	2	0	1.000	1.50	8	0	0	0	4	1	12.0	8	46	2	2	0	0	0	0	4	0	15	0	0
Taschner, Jack, Fresno *	3	0	1.000	1.64	44	0	0	0	26	10	49.1	30	199	9	9	3	1	1	1	24	0	62	4	0
Estes, Shawn, Tucson *	0	0	.000	1.64	2	2	0	0	0	0	11.0	5	42	2	2	1	0	0	0	4	0	9	1	0
Stone, Ricky, Memphis	1	1	.500	1.65	14	0	0	0	12	6	16.1	12	62	5	3	0	0	0	1	2	0	16	0	0
Mercado, Hector, Oklahoma *	4	0	1.000	1.71	22	0	0	0	7	1	31.2	31	136	8	6	1	0	0	0	19	2	31	0	0
Rheinecker, John, Sacramento *	4	0	1.000	1.77	7	7	0	0	0	0	45.2	29	179	15	9	0	0	2	3	14	0	24	0	0
Cassidy, Scott, Portland	0	1	.000	1.89	17	0	0	0	13	11	19.0	10	73	5	4	2	2	1	1	7	1	19	0	0
Accardo, Jeremy, Fresno	2	0	1.000	1.95	25	0	0	0	11	3	32.1	25	127	7	7	0	1	0	0	10	1	30	2	0
Van Buren, Jermaine, Iowa	2	3	.400	1.98	52	0	0	0	43	25	54.2	33	208	13	12	5	5	1	3	22	2	65	1	0
Burns, Mike, Round Rock	2	1	.667	2.10	25	0	0	0	24	13	30.0	22	114	7	7	4	1	0	0	4	0	34	2	0
Miadich, Bart, Albuquerque	3	2	.600	2.20	29	0	0	0	21	11	32.2	23	144	10	8	2	1	2	1	20	1	59	7	0
Lopez, Javier, Tucson *	2	0	1.000	2.22	27	0	0	0	8	2	24.1	17	95	7	6	0	2	2	1	12	1	16	1	0
Hernandez, Felix, Tacoma	9	4	.692	2.25	19	14	1	0	0	0	88.0	62	369	24	22	3	1	2	3	48	0	100	2	2
Sarfate, Dennis, Nashville	0	1	.000	2.25	2	1	0	0	1	0	12.0	6	46	3	3	1	0	1	4	0	10	0	0
Carrasco, Daniel, Omaha	3	2	.600	2.28	11	3	0	0	5	0	27.2	24	116	9	7	1	1	4	3	11	1	21	2	0
Sherrill, George, Tacoma *	1	3	.250	2.28	22	0	0	0	19	7	23.2	19	97	7	6	0	0	0	6	0	38	1	0

DEPARTMENTAL LEADERS: W—Oxspring, 12. L—three pitchers tied with 13. Pct.—Helling, .750. G—Baker, 59. GS—Fulchino and Wainwright, 29. CG—three pitchers tied with 3. ShO—five pitchers tied with 2. GF—Veras—47. Sv.—Baker, 27. IP—Wainwright, 182. H—Wainwright and Powell, 204. TBF—Wainwright, 793. R—Powell, 114. ER—Powell, 102. HR—four pitchers tied with 27. SAC—Fulchino, 13. SF—five pitchers tied with 8. HB—Eckert, 20. BB—Murphy, 78. IBB—Driskill, 8. SO—Cain, 176. WP—Wainwright, 12. BK—Walrond and Koronka, 3.

ALL PITCHERS

*Lefthanded pitcher.

Pitcher, Team	W	L	Pct.	ERA	G	GS	CG	ShO	GF	Sv.	IP	H	TBF	R	ER	HR	SH	SF	HB	BB	IBB	SO	WP	Bk.
Abreu, Winston, Tucson	2	3	.400	6.48	27	0	0	0	10	2	33.1	37	150	24	24	6	0	0	0	15	0	42	2	0
Accardo, Jeremy, Fresno	2	0	1.000	1.95	25	0	0	0	11	3	32.1	25	127	7	7	0	1	0	0	10	1	30	2	0
Acevedo, Jose, Colorado Springs	1	2	.333	3.29	4	4	0	0	0	0	13.2	17	59	5	5	3	0	1	1	2	0	11	0	0
Adams, Mike, Nashville	3	4	.429	5.75	26	0	0	0	11	2	36.0	35	148	23	23	3	2	3	0	12	0	45	3	0

Pitcher, Team	W	L	Pct.	ERA	G	GS	CG	ShO	GF	Sv.	IP	H	TBF	R	ER	HR	SH	SF	HB	BB	IBB	SO	WP	Bk.
Affeldt, Jeremy, Omaha *	0	1	.000	6.48	9	0	0	0	3	0	8.1	9	37	7	6	1	1	0	0	6	0	9	2	0
Allen, Luke, Salt Lake	0	0	.000	0.00	1	0	0	0	1	0	1.0	1	3	0	0	0	0	0	0	0	0	0	0	0
Almanza, Armando, Fresno-Tucson-Memphis	1	1	.500	4.76	27	0	0	0	8	1	28.1	30	123	18	15	5	1	1	2	11	0	31	8	1
Alvarez, Wilson, Las Vegas *	0	1	.000	2.35	4	4	0	0	0	0	7.2	4	28	2	2	1	1	0	0	2	0	9	0	0
Anderson, Brian, Omaha *	0	0	.000	6.23	1	1	0	0	0	0	4.1	3	18	3	3	1	0	1	0	1	0	2	0	0
Anderson, Jimmy, Iowa-Round Rock	2	2	.500	3.26	5	5	1	1	0	0	30.1	36	133	16	11	2	3	1	0	12	2	14	0	0
Anderson, Luke, Fresno	0	0	.000	10.29	6	0	0	0	4	0	7.0	11	35	8	8	2	0	0	0	4	0	7	0	0
Anderson, Matt, Colorado Springs	3	3	.500	4.21	46	0	0	0	36	9	47.0	36	193	23	22	5	1	1	1	21	0	46	7	2
Andrews, Clayton, Salt Lake *	8	8	.500	6.31	28	20	0	0	0	0	122.2	165	554	97	86	16	3	6	3	45	0	58	4	0
Aquino, Greg, Tucson	1	0	1.000	1.04	6	0	0	0	4	0	8.2	4	31	1	1	0	0	0	0	0	0	7	0	0
Arias, Oliver, Tacoma	0	0	.000	18.00	1	0	0	0	1	0	1.0	2	5	2	2	2	0	0	0	0	0	0	0	0
Armas, Tony, New Orleans	1	2	.333	4.38	5	5	0	0	0	0	24.2	26	110	13	12	3	2	0	3	10	3	21	2	1
Asencio, Miguel, Portland	0	3	.000	9.42	3	3	0	0	0	0	14.1	27	73	17	15	1	0	1	0	6	1	7	0	0
Ashby, Andy, Portland	0	0	.000	3.00	1	1	0	0	0	0	3.0	2	11	1	1	1	0	0	0	0	0	3	0	0
Astacio, Ezequiel, Round Rock	4	4	.500	3.02	13	12	0	0	1	1	65.2	53	262	25	22	6	2	1	8	12	0	57	0	0
Astacio, Pedro, Portland	0	1	.000	15.75	1	1	0	0	0	0	4.0	10	22	7	7	0	0	1	1	0	0	1	0	0
Atchison, Scott, Tacoma	0	0	.000	4.15	10	0	0	0	3	0	13.0	13	56	6	6	0	0	0	0	5	0	17	1	0
Baek, Cha Seung, Tacoma	8	8	.500	6.41	25	21	0	0	2	0	113.2	147	507	87	81	19	5	1	1	36	0	73	6	0
Baerlocher, Ryan, Omaha	0	1	.000	6.00	3	3	0	0	0	0	9.0	10	43	6	6	1	0	1	0	9	0	9	1	0
Baez, Federico, Iowa	0	0	.000	8.31	4	0	0	0	1	0	4.1	5	23	4	4	0	0	2	3	0	6	0	0	0
Baker, Bradley, Portland	4	5	.444	4.75	59	0	0	0	41	27	66.1	69	293	36	35	9	3	4	3	32	4	75	6	0
Barnwell, Christopher, Nashville	1	0	1.000	0.00	4	0	0	0	4	0	4.2	3	21	0	0	0	0	0	0	2	0	3	0	0
Bartosh, Cliff, Iowa *	1	2	.333	5.08	22	0	0	0	7	1	28.1	40	134	18	16	3	3	0	1	16	2	26	3	1
Bauer, Peter, Albuquerque-Round Rock	4	5	.444	6.29	16	15	0	0	1	0	78.2	94	358	63	55	14	2	1	10	34	0	46	4	0
Bautista, Denny, Omaha	0	1	.000	2.77	6	6	0	0	0	0	13.0	8	53	4	4	0	1	0	1	6	0	12	1	0
Bazzell, Shane, Oklahoma	0	1	.000	46.29	1	1	0	0	0	0	2.1	10	23	12	12	1	0	0	1	5	0	3	0	0
Beck, Bradley, Salt Lake *	0	0	.000	0.00	1	0	0	0	0	0	1.0	1	3	0	0	0	0	0	0	0	0	1	0	0
Bennett, Jeff, Nashville	2	3	.400	3.03	49	0	0	0	31	13	62.1	44	256	24	21	6	3	3	5	25	0	56	7	0
Benoit, Joaquin, Oklahoma	0	1	.000	5.40	3	1	0	0	0	0	5.0	4	22	3	3	1	0	1	4	0	2	1	0	0
Bentz, Chad, Albuquerque *	0	1	.000	4.01	31	0	0	0	8	1	33.2	36	147	20	15	4	2	0	1	14	0	32	2	0
Bergman, Dusty, Salt Lake-Fresno	8	5	.615	3.77	47	0	0	0	23	8	74.0	85	317	31	31	10	3	0	1	21	0	59	3	0
Bergmann, Jay, New Orleans	3	2	.600	3.16	20	0	0	0	9	2	37.0	26	147	15	13	5	3	3	3	13	1	39	1	0
Bevis, P. J., Colorado Springs	2	1	.667	11.57	13	0	0	0	7	0	21.0	34	111	29	27	5	0	1	4	15	0	14	1	0
Blank, Matt, Albuquerque *	3	0	1.000	2.91	13	3	0	0	1	0	34.0	35	135	12	11	1	1	1	0	10	1	19	1	0
Bonine, Eddie, Portland	1	0	1.000	0.00	1	0	0	0	0	0	2.0	0	7	0	0	0	0	0	0	0	0	5	0	0
Bootcheck, Chris, Salt Lake	7	4	.636	5.42	21	21	0	0	0	0	116.1	144	516	75	70	13	6	4	1	50	0	90	4	0
Borbon, Pedro, Salt Lake *	0	0	.000	6.75	8	0	0	0	3	0	5.1	7	28	4	4	1	0	1	3	0	4	0	0	0
Borland, Toby, Memphis	1	2	.333	7.71	19	0	0	0	12	6	18.2	35	93	16	16	2	1	1	1	7	1	16	2	0
Borowski, Joe, Iowa	0	0	.000	2.25	7	0	0	0	3	0	8.0	3	31	4	2	2	0	0	0	3	0	4	0	0
Bouknight, Kip, New Orleans	3	2	.600	3.42	9	8	0	0	0	0	52.2	52	220	22	20	9	2	0	3	18	0	34	1	0
Bowers, Timothy, New Orleans	0	0	.000	2.45	3	0	0	0	3	0	3.2	2	15	1	1	1	0	0	1	1	0	1	1	0
Bradford, Chad, Sacramento	0	0	.000	6.00	3	1	0	0	0	0	3.0	4	12	2	2	1	0	0	0	0	0	1	0	0
Brandt, Adam, Tacoma *	0	0	.000	0.00	1	0	0	0	1	0	1.0	0	3	0	0	0	0	0	0	0	0	0	0	0
Bray, Bill, New Orleans *	1	4	.200	5.06	23	0	0	0	12	2	21.1	23	98	16	12	3	2	2	2	9	3	25	1	0
Bray, Stephen, Omaha	0	0	.000	4.50	1	0	0	0	0	0	2.0	2	10	1	1	0	0	1	1	0	4	0	0	0
Breslow, Craig, Portland *	0	1	.000	4.00	7	0	0	0	6	0	9.0	11	37	4	4	1	0	1	0	1	0	9	0	0
Bridges, Donnie, New Orleans	2	6	.250	5.68	13	12	0	0	0	0	63.1	72	304	46	40	9	0	1	7	42	1	52	3	0
Brooks, Frank, Las Vegas *	0	0	.000	0.00	1	0	0	0	0	0	1.2	2	9	2	0	0	0	0	1	1	0	0	2	0
Broshuis, Garrett, Fresno	0	1	.000	5.25	2	2	0	0	0	0	12.0	17	52	9	7	1	0	1	0	2	0	2	1	0
Brownlie, Robert, Iowa	6	7	.462	4.74	27	14	0	0	0	0	104.1	98	436	56	55	11	3	4	2	42	1	73	4	1
Brunet, Michael, Salt Lake	5	3	.625	7.53	19	0	0	0	10	0	28.2	37	130	25	24	4	2	2	2	12	0	25	6	0
Bruney, Brian, Tucson	1	0	1.000	1.93	4	0	0	0	2	0	4.2	3	23	3	1	0	0	1	1	5	0	3	0	0
Buchanan, Brian, Colorado Springs	0	0	.000	0.00	1	0	0	0	0	0	1.0	1	4	0	0	0	0	0	0	0	0	0	0	0
Buchholz, Taylor, Round Rock	6	1	1.000	4.81	20	14	0	0	4	0	76.2	79	320	41	41	14	3	2	4	27	0	45	2	0
Buglovsky, Christopher, Tacoma	4	5	.444	4.24	35	13	0	0	9	0	110.1	120	474	55	52	7	5	6	0	40	2	72	3	0
Bulger, Jason, Tucson	3	6	.333	3.54	56	0	0	0	18	4	56.0	50	237	28	22	3	4	3	2	27	1	55	3	1
Bump, Nate, Albuquerque	1	0	1.000	1.80	1	1	0	0	0	0	5.0	4	19	1	1	0	0	0	0	0	0	6	0	0
Bumstead, Michael, Portland-Tacoma	2	3	.400	4.75	25	4	0	0	6	0	47.1	54	212	26	25	4	1	2	5	18	0	23	0	0
Burba, Dave, Round Rock	4	3	.571	4.58	18	1	0	0	4	0	35.1	46	158	19	18	1	2	2	0	10	1	22	1	1
Burns, Mike, Round Rock	2	1	.667	2.10	25	0	0	0	24	13	30.0	22	114	7	7	4	1	0	0	0	0	34	2	0
Cain, Matt, Fresno	10	5	.667	4.39	26	26	1	0	0	0	145.2	118	623	77	71	22	4	4	5	73	0	176	5	0
Calero, Kiko, Sacramento	0	0	.000	9.00	2	2	0	0	0	0	2.0	4	10	2	2	0	0	0	0	0	0	2	0	0
Cali, Carmen, Memphis	4	5	.444	5.40	50	0	0	0	...	2	58.1	74	270	47	35	6	...	...	...	28	2	45		
Cali, Carmen, Memphis	4	5	.444	5.40	50	0	0	0	19	2	58.1	74	275	47	35	6	1	2	3	28	2	45	4	0
Camp, Shawn, Omaha	3	6	.333	3.86	21	7	0	0	7	1	67.2	71	285	36	29	9	2	2	3	22	1	42	2	0
Campillo, Jorge, Tacoma	4	1	.800	2.71	12	12	0	0	0	0	66.1	63	262	21	20	3	1	0	1	18	0	43	3	0
Cannon, Jonathan, Tucson *	3	5	.375	4.17	15	13	0	0	0	0	73.1	72	319	46	34	11	7	0	1	43	1	44	9	0
Capellan, Jose, Nashville	5	3	.625	3.87	36	12	0	0	18	6	90.2	88	392	42	39	4	2	4	3	42	2	76	2	0
Carlyle, Buddy, Las Vegas	1	2	.333	4.88	20	6	0	0	7	2	48.0	51	210	28	26	7	3	2	5	21	0	53	0	0
Carrasco, Daniel, Omaha	3	2	.600	2.28	11	3	0	0	5	0	27.2	24	116	9	7	1	4	3	3	11	1	21	2	0
Carrasco, Hector, New Orleans	1	0	1.000	0.00	6	0	0	0	6	4	8.0	4	31	1	0	0	1	0	1	2	0	10	0	0
Cassel, Joseph, Portland	3	2	.600	4.62	23	3	0	0	8	0	39.0	54	181	25	20	2	2	1	2	17	2	21	2	1
Cassidy, Scott, Portland	0	1	.000	1.89	17	0	0	0	13	11	19.0	10	73	5	4	2	2	1	1	7	1	19	0	0
Castillo, Frank, Albuquerque	9	11	.450	5.53	27	24	0	0	0	0	143.1	161	632	102	88	20	7	4	10	58	3	80	4	0
Cerda, Jaime, Omaha *	4	1	.800	5.26	35	0	0	0	11	2	49.2	48	217	33	29	6	0	2	1	21	1	47	5	0
Chacon, Shawn, Colorado Springs	0	2	.000	9.95	3	3	0	0	0	0	12.2	19	61	14	14	3	0	1	0	4	0	11	1	0
Chavez, Wilton, Colorado Springs	5	7	.417	5.02	28	15	0	0	2	0	113.0	137	511	73	63	7	6	5	4	44	2	79	5	0
Chiasson, Scott, Colorado Springs	0	2	.000	9.00	11	0	0	0	6	0	16.0	25	82	17	16	6	0	0	0	6	0	18	1	0
Choate, Randy, Tucson *	1	1	.500	3.38	47	0	0	0	16	3	40.0	44	182	22	15	4	2	0	2	22	1	20	2	0
Clontz, Brad, Albuquerque	1	0	1.000	0.69	11	0	0	0	5	3	13.0	9	47	1	1	0	0	0	1	0	0	11	0	0

Pitcher, Team	W	L	Pct.	ERA	G	GS	CG	ShO	GF	Sv.	IP	H	TBF	R	ER	HR	SH	SF	HB	BB	IBB	SO	WP	Bk.
Collazo, William, Salt Lake *	0	1	.000	7.71	11	1	0	0	2	0	23.1	29	101	20	20	7	2	2	4	9	0	12	2	0
Cook, Aaron, Colorado Springs	1	0	1.000	5.51	3	3	0	0	0	0	16.1	18	70	10	10	0	2	1	1	7	0	11	2	0
Cooper, Brian, Fresno	7	8	.467	4.53	29	21	0	0	1	0	137.0	139	580	72	69	23	9	7	4	54	1	82	3	0
Corcoran, Roy, New Orleans	4	4	.500	4.85	52	1	0	0	19	3	68.2	67	314	51	37	7	5	3	8	36	2	55	3	1
Corey, Bryan, Albuquerque	3	6	.333	7.65	44	1	0	0	13	0	60.0	78	274	52	51	11	3	2	2	20	1	44	1	0
Cormier, Lance, Tucson	0	1	.000	14.73	1	1	0	0	0	0	3.2	6	20	6	6	1	0	1	0	5	0	5	1	0
Correia, Kevin, Fresno	3	2	.600	6.07	31	3	0	0	19	7	46.0	50	210	38	31	6	2	3	1	23	0	35	0	0
Cortes, David, Colorado Springs	1	0	1.000	4.02	12	0	0	0	6	1	15.2	15	69	9	7	3	0	2	0	7	0	15	0	0
Crabtree, Tim, Oklahoma	0	0	.000	0.00	1	0	0	0	0	0	1.0	2	5	0	0	0	0	0	0	0	0	1	0	0
Crockett, William, Colorado Springs	0	0	.000	7.36	1	1	0	0	0	0	3.2	6	17	3	3	0	0	1	0	1	0	2	0	0
Crowell, Jim, Albuquerque *	2	4	.333	2.67	55	0	0	0	28	12	60.2	54	241	19	18	6	6	0	3	14	2	44	3	0
Cruceta, Francisco, Tacoma	1	1	.500	5.00	2	2	0	0	0	0	9.0	11	40	6	5	3	0	0	3	0	10	3	0
Cruz, Juan, Sacramento	5	1	.833	2.40	13	13	0	0	...	0	75.0	51	294	23	20	4	...	...	...	28	0	90	...	...
Cruz, Juan, Sacramento	5	1	.833	2.40	13	13	0	0	0	0	75.0	51	302	23	20	4	3	3	5	28	0	90	4	0
Cummings, Jeremy, Memphis	7	1	.875	2.77	14	6	0	0	2	0	52.0	38	208	16	16	6	2	1	3	20	2	41	2	0
Cunnane, Will, Iowa-Round Rock	1	5	.167	5.07	51	0	0	0	31	8	65.2	79	294	40	37	10	3	3	1	27	5	54	4	0
Cyr, Eric, Salt Lake *	5	5	.500	5.64	38	9	0	0	8	1	99.0	130	446	71	62	14	2	4	4	28	3	61	4	0
Dannemiller, Beau, Las Vegas	0	0	.000	6.81	29	0	0	0	10	1	37.0	42	171	28	28	7	2	1	2	25	1	32	3	0
Davis, Kane, Nashville	4	2	.667	2.44	45	0	0	0	16	1	62.2	49	253	18	17	5	2	3	0	23	0	81	2	0
Dawley, Joe, Portland-Iowa	2	1	.667	8.44	17	0	0	0	6	0	21.1	26	112	21	20	1	0	1	1	23	1	22	1	0
Day, Zach, Colorado Springs	2	3	.400	5.89	7	7	0	0	0	0	36.2	46	170	29	24	4	2	1	3	15	0	17	4	2
Deago, Roger, Portland *	0	2	.000	11.42	2	2	0	0	0	0	8.2	18	47	11	11	2	0	0	0	5	0	5	0	0
DeHoyos, Gabriel, Omaha	0	0	.000	23.14	2	0	0	0	0	0	2.1	3	16	7	6	1	0	0	0	5	0	0	0	0
de los Santos, Valerio, Albuquerque *	0	0	.000	1.69	6	0	0	0	2	1	5.1	7	25	1	1	0	0	0	1	1	0	6	1	0
Delucchi, Dustin, Portland *	0	0	.000	0.00	1	0	0	0	1	0	1.0	0	4	0	0	0	0	0	0	1	0	0	0	0
Dement, Daniel, New Orleans	0	0	.000	5.40	2	0	0	0	2	0	1.2	2	8	1	1	0	0	0	0	1	0	0	0	0
Dessens, Elmer, Las Vegas	0	0	.000	3.38	3	3	0	0	0	0	8.0	6	30	3	3	1	1	0	2	0	6	0	0
Dickey, R.A., Oklahoma	10	6	.625	5.99	19	17	1	0	0	0	121.2	152	541	88	81	12	4	0	8	39	0	81	9	2
DiFelice, Mark, New Orleans	1	2	.333	8.40	14	2	0	0	4	0	30.0	39	141	35	28	10	3	3	0	13	1	21	1	0
Dohmann, Scott, Colorado Springs	2	1	.667	4.38	34	0	0	0	10	1	39.0	41	176	19	19	5	0	3	3	16	1	53	3	1
Dominguez, Juan, Oklahoma	2	1	.667	4.25	7	7	0	0	0	0	36.0	38	154	20	17	6	0	0	0	14	0	24	2	0
Dorman, Richard, Tacoma	4	4	.500	6.28	10	8	0	0	0	0	38.2	33	168	27	27	6	2	0	1	26	0	22	1	0
Drew, Tim, Colorado Springs	4	3	.571	7.55	11	11	1	0	0	0	56.0	71	254	48	47	11	3	1	2	22	0	56	3	1
Driskill, Travis, Round Rock	9	5	.643	4.37	47	3	0	0	16	4	101.0	99	419	52	49	16	5	5	2	32	8	84	2	0
Duckworth, Brandon, Round Rock	8	6	.571	4.62	20	19	0	0	1	0	115.0	138	501	68	59	17	3	3	3	37	2	89	4	0
Dunn, Scott, Salt Lake	5	7	.417	3.82	47	6	0	0	29	9	92.0	83	385	44	39	7	6	0	1	41	1	98	5	0
Duran, Enmanuel, Tucson	0	0	.000	0.00	1	0	0	0	1	0	1.0	1	4	0	0	0	0	0	0	0	0	1	0	0
Durbin, Chad, New Orleans	4	5	.444	5.77	26	20	0	0	3	0	115.1	121	503	78	74	24	4	3	6	48	3	99	4	0
Eaton, Adam, Portland	0	0	.000	5.63	2	2	0	0	0	0	8.0	11	34	5	5	3	1	0	1	0	4	0	0
Ebert, Derrin, Omaha *	0	0	.000	12.27	2	0	0	0	0	0	3.2	5	20	5	5	0	0	0	0	4	0	1	0	0
Eckert, Harold, Las Vegas	5	10	.333	6.38	33	20	1	0	3	1	135.1	159	634	105	96	23	8	8	20	63	4	121	7	1
Eischen, Joey, New Orleans *	0	0	.000	1.35	6	4	0	0	0	0	6.2	4	28	1	1	0	0	1	3	0	6	1	0
Elder, Dave, Omaha	2	0	1.000	0.00	11	0	0	0	5	0	16.0	8	64	2	0	0	1	0	0	7	0	16	2	0
Emanuel, Dennis, Portland	2	3	.400	5.29	37	6	0	0	7	0	64.2	64	285	49	38	12	2	4	3	25	1	65	7	1
Embry, Byron, Omaha	1	0	1.000	5.02	16	0	0	0	8	0	14.1	19	65	9	8	3	1	2	1	5	0	12	1	0
Erickson, Scott, Las Vegas	2	4	.333	7.20	7	7	0	0	0	0	40.0	47	187	34	32	6	2	2	4	21	0	26	2	0
Escobar, Kelvim, Salt Lake	1	0	1.000	2.51	4	4	0	0	0	0	14.1	14	65	4	4	2	0	0	1	8	0	22	1	0
Espineli, Eugene, Fresno *	1	1	.500	6.38	12	0	0	0	2	0	18.1	22	81	13	13	3	2	0	1	8	0	12	0	1
Esposito, Mike, Colorado Springs	8	9	.471	5.49	27	27	0	0	0	0	155.2	197	693	110	95	20	7	4	8	41	3	94	7	0
Estes, Shawn, Tucson *	0	0	.000	1.64	2	2	0	0	0	0	11.0	5	42	2	2	1	0	0	0	4	0	9	1	0
Etherton, Seth, Sacramento	7	7	.500	2.72	20	19	0	0	1	0	112.1	93	458	44	34	11	3	2	3	30	1	99	2	1
Evert, Brett, Tacoma-Nashville	2	2	.500	5.36	21	3	0	0	5	0	45.1	50	207	30	27	4	3	2	3	20	0	49	6	0
Falkenborg, Brian, Portland-Memphis ..	4	4	.500	4.15	41	0	0	0	17	6	52.0	45	222	28	24	3	3	2	3	26	1	40	0	0
Farmer, Thomas, Las Vegas	1	2	.333	15.19	20	0	0	0	9	0	21.1	45	133	41	36	4	0	1	1	21	2	16	3	1
Field, Nate, Omaha	1	0	1.000	4.91	16	0	0	0	6	0	22.0	26	103	12	12	1	2	1	0	14	1	24	2	1
Fikac, Jeremy, Fresno	4	10	.286	4.42	50	6	0	0	11	1	99.2	112	444	57	49	17	6	4	3	35	1	86	4	1
Flannery, Michael, Albuquerque-Tacoma	1	0	1.000	6.56	20	0	0	0	5	0	23.1	25	111	17	17	3	0	2	0	18	0	18	0	0
Flores, Randy, Memphis *	1	0	1.000	6.43	6	0	0	0	1	0	7.0	8	30	6	5	1	1	2	1	0	0	6	0	0
Flores, Ron, Sacramento *	5	3	.625	2.39	52	0	0	0	16	3	60.1	46	247	18	16	5	5	1	0	30	6	66	3	0
Flury, Patrick, Albuquerque *	1	1	.500	5.53	22	0	0	0	8	0	27.2	27	126	24	17	4	4	3	4	19	0	21	2	0
Foppert, Jesse, Fresno-Tacoma	3	2	.600	4.03	16	15	0	0	0	0	58.0	53	262	29	26	5	3	1	4	35	0	54	2	0
Ford, Matthew, Omaha *	0	1	.000	2.61	9	0	0	0	1	0	10.1	9	43	3	3	1	0	1	0	6	0	5	0	1
Francisco, Frank, Oklahoma	0	0	.000	3.00	2	0	0	0	1	1	3.0	2	13	1	1	0	0	1	0	2	0	4	0	0
Freed, Mark, Tucson *	8	6	.571	4.86	34	13	0	0	5	0	129.2	149	558	75	70	14	6	3	6	39	0	83	1	1
Fruto, Emiliano, Tacoma	1	2	.333	13.09	9	0	0	0	4	0	11.0	11	56	17	16	1	1	1	3	11	0	12	2	0
Fuell, Jerrod, Albuquerque	0	1	.000	5.68	8	0	0	0	4	0	6.1	8	29	4	4	2	1	0	0	4	0	4	1	0
Fulchino, Jeffrey, Albuquerque	11	7	.611	5.06	29	29	0	0	0	0	153.0	179	683	102	86	21	13	3	11	67	3	101	9	0
Fussell, Chris, Round Rock	1	6	.143	6.83	20	8	0	0	7	0	54.0	57	254	42	41	9	2	3	3	50	1	30	7	0
Gagne, Eric, Las Vegas	0	0	.000	0.00	3	0	0	0	1	0	4.0	0	12	0	0	0	0	0	0	0	0	7	0	0
Gallo, Mike, Round Rock *	4	2	.667	3.64	37	1	0	0	6	0	54.1	56	233	29	22	2	5	5	1	20	4	33	1	0
Garcia, Jairo, Sacramento	3	6	.333	4.47	44	0	0	0	37	20	48.1	45	210	30	24	6	2	1	1	20	1	73	5	0
Gelinas, Karl, Salt Lake *	1	0	1.000	1.80	3	0	0	0	2	0	5.0	5	19	1	1	1	0	0	0	0	0	3	0	0
George, Chris, Omaha *	8	8	.500	5.63	32	20	0	0	3	0	147.0	175	653	97	92	27	3	4	6	51	0	103	8	0
Germano, Justin, Portland	7	6	.538	3.70	19	19	1	1	0	0	112.0	111	466	56	46	13	3	1	5	32	1	100	2	0
Gil, David, New Orleans	1	3	.250	3.55	15	2	0	0	1	0	38.0	34	158	18	15	4	0	2	2	12	0	29	1	1
Giron, Roberto, Round Rock	4	3	.571	3.95	22	10	0	0	6	1	66.0	64	278	31	29	5	5	1	3	25	2	56	1	1
Gissell, Chris, Memphis	8	8	.500	3.54	23	23	2	0	0	0	137.1	134	569	63	54	16	10	3	6	36	2	123	2	0
Glover, Gary, Nashville	6	4	.600	3.03	17	16	1	0	1	0	92.0	91	385	39	31	9	3	2	1	29	1	75	5	0
Glynn, Ryan, Sacramento	3	1	.750	2.78	11	11	0	0	0	0	55.0	46	229	20	17	4	1	1	1	23	1	54	2	0
Gobble, Jimmy, Omaha *	2	7	.222	6.63	12	12	0	0	0	0	58.1	76	269	48	43	8	0	4	2	21	0	45	5	0

Pitcher, Team	W	L	Pct.	ERA	G	GS	CG	ShO	GF	Sv.	IP	H	TBF	R	ER	HR	SH	SF	HB	BB	IBB	SO	WP	Bk.
Gomez, Rodolfo, Omaha	0	0	.000	0.00	1	0	0	0	1	0	2.0	1	7	0	0	0	0	0	0	0	0	1	0	0
Gonzalez, Alfredo, Las Vegas	2	2	.500	4.91	46	0	0	0	8	3	66.0	72	297	39	36	10	4	2	3	34	1	43	4	0
Gonzalez, Edgar, Tucson	11	6	.647	4.37	28	24	0	0	1	0	167.0	185	706	94	81	20	10	8	7	38	0	116	3	0
Gonzalez, Luis, Las Vegas *	0	1	.000	9.31	10	0	0	0	5	0	9.2	13	49	10	10	3	0	0	0	11	0	10	1	1
Gosling, Mike, Tucson *	4	6	.400	5.95	18	17	0	0	0	0	92.1	129	427	70	61	11	5	2	2	30	0	76	5	1
Gothreaux, Jared, Round Rock	3	8	.273	4.29	15	15	0	0	0	0	86.0	87	356	45	41	8	4	1	2	29	3	47	1	0
Gracesqui, Franklyn, Albuquerque *	0	0	.000	5.56	16	0	0	0	4	1	11.1	11	53	8	7	2	1	0	0	10	1	12	4	0
Green, Sean, Tacoma	4	2	.667	3.65	33	0	0	0	14	1	49.1	40	216	23	20	1	1	2	4	29	0	44	8	0
Gregg, Kevin, Salt Lake	3	1	.750	3.89	7	6	0	0	0	0	34.2	36	145	15	15	2	0	1	2	10	0	36	3	0
Griffiths, Jeremy, Round Rock	0	1	.000	11.79	9	1	0	0	2	0	23.2	30	125	34	31	2	0	4	0	26	0	8	2	0
Gryboski, Kevin, Oklahoma	0	2	.000	5.23	9	0	0	0	4	0	10.1	14	50	7	6	2	1	0	1	6	1	5	1	0
Gwyn, Marcus, Sacramento	2	2	.500	5.66	34	0	0	0	11	3	41.1	41	210	28	26	1	3	6	10	37	3	37	7	0
Haines, Joseph, Iowa	2	1	.667	2.36	21	0	0	0	10	0	26.2	26	106	9	7	2	3	1	0	5	1	29	0	0
Halama, John, New Orleans *	1	0	1.000	1.13	2	2	0	0	0	0	8.0	6	31	2	1	0	1	0	0	0	0	1	0	0
Hampson, Justin, Colorado Springs *	5	13	.278	5.99	27	26	1	0	0	0	144.1	167	666	109	96	18	6	3	11	71	0	93	3	2
Harden, Rich, Sacramento	0	0	.000	0.00	1	1	0	0	0	0	3.0	1	10	0	0	0	0	0	0	0	0	7	0	0
Harikkala, Tim, Sacramento	1	2	.333	1.27	11	0	0	0	6	3	21.1	13	79	5	3	1	4	0	0	7	3	14	0	0
Harris, Jeff, Tacoma	5	2	.714	2.78	16	9	0	0	3	1	68.0	50	262	22	21	8	3	2	1	17	0	56	0	0
Hart, Corey, Nashville	0	0	.000	0.00	1	0	0	0	0	0	1.0	0	4	0	0	0	0	0	1	0	1	1	1	0
Hawkins, LaTroy, Fresno	0	0	.000	0.00	2	0	0	0	0	0	2.0	2	8	0	0	0	0	0	0	0	0	1	0	0
Heaverlo, Jeff, Tacoma	6	3	.667	4.61	46	0	0	0	11	4	82.0	92	371	49	42	3	4	1	5	44	1	71	6	0
Helling, Rick, Nashville	9	3	.750	4.13	21	21	0	0	0	0	130.2	128	562	74	60	12	8	5	7	50	1	105	5	1
Hendrickson, Ben, Nashville	6	12	.333	4.97	28	27	1	0	1	0	155.1	176	672	100	86	17	9	6	6	58	2	122	9	0
Hennessey, Brad, Fresno	4	2	.667	5.19	11	11	0	0	0	0	67.2	75	298	40	39	7	3	3	4	22	1	46	3	2
Hensley, Clay, Portland	2	2	.500	2.99	15	14	0	0	0	0	90.1	63	347	31	30	8	3	3	2	22	0	71	1	1
Herges, Matt, Tucson	1	2	.333	3.14	26	0	0	0	9	2	28.2	39	124	13	10	3	1	0	1	8	0	29	1	0
Hernandez, Carlos, Round Rock *	5	8	.385	5.56	21	21	0	0	0	0	89.0	99	403	57	55	17	1	1	5	54	2	66	1	1
Hernandez, Felix, Tacoma	9	4	.692	2.25	19	14	1	0	0	0	88.0	62	369	24	22	3	1	2	3	48	0	100	2	2
Hill, Rich, Iowa *	6	1	.857	3.60	11	10	1	0	0	0	65.0	53	262	28	26	11	0	1	4	14	0	92	2	0
Hodge, Kevin, Round Rock	0	0	.000	3.68	6	0	0	0	3	0	7.1	7	29	3	3	1	0	1	0	1	0	3	0	0
Horgan, Joe, New Orleans *	4	3	.571	4.12	46	2	0	0	14	3	63.1	68	280	35	29	9	7	0	5	30	3	48	2	0
House, Craig, Oklahoma	1	0	1.000	9.53	4	0	0	0	1	0	5.2	5	31	6	6	1	0	0	2	8	0	7	1	0
Housman, Jeff, Nashville *	5	12	.294	6.54	28	24	0	0	0	0	130.2	155	587	99	95	27	2	2	4	72	3	110	1	1
Howard, Ben, Albuquerque	6	3	.667	4.63	54	3	0	0	12	2	83.2	85	367	49	43	13	4	2	5	29	1	87	2	0
Howell, J.P., Omaha *	3	1	.750	4.06	7	7	0	0	0	0	37.2	40	160	19	17	1	2	0	1	19	0	29	3	0
Hudgins, John, Oklahoma	3	7	.300	5.87	19	19	1	0	0	0	102.2	127	461	74	67	12	4	3	4	37	1	77	6	2
Hughes, Travis, New Orleans	2	5	.286	3.02	52	0	0	0	27	13	59.2	47	249	25	20	3	1	0	4	25	1	73	4	0
Huisman, Justin, Omaha	8	2	.800	3.92	42	1	0	0	17	1	78.0	89	361	41	34	12	2	3	0	40	1	57	4	0
Hull, Eric, Las Vegas	0	1	.000	7.88	2	2	0	0	0	0	8.0	9	41	11	7	0	0	1	0	8	1	7	0	0
Hunter, Christopher, Salt Lake	1	2	.333	5.86	8	4	0	0	0	0	27.2	40	136	19	18	1	1	0	1	18	0	12	4	0
Jackson, Edwin, Las Vegas	3	7	.300	8.62	12	11	1	0	0	0	55.1	76	275	61	53	13	2	1	5	37	2	33	2	0
Jackson, Steve, Sacramento	0	0	.000	9.00	1	0	0	0	1	0	1.2	2	6	1	1	0	0	0	1	0	1	1	0	0
Jarvis, Kevin, Memphis	11	6	.647	3.38	26	25	1	0	0	0	157.0	164	647	63	59	19	5	4	2	39	1	112	4	0
Jensen, Ryan, Omaha	2	11	.154	7.20	18	18	0	0	0	0	90.0	123	424	80	72	12	1	4	3	38	1	55	6	0
Jimenez, Cesar, Tacoma *	0	0	.000	9.39	4	0	0	0	2	0	7.2	9	33	8	8	5	0	1	0	1	0	9	0	0
Jimenez, Kelvin, Oklahoma	4	6	.400	3.63	37	5	0	0	11	3	79.1	79	342	40	32	6	3	3	4	33	3	64	4	1
Johnson, Adam, Sacramento	1	0	1.000	6.23	4	4	0	0	0	0	21.2	29	97	17	15	1	2	0	1	4	0	17	2	0
Johnson, Tyler, Memphis *	2	1	.667	4.27	57	0	0	0	15	7	59.0	51	249	31	28	6	1	0	3	26	2	77	2	0
Jones, Greg, Salt Lake	1	2	.333	3.20	23	0	0	0	23	10	25.1	20	99	9	9	3	0	0	0	6	0	25	1	0
Journell, Jimmy, Memphis	1	4	.200	4.68	34	0	0	0	12	1	42.1	39	198	25	22	5	1	0	1	38	1	49	10	0
Karp, Joshua, New Orleans	3	1	.750	5.75	21	1	0	0	8	0	36.0	37	158	26	23	8	3	5	3	14	0	29	3	0
Karsay, Steve, Oklahoma	0	1	.000	13.50	4	0	0	0	0	0	4.0	11	25	9	6	0	0	0	0	1	0	5	1	0
Kent, Steve, Colorado Springs *	1	0	1.000	19.44	6	0	0	0	2	0	8.1	18	52	19	18	2	0	1	1	9	0	3	1	0
Kershner, Jason, Portland *	5	2	.714	3.15	46	0	0	0	11	1	60.0	50	234	22	21	4	1	3	0	11	1	44	3	0
Key, Christopher, Tacoma *	0	0	.000	3.60	3	0	0	0	1	0	10.0	10	41	5	4	2	0	1	1	1	0	4	1	0
Kida, Masao, Tacoma	3	6	.333	4.08	53	0	0	0	38	22	79.1	72	326	37	36	6	4	4	4	27	1	66	6	0
Kieschnick, Brooks, Round Rock	2	4	.333	5.72	45	0	0	0	11	1	56.2	77	265	45	36	13	2	1	4	26	5	34	3	0
Kim, Sun-Woo, New Orleans	4	2	.667	2.76	9	9	0	0	0	0	49.0	46	202	23	15	4	2	0	2	15	0	38	2	0
Kinney, Joshua, Memphis	1	2	.333	7.36	26	0	0	0	8	0	25.2	40	135	21	21	4	0	1	2	19	1	25	4	0
Kinney, Matt, Fresno	7	8	.467	5.21	19	19	1	0	0	0	114.0	117	483	68	66	18	7	5	2	45	0	110	6	0
Knox, Ryan, Nashville	0	0	.000	0.00	1	0	0	0	0	0	1.0	0	4	0	0	0	0	0	0	0	0	0	0	0
Koplove, Mike, Tucson	0	2	.000	13.00	9	0	0	0	3	0	9.0	12	47	13	13	1	1	0	2	7	0	6	0	0
Koronka, John, Iowa *	9	11	.450	4.24	23	21	0	0	0	0	136.0	135	562	65	64	12	8	2	3	48	0	96	6	3
Lee, Corey, Salt Lake *	6	2	.750	2.72	14	13	0	0	0	0	79.1	62	329	25	24	5	1	1	2	40	0	77	1	0
Lee, Dave, Fresno-Memphis	0	3	.000	12.08	12	0	0	0	4	0	12.2	23	68	20	17	3	1	0	2	7	0	8	1	0
Lee, Robert, Oklahoma *	5	2	.714	3.86	14	14	1	0	0	0	88.2	91	358	39	38	7	1	2	5	20	0	49	1	0
Leek, Randy, Memphis *	0	1	.000	1.50	1	1	0	0	0	0	6.0	6	23	1	1	0	1	0	0	0	0	2	0	0
Lehr, Justin, Nashville	7	7	.500	3.99	27	11	0	0	4	1	88.0	102	388	49	39	8	4	2	2	32	2	68	3	0
Leicester, Jon, Iowa	3	8	.273	5.51	24	16	0	0	2	1	98.0	115	434	65	60	17	1	1	0	42	1	73	7	0
Levine, Al, Fresno	0	0	.000	2.84	9	0	0	0	3	1	12.2	12	55	5	4	0	2	1	1	6	1	6	0	0
Ligtenberg, Kerry, Tucson	4	3	.571	3.24	38	3	0	0	11	1	50.0	51	201	18	18	4	1	1	1	7	1	50	0	0
Livingston, Robert, Tacoma *	6	2	.750	4.70	10	10	0	0	0	0	51.2	53	221	31	27	2	3	1	1	15	0	41	1	0
Lizarraga, Sergio, Tucson	0	1	.000	7.94	5	2	0	0	0	0	11.1	18	58	10	10	2	0	0	0	7	0	10	1	0
Loe, Kameron, Oklahoma	2	1	.667	5.08	5	5	0	0	0	0	28.1	32	124	17	16	5	0	0	0	10	1	23	1	0
Lopez, Albie, Tacoma	0	1	.000	12.60	3	0	0	0	0	0	5.0	9	27	8	7	3	0	0	0	3	0	3	0	0
Lopez, Aquilino, Las Vegas-Colorado Springs	5	4	.556	4.79	41	0	0	0	23	5	56.1	54	231	34	30	11	1	2	2	10	3	57	1	0
Lopez, Javier, Tucson *	0	1	.000	2.22	27	0	0	0	8	2	24.1	17	95	7	6	0	2	1	1	12	1	16	1	0
Lorraine, Andrew, Tacoma *	9	8	.529	4.79	33	22	2	2	0	0	141.0	162	607	80	75	11	3	7	4	52	0	78	2	0
Lynch, Kevin, Salt Lake	0	0	.000	0.00	2	0	0	0	0	0	2.2	6	13	0	0	0	1	0	0	0	0	3	0	0
Lyon, Brandon, Tucson	0	1	.000	5.40	5	4	0	0	0	0	5.0	5	20	3	3	0	0	0	0	0	0	4	0	0

Pitcher, Team	W	L	Pct.	ERA	G	GS	CG	ShO	GF	Sv.	IP	H	TBF	R	ER	HR	SH	SF	HB	BB	IBB	SO	WP	Bk.
Mabeus, Christopher, Sacramento	9	2	.818	4.21	42	0	0	0	18	1	62.0	61	269	31	29	4	5	5	2	24	5	72	3	0
MacRae, Scott, Round Rock	3	0	1.000	3.21	16	1	0	0	4	0	42.0	38	173	16	15	4	0	0	2	15	2	20	1	0
Mahay, Ron, Oklahoma *	0	0	.000	0.00	3	0	0	0	1	0	3.2	2	13	0	0	0	0	0	0	1	0	5	0	0
Mahomes, Pat, Las Vegas	9	9	.500	5.35	40	15	0	0	15	1	133.0	158	606	87	79	23	6	8	6	67	4	94	0	0
Majewski, Gary, New Orleans	0	0	.000	4.26	3	0	0	0	0	0	6.1	7	26	3	3	0	0	0	0	2	0	2	0	0
Martin, Tom, Round Rock *	0	0	.000	3.62	20	0	0	0	13	5	27.1	33	122	11	11	4	2	1	1	13	2	13	0	0
Martinez, Carlos, Albuquerque	0	0	.000	9.00	2	0	0	0	0	0	2.0	4	10	2	2	1	0	0	0	0	0	0	0	0
Mathews, T.J., Round Rock	1	1	.500	4.03	22	0	0	0	4	0	29.0	33	123	13	13	4	0	0	2	6	1	22	0	0
Mattioni, Nicholas, Sacramento	0	1	.000	11.42	7	0	0	0	2	0	8.2	13	44	12	11	4	2	1	0	7	0	3	2	0
McClaskey, Timothy, Round Rock	0	2	.000	9.28	2	2	0	0	0	0	10.2	14	52	11	11	2	0	0	0	6	1	8	0	0
McClellan, Zachary, Colorado Springs	3	3	.500	5.96	44	2	0	0	9	0	71.0	91	322	48	47	10	2	2	3	26	2	67	3	0
McDaniel, Denton, Round Rock *	1	0	1.000	6.00	18	0	0	0	4	1	27.0	34	118	19	18	7	0	3	2	8	0	10	0	0
McGlinchy, Kevin, Iowa	0	1	.000	5.52	18	1	0	0	4	0	29.1	32	125	21	18	5	3	1	1	11	1	18	0	0
McLeary, Marty, Portland	5	8	.385	4.75	41	12	1	1	10	0	110.0	122	493	68	58	10	4	2	5	51	1	104	5	0
Medders, Brandon, Tucson	3	2	.600	2.48	36	0	0	0	24	8	36.1	31	155	11	10	3	2	1	1	18	3	44	6	0
Mendez, Adalberto, Iowa	0	0	.000	0.00	3	0	0	0	3	0	3.0	1	11	0	0	0	0	0	0	1	0	3	0	0
Mercado, Hector, Oklahoma *	4	0	1.000	1.71	22	0	0	0	7	1	31.2	31	136	8	6	1	0	0	0	19	2	31	0	0
Mercedes, Jose, Iowa	1	1	.500	6.75	10	0	0	0	0	0	13.1	19	65	13	10	4	0	1	0	7	2	14	1	0
Messenger, Randy, Albuquerque	4	2	.667	3.88	39	0	0	0	15	7	48.2	46	203	25	21	5	1	1	2	17	1	35	1	0
Meyer, Dan, Sacramento *	2	8	.200	5.36	19	17	0	0	0	0	89.0	101	400	64	53	15	2	2	2	43	0	63	2	0
Meyers, Mike, Nashville	7	4	.636	5.31	33	7	0	0	9	0	79.2	87	361	51	47	16	4	1	5	40	1	75	5	0
Miadich, Bart, Albuquerque	3	2	.600	2.20	29	0	0	0	21	11	32.2	23	144	10	8	2	1	2	1	20	1	59	7	0
Miceli, Dan, Colorado Springs	0	0	.000	5.40	5	0	0	0	1	0	5.0	4	23	3	3	1	0	0	1	2	0	8	0	0
Michalak, Chris, Tucson *	9	13	.409	4.47	26	25	3	0	0	0	165.0	174	688	88	82	27	4	6	6	42	0	74	0	1
Misch, Patrick, Fresno *	3	9	.250	6.35	19	19	1	0	0	0	102.0	135	465	80	72	18	11	4	6	40	0	69	2	1
Mitre, Sergio, Iowa	5	6	.455	4.33	13	13	1	0	0	0	70.2	72	299	34	34	5	3	2	1	22	0	55	4	2
Molina, Gabe, Colorado Springs	1	2	.333	3.86	12	0	0	0	6	0	16.1	16	72	11	7	1	0	2	1	8	0	11	5	0
Montero, Agustin, Oklahoma	0	0	.000	5.40	4	0	0	0	1	0	5.0	6	22	3	3	0	1	0	1	3	0	4	0	0
Moreno, Victor, Sacramento	4	2	.667	4.50	49	0	0	0	10	2	74.0	72	331	37	37	4	0	3	3	46	5	71	2	0
Moriarty, Mike, Iowa	0	0	.000	0.00	2	0	0	0	2	0	1.2	3	10	0	0	0	0	0	0	2	0	0	0	0
Moseley, Dustin, Salt Lake	4	6	.400	5.03	17	17	0	0	0	0	82.1	102	370	51	46	11	1	8	5	30	1	38	1	2
Moss, Damian, Tacoma *	9	7	.563	3.73	25	24	1	1	0	0	137.2	125	600	68	57	9	5	7	10	75	0	93	7	0
Muessig, Jeffrey, Sacramento	0	0	.000	9.00	1	0	0	0	1	0	1.0	2	6	1	1	0	0	0	0	1	0	0	0	0
Mullen, Scott, Tacoma *	0	0	.000	0.00	1	0	0	0	1	0	1.0	1	4	0	0	0	0	0	0	1	0	2	0	0
Munter, Scott, Fresno	1	3	.250	5.11	12	0	0	0	5	0	12.1	17	53	8	7	0	1	2	0	4	0	5	1	0
Murphy, William, Tucson *	6	8	.429	5.65	23	21	0	0	0	0	121.0	135	564	81	76	14	6	4	7	78	0	87	7	1
Murray, Arlington, Oklahoma *	1	0	1.000	6.30	2	2	0	0	0	0	10.0	11	42	7	7	4	0	0	2	0	0	11	0	0
Myers, Corey, Tucson	0	0	.000	0.00	1	0	0	0	1	0	0.1	2	3	0	0	0	0	0	0	0	0	0	0	0
Nageotte, Clint, Tacoma	2	1	.667	2.65	19	0	0	0	6	2	34.0	21	143	16	10	2	0	1	1	22	0	35	2	0
Nall, Thomas, Las Vegas	6	7	.462	7.17	29	15	0	0	7	0	108.0	154	518	95	86	20	4	6	9	47	2	96	8	0
Nance, Shane, Tucson-Omaha	3	4	.429	5.16	45	0	0	0	13	2	59.1	56	254	34	34	9	4	2	2	28	0	56	3	0
Narveson, Christopher, Memphis *	0	1	.000	12.15	2	2	0	0	0	0	6.2	11	37	9	9	2	0	0	1	7	0	8	0	0
Neal, Blaine, Colorado Springs	0	0	.000	0.00	1	0	0	0	1	0	1.0	1	4	0	0	0	0	0	0	0	0	0	0	0
Neu, Michael, Las Vegas	2	3	.400	5.56	35	9	0	0	10	1	89.0	101	419	62	55	11	5	6	7	62	3	54	8	1
Nieve, Fernando, Round Rock	4	4	.500	4.83	13	13	2	2	0	0	82.0	92	370	45	44	10	2	5	5	33	2	75	3	0
Nina, Elvin, Tucson	1	0	1.000	5.91	12	1	0	0	2	0	21.1	30	104	15	14	5	0	1	2	12	0	17	2	0
Nitkowski, C.J., New Orleans *	2	2	.500	3.62	27	0	0	0	8	4	32.1	36	139	15	13	3	2	2	5	7	0	24	0	0
Nolen, Walt, Iowa *	0	0	.000	6.23	3	0	0	0	0	0	4.1	5	17	3	3	1	0	1	0	0	0	4	1	0
Norton, Phil, Round Rock-Iowa	3	5	.375	5.97	33	7	0	0	4	0	63.1	62	274	46	42	11	3	4	1	34	2	46	1	0
Novoa, Roberto, Iowa	2	2	.500	3.29	19	0	0	0	7	4	27.1	20	108	11	10	1	3	1	4	11	1	18	2	0
Nunez, Vladimir, Oklahoma-Memphis-Tucson	3	4	.429	3.92	49	0	0	0	33	12	57.1	55	243	27	25	6	2	3	2	23	0	56	5	0
Nussbeck, Mark, Memphis *	3	6	.333	3.42	19	8	0	0	6	2	68.1	66	274	27	26	6	2	2	1	11	0	59	1	0
Obermueller, Wes, Nashville	3	1	.750	2.55	9	8	0	0	1	1	42.1	39	168	14	12	1	1	1	0	14	0	39	0	0
Ohman, Will, Iowa *	1	0	1.000	4.15	8	0	0	0	6	1	8.2	4	31	4	4	2	0	0	2	0	0	12	0	0
Oliver, Darren, Tucson-Iowa	1	3	.250	9.38	7	7	0	0	0	0	31.2	61	158	34	33	6	1	2	1	8	0	18	0	0
Olson, Jason, Salt Lake	0	0	.000	9.00	3	0	0	0	1	0	3.0	4	15	3	3	1	0	1	0	2	0	2	2	0
O'Malley, Ryan, Iowa *	3	2	.600	6.33	7	4	0	0	0	0	27.0	40	127	19	19	6	3	1	1	11	2	26	0	0
Oropesa, Eddie, Iowa *	0	1	.000	7.36	7	0	0	0	1	0	7.1	12	40	8	6	1	1	0	1	7	0	10	1	0
Ortiz, Russ, Tucson	0	1	.000	13.00	2	2	0	0	0	0	9.0	14	46	14	13	4	0	0	0	5	0	5	0	0
Osborne, Donovan, Albuquerque *	5	3	.625	4.87	14	14	0	0	0	0	81.1	91	356	49	44	12	1	5	6	27	1	53	0	0
Osoria, Franquelis, Las Vegas	6	4	.600	2.62	40	0	0	0	21	9	55.0	63	229	18	16	3	1	1	4	13	6	35	3	0
Osuna, Antonio, New Orleans	0	0	.000	0.00	2	0	0	0	0	0	3.0	1	10	0	0	0	0	0	0	1	0	4	0	0
Oxspring, Chris, Portland	12	6	.667	4.03	26	26	3	2	0	0	160.2	148	657	81	72	15	5	5	2	42	0	125	5	0
Parker, Christian, Colorado Springs	2	5	.286	6.47	12	11	1	0	0	0	65.1	92	296	52	47	7	5	1	0	27	1	24	4	0
Paronto, Chad, Nashville	3	1	.750	2.75	27	0	0	0	16	6	39.1	40	175	17	12	1	3	1	3	19	3	38	0	0
Patterson, Danny, Portland	1	1	.500	9.82	9	0	0	0	2	0	11.0	17	54	13	12	1	1	0	0	5	0	4	0	1
Pearce, Josh, Memphis	2	3	.400	4.31	24	1	0	0	9	0	39.2	48	164	24	19	9	4	2	1	7	1	31	0	0
Penny, Brad, Las Vegas	1	0	1.000	3.00	1	1	0	0	0	0	6.0	5	25	2	2	1	0	0	0	2	0	9	0	0
Peralta, Joel, Salt Lake	4	1	.800	2.70	19	0	0	0	19	10	20.0	11	80	6	6	0	0	2	3	6	0	18	0	0
Perez, Odalis, Las Vegas *	1	0	1.000	4.30	4	4	0	0	0	0	14.2	14	59	7	7	1	1	0	0	4	0	11	0	0
Perisho, Matt, Albuquerque *	0	2	.000	11.93	17	1	0	0	3	1	14.1	25	71	20	19	4	2	0	0	7	0	10	0	0
Petersen, Jeffrey, Fresno	0	0	.000	0.00	2	0	0	0	2	0	3.0	1	10	0	0	0	0	0	0	1	0	3	0	0
Peterson, Adam, Tucson	0	0	.000	12.00	3	0	0	0	1	0	3.0	5	20	6	4	1	0	0	0	6	0	4	2	0
Phelps, Tommy, Nashville *	1	0	1.000	1.13	5	4	0	0	0	0	16.0	13	60	3	2	0	0	0	0	2	0	14	0	0
Phelps, Travis, Colorado Springs-Iowa	3	1	.750	7.68	25	0	0	0	9	1	41.0	55	201	36	35	13	3	6	2	26	2	36	0	0
Pickler, Jeff, Colorado Springs	0	0	.000	0.00	1	0	0	0	1	0	1.0	0	5	0	0	0	1	0	0	1	0	0	0	0
Pignatiello, Carmen, Iowa *	1	5	.167	5.51	22	5	0	0	6	0	47.1	52	212	34	29	6	1	0	2	20	2	43	2	0
Pineiro, Joel, Tacoma	0	0	.000	1.29	1	1	0	0	0	0	7.0	5	26	1	1	1	0	0	0	0	0	5	0	0
Pinto, Renyel, Iowa *	1	2	.333	9.53	6	6	0	0	0	0	22.2	31	117	30	24	3	4	2	2	24	0	24	0	0
Pizzaro, Melvin, Tacoma *	0	0	.000	5.40	2	0	0	0	1	0	1.2	1	9	1	1	0	0	1	0	3	0	2	0	0

Pitcher, Team	W	L	Pct.	ERA	G	GS	CG	ShO	GF	Sv.	IP	H	TBF	R	ER	HR	SH	SF	HB	BB	IBB	SO	WP	Bk.
Polanco, Phillip, Portland	0	0	.000	9.00	1	0	0	0	0	0	1.0	2	5	1	1	0	0	1	0	0	0	0	0	0
Pote, Lou, Oklahoma	2	1	.667	3.38	14	4	0	0	3	1	42.2	45	196	18	16	2	1	4	1	27	0	35	1	0
Powell, Brian, New Orleans	7	13	.350	5.82	29	26	1	0	0	0	157.2	204	692	114	102	18	12	4	3	42	1	77	7	0
Pratt, Andy, Nashville *	4	4	.500	8.35	23	8	0	0	2	0	50.2	66	258	54	47	11	2	1	5	40	0	51	5	0
Prieto, Ariel, Albuquerque	9	5	.643	3.78	25	21	1	0	1	0	133.1	144	556	65	56	13	7	4	7	37	0	98	4	1
Prinz, Bret, Salt Lake	0	0	.000	5.59	5	0	0	0	1	1	9.2	12	47	7	6	1	0	0	0	6	0	8	0	0
Prior, Mark, Iowa	0	1	.000	10.50	1	1	0	0	0	0	6.0	9	28	7	7	0	1	1	1	7	0	0	0	0
Puffer, Brandon, Fresno	6	5	.545	5.52	54	0	0	0	12	0	73.1	85	323	54	45	9	6	1	12	23	3	48	3	1
Pulsipher, Bill, Memphis *	6	7	.462	4.49	25	18	0	0	1	0	124.1	152	538	72	62	17	6	2	2	29	2	96	3	0
Rall, Tim, Tacoma *	0	0	.000	9.00	3	0	0	0	2	0	5.0	7	25	5	5	0	0	1	0	3	0	2	0	0
Ramirez, Edwar, Salt Lake	0	0	.000	0.00	1	0	0	0	0	0	2.0	0	6	0	0	0	0	0	0	0	0	2	0	0
Ramirez, Erasmo, Oklahoma *	0	0	.000	3.79	16	0	0	0	8	1	19.0	19	84	10	8	3	0	1	3	5	0	11	0	0
Ramirez, Santiago, Oklahoma	5	5	.500	5.21	50	1	0	0	41	17	67.1	81	295	43	39	11	4	2	1	21	3	53	2	1
Ramos, Mario, Sacramento *	4	6	.400	5.21	49	7	0	0	8	0	86.1	107	402	59	50	13	5	5	4	37	0	78	3	1
Randall, Scott, Colorado Springs	1	1	.500	6.75	10	0	0	0	3	0	18.2	20	88	14	14	3	1	3	0	12	1	15	1	0
Randolph, Stephen, New Orleans-Fresno	3	3	.500	6.03	36	6	0	0	5	0	68.2	49	314	50	46	12	3	1	4	66	1	84	3	0
Rauch, Jon, New Orleans	1	1	.500	2.53	7	5	0	0	1	0	21.1	19	84	7	6	3	0	0	0	2	0	25	2	0
Reames, Britt, Sacramento	6	6	.500	3.31	42	7	0	0	16	8	92.1	91	403	46	34	3	5	3	6	35	3	85	7	0
Redding, Tim, Portland	0	0	.000	0.90	2	2	0	0	0	0	10.0	7	38	1	1	0	0	0	1	2	0	5	0	1
Regilio, Nick, Oklahoma	0	0	.000	0.00	1	0	0	0	0	0	2.0	1	7	0	0	0	0	0	1	0	0	2	1	0
Reichert, Dan, Tacoma	1	0	1.000	11.25	2	1	0	0	1	0	4.0	7	25	7	5	1	0	0	0	4	0	3	0	0
Reina, Jesus, Fresno *	0	0	.000	6.23	1	1	0	0	0	0	4.1	3	21	3	3	0	0	0	0	6	0	3	3	0
Reyes, Anthony, Memphis	7	6	.538	3.64	23	23	2	1	0	0	128.2	105	516	55	52	13	5	4	4	34	1	136	3	0
Rheinecker, John, Sacramento *	4	0	1.000	1.77	7	7	0	0	0	0	45.2	29	179	15	9	0	0	2	3	14	0	24	0	0
Riedling, John, Albuquerque	4	1	1.000	3.00	14	0	0	0	7	3	21.0	19	86	9	7	0	2	0	1	9	1	15	1	0
Riley, Matt, Oklahoma *	0	1	.000	8.25	4	4	0	0	0	0	12.0	12	57	11	11	3	0	1	0	7	0	15	2	0
Robertson, James, Sacramento	0	0	.000	1.80	3	0	0	0	1	0	5.0	2	21	1	1	0	1	0	1	3	1	5	0	0
Rodriguez, Jose, Albuquerque *	0	0	.000	6.23	14	0	0	0	1	0	13.0	16	63	10	9	1	0	0	2	8	0	10	0	0
Rodriguez, Nerio, Memphis	0	3	.000	6.95	4	4	0	0	0	0	22.0	33	102	18	17	6	1	0	3	3	0	11	2	0
Rodriguez, Orlando, Las Vegas *	0	0	.000	6.23	5	0	0	0	2	0	4.1	1	21	3	3	0	0	0	9	0	3	0	0	0
Rodriguez, Ricardo, Oklahoma	7	3	.700	2.91	13	12	3	2	0	0	80.1	64	321	30	26	8	1	2	6	23	0	48	0	0
Rodriguez, Wandy, Round Rock *	4	2	.667	3.69	8	8	0	0	0	0	46.1	43	196	20	19	7	0	1	4	16	0	48	1	0
Rodriguez, Wilfredo, Oklahoma *	0	0	.000	1.42	2	2	0	0	0	0	6.1	5	26	2	1	1	0	0	0	2	0	8	0	0
Rohlicek, Russel, Iowa *	3	1	.750	4.33	55	0	0	0	14	3	62.1	48	283	35	30	5	6	2	11	45	1	54	6	0
Roney, Matt, Oklahoma	4	1	.800	3.03	24	0	0	0	12	1	32.2	34	140	11	11	3	1	4	3	8	1	32	1	0
Rouwenhorst, Jonathon, Salt Lake *	4	3	.571	5.27	25	0	0	0	11	1	42.2	60	199	25	25	3	2	3	2	17	0	31	5	0
Rowe, Steven, Oklahoma	1	0	1.000	3.75	8	0	0	0	3	1	12.0	9	44	5	5	1	1	0	0	1	0	10	0	0
Rupe, Josh, Oklahoma	6	7	.462	6.25	17	17	0	0	0	0	93.2	116	428	75	65	12	6	3	8	38	1	62	4	1
Rupe, Ryan, Las Vegas	4	6	.400	6.42	23	11	1	0	0	0	75.2	94	338	60	54	13	2	3	1	24	1	74	1	1
Rust, Evan, Memphis	1	0	1.000	5.40	13	0	0	0	3	0	16.2	16	74	12	10	1	0	1	0	11	0	10	2	0
Saipe, Mike, Sacramento	4	2	.667	2.80	27	4	0	0	3	0	61.0	58	258	26	19	4	1	3	0	17	1	51	4	0
Santana, Ervin, Salt Lake	1	0	1.000	4.19	3	3	0	0	0	0	19.1	19	78	11	9	2	0	1	2	2	0	17	0	0
Santana, Julio, Nashville	2	0	1.000	1.50	8	0	0	0	4	1	12.0	8	46	2	2	0	0	0	4	0	15	0	0	0
Santos, Alexandre, Sacramento	0	0	.000	0.00	3	0	0	0	2	0	4.1	0	13	0	0	0	0	0	0	0	0	0	0	0
Sarfate, Dennis, Nashville	0	1	.000	2.25	5	0	0	0	1	0	12.0	6	46	3	3	1	0	1	4	0	10	0	0	0
Saunders, Joe, Salt Lake *	3	3	.500	4.58	9	9	1	1	0	0	55.0	65	240	38	28	3	4	4	1	21	0	29	1	0
Scarborough, Stephen, Nashville	1	0	1.000	9.00	4	0	0	0	4	0	5.0	13	27	5	5	0	0	0	1	0	3	0	0	0
Schmoll, Steve, Las Vegas	0	3	.000	4.78	22	0	0	0	9	5	26.1	24	113	15	14	1	1	3	2	13	1	31	0	0
Schneider, Scott, Salt Lake	2	2	.500	8.59	36	4	0	0	7	0	73.1	102	356	74	70	12	4	3	5	39	0	47	8	0
Schroder, Christopher, New Orleans	2	0	1.000	7.83	19	0	0	0	8	4	23.0	21	107	21	20	6	2	0	4	15	1	29	1	1
Seay, Bobby, Colorado Springs *	1	0	1.000	2.38	17	0	0	0	12	3	22.2	23	97	8	6	2	1	1	1	10	0	24	0	0
Sedlacek, Shawn, Colorado Springs-Memphis	1	2	.333	9.00	6	4	0	0	1	0	20.0	26	97	22	20	3	0	0	2	12	0	16	1	0
Sele, Aaron, Oklahoma	1	1	.500	8.03	2	2	0	0	0	0	12.1	22	58	12	11	2	0	1	0	2	0	6	0	0
Serrano, Alex, Colorado Springs	4	3	.571	5.85	21	0	0	0	6	0	32.1	33	141	25	21	6	2	0	1	11	1	24	1	0
Serrano, Jimmy, Sacramento	8	3	.727	3.91	16	16	0	0	0	0	92.0	85	392	42	40	7	0	6	1	41	0	89	4	0
Sessions, Douglass, Salt Lake	0	4	.000	7.30	8	8	0	0	0	0	40.2	53	184	36	33	10	0	3	1	16	0	17	1	0
Sherrill, George, Tacoma *	1	3	.250	2.28	22	0	0	0	19	7	23.2	19	97	7	6	0	0	0	6	0	38	1	0	0
Shibilo, Andy, Sacramento	0	0	.000	3.00	3	0	0	0	3	0	3.0	3	12	1	1	0	0	0	0	0	0	4	0	0
Silva, Jesus, Tucson	0	0	.000	13.50	2	0	0	0	0	0	2.2	5	16	4	4	0	0	0	1	3	0	2	0	0
Smith, Dan, New Orleans	1	3	.250	10.73	24	0	0	0	9	1	26.0	47	144	32	31	7	0	1	3	18	2	13	2	0
Smith, Travis, Albuquerque	7	8	.467	4.08	18	17	0	0	0	0	103.2	107	436	54	47	12	2	1	5	31	1	73	5	0
Smyth, Steve, Sacramento *	1	1	.500	10.07	10	4	0	0	2	0	22.1	36	117	27	25	2	0	3	0	17	1	20	1	0
Snare, Ryan, Oklahoma-Portland	5	7	.417	6.23	23	13	0	0	3	2	91.0	117	414	69	63	14	1	3	3	39	0	58	9	0
Snyder, Kyle, Omaha	2	3	.400	3.55	15	12	0	0	0	0	66.0	61	280	32	26	3	2	5	3	22	0	48	2	1
Sodowsky, Clint, Albuquerque	0	0	.000	9.00	6	0	0	0	3	0	5.0	10	28	6	5	1	0	0	3	0	1	0	0	0
Song, Seung, Fresno	2	4	.333	4.42	10	10	0	0	0	0	55.0	50	244	32	27	6	4	1	2	36	0	37	4	0
Songster, Judson, Colorado Springs	0	0	.000	3.86	1	0	0	0	0	0	2.1	2	10	1	1	0	0	1	0	1	0	0	0	0
Sonnier, Shawn, Omaha	3	0	1.000	4.81	19	0	0	0	5	1	33.2	34	145	18	18	7	0	3	0	13	0	37	0	0
Soriano, Rafael, Tacoma	1	0	1.000	0.00	7	0	0	0	3	0	5.1	3	20	0	0	0	0	0	1	0	11	0	0	0
Sparks, Steve, Portland-Sacramento	7	5	.583	5.92	15	14	0	0	0	0	83.2	102	375	58	55	11	6	5	2	32	1	40	5	0
Speier, Ryan, Colorado Springs	2	2	.500	4.99	45	0	0	0	22	6	52.1	70	240	30	29	2	4	0	8	18	0	45	6	0
Spiehs, Randall, Colorado Springs *	1	1	.500	5.28	22	0	0	0	7	2	30.2	32	140	19	18	4	2	1	0	19	1	22	1	0
Stamler, Keith, Oklahoma-Sacramento	3	1	.750	7.56	22	0	0	0	11	5	25.0	40	130	23	21	4	1	0	3	14	1	20	1	0
Standridge, Jason, Oklahoma	5	3	.625	4.50	15	10	0	0	0	0	76.0	83	328	41	38	3	2	2	2	36	0	47	3	0
Stark, Denny, Colorado Springs	2	5	.286	6.58	11	11	0	0	0	0	52.0	54	237	41	38	4	2	1	4	33	1	38	4	0
Stauffer, Tim, Portland	3	5	.375	5.14	13	13	1	1	0	0	75.1	90	329	48	43	5	3	3	5	17	0	64	3	0
Stemle, Steve, Omaha	1	1	.500	0.45	14	0	0	0	5	3	20.0	13	73	3	1	0	1	2	0	3	0	12	0	0
Stetter, Mitchel, Nashville *	1	1	.500	4.26	27	0	0	0	4	0	25.1	23	109	16	12	5	2	1	0	11	1	23	2	0
Stewart, Scott, Portland *	1	5	.167	6.65	17	0	0	0	7	0	21.2	22	94	17	16	2	0	0	0	10	2	16	1	1
Stockman, Phillip, Tucson	1	1	.500	6.25	17	4	0	0	1	0	31.2	35	154	29	22	4	3	3	1	27	0	16	1	0

Pitcher, Team	W	L	Pct.	ERA	G	GS	CG	ShO	GF	Sv.	IP	H	TBF	R	ER	HR	SH	SF	HB	BB	IBB	SO	WP	Bk.
Stone, Ricky, Memphis	1	1	.500	1.65	14	0	0	0	12	6	16.1	12	62	5	3	0	0	0	1	2	0	16	0	0
Strickland, Scott, Round Rock	2	0	1.000	2.37	15	0	0	0	9	5	19.0	11	72	5	5	2	0	1	1	4	0	20	0	0
Stults, Eric, Las Vegas *	3	7	.300	6.58	15	14	0	0	0	0	78.0	107	359	60	57	15	1	2	1	24	0	60	1	0
Sullivan, Scott, Omaha	1	0	1.000	9.00	2	0	0	0	0	0	2.0	3	9	2	2	0	0	0	0	1	0	1	0	0
Sweeney, Brian, Portland	4	5	.444	3.98	20	16	0	0	2	0	110.2	121	453	51	49	15	6	2	4	16	0	72	3	1
Sylvester, Billy, Sacramento	0	0	.000	11.57	12	0	0	0	2	0	14.0	17	81	19	18	1	0	1	4	20	2	13	3	0
Tamayo, Ignacio, Omaha	9	8	.529	5.28	30	27	0	0	0	0	160.1	192	698	99	94	27	5	2	6	50	0	103	2	1
Tankersley, Dennis, Omaha	9	8	.529	4.24	32	23	1	0	0	0	136.0	148	608	72	64	15	1	4	9	59	0	104	4	0
Taschner, Jack, Fresno *	3	0	1.000	1.64	44	0	0	0	26	10	49.1	30	199	9	9	3	1	1	1	24	0	62	4	0
Tavares, Anderson, Iowa	0	1	.000	10.80	2	1	0	0	0	0	3.1	7	17	4	4	0	0	0	1	0	4	0	0
Tejera, Michael, Oklahoma *	3	2	.600	3.79	43	2	0	0	11	2	59.1	52	257	28	25	5	3	2	8	29	5	52	4	0
Teut, Nathan, Iowa *	0	0	.000	0.00	2	0	0	0	0	0	2.2	2	8	0	0	0	0	0	0	0	0	1	0	0
Thomas, Evan, Salt Lake	7	5	.583	6.73	20	14	0	0	2	0	92.1	131	432	75	69	16	7	6	8	30	0	48	3	0
Thomas, Jared, Tacoma *	2	2	.500	4.87	27	0	0	0	11	0	44.1	54	219	27	24	10	1	3	2	35	0	48	2	1
Thompson, Brad, Memphis	2	1	.667	3.29	9	0	0	0	4	0	13.2	12	58	5	5	1	2	0	1	7	5	11	0	1
Thompson, Chris, Tucson	0	0	.000	0.00	1	0	0	0	0	0	1.0	1	4	0	0	0	0	0	0	0	0	1	0	0
Thompson, Derek, Las Vegas *	1	2	.333	3.43	4	3	0	0	1	0	21.0	21	90	11	8	1	1	2	0	11	0	17	1	0
Thompson, Justin, Oklahoma *	2	2	.500	4.70	25	1	0	0	3	0	44.0	47	179	24	23	3	1	2	1	7	3	29	1	0
Thompson, Michael, Portland	4	2	.667	3.15	9	9	0	0	0	0	60.0	58	238	22	21	6	2	0	0	13	0	25	1	0
Tolar, Kevin, Tucson *	6	0	1.000	3.86	27	0	0	0	11	2	32.2	29	139	21	14	3	0	2	1	15	1	26	2	0
Tollberg, Brian, Round Rock	4	3	.571	4.66	10	10	0	0	0	0	63.2	71	260	34	33	11	3	3	4	12	2	41	1	0
Totten, Heath, Las Vegas	7	9	.438	7.12	20	18	0	0	0	0	103.2	149	474	98	82	18	6	2	5	28	1	71	2	0
Tovar, Angel, Portland	2	3	.400	6.65	16	0	0	0	7	0	21.2	31	105	20	16	5	1	1	2	14	1	11	1	1
Tsao, Chin-hui, Colorado Springs	0	0	.000	0.00	1	1	0	0	0	0	1.0	1	4	0	0	0	0	0	0	0	0	1	0	0
Tucker, T.J., New Orleans	0	0	.000	0.00	2	2	0	0	0	0	4.0	2	13	0	0	0	0	0	0	0	0	2	0	0
Ugueto, Luis, Omaha	0	0	.000	0.00	1	0	0	0	0	0	1.0	0	4	0	0	0	0	0	1	0	1	0	0
Valdes, Raul, Iowa *	6	7	.462	5.93	25	17	0	0	3	1	98.2	135	453	71	65	7	8	4	1	39	1	73	5	2
Valdez, Ismael, Albuquerque *	1	0	1.000	0.00	1	1	0	0	0	0	6.0	3	23	0	0	0	0	0	0	4	0	4	0	0
Valverde, Jose, Tucson	0	0	.000	0.00	2	0	0	0	0	0	2.0	1	8	0	0	0	0	0	0	1	0	3	0	0
Van Buren, Jermaine, Iowa	2	3	.400	1.98	52	0	0	0	43	25	54.2	33	208	13	12	5	5	1	3	22	2	65	1	0
Vargas, Claudio, New Orleans	2	2	.500	4.18	5	5	0	0	0	0	28.0	24	118	13	13	4	2	2	0	12	0	35	2	0
Venafro, Mike, Las Vegas *	0	1	.000	6.85	53	0	0	0	13	1	44.2	60	219	38	34	4	5	0	5	35	5	24	0	0
Veras, Jose, Oklahoma	3	5	.375	3.79	57	0	0	0	47	24	61.2	63	274	27	26	4	2	2	2	33	3	72	5	2
Villafuerte, Brandon, Fresno	6	3	.667	3.91	57	0	0	0	21	3	76.0	83	329	38	33	5	2	5	0	32	0	57	4	0
Villarreal, Oscar, Tucson	0	3	.000	5.19	12	8	0	0	0	0	17.1	19	72	12	10	1	0	3	0	4	0	8	1	0
Wainwright, Adam, Memphis	10	10	.500	4.40	29	29	0	0	0	0	182.0	204	786	98	89	18	7	6	5	51	6	147	12	1
Walrond, Les, Albuquerque *	5	4	.555	4.57	15	15	2	2	0	0	86.2	97	371	50	44	13	2	0	1	37	0	61	2	3
Wasdin, John, Oklahoma	9	2	.818	4.93	13	11	0	0	0	0	73.0	84	322	43	40	11	0	2	2	24	1	57	2	0
Watson, Mark, Salt Lake *	0	0	.000	5.06	6	0	0	0	0	0	10.2	14	54	10	6	1	0	0	1	6	0	9	2	0
Wayne, Justin, Las Vegas	0	1	.000	14.40	4	0	0	0	0	0	5.0	5	29	8	8	1	0	0	0	10	0	3	0	0
Weibl, Clint, Nashville	2	5	.286	5.15	39	3	0	0	11	2	73.1	81	343	49	42	8	3	8	2	45	1	55	8	1
Wellemeyer, Todd, Iowa *	3	2	.600	3.02	12	12	0	0	0	0	53.2	47	227	21	18	2	2	2	2	25	0	48	2	0
Whitaker, Brian, Portland	0	0	.000	9.00	2	1	0	0	0	0	6.0	12	29	6	6	1	0	0	0	1	0	4	0	0
White, Gabe, Memphis *	0	0	.000	0.00	8	0	0	0	5	1	7.1	4	27	0	0	0	0	0	1	0	8	0	0
White, Matt, New Orleans *	8	6	.571	3.72	35	16	0	0	3	0	125.2	122	531	62	52	7	3	3	2	45	0	102	9	2
Wilkerson, George, Omaha	2	3	.400	4.99	36	1	0	0	16	3	57.2	66	251	35	32	8	0	3	4	11	0	31	4	0
Williams, Jerome, Fresno-Iowa	2	5	.286	6.21	10	10	0	0	0	0	55.0	74	261	44	38	5	2	2	5	23	0	32	7	1
Williams, Randy, Portland-Colorado Springs ..	3	3	.500	4.39	38	0	0	0	12	4	41.0	31	170	24	20	2	4	1	2	19	0	43	2	1
Williamson, Scott, Iowa	1	0	1.000	3.86	6	0	0	0	2	0	7.0	4	29	3	3	1	0	0	0	3	0	10	0	0
Wilson, Brian, Fresno	1	1	.500	3.97	9	0	0	0	2	0	11.1	8	51	7	5	0	1	1	0	8	0	13	1	0
Witasick, Jay, Colorado Springs	0	0	.000	3.60	8	0	0	0	2	0	10.0	10	43	5	4	0	1	0	0	5	0	14	2	0
Woerman, Joseph, Tacoma	0	0	.000	12.00	2	0	0	0	2	0	3.0	2	17	4	4	1	0	0	0	7	0	2	1	0
Wood, Kerry, Iowa	0	0	.000	2.84	3	3	0	0	0	0	12.2	11	54	4	4	1	0	1	1	6	0	18	0	0
Wood, Mike, Omaha	0	0	.000	2.00	2	2	0	0	0	0	9.0	10	37	2	2	0	0	0	0	2	0	8	0	0
Woods, Jake, Salt Lake *	3	1	.750	5.89	15	5	0	0	2	0	36.2	50	179	27	24	7	1	1	2	17	2	36	1	0
Wylie, Mitch, Fresno	3	5	.375	4.50	22	9	0	0	9	2	66.0	68	278	36	33	6	4	0	2	15	0	58	3	0
Yarnall, Ed, New Orleans *	4	6	.400	5.59	19	14	0	0	2	0	77.1	87	344	49	48	12	4	0	3	33	0	81	6	0
Young, Jason, Colorado Springs	8	8	.529	6.39	21	20	0	0	0	0	105.2	127	471	76	75	16	10	1	11	44	0	92	6	0
Ziegler, Michael, Sacramento	6	6	.500	5.01	22	20	0	0	1	0	115.0	159	519	78	64	11	7	7	4	33	1	65	8	0
Zoccolillo, Peter, Memphis	0	0	.000	0.00	1	0	0	0	1	0	1.0	1	4	0	0	0	0	0	0	0	0	0	0	0
Zumwalt, Sean, Nashville	1	0	1.000	4.61	9	0	0	0	2	1	13.2	11	59	7	7	1	1	1	3	8	0	11	1	0

PITCHERS WITH TWO OR MORE TEAMS

Pitcher, Team	W	L	Pct.	ERA	G	GS	CG	ShO	GF	Sv.	IP	H	TBF	R	ER	HR	SH	SF	HB	BB	IBB	SO	WP	Bk.
Almanza, Armando, Fresno *	0	1	.000	13.50	2	0	0	0	0	0	3.1	5	15	5	5	1	1	0	0	2	0	3	1	1
Almanza, Armando, Tucson *	1	0	1.000	1.80	15	0	0	0	3	1	15.0	12	63	6	3	2	0	1	0	7	0	19	2	0
Almanza, Armando, Memphis *	1	0	1.000	6.30	10	0	0	0	5	0	10.0	13	45	7	7	2	0	0	2	2	0	9	5	0
Anderson, Jimmy, Iowa *	0	0	.000	3.38	1	1	0	0	0	0	5.1	6	23	2	2	1	1	0	0	2	0	2	0	0
Anderson, Jimmy, Round Rock *	2	2	.500	3.24	4	4	1	1	0	0	25.0	30	110	14	9	1	2	0	0	10	2	12	0	0
Bauer, Peter, Albuquerque	3	5	.375	6.91	15	14	0	0	1	0	71.2	88	333	63	55	14	2	1	10	33	0	43	4	0
Bauer, Peter, Round Rock	1	0	1.000	0.00	1	1	0	0	0	0	7.0	6	25	0	0	0	0	0	0	1	0	3	0	0
Bergman, Dusty, Salt Lake *	8	5	.615	3.17	44	0	0	0	22	8	71.0	77	298	25	25	10	3	0	0	18	0	55	3	0
Bergman, Dusty, Fresno *	0	0	.000	18.00	3	0	0	0	1	0	3.0	8	19	6	6	0	0	0	0	3	0	4	0	0
Bumstead, Michael, Portland	2	2	.500	5.26	12	4	0	0	2	0	25.2	32	121	16	15	3	1	0	4	10	0	14	0	0
Bumstead, Michael, Tacoma	1	1	.500	4.15	13	0	0	0	4	0	21.2	22	91	10	10	1	0	2	1	8	0	18	1	0
Cunnane, Will, Iowa	1	1	.500	6.32	24	0	0	0	10	0	37.0	49	172	29	26	8	1	1	1	17	3	33	4	0
Cunnane, Will, Round Rock	0	4	.000	3.45	27	0	0	0	21	8	28.2	30	122	11	11	2	2	2	0	10	2	21	0	0
Dawley, Joe, Portland	1	0	1.000	7.31	13	0	0	0	5	0	16.0	16	80	14	13	1	0	1	1	16	0	17	0	0
Dawley, Joe, Iowa	1	1	.500	11.81	4	0	0	0	1	0	5.1	10	32	7	7	0	0	0	0	7	1	5	1	0
Evert, Brett, Tacoma *	0	0	.000	6.75	8	1	0	0	3	0	13.1	19	64	11	10	1	2	0	3	5	0	8	2	0

Pitcher, Team	W	L	Pct.	ERA	G	GS	CG	ShO	GF	Sv.	IP	H	TBF	R	ER	HR	SH	SF	HB	BB	IBB	SO	WP	Bk.
Evert, Brett, Nashville *	2	2	.500	4.78	13	2	0	0	2	0	32.0	31	143	19	17	3	1	2	15	0	41	4	0
Falkenborg, Brian, Portland	3	4	.429	5.25	28	0	0	0	9	1	36.0	35	160	25	21	2	3	1	2	21	1	26	0	0
Falkenborg, Brian, Memphis	1	0	1.000	1.69	13	0	0	0	8	5	16.0	10	62	3	3	1	0	1	1	5	0	14	0	0
Flannery, Michael, Albuquerque	0	0	1.000	5.40	14	0	0	0	4	0	16.2	16	77	10	10	3	0	1	0	12	0	11	0	0
Flannery, Michael, Tacoma	0	0	.000	9.45	6	0	0	0	1	0	6.2	9	34	7	7	0	0	1	0	6	0	7	0	0
Foppert, Jesse, Fresno	3	1	.750	4.50	10	9	0	0	0	0	44.0	43	202	25	22	5	2	1	2	27	0	41	1	0
Foppert, Jesse, Tacoma	0	1	.000	2.57	6	6	0	0	0	0	14.0	10	60	4	4	0	1	0	2	8	0	13	1	0
Lee, Dave, Fresno	0	2	.000	9.58	8	0	0	0	3	0	10.1	16	52	14	11	3	0	0	2	4	0	7	1	0
Lee, Dave, Memphis	0	1	.000	23.14	4	0	0	0	1	0	2.1	7	16	6	6	0	1	0	0	3	0	1	0	0
Lopez, Aquilino, Las Vegas	3	4	.429	5.89	27	0	0	0	19	5	36.2	40	154	24	24	9	1	1	2	6	3	32	0	0
Lopez, Aquilino, Colorado Springs	2	0	1.000	2.75	14	0	0	0	4	0	19.2	14	77	10	6	2	0	1	0	4	0	25	1	0
Nance, Shane, Tucson *	0	2	.000	3.63	22	0	0	0	11	2	22.1	16	91	9	9	2	3	1	1	11	0	25	2	0
Nance, Shane, Omaha	3	2	.600	6.08	23	0	0	0	2	0	37.0	40	163	25	25	7	1	1	1	17	0	31	1	0
Norton, Phil, Round Rock *	0	1	.000	10.50	8	0	0	0	1	0	6.0	7	33	10	7	0	2	0	0	10	1	3	0	0
Norton, Phil, Iowa *	3	4	.429	5.49	25	7	0	0	3	0	57.1	55	241	36	35	11	1	4	1	24	1	43	1	0
Nunez, Vladimir, Oklahoma	1	1	.500	4.91	17	0	0	0	13	4	22.0	27	95	12	12	1	0	1	0	7	0	17	1	0
Nunez, Vladimir, Memphis	1	1	.500	2.14	17	0	0	0	13	7	21.0	14	86	7	5	1	1	1	1	10	0	26	2	0
Nunez, Vladimir, Tucson	1	2	.333	5.02	15	0	0	0	7	1	14.1	14	62	8	8	4	1	1	1	6	0	13	2	0
Oliver, Darren, Tucson *	1	0	1.000	6.38	4	4	0	0	0	0	18.1	33	88	14	13	3	0	0	1	3	0	8	0	0
Oliver, Darren, Iowa *	0	3	.000	13.50	3	3	0	0	0	0	13.1	28	70	20	20	3	1	2	0	5	0	10	0	0
Phelps, Travis, Colorado Springs	1	1	.500	13.50	7	0	0	0	0	0	12.0	26	68	18	18	6	2	3	0	9	0	8	0	0
Phelps, Travis, Iowa	2	0	1.000	5.28	18	0	0	0	9	0	29.0	29	133	18	17	7	1	3	2	17	2	28	0	0
Randolph, Stephen, New Orleans *	2	2	.500	9.62	14	4	0	0	0	0	29.0	26	141	32	31	8	3	0	3	31	1	34	3	0
Randolph, Stephen, Fresno *	2	2	.500	3.40	22	2	0	0	5	0	39.2	23	173	18	15	4	0	1	1	35	0	50	0	0
Sedlacek, Shawn, Colorado Springs	0	0	.000	3.60	1	1	0	0	0	0	5.0	3	19	2	2	1	0	0	0	1	0	5	0	0
Sedlacek, Shawn, Memphis	1	2	.333	10.80	5	3	0	0	1	0	15.0	23	78	20	18	2	0	0	2	11	0	11	1	0
Snare, Ryan, Oklahoma *	1	5	.167	6.38	17	7	0	0	3	2	60.2	80	281	49	43	8	1	2	3	28	0	35	6	0
Snare, Ryan, Portland *	4	2	.667	5.93	6	6	0	0	0	0	30.1	37	133	20	20	6	0	1	0	11	0	23	3	0
Sparks, Steve, Portland	2	0	1.000	2.04	3	3	0	0	0	0	17.2	15	74	6	4	1	1	1	0	6	0	9	1	0
Sparks, Steve, Sacramento	5	5	.500	6.95	12	11	0	0	0	0	66.0	87	301	52	51	10	5	4	2	26	1	31	4	0
Spiehs, Randall, Portland	1	1	.500	4.70	12	0	0	0	3	1	15.1	15	67	9	8	4	2	0	0	9	1	11	0	0
Spiehs, Randall, Fresno	0	0	.000	5.87	10	0	0	0	4	1	15.1	17	73	10	10	0	0	1	0	10	0	11	1	0
Stamler, Keith, Oklahoma	3	1	.750	7.32	16	0	0	0	8	5	19.2	27	96	16	16	4	1	0	2	11	1	16	0	0
Stamler, Keith, Sacramento	0	0	.000	8.44	6	0	0	0	3	0	5.1	13	34	7	5	0	0	1	3	0	4	1	0
Williams, Jerome, Fresno	1	4	.200	9.39	6	6	0	0	0	0	30.2	47	151	34	32	3	1	2	3	17	0	15	2	1
Williams, Jerome, Iowa	1	1	.500	2.22	4	4	0	0	0	0	24.1	27	110	10	6	2	1	0	2	6	0	17	5	0
Williams, Randy, Portland *	1	1	.500	6.39	12	0	0	0	2	0	12.2	13	57	10	9	1	2	0	0	9	0	7	1	1
Williams, Randy, Colorado Springs *	2	2	.500	3.49	26	0	0	0	14	4	28.1	18	113	14	11	1	2	1	2	10	0	36	1	0

COMBINATION SHUTOUTS: Albuquerque (2) -- Fulchino-Howard-Messenger-Crowell, Valdez-Bentz-Howard. Colorado Springs (2) -- Chavez-McClellan-Speier, Hampson-Neal. Fresno (7) -- Foppert-Randolph-Fikac-Munter-Correia, Cain-Fikac-Munter, Cain-Puffer-Correia, Foppert-Villafuerte-Puffer-Taschner, Cain-Accardo, Kinney-Spiehs, Wylie-Fikac. Iowa (10) -- Mitre-Van Buren-Ohman, Koronka-Borowski, Koronka-Borowski, Mitre-Phelps-Rohlicek-Novoa, Leicester-Norton-Novoa-Van Buren, Valdes-Cunnane, Koronka-Van Buren, Wellemeyer-Haines-Van Buren, Mitre-Pignatiello-Norton-Valdes, Valdes-Baez-Rohlicek. Las Vegas (3) -- Jackson-Venafro-Neu, Eckert-Osoria-Lopez, Perez-Gonzalez-Neu-Schmoll. Memphis (7) -- Gissell-Cali-Borland, Jarvis-Thompson-Cali-Journell-Borland, Gissell-Johnson-Pulsipher-Borland, Reyes-Falkenborg-Stone, Wainwright-Falkenborg, Cummings-Johnson, Jarvis-Johnson-Falkenborg. Nashville (3) -- Pratt-Weibl, Obermueller-Davis-Capellan, Glover-Zumwalt-Adams. New Orleans (4) -- Kim-Powell-Corcoran-Carrasco, Kim-Hughes-White, Bridges-DiFelice, White-Corcoran. Oklahoma (3) -- Rodriguez-Pote, Dominguez-Thompson-Roney, Rupe-Gryboski-Ramirez. Omaha (8) -- George-Stemle-Embry, Tankersley-Camp, Snyder-Tankersley-Cerda-Wilkerson, Bautista-Nance-Cerda-Huisman-Ramirez, Snyder-Sonnier, Tamayo-Cerda, Howell-Nance-Huisman-Ramirez, George-Elder. Portland (5) -- Stauffer-Baker, Emanuel-Falkenborg-Kershner, Cassel-Kershner-Cassidy. Round Rock (6) -- Rodriguez-Gallo-Norton-Burns, Gothreaux-Norton-Burns, Gothreaux-Driskill-Burns, Buchholz-Martin, Astacio-Giron-Martin, Bauer-Buchholz. Sacramento (8) -- Rheinecker-Reames, Serrano-Moreno-Smyth, Ramos-Gwyn, Etherton-Saipe-Stamler, Etherton-Mabeus-Stamler, Cruz-Mabeus-Flores, Cruz-Mabeus, Glynn-Mabeus-Reames-Garcia. Salt Lake (2) -- Dunn-Bergman-Peralta, Gregg-Cyr-Jones. Tacoma (14) -- Baek-Heaverlo-Buglovsky-Evert, Hernandez-Buglovsky-Lorraine-Sherrill, Dorman-Kida-Sherrill, Campillo-Sherrill, Hernandez-Kida-Sherrill, Hernandez-Heaverlo-Sherrill, Moss-Harris-Kida, Hernandez-Buglovsky-Green-Kida, Hernandez-Green-Kida, Moss-Nageotte, Campillo-Nageotte-Kida, Harris-Lorraine-Buglovsky, Livingston-Soriano-Fruto, Moss-Atchison-Fruto. Tucson (6) -- Gonzalez-Valverde-Tolar, Freed-Abreu-Bulger, Freed-Lopez, Michalak-Bulger, Lyon-Villarreal-Freed-Ligtenberg, Gonzalez-Lopez-Bulger-Choate.

2005 FIELDING

TEAM

Team	G	PO	A	E	TC	DP	TP	PB	Pct.
Tacoma	144	3805	1569	101	5475	144	0	10	.982
Iowa	139	3618	1459	100	5177	147	0	14	.981
Portland	143	3729	1362	106	5197	129	0	10	.980
Round Rock	144	3822	1503	107	5432	166	0	14	.980
Memphis	143	3763	1369	108	5240	133	0	13	.979
Albuquerque	144	3819	1661	125	5605	175	0	20	.978
Omaha	144	3760	1466	116	5342	133	0	13	.978
Tucson	144	3787	1578	123	5488	148	0	11	.978
Fresno	144	3880	1343	125	5348	136	0	13	.977
Oklahoma	143	3803	1584	129	5516	176	1	12	.977
Salt Lake	144	3711	1509	124	5344	182	0	7	.977
Las Vegas	143	3729	1485	130	5344	163	0	9	.976
New Orleans	140	3662	1366	125	5153	135	0	13	.976
Colorado Springs	143	3665	1525	132	5322	125	0	13	.975
Sacramento	144	3874	1316	131	5321	103	0	18	.975
Nashville	144	3769	1473	146	5388	140	1	19	.973

INDIVIDUAL

FIRST BASEMEN

NOTE: All caps denotes fielding-percentage leader based on 72 games for catchers, 96 for all other non-pitchers and 115 innings for pitchers. *Throws lefthanded.

Player, Team	Pct.	G	PO	A	E	TC	DP
Alexander, Manny, Oklahoma	.988	9	80	5	1	86	7
Ardoin, Danny, Colorado Springs	.000	1	0	0	1	1	0
Ashby, Christopher, Albuquerque	.994	17	143	10	1	154	16
Barnes, Larry, Albuquerque *	.977	16	155	12	4	171	20
Barnwell, Christopher, Nashville	1.000	2	19	1	0	20	2
Bell, Rick, Iowa	.962	6	25	0	1	26	3
Bozied, Robert, Portland	.988	9	74	5	1	80	10
Broadway, Larry, New Orleans *	.991	18	101	14	1	116	11
Brown, Andrew, Tacoma	1.000	12	77	10	0	87	11
Buchanan, Brian, Colorado Springs	.992	16	118	11	1	130	7
Budde, Ryan, Salt Lake	.978	9	85	4	2	91	15
Cancel, Robinson, Memphis	1.000	2	2	0	0	2	0
Carroll, Wesley, New Orleans	1.000	4	8	0	0	8	1
Cepicky, Matt, New Orleans	.965	36	232	15	9	256	23
Cervenak, Michael, Fresno	.993	75	533	39	4	576	64
Christianson, Ryan, Tacoma	1.000	2	11	1	0	12	2
Colamarino, Brant, Sacramento *	.990	71	562	33	6	601	41
Colbrunn, Greg, Oklahoma	.981	4	49	3	1	53	2
Conway, Daniel, Colorado Springs	1.000	2	18	0	0	18	2
Cota, Jesus, Tucson	1.000	28	249	11	0	260	23
Cresse, Bradley, Memphis	1.000	1	2	0	0	2	1
Dallimore, Brian, Fresno	1.000	1	1	0	0	1	0
Davis, J.J., New Orleans	.929	1	11	2	1	14	0
Dement, Daniel, New Orleans	1.000	1	12	1	0	13	2
Dobbs, Greg, Tacoma	.987	32	287	20	4	311	29
Doster, Dave, Tucson	1.000	2	11	2	0	13	1

Player, Team	Pct.	G	PO	A	E	TC	DP
Duncan, Chris, Memphis	.980	104	771	66	17	854	77
Durrington, Trent, Nashville	1.000	12	94	5	0	99	11
Edwards, Mike, Las Vegas	.991	14	97	10	1	108	2
Fick, Robert, Portland	.986	8	65	8	1	74	6
Gall, John, Memphis	.983	46	279	18	5	302	34
Garrett, Shawn, Sacramento	1.000	19	123	12	0	135	16
Gerber, Joseph, Portland *	.988	12	71	8	1	80	6
Gonzalez, Adrian, Oklahoma *	.994	82	747	64	5	816	101
Grabowski, Jason, Las Vegas	1.000	1	2	0	0	2	0
Haad, Yamid, Fresno	1.000	1	2	0	0	2	0
Halter, Shane, Iowa	1.000	1	6	0	0	6	1
Hansen, Dave, Tacoma	1.000	1	6	1	0	7	1
Hansen, Jed, Fresno	1.000	1	1	0	0	1	0
Hart, Corey, Nashville	1.000	4	20	5	0	25	1
Harvey, Ken, Omaha	.989	18	169	7	2	178	14
Haynes, Charles, New Orleans	.909	2	10	0	1	11	1
Helton, Todd, Colorado Springs *	1.000	2	16	0	0	16	1
Hocking, Denny, Omaha	1.000	3	20	0	0	20	4
HOFFPAUIR, JAMES, Iowa *	.999	98	752	52	1	805	84
Huber, Justin, Omaha	.990	31	260	23	3	286	25
Huffman, Royce, Round Rock	.996	63	473	30	2	505	54
Jackson, Conor, Tucson	.990	73	625	53	7	685	65
Jackson, Steve, Sacramento	.980	8	44	6	1	51	3
Johnson, Dan, Sacramento	.990	45	361	23	4	388	25
Johnson, Mark, Iowa	1.000	2	0	1	0	1	0
Johnson, Nick, New Orleans *	1.000	3	10	3	0	13	2
Kelton, David, Iowa	1.000	10	60	3	0	63	5
Knott, Jon, Portland	.984	40	287	22	5	314	33
Kotchman, Casey, Salt Lake *	.995	89	790	59	4	853	103
Kuzmic, Craig, New Orleans	1.000	5	24	3	0	27	1
Matranga, Dave, Salt Lake	1.000	1	3	1	0	4	1
McAnulty, Paul, Portland	.989	21	163	11	2	176	17
McClain, Scott, Iowa	.989	45	328	23	4	355	44
McDonald, Keith, Oklahoma	1.000	1	3	2	0	5	0
Melo, Juan, New Orleans	.993	22	135	15	1	151	17
Munhall, Brian, Fresno	.500	1	0	1	1	2	0
Myers, Corey, Tucson	.995	41	357	29	2	388	34
Myrow, Brian, Las Vegas	.991	104	798	102	8	908	105
Nakamura, Norihiro, Las Vegas	.967	35	265	25	10	300	35
Nelson, Brad, Nashville	.968	5	26	4	1	31	2
Nevin, Phil, Portland	1.000	2	3	0	0	3	1
Niekro, Lance, Fresno	1.000	1	5	0	0	5	2
Nieves, Melvin, New Orleans	1.000	1	4	0	0	4	0
Ojeda, Miguel, Tacoma	1.000	1	7	1	0	8	1
Olson, Tim, Colorado Springs	1.000	3	22	1	0	23	1
Orie, Kevin, Nashville-New Orleans	.994	46	304	33	2	339	33
Osik, Keith, New Orleans	...	1	0	0	0	0	0
Pellow, Kit, Tacoma	1.000	1	8	0	0	8	2
Pickering, Calvin, Omaha *	.975	9	74	3	2	79	7
Pickler, Jeff, Colorado Springs	.957	6	41	4	2	47	10
Quinlan, Robb, Salt Lake	.983	6	54	3	1	58	10
Ransom, Cody, Iowa	1.000	1	1	0	0	1	0
Richard, Chris, Oklahoma *	.991	48	427	31	4	462	58
Rifkin, Aaron, Tacoma *	.994	91	808	48	5	861	70
Risinger, Benjamin, Portland	1.000	13	101	10	0	111	10
Rivera, Carlos, Round Rock *	.993	98	713	49	5	767	92
Rivera, Michael, Iowa	1.000	3	11	0	0	11	0
Rose, Mike, Las Vegas	.800	1	3	1	1	5	2
Rottino, Vincent, Nashville	1.000	1	3	0	0	3	1
Sain, Gregory, Portland	.990	46	365	28	4	397	36
Santos, Chad, Omaha *	.991	83	701	46	7	754	75
Sears, Todd, Albuquerque	.991	74	635	56	6	697	67
Self, Todd, Round Rock	1.000	2	4	0	0	4	1
Shealy, Ryan, Colorado Springs	.987	101	885	90	13	988	79
Short, Rick, New Orleans	.991	47	288	38	3	329	34
Smith, Bobby, Sacramento	1.000	8	61	3	0	64	8
Smith, Casey, Salt Lake	.994	19	144	14	1	159	19
Sorensen, Zach, Salt Lake	1.000	24	158	14	0	172	19
Spiezio, Scott, Tacoma	1.000	8	82	6	0	88	12
Stokes, Jason, Albuquerque	.981	11	95	7	2	104	12
Swisher, Nicholas, Sacramento *	1.000	1	9	0	0	9	1
Terveen, Bryce, Tacoma	1.000	1	2	0	0	2	0
Torcato, Tony, Fresno	.994	76	554	62	4	620	53
Tracy, Andy, Colorado Springs	1.000	2	18	0	0	18	2
Tremie, Chris, Round Rock	1.000	1	2	0	0	2	0
Wathan, Derek, Albuquerque	1.000	1	5	0	0	5	1
Wilson, Tom, Colorado Springs	1.000	16	128	9	0	137	14
Wood, Jason, Albuquerque	.994	36	285	23	2	310	46
Zinter, Alan, Tucson	1.000	9	60	2	0	62	10
Zoccolillo, Peter, Memphis	.988	10	70	9	1	80	6
Zuniga, Jose, Nashville	.990	25	170	28	2	200	20

FIRST BASEMEN WITH TWO OR MORE TEAMS

Player, Team	Pct.	G	PO	A	E	TC	DP
Orie, Kevin, Nashville	1.000	10	60	9	0	69	5
Orie, Kevin, New Orleans	.993	36	244	24	2	270	28

SECOND BASEMEN

Player, Team	Pct.	G	PO	A	E	TC	DP
Alexander, Manny, Oklahoma	1.000	1	0	5	0	5	1
Appert, Luke, Sacramento	1.000	1	0	1	0	1	0
Athas, Jamie, Fresno	1.000	5	7	9	0	16	3
Aybar, Willy, Las Vegas	.974	28	45	68	3	116	17
Barden, Brian, Tucson	.971	20	39	60	3	102	14
Barfield, Joshua, Portland	.980	137	264	365	13	642	83
Barnwell, Christopher, Nashville	.981	11	27	24	1	52	6
Beattie, Andrew, Sacramento	.971	66	132	165	9	306	36
Bell, Mike, Memphis	1.000	2	4	6	0	10	2
Betancourt, Yuniesky, Tacoma	1.000	1	2	4	0	6	2
Blakeley, Eric, Tacoma	.947	4	8	10	1	19	2
Bowers, Timothy, New Orleans	...	2	0	0	0	0	0
Brown, Andrew, Tacoma	1.000	4	6	8	0	14	1
Brown, Nebasett, Tucson	.750	1	1	2	1	4	0
Burke, Chris, Round Rock	.989	19	45	48	1	94	15
Bynum, Freddie, Sacramento	1.000	1	1	1	0	2	0
Callaspo, Alberto, Salt Lake	.978	48	91	127	5	223	41
Carroll, Wesley, New Orleans	.982	15	31	25	1	57	8
Casilla, Alexi, Salt Lake	.982	11	23	33	1	57	11
Cepicky, Matt, New Orleans	...	1	0	0	0	0	0
Chavez, Angel, Fresno	1.000	11	21	40	0	61	9
Clark, Jermaine, Sacramento	.996	54	87	143	1	231	27
CONRAD, BROOKS, Round Rock	.987	108	217	335	7	559	80
Dallimore, Brian, Fresno	1.000	43	99	104	0	203	26
Delarosa, Tomas, Colorado Springs	1.000	4	15	5	0	20	3
Delgado, Wilson, Albuquerque	.980	81	160	242	8	410	63
Dement, Daniel, New Orleans	.974	14	17	21	1	39	2
De Renne, Keoni, Tucson	.974	51	87	138	6	231	30
Dillon, Joe, Albuquerque	1.000	3	4	7	0	11	0
Doster, Dave, Tucson	1.000	11	21	24	0	45	7
Durrington, Trent, Nashville	1.000	13	25	30	0	55	5
Eckelman, Thomas, Round Rock	1.000	1	2	3	0	5	2
Erickson, Matt, Albuquerque	.981	13	16	36	1	53	5
Flores, Jose, Las Vegas	.897	7	10	16	3	29	5
Fontenot, Mike, Iowa	.984	63	145	162	5	312	48
Fox, Andy, Salt Lake	.984	14	20	41	1	62	8
Frandsen, Kevin, Fresno	.940	20	36	58	6	100	13
Frese, Nate, Iowa	.800	3	3	1	1	5	1
Furmaniak, J.J., Portland	1.000	3	7	10	0	17	3
Garabito, Eddy, Colorado Springs	.966	31	61	111	6	178	19
Gemoll, Justin, Omaha	.980	83	168	232	8	408	48
German, Esteban, Oklahoma	.981	11	20	31	1	52	9
Ginter, Keith, Sacramento	1.000	4	4	11	0	15	1
Gomez, Francis, Sacramento	.889	3	7	9	2	18	1
Gomez, Rodolfo, Omaha	.974	8	14	23	1	38	9
Gonzalez, Edgar, New Orleans	.909	2	5	5	1	11	2
Green, Andy, Tucson	.981	64	139	166	6	311	45
Guerrero, Wilton, Memphis	1.000	14	13	23	0	36	4
Hairston, Jerry, Iowa	1.000	2	5	5	0	10	1
Hairston, Scott, Tucson	1.000	1	1	0	0	1	0
Hansen, Jed, Fresno	.667	1	1	1	1	3	1
Harris, Brendan, New Orleans	.988	85	170	234	5	409	66
Hart, Bo, Memphis	.992	86	155	213	3	371	53
Hart, Corey, Nashville	.988	20	26	57	1	84	13
Hocking, Denny, Omaha	.972	29	55	85	4	144	20
Huffman, Royce, Round Rock	.985	13	29	37	1	67	11
Hummel, Tim, Memphis	.972	7	16	19	1	36	5
Infante, Larry, Salt Lake	1.000	5	0	2	0	2	0
Izturis, Maicer, Salt Lake	1.000	1	1	0	0	1	0
Jackson, Damian, Portland	.833	1	2	3	1	6	1
Jaramillo, Milko, Memphis	1.000	2	1	1	0	2	0
Kata, Matt, Tucson	.945	14	30	39	4	73	13
Kennedy, Adam, Salt Lake	1.000	3	5	11	0	16	5
Kinsler, Ian, Oklahoma	.972	126	276	413	20	709	112
Klassen, Danny, Round Rock	1.000	9	17	24	0	41	5
Lewis, Richard, Iowa	.991	75	140	179	3	322	50
Lopez, Jose, Tacoma	.972	44	84	124	6	214	30
Lopez, Mickey, Fresno	.970	75	155	198	11	364	51
Loretta, Mark, Portland	1.000	2	4	5	0	9	1
Luna, Hector, Memphis	.981	47	94	112	4	210	35
Mateo, Henry, New Orleans	1.000	8	19	14	0	33	3
Matranga, Dave, Salt Lake	1.000	9	13	32	0	45	5
McDougall, Marshall, Oklahoma	1.000	2	3	5	0	8	3
McEwing, Joe, Omaha	1.000	1	4	4	0	8	1

Player, Team	Pct.	G	PO	A	E	TC	DP
Melo, Juan, New Orleans	.929	4	7	6	1	14	4
Merloni, Lou, Salt Lake	1.000	1	1	4	0	5	2
Merrill, Ronald, Portland	1.000	1	0	1	0	1	0
Meyer, Drew, Oklahoma	.800	1	2	2	1	5	0
Miles, Aaron, Colorado Springs	.978	8	14	30	1	45	4
Morris, Warren, Nashville	.981	53	81	128	4	213	29
Morrissey, Adam, Sacramento	1.000	8	15	20	0	35	4
Nicholson, Thomas, Colorado Springs	1.000	7	4	21	0	25	3
Niles, Frank, Albuquerque	.986	14	24	47	1	72	20
Olson, Tim, Colorado Springs	.973	20	47	60	3	110	12
Pavkovich, Adam, Salt Lake	1.000	1	1	1	0	2	1
Pena, Elvis, Colorado Springs	.965	56	108	167	10	285	30
Pickler, Jeff, Colorado Springs	.967	24	51	67	4	122	13
Ransom, Cody, Oklahoma-Iowa	1.000	7	12	15	0	27	5
Relaford, Desi, Colorado Springs	1.000	1	1	3	0	4	1
Rouse, Michael, Sacramento	.981	11	28	23	1	52	6
Santiago, Ramon, Tacoma	.993	94	174	277	3	454	69
Scales, Bobby, Portland	1.000	2	5	7	0	12	1
Schrager, Anthony, Las Vegas	.920	11	18	28	4	50	6
Short, Rick, New Orleans	.983	30	50	63	2	115	13
Smith, Casey, Salt Lake	1.000	14	21	35	0	56	11
Sorensen, Zach, Salt Lake	1.000	5	6	9	0	15	1
Specht, Brian, Salt Lake	.963	44	89	119	8	216	45
Tena, Hector, Colorado Springs	1.000	1	3	2	0	5	0
Theodorou, Nicholas, Las Vegas	1.000	8	7	18	0	25	4
Thurston, Joe, Las Vegas	.981	75	151	202	7	360	46
Ugueto, Luis, Omaha	1.000	29	54	70	0	124	17
Valbuena, Luis, Tacoma	...	1	0	0	0	0	0
Valentin, Jose, Las Vegas	...	1	0	0	0	0	0
Walker, Todd, Iowa	1.000	6	8	17	0	25	4
Wathan, Derek, Albuquerque	.972	33	71	101	5	177	30
Weeks, Rickie, Nashville	.961	55	108	136	10	254	32
Wilson, Josh, Albuquerque	1.000	2	6	3	0	9	1
Wood, Jason, Albuquerque	1.000	14	29	25	0	54	10
Young, Delwyn, Las Vegas	.980	36	85	115	4	204	38
Young, Eric, Portland	1.000	2	2	7	0	9	1

SECOND BASEMEN WITH TWO OR MORE TEAMS

Player, Team	Pct.	G	PO	A	E	TC	DP
Ransom, Cody, Oklahoma	1.000	2	7	7	0	14	2
Ransom, Cody, Iowa	1.000	5	5	8	0	13	3

THIRD BASEMEN

Player, Team	Pct.	G	PO	A	E	TC	DP
Alexander, Manny, Oklahoma	.915	23	16	38	5	59	6
Alfonzo, Edgardo, Fresno	1.000	2	2	2	0	4	0
Allen, Luke, Salt Lake	.000	1	0	0	1	1	0
Arteaga, Joshua, Iowa	...	1	0	0	0	0	0
Atkins, Garrett, Colorado Springs	.917	5	1	10	1	12	1
Aybar, Willy, Las Vegas	.963	78	42	141	7	190	17
Baker, Jeff, Colorado Springs	.917	59	32	112	13	157	8
Barden, Brian, Tucson	.963	115	87	253	13	353	27
Barnwell, Christopher, Nashville	.941	49	22	89	7	118	11
Beattie, Andrew, Sacramento	.973	19	9	27	1	37	0
Bell, Mike, Memphis	.333	1	0	1	2	3	0
Bell, Rick, Iowa	.889	3	0	8	1	9	1
Blanco, Tony, New Orleans	.909	15	14	36	5	55	1
Bocachica, Hiram, Sacramento	1.000	3	2	5	0	7	0
Bowers, Timothy, New Orleans	1.000	4	2	6	0	8	0
Branyan, Russell, Nashville	...	2	0	0	0	0	0
Brewer, Jace, Oklahoma	1.000	9	5	20	0	25	4
Brown, Andrew, Tacoma	.932	67	51	126	13	190	9
Budde, Ryan, Salt Lake	1.000	1	0	1	0	1	0
Burroughs, Sean, Portland	.949	32	23	51	4	78	7
Cabrera, Mayke, Las Vegas	1.000	2	2	3	0	5	0
Caldera, Jose, Salt Lake	...	3	0	0	0	0	0
Cameron, Troy, Portland	1.000	2	3	3	0	6	1
Carroll, Wesley, New Orleans	.949	14	11	26	2	39	6
Cepicky, Matt, New Orleans	...	1	0	0	0	0	0
Cervenak, Michael, Fresno	.925	50	37	74	9	120	7
Chavez, Angel, Fresno	.000	1	0	0	1	1	0
Cirillo, Jeff, Nashville	.875	8	2	5	1	8	2
Clark, Jermaine, Sacramento	.963	9	7	19	1	27	0
COOLBAUGH, MIKE, Round Rock	.968	114	98	240	11	349	24
Dallimore, Brian, Fresno	.929	49	35	83	9	127	7
Delarosa, Tomas, Colorado Springs	.979	16	13	33	1	47	4
Delgado, Wilson, Albuquerque	1.000	1	0	1	0	1	0
Dement, Daniel, New Orleans	.875	7	2	5	1	8	0
De Renne, Keoni, Tucson	1.000	3	1	6	0	7	0
Dillon, Joe, Albuquerque	.941	81	56	168	14	238	25
Dobbs, Greg, Tacoma	.852	10	6	17	4	27	1
Doster, Dave, Tucson	.750	2	0	3	1	4	0
Durrington, Trent, Nashville	.913	39	26	68	9	103	7
Eckelman, Thomas, Round Rock	.964	14	7	20	1	28	1
Edwards, Mike, Las Vegas	1.000	5	2	4	0	6	1
Erickson, Matt, Nashville-Albuquerque	1.000	7	2	5	0	7	0
Fontenot, Mike, Iowa	.918	41	22	68	8	98	8
Fox, Andy, Salt Lake	1.000	1	0	1	0	1	0
Frese, Nate, Iowa	.944	30	11	57	4	72	5
Furmaniak, J.J., Portland	.942	55	41	105	9	155	8
Gall, John, Memphis	1.000	2	1	1	0	2	0
Garcia, Jesse, Portland	.933	10	4	10	1	15	0
Gemoll, Justin, Omaha	.963	30	18	60	3	81	5
German, Esteban, Oklahoma	.954	75	44	123	8	175	15
Ginter, Keith, Sacramento	.958	9	6	17	1	24	3
Gomez, Rodolfo, Omaha	.500	1	0	1	1	2	0
Gonzalez, Edgar, New Orleans	.966	15	10	18	1	29	3
Green, Andy, Tucson	.946	14	10	25	2	37	3
Guerrero, Wilton, Memphis	1.000	9	5	11	0	16	0
Halter, Shane, Iowa	.750	4	0	3	1	4	0
Hansen, Dave, Tacoma	.750	1	2	1	1	4	0
Hansen, Jed, Fresno	.962	39	20	56	3	79	4
Harris, Brendan, New Orleans	.919	44	29	84	10	123	12
Hart, Bo, Memphis	.951	30	20	57	4	81	7
Hart, Corey, Nashville	1.000	4	1	2	0	3	0
Hocking, Denny, Omaha	.500	1	2	0	2	4	0
Hodges, Scott, New Orleans	1.000	3	0	9	0	9	2
Huffman, Royce, Round Rock	.818	15	7	20	6	33	4
Hummel, Tim, Memphis	.968	45	30	62	3	95	7
Izturis, Maicer, Salt Lake	1.000	2	0	2	0	2	0
Jackson, Damian, Portland	.909	4	5	5	1	11	1
Jaramillo, Milko, Memphis	1.000	3	2	1	0	3	0
Johnson, Mark, Iowa	1.000	1	1	1	0	2	0
Kata, Matt, Tucson	.900	6	3	15	2	20	2
Kinsler, Ian, Oklahoma	1.000	1	1	4	0	5	0
Klassen, Danny, Round Rock	.950	7	6	13	1	20	1
Kuzmic, Craig, New Orleans	...	1	0	0	0	0	0
Leone, Justin, Tacoma	.913	63	34	134	16	184	10
Lewis, Richard, Iowa	1.000	2	1	4	0	5	0
Lopez, Mickey, Fresno	.893	16	7	18	3	28	1
Matranga, Dave, Salt Lake	.957	11	5	17	1	23	4
McClain, Scott, Iowa	.951	69	42	113	8	163	15
McDougall, Marshall, Oklahoma	.962	31	21	81	4	106	7
McEwing, Joe, Omaha	.875	5	1	6	1	8	1
McKay, Cody, Memphis	.909	4	2	8	1	11	0
McPherson, Dallas, Salt Lake	.931	11	5	22	2	29	0
Melo, Juan, New Orleans	.945	28	20	32	3	55	7
Merloni, Lou, Salt Lake	1.000	3	0	3	0	3	0
Merrill, Ronald, Portland	.917	4	3	8	1	12	0
Meyer, Drew, Oklahoma	1.000	1	0	1	0	1	0
Morris, Warren, Nashville	1.000	4	4	5	0	9	1
Morrissey, Adam, Sacramento	.953	18	11	30	2	43	2
Myers, Corey, Tucson	.957	10	6	16	1	23	2
Myrow, Brian, Las Vegas	1.000	1	1	1	0	2	0
Nakamura, Norihiro, Las Vegas	.932	51	29	95	9	133	20
Nicholson, Thomas, Colorado Springs	.844	13	5	22	5	32	2
Niles, Frank, Albuquerque	.000	1	0	0	1	1	0
Olson, Tim, Colorado Springs	.970	33	26	39	2	67	6
Orie, Kevin, Nashville-New Orleans	.957	34	16	51	3	70	5
Pavkovich, Adam, Salt Lake	.947	103	81	207	16	304	24
Pena, Elvis, Colorado Springs	.714	2	1	4	2	7	0
Perez, Antonio, Las Vegas	.926	14	9	16	2	27	3
Quinlan, Robb, Salt Lake	1.000	5	4	8	0	12	1
Ransom, Cody, Oklahoma-Iowa	.938	19	10	35	3	48	2
Relaford, Desi, Colorado Springs	1.000	1	0	2	0	2	0
Risinger, Benjamin, Portland	.975	16	16	23	1	40	4
Rohan, James, Las Vegas	...	2	0	0	0	0	0
Rottino, Vincent, Nashville	1.000	5	3	11	0	14	1
Santiago, Ramon, Tacoma	.867	5	2	11	2	13	3
Scales, Bobby, Portland	.905	28	21	46	7	74	7
Scarborough, Stephen, Nashville	...	1	0	0	0	0	0
Schrager, Anthony, Las Vegas	.750	4	0	3	1	4	0
Seabol, Scott, Memphis	.951	52	44	91	7	142	9
Short, Rick, New Orleans	.913	26	8	55	6	69	3
Smith, Bobby, Sacramento	.915	91	56	193	23	272	17
Smith, Casey, Salt Lake	.929	10	4	22	2	28	4
Sorensen, Zach, Salt Lake	1.000	3	1	8	0	9	2
Specht, Brian, Salt Lake	.875	6	4	10	2	16	0
Spiezio, Scott, Tacoma	1.000	2	1	4	0	5	1
Teahen, Mark, Omaha	.923	5	4	8	1	13	0

Player, Team	Pct.	G	PO	A	E	TC	DP
Tena, Hector, Colorado Springs	1.000	9	2	4	0	6	0
Theodorou, Nicholas, Las Vegas	.824	7	4	10	3	17	2
Tracy, Andy, Colorado Springs	.972	10	9	26	1	36	2
Truby, Chris, Omaha	.958	104	63	185	11	259	19
Valentin, Jose, Las Vegas	1.000	4	0	6	0	6	0
Walter, Scott, Omaha	.000	2	0	0	2	2	0
Willingham, Josh, Albuquerque	1.000	5	2	7	0	9	1
Wilson, Tom, Colorado Springs	.800	3	1	3	1	5	0
Wood, Jason, Albuquerque	.963	67	39	141	7	187	11
Zinter, Alan, Tucson	1.000	1	1	1	0	2	1
Zoccolillo, Peter, Memphis	.909	7	6	14	2	22	3
Zuniga, Jose, Nashville	.904	38	19	56	8	83	6

THIRD BASEMEN WITH TWO OR MORE TEAMS

Player, Team	Pct.	G	PO	A	E	TC	DP
Erickson, Matt, Nashville	1.000	6	0	5	0	5	0
Erickson, Matt, Albuquerque	1.000	1	2	0	0	2	0
Orie, Kevin, Nashville	.974	22	9	29	1	39	4
Orie, Kevin, Iowa	.935	12	7	22	2	31	1
Ransom, Cody, Oklahoma	.850	5	4	13	3	20	2
Ransom, Cody, Iowa	1.000	14	6	22	0	28	0

SHORTSTOPS

Player, Team	Pct.	G	PO	A	E	TC	DP
Alexander, Manny, Oklahoma-Portland	.955	72	113	224	16	353	63
Arteaga, Joshua, Iowa	1.000	2	1	0	0	1	0
Athas, Jamie, Fresno	.923	22	19	53	6	78	15
Barden, Brian, Tucson	1.000	2	1	4	0	5	1
Barnwell, Christopher, Nashville	.935	28	41	75	8	124	18
Beattie, Andrew, Sacramento	1.000	7	5	14	0	19	3
Betancourt, Yuniesky, Tacoma	.989	48	83	183	3	269	48
Blanco, Andres, Omaha	.944	35	46	123	10	179	27
BOWERS, TIMOTHY, New Orleans	.974	111	132	248	10	390	54
Brewer, Jace, Oklahoma	.972	12	20	50	2	72	14
Bynum, Freddie, Sacramento	.904	22	28	47	8	83	8
Cabrera, Asdrubal, Tacoma	1.000	6	11	13	0	24	5
Caldera, Jose, Salt Lake	.600	3	2	4	4	10	0
Carroll, Wesley, New Orleans	.909	8	2	8	1	11	3
Casilla, Alexi, Salt Lake	.833	2	0	5	1	6	0
Cedeno, Ronny, Iowa	.961	65	100	198	12	310	50
Chavez, Angel, Fresno	.967	77	115	177	10	302	51
Crosby, Bobby, Sacramento	1.000	2	3	4	0	7	2
Dallimore, Brian, Fresno	.915	10	20	23	4	47	6
Delarosa, Tomas, Colorado Springs	.965	63	100	177	10	287	37
Delgado, Wilson, Albuquerque	1.000	7	8	19	0	27	5
Dement, Daniel, New Orleans	...	1	0	0	0	0	0
De Renne, Keoni, Tucson	1.000	10	7	11	0	18	5
Dominguez, Jeffrey, Tacoma	1.000	1	2	1	0	3	1
Durrington, Trent, Nashville	.917	8	12	21	3	36	4
Eckelman, Thomas, Round Rock	.907	21	33	45	8	86	17
Flores, Jose, Las Vegas	.949	74	114	167	15	296	39
Fontenot, Mike, Iowa	1.000	3	3	2	0	5	0
Frese, Nate, Iowa	.965	27	39	70	4	113	14
Furmaniak, J.J., Portland	.954	38	47	78	6	131	15
Garabito, Eddy, Colorado Springs	.952	36	50	108	8	166	22
Garcia, Jesse, Portland	.967	49	59	117	6	182	33
German, Esteban, Oklahoma	.925	14	24	50	6	80	11
Gomez, Rodolfo, Omaha	.941	5	5	11	1	17	1
Gonzalez, Edgar, New Orleans	1.000	1	0	1	0	1	0
Green, Andy, Tucson	.966	6	11	17	1	29	4
Guerrero, Wilton, Memphis	...	1	0	0	0	0	0
Halter, Shane, Iowa	.977	12	13	30	1	44	5
Hansen, Jed, Fresno	.925	10	16	21	3	40	6
Hart, Bo, Memphis	1.000	9	6	15	0	21	1
Hart, Corey, Nashville	1.000	1	1	1	0	2	1
Hocking, Denny, Memphis	.961	12	23	26	2	51	3
Infante, Larry, Salt Lake	1.000	2	1	3	0	4	1
Izturis, Maicer, Salt Lake	1.000	6	3	8	0	11	2
Jackson, Damian, Portland	.944	5	7	10	1	18	2
Jaramillo, Milko, Memphis	.935	14	9	20	2	31	4
Kata, Matt, Tucson	.941	11	16	32	3	51	6
Kinsler, Ian, Oklahoma	.900	3	5	4	1	10	2
Klassen, Danny, Round Rock	.973	63	101	184	8	293	47
Labandeira, Josh, New Orleans	.949	9	14	23	2	39	8
Leone, Justin, Tacoma	.957	12	13	32	2	47	6
Lopez, Mickey, Fresno	.919	19	21	47	6	74	10
Luna, Hector, Memphis	.977	12	17	25	1	43	5
Machado, Anderson, Colorado Springs	.919	22	28	40	6	74	10
Matranga, Dave, Salt Lake	.958	37	57	102	7	166	26

Player, Team	Pct.	G	PO	A	E	TC	DP
McClain, Scott, Iowa	1.000	3	4	2	0	6	1
McDougall, Marshall, Oklahoma	1.000	4	7	16	0	23	4
Melo, Juan, New Orleans	.959	44	53	89	6	148	19
Mendez, Donaldo, Fresno	.882	17	21	39	8	68	9
Merrill, Ronald, Portland	.931	10	11	16	2	29	5
Meyer, Drew, Oklahoma	.964	29	36	99	5	140	24
Moriarty, Mike, Iowa	.955	16	21	43	3	67	9
Morse, Mike, Tacoma	.981	49	61	143	4	208	25
Nakamura, Norihiro, Las Vegas	.979	14	22	25	1	48	8
Nelson, John, Memphis	.971	126	178	326	15	519	79
Olson, Tim, Colorado Springs	.966	15	23	34	2	59	9
Pavkovich, Adam, Salt Lake	.667	1	1	1	1	3	0
Perez, Antonio, Las Vegas	1.000	2	2	5	0	7	1
Pickler, Jeff, Colorado Springs	1.000	1	0	1	0	1	0
Prieto, Alex, Omaha	.973	46	60	158	6	224	35
Quintanilla, Omar, Colorado Springs	1.000	13	17	46	0	63	8
Ransom, Cody, Oklahoma-Iowa	.968	46	75	138	7	220	33
Relaford, Desi, Colorado Springs	.875	1	4	3	1	8	1
Rouse, Michael, Sacramento	.962	118	200	261	18	479	54
Santiago, Ramon, Tacoma	.992	30	33	98	1	132	17
Santos, Sergio, Tucson	.953	128	152	371	26	549	76
Scarborough, Stephen, Nashville	.959	121	155	340	21	516	66
Schrager, Anthony, Las Vegas	.972	53	70	137	6	213	36
Smith, Casey, Salt Lake	.941	34	44	115	10	169	32
Sorensen, Zach, Salt Lake	.985	47	73	125	3	201	37
Specht, Brian, Salt Lake	.959	22	37	57	4	98	15
Theodorou, Nicholas, Las Vegas	.923	11	21	27	4	52	10
Ugueto, Luis, Omaha	.954	52	95	131	11	237	28
Valdez, Wilson, Tacoma-Portland	.977	47	88	120	5	213	28
Wathan, Derek, Albuquerque	1.000	4	8	10	0	18	6
Whiteman, Tommy, Round Rock	.954	69	105	183	14	302	53
Wilson, Josh, Albuquerque	.973	136	226	452	19	697	112
Wood, Jason, Albuquerque	1.000	3	3	6	0	9	1
Wood, Richard, Salt Lake	.909	4	6	14	2	22	6

SHORTSTOPS WITH TWO OR MORE TEAMS

Player, Team	Pct.	G	PO	A	E	TC	DP
Alexander, Manny, Oklahoma	.956	68	110	213	15	338	62
Alexander, Manny, Portland	.933	4	3	11	1	15	1
Ransom, Cody, Oklahoma	.963	16	28	49	3	80	10
Ransom, Cody, Iowa	.971	30	47	89	4	140	23
Valdez, Wilson, Tacoma	.833	1	1	4	1	6	0
Valdez, Wilson, Portland	.981	46	87	116	4	207	28

OUTFIELDERS

Player, Team	Pct.	G	PO	A	E	TC	DP
Aguila, Chris, Albuquerque	1.000	33	72	0	0	72	0
Aldridge, Cory, Omaha	1.000	24	41	0	0	41	0
Alexander, Manny, Oklahoma	.909	3	10	0	1	11	0
Allen, Chad, Oklahoma-Memphis	.991	64	102	6	1	109	0
Allen, Luke, Salt Lake	.981	94	189	13	4	206	3
Ashby, Christopher, Albuquerque	.500	3	1	0	1	2	0
Auty, Timothy, Tacoma	1.000	1	4	0	0	4	0
Bacon, Dwaine, Iowa	.941	14	15	1	1	17	0
Barnes, Larry, Albuquerque *	.969	42	58	4	2	64	1
Beattie, Andrew, Sacramento	.944	16	33	1	2	36	1
Bell, Mike, Memphis	1.000	2	1	0	0	1	0
Berger, Brandon, Memphis	.990	62	98	1	1	100	0
Berkman, Lance, Round Rock *	1.000	4	3	1	0	4	0
Bigbie, Larry, Colorado Springs	1.000	3	5	0	0	5	0
Blanco, Tony, New Orleans	...	1	0	0	0	0	0
Bohn, Thomas, Tacoma	.983	22	57	2	1	60	1
Botts, Jason, Oklahoma	.948	82	123	4	7	134	0
Bradford Jr., Samuel, Tacoma	.667	3	2	0	1	3	0
Bradley, Milton, Las Vegas	1.000	5	2	0	0	2	0
Branyan, Russell, Nashville	1.000	4	5	0	0	5	0
Brown, Adrian, Omaha	.986	139	336	6	5	347	1
Brown, Dee, New Orleans	1.000	16	32	0	0	32	0
Brown, Nebasett, Tucson	1.000	2	1	0	0	1	0
Buchanan, Brian, Colorado Springs	.967	36	55	3	2	60	0
Burke, Chris, Round Rock	1.000	6	10	0	0	10	0
Bynum, Freddie, Sacramento	.983	77	170	4	3	177	1
Byrd, Marlon, New Orleans	1.000	19	40	1	0	41	1
Camilo, Juan, Tucson	1.000	5	4	0	0	4	0
Carroll, Wesley, New Orleans	1.000	3	1	0	0	1	0
Cedeno, Roger, Memphis	1.000	6	7	1	0	8	0
Cepicky, Matt, New Orleans	.989	51	88	0	1	89	0
Chavez, Endy, New Orleans *	.983	23	54	4	1	59	1
Chen, Chin-Feng, Las Vegas	.950	82	122	11	7	140	4

Player, Team	Pct.	G	PO	A	E	TC	DP
Choo, Shin-Soo, Tacoma *	.991	112	200	24	2	226	3
Clark, Doug, Fresno	.992	103	241	8	2	251	2
Clark, Jermaine, Sacramento	1.000	4	7	1	0	8	0
Colangelo, Mike, Albuquerque	.969	84	90	5	3	98	0
Conti, Jason, Oklahoma	.984	112	229	13	4	246	2
Costa, Shane, Omaha	1.000	4	9	0	0	9	0
Cota, Jesus, Tucson	1.000	4	7	0	0	7	0
Cruz , Jose, Tucson	1.000	1	2	0	0	2	0
Cruz, Nelson, Nashville	.983	58	107	9	2	118	3
Cust, Jack, Sacramento	.971	77	129	4	4	137	0
Davis, J.J., New Orleans-Colorado Springs	.968	58	86	5	3	94	0
Delucchi, Dustin, Tacoma-Portland	.994	76	171	6	1	178	1
Dement, Daniel, New Orleans	1.000	12	14	2	0	16	0
DeVore, Doug, Tucson-Fresno	.969	79	123	4	4	131	0
Diaz, Matt, Omaha	.969	65	119	6	4	129	2
Dillon, Joe, Albuquerque	1.000	19	27	1	0	28	0
Dobbs, Greg, Tacoma	1.000	1	2	0	0	2	0
Donovan, Todd, Las Vegas	1.000	13	25	1	0	26	0
Doster, Dave, Tucson	1.000	2	6	1	0	7	0
Dubois, Jason, Iowa	1.000	4	11	0	0	11	0
Duncan, Chris, Memphis	.929	19	25	1	2	28	1
Durrington, Trent, Nashville	.960	17	21	3	1	25	1
Echevarria, Angel, Iowa	.950	14	18	1	1	20	1
Edwards, Mike, Las Vegas	1.000	15	22	0	0	22	0
Eldridge, Rashad, Oklahoma	.982	79	165	3	3	171	1
Ellison, Jason, Fresno	1.000	8	27	1	0	28	1
Ethier, Andre, Sacramento	.800	4	3	1	1	5	0
Fitzpatrick, Reginald, New Orleans *	1.000	4	9	0	0	9	0
Fontenot, Mike, Iowa	...	1	0	0	0	0	0
Freeman, Choo, Colorado Springs	.989	95	181	3	2	186	0
Gall, John, Memphis	.978	62	86	1	2	89	1
Garrett, Shawn, Sacramento	.983	88	162	8	3	173	3
Gerber, Joseph, Portland *	...	1	0	0	0	0	0
German, Esteban, Oklahoma	1.000	5	8	0	0	8	0
Gipson, Charles, Round Rock	.980	101	235	11	5	251	6
Godwin, Tyrell, New Orleans	.959	122	225	8	10	243	1
Gonzalez, Edgar, New Orleans	...	1	0	0	0	0	0
Gonzalez, Raul, Memphis	.987	84	141	8	2	151	0
Gordon, Brian, Salt Lake	.959	80	136	5	6	147	1
Gorneault, Nicolas, Salt Lake	.980	120	228	12	5	245	1
Grabowski, Jason, Las Vegas	.938	32	41	4	3	48	0
Green, Andy, Tucson	.977	47	82	3	2	87	0
Grieve, Ben, Iowa	.980	65	94	2	2	98	0
Grissom, Marquis, Fresno	1.000	3	8	0	0	8	0
Guerrero, Cristian, New Orleans	1.000	4	7	0	0	7	0
Guerrero, Wilton, Memphis	...	1	0	0	0	0	0
Guiel, Aaron, Omaha	.993	127	255	18	2	275	3
Hairston, Jerry, Iowa	1.000	2	3	0	0	3	0
Hairston, Scott, Tucson	.979	50	88	4	2	94	0
Halter, Shane, Iowa	1.000	1	2	0	0	2	0
Hammock, Robby, Tucson	1.000	3	11	0	0	11	0
Hammonds, Jeffrey, New Orleans	1.000	16	21	0	0	21	0
Hansen, Jed, Fresno	1.000	9	16	0	0	16	0
Harris, Brendan, New Orleans	1.000	1	1	0	0	1	0
Hart, Corey, Nashville	.985	104	189	8	3	200	2
Hawpe, Brad, Colorado Springs *	1.000	5	6	0	0	6	0
Haynes, Charles, Memphis-New Orleans	.938	8	13	2	1	16	1
Herrera, Javier, Sacramento	1.000	5	9	0	0	9	0
Hocking, Denny, Iowa	1.000	11	18	2	0	20	0
Hoffpauir, James, Iowa *	.929	15	13	0	1	14	0
Housman, Jeff, Nashville *	...	1	0	0	0	0	0
Hubbard, Trenidad, Round Rock-Iowa	.986	74	138	6	2	146	0
Hyzdu, Adam, Portland	.993	62	141	7	1	149	3
Jackson, Conor, Tucson	.929	17	26	0	2	28	0
Jackson, Damian, Portland	1.000	4	7	0	0	7	0
Jackson, Derry, Las Vegas	1.000	9	18	0	0	18	0
Jacobs, Gregory, Tacoma *	1.000	6	13	0	0	13	0
Jimerson, Charlton, Round Rock	.950	6	19	0	1	20	0
Johnson, Ben, Portland	.981	107	205	6	4	215	0
Johnson, Dan, Sacramento	1.000	2	4	0	0	4	0
Jones, Jaime, Omaha *	.966	51	82	4	3	89	2
Jones, Kennard, Portland *	1.000	8	14	0	0	14	0
Kata, Matt, Tucson	1.000	14	29	0	0	29	0
Kelly, Kenny, New Orleans	.974	19	35	2	1	38	0
Kelton, David, Iowa	.983	107	163	7	3	173	1
Kirby, Brian, Colorado Springs	1.000	1	1	0	0	1	0
Klassen, Danny, Round Rock	1.000	3	5	0	0	5	0
Knott, Jon, Portland	.976	85	149	11	4	164	0
Knox, Ryan, Nashville	.988	79	159	6	2	167	0
Kroeger, Josh, Tucson *	.968	124	234	8	8	250	2
Krynzel, Dave, Nashville *	.959	109	231	5	10	246	3
Leone, Justin, Tacoma	.880	13	19	3	3	25	0
Linden, Todd, Fresno	.977	87	168	5	4	177	1
Little, Mark, Albuquerque	.983	74	166	12	3	181	5
Matos, Pascual, Colorado Springs	1.000	2	5	0	0	5	0
McAnulty, Paul, Portland	1.000	15	36	1	0	37	0
McDougall, Marshall, Oklahoma	.957	14	21	1	1	23	0
Meyer, Drew, Oklahoma	.957	11	22	0	1	23	0
Michaelis, Derek, Las Vegas *	1.000	6	6	0	0	6	0
Mohr, Dustan, Colorado Springs	1.000	3	7	0	0	7	0
Murray, Calvin, Iowa	.983	131	229	6	4	239	1
Murton, Matt, Iowa	.923	9	12	0	1	13	0
Myrow, Brian, Las Vegas	.900	11	9	0	1	10	0
Nelson, Brad, Nashville	.972	68	99	6	3	108	2
Nelson, John, Memphis	...	1	0	0	0	0	0
Nieves, Melvin, New Orleans	1.000	17	27	0	0	27	0
Nix, Laynce, Oklahoma *	1.000	10	21	1	0	22	0
Nixon, Michael, Las Vegas	1.000	10	10	1	0	11	0
Nunez, Abraham, Tacoma	.979	118	227	6	5	238	0
Ojeda, Miguel, Portland	1.000	1	1	0	0	1	0
Olson, Tim, Colorado Springs	.960	20	24	0	1	25	0
Padgett, Matthew, Albuquerque *	.976	120	193	11	5	209	2
Patterson, Corey, New Orleans	1.000	23	60	3	0	63	1
Pena, Elvis, Colorado Springs	1.000	14	12	0	0	12	0
Pickler, Jeff, Colorado Springs	.970	74	116	12	4	132	2
Piedra, Jorge, Colorado Springs *	.960	46	67	5	3	75	2
Porter, Colin, Tucson *	1.000	19	30	1	0	31	0
Pride, Curtis, Salt Lake	.978	45	87	0	2	89	0
Prieto, Chris, Salt Lake *	1.000	94	241	7	0	248	3
Quentin, Carlos, Tucson	.996	125	256	11	1	268	4
Ramirez, Julio, Fresno	.987	103	220	8	3	231	2
Reed, Eric, Albuquerque *	.989	39	91	1	1	93	1
Repko, Jason, Las Vegas	1.000	7	15	0	0	15	0
Reynolds, Wilton, Round Rock	1.000	3	4	0	0	4	0
Richard, Chris, Oklahoma *	.956	25	42	1	2	45	0
Rivera, Carlos, Round Rock *	1.000	22	21	2	0	23	0
Robinson, Kerry, Portland *	.992	58	125	5	1	131	1
Rodriguez, John, Memphis	.983	31	56	1	1	58	0
Rohan, James, Las Vegas	1.000	4	5	1	0	6	0
Romano, Jason, Albuquerque	1.000	1	1	0	0	1	0
Rose, Mike, Las Vegas	1.000	7	18	0	0	18	0
Ross, Cody, Las Vegas *	.995	110	209	7	1	217	2
Rottino, Vincent, Nashville	1.000	1	2	0	0	2	0
Salazar, Jeffrey, Colorado Springs *	1.000	57	130	4	0	134	1
Sanchez, Alex, Fresno *	1.000	2	3	0	0	3	0
Santos, Chad, Omaha *	.947	16	36	0	2	38	0
Scales, Bobby, Portland	.989	46	90	2	1	93	1
Scarborough, Stephen, Nashville	1.000	1	2	0	0	2	0
Schrager, Anthony, Las Vegas	1.000	8	10	0	0	10	0
SCHUMAKER, SKIP, Memphis	.996	111	274	6	1	281	0
Scott, Luke, Round Rock	.996	100	222	3	1	226	0
Self, Todd, Round Rock	.977	95	161	9	4	174	1
Shabala, Adam, Fresno	.989	84	182	5	2	189	2
Shanks, James, Albuquerque	.943	18	32	1	2	35	1
Shealy, Ryan, Colorado Springs	1.000	1	1	0	0	1	0
Short, Rick, New Orleans	1.000	4	9	0	0	9	0
Smith, William, Oklahoma	.986	35	70	2	1	73	0
Snelling, Chris, Tacoma *	.976	51	78	4	2	84	0
Sorensen, Zach, Salt Lake	1.000	5	9	0	0	9	0
Spiezio, Scott, Tacoma	1.000	1	2	0	0	2	0
Spilborghs, Ryan, Colorado Springs	.979	60	88	6	2	96	2
Stanley, Henri, Las Vegas *	.963	87	181	1	7	189	0
Strong, Jamal, Tacoma	.976	87	197	4	5	206	1
Swisher, Nicholas, Sacramento *	1.000	2	1	0	0	1	0
Taylor, Reggie, Colorado Springs-Memphis	.985	31	65	2	1	68	0
Terrero, Luis, Tucson	1.000	7	9	0	0	9	0
Theodorou, Nicholas, Las Vegas	.976	52	76	6	2	84	1
Thigpen, Judson, Colorado Springs	1.000	12	11	0	0	11	0
Thomas, Charles, Sacramento *	.984	72	184	1	3	188	0
Torcato, Tony, Fresno	.923	15	24	0	2	26	0
Torres, Andres, Oklahoma	.900	15	17	1	2	20	1
Tracy, Andy, Colorado Springs	...	1	0	0	0	0	0
Ugueto, Luis, Omaha	.667	1	2	0	1	3	0
Valentin, Jose, Las Vegas	1.000	4	7	2	0	9	0
Wathan, Derek, Albuquerque	1.000	23	43	0	0	43	0
Watson, Brandon, New Orleans	.986	87	197	8	3	208	2
Werth, Jayson, Las Vegas	.957	15	20	2	1	23	0
Wesson, Barry, Round Rock	.978	119	246	17	6	269	5
Wilson, Tom, Colorado Springs	1.000	2	1	0	0	1	0
Yan, Ruddy, Oklahoma	1.000	5	14	0	0	14	0
Zoccolillo, Peter, Memphis	.953	46	60	1	3	64	0
Zumwalt, Sean, Nashville	...	1	0	0	0	0	0

OUTFIELDERS WITH TWO OR MORE TEAMS

Player, Team	Pct.	G	PO	A	E	TC	DP
Allen, Chad, Oklahoma	.985	39	62	3	1	66	0
Allen, Chad, Memphis	1.000	25	40	3	0	43	0
Davis, J.J., New Orleans	.958	41	66	3	3	72	0
Davis, J.J., Colorado Springs	1.000	17	20	2	0	22	0
Delucchi, Dustin, Tacoma *	.977	20	43	0	1	44	0
Delucchi, Dustin, Portland *	1.000	56	128	6	0	134	1
DeVore, Doug, Tucson *	.952	38	59	1	3	63	0
DeVore, Doug, Fresno *	.985	41	64	3	1	68	0
Haynes, Charles, Memphis	...	1	0	0	0	0	0
Haynes, Charles, New Orleans	.938	7	13	2	1	16	1
Hubbard, Trenidad, Round Rock	1.000	16	39	1	0	40	0
Hubbard, Trenidad, Iowa	.981	58	99	5	2	106	0
Taylor, Reggie, Colorado Springs	1.000	1	2	0	0	2	0
Taylor, Reggie, Memphis	.985	30	63	2	1	66	0

CATCHERS

Player, Team	Pct.	G	PO	A	E	TC	DP
Alfonzo, Eliezer, Fresno	1.000	4	26	1	0	27	0
Ansman, Craig, Tucson	.984	10	59	4	1	64	0
Apodaca, Juan, Las Vegas	1.000	2	14	0	0	14	1
Ardoin, Danny, Colorado Springs	.997	40	286	23	1	310	3
Ashby, Christopher, Albuquerque	.972	27	162	14	5	181	0
Baker, John, Sacramento	.995	102	743	56	4	803	4
Borders, Pat, Nashville	.976	25	192	10	5	207	2
Brito, Juan, Tucson	.998	70	452	35	1	488	1
Budde, Ryan, Salt Lake	.993	46	275	20	2	297	3
Cancel, Robinson, Memphis	.988	26	222	17	3	242	1
Cardona, Javier, Memphis	.978	7	41	3	1	45	0
Castillo, Alberto, Sacramento	.964	4	26	1	1	28	0
Chavez, Raul, Round Rock	.992	34	223	19	2	244	4
Christianson, Ryan, Tacoma	.994	61	441	22	3	466	9
Conway, Daniel, Colorado Springs	.989	41	258	19	3	280	3
Cresse, Bradley, Memphis	.989	39	260	19	3	282	1
Del Chiaro, Brenton, Salt Lake	1.000	2	3	0	0	3	0
Duenas, Tomas, Omaha	.963	4	21	5	1	27	0
Eckelman, Thomas, Round Rock	.984	11	58	5	1	64	0
Esposito, Brian, Oklahoma	.984	7	61	2	1	64	1
Evans, Lee, Portland	.986	11	68	5	1	74	1
Fick, Robert, Portland	1.000	2	14	1	0	15	0
Gil, Rotsen, Las Vegas	.960	4	22	2	1	25	0
Gonzalez, Wiki, Tacoma	.993	39	264	19	2	285	2
Greene, Todd, Colorado Springs	.980	10	46	2	1	49	0
Gregorio, Tom, Sacramento	.991	29	210	11	2	223	2
Gutierrez, Gabriel, Las Vegas	.926	4	23	2	2	27	0
Haad, Yamid, Fresno	.991	57	429	22	4	455	3
Halter, Shane, Iowa	...	1	0	0	0	0	0
Hernandez, Michel, Portland	.992	79	541	56	5	602	6
Hill, Koyie, Tucson	.993	43	247	19	2	268	4
Huffman, Royce, Round Rock	.895	3	17	0	2	19	0
Jackson, Steve, Sacramento	.984	25	177	10	3	190	1
Johnson, Mark, Iowa	.988	53	378	24	5	407	2
Jorgensen, Ryan, Albuquerque	.990	45	263	28	3	294	1
Kuzmic, Craig, New Orleans	.993	46	270	11	2	283	3
Laird, Gerald, Oklahoma	.988	73	463	50	6	519	5
Mahoney, Mike, Memphis	.996	71	487	50	2	539	3
Martinez, Brett, Salt Lake	.929	4	12	1	1	14	0
Mathis, Jeff, Salt Lake	.986	94	598	47	9	654	5
Matos, Pascual, Colorado Springs	.984	46	275	25	5	305	1
McDonald, Keith, Oklahoma	.990	65	462	24	5	491	1
McKay, Cody, Memphis	.967	10	58	1	2	61	0
Mosquera, Julio, Nashville	.983	62	483	49	9	541	8
Moylan, Daniel, Memphis	.979	5	42	4	1	47	0
Munhall, Brian, Fresno	1.000	12	91	6	0	97	1
Myers, Corey, Tucson	.986	22	127	9	2	138	4
Navarro, Dioner, Las Vegas	.998	66	452	39	1	492	10
Nixon, Michael, Las Vegas	.995	32	180	17	1	198	0
Ojeda, Miguel, Portland-Tacoma	.993	19	130	14	1	145	0
Olivo, Miguel, Tacoma	1.000	14	91	7	0	98	1
ORTIZ, HECTOR, New Orleans	.997	73	561	25	2	588	7
Osik, Keith, New Orleans	1.000	14	70	5	0	75	1
Pachot, John, Albuquerque	.995	28	169	25	1	195	3
Paul, Josh, Salt Lake	1.000	4	28	1	0	29	0
Phillips, Paul, Omaha	.990	83	550	53	6	609	4
Price, Jared, Omaha	.978	24	169	9	4	182	0
Quintero, Humberto, Round Rock	.994	51	280	33	2	315	4
Risinger, Benjamin, Portland	1.000	14	98	10	0	108	0
Rivera, Michael, Nashville	.988	55	450	31	6	487	5
Rivera, Rene, Tacoma	1.000	13	78	8	0	86	1
Rose, Mike, Las Vegas	.997	46	314	19	1	334	4

Player, Team	Pct.	G	PO	A	E	TC	DP
Ross, David, Portland	1.000	6	48	2	0	50	0
Rottino, Vincent, Nashville	1.000	2	21	1	0	22	1
Santiago, Ramon, Tacoma	1.000	1	1	0	0	1	0
Short, Rick, New Orleans	1.000	2	1	0	0	1	0
Soto, Geovany, Iowa	.995	87	672	62	4	738	8
Stinnett, Kelly, Tucson	.973	10	69	4	2	75	1
Terveen, Bryce, Tacoma	.993	18	116	17	1	134	2
Theodorou, Nicholas, Las Vegas	1.000	1	3	0	0	3	0
Tremie, Chris, Round Rock	.993	58	363	40	3	406	6
Trzesniak, Nicholas, Portland	.986	20	134	8	2	144	0
Walter, Scott, Omaha	.991	33	221	7	2	230	0
Willingham, Josh, Albuquerque	.988	60	387	26	5	418	4
Wilson, John, New Orleans	.994	24	149	8	1	158	1
Wilson, Tom, Colorado Springs	.992	22	119	12	1	132	2

CATCHERS WITH TWO OR MORE TEAMS

Player, Team	Pct.	G	PO	A	E	TC	DP
Ojeda, Miguel, Portland	.991	14	94	11	1	106	0
Ojeda, Miguel, Tacoma	1.000	5	36	3	0	39	0

PITCHERS

Player, Team	Pct.	G	PO	A	E	TC	DP
Abreu, Winston, Tucson	1.000	27	2	3	0	5	0
Accardo, Jeremy, Fresno	1.000	25	2	4	0	6	0
Acevedo, Jose, Colorado Springs	1.000	4	1	1	0	2	0
Adams, Mike, Nashville	1.000	26	3	2	0	5	0
Affeldt, Jeremy, Omaha *	1.000	9	0	1	0	1	0
Allen, Luke, Salt Lake	...	1	0	0	0	0	0
Almanza, Armando, Fresno-Tucson-Memphis	1.000	27	0	3	0	3	0
Alvarez, Wilson, Las Vegas *	1.000	4	0	1	0	1	0
Anderson, Brian, Omaha *	...	1	0	0	0	0	0
Anderson, Jimmy, Iowa-Round Rock	.875	5	0	7	1	8	1
Anderson, Luke, Fresno	1.000	6	1	0	0	1	0
Anderson, Matt, Colorado Springs	1.000	46	3	2	0	5	0
Andrews, Clayton, Salt Lake *	.952	28	2	18	1	21	0
Aquino, Greg, Tucson	1.000	6	1	0	0	1	0
Arias, Oliver, Tacoma	1.000	1	0	1	0	1	0
Armas, Tony, New Orleans	1.000	5	1	4	0	5	1
Asencio, Miguel, Portland	1.000	3	3	0	0	3	0
Ashby, Andy, Portland	1.000	1	1	0	0	1	0
Astacio, Ezequiel, Round Rock	1.000	13	4	13	0	17	1
Astacio, Pedro, Portland	...	1	0	0	0	0	0
Atchison, Scott, Tacoma	1.000	10	0	2	0	2	0
Baek, Cha Seung, Tacoma	.947	25	8	10	1	19	0
Baerlocher, Ryan, Omaha	1.000	3	0	1	0	1	1
Baez, Federico, Iowa	1.000	4	0	1	0	1	0
Baker, Bradley, Portland	1.000	59	2	5	0	7	0
Barnwell, Christopher, Nashville	...	4	0	0	0	0	0
Bartosh, Cliff, Iowa *	1.000	22	1	7	0	8	1
Barzilla, Philip, Round Rock *	...	1	0	0	0	0	0
Bauer, Peter, Albuquerque-Round Rock	.938	16	10	5	1	16	0
Bautista, Denny, Omaha	...	6	0	0	0	0	0
Bazzell, Shane, Oklahoma	...	1	0	0	0	0	0
Beck, Bradley, Salt Lake *	...	1	0	0	0	0	0
Bennett, Jeff, Nashville	.875	49	8	6	2	16	0
Benoit, Joaquin, Oklahoma	1.000	3	0	2	0	2	1
Bentz, Chad, Albuquerque *	.875	31	4	3	1	8	0
Bergman, Dusty, Salt Lake-Fresno	.800	47	5	3	2	10	0
Bergmann, Jay, New Orleans	.800	20	2	2	1	5	0
Bevis, P. J., Colorado Springs	1.000	13	0	2	0	2	1
Blank, Matt, Albuquerque *	1.000	13	2	5	0	7	2
Bonine, Eddie, Portland	...	1	0	0	0	0	0
Bootcheck, Chris, Salt Lake	.938	21	14	16	2	32	0
Borbon, Pedro, Salt Lake *	...	8	0	0	0	0	0
Borland, Toby, Memphis	1.000	19	2	1	0	3	0
Borowski, Joe, Iowa	1.000	7	1	1	0	2	0
Bouknight, Kip, New Orleans	.941	9	8	8	1	17	0
Bowers, Timothy, New Orleans	1.000	3	1	1	0	2	0
Bradford, Chad, Sacramento	1.000	3	0	1	0	1	0
Brandt, Adam, Tacoma *	...	1	0	0	0	0	0
Bray, Bill, New Orleans	1.000	23	0	1	0	1	0
Bray, Stephen, Omaha	...	1	0	0	0	0	0
Breslow, Craig, Portland *	1.000	7	2	5	0	7	0
Bridges, Donnie, New Orleans	1.000	13	4	4	0	8	0
Brooks, Frank, Las Vegas *	...	1	0	0	0	0	0
Broshuis, Garrett, Fresno	1.000	2	1	3	0	4	0
Brownlie, Robert, Iowa	1.000	27	12	14	0	26	3
Brunet, Michael, Salt Lake	.750	19	0	3	1	4	0
Bruney, Brian, Tucson	1.000	4	0	2	0	2	0
Buchanan, Brian, Colorado Springs	1.000	0	1	0	0	1	0

Player, Team	Pct.	G	PO	A	E	TC	DP
Buchholz, Taylor, Round Rock	1.000	20	7	6	0	13	2
Buglovsky, Christopher, Tacoma	1.000	35	6	12	0	18	1
Bulger, Jason, Tucson	.875	56	2	5	1	8	0
Bump, Nate, Albuquerque	...	1	0	0	0	0	0
Bumstead, Michael, Portland-Tacoma	.857	25	5	7	2	14	0
Burba, Dave, Round Rock	1.000	18	4	3	0	7	0
Burns, Mike, Round Rock	1.000	25	1	1	0	2	1
Cain, Matt, Fresno	.864	26	6	13	3	22	1
Calero, Kiko, Sacramento	...	2	0	0	0	0	0
Cali, Carmen, Memphis *	1.000	50	0	8	0	8	2
Camp, Shawn, Omaha	1.000	21	4	5	0	9	1
Campillo, Jorge, Tacoma	1.000	12	5	10	0	15	2
Cannon, Jonathan, Tucson *	.960	15	8	16	1	25	1
Capellan, Jose, Nashville	.938	36	7	8	1	16	2
Carlyle, Buddy, Las Vegas	1.000	20	5	6	0	11	0
Carrasco, Daniel, Omaha	1.000	11	2	5	0	7	0
Carrasco, Hector, New Orleans	.000	6	0	0	1	1	0
Cassel, Joseph, Portland	.667	23	2	6	4	12	0
Cassidy, Scott, Portland	.667	17	0	2	1	3	0
Castillo, Frank, Albuquerque	.976	27	12	28	1	41	0
Cerda, Jaime, Omaha *	.923	35	2	10	1	13	0
Chacon, Shawn, Colorado Springs	1.000	3	0	1	0	1	0
Chavez, Wilton, Colorado Springs	.929	28	7	19	2	28	2
Chiasson, Scott, Colorado Springs	1.000	11	3	2	0	5	0
Choate, Randy, Tucson *	1.000	47	2	12	0	14	1
Clontz, Brad, Albuquerque	1.000	11	0	1	0	1	0
Collazo, William, Salt Lake *	1.000	11	2	9	0	11	1
Cook, Aaron, Colorado Springs	1.000	3	3	4	0	7	1
COOPER, BRIAN, Fresno	1.000	29	9	18	0	27	1
Corcoran, Roy, New Orleans	.692	52	3	6	4	13	0
Corey, Bryan, Albuquerque	1.000	44	3	7	0	10	0
Cormier, Lance, Tucson	...	1	0	0	0	0	0
Correia, Kevin, Fresno	.714	31	3	2	2	7	0
Cortes, David, Colorado Springs	1.000	12	0	1	0	1	0
Crabtree, Tim, Oklahoma	...	1	0	0	0	0	0
Crockett, William, Colorado Springs	...	1	0	0	0	0	0
Crowell, Jim, Albuquerque *	1.000	55	2	8	0	10	0
Cruceta, Francisco, Tacoma	1.000	2	1	1	0	2	0
Cruz, Juan, Sacramento	.923	13	1	11	1	13	1
Cummings, Jeremy, Memphis	1.000	14	5	5	0	10	1
Cunnane, Will, Iowa-Round Rock	.929	51	5	8	1	14	1
Cyr, Eric, Salt Lake *	.889	38	6	18	3	27	3
Dannemiller, Beau, Las Vegas	1.000	29	1	4	0	5	1
Davis, Kane, Nashville	.857	45	5	7	2	14	1
Dawley, Joe, Portland-Iowa	1.000	17	1	1	0	2	0
Day, Zach, Colorado Springs	1.000	7	4	2	0	6	0
Deago, Roger, Portland *	...	2	0	0	0	0	0
DeHoyos, Gabriel, Omaha	...	2	0	0	0	0	0
de los Santos, Valerio, Albuquerque *	...	6	0	0	0	0	0
Delucchi, Dustin, Portland *	...	1	0	0	0	0	0
Dement, Daniel, New Orleans	...	2	0	0	0	0	0
Dessens, Elmer, Las Vegas	1.000	3	1	0	0	1	0
Dickey, R.A., Oklahoma	.960	19	7	17	1	25	0
DiFelice, Mark, New Orleans	.833	14	3	2	1	6	0
Dohmann, Scott, Colorado Springs	1.000	34	4	2	0	6	0
Dominguez, Juan, Oklahoma	.857	7	3	3	1	7	0
Dorman, Richard, Tacoma	1.000	10	4	6	0	10	1
Drew, Tim, Colorado Springs	1.000	11	3	10	0	13	0
Driskill, Travis, Round Rock	.833	47	4	6	2	12	0
Duckworth, Brandon, Round Rock	.889	20	6	10	2	18	0
Dunn, Scott, Salt Lake	1.000	47	3	11	0	14	1
Duran, Enmanuel, Tucson	...	1	0	0	0	0	0
Durbin, Chad, New Orleans	1.000	26	10	10	0	20	2
Eaton, Adam, Portland	.667	2	0	2	1	3	0
Ebert, Derrin, Omaha *	1.000	2	0	2	0	2	0
Eckert, Harold, Las Vegas	.943	33	11	22	2	35	1
Eischen, Joey, New Orleans *	1.000	6	1	0	0	1	0
Elder, Dave, Omaha	1.000	11	3	2	0	5	0
Emanuel, Dennis, Portland	.923	37	5	7	1	13	0
Embry, Byron, Omaha	1.000	16	0	1	0	1	0
Erickson, Scott, Las Vegas	1.000	7	4	3	0	7	0
Escobar, Kelvim, Salt Lake	...	4	0	0	0	0	0
Espineli, Eugene, Fresno *	1.000	12	1	3	0	4	0
Esposito, Mike, Colorado Springs	.956	27	19	24	2	45	0
Estes, Shawn, Tucson *	1.000	2	1	3	0	4	0
Etherton, Seth, Sacramento	1.000	20	5	8	0	13	0
Evert, Brett, Tacoma-Nashville	1.000	21	3	3	0	6	0
Falkenborg, Brian, Portland-Memphis	.900	41	3	6	1	10	0
Farmer, Thomas, Las Vegas	1.000	20	3	2	0	5	0
Field, Nate, Omaha	1.000	16	1	2	0	3	0
Fikac, Jeremy, Fresno	.840	50	9	12	4	25	1
Flannery, Michael, Albuquerque-Tacoma	1.000	20	2	2	0	4	0
Flores, Randy, Memphis *	1.000	6	0	2	0	2	0
Flores, Ron, Sacramento *	.818	52	1	8	2	11	0
Flury, Patrick, Albuquerque	.600	22	2	1	2	5	0
Foppert, Jesse, Fresno-Tacoma	1.000	16	3	6	0	9	0
Ford, Matthew, Omaha *	1.000	9	2	2	0	4	1
Francisco, Frank, Oklahoma	1.000	2	1	0	0	1	0
Freed, Mark, Tucson	.929	34	4	22	2	28	2
Fruto, Emiliano, Tacoma	1.000	9	0	1	0	1	0
Fuell, Jerrod, Albuquerque	1.000	8	0	1	0	1	0
Fulchino, Jeffrey, Albuquerque	.885	29	9	14	3	26	1
Fussell, Chris, Round Rock	.875	20	2	5	1	8	1
Gagne, Eric, Las Vegas	...	3	0	0	0	0	0
Gallo, Mike, Round Rock	.889	37	0	8	1	9	1
Garcia, Jairo, Sacramento	1.000	44	1	5	0	6	0
Gelinas, Karl, Salt Lake	1.000	3	0	1	0	1	0
George, Chris, Omaha *	.880	32	10	12	3	25	2
Germano, Justin, Portland	1.000	19	6	12	0	18	1
Gil, David, New Orleans	.875	15	2	5	1	8	1
Giron, Roberto, Round Rock	.923	22	1	11	1	13	1
Gissell, Chris, Memphis	.957	23	11	11	1	23	1
Glover, Gary, Nashville	1.000	17	11	11	0	22	2
Glynn, Ryan, Sacramento	.857	11	2	4	1	7	0
Gobble, Jimmy, Omaha *	.833	12	0	5	1	6	1
Gomez, Rodolfo, Omaha	1.000	1	0	1	0	1	0
Gonzalez, Alfredo, Las Vegas	1.000	46	3	9	0	12	0
Gonzalez, Edgar, Tucson	.921	28	13	22	3	38	0
Gonzalez, Luis, Las Vegas *	1.000	10	0	2	0	2	0
Gosling, Mike, Tucson *	.840	18	5	16	4	25	0
Gothreaux, Jared, Round Rock	.923	15	1	11	1	13	1
Gracesqui, Franklyn, Albuquerque *	1.000	16	0	1	0	1	0
Green, Sean, Tacoma	1.000	33	3	8	0	11	1
Gregg, Kevin, Salt Lake	1.000	7	2	4	0	6	0
Griffiths, Jeremy, Round Rock	1.000	9	2	0	0	2	0
Gryboski, Kevin, Albuquerque	1.000	9	1	0	0	1	0
Gwyn, Marcus, Sacramento	.800	34	1	3	1	5	0
Haines, Joseph, Iowa	1.000	21	3	4	0	7	1
Halama, John, New Orleans *	1.000	2	1	1	0	2	0
Hampson, Justin, Colorado Springs *	.893	27	7	18	3	28	0
Harden, Rich, Sacramento	...	1	0	0	0	0	0
Harikkala, Tim, Sacramento	1.000	11	3	5	0	8	0
Harris, Jeff, Tacoma	1.000	16	3	12	0	15	0
Hart, Corey, Nashville	...	1	0	0	0	0	0
Hawkins, LaTroy, Fresno	...	2	0	0	0	0	0
Heaverlo, Jeff, Tacoma	.895	46	7	10	2	19	0
Helling, Rick, Nashville	.935	21	14	15	2	31	0
Hendrickson, Ben, Nashville	.935	28	14	29	3	46	3
Hennessey, Brad, Fresno	.933	11	5	9	1	15	0
Hensley, Clay, Portland	1.000	15	10	19	0	29	0
Herges, Matt, Tucson	1.000	26	1	4	0	5	0
Hernandez, Carlos, Round Rock *	1.000	21	5	11	0	16	2
Hernandez, Felix, Tacoma	.952	19	10	10	1	21	2
Hill, Rich, Iowa *	.909	11	0	10	1	11	0
Hodge, Kevin, Round Rock	1.000	6	0	1	0	1	0
Horgan, Joe, New Orleans *	.929	46	5	8	1	14	0
House, Craig, Oklahoma	1.000	4	1	0	0	1	0
Housman, Jeff, Nashville *	1.000	28	5	17	0	22	1
Howard, Ben, Albuquerque	1.000	54	2	9	0	11	0
Howell, J.P., Omaha *	1.000	7	2	6	0	8	0
Hudgins, John, Oklahoma	.909	19	5	15	2	22	0
Hughes, Travis, New Orleans	.786	52	4	7	3	14	1
Huisman, Justin, Omaha	1.000	42	4	14	0	18	0
Hull, Eric, Las Vegas	.500	2	1	0	1	2	0
Hunter, Christopher, Salt Lake	.833	8	2	3	1	6	0
Jackson, Edwin, Las Vegas	.909	12	6	4	1	11	0
Jackson, Steve, Sacramento	...	1	0	0	0	0	0
Jarvis, Kevin, Memphis	.980	26	15	34	1	50	6
Jensen, Ryan, Omaha	1.000	18	4	11	0	15	1
Jimenez, Cesar, Tacoma *	1.000	4	0	1	0	1	0
Jimenez, Kelvin, Oklahoma	.947	37	4	14	1	19	2
Johnson, Adam, Sacramento	.667	4	2	2	2	6	0
Johnson, Tyler, Memphis *	.900	57	3	6	1	10	1
Jones, Greg, Salt Lake	1.000	23	2	1	0	3	0
Journell, Jimmy, Memphis	1.000	34	3	2	0	5	0
Karp, Joshua, New Orleans	1.000	21	1	1	0	2	0
Karsay, Steve, Oklahoma	1.000	4	1	0	0	1	0
Kent, Steve, Colorado Springs *	1.000	6	1	1	0	2	0
Kershner, Jason, Portland *	.800	46	6	2	2	10	0
Key, Christopher, Tacoma *	1.000	3	3	2	0	5	0

Player, Team	Pct.	G	PO	A	E	TC	DP
Kida, Masao, Tacoma	1.000	53	4	17	0	21	1
Kieschnick, Brooks, Round Rock	.889	45	3	5	1	9	0
Kim, Sun-Woo, New Orleans	.778	9	4	3	2	9	1
Kinney, Joshua, Memphis	1.000	26	0	7	0	7	1
Kinney, Matt, Fresno	1.000	19	7	15	0	22	0
Knox, Ryan, Nashville	1.000	1	0	1	0	1	0
Koplove, Mike, Tucson	.750	9	2	1	1	4	1
KORONKA, JOHN, Iowa *	1.000	23	4	23	0	27	1
Lee, Corey, Salt Lake *	.933	14	5	9	1	15	0
Lee, Dave, Fresno-Memphis	1.000	12	1	1	0	2	0
Lee, Robert, Oklahoma *	1.000	14	6	11	0	17	2
Leek, Randy, Memphis *	1.000	1	0	1	0	1	0
Lehr, Justin, Nashville	.926	27	5	20	2	27	1
Leicester, Jon, Iowa	.909	24	6	14	2	22	0
Levine, Al, Fresno	1.000	9	0	2	0	2	0
Ligtenberg, Kerry, Tucson	1.000	38	3	2	0	5	0
Livingston, Robert, Tacoma *	.929	10	4	9	1	14	0
Lizarraga, Sergio, Tucson	1.000	5	3	0	0	3	0
Loe, Kameron, Oklahoma	1.000	5	2	4	0	6	0
Lopez, Albie, Tacoma	...	3	0	0	0	0	0
Lopez, Aquilino, Las Vegas-Colorado Springs	1.000	41	8	4	0	12	1
Lopez, Javier, Tucson *	.950	27	5	14	1	20	3
Lorraine, Andrew, Tacoma *	1.000	33	6	17	0	23	3
Lynch, Kevin, Salt Lake	1.000	2	0	1	0	1	0
Lyon, Brandon, Tucson	1.000	5	0	1	0	1	0
Mabeus, Christopher, Sacramento	.857	42	6	6	2	14	0
MacRae, Scott, Round Rock	1.000	16	2	7	0	9	0
Mahay, Ron, Oklahoma *	...	3	0	0	0	0	0
Mahomes, Pat, Las Vegas	.944	40	19	15	2	36	2
Majewski, Gary, New Orleans	1.000	3	2	1	0	3	0
Martin, Tom, Round Rock *	1.000	20	1	6	0	7	1
Martinez, Carlos, Albuquerque	1.000	2	0	1	0	1	0
Mathews, T.J., Round Rock	...	22	0	0	0	0	0
Mattioni, Nicholas, Sacramento	.750	7	0	3	1	4	0
McClaskey, Timothy, Round Rock	1.000	2	0	3	0	3	0
McClellan, Zachary, Colorado Springs	.900	44	4	5	1	10	1
McDaniel, Denton, Round Rock *	.667	18	0	2	1	3	0
McGlinchy, Kevin, Iowa	.900	18	5	4	1	10	1
McLeary, Marty, Portland	.947	41	10	8	1	19	1
Medders, Brandon, Tucson	1.000	36	0	7	0	7	0
Mendez, Adalberto, Iowa	...	3	0	0	0	0	0
Mercado, Hector, Oklahoma *	1.000	22	0	4	0	4	0
Mercedes, Jose, Iowa	1.000	10	0	1	0	1	0
Messenger, Randy, Albuquerque	.889	39	2	6	1	9	0
Meyer, Dan, Sacramento *	.867	19	6	7	2	15	0
Meyers, Mike, Nashville	1.000	33	6	11	0	17	1
Miadich, Bart, Albuquerque	.600	29	2	1	2	5	0
Miceli, Dan, Colorado Springs	...	5	0	0	0	0	0
Michalak, Chris, Tucson *	.976	26	11	30	1	42	2
Misch, Patrick, Fresno *	1.000	19	7	16	0	23	2
Mitre, Sergio, Iowa	.955	13	5	16	1	22	0
Molina, Gabe, Colorado Springs	1.000	12	1	2	0	3	1
Montero, Agustin, Oklahoma	1.000	4	0	1	0	1	0
Moreno, Victor, Sacramento	1.000	49	5	2	0	7	2
Moriarty, Mike, Iowa	...	2	0	0	0	0	0
Moseley, Dustin, Salt Lake	.947	17	6	12	1	19	2
Moss, Damian, Tacoma *	.960	25	3	21	1	25	0
Muessig, Jeffrey, Sacramento	...	1	0	0	0	0	0
Mullen, Scott, Tacoma *	...	1	0	0	0	0	0
Munter, Scott, Fresno	1.000	12	1	3	0	4	0
Murphy, William, Tucson *	.929	23	4	22	2	28	0
Murray, Arlington, Oklahoma *	...	2	0	0	0	0	0
Myers, Corey, Tucson	...	1	0	0	0	0	0
Nageotte, Clint, Tacoma	.875	19	1	6	1	8	0
Nall, Thomas, Las Vegas	.935	29	19	10	2	31	1
Nance, Shane, Tucson-Omaha	1.000	45	2	10	0	12	0
Narveson, Christopher, Memphis *	1.000	2	0	2	0	2	0
Neal, Blaine, Colorado Springs	...	1	0	0	0	0	0
Neu, Michael, Las Vegas	.960	35	12	12	1	25	3
Nieve, Fernando, Round Rock	.800	13	4	4	2	10	0
Nina, Elvin, Tucson	1.000	12	2	0	0	2	0
Nitkowski, C.J., New Orleans *	1.000	27	1	8	0	9	0
Nolen, Walt, Iowa	1.000	3	1	0	0	1	0
Norton, Phil, Round Rock-Iowa	.850	33	6	11	3	20	2
Novoa, Roberto, Iowa	1.000	19	0	7	0	7	0
Nunez, Vladimir, Oklahoma-Memphis-Tucson	1.000	49	2	4	0	6	2
Nussbeck, Mark, Memphis *	.833	19	3	2	1	6	0
Obermueller, Wes, Nashville	1.000	9	3	4	0	7	0
Ohman, Will, Iowa *	1.000	8	0	1	0	1	0
Oliver, Darren, Tucson-Iowa	1.000	7	1	8	0	9	1
Olson, Jason, Salt Lake	...	3	0	0	0	0	0
O'Malley, Ryan, Iowa *	.667	7	1	1	1	3	0
Oropesa, Eddie, Iowa *	...	7	0	0	0	0	0
Ortiz, Russ, Tucson	1.000	2	1	0	0	1	0
Osborne, Donovan, Albuquerque *	.933	14	3	11	1	15	1
Osoria, Franquelis, Las Vegas	1.000	40	3	4	0	7	1
Osuna, Antonio, New Orleans	.000	2	0	0	1	1	0
Oxspring, Chris, Portland	1.000	26	6	19	0	25	3
Parker, Christian, Colorado Springs	1.000	12	8	8	0	16	0
Paronto, Chad, Nashville	1.000	27	5	5	0	10	1
Patterson, Danny, Portland	1.000	9	1	2	0	3	0
Pearce, Josh, Memphis	1.000	24	3	3	0	6	0
Penny, Brad, Las Vegas	1.000	1	1	0	0	1	0
Peralta, Joel, Salt Lake *	1.000	19	2	0	0	2	0
Perez, Odalis, Las Vegas *	1.000	4	1	0	0	1	0
Perisho, Matt, Albuquerque *	.000	17	0	0	2	2	0
Petersen, Jeffrey, Fresno	...	2	0	0	0	0	0
Peterson, Adam, Tucson	.000	3	0	0	2	2	0
Phelps, Tommy, Nashville *	1.000	5	1	0	0	1	0
Phelps, Travis, Colorado Springs-Iowa	.833	25	0	5	1	6	0
Pickler, Jeff, Colorado Springs	1.000	1	1	0	0	1	0
Pignatiello, Carmen, Iowa *	1.000	22	1	7	0	8	1
Pineiro, Joel, Tacoma	1.000	1	0	1	0	1	0
Pinto, Renyel, Iowa *	1.000	6	0	4	0	4	0
Pizzaro, Melvin, Tacoma *	...	2	0	0	0	0	0
Polanco, Phillip, Portland	...	1	0	0	0	0	0
Pote, Lou, Oklahoma	1.000	14	2	0	0	2	0
Powell, Brian, New Orleans	.939	29	21	25	3	49	1
Pratt, Andy, Nashville *	.667	23	0	4	2	6	0
Prieto, Ariel, Albuquerque	.907	25	15	24	4	43	2
Prinz, Bret, Salt Lake	1.000	5	1	1	0	2	0
Prior, Mark, Iowa	...	1	0	0	0	0	0
Puffer, Brandon, Fresno	.875	54	3	4	1	8	0
Pulsipher, Bill, Memphis *	.600	25	0	9	6	15	2
Rall, Tim, Tacoma *	1.000	3	0	2	0	2	0
Ramirez, Edwar, Salt Lake	...	1	0	0	0	0	0
Ramirez, Erasmo, Oklahoma *	1.000	16	2	3	0	5	0
Ramirez, Santiago, Omaha	1.000	50	4	6	0	10	2
Ramos, Mario, Sacramento *	.750	49	3	6	3	12	0
Randall, Scott, Colorado Springs	.667	10	1	1	1	3	0
Randolph, Stephen, New Orleans-Fresno	1.000	36	3	6	0	9	2
Rauch, Jon, New Orleans	.500	7	1	0	1	2	0
Reames, Britt, Sacramento	.861	42	8	23	5	36	3
Redding, Tim, Portland	1.000	2	0	2	0	2	0
Regilio, Nick, Oklahoma	...	1	0	0	0	0	0
Reichert, Dan, Tacoma	...	2	0	0	0	0	0
Reina, Jesus, Fresno *	...	1	0	0	0	0	0
Reyes, Anthony, Memphis	.967	23	9	20	1	30	0
Rheinecker, John, Sacramento *	.846	7	3	8	2	13	0
Riedling, John, Albuquerque	.833	14	4	6	2	12	1
Riley, Matt, Oklahoma *	1.000	4	0	3	0	3	0
Robertson, James, Sacramento	1.000	3	0	1	0	1	0
Rodriguez, Jose, Albuquerque *	...	14	0	0	0	0	0
Rodriguez, Nerio, Memphis	.750	4	0	3	1	4	0
Rodriguez, Orlando, Las Vegas *	...	5	0	0	0	0	0
Rodriguez, Ricardo, Oklahoma	.938	13	12	3	1	16	0
Rodriguez, Wandy, Round Rock *	1.000	8	0	2	0	2	0
Rodriguez, Wilfredo, Oklahoma *	...	2	0	0	0	0	0
Rohlicek, Russel, Iowa *	.933	55	3	11	1	15	1
Roney, John, Oklahoma	.833	24	1	4	1	6	0
Rouwenhorst, Jonathon, Salt Lake *	1.000	25	2	6	0	8	1
Rowe, Steven, Oklahoma	1.000	8	1	3	0	4	0
Rupe, Josh, Oklahoma	.909	17	4	16	2	22	1
Rupe, Ryan, Las Vegas	.957	23	13	9	1	23	1
Rust, Evan, Memphis	.857	13	3	3	1	7	0
Saipe, Mike, Sacramento	1.000	27	6	6	0	12	0
Santana, Ervin, Salt Lake	1.000	3	1	0	0	1	1
Santana, Julio, Nashville	1.000	8	0	1	0	1	0
Santos, Alexandre, Sacramento	...	3	0	0	0	0	0
Sarfate, Dennis, Nashville	.500	2	1	0	1	2	0
Saunders, Joe, Salt Lake *	.944	9	2	15	1	18	2
Scarborough, Stephen, Nashville	1.000	4	0	2	0	2	0
Schmoll, Steve, Las Vegas	1.000	22	1	2	0	3	0
Schneider, Scott, Salt Lake	.875	36	6	8	2	16	2
Schroder, Christopher, New Orleans	1.000	19	2	2	0	4	0
Seay, Bobby, Colorado Springs *	1.000	17	1	3	0	4	0
Sedlacek, Shawn, Colorado Springs-Memphis	1.000	6	3	0	0	3	1
Sele, Aaron, Oklahoma	1.000	2	0	2	0	2	0
Serrano, Alex, Colorado Springs	1.000	21	2	7	0	9	0
Serrano, Jimmy, Sacramento	1.000	16	6	9	0	15	0

Player, Team	Pct.	G	PO	A	E	TC	DP
Sessions, Douglass, Salt Lake	.917	8	5	6	1	12	2
Sherrill, George, Tacoma *	1.000	22	1	3	0	4	0
Shibilo, Andy, Sacramento	...	3	0	0	0	0	0
Silva, Jesus, Tucson	1.000	2	0	1	0	1	0
Smith, Dan, New Orleans	1.000	24	1	2	0	3	0
Smith, Travis, Albuquerque	.923	18	16	8	2	26	2
Smyth, Steve, Sacramento *	...	10	0	0	0	0	0
Snare, Ryan, Oklahoma-Portland	1.000	23	4	6	0	10	0
Snyder, Kyle, Omaha	.909	15	5	5	1	11	0
Sodowsky, Clint, Albuquerque	1.000	6	0	1	0	1	0
Song, Seung, Fresno	1.000	10	3	2	0	5	0
Songster, Judson, Colorado Springs	1.000	1	0	1	0	1	0
Sonnier, Shawn, Omaha	1.000	19	1	3	0	4	0
Soriano, Rafael, Tacoma	1.000	5	0	1	0	1	0
Sparks, Steve, Portland-Sacramento	.957	15	5	17	1	23	0
Speier, Ryan, Colorado Springs	.833	45	4	6	2	12	0
Spiehs, Randall, Portland-Fresno	.667	22	1	1	1	3	0
Stamler, Keith, Oklahoma-Sacramento	1.000	22	1	3	0	4	0
Standridge, Jason, Oklahoma	1.000	15	5	5	0	10	1
Stark, Denny, Colorado Springs	.900	11	2	7	1	10	0
Stauffer, Tim, Portland	.952	13	11	9	1	21	0
Stemle, Steve, Omaha	1.000	14	0	3	0	3	2
Stetter, Mitchel, Nashville *	1.000	27	0	2	0	2	0
Stewart, Scott, Portland *	1.000	17	1	3	0	4	1
Stockman, Phillip, Tucson	.667	17	1	1	1	3	0
Stone, Ricky, Memphis	1.000	14	2	2	0	4	0
Strickland, Scott, Round Rock	1.000	15	1	0	0	1	0
Stults, Eric, Las Vegas *	1.000	15	4	11	0	15	1
Sullivan, Scott, Omaha	...	2	0	0	0	0	0
Sweeney, Brian, Portland	1.000	20	11	8	0	19	1
Sylvester, Billy, Sacramento	1.000	12	3	2	0	5	0
Tamayo, Ignacio, Omaha	.941	30	8	24	2	34	1
Tankersley, Dennis, Omaha	1.000	32	9	17	0	26	2
Taschner, Jack, Fresno *	.857	44	3	3	1	7	0
Tavares, Anderson, Iowa	...	2	0	0	0	0	0
Tejera, Michael, Oklahoma *	1.000	43	2	10	0	12	2
Teut, Nathan, Iowa *	...	2	0	0	0	0	0
Thomas, Evan, Salt Lake	1.000	20	4	10	0	14	0
Thomas, Jared, Tacoma *	.500	27	0	1	1	2	0
Thompson, Brad, Memphis	.833	9	3	2	1	6	2
Thompson, Chris, Tucson	...	1	0	0	0	0	0
Thompson, Derek, Las Vegas *	.714	4	1	4	2	7	0
Thompson, Justin, Oklahoma *	1.000	25	4	6	0	10	1
Thompson, Michael, Portland	1.000	9	3	8	0	11	1
Tolar, Kevin, Tucson *	1.000	27	0	3	0	3	1
Tollberg, Brian, Round Rock	.917	10	3	8	1	12	3
Totten, Heath, Las Vegas	1.000	20	7	12	0	19	1
Tovar, Angel, Portland	1.000	16	1	4	0	5	0
Tsao, Chin-hui, Colorado Springs	...	1	0	0	0	0	0
Tucker, T.J., New Orleans	1.000	2	1	1	0	2	0
Ugueto, Luis, Omaha	...	1	0	0	0	0	0
Valdes, Raul, Iowa *	.917	25	3	19	2	24	2
Valdez, Ismael, Albuquerque	1.000	1	0	2	0	2	1
Valverde, Jose, Tucson	...	2	0	0	0	0	0
Van Buren, Jermaine, Iowa	1.000	52	1	7	0	8	1
Vargas, Claudio, New Orleans	1.000	5	3	4	0	7	0
Venafro, Mike, Las Vegas *	.938	53	4	11	1	16	1
Veras, Jose, Oklahoma	1.000	57	4	11	0	15	1
Villafuerte, Brandon, Fresno	1.000	57	14	5	0	19	0
Villarreal, Oscar, Tucson	1.000	12	1	0	0	1	0
Wainwright, Adam, Memphis	.968	29	9	21	1	31	1
Walrond, Les, Albuquerque *	.955	15	5	16	1	22	2
Wasdin, John, Oklahoma	1.000	13	5	7	0	12	1
Watson, Mark, Salt Lake *	...	6	0	0	0	0	0
Wayne, Justin, Las Vegas	1.000	4	1	0	0	1	0
Weibl, Clint, Nashville	.889	39	6	2	1	9	0
Wellemeyer, Todd, Iowa	1.000	12	2	3	0	5	1
Whitaker, Brian, Portland	1.000	2	1	2	0	3	1
White, Gabe, Memphis *	1.000	8	0	2	0	2	0
White, Matt, New Orleans *	.931	35	6	21	2	29	1
Wilkerson, George, Omaha	1.000	36	0	10	0	10	0
Williams, Jerome, Fresno-Iowa	.800	10	2	6	2	10	0
Williams, Randy, Portland-Colorado Springs	.846	38	3	8	2	13	0
Williamson, Scott, Iowa	.500	6	0	1	1	2	0
Wilson, Brian, Fresno	...	9	0	0	0	0	0
Witasick, Jay, Colorado Springs	1.000	8	0	1	0	1	0
Woerman, Joseph, Tacoma	1.000	2	1	1	0	2	0
Wood, Kerry, Iowa	1.000	3	1	1	0	2	0
Wood, Mike, Omaha	1.000	2	2	1	0	3	0
Woods, Jake, Salt Lake *	1.000	15	0	4	0	4	0
Wylie, Mitch, Fresno	1.000	22	4	6	0	10	1
Yarnall, Ed, New Orleans *	1.000	19	1	12	0	13	0
Young, Jason, Colorado Springs	1.000	21	4	24	0	28	3
Ziegler, Michael, Sacramento	1.000	22	8	15	0	23	2
Zoccolillo, Peter, Memphis	...	1	0	0	0	0	0
Zumwalt, Sean, Nashville	1.000	9	1	0	0	1	0

PITCHERS WITH TWO OR MORE TEAMS

Player, Team	Pct.	G	PO	A	E	TC	DP
Almanza, Armando, Fresno *	...	2	0	0	0	0	0
Almanza, Armando, Tucson *	1.000	15	0	2	0	2	0
Almanza, Armando, Memphis	1.000	10	0	1	0	1	0
Anderson, Jimmy, Iowa *	.667	1	0	2	1	3	0
Anderson, Jimmy, Round Rock *	1.000	4	0	5	0	5	1
Bauer, Peter, Albuquerque	.923	15	7	5	1	13	0
Bauer, Peter, Round Rock	1.000	1	3	0	0	3	0
Bergman, Dusty, Salt Lake *	.800	44	5	3	2	10	0
Bergman, Dusty, Fresno *	...	3	0	0	0	0	0
Bumstead, Michael, Portland	.889	12	4	4	1	9	0
Bumstead, Michael, Tacoma	.800	13	1	3	1	5	0
Cunnane, Will, Iowa	.875	24	2	5	1	8	1
Cunnane, Will, Round Rock	1.000	27	3	3	0	6	0
Dawley, Joe, Portland	1.000	13	0	1	0	1	0
Dawley, Joe, Iowa	1.000	4	1	0	0	1	0
Evert, Brett, Tacoma *	...	8	0	0	0	0	0
Evert, Brett, Nashville *	1.000	13	3	3	0	6	0
Falkenborg, Brian, Portland	.857	28	2	4	1	7	0
Falkenborg, Brian, Memphis	1.000	13	1	2	0	3	0
Flannery, Michael, Albuquerque	1.000	14	2	1	0	3	0
Flannery, Michael, Tacoma	1.000	6	0	1	0	1	0
Foppert, Jesse, Fresno	1.000	10	2	2	0	4	0
Foppert, Jesse, Tacoma	1.000	6	1	4	0	5	0
Lee, Dave, Fresno	1.000	8	1	1	0	2	0
Lee, Dave, Memphis	...	4	0	0	0	0	0
Lopez, Aquilino, Las Vegas	1.000	27	5	2	0	7	1
Lopez, Aquilino, Colorado Springs	1.000	14	3	2	0	5	0
Nance, Shane, Tucson *	1.000	22	0	5	0	5	0
Nance, Shane, Omaha *	1.000	23	2	5	0	7	0
Norton, Phil, Round Rock *	.000	8	0	0	2	2	0
Norton, Phil, Iowa *	.944	25	6	11	1	18	2
Nunez, Vladimir, Oklahoma	1.000	17	1	0	0	1	1
Nunez, Vladimir, Memphis	1.000	17	0	2	0	2	1
Nunez, Vladimir, Tucson	1.000	15	1	2	0	3	0
Oliver, Darren, Tucson *	1.000	4	1	2	0	3	0
Oliver, Darren, Iowa *	1.000	3	0	6	0	6	1
Phelps, Travis, Colorado Springs	1.000	7	0	2	0	2	0
Phelps, Travis, Iowa	.750	18	0	3	1	4	0
Randolph, Stephen, New Orleans *	1.000	14	1	3	0	4	0
Randolph, Stephen, Fresno *	1.000	22	2	3	0	5	2
Sedlacek, Shawn, Colorado Springs	...	1	0	0	0	0	0
Sedlacek, Shawn, Memphis	1.000	5	3	0	0	3	1
Snare, Ryan, Oklahoma *	1.000	17	4	5	0	9	0
Snare, Ryan, Portland *	1.000	6	0	1	0	1	0
Sparks, Steve, Portland	1.000	3	2	3	0	5	0
Sparks, Steve, Sacramento	.944	12	3	14	1	18	0
Spiehs, Randall, Portland	1.000	12	1	1	0	2	0
Spiehs, Randall, Fresno	.000	10	0	0	1	1	0
Stamler, Keith, Oklahoma	1.000	16	0	1	0	1	0
Stamler, Keith, Sacramento	1.000	6	1	2	0	3	0
Williams, Jerome, Fresno	.800	6	1	3	1	5	0
Williams, Jerome, Iowa	.800	4	1	3	1	5	0
Williams, Randy, Portland *	.833	12	2	3	1	6	0
Williams, Randy, Colorado Springs *	.857	26	1	5	1	7	0

LEAGUE CHAMPIONS

Year	Team	Pct.	Year	Team	Pct.	Year	Team	Pct.
1903—	Los Angeles	.630	1909—	San Francisco	.623	1918—	Vernon	.569
1904—	Tacoma	.589	1910—	Portland	.567		Los Angeles (2nd)◆	.548
	Tacoma§	.571	1911—	Portland	.589	1919—	Vernon	.613
	Los Angeles§	.571	1912—	Oakland	.591	1920—	Vernon	.556
1905—	Tacoma	.583	1913—	Portland	.559	1921—	Los Angeles	.574
	Los Angeles*	.604	1914—	Portland	.574	1922—	San Francisco	.638
1906—	Portland	.657	1915—	San Francisco	.570	1923—	San Francisco	.617
1907—	Los Angeles	.608	1916—	Los Angeles	.601	1924—	Seattle	.545
1908—	Los Angeles	.585	1917—	San Francisco	.561	1925—	San Francisco	.643

Year	Team	Pct.
1926—	Los Angeles	.599
1927—	Oakland	.615
1928—	San Francisco*	.630
	Sacramento∞	.626
	San Francisco∞	.626
1929—	Mission	.643
	Hollywood*	.592
1930—	Los Angeles	.576
	Hollywood*	.650
1931—	Hollywood	.626
	San Francisco*	.608
1932—	Portland	.587
1933—	Los Angeles	.610
1934—	Los Angeles▼	.786
	Los Angeles▼	.689
1935—	Los Angeles	.648
	San Francisco*	.608
1936—	Portland‡	.549
1937—	Sacramento	.573
	San Diego (3rd)†	.545
1938—	Los Angeles	.590
	Sacramento (3rd)†	.537
1939—	Seattle	.589
	Sacramento (4th)†	.500
1940—	Seattle‡	.629
1941—	Seattle‡	.598
1942—	Sacramento	.590
	Seattle (3rd)†	.539
1943—	Los Angeles	.710
	S. Francisco (2nd)†	.574
1944—	Los Angeles	.586
	S. Francisco (3rd)†	.509
1945—	Portland	.622
	S. Francisco (4th)†	.525
1946—	San Francisco‡	.628
1947—	Los Angeles▲	.567
1948—	Oakland‡	.606
1949—	Hollywood‡	.583
1950—	Oakland	.590
1951—	Seattle‡	.593
1952—	Hollywood	.606
1953—	Hollywood	.589
1954—	San Diego■	.604
1955—	Seattle	.552
1956—	Los Angeles	.637
1957—	San Francisco	.601
1958—	Phoenix	.578
1959—	Salt Lake City	.552
1960—	Spokane	.601
1961—	Tacoma	.630
1962—	San Diego	.604
1963—	Spokane	.620
	Oklahoma City*	.632
1964—	Arkansas	.609
	San Diego*	.576
1965—	Oklahoma City	.628
	Portland	.547
1966—	Seattle*	.561
	Tulsa	.578
1967—	San Diego*	.574
	Spokane	.541
1968—	Tulsa*	.642
	Spokane	.586
1969—	Tacoma*	.589
	Eugene	.603
1970—	Spokane*	.644
	Hawaii	.671
1971—	Salt Lake City	.534
	Tacoma	.545
1972—	Albuquerque	.622
	Eugene	.534
1973—	Tucson	.583
	Spokane*	.563
1974—	Spokane*	.549
	Albuquerque	.535
1975—	Salt Lake City	.556
	Hawaii*	.611
1976—	Salt Lake City	.625
	Hawaii*	.531
1977—	Phoenix*	.579
	Hawaii	.541
1978—	Tacoma††	.584
	Albuquerque††	.557
1979—	Albuquerque	.581
	Salt Lake City‡‡	.541
1980—	Albuquerque	.578
	Hawaii	.539
1981—	Albuquerque*	.712
	Tacoma	.561
1982—	Albuquerque*	.594
	Spokane	.545
1983—	Albuquerque	.594
	Portland*	.528
1984—	Hawaii	.621
	Edmonton*	.486
1985—	Vancouver*	.522
	Phoenix	.563
1986—	Vancouver	.616
	Las Vegas*	.563
1987—	Calgary	.596
	Albuquerque*	.542
1988—	Vancouver	.599
	Las Vegas*	.529
1989—	Albuquerque	.563
	Vancouver*	.514
1990—	Albuquerque*	.641
	Edmonton	.553
1991—	Albuquerque	.580
	Tucson*	.564
1992—	Colorado Springs*	.596
	Portland	.576
1993—	Portland	.608
	Tucson*	.580
1994—	Albuquerque*	.597
	Vancouver	.542
1995—	Salt Lake	.549
	Colorado Springs*	.538
1996—	Edmonton*	.592
	Phoenix	.479
1997—	Phoenix	.615
	Edmonton*	.556
1998—	Iowa	.590
	New Orleans†	.535
1999—	Vancouver‡	.592
2000—	Salt Lake	.629
	Memphis‡	.576
2001—	Tacoma§§	.590
	New Orleans§§	.590
2002—	Las Vegas	.590
	Edmonton†	.579
2003—	Sacramento‡	.639
2004—	Sacramento†	.549
2005—	Nashville†	.521

*Won split-season playoff. †Won four-team playoff. ‡Won pennant and four-team playoff. §Tied for second-half title with Tacoma winning playoff. ∞Tied for second-half title, with Sacramento winning playoff. ▲Ended regular season in tie with San Francisco and won one-game playoff for pennant, then won four-club playoff. ◆Won playoff from first-place Vernon and awarded championship . ■Defeated Hollywood in one-game playoff for pennant. ▼Won both halves, no playoff. *League was divided into Northern, Southern divisions in 1963, 1969-70-71, and Eastern, Western divisions in 1964 through 1968 and 1972 through 1977, won two-team playoff. ††League divided into Eastern and Western divisions, Tacoma and Albuquerque declared co-champions following cancellation of four-team playoff due to continuing rain and wet grounds. ‡‡Won second-half title and defeated Hawaii in four-team playoff. §§Were entering finals of four-team playoff and were declared co-champions when Professional Baseball declared a stoppage of play.

EASTERN LEAGUE

LEAGUE OFFICE

President
Joe McEacharn

Address
30 Danforth St., Suite 208
Portland, ME 04101

Phone
207-761-2700

TEAMS

AKRON AEROS
General manager/vice president
Jeff Auman
Manager
Tim Bogar
Ballpark (capacity, surface)
Canal Park (9,097, grass)
Affiliation
Indians
Address
300 S. Main St.
Akron, OH 44308
Phone
330-253-5151

ALTOONA CURVE
General manager
Todd Parnell
Manager
Tim Leiper
Ballpark (capacity, surface)
Blair County Ballpark (7,200, grass)
Affiliation
Pirates
Address
1000 Park Avenue
Altoona, PA 16602
Phone
814-943-5400

BINGHAMTON METS
General manager
Scott Brown
Manager
To be announced
Ballpark (capacity, surface)
NYSEG Stadium (6,012, grass)
Affiliation
Mets
Address
211 Henry Street
Binghamton, NY 13901
Phone
607-723-6387

BOWIE BAYSOX
General manager
Brian Shallcross
Manager
Don Werner
Ballpark (capacity, surface)
Prince George's Stadium
(10,000, grass)
Affiliation
Orioles
Address
4101 NE Crain Highway
Bowie, MD 20716
Phone
301-805-6000

CONNECTICUT DEFENDERS
General manager
Jim Beaudoin
Manager
Dave Machemer
Ballpark (capacity, surface)
Thomas J. Dodd Memorial Stadium
(6,695, grass)
Affiliation
Giants
Address
14 Stott Ave.
Norwich, CT 06360
Phone
860-887-7962

ERIE SEAWOLVES
General manager
John Frey
Manager
Duffy Dyer
Ballpark (capacity, surface)
Jerry Uht Park (6,000, grass)
Affiliation
Tigers
Address
110 E. 10th Street
Erie, PA 16501
Phone
814-456-1300

HARRISBURG SENATORS
General manager
Todd Vander Woude
Manager
John Stearns
Ballpark (capacity, surface)
Commerce Bank Park/City Island (6,300,
grass)
Affiliation
Nationals
Address
RiverSide Stadium/City Island
Harrisburg, PA 17101
Phone
717-231-4444

NEW BRITAIN ROCK CATS
General manager/president
Bill Dowling
Manager
Riccardo Ingram
Ballpark (capacity, surface)
New Britain Stadium (6,146, grass)
Affiliation
Twins
Address
P.O. Box 1718
New Britain, CT 06050
Phone
860-224-8383

NEW HAMPSHIRE FISHER CATS
General manager
Shawn Smith
Manager
Doug Davis
Ballpark (capacity, surface)
Fisher Cats Ballpark (6,500, grass)
Affiliation
Blue Jays
Address
One Line Drive
Manchester, NH 03101
Phone
603-641-2005

PORTLAND SEA DOGS
General manager/president
Charlie Eshbach
Manager
Todd Claus
Ballpark (capacity, surface)
Hadlock Field (7,365, grass)
Affiliation
Red Sox
Address
271 Park Avenue
Portland, ME 04102
Phone
207-874-9300

READING PHILLIES
General manager
Chuck Domino
Manager
P.J. Forbes
Ballpark (capacity, surface)
First Energy Stadium (9,100, grass)
Affiliation
Phillies
Address
Route 61 South/1900 South Centre Ave.
Reading, PA 19605
Phone
610-375-8469

TRENTON THUNDER
General manager
Brad Taylor
Manager
Bill Masse
Ballpark (capacity, surface)
Samuel J. Plumeri Sr. Field at Mercer
County Waterfront Park (6,440, grass)
Affiliation
Yankees
Address
One Thunder Road
Trenton, NJ 08611
Phone
609-394-3300

CLASS AA *Eastern League*

2005 FINAL STANDINGS

NORTHERN DIVISION

Team	W	L	T	Pct.	GB
Trenton Thunder	74	68	-	0.521	2
Norwich Navigators	71	71	-	0.5	5
New Britain Rock Cats	70	72	-	0.493	6
New Hampshire Fisher Cats	68	74	-	0.479	8
Binghamton Mets	63	79	-	0.444	13

SOUTHERN DIVISION

Team	W	L	T	Pct.	GB
Akron Aeros	84	58	-	0.592	...
Altoona Curve	76	66	-	0.535	8
Bowie Baysox	74	68	-	0.521	10
Reading Phillies	69	73	-	0.486	15
Harrisburg Senators	64	78	-	0.451	20
Erie SeaWolves	63	79	-	0.444	21

COMPOSITE

CLUB (AFFILIATE), ABBREV	ARK	ALT	POR	BOW	TRE	NOR	NBR	REA	NHM	HAR	BIN	ERI	W	L	PCT	GB
Akron (Indians), AKR		13	6	13	4	3	4	5	3	11	11	11	84	58	.592	-
Altoona (Pirates), ALT	6	...	4	12	7	5	3	14	3	8	7	7	76	66	.535	8.0
Portland (Red Sox), POR	2	2	...	1	7	13	15	1	18	7	7	3	76	66	.535	8.0
Bowie (Orioles), BOW	7	6	8	...	4	8	5	10	3	8	3	12	74	68	.521	10.0
Trenton (Yankees), TRE	3	5	9	8	...	3	9	5	8	11	6	7	74	68	.521	10.0
Norwich (Giants), NOR	3	3	11	2	6	...	8	5	11	5	11	6	71	71	.500	13.0
New Britain (Twins), NBR	2	3	6	5	5	14	...	9	6	7	8	5	70	72	.493	14.0
Reading (Phillies), REA	10	8	5	6	11	3	5	...	2	5	4	10	69	73	.486	15.0
New Hampshire (Blue Jays), NHM	3	3	4	4	5	14	12	4	...	5	11	3	68	74	.479	16.0
Harrisburg (Nationals), HAR	5	9	1	9	5	2	4	11	4	...	4	10	64	78	.451	20.0
Binghamton (Mets), BIN	6	3	9	3	7	5	6	3	12	4	...	5	63	79	.444	21.0
Erie (Tigers), ERI	11	11	3	5	7	1	1	6	4	7	7	...	63	79	.444	21.0

Major league affiliations in parentheses.

PLAYOFFS: Semifinals: Portland defeated Trenton, three games to two, and Akron defeated Altoona, three games to two. Finals: Akron defeated Portland, three games to one.

REGULAR-SEASON ATTENDANCE: Erie, 233,415. Akron, 455,056. Bowie, 314,277. Altoona, 390,273. New Hampshire, 279,556. Binghamton, 222,243. Norwich, 170,686. Reading, 469,105. New Britain, 337,687. Portland, 396,277. Harrisburg, 264,718. Trenton, 410,926. All-Star Game (at Portland), 6,975. League total, 3,944,185. Postseason (14 games), 61,246.

MANAGERS: Erie, Duffy Dyer. Akron, Torey Lovullo. Bowie, Don Werner. Altoona, Tony Beasley. New Hampshire, Mike Basso. Binghamton, Jack Lind. Norwich, Dave Machemer. Reading, Steve Swisher. New Britain, Stan Cliburn. Portland, Todd Claus. Harrisburg, Keith Bodie. Trenton, Bill Masse.

ALL-STAR TEAM: 1B-Shelley Duncan, Trenton. 2B-Dustin Pedroia, Portland. 3B-Jose Bautista, Altoona. SS-Hanley Ramirez, Portland. UTIL-Don Kelly, Erie. OF-Dan Ortmeier, Norwich. OF-Chris Roberson, Reading. OF-Alexander Romero, New Britain. C-Mike Jacobs, Binghamton. DH-Randy Ruiz, Reading. RHP-Joel Zumaya, Erie. LHP-Jon Lester, Portland. Relief Pitcher-Edwin Almonte, Erie. Most Valuable Player-Mike Jacobs, Binghamton. Pitcher of the Year-Jon Lester, Portland. Playoffs Most Valuable Player-Nathan Panther, Akron. Manager of the Year-Torey Lovullo, Akron.

2005 BATTING

TEAM

Team	G	TPA	AB	R	H	TB	2B	3B	HR	RBI	SH	SF	HP	BB	IBB	SO	SB	CS	GDP	LOB	ShO	Avg.	OBP	Slg.
Binghamton	142	5416	4789	655	1291	2031	269	36	133	610	95	38	61	433	27	1126	107	57	75	2039	6	.270	.335	.424
Akron	142	5434	4824	726	1276	2061	244	44	151	657	59	37	49	420	17	1094	144	66	89	2006	5	..265	.333	.427
New Britain	142	5333	4742	647	1256	1867	266	15	105	599	69	37	82	402	20	922	61	53	109	2084	14	.265	.331	.394
Altoona	142	5449	4801	671	1262	1997	236	34	141	617	66	36	61	485	20	1081	155	46	99	2084	6	.263	.336	.416
Erie	142	5448	4833	666	1271	1936	249	37	114	617	38	43	77	455	17	1076	73	47	90	2227	6	.263	.333	.401
Reading	142	5466	4871	614	1269	1930	225	29	126	569	64	33	63	435	39	1048	101	63	116	2135	10	.261	.327	.396
Norwich	142	5231	4645	615	1187	1751	225	24	97	558	63	37	86	399	18	999	160	67	110	2002	12	.256	.324	.377
Portland	142	5365	4751	643	1217	1911	274	33	118	587	25	47	62	471	21	1004	102	50	105	2110	8	.256	.328	.402
Harrisburg	142	5348	4754	628	1211	1902	241	24	134	580	53	40	60	441	20	989	90	70	96	2007	10	.255	.323	.400
Bowie	142	5323	4724	579	1198	1739	240	23	85	527	60	40	49	450	20	968	86	52	110	2122	9	.254	.322	.368
Trenton	142	5393	4813	653	1212	1878	231	24	129	605	34	38	62	446	16	1047	88	38	117	2181	12	.252	.321	.390
New Hampshire	142	5197	4734	540	1178	1792	254	21	106	499	35	27	38	363	18	1131	63	34	107	1945	16	.249	.306	.379

INDIVIDUAL

TOP QUALIFIERS FOR BATTING CHAMPIONSHIP

Minimum 383 plate appearances. *Lefthanded batter. †Switch-hitter.

Player, Team	G	TPA	AB	R	H	TB	2B	3B	HR	RBI	SH	SF	HP	BB	IBB	SO	SB	CS	GDP	Avg.	OBP	Slg.
Ruiz, Randy, Reading	89	385	344	59	120	230	29	0	27	89	0	5	6	30	11	87	0	2	6	.349	.405	.669
Jacobs, Mike, Binghamton *	117	482	433	66	139	255	37	2	25	93	1	6	7	35	6	94	1	2	11	.321	.376	.589
Roberson, Christopher, Reading	139	611	553	90	172	257	24	8	15	70	5	4	9	40	2	112	34	14	6	.311	.365	.465
Cosby, Robert, New Hampshire	115	458	428	56	132	217	34	0	17	68	2	2	2	24	1	77	2	1	4	.308	.346	.507
Deeds, Douglas, New Britain *	133	561	493	77	150	236	34	2	16	82	1	3	8	56	3	119	2	4	7	.304	.382	.479
Romero, Alexander, New Britain *	139	560	509	65	153	233	31	2	15	77	4	3	8	36	4	69	12	11	12	.301	.354	.458
Bergeron, Peter, Bowie *	91	401	348	54	103	136	14	2	5	33	14	4	1	34	3	82	13	6	1	.296	.357	.391
Valderrama, Carlos, Norwich	130	540	493	61	145	208	33	3	8	58	2	4	6	34	2	84	29	7	11	.294	.345	.422
Fahey, Brandon, Bowie *	139	578	502	63	146	184	21	4	3	47	22	6	4	44	0	71	17	8	12	.291	.349	.367
Tejeda, Juan, Erie	122	523	470	64	137	210	27	2	14	82	0	5	7	41	1	86	2	4	7	.291	.354	.447
Osborn, Patrick, Akron	129	525	478	66	137	187	18	1	10	63	2	1	7	37	0	66	14	4	18	.287	.346	.391
Torres, Eider, Akron †	108	503	452	73	129	184	27	5	6	57	19	5	11	16	0	66	33	9	5	.285	.322	.407
Bautista, Jose, Altoona	117	507	445	63	126	224	27	1	23	90	2	2	10	48	2	101	7	3	9	.283	.364	.503
Durbin, Christopher, Portland	103	440	394	55	111	180	31	1	12	57	1	5	5	35	2	67	3	4	12	.282	.344	.457
Bonifay, Joshua, Altoona	103	416	376	53	106	209	22	3	25	77	0	5	2	33	2	110	0	1	6	.282	.339	.556
Matienzo, Daniel, New Britain	138	586	531	81	150	259	36	2	23	87	0	7	8	40	4	112	1	1	20	.282	.338	.488
Airoso, Alvin, Erie	99	435	381	67	107	204	9	1	22	71	0	4	10	38	1	105	2	2	7	.281	.358	.535

– 443 –

Player, Team	G	TPA	AB	R	H	TB	2B	3B	HR	RBI	SH	SF	HP	BB	IBB	SO	SB	CS	GDP	Avg.	OBP	Slg.
Davis, Rajai, Altoona	123	561	499	82	140	184	22	5	4	34	6	1	12	43	2	76	45	9	6	.281	.351	.369
Fleming, Ryan, Reading *	126	490	431	55	121	182	19	3	12	58	6	3	2	48	2	62	13	10	6	.281	.353	.422
Gonzalez, Edgar, Harrisburg	101	395	340	41	95	150	25	3	8	50	2	6	5	42	1	75	5	7	7	.279	.361	.441
Jimenez, Luis Antonio, New Britain *	116	478	431	61	120	199	29	1	16	69	0	0	2	45	1	104	3	2	11	.278	.349	.462

DEPARTMENTAL LEADERS: G—Duncan, 142. AB—Roberson, 553. R—Roberson, 90. H—Roberson, 172. TB—Duncan, 263. 2B—Jacobs, 37. 3B—Lydon, 13. HR—Duncan, 34. RBI—Jacobs, 93. SH—Fahey, 22. SF—Concepcion Jr. and Moss, 8. HP—Ortmeier, 21. BB—Lewis, 69. IBB—Ruiz, 11. SO—Van Every, 155. SB—Davis, 45. SB—Thompson, 45. CS—Lydon and Roberson, 14. GIDP—Labarbera and Matienzo, 20. OBP—Ruiz, .405. Slg.—Ruiz, .669.

ALL PLAYERS

*Lefthanded batter. †Switch-hitter.

Player, Team	G	TPA	AB	R	H	TB	2B	3B	HR	RBI	SH	SF	HP	BB	IBB	SO	SB	CS	GDP	Avg.	OBP	Slg.
Aardsma, David, Norwich	4	6	5	1	1	2	1	0	0	1	0	0	0	0	0	1	0	0	0	.200	.200	.400
Accardo, Jeremy, Norwich	4	0	0	0	0	0	0	0	0	0	...	0	0	0	0	0	0	0	0	...	...	...
Acuna, Ronald, New Hampshire	108	438	400	48	98	132	27	2	1	31	5	3	5	25	1	89	12	3	15	.245	.296	.330
Airoso, Alvin, Erie	99	435	381	67	107	204	29	1	22	71	0	4	10	38	1	105	2	2	7	.281	.358	.535
Alfonzo, Eliezer, Norwich	49	189	176	30	55	91	9	0	9	31	0	1	4	8	2	39	1	0	5	.313	.354	.517
Almonte, Edwin, Erie	1	0	0	0	0	0	0	0	0	0	...	0	0	0	0	0	0	0	0	...	...	...
Alvarez, Gerardo, Bowie	7	25	23	4	6	8	2	0	0	1	0	0	1	1	0	5	0	1	1	.261	.320	.348
Anderson, Luke, Norwich	4	0	0	0	0	0	0	0	0	0	0	0	0	0	0	0	0	0	0	...	...	...
Arroyo, Rafael, Binghamton	4	14	12	2	2	2	0	0	0	1	0	0	1	1	0	5	0	0	0	.167	.286	.167
Artiles, Carlos, Trenton *	1	0	0	0	0	0	0	0	0	0	0	0	0	0	0	0	0	0	0	...	...	...
Athas, Jamie, Norwich *	45	157	141	19	37	53	6	2	2	8	4	1	1	10	0	34	7	0	2	.262	.314	.376
Aubrey, Robert, Akron *	28	119	106	17	30	49	5	1	4	20	0	3	3	7	2	18	1	0	3	.283	.336	.462
Bacani, David, Binghamton	90	309	262	35	77	114	18	2	5	42	8	3	6	30	0	56	3	6	5	.294	.375	.435
Bailey, Jeffrey, Portland	43	161	132	21	33	61	7	0	7	26	1	0	8	20	0	36	3	1	2	.250	.381	.462
Bailie, Stefan, Portland	35	137	129	9	19	39	5	0	5	11	0	0	1	7	1	47	1	0	7	.147	.197	.302
Baldiris, Aarom, Binghamton	131	557	495	69	136	206	35	1	11	63	9	2	6	45	2	81	7	1	6	.275	.341	.416
Bannister, Brian, Binghamton	6	15	12	1	3	5	2	0	0	3	3	0	0	0	0	2	0	0	0	.250	.250	.417
Barker, Kevin, New Hampshire *	52	217	185	18	47	78	11	1	6	27	0	3	1	28	2	42	1	2	2	.254	.350	.422
Barthelemy, Ryan, Reading *	117	380	358	39	85	150	25	2	12	35	0	3	3	16	2	90	1	1	10	.237	.274	.419
Bauer, Gregory, Reading	2	0	0	0	0	0	0	0	0	0	0	0	0	0	0	0	0	0	0	...	...	...
Bautista, Jose, Altoona	117	507	445	63	126	224	27	1	23	90	2	2	10	48	2	101	7	3	9	.283	.364	.503
Begg, Christopher, Norwich	7	13	9	1	3	3	0	0	0	1	3	0	0	1	0	2	0	0	0	.333	.400	.333
Belcher, Jason, Harrisburg *	14	45	41	2	5	9	1	0	1	4	0	1	1	2	0	8	0	0	2	.122	.178	.220
Bell, Rick, New Britain	44	164	149	14	36	50	6	1	2	13	1	1	1	12	1	36	0	0	5	.242	.301	.336
Benavidez, Julian, Norwich	38	108	103	8	15	33	3	0	5	13	0	0	1	4	1	35	0	1	2	.146	.185	.320
Bergeron, Peter, Bowie *	91	401	348	54	103	136	14	2	5	33	14	4	1	34	3	82	13	6	1	.296	.357	.391
Bergmann, Jay, Harrisburg	5	2	2	0	0	0	0	0	0	0	0	0	0	0	0	2	0	0	0	.000	.000	.000
Boeve, Adam, Altoona	47	185	160	24	46	72	9	1	5	23	1	1	1	22	1	54	5	2	5	.288	.375	.450
Bonifay, Joshua, Altoona	103	416	376	53	106	209	22	3	25	77	0	5	2	33	2	110	0	1	6	.282	.339	.556
Borner, Brady, Altoona *	21	12	9	1	2	2	0	0	0	0	2	0	0	1	0	1	0	0	0	.222	.300	.222
Borowiak, Zachary, Portland	6	20	20	1	3	4	1	0	0	0	0	0	0	0	0	3	1	0	0	.150	.150	.200
Bouknight, Kip, Harrisburg	3	2	2	0	0	0	0	0	0	0	0	0	0	0	0	2	0	0	0	.000	.000	.000
Bourn, Michael, Reading *	135	614	544	80	146	198	18	8	6	44	4	0	3	63	5	123	38	12	2	.268	.348	.364
Bowie, Micah, Harrisburg *	4	1	1	0	0	0	0	0	0	0	0	0	0	0	0	1	0	0	0	.000	.000	.000
Bramasco, Leslie, Reading	3	3	1	1	0	0	0	0	0	0	0	0	1	1	0	0	0	0	0	.000	.667	.000
Bray, Bill, Harrisburg *	1	1	1	0	0	0	0	0	0	0	0	0	0	0	0	0	0	0	0	.000	.000	.000
Bridges, Donnie, Harrisburg	1	3	2	0	0	0	0	0	0	0	1	0	0	0	0	1	0	0	1	.000	.333	.000
Broadway, Larry, Harrisburg *	52	207	186	29	50	100	14	0	12	34	0	3	1	17	1	37	0	0	6	.269	.329	.538
Brown, Dee, Trenton-Harrisburg	56	220	195	20	34	63	8	0	7	22	0	2	7	16	1	50	2	4	3	.174	.259	.323
Brown, Jason, Trenton	51	175	153	20	38	58	6	1	4	19	2	1	2	17	0	46	0	1	6	.248	.329	.379
Buckley, James, Portland	50	149	129	13	25	42	8	0	3	11	0	1	1	18	1	55	1	0	2	.194	.295	.326
Bucktrot, Keith, Reading *	2	4	3	0	0	0	0	0	0	0	0	0	0	1	0	3	0	0	0	.000	.250	.000
Burke, Erick, Reading *	14	4	4	0	0	0	0	0	0	0	0	0	0	0	0	1	0	0	0	.000	.000	.000
Burres, Brian, Norwich *	6	14	10	0	0	0	0	0	0	0	2	0	1	1	0	4	0	0	0	.000	.167	.000
Buscher, Brian, Norwich *	64	247	215	19	49	62	8	1	1	23	0	6	6	20	0	36	5	3	10	.228	.304	.288
Buttler, Victor, Altoona *	25	95	83	15	26	31	3	1	0	7	1	0	1	10	1	10	6	2	1	.313	.394	.373
Butto, Francisco, Reading	12	3	3	0	1	1	0	0	0	0	0	0	0	0	0	2	0	0	0	.333	.333	.333
Cabrera, Melky, Trenton †	106	464	426	57	117	175	22	3	10	60	1	5	4	28	2	72	11	2	11	.275	.322	.411
Caligiuri, Jay, Binghamton	109	424	373	50	88	159	20	3	15	50	1	5	7	38	0	92	1	1	5	.236	.314	.426
Camacaro, Armando, Akron	34	118	105	12	27	39	3	0	3	13	2	1	4	6	0	25	3	2	3	.257	.319	.371
Cameron, Ryan, Reading	24	1	0	0	0	0	0	0	0	0	1	0	0	0	0	0	0	0	0	...	...	...
Candelario, Eddie, Altoona	4	9	8	0	0	0	0	0	0	0	0	0	0	1	0	4	0	0	0	.000	.111	.000
Cannizaro, Andrew, Trenton	54	219	202	28	50	62	12	0	0	20	1	1	4	11	0	19	5	0	4	.248	.298	.307
Cannon, Rhame, New Hampshire *	47	181	170	15	42	78	13	1	7	23	0	0	1	10	1	58	2	0	4	.247	.293	.459
Capps, Matt, Altoona	3	0	0	0	0	0	0	0	0	0	0	0	0	0	0	0	0	0	0	...	...	...
Cardona, Javier, Akron	15	59	52	7	15	27	3	0	3	13	1	1	0	5	0	9	0	0	2	.288	.345	.519
Carson, Matt, Trenton	28	103	99	10	19	27	5	0	1	5	2	0	2	0	0	25	2	3	2	.192	.208	.273
Castellano, John, Reading	6	24	20	2	7	8	1	0	0	3	1	0	0	3	0	4	0	0	0	.350	.435	.400
Castro, Ramon A., Harrisburg	34	146	130	27	37	77	9	2	9	30	1	1	0	14	1	22	1	1	2	.285	.352	.592
Cates, Gary, Bowie	30	105	93	13	21	26	5	0	0	9	0	2	0	10	0	11	5	2	3	.226	.295	.280
Chantres, Carlos, Reading	11	18	14	1	2	6	1	0	1	3	0	0	1	4	0	8	0	0	0	.143	.300	.429
Chaves, Brandon, Altoona †	52	194	172	20	37	47	6	2	0	8	3	0	1	16	1	38	2	2	4	.215	.288	.273
Chavez, Dirimo, Portland	2	5	5	0	0	0	0	0	0	0	0	0	0	0	0	0	0	0	0	.000	.000	.000
Chenard, Kenneth, Binghamton	7	14	13	0	2	2	0	0	0	0	0	0	0	1	0	6	0	0	0	.154	.214	.154
Chiaffredo, Paul, Altoona	8	32	30	4	8	15	4	0	1	7	1	0	0	1	0	11	0	0	0	.267	.290	.500
Chiaravalloti, Vito, New Hampshire	45	168	148	16	35	52	8	0	3	18	0	2	3	15	1	32	1	0	5	.236	.315	.351
Chiasson, Scott, Norwich	2	0	0	0	0	0	0	0	0	0	...	0	0	0	0	0	0	0	0	...	...	...
Childress, Daylan, New Britain	1	1	1	0	0	0	0	0	0	0	0	0	0	0	0	0	0	0	0	.000	.000	.000
Church, Ryan, Harrisburg *	4	18	18	2	5	6	1	0	0	0	0	0	0	0	0	5	0	0	0	.278	.278	.333

Player, Team	G	TPA	AB	R	H	TB	2B	3B	HR	RBI	SH	SF	HP	BB	IBB	SO	SB	CS	GDP	Avg.	OBP	Slg.
Clark, Howie, Altoona *	31	130	110	15	41	50	3	0	2	13	0	1	0	19	0	5	2	1	1	.373	.462	.455
Clements, Zachary, Binghamton	57	187	178	12	40	48	8	0	0	10	3	0	0	6	0	48	0	2	2	.225	.250	.270
Clendenin, Morgan, Bowie *	44	154	150	19	37	66	8	0	7	16	0	0	2	2	0	49	0	0	2	.247	.266	.440
Cliffords, Benjamin, Bowie *	93	379	315	36	76	100	19	1	1	31	8	4	1	51	3	68	8	7	6	.241	.345	.317
Coleman, Michael, Trenton	42	174	151	20	40	77	8	1	9	34	0	3	2	18	0	41	0	0	1	.265	.345	.510
Concepcion, Alberto, Portland	101	375	329	42	82	121	19	1	6	45	2	8	3	33	0	86	3	3	5	.249	.316	.368
Connolly, Michael, Altoona *	7	12	9	0	0	0	0	0	0	0	0	2	0	1	0	2	0	0	0	.000	.100	.000
Cooper, Jason, Akron *	57	245	205	41	52	98	9	2	11	42	0	4	6	30	1	67	3	2	5	.254	.359	.478
Cordero, Wil, Harrisburg	2	8	8	0	4	6	2	0	0	1	0	0	0	0	0	1	0	0	0	.500	.500	.750
Cordido, Julio, Norwich	101	302	272	35	57	84	9	0	6	29	6	3	4	17	2	53	3	2	10	.210	.264	.309
Cortes, Jorge, Altoona *	110	425	363	50	94	132	18	1	6	49	4	5	4	49	4	81	2	1	6	.259	.349	.364
Cortez, Jose, Reading †	4	12	10	0	1	1	0	0	0	0	1	0	0	1	0	3	0	0	1	.100	.182	.100
Cosby, Robert, New Britain	115	458	428	56	132	217	34	0	17	68	2	2	2	24	1	77	2	1	4	.308	.346	.507
Cota, Carlo, New Hampshire	38	158	144	21	36	54	8	2	2	17	2	1	2	9	0	45	1	0	0	.250	.301	.375
Crowe, Trevor, Akron †	3	10	10	1	1	1	0	0	0	0	0	0	0	0	0	3	0	0	0	.100	.100	.100
Crozier, Eric, Trenton *	34	134	121	13	21	36	6	0	3	18	2	1	1	9	0	52	1	2	2	.174	.235	.298
Cruz, Jose, Trenton	3	7	5	1	2	3	1	0	0	1	0	0	1	0	1	0	0	0	.400	.500	.600
Curry, Christopher, Norwich	72	248	228	31	50	89	12	0	9	26	6	0	4	10	1	57	1	1	1	.219	.264	.390
Davenport, Ulyses, New Hampshire *	95	383	359	34	97	151	22	1	10	38	1	1	1	21	1	66	2	2	10	.270	.312	.421
Davis, Allen, Reading *	10	23	13	1	1	1	0	0	0	2	8	0	0	2	0	5	0	0	0	.077	.200	.077
Davis, Rajai, Altoona	123	561	499	82	140	184	22	5	4	34	6	1	12	43	2	76	45	9	6	.281	.351	.369
Day, Zach, Harrisburg	1	2	2	0	1	1	0	0	0	0	0	0	0	0	0	1	0	0	0	.500	.500	.500
Deaton, Kevin, Binghamton	1	1	1	1	1	2	1	0	0	0	0	0	0	0	0	0	0	0	0	1.000	1.000	2.000
Deeds, Douglas, New Britain *	133	561	493	77	150	236	34	2	16	82	1	3	8	56	3	119	2	4	7	.304	.382	.479
Dement, Daniel, Harrisburg	71	298	268	42	88	155	23	1	14	44	2	4	2	22	0	65	2	0	4	.328	.378	.578
Deschaine, James, Reading	125	437	389	47	94	166	22	1	16	62	0	3	9	36	1	67	2	2	13	.242	.318	.427
Devey, Philip, Reading *	1	1	1	0	0	0	0	0	0	0	0	0	0	0	0	0	0	0	0	.000	.000	.000
Ditter, Brad, Harrisburg *	3	12	11	0	3	4	1	0	0	1	0	0	0	1	0	6	0	0	0	.273	.333	.364
Dorta, Melvin, Harrisburg	121	460	408	56	103	152	16	0	11	50	11	3	3	35	1	46	22	13	6	.252	.314	.373
Duenas, Yobal, Trenton	76	271	258	28	70	101	16	3	3	28	0	1	1	11	1	47	0	5	3	.271	.303	.391
Duncan, David, Trenton	142	606	537	86	129	263	28	2	34	92	0	2	11	56	3	140	3	2	14	.240	.323	.490
Duncan, Eric, Trenton *	126	520	451	60	106	184	15	3	19	61	2	4	4	59	3	136	9	3	9	.235	.326	.408
Duncan, Jeff, Binghamton *	87	319	278	33	68	100	9	4	5	26	1	2	1	37	1	63	11	4	6	.245	.333	.360
Durbin, Christopher, Portland	103	440	394	55	111	180	31	1	12	57	1	5	5	35	2	67	3	4	12	.282	.344	.457
Echols, Justin, Harrisburg	11	13	12	0	1	1	0	0	0	0	1	0	0	0	0	4	0	0	0	.083	.083	.083
Edwards, Bryan, Binghamton	9	7	6	0	0	0	0	0	0	0	1	0	0	0	0	2	0	0	0	.000	.000	.000
Eldred, Brad, Altoona	21	93	84	22	28	73	6	0	13	27	0	1	0	8	1	25	1	1	0	.333	.387	.869
Emmerick, Joshua, Harrisburg	44	154	133	9	25	30	5	0	0	7	1	0	3	17	0	51	1	0	6	.188	.294	.226
Espinosa, David, Erie †	112	506	431	66	113	177	21	8	9	40	1	4	4	66	3	109	11	5	1	.262	.362	.411
Evans, Tom, Altoona	100	405	338	62	94	169	24	3	15	55	1	7	8	51	1	91	8	3	14	.278	.379	.500
Fahey, Brandon, Bowie *	139	578	502	63	146	184	21	4	3	47	22	6	4	44	0	71	17	8	12	.291	.349	.367
Feliciano, Jesus, Harrisburg *	87	347	322	50	90	113	13	2	2	24	6	3	2	14	0	35	10	6	7	.280	.311	.351
Fesh, Sean, Reading *	4	1	1	0	0	0	0	0	0	0	0	0	0	0	0	0	0	0	0	.000	.000	.000
Fleming, Ryan, Reading *	126	490	431	55	121	182	19	3	12	58	6	3	2	48	2	62	13	10	6	.281	.353	.422
Francia, Juan, Erie †	72	331	300	38	87	117	9	6	3	27	7	2	5	17	0	43	15	7	2	.290	.336	.390
Francisco, Louis, Akron	83	352	323	45	99	153	19	7	7	46	2	1	2	24	1	59	15	4	4	.307	.357	.474
Frandsen, Kevin, Norwich	33	142	129	22	37	51	8	0	2	20	2	1	6	4	0	14	7	3	3	.287	.336	.395
Freire, Alejandro, Bowie	3	14	13	0	5	5	0	0	0	2	0	1	0	0	0	1	0	0	2	.385	.357	.385
Fulse, Sheldon, Portland †	60	188	166	21	29	48	9	2	2	15	2	2	1	17	0	50	14	7	3	.175	.253	.289
Galarraga, Armando, Harrisburg	3	5	3	0	0	0	0	0	0	1	0	0	1	0	0	2	0	0	0	.000	.250	.000
Garcia, Anderson, Binghamton	9	1	1	0	0	0	0	0	0	0	0	0	0	0	0	1	0	0	0	.000	.000	.000
Garcia, James, Norwich	10	7	4	0	0	0	0	0	0	0	0	0	0	1	0	2	0	0	0	.000	.200	.000
Garcia, Yunir, Binghamton	4	13	12	1	3	4	1	0	0	2	0	0	0	1	0	4	0	0	0	.250	.308	.333
Gettis, Byron, Erie	69	284	252	44	69	110	12	1	9	40	1	0	8	23	2	81	3	3	8	.274	.353	.437
Giarratano, Tony, Erie †	89	389	346	40	92	129	22	3	3	32	3	3	5	32	0	75	12	5	9	.266	.334	.373
Gil, David, Harrisburg	3	2	1	1	1	3	0	1	0	0	1	0	0	0	0	0	0	0	0	1.000	1.000	3.000
Gil, Geronimo, Bowie	3	9	7	2	3	3	0	0	0	1	0	0	1	1	0	1	0	0	0	.429	.556	.429
Gonzalez, Daniel, Reading †	56	203	179	13	39	52	5	1	2	16	2	1	3	18	0	41	0	0	5	.218	.299	.291
Gonzalez, Edgar, Harrisburg	101	395	340	41	95	150	25	3	8	50	2	6	5	42	1	75	5	7	7	.279	.361	.441
Gorzelanny, Tom, Altoona *	11	22	18	1	1	1	0	0	0	0	2	0	0	2	0	11	0	0	0	.056	.150	.056
Gradoville, Timothy, Reading	72	250	229	19	47	61	6	1	2	14	2	3	2	14	0	73	1	0	4	.205	.254	.266
Grindell, Nathan, Reading	49	182	158	16	39	58	10	0	3	16	0	3	1	20	1	35	1	2	5	.247	.330	.367
Guerrero, Cristian, Harrisburg	112	358	329	45	88	152	12	2	16	56	1	0	4	24	4	106	14	5	9	.267	.325	.462
Guillen, Rodolfo, Trenton	28	114	109	12	28	36	2	0	2	8	0	0	0	5	1	20	0	1	5	.257	.289	.330
Gutierrez, Franklin, Akron	95	426	383	70	100	162	25	2	11	42	1	5	7	30	1	77	14	4	7	.261	.322	.423
Gutierrez, Jannio, New Britain	1	1	1	0	0	0	0	0	0	0	0	0	0	0	0	0	0	0	0	.000	.000	.000
Guzman, Javier, Altoona †	68	279	263	27	62	82	9	1	3	24	4	2	0	10	0	46	8	5	9	.236	.262	.312
Hafner, Travis, Akron *	3	11	9	0	0	0	0	0	0	0	0	0	0	2	0	3	0	0	0	.000	.182	.000
Hall, Victor, Binghamton *	64	194	179	20	37	62	6	2	5	21	3	2	2	8	0	51	7	1	0	.207	.246	.346
Hamels, Colbert, Reading *	1	3	3	0	1	1	0	0	0	0	0	0	0	0	0	0	0	0	0	.333	.333	.333
Hamman, Corey, Erie *	1	0	0	0	0	0	0	0	0	0	0	0	0	0	0	0	0	0	0	...	...	...
Hammond, Joseph, Bowie	115	468	424	53	118	169	18	3	9	49	1	5	1	37	3	78	5	2	15	.278	.334	.399
Hammonds, Jeffrey, Harrisburg	2	8	6	1	1	2	1	0	0	1	0	0	1	1	0	1	0	0	1	.167	.375	.333
Hamulack, Tim, Binghamton *	4	0	0	0	0	0	0	0	0	0	0	0	0	0	0	0	0	0	0	...	...	...
Hannahan, John, Erie *	7	26	22	1	3	3	0	0	0	1	0	0	0	4	0	8	0	0	0	.136	.269	.136
Harper, Brett, Binghamton *	67	256	227	37	62	121	11	0	16	42	0	1	2	26	3	85	0	0	6	.273	.352	.533
Harts, Jeremy, Altoona †	10	3	3	0	0	0	0	0	0	0	0	0	0	0	0	0	0	0	0	.000	.000	.000
Hassey, Brad, New Hampshire	96	335	305	30	67	85	14	2	0	15	7	1	0	22	0	56	1	4	3	.220	.271	.279
Haynes, Charles, Harrisburg	101	405	359	63	103	190	18	3	21	63	0	2	6	21	0	54	0	1	12	.274	.321	.505
Hernandez, Anderson, Binghamton †	66	296	273	46	89	126	14	1	7	24	7	1	1	14	2	58	11	9	0	.326	.360	.462
Hernandez, Yoel, Reading	3	0	0	0	0	0	0	0	0	0	0	0	0	0	0	0	0	0	0	...	...	...

Player, Team	G	TPA	AB	R	H	TB	2B	3B	HR	RBI	SH	SF	HP	BB	IBB	SO	SB	CS	GDP	Avg.	OBP	Slg.
Herrera, Javier, Akron	98	367	328	45	74	112	20	0	6	36	7	0	14	18	0	78	3	3	6	.226	.294	.341
Herrera, Jose, Bowie *	5	17	16	0	4	5	1	0	0	1	0	1	0	0	0	3	0	0	0	.250	.235	.313
Hietpas, Joe, Binghamton	65	245	204	18	44	67	8	0	5	24	6	0	9	26	1	56	1	1	2	.216	.331	.328
Hill, Jeremy, Binghamton	10	2	1	1	1	2	1	0	0	0	0	0	0	1	0	0	0	0	0	1.000	1.000	2.000
Hitchcox, Samuel, Reading *	120	416	372	38	87	123	16	1	6	41	5	3	3	33	0	82	3	4	9	.234	.299	.331
Hodges, Scott, Harrisburg *	11	43	38	3	5	5	0	0	0	3	0	2	2	1	0	5	0	0	0	.132	.186	.132
Holm, Stephen, Norwich	11	31	23	4	5	6	1	0	0	2	2	0	2	4	0	7	1	0	1	.217	.379	.261
Hubele, Ryan, Bowie	24	92	79	13	24	41	2	0	5	8	1	0	4	8	1	19	2	1	3	.304	.396	.519
Huggins, Michael, Bowie	118	447	397	34	84	115	15	2	4	35	0	4	3	43	2	101	0	1	10	.212	.291	.290
Humber, Philip, Binghamton	1	1	0	0	0	0	0	0	0	0	1	0	0	0	0	0	0	0	0	...	...	...
Hutchison, Ryan, Reading	3	0	0	0	0	0	0	0	0	0	0	0	0	0	...	0	0	0	...	...	...	...
Hutting, Timothy, Norwich	111	386	320	54	83	110	17	2	2	27	14	1	10	41	0	68	9	3	8	.259	.360	.344
Inglin, Jeffery, Bowie	43	180	149	18	29	42	7	0	2	19	0	4	3	24	1	25	1	2	2	.195	.311	.282
Izquierdo, Hansel, Altoona	9	10	6	1	1	1	0	0	0	0	3	0	0	1	0	2	0	0	0	.167	.286	.167
Jacobs, Mike, Binghamton *	117	482	433	66	139	255	37	2	25	93	1	6	7	35	6	94	1	2	11	.321	.376	.589
Jacobsen, Landon, Altoona	4	2	2	0	1	1	0	0	0	0	0	0	0	0	0	0	0	0	0	.500	.500	.500
Jimenez, Luis Antonio, New Britain *	116	478	431	61	120	199	29	1	16	69	0	0	2	45	2	104	3	2	11	.278	.349	.462
Johnson, James, Altoona †	15	7	5	0	1	1	0	0	0	0	0	0	0	2	0	1	0	0	0	.200	.429	.200
Johnson III, Nelson, Bowie	134	558	507	62	126	196	29	4	11	59	1	4	5	41	2	108	7	5	9	.249	.309	.387
Johnston, Clinton, New Hampshire *	77	316	279	31	69	103	12	2	6	28	1	2	2	32	0	86	0	1	10	.247	.327	.369
Jova, Maikel, New Hampshire	97	401	387	39	100	133	20	2	3	32	1	2	1	10	0	70	2	6	15	.258	.278	.344
Karp, Joshua, Harrisburg	5	11	10	0	2	2	0	0	0	0	1	0	0	0	0	3	0	0	1	.200	.200	.200
Kaye, Justin, Altoona	28	1	1	0	0	0	0	0	0	0	0	0	0	0	0	1	0	0	0	.000	.000	.000
Kelly, Donald, Erie *	82	371	329	54	112	167	22	3	9	54	0	5	1	36	5	43	10	2	6	.340	.402	.508
Kelly, Kenny, Harrisburg	12	52	47	5	10	21	3	1	2	6	0	0	0	5	0	10	2	1	1	.213	.288	.447
Kennedy, Bryan, New Britain *	72	265	230	23	55	67	9	0	1	26	3	3	10	19	0	43	0	0	6	.239	.321	.291
Keylor, Cory, Bowie *	48	178	160	17	34	52	6	0	4	17	0	0	1	17	0	38	0	0	4	.213	.292	.325
Kingsale, Gene, Bowie †	51	202	175	21	40	56	7	3	1	15	3	1	3	20	2	31	4	2	0	.229	.317	.320
Knoedler, Justin, Norwich-Erie	36	103	89	12	21	30	6	0	1	8	1	0	1	12	0	26	0	1	1	.236	.333	.337
Koutnik, Jared, Trenton	15	60	55	7	8	10	2	0	0	2	0	1	1	3	0	15	0	0	2	.145	.200	.182
Kratz, Erik, New Hampshire	91	332	292	27	60	103	10	0	11	34	3	4	6	27	1	86	2	0	7	.205	.283	.353
Kuzmic, Craig, Harrisburg †	42	184	148	19	35	65	6	3	6	32	1	3	1	31	0	50	1	3	1	.236	.366	.439
Labandeira, Josh, Harrisburg	61	251	212	32	57	76	16	0	1	19	1	0	5	33	1	36	6	4	2	.269	.380	.358
Labarbera, Anthony, Norwich	135	533	472	47	125	157	20	0	4	61	4	3	7	47	2	65	14	10	20	.265	.338	.333
Lambin, Chase, Binghamton †	53	204	181	26	60	119	17	0	14	29	2	1	0	20	0	38	2	0	3	.331	.396	.657
Lane, Richard, Harrisburg *	37	154	128	18	29	42	6	2	1	9	0	1	2	23	0	24	0	2	6	.227	.351	.328
Langaigne, Selwyn, New Britain *	34	122	110	9	28	43	6	0	3	12	1	3	1	7	1	31	2	0	0	.255	.298	.391
Larkin, Shaun, Akron *	90	377	331	48	85	156	24	4	13	55	3	3	2	38	0	48	0	2	8	.257	.334	.471
Lee, Seung Hak, Reading	7	11	10	0	0	0	0	0	0	0	1	0	0	0	0	5	0	0	1	.000	.000	.000
Lee, Taber, Altoona †	24	89	79	8	16	26	2	1	2	10	1	1	1	7	0	13	1	0	2	.203	.273	.329
Leon, Carlos, Reading	75	257	225	32	63	79	11	1	1	9	5	1	6	20	3	37	4	9	7	.280	.353	.351
LeVier, Brian, Portland	13	39	37	3	8	10	2	0	0	2	1	0	0	1	0	8	0	0	1	.216	.237	.270
Lewis, Frederick, Norwich *	137	594	512	79	140	203	28	7	7	47	6	4	3	69	2	124	30	13	9	.273	.361	.396
Lindstrom, Matthew, Binghamton	13	4	3	0	0	0	0	0	0	0	0	0	1	0	0	2	0	0	0	.000	.250	.000
Lombardi, Michael, Reading †	1	1	1	0	0	0	0	0	0	0	0	0	0	0	0	1	0	0	0	.000	.000	.000
Lopez, Gabe, Trenton	82	359	296	50	86	117	14	1	5	42	6	6	3	48	2	30	6	3	11	.291	.388	.395
Lopez, Javy, Bowie	4	16	15	1	6	7	1	0	0	3	0	1	0	0	0	3	0	0	0	.400	.375	.467
Lopez, Rafael, Binghamton	13	8	5	0	1	1	0	0	0	0	0	0	0	0	0	2	0	0	0	.200	.200	.200
Lorenzo, Juan, Harrisburg †	17	61	54	7	10	15	0	1	1	5	1	1	1	4	0	11	0	0	2	.185	.250	.278
Lunetta, Anthony, Akron	34	113	103	18	23	29	3	0	1	10	0	1	3	6	1	25	1	1	1	.223	.283	.282
Lunsford, Trey, Norwich	36	124	111	8	19	23	1	0	1	11	2	1	0	10	0	20	0	1	5	.171	.238	.207
Lydon, Wayne, Binghamton †	129	562	491	70	120	167	15	13	2	43	19	2	4	46	3	101	42	14	6	.244	.313	.340
Lytle, Chaz, Altoona *	6	26	23	3	5	6	1	0	0	1	0	0	2	1	0	5	2	0	2	.217	.308	.261
MacLane, Evan, Binghamton *	3	7	6	0	1	1	0	0	0	0	1	0	0	0	0	2	0	0	0	.167	.167	.167
Maholm, Paul, Altoona *	8	15	12	0	2	2	0	0	0	0	1	0	0	2	0	5	0	0	0	.167	.286	.167
Maldonado, Carlos, Altoona	82	321	278	27	70	105	14	0	7	34	5	1	2	35	0	63	0	1	10	.252	.339	.378
Maldonado Oquendo, Ivan, Binghamton	1	0	0	0	0	0	0	0	0	0	0	0	0	0	0	0	0	0	0	...	...	...
Malek, Robert, Binghamton *	116	439	394	47	109	152	23	4	4	37	6	3	4	32	5	80	1	5	9	.277	.335	.386
Maples, Christopher, Erie	93	369	333	41	75	135	24	0	12	54	4	4	8	20	0	98	2	1	6	.225	.282	.405
Markakis, Nicholas, Bowie *	33	143	124	19	42	71	16	2	3	30	0	1	0	18	0	30	0	1	5	.339	.420	.573
Marsters, Brandon, Bowie	111	393	364	43	78	111	18	0	5	22	1	1	6	21	0	73	3	1	9	.214	.268	.305
Martin, Billy, Harrisburg	7	24	22	4	5	7	2	0	0	1	0	0	0	2	0	9	0	0	0	.227	.292	.318
Martin, Gregory, Altoona *	2	0	0	0	0	0	0	0	0	0	0	0	0	0	0	0	0	0	0	...	...	...
Martinez, Octavio, Bowie	14	53	48	8	17	27	5	1	1	9	0	0	3	2	0	4	0	2	3	.354	.415	.563
Mateo, Henry, Harrisburg †	32	140	122	13	20	27	5	1	0	6	2	0	0	16	1	27	11	5	3	.164	.261	.221
Matienzo, Daniel, New Britain	138	586	531	81	150	259	36	2	23	87	0	7	8	40	4	112	1	1	20	.282	.338	.488
Matos, Josue, Reading	2	2	2	0	0	0	0	0	0	0	0	0	0	0	0	1	0	0	0	.000	.000	.000
Matos, Luis, Bowie	5	22	20	4	5	8	0	0	1	2	0	0	1	1	0	1	4	1	1	.250	.318	.400
Matsui, Kazuo, Binghamton †	3	10	9	4	4	5	1	0	0	0	0	0	1	0	0	1	2	0	0	.444	.500	.556
Mauer, Donald, New Britain	25	36	32	4	8	10	2	0	0	1	0	1	0	3	0	5	1	0	3	.250	.314	.313
Maust, David, Harrisburg *	13	12	10	0	1	1	0	0	0	1	0	0	0	2	0	6	0	0	1	.100	.250	.100
Maza, Luis, New Britain	49	215	197	28	49	76	9	0	6	23	1	2	3	12	1	34	0	1	4	.249	.299	.386
Mazone, Brian, Norwich *	6	11	10	1	2	5	0	0	1	2	0	1	0	0	0	1	0	0	1	.200	.182	.500
McCullough, Clayton, Akron *	4	12	11	0	1	1	0	0	0	1	0	0	0	1	0	5	1	0	0	.091	.167	.091
McMillan, Andrew, Harrisburg	20	61	54	4	14	20	1	1	1	7	1	1	0	5	0	15	0	0	1	.259	.317	.370
McNab, Timothy, Binghamton	11	4	4	0	0	0	0	0	0	0	0	0	0	0	0	2	0	0	0	.000	.000	.000
Meath, Matthew, Altoona †	2	5	3	2	1	2	1	0	0	1	0	0	1	1	0	0	0	0	0	.333	.600	.667
Mejia, Gilberto, Erie †	60	239	211	31	40	55	2	0	3	18	6	0	3	19	1	56	2	1	2	.190	.266	.261
Melian, Jackson, Erie *	7	25	23	2	6	8	2	0	0	1	0	1	0	1	0	5	0	0	1	.261	.280	.348
Mendez, Deivi, Trenton	3	8	8	0	0	0	0	0	0	0	0	0	0	0	0	1	0	0	0	.000	.000	.000
Mendez, Victor, Erie †	96	363	325	46	75	123	14	2	10	39	5	0	1	32	2	82	7	5	5	.231	.302	.378

Player, Team	G	TPA	AB	R	H	TB	2B	3B	HR	RBI	SH	SF	HP	BB	IBB	SO	SB	CS	GDP	Avg.	OBP	Slg.
Mercedes, Victor, Altoona-Harrisburg	41	118	111	13	28	42	6	1	2	7	1	0	0	6	1	21	2	0	3	.252	.291	.378
Merchan, Jesus, Reading	48	166	151	18	40	49	7	1	0	12	5	0	4	6	1	16	2	2	7	.265	.311	.325
Milledge, Lastings, Binghamton	48	214	193	33	65	94	17	0	4	24	2	1	4	14	1	47	11	5	1	.337	.392	.487
Minix, Travis, Reading	22	2	0	0	0	0	0	0	0	0	2	0	0	0	0	0	0	0	0	...	...	...
Misch, Patrick, Norwich	2	5	5	2	1	2	1	0	0	0	0	0	0	0	0	1	0	0	0	.200	.200	.400
Molina, Felix, New Britain †	36	141	122	17	35	51	10	0	2	18	6	3	2	8	0	27	0	2	1	.287	.333	.418
Montero, Oscar, Norwich	8	2	2	0	0	0	0	0	0	0	0	0	0	0	0	2	0	0	0	.000	.000	.000
Montes, Alberto, Norwich	9	1	0	0	0	0	0	0	0	0	1	0	0	0	0	0	0	0	0	...	...	...
Morales, Jose, New Britain †	7	21	20	1	5	6	1	0	0	0	0	0	0	1	0	3	0	0	3	.250	.286	.300
Morban, Jose, Akron	65	286	254	35	63	105	11	2	9	33	5	2	1	24	0	79	10	8	3	.248	.313	.413
Moreno, Anthony, Norwich	4	2	2	0	0	0	0	0	0	0	0	0	0	0	0	0	0	0	0	.000	.000	.000
Moreno, Edwin, Reading	3	5	4	0	0	0	0	0	0	0	1	0	0	0	0	3	0	0	0	.000	.000	.000
Morris, Warren, Akron *	5	23	22	1	2	3	1	0	0	2	0	0	0	1	0	4	1	0	1	.091	.130	.136
Moses, Matthew, New Britain *	48	204	186	25	39	68	9	1	6	30	0	1	3	14	0	51	3	2	3	.210	.275	.366
Moss, Brandon, Portland *	135	569	503	87	135	222	31	4	16	61	1	8	3	53	5	129	6	3	6	.268	.337	.441
Mulhern, Ryan, Akron	67	278	244	40	76	145	18	3	15	46	0	2	3	28	1	64	4	2	8	.311	.386	.594
Murphy, David, Portland *	135	542	484	71	133	208	25	4	14	75	1	3	1	46	3	83	13	6	11	.275	.337	.430
Negron, Miguel, New Hampshire *	124	527	489	69	126	189	21	3	12	46	4	1	1	32	3	100	23	12	6	.258	.304	.387
Neshek, Patrick, New Britain	2	0	0	0	0	0	0	0	0	0	0	0	0	0	...	0	0	0	0	...	...	...
Nettles, Marcus, Harrisburg *	7	18	15	0	2	2	0	0	0	1	2	0	0	1	0	7	1	0	0	.133	.188	.133
Neuberger, Scott, Altoona	10	40	38	1	10	10	0	0	0	4	1	0	0	1	0	7	0	0	0	.263	.282	.263
Nieves, Melvin, Harrisburg †	23	97	77	14	20	37	5	0	4	16	0	0	2	18	3	28	1	2	0	.260	.412	.481
Nieves, Raul, Portland †	90	267	235	29	49	65	9	2	1	11	2	2	1	27	0	41	6	1	5	.209	.291	.277
Nivar, Ramon, Bowie	41	166	150	22	37	47	7	0	1	12	2	0	2	12	0	21	11	6	4	.247	.311	.313
Norderum, Jason, Harrisburg *	8	3	3	0	2	3	1	0	0	0	0	0	0	0	0	0	0	0	0	.667	.667	1.000
Norris, Shawn, Harrisburg *	84	320	283	30	66	91	10	0	5	27	5	4	2	26	1	68	0	4	3	.233	.298	.322
Ochoa, Ivan, Akron †	126	475	422	46	112	143	13	6	2	30	8	3	12	30	0	81	16	12	7	.265	.330	.339
Ogiltree, John, Harrisburg	3	0	0	0	0	0	0	0	0	0	0	0	0	0	...	0	0	0	0	...	...	...
O'Keefe, Michael, Portland *	11	45	40	6	7	10	0	0	1	8	0	1	0	4	0	7	0	0	1	.175	.244	.250
Olson, Justin, New Britain	1	0	0	0	0	0	0	0	0	0	0	0	0	0	...	0	0	0	0	...	...	...
Ortmeier, Dan, Norwich †	135	575	503	85	138	233	23	6	20	79	0	3	21	48	3	115	35	12	2	.274	.360	.463
Osborn, Patrick, Akron	129	525	478	66	137	187	18	1	10	63	2	1	7	37	0	66	14	4	18	.287	.346	.391
Palmer, Jonathan, Norwich	2	2	2	0	0	0	0	0	0	0	0	0	0	0	0	1	0	0	0	.000	.000	.000
Pannone, Anthony, Norwich	7	0	0	0	0	0	0	0	0	0	0	0	0	0	0	0	0	0	0	...	...	...
Panther, Nathan, Akron *	22	91	80	13	22	30	3	1	1	6	0	0	1	10	0	15	1	1	2	.275	.363	.375
Parker, Clark, Harrisburg *	4	7	7	0	0	0	0	0	0	0	0	0	0	0	0	5	0	0	0	.000	.000	.000
Patino, Jorge, Erie	6	19	17	1	1	1	0	0	0	0	0	0	2	0	0	5	0	1	0	.059	.158	.059
Pattee, Benjamin, New Britain	42	169	146	22	30	42	12	0	0	12	3	1	4	15	0	20	0	1	2	.205	.295	.288
Paulino, Ronny, Altoona	43	184	168	24	49	73	6	0	6	20	1	0	0	15	1	30	3	0	3	.292	.350	.435
Pedroia, Dustin, Portland	66	298	256	39	83	130	19	2	8	40	2	2	4	34	2	26	7	3	7	.324	.409	.508
Pena, Ramiro, Trenton †	68	255	236	28	59	68	5	2	0	12	8	1	0	10	0	48	4	1	5	.250	.279	.288
Perez, Kenny, Portland †	66	277	253	35	72	95	9	1	4	28	2	3	0	18	1	35	7	3	4	.285	.328	.375
Peterson, Matthew, Altoona	11	27	25	4	4	4	0	0	0	2	1	0	0	1	0	9	0	0	0	.160	.192	.160
Petit, Yusmeiro, Binghamton	6	16	12	1	1	1	0	0	0	1	4	0	0	0	0	4	0	0	0	.083	.083	.083
Phillips, Kyle, New Britain *	22	77	67	6	14	21	1	0	2	8	1	3	0	6	1	17	0	0	0	.209	.263	.313
Pond, Simon, Bowie *	110	454	406	50	108	192	25	1	19	75	0	1	4	43	3	114	8	3	10	.266	.341	.473
Pope, Justin, Trenton †	1	0	0	0	0	0	0	0	0	0	0	0	0	0	...	0	0	0	0	...	...	...
Porter, Colin, Trenton *	15	62	55	5	11	16	2	0	1	5	0	0	0	7	0	23	0	1	0	.200	.290	.291
Portobanco, Luz, Binghamton	11	3	3	0	1	1	0	0	0	0	0	0	0	0	0	2	0	0	0	.333	.333	.333
Pratt, Trent, Reading	74	255	219	27	43	59	8	1	2	18	4	1	5	26	5	43	0	1	7	.196	.295	.269
Prieto, Alex, Reading	16	58	47	5	10	18	2	0	2	7	0	1	0	10	0	8	1	0	2	.213	.345	.383
Rabelo, Michael, Erie †	77	314	282	33	77	103	18	1	2	26	3	2	9	18	1	42	0	1	6	.273	.334	.365
Raggio, Brady, Reading	5	6	4	0	2	2	0	0	0	0	2	0	0	0	0	0	0	0	0	.500	.500	.500
Ragsdale, William, Binghamton	64	248	217	33	49	87	5	3	9	31	5	1	4	21	0	75	4	3	6	.226	.305	.401
Ramirez, Hanley, Portland	122	519	465	66	126	179	21	7	6	52	5	3	7	39	1	62	26	13	12	.271	.335	.385
Ramirez, Ramon, Trenton	1	0	0	0	0	0	0	0	0	0	0	0	0	0	0	0	0	0	0	...	...	...
Rasner, Darrell, Harrisburg	11	28	28	1	6	7	1	0	0	3	0	0	0	0	0	9	0	0	0	.214	.214	.250
Raymundo, Gregg, Altoona	23	61	56	5	13	16	3	0	0	2	1	0	1	3	0	12	0	0	1	.232	.283	.286
Redman, Prentice, Binghamton	45	187	161	30	50	76	12	1	4	29	1	6	2	17	1	37	2	3	7	.311	.371	.472
Richardson, Juan, Reading	122	425	385	51	96	158	15	1	15	51	0	2	4	34	3	108	0	4	15	.249	.315	.410
Riggan, Jerrod, Binghamton	1	0	0	0	0	0	0	0	0	0	0	0	0	0	0	0	0	0	0	...	...	...
Rivera, Saul, Harrisburg	15	2	2	0	0	0	0	0	0	0	0	0	0	0	0	2	0	0	0	.000	.000	.000
Roach, Jason, Altoona	1	2	2	0	0	0	0	0	0	0	0	0	0	0	0	0	0	0	1	.000	.000	.000
Roberson, Christopher, Reading	139	611	553	90	172	257	24	8	15	70	5	4	9	40	2	112	34	14	6	.311	.365	.465
Roberts, Ryan, New Hampshire	92	399	338	54	92	162	19	3	15	44	1	1	4	55	5	94	5	1	6	.272	.379	.479
Rodney, Thomas, Erie	2	1	1	0	0	0	0	0	0	0	0	0	0	0	0	0	0	0	0	.000	.000	.000
Rodriguez, Guillermo, Norwich	6	20	15	1	4	5	1	0	0	1	0	1	1	3	0	4	0	0	0	.267	.400	.333
Rodriguez, Jose, Binghamton	13	1	1	0	0	0	0	0	0	0	0	0	0	0	0	1	0	0	0	.000	.000	.000
Rogers, Omar, Bowie	67	269	239	23	49	72	14	0	3	31	7	0	3	20	0	28	1	1	6	.205	.275	.301
Rojas, Christopher, Reading	9	18	15	0	3	3	0	0	0	2	2	0	0	1	0	3	0	0	0	.200	.250	.200
Roman, Orlando, Binghamton	9	16	14	0	0	0	0	0	0	0	2	0	0	0	0	5	0	0	0	.000	.000	.000
Romero, Alexander, New Britain *	139	560	509	65	153	233	31	2	15	77	4	3	8	36	4	69	12	11	12	.301	.354	.458
Rooi, Vince, Harrisburg	5	20	19	0	6	11	3	1	0	1	0	0	0	1	0	6	0	0	0	.316	.350	.579
Roughton, Jody, Erie *	2	8	7	0	3	4	1	0	0	0	0	0	1	0	0	1	0	0	0	.429	.500	.571
Rueckel, Daniel, Harrisburg	21	5	4	1	0	0	0	0	0	0	0	0	0	1	0	1	0	0	0	.000	.200	.000
Ruiz, Randy, Reading	89	385	344	59	120	230	29	0	27	89	0	5	6	30	11	87	0	2	6	.349	.405	.669
Rundles, Richard, Harrisburg *	10	22	17	2	2	2	0	0	0	2	3	0	1	1	0	6	0	0	0	.118	.211	.118
Sadler, Ray, Altoona	62	227	209	23	51	87	17	2	5	23	1	0	0	17	1	54	4	4	4	.244	.301	.416
Sadler, William, Norwich	12	2	1	1	0	0	0	0	0	0	0	0	0	1	0	0	0	0	0	.000	.500	.000
Sanchez, Humberto, Erie	1	1	1	0	0	0	0	0	0	0	0	0	0	0	0	1	0	0	0	.000	.000	.000
Sanchez, Romulo, Altoona	1	1	1	0	0	0	0	0	0	0	0	0	0	0	0	1	0	0	0	.000	.000	.000

Player, Team	G	TPA	AB	R	H	TB	2B	3B	HR	RBI	SH	SF	HP	BB	IBB	SO	SB	CS	GDP	Avg.	OBP	Slg.
Sandberg, Jared, Portland	130	538	463	64	108	191	29	0	18	71	1	2	10	62	4	131	3	3	15	.233	.335	.413
Sanders, Anthony, New Hampshire	22	89	82	8	20	27	4	0	1	8	1	0	1	5	0	19	1	0	3	.244	.295	.329
Santos, Omir, Trenton	111	425	401	44	101	148	17	0	10	48	1	3	9	11	1	75	0	1	12	.252	.285	.369
Sardinha, Bronson, Trenton *	133	569	503	63	130	200	30	2	12	68	1	3	7	55	1	115	11	5	14	.258	.338	.398
Scanlon, Matthew, New Britain *	7	22	19	2	3	3	0	0	0	1	0	0	0	3	1	4	0	0	1	.158	.273	.158
Schroder, Christopher, Harrisburg	5	0	0	0	0	0	0	0	0	0	0	0	0	0	0	0	0	0	0	...	...	...
Sequea, Jacobo, Harrisburg	7	1	1	0	0	0	0	0	0	0	0	0	0	0	0	0	0	0	0	.000	.000	.000
Shafer, Adam, Reading *	3	0	0	0	0	0	0	0	0	0	0	0	0	0	0	0	0	0	0	...	...	...
Shaffar, Benjamin, Altoona †	22	7	5	0	0	0	0	0	0	0	2	0	0	0	0	0	0	0	0	.000	.000	.000
Sharpless, Joshua, Altoona	2	0	0	0	0	0	0	0	0	0	0	0	0	0	0	0	0	0	0	...	...	...
Sherrill, James, Akron †	21	70	60	8	15	25	3	2	1	5	1	2	1	6	1	16	0	2	0	.250	.319	.417
Sierra, Eduardo, Trenton	2	0	0	0	0	0	0	0	0	0	0	0	0	0	0	0	0	0	0	...	...	...
Simon, Alfredo, Norwich	14	7	5	1	0	0	0	0	0	0	0	0	1	1	0	2	0	0	0	.000	.286	.000
Singleton, Justin, New Hampshire *	21	89	80	9	17	31	3	1	3	9	0	1	1	7	0	29	2	1	1	.213	.281	.388
Skaggs, Jon, Trenton	1	0	0	0	0	0	0	0	0	0	0	0	0	0	0	0	0	0	0	...	...	...
Slack, Jonathan, Binghamton *	23	80	67	7	15	17	2	0	0	7	6	1	0	6	0	16	1	0	0	.224	.284	.254
Smith, Mike, Reading	9	23	19	1	4	6	2	0	0	3	0	0	1	0	0	2	0	0	0	.211	.250	.316
Snusz, Christopher, Altoona	22	72	66	5	17	23	3	0	1	1	2	0	0	4	1	13	0	0	2	.258	.300	.348
Snyder, Bradley, Akron *	75	337	304	56	85	164	21	5	16	54	1	1	6	25	4	94	5	3	3	.280	.345	.539
Song, Seung, Norwich	2	4	4	0	2	3	1	0	0	2	0	0	0	0	0	2	0	0	0	.500	.500	.750
Sosa, Juan, Reading	40	167	155	18	44	60	4	0	4	19	1	0	1	10	3	25	1	0	10	.284	.331	.387
Span, Keiunta, New Britain *	68	304	267	47	76	92	6	5	0	26	5	2	8	22	1	41	10	8	2	.285	.355	.345
Spann, Charles, Portland	9	34	29	1	6	8	2	0	0	1	2	0	0	3	0	8	1	1	0	.207	.281	.276
Speigner, Jimmy, New Britain	2	0	0	0	0	0	0	0	0	0	0	0	0	0	0	0	0	0	0	...	...	...
Stansberry, Craig, Altoona	116	483	421	62	100	198	22	11	18	67	5	7	6	44	0	114	14	5	9	.238	.314	.470
Stevenson, Jason, Harrisburg *	5	10	9	2	1	1	0	0	0	0	0	0	0	1	0	3	0	0	0	.111	.200	.111
Stewart, Paul, Altoona	10	18	16	1	2	3	1	0	0	1	1	0	0	1	0	10	0	0	0	.125	.176	.188
Stotts, Jarrett, Trenton	103	393	349	51	77	95	10	1	2	30	4	3	4	33	0	52	9	2	10	.221	.293	.272
St. Pierre, Maxim, Erie	95	388	360	46	100	133	18	0	5	46	1	3	1	23	0	55	1	1	14	.278	.320	.369
Sylvester, Billy, Harrisburg	13	2	2	0	0	0	0	0	0	0	0	0	0	0	0	1	0	0	0	.000	.000	.000
Tablado, Raul, New Hampshire	102	393	363	33	73	103	13	1	5	35	2	3	3	22	2	128	6	1	9	.201	.251	.284
Taylor, Samuel, New Britain †	32	122	105	14	29	36	4	0	1	9	3	1	1	11	1	14	1	5	2	.276	.347	.343
Tejeda, Juan, Erie	122	523	470	64	137	210	27	2	14	82	0	5	7	41	1	86	2	4	7	.291	.354	.447
Thigpen, Curtis, New Britain	39	157	141	18	40	60	8	0	4	15	4	0	3	9	0	19	0	0	1	.284	.340	.426
Thomas, John, New Britain *	1	0	0	0	0	0	0	0	0	0	0	0	0	0	0	0	0	0	0	...	...	...
Thompson, Kevin, Trenton	81	377	313	59	103	177	28	5	12	43	2	3	6	53	1	68	25	6	5	.329	.432	.565
Thompson, Rich, Altoona *	94	395	346	58	89	119	11	5	3	30	10	1	8	30	1	60	45	6	4	.257	.330	.344
Thompson, Travis, Reading	2	0	0	0	0	0	0	0	0	0	0	0	0	0	0	0	0	0	0	...	...	...
Threets, Erick, Norwich *	9	2	2	0	1	2	1	0	0	0	0	0	0	0	0	1	0	0	0	.500	.500	1.000
Tomlin, James, New Britain	119	387	343	50	94	132	21	1	5	34	17	0	1	26	0	50	10	5	10	.274	.327	.385
Torres, Eider, Akron †	108	503	452	73	129	184	27	5	6	57	19	5	11	16	0	66	33	4	5	.285	.322	.407
Torres, Gabriel, New Britain	66	206	178	15	43	57	8	0	2	20	3	1	8	16	0	23	1	1	8	.242	.330	.320
Tousa, Scott, Erie *	60	250	212	30	52	72	4	2	4	31	2	3	9	24	0	34	0	3	4	.245	.343	.340
Triplett, Calvin, Binghamton	18	70	63	11	21	30	6	0	1	7	0	1	0	6	1	9	0	0	0	.333	.386	.476
Trumble, Daniel, Norwich *	21	47	37	6	8	14	3	0	1	3	1	0	0	9	0	11	1	0	2	.216	.370	.378
Umbria, Jose, New Hampshire	28	98	92	7	17	22	5	0	0	7	1	0	0	5	0	22	0	0	6	.185	.227	.239
Urdaneta, Lino, Binghamton	1	0	0	0	0	0	0	0	0	0	0	0	0	0	0	0	0	0	0	...	...	...
Valderrama, Carlos, Norwich	130	540	493	61	145	208	33	3	8	58	2	4	6	34	2	84	29	7	11	.294	.345	.422
Valdes, Marc, Trenton	1	0	0	0	0	0	0	0	0	0	0	0	0	0	0	0	0	0	0	...	...	...
Valdez, Merkin, Norwich	6	11	10	0	0	0	0	0	0	0	0	1	0	0	0	4	0	0	0	.000	.000	.000
Van Der Bosch, Matthew, Portland *	11	49	46	3	11	14	1	1	0	3	0	0	1	2	0	14	1	0	0	.239	.286	.304
Van Every, Jonathan, Akron *	118	466	389	71	95	194	14	2	27	64	3	1	7	66	5	155	16	6	3	.244	.363	.499
Velazquez, Gilbert, New Britain	81	323	286	36	66	82	13	0	1	28	6	3	6	22	0	52	3	3	2	.231	.297	.287
Verbryke, Eric, Trenton *	5	19	14	3	2	2	0	0	0	2	1	0	0	4	0	3	2	0	0	.143	.333	.143
Vericker, Brad, Norwich *	30	81	74	7	20	22	2	0	0	8	0	0	1	6	0	19	0	0	2	.270	.333	.297
Villegas, Felix, Reading	14	1	1	0	0	0	0	0	0	0	0	0	0	0	0	0	0	0	0	.000	.000	.000
Von Schell, Eric, Norwich	134	555	512	52	123	191	24	1	14	75	2	6	6	29	3	131	5	4	10	.240	.286	.373
Vroman, Douglas, Harrisburg	3	12	9	0	0	0	0	0	0	0	0	0	1	2	0	4	0	0	0	.000	.250	.000
Walsh, Nick, Trenton *	8	22	20	4	9	10	1	0	0	2	0	0	0	2	0	2	0	0	0	.450	.500	.500
Walter, Paul, Norwich	83	250	228	38	64	96	13	2	5	31	1	1	1	19	0	58	10	6	6	.281	.337	.421
Watkins, Thomas, New Britain	116	368	319	50	73	104	19	0	4	24	13	0	5	31	0	65	12	7	7	.229	.307	.326
Watson, Brandon, Harrisburg *	34	156	146	13	36	37	1	0	0	6	1	0	2	7	0	21	7	5	2	.247	.290	.253
Watts, Derran, Binghamton	2	6	5	1	2	5	0	0	1	1	0	0	0	1	0	1	0	0	0	.400	.500	1.000
Waugh, Jason, New Hampshire	13	44	40	6	7	8	1	0	0	4	0	0	1	3	0	8	0	0	0	.175	.250	.200
West, Jeremy, Portland	127	533	472	48	126	194	32	3	10	50	0	6	14	41	1	76	1	0	11	.267	.340	.411
Whittaker, Timothy, New Hampshire	2	6	6	0	1	1	0	0	0	0	0	0	0	0	0	3	0	0	0	.167	.167	.167
Wilson, Andy, Altoona *	7	21	17	1	4	4	0	0	0	1	1	0	0	3	0	4	0	0	0	.235	.350	.235
Wilson, Brian, Norwich	5	0	0	0	0	0	0	0	0	0	0	0	0	0	0	0	0	0	0	...	...	...
Wilson, Jeffrey, Reading	15	4	3	1	1	1	0	0	0	0	0	0	0	1	0	1	0	0	0	.333	.500	.333
Wilson, John, Harrisburg	75	272	240	30	64	88	9	0	5	31	6	2	5	19	2	23	1	2	4	.267	.331	.367
Woods, Michael, Erie	130	515	451	52	104	158	18	6	8	47	4	7	3	50	1	119	5	5	11	.231	.307	.350
Youman, Shane, Altoona *	18	10	9	0	1	1	0	0	0	0	0	0	0	0	0	5	0	0	0	.111	.111	.111
Youngbauer, Scott, Akron-Portland	86	351	317	42	84	144	18	6	10	39	6	2	4	22	0	79	8	3	1	.265	.319	.454
Zaun, Gregg, New Hampshire †	2	8	6	1	2	3	1	0	0	0	0	0	0	2	0	2	0	0	0	.333	.500	.500
Zimmerman, Ryan, Harrisburg	63	252	233	40	76	123	20	0	9	32	1	1	2	15	3	34	1	5	3	.326	.371	.528

PLAYERS WITH TWO OR MORE TEAMS

Player, Team	G	TPA	AB	R	H	TB	2B	3B	HR	RBI	SH	SF	HP	BB	IBB	SO	SB	CS	GDP	Avg.	OBP	Slg.
Brown, Dee, Trenton *	13	57	51	4	6	13	1	0	2	6	0	0	1	5	1	17	0	0	1	.118	.211	.255
Brown, Dee, Harrisburg *	43	163	144	16	28	50	7	0	5	16	0	2	6	11	0	33	2	4	2	.194	.276	.347
Knoedler, Justin, Norwich	4	12	10	2	3	3	0	0	0	0	...	0	0	2	...	0	2	1	0	.300	.417	.300

Player, Team	G	TPA	AB	R	H	TB	2B	3B	HR	RBI	SH	SF	HP	BB	IBB	SO	SB	CS	GDP	Avg.	OBP	Slg.
Knoedler, Justin, Erie	32	91	79	10	18	27	6	0	1	8	1	0	1	10	0	26	1	0	1	.228	.322	.342
Mercedes, Victor, Altoona †	12	45	43	7	14	24	2	1	2	6	0	0	0	2	0	5	0	0	2	.326	.356	.558
Mercedes, Victor, Harrisburg †	29	73	68	6	14	18	4	0	0	1	1	0	0	4	1	16	2	0	1	.206	.250	.265
Youngbauer, Scott, Akron †	41	171	153	13	33	54	4	1	5	19	4	1	2	11	0	40	3	1	0	.216	.275	.353
Youngbauer, Scott, Portland †	45	180	164	29	51	90	14	5	5	20	2	1	2	11	0	39	5	2	1	.311	.360	.549

GRAND SLAMS—E. Alfonzo, S. Duncan, M. Jacobs, D. Kelly, 2 each; R. Acuna, K. Airoso, J. Bailey, J. Benavidez, V. Chiaravalloti, M. Clendenin, J. Cooper, B. Eldred, B. Fahey, R. Fleming, B. Gettis, M. Huggins, L. Jimenez, C. Kuzmic, S. Larkin, C. Maldonado, C. Maples, J. Morban, M. Moses, R. Mulhern, P. Redman, C. Roberson, R. Ruiz, J. Sandberg, J. Tejeda, R. Thompson, J. Tomlin, R. Triplett, C. Valderrama, J. Van Every, T. Von Schell, 1 each.

AWARDED FIRST BASE ON CATCHER'S INTERFERENCE—D. Murphy 7 (D. McMillan, J. Emmerick, J. Herrera, O. Santos, T. Gradoville, T. Lunsford, T. Pratt); K. Airoso 2 (J. Brown, J. Herrera); B. Moss (A. Camacaro); R. Mulhern (J. Wilson); K. Perez (O. Santos); J. Taylor (A. Concepcion Jr.); C. Valderrama (T. Gradoville).

2005 PITCHING

TEAM

Team	W	L	Pct.	ERA	G	CG	ShO	Sv.	IP	H	TBF	R	ER	HR	SH	SF	HB	BB	IBB	SO	WP	Bk.
Akron	84	58	.592	3.40	142	3	10	36	1266.1	1183	5372	574	479	94	56	29	79	389	17	1001	72	11
Bowie	74	68	.521	3.54	142	2	11	39	1249.1	1128	5261	564	492	112	57	34	73	464	15	1168	65	5
New Hampshire	68	74	.479	3.57	142	5	10	43	1240.2	1188	5157	568	492	114	44	43	48	317	16	1133	44	2
Reading	69	73	.486	3.77	142	5	2	33	1276	1270	5454	609	535	134	54	43	74	410	13	957	58	5
Portland	76	66	.535	3.82	142	6	16	39	1238.1	1182	5296	635	526	113	59	45	59	463	40	1063	71	8
Trenton	74	68	.521	3.86	142	0	13	38	1259.2	1226	5472	641	540	110	54	37	59	527	19	1126	64	7
Norwich	71	71	.500	3.96	142	2	13	41	1231	1243	5301	614	541	111	67	36	63	426	10	971	67	6
Altoona	74	66	.535	4.00	142	2	5	44	1258.2	1266	5497	662	560	112	73	39	47	486	18	1042	75	4
New Britain	70	72	.493	4.10	142	7	7	36	1234	1212	5290	662	562	116	50	35	66	428	31	1005	42	4
Harrisburg	64	78	.451	4.24	142	6	8	28	1251.2	1312	5452	679	590	138	69	35	83	403	36	984	54	6
Binghamton	63	79	.444	4.40	142	6	8	26	1238	1298	5451	717	605	134	42	37	70	465	28	1083	71	6
Erie	63	79	.444	4.52	142	1	11	42	1233.2	1320	5400	722	620	151	36	40	73	422	10	951	49	10

INDIVIDUAL

TOP QUALIFIERS FOR EARNED-RUN AVERAGE TITLE

Minimum 114 innings. *Lefthanded pitcher.

Pitcher, Team	W	L	Pct.	ERA	G	GS	CG	ShO	GF	Sv.	IP	H	TBF	R	ER	HR	SH	SF	HB	BB	IBB	SO	WP	Bk.
Lester, Jonathan, Portland *	11	6	.647	2.61	26	26	3	1	0	0	148.1	114	596	52	43	10	6	4	4	57	3	163	10	1
Petit, Yusmeiro, Binghamton *	9	3	.750	2.91	21	21	2	0	0	0	117.2	90	453	41	38	15	3	2	2	18	1	130	0	0
Desalvo, Matthew, Trenton	9	5	.643	3.02	25	24	0	0	1	0	149.0	106	604	55	50	8	5	4	9	67	1	151	11	0
Morris, Cory, Bowie	8	5	.615	3.03	29	25	0	0	2	0	142.2	116	595	50	48	11	5	1	3	78	4	159	6	1
Begg, Christopher, Norwich	8	7	.533	3.07	23	21	0	0	0	0	138.0	142	561	57	47	9	6	1	1	23	1	86	2	0
Mazone, Brian, Norwich *	11	8	.579	3.10	30	20	0	0	3	1	127.2	122	515	52	44	9	11	3	6	34	1	89	3	1
Denham, Daniel, Akron	9	7	.563	3.15	21	21	1	0	0	0	140.0	115	565	55	49	6	4	5	13	30	1	108	6	1
DuBose, Eric, Bowie *	8	10	.444	3.25	21	20	0	0	0	0	122.0	113	496	52	44	10	6	5	4	29	0	114	5	1
Gorzelanny, Tom, Altoona *	8	5	.615	3.26	23	23	1	1	0	0	129.2	114	537	50	47	6	5	3	5	46	1	124	5	0
Rasner, Darrell, Harrisburg	6	7	.462	3.59	27	26	1	0	0	0	150.1	150	621	66	60	10	7	5	10	29	2	96	2	0
Davis, Allen, Reading *	13	9	.591	3.64	27	25	3	0	1	0	183.0	208	751	79	74	20	9	6	8	22	0	97	3	0
Dittler, Jake, Akron	10	9	.526	3.64	27	27	0	0	1	0	173.0	187	765	94	70	12	4	3	8	61	0	107	10	2
Edwards, Bryan, Binghamton	6	6	.500	3.65	35	13	0	0	7	1	118.1	124	514	53	48	8	6	4	6	46	5	85	9	2
Pauley, David, Portland	9	7	.563	3.81	27	27	1	0	0	0	156.0	169	660	86	66	18	5	5	5	34	2	104	6	0
Banks, Joshua, New Hampshire	8	12	.400	3.83	27	27	2	0	0	0	162.1	159	640	76	69	18	4	7	0	11	0	145	3	0
Birkins, Kurt, Bowie *	7	11	.389	3.91	26	24	0	0	0	0	129.0	134	552	69	56	8	5	2	11	42	0	114	10	0
Rojas, Christopher, Reading	12	6	.667	3.92	22	22	1	0	0	0	131.0	126	546	62	57	17	5	4	8	36	0	107	9	0
Perkins, Vince, New Hampshire	7	7	.500	4.03	26	24	0	0	1	0	131.2	124	559	65	59	9	7	5	7	51	0	111	7	0
Ramirez, Ismael, New Hampshire	8	13	.381	4.12	27	27	0	0	0	0	150.2	155	623	75	69	19	8	7	3	32	1	125	0	1
Speigner, Jimmy, New Britain	6	10	.375	4.13	23	23	2	1	0	0	143.2	149	599	75	66	14	6	2	12	28	1	94	2	1
Karstens, Jeffrey, Trenton	12	11	.522	4.15	28	27	0	0	0	0	169.0	192	724	91	78	16	3	5	3	42	1	147	8	1

DEPARTMENTAL LEADERS—W—Davis, 13. L—Smith, 14. Pct.—Petit, .750. G—Cameron, 58. GS—Smith, 28. CG—Lester and Davis, 3. ShO—12 pitchers tied with 1. GF—Pope, 54. Sv.—Almonte, 33. IP—Davis, 183. H—Davis, 208. TBF—Dittler, 769. R—Peterson, 102. ER—Peterson, 88. HR—Johnson, 23. SAC—Mazone, 11. SF—Chantres, 8. HB—Smith, 23. BB—Smith, 82. IBB—Rivera and Rueckel, 5. SO—Lester, 163. WP—Smith, 14. BK—Zumaya and Montes, 4.

ALL PITCHERS

*Lefthanded pitcher.

Pitcher, Team	W	L	Pct.	ERA	G	GS	CG	ShO	GF	Sv.	IP	H	TBF	R	ER	HR	SH	SF	HB	BB	IBB	SO	WP	Bk.
Aardsma, David, Norwich	6	2	.750	2.93	9	8	0	0	0	0	46.0	44	185	17	15	2	4	0	0	13	0	30	2	0
Abbott, James, New Britain	7	3	.700	5.31	24	12	1	0	9	0	96.2	104	414	59	57	7	3	3	10	26	2	71	4	0
Accardo, Jeremy, Norwich	1	0	1.000	0.93	8	0	0	0	6	4	9.2	8	39	3	1	0	0	0	1	0	15	0	0
Almonte, Edwin, Erie *	1	5	.167	4.97	52	0	0	0	47	33	50.2	57	220	31	28	10	1	0	2	14	1	50	0	0
Anderson, Luke, Norwich	0	2	.000	7.24	8	0	0	0	4	0	13.2	18	59	11	11	4	1	1	0	2	1	14	0	0
Andrade, Stephen, New Hampshire	3	2	.600	1.97	35	0	0	0	14	3	50.1	23	191	12	11	3	2	1	2	16	2	71	4	0
Artiles, Carlos, Trenton *	3	2	.600	3.55	32	0	0	0	12	0	45.2	49	212	27	18	4	1	1	3	29	2	37	3	0
Bacani, David, Binghamton	0	0	.000	0.00	4	0	0	0	4	0	4.0	1	13	0	0	0	0	0	1	0	0	2	0	0
Bailie, Matthew, Bowie	2	3	.400	5.40	6	5	1	1	0	0	28.1	26	121	17	17	5	1	0	2	10	0	18	1	0
Banks, Joshua, New Hampshire	8	12	.400	3.83	27	27	2	0	0	0	162.1	159	640	76	69	18	4	7	0	11	0	145	3	0
Bannister, Brian, Binghamton	9	4	.692	2.56	18	18	1	1	0	0	109.0	91	427	36	31	11	1	1	6	27	0	94	2	1
Barker, Kevin, New Hampshire *	0	0	.000	9.00	1	0	0	0	0	0	1.0	2	5	1	1	0	0	0	0	1	0	1	1	0
Barrett, William, New Britain *	1	0	1.000	0.51	10	0	0	0	2	0	17.2	11	69	4	1	0	0	0	7	1	25	0	0
Bauer, Gregory, Reading	0	1	.000	1.29	5	0	0	0	2	0	7.0	6	29	2	1	0	0	0	4	1	4	0	0
Bay, Ronald, Akron	3	3	.500	4.76	8	0	0	0	0	0	45.1	45	186	24	24	5	2	1	2	13	0	40	2	0

Pitcher, Team	W	L	Pct.	ERA	G	GS	CG	ShO	GF	Sv.	IP	H	TBF	R	ER	HR	SH	SF	HB	BB	IBB	SO	WP	Bk.
Beam, Randall, Portland *	2	3	.400	2.53	34	0	0	0	10	2	46.1	35	191	18	13	3	3	2	3	20	4	49	1	0
Bedard, Erik, Bowie *	0	1	.000	9.00	1	1	0	0	0	0	2.0	2	9	2	2	0	0	0	1	0	4	0	1
Beech, Matt, Erie *	2	3	.400	4.68	6	5	1	0	0	0	32.2	34	148	19	17	4	0	0	5	18	0	23	3	0
Begg, Christopher, Norwich	8	7	.533	3.07	23	21	0	0	0	0	138.0	142	561	57	47	9	6	1	1	23	1	86	2	0
Bergmann, Jay, Harrisburg	2	0	1.000	1.22	21	0	0	0	8	5	37.0	27	152	7	5	3	0	0	2	16	1	37	2	0
Bierd, Randor, Erie	1	3	.250	5.40	4	4	0	0	0	0	21.2	28	103	19	13	2	1	3	3	8	0	10	2	0
Birkins, Kurt, Bowie *	7	11	.389	3.91	26	24	0	0	0	0	129.0	134	552	69	56	8	5	2	11	42	0	114	10	0
Birtwell, John, Erie	0	2	.000	4.46	29	0	0	0	13	0	40.1	40	178	23	20	6	0	1	6	16	0	23	2	0
Blackburn, Robert, New Britain	2	4	.333	1.84	7	7	2	1	0	0	49.0	35	183	16	10	1	3	1	2	10	1	27	1	0
Borner, Brady, Altoona *	6	1	.857	2.08	48	0	0	0	14	0	90.2	77	349	22	21	8	5	1	2	13	2	90	1	0
Borrell, Daniel, Trenton *	1	1	.500	6.34	10	7	0	0	0	0	38.1	49	176	30	27	8	1	2	0	16	0	32	3	1
Bouknight, Kip, Harrisburg	4	4	.500	4.01	20	13	0	0	1	0	89.2	92	382	46	40	10	2	3	3	32	2	60	4	0
Bowie, Micah, Harrisburg *	1	1	.500	4.41	10	0	0	0	5	1	16.1	16	67	8	8	1	0	1	0	3	0	19	0	0
Bray, Bill, Harrisburg *	1	0	1.000	6.35	3	0	0	0	1	1	5.2	10	27	4	4	1	0	0	1	0	0	6	0	0
Bridges, Donnie, Harrisburg	1	3	.250	4.21	5	5	0	0	0	0	25.2	34	124	18	12	1	0	2	3	8	0	18	1	0
Brooks, Conor, Portland	4	2	.667	4.85	52	0	0	0	15	2	68.2	76	289	40	37	4	4	4	5	18	1	42	3	1
Brooks, Jacob, Akron	0	0	.000	5.06	6	0	0	0	2	0	5.1	4	23	3	3	0	1	1	2	1	0	2	1	1
Bruback, Matt, Bowie	5	2	.714	4.14	22	10	0	0	1	0	82.2	79	348	44	38	9	0	6	10	20	2	71	1	0
Brunet, Michael, Trenton	2	1	.667	3.43	15	0	0	0	7	0	21.0	23	94	10	8	0	1	0	3	6	0	21	1	0
Bucktrot, Keith, Reading	3	4	.429	5.52	11	11	0	0	0	0	62.0	76	281	40	38	10	2	2	4	26	0	34	3	1
Bumatay, Michael, Erie *	2	4	.333	4.08	50	0	0	0	19	2	64.0	56	283	33	29	8	1	2	4	36	1	72	1	1
Burke, Erick, Reading *	3	2	.600	3.15	26	0	0	0	10	2	40.0	32	162	14	14	1	2	3	0	12	1	47	2	0
Burres, Brian, Norwich *	9	6	.600	4.20	26	24	0	0	1	0	128.2	130	563	66	60	13	6	3	10	57	1	105	8	1
Butto, Francisco, Reading	2	5	.286	3.65	36	1	0	0	16	3	56.2	57	251	35	23	9	1	1	5	21	0	55	2	0
Buzachero, Edward, New Hampshire	4	5	.444	3.97	46	2	0	0	11	0	81.2	82	352	44	36	13	2	1	7	31	3	84	7	0
Byard, David, Binghamton	0	0	.000	0.00	1	0	0	0	1	0	2.0	1	9	0	0	0	0	0	2	0	0	0	0	0
Bynum, Mike, Erie *	3	0	1.000	2.40	5	5	0	0	0	0	30.0	21	118	8	8	2	2	1	0	9	0	34	1	1
Cabrera, Daniel, Bowie	1	0	1.000	3.00	1	1	0	0	0	0	6.0	8	27	3	2	1	0	0	2	0	0	7	2	0
Cameron, Kevin, New Britain	6	2	.750	2.72	43	0	0	0	17	6	79.1	76	341	38	24	8	2	2	1	27	1	60	1	1
Cameron, Kevin, New Britain	6	5	.545	2.55	58	0	0	0	45	19	88.1	70	361	27	25	11	3	2	4	31	2	99	6	0
Candelario, Eddie, Altoona	3	4	.429	3.12	13	13	0	0	0	0	75.0	76	312	33	26	5	4	4	3	15	0	59	7	1
Capps, Matt, Altoona	0	2	.000	2.70	17	0	0	0	12	7	20.0	21	85	8	6	2	0	0	0	1	0	26	0	1
Carlson, Jesse, New Hampshire *	3	2	.600	1.83	39	0	0	0	13	5	39.1	28	147	8	8	2	1	1	3	5	0	42	0	1
Carmona, Fausto, Akron	6	5	.545	4.07	14	14	0	0	0	0	90.2	100	392	46	41	7	5	2	8	20	1	57	2	0
Chantres, Carlos, Reading	5	12	.294	4.64	26	24	0	0	1	0	141.2	160	621	90	73	18	8	8	7	55	0	76	6	1
Chenard, Kenneth, Binghamton *	7	8	.467	5.12	22	22	1	0	0	0	103.2	107	462	69	59	15	4	2	8	45	0	95	10	0
Chiasson, Scott, Norwich	0	0	.000	5.68	15	0	0	0	5	0	19.0	15	85	12	12	1	0	2	1	13	0	25	3	0
Childress, Daylan, New Britain	3	4	.429	5.19	29	6	0	0	13	2	67.2	60	289	40	39	7	2	3	9	29	1	59	2	0
Cliffords, Benjamin, Bowie	0	0	.000	0.00	1	0	0	0	1	0	0.2	0	3	0	0	0	0	0	1	0	0	0	0	0
Connolly, Michael, Altoona *	5	6	.455	3.32	15	15	1	0	0	0	84.0	90	361	35	31	4	3	3	2	24	0	60	1	0
Cooper, Christopher, Akron *	4	1	.800	2.08	43	0	0	0	28	8	56.1	50	232	19	13	3	2	2	1	18	2	60	2	0
Cordido, Julio, Norwich *	0	0	.000	3.86	2	0	0	0	2	0	2.1	4	13	1	1	0	0	0	0	2	0	1	0	0
Cordova, Vincent, Binghamton	0	1	.000	2.57	1	1	0	0	0	0	7.0	4	30	2	2	0	0	0	1	2	0	7	1	0
Cornejo, Nate, Erie	4	12	.250	4.59	19	19	0	0	0	0	102.0	126	430	57	52	15	0	2	1	17	0	48	4	0
Cullen, Ryan, Binghamton *	0	0	.000	9.00	1	0	0	0	0	0	2.0	3	10	2	2	1	0	0	0	1	1	3	0	0
Davis, Allen, Reading *	13	9	.591	3.64	27	25	3	0	1	0	183.0	208	751	79	74	20	9	6	8	22	0	97	3	0
Day, Zach, Harrisburg	1	0	1.000	2.77	3	3	0	0	0	0	13.0	14	50	4	4	1	2	0	0	1	0	10	1	0
Deaton, Kevin, Binghamton	3	4	.429	4.19	11	10	0	0	0	0	53.2	56	227	31	25	7	0	0	0	13	0	55	1	0
De Jong, Jordan, New Hampshire	1	4	.200	5.88	45	0	0	0	18	2	67.1	82	297	49	44	5	3	3	3	21	1	63	7	0
De La Cruz, Eulogio, Erie	0	1	.000	16.20	1	0	0	0	0	0	1.2	2	11	3	3	0	0	0	0	4	0	0	0	0
Delcarmen, Manny, Portland	4	4	.500	3.23	31	0	0	0	8	3	39.0	31	166	23	14	3	3	0	0	20	1	49	6	0
Denham, Daniel, Akron	9	7	.563	3.15	21	21	1	0	0	0	140.0	115	565	55	49	6	4	5	13	30	1	108	6	0
Desalvo, Matthew, Trenton	9	5	.643	3.02	25	24	0	0	1	0	149.0	106	604	55	50	8	5	4	9	67	1	151	11	0
Deschenes, Mark, Portland	4	3	.571	3.74	39	0	0	0	25	8	43.1	42	198	24	18	4	3	2	2	24	5	54	1	0
Devey, Philip, Portland-Reading	2	7	.222	4.88	38	2	0	0	12	0	51.2	55	228	32	28	5	4	3	3	21	4	49	4	0
Diaz, Jose, Akron	0	0	.000	0.00	4	0	0	0	2	1	15.2	5	53	0	0	0	0	0	0	3	0	19	1	0
Dittler, Jake, Akron	10	9	.526	3.64	28	27	0	0	1	0	173.0	187	765	94	70	12	4	3	8	61	0	107	10	2
DuBose, Eric, Bowie *	8	10	.444	3.25	21	20	0	0	0	0	122.0	113	496	52	44	10	6	5	4	29	0	114	5	1
Echols, Justin, Harrisburg	9	7	.563	5.20	31	17	0	0	4	0	116.0	138	531	78	67	21	1	1	7	40	2	120	8	1
Edwards, Bryan, Binghamton	6	6	.500	3.65	35	13	0	0	7	1	118.1	124	514	53	48	8	6	4	6	46	5	85	9	2
Eisentrager, Daniel, Akron	0	0	.000	6.00	1	1	0	0	0	0	3.0	4	14	3	2	1	0	0	1	1	0	1	0	0
Evans, Kyle, Akron	1	1	.500	5.73	7	0	0	0	2	0	11.0	13	48	7	7	2	2	0	0	6	1	7	1	0
Evans, Tom, Altoona	0	0	.000	0.00	1	0	0	0	1	0	0.1	1	2	0	0	0	0	0	0	0	0	1	1	0
Ferrari, Anthony, Harrisburg *	0	0	.000	3.38	1	0	0	0	1	0	2.2	3	10	1	1	0	0	0	0	1	0	3	1	0
Fesh, Sean, Reading *	2	0	1.000	1.48	20	0	0	0	9	0	24.1	23	98	7	4	0	1	0	2	5	1	15	0	0
Fisher, Peter, Portland	0	0	.000	9.82	7	0	0	0	2	0	7.1	14	40	8	8	2	1	0	0	5	2	4	0	0
Foley, Travis, Akron	6	2	.750	3.86	36	0	0	0	19	1	53.2	53	230	30	23	5	4	0	0	26	3	40	7	1
Forystek, Brian, Bowie *	2	5	.286	4.22	14	14	0	0	0	0	70.1	81	300	42	33	9	1	1	3	23	0	66	1	0
Gabbard, Kason, Portland *	9	11	.450	4.61	27	25	0	0	0	0	132.2	128	575	80	68	10	5	4	4	65	1	96	9	1
Galarraga, Armando, Harrisburg	3	4	.429	5.19	13	13	1	1	0	0	76.1	80	319	47	44	10	5	3	4	21	0	58	2	1
Garcia, Anderson, Binghamton	4	2	.667	4.97	30	1	0	0	17	5	50.2	59	219	32	28	8	2	2	0	20	2	41	1	1
Garcia, James, Norwich	6	7	.462	4.93	32	15	0	0	4	0	95.0	112	426	56	52	20	2	1	6	35	1	74	0	0
Geary, Geoff, Reading	0	0	.000	0.00	1	0	0	0	0	0	2.0	0	6	0	0	0	0	0	0	0	0	2	0	0
Gil, David, Harrisburg	1	1	.500	3.03	14	2	0	0	6	1	32.2	28	134	12	11	2	2	2	5	9	2	29	3	0
Gomez, Mariano, Akron *	4	3	.571	6.30	18	4	1	0	3	0	40.0	45	188	35	28	4	1	0	4	20	0	27	6	2
Gonzalez, Alexander, Portland	0	0	.000	5.40	1	0	0	0	1	0	3.1	2	14	2	2	1	0	0	0	2	0	3	1	0
Gonzalez, Somer, Harrisburg	0	0	.000	0.00	1	0	0	0	0	0	3.0	1	11	0	0	0	0	0	0	1	0	2	0	0
Gorzelanny, Tom, Altoona *	8	5	.615	3.26	23	23	1	1	0	0	129.2	114	537	50	47	6	5	3	5	46	1	124	5	0
Granado, Jan, New Britain *	2	2	.500	5.61	12	2	0	0	5	0	25.2	28	110	17	16	3	3	2	1	9	0	19	1	0
Green, Steve, Akron	2	2	.500	3.45	26	0	0	0	7	1	44.1	36	190	22	17	4	2	4	23	0	45	6	0
Grimsley, Jason, Bowie	2	0	1.000	1.13	8	2	0	0	4	0	8.0	4	32	1	1	0	0	0	0	4	1	4	0	0

Pitcher, Team	W	L	Pct.	ERA	G	GS	CG	ShO	GF	Sv.	IP	H	TBF	R	ER	HR	SH	SF	HB	BB	IBB	SO	WP	Bk.
Gronkiewicz, Lee, New Hampshire	2	0	1.000	1.41	38	0	0	0	34	24	38.1	24	145	7	6	2	2	1	0	10	1	45	0	0
Guerrero, Cristian, Harrisburg	0	0	.000	0.00	1	0	0	0	1	0	1.0	0	4	0	0	0	0	0	0	1	0	1	0	0
Gutierrez, Jannio, New Britain	1	0	1.000	2.70	9	0	0	0	3	0	13.1	11	56	4	4	3	1	0	0	6	1	12	2	0
Haines, Joseph, Portland	0	1	.000	0.87	6	0	0	0	1	0	10.1	6	37	1	1	1	0	0	0	3	0	8	1	0
Hamels, Colbert, Reading *	2	0	1.000	2.37	3	3	0	0	0	0	19.0	10	76	6	5	2	1	0	1	12	0	19	2	0
Hamman, Corey, Erie *	3	5	.375	4.29	45	5	0	0	19	3	92.1	109	398	56	44	8	2	3	4	17	1	60	5	1
Hammond, Joseph, Bowie	0	0	.000	11.57	3	0	0	0	2	0	2.1	6	13	3	3	1	0	0	0	0	0	1	0	0
Hamulack, Tim, Binghamton *	2	2	.500	1.26	21	0	0	0	14	6	28.2	20	113	7	4	0	1	0	0	6	1	27	0	0
Hansen, Craig, Portland	0	0	.000	0.00	8	0	0	0	2	1	9.2	9	38	0	0	0	0	0	0	1	0	10	0	0
Hanson, Mark, Akron	1	0	1.000	8.00	2	0	0	0	2	0	9.0	7	48	9	8	1	0	2	3	8	0	2	4	0
Happ, James, Reading *	1	0	1.000	1.50	1	1	0	0	0	0	6.0	3	23	1	1	0	1	0	0	2	0	8	1	0
Harts, Jeremy, Altoona *	1	2	.333	8.08	29	0	0	0	11	0	39.0	33	200	42	35	4	2	3	5	53	1	46	4	0
Hassey, Brad, New Hampshire	0	0	.000	0.00	1	0	0	0	1	0	1.0	1	3	0	0	0	0	0	0	0	0	1	0	0
Henkel, Robert, Erie *	6	7	.462	5.70	18	14	0	0	0	0	79.0	104	359	60	50	14	5	2	2	30	0	53	3	0
Henn, Sean, Trenton *	2	1	.667	0.71	4	4	0	0	0	0	25.1	16	94	2	2	1	0	0	0	9	0	21	2	0
Hensen, Brian, Erie *	0	0	.000	0.00	2	0	0	0	2	0	2.0	2	9	0	0	0	0	0	1	1	0	0	0	0
Hernandez, Michael, Akron *	0	0	.000	6.23	4	0	0	0	2	0	4.1	4	17	3	3	1	0	0	0	1	0	3	1	0
Hernandez, Yoel, Reading	2	0	1.000	1.32	9	0	0	0	2	0	13.2	12	59	2	2	0	1	0	1	6	2	15	0	0
Hertzler, Barry, Portland	0	0	.000	5.14	3	0	0	0	1	0	7.0	11	33	5	4	0	0	0	0	3	1	6	3	0
Hill, Jeremy, Binghamton	1	3	.250	4.29	19	0	0	0	15	4	21.0	29	104	13	10	1	1	0	0	10	1	20	1	0
Houston, Ryan, New Hampshire	3	2	.600	2.68	33	1	0	0	19	7	40.1	26	156	13	12	3	3	1	0	13	4	50	1	0
Humber, Philip, Binghamton	0	1	.000	6.75	1	1	0	0	0	0	4.0	4	18	3	3	0	0	0	0	2	0	2	0	0
Hundley, Jeffrey, Bowie *	0	0	.000	7.85	11	0	0	0	1	0	18.1	29	93	19	16	3	1	0	4	9	0	15	0	1
Hutchison, Ryan, Reading	0	1	.000	9.00	3	0	0	0	0	0	3.0	3	13	3	3	1	0	0	0	1	0	2	0	1
Isaacson, Charlie, Trenton	6	4	.600	3.26	22	13	0	0	2	0	91.0	102	403	42	33	7	4	0	2	36	1	87	0	0
Izquierdo, Hansel, Altoona	7	5	.583	4.51	24	17	0	0	1	0	103.2	104	449	61	52	6	4	3	6	41	0	84	7	0
Jackson, Kyle, Portland	0	0	.000	6.43	3	0	0	0	2	1	7.0	10	31	5	5	4	0	0	0	0	0	7	2	0
Jackson, Zach, New Hampshire *	4	3	.571	4.00	9	9	0	0	0	0	54.0	57	224	27	24	3	3	3	12	0	43	0	0
Jacobsen, Landon, Altoona	2	0	1.000	3.86	11	0	0	0	2	1	23.1	21	103	14	10	1	1	1	1	11	0	23	2	0
Janssen, Robert, New Hampshire	3	3	.500	2.93	9	9	0	0	0	0	43.0	49	176	20	14	3	1	0	2	4	0	47	2	0
Johnson, James, Altoona *	5	4	.556	3.33	31	1	0	0	9	1	51.1	50	219	25	19	4	5	1	0	16	2	54	8	0
Johnson, James, Bowie	0	0	.000	0.00	1	1	0	0	0	0	7.0	3	25	0	0	0	1	0	1	2	0	6	0	0
Johnson, Jeremy, Erie	9	8	.529	4.91	24	24	0	0	0	0	132.0	161	585	91	72	23	5	1	6	42	0	82	3	0
Johnson, Mark, Erie	4	3	.571	5.06	32	7	0	0	9	0	80.0	89	346	50	45	11	2	2	6	15	2	50	2	0
Jordan, Robert, Portland *	0	0	.000	0.00	1	0	0	0	0	0	0.1	1	4	1	0	0	0	0	0	1	0	1	0	0
Julianel, Benjamin, Trenton *	5	3	.625	3.90	46	2	0	0	14	1	87.2	88	398	43	38	7	3	3	7	50	5	106	7	1
Junge, Eric, Binghamton	1	1	.500	4.15	3	0	0	0	1	0	13.0	14	55	7	6	0	0	1	0	2	0	14	0	0
Karp, Joshua, Harrisburg	2	5	.286	4.68	11	10	0	0	0	0	57.2	57	252	32	30	6	6	1	8	23	1	40	3	0
Karstens, Jeffrey, Trenton	12	11	.522	4.15	28	27	0	0	0	0	169.0	192	724	91	78	16	3	5	3	42	1	147	8	1
Kaye, Justin, Altoona	3	3	.500	4.09	53	0	0	0	42	22	61.2	63	274	29	28	4	0	1	1	29	3	54	4	0
Keefer, Ryan, Bowie	7	3	.700	3.20	54	1	0	0	18	1	84.1	64	340	33	30	7	4	1	4	32	1	92	2	0
Kennard, Jeffery, Trenton	0	1	.000	0.00	5	0	0	0	1	0	6.2	6	30	1	0	0	1	0	1	5	0	4	1	0
King, Jeremy, Trenton	0	0	.000	2.31	5	0	0	0	1	0	11.2	7	49	3	3	1	0	0	1	7	0	9	0	0
Kleine, Victor, Akron *	1	6	.143	4.40	27	5	0	0	16	0	61.1	63	268	33	30	5	6	2	6	24	4	38	4	0
Knippschild, Charles, Akron *	0	0	.000	0.00	2	0	0	0	2	0	3.0	1	11	0	0	0	0	0	0	2	0	1	0	0
Kobow, Michael, Erie	0	0	.000	10.12	3	0	0	0	0	0	2.2	4	16	3	3	0	0	0	0	4	0	2	0	0
Korecky, Robert, New Britain *	0	0	.000	6.75	2	0	0	0	1	0	1.1	2	7	1	1	0	0	0	0	1	0	1	0	0
Laffey, Aaron, Akron *	1	0	1.000	3.60	1	1	0	0	0	0	5.0	8	24	2	2	0	0	0	0	2	0	6	1	0
Lara, Juan, Akron *	1	2	.333	4.56	18	0	0	0	8	5	23.2	27	110	15	12	1	2	2	1	14	3	16	3	1
Larrison, Preston, Erie	4	3	.571	5.23	7	7	0	0	0	0	32.2	38	145	21	19	3	2	0	5	9	1	11	1	0
Lavigne, Tim, Binghamton	0	0	.000	1.04	8	0	0	0	8	5	8.2	8	37	1	1	0	1	0	0	3	1	7	0	0
Lee, Seung Hak, Reading	3	1	.750	1.97	14	11	0	0	1	0	64.0	58	267	17	14	2	3	1	2	24	0	50	3	0
Lester, Jonathan, Portland *	11	6	.647	2.61	26	26	3	1	0	0	148.1	114	596	52	43	10	6	4	4	57	3	163	10	1
Lindstrom, Matthew, Binghamton	2	5	.286	5.40	35	10	0	0	11	0	73.1	90	363	61	44	11	3	5	5	55	2	58	11	1
Liriano, Francisco, New Britain *	3	5	.375	3.64	13	13	0	0	0	0	76.2	70	317	36	31	6	0	0	2	26	0	92	4	1
Lopez, Rafael, Binghamton	2	10	.167	5.98	32	6	0	0	5	0	84.1	109	395	64	56	9	2	5	9	35	2	59	5	0
MacLane, Evan, Binghamton *	3	2	.600	4.14	9	9	1	1	0	0	58.2	63	248	31	27	7	1	1	9	0	48	1	0
Maduro, Calvin, Trenton	4	2	.667	3.18	7	7	0	0	0	0	34.0	33	139	17	12	2	3	2	3	9	0	21	2	0
Maholm, Paul, Altoona *	6	2	.750	3.20	16	16	0	0	0	0	81.2	73	332	32	29	5	9	3	2	26	2	75	3	0
Maldonado Oquendo, Ivan, Binghamton	1	1	.500	4.26	5	1	0	0	2	0	12.2	12	54	6	6	1	1	2	3	0	13	0	0
Mann, Jim, Portland	3	1	.750	1.80	23	0	0	0	21	12	25.0	12	98	6	5	0	1	0	13	2	34	1	0
Manning, Charles, Trenton *	4	3	.571	3.33	45	0	0	0	16	2	73.0	64	319	33	27	6	2	3	6	37	2	67	3	0
Manning, David, Bowie	1	1	.500	12.71	8	0	0	0	1	0	5.2	8	30	8	8	0	1	0	0	6	4	2	0
Maples, Christopher, Erie	0	0	.000	27.00	1	0	0	0	0	0	0.2	1	7	2	2	0	0	1	0	4	0	0	0	0
Marcum, Shawn, New Hampshire	7	1	.875	2.53	9	9	1	1	0	0	53.1	44	206	15	15	5	2	2	2	10	0	40	1	0
Martin, Gregory, Altoona *	0	1	.000	16.87	3	0	0	0	2	0	2.2	5	14	5	5	0	0	0	1	0	0	1	1	0
Martin, John, Akron	3	1	.750	2.38	10	10	0	0	0	0	56.2	42	221	17	15	3	1	1	3	8	0	63	1	0
Martinez, Edgar Ramon, Portland	0	0	.000	1.50	15	0	0	0	3	1	18.0	12	72	3	3	0	0	1	0	8	0	13	1	2
Mastny, Thomas, Akron	1	1	.500	2.18	5	3	0	0	1	0	20.2	18	87	7	5	0	0	0	2	5	0	18	1	0
Matos, Josue, New Hampshire-Reading	3	1	.750	1.31	16	4	0	0	2	0	48.0	32	179	7	7	2	0	0	0	5	0	48	0	0
Maust, David, Harrisburg *	5	4	.556	2.32	26	14	2	1	8	0	100.2	79	381	31	26	7	8	1	8	14	2	78	1	0
Mazone, Brian, Norwich *	11	8	.579	3.10	30	20	0	0	3	1	127.2	122	515	52	44	9	11	3	6	34	1	89	3	1
McCurdy, Nicholas, Bowie	5	5	.500	4.22	30	2	0	0	7	2	64.0	70	274	37	30	10	4	2	4	15	0	48	3	0
McGinley, Blake, Binghamton *	1	0	1.000	2.25	2	0	0	0	0	0	4.0	4	16	1	1	0	0	0	0	0	4	0	0
McGowan, Dustin, New Hampshire	0	2	.000	3.34	6	6	0	0	0	0	35.0	35	147	16	13	6	1	3	1	10	0	33	1	0
McNab, Timothy, Akron *	2	4	.333	5.61	42	2	0	0	16	1	85.0	105	382	63	53	6	3	1	7	21	2	64	5	1
Mercado, Arnoldo, Norwich	0	0	.000	7.20	4	0	0	0	1	0	5.0	9	22	4	4	1	0	0	0	1	0	5	0	0
Mercedes, Victor, Harrisburg	0	0	.000	0.00	2	0	0	0	2	0	2.0	1	8	1	0	0	0	0	1	0	0	0	0
Meredith, Cla, Portland	1	0	1.000	0.00	12	0	0	0	11	9	15.0	5	51	0	0	0	1	1	0	3	1	12	0	0
Miller, Colby, New Britain	2	7	.222	3.60	12	12	1	0	0	0	70.0	70	288	33	28	7	2	3	2	19	1	41	1	0
Miller, Jason, New Britain *	1	2	.333	2.72	26	0	0	0	11	4	49.2	34	204	17	15	5	3	1	0	22	2	56	0	0

Pitcher, Team	W	L	Pct.	ERA	G	GS	CG	ShO	GF	Sv.	IP	H	TBF	R	ER	HR	SH	SF	HB	BB	IBB	SO	WP	Bk.
Miller, Matt, Akron	0	0	.000	0.00	1	0	0	0	0	0	1.0	0	3	0	0	0	0	0	0	0	0	0	0	0
Minix, Travis, Reading	1	1	.500	1.84	39	0	0	0	17	7	58.2	44	232	13	12	3	2	2	1	15	3	55	3	0
Misch, Patrick, Norwich *	4	2	.667	3.52	9	9	1	0	0	0	61.1	63	245	25	24	7	3	2	3	7	0	43	0	0
Montero, Oscar, Norwich	5	4	.556	3.88	36	0	0	0	15	0	51.0	45	219	23	22	7	3	2	2	28	1	62	8	0
Montes, Alberto, Norwich	0	2	.000	7.36	23	0	0	0	7	0	36.2	54	165	30	30	6	4	1	3	9	1	26	0	4
Moreno, Anthony, Norwich	2	4	.333	5.01	18	7	0	0	4	0	50.1	59	227	37	28	4	5	1	1	22	0	33	3	0
Moreno, Edwin, Reading	1	3	.250	4.35	4	4	0	0	0	0	20.2	20	86	10	10	4	0	0	2	2	0	17	0	0
Morris, Cory, Bowie	8	5	.615	3.03	29	25	0	0	2	0	142.2	116	595	50	48	11	5	1	3	78	4	159	6	1
Mujica, Edward, Akron	2	1	.667	2.88	27	0	0	0	18	10	34.1	36	137	11	11	2	4	0	0	5	0	33	3	1
Mumma, Bradley, New Hampshire *	0	1	.000	4.05	7	0	0	0	6	0	6.2	6	28	4	3	0	0	2	0	2	0	6	0	0
Neshek, Patrick, New Britain	6	4	.600	2.19	55	0	0	0	48	24	82.1	69	331	25	20	9	4	2	2	21	3	95	3	0
Nieves, Raul, Portland	0	0	.000	13.50	1	0	0	0	1	0	1.1	2	11	2	2	0	0	0	0	5	0	0	0	0
Norderum, Jason, Harrisburg *	3	3	.500	4.60	25	0	0	0	9	2	47.0	49	215	31	24	3	5	2	8	25	2	33	1	1
Ogiltree, John, New Hampshire-Harrisburg	1	0	1.000	1.93	7	0	0	0	0	0	9.1	7	39	2	2	0	0	1	3	0	6	1	0
Olson, Justin, New Britain	9	8	.529	4.79	31	15	0	0	6	0	109.0	94	462	67	58	17	4	2	5	49	2	103	3	0
Pahucki, David, Portland	3	1	.750	7.31	13	1	0	0	3	0	16.0	16	83	16	13	2	1	0	1	20	1	15	5	0
Palmer, Jonathan, Norwich	0	1	.000	2.67	11	2	0	0	4	1	27.0	22	118	14	8	2	0	2	3	9	0	20	2	0
Pannone, Anthony, Norwich	1	2	.333	5.70	24	1	0	0	12	1	36.1	41	167	28	23	2	6	0	1	23	1	17	3	0
Papelbon, Jonathan, Portland	5	2	.714	2.48	14	14	0	0	0	0	87.0	59	337	28	24	9	4	3	5	23	3	83	2	1
Parcus, William, Reading *	0	0	.000	9.64	4	0	0	0	2	0	4.2	6	23	5	5	1	0	0	0	3	0	1	0	0
Parrish, John, Bowie *	0	0	.000	2.89	5	0	0	0	0	0	9.1	7	41	3	3	0	1	0	2	6	0	13	2	0
Pauley, David, Portland	9	7	.563	3.81	27	27	1	0	0	0	156.0	169	660	86	66	18	5	5	5	34	3	104	6	0
Pearson, Jason, Portland-Bowie	1	1	.500	4.15	19	0	0	0	9	0	21.2	24	95	11	10	3	0	0	2	9	1	24	1	0
Pekarek, Justin, Akron *	1	0	1.000	0.00	1	1	0	0	0	0	5.0	6	20	0	0	0	0	0	0	2	0	2	0	0
Penn, Hayden, Bowie	7	6	.538	3.83	20	19	1	0	0	0	110.1	101	452	51	47	11	1	7	1	37	0	120	6	0
Pennington, Jeffery, Akron	2	1	.667	4.19	19	0	0	0	18	9	19.1	18	92	10	9	2	2	0	3	15	0	21	1	0
Perez, Rafael, Akron *	4	3	.571	1.76	15	8	0	0	3	1	66.2	53	264	22	13	5	4	3	2	12	0	46	3	0
Perkins, Glen, New Britain *	4	4	.500	4.90	14	14	0	0	0	0	79.0	80	349	45	43	4	2	2	8	35	1	67	3	1
Perkins, Vince, New Hampshire	7	7	.500	4.03	26	24	0	0	1	0	131.2	124	559	65	59	9	6	5	7	51	0	111	7	0
Peterson, Adam, Erie	4	3	.571	6.58	47	0	0	0	10	0	64.1	78	305	51	47	8	1	5	4	35	0	54	9	1
Peterson, Matthew, Altoona	11	9	.550	5.51	27	26	0	0	0	0	143.2	156	646	102	88	19	10	5	11	74	1	87	11	1
Petit, Yusmeiro, Binghamton	9	3	.750	2.91	21	21	2	0	0	0	117.2	90	453	41	38	15	3	2	2	18	1	130	0	0
Piersoll, Chris, Bowie	5	1	.833	1.61	27	0	0	0	7	1	50.1	29	196	12	9	3	0	0	5	13	2	63	2	1
Pope, Justin, Trenton	6	4	.600	2.81	57	0	0	0	54	29	77.0	65	299	29	24	2	10	1	1	20	5	55	3	0
Portobanco, Luz, Binghamton	2	12	.143	7.56	40	7	0	0	15	2	75.0	101	370	73	63	9	5	4	7	48	3	49	8	0
Purcey, David, New Hampshire *	4	3	.571	2.93	8	8	1	0	0	0	43.0	32	184	17	14	2	0	2	1	25	0	45	4	0
Raggio, Brady, Reading	1	2	.333	5.34	8	4	0	0	1	0	30.1	38	125	18	18	2	2	0	0	6	0	19	0	0
Ramirez, Ismael, New Hampshire	8	13	.381	4.12	27	27	0	0	0	0	150.2	155	623	75	69	19	8	7	3	32	1	125	0	1
Ramirez, Ramon, Trenton	6	5	.545	3.84	15	15	0	0	0	0	89.0	79	374	44	38	10	1	3	1	35	0	82	4	1
Randazzo, Jeffrey, New Britain *	0	1	.000	4.91	2	0	0	0	1	0	3.2	4	15	2	2	0	1	1	0	2	1	1	0	0
Rasner, Darrell, Harrisburg	6	7	.462	3.59	27	26	1	0	0	0	150.1	150	621	66	60	10	7	5	10	29	2	96	2	0
Ray, Chris, Bowie	1	2	.333	0.96	31	0	0	0	28	18	37.1	17	133	5	4	3	1	2	3	7	0	40	1	0
Reed, Brian, New Hampshire	0	1	.000	4.91	8	0	0	0	3	0	11.0	13	51	6	6	1	0	0	0	6	0	10	3	0
Reimers, Cameron, New Hampshire	6	7	.462	4.15	19	16	1	1	1	0	106.1	134	472	71	49	6	2	1	6	20	0	55	0	0
Rhodes, Arthur, Akron *	0	0	.000	0.00	1	1	0	0	0	0	1.0	0	3	0	0	0	0	0	0	0	0	0	0	0
Rice, Scott, Bowie *	4	1	.800	3.27	57	0	0	0	19	1	74.1	68	312	29	27	4	5	3	8	32	2	42	8	0
Riggan, Jerrod, Binghamton	0	1	.000	5.79	4	0	0	0	3	0	4.2	7	24	4	3	0	0	0	0	3	2	3	0	0
Rivera, Saul, Harrisburg	3	3	.500	2.47	40	0	0	0	29	9	76.2	72	319	30	21	3	7	0	3	20	6	70	3	0
Rleal, Sendy, Bowie	4	4	.500	2.04	56	0	0	0	38	16	70.2	46	268	19	16	4	8	3	1	18	3	75	2	0
Roach, Jason, Altoona	1	3	.250	4.42	10	4	0	0	4	2	36.2	45	163	21	18	7	2	3	3	11	0	19	3	0
Roberts, Grant, Trenton	1	1	.500	5.25	9	3	0	0	4	0	24.0	25	111	14	14	2	2	0	1	17	1	20	2	0
Rodney, Thomas, Erie	5	3	.625	3.99	45	1	0	0	14	3	79.0	91	352	42	35	5	3	4	7	29	1	53	1	0
Rodriguez, Felix, Trenton	0	0	.000	0.00	2	2	0	0	0	0	3.0	1	11	0	0	0	0	0	0	3	0	3	0	0
Rodriguez, Jose, Binghamton	3	5	.375	3.96	33	0	0	0	14	2	61.1	63	275	37	27	3	4	1	7	30	1	59	7	0
Roehl, Scott, Akron	0	1	.000	7.71	2	0	0	0	2	0	2.1	4	12	2	2	2	0	0	0	1	1	3	0	1
Rojas, Christopher, Reading	12	6	.667	3.92	22	22	1	0	0	0	131.0	126	546	62	57	17	5	4	8	36	0	107	9	0
Roman, Orlando, Binghamton	4	4	.500	4.95	31	18	0	0	3	0	120.0	123	531	75	66	18	3	7	9	58	3	136	9	0
Roney, Matt, Erie	0	1	.000	1.25	11	0	0	0	4	1	21.2	13	86	3	3	1	2	1	4	6	1	23	0	0
Rueckel, Daniel, Harrisburg	9	6	.600	4.16	53	0	0	0	28	7	80.0	86	337	41	37	7	8	6	1	21	6	72	6	1
Rundles, Richard, Harrisburg *	6	13	.316	4.18	27	26	2	0	0	0	159.1	177	689	95	74	14	6	2	6	49	2	91	5	0
Sabathia, C.C., Akron *	0	1	.000	1.00	2	2	0	0	0	0	9.0	4	36	3	1	0	1	0	1	2	0	9	1	0
Sadler, William, Norwich	6	5	.545	3.31	47	0	0	0	22	5	84.1	64	360	34	31	4	2	7	12	33	0	81	9	0
Sanchez, Anibal, Portland	3	5	.375	3.45	11	11	0	0	0	0	57.1	53	240	28	22	5	1	2	5	16	2	63	4	1
Sanchez, Humberto, Erie	3	5	.375	5.57	15	11	0	0	0	0	64.2	72	286	42	40	10	1	3	2	27	1	65	5	1
Sanchez, Romulo, Altoona	1	0	1.000	3.60	2	2	0	0	0	0	10.0	11	44	4	4	2	0	1	0	4	0	5	1	0
Schmitt, Eric, Trenton	1	2	.333	5.17	16	6	0	0	2	0	47.0	51	191	27	27	6	3	3	1	7	0	34	2	0
Schroder, Christopher, Harrisburg	2	3	.400	4.70	16	0	0	0	5	0	23.0	20	97	13	12	4	3	1	1	11	3	28	1	0
Sequea, Jacobo, Harrisburg	1	1	.500	6.68	20	0	0	0	12	2	33.2	52	161	27	25	11	3	3	1	13	1	19	3	0
Shafer, Adam, Reading	0	1	.000	2.65	11	0	0	0	4	1	17.0	13	69	8	5	2	0	0	1	5	0	19	0	0
Shaffar, Benjamin, Altoona	2	3	.400	3.44	44	0	0	0	24	9	73.1	73	314	33	28	6	6	2	2	26	2	69	5	1
Sharpless, Joshua, Altoona	1	0	1.000	2.89	7	0	0	0	2	0	9.1	6	39	3	3	0	1	0	0	3	0	13	1	0
Shoemaker, Scott, Portland	0	0	.000	12.27	1	1	0	0	0	0	3.2	6	18	5	5	1	0	0	0	2	0	5	0	0
Shuey, Paul, Akron	0	0	.000	4.50	1	0	0	0	1	0	2.0	2	9	1	1	0	0	0	0	2	0	2	0	0
Sierra, Eduardo, Trenton	3	1	.750	3.28	33	0	0	0	9	2	57.2	37	242	26	21	4	4	2	4	38	1	50	3	0
Simon, Alfredo, Norwich	3	8	.273	5.03	43	9	0	0	28	19	91.1	104	387	54	51	6	8	3	5	24	2	60	5	0
Simonitsch, Errol, New Britain *	6	5	.545	4.12	14	14	0	0	0	0	78.2	92	352	51	36	6	3	1	4	28	2	52	1	0

Pitcher, Team	W	L	Pct.	ERA	G	GS	CG	ShO	GF	Sv.	IP	H	TBF	R	ER	HR	SH	SF	HB	BB	IBB	SO	WP	Bk.
Skaggs, Jon, Trenton	2	7	.222	6.16	22	15	0	0	5	1	80.1	99	375	67	55	14	4	3	5	38	0	48	3	1
Slocum, Brian, Akron	7	5	.583	4.40	21	18	1	0	2	0	102.1	98	430	52	50	9	6	3	6	36	0	95	2	0
Small, Aaron, Trenton	1	0	1.000	3.60	1	1	0	0	0	0	5.0	7	23	3	2	1	0	0	0	1	0	3	1	0
Smith, Christopher, Portland	4	4	.500	5.23	15	15	0	0	0	0	75.2	95	325	46	44	13	6	4	4	15	1	49	3	0
Smith, Matthew, Trenton *	3	4	.429	2.80	22	4	0	0	5	2	54.2	46	225	24	17	2	2	2	0	23	0	59	3	1
Smith, Mike, Reading	5	14	.263	4.48	28	28	1	0	0	0	170.2	162	747	97	85	18	10	5	23	82	0	113	14	1
Snusz, Christopher, Altoona	0	0	.000	0.00	1	0	0	0	1	0	1.0	2	5	1	0	0	0	0	0	0	0	0	0	0
Song, Seung, Norwich	3	2	.600	2.48	6	6	0	0	0	0	36.1	34	145	10	10	4	2	0	0	7	0	29	5	0
Sowers, Jeremy, Akron	5	1	.833	2.08	13	13	0	0	...	0	82.1	74	316	25	19	8	...	...	...	9	1	70	...	...
Speigner, Jimmy, New Britain	6	10	.375	4.13	23	23	2	1	0	0	143.2	149	599	75	66	14	6	2	12	28	1	94	2	1
Stahl, Mark, Bowie *	3	6	.333	4.04	18	17	0	0	0	0	89.0	83	394	46	40	5	7	0	4	58	0	52	5	0
Stanford, Jason, Akron *	2	0	1.000	2.45	8	0	0	0	3	0	14.2	15	63	5	4	1	2	0	4	4	0	13	0	0
Stevenson, Jason, Harrisburg *	1	9	.100	10.57	13	12	0	0	0	0	53.2	80	268	65	63	15	4	2	8	32	1	37	2	0
Stewart, Paul, Altoona	6	10	.375	4.92	26	20	0	0	1	0	120.2	143	531	78	66	19	7	5	1	44	1	76	5	0
Stotts, Jarrett, Trenton	0	0	.000	9.00	1	0	0	0	1	0	1.0	1	6	1	1	0	1	0	1	1	0	0	0	0
Strayhorn, Kole, Binghamton	0	0	.000	0.00	1	0	0	0	0	0	2.0	0	6	0	0	0	0	0	0	0	0	1	0	0
Sturge, Justin, Portland *	2	1	.667	4.88	33	0	0	0	8	0	48.0	52	208	30	26	3	1	4	3	16	2	33	7	0
Sweeney, Matthew, Reading	1	0	1.000	3.00	1	1	0	0	0	0	6.0	4	26	2	2	0	0	1	0	3	0	5	0	0
Sylvester, Billy, Harrisburg	2	4	.333	4.35	26	1	0	0	15	0	41.1	40	191	20	20	8	0	0	5	29	3	52	5	2
Thomas, John, New Britain *	5	4	.556	6.92	39	8	0	0	12	0	79.1	114	381	71	61	14	3	4	2	37	5	52	4	0
Thompson, Travis, Akron-Reading	4	1	.800	2.30	26	0	0	0	9	1	43.0	35	168	13	11	1	0	1	1	11	0	26	2	2
Thorp, Paul, Trenton	0	0	.000	0.00	2	0	0	0	2	1	3.0	1	11	0	0	0	0	0	0	0	0	1	0	0
Thorpe, Tracy, New Hampshire	2	2	.500	3.89	26	0	0	0	6	1	37.0	30	152	18	16	9	3	2	4	17	2	36	2	0
Threets, Erick, Norwich *	1	2	.333	5.06	30	0	0	0	7	2	42.2	43	199	28	24	2	1	0	2	31	0	35	6	0
Tomori, Denney, Portland	2	3	.400	3.42	19	6	1	0	2	0	52.2	65	224	31	20	3	6	1	4	12	1	35	2	1
Torres, Melquicedec, Bowie	2	2	.500	5.28	25	0	0	0	11	0	29.0	31	130	18	17	7	4	1	2	18	0	33	6	1
Tousa, Scott, Erie	0	0	.000	0.00	1	0	0	0	1	0	0.1	0	1	0	0	0	0	0	0	0	0	0	0	0
Traber, Billy, Akron *	3	2	.600	2.65	5	5	0	0	0	0	34.0	25	133	11	10	2	0	0	1	5	0	27	0	0
Trachsel, Steve, Binghamton	1	0	1.000	3.00	2	2	1	0	0	0	12.0	8	46	4	4	2	1	0	0	4	0	7	0	0
Urdaneta, Lino, Binghamton	0	0	.000	5.40	1	0	0	0	0	0	1.2	2	8	1	1	0	0	0	1	1	0	0	0	0
Valdes, Marc, Trenton	1	3	.250	5.28	10	1	0	0	6	0	15.1	18	68	11	9	0	3	0	3	5	0	14	0	0
Valdez, Merkin, Norwich *	5	6	.455	3.53	24	19	1	0	1	0	107.0	99	451	48	42	7	3	5	8	45	0	96	8	0
Van Dusen, Derrick, Akron *	1	0	1.000	1.69	4	0	0	0	2	0	5.1	6	23	1	1	1	0	0	0	2	0	4	0	0
Vasquez, Virgil, Erie	2	8	.200	5.27	15	15	0	0	0	0	83.2	93	356	59	49	10	5	5	6	14	0	53	1	0
Verlander, Justin, Erie	2	0	1.000	0.28	7	7	0	0	0	0	32.2	11	115	1	1	1	1	0	7	0	0	32	0	1
Vermilyea, James, New Hampshire	3	3	.500	2.60	27	4	0	0	6	1	65.2	67	272	21	19	5	1	1	3	16	2	52	0	0
Villegas, Felix, Reading	2	2	.500	5.67	26	0	0	0	11	0	33.1	40	149	21	21	3	0	3	1	15	2	25	1	0
Walk, Mitchell, Norwich *	0	1	.000	4.50	1	1	0	0	0	0	6.0	5	24	3	3	1	0	0	0	2	0	3	0	0
Waugh, Jason, New Hampshire	0	0	.000	0.00	1	0	0	0	1	0	1.0	0	3	0	0	0	0	0	0	0	0	0	0	0
Weis, John, Erie *	0	0	.000	4.60	10	0	0	0	3	0	15.2	19	70	8	8	2	1	0	2	8	1	12	0	0
White, Steven, Trenton	2	7	.222	6.44	11	11	0	0	0	0	50.1	61	238	41	36	9	1	2	4	26	0	54	2	1
Wilson, Brian, Norwich	0	0	.000	0.57	15	0	0	0	15	8	15.2	6	58	1	1	0	0	0	0	5	0	22	0	0
Wilson, Jeffrey, Reading *	0	2	.000	7.76	22	1	0	0	6	0	29.0	40	139	28	25	6	2	1	3	12	1	28	0	1
Wolfe, Brian, New Britain	1	0	1.000	7.04	5	0	0	0	2	0	7.2	10	37	6	6	0	0	0	7	1	4	0	0	0
Worrell, Tim, Reading	0	0	.000	0.00	2	1	0	0	1	0	3.0	0	10	0	0	0	0	0	0	1	0	3	0	0
Yeatman, Matthew, New Britain	5	7	.417	4.08	28	16	1	0	5	0	103.2	99	436	55	47	5	8	5	6	39	5	74	10	0
Youman, Shane, Altoona *	8	6	.571	3.92	44	5	0	0	15	2	101.0	102	445	54	44	10	10	0	2	48	4	77	5	0
Zink, Charles, Portland	8	5	.615	4.87	29	15	1	1	7	0	105.1	102	460	65	57	12	4	7	9	53	1	70	0	0
Zumaya, Joel, Erie	8	3	.727	2.77	18	18	0	0	0	0	107.1	71	437	40	33	8	1	4	2	52	0	143	4	4

PITCHERS WITH TWO OR MORE TEAMS

Pitcher, Team	W	L	Pct.	ERA	G	GS	CG	ShO	GF	Sv.	IP	H	TBF	R	ER	HR	SH	SF	HB	BB	IBB	SO	WP	Bk.
Devey, Philip, Portland *	1	6	.143	3.79	30	1	0	0	7	0	38.0	34	162	20	16	3	3	1	3	16	4	38	2	0
Devey, Philip, Reading *	1	1	.500	7.90	8	1	0	0	5	0	13.2	21	66	12	12	2	1	2	0	5	0	11	2	0
Matos, Josue, New Hampshire	0	1	.000	1.45	9	0	0	0	2	0	18.2	14	71	3	3	0	0	0	3	0	0	27	0	0
Matos, Josue, Reading	3	0	1.000	1.23	7	4	0	0	0	0	29.1	18	108	4	4	2	0	0	0	2	0	21	0	0
Ogiltree, John, New Hampshire	0	0	.000	0.00	2	0	0	0	0	0	2.0	1	9	0	0	0	0	0	0	1	1	1	0	0
Ogiltree, John, Harrisburg	1	0	1.000	2.45	5	0	0	0	0	0	7.1	6	30	2	2	0	0	0	2	5	0	5	0	0
Pearson, Jason, Portland *	1	1	.500	5.06	14	0	0	0	6	0	16.0	21	75	10	9	2	0	0	1	8	1	17	1	0
Pearson, Jason, Bowie *	0	0	.000	1.59	5	0	0	0	3	0	5.2	3	20	1	1	1	0	0	1	1	0	7	0	0
Thompson, Travis, Akron	4	0	1.000	1.80	15	0	0	0	5	0	25.0	15	95	7	5	1	0	0	1	8	0	16	1	2
Thompson, Travis, Reading	0	1	.000	3.00	11	0	0	0	4	1	18.0	20	73	6	6	0	0	1	0	3	0	10	1	0

COMBINATION SHUTOUTS: Akron (10) -- Denham-Green-Kleine, Carmona-Thompson-Pennington, Denham-Green-Mastny, Traber-Green, Sowers-Gomez, Denham-Cooper-Mujica, Bay-Knippschild, Denham-Foley-Lara, Perez-Foley, Sowers-Mujica. Altoona (4) -- Izquierdo-Jacobsen, Maholm-Shaffar, Candelario-Borner-Kaye, Peterson-Shaffar. Binghamton (6) -- Bannister-Roman-McNab, Chenard-Rodriguez-Hamulack, Bannister-Lopez, Edwards-Riggan-Garcia, Petit-Hill, McNab-Strayhorn-Garcia. Bowie (10) -- Bruback-Rice-Rleal-Ray, DuBose-Ray, Stahl-Keefer-Rleal-Ray, Birkins-Parrish-Rleal, Johnson-Torres-Rleal-McCurdy, Morris-Grimsley-Torres, DuBose-Grimsley, Stahl-Keefer-Ray, Birkins-Bruback-Rice, Morris-Piersoll. Erie (11) -- Bynum-Rodney, Johnson-Roney-Almonte, Vasquez-Almonte, Zumaya-Almonte, Zumaya-Hamman-Bumatay-Almonte, Verlander-Johnson, Johnson-Hamman-Rodney-Almonte, Verlander-Johnson-Peterson, Johnson-Bumatay-Almonte, Larrison-Hamman. Harrisburg (6) -- Bridges-Norderum, Rundles-Rueckel, Rasner-Stevenson-Bergmann, Rundles-Bergmann, Maust-Echols, Maust-Bowie. New Britain (5) -- Miller-Cameron-Thomas, Olson-Thomas-Neshek, Miller-Miller, Yeatman-Cameron, Abbott-Childress. New Hampshire (8) -- Ramirez-Vermilyea-Gronkiewicz, Banks-De Jong-Gronkiewicz, Banks-Vermilyea-Gronkiewicz, Vermilyea-Thorpe, Janssen-Perkins-Carlson-Gronkiewicz, Perkins-Buzachero-Mumma, Purcey-De Jong-Carlson, Perkins-De Jong-Houston. Norwich (13) -- Mazone-Aardsma-Accardo, Aardsma-Sadler-Accardo, Begg-Sadler, Garcia-Burres-Pannone, Garcia-Threets-Simon, Burres-Montes-Montero-Sadler, Song-Montero-Wilson, Misch-Chiasson-Wilson, Mazone-Wilson, Mazone-Montero-Simon, Misch-Chiasson, Moreno-Sadler-Simon, Mazone-Sadler-Montero. Portland (14) -- Gabbard-Brooks, Zink-Devey-Haines-Meredith, Papelbon-Pahucki, Smith-Sturge-Brooks, Zink-Deschenes, Gabbard-Beam-Deschenes, Lester-Tomori-Deschenes, Sanchez-Sturge-Pearson-Mann, Gabbard-Beam-Deschenes-Mann, Sanchez-Pearson-Deschenes, Tomori-Beam-Mann, Sanchez-Martinez-Mann, Gabbard-Martinez-Hansen-Mann, Lester-Hertzler. Reading (2) -- Rojas-Cameron, Matos-Devey-Cameron. Trenton (13) -- Henn-Julianel-Pope, Desalvo-Smith-Julianel, Henn-Sierra-Pope, Desalvo-Sierra-Pope, Karstens-Artiles, Skaggs-Julianel-Pope, Isaacson-Pope, Rodriguez-Desalvo, Borrell-Julianel-Brunet, White-Artiles, Maduro-Brunet-Pope, Desalvo-Manning, Maduro-Brunet-Kennard-Thorp.

NO-HIT GAMES: Bailie, Bowie, defeated Erie, 5-0, August 14.

TEAM

Team	G	PO	A	E	TC	DP	TP	PB	Pct.
Bowie	142	3748	1484	125	5357	118	0	13	.977
Akron	142	3799	1541	133	5473	110	0	21	.976
New Hampshire ..	142	3722	1411	126	5259	129	0	17	.976
Norwich	142	3693	1510	126	5329	129	0	22	.976
Harrisburg	142	3755	1512	137	5404	135	0	15	.975
Reading	142	3827	1444	137	5408	134	1	21	.975
Trenton	142	3779	1515	138	5432	146	0	12	.975
New Britain	142	3702	1392	142	5236	126	0	18	.973
Erie	142	3701	1464	154	5319	123	1	15	.971
Portland	142	3715	1407	151	5273	125	0	16	.971
Altoona	142	3776	1483	161	5420	120	0	15	.970
Binghamton	142	3714	1331	169	5214	113	0	18	.968

INDIVIDUAL

FIRST BASEMEN

NOTE: All caps denotes fielding-percentage leader based on 72 games for catchers, 96 for all other non-pitchers and 115 innings for pitchers. *Throws lefthanded.

Player, Team	Pct.	G	PO	A	E	TC	DP
Aubrey, Robert, Akron *	.996	25	218	12	1	231	21
Bailey, Jeffrey, Portland	.977	11	78	8	2	88	6
Bailie, Stefan, Portland	.985	9	62	2	1	65	7
Barker, Kevin, New Hampshire *	.990	9	90	7	1	98	5
Barthelemy, Ryan, Reading	.997	84	618	48	2	668	51
Bell, Rick, New Britain	1.000	5	13	1	0	14	4
Benavidez, Julian, Norwich	1.000	5	50	3	0	53	3
Bonifay, Joshua, Altoona	.995	88	698	66	4	768	54
Broadway, Larry, Harrisburg *	.992	48	369	20	3	392	36
Caligiuri, Jay, Binghamton	.991	37	200	28	2	230	18
Cannon, Rhame, New Hampshire	.988	30	215	33	3	251	19
Chiaravalloti, Vito, New Hampshire	.990	44	377	25	4	406	45
Concepcion, Alberto, Portland	1.000	1	1	0	0	1	0
Cordido, Julio, Norwich	1.000	4	10	2	0	12	2
Cosby, Robert, New Hampshire	1.000	1	3	0	0	3	0
Crozier, Eric, Trenton *	.933	5	26	2	2	30	4
Deeds, Douglas, New Britain *	1.000	1	2	1	0	3	1
Dement, Daniel, Harrisburg	.996	27	211	20	1	232	14
Dorta, Melvin, Harrisburg	.989	11	88	5	1	94	10
Duenas, Yobal, Trenton	1.000	3	12	1	0	13	0
Duncan, David, Trenton	.987	138	1178	78	16	1272	123
Eldred, Brad, Altoona	.989	19	177	3	2	182	15
Evans, Tom, Altoona	.983	39	319	25	6	350	33
Fleming, Ryan, Reading *	1.000	1	6	0	0	6	0
Freire, Alejandro, Bowie	1.000	1	7	1	0	8	0
Garcia, Yunir, Binghamton	1.000	1	6	0	0	6	1
Gettis, Byron, Erie	1.000	1	5	0	0	5	2
Gonzalez, Edgar, Harrisburg	.941	2	15	1	1	17	2
Gradoville, Timothy, Reading	1.000	1	1	0	0	1	0
Grindell, Nathan, Reading	1.000	3	11	2	0	13	2
Hammond, Joseph, Bowie	.875	2	13	1	2	16	0
Harper, Brett, Binghamton	.983	53	377	34	7	418	35
Herrera, Javier, Akron	...	1	0	0	0	0	0
Hietpas, Joe, Binghamton	.978	13	86	4	2	92	3
Hodges, Scott, Harrisburg	1.000	10	90	6	0	96	10
HUGGINS, MICHAEL, Bowie	.992	115	950	77	8	1035	82
Jacobs, Mike, Binghamton	.985	54	439	22	7	468	37
Jimenez, Luis Antonio, New Britain *	.980	64	462	39	10	511	45
Johnston, Clinton, New Hampshire *	.992	60	470	39	4	513	46
Knoedler, Justin, Erie	1.000	4	24	1	0	25	3
Kuzmic, Craig, Harrisburg	1.000	7	44	3	0	47	5
Lane, Richard, Harrisburg *	1.000	31	276	27	0	303	29
Larkin, Shaun, Akron	.995	59	554	37	3	594	41
Maples, Christopher, Erie	1.000	23	150	11	0	161	16
Martin, Billy, Harrisburg	1.000	6	50	2	0	52	8
Martinez, Octavio, Bowie	1.000	1	7	0	0	7	1
Matienzo, Daniel, New Britain	.990	81	640	48	7	695	63
Moses, Matthew, New Britain	1.000	1	2	0	0	2	0
Mulhern, Ryan, Akron	.988	47	395	29	5	429	28
O'Keefe, Michael, Portland *	1.000	6	67	1	0	68	4
Pond, Simon, Bowie	.996	30	236	16	1	253	22
Rabelo, Michael, Erie	.992	16	115	9	1	125	6
Richardson, Juan, Reading	1.000	16	103	11	0	114	11
Roughton, Jody, Erie	1.000	2	16	1	0	17	2

Player, Team	Pct.	G	PO	A	E	TC	DP
Ruiz, Randy, Reading	.976	55	435	19	11	465	51
Sandberg, Jared, Portland	.986	46	318	32	5	355	33
Tejeda, Juan, Erie	.987	104	860	49	12	921	82
Verbryke, Eric, Trenton *	1.000	1	10	0	0	10	1
Vericker, Brad, Norwich *	1.000	9	49	5	0	54	6
Von Schell, Eric, Norwich	.991	131	1115	109	11	1235	111
West, Jeremy, Portland	.990	79	632	43	7	682	64
Wilson, John, Harrisburg	.974	9	69	7	2	78	4
Youngbauer, Scott, Akron	.986	16	136	10	2	148	6

SECOND BASEMEN

Player, Team	Pct.	G	PO	A	E	TC	DP
Acuna, Ronald, New Hampshire	1.000	1	1	0	0	1	0
Alvarez, Gerardo, Bowie	.947	4	6	12	1	19	2
Athas, Jamie, Norwich	1.000	2	2	3	0	5	0
Bacani, David, Binghamton	.960	20	34	38	3	75	8
Baldiris, Aarom, Binghamton	.964	117	219	296	19	534	57
Borowiak, Zachary, Portland	1.000	2	4	10	0	14	0
Castro, Ramon A., Harrisburg	.750	1	1	2	1	4	0
Cates, Gary, Bowie	.957	20	29	38	3	70	7
Chavez, Dirimo, Portland	1.000	2	1	3	0	4	0
Cordido, Julio, Norwich	.958	5	11	12	1	24	5
Cota, Carlo, New Hampshire	.976	34	60	102	4	166	31
Cruz, Jose, Trenton	1.000	1	0	1	0	1	0
Dement, Daniel, Harrisburg	1.000	12	21	41	0	62	9
Ditter, Brad, Harrisburg	1.000	1	1	1	0	2	1
Dorta, Melvin, Harrisburg	.987	18	32	43	1	76	7
Duenas, Yobal, Trenton	.977	14	20	22	1	43	7
Evans, Tom, Altoona	.931	6	11	16	2	29	7
Francia, Juan, Erie	.965	66	145	162	11	318	33
Frandsen, Kevin, Norwich	.993	26	55	78	1	134	19
Gonzalez, Edgar, Harrisburg	.956	66	122	206	15	343	47
Hammond, Joseph, Bowie	.987	76	113	202	4	319	53
Hassey, Brad, New Hampshire	.989	23	31	56	1	88	12
Hernandez, Anderson, Binghamton	.979	8	21	26	1	48	7
HITCHCOX, SAMUEL, Reading	.989	111	215	312	6	533	74
Hutting, Timothy, Norwich	1.000	4	10	9	0	19	3
Koutrik, Jared, Trenton	1.000	1	1	1	0	2	0
Kuzmic, Craig, Harrisburg	1.000	1	1	2	0	3	1
Labandeira, Josh, Harrisburg	1.000	1	0	3	0	3	0
Labarbera, Anthony, Norwich	.977	110	206	335	13	554	77
Lambin, Chase, Binghamton	.778	2	3	4	2	9	2
Larkin, Shaun, Akron	.957	6	11	11	1	23	2
Lee, Taber, Altoona	1.000	8	15	15	0	30	0
Leon, Carlos, Reading	.974	28	46	68	3	117	12
LeVier, Bret, Portland	...	1	0	0	0	0	0
Lopez, Gabe, Trenton	.982	80	162	230	7	399	56
Lorenzo, Juan, Harrisburg	...	1	0	0	0	0	0
Lunetta, Anthony, Akron	.971	17	25	41	2	68	10
Maples, Christopher, Erie	.949	8	17	20	2	39	7
Mateo, Henry, Harrisburg	.972	28	55	82	4	141	15
Matsui, Kazuo, Binghamton	1.000	3	2	12	0	14	2
Mauer, Donald, New Britain	1.000	4	3	7	0	10	3
Maza, Luis, New Britain	.987	49	90	145	3	238	40
Mejia, Gilberto, Erie	.974	55	133	170	8	311	42
Mercedes, Victor, Altoona-Harrisburg	.955	29	46	82	6	134	19
Merchan, Jesus, Reading	1.000	3	4	8	0	12	3
Molina, Felix, New Britain	1.000	13	14	23	0	37	6
Morban, Jose, Akron	.971	20	43	57	3	103	12
Morris, Warren, Akron	1.000	3	4	13	0	17	2
Moses, Matthew, New Britain	1.000	1	0	1	0	1	0
Nieves, Raul, Portland	.988	17	44	41	1	86	14
Norris, Shawn, Harrisburg	1.000	7	16	13	0	29	5
Parker, Clark, Harrisburg	1.000	1	2	0	0	3	1
Pattee, Benjamin, New Britain	.961	42	74	100	7	181	19
Pedroia, Dustin, Portland	.980	58	91	160	5	256	41
Perez, Kenny, Portland	.959	22	41	30	3	74	9
Prieto, Alex, Reading	1.000	7	16	12	0	28	4
Ramirez, Hanley, Portland	.875	5	9	12	3	24	4
Raymundo, Gregg, Altoona	1.000	5	4	10	0	14	1
Roberts, Ryan, New Hampshire	.988	91	160	238	5	403	53
Rogers, Omar, Bowie	.979	49	78	105	4	187	26
Smith, Mike, Reading	.500	1	1	0	1	2	0
Sosa, Juan, Reading	1.000	9	17	25	0	42	2
Stansberry, Craig, Altoona	.974	115	255	308	15	578	68
Stotts, Jarrett, Trenton	.983	56	115	168	5	288	49
Torres, Eider, Akron	.973	102	184	313	14	511	46

Player, Team	Pct.	G	PO	A	E	TC	DP
Tousa, Scott, Erie	1.000	1	4	3	0	7	0
Velazquez, Gilbert, New Britain	.964	19	46	35	3	84	12
Walsh, Nick, Trenton	...	1	0	0	0	0	0
Watkins, Thomas, New Britain	.975	25	58	58	3	119	17
Wilson, Andy, Altoona	1.000	1	1	2	0	3	1
Woods, Michael, Erie	1.000	18	28	40	0	68	8
Youngbauer, Scott, Akron-Portland	.962	44	82	120	8	210	32

SECOND BASEMEN WITH TWO OR MORE TEAMS

Player, Team	Pct.	G	PO	A	E	TC	DP
Mercedes, Victor, Altoona	.940	12	13	34	3	50	6
Mercedes, Victor, Harrisburg	.964	17	33	48	3	84	13
Youngbauer, Scott, Akron	...	1	0	0	0	0	0
Youngbauer, Scott, Portland	.962	43	82	120	8	210	32

THIRD BASEMEN

Player, Team	Pct.	G	PO	A	E	TC	DP
Alvarez, Gerardo, Bowie	.800	3	3	5	2	10	0
Athas, Jamie, Norwich	1.000	4	4	2	0	6	0
Bacani, David, Binghamton	.884	36	22	39	8	69	1
Barthelemy, Ryan, Reading	...	2	0	0	0	0	0
Bautista, Jose, Altoona	.924	116	72	221	24	317	15
Bell, Rick, New Britain	.932	41	25	84	8	117	6
Benavidez, Julian, Norwich	.939	13	9	22	2	33	7
Borowiak, Zachary, Portland	.500	2	1	0	1	2	0
Bramasco, Leslie, Reading	...	2	0	0	0	0	0
Buscher, Brian, Norwich	.939	42	18	74	6	98	8
Caligiuri, Jay, Binghamton	.936	78	49	113	11	173	8
Concepcion, Alberto, Portland	.875	3	1	6	1	8	0
Cordido, Julio, Norwich	.942	67	30	100	8	138	14
Cosby, Robert, New Hampshire	.917	110	57	186	22	265	20
Cota, Carlo, New Hampshire	1.000	3	0	1	0	1	0
Dement, Daniel, Harrisburg	1.000	1	3	0	0	3	1
Deschaine, James, Reading	.944	25	9	42	3	54	4
Dorta, Melvin, Harrisburg	1.000	5	2	8	0	10	1
Duenas, Yobal, Trenton	.875	21	8	34	6	48	2
Duncan, Eric, Trenton	.908	116	61	204	27	292	18
Evans, Tom, Altoona	.839	26	10	42	10	62	1
Frandsen, Kevin, Norwich	1.000	1	0	1	0	1	0
Gonzalez, Edgar, Harrisburg	.938	12	7	23	2	32	1
Grindell, Nathan, Reading	.887	31	23	63	11	97	9
Hammond, Joseph, Bowie	.950	17	7	31	2	40	2
Hannahan, John, Erie	.967	6	15	14	1	30	1
Hassey, Brad, New Hampshire	.970	30	19	46	2	67	6
Hitchcox, Samuel, Reading	1.000	2	0	2	0	2	0
Holm, Stephen, Norwich	1.000	6	4	7	0	11	1
Hutting, Timothy, Norwich	.870	12	10	10	3	23	0
JOHNSON III, NELSON, Bowie	.952	124	89	231	16	336	17
Kelly, Donald, Erie	.875	57	34	92	18	144	7
Labandeira, Josh, Harrisburg	1.000	7	4	11	0	15	1
Labarbera, Anthony, Norwich	.960	21	11	37	2	50	8
Lambin, Chase, Binghamton	.922	31	17	54	6	77	5
Larkin, Shaun, Akron	.909	11	2	18	2	22	0
Leon, Carlos, Reading	.895	20	0	17	2	19	3
LeVier, Bret, Portland	.947	11	3	15	1	19	3
Lunetta, Anthony, Akron	...	1	0	0	0	0	0
Maples, Christopher, Erie	.925	37	31	80	9	120	7
Matienzo, Daniel, New Britain	.810	9	5	12	4	21	2
Mauer, Donald, New Britain	.889	9	5	11	2	18	0
Mendez, Victor, Erie	1.000	1	2	3	0	5	0
Mercedes, Victor, Harrisburg	.500	2	0	1	1	2	0
Molina, Felix, New Britain	.938	23	9	36	3	48	3
Morales, Jose, New Britain	.800	1	0	4	1	5	0
Morban, Jose, Akron	.921	12	8	27	3	38	2
Moses, Matthew, New Britain	.931	48	29	92	9	130	9
Nieves, Raul, Portland	.925	44	22	89	9	120	7
Norris, Shawn, Harrisburg	.910	65	54	137	19	210	18
Osborn, Patrick, Akron	.928	119	75	248	25	348	16
Perez, Kenny, Portland	.936	20	12	32	3	47	2
Prieto, Alex, Reading	.875	2	0	7	1	8	0
Rabelo, Michael, Erie	1.000	2	0	1	0	1	0
Ramirez, Hanley, Portland	1.000	1	0	2	0	2	0
Raymundo, Gregg, Altoona	.000	2	0	0	1	1	0
Richardson, Juan, Reading	.911	82	58	136	19	213	12
Rooi, Vince, Harrisburg	1.000	5	2	9	0	11	1
Sandberg, Jared, Portland	.902	67	48	126	19	193	14
Sosa, Juan, Reading	.778	5	4	3	2	9	1
Spann, Charles, Portland	.903	9	10	18	3	31	8
Stotts, Jarrett, Trenton	.962	13	9	16	1	26	1
Tousa, Scott, Erie	.950	45	35	99	7	141	8

Player, Team	Pct.	G	PO	A	E	TC	DP
Triplett, Calvin, Binghamton	.936	17	9	35	3	47	1
Watkins, Thomas, New Britain	.925	26	14	35	4	53	10
Wilson, Andy, Altoona	.700	3	4	3	3	10	1
Youngbauer, Scott, Akron-Portland	.909	7	4	6	1	11	0
Zimmerman, Ryan, Harrisburg	.961	55	45	101	6	152	6

THIRD BASEMEN WITH TWO OR MORE TEAMS

Player, Team	Pct.	G	PO	A	E	TC	DP
Youngbauer, Scott, Akron	.909	6	4	6	1	11	0
Youngbauer, Scott, Portland	...	1	0	0	0	0	0

SHORTSTOPS

Player, Team	Pct.	G	PO	A	E	TC	DP
Athas, Jamie, Norwich	.929	38	41	89	10	140	20
Bacani, David, Binghamton	.960	23	37	60	4	101	16
Benavidez, Julian, Norwich	...	1	0	0	0	0	0
Borowiak, Zachary, Portland	1.000	3	1	4	0	5	2
Bramasco, Leslie, Reading	...	1	0	0	0	0	0
Cannizaro, Andrew, Trenton	.969	54	69	147	7	223	42
Castro, Ramon A., Harrisburg	.960	32	56	89	6	151	23
Chaves, Brandon, Altoona	.914	52	68	133	19	220	24
Cordido, Julio, Norwich	.981	14	19	32	1	52	3
Cruz, Jose, Trenton	...	1	0	0	0	0	0
Dorta, Melvin, Harrisburg	.958	32	43	70	5	118	19
Evans, Tom, Altoona	1.000	2	3	6	0	9	0
Fahey, Brandon, Bowie	.962	139	221	413	25	659	84
Francia, Juan, Erie	.806	6	6	19	6	31	3
Frandsen, Kevin, Norwich	1.000	5	11	10	0	21	3
Giarratano, Tony, Erie	.954	89	120	255	18	393	47
Gonzalez, Daniel, Reading	.942	47	75	121	12	208	29
Guzman, Javier, Altoona	.972	68	94	221	9	324	48
Hammond, Joseph, Bowie	1.000	4	5	9	0	14	2
Hassey, Brad, New Hampshire	.971	42	50	119	5	174	25
Hernandez, Anderson, Binghamton	.938	57	72	125	13	210	27
Hutting, Timothy, Norwich	.953	93	143	262	20	425	55
Kelly, Donald, Erie	.939	24	36	56	6	98	15
Koutnik, Jared, Trenton	.750	1	0	3	1	4	1
Labandeira, Josh, Harrisburg	.959	52	82	129	9	220	31
Lambin, Chase, Binghamton	.897	8	15	20	4	39	6
Lee, Taber, Altoona	1.000	15	20	39	0	59	8
Leon, Carlos, Reading	.942	29	64	66	8	138	19
Lorenzo, Juan, Harrisburg	.917	14	10	34	4	48	10
Lunetta, Anthony, Akron	.896	13	13	30	5	48	2
Maples, Christopher, Erie	1.000	2	4	6	0	10	2
Mauer, Donald, New Britain	1.000	1	1	0	0	1	0
Mejia, Gilberto, Erie	.926	7	10	15	2	27	2
Mendez, Deivi, Trenton	.667	1	2	0	1	3	0
Mercedes, Victor, Harrisburg	.909	1	2	8	1	11	2
Merchan, Jesus, Reading	.948	43	51	112	9	172	26
Molina, Felix, New Britain	.750	1	2	1	1	4	0
Morban, Jose, Akron	.917	8	10	12	2	24	4
Nieves, Raul, Portland	.923	7	9	15	2	26	6
Norris, Shawn, Harrisburg	.975	9	11	28	1	40	4
OCHOA, IVAN, Akron	.970	126	203	375	18	596	69
Patino, Jorge, Erie	.960	5	8	16	1	25	2
Pedroia, Dustin, Portland	1.000	6	7	17	0	24	1
Pena, Ramiro, Trenton	.951	68	86	204	15	305	47
Perez, Kenny, Portland	.924	21	35	50	7	92	12
Prieto, Alex, Reading	1.000	6	9	11	0	20	2
Ragsdale, William, Binghamton	.947	63	105	165	15	285	28
Ramirez, Hanley, Portland	.960	115	156	305	19	480	57
Raymundo, Gregg, Altoona	1.000	9	20	14	0	34	7
Sosa, Juan, Reading	1.000	27	38	78	0	116	10
Spann, Charles, Portland	1.000	1	1	0	0	1	0
Stotts, Jarrett, Trenton	.948	23	31	61	5	97	15
Tablado, Raul, New Hampshire	.935	100	126	274	28	428	61
Taylor, Samuel, New Britain	.935	32	59	85	10	154	17
Tousa, Scott, Erie	.958	14	25	44	3	72	10
Velazquez, Gilbert, New Britain	.952	62	92	165	13	270	40
Watkins, Thomas, New Britain	.951	55	78	118	10	206	22
Zimmerman, Ryan, Harrisburg	.879	8	12	17	4	33	3

OUTFIELDERS

Player, Team	Pct.	G	PO	A	E	TC	DP
Acuna, Ronald, New Hampshire	.978	96	173	6	4	183	1
Airoso, Alvin, Erie	1.000	10	21	1	0	22	0
Bailey, Jeffrey, Portland	1.000	5	8	0	0	8	0
Baldiris, Aarom, Binghamton	...	1	0	0	0	0	0
Barthelemy, Ryan, Reading	1.000	2	3	0	0	3	0

CLASS AA Eastern League

Player, Team	Pct.	G	PO	A	E	TC	DP
Belcher, Jason, Harrisburg	.833	6	5	0	1	6	0
Bergeron, Peter, Bowie	.982	89	158	9	3	170	0
Boeve, Adam, Altoona	.947	43	71	1	4	76	0
Bonifay, Joshua, Altoona	1.000	4	1	0	0	1	0
BOURN, MICHAEL, Reading	.997	133	310	21	1	332	9
Brown, Dee, Harrisburg	.947	28	35	1	2	38	0
Buttler, Victor, Harrisburg	.969	20	28	3	1	32	0
Cabrera, Melky, Trenton *	.985	105	256	7	4	267	1
Carson, Matt, Trenton	1.000	26	43	1	0	44	1
Castellano, John, Reading	1.000	2	3	0	0	3	0
Church, Ryan, Harrisburg *	1.000	4	8	0	0	8	0
Clark, Howie, Altoona	.917	10	11	0	1	12	0
Cliffords, Benjamin, Bowie	.962	86	121	6	5	132	0
Coleman, Michael, Trenton	1.000	11	19	1	0	20	0
Cooper, Jason, Akron *	.990	50	104	0	1	105	0
Cordido, Julio, Norwich	1.000	12	22	0	0	22	0
Cortes, Jorge, Altoona *	.972	93	168	8	5	181	1
Crowe, Trevor, Akron	1.000	3	2	0	0	2	0
Crozier, Eric, Trenton *	.966	21	25	3	1	29	0
Davenport, Ulyses, New Hampshire	.988	86	145	14	2	161	2
Davis, Rajai, Altoona	.966	118	276	10	10	296	3
Deeds, Douglas, New Britain *	.988	125	235	2	3	240	0
Dement, Daniel, Harrisburg	1.000	34	54	1	0	55	0
Deschaine, James, Reading	.977	52	79	5	2	86	1
Dorta, Melvin, Harrisburg	.980	49	94	5	2	101	0
Duenas, Yobal, Trenton	.875	7	6	1	1	8	0
Duncan, Jeff, Binghamton *	.986	77	135	1	2	138	1
Durbin, Christopher, Portland	.957	95	170	10	8	188	1
Espinosa, David, Erie	.977	106	160	11	4	175	4
Feliciano, Jesus, Harrisburg *	.989	85	175	3	2	180	0
Fleming, Ryan, Reading *	.986	116	211	5	3	219	0
Francisco, Louis, Akron	.991	70	105	1	1	107	0
Fulse, Sheldon, Portland	.976	46	81	0	2	83	0
Gettis, Byron, Erie	.941	62	118	9	8	135	2
Gonzalez, Edgar, Harrisburg	1.000	2	1	0	0	1	0
Grindell, Nathan, Reading	1.000	4	8	0	0	8	0
Guerrero, Cristian, Harrisburg	.980	95	191	9	4	204	5
Guillen, Rodolfo, Trenton	.962	28	50	0	2	52	0
Gutierrez, Franklin, Akron	.995	83	183	2	1	186	2
Hall, Victor, Binghamton *	.965	47	80	3	3	86	0
Hammond, Joseph, Bowie	1.000	7	8	0	0	8	0
Hammonds, Jeffrey, Harrisburg	...	1	0	0	0	0	0
Hassey, Brad, New Hampshire	...	1	0	0	0	0	0
Haynes, Charles, Harrisburg	.993	77	133	4	1	138	0
Herrera, Jose, Bowie *	1.000	3	7	0	0	7	0
Inglin, Jeffery, Bowie	.950	36	52	5	3	60	0
Jacobs, Mike, Binghamton	...	1	0	0	0	0	0
Jova, Maikel, New Hampshire	.988	79	156	8	2	166	2
Kelly, Kenny, Harrisburg	.939	12	29	2	2	33	1
Keylor, Cory, Bowie	.935	30	43	0	3	46	0
Kingsale, Gene, Bowie	.944	50	97	4	6	107	0
Knoedler, Justin, Erie	1.000	24	43	3	0	46	0
Koutnik, Jared, Trenton	1.000	5	8	0	0	8	0
Kuzmic, Craig, Harrisburg	1.000	3	6	0	0	6	0
Lambin, Chase, Binghamton	1.000	4	3	0	0	3	0
Lane, Richard, Harrisburg *	1.000	5	6	1	0	7	0
Langaigne, Selwyn, New Britain *	1.000	11	18	1	0	19	0
LeVier, Bret, Portland	.667	1	2	0	1	3	0
Lewis, Frederick, Norwich	.948	127	252	3	14	269	0
Lydon, Wayne, Binghamton	.959	121	253	4	11	268	1
Lytle, Chaz, Altoona *	1.000	4	9	0	0	9	0
Malek, Robert, Binghamton	.962	108	189	12	8	209	0
Maples, Christopher, Erie	.955	30	39	3	2	44	0
Markakis, Nicholas, Bowie *	1.000	33	66	0	0	66	0
Martin, Billy, Harrisburg	...	1	0	0	0	0	0
Matos, Luis, Bowie	1.000	3	9	1	0	10	1
Meath, Matthew, Altoona	...	1	0	0	0	0	0
Melian, Jackson, Erie	1.000	5	9	0	0	9	0
Mendez, Victor, Erie	.978	94	256	9	6	271	1
Milledge, Lastings, Binghamton	.979	44	90	3	2	95	0
Morban, Jose, Akron	1.000	15	18	0	0	18	0
Moss, Brandon, Portland	.968	126	226	13	8	247	3
Murphy, David, Portland *	.985	131	254	4	4	262	2
Negron, Miguel, New Hampshire *	.975	124	262	7	7	276	2
Nettles, Marcus, Harrisburg *	1.000	6	14	0	0	14	0
Neuberger, Scott, Altoona	1.000	9	20	1	0	21	0
Nieves, Melvin, Harrisburg	1.000	20	37	1	0	38	0
Nieves, Raul, Portland	1.000	18	27	0	0	27	0
Nivar, Ramon, Bowie	.941	40	74	6	5	85	1
O'Keefe, Michael, Portland *	1.000	3	6	0	0	6	0
Ortmeier, Dan, Norwich *	.983	127	223	13	4	240	2

Player, Team	Pct.	G	PO	A	E	TC	DP
Panther, Nathan, Akron *	1.000	20	38	1	0	39	1
Pond, Simon, Bowie	.976	62	78	5	2	85	0
Porter, Colin, Trenton *	.941	15	30	2	2	34	0
Redman, Prentice, Binghamton	.909	29	39	1	4	44	1
Roberson, Christopher, Reading	.982	134	320	16	6	342	4
Romero, Alexander, New Britain *	.975	134	258	13	7	278	1
Ruiz, Randy, Reading	.882	10	15	0	2	17	0
Sadler, Ray, Altoona	.970	53	91	7	3	101	3
Sandberg, Jared, Portland	.923	12	12	0	1	13	0
Sanders, Anthony, New Hampshire	.818	13	17	1	4	22	0
Sardinha, Bronson, Trenton	.969	123	180	9	6	195	3
Scanlon, Matthew, New Britain	1.000	2	3	0	0	3	0
Sherrill, James, Akron	.972	18	35	0	1	36	0
Singleton, Justin, New Hampshire	.975	21	37	2	1	40	0
Slack, Jonathan, Binghamton *	1.000	21	28	4	0	32	1
Snyder, Bradley, Akron *	.961	68	143	6	6	155	2
Span, Keiunta, New Britain *	.976	66	160	5	4	169	1
Stotts, Jarrett, Trenton	.875	14	7	0	1	8	0
Thompson, Kevin, Trenton	.977	75	125	4	3	132	0
Thompson, Rich, Altoona	.989	86	171	7	2	180	1
Tomlin, James, New Britain	.981	102	199	6	4	209	1
Trumble, Daniel, Norwich	1.000	5	8	0	0	8	0
Valderrama, Carlos, Norwich	.983	120	219	6	4	229	1
Van Der Bosch, Matthew, Portland *	1.000	9	14	3	0	17	1
Van Every, Jonathan, Akron *	.982	106	214	8	4	226	3
Verbryke, Eric, Trenton *	1.000	4	5	1	0	6	1
Vroman, Douglas, Harrisburg	1.000	2	3	1	0	4	0
Walsh, Nick, Trenton	1.000	4	6	1	0	7	0
Walter, Paul, Norwich	.989	48	90	1	1	92	0
Watkins, Thomas, New Britain *	1.000	2	3	0	0	3	0
Watson, Brandon, Harrisburg	.973	32	69	2	2	73	0
Watts, Derran, Binghamton	.667	2	2	0	1	3	0
Waugh, Jason, New Hampshire	1.000	12	20	0	0	20	1
Woods, Michael, Erie	.972	111	198	7	6	211	1

CATCHERS

Player, Team	Pct.	G	PO	A	E	TC	DP
Alfonzo, Eliezer, Norwich	.990	38	268	26	3	297	3
Arroyo, Rafael, Binghamton	1.000	3	27	4	0	31	1
Bailey, Jeffrey, Portland	.982	13	101	8	2	111	0
Belcher, Jason, Harrisburg	1.000	1	6	2	0	8	1
Brown, Jason, Trenton	.988	44	307	30	4	341	7
Buckley, James, Portland	.982	45	312	20	6	338	2
Camacaro, Armando, Akron	.996	34	223	30	1	254	4
Cardona, Javier, Akron	.972	15	94	12	3	109	2
Castellano, John, Reading	1.000	4	32	0	0	32	0
Chiaffredo, Paul, Altoona	1.000	8	62	3	0	65	0
Clements, Zachary, Binghamton	.986	50	324	24	5	353	5
Clendenin, Morgan, Bowie	.992	20	119	5	1	125	1
Concepcion, Alberto, Portland	.988	92	700	55	9	764	4
Cortez, Jose, Reading	.962	3	23	2	1	26	0
Curry, Christopher, Norwich	.982	68	411	36	8	455	4
Emmerick, Joshua, Harrisburg	.984	44	275	24	5	304	2
Garcia, Yunir, Binghamton	1.000	3	22	0	0	22	0
Gil, Geronimo, Bowie	1.000	3	18	2	0	20	1
Gradoville, Timothy, Reading	.984	69	441	54	8	503	4
Herrera, Javier, Akron	.987	96	653	48	9	710	4
Hietpas, Joe, Binghamton	.989	54	398	32	5	435	6
Hitchcox, Samuel, Reading	1.000	1	5	0	0	5	0
Holm, Stephen, Norwich	1.000	4	27	3	0	30	0
Hubele, Ryan, Bowie	1.000	14	107	9	0	116	1
Jacobs, Mike, Binghamton	.981	43	341	12	7	360	1
Kennedy, Bryan, New Britain	.988	70	463	33	6	502	2
KRATZ, ERIK, New Hampshire	.992	89	648	63	6	717	4
Kuzmic, Craig, Harrisburg	.976	24	153	8	4	165	1
Leon, Carlos, Reading	1.000	1	1	0	0	1	0
Lombardi, Michael, Reading	...	1	0	0	0	0	0
Lopez, Javy, Bowie	1.000	2	14	0	0	14	0
Lunsford, Trey, Norwich	.988	36	228	12	3	243	0
Maldonado, Carlos, Altoona	.982	79	571	42	11	624	10
Marsters, Brandon, Bowie	.991	107	865	83	9	957	5
Martinez, Octavio, Bowie	.988	10	68	12	1	81	1
McCullough, Clayton, Akron	1.000	4	32	1	0	33	1
McMillan, Andrew, Harrisburg	.992	18	112	14	1	127	2
Morales, Jose, New Britain	.970	4	31	1	1	33	0
Paulino, Ronny, Altoona	.991	40	314	27	3	344	5
Phillips, Kyle, New Britain	.994	22	141	15	1	157	2
Pratt, Trent, Reading	.987	72	507	33	7	547	7
Rabelo, Michael, Erie	.986	55	376	38	6	420	2
Rodriguez, Guillermo, Norwich	1.000	5	30	2	0	32	0

Player, Team	Pct.	G	PO	A	E	TC	DP
Santos, Omir, Trenton	.989	104	842	77	10	929	10
Snusz, Christopher, Altoona	.993	21	120	13	1	134	0
St. Pierre, Maxim, Erie	.990	89	591	72	7	670	9
Thigpen, Curtis, New Hampshire	.994	30	297	23	2	322	1
Torres, Gabriel, New Britain	.988	61	381	42	5	428	5
Umbria, Jose, New Hampshire	1.000	26	188	6	0	194	1
Whittaker, Timothy, New Hampshire	1.000	2	11	0	0	11	0
Wilson, John, Harrisburg	.988	69	433	47	6	486	8
Zaun, Gregg, New Hampshire	1.000	1	4	0	0	4	0

PITCHERS

Player, Team	Pct.	G	PO	A	E	TC	DP
Aardsma, David, Norwich	.889	9	3	5	1	9	0
Abbott, James, New Britain	.941	24	4	12	1	17	0
Accardo, Jeremy, Norwich	1.000	8	0	1	0	1	0
Almonte, Edwin, Erie	1.000	52	3	5	0	8	0
Anderson, Luke, Norwich	1.000	8	1	1	0	2	0
Andrade, Stephen, New Hampshire	1.000	35	8	4	0	12	0
Artiles, Carlos, Trenton *	.833	32	1	4	1	6	0
Bacani, David, Binghamton	1.000	4	1	0	0	1	0
Bailie, Matthew, Bowie	1.000	6	1	4	0	5	0
Banks, Joshua, New Hampshire	.925	27	17	20	3	40	1
Bannister, Brian, Binghamton	.974	18	11	26	1	38	2
Barker, Kevin, New Hampshire *	...	1	0	0	0	0	0
Barrett, William, New Britain *	.667	10	1	3	2	6	0
Bauer, Gregory, Reading	1.000	5	0	2	0	2	0
Bay, Ronald, Akron	1.000	8	0	6	0	6	0
Beam, Randall, Portland *	1.000	34	3	2	0	5	1
Bedard, Erik, Bowie *	...	1	0	0	0	0	0
Beech, Matt, Erie *	1.000	6	1	2	0	3	1
Begg, Christopher, Norwich	1.000	23	11	28	0	39	0
Bergmann, Jay, Harrisburg	1.000	21	4	2	0	6	0
Bierd, Randor, Erie	1.000	4	2	2	0	4	0
Birkins, Kurt, Bowie *	.943	26	7	26	2	35	2
Birtwell, John, Erie	1.000	29	7	4	0	11	1
Blackburn, Robert, New Britain	.889	7	4	4	1	9	0
Borner, Brady, Altoona *	.895	48	3	14	2	19	1
Borrell, Daniel, Trenton *	.857	10	1	5	1	7	0
Bouknight, Kip, Harrisburg	1.000	20	9	14	0	23	4
Bowie, Micah, Harrisburg *	1.000	10	1	1	0	2	0
Bray, Bill, Harrisburg *	...	3	0	0	0	0	0
Bridges, Donnie, Harrisburg	1.000	5	3	3	0	6	0
Brooks, Conor, Portland	.947	52	3	15	1	19	0
Brooks, Jacob, Akron	1.000	6	0	1	0	1	0
Bruback, Matt, Bowie	.875	22	5	9	2	16	1
Brunet, Michael, Trenton	1.000	15	1	1	0	2	0
Bucktrot, Keith, Reading	.727	11	3	5	3	11	0
Bumatay, Michael, Erie *	.857	50	2	4	1	7	0
Burke, Erick, Reading *	1.000	26	2	4	0	6	0
Burres, Brian, Norwich *	1.000	26	9	16	0	25	0
Butto, Francisco, Reading	.500	36	2	0	2	4	0
Buzachero, Edward, New Hampshire	.958	46	9	14	1	24	0
Byard, David, Binghamton	...	1	0	0	0	0	0
Bynum, Mike, Erie *	1.000	5	1	2	0	3	0
Cabrera, Daniel, Bowie	1.000	4	0	1	0	1	0
Cameron, Kevin, New Britain	.917	43	10	12	2	24	0
Cameron, Ryan, Reading	1.000	58	8	8	0	16	0
Candelario, Eddie, Altoona	.905	13	7	12	2	21	2
Capps, Matt, Altoona	1.000	17	1	1	0	2	0
Carlson, Jesse, New Hampshire *	1.000	39	4	5	0	9	0
Carmona, Fausto, Akron	1.000	14	6	22	0	28	2
Chantres, Carlos, Reading	.854	26	15	26	7	48	2
Chenard, Kenneth, Binghamton	.923	22	6	6	1	13	0
Chiasson, Scott, Norwich	1.000	15	2	3	0	5	0
Childress, Daylan, New Britain	1.000	29	6	7	0	13	1
Cliffords, Benjamin, Bowie	1.000	1	0	1	0	1	0
Connolly, Christopher, Akron *	1.000	15	2	11	0	13	1
Cooper, Christopher, Akron *	1.000	43	1	7	0	8	1
Cordido, Julio, Norwich	1.000	2	0	2	0	2	0
Cordova, Vincent, Binghamton	...	1	0	0	0	0	0
Cornejo, Nate, Erie	.900	19	3	15	2	20	2
Cullen, Ryan, Binghamton *	1.000	1	0	1	0	1	0
Davis, Allen, Reading *	.952	27	3	17	1	21	1
Day, Zach, Harrisburg	1.000	3	1	1	0	2	0
Deaton, Kevin, Binghamton	1.000	11	3	1	0	4	0
De Jong, Jordan, New Hampshire	.917	45	6	5	1	12	0
De La Cruz, Eulogio, Erie	1.000	1	0	1	0	1	0
Delcarmen, Manny, Portland	1.000	31	0	6	0	6	0
Denham, Daniel, Akron	.913	21	4	17	2	23	1
Desalvo, Matthew, Trenton	.980	25	16	33	1	50	1

Player, Team	Pct.	G	PO	A	E	TC	DP
Deschenes, Mark, Portland	1.000	39	0	3	0	3	0
Devey, Philip, Portland-Reading	.857	38	1	11	2	14	0
Diaz, Jose, Akron	1.000	8	0	2	0	2	0
Dittler, Jake, Akron	.956	28	14	29	2	45	1
DuBose, Eric, Bowie *	.944	21	5	29	2	36	1
Echols, Justin, Harrisburg	.786	31	3	8	3	14	1
Edwards, Bryan, Binghamton	.857	35	4	20	4	28	0
Eisentrager, Daniel, Akron	...	1	0	0	0	0	0
Evans, Kyle, Akron	1.000	7	0	2	0	2	0
Evans, Tom, Altoona	...	1	0	0	0	0	0
Ferrari, Anthony, Harrisburg *	...	1	0	0	0	0	0
Fesh, Sean, Reading *	1.000	20	0	2	0	2	0
Fisher, Peter, Portland	...	7	0	0	0	0	0
Foley, Travis, Akron	.833	36	2	3	1	6	0
Forystek, Brian, Bowie *	.882	14	6	9	2	17	0
Gabbard, Kason, Portland *	1.000	27	4	22	0	26	0
Galarraga, Armando, Harrisburg	.933	13	4	10	1	15	1
Garcia, Anderson, Binghamton	.875	30	1	6	1	8	1
Garcia, James, Norwich	.895	32	6	11	2	19	0
Geary, Geoff, Reading	1.000	1	1	0	0	1	0
Gil, David, Harrisburg	.833	14	1	4	1	6	0
Gomez, Mariano, Akron *	.857	18	1	5	1	7	1
Gonzalez, Alexander, Portland	...	1	0	0	0	0	0
Gonzalez, Somer, Harrisburg	...	1	0	0	0	0	0
Gorzelanny, Tom, Altoona *	.943	23	7	26	2	35	0
Granado, Jan, New Britain *	1.000	12	1	4	0	5	0
Green, Steve, Akron	.800	26	5	3	2	10	0
Grimsley, Jason, Bowie	1.000	8	0	3	0	3	0
Gronkiewicz, Lee, New Hampshire	.833	38	1	4	1	6	0
Guerrero, Cristian, Harrisburg	...	1	0	0	0	0	0
Gutierrez, Jannio, New Britain	1.000	9	2	1	0	3	0
Haines, Joseph, Portland	1.000	6	2	1	0	3	0
Hamels, Colbert, Reading *	.667	3	0	2	1	3	0
Hamman, Corey, Erie *	1.000	45	4	6	0	10	0
Hammond, Joseph, Bowie	...	3	0	0	0	0	0
Hamulack, Tim, Binghamton *	1.000	21	1	6	0	7	0
Hansen, Craig, Portland	...	8	0	0	0	0	0
Hanson, Mark, Akron	1.000	2	1	1	0	2	0
Happ, James, Reading *	...	1	0	0	0	0	0
Harts, Jeremy, Altoona *	1.000	29	3	6	0	9	0
Hassey, Brad, New Hampshire	1.000	1	0	1	0	1	1
Henkel, Robert, Erie *	1.000	18	3	9	0	12	0
Henn, Sean, Trenton *	1.000	4	0	4	0	4	0
Hensen, Brian, Erie *	...	2	0	0	0	0	0
Hernandez, Michael, Akron *	1.000	4	0	1	0	1	0
Hernandez, Yoel, Reading	1.000	9	0	2	0	2	0
Hertzler, Barry, Portland	1.000	3	0	1	0	1	0
Hill, Jeremy, Binghamton	1.000	19	0	1	0	1	0
Houston, Ryan, New Hampshire	.889	33	4	4	1	9	0
Humber, Philip, Binghamton	1.000	1	0	1	0	1	0
Hundley, Jeffrey, Bowie *	.667	11	0	2	1	3	0
Hutchison, Ryan, Reading	1.000	3	1	0	0	1	0
Isaacson, Charlie, Trenton	1.000	22	4	14	0	18	0
Izquierdo, Hansel, Altoona	.920	24	6	17	2	25	3
Jackson, Kyle, Portland	...	3	0	0	0	0	0
Jackson, Zach, New Hampshire *	.933	9	6	8	1	15	1
Jacobsen, Landon, Altoona	.500	11	0	1	1	2	0
Janssen, Robert, New Hampshire	.889	9	3	5	1	9	0
Johnson, James, Altoona *	.929	31	5	8	1	14	0
Johnson, James, Bowie	1.000	1	0	1	0	1	0
Johnson, Jeremy, Erie	.967	24	8	21	1	30	4
Johnson, Mark, Erie	1.000	32	11	9	0	20	1
Jordan, Robert, Portland *	...	1	0	0	0	0	0
Julianel, Benjamin, Trenton *	1.000	46	4	11	0	15	0
Junge, Eric, Binghamton	1.000	3	0	3	0	3	0
Karp, Joshua, Harrisburg	.923	11	3	9	1	13	0
Karstens, Jeffrey, Trenton	.941	28	9	23	2	34	1
Kaye, Justin, Altoona	1.000	53	8	8	0	16	1
Keefer, Ryan, Bowie	1.000	54	6	10	0	16	2
Kennard, Jeffery, Trenton	1.000	5	0	2	0	2	0
King, Jeremy, Trenton	1.000	5	1	3	0	4	0
Kleine, Victor, Akron *	1.000	27	2	14	0	16	1
Knippschild, Charles, Akron *	1.000	2	0	1	0	1	0
Kobow, Michael, Erie	...	3	0	0	0	0	0
Korecky, Robert, New Britain	1.000	2	0	1	0	1	0
Laffey, Aaron, Akron *	1.000	1	1	0	0	1	0
Lara, Juan, Akron *	.600	18	0	3	2	5	0
Larrison, Preston, Erie	1.000	7	3	8	0	11	0
Lavigne, Tim, Binghamton *	1.000	8	0	2	0	2	0
Lee, Seung Hak, Reading	1.000	14	1	4	0	5	1
Lester, Jonathan, Portland *	1.000	26	2	18	0	20	1

Player, Team	Pct.	G	PO	A	E	TC	DP
Lindstrom, Matthew, Binghamton	.667	35	3	7	5	15	3
Liriano, Francisco, New Britain *	1.000	13	2	9	0	11	0
Lopez, Rafael, Binghamton	1.000	32	5	6	0	11	1
MacLane, Evan, Binghamton *	1.000	9	1	5	0	6	0
Maduro, Calvin, Trenton	1.000	7	5	4	0	9	0
Maholm, Paul, Altoona *	.923	16	1	23	2	26	0
Maldonado Oquendo, Ivan, Binghamton	1.000	5	0	2	0	2	0
Mann, Jim, Portland	.750	23	2	1	1	4	0
Manning, Charles, Trenton *	1.000	45	2	12	0	14	1
Manning, David, Bowie	...	8	0	0	0	0	0
Maples, Christopher, Erie	...	1	0	0	0	0	0
Marcum, Shawn, New Hampshire	1.000	9	3	5	0	8	0
Martin, Gregory, Altoona *	1.000	3	0	1	0	1	0
Martin, John, Akron	.846	10	4	7	2	13	0
Martinez, Edgar Ramon, Portland	1.000	15	1	0	0	1	0
Mastny, Thomas, Akron	1.000	5	2	0	0	2	1
Matos, Josue, New Hampshire-Reading	.800	16	2	2	1	5	0
Maust, David, Harrisburg *	.939	26	11	20	2	33	1
Mazone, Brian, Norwich *	.966	30	4	24	1	29	0
McCurdy, Nicholas, Bowie	1.000	30	5	9	0	14	0
McGinley, Blake, Binghamton *	...	2	0	0	0	0	0
McGowan, Dustin, New Hampshire	.800	6	2	2	1	5	0
McNab, Timothy, Binghamton	1.000	42	5	15	0	20	2
Mercado, Arnoldo, Norwich	...	4	0	0	0	0	0
Mercedes, Victor, Harrisburg	...	2	0	0	0	0	0
Meredith, Cla, Portland	1.000	12	2	2	0	4	0
Miller, Colby, New Britain	1.000	12	8	14	0	22	0
Miller, Jason, New Britain *	1.000	26	2	4	0	6	0
Miller, Matt, Akron	...	1	0	0	0	0	0
Minix, Travis, Reading	1.000	39	4	4	0	8	1
Misch, Patrick, Norwich *	1.000	9	3	11	0	14	2
Montero, Oscar, Norwich	.900	36	3	6	1	10	0
Montes, Alberto, Norwich	1.000	23	5	11	0	16	1
Moreno, Anthony, Norwich	1.000	18	7	10	0	17	0
Moreno, Edwin, Reading	1.000	4	2	5	0	7	0
Morris, Cory, Bowie	.968	29	10	20	1	31	0
Mujica, Edward, Akron	1.000	27	1	8	0	9	0
Mumma, Bradley, New Hampshire *	1.000	7	2	1	0	3	0
Neshek, Patrick, New Britain	1.000	55	5	11	0	16	0
Nieves, Raul, Portland	...	1	0	0	0	0	0
Norderum, Jason, Harrisburg *	.786	25	3	8	3	14	1
Ogiltree, John, New Hampshire-Harrisburg	1.000	7	2	2	0	4	0
Olson, Justin, New Britain	1.000	31	8	16	0	24	1
Pahucki, David, Portland	1.000	13	1	0	0	1	0
Palmer, Jonathan, Norwich	1.000	11	3	7	0	10	0
Pannone, Anthony, Norwich	.929	24	3	10	1	14	1
Papelbon, Jonathan, Portland	.909	14	5	5	1	11	0
Parcus, William, Reading *	...	4	0	0	0	0	0
Parrish, John, Bowie *	.500	5	1	0	1	2	0
Pauley, David, Portland	.967	27	14	15	1	30	1
Pearson, Jason, Portland-Bowie	1.000	19	2	3	0	5	0
Pekarek, Justin, Akron *	...	1	0	0	0	0	0
Penn, Hayden, Bowie	.955	20	10	11	1	22	3
Pennington, Jeffery, Akron	.750	19	0	3	1	4	0
Perez, Rafael, Akron *	.857	15	5	13	3	21	0
Perkins, Glen, New Britain *	1.000	14	3	18	0	21	3
Perkins, Vince, New Hampshire	.875	26	8	13	3	24	1
Peterson, Adam, Erie	.917	47	0	11	1	12	0
Peterson, Matthew, Altoona	.900	27	11	25	4	40	1
Petit, Yusmeiro, Binghamton	1.000	21	4	13	0	17	0
Piersoll, Chris, Bowie	1.000	27	3	5	0	8	0
Pope, Justin, Trenton	1.000	57	8	19	0	27	1
Portobanco, Luz, Binghamton	1.000	40	6	8	0	14	0
Purcey, David, New Hampshire *	1.000	8	2	4	0	6	0
Raggio, Brady, Reading	1.000	8	2	4	0	6	0
Ramirez, Ismael, New Hampshire	1.000	27	13	22	0	35	1
Ramirez, Ramon, Trenton	1.000	15	6	10	0	16	1
Randazzo, Jeffrey, New Britain *	...	2	0	0	0	0	0
RASNER, DARRELL, Harrisburg	1.000	27	17	24	0	41	2
Ray, Chris, Bowie	1.000	31	0	7	0	7	0
Reed, Brian, New Hampshire	1.000	8	0	1	0	1	0
Reimers, Cameron, New Hampshire	.852	19	8	15	4	27	2
Rhodes, Arthur, Akron *	1.000	1	0	1	0	1	0
Rice, Scott, Bowie *	.950	57	6	13	1	20	1
Riggan, Jerrod, Binghamton	1.000	4	1	0	0	1	0
Rivera, Saul, Harrisburg	1.000	40	8	15	0	23	2
Rleal, Sendy, Bowie	.895	56	7	10	2	19	0
Roach, Jason, Altoona	1.000	10	5	11	0	16	1
Roberts, Grant, Trenton	.909	9	3	7	1	11	0
Rodney, Thomas, Erie	1.000	45	2	13	0	15	2
Rodriguez, Felix, Trenton	...	2	0	0	0	0	0

Player, Team	Pct.	G	PO	A	E	TC	DP
Rodriguez, Jose, Binghamton	1.000	33	10	7	0	17	1
Roehl, Scott, Akron	1.000	2	0	1	0	1	0
Rojas, Christopher, Reading	.957	22	6	16	1	23	0
Roman, Orlando, Binghamton	.920	31	6	17	2	25	0
Roney, Matt, Erie	1.000	11	2	2	0	4	0
Rueckel, Daniel, Harrisburg	1.000	53	4	8	0	12	0
Rundles, Richard, Harrisburg *	.956	27	8	35	2	45	2
Sabathia, C.C., Akron *	1.000	2	0	3	0	3	0
Sadler, William, Norwich	1.000	47	4	8	0	12	0
Sanchez, Anibal, Portland	.929	11	8	5	1	14	0
Sanchez, Humberto, Erie	.857	15	2	4	1	7	0
Sanchez, Romulo, Altoona	1.000	2	0	2	0	2	0
Schmitt, Eric, Trenton	1.000	16	3	10	0	13	1
Schroder, Christopher, Harrisburg	.800	16	1	3	1	5	0
Sequea, Jacobo, Harrisburg	1.000	20	0	7	0	7	0
Shafer, Adam, Reading	1.000	11	1	0	0	1	0
Shaffar, Benjamin, Altoona	.882	44	6	9	2	17	1
Sharpless, Joshua, Altoona	1.000	7	0	1	0	1	0
Shoemaker, Scott, Portland	...	1	0	0	0	0	0
Shuey, Paul, Akron	...	1	0	0	0	0	0
Sierra, Eduardo, Trenton	1.000	33	0	11	0	11	1
Simon, Alfredo, Norwich	.912	43	13	18	3	34	3
Simonitsch, Errol, New Britain *	1.000	14	5	9	0	14	1
Skaggs, Jon, Trenton	.926	22	7	18	2	27	3
Slocum, Brian, Akron	.958	21	9	14	1	24	0
Small, Aaron, Trenton	...	1	0	0	0	0	0
Smith, Christopher, Portland	.941	15	6	10	1	17	1
Smith, Matthew, Trenton *	1.000	22	1	10	0	11	1
Smith, Mike, Reading	.980	28	11	37	1	49	2
Snusz, Christopher, Altoona	...	1	0	0	0	0	0
Song, Seung, Norwich	.923	6	4	8	1	13	0
Speigner, Jimmy, New Britain	.960	23	19	29	2	50	1
Stahl, Mark, Bowie *	.879	18	6	23	4	33	1
Stanford, Jason, Akron *	1.000	8	4	3	0	7	0
Stevenson, Jason, Harrisburg *	.938	13	4	11	1	16	1
Stewart, Paul, Altoona	.882	26	5	10	2	17	1
Stotts, Jarrett, Trenton	...	1	0	0	0	0	0
Strayhorn, Kole, Binghamton	...	1	0	0	0	0	0
Sturge, Justin, Portland *	1.000	33	1	9	0	10	0
Sweeney, Matthew, Reading	...	1	0	0	0	0	0
Sylvester, Billy, Harrisburg	1.000	26	2	3	0	5	0
Thomas, John, New Britain *	.889	39	3	13	2	18	1
Thompson, Travis, Akron-Reading	.889	26	1	7	1	9	1
Thorp, Paul, Trenton	1.000	2	1	1	0	2	0
Thorpe, Tracy, New Hampshire	.917	26	2	9	1	12	2
Threets, Erick, Norwich *	.900	30	2	7	1	10	0
Tomori, Denney, Portland	1.000	19	0	14	0	14	2
Torres, Melquicedec, Bowie	1.000	25	2	2	0	4	0
Tousa, Scott, Erie	...	1	0	0	0	0	0
Traber, Billy, Akron *	1.000	5	4	3	0	7	0
Trachsel, Steve, Binghamton	1.000	2	2	3	0	5	0
Urdaneta, Lino, Binghamton	...	1	0	0	0	0	0
Valdes, Marc, Trenton	1.000	10	3	2	0	5	0
Valdez, Merkin, Norwich	1.000	24	8	16	0	24	1
Van Dusen, Derrick, Akron *	1.000	4	1	1	0	2	0
Vasquez, Virgil, Erie	.944	15	6	11	1	18	0
Verlander, Justin, Erie	.889	7	2	6	1	9	0
Vermilyea, James, New Hampshire	.947	27	6	12	1	19	0
Villegas, Felix, Reading	1.000	26	1	2	0	3	0
Walk, Mitchell, Norwich *	...	1	0	0	0	0	0
Waugh, Jason, New Hampshire	...	1	0	0	0	0	0
Weis, John, Erie *	1.000	10	1	0	0	1	0
White, Steven, Trenton	.750	11	4	2	2	8	0
Wilson, Brian, Norwich	1.000	15	1	0	0	1	0
Wilson, Jeffrey, Reading *	1.000	22	0	1	0	1	0
Wolfe, Brian, New Britain	.000	5	0	0	1	1	0
Worrell, Tim, Reading	...	2	0	0	0	0	0
Yeatman, Matthew, New Britain	.833	28	5	5	2	12	0
Youman, Shane, Altoona *	.929	44	9	17	2	28	0
Zink, Charles, Portland	.917	29	9	13	2	24	1
Zumaya, Joel, Erie	.875	18	4	10	2	16	1

PITCHERS WITH TWO OR MORE TEAMS

Player, Team	Pct.	G	PO	A	E	TC	DP
Devey, Philip, Portland *	.833	30	1	9	2	12	0
Devey, Philip, Reading *	1.000	8	0	2	0	2	0
Matos, Josue, New Hampshire	1.000	9	0	1	0	1	0
Matos, Josue, Reading	.750	7	2	1	1	4	0
Ogiltree, John, New Hampshire	1.000	2	1	0	0	1	0
Ogiltree, John, Harrisburg	1.000	5	1	2	0	3	0
Pearson, Jason, Portland *	1.000	14	2	2	0	4	0
Pearson, Jason, Bowie *	1.000	5	0	1	0	1	0
Thompson, Travis, Akron	.875	15	1	6	1	8	1
Thompson, Travis, Reading	1.000	11	0	1	0	1	0

Year	Team	Pct.
1923—	Williamsport	.661
1924—	Williamsport	.654
1925—	York§	.583
	Williamsport§	.583
1926—	Scranton	.627
1927—	Harrisburg	.630
1928—	Harrisburg	.603
1929—	Binghamton	.597
1930—	Wilkes-Barre	.572
1931—	Harrisburg	.597
1932—	Wilkes-Barre	.561
1933—	Binghamton	.690
1934—	Binghamton	.694
	Williamsport*	.603
1935—	Scranton	.657
	Binghamton*	.580
1936—	Scranton*	.609
	Elmira	.629
1937—	Elmira†	.622
1938—	Binghamton	.622
	Elmira (3rd)‡	.522
1939—	Scranton†	.571
1940—	Scranton	.568
	Binghamton (2nd)‡	.554
1941—	Wilkes-Barre	.630
	Elmira (3rd)‡	.514
1942—	Albany	.600
	Scranton (2nd)‡	.593
1943—	Scranton	.630
	Elmira (2nd)‡	.568
1944—	Hartford	.723
	Binghamton (4th)‡	.474
1945—	Utica	.615
	Albany (3rd)‡	.564
1946—	Scranton†	.691
1947—	Utica†	.652
1948—	Scranton†	.636
1949—	Albany	.664
	Binghamton (4th)‡	.500
1950—	Wilkes-Barre‡	.652
1951—	Wilkes-Barre‡	.612
	Scranton (2nd)†	.562
1952—	Albany	.603
	Binghamton (2nd)‡	.562
1953—	Reading	.682
	Binghamton (2nd)‡	.636
1954—	Wilkes-Barre	.576
	Albany (3rd)‡	.540
1955—	Reading	.613
	Allentown (2nd)‡	.565
1956—	Schenectady†	.609
1957—	Binghamton	.607
	Reading (3rd)‡	.529

Year	Team	Pct.
1958—	Lancaster∞	.568
	Binghamton (6th)‡	.493
1959—	Springfield†	.607
1960—	Williamsport▲	.551
	Springfield (3rd)▲	.496
1961—	Springfield	.612
1962—	Williamsport	.593
	Elmira (2nd)‡	.514
1963—	Charleston	.593
1964—	Elmira	.586
1965—	Pittsfield	.607
1966—	Elmira	.633
1967—	Binghamton◆	.586
	Elmira	.532
1968—	Pittsfield	.604
	Reading (2nd)‡	.579
1969—	York	.640
1970—	Waterbury■	.560
	Reading■	.553
1971—	Three Rivers	.569
	Elmira▼	.561
1972—	West Haven▼	.600
	Three Rivers	.559
1973—	Reading▼	.551
	Pittsfield	.551
1974—	Thetford Miners (2nd)*	.536
	Pittsfield (2nd)	.496
1975—	Reading	.613
	Bristol*	.587
1976—	Three Rivers	.601
	West Haven††	.576
1977—	West Haven‡‡	.623
	Three Rivers	.551
1978—	Reading	.642
	Bristol*	.580
1979—	West Haven§§	.597
1980—	Holyoke*	.561
	Waterbury	.540
1981—	Glens Falls	.615
	Bristol*	.577
1982—	West Haven*	.614
	Lynn	.590
1983—	Lynn	.554
	New Britain‡	.518
1984—	Waterbury	.543
	Vermont‡	.536
1985—	Albany	.540
	Vermont‡	.514
1986—	Reading	.566
	Vermont‡	.554
1987—	Pittsfield	.630
	Harrisburg‡	.550
1988—	Glens Falls	.584
	Albany‡	.522
1989—	Albany‡	.657

Year	Team	Pct.
	Harrisburg	.522
1990—	Albany	.568
	London‡	.547
1991—	Harrisburg	.621
	Albany‡	.543
1992—	Canton/Akron	.580
	Binghamton‡	.572
1993—	Harrisburg‡	.681
	Canton/Akron	.543
1994—	Harrisburg	.633
	Binghamton‡	.582
1995—	New Haven	.556
	Reading‡	.514
1996—	Portland	.589
	Harrisburg‡	.521
1997—	Harrisburg‡	.606
	Portland	.556
1998—	New Britain	.585
	Harrisburg‡	.514
1999—	Trenton	.648
	Harrisburg‡	.535
2000—	Reading	.599
	New Haven‡	.577
2001—	New Britain∞∞∞	.613
	Reading∞∞∞	.542
2002—	Akron	.660
	Norwich‡	.543
2003—	Akron†	.624
2004—	New Hampshire‡	.596
2005—	Akron	.592

*Won split-season playoff. †Won championship and four-team playoff. ‡Won four-team playoff. §Tied for pennant, York winning playoff. ∞League was divided into Northern, Southern divisions and played a split season; Lancaster was overall season leader. ▲Playoff finals canceled after one game because of rain with Williamsport and Springfield declared playoff co-champions. ◆League was divided into Eastern, Western divisions; Binghamton won playoff. ■Tied for pennant, Waterbury winning playoff. ▼League was divided into American, National divisions; won playoff. *League was divided into American and National divisions; won four-team playoff. ††League was divided into Northern, Southern divisions, won playoff. ‡‡League was divided into New England and Canadian-American divisions; won playoff. §§Won both halves of split season (no playoffs). ∞∞∞Teams were entering finals of four-team playoff and were declared co-champions when Professional Baseball declared a stoppage of play. (NOTE—Known as New York-Pennsylvania League prior to 1938.)

CLASS AA Eastern League

– 459 –

SOUTHERN LEAGUE

LEAGUE OFFICE

President
Don Mincher
Vice president/operations
Lori Webb

Media coordinator
Janelle Kwietkauski
Address
2551 Roswell Road, Suite 330
Marietta, GA 30062

Phone
770-321-0400

TEAMS

BIRMINGHAM BARONS
General manager
Jonathan Nelson
Manager
Chris Cron
Ballpark (capacity, surface)
Hoover Metropolitan Stadium
(10,800, grass)
Affiliation
White Sox
Address
P.O. Box 360007
Birmingham, AL 35236
Phone
205-988-3200

CAROLINA MUDCATS
General manager
Joe Kremer
Manager
Luis Dorante
Ballpark (capacity, surface)
Five County Stadium (6,500, grass)
Affiliation
Marlins
Address
P.O. Drawer 1218
Zebulon, NC 27597
Phone
919-269-2287

CHATTANOOGA LOOKOUTS
President/general manager
J. Frank Burke
Manager
Jayhawk Owens
Ballpark (capacity, surface)
BellSouth Park (6,362, grass)
Affiliation
Reds
Address
201 Power Alley
Chattanooga, TN 37402
Phone
423-267-2208

HUNTSVILLE STARS
General manager
Tom Van Schaack
Manager
Don Money

Ballpark (capacity, surface)
Joe W. Davis Stadium (10,400, grass)
Affiliation
Brewers
Address
3125 Leeman Ferry Road
Huntsville, AL 35801
Phone
256-882-2562

JACKSONVILLE SUNS
Vice president/general manager
Peter Bragan Jr.
Manager
John Shoemaker
Ballpark (capacity, surface)
Baseball Grounds of Jacksonville (11,000, grass)
Affiliation
Dodgers
Address
301 A. Philip Randolph Blvd.
Jacksonville, FL 32202
Phone
904-358-2846

MISSISSIPPI BRAVES
General manager
Steve DeSalvo
Manager
Jeff Blauser
Ballpark (capacity, surface)
Trustmark Park (6,006, grass)
Affiliation
Braves
Address
P.O. Box 97389
Pearl, MS 39288
Phone
888-272-8374

MOBILE BAYBEARS
General manager
Travis Toth
Manager
Gary Jones
Ballpark (capacity, surface)
Hank Aaron Stadium (6,000, grass)
Affiliation
Padres

Address
755 Bolling Brothers Blvd.
Mobile, AL 36606
Phone
251-479-2327

MONTGOMERY BISCUITS
General manager
Greg Rauch
Manager
To be announced
Ballpark (capacity, surface)
Montgomery Riverwalk Stadium
(7,000, grass)
Affiliation
Devil Rays
Address
200 Coosa St.
Montgomery, AL 36104
Phone
334-323-2255

TENNESSEE SMOKIES
General manager
Brian Cox
Manager
Bill Plummer
Ballpark (capacity, surface)
Smokies Park (6,000, grass)
Affiliation
Diamondbacks
Address
3540 Line Drive
Kodak, TN 37764
Phone
865-637-9494

WEST TENN DIAMOND JAXX
General manager
Jeff Parker
Manager
Bobby Dickerson
Ballpark (capacity, surface)
Pringles Park (6,000, grass)
Affiliation
Cubs
Address
4 Fun Place
Jackson, TN 38305
Phone
731-664-2020

CLASS AA *Southern League*

FIRST HALF

NORTHERN DIVISION

Team	W	L	T	Pct.	GB
West Tenn Diamond Jaxx	44	25	-	0.638	...
Carolina Mudcats	41	27	-	0.603	2.5
Tennessee Smokies	33	37	-	0.471	11.5
Huntsville Stars	29	40	-	0.42	15
Chattanooga Lookouts	27	42	-	0.391	17

SOUTHERN DIVISION

Team	W	L	T	Pct.	GB
Jacksonville Suns	38	32	-	0.543	...
Birmingham Barons	36	33	-	0.522	1.5
Mississippi Braves	36	34	-	0.514	2
Montgomery Biscuits	35	35	-	0.5	3
Mobile BayBears	28	42	-	0.4	10

SECOND HALF

NORTHERN DIVISION

Team	W	L	T	Pct.	GB
West Tenn Diamond Jaxx	39	31	-	0.557	...
Carolina Mudcats	36	30	-	0.545	1
Tennessee Smokies	31	39	-	0.443	8
Huntsville Stars	31	39	-	0.443	8
Chattanooga Lookouts	26	41	-	0.388	11.5

SOUTHERN DIVISION

Team	W	L	T	Pct.	GB
Birmingham Barons	46	24	-	0.657	...
Jacksonville Suns	41	29	-	0.586	5
Montgomery Biscuits	32	35	-	0.478	12.5
Mississippi Braves	28	34	-	0.452	14
Mobile BayBears	30	38	-	0.441	15

COMPOSITE

CLUB (AFFILIATE), ABBREV	WTM	BIR	CAR	JAX	MON	MIS	TEN	HUN	MOB	CHA	W	L	PCT	GB
West Tenn (Cubs), WTN	...	8	7	2	7	12	15	10	12	10	83	56	.597	-
Birmingham (White Sox), BIR	5	...	7	13	13	8	10	9	8	9	82	57	.590	1.0
Carolina (Marlins), CAR	9	2	...	8	3	3	13	9	4	26	77	57	.575	3.5
Jacksonville (Dodgers), JAX	6	10	12	...	10	7	4	6	15	9	79	61	.564	4.5
Montgomery (Devil Rays), MON	2	7	4	16	...	15	9	1	11	2	67	70	.489	15.0
Mississippi (Braves), MIS	10	5	1	8	8	...	5	15	7	5	64	68	.485	15.5
Tennessee (Diamondbacks), TEN	5	8	7	2	12	2	...	9	6	13	64	76	.457	19.5
Huntsville (Brewers), HUN	6	2	5	4	5	6	12	...	12	8	60	79	.432	23.0
Mobile (Padres), MOB	6	7	3	7	10	9	4	11	...	1	58	80	.420	24.5
Chattanooga (Reds), CHA	7	8	11	1	2	6	4	9	5	...	53	83	.390	28.5

Major league affiliations in parentheses.

PLAYOFFS: Semifinals: West Tenn defeated Carolina, three games to none, and Jacksonville defeated Birmingham, three games to none. Finals: Jacksonville defeated West Tenn, three games to one.

REGULAR-SEASON ATTENDANCE: West Tenn, 105,893. Birmingham, 271,031. Carolina, 252,178. Mobile, 187,505. Montgomery, 303,054. Mississippi, 242,423. Chattanooga, 240,075. Tennessee, 241,163. Huntsville, 213,552. Jacksonville, 359,957. All-Star Game (at Mobile), 5,587. League total, 2,416,831. Postseason (10 games), 19,392.

MANAGERS: West Tenn, Bobby Dickerson. Birmingham, Razor Shines. Carolina, Gary Allenson. Mobile, Gary Jones. Montgomery, Charlie Montoyo. Mississippi, Brian Snitker. Chattanooga, Jayhawk Owens. Tennessee, Tony Perezchica. Huntsville, Don Money. Jacksonville, John Shoemaker.

ALL-STAR TEAM: 1B-Casey Rogowski, Birmingham. 2B-Dan Uggla, Tennessee. 3B-Rico Washington, Montgomery. SS-Joel Guzman, Jacksonville. OF-Jeremy Hermida, Carolina. OF-Matt Murton, West Tenn. OF-Jerry Owens, Birmingham. OF-Delmon Young, Montgomery. C-Russell Martin, Jacksonville. DH-Brandon Sing, West Tenn. RHP-Ricky Nolasco, West Tenn. LHP-Renyel Pinto, West Tenn. Relief Pitcher-Chris Resop, Carolina. Most Valuable Player-Delmon Young, Montgomery. Most Outstanding Pitcher-Ricky Nolasco, West Tenn. Best Hustler-Todd Donovan, Jacksonville. Best Utility Player-Dan Uggla, Tennessee. Manager of the Year-Razor Shines, Birmingham.

2005 BATTING

TEAM

Team	G	TPA	AB	R	H	TB	2B	3B	HR	RBI	SH	SF	HP	BB	IBB	SO	SB	CS	GDP	LOB	ShO	Avg.	OBP	Slg.
Birmingham	139	5361	4650	730	1297	1945	267	30	107	664	86	50	70	505	23	966	127	73	87	2145	9	.279	.355	.418
Jacksonville	140	5378	4691	704	1292	1932	248	25	114	649	51	36	65	534	30	1063	116	48	103	2220	3	.275	.355	.412
Montgomery	137	5159	4629	662	1261	1910	226	33	119	614	29	46	62	393	18	978	143	52	121	1927	8	.272	.335	.413
Chattanooga	136	5311	4700	623	1268	1858	268	23	92	570	66	45	55	445	23	913	125	46	112	2158	12	.270	.337	.395
Huntsville	139	5292	4646	591	1255	1751	231	38	63	536	94	36	44	471	24	943	105	51	139	2118	12	.270	.341	.377
West Tenn	139	5305	4639	623	1254	1862	251	42	91	571	67	46	34	519	36	913	151	71	105	2106	6	.270	.345	.401
Carolina	134	5085	4451	563	1186	1759	244	22	95	518	72	32	55	475	22	1045	111	51	90	2010	5	.266	.342	.395
Mississippi	132	4986	4391	545	1133	1662	214	45	75	486	70	35	53	437	31	949	104	60	87	1906	7	.258	.330	.379
Tennessee	140	5229	4621	617	1187	1783	219	28	107	575	72	27	54	449	32	979	170	88	99	1985	12	.257	.328	.386
Mobile	138	5259	4606	571	1123	1649	203	25	91	515	62	33	49	507	14	1157	75	41	81	2124	14	.244	.323	.358

INDIVIDUAL

TOP QUALIFIERS FOR BATTING CHAMPIONSHIP

Minimum 378 plate appearances. *Lefthanded batter. †Switch-hitter.

Player, Team	G	TPA	AB	R	H	TB	2B	3B	HR	RBI	SH	SF	HP	BB	IBB	SO	SB	CS	GDP	Avg.	OBP	Slg.
Owens, Jerry, Birmingham *	130	587	522	99	173	212	21	6	2	52	9	2	2	52	4	72	38	20	5	.331	.393	.406
Hanigan, Ryan, Chattanooga	100	390	333	45	107	135	14	1	4	29	2	0	5	50	1	41	4	1	8	.321	.418	.405
Martin, Russell, Jacksonville	129	505	409	83	127	173	17	1	9	61	5	3	10	78	0	69	15	7	14	.311	.430	.423
Hopper, Norris, Chattanooga	116	487	451	70	140	166	15	4	1	37	4	1	4	27	2	38	25	7	12	.310	.354	.368
Thorman, Scott, Mississippi *	90	383	348	49	106	176	21	2	15	65	0	3	4	28	5	76	2	2	3	.305	.360	.506
Theriot, Ryan, West Tenn	120	503	448	52	136	175	28	4	1	53	4	5	1	45	2	38	24	10	9	.304	.365	.391
Gemoll, Brandon, Huntsville *	120	473	432	53	131	189	27	5	7	59	3	4	4	30	2	104	3	3	16	.303	.351	.438
Weber, Jonathan, Jacksonville *	117	503	450	81	135	205	27	5	11	68	2	1	5	45	6	78	10	6	5	.300	.369	.456
Cruz, Enrique, Huntsville	137	541	496	68	149	231	34	3	14	60	2	1	5	37	6	107	4	4	14	.300	.354	.466
Washington, Rico, Montgomery *	126	532	454	84	136	227	30	2	19	77	0	8	7	63	1	63	6	5	6	.300	.387	.500
Sweeney, Ryan, Birmingham *	113	483	429	64	128	159	22	3	1	47	7	5	7	35	4	53	6	6	5	.298	.357	.371

Player, Team	G	TPA	AB	R	H	TB	2B	3B	HR	RBI	SH	SF	HP	BB	IBB	SO	SB	CS	GDP	Avg.	OBP	Slg.
Uggla, Daniel, Tennessee	135	571	498	88	148	250	33	3	21	87	3	2	14	52	5	103	15	8	10	.297	.378	.502
McGehee, Casey, West Tenn	124	505	455	67	135	192	31	1	8	72	0	6	1	43	5	64	2	2	20	.297	.354	.422
Young, Delwyn, Jacksonville †	95	407	371	52	110	185	25	1	16	62	1	4	3	27	4	86	1	3	9	.296	.346	.499
Howard, Kevin, Chattanooga *	129	522	479	63	142	205	23	2	12	70	2	3	5	33	4	64	13	8	16	.296	.346	.428
Hill, Jason, Carolina	116	454	416	50	123	212	33	1	18	74	1	3	3	31	2	63	2	1	16	.296	.347	.510
Shanks, James, Carolina	98	418	371	55	110	168	19	6	9	51	2	4	6	35	1	103	16	10	2	.296	.363	.453
Rottino, Vincent, Huntsville	120	516	469	63	139	189	20	6	6	52	0	5	2	40	1	68	2	1	14	.296	.351	.403
Hermida, Jeremy, Carolina *	118	507	386	77	113	200	29	2	18	63	1	2	7	111	5	89	23	2	8	.293	.457	.518
Rogowski, Casey, Birmingham *	134	583	505	83	148	224	37	6	9	78	3	6	11	58	3	111	20	12	14	.293	.374	.444
Dukes, Elijah, Montgomery †	120	498	446	73	128	213	21	5	18	73	0	3	4	45	2	83	19	9	13	.287	.355	.478

DEPARTMENTAL LEADERS: G—Loney, 138. AB—Owens, 522. R—Young, 100. H—Owens, 173. TB—Young, 254. 2B—Young, 41. 3B—Blanco, 12. HR—Sing and Young, 26. RBI—Blakely, 89. SH—Crabbe, 20. SF—four players with 8. HP—Timmons, 21. BB—Hermida, 111. IBB—Reyes, 10. SO—Smith, 144. SB—Donovan, 62. CS—Owens, 20. GIDP—McGehee, 20. OBP—Hermida, .457. Slg.—Young, .545.

ALL PLAYERS

*Lefthanded batter. †Switch-hitter.

Player, Team	G	TPA	AB	R	H	TB	2B	3B	HR	RBI	SH	SF	HP	BB	IBB	SO	SB	CS	GDP	Avg.	OBP	Slg.
Aardsma, David, West Tenn	29	7	6	0	0	0	0	0	0	0	0	1	0	0	0	1	0	0	1	.000	.000	.000
Abercrombie, Reginald, Carolina	49	197	178	28	45	86	7	2	10	23	0	2	6	11	0	40	7	5	1	.253	.315	.483
Abraham, Paul, Mobile	25	7	5	0	0	0	0	0	0	0	1	0	1	0	1	0	3	0	0	.000	.143	.000
Abreu, Etanislao, Jacksonville	24	102	96	10	24	31	3	2	0	9	0	1	1	4	0	21	0	2	2	.250	.284	.323
Aceves, Jonathan, Birmingham	70	254	217	32	58	95	14	1	7	34	3	1	7	26	1	47	0	1	8	.267	.363	.438
Acosta, Christian, Birmingham	2	8	7	1	0	0	0	0	0	0	0	0	0	1	0	1	0	0	0	.000	.125	.000
Aguilar, Raymond, Carolina †	11	26	17	1	4	4	0	0	0	1	5	0	0	4	0	3	0	0	1	.235	.381	.235
Almanza, Armando, Tennessee *	4	0	0	0	0	0	0	0	0	0	0	...	0	0	0	0	0	0	0	...	...	...
Alvarez, Carlos, Jacksonville *	19	7	5	0	1	1	0	0	0	1	2	0	0	0	2	0	0	0	0	.200	.200	.200
Alvarez, Nicolas, Jacksonville	98	269	237	27	70	87	11	0	2	35	0	4	2	26	0	32	2	0	10	.295	.364	.367
Anderson, Bryan, Chattanooga	113	300	261	27	48	78	18	0	4	22	6	2	5	26	0	69	1	2	7	.184	.269	.299
Anderson, Dennis, Carolina †	67	208	177	22	59	74	12	0	1	26	5	1	3	22	3	22	1	2	4	.333	.414	.418
Andino, Robert, Carolina	127	570	516	63	139	184	30	0	5	48	8	3	6	37	0	111	22	7	11	.269	.324	.357
Andrew, Jason, Chattanooga	41	17	14	2	3	6	1	1	0	0	1	0	0	2	0	5	0	0	0	.214	.313	.429
Arteaga, Joshua, Mississippi	42	112	101	7	25	31	6	0	0	11	1	1	0	9	0	26	0	2	3	.248	.306	.307
Asadoorian, Eric, Chattanooga	93	322	295	44	80	124	20	3	6	39	6	2	5	14	3	79	11	4	9	.271	.313	.420
Ashby, Christopher, Carolina	23	84	81	7	20	32	3	0	3	9	0	0	1	2	0	8	0	0	5	.247	.274	.395
Atlee, Thomas, West Tenn	25	3	1	1	0	0	0	0	0	0	0	1	0	0	1	0	0	0	0	.000	.500	.000
Avias, Aaron, Tennessee	41	134	113	15	27	38	5	0	2	18	0	2	1	18	2	21	5	2	2	.239	.343	.336
Bacon, Dwaine, West Tenn †	98	347	292	57	78	108	10	7	2	15	4	0	5	46	0	90	37	14	3	.267	.376	.370
Baez, Federico, West Tenn	34	6	5	0	0	0	0	0	0	0	1	0	0	0	0	4	0	0	1	.000	.000	.000
Baker, Casey, Mobile	101	312	271	39	59	73	9	1	1	14	7	1	3	30	0	64	9	2	4	.218	.302	.269
Baker, Ryan, Carolina	22	3	3	0	0	0	0	0	0	0	0	0	0	0	0	2	0	0	0	.000	.000	.000
Baker, Steve, Mobile	66	274	260	26	75	110	13	2	6	33	0	1	3	10	0	70	4	2	1	.288	.321	.423
Ball, Jarred, Tennessee †	128	492	399	69	101	145	19	2	7	34	8	1	6	74	4	115	39	18	8	.253	.377	.363
Ballouli, Khalid, Huntsville	22	22	21	0	3	3	0	0	0	0	1	0	0	0	0	9	0	0	1	.143	.143	.143
Bankston, Wesley, Montgomery	82	337	301	42	88	145	17	2	12	47	0	2	4	30	3	64	3	3	8	.292	.362	.482
Bannon, Jeff, Chattanooga	93	404	365	51	97	164	23	1	14	60	3	6	4	26	1	72	14	1	10	.266	.317	.449
Barnes, John, Mississippi	3	10	10	2	4	4	0	0	0	0	0	0	0	0	0	0	0	0	0	.400	.400	.400
Barnwell, Christopher, Huntsville	15	38	35	6	9	16	2	1	1	4	0	1	1	1	0	7	1	0	0	.257	.289	.457
Barreto, Joel, Chattanooga	3	0	0	0	0	0	0	0	0	0	0	...	0	0	0	...	0	0	0	...	...	...
Barry, Kevin, Mississippi	3	2	2	0	0	0	0	0	0	0	0	0	0	0	0	2	0	0	0	.000	.000	.000
Bartlett, Richard, Jacksonville	24	9	7	1	1	1	0	0	0	0	0	0	1	0	0	1	0	0	0	.143	.250	.143
Basham, Robert, Chattanooga	8	15	13	1	2	4	2	0	0	0	0	2	0	0	0	5	0	0	0	.154	.154	.308
Basner, Ryan, Mississippi	25	19	16	1	1	1	0	0	0	0	2	0	0	1	0	7	0	0	0	.063	.118	.063
Bass, Adam, Tennessee	18	44	37	2	4	5	1	0	0	6	0	1	0	0	0	7	0	0	1	.108	.132	.135
Bass, Christopher, Carolina	116	351	313	36	79	119	25	0	5	36	2	2	0	34	2	74	1	4	7	.252	.324	.380
Bauer, Peter, Carolina *	1	1	1	0	0	0	0	0	0	0	0	0	0	0	0	0	0	0	0	.000	.000	.000
Bazardo, Yorman, Carolina	16	31	23	3	4	8	1	0	1	2	5	0	1	2	0	13	0	0	3	.174	.269	.348
Bell, Rick, Chattanooga	29	102	93	10	20	33	7	0	2	16	2	4	0	3	0	19	0	0	3	.215	.230	.355
Bentz, Chad, Carolina	6	0	0	0	0	0	0	0	0	0	0	...	0	0	0	0	0	0	0	...	...	...
Bernard, Miguel, Mississippi	20	81	76	7	18	22	2	1	0	13	0	0	5	2	0	15	1	0	3	.237	.284	.289
Bibbs, Kennard, Huntsville *	105	411	359	45	100	133	18	6	1	25	12	4	2	34	0	47	23	9	5	.279	.341	.370
Biggs, Billy, Tennessee	8	1	1	0	0	0	0	0	0	0	0	0	0	0	0	0	0	0	0	.000	.000	.000
Billingsley, Chad, Jacksonville	18	38	34	2	6	7	1	0	0	1	2	0	0	2	0	12	0	0	0	.176	.222	.206
Blakely, Darren, Birmingham †	128	520	460	71	130	219	29	3	18	89	3	8	4	45	4	122	5	5	7	.283	.346	.476
Blanco, Gregor, Mississippi *	123	486	401	64	101	154	11	12	6	37	7	3	2	73	2	124	28	12	8	.252	.367	.384
Bobbitt, Seth, Mississippi	2	1	1	0	0	0	0	0	0	0	0	0	0	0	0	0	0	0	0	.000	.000	.000
Bostick II, Adam, Carolina *	8	14	13	2	2	3	1	0	0	0	1	0	0	0	0	5	0	0	0	.154	.154	.231
Bott, Glenn, Jacksonville *	16	6	4	0	2	2	0	0	0	1	2	0	0	0	0	0	0	0	0	.500	.500	.500
Boyer, Blaine, Mississippi	7	9	8	0	0	0	0	0	0	0	0	1	0	0	0	5	0	0	0	.000	.000	.000
Bozied, Robert, Mobile	12	49	45	9	15	24	0	0	3	12	0	0	1	3	0	9	0	0	0	.333	.388	.533
Bradley, David, Huntsville	30	25	18	1	2	2	0	0	0	0	5	0	0	2	0	8	0	0	0	.111	.200	.111
Breslow, Craig, Mobile *	33	3	3	0	0	0	0	0	0	0	0	0	0	0	0	1	0	0	0	.000	.000	.000
Brown, Nebasett, Tennessee *	49	164	146	18	38	49	8	0	1	17	3	0	1	14	0	26	9	3	4	.260	.329	.336
Broxton, Jonathan, Jacksonville	20	22	16	1	3	3	0	0	0	0	5	0	0	1	0	6	0	0	0	.188	.235	.188
Bruksch, Jeffrey, Chattanooga	23	21	17	1	1	1	0	0	0	0	3	0	0	1	0	11	0	0	1	.059	.111	.059
Bumstead, Michael, Mobile	3	7	6	0	0	0	0	0	0	0	0	1	0	0	0	4	0	0	0	.000	.000	.000
Burgamy, Brian, Mobile †	56	205	176	15	35	51	6	2	2	15	2	0	0	27	1	45	2	0	0	.199	.305	.290
Burrus, Josh, Mississippi	46	196	172	21	38	63	6	2	5	21	0	1	1	22	1	53	9	4	1	.221	.311	.366
Bush, Paul, Mississippi	17	14	12	1	1	1	0	0	0	0	2	0	0	0	0	7	0	0	1	.083	.083	.083
Butler, Brent, Montgomery	34	144	121	22	32	59	7	1	6	21	3	2	3	15	0	14	2	0	3	.264	.355	.488
Cameron, Troy, Mobile †	14	32	29	2	4	5	1	0	0	5	0	0	0	3	0	9	0	0	1	.138	.219	.172

Player, Team	G	TPA	AB	R	H	TB	2B	3B	HR	RBI	SH	SF	HP	BB	IBB	SO	SB	CS	GDP	Avg.	OBP	Slg.
Caraccioli, Lance, Chattanooga *	14	19	16	1	1	1	0	0	0	1	2	1	0	0	0	9	0	0	0	.063	.059	.063
Carlin, Luke, Mobile †	88	268	230	24	59	75	8	1	2	25	1	1	1	35	3	46	3	3	4	.257	.356	.326
Carrillo, Cesar, Mobile	3	7	7	0	0	0	0	0	0	0	0	0	0	0	0	5	0	0	0	.000	.000	.000
Carter, William, Tennessee *	36	151	128	21	38	72	4	0	10	30	0	1	3	19	4	11	0	3	1	.297	.397	.563
Cassel, Joseph, Mobile	22	9	6	0	0	0	0	0	0	0	1	0	1	1	0	4	0	0	0	.000	.250	.000
Castro, Juan, Huntsville	45	135	120	18	27	33	6	0	0	14	3	3	1	8	0	32	1	0	2	.225	.273	.275
Cave, Kevin, Carolina	35	1	0	1	0	0	0	0	0	0	0	0	0	1	0	0	0	0	0	...	1.000	...
Cherry, Rocky, West Tenn	2	3	3	0	0	0	0	0	0	0	0	0	0	0	0	2	0	0	0	.000	.000	.000
Cherry, William, Chattanooga	7	0	0	0	0	0	0	0	0	0	0	0	0	0	0	0	0	0	0	...	...	...
Chick, Travis, Mobile-Chattanooga	23	43	35	2	6	12	3	0	1	1	6	0	0	2	0	15	0	0	0	.171	.216	.343
Chico, Matthew, Tennessee *	9	16	15	0	2	3	1	0	0	2	1	0	0	0	0	4	0	0	0	.133	.133	.200
Clements, Jason, Mobile †	70	207	182	25	41	59	5	2	3	18	5	1	2	17	1	48	2	1	4	.225	.297	.324
Coats, Buck, West Tenn *	127	484	439	47	124	171	32	6	1	49	1	4	2	38	1	80	17	5	10	.282	.340	.390
Coenen, Matthew, Mississippi *	16	34	22	1	5	5	0	0	0	2	8	0	0	4	0	4	0	0	0	.227	.346	.227
Colon, Roman, Mississippi	2	3	3	0	1	1	0	0	0	0	0	0	0	0	0	2	0	0	0	.333	.333	.333
Connolly, Jonathan, West Tenn	8	8	5	1	0	0	0	0	0	0	1	0	0	2	0	2	0	0	1	.000	.286	.000
Cortez, Fernando, Montgomery *	55	240	219	39	73	92	11	4	0	23	1	3	2	15	0	42	12	3	3	.333	.377	.420
Costello, Ryan, Huntsville *	8	9	9	0	0	0	0	0	0	0	0	0	0	0	0	5	0	0	1	.000	.000	.000
Cota, Jesus, Tennessee *	95	388	349	40	93	149	14	0	14	68	0	6	5	28	5	46	2	2	9	.266	.325	.427
Crabbe, Callix, Huntsville †	119	475	387	42	94	120	15	4	1	33	20	1	2	65	4	65	18	6	17	.243	.354	.310
Craig, Matthew, West Tenn †	99	371	327	51	90	150	24	0	12	57	0	8	4	32	3	62	7	4	9	.275	.340	.459
Creighton, Matt, West Tenn	42	109	102	11	25	38	7	0	2	11	0	0	1	6	0	18	0	1	2	.245	.294	.373
Cruz, Arian, Chattanooga *	11	1	1	0	0	0	0	0	0	0	0	0	0	0	0	1	0	0	0	.000	.000	.000
Cruz, Enrique, Huntsville	137	541	496	68	149	231	34	3	14	60	2	1	5	37	6	107	4	4	14	.300	.354	.466
Cruz, Nelson, Huntsville	68	286	248	45	76	143	19	0	16	54	0	3	4	31	0	71	10	3	7	.306	.388	.577
Curry, Michael, Montgomery *	49	206	186	39	47	65	10	1	2	11	0	0	3	17	0	47	15	5	5	.253	.325	.349
Curtis, Daniel, Mississippi	4	3	3	0	0	0	0	0	0	0	0	0	0	0	0	1	0	0	0	.000	.000	.000
Daigle, Casey, Tennessee	44	3	3	0	1	1	0	0	0	0	0	0	0	0	0	2	0	0	0	.333	.333	.333
Dannemiller, Beau, Jacksonville	18	3	2	0	0	0	0	0	0	0	1	0	0	0	0	2	0	0	0	.000	.000	.000
D'Antona, James, Tennessee	125	458	410	58	102	158	25	2	9	49	2	1	1	44	2	67	5	6	10	.249	.322	.385
Deago, Roger, Mobile	4	5	4	0	0	0	0	0	0	0	0	0	0	1	0	1	0	0	0	.000	.000	.000
Dehart, James, Mississippi *	30	14	13	0	2	2	0	0	0	0	1	0	0	0	0	3	0	0	1	.154	.154	.154
Delucchi, Dustin, Mobile *	34	131	107	11	30	35	5	0	0	8	3	0	4	16	0	24	4	2	3	.280	.394	.327
DeMarco, Mathew, Carolina *	14	29	24	1	5	6	1	0	0	0	0	0	0	3	2	4	0	0	0	.208	.345	.250
Demontel II, James, Carolina	2	0	0	0	0	0	0	0	0	0	0	0	0	0	...	0	0	0	0	...	...	...
Denorfia, Chris, Chattanooga	46	209	188	40	62	106	17	3	7	26	2	0	2	17	1	38	4	3	1	.330	.391	.564
Devine, Joey, Mississippi	12	1	1	0	0	0	0	0	0	0	0	0	0	0	0	0	0	0	0	.000	.000	.000
DeWitt, Matt, Huntsville	26	3	3	0	0	0	0	0	0	0	0	0	0	0	0	1	0	0	0	.000	.000	.000
Dirosa, Michael, Tennessee	39	106	92	9	22	33	2	0	3	8	0	0	0	14	0	33	1	1	0	.239	.340	.359
Dizard, Fraser, Birmingham *	1	0	0	0	0	0	0	0	0	0	0	0	0	0	0	0	0	0	0	...	...	...
Donovan, Todd, Jacksonville	119	522	459	89	126	186	16	10	8	36	6	0	14	43	0	89	62	13	7	.275	.355	.405
Drew, Stephen, Tennessee *	27	113	101	11	22	39	5	0	4	13	0	0	0	12	0	24	2	3	1	.218	.301	.386
Dukes, Elijah, Montgomery †	120	498	446	73	128	213	21	5	18	73	0	3	4	45	2	83	19	9	13	.287	.355	.478
Dumatrait, Phillip, Chattanooga	20	37	29	1	2	3	1	0	0	2	7	0	0	1	0	15	0	0	1	.069	.100	.103
Duncan, Jeff, Mobile *	22	84	70	12	21	34	3	2	2	7	2	1	2	9	1	20	1	1	1	.300	.390	.486
Duran, Carlos, Mississippi *	63	165	158	12	42	63	8	5	1	11	1	2	0	4	2	31	0	2	3	.266	.280	.399
Eckenstahler, Eric, Chattanooga *	28	1	1	0	0	0	0	0	0	0	0	0	0	0	0	0	0	0	0	.000	.000	.000
Eveland, Dana, Huntsville *	16	40	36	3	4	6	2	0	0	2	2	0	0	2	0	8	0	0	0	.111	.158	.167
Evert, Brett, Huntsville *	13	4	3	0	1	1	0	0	0	0	1	0	0	1	0	1	0	0	0	.333	.500	.333
Ezi, Travis, Huntsville *	17	37	31	7	7	10	1	1	0	3	0	1	1	4	0	10	1	2	0	.226	.324	.323
Fernandez, Alexander, Chattanooga *	42	165	150	18	49	61	6	0	2	23	1	2	0	12	2	25	4	1	1	.327	.372	.407
Ferreras, Yorkin, West Tenn *	24	2	2	0	0	0	0	0	0	0	0	0	0	0	0	0	0	0	0	.000	.000	.000
Fields, Joshua, Birmingham	134	560	477	76	120	195	27	0	16	79	9	6	13	55	2	142	7	6	4	.252	.341	.409
Flannery, Michael, Carolina	26	0	0	0	0	0	0	0	0	0	0	0	0	0	...	0	0	0	0	...	...	...
Flury, Patrick, Carolina	3	0	0	0	0	0	0	0	0	0	0	0	0	0	0	0	0	0	0	...	...	...
Ford, Matthew, Huntsville †	16	0	0	0	0	0	0	0	0	0	0	0	0	0	...	0	0	0	0	...	...	...
Franco, Iker, Mississippi	48	191	179	14	53	69	7	0	3	23	2	2	0	8	0	31	0	3	5	.296	.323	.385
Francoeur, Jeff, Mississippi	84	367	335	40	92	163	28	2	13	62	0	6	5	21	5	76	13	4	7	.275	.322	.487
Freel, Ryan, Chattanooga	5	24	17	3	3	3	0	0	0	1	0	1	0	3	0	5	0	1	1	.176	.286	.176
Frese, Nate, West Tenn	14	36	32	3	12	20	2	0	2	7	0	0	0	4	1	5	0	0	1	.375	.444	.625
Fuell, Jerrod, Carolina	36	1	1	0	0	0	0	0	0	0	0	0	0	0	0	0	0	0	0	.000	.000	.000
Gamble, Jerome, Huntsville	27	5	5	1	1	1	0	0	0	1	0	0	0	0	0	2	0	1	0	.200	.200	.200
Gann, James, Montgomery	5	22	21	0	2	3	1	0	0	0	0	0	0	1	0	6	0	0	2	.095	.136	.143
Garcia, Cipriano, Birmingham	4	12	11	2	4	4	0	0	0	0	0	0	1	0	0	6	0	0	0	.364	.417	.364
Garcia, Jesse, Mobile	7	34	31	4	6	11	2	0	1	3	1	1	1	0	0	4	0	0	0	.194	.212	.355
Garcia, Sergio, Jacksonville	80	273	234	30	58	78	8	0	4	38	5	1	7	26	3	44	1	1	2	.248	.340	.333
Garciaparra, Nomar, West Tenn	4	15	13	2	3	3	0	0	0	0	0	0	1	1	0	1	0	0	0	.231	.333	.231
Gardner, Richard, Chattanooga	10	18	15	2	4	5	1	0	0	1	0	0	0	3	0	6	0	0	0	.267	.389	.333
Gemoll, Brandon, Huntsville *	120	473	432	53	131	189	27	5	7	59	3	4	4	30	2	104	3	3	16	.303	.351	.438
Gerber, Joseph, Mobile *	83	320	271	41	75	138	15	0	16	41	4	1	6	38	0	88	0	1	3	.277	.377	.509
Giambi, Jeremy, Birmingham *	5	13	11	1	3	4	1	0	0	2	0	0	0	2	0	3	0	0	0	.273	.385	.364
Gibson, Derrick, Mississippi	6	15	15	1	2	3	1	0	0	2	0	0	0	0	0	4	0	0	0	.133	.133	.200
Gil, Jerry, Tennessee	55	212	199	28	51	94	7	3	10	29	4	0	1	8	1	52	10	7	3	.256	.288	.472
Gonzalez, Adolfo, Jacksonville †	14	45	41	3	11	17	3	0	1	3	1	1	0	2	2	11	0	0	0	.268	.295	.415
Gonzalez, Alfredo, Jacksonville	3	0	0	0	0	0	0	0	0	0	0	0	0	0	0	0	0	0	0	...	...	...
Gonzalez, Angel, Birmingham	123	511	434	50	119	154	19	2	4	63	5	7	4	61	1	91	6	6	9	.274	.364	.355
Gonzalez, Enrique, Tennessee	20	47	37	2	7	7	0	0	0	2	10	0	0	0	0	6	0	0	0	.189	.189	.189
Gonzalez, Luis, Jacksonville *	30	5	5	0	2	2	0	0	0	0	0	0	0	0	0	3	0	0	0	.400	.400	.400
Goocher, Clint, Tennessee *	19	37	25	2	7	11	4	0	0	1	11	0	0	1	0	6	0	0	0	.280	.308	.440
Gray, Antoin, Birmingham	76	269	230	37	55	92	14	1	7	30	6	2	4	27	0	65	1	1	2	.239	.327	.400
Green, Chad, Carolina †	1	0	0	0	0	0	0	0	0	0	0	0	0	0	0	0	0	0	0	...	...	...

– 463 –

Player, Team	G	TPA	AB	R	H	TB	2B	3B	HR	RBI	SH	SF	HP	BB	IBB	SO	SB	CS	GDP	Avg.	OBP	Slg.
Greenberg, Adam, West Tenn *	95	382	305	51	82	124	12	9	4	33	14	3	4	56	2	68	15	4	1	.269	.386	.407
Gutierrez, Jesse, Chattanooga	26	114	100	11	31	53	8	1	4	25	0	4	2	8	0	20	0	0	2	.310	.360	.530
Guzman, Joel, Jacksonville	122	496	442	63	127	210	31	2	16	75	0	7	5	42	3	128	7	3	10	.287	.351	.475
Gwaltney, William, West Tenn *	1	0	0	0	0	0	0	0	0	0	0	0	0	0	0	0	0	0	0	...	...	...
Gwynn, Anthony, Huntsville *	133	601	509	83	138	172	21	5	1	41	9	2	5	76	1	75	34	15	11	.271	.370	.338
Habel, Joshua, Huntsville *	19	15	12	0	0	0	0	0	0	0	3	0	0	0	0	7	0	0	0	.000	.000	.000
Haeger, Charles, Birmingham	3	5	4	0	1	1	0	0	0	0	1	0	0	0	0	1	0	0	0	.250	.250	.250
Haggerty, Cory, Birmingham *	46	132	111	12	24	35	3	1	2	14	3	1	0	17	1	26	2	1	4	.216	.318	.315
Haines, Joseph, West Tenn	19	1	0	1	0	0	0	0	0	1	0	0	0	1	0	0	0	0	0	...	1.000	...
Haley, Adam, Tennessee *	124	419	377	56	108	140	16	2	4	28	6	0	5	31	3	72	13	8	8	.286	.349	.371
Hall, Josh, Chattanooga	15	37	31	2	5	5	0	0	0	2	5	0	0	1	0	15	0	0	1	.161	.188	.161
Hanigan, Ryan, Chattanooga	100	390	333	45	107	135	14	1	4	29	2	0	5	50	1	41	4	1	8	.321	.418	.405
Hanrahan, Joel, Jacksonville	14	24	18	0	1	1	0	0	0	2	4	1	0	1	0	5	0	0	0	.056	.100	.056
Heether, Adam, Huntsville	14	56	51	11	16	21	5	0	0	9	0	2	1	2	0	8	2	1	4	.314	.339	.412
Hermida, Jeremy, Carolina *	118	507	386	77	113	200	29	2	18	63	1	2	7	111	5	89	23	2	8	.293	.457	.518
Hernandez, Luis, Mississippi †	122	469	415	47	101	129	12	5	2	32	6	3	4	41	2	56	5	5	11	.243	.315	.311
Hill, Jason, Carolina	116	454	416	50	123	212	33	1	18	74	1	3	3	31	2	63	2	1	16	.296	.347	.510
Hill, Rich, West Tenn *	6	17	14	1	1	1	0	0	0	0	2	0	0	1	0	6	0	0	0	.071	.133	.071
Hoerman, Jared, West Tenn	1	0	0	0	0	0	0	0	0	0	0	0	0	0	0	0	0	0	0	...	...	...
Hoffpauir, James, West Tenn *	7	25	25	1	4	7	0	0	1	2	0	0	0	0	0	6	0	0	1	.160	.160	.280
Hopper, Norris, Chattanooga	116	487	451	70	140	166	15	4	1	37	4	1	4	27	2	38	25	7	12	.310	.354	.368
Howard, Kevin, Chattanooga *	129	522	479	63	142	205	23	2	12	70	2	3	5	33	4	64	13	8	16	.296	.346	.428
Hudson, Luke, Chattanooga	1	2	2	0	0	0	0	0	0	0	0	0	0	0	0	1	0	0	0	.000	.000	.000
Hull, Eric, Jacksonville	19	33	24	4	2	2	0	0	0	0	4	0	0	5	0	11	0	0	0	.083	.241	.083
Isenia, Chairon, Montgomery	104	420	390	45	95	146	22	1	9	68	1	4	8	17	2	63	2	1	14	.244	.286	.374
Jackson, Edwin, Jacksonville	9	17	12	0	1	1	0	0	0	2	3	1	1	0	0	5	0	0	0	.083	.143	.083
James, Chuck, Mississippi *	12	25	20	3	5	5	0	0	0	2	3	0	0	2	0	10	0	0	0	.250	.318	.250
Jimenez, D'Angelo, Chattanooga †	90	399	327	55	91	138	20	0	9	45	0	3	0	69	2	34	16	4	4	.278	.401	.422
Johnson, Elliot, Montgomery †	63	283	264	31	69	99	9	6	3	21	1	1	4	13	0	68	15	5	3	.261	.305	.375
Johnson, Josh, Carolina	23	48	37	3	6	9	0	0	1	5	6	1	0	4	0	16	0	0	0	.162	.238	.243
Jones, Geoffrey, Mobile *	42	6	6	0	0	0	0	0	0	0	0	0	0	0	0	5	0	0	0	.000	.000	.000
Jones, Kennard, Mobile *	124	568	487	62	137	171	23	4	1	60	5	1	3	71	1	112	23	14	11	.281	.375	.351
Joseph, Onil, Mississippi	121	470	426	45	106	146	21	5	3	53	9	2	4	29	2	121	18	8	5	.249	.302	.343
Juarez, William, Jacksonville	24	15	14	0	0	0	0	0	0	1	1	0	0	0	0	6	0	0	0	.000	.000	.000
Kensing, Logan, Carolina	6	15	12	2	3	3	0	0	0	3	3	0	0	0	0	3	0	0	1	.250	.250	.250
Kent, Steve, Mississippi †	27	2	2	0	2	2	0	0	0	0	0	0	0	0	0	0	0	0	0	1.000	1.000	1.000
Kopitzke, Casey, West Tenn	55	194	177	12	39	44	3	1	0	10	2	1	1	13	1	28	1	1	5	.220	.276	.249
Kottaras, George, Mobile *	29	121	101	16	29	42	7	0	2	15	0	1	0	19	1	23	0	0	1	.287	.397	.416
Kozlowski, Ben, Chattanooga *	15	32	28	1	1	2	1	0	0	1	2	0	0	2	0	9	0	0	0	.036	.100	.071
Kuo, Hong-Chih, Jacksonville *	12	4	4	0	0	0	0	0	0	0	0	0	0	0	0	1	0	0	0	.000	.000	.000
Lamura, William, Birmingham	3	0	0	0	0	0	0	0	0	0	0	0	0	0	0	0	0	0	0	...	...	...
Langill, Eric, Jacksonville	35	104	94	5	25	25	0	0	0	5	3	0	0	7	0	23	0	1	1	.266	.317	.266
LaRoche, Andy, Jacksonville	64	264	227	41	62	101	12	0	9	43	0	2	3	32	2	54	2	2	9	.273	.367	.445
Lerew, Anthony, Mississippi *	11	26	24	4	8	10	0	1	0	3	2	0	0	0	0	7	1	0	0	.333	.333	.417
Lewis, Richard, West Tenn	28	83	69	8	17	23	1	1	1	7	0	0	1	13	1	18	2	1	1	.246	.373	.333
Lizarraga, Sergio, Tennessee	10	2	2	0	0	0	0	0	0	0	0	0	0	0	0	0	0	0	0	.000	.000	.000
Lockwood, Luke, Carolina *	33	30	27	2	4	7	0	0	1	3	2	0	0	1	0	16	0	0	0	.148	.179	.259
Loney, James, Jacksonville *	138	572	504	74	143	211	31	2	11	65	1	6	2	59	8	87	1	4	13	.284	.357	.419
Lopez, Pedro, Birmingham	68	271	239	26	57	75	7	1	3	24	13	2	4	13	0	29	0	2	10	.238	.287	.314
Mallett, Justin, Chattanooga	2	2	1	0	1	1	0	0	0	1	1	0	0	0	0	0	0	0	0	1.000	1.000	1.000
Malone, Corwin, Birmingham *	2	1	1	0	0	0	0	0	0	0	0	0	0	0	0	0	0	0	0	.000	.000	.000
Maniscalco, Matthew, Montgomery	71	277	243	31	68	78	10	0	0	12	4	1	2	27	0	48	5	3	5	.280	.355	.321
Marmol, Carlos, West Tenn	12	25	21	3	3	3	0	0	0	1	3	0	0	1	0	6	0	0	0	.143	.182	.143
Marshall, Sean, West Tenn *	4	9	7	0	1	1	0	0	0	0	1	0	0	1	0	5	0	0	0	.143	.250	.143
Martin, Russell, Jacksonville	129	505	409	83	127	173	17	1	9	61	5	3	10	78	0	69	15	7	14	.311	.430	.423
Martinez, Carlos, Carolina	1	0	0	0	0	0	0	0	0	0	0	0	0	0	0	0	0	0	0	...	...	...
Martinez, Gabriel, Montgomery *	87	328	288	31	67	107	14	1	8	45	2	4	5	29	2	76	0	1	10	.233	.310	.372
Mateo, Luis, Montgomery	86	278	269	24	62	88	8	3	4	28	0	1	1	7	1	91	3	3	7	.230	.252	.327
Mateo, Nathanel, Mobile	39	5	4	1	1	2	1	0	0	1	0	0	0	1	0	1	0	0	0	.250	.400	.500
McAnulty, Paul, Mobile *	79	341	298	39	84	135	17	2	10	42	0	3	6	34	3	66	5	2	3	.282	.364	.453
McBride, Macay, Mississippi *	4	4	3	0	0	0	0	0	0	0	1	0	0	0	0	0	0	0	1	.000	.000	.000
McCann, Brian, Mississippi *	48	198	166	27	44	79	13	2	6	26	0	5	2	25	3	26	2	3	2	.265	.359	.476
McGehee, Casey, West Tenn	124	505	455	67	135	192	31	1	8	72	0	6	1	43	5	64	2	2	20	.297	.354	.422
McGlinchy, Kevin, West Tenn.	8	0	0	0	0	0	0	0	0	0	0	0	0	0	0	0	0	0	0	...	...	...
McNutt, Michael, Carolina	28	4	4	0	0	0	0	0	0	0	0	0	0	0	0	3	0	0	0	.000	.000	.000
Meadows, Tydus, Jacksonville	108	409	325	59	89	161	27	0	15	65	0	2	3	79	1	96	3	1	8	.274	.418	.495
Meaux, Ryan, Birmingham-Mobile	13	1	1	0	0	0	0	0	0	0	0	0	0	0	0	0	0	0	0	.000	.000	.000
Medero-Stultz, Carlos, Jacksonville.	2	2	2	0	1	2	1	0	0	0	0	0	0	0	0	0	0	0	0	.500	.500	1.000
Merrill, Ronald, Mobile †	120	524	455	65	112	170	24	5	8	58	6	7	4	52	1	81	8	4	8	.246	.324	.374
Merritt, Graig, Montgomery	21	56	48	1	5	6	1	0	0	1	2	0	1	5	0	14	1	0	2	.104	.204	.125
Meyers, Mike, Huntsville	8	3	3	0	0	0	0	0	0	0	0	0	0	0	0	0	0	0	0	.000	.000	.000
Michaelis, Derek, Jacksonville *	45	128	114	13	27	37	7	0	1	11	0	0	0	14	0	42	1	2	1	.237	.320	.325
Miller, Greg, Jacksonville *	6	3	3	0	0	0	0	0	0	0	0	0	0	0	0	2	0	0	0	.000	.000	.000
Miller, Ryan, Huntsville	2	0	0	0	0	0	0	0	0	0	0	0	0	0	0	0	0	0	0	...	...	...
Miner, Zachary, Mississippi	2	4	4	0	1	1	0	0	0	0	0	0	0	0	0	3	0	0	0	.250	.250	.250
Mitchell, Russell, Jacksonville.	3	5	5	1	1	2	1	0	0	3	0	0	0	0	0	4	0	0	0	.200	.200	.400
Molina, Angel, Carolina	11	43	39	3	13	19	3	0	1	9	0	0	0	4	0	8	0	0	0	.333	.395	.487
Molldrem, Craig, Carolina	1	1	1	0	0	0	0	0	0	0	0	0	0	0	0	1	0	0	0	.000	.000	.000
Montanez, Luis, West Tenn	45	171	153	20	41	58	9	1	2	14	2	2	2	12	1	21	0	2	1	.268	.325	.379
Montero, Miguel, Tennessee *	30	120	108	13	27	38	1	2	2	13	1	1	3	7	0	26	1	0	2	.250	.311	.352
Moore, Robert, Carolina *	82	271	245	39	66	99	11	5	4	24	2	0	2	22	1	64	6	2	3	.269	.335	.404

Player, Team	G	TPA	AB	R	H	TB	2B	3B	HR	RBI	SH	SF	HP	BB	IBB	SO	SB	CS	GDP	Avg.	OBP	Slg.
Moran, Javon, Chattanooga	23	88	83	14	25	32	5	1	0	2	0	0	0	5	1	21	7	4	1	.301	.341	.386
Morgan, Matthew, Tennessee	90	295	270	19	74	98	13	1	3	35	5	1	2	17	0	39	0	4	4	.274	.321	.363
Muniz, Juan Carlos, Carolina	106	337	304	35	85	133	19	1	9	43	1	4	5	23	1	77	4	6	4	.280	.336	.438
Murton, Matt, West Tenn *	78	350	313	46	107	156	17	4	8	46	3	1	4	29	3	42	18	5	11	.342	.403	.498
Nelson, Brad, Huntsville *	55	238	208	27	61	89	8	1	6	38	0	3	1	26	5	42	1	2	5	.293	.370	.428
Nelson, Bubba, Chattanooga	35	2	2	0	0	0	0	0	0	0	0	0	0	0	0	2	0	0	0	.000	.000	.000
Neuberger, Scott, Montgomery	31	114	104	13	24	45	6	0	5	15	0	2	3	5	0	25	1	1	4	.231	.281	.433
Nichols, Leslie, Chattanooga	38	129	115	12	22	38	4	0	4	18	0	3	0	11	1	37	0	0	5	.191	.256	.330
Nicholson, David, Jacksonville	17	36	34	4	4	5	1	0	0	1	0	0	0	2	0	13	0	0	0	.118	.167	.147
Nicholson, Thomas, Birmingham *	4	17	15	2	4	6	2	0	0	3	0	1	0	1	0	2	0	0	1	.267	.294	.400
Niles, Frank, Carolina †	93	333	273	34	73	96	15	1	2	25	5	3	3	49	2	68	4	3	5	.267	.381	.352
Nina, Elvin, Tennessee	2	0	0	0	0	0	0	0	0	0	...	0	0	0	...	0	0	0	0	...	...	...
Nippert, Dustin, Tennessee	13	28	26	0	0	0	0	0	0	0	...	0	0	2	...	17	0	0	0	.000	.071	.000
Nixon, Michael, Jacksonville	6	22	20	0	3	3	0	0	0	0	0	0	0	2	0	4	0	0	0	.150	.227	.150
Nolasco, Ricky, West Tenn.	23	56	50	1	6	7	1	0	0	3	4	0	0	2	0	22	0	0	1	.120	.154	.140
O'Connor, Brian, Mississippi	21	32	31	1	6	7	1	0	0	0	...	0	0	1	...	8	0	0	1	.194	.219	.226
Ojeda, Alvis, Jacksonville	3	1	1	0	0	0	0	0	0	0	0	0	0	0	0	1	0	0	0	.000	.000	.000
O'Keefe, Michael, Mississippi *	6	18	15	3	3	4	1	0	0	1	0	0	0	3	0	2	0	0	0	.200	.333	.267
Olsen, Scott, Carolina *	12	25	25	0	0	0	0	0	0	0	0	0	0	0	0	12	0	0	0	.000	.000	.000
Olson, Jason, Jacksonville	23	3	3	0	0	0	0	0	0	0	0	0	0	0	0	3	0	0	0	.000	.000	.000
O'Malley, Ryan, West Tenn	26	21	16	2	2	5	0	0	1	1	5	0	0	0	0	6	0	0	0	.125	.125	.313
Orenduff, Justin, Jacksonville	10	20	20	0	2	3	1	0	0	1	0	0	0	0	0	6	0	0	0	.100	.100	.150
Ortiz, Javier, Birmingham	2	1	1	0	0	0	0	0	0	0	0	0	0	0	0	0	0	0	0	.000	.000	.000
O'Toole, Paul, West Tenn *	12	43	36	4	3	4	1	0	0	4	0	1	2	4	0	11	1	1	0	.083	.209	.111
Overman, Matthew, Carolina	6	1	1	0	0	0	0	0	0	0	0	0	0	1	0	0	0	0	0	.000	.000	.000
Owens, Jerry, Birmingham *	130	587	522	99	173	212	21	6	2	52	9	2	2	52	4	72	38	20	5	.331	.393	.406
Oyervidez, Jose, Mobile	22	47	43	1	5	7	2	0	0	2	2	0	0	2	0	18	0	0	1	.116	.156	.163
Parra, Manuel, Huntsville	15	34	29	3	4	10	1	1	1	2	5	0	0	0	0	16	0	0	0	.138	.138	.345
Patchett, Gary, Chattanooga	48	121	107	7	23	29	6	0	0	8	2	2	6	4	1	26	0	0	5	.215	.277	.271
Patterson, Eric, West Tenn *	9	37	30	5	6	8	2	0	0	2	0	1	0	6	0	7	3	2	0	.200	.324	.267
Pena, Tony, Tennessee	17	34	30	1	3	6	0	0	1	2	4	0	0	0	0	14	0	0	1	.100	.100	.200
Perez, Beltran, Jacksonville	14	3	3	0	0	0	0	0	0	0	0	0	0	0	0	1	0	0	0	.000	.000	.000
Perez, Eduardo, Jacksonville †	2	4	4	0	0	0	0	0	0	0	0	0	0	0	0	2	0	0	0	.000	.000	.000
Perez, Tomas, Chattanooga †	40	161	136	20	37	60	9	1	4	12	0	0	2	23	0	40	9	3	3	.272	.385	.441
Peterson, Brian, Chattanooga	100	383	348	37	94	143	25	3	6	40	5	2	4	24	1	56	0	0	11	.270	.323	.411
Phelps, Travis, Chattanooga	7	2	2	0	0	0	0	0	0	0	0	0	0	0	0	1	0	0	0	.000	.000	.000
Phillips, Heath Michael, Birmingham *	2	4	4	0	0	0	0	0	0	0	0	0	0	0	0	2	0	0	1	.000	.000	.000
Pie, Felix, West Tenn *	59	262	240	41	73	133	17	5	11	25	1	3	2	16	1	53	13	9	1	.304	.349	.554
Pignatiello, Carmen, West Tenn *	15	23	22	1	1	1	0	0	0	2	1	0	0	0	0	8	0	0	0	.045	.045	.045
Pinto, Renyel, West Tenn *	20	43	35	3	0	0	0	0	0	4	0	0	4	4	0	24	0	0	1	.000	.103	.000
Pollok, Dwayne, Birmingham	3	1	0	0	0	0	0	0	0	0	1	0	0	0	0	0	0	0	0	...	...	...
Porzio, Mike, Mississippi *	10	4	4	0	0	0	0	0	0	0	0	0	0	0	0	4	0	0	0	.000	.000	.000
Powell, Jay, Mississippi	8	1	1	0	0	0	0	0	0	0	0	0	0	0	0	1	0	0	0	.000	.000	.000
Prado, Martin, Mississippi	39	162	143	17	40	52	7	1	1	11	1	1	0	17	1	17	3	3	5	.280	.354	.364
Pratt, Andy, Huntsville *	17	5	5	1	1	1	0	0	0	0	0	0	0	0	0	3	0	0	0	.200	.200	.200
Pridie, Jason, Montgomery *	28	104	94	15	20	37	4	2	3	8	2	0	0	8	0	29	5	1	3	.213	.275	.394
Purdom, John, Chattanooga	4	9	9	0	2	2	0	0	0	2	0	0	0	0	0	3	0	0	0	.222	.222	.222
Pyzik, Steven, Mississippi	2	8	8	1	4	5	1	0	0	1	0	0	0	0	0	1	0	0	0	.500	.500	.625
Raburn, John, Montgomery †	112	454	401	62	114	135	16	1	1	31	9	2	3	39	2	65	27	1	8	.284	.351	.337
Ramos, Peeter, Mobile	31	113	104	8	18	22	1	0	1	8	0	0	3	6	0	20	2	0	3	.173	.239	.212
Ramos, Victor, West Tenn *	15	1	0	0	0	0	0	0	0	0	0	0	0	1	0	0	0	0	0	...	1.000	...
Reece, Eric, Montgomery *	17	60	56	4	10	16	3	0	1	5	0	0	0	4	0	20	0	0	2	.179	.233	.286
Reed, Eric, Carolina *	71	298	271	35	69	81	9	0	1	15	3	3	4	17	1	62	23	8	2	.255	.305	.299
Renick, Joshua, Chattanooga	25	37	34	4	4	4	0	0	0	2	1	0	0	2	0	10	0	0	1	.118	.167	.118
Resop, Chris, Carolina	40	2	1	1	1	3	0	1	0	3	1	0	0	0	0	0	0	0	0	1.000	1.000	3.000
Reyes, Guillermo, Birmingham †	48	175	150	28	42	58	7	3	1	18	5	4	1	15	0	18	7	3	6	.280	.341	.387
Reyes, Jose, West Tenn †	97	355	319	27	82	101	10	0	3	50	5	3	1	27	10	48	6	3	16	.257	.314	.317
Reynoso, Paulino, Birmingham *	1	0	0	0	0	0	0	0	0	0	0	0	0	0	0	0	0	0	0	...	...	...
Richardson, Jason, Mississippi	10	4	3	0	0	0	0	0	0	0	1	0	0	0	0	2	0	0	0	.000	.000	.000
Richardson, Michael, Mobile	68	171	142	19	23	32	3	0	2	12	2	0	1	26	1	53	0	1	2	.162	.296	.225
Riggans, Shawn, Montgomery	89	350	313	40	97	142	21	0	8	53	2	5	4	26	0	69	1	2	11	.310	.365	.454
Roberts, Ralph, Mississippi	1	0	0	0	0	0	0	0	0	0	0	0	0	0	0	0	0	0	0	...	...	...
Rodriguez, Guilder, Huntsville †	65	161	133	17	40	45	3	1	0	7	8	0	0	19	0	28	3	0	4	.301	.388	.338
Rodriguez, Jose, Carolina *	5	0	0	0	0	0	0	0	0	0	0	0	0	0	0	0	0	0	0	...	...	...
Rodriguez, Orlando, Jacksonville *	6	0	0	0	0	0	0	0	0	0	0	0	0	0	0	0	0	0	0	...	...	...
Rogers, Tanner, Carolina	3	3	3	0	0	0	0	0	0	0	0	0	0	0	0	0	0	0	0	.000	.000	.000
Rogowski, Casey, Birmingham *	134	583	505	83	148	224	37	6	9	78	3	6	11	58	3	111	20	12	14	.293	.374	.444
Rohan, James, Jacksonville	22	57	54	8	16	18	2	0	0	4	1	0	0	2	0	8	1	0	1	.296	.321	.333
Rohleder, Andrew, Carolina	3	3	3	0	0	0	0	0	0	0	0	0	0	0	0	2	0	0	0	.000	.000	.000
Rosa, Wally, Birmingham	16	50	44	7	12	14	2	0	0	3	1	0	2	3	0	8	0	1	0	.273	.347	.318
Rosamond, George, Mississippi	74	276	244	37	55	94	10	1	9	26	2	2	2	26	0	66	5	2	9	.225	.303	.385
Rottino, Vincent, Huntsville	120	516	469	63	139	189	20	6	6	52	0	5	2	40	1	68	2	1	14	.296	.351	.403
Ruggiano, Justin, Jacksonville	53	185	161	23	55	85	10	1	6	29	0	1	6	17	0	56	8	3	1	.342	.422	.528
Ruiz, Alvaro, Chattanooga *	74	308	272	37	78	93	10	1	1	19	2	2	3	29	1	28	14	6	3	.287	.359	.342
Rundgren, Rex, Carolina	111	403	363	26	84	99	6	3	1	21	7	1	4	28	4	75	1	1	11	.231	.293	.273
Russ, James, Carolina	1	2	0	0	0	0	0	0	0	0	0	0	0	1	0	0	0	0	0	...	1.000	...
Ryu, Jae-kuk, West Tenn.	23	57	50	2	12	15	3	0	0	8	5	0	0	2	0	11	0	0	1	.240	.269	.300
Sain, Gregory, Mobile	64	251	223	27	58	84	11	0	5	25	1	6	0	21	0	48	0	3	7	.260	.316	.377
Saladin, Miguel, Chattanooga	9	1	1	0	0	0	0	0	0	0	0	0	0	0	0	1	0	0	0	.000	.000	.000
Salmon, Bradley, Chattanooga *	30	9	6	0	2	2	0	0	0	3	3	0	2	0	1	0	2	0	0	.333	.333	.333
Sarfate, Dennis, Huntsville	19	38	35	3	3	9	0	0	2	5	2	0	0	1	0	18	0	0	1	.086	.111	.257

Player, Team	G	TPA	AB	R	H	TB	2B	3B	HR	RBI	SH	SF	HP	BB	IBB	SO	SB	CS	GDP	Avg.	OBP	Sig.
Schmidt, Jeremy, Chattanooga	39	6	6	0	0	0	0	0	0	0	0	0	0	0	0	6	0	0	0	.000	.000	.000
Schuerholz, Jonathan, Mississippi	86	335	302	38	84	112	12	2	4	21	1	0	5	27	2	51	8	1	4	.278	.347	.371
Schultz, Michael, Tennessee	47	1	1	0	0	0	0	0	0	0	0	0	0	0	0	1	0	0	0	.000	.000	.000
Searles, Jonathan, West Tenn	50	13	11	0	2	2	0	0	0	0	1	0	0	1	0	4	0	0	0	.182	.250	.182
Sears, Todd, Carolina *	31	111	101	16	32	49	8	0	3	19	0	0	0	10	0	22	0	0	5	.317	.378	.485
Serrano, Raymond, Mississippi	33	97	88	7	25	35	6	2	0	11	0	1	1	7	0	10	1	0	0	.284	.340	.398
Shafer, David, Chattanooga	29	2	2	0	0	0	0	0	0	0	0	0	0	0	0	1	0	0	0	.000	.000	.000
Shanks, James, Carolina	98	418	371	55	110	168	19	6	9	51	2	4	6	35	1	103	16	10	2	.296	.363	.453
Shipman, Andrew, West Tenn	51	1	1	0	0	0	0	0	0	0	0	0	0	0	0	0	0	0	0	.000	.000	.000
Sikaras, Panagiotis, Tennessee	33	8	8	0	0	0	0	0	0	0	0	0	0	0	0	6	0	0	0	.000	.000	.000
Silva, Jesus, Tennessee	1	0	0	0	0	0	0	0	0	0	...	0	0	0	0	0	0	0	0	...	...	...
Simpson, Gerrit, Huntsville	12	3	3	0	0	0	0	0	0	0	0	0	0	0	0	2	0	0	0	.000	.000	.000
Sing, Brandon, West Tenn	127	508	409	74	113	220	29	0	26	71	0	7	1	91	5	110	2	5	6	.276	.404	.538
Sisk, Aaron, West Tenn	48	158	137	18	33	59	6	1	6	19	1	1	0	19	0	32	1	1	3	.241	.331	.431
Sitzman, James, Montgomery *	29	82	77	7	13	15	2	0	0	4	2	0	1	2	0	24	1	1	1	.169	.200	.195
Slaten, Douglas, Tennessee *	43	4	3	0	1	1	0	0	0	1	1	0	0	0	0	0	0	0	0	.333	.333	.333
Smith, Corey, Mobile	135	571	516	64	131	219	30	2	18	73	0	5	4	46	1	144	4	3	11	.254	.317	.424
Smitherman, Stephen, Chattanooga	86	372	313	45	87	152	30	1	11	62	0	5	6	48	2	78	3	1	5	.278	.379	.486
Snare, Ryan, Mobile *	1	2	2	0	1	1	0	0	0	0	0	0	0	0	0	1	0	0	0	.500	.500	.500
Sodowsky, Clint, Carolina *	11	2	2	0	0	0	0	0	0	0	0	0	0	0	0	0	0	0	0	.000	.000	.000
Soto, Jesus, Jacksonville †	3	5	5	0	0	0	0	0	0	0	0	0	0	0	0	5	0	0	0	.000	.000	.000
Spearman, Jemel, West Tenn	14	47	46	6	16	23	3	2	0	6	0	0	1	0	0	6	2	1	0	.348	.362	.500
Spiehs, Randall, Mobile	10	3	2	0	1	1	0	0	0	0	1	0	0	0	0	1	0	0	0	.500	.500	.500
Sprout, Brian, Jacksonville	57	226	205	30	52	80	11	1	5	23	0	1	3	17	1	32	2	0	10	.254	.319	.390
Stamler, Keith, Huntsville *	17	8	8	0	1	1	0	0	0	0	0	0	0	0	0	6	0	0	0	.125	.125	.125
Stanfield, James, Huntsville	3	5	4	0	0	0	0	0	0	0	1	0	1	0	0	3	0	0	1	.000	.000	.000
Steidlmayer, Luke, Mobile	2	4	4	0	1	1	0	0	0	0	0	0	0	0	0	1	0	0	0	.250	.250	.250
Steinborn, Christopher, Mobile *	3	1	1	0	0	0	0	0	0	0	0	0	0	0	0	0	0	0	0	.000	.000	.000
Stetter, Mitchel, Huntsville *	30	7	5	1	2	2	0	0	0	0	3	1	0	1	0	1	0	0	0	.400	.500	.400
Stewart, Chris, Birmingham	95	350	311	39	89	143	21	0	11	51	10	2	3	24	2	37	3	3	7	.286	.341	.460
Stockman, Phillip, Tennessee	22	3	3	0	0	0	0	0	0	0	0	0	0	0	0	2	0	0	0	.000	.000	.000
Stults, Eric, Jacksonville *	8	17	16	0	4	6	2	0	0	4	1	0	0	0	0	6	0	0	0	.250	.250	.375
Sweeney, Ryan, Birmingham *	113	483	429	64	128	159	22	3	1	47	7	5	7	35	4	53	6	6	5	.298	.357	.371
Taubenheim, Ty, Mobile	10	20	17	0	1	1	0	0	0	0	3	0	0	0	0	5	0	0	1	.059	.059	.059
Thayer, Dale, Mobile	45	1	1	0	0	0	0	0	0	0	0	0	0	0	0	0	0	0	0	.000	.000	.000
Theriot, Ryan, West Tenn	120	503	448	52	136	175	28	4	1	53	4	5	1	45	2	38	24	10	9	.304	.365	.391
Thompson, Chris, Tennessee	2	0	0	0	0	0	0	0	0	0	...	0	0	0	0	0	0	0	0	...	...	...
Thompson, Derek, Jacksonville *	5	7	7	0	1	1	0	0	0	0	0	0	0	0	0	3	0	0	GDP	.143	.143	.143
Thompson, Michael, Mobile	14	32	30	0	5	6	1	0	0	2	1	0	0	1	0	12	0	0	0	.167	.194	.200
Thompson, Sean, Mobile *	13	31	28	6	7	7	0	0	0	1	2	0	0	1	0	11	0	0	0	.250	.276	.250
Thorman, Scott, Mississippi *	90	383	348	49	106	176	21	2	15	65	0	3	4	28	5	76	2	2	3	.305	.360	.506
Timmons, Wesley, Mississippi	119	519	427	73	116	172	31	2	7	34	6	3	21	62	2	46	4	7	10	.272	.388	.403
Tovar, Angel, Mobile	5	2	2	1	1	1	0	0	0	0	0	0	0	0	0	0	0	0	0	.500	.500	.500
Tracey, Sean, Birmingham *	1	1	1	0	1	1	0	0	0	0	0	0	0	0	0	0	0	0	0	1.000	1.000	1.000
Trzesniak, Nicholas, Mobile	67	259	233	37	58	88	13	1	5	25	1	1	2	22	0	61	7	0	6	.249	.318	.378
Tucker, Glenn, Mississippi †	39	4	3	1	1	1	0	0	0	1	1	0	0	0	0	1	0	0	0	.333	.333	.333
Tucker, Michael, Carolina	64	207	180	19	42	59	11	0	2	19	2	3	1	21	0	61	1	0	3	.233	.312	.328
Tucker, Rusty, Mobile *	41	5	4	1	0	0	0	0	0	0	0	0	0	1	0	2	0	0	0	.000	.200	.000
Uggla, Daniel, Tennessee	135	571	498	88	148	250	33	3	21	87	3	2	14	52	5	103	15	8	10	.297	.378	.502
Ungs, Nicholas, Carolina	20	39	29	2	5	6	1	0	0	2	7	0	0	3	0	11	0	0	1	.172	.250	.207
Valdes, Raul, West Tenn *	3	4	4	0	1	1	0	0	0	0	0	0	0	0	0	2	0	0	0	.250	.250	.250
Valdez, Edward, Chattanooga	12	20	16	0	0	0	0	0	0	0	3	0	1	0	0	10	0	0	1	.000	.059	.000
Vanden Berg, John, Huntsville	81	254	214	22	54	78	16	1	2	26	4	0	1	35	2	62	1	0	11	.252	.360	.364
Van Hekken, Andy, Mississippi-Chattanooga	4	9	7	1	0	0	0	0	0	0	1	0	0	1	0	6	0	0	0	.000	.125	.000
Van Iderstine, Ben, Huntsville	84	250	229	24	60	79	7	3	2	35	2	2	2	15	1	35	2	2	9	.262	.310	.345
Vargas, Jason, Carolina *	3	6	5	0	0	0	0	0	0	0	1	0	0	0	0	2	0	0	0	.000	.000	.000
Varner, Gary, Tennessee	128	478	421	64	117	160	30	2	3	41	0	2	3	52	3	80	19	7	11	.278	.360	.380
Vasquez, Jorge, Mississippi	22	0	0	0	0	0	0	0	0	0	...	0	0	0	...	0	0	0	0	...	...	...
Velazquez, Juan, Mississippi †	52	179	154	19	39	47	8	0	0	13	4	0	1	20	2	29	3	2	2	.253	.343	.305
Vick, Hunter, Montgomery †	2	4	4	0	0	0	0	0	0	0	0	0	0	0	0	1	0	0	0	.000	.000	.000
Villanueva, Carlos, Huntsville †	4	8	8	0	1	1	0	0	0	0	0	0	0	0	0	4	0	0	0	.125	.125	.125
Villatoro, Wilmer, Mobile	7	0	0	0	0	0	0	0	0	0	0	0	0	0	0	0	0	0	GDP	...	...	...
Ward, Jeremy, Mississippi	11	1	1	0	0	0	0	0	0	0	0	0	0	0	0	1	0	0	0	.000	.000	.000
Washington, Rico, Montgomery *	126	532	454	84	136	227	30	2	19	77	0	8	7	63	1	63	6	5	6	.300	.387	.500
Weber, Ben, Chattanooga	7	0	0	0	0	0	0	0	0	0	0	0	0	0	0	0	0	0	0	...	...	...
Weber, Jonathan, Jacksonville *	117	503	450	81	135	205	27	5	11	68	2	1	5	45	6	78	10	6	5	.300	.369	.456
Wechsler, Justin, Tennessee	31	1	1	0	0	0	0	0	0	0	0	0	0	0	0	0	0	0	0	.000	.000	.000
Wells, Jared, Mobile	5	11	9	0	1	1	0	0	0	1	2	0	0	0	0	3	0	0	0	.111	.111	.111
Wells, Randy, West Tenn	6	0	0	0	0	0	0	0	0	0	0	0	0	0	0	0	0	0	0	...	...	...
Weston, Gordon, West Tenn *	11	20	19	4	6	9	3	0	0	2	0	0	0	1	0	3	0	0	2	.316	.350	.474
Whitaker, Brian, Mobile	21	47	37	2	4	4	0	0	0	2	6	0	0	4	0	10	0	0	0	.108	.195	.108
White, Sean, Mississippi	5	12	10	0	0	0	0	0	0	0	1	0	0	1	0	6	0	0	0	.000	.091	.000
White, William, Tennessee *	46	1	1	0	0	0	0	0	0	0	0	0	0	0	0	0	0	0	0	.000	.000	.000
Williams, Marland, Tennessee	121	426	381	55	89	137	13	7	1	46	2	6	0	37	3	108	38	7	2	.234	.297	.360
Winchester, Jeffrey, Huntsville	78	297	265	27	70	85	15	0	0	29	3	0	9	20	0	40	0	2	10	.264	.337	.321
Wolf, Ross, Carolina	48	6	5	0	0	0	0	0	0	0	1	0	0	0	0	3	0	0	0	.000	.000	.000
Wolfe, Brian, Huntsville	12	2	1	0	0	0	0	0	0	0	1	0	0	0	0	0	0	0	0	.000	.000	.000
Woolard, Glenn, Huntsville	27	44	38	3	8	11	3	0	0	2	2	0	0	4	0	13	0	0	1	.211	.286	.289
Wright, Matthew, Mississippi	11	24	19	1	2	3	1	0	0	2	4	0	0	1	0	11	0	0	0	.105	.150	.158
Young, Christopher, Birmingham	126	553	466	100	129	254	41	3	26	77	1	3	7	70	1	129	32	6	4	.277	.377	.545
Young, Delmon, Montgomery	84	370	330	59	111	192	13	4	20	71	0	8	7	25	5	66	25	8	10	.336	.386	.582

Player, Team	G	TPA	AB	R	H	TB	2B	3B	HR	RBI	SH	SF	HP	BB	IBB	SO	SB	CS	GDP	Avg.	OBP	Slg.
Young, Delwyn, Jacksonville †	95	407	371	52	110	185	25	1	16	62	1	4	3	27	4	86	1	3	9	.296	.346	.499
Yourkin, Matthew, Carolina	9	0	0	0	0	0	0	0	0	0	...	0	0	0	...	0	0	0	0	...	...	...
Zeringue, Jonathan, Tennessee	126	471	436	46	105	149	18	4	6	51	4	4	8	19	0	86	11	8	12	.241	.283	.342
Zumwalt, Sean, Huntsville	27	11	7	0	3	4	1	0	0	2	3	0	1	0	0	1	0	0	0	.429	.500	.571
Zuniga, Jose, Huntsville	57	212	190	17	49	65	7	0	3	28	0	3	2	17	2	27	0	0	1	.258	.321	.342

PLAYERS WITH TWO OR MORE TEAMS

Player, Team	G	TPA	AB	R	H	TB	2B	3B	HR	RBI	SH	SF	HP	BB	IBB	SO	SB	CS	GDP	Avg.	OBP	Slg.
Chick, Travis, Mobile	14	24	19	0	2	3	1	0	0	4	0	1	0	9	0	9	0	0	0	.105	.150	.158
Chick, Travis, Chattanooga	9	19	16	2	4	9	2	0	1	1	2	0	1	0	6	0	0	0	0	.250	.294	.563
Meaux, Ryan, Birmingham *	3	0	0	0	0	0	0	0	0	0	...	0	0	0		0	0	0	0	...	...	...
Meaux, Ryan, Mobile *	10	1	1	0	0	0	0	0	0	0	0	0	0	0	0	0	0	0	0	.000	.000	.000
Van Hekken, Andy, Mississippi	2	4	2	1	0	0	0	0	0	0	1	0	1	0	2	0	0	0	0	.000	.333	.000
Van Hekken, Andy, Chattanooga	2	5	5	0	0	0	0	0	0	0	0	0	0	0	0	4	0	0	0	.000	.000	.000

GRAND SLAMS—S. Smitherman,. 3; R. Andino, C. Ashby, S. Baker, R. Bell, C. Carter, J. Cota, E. Dukes, J. Fields, I. Franco, S. Garcia, J. Gerber, J. Guzman, R. Hanigan, J. Hermida, N. Hopper, K. Howard, C. McGehee, T. Meadows, J. Muniz, K. Nichols, J. Ruggiano, C. Stewart, N. Trzesniak, D. Uggla, J. Weber, M. Williams, D. Young, 1 each.

AWARDED FIRST BASE ON CATCHER'S INTERFERENCE—J. Ball 4 (J. Aceves, J. Vanden Berg, M. Bernard, R. Hanigan); D. Uggla 2 (B. Peterson, J. Vanden Berg,); D. DIlucchi (R. Martin); K. Jones (J. Winchester); G. Rodriguez (M. Bernard); D. Young (B. McCann).

2005 PITCHING

Team	W	L	Pct.	ERA	G	CG	ShO	Sv.	IP	H	TBF	R	ER	HR	SH	SF	HB	BB	IBB	SO	WP	Bk.
West Tenn	83	56	.597	3.35	139	3	13	42	1231.2	1148	5225	517	459	84	84	27	57	450	26	1111	47	6
Carolina	77	57	.575	3.72	134	5	10	47	1175.1	1144	5022	548	486	85	63	46	41	408	30	945	63	3
Jacksonville	79	61	.564	3.91	140	3	13	36	1223.2	1118	5287	603	532	105	55	37	38	550	22	1144	80	4
Mississippi	64	68	.485	3.98	132	2	13	29	1154.1	1136	4945	569	510	76	77	35	43	445	30	916	55	2
Birmingham	82	57	.590	4.08	139	7	8	45	1215.1	1273	5346	642	551	88	53	45	61	544	41	930	61	5
Mobile	58	80	.420	4.15	138	5	3	29	1206.2	1269	5290	655	557	91	70	39	63	508	36	965	83	9
Huntsville	60	79	.432	4.26	139	2	3	34	1217.2	1317	5416	690	576	106	68	30	49	457	21	1008	82	7
Tennessee	64	76	.457	4.28	140	10	14	30	1222.1	1330	5365	693	581	103	74	46	67	440	18	945	67	5
Montgomery	67	70	.489	4.30	137	6	7	31	1190.2	1262	5162	655	569	112	45	36	59	409	8	946	68	6
Chattanooga	53	83	.390	4.34	136	0	4	23	1203	1259	5307	657	580	104	80	45	63	524	21	996	91	9

INDIVIDUAL

TOP QUALIFIERS FOR EARNED-RUN AVERAGE TITLE

Minimum 112 innings. *Lefthanded pitcher.

Pitcher, Team	W	L	Pct.	ERA	G	GS	CG	ShO	GF	Sv.	IP	H	TBF	R	ER	HR	SH	SF	HB	BB	IBB	SO	WP	Bk.
Nippert, Dustin, Tennessee	8	3	.727	2.36	18	18	3	2	...	0	118.1	95	462	33	31	4				42	1	97		0
Pinto, Renyel, West Tenn *	10	3	.769	2.71	22	21	1	1	0	0	129.2	101	522	43	39	3	6	2	9	58	0	123	3	0
Nolasco, Ricky, West Tenn	14	3	.824	2.89	27	27	1	0	0	0	161.2	151	676	57	52	13	11	2	11	46	1	173	4	2
Dumatrait, Phillip, Chattanooga *	4	12	.250	3.17	24	24	0	0	0	0	127.2	115	545	58	45	4	6	4	2	70	4	101	13	0
Thompson, Michael, Mobile	6	6	.500	3.22	18	18	2	1	0	0	114.2	116	466	50	41	6	6	2	5	27	0	68	5	0
Lockwood, Luke, Carolina *	2	8	.200	3.24	34	15	1	0	3	1	114.0	110	453	45	41	6	8	9	2	23	3	79	2	0
Ryu, Jae-kuk, West Tenn	11	8	.579	3.34	27	27	1	1	0	0	169.2	154	686	67	63	12	15	4	6	49	1	133	9	0
Hull, Eric, Jacksonville	7	7	.500	3.38	27	18	1	1	4	3	117.0	105	491	50	44	9	5	2	2	44	0	117	7	0
Gonzalez, Enrique, Tennessee	11	8	.579	3.46	27	27	2	2	0	0	161.1	160	670	76	62	8	6	6	6	52	0	146	9	0
Billingsley, Chad, Jacksonville	13	6	.684	3.51	28	26	2	1	0	0	146.0	116	596	60	57	12	5	2	4	50	0	162	10	0
Hall, Josh, Chattanooga	5	6	.455	3.53	18	18	0	0	0	0	112.1	115	466	49	44	7	7	1	3	35	2	92	10	0
O'Connor, Brian, Mississippi	9	7	.563	3.65	30	19	0	0	0	0	133.1	127	560	66	54	7	...			63	1	98		
Ungs, Nicholas, Carolina	7	5	.583	3.68	22	22	1	1	0	0	120.0	123	502	57	49	8	4	6	3	34	3	79	4	0
Oyervidez, Jose, Mobile	7	9	.438	3.81	27	27	0	0	0	0	153.2	129	652	77	65	16	12	6	7	82	5	130	9	1
Johnson, Josh, Carolina	12	4	.750	3.87	26	26	1	0	0	0	139.2	139	589	67	60	4	9	2	4	50	4	113	7	1
Sarfate, Dennis, Huntsville	9	9	.500	3.88	24	24	1	1	0	0	130.0	120	562	65	56	13	5	4	10	59	1	110	11	1
Bass, Adam, Tennessee	5	10	.333	3.99	27	27	1	0	0	0	158.0	158	664	75	70	14	8	6	10	40	1	120	7	0
Phillips, Heath Michael, Birmingham *	9	5	.643	4.07	22	21	2	0	0	0	135.0	161	561	64	61	12	6	5	3	30	2	78	4	1
Tracey, Sean, Birmingham	14	6	.700	4.07	28	28	2	0	0	0	163.2	154	695	80	74	13	3	5	14	76	1	106	12	0
Whitaker, Brian, Mobile	8	13	.381	4.33	25	25	0	0	0	0	147.2	180	651	85	71	4	8	1	12	53	7	101	6	1
Pena, Tony, Tennessee	7	13	.350	4.43	25	25	2	1	0	0	148.1	165	637	86	73	17	4	4	10	40	1	95	5	0

DEPARTMENTAL LEADERS: W—Tracey and Nolasco, 14. L—Whitaker and Pena, 13. Pct.—Nolasco, .824. G—Schultz, 63. GS—Tracey, 28. CG—three pitchers tied with 3. ShO—three pitchers tied with 2. GF—Thayer, 50. Sv.—Thayer, 27. IP—Ryu, 169.2. H—Goocher, 185. TBF—Ryu, 701. R—Goocher, 105. ER—Goocher, 84. HR—Autrey, 24. SAC—Ryu, 15. SF—Lockwood, 9. HB—Tracey, 14. BB—Oyervidez, 82. IBB—Whitaker and Searles, 7. SO—Nolasco, 173. WP—Dumatrait, 13. BK—Schmidt, 5.

ALL PITCHERS

*Lefthanded pitcher.

Pitcher, Team	W	L	Pct.	ERA	G	GS	CG	ShO	GF	Sv.	IP	H	TBF	R	ER	HR	SH	SF	HB	BB	IBB	SO	WP	Bk.
Aardsma, David, West Tenn	4	1	.800	3.91	33	3	0	0	8	2	50.2	48	223	22	22	3	2	2	4	32	3	43	1	0
Abraham, Paul, Mobile	2	1	.667	3.98	30	0	0	0	10	0	40.2	46	177	21	18	3	4	3	1	13	3	24	5	1
Aguilar, Raymond, Carolina *	5	2	.714	3.20	13	13	1	0	0	0	84.1	70	333	32	30	6	4	1	2	17	1	49	0	0
Almanza, Armando, Tennessee *	1	0	1.000	4.91	6	0	0	0	5	1	7.1	9	35	5	4	1	1	0	0	4	0	7	1	0
Alvarez, Carlos, Jacksonville *	4	0	1.000	3.99	25	0	0	0	10	0	38.1	38	160	18	17	4	2	0	0	16	0	31	3	0
Andrew, Jason, Chattanooga	3	4	.429	3.59	48	2	0	0	11	0	80.1	78	337	39	32	4	4	5	2	28	4	63	1	0
Atlee, Thomas, West Tenn	3	1	.750	3.63	29	0	0	0	11	3	34.2	39	153	21	14	3	0	0	0	10	2	20	2	0
Autrey, Jeffrey, Montgomery	3	11	.214	5.71	21	17	1	1	1	0	108.2	149	494	82	69	24	2	2	4	32	0	65	6	0
Baez, Federico, West Tenn	4	3	.571	4.58	41	2	0	0	15	2	55.0	68	250	29	28	4	5	2	2	30	5	35	4	0
Baker, Ryan, Carolina	3	2	.600	4.31	25	0	0	0	6	0	39.2	42	174	21	19	4	6	2	1	24	3	29	0	0

– 467 –

Pitcher, Team	W	L	Pct.	ERA	G	GS	CG	ShO	GF	Sv.	IP	H	TBF	R	ER	HR	SH	SF	HB	BB	IBB	SO	WP	Bk.
Ballouli, Khalid, Huntsville	4	7	.364	4.82	24	9	0	0	5	2	74.2	94	340	49	40	5	6	1	5	23	0	61	5	0
Barreto, Joel, Chattanooga	3	0	1.000	3.60	3	0	0	0	0	0	5.0	5	22	2	2	0	0	0	0	4	0	3	3	0
Barry, Kevin, Mississippi	0	0	.000	1.23	3	0	0	0	0	0	7.1	3	31	1	1	0	0	0	0	6	0	7	0	0
Bartlett, Richard, Jacksonville	3	3	.500	4.88	35	1	0	0	12	3	59.0	63	276	39	32	3	2	2	3	43	3	30	4	1
Basham, Robert, Chattanooga	5	3	.625	2.98	10	10	0	0	0	0	51.1	52	204	20	17	5	1	1	5	9	0	46	3	0
Basner, Ryan, Mississippi	2	10	.167	5.34	35	11	1	0	7	1	96.0	114	414	61	57	8	6	3	6	23	4	64	5	0
Bass, Adam, Tennessee	5	10	.333	3.99	27	27	1	0	0	0	158.0	158	664	75	70	14	8	6	10	40	1	120	7	0
Bauer, Peter, Carolina	0	1	.000	7.20	1	1	0	0	0	0	5.0	10	24	4	4	1	0	0	1	1	1	2	1	0
Bazardo, Yorman, Carolina	8	7	.533	3.99	19	19	0	0	0	0	108.1	108	460	60	48	12	9	5	8	36	3	73	8	1
Bentz, Chad, Carolina *	1	0	1.000	1.29	7	0	0	0	2	0	7.0	6	31	3	1	0	0	0	0	4	0	5	0	0
Biggs, Billy, Tennessee	0	1	.000	3.97	9	0	0	0	4	0	11.1	13	53	7	5	3	0	0	0	6	1	6	0	0
Billingsley, Chad, Jacksonville	13	6	.684	3.51	28	26	2	1	0	0	146.0	116	596	60	57	12	5	2	4	50	0	162	10	0
Bobbitt, Seth, Mississippi	0	0	.000	1.80	2	0	0	0	0	0	5.0	1	17	1	1	0	0	0	0	2	0	3	0	0
Bostick II, Adam, Carolina *	4	3	.571	4.67	9	9	0	0	0	0	44.1	42	198	26	23	3	1	2	3	25	0	39	7	0
Bott, Glenn, Jacksonville *	2	4	.333	5.12	25	1	0	0	11	1	38.2	34	173	24	22	6	2	0	1	25	2	42	4	0
Boyer, Blaine, Mississippi	2	4	.333	5.03	14	8	0	0	2	0	48.1	62	216	28	27	4	3	3	2	18	3	40	0	0
Bradley, David, Huntsville	6	5	.545	3.35	35	14	1	0	7	0	104.2	99	434	48	39	9	8	4	5	32	2	83	5	0
Brazelton, Dewon, Montgomery	0	0	.000	0.00	1	1	0	0	0	0	3.0	2	11	0	0	0	0	0	0	0	0	6	0	0
Breslow, Craig, Mobile *	2	1	.667	2.75	40	0	0	0	5	0	52.1	38	198	16	16	3	4	1	1	17	2	47	2	0
Broxton, Jonathan, Jacksonville	5	3	.625	3.17	33	13	0	0	15	5	96.2	79	389	36	34	4	3	2	1	31	0	107	7	0
Bruksch, Jeffrey, Chattanooga	3	9	.250	4.81	28	14	0	0	3	0	91.2	86	412	56	49	10	8	6	3	67	2	84	11	1
Bullard, James, Birmingham *	2	3	.400	6.85	8	6	0	0	1	0	23.2	30	105	18	18	2	3	1	0	10	0	19	2	0
Bumstead, Michael, Mobile	0	1	.000	3.94	3	3	0	0	0	0	16.0	14	65	8	7	0	2	1	0	5	0	10	1	0
Bush, Paul, Mississippi	2	0	1.000	2.39	19	5	0	0	2	1	52.2	29	208	17	14	2	3	3	3	22	1	52	2	0
Caraccioli, Lance, Chattanooga *	5	5	.500	3.97	15	10	0	0	2	0	68.0	65	290	35	30	6	4	3	4	31	2	61	5	0
Carrillo, Cesar, Mobile	4	0	1.000	3.23	5	5	0	0	0	0	30.2	23	121	11	11	2	1	0	1	7	0	35	1	0
Cassel, Joseph, Mobile	3	3	.500	3.54	24	3	0	0	9	1	43.0	45	183	18	16	1	1	0	2	16	4	29	5	0
Castro, Juan, Huntsville	0	0	.000	20.25	2	0	0	0	2	0	1.1	4	11	4	3	0	0	0	1	1	0	3	0	0
Cave, Kevin, Carolina	5	3	.625	4.04	37	0	0	0	11	1	42.1	32	183	19	19	1	1	1	3	24	2	35	3	0
Cherry, Rocky, West Tenn	0	0	.000	2.89	3	3	0	0	0	0	9.1	8	40	5	3	0	1	0	1	4	0	9	0	0
Cherry, William, Chattanooga	0	2	.000	7.71	7	0	0	0	4	0	9.1	15	49	10	8	3	1	0	0	3	0	8	0	0
Chick, Travis, Mobile-Chattanooga	4	11	.267	5.14	27	27	1	0	0	0	143.2	154	633	90	82	17	8	5	3	67	3	113	10	1
Chico, Matthew, Tennessee *	1	7	.125	5.98	10	10	0	0	0	0	52.2	75	241	44	35	8	5	4	2	15	1	35	2	2
Coenen, Matthew, Mississippi *	3	9	.250	5.27	19	18	0	0	0	0	95.2	112	412	64	56	8	12	1	1	43	1	52	5	0
Colome, Jesus, Montgomery	0	0	.000	0.00	3	0	0	0	0	0	4.0	2	14	0	0	0	0	0	0	0	0	3	0	0
Colon, Roman, Mississippi	0	0	.000	1.17	2	2	0	0	0	0	7.2	6	29	1	1	0	0	0	0	2	0	7	0	0
Connolly, Jonathan, West Tenn *	3	2	.600	4.44	9	4	0	0	1	0	26.1	29	115	17	13	3	1	3	0	9	0	20	0	0
Costello, Ryan, Huntsville *	0	5	.000	10.13	9	7	0	0	1	0	32.0	54	165	39	36	5	1	0	3	14	1	20	4	0
Cromer, Jason, Montgomery	5	7	.417	4.64	21	21	1	0	...	0	118.1	128	491	67	61	15	...	...	0	33	0	68	...	...
Cruz, Arian, Chattanooga *	3	1	.750	3.26	13	0	0	0	6	0	19.1	23	84	9	7	1	3	1	1	6	0	16	1	0
Curtis, Daniel, Mississippi	2	2	.500	2.67	9	3	0	0	2	0	30.1	30	121	9	9	0	1	0	3	8	0	25	1	0
Daigle, Casey, Tennessee	9	3	.750	2.67	58	2	0	0	45	19	64.0	75	279	24	19	3	7	1	1	18	4	50	5	0
Dannemiller, Beau, Jacksonville	1	3	.250	4.81	27	0	0	0	15	4	43.0	32	188	24	23	4	3	3	3	28	3	37	1	0
Deago, Roger, Mobile *	1	0	1.000	1.38	3	3	0	0	0	0	13.0	10	56	3	2	0	0	0	0	8	0	15	1	1
Dehart, James, Mississippi *	4	2	.667	5.87	38	1	0	0	15	0	61.1	67	271	41	40	10	5	1	1	31	2	38	4	1
Demontel II, James, Carolina	0	0	.000	9.00	2	0	0	0	0	0	2.0	1	12	2	2	0	0	1	0	5	1	1	1	0
Devine, Joey, Mississippi	1	1	.500	2.70	18	0	0	0	15	5	20.0	19	93	13	6	2	2	0	5	12	1	28	1	0
DeWitt, Matt, Huntsville	1	3	.250	4.65	26	0	0	0	12	5	31.0	46	149	25	16	2	1	2	0	11	1	31	3	0
Diaz, Jose, Montgomery	2	2	.500	9.13	18	0	0	0	9	0	23.2	22	114	24	24	2	1	1	4	20	0	22	4	0
Dizard, Fraser, Birmingham *	0	0	.000	3.38	5	0	0	0	1	0	8.0	9	39	5	3	1	0	2	0	5	0	11	0	0
Dumatrait, Phillip, Chattanooga *	4	12	.250	3.17	24	24	0	0	0	0	127.2	115	545	58	45	4	6	4	2	70	4	101	13	0
Eckenstahler, Eric, Chattanooga *	0	0	.000	9.24	35	0	0	0	15	0	37.0	53	203	42	38	4	2	4	6	41	0	29	8	0
Eveland, Dana, Huntsville *	10	4	.714	2.72	18	18	0	0	0	0	109.0	96	449	42	33	4	4	2	4	38	1	98	6	2
Evert, Brett, Huntsville	0	0	.000	2.97	16	0	0	0	10	1	30.1	31	129	13	10	6	0	0	0	7	0	32	1	0
Ferreras, Yorkin, West Tenn *	2	4	.333	5.52	30	0	0	0	11	2	29.1	43	138	26	18	5	2	1	2	6	1	31	1	0
Flannery, Michael, Carolina	1	3	.250	2.21	31	0	0	0	22	13	36.2	30	142	9	9	2	1	0	1	6	1	39	1	0
Flinn, Christopher, Montgomery	5	6	.455	5.00	36	4	0	0	7	2	77.1	89	343	51	43	3	3	5	8	24	0	61	0	1
Flury, Patrick, Carolina	1	0	1.000	0.00	3	0	0	0	0	0	2.2	1	10	0	0	0	0	0	0	2	0	3	0	0
Ford, Matthew, Huntsville *	1	3	.250	5.40	17	0	0	0	2	0	21.2	34	115	20	13	2	2	2	0	14	1	19	3	0
Frese, Nate, West Tenn	0	0	.000	0.00	1	0	0	0	1	0	1.0	0	3	0	0	0	0	0	0	0	0	1	0	0
Fuell, Jerrod, Carolina	4	2	.667	3.31	39	0	0	0	15	4	54.1	50	230	21	20	3	3	3	2	20	0	43	4	1
Gamble, Jerome, Huntsville	4	1	.800	6.33	31	0	0	0	17	5	42.2	51	190	30	30	2	1	0	0	12	2	48	2	0
Garcia, Gerardo, Montgomery	0	2	.000	8.31	2	2	0	0	0	0	8.2	19	45	13	8	1	0	0	1	0	0	5	0	0
Gardner, Richard, Chattanooga *	3	6	.333	5.73	13	13	0	0	0	0	66.0	80	290	46	42	6	5	4	3	24	1	47	5	0
Glen, William, Birmingham	1	0	1.000	8.84	11	0	0	0	2	0	19.1	29	96	20	19	3	0	1	1	11	3	16	1	0
Gonzalez, Alfredo, Jacksonville	2	1	.667	3.86	5	0	0	0	1	0	7.0	4	28	4	3	0	1	0	0	4	0	8	1	0
Gonzalez, Enrique, Tennessee	11	8	.579	3.46	27	27	2	2	0	0	161.1	160	670	76	62	8	6	6	6	52	0	146	9	0
Gonzalez, Luis, Jacksonville *	7	2	.778	2.21	41	0	0	0	26	7	61.0	35	249	17	15	1	3	0	3	34	3	46	4	0
Goocher, Clint, Tennessee *	9	11	.450	5.37	27	25	2	1	0	0	140.2	185	618	105	84	20	12	4	5	37	0	77	4	0
Gwaltney, William, West Tenn	0	0	.000	0.00	1	0	0	0	0	0	1.0	1	3	0	0	0	1	0	0	0	0	0	0	0
Habel, Joshua, Huntsville *	3	7	.300	5.65	21	9	0	0	3	0	65.1	85	301	54	41	12	6	2	2	28	0	47	2	1
Haeger, Charles, Birmingham	6	3	.667	3.78	13	13	3	0	0	0	85.2	84	370	43	36	1	4	1	5	45	1	48	4	0
Haigwood, Daniel, Birmingham *	6	1	.857	1.74	11	11	0	0	0	0	67.1	39	265	14	13	0	3	0	4	31	1	76	4	0
Haines, Joseph, West Tenn	4	2	.667	1.78	23	0	0	0	20	13	25.1	24	100	7	5	0	3	1	1	2	0	20	5	0
Haley, Adam, Tennessee	0	0	.000	27.00	1	0	0	0	1	0	1.0	3	8	3	3	0	1	0	1	2	0	1	1	0
Hall, Josh, Chattanooga	5	6	.455	3.53	18	18	0	0	0	0	112.1	115	466	49	44	7	7	1	3	35	2	92	10	0
Hammel, Jason, Montgomery	8	2	.800	2.66	12	12	3	0	0	0	81.1	70	321	26	24	5	1	2	2	19	0	76	2	1
Hanrahan, Joel, Jacksonville	9	8	.529	4.92	23	21	0	0	0	0	111.2	118	492	71	61	17	6	4	1	55	1	102	9	0
Hayhurst, Dirk, Mobile	1	0	1.000	5.27	1	1	1	0	0	0	7.0	5	26	2	2	1	0	0	0	4	0	4	1	0
Henderson, Brian, Montgomery *	5	1	.833	3.60	48	0	0	0	18	1	55.0	62	244	29	22	3	3	2	1	21	2	49	2	0
Hill, Rich, West Tenn *	4	3	.571	3.28	10	10	0	0	0	0	57.2	42	233	22	21	9	1	0	2	21	0	90	0	0

Pitcher, Team	W	L	Pct.	ERA	G	GS	CG	ShO	GF	Sv.	IP	H	TBF	R	ER	HR	SH	SF	HB	BB	IBB	SO	WP	Bk.
Hines, Carlos, Montgomery	0	2	.000	3.71	22	0	0	0	13	6	34.0	28	137	17	14	1	4	3	0	16	0	24	2	0
Hoerman, Jared, West Tenn	0	0	.000	0.00	2	0	0	0	0	0	1.1	0	4	0	0	0	1	0	0	2	0	1	0	0
Honel, Kristopher, Birmingham	5	7	.417	5.88	21	18	0	0	3	0	93.1	101	439	68	61	10	4	4	8	64	2	70	1	0
Hudson, Luke, Chattanooga	0	1	.000	5.40	1	1	0	0	0	0	6.2	6	28	4	4	2	0	0	1	1	0	7	0	0
Hull, Eric, Jacksonville	7	7	.500	3.38	27	18	1	1	4	3	117.0	105	491	50	44	9	5	2	2	44	0	117	7	0
Jackson, Edwin, Jacksonville	6	4	.600	3.48	11	11	0	0	0	0	62.0	52	254	31	24	7	3	2	2	18	0	44	4	0
James, Chuck, Mississippi *	9	1	.900	2.09	16	16	0	0	0	0	86.0	62	331	25	20	4	6	0	2	18	0	104	4	0
Jenks, Bobby, Birmingham	1	2	.333	2.85	35	0	0	0	32	19	41.0	34	177	17	13	1	1	1	1	4	20	1	48	6	0
Johnson, Josh, Carolina	12	4	.750	3.87	26	26	1	0	0	0	139.2	139	589	67	60	4	9	2	4	50	4	113	7	1
Jones, Geoffrey, Mobile *	3	5	.375	4.37	55	0	0	0	15	0	70.0	76	314	43	34	2	5	2	10	32	4	60	2	0
Juarez, William, Jacksonville	6	5	.545	4.59	38	14	0	0	7	0	104.0	116	460	60	53	11	7	6	5	48	2	75	2	1
Kensing, Logan, Carolina	4	1	.800	3.18	7	7	0	0	0	0	39.2	35	173	16	14	4	2	1	5	14	0	33	3	0
Kent, Steve, Mississippi *	2	5	.286	4.28	33	0	0	0	12	3	40.0	43	173	21	19	1	3	1	0	18	5	29	3	0
Kozlowski, Ben, Chattanooga *	4	4	.500	4.04	20	20	0	0	0	0	111.1	129	484	58	50	10	9	2	6	31	1	82	7	1
Kuo, Hong-Chih, Jacksonville *	1	1	.500	1.91	17	0	0	0	9	3	28.1	22	117	7	6	1	0	1	0	11	1	44	3	0
Lamura, William, Birmingham	5	2	.714	4.79	55	0	0	0	17	1	71.1	73	337	46	38	5	4	3	2	57	6	79	6	0
Lerew, Anthony, Mississippi	6	2	.750	3.93	14	14	1	0	0	0	75.2	70	319	34	33	6	4	1	2	32	1	64	1	0
Lizarraga, Sergio, Jacksonville	0	1	.000	6.63	12	2	0	0	3	0	19.0	31	91	17	14	3	0	0	1	3	0	16	1	0
Lockwood, Brian, Montgomery	3	6	.333	7.18	24	11	0	0	4	0	77.2	112	364	72	62	13	3	0	7	27	2	73	4	0
Lockwood, Luke, Carolina *	2	8	.200	3.24	34	15	1	0	3	1	114.0	110	453	45	41	6	8	9	2	23	3	79	2	0
Lubisich, Nikolas, Birmingham *	9	4	.692	3.00	21	18	0	0	1	1	105.0	111	427	43	35	8	5	6	2	22	4	49	0	1
Lugo, Ruddy, Montgomery	1	1	.500	1.12	26	0	0	0	13	2	40.1	25	172	12	5	1	0	0	1	23	0	48	8	0
Machi, Jean, Montgomery	0	0	.000	54.00	1	0	0	0	0	0	0.2	4	7	4	4	1	0	0	0	1	0	1	0	0
Magrane, James, Montgomery	2	5	.286	5.40	9	8	0	0	0	0	50.0	63	225	31	30	2	1	3	1	21	0	26	2	0
Mallett, Justin, Chattanooga	0	0	.000	5.91	3	2	0	0	0	0	10.2	12	47	7	7	3	1	0	1	5	0	9	0	0
Malone, Corwin, Birmingham *	5	5	.500	4.53	33	13	0	0	5	1	97.1	100	433	55	49	6	7	5	6	55	3	81	4	1
Marmol, Carlos, West Tenn.	3	4	.429	3.65	14	14	0	0	0	0	81.1	70	343	33	33	10	6	2	8	40	0	70	1	1
Marshall, Sean, West Tenn *	0	1	.000	2.52	4	4	0	0	0	0	25.0	16	95	7	7	1	1	0	1	5	0	24	2	1
Martinez, Carlos, Carolina	0	0	.000	9.00	1	0	0	0	1	1	1.0	1	5	1	1	0	0	0	0	1	0	1	0	0
Mateo, Nathanel, Mobile	3	4	.429	3.08	48	0	0	0	14	1	52.2	57	223	22	18	2	5	1	0	15	1	39	0	0
McBride, Macay, Mississippi *	3	1	.750	3.65	6	3	0	0	1	0	24.2	21	102	11	10	2	1	0	0	12	1	16	1	0
McGlinchy, Kevin, West Tenn	0	1	.000	4.32	9	0	0	0	8	3	8.1	12	42	6	4	0	0	0	4	0	7	0	1
McNutt, Michael, Carolina	3	2	.600	3.83	31	0	0	0	8	1	54.0	46	222	23	23	9	3	1	0	24	1	37	4	0
Meaux, Ryan, Birmingham-Mobile	7	2	.778	3.00	53	0	0	0	19	3	84.0	93	357	34	28	4	3	4	1	20	4	76	1	0
Meyers, Mike, Huntsville	0	0	.000	1.71	11	0	0	0	6	1	21.0	21	89	9	4	0	1	0	0	4	0	16	0	0
Miller, Greg, Jacksonville *	0	0	.000	2.77	12	0	0	0	2	2	13.0	14	68	6	4	1	0	0	2	15	1	17	1	0
Miller, Ryan, Huntsville	0	0	.000	5.40	4	0	0	0	2	1	5.0	3	19	3	3	2	0	0	1	0	4	0	0
Miner, Zachary, Mississippi	0	1	.000	4.32	4	2	0	0	1	1	16.2	21	73	10	8	0	1	0	5	0	18	2	0
Molldrem, Craig, Carolina	0	1	.000	7.71	1	1	0	0	0	0	4.2	5	24	4	4	1	0	0	5	0	4	0	0
Nelson, Bubba, Chattanooga	2	4	.333	4.61	42	0	0	0	30	12	68.1	67	297	38	35	5	5	1	7	27	0	70	4	0
Nichols, Leslie, Chattanooga	0	0	.000	0.00	2	0	0	0	2	0	2.0	1	8	0	0	0	0	0	0	2	0	0	0	0
Niemann, Jeffrey, Montgomery	0	1	.000	4.35	6	3	0	0	1	0	10.1	7	43	7	5	0	0	0	5	0	14	0	0
Nina, Elvin, Tennessee	0	1	.000	6.43	4	1	0	0	0	0	7.0	10	33	5	5	0	0	0	2	4	1	4	0	0
Nippert, Dustin, Tennessee	8	3	.727	2.36	18	18	3	2	...	0	118.1	95	462	33	31	4	...	...	...	42	1	97	...	0
Nolasco, Ricky, West Tenn	14	3	.824	2.89	27	27	1	0	0	0	161.2	151	676	57	52	13	11	2	11	46	1	173	4	2
O'Connor, Brian, Mississippi	9	7	.563	3.65	30	19	0	0	...	0	133.1	127	560	66	54	7	...	...	...	63	1	98	...	0
Ojeda, Alvis, Jacksonville	1	0	1.000	2.38	7	1	0	0	2	0	11.1	10	43	3	3	0	1	0	0	2	0	9	0	1
Olsen, Scott, Carolina *	6	4	.600	3.92	14	14	1	1	0	0	80.1	75	334	38	35	7	3	5	3	27	0	94	6	0
Olson, Jason, Jacksonville	1	3	.250	5.86	36	0	0	0	13	5	66.0	67	307	44	43	8	2	4	6	39	3	62	4	0
O'Malley, Ryan, West Tenn *	3	3	.500	3.91	31	9	0	0	5	0	78.1	78	333	41	34	7	3	2	2	25	1	55	3	0
Orenduff, Justin, Jacksonville	5	2	.714	4.07	14	13	0	0	0	0	66.1	59	274	33	30	6	1	4	1	24	0	65	8	1
Ortiz, Javier, Birmingham	2	1	.667	3.52	5	0	0	0	2	0	7.2	8	35	4	3	1	0	0	4	3	7	1	0
Orvella, Chad, Montgomery	0	0	.000	0.36	16	0	0	0	15	9	25.0	15	95	1	1	0	1	0	0	6	0	29	1	0
Overman, Matthew, Carolina	1	0	1.000	0.00	6	0	0	0	1	0	6.2	8	24	0	0	0	1	0	0	0	8	0	0
Oyervidez, Jose, Mobile	7	9	.438	3.81	27	27	0	0	0	0	153.2	129	652	77	65	16	12	6	7	82	5	130	9	1
Pacheco, Enemencio, Birmingham	0	1	.000	6.97	3	3	0	0	0	0	10.1	16	49	8	8	0	0	1	5	0	9	0	0
Parker, Joshua, Montgomery	2	8	.200	4.76	43	0	0	0	23	4	58.2	60	250	35	31	6	5	3	3	16	2	32	6	1
Parra, Manuel, Huntsville *	5	6	.455	3.96	16	16	0	0	0	0	91.0	101	399	47	40	4	5	0	2	21	0	86	7	3
Peguero, Tony, Montgomery	5	1	.833	4.01	9	9	0	0	0	0	51.2	59	227	26	23	4	2	0	5	15	0	37	1	1
Pena, Tony, Tennessee	7	13	.350	4.43	25	25	2	1	0	0	148.1	165	637	86	73	17	4	4	10	40	1	95	5	0
Perez, Beltran, Montgomery	2	3	.400	2.90	17	1	0	0	6	3	31.0	22	127	11	10	1	1	0	1	16	2	32	2	0
Phelps, Travis, Chattanooga	0	1	.000	5.40	7	0	0	0	6	0	10.0	14	42	6	6	1	0	1	0	3	0	10	2	0
Phillips, Heath Michael, Birmingham * ..	9	5	.643	4.07	22	21	2	0	0	0	135.0	161	561	64	61	12	6	5	3	30	2	78	4	1
Phillips, Jason C., Montgomery	1	0	1.000	5.40	1	1	0	0	0	0	5.0	8	22	3	3	2	0	0	2	0	1	0	0
Pignatiello, Carmen, West Tenn *	5	4	.556	2.68	16	10	0	0	1	0	80.2	67	325	26	24	3	5	1	2	28	1	77	3	0
Pinto, Renyel, West Tenn *	10	3	.769	2.71	22	21	1	0	0	0	129.2	101	522	43	39	3	6	2	9	58	0	123	3	0
Pollok, Dwayne, Birmingham	4	5	.444	3.08	56	0	0	0	32	11	87.2	88	369	42	30	7	1	4	4	19	2	58	2	0
Porzio, Mike, Mississippi *	2	3	.400	4.26	14	4	0	0	0	0	31.2	36	137	15	15	3	1	2	1	12	1	20	1	1
Powell, Jay, Mississippi	2	0	1.000	0.64	11	0	0	0	3	0	14.0	6	48	1	1	0	2	0	1	3	1	6	0	0
Pratt, Andy, Huntsville *	0	1	.000	2.96	21	0	0	0	9	2	27.1	22	131	11	9	3	0	0	3	24	1	33	10	0
Raburn, John, Montgomery	0	0	.000	0.00	2	0	0	0	2	0	2.0	2	7	0	0	0	0	0	0	1	0	1	0	0
Ramos, Victor, West Tenn	2	3	.400	3.24	19	0	0	0	5	0	25.0	21	100	9	9	1	4	0	0	12	1	18	2	0
Renick, Joshua, Chattanooga	0	0	.000	27.00	1	0	0	0	1	0	1.0	3	7	3	3	0	0	0	1	0	0	0	0	0
Resop, Chris, Carolina	3	2	.600	2.57	43	0	0	0	40	24	49.0	47	211	15	14	2	1	1	0	16	1	56	4	0
Reynoso, Paulino, Birmingham *	4	4	.500	3.92	54	0	0	0	16	8	57.1	63	266	37	25	6	6	1	3	41	2	46	5	1
Richardson, Jason, Mississippi	0	2	.000	4.11	17	0	0	0	6	0	30.2	34	134	17	14	3	2	0	1	11	0	29	1	0
Richardson, Michael, Mobile	0	0	.000	3.00	3	0	0	0	3	0	3.0	0	13	1	1	0	0	0	0	4	0	3	2	0
Roberts, Ralph, Mississippi	0	0	.000	0.00	1	0	0	0	0	0	1.2	0	6	0	0	0	0	0	0	1	0	0	0	0
Rodriguez, Jose, Carolina *	0	0	.000	7.71	6	0	0	0	1	1	4.2	6	22	4	4	2	0	0	0	1	0	5	0	0
Rodriguez, Orlando, Jacksonville *	0	0	.000	5.54	8	0	0	0	3	0	13.0	14	64	11	8	1	2	3	0	11	0	13	0	0
Russ, James, Carolina	1	0	1.000	0.00	1	1	0	0	0	0	5.0	4	20	0	0	0	0	0	0	0	0	5	0	0

Pitcher, Team	W	L	Pct.	ERA	G	GS	CG	ShO	GF	Sv.	IP	H	TBF	R	ER	HR	SH	SF	HB	BB	IBB	SO	WP	Bk.
Ryu, Jae-kuk, West Tenn	11	8	.579	3.34	27	27	1	1	0	0	169.2	154	686	67	63	12	15	4	6	49	1	133	9	0
Saladin, Miguel, Chattanooga	0	0	.000	3.45	10	0	0	0	2	1	15.2	19	70	6	6	2	0	2	1	5	0	15	0	0
Salas, Juan, Montgomery	1	0	1.000	3.68	15	0	0	0	6	0	22.0	25	104	12	9	2	0	1	2	12	0	18	5	1
Salmon, Bradley, Chattanooga	3	8	.273	3.34	38	0	0	0	13	4	72.2	66	302	31	27	3	8	1	3	31	1	71	7	0
Sarfate, Dennis, Huntsville	9	9	.500	3.88	24	24	1	0	0	0	130.0	120	562	65	56	13	5	4	10	59	1	110	11	1
Schmidt, Jeremy, Chattanooga	3	5	.375	4.36	46	0	0	0	16	0	64.0	64	267	35	31	6	2	1	1	23	1	56	3	5
Schultz, Michael, Tennessee	4	6	.400	3.58	63	0	0	0	26	6	65.1	70	287	31	26	3	7	3	0	41	4	68	11	0
Searles, Jonathan, West Tenn	6	3	.667	3.35	59	0	0	0	18	1	80.2	74	336	30	30	5	6	2	3	29	7	72	3	1
Seddon, Christopher, Montgomery *	6	1	.857	4.82	10	10	0	0	0	0	52.1	58	226	31	28	4	5	1	1	20	0	46	4	0
Shafer, David, Chattanooga	1	6	.143	4.08	34	0	0	0	25	6	39.2	31	171	21	18	3	5	1	3	24	2	41	0	1
Shields, James, Montgomery	7	5	.583	2.80	17	16	0	0	1	0	109.1	95	429	36	34	6	5	2	6	31	0	104	7	0
Shipman, Andrew, West Tenn	3	6	.333	3.17	59	0	0	0	30	15	65.1	60	279	32	23	1	7	1	2	27	2	68	2	0
Sikaras, Panagiotis, Tennessee	2	3	.400	6.12	44	1	0	0	17	2	64.2	77	300	47	44	7	3	3	6	32	1	38	2	1
Silva, Jesus, Tennessee	1	0	1.000	6.35	2	1	0	0	0	0	5.2	9	25	4	4	0	1	0	0	1	0	5	1	0
Simpson, Gerrit, Huntsville	1	0	1.000	2.29	13	0	0	0	10	5	19.2	17	83	5	5	0	0	1	1	7	0	15	3	0
Slaten, Douglas, Tennessee *	2	2	.500	4.26	58	0	0	0	6	1	61.1	61	265	45	29	2	5	3	3	26	0	72	3	2
Smith, Cam, Montgomery	4	2	.667	2.01	20	0	0	0	16	7	22.1	12	95	7	5	1	2	0	2	17	0	26	1	0
Snare, Ryan, Mobile *	0	2	.000	6.23	2	2	1	0	0	0	13.0	16	56	9	9	3	0	3	0	3	0	8	3	0
Sodowsky, Clint, Carolina	0	1	.000	5.03	12	1	0	0	1	0	19.2	20	82	12	11	0	1	1	1	4	0	24	3	0
Spiehs, Randall, Mobile	0	1	.000	7.98	10	0	0	0	1	0	14.2	19	68	18	13	4	1	0	3	3	1	9	0	0
Stamler, Keith, Huntsville	0	1	.000	3.73	23	1	0	0	8	1	50.2	55	220	29	21	3	5	1	1	19	2	27	1	0
Steidlmayer, Luke, Mobile	0	3	.000	6.32	3	3	0	0	0	0	15.2	23	78	14	11	2	0	1	1	7	0	13	2	1
Steinborn, Christopher, Mobile *	0	1	.000	8.31	3	0	0	0	1	0	4.1	4	20	4	4	1	0	0	0	4	0	4	0	0
Stetter, Mitchel, Huntsville *	2	3	.400	2.61	32	0	0	0	22	8	51.2	46	204	15	15	3	1	0	2	11	1	47	0	0
Stockman, Phillip, Tennessee	1	3	.250	3.34	47	1	0	0	7	1	35.0	31	162	16	13	2	4	3	4	24	2	30	2	0
Stokes, Brian, Montgomery	4	6	.400	3.47	16	16	1	0	0	0	93.1	82	376	36	36	8	3	1	2	28	2	70	4	0
Stults, Eric, Jacksonville *	4	3	.571	3.31	12	12	0	0	0	0	68.0	73	289	33	25	6	2	1	0	14	0	58	2	0
Switzer, Jon, Montgomery *	3	1	.750	3.45	6	6	0	0	0	0	31.1	33	135	14	12	2	0	2	5	5	0	20	0	1
Taubenheim, Ty, Huntsville	2	6	.250	4.36	11	11	0	0	0	0	64.0	64	267	36	31	7	8	4	1	24	1	44	3	0
Tavares, Anderson, West Tenn	0	0	.000	0.00	1	0	0	0	0	0	2.0	1	7	0	0	0	0	0	0	1	0	0	0	0
Thayer, Dale, Mobile	3	5	.375	2.34	56	0	0	0	50	27	57.2	60	244	16	15	5	5	2	1	26	2	59	1	0
Thompson, Chris, Tennessee	0	0	.000	2.45	3	0	0	0	1	0	3.2	1	14	1	1	0	0	0	1	1	0	2	0	0
Thompson, Derek, Jacksonville *	0	2	.000	3.89	8	8	0	0	0	0	41.2	45	182	20	18	3	3	1	3	19	0	43	3	0
Thompson, Michael, Mobile	6	6	.500	3.22	18	18	2	1	0	0	114.2	116	466	50	41	6	6	2	5	27	0	68	5	0
Thompson, Sean, Mobile *	4	5	.444	4.67	20	20	0	0	0	0	113.2	127	495	67	59	10	4	4	4	55	1	94	7	3
Thomson, John, Mississippi	1	0	1.000	1.50	1	1	0	0	0	0	6.0	4	21	1	1	0	0	0	0	0	0	4	1	0
Torres, Andy, Carolina	0	0	.000	3.86	1	1	0	0	0	0	4.2	4	20	4	2	1	0	0	0	2	0	2	0	0
Tovar, Angel, Mobile	2	1	.667	6.57	8	1	0	0	0	0	12.1	19	64	12	9	1	0	0	0	8	0	10	6	0
Tracey, Sean, Birmingham	14	6	.700	4.07	28	28	2	0	0	0	163.2	154	695	80	74	13	3	5	14	76	1	106	12	0
Tucker, Glenn, Mississippi	4	2	.667	3.09	49	0	0	0	27	5	64.0	64	264	24	22	4	5	3	4	22	3	42	0	0
Tucker, Michael, Carolina	0	0	.000	4.50	2	0	0	0	2	0	2.0	3	9	1	1	0	0	0	0	0	0	1	0	0
Tucker, Rusty, Mobile *	3	2	.600	5.31	52	0	0	0	16	0	62.2	66	299	42	37	4	3	6	8	49	2	69	11	0
Ulacia, Dennis, Birmingham *	0	0	.000	0.00	2	0	0	0	0	0	4.0	3	16	0	0	0	0	0	0	0	0	3	2	0
Ungs, Nicholas, Carolina	7	5	.583	3.68	22	22	1	1	0	0	120.0	123	502	57	49	8	4	6	3	34	3	79	4	0
Valdes, Raul, West Tenn *	2	0	1.000	5.09	5	5	0	0	0	0	23.0	28	92	13	13	1	1	1	3	3	0	18	2	0
Valdez, Edward, Chattanooga	1	3	.250	6.94	12	11	0	0	0	0	58.1	85	275	48	45	10	5	4	8	24	0	47	2	0
Van Hekken, Andy, Mississippi-Chattanooga	2	0	1.000	4.41	6	6	0	0	0	0	32.2	41	148	16	16	3	2	1	1	15	0	18	1	0
Vargas, Jason, Carolina *	1	0	1.000	2.84	3	3	0	0	0	0	19.0	13	74	6	6	3	1	0	0	7	0	25	0	0
Vasquez, Jorge, Mississippi	2	1	.667	1.12	29	0	0	0	24	10	40.1	22	151	7	5	1	3	2	3	11	2	45	4	0
Velazquez, Juan, Mississippi	0	0	.000	13.50	2	0	0	0	2	0	1.1	1	7	2	2	1	0	0	0	2	0	1	2	0
Villacis, Eduardo, Birmingham	2	5	.286	7.06	9	8	0	0	1	1	43.1	64	208	40	34	10	2	1	0	18	4	37	1	1
Villanueva, Carlos, Huntsville	1	3	.250	7.40	4	4	0	0	0	0	20.2	21	93	18	17	3	1	1	1	9	0	14	1	0
Villatoro, Wilmer, Mobile	0	3	.000	15.55	10	1	0	0	4	0	11.0	22	68	19	19	4	1	1	4	12	1	8	3	1
Walton, Samuel, Montgomery *	0	0	.000	6.57	13	0	0	0	2	0	24.2	31	117	19	18	6	1	2	1	15	0	22	6	0
Ward, Jeremy, Mississippi	0	2	.000	2.63	12	0	0	0	8	2	13.2	16	58	4	4	0	0	0	1	1	0	18	0	0
Wassermann, Ehren, Birmingham	2	0	1.000	2.14	14	0	0	0	5	0	21.0	23	89	6	5	0	1	1	2	7	1	18	2	0
Weber, Ben, Chattanooga	1	1	.500	2.31	9	0	0	0	0	0	11.2	9	47	3	3	2	1	0	1	3	0	5	2	0
Weber, Jonathan, Jacksonville *	0	1	.000	13.50	1	0	0	0	1	0	0.2	0	4	1	1	0	1	0	0	3	1	0	1	0
Wechsler, Justin, Tennessee	3	2	.600	6.14	42	0	0	0	8	0	55.2	62	249	41	38	7	3	5	5	26	1	43	6	0
Wells, Jared, Mobile	2	5	.286	4.40	7	7	0	0	0	0	43.0	51	184	25	21	3	3	2	0	16	1	22	4	0
Wells, Randy, West Tenn	0	1	.000	3.86	6	0	0	0	4	0	9.1	13	43	4	4	0	2	1	0	7	1	8	0	0
Whitaker, Brian, Mobile	8	13	.381	4.33	25	25	0	0	0	0	147.2	180	651	85	71	4	8	1	12	53	7	101	6	1
White, Sean, Mississippi	2	5	.286	4.11	8	8	0	0	0	0	50.1	43	208	25	23	2	2	0	4	18	2	33	7	0
White, William, Tennessee *	0	2	.000	4.50	60	0	0	0	7	0	42.0	40	189	28	21	1	2	1	4	26	0	33	4	0
Winchester, Jeffrey, Huntsville	0	1	.000	6.75	2	0	0	0	2	0	1.1	2	9	1	1	0	0	0	4	1	1	0	0	0
Wolf, Ross, Carolina	5	4	.556	4.96	54	1	0	0	15	1	78.0	106	367	54	43	6	4	5	1	31	4	59	4	0
Wolfe, Brian, Huntsville	3	1	.750	3.38	16	0	0	0	7	0	24.0	32	113	12	9	1	2	1	1	8	2	19	3	0
Woolard, Glenn, Huntsville	7	11	.389	4.91	29	26	0	0	0	0	146.2	160	648	87	80	15	8	4	5	64	4	113	10	0
Wright, Matthew, Mississippi	6	8	.429	6.11	17	14	0	0	2	1	84.0	101	381	60	57	7	4	5	1	37	1	63	5	0
Yofu, Tetsu, Birmingham	0	1	.000	7.11	2	0	0	0	0	0	6.1	6	29	5	5	0	0	0	1	6	1	7	3	0
Yourkin, Matthew, Carolina *	0	2	.000	4.05	11	0	0	0	1	0	6.2	7	31	4	3	0	1	0	0	4	2	4	0	0
Zumwalt, Sean, Huntsville	1	2	.333	4.15	28	0	0	0	12	3	52.0	49	225	28	24	5	2	1	2	22	0	37	2	0

PITCHERS WITH TWO OR MORE TEAMS

Pitcher, Team	W	L	Pct.	ERA	G	GS	CG	ShO	GF	Sv.	IP	H	TBF	R	ER	HR	SH	SF	HB	BB	IBB	SO	WP	Bk.
Chick, Travis, Mobile	2	9	.182	5.27	19	19	1	0	0	0	97.1	107	429	65	57	12	5	2	3	40	2	92	6	0
Chick, Travis, Chattanooga	2	2	.500	4.86	8	8	0	0	0	0	46.1	47	204	25	25	5	3	0	0	27	1	21	4	1
Meaux, Ryan, Birmingham *	5	2	.714	2.96	38	0	0	0	14	3	67.0	77	287	27	22	2	3	3	1	18	4	64	1	0
Meaux, Ryan, Mobile *	2	0	1.000	3.18	15	0	0	0	5	0	17.0	16	70	7	6	2	1	1	0	2	0	12	0	0
Van Hekken, Andy, Mississippi *	0	0	.000	5.63	3	3	0	0	0	0	16.0	22	74	10	10	1	2	1	0	12	0	8	1	0
Van Hekken, Andy, Chattanooga *	2	0	1.000	3.24	3	3	0	0	0	0	16.2	19	74	6	6	2	0	0	1	3	0	10	0	0

COMBINATION SHUTOUTS: Birmingham (6) -- Lubisich-Lamura-Reynoso-Jenks, Phillips-Jenks, Haeger-Jenks, Tracey-Pollok-Wassermann, Haigwood-Reynoso, Honel-Malone-Pollok. Carolina (8) -- Johnson-Bentz-Fuell-Rodriguez-Resop, Kensing-Lockwood-Fuell-Rodriguez-Resop, Johnson-Lockwood-Baker, Ungs-Wolf-Resop, Olsen-Wolf-McNutt-Cave-Resop, Ungs-Yourkin-Resop, Johnson-Sodowsky-Cave, Russ-McNutt-Yourkin-Resop. Chattanooga (4) -- Caraccioli-Schmidt-Salmon, Dumatrait-Shafer-Nelson, Hall-Bruksch-Eckenstahler-Shafer, Dumatrait-Salmon-Cruz. Huntsville (3) -- Sarfate-Habel-Gamble, Eveland-Stetter, Sarfate-Wolfe-Gamble-Simpson. Jacksonville (11) -- Billingsley-Gonzalez-Bott-Dannemiller, Hull-Gonzalez-Bartlett, Billingsley-Dannemiller, Thompson-Juarez-Gonzalez, Broxton-Bartlett-Bott, Hanrahan-Dannemiller-Juarez, Billingsley-Rodriguez, Hanrahan-Kuo-Broxton, Jackson-Miller, Billingsley-Miller-Hull, Billingsley-Bartlett. Mississippi (13) -- Wright-Basner-Vasquez, Lerew-Basner, Wright-Boyer, James-Richardson-Powell, White-Curtis-Devine, James-Barry-Tucker, James-Tucker-Richardson, James-Tucker-Kent, O'Connor-Dehart, Wright-Kent-Bush-Ward, Coenen-Kent, O'Connor-Dehart, Wright-Kent-Bush-Ward, James-Richardson-Powell, White-Curtis-Devine, James-Barry-Tucker, James-Tucker-Richardson, James-Tucker-Kent, O'Connor-Dehart, Oyervidez-Abraham-Thayer. Montgomery (6) -- Switzer-Flinn, Seddon-Flinn, Flinn-Colome-Smith, Shields-Henderson, Magrane-Lugo, Shields-Smith. Tennessee (8) -- Bass-Schultz-Slaten, Pena-Sikaras-White-Schultz-Daigle, Gonzalez-White-Sikaras, Pena-Schultz-Daigle, Pena-Schultz-White-Daigle, Gonzalez-Schultz-White-Daigle, Goocher-Daigle, Bass-Goocher-Daigle. West Tenn (11) -- Nolasco-O'Malley-Ferreras-Haines, Hill-Searles-Baez-Ferreras-O'Malley, Pignatiello-Haines, Pinto-Haines, Ryu-Shipman, Marmol-Searles-Shipman, Baez-Ramos-Atlee, Nolasco-Atlee-Shipman, Pinto-Aardsma-Shipman, Nolasco-Atlee-Searles-Shipman, Marmol-Wells-Aardsma-Atlee.

NO-HIT GAMES: Ungs, Carolina, defeated West Tennessee, 2-0, July 29.

2005 FIELDING

TEAM

Team	G	PO	A	E	TC	DP	TP	PB	Pct.
Carolina	134	3526	1443	116	5085	117	0	11	.977
West Tenn	139	3695	1395	126	5216	127	0	2	.976
Birmingham	139	3646	1479	131	5256	151	0	30	.975
Mississippi	132	3463	1454	126	5043	127	0	6	.975
Jacksonville	140	3671	1255	135	5061	86	0	18	.973
Chattanooga	136	3609	1489	145	5243	133	0	9	.972
Mobile	138	3620	1558	147	5325	157	0	8	.972
Montgomery	137	3572	1415	147	5134	130	0	18	.971
Huntsville	139	3652	1463	161	5276	106	1	31	.969
Tennessee	140	3667	1482	162	5311	136	0	9	.969

INDIVIDUAL

FIRST BASEMEN

NOTE: All caps denotes fielding-percentage leader based on 70 games for catchers, 93 for all other non-pitchers and 112 innings for pitchers. *Throws lefthanded.

Player, Team	Pct.	G	PO	A	E	TC	DP
Aceves, Jonathan, Birmingham	.984	11	57	4	1	62	7
Alvarez, Nicolas, Jacksonville	1.000	7	36	1	0	37	5
Anderson, Bryan, Chattanooga	.986	30	200	14	3	217	17
Arteaga, Joshua, Mississippi	1.000	1	4	0	0	4	0
Ashby, Christopher, Carolina	1.000	1	1	0	0	1	0
Bankston, Wesley, Montgomery	.991	68	602	32	6	640	51
Bass, Christopher, Carolina	.997	38	332	13	1	346	24
Bell, Rick, Chattanooga	1.000	3	16	0	0	16	6
Bozied, Robert, Mobile	.988	9	75	10	1	86	4
Carter, William, Tennessee *	.979	22	170	17	4	191	21
Cota, Jesus, Tennessee	.989	89	737	69	9	815	73
Craig, Matthew, West Tenn	.986	49	393	33	6	432	41
D'Antona, James, Tennessee	.991	14	109	4	1	114	11
Fields, Joshua, Birmingham	.875	2	6	1	1	8	1
Franco, Iker, Mississippi	...	1	0	0	0	0	0
Gemoll, Brandon, Huntsville *	.983	109	873	62	16	951	76
Gerber, Joseph, Mobile *	.988	69	591	66	8	665	73
Gutierrez, Jesse, Chattanooga	.986	26	197	22	3	222	26
Haley, Adam, Tennessee	1.000	1	2	0	0	2	0
Hanigan, Ryan, Chattanooga	.998	47	410	25	1	436	33
Hill, Jason, Carolina	.986	34	258	17	4	279	20
Hoffpauir, James, West Tenn *	1.000	3	28	0	0	28	3
Isenia, Chairon, Montgomery	1.000	10	64	4	0	68	4
Langill, Eric, Jacksonville	1.000	4	11	0	0	11	1
LaRoche, Andy, Jacksonville	...	1	0	0	0	0	0
LONEY, JAMES, Jacksonville *	.993	136	948	92	7	1047	61
Martinez, Gabriel, Montgomery	.993	49	414	15	3	432	47
McAnulty, Paul, Mobile	1.000	9	60	6	0	66	6
McGehee, Casey, West Tenn	1.000	9	66	7	0	73	6
Michaelis, Derek, Jacksonville *	1.000	4	29	3	0	32	4
Montero, Miguel, Tennessee	...	1	0	0	0	0	0
Moore, Robert, Carolina	1.000	22	164	10	0	174	6
Morgan, Matthew, Tennessee	.984	9	56	6	1	63	7
Nichols, Leslie, Chattanooga	.990	23	193	9	2	204	16
Niles, Frank, Carolina	1.000	4	26	1	0	27	0
Nixon, Michael, Jacksonville	1.000	1	2	0	0	2	0
O'Toole, Paul, West Tenn	.980	6	46	2	1	49	9
Peterson, Brian, Chattanooga	1.000	2	9	0	0	9	0
Raburn, John, Montgomery	1.000	1	9	1	0	10	0
Reece, Eric, Montgomery	1.000	6	43	2	0	45	4
Reyes, Jose, West Tenn.	1.000	2	17	1	0	18	1
Richardson, Michael, Mobile	1.000	1	2	0	0	2	0

Player, Team	Pct.	G	PO	A	E	TC	DP
Rogowski, Casey, Birmingham *	.991	133	1126	87	11	1224	133
Rosamond, George, Mississippi	.984	42	336	26	6	368	36
Rottino, Vincent, Huntsville	.995	21	170	11	1	182	12
Sain, Gregory, Mobile	.992	52	436	39	4	479	58
Sears, Todd, Carolina	.996	25	218	19	1	238	23
Sing, Brandon, West Tenn	.989	84	606	34	7	647	46
Sitzman, James, Montgomery *	1.000	1	1	0	0	1	0
Smitherman, Stephen, Chattanooga	.966	20	163	7	6	176	16
Thorman, Scott, Mississippi	.990	90	830	47	9	886	82
Timmons, Wesley, Mississippi	1.000	1	1	0	0	1	0
Trzesniak, Nicholas, Mobile	1.000	4	21	4	0	25	2
Tucker, Michael, Carolina	.992	32	235	22	2	259	28
Uggla, Daniel, Tennessee	.988	10	81	3	1	85	9
Vanden Berg, John, Huntsville	.991	12	110	6	1	117	7
Varner, Gary, Tennessee	1.000	1	3	0	0	3	0
Washington, Rico, Montgomery	.989	11	88	5	1	94	8
Williams, Marland, Tennessee	1.000	1	3	0	0	3	0

SECOND BASEMEN

Player, Team	Pct.	G	PO	A	E	TC	DP
Abreu, Etanislao, Jacksonville	.954	21	47	36	4	87	7
Acosta, Christian, Birmingham	1.000	1	0	1	0	1	0
Anderson, Bryan, Chattanooga	.970	12	11	21	1	33	5
Andino, Robert, Carolina	1.000	1	3	3	0	6	0
Arteaga, Joshua, Mississippi	.960	8	12	12	1	25	0
Baker, Casey, Mobile	.967	51	102	135	8	245	38
Barnwell, Christopher, Huntsville	.952	5	11	9	1	21	3
Brown, Nebasett, Tennessee	.950	35	60	92	8	160	20
Burgamy, Brian, Mobile	.889	2	2	6	1	9	2
Butler, Brent, Montgomery	1.000	1	6	1	0	7	2
Cameron, Troy, Mobile	.900	3	2	7	1	10	0
Castro, Juan, Huntsville	1.000	4	7	12	0	19	1
Clements, Jason, Mobile	.945	40	63	91	9	163	15
Cortez, Fernando, Montgomery	.966	36	64	108	6	178	18
Crabbe, Callix, Huntsville	.974	107	227	288	14	529	56
Creighton, Matt, West Tenn	.938	3	8	7	1	16	3
Donovan, Todd, Jacksonville	1.000	1	0	1	0	1	0
Freel, Ryan, Chattanooga	1.000	2	2	4	0	6	2
Frese, Nate, West Tenn	1.000	2	4	7	0	11	2
Garcia, Sergio, Jacksonville	.947	16	21	33	3	57	6
Gonzalez, Adolfo, Jacksonville	.952	10	21	19	2	42	2
Gonzalez, Angel, Jacksonville	.988	48	118	122	3	243	48
Gray, Antoin, Birmingham	.936	55	82	137	15	234	33
Haggerty, Cory, Birmingham	.949	20	29	45	4	78	12
Haley, Adam, Tennessee	.983	12	23	36	1	60	12
Hopper, Norris, Chattanooga	1.000	1	0	1	0	1	0
Howard, Kevin, Chattanooga	.960	119	239	332	24	595	84
Jimenez, D'Angelo, Chattanooga	1.000	9	19	23	0	42	8
Johnson, Elliot, Montgomery	.956	61	121	162	13	296	43
Lewis, Richard, West Tenn	.988	20	36	45	1	82	15
Martinez, Gabriel, Montgomery	1.000	1	1	2	0	3	1
McGehee, Casey, West Tenn	1.000	2	1	5	0	6	0
Merrill, Ronald, Mobile	.978	32	56	126	4	186	23
Mitchell, Russell, Jacksonville	...	1	0	0	0	0	0
Moore, Robert, Carolina	.952	27	52	67	6	125	15
Morgan, Matthew, Tennessee	1.000	5	10	11	0	21	5
Nicholson, David, Jacksonville	1.000	7	6	8	0	14	2
Nicholson, Thomas, Birmingham	1.000	4	5	15	0	20	4
Niles, Frank, Carolina	.984	19	26	37	1	64	7
Patterson, Eric, West Tenn	.977	9	19	23	1	43	3
Prado, Martin, Mississippi	.989	39	80	105	2	187	30
Raburn, John, Montgomery	.959	38	66	99	7	172	23
Ramos, Peeter, Mobile	.976	27	49	74	3	126	21
Renick, Joshua, Chattanooga	.917	6	4	7	1	12	0

CLASS AA Southern League

Player, Team	Pct.	G	PO	A	E	TC	DP
Reyes, Guillermo, Birmingham	.990	24	36	61	1	98	14
Richardson, Michael, Mobile	1.000	1	1	3	0	4	0
Rodriguez, Guilder, Huntsville	.963	30	67	91	6	164	17
Rohan, James, Jacksonville	.941	5	10	6	1	17	3
RUNDGREN, REX, Carolina	.974	102	185	265	12	462	62
Schuerholz, Jonathan, Mississippi	.974	81	146	259	11	416	60
Sisk, Aaron, West Tenn	.989	20	34	57	1	92	11
Soto, Jesus, Jacksonville	.750	1	3	3	2	8	2
Spearman, Jemel, West Tenn	1.000	11	15	15	0	30	2
Theriot, Ryan, West Tenn	.982	86	178	202	7	387	47
Tucker, Michael, Carolina	1.000	3	0	2	0	2	0
Uggla, Daniel, Tennessee	.959	97	192	232	18	442	62
Velazquez, Juan, Mississippi	1.000	14	19	38	0	57	9
Vick, Hunter, Montgomery	1.000	1	1	1	0	2	0
Washington, Rico, Montgomery	1.000	4	12	13	0	25	3
Young, Delwyn, Jacksonville	.965	90	139	189	12	340	26

THIRD BASEMEN

Player, Team	Pct.	G	PO	A	E	TC	DP
Alvarez, Nicolas, Jacksonville	.714	8	4	6	4	14	0
Anderson, Bryan, Chattanooga	.950	16	7	31	2	40	3
Arteaga, Joshua, Mississippi	.909	11	6	14	2	22	2
Bannon, Jeff, Chattanooga	.907	55	29	118	15	162	9
Barnwell, Christopher, Huntsville	1.000	3	2	3	0	5	0
Bass, Christopher, Carolina	.908	47	29	80	11	120	8
Bell, Rick, Chattanooga	1.000	25	14	39	0	53	3
Cameron, Troy, Mobile	1.000	1	0	1	0	1	0
Castro, Juan, Huntsville	.857	13	12	30	7	49	2
Clements, Jason, Mobile	.929	3	4	9	1	14	2
Craig, Matthew, West Tenn	.950	24	17	40	3	60	3
Cruz, Luis, Mobile	1.000	1	2	5	0	7	2
D'Antona, James, Tennessee	.933	100	65	172	17	254	17
DeMarco, Mathew, Carolina	.938	7	6	9	1	16	0
Fields, Joshua, Birmingham	.933	133	95	239	24	358	22
Freel, Ryan, Chattanooga	1.000	1	0	3	0	3	0
Garcia, Sergio, Jacksonville	.833	10	1	4	1	6	0
Gil, Jerry, Tennessee	1.000	2	0	3	0	3	0
Gonzalez, Angel, Birmingham	1.000	5	3	5	0	8	1
Guzman, Joel, Jacksonville	.889	21	10	22	4	36	3
Haley, Adam, Tennessee	.951	31	28	49	4	81	8
Heether, Adam, Huntsville	.840	13	17	25	8	50	5
Hill, Jason, Carolina	1.000	2	0	2	0	2	0
Howard, Kevin, Chattanooga	...	1	0	0	0	0	0
LaRoche, Andy, Jacksonville	.941	63	43	85	8	136	11
Lewis, Richard, West Tenn	.800	2	0	4	1	5	0
Martinez, Gabriel, Montgomery	.943	15	9	24	2	35	1
MCGEHEE, CASEY, West Tenn	.953	110	67	199	13	279	27
Mitchell, Russell, Jacksonville	1.000	2	0	1	0	1	1
Moore, Robert, Carolina	.833	14	2	18	4	24	0
Morgan, Matthew, Tennessee	.955	12	8	13	1	22	3
Niles, Frank, Carolina	.984	63	40	143	3	186	16
Patchett, Gary, Chattanooga	.933	11	8	20	2	30	1
Perez, Eduardo, Jacksonville	1.000	2	1	4	0	5	0
Perez, Tomas, Chattanooga	.899	34	19	52	8	79	2
Raburn, John, Montgomery	.903	34	28	56	9	93	8
Reece, Eric, Montgomery	1.000	1	3	2	0	5	0
Renick, Joshua, Chattanooga	1.000	3	0	3	0	3	0
Reyes, Guillermo, Birmingham	1.000	11	6	18	0	24	2
Rohan, James, Jacksonville	.833	6	2	3	1	6	1
Rottino, Vincent, Huntsville	.947	63	42	119	9	170	5
Sisk, Aaron, West Tenn	.957	8	6	16	1	23	2
Smith, Corey, Mobile	.903	134	106	221	35	362	26
Spearman, Jemel, West Tenn	1.000	1	0	5	0	5	0
Sprout, Brian, Jacksonville	.942	52	22	75	6	103	6
Theriot, Ryan, West Tenn	1.000	5	0	7	0	7	0
Timmons, Wesley, Mississippi	.949	113	88	228	17	333	19
Tucker, Michael, Carolina	.948	22	11	44	3	58	1
Uggla, Daniel, Tennessee	.971	11	10	23	1	34	1
Velazquez, Juan, Mississippi	.889	17	7	25	4	36	2
Washington, Rico, Montgomery	.946	96	57	172	13	242	18
Young, Delwyn, Jacksonville	1.000	1	0	1	0	1	0
Zuniga, Jose, Huntsville	.924	51	25	121	12	158	10

SHORTSTOPS

Player, Team	Pct.	G	PO	A	E	TC	DP
Abreu, Etanislao, Jacksonville	1.000	4	5	4	0	9	2
Anderson, Bryan, Chattanooga	1.000	13	18	20	0	38	6
Andino, Robert, Carolina	.951	126	150	378	27	555	70
Arteaga, Joshua, Mississippi	1.000	9	5	19	0	24	3
Baker, Casey, Mobile	1.000	3	3	6	0	9	1

Player, Team	Pct.	G	PO	A	E	TC	DP
Bannon, Jeff, Chattanooga	.976	38	57	105	4	166	25
Butler, Brent, Montgomery	.949	29	43	88	7	138	18
Castro, Juan, Huntsville	.857	1	0	6	1	7	1
Clements, Jason, Mobile	.875	3	4	3	1	8	0
Coats, Buck, West Tenn	.913	94	112	236	33	381	40
Cortez, Fernando, Montgomery	.987	17	23	52	1	76	9
Cruz, Enrique, Huntsville	.939	135	188	386	37	611	63
Cruz, Luis, Mobile	.960	42	59	110	7	176	32
Drew, Stephen, Tennessee	.935	27	36	80	8	124	16
Frese, Nate, West Tenn	.909	6	7	13	2	22	2
Garcia, Jesse, Mobile	.923	6	12	24	3	39	4
Garcia, Sergio, Jacksonville	.985	38	40	90	2	132	8
Garciaparra, Nomar, West Tenn	.933	4	7	7	1	15	4
Gil, Jerry, Tennessee	.963	52	76	160	9	245	28
Gonzalez, Adolfo, Jacksonville	.667	1	1	1	1	3	0
Gonzalez, Angel, Birmingham	.926	61	91	170	21	282	40
Guzman, Joel, Jacksonville	.934	99	116	238	25	379	35
Haley, Adam, Tennessee	.946	56	94	153	14	261	35
HERNANDEZ, LUIS, Mississippi	.961	117	176	337	21	534	77
Jimenez, D'Angelo, Chattanooga	.976	73	107	215	8	330	43
Johnson, Elliot, Montgomery	.333	1	1	0	2	3	0
Lopez, Pedro, Birmingham	.970	68	106	216	10	332	59
Maniscalco, Matthew, Montgomery	.983	71	122	218	6	346	41
Martinez, Gabriel, Montgomery	1.000	1	0	2	0	2	0
Merrill, Ronald, Mobile	.976	93	122	249	9	380	60
Nicholson, David, Jacksonville	.933	6	3	11	1	15	1
Niles, Frank, Carolina	.900	2	5	4	1	10	1
Patchett, Gary, Chattanooga	.982	17	16	39	1	56	6
Perez, Tomas, Chattanooga	.857	6	7	5	2	14	2
Raburn, John, Montgomery	.925	22	26	60	7	93	14
Ramos, Peeter, Mobile	1.000	3	7	7	0	14	2
Reyes, Guillermo, Birmingham	.948	13	16	39	3	58	3
Rodriguez, Guilder, Huntsville	.938	5	7	8	1	16	1
Rohan, James, Jacksonville	.974	8	14	23	1	38	5
Rundgren, Rex, Carolina	.972	10	9	26	1	36	7
Sisk, Aaron, West Tenn	.978	13	13	31	1	45	6
Theriot, Ryan, West Tenn	.953	36	38	83	6	127	21
Uggla, Daniel, Tennessee	.896	10	15	28	5	48	5
Velazquez, Juan, Mississippi	.946	14	17	36	3	56	8
Vick, Hunter, Montgomery	...	1	0	0	0	0	0

OUTFIELDERS

Player, Team	Pct.	G	PO	A	E	TC	DP
Abercrombie, Reginald, Carolina	.966	46	112	2	4	118	0
Alvarez, Nicolas, Jacksonville	1.000	36	61	4	0	65	0
Anderson, Bryan, Chattanooga	1.000	9	7	0	0	7	0
Asadoorian, Eric, Chattanooga	.985	78	187	7	3	197	5
Avlas, Aaron, Tennessee	...	1	0	0	0	0	0
Bacon, Dwaine, West Tenn	.993	79	147	3	1	151	0
Baker, Casey, Mobile	.981	35	49	2	1	52	1
Baker, Steve, Mobile	.976	65	119	2	3	124	0
Ball, Jarred, Tennessee	.979	119	225	10	5	240	1
Bankston, Wesley, Montgomery	1.000	2	1	0	0	1	0
Barnes, John, Mississippi	1.000	2	5	1	0	6	0
Bibbs, Kennard, Huntsville *	.983	101	171	6	3	180	4
Blakely, Darren, Birmingham	.992	71	123	6	1	130	1
Blanco, Gregor, Mississippi *	.969	112	234	14	8	256	5
Burgamy, Brian, Mobile	.985	47	65	1	1	67	1
Burrus, Josh, Mississippi	1.000	43	78	0	0	78	1
Cameron, Troy, Mobile	1.000	3	4	0	0	4	0
Carter, William, Tennessee *	1.000	5	3	1	0	4	0
Castro, Juan, Huntsville	1.000	6	16	0	0	16	0
Clements, Jason, Mobile	.833	8	4	1	1	6	0
Coats, Buck, West Tenn	.984	24	60	3	1	64	1
Creighton, Matt, West Tenn	.939	23	30	1	2	33	0
Cruz, Nelson, Huntsville	.967	66	109	8	4	121	1
Curry, Michael, Montgomery	.988	47	79	2	1	82	1
Delucchi, Dustin, Mobile *	1.000	32	61	2	0	63	0
Denorfia, Chris, Chattanooga	.979	44	92	3	2	97	1
Donovan, Todd, Jacksonville	.990	117	287	4	3	294	1
Dukes, Elijah, Montgomery	.964	106	208	8	8	224	1
Duncan, Jeff, Mobile *	1.000	20	29	0	0	29	0
Duran, Carlos, Mississippi *	.985	41	64	2	1	67	0
Ezi, Travis, Huntsville *	1.000	11	17	0	0	17	0
Fernandez, Alexander, Chattanooga *	.983	36	53	5	1	59	0
Francoeur, Jeff, Mississippi	.981	83	144	10	3	157	0
Freel, Ryan, Chattanooga	1.000	2	6	0	0	6	0
Gann, James, Montgomery	1.000	5	5	0	0	5	0
Garcia, Sergio, Jacksonville	.972	16	30	5	1	36	2
Gemoll, Brandon, Huntsville *	1.000	1	1	0	0	1	0

(Fielding — continued)

Player, Team	Pct.	G	PO	A	E	TC	DP
Gerber, Joseph, Mobile *	1.000	2	1	1	0	2	0
Gonzalez, Adolfo, Jacksonville	1.000	1	3	0	0	3	0
Gonzalez, Luis, Jacksonville *	...	1	0	0	0	0	0
Greenberg, Adam, West Tenn *	.988	90	164	3	2	169	0
Gwynn, Anthony, Huntsville	.984	133	294	8	5	307	3
Habel, Joshua, Huntsville *	...	1	0	0	0	0	0
Haggerty, Cory, Birmingham	1.000	1	2	0	0	2	0
Haley, Adam, Tennessee	1.000	4	1	0	0	1	0
Hermida, Jeremy, Carolina	.982	114	212	6	4	222	3
Hoffpauir, James, West Tenn *	.750	3	3	0	1	4	0
Hopper, Norris, Chattanooga	.973	102	199	15	6	220	3
Jones, Kennard, Mobile *	.971	123	257	8	8	273	3
Joseph, Onil, Mississippi	.974	109	174	10	5	189	1
Loney, James, Jacksonville *	1.000	3	1	0	0	1	0
Martin, Russell, Jacksonville	...	1	0	0	0	0	0
Martinez, Gabriel, Montgomery	.972	27	31	4	1	36	1
Mateo, Luis, Montgomery	.958	77	108	7	5	120	1
McAnulty, Paul, Mobile	.962	71	117	8	5	130	1
MEADOWS, TYDUS, Jacksonville	.993	95	139	3	1	143	0
Michaelis, Derek, Jacksonville *	1.000	21	21	2	0	23	0
Molina, Angel, Carolina	1.000	10	16	0	0	16	0
Montanez, Luis, West Tenn	.988	45	75	7	1	83	1
Moore, Robert, Carolina	1.000	10	10	1	0	11	0
Moran, Javon, Chattanooga	1.000	20	49	5	0	54	3
Muniz, Juan Carlos, Carolina	.965	75	106	5	4	115	1
Murton, Matt, West Tenn	.971	77	130	5	4	139	2
Nelson, Brad, Huntsville	.971	53	99	3	3	105	0
Neuberger, Scott, Montgomery	.981	31	45	6	1	52	1
Nicholson, David, Jacksonville	1.000	2	1	0	0	1	0
Nixon, Michael, Jacksonville	1.000	1	1	0	0	1	0
O'Keefe, Michael, Mississippi *	.857	3	6	0	1	7	0
O'Toole, Paul, West Tenn	1.000	1	2	0	0	2	0
Owens, Jerry, Birmingham *	.987	120	209	11	3	223	0
Perez, Tomas, Chattanooga	...	1	0	0	0	0	0
Pie, Felix, West Tenn *	.965	58	105	5	4	114	1
Pratt, Andy, Huntsville *	...	1	0	0	0	0	0
Pridie, Jason, Montgomery	.982	27	55	0	1	56	0
Raburn, John, Montgomery	.870	10	18	2	3	23	1
Reed, Eric, Carolina *	.994	67	150	4	1	155	1
Richardson, Michael, Mobile	1.000	36	43	3	0	46	1
Rogowski, Casey, Birmingham *	1.000	1	1	0	0	1	0
Rosamond, George, Mississippi	.927	20	36	2	3	41	0
Rottino, Vincent, Huntsville	.900	9	17	1	2	20	0
Ruggiano, Justin, Jacksonville	.978	49	84	3	2	89	1
Ruiz, Alvaro, Chattanooga	.984	69	115	6	2	123	1
Shanks, James, Carolina	.978	95	128	4	3	135	1
Sing, Brandon, West Tenn	.932	45	63	5	5	73	3
Sisk, Aaron, West Tenn	1.000	1	2	0	0	2	0
Sitzman, James, Montgomery *	.979	26	46	0	1	47	0
Smitherman, Stephen, Chattanooga	.956	65	82	5	4	91	0
Sprout, Brian, Jacksonville	1.000	10	10	0	0	10	0
Sweeney, Ryan, Birmingham *	.987	107	212	12	3	227	1
Van Iderstine, Ben, Huntsville *	.978	60	84	3	2	89	1
Varner, Gary, Tennessee	1.000	93	137	9	0	146	1
Velazquez, Juan, Mississippi	1.000	1	5	0	0	5	0
Weber, Jonathan, Jacksonville *	.972	115	226	19	7	252	7
Weston, Gordon, West Tenn *	1.000	4	11	0	0	11	0
Williams, Marland, Tennessee	.979	104	221	10	5	236	5
Young, Christopher, Birmingham	.990	123	289	6	3	298	2
Young, Delmon, Montgomery	.952	78	135	5	7	147	0
Young, Delwyn, Jacksonville	1.000	1	1	0	0	1	0
Zeringue, Jonathan, Tennessee	.955	119	239	18	12	269	4

CATCHERS

Player, Team	Pct.	G	PO	A	E	TC	DP
Aceves, Jonathan, Birmingham	.994	51	302	25	2	329	2
Anderson, Dennis, Carolina	.984	53	345	23	6	374	3
Ashby, Christopher, Carolina	1.000	22	176	9	0	185	1
Avlas, Aaron, Tennessee	.976	35	218	23	6	247	3
Bernard, Miguel, Mississippi	.965	20	150	15	6	171	1
Carlin, Luke, Mobile	.984	58	396	46	7	449	8
Dirosa, Michael, Tennessee	.990	27	175	19	2	196	1
Franco, Iker, Mississippi	.980	43	318	29	7	354	1
Garcia, Cipriano, Birmingham	1.000	3	7	0	0	7	0
Hanigan, Ryan, Chattanooga	.986	46	314	32	5	351	4
Hill, Jason, Carolina	.990	71	440	36	5	481	3
Isenia, Chairon, Montgomery	.981	57	378	30	8	416	2
Kopitzke, Casey, West Tenn	.998	52	379	29	1	409	6
Kottaras, George, Mobile	.995	25	161	21	1	183	0
Langill, Eric, Jacksonville	.985	27	187	7	3	197	1

(Catchers — continued)

Player, Team	Pct.	G	PO	A	E	TC	DP
Martin, Russell, Jacksonville	.989	117	960	90	12	1062	4
McCann, Brian, Mississippi	.997	45	300	31	1	332	3
Medero-Stullz, Carlos, Jacksonville	...	1	0	0	0	0	0
Merritt, Graig, Montgomery	1.000	20	116	18	0	134	2
Montero, Miguel, Tennessee	.983	29	211	18	4	233	3
Morgan, Matthew, Tennessee	.990	59	371	43	4	418	6
Nixon, Michael, Jacksonville	.906	4	25	4	3	32	0
O'Toole, Paul, West Tenn	.975	4	35	4	1	40	1
Peterson, Brian, Chattanooga	.991	92	682	82	7	771	10
Purdom, John, Chattanooga	1.000	3	7	1	0	8	0
Pyzik, Steven, Mississippi	1.000	2	11	1	0	12	0
Reece, Eric, Montgomery	1.000	1	1	1	0	2	0
REYES, JOSE, West Tenn	.994	91	712	75	5	792	13
Richardson, Michael, Mobile	1.000	3	7	0	0	7	0
Riggans, Shawn, Montgomery	.983	69	481	42	9	532	7
Rosa, Wally, Birmingham	.965	10	51	4	2	57	0
Rottino, Vincent, Huntsville	.995	22	176	10	1	187	2
Serrano, Raymond, Mississippi	.983	26	159	11	3	173	0
Stanfield, James, Huntsville	1.000	1	7	1	0	8	0
Stewart, Chris, Birmingham	.988	90	601	55	8	664	8
Trzesniak, Nicholas, Mobile	.990	60	437	46	5	488	5
Vanden Berg, John, Huntsville	.992	48	336	27	3	366	3
Winchester, Jeffrey, Huntsville	.993	72	497	52	4	553	3

PITCHERS

Player, Team	Pct.	G	PO	A	E	TC	DP
Aardsma, David, West Tenn	1.000	33	4	7	0	11	0
Abraham, Paul, Mobile	.789	30	5	10	4	19	0
Aguilar, Raymond, Carolina *	.929	13	3	10	1	14	0
Almanza, Armando, Tennessee *	1.000	6	0	1	0	1	0
Alvarez, Carlos, Jacksonville *	1.000	25	2	9	0	11	1
Andrew, Jason, Chattanooga	.957	48	5	17	1	23	1
Atlee, Thomas, West Tenn	1.000	29	1	1	0	2	0
Autrey, Jeffrey, Montgomery	.882	21	2	13	2	17	0
Baez, Federico, West Tenn	1.000	41	3	7	0	10	3
Baker, Ryan, Carolina	.900	25	4	5	1	10	1
Ballouli, Khalid, Huntsville	.857	24	7	11	3	21	0
Barreto, Joel, Chattanooga	1.000	3	1	0	0	1	0
Barry, Kevin, Mississippi	1.000	3	1	1	0	2	0
Bartlett, Richard, Jacksonville	1.000	35	3	7	0	10	0
Basham, Robert, Chattanooga	1.000	10	2	7	0	9	0
Basner, Ryan, Mississippi	.810	35	3	14	4	21	0
Bass, Adam, Tennessee	.939	27	13	18	2	33	0
Bauer, Peter, Carolina	1.000	1	0	3	0	3	0
Bazardo, Yorman, Carolina	.972	19	11	24	1	36	1
Bentz, Chad, Carolina *	1.000	7	0	1	0	1	0
Biggs, Billy, Tennessee	.667	9	2	0	1	3	0
Billingsley, Chad, Jacksonville	.966	28	13	15	1	29	2
Bobbitt, Seth, Mississippi	1.000	2	0	2	0	2	0
Bostick II, Adam, Carolina *	.917	9	2	9	1	12	0
Bott, Glenn, Jacksonville *	.857	25	3	3	1	7	0
Boyer, Blaine, Mississippi	.929	14	2	11	1	14	2
Bradley, David, Huntsville	.824	35	1	13	3	17	1
Brazelton, Dewon, Montgomery	...	1	0	0	0	0	0
Breslow, Craig, Mobile *	1.000	40	2	13	0	15	0
Broxton, Jonathan, Jacksonville	.957	33	8	14	1	23	1
Bruksch, Jeffrey, Chattanooga	.875	28	4	17	3	24	0
Bullard, James, Birmingham *	1.000	8	0	2	0	2	0
Bumstead, Michael, Mobile	.889	3	4	4	1	9	0
Bush, Paul, Mississippi	1.000	19	2	4	0	6	0
Caraccioli, Lance, Chattanooga *	1.000	15	3	12	0	15	0
Carrillo, Cesar, Mobile	1.000	5	1	8	0	9	0
Cassel, Joseph, Mobile	.765	24	4	9	4	17	0
Castro, Juan, Huntsville	...	2	0	0	0	0	0
Cave, Kevin, Carolina	1.000	37	3	9	0	12	0
Cherry, Rocky, West Tenn	1.000	3	0	4	0	4	0
Cherry, William, Chattanooga	1.000	7	2	1	0	3	0
Chick, Travis, Mobile-Chattanooga	.840	27	5	16	4	25	0
Chico, Matthew, Tennessee *	.917	10	0	11	1	12	1
Coenen, Matthew, Mississippi *	.969	19	5	26	1	32	1
Colome, Jesus, Montgomery	1.000	3	0	1	0	1	0
Colon, Roman, Mississippi	1.000	2	0	1	0	1	0
Connolly, Jonathan, West Tenn *	1.000	9	0	3	0	3	0
Costello, Ryan, Huntsville *	1.000	9	0	9	0	9	0
Cruz, Arian, Chattanooga *	.778	13	1	6	2	9	1
Curtis, Daniel, Mississippi	.500	9	0	2	2	4	0
Daigle, Casey, Tennessee	.933	58	7	7	1	15	0
Dannemiller, Beau, Jacksonville	.857	27	3	3	1	7	0
Deago, Roger, Mobile *	1.000	3	0	3	0	3	0
Dehart, James, Mississippi *	1.000	38	4	13	0	17	2

Player, Team	Pct.	G	PO	A	E	TC	DP
Demontel II, James, Carolina	...	2	0	0	0	0	0
Devine, Joey, Mississippi	1.000	18	0	4	0	4	0
DeWitt, Matt, Huntsville	.900	26	5	4	1	10	2
Diaz, Jose, Montgomery	1.000	18	4	4	0	8	2
Dizard, Fraser, Birmingham *	...	5	0	0	0	0	0
Dumatrait, Phillip, Chattanooga *	1.000	24	5	19	0	24	0
Eckenstahler, Eric, Chattanooga *	.889	35	2	6	1	9	0
Eveland, Dana, Huntsville *	1.000	18	7	14	0	21	1
Evert, Brett, Huntsville *	1.000	16	3	0	0	3	0
Ferreras, Yorkin, West Tenn *	1.000	30	0	3	0	3	0
Flannery, Michael, Carolina	1.000	31	4	1	0	5	0
Flinn, Christopher, Montgomery	.875	36	6	8	2	16	3
Flury, Patrick, Carolina	1.000	3	1	1	0	2	1
Ford, Matthew, Huntsville *	1.000	17	2	4	0	6	0
Frese, Nate, West Tenn	...	1	0	0	0	0	0
Fuell, Jerrod, Carolina	.917	39	3	8	1	12	1
Gamble, Jerome, Huntsville	1.000	31	4	6	0	10	0
Garcia, Gerardo, Montgomery	.500	2	0	1	1	2	0
Gardner, Richard, Chattanooga	.917	13	4	18	2	24	2
Glen, William, Birmingham	.750	11	2	1	1	4	0
Gonzalez, Alfredo, Jacksonville	1.000	5	0	2	0	2	0
Gonzalez, Enrique, Tennessee	.925	27	20	17	3	40	3
Gonzalez, Luis, Jacksonville	1.000	41	1	9	0	10	0
Goocher, Clint, Tennessee *	.922	27	16	31	4	51	1
Gwaltney, William, West Tenn	1.000	1	0	1	0	1	0
Habel, Joshua, Huntsville *	.870	21	7	13	3	23	1
Haeger, Charles, Birmingham	.950	13	4	15	1	20	1
Haigwood, Daniel, Huntsville *	1.000	11	2	11	0	13	0
Haines, Joseph, West Tenn	1.000	23	3	5	0	8	0
Haley, Adam, Tennessee	...	1	0	0	0	0	0
Hall, Josh, Chattanooga	.943	18	5	28	2	35	0
Hammel, Jason, Montgomery	1.000	12	5	9	0	14	2
Hanrahan, Joel, Jacksonville	.947	23	9	9	1	19	0
Hayhurst, Dirk, Mobile	...	1	0	0	0	0	0
Henderson, Brian, Montgomery *	.786	48	5	6	3	14	1
Hill, Rich, West Tenn *	.714	10	0	5	2	7	0
Hines, Carlos, Montgomery	1.000	22	2	5	0	7	0
Hoerman, Jared, West Tenn	1.000	2	0	2	0	2	0
Honel, Kristopher, Birmingham	.900	21	8	10	2	20	0
Hudson, Luke, Chattanooga	1.000	1	0	3	0	3	0
Hull, Eric, Jacksonville	.974	27	15	22	1	38	1
Jackson, Edwin, Jacksonville	.857	11	7	11	3	21	3
James, Chuck, Mississippi *	1.000	16	2	10	0	12	1
Jenks, Bobby, Birmingham	1.000	35	5	6	0	11	1
JOHNSON, JOSH, Carolina	1.000	26	12	28	0	40	5
Jones, Geoffrey, Mobile *	1.000	55	7	16	0	23	1
Juarez, William, Jacksonville	.926	38	8	17	2	27	1
Kensing, Logan, Carolina	.867	7	1	12	2	15	1
Kent, Steve, Mississippi *	.900	33	4	5	1	10	0
Kozlowski, Ben, Chattanooga *	.778	20	12	16	8	36	0
Kuo, Hong-Chih, Jacksonville *	.667	17	1	1	1	3	0
Lamura, William, Birmingham	.875	55	1	6	1	8	2
Lerew, Anthony, Mississippi	1.000	14	6	12	0	18	1
Lizarraga, Sergio, Tennessee	1.000	12	1	1	0	2	0
Lockwood, Brian, Montgomery	.952	24	1	19	1	21	0
Lockwood, Luke, Carolina *	.962	34	6	19	1	26	2
Lubisich, Nikolas, Birmingham *	.941	21	9	23	2	34	2
Lugo, Ruddy, Montgomery	.833	26	2	3	1	6	1
Machi, Jean, Montgomery	...	1	0	0	0	0	0
Magrane, James, Montgomery *	1.000	9	2	9	0	11	0
Mallett, Justin, Chattanooga	1.000	3	0	1	0	1	0
Malone, Corwin, Birmingham *	1.000	33	2	16	0	18	1
Marmol, Carlos, West Tenn	.957	14	6	16	1	23	2
Marshall, Sean, West Tenn *	1.000	4	0	2	0	2	0
Martinez, Carlos, Carolina	...	1	0	0	0	0	0
Mateo, Nathanel, Mobile	.923	48	2	10	1	13	0
McBride, Macay, Mississippi *	1.000	6	0	5	0	5	0
McGlinchy, Kevin, West Tenn	1.000	9	0	1	0	1	0
McNutt, Michael, Carolina	1.000	31	4	8	0	12	0
Meaux, Ryan, Birmingham-Mobile	1.000	53	6	12	0	18	2
Meyers, Mike, Huntsville	1.000	11	2	3	0	5	0
Miller, Greg, Jacksonville *	1.000	12	1	1	0	2	0
Miller, Ryan, Huntsville	...	4	0	0	0	0	0
Miner, Zachary, Mississippi	1.000	4	0	1	0	1	0
Molldrem, Craig, Carolina	...	1	0	0	0	0	0
Nelson, Bubba, Chattanooga	.455	42	1	4	6	11	0
Nichols, Leslie, Chattanooga	1.000	2	0	1	0	1	0
Niemann, Jeffrey, Montgomery	...	6	0	0	0	0	0
Nina, Elvin, Tennessee	.000	4	0	0	2	2	0
Nolasco, Ricky, West Tenn	.929	27	7	19	2	28	0
Ojeda, Alvis, Jacksonville	1.000	7	2	3	0	5	1

Player, Team	Pct.	G	PO	A	E	TC	DP
Olsen, Scott, Carolina *	1.000	14	3	7	0	10	0
Olson, Jason, Jacksonville	1.000	36	5	6	0	11	1
O'Malley, Ryan, West Tenn *	.947	31	8	10	1	19	4
Orenduff, Justin, Jacksonville	1.000	14	2	3	0	5	0
Ortiz, Javier, Birmingham	1.000	5	1	1	0	2	0
Orvella, Chad, Montgomery	1.000	16	0	1	0	1	0
Overman, Matthew, Carolina	1.000	6	1	1	0	2	0
Oyervidez, Jose, Mobile	.977	27	13	30	1	44	2
Pacheco, Enemencio, Birmingham	1.000	3	0	1	0	1	0
Parker, Joshua, Montgomery	1.000	43	3	13	0	16	0
Parra, Manuel, Huntsville *	.900	16	7	11	2	20	1
Peguero, Tony, Montgomery	.857	9	3	3	1	7	0
Pena, Tony, Tennessee	.939	25	8	23	2	33	1
Perez, Beltran, Jacksonville	.889	17	6	2	1	9	0
Phelps, Travis, Chattanooga	1.000	7	3	2	0	5	0
Phillips, Heath Michael, Birmingham *	.978	22	6	38	1	45	1
Phillips, Jason C., Montgomery	1.000	1	0	2	0	2	1
Pignatiello, Carmen, West Tenn *	.867	16	3	10	2	15	1
Pinto, Renyel, West Tenn *	1.000	22	3	21	0	24	1
Pollok, Dwayne, Birmingham	.905	56	4	15	2	21	2
Porzio, Mike, Mississippi *	1.000	14	0	3	0	3	0
Powell, Jay, Mississippi	.800	11	0	4	1	5	0
Pratt, Andy, Huntsville *	1.000	21	0	1	0	1	0
Raburn, John, Montgomery	...	2	0	0	0	0	0
Ramos, Victor, West Tenn	.875	19	0	7	1	8	0
Renick, Joshua, Chattanooga	...	1	0	0	0	0	0
Resop, Chris, Carolina	1.000	43	3	4	0	7	0
Reynoso, Paulino, Birmingham *	1.000	54	5	8	0	13	1
Richardson, Jason, Mississippi	1.000	17	1	5	0	6	0
Richardson, Michael, Mobile	1.000	3	1	0	0	1	0
Roberts, Ralph, Mississippi	...	1	0	0	0	0	0
Rodriguez, Jose, Carolina *	1.000	6	0	1	0	1	0
Rodriguez, Orlando, Jacksonville *	1.000	8	0	2	0	2	0
Russ, James, Carolina	...	1	0	0	0	0	0
Ryu, Jae-kuk, West Tenn.	.930	27	11	29	3	43	2
Saladin, Miguel, Chattanooga	1.000	10	1	4	0	5	0
Salas, Juan, Montgomery	.714	15	2	3	2	7	1
Salmon, Bradley, Chattanooga	1.000	38	6	15	0	21	0
Sarfate, Dennis, Huntsville	.792	24	2	17	5	24	0
Schmidt, Jeremy, Chattanooga	1.000	46	3	8	0	11	1
Schultz, Michael, Tennessee	.938	63	1	14	1	16	0
Searles, Jonathan, West Tenn	1.000	59	3	6	0	9	0
Seddon, Christopher, Montgomery *	.900	10	4	5	1	10	0
Shafer, David, Chattanooga	.933	34	3	11	1	15	0
Shields, James, Montgomery	.967	17	6	23	1	30	0
Shipman, Andrew, West Tenn	1.000	59	4	13	0	17	0
Sikaras, Panagiotis, Tennessee	1.000	44	5	8	0	13	0
Silva, Jesus, Tennessee	...	2	0	0	0	0	0
Simpson, Gerrit, Huntsville	1.000	13	2	5	0	7	0
Slaten, Douglas, Tennessee *	.882	58	6	9	2	17	1
Smith, Cam, Montgomery	1.000	20	0	2	0	2	0
Snare, Ryan, Mobile *	1.000	2	0	2	0	2	0
Sodowsky, Clint, Carolina	1.000	12	0	2	0	2	0
Spiehs, Randall, Mobile	1.000	10	3	2	0	5	0
Stamler, Keith, Huntsville	1.000	23	2	11	0	13	0
Steidlmayer, Luke, Mobile	.714	3	2	3	2	7	0
Steinborn, Christopher, Mobile *	1.000	3	0	1	0	1	0
Stetter, Mitchel, Huntsville *	1.000	32	3	9	0	12	0
Stockman, Phillip, Tennessee	1.000	47	1	5	0	6	0
Stokes, Brian, Montgomery	.909	16	7	13	2	22	2
Stults, Eric, Jacksonville *	.842	12	6	10	3	19	0
Switzer, Jon, Montgomery *	1.000	6	0	6	0	6	0
Taubenheim, Ty, Huntsville	.818	11	1	8	2	11	0
Tavares, Anderson, West Tenn.	1.000	1	0	1	0	1	1
Thayer, Dale, Mobile	1.000	56	7	8	0	15	1
Thompson, Chris, Tennessee.	...	3	0	0	0	0	0
Thompson, Derek, Jacksonville *	.833	8	4	6	2	12	0
Thompson, Michael, Mobile	.966	18	8	20	1	29	2
Thompson, Sean, Mobile *	.970	20	8	24	1	33	3
Thomson, John, Mississippi	1.000	1	3	0	0	3	0
Torres, Andy, Carolina	1.000	1	0	1	0	1	0
Tovar, Angel, Mobile	1.000	8	2	1	0	3	1
Tracey, Sean, Birmingham	.906	28	10	19	3	32	2
Tucker, Glenn, Mississippi	1.000	49	3	14	0	17	2
Tucker, Michael, Carolina	...	2	0	0	0	0	0
Tucker, Rusty, Mobile *	.875	52	1	6	1	8	1
Ulacia, Dennis, Birmingham *	1.000	2	0	2	0	2	0
Ungs, Nicholas, Carolina	.917	22	10	23	3	36	1
Valdes, Raul, West Tenn *	1.000	5	1	1	0	2	1
Valdez, Edward, Chattanooga	.846	12	4	7	2	13	2
Van Hekken, Andy, Mississippi-Chattanooga	1.000	6	1	6	0	7	1

Player, Team	Pct.	G	PO	A	E	TC	DP
Vargas, Jason, Carolina *	1.000	3	0	1	0	1	0
Vasquez, Jorge, Mississippi	1.000	29	3	4	0	7	0
Velazquez, Juan, Mississippi	...	2	0	0	0	0	0
Villacis, Eduardo, Birmingham	.952	9	7	13	1	21	0
Villanueva, Carlos, Huntsville	1.000	4	1	1	0	2	0
Villatoro, Wilmer, Mobile	1.000	10	3	0	0	3	0
Walton, Samuel, Montgomery *	1.000	13	0	3	0	3	0
Ward, Jeremy, Mississippi	1.000	12	0	2	0	2	1
Wassermann, Ehren, Birmingham	.750	14	1	2	1	4	0
Weber, Ben, Chattanooga	.667	9	2	2	2	6	0
Weber, Jonathan, Jacksonville *	...	1	0	0	0	0	0
Wechsler, Justin, Tennessee	1.000	42	0	11	0	11	0
Wells, Jared, Mobile	1.000	7	4	8	0	12	0
Wells, Randy, West Tenn	1.000	6	2	2	0	4	0
Whitaker, Brian, Mobile	.944	25	10	24	2	36	4
White, Sean, Mississippi	.909	8	3	7	1	11	0
White, William, Tennessee *	1.000	60	2	4	0	6	0

Player, Team	Pct.	G	PO	A	E	TC	DP
Winchester, Jeffrey, Huntsville	1.000	2	0	1	0	1	0
Wolf, Ross, Carolina	1.000	54	8	13	0	21	0
Wolfe, Brian, Huntsville	1.000	16	1	2	0	3	1
Woolard, Glenn, Huntsville	.963	29	8	18	1	27	0
Wright, Matthew, Mississippi	.938	17	5	10	1	16	0
Yofu, Tetsu, Birmingham	1.000	2	1	2	0	3	0
Yourkin, Matthew, Carolina *	1.000	11	0	2	0	2	0
Zumwalt, Sean, Huntsville	1.000	28	5	6	0	11	0

PITCHERS WITH TWO OR MORE TEAMS

Player, Team	Pct.	G	PO	A	E	TC	DP
Chick, Travis, Mobile	.867	19	3	10	2	15	0
Chick, Travis, Chattanooga	.800	8	2	6	2	10	0
Meaux, Ryan, Birmingham *	1.000	38	5	9	0	14	1
Meaux, Ryan, Mobile *	1.000	15	1	3	0	4	1
Van Hekken, Andy, Mississippi *	1.000	3	1	4	0	5	1
Van Hekken, Andy, Chattanooga *	1.000	3	0	2	0	2	0

LEAGUE CHAMPIONS

Year	Team	Pct.
1904—	Macon	.598
1905—	Macon	.625
1906—	Savannah	.637
1907—	Charleston	.620
1908—	Jacksonville	.694
1909—	Chattanooga*	.738
	Augusta	.702
1910—	Columbus	.588
1911—	Columbus*	.681
	Columbia	.710
1912—	Jacksonville*	.679
	Columbus	.632
1913—	Savannah	.754
	Savannah	.593
1914—	Savannah*	.667
	Albany	.650
1915—	Macon	.588
	Savannah	.686
1916—	Augusta*	.617
	Columbia	.631
1917—	Charleston	.741
	Columbia*	.667
1918—	Did not operate	
1919—	Columbia	.585
1920—	Columbia	.633
1921—	Columbia	.642
1922—	Charleston	.625
1923—	Charlotte*	.653
	Macon	.580
1924—	Augusta	.612
1925—	Spartanburg	.620
1926—	Greenville	.662
1927—	Greenville	.622
1928—	Asheville	.664
1929—	Asheville	.605
	Knoxville*	.634
1930—	Greenville*	.620
	Macon	.643
1931-35—Did not operate.		
1936—	Jacksonville	.652
	Columbus*	.650
1937—	Columbus	.572
	Savannah (3rd)†	.565
1938—	Savannah	.574
	Macon (2nd)†	.570
1939—	Columbus	.601
	Augusta (2nd)†	.597
1940—	Savannah	.627
	Columbus (2nd)†	.583
1941—	Macon	.643
	Columbia (2nd)†	.636
1942—	Charleston	.620
	Macon (2nd)†	.585
1943-45—Did not operate.		
1946—	Columbus	.568
	Augusta (4th)†	.547
1947—	Columbus	.575
	Savannah (2nd)†	.563
1948—	Charleston	.572
	Greenville (3rd)†	.549
1949—	Macon‡	.623

Year	Team	Pct.
1950—	Macon‡	.588
1951—	Montgomery	.607
1952—	Columbia	.649
	Montgomery (3rd)†	.558
1953—	Jacksonville	.679
	Savannah (2nd)†	.571
1954—	Jacksonville	.593
	Savannah (2nd)†	.571
1955—	Columbia	.636
	Augusta (3rd)†	.543
1956—	Jacksonville‡	.621
1957—	Augusta	.636
	Charlotte (2nd)†	.562
1958—	Augusta	.550
	Macon (3rd)†	.500
1959—	Knoxville	.557
	Gastonia (4th)†	.504
1960—	Columbia	.597
	Savannah (3rd)†	.561
1961—	Asheville	.635
1962—	Savannah	.662
	Macon (3rd)†	.576
1963—	Augusta*	.661
	Lynchburg	.662
1964—	Lynchburg	.579
1965—	Columbus	.572
1966—	Mobile	.629
1967—	Birmingham	.604
1968—	Asheville	.614
1969—	Charlotte	.579
1970—	Columbus	.569
1971—	Did not operate as league—clubs were members of Dixie Association.	
1972—	Asheville	.583
	Montgomery§	.561
1973—	Montgomery§	.580
	Jacksonville	.559
1974—	Jacksonville	.565
	Knoxville§	.533
1975—	Orlando	.587
	Montgomery§	.545
1976—	Montgomery∞	.591
	Orlando	.540
1977—	Montgomery∞	.628
	Jacksonville	.522
1978—	Knoxville∞	.611
	Savannah	.500
1979—	Columbus	.587
	Nashville∞	.576
1980—	Memphis	.576
	Charlotte∞	.500
1981—	Nashville	.566
	Orlando∞	.556
1982—	Jacksonville	.576
	Nashville∞	.535
1983—	Birmingham∞	.628
	Jacksonville	.531
1984—	Charlotte∞	.510
	Knoxville	.483
1985—	Charlotte	.545
	Huntsville∞	.542

Year	Team	Pct.
1986—	Huntsville	.553
	Columbus∞	.500
1987—	Charlotte	.586
	Birmingham∞	.476
1988—	Greenville	.604
	Chattanooga∞	.566
1989—	Birmingham∞	.615
	Greenville	.504
1990—	Orlando	.590
	Memphis∞	.507
1991—	Greenville	.611
	Orlando∞	.535
1992—	Greenville∞	.699
	Chattanooga	.629
1993—	Birmingham∞	.549
	Knoxville	.500
1994—	Huntsville∞	.587
	Carolina	.529
1995—	Carolina∞	.618
	Chattanooga	.580
1996—	Chattanooga∞	.579
	Jacksonville∞	.543
1997—	Huntsville	.554
	Greenville∞	.529
1998—	Mobile∞	.614
	Jacksonville	.614
1999—	West Tenn	.596
	Orlando∞	.507
2000—	West Tenn∞	.580
	Jacksonville	.493
2001—	Jacksonville▲	.597
	Huntsville▲	.543
2002—	Birmingham∞	.564
2003—	Carolina∞	.580
2004—	Mobile▲▲	.521
	Tennessee▲▲	.493
2005—	Jacksonville#	.564

*Won split season playoff. †Won four-club playoff. ‡Won championship and four-club playoff. §League was divided into Eastern and Western divisions; won playoff. ∞League was divided into Eastern and Western divisions and played split season; won playoff. ▲Were entering finals of four-team playoff and were declared co-champions when Professional Baseball declared a stoppage of play.▲▲Were entering finals of four-team playoff and were declared co-champions when the championship series was canceled because of the threat of a hurricane. #League was divided into Northern and Southern divisions and played split season; won playoff.

CLASS AA Southern League

– 475 –

TEXAS LEAGUE

LEAGUE OFFICE

President/treasurer
Tom Kayser

Address
2442 Facet Oak
San Antonio, TX 78232

Phone
210-545-5297

TEAMS

ARKANSAS TRAVELERS
Vice president/general manager
Bill Valentine
Manager
Tyrone Boykin
Ballpark (capacity, surface)
Ray Winder Field (6,086, grass)
Affiliation
Angels
Address
P.O. Box 55066
Little Rock, AR 72215
Phone
501-664-1555

CORPUS CHRISTI HOOKS
President/general manager
J.J. Gottsch
Manager
Dave Clark
Ballpark (capacity, surface)
Whataburger Field (7,500, grass)
Affiliation
Astros
Address
734 E. Port Ave.
Corpus Christi, TX 78401
Phone
361-866-8326

FRISCO ROUGHRIDERS
General manager/president
Mike McCall
Manager
Darryl Kennedy
Ballpark (capacity, surface)
Dr Pepper/Seven Up Ballpark (8,000, grass)
Affiliation
Rangers
Address
7300 Roughriders Trail
Frisco, TX 75034

Phone
972-731-9200

MIDLAND ROCKHOUNDS
General manager
Monty Hoppel
Manager
Von Hayes
Ballpark (capacity, surface)
City Bank Ballpark (5,000, grass)
Affiliation
Athletics
Address
5514 Champions Dr.
Midland, TX 79706
Phone
432-520-2255

SAN ANTONIO MISSIONS
President
Burl Yarbrough
Manager
Daren Brown
Ballpark (capacity, surface)
Nelson Wolff Stadium (6,300, grass)
Affiliation
Mariners
Address
5757 Highway 90 West
San Antonio, TX 78227
Phone
210-675-7275

SPRINGFIELD CARDINALS
General manager
Matt Gifford
Manager
Chris Maloney
Ballpark (capacity, surface)
Hammons Field (7,500, grass)
Affiliation
Cardinals

Address
955 E.Trafficway
Springfield, MO 65802
Phone
417-863-2143

TULSA DRILLERS
Executive v.p./general manager
Chuck Lamson
Manager
Stu Cole
Ballpark (capacity, surface)
Drillers Stadium (10,997, grass)
Affiliation
Rockies
Address
4802 E. 15th St.
Tulsa, OK 74112
Phone
918-744-5998

WICHITA WRANGLERS
General manager
Eric Edelstein
Manager
Frank White
Ballpark (capacity, surface)
Lawrence-Dumont Stadium (6,111, artificial infield, grass outfield)
Affiliation
Royals
Address
300 S. Sycamore
Wichita, KS 67213
Phone
316-267-3372

2005 FINAL STANDINGS

FIRST HALF

EAST DIVISION

Team	W	L	T	Pct.	GB
Tulsa Drillers	43	27	-	0.614	...
Springfield Cardinals	35	35	-	0.5	8
Wichita Wranglers	35	35	-	0.5	8
Arkansas Travelers	34	36	-	0.486	9

WEST DIVISION

Team	W	L	T	Pct.	GB
Midland RockHounds	39	31	-	0.557	...
San Antonio Missions	38	32	-	0.543	1
Frisco RoughRiders	29	41	-	0.414	10
Corpus Christi Hooks	27	43	-	0.386	12

SECOND HALF

EAST DIVISION

Team	W	L	T	Pct.	GB
Arkansas Travelers	37	33	-	0.529	...
Springfield Cardinals	35	35	-	0.5	2
Wichita Wranglers	33	37	-	0.471	4
Tulsa Drillers	32	38	-	0.457	5

WEST DIVISION

Team	W	L	T	Pct.	GB
Midland RockHounds	39	31	-	0.557	...
San Antonio Missions	38	32	-	0.543	1
Corpus Christi Hooks	37	33	-	0.529	2
Frisco RoughRiders	29	41	-	0.414	10

CLASS AA Texas League

COMPOSITE

CLUB (AFFILIATE), ABBREV	MID	SAN	TUL	ARK	SPR	WIC	COR	FRI	W	L	PCT	GB
Midland (Athletics), MID		16	12	9	6	6	15	14	78	62	.557	-
San Antonio (Mariners), SAN	12	...	7	10	8	7	18	14	76	64	.543	2.0
Tulsa (Rockies), TUL	2	7	...	16	14	16	8	12	75	65	.536	3.0
Arkansas (Angels), ARK	5	4	12	...	16	17	9	8	71	69	.507	7.0
Springfield (Cardinals), SPR	8	6	14	12	...	13	8	9	70	70	.500	8.0
Wichita (Royals), WIC	8	7	12	11	15	...	6	9	68	72	.486	10.0
Corpus Christi (Astros), COR	13	10	6	5	6	8	...	16	64	76	.457	14.0
Frisco (Rangers), FRI	14	14	2	6	5	5	12	...	58	82	.414	20.0

Major league affiliations in parentheses.

PLAYOFFS: Semifinals: Arkansas defeated Tulsa, three games to none, and Midland defeated San Antonio, three games to two. Finals: Midland defeated Arkansas, three games to one.

REGULAR-SEASON ATTENDANCE: Midland, 252,059. Tulsa, 335,018. Springfield, 526,630. Corpus Christi, 505,189. San Antonio, 272,922. Frisco 581,074. Arkansas, 196,366. Wichita, 165,077. All-Star Game (at Frisco), 10,398. League total, 2,834,335. Postseason (12 games), 30,451.

MANAGERS: Midland, Von Hayes. Tulsa, Tom Runnells. Springfield, Chris Maloney. Corpus Christi, Dave Clark. San Antonio, Dave Brundage. Frisco, Darryl Kennedy. Arkansas, Tom Gamboa. Wichita, Frank White.

ALL-STAR TEAM: 1B-Justin Huber, Wichita. 2B-Alberto Callaspo, Arkansas. 3B-Travis Hanson, Springfield. SS-Erick Aybar, Arkansas. OF-T.J. Bohn Jr., San Antonio. OF-Andre Ethier, Midland. OF-Tyler Minges, Springfield. C-Mike Napoli, Arkansas. DH-Jason Perry, Midland. UTIL-Mike Aviles, Wichita. P-Jonathan Asahina, Tulsa. P-Jason Hirsh, Corpus Christi. P-Randy Leek, Springfield. P-Bobby Livingston, San Antonio. P-Fernando Nieve, Corpus Christi. P-Sandy Nin, Tulsa. Player of the Year-Andre Ethier, Midland. Pitcher of the Year-Jason Hirsh, Corpus Christi. Manager of the Year-Von Hayes, Midland.

2005 BATTING

TEAM

Team	G	TPA	AB	R	H	TB	2B	3B	HR	RBI	SH	SF	HP	BB	IBB	SO	SB	CS	GDP	LOB	ShO	Avg.	OBP	Slg.
Arkansas	140	5254	4679	760	1314	2102	240	46	152	700	30	59	76	410	10	835	171	89	91	1879	6	.281	.345	.449
Midland	140	5488	4823	773	1353	2116	283	30	140	717	23	54	63	524	15	957	41	38	146	2209	4	.281	.355	.439
Wichita	140	5369	4791	744	1330	2068	252	39	136	698	37	45	55	439	23	755	99	45	121	2054	5	.278	.342	.432
Springfield	140	5417	4855	691	1318	2057	254	22	147	645	53	28	53	425	21	954	73	46	121	2054	4	.271	.335	.424
Frisco	141	5422	4875	632	1318	1869	228	31	87	574	38	47	53	408	12	891	129	61	116	2103	12	.270	.330	.383
San Antonio	140	5315	4840	630	1302	1951	232	39	113	576	47	31	50	347	23	1024	146	84	100	1945	5	.269	.323	.403
Corpus Christi	141	5307	4779	530	1228	1797	221	30	96	495	56	37	55	378	21	973	143	74	88	1984	11	.257	.316	.376
Tulsa	140	5299	4611	649	1148	1778	223	31	115	598	51	47	60	525	19	1054	101	60	93	2041	6	.249	.331	.386

INDIVIDUAL

TOP QUALIFIERS FOR BATTING CHAMPIONSHIP

Minimum 378 plate appearances. *Lefthanded batter. †Switch-hitter.

Player, Team	G	TPA	AB	R	H	TB	2B	3B	HR	RBI	SH	SF	HP	BB	IBB	SO	SB	CS	GDP	Avg.	OBP	Slg.
Huber, Justin, Wichita	88	396	335	68	115	191	22	3	16	74	0	5	5	51	2	70	7	3	11	.343	.432	.570
Minges, Tyler, Springfield	116	486	429	98	139	242	34	6	19	60	1	5	4	47	4	61	5	4	11	.324	.392	.564
Ethier, Andre, Midland *	131	572	505	104	161	251	30	3	18	80	0	8	11	48	4	93	1	4	18	.319	.385	.497
Stavisky, Brian, Midland *	135	586	510	84	161	242	36	6	11	88	0	4	3	69	1	84	0	5	23	.316	.398	.475
Arias, Joaquin, Frisco	120	526	499	65	157	211	23	8	5	56	3	6	1	17	1	46	20	10	5	.315	.335	.423
Pressley, Joshua, Wichita *	119	510	440	74	137	228	25	0	22	88	0	3	7	60	6	71	0	2	8	.311	.400	.518
Bohn, Thomas, San Antonio	113	486	438	67	135	205	30	2	12	57	7	1	5	35	1	96	27	9	8	.308	.365	.468
Willits, Reggie, Arkansas †	123	561	487	75	148	189	23	6	2	46	4	8	8	54	0	78	40	14	5	.304	.377	.388
Aybar, Erick, Arkansas †	134	590	535	101	162	238	29	10	9	54	4	8	14	29	0	51	49	23	13	.303	.350	.445
Yan, Ruddy, Frisco †	116	543	483	77	145	179	15	5	3	45	10	0	3	47	1	38	41	11	17	.300	.366	.371
Herr, Aaron, Springfield	112	456	426	56	127	212	20	1	21	81	4	1	10	15	2	108	2	3	12	.298	.336	.498
Callaspo, Alberto, Arkansas †	89	385	350	53	104	142	8	0	10	49	1	5	1	28	1	17	9	8	4	.297	.346	.406
Bubela, Jaime, San Antonio *	130	565	520	84	152	209	20	5	9	57	4	2	5	34	4	118	40	6	12	.292	.340	.402
Stanley, Stephen, Midland *	128	588	514	87	149	201	26	4	6	46	6	5	2	61	3	62	8	8	11	.290	.364	.391
Murphy, Thomas, Arkansas †	135	557	500	85	144	241	24	11	17	76	2	7	5	43	2	97	26	12	11	.288	.346	.482
Eylward, Thomas, Arkansas *	123	469	418	62	120	192	26	2	14	72	3	5	6	37	2	58	3	5	12	.287	.350	.459
Porter, Gregory, Arkansas *	129	480	448	63	128	193	24	4	11	56	0	6	4	22	2	84	2	6	6	.286	.321	.431
King, Brennan, Wichita	118	478	435	58	124	183	28	2	9	56	6	3	5	29	1	68	5	1	12	.285	.335	.421
Hanson, Travis, Springfield *	137	609	546	82	155	250	29	3	20	97	1	6	2	54	6	99	2	2	18	.284	.347	.458
Senreiso, Juan, Frisco	132	553	497	54	141	191	25	5	15	55	2	5	4	45	1	125	16	8	13	.284	.345	.384
Harris, Edward, San Antonio *	120	490	457	68	129	172	21	2	6	42	5	2	4	22	1	72	15	15	8	.282	.320	.376

DEPARTMENTAL LEADERS: G—Hanson, 137. AB—Hanson, 546. R—Ethier, 104. H—Aybar, 162. TB—Ethier, 251. 2B—Saccomanno and Stavisky, 36. 3B—Murphy, 11. HR—Napoli, 31. RBI—Napoli, 99. SH—Bernier and Guzman, 11. SF—Espy, 10. HP—Aybar, 14. BB—Napoli, 88. IBB—Slavik, 7. SO—Hoorelbeke, 156. SB—Anderson, 50. CS—Aybar, 23. GIDP—Stavisky, 23. OBP—Huber, .432. Slg.—Huber, .570.

ALL PLAYERS

*Lefthanded batter. †Switch-hitter.

Player, Team	G	TPA	AB	R	H	TB	2B	3B	HR	RBI	SH	SF	HP	BB	IBB	SO	SB	CS	GDP	Avg.	OBP	Slg.
Abruzzo, Jared, Frisco †	46	174	153	17	32	48	4	0	4	13	0	1	1	19	3	51	0	1	3	.209	.299	.314
Aldridge, Cory, Wichita *	98	423	388	66	105	214	20	4	27	77	1	3	2	29	3	94	9	4	5	.271	.322	.552
Allegra, Matthew, Midland	56	219	203	19	38	64	8	0	6	23	1	3	2	10	2	75	0	0	4	.187	.229	.315
Allen, Blake, Corpus Christi	3	1	0	0	0	0	0	0	0	0	1	0	0	0	0	0	0	0	0	...	...	...
Alvarez, Oscar, Wichita *	8	11	11	0	1	1	0	0	0	0	0	0	0	0	0	4	0	0	0	.091	.091	.091
Anderson, Joshua, Corpus Christi *	127	573	524	67	148	185	16	9	1	26	10	2	8	29	2	80	50	19	5	.282	.329	.353
Ankiel, Rick, Springfield *	34	146	136	18	33	70	7	0	10	30	0	0	0	10	0	29	0	0	4	.243	.295	.515
Arakawa, Yusuke, Tulsa	13	1	1	0	0	0	0	0	0	0	0	0	0	0	0	1	0	0	0	.000	.000	.000
Arias, Joaquin, Frisco	120	526	499	65	157	211	23	8	5	56	3	6	1	17	1	46	20	10	5	.315	.335	.423
Asahina, Jonathan, Tulsa †	13	25	24	0	3	3	0	0	0	1	0	0	1	0	1	7	0	0	0	.125	.160	.125

CLASS AA Texas League

Player, Team	G	TPA	AB	R	H	TB	2B	3B	HR	RBI	SH	SF	HP	BB	IBB	SO	SB	CS	GDP	Avg.	OBP	Slg.
Aspito, Jason, Arkansas *	52	176	157	25	42	74	8	0	8	32	0	3	4	12	0	28	1	2	1	.268	.330	.471
Aviles, Michael, Wichita	133	559	521	79	146	233	33	6	14	80	2	5	1	30	1	64	11	6	16	.280	.318	.447
Axelson, Joshua, Springfield	7	2	2	0	0	0	0	0	0	0	0	0	0	0	0	1	0	0	0	.000	.000	.000
Aybar, Erick, Arkansas †	134	590	535	101	162	238	29	10	9	54	4	8	14	29	0	51	49	23	13	.303	.350	.445
Bagwell, Jeff, Corpus Christi	3	12	9	1	2	2	0	0	0	1	0	0	0	3	0	3	0	0	1	.222	.417	.222
Barker, Sean, Tulsa	125	517	468	72	122	204	24	8	14	76	2	2	4	37	2	133	15	7	10	.261	.319	.436
Barmes, Clint, Tulsa	8	35	34	6	11	12	1	0	0	0	0	0	0	1	0	3	1	0	2	.324	.343	.353
Barton, Daric, Midland *	56	249	212	38	67	104	20	1	5	37	0	2	0	35	1	30	1	1	5	.316	.410	.491
Barzilla, Philip, Corpus Christi *	8	8	8	0	0	0	0	0	0	1	0	0	0	0	0	2	0	0	0	.000	.000	.000
Bauer, Peter, Corpus Christi *	2	4	2	1	0	0	0	0	0	0	0	0	0	2	0	1	0	0	0	.000	.500	.000
Beattie, Andrew, Midland †	22	100	82	13	24	39	6	0	3	17	1	0	0	17	0	22	1	0	2	.293	.414	.476
Beckstead, Jentry, Tulsa	19	3	3	0	0	0	0	0	0	0	0	0	0	0	0	1	0	0	0	.000	.000	.000
Benes, Alan, Springfield	2	0	0	0	0	0	0	0	0	0	0	0	0	0	...	0	0	0	0	...	...	...
Bernier, Douglas, Tulsa †	117	441	369	33	75	102	14	2	3	39	11	7	8	46	0	103	1	4	10	.203	.300	.276
Betancourt, Yuniesky, San Antonio	52	239	227	25	62	93	10	3	5	20	0	2	1	9	1	18	12	7	2	.273	.301	.410
Bevis, P. J., Tulsa	9	0	0	0	0	0	0	0	0	0	0	0	0	0	...	0	0	0	0	...	...	...
Blair, Thomas, Springfield	3	7	4	1	1	1	0	0	0	1	1	0	0	2	0	1	0	0	0	.250	.500	.250
Blakeley, Eric, San Antonio	20	59	57	1	12	13	1	0	0	4	1	0	0	1	0	7	1	1	1	.211	.224	.228
Blanco, Andres, Wichita †	9	41	37	5	7	10	0	0	1	5	1	0	0	3	0	7	0	0	0	.189	.250	.270
Bohn, Thomas, San Antonio	113	486	438	67	135	205	30	2	12	57	7	1	5	35	0	96	27	9	8	.308	.365	.468
Bolivar, Cesar, Springfield	121	466	425	60	115	173	22	3	10	62	1	2	4	34	3	81	17	8	16	.271	.329	.407
Boyd, Shaun, Springfield	127	562	502	82	138	185	22	2	7	60	9	3	3	45	0	97	14	8	7	.275	.336	.369
Brewer, Jace, Frisco	75	290	264	39	77	98	13	1	2	22	8	2	1	15	0	43	8	5	10	.292	.330	.371
Brown, Jeremy, Midland	115	462	394	65	103	192	27	1	20	72	0	5	11	52	0	88	0	0	17	.261	.359	.487
Bubela, Jaime, San Antonio *	130	565	520	84	152	209	20	5	9	57	4	2	5	34	4	118	40	6	12	.292	.340	.402
Butler, Billy, Wichita	29	119	112	14	35	59	9	0	5	19	0	0	0	7	3	18	0	0	3	.313	.353	.527
Caldera, Jose, Arkansas	4	1	1	3	1	1	0	0	0	0	0	0	0	0	0	1	0	0	0	1.000	1.000	1.000
Callaspo, Alberto, Arkansas †	89	385	350	53	104	142	8	0	10	49	1	5	1	28	1	17	9	8	4	.297	.346	.406
Cancel, Robinson, Springfield	65	265	230	31	66	103	13	0	8	26	1	4	1	29	2	36	4	2	4	.287	.364	.448
Cardona, Javier, Tulsa	13	48	44	1	8	10	2	0	0	4	1	0	0	3	0	9	0	0	1	.182	.234	.227
Casilla, Alexi, Arkansas †	7	21	19	4	4	4	0	0	0	4	0	0	0	2	0	3	1	1	0	.211	.286	.211
Castro, Ismael, San Antonio	115	444	421	41	111	164	24	1	9	51	3	5	3	12	1	43	6	9	13	.264	.286	.390
Cavazos, Andres, Springfield	8	0	0	0	0	0	0	0	0	0	0	0	0	0	...	0	0	0	0	...	...	...
Chavez, Jesse, Frisco	1	1	1	0	0	0	0	0	0	0	0	0	0	0	0	1	0	0	0	.000	.000	.000
Clements, Jason, Corpus Christi †	15	44	43	5	13	18	3	1	0	7	0	0	0	1	0	7	0	0	0	.302	.318	.419
Cleveland, Jeremy, Frisco	60	231	198	31	50	59	9	0	0	13	0	1	1	31	1	45	2	1	4	.253	.355	.298
Colamarino, Brant, Midland *	46	207	187	31	60	111	13	4	10	45	0	2	0	18	1	34	0	0	3	.321	.377	.594
Colina, Alvin, Tulsa	59	234	207	23	53	85	5	0	9	35	1	2	4	20	1	42	0	2	8	.256	.330	.411
Conrad, Brooks, Corpus Christi †	22	94	77	13	18	32	6	1	2	11	0	0	1	16	1	15	8	0	1	.234	.372	.416
Conway, Daniel, Tulsa	51	202	170	22	42	70	11	1	5	28	1	2	4	25	0	42	0	0	3	.247	.353	.412
Cook, Aaron, Tulsa	1	2	2	0	1	1	0	0	0	0	0	0	0	0	0	0	0	0	0	.500	.500	.500
Cook, Jeremy, Springfield	11	6	5	0	0	0	0	0	0	0	1	0	0	0	0	2	0	0	0	.000	.000	.000
Costa, Shane, Wichita *	75	316	277	37	78	124	18	2	8	43	1	6	8	24	2	23	5	1	10	.282	.349	.448
Cotton, Nathan, Springfield *	3	0	0	0	0	0	0	0	0	0	0	0	0	0	...	0	0	0	0	...	...	...
Coughlan, Cameron, Corpus Christi †	76	306	252	36	66	91	12	2	3	26	7	2	2	43	0	48	17	10	1	.262	.371	.361
Craig, Casey, San Antonio *	4	2	2	0	0	0	0	0	0	0	0	0	0	0	0	1	0	2	0	.000	.000	.000
Cresse, Bradley, Springfield	11	45	39	3	8	12	4	0	0	6	0	0	1	5	0	11	0	0	2	.205	.311	.308
Crockett, William, Tulsa	6	3	2	0	0	0	0	0	0	0	0	0	0	1	0	1	0	0	0	.000	.333	.000
Cummings, Jeremy, Springfield	4	9	8	2	2	4	0	1	0	1	1	0	0	0	0	3	0	0	1	.250	.250	.500
Czarniecki, Jordan, Tulsa	46	163	145	17	37	56	7	0	4	14	1	0	3	14	0	29	4	3	3	.255	.333	.386
Del Chiaro, Brenton, Arkansas	49	136	117	13	19	40	7	1	4	16	4	3	2	10	0	50	0	0	2	.162	.235	.342
DeMarco, Mathew, Springfield *	17	59	50	4	9	10	1	0	0	1	2	0	1	6	0	6	0	1	1	.180	.281	.200
Diaz, Juan, Springfield	57	219	198	27	61	113	13	0	13	38	0	0	4	17	0	43	0	0	7	.308	.374	.571
Diaz, Matt, Wichita	7	30	26	6	7	10	0	0	1	6	0	1	0	3	0	5	1	0	1	.269	.333	.385
Dickinson, Andy, Midland *	1	0	0	0	0	0	0	0	0	0	0	0	0	0	...	0	0	0	0	...	...	...
Doyne, Michael, Springfield	13	1	1	0	0	0	0	0	0	0	0	0	0	0	0	1	0	0	0	.000	.000	.000
Draper, John, Wichita	62	213	182	30	45	60	10	1	1	14	0	0	2	29	0	38	10	3	3	.247	.357	.330
Duff, Timothy, Arkansas	7	18	18	1	4	5	1	0	0	1	0	0	0	0	0	4	0	0	0	.222	.222	.278
Eckelman, Thomas, Corpus Christi	26	92	84	6	23	29	3	0	1	6	0	1	3	4	0	9	0	1	0	.274	.326	.345
Eldridge, Rashad, Frisco †	11	52	38	10	13	20	7	0	0	10	0	0	2	12	1	10	2	1	1	.342	.519	.526
Emmons, John, San Antonio *	4	3	3	1	2	3	1	0	0	0	0	0	0	0	0	1	0	0	0	.667	.667	1.000
Escobar, Gustavo, Tulsa	43	133	125	17	28	31	3	0	0	9	0	2	1	5	0	31	10	2	2	.224	.256	.248
Esposito, Brian, Frisco	38	147	136	12	31	38	7	0	0	5	2	0	2	7	0	33	1	0	2	.228	.276	.279
Espy, Nathan, San Antonio	122	525	440	70	121	199	27	6	13	61	1	10	8	66	5	100	11	6	11	.275	.372	.452
Estrada, Kevin, Springfield †	90	328	292	39	86	124	19	2	5	19	8	0	0	27	1	51	18	7	6	.295	.354	.425
Ethier, Andre, Midland *	131	572	505	104	161	251	30	3	18	80	0	8	11	48	4	93	1	4	18	.319	.385	.497
Eylward, Thomas, Arkansas	123	469	418	62	120	192	26	2	14	72	3	5	6	37	2	58	3	5	12	.287	.350	.459
Fagan, John, Corpus Christi	68	202	173	18	44	59	4	1	3	15	0	0	7	22	1	50	4	0	1	.254	.361	.341
Falu, Irving, Wichita †	6	18	17	1	4	5	1	0	0	2	0	0	0	1	0	0	0	0	1	.235	.278	.294
Fatheree, Danny, Corpus Christi	1	2	0	0	0	0	0	0	0	0	0	0	1	0	1	0	0	0	0	...	1.000	...
Feldman, Scott, Frisco *	1	0	0	0	0	0	0	0	0	0	0	0	0	0	...	0	0	0	0	...	...	...
Ferrari, Anthony, Springfield *	8	0	0	0	0	0	0	0	0	0	0	0	0	0	...	0	0	0	0	...	...	...
Fox, Adam, Frisco	46	172	149	23	38	57	5	1	4	26	0	1	3	19	0	29	3	0	2	.255	.349	.383
Gates, James, Arkansas	115	432	381	59	94	170	22	3	16	58	2	4	10	35	1	97	1	0	8	.247	.323	.446
Gimenez, Hector, Corpus Christi †‡	121	498	454	47	124	181	19	1	12	58	7	3	2	32	2	88	2	3	8	.273	.322	.399
Giron, Roberto, Corpus Christi	6	0	0	0	0	0	0	0	0	0	0	0	0	0	0	0	0	0	0	...	...	...
Gold, Nathan, Frisco	23	84	79	9	18	21	3	0	0	11	0	0	2	3	0	16	0	0	2	.228	.274	.266
Gomez, Francis, Midland	68	242	224	27	50	78	12	2	4	20	3	4	3	8	0	62	2	3	10	.223	.255	.348
Gomez, Rodolfo, Wichita	39	148	130	16	34	44	7	0	1	14	1	2	2	13	0	15	2	1	6	.262	.333	.338
Gorecki, Reid, Springfield	46	182	159	12	29	44	6	0	3	16	4	1	0	18	0	38	1	3	2	.182	.264	.277
Gotay, Ruben, Wichita †	28	122	110	22	27	44	8	0	3	8	0	0	0	12	0	13	0	2	2	.245	.320	.400
Groves, Timothy, Wichita †	86	316	273	43	64	79	9	0	2	25	7	3	4	29	1	50	2	2	6	.234	.314	.289

Player, Team	G	TPA	AB	R	H	TB	2B	3B	HR	RBI	SH	SF	HP	BB	IBB	SO	SB	CS	GDP	Avg.	OBP	Slg.
Guance, Luis, Tulsa	65	256	216	27	48	79	16	0	5	23	4	4	1	31	0	59	4	3	2	.222	.317	.366
Guzman, Jesus, San Antonio	119	514	453	61	117	178	18	8	9	53	11	1	4	45	0	101	6	11	10	.258	.330	.393
Haerther, Cody, Springfield *	65	219	208	30	62	104	10	1	10	37	0	0	2	9	0	44	0	1	4	.298	.333	.500
Hanson, Travis, Springfield *	137	609	546	82	155	250	29	3	20	97	1	6	2	54	6	99	2	2	18	.284	.347	.458
Harris, Edward, San Antonio *	120	490	457	68	129	172	21	2	6	42	5	2	4	22	1	72	15	15	8	.282	.320	.376
Hart, Jason, Midland	128	534	480	59	118	211	28	1	21	77	0	5	9	40	0	103	0	1	14	.246	.313	.440
Herr, Aaron, Springfield	112	456	426	56	127	212	20	1	21	81	4	1	10	15	2	108	2	3	12	.298	.336	.498
Higashi, Jonathan, Frisco	1	3	3	0	0	0	0	0	0	0	0	0	0	0	0	1	0	0	0	.000	.000	.000
Hirsh, Jason, Corpus Christi	4	11	10	2	1	1	0	0	0	1	0	0	0	1	0	7	0	0	0	.100	.182	.100
Hodge, Kevin, Corpus Christi	3	1	1	0	0	0	0	0	0	0	0	0	0	0	0	0	0	0	0	.000	.000	.000
Holliday, Matt, Tulsa	7	28	26	6	14	20	3	0	1	6	0	1	0	1	0	3	1	0	0	.538	.536	.769
Hoorelbeke, Jesse, San Antonio	119	503	450	62	112	203	25	0	22	81	0	1	5	47	5	156	2	0	8	.249	.326	.451
Huber, Justin, Wichita	88	396	335	68	115	191	22	3	16	74	0	5	5	51	2	70	7	3	11	.343	.432	.570
Iannetta, Christopher, Tulsa	19	70	60	7	14	25	3	1	2	11	0	1	1	8	0	15	0	0	5	.233	.329	.417
Jackson, Steve, Midland	11	40	33	7	10	22	2	2	2	6	1	0	0	6	0	8	0	0	2	.303	.410	.667
Jaramillo, Milko, Springfield †	59	186	175	16	41	57	13	0	1	7	2	0	1	8	2	37	1	1	3	.234	.272	.326
Jimenez, Ubaldo, Tulsa	5	8	7	0	2	2	0	0	0	0	1	0	0	0	0	4	0	0	0	.286	.286	.286
Jimerson, Charlton, Corpus Christi	115	467	425	67	110	188	24	3	16	44	3	2	8	29	4	145	27	10	0	.259	.317	.442
Johnson, Gabriel, Springfield	51	211	183	15	46	73	6	0	7	31	2	2	5	19	0	53	0	0	3	.251	.335	.399
Jones, Adam, San Antonio	63	257	228	33	68	105	10	3	7	20	2	2	3	22	1	48	9	4	4	.298	.365	.461
Keim, Adam, Wichita	17	75	69	11	23	36	1	0	4	18	1	2	0	3	0	12	1	1	1	.333	.351	.522
Kendrick, Howard, Arkansas	46	204	190	35	65	110	20	2	7	42	0	1	7	6	0	20	12	4	7	.342	.382	.579
Kieschnick, Brooks, Corpus Christi *	2	5	3	1	2	2	0	0	0	2	0	1	0	1	0	0	0	0	0	.667	.600	.667
Kiger, Mark, Midland	131	542	460	68	123	169	31	0	5	45	6	6	2	68	0	94	9	4	11	.267	.360	.367
King, Brennan, Wichita	118	478	435	58	124	183	28	2	9	56	6	3	5	29	1	68	5	1	12	.285	.335	.421
Kinney, Joshua, Springfield	12	1	1	0	0	0	0	0	0	0	0	0	0	0	0	0	0	0	0	.000	.000	.000
Koshansky, Joseph, Tulsa *	12	48	45	5	12	21	3	0	2	12	0	1	0	2	0	15	0	0	0	.267	.292	.467
Lambert, Christopher, Springfield	5	11	9	0	0	0	0	0	0	0	2	0	0	0	0	5	0	0	0	.000	.000	.000
Larson, Brandon, Frisco	34	150	135	20	39	70	10	0	7	34	0	1	5	9	1	33	0	0	1	.289	.353	.519
Laya, Rayner, Springfield	12	29	28	5	11	14	1	1	0	4	0	0	0	1	0	1	0	1	0	.393	.414	.500
Leahy, Ryan, Arkansas	43	137	121	12	28	37	4	1	1	10	6	0	4	6	0	17	0	2	5	.231	.290	.306
Leek, Randy, Springfield *	16	22	16	4	4	9	2	0	1	2	2	0	0	3	0	5	0	0	0	.250	.368	.563
MacRae, Scott, Corpus Christi	5	2	2	0	0	0	0	0	0	0	0	0	0	0	0	0	0	0	0	.000	.000	.000
Macri, Matthew, Tulsa	1	4	3	1	0	0	0	0	0	0	0	0	0	1	0	0	0	0	0	.000	.250	.000
Maduro, Jorge, Wichita	2	8	7	0	1	1	0	0	0	0	0	0	0	1	0	1	0	0	1	.143	.250	.143
Maier, Mitchell, Wichita *	80	342	322	55	82	134	21	5	7	49	0	3	2	15	1	47	10	3	4	.255	.289	.416
Mansfield, Monte, Corpus Christi	10	1	1	0	0	0	0	0	0	0	0	0	0	0	0	0	0	0	0	.000	.000	.000
Matranga, Dave, Arkansas	9	28	26	4	5	10	2	0	1	2	0	1	0	1	0	6	0	1	0	.192	.214	.385
Matthews, Gary, Frisco †	1	5	5	0	2	2	0	0	0	1	0	0	0	0	0	1	0	0	0	.400	.400	.400
McClaskey, Timothy, Corpus Christi †	4	8	7	0	0	0	0	0	0	0	1	0	0	0	0	2	0	0	0	.000	.000	.000
McCoy, Michael, Springfield	5	16	14	1	2	2	0	0	0	1	0	1	1	0	0	5	1	0	0	.143	.188	.143
McLemore, Mark, Corpus Christi *	4	5	3	0	0	0	0	0	0	0	1	0	0	1	0	2	0	0	0	.000	.250	.000
McNeal, Aaron, Tulsa	28	103	93	8	14	22	2	0	2	6	0	1	1	8	0	28	0	0	2	.151	.223	.237
Mears, Chris, Springfield	5	0	0	0	0	0	0	0	0	0	0	0	0	0	0	0	0	0	0	...	...	...
Mehl, Truan, Frisco *	2	2	2	0	0	0	0	0	0	0	0	0	0	0	0	2	0	0	0	.000	.000	.000
Melillo, Kevin, Midland *	35	147	131	33	37	68	10	0	7	34	0	2	0	14	1	23	9	2	4	.282	.347	.519
Menchaca, Eriberto, San Antonio	71	247	226	23	51	56	5	0	0	9	6	0	1	14	0	47	4	4	8	.226	.274	.248
Mendoza, Marcos, Tulsa *	4	0	0	0	0	0	0	0	0	0	0	0	0	0	0	0	0	0	0	...	...	...
Merchant, Jamie, Corpus Christi	4	2	2	0	1	1	0	0	0	0	0	0	0	0	0	0	0	0	0	.500	.500	.500
Meyer, Drew, Frisco *	83	358	321	49	103	134	14	4	3	45	3	5	3	26	3	55	12	2	3	.321	.372	.417
Miller, Anthony, Tulsa	129	562	460	102	129	212	17	6	18	58	9	1	5	87	1	116	26	14	6	.280	.400	.461
Miller, James, Tulsa	6	1	1	0	0	0	0	0	0	0	0	0	0	0	0	1	0	0	0	.000	.000	.000
Minges, Tyler, Springfield	116	486	429	98	139	242	34	6	19	60	1	5	4	47	4	61	5	4	11	.324	.392	.564
Moon, Brian, San Antonio †	52	183	161	12	37	49	6	0	2	14	4	0	5	13	1	27	0	1	2	.230	.307	.304
Morales, Kendry, Arkansas †	74	301	281	47	86	149	12	0	17	54	0	1	2	17	1	43	2	0	7	.306	.349	.530
Morris, Jed, Midland *	4	19	18	1	2	3	1	0	0	0	0	0	0	1	0	2	0	0	1	.111	.158	.167
Morris, Kenneth, Arkansas †	52	149	128	13	35	44	3	3	0	12	4	0	0	17	0	28	10	6	0	.273	.359	.344
Morrissey, Adam, Midland	34	127	121	16	29	40	3	1	2	15	1	0	0	5	0	38	0	1	1	.240	.270	.331
Motte, Jason, Springfield	1	4	3	1	1	1	0	0	0	1	0	0	0	1	0	1	0	0	0	.333	.500	.333
Moylan, Daniel, Springfield *	65	231	195	29	41	57	8	1	2	18	1	0	0	35	1	34	1	3	11	.210	.330	.292
Murphy, Donnie, Wichita	50	235	214	33	67	112	13	1	10	32	3	1	4	13	0	32	1	1	6	.313	.362	.523
Murphy, Thomas, Arkansas †	135	557	500	85	144	241	24	11	17	76	2	7	5	43	2	97	26	12	11	.288	.346	.482
Myers, Clinton, Midland	57	226	203	31	69	101	11	0	7	42	0	4	5	14	1	11	0	0	7	.340	.389	.498
Napoli, Michael, Arkansas	131	541	459	96	104	223	22	2	31	99	0	5	9	88	1	140	12	4	8	.237	.372	.508
Navarrete, Raymond, Corpus Christi	52	208	194	23	45	72	12	0	5	16	1	1	5	7	0	30	1	3	5	.232	.275	.371
Neal, Blaine, Tulsa *	2	0	0	0	0	0	0	0	0	0	0	0	0	0	0	0	0	0	0	...	...	...
Nelson, Joe, Springfield	1	0	0	0	0	0	0	0	0	0	0	0	0	0	0	0	0	0	0	...	...	...
Nelson, Jonathan, San Antonio	98	398	375	44	88	159	12	7	15	62	0	5	3	15	1	129	10	9	5	.235	.266	.424
Nesbit, Michael, San Antonio	8	19	18	2	4	4	0	0	0	1	0	0	0	1	0	4	1	0	0	.222	.263	.222
Nicholson, Thomas, Tulsa *	17	58	49	7	14	18	4	0	0	5	1	0	0	8	0	6	1	0	1	.286	.386	.367
Nickeas, Michael, Frisco	68	268	242	22	49	73	7	1	5	24	2	3	1	20	0	43	1	1	6	.202	.263	.302
Nieve, Fernando, Corpus Christi	3	7	7	0	0	0	0	0	0	0	0	0	0	0	0	3	0	0	0	.000	.000	.000
Nin, Sandy, Tulsa	5	8	8	0	0	0	0	0	0	0	0	0	0	0	0	6	0	0	0	.000	.000	.000
Nix, Jayson, Tulsa	131	552	501	68	118	178	27	0	11	47	4	6	11	29	1	92	10	6	8	.236	.289	.355
Norris, Steven, Corpus Christi	106	388	355	28	79	134	16	0	13	50	0	5	0	27	1	42	0	1	13	.223	.274	.377
Nussbeck, Mark, Springfield	2	1	1	0	0	0	0	0	0	0	0	0	0	0	0	0	0	0	0	.000	.000	.000
Oliveros, Luis, San Antonio	40	150	144	15	41	57	8	1	2	23	2	0	2	2	0	20	0	0	2	.285	.304	.396
Ool, Kevin, Springfield *	3	0	0	0	0	0	0	0	0	0	0	0	0	0	0	0	0	0	0	...	...	...
O'Sullivan, Mark, Arkansas	2	0	0	0	0	0	0	0	0	0	0	0	0	0	0	0	0	0	0	...	...	...
Pagnozzi, Matthew, Springfield	15	41	36	3	5	6	1	0	0	1	0	1	0	3	0	8	0	0	2	.139	.225	.167
Pals, Jordan, Tulsa	10	22	18	1	1	4	0	0	1	2	4	0	0	0	0	10	0	0	0	.056	.056	.222
Parker, Christian, Tulsa	4	8	8	0	1	1	0	0	0	0	0	0	0	0	0	3	0	0	0	.125	.125	.125
Parker, Tyler, Springfield	13	43	38	5	10	16	3	0	1	5	1	0	1	3	0	10	0	1	1	.263	.333	.421

Player, Team	G	TPA	AB	R	H	TB	2B	3B	HR	RBI	SH	SF	HP	BB	IBB	SO	SB	CS	GDP	Avg.	OBP	Slg.
Parker, Zachary, Tulsa	9	16	15	2	1	1	0	0	0	1	1	0	0	0	0	4	0	0	1	.067	.067	.067
Pavkovich, Adam, Arkansas	8	27	27	2	11	19	3	1	1	3	0	0	0	0	0	3	1	1	0	.407	.407	.704
Peavey, Patrick, Corpus Christi	12	38	31	0	2	2	0	0	0	1	2	0	2	3	0	8	0	0	1	.065	.194	.065
Peguero, Jailen, Corpus Christi	11	1	1	0	0	0	0	0	0	0	0	0	0	0	0	0	0	0	0	.000	.000	.000
Perez, Nestor, Tulsa	10	31	28	1	4	4	0	0	0	0	0	1	0	2	0	2	0	0	1	.143	.200	.143
Perry, Jason, Midland *	124	498	435	68	112	207	21	4	22	77	0	4	13	45	0	126	1	4	9	.257	.342	.476
Phillips, J.R., Corpus Christi *	43	180	156	20	46	75	5	0	8	20	0	3	0	21	3	42	2	2	2	.295	.372	.481
Pomeranz, Stuart, Springfield	3	4	4	0	0	0	0	0	0	0	0	0	0	0	0	2	0	0	0	.000	.000	.000
Porter, Gregory, Arkansas	129	480	448	63	128	193	24	4	11	56	0	6	4	22	2	84	2	6	6	.286	.321	.431
Pressley, Joshua, Wichita *	119	510	440	74	137	228	25	0	22	88	0	3	7	60	6	71	0	2	8	.311	.400	.518
Price, Jared, Wichita	4	10	10	1	3	7	1	0	1	2	0	0	0	0	0	4	0	0	0	.300	.300	.700
Quintanilla, Omar, Midland *	78	321	294	46	86	116	14	2	4	25	1	1	2	23	1	40	2	3	5	.293	.347	.395
Quintero, Humberto, Corpus Christi	4	12	11	0	2	3	1	0	0	1	0	0	0	1	1	2	0	0	2	.182	.250	.273
Ramirez, Ramon, Tulsa	4	7	7	2	2	2	0	0	0	0	0	0	0	0	0	1	0	0	0	.286	.286	.286
Ramos, Jason, Arkansas †	1	1	0	0	0	0	0	0	0	0	0	0	1	0	0	0	0	0	0	...	1.000	...
Ramsey, Keith, Tulsa †	1	4	3	0	1	1	0	0	0	0	0	0	0	1	0	0	0	0	0	.333	.333	.333
Randall, Scott, Tulsa	2	3	2	0	0	0	0	0	0	0	1	0	0	0	0	1	0	0	0	.000	.000	.000
Rawson, Anthony, Springfield *	15	0	0	0	0	0	0	0	0	0	0	0	0	0	...	0	0	0	0	...	...	...
Reese, Pokey, San Antonio	2	10	8	1	1	1	0	0	0	0	0	0	0	2	0	1	1	0	0	.125	.300	.125
Reyes, Ivan, Arkansas	8	25	22	5	8	19	2	0	3	10	0	1	0	2	0	8	0	0	0	.364	.400	.864
Richardson, Kevin, Frisco	18	69	59	12	18	28	4	0	2	11	0	0	4	6	0	23	0	1	2	.305	.406	.475
Riggs, Eric, Corpus Christi †	130	524	452	40	118	172	27	3	7	57	8	8	4	52	2	77	5	7	11	.261	.337	.381
Rijo, Fernando, Corpus Christi	6	2	2	0	0	0	0	0	0	0	0	0	0	0	0	0	0	0	0	.000	.000	.000
Rivera, Rene, San Antonio	57	221	212	20	59	81	14	1	2	21	1	0	1	7	2	35	1	0	6	.278	.305	.382
Robinson, Brian, Springfield	12	29	27	1	6	6	0	0	0	3	1	0	0	1	0	3	0	0	1	.222	.250	.222
Robinson, Christopher, Corpus Christi *	69	252	219	19	53	60	4	0	1	16	10	3	0	20	0	51	8	10	4	.242	.302	.274
Rodriguez, Carlos, Corpus Christi	88	329	318	30	78	119	12	1	9	42	0	1	2	8	0	71	3	4	9	.245	.267	.374
Rodriguez, Michael, Corpus Christi *	116	457	392	51	110	159	16	9	5	50	7	6	4	47	3	50	25	7	4	.281	.359	.406
Rodriguez, Wandy, Corpus Christi †	1	1	1	0	0	0	0	0	0	0	0	0	0	0	0	0	0	0	0	.000	.000	.000
Rouwenhorst, Jonathon, Arkansas *	1	0	0	0	0	0	0	0	0	0	0	0	0	0	...	0	0	0	0	...	...	...
Ruan, Wilkin, Wichita	76	267	244	31	62	72	4	3	0	20	4	2	2	14	1	19	18	7	5	.254	.298	.295
Rust, Evan, Springfield	2	0	0	0	0	0	0	0	0	0	0	0	0	0	0	0	0	0	0	...	...	...
Ryan, Brendan, Springfield	43	174	154	28	42	58	8	1	2	9	2	1	2	15	0	19	6	0	3	.273	.343	.377
Saccomanno, Mark, Corpus Christi	134	546	514	66	143	217	36	1	12	51	0	1	4	27	1	108	5	3	11	.278	.319	.422
Salazar, Jeffrey, Tulsa *	69	319	266	47	74	109	13	2	6	35	4	3	2	44	4	49	12	8	1	.278	.381	.410
Sampson, Christopher, Corpus Christi	11	11	10	1	1	1	0	0	0	0	1	0	0	0	0	4	0	0	0	.100	.100	.100
Sanchez, Agustin, Tulsa †	62	228	200	22	47	69	14	1	2	24	1	2	1	24	0	37	0	3	2	.235	.317	.345
Santana, Emmanuel, Arkansas *	5	15	14	2	2	2	0	0	0	4	0	1	0	0	0	3	1	0	2	.143	.133	.143
Scalamandre, Richard, Springfield	4	0	0	0	0	0	0	0	0	0	0	0	0	0	...	0	0	0	0	...	...	...
Schutzenhofer, Andrew, Springfield *	63	220	193	25	52	67	9	0	2	17	2	2	8	15	0	28	2	1	3	.269	.344	.347
Seay, Bobby, Tulsa *	2	0	0	0	0	0	0	0	0	0	0	0	0	0	0	0	0	0	0	...	...	...
Senreiso, Juan, Frisco	132	553	497	54	141	191	25	5	5	35	2	5	4	45	1	125	16	8	13	.284	.345	.384
Serrano, Alex, Tulsa	5	0	0	0	0	0	0	0	0	0	0	0	0	0	...	0	0	0	0	...	...	...
Sierra, Eduardo, Tulsa	7	1	1	0	0	0	0	0	0	0	0	0	0	0	0	1	0	0	0	.000	.000	.000
Simpson, Gerrit, Tulsa	9	1	1	1	0	0	0	0	0	0	0	0	0	0	0	0	0	0	0	.000	.000	.000
Sinisi, Vincent, Frisco *	65	271	248	27	64	85	9	0	4	29	0	5	2	15	0	39	4	4	10	.258	.300	.343
Slavik, Richard, Tulsa *	131	535	458	59	108	169	21	5	10	70	3	7	6	61	7	92	4	2	11	.236	.329	.369
Smith, Dustin, Frisco	20	68	63	11	15	22	4	0	1	5	1	0	1	3	0	7	0	0	4	.238	.284	.349
Smith, William, Frisco *	40	165	154	18	35	62	8	2	5	20	0	1	0	10	0	34	0	0	5	.227	.273	.403
Songster, Judson, Tulsa	15	3	3	0	1	1	0	0	0	0	0	0	0	0	0	2	0	0	0	.333	.333	.333
Spanos, Vasili, Midland	43	174	149	20	35	59	6	0	6	27	0	4	9	12	0	40	1	0	8	.235	.322	.396
Spilborghs, Ryan, Tulsa	71	301	255	52	87	134	23	3	6	54	0	2	2	42	2	49	10	3	8	.341	.435	.525
Stanley, Stephen, Midland *	128	588	514	87	149	201	26	4	6	46	6	5	2	61	3	62	8	8	11	.290	.364	.391
Stavisky, Brian, Midland *	135	586	510	84	161	242	36	4	11	88	0	4	3	69	1	84	0	5	23	.316	.398	.475
Stertzbach, Von, Arkansas	3	0	0	0	0	0	0	0	0	0	0	0	0	0	...	0	0	0	0	...	...	...
Stocker, Myreon, Wichita †	80	317	277	35	68	100	6	10	2	27	7	3	3	27	0	42	16	6	7	.245	.316	.361
Stocks, Nicholas, Springfield	6	0	0	0	0	0	0	0	0	0	0	0	0	0	...	0	0	0	0	...	...	...
Taylor, Thomas, Frisco	108	450	414	41	107	169	21	1	13	66	0	9	6	21	0	65	2	5	11	.258	.298	.408
Tena, Hector, Tulsa	31	91	84	8	21	32	2	0	3	5	1	0	1	5	0	24	0	1	1	.250	.300	.381
Thigpen, Judson, Tulsa	61	235	207	32	55	100	8	2	11	33	2	3	5	18	1	40	3	2	3	.266	.335	.483
Tupman, Mathew, Wichita *	109	426	365	59	96	122	16	2	2	32	3	3	8	46	2	62	1	2	13	.263	.355	.334
Turner, Lloyd, Midland	48	169	148	9	37	49	6	0	2	18	3	0	0	18	0	25	6	3	5	.250	.331	.331
Ulloa, Enmanuel, Tulsa	4	11	10	1	1	4	0	0	1	2	0	0	0	1	0	5	0	0	1	.100	.182	.400
Wallace, Shane, Springfield *	4	0	0	0	0	0	0	0	0	0	0	0	0	0	...	0	0	0	0	...	...	...
Whiteman, Tommy, Corpus Christi	41	173	152	13	38	50	9	0	1	15	2	0	1	18	0	40	3	4	4	.250	.333	.329
Wilhite, Matthew, Arkansas	3	0	0	0	0	0	0	0	0	0	0	0	0	0	0	0	0	0	0	...	...	...
Williams, Aaron, Corpus Christi	7	0	0	0	0	0	0	0	0	0	0	0	0	0	...	0	0	0	0	...	...	...
Willits, Reggie, Arkansas †	123	561	487	75	148	189	23	6	2	46	4	8	8	54	0	78	40	14	5	.304	.377	.388
Wright, Gavin, Corpus Christi	4	12	10	1	2	3	1	0	0	1	0	1	0	1	0	6	0	0	0	.200	.273	.300
Yan, Ruddy, Frisco †	116	543	483	77	145	179	15	5	3	45	10	0	3	47	1	38	41	11	17	.300	.366	.371
Young, Christopher, Tulsa	12	0	0	0	0	0	0	0	0	0	0	0	0	0	0	0	0	0	0	...	...	...
Zamora, Junior, Corpus Christi	45	134	126	10	25	32	7	0	0	4	0	0	3	5	0	31	0	0	6	.198	.246	.254
Zoccolillo, Peter, Springfield *	23	94	89	12	24	39	3	0	4	13	0	2	0	3	0	17	0	0	2	.270	.309	.438

GRAND SLAMS—M. Maier, 3; T. Murphy, 2; A. Blanco, S. Boyd, J. Brown, B. Butler, A. Callaspo, D. Conway, J. Czarniecki, J. Diaz, A. Ethier, A. Fox, T. Hanson, M. Holliday, J. Hoorelbeke, G. Johnson, M. Kiger, K. Melillo, T. Miller, T. Minges, D. Norris, J. Perry, J. Pressley, M. Saccomanno, J. Salazar, S. Stanley, 1 each.

AWARDED FIRST BASE ON CATCHER'S INTERFERENCE—S. Barker 4 (H. Gimenez, L. Oliveros, M. Napoli, M. Nickeas); K. Estrada (M. Tupman); R. Leek (H. Gimenez); J. Nix (M. Napoli); D. Norris (B. Esposito); M. Pagnozzi (M. Napoli); J. Perry (J. Draper); M. Rodriguez (B. Esposito); W. Ruan (B. Esposito); V. Sinisi (L. Oliveros); M. Tupman (A. Colina).

2005 PITCHING
TEAM

Team	W	L	Pct.	ERA	G	CG	ShO	Sv.	IP	H	TBF	R	ER	HR	SH	SF	HB	BB	IBB	SO	WP	Bk.
Corpus Christi	64	76	.457	3.34	141	6	10	23	1257	1147	5233	551	466	106	47	29	59	362	21	1036	51	4
San Antonio	76	64	.543	3.74	140	1	9	48	1252.2	1286	5379	614	521	96	50	50	43	441	14	979	76	15

Team	W	L	Pct.	ERA	G	CG	ShO	Sv.	IP	H	TBF	R	ER	HR	SH	SF	HB	BB	IBB	SO	WP	Bk.
Tulsa	75	65	.536	4.02	140	8	7	39	1234.2	1251	5233	622	551	127	53	39	75	352	12	852	77	12
Midland	78	62	.557	4.26	140	0	8	42	1243.2	1318	5442	678	589	105	46	50	43	464	24	964	59	9
Arkansas	71	69	.507	4.56	140	4	8	32	1209.1	1321	5280	701	613	143	30	32	60	451	11	848	54	6
Springfield	70	70	.500	4.57	140	3	4	37	1247.1	1325	5475	732	634	153	41	57	63	457	21	884	73	7
Frisco	58	82	.414	4.70	141	3	4	32	1250.1	1352	5452	745	653	142	32	50	53	463	25	990	73	7
Wichita	68	72	.486	4.92	140	3	4	35	1215	1311	5377	766	664	114	36	41	69	466	16	890	84	9

INDIVIDUAL

TOP QUALIFIERS FOR EARNED-RUN AVERAGE TITLE

Minimum 112 innings. *Lefthanded pitcher.

Pitcher, Team	W	L	Pct.	ERA	G	GS	CG	ShO	GF	Sv.	IP	H	TBF	R	ER	HR	SH	SF	HB	BB	IBB	SO	WP	Bk.
Livingston, Robert, San Antonio *	8	4	.667	2.86	18	18	0	0	0	0	116.1	103	460	45	37	7	7	5	2	27	0	78	2	1
Hirsh, Jason, Corpus Christi	13	8	.619	2.87	29	29	1	1	0	0	172.1	137	689	63	55	12	4	7	12	42	0	165	7	1
Barzilla, Philip, Corpus Christi *	7	7	.500	3.03	41	14	0	0	8	0	113.0	126	484	49	38	6	6	1	4	30	5	87	6	0
Sampson, Christopher, Corpus Christi ..	4	12	.250	3.12	32	19	2	1	9	4	150.0	147	602	67	52	11	4	4	4	19	2	92	2	0
Nin, Sandy, Tulsa	10	6	.625	3.19	20	20	4	0	0	0	129.2	109	504	50	46	15	4	3	2	16	0	80	2	3
McClaskey, Timothy, Corpus Christi	8	10	.444	3.33	27	26	2	0	0	0	159.2	141	637	67	59	16	4	1	11	21	1	105	2	0
Oldham, Thomas, San Antonio *	13	7	.650	3.67	27	26	0	0	0	0	154.2	179	670	79	63	15	5	6	6	45	3	115	3	2
Olenberger, Kasey, Arkansas	9	7	.563	3.71	32	17	0	0	4	0	123.2	135	533	64	51	14	1	6	5	37	0	69	6	1
Parker, Zachary, Tulsa *	12	10	.545	3.79	27	27	0	0	0	0	161.2	171	678	83	68	15	6	4	18	35	1	87	7	0
Leek, Randy, Springfield *	15	7	.682	3.83	28	27	3	2	0	0	185.2	190	752	85	79	29	8	4	6	29	0	102	2	0
Pals, Jordan, Springfield	7	11	.389	3.83	27	27	0	0	0	0	159.2	162	670	87	68	16	2	6	3	41	0	102	3	1
Sandoval, Juan, San Antonio	9	11	.450	4.03	28	28	0	0	0	0	160.2	196	710	88	72	6	4	13	8	46	0	99	8	3
Asahina, Jonathan, Tulsa	12	10	.545	4.19	26	26	4	1	0	0	169.2	189	707	88	79	16	8	9	12	34	2	94	12	5
Rowland-Smith, Ryan, San Antonio *	6	7	.462	4.35	33	17	0	0	4	0	122.0	133	532	72	59	7	5	6	5	51	0	102	15	2
Shell, Steven, Arkansas	10	8	.556	4.57	27	27	1	1	0	0	159.2	175	687	90	81	18	5	2	9	58	0	126	10	0
Bondurant, Steven, Midland *	12	9	.571	4.58	28	28	0	0	0	0	165.0	171	699	94	84	20	11	6	4	59	0	128	2	0
Davidson, Daniel, Arkansas *	13	5	.722	4.72	28	26	1	1	0	0	154.1	179	674	94	81	22	5	4	5	45	0	110	6	1
Huber, Jonathan, San Antonio	7	8	.467	4.74	26	26	1	1	0	0	148.0	159	635	87	78	11	4	3	6	49	1	112	7	2
Bass, Brian, Wichita	12	8	.600	5.24	27	27	0	0	0	0	165.0	185	710	106	96	14	3	8	3	53	0	102	10	0
Middleton, Kyle, Wichita	10	9	.526	5.31	28	28	1	0	0	0	171.1	218	760	118	101	22	6	4	15	37	0	109	6	1
Dickinson, Andy, Midland *	6	10	.375	5.91	27	26	0	0	0	0	120.1	167	568	91	79	11	5	6	5	54	1	53	8	1

DEPARTMENTAL LEADERS: W—Leek, 15. L—Masset and Sampson, 12. Pct.—Davidson, .722. G—Wilhite, 56. GS—Hirsh, 29. CG—Asahina and Nin, 4. ShO—Leek, 2. GF—Bevis, 39. Sv.—Bevis, 21. IP—Leek, 185.2. H—Middleton, 218. TBF—Middleton, 767. R—Masset, 124. ER—Masset, 108. HR—Leek, 29. SAC—Bondurant, 11. SF—Sandoval, 13. HB—Parker, 18. BB—Masset, 61. IBB—Feldman, 8. SO—Hirsh, 165. WP—Griffin, 16. BK—Asahina, 5.

ALL PITCHERS

*Lefthanded pitcher.

Pitcher, Team	W	L	Pct.	ERA	G	GS	CG	ShO	GF	Sv.	IP	H	TBF	R	ER	HR	SH	SF	HB	BB	IBB	SO	WP	Bk.
Allen, Blake, Corpus Christi *	1	3	.250	5.36	16	6	0	0	3	0	42.0	44	188	28	25	4	0	2	1	18	1	31	4	0
Alvarez, Oscar, Springfield *	6	2	.750	3.40	29	14	0	0	2	0	106.0	112	453	47	40	11	3	4	5	40	0	59	1	1
Anderson, Brian, Wichita	0	0	.000	13.50	1	1	0	0	0	0	1.1	5	10	3	2	1	0	0	0	0	0	2	0	0
Andrews, Clayton, Arkansas *	1	0	1.000	0.00	2	1	0	0	1	1	9.2	4	37	0	0	0	0	0	0	7	0	6	0	0
Arakawa, Yusuke, Tulsa	4	4	.500	5.09	41	0	0	0	17	0	53.0	57	233	33	30	9	3	1	6	21	0	40	6	0
Arredondo, Jose, Arkansas	0	0	.000	3.38	5	0	0	0	3	0	5.1	5	22	2	2	0	0	0	4	0	0	4	1	0
Asahina, Jonathan, Tulsa	12	10	.545	4.19	26	26	4	1	0	0	169.2	189	707	88	79	16	8	9	12	34	2	94	12	5
Atchison, Scott, San Antonio	0	0	.000	0.00	5	0	0	0	3	0	6.0	3	23	0	0	0	0	0	0	2	0	8	0	0
Austen, David, Arkansas	4	3	.571	4.05	27	0	0	0	10	0	46.2	43	185	24	21	4	4	1	4	12	3	30	2	0
Axelson, Joshua, Springfield	1	2	.333	8.45	28	2	0	0	5	0	49.0	62	231	50	46	8	1	4	4	30	0	46	12	0
Backe, Brandon, Corpus Christi	0	1	.000	2.25	2	2	0	0	0	0	8.0	4	29	2	2	1	0	0	1	0	0	11	1	0
Baerlocher, Ryan, Wichita	7	5	.583	3.44	15	15	2	1	0	0	89.0	76	366	37	34	5	4	3	6	27	0	63	5	0
Barzilla, Philip, Corpus Christi *	7	7	.500	3.03	41	14	0	0	8	0	113.0	126	484	49	38	6	6	1	4	30	5	87	6	0
Bass, Brian, Wichita	12	8	.600	5.24	27	27	0	0	0	0	165.0	185	710	106	96	14	3	8	3	53	0	102	10	0
Bauer, Peter, Corpus Christi	3	4	.429	3.31	11	8	0	0	2	1	51.2	46	210	25	19	5	2	1	1	9	0	39	3	0
Bayliss, Jonah, Wichita	1	2	.333	2.84	30	0	0	0	15	8	57.0	43	236	19	18	5	0	1	2	26	0	63	5	0
Bazardo, Yorman, San Antonio	3	1	.750	4.28	6	6	0	0	0	0	33.2	38	141	16	16	4	0	1	0	11	0	26	0	2
Bazzell, Shane, Frisco	4	5	.444	4.87	35	8	0	0	8	2	98.0	117	421	56	53	11	1	4	1	27	0	60	1	1
Beckstead, Jentry, Tulsa	5	3	.625	4.10	51	0	0	0	20	3	68.0	79	291	34	31	4	3	4	5	15	0	45	4	0
Benes, Alan, Springfield	1	0	1.000	5.49	15	0	0	0	3	0	19.2	20	86	13	12	5	0	0	0	7	0	16	3	0
Bevis, P. J., Tulsa	0	5	.000	4.26	41	0	0	0	39	21	38.0	38	160	19	18	4	3	0	2	14	3	17	2	1
Bittner, Timothy, Arkansas *	1	7	.125	6.33	14	14	0	0	0	0	58.1	76	264	43	41	5	2	1	2	33	0	41	3	0
Blair, Thomas, Springfield *	1	6	.143	8.50	8	8	0	0	0	0	36.0	55	174	35	34	7	2	1	2	20	0	21	2	1
Bondurant, Steven, Midland *	12	9	.571	4.58	28	28	0	0	0	0	165.0	171	699	94	84	20	11	6	4	59	0	128	2	0
Borbon, Pedro, Arkansas *	0	0	.000	0.00	6	0	0	0	1	0	4.1	1	13	0	0	0	0	0	1	0	0	3	0	0
Bourgeois, Nicholas, San Antonio *	0	1	.000	7.50	2	2	0	0	0	0	6.0	6	29	5	5	1	2	0	1	6	0	9	0	0
Braden, Dallas, Midland *	9	5	.643	3.90	16	16	0	0	0	0	97.0	104	408	43	42	5	5	5	1	32	1	71	8	3
Brannon, Nicholas, Midland *	1	1	.500	4.21	26	1	0	0	8	0	36.1	32	170	23	17	3	2	1	2	33	3	31	2	1
Braun, Ryan, Wichita	0	1	.000	17.36	6	0	0	0	3	0	4.2	15	30	9	9	0	0	0	0	7	1	1	1	0
Bray, Stephen, Wichita	1	1	.500	4.40	20	0	0	0	6	0	30.2	34	138	22	15	3	0	0	0	11	0	26	1	0
Bumstead, Michael, San Antonio	0	2	.000	7.11	7	4	0	0	0	0	19.0	28	97	18	15	1	2	3	0	17	1	9	4	0
Burcie, Jarrad, Frisco	0	0	.000	11.57	1	0	0	0	0	0	2.1	3	11	3	3	1	0	0	0	1	0	2	0	0
Burgos, Ambiorix, Wichita	1	1	.500	4.97	12	0	0	0	6	1	12.2	8	56	7	7	1	0	0	0	8	0	19	2	0
Cavazos, Andres, Springfield	1	2	.333	4.03	23	0	0	0	4	1	29.0	27	119	15	13	4	2	1	2	7	3	24	0	0
Cedeno, Juan, Wichita *	0	2	.000	7.20	11	1	0	0	5	0	20.0	21	92	17	16	4	0	0	2	11	0	16	2	0
Chavez, Jesse, Frisco	4	3	.571	5.68	31	0	0	0	9	0	57.0	71	255	43	36	10	1	3	2	25	2	27	7	0
Collazo, William, Arkansas *	1	5	.167	6.78	26	10	0	0	1	0	71.2	85	326	60	54	16	3	3	4	29	1	58	1	0
Cook, Aaron, Tulsa	0	1	.000	17.18	1	1	0	0	0	0	3.2	10	22	9	7	2	0	0	0	1	0	1	1	0

Pitcher, Team	W	L	Pct.	ERA	G	GS	CG	ShO	GF	Sv.	IP	H	TBF	R	ER	HR	SH	SF	HB	BB	IBB	SO	WP	Bk.
Cook, Jeremy, Springfield	3	8	.273	5.57	37	11	0	0	5	0	103.1	140	469	78	64	12	5	3	4	26	1	54	10	0
Cortez, Renee, San Antonio	5	3	.625	3.96	44	1	0	0	21	10	63.2	61	268	32	28	4	5	3	1	23	1	62	9	0
Cotton, Nathan, Springfield	1	1	.500	6.97	8	0	0	0	3	0	10.1	13	50	10	8	1	1	4	1	6	0	4	0	0
Crabtree, Tim, Frisco	2	0	1.000	0.66	11	0	0	0	6	1	13.2	10	57	4	1	0	1	0	0	4	0	10	0	0
Crockett, William, Tulsa	0	0	.000	4.00	18	2	0	0	2	0	36.0	44	154	19	16	1	1	1	4	11	1	20	1	1
Crowell, Kyle, Midland	3	1	.750	3.44	39	1	0	0	15	0	65.1	64	276	26	25	7	1	1	3	21	0	49	5	1
Cummings, Jeremy, Springfield	5	3	.625	4.50	12	12	0	0	0	0	70.0	67	296	39	35	9	3	1	6	19	0	56	0	1
Damico, Yovany, Wichita	0	1	.000	17.18	1	1	0	0	0	0	3.2	7	20	7	7	1	0	0	0	3	0	3	1	0
Danks, John, Frisco *	4	10	.286	5.49	18	17	0	0	0	0	98.1	117	435	66	60	12	2	2	5	34	1	85	3	0
Davidson, Daniel, Arkansas *	13	5	.722	4.72	28	26	1	0	0	0	154.1	179	674	94	81	22	5	4	5	45	0	110	6	1
Demaria, Chris, Wichita	0	1	.000	1.76	10	0	0	0	6	1	15.1	12	57	3	3	3	1	0	0	2	0	19	1	0
Diamond, Thomas, Frisco	5	4	.556	5.35	14	14	0	0	0	0	69.0	66	311	44	41	8	0	4	4	38	0	68	10	0
Dickinson, Andy, Midland *	6	10	.375	5.91	27	26	0	0	0	0	120.1	167	568	91	79	11	5	6	5	54	1	53	8	1
Dominguez, Juan, Frisco	2	0	1.000	2.63	15	2	0	0	5	2	37.2	30	150	14	11	4	0	1	1	9	1	31	4	0
Done, Juan, San Antonio	1	0	1.000	16.43	7	0	0	0	3	0	7.2	16	41	14	14	2	0	1	1	2	0	6	0	0
Dorman, Richard, San Antonio	3	0	1.000	0.45	3	3	0	0	0	0	20.0	7	74	1	1	0	0	0	0	12	1	24	1	0
Doyne, Michael, Springfield	2	1	.667	1.95	48	0	0	0	31	19	55.1	37	240	14	12	5	1	2	5	36	4	53	5	0
Ebert, Derrin, Wichita *	7	3	.700	4.89	27	16	0	0	6	1	105.0	123	464	69	57	10	3	1	3	35	1	54	4	0
Eldred, Cal, Springfield	1	0	1.000	0.00	3	0	0	0	2	0	6.0	5	21	0	0	0	0	0	0	0	0	1	0	0
Endicott, Drew, Wichita	1	0	1.000	1.50	2	0	0	0	2	0	6.0	1	26	1	1	0	0	1	1	6	0	1	0	0
Estrada, Kevin, Springfield	0	0	.000	81.00	1	0	0	0	0	0	0.1	1	4	3	3	1	0	0	0	1	0	2	1	0
Fahrner, Evan, Midland	7	2	.778	2.48	45	0	0	0	17	3	76.1	71	321	27	21	4	4	2	1	28	4	68	5	1
Feldman, Scott, Frisco	1	2	.333	2.36	46	0	0	0	33	14	61.0	43	236	18	16	3	3	0	0	23	8	41	4	0
Ferrari, Anthony, Springfield *	2	3	.400	4.50	29	0	0	0	10	0	24.0	22	121	18	12	2	3	0	4	24	3	24	1	0
Flannery, Michael, San Antonio	0	0	.000	4.26	6	0	0	0	5	3	6.1	7	27	3	3	0	0	1	0	2	0	5	1	0
Francisco, Frank, Frisco	0	1	.000	8.10	4	3	0	0	0	0	3.1	4	17	6	3	0	1	3	0	2	0	3	1	1
Fruto, Emiliano, San Antonio	2	3	.400	2.57	40	0	0	0	24	12	66.2	56	268	22	19	6	1	3	1	22	0	63	4	0
Garcia, Jairo, Midland	0	0	.000	1.08	10	0	0	0	7	6	16.2	9	68	3	2	1	1	0	0	9	0	30	1	0
Giron, Roberto, Corpus Christi	2	3	.400	3.07	21	0	0	0	14	0	29.1	27	118	11	10	3	2	0	3	6	0	28	0	0
Gomez, Rodolfo, Wichita	1	0	1.000	0.00	3	0	0	0	3	0	4.1	3	17	0	0	0	0	0	0	1	1	3	0	0
Green, Sean, San Antonio	0	1	.000	2.96	21	0	0	0	19	14	24.1	17	99	11	8	1	1	0	1	8	1	18	6	0
Griffin, Jonathan, Wichita	1	1	.500	4.02	37	0	0	0	13	1	56.0	45	252	30	25	4	1	1	8	43	2	36	16	2
Gwyn, Marcus, Midland	0	1	.000	2.86	19	0	0	0	3	0	28.1	24	123	9	9	1	0	2	4	17	1	21	4	0
Harris, Jeff, San Antonio	5	0	1.000	2.10	11	2	0	0	4	0	34.1	25	137	9	8	4	2	1	3	8	1	31	0	0
Hicklen, Patrick, Wichita	0	1	.000	14.73	1	1	0	0	0	0	3.2	5	19	6	6	1	0	0	0	5	0	4	0	0
Hirsh, Jason, Corpus Christi	13	8	.619	2.87	29	29	1	1	0	0	172.1	137	689	63	55	12	4	7	12	42	0	165	7	1
Hodge, Kevin, Corpus Christi	1	4	.200	5.48	14	0	0	0	7	2	23.0	23	100	15	14	3	1	1	1	8	1	25	2	0
Hoelscher, Nathan, Wichita *	3	2	.600	5.63	51	1	0	0	21	4	54.1	62	253	38	34	4	3	1	7	25	4	40	4	0
Howell, J.P., Wichita *	2	0	1.000	2.50	3	3	0	0	0	0	18.0	12	70	5	5	2	0	0	1	5	0	23	2	0
Huber, Jonathan, San Antonio	7	8	.467	4.74	26	26	1	1	0	0	148.0	159	635	87	78	11	4	3	6	49	1	112	7	2
Hudgins, John, Frisco	1	2	.333	4.67	3	2	0	0	0	0	17.1	15	75	9	9	1	2	0	2	8	1	11	0	1
James, Delvin, Arkansas	3	4	.429	5.58	17	8	0	0	0	0	59.2	77	267	40	37	6	2	1	1	25	1	30	2	0
Jimenez, Cesar, San Antonio *	3	5	.375	2.62	45	1	0	0	19	4	68.2	64	284	21	20	3	4	2	2	24	0	54	4	0
Jimenez, Kelvin, Frisco	0	0	.000	3.46	6	0	0	0	3	2	13.0	12	56	5	5	0	1	2	2	6	0	12	2	0
Jimenez, Ubaldo, Tulsa	2	5	.286	5.43	12	11	0	0	0	0	63.0	58	279	40	38	12	0	5	4	31	0	53	7	0
Jones, Greg, Arkansas	0	1	.000	2.70	3	0	0	0	3	0	3.1	2	13	1	1	0	0	0	0	1	0	2	0	0
Karsay, Steve, Frisco	1	2	.333	3.64	19	0	0	0	4	0	29.2	29	124	18	12	2	2	1	0	6	2	30	1	0
Key, Christopher, San Antonio *	4	1	.800	2.42	23	0	0	0	6	3	52.0	55	206	15	14	5	1	1	1	8	0	27	1	1
Kieschnick, Brooks, Corpus Christi	0	0	.000	1.08	5	0	0	0	1	0	8.1	10	36	2	1	0	0	0	1	2	0	5	1	0
Kinney, Joshua, Springfield	5	2	.714	1.29	32	0	0	0	22	11	42.0	28	165	9	6	2	0	2	0	12	0	42	1	0
Kohn, Shawn, Midland	4	3	.571	2.89	55	0	0	0	16	8	84.0	64	326	28	27	5	2	7	2	20	3	92	0	0
Komine, Shane, Midland	2	1	.667	3.16	5	5	0	0	0	0	31.1	27	124	12	11	5	0	0	2	7	0	33	1	0
Lambert, Christopher, Springfield	3	8	.273	6.35	18	18	0	0	0	0	85.0	97	401	69	60	10	2	10	10	48	0	69	7	3
Landeros, Leonard, Midland *	2	2	.500	5.68	18	3	0	0	5	0	31.2	44	145	21	20	3	1	0	0	11	0	20	0	0
Leahy, Ryan, Arkansas	0	0	.000	22.50	1	0	0	0	1	0	2.0	3	13	5	5	0	0	1	1	3	0	2	0	0
Leek, Randy, Springfield *	15	7	.682	3.83	28	27	3	2	0	0	185.2	190	752	85	79	29	8	4	6	29	0	102	2	0
Littleton, Wes, Frisco	2	3	.400	3.97	48	0	0	0	27	3	81.2	93	348	37	36	9	2	4	3	24	7	71	3	1
Livingston, Robert, San Antonio *	8	4	.667	2.86	18	18	0	0	0	0	116.1	103	460	45	37	7	7	5	2	27	0	78	2	1
Lorenzo, Mathew, Frisco	3	5	.375	7.14	10	9	0	0	0	0	46.2	71	225	39	37	9	2	1	1	22	0	28	1	1
Lowery, Devon, Wichita	0	4	.000	24.84	4	4	0	0	0	0	8.1	21	57	24	23	1	0	3	0	14	0	5	2	2
Lynch, Kevin, Arkansas	0	0	.000	11.25	2	0	0	0	1	0	4.0	7	21	5	5	2	0	0	0	2	0	0	0	0
Lynch, Matthew, Midland *	7	7	.500	4.40	35	15	0	0	6	1	110.1	126	487	71	54	7	5	3	2	38	3	65	1	0
MacRae, Scott, Corpus Christi	3	3	.500	2.70	16	4	0	0	2	1	46.2	51	193	19	14	2	2	0	0	9	0	29	3	0
Mahay, Ron, Frisco *	1	3	.250	7.78	5	5	0	0	0	0	19.2	24	92	19	17	3	0	1	2	9	0	20	1	0
Mansfield, Monte, Corpus Christi	3	2	.600	3.82	43	0	0	0	26	0	75.1	65	319	35	32	7	5	3	5	33	2	78	6	2
Marcano, Luis, Frisco	0	1	.000	6.06	10	0	0	0	3	0	16.1	17	74	12	11	6	0	1	0	10	0	6	1	0
Markray, Thaddius, Wichita	4	7	.364	5.26	22	11	0	0	2	1	65.0	62	270	43	38	10	1	4	3	20	0	44	1	1
Masset, Nicholas, Frisco	7	12	.368	6.18	29	27	1	0	1	0	157.1	197	703	124	108	19	3	4	9	61	1	105	9	2
Mateo, Nathanel, San Antonio	0	4	.000	6.61	14	1	0	0	4	0	16.1	20	80	17	12	4	2	0	0	10	1	21	1	1
Mattioni, Nicholas, Midland	2	4	.333	2.58	42	0	0	0	15	4	69.2	56	285	24	20	6	3	0	5	21	3	71	7	0
McClaskey, Timothy, Corpus Christi	8	10	.444	3.33	27	26	2	0	0	0	159.2	141	637	67	59	16	4	1	11	21	1	105	2	0
McGill, Max, Wichita	3	4	.429	5.01	29	1	0	0	10	2	46.2	51	217	30	26	4	3	2	5	27	2	40	4	0
McLemore, Mark, Corpus Christi *	5	6	.455	2.81	15	15	1	0	0	0	73.2	59	304	34	23	5	3	0	2	34	0	65	1	0
Mears, Chris, Springfield	0	2	.000	5.25	13	0	0	0	5	0	12.0	13	52	7	7	0	1	1	1	5	3	6	0	0
Mendoza, Marcos, Tulsa *	0	0	.000	7.15	10	0	0	0	1	0	11.1	16	53	9	9	3	0	0	1	4	0	12	3	0
Merchant, Jamie, Corpus Christi	3	3	.500	4.26	24	1	0	0	4	2	50.2	43	212	25	24	7	2	0	2	21	0	46	0	0
Middleton, Kyle, Wichita	10	9	.526	5.31	28	28	1	0	0	0	171.1	218	760	118	101	22	6	4	15	37	0	109	6	1
Miller, James, Tulsa	1	1	.500	0.60	16	0	0	0	13	9	15.0	6	61	5	1	2	0	0	2	8	0	19	2	0
Miller, Joshua, Corpus Christi	0	1	.000	7.04	3	0	0	0	0	0	7.2	9	33	6	6	1	0	0	0	1	0	5	0	0
Montero, Agustin, Frisco	2	4	.333	5.46	40	0	0	0	18	2	61.0	64	281	40	37	9	3	3	2	33	1	69	10	1
Moylan, Daniel, Springfield	0	0	.000	0.00	1	0	0	0	1	0	1.0	0	5	0	0	0	0	0	0	2	0	0	0	0
Murray, Arlington, Frisco *	4	4	.500	3.26	11	10	0	0	0	0	58.0	62	238	27	21	3	1	4	1	15	0	49	1	0
Nannini, Michael, Midland	8	1	.889	5.79	13	13	0	0	0	0	74.2	80	315	51	48	10	3	8	2	13	0	44	3	1
Neal, Blaine, Tulsa	0	1	.000	9.00	4	1	0	0	0	0	3.0	4	14	4	3	1	0	0	0	1	0	2	1	0
Nelson, Joe, Springfield	0	0	.000	2.03	9	0	0	0	6	1	13.1	4	51	3	3	1	1	0	1	7	0	22	1	0
Nieve, Fernando, Corpus Christi	4	3	.571	2.65	14	14	0	0	0	0	85.0	62	337	27	25	7	2	3	3	29	0	96	4	0
Nin, Sandy, Tulsa	10	6	.625	3.19	20	20	4	0	0	0	129.2	109	504	50	46	15	4	3	2	16	0	80	2	3

Pitcher, Team	W	L	Pct.	ERA	G	GS	CG	ShO	GF	Sv.	IP	H	TBF	R	ER	HR	SH	SF	HB	BB	IBB	SO	WP	Bk.
Nunez, Leo, Wichita	1	0	1.000	0.69	12	0	0	0	11	4	13.0	8	49	3	1	1	0	0	0	2	0	14	1	0
Nussbeck, Mark, Springfield *	3	0	1.000	3.12	6	2	0	0	2	0	17.1	17	68	6	6	3	1	2	0	3	2	14	4	0
Obenchain, Stephen, Midland	4	3	.571	5.92	11	11	0	0	0	0	51.2	67	245	40	34	4	0	1	0	29	0	37	3	0
Oldham, Thomas, San Antonio *	13	7	.650	3.67	27	26	0	0	0	0	154.2	179	670	79	63	15	5	6	6	45	3	115	3	2
Olenberger, Kasey, Arkansas	9	7	.563	3.71	32	17	0	0	4	0	123.2	135	533	64	51	14	1	6	5	37	0	69	6	1
Olson, Jason, Arkansas	0	0	.000	4.50	4	0	0	0	2	1	6.0	9	27	3	3	1	0	0	1	1	0	0	1	0
Ool, Kevin, Springfield *	1	0	1.000	6.63	14	0	0	0	3	0	19.0	26	93	16	14	1	0	1	0	8	0	13	3	0
O'Sullivan, Mark, Arkansas	1	4	.200	6.16	45	4	0	0	11	0	76.0	92	346	59	52	10	2	3	5	38	0	45	8	2
Pals, Jordan, Springfield	7	11	.389	3.83	27	27	0	0	0	0	159.2	162	670	87	68	16	2	6	3	41	0	102	3	1
Parker, Christian, Tulsa	4	1	.800	2.06	12	12	0	0	0	0	70.0	57	273	18	16	1	4	0	0	17	0	50	2	0
Parker, Zachary, Tulsa *	12	10	.545	3.79	27	27	0	0	0	0	161.2	171	678	83	68	15	6	4	18	35	1	87	7	0
Pearce, Josh, Springfield	0	0	.000	2.50	7	0	0	0	3	0	18.0	12	66	6	5	3	0	0	1	2	0	14	2	0
Peguero, Jailen, Corpus Christi	2	2	.500	2.94	50	0	0	0	36	12	64.1	62	276	25	21	3	4	3	4	25	5	63	3	0
Perry, Brandon, Wichita *	0	1	.000	5.40	1	0	0	0	1	0	1.2	3	9	2	1	0	2	0	0	2	0	0	1	0
Pizzaro, Melvin, San Antonio *	2	1	.667	2.57	4	0	0	0	2	0	7.0	5	26	3	2	1	0	0	0	1	0	3	0	0
Pomeranz, Stuart, Springfield	5	6	.455	5.29	18	18	0	0	0	0	98.2	110	447	65	58	12	2	6	5	40	0	66	6	0
Pullin, Aaron, Arkansas	5	6	.455	5.03	51	0	0	0	24	5	77.0	80	342	45	43	13	1	1	2	34	4	53	4	0
Pulsipher, Bill, Springfield *	1	0	1.000	2.70	1	1	0	0	0	0	6.2	8	28	2	2	2	0	0	0	1	0	7	1	0
Rall, Tim, San Antonio *	2	3	.400	3.81	41	0	0	0	14	0	59.0	45	253	27	25	6	2	0	3	34	4	61	4	0
Ramirez, Ramon, Tulsa	2	1	.667	5.33	9	3	0	0	2	0	25.1	27	109	17	15	6	1	1	1	8	0	23	3	0
Ramsey, Keith, Tulsa *	1	3	.250	7.68	10	10	0	0	0	0	41.0	58	189	37	35	8	2	0	1	19	0	23	3	0
Randall, Scott, Tulsa	3	4	.429	4.84	9	9	0	0	0	0	44.2	49	198	31	24	1	2	4	3	22	1	36	5	0
Rawson, Anthony, Springfield *	4	3	.571	4.35	38	0	0	0	13	1	41.1	45	184	21	20	7	2	3	0	21	4	37	2	0
Riggs, Eric, Corpus Christi	0	1	.000	45.00	1	0	0	0	1	0	1.0	3	7	5	5	0	1	0	0	3	1	0	0	0
Rijo, Fernando, Corpus Christi	3	2	.600	4.40	34	2	0	0	10	1	61.1	58	267	35	30	11	3	3	2	34	1	44	4	0
Roberts, Mark, Frisco	2	1	.667	4.26	10	0	0	0	4	2	19.0	16	78	9	9	2	0	0	3	5	0	14	3	0
Robinson, Brian, Springfield	0	0	.000	0.00	1	0	0	0	1	0	1.0	0	3	0	0	0	0	0	0	0	0	0	0	0
Rodriguez, Wandy, Corpus Christi *	0	0	.000	2.70	1	1	0	0	0	0	3.1	3	13	1	1	0	0	0	0	2	1	3	0	0
Rodriguez, Wilfredo, Frisco *	4	5	.444	3.80	12	12	1	0	0	0	68.2	59	288	34	29	5	2	3	7	31	0	64	3	0
Rouwenhorst, Jonathon, Arkansas *	3	1	.750	1.59	22	0	0	0	6	2	22.2	13	91	4	4	2	2	0	4	10	0	19	0	0
Rowe, Steven, Frisco	1	2	.333	6.14	18	0	0	0	5	1	29.1	40	128	22	20	4	1	4	0	6	1	15	3	0
Rowland-Smith, Ryan, San Antonio *	6	7	.462	4.35	33	17	0	0	4	0	122.0	133	532	72	59	7	5	6	5	51	0	102	15	2
Rupe, Josh, Frisco	4	3	.571	3.74	11	10	0	0	0	0	65.0	64	276	29	27	7	2	1	4	26	0	55	3	1
Rust, Evan, Springfield	2	1	.667	4.50	17	0	0	0	8	4	18.0	21	82	11	9	1	0	0	0	7	0	17	3	0
Sampson, Christopher, Corpus Christi	4	12	.250	3.12	32	19	2	1	9	4	150.0	147	602	67	52	11	4	4	4	19	2	92	2	0
Sandoval, Juan, San Antonio	9	11	.450	4.03	28	28	0	0	0	0	160.2	196	710	88	72	6	4	13	8	46	0	99	8	3
Santana, Ervin, Arkansas	5	1	.833	2.31	7	7	0	0	0	0	39.0	34	162	12	10	2	0	0	2	15	0	32	1	0
Santos, Alexandre, Midland	2	3	.400	2.95	37	0	0	0	35	19	42.2	33	174	14	14	2	2	1	1	15	2	46	4	0
Saunders, Joe, Arkansas *	7	4	.636	3.49	18	18	2	1	0	0	105.2	107	444	52	41	9	0	2	3	32	0	80	2	0
Scalamandre, Richard, Springfield	0	0	.000	4.05	7	0	0	0	1	0	6.2	9	33	3	3	0	1	0	0	7	1	5	0	0
Seay, Bobby, Tulsa *	1	0	1.000	1.80	4	0	0	0	2	1	5.0	3	17	1	1	0	0	0	1	0	0	3	0	0
Serrano, Alex, Tulsa-Arkansas	2	3	.400	1.34	35	0	0	0	30	15	40.1	34	154	10	6	2	2	0	1	7	0	23	0	1
Shell, Steven, Arkansas	10	8	.556	4.57	27	27	1	1	0	0	159.2	175	687	90	81	18	5	2	9	58	0	126	10	0
Sierra, Eduardo, Tulsa	0	3	.000	10.20	13	0	0	0	5	0	15.0	23	74	17	17	3	3	0	0	13	2	7	2	0
Simpson, Gerrit, Tulsa	3	0	1.000	3.83	27	1	0	0	4	0	42.1	48	195	23	18	3	2	3	3	19	0	32	2	0
Snare, Ryan, Frisco *	1	1	.500	0.79	9	0	0	0	5	0	11.1	5	43	1	1	0	0	0	0	5	0	11	1	0
Snyder, Kyle, Wichita	1	0	1.000	5.40	1	1	0	0	0	0	5.0	5	21	3	3	1	0	1	0	1	0	1	0	0
Songster, Judson, Tulsa	3	2	.600	2.10	50	0	0	0	9	0	68.2	54	273	18	16	5	6	2	1	21	2	67	3	0
Sonnier, Shawn, Wichita	3	0	1.000	2.18	18	0	0	0	11	5	33.0	26	133	9	8	0	2	2	1	12	3	46	3	0
Soriano, Rafael, San Antonio	0	0	.000	0.00	1	1	0	0	0	0	1.0	0	3	0	0	0	0	0	1	0	0	0	0	0
Spiehs, Randall, San Antonio	2	1	.667	2.81	17	0	0	0	7	2	25.2	21	100	8	8	3	1	1	0	7	0	15	2	0
Stertzbach, Von, Arkansas	3	5	.375	5.23	44	0	0	0	32	10	51.2	60	241	36	30	8	0	5	7	25	2	42	5	0
Stocks, Nicholas, Springfield	0	1	.000	12.71	8	0	0	0	1	0	5.2	9	31	11	8	1	0	0	2	4	0	6	0	0
Stodolka, Michael, Wichita *	4	11	.267	5.92	25	24	0	0	0	0	124.2	153	552	93	82	12	3	3	5	36	0	66	3	1
Thomas, Jared, San Antonio *	1	1	.500	5.24	11	4	0	0	3	0	22.1	30	115	14	13	3	2	0	1	19	0	21	1	0
Thompson, Justin, Frisco *	2	0	1.000	2.84	12	0	0	0	8	2	12.2	14	55	5	4	1	0	1	0	2	0	11	0	0
Ulloa, Enmanuel, Tulsa	8	3	.727	2.96	18	17	0	0	0	0	103.1	88	418	37	34	9	4	1	7	24	0	101	4	2
Volquez, Edison, Frisco	1	5	.167	4.14	10	10	1	1	0	0	58.2	58	244	29	27	6	1	1	1	17	0	49	1	0
Wallace, Shane, Springfield *	0	1	.000	9.82	7	0	0	0	2	0	7.1	13	39	9	8	0	0	2	1	4	0	2	3	0
Weaver, Jered, Arkansas	3	3	.500	3.98	8	8	0	0	0	0	43.0	43	192	22	19	5	0	1	0	19	0	46	1	0
Weis, John, Midland *	1	1	.500	3.27	29	0	0	0	13	1	33.0	32	157	18	12	2	0	1	3	22	2	25	2	1
Wilhite, Matthew, Arkansas	1	2	.333	4.07	56	0	0	0	14	2	59.2	67	242	31	27	5	2	1	3	15	0	32	1	1
Wilkerson, George, Wichita	1	4	.200	6.53	14	3	0	0	5	0	20.2	34	106	26	15	0	1	2	0	7	0	14	1	1
Williams, Aaron, Corpus Christi	2	1	.667	2.64	22	0	0	0	12	0	30.2	27	130	10	9	2	2	0	3	15	1	19	2	1
Wilson, C.J., Frisco *	0	4	.000	4.43	12	12	0	0	0	0	44.2	51	195	32	22	7	1	2	3	14	0	43	0	0
Wilson, Philip, San Antonio	0	0	.000	5.56	4	0	0	0	1	0	11.1	12	49	7	7	2	0	0	0	7	0	10	3	1
Windsor, Jason, Midland	3	6	.333	5.72	11	11	0	0	0	0	56.2	69	259	40	36	5	0	5	3	23	1	39	0	0
Young, Christopher, Tulsa	3	2	.600	4.75	35	0	0	0	10	1	53.0	53	228	29	28	6	0	1	2	17	0	35	5	0
Ziegler, Brad, Midland	2	1	.667	6.86	4	4	0	0	0	0	21.0	27	95	16	16	1	1	1	3	4	0	20	1	0
Ziegler, Michael, Midland	3	1	.750	6.54	6	6	0	0	0	0	31.2	51	151	27	23	3	0	0	0	8	0	21	2	0

PITCHERS WITH TWO OR MORE TEAMS

Pitcher, Team	W	L	Pct.	ERA	G	GS	CG	ShO	GF	Sv.	IP	H	TBF	R	ER	HR	SH	SF	HB	BB	IBB	SO	WP	Bk.
Serrano, Alex, Tulsa	1	0	1.000	0.63	11	0	0	0	8	4	14.1	10	49	1	1	1	1	0	0	1	0	5	0	0
Serrano, Alex, Arkansas	1	3	.250	1.73	24	0	0	0	22	11	26.0	24	105	9	5	1	1	0	1	6	0	18	0	1

COMBINATION SHUTOUTS: Arkansas (6) -- Santana-Olenberger-Rouwenhorst, Olenberger-Wilhite-Rouwenhorst-Pullin, Olenberger-Rouwenhorst-Wilhite-Stertzbach, Andrews-Pullin, Olenberger-Serrano, Davidson-Pullin-O'Sullivan. Corpus Christi (8) -- McClaskey-Mansfield, Nieve-Mansfield-Rijo, Barzilla-MacRae, Hirsh-Peguero, Hirsh-Williams-Peguero, Barzilla-Miller-Mansfield, Hirsh-McClaskey-Sampson, Hirsh-Williams-Sampson-Peguero-Mansfield. Frisco (3) -- Rupe-Thompson-Littleton-Bazzell, Wilson-Bazzell-Chavez-Feldman, Murray-Karsay-Feldman. Midland (8) -- Dickinson-Mattioni-Garcia, Bondurant-Weis, Obenchain-Fahmer, Landeros-Kohn-Mattioni-Crowell, Braden-Santos, Windsor-Weis-Lynch-Brannon, Dickinson-Mattioni-Lynch-Santos, Komine-Kohn-Crowell. San Antonio (8) -- Oldham-Rall-Green, Bourgeois-Pizzaro-Fruto-Green, Rowland-Smith-Cortez, Harris-Fruto, Livingston-Fruto, Sandoval-Fruto, Dorman-Key-Cortez, Dorman-Rowland-Smith. Springfield (2) -- Cook-Rawson-Stocks-Kinney, Cummings-Doyne-Rust. Tulsa (6) -- Randall-Mendoza-Serrano-Beckstead, Parker-Songster-Bevis, Ulloa-Simpson-Young-Bevis, Ulloa-Beckstead-Bevis, Nin-Beckstead, Parker-Songster-Miller. Wichita (3) -- Middleton-Bayliss-Braun, Baerlocher-Griffin-Armitage-Bayliss, Stodolka-Griffin-McGill.

NO-HIT GAMES: Murray (6 innings), Karsay (2 innings) and Feldman (1 inning), Frisco, defeated Corpus Christi, 3-0, July 28.

TEAM

Team	G	PO	A	E	TC	DP	TP	PB	Pct.
Frisco	141	3751	1552	132	5435	158	1	11	.976
Midland	140	3731	1494	127	5352	112	0	12	.976
Tulsa	140	3704	1595	134	5433	136	1	6	.975
San Antonio	140	3758	1483	146	5387	142	0	18	.973
Arkansas	140	3629	1520	147	5296	175	0	18	.972
Corpus Christi	141	3771	1501	153	5425	118	1	10	.972
Wichita	140	3645	1509	147	5301	126	0	14	.972
Springfield	140	3741	1529	171	5441	127	0	22	.969

INDIVIDUAL

FIRST BASEMEN

NOTE: All caps denotes fielding-percentage leader based on 70 games for catchers, 93 for all other non-pitchers and 112 innings for pitchers. *Throws lefthanded.

Player, Team	Pct.	G	PO	A	E	TC	DP
Abruzzo, Jared, Frisco	.965	9	82	1	3	86	9
Allegra, Matthew, Midland	.990	18	191	10	2	203	10
Barton, Daric, Midland	.990	55	448	26	5	479	35
Bernier, Douglas, Tulsa	...	1	0	0	0	0	0
Brewer, Jace, Frisco	1.000	1	11	2	0	13	0
Brown, Jeremy, Midland	.975	4	39	0	1	40	3
Cardona, Javier, Tulsa	.981	6	48	4	1	53	5
Colamarino, Brant, Midland *	.998	46	416	18	1	435	33
Colina, Alvin, Tulsa	.974	16	143	8	4	155	12
Diaz, Juan, Springfield	.978	31	247	21	6	274	21
Espy, Nathan, San Antonio	.989	51	416	34	5	455	34
Estrada, Kevin, Springfield	1.000	5	33	3	0	36	5
Eylward, Thomas, Arkansas	.992	72	583	50	5	638	81
Fagan, John, Corpus Christi	1.000	9	43	4	0	47	3
Gimenez, Hector, Corpus Christi	.992	15	126	5	1	132	16
Gold, Nathan, Frisco	.993	17	125	13	1	139	18
Gomez, Rodolfo, Wichita	1.000	3	21	1	0	22	3
Groves, Timothy, Wichita	1.000	4	23	1	0	24	0
Hanson, Travis, Springfield	1.000	1	1	0	0	1	0
HART, JASON, Frisco	.995	114	1049	60	6	1115	106
Hoorelbeke, Jesse, San Antonio	.991	92	807	58	8	873	91
Huber, Justin, Wichita	.981	66	591	36	12	639	49
Jackson, Steve, Midland	1.000	2	18	2	0	20	3
Johnson, Gabriel, Springfield	.981	40	343	23	7	373	29
King, Brennan, Wichita	.988	9	80	5	1	86	6
Koshansky, Joseph, Tulsa *	1.000	12	98	10	0	108	11
Larson, Brandon, Frisco	1.000	2	18	3	0	21	4
McNeal, Aaron, Tulsa	.992	22	229	30	2	261	21
Menchaca, Eriberto, San Antonio	1.000	3	3	1	0	4	0
Minges, Tyler, Springfield	1.000	3	17	1	0	18	2
Morales, Kendry, Arkansas	.987	60	504	41	7	552	64
Murphy, Thomas, Arkansas	.900	1	9	0	1	10	2
Myers, Clinton, Midland	1.000	3	25	0	0	25	3
Napoli, Michael, Arkansas	1.000	3	16	1	0	17	4
Norris, Steven, Corpus Christi	.985	25	191	8	3	202	19
Peavey, Patrick, Corpus Christi	1.000	1	5	2	0	7	1
Phillips, J.R., Corpus Christi *	.989	36	347	20	4	371	26
Porter, Gregory, Arkansas	.966	11	81	5	3	89	8
Pressley, Joshua, Wichita	.976	63	527	40	14	581	49
Richardson, Kevin, Frisco	1.000	1	1	0	0	1	0
Robinson, Brian, Springfield	1.000	5	54	2	0	56	3
Saccomanno, Mark, Corpus Christi	.996	48	444	22	2	468	30
Sanchez, Agustin, Tulsa	.994	19	159	14	1	174	17
Schutzenhofer, Andrew, Springfield *	.996	57	476	25	2	503	42
Slavik, Richard, Tulsa	.993	72	612	57	5	674	61
Spanos, Vasili, Midland	.982	11	108	4	2	114	11
Stavisky, Brian, Midland	.909	1	10	0	1	11	0
Taylor, Thomas, Frisco	.976	5	40	1	1	42	5
Turner, Lloyd, Midland	1.000	1	9	1	0	10	3
Zamora, Junior, Corpus Christi	.986	20	128	10	2	140	13
Zoccolillo, Peter, Springfield	.992	14	115	4	1	120	15

SECOND BASEMEN

Player, Team	Pct.	G	PO	A	E	TC	DP
Aviles, Michael, Wichita	.943	12	19	31	3	53	6
Beattie, Andrew, Midland	1.000	1	2	0	0	2	0
Bernier, Douglas, Tulsa	1.000	2	2	5	0	7	1
Betancourt, Yuniesky, San Antonio	1.000	1	3	1	0	4	1

Player, Team	Pct.	G	PO	A	E	TC	DP
Blakeley, Eric, San Antonio	.961	12	12	37	2	51	7
Brewer, Jace, Frisco	.969	51	68	153	7	228	32
Caldera, Jose, Arkansas	1.000	1	1	2	0	3	1
Callaspo, Alberto, Arkansas	.983	89	172	245	7	424	73
Casilla, Alexi, Arkansas	1.000	1	0	1	0	1	0
CASTRO, ISMAEL, San Antonio	.978	111	205	362	13	580	82
Clements, Jason, Corpus Christi	.930	12	24	29	4	57	4
Conrad, Brooks, Corpus Christi	.972	22	39	64	3	106	14
Coughlan, Cameron, Frisco *	.960	22	35	61	4	100	14
DeMarco, Mathew, Springfield	.969	13	22	41	2	65	6
Estrada, Kevin, Springfield	.971	14	25	41	2	68	6
Eylward, Thomas, Arkansas	1.000	1	2	2	0	4	1
Fox, Adam, Frisco	.973	11	13	23	1	37	6
Gomez, Francis, Midland	1.000	9	25	20	0	45	6
Gomez, Rodolfo, Wichita	.950	22	40	56	5	101	12
Gotay, Ruben, Wichita	1.000	27	50	72	0	122	14
Groves, Timothy, Wichita	.981	45	86	120	4	210	18
Guance, Luis, Tulsa	.905	6	10	9	2	21	1
Hanson, Travis, Springfield	1.000	1	0	3	0	3	0
Herr, Aaron, Springfield	.959	112	202	308	22	532	74
Keim, Kevin, Wichita	.980	11	20	28	1	49	8
Kendrick, Howard, Arkansas	.974	46	77	146	6	229	38
Kiger, Mark, Midland	.988	74	141	192	4	337	41
Laya, Rayner, Springfield	1.000	5	10	18	0	28	1
Leahy, Ryan, Arkansas	1.000	6	7	11	0	18	2
Matranga, Dave, Arkansas	1.000	2	1	5	0	6	1
McCoy, Michael, Springfield	1.000	1	2	1	0	3	1
Melillo, Kevin, Midland	.986	34	59	87	2	148	25
Menchaca, Eriberto, San Antonio	.962	20	32	43	3	78	12
Meyer, Drew, Frisco	.976	69	115	213	8	336	51
Morrissey, Adam, Midland	.939	14	19	27	3	49	5
Murphy, Donnie, Wichita	.988	30	48	110	2	160	18
Navarrete, Raymond, Corpus Christi	.971	29	45	88	4	137	11
Nicholson, Thomas, Tulsa	1.000	1	4	2	0	6	1
Nix, Jayson, Tulsa	.975	131	274	433	18	725	85
Quintanilla, Omar, Midland	.923	5	14	10	2	26	3
Reyes, Ivan, Arkansas	1.000	1	2	1	0	3	1
Riggs, Don, Corpus Christi	.975	72	127	226	9	362	48
Robinson, Christopher, Corpus Christi	.922	13	38	33	6	77	12
Taylor, Thomas, Frisco	.800	2	1	3	1	5	2
Tena, Hector, Tulsa	1.000	4	6	11	0	17	3
Turner, Lloyd, Midland	.957	15	35	31	3	69	7

THIRD BASEMEN

Player, Team	Pct.	G	PO	A	E	TC	DP
Allegra, Matthew, Midland	.864	9	5	14	3	22	1
Aviles, Michael, Wichita	.922	20	17	42	5	64	7
Beattie, Andrew, Midland	.915	18	10	44	5	59	3
Bernier, Douglas, Tulsa	1.000	1	2	0	0	2	0
Blakeley, Eric, San Antonio	.833	5	2	8	2	12	0
Brewer, Jace, Frisco	.875	4	1	13	2	16	2
Eckelman, Thomas, Corpus Christi	.917	8	5	6	1	12	1
Escobar, Gustavo, Tulsa	.939	26	10	36	3	49	3
Estrada, Kevin, Springfield	.889	5	1	7	1	9	1
Eylward, Thomas, Arkansas	.850	10	5	12	3	20	1
Fox, Adam, Frisco	.959	35	19	51	3	73	5
Gomez, Francis, Midland	.957	54	24	109	6	139	15
Gomez, Rodolfo, Wichita	.889	5	0	8	1	9	1
Groves, Timothy, Wichita	.846	10	3	8	2	13	1
Guance, Luis, Tulsa	.904	50	24	79	11	114	7
Guzman, Jesus, San Antonio	.909	118	71	170	24	265	28
Hanson, Travis, Springfield	.909	136	95	264	36	395	20
Keim, Adam, Wichita	.867	4	6	7	2	15	0
KING, BRENNAN, Wichita	.951	107	60	195	13	268	14
Larson, Brandon, Frisco	.977	13	10	32	1	43	6
Laya, Rayner, Springfield	...	1	0	0	0	0	0
Leahy, Ryan, Arkansas	.985	28	21	44	1	66	12
Maier, Mitchell, Wichita	1.000	1	0	3	0	3	0
Matranga, Dave, Arkansas	.952	7	7	13	1	21	1
Menchaca, Eriberto, San Antonio	.957	21	11	33	2	46	4
Meyer, Drew, Frisco	1.000	7	1	10	0	11	0
Morrissey, Adam, Midland	.900	19	4	32	4	40	2
Navarrete, Raymond, Corpus Christi	.903	15	8	20	3	31	1
Nicholson, Thomas, Tulsa	.880	8	4	18	3	25	4
Pavkovich, Adam, Arkansas	1.000	8	5	20	0	25	1
Peavey, Patrick, Corpus Christi	.889	5	1	7	1	9	0

Player, Team	Pct.	G	PO	A	E	TC	DP
Perry, Jason, Midland	1.000	1	0	1	0	1	0
Porter, Gregory, Arkansas	.904	96	85	169	27	281	25
Reyes, Ivan, Arkansas	.882	4	4	11	2	17	1
Riggs, Eric, Corpus Christi	1.000	3	0	3	0	3	1
Saccomanno, Mark, Corpus Christi	.902	79	39	135	19	193	13
Slavik, Richard, Tulsa	.946	63	47	112	9	168	8
Spanos, Vasili, Midland	.932	31	18	50	5	73	2
Taylor, Thomas, Frisco	.943	88	40	159	12	211	9
Tena, Hector, Tulsa	1.000	5	2	12	0	14	2
Turner, Lloyd, Midland	.881	24	15	44	8	67	2
Whiteman, Tommy, Corpus Christi	.946	20	11	42	3	56	2
Zamora, Junior, Corpus Christi	.860	22	9	40	8	57	2

SHORTSTOPS

Player, Team	Pct.	G	PO	A	E	TC	DP
Arias, Joaquin, Frisco	.952	118	201	373	29	603	90
Aviles, Michael, Wichita	.934	102	171	295	33	499	62
Aybar, Erick, Arkansas	.953	134	243	403	32	678	108
Barmes, Clint, Tulsa	.957	6	4	18	1	23	3
Beattie, Andrew, Midland	.800	2	2	6	2	10	3
BERNIER, DOUGLAS, Tulsa	.974	114	178	356	14	548	77
Betancourt, Yuniesky, San Antonio	.980	51	89	152	5	246	23
Blanco, Andres, Wichita	1.000	9	9	29	0	38	2
Bolivar, Cesar, Springfield	...	1	0	0	0	0	0
Brewer, Jace, Frisco	1.000	11	15	29	0	44	8
Casilla, Alexi, Arkansas	.833	3	5	10	3	18	4
Clements, Jason, Corpus Christi	.667	2	1	1	1	3	0
Eckelman, Thomas, Corpus Christi	1.000	16	13	23	0	36	5
Escobar, Gustavo, Tulsa	.900	2	4	5	1	10	0
Estrada, Kevin, Springfield	.943	50	76	124	12	212	18
Falu, Irving, Wichita	.923	6	7	17	2	26	4
Gomez, Francis, Midland	.918	12	15	30	4	49	7
Groves, Timothy, Wichita	.972	7	13	22	1	36	2
Guance, Luis, Tulsa	.889	3	0	8	1	9	1
Jaramillo, Milko, Springfield	.973	55	79	172	7	258	34
Jones, Adam, San Antonio	.959	61	115	165	12	292	39
Kiger, Mark, Midland	.969	61	79	175	8	262	32
Laya, Rayner, Springfield	1.000	4	6	5	0	11	1
Leahy, Ryan, Arkansas	1.000	1	0	4	0	4	0
Macri, Matthew, Tulsa	1.000	1	1	2	0	3	0
Matranga, Dave, Arkansas	.800	1	1	3	1	5	0
McCoy, Michael, Springfield	1.000	2	4	4	0	8	1
Menchaca, Eriberto, San Antonio	.977	29	44	81	3	128	19
Meyer, Drew, Frisco	.966	12	24	32	2	58	9
Murphy, Donnie, Wichita	.964	20	34	72	4	110	13
Nicholson, Thomas, Tulsa	.952	4	7	13	1	21	3
Pavkovich, Adam, Arkansas	1.000	1	0	1	0	1	0
Perez, Nestor, Tulsa	.946	8	14	21	2	37	6
Quintanilla, Omar, Midland	.963	74	81	229	12	322	33
Reese, Pokey, San Antonio	1.000	1	2	3	0	5	1
Reyes, Ivan, Arkansas	.875	3	1	6	1	8	1
Riggs, Eric, Corpus Christi	.978	52	71	147	5	223	24
Robinson, Christopher, Corpus Christi	.917	53	80	174	23	277	36
Ryan, Brendan, Springfield	.942	43	69	125	12	206	20
Slavik, Richard, Tulsa	.000	2	0	0	1	1	0
Taylor, Thomas, Frisco	1.000	4	5	6	0	11	2
Tena, Hector, Tulsa	.969	10	12	19	1	32	5
Whiteman, Tommy, Corpus Christi	.969	24	32	62	3	97	14
Zamora, Junior, Corpus Christi	...	1	0	0	0	0	0

OUTFIELDERS

Player, Team	Pct.	G	PO	A	E	TC	DP
Aldridge, Cory, Wichita	.980	77	148	1	3	152	0
Allega, Matthew, Midland	1.000	24	42	1	0	43	0
Anderson, Joshua, Corpus Christi	.973	126	287	6	8	301	0
Ankiel, Rick, Springfield *	.981	25	48	3	1	52	1
Aspito, Jason, Arkansas	.978	49	86	4	2	92	0
Barker, Sean, Tulsa	.980	112	189	11	4	204	1
Barton, Daric, Midland	...	1	0	0	0	0	0
Beattie, Andrew, Midland	1.000	1	2	0	0	2	0
Bohn, Thomas, San Antonio	.985	107	247	14	4	265	4
Bolivar, Cesar, Springfield	.980	97	141	8	3	152	1
Boyd, Shaun, Springfield	.968	121	295	10	10	315	4
Brewer, Jace, Frisco	...	1	0	0	0	0	0
Bubela, Jaime, San Antonio	.969	116	247	6	8	261	2
Butler, Billy, Wichita	.914	26	31	1	3	35	0
Cleveland, Jeremy, Frisco	.981	59	100	4	2	106	0
Costa, Shane, Wichita	.975	72	117	2	3	122	1
Coughlan, Cameron, Frisco *	1.000	40	86	3	0	89	3
Craig, Casey, San Antonio	...	1	0	0	0	0	0

Player, Team	Pct.	G	PO	A	E	TC	DP
Czarniecki, Jordan, Tulsa	1.000	42	95	5	0	100	1
Diaz, Matt, Wichita	1.000	5	11	1	0	12	0
Draper, John, Wichita	.957	17	20	2	1	23	2
Eckelman, Thomas, Corpus Christi	1.000	1	3	0	0	3	0
Eldridge, Rashad, Frisco	1.000	7	10	0	0	10	0
Emmons, John, San Antonio	...	1	0	0	0	0	0
Estrada, Kevin, Springfield	1.000	14	26	2	0	28	0
Ethier, Andre, Midland	.990	127	275	16	3	294	2
Eylward, Thomas, Arkansas	1.000	7	10	0	0	10	0
Fagan, John, Corpus Christi	.962	33	48	2	2	52	1
Gates, James, Arkansas	.972	92	135	3	4	142	0
Gorecki, Reid, Springfield	.981	44	100	3	2	105	0
Groves, Timothy, Wichita	1.000	13	22	1	0	23	0
Guance, Luis, Tulsa	1.000	4	8	0	0	8	0
Haerther, Cody, Springfield	.926	36	48	2	4	54	0
Harris, Edward, San Antonio	.996	115	240	12	1	253	4
Hart, Jason, Frisco	1.000	1	1	0	0	1	0
Holliday, Matt, Tulsa	1.000	7	12	0	0	12	0
Hoorelbeke, Jesse, San Antonio	1.000	1	3	0	0	3	0
Jimerson, Charlton, Corpus Christi	.971	112	227	10	7	244	2
Jones, Adam, San Antonio	1.000	2	1	0	0	1	0
Leahy, Ryan, Arkansas	1.000	5	5	1	0	6	0
Maier, Mitchell, Wichita	.984	79	176	4	3	183	1
Matthews, Gary, Frisco	.500	1	1	0	1	2	0
Mehl, Truan, Frisco	1.000	2	1	0	0	1	0
Meyer, Drew, Frisco	...	1	0	0	0	0	0
Miller, Anthony, Tulsa	.958	115	238	12	11	261	2
Minges, Tyler, Springfield	.971	94	195	7	6	208	0
Morales, Kendry, Arkansas	1.000	1	3	1	0	4	1
Morris, Kenneth, Arkansas	.972	33	64	5	2	71	0
Murphy, Thomas, Arkansas	.990	130	283	18	3	304	7
Navarrete, Raymond, Corpus Christi	1.000	7	9	0	0	9	0
Nelson, Jonathan, San Antonio	.958	78	127	11	6	144	3
Nesbit, Michael, San Antonio	1.000	7	13	1	0	14	0
Parker, Tyler, Springfield	.958	10	23	0	1	24	0
Perry, Jason, Midland	.984	93	183	6	3	192	2
Porter, Gregory, Arkansas	1.000	1	1	0	0	1	0
Rodriguez, Carlos, Corpus Christi	.949	48	70	4	4	78	0
Rodriguez, Michael, Corpus Christi *	.994	109	169	7	1	177	1
Ruan, Wilkin, Wichita	1.000	67	141	8	0	149	2
Salazar, Jeffrey, Tulsa *	.994	66	155	6	1	162	1
Senreiso, Juan, Frisco	.958	129	259	15	12	286	5
Sinisi, Vincent, Frisco *	.967	59	87	1	3	91	1
Smith, William, Frisco	1.000	19	36	1	0	37	0
Spilborghs, Ryan, Tulsa	.991	50	97	12	1	110	3
STANLEY, STEPHEN, Midland *	.997	125	297	9	1	307	2
Stavisky, Brian, Midland	.989	55	92	1	1	94	0
Stocker, Myreon, Wichita	.988	75	166	3	2	171	0
Tena, Hector, Tulsa	.875	3	6	1	1	8	0
Thigpen, Judson, Tulsa	.973	28	35	1	1	37	0
Turner, Lloyd, Midland	...	2	0	0	0	0	0
Willits, Reggie, Arkansas	.986	120	269	8	4	281	1
Wright, Gavin, Corpus Christi	1.000	2	4	0	0	4	0
Yan, Ruddy, Frisco	.976	113	230	9	6	245	2
Zoccolillo, Peter, Springfield	1.000	8	19	0	0	19	0

CATCHERS

Player, Team	Pct.	G	PO	A	E	TC	DP
Abruzzo, Jared, Frisco	1.000	1	7	1	0	8	0
Brown, Jeremy, Midland	.984	106	691	58	12	761	6
Cancel, Robinson, Springfield	.989	60	402	48	5	455	2
Cardona, Javier, Tulsa	1.000	6	36	2	0	38	1
Colina, Alvin, Tulsa	.982	42	249	27	5	281	2
Conway, Daniel, Tulsa	.967	48	296	29	11	336	2
Cresse, Bradley, Springfield	.983	11	54	5	1	60	0
Del Chiaro, Brenton, Arkansas	.995	39	179	10	1	190	4
Draper, John, Wichita	.996	40	230	20	1	251	2
Duff, Timothy, Arkansas	1.000	7	34	6	0	40	0
Eckelman, Thomas, Corpus Christi	...	1	0	0	0	0	0
Esposito, Brian, Frisco	.972	38	222	22	7	251	2
GIMENEZ, HECTOR, Corpus Christi	.990	87	640	75	7	722	3
Higashi, Jonathan, Frisco	1.000	1	7	0	0	7	0
Iannetta, Christopher, Tulsa	.980	16	86	10	2	98	1
Jackson, Steve, Midland	.962	8	48	3	2	53	0
Johnson, Gabriel, Springfield	.982	10	48	8	1	57	1
Maduro, Jorge, Wichita	.923	2	10	2	1	13	0
Moon, Brian, San Antonio	.989	52	331	45	4	380	3
Morris, Jed, Midland	1.000	4	31	4	0	35	0
Motte, Jason, Springfield	1.000	1	8	5	0	13	1
Moylan, Daniel, Springfield	.981	56	330	28	7	365	4

CLASS AA Texas League

Player, Team	Pct.	G	PO	A	E	TC	DP
Myers, Clinton, Midland	.991	31	197	16	2	215	1
Napoli, Michael, Arkansas	.981	109	638	76	14	728	7
Nickeas, Michael, Frisco	.995	68	521	50	3	574	5
Norris, Steven, Corpus Christi	.995	55	402	29	2	433	3
Oliveros, Luis, San Antonio	.984	39	291	26	5	322	5
Pagnozzi, Matthew, Springfield	.971	11	61	5	2	68	0
Price, Jared, Wichita	.944	4	15	2	1	18	0
Quintero, Humberto, Corpus Christi	1.000	3	24	4	0	28	1
Richardson, Kevin, Frisco	.993	16	123	10	1	134	1
Rivera, Rene, San Antonio	.990	57	367	44	4	415	4
Sanchez, Agustin, Tulsa	.992	35	217	17	2	236	2
Santana, Emmanuel, Arkansas	1.000	3	18	2	0	20	0
Smith, Dustin, Frisco	.986	20	130	8	2	140	2
Tupman, Mathew, Wichita	.986	102	648	82	10	740	12

PITCHERS

Player, Team	Pct.	G	PO	A	E	TC	DP
Allen, Blake, Corpus Christi *	1.000	16	0	4	0	4	0
Alvarez, Oscar, Springfield *	.923	29	4	20	2	26	1
Anderson, Brian, Wichita *	...	1	0	0	0	0	0
Andrews, Clayton, Arkansas *	1.000	2	1	2	0	3	0
Arakawa, Yusuke, Tulsa	.941	41	5	11	1	17	0
Armitage, Barry, Wichita	1.000	41	5	13	0	18	1
Arredondo, Jose, Arkansas	...	5	0	0	0	0	0
Asahina, Jonathan, Tulsa	.978	26	15	29	1	45	3
Atchison, Scott, San Antonio	...	5	0	0	0	0	0
Austen, David, Arkansas	1.000	27	3	10	0	13	0
Axelson, Joshua, Springfield	1.000	28	5	4	0	9	1
Backe, Brandon, Corpus Christi	1.000	2	0	1	0	1	0
Baerlocher, Ryan, Wichita	.950	15	6	13	1	20	0
Barzilla, Philip, Corpus Christi *	.862	41	7	18	4	29	1
Bass, Brian, Wichita	.950	27	12	26	2	40	3
Bauer, Peter, Corpus Christi	.929	11	4	9	1	14	1
Bayliss, Jonah, Wichita	.800	30	2	2	1	5	0
Bazardo, Yorman, San Antonio	1.000	6	5	1	0	6	2
Bazzell, Shane, Frisco	1.000	35	5	9	0	14	0
Beckstead, Jentry, Tulsa	1.000	51	3	14	0	17	3
Benes, Alan, Springfield	1.000	15	1	1	0	2	0
Bevis, P. J., Tulsa	1.000	41	1	4	0	5	0
Bittner, Timothy, Arkansas *	1.000	14	1	14	0	15	0
Blair, Thomas, Springfield *	1.000	8	0	8	0	8	0
Bondurant, Steven, Midland *	.880	28	3	19	3	25	2
Borbon, Pedro, Arkansas *	1.000	6	0	1	0	1	0
Bourgeois, Nicholas, San Antonio *	1.000	2	0	1	0	1	0
Braden, Dallas, Midland *	.853	16	6	23	5	34	1
Brannon, Nicholas, Midland *	.857	26	1	5	1	7	1
Braun, Ryan, Wichita	1.000	6	0	1	0	1	0
Bray, Stephen, Wichita	.667	20	0	2	1	3	0
Bumstead, Michael, San Antonio	.625	7	3	2	3	8	0
Burcie, Jarrad, Frisco	...	1	0	0	0	0	0
Burgos, Ambiorix, Wichita	1.000	12	0	1	0	1	0
Cavazos, Andres, Springfield	1.000	23	3	3	0	6	0
Cedeno, Juan, Wichita *	1.000	11	1	2	0	3	0
Chavez, Jesse, Frisco	1.000	31	1	11	0	12	0
Collazo, William, Arkansas *	.833	26	4	16	4	24	2
Cook, Aaron, Tulsa	1.000	1	0	1	0	1	0
Cook, Jeremy, Corpus Christi	.889	37	5	19	3	27	2
Cortez, Renee, San Antonio	1.000	44	5	6	0	11	1
Cotton, Nathan, Springfield	1.000	8	3	2	0	5	1
Crabtree, Tim, Wichita	.800	11	2	2	1	5	0
Crockett, William, Tulsa	.875	18	2	5	1	8	2
Crowell, Kyle, Midland	.905	39	4	15	2	21	1
Cummings, Jeremy, Springfield	.833	12	2	13	3	18	2
Damico, Yovany, Wichita	1.000	1	0	1	0	1	0
Danks, John, Frisco *	.955	18	4	17	1	22	2
Davidson, Daniel, Arkansas *	.969	28	7	24	1	32	2
Demaria, Chris, Wichita	1.000	10	1	3	0	4	0
Diamond, Thomas, Frisco	.800	14	1	3	1	5	0
Dickinson, Andy, Midland *	.978	27	8	36	1	45	1
Dominguez, Juan, Frisco	.800	15	0	4	1	5	0
Done, Juan, San Antonio	1.000	7	1	1	0	2	0
Dorman, Richard, San Antonio	1.000	3	0	1	0	1	0
Doyne, Michael, Springfield	1.000	48	4	2	0	6	0
Ebert, Derrin, Wichita *	.938	27	10	20	2	32	4
Eldred, Cal, Springfield	1.000	3	0	2	0	2	0
Endicott, Drew, Wichita	1.000	2	0	2	0	2	0
Estrada, Kevin, Springfield	...	1	0	0	0	0	0
Fahrner, Evan, Midland	.870	45	3	17	3	23	0
Feldman, Scott, Frisco	1.000	46	5	11	0	16	0
Ferrari, Anthony, Springfield *	1.000	29	0	4	0	4	1
Flannery, Michael, San Antonio	...	6	0	0	0	0	0
Francisco, Frank, Frisco	.500	4	0	1	1	2	0
Fruto, Emiliano, San Antonio	.889	40	5	11	2	18	1
Garcia, Jairo, Midland	1.000	10	0	2	0	2	0
Giron, Roberto, Corpus Christi	1.000	21	1	5	0	6	1
Gomez, Rodolfo, Wichita	1.000	3	0	1	0	1	0
Green, Sean, San Antonio	.800	21	3	5	2	10	0
Griffin, Jonathan, Wichita	1.000	37	8	6	0	14	0
Gwyn, Marcus, Midland	1.000	19	2	3	0	5	1
Harris, Jeff, San Antonio	.833	11	2	8	2	12	0
Hicklen, Patrick, Wichita	...	1	0	0	0	0	0
Hirsh, Jason, Corpus Christi	.912	29	9	22	3	34	0
Hodge, Kevin, Corpus Christi	1.000	14	0	2	0	2	0
Hoelscher, Nathan, Wichita *	1.000	51	3	10	0	13	0
Howell, J.P., Wichita *	1.000	3	0	2	0	2	0
Huber, Jonathan, San Antonio	.897	26	10	16	3	29	1
Hudgins, John, Frisco	1.000	3	1	6	0	7	0
James, Delvin, Arkansas	1.000	17	1	8	0	9	1
Jimenez, Cesar, San Antonio *	.955	45	2	19	1	22	0
Jimenez, Kelvin, Frisco	1.000	6	0	3	0	3	0
Jimenez, Ubaldo, Tulsa	1.000	12	3	5	0	8	0
Jones, Greg, Arkansas		3	0	0	0	0	0
Karsay, Steve, Frisco	1.000	19	1	4	0	5	1
Key, Christopher, San Antonio *	.933	23	2	12	1	15	3
Kieschnick, Brooks, Corpus Christi	1.000	5	0	1	0	1	0
Kinney, Joshua, Springfield	1.000	32	3	9	0	12	1
Kohn, Shawn, Midland	1.000	55	1	15	0	16	2
Komine, Shane, Midland	1.000	5	0	5	0	5	0
Lambert, Christopher, Springfield	.917	18	2	9	1	12	0
Landeros, Leonard, Midland *	1.000	18	1	6	0	7	0
Leahy, Ryan, Arkansas	1.000	1	0	1	0	1	0
Leek, Randy, Springfield *	.982	28	13	43	1	57	2
Littleton, Wes, Frisco	1.000	48	5	22	0	27	2
Livingston, Robert, San Antonio *	.956	18	13	30	2	45	0
Lorenzo, Mathew, Frisco	1.000	10	2	9	0	11	0
Lowery, Devon, Wichita	.667	4	0	2	1	3	0
Lynch, Kevin, Arkansas	.667	2	0	2	1	3	0
Lynch, Matthew, Midland *	.921	35	9	26	3	38	1
MacRae, Scott, Corpus Christi	1.000	16	5	12	0	17	0
Mahay, Ron, Frisco *	1.000	5	1	2	0	3	0
Mansfield, Monte, Corpus Christi	.941	43	4	12	1	17	2
Marcano, Luis, Frisco	1.000	10	0	1	0	1	0
Markray, Thaddius, Wichita	.900	22	6	3	1	10	2
Masset, Nicholas, Frisco	.895	29	13	21	4	38	4
Mateo, Nathanel, San Antonio	.750	14	1	5	2	8	0
Mattioni, Nicholas, Midland	1.000	42	5	9	0	14	1
McClaskey, Timothy, Corpus Christi	.968	27	4	26	1	31	1
McGill, Max, Wichita	.900	29	2	7	1	10	0
McLemore, Mark, Corpus Christi *	.750	15	1	8	3	12	2
Mears, Chris, Springfield	1.000	13	1	2	0	3	0
Mendoza, Marcos, Tulsa *	1.000	10	2	1	0	3	0
Merchant, Jamie, Corpus Christi	.929	24	1	12	1	14	0
Middleton, Kyle, Wichita	.978	28	13	32	1	46	2
Miller, James, Tulsa	1.000	16	1	0	0	1	0
Miller, Joshua, Corpus Christi	...	3	0	0	0	0	0
Montero, Agustin, Frisco	.909	40	3	7	1	11	0
Moylan, Daniel, Springfield	...	1	0	0	0	0	0
Murray, Arlington, Frisco *	.944	11	2	15	1	18	1
Nannini, Michael, Midland	.938	13	5	10	1	16	0
Neal, Blaine, Tulsa	1.000	4	0	1	0	1	0
Nelson, Joe, Wichita	1.000	9	3	1	0	4	0
Nieve, Fernando, Corpus Christi	1.000	14	3	10	0	13	0
Nin, Sandy, Tulsa	1.000	20	5	15	0	20	0
Nunez, Leo, Wichita	1.000	12	2	0	0	2	0
Nussbeck, Mark, Springfield *	1.000	6	0	1	0	1	0
Obenchain, Stephen, Midland	1.000	11	4	5	0	9	1
Oldham, Thomas, San Antonio *	.810	27	3	14	4	21	1
Olenberger, Kasey, Arkansas	.963	32	8	18	1	27	1
Olson, Jason, Arkansas	...	4	0	0	0	0	0
Ool, Kevin, Springfield *	1.000	14	0	2	0	2	0
O'Sullivan, Mark, Arkansas	.909	45	5	5	1	11	1
Pals, Jordan, Springfield	.895	27	13	21	4	38	3
Parker, Christian, Tulsa	.963	12	12	14	1	27	2
Parker, Zachary, Tulsa *	.833	27	4	26	6	36	1
Pearce, Josh, Springfield	1.000	7	0	1	0	1	0
Peguero, Jailen, Corpus Christi	.889	50	3	5	1	9	0
Perry, Brandon, Wichita *	.500	10	0	1	1	2	0
Pizzaro, Melvin, San Antonio *	1.000	4	0	1	0	1	0
Pomeranz, Stuart, Springfield	.933	18	2	12	1	15	0
Pullin, Aaron, Arkansas	.846	51	7	4	2	13	1
Pulsipher, Bill, Springfield *	1.000	1	0	2	0	2	0

Player, Team	Pct.	G	PO	A	E	TC	DP
Rall, Tim, San Antonio *	.938	41	4	11	1	16	0
Ramirez, Ramon, Tulsa	.714	9	3	2	2	7	0
Ramsey, Keith, Tulsa *	1.000	10	0	5	0	5	0
Randall, Scott, Tulsa	1.000	9	7	6	0	13	0
Rawson, Anthony, Springfield *	1.000	38	2	12	0	14	1
Riggs, Eric, Corpus Christi	1.000	1	0	1	0	1	0
Rijo, Fernando, Corpus Christi	1.000	34	4	6	0	10	1
Roberts, Mark, Frisco	1.000	10	1	1	0	2	0
Robinson, Brian, Springfield	...	1	0	0	0	0	0
Rodriguez, Wandy, Corpus Christi *	...	1	0	0	0	0	0
Rodriguez, Wilfredo, Frisco *	1.000	12	1	6	0	7	1
Rouwenhorst, Jonathon, Arkansas *	1.000	22	3	3	0	6	0
Rowe, Steven, Frisco	1.000	18	1	4	0	5	0
Rowland-Smith, Ryan, San Antonio *	.833	33	6	9	3	18	0
Rupe, Josh, Frisco	1.000	11	2	9	0	11	1
Rust, Evan, Springfield	.833	17	0	5	1	6	0
Sampson, Christopher, Corpus Christi	.980	32	13	36	1	50	2
Sandoval, Juan, San Antonio	.719	28	7	16	9	32	0
Santana, Ervin, Arkansas	.900	7	5	4	1	10	3
Santos, Alexandre, Midland	1.000	37	0	6	0	6	0
Saunders, Joe, Arkansas *	.957	18	4	18	1	23	0
Scalamandre, Richard, Springfield	1.000	7	0	1	0	1	0
Seay, Bobby, Tulsa *	1.000	4	2	2	0	4	0
Serrano, Alex, Tulsa-Arkansas	1.000	35	2	6	0	8	1
Shell, Steven, Arkansas	.973	27	13	23	1	37	2
Sierra, Eduardo, Tulsa	1.000	13	2	2	0	4	1
Simpson, Gerrit, Tulsa	1.000	27	1	4	0	5	0
Snare, Ryan, Frisco *	1.000	9	0	2	0	2	0
Snyder, Kyle, Wichita	1.000	1	3	1	0	4	0

Player, Team	Pct.	G	PO	A	E	TC	DP
Songster, Judson, Tulsa	.923	50	3	9	1	13	0
Sonnier, Shawn, Wichita	.857	18	3	3	1	7	0
Soriano, Rafael, San Antonio	...	1	0	0	0	0	0
Spiehs, Randall, San Antonio	1.000	17	5	2	0	7	0
Stertzbach, Von, Arkansas	.778	44	5	2	2	9	1
Stocks, Nicholas, Springfield	1.000	8	0	1	0	1	0
STODOLKA, MICHAEL, Wichita *	1.000	25	6	23	0	29	1
Thomas, Jared, San Antonio *	1.000	11	0	5	0	5	0
Thompson, Justin, Frisco *	1.000	12	3	1	0	4	0
Ulloa, Enmanuel, Tulsa	1.000	18	9	8	0	17	0
Volquez, Edison, Frisco	.875	10	2	5	1	8	0
Wallace, Shane, Springfield *	.600	7	0	3	2	5	1
Weaver, Jered, Arkansas	.500	8	1	1	2	4	0
Weis, John, Midland *	.750	29	2	1	1	4	0
Wilhite, Matthew, Arkansas	1.000	56	4	23	0	27	4
Wilkerson, George, Wichita	.875	14	2	5	1	8	0
Williams, Aaron, Corpus Christi	.833	22	2	3	1	6	0
Wilson, C.J., Frisco *	.857	12	0	12	2	14	1
Wilson, Philip, San Antonio	1.000	4	2	0	0	2	0
Windsor, Jason, Midland	1.000	11	2	8	0	10	1
Young, Christopher, Tulsa	.952	35	9	11	1	21	0
Ziegler, Brad, Midland	1.000	4	3	2	0	5	0
Ziegler, Michael, Midland	1.000	6	2	5	0	7	1

PITCHERS WITH TWO OR MORE TEAMS

Player, Team	Pct.	G	PO	A	E	TC	DP
Serrano, Alex, Tulsa	1.000	11	2	5	0	7	0
Serrano, Alex, Arkansas	1.000	24	0	1	0	1	1

LEAGUE CHAMPIONS

Year	Team	Pct.
1888—	Dallas	.671
1889—	Houston	.551
1890—	Galveston	.705
1892—	Houston	.741
	Houston	.613
1895—	Dallas	.754
	Fort Worth*	.750
1896—	Fort Worth	.757
	Houston*	.679
	Galveston	.548
1897—	San Antonio†	.657
	Galveston†	.717
1898—	League disbanded.	
1899—	Galveston	.632
	Galveston	.762
1900-01—	Did not operate.	
1902—	Corsicana	.866
	Corsicana	.682
1903—	Paris-Waco	.615
	Dallas*	.648
1904—	Corsicana*	.615
	Fort Worth	.800
1905—	Fort Worth	.545
1906—	Fort Worth	.677
	Cleburne∞	.609
1907—	Austin	.629
1908—	San Antonio	.664
1909—	Houston	.601
1910—	Dallas†	.586
	Houston†	.586
1911—	Austin	.575
1912—	Houston	.626
1913—	Houston	.620
1914—	Houston†	.671
	Waco†	.671
1915—	Waco	.592
1916—	Waco	.587
1917—	Dallas	.600
1918—	Dallas	.584
1919—	Shreveport*	.677
	Fort Worth	.651
1920—	Fort Worth	.703
	Fort Worth	.750
1921—	Fort Worth	.691
	Fort Worth	.662
1922—	Fort Worth	.694
	Fort Worth	.711
1923—	Fort Worth	.632

Year	Team	Pct.
1924—	Fort Worth	.689
	Fort Worth	.763
1925—	Fort Worth	.711
	Fort Worth▲	.653
1926—	Dallas	.574
1927—	Wichita Falls	.654
1928—	Houston*	.679
	Wichita Falls	.731
1929—	Dallas*	.588
	Wichita Falls	.620
1930—	Wichita Falls	.697
	Fort Worth*	.632
1931—	Houston◆	.625
	Houston	.734
1932—	Beaumont*	.640
	Dallas	.727
1933—	Houston	.623
	San Antonio (4th)§	.523
1934—	Galveston‡	.579
1935—	Oklahoma City‡	.590
1936—	Dallas	.604
	Tulsa (3rd)§	.519
1937—	Oklahoma City	.635
	Fort Worth (3rd)§	.535
1938—	Beaumont	.635
1939—	Houston	.606
	Fort Worth (4th)§	.540
1940—	Houston‡	.652
1941—	Houston	.673
	Dallas (4th)§	.519
1942—	Beaumont	.605
	Shreveport (2nd)§	.576
1943-44-45—	Did not operate.	
1946—	Fort Worth	.656
	Dallas (2nd)§	.591
1947—	Houston‡	.623
1948—	Fort Worth‡	.601
1949—	Fort Worth	.649
	Tulsa (2nd)§	.584
1950—	Beaumont	.595
	San Antonio (4th)§	.513
1951—	Houston‡	.619
1952—	Dallas	.571
	Shreveport (3rd)§	.522
1953—	Dallas‡	.571
1954—	Shreveport	.559
	Houston (2nd)§	.553

Year	Team	Pct.
1955—	Dallas	.581
	Shreveport (3rd)§	.540
1956—	Houston‡	.623
1957—	Dallas	.662
	Houston (2nd)§	.630
1958—	Fort Worth	.582
	Cor. Christi (3rd)§	.507
1959—	Victoria	.589
	Austin (2nd)§	.548
1960—	Rio Grande Valley	.590
	Tulsa (3rd)	.528
1961—	Amarillo	.643
	San Antonio (3rd)§	.532
1962—	El Paso	.571
	Tulsa (2nd)§	.550
1963—	San Antonio	.564
	Tulsa (3rd)§	.529
1964—	San Antonio‡	.607
1965—	Tulsa	.574
	Albuquerque■	.550
1966—	Arkansas	.579
1967—	Albuquerque	.557
1968—	Arkansas	.586
	El Paso■	.562
1969—	Amarillo	.593
	Memphis■	.504
1970—	Albuquerque◆	.615
	Memphis	.507
1971—	Did not operate as league—clubs were members of Dixie Association.	
1972—	Alexandria	.600
	El Paso■	.557
1973—	San Antonio	.590
	Memphis■	.558
1974—	Victoria■	.581
	El Paso	.555
1975—	Lafayette▼	.558
	Midland▼	.604
1976—	Amarillo■	.600
	Shreveport	.515
1977—	El Paso	.600
	Arkansas*	.485
1978—	El Paso *	.593
	Jackson	.567
1979—	Arkansas*	.571
	Midland	.563
1980—	Arkansas*	.596
	San Antonio	.544

CLASS AA *Texas League*

– 487 –

Year	Team	Pct.
1981—	San Antonio	.571
	Jackson*	.507
1982—	El Paso	.559
	Tulsa*	.515
1983—	Jackson	.507
	Beaumont*	.500
1984—	Beaumont	.654
	Jackson*	.610
1985—	El Paso	.632
	Jackson*	.537
1986—	El Paso*	.630
	Jackson	.533
1987—	Wichita*	.515
	Jackson	.515
1988—	El Paso	.552
	Tulsa*	.522
1989—	Arkansas*	.585
	Wichita	.537
1990—	San Antonio	.582
	Shreveport*	.489
1991—	Shreveport*	.632
	El Paso	.596

Year	Team	Pct.
1992—	Shreveport	.566
	Wichita*	.515
1993—	El Paso	.563
	Jackson*	.541
1994—	El Paso*	.647
	Jackson	.548
1995—	Shreveport*	.652
	Midland	.485
1996—	Jackson*	.547
	Wichita	.500
1997—	San Antonio*	.604
	Shreveport	.551
1998—	Arkansas	.571
	Tulsa*	.557
1999—	Wichita*	.593
2000—	Round Rock*	.593
2001—	Round Rock	.614
	Arkansas††	.485
2002—	Wichita	.576
	San Antonio§	.486
2003—	San Antonio§§	.633
2004—	Frisco**	.579
2005—	Midland§	.557

*Won split-season playoff. †Won playoff for title. ‡Finished first and won four-club playoff. §Won four-club playoff. §§Won both halves of split season, received a bye into playoffs and won three-team playoff. ∞Title to Cleburne by default. ▲Tied with Dallas in second half and won playoff for championship. ◆Tied with Beaumont at end of first half and won title in best-of-five series played as part of second-half schedule. ■League divided into Eastern, Western divisions; won two-team playoff. ▼League divided into Eastern, Western divisions; declared co-champions when playoffs were not completed. *League divided into Eastern and Western divisions and played split season; won playoffs. NOTE—Championship awarded to winner of four-team playoff, 1933-51; first-place team and playoff winner co-champions, 1952-64. ††Was leading final round of split-season playoff, two games to none, and was declared champion when Professional Baseball declared a stoppage of play. **Won three-club playoff.

CALIFORNIA LEAGUE

LEAGUE OFFICE

President
Joe Gagliardi
Address
2380 S. Bascom Ave., Suite 200
Campbell, CA 95008
Phone
408-369-8038

Teams (affiliation)
Bakersfield Blaze (Rangers)
High Desert Mavericks (Royals)
Inland Empire 66ers of San Bernardino
(Mariners)
Lake Elsinore Storm (Padres)
Lancaster JetHawks (Diamondbacks)

Modesto Nuts (Rockies)
Rancho Cucamonga Quakes (Angels)
San Jose Giants (Giants)
Stockton Ports (Athletics)
Visalia Oaks (Devil Rays)

2005 FINAL STANDINGS

FIRST HALF

NORTHERN DIVISION

Team	W	L	T	Pct.	GB
San Jose Giants	44	26	-	.629	-
Modesto Nuts	38	32	-	.543	6
Stockton Ports	36	34	-	.514	8
Bakersfield Blaze	35	35	-	.500	9
Visalia Oaks	26	44	-	.371	18

SOUTHERN DIVISION

Team	W	L	T	Pct.	GB
Lake Elsinore Storm	41	28	-	.594	-
Lancaster JetHawks	37	33	-	.529	4.5
High Desert Mavericks	36	34	-	.514	5.5
Rancho Cucamonga Quakes	28	41	-	.406	13
Inland Empire 66ers	28	42	-	.400	13.5

SECOND HALF

NORTHERN DIVISION

Team	W	L	T	Pct.	GB
Stockton Ports	42	28	-	.600	-
San Jose Giants	41	29	-	.586	1
Modesto Nuts	34	35	-	.493	7.5
Bakersfield Blaze	33	37	-	.471	9
Visalia Oaks	29	41	-	.414	13

SOUTHERN DIVISION

Team	W	L	T	Pct.	GB
High Desert Mavericks	39	31	-	.557	-
Lancaster JetHawks	38	32	-	.543	1
Rancho Cucamonga Quakes	34	36	-	.486	5
Inland Empire 66ers	30	40	-	.429	9
Lake Elsinore Storm	29	40	-	.420	9.5

COMPOSITE

CLUB (AFFILIATE), ABBREV	SJO	STO	HDM	LNC	MOD	LAK	BAK	RCQ	INL	VIS	W	L	PCT	GB
San Jose (Giants), SJO		16	5	5	15	5	17	4	6	12	85	55	.607	-
Stockton (Athletics),STO ...13		...	1	5	13	6	11	6	8	15	78	62	.557	7.0
High Desert (Royals), HDM 4	5	...		14	5	11	6	17	7	6	75	65	.536	10.0
Lancaster (Diamondbacks), LNC 4	4	11	4		5	16	7	11	12	5	75	65	.536	10.0
Modesto (Rockies), MOD 9	11	4	4	...		5	12	3	8	16	72	67	.518	12.5
Lake Elsinore (Padres), LAK............4	3	13	4	3	...		5	14	19	5	70	68	.507	14.0
Bakersfield (Rangers), BAK 8	10	3	6	9	4		5	6	17	68	72	.486	17.0
Rancho Cucamonga (Angels), RCQ 2	3	11	10	6	11	3	...		13	3	62	77	.446	22.5
Inland Empire (Mariners), INL 3	1	14	13	1	6	3	11	...		6	58	82	.414	27.0
Visalia (Devil Rays), VIS 8	9	3	4	10	4	8	6	3	...		55	85	.393	30.0

Major league affiliations in parentheses.

PLAYOFFS: Division Series: Modesto defeated Stockton, two games to none, and Lancaster defeated High Desert, two games to one. Semifinals: San Jose defeated Modesto, three games to none, and Lake Elsinore defeated Lancaster, three games to none. Finals: San Jose defeated Lake Elsinore, three games to two.

REGULAR-SEASON ATTENDANCE: Lake Elsinore, 222,624. Inland Empire, 211,117. Bakersfield, 76,738. San Jose, 150,338. Lancaster, 123,601. High Desert, 118,387. Modesto, 136,612. Visalia, 63,475. Stockton, 205,819. Rancho Cucamonga, 272,855. League total, 1,581,566. Postseason (16 games), 29,982.

MANAGERS: Lake Elsinore, Rick Renteria. Inland Empire, Daren Brown. Bakersfield, Arnie Beyeler. San Jose, Lenn Sakata. Lancaster, Bill Plummer. High Desert, Mel Queen. Modesto, Stu Cole. Visalia, Steve Livesey. Stockton, Todd Stevenson. Rancho Cucamonga, Tyrone Boykin.

ALL-STAR TEAM: 1B-Bryan Lahair, Inland Empire. 2B-Howie Kendrick, Rancho Cucamonga. 3B-Ian Stewart, Modesto. SS-Brandon Wood, Rancho Cucamonga. OF-Joe Gaetti, Modesto. OF-Kevin Mahar, Bakersfield. OF-Eddy Martinez-Esteve, San Jose. UTIL-Brandon Powell, High Desert. C-Miguel Montero, Lancaster. DH-Billy Butler, High Desert. P-Thomas Diamond, Bakersfield. P-John Gragg III, High Desert. P-Garrett Mock, Lancaster. P-Jared Wells, Lake Elsinore. Most Valuable Player-Brandon Wood, Rancho Cucamonga. Rookie of the Year-Billy Butler, High Desert. Pitcher of the Year-Jared Wells, Lake Elsinore. Manager of the Year-Lenn Sakata, San Jose.

2005 BATTING

TEAM

Team	G	TPA	AB	R	H	TB	2B	3B	HR	RBI	SH	SF	HP	BB	IBB	SO	SB	CS	GDP	LOB	ShO	Avg.	OBP	Slg.
Lancaster	140	5744	5013	917	1512	2470	346	45	174	840	76	55	89	511	12	904	48	36	106	2299	3	.302	.373	.493
High Desert	140	5713	5106	918	1536	2557	340	36	203	850	18	34	47	508	11	1050	77	34	94	2350	5	.301	.367	.501
San Jose	140	5472	4848	813	1430	2239	292	44	143	747	33	55	86	450	7	1035	96	65	119	2126	4	.295	.361	.462
Lake Elsinore	138	5630	4926	798	1407	2153	277	47	125	736	50	37	71	541	22	1018	95	52	103	2374	4	.286	.362	.437
Visalia	140	5459	4828	717	1375	2058	283	29	114	663	40	46	74	469	8	1039	112	67	117	2197	5	.285	.354	.426
Inland Empire	140	5590	5004	753	1412	2132	282	45	116	691	33	41	61	451	7	1042	104	55	120	2275	5	.282	.346	.426
Modesto	139	5447	4792	793	1347	2131	312	56	120	739	52	34	64	504	7	1157	42	50	120	2176	1	.281	.355	.445
Stockton	140	5611	4835	835	1355	2208	318	38	153	772	29	46	70	629	2	1042	60	42	118	2403	2	.280	.368	.457
Rancho Cucamonga	139	5471	4916	750	1352	2179	297	40	150	683	30	48	85	392	18	1086	77	50	84	2138	3	.275	.336	.443
Bakersfield	140	5438	4830	728	1325	2047	269	39	125	671	21	32	101	452	5	1025	106	45	117	2184	5	.274	.347	.424

TOP QUALIFIERS FOR BATTING CHAMPIONSHIP

Minimum 378 plate appearances. *Lefthanded batter. †Switch-hitter.

Player, Team	G	TPA	AB	R	H	TB	2B	3B	HR	RBI	SH	SF	HP	BB	IBB	SO	SB	CS	GDP	Avg.	OBP	Slg.
Montero, Miguel, Lancaster *	85	399	355	73	124	222	24	1	24	82	2	6	10	26	0	52	1	2	5	.349	.403	.625
Butler, Billy, High Desert	92	430	379	70	132	241	30	2	25	91	0	3	6	42	3	80	0	0	12	.348	.419	.636
Gaetti, Joseph, Modesto	113	463	395	90	131	239	29	8	21	87	4	3	9	52	2	114	5	7	1	.332	.418	.605
Gomes, Joseph, Visalia	133	597	530	77	172	244	34	1	12	86	1	10	3	53	0	92	4	5	17	.325	.383	.460
Wood, Richard, Rancho Cucamonga	130	595	536	109	172	360	51	4	43	115	2	2	7	48	5	128	7	3	12	.321	.383	.672
Schierholtz, Nathan, San Jose *	128	548	502	83	160	258	37	8	15	86	3	5	6	32	0	132	5	7	10	.319	.363	.514
Garrabrants, Steve, Lancaster	95	420	358	79	114	173	28	5	7	58	7	4	12	39	0	45	8	4	6	.318	.400	.483
Mahar, Kevin, Bakersfield	110	513	447	98	141	227	27	4	17	63	0	4	15	47	2	109	17	10	10	.315	.396	.508
Cook, Jeff, Lancaster *	129	592	526	96	165	279	43	7	19	89	13	6	1	46	2	75	2	4	14	.314	.366	.530
Arroyo, Carlos, Inland Empire *	98	434	402	50	126	147	17	2	0	62	3	3	0	26	1	37	13	5	15	.313	.353	.366
Sanchez, Angel, High Desert	133	639	585	102	183	239	33	4	5	70	7	5	3	39	0	54	10	5	11	.313	.356	.409
Martinez-Esteve, Eduardo, San Jose *	132	579	479	89	150	251	44	3	17	94	0	3	8	89	2	82	4	2	16	.313	.427	.524
Lahair, Bryan, Inland Empire *	126	569	509	81	158	256	28	2	22	113	0	6	3	51	4	125	0	1	19	.310	.373	.503
Colonel, Christian, Modesto	96	425	364	73	113	172	32	3	7	60	1	5	8	47	2	66	1	3	12	.310	.396	.473
Varela, Edgar, Lancaster *	106	432	395	58	122	183	30	2	9	60	4	9	6	18	1	74	1	2	9	.309	.341	.463
Putnam, Daniel, Stockton *	131	594	514	97	158	246	37	3	15	100	1	7	6	66	1	92	1	3	13	.307	.388	.479
Dufner, Kristofor, Visalia †	102	443	382	62	116	168	21	5	7	48	9	2	6	44	1	90	5	5	6	.304	.382	.440
Kaaihue, Micah, High Desert *	132	605	493	84	150	245	31	2	20	90	0	3	12	97	2	97	2	1	12	.304	.428	.497
Rogelstad, Matthew, Inland Empire *	111	495	438	71	133	163	23	2	1	47	10	2	1	44	1	52	3	2	8	.304	.367	.372
Stephens, Leon, High Desert *	120	535	485	96	147	234	33	6	14	67	2	2	3	43	1	102	12	3	4	.303	.362	.482
Kottaras, Sandy, Lake Elsinore *	91	394	337	54	102	158	29	0	9	50	2	4	1	50	2	60	2	1	6	.303	.390	.469

DEPARTMENTAL LEADERS: G—Majewski, 136. AB—Sanchez, 585. R—Wood, 109. H—Sanchez, 183. TB—Wood, 360. 2B—Wood, 51. 3B—Timpner, 12. HR—Wood, 43. RBI—Lubanski, 116. SH—Cook, 13. SF—Gomes, 10. HP—Kreuzer, 19. BB—Kaaihue, 97. IBB—Valenzuela Jr., 6. SO—Bonvechio, 163. SB—Timpner, 34. CS—Macias, 15. GIDP—Jennings, 21. Slg.—Wood, .672. OBP—Kaaihue, .428.

ALL PLAYERS

*Lefthanded batter. †Switch-hitter.

Player, Team	G	TPA	AB	R	H	TB	2B	3B	HR	RBI	SH	SF	HP	BB	IBB	SO	SB	CS	GDP	Avg.	OBP	Slg.
Abruzzo, Jared, Bakersfield †	9	34	30	0	2	3	1	0	0	3	0	1	0	3	0	12	0	0	1	.067	.147	.100
Adams, Skipton, Lake Elsinore	82	273	245	30	66	102	19	1	5	38	6	2	3	17	1	65	6	4	3	.269	.322	.416
Alfonzo, Eliezer, San Jose	53	217	196	35	70	125	16	0	13	45	0	2	8	11	0	49	1	3	2	.357	.410	.638
Allegra, Matthew, Stockton	50	213	182	29	47	87	11	1	9	36	0	0	4	27	0	62	1	1	2	.258	.366	.478
Appert, Luke, Stockton *	113	494	410	72	103	180	27	7	12	72	7	3	5	69	1	65	1	3	10	.251	.363	.439
Aracena, Sandy, Visalia	57	213	198	24	56	76	14	0	2	22	1	1	2	11	0	42	3	1	4	.283	.325	.384
Arhart, Joshua, Visalia	99	415	379	51	110	161	24	0	9	56	1	8	3	24	0	60	0	0	9	.290	.331	.425
Arias, Roberto, Stockton	3	16	11	4	3	3	0	0	0	2	1	0	0	4	0	2	0	0	0	.273	.467	.273
Arroyo, Carlos, Inland Empire *	98	434	402	50	126	147	17	2	0	62	3	3	0	26	1	37	13	5	15	.313	.353	.366
Asanovich, Robert, Visalia	40	162	145	23	49	71	10	0	4	14	0	1	1	15	0	32	2	5	6	.338	.401	.490
Avlas, Aaron, Lancaster	37	161	147	29	54	83	12	1	5	24	3	1	0	10	0	25	1	1	3	.367	.405	.565
Baker, Steve, Lake Elsinore	54	237	221	33	76	107	17	1	4	37	1	0	2	13	1	46	6	2	5	.344	.386	.484
Balentien, Wladimir, Inland Empire	123	539	492	76	143	272	38	8	25	93	1	7	6	33	0	160	9	2	7	.291	.338	.553
Balkcom, Brandon, Rancho Cucamonga	87	352	320	37	78	119	19	2	6	35	5	2	3	22	0	102	0	2	9	.244	.297	.372
Bankston, Wesley, Visalia	17	78	62	15	24	39	4	1	3	23	0	0	1	15	1	17	0	2	1	.387	.513	.629
Barton, Daric, Stockton *	79	362	292	60	93	137	16	2	8	52	0	4	3	62	0	49	0	1	6	.318	.438	.469
Batista, Alexander, High Desert	25	95	89	9	18	26	5	0	1	10	0	0	2	4	0	28	1	0	3	.202	.253	.292
Bethel, Ryan, Visalia †	6	18	14	1	3	3	0	0	0	1	0	1	0	2	0	4	0	0	0	.214	.353	.214
Blakeley, Eric, Inland Empire	14	62	57	10	15	29	3	1	3	11	0	0	3	2	0	8	0	0	0	.263	.323	.509
Blanco, Andres, High Desert †	3	10	10	0	5	6	1	0	0	3	0	0	0	0	0	1	1	2	0	.500	.500	.600
Blood, Randy, Modesto *	101	413	367	53	92	140	25	4	5	54	4	3	3	35	0	76	0	4	8	.251	.319	.381
Blum, Geoff, Lake Elsinore †	2	9	8	3	2	8	0	0	2	5	0	0	0	1	0	2	0	0	0	.250	.333	1.000
Bonine, Eddie, Lake Elsinore	1	1	1	0	0	0	0	0	0	0	0	0	0	0	0	0	0	0	0	.000	.000	.000
Bonvechio, Brett, Lake Elsinore *	131	579	480	85	128	221	24	6	19	73	3	2	6	86	2	163	1	2	8	.267	.385	.460
Boucher, Sebastien, Inland Empire *	52	255	213	54	75	101	14	3	2	21	1	1	4	36	0	49	15	3	1	.352	.453	.474
Bourassa, Adam, Bakersfield-Lake Elsinore	78	341	297	42	90	113	13	2	2	21	5	2	1	36	1	31	11	6	5	.303	.378	.380
Bowker, John, San Jose *	121	513	464	66	124	192	27	1	13	67	2	8	3	36	0	108	3	7	14	.267	.319	.414
Bradford Jr., Samuel, Inland Empire †	28	112	95	11	16	29	2	1	3	9	1	1	2	13	1	25	3	2	2	.168	.279	.305
Brito, Javier, Lancaster	25	101	89	17	26	38	6	0	2	11	0	0	2	10	0	17	0	0	1	.292	.376	.427
Brown, Matthew, Rancho Cucamonga	125	547	488	68	128	211	39	4	12	65	3	5	11	40	0	125	4	5	10	.262	.329	.432
Brown, Nebasett, Lancaster *	45	202	168	33	46	61	7	1	2	24	2	3	1	28	0	32	5	4	5	.274	.375	.363
Bruce, Derek, Lancaster	30	98	88	19	30	49	10	0	3	13	4	1	1	4	0	21	0	0	4	.341	.372	.557
Burgamy, Brian, Lake Elsinore †	59	265	234	43	69	110	12	4	7	40	3	2	1	25	1	47	4	3	7	.295	.363	.470
Buscher, Brian, San Jose *	55	237	206	37	58	87	12	1	5	29	0	2	2	27	0	47	0	2	7	.282	.367	.422
Butler, Billy, High Desert	92	430	379	70	132	241	30	2	25	91	0	3	6	42	3	80	0	0	12	.348	.419	.636
Cabrera, Asdrubal, Inland Empire †	55	244	225	31	64	94	15	6	1	26	1	3	0	15	0	47	3	1	8	.284	.325	.418
Carter, William, Lancaster *	103	470	412	71	122	215	26	2	21	85	0	6	6	46	4	66	0	0	12	.296	.370	.522
Chang, Raymond, Lake Elsinore	3	4	4	2	2	2	0	0	0	0	0	0	0	0	0	0	0	0	0	.500	.500	.500
Chavez, Angel, San Jose	30	126	120	22	34	53	2	1	5	19	0	1	0	5	0	21	4	0	7	.283	.310	.442
Cho, Hyung, Inland Empire	11	46	39	5	10	10	0	0	0	3	0	0	1	6	0	2	0	0	3	.256	.370	.256
Ciriaco, Juan, Lake Elsinore	120	511	466	73	131	199	29	6	9	77	7	2	3	33	1	84	17	10	9	.281	.331	.427
Cleveland, Jeremy, Bakersfield	58	257	224	31	59	85	9	1	5	28	0	5	7	21	0	42	3	3	4	.263	.339	.379
Colina, Alvin, Modesto	9	37	34	2	9	12	3	0	0	3	0	0	0	3	0	14	0	1	0	.265	.324	.353
Collins, Christopher, Inland Empire	47	186	167	22	43	54	8	0	1	19	0	1	1	17	0	29	1	0	6	.257	.328	.323
Colonel, Christian, Modesto	96	425	364	73	113	172	32	3	7	60	1	5	8	47	2	66	1	3	12	.310	.396	.473
Colton, Christopher, Inland Empire	51	184	169	24	41	65	10	1	4	23	2	0	3	10	0	36	5	5	3	.243	.297	.385

Player, Team	G	TPA	AB	R	H	TB	2B	3B	HR	RBI	SH	SF	HP	BB	IBB	SO	SB	CS	GDP	Avg.	OBP	Slg.
Contreras, Anthony, San Jose *	17	60	56	5	12	15	3	0	0	3	0	1	0	3	0	11	1	0	2	.214	.250	.268
Cook, Jeff, Lancaster *	129	592	526	96	165	279	43	7	19	89	13	6	1	46	2	75	2	4	14	.314	.366	.530
Cornejo, Eduardo, Stockton *	89	358	316	45	96	116	14	0	2	38	6	2	3	31	0	34	2	3	10	.304	.369	.367
Craig, Casey, Inland Empire *	8	32	29	2	10	13	1	1	0	3	0	0	0	3	0	6	0	1	0	.345	.406	.448
Crosby, Bobby, Stockton	3	11	9	1	3	4	1	0	0	1	0	0	0	2	0	1	0	0	0	.333	.455	.444
Cuevas, Aneudi, Visalia	120	483	413	72	116	214	24	4	22	75	3	2	8	57	1	141	9	4	9	.281	.377	.518
Czarniecki, Jordan, Modesto	46	207	170	38	54	89	15	1	6	23	3	1	2	31	1	33	1	5	3	.318	.426	.524
Davies, Michael, Modesto *	108	432	407	53	113	188	23	5	14	62	3	0	0	22	0	145	2	4	14	.278	.315	.462
Davis, John-paul, Visalia	121	521	448	68	125	192	28	0	13	59	0	3	16	54	1	103	5	2	13	.279	.374	.429
Day, Devin, Rancho Cucamonga	60	230	215	34	61	91	13	1	5	22	0	2	0	13	0	55	3	3	1	.284	.322	.423
Dean, Erik, Modesto *	79	321	288	48	78	117	15	3	6	43	2	0	8	23	0	67	3	5	8	.271	.342	.406
De Renne, Keoni, Lancaster †	10	50	41	10	12	13	1	0	0	4	0	0	0	9	0	3	1	0	0	.293	.420	.317
Dobson, Patrick, San Jose	87	269	232	41	65	96	13	3	4	27	4	0	3	30	0	60	2	4	5	.280	.370	.414
Dominguez, Jeffrey, Inland Empire †	6	22	18	4	6	7	1	0	0	1	0	0	0	4	0	3	0	0	1	.333	.455	.389
Donachie, Adam, High Desert	95	394	347	64	102	162	24	0	12	48	2	0	2	43	0	78	1	0	8	.294	.375	.467
Dowdy, Brett, Lake Elsinore	21	93	83	7	22	30	5	0	1	5	1	1	1	7	0	13	0	0	4	.265	.326	.361
Downing, Ramon, Lancaster †	2	5	5	0	1	1	0	0	0	0	0	0	0	0	0	1	0	0	0	.200	.200	.200
Draper, John, High Desert	5	18	15	3	5	11	2	2	0	0	0	0	0	3	0	2	0	0	1	.333	.444	.733
Drew, Stephen, Lancaster *	38	177	149	33	58	110	16	3	10	39	0	0	2	26	2	25	1	1	1	.389	.486	.738
Duff, Timothy, Rancho Cucamonga	22	76	63	10	12	21	3	0	2	4	1	0	2	10	0	14	0	2	4	.190	.320	.333
Dufner, Kristofor, Visalia †	102	443	382	62	116	168	21	5	7	48	9	2	6	44	1	90	5	5	6	.304	.382	.440
Espino, Damaso, High Desert	25	103	91	10	21	25	1	0	1	12	1	1	1	9	0	8	1	0	2	.231	.304	.275
Everett, Brady, High Desert	6	22	18	3	5	6	1	0	0	2	0	2	0	2	0	2	0	0	1	.278	.318	.333
Felix, Maximo, San Jose	4	6	4	2	0	0	0	0	0	0	1	0	0	2	0	3	0	0	0	.000	.333	.000
Ferrer, Simon, Modesto †	58	217	191	20	40	52	8	2	0	21	7	2	1	16	0	59	0	1	2	.209	.271	.272
Finley, Steve, Rancho Cucamonga *	1	5	4	2	2	3	1	0	0	0	0	0	0	1	0	0	0	0	0	.500	.600	.750
Frandsen, Kevin, San Jose	75	335	291	57	102	136	22	3	2	40	2	1	15	26	0	22	13	11	12	.351	.429	.467
Frazier, Alex, Lancaster	98	455	388	72	103	187	19	4	19	69	0	3	15	49	1	96	5	4	10	.265	.367	.482
Fryer, Brian, Lake Elsinore	11	26	25	7	3	6	1	1	0	1	0	0	0	1	0	5	0	0	0	.120	.154	.240
Fuller, Cody, Rancho Cucamonga	32	134	115	19	31	55	13	1	3	11	2	0	7	10	0	44	4	1	1	.270	.364	.478
Gaetti, Joseph, Modesto	113	463	395	90	131	239	29	8	21	87	4	3	9	52	2	114	5	7	1	.332	.418	.605
Gaffney, Michael, High Desert	44	148	134	14	40	48	6	1	0	8	4	0	2	8	0	17	1	3	4	.299	.347	.358
Garbe, B.J., Inland Empire	80	336	305	41	84	130	17	1	9	41	2	1	3	25	0	48	8	5	6	.275	.335	.426
Garcia, Lino, Lancaster	18	71	63	3	10	10	0	0	0	6	3	0	1	4	1	12	2	2	0	.159	.221	.159
Garciaparra, Michael, Inland Empire	84	388	336	60	100	139	15	3	6	33	3	0	14	35	0	64	10	8	6	.298	.387	.414
Garrabrants, Steve, Lancaster	95	420	358	79	114	173	28	5	7	58	7	4	12	39	0	45	8	4	6	.318	.400	.483
Garthwaite, Jay, Lancaster	124	540	487	81	146	253	36	4	21	102	5	7	8	33	0	131	1	3	8	.300	.350	.520
Gergel, Kevin, Inland Empire *	5	21	20	1	5	7	2	0	0	3	0	0	0	1	0	5	0	0	0	.250	.286	.350
Gold, Nathan, Bakersfield	101	433	381	63	107	201	27	2	21	69	1	3	6	42	0	65	2	2	19	.281	.359	.528
Gomes, Joseph, Visalia	133	597	530	77	172	244	34	1	12	86	1	10	3	53	0	92	4	5	17	.325	.383	.460
Gomez, Francis, Stockton	51	208	186	22	50	81	13	0	6	27	2	2	2	16	0	42	7	1	2	.269	.330	.435
Gonzalez, Bernard, Modesto	20	79	72	3	17	28	4	2	1	9	0	0	1	6	0	15	0	1	5	.236	.304	.389
Gonzalez, Juan, Inland Empire †	22	89	85	10	18	26	1	2	1	5	0	0	1	3	0	16	4	3	1	.212	.247	.306
Gonzalez, Luis, High Desert	6	19	14	5	4	5	1	0	0	1	0	0	0	5	0	5	0	0	0	.286	.474	.357
Grayson, Larry, Bakersfield	106	475	421	63	117	193	33	2	13	61	0	2	8	44	0	117	11	4	3	.278	.356	.458
Greene, Khalil, Lake Elsinore	4	15	12	4	6	7	1	0	0	3	0	0	1	2	0	1	0	0	0	.500	.600	.583
Guance, Luis, Modesto	47	206	180	26	49	66	11	3	0	16	3	0	3	20	0	44	6	6	1	.272	.355	.367
Guarno, Richard, Modesto	57	218	188	26	48	61	10	0	1	23	5	1	7	17	0	41	0	1	4	.255	.338	.324
Hagen, Matthew, Inland Empire	35	114	108	8	20	31	6	1	1	8	0	1	1	4	0	30	2	1	3	.185	.219	.287
Haines, Kyle, San Jose *	17	57	51	6	9	11	2	0	0	5	0	0	2	4	0	7	2	0	2	.176	.263	.216
Hargrove, Andrew, Inland Empire	6	23	20	2	4	7	0	0	1	1	0	0	0	3	0	8	0	0	0	.200	.304	.350
Harrison, Benjamin, Bakersfield	12	49	44	4	14	19	2	0	1	7	0	1	1	3	0	13	2	1	3	.318	.367	.432
Hatcher, Justin, Bakersfield	85	347	311	42	84	101	14	0	1	31	3	1	8	23	1	56	4	2	8	.270	.335	.325
Heid, Trevor, Inland Empire	12	39	34	5	7	13	3	0	1	1	1	0	0	4	0	10	0	0	0	.206	.289	.382
Herrera, Jonathan, Modesto †	73	345	310	48	80	103	9	4	2	30	8	1	3	23	0	52	9	4	9	.258	.315	.332
Hornstaj, Aaron, San Jose *	9	35	33	0	4	6	2	0	0	2	2	0	0	0	0	9	0	0	1	.121	.121	.182
Howard, Joshua, Lake Elsinore *	6	23	19	3	5	7	0	1	0	4	1	0	1	2	0	4	2	0	1	.263	.364	.368
Hughes, Michael, Rancho Cucamonga	12	47	44	3	6	8	0	1	0	4	0	0	1	2	0	13	1	0	1	.136	.191	.182
Hurba, Craig, Bakersfield	34	131	126	6	36	42	6	0	0	11	0	0	0	5	0	24	1	0	3	.286	.313	.333
Iannetta, Christopher, Modesto	74	312	261	51	72	128	17	3	11	58	0	4	2	45	1	61	1	2	9	.276	.381	.490
Ishikawa, Travis, San Jose *	127	516	432	87	122	230	28	7	22	79	2	5	7	70	3	129	1	4	1	.282	.387	.532
Jacobsen, Bucky, Inland Empire	6	29	21	7	12	23	2	0	3	9	0	1	1	6	0	2	0	0	0	.571	.655	1.095
Jennings, Jeffrey, San Jose	128	548	504	64	145	199	22	1	10	67	6	9	6	23	1	77	7	5	21	.288	.321	.395
Johnson, Craig, Lake Elsinore *	55	201	172	25	38	53	7	1	2	17	1	1	4	23	0	37	2	0	4	.221	.325	.308
Johnson, Elliot, Visalia †	56	257	227	42	62	102	10	3	8	33	2	0	3	24	1	49	28	5	2	.273	.350	.449
Johnson, Michael, Rancho Cucamonga †	78	312	277	38	75	131	19	2	11	36	0	3	10	22	0	58	1	1	3	.271	.343	.473
Johnson, Robert, Inland Empire	19	86	70	15	22	31	3	0	2	12	2	4	0	10	0	14	2	0	1	.314	.381	.443
Johnson, William, Lake Elsinore *	73	333	288	59	85	178	20	5	21	76	0	6	8	37	4	89	0	3	4	.295	.374	.618
Jones, Adam, Inland Empire	68	315	271	43	80	134	20	5	8	46	2	5	8	29	0	64	4	5	4	.295	.374	.494
Kaaihue, Micah, High Desert *	132	605	493	84	150	245	31	2	20	90	0	3	12	97	2	97	2	1	12	.304	.428	.497
Kaplan, Jonathan, Lancaster	21	58	46	11	7	10	3	0	0	3	0	2	7	0	0	11	2	0	2	.152	.291	.217
Keim, Adam, High Desert	85	374	351	59	99	198	19	1	26	68	1	1	1	20	0	73	0	0	8	.282	.322	.564
Kendrick, Howard, Rancho Cucamonga	63	304	279	69	107	178	23	6	12	47	0	4	7	14	0	42	13	4	5	.384	.421	.638
Kennedy, Adam, Rancho Cucamonga *	2	6	5	1	2	2	0	0	0	0	0	0	1	0	1	1	1	1	0	.400	.500	.400
Kerbs, Reuben, Lancaster *	1	0	0	0	0	0	0	0	0	0	0	0	0	0	…	0	0	0	0	…	…	…
Kolkhorst, Christopher, Lake Elsinore *	26	126	107	18	35	49	6	4	0	6	2	0	2	15	0	21	2	0	2	.327	.419	.458
Kottaras, George, Lake Elsinore *	91	394	337	54	102	158	29	0	9	50	2	4	1	50	0	66	2	1	6	.303	.390	.469
Kreuzer, Joshua, Bakersfield	113	475	400	63	104	164	25	1	11	74	2	4	19	49	0	89	3	2	5	.260	.364	.410
Lahair, Bryan, Inland Empire *	126	569	509	81	158	256	28	2	22	113	0	6	3	51	4	125	0	1	19	.310	.373	.503
Leahy, Ryan, Rancho Cucamonga	39	182	150	27	38	48	5	1	1	18	2	4	4	22	0	20	4	4	5	.253	.356	.320

Player, Team	G	TPA	AB	R	H	TB	2B	3B	HR	RBI	SH	SF	HP	BB	IBB	SO	SB	CS	GDP	Avg.	OBP	Slg.
Leandro, Francisco, Visalia *	60	294	248	53	88	141	23	3	8	40	0	2	7	37	2	24	9	7	4	.355	.449	.569
Ledbetter, Curtis, Inland Empire	4	17	16	0	1	1	0	0	0	0	0	0	0	1	0	5	0	0	2	.063	.118	.063
Lenoir, Robert, Bakersfield	78	285	260	30	51	73	4	3	4	27	3	1	4	17	0	80	9	2	5	.196	.255	.281
Lopez, Baltazar, Rancho Cucamonga *	52	215	194	15	50	62	12	0	0	25	1	3	0	17	1	57	3	2	1	.258	.313	.320
Lubanski, Christopher, High Desert *	126	581	531	91	160	294	38	6	28	116	0	7	5	38	0	131	14	1	1	.301	.349	.554
Macias, Andres, Lake Elsinore *	128	551	492	79	142	195	23	6	6	66	5	2	6	46	3	78	15	15	7	.289	.355	.396
Macri, Matthew, Modesto	64	292	244	40	69	108	16	1	7	34	6	2	7	33	0	67	6	1	3	.283	.381	.443
Maestrales, Peter, High Desert †	54	275	225	55	75	120	18	3	7	33	0	2	1	47	0	41	6	3	2	.333	.447	.533
Mahar, Kevin, Bakersfield	110	513	447	98	141	227	27	4	17	63	0	4	15	47	2	109	17	10	10	.315	.396	.508
Maier, Mitchell, High Desert *	50	227	211	42	71	123	26	1	8	32	0	3	1	12	1	43	6	1	5	.336	.370	.583
Majewski, Dustin, Stockton *	136	605	533	91	145	254	43	3	20	73	4	4	4	60	0	130	13	7	10	.272	.348	.477
Maniscalco, Matthew, Visalia	52	238	209	31	58	71	7	0	2	21	2	4	0	23	0	33	21	6	3	.278	.343	.340
Martinez, Gabriel, Visalia *	24	111	100	15	28	47	7	0	4	9	1	1	2	7	0	27	0	0	1	.280	.336	.470
Martinez-Esteve, Eduardo, San Jose	132	579	479	89	150	251	44	3	17	94	0	3	8	89	2	82	4	2	16	.313	.427	.524
Mask, Michael, Bakersfield *	9	21	14	3	2	2	0	0	0	2	0	0	0	7	0	2	1	1	0	.143	.429	.143
McCurdy, John, Stockton	94	382	341	47	86	132	16	3	8	44	2	3	2	34	0	85	3	4	13	.252	.321	.387
McMains, Derin, San Jose †	22	93	83	17	27	36	3	0	2	10	0	2	1	7	0	12	2	3	1	.325	.376	.434
McPherson, Dallas, Rancho Cucamonga *	5	20	16	3	7	15	2	0	2	5	0	0	1	3	2	4	1	1	0	.438	.550	.938
Melgarejo, Ransel, Rancho Cucamonga	13	51	45	2	8	10	2	0	0	3	0	0	2	4	0	10	2	1	2	.178	.275	.222
Melillo, Kevin, Stockton *	22	104	90	21	36	72	7	1	9	23	0	1	1	12	0	18	2	0	2	.400	.471	.800
Metcalf, Travis, Bakersfield	132	566	505	80	147	259	32	7	22	94	1	5	6	49	0	129	8	2	14	.291	.358	.513
Miller, Matthew, Modesto	1	5	5	0	2	2	0	0	0	1	0	0	0	0	0	0	0	0	0	.400	.400	.400
Montero, Miguel, Lancaster *	85	399	355	73	124	222	24	1	24	82	2	6	10	26	0	52	1	2	5	.349	.403	.625
Monzon, Erick, Inland Empire	94	392	350	53	95	163	25	2	13	49	1	3	3	35	0	80	7	1	7	.271	.340	.466
Morales, Kendry, Rancho Cucamonga †	22	100	90	18	31	49	3	0	5	17	0	1	3	6	0	11	0	0	3	.344	.400	.544
Morris, Jed, Stockton *	75	306	268	49	81	151	26	1	14	55	0	4	3	31	0	59	1	3	8	.302	.376	.563
Morton, Kristopher, Lake Elsinore	26	113	96	19	31	62	4	0	9	19	0	2	1	14	0	30	0	1	1	.323	.407	.646
Moye, Alan, High Desert	76	343	320	68	99	182	15	4	20	64	0	1	2	20	1	97	10	6	4	.309	.353	.569
Munhall, Brian, San Jose	31	122	105	21	33	57	6	0	6	25	1	1	7	8	0	28	1	1	5	.314	.397	.543
Nesbit, Michael, Inland Empire	65	243	218	37	62	88	17	3	1	14	0	2	2	21	0	64	15	8	3	.284	.350	.404
Nunez, Argelis, Lancaster	4	11	11	0	1	2	1	0	0	0	0	0	0	0	0	7	0	0	0	.091	.091	.182
Oliveros, Luis, Inland Empire	18	75	72	6	15	23	0	1	2	11	1	0	1	1	0	11	0	0	2	.208	.230	.319
Owings, Micah, Lancaster	1	1	1	0	1	1	0	0	0	1	0	0	0	0	0	0	0	0	0	1.000	1.000	1.000
Pagan, Andres, Lake Elsinore	47	148	139	16	32	52	6	1	4	23	1	1	1	6	0	30	3	0	5	.230	.265	.374
Pali, Matthew, Rancho Cucamonga *	135	589	513	81	132	188	18	1	12	77	5	7	9	55	4	86	15	5	4	.257	.336	.366
Peel, Aaron, Rancho Cucamonga	51	248	222	46	69	122	12	4	11	35	0	2	9	15	0	57	1	2	1	.311	.375	.550
Pence, Howard, Lake Elsinore	2	0	0	0	0	0	0	0	0	0	...	0	0	0	...	0	0	0	0	...	...	...
Perez, Josue, Bakersfield †	6	16	14	3	1	1	0	0	0	1	0	0	0	2	0	6	0	0	0	.071	.188	.071
Perez, Kenny, Lancaster †	22	107	97	25	31	43	7	1	1	10	1	0	0	9	0	15	0	0	4	.320	.377	.443
Perez, Luis, Stockton	31	126	116	16	35	54	9	2	2	18	0	2	0	8	0	20	0	2	5	.302	.341	.466
Perez, Nestor, Visalia	16	65	56	2	11	14	3	0	0	1	2	0	1	6	0	14	1	1	2	.196	.286	.250
Pickens, Jordan, Lake Elsinore	77	328	277	42	68	119	19	1	10	46	2	1	16	32	0	75	2	2	4	.245	.356	.430
Powell, Brandon, High Desert *	106	431	397	74	114	203	29	3	18	69	0	2	4	28	1	97	6	4	4	.287	.339	.511
Price, Jared, High Desert	30	112	107	21	34	77	10	0	11	32	0	0	1	4	0	31	1	0	3	.318	.348	.720
Pridie, Jason, Visalia *	1	2	2	0	1	1	0	0	0	0	0	0	0	0	0	0	0	0	0	.500	.500	.500
Putnam, Daniel, Stockton *	131	594	514	97	158	246	37	3	15	100	1	7	6	66	1	92	1	3	13	.307	.388	.479
Ramos, Carlos, Visalia *	95	366	335	48	94	119	10	3	3	36	11	2	6	12	0	29	6	7	9	.281	.315	.355
Ramos, Peeter, Lake Elsinore	100	477	424	69	118	142	14	2	2	46	10	2	5	36	0	58	18	3	12	.278	.340	.335
Reese, Pokey, Inland Empire	3	15	12	2	3	5	2	0	0	3	1	0	0	2	0	1	0	0	0	.250	.357	.417
Remole, Clifton, Rancho Cucamonga *	49	216	200	27	60	84	11	2	3	24	1	3	0	12	2	19	3	1	5	.300	.335	.420
Reyes, Ivan, Rancho Cucamonga	33	127	113	14	21	37	2	1	4	15	1	1	1	11	0	41	1	1	4	.186	.262	.327
Richar, Danny, Lancaster *	121	503	454	78	136	244	32	8	20	79	10	4	3	32	0	64	9	3	10	.300	.347	.537
Rico, Matt, Visalia	48	170	157	17	32	50	12	0	2	19	0	0	1	12	0	50	2	3	3	.204	.265	.318
Ringe, Craig, Bakersfield	116	469	399	54	102	136	14	4	4	35	4	3	10	53	0	84	6	3	10	.256	.355	.341
Roberts, Dave, Lake Elsinore *	3	13	10	2	2	3	1	0	0	0	0	0	0	3	0	1	0	1	0	.200	.385	.300
Robnett, Richard, Stockton *	115	519	457	77	111	201	30	0	20	74	1	4	1	56	0	151	8	4	5	.243	.324	.440
Rodriguez, Guillermo, San Jose	67	241	209	36	57	104	14	3	9	43	3	7	10	12	0	50	5	1	5	.273	.332	.498
Rogelstad, Matthew, Inland Empire *	111	495	438	71	133	163	23	2	1	47	10	2	1	44	1	52	3	2	8	.304	.367	.372
Rosario, Anderson, Rancho Cucamonga	14	52	49	3	6	7	1	0	0	1	1	0	1	1	0	20	0	0	0	.122	.157	.143
Rose, Brian, Lancaster	72	297	253	37	73	113	22	0	6	37	7	3	12	22	0	44	0	1	7	.289	.369	.447
Ruchti, Justin, Inland Empire	60	213	199	21	42	68	8	0	6	24	1	0	3	10	0	38	0	2	12	.211	.259	.342
Salazar, Darwinson, High Desert	14	55	44	5	8	13	2	0	1	3	0	0	0	11	0	18	0	0	1	.182	.345	.295
Sanchez, Angel, High Desert	133	639	585	102	183	239	33	4	5	70	7	5	3	39	0	54	10	5	11	.313	.356	.409
Sandoval, Abigail, Bakersfield	99	403	384	43	97	130	16	1	5	39	4	1	3	11	0	78	5	6	10	.253	.278	.339
Santana, Emmanuel, Rancho Cucamonga *	2	6	4	0	0	0	0	0	0	0	0	0	0	2	0	1	0	0	0	.000	.333	.000
Schierholtz, Nathan, San Jose *	128	548	502	83	160	258	37	8	15	86	3	5	6	32	0	132	5	7	10	.319	.363	.514
Schindewolf, Donald, Lancaster *	109	492	391	76	107	148	19	5	4	33	9	2	3	87	0	67	7	3	2	.274	.408	.379
Schleicher, Mark, Visalia	86	309	288	35	58	99	14	0	9	38	1	4	5	11	0	104	1	3	5	.201	.240	.344
Schweiger, Brian, Inland Empire	1	4	3	0	0	0	0	0	0	0	0	0	0	1	0	2	0	0	0	.000	.250	.000
Sevilla, Walter, High Desert	68	270	234	40	58	91	15	0	6	27	1	2	1	32	0	42	3	4	8	.248	.338	.389
Shankle, Robert, Rancho Cucamonga	5	21	16	1	4	5	1	0	0	1	0	0	0	5	1	7	0	0	2	.250	.429	.313
Simmons, Coltyn, Visalia	81	319	274	31	70	95	18	2	1	38	2	4	5	34	1	41	0	2	15	.255	.344	.347
Simon, Brandon, Lancaster *	23	89	78	12	20	25	3	1	0	6	3	0	4	4	0	20	2	2	3	.256	.326	.321
Sinisi, Vincent, Bakersfield *	35	153	135	25	49	81	10	2	6	22	0	0	1	17	1	19	5	0	3	.363	.438	.600
Sitzman, James, Visalia *	59	254	224	29	60	86	13	5	1	26	1	1	2	25	0	57	14	4	3	.268	.345	.384
Smith, Dustin, Bakersfield	36	147	122	20	40	65	11	1	4	22	0	0	9	16	0	22	1	1	2	.328	.442	.533
Smith, Garry, Modesto *	129	585	533	87	160	244	45	6	9	72	4	3	1	44	1	115	5	3	16	.300	.353	.458
Spanos, Vasili, Stockton	77	344	281	51	87	143	21	4	9	57	0	2	14	46	0	73	5	2	11	.310	.429	.509
Statia, Hainley, Rancho Cucamonga †	23	112	106	12	26	31	2	0	1	8	0	0	1	5	0	13	6	3	2	.245	.286	.292
St. Clair, Jason, Visalia	45	144	137	21	42	65	7	2	4	19	2	1	1	3	0	30	2	5	5	.307	.324	.474
Stephens, Leon, High Desert *	120	535	485	96	147	234	33	6	14	67	2	2	3	43	1	102	12	3	4	.303	.362	.482
Stewart, Ian, Modesto *	112	499	435	83	119	216	32	7	17	86	0	7	5	52	0	113	2	2	13	.274	.353	.497
Stinnett, Kelly, Lancaster	3	13	11	4	3	7	1	0	1	5	0	0	0	2	1	1	0	0	0	.273	.385	.636
Stocker, Myreon, High Desert †	7	27	26	3	6	8	0	1	0	4	0	0	0	1	0	3	2	1	0	.231	.259	.308
Sugden, Jason Andrew, Rancho Cucamonga †	83	347	316	35	78	114	13	7	3	35	6	6	4	15	1	81	4	7	3	.247	.284	.361
Suzuki, Kurt, Stockton	114	523	441	85	122	194	26	5	12	65	2	5	12	63	0	61	5	3	16	.277	.378	.440

Player, Team	G	TPA	AB	R	H	TB	2B	3B	HR	RBI	SH	SF	HP	BB	IBB	SO	SB	CS	GDP	Avg.	OBP	Slg.
Thayer, Matthew, Lake Elsinore	23	71	58	10	17	23	1	1	1	6	1	0	2	10	0	11	2	0	0	.293	.414	.397
Thigpen, Judson, Modesto	45	196	171	23	52	77	9	2	4	27	1	2	1	21	0	35	0	0	7	.304	.379	.450
Timpner, Clay, San Jose *	126	591	549	85	160	218	22	12	4	39	2	3	3	34	1	93	34	13	7	.291	.334	.397
Trytten, Ryan, Lake Elsinore	1	0	0	0	0	0	0	0	0	0	...	0	0	0	0	0	0	0	0	...	...	...
Tulowitzki, Troy, Modesto	22	105	94	17	25	43	6	0	4	14	0	0	2	9	0	18	1	0	2	.266	.343	.457
Turner, Lloyd, Stockton	63	290	252	49	71	112	13	5	6	23	2	2	8	26	0	54	11	5	2	.282	.365	.444
Turner, Timothy, Lake Elsinore	4	5	4	1	1	1	0	0	0	0	0	0	0	1	0	1	0	0	0	.250	.400	.250
Valenzuela Jr., Fernando, Lake Elsinore *	133	608	530	78	157	229	28	4	12	83	0	5	12	56	6	84	5	0	17	.296	.373	.432
Varela, Edgar, Lancaster *	106	432	395	58	122	183	30	2	9	60	4	9	6	18	1	74	1	2	9	.309	.341	.463
Villatoro, Wilmer, Lake Elsinore	1	0	0	0	0	0	0	0	0	0	...	0	0	0	0	0	0	0	0	...	...	...
Wagner, Michael, San Jose	8	31	28	4	9	15	3	0	1	4	0	0	1	2	0	8	0	0	0	.321	.387	.536
Wald, Jacob, San Jose	86	348	304	56	89	150	14	1	15	62	6	5	4	29	0	87	11	2	1	.293	.357	.493
Washington, Johnny, Bakersfield	4	13	12	1	1	1	0	0	0	3	0	0	0	1	0	5	0	0	2	.083	.154	.083
Wayment, Kory, Stockton	25	93	81	10	15	19	4	0	0	6	1	1	0	10	0	21	0	0	2	.185	.272	.235
Webster, Anthony, Bakersfield *	122	536	498	93	150	241	36	11	11	73	2	1	4	31	1	55	25	5	14	.301	.346	.484
Weed, James, Rancho Cucamonga †	19	76	70	10	13	17	0	2	0	2	0	0	0	6	1	16	1	0	1	.186	.250	.243
Wilson, Kyle, Modesto	21	85	78	12	22	42	3	1	5	15	1	0	1	5	0	22	0	0	2	.282	.333	.538
Wilson, Neil, Modesto	1	5	5	0	2	4	0	1	0	1	0	0	0	0	0	0	0	0	1	.400	.400	.800
Wilson, Robert, Rancho Cucamonga	115	501	466	66	135	211	32	1	14	77	0	3	2	30	0	61	2	1	5	.290	.333	.453
Winslow, Benjamin, Stockton	23	63	55	9	13	22	4	1	1	6	0	0	2	6	0	23	0	0	1	.236	.333	.400
Wood, Richard, Rancho Cucamonga	130	595	536	109	172	360	51	4	43	115	2	2	7	48	5	128	7	3	12	.321	.383	.672
Zorn, Dean, Inland Empire †	5	11	11	1	2	3	1	0	0	0	0	0	0	0	0	1	0	0	0	.182	.182	.273

PLAYERS WITH TWO OR MORE TEAMS

Player, Team	G	TPA	AB	R	H	TB	2B	3B	HR	RBI	SH	SF	HP	BB	IBB	SO	SB	CS	GDP	Avg.	OBP	Slg.
Bourassa, Adam, Bakersfield *	30	115	103	6	21	23	2	0	0	6	1	0	0	11	0	18	3	1	1	.204	.281	.223
Bourassa, Adam, Lake Elsinore *	48	226	194	36	69	90	11	2	2	16	5	4	2	21	1	25	13	8	5	.356	.428	.464

GRAND SLAMS—J. Wald, 3; B. Butler, J. Gaetti, M. Johnson, E. Monzon, D. Richar, 2 each; L. Appert, B. Balkcom, W. Bankston, R. Blood, B. Bonvechio, J. Bowker, C. Carter, J. Ciriaco, A. Cuevas, S. Garrabrants, F. Gomez, C. Iannetta, T. Ishikawa, B. Johnson, A. Keim, B. Lahair, B. Lenoir, C. Lubanski, D. Macias, M. Macri, K. Mahar, M. Pali, J. Price, D. Putnam, I. Reyes, M. Schleicher, V. Spanos, I. Stewart, K. Suzuki, A. Webster, 1 each.

AWARDED FIRST BASE ON CATCHER'S INTERFERENCE—F. Valenzuela Jr. 5 (E. Alfonzo, G. Rodriguez, J. Ruchti, K. Suzuki, L. Gonzalez); D. Barton (E. Alfonzo); R. Blood (L. Oliveros); J. Hatcher (R. Guarno); E. Johnson (T. Duff); J. Kreuzer (K. Suzuki); J. Sitzman (K. Suzuki); V. Spanos (E. Alfonzo).

2005 PITCHING

TEAM

Team	W	L	Pct.	ERA	G	CG	ShO	Sv.	IP	H	TBF	R	ER	HR	SH	SF	HB	BB	IBB	SO	WP	Bk.
San Jose	85	55	.607	4.24	140	0	8	40	1238.2	1232	5411	666	583	122	32	47	60	506	4	1139	89	4
Bakersfield	68	72	.486	4.60	140	3	3	38	1229.2	1325	5423	708	628	154	41	44	80	461	3	1049	64	9
Modesto	72	67	.518	4.75	139	1	4	38	1223	1366	5428	757	646	105	33	40	79	453	4	1006	87	2
Inland Empire	58	82	.414	4.86	140	1	4	22	1245.2	1454	5679	798	673	128	59	35	109	517	16	1039	82	7
Stockton	78	62	.557	4.86	140	1	5	51	1228	1391	5480	791	663	141	36	33	58	437	15	1182	94	9
Lake Elsinore	70	68	.507	5.05	138	2	4	34	1239	1413	5580	842	695	132	40	53	56	465	10	927	71	6
Lancaster	75	65	.536	5.22	140	1	0	36	1252.1	1525	5708	849	726	176	31	44	71	429	14	1003	84	4
High Desert	75	65	.536	5.40	140	1	4	35	1235	1531	5649	899	741	173	31	36	84	477	21	922	87	9
Visalia	55	85	.393	5.52	140	1	3	21	1220.1	1436	5596	858	749	142	38	52	81	538	8	1109	99	9
Rancho Cucamonga	62	77	.446	5.55	139	0	2	29	1231.2	1378	5621	854	759	150	41	44	70	624	4	1022	97	4

INDIVIDUAL

TOP QUALIFIERS FOR EARNED-RUN AVERAGE TITLE

Minimum 112 innings. *Lefthanded pitcher.

Pitcher, Team	W	L	Pct.	ERA	G	GS	CG	ShO	GF	Sv.	IP	H	TBF	R	ER	HR	SH	SF	HB	BB	IBB	SO	WP	Bk.
Wells, Jared, Lake Elsinore	11	3	.786	3.44	19	19	2	1	0	0	120.1	116	491	51	46	6	1	6	7	26	0	80	5	1
Smith, Cody, Bakersfield	6	3	.667	3.88	30	18	0	0	7	2	123.0	155	543	62	53	5	2	6	7	43	0	67	4	0
Feierabend, Ryan, Inland Empire *	9	7	.533	3.88	29	29	0	0	0	0	150.2	186	660	80	65	16	5	1	8	51	0	122	3	0
Mock, Garrett, Lancaster	14	7	.667	4.18	28	28	0	0	0	0	174.1	202	755	95	81	19	2	2	9	33	1	160	7	0
Mackintosh, Jason, Inland Empire *	10	11	.476	4.26	29	28	1	0	0	0	179.2	206	779	97	85	12	7	6	17	57	0	141	8	1
Gragg III, John, High Desert *	13	5	.722	4.36	27	27	1	1	0	0	148.2	178	667	92	72	18	2	5	13	47	0	95	4	0
Broshuis, Garrett, San Jose	12	9	.571	4.40	26	26	0	0	0	0	151.1	173	652	80	74	16	6	3	7	35	1	124	7	0
Morillo, Juan, Modesto	6	5	.545	4.41	20	20	0	0	0	0	112.1	107	490	69	55	10	3	2	8	65	0	101	13	1
Register, Steven, Modesto	9	11	.450	4.44	27	27	1	0	0	0	156.0	184	672	98	77	16	3	4	1	35	0	108	6	0
Kaiser, Marc, Modesto	7	6	.538	4.45	22	20	0	0	1	0	127.1	160	548	81	63	12	5	2	7	26	0	82	9	0
Sadowski, Ryan, San Jose	9	6	.600	4.64	24	23	0	0	0	0	126.0	120	541	70	65	12	0	5	9	42	0	118	15	0
Castellanos, Jonathan, Lancaster	10	3	.769	4.65	28	28	0	0	0	0	160.2	186	708	96	83	24	1	3	8	41	0	116	9	0
Ziegler, Brad, Stockton	9	7	.563	4.66	24	24	0	0	0	0	141.0	166	604	84	73	13	1	2	6	20	0	144	4	0
Moorhead, Michael, Inland Empire *	6	9	.400	4.75	26	25	0	0	0	0	142.0	163	624	91	75	13	3	10	11	36	0	120	7	0
Holcomb, James, Rancho Cucamonga	10	7	.588	5.02	27	26	0	0	0	0	141.2	153	617	93	79	16	5	7	11	50	0	128	11	1
Hunter, Christopher, Rancho Cucamonga	6	8	.429	5.11	21	20	0	0	0	0	118.0	130	536	77	67	10	2	2	6	60	0	72	8	1
Prochaska, Michael, Visalia *	4	12	.250	5.12	26	25	0	0	0	0	147.2	171	640	97	84	24	5	2	3	49	1	103	10	1
Floyd, Jesse, San Jose	12	6	.667	5.18	27	26	0	0	0	0	140.2	155	625	93	81	20	4	5	2	59	0	121	2	0
Thompson, Richard, Rancho Cucamonga	6	8	.429	5.27	42	15	0	0	14	3	121.1	132	537	76	71	20	2	5	2	53	1	92	12	2
Flanagan, Jeremy, Visalia	7	7	.462	5.43	25	23	1	0	0	0	126.0	170	587	93	76	16	2	6	5	57	0	84	6	1
Lopez, Javier Arturo, Lake Elsinore *	5	11	.313	5.85	27	27	0	0	0	0	140.0	174	637	108	91	13	4	3	8	49	1	94	7	1

DEPARTMENTAL LEADERS: W—Mock, 14. L—Marsden and Prochaska, 12. Pct.—Wells, .786. G—Rosales, 61. GS—Feierabend, 29. CG—Wells, 2. ShO—three pitchers tied with 1. GF—Rosales, 56. Sv.—Rosales, 27. IP—Mackintosh, 179.2. H—Mackintosh, 206. TBF—Mackintosh, 786. R—Herrera, 118. ER—Herrera, 101. HR—Castellanos and Prochaska, 24. SAC—four pitchers tied with 7. SF—Moorhead, 10. HB—Mackintosh and Scarbery, 17. BB—Morillo, 65. IBB—Muessig, 5. SO—Mock, 160. WP—Machi, 16. BK—Reina, 3.

ADVANCED CLASS A California League

ALL PITCHERS

*Lefthanded pitcher.

Pitcher, Team	W	L	Pct.	ERA	G	GS	CG	ShO	GF	Sv.	IP	H	TBF	R	ER	HR	SH	SF	HB	BB	IBB	SO	WP	Bk.
Abbott, Justin, Bakersfield	1	0	1.000	4.50	2	0	0	0	1	0	4.0	5	19	2	2	1	0	0	0	3	0	3	0	0
Abraham, Paul, Lake Elsinore	2	1	.667	1.07	35	0	0	0	12	4	42.0	29	156	8	5	1	4	1	0	10	1	36	1	0
Abruzzo, Jared, Bakersfield	0	0	.000	0.00	1	0	0	0	0	0	0.2	0	2	0	0	0	0	0	0	0	0	0	0	0
Accardo, Jeremy, San Jose	0	0	.000	0.00	2	0	0	0	2	1	2.0	1	9	0	0	0	0	0	1	1	0	3	0	0
Acevedo, Danielin, Stockton	1	3	.250	8.00	8	6	0	0	0	0	36.0	56	182	43	32	4	4	2	2	16	0	24	3	2
Ackerman, Eric, High Desert *	3	2	.600	5.54	31	0	0	0	9	1	50.1	61	230	36	31	7	1	3	8	13	0	30	3	1
Acosta, Nibaldo, Inland Empire	3	5	.375	5.83	39	3	0	0	12	2	80.1	106	374	63	52	8	7	5	12	29	1	65	9	0
Allen, Max, Visalia	1	4	.200	5.03	30	1	0	0	13	2	77.0	94	329	44	43	10	2	3	2	16	0	58	7	0
Anderson, Luke, San Jose	0	1	.000	31.50	1	1	0	0	0	0	2.0	7	15	7	7	3	0	0	0	2	0	1	0	0
Arias, Alberto, Modesto	4	4	.500	4.37	37	7	0	0	4	2	90.2	99	392	48	44	4	2	3	6	25	0	53	6	0
Arias, Oliver, Inland Empire	0	0	.000	6.64	14	0	0	0	6	0	20.1	26	98	16	15	4	0	0	0	16	0	24	3	0
Asencio, Miguel, Lake Elsinore	1	0	1.000	1.80	1	1	0	0	0	0	5.0	2	20	1	1	0	0	0	0	4	0	2	0	0
Ashby, Andy, Lake Elsinore	0	0	.000	0.00	1	1	0	0	0	0	3.0	3	13	1	0	0	0	0	0	0	0	1	0	0
Atencio, Alonzo, High Desert	3	1	.750	5.65	19	1	0	0	5	0	36.2	43	178	28	23	4	2	0	4	24	4	36	7	1
Austen, David, Rancho Cucamonga	3	2	.600	1.80	29	0	0	0	16	4	45.0	33	178	12	9	1	3	1	2	14	1	38	3	0
Avendano, Elvis, Stockton	2	4	.333	5.49	39	0	0	0	14	0	57.1	71	255	37	35	7	2	0	4	18	1	51	10	1
Baca, Daniel, Lake Elsinore	0	0	.000	10.97	6	0	0	0	1	0	10.2	23	59	13	13	1	0	1	1	7	0	5	1	0
Balbuena, Caleb, Modesto	2	0	1.000	2.65	12	0	0	0	3	0	17.0	21	77	6	5	0	1	0	2	4	0	15	2	0
Barratt, Jonathan, Visalia *	2	6	.250	6.59	36	5	0	0	16	1	71.0	85	348	59	52	9	1	1	5	52	1	79	5	1
Bateman, Joe, San Jose	3	4	.429	1.91	56	0	0	0	39	21	75.1	54	303	20	16	1	0	3	3	22	0	80	1	0
Beerer, Scott, Modesto	1	0	1.000	17.18	5	0	0	0	3	0	3.2	6	21	7	7	1	1	0	2	3	0	3	1	0
Benitez, Armando, San Jose	0	0	.000	0.00	2	2	0	0	0	0	2.0	0	6	0	0	0	0	0	0	1	0	0	0	0
Biggs, Billy, Lancaster	3	6	.333	6.04	39	0	0	0	12	1	44.2	66	208	34	30	5	4	3	0	16	4	26	0	0
Bilke, Austin, Inland Empire	0	1	.000	81.00	1	0	0	0	0	0	0.1	3	5	3	3	1	0	0	0	1	0	1	1	0
Blackwell, Brad, Lake Elsinore	0	0	.000	4.22	15	0	0	0	5	0	21.1	22	92	11	10	0	1	0	0	9	0	14	2	0
Blackwell, Chad, High Desert	0	0	.000	13.50	1	0	0	0	0	0	2.0	4	11	3	3	1	0	0	0	0	0	5	0	0
Bonine, Eddie, Lake Elsinore	5	6	.455	6.47	36	10	0	0	7	0	104.1	142	491	88	75	14	3	5	4	42	2	77	8	0
Bono, Kyle, Lancaster	1	0	1.000	7.04	6	0	0	0	1	0	7.2	7	36	7	6	2	0	0	0	5	0	9	2	0
Bourgeois, Nicholas, Inland Empire *	2	4	.333	3.59	27	0	0	0	5	1	47.2	41	209	25	19	4	3	1	3	31	1	45	5	0
Boyd, Jason, Bakersfield	1	3	.250	5.35	17	0	0	0	6	1	33.2	39	151	20	20	5	4	1	3	10	0	23	6	0
Braden, Dallas, Stockton *	6	0	1.000	2.68	7	7	1	0	0	0	43.2	31	168	14	13	4	2	0	3	11	0	64	4	2
Bradford, Chad, Stockton	0	0	.000	3.86	3	0	0	0	2	0	2.1	3	11	1	1	0	0	0	1	0	1	0	0
Brannon, Clint, Bakersfield *	9	7	.563	4.45	29	14	1	0	6	0	111.1	107	483	63	55	13	3	6	9	40	0	81	6	2
Braun, Ryan, High Desert	1	0	1.000	4.50	2	0	0	0	0	0	4.0	3	16	2	2	0	0	0	0	2	0	6	0	0
Bray, Stephen, High Desert	3	1	.750	4.93	26	0	0	0	24	9	34.2	37	146	21	19	9	0	0	0	8	3	39	1	0
Broshuis, Garrett, San Jose	12	9	.571	4.40	26	26	0	0	0	0	151.1	173	652	80	74	16	6	3	7	35	1	124	7	0
Buckley, Larry, Rancho Cucamonga	4	4	.500	4.20	54	0	0	0	21	3	79.1	76	360	43	37	7	3	2	6	52	0	96	4	0
Buckner, William, High Desert	5	6	.455	5.36	17	17	0	0	0	0	94.0	105	420	65	56	10	1	2	4	46	0	92	14	2
Burch, Robert, Modesto	7	3	.700	2.85	49	0	0	0	19	4	60.0	49	254	22	19	1	3	2	6	25	1	73	7	0
Burton, Levi, Stockton	4	4	.500	2.60	52	0	0	0	35	24	55.1	44	232	21	16	2	2	0	4	20	1	67	8	1
Cabaniel, Tomas, Stockton	1	0	1.000	12.60	4	0	0	0	3	0	5.0	7	27	7	7	1	0	0	0	5	0	2	0	0
Carrillo, Cesar, Lake Elsinore	1	2	.333	7.01	7	7	0	0	0	0	25.2	30	120	21	20	3	0	1	3	9	0	29	1	0
Castellanos, Jonathan, Lancaster	10	3	.769	4.65	28	28	0	0	0	0	160.2	186	708	96	83	24	1	3	8	41	0	116	9	0
Cate, Troy, Inland Empire *	4	4	.500	2.53	23	0	0	0	10	1	42.2	36	195	21	12	1	3	0	7	25	1	54	5	1
Chamberlain, Stephen, High Desert	3	0	1.000	7.61	44	0	0	0	11	0	75.2	102	361	71	64	15	2	2	7	36	2	41	8	0
Chavez, Jesse, Bakersfield	0	0	.000	2.22	11	0	0	0	5	2	24.1	16	97	6	6	2	0	0	0	9	0	31	1	0
Chico, Matthew, Lancaster *	7	2	.778	3.76	18	18	0	0	0	0	110.0	101	462	50	46	13	0	5	3	39	0	102	4	1
Clarke, Darren, Modesto	0	0	.000	9.00	5	0	0	0	0	0	6.0	13	33	8	6	2	0	0	0	3	0	4	1	0
Coffin, Ryan, Lancaster	4	2	.667	6.28	33	0	0	0	11	2	43.0	51	200	34	30	7	1	1	7	13	0	45	2	0
Coggin, Dave, Visalia	3	2	.600	3.38	18	0	0	0	12	6	29.1	28	127	21	11	2	4	1	1	14	0	27	3	0
Cook, Aaron, Modesto	1	0	1.000	1.80	1	1	0	0	0	0	5.0	5	19	1	1	0	0	0	0	0	0	5	0	0
Corchado, Jose, Stockton	0	1	.000	11.81	4	0	0	0	1	0	5.1	5	28	7	7	1	0	0	1	7	0	4	2	0
Cordeiro, Christopher, Bakersfield	6	3	.667	3.80	41	0	0	0	35	14	66.1	67	290	29	28	3	4	4	7	30	0	52	6	0
Cornejo, Eduardo, Stockton	0	0	.000	27.00	1	0	0	0	1	0	1.0	5	8	3	3	0	0	0	0	0	0	1	0	0
Corpas, Manuel, Modesto	3	2	.600	3.78	47	0	0	0	19	2	69.0	83	297	33	29	2	2	2	3	14	1	52	3	0
Correia, Kevin, San Jose	0	1	.000	2.57	1	1	0	0	0	0	7.0	5	29	2	2	0	0	0	0	5	0	7	2	0
Coughlin, Christopher, High Desert	5	11	.313	7.31	29	11	0	0	1	0	85.0	133	408	88	69	21	1	3	5	29	0	52	0	2
Coutlangus, Jonathan, San Jose *	4	0	1.000	3.04	50	0	0	0	14	3	77.0	64	312	27	26	3	2	5	4	29	0	79	9	0
Cox, Benjamin, San Jose	0	0	.000	4.91	2	0	0	0	1	0	3.2	3	16	3	2	1	0	0	1	1	0	6	0	0
Cremidan, Alexander, Lancaster	1	5	.167	4.58	44	0	0	0	12	0	57.0	55	263	35	29	5	2	1	5	34	3	49	6	0
Crowder, Justin, Stockton *	3	2	.600	2.47	50	1	0	0	12	1	54.2	53	240	21	15	4	2	0	3	23	1	60	3	0
Cruz Chavez, Rafael, Rancho Cucamonga	0	0	.000	3.75	5	0	0	0	0	0	12.0	13	51	5	5	2	0	0	1	1	0	4	1	0
Danks, John, Bakersfield *	3	3	.500	2.50	10	10	0	0	0	0	57.2	50	237	18	16	5	0	0	2	16	0	53	1	0
Davis, John-paul, Visalia	0	0	.000	9.00	1	0	0	0	1	0	2.0	4	10	2	2	0	0	0	0	1	0	0	0	0
DeHoyos, Gabriel, High Desert	2	0	1.000	0.93	7	0	0	0	5	2	9.2	10	38	1	1	0	0	0	1	2	0	7	0	0
DeLoizaga-Carney, Frederic, Rancho Cucamonga	1	1	.500	8.91	23	0	0	0	6	1	33.1	48	165	33	33	9	2	4	2	22	0	29	4	0
Demaria, Chris, High Desert	4	2	.667	2.23	48	0	0	0	42	19	60.2	57	243	19	15	8	2	0	2	10	1	73	2	0
Diamond, Thomas, Bakersfield	8	0	1.000	1.99	14	14	1	0	0	0	81.1	53	319	20	18	3	3	2	9	31	0	101	5	0
Dickinson, Andy, Stockton *	0	0	.000	0.00	1	0	0	0	1	0	0.2	0	4	0	0	0	0	0	0	2	0	1	0	0
Dowdy, Justin, Rancho Cucamonga *	3	4	.429	4.98	46	3	0	0	11	0	77.2	87	351	47	43	13	0	2	2	36	0	64	4	0
Drucker, Scot, Stockton	7	1	.875	5.51	29	9	0	0	4	1	83.1	107	366	54	51	11	4	2	2	26	0	61	3	0
Dufner, Kristofor, Visalia	0	0	.000	54.00	1	0	0	0	1	0	1.0	6	10	6	6	3	0	0	0	0	0	0	0	0
Dunn, Keith, Stockton	11	4	.733	4.56	18	18	0	0	0	0	100.2	112	438	64	51	18	1	3	2	28	0	77	2	1
Dunwell, Christopher, Stockton	9	5	.643	5.63	30	12	0	0	1	0	88.0	115	398	61	55	15	2	4	4	31	1	89	8	0
Eaton, Adam, Lake Elsinore	0	0	.000	0.00	1	1	0	0	0	0	3.0	1	11	0	0	0	0	0	0	2	0	2	0	0
Edwards, William, Rancho Cucamonga	1	7	.125	5.91	17	17	0	0	0	0	91.1	115	431	73	60	12	4	4	8	48	0	66	3	0
Ellison, Derrick, Inland Empire *	0	1	.000	6.97	7	0	0	0	0	0	10.1	14	53	11	8	0	2	0	2	10	0	7	0	0

Pitcher, Team	W	L	Pct.	ERA	G	GS	CG	ShO	GF	Sv.	IP	H	TBF	R	ER	HR	SH	SF	HB	BB	IBB	SO	WP	Bk.
Endicott, Drew, High Desert	2	3	.400	6.40	42	1	0	0	10	1	83.0	117	391	71	59	12	3	4	7	30	2	37	5	1
Escobar, Kelvim, Rancho Cucamonga	0	0	.000	0.00	1	1	0	0	0	0	3.0	1	12	0	0	0	0	0	0	2	0	7	0	0
Espineli, Eugene, San Jose *	4	0	1.000	2.66	40	0	0	0	7	1	64.1	57	266	22	19	2	5	4	2	24	0	55	0	1
Farnum, Matthew, Bakersfield	0	1	.000	12.38	4	0	0	0	0	0	8.0	18	44	11	11	2	0	1	1	1	0	5	0	0
Feierabend, Ryan, Inland Empire *	8	7	.533	3.88	29	29	0	0	0	0	150.2	186	660	80	65	16	5	1	8	51	0	122	3	0
Feldman, Scott, Bakersfield	0	0	.000	0.00	6	0	0	0	6	3	9.0	5	36	2	0	0	0	0	1	2	0	11	1	0
Fernandez, Alfredo, Lake Elsinore	0	0	.000	0.00	3	0	0	0	1	0	3.0	1	13	0	0	0	0	0	0	3	0	1	0	0
Ferrer, Simon, Modesto	0	0	.000	0.00	1	0	0	0	1	0	1.0	1	4	0	0	0	0	0	0	0	0	0	0	0
Fillinger, Chad, Inland Empire	2	5	.286	5.96	15	11	0	0	1	0	71.0	90	318	48	47	16	3	0	4	18	1	61	2	0
Flanagan, Jeremy, Visalia	6	7	.462	5.43	25	23	1	0	0	0	126.0	170	587	93	76	16	2	6	5	57	0	84	6	1
Floyd, Jesse, San Jose	12	6	.667	5.18	27	26	0	0	0	0	140.2	155	625	93	81	20	4	5	2	59	0	121	2	0
Foppert, Jesse, San Jose	1	0	1.000	2.08	3	3	0	0	0	0	8.2	5	36	2	2	0	0	1	0	6	0	9	0	0
Frieri, Ernesto, Lake Elsinore	0	0	.000	2.70	2	0	0	0	0	0	3.1	3	14	1	1	1	0	0	0	1	0	3	0	0
Fritz, Benjamin, Stockton	0	0	.000	8.10	2	2	0	0	0	0	6.2	10	32	6	6	0	0	0	1	2	0	3	0	0
Fulmer, Thomas, Visalia	3	6	.333	5.80	26	20	0	0	3	0	99.1	123	455	68	64	10	3	5	11	32	1	97	4	0
Garthwaite, Jay, Lancaster	0	0	.000	0.00	1	0	0	0	1	0	2.0	2	8	0	0	0	0	0	0	1	0	1	0	0
Giles, Joshua, Bakersfield	0	0	.000	0.00	1	0	0	0	0	0	2.0	1	8	0	0	0	0	0	1	1	0	3	0	0
Girardeau, Maurice, Lake Elsinore	3	9	.250	7.13	20	17	0	0	0	0	88.1	125	421	85	70	18	2	4	3	30	1	50	3	0
Glant, Dustin, Lancaster	0	1	.000	7.19	50	0	0	0	29	16	46.1	74	228	41	37	10	1	3	2	12	0	49	10	0
Gonzalez, Miguel, Rancho Cucamonga	0	0	.000	0.00	2	0	0	0	0	0	4.2	0	15	0	0	0	0	0	0	2	0	3	0	0
Gragg III, John, High Desert *	13	5	.722	4.36	27	27	1	1	0	0	148.2	178	667	92	72	18	2	5	13	47	0	95	4	0
Green, Patrick, High Desert	3	4	.429	4.33	7	7	0	0	0	0	43.2	43	181	27	21	4	1	2	2	8	0	40	3	0
Hamilton, Clayton, Lake Elsinore	2	2	.500	5.14	7	6	0	0	0	0	28.0	39	128	19	16	2	0	3	1	9	1	18	1	0
Hayhurst, Dirk, Lake Elsinore	5	5	.500	5.38	38	7	0	0	7	1	93.2	106	413	66	56	9	1	7	4	27	1	69	3	1
Hedrick, Justin, San Jose	3	4	.429	3.55	51	0	0	0	39	12	58.1	42	240	24	23	7	1	1	1	23	1	75	6	0
Herrera, Cesar, High Desert	7	7	.500	7.27	31	23	0	0	1	0	125.0	177	596	118	101	21	3	7	6	45	0	81	8	0
Herrera, Marcos, Bakersfield	6	4	.600	6.34	24	0	0	0	9	2	49.2	65	228	39	35	14	3	2	2	21	1	41	3	0
Holcomb, James, Rancho Cucamonga	10	7	.588	5.02	27	26	0	0	0	0	141.2	153	617	93	79	16	5	7	11	50	0	128	11	1
Holsten, Ryan, Lancaster	0	0	.000	18.00	3	0	0	0	0	0	3.0	10	20	6	6	1	0	0	1	1	0	1	0	0
Howell, J.P., High Desert *	3	1	.750	1.96	8	8	0	0	0	0	46.0	33	190	16	10	2	0	0	3	24	0	48	5	1
Huerta, Edgar, Lake Elsinore *	1	0	1.000	10.95	8	0	0	0	2	0	12.1	21	60	15	15	0	1	0	0	4	0	14	0	0
Hughes, Dustin, High Desert *	5	7	.417	5.67	19	19	0	0	0	0	92.0	119	427	74	58	13	5	4	5	45	1	87	9	1
Hunter, Christopher, Rancho Cucamonga	6	8	.429	5.11	21	20	0	0	0	0	118.0	130	536	77	67	10	2	2	6	60	0	72	8	1
Ingram, Jesse, Bakersfield	0	2	.000	21.00	8	0	0	0	5	2	6.0	15	40	15	14	1	3	0	0	11	0	8	1	0
Jaile, Christopher, Bakersfield	2	3	.400	4.26	13	13	0	0	0	0	63.1	65	293	37	30	4	0	1	8	35	0	58	2	0
James, Craig, Inland Empire	0	2	.000	2.42	23	0	0	0	23	10	26.0	25	110	8	7	3	1	0	2	8	2	24	2	0
Jepsen, Kevin, Rancho Cucamonga	0	1	.000	10.66	4	4	0	0	0	0	12.2	19	68	18	15	2	0	0	1	10	0	11	0	0
Jimenez, Ubaldo, Modesto	5	3	.625	3.98	14	14	0	0	0	0	72.1	61	309	35	32	5	0	1	5	40	1	78	4	0
Kaanoi, Jason, High Desert	4	8	.333	5.91	18	15	0	0	2	0	85.1	120	406	71	56	10	2	1	10	42	2	37	8	0
Kaiser, Marc, Modesto	7	6	.538	4.45	22	20	0	0	1	0	127.1	160	548	81	63	12	5	2	7	26	0	82	9	0
Kerbs, Reuben, Lancaster *	2	1	.667	4.74	57	0	0	0	10	0	38.0	37	168	26	20	8	3	2	1	19	0	28	1	1
Key, Christopher, Inland Empire *	4	0	1.000	1.80	18	0	0	0	10	2	30.0	44	135	15	6	2	1	0	0	5	2	20	1	0
Kinney, Matt, San Jose	3	0	1.000	2.10	5	5	0	0	0	0	30.0	23	122	8	7	3	0	1	0	14	0	34	0	0
Kinsey, Christopher, Lancaster	3	11	.214	6.56	15	15	0	0	0	0	72.2	112	352	72	53	10	0	3	1	29	0	60	9	0
Klatt, Ryan, Lake Elsinore	2	0	1.000	7.71	17	0	0	0	1	0	23.1	27	104	21	20	6	2	1	1	7	0	17	1	0
Knox, Bradley, Stockton	8	7	.533	4.27	20	20	0	0	0	0	111.2	109	468	59	53	13	0	6	6	34	1	93	4	1
Komine, Shane, Stockton	0	0	.000	4.15	2	2	0	0	0	0	8.2	10	39	4	4	0	0	0	2	3	0	11	3	0
Kranawetter, Josh, Visalia	1	4	.200	6.21	18	0	0	0	8	2	29.0	36	138	22	20	2	2	0	3	17	1	28	2	0
Landeros, Leonard, Stockton *	0	0	.000	1.93	1	1	0	0	0	0	4.2	4	21	1	1	0	0	0	1	4	0	7	0	0
Lebron, Willy, Bakersfield	3	4	.429	5.11	24	5	0	0	8	2	56.1	69	260	40	32	14	1	1	2	25	0	50	4	2
Leon, Brigmer, Stockton	0	4	.000	5.83	27	1	0	0	9	1	46.1	65	218	40	30	7	5	0	0	20	1	39	4	0
Liebeck, Jered, Lancaster	1	1	.500	5.81	18	0	0	0	5	1	26.1	34	129	18	17	1	0	1	2	14	1	24	0	0
Little, Joseph, Visalia *	5	7	.417	7.48	26	11	0	0	6	0	71.0	65	342	63	59	10	1	3	8	63	0	70	12	1
Looper, Aaron, Inland Empire	0	1	.000	3.75	9	0	0	0	1	0	12.0	9	52	8	5	3	0	0	1	5	0	11	2	0
Lopez, Javier Arturo, Lake Elsinore *	5	11	.313	5.85	27	27	0	0	0	0	140.0	174	637	108	91	13	4	3	8	49	1	94	7	1
Lorenzo, Mathew, Bakersfield	1	4	.200	4.02	9	9	0	0	0	0	53.2	60	236	31	24	8	3	1	1	21	0	55	2	1
Lowery, Devon, High Desert	6	3	.667	3.84	14	11	0	0	1	0	70.1	70	290	34	30	8	1	2	0	25	0	50	1	0
Lugo, Ruddy, Visalia	0	0	.000	13.50	1	0	0	0	1	0	2.0	7	13	4	3	0	0	0	0	1	0	0	0	0
Lynn, Kevin, Visalia	2	6	.250	6.81	14	13	0	0	0	0	71.1	101	321	59	54	7	1	4	3	9	0	55	5	0
Machi, Jean, Visalia	3	11	.214	6.03	31	14	0	0	9	3	97.0	113	456	76	65	8	0	5	10	58	0	106	16	1
MacKenzie, Aaron, Rancho Cucamonga	0	3	.000	5.58	49	0	0	0	8	0	79.0	93	371	51	49	8	1	0	5	49	0	62	9	0
Mackintosh, Jason, Inland Empire *	10	11	.476	4.26	29	28	1	0	0	0	179.2	206	779	97	85	12	7	6	17	57	0	141	8	1
Marini, Christopher, Bakersfield *	2	6	.250	6.51	13	9	0	0	3	1	55.1	68	259	43	40	11	3	1	4	27	0	53	3	1
Marsden, Aaron, Modesto *	6	12	.333	6.62	27	24	0	0	0	0	125.0	172	592	110	92	19	2	9	9	53	0	73	9	0
Martinez, Gregorio, San Jose	1	0	1.000	10.66	4	2	0	0	1	0	12.2	25	67	16	15	5	0	1	1	4	0	7	0	0
Martinez, Javier, Lake Elsinore	4	2	.667	4.77	17	17	0	0	0	0	100.0	100	427	59	53	16	1	5	3	29	0	76	3	1
Martinez, Miguel A., Inland Empire *	1	4	.200	7.09	19	6	0	0	4	1	47.0	52	229	42	37	4	4	2	3	36	0	42	4	1
Mattoon, Brian, Bakersfield *	5	5	.500	4.06	38	2	0	0	11	2	88.2	84	372	46	40	13	4	6	4	25	1	67	3	2
Mault, James, Inland Empire	0	0	.000	3.10	14	0	0	0	7	0	20.1	17	85	7	7	1	0	0	0	13	0	13	0	0
McBeth, Marcus, Stockton	0	0	.000	0.00	2	0	0	0	1	0	2.2	1	11	0	0	0	0	0	1	2	0	3	0	0
McNiven, Brooks, San Jose	7	2	.778	4.24	39	6	0	0	7	0	93.1	109	403	49	44	8	1	4	4	30	0	51	5	0
Mendoza, Luis, Lake Elsinore	0	1	.000	9.28	2	2	0	0	0	0	10.2	18	50	14	11	1	1	0	0	4	0	3	1	0
Mendoza, Thomas, Rancho Cucamonga	1	0	1.000	0.00	2	1	0	0	1	1	10.0	4	33	0	0	0	0	0	0	0	0	12	0	0
Merricks, Matthew, Modesto *	0	0	.000	7.71	2	0	0	0	0	0	2.1	4	15	3	2	0	0	1	1	2	0	2	0	0
Miller, James, Modesto	1	3	.250	3.78	48	0	0	0	44	25	47.2	39	201	22	20	3	0	0	1	17	0	68	3	0
Mock, Garrett, Lancaster	14	7	.667	4.18	28	28	0	0	0	0	174.1	202	755	95	81	19	2	2	9	33	1	160	7	0
Moore, James, High Desert	2	4	.333	4.99	40	0	0	0	19	0	57.2	76	271	36	32	5	3	0	6	29	3	33	5	0
Moorhead, Michael, Inland Empire	6	9	.400	4.75	26	25	0	0	0	0	142.0	163	624	91	75	13	3	10	11	36	0	120	7	0
Morel, Edwin, Modesto	1	2	.333	6.29	45	0	0	0	12	1	68.2	81	307	54	48	11	3	4	2	25	0	46	5	0
Morillo, Juan, Modesto	6	5	.545	4.41	20	20	0	0	0	0	112.1	107	490	69	55	10	3	2	8	65	0	101	13	1

Pitcher, Team	W	L	Pct.	ERA	G	GS	CG	ShO	GF	Sv.	IP	H	TBF	R	ER	HR	SH	SF	HB	BB	IBB	SO	WP	Bk.
Morla, Wandy, Bakersfield	0	0	.000	15.00	3	0	0	0	1	1	6.0	8	33	11	10	4	0	0	1	8	0	4	1	0
Muessig, Jeffrey, Stockton	1	5	.167	4.80	49	0	0	0	27	15	60.0	56	267	43	32	6	5	3	0	35	5	80	5	0
Murray, Arlington, Bakersfield *	2	5	.286	5.25	14	11	0	0	0	0	60.0	75	266	38	35	6	0	2	2	13	0	64	2	0
Newman, Joshua, Modesto *	5	2	.714	3.13	41	0	0	0	16	0	63.1	45	267	22	22	5	1	0	0	40	0	99	2	0
Niemann, Jeffrey, Visalia	0	1	.000	3.98	5	5	0	0	0	0	20.1	12	84	10	9	3	0	0	2	10	0	28	1	0
Nin, Sandy, Modesto	4	1	.800	2.55	7	7	0	0	0	0	35.1	30	140	11	10	3	0	2	2	7	0	34	1	0
Nottingham, Shawn, Inland Empire *	4	3	.571	3.86	7	6	0	0	0	0	37.1	48	170	19	16	2	0	2	3	10	0	28	2	1
Nunez, Leo, High Desert	0	0	.000	9.00	8	0	0	0	0	0	13.0	23	64	15	13	2	2	0	0	3	2	15	3	0
Olore, Kevin, Inland Empire	0	0	.000	15.43	1	1	0	0	0	0	2.1	4	15	4	4	2	0	0	0	4	0	3	0	0
Ortiz, Russ, Lancaster	0	1	.000	42.43	1	1	0	0	0	0	2.1	12	19	11	11	2	0	1	0	1	0	1	0	0
Owings, Micah, Lancaster	1	1	.500	2.45	16	0	0	0	1	0	22.0	17	82	6	6	0	1	1	0	4	0	30	0	0
Padgett, Michael, Bakersfield	0	1	.000	4.30	14	0	0	0	10	5	23.0	30	100	13	11	2	1	1	2	5	0	20	0	0
Pali, Matthew, Rancho Cucamonga *	0	0	.000	0.00	1	0	0	0	1	0	0.1	0	2	0	0	0	0	0	0	1	0	0	0	0
Peguero, Tony, Visalia	4	4	.500	5.77	30	6	0	0	19	5	64.0	79	287	48	41	5	3	4	5	20	1	39	4	1
Pence, Howard, Lake Elsinore	4	5	.444	4.56	41	0	0	0	12	1	49.1	56	229	33	25	3	4	2	2	27	1	34	5	0
Pendley, Nathan, San Jose *	1	1	.500	1.86	14	0	0	0	4	1	19.1	7	78	4	4	0	1	0	0	15	0	17	1	0
Petersen, Jeffrey, San Jose	4	4	.500	4.97	40	2	0	0	7	0	67.0	80	311	45	37	5	3	2	7	34	1	61	7	0
Peterson, John, Stockton *	4	6	.400	6.04	15	15	0	0	0	0	79.0	107	371	64	53	10	0	3	5	25	0	59	8	0
Pickens, Joseph, Stockton	1	1	.500	7.59	16	0	0	0	4	0	21.1	28	104	19	18	1	1	1	3	10	0	21	2	1
Posey, Micah, Rancho Cucamonga *	0	2	.000	12.00	6	6	0	0	0	0	18.0	29	98	24	24	1	0	4	2	17	0	14	3	0
Prinz, Bret, Rancho Cucamonga	0	0	.000	1.80	2	0	0	0	0	0	5.0	2	19	1	1	0	0	1	1	3	0	6	0	0
Prochaska, Michael, Visalia *	4	12	.250	5.12	26	25	0	0	0	0	147.2	171	640	97	84	24	5	2	3	49	1	103	10	1
Ramirez, Ivan, Bakersfield *	1	3	.250	4.91	25	0	0	0	16	1	40.1	39	168	25	22	8	2	1	2	15	1	31	1	0
Ramsey, Keith, Lancaster *	0	1	.000	4.50	4	0	0	0	2	0	4.0	3	19	2	2	0	1	0	1	5	1	4	1	0
Ray, Ronald, Rancho Cucamonga	1	2	.333	5.79	20	0	0	0	6	0	32.2	43	157	25	21	5	1	1	2	20	0	24	5	0
Register, Steven, Modesto	9	11	.450	4.44	27	27	1	0	0	0	156.0	184	672	98	77	16	3	4	1	35	0	108	6	0
Reina, Jesus, San Jose *	2	4	.333	5.16	18	13	0	0	2	0	68.0	58	303	48	39	8	0	1	5	42	0	72	6	3
Reynolds, Grant, Stockton	0	0	.000	14.40	4	0	0	0	2	0	5.0	9	28	8	8	3	0	0	0	4	0	3	0	0
Ridgway, Jeffrey, Visalia *	3	4	.429	5.20	24	0	0	0	9	0	45.0	43	211	31	26	2	7	5	3	36	1	56	7	0
Rivera, Mumba, Inland Empire	5	8	.385	7.49	18	17	0	0	0	0	91.1	118	437	79	76	19	1	2	12	50	0	67	10	0
Robertson, James, Stockton	5	2	.714	2.76	32	0	0	0	7	1	42.1	37	188	17	13	1	1	1	2	23	4	68	4	0
Robles, Lawrence, Modesto	4	4	.500	8.07	12	11	0	0	0	0	61.1	90	297	58	55	3	2	3	12	21	0	32	7	1
Rodriguez, Guillermo, San Jose	0	0	.000	0.00	2	0	0	0	2	0	2.0	1	7	0	0	0	0	0	0	0	0	3	0	0
Rodriguez, Manuel, Stockton	0	0	.000	8.10	6	0	0	0	0	0	10.0	16	48	9	9	4	0	1	1	2	0	3	2	0
Rodriguez, Rafael, Rancho Cucamonga	4	4	.500	6.75	14	14	0	0	0	0	72.0	84	326	58	54	11	2	4	1	33	0	44	11	0
Rodriguez, William, Bakersfield *	1	1	.500	10.06	11	0	0	0	7	0	17.0	25	76	20	19	4	3	0	0	8	0	7	0	0
Rosales, Leonel, Lake Elsinore	8	7	.533	3.18	61	0	0	0	56	27	65.0	53	270	26	23	5	5	3	1	24	0	77	1	0
Rowe, Steven, Bakersfield	1	1	.500	5.40	2	0	0	0	1	0	3.1	4	14	2	2	1	0	0	0	0	0	2	0	0
Sadowski, Ryan, San Jose	9	6	.600	4.64	24	23	0	0	0	0	126.0	120	541	70	65	12	0	5	9	42	0	118	15	0
Salas, Juan, Visalia	2	1	.667	3.52	25	0	0	0	11	1	38.1	30	163	19	15	6	2	1	5	18	1	47	6	1
Sanchez, Jose, San Jose	0	0	.000	13.50	7	1	0	0	3	0	9.1	15	52	14	14	2	0	1	0	11	0	10	2	0
Santiago, Tomas, Modesto	3	9	.250	5.02	38	8	0	0	13	4	84.1	94	384	55	47	7	4	5	10	42	1	69	7	0
Santos, Alexandre, Stockton	0	0	.000	0.56	12	0	0	0	9	7	16.0	8	58	2	1	1	0	0	0	2	0	20	0	0
Scarbery, Chad, Lancaster	5	6	.455	6.11	25	24	1	0	0	0	131.0	174	617	103	89	17	6	8	17	53	0	77	12	1
Seanez, Rudy, Lake Elsinore	0	1	.000	36.00	1	0	0	0	0	0	1.0	3	7	4	4	2	0	0	0	1	0	0	0	0
Serrato, Juan, San Jose	5	6	.455	6.10	27	15	0	0	4	0	87.0	97	405	67	59	12	3	4	6	48	0	88	11	0
Shank, Christopher, Stockton	0	2	.000	4.82	8	0	0	0	1	0	9.1	11	42	8	5	1	2	1	0	4	0	10	2	0
Shappi, Austin, Lancaster	5	6	.455	5.10	12	12	0	0	0	0	77.2	94	344	51	44	13	0	3	5	20	1	56	2	1
Sharpe, Steven, Stockton	1	0	1.000	5.40	3	1	0	0	0	0	6.2	4	30	4	4	0	1	0	2	6	0	9	3	0
Silva, Jesus, Lancaster	5	2	.714	6.91	29	3	0	0	6	1	41.2	64	206	40	32	11	1	2	2	16	3	38	2	0
Simard, Michel, Rancho Cucamonga	3	5	.375	7.32	13	13	0	0	0	0	67.2	82	306	62	55	13	3	3	6	32	0	48	3	0
Smith, Cody, Bakersfield	6	3	.667	3.88	30	18	0	0	7	2	123.0	155	543	62	53	5	2	6	7	43	0	67	4	0
Smith, Jesse, Rancho Cucamonga	3	2	.600	4.70	13	2	0	0	2	0	30.2	36	136	18	16	4	0	0	1	9	0	30	2	0
Smith, Samuel, Lancaster	7	6	.538	5.44	41	11	0	0	10	0	101.0	132	464	73	61	21	3	1	4	33	0	66	8	0
Smyth, Steve, Stockton *	3	1	.750	6.02	9	9	0	0	0	0	43.1	53	208	36	29	5	0	2	1	24	0	32	2	0
Song, Seung, San Jose	5	2	.714	1.95	9	6	0	0	0	0	37.0	27	155	11	8	3	2	0	2	17	0	47	8	0
Sonnanstine, Andrew, Visalia	4	1	.800	3.80	10	10	0	0	0	0	64.0	71	266	29	27	5	0	2	1	7	0	75	2	0
Soriano, Rafael, Inland Empire	0	0	.000	0.00	3	3	0	0	0	0	4.0	2	13	0	0	0	0	0	0	0	0	5	0	0
Steele, Michael, Inland Empire	4	5	.444	4.41	30	1	0	0	22	2	49.0	54	215	31	24	7	7	1	2	23	3	42	9	1
Steffek, Brian, High Desert	1	0	1.000	5.60	15	0	0	0	9	3	17.2	20	83	11	11	3	0	0	1	9	1	18	1	0
Steidlmayer, Luke, Lake Elsinore	0	3	.000	4.33	9	8	0	0	0	0	52.0	59	229	37	25	7	1	2	5	10	0	34	3	1
Steinborn, Christopher, Modesto *	3	0	1.000	7.90	11	0	0	0	2	0	13.2	22	72	14	12	1	1	0	2	6	0	8	1	0
Stitt, Brian, Inland Empire	1	2	.333	5.92	15	0	0	0	7	0	24.1	30	112	18	16	1	3	0	2	9	3	22	1	1
Stokes, Brian, Visalia	1	2	.333	4.24	4	4	0	0	0	0	17.0	15	71	8	8	3	0	1	0	5	0	21	0	0
Sullivan, Bradley, Stockton	0	1	.000	7.30	13	2	0	0	3	0	24.2	36	122	26	20	4	1	0	0	21	0	11	7	0
Thompson, Chris, Lancaster	3	1	.750	5.13	27	0	0	0	12	0	33.1	32	147	20	19	3	1	1	3	16	0	24	5	0
Thompson, Richard, Rancho Cucamonga	6	8	.429	5.27	42	15	0	0	14	3	121.1	132	537	76	71	20	2	5	2	53	1	92	12	2
Thompson, Sean, Lake Elsinore *	4	1	.800	2.16	6	6	0	0	0	0	33.1	26	139	15	8	4	0	0	2	13	0	45	2	0
Thurmond, J, San Jose	2	3	.400	6.64	5	4	0	0	0	0	20.1	29	101	18	15	5	0	0	0	11	0	10	1	0
Tierney, Chris, Lake Elsinore *	4	6	.400	6.35	41	9	0	0	3	0	89.1	114	439	81	63	9	4	3	5	61	0	50	9	1
Toledo, Jean, Rancho Cucamonga	2	2	.500	3.28	8	4	0	0	1	0	35.2	41	147	14	13	1	3	0	1	13	0	21	3	0
Torres, Joseph, Rancho Cucamonga *	0	4	.000	18.00	10	6	0	0	1	0	20.0	39	129	43	40	4	2	1	5	31	0	15	4	0
Touchstone, Nicholas, Rancho Cucamonga *	4	2	.667	10.94	23	0	0	0	3	0	26.1	41	145	37	32	5	1	0	2	29	0	23	3	0
Trolia, Aaron, Inland Empire	3	7	.300	4.82	40	10	0	0	11	0	104.2	118	475	71	56	6	6	2	13	49	2	77	1	0
Trytten, Ryan, Lake Elsinore	6	2	.750	3.73	50	0	0	0	12	0	50.2	59	233	28	21	7	2	1	1	23	2	52	6	0
Tsao, Chin-hui, Modesto	0	0	.000	0.00	1	0	0	0	1	0	1.0	0	3	0	0	0	0	0	0	0	0	1	0	0
Vandermeer, Scott, Visalia	6	3	.667	5.77	42	0	0	0	21	0	73.1	105	355	58	47	11	2	4	5	34	0	49	4	2
Villatoro, Wilmer, Lake Elsinore	2	1	.667	3.88	52	0	0	0	17	1	60.1	61	274	36	26	4	3	5	5	34	0	44	8	0
Volquez, Edison, Bakersfield	5	4	.556	4.19	11	11	1	0	0	0	66.2	64	273	34	31	9	2	0	7	12	0	77	3	0
Waddell, Jason, San Jose *	5	1	.833	3.40	26	2	0	0	5	0	47.2	42	194	20	18	4	2	3	1	15	1	44	4	0
Walk, Mitchell, San Jose *	2	1	.667	3.04	12	2	0	0	3	1	26.2	33	127	16	9	2	2	3	4	15	0	17	2	0
Walker, Andrew, Bakersfield	3	3	.500	4.94	9	9	0	0	0	0	54.2	71	239	34	30	7	0	6	3	9	0	35	0	0
Watson, Michael, Lancaster	0	1	.000	6.98	16	0	0	0	4	0	19.1	25	92	16	15	2	3	1	0	11	0	14	3	0
Watson, Tanner, Inland Empire	0	0	.000	27.00	3	0	0	0	0	0	3.2	7	27	11	11	0	1	0	2	6	0	2	3	0
Wayne, Brett, Visalia	5	4	.556	4.46	36	3	0	0	9	1	74.2	78	345	41	37	6	3	5	9	38	1	87	5	0
Wear, Gregory, Inland Empire	1	3	.250	4.73	33	0	0	0	18	3	40.0	45	186	24	21	3	2	2	4	21	1	34	4	0
Weaver, Jered, Rancho Cucamonga	4	1	.800	3.82	7	7	0	0	0	0	33.0	25	131	18	14	3	0	1	1	7	0	49	1	0

Pitcher, Team	W	L	Pct.	ERA	G	GS	CG	ShO	GF	Sv.	IP	H	TBF	R	ER	HR	SH	SF	HB	BB	IBB	SO	WP	Bk.
Wells, Carlton, Lancaster *	3	1	.750	2.70	14	0	0	0	3	0	16.2	16	72	6	5	0	1	0	0	5	0	3	0	0
Wells, Jared, Lake Elsinore	11	3	.786	3.44	19	19	2	1	0	0	120.1	116	491	51	46	6	1	6	7	26	0	80	5	1
West, James, Rancho Cucamonga	0	0	.000	5.40	2	0	0	0	0	0	1.2	2	9	1	1	0	0	0	0	3	0	2	0	0
Wilkinson, Matthew, Lancaster	0	0	.000	3.06	20	0	0	0	20	15	17.2	19	78	7	6	2	0	2	0	8	0	20	1	0
Wilson, C.J., Bakersfield *	0	1	.000	3.29	4	4	0	0	0	0	13.2	10	57	5	5	2	0	0	4	0	14	0	0
Wilson, Philip, Inland Empire	0	0	.000	6.23	5	0	0	0	1	0	8.2	10	42	6	6	0	0	1	1	4	0	9	0	1
Windsor, Jason, Stockton	2	2	.500	3.58	10	10	0	0	0	0	55.1	52	225	28	22	5	0	2	2	8	0	64	1	0
Wing, Ryan, Bakersfield *	2	5	.286	6.93	12	11	0	0	0	0	50.2	57	239	42	39	7	0	2	2	36	0	33	9	1
Ziegler, Brad, Stockton	9	7	.563	4.66	24	24	0	0	0	0	141.0	166	604	84	73	13	1	2	6	20	0	144	4	0
Zimmermann, Robert, Rancho Cucamonga	6	8	.429	3.32	52	0	0	0	48	17	59.2	50	249	25	22	3	7	2	2	27	2	62	3	0

COMBINATION SHUTOUTS: Bakersfield (2) -- Volquez-Chavez, Diamond-Brannon. High Desert (3) -- Hughes-Moore, Herrera-Bray, Buckner-Coughlin-DeHoyos. Inland Empire (4) -- Nottingham-Wear, Mackintosh-Martinez-Steele, Moorhead-Looper-Stitt, Feierabend-Acosta. Lake Elsinore (3) -- Thompson-Villatoro-Huerta, Wells-Trytten-Abraham, Hayhurst-Tierney-Klatt-Trytten-Rosales. Modesto (4) -- Marsden-Steinborn-Morel-Burch-Miller, Arias-Kaiser-Corpas, Kaiser-Santiago-Burch-Miller, Kaiser-Newman. Rancho Cucamonga (2) -- Weaver-Buckley-Zimmermann, Smith-DeLoizaga-Carney-Buckley-Zimmermann. San Jose (8) -- Floyd-Espineli, Sadowski-Espineli, Song-Pendley-Petersen-Hedrick, Foppert-Reina, Reina-Espineli-Bateman, Serrato-Coutlangus-Bateman, Floyd-Waddell-Coutlangus, Broshuis-Coutlangus. Stockton (5) – Knox-Dunwell, Knox-Crowder-Drucker, Ziegler-Leon, Crowder-Muessig-Burton, Sharpe-Muessig-McBeth. Visalia (3) -- Fulmer-Salas-Wayne, Little-Wayne-Barratt, Fulmer-Allen-Coggin.

2005 FIELDING

TEAM

Team	G	PO	A	E	TC	DP	TP	PB	Pct.
San Jose	140	3716	1381	127	5224	122	0	11	.976
Bakersfield	140	3688	1511	134	5333	143	0	18	.975
Modesto	140	3669	1457	145	5271	169	0	27	.972
Rancho Cucamonga	139	3695	1461	147	5303	132	0	19	.972
Visalia	140	3661	1383	147	5191	119	0	34	.972
Inland Empire	140	3736	1517	159	5412	143	2	22	.971
High Desert	140	3705	1668	167	5540	170	0	20	.970
Stockton	140	3684	1318	162	5164	131	0	21	.969
Lancaster	140	3757	1445	174	5376	134	0	15	.968
Lake Elsinore	138	3717	1487	194	5398	131	0	21	.964

INDIVIDUAL

FIRST BASEMEN

NOTE: All caps denotes fielding-percentage leader based on 70 games for catchers, 93 for all other non-pitchers and 112 innings for pitchers. *Throws lefthanded.

Player, Team	Pct.	G	PO	A	E	TC	DP
Adams, Skipton, Lake Elsinore	1.000	7	19	2	0	21	0
Allegra, Matthew, Stockton	.972	40	294	20	9	323	32
Appert, Luke, Stockton	1.000	4	25	5	0	30	4
Bankston, Wesley, Visalia	1.000	15	137	12	0	149	10
Barton, Daric, Stockton	.980	58	421	31	9	461	40
Brito, Javier, Lancaster	.987	18	144	12	2	158	12
Carter, William, Lancaster *	.982	69	553	44	11	608	55
Colonel, Christian, Modesto	.992	13	112	10	1	123	17
Davies, Michael, Modesto *	.991	102	848	82	8	938	106
Davis, John-paul, Visalia	.980	99	730	70	16	816	73
Dean, Erik, Modesto	.993	14	133	8	1	142	19
Dobson, Patrick, San Jose	.992	15	118	4	1	123	13
Dufner, Kristofor, Visalia	.981	17	95	6	2	103	11
Ferrer, Simon, Modesto	1.000	12	69	15	0	84	7
Gaffney, Michael, High Desert	1.000	10	79	8	0	87	16
Garthwaite, Jay, Lancaster	1.000	4	39	5	0	44	2
Gold, Nathan, Bakersfield	.991	55	495	40	5	540	58
Hagen, Matthew, Inland Empire	.983	18	149	20	3	172	22
Hargrove, Andrew, Inland Empire *	.951	6	35	4	2	41	4
Ishikawa, Travis, San Jose *	.993	127	999	98	8	1105	96
Johnson, Craig, Lake Elsinore *	1.000	1	8	1	0	9	0
Johnson, William, Lake Elsinore *	.988	57	481	23	6	510	47
Kaaihue, Micah, High Desert	.986	126	1220	95	19	1334	136
Keim, Adam, High Desert	1.000	1	19	0	0	19	0
Kreuzer, Joshua, Bakersfield	.987	85	740	43	10	793	78
LAHAIR, BRYAN, Inland Empire	.996	117	1003	87	4	1094	90
Ledbetter, Curtis, Inland Empire	1.000	2	9	1	0	10	1
Lopez, Baitazar, Rancho Cucamonga *	.988	36	299	25	4	328	31
Martinez, Gabriel, Visalia	1.000	15	118	15	0	133	11
Montero, Miguel, Lancaster	1.000	1	2	0	0	2	0
Morales, Kendry, Rancho Cucamonga	.973	15	136	7	4	147	14
Morris, Jed, Stockton	.955	8	56	7	3	66	6
Pali, Matthew, Rancho Cucamonga *	.991	49	401	38	4	443	41
Pickens, Jordan, Lake Elsinore	.964	3	26	1	1	28	2
Price, Jared, High Desert	.983	5	46	11	1	58	8
Remole, Clifton, Rancho Cucamonga *	.974	41	346	29	10	385	30
Rogelstad, Matthew, Inland Empire	1.000	2	12	2	0	14	2
Rose, Brian, Lancaster	1.000	1	1	0	0	1	0

Player, Team	Pct.	G	PO	A	E	TC	DP
Sandoval, Abigail, Bakersfield	1.000	1	7	0	0	7	0
Sitzman, James, Visalia *	.833	1	5	0	1	6	0
Spanos, Vasili, Stockton	.996	29	208	14	1	223	27
Turner, Lloyd, Stockton	1.000	2	21	0	0	21	3
Valenzuela Jr., Fernando, Lake Elsinore *	.986	77	722	52	11	785	67
Varela, Edgar, Lancaster	.990	53	444	35	5	484	52
Winslow, Benjamin, Stockton	.967	7	27	2	1	30	2

SECOND BASEMEN

Player, Team	Pct.	G	PO	A	E	TC	DP
Adams, Skipton, Lake Elsinore	.945	22	34	70	6	110	10
Appert, Luke, Stockton	.933	65	110	127	17	254	32
Asanovich, Robert, Visalia	1.000	12	22	38	0	60	11
Bethel, Ryan, Visalia	1.000	2	4	4	0	8	1
Blakeley, Eric, Inland Empire	.926	10	18	45	5	68	6
Blanco, Andres, High Desert	1.000	3	3	7	0	10	2
Blood, Randy, Modesto	.975	79	160	232	10	402	67
Blum, Geoff, Lake Elsinore	1.000	1	4	2	0	6	1
Brown, Nebasett, Lancaster	.987	17	31	47	1	79	11
Bruce, Derek, Lancaster	.929	5	12	14	2	28	4
Chang, Raymond, Lake Elsinore	1.000	1	1	3	0	4	1
Cho, Hyung, Inland Empire	.902	11	19	36	6	61	11
Ciriaco, Juan, Lake Elsinore	1.000	1	2	4	0	6	2
Contreras, Anthony, San Jose	.975	10	16	23	1	40	8
Cornejo, Eduardo, Stockton	.988	17	34	47	1	82	10
Day, Devin, Rancho Cucamonga	.978	9	13	31	1	45	10
Dean, Erik, Modesto	.966	28	70	74	5	149	26
De Renne, Keoni, Lancaster	1.000	1	3	2	0	5	2
Dobson, Patrick, San Jose	.955	4	8	13	1	22	1
Dowdy, Brett, Lake Elsinore	.974	20	42	34	2	78	8
Dufner, Kristofor, Visalia	.938	47	81	102	12	195	18
Ferrer, Simon, Modesto	.857	2	2	10	2	14	1
Frandsen, Kevin, San Jose	.978	62	107	163	6	276	31
Gaffney, Michael, High Desert	.969	5	12	19	1	32	3
Garciaparra, Michael, Inland Empire	.959	83	146	271	18	435	52
Garrabrants, Steve, Lancaster	.917	3	4	7	1	12	0
Gonzalez, Juan, Inland Empire	.984	13	27	34	1	62	8
Guance, Luis, Modesto	.945	14	33	36	4	73	13
Haines, Kyle, San Jose	.962	7	9	16	1	26	5
Herrera, Jonathan, Modesto	.977	19	26	60	2	88	11
Hornostaj, Aaron, San Jose	1.000	2	2	5	0	7	3
Jennings, Jeffrey, San Jose	.974	43	73	114	5	192	28
Johnson, Elliot, Visalia	.940	55	133	132	17	282	36
Keim, Adam, High Desert	.978	46	75	150	5	230	25
Kendrick, Howard, Rancho Cucamonga	.973	59	98	195	8	301	32
Kennedy, Adam, Rancho Cucamonga	1.000	1	2	2	0	4	1
Leahy, Ryan, Rancho Cucamonga	.972	39	66	110	5	181	21
Lenoir, Robert, Lancaster	.949	54	78	163	13	254	30
Maestrales, Peter, High Desert	.970	37	75	119	6	200	29
McMains, Derin, San Jose	.963	20	39	38	3	80	6
Melillo, Kevin, Stockton	.959	21	35	58	4	97	13
Perez, Nestor, Visalia	1.000	1	1	2	0	3	1
Powell, Brandon, High Desert	.930	11	15	25	3	43	5
RAMOS, PEETER, Lake Elsinore	.975	99	211	335	14	560	71
Reyes, Ivan, Rancho Cucamonga	.930	9	15	25	3	43	7
Richar, Danny, Lancaster	.972	49	95	150	7	252	38
Ringe, Craig, Bakersfield	1.000	1	0	4	0	4	0
Rogelstad, Matthew, Inland Empire	.956	26	42	66	5	113	10
Sandoval, Abigail, Bakersfield	.968	86	166	256	14	436	72

ADVANCED CLASS A *California League*

Player, Team	Pct.	G	PO	A	E	TC	DP
Schindewolf, Donald, Lancaster	.965	72	143	215	13	371	39
Schleicher, Mark, Visalia	1.000	3	5	3	0	8	0
Sevilla, Walter, High Desert	.967	45	79	159	8	246	41
Statia, Hainley, Rancho Cucamonga	.983	22	44	72	2	118	14
St. Clair, Jason, Visalia	.941	29	40	55	6	101	12
Turner, Lloyd, Stockton	.945	37	69	87	9	165	30
Wald, Jacob, San Jose	1.000	2	3	2	0	5	0
Washington, Johnny, Bakersfield	.955	4	6	15	1	22	2
Wayment, Kory, Stockton	.500	1	2	0	2	4	0
Zorn, Dean, Inland Empire	1.000	1	2	1	0	3	1

THIRD BASEMEN

Player, Team	Pct.	G	PO	A	E	TC	DP
Adams, Skipton, Lake Elsinore	.762	9	5	11	5	21	1
Appert, Luke, Stockton	.929	14	5	21	2	28	3
Barton, Daric, Stockton	1.000	1	1	0	0	1	0
Blakeley, Eric, Inland Empire	.750	1	0	3	1	4	0
Blood, Randy, Modesto	1.000	2	2	1	0	3	0
Bonvechio, Brett, Lake Elsinore	.905	130	97	235	35	367	25
BROWN, MATTHEW, Rancho Cucamonga	.948	119	92	202	16	310	18
Brown, Nebasett, Lancaster	.925	21	17	45	5	67	5
Bruce, Derek, Lancaster	1.000	6	2	6	0	8	0
Buscher, Brian, San Jose	.879	54	23	79	14	116	9
Butler, Billy, High Desert	.842	41	13	83	18	114	5
Colonel, Christian, Modesto	1.000	3	2	0	0	2	0
Colton, Christopher, Inland Empire	...	1	0	0	0	0	0
Cornejo, Eduardo, Stockton	.971	28	21	46	2	69	3
Cuevas, Aneudi, Visalia	.947	97	60	174	13	247	13
Day, Devin, Rancho Cucamonga	.800	3	0	4	1	5	0
De Renne, Keoni, Lancaster	.889	4	0	8	1	9	0
Dominguez, Jeffrey, Inland Empire	1.000	2	1	1	0	2	0
Dowdy, Brett, Lake Elsinore	.000	1	0	0	1	1	0
Downing, Ramon, Lancaster	...	1	0	0	0	0	0
Dufner, Kristofor, Visalia	.951	32	35	42	4	81	7
Ferrer, Simon, Modesto	.882	7	3	12	2	17	1
Gaffney, Michael, High Desert	.902	22	10	45	6	61	4
Garrabrants, Steve, Lancaster	.875	6	7	14	3	24	1
Garthwaite, Jay, Lancaster	.870	28	10	57	10	77	4
Gonzalez, Juan, Inland Empire	.714	1	1	4	2	7	0
Guance, Luis, Modesto	.915	21	15	50	6	71	5
Hagen, Michael, Inland Empire	.875	5	3	4	1	8	0
Haines, Kyle, San Jose	.900	4	4	5	1	10	0
Hornostaj, Aaron, San Jose	.909	3	2	8	1	11	0
Jennings, Jeffrey, San Jose	.927	79	40	125	13	178	6
Keim, Adam, High Desert	.971	30	16	51	2	69	8
Lenoir, Robert, Bakersfield	.933	9	5	23	2	30	1
Maestrales, Peter, High Desert	.857	2	3	3	1	7	2
Martinez, Gabriel, Visalia	1.000	2	3	5	0	8	0
McCurdy, John, Stockton	.952	54	31	89	6	126	7
McPherson, Dallas, Rancho Cucamonga	.857	4	1	5	1	7	0
Metcalf, Travis, Bakersfield	.945	132	82	244	19	345	26
Monzon, Erick, Inland Empire	.917	73	57	119	16	192	12
Morales, Kendry, Rancho Cucamonga	.900	3	5	4	1	10	1
Morris, Jed, Stockton	1.000	1	0	2	0	2	0
Powell, Brandon, High Desert	.922	39	16	79	8	103	11
Reyes, Ivan, Rancho Cucamonga	.933	11	9	19	2	30	0
Richar, Danny, Lancaster	.905	6	4	15	2	21	4
Rogelstad, Matthew, Inland Empire	.924	64	35	110	12	157	11
Schindewolf, Donald, Lancaster	.947	36	20	51	4	75	5
Schleicher, Mark, Visalia	.931	13	7	20	2	29	2
Sevilla, Walter, High Desert	.953	14	10	31	2	43	2
Simmons, Coltyn, Visalia	1.000	1	0	3	0	3	0
Spanos, Vasili, Stockton	.953	32	21	60	4	85	5
Stewart, Ian, Modesto	.923	107	87	190	23	300	24
Turner, Lloyd, Stockton	.818	13	6	12	4	22	1
Varela, Edgar, Lancaster	.942	49	27	87	7	121	4
Wald, Jacob, San Jose	.900	3	4	5	1	10	0
Winslow, Benjamin, Stockton	.889	3	4	4	1	9	0

SHORTSTOPS

Player, Team	Pct.	G	PO	A	E	TC	DP
Adams, Skipton, Lake Elsinore	.933	23	35	63	7	105	15
Asanovich, Robert, Visalia	.935	29	42	59	7	108	12
Bethel, Ryan, Visalia	1.000	3	1	11	0	12	0
Blum, Geoff, Lake Elsinore	.917	1	5	6	1	12	2
Bruce, Derek, Lancaster	.986	19	22	48	1	71	11
Cabrera, Asdrubal, Inland Empire	.960	54	88	155	10	253	44
Chavez, Angel, San Jose	.974	30	50	100	4	154	24
Ciriaco, Juan, Lake Elsinore	.924	119	182	363	45	590	63
Contreras, Anthony, San Jose	.917	7	10	23	3	36	7

Player, Team	Pct.	G	PO	A	E	TC	DP
Cornejo, Eduardo, Stockton	.960	36	53	117	7	177	21
Crosby, Bobby, Stockton	1.000	2	1	2	0	3	1
Cuevas, Aneudi, Visalia	.860	11	15	22	6	43	3
Day, Devin, Rancho Cucamonga	.950	6	10	9	1	20	2
De Renne, Keoni, Lancaster	1.000	4	4	13	0	17	2
Dominguez, Jeffrey, Inland Empire	1.000	4	6	6	0	12	4
Drew, Stephen, Lancaster	.950	36	52	101	8	161	21
Ferrer, Simon, Modesto	.938	5	13	17	2	32	5
Frandsen, Kevin, San Jose	.967	15	29	30	2	61	6
Gaffney, Michael, High Desert	1.000	5	6	10	0	16	4
Garrabrants, Steve, Lancaster	.833	3	1	4	1	6	0
Gomez, Francis, Stockton	.926	50	74	152	18	244	35
Greene, Khalil, Lake Elsinore	1.000	5	5	9	0	14	0
Guance, Luis, Modesto	.967	6	11	18	1	30	5
Haines, Kyle, San Jose	.958	5	14	9	1	24	3
Herrera, Jonathan, Modesto	.964	51	90	180	10	280	46
Hornostaj, Aaron, San Jose	1.000	4	14	12	0	26	4
Jones, Adam, Inland Empire	.935	64	130	185	22	337	44
Keim, Adam, High Desert	.889	2	5	3	1	9	2
Lenoir, Robert, Bakersfield	.931	13	18	36	4	58	9
Macri, Matthew, Modesto	.965	58	92	158	9	259	50
Maniscalco, Matthew, Visalia	.974	51	92	169	7	268	34
McCurdy, John, Stockton	.961	36	51	96	6	153	17
Monzon, Erick, Inland Empire	1.000	14	24	38	0	62	8
Perez, Kenny, Lancaster	.953	22	34	68	5	107	19
Perez, Nestor, Visalia	.955	15	23	40	3	66	10
Reese, Pokey, Inland Empire	1.000	2	4	8	0	12	2
Reyes, Ivan, Rancho Cucamonga	.894	9	21	21	5	47	7
Richar, Danny, Lancaster	.920	65	102	163	23	288	39
Ringe, Craig, Bakersfield	.959	115	166	343	22	531	76
Rogelstad, Matthew, Inland Empire	...	1	0	0	0	0	0
Sanchez, Angel, High Desert	.964	133	253	451	26	730	110
Sandoval, Abigail, Bakersfield	.971	13	21	45	2	68	9
Schleicher, Mark, Visalia	.984	33	45	76	2	123	16
Sevilla, Walter, High Desert	.929	3	4	9	1	14	0
Statia, Hainley, Rancho Cucamonga	1.000	1	1	3	0	4	1
St. Clair, Jason, Visalia	1.000	1	1	2	0	3	1
Tulowitzki, Troy, Modesto	.948	19	36	56	5	97	13
Wald, Jacob, San Jose	.943	81	124	238	22	384	49
Wayment, Kory, Stockton	.966	19	30	56	3	89	14
Winslow, Benjamin, Stockton	1.000	1	2	4	0	6	2
WOOD, RICHARD, Rancho Cucamonga	.966	124	208	352	20	580	76
Zorn, Dean, Inland Empire	1.000	2	3	6	0	9	0

OUTFIELDERS

Player, Team	Pct.	G	PO	A	E	TC	DP
Adams, Skipton, Lake Elsinore	.905	16	17	2	2	21	1
Allegra, Matthew, Stockton	1.000	9	13	1	0	14	0
Appert, Luke, Stockton	...	1	0	0	0	0	0
Arroyo, Carlos, Inland Empire *	.969	70	124	3	4	131	1
Baker, Steve, Lake Elsinore	.966	54	105	8	4	117	1
Balentien, Wladimir, Inland Empire	.958	85	176	8	8	192	2
Balkcom, Brandon, Rancho Cucamonga	.989	63	91	3	1	95	2
Barton, Daric, Stockton	1.000	1	2	0	0	2	0
Batista, Alexander, High Desert	.960	18	22	2	1	25	0
Blakeley, Eric, Inland Empire	1.000	2	3	0	0	3	0
Boucher, Sebastien, Inland Empire	.964	49	104	3	4	111	1
Bourassa, Adam, Bakersfield-Lake Elsinore	.968	76	138	14	5	157	2
Bowker, John, San Jose *	.971	104	134	2	4	140	2
Bradford Jr., Samuel, Inland Empire	.978	25	43	2	1	46	0
Brito, Javier, Lancaster	1.000	3	2	0	0	2	0
Brown, Nebasett, Lancaster	.867	9	12	1	2	15	0
Burgamy, Brian, Lake Elsinore	.970	52	96	2	3	101	0
Butler, Billy, High Desert	.932	34	38	3	3	44	0
Carter, William, Lancaster *	.974	25	37	0	1	38	0
Cleveland, Jeremy, Bakersfield	.973	41	71	1	2	74	0
Colonel, Christian, Modesto	.963	76	124	5	5	134	0
Colton, Christopher, Inland Empire	.989	50	88	5	1	94	2
Cook, Jeff, Lancaster	.981	129	256	8	5	269	1
Craig, Casey, Inland Empire	.929	8	13	0	1	14	0
Cuevas, Aneudi, Visalia	.500	3	1	0	1	2	0
Czarniecki, Jordan, Modesto	.968	43	90	2	3	95	1
Day, Devin, Rancho Cucamonga	.986	35	68	4	1	73	0
Dobson, Patrick, San Jose	1.000	61	88	5	0	93	0
Dufner, Kristofor, Visalia	.917	6	11	0	1	12	0
Ferrer, Simon, Modesto	.953	23	41	0	2	43	0
Frazier, Alex, Lancaster	.930	61	92	1	7	100	0
Fryer, Brian, Lake Elsinore	.923	8	12	0	1	13	0
Fuller, Cody, Rancho Cucamonga	.986	32	67	1	1	69	0
Gaetti, Joseph, Modesto	.966	108	214	10	8	232	3

Player, Team	Pct.	G	PO	A	E	TC	DP
Garbe, B.J., Inland Empire	.972	76	98	6	3	107	1
Garcia, Lino, Lancaster	.977	18	41	1	1	43	0
Garrabrants, Steve, Lancaster	.991	80	225	7	2	234	1
Garthwaite, Jay, Lancaster	.960	81	110	9	5	124	2
Gomes, Joseph, Visalia	.964	122	176	13	7	196	0
Gonzalez, Bernard, Modesto	.975	16	37	2	1	40	0
Grayson, Larry, Bakersfield	.975	97	146	8	4	158	0
Harrison, Benjamin, Bakersfield	1.000	8	10	0	0	10	0
Heid, Trevor, Inland Empire	.960	10	24	0	1	25	0
Howard, Joshua, Lake Elsinore *	1.000	6	11	1	0	12	0
Hughes, Michael, Rancho Cucamonga	.917	11	18	4	2	24	0
Johnson, Craig, Lancaster *	.986	38	68	4	1	73	1
Johnson, Michael, Rancho Cucamonga	.981	28	48	3	1	52	0
Kaplan, Jonathan, Lancaster	1.000	18	38	1	0	39	0
Kolkhorst, Christopher, Lake Elsinore	.960	26	44	4	2	50	0
Leandro, Francisco, Visalia *	.993	60	132	5	1	138	1
Lubanski, Christopher, High Desert *	.967	121	222	12	8	242	6
Macias, Andres, Lake Elsinore *	.968	126	322	15	11	348	4
Maestrales, Peter, High Desert	1.000	8	7	0	0	7	0
Mahar, Kevin, Bakersfield	.984	107	234	12	4	250	1
Maier, Mitchell, High Desert	.971	48	93	6	3	102	2
Majewski, Dustin, Stockton *	.981	133	295	9	6	310	2
Martinez, Gabriel, Visalia	1.000	8	20	1	0	21	0
Martinez-Esteve, Eduardo, San Jose	1.000	34	55	3	0	58	0
Mask, Michael, Bakersfield *	1.000	7	5	1	0	6	0
Melgarejo, Ransel, Rancho Cucamonga	.950	12	19	0	1	20	0
Miller, Matthew, Modesto	1.000	1	4	0	0	4	0
Morales, Kendry, Rancho Cucamonga	1.000	2	2	0	0	2	0
Morris, Jed, Stockton	1.000	4	5	2	0	7	2
Moye, Alan, High Desert	.934	68	110	3	8	121	1
Nesbit, Michael, Inland Empire	.980	49	92	5	2	99	2
Nunez, Argelis, Lancaster	1.000	3	5	0	0	5	0
Pali, Matthew, Rancho Cucamonga *	.971	77	128	4	4	136	0
Peel, Aaron, Rancho Cucamonga	.972	47	98	5	3	106	2
Perez, Josue, Bakersfield	1.000	3	7	0	0	7	0
Perez, Luis, Stockton	.938	17	30	0	2	32	0
Pickens, Jordan, Lake Elsinore	.964	34	51	2	2	55	0
Powell, Brandon, High Desert	1.000	2	4	1	0	5	0
Pridie, Jason, Visalia	1.000	1	2	0	0	2	0
Putnam, Daniel, Stockton *	.971	129	222	10	7	239	0
Ramos, Carlos, Visalia *	.972	95	201	10	6	217	2
Remole, Clifton, Rancho Cucamonga *	1.000	2	3	0	0	3	0
Richar, Danny, Lancaster	...	2	0	0	0	0	0
Rico, Matt, Visalia	.956	41	58	7	3	68	2
Roberts, Dave, Lake Elsinore *	1.000	3	4	0	0	4	0
Robnett, Richard, Stockton *	.970	113	218	10	7	235	3
Rogelstad, Matthew, Inland Empire	1.000	3	5	0	0	5	0
Rosario, Anderson, Rancho Cucamonga	.974	14	35	2	1	38	1
Salazar, Darwinson, High Desert	.909	11	9	1	1	11	1
Sandoval, Abigail, Bakersfield	...	1	0	0	0	0	0
Schierholtz, Nathan, San Jose	.986	113	191	15	3	209	3
Schleicher, Mark, Visalia	.986	34	69	4	1	74	1
Simmons, Coltyn, Visalia	1.000	4	6	0	0	6	0
Simon, Brandon, Lancaster *	.965	23	54	1	2	57	0
Sinisi, Vincent, Bakersfield *	.964	29	51	2	2	55	0
Sitzman, James, Visalia *	.960	57	115	5	5	125	0
Smith, Garry, Modesto *	.958	124	191	15	9	215	2
Stephens, Leon, High Desert	.952	108	186	14	10	210	1
Stocker, Myreon, High Desert *	1.000	7	11	0	0	11	0
Sugden, Jason Andrew, Rancho Cucamonga	.979	82	184	3	4	191	1
Thayer, Matthew, Lake Elsinore *	.893	19	24	1	3	28	0
Thigpen, Judson, Modesto	1.000	30	37	0	0	37	0
TIMPNER, CLAY, San Jose *	.990	125	308	4	3	315	1
Turner, Lloyd, Stockton	1.000	9	20	0	0	20	0
Turner, Timothy, Lake Elsinore *	...	4	0	0	0	0	0
Wagner, Michael, San Jose	.941	8	15	1	1	17	0
Wayment, Kory, Stockton	1.000	2	1	0	0	1	0
Webster, Anthony, Bakersfield	.974	105	180	11	5	196	5
Weed, James, Rancho Cucamonga	.957	19	42	2	2	46	0
Winslow, Benjamin, Stockton	1.000	12	19	1	0	20	1

OUTFIELDERS WITH TWO OR MORE TEAMS

Player, Team	Pct.	G	PO	A	E	TC	DP
Bourassa, Adam, Bakersfield *	.984	30	59	4	1	64	0
Bourassa, Adam, Lake Elsinore *	.957	46	79	10	4	93	2

CATCHERS

Player, Team	Pct.	G	PO	A	E	TC	DP
Alfonzo, Eliezer, San Jose	.983	47	411	39	8	458	6
Aracena, Sandy, Visalia	.989	41	312	43	4	359	7
ARHART, JOSHUA, Visalia	.994	79	604	57	4	665	5

Player, Team	Pct.	G	PO	A	E	TC	DP
Arias, Roberto, Stockton	1.000	3	21	2	0	23	0
Avlas, Aaron, Lancaster	.986	36	281	11	4	296	2
Barton, Daric, Stockton	1.000	1	1	0	0	1	0
Colina, Alvin, Modesto	.984	7	58	5	1	64	2
Collins, Christopher, Inland Empire	.984	46	332	28	6	366	4
Dean, Erik, Modesto	.962	8	48	3	2	53	0
Donachie, Adam, High Desert	.986	92	620	67	10	697	6
Draper, John, High Desert	.923	1	12	0	1	13	0
Duff, Timothy, Rancho Cucamonga	.981	22	134	18	3	155	0
Espino, Damaso, High Desert	.979	25	170	15	4	189	2
Everett, Brady, High Desert	1.000	5	29	3	0	32	0
Felix, Maximo, San Jose	1.000	4	8	0	0	8	0
Gonzalez, Luis, High Desert	.960	6	23	1	1	25	0
Guarno, Richard, Modesto	.982	56	384	46	8	438	5
Hagen, Matthew, Inland Empire	1.000	5	12	2	0	14	0
Hatcher, Justin, Bakersfield	.987	82	627	57	9	693	8
Hurba, Craig, Bakersfield	1.000	29	212	11	0	223	0
Iannetta, Christopher, Modesto	.989	70	522	40	6	568	3
Jennings, Jeffrey, San Jose	1.000	9	51	0	0	51	0
Johnson, Michael, Rancho Cucamonga	.987	16	140	9	2	151	2
Johnson, Robert, Inland Empire	1.000	19	131	19	0	150	1
Kottaras, George, Lake Elsinore	.986	84	520	48	8	576	4
Ledbetter, Curtis, Inland Empire	1.000	1	9	0	0	9	0
Montero, Miguel, Lancaster	.983	59	439	33	8	480	4
Morris, Jed, Stockton	.993	36	287	16	2	305	0
Morton, Kristopher, Lake Elsinore	.989	25	168	14	2	184	0
Munhall, Brian, San Jose	.994	22	151	10	1	162	0
Oliveros, Luis, Inland Empire	.994	18	162	14	1	177	1
Pagan, Andres, Lake Elsinore	.982	46	255	18	5	278	5
Price, Jared, High Desert	1.000	17	77	12	0	89	0
Rodriguez, Guillermo, San Jose	.990	67	540	51	6	597	2
Rose, Brian, Lancaster	.994	45	291	21	2	314	3
Ruchti, Justin, Inland Empire	.989	60	414	39	5	458	5
Santana, Emmanuel, Rancho Cucamonga	1.000	2	7	1	0	8	0
Schweiger, Brian, Inland Empire	1.000	1	4	2	0	6	0
Simmons, Coltyn, Visalia	.984	28	168	19	3	190	2
Smith, Dustin, Bakersfield	.992	31	231	16	2	249	2
Stinnett, Kelly, Lancaster	1.000	2	9	2	0	11	0
Suzuki, Kurt, Stockton	.984	104	882	50	15	947	7
Wilson, Kyle, Modesto	1.000	1	6	0	0	6	0
Wilson, Neil, Modesto	1.000	1	3	0	0	3	0
Wilson, Robert, Rancho Cucamonga	.984	103	745	104	14	863	9

PITCHERS

Player, Team	Pct.	G	PO	A	E	TC	DP
Abbott, Justin, Bakersfield	...	2	0	0	0	0	0
Abraham, Paul, Lake Elsinore	1.000	35	2	4	0	6	0
Abruzzo, Jared, Bakersfield	...	1	0	0	0	0	0
Accardo, Jeremy, San Jose	...	2	0	0	0	0	0
Acevedo, Danielin, Stockton	1.000	8	2	5	0	7	0
Ackerman, Eric, High Desert *	.944	31	6	11	1	18	1
Acosta, Nibaldo, Inland Empire	1.000	39	3	8	0	11	1
Allen, Max, Visalia	1.000	30	5	7	0	12	1
Anderson, Luke, San Jose	1.000	1	1	0	0	1	0
Arias, Alberto, Modesto	1.000	37	9	10	0	19	0
Arias, Oliver, Inland Empire	.000	14	0	0	1	1	0
Asencio, Miguel, Lake Elsinore *	1.000	1	0	2	0	2	0
Ashby, Andy, Lake Elsinore	...	1	0	0	0	0	0
Atencio, Alonzo, High Desert	.875	19	4	3	1	8	0
Austen, David, Rancho Cucamonga	.778	29	3	4	2	9	0
Avendano, Elvis, Stockton	.917	39	3	8	1	12	1
Baca, Daniel, Lake Elsinore	1.000	6	2	1	0	3	1
Balbuena, Caleb, Modesto	.750	12	2	1	1	4	0
Barratt, Jonathan, Visalia *	.905	36	7	12	2	21	2
Bateman, Joe, San Jose	.833	56	6	4	2	12	1
Beerer, Scott, Modesto	...	5	0	0	0	0	0
Benitez, Armando, San Jose	...	2	0	0	0	0	0
Biggs, Billy, Lancaster	.900	39	1	8	1	10	0
Bilke, Austin, Inland Empire	...	1	0	0	0	0	0
Blackwell, Brad, Lake Elsinore	.750	15	0	3	1	4	0
Blackwell, Chad, High Desert	...	1	0	0	0	0	0
Bonine, Eddie, Lake Elsinore	1.000	36	9	14	0	23	1
Bono, Kyle, Lancaster	...	6	0	0	0	0	0
Bourgeois, Nicholas, Inland Empire *	.857	27	1	5	1	7	2
Boyd, Jason, Bakersfield	1.000	17	4	6	0	10	2
Braden, Dallas, Stockton *	1.000	7	4	6	0	10	0
Bradford, Chad, Stockton	1.000	3	0	2	0	2	0
Brannon, Clint, Bakersfield *	.971	29	5	28	1	34	2
Braun, Ryan, High Desert	...	2	0	0	0	0	0
Bray, Stephen, High Desert	.800	26	2	2	1	5	0

ADVANCED CLASS A *California League*

Player, Team	Pct.	G	PO	A	E	TC	DP
Broshuis, Garrett, San Jose	.923	26	9	15	2	26	3
Buckley, Larry, Rancho Cucamonga	.818	54	10	8	4	22	4
Buckner, William, High Desert	.960	17	14	10	1	25	1
Burch, Robert, Modesto	1.000	49	4	8	0	12	0
Burton, Levi, Stockton	.875	52	6	8	2	16	0
Cabaniel, Tomas, Stockton	...	4	0	0	0	0	0
Carrillo, Cesar, Lake Elsinore	1.000	7	2	2	0	4	0
Castellanos, Jonathan, Lancaster	1.000	28	16	19	0	35	3
Cate, Troy, Inland Empire *	1.000	23	5	8	0	13	1
Chamberlain, Stephen, High Desert	1.000	44	9	9	0	18	2
Chavez, Jesse, Bakersfield	1.000	11	2	1	0	3	0
Chico, Matthew, Lancaster *	.941	18	2	14	1	17	0
Clarke, Darren, Modesto	1.000	5	0	2	0	2	0
Coffin, Ryan, Lancaster	1.000	33	2	4	0	6	0
Coggin, Dave, Visalia	1.000	18	3	6	0	9	0
Cook, Aaron, Modesto	1.000	1	0	1	0	1	0
Corchado, Jose, Stockton	...	4	0	0	0	0	0
Cordeiro, Christopher, Bakersfield	1.000	41	9	9	0	18	1
Cornejo, Eduardo, Stockton	...	1	0	0	0	0	0
Corpas, Manuel, Modesto	1.000	47	8	9	0	17	1
Correia, Kevin, San Jose	1.000	1	0	1	0	1	0
Coughlin, Christopher, High Desert	1.000	29	4	11	0	15	0
Coutlangus, Jonathan, San Jose *	1.000	50	2	17	0	19	0
Cox, Benjamin, San Jose	1.000	2	1	0	0	1	0
Cremidan, Alexander, Lancaster	1.000	44	8	3	0	11	1
Crowder, Justin, Stockton *	.933	50	4	10	1	15	0
Cruz Chavez, Rafael, Rancho Cucamonga	1.000	5	1	2	0	3	0
Danks, John, Bakersfield *	1.000	10	3	10	0	13	0
Davis, John-paul, Visalia	1.000	1	0	1	0	1	0
DeHoyos, Gabriel, High Desert	1.000	7	0	3	0	3	0
DeLoizaga-Carney, Frederic, Rancho Cucamonga	1.000	23	1	3	0	4	0
Demaria, Chris, High Desert	1.000	48	3	10	0	13	1
Diamond, Thomas, Bakersfield	1.000	14	0	7	0	7	1
Dickinson, Andy, Stockton	...	1	0	0	0	0	0
Dowdy, Justin, Rancho Cucamonga *	.923	46	4	8	1	13	1
Drucker, Scot, Stockton	.857	29	1	11	2	14	1
Dufner, Kristofor, Visalia	...	1	0	0	0	0	0
Dunn, Keith, Stockton	1.000	18	4	10	0	14	1
Dunwell, Christopher, Stockton	1.000	30	11	9	0	20	5
Eaton, Adam, Lake Elsinore	...	1	0	0	0	0	0
Edwards, William, Rancho Cucamonga	1.000	17	10	14	0	24	2
Ellison, Derrick, Inland Empire *	1.000	7	1	1	0	2	0
Endicott, Drew, High Desert	1.000	42	4	9	0	13	1
Escobar, Kelvim, Rancho Cucamonga	...	1	0	0	0	0	0
Espineli, Eugene, San Jose *	.923	40	3	9	1	13	1
Farnum, Matthew, Bakersfield	1.000	4	0	2	0	2	0
Feierabend, Ryan, Inland Empire *	.958	29	6	40	2	48	1
Feldman, Scott, Bakersfield	.500	6	1	0	1	2	0
Fernandez, Alfredo, Lake Elsinore	1.000	3	0	1	0	1	0
Ferrer, Simon, Modesto	...	1	0	0	0	0	0
Fillinger, Chad, Inland Empire	.941	15	12	4	1	17	1
Flanagan, Jeremy, Visalia	.850	25	8	9	3	20	0
Floyd, Jesse, San Jose	.952	27	9	11	1	21	1
Foppert, Jesse, San Jose	1.000	3	1	1	0	2	0
Frieri, Ernesto, Lake Elsinore	...	2	0	0	0	0	0
Fritz, Benjamin, Stockton	1.000	2	0	2	0	2	0
Fulmer, Thomas, Visalia	.944	26	5	12	1	18	1
Garthwaite, Jay, Lancaster	...	1	0	0	0	0	0
Giles, Joshua, Bakersfield	...	1	0	0	0	0	0
Girardeau, Maurice, Lake Elsinore	1.000	20	3	16	0	19	1
Glant, Dustin, Lancaster	.833	50	1	4	1	6	1
Gonzalez, Miguel, Rancho Cucamonga	...	2	0	0	0	0	0
Gragg III, John, High Desert *	.973	27	16	20	1	37	5
Green, Patrick, High Desert	1.000	7	5	6	0	11	1
Hamilton, Clayton, Lake Elsinore	1.000	7	0	3	0	3	1
Hayhurst, Dirk, Lake Elsinore	.909	38	4	6	1	11	1
Hedrick, Justin, San Jose	.938	51	5	10	1	16	0
Herrera, Cesar, High Desert	.921	31	12	23	3	38	1
Herrera, Marcos, Bakersfield	.857	24	3	3	1	7	1
Holcomb, James, Rancho Cucamonga	.955	27	4	17	1	22	0
Holsten, Ryan, Lancaster	1.000	3	0	1	0	1	0
Howell, J.P., High Desert *	1.000	8	4	8	0	12	0
Huerta, Edgar, Lake Elsinore *	1.000	8	0	1	0	1	0
Hughes, Dustin, High Desert *	1.000	19	10	19	0	29	1
Hunter, Christopher, Rancho Cucamonga	.926	21	11	14	2	27	0
Ingram, Jesse, Bakersfield	1.000	8	0	1	0	1	0
Jaile, Christopher, Bakersfield	.938	13	5	10	1	16	1
James, Craig, Inland Empire	1.000	23	2	2	0	4	0
Jepsen, Kevin, Rancho Cucamonga	.000	4	0	0	1	1	0
Jimenez, Ubaldo, Modesto	1.000	14	6	3	0	9	1

Player, Team	Pct.	G	PO	A	E	TC	DP
Kaanoi, Jason, High Desert	.944	18	6	11	1	18	0
Kaiser, Marc, Modesto	.895	22	10	7	2	19	1
Kerbs, Reuben, Lancaster *	1.000	57	4	3	0	7	0
Key, Christopher, Inland Empire *	1.000	18	2	3	0	5	1
Kinney, Matt, San Jose	1.000	5	0	2	0	2	0
Kinsey, Christopher, Lancaster	.778	15	6	8	4	18	0
Klatt, Ryan, Lake Elsinore	.000	17	0	0	1	1	0
Knox, Bradley, Stockton	1.000	20	7	16	0	23	2
Komine, Shane, Stockton	...	2	0	0	0	0	0
Kranawetter, Josh, Visalia	1.000	18	5	3	0	8	0
Landeros, Leonard, Stockton *	1.000	1	0	2	0	2	1
Lebron, Willy, Bakersfield	1.000	24	5	3	0	8	0
Leon, Brigmer, Stockton	1.000	27	3	5	0	8	1
Liebeck, Jered, Lancaster	1.000	18	2	3	0	5	0
Little, Joseph, Visalia *	.833	26	4	6	2	12	0
Looper, Aaron, Inland Empire	1.000	9	4	0	0	4	0
Lopez, Javier Arturo, Lake Elsinore *	.889	27	6	10	2	18	1
Lorenzo, Mathew, Bakersfield	.900	9	3	6	1	10	0
Lowery, Devon, High Desert	1.000	14	7	4	0	11	0
Lugo, Ruddy, Visalia	1.000	1	0	1	0	1	0
Lynn, Kevin, Visalia	1.000	14	7	10	0	17	0
Machi, Jean, Visalia	.917	31	9	13	2	24	0
MacKenzie, Aaron, Rancho Cucamonga	.882	49	8	7	2	17	0
Mackintosh, Jason, Inland Empire *	.969	29	11	20	1	32	0
Marini, Christopher, Bakersfield *	1.000	13	3	3	0	6	0
Marsden, Aaron, Modesto	.938	27	13	17	2	32	2
Martinez, Gregorio, San Jose	.500	4	0	1	1	2	0
Martinez, Javier, Lake Elsinore	1.000	17	4	4	0	8	0
Martinez, Miguel A., Inland Empire *	1.000	19	6	11	0	17	0
Mattoon, Brian, Bakersfield *	.920	38	3	20	2	25	2
Mault, James, Inland Empire	1.000	14	4	3	0	7	0
McBeth, Marcus, Stockton	...	2	0	0	0	0	0
McNiven, Brooks, San Jose	.941	39	0	16	1	17	1
Mendoza, Luis, Lake Elsinore	...	2	0	0	0	0	0
Mendoza, Thomas, Rancho Cucamonga	...	2	0	0	0	0	0
Merricks, Matthew, Modesto *	...	2	0	0	0	0	0
Miller, James, Modesto	1.000	48	1	1	0	2	0
Mock, Garrett, Lancaster	.788	28	9	17	7	33	0
Moore, James, High Desert	1.000	40	7	11	0	18	2
Moorhead, Michael, Inland Empire	.931	26	10	17	2	29	3
Morel, Edwin, Modesto	.933	45	9	5	1	15	2
Morillo, Juan, Modesto	.923	20	5	7	1	13	0
Morla, Wandy, Bakersfield	...	3	0	0	0	0	0
Muessig, Jeffrey, Stockton	.929	49	3	10	1	14	0
Murray, Arlington, Bakersfield *	.857	14	1	5	1	7	0
Newman, Joshua, Modesto *	.929	41	7	6	1	14	0
Niemann, Jeffrey, Visalia	1.000	5	3	1	0	4	0
Nin, Sandy, Modesto	1.000	7	4	4	0	8	0
Nottingham, Shawn, Inland Empire *	1.000	7	1	4	0	5	1
Nunez, Leo, High Desert	...	8	0	0	0	0	0
Olore, Kevin, Inland Empire	1.000	1	0	0	0	0	0
Ortiz, Russ, Lancaster	...	1	0	0	0	0	0
Owings, Micah, Lancaster	.800	16	2	2	1	5	0
Padgett, Michael, Bakersfield	.778	14	2	5	2	9	0
Pali, Matthew, Rancho Cucamonga *	...	1	0	0	0	0	0
Peguero, Tony, Visalia	1.000	30	5	8	0	13	0
Pence, Howard, Lake Elsinore	1.000	41	7	6	0	13	0
Pendley, Nathan, San Jose *	1.000	14	1	3	0	4	0
Petersen, Jeffrey, San Jose	1.000	40	6	6	0	12	1
Peterson, John, Stockton *	.733	15	2	9	4	15	1
Pickens, Joseph, Stockton	1.000	16	1	3	0	4	0
Posey, Micah, Rancho Cucamonga *	1.000	6	2	1	0	3	0
Prinz, Bret, Rancho Cucamonga	1.000	2	1	0	0	1	0
Prochaska, Michael, Visalia *	.975	26	12	27	1	40	2
Ramirez, Ivan, Bakersfield	1.000	25	6	5	0	11	2
Ramsey, Keith, Lancaster *	1.000	4	0	1	0	1	0
Ray, Ronald, Rancho Cucamonga	.857	20	4	2	1	7	1
REGISTER, STEVEN, Modesto	1.000	27	18	18	0	36	5
Reina, Jesus, San Jose *	.923	18	5	7	1	13	0
Reynolds, Grant, Stockton	...	4	0	0	0	0	0
Ridgway, Jeffrey, Visalia *	1.000	24	0	10	0	10	1
Rivera, Mumba, Inland Empire	.833	18	6	9	3	18	1
Robertson, James, Stockton	1.000	32	2	2	0	4	0
Robles, Lawrence, Modesto	1.000	12	4	11	0	15	0
Rodriguez, Guillermo, San Jose	1.000	2	1	0	0	1	0
Rodriguez, Manuel, Stockton	1.000	6	1	2	0	3	0
Rodriguez, Rafael, Rancho Cucamonga	.950	14	4	15	1	20	1
Rodriguez, William, Bakersfield *	1.000	11	1	5	0	6	0
Rosales, Leonel, Lake Elsinore	1.000	61	3	8	0	11	0
Rowe, Steven, Bakersfield	1.000	2	1	1	0	2	0

Player, Team	Pct.	G	PO	A	E	TC	DP
Sadowski, Ryan, San Jose	.889	24	11	13	3	27	2
Salas, Juan, Visalia	.875	25	1	6	1	8	1
Sanchez, Jose, San Jose	1.000	7	1	1	0	2	0
Santiago, Tomas, Modesto	.917	38	3	8	1	12	2
Santos, Alexandre, Stockton	1.000	12	1	2	0	3	0
Scarbery, Chad, Lancaster	.963	25	8	18	1	27	0
Seanez, Rudy, Lake Elsinore	...	1	0	0	0	0	0
Serrato, Juan, San Jose	1.000	27	3	8	0	11	0
Shank, Christopher, Stockton	.000	8	0	0	1	1	0
Shappi, Austin, Lancaster	.867	12	7	6	2	15	0
Sharpe, Steven, Stockton	1.000	3	1	0	0	1	0
Silva, Jesus, Lancaster	.818	29	6	3	2	11	1
Simard, Michel, Rancho Cucamonga	.917	13	2	9	1	12	1
Smith, Cody, Bakersfield	1.000	30	6	25	0	31	3
Smith, Jesse, Rancho Cucamonga	1.000	13	6	7	0	13	0
Smith, Samuel, Lancaster	.913	41	14	7	2	23	1
Smyth, Steve, Stockton *	.667	9	1	3	2	6	0
Song, Seung, San Jose	1.000	9	5	3	0	8	0
Sonnanstine, Andrew, Visalia	1.000	10	7	7	0	14	0
Soriano, Rafael, Inland Empire	1.000	3	0	2	0	2	0
Steele, Michael, Inland Empire	1.000	30	2	11	0	13	1
Steffek, Brian, High Desert	...	15	0	0	0	0	0
Steidlmayer, Luke, Lake Elsinore	.917	9	3	8	1	12	1
Steinborn, Christopher, Modesto *	1.000	11	3	2	0	5	0
Stitt, Brian, Inland Empire	1.000	15	1	2	0	3	0
Stokes, Brian, Visalia	1.000	4	2	1	0	3	0
Sullivan, Bradley, Stockton	1.000	13	3	8	0	11	3
Thompson, Chris, Lancaster	.900	27	3	6	1	10	1
Thompson, Richard, Rancho Cucamonga	.958	42	16	7	1	24	1
Thompson, Sean, Lake Elsinore *	1.000	6	2	5	0	7	0

Player, Team	Pct.	G	PO	A	E	TC	DP
Thurmond, J, San Jose	1.000	5	0	3	0	3	0
Tierney, Chris, Lake Elsinore *	.933	41	3	25	2	30	2
Toledo, Jean, Rancho Cucamonga	1.000	8	5	4	0	9	2
Torres, Joseph, Rancho Cucamonga *	.833	10	2	3	1	6	0
Touchstone, Nicholas, Rancho Cucamonga *	.900	23	1	8	1	10	0
Trolia, Aaron, Inland Empire	.933	40	8	20	2	30	2
Trytten, Ryan, Lake Elsinore	.889	50	1	7	1	9	0
Tsao, Chin-hui, Modesto	...	1	0	0	0	0	0
Vandermeer, Scott, Visalia	1.000	42	3	9	0	12	1
Villatoro, Wilmer, Lake Elsinore	1.000	52	3	5	0	8	1
Volquez, Edison, Bakersfield	.833	11	2	3	1	6	0
Waddell, Jason, San Jose *	1.000	26	4	6	0	10	0
Walk, Mitchell, San Jose *	1.000	12	2	4	0	6	1
Walker, Andrew, Bakersfield	1.000	9	2	6	0	8	1
Watson, Michael, Lancaster	1.000	16	0	4	0	4	0
Watson, Tanner, Inland Empire	1.000	3	0	1	0	1	0
Wayne, Brett, Visalia	.929	36	5	8	1	14	0
Wear, Gregory, Inland Empire	.833	33	1	4	1	6	0
Weaver, Jered, Rancho Cucamonga	1.000	7	0	4	0	4	0
Wells, Carlton, Lancaster *	1.000	14	1	5	0	6	0
Wells, Jared, Lake Elsinore	.875	19	8	13	3	24	2
West, James, Rancho Cucamonga	1.000	2	0	1	0	1	1
Wilkinson, Matthew, Lancaster	1.000	20	0	2	0	2	1
Wilson, C.J., Bakersfield *	.857	4	2	4	1	7	0
Wilson, Philip, Inland Empire	1.000	5	2	0	0	2	0
Windsor, Jason, Stockton	1.000	10	0	5	0	5	0
Wing, Ryan, Bakersfield *	.909	12	2	8	1	11	0
Ziegler, Brad, Stockton	1.000	24	6	20	0	26	3
Zimmermann, Robert, Rancho Cucamonga	1.000	52	4	7	0	11	1

LEAGUE CHAMPIONS

Year	Team	Pct.
1914—	Fresno	.571
1915—	Modesto	.857
1916-40—	Did not operate.	
1941—	Fresno	.643
	Santa Barbara (2nd)*	.597
1942—	Santa Barbara†	.642
1943-44-45—	Did not operate.	
1946—	Stockton‡	.600
1947—	Stockton‡	.679
1948—	Fresno	.607
	Santa Barbara (3rd)*	.529
1949—	Bakersfield	.612
	San Jose (4th)*	.543
1950—	Ventura	.607
	Modesto (2nd)*	.586
1951—	Santa Barbara‡	.599
1952—	Fresno‡	.629
1953—	San Jose‡	.664
1954—	Modesto‡	.623
1955—	Stockton	.733
	Fresno§	.718
1956—	Fresno§	.650
1957—	Visalia∞	.622
	Salinas (4th)*	.504
1958—	Fresno*	.639
	Bakersfield	.672
1959—	Bakersfield	.592
	Modesto§	.643
1960—	Reno	.614
	Reno	.657
1961—	Reno	.743
	Reno	.643
1962—	San Jose§	.686
	Reno	.587
1963—	Modesto	.589
	Stockton§	.687
1964—	Fresno	.638
	Fresno	.600
1965—	San Jose	.586
	Stockton§	.614
1966—	Modesto	.577
	Modesto	.671
1967—	San Jose§	.676
	Modesto	.586
1968—	San Jose	.629
	Fresno§	.623
1969—	Stockton§	.600
	Visalia	.614

Year	Team	Pct.
1970—	Bakersfield	.667
	Bakersfield	.671
1971—	Visalia§	.583
	Fresno	.500
1972—	Modesto§	.547
	Bakersfield	.629
1973—	Lodi§	.657
	Bakersfield	.571
1974—	Fresno§	.607
	San Jose	.579
1975—	Reno	.614
	Reno	.614
1976—	Salinas	.650
	Reno§	.547
1977—	Salinas	.564
	Lodi§	.579
1978—	Visalia§	.698
	Lodi	.607
1979—	San Jose§	.636
	Reno	.525
1980—	Stockton§	.638
	Visalia	.507
1981—	Visalia	.621
	Lodi§	.521
1982—	Modesto§	.671
	Visalia	.586
1983—	Visalia	.621
	Redwood§	.529
1984—	Modesto§	.597
	Bakersfield	.486
1985—	Fresno§	.575
	Stockton	.566
1986—	Palm Springs	.613
	Stockton§	.585
1987—	Fresno§	.559
	Reno	.535
1988—	Stockton	.657
	Riverside§	.599
1989—	Stockton	.627
	Bakersfield§	.577
1990—	Visalia	.638
	Stockton§	.582
1991—	San Jose	.676
	High Desert§	.537
1992—	Stockton§	.610
	Visalia	.551
1993—	High Desert§	.620
	Modesto	.529
1994—	Modesto	.706

Year	Team	Pct.
	Rancho Cucamonga§	.566
1995—	San Bernardino§	.612
	San Jose	.550
1996—	San Jose	.636
	Lake Elsinore‡	.550
1997—	High Desert▲	.593
	San Bernardino	.486
1998—	San Jose▲	.593
	Rancho Cucamonga	.550
1999—	Modesto	.629
	San Bernardino▲	.567
2000—	Lancaster	.636
	San Bernardino▲	.550
2001—	Lake Elsinore◆	.650
	San Jose◆	.550
2002—	Stockton▲	.636
2003—	Inland Empire▲	.557
2004—	Modesto	.643
2005—	San Jose▲	.607

*Won four-club playoff. †League disbanded June 28. ‡Won championship and four-club playoff. §Won split-season playoff. ∞Won both halves of split season. ▲Played split season and won six-club playoff. ◆Played split season and were in midst of six-club playoff and declared co-champions when Profes— sional Baseball declared a stoppage of play.

CAROLINA LEAGUE

LEAGUE OFFICE

President/treasurer
John Hopkins
Address
P.O. Box 9503
Greensboro, NC 27429
Phone
336-691-9030

Teams (affiliation)
Frederick Keys (Orioles)
Kinston Indians (Indians)
Lynchburg Hillcats (Pirates)
Myrtle Beach Pelicans (Braves)
Potomac Nationals (Nationals)
Salem Avalanche (Astros)

Wilmington (Del.) Blue Rocks (Red Sox)
Winston-Salem Warthogs (White Sox)

2005 FINAL STANDINGS

FIRST HALF

NORTHERN DIVISION

Team	W	L	T	Pct.	GB
Lynchburg Hillcats	40	30	-	.571	-
Frederick Keys	35	35	-	.500	5
Wilmington Blue Rocks	31	39	-	.443	9
Potomac Nationals	31	39	-	.443	9

SOUTHERN DIVISION

Team	W	L	T	Pct.	GB
Kinston Indians	41	29	-	.586	-
Winston-Salem Warthogs	39	31	-	.557	2
Myrtle Beach Pelicans	33	37	-	.471	8
Salem Avalanche	30	40	-	.429	11

SECOND HALF

NORTHERN DIVISION

Team	W	L	T	Pct.	GB
Frederick Keys	44	26	-	.629	-
Lynchburg Hillcats	38	32	-	.543	6
Potomac Nationals	32	38	-	.457	12
Wilmington Blue Rocks	29	41	-	.414	15

SOUTHERN DIVISION

Team	W	L	T	Pct.	GB
Winston-Salem Warthogs	38	33	-	.535	-
Salem Avalanche	37	34	-	.521	1
Kinston Indians	35	35	-	.500	2.5
Myrtle Beach Pelicans	28	42	-	.400	9.5

COMPOSITE

CLUB (AFFILIATE), ABBREV	FRD	LYN	WSW	KIN	SAL	POT	MYR	WIL	W	L	PCT	GB
Frederick (Orioles), FRD	...	8	10	8	12	12	14	15	79	61	.564	-
Lynchburg (Pirates), LYN 12	...	...	9	8	12	12	11	14	78	62	.557	1.0
Winston-Salem (White Sox), WSW 10	11	...	...	12	13	9	9	13	77	64	.546	2.5
Kinston (Indians), KIN 12	12	8	...	...	11	11	15	7	76	64	.543	3.0
Salem (Astros), SAL 8	8	8	9	...	...	12	9	13	67	74	.475	12.5
Potomac (Nationals), POT 8	8	11	9	8	...	...	11	8	63	77	.450	16.0
Myrtle Beach (Braves), MYR 6	9	11	5	11	9	...	...	10	61	79	.436	18.0
Wilmington (Red Sox), WIL 5	6	7	13	7	12	10	...	...	60	80	.429	19.0

Major league affiliations in parentheses.

PLAYOFFS: Semifinals: Frederick defeated Lynchburg, two games to none, and Kinston defeated Winston-Salem, two games to none. Finals: Frederick defeated Kinston, three games to two.

REGULAR-SEASON ATTENDANCE: Salem, 255,225. Wilmington, 322,287. Potomac, 138,143. Lynchburg, 150,109. Kinston, 103,069. Frederick, 275,663. Myrtle Beach, 198,092. Winston-Salem, 147,194. All-Star Game (at Frederick), 7,734. League total, 1,589,782. Postseason (9 games), 10,728.

MANAGERS: Salem, Ivan DeJesus. Wilmington, Dann Bilardello. Potomac, Bob Henley. Lynchburg, Tim Leiper. Kinston, Luis Rivera. Frederick, Bien Figueroa. Myrtle Beach, Randy Ingle. Winston-Salem, Chris Cron.

ALL-STAR TEAM: 1B-Leo Daigle, Winston-Salem. 2B-Nate Spears, Frederick. 3B-Robert Valido, Winston-Salem. SS-Kory Casto, Potomac. UIF-Pat Magness, Lynchburg. OF-Thomas Collaro, Winston-Salem. OF-Frank Diaz, Potomac. OF-Nick Markakis, Frederick. UOF-Noah Hall, Winston-Salem. C-Jarrod Saltalamacchia, Myrtle Beach. DH-Mario Delgado, Frederick. SP-James Johnson, Frederick. Relief Pitcher-Ehren Wassermann, Winston-Salem. Championship Series Most Valuable Player-Brian Finch, Frederick. Most Valuable Player-Leo Daigle, Winston-Salem. Pitcher of the Year-James Johnson, Frederick. Manager of the Year-Ivan DeJesus, Salem.

2005 BATTING

TEAM

Team	G	TPA	AB	R	H	TB	2B	3B	HR	RBI	SH	SF	HP	BB	IBB	SO	SB	CS	GDP	LOB	ShO	Avg.	OBP	Slg.
Lynchburg	140	5424	4697	741	1323	1970	261	40	102	682	22	43	69	590	7	944	106	45	123	2332	8	.282	.367	.419
Winston-Salem	141	5493	4847	809	1354	2245	297	30	178	744	39	38	79	489	9	889	188	57	103	2052	3	.279	.352	.463
Potomac	140	5369	4736	674	1273	1995	294	31	122	611	44	32	68	489	14	1012	82	51	102	2224	8	.269	.344	.421
Frederick	140	5363	4740	700	1262	2012	258	21	150	658	72	24	82	445	19	1056	82	39	96	2120	10	.266	.338	.424
Salem	141	5253	4573	562	1147	1681	243	24	81	510	63	36	54	526	12	981	82	61	138	2111	11	.251	.333	.368
Kinston	140	5305	4671	656	1170	1842	250	34	118	608	33	46	79	476	10	1075	99	51	97	2060	7	.250	.327	.394
Myrtle Beach	140	5257	4667	596	1161	1723	248	16	94	538	37	38	56	459	20	1137	121	76	95	1912	13	.249	.321	.369
Wilmington	140	5250	4588	619	1130	1733	232	31	103	558	45	48	81	488	7	1114	69	45	91	2065	7	.246	.326	.378

INDIVIDUAL

TOP QUALIFIERS FOR BATTING CHAMPIONSHIP

Minimum 378 plate appearances. *Lefthanded batter. †Switch-hitter.

Player, Team	G	TPA	AB	R	H	TB	2B	3B	HR	RBI	SH	SF	HP	BB	IBB	SO	SB	CS	GDP	Avg.	OBP	Slg.
Daigle, Leo, Winston-Salem	108	473	411	85	140	262	33	1	29	112	0	6	6	50	3	72	10	4	9	.341	.414	.637
Hall, Noah, Winston-Salem	120	537	425	112	141	269	38	6	26	92	1	6	19	86	2	76	24	5	11	.332	.459	.633

Player, Team	G	TPA	AB	R	H	TB	2B	3B	HR	RBI	SH	SF	HP	BB	IBB	SO	SB	CS	GDP	Avg.	OBP	Slg.
Saltalamacchia, Jarrod, Myrtle Beach †	129	529	459	70	144	238	35	1	19	81	1	5	7	57	11	99	4	2	14	.314	.394	.519
Diaz, Frank, Potomac	134	585	554	85	173	276	45	5	16	74	1	3	7	20	1	67	14	9	11	.312	.342	.498
Magness, Patrick, Lynchburg *	133	570	425	98	131	244	39	1	24	92	0	2	2	141	5	114	0	1	6	.308	.481	.574
Delgado, Mario, Frederick *	119	473	435	53	133	240	27	1	26	86	0	0	7	31	7	80	1	0	8	.306	.362	.552
Markakis, Nicholas, Frederick *	91	401	350	59	105	168	25	1	12	62	0	4	4	43	4	65	2	1	6	.300	.379	.480
Pritz, Bryan, Wilmington	97	396	328	51	98	121	15	1	2	25	7	5	3	53	0	53	18	4	2	.299	.396	.369
Spears, Nathaniel, Frederick *	112	498	445	63	131	191	30	6	6	41	14	1	2	36	1	82	8	4	1	.294	.349	.429
Whitesell, Joshua, Potomac *	113	474	389	59	114	204	32	2	18	66	1	1	9	74	3	125	1	1	3	.293	.416	.524
McCuistion, Michael, Lynchburg *	98	382	335	43	98	145	19	2	8	59	0	5	3	39	1	64	5	1	7	.293	.366	.433
Nanita, Ricardo, Winston-Salem *	120	499	415	73	121	188	36	2	9	54	8	4	10	61	2	53	14	11	6	.292	.392	.453
Casto, Kory, Potomac *	135	594	500	86	145	255	36	4	22	90	0	5	5	84	1	98	6	3	5	.290	.394	.510
Valido, Robert, Potomac	119	550	513	86	148	214	28	7	8	59	9	3	4	21	1	64	52	5	9	.288	.320	.417
Manriquez, Salomon, Potomac	119	484	443	64	127	212	36	2	15	68	2	4	5	30	0	86	0	0	13	.287	.336	.479
Fiorentino, Jeff, Frederick *	103	455	413	70	118	210	18	4	22	66	4	0	4	34	2	90	12	6	5	.286	.346	.508
Floyd, Michael, Salem *	119	499	433	63	118	186	24	4	12	62	2	7	6	51	1	112	14	7	15	.273	.352	.430
Asprilla, Avelino, Lynchburg *	112	409	375	51	101	159	20	1	12	56	0	3	5	26	0	78	4	4	13	.269	.323	.424
Rea, Bradley, Lynchburg	118	504	435	58	117	182	37	2	8	58	0	2	6	61	0	78	0	0	23	.269	.365	.418
Schnurstein, Micah, Winston-Salem	132	537	488	78	131	203	21	3	15	68	0	2	7	40	0	98	12	8	15	.268	.331	.416
Esquivel, William, Myrtle Beach	127	527	468	58	124	206	31	0	17	81	0	2	4	49	0	140	9	6	6	.265	.338	.440

DEPARTMENTAL LEADERS: G—Casto, 135. AB—Diaz, 554. R—Hall, 112. H—Diaz, 173. TB—Diaz, 276. 2B—Diaz, 45. 3B—Guzman and Valido, 7. HR—Collaro and Daigle, 29. RBI—Daigle, 112. SH—Spears, 14. SF—three players with 7. HP—Hall, 19. BB—Magness, 141. IBB—Saltalamacchia, 11. SO—Collaro, 153. SB—Valido, 52. CS—Doetsch, 15. GIDP—Rea, 23. Slg.—Daigle, .637. OBP—Magness, .481.

ALL PLAYERS

*Lefthanded batter. †Switch-hitter.

Player, Team	G	TPA	AB	R	H	TB	2B	3B	HR	RBI	SH	SF	HP	BB	IBB	SO	SB	CS	GDP	Avg.	OBP	Slg.
Acosta, Manuel, Myrtle Beach	2	0	0	0	0	0	0	0	0	0	0	0	0	0	...	0	0	0	0	...	...	...
Alcantara, Ervin, Salem	130	482	417	47	102	148	27	2	5	44	5	2	1	57	2	109	17	9	11	.245	.335	.355
Alvarez, Gerardo, Frederick	70	271	227	39	58	92	16	0	6	34	11	1	6	26	0	45	2	6	4	.256	.346	.405
Amador, Christopher, Winston-Salem	64	225	210	34	56	104	13	1	11	35	2	0	3	10	0	52	19	5	1	.267	.309	.495
Arias, Claudio, Wilmington	14	56	53	5	13	27	2	0	4	9	0	1	0	2	0	11	0	1	0	.245	.268	.509
Arko, Thomas, Frederick	19	68	63	5	9	22	4	0	3	5	0	0	0	5	0	25	1	0	0	.143	.206	.349
Ash, Jonathan, Salem *	59	248	225	32	72	98	19	2	1	25	4	2	3	14	1	15	3	5	1	.320	.365	.436
Asprilla, Avelino, Lynchburg	112	409	375	51	101	159	20	1	12	56	0	3	5	26	0	78	4	4	13	.269	.323	.424
Barksdale, James, Myrtle Beach	8	29	26	3	5	6	1	0	0	2	0	0	0	3	0	3	0	0	1	.192	.276	.231
Barton, Brian, Kinston	64	273	223	42	61	97	15	6	3	32	1	0	15	34	2	57	13	8	6	.274	.404	.435
Bass, Allan, Frederick †	117	409	352	59	85	143	24	0	12	51	8	2	6	41	0	135	11	4	5	.241	.329	.406
Belcher, Jason, Potomac *	55	200	176	21	44	67	8	0	5	20	2	3	2	17	2	30	0	1	6	.250	.318	.381
Benick, Jonathan, Lynchburg †	50	209	187	16	30	49	7	0	4	30	0	4	2	16	0	44	0	0	11	.160	.230	.262
Bernard, Miguel, Myrtle Beach	18	69	65	9	21	43	10	0	4	14	0	0	3	1	0	8	0	1	1	.323	.362	.662
Bladergroen, Ian, Wilmington *	75	307	263	25	63	87	6	3	4	31	1	3	10	30	0	77	0	1	4	.240	.337	.331
Blakeney, Ted, Myrtle Beach	1	0	0	0	0	0	0	0	0	0	0	0	0	0	...	0	0	0	0	...	...	...
Bocchino, Anthony, Lynchburg *	41	92	78	16	21	28	4	0	1	11	1	2	0	11	0	14	0	2	1	.269	.352	.359
Bock, Brian, Frederick	37	142	134	16	34	48	5	0	3	26	2	0	1	5	0	19	1	0	2	.254	.286	.358
Boeve, Adam, Lynchburg	71	301	249	60	78	134	15	1	13	47	0	4	9	39	0	66	12	0	7	.313	.419	.538
Boran, Patrick, Wilmington †	5	14	12	1	3	4	1	0	0	1	0	0	0	2	0	1	0	0	0	.250	.357	.333
Borowiak, Zachary, Wilmington	114	469	406	72	103	169	27	3	11	59	11	4	15	33	1	72	6	4	10	.254	.330	.416
Brock, Caleb, Kinston	87	355	318	39	75	114	17	2	6	48	2	3	7	25	1	55	3	2	4	.236	.303	.358
Brooks, Cedrick, Kinston	118	469	412	59	99	149	18	1	10	43	4	2	12	39	2	127	8	4	13	.240	.323	.362
Brown, Dustin, Wilmington	62	253	219	32	56	92	12	0	8	36	0	2	1	31	0	52	1	1	7	.256	.348	.420
Brown, Travis, Frederick	118	446	392	41	99	121	11	1	3	40	13	5	7	29	0	63	3	5	9	.253	.312	.309
Burrows, Angelo, Myrtle Beach *	1	0	0	0	0	0	0	0	0	0	0	0	0	0	...	0	0	0	0	...	...	...
Burrus, Josh, Myrtle Beach	76	335	299	54	85	138	20	0	11	53	0	4	4	28	1	75	25	8	5	.284	.349	.462
Butia, Michael, Kinston *	35	144	131	12	26	36	4	0	2	13	0	1	2	10	0	33	0	0	1	.198	.264	.275
Buttler, Victor, Lynchburg *	57	243	231	40	77	111	13	3	5	38	0	1	7	4	0	34	8	2	5	.333	.362	.481
Bynum, Seth, Potomac	35	93	84	16	15	24	4	1	1	6	2	2	5	0	0	20	2	2	3	.179	.237	.286
Campbell, Richard, Potomac	1	0	0	0	0	0	0	0	0	0	0	0	0	0	...	0	0	0	0	...	...	...
Caraballo, Francisco, Salem	14	51	45	8	11	19	2	0	2	12	1	2	2	1	0	9	1	0	3	.244	.280	.422
Casto, Kory, Potomac *	135	594	500	86	145	255	36	4	22	90	0	5	5	84	1	98	6	3	5	.290	.394	.510
Castro, Ramon A., Potomac	10	40	33	6	7	13	1	1	1	5	1	0	1	5	0	5	1	1	1	.212	.333	.394
Chauncey, Clinton, Wilmington	36	109	97	6	14	21	2	1	1	6	3	1	1	7	0	35	1	1	4	.144	.208	.216
Chaves, Brandon, Lynchburg †	61	239	210	34	63	82	8	4	1	25	0	0	1	28	0	46	2	3	9	.300	.385	.390
Chavez, Dirimo, Wilmington	41	146	127	19	26	40	7	2	1	12	1	2	0	16	0	25	1	2	4	.205	.290	.315
Chavez, Ender, Potomac *	112	421	371	54	93	118	11	4	2	28	9	0	2	39	1	64	13	10	1	.251	.325	.318
Chop, Chad, Potomac *	115	448	411	36	107	146	26	2	3	52	3	6	6	22	1	55	1	4	17	.260	.303	.355
Choy Foo, Rodney, Kinston †	65	283	238	38	68	108	15	5	5	31	2	6	3	34	1	56	7	3	7	.286	.374	.454
Cockrell, Michael, Lynchburg	11	44	42	3	7	11	1	0	1	1	0	0	0	2	0	7	0	1	0	.167	.205	.262
Collaro, Thomas, Winston-Salem	133	559	531	68	140	260	27	3	29	100	0	1	2	25	0	153	5	3	10	.264	.299	.490
Conroy, Michael, Kinston *	61	265	232	33	56	103	16	2	9	38	3	1	5	24	2	76	3	2	2	.241	.324	.444
Cordero, Wil, Potomac	2	8	7	2	3	10	1	0	2	5	0	0	0	0	0	0	0	0	0	.429	.500	1.429
Cotto, Luis, Kinston	64	213	198	20	43	58	10	1	1	14	2	0	2	11	0	39	2	3	5	.217	.265	.293
Creek, Gregory, Myrtle Beach *	4	19	16	2	6	8	2	0	0	2	0	0	0	3	1	5	0	1	0	.375	.474	.500
Cronkhite, Ian, Wilmington *	6	18	16	0	4	6	2	0	0	0	0	0	0	2	0	0	0	0	0	.250	.333	.375
Daigle, Leo, Winston-Salem	108	473	411	85	140	262	33	1	29	112	0	6	6	50	1	72	10	4	9	.341	.414	.637
Davidson, Kevin, Salem	86	312	269	25	76	109	16	1	5	41	7	2	3	31	0	45	1	1	5	.283	.361	.405
De La Cruz, Christopher, Kinston †	77	296	274	30	63	72	5	2	0	20	5	2	1	14	0	42	7	5	7	.230	.268	.263
Delgado, Mario, Frederick *	119	473	435	53	133	240	27	1	26	86	0	0	7	31	7	80	1	0	8	.306	.362	.552
Desmond, Ian, Potomac	55	248	219	37	56	84	13	3	3	15	5	1	2	21	0	53	13	6	6	.256	.325	.384
Devries, Jonathan, Wilmington	34	135	113	16	32	54	10	0	4	13	0	0	8	14	0	40	0	0	4	.283	.400	.478
Diaz, Frank, Potomac	134	585	554	85	173	276	45	5	16	74	1	3	7	20	1	67	14	9	11	.312	.342	.498

Player, Team	G	TPA	AB	R	H	TB	2B	3B	HR	RBI	SH	SF	HP	BB	IBB	SO	SB	CS	GDP	Avg.	OBP	Slg.
Digby, Bryan, Myrtle Beach	1	1	1	0	0	0	0	0	0	0	0	0	0	0	0	1	0	0	0	.000	.000	.000
Doetsch, Steven, Myrtle Beach	118	515	461	60	119	158	23	2	4	32	6	2	3	43	0	105	14	15	11	.258	.324	.343
Duran, Carlos, Myrtle Beach *	12	50	47	6	12	14	2	0	0	2	0	0	0	3	1	12	2	0	0	.255	.300	.298
Emmerick, Joshua, Potomac	13	50	43	9	16	20	4	0	0	2	0	0	1	6	0	9	1	0	1	.372	.460	.465
Escobar, Rodrigo, Salem	2	0	0	0	0	0	0	0	0	0	...	0	0	0	0	0	0	0	0	...	...	...
Esquivel, William, Myrtle Beach	127	527	468	58	124	206	31	0	17	81	0	2	8	49	0	140	9	6	14	.265	.343	.440
Fagan, John, Salem	37	146	119	14	31	51	11	0	3	13	1	0	6	19	1	36	4	2	4	.261	.389	.429
Fernando, Osvaldo, Salem	67	239	208	27	43	55	4	1	2	14	8	2	5	16	0	39	12	7	4	.207	.277	.264
Fiorentino, Jeff, Frederick *	103	455	413	70	118	210	18	4	22	66	4	0	4	34	2	90	12	6	5	.286	.346	.508
Florence, Branden, Frederick	78	313	283	50	92	162	18	2	16	51	0	3	11	16	1	29	0	0	9	.325	.380	.572
Floyd, Michael, Salem	119	499	433	63	118	186	24	4	12	62	2	7	6	51	1	112	14	7	15	.273	.352	.430
Freeman, Daniel, Salem	1	0	0	0	0	0	0	0	0	0	...	0	0	0	0	0	0	0	0	...	...	...
Garcia, Cipriano, Winston-Salem	24	42	38	7	12	23	2	0	3	9	0	0	2	2	0	12	0	0	1	.316	.381	.605
Garza, Mario, Salem *	80	315	260	41	76	128	25	0	9	43	2	3	3	47	1	74	5	2	8	.292	.403	.492
Goelz, Bryan, Wilmington *	75	245	207	30	43	62	9	2	2	19	2	6	2	28	1	45	4	5	5	.208	.300	.300
Goleski, Ryan, Kinston	122	507	458	59	97	175	27	0	17	67	0	6	4	39	0	134	6	4	12	.212	.276	.382
Grimm, Eric, Frederick †	11	42	37	3	8	13	2	0	1	2	1	0	1	3	0	10	0	0	1	.216	.293	.351
Guzman, Carlos, Myrtle Beach	34	131	114	8	18	31	10	0	1	12	2	1	2	12	2	57	0	1	2	.158	.248	.272
Guzman, Javier, Lynchburg †	69	279	256	40	83	125	13	7	5	35	1	1	1	20	0	41	13	5	7	.324	.374	.488
Haggerty, Cory, Winston-Salem *	34	98	89	16	22	28	4	1	0	3	2	1	0	6	0	21	2	1	4	.247	.292	.315
Hall, Michael, Wilmington *	71	284	250	31	54	96	16	4	6	25	1	1	0	32	0	98	5	3	2	.216	.304	.384
Hall, Noah, Winston-Salem	120	537	425	112	141	269	38	6	26	92	1	6	19	86	2	76	24	5	11	.332	.459	.633
Harris, Justin, Lynchburg	46	161	150	25	45	56	4	2	1	17	2	2	1	6	0	21	1	0	6	.300	.327	.373
Head, Stephen, Kinston *	47	213	203	31	58	85	15	0	4	36	0	2	0	8	0	33	4	0	4	.286	.310	.419
Hernandez, Diory, Myrtle Beach	73	300	265	30	67	99	15	1	5	30	4	5	8	18	0	53	5	5	5	.253	.314	.374
Hernandez, Jose, Lynchburg	43	162	149	14	40	49	4	1	1	20	2	0	2	9	0	34	2	1	5	.268	.319	.329
Hinton, Travis, Winston-Salem *	112	435	381	55	98	178	34	2	14	67	0	5	5	44	0	80	1	0	2	.257	.338	.467
Hubele, Ryan, Frederick	53	213	195	25	55	83	16	0	4	29	4	2	5	7	0	37	1	0	7	.282	.321	.426
Humphries, Justin, Salem	35	128	112	12	20	34	2	0	4	10	2	0	2	12	1	30	0	0	5	.179	.270	.304
James, Wilson, Myrtle Beach †	77	214	184	25	29	35	3	0	1	9	5	1	4	20	0	27	12	9	3	.158	.254	.190
Jansen, Ardley, Myrtle Beach	52	202	185	18	40	63	6	1	5	20	1	2	2	12	0	57	6	3	2	.216	.269	.341
Jones, Brandon, Myrtle Beach *	17	71	60	7	21	25	4	0	0	5	0	1	1	9	0	9	0	1	1	.350	.437	.417
Jurich, Mark, Myrtle Beach *	37	152	132	13	26	42	8	1	2	13	0	1	2	17	1	39	1	0	2	.197	.296	.318
Kelly, Dustin, Wilmington	11	38	35	5	8	9	1	0	0	3	0	0	2	1	0	5	1	0	1	.229	.289	.257
Kingsbury, Robert, Lynchburg *	86	344	289	42	71	124	18	4	9	55	1	7	5	41	0	69	5	3	6	.246	.342	.429
Kochen, Ryan, Salem	20	71	63	6	9	12	0	0	1	6	0	0	0	8	1	16	0	0	0	.143	.239	.190
Kolb, Daniel, Potomac	1	0	0	0	0	0	0	0	0	0	...	0	0	0	0	0	0	0	0	...	...	...
Kouzmanoff, Kevin, Kinston	68	287	254	47	86	150	20	4	12	58	0	4	5	24	1	51	3	1	6	.339	.401	.591
Lane, Andrew, Potomac	1	4	2	1	0	0	0	0	0	1	1	0	0	1	0	0	0	0	0	.000	.333	.000
Larkin, Shaun, Kinston *	31	140	116	16	33	50	5	3	2	17	0	1	2	21	0	21	3	0	1	.284	.400	.431
Lee, Carlos, Winston-Salem	84	314	294	35	85	138	9	1	14	48	0	2	4	14	1	33	2	1	9	.289	.328	.469
Lee, Taber, Lynchburg †	84	379	311	44	75	104	15	1	4	34	3	0	5	60	0	70	5	4	5	.241	.372	.334
Letson, Wesley, Myrtle Beach *	2	1	1	0	0	0	0	0	0	0	0	0	0	0	0	0	0	0	0	.000	.000	.000
LeVier, Bret, Wilmington	7	26	21	2	5	6	1	0	0	3	0	0	0	5	0	3	0	0	1	.238	.385	.286
Loadenthal, Carl, Myrtle Beach *	60	260	230	47	65	101	13	4	5	20	7	0	3	20	0	46	17	6	3	.283	.348	.439
Lorenzo, Mathew, Myrtle Beach *	1	2	2	0	0	0	0	0	0	0	0	0	0	0	0	0	0	0	0	.000	.000	.000
Lunetta, Anthony, Kinston	32	129	103	20	31	49	9	0	3	14	4	3	4	15	0	13	2	3	1	.301	.400	.476
Lytle, Chaz, Lynchburg *	76	281	247	43	73	82	7	1	0	19	5	1	6	20	0	45	12	5	5	.296	.361	.332
Mackor, Jeffrey, Salem	52	163	146	9	26	37	9	1	0	8	3	1	2	11	0	33	0	2	4	.178	.244	.253
Magness, Patrick, Lynchburg *	133	570	425	98	131	244	39	1	24	92	0	2	2	141	5	114	0	1	6	.308	.481	.574
Manriquez, Salomon, Potomac	119	484	443	64	127	212	36	2	15	68	2	4	5	30	0	86	0	0	13	.287	.336	.479
Markakis, Nicholas, Frederick *	91	401	350	59	105	168	25	1	12	62	0	4	4	43	4	65	2	1	6	.300	.379	.480
Martel Jr, Normand, Winston-Salem *	11	33	29	3	4	4	0	0	0	0	0	0	0	4	0	6	0	0	0	.138	.242	.138
Martin, Billy, Potomac	5	21	16	3	6	11	2	0	1	4	0	1	1	3	0	6	0	0	0	.375	.476	.688
Mateo, Henry, Potomac †	13	58	50	13	14	30	5	1	3	9	2	0	3	3	0	10	2	0	1	.280	.357	.600
Matulich, Mario, Kinston	8	30	29	3	4	9	2	0	1	5	0	0	0	1	0	10	0	1	0	.138	.167	.310
Maysonet, Edwin, Salem	66	281	236	29	46	62	9	2	1	16	12	4	3	26	0	69	4	2	4	.195	.279	.263
McCuistion, Michael, Lynchburg *	98	382	335	43	98	145	19	2	8	59	0	5	3	39	1	64	5	1	7	.293	.366	.433
McCullough, Clayton, Kinston *	2	8	5	1	0	0	0	0	0	0	0	0	0	3	0	4	0	0	0	.000	.375	.000
McCurdy, Joshua, Frederick	63	235	210	27	50	69	9	2	2	23	1	2	4	18	0	41	10	4	6	.238	.308	.329
Meath, Matthew, Lynchburg †	13	40	30	5	8	8	0	0	0	1	2	0	3	5	0	4	0	0	0	.267	.421	.267
Mercedes, Victor, Lynchburg-Potomac	23	90	83	10	18	27	4	1	1	6	1	0	1	5	0	21	3	1	2	.217	.270	.325
Merchant, Jamie, Salem	1	0	0	0	0	0	0	0	0	0	...	0	0	0	0	0	0	0	0	...	...	...
Molina, Gustavo, Winston-Salem	109	392	345	38	90	145	20	1	11	41	8	3	6	30	0	47	1	2	16	.261	.328	.420
Morgan, Nyjer, Lynchburg *	60	277	252	36	72	90	12	3	0	24	3	4	7	11	0	40	24	10	0	.286	.328	.357
Mota, Willy, Wilmington	6	21	18	2	1	4	0	0	1	4	0	0	0	3	0	5	0	0	0	.056	.190	.222
Muecke, Joshua, Salem *	2	1	1	0	0	0	0	0	0	0	0	0	0	0	0	1	0	0	0	.000	.000	.000
Mulhern, Ryan, Kinston	45	185	159	32	51	113	11	0	17	48	0	4	3	19	0	50	2	2	3	.321	.395	.711
Myers, Michael, Winston-Salem	120	505	419	81	107	165	27	2	9	42	6	4	7	69	0	74	37	8	7	.255	.367	.394
Nanita, Ricardo, Winston-Salem *	120	499	415	73	121	188	36	2	9	54	8	4	10	61	2	53	14	11	6	.292	.392	.453
Norderum, Jason, Potomac *	1	0	0	0	0	0	0	0	0	0	...	0	0	0	0	0	0	0	0	...	...	...
Norris, Shawn, Potomac *	39	172	138	23	38	63	10	0	5	19	0	1	1	32	1	27	1	0	6	.275	.413	.457
Ontiveros, Jeffrey, Wilmington	87	361	303	48	76	135	20	0	13	48	0	2	9	47	1	96	0	1	6	.251	.366	.446
Panther, Nathan, Kinston *	102	436	370	60	91	147	14	3	12	41	1	4	4	57	1	73	11	5	5	.246	.349	.397
Peavey, Patrick, Salem	97	378	343	32	78	103	13	0	4	36	1	1	0	33	0	39	1	0	16	.227	.297	.300
Pena, Rodolfo, Lynchburg	9	27	26	2	8	12	1	0	1	1	1	0	0	0	0	8	0	0	1	.308	.308	.462
Pence, Hunter, Salem	41	171	151	24	46	74	8	1	6	30	0	2	0	18	0	37	1	2	6	.305	.374	.490
Pinckney, Brandon, Kinston	87	350	319	39	83	112	19	2	2	26	3	4	1	23	1	31	4	2	9	.260	.308	.351
Pope, Peter, Myrtle Beach	25	95	84	7	14	18	1	0	1	5	0	1	1	9	0	21	0	0	2	.167	.253	.214
Poppert, John, Potomac	2	8	8	0	0	0	0	0	0	0	0	0	0	0	0	1	0	0	0	.000	.000	.000
Powell, Pedro, Lynchburg †	8	37	34	9	10	13	1	1	0	1	0	0	0	3	0	2	2	0	0	.294	.351	.382

Player, Team	G	TPA	AB	R	H	TB	2B	3B	HR	RBI	SH	SF	HP	BB	IBB	SO	SB	CS	GDP	Avg.	OBP	Slg.
Prado, Martin, Myrtle Beach	75	326	297	44	91	122	13	3	4	34	0	5	0	24	0	48	9	6	7	.306	.353	.411
Pritz, Bryan, Wilmington	97	396	328	51	98	121	15	1	2	25	7	5	3	53	0	53	18	4	2	.299	.396	.369
Pudewell, Nathanial, Myrtle Beach	1	0	0	0	0	0	0	0	0	0	0	0	0	0	0	0	0	0	0	...	...	...
Pyzik, Steven, Myrtle Beach	17	54	49	8	12	17	2	0	1	3	0	0	1	4	0	10	0	0	1	.245	.315	.347
Raymundo, Gregg, Lynchburg	3	13	12	1	2	3	1	0	0	3	0	1	0	0	0	1	0	0	0	.167	.154	.250
Rayo, Pedro, Myrtle Beach	1	0	0	0	0	0	0	0	0	0	0	0	0	0	...	0	0	0	0	...	...	...
Rea, Bradley, Lynchburg	118	504	435	58	117	182	37	2	8	58	0	2	6	61	0	78	0	0	23	.269	.365	.418
Reimold, Nolan, Frederick	23	97	83	17	22	46	6	0	6	11	0	0	2	12	0	27	3	0	0	.265	.371	.554
Reyes, Argenis, Kinston †	52	217	202	23	52	61	4	1	1	13	5	1	1	8	0	38	8	3	7	.257	.288	.302
Reynolds, Wilton, Salem	62	244	210	29	55	100	18	3	7	31	1	1	7	25	1	70	4	5	4	.262	.358	.476
Richards, Glen, Myrtle Beach	1	0	0	0	0	0	0	0	0	0	0	...	0	0	0	0	0	0	0	...	...	...
Rine, Jarod, Frederick *	115	418	369	53	77	103	11	3	3	23	6	1	6	36	2	89	21	7	11	.209	.289	.279
Roberts, Ralph, Myrtle Beach	1	1	1	0	0	0	0	0	0	0	0	0	0	0	0	1	0	0	0	.000	.000	.000
Robinson, Christopher, Salem *	46	184	168	13	43	55	5	2	1	11	4	1	1	10	1	27	4	5	3	.256	.300	.327
Robinson, Scott, Salem *	74	325	288	31	80	104	13	1	3	40	2	4	0	31	0	29	2	2	12	.278	.344	.361
Rodriguez, Javier, Potomac	28	104	92	9	26	31	3	1	0	7	1	0	2	9	0	12	8	2	6	.283	.359	.337
Rodriguez, Robert, Potomac	28	77	72	5	11	12	1	0	0	9	1	0	1	3	0	27	0	0	1	.153	.197	.167
Rojas, Ricardo, Kinston	35	98	92	10	20	30	5	1	1	6	3	0	0	3	0	28	5	1	2	.217	.242	.326
Rooi, Vince, Potomac	63	249	220	32	66	101	14	0	7	38	1	1	2	25	1	60	1	0	3	.300	.375	.459
Rozema, Michael, Myrtle Beach *	59	244	211	34	48	63	10	1	1	20	3	1	2	27	1	33	8	3	2	.227	.320	.299
Ruelas, Alonzo, Myrtle Beach	38	119	107	7	15	20	5	0	0	7	1	0	2	9	0	26	1	1	1	.140	.220	.187
Ruiz, Reinaldo, Salem	29	85	81	11	18	24	3	0	1	5	0	0	0	4	0	15	0	0	1	.222	.259	.296
Russell, Michael, Frederick	75	268	229	38	54	98	14	0	10	37	2	0	6	31	1	82	1	0	7	.236	.342	.428
Saltalamacchia, Jarrod, Myrtle Beach †	129	529	459	70	144	238	35	1	19	81	1	5	7	57	11	99	4	2	14	.314	.394	.519
San Pedro, Erick, Potomac	7	24	19	1	2	2	0	0	0	0	0	0	0	5	0	5	0	0	2	.105	.292	.105
Scalabrini, Patrick, Frederick	45	168	151	25	37	54	8	0	3	19	2	1	2	12	1	33	1	0	8	.245	.307	.358
Schade, Scott, Myrtle Beach	95	382	332	46	75	122	17	0	10	48	1	5	1	43	0	130	1	2	6	.226	.312	.367
Schilling, Micah, Kinston *	67	251	220	27	53	74	9	0	4	24	0	1	3	30	0	62	1	2	2	.241	.335	.336
Schnurstein, Micah, Winston-Salem	132	537	488	78	131	203	21	3	15	68	0	2	7	40	0	98	12	8	15	.268	.331	.416
Segovia, Luis, Wilmington †	8	25	24	2	2	2	0	0	0	0	0	0	0	1	0	9	0	0	0	.083	.120	.083
Serrano, Raymond, Myrtle Beach	1	5	5	0	0	0	0	0	0	0	0	0	0	0	0	1	0	0	0	.000	.000	.000
Seuss, Adam, Salem *	39	148	128	10	19	28	3	0	2	8	0	0	7	13	0	30	0	1	11	.148	.264	.219
Shaffer, Joshua, Winston-Salem *	51	133	115	19	23	26	3	0	0	6	1	1	0	16	0	33	3	2	0	.200	.295	.226
Sherrill, James, Kinston †	2	9	7	0	1	1	0	0	0	0	0	0	0	2	0	3	0	1	0	.143	.333	.143
Snyder, Bradley, Kinston *	58	241	209	36	58	90	10	2	6	28	0	2	6	24	1	64	12	1	2	.278	.365	.431
Spann, Charles, Wilmington	111	455	400	55	99	169	23	4	13	48	1	7	8	39	2	106	1	4	12	.248	.322	.423
Spears, Nathaniel, Frederick *	112	498	445	63	131	191	30	6	6	41	14	1	2	36	1	82	8	4	1	.294	.349	.429
Spidale, Michael, Winston-Salem	39	161	144	19	36	38	2	0	0	8	2	0	4	11	0	15	6	2	3	.250	.321	.264
Stansberry, Craig, Lynchburg	24	107	94	17	33	53	7	2	3	19	0	0	2	11	1	13	7	1	1	.351	.430	.564
Stevenson, Jason, Potomac *	2	2	2	1	0	0	0	0	0	0	0	0	0	0	0	0	0	0	0	.000	.000	.000
Stone, Gregory, Wilmington *	15	42	31	5	4	4	0	0	0	1	3	0	1	7	0	12	1	0	0	.129	.308	.129
Suarez, Ignacio, Wilmington	116	441	403	38	94	116	20	1	0	38	5	2	2	29	0	73	9	6	11	.233	.287	.288
Sutton, Stephen, Salem †	43	178	148	22	38	54	5	1	3	12	0	0	1	29	1	34	4	3	3	.257	.382	.365
Thissen, Greg, Potomac	77	307	273	32	62	100	15	1	7	34	5	2	3	24	0	64	2	4	1	.227	.295	.366
Thomas, Benjamin, Myrtle Beach *	72	266	229	16	53	64	7	2	0	19	2	0	1	34	2	53	4	4	6	.231	.333	.279
Torres, Saul, Salem	86	361	322	47	82	113	11	1	6	26	5	3	0	31	0	77	3	4	15	.255	.317	.351
Trejo, Jaime, Myrtle Beach	92	340	320	23	66	84	9	0	3	25	4	2	1	13	0	73	3	2	6	.206	.238	.263
Triplett, Bryan, Salem	22	63	59	5	11	17	4	1	0	4	2	0	0	2	0	18	0	1	0	.186	.213	.288
Ust, Brant, Wilmington	115	485	443	54	116	175	20	0	13	71	1	6	8	27	0	107	1	1	10	.262	.312	.395
Valido, Robert, Winston-Salem	119	550	513	86	148	214	28	7	8	59	9	3	4	21	1	64	52	5	9	.288	.320	.417
Van Der Bosch, Matthew, Wilmington *	69	299	265	45	75	107	11	3	5	28	5	2	0	27	0	69	16	5	5	.283	.347	.404
Velazquez, Juan, Myrtle Beach †	4	15	14	0	3	4	1	0	0	1	0	0	0	1	0	4	0	0	0	.214	.267	.286
Vidro, Jose, Potomac †	5	17	13	3	2	3	1	0	0	3	0	0	0	4	0	2	0	0	0	.154	.353	.231
Walker, Neil, Lynchburg †	9	45	42	4	11	15	2	1	0	12	0	3	0	0	0	12	0	0	0	.262	.244	.357
Wallace, David, Kinston	96	375	311	38	60	108	18	0	10	29	2	2	13	47	0	102	3	2	11	.193	.322	.347
Wargo, Cody, Frederick	4	4	4	0	0	0	0	0	0	0	0	0	0	0	0	2	0	0	1	.000	.000	.000
Waters, Chris, Myrtle Beach *	1	3	3	1	2	2	0	0	0	0	0	0	0	0	0	0	0	0	0	.667	.667	.667
White, Scott, Wilmington	123	502	445	57	106	171	22	2	13	60	2	3	9	43	1	96	0	4	4	.238	.316	.384
Whitesell, Joshua, Potomac *	113	474	389	59	114	204	32	2	18	66	1	1	9	74	3	125	1	1	3	.293	.416	.524
Williams, Aaron, Salem	1	0	0	0	0	0	0	0	0	0	...	0	0	0	0	0	0	0	0	...	...	...
Wilson, Andy, Lynchburg	58	219	185	30	55	70	11	2	0	18	0	1	1	32	0	22	1	1	5	.297	.402	.378
Yepez, Marco, Potomac *	51	182	159	17	43	58	6	3	1	16	5	0	1	17	1	51	8	4	1	.270	.345	.365
Youngbauer, Scott, Wilmington †	27	123	109	18	35	56	5	5	2	18	2	1	2	9	1	21	3	1	1	.321	.380	.514
Yount, Dustin, Frederick *	110	442	368	57	95	149	16	1	12	52	4	2	8	60	0	102	4	2	6	.258	.372	.405
Zobrist, Benjamin, Salem †	42	180	141	25	47	70	12	1	3	13	1	0	1	37	1	17	2	1	3	.333	.475	.496

PLAYERS WITH TWO OR MORE TEAMS

Player, Team	G	TPA	AB	R	H	TB	2B	3B	HR	RBI	SH	SF	HP	BB	IBB	SO	SB	CS	GDP	Avg.	OBP	Slg.
Mercedes, Victor, Lynchburg †	13	60	53	10	14	21	2	1	1	6	1	0	1	5	0	15	3	1	5	.264	.339	.396
Mercedes, Victor, Potomac †	10	30	30	0	4	6	2	0	0	0	0	0	0	0	0	6	0	0	1	.133	.133	.200

GRAND SLAMS—T. Collaro, 2; A. Asprilla, B. Bass, D. Brown, L. Daigle, M. Delgado, F. Diaz, J. Fiorentino, R. Goleski, S. Head, R. Hubele, B. Kingsbury, N. Markakis, M. McCuistion, R. Mulhern, N. Panther, M. Russell, J. Saltalamacchia, P. Scalabrini, J. Whitesell, D. Yount, 1 each.

AWARDED FIRST BASE ON CATCHER'S INTERFERENCE—C. Lytle 2 (J. Saltalamacchia 2); J. Fagan (R. Rodriguez); B. Kingsbury (J. Saltalamacchia); R. Nanita (M. McCuistion).

2005 PITCHING
TEAM

Team	W	L	Pct.	ERA	G	CG	ShO	Sv.	IP	H	TBF	R	ER	HR	SH	SF	HB	BB	IBB	SO	WP	Bk.
Kinston	76	64	.543	3.65	140	1	10	35	1232	1173	5259	586	499	116	36	28	75	450	20	1087	64	1
Salem	67	74	.475	3.77	141	3	10	44	1229.2	1188	5292	596	515	96	43	25	66	479	9	986	87	5
Myrtle Beach	61	79	.436	4.11	140	1	9	27	1233	1236	5371	661	563	107	41	39	45	545	12	993	104	8
Wilmington	60	80	.429	4.36	140	2	11	32	1214.2	1200	5244	684	589	131	60	51	73	412	17	996	74	7

Team	W	L	Pct.	ERA	G	CG	ShO	Sv.	IP	H	TBF	R	ER	HR	SH	SF	HB	BB	IBB	SO	WP	Bk.
Frederick	79	61	.564	4.39	140	4	8	37	1225	1203	5375	684	598	122	35	27	84	544	15	1154	84	4
Winston-Salem	77	64	.546	4.53	141	3	3	37	1244.1	1331	5473	698	626	118	49	50	61	502	6	1046	72	9
Potomac	63	77	.450	4.56	140	7	10	22	1205.2	1203	5321	696	611	128	38	35	81	559	10	1049	118	7
Lynchburg	78	62	.557	4.87	140	5	6	44	1207	1286	5379	752	653	130	53	50	83	471	9	897	70	4

INDIVIDUAL

TOP QUALIFIERS FOR EARNED-RUN AVERAGE TITLE

Minimum 112 innings. *Lefthanded pitcher.

Pitcher, Team	W	L	Pct.	ERA	G	GS	CG	ShO	GF	Sv.	IP	H	TBF	R	ER	HR	SH	SF	HB	BB	IBB	SO	WP	Bk.
Douglass, Chance, Salem	12	9	.571	2.90	27	27	1	0	0	0	167.2	157	692	59	54	7	4	3	15	44	0	128	10	1
Finch, Brian, Frederick	10	10	.500	3.38	27	27	1	0	1	0	154.1	157	660	72	58	13	3	1	6	60	1	124	12	0
Johnson, James, Frederick	12	9	.571	3.49	28	27	2	0	1	1	159.2	139	685	77	62	11	4	1	19	64	2	168	5	1
O'Connor, Michael, Potomac *	10	11	.476	3.54	26	26	2	1	0	0	167.2	144	683	73	66	14	6	4	3	48	0	158	11	1
Smith, Sean, Kinston	5	8	.385	3.60	29	23	0	0	3	2	142.1	123	602	63	57	15	1	3	8	71	1	120	6	0
Muecke, Joshua, Salem *	10	12	.455	3.67	28	28	1	1	0	0	159.1	164	671	81	65	10	6	5	8	47	1	98	12	3
Vaquedano, Jose, Wilmington	8	7	.533	3.75	28	23	0	0	2	1	146.1	120	598	66	61	12	7	4	9	50	1	117	7	1
Pesco, Nicholas, Kinston	11	10	.524	3.82	27	26	0	0	0	0	153.1	168	649	77	65	15	3	3	9	39	0	101	1	0
Rodriguez, Ryan, Winston-Salem *	13	7	.650	4.09	29	29	2	1	0	0	167.1	180	708	87	76	17	7	13	6	49	0	108	4	2
Loewen, Adam, Frederick	10	8	.556	4.12	28	27	1	0	0	0	142.0	130	631	77	65	8	4	1	14	86	0	146	15	1
Van Dusen, Derrick, Lynchburg *	11	6	.647	4.24	22	22	1	0	0	0	123.0	123	540	73	58	16	6	6	15	36	0	92	7	1
Talbot, Mitchell, Salem	8	11	.421	4.34	27	27	1	1	0	0	151.1	169	659	90	73	15	8	2	8	46	0	100	9	1
Price, Jonathan, Potomac *	10	13	.435	4.44	28	28	2	2	0	0	144.0	122	624	83	71	20	3	2	10	81	0	150	11	0
Shortslef, Joshua, Lynchburg *	10	5	.667	4.58	22	22	1	1	0	0	120.0	132	518	69	61	8	5	4	6	44	0	84	4	0
Albers, Matthew, Salem	8	12	.400	4.66	28	27	0	0	0	0	148.2	161	653	86	77	15	2	4	8	62	0	146	7	0
Stevens, Jacob, Myrtle Beach *	10	9	.526	4.93	28	28	0	0	0	0	148.0	167	655	90	81	13	5	6	8	62	0	102	12	4
Hinckley, Michael, Potomac *	3	9	.250	4.93	22	21	1	0	0	0	127.2	151	580	90	70	10	2	5	9	51	0	80	6	2
Starling, Wardell, Lynchburg	10	10	.500	5.22	28	28	1	0	0	0	153.1	168	675	98	89	18	8	7	11	55	1	102	7	0
Mendoza, Luis, Wilmington	4	9	.308	6.34	23	22	1	0	1	0	119.1	145	539	91	84	17	5	8	7	36	0	60	8	0
Whisler, Wesley, Winston-Salem *	4	9	.308	6.73	26	21	1	0	2	1	112.1	153	521	93	84	10	2	2	6	42	0	79	6	0

DEPARTMENTAL LEADERS: W—Rodriguez, 13. L—Price, 13. Pct.—Shortslef, .667. G—Castro, 53. GS—Rodriguez, 29. CG—six pitchers tied with 2. ShO—Price, 2. GF—Salas and Wassermann, 38. Sv.—Wassermann, 20. IP—O'Connor and Douglass, 167.2. H—Rodriguez, 180. TBF—Rodriguez, 715. R—Starling, 98. ER—Starling, 89. HR—Price, 20. SAC—three pitchers tied with 8. SF—Rodriguez, 13. HB—Johnson, 19. BB—Loewen, 86. IBB—Warden, 5. SO—Johnson, 168. WP—Loewen, 15. BK—Stevens, 4.

ALL PITCHERS

*Lefthanded pitcher.

Pitcher, Team	W	L	Pct.	ERA	G	GS	CG	ShO	GF	Sv.	IP	H	TBF	R	ER	HR	SH	SF	HB	BB	IBB	SO	WP	Bk.
Acosta, Manuel, Myrtle Beach	2	2	.500	4.43	18	0	0	0	16	7	22.1	22	98	12	11	1	2	0	2	9	0	18	3	0
Albaladejo, Jonathan, Lynchburg	4	3	.571	3.91	28	6	0	0	6	2	78.1	74	331	40	34	9	2	7	2	21	0	76	2	1
Albers, Matthew, Salem	8	12	.400	4.66	28	27	0	0	0	0	148.2	161	653	86	77	15	2	4	8	62	0	146	7	0
Allen, Blake, Salem *	1	2	.333	3.08	21	0	0	0	10	1	38.0	35	165	15	13	1	3	0	1	16	0	43	7	0
Allen, Wyatt, Lynchburg	0	0	.000	8.38	3	2	0	0	0	0	9.2	17	48	10	9	2	0	1	0	4	0	8	3	0
Alvarez, Gerardo, Frederick	0	0	.000	20.25	1	0	0	0	0	0	1.1	5	9	3	3	1	0	1	0	0	0	1	0	0
Alvarez, Juan, Myrtle Beach *	0	1	.000	4.80	12	6	0	0	2	0	45.0	47	199	25	24	4	1	2	1	29	0	33	5	0
Ascanio, Jose, Myrtle Beach	3	1	.750	6.10	5	3	0	0	2	0	20.2	26	93	17	14	5	1	0	0	9	0	12	2	0
Bakker, Garry, Winston-Salem	1	2	.333	9.09	16	3	0	0	5	0	32.2	54	157	34	33	7	5	1	2	11	1	16	6	0
Barthmaier, James, Salem	1	0	1.000	1.50	1	1	0	0	0	0	6.0	4	28	4	1	1	0	0	3	1	0	6	0	0
Bay, Ronald, Kinston	6	5	.545	3.38	15	15	1	0	0	0	85.1	82	345	35	32	14	2	2	5	15	0	85	0	0
Baysinger, Trent, Frederick *	0	1	.000	18.00	5	0	0	0	4	0	5.0	13	30	10	10	1	0	0	0	2	0	6	0	0
Beam, Randall, Wilmington *	2	3	.400	2.25	19	0	0	0	14	5	28.0	19	117	7	7	2	0	0	1	11	2	28	2	0
Beltre, Jonathan, Salem *	5	1	.833	6.12	36	0	0	0	15	1	60.1	52	261	41	41	10	2	0	2	34	0	55	2	0
Bishop, Matthew, Lynchburg *	0	2	.000	11.08	8	0	0	0	2	0	13.0	26	76	18	16	5	0	1	1	9	0	10	0	0
Blakeney, Ted, Myrtle Beach	2	0	1.000	3.27	24	0	0	0	10	3	41.1	41	183	16	15	2	2	3	2	22	2	36	5	0
Bloom, Kyle, Lynchburg *	3	5	.375	5.86	12	12	0	0	0	0	63.0	61	286	45	41	12	3	1	3	43	0	34	4	0
Bobbitt, Seth, Myrtle Beach	3	0	1.000	4.58	9	0	0	0	2	0	17.2	19	76	10	9	0	0	1	0	8	0	7	0	0
Bono, Kyle, Wilmington	2	2	.500	4.07	24	0	0	0	8	0	48.2	39	218	29	22	5	3	3	7	32	3	56	1	0
Bray, Bill, Potomac *	1	0	1.000	2.13	8	0	0	0	5	3	12.2	8	50	3	3	1	0	0	0	3	0	18	0	0
Britton, Christopher, Frederick	6	0	1.000	1.60	46	0	0	0	15	6	78.2	47	298	15	14	5	0	0	1	23	0	110	1	0
Broadway, Lance, Winston-Salem	1	3	.250	4.58	11	11	0	0	0	0	55.0	68	249	31	28	4	4	0	7	20	0	58	2	0
Bullock, Tyler, Myrtle Beach	0	0	.000	0.00	1	0	0	0	0	0	3.0	2	12	0	0	0	0	0	0	1	0	1	2	1	0
Bunn, William, Potomac	2	6	.250	7.16	13	13	0	0	0	0	60.1	72	291	52	48	8	3	3	2	45	0	65	8	0
Burrows, Angelo, Myrtle Beach *	1	2	.333	3.15	14	0	0	0	6	0	20.0	14	84	11	7	1	0	1	0	10	0	22	2	1
Bush, Paul, Myrtle Beach	1	3	.250	2.32	18	3	0	0	9	4	42.2	36	171	16	11	3	0	1	1	13	1	40	3	0
Campbell, Richard, Potomac	0	2	.000	9.60	12	0	0	0	5	0	15.0	21	78	18	16	3	1	1	3	10	0	13	4	0
Castro, Fabio, Winston-Salem *	5	5	.500	2.28	53	0	0	0	20	6	79.0	58	321	23	20	7	4	4	3	37	0	75	4	0
Caughey, Trevor, Frederick *	5	1	.833	6.31	33	1	0	0	7	1	51.1	61	231	39	36	6	2	2	3	16	1	47	4	1
Cedeno, Juan, Wilmington *	2	6	.250	5.49	22	12	0	0	1	0	80.1	85	358	52	49	11	0	2	1	37	0	71	10	1
Chavez, Dirimo, Wilmington	0	0	.000	0.00	1	0	0	0	1	0	1.0	0	3	0	0	0	0	0	0	0	0	1	0	0
Chop, Chad, Potomac *	0	0	.000	0.00	1	0	0	0	0	0	2.0	0	8	0	0	0	0	0	0	2	0	1	0	0
Collins, Kyle, Kinston	3	4	.429	4.03	21	0	0	0	11	2	29.0	23	132	15	13	1	3	1	3	20	3	24	2	0
Cotto, Luis, Kinston	0	0	.000	0.00	1	0	0	0	0	0	1.0	1	5	0	0	0	0	0	0	0	0	0	0	0
Craig, Dustin, Lynchburg	0	0	.000	0.00	1	0	0	0	0	0	2.0	1	8	0	0	0	0	0	0	2	0	2	0	0
Davila, Marcus, Lynchburg	4	3	.571	5.82	48	0	0	0	17	1	72.2	84	318	50	47	8	7	3	5	24	3	45	7	0
Davis, Matthew, Kinston	5	6	.455	5.55	44	0	0	0	12	1	73.0	91	343	55	45	13	3	1	10	33	4	61	3	0
Delgado, Mario, Frederick *	0	0	.000	0.00	1	0	0	0	1	0	0.2	0	2	0	0	0	0	0	0	0	0	0	0	0
Devine, Joey, Myrtle Beach	0	0	.000	0.00	4	0	0	0	3	1	5.0	0	18	0	0	0	0	0	0	1	0	7	0	0
Dewitt, Anthony, Salem	6	2	.750	4.15	31	0	0	0	13	2	52.0	55	221	27	24	4	0	1	1	19	0	29	3	0
Deza, Fredy, Frederick	5	8	.385	6.12	28	18	0	0	2	0	104.1	134	479	75	71	13	3	3	9	36	0	64	4	0

Pitcher, Team	W	L	Pct.	ERA	G	GS	CG	ShO	GF	Sv.	IP	H	TBF	R	ER	HR	SH	SF	HB	BB	IBB	SO	WP	Bk.
Digby, Bryan, Myrtle Beach	1	4	.200	8.89	25	0	0	0	12	3	28.1	40	154	29	28	3	1	0	4	30	1	28	14	0
Dixon, Zachary, Frederick *	1	7	.125	6.13	14	9	0	0	1	0	54.1	61	252	43	37	8	4	2	5	27	1	38	2	0
Dizard, Fraser, Winston-Salem *	4	7	.364	6.72	31	10	0	0	3	1	85.2	103	389	66	64	11	3	3	2	38	0	87	8	1
Dobies, Andrew, Wilmington *	4	6	.400	4.40	16	16	0	0	0	0	86.0	89	355	54	42	7	6	5	6	18	0	50	2	0
Douglas, Robert, Kinston *	1	2	.333	9.56	12	0	0	0	1	0	16.0	24	81	19	17	2	1	2	1	7	1	16	0	0
Douglass, Chance, Salem	12	9	.571	2.90	27	27	1	0	0	0	167.2	157	692	59	54	7	4	3	15	44	0	128	10	1
Eisentrager, Daniel, Kinston	2	2	.500	5.75	25	0	0	0	11	0	51.2	63	233	33	33	6	0	3	3	17	2	32	1	0
Endl, Brady, Myrtle Beach *	6	7	.462	3.39	20	20	0	0	0	0	109.0	87	462	55	41	8	6	4	0	61	0	101	8	0
Escobar, Rodrigo, Salem	3	4	.429	2.14	47	0	0	0	30	14	75.2	63	318	26	18	6	4	1	3	36	2	76	8	0
Ferrari, Anthony, Potomac *	0	0	.000	1.86	9	0	0	0	3	0	9.2	8	41	2	2	0	1	0	2	6	0	8	1	0
Finch, Brian, Frederick	10	10	.500	3.38	27	27	1	1	0	0	154.1	157	660	72	58	13	3	1	6	60	1	124	12	0
Fisher, Peter, Wilmington	1	4	.200	3.89	26	1	0	0	14	8	41.2	42	177	25	18	3	2	2	2	14	0	26	5	0
Flores, Eugenio, Wilmington	0	0	.000	9.00	2	0	0	0	2	0	2.0	4	10	2	2	0	0	0	0	0	0	1	0	0
Flores, Rafael, Winston-Salem	3	4	.429	4.77	28	9	0	0	6	2	88.2	93	376	52	47	12	4	6	3	27	1	65	2	1
France, Ryan, Potomac	0	0	.000	9.64	3	0	0	0	2	0	4.2	5	22	5	5	0	0	0	0	4	0	3	2	0
Freeman, Daniel, Salem	3	5	.375	3.57	39	0	0	0	25	4	53.0	51	232	24	21	4	3	2	1	29	3	37	3	0
Galarraga, Armando, Potomac	3	4	.429	2.48	14	14	0	0	0	0	80.0	69	336	30	22	7	1	1	10	23	0	79	4	2
Gardner, Jarrett, Wilmington	1	2	.333	6.00	10	7	0	0	1	0	42.0	54	187	28	28	13	1	1	2	7	0	35	0	0
Gomez, Mariano, Kinston *	2	1	.667	2.83	17	1	0	0	4	1	35.0	28	145	13	11	1	2	1	0	17	2	30	4	0
Gonzalez, Giovany, Winston-Salem *	8	3	.727	3.56	13	13	0	0	0	0	73.1	61	295	33	29	5	2	1	1	25	0	79	2	3
Goodman, Christopher, Potomac	1	0	1.000	2.70	10	0	0	0	7	0	16.2	17	64	5	5	0	0	0	2	3	0	6	3	0
Goodson, Matthew, Wilmington	1	1	.500	4.38	9	4	0	0	1	0	24.2	26	113	14	12	3	1	1	2	13	0	24	3	1
Guerrero, Julio, Lynchburg	4	2	.667	5.35	14	1	0	0	4	0	33.2	44	155	25	20	0	2	1	0	9	1	17	0	0
Gutierrez, Juan, Salem	1	1	.500	3.00	3	2	0	0	0	0	12.0	10	51	4	4	1	0	0	0	8	0	9	0	0
Haeger, Charles, Winston-Salem	8	2	.800	3.20	14	13	0	0	1	0	81.2	82	354	33	29	3	3	2	5	40	0	64	2	0
Haehnel, David, Frederick *	3	1	.750	3.41	23	0	0	0	9	2	34.1	27	136	15	13	1	1	0	2	10	1	37	1	0
Haigwood, Daniel, Winston-Salem *	8	2	.800	3.77	15	15	0	0	0	0	76.1	79	339	39	32	8	1	2	6	33	0	84	5	2
Hale, Beau, Frederick	1	2	.333	5.23	22	5	0	0	6	0	53.1	51	230	34	31	7	1	4	4	23	1	48	4	0
Hernandez, Christopher, Lynchburg	6	3	.667	3.82	45	0	0	0	32	16	61.1	62	268	32	26	7	4	2	2	25	2	69	4	0
Hernandez, Fernando, Winston-Salem	4	1	.800	5.14	45	0	0	0	16	1	70.0	83	312	44	40	6	5	4	4	30	0	59	3	0
Hernandez, Jose, Lynchburg	0	0	.000	13.50	2	0	0	0	2	0	2.2	6	14	4	4	2	0	0	0	0	0	0	0	0
Hertzler, Barry, Wilmington	5	3	.625	4.21	33	1	0	0	9	1	83.1	80	351	47	39	4	8	2	4	24	1	58	8	1
Hinckley, Michael, Potomac *	3	9	.250	4.93	22	21	1	0	0	0	127.2	151	580	90	70	10	2	5	9	51	0	80	6	2
Holliday, Brian, Lynchburg *	5	4	.556	5.40	19	19	0	0	0	0	93.1	106	434	66	56	5	3	4	6	54	0	39	10	0
Hottovy, Thomas, Wilmington *	3	12	.200	5.45	25	23	0	0	0	0	104.0	116	461	74	63	18	6	5	7	37	2	82	8	0
Jacobsen, Landon, Lynchburg	3	1	.750	2.10	5	5	0	0	0	0	30.0	29	131	12	7	0	4	2	5	13	0	25	2	0
James, Chuck, Myrtle Beach *	3	3	.500	1.08	7	7	0	0	0	0	41.2	20	152	6	5	1	0	0	0	8	0	59	2	0
James, Michael, Wilmington	0	1	.000	3.06	14	0	0	0	11	3	17.2	9	69	7	6	2	0	1	2	7	2	12	0	0
James, Wilson, Myrtle Beach	0	0	.000	0.00	1	0	0	0	1	0	0.1	0	1	0	0	0	0	0	0	0	0	0	0	0
Jan, Carlos, Frederick *	5	2	.714	3.78	16	11	0	0	2	0	66.2	53	286	33	28	8	0	1	3	45	0	61	5	1
Johnson, James, Frederick	12	9	.571	3.49	28	27	2	0	1	1	159.2	139	685	77	62	11	4	1	19	64	2	168	5	1
Kobow, Michael, Potomac	0	0	.000	5.11	7	0	0	0	3	1	12.1	16	55	7	7	1	0	0	1	4	0	5	0	0
Kolb, Daniel, Potomac	4	3	.571	5.62	43	1	0	0	22	3	73.2	71	316	48	46	13	3	5	6	27	1	69	8	1
Langone, Steve, Wilmington	3	4	.429	3.92	18	5	1	0	8	0	43.2	44	171	21	19	4	3	1	3	5	0	34	4	0
Lara, Juan, Kinston *	0	1	.000	4.04	26	0	0	0	7	0	42.1	40	179	22	19	4	1	0	0	15	1	46	6	0
Letson, Wesley, Myrtle Beach *	2	4	.333	3.92	41	0	0	0	15	1	64.1	75	278	34	28	4	3	2	1	22	1	37	3	0
Linares, Ramon, Lynchburg	0	1	.000	2.33	12	0	0	0	4	1	19.1	14	81	7	5	0	1	0	1	11	0	16	2	2
Liotta, Raymond, Winston-Salem *	6	2	.750	1.45	8	8	0	0	0	0	49.2	46	201	11	8	1	1	2	2	16	0	37	4	0
Lira, Oscar, Potomac	0	0	.000	5.40	3	0	0	0	2	0	5.0	5	23	3	3	2	0	0	1	3	0	2	1	0
Loewen, Adam, Frederick *	10	8	.556	4.12	28	27	1	0	0	0	142.0	130	631	77	65	8	4	1	14	86	0	146	15	1
Logan, Boone, Winston-Salem *	0	0	.000	5.06	4	0	0	0	1	0	5.1	7	27	3	3	2	0	1	0	4	0	5	0	0
Lopez, Orionny, Winston-Salem	2	2	.500	5.14	36	1	0	0	12	2	61.1	56	267	36	35	5	1	2	4	25	0	45	5	0
Lorenzo, Mathew, Myrtle Beach	1	4	.200	3.72	9	5	0	0	2	0	36.1	41	157	20	15	6	2	1	3	13	1	17	2	0
Lubrano, Paul, Kinston *	2	0	1.000	0.00	3	0	0	0	1	0	3.1	4	13	0	0	0	0	0	2	0	0	0	0	0
Martin, Gregory, Lynchburg *	5	2	.714	7.30	23	1	0	0	10	0	40.2	51	193	38	33	5	4	2	2	25	2	43	2	0
Martinez, Edgar Ramon, Wilmington	1	1	.500	2.10	28	0	0	0	18	7	34.1	20	134	10	8	3	0	0	2	12	1	46	1	2
Martinez, Samuel, Potomac	3	2	.600	7.03	14	7	0	0	1	0	48.2	55	234	44	38	8	1	3	5	39	1	34	5	1
Mastny, Thomas, Kinston	7	3	.700	2.35	29	11	0	0	5	2	88.0	78	361	28	23	4	6	1	5	26	0	94	2	0
Mattison, Kieran, Kinston	1	0	1.000	2.25	5	0	0	0	1	1	8.0	8	34	2	2	0	0	0	0	5	0	6	0	0
Maust, David, Potomac *	1	0	1.000	6.64	9	0	0	0	3	0	20.1	27	95	15	15	2	1	1	3	13	1	18	2	0
Mazurek, David, Lynchburg	0	2	.000	6.00	30	1	0	0	15	2	51.0	52	228	39	34	9	3	1	7	19	0	40	4	0
McCurdy, Nicholas, Frederick	2	0	1.000	6.91	12	1	0	0	6	1	28.2	36	132	23	22	5	0	2	4	8	0	26	1	0
Mendoza, Luis, Wilmington	4	9	.308	6.34	23	22	1	0	1	0	119.1	145	539	91	84	17	5	8	7	36	0	60	8	0
Merchant, Jamie, Salem	0	2	.000	4.50	21	2	0	0	6	0	52.0	54	231	27	26	3	2	1	0	22	1	56	8	0
Meredith, Cla, Wilmington	0	0	.000	0.00	1	0	0	0	0	0	1.0	1	4	0	0	0	0	0	0	0	0	2	0	0
Michael, Mark, Lynchburg	1	2	.333	10.29	4	3	0	0	1	0	14.0	24	69	17	16	4	0	0	1	4	0	14	1	0
Miller, Adam, Kinston	2	4	.333	4.83	12	12	0	0	0	0	59.2	76	263	43	32	5	1	2	5	17	0	45	4	0
Miller, Brian, Winston-Salem	0	0	.000	6.19	11	0	0	0	5	0	16.0	15	74	14	11	2	0	1	0	8	0	18	1	0
Miller, Wade, Wilmington	0	0	.000	1.80	1	1	0	0	0	0	5.0	6	19	1	1	1	0	0	0	0	0	6	0	0
Moat, Michael, Winston-Salem	1	2	.333	5.56	12	3	0	0	4	1	22.2	25	104	15	14	5	1	0	0	12	0	15	2	0
Montani, Jeffrey, Frederick	1	2	.333	7.59	31	1	0	0	15	0	51.0	70	244	49	43	10	3	1	3	27	0	40	10	0
Morales, Alexis, Potomac	2	2	.500	3.72	23	0	0	0	13	3	36.1	25	159	15	15	4	1	1	3	26	2	47	7	0
Muecke, Joshua, Salem *	10	12	.455	3.67	28	28	1	1	0	0	159.1	164	671	81	65	10	6	5	8	47	1	98	12	3
Mujica, Edward, Kinston	1	0	1.000	2.08	25	0	0	0	25	14	26.0	17	96	6	6	3	1	0	1	2	0	32	1	0
Neal, Tony, Frederick	3	6	.333	4.85	20	0	0	0	17	8	26.0	29	117	17	14	5	2	0	0	10	3	29	1	0
Newsom, Randall, Wilmington	0	1	.000	0.00	2	0	0	0	2	1	2.2	0	12	1	0	0	0	0	2	2	1	2	1	0
Niesel, Christopher, Kinston	1	1	.500	4.57	10	2	0	0	2	1	21.2	23	99	14	11	2	1	0	1	11	0	18	1	0
Norderum, Jason, Potomac *	1	2	.333	4.37	13	0	0	0	2	1	22.2	31	107	13	11	0	3	1	2	13	0	13	7	0
O'Brien, Patrick, Lynchburg	4	8	.333	5.01	17	16	2	1	0	0	82.2	94	362	51	46	7	0	6	6	26	0	49	5	0
O'Connor, Michael, Potomac *	10	11	.476	3.54	26	26	2	1	0	0	167.2	144	683	73	66	14	6	4	3	48	0	158	11	1
Ogiltree, John, Potomac	5	3	.625	6.57	27	0	0	0	16	2	24.2	27	113	19	18	2	0	0	1	14	0	8	1	0

Pitcher, Team	W	L	Pct.	ERA	G	GS	CG	ShO	GF	Sv.	IP	H	TBF	R	ER	HR	SH	SF	HB	BB	IBB	SO	WP	Bk.
Olson, Garrett, Frederick *	0	0	.000	3.14	3	3	0	0	0	0	14.1	10	61	5	5	0	0	0	2	7	0	19	1	0
Ontiveros, Jeffrey, Wilmington	0	0	.000	6.75	1	0	0	0	1	0	1.1	2	6	1	1	0	0	0	0	0	0	0	0	0
Ortiz, Javier, Winston-Salem	0	1	.000	4.50	3	0	0	0	3	0	4.0	7	21	2	2	1	0	0	0	3	0	3	1	0
Ovalles, Juan, Winston-Salem	5	6	.455	4.15	52	0	0	0	21	3	86.2	86	387	46	40	7	3	3	6	51	2	89	10	0
Ozias, Todd, Lynchburg	1	1	.500	3.38	25	0	0	0	24	13	29.1	20	114	11	11	4	0	0	1	8	0	29	0	0
Pahucki, David, Wilmington	2	1	.667	1.23	4	0	0	0	1	0	7.1	7	28	3	1	0	3	1	0	3	0	6	0	0
Patton, Troy, Salem *	1	4	.200	2.63	10	9	0	0	0	0	41.0	34	162	12	12	2	0	2	2	8	0	38	1	0
Pearson, Willard, Potomac	3	0	1.000	3.86	12	0	0	0	4	0	28.0	24	125	15	12	1	0	1	1	17	0	25	4	0
Pekarek, Justin, Kinston *	2	0	1.000	4.84	5	4	0	0	0	0	22.1	25	96	13	12	2	0	2	0	5	0	21	3	0
Pennington, Jeffery, Kinston	0	0	.000	3.20	25	0	0	0	17	5	25.1	22	119	12	9	3	1	0	2	21	0	28	1	0
Perez, Rafael, Kinston *	8	5	.615	3.36	14	14	0	0	0	0	77.2	54	315	33	29	6	0	2	2	32	0	48	7	0
Perrin, Devin, Potomac	3	7	.300	4.99	28	14	0	0	12	3	92.0	96	414	54	51	7	3	0	7	58	2	66	11	0
Pesco, Nicholas, Kinston	11	10	.524	3.82	27	26	0	0	0	0	153.1	168	649	77	65	15	3	3	9	39	0	101	1	0
Piersoll, Chris, Frederick	5	0	1.000	3.41	17	0	0	0	6	1	29.0	22	117	12	11	3	1	1	1	10	1	34	2	0
Price, Jonathan, Potomac *	10	13	.435	4.44	28	28	2	2	0	0	144.0	122	624	83	71	20	3	2	10	81	0	150	11	0
Pudewell, Nathanial, Myrtle Beach	0	0	.000	1.04	5	0	0	0	1	0	8.2	8	35	1	1	0	0	0	1	0	0	9	1	0
Quintero, Mayque, Potomac	2	2	.500	4.67	32	3	0	0	10	2	69.1	71	302	40	36	12	2	2	4	23	1	67	10	0
Rayo, Pedro, Wilmington	1	0	1.000	3.86	3	1	0	0	0	0	9.1	8	39	4	4	3	0	0	0	3	0	16	2	0
Reid, Brett, Potomac	4	6	.400	2.76	28	0	0	0	19	2	42.1	38	179	15	13	3	3	2	1	23	2	43	8	0
Richards, Glen, Myrtle Beach *	0	0	.000	18.69	4	0	0	0	1	0	4.1	11	32	10	9	1	0	0	0	9	0	2	2	0
Richardson, Jason, Myrtle Beach	1	2	.333	4.04	19	0	0	0	3	0	35.2	33	151	23	16	2	4	2	3	11	0	34	4	0
Rios, Travis, Wilmington	2	1	.667	8.49	16	0	0	0	7	2	23.1	31	112	23	22	2	2	3	2	14	2	15	1	0
Roberts, Ralph, Myrtle Beach	4	5	.444	2.93	38	4	0	0	20	1	76.2	74	327	37	25	7	5	4	2	37	1	64	3	0
Rodriguez, Ricardo, Myrtle Beach	3	9	.250	5.34	33	9	0	0	10	1	86.0	82	376	56	51	12	2	2	4	47	1	80	8	1
Rodriguez, Ryan, Winston-Salem *	13	7	.650	4.09	29	29	2	1	0	0	167.1	180	708	87	76	17	7	13	6	49	0	108	4	2
Roehl, Scott, Kinston	2	0	1.000	1.04	15	10	0	0	2	0	60.2	41	233	9	7	1	1	0	1	16	0	57	3	0
Rogers, Joseph, Wilmington *	1	1	.500	2.57	6	1	0	0	3	0	14.0	17	62	7	4	2	0	0	1	6	0	8	0	0
Romero, Felix, Wilmington	5	7	.417	2.93	34	3	0	0	16	1	73.2	72	296	28	24	3	6	1	6	11	1	87	2	1
Rudrude, Brett, Wilmington	2	1	.667	0.46	14	0	0	0	5	0	19.2	13	84	3	1	1	0	0	0	14	0	18	1	0
Sabo, Timothy, Winston-Salem	0	0	.000	4.91	7	0	0	0	1	0	11.0	9	49	6	6	1	0	0	0	9	0	4	1	0
Salas, Marino, Frederick	4	2	.667	3.63	50	0	0	0	38	16	62.0	54	264	32	25	7	2	2	2	28	1	63	9	0
Salazar, Richard, Frederick *	2	1	.667	4.47	23	1	0	0	3	0	44.1	44	196	22	22	5	3	3	2	27	1	40	1	0
Sanchez, Anibal, Wilmington	6	1	.857	2.40	14	14	0	0	0	0	78.2	53	316	25	21	7	0	5	3	24	0	95	5	0
Schade, Scott, Myrtle Beach	0	0	.000	0.00	1	0	0	0	1	0	1.1	2	6	0	0	0	0	0	0	0	0	0	0	0
Schreiber, Zachery, Myrtle Beach	0	2	.000	2.84	15	0	0	0	7	0	25.1	15	100	10	8	4	0	0	0	11	0	25	3	0
Schroder, Christopher, Potomac	0	0	.000	0.00	5	0	0	0	2	1	7.0	7	32	3	0	0	1	1	2	0	1	6	1	0
Schroyer, Ryan, Wilmington	1	1	.500	4.50	13	0	0	0	5	1	26.0	30	122	20	13	3	1	1	2	14	0	22	1	0
Shafer, Kurt, Lynchburg	1	0	1.000	5.40	9	1	0	0	2	0	23.1	29	112	17	14	4	0	1	3	9	0	19	3	0
Sharpless, Joshua, Lynchburg	3	0	1.000	0.00	17	0	0	0	9	5	27.0	7	97	1	0	0	0	0	0	11	0	46	0	0
Shoemaker, Scott, Wilmington	1	3	.250	7.94	5	5	0	0	0	0	22.2	34	108	22	20	5	0	2	1	9	0	13	2	0
Shortell, Rory, Salem	7	7	.500	3.87	22	18	0	0	0	0	109.1	94	465	51	47	8	4	5	11	53	0	60	10	0
Shortslef, Joshua, Lynchburg *	10	5	.667	4.58	22	22	1	1	0	0	120.0	132	518	69	61	8	5	4	6	44	0	84	4	0
Sipp, Tony, Kinston *	2	2	.500	2.66	22	5	0	0	8	2	47.1	34	192	19	14	4	4	1	2	23	1	59	3	0
Smith, Daniel, Myrtle Beach *	2	2	.500	2.61	25	0	0	0	14	6	38.0	33	160	11	11	1	0	0	1	17	2	32	3	0
Smith, Sean, Kinston	5	8	.385	3.60	29	23	0	0	3	2	142.1	123	602	63	57	15	1	3	8	71	1	120	6	0
Soto, Jesus, Kinston	0	0	.000	0.00	1	0	0	0	0	0	2.1	1	8	0	0	0	0	0	0	0	0	4	0	0
Sowers, Jeremy, Kinston	8	3	.727	2.78	13	13	0	0	0	0	71.1	60	288	25	22	5	...	...	0	19	0	75	...	...
Stahl, Mark, Frederick	4	1	.800	2.77	9	9	0	0	0	0	52.0	48	220	19	16	3	2	1	0	26	1	43	2	0
Starling, Wardell, Lynchburg	10	10	.500	5.22	28	28	1	0	0	0	153.1	168	675	98	89	18	8	7	11	55	1	102	7	0
Stevens, Jacob, Myrtle Beach *	10	9	.526	4.93	28	28	0	0	0	0	148.0	167	655	90	81	13	5	6	8	62	0	102	12	4
Stevenson, Jason, Potomac *	5	5	.500	4.23	15	13	2	1	1	0	83.0	93	351	44	39	10	4	2	4	21	0	61	4	0
Stiehl, Robert, Salem	1	0	1.000	5.11	22	1	0	0	8	1	37.0	36	168	24	21	5	1	0	0	26	0	40	5	0
Sturge, Justin, Wilmington *	3	1	.750	3.58	13	2	0	0	4	1	32.2	33	130	15	13	2	4	3	1	6	0	18	2	0
Tabeek, Kyle, Wilmington	0	1	.000	19.64	4	0	0	0	3	1	3.2	9	24	8	8	0	1	0	0	6	1	3	0	0
Talbot, Mitchell, Salem	8	11	.421	4.34	27	27	1	1	0	0	151.1	169	659	90	73	15	8	2	8	46	0	100	9	1
Tiller, James, Charlotte	0	0	.000	12.91	5	0	0	0	2	0	7.2	8	42	11	11	1	0	1	4	7	0	2	4	0
Torrealba, Yoann, Lynchburg	3	1	.750	4.07	16	1	0	0	3	2	48.2	54	212	24	22	4	0	0	5	14	0	24	2	0
Torres, Melquicedec, Frederick	0	0	.000	2.25	3	0	0	0	1	1	4.0	4	18	1	1	1	0	0	0	2	1	8	0	0
Traber, Billy, Kinston *	2	2	.500	4.98	4	4	0	0	0	0	21.2	19	86	12	12	2	1	1	0	6	0	13	1	1
Tucker, Glenn, Myrtle Beach	0	1	.000	16.20	1	0	0	0	0	0	1.2	3	8	3	3	1	1	0	0	1	0	0	0	0
Van Dusen, Derrick, Lynchburg *	11	6	.647	4.24	22	22	1	0	0	0	123.0	123	540	73	58	16	6	6	15	36	0	92	7	1
Vaquedano, Jose, Wilmington	8	7	.533	3.75	28	23	0	0	2	1	146.1	120	598	66	61	12	7	4	9	50	1	117	7	1
Villa, Kelvin, Myrtle Beach *	2	10	.167	5.13	22	19	0	0	0	0	100.0	112	453	65	57	10	2	3	2	48	0	78	5	2
Warden, James, Kinston	3	5	.375	3.72	46	0	0	0	28	4	67.2	68	302	38	28	8	4	2	12	32	5	72	11	0
Wassermann, Ehren, Winston-Salem	4	2	.667	1.37	42	0	0	0	38	20	46.0	41	180	10	7	0	3	3	2	9	2	37	3	0
Waters, Chris, Myrtle Beach *	4	5	.444	4.27	17	17	1	0	0	0	103.1	106	433	54	49	10	1	5	4	31	2	67	0	0
Whisler, Wesley, Winston-Salem *	4	9	.308	6.73	26	21	1	0	2	1	112.1	153	521	93	84	10	2	6	42	0	0	79	6	0
White, Sean, Myrtle Beach	9	3	.750	3.71	18	18	0	0	0	0	97.0	112	414	46	40	5	3	1	5	29	0	65	11	0
Wigdahl, Jeffrey, Salem *	0	1	.000	3.98	22	0	0	0	9	4	31.2	30	139	16	14	2	1	0	0	18	1	30	1	0
Williams, Aaron, Salem	0	1	.000	2.34	27	0	0	0	22	17	34.2	19	133	9	9	2	1	0	3	10	1	35	1	0
Wing, Ryan, Winston-Salem *	0	4	.000	8.69	5	5	0	0	0	0	19.2	25	93	20	19	4	0	0	2	13	0	19	1	0
Young, Christopher, Lynchburg	0	0	.000	3.00	10	0	0	0	4	2	15.0	9	55	5	5	1	1	1	1	5	0	14	1	0

COMBINATION SHUTOUTS: Frederick (7) -- Stahl-Neal, Johnson-Salas-Montani, Loewen-Salas-Neal, Loewen-Britton-Salas, Finch-Salas, Olson-Salazar-Caughey, Jan-Britton. Kinston (10) -- Pesco-Lara, Perez-Smith, Sowers-Smith-Mujica, Bay-Gomez, Sowers-Gomez-Mujica, Perez-Mastny, Smith-Mastny-Pennington, Miller-Lara-Warden-Pennington, Niesel-Douglas-Warden, Roehl-Warden-Sipp. Lynchburg (4) -- Starling-Sharpless-Mazurek, Starling-Sharpless, Starling-Sharpless, O'Brien-Hernandez. Myrtle Beach (9) -- Endl-Richardson, James-Digby-Roberts, Endl-Bush, Bush-Digby-Letson, White-Roberts, Waters-Richardson, Stevens-Smith-Acosta, Endl-Smith-Acosta, Stevens-Acosta. Potomac (6) -- Martinez-Quintero, Price-Lira, Hinckley-Goodman, Price-Quintero, Hinckley-Reid, Quintero-Schroder-Perrin. Salem (8) -- Muecke-Dewitt-Williams, Shortell-Williams, Douglass-Williams, Douglass-Stiehl, Shortell-Dewitt, Muecke-Freeman-Williams, Douglass-Escobar, Albers-Wigdahl. Wilmington (11) -- Sanchez-Romero-Fisher, Hottovy-Vaquedano, Vaquedano-Fisher, Mendoza-Beam, Hottovy-Romero-Beam, Gardner-Bono, Hertzler-Langone-Beam, Goodson-Rios-Martinez, Hottovy-Romero-Schroyer, Hottovy-Rudrude-Sturge, Sturge-Schroyer. Winston-Salem (2) -- Gonzalez-Hernandez, Liotta-Ovalles.

TEAM

Team	G	PO	A	E	TC	DP	TP	PB	Pct.
Winston-Salem	141	3732	1429	113	5274	127	1	37	.979
Salem	141	3691	1569	129	5389	131	0	18	.976
Kinston	140	3695	1452	130	5277	135	0	21	.975
Frederick	140	3675	1400	133	5208	127	0	28	.974
Myrtle Beach	140	3699	1435	148	5282	149	0	15	.972
Potomac	140	3617	1425	147	5189	151	0	24	.972
Lynchburg	140	3622	1526	157	5305	122	0	28	.970
Wilmington	140	3644	1401	162	5207	116	0	28	.969

INDIVIDUAL

FIRST BASEMEN

NOTE: All caps denotes fielding-percentage leader based on 70 games for catchers, 93 for all other non-pitchers and 112 innings for pitchers. *Throws lefthanded.

Player, Team	Pct.	G	PO	A	E	TC	DP
Alvarez, Gerardo, Frederick	...	1	0	0	0	0	0
Belcher, Jason, Potomac	1.000	1	2	0	0	2	0
Benick, Jonathan, Lynchburg	.989	46	407	28	5	440	39
Bladergroen, Ian, Wilmington *	.984	64	519	28	9	556	40
Brock, Caleb, Kinston	.991	23	191	18	2	211	14
Chavez, Dirimo, Wilmington	1.000	7	51	5	0	56	5
Chop, Chad, Potomac *	.990	51	353	34	4	391	42
Choy Foo, Rodney, Kinston	.993	18	138	8	1	147	14
Daigle, Leo, Winston-Salem	.992	87	681	44	6	731	62
Delgado, Mario, Frederick *	.979	45	346	26	8	380	31
Fagan, John, Salem	1.000	1	2	0	0	2	0
Garza, Mario, Salem	.988	8	77	5	1	83	3
Guzman, Carlos, Myrtle Beach	.975	23	189	10	5	204	19
Harris, Justin, Lynchburg	1.000	2	6	0	0	6	0
Head, Stephen, Kinston *	.994	43	329	27	2	358	42
Hinton, Travis, Winston-Salem *	.996	62	472	37	2	511	44
Hubele, Ryan, Frederick	1.000	1	1	0	0	1	0
Humphries, Justin, Salem	.994	33	304	12	2	318	18
Jurich, Mark, Myrtle Beach *	.973	29	240	9	7	256	31
Larkin, Shaun, Kinston	.969	13	111	13	4	128	12
Lee, Carlos, Winston-Salem	.875	2	6	1	1	8	0
Lunetta, Anthony, Kinston	.980	6	47	2	1	50	4
Magness, Patrick, Lynchburg	.992	39	359	21	3	383	29
Martin, Billy, Potomac	.979	5	45	1	1	47	6
Matulich, Mario, Kinston	1.000	6	46	1	0	47	4
Molina, Gustavo, Winston-Salem	.923	2	12	0	1	13	0
Mulhern, Ryan, Salem	.987	34	292	21	4	317	27
Myers, Michael, Winston-Salem	1.000	3	15	0	0	15	0
Ontiveros, Jeffrey, Wilmington	.994	18	152	13	1	166	16
Peavey, Patrick, Salem	1.000	31	249	18	0	267	33
Rea, Bradley, Lynchburg	.991	57	512	30	5	547	43
Robinson, Scott, Salem *	.997	74	660	58	2	720	58
Rooi, Vince, Potomac	1.000	4	30	3	0	33	6
Rozema, Michael, Myrtle Beach	1.000	3	8	1	0	9	0
Scalabrini, Patrick, Frederick	1.000	4	30	3	0	33	3
Schade, Scott, Myrtle Beach	.993	80	649	45	5	699	74
Shaffer, Joshua, Winston-Salem	...	1	0	0	0	0	0
Thissen, Greg, Potomac	1.000	2	2	0	0	2	0
Thomas, Benjamin, Myrtle Beach	.976	15	78	5	2	85	7
Ust, Brant, Wilmington	1.000	12	95	10	0	105	11
White, Scott, Wilmington *	.992	44	362	29	3	394	31
Whitesell, Joshua, Potomac *	.992	87	696	47	6	749	83
YOUNT, DUSTIN, Frederick	.991	95	784	29	7	820	80

SECOND BASEMEN

Player, Team	Pct.	G	PO	A	E	TC	DP
Alvarez, Gerardo, Frederick	.990	25	40	61	1	102	16
Amador, Christopher, Winston-Salem	.966	24	53	60	4	117	13
Ash, Jonathan, Salem	.981	58	96	160	5	261	41
Borowiak, Zachary, Wilmington	.974	71	104	198	8	310	36
Bynum, Seth, Potomac	1.000	1	4	6	0	10	3
Casto, Kory, Potomac *	1.000	1	0	1	0	1	0
Chavez, Dirimo, Wilmington	.978	23	42	46	2	90	10
Choy Foo, Rodney, Kinston	1.000	2	3	5	0	8	2
Cotto, Luis, Kinston	.957	10	14	31	2	47	7
De La Cruz, Christopher, Kinston	.923	14	21	39	5	65	13
Fernando, Osvaldo, Salem	.976	23	52	70	3	125	18
Grimm, Eric, Frederick	.933	7	12	16	2	30	4

Player, Team	Pct.	G	PO	A	E	TC	DP
Haggerty, Cory, Winston-Salem	.974	29	47	66	3	116	12
Harris, Justin, Lynchburg	.991	24	51	54	1	106	17
James, Wilson, Myrtle Beach	.966	34	65	78	5	148	17
Kelly, Dustin, Wilmington	.956	11	18	25	2	45	6
Lee, Taber, Lynchburg	.977	73	119	215	8	342	42
LeVier, Bret, Wilmington	1.000	4	12	7	0	19	2
Lunetta, Anthony, Kinston	.983	12	29	28	1	58	10
Mateo, Henry, Potomac	.974	8	15	22	1	38	7
Mercedes, Victor, Lynchburg-Potomac	.951	18	39	39	4	82	18
Myers, Michael, Winston-Salem	.992	58	95	147	2	244	33
Norris, Shawn, Potomac	.983	34	76	93	3	172	26
Peavey, Patrick, Salem	1.000	4	4	9	0	13	0
Pinckney, Brandon, Kinston	1.000	13	29	36	0	65	8
Prado, Martin, Myrtle Beach	.974	72	141	201	9	351	59
Raymundo, Gregg, Lynchburg	.833	2	6	4	2	12	1
Reyes, Argenis, Kinston	.989	39	72	109	2	183	25
Robinson, Christopher, Salem	.949	37	72	96	9	177	15
Rodriguez, Javier, Potomac	.932	13	14	27	3	44	9
Rooi, Vince, Potomac	.981	11	13	38	1	52	8
Rozema, Michael, Myrtle Beach	.982	35	70	93	3	166	23
Scalabrini, Patrick, Frederick	.920	7	6	17	2	25	2
Schilling, Micah, Kinston	.965	59	116	156	10	282	32
Schnurstein, Micah, Winston-Salem	.961	13	26	23	2	51	5
Segovia, Luis, Wilmington	1.000	6	13	11	0	24	1
Shaffer, Joshua, Winston-Salem	.970	39	55	73	4	132	15
SPEARS, NATHANIEL, Frederick	.981	105	195	308	10	513	79
Stansberry, Craig, Lynchburg	.952	24	38	62	5	105	11
Sutton, Stephen, Salem	.973	25	44	65	3	112	15
Thissen, Greg, Potomac	.968	72	134	170	10	314	50
Trejo, Jaime, Myrtle Beach	1.000	1	3	2	0	5	1
Triplett, Bryan, Salem	1.000	3	2	7	0	9	1
Ust, Brant, Wilmington	.983	13	23	36	1	60	7
Velazquez, Juan, Myrtle Beach	1.000	3	5	9	0	14	2
Vidro, Jose, Potomac	1.000	2	3	1	0	4	0
Wilson, Andy, Lynchburg	1.000	9	30	18	0	48	5
Yepez, Marco, Potomac	.980	10	19	30	1	50	8
Youngbauer, Scott, Wilmington	.962	22	34	67	4	105	17

SECOND BASEMEN WITH TWO OR MORE TEAMS

Player, Team	Pct.	G	PO	A	E	TC	DP
Mercedes, Victor, Lynchburg	.934	13	28	29	4	61	11
Mercedes, Victor, Potomac	1.000	5	11	10	0	21	7

THIRD BASEMEN

Player, Team	Pct.	G	PO	A	E	TC	DP
Alvarez, Gerardo, Frederick	.963	17	6	20	1	27	1
Asprilla, Avelino, Lynchburg	.938	110	72	243	21	336	20
Bass, Allan, Frederick	.906	106	70	171	25	266	14
Borowiak, Zachary, Wilmington	.915	16	7	36	4	47	0
CASTO, KORY, Potomac	.956	132	74	271	16	361	39
Choy Foo, Rodney, Kinston	.963	31	17	61	3	81	3
Cockrell, Michael, Lynchburg	.903	11	14	14	3	31	1
Cotto, Luis, Kinston	.949	36	23	71	5	99	9
Creek, Gregory, Myrtle Beach	.917	4	2	9	1	12	0
Daigle, Leo, Winston-Salem	.794	16	5	22	7	34	1
Grimm, Eric, Frederick	1.000	1	0	2	0	2	0
Harris, Justin, Lynchburg	.939	12	5	26	2	33	3
Hubele, Ryan, Frederick	.889	3	4	4	1	9	0
James, Wilson, Myrtle Beach	1.000	3	0	1	0	1	0
Kouzmanoff, Kevin, Kinston	.925	56	40	108	12	160	14
Lane, Andrew, Potomac	1.000	1	1	0	0	1	0
Larkin, Shaun, Kinston	.964	7	6	21	1	28	3
LeVier, Bret, Wilmington	1.000	3	3	5	0	8	1
Lunetta, Anthony, Kinston	.846	12	5	17	4	26	1
Molina, Gustavo, Winston-Salem	1.000	3	0	4	0	4	0
Myers, Michael, Winston-Salem	1.000	5	4	11	0	15	1
Peavey, Patrick, Salem	.934	48	30	97	9	136	4
Pope, Peter, Myrtle Beach	.921	25	26	56	7	89	6
Raymundo, Gregg, Lynchburg	.000	1	0	0	2	2	0
Reyes, Argenis, Kinston	.895	8	7	10	2	19	1
Rooi, Vince, Potomac	1.000	6	3	8	0	11	0
Rozema, Michael, Myrtle Beach	.857	8	5	7	2	14	0
Scalabrini, Patrick, Frederick	.925	18	14	35	4	53	5
Schade, Scott, Myrtle Beach	.917	6	2	9	1	12	0
Schnurstein, Micah, Winston-Salem	.929	122	83	192	21	296	16
Shaffer, Joshua, Winston-Salem	1.000	7	1	6	0	7	0
Spann, Charles, Wilmington	.909	72	48	152	20	220	17

Player, Team	Pct.	G	PO	A	E	TC	DP
Thomas, Benjamin, Myrtle Beach	.933	57	32	94	9	135	17
Torres, Saul, Salem	.903	86	46	188	25	259	19
Trejo, Jaime, Myrtle Beach	.929	47	39	78	9	126	13
Triplett, Bryan, Salem	.919	15	5	29	3	37	1
Velazquez, Juan, Myrtle Beach	1.000	1	1	0	0	1	0
White, Scott, Wilmington *	.929	53	38	93	10	141	3
Wilson, Andy, Lynchburg	.950	18	10	28	2	40	0
Yepez, Marco, Potomac	.857	3	2	4	1	7	1

SHORTSTOPS

Player, Team	Pct.	G	PO	A	E	TC	DP
Alvarez, Gerardo, Frederick	.963	25	30	75	4	109	19
Asprilla, Avelino, Lynchburg	1.000	1	0	1	0	1	0
Borowiak, Zachary, Wilmington	.952	30	45	74	6	125	13
Brown, Travis, Frederick	.966	115	189	348	19	556	78
Bynum, Seth, Potomac	.910	28	34	57	9	100	19
Castro, Ramon A., Potomac	.971	10	19	14	1	34	3
Chaves, Brandon, Lynchburg	.956	61	82	198	13	293	36
Cotto, Luis, Kinston	.954	18	24	38	3	65	6
De La Cruz, Christopher, Kinston	.957	61	76	166	11	253	34
Desmond, Ian, Potomac	.931	55	108	147	19	274	36
Fernando, Osvaldo, Salem	.943	42	52	97	9	158	17
Guzman, Javier, Lynchburg	.927	69	92	213	24	329	39
Haggerty, Cory, Winston-Salem	...	1	0	0	0	0	0
Hernandez, Diory, Myrtle Beach	.983	71	118	179	5	302	45
James, Wilson, Myrtle Beach	.975	17	25	53	2	80	11
Lee, Taber, Lynchburg	.949	13	15	41	3	59	9
Maysonet, Edwin, Salem	.950	66	83	203	15	301	38
Myers, Michael, Winston-Salem	.929	25	36	56	7	99	13
Norris, Shawn, Potomac	.923	4	2	10	1	13	0
Peavey, Patrick, Salem	...	1	0	0	0	0	0
Pinckney, Brandon, Kinston	.954	68	85	162	12	259	43
Robinson, Christopher, Salem	.955	6	6	15	1	22	2
Rodriguez, Javier, Potomac	.897	14	19	33	6	58	5
Rozema, Michael, Myrtle Beach	.962	13	10	40	2	52	6
Segovia, Luis, Wilmington	.909	3	1	9	1	11	1
Shaffer, Joshua, Winston-Salem	.818	2	4	5	2	11	2
Spears, Nathaniel, Frederick	.842	6	3	13	3	19	1
Suarez, Ignacio, Wilmington	.932	115	147	289	32	468	65
Trejo, Jaime, Myrtle Beach	.952	47	65	153	11	229	36
Triplett, Bryan, Salem	.833	1	2	3	1	6	0
VALIDO, ROBERT, Winston-Salem	.978	118	166	362	12	540	84
Yepez, Marco, Potomac	.966	37	51	117	6	174	19
Zobrist, Benjamin, Salem	.983	39	55	121	3	179	25

OUTFIELDERS

Player, Team	Pct.	G	PO	A	E	TC	DP
ALCANTARA, ERVIN, Salem	.996	126	233	14	1	248	3
Amador, Christopher, Winston-Salem	.963	35	77	0	3	80	0
Arias, Claudio, Wilmington	.941	7	16	0	1	17	0
Barton, Brian, Kinston	.992	55	120	4	1	125	1
Belcher, Jason, Potomac	1.000	19	17	0	0	17	0
Bocchino, Anthony, Lynchburg *	.961	38	47	2	2	51	1
Boeve, Adam, Lynchburg	.986	66	131	5	2	138	1
Boran, Patrick, Wilmington	1.000	4	4	0	0	4	0
Borowiak, Zachary, Wilmington	1.000	2	4	0	0	4	0
Brock, Caleb, Kinston	1.000	6	13	0	0	13	0
Brooks, Cedrick, Potomac	.966	111	164	6	6	176	0
Brown, Dustin, Wilmington	.986	34	68	3	1	72	0
Burrus, Josh, Myrtle Beach	.960	67	115	6	5	126	3
Butia, Michael, Kinston	.976	26	39	2	1	42	0
Buttler, Victor, Lynchburg *	.991	56	97	8	1	106	2
Caraballo, Francisco, Salem	1.000	14	19	1	0	20	0
Casto, Kory, Potomac	...	1	0	0	0	0	0
Chavez, Dirimo, Wilmington	1.000	3	0	1	0	1	0
Chavez, Ender, Potomac *	.984	107	173	14	3	190	2
Chop, Chad, Potomac *	.982	64	103	4	2	109	1
Collaro, Thomas, Winston-Salem	.972	120	228	13	7	248	3
Conroy, Michael, Kinston *	.953	44	74	7	4	85	1
Cotto, Luis, Kinston	1.000	1	4	0	0	4	0
Cronkhite, Ian, Wilmington *	1.000	3	6	0	0	6	0
Daigle, Leo, Winston-Salem	1.000	1	0	1	0	1	0
Davidson, Kevin, Salem	1.000	3	2	0	0	2	0
Delgado, Mario, Frederick *	.917	14	10	1	1	12	0
Diaz, Frank, Potomac	.977	134	285	17	7	309	4
Doetsch, Steven, Myrtle Beach	.970	107	249	8	8	265	4
Duran, Carlos, Myrtle Beach *	.963	11	24	2	1	27	0
Esquivel, William, Myrtle Beach	.951	114	222	12	12	246	2
Fagan, John, Salem	.984	36	62	1	1	64	0
Fiorentino, Jeff, Frederick	.968	102	174	8	6	188	1
Florence, Branden, Frederick	.963	21	26	0	1	27	0
Floyd, Michael, Salem	.986	115	201	8	3	212	1
Garza, Mario, Salem	...	1	0	0	0	0	0
Goelz, Bryan, Wilmington *	.993	73	129	4	1	134	1
Goleski, Ryan, Kinston	.972	111	197	12	6	215	3
Hall, Michael, Wilmington *	.969	67	121	6	4	131	2
Hall, Noah, Winston-Salem	.987	88	145	5	2	152	1
Harris, Justin, Lynchburg	1.000	7	10	0	0	10	0
Hubele, Ryan, Frederick	.941	13	15	1	1	17	0
James, Wilson, Myrtle Beach	.833	8	14	1	3	18	0
Jansen, Ardley, Myrtle Beach	.971	47	96	6	3	105	1
Jones, Brandon, Myrtle Beach	1.000	15	42	0	0	42	0
Kingsbury, Robert, Lynchburg *	.983	82	173	5	3	181	3
Kochen, Ryan, Salem	1.000	16	18	0	0	18	0
Loadenthal, Carl, Myrtle Beach *	.960	57	114	7	5	126	1
Lytle, Chaz, Lynchburg *	.959	68	111	6	5	122	3
Magness, Patrick, Salem	.958	37	44	2	2	48	1
Markakis, Nicholas, Frederick *	.971	88	165	2	5	172	0
Martel Jr, Normand, Winston-Salem	1.000	8	12	1	0	13	1
McCurdy, Joshua, Frederick	.979	58	91	3	2	96	0
Meath, Matthew, Lynchburg	1.000	11	14	0	0	14	0
Morgan, Nyjer, Lynchburg *	.965	58	138	1	5	144	0
Mota, Willy, Wilmington	1.000	6	13	0	0	13	0
Myers, Michael, Winston-Salem	.977	36	83	2	2	87	1
Nanita, Ricardo, Winston-Salem *	.977	115	250	7	6	263	1
Ontiveros, Jeffrey, Wilmington	1.000	1	1	0	0	1	0
Panther, Nathan, Kinston *	.983	98	167	8	3	178	1
Pence, Hunter, Salem	1.000	37	66	6	0	72	1
Powell, Pedro, Lynchburg	1.000	8	9	1	0	10	0
Pritz, Bryan, Wilmington	.971	89	189	9	6	204	3
Reimold, Nolan, Frederick	.955	23	41	1	2	44	0
Reyes, Argenis, Kinston	1.000	6	17	0	0	17	0
Reynolds, Wilton, Salem	.990	53	92	5	1	98	0
Rine, Jarod, Frederick	.985	108	191	7	3	201	0
Rojas, Ricardo, Kinston	.985	34	63	2	1	66	0
Scalabrini, Patrick, Frederick.	1.000	10	13	2	0	15	0
Seuss, Adam, Salem	.985	36	62	4	1	67	1
Sherrill, James, Kinston	1.000	1	3	0	0	3	0
Snyder, Bradley, Kinston *	.990	50	99	3	1	103	1
Spidale, Michael, Winston-Salem	.986	36	71	0	1	72	0
Stone, Gregory, Wilmington	1.000	14	21	2	0	23	0
Thissen, Greg, Potomac	.867	8	12	1	2	15	0
Triplett, Bryan, Salem	1.000	1	3	0	0	3	0
Ust, Brant, Wilmington	.984	79	115	5	2	122	4
Van Der Bosch, Matthew, Wilmington *	.977	67	165	4	4	173	0
Wilson, Andy, Lynchburg	1.000	25	42	1	0	43	1

CATCHERS

Player, Team	Pct.	G	PO	A	E	TC	DP
Arko, Thomas, Frederick	.986	16	129	7	2	138	1
Barksdale, James, Myrtle Beach	1.000	1	9	0	0	9	0
Belcher, Jason, Potomac	.973	17	100	8	3	111	2
Bernard, Miguel, Myrtle Beach	.986	9	63	6	1	70	0
Bock, Brian, Frederick	.988	37	307	25	4	336	5
Brock, Caleb, Kinston	1.000	43	333	29	0	362	3
Brown, Dustin, Wilmington	.971	29	182	21	6	209	2
Chauncey, Clinton, Wilmington	.992	34	228	20	2	250	3
Davidson, Kevin, Salem	.982	78	484	62	10	556	6
Delgado, Mario, Frederick *	1.000	1	1	0	0	1	0
Devries, Jonathan, Wilmington	.978	33	203	21	5	229	3
Emmerick, Joshua, Potomac	1.000	11	95	9	0	104	0
Garcia, Cipriano, Winston-Salem	.975	20	70	9	2	81	1
Hernandez, Jose, Lynchburg	.993	42	248	26	2	276	4
Hubele, Ryan, Frederick	.996	30	245	16	1	262	4
Lee, Carlos, Winston-Salem	.996	36	229	26	1	256	4
Mackor, Jeffrey, Salem	.995	49	342	27	2	371	3
Manriquez, Salomon, Potomac	.992	87	656	51	6	713	7
McCuistion, Michael, Lynchburg	.984	88	565	67	10	642	2
McCullough, Clayton, Kinston	1.000	2	14	1	0	15	0
MOLINA, GUSTAVO, Winston-Salem	.993	107	744	107	6	857	9
Ontiveros, Jeffrey, Wilmington	.988	53	390	25	5	420	3
Pena, Rodolfo, Lynchburg	.966	8	51	5	2	58	1
Poppert, John, Potomac	1.000	2	14	3	0	17	1
Pyzik, Steven, Myrtle Beach	1.000	12	69	5	0	74	0
Rodriguez, Robert, Potomac	.969	27	142	13	5	160	0
Ruelas, Alonzo, Myrtle Beach	.996	35	227	31	1	259	3
Ruiz, Reinaldo, Salem	1.000	28	173	12	0	185	4
Russell, Michael, Frederick	.992	64	491	33	4	528	2
Saltalamacchia, Jarrod, Myrtle Beach	.986	93	639	49	10	698	7
San Pedro, Erick, Potomac	.982	7	49	6	1	56	0
Walker, Neil, Lynchburg	1.000	4	32	2	0	34	0

Player, Team	Pct.	G	PO	A	E	TC	DP
Wallace, David, Kinston	.988	95	737	76	10	823	8
Wargo, Cody, Frederick	1.000	1	3	0	0	3	0

PITCHERS

Player, Team	Pct.	G	PO	A	E	TC	DP
Acosta, Manuel, Myrtle Beach	1.000	18	1	11	0	12	1
Albaladejo, Jonathan, Lynchburg	1.000	28	6	7	0	13	0
Albers, Matthew, Salem	.946	28	14	21	2	37	3
Allen, Blake, Salem *	.833	21	2	3	1	6	0
Allen, Wyatt, Lynchburg	.000	3	0	0	1	1	0
Alvarez, Gerardo, Frederick	...	1	0	0	0	0	0
Alvarez, Juan, Myrtle Beach *	.857	12	0	6	1	7	0
Ascanio, Jose, Myrtle Beach	1.000	5	0	6	0	6	0
Bakker, Garry, Myrtle Beach	1.000	16	1	5	0	6	0
Barthmaier, James, Salem	1.000	1	1	0	0	1	0
Bay, Ronald, Kinston	.913	15	4	17	2	23	0
Baysinger, Trent, Frederick *	...	5	0	0	0	0	0
Beam, Randall, Wilmington	.500	19	0	2	2	4	0
Beltre, Jonathan, Salem *	1.000	36	2	5	0	7	0
Bishop, Matthew, Lynchburg	.750	8	0	3	1	4	0
Blakeney, Ted, Myrtle Beach	1.000	24	4	5	0	9	1
Bloom, Kyle, Lynchburg *	.882	12	3	12	2	17	0
Bobbitt, Seth, Myrtle Beach	1.000	9	0	4	0	4	0
Bono, Kyle, Wilmington	.900	24	0	9	1	10	0
Bray, Bill, Potomac *	1.000	8	1	3	0	4	0
Britton, Christopher, Frederick	1.000	46	1	5	0	6	0
Broadway, Lance, Winston-Salem	1.000	11	1	5	0	6	0
Bullock, Tyler, Myrtle Beach	...	1	0	0	0	0	0
Bunn, William, Potomac	1.000	13	9	6	0	15	0
Burrows, Angelo, Myrtle Beach	1.000	14	1	2	0	3	0
Bush, Paul, Myrtle Beach	.500	18	0	1	1	2	0
Campbell, Richard, Potomac	1.000	12	2	2	0	4	0
Castro, Fabio, Winston-Salem *	1.000	53	2	7	0	9	1
Caughey, Trevor, Frederick *	.909	33	2	8	1	11	0
Cedeno, Juan, Wilmington *	.917	22	6	5	1	12	0
Chavez, Dirimo, Wilmington	...	1	0	0	0	0	0
Chop, Chad, Potomac *	...	1	0	0	0	0	0
Collins, Kyle, Kinston	1.000	21	3	3	0	6	0
Cotto, Luis, Kinston	...	1	0	0	0	0	0
Craig, Dustin, Lynchburg	...	1	0	0	0	0	0
Davila, Marcus, Lynchburg	1.000	46	3	16	0	19	0
Davis, Matthew, Kinston	.917	44	5	6	1	12	0
Delgado, Mario, Frederick *	...	1	0	0	0	0	0
Devine, Joey, Myrtle Beach	1.000	4	0	1	0	1	0
Dewitt, Anthony, Salem	1.000	31	4	4	0	8	0
Deza, Fredy, Frederick	.950	28	4	15	1	20	0
Digby, Bryan, Myrtle Beach	.833	25	0	5	1	6	0
Dixon, Zachary, Frederick *	.923	14	3	9	1	13	0
Dizard, Fraser, Winston-Salem *	1.000	31	1	9	0	10	1
Dobies, Andrew, Wilmington *	1.000	16	2	11	0	13	1
Douglas, Robert, Kinston *	1.000	12	2	0	0	2	0
Douglass, Chance, Salem	.953	27	13	28	2	43	3
Eisentrager, Daniel, Kinston	1.000	25	6	10	0	16	1
Endl, Brady, Myrtle Beach *	.933	20	0	14	1	15	0
Escobar, Rodrigo, Salem	1.000	47	9	10	0	19	1
Ferrari, Anthony, Potomac *	1.000	9	3	1	0	4	0
Finch, Brian, Frederick	.971	27	12	21	1	34	3
Fisher, Peter, Wilmington	.778	26	2	5	2	9	2
Flores, Eugenio, Wilmington	1.000	2	0	1	0	1	0
Flores, Rafael, Winston-Salem	.947	28	7	11	1	19	0
France, Ryan, Potomac	1.000	3	1	0	0	1	0
Freeman, Daniel, Salem	.857	39	4	8	2	14	0
Galarraga, Armando, Potomac	.944	14	5	12	1	18	0
Gardner, Jarrett, Wilmington	1.000	10	1	7	0	8	0
Gomez, Mariano, Kinston *	1.000	17	1	3	0	4	0
Gonzalez, Giovany, Winston-Salem *	.929	13	2	11	1	14	0
Goodman, Christopher, Potomac	1.000	10	0	3	0	3	0
Goodson, Matthew, Wilmington	.875	9	3	4	1	8	0
Guerrero, Julio, Lynchburg	1.000	14	2	3	0	5	0
Gutierrez, Juan, Salem	1.000	3	1	0	0	1	0
Haeger, Charles, Winston-Salem	1.000	14	3	15	0	18	0
Haehnel, David, Frederick *	1.000	23	2	3	0	5	0
Haigwood, Daniel, Winston-Salem *	.833	15	5	5	2	12	0
Hale, Beau, Frederick	1.000	22	0	2	0	2	0
Hernandez, Christopher, Lynchburg	1.000	45	3	2	0	5	0
Hernandez, Fernando, Winston-Salem	1.000	45	4	6	0	10	1
Hernandez, Jose, Lynchburg	...	2	0	0	0	0	0
Hertzler, Barry, Wilmington	.889	33	10	14	3	27	1
Hinckley, Michael, Potomac *	.778	22	5	16	6	27	0
Holliday, Brian, Lynchburg *	.957	19	4	18	1	23	0

Player, Team	Pct.	G	PO	A	E	TC	DP
Hottovy, Thomas, Wilmington *	.870	25	2	18	3	23	0
Jacobsen, Landon, Lynchburg	1.000	5	3	4	0	7	1
James, Chuck, Myrtle Beach *	1.000	7	1	4	0	5	0
James, Michael, Lynchburg	1.000	14	1	3	0	4	0
James, Wilson, Myrtle Beach	...	1	0	0	0	0	0
Jan, Carlos, Frederick *	.818	16	1	8	2	11	1
Johnson, James, Frederick	1.000	28	5	17	0	22	0
Kobow, Michael, Potomac	1.000	7	2	0	0	2	0
Kolb, Daniel, Potomac	.909	43	3	7	1	11	1
Langone, Steve, Wilmington	.875	18	0	7	1	8	0
Lara, Juan, Kinston *	1.000	26	3	7	0	10	0
Letson, Wesley, Myrtle Beach *	.941	41	3	13	1	17	1
Linares, Ramon, Lynchburg	.667	12	1	1	1	3	0
Liotta, Raymond, Winston-Salem *	1.000	8	2	4	0	6	0
Lira, Oscar, Potomac	...	3	0	0	0	0	0
Loewen, Adam, Frederick *	.925	28	4	33	3	40	3
Logan, Boone, Winston-Salem *	...	4	0	0	0	0	0
Lopez, Orionny, Winston-Salem	1.000	36	4	9	0	13	0
Lorenzo, Mathew, Myrtle Beach	.833	9	2	3	1	6	0
Lubrano, Paul, Kinston *	1.000	3	0	2	0	2	0
Martin, Gregory, Lynchburg *	.909	23	2	8	1	11	0
Martinez, Edgar Ramon, Wilmington	1.000	28	0	2	0	2	0
Martinez, Samuel, Potomac	.889	14	2	6	1	9	0
Mastny, Thomas, Kinston	.958	29	7	16	1	24	1
Mattison, Kieran, Kinston	...	5	0	0	0	0	0
Maust, David, Potomac *	1.000	9	3	3	0	6	0
Mazurek, David, Lynchburg	.625	30	3	7	6	16	1
McCurdy, Nicholas, Frederick	1.000	12	1	5	0	6	0
Mendoza, Luis, Wilmington	.909	23	16	14	3	33	0
Merchant, Jamie, Salem	.786	21	4	7	3	14	0
Meredith, Cla, Wilmington	...	1	0	0	0	0	0
Michael, Mark, Lynchburg	1.000	4	2	2	0	4	0
Miller, Adam, Kinston	.846	12	8	3	2	13	1
Miller, Brian, Winston-Salem	1.000	11	2	1	0	3	0
Miller, Wade, Wilmington	1.000	1	0	1	0	1	0
Moat, Michael, Winston-Salem	1.000	12	2	3	0	5	0
Montani, Jeffrey, Frederick	.818	31	3	6	2	11	0
Morales, Alexis, Potomac	.500	23	1	1	2	4	0
Muecke, Joshua, Salem *	.907	28	16	33	5	54	0
Mujica, Edward, Kinston	.857	25	1	5	1	7	0
Neal, Tony, Frederick	1.000	20	1	4	0	5	0
Newsom, Randall, Wilmington	1.000	2	1	0	0	1	0
Niesel, Christopher, Kinston	1.000	10	1	5	0	6	0
Norderum, Jason, Potomac *	.833	13	0	5	1	6	0
O'Brien, Patrick, Lynchburg	1.000	17	4	6	0	10	1
O'Connor, Michael, Potomac *	.826	26	5	14	4	23	0
Ogiltree, John, Potomac	1.000	27	2	4	0	6	0
Olson, Garrett, Frederick *	1.000	3	0	1	0	1	0
Ontiveros, Jeffrey, Wilmington	...	1	0	0	0	0	0
Ortiz, Javier, Winston-Salem	...	3	0	0	0	0	0
Ovalles, Juan, Winston-Salem	1.000	52	8	8	0	16	2
Ozias, Todd, Lynchburg	1.000	25	1	6	0	7	1
Pahucki, David, Wilmington	.667	4	2	0	1	3	0
Patton, Troy, Salem *	1.000	10	0	9	0	9	0
Pearson, Willard, Potomac	.857	12	2	4	1	7	0
Pekarek, Justin, Kinston *	.750	5	2	1	1	4	0
Pennington, Jeffery, Kinston	1.000	25	1	1	0	2	0
Perez, Rafael, Kinston *	.913	14	7	14	2	23	1
Perrin, Devin, Potomac	.952	28	9	11	1	21	0
Pesco, Nicholas, Kinston	.931	27	16	11	2	29	1
Piersoll, Chris, Frederick	1.000	17	1	3	0	4	1
Price, Jonathan, Potomac *	.926	28	6	19	2	27	1
Pudewell, Nathanial, Myrtle Beach	1.000	5	1	1	0	2	0
Quintero, Mayque, Potomac	1.000	32	5	7	0	12	2
Rayo, Pedro, Myrtle Beach	1.000	3	0	3	0	3	0
Reid, Brett, Potomac	.900	28	5	4	1	10	0
Richards, Glen, Myrtle Beach *	.000	4	0	0	1	1	0
Richardson, Jason, Myrtle Beach	1.000	19	2	7	0	9	1
Rios, Travis, Wilmington	.750	16	0	3	1	4	0
Roberts, Ralph, Myrtle Beach	.917	38	4	7	1	12	2
Rodriguez, Ricardo, Myrtle Beach	.923	33	4	8	1	13	2
Rodriguez, Ryan, Winston-Salem *	.970	29	8	24	1	33	1
Roehl, Scott, Kinston	1.000	15	6	6	0	12	2
Rogers, Joseph, Wilmington *	1.000	6	0	2	0	2	0
Romero, Felix, Wilmington	1.000	34	5	10	0	15	0
Rudrude, Brett, Wilmington	...	14	0	0	0	0	0
Sabo, Timothy, Winston-Salem	1.000	7	3	1	0	4	0
Salas, Marino, Frederick	1.000	50	1	4	0	5	0
Salazar, Richard, Frederick *	1.000	23	2	11	0	13	0
Sanchez, Anibal, Wilmington	.857	14	11	1	2	14	0
Schade, Scott, Myrtle Beach	...	1	0	0	0	0	0

Player, Team	Pct.	G	PO	A	E	TC	DP
Schreiber, Zachery, Myrtle Beach	1.000	15	1	2	0	3	0
Schroder, Christopher, Potomac	1.000	5	2	0	0	2	1
Schroyer, Ryan, Wilmington	1.000	13	4	1	0	5	0
Shafer, Kurt, Lynchburg	1.000	9	2	1	0	3	0
Sharpless, Joshua, Lynchburg	1.000	17	0	1	0	1	0
Shoemaker, Scott, Wilmington	1.000	5	1	2	0	3	0
Shortell, Rory, Salem	.950	22	8	11	1	20	0
Shortslef, Joshua, Lynchburg *	.929	22	5	21	2	28	0
Sipp, Tony, Kinston *	1.000	22	1	6	0	7	0
Smith, Daniel, Myrtle Beach *	1.000	25	0	4	0	4	0
Smith, Sean, Kinston	.967	29	12	17	1	30	3
Soto, Jesus, Kinston	...	1	0	0	0	0	0
Stahl, Mark, Frederick *	.769	9	0	10	3	13	0
Starling, Wardell, Lynchburg	.897	28	10	25	4	39	0
Stevens, Jacob, Myrtle Beach *	.955	28	4	17	1	22	2
Stevenson, Jason, Potomac *	.926	15	4	21	2	27	0
Stiehl, Robert, Salem	.833	22	1	4	1	6	1
Sturge, Justin, Wilmington *	.833	13	1	4	1	6	1
Tabeek, Kyle, Wilmington	...	4	0	0	0	0	0
Talbot, Mitchell, Salem	.951	27	12	27	2	41	1
Tiller, James, Frederick	1.000	5	0	1	0	1	0
Torrealba, Yoann, Lynchburg	1.000	16	4	9	0	13	2
Torres, Melquicedec, Frederick	...	3	0	0	0	0	0
Traber, Billy, Kinston *	1.000	4	2	4	0	6	0
Tucker, Glenn, Myrtle Beach	1.000	1	0	1	0	1	0
Van Dusen, Derrick, Lynchburg *	.955	22	4	17	1	22	0
VAQUEDANO, JOSE, Wilmington	1.000	28	7	21	0	28	1
Villa, Kelvin, Myrtle Beach *	.923	22	3	9	1	13	0
Warden, James, Kinston	.700	46	2	5	3	10	0
Wassermann, Ehren, Winston-Salem	1.000	42	3	11	0	14	1
Waters, Chris, Myrtle Beach *	.952	17	5	15	1	21	4
Whisler, Wesley, Winston-Salem *	.867	26	3	10	2	15	3
White, Sean, Myrtle Beach	.933	18	7	21	2	30	4
Wigdahl, Jeffrey, Salem *	1.000	22	1	2	0	3	1
Williams, Aaron, Salem	1.000	27	1	4	0	5	0
Wing, Ryan, Winston-Salem *	.714	5	1	4	2	7	0
Young, Christopher, Lynchburg	1.000	10	2	1	0	3	1

LEAGUE CHAMPIONS

Year	Team	Pct.
1945—	Danville	.681
1946—	Greensboro	.599
	Raleigh (2nd)†	.563
1947—	Burlington	.613
	Raleigh (3rd)†	.574
1948—	Raleigh	.592
	Martinsville (2nd)†	.570
1949—	Danville	.601
	Burlington (4th)†	.500
1950—	Winston-Salem*	.693
1951—	Durham	.600
	Winston-Salem (2nd)†	.583
1952—	Raleigh	.581
	Reidsville (4th)†	.536
1953—	Raleigh	.593
	Danville (2nd)†	.572
1954—	Fayetteville*	.628
1955—	HP-Thomasville	.580
	Danville (2nd)†	.533
1956—	HP-Thomasville	.591
	Fayetteville (4th)§	.523
1957—	Durham	.632
	HP-Thomasville	.622
1958—	Danville	.576
	Burlington (4th)†	.511
1959—	Raleigh	.600
	Wilson (2nd)†	.550
1960—	Greensboro‡	.636
	Burlington	.586
1961—	Wilson	.594
1962—	Durham	.636
	Wilson	.600
	Kinston (2nd)†	.593
1963—	Kinston§	.538
	Greensboro§	.590
	Wilson (2nd)†	.535
1964—	Kinston§	.572
	Winston-Salem§†	.590
1965—	Peninsula§	.597
	Durham§	.580
	Tidewater†	.528
1966—	Kinston§	.547
	Winston-Salem§	.586
	Rocky Mount†	.533
1967—	Durham∞(West.)	.536
	Raleigh (East.)	.542
1968—	Salem (West.)	.607
	Ral-Dur (East.)	.597
	HP-Thom.▲(W.)	.493
1969—	Rocky M (East.)	.569
	Salem (West.)	.542
	Ral-Dur◆(East.)	.560
1970—	Winston-Salem‡	.586
	Burlington	.597
1971—	Peninsula‡	.647
	Kinston	.623
1972—	Salem‡	.657
	Burlington	.632
1973—	Lynchburg	.588
	Winston-Salem‡	.557
1974—	Salem	.671
	Salem	.582
1975—	Rocky Mount	.667
	Rocky Mount	.614
1976—	Winston-Salem	.618
	Winston-Salem	.551
1977—	Lynchburg	.591
	Peninsula‡	.556
1978—	Peninsula	.696
	Lynchburg‡	.614
1979—	Winston-Salem■	.607
1980—	Peninsula‡	.714
	Durham	.600
1981—	Peninsula	.522
	Hagerstown‡	.507
1982—	Alexandria‡	.597
	Durham	.588
1983—	Lynchburg‡	.691
	Winston-Salem	.529
1984—	Lynchburg‡	.645
	Durham	.486
1985—	Lynchburg	.679
	Winston-Salem‡	.417
1986—	Hagerstown	.655
	Winston-Salem‡	.594
1987—	Salem‡	.576
	Kinston	.536
1988—	Kinston§	.629
	Lynchburg	.486
1989—	Durham	.609
	Prince William‡	.522
1990—	Kinston	.652
	Frederick‡	.544
1991—	Kinston‡	.645
	Lynchburg	.482
1992—	Lynchburg	.570
	Peninsula‡	.536
1993—	Wilmington	.532
	Winston-Salem‡	.514
1994—	Wilmington‡	.681
	Winston-Salem	.555
1995—	Wilmington	.601
	Kinston‡	.591
1996—	Wilmington▼	.571
	Kinston	.551
1997—	Kinston	.621
	Lynchburg†	.586
1998—	Wilmington▼	.614
	Winston-Salem	.568
1999—	Kinston	.577
	Myrtle Beach*	.568
	Wilmington*	.568
2000—	Myrtle Beach▼	.629
2001—	Kinston	.636
	Salem▼	.507
2002—	Wilmington	.636
	Lynchburg▼	.621
2003—	Wilmington	.571
	Winston-Salem▼	.514
2004—	Kinston▼	.638
2005—	Frederick▼	.564

*Won championship and four-club playoff. †Won four-club playoff. ‡Won split-season playoff. §League was divided into Eastern, Western divisions. ∞Won eight-club, two-division playoff. ▲Won eight-club, two-division playoff against Raleigh-Durham. ◆Won eight-club, two-division playoff against Burlington. ■Won both halves of split season (no playoffs). ▼League divided into Northern and Southern divisions and played a split-season, won playoffs. *Declared co-champions after final series cancelled due to hurricane.

FLORIDA STATE LEAGUE

LEAGUE OFFICE

President
Chuck Murphy
Address
P.O. Box 349
Daytona Beach, FL 32115
Phone
386-252-7479

Teams (affiliation)
Brevard County Manatees (Brewers)
Clearwater Threshers (Phillies)
Daytona Cubs (Cubs)
Dunedin Blue Jays (Blue Jays)
Fort Myers Miracle (Twins)
Jupiter Hammerheads (Marlins)
Lakeland Tigers (Tigers)

Palm Beach Cardinals (Cardinals)
St. Lucie Mets (Mets)
Sarasota Reds (Reds)
Tampa Yankees (Yankees)
Vero Beach Dodgers (Dodgers)

2005 FINAL STANDINGS

FIRST HALF

EAST DIVISION

Team	W	L	T	Pct.	GB
Vero Beach Dodgers	40	26	-	.606	-
Daytona Cubs	35	32	-	.522	5.5
Jupiter Hammerheads	35	33	-	.515	6
St. Lucie Mets	30	35	-	.462	9.5
Palm Beach Cardinals	30	40	-	.429	12
Brevard County Manatees	26	42	-	.382	15

WEST DIVISION

Team	W	L	T	Pct.	GB
Lakeland Tigers	45	22	-	.672	-
Dunedin Blue Jays	40	28	-	.588	5.5
Fort Myers Miracle	37	27	-	.578	6.5
Sarasota Reds	34	31	-	.523	10
Tampa Yankees	31	34	-	.477	13
Clearwater Threshers	17	50	-	.254	28

SECOND HALF

EAST DIVISION

Team	W	L	T	Pct.	GB
Palm Beach Cardinals	39	31	-	.557	-
Vero Beach Dodgers	37	30	-	.552	.5
Brevard County Manatees	37	31	-	.544	1
St. Lucie Mets	36	33	-	.522	2.5
Daytona Cubs	34	34	-	.500	4
Jupiter Hammerheads	29	38	-	.433	8.5

WEST DIVISION

Team	W	L	T	Pct.	GB
Lakeland Tigers	40	26	-	.606	-
Dunedin Blue Jays	41	29	-	.586	1
Fort Myers Miracle	37	32	-	.536	4.5
Sarasota Reds	31	36	-	.463	9.5
Tampa Yankees	24	44	-	.353	17
Clearwater Threshers	24	45	-	.348	17.5

COMPOSITE

CLUB (AFFILIATE), ABBREV	LAK	DUN	VER	FTM	DAY	PBC	SLU	SAR	JUP	BRE	TAM	CLE	W	L	PCT	GB
Lakeland (Tigers), LAK		7	2	13	5	2	5	9	5	6	16	15	85	48	.639	-
Dunedin (Blue Jays), DUN 11	...	3	7	5	5	5	10	6	4	13	13	82	58	.586	6.5
Vero Beach (Dodgers), VER 6	5	...	5	8	10	9	3	12	7	6	6	77	56	.579	8.0
Fort Myers (Twins), FTM 5	11	3	...	3	4	2	9	3	6	13	15	74	59	.556	11.0
Daytona (Cubs), DAY 1	3	10	5	...	13	8	4	8	9	2	6	69	66	.511	17.0
Palm Beach (Cardinals), PBC 6	3	8	4	5	...	11	4	11	9	5	3	69	71	.493	19.5
St. Lucie (Mets), SLU 3	3	8	4	9	7	...	3	9	10	3	7	66	68	.493	19.5
Sarasota (Reds), SAR 6	8	4	8	3	4	5	...	4	4	7	12	65	67	.492	19.5
Jupiter (Marlins), JUP 3	2	5	5	10	9	9	4	...	11	3	3	64	71	.474	22.0
Brevard County (Brewers), BRE 2	4	9	2	10	9	8	4	7	...	3	5	63	73	.463	23.5
Tampa (Yankees), TAM 3	5	2	3	6	3	5	11	3	5	...	10	56	79	.415	30.0
Clearwater (Phillies), CLE 2	7	2	3	2	5	1	6	3	2	8	...	41	95	.301	45.5

Major league affiliations in parentheses.

PLAYOFFS: Semifinals: Lakeland defeated Dunedin, two games to none, and Palm Beach defeated Vero Beach, two games to one. Finals: Palm Beach defeated Lakeland, three games to two.

REGULAR-SEASON ATTENDANCE: Palm Beach, 98,841. Dunedin, 40,479. Daytona, 127,060. Vero Beach, 55,737. Jupiter, 88,580. Brevard County, 101,847. St. Lucie, 91,382. Fort Myers, 112,272. Sarasota, 28,122. Clearwater, 130,446. Lakeland, 32,912. Tampa, 78,155. All-Star Game (at Clearwater), 5,547. League total, 985,833. Postseason (10 games), 9,276.

MANAGERS: Palm Beach, Ron Warner. Dunedin, Omar Malave. Daytona, Richie Zisk. Vero Beach, Scott Little. Jupiter, Tim Cossins. Brevard County, John Tamargo. St. Lucie, Tim Teufel. Fort Myers, Riccardo Ingram. Sarasota, Edgar Caceres. Clearwater, Greg Legg. Lakeland, Mike Rojas. Tampa, Joe Breeden.

ALL-STAR TEAM: 1B-Andy Wilson, St. Lucie. 2B-Tony Abreu, Vero Beach. 3B-Andy LaRoche, Vero Beach. SS-Chin-lung Hu, Vero Beach. IF-Adam Heether, Brevard County. LF-Adam Lind, Dunedin. CF-Christopher Walker, Daytona. OF-Vincent Blue, Lakeland. OF-Brent Clevlen, Lakeland. C-Robinzon Diaz, Dunedin. C-Danilo Sanchez, Lakeland. DH-Matt Kemp, Vero Beach. SP-Nathan Bumstead, Lakeland. SP-Tim Dillard, Brevard County. SP-Jordan Tata, Lakeland. SP-Carlos Villanueva, Brevard County. Relief Pitcher-Paul Thorp, Tampa. Relief Pitcher-Mark Worrell, Palm Beach. Most Valuable Player-Brent Clevlen, Lakeland. Most Valuable Pitcher-Jordan Tata, Lakeland.

2005 BATTING

TEAM

Team	G	TPA	AB	R	H	TB	2B	3B	HR	RBI	SH	SF	HP	BB	IBB	SO	SB	CS	GDP	LOB	ShO	Avg.	OBP	Slg.
Vero Beach	133	4987	4459	708	1271	1936	233	30	124	647	26	41	61	399	20	852	116	52	98	1959	9	.285	.349	.434
Dunedin	140	5420	4838	751	1375	2043	278	30	110	692	21	41	61	456	20	847	30	20	151	2118	8	.284	.351	.422
Lakeland	133	5112	4548	700	1256	1918	205	35	129	644	25	37	66	435	29	977	166	88	80	1960	2	.276	.345	.422
Daytona	135	4939	4432	602	1160	1788	225	29	115	561	21	44	68	374	19	973	131	67	105	1860	7	.262	.326	.403
Brevard County	136	5018	4519	551	1170	1650	192	48	64	486	45	40	86	327	15	960	104	70	100	1954	11	.259	.318	.365
Jupiter	135	5158	4579	606	1175	1653	212	28	70	542	42	39	63	435	18	1060	148	56	108	2004	8	.257	.327	.361
Fort Myers	133	4853	4298	554	1097	1504	183	28	56	486	46	38	76	395	11	927	123	57	85	1924	12	.255	.326	.350

Team	G	TPA	AB	R	H	TB	2B	3B	HR	RBI	SH	SF	HP	BB	IBB	SO	SB	CS	GDP	LOB	ShO	Avg.	OBP	Slg.
Clearwater	136	5082	4490	566	1140	1655	216	19	87	508	47	37	70	436	15	872	110	61	107	1994	11	.254	.327	.369
St. Lucie	134	5045	4443	641	1129	1820	224	28	137	585	44	34	79	443	28	1209	116	83	81	1864	8	.254	.330	.410
Sarasota	132	4854	4351	570	1087	1626	199	32	92	507	28	39	52	384	12	1104	119	52	69	1917	13	.250	.316	.374
Tampa	135	4963	4429	526	1089	1553	203	30	67	479	16	37	64	415	8	841	96	39	118	2019	11	.246	.317	.351
Palm Beach......	140	5183	4600	594	1124	1669	230	27	87	544	46	27	75	435	18	1061	155	49	95	2014	9	.244	.318	.363

INDIVIDUAL

TOP QUALIFIERS FOR BATTING CHAMPIONSHIP

Minimum 378 plate appearances. *Lefthanded batter. †Switch-hitter.

Player, Team	G	TPA	AB	R	H	TB	2B	3B	HR	RBI	SH	SF	HP	BB	IBB	SO	SB	CS	GDP	Avg.	OBP	Slg.
Abreu, Etanislao, Vero Beach	96	421	394	54	129	178	23	7	4	43	3	4	5	15	1	56	14	10	9	.327	.356	.452
Lind, Adam, Dunedin *	126	554	495	80	155	241	42	4	12	84	0	6	4	49	7	77	2	1	12	.313	.375	.487
Hu, Chin-lung, Vero Beach	116	505	470	80	147	202	29	1	8	56	7	2	7	19	1	40	23	6	6	.313	.347	.430
Anderson, Drew, Brevard County *	129	558	508	69	158	207	17	7	6	62	2	6	3	39	6	95	19	8	7	.311	.360	.407
Kemp, Matthew, Vero Beach	109	454	418	76	128	238	21	4	27	90	1	5	5	25	2	92	23	6	8	.306	.349	.569
Christian, Justin, Tampa	95	416	372	52	114	177	27	6	8	37	4	1	6	33	0	47	38	5	2	.306	.371	.476
Heether, Adam, Brevard County	93	389	338	48	103	152	27	2	6	54	0	4	13	34	2	48	3	1	13	.305	.386	.450
Clevlen, Brent, Lakeland	130	568	494	77	149	239	28	4	18	102	2	2	5	65	8	118	14	5	16	.302	.387	.484
Nicholson, Derek, Lakeland *	119	497	427	78	127	213	24	4	18	66	0	7	4	59	9	77	13	0	5	.297	.382	.499
Blue, Vincent, Lakeland *	124	556	498	67	148	171	17	3	0	50	6	4	1	47	2	84	40	29	10	.297	.356	.343
Tugwell, Marc, Clearwater	110	429	383	52	113	155	21	0	7	43	5	2	10	29	3	57	2	7	10	.295	.358	.405
Diaz, Robinson, Dunedin	100	414	388	47	114	146	17	6	1	65	2	4	5	15	0	28	5	2	11	.294	.325	.376
Smith, David Lawrence, Dunedin	106	435	391	65	115	185	24	2	14	73	0	7	2	35	0	73	4	2	13	.294	.349	.473
Bear, Ryan, Jupiter	129	531	472	76	139	179	25	3	3	46	2	5	7	45	1	72	23	4	12	.294	.361	.379
Dunlap, Cory, Vero Beach *	121	505	430	61	125	171	25	0	7	77	0	7	3	65	2	64	5	2	9	.291	.382	.398
Raglani, John, Vero Beach *	124	491	419	82	121	208	20	5	19	77	0	5	7	60	2	98	9	2	6	.289	.383	.496
Oeltjen, Trent, Fort Myers *	98	395	341	44	98	135	17	4	4	43	5	3	20	26	0	77	21	9	3	.287	.369	.396
De Aza, Alejandro, Jupiter *	123	554	472	75	135	186	24	9	3	37	11	5	8	58	3	87	34	17	8	.286	.370	.394
Randel, Kevin, Jupiter *	114	465	393	59	112	160	19	1	9	50	7	1	6	58	3	95	15	3	11	.285	.384	.407
Wilson, Andrew, St. Lucie	127	540	464	81	132	247	25	3	28	89	0	8	0	68	10	88	8	4	5	.284	.370	.532
Walker, Christopher, Daytona	133	587	526	97	152	219	21	14	6	57	0	1	1	60	21	111	60	21	4	.284	.344	.409

DEPARTMENTAL LEADERS: G—Blalock, 134. AB—Walker, 536. R—Walker, 97. H—Anderson, 158. TB—Wilson, 247. 2B—Lind, 42. 3B—Walker, 14. HR—Wilson, 28. RBI—Clevlen, 102. SH—Tolbert, 15. SF—Moore and Votto, 9. HP—Sollmann, 26. BB—Wilson, 68. IBB—Wilson, 10. SO—Whitrock, 158. SB—Walker, 60. CS—Blue, 29. GIDP—Dopirak, 20. Slg.—Kemp, .569. OBP—Clevlen, .387.

ALL PLAYERS

*Lefthanded batter. †Switch-hitter.

Player, Team	G	TPA	AB	R	H	TB	2B	3B	HR	RBI	SH	SF	HP	BB	IBB	SO	SB	CS	GDP	Avg.	OBP	Slg.
Abercrombie, Reginald, Jupiter	76	321	299	51	82	145	12	3	15	45	2	1	5	14	2	87	19	6	5	.274	.317	.485
Abreu, Etanislao, Vero Beach	96	421	394	54	129	178	23	7	4	43	3	4	5	15	1	56	14	10	9	.327	.356	.452
Alexander, Mark, Vero Beach	1	0	0	0	0	0	0	0	0	0	...	0	0	0	...	0	0	0	0	...	...	...
Allen, Roderick, Tampa	14	42	39	4	11	15	1	0	1	4	0	1	0	2	0	9	1	1	2	.282	.310	.385
Almario-Cabrera, Yosvany, Tampa	50	208	192	25	55	67	7	1	1	18	0	1	2	12	0	31	5	0	8	.286	.333	.349
Anderson, Drew, Brevard County *	129	558	508	69	158	207	17	7	6	62	2	6	3	39	6	95	19	8	7	.311	.360	.407
Andrus, Erold, Tampa †	125	513	461	53	111	154	24	2	5	49	1	3	6	42	2	88	5	3	8	.241	.311	.334
Arlis, Patrick, Jupiter	91	342	305	38	74	105	9	2	6	35	8	4	0	25	1	72	9	1	13	.243	.296	.344
Arnerich, Anthony, Jupiter	29	112	99	8	21	24	3	0	0	14	1	0	3	9	0	29	1	0	1	.212	.297	.242
Arneson, Justin, Fort Myers †	56	198	171	23	34	49	4	1	3	22	0	3	5	19	1	62	6	1	1	.199	.293	.287
Arnold, Eric, Dunedin	100	424	379	70	104	191	28	1	19	72	0	3	5	36	3	108	1	0	10	.274	.343	.504
Arteaga, Felix, Clearwater	1	0	0	0	0	0	0	0	0	0	...	0	0	0	...	0	0	0	0	...	...	...
Arteaga, Joshua, Daytona	5	21	21	3	4	4	0	0	0	1	0	0	0	0	0	2	0	0	2	.190	.190	.190
Batista, Norberto, Jupiter	7	10	9	2	3	4	1	0	0	3	0	0	0	1	0	2	1	0	0	.333	.400	.444
Batista, Wilson, St. Lucie †	61	277	248	33	68	98	7	4	5	22	2	5	2	20	2	37	12	13	5	.274	.327	.395
Bear, Ryan, Jupiter	129	531	472	76	139	179	25	3	3	46	2	5	7	45	1	72	23	4	12	.294	.361	.379
Bellorin, Edwin, Vero Beach	87	329	308	36	84	115	18	2	3	33	1	2	4	14	2	44	1	1	9	.273	.311	.373
Blake, Jupiter	3	9	8	0	1	1	0	0	0	0	0	0	0	1	0	2	0	0	1	.125	.222	.125
Blalock, Jake, Clearwater	134	571	502	50	140	195	22	0	11	65	0	4	5	60	1	100	10	1	15	.279	.359	.388
Blevins, John, Brevard County *	1	3	3	0	1	1	0	0	0	0	0	0	0	0	0	1	0	0	0	.333	.333	.333
Blue, Vincent, Lakeland *	124	556	498	67	148	171	17	3	0	50	6	4	1	47	2	84	40	29	10	.297	.356	.343
Bolivar, Luis, Sarasota †	103	403	366	45	89	122	19	4	2	27	6	2	11	18	3	62	17	4	8	.243	.297	.333
Bowman, Shawn, St. Lucie	87	355	326	44	72	140	15	1	17	53	1	0	6	22	1	110	4	1	8	.221	.282	.429
Boyer, Kyle, Daytona	39	120	111	15	21	34	4	0	3	13	0	0	3	5	2	35	2	0	5	.189	.250	.306
Brady, Joshua, Brevard County	27	101	96	7	14	21	1	0	2	8	0	0	3	2	0	22	1	1	2	.146	.188	.219
Bramasco, Leslie, Clearwater	108	373	323	45	72	104	19	2	3	40	7	4	7	32	1	88	6	3	7	.223	.303	.322
Brinkley, Dante, St. Lucie	54	228	192	36	51	75	5	2	5	24	2	2	8	24	3	64	9	6	3	.266	.367	.391
Brock, Matthew, Jupiter	83	253	231	23	45	68	9	1	4	17	0	2	5	15	0	70	4	6	4	.195	.257	.294
Brown, Gregory, Jupiter	27	69	56	5	11	13	2	0	0	9	1	1	0	11	0	17	0	0	0	.196	.324	.232
Bruce, Cole, Vero Beach	56	199	178	26	44	70	6	1	6	21	2	4	1	14	0	56	6	0	3	.247	.299	.393
Burgos, Jose, Fort Myers	34	114	101	8	17	21	1	0	1	8	0	0	2	11	0	24	2	0	0	.168	.263	.208
Cabrera, Mayke, Vero Beach *	48	155	135	12	37	39	2	0	0	16	0	0	1	19	1	33	0	2	5	.274	.368	.289
Cairo, Miguel, St. Lucie	1	4	4	0	1	1	0	0	0	0	0	0	0	0	0	0	0	0	0	.250	.250	.250
Cameron, Mike, St. Lucie	4	15	10	3	3	5	2	0	0	0	0	0	0	2	3	0	3	0	0	.300	.533	.500
Campana, Wandel, Brevard County	86	334	318	31	86	120	18	2	4	37	4	3	2	7	1	31	0	5	11	.270	.284	.377
Campusano, Jose, Jupiter †	89	320	300	37	83	98	9	3	0	32	5	2	4	9	0	67	13	5	5	.277	.305	.327
Cannon, Rhame, Dunedin *	29	129	112	28	43	93	4	2	14	39	0	0	1	16	2	32	0	1	2	.384	.465	.830
Carroll, Mark, Tampa	9	30	26	3	9	13	1	0	1	2	2	0	0	2	0	3	0	0	1	.346	.393	.500
Carson, Matt, Tampa....................	84	364	321	43	81	125	14	3	8	39	0	4	8	31	0	88	10	2	6	.252	.330	.389
Carter, Joshua, Clearwater	27	114	110	11	24	35	2	0	3	18	0	1	1	2	0	11	1	1	1	.218	.237	.318

Player, Team	G	TPA	AB	R	H	TB	2B	3B	HR	RBI	SH	SF	HP	BB	IBB	SO	SB	CS	GDP	Avg.	OBP	Slg.
Chapman, Travis, Sarasota	13	52	48	4	13	17	1	0	1	6	0	0	0	4	0	5	0	3	0	.271	.327	.354
Chavez, Ozzie, Brevard County †	125	492	451	39	105	146	17	6	4	35	5	1	3	32	1	73	8	9	12	.233	.287	.324
Chiaravalloti, Vito, Dunedin	42	168	146	22	31	52	7	1	4	18	0	0	2	18	0	39	0	0	5	.212	.307	.356
Chirinos, Robinson, Daytona	74	253	231	30	63	90	6	0	7	27	1	2	3	16	0	42	3	4	5	.273	.325	.390
Christian, Justin, Tampa	95	416	372	52	114	177	27	6	8	37	4	1	6	33	0	47	38	5	2	.306	.371	.476
Clements, Zachary, St. Lucie	7	24	23	4	4	5	1	0	0	5	0	0	0	1	0	8	0	0	2	.174	.208	.217
Cleveland, Russell, Lakeland	44	124	113	14	31	44	3	2	2	10	3	0	0	8	0	22	3	1	2	.274	.322	.389
Clevlen, Brent, Lakeland	130	568	494	77	149	239	28	4	18	102	2	2	5	65	8	118	14	5	16	.302	.387	.484
Collins, Kevin, Daytona *	85	338	294	42	78	149	15	1	18	52	0	5	3	36	3	114	0	3	1	.265	.346	.507
Conley, Evan, Sarasota	2	6	6	0	2	2	0	0	0	0	0	0	0	0	0	1	0	0	0	.333	.333	.333
Corona, Reegie, Tampa †	3	14	12	1	0	0	0	0	0	0	0	0	0	2	0	3	0	0	0	.000	.143	.000
Corredor, Nestor, Brevard County	15	52	47	5	13	15	2	0	0	4	0	1	1	3	0	7	0	0	0	.277	.327	.319
Correll, Richard, Clearwater	117	459	415	41	117	178	21	2	12	54	2	3	2	37	0	68	3	7	13	.282	.341	.429
Cortez, Jose, Clearwater †	46	156	139	9	19	24	2	0	1	8	1	1	2	13	0	30	1	1	4	.137	.219	.173
Cota, Carlo, Dunedin	68	311	276	47	84	138	20	2	10	35	1	2	4	28	0	65	0	1	7	.304	.374	.500
Cotto, Pedro, Lakeland *	9	19	17	3	4	4	0	0	0	1	1	0	0	1	0	1	0	0	0	.235	.278	.235
Creighton, Matt, Daytona	27	102	93	10	24	38	5	0	3	10	0	0	4	5	0	14	0	1	3	.258	.324	.409
Cruz, Jose, Tampa-Daytona *	56	187	162	21	30	47	5	0	4	19	2	2	3	18	0	40	6	0	6	.185	.276	.290
Culpepper, Jeffrey, Daytona *	38	124	108	14	37	47	7	0	1	10	2	0	5	9	2	15	1	5	2	.343	.418	.435
Cummins, Daniel, St. Lucie	1	0	0	0	0	0	0	0	0	0	0	0	0	0	...	0	0	0	0	...	...	...
Davidson, Seth, Clearwater †	14	57	48	5	12	16	2	1	0	7	1	2	4	2	0	5	3	1	0	.250	.321	.333
Davidson, Tyler, St. Lucie	39	143	124	14	20	29	3	0	2	8	1	1	5	12	1	46	1	1	2	.161	.261	.234
De Aza, Alejandro, Jupiter *	123	554	472	75	135	186	24	9	3	37	11	5	8	58	3	87	34	17	8	.286	.370	.394
Deevers, Robby, Brevard County	60	187	177	11	30	41	7	2	0	10	5	0	2	3	0	57	4	2	8	.169	.192	.232
De La Cruz, Carlos, Brevard County	36	118	107	4	22	28	3	0	1	12	3	1	3	4	0	34	1	1	2	.206	.252	.262
DeMarco, Mathew, Palm Beach-Jupiter	59	222	204	29	46	52	6	0	0	11	1	0	4	13	2	25	3	0	4	.225	.285	.255
Demontel II, James, Jupiter	1	0	0	0	0	0	0	0	0	0	0	...	0	0	0	0	0	0	0	...	...	...
Denker, Travis, Vero Beach	31	125	108	14	20	29	3	0	2	9	0	0	2	15	0	26	1	2	2	.185	.296	.269
de San Miguel, Allan, Fort Myers	11	39	33	3	8	10	2	0	0	4	0	1	1	4	0	11	0	0	0	.242	.333	.303
Dewitt, Blake, Vero Beach *	8	32	31	4	13	19	3	0	1	7	0	0	0	1	0	3	0	0	0	.419	.438	.613
Diaz, Robinzon, Dunedin	100	414	388	47	114	146	17	6	1	65	2	4	5	15	0	28	5	2	11	.294	.325	.376
Dickerson, Christopher, Sarasota *	119	505	436	68	103	167	17	7	11	43	7	3	6	53	2	124	19	3	2	.236	.325	.383
Diggins, Ben, Brevard County	6	21	18	4	4	6	0	1	0	1	0	0	1	2	0	9	1	0	0	.222	.333	.333
Dopirak, Brian, Daytona	132	553	507	53	119	193	26	0	16	76	0	5	4	37	4	107	1	4	20	.235	.289	.381
Dragicevich, Scott, Dunedin	83	293	264	38	66	92	13	2	3	30	0	1	2	26	1	61	0	0	8	.250	.321	.348
Dryer, Matthew, Palm Beach	121	487	433	58	95	180	20	1	21	76	0	5	4	45	4	130	3	1	10	.219	.296	.416
Dunlap, Cory, Vero Beach *	121	505	430	61	125	171	25	0	7	77	0	7	3	65	2	64	5	2	9	.291	.382	.398
Dunn, Michael, Tampa *	28	102	90	8	15	20	5	0	0	6	0	0	1	11	0	28	2	2	2	.167	.265	.222
Dyson, Colie, Vero Beach *	10	35	31	6	5	6	1	0	0	5	0	1	0	3	0	6	0	0	0	.161	.229	.194
Ehlers, Cody, Tampa *	35	139	129	14	31	50	10	0	3	11	0	0	0	10	1	20	1	1	3	.240	.295	.388
Ellis, Andrew, Vero Beach	57	206	176	27	45	62	8	0	3	22	1	1	6	22	0	26	1	3	3	.256	.356	.352
Ellison, Joshua, Tampa	27	111	101	16	21	25	4	0	0	9	1	1	1	7	0	17	3	2	6	.208	.264	.248
Eure, Jeffrey, Brevard County	130	515	467	64	107	193	31	2	17	66	0	3	13	31	1	140	2	3	5	.229	.294	.413
Evans, Michael, Palm Beach	114	425	385	34	85	127	16	1	8	47	1	3	7	29	1	110	12	6	5	.221	.285	.330
Ezi, Travis, Brevard County †	102	433	389	62	106	149	12	11	3	27	10	3	4	27	0	120	22	11	1	.272	.324	.383
Faison, Vincent, Tampa *	14	65	60	4	23	39	5	4	1	14	0	1	0	4	0	10	5	1	1	.383	.415	.650
Fermin, Angelo, Fort Myers *	35	125	112	14	28	37	5	2	0	10	0	2	4	7	0	25	0	1	2	.250	.312	.330
Festa, Anthony, Brevard County *	12	42	35	3	9	12	0	0	1	4	0	0	2	5	1	3	1	0	1	.257	.381	.343
Figueroa, Juan, Jupiter *	80	324	293	30	76	93	15	1	0	33	0	3	2	26	2	72	3	1	6	.259	.321	.317
Floyd, Michael, Clearwater	7	28	22	3	3	4	1	0	0	2	0	0	2	4	0	3	0	1	0	.136	.321	.182
Fox, Jacob, Daytona	83	309	270	37	76	123	20	0	9	40	1	4	8	26	3	48	5	2	8	.281	.357	.456
Francia, Juan, Lakeland †	60	290	255	39	83	97	5	0	3	29	2	1	5	27	2	34	26	10	1	.325	.399	.380
Garcia, Emmanuel, St. Lucie *	2	9	9	1	2	3	1	0	0	0	0	0	0	0	0	2	0	0	0	.222	.222	.333
Garcia, Yunir, St. Lucie	59	211	170	27	29	50	5	2	4	18	2	1	9	29	0	70	5	0	6	.171	.321	.294
Geiger, Kyle, Fort Myers	81	324	292	34	75	101	8	0	6	33	0	1	7	24	0	55	1	3	12	.257	.327	.346
Gentry, Philip, Sarasota *	31	133	128	14	29	42	7	0	2	13	1	1	0	3	0	22	1	2	1	.227	.242	.328
Gonzalez, Juan, Lakeland †	64	243	219	30	60	77	6	4	1	12	5	1	1	17	0	33	5	5	3	.274	.328	.352
Gorecki, Reid, Palm Beach	64	275	234	38	67	107	18	2	6	41	2	4	3	32	1	55	24	7	5	.286	.374	.457
Graham, Andrew, Lakeland	7	14	14	1	4	4	0	0	0	2	0	0	0	0	0	2	0	0	0	.286	.286	.286
Granato, Anthony, Daytona †	34	114	93	14	21	25	4	0	0	4	1	0	0	20	0	22	9	3	2	.226	.363	.269
Gredvig, Doug, Clearwater	20	81	65	11	16	23	1	0	2	9	0	1	1	14	0	20	0	1	3	.246	.383	.354
Greene, James, Palm Beach	20	92	85	17	23	33	4	0	2	5	0	0	2	5	0	28	6	0	1	.271	.326	.388
Greenwood, Jared, Tampa *	11	42	38	0	4	5	1	0	0	4	0	0	0	4	0	14	0	0	0	.105	.190	.132
Guevara, Orlando, Clearwater †	1	1	1	0	0	0	0	0	0	0	0	0	0	0	0	1	0	0	0	.000	.000	.000
Guillen, Rodolfo, Tampa	100	417	389	51	101	141	14	4	6	39	0	2	7	19	0	70	10	5	12	.260	.305	.362
Haag, Ryan, Tampa *	18	68	56	5	13	16	1	1	0	6	0	0	0	12	0	9	2	2	1	.232	.368	.286
Haerther, Cody, Palm Beach *	47	192	173	29	55	101	8	7	8	30	0	1	1	17	1	31	8	3	4	.318	.380	.584
Hansen, Bryan, Clearwater *	90	376	331	44	88	126	12	1	8	38	0	3	5	37	4	44	0	0	10	.266	.346	.381
Harper, Brett, St. Lucie *	62	264	239	35	67	140	11	1	20	60	0	3	1	21	3	64	0	1	5	.280	.337	.586
Harvey, Ryan, St. Lucie	16	60	55	4	17	20	3	0	0	10	0	0	2	3	0	8	2	1	0	.309	.367	.364
Hathaway, Aaron, St. Lucie	38	156	135	22	42	50	8	0	0	15	3	2	0	16	0	33	3	2	4	.311	.379	.370
Hattig, John, Dunedin †	11	48	44	8	17	20	3	0	0	5	0	1	0	3	0	7	0	0	2	.386	.417	.455
Hayes, Calvin, Palm Beach	51	202	181	23	39	55	7	3	1	16	2	1	5	13	0	44	6	3	2	.215	.285	.304
Heether, Adam, Brevard County	93	389	338	48	103	152	27	2	6	54	0	4	13	34	2	48	3	1	13	.305	.386	.450
Hill, Jamar, St. Lucie	125	514	456	64	115	189	23	3	15	64	5	2	4	47	3	151	13	9	6	.252	.326	.414
Himes, Benjamin, Sarasota *	71	271	244	44	78	130	19	3	9	53	2	3	2	20	2	71	6	1	3	.320	.372	.533
Hoffmann, Jamie, Vero Beach	46	178	166	26	40	53	6	2	1	10	0	1	1	10	0	45	3	1	5	.241	.287	.319
Hoffpauir, Jarrett, Palm Beach	63	265	226	23	58	70	10	1	0	19	5	2	0	32	0	26	11	5	2	.257	.346	.310
Hollingsworth, Josh, Tampa	18	62	60	8	14	26	0	0	4	12	1	0	0	1	0	13	0	0	1	.233	.246	.433
Hu, Chin-lung, Vero Beach	116	505	470	80	147	202	29	1	8	56	7	2	7	19	1	40	23	6	6	.313	.347	.430
Hudson, William, Sarasota †	52	153	136	11	24	30	3	0	1	4	1	0	2	14	0	49	3	3	1	.176	.263	.221

– 515 –

Player, Team	G	TPA	AB	R	H	TB	2B	3B	HR	RBI	SH	SF	HP	BB	IBB	SO	SB	CS	GDP	Avg.	OBP	Slg.
Hughes, Luke, Fort Myers	23	92	84	9	17	22	3	1	0	7	2	3	1	2	0	15	0	0	3	.202	.222	.262
Hunt, Kelly, Lakeland	128	541	501	59	108	188	26	0	18	86	0	8	3	29	2	122	6	10	13	.216	.259	.375
Isaacson, Gregory, Clearwater *	53	138	116	20	30	38	6	1	0	13	4	0	0	18	0	31	2	2	2	.259	.358	.328
Johnson, Jonathan, Daytona	121	448	417	52	109	178	29	5	10	50	2	2	3	24	0	77	12	5	15	.261	.305	.427
Johnston, Clinton, Dunedin *	42	183	158	29	49	71	10	0	4	21	0	1	2	22	0	39	0	0	8	.310	.399	.449
Kaplan, Jonathan, Palm Beach	15	59	53	8	10	15	2	0	1	3	0	0	2	4	0	12	3	2	0	.189	.271	.283
Kartler, Bryce, Tampa *	43	149	122	13	23	28	2	0	1	9	1	1	2	23	1	30	4	4	1	.189	.324	.230
Kelly, Kenny, Sarasota	3	13	12	1	2	3	1	0	0	0	0	0	0	1	0	2	0	0	0	.167	.231	.250
Kemp, Matthew, Vero Beach	109	454	418	76	128	238	21	4	27	90	1	5	5	25	2	92	23	6	8	.306	.349	.569
Kirkland, Kody, Lakeland	125	497	443	78	118	208	24	9	16	65	0	2	16	36	1	102	12	3	6	.266	.342	.470
Klemm, Christopher, Clearwater *	14	50	47	5	9	10	1	0	0	1	0	0	2	1	0	8	1	1	3	.191	.240	.213
Knoedler, Justin, Lakeland	40	107	89	18	25	31	6	0	0	9	1	1	0	16	1	21	3	1	1	.281	.387	.348
Koutnik, Jared, Tampa	33	122	116	7	28	39	2	0	3	19	1	1	1	3	0	26	1	2	3	.241	.264	.336
LaRoche, Andy, Vero Beach	63	271	249	54	83	162	14	1	21	51	0	2	1	19	3	38	6	1	6	.333	.380	.651
Larsen, Andrew, Daytona	4	13	12	1	4	9	1	2	0	3	0	0	0	1	0	4	3	1	0	.333	.385	.750
Laurin, Dominique, Vero Beach	16	40	34	3	4	6	2	0	0	0	3	0	0	3	0	18	0	0	2	.118	.189	.176
Laya, Rayner, Palm Beach	75	287	267	29	68	82	9	1	1	26	5	1	1	13	0	21	10	4	14	.255	.291	.307
Lee, Seung Hak, Clearwater	1	0	0	0	0	0	0	0	0	0	0	0	0	0	...	0	0	0	0	...	...	...
Leger, Jose, Fort Myers	51	200	179	18	50	63	10	0	1	24	1	5	2	13	0	39	3	3	4	.279	.327	.352
Leon, Carlos, Clearwater	24	88	77	11	21	22	1	0	0	3	3	0	3	5	0	13	6	3	0	.273	.341	.286
Lewis, Richard, Daytona	3	13	11	1	2	5	1	1	0	0	0	0	0	2	0	6	0	0	0	.182	.308	.455
Linares, Miguel, Lakeland	1	0	0	0	0	0	0	0	0	0	0	0	0	0	...	0	0	0	0	...	...	...
Lind, Adam, Dunedin *	126	554	495	80	155	241	42	4	12	84	0	6	4	49	7	77	2	1	12	.313	.375	.487
Lindsey, John, Jupiter	30	111	96	13	21	32	8	0	1	16	0	0	4	11	0	22	0	0	5	.219	.324	.333
Littleton, Brandon, Clearwater †	80	309	268	32	69	88	8	4	1	24	9	0	1	31	1	50	20	9	2	.257	.337	.328
Lombardi, Michael, Clearwater †	4	8	7	0	0	0	0	0	0	0	0	0	0	1	0	3	0	0	0	.000	.125	.000
Made, Hector, Tampa	43	184	170	17	37	44	5	1	0	22	0	2	0	12	0	27	1	1	4	.218	.266	.259
Maldonado, Brahiam, St. Lucie	6	21	16	4	5	6	1	0	0	3	2	0	1	2	0	6	0	0	0	.313	.421	.375
Maldonado Oquendo, Ivan, St. Lucie	1	0	0	0	0	0	0	0	0	0	0	0	0	0	...	0	0	0	0	...	...	...
Malo, Jonathan, St. Lucie	5	16	14	1	2	3	1	0	0	2	0	0	0	2	0	4	1	0	0	.143	.250	.214
Marcelli, Brandon, Palm Beach	18	64	58	4	10	12	2	0	0	4	1	0	2	3	0	13	0	1	2	.172	.238	.207
Martin, Brian, Palm Beach	60	250	222	36	66	97	16	0	5	38	2	2	2	22	1	67	6	1	6	.297	.363	.437
Martinez, Joan, St. Lucie †	2	5	4	1	1	1	0	0	0	1	0	0	0	1	0	2	0	0	0	.250	.400	.250
Mather, Joseph, Palm Beach	57	225	200	37	55	95	12	2	8	27	3	1	9	12	1	39	4	0	5	.275	.342	.475
Mauer, Donald, Fort Myers	19	76	69	11	22	25	3	0	0	8	2	0	2	3	0	8	0	0	2	.319	.365	.362
Mayorson, Manuel, Dunedin	121	481	441	59	118	160	23	5	3	48	11	2	3	24	0	34	7	3	17	.268	.309	.363
McCoy, Michael, Palm Beach	86	332	282	47	76	96	13	2	1	27	8	3	3	36	1	56	18	3	2	.270	.355	.340
McCraw, Sean, St. Lucie *	1	3	2	1	1	1	0	0	0	0	0	0	0	1	0	1	0	0	0	.500	.667	.500
McKinney, Garth, Lakeland	115	439	401	70	97	189	17	3	23	71	0	3	9	26	0	151	16	5	6	.242	.301	.471
McQuade, Anthony, Palm Beach †	32	115	100	17	25	39	4	2	2	13	1	2	3	9	1	21	4	0	2	.250	.325	.390
Medina, Rodney, Dunedin †	45	179	169	22	46	59	8	1	1	20	2	0	2	6	0	16	1	3	2	.272	.305	.349
Medlin, Clifton, Brevard County	48	187	162	24	41	68	9	0	6	27	1	2	4	18	0	52	0	1	3	.253	.339	.420
Mejia, Gilberto, Lakeland †	64	284	260	32	69	87	8	2	2	21	2	0	3	19	0	64	10	8	5	.265	.323	.335
Mejia, Jorge, Sarasota	29	104	90	13	23	28	3	1	0	5	2	0	1	11	0	25	7	2	2	.256	.343	.311
Mendez, Deivi, Tampa	27	91	82	6	19	22	3	0	0	8	1	1	0	7	0	16	0	1	7	.232	.289	.268
Mendez, Jose, Palm Beach	1	3	3	0	0	0	0	0	0	0	0	0	0	0	0	1	0	0	0	.000	.000	.000
Merchan, Jesus, Fort Myers	12	45	39	5	7	8	1	0	0	7	1	0	1	4	0	2	0	2	0	.179	.273	.205
Messner, Nathan, Jupiter	4	6	4	1	0	0	0	0	0	0	0	0	0	2	0	2	1	0	0	.000	.333	.000
Mientkiewicz, Doug, St. Lucie *	8	34	27	3	7	11	4	0	0	2	0	0	0	7	4	7	0	0	0	.259	.412	.407
Milledge, Lastings, St. Lucie	62	269	232	48	70	97	15	0	4	22	4	1	13	19	1	41	18	13	5	.302	.385	.418
Mitchell, Lee, Jupiter	126	532	468	65	106	177	27	1	14	60	2	3	8	51	2	142	4	1	13	.226	.311	.378
Mitchell, Russell, Vero Beach	13	37	33	5	10	14	1	0	1	4	1	1	0	2	0	6	0	0	2	.303	.333	.424
Molina, Angel, Jupiter	120	514	456	59	119	175	23	3	9	84	0	7	3	48	2	89	7	7	12	.261	.331	.384
Molina, Felix, Fort Myers †	46	172	155	23	40	53	9	2	0	9	0	0	1	16	0	16	1	2	3	.258	.331	.342
Monegan, Anthony, Palm Beach *	24	100	95	8	18	24	4	1	0	5	1	0	0	4	0	21	4	0	1	.189	.222	.253
Moni-Erigbali, Victor, Clearwater	16	61	55	7	11	17	0	0	2	7	0	0	1	5	0	14	0	1	3	.200	.279	.309
Moore, Robert, Jupiter *	37	165	146	15	42	52	8	1	0	21	1	0	2	16	1	30	6	3	1	.288	.366	.356
Moore, Scott, Daytona *	128	536	466	77	131	226	31	2	20	82	0	9	6	55	4	134	22	7	7	.281	.358	.485
Moran, Javon, Sarasota	53	231	210	35	69	83	4	2	2	23	1	2	4	14	0	32	13	7	3	.329	.378	.395
Moses, Matthew, Fort Myers *	73	298	265	37	81	120	16	1	7	42	0	2	3	28	6	59	13	4	3	.306	.376	.453
Moss, Steve, Brevard County	118	488	442	62	124	184	19	7	9	51	3	6	1	36	1	113	18	12	10	.281	.332	.416
Moss, Timothy, Clearwater	123	536	469	87	126	217	30	5	17	61	4	4	14	45	1	129	28	10	8	.269	.348	.463
Motooka, Rafael, Sarasota	10	32	30	2	6	9	0	0	1	2	0	0	0	2	0	5	0	0	1	.200	.250	.300
Motte, Jason, Palm Beach	40	128	122	7	21	34	4	0	3	10	2	0	0	4	0	41	1	0	3	.172	.198	.279
Murray, Joshua, Brevard County	5	20	18	6	8	8	0	0	0	0	0	0	0	2	0	4	0	0	0	.444	.500	.444
Nichols, Leslie, Clearwater	35	130	113	8	21	24	3	0	0	7	0	1	0	16	0	24	0	0	8	.186	.285	.212
Nicholson, Derek, Lakeland *	119	497	427	78	127	213	24	4	18	66	0	7	4	59	9	77	13	0	5	.297	.382	.499
Nixon, Michael, Vero Beach	23	78	65	13	15	26	5	0	2	11	1	0	1	11	0	21	1	2	1	.231	.351	.400
Norman, Zachary, Clearwater	72	265	241	28	54	85	16	0	5	28	4	1	3	16	1	61	1	3	3	.224	.280	.353
Nunez, Luis, Tampa	1	5	5	0	2	3	1	0	0	0	0	0	0	0	0	2	1	0	0	.400	.400	.600
Ochoa, Blake, Jupiter	1	1	1	0	0	0	0	0	0	0	0	0	0	0	0	0	0	0	0	.000	.000	.000
Oeltjen, Trent, Fort Myers *	98	395	341	44	98	135	17	4	4	43	5	3	20	26	1	77	21	9	3	.287	.369	.396
Olmstead, Walter, Sarasota †	36	130	123	8	30	48	4	1	4	16	0	2	0	5	0	37	1	0	4	.244	.269	.390
O'Toole, Paul, Daytona *	55	188	164	23	45	63	7	1	3	19	1	5	4	14	0	40	1	3	3	.274	.337	.384
Padilla, Jorge, Clearwater	14	64	59	9	18	22	4	0	0	6	0	0	2	3	0	7	1	0	1	.305	.359	.373
Pagnozzi, Matthew, Palm Beach	61	211	187	14	36	50	10	1	0	18	2	0	2	20	1	49	3	2	6	.193	.278	.267
Palmisano, Louis, Brevard County	118	475	432	47	110	155	16	7	5	49	1	3	5	34	0	65	3	1	19	.255	.314	.359
Parker, Tyler, Palm Beach	93	368	325	46	87	140	20	3	9	54	2	0	5	36	0	102	15	3	4	.268	.350	.431
Patrick, Brian, Dunedin †	53	201	174	29	51	65	11	0	1	15	0	2	1	24	0	27	0	0	7	.293	.378	.374
Pattee, Benjamin, Fort Myers	22	92	81	17	27	32	1	2	0	9	0	0	1	10	0	9	6	1	2	.333	.413	.395
Paul, Matthew, Vero Beach	4	8	8	0	0	0	0	0	0	0	0	0	0	0	0	3	0	0	0	.000	.000	.000

Player, Team	G	TPA	AB	R	H	TB	2B	3B	HR	RBI	SH	SF	HP	BB	IBB	SO	SB	CS	GDP	Avg.	OBP	Slg.
Paul, Xavier, Vero Beach *	85	330	288	42	71	113	15	3	7	41	4	2	4	32	2	81	1	5	3	.247	.328	.392
Pena, Ramiro, Tampa †	23	86	73	11	18	27	4	1	1	6	2	2	0	9	0	12	1	0	4	.247	.321	.370
Perez, Miguel, Sarasota	80	312	291	36	78	101	11	0	4	33	1	3	1	16	1	63	7	1	3	.268	.305	.347
Perodin, Ronald, Fort Myers *	103	365	318	41	72	81	9	0	0	21	8	2	5	32	0	56	13	6	5	.226	.305	.255
Peterson, Brock, Fort Myers	119	485	424	49	106	170	22	3	12	60	0	6	9	46	1	102	1	2	18	.250	.332	.401
Phillips, Kyle, Fort Myers *	83	315	278	20	64	84	12	1	2	32	1	3	2	31	2	47	2	0	8	.230	.309	.302
Piazza, Anthony, St. Lucie	33	102	93	12	21	28	4	0	1	4	1	0	0	8	0	24	2	0	3	.226	.287	.301
Piepkorn, Jeremiah, Sarasota	27	100	89	12	20	37	2	3	3	13	0	2	1	8	0	13	1	2	1	.225	.290	.416
Plumley, Grant, Tampa	43	157	140	18	35	40	3	1	0	15	0	4	3	10	0	22	0	0	6	.250	.306	.286
Plummer, Jarod, Vero Beach	1	0	0	0	0	0	0	0	0	0	0	0	0	0	...	0	0	0	0	...	...	...
Plumsky, Richard, Clearwater	6	15	13	1	3	5	2	0	0	0	1	0	0	1	0	6	0	0	1	.231	.286	.385
Psomas, William, St. Lucie	34	135	118	15	36	49	10	0	1	15	2	0	0	15	0	29	1	1	4	.305	.383	.415
Quiroz, Guillermo, Dunedin	11	43	38	4	9	16	1	0	2	6	0	0	3	2	0	8	0	0	1	.237	.326	.421
Raglani, John, Vero Beach *	124	491	419	82	121	208	20	5	19	77	0	5	7	60	2	98	9	2	6	.289	.383	.496
Ragsdale, William, St. Lucie	68	312	273	51	71	133	16	8	10	38	1	1	4	33	0	94	8	7	0	.260	.347	.487
Randel, Kevin, Jupiter *	114	465	393	59	112	160	19	1	9	50	7	1	6	58	3	95	15	3	11	.285	.384	.407
Reiman, Joey, Dunedin	77	322	282	39	83	116	16	1	5	36	1	1	5	33	1	71	1	3	12	.294	.377	.411
Reynolds, Wilton, Lakeland	15	34	34	3	7	12	5	0	0	4	0	0	0	0	0	13	1	1	2	.206	.206	.353
Rich, Dominic, Palm Beach *	3	9	8	0	1	1	0	0	0	0	0	0	0	1	0	1	0	0	0	.125	.222	.125
Richie, Anthony, Daytona	78	279	257	29	72	102	18	0	4	27	1	5	1	15	1	45	1	1	4	.280	.317	.397
Rios, Kevin, St. Lucie	94	351	332	33	84	119	18	1	5	35	1	3	4	11	0	82	2	4	7	.253	.283	.358
Rivera, Ruben, Tampa	6	19	17	2	2	2	0	0	0	1	0	0	0	2	0	6	0	0	0	.118	.211	.118
Roa, Joel, Lakeland	1	0	0	0	0	0	0	0	0	0	...	0	0	0	...	0	0	0	0	...	...	...
Roberts, Ryan, Dunedin	42	192	164	33	47	83	9	0	9	35	0	2	2	24	0	27	6	1	5	.287	.380	.506
Robles, Luis, Tampa	9	23	23	2	4	4	0	0	0	1	0	0	0	0	0	6	0	0	0	.174	.174	.174
Rodland, Eric, Lakeland *	72	258	230	33	64	95	12	2	5	28	1	2	3	22	2	42	8	5	4	.278	.346	.413
Rodriguez, Carlos, Clearwater †	88	334	293	39	69	89	14	0	2	21	5	2	5	29	1	46	14	7	8	.235	.313	.304
Rohan, James, Vero Beach	70	251	223	33	61	82	12	0	3	33	1	3	4	20	2	20	6	3	13	.274	.340	.368
Rohleder, Andrew, Jupiter	87	297	271	25	58	83	13	0	4	27	0	5	4	17	0	70	5	2	6	.214	.266	.306
Rojas, Carlos, Daytona	111	447	398	47	97	103	6	0	0	29	6	2	6	35	0	68	4	7	9	.244	.313	.259
Rojas, Thomas, Tampa	81	307	272	34	75	105	13	1	5	35	0	3	6	26	0	60	0	1	12	.276	.349	.386
Rojo, Billy Garrison, Sarasota	2	6	6	0	1	1	0	0	0	0	0	0	0	0	0	3	0	0	0	.167	.167	.167
Rosenthal, Benjamin, Palm Beach *	8	21	19	3	3	3	0	0	0	0	0	0	0	2	0	1	1	0	1	.158	.238	.158
Ruggiano, Justin, Vero Beach	71	281	242	47	75	125	15	4	9	37	0	1	9	28	2	65	16	5	6	.310	.400	.517
Ruiz, Alvaro, Sarasota *	54	222	186	40	58	81	10	2	3	24	0	1	2	33	0	20	17	2	5	.312	.419	.435
Russ, Ryan, Vero Beach †	16	56	53	7	14	18	4	0	0	4	1	0	0	2	0	11	0	1	0	.264	.291	.340
Ryan, Brendan, Palm Beach	49	207	188	29	57	77	17	0	1	16	4	0	0	15	0	20	8	1	4	.303	.355	.410
Salas, Francisco, Daytona	78	281	254	32	67	118	17	2	10	36	4	3	6	14	0	42	1	0	10	.264	.314	.465
Sanchez, Danilo, Lakeland	103	400	349	58	99	183	18	0	22	68	0	5	7	38	1	52	0	1	5	.284	.361	.524
Santiago, Benito, St. Lucie	3	10	9	1	3	4	1	0	0	1	0	0	0	1	0	0	0	0	2	.333	.400	.444
Santor, Johnathon, Palm Beach †	98	355	321	30	70	111	18	1	7	35	1	0	6	27	1	92	1	3	4	.218	.291	.346
Schade, Ryan, Jupiter	28	52	45	3	10	11	1	0	0	1	1	0	0	6	0	11	1	0	1	.222	.314	.244
Schneider, John, Dunedin	22	71	56	8	18	27	3	0	2	10	1	1	3	10	1	16	0	0	1	.321	.443	.482
Schramek, Mark, Sarasota *	118	459	416	52	89	147	23	1	11	51	0	3	3	37	2	143	5	0	5	.214	.281	.353
Schutzenhofer, Andrew, Palm Beach *	57	238	191	29	49	55	6	0	0	13	3	2	13	29	4	32	2	1	7	.257	.387	.288
Segovia, Zachary, Clearwater	1	0	0	0	0	0	0	0	0	0	...	0	0	0	...	0	0	0	0	...	...	...
Sellier, Brian, Clearwater *	99	419	379	46	101	171	28	3	12	50	1	8	0	29	2	51	11	2	5	.266	.313	.451
Sena, Emmanuel, Dunedin †	3	11	8	1	1	1	0	0	0	0	0	0	1	2	0	3	0	1	1	.125	.364	.125
Serfass, Jacob, Brevard County *	10	34	31	3	4	5	1	0	0	1	0	0	0	3	0	16	0	0	0	.129	.206	.161
Shafer, Adam, Clearwater *	1	0	0	0	0	0	0	0	0	0	0	0	0	0	0	0	0	0	0	...	...	...
Skelton, James, Lakeland *	1	1	1	0	0	0	0	0	0	0	0	0	0	0	0	1	0	0	0	.000	.000	.000
Slack, Jonathan, St. Lucie *	77	303	275	33	71	97	15	1	3	24	3	1	0	24	0	52	14	5	2	.258	.317	.353
Smith, David Lawrence, Dunedin *	106	435	391	65	115	185	24	2	14	73	0	7	2	35	0	73	4	2	13	.294	.349	.473
Smith, Kyle, Sarasota	72	254	219	20	48	73	8	1	5	20	1	2	5	27	0	92	2	3	4	.219	.316	.333
Smolarski, Freddy, Jupiter	1	4	4	0	1	1	0	0	0	0	0	0	0	0	0	0	0	0	0	.250	.250	.250
Snyder, Michael, Dunedin *	48	195	177	25	40	56	4	0	4	20	0	0	1	17	2	51	1	0	4	.226	.297	.316
Sollmann, Steven, Brevard County	127	517	430	61	117	131	12	1	0	34	11	6	26	44	1	60	21	15	5	.272	.370	.305
Sosa, Juan, Clearwater	1	2	2	0	0	0	0	0	0	0	0	0	0	0	0	1	0	0	0	.000	.000	.000
Span, Keiunta, Fort Myers *	49	212	186	38	63	75	3	3	1	19	2	1	1	22	0	25	13	4	3	.339	.410	.403
Sprowl, Jon, Tampa *	63	216	184	19	42	59	7	2	2	22	0	1	4	27	0	29	1	2	6	.228	.338	.321
Stewart, Caleb, St. Lucie	17	70	56	12	16	31	6	0	3	7	3	1	3	7	0	13	3	1	0	.286	.388	.554
Sulbaran, Orlando, Sarasota	4	13	11	0	1	2	1	0	0	0	0	0	0	2	0	2	0	0	0	.091	.231	.182
Taylor, Samuel, Fort Myers †	72	299	262	37	67	81	10	2	0	23	6	2	1	28	0	34	10	9	6	.256	.328	.309
Tejeda, Ferdin, Tampa	9	34	29	5	6	9	3	0	0	4	0	2	0	3	0	8	0	0	2	.207	.265	.310
Thome, Jim, Clearwater *	5	18	12	2	4	7	0	0	1	3	0	0	0	6	0	1	0	0	0	.333	.556	.583
Thompson, Andrew, Fort Myers	4	14	13	2	4	5	1	0	0	1	0	0	0	1	0	4	0	0	0	.308	.357	.385
Tiburcio, Hector, Sarasota †	116	430	400	56	104	149	13	4	8	42	3	2	1	23	0	89	12	9	7	.259	.300	.372
Tierce, Jonathan, Tampa *	20	82	68	9	14	22	3	1	1	7	1	0	1	12	1	13	1	0	0	.206	.333	.324
Tingler, Jayce, Dunedin *	121	538	465	67	123	148	16	3	1	28	3	4	13	53	2	31	2	2	16	.265	.353	.318
Tolbert, Christopher, Fort Myers †	111	472	417	55	111	152	20	6	3	46	15	2	3	35	1	80	11	4	3	.266	.326	.365
Toops, Brady, Palm Beach *	25	89	76	6	12	14	2	0	0	8	1	0	1	11	0	18	3	1	2	.158	.273	.184
Tousa, Scott, Lakeland *	59	240	203	40	63	76	6	2	1	20	2	1	9	25	1	39	8	4	4	.310	.408	.374
Tucker, Michael, Jupiter	12	43	35	7	8	16	2	0	2	5	0	0	0	8	0	7	0	0	1	.229	.372	.457
Tugwell, Marc, Clearwater	110	429	383	52	113	155	21	0	7	43	5	2	10	29	3	57	2	7	10	.295	.358	.405
Turay, Alhaji, St. Lucie	42	163	145	15	28	47	7	0	4	13	5	0	4	7	0	54	4	6	2	.193	.250	.324
Urgelles, Jeffrey, Sarasota	63	229	202	19	45	65	14	0	2	23	1	3	6	17	0	40	0	1	3	.223	.298	.322
Urick, John, Tampa *	94	380	340	38	81	139	23	1	11	46	0	1	7	32	2	56	0	0	5	.238	.316	.409
Van Iderstine, Ben, Brevard County	13	52	50	1	8	8	0	0	0	4	0	1	0	1	0	10	0	0	1	.160	.173	.160
Vavao, Jason, Sarasota	67	267	237	26	56	92	16	1	6	26	1	1	4	24	0	82	4	4	7	.236	.316	.388
Verbryke, Eric, Tampa *	12	49	42	5	8	12	1	0	1	2	0	1	1	4	0	9	0	2	2	.190	.271	.286
Votto, Joseph, Sarasota *	124	529	464	64	119	197	23	2	17	83	1	9	3	52	2	122	4	5	9	.256	.330	.425

Player, Team	G	TPA	AB	R	H	TB	2B	3B	HR	RBI	SH	SF	HP	BB	IBB	SO	SB	CS	GDP	Avg.	OBP	Slg.
Walker, Christopher, Daytona	133	587	536	97	152	219	21	14	6	57	0	1	9	41	1	111	60	21	4	.284	.344	.409
Walsh, Nick, Tampa *	26	106	88	9	20	23	0	0	1	5	0	1	1	16	1	13	4	2	1	.227	.349	.261
Watts, Derran, St. Lucie	28	115	97	14	26	34	4	2	0	14	3	0	4	11	0	19	3	4	1	.268	.366	.351
Waugh, Jason, Dunedin	21	80	75	12	23	35	12	0	0	10	0	3	0	2	1	10	0	0	3	.307	.313	.467
Weston, Gordon, Daytona *	7	21	19	5	8	15	2	1	1	6	0	0	1	1	0	2	0	0	1	.421	.476	.789
Westphal, Joshua, Daytona	17	41	38	4	4	4	0	0	0	1	0	0	0	3	0	15	0	0	0	.105	.171	.105
Whealy, Blake, St. Lucie	88	333	292	29	62	105	13	0	10	36	3	3	7	28	0	96	3	4	9	.212	.294	.360
Whitrock, Scott, Fort Myers	111	413	379	56	84	151	22	0	15	50	3	1	5	25	0	158	25	5	5	.222	.278	.398
Whittaker, Timothy, Dunedin	39	148	136	18	38	48	7	0	1	22	0	1	0	11	0	24	0	0	4	.279	.331	.353
Williams, Simon, Palm Beach	20	75	69	6	18	26	2	0	2	8	0	0	1	5	0	18	1	2	2	.261	.320	.377
Willingham, Josh, Jupiter	2	10	9	1	2	3	1	0	0	1	0	0	1	0	0	2	0	0	0	.222	.300	.333
Wilson, Andrew, St. Lucie	127	540	464	81	132	247	25	3	28	89	0	8	0	68	10	88	8	4	5	.284	.370	.532
Wilson, Brandon, St. Lucie	2	3	3	0	2	2	0	0	0	0	0	0	0	0	0	0	0	0	0	.667	.667	.667
Zamojc, Mitchell, Fort Myers *	30	108	99	12	22	29	4	0	1	8	0	1	0	8	0	19	1	1	2	.222	.278	.293
Zamora, Hector, Tampa *	87	324	282	39	68	98	19	1	3	28	1	2	6	33	0	66	0	0	11	.241	.331	.348

PLAYERS WITH TWO OR MORE TEAMS

Player, Team	G	TPA	AB	R	H	TB	2B	3B	HR	RBI	SH	SF	HP	BB	IBB	SO	SB	CS	GDP	Avg.	OBP	Slg.
Cruz, Jose, Tampa	9	36	30	5	4	4	0	0	0	1	0	1	1	4	0	10	0	0	2	.133	.250	.133
Cruz, Jose, Daytona	47	151	132	16	26	43	5	0	4	18	2	1	2	14	0	30	6	0	4	.197	.282	.326
DeMarco, Mathew, Palm Beach *	30	109	97	16	20	25	5	0	0	5	0	0	3	9	1	12	1	0	1	.206	.294	.258
DeMarco, Mathew, Jupiter *	29	113	107	13	26	27	1	0	0	6	1	0	1	4	1	13	2	0	3	.243	.277	.252

GRAND SLAMS—A. Raglani, 3; B. Himes, 2; T. Abreu, E. Arnold, E. Bellorin, S. Bowman, J. Brady, C. Cannon, M. Dryer, C. Dunlap, J. Fox, B. Hansen, M. Kemp, J. Koutnik, A. LaRoche, B. Martin, J. Mather, R. Medina, T. Moss, T. Oeltjen, T. Parker, X. Paul, K. Phillips, I. Salas, M. Schramek, M. Snyder, H. Tiburcio, J. Votto, C. Walker, A. Wilson, 1 each.

AWARDED FIRST BASE ON CATCHER'S INTERFERENCE—V. Chiaravalloti 2 (A. de San Miguel, K. Geiger); B. Sellier 2 (J. Reiman, M. Perez); A. Turay 2 (J. Urgelles, P. Arlis); Y. Almario-Cabrera (C. Medlin); E. Arnold (M. Tugwell); J. Eure (Z. Norman); J. Ruggiano (L. Palmisano); D. Sanchez (J. Motte); E. Verbryke (K. Phillips).

2005 PITCHING

TEAM

Team	W	L	Pct.	ERA	G	CG	ShO	Sv.	IP	H	TBF	R	ER	HR	SH	SF	HB	BB	IBB	SO	WP	Bk.
Fort Myers	74	59	.556	3.35	133	10	13	34	1140.1	1077	4820	509	425	85	28	29	54	395	6	1003	62	17
Lakeland	85	48	.639	3.37	133	8	11	38	1181	1095	4956	514	442	84	43	34	67	400	26	934	77	6
Dunedin	82	58	.586	3.56	140	0	9	28	1227.2	1229	5266	607	486	93	35	35	72	392	15	1013	73	11
Brevard County	63	73	.463	3.65	136	8	10	32	1182.1	1080	4963	563	480	101	31	31	68	393	17	1056	90	14
Sarasota	65	67	.492	3.84	132	2	5	33	1137.2	1141	4917	597	485	79	24	32	69	417	14	987	66	17
Palm Beach	69	71	.493	3.94	140	3	14	40	1213.1	1234	5207	635	531	77	48	35	82	402	9	864	82	13
Daytona	69	66	.511	3.97	135	4	12	33	1159.2	1180	4997	602	511	89	34	29	48	423	35	1080	70	12
Vero Beach	77	56	.579	4.12	133	3	10	34	1139.2	1096	4909	586	522	109	30	37	62	473	11	1062	71	8
St. Lucie	66	68	.493	4.27	134	5	10	29	1166.2	1205	5055	641	554	105	29	39	92	351	24	901	65	13
Jupiter	64	71	.474	4.39	135	2	6	38	1201	1231	5262	677	586	96	40	56	72	454	7	1019	77	16
Tampa	56	79	.415	4.44	135	1	8	30	1154	1170	4998	650	569	91	33	52	61	382	24	936	58	12
Clearwater	41	95	.301	5.26	136	3	1	20	1168.1	1335	5264	788	683	129	32	45	74	452	25	828	79	8

INDIVIDUAL

TOP QUALIFIERS FOR EARNED-RUN AVERAGE TITLE

Minimum 112 innings. *Lefthanded pitcher.

Pitcher, Team	W	L	Pct.	ERA	G	GS	CG	ShO	GF	Sv.	IP	H	TBF	R	ER	HR	SH	SF	HB	BB	IBB	SO	WP	Bk.
Villanueva, Carlos, Brevard County	8	1	.889	2.32	21	21	0	0	0	0	112.1	78	438	31	29	11	0	2	3	32	0	124	8	4
Dillard, Timothy, Brevard County	12	10	.545	2.48	28	28	5	2	0	0	185.1	150	735	64	51	9	5	7	13	31	0	128	13	0
Bumstead, Nathan, Lakeland	12	4	.750	2.58	25	25	2	0	0	0	160.2	136	665	61	46	11	2	5	4	58	2	111	10	0
Harben, Adam, Fort Myers	10	5	.667	2.66	25	25	2	2	0	0	135.1	102	561	52	40	6	3	1	5	62	0	119	11	2
Tata, Jordan, Lakeland	13	2	.867	2.79	25	25	2	2	0	0	155.0	138	628	55	48	12	2	1	8	41	1	134	11	1
Mildren, Paul, Jupiter *	10	3	.769	3.08	29	20	0	0	1	0	140.1	115	565	55	48	13	1	8	5	42	0	111	0	0
Clippard, Tyler, Tampa	10	9	.526	3.18	26	25	0	0	1	0	147.1	118	587	56	52	12	2	5	9	34	1	169	5	1
MacLane, Evan, St. Lucie *	8	5	.615	3.20	19	19	1	0	0	0	112.1	96	449	51	40	14	2	3	2	15	0	92	6	1
Muegge, Danny, Vero Beach	8	2	.800	3.38	31	18	0	0	1	0	127.2	124	531	53	48	11	1	3	7	34	0	91	5	1
Romero, Davis, Dunedin *	9	6	.600	3.47	34	18	0	0	4	1	124.2	133	525	60	48	10	3	2	1	34	0	136	5	1
Russ, James, Jupiter	11	8	.579	3.51	27	26	0	0	0	0	161.2	133	657	72	63	7	4	10	12	48	0	143	6	1
Isenberg, John, Dunedin *	12	8	.600	3.54	26	26	0	0	0	0	145.0	147	609	67	57	13	3	4	9	32	0	90	9	1
Tyler, Scott, Fort Myers	7	8	.467	3.95	23	23	0	0	0	0	118.1	106	486	61	52	18	4	2	3	48	0	109	7	2
Cordova, Vincent, St. Lucie	8	9	.471	4.01	25	25	2	2	0	0	141.1	150	596	78	63	14	3	6	9	26	0	110	2	1
Mathieson, Scott, Clearwater	3	8	.273	4.14	23	23	1	0	0	0	121.2	111	504	62	56	17	4	5	5	34	0	118	7	0
MacDonald, Michael, Dunedin	9	6	.600	4.24	25	23	0	0	1	0	127.1	136	549	76	60	4	4	3	13	40	2	87	5	0
Garcia, Jose, Palm Beach	7	5	.583	4.35	30	20	0	0	0	0	134.1	147	579	74	65	11	3	2	12	41	0	122	4	0
Mathes, Alfred, Daytona *	11	8	.579	4.49	24	24	1	0	0	0	132.1	161	580	77	66	9	1	1	5	37	4	97	5	1
Carlsen, Clary, Clearwater	4	7	.364	4.59	32	15	0	0	5	0	115.2	132	520	77	59	7	3	6	5	46	2	56	6	0
Smith, Charles, St. Lucie	4	4	.500	4.94	24	20	0	0	0	0	116.2	129	507	70	64	12	4	7	6	40	3	59	10	0
Pimentel, Julio Cesar, Vero Beach	8	10	.444	5.08	26	24	1	0	0	0	124.0	149	543	79	70	9	3	5	7	43	0	105	13	0

DEPARTMENTAL LEADERS: W—Tata, 13. L—Segovia, 14. Pct.—Villanueva, .889. G—Lewis, 55. GS—Dillard, 28. CG—Dillard, 5. ShO—four pitchers tied with 2. GF—Worrell, 52. Sv.—Worrell, 35. IP—Dillard, 185.1. H—Jones, 171. TBF—Dillard, 740. R—Segovia, 98. ER—Segovia, 89. HR—Segovia and Tyler, 18. SAC—Reed and Moscat, 6. SF—Russ, 10. HB—Segovia, 17. BB—Pelland, 63. IBB—three pitchers tied with 5. SO—Clippard, 169. WP—Baxter, 15. BK—Batista, 7.

ALL PITCHERS

*Lefthanded pitcher.

Pitcher, Team	W	L	Pct.	ERA	G	GS	CG	ShO	GF	Sv.	IP	H	TBF	R	ER	HR	SH	SF	HB	BB	IBB	SO	WP	Bk.
Adamczyk, Tyler, Palm Beach	3	7	.300	6.68	14	13	0	0	0	0	67.1	83	317	57	50	10	0	3	7	32	0	33	7	0
Adames, Geovanny, Sarasota	0	0	.000	38.57	2	0	0	0	0	0	2.1	7	22	11	10	1	0	1	2	4	0	3	1	0

Pitcher, Team	W	L	Pct.	ERA	G	GS	CG	ShO	GF	Sv.	IP	H	TBF	R	ER	HR	SH	SF	HB	BB	IBB	SO	WP	Bk.
Aguilar, Raymond, Jupiter *	1	0	1.000	5.40	1	1	0	0	0	0	5.0	6	23	3	3	0	0	0	0	2	0	2	1	0
Alexander, Mark, Vero Beach	5	4	.556	3.03	52	0	0	0	48	23	65.1	64	278	25	22	6	1	4	1	23	0	91	4	0
Alfonseca, Antonio, Jupiter	0	0	.000	3.00	3	1	0	0	0	0	3.0	3	10	1	1	0	0	0	0	0	0	4	0	0
Alvarez, Juan, Clearwater	0	0	.000	6.75	3	0	0	0	1	0	4.0	5	22	3	3	0	0	0	0	5	0	3	0	1
Alvarez, Oscar, Palm Beach *	3	2	.600	1.80	7	4	0	0	0	0	35.0	30	134	9	7	0	3	0	1	10	0	21	0	0
Anderson, Ryan, Brevard County *	0	1	.000	6.30	6	6	0	0	0	0	10.0	10	48	9	7	1	0	0	0	3	0	17	4	0
Arteaga, Erick, Clearwater	2	4	.333	5.91	32	7	0	0	13	2	77.2	108	362	62	51	6	1	2	3	21	5	28	5	0
Artiles, Carlos, Tampa *	0	1	.000	7.71	9	0	0	0	3	0	9.1	12	46	8	8	1	0	1	4	0	6	1	0
Atlee, Thomas, Daytona	1	3	.250	2.61	20	0	0	0	18	8	20.2	18	86	11	6	1	3	1	0	8	1	15	2	0
Axelson, Joshua, Palm Beach	5	2	.714	4.10	9	9	1	0	0	0	52.2	47	223	27	24	5	0	3	3	19	0	32	3	0
Baez, Federico, Daytona	0	0	.000	3.86	3	0	0	0	0	0	9.1	8	37	4	4	1	0	0	0	3	0	14	1	0
Bailey, Chad, Vero Beach *	0	0	.000	13.06	7	0	0	0	2	0	10.1	19	58	17	15	4	0	0	1	6	0	9	2	0
Baker, Ryan, Jupiter	0	0	.000	1.08	6	0	0	0	3	2	8.1	7	31	1	1	0	0	0	1	0	4	0	0
Baldwin, Ancil, Lakeland	1	1	.500	5.30	12	0	0	0	3	0	18.2	17	82	14	11	0	1	1	3	10	1	13	2	0
Barrack, Jacob, Clearwater	1	1	.500	3.72	7	0	0	0	4	0	9.2	10	42	4	4	1	0	1	0	4	0	11	2	0
Barreto, Joel, Sarasota	3	1	.750	2.45	18	0	0	0	13	5	25.2	16	106	8	7	3	1	1	0	17	1	31	2	0
Basham, Robert, Sarasota	5	2	.714	3.75	10	10	0	0	0	0	50.1	60	205	22	21	3	2	4	1	6	0	42	2	0
Batista, Roberto, Palm Beach	4	2	.667	3.29	43	8	0	0	9	1	101.1	96	422	50	37	3	4	1	10	31	0	36	6	7
Bauer, Gregory, Clearwater	2	6	.250	5.32	24	4	0	0	10	2	45.2	63	217	34	27	3	0	0	2	18	2	32	2	1
Baxter, Allen, Jupiter	0	5	.000	7.15	12	5	0	0	3	0	34.0	52	174	27	27	4	2	0	0	28	1	38	15	3
Beam, Theodore, Tampa	1	1	.500	3.12	12	0	0	0	5	1	17.1	14	72	7	6	2	0	0	0	7	1	27	0	0
Bechtel, Charles, Palm Beach	1	2	.333	7.71	5	4	0	0	0	0	16.1	24	88	20	14	1	0	2	2	13	0	11	1	0
Belson, Gregory, St. Lucie	3	2	.600	5.09	25	2	0	0	8	0	53.0	69	244	31	30	7	0	0	4	17	1	28	2	1
Benson, Kris, St. Lucie	0	0	.000	0.00	1	1	0	0	0	0	3.0	0	10	0	0	0	0	0	1	0	0	4	0	0
Berroa, Yesson, Dunedin	0	2	.000	9.45	9	0	0	0	4	0	13.1	20	67	15	14	2	0	1	2	4	0	9	1	0
Bierd, Randor, Lakeland	1	3	.250	5.66	4	4	0	0	0	0	20.2	22	88	14	13	4	0	0	2	4	0	18	1	0
Blackburn, Robert, Fort Myers	7	5	.583	3.36	15	15	1	0	0	0	93.2	95	381	43	35	5	0	2	5	16	0	55	1	0
Blair, Thomas, Palm Beach *	2	3	.400	6.10	6	6	0	0	0	0	31.0	34	135	21	21	6	0	0	0	12	0	24	0	0
Blasdell, Jared, Clearwater	0	1	.000	7.94	8	0	0	0	3	0	11.1	16	57	14	10	3	1	1	1	9	0	9	1	0
Boehringer, Brian, Tampa	0	0	.000	1.80	2	2	0	0	0	0	5.0	1	16	1	1	0	1	0	0	2	0	2	0	0
Bong, Jung Keun, Sarasota *	0	0	.000	4.50	1	1	0	0	0	0	4.0	4	17	3	2	0	0	0	1	0	1	0	0
Borrell, Daniel, Tampa *	0	0	.000	4.25	6	6	0	0	0	0	29.2	24	118	14	14	1	0	0	3	7	0	21	2	0
Bostick II, Adam, Jupiter *	4	5	.444	3.84	17	17	0	0	0	0	91.1	95	397	47	39	7	2	5	4	36	0	94	5	1
Bott, Glenn, Vero Beach *	0	2	.000	5.08	14	3	0	0	3	0	28.1	24	134	17	16	3	0	0	1	24	1	36	2	0
Bramasco, Leslie, Clearwater	0	0	.000	6.75	2	0	0	0	2	0	1.1	2	7	1	1	0	0	0	1	0	3	0	0
Brandenburg, Adam, Jupiter *	0	1	.000	2.66	7	2	0	0	1	0	20.1	20	91	11	6	0	4	3	1	10	0	16	1	2
Brumit, Mathew, Tampa	1	2	.333	5.59	20	1	0	0	7	0	38.2	51	181	29	24	3	0	2	1	11	1	29	2	0
Bucktrot, Keith, Clearwater	1	1	.500	4.60	3	3	0	0	0	0	15.2	12	64	8	8	3	0	2	0	7	0	9	1	0
Bumstead, Nathan, Lakeland	12	4	.750	2.58	25	25	2	0	0	0	160.2	136	665	61	46	11	2	5	4	58	2	111	10	0
Burrows, Angelo, Daytona	0	0	.000	0.00	3	0	0	0	1	0	4.0	2	15	0	0	0	0	0	1	0	6	0	0
Butto, Francisco, Clearwater	1	2	.333	3.49	17	0	0	0	13	3	28.1	28	121	12	11	1	0	0	0	7	1	33	3	1
Buzachero, Edward, Dunedin	0	1	.000	4.50	2	0	0	0	2	1	2.0	2	7	1	1	1	0	0	0	0	0	2	0	0
Camacho, Edward, St. Lucie *	2	4	.333	2.74	45	0	0	0	33	10	49.1	49	211	17	15	2	0	0	2	21	2	40	3	0
Cannon, Edward, Dunedin	0	0	.000	7.71	1	0	0	0	0	0	2.1	4	10	2	2	0	1	0	0	0	0	2	0	0
Carlsen, Clary, Clearwater	4	7	.364	4.59	32	15	0	0	5	0	115.2	132	520	77	59	7	3	6	5	46	2	56	6	0
Castillo, Jonathan, St. Lucie	0	1	.000	20.25	1	0	0	0	0	0	2.2	3	13	6	6	1	1	0	0	4	0	0	2	0
Castle, Heath, Tampa	3	2	.600	2.55	36	0	0	0	7	1	35.1	42	164	21	10	1	4	4	1	15	1	25	3	1
Cavazos, Andres, Palm Beach	1	5	.167	3.41	28	0	0	0	12	1	31.2	36	136	20	12	1	1	0	0	7	1	43	0	1
Cave, Kevin, Jupiter	0	0	.000	4.35	11	0	0	0	8	7	10.1	9	48	6	5	3	0	0	2	5	0	9	0	0
Cherry, William, Sarasota	1	0	1.000	1.96	13	0	0	0	7	1	18.1	14	81	6	4	1	0	0	0	10	0	19	0	2
Clippard, Tyler, Tampa	10	9	.526	3.18	26	25	0	0	1	0	147.1	118	587	56	52	12	2	5	9	34	1	169	5	1
Cordova, Vincent, St. Lucie	8	9	.471	4.01	25	25	2	2	0	0	141.1	150	596	78	63	14	3	6	9	26	0	110	2	1
Core, Daniel, Dunedin	0	0	.000	7.24	9	0	0	0	2	1	13.2	15	62	11	11	5	0	0	1	10	0	16	1	0
Costello, Ryan, Brevard County *	6	6	.500	3.21	24	14	1	0	4	2	101.0	79	414	43	36	8	2	4	4	34	1	99	5	1
Cotton, Nathan, Palm Beach	0	0	.000	10.80	2	0	0	0	1	0	1.2	3	9	2	2	0	0	0	0	1	0	1	0	0
Cox, James, Tampa	1	2	.333	2.60	16	0	0	0	2	0	27.2	20	106	9	8	1	0	1	3	5	0	27	1	0
Crawford, Tristan, Fort Myers	6	5	.545	4.15	32	7	0	0	9	2	80.1	89	352	44	37	11	3	2	5	23	0	88	6	0
Crews, Jordan, Daytona	0	0	.000	6.23	10	0	0	0	3	0	13.0	19	63	10	9	2	0	0	3	1	1	9	1	0
Cueto, Johnny, Sarasota	0	1	.000	3.00	2	1	0	0	0	0	6.0	5	25	2	2	0	0	0	2	1	6	2	0
Cullen, Ryan, St. Lucie *	0	1	.000	8.76	13	0	0	0	3	0	12.1	27	64	13	12	1	1	2	1	7	0	0	0
Currier, Rik, Clearwater	1	1	.500	6.05	16	0	0	0	10	1	19.1	22	101	13	13	2	1	0	1	22	0	17	2	0
De La Cruz, Eulogio, Lakeland	4	3	.571	3.39	40	10	0	0	15	0	95.2	66	390	46	36	5	5	3	5	36	2	97	13	0
De La Cruz, Jose, Jupiter	0	0	15.00	2	0	0	0	1	0	3.0	5	19	5	5	0	0	1	1	4	0	2	1	0
de los Santos, Valerio, Jupiter *	0	0	.000	0.00	3	0	0	0	0	0	4.0	4	18	0	0	0	0	2	0	4	0	0
Demontel II, James, Jupiter	1	4	.200	5.36	32	0	0	0	7	0	47.0	63	218	32	28	4	1	4	5	17	0	39	5	0
De Paula, Jorge, Tampa	0	2	.000	4.58	4	4	0	0	0	0	17.2	14	70	9	9	2	0	0	4	0	14	1	0
DePaula, Julio, Fort Myers	4	3	.571	2.24	36	0	0	0	15	4	64.1	52	262	18	16	0	1	0	7	25	1	51	2	4
Diaz, Jose, Vero Beach	0	1	.000	0.00	14	0	0	0	4	0	15.2	6	62	3	0	0	1	0	12	2	18	1	0
Diggins, Ben, Brevard County	0	1	.000	5.27	12	2	0	0	2	0	13.2	11	68	8	8	0	0	1	7	0	13	3	0
Dillard, Timothy, Brevard County	12	10	.545	2.48	28	28	5	2	0	0	185.1	150	735	64	51	9	5	7	13	31	0	128	13	0
Dove, Dennis, Palm Beach	2	4	.333	4.85	8	8	0	0	0	0	42.2	48	188	24	23	1	1	3	15	0	23	6	0
Doyne, Michael, Palm Beach	1	0	1.000	0.00	6	0	0	0	4	0	9.0	3	32	0	0	0	0	0	0	2	0	11	0	0
Dumatrait, Phillip, Sarasota *	0	0	.000	2.70	3	2	0	0	0	0	10.0	8	41	4	3	0	0	0	3	0	13	0	0
Durost, Kenneth, Brevard County	1	9	.100	5.57	29	11	0	0	4	0	84.0	91	375	62	52	14	2	3	4	41	1	90	6	0
Edens, Kyle, Sarasota	8	3	.727	2.62	37	0	0	0	11	3	82.1	79	348	33	24	4	1	2	10	27	1	64	4	1
Edlich, Kyle, Fort Myers *	0	1	.000	6.75	2	0	0	0	0	0	2.2	3	14	2	2	0	0	0	0	3	0	3	0	0
Evangelista, Nicholas, Clearwater	7	6	.538	3.03	37	0	0	0	15	2	68.1	54	269	26	23	5	4	3	3	20	3	68	1	0
Evert, Brett, Brevard County *	0	2	.000	5.06	7	0	0	0	6	2	10.2	9	45	6	6	1	0	0	1	4	0	7	0	0
Fermin, Angelo, Fort Myers	0	0	.000	0.00	1	0	0	0	1	0	1.0	0	3	0	0	0	0	0	0	0	0	0	0	0
Ferreras, Yorkin, Daytona *	3	5	.375	5.21	14	13	1	0	0	0	65.2	58	275	39	38	3	1	3	2	26	2	75	5	0

– 519 –

Pitcher, Team	W	L	Pct.	ERA	G	GS	CG	ShO	GF	Sv.	IP	H	TBF	R	ER	HR	SH	SF	HB	BB	IBB	SO	WP	Bk.
Figueroa, Jonathan, Vero Beach *	4	3	.571	6.00	22	16	0	0	3	0	81.0	81	365	54	54	14	2	4	4	53	0	52	3	1
Flury, Patrick, Jupiter	0	0	.000	1.23	8	0	0	0	1	0	7.1	4	30	2	1	0	1	0	0	5	0	5	0	0
Foli, Daniel, St. Lucie	5	2	.714	3.74	37	0	0	0	16	6	67.1	68	282	29	28	5	2	2	6	21	4	53	6	0
French, Lucas, Lakeland *	3	1	.750	4.43	4	4	0	0	0	0	22.1	29	103	14	11	3	0	0	0	9	0	17	1	1
Galbizo, Rafael, Jupiter	0	0	.000	2.25	3	0	0	0	0	0	4.0	2	18	2	1	0	0	0	0	4	0	6	1	1
Gallagher, Sean, Daytona	0	0	.000	1.80	1	1	0	0	0	0	5.0	6	21	1	1	0	0	0	0	0	0	7	0	0
Garcia, Anderson, St. Lucie	2	2	.500	2.70	16	0	0	0	9	3	26.2	21	110	9	8	2	2	1	1	9	1	20	2	1
Garcia, Jose, Palm Beach	7	5	.583	4.35	30	20	0	0	0	0	134.1	147	579	74	65	11	3	2	12	41	0	122	4	0
Garcia, Jose, Jupiter	0	0	.000	18.00	1	1	0	0	0	0	2.0	2	10	4	4	0	0	1	0	2	0	0	0	3
Gardner, Michael, Tampa	3	1	.750	3.38	21	0	0	0	9	1	34.2	35	151	16	13	1	0	1	2	10	2	31	3	0
Garmon, Ryan, Sarasota *	0	0	.000	3.09	8	0	0	0	6	0	11.2	14	59	8	4	0	0	1	0	10	0	2	1	0
Garza, Justin, Palm Beach	0	0	.000	3.57	29	0	0	0	7	0	40.1	41	171	17	16	1	3	2	2	13	1	26	5	0
Gerk, Jordan, Daytona *	4	4	.500	3.72	52	0	0	0	9	0	65.1	66	279	36	27	4	3	3	2	26	3	53	2	1
Glaser, Eric, Clearwater	0	7	.000	7.44	9	8	0	0	1	0	42.1	62	194	35	35	9	0	0	2	8	0	29	4	0
Gogal, Jeffrey, Jupiter *	2	4	.333	5.69	13	10	0	0	2	0	61.2	83	279	40	39	4	1	2	8	11	0	49	2	0
Gomez, Abel, Tampa *	2	5	.286	3.79	15	13	0	0	0	0	80.2	70	357	43	34	2	3	3	51	0	69	2	0
Granado, Jan, Fort Myers *	6	6	.500	2.92	25	2	0	0	10	2	49.1	52	209	25	16	5	1	3	2	13	1	31	4	3
Gray, Joshua, Fort Myers *	1	3	.250	3.34	32	3	0	0	8	1	62.0	59	265	27	23	5	3	3	2	28	0	49	4	2
Griffin, David, Sarasota *	0	0	.000	18.00	2	0	0	0	1	0	3.0	7	19	6	6	1	0	0	0	3	0	1	0	0
Gross, Kristopher, Daytona	0	1	.000	6.75	6	0	0	0	2	0	8.0	14	42	7	6	3	0	0	0	5	0	6	0	0
Grybash, Daniel, Brevard County *	0	1	.000	8.24	17	0	0	0	4	1	19.2	32	100	21	18	2	1	0	1	11	0	25	4	0
Guevara, Jose, Sarasota	4	3	.571	2.45	44	0	0	0	29	14	51.1	39	208	17	14	2	3	0	2	14	0	65	6	0
Gutierrez, Jannio, Fort Myers	1	1	.500	1.78	15	0	0	0	11	6	25.1	22	106	7	5	2	1	0	1	10	2	39	1	1
Gwaltney, William, Daytona	2	3	.400	2.63	22	5	0	0	7	3	51.1	39	209	22	15	4	0	2	4	16	1	55	3	1
Habel, Joshua, Brevard County *	5	4	.556	2.56	11	10	0	0	0	0	63.1	45	250	23	18	7	1	1	1	17	0	60	4	1
Haberer, Eric, Palm Beach *	8	6	.571	3.71	17	17	1	0	0	0	94.2	96	394	42	39	2	5	1	3	35	0	58	6	0
Hall, Jeremy, Brevard County	2	3	.400	4.04	45	3	0	0	9	0	89.0	87	387	46	40	12	1	2	5	40	2	83	5	0
Hall, Josh, Sarasota	0	3	.000	6.83	7	7	0	0	0	0	29.0	46	144	30	22	5	0	0	0	14	1	21	2	0
Hamels, Colbert, Clearwater *	2	0	1.000	2.25	3	3	0	0	0	0	16.0	7	59	5	4	0	1	1	0	7	0	18	4	0
Hammond, Steven, Brevard County *	1	3	.250	2.78	8	7	0	0	0	0	35.2	33	147	17	11	2	1	3	0	9	1	30	0	1
Hanrahan, Joel, Vero Beach	1	0	1.000	5.91	5	5	0	0	0	0	21.1	25	97	15	14	5	0	0	0	11	0	25	2	0
Harang, Daryl, Dunedin *	1	1	.500	4.01	14	0	0	0	2	0	24.2	24	108	12	11	3	1	1	1	13	1	13	2	0
Harben, Adam, Fort Myers	10	5	.667	2.66	25	25	2	2	0	0	135.1	102	561	52	40	6	3	1	5	62	0	119	11	2
Harmsen, Brandon, Tampa	1	8	.111	6.26	19	6	0	0	5	0	46.0	63	213	39	32	8	2	7	3	14	2	28	2	2
Harper, Jeremy, Dunedin *	4	0	1.000	2.93	26	0	0	0	3	1	43.0	44	196	18	14	3	1	3	1	26	1	33	6	2
Hendley, Blake, Sarasota	0	1	1.000	4.24	10	0	0	0	3	1	17.0	15	71	8	8	1	0	0	0	5	0	18	1	0
Henkenjohann, Tim, Fort Myers	0	0	.000	5.06	7	0	0	0	3	0	10.2	10	49	6	6	1	0	0	1	9	0	9	1	1
Hensen, Brian, Lakeland *	2	1	.667	3.77	43	0	0	0	17	0	62.0	69	264	28	26	7	5	5	3	17	3	36	1	0
Heredia, Felix, St. Lucie *	0	1	.000	13.50	5	0	0	0	4	0	6.0	9	19	6	6	0	2	0	1	2	0	3	1	1
Hernandez, Gabriel, St. Lucie	2	5	.286	5.74	10	10	0	0	0	0	42.1	48	185	28	27	1	0	1	13	10	0	32	4	3
Hernandez, Yoel, Clearwater	1	1	.500	11.81	4	0	0	0	1	0	5.1	8	29	10	7	1	1	0	1	3	0	7	1	0
Hill, Danny, Dunedin	3	2	.600	3.22	33	0	0	0	15	3	50.1	47	216	25	18	2	3	2	5	21	4	29	6	0
Hill, Jeremy, St. Lucie	0	0	.000	2.35	7	0	0	0	2	1	7.2	8	34	4	2	1	0	1	0	3	0	5	0	0
Hill, Joshua, Fort Myers	0	0	.000	6.97	7	0	0	0	4	0	10.1	9	50	9	8	1	0	1	1	9	0	12	1	0
Hoff, Brian, Jupiter	2	4	.333	4.72	28	0	0	0	4	0	34.1	49	165	22	18	2	1	3	2	9	0	33	1	0
Holdzkom, Lincoln, Jupiter	0	1	.000	5.79	9	0	0	0	3	1	9.1	7	39	6	6	0	1	0	0	5	0	9	1	1
Homer, Christopher, Lakeland	7	4	.636	3.09	54	0	0	0	50	29	64.0	55	258	25	22	4	5	2	2	25	5	50	4	0
Honsa, Christopher, Clearwater *	4	5	.444	4.71	25	5	1	0	4	0	63.0	64	269	37	33	2	0	2	4	20	1	39	1	0
Hoorelbeke, Casey, Vero Beach	9	3	.750	2.40	42	1	0	0	15	4	82.2	74	342	25	22	0	4	2	12	35	2	58	7	1
Hudson, William, Sarasota	0	0	.000	0.00	2	0	0	0	2	0	2.0	1	7	0	0	0	0	0	0	1	0	2	0	0
Hughes, Philip, Tampa	2	0	1.000	3.06	5	4	0	0	0	0	17.2	8	64	6	6	0	1	0	3	4	0	21	0	0
Humber, Philip, St. Lucie	2	6	.250	4.99	14	14	0	0	0	0	70.1	74	300	41	39	6	1	3	8	18	0	65	2	0
Iehl, Jason, Jupiter	1	5	.167	5.67	23	7	0	0	5	0	54.0	75	260	41	34	6	1	3	4	23	0	45	6	1
Isenberg, Kurt, Dunedin *	12	8	.600	3.54	26	26	0	0	0	0	145.0	147	609	67	57	13	3	4	9	32	0	90	9	1
Ishii, Kazuhisa, St. Lucie *	0	0	.000	0.00	1	1	0	0	0	0	4.0	0	12	0	0	0	0	0	0	1	0	3	0	0
Jackson, Zach, Dunedin *	8	1	.889	2.88	10	10	0	0	0	0	59.1	56	236	25	19	3	2	3	0	6	0	48	0	0
James, Justin, Dunedin	4	7	.364	2.87	44	5	0	0	8	0	94.0	107	401	44	30	6	2	2	4	21	0	56	3	1
Janssen, Robert, Dunedin	6	1	.857	2.26	10	10	0	0	0	0	59.2	46	228	16	15	2	1	1	2	12	0	51	1	0
Japa, Rolando, Tampa	0	0	.000	0.00	1	0	0	0	1	0	4.0	1	12	0	0	0	0	0	0	0	0	2	0	0
Jones, Blake, Jupiter	1	2	.333	6.43	16	0	0	0	7	0	21.0	30	101	16	15	3	0	0	1	7	1	14	1	0
Jones, Jason, Tampa	5	13	.278	5.68	26	24	1	0	0	0	128.1	171	559	89	81	11	3	5	4	20	3	76	2	1
Jones, Justin, Fort Myers *	7	3	.700	3.01	13	13	2	0	0	0	77.2	78	325	28	26	5	3	3	28	0	54	5	1
Kauten, Joshua, Lakeland	4	2	.667	2.84	6	6	1	0	0	0	38.0	31	156	13	12	1	0	2	17	0	18	1	0
Kendrick, Kyle, Clearwater	0	1	.000	0.00	1	1	0	0	0	0	4.0	5	18	1	0	0	0	1	2	0	1	0	0
Kennard, Jeffery, Tampa	7	3	.700	3.40	42	0	0	0	15	0	53.0	40	222	23	20	3	2	3	25	3	49	6	1
King, Bryan, St. Lucie	0	0	.000	11.70	6	0	0	0	1	0	10.0	14	54	14	13	2	0	1	1	9	0	11	0	0
King, Jeremy, Tampa	5	5	.500	3.61	24	16	0	0	1	0	99.2	93	422	49	40	8	0	3	4	30	2	83	6	3
Knoff, Justin, Palm Beach	0	0	.000	7.36	2	1	0	0	0	0	7.1	10	32	6	6	1	0	1	1	3	1	0	0	0
Knox, Michael, Tampa	1	0	1.000	11.50	14	0	0	0	6	0	18.0	31	92	23	23	2	1	1	0	9	1	14	1	0
Kobow, Michael, Lakeland	1	1	.500	4.80	14	0	0	0	4	0	15.0	14	68	9	8	1	1	2	11	1	12	2	0
Koehler, Kurt, Jupiter	1	0	1.000	1.50	3	0	0	0	2	1	6.0	2	22	2	1	0	1	0	3	1	9	0	0
Kuo, Hong-Chih, Vero Beach *	1	1	.500	2.08	11	3	0	0	0	0	26.0	19	107	7	6	2	0	1	2	10	0	42	1	0
Lambert, Christopher, Palm Beach	7	1	.875	2.63	10	10	0	0	0	0	54.2	53	229	20	16	4	2	1	5	15	0	46	6	1
Lanier, Thomas, Sarasota	0	0	.000	0.00	2	1	0	0	0	0	5.0	2	21	0	0	0	0	0	4	0	2	1	0
Larrison, Preston, Lakeland	1	2	.333	4.70	9	9	0	0	0	0	38.1	48	167	22	20	0	2	2	12	0	25	4	1
Layden, Timothy, Daytona *	1	0	1.000	1.35	3	0	0	0	0	0	6.2	5	23	1	1	1	0	0	0	1	0	4	1	0
Lee, Seung Hak, Clearwater	0	1	.000	1.80	2	1	0	0	1	0	5.0	5	21	2	1	1	0	0	0	1	0	5	0	0
Leger, Jose, Fort Myers	0	0	.000	0.00	1	0	0	0	1	0	1.0	0	3	0	0	0	0	0	0	1	0	0	0	0
Lerch, Zachary, Jupiter	2	1	.667	8.66	7	2	0	0	3	1	17.2	20	79	18	17	2	0	1	1	4	0	15	1	0
Lewis, Jeremy, Brevard County *	6	7	.462	2.95	55	0	0	0	30	10	79.1	69	323	31	26	5	5	2	3	23	3	73	2	0
Lohse, Erik, Sarasota	10	5	.667	4.69	39	2	0	0	14	0	80.2	90	355	49	42	10	2	3	9	25	1	66	7	0

Pitcher, Team	W	L	Pct.	ERA	G	GS	CG	ShO	GF	Sv.	IP	H	TBF	R	ER	HR	SH	SF	HB	BB	IBB	SO	WP	Bk.
Lopez, Rafael, St. Lucie	1	0	1.000	4.00	5	0	0	0	2	0	9.0	10	38	4	4	1	1	0	1	1	0	4	0	0
Lundgren, Wayne, Palm Beach	3	3	.500	4.15	25	0	0	0	5	0	43.1	53	176	22	20	3	5	2	0	8	0	19	1	1
MacDonald, Michael, Dunedin	9	6	.600	4.24	25	23	0	0	1	0	127.1	136	549	76	60	4	4	3	13	40	2	87	5	0
MacLane, Evan, St. Lucie *	8	5	.615	3.20	19	19	1	0	0	0	112.1	96	449	51	40	14	2	3	2	15	0	92	6	1
Maduro, Calvin, Tampa	0	1	.000	4.50	3	1	0	0	1	0	8.0	11	39	4	4	1	0	0	2	2	0	7	0	0
Maldonado Oquendo, Ivan, St. Lucie	4	5	.444	5.46	27	3	0	0	10	1	59.1	62	267	43	36	6	3	2	7	23	2	43	4	3
Mallett, Justin, Sarasota	2	3	.400	2.87	16	5	0	0	3	1	53.1	44	220	23	17	3	2	3	4	18	0	60	3	1
Marmol, Carlos, Daytona	6	2	.750	2.99	13	13	0	0	0	0	72.1	60	305	30	24	7	1	1	3	37	1	71	5	1
Marshall, Sean, Daytona *	4	4	.500	2.74	12	12	1	0	0	0	69.0	63	283	24	21	7	1	0	1	26	0	61	7	1
Martin, Adrian, Dunedin	0	0	.000	7.71	5	0	0	0	4	0	7.0	10	33	6	6	1	0	0	1	1	1	1	1	0
Martin, Forrest, Brevard County	3	3	.500	6.15	12	4	0	0	4	0	33.2	46	160	27	23	5	1	1	4	18	0	30	4	1
Martinez, Carlos, Jupiter	4	5	.444	3.12	47	0	0	0	37	22	60.2	52	257	25	21	5	3	2	3	22	1	65	0	2
Martinez, Cristhian, Lakeland	2	0	1.000	4.91	3	2	0	0	0	0	11.0	11	49	6	6	0	0	0	2	4	0	9	0	0
Mateo, Juan, Daytona	10	5	.667	3.21	32	16	1	1	11	2	109.1	99	445	47	39	9	2	3	3	27	2	123	2	0
Mathes, Alfred, Daytona *	11	8	.579	4.49	24	24	1	0	0	0	132.1	161	580	77	66	9	1	1	5	37	4	97	5	1
Mathieson, Scott, Clearwater	3	8	.273	4.14	23	23	1	0	0	0	121.2	111	504	62	56	17	4	5	5	34	0	118	7	0
Mattox, David, Sarasota	4	8	.333	5.94	16	16	0	0	0	0	72.2	76	327	57	48	6	2	2	8	37	0	62	3	2
McCormack, Zachariah, Jupiter *	1	1	.500	6.23	4	0	0	0	1	0	4.1	2	17	3	3	1	0	0	0	2	0	3	1	0
McCoy, Michael, Palm Beach	0	0	.000	9.00	1	0	0	0	1	0	1.0	2	7	1	1	0	0	0	1	1	0	0	0	0
McDowell, Kevin, Lakeland *	2	6	.250	6.06	35	12	0	0	6	0	84.2	97	381	64	57	8	5	2	7	42	2	63	1	0
McGowan, Dustin, Dunedin	0	1	.000	4.29	5	5	0	0	0	0	21.0	21	90	12	10	2	0	0	2	5	0	20	0	1
McNutt, Michael, Jupiter	1	2	.333	4.13	13	0	0	0	3	0	24.0	22	105	11	11	4	3	0	2	11	1	24	3	0
Medlock, Calvin, Sarasota	6	3	.667	3.06	25	17	0	0	3	0	108.2	95	432	42	37	6	2	2	2	22	1	98	2	1
Megrew, Michael, Vero Beach *	0	2	.000	20.25	2	2	0	0	0	0	4.0	9	23	9	9	1	0	0	0	2	0	2	0	0
Mejias, Jose Angel, Clearwater	0	0	.000	9.00	1	0	0	0	0	0	2.0	3	11	2	2	0	0	0	0	2	0	2	0	0
Mendez, Adalberto, Daytona	1	1	.500	6.67	23	0	0	0	10	3	28.1	37	146	24	21	2	1	2	0	25	4	32	2	0
Mendez, Jesus, Tampa	0	0	.000	0.00	1	0	0	0	1	0	2.0	2	8	0	0	0	0	0	0	0	0	0	0	0
Merricks, Matthew, Vero Beach *	2	1	.667	4.88	10	4	0	0	1	0	27.2	23	116	18	15	6	1	0	1	10	0	27	1	0
Michael, Mark, Palm Beach	4	5	.444	4.04	18	17	0	0	0	0	82.1	68	355	47	37	7	0	3	14	35	2	57	10	1
Mijares, Jose, Fort Myers *	1	0	1.000	1.50	5	1	0	0	1	0	12.0	5	48	4	2	1	0	0		5	0	17	0	0
Mildren, Paul, Jupiter *	10	3	.769	3.08	29	20	0	0	1	0	140.1	115	565	55	48	13	1	8	5	42	0	111	0	0
Miller, Greg, Vero Beach *	1	0	1.000	0.93	5	3	0	0	0	0	9.2	4	37	1	1	0	0	0	1	7	0	10	1	0
Miller, Ryan, Brevard County	0	0	.000	0.00	2	0	0	0	2	1	2.0	0	6	0	0	0	0	0	0	1	0	1	0	0
Molldrem, Craig, Jupiter	0	2	.000	6.26	5	4	0	0	0	0	23.0	40	119	20	16	0	1	2	2	12	0	10	4	0
Morales, Jorge, Tampa	0	1	.000	3.38	11	0	0	0	4	0	18.2	15	75	7	7	1	1	0	1	4	0	23	3	0
Morenko, Brad, Sarasota	2	2	.500	4.98	9	1	0	0	3	2	21.2	29	97	14	12	4	0	0	1	3	0	6	1	0
Morris, Matt, Palm Beach	0	1	.000	6.52	2	2	0	0	0	0	9.2	12	43	7	7	0	0	1	0	2	0	15	0	0
Moscat, Marvin, Tampa	3	1	.750	3.29	31	0	0	0	10	1	54.2	59	235	26	20	4	2	2		20	2	35	3	0
Mota, Guillermo, Jupiter	0	0	.000	0.00	2	2	0	0	0	0	2.2	3	10	1	0	0	0	0	0	0	0	4	0	0
Muegge, Danny, Vero Beach	8	2	.800	3.38	31	18	0	0	1	0	127.2	124	531	53	48	11	1	3	7	34	0	91	5	1
Mumma, Bradley, Dunedin *	3	2	.600	4.09	45	0	0	0	16	2	61.2	60	270	35	28	7	2	1	7	20	2	69	4	0
Muniz, Carlos, St. Lucie	3	0	1.000	5.82	14	0	0	0	3	0	17.0	13	72	11	11	3	1	1	0	9	1	19	1	0
Nall, Brandon, St. Lucie	0	0	.000	11.57	2	0	0	0	1	0	2.1	3	13	3	3	0	0	0	0	3	0	1	2	0
Nicholson, Derek, Lakeland	0	0	.000	27.00	1	0	0	0	1	0	1.0	2	7	3	3	1	0	0	0	2	0	0	0	0
O'Brien, Weston, Daytona	2	2	.500	5.64	21	0	0	0	5	0	30.1	34	144	21	19	3	2	1	2	20	3	29	7	1
Ojeda, Alvis, Vero Beach	5	1	.833	3.36	28	2	0	0	4	1	61.2	47	246	27	23	1	2	2	6	20	1	36	1	1
Olivera, Manuel, Jupiter *	3	4	.429	3.94	35	8	1	0	14	0	75.1	68	316	43	33	4	2	1	3	34	1	56	6	0
O'Neal, Charles, Sarasota *	0	0	.000	5.87	10	0	0	0	6	0	15.1	14	67	12	10	1	1	1	0	9	1	13	5	0
Ool, Kevin, Palm Beach *	1	0	1.000	1.37	12	0	0	0	2	0	19.2	16	76	5	3	0	2	1	0	3	1	17	1	1
Orenduff, Justin, Vero Beach	5	3	.625	2.24	12	12	1	1	0	0	60.1	35	237	21	15	3	0	2	0	26	0	81	3	0
Ortiz, Ramon, Sarasota	0	1	.000	9.00	1	1	0	0	0	0	3.0	7	17	4	3	1	0	0	0	0	0	3	0	0
Ostlund, Ian, Lakeland *	4	3	.571	2.93	19	0	0	0	4	0	27.2	29	108	11	9	4	3	3	0	3	2	18	1	1
Overman, Matthew, Jupiter	5	1	.833	5.35	27	0	0	0	11	1	38.2	42	174	27	23	5	2	2	2	19	0	20	3	0
Owens, Henry, St. Lucie	2	5	.286	3.15	38	1	0	0	16	4	54.1	49	240	29	19	2	0	1	5	24	2	74	7	0
Padilla, Vicente, Clearwater	0	1	.000	1.80	1	1	0	0	0	0	5.0	4	21	1	1	0	0	0	0	1	0	3	0	0
Paduch, James, Sarasota	4	9	.308	3.81	23	17	1	0	3	1	104.0	104	430	51	44	6	2	4	4	25	2	66	1	1
Parcus, William, Clearwater *	1	2	.333	4.17	38	0	0	0	14	1	54.0	59	232	29	25	6	1	3	0	22	2	53	3	0
Parisi, Michael, Palm Beach	5	6	.455	3.23	13	13	1	0	0	0	78.0	79	326	31	28	6	3	1	4	22	0	63	3	0
Pavano, Carl, Tampa	0	1	.000	4.50	1	1	0	0	0	0	6.0	6	24	3	3	1	0	0	0	0	0	3	0	0
Pelland, Tyler, Sarasota *	5	8	.385	4.05	30	15	0	0	5	0	102.1	103	455	52	46	5	2	3	8	63	2	103	6	1
Pena, Luismar, Brevard County	2	6	.250	4.26	15	12	0	0	0	0	76.0	72	314	39	36	6	1	0	7	28	1	51	5	0
Penny, Brad, Vero Beach	1	0	1.000	1.80	1	1	0	0	0	0	5.0	2	17	1	1	1	0	0	0	1	0	3	0	0
Perez, Beltran, Vero Beach	3	2	.600	3.78	19	0	0	0	9	0	33.1	31	139	15	14	3	1	1	2	15	0	33	1	0
Perez, Jose Miguel, Clearwater	0	0	.000	6.75	3	0	0	0	1	0	5.1	10	31	6	4	0	0	0	1	4	0	1	0	0
Perkins, Glen, Fort Myers *	3	2	.600	2.13	10	9	2	1	0	0	55.0	41	217	14	13	2	1	3	1	13	1	66	2	0
Petrick, William, Daytona	1	4	.200	5.59	9	9	0	0	0	0	37.0	39	168	23	23	0	4	0	7	19	0	25	3	0
Phelps, Michael, Daytona	1	0	1.000	4.76	4	0	0	0	3	1	5.2	2	24	3	3	0	0	0	0	4	0	8	0	0
Pilkington, Brian, Vero Beach	7	9	.438	3.71	19	17	1	0	1	0	106.2	112	449	54	44	10	5	2	4	24	2	70	2	1
Pimentel, Julio Cesar, Vero Beach	8	10	.444	5.08	26	24	1	0	0	0	124.0	149	543	79	70	9	3	5	7	43	0	105	13	0
Pinango, Miguel, St. Lucie	3	2	.600	4.13	12	11	0	0	0	0	61.0	75	268	30	28	5	0	2	6	11	1	26	0	1
Plummer, Jarod, Vero Beach	1	1	.500	3.20	9	1	0	0	4	0	25.1	22	103	9	9	1	2	2		7	1	23	0	1
Polanco, Alfredo, Daytona	2	2	.500	11.49	13	1	0	0	4	0	15.2	20	86	21	20	2	1	0	2	23	3	11	1	0
Pomeranz, Stuart, Palm Beach	2	5	.286	3.35	8	8	0	0	0	0	48.1	56	205	26	18	1	3	3	3	10	0	29	2	0
Powers, Joseph, Sarasota	0	1	.000	8.25	4	1	0	0	0	0	12.0	14	60	15	11	1	0	3	0	8	2	1	1	0
Prahm, Ryan, Dunedin	0	0	.000	18.00	2	0	0	0	1	0	1.0	3	10	2	2	0	0	0	0	4	0	0	0	0
Purcey, David, Dunedin *	5	4	.556	3.63	21	21	0	0	0	0	94.1	80	420	51	38	8	2	4	10	56	1	116	6	0
Quezada, Elvys, Tampa	4	1	.800	5.94	19	4	0	0	4	1	47.0	50	216	33	31	5	1	2	3	26	2	49	6	0
Rainville, Jay, Fort Myers	4	3	.571	2.67	9	9	1	0	0	0	54.0	54	223	22	16	7	0	0	6	6	0	35	2	0
Ramirez, Greg, St. Lucie	4	5	.444	4.17	18	12	0	0	0	0	69.0	66	294	38	32	6	3	1	3	21	1	64	1	0
Ramsey, Keith, Clearwater *	2	4	.333	5.07	12	10	0	0	1	0	60.1	59	267	42	34	11	0	4	4	31	1	32	4	1
Randazzo, Jeffrey, Palm Beach *	0	1	.000	9.31	8	0	0	0	5	1	9.2	14	49	11	10	1	0	1	1	5	1	8	2	0

Pitcher, Team	W	L	Pct.	ERA	G	GS	CG	ShO	GF	Sv.	IP	H	TBF	R	ER	HR	SH	SF	HB	BB	IBB	SO	WP	Bk.
Rapada, Clayton, Daytona *	1	3	.250	3.83	27	0	0	0	12	5	42.1	40	182	21	18	2	4	0	3	16	4	61	2	2
Rasowsky, Avi, Jupiter *	0	0	.000	0.00	1	0	0	0	0	0	1.0	0	3	0	0	0	0	0	0	0	0	0	0	0
Rawson, Anthony, Palm Beach *	2	1	.667	2.78	18	0	0	0	6	0	22.2	24	91	8	7	2	3	0	2	4	0	19	1	0
Reed, Brian, Dunedin	3	4	.429	2.84	40	0	0	0	17	4	63.1	53	254	25	20	4	6	3	3	18	1	48	1	0
Ribas, Gabriel, Clearwater	3	1	.750	4.53	11	7	0	0	2	0	43.2	51	194	25	22	7	3	2	4	13	0	27	5	1
Richardson, Robert, Clearwater *	0	1	.000	7.65	15	0	0	0	3	1	20.0	17	88	18	17	1	2	0	2	12	2	13	0	0
Riggan, Jerrod, St. Lucie	1	0	1.000	3.86	4	0	0	0	1	0	4.2	3	17	2	2	1	0	0	0	0	0	4	2	0
Rincon, Daniel, Sarasota	3	2	.600	5.17	16	3	0	0	5	0	47.0	55	215	30	27	6	1	2	3	16	0	46	3	1
Rival, Kevin, Brevard County	0	1	.000	6.43	6	0	0	0	2	0	7.0	9	34	5	5	0	0	1	0	5	1	9	0	1
Rodriguez, Jermy, Lakeland	4	5	.444	4.73	21	11	0	0	2	0	64.2	60	274	40	34	7	1	1	6	24	1	50	5	1
Rodriguez, Jose, St. Lucie	0	0	.000	2.70	3	0	0	0	3	2	3.1	2	12	1	1	0	0	0	0	1	0	3	1	0
Rodriguez, Mike, Vero Beach	0	0	.000	9.95	10	0	0	0	4	0	12.2	18	67	17	14	3	0	1	1	10	0	13	5	0
Rodriguez, Orlando, Vero Beach *	1	0	1.000	4.15	12	0	0	0	7	1	17.1	14	76	9	8	2	0	1	0	9	0	25	1	0
Rogers, Brian, Lakeland	4	1	.800	2.06	52	1	0	0	10	2	65.2	50	262	16	15	2	1	2	3	21	1	65	6	0
Rohan, James, Vero Beach	0	0	.000	18.00	1	0	0	0	1	0	1.0	2	7	2	2	0	0	0	1	1	0	1	0	0
Romero, Davis, Dunedin *	9	6	.600	3.47	34	18	0	0	4	1	124.2	133	525	60	48	10	3	2	1	34	0	136	5	1
Romero, Ricardo, Dunedin	1	0	1.000	3.82	8	8	0	0	0	0	30.2	36	134	13	13	2	0	0	0	7	0	22	5	1
Rosario, Carlos, Tampa	0	0	.000	18.41	5	0	0	0	2	0	7.1	12	47	16	15	2	1	1	1	13	0	1	0	0
Russ, Christopher, Palm Beach	2	3	.400	5.35	29	0	0	0	14	0	37.0	44	162	29	22	1	0	0	2	11	0	19	3	1
Russ, James, Jupiter	11	8	.579	3.51	27	26	0	0	0	0	161.2	133	657	72	63	7	4	10	12	48	1	143	6	1
Sanchez, Felix, Lakeland *	2	1	.667	2.93	22	0	0	0	7	2	27.2	28	121	11	9	2	0	2	1	12	0	13	3	0
Savickas, Russell, Dunedin	1	0	1.000	0.00	1	0	0	0	1	0	1.0	1	6	0	0	0	0	0	0	2	0	0	0	0
Sawatski, John, Fort Myers *	3	3	.500	3.94	43	0	0	0	36	13	61.2	71	272	35	27	5	2	2	2	21	0	50	2	0
Scalamandre, Richard, Palm Beach	3	2	.600	3.15	47	0	0	0	14	2	54.1	51	226	23	19	3	4	2	2	22	1	45	3	0
Schade, Ryan, Jupiter	0	0	.000	12.00	3	0	0	0	3	0	3.0	5	17	4	4	3	0	0	0	5	0	1	0	0
Schappert, Paul, Daytona *	0	0	.000	0.82	21	0	0	0	10	4	43.2	36	171	5	4	2	1	1	1	8	1	29	2	1
Schmidt, Jeremy, Sarasota	0	3	.000	2.61	7	0	0	0	2	0	10.1	10	45	5	3	0	1	0	0	5	0	9	0	1
Schultz, Cory, Clearwater	0	0	.000	4.05	3	0	0	0	0	0	6.2	9	32	5	3	0	0	1	0	5	0	7	1	0
Schutt, Christopher, Fort Myers	4	4	.500	3.24	38	3	0	0	16	5	66.2	60	284	30	24	1	1	3	1	30	1	70	6	0
Schweitzer, Stephen, Palm Beach *	0	2	.000	4.07	22	0	0	0	5	0	24.1	23	106	14	11	1	3	2	1	12	0	23	4	1
Segovia, Zachary, Clearwater	4	14	.222	5.54	27	27	0	0	0	0	144.2	168	648	98	89	18	5	6	17	48	0	83	9	1
Sevier, Nathan, Daytona	3	0	1.000	3.88	31	3	0	0	18	5	51.0	50	208	24	22	4	0	3	0	10	1	48	7	2
Shafer, Adam, Clearwater	0	5	.000	5.09	20	0	0	0	17	8	23.0	25	106	16	13	1	1	0	1	9	2	31	4	0
Shafer, David, Sarasota	1	0	1.000	0.00	10	0	0	0	10	5	13.2	9	52	0	0	0	1	1	1	2	1	18	2	0
Shaver, Christopher, Daytona *	2	3	.400	2.12	6	6	0	0	0	0	34.0	33	138	15	8	2	2	2	1	7	1	19	0	0
Simmons, Justin, Vero Beach *	4	2	.667	4.42	44	0	0	0	10	1	57.0	63	258	29	28	4	2	2	2	30	1	51	4	2
Simonitsch, Errol, Fort Myers *	8	3	.727	2.69	14	13	2	1	0	0	80.1	70	313	27	24	5	2	1	3	12	0	72	2	0
Skaggs, Jon, Tampa	0	3	.000	6.00	6	6	0	0	0	0	27.0	32	135	19	18	1	0	5	2	22	0	13	1	1
Slack, Nicholas, Brevard County	3	4	.429	6.54	39	0	0	0	26	5	52.1	60	223	43	38	6	4	1	4	14	2	46	3	0
Smith, Brett, Tampa	4	7	.364	5.21	14	13	0	0	0	0	74.1	71	305	44	43	9	0	4	4	17	0	34	2	0
Smith, Charles, St. Lucie	4	4	.500	4.94	24	20	0	0	0	0	116.2	129	507	70	64	12	4	7	6	40	3	59	10	0
Smith, Joshua, Tampa	0	0	.000	7.30	9	1	0	0	3	0	12.1	23	70	14	10	1	1	0	8	1	7	2	0
Solis, Hairo, Tampa	0	0	.000	2.25	2	0	0	0	1	0	4.0	4	17	1	1	1	0	0	0	0	0	1	1	0
Sopko, Mark, Dunedin	0	1	.000	7.20	13	0	0	0	6	1	15.0	23	75	14	12	1	0	0	2	8	0	14	2	0
Soto, Darwin, Brevard County	0	2	.000	6.26	17	0	0	0	6	0	23.0	33	112	18	16	0	0	2	10	1	22	5	2
Soto, Edgar, Tampa *	0	1	.000	9.39	2	2	0	0	0	0	7.2	13	36	8	8	1	0	0	1	0	8	0	0
Spooneybarger, Tim, Jupiter	0	0	.000	3.00	4	1	0	0	0	0	3.0	1	16	1	1	0	0	2	4	0	2	1	0
Squires, Matthew, Clearwater *	0	2	.000	4.88	22	0	0	0	5	0	31.1	32	144	19	17	1	1	2	5	19	2	26	3	2
Stiles, Brad, Daytona *	0	0	.000	3.86	5	0	0	0	0	0	9.1	9	43	4	4	0	0	1	0	10	0	5	0	0
Stockman, Landon, Brevard County	3	4	.429	3.60	31	0	0	0	12	1	40.0	43	171	20	16	4	4	1	4	15	3	36	5	0
Strayhorn, Kole, St. Lucie	5	3	.625	4.46	33	0	0	0	14	2	38.1	44	182	25	19	4	2	3	4	22	4	31	1	0
Strelitz, Brian, Jupiter	1	1	.500	11.37	5	0	0	0	1	0	6.1	10	32	9	8	1	0	0	0	3	0	2	0	0
Strickland, Scott, St. Lucie	0	0	.000	10.80	1	0	0	0	0	0	1.2	4	9	2	2	1	0	0	0	0	0	2	0	0
Sturtze, Tanyon, Tampa	0	1	.000	6.00	2	2	0	0	0	0	3.0	4	14	2	2	0	0	0	0	0	0	4	0	0
Swarzak, Anthony, Fort Myers	3	4	.429	3.66	10	10	0	0	0	0	59.0	72	254	25	24	3	3	2	1	11	0	55	1	1
Sweeney, Matthew, Clearwater	1	8	.111	6.62	14	12	1	0	1	0	68.0	99	311	55	50	13	2	5	6	19	0	31	6	0
Swindell, Michael, St. Lucie	0	2	.000	2.90	6	5	0	0	1	0	31.0	28	133	12	10	1	0	4	8	0	15	0	1
Tankersley, Taylor, Jupiter *	1	0	1.000	3.38	4	4	1	0	0	0	24.0	21	95	10	9	1	0	1	0	9	0	19	0	0
Tata, Jordan, Lakeland	13	2	.867	2.79	25	25	2	2	0	0	155.0	138	628	55	48	12	2	1	8	41	1	134	11	1
Tate, Derek, Dunedin *	0	0	.000	0.00	1	0	0	0	0	0	1.1	1	5	0	0	0	0	0	0	0	0	0	0	0
Taubenheim, Ty, Brevard County	10	2	.833	2.63	16	16	2	1	0	0	106.0	86	420	34	31	7	3	1	9	26	0	75	8	0
Tautor, Peter, Fort Myers	0	0	.000	14.77	16	0	0	0	7	1	17.2	25	103	30	29	2	0	1	4	22	0	16	3	0
Tavares, Anderson, Daytona	4	11	.267	5.40	27	20	0	0	2	0	113.1	145	495	81	68	14	4	7	3	35	2	92	5	1
Tavarez, Milton, Dunedin	4	7	.364	3.36	51	0	0	0	46	13	59.0	56	250	27	22	4	3	4	3	21	2	50	4	3
Teekel, Joshua, Jupiter	1	3	.250	8.06	5	5	0	0	0	0	22.1	31	115	24	20	2	1	2	4	15	0	11	5	0
Thatcher, Joeseph, Brevard County *	0	0	.000	0.00	7	0	0	0	4	2	9.0	6	32	0	0	0	0	0	0	0	14	3	0
Thomas, Eric, Brevard County	0	2	.000	17.55	4	2	0	0	0	0	6.2	12	37	13	13	1	0	1	1	6	0	1	2	3
Thorp, Paul, Tampa	2	4	.333	4.10	50	0	0	0	46	25	48.1	43	200	25	22	5	3	1	1	12	2	38	3	2
Thorpe, Tracy, Dunedin	2	1	.667	3.67	25	0	0	0	9	1	34.1	32	145	14	14	4	1	0	3	10	0	33	8	1
Tiffany, Charles, Vero Beach *	11	7	.611	3.93	22	21	0	0	0	0	110.0	91	456	52	48	17	3	4	6	43	1	134	6	0
Till, Brock, Sarasota	4	6	.400	4.09	29	16	0	0	3	0	105.2	116	464	64	48	7	1	1	5	42	2	77	8	4
Tillman, Derek, Jupiter	2	1	.667	5.23	23	0	0	0	8	3	31.0	26	132	21	18	1	3	2	5	12	1	22	4	0
Timm, Jordan, Dunedin *	0	0	.000	16.20	1	0	0	0	1	0	1.2	2	8	3	3	1	0	0	0	1	0	1	0	0
Tompkins, Jacob, Clearwater	0	0	.000	9.53	5	0	0	0	2	0	5.2	10	35	7	6	0	0	0	1	7	0	4	0	0
Torres, Andy, Jupiter	4	1	.800	3.53	6	6	0	0	0	0	35.2	36	148	15	14	4	1	2	0	12	0	27	0	0
Torres, Jaymes, Palm Beach	1	0	1.000	0.00	3	0	0	0	1	0	6.0	0	18	0	0	0	1	0	1	0	6	0	0
Trachsel, Steve, St. Lucie	0	1	.000	1.35	2	2	0	0	0	0	6.2	5	26	2	1	0	0	0	1	1	0	5	1	0
Treanor, Bryan, Jupiter	0	0	.000	0.00	1	0	0	0	0	0	3.0	0	9	0	0	0	0	0	0	0	0	1	0	0
Tressler, Aaron, Dunedin	0	0	.000	16.20	2	0	0	0	1	0	1.2	3	9	3	3	1	0	0	0	1	0	2	0	0
Tyler, Scott, Fort Myers	7	8	.467	3.95	23	23	0	0	0	0	118.1	106	486	61	52	18	4	2	3	48	0	109	7	2
Urdaneta, Lino, St. Lucie	0	0	.000	1.93	3	0	0	0	1	0	4.2	2	18	1	1	0	0	0	0	1	0	4	0	0

ADVANCED CLASS A *Florida State League*

Pitcher, Team	W	L	Pct.	ERA	G	GS	CG	ShO	GF	Sv.	IP	H	TBF	R	ER	HR	SH	SF	HB	BB	IBB	SO	WP	Bk.
Valdez, Edward, Sarasota	3	2	.600	1.95	14	13	1	0	1	0	69.1	58	281	21	15	2	0	2	5	21	0	62	1	1
Valdez, Ismael, Jupiter	1	1	.500	7.88	2	2	0	0	0	0	8.0	7	33	7	7	1	0	0	0	2	0	5	1	0
Vanden Hurk, Henricus, Jupiter	0	1	.000	4.05	2	2	0	0	0	0	6.2	7	28	4	3	0	0	0	1	0	0	6	0	0
Vargas, Jason, Jupiter *	2	3	.400	3.42	9	9	0	0	0	0	55.1	47	224	24	21	6	2	1	0	14	0	60	0	0
Vasquez, Virgil, Lakeland	4	1	.800	4.21	8	8	1	1	0	0	47.0	52	190	23	22	6	1	0	3	7	0	31	2	0
Verlander, Justin, Lakeland	9	2	.818	1.67	13	13	2	0	0	0	86.0	70	334	19	16	3	4	3	7	19	0	104	8	2
Villanueva, Carlos, Brevard County	8	1	.889	2.32	21	21	0	0	0	0	112.1	78	438	31	29	11	0	2	3	32	0	124	8	4
Waldie, Andrew, Clearwater	0	0	.000	0.00	2	0	0	0	0	0	4.1	5	23	2	0	0	0	0	0	3	0	3	1	0
Walker, Brian, St. Lucie *	3	1	.750	4.80	17	1	0	0	3	0	30.0	33	135	17	16	4	0	0	2	15	0	25	4	0
Wallace, Shane, Palm Beach *	0	0	.000	18.00	1	0	0	0	1	0	1.0	3	6	2	2	0	0	0	0	0	0	1	1	0
Webb, Alan, Clearwater *	1	2	.333	11.66	13	6	0	0	4	0	29.1	47	151	39	38	6	1	2	4	17	2	19	1	0
Weber, Matthew, Daytona	0	2	.000	12.71	2	2	0	0	0	0	5.2	16	37	10	8	1	0	0	0	3	0	4	1	0
Wells, Randy, Daytona	10	2	.833	2.74	41	10	0	0	12	2	98.2	93	404	33	30	5	3	0	3	22	1	106	5	0
White, Steven, Tampa	0	0	.000	3.09	3	2	0	0	0	0	11.2	8	44	4	4	1	1	0	1	2	0	8	0	0
Williams, Matthew, Fort Myers	0	0	.000	0.00	1	0	0	0	1	0	2.0	2	9	0	0	0	0	0	0	1	0	2	0	0
Wilson, Kyle, Vero Beach	0	2	.000	8.05	18	0	0	0	12	4	19.0	30	94	20	17	3	1	0	1	7	0	18	4	0
Wolfe, Brian, Brevard County	1	1	.500	0.79	18	0	0	0	13	8	22.2	19	91	3	2	0	0	0	8	1	22	1	0
Woodrow, Christopher, Clearwater	0	3	.000	14.34	3	3	0	0	0	0	10.2	23	60	18	17	4	0	0	1	5	0	7	2	0
Worrell, Mark, Palm Beach	2	3	.400	2.25	53	0	0	0	52	35	56.0	38	223	20	14	6	2	1	4	19	2	53	6	0
Worthington, Timothy, St. Lucie	4	2	.667	2.98	13	7	2	1	2	0	51.1	39	206	21	17	3	1	2	4	13	1	49	1	0
Wright, Dequam, Vero Beach *	0	0	.000	9.45	6	0	0	0	1	0	6.2	8	37	7	7	0	0	0	0	10	0	8	0	0
Wright, Jaret, Tampa	1	0	1.000	1.50	2	2	0	0	0	0	12.0	9	48	2	2	0	1	1	3	3	0	12	0	0
Wylie, Jason, Daytona	0	1	.000	4.26	10	0	0	0	4	0	12.2	8	54	8	6	0	0	1	2	5	0	15	1	0
Yates, Kyle, Dunedin	7	3	.700	1.91	14	14	0	0	0	0	75.1	69	307	30	16	4	0	1	2	19	0	67	1	0
Yourkin, Matthew, Jupiter *	2	2	.500	4.30	22	0	0	0	5	0	29.1	25	123	15	14	2	2	1	0	11	0	30	2	1
Zell, Daniel, Lakeland *	5	5	.500	2.15	49	3	0	0	10	0	75.1	71	318	20	18	3	4	1	5	26	5	50	1	0

COMBINATION SHUTOUTS: Brevard County (7) -- Habel-Lewis, Villanueva-Lewis-Wolfe, Taubenheim-Slack, Habel-Lewis, Pena-Slack-Lewis, Dillard-Lewis, Villanueva-Durost-Hall-Soto. Clearwater (1) -- Bucktrot-Parcus-Currier. Daytona (11) -- Marmol-Gerk-O'Brien-Mateo, Marshall-Atlee-Mateo, Marshall-Wells, Petrick-Tavares, Mateo-Gerk-Sevier, Wells-Gwaltney-Rapada-Sevier, Mathes-Rapada, Mateo-Gwaltney-Rapada, Wells-Schappert-Gwaltney, Mateo-Crews-Gerk-Gwaltney, Wells-Gerk-Gwaltney. Dunedin (9) -- MacDonald-Mumma, Isenberg-Reed, MacDonald-Mumma-Tavarez, Jackson-Thorpe, Purcey-Thorpe, Janssen-James-Reed, Romero-Reed, Romero-Hill, Isenberg-Reed-Mumma. Fort Myers (9) -- Simonitsch-Sawatski, Harben-Schutt-Granado-Sawatski, Tyler-Schutt-DePaula, Harben-Sawatski, Harben-Sawatski, Schutt-Simonitsch-DePaula-Gutierrez, Jones-DePaula, Tyler-Crawford, Swarzak-Gray. Jupiter (6) -- Mildern-Hoff-Overman-Tillman, Russ-Demontel II, Vanden Hurk-Hoff-Yourkin-Martinez, Mildern-Hoff-Holdzkom, Russ-Jones-Martinez, Mildern-Jones-Overman. Lakeland (7) -- Bumstead-McDowell-Rogers, Tata-McDowell, Tata-Ostlund-Rogers-Zell, Tata-De La Cruz, Rodriguez-Sanchez-Rogers-Ostlund-Homer, Bumstead-De La Cruz-Zell-Rogers, Tata-Rogers-Homer. Palm Beach (14) -- Lambert-Lundgren-Scalamandre-Worrell, Lambert-Randazzo-Cavazos, Garcia-Lundgren-Cavazos-Worrell, Pomeranz-Cavazos-Worrell, Blair-Russ-Schweitzer-Worrell, Haberer-Russ, Haberer-Cavazos-Worrell, Parisi-Scalamandre, Garcia-Worrell, Axelson-Ool-Scalamandre, Parisi-Worrell, Parisi-Worrell, Alvarez-Scalamandre-Worrell, Alvarez-Scalamandre-Worrell. Sarasota (5) -- Pelland-Cherry-Rincon-Guevara, Basham-Till-Barreto, Medlock-Till-Barreto, Mattox-Paduch, Valdez-Lohse-Hendley-Guevara. St. Lucie (7) -- Ramirez-Walker-Garcia, MacLane-Foli-King, Cordova-Foli, MacLane-Hill, Cordova-Strayhorn-Maldonado Oquendo, Pinango-Riggan-Cullen-Strayhorn-Foli, Pinango-Nall. Tampa (8) -- Jones-Kennard-Moscat, Gomez-Kennard-Thorp, King-Thorp, Clippard-Beam, Smith-Smith-Beam, Clippard-Smith, King-Cox, King-Gardner-Thorp. Vero Beach (9) -- Tiffany-Muegge-Alexander-Wilson, Tiffany-Muegge-Rodriguez, Orenduff-Alexander, Kuo-Ojeda-Alexander, Orenduff-Perez-Hoorelbeke, Figueroa-Merricks-Ojeda-Rodriguez, Muegge-Alexander, Muegge-Rodriguez-Simmons-Perez, Pimentel-Bott-Figueroa.

2005 FIELDING

TEAM

Team	G	PO	A	E	TC	DP	TP	PB	Pct.
Lakeland	133	3543	1444	110	5097	151	1	17	.978
Brevard County	136	3547	1351	115	5013	137	0	11	.977
Daytona	135	3479	1404	131	5014	120	0	16	.974
Tampa	135	3462	1299	133	4894	77	0	23	.973
Vero Beach	133	3418	1311	130	4859	121	0	9	.973
Dunedin	140	3683	1602	152	5437	125	0	31	.972
Fort Myers	133	3421	1329	136	4886	131	0	21	.972
Palm Beach	140	3640	1597	153	5390	161	0	16	.972
Clearwater	136	3505	1401	153	5059	122	1	37	.970
St. Lucie	134	3499	1350	152	5001	121	1	19	.970
Sarasota	132	3413	1355	155	4923	121	0	20	.969
Jupiter	135	3603	1331	166	5100	112	0	18	.967

INDIVIDUAL

FIRST BASEMEN

NOTE: All caps denotes fielding-percentage leader based on 70 games for catchers, 93 for all other non-pitchers and 112 innings for pitchers. *Throws lefthanded.

Player, Team	Pct.	G	PO	A	E	TC	DP
Andrus, Erold, Tampa *	.982	15	105	7	2	114	3
Bear, Ryan, Jupiter	.990	74	582	18	6	606	47
Boyer, Kyle, Daytona	1.000	1	8	0	0	8	1
Brady, Joshua, Brevard County	.983	21	169	9	3	181	19
Bramasco, Leslie, Clearwater	1.000	1	3	0	0	3	0
Bruce, Cole, Vero Beach	.990	14	90	13	1	104	11
Burgos, Jose, Fort Myers	1.000	17	150	8	0	158	16
Cabrera, Mayke, Vero Beach	.967	10	54	4	2	60	5
Cannon, Rhame, Dunedin	.993	15	127	23	1	151	8
Chiaravalloti, Vito, Dunedin	.991	19	198	14	2	214	14
Collins, Kevin, Daytona *	.984	13	120	7	2	129	15
Creighton, Matt, Daytona	1.000	5	35	5	0	40	6
Cummins, Daniel, St. Lucie	1.000	1	1	1	0	2	0
Davidson, Tyler, St. Lucie	1.000	15	124	3	0	127	16

Player, Team	Pct.	G	PO	A	E	TC	DP
De La Cruz, Carlos, Brevard County	1.000	12	83	8	0	91	8
DeMarco, Mathew, Palm Beach-Jupiter	.992	14	120	4	1	125	11
Diggins, Ben, Brevard County	.833	1	5	0	1	6	0
Dopirak, Brian, Daytona	.984	117	963	58	17	1038	84
Dryer, Matthew, Palm Beach	.900	1	9	0	1	10	0
Dunlap, Cory, Vero Beach *	.985	98	748	46	12	806	89
Dyson, Colie, Vero Beach *	1.000	2	10	0	0	10	2
Ehlers, Cody, Tampa *	.989	32	243	24	3	270	20
Eure, Jeffrey, Brevard County	.990	109	896	39	9	944	90
Figueroa, Juan, Jupiter *	.973	57	448	17	13	478	41
Gredvig, Doug, Clearwater	.966	19	182	16	7	205	15
Greenwood, Jared, Tampa	1.000	1	6	0	0	6	0
Hansen, Bryan, Clearwater *	.990	90	754	60	8	822	65
Harper, Brett, St. Lucie	.988	48	375	26	5	406	36
HUNT, KELLY, Lakeland	.992	125	1092	117	10	1219	129
Isaacson, Gregory, Clearwater	.980	9	47	2	1	50	4
Johnston, Clinton, Dunedin *	.985	35	309	30	5	344	28
Klemm, Christopher, Clearwater *	.957	3	18	4	1	23	3
Knoedler, Justin, Lakeland		1	0	0	0	0	0
Laurin, Dominique, Vero Beach	1.000	5	24	2	0	26	0
Lindsey, John, Jupiter	.985	9	62	4	1	67	5
Mauer, Donald, Fort Myers	1.000	9	73	5	0	78	5
Mejia, Jorge, Sarasota	1.000	2	7	1	0	8	0
Messner, Nathan, Jupiter	.889	3	8	0	1	9	0
Mientkiewicz, Doug, St. Lucie	.985	6	63	4	1	68	3
Mitchell, Russell, Vero Beach	.943	4	32	1	2	35	0
Moore, Robert, Jupiter	1.000	3	21	1	0	22	3
Nichols, Leslie, Clearwater	.980	13	97	3	2	102	11
Nicholson, Derek, Lakeland	1.000	9	83	7	0	90	10
Nixon, Michael, Vero Beach	1.000	4	23	2	0	25	2
Norman, Zachary, Clearwater	1.000	2	13	2	0	15	2
Olmstead, Walter, Sarasota	1.000	5	37	2	0	39	2
Peterson, Brock, Fort Myers	.988	96	772	53	10	835	89
Phillips, Kyle, Fort Myers	1.000	1	2	0	0	2	0
Piepkorn, Jeremiah, Sarasota	.929	2	13	0	1	14	1
Reiman, Joey, Dunedin	.996	47	463	31	2	496	36
Rios, Kevin, St. Lucie	1.000	3	11	0	0	11	0

Player, Team	Pct.	G	PO	A	E	TC	DP
Rodland, Eric, Lakeland	1.000	2	1	2	0	3	1
Rohan, James, Vero Beach	.976	8	37	4	1	42	5
Rosenthal, Benjamin, Palm Beach	1.000	1	3	0	0	3	0
Salas, Francisco, Daytona	1.000	3	4	0	0	4	0
Santor, Johnathon, Palm Beach	.987	79	704	59	10	773	76
Schutzenhofer, Andrew, Palm Beach *	.996	53	490	44	2	536	58
Snyder, Michael, Dunedin	.996	24	209	26	1	236	23
Sulbaran, Orlando, Sarasota	1.000	1	13	1	0	14	0
Tucker, Michael, Jupiter	1.000	1	6	1	0	7	2
Tugwell, Marc, Clearwater	1.000	9	59	7	0	66	4
Urgelles, Jeffrey, Sarasota	.969	4	29	2	1	32	2
Urick, John, Tampa *	.988	85	724	39	9	772	46
Vavao, Jason, Sarasota	.980	15	134	10	3	147	18
Verbryke, Eric, Tampa *	1.000	4	38	1	0	39	2
Votto, Joseph, Sarasota	.991	107	851	75	8	934	84
Whealy, Blake, St. Lucie	1.000	9	53	3	0	56	7
Wilson, Andrew, St. Lucie	.986	59	537	30	8	575	48
Zamojc, Mitchell, Fort Myers	.973	14	104	3	3	110	10

FIRST BASEMEN WITH TWO OR MORE TEAMS

Player, Team	Pct.	G	PO	A	E	TC	DP
DeMarco, Mathew, Palm Beach	.992	13	117	4	1	122	11
DeMarco, Mathew, Jupiter	1.000	1	3	0	0	3	0

SECOND BASEMEN

Player, Team	Pct.	G	PO	A	E	TC	DP
Abreu, Etanislao, Vero Beach	.977	88	181	206	9	396	49
Arteaga, Joshua, Daytona	1.000	3	4	10	0	14	3
Batista, Norberto, Jupiter	1.000	4	2	1	0	3	0
BOLIVAR, LUIS, Sarasota	.977	100	164	262	10	436	53
Bramasco, Leslie, Clearwater	1.000	3	2	6	0	8	2
Brock, Matthew, Jupiter	.951	13	26	13	2	41	5
Bruce, Cole, Vero Beach	1.000	3	2	4	0	6	0
Cabrera, Mayke, Vero Beach	...	1	0	0	0	0	0
Campana, Wandel, Brevard County	.967	13	28	31	2	61	7
Chapman, Travis, Sarasota	1.000	1	3	5	0	8	2
Chirinos, Robinson, Daytona	.962	69	135	191	13	339	42
Christian, Justin, Tampa	.962	94	145	238	15	398	33
Conley, Evan, Sarasota	1.000	2	1	12	0	13	0
Corona, Reegie, Tampa	1.000	3	9	11	0	20	1
Cota, Carlo, Dunedin	.950	68	131	211	18	360	34
Creighton, Matt, Daytona	.800	1	1	3	1	5	0
Cruz, Jose, Tampa-Daytona	.975	39	63	94	4	161	25
Davidson, Seth, Clearwater	1.000	2	3	7	0	10	0
DeMarco, Mathew, Palm Beach-Jupiter	1.000	11	19	24	0	43	4
Denker, Travis, Vero Beach	.964	28	45	88	5	138	17
Dragicevich, Scott, Dunedin	.984	12	24	39	1	64	8
Fermin, Angelo, Fort Myers	.980	12	19	30	1	50	5
Francia, Juan, Lakeland	.976	60	125	206	8	339	51
Gonzalez, Juan, Lakeland	1.000	2	1	6	0	7	1
Granato, Anthony, Daytona	.978	12	20	24	1	45	6
Hayes, Calvin, Palm Beach	.942	47	101	128	14	243	33
Hoffpauir, Jarrett, Palm Beach	.970	62	117	203	10	330	55
Hudson, William, Sarasota	.973	9	12	24	1	37	7
Hughes, Luke, Fort Myers	.948	21	33	58	5	96	17
Isaacson, Gregory, Clearwater	.970	12	15	17	1	33	3
Koutnik, Jared, Tampa	1.000	8	12	17	0	29	3
Laurin, Dominique, Vero Beach	1.000	6	13	6	0	19	1
Laya, Rayner, Palm Beach	1.000	7	13	16	0	29	7
Leger, Jose, Fort Myers	1.000	4	10	11	0	21	4
Leon, Carlos, Clearwater	1.000	1	1	0	0	1	0
Lewis, Richard, Daytona	1.000	1	0	2	0	2	0
Mayorson, Manuel, Dunedin	.974	9	15	23	1	39	4
McCoy, Michael, Palm Beach	.944	25	43	59	6	108	19
Mejia, Gilberto, Lakeland	.969	48	89	158	8	255	31
Mejia, Jorge, Sarasota	.957	19	26	40	3	69	9
Mendez, Deivi, Tampa	.857	2	3	3	1	7	0
Mitchell, Russell, Vero Beach	1.000	1	0	3	0	3	0
Molina, Felix, Fort Myers	.961	33	55	94	6	155	27
Moore, Robert, Jupiter	1.000	8	24	30	0	54	5
Moss, Timothy, Clearwater	.967	120	220	329	19	568	74
Patrick, Brian, Dunedin	.968	15	20	41	2	63	6
Pattee, Benjamin, Fort Myers	1.000	4	7	9	0	16	5
Randel, Kevin, Jupiter	.956	102	211	224	20	455	51
Rich, Dominic, Palm Beach	1.000	2	2	6	0	8	0
Rios, Kevin, St. Lucie	.974	84	150	218	10	378	50
Roberts, Ryan, Dunedin	.949	41	86	120	11	217	34
Rodland, Eric, Lakeland	.992	30	47	73	1	121	23
Rodriguez, Carlos, Clearwater	.975	9	19	20	1	40	4
Rohan, James, Vero Beach	.989	19	34	54	1	89	17

Player, Team	Pct.	G	PO	A	E	TC	DP
Rojo, Billy Garrison, Sarasota	1.000	2	2	4	0	6	1
Salas, Francisco, Daytona	1.000	23	54	61	0	115	21
Schade, Ryan, Jupiter	.960	22	24	24	2	50	3
Sollmann, Steven, Brevard County	.969	124	233	359	19	611	94
Tejeda, Ferdin, Tampa	.886	8	14	17	4	35	2
Thompson, Andrew, Fort Myers	.955	4	3	18	1	22	1
Tiburcio, Hector, Sarasota	.864	4	10	9	3	22	4
Tolbert, Christopher, Fort Myers	.973	58	95	155	7	257	43
Walsh, Nick, Tampa	.988	20	29	54	1	84	11
Whealy, Blake, St. Lucie	.934	54	90	135	16	241	26

SECOND BASEMEN WITH TWO OR MORE TEAMS

Player, Team	Pct.	G	PO	A	E	TC	DP
Cruz, Jose, Tampa	.933	3	2	12	1	15	0
Cruz, Jose, Daytona	.979	36	61	82	3	146	25
DeMarco, Mathew, Palm Beach	1.000	1	1	0	0	1	0
DeMarco, Mathew, Jupiter	1.000	10	18	24	0	42	4

THIRD BASEMEN

Player, Team	Pct.	G	PO	A	E	TC	DP
Arnold, Eric, Dunedin	.911	90	46	190	23	259	21
Arteaga, Joshua, Daytona	1.000	1	1	2	0	3	0
Batista, Norberto, Jupiter	...	1	0	0	0	0	0
Bowman, Shawn, St. Lucie	.928	87	59	186	19	264	19
Bramasco, Leslie, Clearwater	.959	17	14	33	2	49	6
Brock, Matthew, Jupiter	.905	13	3	16	2	21	0
Bruce, Cole, Vero Beach	.895	32	6	45	6	57	3
Burgos, Jose, Fort Myers	.941	15	5	27	2	34	3
Cabrera, Mayke, Vero Beach	.905	13	7	12	2	21	1
Campana, Wandel, Brevard County	.854	23	10	25	6	41	4
Carroll, Mark, Tampa	.889	7	3	5	1	9	0
Chapman, Travis, Sarasota	1.000	2	0	4	0	4	1
Cleveland, Russell, Lakeland	1.000	1	0	3	0	3	1
Correll, Richard, Clearwater	.667	1	0	2	1	3	1
Cruz, Jose, Daytona	.778	3	2	5	2	9	0
Davidson, Seth, Clearwater	.926	7	11	14	2	27	2
De La Cruz, Carlos, Brevard County	.889	7	1	7	1	9	0
DeMarco, Mathew, Palm Beach-Jupiter	.933	18	7	21	2	30	2
Dewitt, Blake, Vero Beach	1.000	8	5	7	0	12	0
Dragicevich, Scott, Dunedin	.953	41	22	79	5	106	6
Dryer, Matthew, Palm Beach	.931	102	60	195	19	274	21
Eure, Jeffrey, Brevard County	.786	10	8	14	6	28	1
Fermin, Angelo, Fort Myers	.909	8	5	15	2	22	2
Festa, Anthony, Brevard County	.842	7	2	14	3	19	1
Garcia, Emmanuel, St. Lucie	1.000	1	2	0	0	2	0
Gonzalez, Juan, Lakeland	1.000	1	0	4	0	4	1
Hathaway, Aaron, St. Lucie	1.000	7	7	14	0	21	3
Hattig, John, Dunedin	.909	8	3	27	3	33	6
Heether, Adam, Brevard County	.943	90	51	166	13	230	15
Hollingsworth, Josh, Tampa	.885	16	5	18	3	26	0
Hudson, William, Sarasota	.880	14	4	18	3	25	1
Isaacson, Gregory, Clearwater	.778	16	9	12	6	27	0
Kirkland, Kody, Lakeland	.924	122	77	237	26	340	32
Koutnik, Jared, Tampa	.886	15	10	29	5	44	1
LaRoche, Andy, Vero Beach	.920	55	45	105	13	163	8
Larsen, Andrew, Daytona	1.000	1	0	1	0	1	0
Laurin, Dominique, Vero Beach	...	1	0	0	0	0	0
Leger, Jose, Fort Myers	.933	16	26	86	8	120	9
Leon, Carlos, Clearwater	.931	13	5	22	2	29	2
Malo, Jonathan, St. Lucie	1.000	1	0	3	0	3	0
Mather, Joseph, Palm Beach	.667	1	0	2	1	3	0
Mauer, Donald, Fort Myers	1.000	2	1	2	0	3	0
McCoy, Michael, Palm Beach	.951	25	14	44	3	61	2
Mejia, Jorge, Sarasota	1.000	2	1	4	0	5	0
Mendez, Deivi, Tampa	1.000	11	3	19	0	22	1
Merchan, Jesus, Fort Myers	1.000	1	0	4	0	4	0
MITCHELL, LEE, Jupiter	.938	124	86	245	22	353	24
Mitchell, Russell, Vero Beach	.800	5	2	6	2	10	0
Molina, Felix, Fort Myers	1.000	3	2	8	0	10	1
Moore, Robert, Jupiter	1.000	1	2	3	0	5	0
Moore, Scott, Daytona	.904	120	79	205	30	314	13
Moses, Matthew, Fort Myers	.945	59	24	97	7	128	11
Murray, Joshua, Brevard County	1.000	4	2	5	0	7	0
Norman, Zachary, Clearwater	.833	10	4	16	4	24	0
Nunez, Luis, Tampa	1.000	1	1	0	0	1	0
Olmstead, Walter, Sarasota	.714	3	2	3	2	7	0
Patrick, Brian, Dunedin	.636	4	1	6	4	11	1
Pattee, Benjamin, Fort Myers	1.000	4	3	9	0	12	1
Piepkorn, Jeremiah, Sarasota	.667	1	1	1	1	3	1
Plumley, Grant, Tampa	1.000	10	3	16	0	19	1

Player, Team	Pct.	G	PO	A	E	TC	DP
Psomas, William, St. Lucie	.926	34	20	68	7	95	6
Rios, Kevin, St. Lucie	1.000	5	1	9	0	10	0
Rodland, Eric, Lakeland	.931	13	2	25	2	29	2
Rodriguez, Carlos, Clearwater	.896	29	16	44	7	67	5
Rohan, James, Vero Beach	.943	28	17	49	4	70	5
Salas, Francisco, Daytona	.972	17	8	27	1	36	3
Santor, Johnathon, Palm Beach	.867	5	2	11	2	15	3
Schramek, Mark, Sarasota	.908	116	65	213	28	306	20
Sena, Emmanuel, Dunedin	1.000	2	2	4	0	6	1
Sosa, Juan, Clearwater	1.000	1	0	3	0	3	0
Sprowl, Jon, Tampa	...	1	0	0	0	0	0
Tucker, Michael, Jupiter	.929	4	2	11	1	14	2
Tugwell, Marc, Clearwater	.940	54	30	96	8	134	11
Wilson, Andrew, St. Lucie	1.000	3	1	1	0	2	0
Zamora, Hector, Tampa	.947	82	57	158	12	227	6

THIRD BASEMEN WITH TWO OR MORE TEAMS

Player, Team	Pct.	G	PO	A	E	TC	DP
DeMarco, Mathew, Palm Beach	.917	14	6	16	2	24	2
DeMarco, Mathew, Jupiter	1.000	4	1	5	0	6	0

SHORTSTOPS

Player, Team	Pct.	G	PO	A	E	TC	DP
Abreu, Etanislao, Vero Beach	1.000	9	15	19	0	34	6
Arteaga, Joshua, Daytona	1.000	2	2	4	0	6	1
Batista, Wilson, St. Lucie	.944	61	96	157	15	268	35
Bolivar, Luis, Sarasota	1.000	2	1	10	0	11	2
Bramasco, Leslie, Clearwater	.952	85	131	265	20	416	45
Brock, Matthew, Jupiter	.971	59	70	163	7	240	25
Bruce, Cole, Vero Beach	1.000	3	4	2	0	6	0
Campana, Wandel, Brevard County	.944	15	20	47	4	71	7
Campusano, Jose, Jupiter	.906	86	117	238	37	392	43
Carroll, Mark, Tampa	1.000	1	1	0	0	1	0
Chavez, Ozzie, Brevard County	.960	121	161	370	22	553	91
Chirinos, Robinson, Daytona	1.000	1	0	1	0	1	0
Cruz, Jose, Daytona	.750	1	0	3	1	4	0
Davidson, Seth, Clearwater	.938	3	3	12	1	16	2
DeMarco, Mathew, Palm Beach-Jupiter	.950	3	7	12	1	20	3
Dragicevich, Scott, Dunedin	.938	30	41	79	8	128	19
Fermin, Angelo, Fort Myers	.954	14	22	40	3	65	5
Garcia, Emmanuel, St. Lucie	.750	1	1	2	1	4	0
Gonzalez, Juan, Lakeland	.971	56	95	141	7	243	38
Granato, Anthony, Daytona	.938	4	7	8	1	16	1
Greene, James, Palm Beach	.913	20	32	62	9	103	19
Haag, Ryan, Tampa	1.000	18	23	55	0	78	8
Hollingsworth, Josh, Tampa	.875	3	1	6	1	8	0
Hu, Chin-lung, Vero Beach	.958	116	157	340	22	519	70
Hudson, William, Sarasota	.899	19	20	51	8	79	10
Kirkland, Kody, Lakeland	1.000	1	2	2	0	4	1
Koutnik, Jared, Tampa	.960	7	6	18	1	25	2
Laurin, Dominique, Vero Beach	1.000	1	1	6	0	7	1
Laya, Rayner, Palm Beach	.975	64	107	210	8	325	41
Leon, Carlos, Clearwater	1.000	3	7	4	0	11	1
Made, Hector, Tampa	.922	43	75	126	17	218	17
Malo, Jonathan, St. Lucie	.944	4	5	12	1	18	1
Mayorson, Manuel, Dunedin	.967	114	159	363	18	540	56
McCoy, Michael, Palm Beach	.944	11	17	34	3	54	4
Mejia, Gilberto, Lakeland	.905	18	21	46	7	74	12
Mejia, Jorge, Sarasota	1.000	6	5	16	0	21	1
Mendez, Deivi, Tampa	.952	10	15	25	2	42	8
Merchan, Jesus, Fort Myers	.943	10	17	33	3	53	9
Murray, Joshua, Brevard County	1.000	1	3	1	0	4	0
Pena, Ramiro, Tampa	.965	23	32	78	4	114	11
Plumley, Grant, Tampa	.943	35	51	98	9	158	11
Ragsdale, William, St. Lucie	.949	68	111	225	18	354	42
Rios, Kevin, St. Lucie	.833	1	1	4	1	6	1
Rodland, Eric, Lakeland	.833	2	1	4	1	6	0
Rodriguez, Carlos, Clearwater	.939	53	76	124	13	213	26
Rohan, James, Vero Beach	.857	11	15	15	5	35	5
ROJAS, CARLOS, Daytona	.968	111	151	360	17	528	72
Ryan, Brendan, Palm Beach	.938	49	77	179	17	273	41
Salas, Francisco, Daytona	.964	30	18	62	3	83	11
Schade, Ryan, Jupiter	1.000	1	0	3	0	3	0
Sena, Emmanuel, Dunedin	.750	1	2	1	1	4	1
Taylor, Samuel, Fort Myers	.959	64	89	169	11	269	48
Tiburcio, Hector, Sarasota	.943	111	198	313	31	542	67
Tolbert, Christopher, Fort Myers	.931	47	64	137	15	216	31
Tousa, Scott, Lakeland	.980	58	76	173	5	254	44

SHORTSTOPS WITH TWO OR MORE TEAMS

Player, Team	Pct.	G	PO	A	E	TC	DP
DeMarco, Mathew, Palm Beach	1.000	1	3	6	0	9	1
DeMarco, Mathew, Jupiter	.909	2	4	6	1	11	2

OUTFIELDERS

Player, Team	Pct.	G	PO	A	E	TC	DP
Abercrombie, Reginald, Jupiter	.977	75	202	6	5	213	2
Allen, Roderick, Tampa	1.000	12	13	0	0	13	0
Almario-Cabrera, Yosvany, Tampa	.879	21	29	0	4	33	0
Anderson, Drew, Brevard County	.986	127	201	10	3	214	3
Andrus, Erold, Tampa *	.990	108	195	4	2	201	0
Arneson, Justin, Fort Myers	.989	47	90	3	1	94	1
Batista, Norberto, Jupiter	1.000	1	1	0	0	1	0
Bear, Ryan, Jupiter	.983	31	56	1	1	58	0
Blalock, Jake, Clearwater	.987	125	215	10	3	228	4
Blue, Vincent, Lakeland	.983	123	293	5	5	303	2
Boyer, Kyle, Daytona	1.000	34	43	0	0	43	0
Brady, Joshua, Brevard County	1.000	2	2	0	0	2	0
Brinkley, Dante, St. Lucie	.978	52	86	3	2	91	0
Burgos, Jose, Fort Myers	.750	2	3	0	1	4	0
Cameron, Mike, St. Lucie	1.000	4	2	0	0	2	0
Carroll, Mark, Tampa	1.000	1	4	0	0	4	0
Carson, Matt, Tampa	.988	69	156	10	2	168	2
Carter, Joshua, Clearwater	.959	27	68	3	3	74	0
Clevlen, Brent, Lakeland	.979	129	259	16	6	281	5
Collins, Kevin, Daytona *	.968	51	58	2	2	62	0
Correll, Richard, Clearwater	.974	78	141	11	4	156	6
Cotto, Pedro, Lakeland *	.889	7	7	1	1	9	0
Creighton, Matt, Daytona	.947	15	17	1	1	19	1
Cruz, Jose, Daytona	...	1	0	0	0	0	0
Culpepper, Jeffrey, Daytona	.980	37	48	1	1	50	0
Davidson, Tyler, St. Lucie	1.000	2	1	0	0	1	0
De Aza, Alejandro, Jupiter *	.976	111	234	9	6	249	3
Deevers, Robby, Brevard County	.989	52	83	7	1	91	5
De La Cruz, Carlos, Brevard County	1.000	10	15	0	0	15	0
Dickerson, Christopher, Sarasota *	.963	112	231	5	9	245	1
Dunlap, Cory, Vero Beach *	1.000	1	1	0	0	1	0
Dunn, Michael, Tampa *	.982	26	53	2	1	56	0
Dyson, Colie, Vero Beach *	1.000	4	6	1	0	7	0
Ellison, Joshua, Tampa	1.000	9	14	0	0	14	0
Eure, Jeffrey, Brevard County	1.000	1	1	0	0	1	0
Evans, Michael, Palm Beach	.958	110	171	13	8	192	3
Ezi, Travis, Brevard County *	.990	97	195	7	2	204	3
Faison, Vincent, Tampa	1.000	14	42	2	0	44	0
Figueroa, Juan, Jupiter *	1.000	4	7	0	0	7	0
Floyd, Michael, Clearwater	.917	5	9	2	1	12	0
Fox, Jacob, Daytona	.000	1	0	0	1	1	0
Gentry, Philip, Sarasota	1.000	30	62	2	0	64	0
Gorecki, Reid, Palm Beach	1.000	63	131	7	0	138	1
Granato, Anthony, Daytona	.667	4	2	0	1	3	0
Guillen, Rodolfo, Tampa	.969	98	214	6	7	227	2
Haerther, Cody, Palm Beach	.967	16	28	1	1	30	0
Harvey, Ryan, St. Lucie	1.000	10	12	0	0	12	0
Hill, Jamar, St. Lucie	.979	122	277	7	6	290	3
Himes, Benjamin, Sarasota	.946	68	98	7	6	111	3
Hoffmann, Jamie, Vero Beach	1.000	42	84	0	0	84	0
Hudson, William, Sarasota	1.000	8	5	0	0	5	0
Isaacson, Gregory, Clearwater	1.000	2	1	0	0	1	0
Johnson, Jonathan, Daytona	.971	114	220	11	7	238	5
Kaplan, Jonathan, Palm Beach	.938	14	29	1	2	32	0
Kartler, Bryce, Tampa *	1.000	28	51	1	0	52	0
Kelly, Kenny, Sarasota	1.000	3	4	1	0	5	0
Kemp, Matthew, Vero Beach	.976	103	198	4	5	207	0
Klemm, Christopher, Clearwater *	1.000	10	18	1	0	19	0
Knoedler, Justin, Palm Beach	.915	28	41	2	4	47	0
Koutnik, Jared, Tampa	...	1	0	0	0	0	0
Larsen, Andrew, Daytona	1.000	3	1	1	0	2	0
Laurin, Dominique, Vero Beach	1.000	3	4	0	0	4	0
Laya, Rayner, Palm Beach	1.000	2	3	0	0	3	0
Leon, Carlos, Clearwater	1.000	4	9	0	0	9	0
Lind, Adam, Dunedin *	.962	120	148	3	6	157	1
Littleton, Brandon, Clearwater *	.984	77	184	1	3	188	0
Maldonado, Brahiam, St. Lucie	.857	5	6	0	1	7	0
Martin, Brian, Palm Beach	1.000	7	12	0	0	12	0
Mather, Joseph, Palm Beach	.969	55	85	9	3	97	3
McCoy, Michael, Palm Beach	.978	23	38	7	1	46	1
McKinney, Garth, Lakeland	.972	115	162	14	5	181	1
McQuade, Anthony, Palm Beach	.974	20	37	1	1	39	0
Medina, Rodney, Dunedin	.974	43	72	3	2	77	0
Milledge, Lastings, St. Lucie	.968	61	146	3	5	154	1

Player, Team	Pct.	G	PO	A	E	TC	DP
Molina, Angel, Jupiter	.995	103	183	9	1	193	1
Monegan, Anthony, Palm Beach	.978	24	44	0	1	45	0
Moni-Erigbali, Victor, Clearwater	.980	16	50	0	1	51	0
Moore, Robert, Jupiter	.942	25	45	4	3	52	1
Moran, Javon, Sarasota	.961	51	93	5	4	102	3
MOSS, STEVE, Brevard County	.996	115	250	9	1	260	2
Nicholson, Derek, Lakeland	1.000	10	16	1	0	17	0
Nixon, Michael, Vero Beach	1.000	12	10	0	0	10	0
Oeltjen, Trent, Fort Myers *	.987	86	148	3	2	153	1
Olmstead, Walter, Sarasota	.923	9	12	0	1	13	0
O'Toole, Paul, Daytona	1.000	28	29	1	0	30	0
Padilla, Jorge, Clearwater	1.000	14	25	2	0	27	2
Pagnozzi, Matthew, Palm Beach	...	2	0	0	0	0	0
Parker, Tyler, Palm Beach	.978	79	128	7	3	138	2
Patrick, Brian, Dunedin	1.000	26	37	1	0	38	0
Pattee, Benjamin, Fort Myers	1.000	9	19	0	0	19	0
Paul, Matthew, Vero Beach	1.000	1	4	0	0	4	0
Paul, Xavier, Vero Beach	.923	56	76	8	7	91	0
Perodin, Ronald, Fort Myers *	.967	100	202	4	7	213	2
Piepkorn, Jeremiah, Sarasota	1.000	21	22	3	0	25	0
Plumsky, Richard, Clearwater	.923	6	11	1	1	13	0
Raglani, John, Vero Beach *	.983	103	169	5	3	177	1
Reynolds, Wilton, Lakeland	1.000	4	2	0	0	2	0
Rivera, Ruben, Tampa	1.000	6	9	0	0	9	0
Rohan, James, Vero Beach	1.000	12	8	0	0	8	0
Rohleder, Andrew, Jupiter	.982	76	105	3	2	110	0
Ruggiano, Justin, Vero Beach	.955	66	101	4	5	110	0
Ruiz, Alvaro, Sarasota	.980	50	95	4	2	101	1
Russ, Ryan, Vero Beach	1.000	15	27	2	0	29	0
Schade, Ryan, Jupiter	1.000	1	0	1	0	1	0
Schutzenhofer, Andrew, Palm Beach *	1.000	1	2	0	0	2	0
Sellier, Brian, Clearwater	.992	56	123	5	1	129	2
Serfass, Jacob, Brevard County	1.000	6	6	0	0	6	0
Slack, Jonathan, St. Lucie *	1.000	69	119	3	0	122	1
Smith, David Lawrence, Dunedin	.963	104	170	14	7	191	6
Smith, Kyle, Sarasota	.975	55	77	1	2	80	0
Span, Keiunta, Fort Myers *	.976	48	75	5	2	82	1
Stewart, Caleb, St. Lucie	1.000	15	28	1	0	29	0
Taylor, Samuel, Fort Myers	1.000	1	1	0	0	1	0
Tierce, Jonathan, Tampa *	1.000	20	42	3	0	45	1
Tingler, Jayce, Dunedin *	.992	121	233	9	2	244	3
Turay, Alhaji, St. Lucie	.960	36	47	1	2	50	0
Van Iderstine, Ben, Brevard County *	1.000	7	17	0	0	17	0
Vavao, Jason, Sarasota	.917	10	11	0	1	12	0
Walker, Christopher, Daytona	.996	130	232	8	1	241	0
Walsh, Nick, Tampa	1.000	1	1	0	0	1	0
Watts, Derran, St. Lucie	.967	28	55	3	2	60	0
Waugh, Jason, Dunedin	1.000	20	31	3	0	34	0
Weston, Gordon, Daytona *	1.000	3	4	0	0	4	0
Westphal, Joshua, Daytona	1.000	16	16	0	0	16	0
Whitrock, Scott, Fort Myers	.976	109	223	17	6	246	4
Williams, Simon, Palm Beach *	.956	20	43	0	2	45	0
Wilson, Andrew, St. Lucie	.966	13	27	1	1	29	0
Zamojc, Mitchell, Fort Myers	1.000	10	12	0	0	12	0

CATCHERS

Player, Team	Pct.	G	PO	A	E	TC	DP
Arlis, Patrick, Jupiter	.982	90	632	68	13	713	7
Americh, Anthony, Jupiter	.984	29	224	24	4	252	4
BELLORIN, EDWIN, Vero Beach	.997	82	635	52	2	689	3
Blake, Ryan, Jupiter	1.000	1	4	0	0	4	0
Blevins, John, Brevard County	1.000	1	9	0	0	9	0
Brown, Gregory, Jupiter	.987	25	143	11	2	156	0
Clements, Zachary, St. Lucie	.974	6	30	8	1	39	1
Cleveland, Russell, Lakeland	.996	41	210	16	1	227	0
Corredor, Nestor, Brevard County	.993	15	117	18	1	136	1
Cortez, Jose, Clearwater	.968	45	223	22	8	253	1
de San Miguel, Allan, Fort Myers	.973	11	63	8	2	73	0
Diaz, Robinzon, Dunedin	.978	87	599	59	15	673	6
Ellis, Andrew, Vero Beach	.990	54	443	44	5	492	2
Fox, Jacob, Daytona	.992	63	470	47	4	521	3
Garcia, Yunir, St. Lucie	.991	59	421	41	4	466	3
Geiger, Kyle, Fort Myers	.985	59	425	26	7	458	2
Graham, Andrew, Lakeland	1.000	7	25	3	0	28	0
Granato, Anthony, Daytona	1.000	1	2	0	0	2	0
Greenwood, Jared, Tampa	1.000	8	73	3	0	76	0
Guevara, Orlando, Clearwater	...	1	0	0	0	0	0
Hathaway, Aaron, St. Lucie	.985	27	171	26	3	200	0
Kartler, Bryce, Tampa *	.000	1	0	0	1	1	0
Lombardi, Michael, Clearwater	1.000	3	7	0	0	7	0

Player, Team	Pct.	G	PO	A	E	TC	DP
Marcelli, Brandon, Palm Beach	.981	18	99	5	2	106	1
Martinez, Joan, St. Lucie	1.000	2	8	0	0	8	0
McCraw, Sean, St. Lucie	1.000	1	3	0	0	3	0
Medlin, Clifton, Brevard County	.985	35	254	11	4	269	2
Mendez, Jose, Palm Beach	1.000	1	6	2	0	8	0
Motooka, Rafael, Sarasota	.985	9	61	3	1	65	0
Motte, Jason, Palm Beach	.988	40	230	25	3	258	0
Nixon, Michael, Vero Beach	1.000	3	20	1	0	21	0
Norman, Zachary, Clearwater	.986	59	371	48	6	425	5
Ochoa, Blake, Jupiter	...	1	0	0	0	0	0
O'Toole, Paul, Daytona	.981	9	49	3	1	53	1
Pagnozzi, Matthew, Palm Beach	.990	60	368	32	4	404	5
Palmisano, Louis, Brevard County	.995	89	674	71	4	749	9
Parker, Tyler, Palm Beach	1.000	4	10	0	0	10	0
Perez, Miguel, Sarasota	.987	77	588	70	9	667	7
Phillips, Kyle, Fort Myers	.995	70	514	55	3	572	3
Piazza, Anthony, St. Lucie	.970	29	156	8	5	169	1
Quiroz, Guillermo, Dunedin	1.000	4	22	5	0	27	0
Reiman, Joey, Dunedin	.976	6	39	2	1	42	0
Richie, Anthony, Daytona	.995	71	568	44	3	615	6
Roa, Joel, Lakeland	1.000	1	2	0	0	2	0
Robles, Luis, Tampa	.958	8	42	4	2	48	0
Rojas, Thomas, Tampa	.991	74	510	36	5	551	4
Rosenthal, Benjamin, Palm Beach	1.000	4	18	1	0	19	1
Sanchez, Danilo, Lakeland	.996	103	711	56	3	770	10
Santiago, Benito, St. Lucie	1.000	2	9	2	0	11	0
Schneider, John, Dunedin	.981	16	98	8	2	108	0
Skelton, James, Lakeland	...	1	0	0	0	0	0
Sprowl, Jon, Tampa	.989	54	341	25	4	370	1
Toops, Brady, Palm Beach	.988	25	154	15	2	171	2
Tugwell, Marc, Clearwater	.989	43	242	34	3	279	6
Urgelles, Jeffrey, Sarasota	.985	51	375	30	6	411	1
Whittaker, Timothy, Dunedin	.993	36	264	18	2	284	3
Willingham, Josh, Jupiter	1.000	2	14	0	0	14	0
Wilson, Andrew, St. Lucie	.985	20	116	18	2	136	2
Wilson, Brandon, St. Lucie	1.000	2	11	1	0	12	0

PITCHERS

Player, Team	Pct.	G	PO	A	E	TC	DP
Adamczyk, Tyler, Palm Beach	1.000	14	5	13	0	18	0
Adames, Geovanny, Sarasota	...	2	0	0	0	0	0
Aguilar, Raymond, Jupiter *	...	1	0	0	0	0	0
Alexander, Mark, Vero Beach	.800	52	2	2	1	5	0
Alfonseca, Antonio, Jupiter	...	3	0	0	0	0	0
Almenar, Aristides, St. Lucie	...	1	0	0	0	0	0
Alvarez, Juan, Clearwater	...	3	0	0	0	0	0
Alvarez, Oscar, Palm Beach *	.923	7	2	10	1	13	0
Anderson, Ryan, Brevard County *	1.000	6	0	2	0	2	0
Arteaga, Erick, Clearwater	.938	32	6	9	1	16	0
Artiles, Carlos, Tampa *	1.000	9	0	1	0	1	0
Atlee, Thomas, Daytona	1.000	20	3	1	0	4	0
Axelson, Joshua, Palm Beach	.917	9	7	4	1	12	0
Baez, Federico, Daytona	1.000	3	0	2	0	2	0
Bailey, Chad, Vero Beach *	...	7	0	0	0	0	0
Baker, Ryan, Jupiter	1.000	6	2	0	0	2	0
Baldwin, Ancil, Lakeland	1.000	12	2	1	0	3	1
Barrack, Jacob, Clearwater	...	7	0	0	0	0	0
Barreto, Joel, Sarasota	.833	18	2	3	1	6	0
Basham, Robert, Sarasota	.727	10	2	6	3	11	1
Batista, Roberto, Palm Beach	.850	43	3	14	3	20	0
Bauer, Gregory, Clearwater	1.000	24	2	9	0	11	1
Baxter, Allen, Jupiter	.857	12	3	3	1	7	0
Beam, Theodore, Tampa	1.000	12	1	0	0	1	0
Bechtel, Charles, Palm Beach	1.000	5	1	1	0	2	0
Belson, Gregory, St. Lucie	1.000	25	5	2	0	7	0
Benson, Kris, St. Lucie	1.000	1	1	0	0	1	0
Berroa, Yesson, Dunedin	1.000	9	1	1	0	2	0
Bierd, Randor, Lakeland	1.000	4	1	2	0	3	1
Blackburn, Robert, Fort Myers	.900	15	8	10	2	20	2
Blair, Thomas, Palm Beach *	1.000	6	0	8	0	8	0
Blasdell, Jared, Clearwater	...	8	0	0	0	0	0
Boehringer, Brian, Tampa	1.000	2	0	1	0	1	0
Bong, Jung Keun, Sarasota *	.000	1	0	0	1	1	0
Borrell, Daniel, Tampa *	.667	6	3	3	3	9	0
Bostick II, Adam, Jupiter *	.786	17	2	9	3	14	0
Bott, Glenn, Vero Beach *	1.000	14	1	3	0	4	0
Bramasco, Leslie, Clearwater	...	2	0	0	0	0	0
Brandenburg, Adam, Jupiter *	.833	7	0	5	1	6	1
Brumit, Mathew, Tampa	1.000	20	3	3	0	6	0
Bucktrot, Keith, Clearwater	1.000	3	2	0	0	2	0

Player, Team	Pct.	G	PO	A	E	TC	DP
BUMSTEAD, NATHAN, Lakeland	1.000	25	20	13	0	33	0
Burrows, Angelo, Daytona	1.000	3	0	1	0	1	0
Butto, Francisco, Clearwater	1.000	17	0	5	0	5	0
Buzachero, Edward, Dunedin	...	2	0	0	0	0	0
Camacho, Edward, St. Lucie *	1.000	45	3	6	0	9	1
Cannon, Edward, Dunedin	1.000	1	1	1	0	2	0
Carlsen, Clary, Clearwater	.938	32	12	18	2	32	1
Castillo, Jonathan, St. Lucie	...	1	0	0	0	0	0
Castle, Heath, Tampa *	.929	36	2	11	1	14	0
Cavazos, Andres, Palm Beach	.800	28	2	2	1	5	0
Cave, Kevin, Jupiter	1.000	11	1	0	0	1	0
Cherry, William, Sarasota	1.000	13	3	0	0	3	0
Clippard, Tyler, Tampa	.875	26	4	10	2	16	2
Cordova, Vincent, St. Lucie	.875	25	5	16	3	24	2
Core, Daniel, Dunedin	...	9	0	0	0	0	0
Costello, Ryan, Brevard County *	1.000	24	4	10	0	14	1
Cotton, Nathan, Palm Beach	...	2	0	0	0	0	0
Cox, James, Tampa	1.000	16	0	8	0	8	1
Cox, Michael, St. Lucie	...	1	0	0	0	0	0
Crawford, Tristan, Fort Myers	.769	32	3	7	3	13	0
Crews, Jordan, Daytona	1.000	10	0	1	0	1	0
Cueto, Johnny, Sarasota	1.000	2	0	1	0	1	0
Cullen, Ryan, St. Lucie *	1.000	13	0	2	0	2	0
Currier, Rik, Clearwater	.667	16	1	1	1	3	0
De La Cruz, Eulogio, Lakeland	.947	40	10	8	1	19	1
De La Cruz, Jose, Jupiter	...	2	0	0	0	0	0
de los Santos, Valerio, Jupiter *	...	3	0	0	0	0	0
Demontel II, James, Jupiter	.778	32	2	5	2	9	2
De Paula, Jorge, Tampa	1.000	4	1	1	0	2	0
DePaula, Julio, Fort Myers	.875	36	5	9	2	16	1
Diaz, Jose, Vero Beach	.750	14	1	2	1	4	0
Diggins, Ben, Brevard County	1.000	12	1	0	0	1	0
Dillard, Timothy, Brevard County	.909	28	16	24	4	44	1
Dove, Dennis, Palm Beach	1.000	8	5	5	0	10	1
Doyne, Michael, Palm Beach	1.000	6	0	1	0	1	0
Dumatrait, Phillip, Sarasota *	1.000	3	0	1	0	1	0
Durost, Kenneth, Brevard County	.938	29	3	12	1	16	0
Edens, Kyle, Sarasota	1.000	37	5	14	0	19	1
Edlich, Kyle, Fort Myers *	...	2	0	0	0	0	0
Evangelista, Nicholas, Clearwater	1.000	37	3	13	0	16	0
Evert, Brett, Brevard County *	1.000	7	1	0	0	1	0
Fermin, Angelo, Fort Myers	...	1	0	0	0	0	0
Ferreras, Yorkin, Daytona *	.750	14	0	6	2	8	0
Figueroa, Jonathan, Vero Beach *	1.000	22	3	16	0	19	1
Flury, Patrick, Jupiter	1.000	8	0	1	0	1	0
Foli, Daniel, St. Lucie	1.000	37	2	6	0	8	0
French, Lucas, Lakeland *	1.000	4	3	0	0	3	0
Galbizo, Rafael, Jupiter	...	3	0	0	0	0	0
Gallagher, Sean, Daytona	...	1	0	0	0	0	0
Garcia, Anderson, St. Lucie	1.000	16	2	1	0	3	0
Garcia, Jose, Palm Beach	1.000	30	9	16	0	25	0
Garcia, Jose, Jupiter	...	1	0	0	0	0	0
Gardner, Michael, Tampa	1.000	21	2	2	0	4	0
Garmon, Bryan, Sarasota *	.750	8	2	1	1	4	0
Garza, Justin, Palm Beach	1.000	29	4	6	0	10	1
Gerk, Jordan, Daytona *	.933	52	1	13	1	15	0
Glaser, Eric, Clearwater	.833	9	2	3	1	6	0
Gogal, Jeffrey, Jupiter *	.923	13	2	10	1	13	0
Gomez, Abel, Tampa *	.800	15	2	10	3	15	2
Granado, Jan, Fort Myers *	.778	25	1	6	2	9	1
Gray, Joshua, Fort Myers *	1.000	32	3	15	0	18	0
Griffin, David, Sarasota *	...	2	0	0	0	0	0
Gross, Kristopher, Daytona	...	6	0	0	0	0	0
Grybash, Daniel, Brevard County	.667	17	0	2	1	3	0
Guevara, Jose, Sarasota	1.000	44	2	6	0	8	1
Gutierrez, Jannio, Fort Myers	.857	15	1	5	1	7	0
Gwaltney, William, Daytona	1.000	22	3	10	0	13	0
Habel, Joshua, Brevard County *	1.000	11	1	4	0	5	0
Haberer, Eric, Palm Beach *	1.000	17	4	16	0	20	2
Hall, Jeremy, Brevard County	.800	45	1	3	1	5	0
Hall, Josh, Sarasota	1.000	7	2	7	0	9	0
Hamels, Colbert, Clearwater *	1.000	3	1	2	0	3	0
Hammond, Steven, Brevard County *	.857	8	3	3	1	7	0
Hanrahan, Joel, Vero Beach	1.000	5	3	2	0	5	1
Harang, Daryl, Dunedin	.900	14	6	3	1	10	0
Harben, Adam, Fort Myers	.929	25	7	19	2	28	1
Harmsen, Brandon, Tampa	1.000	19	0	3	0	3	0
Harper, Jeremy, Dunedin	1.000	26	3	2	0	5	0
Hendley, Blake, Sarasota	1.000	10	4	2	0	6	0
Henkenjohann, Tim, Fort Myers	.667	7	1	1	1	3	0
Hensen, Brian, Lakeland *	1.000	43	2	8	0	10	1
Heredia, Felix, St. Lucie *	1.000	5	2	1	0	3	0
Hernandez, Gabriel, St. Lucie	.875	10	3	4	1	8	0
Hernandez, Yoel, Clearwater	1.000	4	1	0	0	1	0
Hill, Danny, Dunedin	1.000	33	8	4	0	12	1
Hill, Jeremy, St. Lucie	1.000	7	0	2	0	2	0
Hill, Joshua, Fort Myers	1.000	7	1	0	0	1	0
Hoff, Brian, Jupiter	1.000	28	2	4	0	6	0
Holdzkom, Lincoln, Jupiter	1.000	9	0	1	0	1	0
Homer, Christopher, Lakeland	1.000	54	1	4	0	5	0
Honsa, Christopher, Clearwater	.929	25	3	10	1	14	0
Hoorelbeke, Casey, Vero Beach	.923	42	7	17	2	26	1
Hudson, William, Sarasota	1.000	2	1	1	0	2	1
Hughes, Philip, Tampa	1.000	5	2	1	0	3	1
Humber, Philip, St. Lucie	1.000	14	3	7	0	10	0
Iehl, Jason, Jupiter	.667	23	0	6	3	9	1
Isenberg, Kurt, Dunedin *	1.000	26	9	21	0	30	1
Ishii, Kazuhisa, St. Lucie *	1.000	1	0	1	0	1	0
Jackson, Zach, Dunedin *	1.000	10	4	15	0	19	0
James, Justin, Dunedin	.909	44	12	8	2	22	0
Janssen, Robert, Dunedin	1.000	10	10	9	0	19	0
Japa, Rolando, Tampa	1.000	1	2	1	0	3	0
Jones, Blake, Jupiter	1.000	16	0	2	0	2	0
Jones, Jason, Tampa	.962	26	6	19	1	26	0
Jones, Justin, Fort Myers *	.870	13	7	13	3	23	0
Kauten, Joshua, Lakeland	1.000	6	3	9	0	12	1
Kendrick, Kyle, Clearwater	1.000	1	1	0	0	1	0
Kennard, Jeffery, Tampa	1.000	42	4	1	0	5	0
King, Bryan, St. Lucie	.000	6	0	0	1	1	0
King, Jeremy, Tampa	1.000	24	2	10	0	12	0
Knoff, Justin, Palm Beach	...	2	0	0	0	0	0
Knox, Michael, Tampa	1.000	14	1	4	0	5	0
Kobow, Michael, Lakeland	1.000	14	0	1	0	1	0
Koehler, Kurt, Jupiter	1.000	3	0	1	0	1	0
Kuo, Hong-Chih, Vero Beach *	1.000	11	1	1	0	2	0
Lambert, Christopher, Palm Beach	1.000	10	2	9	0	11	0
Lanier, Thomas, Sarasota	1.000	2	2	2	0	4	0
Larrison, Preston, Lakeland	.875	9	4	3	1	8	0
Layden, Timothy, Daytona *	1.000	3	1	0	0	1	0
Lee, Seung Hak, Clearwater	1.000	2	1	1	0	2	1
Leger, Jose, Fort Myers	...	1	0	0	0	0	0
Lerch, Zachary, Jupiter	1.000	7	1	4	0	5	0
Lewis, Jeremy, Brevard County *	.833	55	0	5	1	6	0
Lohse, Erik, Sarasota	.950	39	4	15	1	20	3
Lopez, Rafael, St. Lucie	1.000	5	2	1	0	3	0
Lundgren, Wayne, Palm Beach	1.000	25	6	3	0	9	0
MacDonald, Michael, Dunedin	.966	25	3	25	1	29	0
MacLane, Evan, St. Lucie *	.875	19	3	18	3	24	1
Maduro, Calvin, Tampa	1.000	3	1	0	0	1	0
Maldonado Oquendo, Ivan, St. Lucie	.769	27	3	7	3	13	0
Mallett, Justin, Sarasota	1.000	16	3	3	0	6	0
Mannix, Kevin, St. Lucie	...	1	0	0	0	0	0
Marmol, Carlos, Daytona	1.000	13	5	8	0	13	0
Marshall, Sean, Daytona *	.929	12	3	10	1	14	0
Martin, Adrian, Dunedin	1.000	5	1	0	0	1	0
Martin, Forrest, Brevard County	1.000	12	3	6	0	9	0
Martinez, Carlos, Jupiter	1.000	47	2	10	0	12	0
Martinez, Cristhian, Lakeland	...	3	0	0	0	0	0
Mateo, Juan, Daytona	.846	32	1	10	2	13	0
Mathes, Alfred, Daytona *	.897	24	7	28	4	39	1
Mathieson, Scott, Clearwater	.700	23	3	4	3	10	0
Mattox, David, Sarasota	.889	16	5	11	2	18	0
McCormack, Zachariah, Jupiter *	1.000	4	0	1	0	1	0
McCoy, Michael, Palm Beach	...	1	0	0	0	0	0
McDowell, Kevin, Lakeland *	.889	35	3	13	2	18	2
McGowan, Dustin, Dunedin	1.000	5	2	2	0	4	0
McNutt, Michael, Jupiter	.750	13	0	3	1	4	0
Medlock, Calvin, Sarasota	1.000	25	3	11	0	14	1
Megrew, Michael, Vero Beach *	1.000	2	0	1	0	1	0
Mejias, Jose Angel, Clearwater	1.000	1	1	0	0	1	0
Mendez, Adalberto, Daytona	1.000	23	2	4	0	6	0
Mendez, Jesus, Tampa	1.000	1	0	1	0	1	0
Merricks, Matthew, Vero Beach *	.750	10	1	2	1	4	0
Michael, Mark, Palm Beach	.870	18	9	11	3	23	0
Mijares, Jose, Fort Myers *	1.000	5	0	2	0	2	0
Mildren, Paul, Jupiter *	1.000	29	3	15	0	18	0
Miller, Greg, Vero Beach *	1.000	5	1	3	0	4	0
Miller, Ryan, Brevard County	...	2	0	0	0	0	0
Molldrem, Craig, Jupiter	1.000	5	1	1	0	2	0
Morales, Jorge, Tampa	1.000	11	1	1	0	2	0
Morenko, Brad, Sarasota	1.000	9	3	0	0	3	0
Morris, Matt, Palm Beach	1.000	2	1	3	0	4	0
Moscat, Marvin, Tampa	.889	31	2	14	2	18	0

ADVANCED CLASS A Florida State League

Player, Team	Pct.	G	PO	A	E	TC	DP
Mota, Guillermo, Jupiter	...	2	0	0	0	0	0
Muegge, Danny, Vero Beach	.953	31	14	27	2	43	4
Mumma, Bradley, Dunedin *	1.000	45	11	12	0	23	1
Muñiz, Carlos, St. Lucie	1.000	14	1	2	0	3	0
Nall, Brandon, St. Lucie	1.000	2	0	1	0	1	0
Nicholson, Derek, Lakeland	...	1	0	0	0	0	0
O'Brien, Weston, Daytona	1.000	21	2	6	0	8	0
Ojeda, Alvis, Vero Beach	1.000	28	3	4	0	7	0
Olivera, Manuel, Jupiter *	.950	35	1	18	1	20	1
O'Neal, Charles, Sarasota *	1.000	10	0	2	0	2	0
Orenduff, Justin, Vero Beach	.857	12	3	3	1	7	0
Ortiz, Ramon, Sarasota	1.000	1	0	1	0	1	0
Ostlund, Ian, Lakeland *	1.000	19	0	4	0	4	0
Overman, Matthew, Jupiter	1.000	27	1	7	0	8	2
Owens, Henry, St. Lucie	1.000	38	3	3	0	6	0
Padilla, Vicente, Clearwater	.750	1	2	1	1	4	0
Paduch, James, Sarasota	.962	23	9	16	1	26	3
Parcus, William, Clearwater *	1.000	38	6	8	0	14	0
Parisi, Michael, Palm Beach	.958	13	8	15	1	24	2
Pavano, Carl, Tampa	1.000	1	2	0	0	2	0
Pelland, Tyler, Sarasota *	1.000	30	2	15	0	17	0
Pena, Luismar, Brevard County	.944	15	7	10	1	18	0
Penny, Brad, Vero Beach	...	1	0	0	0	0	0
Perez, Beltran, Vero Beach	1.000	19	1	3	0	4	1
Perez, Jose Miguel, Clearwater	...	3	0	0	0	0	0
Perkins, Glen, Fort Myers *	.667	10	0	2	1	3	0
Petrick, William, Daytona	1.000	9	3	7	0	10	0
Phelps, Michael, Daytona	1.000	4	1	1	0	2	0
Pilkington, Brian, Vero Beach	1.000	19	8	20	0	28	4
Pimentel, Julio Cesar, Vero Beach	.944	26	8	9	1	18	1
Pinango, Miguel, St. Lucie	.923	12	4	8	1	13	0
Plummer, Jarod, Vero Beach	1.000	9	1	3	0	4	0
Polanco, Alfredo, Daytona	1.000	13	1	4	0	5	0
Pomeranz, Stuart, Palm Beach	1.000	8	4	10	0	14	0
Powers, Joseph, Sarasota	1.000	4	0	1	0	1	0
Prahm, Ryan, Dunedin	...	2	0	0	0	0	0
Purcey, David, Dunedin *	1.000	21	5	13	0	18	0
Quezada, Elvys, Tampa	1.000	19	0	5	0	5	0
Rainville, Jay, Fort Myers	1.000	9	3	3	0	6	0
Ramirez, Greg, St. Lucie	.857	18	2	4	1	7	0
Ramsey, Keith, Clearwater *	1.000	12	2	12	0	14	2
Randazzo, Jeffrey, Palm Beach *	1.000	8	1	1	0	2	0
Rapada, Clayton, Daytona *	1.000	27	1	7	0	8	0
Rasowsky, Avi, Jupiter *	...	1	0	0	0	0	0
Rawson, Anthony, Palm Beach *	.833	18	0	5	1	6	0
Reed, Brian, Dunedin	.933	40	4	10	1	15	0
Ribas, Gabriel, Clearwater	1.000	11	2	9	0	11	0
Richardson, Robert, Clearwater *	1.000	15	3	2	0	5	0
Riggan, Jerrod, St. Lucie	1.000	4	0	2	0	2	0
Rincon, Daniel, Sarasota	.889	16	5	3	1	9	0
Rival, Kevin, Brevard County	1.000	6	0	3	0	3	0
Rodriguez, Jermy, Lakeland	.833	21	1	4	1	6	1
Rodriguez, Jose, St. Lucie	...	3	0	0	0	0	0
Rodriguez, Mike, Vero Beach	.500	10	0	1	1	2	0
Rodriguez, Orlando, Vero Beach *	1.000	12	1	1	0	2	1
Rogers, Brian, Lakeland	.929	52	6	7	1	14	2
Rohan, James, Vero Beach	...	1	0	0	0	0	0
Romero, Davis, Dunedin *	.943	34	9	24	2	35	0
Romero, Ricardo, Dunedin *	1.000	8	3	4	0	7	0
Rosario, Carlos, Tampa	1.000	5	0	1	0	1	0
Russ, Christopher, Palm Beach	.933	29	3	11	1	15	0
Russ, James, Jupiter	.955	27	5	16	1	22	3
Sanchez, Felix, Lakeland *	1.000	22	3	1	0	4	1
Savickas, Russell, Dunedin	...	1	0	0	0	0	0
Sawatski, John, Fort Myers *	.769	43	3	7	3	13	0
Scalamandre, Richard, Palm Beach	1.000	47	3	5	0	8	1
Schade, Ryan, Jupiter	...	3	0	0	0	0	0
Schappert, Paul, Daytona *	.833	21	1	4	1	6	0
Schmidt, Jeremy, Sarasota	1.000	7	0	2	0	2	0
Schultz, Cory, Clearwater	...	3	0	0	0	0	0
Schutt, Christopher, Fort Myers	1.000	38	4	13	0	17	1
Schweitzer, Stephen, Palm Beach *	1.000	22	0	4	0	4	0
Segovia, Zachary, Clearwater	.958	27	4	19	1	24	0
Sevier, Nathan, Daytona	.867	31	5	8	2	15	0
Shafer, Adam, Clearwater	.667	20	0	2	1	3	0
Shafer, David, Sarasota	1.000	10	1	1	0	2	0
Shaver, Christopher, Daytona *	1.000	6	0	5	0	5	0
Shaver, Justin, Vero Beach *	.917	44	2	9	1	12	1
Simmons, Justin, Vero Beach	1.000	14	4	11	0	15	0
Simonitsch, Errol, Fort Myers *	1.000	14	4	11	0	15	0
Skaggs, Jon, Tampa	1.000	6	3	3	0	6	0
Slack, Nicholas, Brevard County	1.000	39	1	5	0	6	0
Smith, Brett, Tampa	.923	14	5	7	1	13	0
Smith, Charles, St. Lucie	.947	24	8	10	1	19	4
Smith, Joshua, Tampa	...	9	0	0	0	0	0
Solis, Hairo, Tampa	...	2	0	0	0	0	0
Sopko, Mark, Dunedin	...	13	0	0	0	0	0
Soto, Darwin, Brevard County	1.000	17	1	4	0	5	0
Soto, Edgar, Tampa	...	2	0	0	0	0	0
Spooneybarger, Tim, Jupiter	1.000	4	0	1	0	1	0
Squires, Matthew, Clearwater *	1.000	22	0	1	0	1	0
Stiles, Brad, Daytona *	1.000	5	0	1	0	1	0
Stockman, Landon, Brevard County	1.000	31	1	4	0	5	0
Strayhorn, Kole, St. Lucie	.800	33	1	3	1	5	0
Strelitz, Brian, Jupiter	...	5	0	0	0	0	0
Strickland, Scott, St. Lucie	1.000	1	1	1	0	2	0
Sturtze, Tanyon, Tampa	1.000	2	0	1	0	1	0
Swarzak, Anthony, Fort Myers	1.000	10	4	5	0	9	0
Sweeney, Matthew, Clearwater	1.000	14	7	6	0	13	0
Swindell, Michael, St. Lucie	1.000	6	3	7	0	10	0
Tankersley, Taylor, Jupiter *	1.000	4	0	8	0	8	1
Tata, Jordan, Lakeland	.955	25	20	22	2	44	1
Tate, Derek, Dunedin *	...	1	0	0	0	0	0
Taubenheim, Ty, Brevard County	1.000	16	3	10	0	13	1
Tautor, Peter, Fort Myers	.667	16	1	1	1	3	0
Tavares, Anderson, Daytona	.875	27	3	11	2	16	2
Tavarez, Milton, Dunedin	1.000	51	7	3	0	10	0
Teekel, Joshua, Jupiter	1.000	5	0	2	0	2	0
Thatcher, Joeseph, Brevard County *	1.000	7	0	1	0	1	0
Thomas, Eric, Brevard County	...	4	0	0	0	0	0
Thorp, Paul, Tampa	.889	50	4	4	1	9	1
Thorpe, Tracy, Dunedin	1.000	25	3	4	0	7	0
Tiffany, Charles, Vero Beach *	.828	22	3	21	5	29	1
Till, Brock, Sarasota	1.000	29	13	5	0	18	1
Tillman, Derek, Jupiter	1.000	23	2	1	0	3	0
Timm, Jordan, Dunedin *	1.000	1	1	0	0	1	0
Tompkins, Jacob, Clearwater	...	5	0	0	0	0	0
Torres, Andy, Jupiter	1.000	6	1	4	0	5	0
Torres, Jaymes, Palm Beach	1.000	3	0	5	0	5	0
Trachsel, Steve, St. Lucie	1.000	2	0	1	0	1	0
Treanor, Bryan, Jupiter	...	1	0	0	0	0	0
Tressler, Aaron, Dunedin	1.000	2	1	0	0	1	0
Tyler, Scott, Fort Myers	1.000	23	9	8	0	17	1
Urdaneta, Lino, St. Lucie	...	3	0	0	0	0	0
Valdez, Edward, Sarasota	1.000	14	7	14	0	21	3
Valdez, Ismael, Jupiter	...	2	0	0	0	0	0
Vanden Hurk, Henricus, Jupiter	1.000	2	0	1	0	1	0
Vargas, Jason, Jupiter *	1.000	9	2	5	0	7	0
Vasquez, Virgil, Lakeland	1.000	8	3	3	0	6	0
Verlander, Justin, Lakeland	.920	13	11	12	2	25	0
Villanueva, Carlos, Brevard County	1.000	21	4	12	0	16	1
Waldie, Andrew, Clearwater	.000	2	0	0	1	1	0
Walker, Brian, St. Lucie *	.800	17	1	3	1	5	0
Wallace, Shane, Palm Beach *	...	1	0	0	0	0	0
Webb, Alan, Clearwater *	1.000	13	4	5	0	9	0
Weber, Matthew, Daytona	1.000	2	1	2	0	3	0
Wells, Randy, Daytona	.867	41	2	11	2	15	1
White, Steven, Tampa	1.000	3	2	1	0	3	0
Williams, Matthew, Fort Myers	...	1	0	0	0	0	0
Wilson, Kyle, Vero Beach	1.000	18	1	1	0	2	0
Wolfe, Brian, Brevard County	1.000	18	1	3	0	4	0
Woodrow, Christopher, Clearwater	1.000	3	0	1	0	1	0
Worrell, Mark, Palm Beach	1.000	53	7	9	0	16	0
Worthington, Timothy, St. Lucie	1.000	13	2	4	0	6	0
Wright, Dequam, Vero Beach *	...	6	0	0	0	0	0
Wright, Jaret, Tampa	1.000	2	2	2	0	4	0
Wylie, Jason, Daytona	1.000	10	1	3	0	4	0
Yates, Kyle, Dunedin	.895	14	8	9	2	19	1
Yourkin, Matthew, Jupiter *	1.000	22	0	4	0	4	0
Zell, Daniel, Lakeland *	1.000	49	10	11	0	21	1

LEAGUE CHAMPIONS

Year	Team	Pct.	Year	Team	Pct.	Year	Team	Pct.
1919—	Sanford*	.605		St. Petersburg	.618		Tampa†	.696
	Orlando*	.703	1923—	Orlando	.667	1926—	Sanford	.647
1920—	Tampa	.654		Orlando	.678		Sanford	.623
	Tampa	.722	1924—	Lakeland	.695	1927—	Orlando†	.600
1921—	Orlando	.635		Lakeland	.683		Miami	.661
1922—	St. Petersburg	.503	1925—	St. Petersburg	.667	1928-35—	Did not operate.	

Year	Team	Pct.
1936—	Gainesville	.542
	St. Augustine (4th)†	.492
1937—	Gainesville§	.616
1938—	Leesburg	.626
	Gainesville (2nd)‡	.615
1939—	Sanford§	.787
1940—	Daytona Beach	.619
	Orlando (4th)‡	.507
1941—	St. Augustine	.659
	Leesburg (4th)‡	.488
1942-45—	Did not operate.	
1946—	Orlando§	.681
1947—	St. Augustine	.625
	St. Augustine (2nd)‡	.584
1948—	Orlando	.643
	Daytona Beach (2nd)‡	.616
1949—	Gainesville	.635
	St. Augustine (3rd)‡	.556
1950—	Orlando	.629
	DeLand (3rd)‡	.590
1951—	DeLand§	.643
1952—	DeLand∞	.704
	Palatka (3rd)‡	.569
1953—	Daytona Beach†	.657
	DeLand	.703
1954—	Jacksonville Beach	.629
	Lakeland†	.594
1955—	Orlando	.671
	Orlando	.643
1956—	Cocoa	.614
	Cocoa	.671
1957—	Palatka	.629
	Tampa†	.681
1958—	St. Petersburg	.732
	St. Petersburg	.681
1959—	Tampa	.591
	St. Petersburg†	.612
1960—	Lakeland	.731
	Palatka†	.614
1961—	Tampa†	.710
	Sarasota	.696
1962—	Sarasota	.689
	Fort Lauderdale†	.623
1963—	Sarasota	.645
	Sarasota	.667
1964—	Fort Lauderdale†	.629
	St. Petersburg	.594
1965—	Fort Lauderdale	.627
	Fort Lauderdale	.634
1966—	Leesburg†	.781
	St. Petersburg	.700
1967—	St. Petersburg▲	.691
	Orlando	.638
1968—	Miami	.613
	Orlando◆	.579
1969—	Miami■	.606
	Orlando	.606
1970—	Miami▼	.662
	St. Petersburg	.600
1971—	Miami▼	.667

Year	Team	Pct.
	Daytona Beach	.586
1972—	Miami*	.562
	Daytona Beach	.606
1973—	St. Petersburg††	.575
	West Palm Beach	.580
1974—	West Palm Beach††	.598
	Fort Lauderdale	.626
1975—	St. Petersburg††	.652
	Miami	.581
1976—	Tampa	.559
	Lakeland††	.536
1977—	Lakeland††	.616
	West Palm Beach	.583
1978—	Lakeland	.565
	Miami§	.539
1979—	Fort Lauderdale	.643
	Winter Haven‡‡	.577
1980—	Daytona Beach	.628
	Fort Lauderdale††	.606
1981—	Fort Myers	.554
	Daytona Beach§§	.504
1982—	Fort Lauderdale§§	.621
	Tampa	.546
1983—	Daytona Beach	.634
	Vero Beach§§	.515
1984—	Tampa	.532
	Fort Lauderdale§§	.521
1985—	Fort Myers∞∞	.590
	Fort Lauderdale	.550
1986—	St. Petersburg∞∞	.647
	West Palm Beach	.593
1987—	Fort Lauderdale∞∞	.616
	Osceola	.576
1988—	Osceola	.606
	St. Lucie▲▲	.532
1989—	Port Charlotte▲▲	.540
	St. Petersburg	.540
1990—	West Palm Beach	.697
	Vero Beach▲▲	.585
1991—	Clearwater	.623
	West Palm Beach▲▲	.550
1992—	Sarasota	.639
	Lakeland◆◆	.530
1993—	St. Lucie	.600
	Clearwater§§	.556
1994—	Tampa§§	.606
	Brevard County	.561
1995—	Daytona§§	.644
	Fort Myers	.577
1996—	Tampa	.627
	St. Lucie§§	.534
1997—	St. Petersburg■■	.591
	Vero Beach	.511
1998—	Charlotte	.594
	St. Lucie■■	.515
1999—	Dunedin	.628
	Kissimmee■■	.578
2000—	Dunedin	.609

Year	Team	Pct.
	Daytona■■	.547
2001—	Brevard County▼▼	.593
	Tampa▼▼	.554
2002—	Charlotte■■	.600
2003—	St. Lucie■■	.554
2004—	Daytona▼▼▼	.555
	Tampa▼▼▼	.564
2005—	Palm Beach■ ■	.493

*Split-season playoff abandoned after each team won three games. †Won split-season playoff. ‡Won four-club playoff. §Won championship and four-club playoff. ∞Won both halves of split season. ▲League divided into Eastern and Western divisions with split season. St. Petersburg and Orlando won both halves of split season; St. Petersburg won playoff. ◆League divided into Eastern and Western divisions. Miami won regular-season pennant on basis of highest won-lost percentage. Orlando won four-club playoff involving first two teams in each division. ■ League divided into Southern and Central divisions. Miami won playoff between division leaders. (NOTE—Pennant awarded to playoff winner in 1936.) ▼League divided into Eastern and Western divisions. Miami won regular-season pennant on basis of highest won-loss percentage, and also won four-club playoff involving first two teams in each division. *League divided into Eastern and Western divisions. Won four-club playoff involving first two teams in each division. ††League divided into Northern and Southern divisions. Won four-club playoff involving first two teams in each division. ‡‡League divided into Northern and Southern divisions. Same two clubs won both halves; won playoffs. §§Won split-season playoff. ∞∞League divided into Western, Central and Southern divisions. Won four-club playoff. ▲▲League divided into Eastern, Western and Central divisions; played split-season. Won six-club playoff. ◆◆League divided into Eastern, Western and Central divisions; played split-season. Won eight-club playoff.

■ ■ League divided into East and West divisions and played split season; won four-club playoff. ▼▼League divided into East and West divisions and played split season; teams were about to start final round of playoffs, but were declared co-champions when Professional Baseball declared a stoppage of play. ▼▼▼League divided into East and West divisions and played split season; teams declared co-champions when championship series is canceled because of a hurricane threat.

MIDWEST LEAGUE

CLASS A *Midwest League*

LEAGUE OFFICE

President
George H. Spelius

Address
P.O. Box 936
Beloit, WI 53512

Phone
608-364-1188

Teams (affiliation)
Beloit Snappers (Twins)
Burlington Bees (Royals)
Cedar Rapids Kernels (Angels)
Clinton LumberKings (Rangers)
Dayton Dragons (Reds)
Fort Wayne Wizards (Padres)
Kane County Cougars (A's)
Lansing Lugnuts (Blue Jays)

Peoria Chiefs (Cubs)
Swing of the Quad Cities (Cardinals)
South Bend Silver Hawks (Diamondbacks)
Southwest Michigan Devil Rays (Devil Rays)
West Michigan Whitecaps (Tigers)
Wisconsin Timber Rattlers (Mariners)

2005 FINAL STANDINGS

FIRST HALF

EASTERN DIVISION

Team	W	L	T	Pct.	GB
South Bend Silver Hawks	41	29	-	.586	-
Fort Wayne Wizards	38	32	-	.543	3
Lansing Lugnuts	37	32	-	.536	3.5
Southwest Michigan Devil Rays	33	36	-	.478	7.5
West Michigan Whitecaps	33	37	-	.471	8
Dayton Dragons	30	40	-	.429	11

WESTERN DIVISION

Team	W	L	T	Pct.	GB
Wisconsin Timber Rattlers	39	31	-	.557	-
Clinton LumberKings	38	32	-	.543	1
Swing of the Quad Cities	36	33	-	.522	2.5
Peoria Chiefs	35	35	-	.500	4
Burlington Bees	34	36	-	.486	5
Beloit Snappers	33	37	-	.471	6
Kane County Cougars	31	38	-	.449	7.5
Cedar Rapids Kernels	30	40	-	.429	9

SECOND HALF

EASTERN DIVISION

Team	W	L	T	Pct.	GB
South Bend Silver Hawks	43	27	-	.614	-
West Michigan Whitecaps	40	30	-	.571	3
Southwest Michigan Devil Rays	39	31	-	.557	4
Lansing Lugnuts	33	37	-	.471	10
Dayton Dragons	30	39	-	.435	12.5
Fort Wayne Wizards	27	43	-	.386	16

WESTERN DIVISION

Team	W	L	T	Pct.	GB
Wisconsin Timber Rattlers	37	32	-	.536	-
Kane County Cougars	36	34	-	.514	1.5
Beloit Snappers	36	34	-	.514	1.5
Swing of the Quad Cities	36	34	-	.514	1.5
Cedar Rapids Kernels	35	35	-	.500	2.5
Peoria Chiefs	33	37	-	.471	4.5
Clinton LumberKings	33	37	-	.471	4.5
Burlington Bees	31	39	-	.443	6.5

COMPOSITE

CLUB (AFFILIATE), ABBREV	SOU	WIS	WMI	QC	SWM	CLI	LAN	BEL	PEO	KCC	BUR	CED	FTW	DAY	W	L	PCT	GB
South Bend (Diamondbacks), SOU	...	4	8	5	8	8	8	5	6	3	5	5	8	11	84	56	.600	-
Wisconsin (Mariners), WIS	4	...	4	8	3	7	3	8	8	9	8	6	6	2	76	63	.547	7.5
West Michigan (Tigers), WMI	8	4	...	4	9	5	7	5	4	4	4	2	9	8	73	67	.521	11.0
Quad Cities (Cardinals), QC	3	9	4	...	2	5	4	6	7	7	7	10	3	5	72	67	.518	11.5
Southwest Michigan (Devil Rays), SWM	4	5	11	6	...	2	9	5	4	5	5	5	4	7	72	67	.518	11.5
Clinton (Rangers), CLI	0	4	3	7	6	...	4	6	6	7	12	6	3	7	71	69	.507	13.0
Lansing (Blue Jays), LAN	3	5	8	4	8	4	...	4	6	3	3	3	11	8	70	69	.504	13.5
Beloit (Twins), BEL	3	8	3	6	3	6	4	...	4	9	6	9	4	4	69	71	.493	15.0
Peoria (Cubs), PEO	2	4	4	8	4	5	2	8	...	5	5	10	4	7	68	72	.486	16.0
Kane County (Athletics), KCC	5	3	4	4	3	5	5	7	11	...	5	7	2	6	67	72	.482	16.5
Burlington (Royals), BUR	3	4	4	1	3	11	5	6	6	7	...	5	5	5	65	75	.464	19.0
Cedar Rapids (Angels), CED	3	6	6	6	3	5	5	3	5	5	9	...	6	3	65	75	.464	19.0
Fort Wayne (Padres), FTW	10	2	3	5	10	5	5	4	4	6	3	2	...	6	65	75	.464	19.0
Dayton (Reds), DAY	8	5	5	3	5	1	8	4	1	2	3	5	10	...	60	79	.432	23.5

Major league affiliations in parentheses.

PLAYOFFS: Division Series: South Bend defeated Southwest Michigan, two games to none; Clinton defeated Quad Cities, two games to none; West Michigan defeated Fort Wayne, two games to none; Wisconsin defeated Beloit, two games to one. Semifinals: South Bend defeated West Michigan, two games to none, and Wisconsin defeated Clinton, two games to none. Finals: South Bend defeated Wisconsin, three games to two.

REGULAR-SEASON ATTENDANCE: Burlington, 70,807. Peoria, 256,612. Kane County, 518,394. Southwest Michigan, 105,340. Dayton, 572,053. Cedar Rapids, 184,190. Lansing, 354,855. Clinton, 95,775. South Bend, 208,590. Beloit, 93,399. Quad Cities, 165,878. Wisconsin, 211,927. West Michigan, 370,153. Fort Wayne, 278,631. All-Star Game (at Peoria), 5,707. League total, 3,486,604. Postseason (18 games), 21,731.

MANAGERS: Burlington, Jim Gabella. Peoria, Julio Garcia. Kane County, Dave Joppie. SW Michigan, Joe Szekely. Dayton, Alonzo Powell. Cedar Rapids, Bobby Magallanes. Lansing, Ken Navarrette. Clinton, Carlos Subero. South Bend, Mark Haley. Beloit, Kevin Boles. Quad Cities, Joe Cunningham. Wisconsin, Scott Steinmann. West Michigan, Matt Walbeck. Fort Wayne, Randy Ready.

ALL-STAR TEAM: 1B-Tonys Gutierrez, Dayton, and Cesar Nicolas, South Bend. 2B-Eric Patterson, Peoria. 3B-David Winfree, Beloit. SS-Matt Tuiasosopo, Wisconsin. OF-Carlos Gonzales, South Bend. OF-Ryan Harvey, Peoria. OF-Javier Herrera, Kane County. C-Michael Collins, Cedar Rapids. DH-John Jaso, Southwest Michigan. RHP-Sean Gallagher, Peoria. LHP-Chi-Hung Cheng, Lansing. RHR-Matt Elliott, South Bend. LHR-Kevin Ool, Quad Cities. Most Valuable Player-Carlos Gonzales, South Bend. Prospect of the Year-Carlos Gonzales, South Bend. Manager of the Year-Mark Haley, South Bend.

2005 BATTING

TEAM

Team	G	TPA	AB	R	H	TB	2B	3B	HR	RBI	SH	SF	HP	BB	IBB	SO	SB	CS	GDP	LOB	ShO	Avg.	OBP	Slg.
South Bend	140	5476	4824	800	1355	2085	274	45	122	715	55	51	70	473	19	827	121	62	121	2153	3	.281	.350	.432
Wisconsin	139	5499	4833	788	1331	1977	267	38	101	712	27	52	65	521	13	942	142	54	83	2151	3	.275	.350	.409

Team	G	TPA	AB	R	H	TB	2B	3B	HR	RBI	SH	SF	HP	BB	IBB	SO	SB	CS	GDP	LOB	ShO	Avg.	OBP	Slg.
Southwest Michigan	139	5268	4674	668	1268	1867	262	32	91	601	29	62	59	444	14	901	148	60	129	2146	1	.271	.338	.399
Peoria	140	5331	4728	695	1259	1900	258	46	97	629	23	45	84	447	13	1014	137	62	113	2180	9	.266	.337	.402
Quad Cities	139	5398	4704	738	1247	1890	248	28	113	663	56	46	68	523	25	827	126	46	110	2110	7	.265	.344	.402
Kane County	139	5508	4777	750	1246	1917	266	24	119	661	22	53	51	602	18	1000	120	34	114	2286	10	.261	.346	.401
Dayton	139	5357	4762	665	1240	1920	239	45	117	617	39	42	88	426	10	1097	116	51	79	2075	9	.260	.330	.403
Clinton	140	5525	4802	739	1244	1913	263	35	112	645	39	45	61	576	12	1041	147	71	84	2157	7	.259	.343	.398
Lansing	139	5322	4644	684	1195	1748	239	31	84	619	18	41	62	554	18	938	108	49	112	2172	4	.257	.342	.376
Beloit	140	5455	4805	695	1211	1810	219	43	98	634	25	50	82	493	7	981	102	35	81	2185	9	.252	.329	.377
Fort Wayne	140	5342	4741	599	1197	1708	234	26	75	534	19	44	52	482	12	897	107	40	109	2300	10	.252	.325	.360
Cedar Rapids	140	5215	4582	620	1148	1776	241	33	107	557	42	41	87	463	16	1098	202	91	88	1931	5	.251	.328	.388
West Michigan	140	5355	4772	600	1200	1699	240	32	65	527	49	42	72	419	16	1108	111	59	98	2088	10	.251	.319	.356
Burlington	140	5270	4623	592	1129	1589	203	25	69	520	42	37	87	478	12	931	178	82	103	1980	7	.244	.324	.344

INDIVIDUAL

TOP QUALIFIERS FOR BATTING CHAMPIONSHIP

Minimum 378 plate appearances. *Lefthanded batter. †Switch-hitter.

Player, Team	G	TPA	AB	R	H	TB	2B	3B	HR	RBI	SH	SF	HP	BB	IBB	SO	SB	CS	GDP	Avg.	OBP	Slg.
Patterson, Eric, Peoria *	110	500	432	90	144	231	26	11	13	71	4	7	4	53	3	94	40	11	7	.333	.405	.535
Gutierrez, Tonys, Dayton *	109	465	410	65	133	185	21	5	7	48	0	4	11	40	1	71	6	0	7	.324	.396	.451
Collins, Michael, Cedar Rapids	100	426	363	64	116	175	32	3	7	64	1	3	25	34	1	44	16	8	5	.320	.412	.482
Gonzales, Alberto, South Bend	95	387	352	60	112	150	21	7	1	42	5	5	5	20	1	42	12	5	7	.318	.359	.426
Johnson, Brent, Wisconsin	109	444	378	77	117	143	21	1	1	44	2	3	6	55	1	57	22	8	14	.310	.403	.378
Gonzales, Carlos, South Bend	129	569	515	91	158	252	28	6	18	92	0	1	5	48	8	86	7	3	12	.307	.371	.489
McIntyre, Nicholas, West Michigan †	118	501	442	61	134	189	30	2	7	45	7	6	4	42	3	85	11	9	6	.303	.364	.428
Fasano, James, Clinton *	98	439	394	65	119	180	21	5	10	74	0	5	4	36	3	62	2	1	10	.302	.362	.457
Nicolas, Cesar, South Bend	91	400	325	70	98	193	30	1	21	70	0	2	15	58	0	60	1	0	7	.302	.428	.594
Castillo, Wilkin, South Bend †	113	462	411	65	124	169	21	3	6	53	16	4	4	26	0	38	9	9	11	.302	.346	.411
Ciofrone, Peter, Fort Wayne	104	458	395	56	119	158	20	2	5	59	0	3	10	50	1	53	7	1	8	.301	.391	.400
Fuld, Samuel, Peoria *	125	508	443	82	133	192	32	6	5	37	4	4	7	50	0	44	18	11	16	.300	.377	.433
Hubbard, Thomas, Wisconsin *	110	457	391	76	116	194	25	1	17	77	2	4	6	54	2	95	4	2	2	.297	.387	.496
Murillo, Agustin, South Bend	126	565	494	94	146	237	34	3	17	82	1	8	8	53	3	80	5	1	21	.296	.368	.480
Winfree, David, Beloit	135	601	562	80	165	254	31	5	16	101	0	6	11	22	2	93	3	2	12	.294	.329	.452
Chen, Yung Chi, Wisconsin	121	549	503	77	147	209	27	7	7	80	1	6	2	37	1	76	15	6	9	.292	.339	.416
Lucas, Edward, Burlington	113	474	425	52	124	147	12	4	1	36	7	0	2	40	1	67	29	10	2	.292	.355	.346
Shepherd, Matthew, Quad Cities †	130	585	479	78	140	177	26	4	1	57	16	1	2	87	4	72	21	9	10	.292	.402	.370
Armstrong, Jason, Lansing	118	526	484	63	140	160	20	0	0	52	0	5	7	29	0	61	9	3	6	.289	.335	.331
Snavely, Christian, Lansing *	117	481	408	67	117	181	27	2	11	56	1	2	3	67	1	80	4	5	11	.287	.390	.444
Frazier, Jeffrey, West Michigan	137	602	537	79	154	243	45	4	12	81	1	8	10	46	3	86	16	3	17	.287	.349	.453

DEPARTMENTAL LEADERS: G—Frazier, 137. AB—Winfree, 562. R—Murillo, 94. H—Winfree, 165. TB—Winfree, 254. 2B—Frazier, 45. 3B—Burns and Perez, 13. HR—Harvey, 24. RBI—Winfree, 101. SH—Castillo and Shepherd, 16. SF—Navarro, 10. HP—Collins, 25. BB—Hulett Jr., 90. IBB—Gonzales, 8. SO—Ramirez, 143. SB—Perez, 57. CS—Bonifacio and Perez, 17. GIDP—Nielsen, 25. Slg.—Nicolas, .594. OBP—Nicolas, .428.

ALL PLAYERS

*Lefthanded batter. †Switch-hitter.

Player, Team	G	TPA	AB	R	H	TB	2B	3B	HR	RBI	SH	SF	HP	BB	IBB	SO	SB	CS	GDP	Avg.	OBP	Slg.
Alley, Joshua, Fort Wayne *	45	210	167	26	44	53	3	0	2	11	0	0	2	40	0	26	5	4	6	.263	.411	.317
Anderson, Charles, Lansing *	50	200	159	26	41	75	16	0	6	34	0	0	5	36	1	36	1	0	2	.258	.410	.472
Anderson, Drew, Dayton †	105	443	407	59	100	151	15	9	6	37	3	2	0	31	1	96	15	9	6	.246	.298	.371
Ankiel, Rick, Quad Cities *	51	223	185	33	50	95	10	1	11	45	0	6	5	27	1	37	0	0	4	.270	.368	.514
Arias, Roberto, Kane County	8	25	21	1	2	3	1	0	0	1	0	0	0	4	0	6	0	0	0	.095	.240	.143
Armstrong, Jason, Lansing	118	526	484	63	140	160	20	0	0	52	0	5	7	29	0	61	9	3	6	.289	.335	.331
Arroyo, Jack, Wisconsin	81	286	247	36	51	73	11	4	1	31	4	3	6	26	0	57	11	3	4	.206	.294	.296
Arteaga, Joshua, Peoria	32	137	129	15	33	50	9	1	2	23	1	1	2	4	0	17	2	2	8	.256	.287	.388
Baez, Lizahio, Clinton †	49	196	181	19	40	69	14	0	5	24	0	0	2	13	0	32	1	2	5	.221	.281	.381
Balcom, Jasha, Peoria	6	15	13	1	3	4	1	0	0	0	0	0	0	2	0	4	0	1	1	.231	.333	.308
Baxter, Michael, Fort Wayne *	45	195	183	11	40	57	12	1	1	17	0	0	0	12	0	29	4	1	4	.219	.267	.311
Belcher, Brandon, Dayton	25	101	89	14	26	36	7	0	1	8	0	1	0	11	1	12	2	2	2	.292	.366	.404
Benjamin, Casey, Clinton	114	441	351	60	94	135	18	4	5	39	8	5	4	73	0	65	7	7	4	.268	.395	.385
Bernard, Oscar, Peoria	66	249	225	29	53	70	11	0	2	23	1	2	7	13	0	40	2	4	7	.236	.296	.311
Blasi, Nicholas, Kane County	116	468	411	57	108	145	25	0	4	52	3	4	3	47	1	81	19	1	1	.263	.340	.353
Blevins, Jerry, Peoria *	1	0	0	0	0	0	0	0	0	0	0	0	0	0	...	0	0	0	0	...	...	...
Boggs, Brandon, Clinton †	85	363	309	54	76	135	16	2	13	51	0	2	2	50	1	69	14	6	3	.246	.353	.437
Bonifacio, Emilio, South Bend †	127	592	522	81	141	172	14	7	1	44	7	4	2	56	0	90	55	17	9	.270	.341	.330
Boucher, Sebastien, Wisconsin *	48	208	178	37	58	82	14	2	2	31	1	2	1	26	0	34	11	1	4	.326	.411	.461
Boyer, William, Cedar Rapids †	21	74	71	8	13	26	5	1	2	11	0	0	1	2	0	31	3	2	1	.183	.216	.366
Brito, Javier, Kane County	78	338	284	43	84	119	18	1	5	52	1	6	6	41	1	37	1	2	9	.296	.389	.419
Brown, Andrew, Quad Cities *	7	18	17	1	3	5	0	1	0	0	0	0	0	1	0	9	0	0	0	.176	.222	.294
Brown, Christopher, Beloit	87	366	332	46	88	150	19	5	11	39	1	2	1	30	0	104	4	2	6	.265	.326	.452
Brown, Russell, Burlington	124	494	445	54	119	196	29	0	16	70	0	7	3	39	4	95	1	2	7	.267	.326	.440
Buck, Travis, Kane County *	32	144	123	17	42	58	13	0	1	22	1	1	0	19	1	19	3	1	4	.341	.427	.472
Buhagiar, Joshua, South Bend *	17	58	51	0	5	6	1	0	0	1	2	1	0	4	0	8	0	0	2	.098	.161	.118
Burns, Deacon, Beloit *	132	595	527	90	143	241	36	13	12	78	1	5	12	50	1	92	13	3	6	.271	.345	.457
Burt, Landon, Beloit *	62	270	241	37	58	72	10	2	0	24	5	1	1	22	0	22	3	2	7	.241	.306	.299
Bush, Matthew, Fort Wayne	126	495	453	56	100	125	13	3	2	32	1	3	5	33	1	76	8	4	15	.221	.279	.276
Cabrera, Asdrubal, Wisconsin †	51	229	192	26	61	91	12	3	4	30	2	3	1	30	1	32	2	6	6	.318	.407	.474
Caldera, Jose, Cedar Rapids	5	12	12	0	1	1	0	0	0	1	0	0	0	0	0	2	0	0	2	.083	.083	.083
Cannon, Rhame, Lansing *	46	191	168	22	45	91	9	2	11	36	0	1	2	20	5	47	0	0	1	.268	.351	.542

Player, Team	G	TPA	AB	R	H	TB	2B	3B	HR	RBI	SH	SF	HP	BB	IBB	SO	SB	CS	GDP	Avg.	OBP	Slg.
Cashman, Brandon, Clinton	111	488	434	64	101	173	26	5	12	47	5	1	10	36	0	117	21	7	7	.233	.306	.399
Casilla, Alexi, Cedar Rapids †	78	347	308	62	100	126	11	3	3	17	3	1	6	29	0	31	47	12	6	.325	.392	.409
Castillo, David, Kane County	32	109	93	17	19	27	5	0	1	9	0	1	3	11	0	22	0	0	4	.204	.306	.290
Castillo, Wilkin, South Bend †	113	462	411	65	124	169	21	3	6	53	16	4	4	26	0	38	9	9	11	.302	.346	.411
Cavanaugh, Brian, Fort Wayne *	7	25	20	1	3	4	1	0	0	2	0	0	0	5	0	11	0	0	0	.150	.320	.200
Chapman, Travis, Kane County	45	128	108	8	12	17	5	0	0	10	1	2	1	16	0	24	0	1	3	.111	.228	.157
Chen, Yung Chi, Wisconsin	121	549	503	77	147	209	27	7	7	80	1	6	2	37	1	76	15	6	9	.292	.339	.416
Ciofrone, Peter, Fort Wayne	104	458	395	56	119	158	20	2	5	59	0	3	10	50	0	53	7	1	8	.301	.391	.400
Clark, Douglas, Clinton	6	26	17	4	1	2	1	0	0	2	0	2	1	6	0	5	0	0	0	.059	.308	.118
Clement, Jeffrey, Wisconsin *	30	127	113	17	36	59	5	0	6	20	0	1	1	12	0	25	1	2	0	.319	.386	.522
Collins, Michael, Cedar Rapids	100	426	363	64	116	175	32	3	7	64	1	3	25	34	1	44	16	8	5	.320	.412	.482
Colton, Christopher, Wisconsin	52	220	203	46	68	118	8	3	12	37	1	2	1	13	0	36	10	3	6	.335	.374	.581
Colvin, Brooks, West Michigan	111	482	417	50	96	127	20	1	3	33	6	3	3	53	1	79	9	8	6	.230	.319	.305
Conley, Evan, Dayton	22	74	61	7	11	16	2	0	1	8	0	1	2	10	0	17	0	0	1	.180	.311	.262
Corbeil, Alfred, Peoria *	2	4	4	0	0	0	0	0	0	0	0	0	0	0	0	1	0	0	0	.000	.000	.000
Corrente, Damaso, Lansing	65	232	200	30	40	53	8	1	1	23	2	4	5	21	0	58	1	1	4	.200	.287	.265
Coughlan, Cameron, Clinton †	39	166	134	30	47	64	4	2	3	16	6	1	1	24	1	21	20	5	2	.351	.450	.478
Cure, Cody, Burlington	55	209	191	15	46	62	9	2	1	17	1	0	1	16	0	38	11	2	5	.241	.303	.325
Dale, Lachlan, Fort Wayne	89	360	328	41	62	116	18	0	12	37	0	8	2	22	0	108	0	0	9	.189	.239	.354
Danielson, Sean, Quad Cities †	6	27	24	5	8	12	0	2	0	1	0	0	0	3	0	3	1	1	0	.333	.407	.500
Davidson, Drew, Fort Wayne	21	92	84	9	22	39	2	0	5	15	1	2	4	1	0	21	0	0	0	.262	.297	.464
Delgado, Jose, Quad Cities †	4	8	7	1	1	1	0	0	0	1	0	0	0	1	0	3	0	0	0	.143	.250	.143
Del Rosario, Felipe, Burlington	26	88	78	9	20	32	6	0	2	9	0	0	0	10	0	19	1	2	0	.256	.341	.410
Dini, Gregory, Cedar Rapids	9	34	29	1	5	7	2	0	0	1	1	0	2	2	0	6	0	0	1	.172	.273	.241
Dlugach, Brent, West Michigan	124	522	488	54	138	189	26	5	5	61	4	4	7	19	0	121	13	5	10	.283	.317	.387
Douillard, Jonathan, Peoria *	9	32	30	2	6	10	1	0	1	3	0	0	0	2	0	4	0	0	2	.200	.250	.333
Dowdy, Brett, Fort Wayne	77	337	301	47	82	116	10	9	2	41	1	2	1	32	1	44	7	0	4	.272	.342	.385
Duenas, Tomas, Cedar Rapids	55	213	191	20	40	66	6	1	6	19	2	0	5	15	1	56	4	0	3	.209	.284	.346
Duff, Timothy, Cedar Rapids	13	52	47	3	8	8	0	0	0	0	0	0	0	5	0	15	1	0	3	.170	.250	.170
Ellis, Jared, Burlington	14	44	38	4	6	8	2	0	0	3	1	0	0	5	0	21	2	0	2	.158	.256	.211
Espino, Damaso, Burlington	74	313	278	26	73	79	6	0	0	41	0	5	3	27	2	27	3	1	6	.263	.329	.284
Everidge, Thomas, Kane County	114	430	365	59	102	176	26	3	14	66	0	8	1	56	1	73	1	0	10	.279	.370	.482
Falcon, Omar, Wisconsin †	42	166	136	22	37	60	11	0	4	22	1	1	3	25	1	48	0	3	0	.272	.394	.441
Falu, Irving, Burlington †	119	525	445	71	113	146	20	5	1	28	9	7	3	61	0	39	34	15	8	.254	.343	.328
Fasano, James, Clinton *	98	439	394	65	119	180	21	5	10	74	0	5	4	36	3	62	2	1	10	.302	.362	.457
Feiner, Korey, Beloit	63	250	202	25	38	47	4	1	1	18	2	2	7	37	1	36	0	0	5	.188	.331	.233
Fermin, Angelo, Beloit †	42	178	143	23	32	39	5	1	0	11	0	0	2	33	0	40	9	3	3	.224	.376	.273
Ferris, Michael, Quad Cities *	127	519	439	65	101	175	26	0	16	69	3	5	2	69	6	88	2	3	8	.230	.334	.399
Figueroa, Baudilio, Fort Wayne	51	184	171	21	40	47	4	0	1	12	1	3	1	8	0	39	0	3	3	.234	.268	.275
Flowers, Clarence, Peoria	105	396	366	44	87	129	10	4	8	49	0	4	7	19	0	121	10	1	4	.238	.286	.353
Fox, Adam, Clinton	75	327	282	42	72	110	12	1	8	36	1	5	2	37	1	39	11	9	7	.255	.340	.390
Francisco, Alfredo, Peoria	4	13	13	0	2	2	0	0	0	0	0	0	0	0	0	1	0	0	1	.154	.154	.154
Frazier, Jeffrey, West Michigan	137	602	537	79	154	243	45	4	12	81	1	8	10	46	3	86	16	3	17	.287	.349	.453
Frostad, Emerson, Clinton *	114	488	432	72	116	194	26	2	16	62	2	2	4	48	2	75	6	5	11	.269	.346	.449
Fryer, Brian, Fort Wayne	31	114	104	12	29	39	2	1	2	11	1	1	1	7	0	19	6	3	6	.279	.327	.375
Fuld, Samuel, Peoria *	125	508	443	82	133	192	32	6	5	37	4	4	7	50	0	44	18	11	16	.300	.377	.433
Gac, Ian, Clinton	91	371	346	42	83	149	24	3	12	57	1	1	4	19	0	108	2	3	8	.240	.286	.431
Garcia, Alberto, Peoria	58	230	209	19	66	79	8	1	1	25	1	1	2	15	1	29	1	1	6	.316	.366	.378
Garciaparra, Nomar, Peoria	2	7	5	1	1	1	0	0	0	2	0	0	0	2	0	0	0	0	0	.200	.429	.200
Gentry, Philip, Dayton *	88	404	365	51	99	151	23	7	5	47	5	4	7	23	0	79	13	5	3	.271	.323	.414
Giannotti, Richard, Cedar Rapids †	104	389	353	42	83	114	18	2	3	28	6	2	5	23	1	107	17	11	8	.235	.290	.323
Gonzales, Alberto, South Bend	95	387	352	60	112	150	21	7	1	42	5	5	5	20	1	42	12	5	7	.318	.359	.426
Gonzales, Carlos, South Bend *	129	569	515	91	158	252	28	6	18	92	0	1	5	48	8	86	7	3	12	.307	.371	.489
Gonzalez, Julio, Dayton	4	11	11	0	1	1	0	0	0	0	0	0	0	0	0	5	0	0	0	.091	.091	.091
Graham, Andrew, West Michigan	32	110	100	6	19	23	4	0	0	10	3	1	3	3	0	21	2	1	3	.190	.234	.230
Grana, Robert, Burlington	42	129	113	11	19	20	1	0	0	8	4	1	0	11	0	29	1	2	2	.168	.240	.177
Granato, Anthony, Peoria †	75	302	254	46	72	102	10	4	4	35	1	3	3	41	1	55	15	4	6	.283	.385	.402
Green, Brandon, Wisconsin †	99	395	356	39	77	102	14	4	1	45	1	4	2	32	1	62	3	0	4	.216	.282	.287
Gulick, Travis, South Bend	69	267	244	28	53	81	13	3	3	30	2	0	1	20	1	56	2	5	9	.217	.279	.332
Gutierrez, Tonys, Dayton *	109	465	410	65	133	185	21	5	7	48	0	4	11	40	1	71	6	0	7	.324	.396	.451
Hall, David, Wisconsin	13	42	38	6	9	11	2	0	0	1	1	0	2	1	0	11	2	0	0	.237	.293	.289
Hammond, Derry, Quad Cities	43	172	156	23	35	65	7	1	7	27	0	1	3	12	0	43	2	1	5	.224	.291	.417
Harris, Steven, Peoria	8	35	34	2	7	13	3	0	1	5	0	1	0	0	0	6	3	0	1	.206	.200	.382
Harrison, Benjamin, Clinton	83	346	308	56	77	113	14	2	6	37	2	2	3	31	1	72	13	3	3	.250	.323	.367
Harvey, Ryan, Peoria	117	507	467	71	120	226	30	2	24	100	1	6	9	24	5	137	8	4	4	.257	.302	.484
Hayes, Calvin, Quad Cities	28	102	95	11	23	24	1	0	0	12	2	1	1	3	0	21	1	0	2	.242	.270	.253
Headley, Chase, Fort Wayne †	4	16	15	2	3	3	0	0	0	1	0	0	0	1	0	4	0	0	1	.200	.250	.200
Heckman, John, Wisconsin	3	9	8	1	1	1	0	0	0	0	0	0	0	1	0	3	0	0	0	.125	.222	.125
Herbert, Samuel, Quad Cities	5	20	17	1	3	4	1	0	0	2	1	0	0	2	0	2	1	0	0	.176	.263	.235
Hernandez, Habelito, Dayton	47	191	181	18	51	76	14	1	3	23	5	0	2	3	0	31	3	3	0	.282	.301	.420
Herrera, Javier, Kane County	94	424	360	70	99	160	18	2	13	62	0	3	12	47	2	110	26	5	8	.275	.374	.444
Hetherington, Luke, Lansing	72	264	207	40	55	69	10	2	0	21	0	1	7	49	1	55	10	3	3	.266	.420	.333
Hicks, David, Lansing *	107	404	368	51	89	130	15	4	6	39	1	2	4	29	3	47	1	5	15	.242	.303	.353
Himes, Benjamin, Dayton *	27	124	106	18	27	44	11	0	2	18	0	0	2	16	1	33	1	2	2	.255	.363	.415
Hoffpauir, Jarrett, Quad Cities	61	256	227	27	71	94	15	1	2	28	1	3	4	21	1	14	5	1	3	.313	.376	.414
Hubbard, Thomas, Wisconsin *	110	457	391	76	116	194	25	1	17	77	2	4	6	54	2	95	4	2	2	.297	.387	.496
Hughes, Luke, Beloit	72	325	292	42	75	114	14	2	7	42	2	3	7	21	0	63	4	2	6	.257	.319	.390
Hulett, Timothy, Clinton *	106	491	385	70	102	133	22	3	1	45	9	5	2	90	0	87	20	6	7	.265	.402	.345
Hundley, Nicholas, Fort Wayne	10	42	36	2	8	10	2	0	0	5	0	1	1	4	0	9	0	0	0	.222	.310	.278
Hurba, Craig, Clinton	45	171	154	21	47	72	11	1	4	29	0	2	1	14	0	34	1	3	4	.305	.363	.468

Player, Team	G	TPA	AB	R	H	TB	2B	3B	HR	RBI	SH	SF	HP	BB	IBB	SO	SB	CS	GDP	Avg.	OBP	Slg.
Janish, Paul, Dayton	55	254	208	30	51	80	10	2	5	29	8	4	5	29	2	38	5	2	1	.245	.346	.385
Johnson, Brent, Wisconsin	109	444	378	64	117	143	21	1	1	44	2	3	6	55	1	57	22	8	14	.310	.403	.378
Johnson, Craig, Fort Wayne *	10	40	32	4	5	9	2	1	0	1	1	0	1	6	0	6	0	0	0	.156	.308	.281
Johnson, Michael, Cedar Rapids †	22	86	72	9	18	31	5	1	2	14	0	3	1	10	0	14	2	0	1	.250	.337	.431
Johnson, Robert, Wisconsin	77	335	305	41	83	131	19	1	9	51	3	4	3	20	0	31	10	3	8	.272	.319	.430
Johnston, Trey, Fort Wayne	1	4	3	1	0	0	0	0	0	0	0	0	0	1	1	1	0	0	0	.000	.250	.000
Joseph, Alfred, Peoria	7	30	27	2	8	9	1	0	0	2	0	0	1	2	0	4	0	1	0	.296	.367	.333
Justice, Justin, West Michigan *	78	307	287	37	66	92	10	5	2	24	1	1	3	15	0	63	5	1	3	.230	.275	.321
Kazmar, Sean, Fort Wayne	125	519	469	47	125	181	26	0	10	48	2	3	1	44	2	69	7	4	8	.267	.329	.386
Kelly, Paul, Beloit	5	20	16	2	5	10	2	0	1	4	1	1	0	2	0	3	0	0	0	.313	.368	.625
Key, Bradley, Dayton	68	274	256	25	62	84	4	0	6	31	0	2	0	16	0	76	0	0	8	.242	.285	.328
Killian, William, Fort Wayne *	1	0	0	0	0	0	0	0	0	0	...	0	0	0	...	0	0	0	0	...	...	...
Kim, Edward, Kane County *	77	275	246	39	61	111	14	0	12	54	0	6	3	20	3	50	1	0	8	.248	.305	.451
Klosterman, Ryan, Lansing	129	531	452	85	109	182	26	4	13	69	2	4	10	62	2	99	30	4	6	.241	.343	.403
Kolkhorst, Christopher, Fort Wayne *	100	472	393	65	111	137	21	1	1	30	4	2	7	65	2	57	19	6	15	.282	.392	.349
Kroski, Christopher, Dayton *	59	238	211	29	57	92	11	3	6	32	0	1	2	24	0	48	3	1	2	.270	.349	.436
Larsen, Andrew, Peoria	120	490	424	52	104	152	25	4	5	48	1	4	19	42	1	108	9	6	4	.245	.337	.358
Lauderdale, Matthew, Fort Wayne	75	319	273	35	77	136	25	2	10	54	0	5	3	38	3	52	2	1	7	.282	.370	.498
Lawhorn, Trevor, Dayton	84	333	303	39	79	124	19	4	6	45	6	7	4	13	1	63	11	6	3	.261	.294	.409
Layden, Timothy, Peoria *	1	0	0	0	0	0	0	0	0	0	...	0	0	0	...	0	0	0	0	...	...	...
Leblanc, Joshua, Cedar Rapids *	63	264	230	30	63	85	12	5	0	27	3	3	1	27	4	66	18	5	5	.274	.349	.370
Lee, Joshua, West Michigan *	104	430	397	35	95	132	14	1	7	63	0	4	4	24	1	116	0	3	10	.239	.287	.332
Lemanczyk, Matthew, Quad Cities	115	483	413	92	110	167	20	5	9	47	12	3	10	45	0	62	48	6	8	.266	.350	.404
Leslie, Myron, Kane County †	131	557	472	77	130	211	32	2	15	68	0	5	2	78	4	89	2	1	15	.275	.377	.447
Lewis, Kenneth, Dayton *	26	101	90	9	19	28	2	2	1	6	1	0	2	8	0	25	11	6	1	.211	.290	.311
Lex, Joshua, Lansing	22	77	65	12	16	22	3	0	1	8	1	0	2	9	0	18	0	0	4	.246	.355	.338
Lisson, Mario, Burlington	78	324	260	57	65	106	15	4	6	36	3	2	6	53	3	68	23	4	11	.250	.386	.408
Lobaton, Jose, Fort Wayne †	9	37	34	2	6	7	1	0	0	1	1	0	0	2	0	5	0	0	2	.176	.222	.206
Lockin, William, South Bend	28	104	91	18	26	31	5	0	0	11	1	1	3	8	0	9	1	2	1	.286	.359	.341
Long, Wesley, Kane County	29	94	83	10	16	22	1	1	1	6	0	1	0	10	0	16	1	0	3	.193	.277	.265
Lucas, Edward, Burlington	113	474	425	52	124	147	12	4	1	36	7	0	2	40	1	67	29	10	2	.292	.355	.346
Lucena, Juan, Quad Cities	99	360	332	39	100	116	10	0	2	43	7	5	4	12	0	11	9	5	8	.301	.329	.349
Madrigal, Warner A., Cedar Rapids	111	432	405	43	100	170	21	2	15	53	1	2	2	22	2	90	6	7	7	.247	.288	.420
Maduro, Jorge, Burlington	7	21	17	2	2	3	1	0	0	1	0	0	0	1	0	2	0	0	1	.118	.167	.176
Maestrales, Peter, Burlington †	16	69	57	11	18	23	3	1	0	6	0	0	2	10	0	9	3	1	2	.316	.435	.404
Mallory, Michael, Peoria	29	121	99	17	29	42	4	0	3	14	0	2	2	18	0	25	2	1	3	.293	.405	.424
Martinez, Alberto, Clinton	21	80	75	11	23	26	3	0	0	11	1	0	0	4	1	16	0	0	1	.307	.342	.347
Martinez, Brett, Cedar Rapids	3	9	8	1	1	1	0	0	0	0	0	0	0	1	0	2	1	0	0	.125	.222	.125
Mather, Joseph, Quad Cities	54	234	209	30	46	92	15	2	9	33	0	2	3	20	3	49	0	0	8	.220	.295	.440
Mathews, Aaron, Lansing	70	232	204	28	59	92	11	5	4	30	2	4	1	21	0	40	11	3	7	.289	.352	.451
McBeth, Marcus, Kane County	1	0	0	0	0	0	0	0	0	0	0	0	0	0	0	0	0	0	0	...	...	...
Mc Fall, Robert, Burlington	103	421	364	53	85	146	17	1	14	58	1	7	18	31	0	113	17	3	6	.234	.319	.401
McIntyre, Nicholas, West Michigan †	118	501	442	61	134	189	30	2	7	45	7	6	4	42	3	85	11	9	6	.303	.364	.428
Mejia, Jorge, Dayton	49	182	157	22	31	41	5	1	1	14	1	2	0	22	0	35	4	3	3	.197	.293	.261
Melillo, Kevin, Kane County *	78	342	280	47	80	128	18	3	8	36	1	5	3	53	1	40	10	4	5	.286	.399	.457
Mendez, Jose, Quad Cities	1	1	1	0	1	2	1	0	0	0	0	0	0	0	0	0	0	0	0	1.000	1.000	2.000
Mercado, Orlando, South Bend	67	272	225	31	56	84	10	0	6	35	6	5	2	34	0	34	1	2	6	.249	.346	.373
Milons, Jereme, South Bend	123	536	491	81	130	204	28	8	10	66	3	7	3	32	0	114	11	6	13	.265	.310	.415
Montanez, Luis, Peoria	82	361	315	54	96	164	28	2	12	48	2	2	10	32	1	46	10	4	6	.305	.384	.521
Mora, Ruben, Fort Wayne †	32	125	111	11	22	30	3	1	1	7	2	0	0	12	0	19	3	1	4	.198	.276	.270
Morton, Kristopher, Fort Wayne	63	266	222	27	58	103	15	0	10	46	0	5	3	35	1	57	0	0	4	.261	.362	.464
Mosby, Robert, Dayton	52	208	188	25	46	81	8	0	9	28	0	3	3	14	1	60	0	0	5	.245	.303	.431
Mottram, Allen, South Bend	59	245	217	51	67	134	20	1	15	39	0	3	2	23	2	32	1	3	4	.309	.376	.618
Moye, Alan, Burlington	46	181	162	26	42	64	8	1	4	32	2	3	3	11	0	57	10	5	2	.259	.313	.395
Mullinax, Jacob, Quad Cities	99	398	357	56	101	139	21	4	3	49	1	3	10	27	1	61	9	5	10	.283	.348	.389
Murillo, Agustin, South Bend	126	565	494	94	146	237	34	3	17	82	1	8	8	53	3	80	5	1	21	.296	.368	.480
Navarro, Oswaldo, Wisconsin †	120	509	450	57	121	177	29	0	9	69	4	10	6	39	0	60	11	7	9	.269	.329	.393
Nicolas, Cesar, South Bend	91	400	325	70	98	193	30	1	21	70	0	2	15	58	0	60	1	0	7	.302	.428	.594
Nielsen, Eric, Lansing	128	546	480	66	128	180	27	2	7	59	0	6	6	53	2	74	7	8	25	.267	.343	.375
Nolen, Walt, Peoria	1	0	0	0	0	0	0	0	0	0	0	0	0	0	0	0	0	0	0	...	...	...
Norman, Derek, Burlington	30	109	96	13	26	30	4	0	0	9	0	0	0	13	0	12	1	5	2	.271	.358	.313
O'Flaherty, Eric, Wisconsin *	1	0	0	0	0	0	0	0	0	0	0	0	0	0	0	0	0	0	0	...	...	...
Padron, Raul, Kane County *	113	431	394	40	102	141	17	2	6	57	0	7	3	27	3	78	0	0	5	.259	.306	.358
Palmer, Cody, Quad Cities	31	110	98	8	16	27	5	0	2	5	2	1	1	8	0	44	0	1	3	.163	.231	.276
Parrish, Matthew, West Michigan	76	300	263	30	60	81	15	0	2	28	1	2	8	26	2	87	4	6	7	.228	.314	.308
Patrick, Brian, Lansing †	14	54	48	8	9	12	3	0	0	7	0	0	1	5	0	12	0	0	2	.188	.278	.250
Patrick, Christopher, Quad Cities	79	292	251	43	77	116	18	0	7	50	2	5	6	28	1	34	2	0	5	.307	.383	.462
Patterson, Eric, Peoria *	110	500	432	90	144	231	26	11	13	71	4	7	4	53	3	94	40	11	7	.333	.405	.535
Patterson, Tarrence, Beloit	91	354	307	55	78	106	14	1	4	38	1	7	7	32	1	69	18	4	1	.254	.331	.345
Patton, Preston, Lansing *	58	197	180	23	36	63	9	0	6	22	0	2	1	14	1	55	0	3	3	.200	.259	.350
Peel, Aaron, Cedar Rapids	52	216	182	31	56	93	13	0	8	34	0	2	11	21	2	46	6	4	5	.308	.407	.511
Pennington, Clifton, Kane County †	69	334	290	49	80	104	15	0	3	29	2	1	2	39	0	47	25	6	4	.276	.364	.359
Peralta, Juan, Lansing †	57	195	176	25	50	64	5	3	1	35	4	0	1	14	0	37	8	1	6	.284	.340	.364
Perez, Fernando, Burlington	29	123	115	10	29	47	6	0	4	16	0	1	7	...	0	25	4	1	0	.252	.301	.409
Perez, Luis, South Bend	56	258	245	38	70	111	13	2	8	39	0	2	0	11	1	30	4	1	9	.286	.314	.453
Petit, Gregorio, Kane County	87	318	287	55	83	128	10	4	9	38	3	3	1	26	0	44	8	2	9	.289	.349	.446
Pickrel, Jeremy, Beloit *	108	459	393	52	109	177	18	7	12	65	0	5	11	50	1	121	15	5	5	.277	.370	.450
Piepkorn, Jeremiah, Dayton	107	467	421	68	112	208	24	3	22	77	1	4	11	30	1	94	4	3	5	.266	.328	.494
Pineda, Jose, Kane County	76	322	278	43	71	108	15	2	6	43	6	6	4	37	0	72	5	2	4	.255	.354	.388
Plouffe, Trevor, Beloit	127	532	466	58	104	161	18	0	13	60	5	7	4	50	0	78	8	4	7	.223	.300	.345

Player, Team	G	TPA	AB	R	H	TB	2B	3B	HR	RBI	SH	SF	HP	BB	IBB	SO	SB	CS	GDP	Avg.	OBP	Slg.
Puello, Elvin, Peoria	6	23	21	0	5	7	2	0	0	2	0	0	1	1	0	6	0	0	0	.238	.304	.333
Purdom, John, Dayton	89	367	318	36	88	113	19	0	2	39	1	2	13	33	1	52	1	0	8	.277	.366	.355
Quintana, Alberto, Lansing	5	14	13	2	1	1	0	0	0	0	0	0	0	1	0	4	0	0	0	.077	.143	.077
Ramirez, Wilkin, West Michigan	131	541	493	69	129	202	21	2	16	65	1	5	7	35	1	143	21	8	9	.262	.317	.410
Ramirez, Yordany, Fort Wayne	104	396	369	50	82	131	19	3	8	46	1	4	4	18	0	71	15	5	5	.222	.263	.355
Ramos, Jason, Cedar Rapids †	26	93	85	5	14	20	3	0	1	6	0	0	0	8	0	21	2	1	2	.165	.237	.235
Reed, Mark, Peoria *	14	54	52	2	7	10	1	1	0	6	0	0	1	1	0	12	0	0	2	.135	.167	.192
Reiman, Joey, Lansing	9	28	27	2	4	4	0	0	0	3	0	0	0	1	1	8	0	0	0	.148	.179	.148
Remole, Clifton, Cedar Rapids *	5	14	13	1	4	5	1	0	0	0	0	0	0	1	0	0	1	0	0	.308	.357	.385
Renz, Jordan Tyler, Cedar Rapids †	103	398	353	29	70	107	10	0	9	55	1	8	1	35	1	126	7	5	6	.198	.267	.303
Reynolds, Mark, South Bend	118	484	434	65	110	197	26	2	19	76	5	2	6	37	2	107	4	1	7	.253	.319	.454
Richardson, Kevin, Clinton	56	236	202	28	54	82	8	1	6	37	0	1	10	23	0	56	3	2	2	.267	.369	.406
Rick, Samuel, Peoria *	77	278	249	32	49	75	11	3	3	32	0	0	1	28	0	67	0	1	9	.197	.281	.301
Rios, Jose, Peoria	28	106	95	9	23	25	2	0	0	6	1	1	3	6	0	9	0	2	4	.242	.305	.263
Rivera, Luis, Peoria	25	72	69	7	24	24	0	0	0	12	1	0	0	2	0	7	3	1	1	.348	.366	.348
Robinson, Christopher, West Michigan	41	165	148	16	38	54	8	1	2	18	1	0	1	15	0	39	0	0	5	.257	.329	.365
Rodriguez, Sean, Cedar Rapids	124	546	448	86	112	189	29	3	14	45	9	2	9	78	0	85	27	11	6	.250	.371	.422
Rodriguez, Yuber, Lansing †	111	433	375	52	75	104	15	1	4	43	3	4	4	47	0	114	13	8	5	.200	.293	.277
Rosales, Adam, Dayton	32	148	134	24	44	79	8	0	9	21	0	2	2	10	0	24	3	1	3	.328	.378	.590
Roughton, Jody, West Michigan	46	175	164	5	30	39	5	2	0	8	1	0	0	10	1	27	0	1	5	.183	.230	.238
Rowe, Adam, Burlington *	2	0	0	1	0	0	0	0	0	0	0	0	0	0	0	0	0	0	0	...	...	...
Rowlett, Casey, Quad Cities	21	67	61	5	13	19	3	0	1	10	0	0	0	6	0	10	0	0	2	.213	.284	.311
Ruiz, Ryan, Kane County	93	350	283	60	70	121	16	1	11	45	5	4	5	53	0	68	8	5	8	.247	.371	.428
Rutgers, Paul, Beloit	70	262	230	22	53	67	6	1	2	30	2	4	4	22	0	38	4	2	4	.230	.304	.291
Ryan, Dusty, West Michigan	75	271	241	21	44	67	11	0	4	21	4	2	2	22	0	70	3	3	6	.183	.255	.278
Sabino, Luis, West Michigan †	118	485	399	77	95	136	18	4	5	49	4	4	8	70	1	111	11	5	6	.238	.360	.341
Salazar, Darwinson, Burlington	66	231	198	23	33	45	6	0	2	16	5	0	6	22	0	71	5	5	8	.167	.270	.227
Sanchez, Javier, Beloit	84	313	271	45	68	83	12	0	1	27	0	2	6	34	0	33	8	0	4	.251	.345	.306
Sanders, Anthony, Lansing	10	42	36	4	10	12	2	0	0	3	0	0	0	6	0	5	1	0	0	.278	.381	.333
Sandoval, Freddy, Cedar Rapids †	117	497	427	54	120	174	34	4	4	63	6	7	4	53	3	58	17	12	11	.281	.360	.407
Sandoval, Mayker, Dayton	26	99	85	11	14	22	4	2	0	4	1	0	4	9	0	39	2	1	1	.165	.276	.259
Schappert, Paul, Peoria *	1	0	0	0	0	0	0	0	0	0	...	0	0	0	...	0	0	0	0	...	...	...
Schmidt, Jesse, Peoria †	50	210	175	27	43	69	13	2	3	22	1	2	2	30	1	40	5	1	3	.246	.359	.394
Schweiger, Brian, Wisconsin	6	23	19	1	6	7	1	0	0	5	0	0	0	4	1	2	0	0	0	.316	.435	.368
Shepherd, Matthew, Quad Cities †	130	585	479	78	140	177	26	4	1	57	16	1	2	87	4	72	21	9	10	.292	.402	.370
Simokaitis, Joseph, Peoria	51	194	168	20	32	38	2	2	0	13	0	2	0	24	0	34	2	0	8	.190	.289	.226
Simon, Brandon, South Bend *	58	197	168	22	45	56	5	3	0	22	6	2	8	13	1	34	11	6	3	.268	.346	.333
Sisk, Aaron, Peoria	39	176	152	36	48	86	13	2	7	29	1	1	2	20	0	42	5	5	2	.316	.400	.566
Smith, Aaron, Peoria	78	281	259	35	64	90	15	1	3	22	3	2	1	16	0	61	2	1	6	.247	.291	.347
Smith, Matthew, Clinton *	10	46	36	7	9	10	1	0	0	4	1	1	0	8	0	6	0	0	0	.250	.378	.278
Snavely, Christian, Lansing *	117	481	408	67	117	181	27	2	11	56	1	2	3	67	1	80	4	5	11	.287	.390	.444
Solis, Heriberto, Burlington	107	411	343	39	70	116	19	0	9	47	3	2	11	52	1	89	1	1	11	.204	.326	.338
Soto, Luis, Wisconsin	23	77	73	5	12	16	2	1	0	7	0	0	0	4	0	17	0	0	2	.164	.208	.219
Springer, Kenard, Burlington	115	434	387	44	90	111	12	0	3	30	3	2	17	25	0	53	20	8	9	.233	.306	.287
Stavinoha, Nicholas, Quad Cities	65	279	250	54	86	141	9	2	14	53	0	4	2	23	1	25	4	0	7	.344	.398	.564
Strait, William, Dayton	116	474	413	63	110	176	16	4	14	60	7	1	15	38	0	102	25	7	6	.266	.349	.426
Susdorf, William, Clinton	85	347	328	37	91	133	24	0	6	37	3	4	3	9	1	49	17	6	8	.277	.299	.405
Sutton, Nathanael, Cedar Rapids *	91	368	314	41	76	101	12	5	1	25	7	3	4	40	0	60	15	6	4	.242	.332	.322
Swackhamer, Wesley, Quad Cities *	91	307	284	43	68	105	15	2	6	30	2	3	0	18	4	45	5	3	5	.239	.282	.370
Szymanski, Brandon, Dayton †	50	214	191	32	50	90	8	1	10	26	0	2	0	21	0	57	7	1	6	.262	.332	.471
Tatum, Craig, Dayton	37	151	128	16	24	36	7	1	1	12	0	0	2	21	0	30	0	2	2	.188	.311	.281
Thayer, Matthew, Fort Wayne	37	164	136	21	48	64	10	0	2	19	3	0	3	21	1	25	6	2	3	.353	.450	.471
Thigpen, Curtis, Lansing	79	352	293	41	84	121	18	2	5	35	2	2	1	54	0	34	5	0	10	.287	.397	.413
Thomas, Michael, West Michigan *	51	221	194	39	55	73	8	5	0	11	2	2	2	21	3	37	11	3	3	.284	.356	.376
Tietje, Chalon, Kane County	42	162	143	20	33	45	7	1	1	18	3	0	5	11	0	30	2	1	7	.231	.308	.315
Tolleson, Steven, Beloit	31	125	102	16	18	29	2	0	3	10	3	0	3	17	0	23	3	0	3	.176	.311	.284
Toops, Brady, Quad Cities *	49	161	138	21	28	46	7	1	3	8	3	0	4	16	0	28	3	3	3	.203	.304	.333
Toussaint, Andrew, Cedar Rapids	109	448	391	68	102	196	25	3	21	68	2	3	7	45	1	125	11	5	5	.261	.345	.501
Tritle, Christopher, Kane County	34	123	102	16	22	36	5	0	3	11	0	0	21	1	52	5	3	2	.216	.350	.353
Trout, Jared, Kane County	1	0	0	0	0	0	0	0	0	0	0	0	0	0	0	0	0	0	0	...	...	...
Tuiasosopo, Matthew, Wisconsin	107	464	409	72	113	158	21	3	6	45	1	1	9	44	2	96	8	5	7	.276	.359	.386
Valentin, Geraldo, Burlington	121	528	477	58	112	150	19	5	3	43	3	0	10	38	0	55	10	14	18	.235	.305	.314
Vazquez, Kelvin, Fort Wayne †	14	54	50	9	16	21	5	0	0	7	0	0	0	4	0	12	0	0	0	.320	.370	.420
Vega, Miguel, Burlington	38	142	134	13	37	58	8	2	3	14	0	1	1	6	1	42	2	1	1	.276	.310	.433
Velez, Eugenio, Lansing †	67	254	239	25	68	97	11	3	4	34	0	4	2	9	0	40	7	5	2	.285	.311	.406
Verbryke, Eric, Quad Cities *	63	267	233	31	64	105	14	0	9	39	0	2	3	29	2	49	4	3	6	.275	.360	.451
Vincent, Tom, Fort Wayne *	98	418	392	43	95	122	20	2	1	32	0	2	3	21	0	84	18	5	5	.242	.285	.311
Walston, Christopher, Cedar Rapids	79	297	280	22	46	81	2	0	11	26	0	2	3	12	0	113	1	2	5	.164	.205	.289
Washington, Johnny, Clinton	31	112	98	7	19	25	3	0	1	5	0	0	1	13	0	37	3	0	2	.194	.295	.255
Wayment, Kory, Kane County	58	214	193	27	44	65	10	1	3	20	3	1	1	16	0	49	0	1	5	.228	.289	.337
White, Dwayne, Beloit *	78	299	268	35	70	89	11	1	2	30	1	3	2	25	0	44	2	4	4	.261	.326	.332
Williams, Adam, Quad Cities	64	220	181	38	52	85	13	1	6	27	1	0	6	32	0	55	8	5	4	.287	.411	.470
Wilson, Michael Ladon, Wisconsin †	127	542	463	93	123	215	29	3	19	84	1	6	15	57	2	107	10	2	6	.266	.360	.464
Winfree, David, Beloit	135	601	562	80	165	254	31	5	16	101	0	6	11	22	2	93	3	2	12	.294	.329	.452
Wishy, Andrew, Clinton *	102	391	336	50	73	108	15	4	4	32	0	6	7	42	1	91	6	6	0	.217	.312	.321
Wolfe, Joseph, Lansing *	24	69	62	12	19	35	4	0	4	10	0	0	0	7	0	14	0	0	0	.306	.377	.565
Womack, Joshua, Wisconsin *	102	417	371	59	95	130	16	5	3	33	2	2	1	41	1	93	22	3	2	.256	.330	.350
Woodard, Johnny, Beloit *	60	245	217	36	51	86	9	1	8	27	1	1	2	24	0	65	0	0	4	.235	.316	.396
Wyman, Spencer, Quad Cities *	35	141	117	16	23	32	6	0	1	10	2	0	1	21	1	22	0	0	6	.197	.324	.274
Yarbrough, Brandon, Quad Cities *	38	148	133	17	27	46	5	1	4	17	1	1	1	12	0	40	1	0	3	.203	.272	.346

Player, Team	G	TPA	AB	R	H	TB	2B	3B	HR	RBI	SH	SF	HP	BB	IBB	SO	SB	CS	GDP	Avg.	OBP	Slg.
Young, Stephen, West Michigan †	63	243	202	21	47	52	5	0	0	10	13	0	10	18	0	23	5	3	2	.233	.326	.257
Zamojc, Mitchell, Beloit *	62	261	236	31	56	85	8	3	5	30	0	1	2	22	1	57	8	2	4	.237	.307	.360
Ziemendorf, Chad, Dayton	9	34	29	4	5	6	1	0	0	4	0	0	1	4	0	10	0	0	0	.172	.294	.207

GRAND SLAMS—B. Flowers, C. Nicolas, J. Piepkorn, 2 each; R. Ankiel, L. Baez, E. Bonifacio, J. Brito, T. Buck, W. Castillo, B. Colvin, S. Cumberland, T. Everidge, J. Frazier, A. Granato, J. Herrera, R. Klosterman, C. Kolkhorst, J. Lee, J. Lucena, B. Mc Fall, J. Mejia, O. Mercado, J. Mullinax, A. Murillo, O. Navarro, R. Padron, C. Patrick, P. Rutgers, D. Ryan, E. Thigpen, E. Verbryke, D. Winfree, J. Wolfe, B. Yarbrough, M. Zamojc, 1 each.

AWARDED FIRST BASE ON CATCHER'S INTERFERENCE—J. Maduro 3 (C. Clark, K. Richardson, M. Collins); B. Cashman 2 (B. Yarbrough, J. Maduro); A. Garcia 2 (B. Yarbrough, M. Collins); J. Herrera 2 (C. Robinson, O. Bernard); J. Alley (O. Mercado); J. Armstrong (J. Jaso); O. Bernard (C. Robinson); E. Bonifacio (C. Tatum); A. Cabrera (T. Duenas); D. Castillo (M. Collins); W. Castillo (R. Grana); M. Ferris (R. Padron); B. Flowers (D. Corrente); R. Klosterman (C. Tatum); C. Kolkhorst (C. Tatum); J. Lee (C. Tatum); C. Morton (B. Yarbrough); A. Murillo (R. Padron); E. Nielsen (O. Bernard); M. Thayer (R. Gonzalez).

2005 PITCHING

TEAM

Team	W	L	Pct.	ERA	G	CG	ShO	Sv.	IP	H	TBF	R	ER	HR	SH	SF	HB	BB	IBB	SO	WP	Bk.
West Michigan	73	67	.521	3.63	140	5	8	37	1258.1	1182	5332	604	507	76	34	44	63	414	14	942	94	7
Burlington	65	75	.464	4.02	140	1	7	30	1240	1292	5445	679	554	81	31	49	62	465	21	1005	129	6
Fort Wayne	65	75	.464	4.02	140	2	6	39	1221	1247	5263	642	546	97	45	38	50	412	11	934	52	2
Southwest Michigan	72	67	.518	4.02	139	1	9	36	1206	1103	5175	639	539	88	34	43	50	543	4	978	90	15
Beloit	69	71	.493	4.11	140	3	6	36	1247	1167	5406	645	569	118	38	34	61	514	20	1186	77	9
Clinton	71	69	.507	4.13	140	2	9	28	1259.1	1274	5464	686	578	83	37	43	76	437	11	960	72	8
South Bend	84	56	.600	4.14	140	4	8	39	1246	1283	5434	667	573	83	40	64	54	471	19	1031	97	7
Lansing	70	69	.504	4.17	139	1	3	36	1213	1224	5210	634	562	111	19	47	67	434	12	1001	60	9
Quad Cities	72	67	.518	4.32	139	3	4	39	1224.1	1199	5418	700	587	103	23	42	86	520	25	932	96	6
Cedar Rapids	65	75	.464	4.42	140	1	9	37	1217.2	1247	5336	711	598	99	26	39	79	501	21	922	78	10
Peoria	68	72	.486	4.49	140	3	7	37	1216.1	1236	5364	708	607	92	37	49	83	486	13	976	86	6
Kane County	67	72	.482	4.54	139	1	3	36	1234	1261	5472	740	623	105	45	59	84	532	18	934	115	9
Wisconsin	76	63	.547	4.88	139	1	8	35	1234	1297	5533	790	669	116	40	53	99	572	6	881	112	10
Dayton	60	79	.432	4.92	139	1	6	32	1213.2	1258	5469	788	663	118	36	47	74	600	10	920	111	13

INDIVIDUAL

TOP QUALIFIERS FOR EARNED-RUN AVERAGE TITLE

Minimum 112 innings. *Lefthanded pitcher.

Pitcher, Team	W	L	Pct.	ERA	G	GS	CG	ShO	GF	Sv.	IP	H	TBF	R	ER	HR	SH	SF	HB	BB	IBB	SO	WP	Bk.
Aselton, Kyle, Beloit *	6	2	.750	2.49	41	10	0	0	15	2	112.0	80	472	38	31	9	1	4	4	61	3	113	5	1
Gallagher, Sean, Peoria	14	5	.737	2.71	26	26	0	0	0	0	146.0	107	594	53	44	10	6	5	15	55	0	139	5	0
Hamilton, Clayton, Fort Wayne	9	6	.600	2.88	20	20	0	0	0	0	122.0	101	491	44	39	9	4	5	4	36	0	86	4	0
Walker, Andrew, Clinton	4	8	.333	2.93	19	19	2	0	0	0	123.0	123	502	54	40	7	2	1	1	24	4	58	2	1
Cheng, Chi-Hung, Lansing *	7	6	.538	3.15	26	25	0	0	0	0	137.0	109	586	61	48	8	0	2	6	72	0	142	7	2
Jurrjens, Jair, West Michigan	12	6	.667	3.41	26	26	0	0	0	0	142.2	132	583	62	54	5	3	4	6	36	1	108	12	3
Trahern, Dallas, West Michigan	7	11	.389	3.58	26	26	2	0	0	0	156.0	158	660	78	62	9	2	5	9	50	1	66	15	1
Ekstrom, Michael, Fort Wayne	13	6	.684	3.70	28	28	1	1	0	0	167.2	167	697	76	69	11	6	6	5	36	0	112	4	0
Hurley, Eric, Clinton	12	6	.667	3.77	28	28	0	0	0	0	155.1	135	651	72	65	11	2	7	8	59	0	152	11	0
Gelinas, Karl, Cedar Rapids	11	8	.579	3.81	26	25	1	1	1	0	151.0	180	641	77	64	14	4	4	5	20	0	78	5	2
Kolberg, Koley, South Bend	6	7	.462	3.90	20	20	0	0	0	0	115.1	111	486	58	50	13	1	1	7	36	1	110	7	0
Weber, Matthew, Peoria	7	9	.438	3.91	25	24	1	0	1	0	142.2	173	616	71	62	12	3	3	8	27	0	85	5	0
Scherer, Matthew, Quad Cities	9	8	.529	3.96	24	24	0	0	0	0	134.0	146	601	74	59	15	1	6	7	43	0	96	10	0
Cota, Luis, Burlington	5	8	.385	4.01	26	26	0	0	0	0	148.0	143	642	75	66	10	1	5	8	63	1	137	17	1
Schlact, Michael, Clinton	10	7	.588	4.17	28	28	0	0	0	0	168.1	184	705	85	78	10	3	4	8	37	0	90	9	2
Rodriguez, Fernando, Cedar Rapids	8	10	.444	4.18	28	28	4	0	0	0	157.1	161	673	87	73	8	2	3	13	49	3	128	2	1
Hicklen, Patrick, Burlington	6	8	.429	4.19	25	20	0	0	3	0	135.1	156	611	82	63	15	4	6	10	52	2	79	11	1
Ford, Ryan, Kane County *	14	7	.667	4.26	26	26	0	0	0	0	143.2	141	609	83	68	10	6	7	12	58	1	85	12	0
Kown, Andrew, West Michigan	8	11	.421	4.36	26	26	1	0	0	0	150.2	152	653	83	73	13	3	5	10	52	1	98	6	1
Raab, Kellen, South Bend *	7	6	.538	4.44	27	22	1	0	1	0	150.0	170	635	83	74	10	4	6	2	36	2	133	8	2
Ramirez, Ramon, Dayton	5	7	.417	4.50	30	19	0	0	2	0	114.0	114	502	69	57	8	0	7	15	50	0	90	9	1

DEPARTMENTAL LEADERS: W—Ford and Gallagher, 14. L—Jensen, 13. Pct.—Aselton, .750. G—Tomey, 59. GS—six pitchers tied with 28. CG—Rodriguez Jr., 4. ShO—seven pitchers tied with 1. GF—Varner, 47. Sv.—Varner, 34. IP—Schlact, 168.1. H—Jackson, 205. TBF—three pitchers tied with 708. R—Jensen, 115. ER—Jensen, 97. HR—Core, 22. SAC—Blevins, 9. SF—Webb and Jackson, 10. HB—Bello, 17. BB—Cheng, 72. IBB—Torres, 7. SO—Hurley, 152. WP—Sharpe, 25. BK—Bailey, 5.

ALL PITCHERS

*Lefthanded pitcher.

Pitcher, Team	W	L	Pct.	ERA	G	GS	CG	ShO	GF	Sv.	IP	H	TBF	R	ER	HR	SH	SF	HB	BB	IBB	SO	WP	Bk.
Abrams, Casey, Wisconsin *	4	7	.364	6.04	17	16	0	0	0	0	76.0	84	369	66	51	8	2	6	6	63	0	35	12	0
Abreu, Francis, Cedar Rapids	0	1	.000	6.52	10	1	0	0	1	0	19.1	32	96	19	14	1	1	4	3	7	0	8	1	0
Adamczyk, Tyler, Quad Cities	4	3	.571	7.83	15	9	0	0	2	0	54.0	68	253	51	47	8	2	3	3	26	1	25	6	1
Aguero, Miguel, Quad Cities	0	1	.000	19.29	2	0	0	0	0	0	2.1	6	14	5	5	2	0	1	0	1	0	0	0	0
Altman, Kevin, Clinton	7	6	.538	7.01	32	1	0	0	14	3	78.1	110	363	72	61	5	4	6	8	18	1	62	3	1
Andersen, Phillip, Quad Cities	5	1	.833	2.96	17	17	0	0	0	0	100.1	79	420	41	33	9	0	5	12	37	1	86	3	0
Ardoin, Kevin, West Michigan	5	1	.833	2.84	22	0	0	0	0	0	44.1	33	183	19	14	3	2	1	3	16	0	47	5	0
Arnold, Mitchell Scott, Cedar Rapids	0	2	.000	6.94	12	0	0	0	7	4	11.2	14	59	9	9	0	0	1	1	10	1	11	7	0
Aselton, Kyle, Beloit *	6	2	.750	2.49	41	10	0	0	15	2	112.0	80	472	38	31	9	1	4	4	61	3	113	5	1
Atencio, Alonzo, Burlington	5	2	.714	4.15	17	2	0	0	8	0	43.1	33	187	22	20	0	1	4	7	18	1	40	7	0
Avery, James, Dayton	1	1	.500	3.94	5	2	0	0	1	0	16.0	17	68	8	7	1	0	0	0	6	0	8	5	0
Baez, Edgar, Peoria	0	0	.000	0.00	4	0	0	0	2	0	3	1	29	1	0	0	0	2	0	7	0	2	0	0
Bailey, David, Dayton	8	4	.667	4.43	28	21	0	0	1	0	103.2	89	454	64	51	5	4	8	6	62	0	125	11	5
Bannister, John, Clinton	8	10	.444	4.58	29	28	0	0	1	0	157.1	171	695	98	80	13	2	3	13	58	1	127	5	1

Pitcher, Team	W	L	Pct.	ERA	G	GS	CG	ShO	GF	Sv.	IP	H	TBF	R	ER	HR	SH	SF	HB	BB	IBB	SO	WP	Bk.
Begnaud, Russell, Burlington	0	1	.000	4.28	15	1	0	0	12	1	27.1	33	125	14	13	4	0	1	1	12	0	10	4	0
Bello, Cibney, Wisconsin	4	4	.500	5.02	37	8	0	0	6	1	95.0	88	441	58	53	8	5	2	17	69	1	75	10	0
Berg, Justin, Peoria	0	0	.000	9.45	2	1	0	0	0	0	6.2	9	32	7	7	0	0	1	0	6	0	3	2	0
Bergdall, Kendall, Wisconsin *	0	1	.000	4.13	18	0	0	0	4	0	32.2	33	158	24	15	3	0	1	2	31	1	23	7	0
Berroa, Yesson, Lansing	0	1	.000	5.87	5	0	0	0	5	0	7.2	10	40	5	5	0	0	0	1	7	0	7	1	0
Bierd, Randor, West Michigan	4	1	.800	2.64	7	7	0	0	0	0	44.1	30	169	14	13	2	1	1	3	10	0	42	3	2
Billek, Michael, Peoria	2	0	1.000	4.06	8	8	0	0	0	0	37.2	33	152	18	17	6	0	0	1	10	0	25	1	0
Blackford, Todd, Peoria	1	0	1.000	0.00	1	1	0	0	0	0	5.0	3	18	0	0	0	0	0	0	2	0	1	0	0
Blackwell, Chad, Burlington	7	4	.636	2.23	48	0	0	0	42	14	68.2	62	290	21	17	4	5	0	6	27	1	74	5	0
Blair, Thomas, Quad Cities *	0	0	.000	9.00	4	0	0	0	1	0	3.0	4	16	3	3	0	0	0	1	2	0	3	1	0
Blanco, Ivan, Wisconsin	3	3	.500	6.93	28	6	0	0	10	0	62.1	67	278	54	48	9	6	5	6	30	0	53	17	3
Blevins, Jerry, Peoria *	3	7	.300	5.54	48	2	0	0	29	14	76.1	75	335	51	47	6	9	3	5	38	2	96	5	0
Bohorquez, Carlos, Dayton	2	5	.286	4.52	37	5	0	0	13	1	75.2	73	341	44	38	8	4	0	7	35	2	65	11	0
Brandt, Adam, Wisconsin *	1	0	1.000	8.59	11	0	0	0	6	1	14.2	23	71	14	14	4	0	1	0	9	0	5	1	0
Brito, Luis, Peoria	1	0	1.000	11.74	6	0	0	0	2	0	7.2	14	42	11	10	1	0	1	1	3	0	6	1	0
Brown, Justin, Quad Cities	0	1	.000	94.50	3	2	0	0	0	0	1.1	6	22	14	14	0	0	1	1	11	0	2	2	0
Buckner, William, Burlington	3	7	.300	3.88	11	11	0	0	0	0	60.1	66	268	36	26	9	1	3	2	17	0	60	3	0
Cabaniel, Tomas, Kane County	1	3	.250	4.43	31	0	0	0	13	2	40.2	38	184	24	20	4	2	3	0	30	1	32	3	1
Cairns, Jason, Quad Cities	0	3	.000	2.65	22	1	0	0	11	8	34.0	31	151	14	10	3	1	0	2	19	3	17	1	0
Campbell, Matthew, Burlington *	1	5	.167	4.66	13	12	0	0	0	0	63.2	74	295	41	33	3	1	1	3	37	1	48	11	0
Campusano, Edward, Peoria *	2	2	.500	2.63	19	0	0	0	6	1	27.1	25	120	11	8	0	2	0	2	14	0	23	0	0
Carlson, Zane, Burlington	2	1	.667	5.82	13	0	0	0	3	0	21.2	28	108	18	14	0	0	2	2	15	1	12	8	0
Carter, Brenton, Fort Wayne *	2	0	1.000	0.75	2	2	0	0	0	0	12.0	7	42	1	1	1	0	0	0	1	0	13	0	0
Cheng, Chi-Hung, Lansing *	7	6	.538	3.15	26	25	0	0	0	0	137.0	109	586	61	48	8	0	2	6	72	0	142	7	2
Cherry, William, Dayton	1	0	1.000	1.95	17	0	0	0	4	0	27.2	13	104	8	6	3	2	1	1	9	1	24	0	2
Christensen, Daniel, Burlington *	3	7	.300	3.54	26	21	0	0	3	1	109.1	100	481	54	43	9	2	3	5	53	1	110	6	1
Clelland, Edward, West Michigan *	7	2	.778	3.40	37	0	0	0	16	1	42.1	39	168	16	16	3	4	4	0	8	1	37	1	0
Coffin, Ryan, South Bend	1	0	1.000	3.32	14	0	0	0	4	0	19.0	12	78	7	7	3	1	0	0	10	0	21	0	0
Cooper, Michael, Quad Cities	1	4	.200	6.70	10	10	0	0	0	0	48.1	58	224	40	36	6	0	4	3	19	1	32	1	1
Corchado, Jose, Kane County	0	2	.000	7.30	12	0	0	0	5	1	12.1	10	66	11	10	0	3	3	21	1	13	9	0
Cordeiro, Christopher, Clinton	0	0	.000	1.50	6	0	0	0	6	3	6.0	5	22	1	1	0	0	0	0	1	0	4	0	0
Cordero, Jose, Beloit	0	1	.000	4.70	7	0	0	0	6	1	7.2	9	37	4	4	0	0	0	1	5	1	8	3	0
Cordova, Francisco, Cedar Rapids	4	5	.444	4.35	29	9	0	0	9	4	89.0	80	382	48	43	8	1	0	3	36	1	67	10	0
Core, Daniel, Lansing	8	9	.471	6.32	21	21	0	0	0	0	105.1	120	472	80	74	22	1	6	3	42	1	73	5	0
Cota, Luis, Burlington	5	8	.385	4.01	26	26	0	0	0	0	148.0	143	642	75	66	10	1	5	8	63	1	137	17	1
Crist, Kyle, Burlington	9	3	.750	4.73	16	10	1	0	1	0	70.1	73	304	39	37	3	0	4	5	22	1	44	5	0
Culpepper, Kevin, Beloit *	7	6	.538	4.45	49	0	0	0	19	1	85.0	92	370	47	42	9	6	2	4	31	3	74	3	0
Damico, Yovany, Burlington	2	3	.400	4.66	35	0	0	0	16	3	75.1	77	326	47	39	5	1	2	2	25	0	72	7	2
Day, Amos, Lansing	0	0	.000	4.05	9	0	0	0	3	0	13.1	15	62	6	6	2	0	1	2	9	0	14	4	0
DeHoyos, Gabriel, Burlington	4	1	.800	1.56	28	3	0	0	9	3	69.1	51	282	24	12	2	1	2	1	27	1	81	12	1
Delgadillo, Hector, Lansing	0	0	.000	3.60	1	1	0	0	0	0	5.0	4	23	3	2	0	0	1	4	0	1	0	0
DeLoizaga-Carney, Frederic, Cedar Rapids	0	0	.000	3.57	21	0	0	0	13	7	22.2	24	94	10	9	1	2	0	2	6	1	20	1	1
Dickerson, Roy, Quad Cities *	2	2	.500	4.91	22	0	0	0	8	0	22.0	19	114	20	12	1	0	0	4	21	3	15	3	0
Dickson, Andrew, Peoria	0	2	.000	4.45	25	0	0	0	14	4	32.1	28	144	17	16	2	1	2	0	24	3	26	2	1
Dolsi, Freddy, West Michigan	1	0	1.000	2.43	23	0	0	0	6	0	37.0	36	163	16	10	5	0	2	1	14	0	27	7	0
Dossett, William, Burlington	1	1	.500	4.07	4	4	0	0	0	0	24.1	27	100	11	11	0	1	1	0	5	0	13	2	0
Douglas, James, Cedar Rapids *	1	2	.333	7.88	24	0	0	0	7	0	32.0	37	166	41	28	7	0	2	9	27	0	21	5	0
Dove, Dennis, Quad Cities	7	5	.583	3.88	18	18	2	1	0	0	102.0	93	420	47	44	6	2	3	2	30	0	72	5	1
Downs, Darin, Peoria *	0	2	.000	18.47	2	2	0	0	0	0	6.1	12	36	14	13	1	0	1	4	0	3	1	0
Doyne, Michael, Quad Cities	0	0	.000	0.00	2	0	0	0	1	0	2.1	0	7	0	0	0	0	0	0	0	0	5	0	0
Drucker, Scot, Kane County	2	3	.400	2.86	21	0	0	0	14	11	22.0	22	98	13	7	1	5	1	2	9	2	24	2	0
Duguay, Steven, Beloit	1	2	.333	1.91	17	0	0	0	13	4	28.1	12	108	6	6	1	1	0	1	15	1	35	0	0
Duran, Enmanuel, South Bend	0	3	.000	8.06	10	4	0	0	3	0	22.1	32	108	21	20	0	0	2	2	11	0	14	2	0
Edwards, William, Cedar Rapids	5	1	.833	3.20	10	9	0	0	0	0	56.1	46	230	25	20	4	2	2	9	20	1	43	2	1
Ekstrom, Michael, Fort Wayne	13	6	.684	3.70	28	28	1	1	0	0	167.2	167	697	76	69	11	6	6	5	36	0	112	4	0
Elliott, Matthew, South Bend	3	4	.429	2.14	53	0	0	0	45	32	54.2	35	219	18	13	1	4	4	2	22	0	71	4	0
Ellis, Jonathon, Fort Wayne	5	3	.625	3.89	43	5	0	0	7	0	78.2	82	338	41	34	8	5	5	3	24	0	69	2	0
Espinoza, Gustavo, Cedar Rapids *	1	0	1.000	1.69	1	1	0	0	0	0	5.1	5	23	2	1	1	0	1	0	3	0	0
Estrada, Jesus, Peoria	6	12	.333	5.35	27	27	1	0	0	0	151.1	193	686	104	90	15	2	6	12	41	1	65	4	1
Evans, Ronald, Kane County	6	6	.500	4.44	15	15	1	0	0	0	91.1	85	401	50	43	15	2	3	9	35	0	70	4	0
Falkenbach, Thomas, Lansing	1	1	.500	13.50	2	0	0	0	2	0	2.0	6	12	3	3	0	0	0	0	0	0	3	0	0
Farfan, Alexander, Dayton	2	7	.222	7.69	44	0	0	0	14	0	57.1	68	294	57	49	4	5	5	7	58	1	29	12	0
Farnum, Matthew, Clinton	3	1	.750	3.18	17	0	0	0	10	0	28.1	25	114	11	10	1	1	0	4	25	2	0
Fenton, Willson, Peoria	0	0	.000	11.37	6	0	0	0	2	0	6.1	12	37	8	8	1	0	0	5	1	7	1	0
Fillinger, Chad, Wisconsin	2	3	.400	2.70	23	1	0	0	9	3	43.1	37	174	13	13	3	3	1	0	13	1	53	2	0
Finigan, Patrick, West Michigan	2	2	.500	2.39	25	0	0	0	10	4	37.2	35	154	11	10	0	0	2	1	7	1	32	0	0
Ford, Ryan, Kane County *	14	7	.667	4.26	26	26	0	0	0	0	143.2	141	609	83	68	10	6	7	12	58	1	85	12	0
Francisco, Alfredo, Peoria	1	0	1.000	3.07	6	0	0	0	3	0	14.2	14	62	5	5	0	0	0	7	0	14	2	0
French, Lucas, West Michigan *	1	2	.333	5.45	6	6	0	0	0	0	34.2	42	157	23	21	4	2	1	1	14	0	24	7	0
Frias, Juan, Dayton *	1	5	.167	4.19	14	8	0	0	3	1	53.2	49	231	31	25	4	0	1	8	20	0	30	4	1
Frye, Randall, Wisconsin	2	4	.333	8.12	11	10	0	0	0	0	44.1	57	231	43	40	6	1	3	4	38	0	19	3	1
Fyvie, Daniel, Kane County	2	0	1.000	2.01	13	0	0	0	7	1	22.1	18	91	8	5	0	2	2	0	6	1	22	4	0
Gallagher, Sean, Peoria	14	5	.737	2.71	26	26	0	0	0	0	146.0	107	594	53	44	10	6	5	15	55	0	139	5	0
Garcia, Angel, Beloit	2	0	1.000	4.26	17	3	0	0	6	0	25.1	14	110	13	12	2	0	0	3	20	1	33	2	0
Garcia, Geivy, Fort Wayne	2	2	.500	5.01	41	0	0	0	11	0	55.2	57	251	43	31	5	1	2	0	27	2	44	4	0
Garrison, Aaron, Dayton	1	1	.500	7.04	8	2	0	0	1	0	15.1	19	81	14	12	0	0	1	2	12	1	12	6	0
Garza, Matthew, Beloit	3	3	.500	3.54	10	10	0	0	0	0	56.0	53	231	24	22	5	1	4	4	15	0	64	1	0
Geer, Joshua, Fort Wayne	1	1	.500	4.25	5	5	0	0	0	0	29.2	29	123	16	14	3	2	1	1	9	0	23	0	0
Gelinas, Karl, Cedar Rapids	11	8	.579	3.81	26	25	1	1	1	0	151.0	180	641	77	64	14	4	5	20	0	78	5	2
George, Jonathan, Dayton	5	8	.385	5.33	35	12	0	0	1	0	98.0	129	427	66	58	9	1	6	2	17	0	52	3	1
Giles, Joshua, Clinton	0	2	.000	9.56	11	0	0	0	6	1	16.0	15	86	20	17	2	0	4	2	18	0	12	2	0

Pitcher, Team	W	L	Pct.	ERA	G	GS	CG	ShO	GF	Sv.	IP	H	TBF	R	ER	HR	SH	SF	HB	BB	IBB	SO	WP	Bk.
Girardeau, Maurice, Fort Wayne	1	1	.500	4.15	6	6	0	0	0	0	30.1	34	130	17	14	3	1	0	3	6	0	22	0	1
Gonzalez, Miguel, Cedar Rapids	2	5	.286	4.70	28	0	0	0	21	8	44.0	47	190	30	23	4	3	1	4	8	3	42	6	0
Gonzalez, Rafael, Dayton	3	5	.375	9.35	10	5	0	0	0	0	26.0	24	123	29	27	5	0	0	3	24	0	22	2	0
Grasley, Stephen, Wisconsin	9	0	1.000	3.71	44	0	0	0	14	3	89.2	84	381	44	37	5	1	5	8	34	1	70	4	0
Green, Nicholas, Cedar Rapids	3	3	.500	3.58	26	8	1	0	4	2	100.2	95	401	47	40	11	0	5	0	14	0	74	5	0
Green, Patrick, Burlington	6	7	.462	4.09	19	18	0	0	1	0	103.1	124	437	60	47	4	4	6	0	22	2	60	2	0
Gross, Timothy, Quad Cities	2	6	.250	4.53	36	0	0	0	11	0	49.2	50	227	35	25	3	1	1	2	25	2	29	2	0
Guerrero, Hipolito, South Bend *	4	3	.571	2.67	46	0	0	0	13	1	64.0	51	270	20	19	3	3	1	4	31	2	45	2	0
Guzman, Angel, Peoria	0	1	.000	4.26	2	2	0	0	0	0	6.1	10	30	5	3	1	0	0	1	0	0	7	0	0
Gwaltney, William, Peoria	4	1	.800	2.56	10	10	0	0	0	0	56.1	45	235	17	16	1	1	1	3	17	0	50	5	0
Haberer, Eric, Quad Cities *	4	2	.667	2.11	9	9	0	0	0	0	55.1	52	230	20	13	0	1	2	1	17	0	33	2	0
Hahn, Jeffrey, West Michigan	4	2	.667	3.25	6	6	0	0	0	0	36.0	36	146	14	13	0	1	1	0	9	0	14	3	0
Hamilton, Clayton, Fort Wayne	9	6	.600	2.88	20	20	0	0	0	0	122.0	101	491	44	39	9	4	5	4	36	0	86	4	0
Harang, Daryl, Lansing *	2	0	1.000	3.21	16	1	0	0	7	2	28.0	27	117	11	10	3	1	1	0	12	2	22	1	0
Harper, Jeremy, Lansing	1	4	.200	3.82	19	0	0	0	13	4	33.0	33	144	15	14	3	3	3	3	14	2	38	4	1
Harrison, Benjamin, Lansing *	0	0	.000	0.00	1	0	0	0	1	1	4.0	2	14	0	0	0	0	0	0	0	0	3	0	0
Hendley, Blake, Dayton	7	0	1.000	2.12	38	0	0	0	30	14	51.0	31	195	12	12	2	0	2	1	12	1	45	4	0
Heuser, James, Kane County *	0	2	.000	4.30	18	0	0	0	2	0	14.2	11	70	8	7	0	2	0	2	16	2	10	2	1
Hicklen, Patrick, Burlington	6	8	.429	4.19	25	20	0	0	3	0	135.1	156	611	82	63	15	4	6	10	52	2	79	11	1
Hill, Danny, Lansing	1	2	.333	2.04	17	0	0	0	16	11	17.2	16	76	8	4	0	1	1	1	7	0	12	1	0
Hill, Joshua, Beloit	4	7	.364	3.66	35	10	0	0	8	4	105.2	89	442	45	43	4	2	1	5	46	2	82	10	1
Hill, Rich, Peoria *	1	0	1.000	1.13	1	1	0	0	0	0	8.0	5	28	2	1	0	0	0	0	0	0	12	0	0
Howard, Adam, South Bend	2	2	.500	2.56	20	1	0	0	3	0	31.2	29	128	11	9	2	1	2	1	11	0	16	2	0
Hunton, Jonathan, Peoria	0	2	.000	7.42	25	0	0	0	10	3	30.1	38	152	28	25	3	1	5	4	17	0	30	3	2
Hurley, Eric, Clinton	12	6	.667	3.77	28	28	0	0	0	0	155.1	135	651	72	65	11	2	7	8	59	0	152	11	0
Hyle, Michael, Peoria	1	0	1.000	15.63	4	0	0	0	1	0	6.1	14	35	11	11	5	0	0	0	3	0	0	0	0
Jackson, Steven, South Bend	10	5	.667	5.33	28	28	0	0	0	0	158.2	205	707	109	94	14	1	10	2	57	2	89	12	0
Jaile, Christopher, Clinton	1	1	.500	3.60	17	0	0	0	7	3	45.0	49	198	21	18	5	0	1	2	13	1	42	5	0
James, Craig, Wisconsin	2	1	.667	0.88	26	0	0	0	26	9	30.2	18	110	3	3	1	2	0	0	5	0	31	1	0
Jamison, Neil, Fort Wayne	1	1	.500	2.70	7	0	0	0	3	0	10.0	11	44	3	3	0	1	0	0	5	2	12	0	0
Janssen, Robert, Lansing	4	0	1.000	1.37	7	7	0	0	0	0	46.0	27	163	8	7	0	0	3	1	4	0	38	1	0
Jensen, Aaron, Wisconsin	10	13	.435	5.56	28	27	1	1	0	0	157.0	190	701	115	97	21	7	7	11	55	0	87	7	1
Jimenez Angulo, Fabian Enrique, Fort Wayne *	4	11	.267	7.03	20	20	0	0	0	0	89.2	120	432	80	70	8	7	2	8	59	0	38	8	0
Johnson, Grant, Peoria	3	8	.273	3.82	14	14	1	0	0	0	73.0	65	303	45	31	7	2	5	3	26	0	52	6	0
Jones, Michael, Peoria	2	3	.400	9.11	18	0	0	0	4	1	26.2	48	133	29	27	1	0	3	0	10	1	19	5	0
Jordan, Justin, Wisconsin	3	1	.750	6.68	17	0	0	0	8	1	32.1	46	150	28	24	3	0	2	1	7	0	29	2	0
Jurrjens, Jair, West Michigan	12	6	.667	3.41	26	26	0	0	0	0	142.2	132	583	62	54	5	3	4	6	36	1	108	12	3
Kauten, Joshua, West Michigan	4	3	.571	3.32	14	14	2	0	0	0	78.2	76	312	33	29	7	2	1	5	12	0	49	3	0
Keng, Po-Hsuan, Lansing	5	5	.500	5.08	28	10	0	0	1	0	79.2	98	355	54	45	12	2	5	6	21	0	54	9	2
Key, Bradley, Dayton	0	0	.000	18.00	1	0	0	0	1	0	1.0	2	8	2	2	0	0	0	1	2	0	0	1	0
Kinsey, Christopher, South Bend	4	4	.500	5.31	13	13	0	0	0	0	78.0	88	348	55	46	5	2	8	7	27	0	48	12	0
Kintzler, Brandon, Fort Wayne	1	2	.333	3.09	19	0	0	0	9	0	23.1	20	96	12	8	2	1	0	2	7	0	19	0	0
Klatt, Ryan, Fort Wayne	0	2	.000	2.87	16	0	0	0	5	1	15.2	18	70	7	5	1	0	0	0	5	1	14	2	0
Knoff, Justin, Quad Cities	2	0	1.000	4.18	22	0	0	0	3	0	28.0	23	127	17	13	4	0	1	1	18	0	31	4	0
Kolberg, Koley, South Bend	6	7	.462	3.90	20	20	0	0	0	0	115.1	111	486	58	50	13	1	1	7	36	1	110	7	0
Kometani, Paul, Clinton	3	2	.600	2.40	13	9	0	0	2	1	56.1	56	236	21	15	5	1	2	1	13	0	46	4	0
Konecny, Daniel, West Michigan	2	6	.250	3.28	22	2	0	0	6	0	49.1	49	214	31	18	0	2	2	0	22	0	16	0	0
Kown, Andrew, West Michigan	8	11	.421	4.36	26	26	1	0	0	0	150.2	152	653	83	73	13	3	5	10	52	1	98	6	1
LaMacchia, Marc, Clinton	4	2	.667	3.73	32	0	0	0	17	4	62.2	48	260	28	26	4	4	3	4	26	1	53	1	0
Langdon, Donny, Wisconsin *	0	3	.000	4.75	18	1	0	0	5	1	30.1	34	143	18	16	2	0	0	3	21	0	23	4	1
Layden, Timothy, Peoria *	4	4	.500	4.62	38	0	0	0	17	4	50.2	43	221	30	26	2	3	0	6	22	2	53	13	0
Layman, William, Cedar Rapids	0	2	.000	7.31	7	3	0	0	0	0	16.0	11	79	15	13	0	0	0	2	22	0	17	3	0
Lewis, Lavon, West Michigan	2	0	1.000	2.38	24	1	0	0	5	1	45.1	33	181	13	12	2	2	2	2	17	2	31	5	0
Lockwood, Jonathan, Wisconsin	3	0	1.000	2.12	15	0	0	0	8	3	29.2	18	123	12	7	0	0	1	1	14	0	43	5	0
Lowe, Mark, Wisconsin	6	6	.500	5.47	22	22	0	0	0	0	103.2	107	468	72	63	12	1	2	11	49	0	72	5	0
Lujan, John, Clinton	4	4	.500	2.80	31	0	0	0	25	5	64.1	57	270	26	20	1	6	0	4	27	0	56	7	1
Lundgren, Wayne, Quad Cities	1	0	1.000	8.76	10	0	0	0	1	0	12.1	16	57	12	12	0	0	0	0	6	0	7	4	0
Mahoney, Collin, West Michigan	0	2	.000	5.24	25	0	0	0	18	10	22.1	20	106	16	13	0	1	1	1	21	1	23	0	0
Martin, Adrian, Lansing	0	0	.000	7.71	5	1	0	0	2	0	9.1	17	42	8	8	4	0	2	0	0	0	6	0	0
Martinez, Jonathan, Beloit	5	2	.714	1.83	53	0	0	0	37	20	88.1	63	361	26	18	5	4	2	4	31	2	92	8	0
Martinez, Roman, Wisconsin	0	2	.000	3.66	19	1	0	0	6	0	39.1	39	172	20	16	3	0	1	5	17	0	29	2	0
Martinez, Shawn, Kane County	0	0	.000	4.70	14	0	0	0	5	0	23.0	26	107	13	12	2	0	0	1	11	0	15	4	0
Mauer, William, Beloit	0	0	.000	20.25	1	0	0	0	0	0	1.1	2	9	3	3	0	0	0	0	3	0	3	0	0
McBeth, Marcus, Kane County	1	2	.333	5.03	16	0	0	0	11	1	19.2	20	91	11	11	2	0	2	0	13	0	21	4	0
McClellan, Kyle, Quad Cities	1	4	.200	4.83	17	8	0	0	4	1	54.0	59	242	33	29	4	1	4	6	26	1	36	7	0
McCormick, Mark, Quad Cities	1	2	.333	5.48	9	9	0	0	0	0	42.2	41	195	27	26	4	0	0	5	28	0	45	4	1
McLaughlin, Joey, Lansing	2	2	.500	3.13	42	0	0	0	28	7	46.0	36	194	17	16	3	0	1	1	24	1	45	1	1
Meacham, Cory, Quad Cities	2	2	.500	5.47	18	0	0	0	2	0	24.2	24	110	17	15	1	1	0	1	13	1	19	4	0
Medina, Dennis, Quad Cities	1	2	.333	1.95	20	1	0	0	4	0	32.1	20	128	9	7	1	0	0	4	9	1	39	5	0
Medlin, Richard, South Bend	1	1	.500	7.88	9	0	0	0	5	0	8.0	12	41	7	7	1	1	2	0	7	1	6	2	0
Meek, Evan, Beloit	0	1	.000	10.00	13	0	0	0	2	0	18.0	15	106	26	20	0	1	3	2	36	0	11	8	1
Mendez, Adalberto, Peoria	2	1	.667	3.10	22	0	0	0	14	6	29.0	26	122	10	10	1	0	0	2	10	0	24	2	0
Mijares, Jose, Beloit *	6	3	.667	4.31	20	6	0	0	5	2	54.1	43	239	28	26	6	1	1	2	40	0	78	3	1
Miller, Brian, Quad Cities	0	1	.000	6.00	14	0	0	0	3	0	24.0	23	106	19	16	7	0	1	3	7	0	23	0	0
Mitchell, Michael, Kane County	0	0	.000	3.24	19	0	0	0	4	3	25.0	24	107	11	9	2	2	1	2	11	1	19	5	0
Moore, James, Burlington	0	1	.000	3.94	7	0	0	0	3	1	16.0	20	70	9	7	1	0	0	2	5	2	21	1	0
Morenko, Brad, Dayton	6	1	.857	2.49	16	5	0	0	7	1	61.1	62	258	25	17	7	2	0	1	9	0	34	0	3
Morillo, Lennyn, Cedar Rapids	0	1	.000	8.68	3	1	0	0	0	0	9.1	10	48	11	9	0	0	1	1	10	0	6	5	0
Morlan, Eduardo, Beloit	4	4	.500	4.38	10	10	0	0	0	0	51.1	39	223	25	25	5	2	0	4	31	0	55	2	0
Morrison, James, Dayton	0	5	.000	5.46	31	3	1	0	13	6	62.2	76	284	52	38	7	3	0	4	21	0	44	4	0
Mutter, Casey, Cedar Rapids	2	1	.667	2.63	19	0	0	0	5	0	27.1	19	117	11	8	3	0	1	0	19	0	20	1	0

Pitcher, Team	W	L	Pct.	ERA	G	GS	CG	ShO	GF	Sv.	IP	H	TBF	R	ER	HR	SH	SF	HB	BB	IBB	SO	WP	Bk.
Nolen, Walt, Peoria	7	4	.636	4.61	37	2	0	0	10	0	66.1	61	319	47	34	2	2	8	48	2	60	10	0
Nottingham, Shawn, Wisconsin *	0	1	.000	9.53	3	3	0	0	0	0	11.1	15	57	12	12	0	0	1	3	7	10	2	0
O'Flaherty, Eric, Wisconsin *	4	4	.500	3.75	45	0	0	0	31	13	69.2	73	305	35	29	2	3	0	3	30	1	51	7	1
Ohlendorf, Curtis, South Bend	11	10	.524	4.53	27	26	1	1	1	0	157.0	181	695	97	79	10	4	4	10	48	0	144	9	0
Oliveros, Rayner, Burlington	0	0	.000	6.43	2	1	0	0	0	0	7.0	12	33	5	5	0	2	*1	0	3	0	2	0	0
Ool, Kevin, Quad Cities *	9	2	.818	2.15	30	0	0	0	13	3	37.2	25	141	10	9	1	1	1	3	8	1	22	5	0
Ostlund, Ian, West Michigan *	2	3	.400	2.40	32	0	0	0	7	2	48.2	32	183	15	13	3	3	4	2	5	1	54	0	0
Padgett, Michael, Clinton	3	5	.375	2.31	23	0	0	0	17	4	50.2	47	207	14	13	1	3	1	3	12	2	39	1	0
Parisi, Michael, Quad Cities	5	5	.500	4.08	14	14	0	0	0	0	86.0	98	376	42	39	5	3	4	4	25	0	66	2	2
Paz, Jackson, Quad Cities *	1	0	1.000	2.45	6	0	0	0	0	0	7.1	5	31	4	2	1	0	0	3	0	12	1	0
Peralta, Tony, West Michigan *	1	2	.333	7.71	22	0	0	0	6	0	30.1	34	137	28	26	3	1	1	2	7	1	28	5	0
Perez, Henry, Fort Wayne	0	2	.000	8.18	11	0	0	0	4	0	11.0	17	54	11	10	2	0	1	0	5	0	11	0	0
Perez, Juan, Lansing	7	6	.538	4.25	34	9	0	0	5	0	101.2	118	445	54	48	8	2	1	6	35	1	60	4	0
Perez, Keith, Kane County	2	0	1.000	6.39	26	0	0	0	5	1	31.0	37	146	24	22	1	0	1	0	20	0	26	6	0
Perez, Roberto, Clinton	2	2	.500	4.02	26	0	0	0	16	3	47.0	41	204	26	21	4	2	0	5	26	0	44	1	0
Perrault, Joshua, South Bend	7	2	.778	2.07	45	2	0	0	9	0	78.1	61	306	24	18	4	7	5	2	19	2	63	4	0
Peterson, John, Kane County *	3	3	.500	3.13	16	8	0	0	2	0	63.1	65	258	25	22	4	2	2	5	11	0	54	4	0
Pettit, William, Beloit	0	0	.000	4.22	6	0	0	0	3	0	10.2	11	46	5	5	2	1	0	0	8	1	9	0	0
Phelps, Michael, Peoria	0	1	.000	1.59	12	0	0	0	5	1	17.0	12	64	5	3	0	1	0	0	3	0	17	2	0
Phillips, Zachary, Clinton *	0	0	.000	6.75	2	0	0	0	0	0	4.0	7	18	3	3	0	1	0	0	0	0	4	0	0
Pickens, Joseph, Kane County	5	2	.714	4.92	33	0	0	0	14	2	56.2	59	253	37	31	3	3	3	5	27	3	37	2	1
Polanco, Alfredo, Peoria	3	0	1.000	5.59	22	1	0	0	7	0	37.0	34	166	24	23	2	2	0	3	23	0	44	6	2
Polanco, Phillip, Fort Wayne	1	3	.250	6.20	26	1	0	0	3	0	45.0	51	199	33	31	5	3	4	1	23	0	33	4	0
Powers, Joseph, Dayton	2	0	1.000	6.43	5	2	0	0	0	0	14.0	10	59	11	10	3	0	0	1	8	0	8	1	0
Purdum, John, Dayton	0	0	.000	27.00	1	0	0	0	1	0	1.0	4	8	3	3	0	0	1	0	1	0	0	0	0
Raab, Kellen, South Bend *	7	6	.538	4.44	27	22	1	0	1	0	150.0	170	635	83	74	10	4	6	2	36	2	133	8	0
Rainville, Jay, Beloit	8	2	.800	3.77	16	16	0	0	0	0	88.1	83	376	39	37	14	0	4	4	27	0	77	3	3
Rainwater, Joshua, West Michigan	3	7	.300	4.24	16	16	0	0	0	0	80.2	84	342	45	38	8	1	1	5	20	1	75	3	0
Ramirez, Ramon, Dayton	5	7	.417	4.50	30	19	0	0	2	0	114.0	114	502	69	57	8	0	7	15	50	0	90	9	1
Ramos, Cesar, Fort Wayne *	3	2	.600	4.19	7	7	1	0	0	0	38.2	42	160	19	18	0	0	3	1	7	0	32	2	0
Ramos, Victor, Peoria	0	1	.000	2.70	5	0	0	0	1	0	6.2	5	27	3	2	1	0	0	0	3	1	5	0	0
Randazzo, Jeffrey, Quad Cities *	0	0	.000	6.17	7	0	0	0	1	0	11.2	12	58	8	8	3	0	0	2	8	0	12	1	0
Ray, Ronald, Cedar Rapids	6	3	.667	3.42	19	9	0	0	2	1	71.0	69	294	29	27	2	1	3	2	30	1	43	2	0
Rico, Erik, Lansing *	1	1	.500	9.20	7	0	0	0	2	0	14.2	22	73	15	15	2	0	0	9	0	12	1	0
Righter, Matthew, West Michigan	4	1	.800	3.14	27	10	0	0	5	0	77.1	79	331	33	27	5	1	2	2	24	0	48	4	0
Rivera, Mumba, Wisconsin *	7	0	1.000	3.22	10	10	0	0	0	0	58.2	46	237	25	21	3	3	6	2	26	0	30	3	0
Roberts, Mark, Clinton	2	1	.667	1.45	10	0	0	0	7	1	18.2	7	72	3	3	0	1	0	10	0	16	1	0
Robertson, James, Kane County	2	2	.500	2.93	20	0	0	0	6	1	27.2	23	116	10	9	0	2	0	3	14	0	47	3	1
Robertson, Quinton, Quad Cities	1	2	.333	6.07	22	7	0	0	2	0	46.0	63	212	36	31	4	2	2	4	11	0	34	5	0
Rocha, Angel, South Bend *	2	1	.667	6.98	13	9	0	0	1	0	40.0	41	198	33	31	3	0	4	36	1	43	6	3
Rodriguez, Fernando, Cedar Rapids	8	10	.444	4.18	28	28	0	0	0	0	157.1	161	673	87	73	8	2	3	13	49	3	128	2	1
Rodriguez, Rafael, Cedar Rapids	5	2	.714	2.78	13	13	0	0	0	0	74.1	61	309	24	23	5	1	1	4	27	0	74	2	1
Rogers, Kyle, Clinton	6	10	.375	6.01	28	27	0	0	0	0	130.1	143	603	103	87	12	4	6	14	67	1	95	17	2
Rogers, Michael, Kane County	6	8	.429	4.90	26	26	0	0	0	0	137.2	147	599	83	75	15	2	4	7	51	1	111	4	0
Rosen, Mark, South Bend *	6	1	.857	4.87	46	0	0	0	19	2	44.1	39	211	25	24	2	0	1	0	41	2	42	7	0
Rowe, Adam, Burlington *	6	6	.500	4.78	45	0	0	0	29	7	75.1	87	323	46	40	5	3	3	1	21	5	62	8	0
Roy, Scott, Lansing	3	4	.429	3.76	25	0	0	0	15	0	38.1	29	161	21	16	3	1	3	12	2	34	2	0
Sanders, Jared, Dayton	1	6	.143	4.28	42	0	0	0	26	6	61.0	77	289	42	29	7	2	4	2	31	3	31	8	0
Santiago, Julio, Wisconsin *	7	3	.700	4.44	17	17	0	0	0	0	99.1	110	424	58	49	10	3	7	3	23	0	66	5	2
Santo, Joel, Fort Wayne	4	11	.267	4.75	27	27	0	0	0	0	140.1	156	619	90	74	14	2	2	9	51	0	86	5	1
Savickas, Russell, Lansing	6	7	.462	4.96	19	19	0	0	0	0	90.2	111	399	57	50	4	1	2	1	37	0	70	5	0
Sborz, John, West Michigan	1	1	.500	7.90	21	0	0	0	10	0	27.1	36	146	27	24	2	1	2	9	23	1	31	6	0
Schambough, Douglas, Burlington	2	2	.500	4.32	14	0	0	0	4	0	33.1	28	146	20	16	1	3	1	2	18	2	29	5	0
Schappert, Paul, Peoria	1	0	1.000	4.50	20	0	0	0	3	0	24.0	26	102	15	12	1	1	2	0	8	0	18	1	0
Scherer, Matthew, Quad Cities	9	8	.529	3.96	24	24	0	0	0	0	134.0	146	601	74	59	15	1	6	7	43	0	96	10	0
Schlact, Michael, Clinton	10	7	.588	4.17	28	28	0	0	0	0	168.1	184	705	85	78	10	3	4	8	37	0	90	9	2
Scott, Joseph, Kane County	5	2	.714	4.66	14	9	0	0	2	1	58.0	61	264	37	30	5	0	3	6	30	0	35	2	0
Segovia, Omar, Dayton *	1	2	.333	5.10	10	4	0	0	2	2	30.0	27	132	17	17	7	0	1	1	21	0	29	1	0
Semerano, Robert, Kane County	4	2	.667	3.28	39	0	0	0	25	10	46.2	38	191	17	17	3	1	1	0	18	1	48	2	1
Shappi, Austin, South Bend	11	1	.917	2.86	15	15	2	0	0	0	103.2	98	413	38	33	7	5	3	3	15	0	59	0	0
Sharpe, Steven, Kane County	3	4	.429	5.85	18	10	0	0	2	0	60.0	68	280	50	39	5	2	4	10	39	0	33	25	0
Shaver, Christopher, Peoria *	3	7	.300	4.31	19	19	0	0	0	0	102.1	92	433	59	49	9	5	5	45	0	76	4	0
Sherman, Justin, Burlington	3	8	.273	4.90	21	11	0	0	4	0	86.1	96	375	54	47	6	1	4	5	21	0	51	15	0
Shinskie, David, Beloit	2	8	.200	7.22	29	10	0	0	8	1	77.1	111	363	72	62	11	0	4	2	24	1	51	8	0
Sillman, Michael, Quad Cities	8	2	.800	2.74	56	0	0	0	39	22	65.2	39	282	23	20	3	2	1	4	49	3	77	5	0
Silva, Carlos, Beloit	0	0	.000	1.80	1	1	0	0	0	0	5.0	5	19	1	1	0	0	0	0	3	0	0	0	0
Simard, Michel, Cedar Rapids	6	4	.600	3.80	20	5	1	0	8	2	64.0	55	267	27	27	7	0	1	5	23	1	60	1	0
Slowey, Kevin, Beloit	3	2	.600	2.24	13	9	1	1	2	0	64.1	42	242	18	16	4	1	2	2	8	2	69	0	0
Smit, Alexander, Beloit *	1	9	.100	5.98	14	10	0	0	1	0	49.2	58	235	41	33	9	3	1	1	28	1	54	5	0
Smith, Aaron, Peoria	0	0	.000	0.00	2	0	0	0	2	0	1.1	2	5	0	0	0	0	1	0	0	0	0	0	0
Smith, Donnie, Quad Cities	1	2	.333	6.00	5	5	0	0	0	0	24.0	24	109	20	16	2	0	0	3	11	0	15	2	0
Smith, Jesse, Cedar Rapids	4	6	.400	4.97	23	15	1	0	2	1	99.2	112	433	68	55	6	3	2	7	32	1	75	2	4
Snyder, Jason, Wisconsin	9	7	.563	4.82	27	17	0	0	5	0	114.0	128	500	76	61	13	3	2	13	31	1	77	13	1
Solis, Heriberto, Burlington	0	0	.000	5.40	1	0	0	0	1	0	1.2	2	9	1	1	0	0	0	0	2	0	0	0	0
Sopko, Mark, Lansing	0	1	.000	2.94	23	0	0	0	14	4	33.2	38	147	14	11	1	3	2	3	14	1	24	3	1
Stanton, Travis, Cedar Rapids	4	4	.500	4.62	35	0	0	0	18	4	50.2	67	233	33	26	5	3	2	3	20	2	43	2	0
Steidlmayer, Luke, Fort Wayne	7	2	.778	2.28	16	8	0	0	1	0	59.1	46	245	17	15	3	1	3	4	21	0	53	3	0
Steik, Richard, Fort Wayne	0	6	.000	2.40	54	0	0	0	18	3	60.0	54	244	17	16	5	5	0	1	24	4	53	1	0
Stein, Todd, South Bend *	3	2	.600	3.83	45	0	0	0	15	1	49.1	45	221	28	21	3	2	3	3	17	5	48	7	1
Steinborn, Christopher, Fort Wayne *	1	4	.200	4.18	19	7	0	0	2	0	56.0	65	246	34	26	4	1	2	3	16	0	24	5	0
Sterry, Vern, Fort Wayne	4	3	.571	4.58	20	4	0	0	1	0	55.0	58	236	33	28	5	0	1	3	13	0	50	5	1

Pitcher, Team	W	L	Pct.	ERA	G	GS	CG	ShO	GF	Sv.	IP	H	TBF	R	ER	HR	SH	SF	HB	BB	IBB	SO	WP	Bk.
Stott, Zachary, Dayton	2	2	.500	4.16	40	2	0	0	14	0	71.1	89	320	37	33	8	2	2	1	29	0	48	3	0
Stutes, Kyle, Fort Wayne *	1	2	.333	2.42	45	0	0	0	22	1	52.0	52	222	22	14	3	1	0	1	16	1	61	1	0
Swarzak, Anthony, Beloit	9	5	.643	4.04	18	18	0	0	0	0	91.1	81	382	48	41	7	4	2	7	32	0	101	3	1
Teasley, Jeffrey, Peoria	0	0	.000	3.86	4	0	0	0	4	3	4.2	4	23	2	2	1	0	0	1	3	0	7	0	0
Templet, Jordy, Lansing	6	6	.500	4.15	40	0	0	0	9	0	89.0	98	386	44	41	6	3	2	7	31	2	69	4	0
Tharpe, Derek, Kane County *	2	7	.222	4.67	36	12	0	0	8	0	90.2	96	386	56	47	9	2	3	2	26	1	67	4	2
Thigpen, Joshua, Dayton	4	4	.500	4.99	13	5	0	0	0	0	39.2	34	181	24	22	2	1	2	2	30	0	40	5	0
Thompson, Nicolas, Peoria	0	0	.000	27.00	3	0	0	0	0	0	1.2	4	16	5	5	1	0	1	2	5	0	2	0	0
Tichota, Clay, Kane County	0	1	.000	7.76	18	0	0	0	3	0	26.2	34	131	27	23	2	0	2	2	16	0	23	1	1
Timm, Jordan, Lansing *	2	0	1.000	2.47	18	4	0	0	9	5	47.1	39	193	16	13	2	0	3	1	16	0	44	2	0
Tomey, Anthony, West Michigan	3	4	.429	2.98	59	0	0	0	24	8	60.1	42	265	26	20	2	2	2	1	45	2	70	6	0
Torres, Jaymes, Quad Cities	4	3	.571	3.31	56	0	0	0	26	5	70.2	67	311	33	26	5	3	0	7	27	7	56	5	0
Torres, Joseph, Cedar Rapids *	1	6	.143	8.50	20	9	0	0	3	0	36.0	32	187	38	34	2	1	0	2	61	0	25	8	0
Touchet, Daniel, Clinton	0	1	.000	3.42	12	0	0	0	3	0	26.1	30	118	16	10	0	2	2	8	0	16	0	0
Touchstone, Nicholas, Cedar Rapids *	1	4	.200	7.83	11	4	0	0	1	0	23.0	27	121	23	20	3	1	1	4	29	0	18	2	0
Trahern, Dallas, West Michigan	7	11	.389	3.58	26	26	2	0	0	0	156.0	158	660	78	62	9	2	5	9	50	1	66	15	1
Trent, Matthew, Quad Cities	1	0	1.000	4.11	11	0	0	0	4	0	15.1	13	66	8	7	2	1	1	1	9	0	9	3	0
Tressler, Aaron, Lansing	3	1	.750	2.06	17	0	0	0	6	2	39.1	32	155	9	9	1	1	0	5	7	0	28	2	0
Trout, Jared, Kane County	4	5	.444	4.78	38	10	0	0	10	2	92.1	99	411	60	49	6	2	7	4	29	1	58	6	0
Trytten, Ryan, Fort Wayne	1	0	1.000	1.20	10	0	0	0	5	0	15.0	13	55	2	2	0	2	1	0	3	0	17	1	0
Ursin, Damian, Dayton	0	4	.000	5.16	9	4	0	0	1	0	29.2	33	136	21	17	1	3	0	0	20	0	19	2	0
Valiquette, Philippe-Alexandre, Dayton *	2	5	.286	6.30	19	16	0	0	1	0	64.1	81	306	54	45	3	4	4	1	44	0	42	7	0
Varner, Matthew, Fort Wayne	4	5	.444	4.00	54	0	0	0	47	34	54.0	47	224	24	24	5	2	0	1	18	1	62	1	0
Vasquez, Esmerling, South Bend	6	4	.600	3.64	53	0	0	0	17	3	71.2	63	323	33	29	2	4	6	5	47	1	79	13	1
Vazquez, Camilo, Dayton *	4	4	.500	5.18	29	18	0	0	1	0	99.0	91	443	63	57	10	1	2	4	62	0	88	9	0
Vera, Edwin, Clinton	2	1	.667	3.80	11	0	0	0	7	0	21.1	21	101	12	9	2	0	1	1	16	0	19	1	0
Waldrop, Steven, Beloit	6	11	.353	4.98	27	27	2	1	0	0	151.2	182	662	93	84	17	5	5	8	23	1	108	9	0
Walker, Andrew, Clinton	4	8	.333	2.93	19	19	2	0	0	0	123.0	123	502	54	40	7	2	1	1	24	4	58	2	1
Waters, Christopher, Cedar Rapids	1	5	.167	5.05	49	0	0	0	30	4	57.0	63	263	37	32	7	1	5	2	30	6	46	6	0
Webb, Ryan, Kane County	5	11	.313	4.76	24	23	0	0	0	0	128.2	139	556	82	68	16	5	10	9	41	2	84	7	1
Webber, Nicholas, Quad Cities	0	4	.000	3.41	5	5	1	0	0	0	29.0	28	122	15	11	1	1	1	0	9	0	11	3	0
Weber, Ben, Dayton	0	0	.000	0.00	2	0	0	0	1	0	3.0	1	10	0	0	0	0	0	0	0	0	4	0	0
Weber, Matthew, Peoria	7	9	.438	3.91	25	24	1	0	1	0	142.2	173	616	71	62	12	3	3	8	27	0	85	5	0
Whelan, Kevin, West Michigan	0	0	.000	0.73	14	0	0	0	14	11	12.1	4	43	1	1	0	0	0	0	2	0	22	1	0
Wideman, Aaron, Lansing *	7	10	.412	4.91	27	27	0	0	0	0	143.0	135	594	84	78	21	0	6	10	38	0	121	3	2
Williams, John, Beloit *	4	3	.400	4.54	38	0	0	0	12	1	75.1	83	335	43	38	7	2	2	3	30	1	66	4	1
Wilson, Joseph, Dayton *	2	3	.400	8.20	12	6	0	0	1	0	37.1	45	174	35	34	14	2	2	5	18	0	31	3	0
Wood, Kerry, Peoria	0	0	.000	0.00	2	0	0	0	2	0	2.1	1	8	0	0	0	0	0	0	0	0	5	0	0
Yates, Kyle, Lansing	4	3	.571	4.43	14	14	1	0	0	0	81.1	82	337	41	40	6	0	3	6	19	0	81	0	0
Zick, Jeremy, Quad Cities	0	0	.000	6.23	2	0	0	0	0	0	4.1	7	20	3	3	2	0	0	2	3	0	3	0	0

COMBINATION SHUTOUTS: Beloit (4) -- Rainville-Martinez-Aselton, Swarzak-Culpepper-Shinskie, Garza-Mijares-Martinez, Garza-Hill. Burlington (7) -- Cota-Atencio, Cota-Damico, Hicklen-Christensen, Campbell-Blackwell, Atencio-Blackwell, Crist-Damico, Cota-Rowe. Cedar Rapids (8) -- Touchstone-DeLoizaga-Carney-Douglas, Smith-Green, Smith-Stanton-DeLoizaga-Carney, Simard-Waters, Green-Simard, Green-Simard, Gelinas-DeLoizaga-Carney, Rodriguez-Mutter-Gonzalez. Clinton (9) -- Hurley-Jaile, Walker-LaMacchia, Hurley-Jaile, Walker-Farnum, Hurley-Padgett, Bannister-Kometani, Kometani-Touchet-Roberts, Kometani-Lujan, Schlact-LaMacchia. Dayton (6) -- Ramirez-Gonzalez-Sanders, Bailey-Morenko-Sanders, Vazquez-Morrison, Bailey-George-Hendley, Bailey-George-Segovia, Fisanders-Avery-Morrison. Fort Wayne (5) -- Steidlmayer-Sterry-Steik-Varner, Hamilton-Steik-Varner, Jimenez Angulo-Varner, Ramos-Kintzler-Varner, Carter-Jamison-Varner. Kane County (3) -- Rogers-Scott, Webb-Martinez-Pickens, Scott-Peterson. Lansing (3) -- Janssen-McLaughlin-Hill, Cheng-Hill, Cheng-Tressler-Roy. Peoria (7) -- Gwaltney-Blevins, Gallagher-Hunton, Gallagher-Schappert-Nolen-Blevins, Weber-Layden-Hunton, Johnson-Mendez-Blevins, Nolen-Ramos-Mendez, Johnson-Mendez-Jones. Quad Cities (3) -- Haberer-Doyne-Gross-Sillman, Parisi-Ool-Sillman, Scherer-Miller-Lundgren. South Bend (7) -- Jackson-Elliott, Kolberg-Vasquez-Perrault-Rosen, Kolberg-Elliott, Kinsey-Rosen-Elliott, Kolberg-Elliott-Rosen, Perrault-Vasquez-Elliott, Kolberg-Guerrero-Vasquez. Southwest Michigan (9) -- De La Cruz-Wagner-Walker-Perez, Houser-Bitter, Sonnanstine-Wagner, Gonzalez-Larson-De La Cruz, Sonnanstine-De La Cruz, Sonnanstine-Perez, Houser-De Los Santos, Lavergne-De Los Santos-Bitter, Houser-De Los Santos. West Michigan (8) -- Kown-Ostlund-Mahoney, Rainwater-Clelland-Tomey-Ostlund-Mahoney, Righter-Tomey, Kown-Finigan-Tomey, Trahern-Tomey-Finigan, Jurrjens-Dolsi-Ardoin, Hahn-Tomey-Dolsi-Whelan, Rainwater-Lewis-Ardoin-Whelan. Wisconsin (7) -- Jensen-Grasley-Fillinger, Snyder-Bello-James, Lowe-Bello-Grasley-Bergdall-James, Blanco-Brandt, Jensen-Snyder, Santiago-Blanco, Jensen-Blanco-O'Flaherty.

NO-HIT GAMES: Gallagher (6 innings), Nolan (3 innings) and Hunton (1 inning), Peoria, defeated Cedar Rapids, 3-2, April 20; Gonzalez (5 innings), Larson (2 innings) and De La Cruz (2 innings), Southwest Michigan, defeated Beloit, 7-0, May 28.

2005 FIELDING

TEAM

Team	G	PO	A	E	TC	DP	TP	PB	Pct.
Lansing	139	3638	1448	141	5227	111	0	30	.973
Beloit	140	3741	1325	153	5219	113	0	15	.971
Clinton	140	3778	1457	158	5393	118	0	22	.971
West Michigan	140	3775	1586	160	5521	135	0	19	.971
South Bend	140	3738	1593	165	5496	129	0	22	.970
Southwest Michigan	139	3616	1386	153	5155	125	1	23	.970
Peoria	140	3649	1449	162	5260	121	1	24	.969
Fort Wayne	140	3663	1439	171	5273	134	0	21	.968
Kane County	139	3702	1473	170	5345	108	0	26	.968
Wisconsin	139	3702	1439	172	5313	139	0	19	.968
Dayton	139	3641	1479	184	5304	126	0	18	.965
Burlington	140	3720	1495	193	5408	120	0	26	.964
Quad Cities	139	3673	1462	191	5326	128	0	17	.964
Cedar Rapids	140	3653	1502	198	5353	153	0	12	.963

INDIVIDUAL

FIRST BASEMEN

NOTE: All caps denotes fielding-percentage leader based on 70 games for catchers, 93 for all other non-pitchers and 112 innings for pitchers. *Throws lefthanded.

Player, Team	Pct.	G	PO	A	E	TC	DP
Anderson, Charles, Lansing	.993	17	127	12	1	140	5
Anderson, Drew, Dayton	1.000	1	8	1	0	9	1
Baxter, Michael, Fort Wayne	.993	45	365	34	3	402	38
Bernard, Oscar, Peoria	1.000	3	12	1	0	13	0
Brito, Javier, South Bend	.989	42	342	23	4	369	36
Brown, Christopher, Beloit	.982	38	258	16	5	279	26
Brown, Russell, Burlington	.981	63	540	37	11	588	36
Cannon, Rhame, Lansing	.989	31	249	20	3	272	23
Ciofrone, Peter, Fort Wayne	.971	8	62	6	2	70	9
Collins, Michael, Cedar Rapids	.989	40	352	15	4	371	41
Conley, Evan, Dayton	.926	3	24	1	2	27	0
Dale, Lachlan, Fort Wayne	.988	87	773	43	10	826	78
Douillard, Jonathan, Peoria	1.000	1	10	0	0	10	0
Espino, Damaso, Burlington	1.000	6	49	3	0	52	3
Everidge, Thomas, Kane County	.988	95	693	55	9	757	60
Fasano, Sal, Clinton	.992	64	580	40	5	625	53
Ferris, Michael, Quad Cities *	.991	123	1046	86	10	1142	96
Figueroa, Baudilio, Fort Wayne	1.000	1	10	0	0	10	0
Francisco, Alfredo, Peoria	1.000	1	11	0	0	11	0
Frazier, Jeffrey, West Michigan	1.000	1	0	1	0	1	0
Frostad, Emerson, Clinton	1.000	3	5	0	0	5	0

- 539 -

Player, Team	Pct.	G	PO	A	E	TC	DP
Gac, Ian, Clinton	.987	78	634	41	9	684	53
Garcia, Alberto, Peoria	.989	55	441	23	5	469	36
Granato, Anthony, Peoria	.989	20	170	11	2	183	19
Green, Brandon, Wisconsin	.990	47	361	42	4	407	39
Gutierrez, Tonys, Dayton *	.987	98	855	58	12	925	81
HICKS, DAVID, Lansing *	.996	103	794	55	3	852	72
Hubbard, Thomas, Wisconsin	.986	82	659	47	10	716	72
Johnson, Brent, Wisconsin	.973	5	36	0	1	37	2
Johnson, Michael, Cedar Rapids	.969	19	140	16	5	161	19
Kim, Edward, Kane County	.987	57	410	33	6	449	33
Kroski, Christopher, Dayton	.925	6	47	2	4	53	5
Larsen, Andrew, Peoria	.978	62	512	32	12	556	44
Lee, Joshua, West Michigan	.990	103	993	61	11	1065	87
Lucas, Edward, Burlington	1.000	14	84	11	0	95	12
Martinez, Brett, Cedar Rapids	...	1	0	0	0	0	0
Mather, Joseph, Cedar Rapids	.963	14	100	3	4	107	15
McIntyre, Nicholas, West Michigan	1.000	1	7	2	0	9	0
Melillo, Kevin, Kane County	1.000	1	6	2	0	8	1
Morton, Kristopher, Fort Wayne	1.000	1	6	0	0	6	0
Mosby, Robert, Dayton	.980	22	183	10	4	197	20
Mottram, Allen, South Bend	1.000	4	29	3	0	32	1
Mullinax, Jacob, Quad Cities	1.000	6	32	3	0	35	1
Murillo, Agustin, South Bend	1.000	13	110	9	0	119	8
Nicolas, Cesar, South Bend	.985	85	807	66	13	886	73
Padron, Raul, Kane County	.981	7	48	4	1	53	3
Piepkorn, Jeremiah, Dayton	.975	7	38	1	1	40	5
Purdom, John, Dayton	1.000	8	73	3	0	76	5
Reiman, Joey, Lansing	1.000	1	7	1	0	8	1
Remole, Clifton, Cedar Rapids *	1.000	4	19	2	0	21	6
Rick, Samuel, Peoria	.971	10	64	3	2	69	6
Roughton, Jody, West Michigan	.994	37	324	21	2	347	39
Sandoval, Freddy, Cedar Rapids	1.000	6	25	1	0	26	2
Smith, Aaron, Peoria	1.000	3	14	0	0	14	3
Solis, Heriberto, Burlington	.990	32	279	16	3	298	21
Soto, Luis, Wisconsin	1.000	12	91	7	0	98	11
Stavinoha, Nicholas, Quad Cities	1.000	7	50	2	0	52	5
Sutton, Nathanael, Cedar Rapids	1.000	1	7	0	0	7	1
Vega, Miguel, Burlington	.984	34	286	16	5	307	33
Walston, Christopher, Cedar Rapids	.979	75	701	43	16	760	69
Williams, Simon, Quad Cities *	1.000	1	1	0	0	1	0
Winfree, David, Beloit	...	1	0	0	0	0	0
Woodard, Johnny, Beloit	.985	51	427	19	7	453	41
Zamojc, Mitchell, Beloit	.986	54	460	29	7	496	32
Maestrales, Peter, Burlington	1.000	8	10	18	0	28	1
McIntyre, Nicholas, West Michigan	.900	2	5	4	1	10	0
Mejia, Jorge, Dayton	.956	10	19	24	2	45	6
Melillo, Kevin, Kane County	.968	68	135	167	10	312	37
Navarro, Oswaldo, Wisconsin	.974	57	145	157	8	310	38
Patrick, Brian, Lansing	1.000	3	6	8	0	14	2
Patrick, Christopher, Quad Cities	.953	16	20	41	3	64	8
PATTERSON, ERIC, Peoria	.982	106	183	315	9	507	61
Peralta, Juan, Lansing	.986	56	113	161	4	278	27
Petit, Gregorio, Kane County	.980	43	94	102	4	200	26
Ramos, Jason, Cedar Rapids	.969	12	24	38	2	64	9
Rios, Jose, Peoria	1.000	4	6	5	0	11	1
Rivera, Luis, Peoria	1.000	3	1	4	0	5	0
Rodriguez, Sean, Cedar Rapids	.974	12	29	45	2	76	16
Rowlett, Casey, Quad Cities	1.000	1	0	1	0	1	0
Ruiz, Ryan, Kane County	.936	37	89	71	11	171	22
Rutgers, Paul, Beloit	.978	24	39	48	2	89	12
Sandoval, Mayker, Dayton	.945	21	43	61	6	110	13
Shepherd, Matthew, Quad Cities	.956	49	99	142	11	252	28
Smith, Aaron, Peoria	.978	20	46	41	2	89	11
Smith, Matthew, Clinton	1.000	5	8	9	0	17	3
Solis, Heriberto, Burlington	1.000	25	66	74	0	140	25
Sutton, Nathanael, Cedar Rapids	.975	70	110	197	8	315	43
Tolleson, Steven, Beloit	.981	27	38	67	2	107	14
Valentin, Geraldo, Burlington	.986	35	53	90	2	145	10
Vazquez, Kelvin, Fort Wayne	.900	5	6	12	2	20	3
Velez, Eugenio, Lansing	.972	65	132	147	8	287	25
Washington, Johnny, Clinton	.971	27	55	81	4	140	12
Young, Stephen, West Michigan	.980	56	113	184	6	303	41

SECOND BASEMEN

Player, Team	Pct.	G	PO	A	E	TC	DP
Anderson, Drew, Dayton	.970	39	69	93	5	167	16
Armstrong, Jason, Lansing	.946	22	39	48	5	92	7
Arroyo, Jack, Wisconsin	.945	25	41	45	5	91	11
Arteaga, Joshua, Peoria	.938	4	6	9	1	16	1
Bonifacio, Emilio, South Bend	.964	119	222	386	23	631	74
Boyer, William, Cedar Rapids	1.000	7	9	17	0	26	5
Cabrera, Asdrubal, Wisconsin	.993	30	64	73	1	138	19
Casilla, Alexi, Cedar Rapids	.953	37	70	112	9	191	27
Chen, Yung Chi, Wisconsin	.982	35	59	104	3	166	29
Colvin, Brooks, West Michigan	.971	85	170	260	13	443	57
Conley, Evan, Dayton	1.000	5	11	10	0	21	2
Coughlan, Cameron, Clinton *	1.000	1	1	2	0	3	0
Delgado, Jose, Quad Cities	1.000	1	1	2	0	3	0
Falu, Irving, Burlington	.968	56	113	159	9	281	36
Fermin, Angelo, Beloit	.964	26	36	72	4	112	14
Figueroa, Baudilio, Fort Wayne	.959	11	20	27	2	49	3
Fox, Adam, Clinton	.987	15	29	46	1	76	11
Frostad, Emerson, Clinton	1.000	1	0	3	0	3	0
Gonzales, Alberto, South Bend	1.000	6	9	15	0	24	3
Granato, Anthony, Peoria	1.000	12	27	26	0	53	9
Green, Brandon, Wisconsin	...	1	0	0	0	0	0
Gutierrez, Tonys, Dayton *	1.000	1	2	2	0	4	2
Hayes, Calvin, Quad Cities	.942	21	47	50	6	103	10
Heckman, John, Wisconsin	...	1	0	0	0	0	0
Hoffpauir, Jarrett, Quad Cities	.981	61	119	185	6	310	46
Hughes, Luke, Beloit	.966	67	116	167	10	293	42
Hulett, Timothy, Clinton	.963	99	202	289	19	510	59
Kazmar, Sean, Fort Wayne	.973	125	243	375	17	635	92
Kelly, Paul, Beloit	.964	5	12	15	1	28	4
Lawhorn, Trevor, Dayton	.962	69	151	176	13	340	42
Leblanc, Joshua, Cedar Rapids	.872	8	14	20	5	39	6
Lockin, William, South Bend	.974	16	31	45	2	78	14
Long, Wesley, Kane County	1.000	1	1	1	0	2	1
Lucena, Juan, Quad Cities	1.000	2	0	3	0	3	0

THIRD BASEMEN

Player, Team	Pct.	G	PO	A	E	TC	DP
Anderson, Drew, Dayton	.875	7	4	10	2	16	0
Armstrong, Jason, Lansing	.922	84	69	157	19	245	14
Arteaga, Joshua, Peoria	.895	17	8	26	4	38	2
Bernard, Oscar, Peoria	1.000	1	0	2	0	2	0
Boyer, William, Cedar Rapids	.929	4	4	9	1	14	1
Brown, Christopher, Beloit	1.000	3	1	8	0	9	0
Cabrera, Asdrubal, Wisconsin	1.000	6	5	13	0	18	1
Castillo, Wilkin, South Bend	.750	3	2	1	1	4	1
Chen, Yung Chi, Wisconsin	.939	80	54	161	14	229	14
Ciofrone, Peter, Fort Wayne	.895	40	25	60	10	95	5
Colvin, Brooks, West Michigan	.915	15	12	31	4	47	1
Conley, Evan, Dayton	.862	12	5	20	4	29	0
Coughlan, Cameron, Clinton *	...	1	0	0	0	0	0
Dowdy, Brett, Fort Wayne	.933	75	60	120	13	193	18
Espino, Damaso, Burlington	.750	2	1	2	1	4	0
Fermin, Angelo, Beloit	1.000	2	0	1	0	1	0
Figueroa, Baudilio, Fort Wayne	.922	20	13	46	5	64	5
Fox, Adam, Clinton	1.000	27	16	67	0	83	5
Francisco, Alfredo, Peoria	.667	1	2	2	2	6	1
Frostad, Emerson, Clinton	.927	107	77	201	22	300	18
Gac, Ian, Clinton	.727	5	2	6	3	11	0
Garcia, Alberto, Peoria	1.000	3	1	10	0	11	1
Gonzales, Alberto, South Bend	1.000	1	0	1	0	1	0
Granato, Anthony, Peoria	.851	14	9	31	7	47	3
Green, Brandon, Wisconsin	.892	37	21	70	11	102	15
Headley, Chase, Fort Wayne	.800	4	3	5	2	10	0
Heckman, John, Wisconsin	.500	1	0	1	1	2	0
Hernandez, Habelito, Dayton	.930	16	9	31	3	43	2
Hulett, Timothy, Clinton	1.000	3	0	5	0	5	0
Johnson, Brent, Wisconsin	.925	21	11	26	3	40	2
Kelly, Paul, Beloit	...	1	0	0	0	0	0
Key, Bradley, Dayton	.879	68	39	121	22	182	13
Larsen, Andrew, Peoria	.932	45	25	84	8	117	6
Lawhorn, Trevor, Dayton	.727	3	2	6	3	11	2
Leslie, Myron, Kane County	.915	118	89	234	30	353	12
Lisson, Mario, Burlington	.910	62	51	130	18	199	12
Lockin, William, South Bend	1.000	2	0	2	0	2	0
Long, Wesley, Kane County	.816	14	5	26	7	38	2
Lucas, Edward, Burlington	.899	53	34	99	15	148	3
Maestrales, Peter, Burlington	...	1	0	0	0	0	0
McIntyre, Nicholas, West Michigan	.933	74	51	145	14	210	15
Mejia, Jorge, Dayton	1.000	3	0	11	0	11	0
Mullinax, Jacob, Quad Cities	.869	79	55	164	33	252	18
Murillo, Agustin, South Bend	.928	105	68	190	20	278	18
Navarro, Oswaldo, Wisconsin	.800	2	2	2	1	5	0
Patrick, Christopher, Quad Cities	.963	30	20	58	3	81	4
Petit, Gregorio, Kane County	.935	10	5	24	2	31	2
Piepkorn, Jeremiah, Dayton	.879	27	18	69	12	99	1

Player, Team	Pct.	G	PO	A	E	TC	DP
Puello, Elvin, Peoria	.727	6	5	3	3	11	0
Purdom, John, Dayton	.800	7	5	7	3	15	0
Ramirez, Wilkin, West Michigan	.843	57	34	106	26	166	8
Ramos, Jason, Cedar Rapids	.889	11	5	19	3	27	1
Reynolds, Mark, South Bend	.872	34	15	53	10	78	3
Rios, Jose, Peoria	1.000	1	0	4	0	4	0
Rivera, Luis, Peoria	.956	19	9	34	2	45	2
Rodriguez, Sean, Cedar Rapids	.852	14	9	14	4	27	3
Rowlett, Casey, Quad Cities	.800	8	4	8	3	15	0
Rutgers, Paul, Beloit	1.000	3	2	2	0	4	0
SANDOVAL, FREDDY, Cedar Rapids	.947	113	75	245	18	338	21
Sandoval, Mayker, Dayton	1.000	2	0	5	0	5	0
Shepherd, Matthew, Quad Cities	.917	32	19	58	7	84	4
Sisk, Aaron, Peoria	.929	12	7	19	2	28	2
Smith, Aaron, Peoria	.904	39	19	56	8	83	6
Smith, Matthew, Clinton	.909	3	2	8	1	11	0
Snavely, Christian, Lansing	.889	61	32	96	16	144	7
Solis, Heriberto, Burlington	.917	26	25	52	7	84	2
Sutton, Nathanael, Cedar Rapids	1.000	5	4	10	0	14	1
Tuiasosopo, Matthew, Wisconsin	1.000	1	1	2	0	3	0
Valentin, Geraldo, Burlington	.933	4	3	11	1	15	0
Vazquez, Kelvin, Fort Wayne	.714	3	2	3	2	7	0
Velez, Eugenio, Lansing	1.000	2	0	4	0	4	0
Wayment, Kory, Kane County	1.000	2	0	6	0	6	0
Winfree, David, Beloit	.895	133	80	211	34	325	18

SHORTSTOPS

Player, Team	Pct.	G	PO	A	E	TC	DP
Anderson, Drew, Dayton	.942	27	42	89	8	139	21
Armstrong, Jason, Lansing	.970	14	23	42	2	67	10
Arteaga, Joshua, Peoria	.937	13	21	38	4	63	9
Benjamin, Casey, Clinton	.953	112	175	312	24	511	52
Boyer, William, Cedar Rapids	.892	8	14	19	4	37	4
Bush, Matthew, Fort Wayne	.941	125	185	422	38	645	83
Cabrera, Asdrubal, Wisconsin	.927	11	15	23	3	41	6
Caldera, Jose, Cedar Rapids	.952	5	8	12	1	21	3
Casilla, Alexi, Cedar Rapids	.969	41	74	113	6	193	33
Chen, Yung Chi, Wisconsin	...	1	0	0	0	0	0
Colvin, Brooks, West Michigan	.977	8	17	25	1	43	3
Dlugach, Brent, West Michigan	.955	121	176	457	30	663	81
Falu, Irving, Burlington	.958	62	90	186	12	288	27
Fermin, Angelo, Beloit	.975	14	29	48	2	79	10
Figueroa, Baudilio, Fort Wayne	.903	17	21	44	7	72	8
Fox, Adam, Clinton	.979	22	33	59	2	94	17
Frostad, Emerson, Clinton	1.000	3	2	5	0	7	1
Garciaparra, Nomar, Peoria	1.000	2	1	3	0	4	2
Gonzales, Alberto, South Bend	.975	84	126	307	11	444	62
Granato, Anthony, Peoria	.975	26	32	86	3	121	12
Hulett, Timothy, Clinton	1.000	8	19	24	0	43	3
Janish, Paul, Dayton	.963	55	96	188	11	295	34
KLOSTERMAN, RYAN, Lansing	.958	128	209	361	25	595	65
Lawhorn, Trevor, Dayton	.667	1	3	1	2	6	1
Lisson, Mario, Burlington	.977	7	17	25	1	43	4
Lockin, William, South Bend	1.000	3	0	9	0	9	1
Lucas, Edward, Burlington	.929	38	46	111	12	169	22
Lucena, Juan, Quad Cities	.942	93	98	244	21	363	47
McIntyre, Nicholas, West Michigan	.946	13	20	33	3	56	10
Mejia, Jorge, Dayton	.973	27	40	69	3	112	15
Melillo, Kevin, Kane County	1.000	1	0	2	0	2	0
Navarro, Oswaldo, Wisconsin	.935	53	105	152	18	275	42
Pennington, Clifton, Kane County	.958	65	99	194	13	306	31
Peralta, Juan, Lansing	1.000	1	0	1	0	1	0
Petit, Gregorio, Kane County	.951	29	50	87	7	144	21
Plouffe, Trevor, Beloit	.933	125	168	319	35	522	67
Ramos, Jason, Cedar Rapids	.880	4	7	15	3	25	3
Reynolds, Mark, South Bend	.922	56	75	163	20	258	29
Rios, Jose, Peoria	.893	23	33	67	12	112	9
Rivera, Luis, Peoria	1.000	4	3	7	0	10	1
Rodriguez, Sean, Cedar Rapids	.964	85	169	238	15	422	63
Rosales, Adam, Dayton	.957	32	48	87	6	141	16
Ruiz, Ryan, Kane County	.987	23	21	57	1	79	11
Rutgers, Paul, Beloit	.750	1	1	2	1	4	0
Shepherd, Matthew, Quad Cities	.935	61	91	153	17	261	37
Simokaitis, Joseph, Peoria	.945	51	59	163	13	235	33
Sisk, Aaron, Peoria	.946	21	24	63	5	92	10
Smith, Aaron, Peoria	.950	7	3	16	1	20	0
Smith, Matthew, Clinton	.923	4	3	9	1	13	1
Tolleson, Steven, Beloit	.941	5	3	13	1	17	3
Tuiasosopo, Matthew, Wisconsin	.922	79	118	190	26	334	36
Valentin, Geraldo, Burlington	.923	28	35	73	9	117	22
Wayment, Kory, Kane County	.951	29	35	100	7	142	21

OUTFIELDERS

Player, Team	Pct.	G	PO	A	E	TC	DP
Alley, Joshua, Fort Wayne *	.964	41	80	0	3	83	0
Anderson, Drew, Dayton	1.000	33	61	3	0	64	1
Ankiel, Rick, Quad Cities *	.949	30	54	2	3	59	0
Arroyo, Jack, Wisconsin	.990	44	94	9	1	104	2
Balcom, Jasha, Peoria	.875	4	7	0	1	8	0
Belcher, Jordan, Dayton	.954	25	59	3	3	65	0
Benjamin, Casey, Clinton	1.000	1	1	0	0	1	0
BLASI, NICHOLAS, Kane County	.991	111	204	7	2	213	1
Boggs, Brandon, Clinton	.967	76	172	5	6	183	1
Boucher, Sebastien, Wisconsin	.990	44	93	7	1	101	0
Brito, Javier, South Bend	.951	28	37	2	2	41	0
Brown, Andrew, Quad Cities *	...	1	0	0	0	0	0
Buck, Travis, Kane County	.985	30	64	0	1	65	0
Buhagiar, Joshua, South Bend *	.973	17	35	1	1	37	0
Burns, Deacon, Beloit *	.981	111	199	6	4	209	0
Burt, Landon, Beloit *	.972	60	102	3	3	108	2
Cannon, Rhame, Lansing	1.000	1	1	0	0	1	0
Cashman, Brandon, Clinton	.962	109	241	9	10	260	2
Castillo, Wilkin, South Bend	.981	28	50	3	1	54	0
Cavanaugh, Brian, Fort Wayne	.909	6	10	0	1	11	0
Colton, Christopher, Wisconsin	.985	46	127	4	2	133	2
Coughlan, Cameron, Clinton *	.963	36	74	3	3	80	1
Cure, Cody, Burlington	.967	52	114	3	4	121	1
Danielson, Sean, Quad Cities	1.000	6	15	0	0	15	0
Davidson, Drew, Fort Wayne	1.000	10	16	0	0	16	0
Ellis, Jared, Burlington	1.000	13	15	0	0	15	0
Flowers, Clarence, Peoria	.936	74	126	6	9	141	0
Frazier, Jeffrey, West Michigan	.977	127	205	8	5	218	0
Fryer, Brian, Fort Wayne	.966	18	28	0	1	29	0
Fuld, Samuel, Peoria *	.981	123	308	7	6	321	4
Gentry, Philip, Dayton	1.000	83	131	6	0	137	2
Giannotti, Richard, Cedar Rapids	.954	99	200	7	10	217	4
Gonzales, Carlos, South Bend *	.973	127	239	13	7	259	3
Gulick, Travis, South Bend	.991	60	108	3	1	112	0
Gutierrez, Tonys, Dayton *	.750	2	3	0	1	4	0
Hall, David, Wisconsin	.800	8	8	0	2	10	0
Hammond, Derry, Quad Cities	1.000	6	5	0	0	5	0
Harris, Steven, Peoria	1.000	5	8	0	0	8	0
Harrison, Benjamin, Clinton	.927	67	121	6	10	137	0
Harvey, Ryan, Peoria	.988	94	148	10	2	160	3
Hayes, Calvin, Quad Cities	1.000	1	1	0	0	1	0
Herbert, Samuel, Quad Cities	1.000	5	4	0	0	4	0
Herrera, Javier, Kane County	.967	88	222	10	8	240	0
Hetherington, Luke, Lansing	.990	59	90	5	1	96	1
Himes, Benjamin, Dayton	.944	27	34	0	2	36	0
Hoffpauir, Jarrett, Quad Cities	...	2	0	0	0	0	0
Hubbard, Thomas, Wisconsin	1.000	3	3	1	0	4	1
Hurba, Craig, Clinton	...	1	0	0	0	0	0
Johnson, Brent, Wisconsin	.994	76	160	9	1	170	1
Johnson, Craig, Fort Wayne *	.875	5	7	0	1	8	0
Johnson, Robert, Wisconsin	...	1	0	0	0	0	0
Joseph, Alfred, Peoria	1.000	7	16	0	0	16	0
Justice, Justin, West Michigan *	.989	77	185	3	2	190	1
Kolkhorst, Christopher, Fort Wayne	.985	95	129	5	2	136	1
Kroski, Christopher, Dayton	...	1	0	0	0	0	0
Larsen, Andrew, Peoria	.938	19	27	3	2	32	1
Leblanc, Joshua, Cedar Rapids	.976	50	118	2	3	123	1
Lemanczyk, Matthew, Quad Cities	.987	105	227	4	3	234	1
Lewis, Kenneth, Dayton *	1.000	26	47	1	0	48	0
Lucas, Edward, Burlington	.846	7	10	1	2	13	0
Madrigal, Warner A., Cedar Rapids	.955	82	140	8	7	155	3
Maestrales, Peter, Burlington	1.000	5	7	0	0	7	0
Mallory, Michael, Peoria	1.000	3	5	0	0	5	0
Mather, Joseph, Quad Cities	1.000	42	82	4	0	86	1
Mathews, Aaron, Lansing	.991	63	106	8	1	115	0
Mc Fall, Robert, Burlington	.963	97	173	7	7	187	1
McIntyre, Nicholas, West Michigan	1.000	2	3	0	0	3	0
Milons, Jereme, South Bend	.972	116	234	6	7	247	1
Montanez, Luis, Peoria	1.000	76	115	7	0	122	2
Mora, Ruben, Fort Wayne	.986	32	70	1	1	72	0
Moye, Alan, Burlington	.975	45	76	2	2	80	1
Nielsen, Eric, Lansing	.986	120	195	11	3	209	1
Norman, Derek, Burlington	1.000	4	6	2	0	8	0
Parrish, Matthew, West Michigan	.967	58	84	3	3	90	3
Patrick, Brian, Lansing	.909	8	9	1	1	11	0
Patterson, Tarrence, Beloit	.988	83	159	6	2	167	2
Patton, Preston, Lansing *	.961	55	67	6	3	76	2
Peel, Aaron, Cedar Rapids	.943	30	32	1	2	35	0
Perez, Luis, Kane County	.990	48	95	5	1	101	1

CLASS A Midwest League

Player, Team	Pct.	G	PO	A	E	TC	DP
Pickrel, Jeremy, Beloit	.986	94	207	2	3	212	0
Piepkorn, Jeremiah, Dayton	.955	73	122	6	6	134	0
Pineda, Jose, Kane County	.971	59	128	4	4	136	1
Purdom, John, Dayton	...	1	0	0	0	0	0
Ramirez, Yordany, Fort Wayne	.963	104	294	20	12	326	1
Remole, Clifton, Cedar Rapids *	1.000	1	4	0	0	4	0
Renz, Jordan Tyler, Cedar Rapids	.973	68	103	5	3	111	1
Rodriguez, Sean, Cedar Rapids	.980	14	46	4	1	51	0
Rodriguez, Yuber, Lansing	.972	108	237	4	7	248	3
Rowlett, Casey, Quad Cities	1.000	12	21	1	0	22	0
Ruiz, Ryan, Kane County	...	1	0	0	0	0	0
Rutgers, Paul, Beloit	1.000	36	56	0	0	56	0
Sabino, Luis, West Michigan	.968	113	233	6	8	247	3
Salazar, Darwinson, Burlington	.962	57	97	3	4	104	1
Sanders, Anthony, Lansing	1.000	6	6	0	0	6	0
Schmidt, Jesse, Peoria	1.000	38	80	2	0	82	1
Simon, Brandon, South Bend *	.951	54	94	3	5	102	2
Snavely, Christian, Lansing	1.000	25	30	0	0	30	0
Springer, Kenard, Burlington	.955	101	171	22	9	202	4
Stavinoha, Nicholas, Quad Cities	.991	55	103	5	1	109	1
Strait, William, Dayton	.978	112	257	13	6	276	2
Susdorf, William, Clinton	.973	70	140	4	4	148	3
Swackhamer, Wesley, Quad Cities *	.980	68	96	4	2	102	0
Szymanski, Brandon, Dayton	.969	44	91	3	3	97	2
Thayer, Matthew, Fort Wayne *	1.000	25	42	1	0	43	0
Thomas, Michael, West Michigan	.991	50	110	4	1	115	0
Tietje, Chalon, Kane County	1.000	36	54	3	0	57	1
Toussaint, Andrew, Cedar Rapids	.963	79	122	8	5	135	0
Tritle, Christopher, Kane County	1.000	33	71	0	0	71	0
Valentin, Geraldo, Burlington	.974	51	106	8	3	117	1
Vazquez, Kelvin, Fort Wayne	1.000	1	1	0	0	1	0
Verbryke, Eric, Quad Cities *	.961	55	98	1	4	103	0
Vincent, Tom, Fort Wayne	.975	87	149	6	4	159	1
Wayment, Kory, Kane County	1.000	28	44	3	0	47	1
White, Dwayne, Beloit *	1.000	48	70	1	0	71	0
Williams, Simon, Quad Cities *	.992	62	129	0	1	130	0
Wilson, Michael Ladon, Wisconsin	.982	122	263	14	5	282	5
Wishy, Andrew, Clinton	.972	78	126	11	4	141	1
Womack, Joshua, Wisconsin *	.974	93	180	6	5	191	1
Zamojc, Mitchell, Beloit	1.000	1	2	0	0	2	0

CATCHERS

Player, Team	Pct.	G	PO	A	E	TC	DP
Anderson, Charles, Lansing	...	1	0	0	0	0	0
Arias, Roberto, Kane County	.967	6	29	0	1	30	0
Baez, Lizahio, Clinton	.971	30	154	13	5	172	1
Bernard, Oscar, Peoria	.972	62	405	39	13	457	4
Castillo, David, Kane County	.981	29	190	21	4	215	2
Castillo, Wilkin, South Bend	.983	60	417	42	8	467	4
Chapman, Travis, Kane County	.989	45	255	23	3	281	0
Clark, Douglas, Clinton	.981	6	45	8	1	54	0
Clement, Jeffrey, Wisconsin	.988	20	148	13	2	163	4
Collins, Michael, Cedar Rapids	.974	59	387	31	11	429	3
Corrente, David, Lansing	.984	62	390	50	7	447	1
Del Rosario, Felipe, Burlington	.953	16	113	9	6	128	0
Dini, Gregory, Cedar Rapids	.986	9	65	5	1	71	1
Douillard, Jonathan, Peoria	1.000	8	47	5	0	52	0
Duenas, Tomas, Cedar Rapids	.964	55	397	61	17	475	4
Duff, Timothy, Cedar Rapids	.975	12	68	11	2	81	0
Espino, Damaso, Burlington	.983	64	422	41	8	471	3
Falcon, Omar, Wisconsin	.981	41	232	24	5	261	3
Feiner, Korey, Beloit	.991	63	524	55	5	584	7
Gonzalez, Julio, Dayton	.929	4	22	4	2	28	0
Graham, Andrew, West Michigan	.987	32	205	17	3	225	2
Grana, Robert, Burlington	.990	41	277	24	3	304	2
Hundley, Nicholas, Fort Wayne	.973	8	66	7	2	75	0
Hurba, Craig, Clinton	.996	40	262	18	1	281	2
Johnson, Michael, Cedar Rapids	.955	3	20	1	1	22	0
Johnson, Robert, Wisconsin	.986	75	489	65	8	562	4
Killian, William, Fort Wayne	1.000	1	1	0	0	1	0
Kroski, Christopher, Dayton	1.000	26	185	20	0	205	1
Lauderdale, Matthew, Fort Wayne	.977	65	430	36	11	477	2
Lex, Joshua, Lansing	1.000	14	107	10	0	117	0
Lobaton, Jose, Fort Wayne	.985	9	64	3	1	68	0
Maduro, Jorge, Burlington	.968	7	53	7	2	62	0
Martinez, Alberto, Clinton	.989	21	156	23	2	181	1
Martinez, Brett, Cedar Rapids	1.000	2	9	0	0	9	0
Mendez, Jose, Quad Cities	1.000	1	4	0	0	4	0

Player, Team	Pct.	G	PO	A	E	TC	DP
Mercado, Orlando, South Bend	.984	59	440	47	8	495	1
Morton, Kristopher, Fort Wayne	.984	59	415	27	7	449	3
Mottram, Allen, South Bend	.995	26	160	22	1	183	2
Norman, Derek, Burlington	.990	24	170	21	2	193	2
Padron, Raul, Kane County	.980	87	486	40	11	537	3
Palmer, Cody, Quad Cities	.985	31	181	16	3	200	1
Purdom, John, Dayton	.988	69	429	51	6	486	5
Quintana, Alberto, Lansing	1.000	3	20	2	0	22	0
Reed, Mark, Peoria	.991	14	104	10	1	115	0
Reiman, Joey, Lansing	1.000	6	31	5	0	36	0
Richardson, Kevin, Clinton	.990	51	370	24	4	398	3
Rick, Samuel, Peoria	.994	63	432	43	3	478	5
Robinson, Christopher, West Michigan	.987	41	286	21	4	311	1
RYAN, DUSTY, West Michigan	.990	75	459	58	5	522	1
Sanchez, Javier, Beloit	.985	84	691	56	11	758	3
Schweiger, Brian, Wisconsin	.974	6	31	6	1	38	0
Soto, Luis, Wisconsin	1.000	1	2	0	0	2	0
Tatum, Craig, Dayton	.968	36	243	31	9	283	2
Thigpen, Curtis, Lansing	.986	60	451	58	7	516	6
Toops, Brady, Quad Cities	.985	47	304	25	5	334	4
Wolfe, Joseph, Lansing	1.000	3	15	3	0	18	0
Wyman, Spencer, Quad Cities	.983	35	223	14	4	241	0
Yarbrough, Brandon, Quad Cities	.964	37	246	21	10	277	2
Ziemendorf, Chad, Dayton	.985	9	56	11	1	68	0

PITCHERS

Player, Team	Pct.	G	PO	A	E	TC	DP
Abrams, Casey, Wisconsin *	.882	17	4	11	2	17	2
Abreu, Francis, Cedar Rapids	1.000	10	0	2	0	2	0
Adamczyk, Tyler, Quad Cities	.938	15	6	9	1	16	1
Aguero, Miguel, Quad Cities	1.000	2	0	1	0	1	0
Altman, Kevin, Clinton	.923	32	4	8	1	13	2
Andersen, Phillip, Quad Cities	.750	17	7	5	4	16	0
Ardoin, Kevin, West Michigan	1.000	22	4	6	0	10	0
Arnold, Mitchell Scott, Cedar Rapids	1.000	12	0	2	0	2	0
Aselton, Kyle, Beloit *	.941	41	4	12	1	17	0
Atencio, Alonzo, Burlington	1.000	17	3	7	0	10	0
Avery, James, Dayton	1.000	5	0	5	0	5	0
Baez, Edgar, Peoria	1.000	4	0	2	0	2	0
Bailey, David, Dayton	.818	28	6	12	4	22	1
Bannister, John, Clinton	.926	29	9	16	2	27	1
Begnaud, Russell, Burlington	.800	15	2	2	1	5	1
Bello, Cibney, Wisconsin	.952	37	6	14	1	21	0
Berg, Justin, Peoria	...	2	0	0	0	0	0
Bergdall, Kendall, Wisconsin *	.818	18	3	6	2	11	1
Berroa, Yesson, Lansing	1.000	5	0	2	0	2	0
Bierd, Randor, West Michigan	1.000	7	0	4	0	4	0
Billek, Michael, Peoria	.800	8	2	2	1	5	1
Blackford, Todd, Peoria	...	1	0	0	0	0	0
Blackwell, Chad, Burlington	1.000	48	6	7	0	13	0
Blair, Thomas, Quad Cities *	...	4	0	0	0	0	0
Blanco, Ivan, Wisconsin	.929	28	4	9	1	14	0
Blevins, Jerry, Peoria *	.917	48	1	10	1	12	0
Bohorquez, Carlos, Dayton	.933	37	6	8	1	15	0
Brandt, Adam, Wisconsin *	1.000	11	1	1	0	2	0
Brito, Luis, Peoria	.500	6	0	1	1	2	0
Brown, Justin, Quad Cities	1.000	3	0	1	0	1	0
Buckner, William, Burlington	.889	11	4	4	1	9	1
Cabaniel, Tomas, Kane County	1.000	31	3	5	0	8	0
Cairns, Jason, Quad Cities	.700	22	3	4	3	10	1
Campbell, Matthew, Burlington *	.750	13	2	4	2	8	0
Campusano, Edward, Peoria *	1.000	19	1	4	0	5	0
Carlson, Zane, Burlington	1.000	13	3	3	0	6	0
Carter, Brenton, Fort Wayne *	1.000	2	0	4	0	4	0
Cheng, Chi-Hung, Lansing *	.885	26	5	18	3	26	0
Cherry, William, Dayton	1.000	17	3	3	0	6	0
Christensen, Daniel, Burlington *	.786	26	0	11	3	14	0
Clelland, Edward, West Michigan *	1.000	37	4	5	0	9	0
Coffin, Ryan, South Bend	1.000	14	1	0	0	1	0
Cooper, Michael, Quad Cities	1.000	10	3	4	0	7	1
Corchado, Jose, Kane County	1.000	12	1	2	0	3	0
Cordeiro, Christopher, Clinton	...	6	0	0	0	0	0
Cordero, Jose, Beloit	...	7	0	0	0	0	0
Cordova, Francisco, Cedar Rapids	.938	29	5	10	1	16	1
Core, Daniel, Lansing	.931	21	9	18	2	29	2
Cota, Luis, Burlington	.941	26	13	19	2	34	1

Player, Team	Pct.	G	PO	A	E	TC	DP
Crist, Kyle, Burlington	1.000	16	2	6	0	8	0
Culpepper, Kevin, Beloit *	.941	49	4	12	1	17	0
Damico, Yovany, Burlington	.833	35	0	10	2	12	1
Day, Amos, Lansing	.500	9	0	1	1	2	0
DeHoyos, Gabriel, Burlington	1.000	28	5	9	0	14	1
Delgadillo, Hector, Lansing	1.000	1	1	0	0	1	0
DeLoizaga-Carney, Frederic, Cedar Rapids	.800	21	0	4	1	5	0
Dickerson, Roy, Quad Cities *	.800	22	0	4	1	5	0
Dickson, Andrew, Peoria	1.000	25	3	7	0	10	1
Dolsi, Freddy, West Michigan	.778	23	1	6	2	9	1
Dossett, William, Burlington	.714	4	2	3	2	7	0
Douglas, James, Cedar Rapids *	.625	24	4	1	3	8	1
Dove, Dennis, Quad Cities	.920	18	11	12	2	25	0
Downs, Darin, Peoria *	.500	2	0	1	1	2	0
Doyne, Michael, Quad Cities	...	2	0	0	0	0	0
Drucker, Scot, Kane County	.857	21	0	6	1	7	0
Duguay, Steven, Beloit	1.000	17	2	0	0	2	0
Duran, Enmanuel, South Bend	.857	10	1	5	1	7	1
Edwards, William, Cedar Rapids	1.000	10	8	7	0	15	1
Ekstrom, Michael, Fort Wayne	.935	28	12	17	2	31	1
Elliott, Matthew, South Bend	1.000	53	5	7	0	12	0
Ellis, Jonathon, Fort Wayne	.905	43	5	14	2	21	3
Espinoza, Gustavo, Cedar Rapids *	...	1	0	0	0	0	0
Estrada, Jesus, Peoria	.967	27	14	15	1	30	1
Evans, Ronald, Kane County	.857	15	7	5	2	14	0
Falkenbach, Thomas, Lansing	...	2	0	0	0	0	0
Farfan, Alexander, Dayton	.938	44	2	13	1	16	0
Farnum, Matthew, Clinton	1.000	17	3	1	0	4	1
Fenton, Willson, Peoria	...	6	0	0	0	0	0
Fillinger, Chad, Wisconsin	.900	23	3	6	1	10	0
Finigan, Patrick, West Michigan	.917	25	4	7	1	12	1
Ford, Ryan, Kane County *	.960	26	7	41	2	50	1
Francisco, Alfredo, Peoria	1.000	6	0	1	0	1	0
French, Lucas, West Michigan *	1.000	6	2	2	0	4	0
Frias, Juan, Dayton *	.944	14	7	10	1	18	2
Frye, Randall, Wisconsin	.909	11	4	6	1	11	0
Fyvie, Daniel, Kane County	1.000	13	2	4	0	6	0
Gallagher, Sean, Peoria	.889	26	3	21	3	27	2
Garcia, Angel, Beloit	.667	17	1	1	1	3	0
Garcia, Geivy, Fort Wayne	.750	41	0	3	1	4	0
Garrison, Aaron, Dayton	.800	8	0	4	1	5	0
Garza, Matthew, Beloit	1.000	10	1	7	0	8	0
Geer, Joshua, Fort Wayne	1.000	5	3	4	0	7	0
Gelinas, Karl, Cedar Rapids	.839	26	10	16	5	31	0
George, Jonathan, Dayton	1.000	35	8	10	0	18	1
Giles, Joshua, Clinton	1.000	11	2	3	0	5	0
Girardeau, Maurice, Fort Wayne	1.000	6	2	3	0	5	0
Gonzalez, Miguel, Cedar Rapids	1.000	28	3	9	0	12	1
Gonzalez, Rafael, Dayton	.750	10	0	3	1	4	0
Grasley, Stephen, Wisconsin	1.000	44	6	12	0	18	0
Green, Nicholas, Cedar Rapids	.947	26	8	10	1	19	2
Green, Patrick, Burlington	.931	19	13	14	2	29	0
Gross, Timothy, Quad Cities	1.000	36	4	9	0	13	0
Guerrero, Hipolito, South Bend *	1.000	46	3	8	0	11	0
Guzman, Angel, Peoria	...	2	0	0	0	0	0
Gwaltney, William, Peoria	1.000	10	2	8	0	10	0
Haberer, Eric, Quad Cities *	.765	9	4	9	4	17	1
Hahn, Jeffrey, West Michigan	1.000	6	3	3	0	6	0
HAMILTON, CLAYTON, Fort Wayne	1.000	20	8	16	0	24	1
Harang, Daryl, Lansing *	1.000	16	1	3	0	4	0
Harper, Jeremy, Lansing	1.000	19	2	5	0	7	0
Harrison, Benjamin, Lansing *	...	1	0	0	0	0	0
Hendley, Blake, Dayton	1.000	38	2	4	0	6	1
Heuser, James, Kane County *	.667	18	0	4	2	6	0
Hicklen, Patrick, Burlington	.840	25	6	15	4	25	0
Hill, Danny, Lansing	1.000	17	1	3	0	4	0
Hill, Joshua, Beloit	1.000	35	4	12	0	16	1
Hill, Rich, Peoria *	...	1	0	0	0	0	0
Howard, Adam, South Bend	1.000	20	4	1	0	5	0
Hunton, Jonathan, Peoria	.833	25	0	5	1	6	0
Hurley, Eric, Clinton	.920	28	9	14	2	25	1
Hyle, Michael, Peoria	1.000	4	1	2	0	3	1
Jackson, Steven, South Bend	.976	28	15	26	1	42	2
Jaile, Christopher, Clinton	1.000	17	3	2	0	5	0
James, Craig, Wisconsin	1.000	26	0	6	0	6	0
Jamison, Neil, Fort Wayne	1.000	7	0	1	0	1	0
Janssen, Robert, Lansing	1.000	7	4	7	0	11	0
Jensen, Aaron, Wisconsin	.875	28	9	19	4	32	2
Jimenez Angulo, Fabian Enrique, Fort Wayne *	1.000	20	4	17	0	21	0
Johnson, Grant, Peoria	1.000	14	4	10	0	14	0
Jones, Michael, Peoria	1.000	18	1	3	0	4	0
Jordan, Justin, Wisconsin	1.000	17	1	4	0	5	1
Jurrens, Jair, West Michigan	.962	26	6	19	1	26	0
Kauten, Joshua, West Michigan	1.000	14	5	7	0	12	3
Keng, Po-Hsuan, Lansing	.875	28	4	10	2	16	1
Key, Bradley, Dayton	...	1	0	0	0	0	0
Kinsey, Christopher, South Bend	.900	13	7	11	2	20	1
Kintzler, Brandon, Fort Wayne	1.000	19	1	3	0	4	0
Klatt, Ryan, Fort Wayne	1.000	16	1	1	0	2	0
Knoff, Justin, Quad Cities	.857	22	2	4	1	7	0
Kolberg, Koley, South Bend	.889	20	8	16	3	27	3
Kometani, Paul, Clinton	.750	13	1	2	1	4	0
Konecny, Daniel, West Michigan	.889	22	5	3	1	9	0
Kown, Andrew, West Michigan	1.000	26	7	10	0	17	0
LaMacchia, Marc, Clinton	1.000	32	3	10	0	13	1
Langdon, Donny, Wisconsin *	1.000	18	1	1	0	2	0
Layden, Timothy, Peoria *	.867	38	4	9	2	15	0
Layman, William, Cedar Rapids	.400	7	0	2	3	5	0
Lewis, Lavon, Beloit *	.857	24	2	4	1	7	0
Lockwood, Jonathan, Wisconsin	1.000	15	3	1	0	4	0
Lowe, Mark, Wisconsin	.829	22	17	12	6	35	0
Lujan, John, Clinton	.933	31	3	11	1	15	0
Lundgren, Wayne, Quad Cities	1.000	10	1	2	0	3	0
Mahoney, Collin, West Michigan	1.000	25	1	4	0	5	0
Martin, Adrian, Lansing	1.000	5	1	1	0	2	0
Martinez, Jonathan, Beloit	.905	53	5	14	2	21	1
Martinez, Roman, Wisconsin	.600	19	2	1	2	5	0
Martinez, Shawn, Kane County	1.000	14	2	1	0	3	0
Mauer, William, Beloit	...	1	0	0	0	0	0
McBeth, Marcus, Kane County	1.000	16	1	1	0	2	0
McClellan, Kyle, Quad Cities	1.000	17	4	10	0	14	0
McCormick, Mark, Quad Cities	.778	9	3	4	2	9	0
McLaughlin, Joey, Lansing	.889	42	5	3	1	9	0
Meacham, Cory, Quad Cities	1.000	18	0	3	0	3	0
Medina, Dennis, Quad Cities	1.000	20	1	3	0	4	0
Medlin, Richard, South Bend	1.000	9	1	1	0	2	0
Meek, Evan, Beloit	1.000	13	1	4	0	5	2
Mendez, Adalberto, Peoria	1.000	22	4	0	0	4	2
Mijares, Jose, Beloit *	.889	20	0	8	1	9	2
Miller, Brian, Quad Cities	1.000	14	1	0	0	1	0
Mitchell, Michael, Kane County	.700	19	3	4	3	10	0
Moore, James, Burlington	.833	7	3	2	1	6	0
Morenko, Brad, Dayton	1.000	16	7	13	0	20	3
Morillo, Lennyn, Cedar Rapids	1.000	3	1	3	0	4	1
Morlan, Eduardo, Beloit	.867	10	5	8	2	15	2
Morrison, James, Dayton	1.000	31	3	16	0	19	1
Mutter, Casey, Cedar Rapids	.333	19	0	1	2	3	0
Nolen, Walt, Peoria	.800	37	4	4	2	10	0
Nottingham, Shawn, Wisconsin *	1.000	3	2	3	0	5	0
O'Flaherty, Eric, Wisconsin *	.913	45	5	16	2	23	0
Ohlendorf, Curtis, South Bend	.853	27	8	21	5	34	0
Oliveros, Rayner, Burlington	1.000	2	0	2	0	2	0
Ool, Kevin, Quad Cities *	1.000	30	4	11	0	15	0
Ostlund, Ian, West Michigan *	.889	32	0	8	1	9	0
Padgett, Michael, Clinton	1.000	23	2	7	0	9	1
Parisi, Michael, Quad Cities	.909	14	3	17	2	22	0
Paz, Jackson, Quad Cities *	1.000	6	0	1	0	1	0
Peralta, Tony, West Michigan *	.500	22	0	3	3	6	0
Perez, Henry, Fort Wayne	...	11	0	0	0	0	0
Perez, Juan, Lansing	.880	34	6	16	3	25	0
Perez, Keith, Kane County	.600	26	2	4	4	10	0
Perez, Roberto, Clinton	1.000	26	3	3	0	6	0
Perrault, Joshua, South Bend	.967	45	14	15	1	30	2
Peterson, John, Kane County *	.875	16	5	9	2	16	0
Pettit, William, Beloit	1.000	6	1	3	0	4	1
Phelps, Michael, Peoria	...	12	0	0	0	0	0
Phillips, Zachary, Clinton *	.000	2	0	0	1	1	0
Pickens, Joseph, Kane County	1.000	33	6	7	0	13	0
Polanco, Alfredo, Peoria	.857	22	2	4	1	7	0
Polanco, Phillip, Fort Wayne	1.000	26	2	3	0	5	1

Player, Team	Pct.	G	PO	A	E	TC	DP
Powers, Joseph, Dayton	1.000	5	1	0	0	1	0
Purdum, John, Dayton	...	1	0	0	0	0	0
Raab, Kellen, South Bend *	.926	27	4	21	2	27	2
Rainville, Jay, Beloit	1.000	16	2	3	0	5	0
Rainwater, Joshua, West Michigan	.875	16	9	5	2	16	2
Ramirez, Ramon, Dayton	.955	30	4	17	1	22	4
Ramos, Cesar, Fort Wayne *	1.000	7	2	4	0	6	0
Ramos, Victor, Peoria	1.000	5	0	1	0	1	0
Randazzo, Jeffrey, Quad Cities *	1.000	7	0	1	0	1	0
Ray, Ronald, Cedar Rapids	1.000	19	8	7	0	15	1
Rico, Erik, Lansing *	1.000	7	1	3	0	4	0
Righter, Matthew, West Michigan	.909	27	4	6	1	11	1
Rivera, Mumba, Wisconsin	.923	10	4	8	1	13	0
Roberts, Mark, Clinton	1.000	10	1	1	0	2	0
Robertson, James, Kane County	1.000	20	1	2	0	3	0
Robertson, Quinton, Quad Cities	.900	22	2	7	1	10	2
Rocha, Angel, South Bend *	1.000	13	0	3	0	3	0
Rodriguez, Fernando, Cedar Rapids	.871	28	9	18	4	31	0
Rodriguez, Rafael, Cedar Rapids	.850	13	3	14	3	20	0
Rogers, Kyle, Clinton	.857	28	5	13	3	21	1
Rogers, Michael, Kane County	.917	26	7	15	2	24	0
Rosen, Mark, South Bend	.800	46	1	7	2	10	0
Rowe, Adam, Burlington *	.950	45	7	12	1	20	2
Roy, Scott, Lansing	.900	25	4	5	1	10	0
Sanders, Jared, Dayton	.957	42	5	17	1	23	1
Santiago, Julio, Wisconsin *	.684	17	1	12	6	19	1
Santo, Joel, Fort Wayne	.952	27	9	11	1	21	1
Savickas, Russell, Lansing	.862	19	6	19	4	29	1
Sborz, John, West Michigan	.833	21	3	2	1	6	0
Schambough, Douglas, Burlington	1.000	14	1	7	0	8	1
Schappert, Paul, Peoria *	1.000	20	0	3	0	3	0
Scherer, Matthew, Quad Cities	.786	24	9	13	6	28	0
Schlact, Michael, Clinton	.973	28	14	22	1	37	0
Scott, Joseph, Kane County	1.000	14	2	7	0	9	0
Segovia, Omar, Dayton *	1.000	10	1	1	0	2	1
Semerano, Robert, Kane County	1.000	39	4	5	0	9	2
Shappi, Austin, South Bend	.967	15	10	19	1	30	3
Sharpe, Steven, Kane County	.870	18	7	13	3	23	3
Shaver, Christopher, Peoria *	.929	19	4	9	1	14	0
Sherman, Justin, Burlington	.923	21	5	7	1	13	1
Shinskie, David, Beloit	.875	29	4	17	3	24	1
Sillman, Michael, Quad Cities	.889	56	4	4	1	9	0
Silva, Carlos, Beloit	1.000	1	2	1	0	3	0
Simard, Michel, Cedar Rapids	.778	20	3	4	2	9	0
Slowey, Kevin, Beloit	1.000	13	2	6	0	8	0
Smit, Alexander, Beloit *	1.000	14	2	5	0	7	0
Smith, Aaron, Peoria	...	2	0	0	0	0	0
Smith, Donnie, Quad Cities	.750	5	0	3	1	4	0
Smith, Jesse, Cedar Rapids	.952	23	5	15	1	21	0
Snyder, Jason, Wisconsin	.963	27	8	18	1	27	0
Solis, Heriberto, Burlington	1.000	1	1	0	0	1	0
Sopko, Mark, Lansing	1.000	23	1	3	0	4	0
Stanton, Travis, Cedar Rapids	1.000	35	1	9	0	10	1
Steidlmayer, Luke, Fort Wayne	1.000	16	4	6	0	10	0
Steik, Richard, Fort Wayne	1.000	54	2	5	0	7	0
Stein, Todd, South Bend *	1.000	45	2	6	0	8	0
Steinborn, Christopher, Fort Wayne *	.833	19	2	8	2	12	1
Sterry, Vern, Fort Wayne	.727	20	4	4	3	11	1
Stott, Zachary, Dayton	1.000	40	2	10	0	12	1
Stutes, Kyle, Fort Wayne *	1.000	45	2	5	0	7	0
Swarzak, Anthony, Beloit	.933	18	3	11	1	15	3
Teasley, Jeffrey, Peoria	...	4	0	0	0	0	0
Templet, Jordy, Lansing	1.000	40	9	18	0	27	1
Tharpe, Derek, Kane County *	1.000	36	3	21	0	24	1
Thigpen, Joshua, Dayton	.667	13	0	2	1	3	0
Thompson, Nicolas, Peoria	...	3	0	0	0	0	0
Tichota, Clay, Kane County	.875	18	2	5	1	8	0
Timm, Jordan, Lansing *	.900	18	3	6	1	10	0
Tomey, Anthony, West Michigan	.889	59	3	5	1	9	0
Torres, Jaymes, Quad Cities	.944	56	4	13	1	18	0
Torres, Joseph, Cedar Rapids *	.923	20	3	9	1	13	3
Touchet, Daniel, Clinton	.800	12	2	2	1	5	0
Touchstone, Nicholas, Cedar Rapids *	.818	11	0	9	2	11	1
Trahern, Dallas, West Michigan	.938	26	19	26	3	48	3
Trent, Matthew, Quad Cities	.750	11	0	3	1	4	0
Tressler, Aaron, Lansing	1.000	17	1	3	0	4	0
Trout, Jared, Kane County	.957	38	8	14	1	23	0
Trytten, Ryan, Fort Wayne	1.000	10	1	3	0	4	0
Ursin, Damian, Dayton	.875	9	3	4	1	8	0
Valiquette, Philippe-Alexandre, Dayton *	.857	19	3	9	2	14	0
Varner, Matthew, Fort Wayne	.875	54	3	4	1	8	0
Vasquez, Esmerling, South Bend	.882	53	4	11	2	17	0
Vazquez, Camilo, Dayton *	.846	29	4	7	2	13	0
Vera, Edwin, Clinton	.500	11	1	0	1	2	1
Waldrop, Steven, Beloit	.977	27	17	25	1	43	0
Walker, Andrew, Clinton	.864	19	8	11	3	22	0
Waters, Christopher, Cedar Rapids	1.000	49	2	6	0	8	0
Webb, Ryan, Kane County	.857	24	7	17	4	28	1
Webber, Nicholas, Quad Cities	1.000	5	2	5	0	7	0
Weber, Ben, Dayton	1.000	2	0	1	0	1	0
Weber, Matthew, Peoria	.857	25	7	11	3	21	1
Whelan, Kevin, West Michigan	1.000	14	1	1	0	2	0
Wideman, Aaron, Lansing *	.833	27	8	22	6	36	1
Williams, John, Beloit *	.917	38	1	10	1	12	2
Wilson, Joseph, Dayton *	1.000	12	0	2	0	2	0
Wood, Kerry, Peoria	...	2	0	0	0	0	0
Yates, Kyle, Lansing	.944	14	11	6	1	18	2
Zick, Jeremy, Quad Cities	...	2	0	0	0	0	0

LEAGUE CHAMPIONS

Year	Team	Pct.
1947—	Belleville	.667
	Belleville	.672
1948—	West Frankfort*	.708
1949—	Centralia	.627
	Paducah (4th)†	.454
1950—	Centralia‡	.675
1951—	Paris§	.700
	Danville (4th)†	.432
1952—	Danville∞	.685
	Decatur (3rd)†	.584
1953—	Decatur*	.576
1954—	Decatur	.587
	Danville (2nd)‡	.528
1955—	Dubuque*	.587
1956—	Paris▲	.656
	Dubuque	.603
1957—	Decatur▲	.683
	Clinton	.623
1958—	Michigan City	.623
	Waterloo◆	.613
1959—	Waterloo	.613
	Waterloo	.613
1960—	Waterloo	.629
	Waterloo	.677
1961—	Waterloo	.613
	Quincy◆	.594
1962—	Dubuque◆	.667
	Waterloo	.625
1963—	Clinton	.710
	Clinton	.629
1964—	Clinton	.667
	Fox Cities◆	.667
1965—	Burlington	.667
	Burlington	.677
1966—	Fox Cities◆	.689
	Cedar Rapids	.762
1967—	Wisconsin Rapids	.685
	Appleton◆	.587
1968—	Decatur	.656
	Quad Cities◆	.648
1969—	Appleton	.648
	Appleton	.690
1970—	Quincy◆	.691
	Quad Cities	.581
1971—	Appleton	.642
	Quad Cities■	.548
1972—	Appleton	.598
	Danville■	.584
1973—	Wisconsin Rapids■	.562
	Danville	.537
1974—	Appleton	.593
	Danville■	.517
1975—	Waterloo■	.727
	Quad Cities	.624
1976—	Waterloo■	.600
	Cedar Rapids	.595
1977—	Waterloo	.580
	Burlington■	.511
1978—	Appleton■	.708
	Burlington	.500
1979—	Waterloo	.600
	Quad Cities■	.579
1980—	Waterloo■	.610
	Quad Cities	.532
1981—	Wausau■	.636
	Quad Cities	.570
1982—	Madison	.626
	Appleton▼	.579
1983—	Appleton*	.635
	Springfield	.576
1984—	Appleton*	.640
	Springfield	.504
1985—	Kenosha▼	.568
	Peoria	.536
1986—	Springfield	.621
	Waterloo▼	.557
1987—	Springfield	.671

Year	Team	Pct.
	Kenosha▼	.586
1988—	Cedar Rapids■	.621
	Kenosha	.579
1989—	South Bend■	.644
	Springfield	.541
1990—	Cedar Rapids	.657
	Quad City■	.579
1991—	Clinton■	.583
	Madison	.558
1992—	Quad City	.664
	Cedar Rapids■	.594
1993—	Clinton	.597
	South Bend■	.566
1994—	Rockford	.640
	Cedar Rapids■	.554
1995—	Beloit††	.633
	Michigan	.543
1996—	Wisconsin	.570

Year	Team	Pct.
	West Michigan††	.558
1997—	Kane County	.507
	Lansing**	.504
1998—	West Michigan††	.593
1999—	Kane County	.569
	Burlington**	.511
2000—	West Michigan	.629
	Michigan‡‡	.594
2001—	Kane County▲▲	.638
2002—	Peoria‡‡	.616
2003—	Lansing‡‡	.511
2004—	West Michigan‡‡	.496
2005—	South Bend‡‡	.600

*Won championship and four-club playoff. †Won four-club playoff. ‡Playoff finals canceled because of bad weather. §Won both halves of split season. ∞Won first half of split season and tied Paris for second-half title. ▲Won first-half title and four-team playoff. ◆Won split season playoff. ■League divided into Northern and Southern divisions and played split season. Playoff winner. ▼League divided into Northern, Central and Southern divisions. Playoff winner. *League divided into Northern, Central and Southern divisions; regular season and playoff winner. ††League divided into Eastern, Central and Western divisions; regular season and playoff winner. **League divided into Eastern, Central and Western divisions, playoff winner. ‡‡League divided into Eastern and Western divisions and played split season. Playoff winner. (NOTE—Known as Illinois State League in 1947-48 and Mississippi-Ohio Valley League from 1949 through 1955.) ▲▲League divided into Eastern and Western divisions and played split season; was leading final series of four-team playoff and was declared champion when Professional Baseball declared a stoppage of play.

SOUTH ATLANTIC LEAGUE

LEAGUE OFFICE

President/secretary-treasurer
John Moss

Address
P.O. Box 38
504 Crescent Hill
Kings Mountain, NC 28086

Phone
704-739-3466

Teams (affiliation)
Asheville Tourists (Rockies)
Augusta GreenJackets (Giants)
Charleston (S.C.) RiverDogs (Yankees)
Columbus Catfish (Dodgers)
Delmarva Shorebirds (Orioles)
Greensboro Grasshoppers (Marlins)
Greenville Drive (Red Sox)
Hagerstown Suns (Mets)

Hickory Crawdads (Pirates)
Kannapolis Intimidators (White Sox)
Lake County Captains (Indians)
Lakewood BlueClaws (Phillies)
Lexington Legends (Astros)
Rome Braves (Braves)
Savannah Sand Gnats (Nationals)
West Virginia Power (Brewers)

2005 FINAL STANDINGS

FIRST HALF

NORTHERN DIVISION

Team	W	L	T	Pct.	GB
Lexington Legends	42	28	-	0.6	...
Hagerstown Suns	42	28	-	0.6	...
Lake County Captains	40	30	-	0.571	2
Greensboro Grasshoppers	35	34	-	0.507	6.5
Delmarva Shorebirds	30	40	-	0.429	12
Lakewood BlueClaws	25	45	-	0.357	17
West Virginia Power	25	45	-	0.357	17
Hickory Crawdads	22	44	-	0.333	18

SOUTHERN DIVISION

Team	W	L	T	Pct.	GB
Charleston RiverDogs	43	26	-	0.623	...
Augusta GreenJackets	40	27	-	0.597	2
Rome Braves	39	29	-	0.574	3.5
Asheville Tourists	38	31	-	0.551	5
Kannapolis Intimidators	36	33	-	0.522	7
Greenville Bombers	35	33	-	0.515	7.5
Savannah Sand Gnats	31	37	-	0.456	11.5
Columbus Catfish	28	41	-	0.406	15

SECOND HALF

NORTHERN DIVISION

Team	W	L	T	Pct.	GB
Delmarva Shorebirds	42	27	-	0.609	...
Lexington Legends	39	30	-	0.565	3
West Virginia Power	35	33	-	0.515	6.5
Lake County Captains	32	36	-	0.471	9.5
Hickory Crawdads	32	36	-	0.471	9.5
Greensboro Grasshoppers	32	37	-	0.464	10
Lakewood BlueClaws	31	38	-	0.449	11
Hagerstown Suns	29	38	-	0.433	12

SOUTHERN DIVISION

Team	W	L	T	Pct.	GB
Kannapolis Intimidators	38	26	-	0.594	...
Charleston RiverDogs	37	32	-	0.536	3.5
Augusta GreenJackets	37	32	-	0.536	3.5
Greenville Bombers	37	33	-	0.529	4
Rome Braves	33	36	-	0.478	7.5
Asheville Tourists	33	36	-	0.478	7.5
Savannah Sand Gnats	31	39	-	0.443	10
Columbus Catfish	29	38	-	0.433	1.5

COMPOSITE

CLUB (AFFILIATE), ABBREV	LEX	CHA	AUG	KAN	ROM	GRE	LCO	HAG	DEL	ASH	GBO	SAV	WVA	COL	HIC	LAK	W	L	PCT	GB
Lexington (Astros), LEX	-	-	4	-	-	14	13	5	6	4	-	20	-	5	10	81	58	.583	...	
Charleston (Yankees), CHA	...	15	2	11	13	-	-	1	6	10	-	15	4	3	80	58	.580	0.5		
Augusta (Giants), AUG	12	...	4	15	8	-	-	3	6	14	-	12	3	-	77	59	.566	2.5		
Kannapolis (White Sox), KAN	4	6	3	...	3	4	3	3	5	6	9	7	6	5	7	3	74	59	.556	4.0
Rome (Braves), ROM	-	8	10	5	...	-	13	-	-	5	5	7	-	13	6	-	72	65	.526	8.0
Greenville (Red Sox), GRE	-	7	8	4	11	...	-	-	5	5	16	-	11	5	-	72	66	.522	8.5	
Lake County (Indians), LCO	6	-	-	3	-	-	...	13	13	5	4	-	7	-	6	15	72	66	.522	8.5
Hagerstown (Mets), HAG	11	-	-	3	-	-	7	...	10	4	3	-	12	-	7	14	71	66	.518	9.0
Delmarva (Orioles), DEL	11	-	-	3	-	-	-	17	8	-	2	3	-	12	-	4	72	67	.518	9.0
Asheville (Rockies), ASH	6	3	5	8	3	3	3	4	5	...	3	5	5	2	10	6	71	67	.514	9.5
Greensboro (Marlins), GBO	4	1	2	7	3	2	4	5	5	11	...	2	4	5	8	4	67	71	.486	13.5
Savannah (Nationals), SAV	-	9	10	1	8	8	-	-	3	6	-	...	13	4	-	62	76	.449	18.5	
West Virginia (Brewers), WVA	12	-	-	2	-	-	9	7	8	3	4	-	...	-	4	11	60	78	.435	20.5
Columbus (Dodgers), COL	-	7	4	3	9	12	-	-	-	5	3	11	-	...	4	-	57	79	.419	22.5
Hickory (Pirates), HIC	2	4	2	6	2	3	2	1	6	6	4	4	3	-	...	5	54	80	.403	24.5
Lakewood (Phillies), LAK	2	1	-	5	-	-	7	12	12	2	4	-	8	-	3	...	56	83	.403	25.0

Major league affiliations in parentheses.

PLAYOFFS: Semifinals: Kannapolis defeated Charleston, two games to none, and Hagerstown defeated Delmarva, two games to one. Finals: Kannapolis defeated Hagerstown, three games to one.

REGULAR-SEASON ATTENDANCE: Charleston, 249,374. Lakewood, 444,607. Greenville, 115,161. Rome, 232,187. Lake County, 394,208. Columbus, 62,547. Hickory, 163,863. Greensboro, 407,711. Augusta, 123,545. Kannapolis, 104,781. Lexington, 388,710. West Virginia, 233,143. Savannah, 72,435. Delmarva, 219,361. Hagerstown, 153,675. Asheville, 155,129. All-Star Game (at Augusta), 4,333. League total, 3,520,437. Postseason (9 games), 14,249.

MANAGERS: Charleston, Bill Mosiello. Lakewood, P.J. Forbes. Greenville, Chad Epperson. Rome, Rocket Wheeler. Lake County, Mike Sarbaugh. Columbus, Travis Barbary. Hickory, Jeff Branson. Greensboro, Brandon Hyde. Augusta, Roberto Kelly. Kannapolis, Nick Capra. Lexington, Tim Bogar. West Virginia, Ramon Aviles. Savannah, Randy Knoor. Delmarva, Gary Kendall. Hagerstown, Gene Richards. Asheville, Joe Mikulik.

ALL-STAR TEAM: 1B-Joseph Koshansky, Asheville. 2B-Travis Denker, Columbus. 3B-Marcus Sanders, Augusta. SS-Andrew Pinckney, Greenville. UIF-Brad McCann, Greensboro. OF-Brian Horwitz, Augusta. OF-Matthew Miller, Asheville. OF-Hunter Pence, Lexington. DH-John Otness, Greenville. UOF-David Cook, Kannapolis. C-Neil Walker, Hickory. RHP-James Barthmaier, Lexington. LHP-Ray Liotta, Kannapolis. Most Valuable Player-Matthew Miller, Asheville. Most Outstanding Pitcher-Ray Liotta, Kannapolis. Most Outstanding Major League Prospect-Hunter Pence, Lexington.

2005 BATTING

TEAM

Team	G	TPA	AB	R	H	TB	2B	3B	HR	RBI	SH	SF	HP	BB	IBB	SO	SB	CS	GDP	LOB	ShO	Avg.	OBP	Slg.
Greenville	138	5285	4668	720	1285	1979	292	39	108	659	6	38	93	479	4	1005	63	21	100	2287	4	.275	.352	.424
Asheville	138	5299	4679	734	1283	2104	286	17	167	675	29	28	76	487	18	1020	89	66	96	2062	9	.274	.350	.450

Team	G	TPA	AB	R	H	TB	2B	3B	HR	RBI	SH	SF	HP	BB	IBB	SO	SB	CS	GDP	LOB	ShO	Avg	OBP	Slg
Augusta	136	5243	4574	673	1227	1740	255	33	64	596	16	38	77	537	9	964	168	63	87	2253	7	.268	.352	.380
Lexington	139	5370	4681	733	1251	2043	271	28	155	685	47	39	101	500	10	1059	152	74	105	2138	5	.267	.348	.436
Rome	137	5223	4640	642	1238	1805	247	37	82	599	41	49	42	444	3	976	81	48	95	2073	7	.267	.333	.389
Hagerstown	137	5251	4620	692	1220	1902	252	35	120	588	64	45	97	424	8	1069	203	119	81	1932	5	.264	.336	.412
Kannapolis	133	5052	4414	610	1153	1708	218	23	97	546	51	32	70	484	12	906	104	39	110	2147	6	.261	.341	.387
Hickory	134	5036	4528	596	1175	1685	181	31	89	537	25	43	85	355	7	915	117	76	81	1925	6	.259	.322	.372
Charleston	138	5222	4641	649	1197	1754	230	36	85	572	32	40	69	440	6	950	187	60	105	2014	7	.258	.329	.378
Columbus	136	5131	4568	623	1180	1782	223	29	107	573	22	40	68	432	7	937	45	33	113	2051	6	.258	.329	.390
Delmarva	139	5388	4700	671	1208	1774	245	33	85	603	68	32	81	504	10	911	100	53	116	2174	5	.257	.337	.377
Lakewood	140	5353	4706	625	1207	1772	242	37	83	552	51	23	79	492	15	1027	72	59	104	2277	12	.256	.335	.377
Lake County	138	5394	4747	667	1204	1745	227	22	90	613	29	44	96	475	11	1001	84	46	99	2225	9	.254	.331	.368
Savannah	138	5148	4518	626	1137	1764	237	30	110	574	17	43	64	501	3	1066	163	60	92	2077	9	.252	.332	.390
Greensboro	138	5226	4642	670	1165	1842	233	18	136	608	15	31	94	441	7	1096	100	57	110	1994	8	.251	.326	.397
West Virginia	139	5174	4583	580	1151	1671	216	35	78	520	60	39	80	412	12	1030	141	77	89	2024	17	.251	.321	.365

INDIVIDUAL

TOP QUALIFIERS FOR BATTING CHAMPIONSHIP

Minimum 378 plate appearances. *Lefthanded batter. †Switch-hitter.

Player, Team	G	TPA	AB	R	H	TB	2B	3B	HR	RBI	SH	SF	HP	BB	IBB	SO	SB	CS	GDP	Avg	OBP	Slg
Horwitz, Brian, Augusta	123	535	470	77	164	216	38	4	2	88	0	7	8	50	2	39	6	6	12	.349	.415	.460
Otness, John, Greenville	117	508	441	59	146	207	25	0	12	67	0	11	21	35	0	42	1	1	10	.331	.398	.469
Miller, Matthew, Asheville	127	549	508	79	168	292	34	0	30	100	0	3	12	26	1	71	9	8	7	.331	.375	.575
Dzurilla, Michael, Lakewood	110	495	434	73	139	216	33	4	12	60	5	3	5	48	0	71	2	4	8	.320	.392	.498
Restko, Jason, Greensboro	115	476	403	69	126	198	21	3	15	70	0	2	18	53	1	91	3	0	9	.313	.414	.491
Young, Matthew, Rome *	114	500	423	85	132	173	15	4	6	52	7	2	7	66	0	65	10	11	3	.312	.412	.409
Pinckney, Andrew, Greenville †	128	556	508	91	158	272	33	9	21	98	0	5	7	36	1	78	6	0	15	.311	.362	.535
Denker, Travis, Columbus	101	434	358	65	111	199	23	1	21	68	0	6	3	67	2	78	2	5	6	.310	.417	.556
Fransz, Jason, Delmarva	103	446	396	70	122	223	33	1	22	111	0	6	13	31	1	77	4	1	8	.308	.372	.563
Jaramillo, Jason, Lakewood †	119	496	448	46	136	196	28	4	8	63	1	1	2	44	3	72	2	3	15	.304	.368	.438
Harman, Bradley, Lakewood	105	472	419	63	127	185	23	1	11	58	1	0	7	45	1	89	5	11	8	.303	.380	.442
Walker, Neil, Hickory †	120	518	485	78	146	219	33	2	12	68	0	7	6	20	2	71	7	4	10	.301	.332	.452
Psomas, William, Hagerstown	99	421	350	66	105	193	27	2	19	54	2	5	2	62	5	79	6	4	8	.300	.403	.551
Sanders, Marcus, Augusta	111	504	420	86	126	168	19	4	5	40	3	3	9	69	0	90	57	9	1	.300	.407	.400
Duncan, Jacob, Delmarva *	110	462	402	73	119	166	20	6	5	39	8	0	3	49	1	66	11	6	11	.296	.377	.413
McCann, Bradley, Greensboro	123	527	478	67	141	264	35	2	28	106	0	3	9	37	2	97	1	1	17	.295	.355	.552
De Los Santos, Jose, Kannapolis	103	426	391	45	115	139	18	3	0	34	10	3	4	18	0	42	1	2	15	.294	.329	.355
Valdez, Jose, Asheville *	115	493	439	75	128	214	19	2	21	56	8	0	1	45	0	64	8	8	4	.292	.359	.487
Finegan, Brian, Lake County	115	505	435	77	127	186	30	1	9	60	5	5	16	44	0	76	16	5	10	.292	.374	.428
Koshansky, Joseph, Asheville *	120	525	453	92	132	273	31	1	36	103	0	8	11	53	7	122	6	6	14	.291	.373	.603
Sosa, Carlos, Augusta	108	444	379	61	110	168	25	3	9	71	0	2	1	62	1	96	4	2	4	.290	.390	.443

DEPARTMENTAL LEADERS: G—Battle, 134. AB—Battle, 525. R—Battle, 97. H—Miller, 168. TB—Miller, 292. 2B—Horwitz, 38. 3B—Battle, 11. HR—Koshansky, 36. RBI—Fransz, 111. SH—Ascencion, 15. SF—Otness, 11. HP—Gimenez, 25. BB—Bernadina, 75. IBB—Koshansky, 7. SO—Battle, 195. SB—Gomez, 64. CS—Gomez, 24. GIDP—Jones, 19. Slg.—Koshansky, .603. OBP—Denker, .417.

ALL PLAYERS

*Lefthanded batter. †Switch-hitter.

Player, Team	G	TPA	AB	R	H	TB	2B	3B	HR	RBI	SH	SF	HP	BB	IBB	SO	SB	CS	GDP	Avg	OBP	Slg
Abreu, Johany, Augusta †	10	29	26	3	8	12	2	1	0	0	1	0	0	2	0	5	1	0	0	.308	.357	.462
Alen, Luis, Greensboro	39	121	116	9	21	25	4	0	0	8	2	0	0	3	0	11	0	0	2	.181	.202	.216
Allen, Trevor, Asheville	21	88	76	9	19	33	2	0	4	11	0	0	1	11	0	31	1	1	2	.250	.352	.434
Almonte, Sandy, Asheville †	28	129	120	21	25	41	2	4	2	9	0	0	1	8	0	30	5	0	3	.208	.264	.342
Apodaca, Juan, Columbus	35	133	123	10	30	47	3	1	4	20	1	2	0	7	0	21	0	1	6	.244	.280	.382
Apodaca, Luis, Savannah	7	28	28	4	6	7	1	0	0	1	0	0	0	0	0	6	0	0	1	.214	.214	.250
Arias, Claudio, Greenville	50	217	199	33	62	120	15	2	13	38	0	2	5	11	0	55	2	0	7	.312	.359	.603
Armitage, Jonathan, Augusta †	120	476	406	63	99	154	23	1	10	54	0	2	6	62	1	89	6	6	11	.244	.351	.379
Armstrong, Melville, Rome *	105	418	378	33	86	135	26	1	7	42	1	7	0	32	0	71	0	2	5	.228	.283	.357
Arroyo, Rafael, Hagerstown	28	113	91	15	20	38	3	0	5	11	2	0	6	14	0	25	0	2	1	.220	.360	.418
Arroyo, Xavier, Greensboro	40	144	115	17	23	28	3	1	0	9	1	0	3	25	1	38	4	3	8	.200	.357	.243
Ascencion, Quincy, Delmarva	126	501	441	59	112	150	21	4	3	44	15	1	13	31	0	75	16	12	5	.254	.321	.340
Ash, Jonathan, Lexington *	67	299	256	44	82	121	11	2	8	38	3	5	10	25	1	20	3	7	5	.320	.395	.473
Babilonia, Edgar, Lexington	39	115	106	11	21	25	4	0	0	7	4	0	0	5	0	12	10	1	1	.198	.234	.236
Bacon, Matthew, Hagerstown *	15	35	30	4	6	8	2	0	0	5	0	1	1	3	0	8	0	0	1	.200	.286	.267
Baez, Edgardo, Savannah	125	509	447	62	110	176	21	6	11	64	1	4	2	55	1	128	11	4	13	.246	.329	.394
Barganier, Brandon, Lexington *	40	165	148	21	44	61	12	1	1	18	4	2	2	9	0	21	4	1	0	.297	.342	.412
Barksdale, James, Rome	16	50	47	2	8	11	0	1	0	6	0	1	1	1	0	24	0	2	0	.170	.200	.234
Barton, Brian, Lake County	35	160	133	31	55	83	14	1	4	32	0	1	8	18	1	21	7	2	5	.414	.506	.624
Batista, Norberto, Greensboro	11	29	24	8	8	9	1	0	0	0	0	0	0	5	0	4	0	1	2	.333	.448	.375
Batista, Wilson, Hagerstown †	68	298	265	41	63	101	11	3	7	28	6	2	1	24	0	46	13	14	5	.238	.301	.381
Batz, Daniel, Columbus	120	481	429	59	120	163	27	2	4	46	0	5	9	38	1	45	5	2	8	.280	.347	.380
Baysinger, Trent, Delmarva *	1	0	0	0	0	0	0	0	0	0	0	0	0	0	0	0	0	0	0	...	...	...
Benavidez, Julian, Augusta	48	192	172	23	38	68	12	0	6	25	0	1	2	17	0	49	0	0	7	.221	.297	.395
Bernadina, Roger, Savannah *	122	505	417	64	97	154	15	3	12	54	2	4	7	75	0	92	35	8	9	.233	.356	.369
Berry, Layne, Kannapolis *	101	413	342	56	91	120	13	2	4	32	4	3	11	52	0	70	15	3	3	.266	.377	.351
Bixler, Brian, Hickory	126	557	502	74	141	195	23	2	9	50	3	3	11	38	0	134	21	10	5	.281	.343	.388
Bocchino, Anthony, Hickory *	65	283	233	44	60	111	13	4	10	45	0	3	10	37	2	45	1	2	4	.258	.378	.476
Bock, Brian, Delmarva	33	137	124	4	32	39	7	0	0	15	1	3	1	8	0	23	2	0	6	.258	.301	.315
Brant, Derek, Lakewood	35	120	107	11	22	28	6	0	0	8	1	0	3	9	0	24	0	0	5	.206	.262	.262
Brice, Thomas, Kannapolis *	20	83	77	13	22	30	5	0	1	7	0	1	1	4	0	11	2	0	0	.286	.325	.390

Player, Team	G	TPA	AB	R	H	TB	2B	3B	HR	RBI	SH	SF	HP	BB	IBB	SO	SB	CS	GDP	Avg.	OBP	Slg.
Brinkley, Dante, Hagerstown	61	265	214	48	78	133	17	4	10	41	1	2	10	38	0	57	20	13	2	.364	.477	.621
Brown, Gregory, Greensboro	30	96	86	9	16	26	4	0	2	12	0	0	4	6	0	22	2	0	3	.186	.271	.302
Brown, Jeremy, Columbus	5	22	20	2	4	4	0	0	0	4	0	0	2	0	0	4	0	0	1	.200	.273	.200
Brown, Kyle, Hagerstown	27	110	91	17	20	31	3	1	2	16	3	4	4	8	0	29	6	2	0	.220	.299	.341
Brown, Terrance, Rome	29	76	69	6	7	9	2	0	0	3	0	0	0	7	0	35	0	0	1	.101	.184	.130
Bruce, Cole, Columbus	22	73	69	10	21	42	4	1	5	11	0	2	0	2	1	20	1	1	1	.304	.315	.609
Buechner, Christopher, Asheville	1	1	1	0	1	1	0	0	0	2	0	0	0	0	0	0	0	0	0	1.000	1.000	1.000
Buller, Dayton, Augusta	20	73	65	7	15	18	3	0	0	4	0	0	1	7	0	26	1	0	1	.231	.315	.277
Burrows, Angelo, Rome *	2	0	0	0	0	0	0	0	0	0	0	0	0	0	0	0	0	0	0	...	...	...
Burt, James, Hagerstown	63	230	192	35	49	76	13	1	4	16	3	2	7	26	0	47	4	5	7	.255	.361	.396
Butia, Michael, Lake County *	74	331	298	45	75	113	18	1	6	48	0	3	2	27	3	71	1	1	5	.252	.315	.379
Buttler, Victor, Hickory *	25	100	92	7	19	21	2	0	0	5	3	0	1	4	0	11	3	1	1	.207	.247	.228
Bynum, Seth, Savannah	50	218	186	32	56	90	13	3	5	29	0	2	1	29	0	40	6	1	3	.301	.394	.484
Caraballo, Francisco, Lexington	112	452	409	63	114	210	23	2	23	69	3	2	8	30	0	119	8	7	9	.279	.339	.513
Carlin, Michael, Hickory	89	354	308	53	98	175	21	4	16	65	0	3	14	29	1	70	6	1	1	.318	.398	.568
Carp, Christopher, Hagerstown *	89	375	313	49	78	149	12	1	19	63	1	5	21	35	3	96	2	2	2	.249	.358	.476
Carroll, Brett, Greensboro	118	449	412	57	100	184	28	1	18	54	3	2	15	17	2	108	10	10	4	.243	.296	.447
Carter, Brandon, Columbus *	75	313	276	38	61	70	6	0	1	33	1	2	4	30	0	33	0	4	9	.221	.304	.254
Carter, Ryan, Columbus	60	235	224	35	63	120	13	1	14	44	0	0	3	8	0	68	4	0	3	.281	.315	.536
Castillo, Javier, Kannapolis	50	206	190	16	43	65	11	1	3	20	2	0	1	13	0	49	2	1	9	.226	.279	.342
Castro, Ofilio, Savannah	113	456	403	43	105	146	24	1	5	43	2	3	1	47	0	91	6	3	6	.261	.337	.362
Cates, Gary, Delmarva	75	338	300	51	84	108	16	1	2	30	7	2	4	25	0	37	12	5	10	.280	.341	.360
Chavez, Dirimo, Greenville	13	60	54	6	14	18	4	0	0	7	0	0	1	5	0	10	0	0	0	.259	.333	.333
Cho, Hyung, Hickory	31	120	108	13	17	19	2	0	0	11	1	3	0	8	0	10	1	0	5	.157	.210	.176
Ciaramella, Matthew, Greenville †	60	247	225	27	68	95	13	1	4	30	0	1	0	21	0	39	2	1	6	.302	.360	.422
Clark, Robert, Lexington	51	190	168	20	40	60	8	0	4	23	0	0	6	16	0	45	3	0	6	.238	.326	.357
Clem, Christopher, Lake County	6	24	19	3	4	4	0	0	0	0	0	0	1	4	0	5	0	0	0	.211	.375	.211
Cleveland, Brian, Greensboro	109	481	444	66	123	172	21	2	8	50	1	2	10	24	0	71	20	7	11	.277	.327	.387
Cockrell, Michael, Hickory	99	410	371	47	99	146	14	6	7	44	3	6	5	25	0	29	7	5	10	.267	.317	.394
Coles, Corey, Hagerstown *	69	281	264	27	81	109	16	0	4	33	3	0	2	12	0	40	11	5	4	.307	.342	.413
Columbus, Jason, Augusta	71	275	240	27	62	82	15	1	1	29	0	3	7	25	0	59	2	2	2	.258	.342	.342
Concepcion, Ambiorix, Hagerstown	130	564	521	68	131	215	29	5	15	61	3	8	9	22	0	136	35	15	9	.251	.289	.413
Conroy, Michael, Lake County *	5	24	21	2	7	8	1	0	0	1	0	0	0	2	1	4	0	0	0	.333	.391	.381
Constanza, Jose, Lake County †	23	88	72	9	17	17	0	0	0	4	1	0	0	15	0	13	2	1	2	.236	.368	.236
Conte, Nick, Augusta	64	223	202	20	47	62	9	0	2	24	1	0	3	17	0	40	2	4	7	.233	.302	.307
Contreras, Jose, Savannah †	13	46	39	5	7	8	1	0	0	1	0	1	0	6	0	14	3	0	0	.179	.283	.205
Cook, David, Kannapolis	109	447	368	75	104	203	21	3	24	65	0	3	4	72	1	105	8	6	7	.283	.403	.552
Coronado, Jose, Hagerstown †	18	81	71	4	16	20	2	1	0	4	3	0	0	7	0	17	1	4	1	.225	.295	.282
Corsaletti, Jeffrey, Greenville *	59	282	249	49	89	122	17	2	4	26	0	1	0	32	0	38	9	4	2	.357	.429	.490
Coultas, Ryan, Hagerstown	89	335	304	43	88	136	22	4	6	36	4	3	4	20	0	57	11	6	4	.289	.338	.447
Creek, Gregory, Rome *	7	28	24	3	8	12	1	0	1	1	0	0	0	4	0	4	1	0	1	.333	.429	.500
Crist, Justin, Columbus	12	37	34	3	6	7	1	0	0	4	0	1	0	2	0	8	0	0	0	.176	.216	.206
Cronkhite, Ian, Hagerstown *	42	174	163	20	42	65	7	5	2	16	0	0	0	11	0	34	2	2	1	.258	.305	.399
Crosland, Jason, Lakewood	6	25	23	2	4	8	1	0	1	2	0	0	1	1	0	7	0	0	0	.174	.240	.348
Crowe, Trevor, Lake County †	44	199	178	18	46	58	8	2	0	23	0	2	1	18	1	25	7	5	4	.258	.327	.326
Cunningham, Aaron, Kannapolis	10	29	26	7	3	3	0	0	0	2	0	0	0	3	0	7	1	0	0	.115	.207	.115
Daley, Matthew, Asheville	1	0	0	0	0	0	0	0	0	0	0	0	0	0	0	0	0	0	0	...	...	...
DAntonio, Trent, Greensboro †	24	80	71	11	20	35	6	0	3	15	0	1	0	8	0	9	1	1	1	.282	.350	.493
Davidson, Tyler, Hagerstown	23	84	78	12	16	26	4	0	2	13	0	0	1	5	0	27	1	0	1	.205	.262	.333
Davis, Bradley, Greensboro	64	253	228	26	52	82	13	1	5	24	3	2	2	17	0	62	0	2	9	.228	.285	.360
De La Cruz, Christopher, Lake County †	17	69	61	5	16	18	2	0	0	6	2	1	0	5	0	9	1	2	1	.262	.313	.295
Delacruz, Miguel, Delmarva	23	86	75	10	20	31	1	2	2	7	0	0	2	9	0	17	0	0	0	.267	.360	.413
Delgado, Dario, Hickory	6	22	18	0	5	5	0	0	0	1	1	0	0	3	0	4	0	1	1	.278	.381	.278
De Los Santos, Jose, Kannapolis	103	426	391	45	115	139	18	3	0	34	10	3	4	18	0	42	1	2	15	.294	.329	.355
Denker, Travis, Columbus	101	434	358	65	111	199	23	1	21	68	0	6	3	67	2	78	2	5	6	.310	.417	.556
Desmond, Ian, Savannah	73	321	296	37	73	99	10	2	4	23	4	1	6	13	0	60	20	6	5	.247	.291	.334
Devries, Jonathan, Greenville	4	16	14	1	3	3	0	0	0	1	0	0	1	1	0	4	0	0	0	.214	.313	.214
Dewitt, Blake, Columbus *	120	522	481	61	136	206	31	3	11	65	0	3	4	34	0	79	0	1	13	.283	.333	.428
Diaz, Rafael, Delmarva	55	182	173	8	32	39	7	0	0	13	3	0	1	5	0	30	1	0	9	.185	.212	.225
Diaz, Raymar, Lexington	1	0	0	0	0	0	0	0	0	0	0	0	0	0	0	0	0	0	0	...	...	...
Disla, Lisandro, Augusta	68	256	233	24	46	54	3	1	1	19	2	3	1	17	0	61	3	2	5	.197	.252	.232
Ditter, Brad, Savannah *	96	382	335	38	87	110	14	3	1	28	0	7	7	33	1	53	11	4	12	.260	.332	.328
Doetsch, Steven, Rome	13	63	55	13	20	28	1	2	1	9	0	0	0	8	0	12	5	0	0	.364	.444	.509
Dragicevich, Jeffrey, Asheville	104	434	374	57	105	150	29	2	4	44	3	3	7	47	0	86	5	4	7	.281	.369	.401
Drobiak, Jayson, Lakewood *	26	105	95	9	18	31	8	1	1	11	0	1	2	7	0	29	1	1	5	.189	.257	.326
Duncan, Jacob, Delmarva *	110	462	402	73	119	166	20	6	5	39	8	0	3	49	1	66	11	6	11	.296	.377	.413
Dzurilla, Michael, Lakewood	110	495	434	73	139	216	33	4	12	60	5	3	5	48	0	71	2	4	8	.320	.392	.498
Easley, Jesse, Greenville	62	247	219	32	51	87	11	2	7	26	0	0	3	25	0	64	4	2	5	.233	.320	.397
Eichas, Keith, Rome	61	243	231	19	49	67	10	1	2	25	1	0	2	8	0	56	1	0	7	.212	.245	.290
Einertson, Mitch, Lexington	101	422	355	52	83	125	19	1	7	45	0	1	14	52	2	99	5	4	8	.234	.353	.352
Elliott, Justin, Hickory	1	5	5	2	3	3	0	0	0	1	0	0	0	0	0	0	0	0	0	.600	.600	.600
Escobar, Yunel, Rome	48	214	198	30	62	93	13	3	4	19	2	0	0	14	0	30	0	2	6	.313	.358	.470
Estrada, Paul, Lexington	1	0	0	0	0	0	0	0	0	0	0	0	0	0	0	0	0	0	0	...	...	...
Figueroa, Francisco, Delmarva	40	181	150	30	46	57	7	2	0	12	2	0	5	24	0	25	6	3	0	.307	.419	.380
Figueroa, Juan, Greensboro *	24	106	86	13	28	35	4	0	1	15	0	0	1	19	0	23	0	1	2	.326	.453	.407
Finan, Ryan, Lexington	10	43	41	3	8	13	2	0	1	9	0	1	0	1	0	17	0	0	0	.195	.209	.317
Finegan, Brian, Lake County	115	505	435	77	127	186	30	1	9	60	5	5	16	44	0	76	16	5	10	.292	.374	.428
Fisher, Kiel, Lakewood *	29	105	98	9	17	21	2	1	0	6	0	0	0	7	2	30	0	3	2	.173	.229	.214
Fisher, Matthew, Hagerstown	45	165	141	24	35	51	6	2	2	14	5	2	0	17	0	26	2	3	3	.248	.325	.362
Fitzpatrick, Reginald, Savannah *	90	336	307	40	77	108	13	0	6	35	1	1	8	18	0	66	23	9	4	.251	.308	.352
Flores, Jesus, Hagerstown	82	337	319	34	69	108	18	0	7	42	1	2	3	12	0	90	2	2	6	.216	.250	.339

Player, Team	G	TPA	AB	R	H	TB	2B	3B	HR	RBI	SH	SF	HP	BB	IBB	SO	SB	CS	GDP	Avg.	OBP	Slg.
Flores, Joshua, Lexington	5	20	18	1	5	7	2	0	0	1	1	0	0	1	0	4	4	0	1	.278	.316	.389
Fransz, Jason, Delmarva	103	446	396	70	122	223	33	1	22	111	0	6	13	31	1	77	4	1	8	.308	.372	.563
Frith, Ryan, Lakewood	110	444	399	54	107	180	24	2	15	54	5	1	10	29	1	112	8	6	3	.268	.333	.451
Fulton, Jonathan, Greensboro	76	293	267	34	62	111	10	2	11	39	0	1	5	20	0	72	1	1	6	.232	.297	.416
Gaerlan, Armand, Hagerstown	50	201	170	28	44	58	7	2	1	14	5	2	3	21	0	39	13	3	4	.259	.347	.341
Galloway, Carl, Lakewood	20	81	76	4	18	22	4	0	0	7	0	0	4	1	0	17	0	0	2	.237	.284	.289
Gamble, Sean, Lakewood *	117	483	427	55	107	141	16	6	2	33	12	2	6	36	1	56	7	6	4	.251	.316	.330
Gamero, Jesus, Hagerstown	16	61	55	8	9	11	2	0	0	2	0	0	2	4	0	9	0	1	2	.164	.246	.200
Garza, Mario, Lexington *	29	105	88	18	19	41	4	0	6	19	0	3	4	10	0	32	0	1	1	.216	.314	.466
Gaston, Jared, Greensboro	75	290	253	41	67	92	11	1	4	17	0	1	7	29	0	46	5	5	5	.265	.355	.364
Gendron, Steve, Greensboro	128	534	485	65	122	173	22	1	9	56	1	4	4	40	0	95	14	5	12	.252	.311	.357
German, Agustin, Savannah	1	3	3	0	0	0	0	0	0	0	0	0	0	0	0	2	0	0	0	.000	.000	.000
Getz, Christopher, Kannapolis *	55	253	214	38	65	85	13	2	1	28	0	1	3	35	1	10	11	4	5	.304	.407	.397
Gimenez, Christopher, Lake County	112	463	384	54	90	155	24	1	13	66	2	4	25	48	0	90	4	3	4	.234	.354	.404
Golson, Gregory, Lakewood	89	409	375	51	99	146	19	8	4	27	2	0	6	26	0	106	25	9	4	.264	.322	.389
Gomez, Carlos, Hagerstown	120	539	487	75	134	183	13	6	8	48	10	1	9	32	0	88	64	24	6	.275	.331	.376
Gonzalez, Bernard, Kannapolis	83	349	315	38	83	121	19	2	5	35	0	1	9	24	0	53	2	1	11	.263	.332	.384
Granadillo, Antonio, Greenville †	67	271	234	43	68	100	11	3	5	31	0	1	9	27	0	52	2	0	6	.291	.384	.427
Gredvig, Doug, Lakewood	79	335	273	44	83	129	16	0	10	50	1	3	6	51	3	49	1	2	14	.304	.420	.473
Grimm, Eric, Delmarva †	38	138	116	18	22	29	4	0	1	11	2	1	0	19	0	27	2	3	3	.190	.301	.250
Guarno, Richard, Asheville	19	80	69	7	18	25	7	0	0	2	1	1	3	6	0	6	1	0	2	.261	.342	.362
Guerrero, Francisco, Delmarva	48	169	153	14	29	37	6	1	0	12	3	0	2	11	0	19	2	2	6	.190	.253	.242
Gutierrez, Gabriel, Columbus	71	260	232	25	60	80	9	1	3	18	2	1	6	18	0	40	0	1	5	.259	.327	.345
Gutierrez, Juan, Delmarva †	84	305	254	36	67	96	13	2	4	35	2	2	1	46	5	49	1	1	6	.264	.376	.378
Guzman, Carlos, Rome	30	123	113	15	22	48	5	0	7	15	0	3	1	6	0	54	3	2	0	.195	.236	.425
Hahn, Donald, Asheville *	130	551	488	70	137	206	32	2	11	59	1	2	5	55	4	96	6	4	11	.281	.358	.422
Haines, Kyle, Augusta *	35	149	132	19	49	59	7	0	1	15	1	1	0	15	0	15	7	4	3	.371	.432	.447
Hansen, Joshua, Kannapolis	126	550	490	69	135	237	28	1	24	90	0	6	6	48	3	130	2	1	13	.276	.344	.484
Hardy, John, Lakewood	39	147	131	12	14	20	4	1	0	6	3	0	1	12	0	28	2	0	5	.107	.188	.153
Harman, Bradley, Lakewood	105	472	419	63	127	185	23	1	11	58	1	0	7	45	1	89	5	11	8	.303	.380	.442
Hathaway, Aaron, Hagerstown	39	150	139	18	36	47	8	0	1	13	1	1	1	8	0	32	0	2	4	.259	.302	.338
Hernandez, Francisco, Kannapolis †	44	171	153	15	34	48	5	0	3	18	0	2	3	13	0	29	0	0	5	.222	.292	.314
Herrera, Jonathan, Asheville †	19	99	87	17	27	29	2	0	0	5	0	1	3	8	0	11	6	6	1	.310	.384	.333
Hoffmann, Jamie, Columbus	79	368	321	53	99	133	13	9	1	24	5	2	1	39	1	73	10	4	6	.308	.383	.414
Hofius, Steven, Hickory *	82	305	266	27	59	79	8	0	4	30	0	4	6	29	0	58	2	1	7	.222	.308	.297
Holm, Stephen, Augusta	56	201	176	16	41	63	7	0	5	31	2	3	3	17	0	36	1	1	2	.233	.307	.358
Holmes, Brett, Hickory	9	41	35	8	12	19	1	0	2	3	0	0	0	6	0	18	1	1	0	.343	.439	.543
Holmes, Justin, Lake County	3	9	9	0	2	2	0	0	0	0	0	0	0	0	0	3	0	0	0	.222	.222	.222
Holt, John, Rome *	123	496	441	60	118	162	23	3	5	50	12	4	2	37	0	89	12	8	8	.268	.324	.367
Hornostaj, Aaron, Augusta *	74	263	237	27	60	90	13	4	3	29	1	1	5	19	0	41	13	7	4	.253	.321	.380
Horwitz, Brian, Augusta	123	535	470	77	164	216	38	4	2	88	0	7	8	50	2	39	6	6	12	.349	.415	.460
Hosgood, Robert, Asheville *	34	130	111	18	26	45	6	2	3	14	0	0	2	17	0	42	4	2	0	.234	.346	.405
Houston, Matthew, Delmarva	77	292	252	29	73	92	10	0	3	26	6	0	7	27	0	31	0	0	14	.290	.374	.365
Humphries, Justin, Lexington	36	149	122	20	33	58	10	0	5	16	0	2	3	22	0	27	0	0	5	.270	.389	.475
Isaacson, Gregory, Lakewood *	21	74	63	8	15	19	4	0	0	13	1	0	0	10	0	16	0	0	0	.238	.342	.302
Ivany, Devin, Savannah	113	446	409	52	107	175	27	1	13	54	1	3	8	25	0	65	7	7	10	.262	.315	.428
Jansen, Ardley, Rome	58	222	199	31	54	97	11	1	10	38	2	3	3	15	0	60	3	1	4	.271	.327	.487
Jaramillo, Jason, Lakewood †	119	496	448	46	136	196	28	4	8	63	1	1	2	44	3	72	2	3	15	.304	.368	.438
Jenkins, Andrew, Greensboro	48	186	168	22	37	55	9	0	3	20	1	1	2	14	0	33	1	3	3	.220	.286	.327
Jeroloman, Charles, Greenville	80	324	259	44	61	96	21	1	4	29	0	1	4	60	0	93	5	1	10	.236	.386	.371
Jimenez, Franklyn, Savannah	27	86	78	7	10	15	0	1	1	5	1	1	0	6	0	24	0	0	0	.128	.188	.192
Johnson, Atlee, Hickory *	97	379	348	38	79	122	12	2	9	44	0	1	6	24	0	88	3	10	5	.227	.288	.351
Jones, Brandon, Rome *	43	189	156	37	48	90	12	3	8	27	0	1	3	29	0	29	4	1	3	.308	.423	.577
Jones, Chipper, Rome †	3	9	6	1	3	3	0	0	0	2	0	0	0	3	0	1	0	0	1	.500	.667	.500
Jordan, Brian, Rome	5	20	16	5	8	12	1	0	1	7	0	2	0	2	1	2	1	0	0	.500	.500	.750
Jurich, Mark, Rome *	52	219	193	33	56	101	8	2	11	37	0	2	1	18	0	39	2	1	3	.290	.350	.523
Kelly, Christopher, Kannapolis *	28	99	91	10	20	37	5	0	4	13	1	1	0	6	0	30	1	1	2	.220	.265	.407
Kelly, Dustin, Greenville	7	29	25	3	4	7	0	0	1	4	0	0	1	3	0	7	0	1	1	.160	.276	.280
King, Clinton, Kannapolis *	92	383	333	40	76	113	18	2	5	41	1	3	6	40	3	83	7	5	14	.228	.319	.339
Kitch, Denver, Delmarva	35	139	132	13	25	34	3	0	2	17	2	0	0	5	0	45	2	3	0	.189	.219	.258
Klemm, Christopher, Lakewood *	87	340	295	43	63	90	12	3	3	32	6	5	5	29	0	73	2	2	3	.214	.290	.305
Klink, Simon, Augusta †	131	551	474	70	120	174	30	0	8	83	0	3	15	59	4	128	1	4	11	.253	.352	.367
Koshansky, Joseph, Asheville *	120	525	463	92	132	273	31	1	36	103	0	8	11	53	7	122	6	6	14	.291	.373	.603
Lane, Richard, Savannah	10	40	36	5	14	23	4	1	1	8	0	0	0	4	0	5	0	1	1	.389	.450	.639
Lara, Christian, Greenville †	112	427	384	64	89	115	14	3	2	31	3	0	3	37	1	90	6	2	7	.232	.304	.299
Laurin, Dominique, Columbus	54	195	168	20	27	46	4	0	5	18	3	4	3	17	0	62	2	1	2	.161	.245	.274
Lerud, Steven, Hickory †	25	87	80	6	7	19	2	2	2	13	0	1	2	4	0	27	0	1	1	.088	.149	.238
LeVier, Bret, Greenville	59	245	229	25	56	78	16	0	2	31	0	2	4	10	0	27	2	1	7	.245	.286	.341
Lisk, Charles, Kannapolis	9	31	25	4	4	5	1	0	0	1	2	0	1	3	0	11	0	0	0	.160	.276	.200
Loadenthal, Carl, Rome *	63	245	210	35	55	73	13	1	1	23	1	2	4	28	0	28	17	4	2	.262	.357	.348
Lomack, Jermal, Hickory †	59	207	181	18	44	50	4	1	0	12	4	0	1	21	0	33	12	10	1	.243	.325	.276
Lombardi, Michael, Lakewood †	14	52	44	6	9	12	3	0	0	9	0	1	0	7	0	13	0	0	3	.205	.308	.273
Longworth, Randall, Lake County	57	214	196	22	49	71	8	1	4	25	0	3	3	12	0	48	3	1	5	.250	.299	.362
Lowrance, Marvin, Savannah *	57	235	212	27	61	90	15	1	4	35	0	1	6	16	0	50	2	1	2	.288	.353	.425
Lucy, Donald, Kannapolis	54	211	178	25	47	55	5	0	1	22	4	3	5	21	0	41	6	3	4	.264	.353	.309
Lunetta, Anthony, Lake County	6	24	19	1	3	4	1	0	0	2	0	1	1	3	0	9	0	0	0	.158	.292	.211
Macia, Wanell, Hickory *	40	133	128	12	34	40	4	1	0	15	0	2	1	2	0	28	3	4	3	.266	.278	.313
Mader, Joshua, Lakewood	62	228	207	24	40	48	6	1	0	16	4	1	2	14	0	51	7	1	4	.193	.254	.232
Maestrales, Peter, Delmarva †	52	240	195	48	59	103	14	3	8	16	1	0	3	39	0	35	6	4	2	.303	.426	.528
Mansolino, Anthony, Hickory	8	34	29	4	6	11	2	0	1	5	0	2	0	3	0	4	0	0	0	.207	.265	.379
Marcial, Robert, Rome	6	20	19	1	5	7	0	1	0	1	0	0	0	1	0	1	1	0	0	.263	.300	.368

Player, Team	G	TPA	AB	R	H	TB	2B	3B	HR	RBI	SH	SF	HP	BB	IBB	SO	SB	CS	GDP	Avg.	OBP	Slg.
Marconi, Robert, Delmarva	38	144	127	15	23	34	5	0	2	9	4	2	1	9	0	34	2	0	2	.181	.237	.268
Martel Jr, Normand, Kannapolis *	9	37	33	3	6	7	1	0	0	2	0	0	0	4	0	6	1	0	0	.182	.270	.212
May, Lucas, Columbus	99	416	385	46	88	133	14	2	9	53	1	7	7	16	1	92	5	2	7	.229	.267	.345
Maysonet, Edwin, Lexington	45	201	173	29	45	70	11	1	4	17	2	1	10	15	0	29	11	4	0	.260	.352	.405
McCann, Bradley, Greensboro	123	527	478	67	141	264	35	2	28	106	0	3	9	37	2	97	1	1	17	.295	.355	.552
McCarthy, Greg, Augusta	13	46	46	1	11	13	2	0	0	3	0	0	0	0	0	13	0	0	1	.239	.239	.283
McCarthy, Ryan, Kannapolis	98	396	354	46	83	130	20	3	7	45	5	2	1	34	0	79	6	2	6	.234	.302	.367
McCurdy, Joshua, Delmarva	29	113	104	13	31	42	5	0	2	15	1	0	0	8	0	16	6	1	4	.298	.348	.404
McGill, Clint, Lexington	75	256	239	27	48	69	6	3	3	16	5	0	3	9	0	69	10	11	7	.201	.239	.289
McMillan, Beau, Greensboro	47	145	117	19	25	36	3	1	2	12	1	2	5	20	0	41	7	1	1	.214	.347	.308
Medero-Stullz, Carlos, Columbus	1	5	3	0	1	1	0	0	0	0	0	0	0	2	0	2	0	0	0	.333	.600	.333
Mercedes, Victor, Hickory †	2	8	8	1	4	4	0	0	0	0	0	0	0	0	0	1	0	1	0	.500	.500	.500
Merchan, Jesus, Lakewood	28	121	112	10	31	38	7	0	0	12	0	1	3	5	1	4	1	2	3	.277	.322	.339
Mihalics, Joseph, Hagerstown	17	55	45	3	12	15	3	0	0	8	4	1	1	4	0	5	0	1	0	.267	.333	.333
Miller, Matthew, Asheville	127	549	508	79	168	292	34	0	30	100	0	3	12	26	1	71	9	8	7	.331	.375	.575
Miller, Randall, Greensboro	115	479	415	69	86	143	14	2	13	34	1	3	3	57	1	139	16	11	5	.207	.305	.345
Moffitt, Andrew, Delmarva	31	117	88	13	19	33	5	0	3	14	0	0	2	27	0	28	4	1	3	.216	.410	.375
Moni-Erigbali, Victor, Lakewood	68	251	195	35	48	67	5	1	4	20	5	1	11	38	1	50	9	7	4	.246	.396	.344
Montgomery, Timothy, Lake County	53	224	201	28	48	79	10	0	7	28	0	4	2	17	0	77	3	1	4	.239	.299	.393
Montz, Luke, Savannah	100	403	343	66	77	160	24	1	19	68	2	5	3	50	0	95	1	1	6	.224	.324	.466
Morales, Franklin, Asheville *	1	3	2	0	0	0	0	0	0	0	0	0	0	0	0	2	0	0	0	.000	.000	.000
Moreno, Junior, Greenville	3	7	7	0	0	0	0	0	0	0	0	0	0	0	0	2	0	0	0	.000	.000	.000
Mortimer, Steve, Savannah *	101	388	328	47	80	133	19	2	10	41	0	5	9	46	1	135	7	2	4	.244	.348	.405
Natale, Jeffrey, Greenville	47	202	160	35	54	87	19	4	2	35	1	2	11	28	0	14	1	0	4	.338	.463	.544
Nelson, Christopher, Asheville	79	349	315	51	76	104	13	3	3	38	0	4	5	25	0	88	7	4	2	.241	.304	.330
Nelson, Justin, Asheville	113	485	413	77	115	216	36	1	21	64	2	3	6	61	4	102	14	6	11	.278	.377	.523
Nicholson, David, Columbus	92	378	345	49	85	109	14	2	2	28	0	1	4	28	0	67	7	5	9	.246	.310	.316
Nino, Denny, Hickory	3	6	6	0	0	0	0	0	0	0	0	0	0	0	0	1	0	0	1	.000	.000	.000
Noviskey, Joshua, Lake County *	63	254	215	37	53	85	8	3	6	38	0	2	2	35	1	46	0	2	4	.247	.354	.395
Nunez, Eduardo, Savannah	1	4	4	0	2	2	0	0	0	0	0	0	0	0	0	0	0	0	0	.500	.500	.500
Nunez, Florentino, Asheville †	76	283	250	43	64	104	10	0	10	36	3	1	1	28	1	54	9	4	6	.256	.332	.416
Obradovich, Mark, Lake County †	9	35	32	3	6	7	1	0	0	1	1	0	0	2	0	8	0	0	0	.188	.235	.219
Orr, Samuel, Lakewood *	129	547	464	64	103	168	21	4	12	64	3	4	4	72	2	122	0	2	12	.222	.329	.362
Ortega, Jose, Lake County	43	138	118	15	26	29	3	0	0	7	0	1	2	17	0	17	1	2	0	.220	.326	.246
Otness, John, Greenville	117	508	441	59	146	207	25	0	12	67	0	11	21	35	0	42	1	1	10	.331	.398	.469
Owings, John, Rome	2	8	7	2	2	3	1	0	0	1	0	0	0	1	0	0	0	0	0	.286	.375	.429
Pacheco, Fernando, Lake County *	119	502	456	47	107	169	21	4	11	68	1	4	5	36	1	113	0	0	13	.235	.295	.371
Paniagua, Salvador, Greenville	72	284	267	34	65	103	12	1	8	37	0	3	1	12	0	91	0	0	2	.243	.276	.386
Pedroza, Sergio, Columbus *	49	201	179	31	37	86	11	1	12	30	0	6	16	0	58	0	0	5	.207	.294	.480
Pence, Hunter, Lexington	80	341	302	59	102	197	14	3	25	60	0	0	1	38	2	53	8	3	2	.338	.413	.652
Perez, Eduardo, Columbus †	10	35	33	0	7	9	2	0	0	4	0	0	1	1	0	10	0	0	2	.212	.257	.273
Perry, Patrick, Greenville *	16	62	54	5	13	17	4	0	0	8	0	2	0	6	0	15	0	0	1	.241	.306	.315
Peterson, James, Columbus *	30	120	103	8	25	35	4	0	2	10	1	1	0	15	0	29	2	0	8	.243	.336	.340
Piazza, Anthony, Hagerstown	5	21	20	1	3	4	1	0	0	1	0	0	0	1	0	9	1	0	0	.150	.190	.200
Pietro, Joseph, Greensboro *	11	45	36	6	6	6	0	0	0	5	0	1	0	8	0	15	5	1	0	.167	.311	.167
Pinckney, Andrew, Greenville †	128	556	508	91	158	272	33	9	21	98	0	5	7	36	1	78	6	0	15	.311	.362	.535
Plumsky, Richard, Lakewood	4	14	12	0	3	3	0	0	0	1	1	0	0	1	0	6	0	0	0	.250	.308	.250
Pope, Peter, Rome	100	436	386	48	107	163	24	7	6	60	1	5	2	42	0	70	0	1	9	.277	.347	.422
Poppert, John, Savannah	15	43	38	2	4	5	1	0	0	0	0	0	2	3	0	11	0	0	1	.105	.209	.132
Powell, Pedro, Hickory †	112	497	445	75	121	138	6	4	1	24	6	1	4	41	0	83	44	16	6	.272	.338	.310
Pritz, Bryan, Greenville	10	41	37	6	11	16	5	0	0	7	0	0	0	4	0	4	0	0	1	.297	.366	.432
Psomas, William, Hagerstown	99	421	350	66	105	193	27	2	19	54	2	5	2	62	5	79	6	4	8	.300	.403	.551
Puente, Juan, Delmarva	9	26	22	1	2	2	0	0	0	2	0	0	0	2	0	10	0	0	0	.091	.167	.091
Pyzik, Steven, Rome	19	58	53	2	15	17	2	0	0	6	1	2	0	2	0	11	0	0	2	.283	.298	.321
Reed, Ryan, Lexington *	29	115	102	12	27	38	5	0	2	14	2	1	0	10	0	41	6	3	1	.265	.327	.373
Reineke, Chad, Lexington	2	0	0	0	0	0	0	0	0	0	0	0	0	0	0	0	0	0	0	...	...	...
Requena, Alex, Augusta †	109	504	449	78	113	153	23	7	1	23	3	1	4	47	0	84	56	14	2	.252	.327	.341
Restko, Jason, Greensboro	115	476	403	69	126	198	21	3	15	70	0	2	18	53	1	91	3	0	9	.313	.414	.491
Restrepo, John, Asheville *	44	176	155	15	33	37	4	0	0	10	1	0	0	20	1	48	4	7	3	.213	.303	.239
Reyes, Argenis, Lake County †	71	339	317	51	102	132	14	5	2	36	3	2	1	16	1	36	16	6	4	.322	.354	.416
Reyes, Milver, Hickory	43	147	133	10	25	34	2	2	1	13	0	1	1	12	0	18	0	0	3	.188	.259	.256
Reynolds, Lagatila, Asheville	3	14	11	0	2	3	1	0	0	0	0	1	0	2	0	3	0	0	0	.182	.308	.273
Richmond, Barry, Columbus *	12	43	39	2	4	5	1	0	0	2	0	0	0	4	0	14	1	0	2	.103	.186	.128
Ricks, Adam, Kannapolis †	87	364	285	41	74	92	9	3	1	23	11	1	5	62	3	46	1	1	11	.260	.399	.323
Rivas, Arturo, Delmarva	125	518	434	78	109	181	29	8	9	62	5	6	12	61	1	94	11	5	11	.251	.355	.417
Roberts, Daron, Kannapolis	22	86	79	5	19	20	1	0	0	5	1	1	1	4	1	23	3	2	1	.241	.282	.253
Robinson, Scott, Lexington *	34	150	127	20	37	58	10	1	3	34	0	1	1	19	1	15	3	2	8	.291	.385	.457
Robledo, Nelson, Asheville	93	371	322	46	77	105	22	0	2	34	5	1	6	37	0	71	1	1	7	.239	.328	.326
Rojas, Ricardo, Lake County	40	158	145	14	33	51	7	1	3	17	5	2	2	4	0	27	6	2	5	.228	.255	.352
Rosa, Wally, Kannapolis	12	37	33	1	6	6	0	0	0	3	1	2	0	0	2	0	10	0	0	1	.182	.229	.182
Rozema, Michael, Rome *	51	225	195	27	53	78	19	3	0	30	3	3	5	18	1	44	13	4	3	.272	.344	.400
Russ, Ryan, Columbus †	98	387	351	48	98	152	20	5	8	49	2	2	8	24	1	66	4	6	8	.279	.338	.433
Sammons, Clint, Rome	121	494	427	60	122	163	29	0	4	62	0	7	5	55	0	66	4	1	15	.286	.368	.382
Sanders, Marcus, Augusta	111	504	420	86	126	168	19	4	5	40	3	3	9	69	0	90	57	9	1	.300	.407	.400
Sandora, Robert, Savannah *	2	4	4	0	0	0	0	0	0	0	0	0	0	0	0	0	0	0	0	.000	.000	.000
Santana, Yury, Hagerstown	8	23	22	4	4	5	1	0	0	0	0	0	0	1	0	10	0	0	0	.182	.217	.227
Santangelo, Louis, Lexington	70	268	239	43	64	124	14	2	14	39	3	1	1	24	0	86	4	3	4	.268	.336	.519
Santiago, John, Hickory	9	29	27	3	5	8	3	0	0	0	0	0	0	2	0	2	0	0	3	.185	.241	.296
Sapp, Steven, Columbus	10	25	23	2	3	4	1	0	0	1	0	0	0	2	0	9	0	0	0	.130	.200	.174
Sardinha, Duke, Asheville	9	35	31	3	4	5	1	0	0	1	0	0	0	4	0	5	0	1	1	.129	.229	.161
Scalabrini, Patrick, Delmarva	62	260	235	29	61	95	13	0	7	37	1	3	6	15	1	52	5	2	4	.260	.317	.404

Player, Team	G	TPA	AB	R	H	TB	2B	3B	HR	RBI	SH	SF	HP	BB	IBB	SO	SB	CS	GDP	Avg.	OBP	Slg.
Schade, Ryan, Greensboro	13	32	28	5	10	12	2	0	0	3	1	0	3	0	0	5	1	1	0	.357	.419	.429
Schwartzbauer, Daniel, Hickory	97	362	324	38	87	121	17	1	5	34	4	3	6	25	0	70	3	5	4	.269	.330	.373
Seifrig, Cole, Greensboro	69	262	237	32	52	92	10	0	10	34	0	3	4	17	0	73	7	2	4	.219	.280	.388
Sewell, Kevin, Greensboro *	49	165	143	23	34	56	10	0	4	24	0	3	2	16	0	35	1	0	5	.238	.317	.392
Sheldon, Ole, Lexington	68	284	247	34	64	91	12	0	5	35	0	5	3	29	0	36	2	5	9	.259	.338	.368
Shier, Peter, Delmarva	37	167	150	18	39	52	5	1	2	13	0	1	2	14	0	28	6	3	2	.260	.329	.347
Silva, Johan, Rome *	38	145	129	14	29	38	3	3	0	18	3	2	1	10	0	35	0	2	2	.225	.282	.295
Smith, Carl, Delmarva	83	337	295	34	67	105	18	1	6	45	0	3	2	37	1	65	0	0	8	.227	.315	.356
Smith, Sean, Kannapolis	110	481	437	63	123	192	25	1	14	62	8	1	9	26	0	71	35	7	3	.281	.334	.439
Smolarski, Freddy, Greensboro	3	11	11	0	2	2	0	0	0	0	0	0	0	0	0	2	0	0	0	.182	.182	.182
Solano, Euvi, Hickory	1	4	3	0	0	0	0	0	0	0	0	0	0	1	0	0	0	0	0	.000	.250	.000
Sorensen, Logan, Greenville *	95	361	315	44	71	99	16	0	4	32	0	2	5	39	1	61	2	2	5	.225	.319	.314
Sosa, Carlos, Augusta	108	444	379	61	110	168	25	3	9	71	0	2	1	62	1	96	4	2	4	.290	.390	.443
Soto, Enyelbert, Lexington *	1	0	0	0	0	0	0	0	0	0	0	0	...	0	0	0	0	0	0	...	...	...
Soto, Luis, Greenville †	23	89	85	6	18	22	4	0	0	10	0	0	4	0	19	1	0	4	.212	.247	.259
Stachowsky, Mitchel, Greenville	37	139	115	18	19	42	8	0	5	16	0	1	7	16	0	49	1	0	3	.165	.302	.365
Steidl, Sam, Columbus *	55	232	193	25	47	54	7	0	0	12	6	1	3	29	0	24	2	0	8	.244	.350	.280
Strop, Pedro, Asheville †	4	13	12	2	2	2	0	0	0	0	1	0	0	0	0	6	0	0	0	.167	.167	.167
Sucre, Antonio, Hickory	107	428	393	38	104	146	12	0	10	54	0	3	10	22	2	109	3	3	10	.265	.318	.372
Sutil, Wladimir, Lexington	6	23	23	2	6	7	1	0	0	3	0	0	0	0	0	5	2	0	1	.261	.261	.304
Sutton, Stephen, Lexington †	62	275	231	46	66	128	19	2	13	42	1	1	6	36	1	51	4	2	5	.286	.394	.554
Szabo, Jordan, Lakewood	3	9	9	2	4	4	0	0	0	0	0	0	0	0	0	2	0	0	0	.444	.444	.444
Szabo, Marshall, Lake County †	105	430	377	60	94	127	15	0	6	35	1	1	11	40	2	54	5	0	6	.249	.338	.337
Terrazas, Ivan, Rome †	87	338	321	42	89	117	17	1	3	41	4	2	1	10	1	48	1	3	9	.277	.299	.364
Thomas, Benjamin, Rome *	11	36	34	6	12	20	2	0	2	8	0	1	0	1	0	4	0	0	0	.353	.361	.588
Thompson, Ryan, Lexington	1	0	0	0	0	0	0	0	0	0	0	0	...	0	0	0	0	0	0	...	...	...
Torbert, Wallace, Lexington	71	280	256	40	77	129	20	4	8	47	0	2	6	16	0	63	13	3	4	.301	.354	.504
Toregas, Wyatt, Lake County	104	459	411	57	95	132	22	0	5	42	2	3	6	37	0	76	0	1	15	.231	.302	.321
Torres, Saul, Lexington	36	147	130	29	36	69	12	0	7	24	0	1	4	12	0	29	1	1	3	.277	.354	.531
Towles, Justin, Lexington	45	193	162	35	56	89	14	2	5	23	5	0	10	16	0	29	11	7	3	.346	.436	.549
Trejo, Jaime, Rome	24	82	75	7	12	15	0	0	1	2	0	0	1	6	0	31	0	0	2	.160	.232	.200
Triplett, Bryan, Lexington	90	377	336	42	72	103	15	2	4	36	6	3	3	29	0	81	21	4	13	.214	.280	.307
Triplett, Calvin, Hagerstown	43	165	136	20	36	58	9	2	3	18	4	2	5	18	0	26	2	4	5	.265	.366	.426
Trumble, Daniel, Augusta	24	86	75	16	15	27	4	1	2	6	0	0	0	11	0	18	4	0	3	.200	.302	.360
Turner, Christopher, Greenville	79	338	301	53	87	155	29	3	11	66	0	2	7	28	1	85	9	1	2	.289	.361	.515
Valdes, Juan, Lake County †	107	426	373	50	82	123	13	2	8	47	6	2	3	41	0	109	12	9	1	.220	.301	.330
Valdez, Jose, Asheville †	115	493	439	75	128	214	19	2	21	56	8	0	1	45	0	64	8	8	4	.292	.359	.487
Van Der Bosch, Matthew, Greenville *	35	159	124	22	36	53	8	3	1	13	2	2	3	28	0	32	8	3	1	.290	.427	.427
Vericker, Brad, Augusta *	51	183	163	14	43	62	7	0	4	20	0	2	0	18	0	22	1	0	7	.264	.333	.380
Vital, Kevin, Lexington *	61	233	197	20	35	61	8	0	6	27	4	1	1	30	1	58	3	0	7	.178	.288	.310
Vroman, Douglas, Savannah	70	256	209	38	53	89	11	2	7	34	1	3	1	39	0	64	9	4	6	.254	.369	.426
Wagner, Michael, Augusta	54	208	171	31	51	82	9	5	4	26	1	4	11	20	1	42	2	1	2	.298	.398	.480
Wald, Jacob, Augusta	14	45	38	10	9	15	4	1	0	6	1	2	1	3	0	11	1	1	2	.237	.295	.395
Walker, Neil, Hickory †	120	518	485	78	146	219	33	2	12	68	0	7	6	20	2	71	7	4	10	.301	.332	.452
Watts, Derran, Hagerstown	65	251	221	31	63	94	17	1	4	40	1	1	4	24	0	55	6	5	4	.285	.364	.425
Webb, Billy, Savannah	102	429	379	59	103	156	22	2	9	45	2	2	3	36	0	62	22	8	9	.272	.338	.412
Webb, Justin, Greensboro	2	7	6	1	1	2	1	0	0	1	0	0	0	1	0	2	1	0	0	.167	.286	.333
Westervelt, Christopher, Columbus	53	216	179	31	47	77	15	0	5	29	0	0	4	33	0	35	0	0	4	.263	.389	.430
White, Dean, Rome	72	261	235	34	56	70	9	1	1	14	3	0	3	20	0	67	3	3	9	.238	.306	.298
Whitney, Matthew, Lake County	74	319	277	38	67	92	7	0	6	27	0	3	5	34	0	64	0	3	6	.242	.332	.332
Wigdahl, Jeffrey, Lexington *	1	0	0	0	0	0	0	0	0	0	0	0	0	0	0	0	0	0	0	...	...	...
Wilson, Kyle, Asheville	40	158	143	19	43	83	10	0	10	36	0	0	4	11	0	34	0	0	4	.301	.367	.580
Wilson, Neil, Asheville	81	333	299	33	81	136	25	1	8	51	2	1	8	23	0	48	3	0	11	.271	.338	.455
Wilson, Thomas, Savannah	1	0	0	0	0	0	0	0	0	0	0	0	0	0	0	0	0	0	0	...	...	...
Witt, Paul, Greensboro	4	15	13	1	3	3	0	0	0	0	0	0	0	2	0	2	0	0	1	.231	.333	.231
Wyrick, Joshua, Hagerstown *	23	91	81	17	24	33	6	0	1	7	2	1	1	6	0	16	3	2	1	.296	.348	.407
Young, Matthew, Rome *	114	505	423	85	132	173	15	4	6	52	7	2	7	66	0	65	10	11	3	.312	.412	.409
Zapata, Jose, Delmarva	14	47	41	4	7	13	1	1	1	9	3	1	1	1	0	11	1	1	2	.171	.205	.317
Zimmerman, Ryan, Savannah	4	17	17	5	8	18	2	1	0	6	0	0	0	0	0	3	0	1	0	.471	.471	1.059
Zobrist, Benjamin, Lexington †	68	310	247	45	75	102	17	2	2	32	4	7	5	47	2	35	16	5	2	.304	.415	.413

GRAND SLAMS—C. Gimenez, 3; J. Fransz, L. Montz, S. Robinson, 2 each; C. Arias, Q. Ascencion, J. Ash, E. Baez, R. Bernadina, F. Caraballo, M. Carp, B. Cleveland, N. Conte, T. Denker, B. Dewitt, C. Ehlers, K. Eichas, M. Einertson, R. Frith, M. Garza, J. Hansen, A. Jansen, J. Koshansky, A. Mannon, L. May, B. McCann, T. Moni-Erigbali, J. Murray, J. Noviskey, S. Orr, F. Pacheco, J. Restko, A. Reyes, G. Richardson, N. Robledo, C. Smith, S. Smith, D. Sutton, C. Turner, K. Vital, C. Westervelt, K. Wilson, 1 each.

AWARDED FIRST BASE ON CATCHER'S INTERFERENCE—M. Jurich 5 (G. Brown, G. Gutierrez, G. McCarthy, I. Rojas, W. Plaza); D. Vroman 3 (F. Hernandez, G. Gutierrez, S. Paniagua); P. Maestrales 2 (A. Hathaway, C. Blevins); S. Robinson 2 (J. Noviskey, N. Corredor);

2005 PITCHING
TEAM

Team	W	L	Pct.	ERA	G	CG	ShO	Sv.	IP	H	TBF	R	ER	HR	SH	SF	HB	BB	IBB	SO	WP	Bk.
Lexington	81	58	.583	3.56	139	2	15	35	1228	1115	5210	574	486	104	46	34	63	477	11	1174	81	12
Kannapolis	74	59	.556	3.57	133	6	14	33	1150	1065	4957	579	456	76	36	34	68	467	11	940	75	12
Lake County	72	66	.522	3.71	138	2	10	40	1231	1196	5293	617	508	102	62	21	99	443	9	994	69	8
Charleston	80	58	.580	3.72	138	3	6	36	1220.2	1171	5250	603	505	67	23	32	51	491	3	1049	73	11
Hagerstown	71	66	.518	3.93	137	3	10	36	1227.2	1140	5360	664	536	114	50	38	121	524	18	1020	79	16
Greenville	72	66	.522	4.04	138	3	3	33	1180	1234	5176	639	530	94	27	48	64	427	6	948	75	6
Rome	72	65	.526	4.07	137	5	8	33	1204.2	1238	5223	619	545	100	24	46	63	425	11	882	63	6
Augusta	77	59	.566	4.13	136	3	3	39	1170	1182	5110	633	537	78	25	37	78	423	4	1074	71	5
Columbus	57	79	.419	4.14	136	5	9	24	1172	1152	5187	667	539	91	25	47	76	538	4	1066	80	4
Delmarva	72	67	.518	4.21	139	1	7	46	1232.2	1322	5488	710	577	75	35	47	70	467	9	1086	95	11

Team	W	L	Pct.	ERA	G	CG	ShO	Sv.	IP	H	TBF	R	ER	HR	SH	SF	HB	BB	IBB	SO	WP	Bk.
West Virginia	60	78	.435	4.30	138	0	5	32	1210.2	1226	5332	695	579	124	51	37	86	491	18	1014	87	4
Savannah	62	76	.449	4.37	138	4	8	35	1169	1175	5093	643	568	126	25	32	91	435	6	854	69	8
Greensboro	67	71	.486	4.38	138	2	4	46	1216.2	1242	5401	721	592	129	40	35	83	525	11	1031	101	7
Hickory	54	80	.403	4.39	134	2	3	27	1174.1	1261	5149	672	573	122	40	34	60	421	10	843	76	5
Lakewood	56	83	.403	4.46	139	10	8	25	1206.2	1262	5254	702	598	103	35	55	97	396	8	905	83	11
Asheville	71	67	.514	5.05	138	2	5	41	1192	1300	5312	773	669	151	29	27	102	457	3	1052	85	13

INDIVIDUAL

TOP QUALIFIERS FOR EARNED-RUN AVERAGE TITLE

Minimum 112 innings. *Lefthanded pitcher.

Pitcher, Team	W	L	Pct.	ERA	G	GS	CG	ShO	GF	Sv.	IP	H	TBF	R	ER	HR	SH	SF	HB	BB	IBB	SO	WP	Bk.
Liotta, Raymond, Kannapolis *	8	3	.727	2.26	20	20	1	0	0	0	115.1	108	468	39	29	5	9	3	2	35	0	107	3	1
Barthmaier, James, Lexington	11	6	.647	2.27	25	25	0	0	0	0	134.2	108	553	41	34	3	2	4	4	55	0	142	7	1
Ramirez, Luis, Delmarva	9	7	.563	2.55	28	27	1	1	0	0	162.1	131	658	53	46	7	2	6	2	54	0	155	5	0
Elbert, Timothy, Columbus *	8	5	.615	2.66	25	24	1	1	0	0	115.0	83	481	37	34	8	0	5	4	57	0	128	5	0
Egbert, John, Kannapolis	10	5	.667	3.12	30	24	4	3	1	0	147.0	127	605	66	51	5	4	2	16	48	0	107	10	0
Gutierrez, Juan, Lexington	9	5	.643	3.21	22	21	1	0	1	0	120.2	106	503	55	43	10	2	6	10	43	0	100	7	2
Laffey, Aaron, Lake County *	7	7	.500	3.22	25	23	1	0	2	1	142.1	123	572	62	51	5	9	1	4	52	0	69	2	2
Harrison, Matthew, Rome *	12	7	.632	3.23	27	27	2	1	0	0	167.0	151	671	65	60	17	1	3	6	30	0	118	3	2
Galvez, Gary, Greenville	10	4	.714	3.35	31	18	0	0	2	0	126.1	118	540	64	47	12	2	6	7	40	0	87	3	3
Parr, James, Rome	13	4	.765	3.41	26	18	0	0	7	3	126.2	134	534	54	48	13	3	7	4	24	0	98	1	0
Harrell, Lucas, Kannapolis	7	11	.389	3.65	26	26	0	0	0	0	133.1	128	605	86	54	8	2	7	11	71	1	85	13	4
Balester, Collin, Savannah	8	6	.571	3.67	24	23	1	0	0	0	125.0	105	520	62	51	11	1	0	6	42	0	95	4	1
Martinez, Ronnie, Lexington	13	3	.813	3.67	27	26	0	0	1	0	152.0	142	628	73	62	14	1	4	4	50	2	113	4	3
Russell, Adam, Kannapolis	9	7	.563	3.78	24	24	0	0	0	0	126.1	116	538	61	53	10	4	5	6	55	0	82	5	0
Malone, Christopher, Columbus	9	7	.563	3.88	31	21	2	0	2	0	141.2	133	590	77	61	10	4	4	8	41	0	127	5	0
Devaney, Michael, Hagerstown	10	4	.714	3.88	32	15	2	0	6	0	137.0	107	563	73	59	9	3	10	51	0	121	8	2
Morales, Ricardo, Savannah *	8	7	.533	3.94	25	25	0	0	0	0	137.0	147	575	66	60	16	2	2	7	39	1	99	4	0
Griffith, Derek, Lakewood *	7	11	.389	3.95	26	26	1	1	0	0	161.2	152	678	79	71	11	1	3	13	59	0	131	8	1
Sanchez, Jonathan, Augusta *	5	7	.417	4.08	25	25	0	0	0	0	125.2	122	531	59	57	8	3	5	7	39	0	166	7	0
Atilano, Luis, Rome	8	9	.471	4.17	24	24	1	0	0	0	136.0	138	572	77	63	17	2	5	7	32	0	66	6	0
Sanchez, Jose, Lexington	11	5	.688	4.20	26	24	0	0	0	0	133.0	147	571	73	62	18	2	4	9	37	0	87	7	0

DEPARTMENTAL LEADERS: W—Martinez and Parr, 13. L—Kloosterman, 19. Pct.—Martinez, .813. G—Nestor, 58. GS—Hart, 28. CG—De La Cruz, 5. ShO—Egbert, 3. GF—Mobley, 47. Sv.—Mobley, 34. IP—Baldwin, 168. H—De La Cruz, 186. TBF—Baldwin, 726. R—De La Cruz, 109. ER—De La Cruz, 92. HR—Lo, 23. SAC—four pitchers tied with 9. SF—three pitchers tied with 8. HB—Miramontes, 19. BB—Harrell, 71. IBB—Mannix and Decarlo, 4. SO—Sanchez, 166. WP—Kloosterman, 17. BK—Morales, 7.

ALL PITCHERS

*Lefthanded pitcher.

Pitcher, Team	W	L	Pct.	ERA	G	GS	CG	ShO	GF	Sv.	IP	H	TBF	R	ER	HR	SH	SF	HB	BB	IBB	SO	WP	Bk.
Acosta, Kelyn, Augusta	0	1	.000	1.42	11	0	0	0	5	0	12.2	10	48	2	2	0	0	0	0	3	0	6	1	0
Akin, Brian, Columbus	1	4	.200	4.35	35	1	0	0	10	2	72.1	77	315	38	35	8	2	1	5	31	0	54	6	0
Alen, Luis, Greensboro	0	0	.000	0.00	1	0	0	0	1	0	0.1	0	1	0	0	0	0	0	0	0	0	1	0	0
Alfonzo, Edgar, Hagerstown *	2	2	.500	0.92	13	0	0	0	7	0	19.2	13	78	3	2	1	1	0	1	5	0	13	1	1
Allen, Kyle, Lakewood *	0	4	.000	4.55	21	0	0	0	10	0	27.2	28	127	17	14	3	2	1	1	18	1	27	8	0
Allison, Jeffrey, Greensboro	5	4	.556	4.18	17	17	0	0	0	0	94.2	86	404	49	44	13	3	3	6	40	0	83	5	1
Almenar, Aristides, Hagerstown	0	0	.000	9.82	2	0	0	0	1	0	3.2	1	16	4	4	0	0	0	0	5	0	2	0	0
Alvarado, Andrew, Lexington	2	0	1.000	3.38	9	0	0	0	3	0	10.2	13	48	4	4	1	1	0	0	6	1	5	0	1
Alvarez, Carlos, Columbus *	2	2	.500	0.93	20	0	0	0	14	3	38.2	24	153	9	4	0	3	2	3	12	0	63	0	1
Alvarez, Juan, Rome *	0	0	.000	0.00	1	0	0	0	0	0	1.0	1	5	0	0	0	0	0	1	1	0	1	0	0
Alvarez, Timothy, Augusta *	1	1	.500	5.08	25	0	0	0	12	1	33.2	40	161	25	19	2	2	0	4	15	2	34	2	0
Anderson, Devin, Rome *	0	2	.000	4.32	16	0	0	0	4	0	25.0	25	112	13	12	0	1	0	0	15	0	14	2	0
Ashabraner, Robert, Lake County	0	1	.000	7.04	7	0	0	0	4	2	7.2	8	39	6	6	1	0	0	4	5	0	3	3	0
Atilano, Luis, Rome	8	9	.471	4.17	24	24	1	0	0	0	136.0	138	572	77	63	17	2	5	7	32	0	66	6	0
Bacot, Paul, Rome	1	2	.333	5.53	9	5	0	0	2	1	40.2	58	184	27	25	3	2	5	0	12	0	12	0	1
Bailey, Chad, Columbus *	2	4	.333	4.93	19	1	0	0	6	0	42.0	57	195	34	23	3	2	1	2	15	0	29	0	0
Bakker, Garry, Kannapolis	5	4	.556	3.69	18	5	0	0	8	3	53.2	47	224	27	22	5	0	0	3	19	1	38	4	0
Baldwin, Ancil, Savannah	4	4	.500	4.14	12	12	1	0	0	0	67.1	64	296	38	31	9	2	0	17	26	0	43	9	0
Baldwin, Andrew, Lakewood	5	12	.294	4.77	27	27	1	0	0	0	168.0	183	721	106	89	16	5	8	12	43	1	100	15	0
Balester, Collin, Savannah	8	6	.571	3.67	24	23	1	0	0	0	125.0	105	520	62	51	11	1	0	6	42	0	95	4	1
Banks, Demetrius, Kannapolis *	0	0	.000	1.93	9	0	0	0	2	0	9.1	6	37	2	2	0	0	0	1	5	0	11	1	0
Barone, Daniel, Greensboro	2	2	.500	4.12	12	6	0	0	2	1	39.1	35	161	19	18	4	3	0	4	10	0	29	3	0
Barrack, Jacob, Lakewood	4	4	.500	2.33	39	0	0	0	34	12	54.0	42	212	19	14	2	3	1	3	10	1	66	2	0
Barthmaier, James, Lexington	11	6	.647	2.27	25	25	0	0	0	0	134.2	108	553	41	34	3	2	4	4	55	0	142	7	1
Batista, Norberto, Greensboro	0	0	.000	0.00	1	0	0	0	1	0	1.0	0	3	0	0	0	0	0	0	0	0	1	0	0
Baxter, Allen, Greensboro	1	3	.250	4.15	11	11	0	0	0	0	56.1	57	257	34	26	8	0	3	1	37	0	53	16	0
Baysinger, Trent, Delmarva	2	0	1.000	3.25	29	0	0	0	7	3	36.0	41	153	16	13	1	1	0	3	5	0	25	2	0
Bedard, Erik, Delmarva *	1	0	1.000	0.00	1	1	0	0	0	0	5.0	3	18	0	0	0	0	0	0	1	0	9	2	0
Beerer, Scott, Asheville	2	3	.400	3.89	45	0	0	0	38	23	46.1	52	202	23	19	3	3	1	0	15	0	44	3	0
Bille, Michael, Greensboro	0	0	.000	81.00	2	0	0	0	0	0	0.2	4	9	6	6	1	1	1	0	3	1	1	1	0
Bisenius, Joseph, Lakewood	6	4	.600	5.88	40	4	1	0	14	4	64.1	66	297	45	42	5	3	4	6	37	2	56	10	3
Bishop, Matthew, Hickory	3	7	.300	4.58	24	1	0	0	12	0	53.0	63	238	34	27	5	5	2	1	22	1	34	3	0
Blackley, Adam, Greenville *	2	7	.222	6.15	14	13	0	0	0	0	60.0	75	277	49	41	11	2	2	1	26	0	42	5	0
Blazek, Christopher, Lexington *	1	0	1.000	6.18	18	0	0	0	5	0	27.2	27	124	20	19	7	2	0	1	16	2	20	6	0
Bloom, Kyle, Hickory *	4	1	.800	1.87	12	12	0	0	0	0	62.2	38	252	15	13	3	0	1	2	33	0	58	0	0
Bobbitt, Seth, Rome	0	0	.000	0.00	2	0	0	0	1	0	3.0	1	12	0	0	0	0	1	0	1	0	0	0	0
Bowman, Charles, Hagerstown	2	2	.500	2.98	26	0	0	0	10	0	54.1	58	236	22	18	4	5	1	9	18	2	30	4	0
Brandenburg, Adam, Greensboro *	5	6	.455	4.70	27	19	0	0	2	1	99.2	128	458	72	52	8	4	7	8	42	1	65	7	0

CLASS A South Atlantic League

Pitcher, Team	W	L	Pct.	ERA	G	GS	CG	ShO	GF	Sv.	IP	H	TBF	R	ER	HR	SH	SF	HB	BB	IBB	SO	WP	Bk.
Brazell, Landon, Greensboro	1	0	1.000	10.24	2	2	0	0	0	0	9.2	15	52	11	11	3	0	1	0	8	0	5	0	0
Brice, Thomas, Kannapolis *	0	0	.000	4.50	7	0	0	0	2	0	4.0	2	19	2	2	0	0	0	0	5	0	4	2	0
Bright, Adam, Asheville *	4	2	.667	3.38	51	0	0	0	20	6	64.0	56	261	26	24	6	2	0	3	28	1	51	3	1
Brooks, Richard, Kannapolis	1	2	.333	9.13	6	5	1	0	0	0	23.2	30	106	26	24	3	1	1	0	10	1	19	4	0
Buechner, Christopher, Asheville	4	3	.571	5.07	53	0	0	0	12	3	65.2	68	298	40	37	8	2	1	8	26	1	68	5	0
Bunkelman, Cody, Lake County	5	5	.500	4.08	16	16	0	0	0	0	79.1	75	348	43	36	5	2	0	10	39	0	61	8	2
Bunn, William, Savannah	3	5	.375	3.86	11	11	1	0	0	0	58.1	51	256	29	25	10	1	3	6	25	0	56	6	0
Burrows, Angelo, Rome	3	1	.750	3.48	16	0	0	0	9	3	20.2	23	94	8	8	0	0	0	0	9	1	18	3	0
Burton, Timothy, Lake County	4	8	.333	3.80	49	1	0	0	11	2	71.0	78	312	39	30	5	5	2	9	20	2	42	2	4
Cabrera, Henry, Greenville	0	4	.000	6.45	6	4	0	0	0	0	22.1	23	105	18	16	3	1	1	3	15	0	27	2	2
Cahill, Casey, Delmarva	6	7	.462	3.42	53	0	0	0	16	5	84.1	78	364	39	32	7	5	5	7	30	2	75	7	0
Campbell, Richard, Savannah	4	2	.667	1.69	36	0	0	0	28	19	48.0	28	188	10	9	2	1	0	2	15	1	50	4	0
Capps, Matt, Hickory	3	4	.429	2.52	35	0	0	0	27	14	53.2	47	206	15	15	0	4	2	2	5	2	39	2	0
Carrasco, Carlos, Lakewood	1	7	.125	7.04	13	13	1	0	0	0	62.2	78	297	50	49	11	0	2	9	28	0	46	1	1
Castillo, Albenis, Columbus	1	5	.167	3.99	38	0	0	0	34	10	56.1	61	254	33	25	4	3	2	1	26	0	48	3	1
Castillo, Arismendy, Columbus	0	2	.000	6.43	3	1	0	0	1	0	7.0	14	39	12	5	0	0	0	1	2	0	6	2	0
Castillo, Jesus, Columbus	1	2	.333	2.96	6	5	0	0	0	0	24.1	18	97	8	8	0	0	0	2	7	0	28	1	0
Castillo, Jonathan, Hagerstown	1	0	1.000	2.57	2	1	0	0	0	0	7.0	4	25	3	2	1	1	0	0	3	0	4	0	0
Castor, Parrish, Greensboro *	1	1	.500	18.00	3	0	0	0	0	0	3.0	9	23	6	6	2	0	0	0	5	0	5	1	0
Cerrato, Justin, Lakewood	0	1	.000	3.24	4	0	0	0	0	0	8.1	8	36	6	3	1	0	1	0	3	0	7	1	0
Cevette, Daniel, Lake County *	5	4	.556	2.73	17	17	0	0	0	0	82.1	74	348	35	25	7	5	2	6	30	0	85	5	0
Coles, Corey, Hagerstown *	0	0	.000	0.00	1	0	0	0	1	0	1.0	1	4	0	0	0	0	0	0	0	0	2	0	0
Collins, Kyle, Lake County	4	5	.444	2.80	36	0	0	0	12	0	45.0	41	193	18	14	5	2	1	6	17	0	39	4	0
Cook, Steven, Savannah	3	4	.429	5.28	20	9	0	0	7	0	61.1	80	264	39	36	10	2	4	4	12	0	30	3	0
Coppinger, Joseph, Delmarva	2	3	.400	5.47	14	9	0	0	2	1	51.0	64	236	37	31	7	2	2	6	18	0	25	8	0
Correa, Jose, Lakewood	0	1	.000	5.63	4	0	0	0	3	0	8.0	11	40	6	5	1	0	0	2	5	0	5	0	0
Cova, Rafael, Hagerstown	5	6	.455	4.60	24	5	0	0	6	1	62.2	62	285	45	32	5	4	6	8	33	3	61	12	2
Covington, Marcus, Rome	0	0	.000	5.87	5	0	0	0	3	0	7.2	7	36	5	5	1	0	0	0	8	0	4	1	0
Cox, Benjamin, Savannah	4	4	.500	3.00	42	0	0	0	27	6	63.0	55	273	24	21	6	5	2	3	33	0	51	2	0
Craig, Dustin, Hickory	4	5	.444	5.14	34	0	0	0	12	2	56.0	56	257	35	32	7	3	2	3	37	1	61	7	0
Daley, Matthew, Asheville	8	2	.800	3.99	45	0	0	0	21	1	79.0	90	347	46	35	10	2	3	12	16	0	49	5	0
Davidson, David, Hickory *	1	2	.333	9.78	10	2	0	0	3	0	19.1	16	95	22	21	4	1	0	3	21	2	23	5	0
Deduno, Samuel, Asheville	8	8	.500	5.62	20	20	1	0	0	0	89.2	82	407	67	56	9	3	1	11	65	0	110	13	1
De La Cruz, Maximino, Lakewood	8	12	.400	5.10	27	27	5	1	0	0	162.1	186	711	109	92	15	3	7	14	48	0	105	9	2
Delgado, George, Asheville	0	1	.000	10.32	10	0	0	0	3	1	11.1	22	60	17	13	2	0	0	0	3	0	13	1	0
Delgado, Jesus, Greenville	7	3	.700	3.50	33	0	0	0	7	2	72.0	57	309	30	28	3	1	3	2	39	1	69	11	0
Devaney, Michael, Hagerstown	10	4	.714	3.88	32	15	2	0	6	0	137.0	107	563	73	59	9	3	3	10	51	0	121	8	2
Diangelo, Jason, Asheville	4	4	.500	5.52	46	0	0	0	15	0	73.1	93	347	59	45	11	1	2	5	29	0	74	10	0
Diaz, Raymar, Lexington	1	3	.250	4.48	43	3	0	0	10	1	82.1	77	358	50	41	15	3	3	3	38	0	87	5	0
Digby, Bryan, Rome	0	0	.000	10.80	2	0	0	0	0	0	1.2	0	10	2	2	0	0	0	0	6	0	1	0	0
Dobies, Andrew, Greenville *	5	3	.625	3.59	10	10	0	0	0	0	57.2	69	244	25	23	5	0	1	1	12	0	52	4	0
Drage, Derek, Hickory	3	5	.375	4.46	37	1	0	0	21	6	74.2	73	319	42	37	13	4	3	5	30	1	58	7	0
Dueitt, Cory, Lakewood	2	6	.250	3.21	49	0	0	0	23	7	73.0	62	305	33	26	8	3	2	6	23	2	48	5	0
Durkin, Matthew, Hagerstown	4	5	.444	3.77	19	14	0	0	1	0	76.1	54	327	42	32	9	1	1	9	54	0	79	3	0
Eager, Blake, Hagerstown	6	3	.667	3.76	21	20	0	0	0	0	105.1	109	445	50	44	13	3	2	9	16	0	83	0	0
Egbert, John, Kannapolis	10	5	.667	3.12	30	24	4	3	1	0	147.0	127	605	66	51	5	4	2	16	48	0	107	10	0
Elbert, Timothy, Columbus *	8	5	.615	2.66	25	24	1	1	0	0	115.0	83	481	37	34	8	0	5	4	57	0	128	5	0
Englebrook, Evan, Lexington	8	6	.571	4.32	30	17	0	0	5	0	114.2	103	509	69	55	10	5	3	9	65	1	101	7	1
Estrada, Paul, Lexington	6	7	.462	2.69	46	3	0	0	13	3	90.1	65	365	31	27	6	5	3	7	34	1	94	13	1
Felfoldi, Jonathan, Savannah *	0	1	.000	5.65	3	3	0	0	0	0	14.1	13	62	9	9	2	0	0	1	9	0	13	1	0
Fernandes, Kyle, Greenville *	1	0	1.000	5.40	1	0	0	0	0	0	3.1	2	12	2	2	2	0	0	0	0	0	2	0	0
Forbes, Derek, Delmarva	0	0	.000	2.41	16	0	0	0	9	1	18.2	13	80	5	5	3	0	0	0	13	0	18	2	0
France, Ryan, Savannah	1	1	.500	3.81	16	2	0	0	1	0	28.1	25	126	13	12	4	2	0	4	15	2	26	5	0
Francisco, Bartolo, Savannah	1	1	.500	4.24	3	3	0	0	0	0	17.0	16	80	8	8	4	0	0	2	15	0	6	0	0
Galvez, Gary, Greenville	10	4	.714	3.35	31	18	0	0	2	0	126.1	118	540	64	47	12	2	6	7	40	0	87	3	3
Gant, James, Lexington	0	0	.000	2.63	17	0	0	0	7	0	27.1	25	113	8	8	1	3	0	2	12	1	26	4	0
Garavito, Jean, Hickory	2	4	.333	5.20	33	0	0	0	13	0	62.1	81	288	39	36	5	3	2	1	27	2	35	8	0
Garcia, Felipe, Hickory	4	5	.444	4.37	36	0	0	0	22	4	57.2	59	256	39	28	7	2	1	2	29	0	53	5	0
Garcia, Harvey, Greenville	3	5	.375	2.01	32	0	0	0	22	6	44.2	49	204	18	10	3	2	3	5	18	0	54	2	0
Garcia, Jose, Greensboro	3	0	1.000	1.27	5	4	0	0	0	0	28.1	11	102	5	4	1	0	1	1	4	0	39	0	0
Gardner, Adam, Augusta *	3	1	.750	3.44	39	1	0	0	16	1	68.0	59	290	32	26	2	2	1	6	25	0	80	5	1
Gardner, Jarrett, Greenville	2	9	.182	5.06	17	17	1	0	0	0	105.0	136	446	63	59	12	3	0	2	14	0	67	6	0
Gervacio, Samuel, Lexington	1	0	1.000	0.96	5	0	0	0	2	0	9.1	4	33	1	1	0	0	0	0	1	0	11	1	2
Gogal, Jeffrey, Greensboro *	2	1	.667	3.10	9	0	0	0	2	0	20.1	15	81	7	7	3	0	0	2	6	0	19	0	0
Gomez, Jose Luis, Hagerstown	1	4	.200	6.75	17	0	0	0	5	0	30.2	29	149	30	23	6	1	0	5	23	0	24	0	6
Gomez, Warmar, Savannah	0	0	.000	4.70	17	0	0	0	6	0	30.2	44	138	17	16	2	1	1	2	4	0	16	1	1
Gonzalez, Giovany, Kannapolis *	5	3	.625	1.87	11	10	0	0	0	0	57.2	36	231	16	12	3	0	1	2	22	0	84	2	3
Gonzalez, Somer, Savannah	4	4	.500	5.82	30	4	0	0	8	0	68.0	74	310	54	44	6	2	1	9	30	0	52	7	0
Goodman, Christopher, Savannah	2	5	.286	5.43	20	6	0	0	5	0	56.1	67	252	45	34	6	0	2	6	11	0	39	4	0
Goodson, Matthew, Greenville	6	4	.600	2.76	17	12	0	0	3	2	78.1	60	311	33	24	4	2	1	3	20	0	60	4	0
Griffith, Derek, Lakewood *	7	11	.389	3.95	26	26	1	1	0	0	161.2	152	678	79	71	11	1	3	13	59	0	131	8	1
Grube, Jarrett, Asheville	5	5	.500	6.02	32	11	0	0	6	0	104.2	119	464	76	70	17	2	4	14	30	1	98	5	1
Gryboski, Kevin, Rome	0	0	.000	0.00	1	1	0	0	0	0	1.0	1	4	0	0	0	0	0	0	0	0	0	0	0
Guanchez, Argimiro, Greenville *	0	0	.000	8.10	3	0	0	0	0	0	3.1	6	24	8	3	0	0	0	0	7	0	1	0	0
Guerra, Javy, Columbus	2	5	.286	4.96	11	11	0	0	0	0	52.2	51	241	35	29	3	0	3	10	23	0	40	2	1
Guerrero, Julio, Hickory	7	3	.700	4.41	17	16	0	0	1	0	96.0	97	393	50	47	14	0	3	2	14	0	61	5	3
Guillory, Matthew, Hickory	4	7	.364	2.64	22	22	0	0	0	0	109.0	106	462	44	32	11	1	5	4	31	0	82	6	0
Gutierrez, Juan, Lexington	9	5	.643	3.21	22	21	1	0	1	0	120.2	106	503	55	43	10	2	6	10	43	0	100	7	2
Guyette, Kevin, Greenville	4	0	1.000	3.26	12	3	0	0	6	1	30.1	30	128	13	11	2	1	1	3	6	0	28	5	0
Haehnel, David, Delmarva *	1	1	.500	0.79	28	0	0	0	26	16	34.0	20	128	3	3	1	3	0	1	10	0	34	4	0
Hammes, Zachary, Columbus	3	4	.429	4.81	22	8	0	0	2	1	63.2	69	310	43	34	7	3	1	4	52	0	46	7	1

Pitcher, Team	W	L	Pct.	ERA	G	GS	CG	ShO	GF	Sv.	IP	H	TBF	R	ER	HR	SH	SF	HB	BB	IBB	SO	WP	Bk.
Hankins, Derek, Hickory	6	6	.500	4.49	27	27	1	0	0	0	156.1	176	688	90	78	17	1	3	6	43	0	118	12	0
Hansen, Matthew, Kannapolis	1	5	.167	6.11	10	7	0	0	1	0	35.1	33	161	29	24	2	2	1	1	29	0	26	5	0
Hanson, Mark, Lake County	0	2	.000	7.71	10	0	0	0	7	1	23.1	34	117	24	20	3	3	1	4	17	0	18	3	0
Happ, James, Lakewood	4	4	.500	2.36	14	12	0	0	0	0	72.1	57	298	26	19	3	1	0	5	26	0	70	4	1
Harrell, Lucas, Kannapolis	7	11	.389	3.65	26	26	0	0	0	0	133.1	128	605	86	54	8	2	7	11	71	1	85	13	4
Harris, Josh, Lake County	1	0	1.000	13.03	9	0	0	0	6	4	9.2	16	58	14	14	0	2	1	1	15	0	7	3	0
Harrison, Matthew, Rome *	12	7	.632	3.23	27	27	2	1	0	0	167.0	151	671	65	60	17	1	3	6	30	0	118	3	2
Hart, Kevin, Delmarva	9	8	.529	4.55	28	28	0	0	0	0	152.1	170	685	101	77	9	2	8	12	54	0	164	14	3
Henderson, James, Savannah	9	11	.450	5.47	26	26	1	1	0	0	149.2	166	654	99	91	20	3	5	7	50	0	76	3	0
Henington, Henry, Delmarva	3	2	.600	2.31	33	0	0	0	30	16	35.0	34	146	15	9	1	0	0	2	7	1	31	2	0
Henry, Paul, Delmarva	4	1	.800	3.34	28	0	0	0	10	0	35.0	30	150	14	13	1	1	1	4	18	0	28	3	0
Herman, Jason, Hickory	1	0	1.000	4.50	1	1	0	0	0	0	6.0	5	24	3	3	2	0	0	0	2	0	2	0	0
Hernandez, Gabriel, Hagerstown	6	1	.857	2.43	18	18	1	1	0	0	92.2	59	369	29	25	4	2	2	8	30	0	99	2	1
Hernandez, Michael, Lake County *	3	2	.600	1.82	18	0	0	0	1	0	34.2	30	147	14	7	2	0	1	5	12	1	35	7	0
Hlebovy, August, Savannah	0	0	.000	1.29	4	0	0	0	1	0	7.0	3	28	1	1	0	0	0	1	4	0	9	0	0
Hochgesang, Nathan, Columbus	1	0	1.000	6.62	6	2	0	0	1	0	17.2	25	87	14	13	1	0	2	0	7	0	26	3	0
Hoff, Brian, Greensboro	0	0	.000	9.53	4	0	0	0	2	0	5.2	13	31	6	6	1	0	0	0	2	0	4	1	0
Hogan, Patrick, Greensboro	1	1	.500	7.66	24	0	0	0	7	1	24.2	39	124	26	21	5	0	1	2	9	1	17	4	0
Honsa, Christopher, Lakewood	0	0	.000	3.38	4	0	0	0	0	0	8.0	9	40	5	3	1	0	2	0	7	0	4	0	0
Hoyman, Justin, Lake County	2	0	1.000	3.00	9	9	0	0	0	0	48.0	44	203	23	16	3	0	0	3	18	0	36	1	0
Humen, David, Greensboro	3	2	.600	3.90	18	9	0	0	5	1	64.2	57	289	30	28	7	1	0	6	33	1	79	4	0
Hurd, John, Kannapolis	7	3	.700	3.54	44	0	0	0	21	4	68.2	56	297	34	27	3	1	1	5	33	0	41	5	0
Jackson, Kyle, Greenville	3	5	.375	4.78	26	5	0	0	12	2	84.2	96	374	51	45	5	1	5	4	25	0	92	7	0
James, Michael, Greenville	1	1	.500	3.77	30	0	0	0	24	11	43.0	41	189	22	18	1	0	1	4	16	0	38	4	0
Jan, Carlos, Delmarva *	1	2	.333	4.37	28	0	0	0	12	1	47.1	36	211	27	23	2	1	2	2	30	1	55	4	2
Jimenez, Rodny, Rome	0	0	.000	4.63	7	0	0	0	2	0	11.2	9	56	6	6	1	1	1	1	14	0	16	4	0
Johnson, Blair, Hickory	1	0	1.000	4.02	3	3	0	0	0	0	15.2	17	66	7	7	0	3	0	1	7	0	6	0	0
Johnson, Blake, Columbus	9	4	.692	3.33	24	17	1	1	0	0	100.0	83	409	47	37	4	3	4	2	36	0	88	6	0
Johnson, Nathan, Lakewood	12	8	.600	5.04	40	11	0	0	8	0	103.2	129	455	67	58	7	5	8	12	16	1	84	9	0
Jordan, Robert, Greenville *	4	3	.571	1.95	17	0	0	0	12	2	32.1	31	132	9	7	0	0	1	1	11	1	28	2	0
Kendrick, Kyle, Lakewood	0	3	.000	9.13	5	5	0	0	0	0	22.2	38	117	24	23	2	0	2	2	10	0	11	1	0
Knippschild, Charles, Lake County *	2	1	.667	4.00	19	1	0	0	4	0	36.0	37	151	16	16	4	1	1	2	7	1	36	1	0
Knox, Matthew, Lake County	0	0	.000	0.00	2	0	0	0	2	1	2.0	1	7	0	0	0	0	0	0	0	0	0	0	0
Koehler, Kurt, Greensboro	2	9	.182	5.23	29	18	0	0	1	0	117.0	152	541	81	68	7	4	2	17	48	2	90	11	1
Laffey, Aaron, Lake County *	7	7	.500	3.22	25	23	1	0	2	0	142.1	123	572	62	51	5	9	1	4	52	0	69	2	2
Lambert, Bryan, Savannah	1	1	.500	6.00	3	0	0	0	1	0	6.0	6	26	4	4	0	0	0	0	2	0	4	1	0
Landing, Jeffrey, Hagerstown	5	5	.500	4.40	14	14	0	0	0	0	75.2	74	323	41	37	7	2	3	7	34	0	45	6	0
Lerch, Zachary, Greensboro	4	4	.500	4.91	14	11	0	0	0	0	69.2	78	308	53	38	9	5	1	1	24	0	37	7	0
Lincoln, Roger, Greenville *	4	2	.667	4.21	9	9	0	0	0	0	51.1	63	225	24	24	5	0	2	0	14	0	51	1	1
Liotta, Raymond, Kannapolis *	8	3	.727	2.26	20	20	1	0	0	0	115.1	108	468	39	29	5	9	3	2	35	0	107	3	1
Lira, Efren, Asheville	0	0	.000	0.00	1	0	0	0	1	0	0.1	0	1	0	0	0	0	0	0	0	0	0	0	0
Lissir, Alexander, Hickory	0	1	.000	36.00	1	0	0	0	1	0	1.0	3	7	4	4	1	0	0	0	1	0	0	0	0
Little, Jeffrey, Kannapolis	5	3	.625	3.70	34	0	0	0	6	0	58.1	60	245	28	24	5	4	0	4	18	1	49	8	0
Liz, Radhames, Delmarva	2	3	.400	4.46	10	10	0	0	0	0	38.1	33	168	23	19	2	2	1	1	23	0	55	5	0
Lo, Ching, Asheville	7	9	.438	5.65	24	24	1	0	0	0	121.0	148	545	90	76	23	5	5	14	38	0	91	4	0
Lofgren, Charles, Lake County *	5	5	.500	2.81	18	18	0	0	0	0	93.0	73	389	31	29	6	4	2	9	43	0	89	8	0
MacKay, Douglas, Augusta	1	0	1.000	1.96	10	0	0	0	2	0	18.1	19	84	6	4	0	1	0	12	0	13	1	0
Maestrales, Peter, Delmarva	0	0	.000	0.00	1	0	0	0	1	0	1.0	0	3	0	0	0	0	0	0	0	0	1	0	0
Malone, Christopher, Columbus	9	7	.563	3.88	31	21	2	0	2	0	141.2	133	590	77	61	10	4	4	8	41	0	127	5	0
Mannix, Kevin, Hagerstown	3	6	.333	5.36	29	9	0	0	12	2	85.2	98	395	63	51	10	5	6	8	40	4	48	3	0
Marceaux, Jacob, Greensboro	0	3	.000	12.36	5	5	0	0	0	0	19.2	40	105	32	27	4	0	1	1	9	0	12	3	0
Marshall, Brian, Greenville *	1	0	1.000	2.08	9	0	0	0	7	1	13.0	5	54	3	3	1	0	0	2	9	0	12	0	0
Martin, Gregory, Hickory *	0	0	.000	3.00	2	0	0	0	1	0	3.0	3	13	2	1	0	0	1	0	0	0	3	0	0
Martin, Sean, Augusta	6	1	.857	3.74	46	0	0	0	18	7	86.2	96	370	39	36	6	3	2	6	19	0	70	2	0
Martinez, Jason, Lakewood *	0	0	.000	8.18	7	0	0	0	1	0	11.0	22	58	14	10	2	0	2	0	1	0	9	2	0
Martinez, Ronnie, Lexington	13	3	.813	3.67	27	26	0	0	1	0	152.0	142	628	73	62	14	1	4	4	50	2	113	4	3
Matos, Osiris, Augusta	8	8	.500	4.99	29	22	0	0	3	0	135.1	162	590	83	75	12	4	6	8	31	0	79	1	1
Mattheus, Ryan, Asheville	7	6	.538	5.82	23	23	0	0	0	0	128.1	142	578	90	83	16	3	3	12	52	0	102	14	0
Mattison, Kieran, Lake County	1	2	.333	3.52	45	0	0	0	40	24	46.0	45	203	20	18	5	2	0	4	23	0	52	2	0
Mayi, Leonardo, Kannapolis	1	1	.500	5.12	41	0	0	0	6	1	31.2	32	141	20	18	5	1	3	4	16	2	29	2	0
McCormack, Zachariah, Greensboro *	4	2	.667	4.61	26	0	0	0	8	2	41.0	41	178	24	21	2	1	1	4	17	0	33	2	0
McGill, Clint, Lexington	0	0	.000	0.00	1	0	0	0	1	0	1.0	0	3	0	0	0	0	0	0	0	0	0	0	0
McKeller, Ryan, Lexington	4	4	.500	4.99	12	11	1	0	0	0	57.2	68	264	36	32	6	1	1	7	23	0	42	6	0
Melendez, German, Lexington	0	0	.000	5.40	2	0	0	0	0	0	1.2	3	12	3	1	0	0	0	3	0	0	0	0	0
Mercado, Arnoldo, Augusta	0	2	.000	3.94	16	1	0	0	2	0	32.0	22	137	14	14	3	0	1	8	14	0	27	5	0
Merrell, Darric, Asheville	3	4	.429	3.76	52	0	0	0	16	6	83.2	78	336	37	35	7	1	2	6	15	0	68	5	2
Michael, Mark, Hickory	0	2	.000	7.07	3	3	0	0	0	0	14.0	19	65	11	11	2	0	1	1	5	0	13	1	0
Miller, Wade, Greenville	0	0	.000	3.86	1	1	0	0	0	0	4.2	4	19	2	2	1	0	0	0	1	0	4	2	0
Minor, Matthew, Augusta	0	1	.000	7.00	8	0	0	0	6	1	9.0	14	47	7	7	2	0	0	1	8	0	4	1	0
Miramontes, Matthew, Hagerstown	3	2	.600	6.48	25	1	0	0	7	1	41.2	38	206	34	30	3	1	1	19	35	1	34	8	1
Moat, Michael, Kannapolis	6	1	.857	2.35	38	0	0	0	17	1	69.0	61	276	26	18	5	0	2	3	9	0	66	0	0
Mobley, Chris, Greensboro	3	5	.375	2.23	54	0	0	0	47	34	60.2	32	244	16	15	7	4	0	4	33	0	74	4	0
Molldrem, Craig, Greensboro	6	1	.857	2.83	16	10	1	0	3	1	63.2	47	266	26	20	5	0	1	5	27	0	47	1	0
Montero, Oscar, Augusta	1	0	1.000	4.91	2	0	0	0	0	0	4.1	1	16	0	0	0	0	0	1	1	0	10	0	0
Morales, Alexis, Savannah	1	1	.500	4.82	18	0	0	0	9	3	28.0	20	128	17	15	2	0	2	5	25	0	22	0	1
Morales, Franklin, Asheville *	8	4	.667	3.08	21	15	0	0	3	1	96.1	73	398	40	33	6	1	1	8	48	0	108	7	7
Morales, Ricardo, Savannah *	8	7	.533	3.94	25	25	0	0	0	0	137.0	147	575	66	60	16	2	2	7	39	1	99	4	0

Pitcher, Team	W	L	Pct.	ERA	G	GS	CG	ShO	GF	Sv.	IP	H	TBF	R	ER	HR	SH	SF	HB	BB	IBB	SO	WP	Bk.
Moreno, Anthony, Augusta	6	0	1.000	3.81	16	0	0	0	7	1	26.0	20	108	13	11	3	0	0	3	12	0	31	2	0
Morillo, Juan, Asheville	1	3	.250	4.54	7	7	0	0	0	0	33.2	40	152	24	17	2	0	0	1	13	0	43	3	0
Morton, Charles, Rome	5	9	.357	5.20	26	22	0	0	4	1	124.2	124	559	84	72	7	2	7	14	62	0	86	12	2
Muniz, Carlos, Hagerstown	3	4	.429	4.78	30	0	0	0	26	14	37.2	37	166	22	20	6	3	1	2	19	2	43	1	2
Munoz, Luis, Hickory	0	0	.000	0.00	1	0	0	0	0	0	2.2	2	12	1	0	0	0	0	0	0	0	4	0	0
Murdy, Garrett, Lexington	3	2	.600	7.82	25	2	0	0	7	1	50.2	70	241	49	44	10	1	3	2	19	0	45	3	0
Musgrave, Mike, Augusta	3	3	.500	4.93	21	17	0	0	0	0	87.2	96	399	59	48	7	0	1	2	43	0	48	9	1
Nail, Brandon, Hagerstown	1	2	.333	7.06	12	2	0	0	4	0	21.2	21	107	20	17	1	4	5	4	19	0	30	6	0
Nelson, Stephen, Columbus	4	4	.500	4.53	19	4	1	0	6	1	49.2	53	212	32	25	9	0	1	4	11	0	26	0	0
Nestor, Scott, Greensboro	4	6	.400	3.96	58	0	0	0	17	2	72.2	59	318	40	32	7	5	3	9	46	1	80	10	2
Newsom, Randall, Greenville	1	0	1.000	5.06	15	0	0	0	9	1	37.1	39	170	26	21	2	1	2	4	15	1	20	2	0
Niesel, Christopher, Lake County	5	3	.625	4.48	19	11	0	0	2	0	74.1	82	321	46	37	8	2	0	7	20	0	69	1	0
Nix, Michael, Rome	1	3	.250	7.17	18	0	0	0	14	5	21.1	24	106	18	17	1	0	0	3	15	2	22	0	0
Nowicki, Nathan, Greensboro	4	3	.571	5.20	29	0	0	0	12	0	45.0	54	205	36	26	6	3	2	3	19	1	24	0	0
Nunez, Florentino, Asheville	0	0	.000	27.00	1	0	0	0	1	0	1.0	3	8	4	3	0	0	1	0	2	0	0	0	0
Obradovich, Mark, Lake County	0	0	.000	0.00	1	0	0	0	1	0	1.0	2	5	0	0	0	0	0	0	1	0	0	0	0
Odom, John, Augusta	1	1	.500	4.91	3	1	0	0	1	0	7.1	9	32	4	4	0	1	0	0	1	0	7	0	0
O'Flaherty, Liam, Columbus *	3	2	.600	5.96	16	0	0	0	6	0	25.2	30	120	17	17	2	1	2	5	16	1	19	2	0
Ortega, Jose, Lake County	0	0	.000	0.00	2	0	0	0	1	0	3.0	3	12	1	0	0	0	0	1	0	0	0	0	0
Owen, William, Delmarva	1	1	.500	8.44	5	0	0	0	2	0	5.1	4	23	5	5	0	0	0	0	3	0	6	1	0
Ozuna, Modesto, Greenville	1	0	1.000	6.35	15	0	0	0	11	1	22.2	29	114	23	16	3	0	5	6	11	0	7	2	0
Paddock, Joshua, Lakewood	1	0	1.000	5.47	19	0	0	0	7	0	26.1	28	111	16	16	1	2	1	2	9	0	24	1	0
Pannone, Anthony, Augusta	2	1	.667	2.90	10	7	0	0	1	1	40.1	37	171	16	13	4	0	0	1	14	0	30	0	0
Parr, James, Rome	13	4	.765	3.41	26	18	0	0	7	3	126.2	134	534	54	48	13	3	7	4	24	0	98	1	0
Patton, David, Asheville	0	3	.000	10.93	4	4	0	0	0	0	14.0	26	78	23	17	4	0	0	1	8	0	9	1	0
Patton, Troy, Lexington *	5	2	.714	1.94	15	15	0	0	0	0	78.2	59	305	24	17	3	4	0	5	20	0	94	0	0
Paul, Jason, Rome	1	2	.333	5.45	28	0	0	0	18	0	34.2	48	163	23	21	8	1	1	1	15	2	30	2	0
Paulino Del Giudice, Felipe, Lexington ..	1	1	.500	1.85	7	5	0	0	0	0	24.1	21	97	8	5	2	3	1	0	6	0	30	2	0
Payano, Nelson, Rome *	0	0	.000	0.00	1	0	0	0	0	0	4.0	3	15	1	0	0	0	0	0	3	0	2	2	0
Pearson, Kyle, Hickory	2	10	.167	6.17	24	15	0	0	4	1	100.2	141	465	79	69	13	2	2	12	34	0	55	3	1
Peralta, Yader, Greenville	0	0	.000	10.38	4	0	0	0	2	0	4.1	7	25	7	5	0	0	1	1	3	0	2	1	0
Perez, Carlos, Delmarva *	11	8	.579	4.28	27	27	0	0	0	0	151.1	168	666	84	72	10	4	5	3	61	0	146	12	2
Perez, Marcelo, Hagerstown	2	6	.250	3.79	43	0	0	0	31	13	59.1	63	277	37	25	7	3	0	1	32	2	53	4	1
Perez, Oneli, Kannapolis	4	2	.667	3.71	36	2	0	0	10	2	80.0	84	357	41	33	7	2	2	6	32	3	62	4	0
Petrick, Russell, Delmarva *	6	3	.667	3.98	47	2	0	0	3	1	74.2	89	338	41	33	1	4	3	2	30	2	58	4	1
Pinto, Julio, Lake County	0	1	.000	3.86	1	0	0	0	0	0	2.1	4	13	1	1	0	0	0	0	3	1	1	0	0
Plexico, Gerald, Savannah *	0	1	.000	5.87	3	0	0	0	1	0	7.2	8	30	5	5	2	0	1	0	0	0	5	0	0
Plummer, Jarod, Columbus	3	2	.600	4.14	9	8	0	0	1	0	54.1	52	224	27	25	5	0	1	4	6	0	49	2	0
Postlewait, Jacob, Asheville *	7	8	.467	5.99	26	26	0	0	0	0	136.2	177	623	96	91	21	4	2	4	49	0	91	4	1
Potter, Joshua, Delmarva	4	3	.571	4.63	42	5	0	0	9	1	83.2	102	376	54	43	5	2	5	3	25	2	67	6	0
Pratt, Jordan, Columbus	0	1	.000	6.06	6	1	0	0	1	0	16.1	13	75	13	11	1	1	0	3	11	0	14	5	0
Quarles, Jason, Hickory	0	3	.000	2.61	19	1	0	0	9	0	38.0	31	167	15	11	2	4	1	3	26	1	45	5	0
Ramirez, Luis, Delmarva	9	7	.563	2.55	28	27	1	1	0	0	162.1	131	658	53	46	7	2	6	2	54	0	155	5	0
Rawl, Aaron, Lakewood	1	0	1.000	3.68	16	0	0	0	7	0	22.0	26	90	9	9	2	1	0	0	6	0	10	1	0
Ray, Ronald, Augusta	0	1	.000	3.38	1	1	0	0	0	0	5.1	6	27	4	2	0	0	0	0	3	0	6	1	0
Reina, Dimas, Columbus	0	3	.000	5.06	11	6	0	0	3	0	32.0	27	152	21	18	2	3	1	4	34	0	20	6	0
Reineke, Chad, Lexington	10	8	.556	3.52	42	11	0	0	16	4	102.1	84	420	46	40	5	5	1	4	49	1	108	6	0
Rengel, Orlando, Hagerstown	2	5	.286	4.97	14	9	0	0	1	0	54.1	64	248	40	30	5	2	2	6	25	0	46	4	0
Richard, Clayton, Kannapolis *	0	1	.000	5.23	3	2	0	0	1	0	10.1	14	44	7	6	1	0	0	0	1	0	8	1	2
Rickert, Brandon, Lake County *	7	1	.875	3.81	35	0	0	0	16	2	54.1	53	230	30	23	8	6	0	3	20	2	43	3	0
Riera, Jorge, Lake County	0	1	.000	5.14	2	1	0	0	1	0	7.0	4	28	4	4	1	0	0	0	5	0	2	1	0
Robinson, Dennis, Greenville	5	10	.333	6.04	25	22	0	0	0	0	110.1	161	528	95	74	11	2	6	12	30	0	56	8	1
Robles, Lawrence, Asheville	3	2	.600	3.00	8	8	0	0	0	0	42.0	31	172	15	14	6	0	1	3	20	0	33	2	0
Rodriguez, Noe, Kannapolis *	0	0	.000	2.63	16	0	0	0	5	0	13.2	12	67	4	4	0	0	1	4	13	0	13	1	2
Roehl, Scott, Lake County	4	3	.571	2.34	24	0	0	0	9	0	42.1	41	175	15	11	2	1	1	5	7	2	35	2	0
Romero, Levi, Lexington	0	0	.000	0.00	2	0	0	0	1	0	3.2	3	16	1	0	0	0	0	3	0	6	0	0
Rose, Kevin, Lakewood	1	0	1.000	4.60	13	0	0	0	3	0	15.2	14	69	8	8	1	1	3	1	12	0	14	1	2
Rote, Ryan, Kannapolis *	0	1	.000	14.63	9	0	0	0	5	0	8.0	12	46	16	13	3	0	0	1	7	0	13	1	0
Rozier, Michael, Greenville *	6	5	.545	3.90	21	20	0	0	1	0	92.1	94	407	50	40	8	3	3	4	49	0	52	6	0
Russell, Adam, Kannapolis	9	7	.563	3.78	24	24	0	0	0	0	126.1	116	538	61	53	10	4	5	6	55	0	82	5	0
Russell, Stephen, Rome	0	2	.000	3.80	10	2	0	0	1	0	23.2	24	110	14	10	2	0	1	4	12	0	28	0	0
Sack, Darren, Augusta	8	7	.533	5.08	26	25	2	1	1	0	125.2	144	556	90	71	10	4	4	11	38	0	114	6	1
Salankey, Caleb, Augusta	12	8	.600	4.20	28	17	0	0	2	0	111.1	93	453	58	52	6	1	5	5	38	0	116	8	0
Salazar, Richard, Delmarva *	1	0	1.000	9.00	3	0	0	0	3	0	4.0	2	21	6	4	1	0	0	2	5	1	5	0	0
Sanchez, Jonathan, Augusta *	5	7	.417	4.08	25	25	0	0	0	0	125.2	122	531	59	57	8	3	5	7	39	0	166	7	0
Sanchez, Jose, Hagerstown	11	5	.688	4.20	26	24	0	0	0	0	133.0	147	571	73	62	18	2	4	9	37	0	87	7	0
Sanchez, Romulo, Hickory	3	3	.500	4.70	10	10	0	0	0	0	53.2	59	232	34	28	5	3	1	10	19	0	24	4	1
Santos, Arthur, Rome	4	2	.667	3.35	27	3	0	0	10	4	51.0	62	226	24	19	1	1	2	1	13	1	35	3	0
Santos, Jarrett, Greensboro	7	4	.636	3.70	52	0	0	0	15	2	82.2	94	363	43	34	4	2	4	2	23	2	52	5	1
Santos, Reid, Delmarva *	5	8	.385	4.94	27	27	0	0	0	0	147.2	168	645	93	81	17	9	5	10	46	0	127	2	0
Schau, Adrian, Lake County	4	4	.500	4.89	38	2	1	0	7	1	77.1	84	329	50	42	6	5	1	7	16	0	53	5	0
Schmidt, Kyle, Delmarva	0	1	.000	4.50	1	0	0	0	1	0	2.0	2	7	1	1	0	1	0	0	0	0	1	0	0
Schreiber, Zachery, Rome	1	3	.250	2.94	27	0	0	0	18	2	33.2	24	144	14	11	0	0	2	4	22	1	31	5	0
Schroyer, Ryan, Greenville	3	3	.500	2.91	26	1	0	0	17	4	58.2	52	243	23	19	1	4	3	4	18	3	45	3	0
Schultz, Cory, Lakewood	0	0	.000	3.86	2	0	0	0	1	0	2.1	3	11	1	1	0	0	0	0	1	0	0	0	0
Schwabe, Ryan, Delmarva *	0	1	.000	5.40	3	0	0	0	1	0	8.1	14	42	9	5	0	1	1	0	3	0	7	0	1
Schwartzbauer, Daniel, Hickory	0	0	.000	0.00	1	0	0	0	1	0	0.1	0	1	0	0	0	0	0	0	0	0	1	0	0

– 555 –

Pitcher, Team	W	L	Pct.	ERA	G	GS	CG	ShO	GF	Sv.	IP	H	TBF	R	ER	HR	SH	SF	HB	BB	IBB	SO	WP	Bk.
Serfass, Joseph, Hagerstown	1	1	.500	1.23	16	0	0	0	9	4	44.0	32	165	6	6	1	3	1	2	9	2	35	0	0
Shafer, Adam, Lakewood	1	0	1.000	2.51	10	0	0	0	3	0	14.1	13	57	5	4	1	0	1	1	2	0	11	0	1
Shafer, Kurt, Hickory	0	5	.000	5.55	5	4	1	0	0	0	24.1	35	115	25	15	3	2	2	0	9	0	11	1	0
Shoemaker, Scott, Greenville	6	3	.667	3.50	16	15	1	0	1	0	79.2	76	343	35	31	6	2	4	6	36	0	69	1	0
Sipp, Tony, Lake County *	4	1	.800	2.22	13	12	0	0	1	0	69.0	47	260	19	17	5	3	1	0	19	0	71	5	0
Smith, Charles, Hagerstown	0	0	.000	0.00	6	0	0	0	0	0	14.0	3	50	0	0	0	0	0	2	2	0	17	0	0
Smith, Christopher, Delmarva *	1	1	.500	8.54	13	0	0	0	3	0	26.1	46	138	26	25	3	0	2	0	15	1	23	2	1
Smith, Daniel, Rome *	3	2	.600	1.89	19	0	0	0	8	5	33.1	24	137	8	7	1	2	1	1	18	2	45	2	0
Smith, H. Clifford, Hickory	0	0	.000	8.68	7	0	0	0	4	0	9.1	16	46	9	9	2	0	0	0	2	0	6	0	0
Sobkow, Philip, Columbus	2	2	.500	8.39	11	2	0	0	3	0	24.2	40	127	24	23	4	0	1	1	17	0	19	1	0
Sosa, Carlos, Augusta *	0	0	.000	0.00	1	0	0	0	1	0	1.0	1	3	0	0	0	0	0	0	0	0	0	0	0
Soto, Enyelbert, Lexington *	2	1	.667	4.44	16	0	0	0	8	2	26.1	36	112	14	13	5	3	0	0	2	0	16	1	0
Soto, Jesus, Lake County	4	1	.800	1.98	21	0	0	0	8	2	27.1	23	102	8	6	2	0	0	0	6	0	17	1	0
Spillers, Larry, Delmarva	1	0	1.000	4.76	12	0	0	0	3	0	17.0	23	84	12	9	0	0	0	1	9	0	6	0	0
Stanford, Jason, Lake County *	0	1	.000	18.00	1	0	0	0	0	0	1.0	3	6	3	2	0	1	0	0	1	0	0	0	0
Startup, William, Rome *	3	2	.600	2.37	25	0	0	0	13	5	38.0	31	149	13	10	3	2	3	0	6	1	30	1	0
Stirm, Brian, Augusta	7	7	.500	3.89	41	4	0	0	17	4	83.1	82	375	41	36	4	0	4	1	46	2	72	10	1
Sweeney, Matthew, Lakewood	3	4	.429	2.43	13	7	1	0	5	1	55.2	41	218	21	15	2	2	4	3	13	0	25	2	0
Talbott, Travis, Greensboro *	0	1	.000	3.00	18	0	0	0	4	0	21.0	13	82	8	7	1	3	1	0	10	0	13	2	1
Tankersley, Taylor, Greensboro *	2	7	.222	5.18	12	12	0	0	0	0	66.0	74	293	45	38	12	0	1	2	25	0	63	3	1
Thompson, Daryl, Savannah	2	3	.400	3.35	11	11	0	0	0	0	53.2	46	225	23	20	3	0	2	1	24	0	48	3	1
Thompson, Ryan, Lexington	3	9	.250	3.89	50	0	0	0	32	11	71.2	78	299	31	31	5	4	4	3	15	2	76	2	1
Thomson, John, Rome	0	0	.000	0.00	1	1	0	0	0	0	4.0	2	15	0	0	0	0	0	0	1	0	1	0	0
Thurmond, J, Augusta	5	4	.556	3.72	19	9	1	0	1	0	65.1	72	285	38	27	6	3	5	4	15	0	59	2	0
Tiller, James, Delmarva	2	5	.286	6.02	11	8	0	0	1	1	49.1	58	230	44	33	3	2	1	7	23	0	36	4	0
Tompkins, Jacob, Lakewood	0	2	.000	3.86	15	0	0	0	8	1	23.1	20	104	17	10	4	0	1	1	16	0	17	2	0
Torrealba, Yoann, Hickory	6	5	.545	3.52	14	14	0	0	0	0	87.0	94	356	38	34	5	1	2	0	14	0	42	0	0
Torres, Carlos, Kannapolis	1	3	.250	3.53	8	8	0	0	0	0	43.1	28	182	20	17	4	0	2	1	23	0	54	3	0
Trahan, David, Savannah	3	10	.231	6.52	34	3	0	0	19	2	58.0	79	282	50	42	5	1	3	4	31	1	34	5	0
Triplett, Bryan, Lexington	0	0	.000	9.00	1	0	0	0	1	0	1.0	2	5	1	1	0	0	0	0	0	0	0	0	0
Troncoso, Ramon, Columbus	2	3	.400	6.69	13	6	0	0	3	1	37.2	58	183	33	28	2	0	5	4	13	0	27	2	0
Valdez, Luis, Lake County	0	0	.000	4.50	1	0	0	0	1	0	4.0	3	16	2	2	2	0	0	0	0	0	2	0	0
Valdez, Luis, Hickory	0	2	.000	7.50	7	2	0	0	1	0	18.0	24	86	19	15	1	1	1	1	9	0	9	2	0
Vanden Hurk, Henricus, Greensboro	1	2	.333	2.45	4	4	1	0	0	0	22.0	17	90	7	6	1	0	0	1	11	0	26	1	0
Vargas, Jason, Greensboro *	4	1	.800	0.80	5	5	0	0	0	0	33.2	16	126	4	3	1	1	0	2	10	0	33	1	0
Vaughan, William, Greenville	2	5	.286	5.81	11	10	1	0	0	0	52.2	72	251	41	34	4	2	3	1	22	0	39	2	0
Venters, Jonathan, Rome *	8	6	.571	3.93	23	12	0	0	8	3	103.0	100	451	51	45	4	3	3	8	52	1	66	12	0
Villa, Kelvin, Rome *	2	1	.667	1.33	7	3	1	1	2	0	27.0	19	104	7	4	1	0	0	0	7	0	25	0	0
Vines, Barry, Rome	6	7	.462	4.80	23	19	1	0	2	0	129.1	156	560	77	69	17	3	5	5	31	0	104	2	1
Wade, Cory, Columbus	0	2	.000	4.05	12	0	0	0	8	2	20.0	29	99	19	9	2	3	3	1	10	1	14	1	0
Ward, Joshua, Rome	0	0	.000	5.40	3	0	0	0	1	0	5.0	6	21	3	3	0	0	0	0	1	0	7	1	0
Weeden, Brandon, Columbus	2	9	.182	5.70	26	18	0	0	2	1	94.2	101	443	67	60	13	0	6	3	69	1	96	14	0
Weintraub, Jason, Hagerstown	1	1	.500	3.04	10	0	0	0	4	0	23.2	24	99	12	8	2	1	0	1	5	0	15	2	0
Whitaker, Roger, Augusta	3	4	.429	4.66	29	6	0	0	11	5	58.0	54	269	36	30	3	0	3	7	39	0	72	8	1
Wigdahl, Jeffrey, Lexington *	1	1	.500	1.83	30	0	0	0	24	13	39.1	21	155	9	8	1	1	1	2	17	0	58	7	0
Wiggins, Johnnie, Rome *	0	1	.000	10.50	12	0	0	0	3	0	18.0	32	98	23	21	1	0	0	2	12	0	9	1	0
Williams, David, Rome	1	0	1.000	3.86	7	0	0	0	2	1	11.2	11	46	5	5	2	0	0	0	0	0	12	0	0
Williams, Joseph, Hagerstown *	0	0	.000	5.06	3	1	0	0	0	0	5.1	7	27	5	3	1	1	0	0	6	0	3	1	0
Wilson, Brian, Augusta	5	1	.833	0.82	26	0	0	0	24	13	33.0	23	131	7	3	0	1	0	3	7	0	30	0	0
Wilson, Kyle, Asheville	0	0	.000	0.00	1	0	0	0	1	0	1.0	0	3	0	0	0	0	0	0	0	0	0	0	0
Wilson, Kyle, Columbus	1	2	.333	2.16	20	0	0	0	19	2	25.0	16	97	6	6	1	0	0	1	9	1	31	2	0
Wilson, Thomas, Savannah *	4	5	.444	3.82	45	0	0	0	18	5	70.2	69	304	34	30	5	1	4	4	21	1	64	6	4
Wood, Adam, Greensboro *	0	0	.000	4.50	2	0	0	0	1	0	2.0	2	10	1	1	0	0	0	1	1	0	3	0	0
Wood, Timothy, Greensboro	1	2	.333	9.28	5	5	0	0	0	0	21.1	29	109	23	22	2	0	1	0	15	0	10	5	0
Woodrow, Christopher, Lakewood	0	0	.000	3.34	10	4	0	0	2	0	35.0	39	146	16	13	4	2	2	3	4	0	28	1	0
Worrell, Tim, Lakewood	0	0	.000	2.08	3	3	0	0	0	0	4.1	7	20	3	1	0	1	0	0	0	0	6	0	0
Worthington, Timothy, Hagerstown	2	2	.500	1.52	15	4	0	0	3	1	41.1	35	176	10	7	1	2	0	1	23	2	46	3	0
Wright, Dequam, Columbus *	1	5	.167	1.93	30	0	0	0	9	1	60.2	38	254	21	13	2	0	1	7	33	0	68	5	0
Yost, Wendell, Savannah *	0	0	.000	2.63	8	0	0	0	3	0	13.2	9	51	5	4	1	1	0	0	2	0	16	1	0
Yourkin, Matthew, Greensboro *	1	1	.500	2.67	21	0	0	0	8	2	30.1	25	124	11	9	5	0	0	1	7	1	33	2	0
Zaleski, Matthew, Kannapolis	4	4	.500	3.38	48	0	0	0	42	22	61.1	73	271	29	23	2	6	3	2	16	2	42	1	0

COMBINATION SHUTOUTS: Asheville (5) -- Deduno-Grube-Buechner-Beerer, Grube-Morales, Morales-Diangelo-Merrell, Lo-Bright-Merrell, Robles-Merrell-Buechner-Beerer. Augusta (2) -- Sanchez-Martin-Minor, Sanchez-Stirm. Charleston (6) -- Smith-Blackwell, Coke-Rival-Beltran-Parker, Hacker-Smith-Martinez-Beltran, Wright-Rival-Gardner, Hacker-Martinez, Marquez-Martinez-Smith-Beam. Columbus (7) -- Castillo-Hammes, Weeden-Wright-Alvarez, Malone-Akin-Alvarez, Malone-Elbert-Castillo, Elbert-Wright, Malone-Akin-Nelson, Plummer-O'Flaherty-Akin. Delmarva (6) -- Ramirez-Potter-Haehnel, Perez-Cahill-Potter, Ramirez-Cahill, Ramirez-Robinson-Cahill-Henington, Potter-Forbes-Baysinger-Henry, Potter-Petrick-Cahill-Henington. Greensboro (4) -- Vargas-Yourkin-Molldrem, Vargas-McCormack-Santos, Vargas-Yourkin-Mobley, Vargas-Mobley. Greenville (3) -- Goodson-Galvez-Garcia, Shoemaker-Ozuna, Goodson-Galvez-James. Hagerstown (9) -- Sanchez-Worthington-Mannix, Landing-Smith-Muniz, Durkin-Miramontes, Sanchez-Worthington, Sanchez-Eager-Gomez, Rengel-Cova-Perez, Rengel-Alfonzo-Serfass, Devaney-Cova-Perez, Devaney-Serfass. Hickory (3) -- Bloom-Capps, Bloom-Capps, Guillory-Pearson. Kannapolis (11) -- Gonzalez-Little-Zaleski, Gonzalez-Zaleski, Liotta-Egbert-Zaleski, Russell-Moat, Harrell-Zaleski-Hurd-Mayi-Perez, Egbert-Moat, Liotta-Little-Mayi-Zaleski, Liotta-Hurd-Mayi-Moat-Zaleski, Liotta-Moat-Mayi-Zaleski, Russell-Perez, Russell-Bakker. Lake County (10) -- Niesel-Hernandez-Knox, Sipp-Laffey, Sipp-Schau-Hernandez-Mattison, Niesel-Mattison-Ashabraner, Laffey-Roehl-Mattison, Cevette-Burton-Collins-Mattison, Santos-Burton, Bunkelman-Burton-Rickert-Soto, Cevette-Schau-Knippschild, Santos-Schau-Soto. Lakewood (6) -- Carrasco-Allen, Happ-Bisenius-Barrack, Sweeney-Dueitt-Bisenius-Barrack, Baldwin-Bisenius, Happ-Johnson-Dueitt-Bisenius, Baldwin-Dueitt. Lexington (15) -- Martinez-Estrada, Diaz-Soto-Thompson, Barthmaier-Soto-Wigdahl, Patton-Diaz-Estrada, Barthmaier-Estrada-Wigdahl, Patton-Reineke, Barthmaier-Estrada-Thompson, Englebrook-Diaz-Murdy, Gutierrez-Estrada-Thompson, Barthmaier-Estrada, Reineke-Gant, Barthmaier-Diaz-Gant, Martinez-Estrada-Thompson, Paulino Del Guidice-Gant-Diaz-Englebrook, Reineke-Gervacio. Rome (6) -- Harrison-Schreiber-Smith, Atilano-Smith, Atilano-Smith, Parr-Burrows, Parr-Schreiber, Harrison-Paul. Savannah (7) -- Thompson-Cox-Campbell, Bunn-Campbell, Morales-Cox-Campbell, Balester-Campbell, Morales-France-Campbell, Morales-Cox, Cook-Morales-Wilson. West Virginia (5) -- Wahpepah-Rogers-Hinton-Beresford, Wahpepah-Stanczyk, Gallardo-Rogers, Wahpepah-Martin-Barnes-Hinton, Gallardo-Decarlo-Hinton.

NO-HIT GAMES: Galvez (2.1 innings), Delgado (0.1 innings) and Jackson (3.1 innings), Greenville, defeated by Savannah, 4-3, May 19; Parr (8 innings) and Burrows (1 inning), Rome, defeated Savannah, 5-0, June 7; Hernandez, Hagerstown, defeated West Virginia, 1-0, June 19.

TEAM

Team	G	PO	A	E	TC	DP	TP	PB	Pct.
Rome	137	3614	1402	132	5148	120	0	24	.974
Asheville	138	3576	1532	148	5256	117	0	34	.972
Charleston	138	3661	1531	148	5340	135	0	31	.972
Greenville	138	3540	1388	144	5072	121	0	40	.972
Hickory	134	3523	1516	153	5192	120	0	29	.971
Lake County	138	3693	1567	155	5415	153	0	33	.971
Lexington	139	3684	1433	159	5276	125	0	28	.970
Savannah	138	3506	1273	146	4925	122	0	18	.970
Augusta	136	3510	1294	166	4970	107	0	14	.967
Columbus	136	3516	1354	166	5036	138	0	20	.967
Greensboro	138	3650	1549	182	5381	132	0	47	.966
Kannapolis	133	3450	1465	172	5087	108	0	29	.966
West Virginia	138	3632	1560	182	5374	132	0	31	.966
Lakewood	139	3620	1430	182	5232	121	0	20	.965
Hagerstown	137	3683	1484	194	5361	135	0	22	.964
Delmarva	139	3697	1391	216	5304	117	1	25	.959

INDIVIDUAL

FIRST BASEMEN

NOTE: All caps denotes fielding-percentage leader based on 70 games for catchers, 93 for all other non-pitchers and 112 innings for pitchers. *Throws lefthanded.

Player, Team	Pct.	G	PO	A	E	TC	DP
Armstrong, Melville, Rome	.967	11	85	4	3	92	8
Bacon, Matthew, Hagerstown	1.000	2	3	0	0	3	0
BATZ, DANIEL, Columbus	.993	111	909	76	7	992	96
Benavidez, Julian, Augusta	.989	48	337	26	4	367	33
Brice, Thomas, Kannapolis *	1.000	3	28	0	0	28	1
Bruce, Cole, Columbus	1.000	9	72	4	0	76	9
Burt, James, Hagerstown *	.991	41	314	26	3	343	25
Carlin, Michael, Hickory	.997	76	712	44	2	758	60
Carp, Christopher, Hagerstown	.984	80	646	48	11	705	71
Chavez, Dirimo, Greenville	1.000	1	12	1	0	13	1
Coles, Corey, Hagerstown *	1.000	2	7	0	0	7	0
Columbus, Jason, Augusta	.988	47	369	35	5	409	27
Creek, Gregory, Rome	.967	3	27	2	1	30	2
Davidson, Tyler, Hagerstown	.985	17	121	14	2	137	13
Delacruz, Miguel, Delmarva	1.000	1	6	0	0	6	1
Delgado, Dario, Hickory	1.000	2	11	1	0	12	3
De Los Santos, Jose, Kannapolis	.909	2	19	1	2	22	3
Ditter, Brad, Savannah	.975	6	33	6	1	40	5
Dragicevich, Jeffrey, Asheville	1.000	13	97	11	0	108	5
Drobiak, Jayson, Lakewood	.973	26	209	11	6	226	16
Dzurilla, Michael, Lakewood	.990	41	352	33	4	389	24
Easley, Jesse, Greenville	1.000	5	39	2	0	41	5
Eichas, Keith, Rome	.994	56	460	33	3	496	46
Einertson, Mitch, Lexington	...	1	0	0	0	0	0
Figueroa, Juan, Greensboro *	.975	21	186	9	5	200	17
Finan, Ryan, Delmarva	1.000	7	50	1	0	51	7
Fisher, Matthew, Hagerstown	.800	1	4	0	1	5	2
Fransz, Jason, Delmarva	.971	14	95	6	3	104	8
Galloway, Carl, Lakewood	.980	6	43	6	1	50	3
Garza, Mario, Lexington	1.000	1	4	0	0	4	0
Gendron, Steve, Greensboro	.986	8	68	4	1	73	4
Gimenez, Christopher, Lake County	1.000	20	169	5	0	174	13
Gonzalez, Bernard, Kannapolis	.857	1	6	0	1	7	0
Gredvig, Doug, Lakewood	.992	57	483	25	4	512	52
Gutierrez, Juan, Delmarva	.966	15	111	4	4	119	11
Guzman, Carlos, Rome	.988	26	236	21	3	260	17
Hansen, Joshua, Kannapolis	.989	78	710	26	8	744	69
Hathaway, Aaron, Hagerstown	1.000	1	6	0	0	6	0
Hofius, Steven, Hickory *	.985	62	493	38	8	539	43
Holm, Stephen, Augusta	1.000	1	5	0	0	5	0
Hornstaj, Aaron, Augusta	1.000	2	7	0	0	7	0
Humphries, Justin, Lexington	.979	28	220	10	5	235	13
Isaacson, Gregory, Lakewood	.952	6	38	2	2	42	1
Jenkins, Andrew, Greensboro	1.000	9	46	3	0	49	7
Jimenez, Franklyn, Savannah	.991	17	105	7	1	113	9
Jurich, Mark, Rome *	.990	25	193	11	2	206	20
Kelly, Christopher, Kannapolis	.987	27	286	9	4	299	15
Klemm, Christopher, Lakewood *	1.000	5	32	3	0	35	2
Koshansky, Joseph, Asheville *	.989	116	1059	84	13	1156	86
Lane, Richard, Savannah *	.967	9	56	3	2	61	7

Player, Team	Pct.	G	PO	A	E	TC	DP
LeVier, Bret, Greenville	.889	1	6	2	1	9	0
McCann, Bradley, Greensboro	.989	103	967	67	11	1045	85
Montz, Luke, Savannah	1.000	21	163	15	0	178	16
Mortimer, Steve, Savannah *	.988	96	735	66	10	811	68
Nicholson, David, Columbus	.993	18	123	10	1	134	17
Otness, John, Greenville	.991	49	406	26	4	436	38
Pacheco, Fernando, Lake County *	.986	119	1162	62	18	1242	123
Paniagua, Salvador, Greenville	1.000	1	3	0	0	3	0
Pinckney, Andrew, Greenville	1.000	3	33	2	0	35	0
Psomas, William, Hagerstown	.966	4	26	2	1	29	2
Restko, Jason, Greensboro	1.000	1	4	0	0	4	0
Ricks, Adam, Kannapolis	.991	23	202	22	2	226	15
Robinson, Scott, Lexington *	.982	32	250	21	5	276	24
Robledo, Nelson, Asheville	1.000	12	112	6	0	118	11
Sardinha, Duke, Asheville	1.000	1	11	0	0	11	1
Scalabrini, Patrick, Delmarva	.992	31	240	16	2	258	25
Sheldon, Ole, Lexington	.993	66	565	44	4	613	57
Smith, Carl, Delmarva	.980	76	605	45	13	663	48
Sorensen, Logan, Greenville *	.997	85	684	58	2	744	68
Sosa, Carlos, Augusta *	.963	31	224	13	9	246	20
Sutton, Stephen, Lexington	1.000	1	6	0	0	6	0
Terrazas, Ivan, Rome	.988	10	73	6	1	80	8
Thomas, Benjamin, Rome	1.000	7	41	4	0	45	2
Vericker, Brad, Augusta *	.983	21	159	16	3	178	14
Vital, Kevin, Lexington	.965	15	130	9	5	144	12
White, Dean, Rome	.981	6	42	9	1	52	5
Wyrick, Joshua, Hagerstown *	1.000	2	15	1	0	16	3

SECOND BASEMEN

Player, Team	Pct.	G	PO	A	E	TC	DP
Abreu, Johany, Augusta	1.000	1	0	1	0	1	0
Almonte, Sandy, Asheville	.985	27	40	90	2	132	15
Ash, Jonathan, Lexington	.979	54	100	134	5	239	31
Babilonia, Edgar, Lexington	.938	9	13	17	2	32	1
Batista, Wilson, Hagerstown	.966	22	47	67	4	118	21
Berry, Layne, Kannapolis	.977	72	125	208	8	341	39
Brown, Terrance, Rome	1.000	5	6	18	0	24	4
Bruce, Cole, Columbus	1.000	2	2	8	0	10	2
Carter, Brandon, Columbus	.960	44	63	127	8	198	29
Castro, Ofilio, Savannah	.933	8	13	15	2	30	4
Cates, Gary, Delmarva	.961	30	63	85	6	154	23
Chavez, Dirimo, Greenville	.971	12	24	42	2	68	9
Clem, Christopher, Lake County	.833	3	5	5	2	12	2
Cleveland, Brian, Greensboro	.988	51	88	161	3	252	26
Cockrell, Michael, Hickory	.975	14	34	45	2	81	11
Contreras, Jose, Savannah	.912	9	9	22	3	34	3
Coultas, Ryan, Hagerstown	.949	36	75	93	9	177	19
Crist, Justin, Columbus	.875	8	9	12	3	24	2
De La Cruz, Christopher, Lake County	.944	7	17	17	2	36	6
De Los Santos, Jose, Kannapolis	1.000	8	10	18	0	28	5
Denker, Travis, Columbus	.972	67	120	226	10	356	54
Diaz, Rafael, Delmarva	.955	4	4	17	1	22	2
Disla, Lisandro, Augusta	.947	65	89	178	15	282	30
Ditter, Brad, Savannah	.978	42	75	99	4	178	16
Dragicevich, Jeffrey, Asheville	.966	28	37	77	4	118	14
Dzurilla, Michael, Lakewood	.972	50	95	114	6	215	28
Figueroa, Francisco, Delmarva	.972	30	52	88	4	144	12
Fisher, Matthew, Hagerstown	.980	34	76	74	3	153	24
Gaerlan, Armand, Hagerstown	.940	34	64	76	9	149	15
Gendron, Steve, Greensboro	...	1	0	0	0	0	0
Getz, Christopher, Kannapolis	.969	36	68	118	6	192	23
Granadillo, Antonio, Greenville	.978	55	106	158	6	270	32
Grimm, Eric, Delmarva	.949	24	27	48	4	79	8
Guerrero, Francisco, Delmarva	.958	27	53	60	5	118	8
Haines, Kyle, Augusta	.984	33	44	80	2	126	18
Hardy, John, Lakewood	.935	8	13	16	2	31	2
Harman, Bradley, Lakewood	.940	26	65	61	8	134	15
Herrera, Jonathan, Asheville	1.000	3	6	8	0	14	0
Holm, Stephen, Augusta	.889	2	6	2	1	9	1
Holmes, Justin, Lake County	1.000	1	0	1	0	1	0
Holt, John, Rome	.972	119	204	311	15	530	62
Hornstaj, Aaron, Augusta	.970	42	48	112	5	165	23
Isaacson, Gregory, Lakewood	...	1	0	0	0	0	0
Jeroloman, Charles, Greenville	.984	27	46	81	2	129	20
Jimenez, Franklyn, Savannah	.889	2	4	4	1	9	0
Kelly, Christopher, Kannapolis	.833	1	3	2	1	6	0
Kelly, Dustin, Greenville	.960	5	8	16	1	25	3

Player, Team	Pct.	G	PO	A	E	TC	DP
Lara, Christian, Greenville	1.000	1	2	4	0	6	1
LeVier, Bret, Greenville	1.000	1	1	2	0	3	0
Lomack, Jermal, Hickory	.947	51	114	135	14	263	24
Lunetta, Anthony, Lake County	1.000	2	3	6	0	9	1
Mader, Joshua, Lakewood	.976	47	92	109	5	206	25
Maestrales, Peter, Delmarva	.889	19	31	41	9	81	7
Marcial, Robert, Rome	1.000	1	1	3	0	4	0
Marconi, Robert, Delmarva	.970	7	17	15	1	33	6
McCarthy, Ryan, Kannapolis	.941	16	36	59	6	101	10
McGill, Clint, Lexington	.961	38	50	73	5	128	19
McMillan, Beau, Greensboro	.915	23	25	40	6	71	11
Mercedes, Victor, Hickory	1.000	1	3	5	0	8	2
Merchan, Jesus, Lakewood	.985	11	24	40	1	65	10
Mihalics, Joseph, Hagerstown	1.000	7	12	13	0	25	2
Natale, Jeffrey, Greenville	.972	38	74	99	5	178	21
Nicholson, David, Columbus	.987	19	22	54	1	77	9
Nunez, Eduardo, Savannah	1.000	1	1	2	0	3	2
Ortega, Jose, Lake County	.988	18	38	46	1	85	10
Psomas, William, Hagerstown	1.000	2	2	5	0	7	1
Reyes, Argenis, Lake County	.966	16	43	43	3	89	17
Reynolds, Lagatila, Asheville	.947	3	5	13	1	19	2
Ricks, Adam, Kannapolis	.963	5	8	18	1	27	4
Sardinha, Duke, Asheville	1.000	3	7	10	0	17	2
Schade, Ryan, Greensboro	.968	7	9	21	1	31	5
Schwartzbauer, Daniel, Hickory	.980	76	155	244	8	407	51
Seifrig, Cole, Greensboro	.983	66	106	180	5	291	37
Sutton, Stephen, Lexington	.958	46	82	101	8	191	32
SZABO, MARSHALL, Lake County	.984	96	175	268	7	450	74
Triplett, Bryan, Lexington	1.000	1	4	2	0	6	1
Triplett, Calvin, Hagerstown	.979	13	16	30	1	47	6
Valdez, Jose, Asheville	.964	76	119	202	12	333	43
Wald, Jacob, Augusta	1.000	3	7	8	0	15	1
Webb, Billy, Savannah	.953	80	147	198	17	362	44
Webb, Justin, Greensboro	.800	1	1	3	1	5	2
White, Dean, Rome	.962	18	21	30	2	53	3
Witt, Paul, Greensboro	1.000	1	1	2	0	3	0
Zapata, Jose, Delmarva	1.000	7	11	17	0	28	5

THIRD BASEMEN

Player, Team	Pct.	G	PO	A	E	TC	DP
Abreu, Johany, Augusta	...	1	0	0	0	0	0
Ash, Jonathan, Lexington	.944	8	5	12	1	18	1
Babilonia, Edgar, Lexington	1.000	4	2	5	0	7	0
Batista, Norberto, Greensboro	.600	1	1	2	2	5	0
Berry, Layne, Kannapolis	.868	26	18	41	9	68	0
Brown, Terrance, Rome	.909	6	4	6	1	11	1
Bynum, Seth, Savannah	1.000	2	1	3	0	4	0
Caraballo, Francisco, Lexington	...	1	0	0	0	0	0
Carp, Christopher, Hagerstown	1.000	1	0	1	0	1	0
Castillo, Javier, Kannapolis	.848	10	7	21	5	33	0
CASTRO, OFILIO, Savannah	.953	100	72	170	12	254	12
Cates, Gary, Delmarva	.921	18	13	22	3	38	2
Cho, Hyung, Hickory	.913	30	23	50	7	80	6
Clem, Christopher, Lake County	1.000	3	1	2	0	3	1
Cockrell, Michael, Hickory	.940	76	64	172	15	251	16
Creek, Gregory, Rome	.778	4	1	6	2	9	0
De La Cruz, Christopher, Lake County	...	1	0	0	0	0	0
Delacruz, Miguel, Delmarva	.690	10	3	17	9	29	0
De Los Santos, Jose, Kannapolis	.892	83	39	127	20	186	7
Dewitt, Blake, Columbus	.918	109	73	172	22	267	16
Diaz, Rafael, Delmarva	.836	28	15	31	9	55	7
Disla, Lisandro, Augusta	1.000	2	1	1	0	2	0
Ditter, Brad, Savannah	.933	32	20	64	6	90	9
Dragicevich, Jeffrey, Asheville	.978	41	31	100	3	134	11
Dzurilla, Michael, Lakewood	1.000	6	8	11	0	19	3
Fisher, Matthew, Hagerstown	.818	4	2	7	2	11	2
Fulton, Jonathan, Greensboro	.832	73	26	118	29	173	4
Gaerlan, Armand, Hagerstown	.897	14	5	30	4	39	1
Gendron, Steve, Greensboro	.949	25	16	58	4	78	3
Gimenez, Christopher, Lake County	.923	47	29	103	11	143	7
Gonzalez, Bernard, Kannapolis	1.000	1	0	1	0	1	0
Granadillo, Antonio, Greenville	.946	10	10	25	2	37	1
Grimm, Eric, Delmarva	.789	8	3	12	4	19	3
Gutierrez, Juan, Delmarva	.837	17	4	32	7	43	2
Hahn, Donald, Asheville	.921	92	54	192	21	267	10
Harman, Bradley, Lakewood	1.000	1	0	2	0	2	0
Hathaway, Aaron, Hagerstown	1.000	4	1	8	0	9	1
Holm, Stephen, Augusta	.000	1	0	0	1	1	0

Player, Team	Pct.	G	PO	A	E	TC	DP
Holmes, Justin, Lake County	1.000	2	3	4	0	7	0
Hornostaj, Aaron, Augusta	...	4	0	0	0	0	0
Isaacson, Gregory, Lakewood	.913	8	5	16	2	23	0
Jenkins, Andrew, Greensboro	.939	38	23	69	6	98	4
Jeroloman, Charles, Greenville	.930	24	15	38	4	57	5
Jimenez, Franklyn, Savannah	.667	2	2	0	1	3	0
Jones, Chipper, Rome	.833	2	1	4	1	6	0
Klink, Simon, Augusta	.904	131	66	198	28	292	16
LeVier, Bret, Greenville	.870	10	6	14	3	23	1
Mader, Joshua, Lakewood	.905	7	4	15	2	21	0
Maestrales, Peter, Delmarva	.952	9	5	15	1	21	1
Mansolino, Anthony, Hickory	.778	8	6	15	6	27	3
Marcial, Robert, Rome	1.000	3	0	5	0	5	0
Marconi, Robert, Delmarva	.904	29	23	62	9	94	6
McCarthy, Ryan, Kannapolis	.800	2	1	3	1	5	0
McGill, Clint, Lexington	.929	9	2	11	1	14	0
McMillan, Beau, Greensboro	.625	6	0	10	6	16	0
Mihalics, Joseph, Hagerstown	.667	1	0	2	1	3	0
Nicholson, David, Columbus	.954	20	18	44	3	65	7
Orr, Samuel, Lakewood	.913	120	113	253	35	401	39
Ortega, Jose, Lake County	.875	10	2	19	3	24	1
Otness, John, Greenville	1.000	4	4	9	0	13	0
Perez, Eduardo, Columbus	.750	7	3	9	4	16	1
Pinckney, Andrew, Greenville	.903	93	53	181	25	259	19
Pope, Peter, Rome	.944	96	75	179	15	269	17
Psomas, William, Hagerstown	.911	93	72	173	24	269	16
Reyes, Argenis, Lake County	.976	29	16	67	2	85	11
Ricks, Adam, Kannapolis	.925	13	3	34	3	40	2
Santana, Yury, Hagerstown	.750	1	2	1	1	4	0
Santiago, John, Hickory	.840	9	3	18	4	25	1
Sardinha, Duke, Asheville	1.000	1	4	1	0	5	0
Scalabrini, Patrick, Delmarva	.938	32	20	70	6	96	3
Schade, Ryan, Greensboro	1.000	1	0	1	0	1	0
Schwartzbauer, Daniel, Hickory	.900	13	11	25	4	40	3
Seifrig, Cole, Greensboro	.600	5	2	4	4	10	0
Solano, Euvi, Hickory	1.000	1	0	2	0	2	0
Strop, Pedro, Asheville	1.000	2	0	3	0	3	2
Sutton, Stephen, Lexington	1.000	1	1	1	0	2	1
Thomas, Benjamin, Rome	1.000	2	0	3	0	3	0
Torres, Saul, Lexington	.906	36	23	64	9	96	2
Trejo, Jaime, Rome	.944	10	5	12	1	18	2
Triplett, Bryan, Lexington	.955	88	62	190	12	264	15
Triplett, Calvin, Hagerstown	.958	25	14	55	3	72	7
Valdez, Jose, Asheville	.833	4	1	4	1	6	0
Webb, Justin, Greensboro	...	1	0	0	0	0	0
White, Dean, Rome	.922	22	13	34	4	51	3
Whitney, Matthew, Lake County	.901	55	32	141	19	192	15
Zapata, Jose, Delmarva	1.000	2	1	0	0	1	0
Zimmerman, Ryan, Savannah	1.000	4	2	12	0	14	1

SHORTSTOPS

Player, Team	Pct.	G	PO	A	E	TC	DP
Abreu, Johany, Augusta	.947	5	7	11	1	19	2
Batista, Norberto, Greensboro	1.000	9	13	21	0	34	9
Batista, Wilson, Hagerstown	.940	46	92	144	15	251	34
Berry, Layne, Kannapolis	1.000	1	0	1	0	1	0
Bixler, Brian, Hickory	.948	126	195	407	33	635	67
Brown, Terrance, Rome	.938	4	6	9	1	16	1
Bruce, Cole, Columbus	.909	8	11	19	3	33	6
Bynum, Seth, Savannah	.966	48	74	125	7	206	30
Carter, Brandon, Columbus	.833	3	4	6	2	12	3
Castillo, Javier, Kannapolis	.934	37	58	126	13	197	17
Castro, Ofilio, Savannah	1.000	3	1	9	0	10	2
Cates, Gary, Delmarva	.991	27	39	69	1	109	12
Cleveland, Brian, Greensboro	.948	42	70	129	11	210	32
Contreras, Jose, Savannah	.933	4	6	8	1	15	0
Coronado, Jose, Hagerstown	.939	18	28	65	6	99	10
Coultas, Ryan, Hagerstown	.925	54	108	175	23	306	44
Crist, Justin, Columbus	1.000	1	0	1	0	1	0
De La Cruz, Christopher, Lake County	1.000	7	11	20	0	31	7
De Los Santos, Jose, Kannapolis	.889	1	3	5	1	9	1
Desmond, Ian, Savannah	.943	72	130	199	20	349	42
Diaz, Rafael, Delmarva	.895	22	28	74	12	114	12
Dragicevich, Jeffrey, Asheville	.929	19	29	49	6	84	7
Escobar, Yunel, Rome	.977	48	96	159	6	261	25
Finegan, Brian, Lake County	.945	111	196	351	32	579	72
Gaerlan, Armand, Hagerstown	.833	1	2	3	1	6	0
Gendron, Steve, Greensboro	.944	88	160	295	27	482	61

Player, Team	Pct.	G	PO	A	E	TC	DP
Getz, Christopher, Kannapolis	.946	19	21	49	4	74	11
Guerrero, Francisco, Delmarva	.925	20	15	34	4	53	6
Haines, Kyle, Augusta	.889	3	1	7	1	9	1
Hardy, John, Lakewood	.960	31	31	89	5	125	9
Harman, Bradley, Lakewood	.936	78	128	225	24	377	43
Herrera, Jonathan, Asheville	.938	15	18	43	4	65	7
Hornostaj, Aaron, Augusta	.938	22	47	58	7	112	18
Jeroloman, Charles, Greenville	.946	25	40	66	6	112	12
Kelly, Dustin, Greenville	1.000	2	5	4	0	9	0
Kitch, Denver, Delmarva	.913	35	66	92	15	173	21
LARA, CHRISTIAN, Greenville	.951	106	165	284	23	472	64
Laurin, Dominique, Columbus	.937	54	81	126	14	221	35
LeVier, Bret, Greenville	.950	7	7	12	1	20	4
Lunetta, Anthony, Lake County	.818	3	4	5	2	11	1
Mader, Joshua, Lakewood	.913	7	8	13	2	23	1
May, Lucas, Columbus	.893	46	87	131	26	244	35
Maysonet, Edwin, Lexington	.987	45	78	142	3	223	26
McCarthy, Ryan, Kannapolis	.957	76	119	256	17	392	53
McGill, Clint, Lexington	.938	21	32	59	6	97	9
McMillan, Beau, Greensboro	.846	3	5	6	2	13	2
Merchan, Jesus, Lakewood	.957	17	28	61	4	93	13
Mihalics, Joseph, Hagerstown	.973	8	13	23	1	37	5
Natale, Jeffrey, Greenville	1.000	1	0	1	0	1	0
Nelson, Christopher, Asheville	.930	69	116	202	24	342	37
Nicholson, David, Columbus	.966	28	38	77	4	119	20
Orr, Samuel, Lakewood	.964	6	10	17	1	28	1
Ortega, Jose, Lake County	.935	13	15	43	4	62	12
Reyes, Argenis, Lake County	1.000	8	15	26	0	41	7
Rozema, Michael, Rome	.951	50	97	175	14	286	36
Sanders, Marcus, Augusta	.940	109	163	291	29	483	59
Santana, Yury, Hagerstown	.923	7	8	16	2	26	3
Schwartzbauer, Daniel, Hickory	.976	11	13	27	1	41	9
Seifrig, Cole, Greensboro	1.000	1	0	2	0	2	0
Shier, Peter, Delmarva	.937	37	67	110	12	189	24
Strop, Pedro, Asheville	.818	2	2	7	2	11	0
Sutil, Wladimir, Lexington	1.000	6	5	15	0	20	3
Sutton, Stephen, Lexington	.960	9	15	33	2	50	5
Szabo, Marshall, Lake County	1.000	1	0	1	0	1	0
Trejo, Jaime, Rome	.986	14	24	44	1	69	10
Triplett, Calvin, Hagerstown	.900	8	4	23	3	30	1
Valdez, Jose, Asheville	.949	36	59	109	9	177	21
Wald, Jacob, Augusta	1.000	1	3	2	0	5	0
Webb, Billy, Savannah	.957	15	24	21	2	47	2
Webb, Justin, Greensboro	1.000	1	3	3	0	6	2
White, Dean, Rome	.935	24	40	60	7	107	14
Witt, Paul, Greensboro	.667	1	2	0	1	3	0
Zapata, Jose, Delmarva	.688	4	5	6	5	16	1
Zobrist, Benjamin, Lexington	.962	63	100	204	12	316	41

OUTFIELDERS

Player, Team	Pct.	G	PO	A	E	TC	DP
Abreu, Johany, Augusta	1.000	3	8	0	0	8	0
Allen, Trevor, Asheville	.912	17	28	3	3	34	3
Arias, Claudio, Greenville	.932	40	64	4	5	73	0
Armitage, Jonathan, Augusta	.974	111	175	9	5	189	1
Arroyo, Xavier, Greensboro	.947	37	54	0	3	57	0
Ascencion, Quincy, Delmarva	.989	121	252	9	3	264	0
Babilonia, Edgar, Lexington	1.000	11	6	0	0	6	0
Baez, Edgardo, Savannah	.962	122	214	12	9	235	3
Barganier, Brandon, Lexington	.970	34	61	3	2	66	0
Barton, Brian, Lake County	.983	31	55	2	1	58	0
Batz, Daniel, Columbus	1.000	3	3	0	0	3	0
Bernadina, Rogearvin, Savannah *	.989	119	270	10	3	283	2
Bocchino, Anthony, Hickory *	.989	54	88	3	1	92	0
Brice, Thomas, Kannapolis *	1.000	3	3	0	0	3	0
Brinkley, Dante, Hagerstown	.986	37	68	3	1	72	1
Brown, Jeremy, Columbus	1.000	5	8	1	0	9	1
Brown, Kyle, Hagerstown	.957	21	42	3	2	47	1
Brown, Terrance, Rome	1.000	10	18	0	0	18	0
Burt, James, Hagerstown *	.950	14	18	1	1	20	0
Butia, Michael, Lake County	1.000	57	85	1	0	86	0
Buttler, Victor, Hickory *	1.000	22	38	2	0	40	0
Caraballo, Francisco, Lexington	.980	109	191	7	4	202	1
Carroll, Brett, Greensboro	.964	114	199	18	8	225	5
Carter, Brandon, Columbus	1.000	13	14	2	0	16	0
Carter, Ryan, Columbus	.982	55	103	5	2	110	1
Cates, Gary, Delmarva	...	1	0	0	0	0	0
Ciaramella, Matthew, Greenville *	.961	56	95	4	4	103	2
Cockrell, Michael, Hickory	.889	4	8	0	1	9	0
Coles, Corey, Hagerstown *	.913	35	41	1	4	46	0
Concepcion, Ambiorix, Hagerstown	.980	123	287	14	6	307	1
Conroy, Michael, Lake County *	.889	4	6	2	1	9	0
Constanza, Jose, Lake County *	.971	23	30	3	1	34	0
Cook, David, Kannapolis	.976	100	154	7	4	165	1
Corsaletti, Jeffrey, Greenville	.992	58	131	0	1	132	0
Cronkhite, Ian, Greenville *	.975	40	78	1	2	81	0
Crosland, Jason, Lakewood	1.000	3	13	0	0	13	0
Crowe, Trevor, Lake County	1.000	43	92	2	0	94	0
Cunningham, Aaron, Kannapolis	1.000	4	5	0	0	5	0
Delacruz, Miguel, Delmarva	.500	3	1	0	1	2	0
Doetsch, Steven, Rome	1.000	12	21	0	0	21	0
Dragicevich, Jeffrey, Asheville	...	1	0	0	0	0	0
Duncan, Jacob, Delmarva *	.983	100	158	11	3	172	0
Easley, Jesse, Greenville	.988	46	76	6	1	83	1
Eichas, Keith, Rome	1.000	1	4	0	0	4	0
Einertson, Mitch, Lexington	.953	99	137	6	7	150	3
Figueroa, Francisco, Delmarva	1.000	12	19	0	0	19	0
Figueroa, Juan, Greensboro *	1.000	2	2	0	0	2	0
Fitzpatrick, Reginald, Savannah *	.970	75	157	6	5	168	0
Flores, Joshua, Lexington	.857	4	6	0	1	7	0
Fransz, Jason, Delmarva	.920	11	22	1	2	25	0
Frith, Ryan, Lakewood	.985	105	245	12	4	261	2
Gamble, Sean, Lakewood *	.978	102	170	8	4	182	1
Gamero, Jesus, Hagerstown	.923	13	12	0	1	13	0
Garza, Mario, Lexington	1.000	12	6	0	0	6	0
Gaston, Jared, Greensboro	1.000	69	95	7	0	102	1
Gimenez, Christopher, Lake County	.981	40	46	6	1	53	1
Golson, Gregory, Lakewood	.991	89	209	7	2	218	2
Gomez, Carlos, Hagerstown	.959	116	227	8	10	245	2
Gonzalez, Bernard, Kannapolis	.990	56	91	7	1	99	0
Hahn, Donald, Asheville	.980	36	48	2	1	51	0
Hansen, Joshua, Kannapolis	1.000	15	20	0	0	20	0
Hoffmann, Jamie, Columbus	.967	79	144	3	5	152	1
Holmes, Brett, Hickory	1.000	9	19	1	0	20	0
Horwitz, Brian, Augusta	.956	116	210	8	10	228	0
Hosgood, Robert, Asheville *	.955	20	21	0	1	22	0
Jansen, Ardley, Rome	.995	57	173	8	1	182	4
Johnson, Atlee, Hickory	.960	75	136	9	6	151	4
Jones, Brandon, Rome	.960	40	71	1	3	75	0
Jordan, Brian, Rome	1.000	1	2	0	0	2	0
Jurich, Mark, Rome *	.953	22	41	0	2	43	0
King, Clinton, Kannapolis	.949	84	126	3	7	136	0
Klemm, Christopher, Lakewood *	.967	68	108	9	4	121	5
LeVier, Bret, Greenville	.971	39	94	5	3	102	1
Loadenthal, Carl, Rome *	.968	58	115	5	4	124	0
Lomack, Jermal, Hickory	1.000	8	12	2	0	14	1
Longworth, Randall, Lake County	.976	52	81	2	2	85	0
Lowrance, Marvin, Savannah	.980	51	94	5	2	101	1
Macia, Wanell, Hickory *	.966	30	54	3	2	59	1
Maestrales, Peter, Delmarva	1.000	14	23	3	0	26	1
Marcial, Robert, Rome	.667	1	2	0	1	3	0
Martel Jr, Normand, Kannapolis	1.000	8	12	0	0	12	0
May, Lucas, Columbus	.935	26	25	4	2	31	0
McCarthy, Ryan, Kannapolis	1.000	3	6	0	0	6	0
McCurdy, Joshua, Delmarva	.979	26	45	1	1	47	0
McGill, Clint, Lexington	1.000	1	2	0	0	2	0
Miller, Matthew, Asheville	.988	121	163	8	2	173	1
Miller, Randall, Greensboro	.983	114	232	6	4	242	2
Moffitt, Andrew, Delmarva	.980	22	47	2	1	50	1
Moni-Erigbali, Victor, Lakewood	.945	56	98	5	6	109	1
Montgomery, Timothy, Lake County	.962	22	25	0	1	26	0
Mortimer, Steve, Savannah *	1.000	1	1	1	0	2	0
Nelson, Justin, Asheville *	.960	102	153	13	7	173	2
Nunez, Florentino, Asheville	1.000	66	118	10	0	128	2
Otness, John, Greenville	1.000	10	12	1	0	13	0
Owings, John, Rome	.750	2	3	0	1	4	0
Pedroza, Sergio, Columbus	.967	45	86	1	3	90	1
Pence, Hunter, Lexington	.992	72	117	5	1	123	2
Peterson, James, Columbus *	.879	22	27	2	4	33	1
Pietro, Joseph, Greensboro	1.000	11	14	1	0	15	0
Plumsky, Richard, Lakewood	1.000	4	6	0	0	6	0
Powell, Pedro, Hickory	.966	111	244	10	9	263	4
Pritz, Bryan, Greenville	1.000	10	13	0	0	13	0
Reed, Ryan, Lexington *	.900	27	48	6	6	60	3
Requena, Alex, Augusta	.968	108	231	8	8	247	1
Restko, Jason, Greensboro	.910	64	78	3	8	89	1

Player, Team	Pct.	G	PO	A	E	TC	DP
Restrepo, John, Asheville *	.966	44	81	4	3	88	0
Reyes, Argenis, Lake County	1.000	11	18	0	0	18	0
Richmond, Barry, Columbus *	1.000	12	17	1	0	18	0
Rivas, Arturo, Delmarva	.966	124	297	17	11	325	7
Roberts, Daron, Kannapolis	.972	22	35	0	1	36	0
Rojas, Ricardo, Lake County	.931	39	65	2	5	72	0
Russ, Ryan, Columbus	.982	96	214	5	4	223	2
Sapp, Steven, Columbus	1.000	6	8	1	0	9	0
Sardinha, Duke, Asheville	1.000	3	7	1	0	8	0
Sewell, Kevin, Greensboro	.982	32	53	1	1	55	0
Silva, John, Rome	.980	36	94	5	2	101	1
Smith, Sean, Kannapolis	.992	110	229	5	2	236	0
Sosa, Carlos, Augusta *	.966	36	56	1	2	59	0
Soto, Luis, Greenville	.923	15	24	0	2	26	0
Steidl, Sam, Columbus *	.976	54	76	7	2	85	1
Sucre, Antonio, Hickory	.979	96	178	5	4	187	0
Szabo, Jordan, Lakewood	1.000	3	6	1	0	7	0
Terrazas, Ivan, Rome	.936	73	127	4	9	140	0
Torbert, Wallace, Lexington	.973	61	100	7	3	110	1
Trumble, Daniel, Augusta	1.000	6	9	0	0	9	0
Turner, Christopher, Greenville	.967	75	140	6	5	151	1
Valdes, Juan, Lake County	.980	103	190	7	4	201	1
Van Der Bosch, Matthew, Greenville *	.973	33	68	3	2	73	1
Vital, Kevin, Lexington	1.000	1	5	0	0	5	0
Vroman, Douglas, Savannah	.993	57	128	5	1	134	1
Wagner, Michael, Augusta	.986	39	69	1	1	71	0
Watts, Derran, Hagerstown	.951	52	73	4	4	81	0
White, Dean, Rome	1.000	1	2	0	0	2	0
Wilson, Kyle, Asheville	1.000	8	14	0	0	14	0
Wyrick, Joshua, Hagerstown *	.885	15	22	1	3	26	0
YOUNG, MATTHEW, Rome	.992	112	229	8	2	239	2

CATCHERS

Player, Team	Pct.	G	PO	A	E	TC	DP
Alen, Luis, Greensboro	.989	39	240	41	3	284	2
Apodaca, Juan, Columbus	.989	35	263	18	3	284	2
Apodaca, Luis, Savannah	1.000	2	8	1	0	9	0
Armstrong, Melville, Rome	.988	42	237	18	3	258	0
Arroyo, Rafael, Hagerstown	.991	26	201	21	2	224	2
Bacon, Matthew, Hagerstown	1.000	8	44	5	0	49	0
Barksdale, James, Rome	1.000	8	36	6	0	42	0
Bock, Brian, Delmarva	.993	32	269	26	2	297	3
Brant, Derek, Lakewood	.963	35	235	25	10	270	2
Brown, Gregory, Greensboro	.987	30	200	20	3	223	0
Buller, Dayton, Augusta	.982	20	151	10	3	164	3
Clark, Robert, Lexington	.973	46	357	36	11	404	7
Conte, Nick, Augusta	.982	63	457	47	9	513	3
DAntonio, Trent, Greensboro	1.000	15	100	8	0	108	0
Davis, Bradley, Greensboro	.982	59	435	48	9	492	5
Devries, Jonathan, Greenville	1.000	3	23	2	0	25	0
Elliott, Justin, Hickory	1.000	1	7	0	0	7	0
Flores, Jesus, Hickory	.987	71	501	50	7	558	10
German, Agustin, Savannah	1.000	1	10	0	0	10	0
Guarno, Richard, Asheville	.991	12	101	13	1	115	0
GUTIERREZ, GABRIEL, Columbus	.993	71	552	53	4	609	4
Gutierrez, Juan, Delmarva	.988	30	216	23	3	242	1
Hathaway, Aaron, Hagerstown	.983	32	242	49	5	296	3
Hernandez, Francisco, Kannapolis	.981	39	279	26	6	311	1
Holm, Stephen, Augusta	.995	47	373	31	2	406	2
Houston, Matthew, Delmarva	.970	76	554	37	18	609	7
Ivany, Devin, Savannah	.983	84	536	42	10	588	8
Jaramillo, Jason, Lakewood	.974	106	656	86	20	762	8
Jenkins, Andrew, Greensboro	1.000	4	20	0	0	20	0
Lerud, Steven, Hickory	.975	14	66	11	2	79	0
Lisk, Charles, Kannapolis	1.000	3	13	3	0	16	0
Lombardi, Michael, Lakewood	1.000	6	25	3	0	28	1
Lucy, Donald, Kannapolis	.991	48	309	26	3	338	2
McCarthy, Greg, Augusta	.973	13	104	3	3	110	0
Medero-Stullz, Carlos, Columbus	1.000	1	10	1	0	11	0
Montz, Luis, Savannah	.987	43	272	22	4	298	4
Moreno, Junior, Greenville	1.000	2	6	1	0	7	0
Nino, Denny, Hickory	1.000	3	16	0	0	16	0
Noviskey, Joshua, Lake County	.967	34	193	12	7	212	2
Obradovich, Mark, Lake County	.989	9	79	9	1	89	1
Otness, John, Greenville	.987	29	218	18	3	239	1
Paniagua, Salvador, Greenville	.975	58	351	35	10	396	3
Perry, Patrick, Greenville	1.000	14	89	7	0	96	1
Piazza, Anthony, Hagerstown	.961	5	41	8	2	51	1
Poppert, John, Savannah	1.000	13	65	5	0	70	2

Player, Team	Pct.	G	PO	A	E	TC	DP
Puente, Juan, Delmarva	.984	7	54	7	1	62	0
Pyzik, Steven, Rome	.990	17	91	4	1	96	1
Reyes, Milver, Hickory	.985	43	233	28	4	265	4
Ricks, Adam, Kannapolis	.987	35	274	26	4	304	5
Robledo, Nelson, Asheville	.991	67	514	54	5	573	7
Rosa, Wally, Kannapolis	.977	12	72	13	2	87	1
Sammons, Clint, Rome	.988	83	531	62	7	600	4
Sandora, Robert, Savannah	1.000	1	2	0	0	2	0
Santangelo, Louis, Lexington	.980	64	544	49	12	605	4
Smolarski, Freddy, Greensboro	1.000	3	29	1	0	30	0
Stachowsky, Mitchel, Greenville	.970	36	242	20	8	270	1
Toregas, Wyatt, Lake County	.989	98	728	103	9	840	10
Towles, Justin, Lexington	.993	36	280	19	2	301	3
Vital, Kevin, Lexington	1.000	2	3	0	0	3	0
Walker, Neil, Hickory	.982	79	521	86	11	618	3
Westervelt, Christopher, Columbus	.985	34	254	15	4	273	2
Wilson, Kyle, Asheville	1.000	12	73	2	0	75	1
Wilson, Neil, Asheville	.995	52	371	26	2	399	4

PITCHERS

Player, Team	Pct.	G	PO	A	E	TC	DP
Acosta, Kelyn, Augusta	1.000	11	1	1	0	2	0
Akin, Brian, Columbus	.857	35	7	11	3	21	0
Alen, Luis, Greensboro	...	1	0	0	0	0	0
Alfonzo, Edgar, Hagerstown *	1.000	13	3	3	0	6	0
Allen, Kyle, Lakewood *	1.000	21	0	4	0	4	1
Allison, Jeffrey, Greensboro	.867	17	6	7	2	15	0
Almenar, Aristides, Hagerstown	1.000	2	0	1	0	1	0
Alvarado, Andrew, Lexington	.667	9	1	1	1	3	0
Alvarez, Carlos, Columbus *	1.000	20	0	8	0	8	1
Alvarez, Juan, Rome *	...	1	0	0	0	0	0
Alvarez, Timothy, Augusta *	1.000	25	1	6	0	7	1
Anderson, Devin, Rome *	1.000	16	3	4	0	7	0
Ashabraner, Robert, Lake County	1.000	7	1	1	0	2	0
Atilano, Luis, Rome	.900	24	11	16	3	30	2
Bacot, Paul, Rome	1.000	9	4	3	0	7	0
Bailey, Chad, Columbus *	1.000	19	0	4	0	4	0
Bakker, Garry, Kannapolis	.909	18	1	9	1	11	0
Baldwin, Ancil, Savannah	.818	12	3	6	2	11	0
Baldwin, Andrew, Lakewood	.929	27	9	17	2	28	0
Balester, Collin, Savannah	.917	24	3	8	1	12	0
Banks, Demetrius, Kannapolis *	1.000	9	1	0	0	1	1
Barone, Daniel, Greensboro	1.000	12	1	4	0	5	0
Barrack, Jacob, Lakewood	1.000	39	3	10	0	13	1
Barthmaier, James, Lexington	1.000	25	6	14	0	20	1
Batista, Norberto, Greensboro	...	1	0	0	0	0	0
Baxter, Allen, Greensboro	.786	11	5	6	3	14	0
Baysinger, Trent, Delmarva *	1.000	29	2	4	0	6	2
Bedard, Erik, Delmarva *	1.000	1	1	1	0	2	0
Beerer, Scott, Asheville	.800	45	1	3	1	5	0
Bille, Michael, Greensboro	...	2	0	0	0	0	0
Bisenius, Joseph, Lakewood	.800	40	2	6	2	10	0
Bishop, Matthew, Hickory	.909	24	4	6	1	11	2
Blackley, Adam, Greenville *	1.000	14	1	5	0	6	0
Blazek, Christopher, Lexington *	...	18	0	0	0	0	0
Bloom, Kyle, Hickory *	1.000	12	2	10	0	12	0
Bobbitt, Seth, Rome	1.000	2	1	1	0	2	0
Bowman, Charles, Hagerstown	.778	26	0	7	2	9	1
Brandenburg, Adam, Greensboro *	.927	27	7	31	3	41	3
Brazell, Landon, Greensboro	.667	2	1	1	1	3	0
Brice, Thomas, Kannapolis *	1.000	7	0	1	0	1	0
Bright, Adam, Asheville	.978	51	11	33	1	45	1
Brooks, Richard, Kannapolis	.750	6	1	2	1	4	0
Buechner, Christopher, Asheville	.929	53	4	9	1	14	0
Bunkelman, Cody, Lake County	1.000	16	3	8	0	11	1
Bunn, William, Savannah	.833	11	6	4	2	12	0
Burrows, Angelo, Rome	1.000	16	1	2	0	3	0
Burton, Timothy, Lake County	.941	49	3	13	1	17	0
Cabrera, Henry, Greenville	.400	6	1	1	3	5	0
Cahill, Casey, Delmarva	1.000	53	6	13	0	19	0
Campbell, Richard, Savannah	.857	36	1	5	1	7	0
Capps, Matt, Hickory	1.000	35	8	7	0	15	2
Carrasco, Carlos, Lakewood	1.000	13	3	8	0	11	1
Castillo, Albenis, Columbus	1.000	38	2	3	0	5	0
Castillo, Arismendy, Columbus	.500	3	0	2	2	4	0
Castillo, Jesus, Columbus	1.000	6	2	2	0	4	0
Castillo, Jonathan, Hagerstown	1.000	2	1	0	0	1	0
Castor, Parrish, Greensboro *	...	3	0	0	0	0	0
Cerrato, Justin, Lakewood	1.000	4	1	0	0	1	0
Cevette, Daniel, Lake County *	.944	17	4	13	1	18	1

Player, Team	Pct.	G	PO	A	E	TC	DP
Coles, Corey, Hagerstown *	...	1	0	0	0	0	0
Collins, Kyle, Lake County	1.000	36	4	9	0	13	1
Cook, Steven, Savannah	1.000	20	8	5	0	13	1
Coppinger, Joseph, Delmarva	1.000	14	5	7	0	12	1
Correa, Jose, Lakewood	1.000	4	0	2	0	2	0
Cova, Rafael, Hagerstown	.813	24	2	11	3	16	2
Covington, Marcus, Rome	...	5	0	0	0	0	0
Cox, Benjamin, Savannah	.750	42	4	2	2	8	1
Craig, Dustin, Hickory	.857	34	2	4	1	7	0
Daley, Matthew, Asheville	1.000	45	9	11	0	20	2
Davidson, David, Hickory *	1.000	10	0	2	0	2	0
Deduno, Samuel, Asheville	.769	20	11	9	6	26	2
De La Cruz, Maximino, Lakewood	.848	27	11	17	5	33	0
Delgado, George, Asheville	...	10	0	0	0	0	0
Delgado, Jesus, Greenville	1.000	33	4	7	0	11	1
Devaney, Michael, Hagerstown	.967	32	16	13	1	30	2
Diangelo, Jason, Asheville	.833	46	3	7	2	12	1
Diaz, Raymar, Lexington	.917	43	4	7	1	12	1
Digby, Bryan, Rome	...	2	0	0	0	0	0
Dobies, Andrew, Greenville *	1.000	10	4	8	0	12	1
Drage, Derek, Hickory	1.000	37	3	12	0	15	1
Dueitt, Cory, Lakewood	.950	49	6	13	1	20	1
Durkin, Matthew, Hagerstown	.875	19	6	8	2	16	0
Eager, Blake, Hagerstown	1.000	21	6	11	0	17	1
Egbert, John, Kannapolis	.936	30	6	38	3	47	0
Elbert, Timothy, Columbus *	.923	25	3	9	1	13	0
Englebrook, Evan, Lexington	.757	30	10	18	9	37	1
Estrada, Paul, Lexington	.833	46	4	11	3	18	2
Felfoldi, Jonathan, Savannah *	1.000	3	1	4	0	5	0
Fernandes, Kyle, Greenville *	1.000	1	0	1	0	1	0
Forbes, Derek, Delmarva	.500	16	0	1	1	2	0
France, Ryan, Savannah	.750	16	4	2	2	8	0
Francisco, Bartolo, Savannah	.750	3	1	2	1	4	1
Galvez, Gary, Greenville	.929	31	6	20	2	28	0
Gant, James, Lexington	.833	17	0	5	1	6	0
Garavito, Jean, Hickory	.900	33	6	12	2	20	2
Garcia, Felipe, Hickory	.786	36	4	7	3	14	1
Garcia, Harvey, Greenville	.923	32	4	8	1	13	0
Garcia, Jose, Greensboro	1.000	5	4	1	0	5	0
Gardner, Adam, Augusta *	1.000	39	9	9	0	18	2
Gardner, Jarrett, Greenville	.950	17	4	15	1	20	2
Gervacio, Samuel, Lexington	1.000	5	0	1	0	1	0
Gogal, Jeffrey, Greensboro *	1.000	9	0	4	0	4	0
Gomez, Jose Luis, Hagerstown	1.000	17	2	3	0	5	1
Gomez, Warmar, Savannah	1.000	17	2	3	0	5	0
Gonzalez, Giovany, Kannapolis *	.833	11	1	4	1	6	0
Gonzalez, Somer, Kannapolis	.846	30	7	4	2	13	3
Goodman, Christopher, Savannah	1.000	20	0	2	0	2	0
Goodson, Matthew, Greenville	1.000	17	6	14	0	20	1
Griffith, Derek, Lakewood *	.936	26	9	35	3	47	1
Grube, Jarrett, Asheville	1.000	32	4	10	0	14	0
Gryboski, Kevin, Rome	1.000	1	0	1	0	1	0
Guanchez, Argimiro, Greenville *	...	3	0	0	0	0	0
Guerra, Javy, Columbus	.875	11	5	2	1	8	0
Guerrero, Julio, Hickory	1.000	17	7	6	0	13	0
Guillory, Matthew, Hickory	.889	22	1	7	1	9	0
Gutierrez, Juan, Lexington	.938	22	13	17	2	32	3
Guyette, Kevin, Greenville	1.000	12	3	5	0	8	0
Haehnel, David, Delmarva *	.833	28	1	4	1	6	0
Hammes, Zachary, Columbus	.950	22	7	12	1	20	1
Hankins, Derek, Hickory	1.000	27	7	16	0	23	0
Hansen, Matthew, Kannapolis	.667	10	2	8	5	15	0
Hanson, Mark, Lake County	...	10	0	0	0	0	0
Happ, James, Lakewood *	.867	14	4	9	2	15	0
Harrell, Lucas, Kannapolis	.838	26	2	29	6	37	2
Harris, Josh, Lake County	1.000	9	1	1	0	2	0
Harrison, Matthew, Rome *	1.000	27	5	11	0	16	1
Hart, Kevin, Delmarva	.875	28	8	20	4	32	1
Henderson, James, Savannah	.943	26	14	19	2	35	0
Henington, Henry, Delmarva	1.000	33	3	7	0	10	1
Henry, Paul, Delmarva	1.000	28	0	4	0	4	0
Herman, Jason, Hickory	1.000	1	1	0	0	1	0
Hernandez, Gabriel, Hagerstown	.957	18	7	15	1	23	0
Hernandez, Michael, Lake County *	1.000	18	1	1	0	2	0
Hlebovy, August, Greenville *	...	4	0	0	0	0	0
Hochgesang, Nathan, Columbus	.667	6	0	2	1	3	0
Hoff, Brian, Greensboro	...	4	0	0	0	0	0
Hogan, Patrick, Greensboro	1.000	24	3	3	0	6	0
Honsa, Christopher, Lakewood	1.000	4	2	1	0	3	0
Hoyman, Justin, Lake County	1.000	9	4	3	0	7	1
Humen, David, Greensboro	1.000	18	1	5	0	6	0
Hurd, John, Kannapolis	.958	44	1	22	1	24	0
Jackson, Kyle, Greenville	.917	26	8	3	1	12	0
James, Michael, Greenville	1.000	30	1	4	0	5	0
James, Rhett, Greensboro	...	1	0	0	0	0	0
Jan, Carlos, Delmarva *	.750	28	2	4	2	8	0
Jimenez, Rodny, Rome	1.000	7	1	1	0	2	0
Johnson, Blair, Hickory	1.000	3	2	3	0	5	0
Johnson, Blake, Columbus	.917	24	16	17	3	36	1
Johnson, Nathan, Lakewood	1.000	40	2	9	0	11	1
Jordan, Robert, Greenville *	.750	17	2	4	2	8	0
Kendrick, Kyle, Lakewood	1.000	5	2	3	0	5	0
Knippschild, Charles, Lake County *	1.000	19	3	3	0	6	0
Knox, Matthew, Lake County	1.000	2	0	1	0	1	0
Koehler, Kurt, Greensboro	.971	29	7	27	1	35	4
Laffey, Aaron, Lake County *	.955	25	4	38	2	44	5
Lambert, Bryan, Savannah	...	3	0	0	0	0	0
Landing, Jeffrey, Hagerstown	.929	14	7	6	1	14	2
Lerch, Zachary, Greensboro	.895	14	6	11	2	19	2
Lincoln, Roger, Greenville *	1.000	9	2	9	0	11	0
Liotta, Raymond, Kannapolis *	.960	20	4	20	1	25	1
Lira, Efren, Asheville	...	1	0	0	0	0	0
Lissir, Alexander, Hickory	1.000	1	1	0	0	1	0
Little, Jeffrey, Kannapolis	.875	34	5	9	2	16	0
Liz, Radhames, Delmarva	.778	10	4	3	2	9	0
Lo, Ching, Asheville	.970	24	13	19	1	33	1
Lofgren, Charles, Lake County *	.941	18	2	14	1	17	0
MacKay, Douglas, Augusta	1.000	10	0	2	0	2	0
Maestrales, Peter, Delmarva	...	1	0	0	0	0	0
Malone, Christopher, Columbus	.935	31	11	18	2	31	1
Mannix, Kevin, Hagerstown	1.000	29	0	7	0	7	1
Marceaux, Jacob, Greensboro	1.000	5	0	1	0	1	0
Marshall, Brian, Greenville *	1.000	9	2	2	0	4	0
Martin, Gregory, Hickory *	...	2	0	0	0	0	0
Martin, Sean, Augusta	.958	46	8	15	1	24	1
Martinez, Jason, Lakewood *	1.000	7	1	1	0	2	1
MARTINEZ, RONNIE, Lexington	1.000	27	13	15	0	28	3
Matos, Osiris, Augusta	.971	29	16	18	1	35	0
Mattheus, Ryan, Asheville	.810	23	7	10	4	21	1
Mattison, Kieran, Lake County	.800	45	1	3	1	5	0
Mayi, Leonardo, Kannapolis *	1.000	41	1	2	0	3	0
McCormack, Zachariah, Greensboro *	1.000	26	2	9	0	11	1
McGill, Clint, Lexington	...	1	0	0	0	0	0
McKeller, Ryan, Lexington	.867	12	4	9	2	15	1
Melendez, German, Lexington	...	2	0	0	0	0	0
Mercado, Arnoldo, Augusta	.833	16	3	2	1	6	0
Merrell, Darric, Asheville	1.000	52	3	15	0	18	2
Michael, Mark, Hickory	...	3	0	0	0	0	0
Miller, Wade, Greenville	1.000	1	2	0	0	2	0
Minor, Matthew, Augusta	1.000	8	2	1	0	3	0
Miramontes, Matthew, Hagerstown	1.000	25	2	6	0	8	2
Moat, Michael, Kannapolis	.875	38	6	8	2	16	0
Mobley, Chris, Greensboro	.944	54	5	12	1	18	1
Molldrem, Craig, Greensboro	1.000	16	4	6	0	10	1
Montero, Oscar, Augusta	...	2	0	0	0	0	0
Morales, Alexis, Savannah	1.000	18	2	5	0	7	2
Morales, Franklin, Asheville *	.886	21	6	25	4	35	1
Morales, Ricardo, Savannah *	.947	25	4	14	1	19	3
Moreno, Anthony, Augusta	1.000	16	3	2	0	5	0
Morillo, Juan, Asheville	1.000	7	0	1	0	1	0
Morton, Charles, Rome	.947	26	4	14	1	19	1
Muniz, Carlos, Hagerstown	1.000	30	1	7	0	8	1
Munoz, Luis, Hickory	...	1	0	0	0	0	0
Murdy, Garrett, Lexington	1.000	25	1	5	0	6	0
Musgrave, Mike, Augusta	1.000	21	5	15	0	20	1
Nall, Brandon, Hagerstown	.875	12	1	6	1	8	0
Nelson, Stephen, Columbus	.778	19	5	2	2	9	0
Nestor, Scott, Greensboro	.786	58	5	6	3	14	0
Newsom, Randall, Greenville	1.000	15	2	7	0	9	0
Niesel, Christopher, Lake County	1.000	19	7	9	0	16	2
Nix, Michael, Rome	.800	18	1	3	1	5	0
Nowicki, Nathan, Greensboro	.917	29	2	9	1	12	1
Nunez, Florentino, Asheville	...	1	0	0	0	0	0
Oakes, Gerard, Rome	...	1	0	0	0	0	0
Obradovich, Mark, Lake County	...	1	0	0	0	0	0
Odom, John, Augusta	1.000	3	2	1	0	3	0
O'Flaherty, Liam, Columbus *	1.000	16	1	4	0	5	2
Ortega, Jose, Lake County	1.000	2	2	0	0	4	1

Player, Team	Pct.	G	PO	A	E	TC	DP
Owen, William, Delmarva	1.000	5	0	1	0	1	0
Ozuna, Modesto, Greenville	1.000	15	0	3	0	3	0
Paddock, Joshua, Lakewood	1.000	19	1	4	0	5	0
Pannone, Anthony, Augusta	.900	10	5	4	1	10	0
Parr, James, Rome	1.000	26	3	8	0	11	0
Patton, David, Asheville	1.000	4	0	3	0	3	0
Patton, Troy, Lexington *	.842	15	5	11	3	19	1
Paul, Jason, Rome	.857	28	3	3	1	7	0
Paulino Del Guidice, Felipe, Lexington	.857	7	1	5	1	7	0
Payano, Nelson, Rome *	.667	1	1	1	1	3	0
Pearson, Kyle, Hickory	.958	24	11	12	1	24	0
Peralta, Yader, Greenville	1.000	4	1	0	0	1	0
Perez, Carlos, Delmarva *	.875	27	4	17	3	24	1
Perez, Marcelo, Hagerstown	1.000	43	3	7	0	10	0
Perez, Oneli, Kannapolis	.889	36	6	10	2	18	1
Petrick, Russell, Delmarva *	.957	47	3	19	1	23	1
Pinto, Julio, Lake County	...	1	0	0	0	0	0
Plexico, Gerald, Savannah *	...	3	0	0	0	0	0
Plummer, Jarod, Columbus	.600	9	1	2	2	5	0
Postlewait, Jacob, Asheville *	.967	26	4	25	1	30	4
Potter, Joshua, Delmarva	1.000	42	6	8	0	14	0
Pratt, Jordan, Columbus	1.000	6	2	2	0	4	0
Quarles, Jason, Hickory	1.000	19	0	6	0	6	0
Ramirez, Luis, Delmarva	1.000	28	5	14	0	19	0
Rawl, Aaron, Lakewood	1.000	16	1	2	0	3	1
Ray, Ronald, Augusta	...	1	0	0	0	0	0
Reina, Dimas, Columbus	.800	11	3	5	2	10	1
Reineke, Chad, Lexington	1.000	42	5	12	0	17	0
Rengel, Orlando, Hagerstown	.857	14	2	4	1	7	0
Richard, Clayton, Kannapolis *	...	3	0	0	0	0	0
Rickert, Brandon, Lake County	.950	35	4	15	1	20	0
Riera, Jorge, Lake County	...	2	0	0	0	0	0
Robinson, Dennis, Delmarva	.852	25	5	18	4	27	2
Robles, Lawrence, Asheville	1.000	8	1	5	0	6	0
Rodriguez, Noe, Kannapolis *	1.000	16	0	1	0	1	0
Roehl, Scott, Lake County	.700	24	5	2	3	10	1
Romero, Levi, Lexington	...	2	0	0	0	0	0
Rose, Kevin, Lakewood	...	13	0	0	0	0	0
Rote, Ryan, Kannapolis	.000	9	0	0	1	1	0
Rozier, Michael, Greenville *	1.000	21	3	12	0	15	0
Russell, Aaron, Kannapolis	.943	24	11	22	2	35	2
Russell, Stephen, Rome	1.000	10	1	0	0	1	0
Sack, Darren, Augusta	.840	26	9	12	4	25	0
Salankey, Caleb, Augusta	.944	28	5	12	1	18	1
Salazar, Richard, Delmarva *	.000	3	0	0	1	1	0
Sanchez, Jonathan, Augusta *	1.000	25	2	8	0	10	0
Sanchez, Jose, Hagerstown	.935	26	12	17	2	31	3
Sanchez, Romulo, Hickory	1.000	10	1	6	0	7	1
Santos, Arthur, Rome	1.000	27	3	3	0	6	0
Santos, Jarrett, Greensboro	1.000	52	4	15	0	19	4
Santos, Reid, Lake County *	.941	27	7	25	2	34	1
Schau, Adrian, Lake County	.923	38	5	7	1	13	1
Schmidt, Kyle, Delmarva	1.000	1	0	1	0	1	0
Schreiber, Zachery, Rome	.900	27	2	7	1	10	0
Schroyer, Ryan, Greenville	1.000	26	6	11	0	17	2
Schultz, Cory, Lakewood	...	2	0	0	0	0	0
Schwabe, Ryan, Delmarva *	1.000	3	1	2	0	3	0
Schwartzbauer, Daniel, Hickory	...	1	0	0	0	0	0
Serfass, Joseph, Hagerstown	1.000	16	5	5	0	10	0
Shafer, Adam, Lakewood	1.000	10	1	1	0	2	0
Shafer, Kurt, Hickory	1.000	5	2	2	0	4	1
Shoemaker, Scott, Greenville	1.000	16	2	4	0	6	0
Sipp, Tony, Lake County *	.800	13	0	12	3	15	0
Smith, Charles, Hagerstown	1.000	6	1	2	0	3	0
Smith, Christopher, Delmarva *	1.000	13	4	5	0	9	0
Smith, Daniel, Rome	1.000	19	0	2	0	2	0
Smith, H. Clifford, Hickory	1.000	7	0	1	0	1	0
Sobkow, Philip, Columbus	1.000	11	2	2	0	4	0
Sosa, Carlos, Augusta *	1.000	1	0	1	0	1	1
Soto, Enyelbert, Lexington *	.800	16	0	4	1	5	0
Soto, Jesus, Lake County	1.000	21	2	1	0	3	1
Spillers, Larry, Delmarva	.875	12	4	3	1	8	0
Stanford, Jason, Lake County *	...	1	0	0	0	0	0
Startup, William, Rome *	1.000	25	3	4	0	7	0
Stirm, Brian, Augusta	.857	41	6	12	3	21	1
Sweeney, Matthew, Lakewood	.917	13	6	5	1	12	1
Talbott, Travis, Greensboro *	1.000	18	2	6	0	8	1
Tankersley, Taylor, Greensboro *	.941	12	6	10	1	17	1
Thompson, Daryl, Savannah	.842	11	5	11	3	19	1
Thompson, Ryan, Lexington	1.000	50	3	8	0	11	0
Thomson, John, Rome	...	1	0	0	0	0	0
Thurmond, J, Augusta	1.000	19	2	4	0	6	0
Tiller, James, Delmarva	.929	11	4	9	1	14	1
Tompkins, Jacob, Lakewood	.750	15	3	0	1	4	0
Torrealba, Yoann, Hickory	1.000	14	4	8	0	12	1
Torres, Carlos, Kannapolis	1.000	8	1	4	0	5	0
Trahan, David, Savannah	.895	34	8	9	2	19	1
Triplett, Bryan, Lexington	...	1	0	0	0	0	0
Troncoso, Ramon, Columbus	.909	13	2	8	1	11	0
Valdez, Luis, Lake County	1.000	1	1	0	0	1	0
Valdez, Luis, Rome	1.000	7	0	1	0	1	0
Vanden Hurk, Henricus, Greensboro	1.000	4	2	1	0	3	1
Vargas, Jason, Greensboro *	1.000	5	2	6	0	8	0
Vaughan, William, Greenville	.889	11	3	5	1	9	0
Venters, Jonathan, Rome *	.923	23	5	19	2	26	2
Villa, Kelvin, Rome *	.909	7	3	7	1	11	1
Vines, Barry, Rome	1.000	23	7	18	0	25	4
Wade, Cory, Columbus	.667	12	1	1	1	3	0
Ward, Joshua, Rome	...	3	0	0	0	0	0
Weeden, Brandon, Columbus	.923	26	4	8	1	13	0
Weintraub, Jason, Hagerstown	1.000	10	0	1	0	1	0
Whitaker, Roger, Augusta	1.000	29	3	8	0	11	1
Wigdahl, Jeffrey, Lexington *	.875	30	2	5	1	8	1
Wiggins, Johnnie, Rome *	.750	12	1	2	1	4	1
Williams, David, Rome	1.000	7	3	3	0	6	0
Williams, Joseph, Hagerstown *	.500	3	0	1	1	2	0
Wilson, Brian, Augusta	1.000	26	2	4	0	6	0
Wilson, Kyle, Asheville	...	1	0	0	0	0	0
Wilson, Kyle, Columbus	.667	20	1	1	1	3	0
Wilson, Thomas, Savannah *	.929	45	3	10	1	14	0
Wood, Adam, Greensboro *	1.000	2	0	1	0	1	0
Wood, Timothy, Greensboro	1.000	5	1	2	0	3	0
Woodrow, Christopher, Lakewood	.800	10	1	3	1	5	0
Worrell, Tim, Lakewood	1.000	3	0	2	0	2	0
Worthington, Timothy, Hagerstown	.667	15	2	0	1	3	0
Wright, Dequam, Columbus *	.909	30	2	8	1	11	0
Yost, Wendell, Savannah *	1.000	8	0	1	0	1	0
Yourkin, Matthew, Greensboro *	1.000	21	1	3	0	4	0
Zaleski, Matthew, Kannapolis	.900	48	3	15	2	20	0

LEAGUE CHAMPIONS

Year	Team	Pct.	Year	Team	Pct.	Year	Team	Pct.
1948—	Lincolnton*	.627	1963—	Greenville†	.576	1971—	Greenwood	.631
1949—	Newton-Conover	.667		Salisbury	.631		Greenwood	.759
	Rutherford Co. (2nd)†	.627	1964—	Rock Hill	.672	1972—	Spartanburg‡	.788
1950—	Newton-Conover	.627		Salisbury‡	.631		Greenville	.652
	Lenoir (2nd)†	.626	1965—	Salisbury	.641	1973—	Spartanburg‡	.646
1951—	Morganton	.645		Rock Hill‡	.603		Gastonia	.619
	Shelby (2nd)†	.604	1966—	Spartanburg	.682	1974—	Gastonia	.606
1952—	Lincolnton	.649		Spartanburg	.767		Gastonia	.672
	Shelby (2nd)†	.645	1967—	Spartanburg	.730	1975—	Spartanburg	.543
1953-59—League inactive.				Spartanburg	.567		Spartanburg	.614
1960—	Lexington	.707	1968—	Spartanburg	.597	1976—	Asheville	.544
	Salisbury (2nd)†	.650		Greenwood‡	.597		Greenwood‡	.600
1961—	Salisbury	.627	1969—	Greenwood‡	.587	1977—	Greenwood	.557
	Shelby (4th)†	.481		Shelby	.565		Gastonia‡	.590
1962—	Statesville	.563	1970—	Greenville	.576	1978—	Greenwood	.614
	Statesville	.700		Greenville	.619		Greenwood	.565

Year	Team	Pct.
1979—	Greenwood‡	.565
	Spartanburg	.525
1980—	Greensboro	.590
	Charleston	.561
1981—	Greensboro‡	.695
	Greenwood	.549
1982—	Greensboro‡	.681
	Florence	.546
1983—	Columbia	.620
	Gastonia‡	.587
1984—	Charleston	.549
	Asheville‡	.510
1985—	Florence‡	.599
	Greensboro	.540
1986—	Columbia‡	.682
	Asheville	.643
1987—	Asheville	.655
	Myrtle Beach‡	.597
1988—	Charleston (S.C.)	.616
	Spartanburg‡	.500

Year	Team	Pct.
1989—	Gastonia	.657
	Augusta‡	.535
1990—	Columbia	.580
	Charleston (W.Va.)‡	.538
1991—	Charleston (W.Va.)	.648
	Columbia‡	.614
1992—	Columbia	.572
	Myrtle Beach‡	.522
1993—	Savannah‡	.662
	Greensboro	.603
1994—	Columbus	.630
	Savannah‡	.599
1995—	Piedmont	.586
	Augusta‡	.551
1996—	Delmarva	.585
	Savannah†	.511
1997—	Delmarva§	.543
	Greensboro	.536
1998—	Columbia§	.638
	Hagerstown	.574

Year	Team	Pct.
1999—	Hagerstown	.600
	Augusta§	.496
2000—	Piedmont	.657
	Delmarva∞	.544
2001—	Lexington††	.657
2002—	Hickory∞	.597
2003—	Rome∞	.561
2004—	Hickory∞	.607
2005—	Kannapolis∞	.556

*Won championship and four-club playoff. †Won four-club playoff. ‡Won split-season playoff. §Won split season, eight-club playoff. ∞Won split season, four-club playoff. ††Was leading final series of split-season, four-club playoff and was declared champion when Professional Baseball declared a stoppage of play. (NOTE— Known as Western Carolina League from 1948 through 1962 and known as Western Carolinas League through 1979.)

NEW YORK-PENN LEAGUE

LEAGUE OFFICE

President
Ben Hayes
Address
One Progress Plaza
200 Central Ave., Suite 2300
St. Petersburg, FL 33701
Phone
727-576-6300

Teams (affiliation)
Aberdeen IronBirds (Orioles)
Auburn Doubledays (Blue Jays)
Batavia Muckdogs (Phillies)
Brooklyn Cyclones (Mets)
Hudson Valley Renegades (Devil Rays)
Jamestown Jammers (Marlins)
Lowell Spinners (Red Sox)

Mahoning Valley Scrappers (Indians)
Oneonta Tigers (Tigers)
State College Spikes (Cardinals)
Staten Island Yankees (Yankees)
Tri-City ValleyCats (Astros)
Vermont Lake Monsters (Nationals)
Williamsport Crosscutters (Pirates)

2005 FINAL STANDINGS

McNAMARA DIVISION

Team	W	L	T	Pct.	GB
Staten Island Yankees	52	24	-	0.684	...
Williamsport Crosscutters	44	32	-	0.579	8
Brooklyn Cyclones	40	36	-	0.526	12
New Jersey Cardinals	37	39	-	0.487	15
Hudson Valley Renegades	31	43	-	0.419	20
Aberdeen IronBirds	27	48	-	0.36	24.5

PINCKNEY DIVISION

Team	W	L	T	Pct.	GB
Auburn Doubledays	45	30	-	0.6	...
Batavia Muckdogs	36	39	-	0.48	9
Mahoning Valley Scrappers	33	43	-	0.434	12.5
Jamestown Jammers	31	44	-	0.413	14

STEDLER DIVISION

Team	W	L	T	Pct.	GB
Oneonta Tigers	48	27	-	0.64	...
Lowell Spinners	42	33	-	0.56	6
Tri-City ValleyCats	34	42	-	0.447	14.5
Vermont Expos	28	48	-	0.368	2.5

COMPOSITE

CLUB (AFFILIATE), ABBREV	STA	ONE	AUB	WPT	LOW	BRO	NJC	BAT	TRI	MVS	HVR	JAM	VER	ABE	W	L	PCT	GB
Staten Island (Yankees), STA	1	2	8	2	7	6	1	2	2	9	3	1	8		52	24	.684	-
Oneonta (Tigers), ONE	2	...	1	0	8	0	3	1	11	2	1	3	13	3	48	27	.640	3.5
Auburn (Blue Jays), AUB	1	2	...	3	1	2	2	10	0	10	1	8	2	3	45	30	.600	6.5
Williamsport (Pirates), WPT	2	3	0	...	1	7	6	2	3	2	7	2	3	6	44	32	.579	8.0
Lowell(Red Sox), LOW	1	8	2	2	...	3	2	2	6	1	1	2	10	2	42	33	.560	9.5
Brooklyn(Mets), BRO	5	3	1	3	0	...	6	2	1	1	8	2	2	6	40	36	.526	12.0
New Jersey(Cardinals), NJC	4	0	1	4	1	4	...	2	2	0	6	2	3	8	37	39	.487	15.0
Batavia (Phillies), BAT	2	1	6	1	1	1	1	...	2	9	2	8	2	0	36	39	.480	15.5
Tri-City (Astros), TRI	1	5	3	0	8	2	1	1	...	2	1	2	7	1	34	42	.447	18.0
Mahoning Valley (Indians), MVS	1	1	6	1	2	2	3	5	1	...	2	7	0	2	33	43	.434	19.0
Hudson Valley (Devil Rays), HVR	1	2	2	3	1	2	6	1	2	1	...	2	2	6	31	43	.419	20.0
Jamestown (Marlins), JAM	0	0	5	1	1	1	1	8	1	9	1	...	1	2	31	44	.413	20.5
Vermont (Nationals), VER	2	1	1	0	6	1	0	1	9	3	1	2	...	1	28	48	.368	24.0
Aberdeen (Orioles), ABE	2	0	0	6	1	4	2	3	2	1	3	1	2	...	27	48	.360	24.5

Major league affiliations in parentheses.

PLAYOFFS: Semifinals: Auburn defeated Oneonta, two games to none, and Staten Island defeated Williamsport, two games to none. Finals: Staten Island defeated Auburn, two games to none.

REGULAR-SEASON ATTENDANCE: New Jersey, 115,129. Williamsport, 79,253. Brooklyn, 285,818. Auburn, 69,716. Vermont, 106,407. Aberdeen, 239,748. Jamestown, 50,460. Batavia, 40,557. Hudson Valley, 158,423. Mahoning Valley, 153,879. Lowell, 185,000. Oneonta, 45,349. Tri-City, 116,674. Staten Island, 155,541. All-Star Game (at Brooklyn), 9,054. League total, 1,801,954. Postseason (6 games), 12,173.

MANAGERS: New Jersey, Mark DeJohn. Williamsport, Tom Prince. Brooklyn, Mookie Wilson. Auburn, Dennis Holmberg. Vermont, Bobby Williams. Aberdeen, Andy Etchebarren. Jamestown, Mike Mordecai. Batavia, Manny Amador. Hudson Valley, Dave Howard. Mahoning Valley, Rouglas Odor. Lowell, Luis Alicea. Oneonta, Tom Brookens. Tri-City, Gregg Langbehn. Staten Island, Andy Stankiewicz.

2005 BATTING
TEAM

Team	G	TPA	AB	R	H	TB	2B	3B	HR	RBI	SH	SF	HP	BB	IBB	SO	SB	CS	GDP	LOB	ShO	Avg.	OBP	Slg.
Tri-City	76	2915	2578	382	723	991	111	20	39	335	22	25	53	236	3	428	85	33	58	1235	5	.280	.350	.384
Oneonta	75	2920	2547	459	695	1057	129	34	55	411	14	32	43	284	7	619	65	27	45	1173	1	.273	.352	.415
New Jersey	75	2933	2603	334	685	947	129	20	31	293	17	23	43	247	6	607	86	39	71	1246	5	.263	.334	.364
Jamestown	75	2836	2555	338	670	963	105	25	46	294	19	15	43	201	3	609	62	44	40	1093	2	.262	.325	.377
Lowell	75	2959	2571	395	672	969	124	22	43	345	10	21	55	302	5	557	68	25	47	1270	1	.261	.349	.377
Batavia	75	2969	2628	383	683	993	138	22	42	343	16	20	45	260	3	576	48	31	55	1182	5	.260	.335	.378
Auburn	75	2918	2558	372	661	1063	165	18	67	338	38	21	38	259	4	666	26	19	49	1183	5	.258	.333	.416
Staten Island	76	2953	2569	373	664	908	117	17	31	333	32	25	62	265	11	452	67	30	57	1230	2	.258	.339	.353
Vermont	76	2889	2536	356	634	920	102	20	48	317	22	17	48	266	1	664	63	33	69	1127	5	.250	.331	.363

Team	G	TPA	AB	R	H	TB	2B	3B	HR	RBI	SH	SF	HP	BB	IBB	SO	SB	CS	GDP	LOB	ShO	Avg.	OBP	Slg.
Mahoning Valley	76	2943	2562	349	627	881	98	21	38	292	25	16	40	299	6	546	90	38	54	1208	6	.245	.331	.344
Williamsport....	76	2947	2580	349	631	885	117	19	33	297	28	25	54	258	2	556	74	41	42	1224	2	.245	.323	.343
Brooklyn	76	2929	2558	332	621	909	118	22	42	295	27	22	32	290	9	512	107	38	48	1190	6	.243	.325	.355
Aberdeen........	75	2861	2514	296	603	862	126	11	37	266	18	24	29	276	10	688	38	24	48	1167	7	.240	.319	.343
Hudson Valley	74	2785	2486	299	581	855	117	14	43	262	14	16	58	211	7	664	42	25	55	1097	7	.234	.307	.344

INDIVIDUAL

TOP QUALIFIERS FOR BATTING CHAMPIONSHIP

Minimum 205 plate appearances. *Lefthanded batter. †Switch-hitter.

Player, Team	G	TPA	AB	R	H	TB	2B	3B	HR	RBI	SH	SF	HP	BB	IBB	SO	SB	CS	GDP	Avg.	OBP	Slg.
Sanchez, Gabriel, Jamestown	62	260	234	34	83	114	16	0	5	42	0	3	4	16	0	24	11	5	6	.355	.401	.487
Patterson, Ryan, Auburn	71	306	274	52	93	163	23	4	13	65	3	5	3	21	4	53	5	2	5	.339	.386	.595
Joyce, Matthew, Oneonta *	65	283	245	51	81	111	10	4	4	45	1	6	1	28	0	29	9	5	4	.331	.397	.453
Lowrie, Jed, Lowell †	53	240	201	36	66	90	12	0	4	32	2	1	2	34	0	30	7	5	3	.328	.429	.448
Rhymes, William, Oneonta *	61	279	250	48	82	105	11	3	2	27	3	0	1	25	0	15	14	3	1	.328	.391	.420
Groce, Edward, Hudson Valley	70	297	258	49	83	127	13	2	9	35	0	2	3	34	4	53	12	4	3	.322	.404	.492
Nunez, Eduardo, Staten Island †	73	310	281	37	88	120	11	6	3	46	6	0	3	20	1	43	6	3	2	.313	.365	.427
Harris, Clay, Batavia	71	319	280	44	87	119	22	2	2	40	0	3	6	30	2	48	1	1	5	.311	.386	.425
Gabriel, Chad, New Jersey	56	228	207	30	64	85	13	1	2	29	4	2	3	12	0	44	6	1	6	.309	.353	.411
Larsen, Kyle, Staten Island *	67	277	240	32	74	111	19	0	6	49	3	3	13	18	4	35	3	2	6	.308	.383	.463
Marconi, Robert, Aberdeen	60	234	205	34	62	93	14	4	3	17	3	1	3	22	1	38	5	1	4	.302	.377	.454
Yema, Yahmed, Lowell *	55	237	219	35	66	90	17	2	1	29	0	1	0	17	0	21	8	1	3	.301	.350	.411
Acey, Jermy, Auburn †	55	218	193	26	58	87	17	0	4	17	3	0	6	16	1	41	0	1	5	.301	.372	.451
Pearce, Steven, Williamsport	72	312	272	48	82	129	26	0	7	52	0	3	2	35	0	43	2	4	9	.301	.381	.474
Harvey, Bryan, Jamestown	65	275	263	34	79	126	14	3	9	38	0	3	0	9	0	60	4	0	3	.300	.320	.479
Plasencia, Francisco, Vermont *	72	318	280	43	84	141	16	4	11	56	2	4	3	29	0	60	14	3	5	.300	.367	.504
Davis, Leonard, Vermont *	67	257	237	34	71	116	8	8	7	35	1	1	6	12	0	64	8	4	9	.300	.348	.489
Reimold, Nolan, Aberdeen	50	212	180	33	53	99	15	2	9	30	0	2	1	29	1	44	2	0	2	.294	.392	.550
Soto, Luis, Lowell †	65	281	246	39	72	106	11	1	7	48	0	1	7	27	2	46	2	3	2	.293	.377	.431
Boone, James, Williamsport †	68	303	278	44	81	125	12	4	8	42	0	2	7	16	0	85	8	4	1	.291	.343	.450
Holden, Joseph, Brooklyn *	64	251	223	33	65	82	7	5	0	15	2	1	0	30	0	22	8	2	2	.291	.361	.368

DEPARTMENTAL LEADERS: G—Peterson, 75. AB—Peterson, 295. R—Hollimon, 66. H—Sellers, 96. TB—Patterson, 163. 2B—Pearce, 26. 3B—Hollimon, 10. HR—Patton, 14. RBI—Patterson, 65. SH—Sena, 9. SF—Johnson, 7. HP—Cunningham, 21. BB—Contreras, 51. IBB—Stewart, 5. SO—Costanzo, 89. SB—Constanza, 24. CS—Burns, 11. GIDP—Marson, 12. OBP—Lowrie, .429. Slg.—Patterson, .595.

ALL PLAYERS

*Lefthanded batter. †Switch-hitter.

Player, Team	G	TPA	AB	R	H	TB	2B	3B	HR	RBI	SH	SF	HP	BB	IBB	SO	SB	CS	GDP	Avg.	OBP	Slg.
Acey, Jermy, Auburn †	55	218	193	26	58	87	17	0	4	17	3	0	6	16	1	41	0	1	5	.301	.372	.451
Allen, Roderick, Staten Island	6	17	17	2	4	6	0	0	1	0	0	0	0	0	0	4	1	0	0	.235	.235	.353
Alvarez, Jean Carlos, Vermont *	7	29	27	2	4	4	0	0	0	1	0	0	1	1	0	9	0	0	0	.148	.207	.148
Anderson, Matthew, Brooklyn	23	100	90	10	25	38	4	0	3	10	0	1	1	8	0	13	0	0	2	.278	.340	.422
Andrews, Robert, Aberdeen	35	164	141	18	32	41	7	1	0	12	2	0	2	19	0	39	8	2	2	.227	.327	.291
Anson, Kyle, Staten Island †	37	165	131	24	33	40	7	0	0	10	3	1	3	27	1	26	7	2	6	.252	.389	.305
Antoniato, Pasquale, Batavia	34	131	121	12	24	28	2	1	0	13	1	2	2	5	0	10	1	1	4	.198	.238	.231
Apodaca, Luis, Vermont	35	129	109	14	28	33	5	0	0	18	1	1	3	15	0	20	1	0	5	.257	.359	.303
Aranda, Mark, Jamestown *	51	198	179	27	36	74	7	2	9	24	0	1	3	15	2	62	2	1	1	.201	.273	.413
Arnedo, Rolando, Vermont	35	142	112	19	32	34	2	0	0	9	2	0	10	18	0	12	0	2	3	.286	.429	.304
Arroyo, Rafael, Brooklyn	19	62	53	8	10	17	5	1	0	4	1	0	1	7	0	17	1	1	3	.189	.295	.321
Avila, Angel, Aberdeen	19	66	63	4	10	11	1	0	0	1	1	0	0	2	0	22	1	2	2	.159	.185	.175
Baez, Wellinson, Batavia	45	196	170	34	55	89	14	1	6	37	0	1	3	22	0	45	2	1	1	.324	.408	.524
Bell, Joshua, Auburn	46	187	181	13	43	70	16	1	3	17	1	0	1	4	0	65	0	1	4	.238	.258	.387
Bergeron, Jabe, Brooklyn	4	15	13	1	2	2	0	0	0	4	0	0	0	2	0	4	0	0	0	.154	.267	.154
Berkenbosch, Kenneth, Jamestown	12	43	39	5	7	9	0	1	0	5	0	0	1	3	0	13	0	0	0	.179	.256	.231
Bernhard, Steven, Auburn	42	96	80	15	17	20	3	0	0	5	2	0	4	9	0	17	2	1	3	.213	.323	.250
Blair, Cameron, Williamsport	64	284	222	38	47	66	11	1	2	26	3	6	10	43	0	46	9	4	1	.212	.356	.297
Blanton, John, Batavia	6	19	15	0	2	3	1	0	0	2	1	0	2	0	0	3	0	0	0	.133	.222	.200
Bohm, Kyle, Auburn	40	112	98	12	23	37	5	0	3	6	0	1	2	11	0	16	0	1	3	.235	.321	.378
Boone, James, Williamsport †	68	303	278	44	81	125	12	4	8	42	0	2	7	16	0	85	8	4	1	.291	.343	.450
Bormaster, Brian, Auburn	41	142	117	19	38	51	8	1	1	18	2	3	2	18	0	22	0	0	3	.325	.414	.436
Bouman, John, Hudson Valley	47	179	163	12	33	49	4	0	4	19	0	1	0	15	0	56	0	2	3	.202	.268	.301
Brown, Jordan, Mahoning Valley *	19	79	75	15	19	29	1	0	3	7	0	1	0	3	1	7	2	1	3	.253	.291	.387
Brown, Kyle, Brooklyn	17	63	53	5	14	18	4	0	0	3	1	0	1	8	0	16	4	3	0	.264	.371	.340
Brown, Willie, Vermont	47	202	184	28	52	89	9	2	8	32	0	1	5	12	1	56	2	3	8	.283	.342	.484
Burgess, Nolan, Lowell *	10	42	39	5	9	16	4	0	1	7	0	0	0	3	0	15	1	0	0	.231	.286	.410
Burke, Joseph, Staten Island *	37	130	118	14	26	33	4	0	1	13	2	2	0	8	0	12	3	1	3	.220	.266	.280
Burns, Gregory, Jamestown *	65	288	241	43	62	74	5	2	1	11	4	1	3	39	1	84	17	11	1	.257	.366	.307
Butera, Andrew, Brooklyn	55	204	175	13	38	52	9	1	1	23	1	4	2	22	0	33	1	0	7	.217	.305	.297
Butler, Jacob, Auburn	11	42	40	5	8	17	1	1	2	6	0	0	0	2	0	7	0	0	2	.200	.238	.425
Cabral, Marcos, Jamestown	24	91	85	9	19	26	1	0	2	6	2	0	1	3	0	16	3	1	1	.224	.258	.306
Canada, Bradley, Staten Island	10	24	23	0	3	3	0	0	0	1	0	0	0	0	0	8	0	0	1	.130	.167	.130
Cardona, David, Hudson Valley	32	116	107	8	27	47	3	1	5	8	1	1	2	5	0	33	1	0	4	.252	.296	.439
Carroll, Mark, Staten Island	20	81	68	10	14	15	1	0	0	4	0	0	2	11	0	15	2	1	2	.206	.333	.221
Casillas, Omar, Mahoning Valley	43	181	161	31	46	67	10	4	1	16	1	2	1	16	0	40	3	1	2	.286	.350	.416
Castro, Jonathan, Vermont †	7	29	26	7	7	11	2	1	0	4	1	0	0	2	0	8	0	1	0	.269	.321	.423
Celigoy, Joshua, Auburn	23	55	48	8	10	13	3	0	0	6	0	0	1	6	0	16	0	0	0	.208	.278	.271
Chavez, Dirimo, Brooklyn	23	87	75	4	14	20	3	0	1	6	5	1	0	6	0	18	3	1	1	.187	.244	.267

SHORT-SEASON CLASS A New York-Penn League

Player, Team	G	TPA	AB	R	H	TB	2B	3B	HR	RBI	SH	SF	HP	BB	IBB	SO	SB	CS	GDP	Avg.	OBP	Slg.
Chavez, Jose, Mahoning Valley †	43	169	148	18	32	37	2	0	1	8	3	0	2	16	0	27	4	4	3	.216	.301	.250
Chourio, Junior, Auburn	2	2	1	1	0	0	0	0	0	0	0	0	1	0	0	0	0	0	0	.000	.500	.000
Clark, John, Mahoning Valley	38	150	131	20	27	37	5	1	1	9	0	0	3	16	0	41	0	1	3	.206	.307	.282
Clem, Christopher, Mahoning Valley	46	191	161	23	36	54	9	0	3	17	1	1	4	24	0	26	2	0	2	.224	.337	.335
Constanza, Jose, Mahoning Valley †	64	304	270	30	71	86	5	5	0	20	1	1	4	28	1	39	24	6	6	.263	.340	.319
Contreras, Jose, Vermont †	64	294	241	49	61	68	7	0	0	16	2	0	0	51	0	57	14	5	2	.253	.384	.282
Conway, Brandon, Vermont *	36	117	105	10	13	14	1	0	0	4	2	1	3	6	0	42	0	1	2	.124	.191	.133
Cooksey, Joseph, Auburn *	52	162	129	20	31	41	4	0	2	11	6	1	2	24	1	32	5	3	2	.240	.365	.318
Cooper, James, Staten Island *	64	285	243	30	60	76	7	3	1	34	3	2	10	27	1	27	5	9	6	.247	.344	.313
Corley, William, Williamsport	68	287	265	29	74	108	10	6	4	35	0	1	5	16	1	56	3	7	4	.279	.331	.408
Cormier, Richard, New Jersey †	4	16	15	1	2	2	0	0	0	2	0	1	0	0	0	2	0	0	0	.133	.125	.133
Corona, Reegie, Staten Island †	72	289	255	32	58	69	11	0	0	20	4	2	1	27	1	32	9	3	2	.227	.302	.271
Costanzo, Michael, Batavia	73	323	281	47	77	133	17	3	11	50	0	4	3	35	0	89	0	1	3	.274	.356	.473
Cotto, Pedro, Oneonta *	9	32	29	2	8	11	1	1	0	5	1	1	0	1	1	4	0	1	2	.276	.290	.379
Crowe, Trevor, Mahoning Valley †	12	58	51	9	13	20	2	1	1	6	0	0	1	6	0	8	4	3	0	.255	.345	.392
Cumberbatch, Cirilo, Mahoning Valley †	45	164	146	21	38	49	2	0	3	21	0	2	3	13	0	41	5	2	4	.260	.329	.336
Cummins, Daniel, Brooklyn	2	7	7	1	3	4	1	0	0	0	0	0	0	0	0	0	0	0	0	.429	.429	.571
Dahlberg, Kyle, Aberdeen	54	170	149	11	26	41	6	0	3	9	3	1	2	15	0	62	1	1	3	.174	.257	.275
Dalton, Brett, Batavia	36	168	144	18	33	41	6	1	0	13	0	0	4	20	1	29	1	3	1	.229	.339	.285
Daniel, Michael, Vermont *	67	280	235	41	61	84	6	4	3	25	4	5	7	29	0	64	6	7	5	.260	.351	.357
Danielson, Sean, New Jersey †	40	147	131	20	45	50	1	2	0	9	2	0	1	13	0	33	19	1	2	.344	.407	.382
DAntonio, Trent, Jamestown †	7	18	14	5	3	4	1	0	0	2	0	1	0	3	0	2	0	0	0	.214	.333	.286
Davis, Leonard, Vermont *	67	257	237	34	71	116	8	8	7	35	1	1	6	12	0	64	8	4	9	.300	.348	.489
Davis, Zachary, Aberdeen *	47	204	178	21	46	64	11	2	1	25	1	3	0	22	1	53	3	5	1	.258	.335	.360
De La Cruz, Carlos, New Jersey *	44	173	160	17	45	59	5	3	1	12	2	1	1	9	1	44	13	6	0	.281	.322	.369
Delaney, Jason, Williamsport	55	223	197	19	42	50	8	0	0	13	4	1	0	19	0	33	2	2	8	.213	.281	.254
de la Rosa, Jairo, Hudson Valley	34	116	109	15	22	28	6	0	0	8	2	0	1	4	0	36	3	1	2	.202	.237	.257
De Leon, Evandy, Mahoning Valley	45	184	146	28	38	65	4	1	7	30	3	2	5	28	0	37	13	4	2	.260	.392	.445
Delgado, Jose, New Jersey †	47	147	123	13	22	28	1	1	1	5	0	0	5	19	0	39	5	4	0	.179	.313	.228
Devoir, Jordan, Staten Island	16	55	51	4	12	15	3	0	0	3	0	0	0	4	0	17	1	0	2	.235	.291	.294
Diaz, Dennis, Batavia	37	134	118	22	35	38	3	0	0	10	1	0	1	14	0	22	12	7	2	.297	.376	.322
Dobson, Sean, New Jersey	44	179	161	17	44	50	2	2	0	13	1	0	3	14	0	30	2	2	5	.273	.343	.311
Durante, Eric, Hudson Valley	51	215	187	19	47	68	12	0	3	17	7	1	7	13	0	38	3	4	3	.251	.322	.364
Edwards, Matt, Batavia	42	175	155	23	29	41	3	0	3	17	0	2	3	15	0	35	0	1	5	.187	.269	.265
Ellington, Matthew, Jamestown *	9	35	31	3	11	14	1	1	0	1	0	0	2	2	0	6	1	0	0	.355	.429	.452
Ellsbury, Jacoby, Lowell *	35	165	139	28	44	60	3	5	1	19	0	1	1	24	0	20	23	3	4	.317	.418	.432
Evans, Nicholas, Brooklyn	57	245	226	30	57	92	11	3	6	33	0	2	0	17	1	34	0	1	3	.252	.302	.407
Farkas, Zak, Lowell	40	143	132	12	23	36	7	0	2	13	1	0	2	8	0	36	2	1	5	.174	.232	.273
Figuereo, Johan, Vermont *	4	15	13	2	1	1	0	0	0	0	0	0	0	1	0	3	0	0	1	.077	.200	.077
Finan, Ryan, Aberdeen *	60	244	213	21	55	76	15	0	2	33	0	5	1	25	0	41	0	1	8	.258	.332	.357
Fisher, Matthew, Brooklyn	2	9	8	2	1	1	0	0	0	0	0	0	0	1	0	2	1	0	0	.125	.222	.125
Fleisher, Mark, Aberdeen	61	267	231	34	64	97	12	0	7	32	0	5	6	25	2	55	0	2	5	.277	.356	.420
Fornasiere, Matthew, Mahoning Valley *	67	297	238	37	61	81	15	1	1	28	2	3	6	48	2	50	5	0	5	.256	.390	.340
Frias, Fernando, Hudson Valley	8	33	28	5	9	14	2	0	1	4	0	0	0	5	0	9	1	1	1	.321	.424	.500
Gabriel, Chad, New Jersey	56	228	207	30	64	85	13	1	2	29	4	2	3	12	0	44	6	1	6	.309	.353	.411
Gaerlan, Armand, Brooklyn	28	112	101	14	22	34	4	1	2	15	1	3	0	7	0	19	8	1	5	.218	.261	.337
Galloway, Carl, Batavia	34	128	120	7	29	44	10	1	1	15	0	1	5	2	0	0	4	0	2	.242	.281	.367
Gamero, Jesus, Brooklyn	53	209	190	21	45	55	3	2	1	20	2	4	3	10	0	26	5	2	6	.237	.280	.289
Garcia, Felipe, Staten Island	50	190	162	30	41	59	7	1	3	17	0	2	10	16	0	38	1	2	3	.253	.353	.364
Garcia, Julio Cesar, Mahoning Valley †	6	23	20	5	5	6	1	0	0	4	0	0	0	3	0	6	0	1	0	.250	.348	.300
Gardner, Brett, Staten Island *	73	335	282	62	80	106	9	1	5	32	3	5	6	39	1	49	19	3	4	.284	.377	.376
Garibaldi, Anthony, Auburn	35	131	116	19	22	39	4	2	3	14	4	0	6	5	0	32	2	1	2	.190	.260	.336
German, Agustin, Vermont	3	12	10	1	1	1	0	0	0	1	1	0	0	1	0	5	0	0	0	.100	.182	.100
Gonzalez, Gregory, Brooklyn *	33	136	124	20	36	42	4	1	0	11	2	0	0	10	0	17	18	3	1	.290	.343	.339
Gonzalez, Hector, Staten Island †	23	82	66	13	11	21	1	3	1	7	3	1	1	11	1	16	2	0	1	.167	.291	.318
Gonzalez, Jesus, Auburn	6	16	15	3	4	4	0	0	0	0	0	0	1	0	0	1	0	2	0	.267	.313	.267
Gosewisch, Ian, Batavia	1	9	9	0	2	3	1	0	0	2	...	0	0	...	0	3	0	0	0	.222	.222	.333
Gosewisch, James, Batavia	9	40	29	2	7	7	0	0	0	3	0	0	2	0	3	0	0	0	1	.241	.290	.241
Grandstrand, Brett, Williamsport	24	93	79	8	18	26	6	1	0	7	1	2	0	11	0	15	3	1	0	.228	.315	.329
Greene, James, New Jersey	35	159	138	28	36	51	12	0	1	18	0	1	5	15	1	37	13	1	7	.261	.352	.370
Groce, Edward, Hudson Valley	70	297	258	49	83	127	13	2	9	35	0	2	3	34	0	53	12	4	3	.322	.404	.492
Grogan, Timothy, Brooklyn *	17	64	49	7	8	13	2	0	1	2	1	0	1	13	0	12	1	0	0	.163	.349	.265
Grullon, Leonardo, Oneonta	30	106	98	17	24	42	6	0	4	19	2	0	4	2	0	39	0	2	1	.245	.288	.429
Guerrero, Francisco, Aberdeen	35	122	112	8	31	36	5	0	0	11	4	1	1	0	0	22	6	1	2	.277	.305	.321
Guerrero, James, Jamestown	62	265	235	35	57	84	12	3	3	26	0	1	9	20	0	56	7	2	4	.243	.325	.357
Guevara, Orlando, Batavia †	14	49	47	6	12	15	1	1	0	5	1	0	0	1	0	12	0	3	3	.255	.271	.319
Gutierrez, Christopher, Auburn	21	69	62	8	14	21	5	1	0	6	3	0	2	2	0	17	0	1	1	.226	.273	.339
Guzman, Francisco, Vermont	9	33	32	8	15	23	2	0	2	7	0	0	1	0	0	4	0	0	0	.469	.485	.719
Hall, James, Hudson Valley *	69	274	250	33	58	85	9	3	4	29	0	1	6	17	3	59	5	3	5	.232	.296	.340
Hardy, John, Batavia	36	151	139	11	41	55	10	2	0	17	2	1	1	8	0	21	3	2	4	.295	.336	.396
Harris, Clay, Batavia	71	319	280	44	87	119	22	2	2	40	0	3	6	30	2	48	1	1	5	.311	.386	.425
Harvey, Bryan, Jamestown	65	275	263	34	79	126	14	3	9	38	0	3	0	9	0	60	4	0	3	.300	.320	.479
Haske, Mark, Oneonta *	45	181	159	29	43	56	6	2	1	27	1	4	3	15	0	25	2	2	5	.270	.337	.352
Hayes, Brett, Jamestown	36	131	117	11	28	39	6	1	1	12	0	1	1	12	0	21	3	3	3	.239	.313	.333
Hayes, Calvin, New Jersey	9	40	37	5	7	7	0	0	0	1	0	0	0	3	0	4	3	0	1	.189	.250	.189
Head, Stephen, Mahoning Valley *	10	45	37	11	16	38	4	0	6	14	0	0	0	8	0	5	0	0	0	.432	.533	1.027
Hicks, Joseph, Williamsport	17	70	64	9	15	18	3	0	0	5	0	0	0	6	0	15	1	0	0	.234	.300	.281
Hiser, Charles, Mahoning Valley	25	106	99	14	26	55	5	3	6	18	0	0	1	6	1	33	1	0	1	.263	.311	.556
Holden, Joseph, Brooklyn *	64	251	223	33	65	82	7	5	0	15	2	1	3	22	0	30	22	8	2	.291	.361	.368
Hollimon, Michael, Oneonta †	72	313	256	66	71	143	13	10	13	53	1	5	2	50	1	76	8	3	5	.277	.389	.559

Player, Team	G	TPA	AB	R	H	TB	2B	3B	HR	RBI	SH	SF	HP	BB	IBB	SO	SB	CS	GDP	Avg.	OBP	Slg.
Howell, John, Vermont *	29	124	113	17	41	55	5	0	3	17	0	2	0	9	0	20	0	1	3	.363	.403	.487
Hughes, John, Hudson Valley *	58	239	219	34	61	103	18	0	8	30	0	1	4	15	0	53	3	2	6	.279	.335	.470
Jamieson, Alex, Hudson Valley	20	69	62	8	21	32	6	1	1	12	0	1	1	5	0	12	0	0	0	.339	.391	.516
Jenkins, Andrew, Jamestown	4	17	14	2	7	9	2	0	0	1	0	1	0	2	0	0	1	0	0	.500	.529	.643
Johnson, Jay, Lowell	60	252	220	35	60	85	12	2	3	38	0	7	2	23	0	40	3	2	2	.273	.337	.386
Johnson, Joshua, Hudson Valley	37	133	118	13	23	35	6	0	2	10	1	1	4	9	0	36	0	0	2	.195	.273	.297
Jones, Christopher, Williamsport	32	126	114	6	26	30	4	0	0	13	1	1	3	7	0	20	2	1	2	.228	.288	.263
Joyce, Matthew, Oneonta *	65	283	245	51	81	111	10	4	4	45	1	6	1	28	0	29	9	5	4	.331	.397	.453
Justice, Justin, Oneonta *	46	190	160	23	44	70	12	4	2	35	0	1	5	24	1	51	3	1	0	.275	.384	.438
Kapler, Gabriel, Lowell	2	9	8	1	1	1	0	0	0	0	0	0	0	1	0	3	0	0	0	.125	.222	.125
Kelly, Dustin, Lowell	44	179	153	21	34	43	6	0	1	15	0	1	1	24	0	27	2	0	3	.222	.330	.281
Kennedy, David, Hudson Valley †	55	246	213	29	48	69	11	5	0	17	0	1	8	24	0	56	4	2	2	.225	.325	.324
Konecny, Daniel, Oneonta	1	0	0	1	0	0	0	0	0	0	0	0	0	0	0	0	0	0	0	...	...	...
Kouzmanoff, Kevin, Mahoning Valley	3	8	7	0	1	1	0	0	0	0	0	0	0	1	0	2	0	0	0	.143	.250	.143
Kutler, Matthew, Jamestown *	8	29	29	8	13	22	4	1	1	9	0	0	0	0	0	2	0	0	1	.448	.448	.759
Lafountain, Jason, Staten Island †	3	9	9	1	3	5	0	1	0	0	0	0	0	0	0	3	0	0	0	.333	.333	.556
Lane, Andrew, Vermont	34	130	113	9	23	28	5	0	0	11	3	0	1	13	0	21	2	0	1	.204	.291	.248
Larish, Jeffrey, Oneonta *	18	79	64	16	19	40	3	0	6	13	0	0	2	13	0	6	0	0	0	.297	.430	.625
Larsen, Kyle, Staten Island *	67	277	240	32	74	111	19	0	6	49	3	3	13	18	4	35	3	2	6	.308	.383	.463
Laster, Jeramy, Oneonta	43	137	120	19	25	38	3	2	2	14	1	2	1	13	0	53	6	2	1	.208	.287	.317
Leonard, Donald, Lowell	22	80	70	8	21	27	1	1	1	7	0	1	0	9	0	9	0	0	4	.300	.375	.386
Lerud, Steven, Williamsport *	10	34	32	3	4	7	0	0	1	2	0	0	0	2	0	14	0	0	1	.125	.176	.219
Lillibridge, Brent, Williamsport	42	191	169	19	41	73	12	4	4	18	4	2	2	14	0	35	10	3	0	.243	.305	.432
Lipsey, Carl, Lowell	4	8	5	2	1	1	0	0	0	0	0	0	0	3	0	2	0	0	0	.200	.500	.200
Lomack, Jermal, Williamsport †	27	119	101	17	26	28	2	0	0	8	5	1	1	11	0	13	19	2	0	.257	.333	.277
Lombardi, Michael, Batavia †	3	10	9	1	1	1	0	0	0	0	0	0	0	1	0	3	0	0	0	.111	.200	.111
Long, Nicholas, Vermont	1	0	0	0	0	0	0	0	0	0	...	0	0	0	0	0	0	0	0	...	...	...
Longworth, Randall, Mahoning Valley	25	105	94	8	22	28	4	1	0	14	1	2	2	6	0	19	5	3	2	.234	.288	.298
Louisa, Lorvin, Vermont	49	187	175	21	37	58	7	1	4	21	1	0	3	8	0	58	7	3	6	.211	.258	.331
Lowrie, Jed, Lowell †	53	240	201	36	66	90	12	0	4	32	2	1	2	34	0	30	7	5	3	.328	.429	.448
Lytle, Andrew, Mahoning Valley	56	230	210	20	54	64	6	2	0	18	3	1	0	16	1	33	6	6	4	.257	.308	.305
MacFarlane, Andrew, Batavia	48	177	167	20	34	52	8	2	2	19	0	2	1	7	0	64	6	3	3	.204	.237	.311
Madden, Scott, New Jersey	3	6	6	0	1	1	0	0	0	1	0	0	0	0	0	2	0	0	0	.167	.167	.167
Malo, Jonathan, Brooklyn	46	168	130	25	30	48	4	4	2	15	2	1	2	33	1	31	7	3	1	.231	.392	.369
Mancebo, Melvin, Vermont	11	32	30	2	5	9	1	0	1	4	0	0	0	2	0	8	0	0	3	.167	.219	.300
Marcelli, Brandon, New Jersey	2	6	6	1	1	1	0	0	0	2	0	0	0	0	0	2	0	0	1	.167	.167	.167
Marconi, Robert, Aberdeen	60	234	205	34	62	93	14	4	3	17	3	1	3	22	1	38	5	1	4	.302	.377	.454
Marson, Louis, Batavia	60	252	220	25	54	86	11	3	5	25	3	1	1	27	0	52	0	1	12	.245	.329	.391
Mathias, Ryder, Hudson Valley	52	208	174	23	41	57	7	0	3	22	1	2	15	16	0	31	2	1	7	.236	.348	.328
Matsui, Kazuo, Brooklyn †	1	5	3	0	0	0	0	0	0	0	0	0	0	2	0	0	0	0	0	.000	.400	.000
Matthews, William, Hudson Valley †	5	9	9	0	0	0	0	0	0	1	0	0	0	0	0	1	0	0	1	.000	.000	.000
Matulia, John, Hudson Valley *	9	42	37	4	7	7	0	0	0	1	1	0	0	4	0	9	0	1	0	.189	.268	.189
Maxey, Jason, Aberdeen *	36	103	90	9	23	34	8	0	1	16	0	0	2	11	2	22	0	0	3	.256	.330	.378
McCutchen, Andrew, Williamsport	13	62	52	12	18	23	3	1	0	5	1	0	1	8	0	6	4	1	0	.346	.443	.442
McMillan, Andrew, Vermont	15	62	51	8	15	22	4	0	1	6	0	2	1	8	0	19	0	0	0	.294	.387	.431
Mendez, Jose, New Jersey	20	65	58	7	12	15	3	0	0	5	2	1	0	4	0	10	0	0	3	.207	.254	.259
Mendez, Rafael, Oneonta	39	136	113	19	21	33	7	1	1	13	0	2	0	20	0	34	0	3	2	.186	.309	.292
Mercurio, Matthew, Lowell	66	279	231	33	52	71	9	2	2	28	3	3	9	33	0	48	2	4	5	.225	.341	.307
Messner, Nathan, Jamestown	36	137	128	11	26	36	4	0	2	14	0	0	1	8	0	35	1	1	4	.203	.255	.281
Metropoulos, Joseph, Auburn	52	197	178	25	52	95	21	2	6	28	0	3	0	15	0	44	0	0	3	.292	.342	.534
Michalski, Joseph, Aberdeen	23	56	49	1	8	9	1	0	0	6	1	0	0	6	0	18	1	0	0	.163	.255	.184
Middleton, Cory, Oneonta	68	291	259	39	64	107	22	0	7	52	2	3	9	19	1	60	3	1	6	.247	.317	.413
Mihalics, Joseph, Brooklyn	12	31	24	4	3	3	0	0	0	2	1	0	0	6	0	6	2	0	1	.125	.300	.125
Morris, Adam, New Jersey	21	79	66	10	16	19	0	0	1	11	0	2	2	9	1	23	0	0	2	.242	.342	.288
Mortensen, Trevor, Mahoning Valley	50	195	172	22	45	56	5	0	2	19	4	1	2	16	0	36	8	1	5	.262	.330	.326
Mota, Willy, Lowell	37	153	127	26	26	37	6	1	1	9	0	1	2	23	0	47	3	2	2	.205	.333	.291
Naccarata, Ivan, Brooklyn *	55	193	158	18	37	61	7	1	5	20	0	1	1	33	2	30	4	3	3	.234	.368	.386
Natale, Jeffrey, Lowell	12	46	41	9	20	25	5	0	0	9	1	0	1	3	0	3	2	0	0	.488	.522	.610
Nelson, Daniel, New Jersey *	52	211	187	24	53	69	10	3	0	22	0	4	3	17	0	31	2	5	6	.283	.346	.369
Newton, Jonathan, New Jersey *	24	82	73	13	19	33	6	1	2	10	0	0	1	8	0	18	1	1	0	.260	.341	.452
Nino, Denny, Williamsport	12	29	26	4	6	7	1	0	0	2	0	0	0	2	0	2	0	0	1	.231	.276	.269
Nunez, Eduardo, Staten Island †	73	310	281	37	88	120	11	6	3	46	6	0	3	20	1	43	6	3	2	.313	.365	.427
Nunez, Eduardo, Vermont	31	102	92	5	12	17	5	0	0	6	0	0	0	10	0	35	3	2	2	.130	.216	.185
Pacheco, Jonel, Brooklyn	54	225	201	34	55	83	10	0	6	30	1	1	5	17	0	35	20	6	4	.274	.344	.413
Padgett, Nathan, Jamestown	6	24	24	1	5	5	0	0	0	1	0	0	0	0	0	8	0	0	0	.208	.208	.208
Patino, Jorge, Oneonta	27	90	81	14	21	25	2	1	0	4	0	1	4	4	0	10	1	1	1	.259	.322	.309
Patterson, Ryan, Auburn	71	306	274	52	93	163	23	4	13	65	3	5	3	21	4	53	5	2	5	.339	.386	.595
Patton, Preston, Auburn *	57	247	220	41	60	122	18	1	14	44	1	1	2	22	0	60	1	0	4	.273	.343	.555
Pearce, Steven, Williamsport	72	312	272	48	82	129	26	0	7	52	0	3	2	35	0	43	2	4	9	.301	.381	.474
Perez, Jose A., Staten Island	28	89	78	15	20	26	4	1	0	13	0	0	0	11	0	17	5	1	1	.256	.348	.333
Perry, Patrick, Lowell *	14	52	44	7	7	11	2	1	0	5	0	0	2	6	0	9	0	0	1	.159	.288	.250
Petersen, Joshua, Brooklyn	46	193	182	27	52	76	13	1	3	22	1	0	4	6	0	34	1	3	4	.286	.323	.418
Peterson, Derrick, Mahoning Valley	60	238	201	19	41	61	12	1	2	31	2	0	1	33	0	36	7	2	6	.204	.319	.303
Pettway, Brian, Auburn	56	219	200	19	45	77	10	2	6	25	0	1	2	16	1	66	0	1	3	.225	.288	.385
Pilittere, Peter, Staten Island	53	203	176	18	44	67	11	0	4	25	3	4	8	12	0	17	0	0	4	.250	.320	.381
Plasencia, Francisco, Vermont *	72	318	280	43	84	141	16	4	11	56	2	4	3	29	0	60	14	3	5	.300	.367	.504
Poni, Francis, Williamsport	12	38	34	2	5	6	1	0	0	2	1	1	2	0	0	11	1	0	0	.147	.189	.176
Poppert, John, Vermont	41	151	136	15	27	45	6	0	4	13	1	0	0	14	0	30	3	0	5	.199	.273	.331
Poterson, Jonathan, Staten Island †	75	322	295	33	73	110	19	0	6	52	1	2	2	22	1	72	2	1	11	.247	.302	.373
Prasch, Edward, Williamsport	26	110	92	11	20	22	2	0	0	7	1	2	3	12	1	17	3	2	0	.217	.321	.239

SHORT-SEASON CLASS A *New York-Penn League*

Player, Team	G	TPA	AB	R	H	TB	2B	3B	HR	RBI	SH	SF	HP	BB	IBB	SO	SB	CS	GDP	Avg.	OBP	Slg.
Pulley, Matthew, Aberdeen *	40	142	130	10	19	24	5	0	0	7	0	1	1	10	1	32	1	0	4	.146	.211	.185
Rainville, Michael, Hudson Valley *	35	120	113	5	16	18	2	0	0	7	0	1	1	5	0	39	1	0	6	.142	.183	.159
Ramos, Dominic, Lowell	65	297	265	42	69	98	8	3	5	29	2	2	2	26	0	56	10	3	4	.260	.329	.370
Reddinger, Brandon, Williamsport	30	108	92	18	15	16	1	0	0	5	0	1	6	9	0	23	1	1	2	.163	.278	.174
Reed, Keith, Aberdeen	16	69	62	10	16	30	2	0	4	11	0	0	0	7	1	18	2	0	0	.258	.333	.484
Reifenberger, David, Mahoning Valley	12	37	34	4	7	8	1	0	0	1	0	0	0	3	0	11	0	1	0	.206	.270	.235
Reimold, Nolan, Aberdeen	50	212	180	33	53	99	15	2	9	30	0	2	1	29	1	44	2	0	2	.294	.392	.550
Rhymes, William, Oneonta *	61	279	250	48	82	105	11	3	2	27	3	0	1	25	0	15	14	3	1	.328	.391	.420
Richmond, Kevin, New Jersey †	20	62	56	6	15	22	2	1	1	7	0	2	2	2	0	13	2	1	0	.268	.306	.393
Roa, Joel, Oneonta	42	151	138	20	33	51	4	1	4	14	0	1	3	9	0	57	0	0	2	.239	.298	.370
Roberson, Ryan, Oneonta	52	214	197	26	56	94	13	2	7	47	0	2	1	14	1	60	0	0	5	.284	.332	.477
Robinson, Christopher, Oneonta	4	15	13	2	2	2	0	0	0	1	0	1	0	1	0	3	0	0	2	.154	.200	.154
Roche, Gary, Jamestown	49	204	187	20	58	68	5	1	1	20	7	1	1	8	0	24	3	1	8	.310	.340	.364
Rodgers, Mark, New Jersey	60	236	202	29	58	89	16	0	5	38	1	3	4	26	0	40	2	1	8	.287	.374	.441
Rogers, Tanner, Jamestown	50	176	150	22	34	50	3	2	3	15	2	1	7	16	0	33	5	9	0	.227	.328	.333
Roth, Anthony, Staten Island	26	90	74	16	20	26	3	0	1	6	1	1	3	11	0	21	1	2	3	.270	.382	.351
Roth, Randy, New Jersey	32	128	119	8	29	46	6	1	3	14	1	1	1	6	0	21	0	2	3	.244	.283	.387
Rousseve, Brandon, Hudson Valley	12	52	47	4	11	13	2	0	0	7	0	0	1	4	0	11	2	2	3	.234	.308	.277
Rowlett, Casey, New Jersey	36	159	139	18	35	45	8	1	0	9	1	0	1	18	0	24	4	4	7	.252	.342	.324
Sanchez, Gabriel, Jamestown	62	260	234	34	83	114	16	0	5	42	0	3	4	16	0	24	11	5	6	.355	.401	.487
Sanchez, Ricardo, Lowell	4	7	5	1	0	0	0	0	0	0	0	0	1	1	0	4	0	0	0	.000	.286	.000
Sandora, Robert, Vermont *	6	20	16	0	4	6	2	0	0	6	0	0	0	4	0	3	0	0	3	.250	.400	.375
Santana, Luis, Brooklyn	8	20	18	0	2	2	0	0	0	1	0	0	0	2	0	6	0	0	0	.111	.200	.111
Santana, Yury, Brooklyn	25	94	83	8	15	17	2	0	0	6	5	0	3	3	0	25	2	0	2	.181	.236	.205
Santiago, John, Williamsport	49	189	170	22	41	58	6	1	3	15	0	0	6	13	0	32	1	2	4	.241	.317	.341
Scott Jr., Lorenzo, Aberdeen *	34	147	133	18	29	44	6	0	3	12	0	0	0	14	0	58	7	4	1	.218	.293	.331
Searage, Alex, Williamsport *	22	78	67	8	9	15	3	0	1	10	3	0	0	8	0	26	0	0	1	.134	.227	.224
Sena, Emmanuel, Auburn †	65	256	225	30	47	62	6	0	3	18	9	1	0	20	0	84	9	3	1	.209	.272	.276
Shafer, Corey, Aberdeen *	39	142	130	13	28	43	5	2	2	19	0	0	1	11	0	29	0	0	3	.215	.282	.331
Sharpe, Michael, Brooklyn *	21	48	41	4	6	6	0	0	0	1	1	0	1	5	0	14	1	1	1	.146	.255	.146
Shofitt, Sean, Auburn *	57	225	188	32	47	65	13	1	1	21	2	1	2	32	0	52	2	2	6	.250	.363	.346
Sivira, Yonathan, New Jersey	61	247	225	27	57	77	12	1	2	17	2	1	2	17	0	42	8	7	9	.253	.310	.342
Skorupski, John, New Jersey	10	35	31	3	6	8	2	0	0	2	0	0	3	1	0	14	0	0	0	.194	.286	.258
Slayden, Jeremy, Batavia *	54	229	194	35	52	90	11	0	9	36	1	1	5	28	0	45	1	0	4	.268	.373	.464
Snyder, Brandon, Aberdeen	8	31	28	4	11	13	2	0	0	6	0	1	0	2	0	7	0	0	0	.393	.419	.464
Solano, Donovan, New Jersey	22	89	77	7	19	24	5	0	0	11	1	0	4	7	0	12	1	1	2	.247	.341	.312
Solano, Euvi, Williamsport	50	201	175	24	47	61	5	0	3	27	2	1	4	19	0	34	1	4	7	.269	.352	.349
Soto, Auddy, Vermont	5	9	6	0	1	1	0	0	0	0	0	0	0	3	0	4	0	0	0	.167	.444	.167
Soto, Luis, Lowell †	65	281	246	39	72	106	11	1	7	48	0	1	7	27	2	46	2	3	2	.293	.377	.431
Spilman, Ryan, Mahoning Valley	6	20	18	0	0	0	0	0	0	0	0	0	0	2	0	8	0	0	1	.000	.100	.000
Spring, Matthew, Hudson Valley	50	201	170	24	32	54	8	1	4	19	0	2	2	27	0	60	2	0	3	.188	.303	.318
Stachowsky, Mitchel, Lowell	36	127	115	17	26	50	3	0	7	15	0	0	8	4	0	55	0	0	3	.226	.299	.435
Stadanlick, Ryan, Aberdeen	1	0	0	0	0	0	0	0	0	0	0	0	0	0	0	0	0	0	0	...	...	...
Steinbach, Ryan, Aberdeen †	65	296	250	32	68	73	5	0	0	9	2	2	6	36	0	65	1	4	4	.272	.374	.292
Stevens, Anthony, Williamsport	16	46	41	7	8	11	1	1	0	1	1	0	2	2	0	16	3	2	1	.195	.267	.268
Stewart, Caleb, Brooklyn	74	317	265	39	72	129	23	2	10	45	0	2	3	47	5	64	6	3	1	.272	.385	.487
Szabo, Jordan, Batavia	37	153	138	21	35	52	8	3	1	14	1	1	2	11	0	30	8	1	3	.254	.316	.377
Thissen, Greg, Vermont	14	59	53	9	15	25	4	0	2	6	1	0	1	4	0	12	3	1	1	.283	.345	.472
Thomas, Brent, Mahoning Valley	20	78	72	8	16	23	5	1	0	4	0	1	2	3	0	25	0	2	2	.222	.269	.319
Thomas, Michael, Oneonta *	18	84	70	19	27	37	5	1	1	14	0	0	2	12	1	11	9	0	0	.386	.488	.529
Thomas, Nicolas, Auburn *	62	236	193	24	49	79	7	1	7	32	1	3	2	37	2	41	0	0	2	.254	.374	.409
Timm, Brandon, Oneonta	50	200	169	28	44	53	5	2	0	14	2	2	2	26	0	50	9	3	4	.260	.359	.314
Timmons, Jeffrey, Brooklyn	10	23	22	2	1	4	0	0	1	1	0	0	0	1	0	13	0	0	0	.045	.087	.182
Torres, Carlos, Vermont	35	135	120	11	23	34	5	0	2	18	0	0	2	13	0	41	0	0	4	.192	.281	.283
Torres, Christopher, Oneonta	23	66	63	9	17	22	2	0	1	8	0	0	0	3	1	24	0	0	1	.270	.303	.349
Travis, David, Vermont *	6	21	20	1	1	1	0	0	0	1	0	0	0	1	0	11	0	0	1	.050	.095	.050
Twomley, Jason, Lowell *	66	281	242	28	61	104	16	3	7	36	2	0	13	24	1	79	2	4	4	.252	.351	.430
Vander Weg, Scott, New Jersey	1	0	0	0	0	0	0	0	0	0	0	0	0	0	0	0	0	0	0	...	...	...
Van Houten, Jeffrey, Jamestown	62	259	226	35	64	107	18	2	7	36	3	1	5	24	0	41	2	5	5	.283	.363	.473
Van Slyke, A.J., New Jersey *	9	39	35	6	12	20	2	0	2	5	0	0	1	3	1	5	0	0	0	.343	.410	.571
Ventura, Leivi, Brooklyn	2	8	7	0	2	2	0	0	0	2	0	0	1	0	0	4	0	0	0	.286	.375	.286
Wabick, David, Brooklyn *	10	40	37	2	6	8	2	0	0	3	0	0	0	2	0	9	0	0	1	.162	.200	.216
Wagner, Mark, Lowell	24	81	69	10	14	18	2	1	0	6	0	1	2	9	0	7	1	1	2	.203	.309	.261
Walton, Jamar, Jamestown *	64	250	227	19	51	69	2	5	2	22	1	0	5	17	0	84	1	3	1	.225	.293	.304
Walton, Neil, Hudson Valley	57	214	200	14	40	47	4	0	1	16	1	1	3	9	0	65	3	2	2	.200	.244	.235
Wargo, Cody, Aberdeen	2	8	5	1	0	0	0	0	0	0	1	0	0	2	0	1	0	0	2	.000	.286	.000
Wiggins, Bradford, Aberdeen *	23	57	55	3	6	10	1	0	1	2	0	0	0	2	0	26	0	1	0	.109	.140	.182
Wilkerson, Matthew, New Jersey	45	184	163	17	39	71	6	1	8	25	0	1	0	20	1	59	2	0	3	.239	.321	.436
Williams, Julian, Batavia	70	315	272	55	74	96	10	3	2	25	5	0	8	30	0	33	13	6	0	.272	.361	.353
Williamson, Schuyler, Oneonta	25	73	64	11	13	16	3	0	0	6	0	1	3	5	0	11	1	0	3	.203	.288	.250
Witt, Paul, Jamestown	35	136	132	14	27	33	4	1	0	9	0	0	0	4	0	38	1	2	2	.205	.228	.250
Woodruff, Ernest, Hudson Valley	9	22	22	0	2	2	0	0	0	0	0	0	0	0	0	7	0	0	2	.091	.091	.091
Woodson, Michael, Mahoning Valley	22	81	71	6	13	16	0	0	1	7	4	0	2	4	0	16	1	0	3	.183	.247	.225
Wulf, Kent, Williamsport †	16	44	38	1	6	6	0	0	0	2	1	0	0	5	0	14	1	1	0	.158	.256	.158
Yarbrough, Brandon, New Jersey *	51	216	188	27	48	75	17	2	2	25	0	3	1	24	1	58	3	3	6	.255	.338	.399
Yema, Yahmed, Lowell *	55	237	219	35	66	90	17	2	1	29	0	1	0	17	0	21	8	1	3	.301	.350	.411
Zapata, Jose, Aberdeen	37	127	110	11	16	24	5	0	1	8	0	0	3	14	1	36	0	0	2	.145	.260	.218

GRAND SLAMS—C. Stewart, 2; D. Brown, J. Cooper, B. Corley, M. Costanzo, M. Cunningham, E. De Leon, C. Harris, M. Hollimon, N. Messner, C. Middleton, F. Plasencia, R. Roberson, R. Searage, E. Solano, M. Wilkerson, 1 each.

AWARDED FIRST BASE ON CATCHER'S INTERFERENCE—G. Sanchez 3 (B. Bormaster, O. Casillas, O. Guevara); J. Delaney 2 (A. Butera, R. Arroyo); M. Bernhard (L. Marson); J. Cooper (M. Mancebo); J. Metropoulos (A. Butera); C. Patton (K. Dahlberg); D. Peterson (L. Marson); E. Sena (T. Rogers).

TEAM

Team	W	L	Pct.	ERA	G	CG	ShO	Sv.	IP	H	TBF	R	ER	HR	SH	SF	HB	BB	IBB	SO	WP	Bk.
Staten Island	52	24	.684	2.85	76	0	6	26	679.2	548	2830	258	215	35	32	18	32	270	8	645	46	11
Williamsport	44	32	.579	3.40	76	0	7	21	679.2	609	2861	312	257	34	22	25	51	243	6	514	34	5
Brooklyn	40	36	.526	3.41	76	1	4	20	678.1	672	2958	324	257	40	14	19	50	265	4	527	41	7
Lowell	42	33	.560	3.70	75	0	7	22	659	661	2865	343	271	40	18	13	40	207	5	575	56	4
Auburn	45	30	.600	3.71	75	0	2	29	673.2	652	2920	346	278	30	13	23	36	242	11	615	77	8
Mahoning Valley	33	43	.434	3.71	76	0	3	19	667.1	666	2891	368	275	54	22	20	47	225	5	613	40	5
Hudson Valley	31	43	.419	3.72	74	1	3	24	650.1	626	2820	344	269	51	19	21	40	234	4	630	47	3
Oneonta	48	27	.640	3.78	75	1	5	21	655	609	2847	327	275	33	24	24	39	282	6	563	75	3
New Jersey	37	39	.487	3.82	76	0	6	19	672	644	2939	346	285	42	21	23	54	259	8	588	56	4
Aberdeen	27	48	.360	3.97	75	1	5	14	664	651	2920	356	293	37	32	18	49	274	8	630	49	9
Batavia	36	39	.480	4.17	75	2	4	20	675.2	721	2997	370	313	38	37	20	42	254	8	580	42	7
Jamestown	31	44	.413	4.59	75	1	2	17	652.1	701	2941	421	333	60	19	26	38	276	4	603	70	7
Vermont	28	48	.368	4.88	76	1	2	7	662.2	758	3038	453	359	38	14	34	55	260	0	461	52	11
Tri-City	34	42	.447	5.57	76	0	3	11	648	632	2930	449	401	68	15	18	70	363	3	600	65	5

INDIVIDUAL

TOP QUALIFIERS FOR EARNED-RUN AVERAGE TITLE

Minimum 61 innings. *Lefthanded pitcher.

Pitcher, Team	W	L	Pct.	ERA	G	GS	CG	ShO	GF	Sv.	IP	H	TBF	R	ER	HR	SH	SF	HB	BB	IBB	SO	WP	Bk.
Parnell, Robert, Brooklyn	2	3	.400	1.73	15	14	0	0	1	0	73.0	48	294	20	14	1	0	2	4	29	1	67	3	0
Redmond, Todd, Williamsport	1	2	.333	1.98	15	14	0	0	0	0	72.2	62	294	22	16	2	1	0	6	21	0	63	2	0
Conroy, James, Staten Island	5	1	.833	2.04	18	9	0	0	1	1	66.1	52	273	20	15	2	3	1	4	20	0	67	6	0
Seccombe, David, Staten Island	8	2	.800	2.15	17	9	0	0	1	1	71.0	45	283	18	17	4	2	0	4	26	0	53	6	0
Phillips, Ryan, Lowell *	7	2	.778	2.28	14	14	0	0	0	0	67.0	45	274	19	17	2	0	0	4	31	0	61	6	1
Mateo, Waner, Brooklyn	4	2	.667	2.56	14	12	0	0	1	0	63.1	59	280	28	18	4	0	1	3	30	0	53	3	0
Davis, Wade, Hudson Valley	7	4	.636	2.72	15	15	0	0	0	0	86.0	75	349	35	26	5	4	0	5	23	0	97	3	0
Ray, Robert, Auburn	4	3	.571	2.77	15	13	0	0	0	0	61.2	46	253	22	19	2	0	3	4	20	0	58	3	1
Stephens, Jason, Staten Island	4	1	.800	2.82	18	10	0	0	2	1	67.0	55	266	25	21	3	4	2	5	19	0	52	3	1
Bauserman, Joseph, Williamsport	6	2	.750	2.84	14	14	0	0	0	0	69.2	64	287	30	22	3	3	3	5	26	0	45	1	1
Landing, Jeffrey, Brooklyn	6	6	.500	2.87	16	16	0	0	1	0	84.2	78	353	35	27	3	2	2	8	27	0	59	4	2
Badenhop, Burke, Oneonta	6	4	.600	2.92	14	14	1	1	0	0	77.0	69	319	32	25	0	2	0	3	26	1	55	2	0
Edell, Ryan, Mahoning Valley *	3	4	.429	2.95	14	11	0	0	0	0	64.0	65	265	26	21	5	1	1	1	18	0	62	3	0
Deters, James, Mahoning Valley	3	4	.429	2.97	14	14	0	0	0	0	69.2	73	301	37	23	1	0	5	2	17	0	49	4	0
Bell, Kristian, Auburn	5	4	.556	3.14	15	15	0	0	0	0	77.1	74	330	38	27	3	5	2	2	33	1	71	12	0
Barb, Andrew, Batavia	3	2	.600	3.23	11	11	0	0	0	0	64.0	59	274	27	23	7	3	3	7	27	0	57	4	1
Yost, Wendell, Vermont *	6	5	.545	3.25	14	14	1	1	0	0	83.0	70	347	36	30	7	2	3	2	30	0	56	1	0
O'Brien, Matt, Oneonta	6	3	.667	3.34	15	15	0	0	0	0	89.0	79	368	42	33	6	1	3	1	24	1	57	3	0
Antelo, Derek, Williamsport	6	3	.667	3.48	13	13	0	0	0	0	67.1	52	269	32	26	3	0	2	6	21	0	52	3	0
Vasquez, Sendy, Oneonta	7	0	1.000	3.63	15	11	0	0	0	0	67.0	53	286	30	27	4	2	4	5	34	0	60	4	0
McGee, Jacob, Hudson Valley *	5	4	.556	3.56	15	14	0	0	0	0	76.2	64	308	32	31	4	1	1	1	23	0	89	5	0

DEPARTMENTAL LEADERS: W—Seccombe, 8. L—Pena, 8. Pct.—Vasquez, 1.000. G—Miller, 29. GS—Landing and Pena, 16. CG—eight pitchers tied with 1. ShO—four pitchers tied with 1. GF—Phillips and Schmidt, 23. Sv.—Feldkamp, 15. IP—Kendrick, 91.1. H—Pena, 97. TBF—Kendrick, 391. R—Pena, 56. ER—Pluta III, 53. HR—Blackley, 11. SAC—five pitchers tied with 5. SF—Reinhard, 6. HB—McKeller, 13. BB—Pluta III, 51. IBB—three pitchers tied with 3. SO—Davis, 97. WP—Bell, 12. BK—Hernandez, 4.

ALL PITCHERS

*Lefthanded pitcher.

Pitcher, Team	W	L	Pct.	ERA	G	GS	CG	ShO	GF	Sv.	IP	H	TBF	R	ER	HR	SH	SF	HB	BB	IBB	SO	WP	Bk.
Aguilar, Salvador, Brooklyn	5	0	1.000	2.24	15	2	0	0	4	1	52.1	49	204	16	13	4	0	0	1	9	0	45	1	0
Alfaro, Gabriel, Auburn	2	4	.333	6.23	18	0	0	0	9	1	30.1	40	140	23	21	3	0	0	0	13	3	36	6	0
Alfonzo, Edgar, Brooklyn *	0	1	.000	5.40	2	0	0	0	1	0	5.0	6	22	3	3	0	1	0	1	1	0	4	0	0
Almenar, Aristides, Brooklyn	0	2	.000	1.76	19	0	0	0	14	4	30.2	19	128	8	6	3	2	1	1	17	0	24	3	1
Amaya, Jose, Mahoning Valley	2	2	.500	4.19	8	1	0	0	1	0	19.1	22	86	14	9	2	1	1	2	5	0	8	0	0
Antelo, Derek, Williamsport	6	3	.667	3.48	13	13	0	0	0	0	67.1	52	269	32	26	3	0	2	6	21	0	52	3	0
Badenhop, Burke, Oneonta	6	4	.600	2.92	14	14	1	1	0	0	77.0	69	319	32	25	0	2	0	3	26	1	55	2	0
Bahr, Jesse, Staten Island *	0	0	.000	0.00	3	0	0	0	1	0	2.1	2	12	0	0	0	1	0	1	0	0	3	0	0
Barb, Andrew, Batavia	3	2	.600	3.23	11	11	0	0	0	0	64.0	59	274	27	23	7	3	3	7	27	0	57	4	1
Barone, Daniel, Jamestown	2	0	1.000	0.46	9	0	0	0	3	2	19.2	14	76	2	1	1	1	0	1	4	0	17	1	0
Bauserman, Joseph, Williamsport	6	2	.750	2.84	14	14	0	0	0	0	69.2	64	287	30	22	3	3	3	5	26	0	45	1	1
Baxter, Jake, Oneonta	2	2	.500	4.45	16	0	0	0	6	2	30.1	30	134	18	15	3	4	4	3	12	0	31	3	0
Baxter, James, Lowell *	0	0	.000	3.27	10	0	0	0	4	0	11.0	8	44	4	4	1	0	0	1	5	0	4	2	0
Bell, Kristian, Auburn	5	4	.556	3.14	15	15	0	0	0	0	77.1	74	330	38	27	3	5	2	2	33	1	71	12	0
Berg, Justin, Staten Island	6	2	.750	3.53	15	9	0	0	2	0	58.2	48	236	26	23	3	2	0	4	20	0	52	0	2
Bergesen, Bradley, Aberdeen	1	3	.250	4.82	15	15	0	0	0	0	71.0	89	309	45	38	5	2	5	1	14	0	54	3	0
Berkenbosch, Kenneth, Jamestown	1	0	1.000	4.81	17	0	0	0	2	1	33.2	29	138	18	18	7	2	1	1	15	0	30	3	0
Berroa, Yesson, Auburn	3	1	.750	4.18	17	0	0	0	13	7	23.2	20	94	11	11	2	0	0	0	4	0	32	1	1
Bigda, Drew, Hudson Valley *	0	4	.000	5.13	24	0	0	0	13	2	33.1	35	155	24	19	0	1	1	2	22	1	42	4	0
Bille, Michael, Jamestown	3	2	.600	3.45	18	0	0	0	6	2	31.1	27	137	17	12	0	3	2	3	12	2	25	4	0
Blackley, Adam, Lowell *	6	3	.667	4.01	15	15	0	0	0	0	74.0	82	327	41	33	11	3	1	3	23	0	86	6	0
Blaine, Davis, Batavia *	2	1	.667	3.26	11	4	0	0	1	1	30.1	27	140	13	11	0	2	1	1	23	0	23	1	0
Blair, Thomas, New Jersey *	0	0	.000	0.96	6	0	0	0	0	0	9.1	5	39	1	1	0	1	0	2	6	0	12	0	0
Boehm, Kyle, Aberdeen	0	1	.000	5.73	19	1	0	0	4	0	33.0	41	147	22	21	7	0	0	5	8	0	24	3	0
Boggs, Mitchell, New Jersey	4	4	.500	3.89	15	14	0	0	0	0	71.2	77	314	38	31	5	1	1	5	24	0	61	4	0

SHORT-SEASON CLASS A *New York-Penn League*

Pitcher, Team	W	L	Pct.	ERA	G	GS	CG	ShO	GF	Sv.	IP	H	TBF	R	ER	HR	SH	SF	HB	BB	IBB	SO	WP	Bk.
Brauer, James, Jamestown	3	2	.600	4.22	10	10	1	0	0	0	42.2	38	186	32	20	1	1	3	0	14	0	31	5	2
Brazell, Landon, Jamestown	2	3	.400	5.09	14	9	0	0	0	0	53.0	56	237	37	30	3	1	5	2	25	0	38	5	1
Brocato, Russell, Aberdeen	1	3	.250	5.88	21	0	0	0	6	0	33.2	41	154	24	22	1	1	2	1	15	1	23	1	0
Brown, Eric, Brooklyn	3	2	.600	3.97	16	0	0	0	9	4	34.0	33	141	16	15	3	0	1	3	7	0	31	2	0
Brown, Justin, New Jersey	1	0	1.000	9.00	2	1	0	0	0	0	5.0	7	23	6	5	0	0	0	0	3	0	4	0	0
Buchholz, Clay, Lowell	0	1	.000	2.61	15	15	0	0	0	0	41.1	34	166	15	12	2	0	1	1	9	0	45	0	1
Cairns, Jason, New Jersey	0	0	.000	0.00	2	0	0	0	0	0	3.0	2	13	0	0	0	0	0	0	0	0	1	0	0
Camilo, Juan, Jamestown	1	2	.333	7.94	10	0	0	0	9	3	11.1	20	56	12	10	3	0	0	0	3	0	9	0	0
Carnline, William, Auburn	4	0	1.000	4.61	21	2	0	0	3	1	41.0	41	180	23	21	1	0	1	2	20	0	36	9	0
Carrasco, Carlos, Batavia	0	3	.000	13.50	4	4	0	0	0	0	15.1	29	82	25	23	8	0	1	2	5	0	12	3	1
Casillas, Ismael, Lowell	2	1	.667	3.09	18	0	0	0	3	0	32.0	31	136	12	11	0	1	2	1	8	0	40	4	0
Castor, Parrish, Jamestown *	0	0	.000	2.25	3	0	0	0	1	0	4.0	4	20	1	1	0	0	0	0	4	0	6	0	0
Chamberlin, Bryce, Aberdeen	1	2	.333	5.64	18	0	0	0	5	1	30.1	35	141	21	19	2	2	0	1	20	0	37	7	0
Claggett, Anthony, Oneonta	0	1	.000	4.03	21	0	0	0	16	7	22.1	23	101	10	10	1	2	2	2	12	1	25	7	0
Clem, Christopher, New Jersey	1	2	.333	5.57	12	4	0	0	3	0	32.1	45	144	23	20	2	1	5	1	9	0	22	0	0
Cobb, Matthew, Hudson Valley *	3	5	.375	3.57	16	3	0	0	4	0	40.1	37	171	21	16	6	2	2	1	10	0	29	4	0
Conroy, James, Staten Island	5	1	.833	2.04	18	9	0	0	1	1	66.1	52	273	20	15	2	3	1	4	20	0	67	6	0
Coonrod, Aaron, Vermont	0	0	.000	10.80	4	0	0	0	1	0	3.1	5	24	5	4	0	0	0	2	8	0	4	0	0
Cooper, Michael, New Jersey	1	2	.333	1.71	4	3	0	0	0	0	21.0	11	77	4	4	1	1	0	0	6	0	18	0	0
Coose, Austin, Hudson Valley	0	1	.000	4.09	11	0	0	0	3	1	11.0	10	49	7	5	1	0	0	0	5	0	14	0	0
Corporan, Willy, Hudson Valley	1	0	1.000	2.01	14	0	0	0	7	2	22.1	17	88	6	5	3	1	0	0	6	0	13	1	0
Correa, Jose, Batavia	1	0	1.000	4.73	18	0	0	0	7	0	26.2	29	119	16	14	2	0	0	1	12	0	21	2	0
Cowley, Thomas, Mahoning Valley *	3	3	.500	3.43	21	0	0	0	7	2	42.0	30	172	19	16	4	1	3	3	20	2	47	0	0
Cox, Timothy, Lowell *	1	1	.500	3.86	2	0	0	0	1	0	7.0	10	35	3	3	1	0	0	0	3	0	10	2	0
Cuffman, Jacob, Williamsport	1	1	.500	3.86	21	0	0	0	12	2	35.0	19	153	17	15	2	3	3	8	25	0	32	4	0
D'Alessandro, Joe, Brooklyn	1	2	.333	5.14	17	0	0	0	10	2	21.0	20	94	16	12	1	1	1	2	10	0	22	2	0
Daniels, Adam, New Jersey *	2	1	.667	4.50	10	5	0	0	1	0	26.0	18	116	14	13	0	0	3	0	18	0	25	6	0
Davidson, David, Williamsport *	1	1	.500	3.18	5	4	0	0	0	0	17.0	14	72	7	6	0	0	2	8	0	23	2	0
Davis, Wade, Hudson Valley	7	4	.636	2.72	15	15	0	0	0	0	86.0	75	349	35	26	5	4	0	5	23	0	97	3	0
Day, Amos, Auburn	0	0	.000	3.00	3	0	0	0	1	0	3.0	4	17	2	1	0	0	0	0	3	0	4	1	0
De Los Santos, Richard, Hudson Valley	1	0	1.000	0.93	6	0	0	0	3	2	9.2	6	37	2	1	0	0	0	2	0	8	2	0
Denney, Kyle, Mahoning Valley	0	0	.000	18.00	1	1	0	0	0	0	1.0	2	6	2	2	1	0	0	0	1	0	2	0	0
Deters, James, Mahoning Valley	3	4	.429	2.97	14	14	0	0	0	0	69.2	73	301	37	23	1	0	5	2	17	0	49	4	0
Diaz, Dennis, Batavia	0	0	.000	18.00	1	0	0	0	0	0	1.0	0	7	2	2	0	0	1	3	0	0	1	0
Dicken, Randy, Auburn	4	2	.667	3.60	14	11	0	0	1	0	60.0	63	264	31	24	5	0	1	3	24	0	66	4	0
Dickerson, Roy, New Jersey *	0	0	.000	4.50	1	0	0	0	0	0	2.0	3	12	1	1	0	0	0	1	3	0	3	0	0
Dixon, Kevin, Mahoning Valley	3	6	.333	4.53	14	14	0	0	0	0	57.2	66	244	34	29	6	0	1	2	11	0	31	3	1
Domangue, Eric, Brooklyn *	1	0	1.000	6.97	15	0	0	0	2	0	20.2	25	107	16	16	0	1	1	6	17	0	12	2	2
Doolittle, Michael, Jamestown	4	5	.444	4.03	22	3	0	0	5	2	58.0	61	253	36	26	4	0	0	1	20	0	71	4	0
Douglas, Robert, Mahoning Valley	1	2	.333	6.94	6	0	0	0	1	0	11.2	10	51	11	9	2	1	0	1	3	0	14	1	0
Dumesnil, Bryan, Aberdeen *	1	3	.250	5.06	18	0	0	0	9	1	26.2	33	133	21	15	4	4	0	4	15	2	18	2	1
Easton, Aaron, Jamestown	0	0	.000	5.16	17	0	0	0	5	0	29.2	27	132	22	17	2	0	2	4	13	0	25	4	0
Eberhardt, Peter, Auburn	0	0	.000	6.00	3	0	0	0	1	0	3.0	2	14	2	2	0	0	0	1	2	0	1	0	0
Edell, Ryan, Mahoning Valley *	3	4	.429	2.95	14	11	0	0	0	0	64.0	65	265	26	21	5	1	1	1	18	0	62	3	0
Eichelberger, Jared, Brooklyn	0	0	.000	0.00	1	0	0	0	0	0	1.2	2	8	0	0	0	0	0	0	1	0	0	0	0
Erbe, Brandon, Aberdeen	1	1	.500	7.71	3	1	0	0	0	0	7.0	6	29	6	6	0	1	1	1	4	0	9	1	0
Estrada, Marco, Vermont	1	3	.250	5.08	9	6	0	0	2	1	33.2	31	153	21	19	4	0	3	16	0	37	1	0
Everitt, Keaton, Staten Island	1	0	1.000	6.00	5	2	0	0	0	0	12.0	10	55	9	8	0	1	0	11	0	8	3	0
Evers, William, Hudson Valley	2	2	.333	4.78	20	0	0	0	9	1	32.0	45	150	26	17	1	1	5	2	8	0	18	3	0
Everts, Clinton, Vermont	0	1	.000	3.79	8	1	0	0	2	0	19.0	21	94	12	8	0	0	1	2	12	0	21	4	0
Falk, Matthew, Hudson Valley	1	1	.500	2.18	12	0	0	0	2	0	20.2	17	89	9	5	1	0	0	1	9	0	29	3	0
Farley, Christopher, New Jersey	1	0	1.000	7.23	5	3	0	0	0	0	18.2	23	87	16	15	1	1	1	0	10	0	18	4	0
Feldkamp, Derek, Hudson Valley	1	2	.333	4.05	23	0	0	0	19	15	26.2	20	110	14	12	3	2	0	2	11	1	35	0	0
Fernandes, Kyle, Lowell *	0	0	.000	13.50	1	0	0	0	0	0	2.0	5	13	3	3	0	0	0	0	1	0	3	1	0
Fisher, Matthew, Hudson Valley	1	1	.500	6.16	15	0	0	0	5	0	19.0	24	89	16	13	3	1	1	5	1	5	4	0
Flores, Eugenio, Lowell	2	1	.667	5.06	14	0	0	0	3	0	21.1	23	94	15	12	0	1	1	3	7	0	14	3	0
Foulke, Keith, Lowell	0	0	.000	7.36	3	0	0	0	0	0	3.2	8	20	4	3	0	0	0	1	0	5	0	0
Fowler, Jonathan, Auburn *	4	2	.667	3.02	15	10	0	0	2	0	56.2	42	240	24	19	1	2	1	2	29	0	55	8	0
Fragoso, Jose, Oneonta	6	2	.750	2.25	13	4	0	0	2	0	44.0	33	184	17	11	0	4	1	4	22	1	50	7	0
Fraser, Loren, Oneonta	2	2	.500	3.45	19	0	0	0	9	4	28.2	33	122	12	11	0	3	1	0	12	1	30	4	0
Frias, Junior, Lowell	0	0	.000	9.00	1	0	0	0	0	0	2.0	3	10	2	2	0	0	0	1	0	2	0	0
Galbizo, Rafael, Jamestown	1	0	1.000	2.77	8	0	0	0	3	0	13.0	15	57	4	4	0	0	0	5	0	18	1	0
Gallaway, Michael, Aberdeen *	0	1	.000	1.59	3	2	0	0	0	0	5.2	5	25	1	1	1	0	0	4	0	6	0	0
Garza, Rodolfo, Vermont	0	0	.000	5.84	9	0	0	0	5	0	12.1	16	57	9	8	3	0	2	5	0	7	3	0
Gil, Roberto, Hudson Valley	1	0	1.000	4.26	6	0	0	0	2	0	12.2	10	52	6	6	2	0	0	2	3	0	14	1	1
Gomez, Warmar, Vermont	3	3	.500	3.76	23	0	0	0	11	1	38.1	46	161	22	16	2	2	1	2	5	0	19	2	2
Goyen, Matthew, Jamestown *	1	5	.167	4.03	10	10	0	0	0	0	44.2	44	200	25	20	8	0	1	4	21	0	44	6	1
Grant, Brian, Auburn	0	1	.000	13.50	5	0	0	0	3	1	10.2	16	55	19	16	2	1	1	2	6	2	8	1	0
Grant, Jessen, New Jersey	1	0	1.000	3.34	24	0	0	0	8	1	32.1	29	152	13	12	2	1	3	2	22	0	26	3	1
Gross, Timothy, New Jersey	0	0	.000	2.70	11	1	0	0	2	0	16.2	13	64	6	5	1	1	0	1	0	17	0	0
Guanchez, Argimiro, Lowell *	1	4	.200	4.25	26	0	0	0	20	8	36.0	47	174	28	17	1	1	0	1	13	0	41	7	0
Guevara, Orlando, Batavia	0	0	.000	0.00	1	0	0	0	0	0	1.0	1	4	0	0	0	0	0	0	1	0	0	0	0
Guyette, Kevin, Lowell	2	1	.667	0.00	6	0	0	0	1	1	11.2	3	38	2	0	0	0	0	1	0	10	1	0
Hahn, Cory, Auburn	0	0	.000	0.00	1	0	0	0	0	0	1.0	2	4	0	0	0	0	0	0	0	0	1	0	0
Hahn, Jeffrey, Oneonta	4	0	1.000	0.00	10	1	0	0	4	0	22.2	20	88	2	0	0	0	0	1	3	0	17	3	0
Hamblet, Reid, Aberdeen	4	4	.500	3.93	22	4	0	0	11	0	52.2	51	231	27	23	3	0	3	21	1	40	5	0
Hancock, Matthew, Lowell *	3	2	.600	5.59	22	0	0	0	10	0	37.0	45	168	25	23	6	1	1	1	11	2	34	0	0
Harker, Brett, Batavia	1	2	.333	5.06	9	7	0	0	0	0	37.1	38	163	23	21	5	1	0	3	12	0	15	0	0
Hawksworth, Blake, New Jersey	0	3	.000	7.98	7	6	0	0	0	0	14.2	18	72	18	13	0	0	1	5	10	1	12	3	0
Haynes, Matthew, Mahoning Valley	1	2	.333	5.77	18	0	0	0	3	2	39.0	39	178	27	25	7	0	2	1	21	0	47	4	1
Hearne, Donald, New Jersey	4	2	.667	2.56	24	1	0	0	6	0	38.2	25	151	15	11	2	0	0	1	12	0	42	7	0

Pitcher, Team	W	L	Pct.	ERA	G	GS	CG	ShO	GF	Sv.	IP	H	TBF	R	ER	HR	SH	SF	HB	BB	IBB	SO	WP	Bk.
Heisel, Ian, Williamsport	2	3	.400	3.86	28	0	0	0	6	0	44.1	43	194	20	19	1	2	2	3	16	0	44	4	0
Henyan, Peter, Batavia	2	0	1.000	4.46	19	1	0	0	0	0	38.1	48	175	19	19	1	1	1	2	18	0	24	5	0
Hernandez, David, Aberdeen	2	4	.333	3.89	12	8	0	0	0	0	41.2	41	187	21	18	2	1	2	7	17	1	47	3	1
Hernandez, Moises, Aberdeen	0	4	.000	3.08	11	7	1	0	1	0	52.2	43	226	21	18	2	1	3	1	24	0	56	4	4
Hill, Ronald, Batavia	2	3	.400	2.96	20	0	0	0	11	4	48.2	50	214	17	16	0	4	0	2	23	2	48	2	0
Hinchman, Grady, Brooklyn *	0	0	.000	3.38	3	0	0	0	1	0	5.1	7	26	2	2	0	0	1	1	4	0	7	0	0
Hiraldo, Nelson, Mahoning Valley	1	1	.500	12.88	18	0	0	0	7	0	21.2	28	113	32	31	8	0	1	5	16	0	15	6	2
Hoey, James, Aberdeen	1	1	.500	4.80	9	0	0	0	2	0	15.0	11	65	10	8	1	2	1	3	10	0	15	1	0
Hooks, Ashley, New Jersey	0	1	.000	7.59	9	0	0	0	2	1	10.2	14	54	11	9	0	2	1	1	7	0	12	2	0
Hope, Travis, Brooklyn	5	1	.833	3.95	22	0	0	0	9	2	41.0	41	183	21	18	2	3	0	5	16	1	26	1	0
Jackson, Aaron, Vermont	3	7	.300	6.13	15	12	0	0	2	0	61.2	76	299	53	42	0	0	4	10	27	0	44	5	0
Japa, Rolando, Staten Island	0	0	.000	16.20	1	0	0	0	0	0	1.2	5	12	4	3	1	0	0	0	1	0	2	0	0
Jecmen, Mark, Mahoning Valley	1	2	.333	3.35	23	0	0	0	3	1	48.1	36	209	27	18	1	3	1	6	28	0	40	5	0
Jones, Christopher, Lowell	3	1	.750	2.59	11	0	0	0	0	0	24.1	23	97	10	7	1	0	1	1	5	0	26	3	0
Jones, David, Lowell *	1	1	.500	3.21	12	1	0	0	1	1	28.0	29	118	12	10	2	0	0	5	0	30	2	0	
Joseph, Jacob, Brooklyn	0	1	.000	1.80	6	0	0	0	2	0	10.0	7	42	2	2	0	1	1	1	6	0	5	1	0
Kamrath, Jeffrey, Hudson Valley	2	4	.333	7.39	9	8	0	0	0	0	35.1	49	170	32	29	5	1	3	3	17	0	28	1	0
Kelly, Dustin, Lowell	0	0	.000	0.00	1	0	0	0	1	0	0.1	0	1	0	0	0	0	0	0	0	0	1	0	0
Kendrick, Kyle, Batavia	5	4	.556	3.74	14	14	1	0	0	0	91.1	94	386	49	38	7	5	1	4	22	0	70	2	1
Kite, Josh, Mahoning Valley *	1	1	.500	7.59	9	0	0	0	5	1	10.2	18	59	17	9	0	0	0	0	9	0	14	2	0
Knippschild, Charles, Mahoning Valley *	0	0	.000	4.50	1	0	0	0	0	0	4.0	3	14	2	2	0	0	0	0	0	0	5	0	0
Knox, Matthew, Mahoning Valley	0	0	.000	3.00	5	0	0	0	3	0	6.0	6	23	2	2	0	0	0	0	0	0	4	0	0
Konecny, Daniel, Oneonta	4	3	.571	6.26	15	11	0	0	2	0	54.2	73	250	43	38	2	1	0	6	18	0	30	6	0
Krebs, Eric, Williamsport	1	1	.500	4.68	7	7	0	0	0	0	32.2	34	148	18	17	1	0	1	2	17	0	14	1	1
Kroenke, Zachary, Staten Island *	1	1	.500	2.54	11	5	0	0	3	2	39.0	30	158	14	11	2	1	3	3	15	0	28	2	0
Landing, Jeffrey, Brooklyn	6	6	.500	2.87	16	16	0	0	0	0	84.2	78	353	35	27	3	2	2	8	27	0	59	4	2
Lannan, John, Vermont *	3	5	.375	5.26	14	11	0	0	1	0	63.1	74	296	46	37	5	0	3	4	31	0	41	5	3
Lara, Toni, Staten Island *	2	5	.286	7.00	17	5	0	0	0	0	45.0	51	210	41	35	6	1	2	1	29	1	42	5	1
Large, Terry, Lowell	0	1	.000	6.23	12	0	0	0	9	5	13.0	20	65	13	9	1	1	0	1	6	2	10	1	0
Lehman, James, Vermont	0	1	.000	6.31	20	0	0	0	10	1	25.2	28	118	20	18	2	0	1	2	9	0	20	6	1
Lerch, Zachary, Jamestown	0	0	.000	0.00	1	0	0	0	0	0	1.0	0	3	0	0	0	0	0	0	0	0	0	0	0
Levinski, Donald, Aberdeen	0	3	.000	19.29	6	0	0	0	2	0	4.2	11	33	14	10	0	1	0	1	6	1	4	2	0
Lewis, Jensen, Mahoning Valley	4	2	.667	3.20	13	11	0	0	0	0	59.0	58	247	24	21	6	2	1	6	11	0	59	2	0
Lewis, Jonathan, Jamestown	1	2	.333	5.85	19	0	0	0	5	0	32.1	43	160	29	21	5	1	3	3	17	0	25	7	0
Lewis, Scott, Mahoning Valley *	0	1	.000	4.60	7	6	0	0	0	0	15.2	13	66	8	8	2	0	0	6	2	0	24	3	0
Lira, Oscar, Vermont	1	2	.333	5.14	16	2	0	0	7	0	28.0	35	133	19	16	1	1	2	4	10	0	10	3	1
Litsch, Jesse, Auburn	1	1	.500	3.60	4	3	0	0	0	0	10.0	11	49	9	4	0	1	2	0	6	0	7	1	0
Liz, Radhames, Aberdeen	5	4	.556	1.77	11	11	0	0	0	0	56.0	36	212	14	11	1	2	0	2	19	0	82	4	3
Loberg, Matthew, Mahoning Valley	0	4	.000	2.29	22	0	0	0	17	7	35.1	32	140	16	9	2	4	0	1	8	0	16	0	0
Long, Nicholas, Vermont	0	0	.000	0.00	5	0	0	0	2	1	7.0	3	25	0	0	0	0	0	1	0	9	2	0	
Lopez, Romelio, Hudson Valley	1	2	.333	1.47	4	4	0	0	0	0	18.1	10	80	8	3	2	0	0	4	10	0	13	1	0
Lozado, Henry, Aberdeen	2	1	.667	3.90	15	0	0	0	2	1	30.0	27	133	18	13	0	3	1	4	14	0	28	1	0
Lugo, Chris, Vermont	2	1	.667	5.13	7	4	0	0	1	0	26.1	32	118	17	15	1	1	0	3	7	0	20	1	0
Lyons, Thomas, Oneonta	0	1	.000	11.85	6	1	0	0	4	0	13.2	19	77	20	18	1	0	1	2	14	0	14	5	0
Mahoney, Collin, Oneonta	0	1	.000	7.82	18	0	0	0	2	0	25.1	22	123	23	22	5	0	3	3	26	0	26	5	0
Maloney, Matthew, Batavia *	2	1	.667	3.89	8	8	0	0	0	0	37.0	38	155	20	16	2	1	2	1	15	0	36	3	0
Manuel, Robert, Brooklyn	0	0	.000	1.80	2	0	0	0	1	0	5.0	5	20	1	1	0	0	0	0	0	0	5	0	0
Marceaux, Jacob, Jamestown	3	5	.375	5.55	10	10	0	0	0	0	47.0	56	215	33	29	5	0	1	6	13	0	32	10	0
Marshall, Brian, Lowell *	3	0	1.000	2.35	11	0	0	0	0	0	23.0	19	99	8	6	1	0	1	4	9	0	31	1	0
Marte, German, Brooklyn	0	0	.000	0.00	1	0	0	0	0	0	1.0	2	5	0	0	0	0	0	0	1	0	0	0	0
Martin, Adrian, Auburn	1	1	.500	3.05	22	2	0	0	7	3	44.1	51	188	19	15	1	0	2	3	2	0	36	5	0
Martinez, Carlos, Vermont	1	7	.125	4.63	13	11	0	0	1	0	68.0	74	299	44	35	2	2	3	5	21	0	39	4	1
Mason, Christopher, Hudson Valley	1	1	.500	2.40	9	0	0	0	3	2	15.0	11	60	4	4	0	2	0	2	8	0	14	1	0
Mateo, Waner, Brooklyn	4	2	.667	2.56	14	12	0	0	1	0	63.1	59	280	28	18	4	0	1	3	30	0	53	3	0
Maxwell, Blake, Lowell	3	3	.500	2.76	26	0	0	0	17	7	45.2	31	180	16	14	1	2	1	3	11	1	29	3	0
McCamie, Zac, Jamestown	0	0	.000	11.05	5	0	0	0	2	0	7.1	16	37	9	9	3	0	1	0	1	0	8	1	0
McCormick, Mark, New Jersey	0	0	.000	0.00	2	2	0	0	0	0	6.0	1	22	0	0	0	0	0	0	3	0	10	1	0
McCrory, Robert, Aberdeen	2	1	.667	3.28	5	5	0	0	0	0	24.2	21	101	9	9	2	0	0	3	8	0	21	3	0
McGee, Jacob, Hudson Valley *	5	4	.556	3.64	15	14	0	0	0	0	76.2	64	308	32	31	4	1	1	1	23	0	89	5	0
Meacham, Cory, New Jersey	0	2	.000	1.98	11	0	0	0	7	1	13.2	6	54	4	3	1	1	1	1	8	0	11	1	0
Meagher, Michael, New Jersey *	0	0	.000	0.00	2	0	0	0	0	0	1.2	1	8	0	0	0	0	0	0	2	0	4	0	0
Mendez, Jose, New Jersey	0	0	.000	9.00	1	0	0	0	0	0	1.0	1	5	1	1	0	0	0	0	1	0	0	0	0
Mendez, Winer, Aberdeen	0	0	.000	0.00	4	0	0	0	2	0	6.0	4	25	0	0	0	1	0	0	5	0	4	0	0
Meyers, Ryan, Brooklyn	1	5	.167	4.08	9	8	0	0	0	0	35.1	40	164	25	16	1	0	4	14	0	18	2	0	
Michael, Mark, Williamsport	1	0	1.000	2.70	2	2	0	0	0	0	10.0	7	38	3	3	1	0	0	1	1	0	7	0	0
Miller, Adam, Mahoning Valley	0	0	.000	5.06	3	3	0	0	0	0	10.2	17	50	6	6	0	0	1	3	4	0	6	0	0
Miller, Kevin, Williamsport	5	1	.833	2.08	29	0	0	0	12	3	39.0	30	146	9	9	2	2	1	0	10	2	24	2	0
Miller, Matt, Mahoning Valley	0	0	.000	54.00	1	1	0	0	0	0	0.2	5	8	4	4	0	0	0	0	1	0	0	0	0
Mitchinson, Scott, Batavia	5	6	.455	5.35	13	13	1	1	0	0	70.2	88	307	49	42	1	5	4	4	16	0	57	3	1
Moeves, Mark, Williamsport	3	4	.429	4.12	24	0	0	0	6	0	39.1	39	179	21	18	1	1	1	5	22	2	32	6	0
Montani, Jeffrey, Brooklyn	0	0	.000	1.00	6	0	0	0	2	2	9.0	8	35	2	1	0	0	0	0	3	0	7	0	0
Morrison, Erik, Staten Island	3	1	.750	2.67	21	0	0	0	5	0	27.0	23	111	11	8	2	4	1	0	11	1	22	1	0
Moscoso, Guillermo, Oneonta	2	2	.500	4.37	11	10	0	0	0	0	47.1	49	202	27	23	4	0	2	1	11	0	44	4	0
Munoz, Luis, Williamsport	6	3	.667	3.81	16	13	0	0	0	0	78.0	69	314	41	33	8	4	3	1	22	0	46	5	1
Ness, Roger, Mahoning Valley	4	2	.667	1.67	14	10	0	0	0	0	59.1	52	245	15	11	0	1	0	4	19	0	68	3	0
Newlin, Darren, Williamsport	3	1	.750	3.53	20	1	0	0	3	1	43.1	49	189	24	17	3	3	4	1	17	1	31	0	0
Newsom, Randall, Lowell	0	0	.000	0.00	1	0	0	0	0	0	2.2	1	11	0	0	0	0	0	0	2	0	4	0	0
Nickerson, Jon-Michael, Jamestown *	2	5	.286	5.93	17	14	0	0	0	0	57.2	59	264	44	38	9	1	1	4	37	0	62	6	1
Norfleet, Mathew, Oneonta	3	1	.750	2.29	18	1	0	0	8	0	39.1	32	167	15	10	1	2	2	17	0	32	2	1	
O'Brien, Matt, Oneonta	6	3	.667	3.34	15	15	0	0	0	0	89.0	79	368	42	33	6	1	3	1	24	1	57	5	0
Ochoa, Nehomar, Vermont	0	2	.000	5.93	23	0	0	0	13	3	30.1	36	149	25	20	4	0	3	5	14	0	27	7	0

Pitcher, Team	W	L	Pct.	ERA	G	GS	CG	ShO	GF	Sv.	IP	H	TBF	R	ER	HR	SH	SF	HB	BB	IBB	SO	WP	Bk.
Olson, Garrett, Aberdeen *	2	1	.667	1.58	11	6	0	0	2	1	40.0	22	149	7	7	1	4	0	2	13	0	40	1	0
Outman, Joshua, Batavia *	2	1	.667	2.76	11	4	0	0	0	0	29.1	23	127	14	9	1	1	0	2	14	0	31	3	0
Overholt, Patrick, Batavia	2	3	.400	2.65	21	0	0	0	15	5	34.0	28	142	12	10	1	5	2	2	13	2	51	4	1
Owen, William, Aberdeen	1	2	.333	1.57	23	0	0	0	21	8	23.0	18	100	8	4	0	1	0	2	13	0	27	2	0
Ozuna, Modesto, Lowell	2	0	1.000	6.35	13	0	0	0	3	0	22.2	25	108	16	16	1	0	0	4	12	0	15	3	0
Palm, Joshua, Vermont	0	1	.000	8.10	3	0	0	0	1	0	3.1	7	18	5	3	0	1	0	1	2	0	3	0	0
Parnell, Robert, Brooklyn	2	3	.400	1.73	15	14	0	0	1	0	73.0	48	294	20	14	1	0	2	4	29	1	67	3	0
Patterson, Garrett, Staten Island *	1	2	.333	3.71	17	11	0	0	1	0	51.0	37	220	22	21	1	2	0	1	38	0	71	9	0
Paulk, Robert, Brooklyn	4	0	1.000	0.95	14	0	0	0	6	4	19.0	16	82	4	2	0	2	0	0	10	0	21	2	0
Pekarek, Justin, Mahoning Valley *	2	1	.667	1.50	9	2	0	0	2	0	30.0	26	122	8	5	0	3	0	0	10	0	43	3	0
Pena, Mario, Lowell *	6	8	.429	4.50	16	16	0	0	0	0	82.0	97	356	56	41	6	5	1	6	10	0	31	9	1
Pendleton, Lance, Staten Island	1	0	1.000	2.33	9	6	0	0	0	0	27.0	27	123	11	7	1	1	0	1	13	0	23	2	1
Peralta, Yader, Lowell	0	0	.000	3.97	6	0	0	0	2	0	11.1	7	47	5	5	0	1	1	2	6	0	11	0	1
Phillips, Paul, Auburn	2	1	.667	2.29	26	0	0	0	23	13	39.1	31	161	14	10	2	2	1	2	13	2	41	4	2
Phillips, Ryan, Lowell *	7	2	.778	2.28	14	14	0	0	0	0	67.0	45	274	19	17	2	0	0	4	31	0	61	6	1
Quijada, Fernando, Batavia	2	3	.400	4.13	23	0	0	0	19	6	32.2	34	146	19	15	0	4	1	3	14	3	39	6	0
Rasowsky, Avi, Jamestown *	0	0	.000	7.36	2	0	0	0	1	0	7.1	10	35	6	6	1	0	0	0	5	0	8	0	0
Rawl, Aaron, Batavia	0	2	.000	3.38	8	0	0	0	4	2	16.0	22	67	7	6	0	0	2	0	0	0	8	0	1
Ray, Robert, Auburn	4	3	.571	2.77	15	13	0	0	0	0	61.2	46	253	22	19	2	0	3	4	20	0	58	3	1
Redmond, Todd, Williamsport	1	2	.333	1.98	15	14	0	0	0	0	72.2	62	294	22	16	2	1	0	6	21	0	63	2	0
Reinhard, Gregory, Hudson Valley	2	3	.400	3.71	12	11	0	0	0	0	53.1	54	225	28	22	5	1	6	5	13	0	63	0	0
Rengel, Orlando, Brooklyn	0	0	.000	3.51	6	6	0	0	0	0	25.2	24	109	12	10	1	1	3	3	9	0	22	5	0
Repole, Michael, New Jersey	7	2	.778	5.30	25	0	0	0	8	1	37.1	49	178	25	22	3	1	1	2	17	2	34	6	1
Reyes, Jorge, Brooklyn	4	5	.444	5.20	13	13	1	0	0	0	62.1	80	279	40	36	5	0	2	2	19	0	35	5	1
Rico, Matt, Hudson Valley	0	0	.000	2.53	8	0	0	0	5	0	10.2	8	43	3	3	2	0	0	2	2	0	9	2	0
Risinger, Kyle, Brooklyn	1	3	.250	4.04	15	0	0	0	5	0	35.2	47	164	23	16	1	0	1	3	15	1	23	2	0
Robertson, Quinton, New Jersey	2	3	.400	3.02	12	7	0	0	0	0	47.2	55	209	19	16	5	0	0	8	7	0	30	2	0
Robertson, Timothy, Oneonta	1	1	.500	2.65	16	0	0	0	7	1	37.1	38	158	13	11	3	1	0	1	12	1	27	5	1
Robinson, Dennis, Aberdeen	1	1	.500	5.06	5	5	0	0	0	0	21.1	22	94	16	12	1	0	1	3	7	0	15	1	0
Roddy, Dustin, Mahoning Valley	3	3	.500	2.70	25	0	0	0	21	6	36.2	35	155	22	11	4	3	2	4	9	2	43	1	0
Rodriguez, Edward, Auburn	3	1	.750	3.49	21	0	0	0	8	3	38.2	41	164	21	15	2	1	3	3	7	2	25	5	1
Rodriguez, Edward, Vermont *	2	1	.667	4.81	20	3	0	0	4	0	48.2	60	217	31	26	3	2	5	1	19	0	29	3	1
Rodriguez, Felix, Staten Island	0	0	.000	3.00	2	2	0	0	0	0	3.0	4	13	1	1	1	0	0	0	0	0	5	0	0
Romero, Ricardo, Auburn *	0	0	.000	0.00	1	1	0	0	0	0	2.0	2	9	0	0	0	0	0	0	1	0	2	1	0
Rosario, Carlos, Staten Island	0	0	.000	3.12	9	0	0	0	3	0	8.2	11	41	3	3	1	0	0	0	7	0	5	3	3
Ruckle, Jacob, Brooklyn	0	0	.000	0.00	2	0	0	0	2	0	2.1	1	8	0	0	0	0	0	0	0	0	2	0	0
Rueger, Bryan, Staten Island *	1	0	1.000	6.00	4	0	0	0	1	0	6.0	8	27	5	4	0	0	0	0	2	0	5	0	0
Rulon, Benjamin, Hudson Valley *	1	0	1.000	2.28	6	3	1	1	0	0	23.2	25	97	9	6	1	1	1	2	5	0	15	0	0
Rusch, Matthew, Oneonta	1	0	1.000	1.80	2	0	0	0	0	0	5.0	6	20	1	1	0	0	0	0	5	0	5	1	0
Sadlowski, Kyle, New Jersey	0	4	.000	7.91	11	6	0	0	1	0	33.0	54	167	34	29	3	1	1	5	11	0	25	2	0
Salas, Joseph, Williamsport *	0	0	.000	3.86	5	0	0	0	1	0	7.0	6	29	3	3	0	0	0	1	1	0	6	0	0
Sborz, John, Oneonta	1	3	.250	4.34	9	7	0	0	0	0	29.0	24	136	15	14	1	3	0	2	27	0	25	9	0
Schellinger, Michael, New Jersey	0	0	.000	5.23	4	0	0	0	1	1	10.1	9	41	6	6	1	0	0	0	3	0	13	0	0
Schmidt, Joshua, Staten Island	5	1	.833	0.27	26	0	0	0	23	13	33.0	14	119	1	1	0	2	1	1	8	2	47	1	1
Schmidt, Kyle, Aberdeen	0	1	.000	5.40	1	1	0	0	0	0	5.0	7	25	4	3	0	0	1	1	0	0	7	1	0
Schroer, Steven, Staten Island	3	3	.500	1.60	23	0	0	0	4	0	39.1	24	151	10	7	2	3	1	2	12	0	39	3	0
Schwabe, Ryan, Aberdeen *	2	6	.250	4.09	18	7	0	0	1	0	55.0	57	239	32	25	2	2	2	2	20	0	41	0	0
Seccombe, David, Staten Island	8	2	.800	2.15	17	9	0	0	1	1	71.0	45	283	18	17	4	2	0	4	26	0	53	6	0
Shefka, Richard, Vermont	1	2	.333	6.53	10	5	0	0	0	0	30.1	46	144	25	22	2	1	4	1	10	0	20	2	0
Shepard, Kevin, Batavia *	2	1	.667	4.76	18	1	0	0	5	0	34.0	43	157	21	18	1	2	1	4	14	1	28	2	0
Solis, Hairo, Staten Island	7	1	.875	3.23	21	0	0	0	6	1	30.2	23	117	12	11	3	2	1	1	8	2	24	0	0
Soriano, Julio, Aberdeen	1	2	.333	0.66	6	2	0	0	2	0	13.2	10	63	5	1	2	0	0	2	8	1	18	0	0
Soto, Auddy, Vermont	0	0	.000	0.00	1	0	0	0	1	0	0.2	0	2	0	0	0	0	0	0	0	0	2	0	0
Sowers, Jeremy, Auburn	4	0	1.000	4.86	19	2	0	0	3	0	37.0	42	170	23	20	1	0	2	4	16	0	27	3	1
Stadanlick, Ryan, Aberdeen	0	1	.000	11.37	4	0	0	0	2	0	6.1	7	31	8	8	0	2	0	0	5	1	7	4	0
Stammen, Craig, Vermont	4	5	.444	4.06	13	7	0	0	3	0	51.0	62	225	36	23	2	0	2	2	12	0	32	3	1
Stanford, Jason, Mahoning Valley *	0	0	.000	0.00	2	2	0	0	0	0	1.2	1	9	0	0	0	0	0	0	2	0	1	0	0
Stephens, Jason, Staten Island	4	1	.800	2.82	18	10	0	0	2	1	67.0	55	266	25	21	3	4	2	5	19	0	52	3	1
Stevens, Daniel, New Jersey *	0	0	.000	2.70	5	0	0	0	2	1	3.1	6	19	2	1	0	0	0	3	3	0	3	1	0
Stewart, Clayton, Batavia	2	3	.400	2.74	14	0	0	0	6	0	23.0	23	96	8	7	0	2	0	0	7	0	17	1	0
Stidfole, Sean, Auburn	4	1	.800	3.79	19	0	0	0	3	0	35.2	26	159	22	15	1	0	0	3	20	1	40	5	0
Stuart, Cory, Staten Island	3	1	.750	0.83	22	0	0	0	19	7	32.2	17	129	8	3	1	1	0	5	13	1	50	0	1
Suero, Nicolas, Williamsport	0	2	.000	4.50	3	1	0	0	1	0	12.0	14	52	8	6	1	0	0	0	2	0	7	0	0
Swanson, Matt, Williamsport	4	2	.667	1.61	19	0	0	0	18	6	28.0	16	109	6	5	2	1	0	4	7	0	30	1	1
Tabeek, Kyle, Lowell	0	0	.000	9.75	7	0	0	0	0	0	12.0	19	65	15	13	1	0	0	2	10	0	6	0	0
Talbott, Travis, Jamestown *	0	2	.000	5.11	7	0	0	0	2	0	12.1	16	56	9	7	0	0	0	0	8	1	8	3	0
Taylor, Jeffrey, Vermont	0	2	.000	9.18	14	0	0	0	3	0	16.2	22	89	23	17	0	1	1	2	13	0	16	0	1
Thompson, Aaron, Jamestown *	1	2	.333	3.10	5	5	0	0	0	0	20.1	25	94	13	7	1	0	1	1	10	0	17	0	0
Timm, Jordan, Auburn *	0	1	.000	6.75	1	1	0	0	0	0	4.0	5	17	3	3	0	1	0	0	1	0	4	1	0
Tomasiewicz, Kevin, Brooklyn *	3	3	.500	5.62	20	5	0	0	6	3	41.2	56	194	32	26	5	0	1	2	18	1	37	3	0
Townsend, Wade, Hudson Valley	0	4	.000	5.49	12	10	0	0	0	0	39.1	44	187	28	24	4	0	1	2	24	0	33	8	1
Trahan, David, Vermont	1	0	1.000	3.00	9	0	0	0	5	0	12.0	14	55	4	4	0	1	1	2	8	0	5	0	0
Trent, Matthew, New Jersey	1	1	.500	0.68	14	0	0	0	14	9	13.1	8	51	1	1	0	1	2	0	6	1	13	0	0
Tressler, Aaron, Auburn	1	0	1.000	0.00	5	0	0	0	1	0	13.1	8	46	0	0	0	0	0	0	1	0	11	0	0
Trias, Orlando, Auburn	4	7	.364	3.89	15	15	0	0	0	0	81.0	85	352	40	35	4	1	3	6	21	0	54	7	2
Tucker, Ryan, Jamestown	1	1	.500	8.36	4	4	0	0	0	0	14.0	21	76	14	13	3	0	1	2	8	0	18	3	0
Vaclavik, Justin, Williamsport	0	1	.000	4.38	20	0	0	0	15	9	24.2	24	107	12	12	0	2	2	3	10	1	28	0	0
Valdez, Luis, Williamsport	4	5	.444	4.53	16	7	0	0	2	0	59.2	67	259	39	30	4	0	2	4	17	0	30	3	1
Vander Weg, Scott, New Jersey	2	2	.500	2.45	24	0	0	0	17	4	25.2	21	112	8	7	0	2	2	2	14	3	29	6	0
Van Houten, Jeffrey, Jamestown	0	0	.000	0.00	2	0	0	0	2	0	1.2	0	5	0	0	0	0	0	0	1	0	3	0	0
Vargas, Albert, Mahoning Valley	1	3	.250	4.43	10	0	0	0	5	0	20.1	26	88	11	10	3	2	0	0	6	0	13	0	0

Pitcher, Team	W	L	Pct.	ERA	G	GS	CG	ShO	GF	Sv.	IP	H	TBF	R	ER	HR	SH	SF	HB	BB	IBB	SO	WP	Bk.
Vasquez, Sendy, Oneonta	7	0	1.000	3.63	15	11	0	0	0	0	67.0	53	286	30	27	4	2	4	5	34	0	60	4	0
Villalona, Guillermo, Staten Island	1	0	1.000	2.30	8	6	0	0	0	0	31.1	29	124	8	8	0	0	2	0	7	0	25	0	1
Volstad, Christopher, Jamestown	3	2	.600	2.13	7	7	0	0	0	0	38.0	43	169	19	9	0	1	1	3	11	0	29	2	1
Wagner, Michael, Staten Island *	0	1	.000	1.59	19	0	0	0	4	0	17.0	18	78	4	3	1	1	1	0	7	1	19	1	0
Wagner, Nicholas, Hudson Valley	1	0	1.000	3.38	9	0	0	0	1	0	13.1	15	62	8	5	3	1	0	1	5	0	10	1	0
Walker, Aaron, Hudson Valley *	1	1	.500	3.38	15	0	0	0	2	1	24.0	23	105	13	9	0	0	0	1	7	0	22	2	0
Walker, Matthew, Hudson Valley	0	0	.000	10.80	1	1	0	0	0	0	3.1	5	19	4	4	0	0	1	0	4	0	5	0	0
Webber, Nicholas, New Jersey	5	2	.714	1.87	10	9	0	0	0	0	53.0	35	211	18	11	2	0	0	1	15	0	43	4	0
Weintraub, Jason, Brooklyn	0	0	.000	4.70	4	0	0	0	2	0	7.2	7	34	4	4	0	0	0	0	5	0	9	0	1
West, Sean, Jamestown *	0	2	.000	5.73	3	3	0	0	0	0	11.0	17	52	7	7	1	0	0	5	0	14	1	0
Whelan, Kevin, Oneonta	1	1	.500	2.25	11	0	0	0	11	4	12.0	2	46	4	3	1	0	0	1	6	0	19	2	1
Wilson, Gibbs, Oneonta	2	0	1.000	2.61	9	0	0	0	6	3	10.1	4	41	3	3	1	1	1	2	6	0	17	3	0
Wlodarczyk, Michael, Hudson Valley *	0	4	.000	1.90	5	5	0	0	0	0	23.2	22	106	9	5	0	0	0	1	12	1	25	1	1
Wood, Adam, Jamestown *	1	1	.500	3.97	25	0	0	0	10	0	34.0	36	149	19	15	0	3	3	1	16	0	30	4	1
Woodson, Michael, Mahoning Valley	0	0	.000	9.00	2	0	0	0	2	0	2.0	2	13	4	2	0	0	1	3	1	0	1	0	1
Wordekemper, Eric, Staten Island	0	2	.000	4.50	2	2	0	0	0	0	10.0	15	40	5	5	1	2	2	0	2	0	3	1	0
Yost, Wendell, Vermont *	6	5	.545	3.25	14	14	1	1	0	0	83.0	70	347	36	30	7	2	3	2	30	0	56	1	0
Zagurski, Michael, Batavia *	3	4	.429	4.60	15	8	0	0	3	0	45.0	47	196	29	23	2	1	1	3	15	0	43	1	1
Zarate, Mauro, Jamestown	1	3	.250	4.28	24	0	0	0	19	7	27.1	24	114	13	13	3	2	1	2	8	1	35	0	0
Zerbe, Chad, Mahoning Valley *	0	0	.000	0.00	1	0	0	0	0	0	1.0	1	4	0	0	0	0	0	0	0	0	0	0	0
Zick, Jeremy, New Jersey	1	0	1.000	2.79	25	0	0	0	0	3	42.0	42	191	26	13	4	2	1	5	14	1	37	2	0
Zink, James, Lowell	0	3	.000	2.63	14	14	0	0	0	0	48.0	46	203	19	14	2	1	2	1	18	0	26	2	0
Zuercher, Zachary, New Jersey *	5	7	.417	3.73	16	14	0	0	0	0	82.0	66	332	36	34	9	4	2	9	25	0	63	2	2

COMBINATION SHUTOUTS: Aberdeen (5) -- Liz-Montani-Olson, Hernandez-Hernandez-Olson-Montani, Olson-Hamblet-Owen, Bergesen-Boehm-Brocato-Chamberlin-Owen, Soriano-Hoey-Lozado-Owen. Auburn (2) -- Fowler-Ray-Tressler, Ray-Martin. Batavia (3) -- Zagurski-Hill-Henyan-Quijada, Outman-Quijada, Blaine-Henyan-Overholt. Brooklyn (4) -- Landing-Hope-Alfonzo, Reyes-Aguilar, Parnell-Risinger-Tomasiewicz, Parnell-Paulk. Hudson Valley (2) -- Reinhard-De Los Santos-Feldkamp, Townsend-Corporan-Feldkamp. Jamestown (2) -- Nickerson-Wood-Zarate, West-Lewis-Wood-Zarate. Lowell (7) -- Pena-Casillas-Guanchez, Blackley-Guyette-Maxwell, Phillips-Marshall-Maxwell-Flores, Buchholz-Jones-Casillas-Guanchez, Blackley-Jones-Large, Pena-Jones-Casillas-Guanchez, Buchholz-Hancock-Jones-Guanchez. Mahoning Valley (3) -- Ness-Loberg, Stanford-Edell-Loberg, Ness-Cowley-Vargas. New Jersey (6) -- Cooper-Meacham-Sadlowski-Trent, Hawksworth-Zuercher-Grant-Zick-Hearne, Webber-Daniels-Gross-Trent, McCormick-Hearne-Daniels-Gross-Meacham, Zuercher-Robertson-Trent, Zuercher-Vander Weg. Oneonta (4) -- Sborz-Fragoso-Vasquez-Claggett, O'Brien-Mahoney-Whelan, Fragoso-Mahoney-Fraser, O'Brien-Wilson. Staten Island (6) -- Rodriguez-Kroenke-Seccombe-Wagner, Seccombe-Kroenke-Schmidt, Berg-Stephens, Conroy-Stuart, Stephens-Wagner-Schmidt, Stephens-Solis-Wagner-Schroer-Schmidt. Tri-City (3) -- McKeller-Sheridan, McKeller-Paulino Del Guidice, Davis-Sarver-Soto. Vermont (1) -- Yost-Lehman-Trahan. Williamsport (7) -- Antelo-Newlin-Salas-Vaclavik, Munoz-Heisel-Moeves-Swanson, Antelo-Moeves-Swanson, Bauserman-Moeves-Swanson, Bauserman-Swanson, Valdez-Miller, Munoz-Heisel-Vaclavik.

NO-HIT GAMES: Ray (5 innings) and Martin (4 innings), Auburn, defeated Batavia, 5-0, August 26.

2005 FIELDING

TEAM

Team	G	PO	A	E	TC	DP	TP	PB	Pct.
Staten Island	20	39	849	74	2962	66	0	20	.975
Tri-City	76	1944	726	68	2738	70	0	18	.975
Oneonta	75	1965	787	84	2836	73	0	13	.970
Batavia	75	2027	816	101	2944	66	0	16	.966
Aberdeen	75	1992	740	99	2831	72	0	28	.965
New Jersey	76	2016	809	103	2928	62	0	20	.965
Williamsport	76	2039	909	111	3059	85	0	22	.964
Lowell	75	1977	835	110	2922	54	0	20	.962
Mahoning Valley	75	2002	767	108	2877	69	0	19	.962
Auburn	75	2021	866	117	3004	59	0	18	.961
Brooklyn	76	2035	876	117	3028	84	0	11	.961
Hudson Valley	74	1950	711	112	2773	51	1	14	.960
Jamestown	75	1985	755	117	2857	71	0	18	.959
Vermont	76	1988	812	126	2926	62	0	17	.957

INDIVIDUAL

FIRST BASEMEN

NOTE: All caps denotes fielding-percentage leader based on 38 games for catchers, 51 for all other non-pitchers or 61 innings for pitchers. *Throws lefthanded.

Player, Team	Pct.	G	PO	A	E	TC	DP
Anderson, Matthew, Brooklyn	1.000	1	10	1	0	11	1
Apodaca, Luis, Vermont	.983	14	107	6	2	115	12
Aranda, Mark, Jamestown *	.984	24	170	12	3	185	14
Arnedo, Rolando, Vermont	.981	31	291	17	6	314	24
Bergeron, Jabe, Brooklyn	1.000	2	18	1	0	19	0
Bohm, Kyle, Auburn	1.000	13	63	5	0	68	5
Bouman, John, Hudson Valley	1.000	2	13	0	0	13	0
Brown, Jordan, Mahoning Valley *	.970	3	28	4	1	33	1
Burgess, John, Lowell *	.990	9	93	4	1	98	11
Celigoy, Joshua, Auburn	.983	20	107	10	2	119	6
Clark, John, Mahoning Valley	.996	30	201	24	1	226	20
Clem, Christopher, Mahoning Valley	1.000	1	5	2	0	7	0
Conway, Brandon, Vermont	1.000	2	12	0	0	12	0
Delgado, Jose, New Jersey	1.000	1	4	0	0	4	0
Edwards, Matt, Batavia	.981	28	240	17	5	262	22
Ellington, Matthew, Jamestown *	.958	9	85	6	4	95	6

Player, Team	Pct.	G	PO	A	E	TC	DP
Evans, Nicholas, Brooklyn	.988	56	537	31	7	575	45
Farkes, Zak, Lowell	.929	2	11	2	1	14	0
Finan, Ryan, Aberdeen	.997	38	318	17	1	336	33
Fleisher, Mark, Aberdeen	.994	39	330	14	2	346	26
Galloway, Carl, Batavia	.993	16	126	7	1	134	13
Garcia, Felipe, Staten Island	.994	22	163	8	1	172	18
Harris, Clay, Batavia	.990	35	287	21	3	311	24
Haske, Mark, Oneonta	1.000	2	8	0	0	8	1
Head, Stephen, Mahoning Valley *	.984	7	57	5	1	63	4
Hiser, Charles, Mahoning Valley	.988	19	149	14	2	165	20
Howell, John, Vermont	1.000	6	52	1	0	53	4
Hughes, John, Hudson Valley *	.990	10	91	8	1	100	8
Jenkins, Andrew, Jamestown	1.000	3	26	1	0	27	2
Johnson, Joshua, Hudson Valley	.985	19	125	10	2	137	8
Kelly, Dustin, Lowell	.962	6	48	3	2	53	1
Larish, Jeffrey, Oneonta	.988	16	144	15	2	161	23
LARSEN, KYLE, Staten Island *	.994	58	505	34	3	542	44
Leonard, Donald, Lowell	1.000	7	63	4	0	67	5
Lytle, Andrew, Mahoning Valley	.989	11	81	10	1	92	9
Mathias, Ryder, Hudson Valley	.978	46	333	26	8	367	33
Maxey, Jason, Aberdeen	1.000	1	4	0	0	4	0
Mendez, Jose, New Jersey	.974	5	33	4	1	38	2
Mendez, Rafael, Oneonta	.989	34	247	16	3	266	22
Mercurio, Matthew, Lowell	.989	20	172	12	2	186	10
Messner, Nathan, Jamestown	.983	34	275	10	5	290	30
Metropoulos, Joseph, Auburn	.983	19	152	21	3	176	9
Pearce, Steven, Williamsport	.987	71	651	58	9	718	65
Petersen, Joshua, Brooklyn	.984	14	108	13	2	123	15
Peterson, Derrick, Mahoning Valley	1.000	7	62	4	0	66	8
Pilittere, Peter, Staten Island	1.000	3	17	1	0	18	0
Poni, Francis, Williamsport	.967	9	81	7	3	91	5
Poterson, Jonathan, Staten Island	1.000	1	1	0	0	1	0
Pulley, Matthew, Aberdeen	...	1	0	0	0	0	0
Reimold, Nolan, Aberdeen	...	1	0	0	0	0	0
Roberson, Ryan, Oneonta	.993	30	247	21	2	270	18
Rodgers, Mark, New Jersey	.988	55	494	19	6	519	42
Roth, Randy, New Jersey	1.000	4	36	2	0	38	1
Sanchez, Gabriel, Jamestown	.981	12	97	9	2	108	10
Skorupski, John, New Jersey	.970	9	59	5	2	66	6
Thissen, Greg, Vermont	.958	3	23	0	1	24	1
Thomas, Nicolas, Auburn	.993	45	375	25	3	403	30
Torres, Carlos, Vermont	.982	24	214	9	4	227	14

Player, Team	Pct.	G	PO	A	E	TC	DP
Travis, David, Vermont	.870	3	19	1	3	23	2
Twomley, Jason, Lowell *	.980	36	310	25	7	342	24
Van Slyke, A.J., New Jersey	1.000	5	36	3	0	39	5
Wabick, David, Brooklyn	1.000	5	51	2	0	53	5
Wilkerson, Matthew, New Jersey	.976	4	39	2	1	42	0

SECOND BASEMEN

Player, Team	Pct.	G	PO	A	E	TC	DP
Acey, Jermy, Auburn	1.000	11	13	24	0	37	5
Antoniato, Pasquale, Batavia	1.000	3	3	7	0	10	1
Bernhard, Steven, Auburn	.925	16	27	35	5	67	5
Blair, Cameron, Williamsport	.966	32	55	118	6	179	33
Bouman, John, Hudson Valley	.913	14	21	21	4	46	2
Castro, Jonathan, Vermont	1.000	5	6	11	0	17	2
Chavez, Dirimo, Brooklyn	1.000	5	12	17	0	29	1
Clem, Christopher, Mahoning Valley	.989	18	43	43	1	87	9
Contreras, Jose, Vermont	.941	3	7	9	1	17	4
Conway, Brandon, Vermont	.931	8	11	16	2	29	2
CORONA, REEGIE, Staten Island	.981	67	157	205	7	369	49
Dalton, Brett, Batavia	.961	34	51	95	6	152	17
Delgado, Jose, New Jersey	.966	43	69	104	6	179	16
Durante, Eric, Hudson Valley	.974	49	107	118	6	231	25
Farkes, Zak, Lowell	.938	6	13	17	2	32	5
Fornasiere, Matthew, Mahoning Valley	.927	40	76	89	13	178	26
Gaerlan, Armand, Brooklyn	.970	27	50	78	4	132	22
Garcia, Julio Cesar, Mahoning Valley	.923	6	17	19	3	39	5
Grandstrand, Brett, Williamsport	.923	4	7	17	2	26	3
Guerrero, Francisco, Aberdeen	.984	31	56	67	2	125	16
Guerrero, James, Jamestown	.956	48	81	138	10	229	24
Gutierrez, Christopher, Auburn	1.000	2	2	9	0	11	2
Hardy, John, Batavia	.943	21	25	41	4	70	5
Harris, Clay, Batavia	.981	23	50	55	2	107	17
Haske, Mark, Oneonta	.932	10	13	28	3	44	2
Hayes, Calvin, New Jersey	1.000	4	8	15	0	23	5
Kelly, Dustin, Lowell	.945	14	16	36	3	55	5
Lafountain, Jason, Staten Island	.667	2	0	2	1	3	0
Lane, Andrew, Vermont	.976	30	56	66	3	125	13
Lipsey, Carl, Lowell	1.000	2	2	2	0	4	1
Lomack, Jermal, Williamsport	.875	3	6	8	2	16	1
Lowrie, Jed, Lowell	1.000	11	28	20	0	48	5
Lytle, Andrew, Mahoning Valley	.898	13	17	27	5	49	3
Malo, Jonathan, Brooklyn	.955	15	30	33	3	66	13
Marconi, Robert, Aberdeen	.982	22	44	67	2	113	13
Matsui, Kazuo, Brooklyn	1.000	1	2	3	0	5	1
Matthews, William, Hudson Valley	.941	5	7	9	1	17	3
Mendez, Rafael, Oneonta	1.000	2	1	3	0	4	1
Mercurio, Matthew, Lowell	.958	11	21	25	2	48	4
Mihalics, Joseph, Brooklyn	1.000	4	7	11	0	18	3
Naccarata, Ivan, Brooklyn	.947	33	51	91	8	150	22
Natale, Jeffrey, Lowell	.980	10	16	34	1	51	5
Nelson, Daniel, New Jersey	.938	5	7	8	1	16	1
Nunez, Eduardo, Vermont	.931	29	47	88	10	145	16
Patino, Jorge, Oneonta	.963	22	29	48	3	80	7
Ramos, Dominic, Lowell	.981	28	56	95	3	154	16
Rhymes, William, Oneonta	.957	51	100	123	10	233	33
Richmond, Kevin, New Jersey	.922	10	26	21	4	51	7
Roche, Gary, Jamestown	.945	31	46	75	7	128	19
Roth, Anthony, Staten Island	.952	10	14	26	2	42	3
Rousseve, Brandon, Hudson Valley	.962	12	22	28	2	52	4
Rowlett, Casey, New Jersey	.951	20	37	60	5	102	15
Santiago, John, Williamsport	.962	28	49	76	5	130	15
Sena, Emmanuel, Auburn	.967	7	9	20	1	30	2
Shoffit, Sean, Auburn	.954	54	88	141	11	240	26
Solano, Donovan, New Jersey	.900	3	2	7	1	10	1
Solano, Euvi, Williamsport	.962	11	20	31	2	53	5
Thissen, Greg, Vermont	.944	7	16	18	2	36	4
Zapata, Jose, Aberdeen	.983	24	42	77	2	121	19

THIRD BASEMEN

Player, Team	Pct.	G	PO	A	E	TC	DP
Acey, Jermy, Auburn	.932	33	19	63	6	88	5
Anderson, Matthew, Brooklyn	.958	22	14	54	3	71	3
Anson, Kyle, Staten Island	.989	36	19	74	1	94	6
Baez, Welinson, Batavia	1.000	4	3	6	0	9	0
Bernhard, Steven, Auburn	...	1	0	0	0	0	0
Blanton, John, Batavia	1.000	1	0	3	0	3	0
Bouman, John, Hudson Valley	.909	14	6	14	2	22	2
Cabral, Marcos, Jamestown	1.000	2	1	2	0	3	0
Canada, Bradley, Staten Island	1.000	2	0	2	0	2	0
Carroll, Mark, Staten Island	.912	18	11	41	5	57	2

Player, Team	Pct.	G	PO	A	E	TC	DP
Celigoy, Joshua, Auburn	.833	3	1	4	1	6	0
Chavez, Jose, Mahoning Valley	.667	1	0	2	1	3	0
Clem, Christopher, Mahoning Valley	.959	20	17	30	2	49	3
Conway, Brandon, Vermont	.902	17	9	37	5	51	1
Costanzo, Michael, Batavia	.906	69	52	150	21	223	15
DAVIS, LEONARD, Vermont	.914	58	51	130	17	198	9
de la Rosa, Jairo, Hudson Valley	.863	31	26	56	13	95	4
Devoir, Jordan, Staten Island	.857	8	4	14	3	21	1
Durante, Eric, Hudson Valley	.667	2	1	1	1	3	0
Farkes, Zak, Lowell	.880	22	12	54	9	75	2
Figueroa, Johan, Vermont	1.000	4	1	7	0	8	1
Gardner, Brett, Staten Island *	...	1	0	0	0	0	0
Garibaldi, Anthony, Auburn	.887	35	16	70	11	97	9
Gonzalez, Hector, Staten Island	.800	1	0	4	1	5	0
Gonzalez, Jesus, Auburn	1.000	3	1	2	0	3	0
Grandstrand, Brett, Williamsport	.952	9	4	16	1	21	0
Grogan, Timothy, Brooklyn	.875	16	6	22	4	32	1
Gutierrez, Christopher, Auburn	.938	11	2	13	1	16	1
Hardy, John, Batavia	...	1	0	0	0	0	0
Harris, Clay, Batavia	.875	5	2	5	1	8	0
Harvey, Bryan, Jamestown	.833	25	9	31	8	48	1
Haske, Mark, Oneonta	.927	12	12	26	3	41	6
Jenkins, Andrew, Jamestown	1.000	1	0	5	0	5	0
Kelly, Dustin, Lowell	.943	19	8	42	3	53	4
Kouzmanoff, Kevin, Mahoning Valley	.750	3	0	6	2	8	0
Lane, Andrew, Vermont	.778	2	2	5	2	9	0
Leonard, Donald, Lowell	.500	1	1	1	2	4	0
Lytle, Andrew, Mahoning Valley	1.000	5	0	6	0	6	0
Marconi, Robert, Aberdeen	.874	38	19	64	12	95	2
Mendez, Jose, New Jersey	1.000	3	0	1	0	1	0
Mercurio, Matthew, Lowell	.842	33	24	61	16	101	4
Middleton, Cory, Oneonta	.905	65	32	130	17	179	9
Morris, Adam, New Jersey	.952	17	6	34	2	42	4
Naccarata, Ivan, Brooklyn	.857	11	9	21	5	35	1
Nelson, Daniel, New Jersey	.889	22	12	60	9	81	6
Padgett, Nathan, Jamestown	.667	1	2	0	1	3	0
Patino, Jorge, Oneonta	.750	4	1	2	1	4	0
Petersen, Joshua, Brooklyn	.888	28	19	68	11	98	6
Peterson, Derrick, Mahoning Valley	.900	51	29	79	12	120	11
Prasch, Edward, Williamsport	.892	25	15	43	7	65	3
Pulley, Matthew, Aberdeen	.880	39	26	55	11	92	7
Rainville, Michael, Hudson Valley	.857	33	21	57	13	91	2
Ramos, Dominic, Lowell	.818	3	0	9	2	11	1
Richmond, Kevin, New Jersey	.600	4	0	6	4	10	1
Roche, Gary, Jamestown	1.000	11	3	19	0	22	2
Rogers, Tanner, Jamestown	.759	9	7	15	7	29	1
Roth, Anthony, Staten Island	.886	16	4	27	4	35	1
Roth, Randy, New Jersey	.938	24	17	43	4	64	0
Rowlett, Casey, New Jersey	1.000	8	3	9	0	12	1
Sanchez, Gabriel, Jamestown	.853	30	18	46	11	75	3
Santiago, John, Williamsport	.957	10	8	14	1	23	3
Sena, Emmanuel, Auburn	.895	6	2	15	2	19	0
Snyder, Brandon, Aberdeen	.500	1	1	0	1	2	0
Solano, Donovan, New Jersey	.957	8	5	17	1	23	1
Solano, Euvi, Williamsport	.865	34	23	54	12	89	9
Ventura, Leivi, Brooklyn	1.000	2	0	1	0	1	0
Zapata, Jose, Aberdeen	.750	2	2	4	2	8	1

SHORTSTOPS

Player, Team	Pct.	G	PO	A	E	TC	DP
Alvarez, Jean Carlos, Vermont	.925	7	16	21	3	40	5
Antoniato, Pasquale, Batavia	.993	32	42	101	1	144	19
Baez, Welinson, Batavia	.892	25	42	57	12	111	10
Bernhard, Steven, Auburn	.903	18	23	42	7	72	9
Blair, Cameron, Williamsport	.957	30	46	108	7	161	15
Blanton, John, Batavia	.875	5	8	13	3	24	3
Bouman, John, Hudson Valley	.914	18	26	48	7	81	8
Cabral, Marcos, Jamestown	.920	22	33	71	9	113	10
Chavez, Dirimo, Brooklyn	.917	18	35	53	8	96	12
Chavez, Jose, Mahoning Valley	.923	42	82	133	18	233	33
Clem, Christopher, Mahoning Valley	...	1	0	0	0	0	0
Contreras, Jose, Vermont	.910	59	80	182	26	288	25
Conway, Brandon, Vermont	.971	7	11	23	1	35	7
Corona, Reegie, Staten Island	.938	4	4	11	1	16	1
Fornasiere, Matthew, Mahoning Valley	.908	18	29	50	8	87	9
Gaerlan, Armand, Brooklyn	1.000	1	1	0	0	1	0
Gonzalez, Jesus, Auburn	.952	4	7	13	1	21	2
Grandstrand, Brett, Williamsport	.926	5	10	15	2	27	3
Greene, James, New Jersey	.946	35	53	105	9	167	17

Player, Team	Pct.	G	PO	A	E	TC	DP
Guerrero, Francisco, Aberdeen	1.000	1	2	1	0	3	2
Guerrero, James, Jamestown	.952	15	15	45	3	63	10
Gutierrez, Christopher, Auburn	.957	12	10	35	2	47	6
Hardy, John, Batavia	.956	16	40	47	4	91	11
Haske, Mark, Oneonta	1.000	9	12	17	0	29	6
Hayes, Brett, Jamestown	.625	1	2	3	3	8	1
HOLLIMON, MICHAEL, Oneonta	.967	68	112	209	11	332	45
Kelly, Dustin, Lowell	.833	3	1	4	1	6	1
Lillibridge, Brent, Williamsport	.942	42	72	141	13	226	43
Lowrie, Jed, Lowell	.945	40	50	123	10	183	17
Lytle, Andrew, Mahoning Valley	.933	17	17	39	4	60	7
Malo, Jonathan, Brooklyn	.937	30	42	106	10	158	18
Mercurio, Matthew, Lowell	1.000	1	2	3	0	5	2
Mihalics, Joseph, Brooklyn	.906	6	10	19	3	32	8
Nelson, Daniel, New Jersey	.961	27	32	66	4	102	16
Nunez, Eduardo, Staten Island	.916	72	101	203	28	332	46
Nunez, Eduardo, Vermont	1.000	1	3	3	0	6	0
Padgett, Nathan, Jamestown	.840	5	6	15	4	25	5
Ramos, Dominic, Lowell	.918	33	51	95	13	159	17
Richmond, Kevin, New Jersey	.833	3	1	4	1	6	1
Rowlett, Casey, New Jersey	.967	5	11	18	1	30	2
Santana, Luis, Brooklyn	.889	2	3	5	1	9	2
Santana, Yury, Brooklyn	.911	25	44	69	11	124	17
Sena, Emmanuel, Auburn	.918	49	55	157	19	231	22
Solano, Donovan, New Jersey	.931	11	20	34	4	58	5
Solano, Euvi, Williamsport	1.000	1	1	0	0	1	0
Steinbach, Ryan, Aberdeen	.919	65	79	170	22	271	36
Thissen, Greg, Vermont	.963	4	7	19	1	27	5
Walton, Neil, Hudson Valley	.932	57	71	149	16	236	28
Wiggins, Bradford, Aberdeen *	...	1	0	0	0	0	0
Witt, Paul, Jamestown	.960	35	44	101	6	151	27
Zapata, Jose, Aberdeen	1.000	10	17	24	0	41	8

OUTFIELDERS

Player, Team	Pct.	G	PO	A	E	TC	DP
Acey, Jermy, Auburn	.875	11	14	0	2	16	0
Allen, Roderick, Staten Island	1.000	2	2	0	0	2	0
Andrews, Robert, Aberdeen	.955	35	63	1	3	67	1
Aranda, Mark, Jamestown *	.975	22	39	0	1	40	0
Arnedo, Rolando, Vermont	1.000	1	2	0	0	2	0
Avila, Angel, Aberdeen	1.000	18	19	2	0	21	0
Berkenbosch, Kenneth, Jamestown	.923	7	12	0	1	13	0
Boone, James, Williamsport	1.000	13	21	2	0	23	0
Brown, Jordan, Mahoning Valley *	.958	15	20	3	1	24	1
Brown, Kyle, Brooklyn	.960	15	22	2	1	25	0
Brown, Willie, Vermont	.958	41	66	2	3	71	0
Burke, Joseph, Staten Island	...	1	0	0	0	0	0
Burns, Gregory, Jamestown *	.980	60	139	5	3	147	1
Butler, Jacob, Auburn	.778	9	12	2	4	18	0
Cardona, David, Hudson Valley	.955	30	60	3	3	66	0
Carroll, Mark, Staten Island	...	2	0	0	0	0	0
Chourio, Junior, Auburn	...	1	0	0	0	0	0
Clark, John, Mahoning Valley	...	1	0	0	0	0	0
Clem, Christopher, Mahoning Valley	1.000	1	2	0	0	2	0
Constanza, Jose, Mahoning Valley *	.984	64	115	5	2	122	0
Cooksey, Joseph, Auburn *	.988	49	80	1	1	82	1
COOPER, JAMES, Staten Island	1.000	60	80	3	0	83	0
Corley, William, Williamsport	.954	65	121	3	6	130	2
Cotto, Pedro, Oneonta *	.900	6	9	0	1	10	0
Crowe, Trevor, Mahoning Valley	.966	12	27	1	1	29	0
Cumberbatch, Cirilo, Mahoning Valley	.955	21	41	1	2	44	1
Daniel, Michael, Vermont	.939	64	100	7	7	114	2
Danielson, Sean, New Jersey	.978	36	82	6	2	90	0
Davis, Zachary, Aberdeen *	.935	47	82	5	6	93	2
De La Cruz, Carlos, New Jersey *	.962	37	48	2	2	52	0
Delaney, Jason, Williamsport	.933	53	81	3	6	90	1
De Leon, Evandy, Mahoning Valley	.971	45	99	2	3	104	0
Devoir, Jordan, Staten Island	1.000	6	12	1	0	13	0
Diaz, Dennis, Batavia	.964	32	52	2	2	56	0
Dobson, Sean, New Jersey *	.961	35	49	0	2	51	0
Edwards, Matt, Batavia	.000	1	0	0	1	1	0
Ellsbury, Jacoby, Lowell *	.984	27	61	0	1	62	0
Frias, Fernando, Hudson Valley	.950	8	19	0	1	20	0
Gabriel, Chad, New Jersey	.968	37	58	2	2	62	0
Gamero, Jesus, Brooklyn	.978	50	82	5	2	89	1
Garcia, Felipe, Staten Island	1.000	3	1	0	0	1	0
GARDNER, BRETT, Staten Island *	1.000	67	123	7	0	130	1
Gonzalez, Gregory, Brooklyn *	.979	32	45	2	1	48	0
Groce, Edward, Hudson Valley	.967	68	141	5	5	151	1
Grullon, Leonardo, Oneonta	.800	21	24	0	6	30	0

Player, Team	Pct.	G	PO	A	E	TC	DP
Guzman, Francisco, Vermont	1.000	9	20	0	0	20	0
Hall, James, Hudson Valley	.931	60	78	3	6	87	1
Harvey, Bryan, Jamestown	1.000	24	34	2	0	36	1
Hayes, Brett, Jamestown	...	1	0	0	0	0	0
Hicks, Joseph, Williamsport	1.000	15	30	0	0	30	0
Holden, Joseph, Brooklyn	.993	58	129	6	1	136	3
Howell, John, Vermont	1.000	4	6	0	0	6	0
Johnson, Jay, Lowell	.985	48	64	3	1	68	1
Joyce, Matthew, Oneonta	.992	63	122	5	1	128	3
Justice, Justin, Oneonta	.978	45	90	1	2	93	1
Kennedy, David, Hudson Valley	.964	54	105	3	4	112	0
Kutler, Matthew, Jamestown *	.923	6	12	0	1	13	0
Laster, Jeramy, Oneonta	.985	38	62	2	1	65	0
Lomack, Jermal, Williamsport	.969	24	58	4	2	64	1
Longworth, Randall, Mahoning Valley	.940	24	44	3	3	50	0
Louisa, Lorvin, Vermont	.937	41	72	2	5	79	0
MacFarlane, Andrew, Batavia *	.974	45	106	7	3	116	1
Matulia, John, Hudson Valley *	1.000	9	13	1	0	14	0
McCutchen, Andrew, Williamsport	1.000	13	29	0	0	29	0
Mortensen, Trevor, Mahoning Valley	.978	40	42	2	1	45	0
Mota, Willy, Lowell	.935	34	55	3	4	62	1
Pacheco, Jonel, Brooklyn	.988	53	74	5	1	80	2
Patterson, Ryan, Auburn	.966	66	109	6	4	119	1
Patton, Preston, Auburn *	.944	50	76	8	5	89	1
Perez, Jose A., Staten Island	.944	22	30	4	2	36	0
Pettway, Brian, Auburn	.958	50	65	3	3	71	0
Plasencia, Francisco, Vermont *	.984	71	181	2	3	186	0
Poterson, Jonathan, Staten Island	.979	70	95	0	2	97	0
Reed, Keith, Aberdeen	1.000	4	9	0	0	9	0
Reimold, Nolan, Aberdeen	.990	46	90	5	1	96	2
Richmond, Kevin, New Jersey	1.000	1	1	0	0	1	0
Rogers, Tanner, Jamestown	.929	9	11	2	1	14	0
Rowlett, Casey, New Jersey	.900	6	9	0	1	10	0
Scott Jr., Lorenzo, Aberdeen *	1.000	32	70	1	0	71	0
Searage, Ryan, Williamsport	.979	22	45	2	1	48	0
Shafer, Corey, Aberdeen *	.981	35	49	2	1	52	1
Sharpe, Michael, Brooklyn	1.000	19	22	2	0	24	1
Sivira, Yonathan, New Jersey	.991	60	108	5	1	114	2
Slayden, Jeremy, Batavia	.922	51	55	4	5	64	0
Solano, Euvi, Williamsport	1.000	2	0	1	0	1	0
Soto, Luis, Lowell	.991	62	107	7	1	115	2
Stevens, Anthony, Williamsport	.947	13	17	1	1	19	0
Stewart, Caleb, Brooklyn	1.000	22	23	2	0	25	0
Szabo, Jordan, Batavia	.984	36	56	6	1	63	2
Thissen, Greg, Vermont	1.000	1	1	0	0	1	0
Thomas, Brent, Mahoning Valley	.976	20	40	1	1	42	0
Thomas, Michael, Oneonta	1.000	18	32	2	0	34	1
Thomas, Nicolas, Auburn	.929	11	13	0	1	14	0
Timm, Brandon, Oneonta	.959	43	66	4	3	73	1
Torres, Christopher, Oneonta	...	1	0	0	0	0	0
Twomley, Jason, Lowell *	1.000	19	18	0	0	18	0
Van Houten, Jeffrey, Jamestown	.991	49	99	6	1	106	2
Walton, Jamar, Jamestown	.940	58	73	6	5	84	2
Wiggins, Bradford, Aberdeen *	1.000	13	20	1	0	21	0
Wilkerson, Matthew, New Jersey	.978	27	44	1	1	46	0
Williams, Julian, Batavia	.988	69	153	10	2	165	4
Wulf, Kent, Williamsport	.958	16	22	1	1	24	1
Yema, Yahmed, Lowell *	.985	45	63	1	1	65	0

CATCHERS

Player, Team	Pct.	G	PO	A	E	TC	DP
Apodaca, Luis, Vermont	.964	11	72	8	3	83	0
Arroyo, Rafael, Brooklyn	.972	18	127	11	4	142	3
BELL, JOSHUA, Auburn	.995	41	340	31	2	373	4
Bohm, Kyle, Auburn	1.000	6	8	1	0	9	0
Bormaster, Brian, Auburn	.983	41	267	20	5	292	2
Burke, Joseph, Staten Island	.996	33	257	24	1	282	1
Butera, Andrew, Brooklyn	.971	54	355	44	12	411	8
Canada, Bradley, Staten Island	1.000	4	13	1	0	14	0
Casillas, Omar, Mahoning Valley	.986	41	312	33	5	350	3
Cormier, Richard, New Jersey	1.000	2	11	3	0	14	0
Cummins, Daniel, Brooklyn	1.000	1	5	1	0	6	0
Dahlberg, Kyle, Aberdeen	.976	54	405	40	11	456	6
DAntonio, Trent, Aberdeen	1.000	7	33	2	0	35	0
German, Agustin, Vermont	1.000	3	12	4	0	16	1
Gosewisch, James, Batavia	1.000	5	61	7	0	68	1
Guerrero, Francisco, Aberdeen	1.000	1	1	0	0	1	0
Guevara, Orlando, Batavia	.990	13	88	8	1	97	1
Hayes, Brett, Jamestown	.987	34	275	18	4	297	2
Jamieson, Alex, Hudson Valley	.984	15	117	6	2	125	0

Player, Team	Pct.	G	PO	A	E	TC	DP
Johnson, Joshua, Hudson Valley	.985	14	117	12	2	131	2
Jones, Christopher, Williamsport	.961	32	211	33	10	254	4
Leonard, Donald, Lowell	.985	8	56	8	1	65	0
Lerud, Steven, Williamsport	1.000	10	63	6	0	69	1
Lombardi, Michael, Batavia	1.000	3	20	1	0	21	0
MacFarlane, Andrew, Batavia *	1.000	1	1	0	0	1	0
Madden, Scott, New Jersey	1.000	3	22	0	0	22	0
Mancebo, Melvin, Vermont	.949	7	37	0	2	39	0
Marcelli, Brandon, New Jersey	1.000	2	12	1	0	13	0
Marson, Louis, Batavia	.979	56	419	42	10	471	4
Maxey, Jason, Aberdeen	1.000	7	37	4	0	41	1
McMillan, Andrew, Vermont	.990	15	91	9	1	101	0
Mendez, Jose, New Jersey	1.000	12	90	6	0	96	1
Michalski, Joseph, Aberdeen	.969	23	114	13	4	131	1
Newton, Jonathan, New Jersey	.978	21	160	14	4	178	2
Nino, Denny, Williamsport	1.000	12	47	9	0	56	2
Perry, Patrick, Lowell	1.000	14	110	12	0	122	0
Pilittere, Peter, Staten Island	.988	49	380	47	5	432	1
Poppert, John, Vermont	.971	41	240	27	8	275	2
Reddinger, Brandon, Williamsport	.995	30	194	23	1	218	3
Reifenberger, David, Mahoning Valley	.988	12	76	4	1	81	0
Roa, Joel, Oneonta	.985	42	298	26	5	329	2
Robinson, Christopher, Oneonta	1.000	4	21	1	0	22	0
Rodgers, Mark, New Jersey	1.000	1	7	1	0	8	0
Rogers, Tanner, Jamestown	.972	31	226	19	7	252	3
Sanchez, Gabriel, Jamestown	.988	11	73	8	1	82	0
Sanchez, Ricardo, Lowell	.933	4	14	0	1	15	0
Sandora, Robert, Vermont	1.000	2	6	0	0	6	0
Santana, Luis, Brooklyn	1.000	3	8	4	0	12	0
Snyder, Brandon, Aberdeen	.980	5	44	5	1	50	0
Soto, Auddy, Vermont	1.000	3	10	1	0	11	0
Spilman, Ryan, Mahoning Valley	.982	6	49	7	1	57	0
Spring, Matthew, Hudson Valley	.984	48	393	44	7	444	0
Stachowsky, Mitchel, Lowell	.974	36	247	17	7	271	1
Timmons, Jeffrey, Brooklyn	1.000	8	46	3	0	49	2
Torres, Christopher, Oneonta	1.000	20	101	10	0	111	0
Wagner, Mark, Lowell	.988	24	145	21	2	168	1
Wargo, Cody, Aberdeen	1.000	2	17	0	0	17	0
Williamson, Schuyler, Oneonta	.981	25	133	18	3	154	1
Woodson, Michael, Mahoning Valley	.990	22	179	13	2	194	2
Yarbrough, Brandon, New Jersey	.966	44	280	34	11	325	3

PITCHERS

Player, Team	Pct.	G	PO	A	E	TC	DP
Aguilar, Salvador, Brooklyn	1.000	15	5	6	0	11	0
Alfaro, Gabriel, Auburn	1.000	18	4	2	0	6	1
Alfonzo, Edgar, Brooklyn *	1.000	2	1	5	0	6	0
Almenar, Aristides, Brooklyn	.800	17	1	3	1	5	0
Amaya, Jose, Mahoning Valley	1.000	8	4	4	0	8	0
Antelo, Derek, Williamsport	1.000	13	7	11	0	18	2
Badenhop, Burke, Oneonta	.870	14	8	12	3	23	4
Bahr, Jesse, Staten Island *	...	3	0	0	0	0	0
Barb, Andrew, Batavia	.933	11	5	9	1	15	0
Barone, Daniel, Jamestown	1.000	9	1	5	0	6	0
Bauserman, Joseph, Williamsport	.833	14	6	9	3	18	1
Baxter, Jake, Oneonta	1.000	16	1	5	0	6	0
Baxter, James, Lowell *	1.000	10	1	0	0	1	0
Bell, Kristian, Auburn	.769	15	7	13	6	26	2
Berg, Justin, Staten Island	1.000	15	3	16	0	19	3
Bergesen, Bradley, Aberdeen	.923	15	3	9	1	13	0
Berkenbosch, Kenneth, Jamestown	1.000	17	1	4	0	5	1
Berroa, Yesson, Auburn	1.000	17	1	1	0	2	0
Bigda, Drew, Hudson Valley *	1.000	24	3	3	0	6	1
Bille, Michael, Jamestown	.900	18	3	6	1	10	0
Blackley, Adam, Lowell *	.905	15	6	13	2	21	0
Blaine, Davis, Batavia *	1.000	11	1	7	0	8	1
Blair, Thomas, New Jersey *	1.000	6	0	1	0	1	0
Boehm, Kyle, Jamestown	.714	19	2	3	2	7	0
Boggs, Mitchell, New Jersey	1.000	15	4	10	0	14	0
Brauer, James, Jamestown	.875	10	5	2	1	8	0
Brazell, Landon, Jamestown	1.000	14	2	3	0	5	0
Brocato, Russell, Aberdeen	.800	21	1	3	1	5	0
Brown, Eric, Brooklyn	1.000	16	2	3	0	5	0
Brown, Justin, New Jersey	.000	2	0	0	1	1	0
Buchholz, Clay, Lowell	1.000	15	1	3	0	4	0
Cairns, Jason, New Jersey	...	2	0	0	0	0	0
Camilo, Juan, Jamestown	1.000	10	0	2	0	2	0
Camline, William, Auburn	.857	21	4	2	1	7	1
Carrasco, Carlos, Batavia	1.000	4	0	1	0	1	0
Casillas, Ismael, Lowell	1.000	18	0	6	0	6	0

Player, Team	Pct.	G	PO	A	E	TC	DP
Castor, Parrish, Jamestown *	...	3	0	0	0	0	0
Chamberlin, Bryce, Aberdeen	1.000	18	1	5	0	6	0
Claggett, Anthony, Oneonta	1.000	21	1	3	0	4	1
Clem, Christopher, New Jersey	.857	12	4	2	1	7	0
Cobb, Matthew, Hudson Valley *	1.000	16	2	4	0	6	0
Conroy, James, Staten Island	1.000	18	2	13	0	15	0
Coonrod, Aaron, Vermont	1.000	4	0	2	0	2	1
Cooper, Michael, New Jersey	1.000	4	1	2	0	3	0
Coose, Austin, Hudson Valley	...	11	0	0	0	0	0
Corporan, Willy, Hudson Valley	.800	14	3	1	1	5	0
Correa, Jose, Batavia	.500	18	1	2	3	6	0
Cowley, Thomas, Mahoning Valley *	.923	21	7	5	1	13	1
Cox, Timothy, Lowell *	1.000	2	0	1	0	1	0
Cuffman, Jacob, Williamsport	.917	21	2	9	1	12	1
D'Alessandro, Joe, Brooklyn	.800	17	1	3	1	5	0
Daniels, Adam, New Jersey *	.857	10	2	4	1	7	0
Davidson, David, Williamsport *	1.000	5	2	1	0	3	1
Davis, Wade, Hudson Valley	.941	15	2	14	1	17	1
Day, Amos, Auburn	...	3	0	0	0	0	0
De Los Santos, Richard, Hudson Valley	1.000	6	0	3	0	3	1
Denney, Nolan, Hudson Valley	...	1	0	0	0	0	0
Deters, James, Mahoning Valley	.929	14	4	9	1	14	1
Diaz, Dennis, Batavia	...	1	0	0	0	0	0
Dicken, Randy, Auburn	1.000	14	4	4	0	8	0
Dickerson, Roy, New Jersey *	...	1	0	0	0	0	0
Dixon, Kevin, Mahoning Valley	1.000	14	6	12	0	18	0
Domangue, Eric, Brooklyn *	1.000	15	1	2	0	3	0
Doolittle, Michael, Jamestown	1.000	22	5	3	0	8	0
Douglas, Robert, Mahoning Valley *	.667	6	1	1	1	3	0
Dumesnil, Bryan, Aberdeen *	1.000	18	2	8	0	10	2
Easton, Aaron, Jamestown	.667	17	0	2	1	3	0
Eberhardt, Peter, Auburn	...	3	0	0	0	0	0
Edell, Ryan, Mahoning Valley *	1.000	14	2	10	0	12	0
Eichelberger, Jared, Brooklyn	...	1	0	0	0	0	0
Erbe, Brandon, Aberdeen	1.000	3	1	1	0	2	0
Estrada, Marco, Vermont	1.000	9	0	3	0	3	0
Everitt, Keaton, Staten Island	.667	5	1	1	1	3	0
Evers, William, Hudson Valley	1.000	20	3	4	0	7	1
Everts, Clinton, Vermont	.000	8	0	0	1	1	0
Falk, Matthew, Hudson Valley	.750	12	1	2	1	4	0
Farley, Christopher, New Jersey	1.000	5	0	1	0	1	0
Feldkamp, Derek, Hudson Valley	1.000	23	2	4	0	6	1
Fernandes, Kyle, Lowell *	...	1	0	0	0	0	0
Fisher, Matthew, Hudson Valley	1.000	15	0	1	0	1	0
Flores, Eugenio, Lowell	1.000	14	2	2	0	4	0
Foulke, Keith, Lowell	1.000	3	0	1	0	1	0
Fowler, Jonathan, Auburn *	.909	15	1	9	1	11	0
Fragoso, Jose, Oneonta	.714	13	2	3	2	7	0
Fraser, Loren, Oneonta	1.000	19	3	5	0	8	0
Frias, Junior, Lowell	...	1	0	0	0	0	0
Galbizo, Rafael, Jamestown	1.000	8	1	0	0	1	0
Gallaway, Michael, Aberdeen *	1.000	3	0	3	0	3	0
Garza, Rodolfo, Vermont	1.000	9	1	0	0	1	0
Gil, Roberto, Hudson Valley	1.000	6	2	0	0	2	0
Gomez, Warmar, Vermont	.889	23	1	7	1	9	1
Goyen, Matthew, Jamestown *	1.000	10	3	4	0	7	0
Grant, Brian, Auburn	1.000	5	1	1	0	2	0
Grant, Jessen, New Jersey	1.000	24	2	2	0	4	0
Gross, Timothy, New Jersey	1.000	11	0	3	0	3	0
Guanchez, Argimiro, Lowell *	.923	26	5	7	1	13	0
Guevara, Orlando, Batavia	...	1	0	0	0	0	0
Guyette, Kevin, Lowell	.500	6	0	1	1	2	0
Hahn, Cory, Auburn	...	1	0	0	0	0	0
Hahn, Jeffrey, Oneonta	1.000	10	4	2	0	6	0
Hamblet, Reid, Aberdeen	1.000	22	0	8	0	8	1
Hancock, Matthew, Lowell *	.857	22	3	3	1	7	0
Harker, Brett, Batavia	1.000	9	4	6	0	10	0
Hawksworth, Blake, New Jersey	1.000	7	0	1	0	1	0
Haynes, Matthew, Mahoning Valley	.667	18	2	2	2	6	0
Hearne, Donald, New Jersey	.500	24	0	3	3	6	1
Heisel, Ian, Williamsport	1.000	28	1	9	0	10	0
Henyan, Peter, Batavia	1.000	19	5	6	0	11	1
Hernandez, David, Aberdeen	.846	12	3	8	2	13	1
Hernandez, Moises, Aberdeen	.875	11	4	10	2	16	0
Hill, Ronald, Batavia	1.000	20	5	12	0	17	0
Hinchman, Grady, Brooklyn *	1.000	3	0	1	0	1	0
Hiraldo, Nelson, Mahoning Valley	1.000	18	0	2	0	2	0
Hoey, James, Aberdeen	.857	9	1	5	1	7	0
Hooks, Ashley, New Jersey	1.000	9	1	3	0	4	0
Hope, Travis, Brooklyn	.846	22	3	8	2	13	0

Player, Team	Pct.	G	PO	A	E	TC	DP
Jackson, Aaron, Vermont	.917	15	6	5	1	12	1
Japa, Rolando, Staten Island	...	1	0	0	0	0	0
Jecmen, Mark, Mahoning Valley	1.000	23	3	11	0	14	1
Jones, Christopher, Lowell	.500	11	1	0	1	2	0
Jones, David, Lowell *	.833	12	1	4	1	6	0
Joseph, Jacob, Brooklyn	1.000	6	0	2	0	2	0
Kamrath, Jeffrey, Hudson Valley	1.000	9	2	4	0	6	0
Kelly, Dustin, Lowell	...	1	0	0	0	0	0
Kendrick, Kyle, Batavia	.900	14	10	17	3	30	1
Kite, Josh, Mahoning Valley *	.800	9	1	3	1	5	1
Knippschild, Charles, Mahoning Valley *	...	1	0	0	0	0	0
Knox, Matthew, Mahoning Valley	1.000	5	0	2	0	2	0
Konecny, Daniel, Oneonta	1.000	15	5	6	0	11	1
Krebs, Eric, Williamsport	1.000	7	3	2	0	5	0
Kroenke, Zachary, Staten Island *	1.000	11	0	2	0	2	0
Landing, Jeffrey, Brooklyn	.941	16	3	13	1	17	1
Lannan, John, Vermont *	.889	14	0	8	1	9	0
Lara, Toni, Staten Island *	1.000	17	0	3	0	3	0
Large, Terry, Lowell	1.000	12	1	3	0	4	0
Lehman, James, Vermont	1.000	20	2	5	0	7	0
Lerch, Zachary, Jamestown	...	1	0	0	0	0	0
Levinski, Donald, Aberdeen	.000	6	0	0	1	1	0
Lewis, Jensen, Mahoning Valley	1.000	13	3	11	0	14	1
Lewis, Jonathan, Jamestown	1.000	19	3	5	0	8	1
Lewis, Scott, Mahoning Valley *	1.000	7	0	3	0	3	0
Lira, Oscar, Vermont	.875	16	1	6	1	8	0
Litsch, Jesse, Auburn	1.000	4	2	3	0	5	0
Liz, Radhames, Aberdeen	.889	11	5	3	1	9	0
Loberg, Matthew, Mahoning Valley	1.000	22	3	5	0	8	1
Long, Nicholas, Vermont	...	5	0	0	0	0	0
Lopez, Romelio, Hudson Valley	.889	4	3	5	1	9	0
Lozado, Henry, Aberdeen	.800	15	1	7	2	10	0
Lugo, Chris, Vermont	1.000	7	1	4	0	5	1
Lyons, Thomas, Oneonta	1.000	6	1	2	0	3	0
Mahoney, Collin, Oneonta	1.000	18	2	3	0	5	0
Maloney, Matthew, Batavia *	1.000	8	1	4	0	5	0
Manuel, Robert, Brooklyn	1.000	2	0	1	0	1	0
Marceaux, Jacob, Jamestown	1.000	10	3	8	0	11	0
Marshall, Brian, Lowell *	1.000	11	0	2	0	2	0
Marte, German, Brooklyn	1.000	1	1	0	0	1	0
Martin, Adrian, Auburn	.909	22	4	6	1	11	0
Martinez, Carlos, Vermont	1.000	13	6	10	0	16	0
Mason, Christopher, Hudson Valley	1.000	9	1	3	0	4	1
Mateo, Waner, Brooklyn	.833	14	3	7	2	12	0
Maxwell, Blake, Lowell	.900	26	3	6	1	10	0
McCamie, Zac, Jamestown	...	5	0	0	0	0	0
McCormick, Mark, New Jersey	...	2	0	0	0	0	0
McCrory, Robert, Aberdeen	1.000	5	3	2	0	5	0
Mcgee, Jacob, Hudson Valley *	1.000	15	3	5	0	8	1
Meacham, Cory, New Jersey	.750	11	1	2	1	4	0
Meagher, Michael, New Jersey *	...	2	0	0	0	0	0
Mendez, Jose, New Jersey	...	1	0	0	0	0	0
Mendez, Winer, Aberdeen	1.000	4	0	2	0	2	0
Meyers, Ryan, Brooklyn	.571	9	1	3	3	7	0
Michael, Mark, Williamsport	1.000	2	2	0	0	2	0
Miller, Adam, Mahoning Valley	1.000	3	2	1	0	3	0
Miller, Kevin, Williamsport	1.000	29	3	6	0	9	0
Miller, Matt, Mahoning Valley	...	1	0	0	0	0	0
Mitchinson, Scott, Batavia	.900	13	2	7	1	10	0
Moeves, Mark, Williamsport	1.000	24	3	8	0	11	4
Montani, Jeffrey, Aberdeen	1.000	6	1	1	0	2	1
Morrison, Erik, Staten Island	1.000	21	3	7	0	10	0
Moscoso, Guillermo, Oneonta	1.000	11	3	3	0	6	0
Munoz, Luis, Williamsport	.909	16	3	17	2	22	1
Ness, Roger, Mahoning Valley	.769	14	4	6	3	13	0
Newlin, Darren, Williamsport	1.000	20	3	5	0	8	0
Newsom, Randall, Lowell	1.000	1	0	1	0	1	0
Nickerson, Jon-Michael, Jamestown *	.667	17	4	6	5	15	0
Norfleet, Mathew, Oneonta	1.000	18	1	4	0	5	0
O'Brien, Matt, Oneonta	.909	15	9	11	2	22	1
Ochoa, Nehomar, Vermont	1.000	23	0	3	0	3	0
Olson, Garrett, Aberdeen *	1.000	11	1	6	0	7	0
Outman, Joshua, Batavia *	1.000	11	0	4	0	4	0
Overholt, Patrick, Batavia	.857	21	2	4	1	7	1
Owen, William, Aberdeen	1.000	23	2	1	0	3	0
Ozuna, Modesto, Lowell	1.000	13	0	2	0	2	0
Palm, Joshua, Vermont	...	3	0	0	0	0	0
Parnell, Robert, Brooklyn	.923	15	2	10	1	13	1
Patterson, Garrett, Staten Island *	1.000	17	5	8	0	13	0
Paulk, Robert, Brooklyn	.500	14	0	2	2	4	0
Pekarek, Justin, Mahoning Valley *	.923	9	1	11	1	13	0
Pena, Mario, Lowell *	.957	16	10	12	1	23	1
Pendleton, Lance, Staten Island	.667	9	3	1	2	6	0
Peralta, Yader, Lowell	1.000	6	0	1	0	1	0
Phillips, Paul, Auburn	.857	26	8	4	2	14	1
Phillips, Ryan, Lowell *	1.000	14	2	18	0	20	0
Quijada, Fernando, Batavia	1.000	23	1	4	0	5	0
Rasowsky, Avi, Jamestown *	1.000	2	0	1	0	1	0
Rawl, Aaron, Batavia	1.000	8	3	2	0	5	0
Ray, Robert, Auburn	.778	15	3	4	2	9	0
Redmond, Todd, Williamsport	.933	15	0	14	1	15	0
Reinhard, Gregory, Hudson Valley	1.000	12	2	8	0	10	0
Rengel, Orlando, Brooklyn	1.000	6	4	3	0	7	0
Repole, Michael, New Jersey	.750	25	1	2	1	4	0
Reyes, Jorge, Brooklyn	.818	13	4	5	2	11	0
Rico, Matt, Hudson Valley	1.000	8	1	1	0	2	0
Risinger, Kyle, Brooklyn	1.000	15	3	7	0	10	1
Robertson, Quinton, New Jersey	.909	12	2	8	1	11	1
Robertson, Timothy, Oneonta	1.000	16	3	8	0	11	2
Robinson, Dennis, Aberdeen	.500	5	0	1	1	2	0
Roddy, Dustin, Mahoning Valley	1.000	25	3	4	0	7	0
Rodriguez, Edward, Auburn	.909	21	4	6	1	11	0
Rodriguez, Edward, Vermont *	1.000	20	3	3	0	6	0
Rodriguez, Felix, Staten Island	...	2	0	0	0	0	0
Romero, Ricardo, Auburn *	1.000	1	0	1	0	1	0
Rosario, Carlos, Staten Island	1.000	9	1	1	0	2	0
Ruckle, Jacob, Brooklyn	1.000	2	1	1	0	2	0
Rueger, Bryan, Staten Island *	1.000	4	1	0	0	1	0
Rulon, Benjamin, Hudson Valley *	1.000	6	0	9	0	9	0
Rusch, Matthew, Oneonta	1.000	2	2	0	0	2	1
Sadlowski, Kyle, New Jersey	1.000	11	0	2	0	2	0
Salas, Joseph, Williamsport *	1.000	5	1	0	0	1	0
Sborz, John, Oneonta	1.000	9	0	8	0	8	0
Schellinger, Michael, New Jersey	1.000	4	0	3	0	3	0
Schmidt, Joshua, Staten Island	.875	26	3	4	1	8	0
Schmidt, Kyle, Aberdeen	1.000	1	0	2	0	2	0
Schroer, Steven, Staten Island	1.000	23	3	9	0	12	1
Schwabe, Ryan, Aberdeen *	1.000	18	0	9	0	9	0
Seccombe, David, Staten Island	.895	17	7	10	2	19	1
Shefka, Richard, Vermont	1.000	10	2	3	0	5	0
Shepard, Kevin, Batavia *	.846	18	3	8	2	13	0
Solis, Hairo, Staten Island	1.000	21	3	2	0	5	0
Soriano, Julio, Aberdeen	.500	6	1	0	1	2	0
Soto, Auddy, Vermont	...	1	0	0	0	0	0
Sowers, Jeremy, Vermont	.923	19	6	6	1	13	1
Stadanlick, Ryan, Aberdeen	1.000	4	0	4	0	4	0
Stammen, Craig, Vermont	1.000	13	3	9	0	12	1
Stanford, Jason, Mahoning Valley *	...	2	0	0	0	0	0
Stephens, Jason, Staten Island	1.000	18	5	20	0	25	2
Stevens, Daniel, New Jersey *	...	5	0	0	0	0	0
Stewart, Clayton, Batavia	1.000	14	2	2	0	4	0
Stidfole, Sean, Auburn	1.000	19	5	4	0	9	0
Stuart, Cory, Staten Island	.900	22	4	5	1	10	1
Suero, Nicolas, Williamsport	1.000	3	1	4	0	5	0
Swanson, Matt, Williamsport	.917	19	5	6	1	12	0
Tabeek, Kyle, Lowell	.600	7	1	2	2	5	0
Talbott, Travis, Jamestown *	1.000	7	3	8	0	11	0
Taylor, Jeffrey, Vermont	1.000	14	0	1	0	1	0
Thompson, Aaron, Jamestown *	1.000	5	0	1	0	1	0
Timm, Jordan, Auburn *	...	1	0	0	0	0	0
Tomasiewicz, Kevin, Brooklyn *	1.000	20	2	4	0	6	0
Townsend, Wade, Hudson Valley	.867	12	6	7	2	15	0
Trahan, David, Vermont	1.000	9	1	4	0	5	1
Trent, Matthew, New Jersey	1.000	14	0	3	0	3	1
Tressler, Aaron, Auburn	1.000	5	2	4	0	6	0
TRIAS, ORLANDO, Auburn	1.000	15	9	20	0	29	0
Tucker, Ryan, Jamestown	1.000	4	0	2	0	2	0
Vaclavik, Justin, Williamsport	1.000	20	3	2	0	5	0
Valdez, Luis, Williamsport	.864	16	7	12	3	22	2
Vander Weg, Scott, New Jersey	1.000	24	0	1	0	1	0
Van Houten, Jeffrey, Jamestown	...	2	0	0	0	0	0
Vargas, Albert, Mahoning Valley	1.000	10	0	4	0	4	2
Vasquez, Sendy, Oneonta	1.000	15	1	4	0	5	0
Villalona, Guillermo, Staten Island	1.000	8	1	4	0	5	0
Volstad, Christopher, Jamestown	1.000	7	2	8	0	10	1
Wagner, Michael, Staten Island *	1.000	19	1	3	0	4	0
Wagner, Nicholas, Hudson Valley	1.000	9	0	2	0	2	0
Walker, Aaron, Hudson Valley *	1.000	15	1	4	0	5	0
Walker, Matthew, Hudson Valley	...	1	0	0	0	0	0
Webber, Nicholas, New Jersey	.875	10	5	9	2	16	1

SHORT-SEASON CLASS A New York-Penn League

Player, Team	Pct.	G	PO	A	E	TC	DP
Weintraub, Jason, Brooklyn	1.000	4	0	1	0	1	0
West, Sean, Jamestown *	.667	3	0	2	1	3	0
Whelan, Kevin, Oneonta	1.000	11	2	0	0	2	0
Wilson, Gibbs, Oneonta	1.000	9	1	1	0	2	0
Wlodarczyk, Michael, Hudson Valley *	1.000	5	0	4	0	4	0
Wood, Adam, Jamestown *	1.000	25	1	7	0	8	0
Woodson, Michael, Mahoning Valley	...	2	0	0	0	0	0
Wordekemper, Eric, Staten Island	1.000	2	0	1	0	1	0
Yost, Wendall, Vermont *	1.000	14	4	8	0	12	1
Zagurski, Michael, Batavia *	.818	15	0	9	2	11	2
Zarate, Mauro, Jamestown	1.000	24	2	4	0	6	1
Zerbe, Chad, Mahoning Valley *	...	1	0	0	0	0	0
Zick, Jeremy, New Jersey	1.000	25	0	8	0	8	1
Zink, James, Lowell	1.000	14	2	4	0	6	0
Zuercher, Zachary, New Jersey *	1.000	16	2	17	0	19	2

LEAGUE CHAMPIONS

Year	Team	Pct.
1939—	Olean*	.631
1940—	Olean*	.625
1941—	Jamestown	.618
	Bradford (2nd)†	.549
1942—	Jamestown*	.672
1943—	Lockport	.591
	Wellsville (3rd)†	.532
1944—	Lockport	.608
	Jamestown (2nd)†	.565
1945—	Batavia*	.677
1946—	Jamestown‡	.672
	Batavia‡	.672
1947—	Jamestown*	.690
1948—	Lockport*	.603
1949—	Bradford*	.635
1950—	Hornell	.653
	Olean (2nd)†	.568
1951—	Olean	.622
	Hornell (3rd)†	.568
1952—	Hamilton	.659
	Jamestown (2nd)†	.643
1953—	Jamestown*	.704
1954—	Corning*	.621
1955—	Hamilton	.656
1956—	Wellsville*	.617
1957—	Wellsville	.632
	Erie (2nd)†	.598
1958—	Wellsville	.556
	Geneva (2nd)†	.548
1959—	Wellsville†	.635
1960—	Erie	.643
	Wellsville (2nd)†	.535
1961—	Geneva	.616
	Olean (4th)†	.512
1962—	Jamestown	.580
	Auburn (3rd)†	.521
1963—	Auburn	.585
	Batavia (3rd)†	.485
1964—	Auburn§	.622
1965—	Binghamton	.677
	Binghamton	.607
1966—	Auburn∞	.620
	Binghamton	.646
1967—	Auburn	.667
1968—	Auburn	.645
	Oneonta (2nd)*	.558
1969—	Oneonta	.662
1970—	Auburn	.623
1971—	Oneonta	.662
1972—	Niagara Falls	.686
1973—	Auburn	.667
1974—	Oneonta	.768
1975—	Newark	.688
	Newark	.714
1976—	Elmira	.727
	Elmira	.703
1977—	Oneonta▲	.671
	Batavia	.600
1978—	Oneonta	.729
	Geneva◆	.718
1979—	Geneva	.725
	Oneonta◆	.618
1980—	Oneonta▲	.662
	Geneva	.649
1981—	Oneonta▲	.658
	Jamestown	.649
1982—	Oneonta	.566
	Niagara Falls▲	.553
1983—	Utica▲	.649
	Newark	.649
1984—	Newark	.622
	Little Falls▲	.587
1985—	Oneonta*	.705
	Auburn	.603
1986—	Oneonta	.766
	St. Catharines◆	.632
1987—	Geneva▲	.632
	Watertown	.579
1988—	Oneonta▲	.632
	Jamestown	.618
1989—	Pittsfield	.697
	Jamestown▲	.579
1990—	Oneonta■	.667
	Geneva	.662
1991—	Pittsfield	.662
	Jamestown■	.654
1992—	Hamilton	.737
	Geneva▼	.547
1993—	Niagara Falls▼	.603
	Pittsfield	.533
1994—	Auburn	.592
	New Jersey▼	.573
1995—	Vermont	.645
	Watertown▼	.630
1996—	Vermont▼	.649
	St. Catharines	.579
1997—	Batavia	.635
	Pittsfield▼	.568
1998—	Hudson Valley	.658
	Oneonta††	.592
	Auburn††	.573
1999—	Mahoning Valley	.566
	Hudson Valley‡‡	.553
2000—	Mahoning Valley	.632
	Staten Island§§	.622
2001—	Brooklyn∞∞	.684
	Williamsport∞∞	.649
2002—	Staten Island▲▲	.649
2003—	Williamsport▲▲	.605
2004—	Mahoning Valley▲▲	.553
2005—	Staten Island▲▲	.684

*Won championship and four-club playoff. †Won four-club playoff. ‡Jamestown and Batavia declared co-champions; Batavia defeated Jamestown in final of four-club playoff. §Won championship and two-club playoff. ∞Won split-season playoff. ▲League divided into Eastern and Western divisions; won playoff. ◆League divided into Wrigley and Yawkey divisions; won playoff. ■League divided into Eastern, Western and Stedler divisions; won playoff. ▼League divided into McNamara, Pinckney and Stedler divisions; won playoff. ††Named co-champions due to final series being rained out. ‡‡League divided into McNamara and Pinckney divisions; won playoff. §§League divided into McNamara and Stedler divisions; won playoff. ∞∞League divided into McNamara and Stedler divisions; Brooklyn was leading final series of four-team playoff over Williamsport, but both teams were declared co-champions when Professional Baseball declared a stoppage of play. (NOTE—Known as Pennsylvania-Ontario-New York League from 1939 through 1956.) ▲▲League divided into McNamara, Pinckney and Stedler divisions; won playoff.

NORTHWEST LEAGUE

LEAGUE OFFICE

President/treasurer
Bob Richmond

Address
P.O. Box 1645
Boise, ID 83701

Phone
208-429-1511

Teams (affiliation)
Boise Hawks (Cubs)
Eugene Emeralds (Padres)
Everett AquaSox (Mariners)
Salem-Keizer Volcanoes (Giants)

Spokane Indians (Rangers)
Tri-City Dust Devils (Rockies)
Vancouver Canadians (Athletics)
Yakima Bears (Diamondbacks)

2005 FINAL STANDINGS

EAST DIVISION

Team	W	L	T	Pct.	GB
Spokane Indians	37	39	-	0.487	...
Tri-City Dust Devils	36	40	-	0.474	1
Boise Hawks	34	42	-	0.447	3
Yakima Bears	30	46	-	0.395	7

WEST DIVISION

Team	W	L	T	Pct.	GB
Vancouver Canadians	46	30	-	0.605	...
Salem-Keizer Volcanoes	45	31	-	0.592	1
Everett AquaSox	42	34	-	0.553	4
Eugene Emeralds	34	42	-	0.447	12

COMPOSITE

CLUB (AFFILIATE), ABBREV	VAN	SKV	EVE	SPO	TRI	BOI	EUG	YAK	W	L	PCT	GB
Vancouver (Athletics), VAN		6	8	5	7	4	9	7	46	30	.605	-
Salem-Keizer (Giants), SKV 6	...		6	4	5	9	9	6	45	31	.592	1.0
Everett (Mariners), EVE 4	6	...		5	5	7	7	8	42	34	.553	4.0
Spokane (Rangers), SPO 5	6	5	...		6	6	5	4	37	39	.487	9.0
Tri-City (Rockies), TRI ...3	5	5	6	...		6	4	7	36	40	.474	10.0
Boise (Cubs), BOI 6	1	3	6	6	...		4	8	34	42	.447	12.0
Eugene (Padres), EUG 3	3	5	5	6	6	...		6	34	42	.447	12.0
Yakima (Diamondbacks), YAK 3	4	2	8	5	4	4	...		30	46	.395	16.0

Major league affiliations in parentheses.

PLAYOFFS: Finals: Finals: Spokane defeated Vancouver, three games to two.

REGULAR-SEASON ATTENDANCE: Everett, 108,884. Yakima, 60,150. Vancouver, 124,708. Tri-City, 63,173. Eugene, 124,512. Boise, 109,746. Spokane, 180,084. Salem-Keizer, 108,413. League total, 879,670. Postseason (5 games), 6,309.

MANAGERS: Everett, Pedro Grifol. Yakima, Jay Gainer. Vancouver, Juan Navarette. Tri-City, Ron Gideon. Eugene, Roy Howell. Boise, Trey Forkerway. Spokane, Greg Riddoch. Salem-Keizer, Steve Decker.

ALL-STAR TEAM: 1B-William Thompson, Salem-Keizer. 2B-Luis Valbuena, Everett. 3B-Pablo Sandoval, Salem-Keizer. SS-German Duran, Spokane. OF-Travis Becktel, Tri-City. OF-Michael Mooney, Salem-Keizer. OF-Steven Murphy, Spokane. C-Joshua Ford, Yakima. DH-Lizahio Baez, Spokane. LHP-Darin Downs, Boise. RHP-Michael Madsen, Vancouver. LHR-Brad Kilby, Vancouver. RHR-Brian Anderson, Salem-Keizer. Most Valuable Player-Steven Murphy, Spokane. Manager of the Year-Steve Decker, Salem-Keizer.

2005 BATTING

TEAM

Team	G	TPA	AB	R	H	TB	2B	3B	HR	RBI	SH	SF	HP	BB	IBB	SO	SB	CS	GDP	LOB	ShO	Avg.	OBP	Slg.
Salem-Keizer	76	3035	2701	398	786	1097	149	17	48	362	34	15	47	238	8	537	57	39	48	1271	3	.291	.357	.406
Everett	76	3002	2624	418	692	1100	149	23	71	374	23	23	55	277	5	653	89	41	43	1187	3	.264	.344	.419
Boise	76	2860	2606	330	678	925	123	8	36	288	31	9	35	179	4	547	76	46	53	1100	4	.260	.315	.355
Spokane	76	2927	2588	380	658	1065	141	25	72	343	18	21	48	251	9	665	65	37	40	1093	4	.254	.329	.412
Vancouver	76	2962	2587	344	653	912	134	10	35	291	24	19	56	276	5	581	72	31	58	1234	2	.252	.335	.353
Yakima	76	2931	2626	315	661	988	149	20	46	283	28	26	47	204	8	619	50	33	45	1133	5	.252	.314	.376
Tri-City	76	2989	2580	349	647	934	134	18	39	310	51	23	56	279	5	661	44	29	43	1232	1	.251	.334	.362
Eugene	76	2940	2560	320	609	877	102	23	40	269	31	21	48	279	5	676	57	32	45	1212	5	.238	.322	.343

INDIVIDUAL

TOP QUALIFIERS FOR BATTING CHAMPIONSHIP

Minimum 205 plate appearances. *Lefthanded batter. †Switch-hitter.

Player, Team	G	TPA	AB	R	H	TB	2B	3B	HR	RBI	SH	SF	HP	BB	IBB	SO	SB	CS	GDP	Avg.	OBP	Slg.
Thompson, William, Salem-Keizer *	48	211	185	25	71	91	12	1	2	35	1	1	1	23	2	22	0	1	1	.384	.452	.492
Mooney, Michael, Salem-Keizer	73	334	304	57	104	157	20	9	5	29	2	3	5	20	2	64	13	4	1	.342	.389	.516
Sandoval, Pablo, Salem-Keizer †	75	327	294	46	97	125	15	2	3	50	3	3	6	21	3	33	2	3	9	.330	.383	.425
Minicozzi, Mark, Salem-Keizer	70	288	243	42	78	104	14	3	2	36	3	3	4	35	0	41	4	7	7	.321	.411	.428
Eastley, Tyler, Everett *	55	245	201	29	64	93	13	2	4	28	1	1	5	37	0	42	8	1	4	.318	.434	.463
Murphy, Steven, Spokane *	62	280	255	45	78	136	23	4	9	37	0	2	3	20	1	71	13	3	3	.306	.361	.533
Hendricks, Arthur, Yakima †	76	329	301	33	89	133	16	2	8	42	0	3	0	25	3	46	2	1	9	.296	.347	.442
Sansoe, Mike, Eugene	49	223	193	32	56	66	8	1	0	20	3	1	6	20	1	48	13	3	5	.290	.373	.342
Dyche, Joseph, Salem-Keizer	70	317	284	43	82	101	6	2	3	26	2	0	6	25	0	44	17	10	2	.289	.359	.356
Boyd, Chad, Vancouver *	56	238	212	28	60	78	15	0	1	27	1	2	1	22	0	24	9	5	2	.283	.350	.368
Gregg, David, Boise *	74	336	300	53	84	96	9	0	1	19	11	0	2	23	0	50	36	12	2	.280	.335	.320
Yens, Jose, Salem-Keizer	61	238	225	34	63	107	13	2	9	42	2	1	2	8	1	46	3	4	3	.280	.309	.476
Thon, Freddie, Spokane *	54	226	208	29	58	108	14	0	12	49	0	2	2	14	4	46	2	1	4	.279	.327	.519
Craig, Casey, Everett *	62	265	241	53	67	102	9	4	6	28	1	0	2	21	0	57	18	4	2	.278	.341	.423
Prettyman, Ronald, Everett *	58	258	234	35	65	98	11	2	6	27	2	1	2	19	0	57	7	3	5	.278	.336	.419

Player, Team	G	TPA	AB	R	H	TB	2B	3B	HR	RBI	SH	SF	HP	BB	IBB	SO	SB	CS	GDP	Avg.	OBP	Slg.
Bruce, Derek, Yakima	75	328	299	40	83	120	28	0	3	27	3	4	7	15	0	57	2	5	2	.278	.323	.401
Downing, Ramon, Yakima †	68	292	256	35	71	113	15	3	7	34	7	5	4	20	1	40	7	4	6	.277	.333	.441
Sellers, Justin, Vancouver	47	207	175	31	48	58	8	1	0	13	4	1	8	19	0	24	8	3	0	.274	.369	.331
Kleen, Steve, Vancouver	58	234	209	30	57	71	11	0	1	14	3	0	5	17	0	35	6	1	7	.273	.342	.340
Santin, Daniel, Everett *	54	219	205	20	56	79	11	0	4	31	0	2	1	11	1	42	0	4	4	.273	.311	.385
Saunders, Michael, Everett *	56	228	196	24	53	93	13	3	7	39	1	2	2	27	1	74	2	7	1	.270	.361	.474

DEPARTMENTAL LEADERS: G—Hendricks, 76. AB—Mooney, 304. R—Mooney, 57. H—Mooney, 104. TB—Mooney, 157. 2B—Bruce, 28. 3B—Mooney, 9. HR—Thon and Valbuena, 12. RBI—Valbuena, 51. SH—Gregg, 11. SF—Downing, 5. HP—Cuadrado, 20. BB—three players with 37. IBB—Thon, 4. SO—Strop, 86. SB—Gregg, 36. CS—Gregg, 12. GIDP—three players with 9. OBP—Thompson, .452. Slg.—Tucker, .580.

ALL PLAYERS

*Lefthanded batter. †Switch-hitter.

Player, Team	G	TPA	AB	R	H	TB	2B	3B	HR	RBI	SH	SF	HP	BB	IBB	SO	SB	CS	GDP	Avg.	OBP	Slg.
Abreu, Johany, Salem-Keizer †	22	54	53	5	10	14	2	1	0	8	0	0	0	1	0	12	3	2	0	.189	.204	.264
Acosta, Jesse, Vancouver	3	13	11	2	2	2	0	0	0	0	1	0	0	1	0	5	0	0	0	.182	.250	.182
Alley, Joshua, Eugene *	14	68	52	11	19	26	5	1	0	6	0	1	0	15	0	9	3	3	2	.365	.500	.500
Babineaux Jr., Erroll, Salem-Keizer	47	164	142	13	29	48	7	0	4	18	1	1	6	14	0	44	0	2	2	.204	.301	.338
Backman II, Walter, Spokane *	16	54	46	6	10	14	2	1	0	2	2	0	0	6	0	15	2	0	0	.217	.308	.304
Baez, Lizahio, Spokane †	38	156	144	21	45	85	5	1	11	33	0	0	5	7	0	28	1	1	4	.313	.365	.590
Baisley, Jeffrey, Vancouver	61	262	218	28	55	90	15	1	6	38	2	3	12	27	2	27	3	5	9	.252	.362	.413
Batten, Joseph, Yakima	9	37	30	5	9	11	2	0	0	1	0	0	1	6	0	9	4	2	0	.300	.432	.367
Bauer, Garrett, Yakima	3	7	7	0	0	0	0	0	0	0	0	0	0	0	0	5	0	0	0	.000	.000	.000
Bieker, Jeffrey, Vancouver	34	136	117	9	28	36	5	0	1	10	2	0	8	9	0	31	1	0	2	.239	.336	.308
Biguenet, Michael, Yakima	41	120	110	14	22	34	3	0	3	7	0	0	1	9	0	51	0	1	1	.200	.267	.309
Blunt, Terrance, Spokane †	47	202	172	34	39	62	5	3	4	22	3	0	6	21	1	31	7	5	3	.227	.332	.360
Boyd, Chad, Vancouver *	56	238	212	28	60	78	15	0	1	27	1	2	1	22	0	24	9	5	2	.283	.350	.368
Bruce, Derek, Yakima	75	328	299	40	83	120	28	0	3	27	3	4	7	15	0	57	2	5	2	.278	.323	.401
Bubalo, Ty, Vancouver	42	144	132	13	27	50	8	0	5	23	0	2	1	9	0	60	0	0	2	.205	.257	.379
Buck, Travis, Vancouver *	9	41	36	7	13	20	1	0	2	9	0	0	0	5	0	8	1	1	3	.361	.439	.556
Burgess, Brandon, Yakima †	33	139	119	21	40	63	10	2	3	18	0	0	6	14	2	34	1	0	3	.336	.432	.529
Busch, Andrew, Salem-Keizer	36	119	105	10	22	33	5	0	2	9	6	0	1	7	0	44	0	0	1	.210	.265	.314
Callahan, Shawn, Vancouver	31	123	102	10	22	33	6	1	1	9	1	2	3	15	1	29	2	1	4	.216	.328	.324
Cavanaugh, Brian, Eugene *	53	213	190	25	44	53	6	0	1	18	0	2	3	17	1	68	2	4	1	.232	.302	.279
Centeno, Jaen, Yakima	66	245	212	21	42	81	12	0	9	32	5	3	3	22	1	67	2	4	3	.198	.279	.382
Cho, Hyung, Everett	5	17	15	3	4	5	1	0	0	2	0	0	1	1	0	2	0	0	0	.267	.353	.333
Cleland, Clinton, Eugene	24	95	85	11	20	31	6	1	1	7	2	0	0	8	0	32	3	0	0	.235	.301	.365
Clement, Jeffrey, Everett *	4	15	11	4	3	4	1	0	0	1	0	1	2	1	0	2	0	0	0	.273	.400	.364
Contreras, Anthony, Salem-Keizer *	22	84	72	10	18	21	3	0	0	4	3	1	1	7	0	8	4	1	4	.250	.321	.292
Contreras, Lester, Yakima	46	165	148	18	33	55	8	1	4	14	1	1	2	13	0	37	1	1	3	.223	.293	.372
Copeland, Benjamin, Salem-Keizer *	29	133	121	25	37	62	5	4	4	23	1	0	0	11	0	25	2	1	1	.306	.364	.512
Crabtree, Benjamin, Spokane	27	93	81	7	19	24	2	0	1	11	1	2	1	8	0	13	1	2	2	.235	.304	.296
Craig, Casey, Everett *	62	265	241	53	67	102	9	4	6	28	1	0	2	21	0	57	18	4	2	.278	.341	.423
Culpepper, Jeffrey, Boise *	20	84	69	10	21	27	3	0	1	7	1	0	4	10	0	9	5	0	2	.304	.422	.391
Davidson, Drew, Eugene	34	153	138	18	41	62	7	1	4	19	1	1	3	10	0	26	2	3	2	.297	.355	.449
Defendis, John, Boise *	44	190	171	23	56	70	8	0	2	20	2	0	0	17	0	21	3	4	4	.327	.388	.409
Del Campo, Manny, Yakima	38	128	119	9	19	28	6	0	1	9	0	0	4	5	0	29	0	0	0	.160	.219	.235
Diaz, Javis, Eugene *	5	23	19	3	4	4	0	0	0	0	0	0	0	4	0	4	2	0	0	.211	.348	.211
Dixon, Dorian, Salem-Keizer *	42	115	101	13	30	39	6	0	1	9	2	0	1	11	0	14	1	0	3	.297	.372	.386
Douillard, Jonathan, Boise *	5	11	9	1	1	1	0	0	0	1	0	1	0	1	0	4	0	0	0	.111	.182	.111
Downing, Ramon, Yakima †	68	292	256	35	71	113	15	3	7	34	7	5	4	20	1	40	7	4	6	.277	.333	.441
Duran, German, Spokane	62	274	252	36	66	99	17	2	4	33	2	1	1	18	0	56	6	4	6	.262	.313	.393
Dyche, Joseph, Salem-Keizer	70	317	284	43	82	101	6	2	3	26	2	0	6	25	0	44	17	10	2	.289	.359	.356
Eastley, Tyler, Everett *	55	245	201	29	64	93	13	2	4	28	1	1	5	37	0	42	8	1	4	.318	.434	.463
Farina, Peter, Boise	13	33	31	0	7	8	1	0	0	1	0	0	0	2	0	8	0	0	1	.226	.273	.258
Flaig, Jeffrey, Everett	64	271	236	38	60	100	19	0	7	38	2	4	11	18	1	48	2	3	5	.254	.331	.424
Ford, Joshua, Yakima	43	185	163	12	46	53	7	0	0	25	0	4	3	15	1	30	0	1	2	.282	.346	.325
Fowles, Matt, Yakima †	1	0	0	0	0	0	0	0	0	0	...	0	0	0	...	0	0	0	0	...	...	...
Garcia, Jose, Vancouver	51	205	183	23	47	67	8	3	2	20	3	2	3	14	1	40	3	2	3	.257	.317	.366
Gary, Robert, Everett	42	156	139	26	33	64	9	2	6	22	1	0	8	8	0	58	2	1	3	.237	.316	.460
Gaskin, Christopher, Boise	65	280	254	30	63	96	15	0	6	39	1	1	9	23	2	50	4	0	5	.256	.341	.390
Gottier, Brandon, Eugene	25	88	78	2	18	25	4	0	1	9	2	1	4	3	0	11	0	0	2	.231	.291	.321
Gregg, David, Boise *	74	336	300	53	84	96	9	0	1	19	11	0	2	23	0	50	36	12	2	.280	.335	.320
Guerrero, Santiago, Eugene	55	224	194	22	49	74	5	7	2	31	1	4	10	15	0	43	9	6	5	.253	.332	.381
Gunther, Barry, Salem-Keizer †	31	101	86	15	29	40	6	1	1	15	1	0	1	13	0	13	1	0	5	.337	.430	.465
Gutierrez, Henry, Salem-Keizer	23	92	81	12	18	25	4	0	1	8	0	0	1	10	0	14	0	0	1	.222	.315	.309
Hall, David, Everett	34	120	102	9	27	31	4	0	0	10	3	1	2	12	0	29	4	2	2	.265	.350	.304
Hawke, Matthew, Spokane *	26	109	88	12	22	44	4	0	6	14	0	3	4	14	1	24	0	0	1	.250	.367	.500
Headley, Chase, Eugene †	57	259	220	29	59	97	14	3	6	33	0	1	4	34	1	48	1	1	6	.268	.375	.441
Heckman, John, Everett	2	7	7	1	2	2	0	0	0	0	0	0	0	0	0	3	0	0	0	.286	.286	.286
Heid, Trevor, Everett	32	113	97	29	29	56	11	2	4	14	1	1	4	10	2	23	10	2	1	.299	.384	.577
Hendricks, Arthur, Yakima †	76	329	301	33	89	133	16	2	8	42	0	3	0	25	3	46	2	1	9	.296	.347	.442
Herren, Karl, Spokane *	57	246	216	22	57	90	15	3	4	27	0	2	0	28	1	63	6	4	0	.264	.346	.417
Higashi, Jonathan, Spokane	27	102	89	10	27	39	10	1	0	11	2	1	5	5	0	20	1	0	2	.303	.370	.438
Hode, Scott, Boise	22	88	82	6	23	29	3	0	1	9	0	0	3	3	0	9	1	1	3	.280	.330	.354
Hooft, Joseph, Spokane	60	237	218	26	49	62	8	1	1	20	1	1	0	16	0	48	3	6	6	.225	.277	.284
Hudson, Robert, Everett	55	205	186	24	47	57	8	1	0	16	6	0	1	12	0	32	6	2	0	.253	.302	.306
Hundley, Nicholas, Eugene	43	184	148	30	37	67	7	1	7	22	0	1	2	33	1	35	1	0	2	.250	.391	.453
Johnston, John, Eugene	47	190	170	15	43	59	8	1	2	23	4	3	0	13	0	41	2	4	4	.253	.301	.347
Jones, Daryl, Eugene *	73	282	255	28	48	68	8	4	1	16	1	0	5	21	1	81	0	2	3	.188	.263	.267
Joseph, Alfred, Boise †	16	66	59	7	16	21	5	0	0	9	2	0	1	4	0	15	2	1	2	.271	.328	.356

Player, Team	G	TPA	AB	R	H	TB	2B	3B	HR	RBI	SH	SF	HP	BB	IBB	SO	SB	CS	GDP	Avg.	OBP	Slg.
Kemp, Joseph, Spokane *	47	172	149	23	39	58	5	4	2	18	1	1	2	19	0	40	9	3	1	.262	.351	.389
Killian, William, Eugene *	14	42	37	0	7	9	0	1	0	4	0	0	1	4	0	13	0	0	1	.189	.286	.243
Kleen, Steve, Vancouver	58	234	209	30	57	71	11	0	1	14	3	0	5	17	0	35	6	1	7	.273	.342	.340
Lobaton, Jose, Eugene †	11	42	32	4	9	11	2	0	0	3	3	0	1	6	0	8	0	0	0	.281	.410	.344
Long, Wesley, Vancouver	13	58	52	8	18	24	6	0	0	5	0	0	1	5	0	8	3	0	0	.346	.414	.462
Maroul, David, Salem-Keizer	44	188	175	20	46	71	8	1	5	27	4	2	3	4	0	61	0	1	6	.263	.288	.406
Martinez, Frank, Vancouver †	14	61	48	6	8	9	1	0	0	3	0	1	0	12	0	18	3	1	1	.167	.328	.188
Massaro, Michael, Vancouver *	58	219	191	35	48	60	5	2	1	15	1	1	0	26	0	51	5	2	4	.251	.339	.314
Mayberry, John, Spokane	71	302	265	51	67	116	16	0	11	26	0	1	10	26	1	71	7	3	1	.253	.341	.438
Mercado, Richard, Yakima	10	37	30	3	7	11	2	1	0	3	0	1	1	5	0	5	0	0	2	.233	.351	.367
Minicozzi, Mark, Salem-Keizer	70	288	243	42	78	104	14	3	2	36	3	3	4	35	0	41	4	7	7	.321	.411	.428
Mooney, Michael, Salem-Keizer	73	334	304	57	104	157	20	9	5	29	2	3	5	20	2	64	13	4	1	.342	.389	.516
Mota, Jonathan, Boise	63	235	212	18	50	59	7	1	0	22	5	0	2	16	0	49	4	5	6	.236	.296	.278
Murphy, Steven, Spokane *	62	280	255	45	78	136	23	4	9	37	0	2	3	20	1	71	13	3	3	.306	.361	.533
Muyco, Dionisio, Boise	37	134	121	10	26	30	1	0	1	8	5	0	0	8	0	31	0	2	2	.215	.264	.248
Olivares, Juan, Yakima	53	210	191	21	43	55	3	3	1	18	2	1	3	13	0	47	6	2	4	.225	.284	.288
Omura, Isaac, Vancouver *	40	151	131	11	26	34	5	0	1	11	2	0	0	18	0	36	2	1	3	.198	.295	.260
Parraz, Ezekiel, Vancouver	26	89	76	10	19	22	3	0	0	6	0	0	3	10	0	20	2	0	0	.250	.360	.289
Paulino, Adalberto, Salem-Keizer	29	53	47	6	12	15	0	0	1	6	1	0	3	2	0	15	0	3	1	.255	.327	.319
Pena, Antonio, Spokane	4	9	8	0	0	0	0	0	0	0	0	0	0	1	0	2	0	0	0	.000	.111	.000
Perez, Wilber, Vancouver †	39	145	132	19	36	50	6	1	2	20	2	1	1	9	0	20	10	4	1	.273	.322	.379
Peterson, David, Spokane	23	82	68	6	10	11	1	0	0	3	3	1	3	7	0	27	1	1	2	.147	.253	.162
Piper-Jordan, Andre, Vancouver	6	12	10	0	2	3	1	0	0	1	0	0	0	2	0	4	1	0	0	.200	.333	.300
Pratt, Haas, Vancouver	59	247	223	30	60	94	16	0	6	29	0	2	5	17	0	51	2	1	7	.269	.332	.422
Prettyman, Ronald, Everett *	58	258	234	35	65	98	11	2	6	27	2	1	2	19	0	57	7	3	5	.278	.336	.419
Puello, Elvin, Boise	61	249	227	32	54	82	15	2	3	20	0	1	6	15	1	54	3	0	8	.238	.301	.361
Quinones, Carlos, Boise †	43	169	161	11	38	42	4	0	0	15	0	1	0	7	0	29	0	3	0	.236	.266	.261
Rahl, Christopher, Spokane	47	198	182	29	49	74	12	5	1	10	3	0	1	12	0	44	10	5	2	.269	.318	.407
Recker, Anthony, Vancouver	43	169	150	16	35	58	8	0	5	18	1	0	2	16	0	40	0	0	5	.233	.315	.387
Reed, Mark, Boise *	55	202	184	32	46	68	10	0	4	18	2	0	1	15	0	53	7	5	6	.250	.310	.370
Reynolds, Kyle, Boise *	52	215	199	28	51	78	6	3	5	24	0	1	3	12	0	52	4	2	2	.256	.307	.392
Richardson, William, Eugene	55	204	178	19	31	44	8	1	1	7	4	1	4	17	0	46	4	1	4	.174	.260	.247
Rios, Jose, Boise	35	101	99	11	32	39	7	0	0	8	1	0	1	0	0	11	1	3	1	.323	.330	.394
Rivera, Jodam, Eugene †	24	99	83	10	20	22	2	0	0	6	4	1	1	10	0	20	0	1	1	.241	.326	.265
Sabatella, Bryan, Everett	53	196	169	28	42	63	5	2	4	24	0	4	3	20	0	45	7	4	7	.249	.332	.373
Sandoval, Pablo, Salem-Keizer †	75	327	294	46	97	125	15	2	3	50	3	3	6	21	3	33	2	3	9	.330	.383	.425
Sansoe, Mike, Eugene	49	223	193	32	56	66	8	1	0	20	3	1	6	20	1	48	13	3	5	.290	.373	.342
Santana, Julio, Spokane †	58	209	192	22	39	48	7	1	0	19	2	3	2	10	0	56	5	3	4	.203	.246	.250
Santin, Daniel, Everett *	54	219	205	20	56	79	11	0	4	31	0	2	1	11	1	42	0	4	4	.273	.311	.385
Santoro, Michael, Salem-Keizer	10	32	27	4	4	5	1	0	0	2	1	0	0	4	0	10	1	0	1	.148	.258	.185
Saunders, Michael, Everett *	56	228	196	24	53	93	13	3	7	39	1	2	2	27	1	74	2	7	1	.270	.361	.474
Schweiger, Brian, Everett	20	73	59	7	8	10	2	0	0	4	1	0	3	10	0	23	3	1	0	.136	.292	.169
Sellers, Justin, Vancouver	47	207	175	31	48	58	8	1	0	13	4	1	8	19	0	24	8	3	0	.274	.369	.331
Septimo, Leyson, Yakima *	67	254	237	20	57	78	11	2	2	21	4	2	1	10	0	51	2	3	4	.241	.272	.329
Smith, John, Eugene	25	89	79	4	8	11	0	0	1	5	0	2	0	8	0	27	0	0	1	.101	.180	.139
Sosa, Ricardo, Yakima	32	133	118	17	30	53	9	1	4	18	1	2	2	10	0	22	2	0	3	.254	.318	.449
Stanton, Christopher, Salem-Keizer	26	104	93	11	23	26	3	0	0	7	1	0	2	8	0	18	3	0	0	.247	.320	.280
Steiner, Chad, Eugene	14	60	56	8	14	20	1	1	1	8	0	0	0	4	0	9	0	0	4	.250	.300	.357
Taylor, Brandon, Boise	57	221	202	28	53	92	16	1	7	30	1	2	2	14	1	53	2	5	5	.262	.314	.455
Teagarden, Taylor, Spokane	31	122	96	23	27	61	5	4	7	16	0	1	2	23	0	32	1	1	1	.281	.426	.635
Thompson, William, Salem-Keizer *	48	211	185	25	71	91	12	1	2	35	1	1	1	23	2	22	0	1	1	.384	.452	.492
Thon, Freddie, Spokane *	54	226	208	29	58	108	14	0	12	49	0	2	2	14	4	46	2	1	4	.279	.327	.519
Tietje, Chalon, Vancouver	32	138	120	17	27	30	3	0	0	12	1	1	3	13	1	30	4	3	5	.225	.314	.250
Todd, Christopher, Salem-Keizer †	34	81	63	7	13	13	0	0	0	8	0	0	4	14	0	9	3	0	0	.206	.383	.206
Tritle, Christopher, Vancouver	18	70	59	11	15	23	3	1	1	8	0	1	0	10	0	20	7	1	0	.254	.357	.390
Tucker, John, Everett	48	206	174	34	45	101	19	2	11	36	1	2	6	23	0	60	4	0	2	.259	.361	.580
Turner, Timothy, Eugene	36	160	151	19	36	59	1	2	6	14	0	0	0	9	0	52	9	1	0	.238	.281	.391
Valbuena, Luis, Everett *	74	325	287	40	75	127	10	3	12	51	1	4	2	31	0	37	14	6	3	.261	.333	.443
Valdez, Jesus, Boise	61	246	234	30	57	87	13	1	5	38	0	2	1	9	0	49	4	3	3	.244	.272	.372
Valichka, Brian, Spokane	7	28	21	5	4	5	1	0	0	2	0	0	1	6	0	4	0	0	0	.190	.393	.238
Vazquez, Kelvin, Eugene †	23	86	63	13	16	24	5	0	1	4	6	1	2	14	0	17	4	2	1	.254	.400	.381
Venable, William, Eugene *	42	156	139	17	30	45	5	2	2	14	0	1	2	14	0	38	2	1	1	.216	.295	.324
Washington, Johnny, Spokane	10	24	20	2	2	3	1	0	0	1	0	1	0	2	0	8	0	0	0	.100	.217	.150
Williams, Kevin, Yakima	33	124	104	17	21	26	5	0	0	4	2	0	8	10	0	45	11	4	1	.202	.320	.250
Wu, Chao Kuan, Everett *	8	30	23	4	5	5	0	0	0	1	0	0	0	7	0	6	1	0	2	.217	.400	.217
Yens, Jose, Salem-Keizer	61	238	225	34	63	107	13	2	9	42	2	1	2	8	1	46	3	4	3	.280	.309	.476
Zorn, Dean, Everett †	12	53	43	3	7	10	3	0	0	2	1	1	1	9	0	13	1	1	1	.167	.314	.238

GRAND SLAMS—R. Eastley, 2; S. Almonte, C. Boyd, A. Busch, D. Carte, J. Centeno, C. Craig, P. Cuadrado, S. Johnston, W. Richardson, F. Thon, 1 each.
AWARDED FIRST BASE ON CATCHER'S INTERFERENCE—B. Cavanaugh (B. Valichka); J. Hooft (M. Del Campo).

2005 PITCHING

TEAM

Team	W	L	Pct.	ERA	G	CG	ShO	Sv.	IP	H	TBF	R	ER	HR	SH	SF	HB	BB	IBB	SO	WP	Bk.
Vancouver	46	30	.605	3	76	0	3	28	688	568	2864	268	229	26	42	13	34	224	5	643	50	9
Salem-Keizer	45	31	.592	3.66	76	0	5	27	683	641	2905	324	278	59	30	18	36	235	10	678	50	6
Tri-City	36	40	.474	3.69	76	0	5	23	674	633	2868	332	276	46	21	22	51	239	1	572	68	6
Eugene	34	42	.447	3.78	76	0	1	21	673	711	2934	361	283	46	29	24	56	182	12	577	47	2
Yakima	30	46	.395	4.09	76	1	2	15	681.1	712	3043	399	310	45	28	22	48	287	3	653	76	9
Spokane	37	39	.487	4.17	76	0	2	18	676.1	718	2988	379	313	50	40	19	53	214	6	605	57	2
Everett	42	34	.553	4.32	76	0	6	21	680.2	694	2985	375	327	58	16	19	65	278	6	604	77	5
Boise	34	42	.447	4.61	76	0	4	17	675.1	707	3059	416	346	52	34	20	49	324	4	597	88	12

INDIVIDUAL

TOP QUALIFIERS FOR EARNED-RUN AVERAGE TITLE

Minimum 61 innings.*Lefthanded pitcher.

Pitcher, Team	W	L	Pct.	ERA	G	GS	CG	ShO	GF	Sv.	IP	H	TBF	R	ER	HR	SH	SF	HB	BB	IBB	SO	WP	Bk.
Madsen, Michael, Vancouver	6	1	.857	1.69	15	12	0	0	1	0	80.0	56	309	21	15	2	4	0	4	14	0	68	6	0
Carter, Brenton, Eugene *	4	2	.667	1.88	13	13	0	0	0	0	72.0	58	277	24	15	3	2	4	3	7	0	66	3	0
McKae, Dave, Salem-Keizer	3	2	.600	2.42	19	4	0	0	4	3	67.0	55	269	27	18	5	3	0	1	17	3	83	7	0
Shull, James, Vancouver	4	3	.571	2.47	14	13	0	0	0	0	73.0	65	293	25	20	3	3	0	4	10	0	81	4	1
Mathis, Douglas, Spokane	4	7	.364	2.68	17	16	0	0	0	0	84.0	78	344	33	25	2	2	0	6	17	0	78	7	0
Romo, Sergio, Salem-Keizer	7	1	.875	2.75	15	14	0	0	0	0	68.2	70	280	24	21	7	3	0	3	9	1	65	1	1
Coffman, Broc, Spokane *	2	2	.500	2.99	17	11	0	0	2	1	69.1	62	290	28	23	2	4	2	1	26	0	63	3	0
Piekarz, Joseph, Vancouver *	3	3	.500	3.38	15	12	0	0	1	0	77.1	67	316	32	29	2	2	1	1	24	0	59	4	0
Fagan, Robert, Everett *	6	2	.750	3.50	15	14	0	0	0	0	82.1	86	355	40	32	5	4	1	4	33	1	50	11	2
Downs, Darin, Boise *	5	4	.556	3.50	14	13	0	0	0	0	61.2	61	261	30	24	5	2	0	4	22	0	63	6	0
Rohrbaugh, Robert, Everett *	5	2	.714	3.84	14	12	0	0	0	0	68.0	68	283	33	29	7	2	1	4	18	0	71	7	0
Yepez, Jesus, Boise *	4	2	.667	3.92	14	13	0	0	0	0	62.0	57	265	31	27	3	3	1	3	28	0	46	8	2
Wright, Kyle, Yakima	1	4	.200	4.22	15	14	0	0	1	0	79.0	88	350	47	37	4	2	1	7	22	1	65	6	1
Howard, Adam, Yakima	4	5	.444	4.29	13	13	0	0	0	0	71.1	88	311	36	34	8	1	3	7	12	0	59	2	0
Newby, Joseph, Vancouver	5	5	.500	4.29	15	15	0	0	0	0	77.2	71	326	39	37	2	2	5	4	24	0	50	7	2
Martinez, Joseph, Salem-Keizer	4	3	.571	4.30	15	13	0	0	1	0	69.0	69	281	33	33	9	4	0	5	15	0	59	4	1
Allen, Nicholas, Everett	6	4	.600	4.59	16	12	0	0	0	0	66.2	82	293	42	34	3	0	3	10	12	1	37	0	0
Krosschell, Benjamin, Eugene	2	7	.222	4.70	16	15	0	0	0	0	76.2	83	330	50	40	4	3	3	4	18	0	59	4	0
Delabar, Steven, Eugene	4	6	.400	4.76	16	16	0	0	0	0	75.2	84	338	45	40	7	2	4	15	18	0	59	4	0
Atkins, Mitchell, Boise	3	6	.333	5.03	15	15	0	0	0	0	73.1	85	333	45	41	8	4	2	9	30	0	59	6	4
Kemlo, Christopher, Yakima	5	7	.417	5.08	16	16	1	0	0	0	88.2	116	406	65	50	6	3	1	1	28	0	47	9	1

DEPARTMENTAL LEADERS: W—Romo, 7. L—Rocha, 8. Pct.—Romo, .875. G—Madden, 38. GS—three pitchers tied with 16. CG—Kemlo, 1. GF—Delgado, 29. Sv.—Anderson, 19. IP—Kemlo, 88.2. H—Kemlo, 116. TBF—Kemlo, 409. R—Kemlo, 65. ER—McConnell, 51. HR—Wilding, 12. SAC—Pfautz, 7. SF—Gold and Newby, 5. HB—Delabar, 15. BB—Rocha, 53. IBB—Madden, 4. SO—Lindsay, 107. WP—Rocha, 17. BK—Atkins, 4.

ALL PITCHERS

*Lefthanded pitcher.

Pitcher, Team	W	L	Pct.	ERA	G	GS	CG	ShO	GF	Sv.	IP	H	TBF	R	ER	HR	SH	SF	HB	BB	IBB	SO	WP	Bk.
Abbott, Justin, Spokane	0	1	.000	5.40	3	0	0	0	1	0	3.1	6	18	5	2	0	2	0	2	0	0	2	2	0
Acevedo, Danielin, Vancouver	4	3	.571	4.81	17	0	0	0	7	1	24.1	28	99	15	13	4	5	0	5	1	1	18	2	1
Allen, Nicholas, Everett	6	4	.600	4.59	16	12	0	0	0	0	66.2	82	293	42	34	3	0	3	10	12	1	37	0	0
Anderson, Brian, Salem-Keizer	3	1	.750	1.95	27	0	0	0	27	19	27.2	16	104	6	6	2	0	1	1	3	0	42	1	0
Arias, Oliver, Everett	0	0	.000	4.91	6	1	0	0	1	0	14.2	20	65	9	8	2	1	0	1	2	0	9	1	0
Asher, David, Everett *	1	5	.167	4.79	18	6	0	0	8	3	35.2	38	151	20	19	2	3	1	3	9	3	40	2	0
Atkins, Mitchell, Boise	3	6	.333	5.03	15	15	0	0	0	0	73.1	85	333	45	41	8	4	2	9	30	0	59	6	4
Avery, Matthew, Boise	1	3	.250	4.62	11	11	0	0	0	0	48.2	53	205	27	25	7	1	3	3	15	0	25	3	0
Baca, Daniel, Eugene	0	1	.000	9.53	7	0	0	0	1	0	11.1	17	56	13	12	2	0	0	1	4	0	11	3	0
Baez, Edgar, Boise	0	0	.000	8.86	20	0	0	0	4	0	21.1	30	107	21	21	2	0	3	4	11	0	16	5	0
Bauer, Garrett, Yakima *	1	0	1.000	5.06	18	0	0	0	6	1	26.2	25	133	15	15	2	2	3	27	1	42	9	0
Beus, Lance, Everett *	1	2	.333	3.68	19	0	0	0	4	1	36.2	37	154	18	15	5	0	2	13	0	34	4	0
Billek, Michael, Boise	0	1	.000	2.65	5	5	0	0	0	0	17.0	16	74	10	5	0	1	1	0	6	0	20	2	0
Brandt, Adam, Everett *	0	0	.000	54.00	1	0	0	0	0	0	0.1	2	5	3	2	0	0	0	1	0	0	0	0	0
Bryant, Stephen, Vancouver	3	3	.500	3.03	21	0	0	0	9	3	29.2	24	118	10	10	1	1	1	1	7	0	34	3	0
Burcie, Jarrad, Spokane	1	0	1.000	5.51	8	0	0	0	2	0	16.1	20	82	16	10	0	2	1	2	9	0	14	1	0
Byrd, Taylor, Spokane	2	1	.667	5.83	17	0	0	0	9	0	29.1	27	131	20	19	7	0	3	1	18	1	30	3	0
Cahill, John, Yakima	0	0	.000	8.25	8	0	0	0	1	0	12.0	20	58	11	11	1	1	0	0	7	0	8	0	1
Carter, Brenton, Eugene *	4	2	.667	1.88	13	13	0	0	0	0	72.0	58	277	24	15	3	2	4	3	7	0	66	3	0
Carter, Eric, Everett	2	2	.500	7.67	14	5	0	0	4	0	31.2	50	163	28	27	6	2	3	5	22	0	26	12	0
Carter, Steven-Ryder, Vancouver	1	1	.500	2.08	6	0	0	0	4	1	13.0	9	56	4	3	0	0	0	2	3	0	11	0	0
Cepeda, Benigno, Salem-Keizer *	1	1	.500	6.43	6	2	0	0	1	0	14.0	13	66	10	10	2	1	1	0	13	0	5	3	0
Chambers, Ryan, Boise *	1	2	.333	4.91	18	0	0	0	4	1	25.2	25	113	14	14	3	2	0	3	9	0	31	4	0
Cody, Buck, Salem-Keizer *	0	2	.000	3.78	15	0	0	0	1	0	16.2	19	75	10	7	3	1	0	1	6	1	22	0	0
Coffman, Broc, Spokane *	2	2	.500	2.99	17	11	0	0	2	1	69.1	62	290	28	23	2	4	2	1	26	0	63	3	0
Colon, Juan, Everett	0	0	.000	5.00	6	0	0	0	5	0	9.0	9	39	5	5	0	0	1	0	5	0	8	2	0
Corchado, Jose, Vancouver	3	2	.600	5.40	17	0	0	0	6	0	25.0	24	113	18	15	2	1	0	2	16	0	34	5	0
Davis, Bradley, Vancouver *	4	1	.800	0.52	23	0	0	0	8	4	34.2	26	141	6	2	1	3	0	3	9	2	44	2	1
Delabar, Steven, Eugene	4	6	.400	4.76	16	16	0	0	0	0	75.2	84	338	45	40	7	2	4	15	18	0	59	4	0
De La O, Danny, Eugene *	0	0	.000	16.20	4	0	0	0	1	0	3.1	7	18	6	6	2	2	0	1	1	0	4	1	0
Doherty, Ryan, Yakima	3	3	.500	3.27	22	0	0	0	6	1	33.0	26	136	16	12	3	2	1	4	9	0	38	3	0
Dove, Bradley, Yakima *	2	4	.333	5.49	9	7	0	0	0	0	39.1	51	180	33	24	3	2	3	0	18	0	30	4	1
Downs, Darin, Boise *	5	4	.556	3.50	14	13	0	0	0	0	61.2	61	261	30	24	5	2	0	4	22	0	63	6	0
Duran, Enmanuel, Yakima	0	1	.000	2.72	24	1	0	0	8	2	36.1	34	154	14	11	0	0	0	2	14	0	25	3	1
Evenson, Roger, Boise	4	4	.500	5.58	24	1	0	0	10	4	40.1	41	171	26	25	3	4	1	2	14	1	39	9	0
Fagan, Robert, Everett *	6	2	.750	3.50	15	14	0	0	0	0	82.1	86	355	40	32	5	4	1	4	33	1	50	11	2
Fairbanks, Scott, Vancouver	0	0	.000	36.00	2	0	0	0	1	0	1.0	0	9	4	4	0	0	0	2	4	0	1	3	0
Fernandez, Alfredo, Eugene	3	2	.600	2.63	33	0	0	0	28	7	37.2	36	164	20	11	1	2	0	3	13	1	35	1	0
Fogle, Nathan, Spokane	1	0	1.000	3.90	20	0	0	0	8	2	30.0	20	126	14	13	4	0	0	3	15	0	45	4	0
Foltin, Wayne, Salem-Keizer	2	1	.667	3.38	17	0	0	0	13	1	21.1	24	93	14	8	1	1	1	0	7	1	20	0	1
Fowles, Matt, Yakima *	2	2	.500	4.15	23	0	0	0	8	2	26.0	26	122	18	12	2	1	1	2	19	0	30	2	0
Frye, Randall, Everett	0	0	.000	4.00	4	0	0	0	1	0	9.0	8	38	4	4	1	0	0	6	0	7	2	0
Garcia, Juan Carlos, Spokane	1	2	.333	6.69	16	3	0	0	8	0	35.0	43	176	29	26	3	3	2	7	23	0	25	8	0
Geer, Joshua, Eugene	3	1	.750	3.69	7	6	0	0	0	0	31.2	35	129	13	13	5	2	1	1	4	0	13	1	0
Gibson, Rollie, Everett *	3	2	.600	4.45	15	2	0	0	5	1	28.1	31	123	14	14	5	1	1	3	12	1	30	3	0

Pitcher, Team	W	L	Pct.	ERA	G	GS	CG	ShO	GF	Sv.	IP	H	TBF	R	ER	HR	SH	SF	HB	BB	IBB	SO	WP	Bk.
Gilmore, Jeffrey, Everett	5	1	.833	3.97	12	8	0	0	0	0	56.2	55	234	25	25	9	1	0	4	13	0	57	5	1
Gold, Adam, Eugene	3	3	.500	4.91	28	0	0	0	5	0	36.2	35	170	23	20	3	1	5	8	22	1	33	3	0
Gray, Jeffrey, Vancouver	4	2	.667	2.51	12	11	0	0	0	0	46.2	33	179	16	13	0	4	0	1	5	0	24	4	1
Griffin, Daniel, Salem-Keizer	3	2	.600	2.39	8	8	0	0	0	0	37.2	33	152	11	10	1	1	1	2	12	0	49	3	0
Guaramato, Edgar, Everett	1	4	.200	3.62	28	0	0	0	11	1	37.1	23	162	20	15	1	0	3	9	24	0	38	3	0
Hagerty, Luke, Boise *	0	1	.000	31.05	14	1	0	0	1	0	6.2	14	67	26	23	0	1	1	4	30	0	4	9	0
Hall, Jesse, Spokane	2	3	.400	6.47	16	5	0	0	2	0	32.0	46	160	29	23	2	0	3	3	15	0	29	5	0
Herrera, John, Vancouver	1	1	.500	6.08	16	0	0	0	9	0	23.2	24	104	16	16	1	3	1	2	14	0	16	5	2
Higelin, Brandon, Eugene *	0	2	.000	5.00	22	0	0	0	5	0	27.0	40	129	18	15	2	1	0	1	11	1	21	1	0
Hinshaw, Alexander, Salem-Keizer *	0	1	.000	3.68	25	0	0	0	2	0	22.0	17	99	9	9	1	3	3	3	18	1	33	2	0
Holden, Kyle, Boise	2	2	.500	7.45	20	1	0	0	7	0	29.0	48	142	30	24	2	2	2	0	9	1	19	8	1
Howard, Arnold, Yakima *	4	5	.444	4.29	13	13	0	0	0	0	71.1	88	311	36	34	8	1	3	7	12	0	59	2	0
Hughey, Arnold, Eugene *	5	1	.833	3.06	26	3	0	0	4	1	47.0	43	193	17	16	4	3	1	1	12	1	58	3	0
Hunton, Jonathan, Boise	1	3	.250	3.20	19	0	0	0	11	4	25.1	22	118	16	9	2	1	0	3	15	2	28	5	0
Hyle, Michael, Boise	3	5	.375	3.18	15	6	0	0	2	0	45.1	37	200	24	16	0	1	1	10	20	0	37	3	0
Jamison, Neil, Eugene	1	2	.333	1.32	25	0	0	0	17	8	27.1	23	115	5	4	0	1	1	4	8	2	31	4	0
Jimenez, Juan, Eugene	0	0	.000	0.00	1	0	0	0	0	0	1.0	1	3	0	0	0	0	0	0	0	0	0	0	0
Jimenez Angulo, Fabian Enrique, Eugene *	1	3	.250	2.22	7	6	0	0	0	0	28.1	31	133	19	7	0	0	0	2	12	0	18	6	0
Jones, Michael, Boise	0	1	.000	0.00	1	0	0	0	0	0	2.0	3	11	2	0	0	0	0	0	1	0	2	0	0
Kahn, Stephen, Everett	3	0	1.000	3.93	17	0	0	0	15	12	18.1	14	81	9	8	1	0	0	0	14	0	22	2	0
Kemlo, Christopher, Yakima	5	7	.417	5.08	16	16	1	0	0	0	88.2	116	406	65	50	6	3	1	5	28	0	47	9	1
Kilby, Brad, Vancouver *	2	0	1.000	1.95	23	0	0	0	18	14	27.2	20	115	7	6	2	0	1	0	11	0	38	1	0
Kintzler, Brandon, Eugene	0	0	.000	0.00	3	0	0	0	0	0	3.1	3	11	0	0	0	1	0	0	0	0	1	0	0
Kleen, Steve, Vancouver	0	0	.000	0.00	1	0	0	0	1	0	0.2	0	2	0	0	0	0	0	0	0	0	1	0	0
Koerber, Scott, Boise *	1	1	.500	3.67	23	0	0	0	4	1	34.1	35	154	15	14	2	2	1	2	20	0	23	0	1
Koliscak, Cory, Everett	2	1	.667	5.06	22	0	0	0	13	3	26.2	27	118	18	15	3	1	0	3	12	0	23	2	1
Kometani, Paul, Spokane	0	0	.000	2.25	2	2	0	0	0	0	8.0	9	35	2	2	0	0	0	2	0	0	10	0	0
Krohe, Matthew, Yakima *	0	2	.000	3.14	20	0	0	0	6	0	28.2	30	122	14	10	2	2	0	1	9	0	18	0	1
Krosschell, Benjamin, Eugene	2	7	.222	4.70	16	15	0	0	0	0	76.2	83	330	50	40	4	3	3	4	18	0	59	4	0
Link, Jon, Eugene	3	3	.500	4.42	25	7	0	0	1	0	59.0	67	247	33	29	5	1	2	2	8	1	44	5	0
Lockwood, Jonathan, Everett	2	0	1.000	0.00	5	0	0	0	1	0	16.0	3	53	0	0	0	0	0	2	1	0	19	0	0
Lopez, Aleurys, Boise *	0	0	.000	9.90	7	0	0	0	1	1	10.0	20	54	11	11	1	0	1	0	6	0	10	0	0
Ludwig, Kellen, Salem-Keizer	1	3	.250	5.19	18	8	0	0	0	0	52.0	63	234	32	30	2	2	1	0	21	0	46	2	0
Madden, John, Eugene	2	5	.286	3.48	38	0	0	0	15	5	41.1	49	193	27	16	1	4	0	4	17	4	55	4	0
Madej, Ronald, Vancouver *	0	0	.000	2.81	17	0	0	0	0	0	25.2	27	112	9	8	0	5	0	2	15	1	28	3	1
Madsen, Michael, Vancouver	6	1	.857	1.69	15	12	0	0	1	0	80.0	56	309	21	15	2	4	0	4	14	0	68	6	0
Maldonado, Juan, Spokane	4	5	.444	5.00	22	1	0	0	11	2	45.0	60	204	28	25	3	6	1	6	9	2	29	1	0
Martinez, Joseph, Salem-Keizer	4	3	.571	4.30	15	13	0	0	0	0	69.0	69	281	33	33	9	4	0	5	15	0	59	4	1
Martinez, Roman, Everett	1	2	.333	4.86	13	4	0	0	1	0	33.1	32	151	19	18	4	0	1	3	17	1	27	5	0
Martinez, Shawn, Vancouver	1	1	.500	4.70	4	0	0	0	1	0	7.2	6	33	5	4	1	1	0	0	5	0	8	0	0
Mathis, Douglas, Spokane	4	7	.364	2.68	17	16	0	0	0	0	84.0	78	344	33	25	2	2	0	6	17	0	78	7	0
Mault, James, Everett	0	1	.000	5.06	5	0	0	0	2	0	5.1	6	25	3	3	0	0	0	0	4	1	5	0	0
McConnell, Kellan, Spokane	6	5	.545	5.86	17	14	0	0	1	0	78.1	93	339	55	51	8	5	4	3	16	0	60	4	0
McElroy, Tanner, Spokane	3	2	.600	2.53	16	3	0	0	4	0	42.2	35	177	15	12	2	1	0	1	15	0	55	3	1
McKae, Dave, Salem-Keizer	3	2	.600	2.42	19	4	0	0	4	3	67.0	55	269	27	18	5	3	0	1	17	3	83	7	0
Millikan, Bryan, Salem-Keizer	1	3	.250	4.84	20	2	0	0	6	1	35.1	39	157	23	19	2	0	2	1	15	0	27	3	1
Minor, Matthew, Salem-Keizer	3	1	.750	2.72	23	0	0	0	8	3	36.1	21	145	11	11	3	3	2	2	18	2	33	5	0
Mitchell, Michael, Vancouver	0	0	.000	0.00	7	0	0	0	6	5	9.1	4	39	1	0	0	1	0	1	4	1	6	1	0
Newby, Joseph, Vancouver	5	5	.500	4.29	15	15	0	0	0	0	77.2	71	326	39	37	2	2	5	4	24	0	50	7	2
Newby, Kyler, Yakima	1	0	1.000	2.18	24	0	0	0	9	2	41.1	25	162	12	10	1	0	2	1	14	0	66	6	1
Nieto, Christopher, Salem-Keizer *	3	0	1.000	1.05	5	5	0	0	0	0	25.2	21	101	4	3	1	0	0	0	7	0	23	2	0
Ortiz, Jose, Boise	0	2	.000	4.43	15	0	0	0	3	0	22.1	28	110	16	11	0	2	2	1	13	0	12	0	1
Pawelek, Mark, Boise *	0	0	.000	0.00	1	1	0	0	0	0	3.0	6	14	1	0	0	1	0	0	1	0	4	0	0
Pereira, Nick, Salem-Keizer	5	3	.625	3.04	14	9	0	0	1	0	50.1	54	213	21	17	0	2	2	2	14	1	41	3	1
Pfautz, Craig, Yakima *	1	6	.143	5.46	20	0	0	0	5	0	28.0	39	133	29	17	2	7	2	0	16	1	16	6	0
Piekarz, Joseph, Vancouver *	3	3	.500	3.38	15	12	0	0	1	0	77.1	67	316	32	29	2	2	1	24	0	59	4	0
Polanco, Phillip, Eugene	1	0	1.000	2.00	6	0	0	0	1	0	9.0	6	36	3	2	0	1	0	2	2	1	5	0	0
Ponce, William, Eugene	2	1	.667	4.15	21	0	0	0	9	0	26.0	30	118	13	12	1	2	1	1	15	0	16	2	2
Putman, Rickey, Salem-Keizer	1	1	.500	5.14	17	0	0	0	7	0	28.0	27	123	20	16	3	3	2	2	14	0	18	4	0
Quinowski, David, Salem-Keizer	2	1	.667	3.21	19	0	0	0	4	0	14.0	12	67	7	5	1	0	0	2	14	0	19	3	0
Raguse, Matthew, Salem-Keizer	4	3	.571	4.91	11	6	0	0	1	0	36.2	33	160	22	20	2	2	0	7	12	0	38	3	0
Ramos, Cesar, Eugene *	0	1	.000	6.53	6	4	0	0	0	0	20.2	27	101	21	15	3	0	2	3	7	0	13	2	0
Ramos, Victor, Boise	1	1	.500	3.68	5	0	0	0	3	0	7.1	5	30	3	3	0	1	0	0	3	0	11	1	0
Ray, Jason, Vancouver	0	1	.000	2.12	20	0	0	0	5	0	29.2	17	130	8	7	1	2	1	2	23	0	56	2	0
Rocha, Angel, Yakima *	3	8	.273	5.43	15	15	0	0	0	0	71.1	62	328	50	43	4	2	1	8	53	0	93	17	2
Rohrbaugh, Robert, Everett *	5	2	.714	3.84	14	12	0	0	0	0	68.0	68	283	33	29	7	2	1	4	18	0	71	7	0
Romo, Sergio, Salem-Keizer	7	1	.875	2.75	15	14	0	0	0	0	68.2	70	280	24	21	7	3	0	3	9	1	65	1	1
Rosebrock, Warren, Spokane	4	1	.800	3.22	14	0	0	0	6	0	22.1	30	100	12	8	3	2	0	4	5	0	11	1	0
Sanchez, Jose, Salem-Keizer	1	1	.500	2.08	8	0	0	0	1	0	17.1	9	65	5	4	2	0	0	1	4	0	13	2	1
Santana, Andy, Boise *	4	1	.800	2.47	19	1	0	0	1	0	43.2	44	196	18	12	3	3	1	0	23	0	45	4	0
Schreppel, Ryan, Yakima *	2	2	.500	3.35	14	7	0	0	1	0	45.2	41	194	23	17	2	2	3	2	17	0	50	3	0
Scott, Joseph, Salem-Keizer	2	0	1.000	2.45	4	4	0	0	0	0	22.0	20	86	6	6	2	2	2	0	6	0	12	3	0
Shields, William, Vancouver	3	3	.500	3.34	12	9	0	0	0	0	59.1	47	242	26	22	2	3	2	1	25	0	54	4	0
Shull, James, Vancouver	4	3	.571	2.47	14	13	0	0	0	0	73.0	65	293	25	20	3	3	0	4	10	0	81	4	1
Smith, David, Spokane *	1	2	.333	1.76	13	8	0	0	1	0	56.1	49	226	14	11	3	2	0	1	14	0	32	2	1
Soriano, Rafael, Everett	0	0	.000	3.00	4	4	0	0	0	0	6.0	6	27	3	2	0	0	0	1	2	0	8	0	1
Taylor, Scott, Boise	0	0	.000	5.63	2	2	0	0	0	0	8.0	7	32	5	5	0	0	0	2	0	0	7	0	0
Teasley, Jeffrey, Boise	1	0	1.000	5.19	10	0	0	0	9	4	26.0	24	110	15	15	4	2	0	1	12	0	28	3	0
Thomas, Justin, Everett *	3	3	.500	3.81	18	6	0	0	2	0	59.0	63	256	31	25	2	0	4	20	0	48	5	0
Thompson, Chris, Yakima	3	0	1.000	1.89	16	0	0	0	12	5	19.0	10	75	5	4	4	1	0	3	5	0	26	1	0

SHORT-SEASON CLASS A *Northwest League*

Pitcher, Team	W	L	Pct.	ERA	G	GS	CG	ShO	GF	Sv.	IP	H	TBF	R	ER	HR	SH	SF	HB	BB	IBB	SO	WP	Bk.
Thompson, Nicolas, Boise	2	1	.667	3.51	25	0	0	0	16	2	33.1	27	142	19	13	5	0	1	0	19	0	34	8	0
Torra, Matthew, Yakima	0	1	.000	1.80	5	2	0	0	1	0	10.0	11	41	3	2	1	2	0	0	4	0	10	0	0
Urquidez, Jason, Yakima	1	1	.500	1.80	11	1	0	0	3	0	15.0	14	69	7	3	0	0	2	3	7	0	19	2	0
Van Buskirk, Thomas, Spokane	2	3	.400	3.18	22	0	0	0	8	0	34.0	25	142	16	12	0	4	1	3	12	2	22	5	0
Vandel, Geoff, Eugene *	0	0	.000	0.90	2	2	0	0	0	0	10.0	8	36	1	1	0	0	0	0	0	0	11	0	0
Varnell, Grant, Eugene	0	2	.000	3.21	8	4	0	0	0	0	28.0	28	108	10	10	3	1	0	0	2	0	24	0	0
Veal, Donald, Boise *	1	2	.333	2.48	7	6	0	0	0	0	29.0	18	116	11	8	2	1	1	0	15	0	34	4	3
Vega, Marwin, Everett	0	2	.000	9.35	3	2	0	0	0	0	8.2	7	44	11	9	0	0	0	2	7	0	9	3	0
Wilding, Taylor, Salem-Keizer	2	1	.667	6.44	15	5	0	0	0	0	43.1	46	191	35	31	12	1	2	3	16	0	42	2	0
Wilkinson, Matthew, Yakima	1	0	1.000	0.90	9	0	0	0	8	2	10.0	6	40	1	1	0	0	0	0	6	0	11	3	0
Williams, Harold, Everett *	1	1	.500	5.79	4	4	0	0	0	0	14.0	11	64	9	9	2	0	0	2	11	0	15	2	0
Wilson, Jon, Spokane	3	1	.750	2.08	29	0	0	0	26	11	34.2	26	127	8	8	4	3	0	0	4	1	49	1	0
Woerman, Joseph, Everett	0	0	.000	4.76	11	2	0	0	3	0	17.0	16	85	11	9	0	1	2	3	20	0	21	6	0
Wright, Kyle, Yakima	1	4	.200	4.22	15	14	0	0	1	0	79.0	88	350	47	37	4	2	1	7	22	1	65	6	1
Yepez, Jesus, Boise *	4	2	.667	3.92	14	13	0	0	0	0	62.0	57	265	31	27	3	3	1	3	28	0	46	8	2
Zamzow, Brett, Spokane	4	4	.200	6.95	14	13	0	0	0	0	55.2	89	270	55	43	7	3	2	10	14	0	53	7	0

COMBINATION SHUTOUTS: Boise (4) -- Santana-Evenson-Ramos-Thompson, Billek-Baez-Santana-Koerber, Atkins-Evenson, Veal-Chambers-Thompson. Everett (6) -- Allen-Colon, Rohrbaugh-Lockwood-Gibson, Fagan-Carter, Rohrbaugh-Thomas-Kahn. Salem-Keizer (5) -- Allen-Asher, Rohrbaugh-Thomas-Kahn, Raguse-McKae, Romo-Minor, Romo-Ludwig-Foltin, Griffin-Foltin, Martinez-Minor-Anderson. Spokane (2) -- Smith-McElroy, Mathis-Maldonado. Tri-City (5) -- Simons-White-Lira-Delgado, Simons-Katz-Lira, Freeman-Fox-Burok, Katz-Stanley-Burok, Lindsay-Ruthven. Vancouver (3) -- Newby-Kilby, Scott-Madej-Herrera, Madsen-Kilby. Yakima (2) -- Howard-Torra-Duran, Wright-Fowles-Doherty-Newby.

2005 FIELDING

TEAM

Team	G	PO	A	E	TC	DP	TP	PB	Pct.
Salem-Keizer	76	2049	765	76	2890	63	0	16	.974
Everett	76	2042	884	88	3014	80	0	11	.971
Tri-City	76	2021	805	87	2913	60	1	13	.970
Vancouver	76	2064	798	91	2953	57	0	14	.969
Eugene	76	2019	805	106	2930	52	0	20	.964
Spokane	76	2029	812	112	2953	49	1	22	.962
Yakima	76	2044	825	113	2982	51	0	15	.962
Boise	76	2026	858	120	3004	72	2	15	.960

INDIVIDUAL

FIRST BASEMEN

NOTE: All caps denotes fielding-percentage leader based on 38 games for catchers, 51 for all other non-pitchers and 61 innings for pitchers. *Throws lefthanded.

Player, Team	Pct.	G	PO	A	E	TC	DP
Babineaux Jr., Erroll, Salem-Keizer	.933	2	13	1	1	15	2
Backman II, Walter, Spokane	1.000	1	11	0	0	11	0
Boyd, Chad, Vancouver *	1.000	2	3	0	0	3	0
Cleland, Clinton, Eugene	.958	2	20	3	1	24	2
Contreras, Lester, Yakima	1.000	8	44	3	0	47	2
Eastley, Tyler, Everett	.977	14	122	6	3	131	9
FLAIG, JEFFREY, Everett	.993	61	528	29	4	561	57
Garcia, Jose, Vancouver	1.000	1	10	0	0	10	0
Gaskin, Christopher, Boise	.982	60	511	42	10	563	48
Gunther, Barry, Salem-Keizer	1.000	1	7	1	0	8	0
Hawke, Matthew, Spokane *	.987	22	214	11	3	228	15
Hendricks, Arthur, Yakima	.989	73	596	56	7	659	39
Jones, Daryl, Eugene	.976	71	601	44	16	661	42
Kemp, Joseph, Spokane *	1.000	4	35	1	0	36	1
Kleen, Steve, Vancouver	.988	46	387	36	5	428	29
Pratt, Haas, Vancouver	.980	31	269	22	6	297	16
Puello, Elvin, Boise	.987	14	144	5	2	151	12
Sabatella, Bryan, Everett	1.000	1	5	2	0	7	1
Sandoval, Pablo, Salem-Keizer	1.000	1	9	0	0	9	0
Smith, John, Eugene	.973	4	36	0	1	37	1
Stanton, Christopher, Salem-Keizer	.988	26	220	19	3	242	23
Taylor, Brandon, Boise	.952	2	19	1	1	21	6
Thompson, William, Salem-Keizer *	.998	48	440	19	1	460	33
Thon, Freddie, Spokane *	.981	50	429	35	9	473	28
Todd, Christopher, Salem-Keizer	1.000	2	4	0	0	4	0
Valdez, Jesus, Boise	1.000	1	13	0	0	13	0
Wu, Chao Kuan, Everett	.959	6	45	2	2	49	5

SECOND BASEMEN

Player, Team	Pct.	G	PO	A	E	TC	DP
Abreu, Johany, Salem-Keizer	1.000	1	0	2	0	2	1
Acosta, Jesse, Vancouver	1.000	3	5	7	0	12	1
Batten, Joseph, Yakima	.941	8	9	23	2	34	3
Biguenet, Michael, Yakima	.923	8	13	23	3	39	5
Blunt, Terrance, Spokane	.917	6	11	22	3	36	5

Player, Team	Pct.	G	PO	A	E	TC	DP
Bruce, Derek, Yakima	.941	23	35	60	6	101	9
Cho, Hyung, Everett	1.000	1	1	2	0	3	0
Cleland, Clinton, Eugene	.953	18	26	56	4	86	8
Contreras, Anthony, Salem-Keizer	.909	2	5	5	1	11	1
Downing, Ramon, Yakima	.970	39	70	94	5	169	17
Eastley, Tyler, Everett	.875	4	5	9	2	16	2
Hode, Scott, Boise	.945	20	43	60	6	109	15
Hooft, Joseph, Spokane	.914	7	9	23	3	35	1
Johnston, John, Eugene	.921	8	15	20	3	38	5
Martinez, Frank, Vancouver	1.000	2	3	4	0	7	0
Minicozzi, Mark, Salem-Keizer	.973	69	83	200	8	291	34
Mota, Jonathan, Boise	.970	20	45	53	3	101	14
Omura, Isaac, Vancouver	.946	36	64	94	9	167	17
Parraz, Ezekiel, Vancouver	.889	2	3	5	1	9	1
Paulino, Adalberto, Salem-Keizer	1.000	5	7	15	0	22	0
Pena, Antonio, Spokane	1.000	3	5	3	0	8	0
Perez, Wilber, Vancouver	.941	33	75	85	10	170	16
Peterson, David, Spokane	.957	19	29	59	4	92	7
Reynolds, Kyle, Boise	.939	17	25	52	5	82	9
Richardson, William, Eugene	1.000	10	21	26	0	47	7
Rios, Jose, Boise	.980	22	51	49	2	102	9
Rivera, Jodam, Eugene	.959	24	39	77	5	121	11
Santana, Julio, Spokane	.938	41	70	97	11	178	17
Todd, Christopher, Salem-Keizer	1.000	8	4	12	0	16	0
VALBUENA, LUIS, Everett	.978	74	149	209	8	366	52
Vazquez, Kelvin, Eugene	.949	17	39	55	5	99	11
Washington, Johnny, Spokane	.971	10	14	19	1	34	2

THIRD BASEMEN

Player, Team	Pct.	G	PO	A	E	TC	DP
Abreu, Johany, Salem-Keizer	.667	2	1	1	1	3	0
Backman II, Walter, Spokane	.833	14	3	17	4	24	0
Baez, Lizahio, Spokane	.920	11	7	16	2	25	0
Baisley, Jeffrey, Vancouver	.937	60	38	125	11	174	9
Biguenet, Michael, Yakima	1.000	9	10	14	0	24	0
Callahan, Shawn, Vancouver *	.875	3	1	6	1	8	1
Cho, Hyung, Everett	1.000	3	2	2	0	4	0
Contreras, Lester, Yakima	.923	34	26	70	8	104	1
Eastley, Tyler, Everett	.875	10	6	15	3	24	5
Headley, Chase, Eugene	.915	57	28	91	11	130	5
Heckman, John, Everett	.909	2	4	6	1	11	0
Hooft, Joseph, Spokane	.900	54	23	76	11	110	6
Johnston, John, Eugene	...	1	0	0	0	0	0
Kemp, Joseph, Spokane *	.500	1	0	1	1	2	0
Long, Wesley, Vancouver	.857	10	9	15	4	28	0
Minicozzi, Mark, Salem-Keizer	.500	1	0	2	2	4	0
Olivares, Juan, Yakima	.944	6	6	11	1	18	1
Parraz, Ezekiel, Vancouver	1.000	2	1	2	0	3	0
Paulino, Adalberto, Salem-Keizer	1.000	2	0	1	0	1	0
Pena, Antonio, Spokane	1.000	1	1	4	0	5	1
Perez, Wilber, Vancouver	1.000	5	2	6	0	8	0
Peterson, David, Spokane	.667	2	3	1	2	6	0
PRETTYMAN, RONALD, Everett	.944	56	46	124	10	180	7
Puello, Elvin, Boise	.895	41	29	73	12	114	10
Rios, Jose, Boise	.667	2	0	2	1	3	1

Player, Team	Pct.	G	PO	A	E	TC	DP
Sabatella, Bryan, Everett	.864	10	6	13	3	22	2
Sandoval, Pablo, Salem-Keizer	.922	70	46	107	13	166	7
Sosa, Ricardo, Yakima	.962	29	23	53	3	79	4
Steiner, Chad, Eugene	.921	14	15	20	3	38	2
Taylor, Brandon, Boise	.924	37	20	89	9	118	5
Todd, Christopher, Salem-Keizer	.800	6	1	3	1	5	0
Vazquez, Kelvin, Eugene	.889	6	1	7	1	9	0

SHORTSTOPS

Player, Team	Pct.	G	PO	A	E	TC	DP
Abreu, Johany, Salem-Keizer	.811	9	8	22	7	37	4
Bruce, Derek, Yakima	.926	50	65	149	17	231	23
Cho, Hyung, Everett	1.000	1	2	6	0	8	1
Contreras, Anthony, Salem-Keizer	.957	20	37	51	4	92	15
Duran, German, Spokane	.936	59	87	176	18	281	27
Eastley, Tyler, Everett	.976	10	10	31	1	42	4
Hode, Scott, Boise	.857	1	3	3	1	7	0
HUDSON, ROBERT, Everett	.963	54	97	190	11	298	42
Johnston, John, Eugene	.935	35	53	91	10	154	16
Maroul, David, Salem-Keizer	.944	43	65	105	10	180	22
Martinez, Frank, Vancouver	.952	12	22	37	3	62	5
Mota, Johnathan, Boise	.927	43	85	119	16	220	24
Olivares, Juan, Yakima	.908	26	45	74	12	131	10
Parraz, Ezekiel, Vancouver	.921	17	30	52	7	89	9
Paulino, Adalberto, Salem-Keizer	1.000	1	0	3	0	3	0
Peterson, David, Eugene	1.000	1	1	3	0	4	1
Prettyman, Ronald, Everett	.944	4	2	15	1	18	4
Reynolds, Kyle, Boise	.906	26	36	90	13	139	15
Richardson, William, Eugene	.959	43	65	123	8	196	15
Rios, Jose, Boise	.944	9	13	38	3	54	6
Santana, Julio, Spokane	.864	20	22	54	12	88	6
Sellers, Justin, Vancouver	.943	47	71	129	12	212	27
Todd, Christopher, Salem-Keizer	.938	15	11	19	2	32	2
Zorn, Dean, Everett	.883	12	18	35	7	60	3

OUTFIELDERS

Player, Team	Pct.	G	PO	A	E	TC	DP
Abreu, Johany, Salem-Keizer	.800	5	4	0	1	5	0
Alley, Joshua, Eugene *	1.000	11	22	0	0	22	0
Babineaux Jr., Erroll, Salem-Keizer	.955	21	20	1	1	22	0
Batten, Joseph, Yakima	...	1	0	0	0	0	0
Bieker, Jeffrey, Vancouver	.968	32	55	5	2	62	1
Biguenet, Michael, Yakima	1.000	6	6	0	0	6	0
Blunt, Terrance, Spokane	.978	36	88	2	2	92	0
Boyd, Chad, Vancouver *	.981	46	50	3	1	54	0
Bubalo, Ty, Vancouver	.857	9	6	0	1	7	0
Buck, Travis, Vancouver	.895	9	16	1	2	19	1
Burgess, Brandon, Yakima	.919	27	30	4	3	37	0
Cavanaugh, Brian, Eugene	.934	36	53	4	4	61	1
Centeno, Jaen, Yakima	.963	64	96	9	4	109	1
Cleland, Clinton, Eugene	1.000	2	1	0	0	1	0
Copeland, Benjamin, Salem-Keizer *	.979	28	45	1	1	47	1
Craig, Casey, Everett	.969	60	116	10	4	130	3
Culpepper, Jeffrey, Boise	.971	19	30	3	1	34	1
Davidson, Drew, Eugene	.957	24	42	2	2	46	1
Defendis, John, Boise	.943	42	50	0	3	53	0
Diaz, Javis, Eugene *	1.000	3	5	0	0	5	0
DYCHE, JOSEPH, Salem-Keizer	.993	68	138	7	1	146	3
Flaig, Jeffrey, Everett	1.000	3	2	0	0	2	0
Garcia, Jose, Vancouver	.987	44	73	2	1	76	0
Gary, Robert, Everett	.957	38	40	4	2	46	0
Gregg, David, Boise	.978	73	130	1	3	134	0
Guerrero, Santiago, Eugene	.979	50	89	4	2	95	1
Hall, David, Everett	.962	31	49	1	2	52	1
Heid, Trevor, Everett	1.000	31	36	4	0	40	1
Herren, Karl, Spokane	.961	55	95	3	4	102	1
Joseph, Alfred, Boise	.958	14	20	3	1	24	0
Kemp, Joseph, Spokane *	1.000	29	49	0	0	49	0
Kleen, Steve, Vancouver	...	1	0	0	0	0	0
Massaro, Michael, Vancouver *	.976	55	81	2	2	85	1
Mayberry, John, Spokane	.990	61	92	3	1	96	1
Mooney, Michael, Salem-Keizer	.969	72	116	11	4	131	2
Murphy, Steven, Spokane	.976	50	78	5	2	85	1
Olivares, Juan, Yakima	.952	13	19	1	1	21	0
Paulino, Adalberto, Salem-Keizer	.889	9	8	0	1	9	0
Piper-Jordan, Andre, Vancouver	1.000	6	2	0	0	2	0
Quinones, Carlos, Boise	1.000	27	29	4	0	33	1
Rahl, Christopher, Yakima	.989	41	81	7	1	89	4

Player, Team	Pct.	G	PO	A	E	TC	DP
Sabatella, Bryan, Everett	.953	29	37	4	2	43	0
Sansoe, Mike, Eugene	.979	44	88	6	2	96	1
Santoro, Michael, Salem-Keizer	1.000	6	11	1	0	12	1
Saunders, Michael, Everett	.967	55	87	2	3	92	1
Septimo, Leyson, Yakima *	.943	63	106	9	7	122	3
Smith, John, Eugene	.667	3	2	0	1	3	0
Tietje, Chalon, Vancouver	1.000	29	60	2	0	62	2
Tritle, Christopher, Vancouver	1.000	17	40	0	0	40	0
Turner, Timothy, Eugene *	.989	36	91	3	1	95	0
Valdez, Jesus, Boise	.979	59	90	2	2	94	0
Venable, William, Eugene *	.915	27	42	1	4	47	0
Williams, Kevin, Yakima	.964	30	78	2	3	83	0
Yens, Jose, Salem-Keizer	.966	37	55	1	2	58	0

CATCHERS

Player, Team	Pct.	G	PO	A	E	TC	DP
Baez, Lizahio, Spokane	.981	18	141	17	3	161	1
Biguenet, Michael, Yakima	1.000	12	56	5	0	61	0
Bubalo, Ty, Vancouver	.986	19	131	14	2	147	1
Busch, Andrew, Salem-Keizer	.996	36	258	19	1	278	0
Callahan, Shawn, Vancouver	.989	24	161	15	2	178	1
Clement, Jeffrey, Everett	1.000	2	15	1	0	16	0
Contreras, Lester, Yakima	1.000	1	2	0	0	2	0
Crabtree, Benjamin, Spokane	.994	23	141	24	1	166	4
Del Campo, Manny, Yakima	.988	34	293	38	4	335	2
Dixon, Dorian, Salem-Keizer	1.000	3	15	1	0	16	0
Douillard, Jonathan, Boise	1.000	4	11	3	0	14	0
Farina, Peter, Boise	.918	9	43	2	4	49	0
Ford, Joshua, Yakima	.986	33	246	32	4	282	0
Gottier, Brandon, Eugene	.973	22	162	17	5	184	2
Gunther, Barry, Salem-Keizer	.991	29	187	29	2	218	1
Gutierrez, Henry, Salem-Keizer	1.000	23	194	11	0	205	0
Higashi, Jonathan, Spokane	1.000	15	91	13	0	104	0
Hundley, Nicholas, Eugene	.978	40	278	37	7	322	2
Killian, William, Eugene	1.000	7	54	1	0	55	0
Lobaton, Jose, Eugene	1.000	11	90	8	0	98	2
Mercado, Richard, Yakima	1.000	8	40	2	0	42	1
Muyco, Dionisio, Boise	.989	33	250	30	3	283	2
RECKER, ANTHONY, Vancouver	.995	39	343	24	2	369	2
Reed, Mark, Boise	.979	40	301	30	7	338	2
Sandoval, Pablo, Salem-Keizer	1.000	1	10	1	0	11	0
Santin, Daniel, Everett *	.983	19	159	19	3	181	2
Schweiger, Brian, Everett	.993	19	128	13	1	142	1
Teagarden, Taylor, Spokane	1.000	22	173	15	0	188	1
Tucker, John, Everett	.991	40	303	29	3	335	2
Valichka, Brian, Spokane	.955	7	57	6	3	66	0

PITCHERS

Player, Team	Pct.	G	PO	A	E	TC	DP
Abbott, Justin, Spokane	1.000	3	2	1	0	3	0
Acevedo, Danielin, Vancouver	1.000	17	0	3	0	3	0
Allen, Nicholas, Everett	1.000	16	2	7	0	9	1
Anderson, Brian, Salem-Keizer	1.000	27	1	2	0	3	0
Arias, Oliver, Everett	.875	6	2	5	1	8	0
Asher, David, Everett *	.900	18	1	8	1	10	0
Atkins, Mitchell, Boise	.895	15	3	14	2	19	1
Avery, Matthew, Boise	1.000	11	4	5	0	9	1
Baca, Daniel, Eugene	1.000	7	3	2	0	5	0
Baez, Edgar, Boise	1.000	20	1	3	0	4	0
Bauer, Garrett, Yakima *	1.000	18	2	1	0	3	0
Beus, Lance, Everett *	.714	19	1	4	2	7	0
Billek, Michael, Boise	1.000	5	0	1	0	1	0
Brandt, Adam, Everett *	.000	1	0	0	1	1	0
Bryant, Stephen, Everett	1.000	21	1	4	0	5	0
Burcie, Jarrad, Spokane	1.000	8	0	3	0	3	0
Byrd, Taylor, Spokane	1.000	17	3	6	0	9	0
Cahill, John, Yakima	1.000	8	0	1	0	1	0
Carter, Brenton, Eugene *	1.000	13	4	9	0	13	1
Carter, Eric, Everett	1.000	14	0	3	0	3	0
Carter, Steven-Ryder, Vancouver	1.000	6	0	2	0	2	0
Cepeda, Benigno, Salem-Keizer	1.000	6	0	3	0	3	0
Chambers, Ryan, Boise *	1.000	18	1	5	0	6	0
Cody, Buck, Salem-Keizer *	1.000	15	0	2	0	2	0
Coffman, Broc, Spokane *	1.000	17	3	9	0	12	1
Colon, Juan, Everett	1.000	6	1	0	0	1	0
Corchado, Jose, Spokane	1.000	17	3	3	0	6	2
Davis, Bradley, Vancouver *	1.000	23	3	6	0	9	0
Delabar, Steven, Eugene	.947	16	6	12	1	19	2
De La O, Danny, Eugene *	.500	4	0	1	1	2	0
Doherty, Ryan, Yakima	.818	22	4	5	2	11	0

Player, Team	Pct.	G	PO	A	E	TC	DP
Dove, Bradley, Yakima *	.917	9	3	8	1	12	0
Downs, Darin, Boise *	1.000	14	2	12	0	14	0
Duran, Enmanuel, Yakima	1.000	24	3	3	0	6	0
Evenson, Roger, Boise	.923	24	6	6	1	13	1
Fagan, Robert, Everett *	.880	15	2	20	3	25	1
Fairbanks, Scott, Vancouver	...	2	0	0	0	0	0
Fernandez, Alfredo, Eugene	.909	33	3	7	1	11	0
Fogle, Nathan, Spokane	1.000	20	2	3	0	5	0
Foltin, Wayne, Salem-Keizer	.800	17	1	3	1	5	0
Fowles, Matt, Yakima	.667	23	3	1	2	6	1
Frye, Randall, Everett	1.000	4	0	1	0	1	0
Garcia, Juan Carlos, Spokane	.875	16	1	6	1	8	1
Geer, Joshua, Eugene	1.000	7	2	8	0	10	0
Gibson, Rollie, Everett *	.875	15	0	7	1	8	1
Gilmore, Jeffrey, Everett	1.000	12	2	3	0	5	0
Gold, Adam, Eugene	.750	28	1	2	1	4	1
Gray, Jeffrey, Vancouver	1.000	12	3	10	0	13	1
Griffin, Daniel, Salem-Keizer	.857	8	1	5	1	7	1
Guaramato, Edgar, Everett	.800	28	2	2	1	5	2
Hagerty, Luke, Boise *	.500	14	1	1	2	4	0
Hall, Jesse, Spokane	.429	16	0	3	4	7	0
Herrera, John, Vancouver	.900	16	4	5	1	10	0
Higelin, Brandon, Eugene *	1.000	22	3	5	0	8	0
Hinshaw, Alexander, Salem-Keizer *	1.000	25	1	5	0	6	0
Holden, Kyle, Boise	1.000	20	1	7	0	8	0
Howard, Adam, Yakima	1.000	13	5	8	0	13	1
Hughey, Arnold, Eugene *	1.000	26	3	7	0	10	1
Hunton, Jonathan, Boise	1.000	19	2	4	0	6	1
Hyle, Michael, Boise	1.000	15	6	7	0	13	1
Jamison, Neil, Eugene	1.000	25	1	3	0	4	0
Jimenez, Juan, Eugene	...	1	0	0	0	0	0
Jimenez Angulo, Fabian Enrique, Eugene *	1.000	7	1	2	0	3	0
Jones, Michael, Boise	1.000	1	0	1	0	1	0
Kahn, Stephen, Everett	1.000	17	0	2	0	2	0
Kemlo, Christopher, Yakima	.960	16	12	12	1	25	0
Kilby, Brad, Vancouver *	1.000	23	0	1	0	1	0
Kintzler, Brandon, Eugene	1.000	3	0	3	0	3	0
Kleen, Steve, Vancouver	...	1	0	0	0	0	0
Koerber, Scott, Boise *	1.000	23	2	6	0	8	3
Koliscak, Cory, Everett	.929	22	1	12	1	14	0
Kometani, Paul, Spokane	1.000	2	0	1	0	1	0
Krohe, Matthew, Yakima *	1.000	20	0	5	0	5	0
Krosschell, Brnjamin, Eugene	1.000	16	2	9	0	11	1
Link, Jon, Eugene	.864	25	5	14	3	22	0
Lockwood, Jonathan, Everett	1.000	5	0	1	0	1	0
Lopez, Aleurys, Boise *	.500	7	0	1	1	2	0
Ludwig, Kellen, Salem-Keizer	1.000	18	3	10	0	13	1
Madden, John, Eugene	.900	38	1	8	1	10	1
Madej, Ronald, Vancouver *	.800	17	0	4	1	5	0
Madsen, Michael, Vancouver	.833	15	3	7	2	12	0
Maldonado, Juan, Spokane	1.000	22	4	14	0	18	0
Martinez, Joseph, Salem-Keizer	1.000	15	7	12	0	19	1
Martinez, Roman, Everett	1.000	13	1	4	0	5	0
Martinez, Shawn, Vancouver	1.000	4	0	1	0	1	0
Mathis, Douglas, Spokane	1.000	17	4	13	0	17	0
Mault, James, Everett	1.000	5	1	1	0	2	0
McConnell, Kellan, Spokane	.947	17	10	8	1	19	1
McElroy, Tanner, Spokane	.875	16	4	3	1	8	0
McKae, Dave, Salem-Keizer	.833	19	4	6	2	12	0
Millikan, Bryan, Salem-Keizer	.857	20	0	6	1	7	2
Minor, Matthew, Salem-Keizer	1.000	23	1	4	0	5	0
Mitchell, Michael, Vancouver	1.000	7	1	2	0	3	0
NEWBY, JOSEPH, Vancouver	1.000	15	13	20	0	33	2
Newby, Kyler, Yakima	1.000	24	2	1	0	3	0
Nieto, Christopher, Salem-Keizer *	1.000	5	0	2	0	2	1
Ortiz, Jose, Boise	.500	15	0	1	1	2	0
Pawelek, Mark, Boise *	1.000	1	0	1	0	1	0
Pereira, Nick, Salem-Keizer	1.000	14	1	7	0	8	0
Pfautz, Craig, Yakima	.667	20	2	6	4	12	0
Piekarz, Joseph, Vancouver *	.920	15	8	15	2	25	1
Polanco, Phillip, Eugene	1.000	6	1	2	0	3	0
Ponce, William, Eugene	1.000	21	2	3	0	5	0
Putman, Rickey, Salem-Keizer	1.000	17	0	3	0	3	0
Quinowski, David, Salem-Keizer *	1.000	19	0	2	0	2	0
Raguse, Matthew, Everett	.500	11	1	2	3	6	0
Ramos, Cesar, Eugene *	.750	6	1	5	2	8	0
Ramos, Victor, Boise	1.000	5	1	2	0	3	0
Ray, Jason, Vancouver	1.000	20	1	1	0	2	0
Rocha, Angel, Yakima *	.615	15	1	7	5	13	0
Rohrbaugh, Robert, Everett *	1.000	14	2	10	0	12	1
Romo, Sergio, Salem-Keizer	1.000	15	3	12	0	15	0
Rosebrock, Warren, Spokane	1.000	14	2	4	0	6	0
Sanchez, Jose, Salem-Keizer	1.000	8	2	1	0	3	0
Santana, Andy, Boise *	.889	19	4	4	1	9	0
Schreppel, Ryan, Yakima *	.667	14	1	7	4	12	0
Scott, Joseph, Vancouver	1.000	4	1	3	0	4	0
Shields, William, Vancouver	.923	12	4	8	1	13	2
Shull, James, Vancouver	1.000	14	8	10	0	18	3
Smith, David, Spokane *	.889	13	2	6	1	9	0
Soriano, Rafael, Everett	...	4	0	0	0	0	0
Taylor, Scott, Boise	1.000	2	0	1	0	1	0
Teasley, Jeffrey, Boise	1.000	20	0	2	0	2	0
Thomas, Justin, Everett *	.917	18	3	8	1	12	1
Thompson, Chris, Yakima	1.000	16	1	1	0	2	0
Thompson, Nicolas, Boise	1.000	25	0	3	0	3	1
Torra, Matthew, Yakima	.833	5	2	3	1	6	0
Urquidez, Jason, Yakima	.500	11	0	1	1	2	0
Van Buskirk, Thomas, Spokane	.875	22	4	10	2	16	0
Vandel, Geoff, Eugene *	1.000	2	0	1	0	1	0
Varnell, Grant, Eugene	1.000	8	2	6	0	8	0
Veal, Donald, Boise *	.600	7	0	3	2	5	0
Vega, Marwin, Everett	1.000	3	1	1	0	2	0
Wilding, Taylor, Salem-Keizer	1.000	15	1	7	0	8	0
Wilkinson, Matthew, Yakima	1.000	9	1	2	0	3	1
Williams, Harold, Everett *	...	4	0	0	0	0	0
Wilson, Jon, Spokane	1.000	29	3	7	0	10	0
Woerman, Joseph, Everett	1.000	11	0	2	0	2	0
Wright, Kyle, Yakima	.955	15	7	14	1	22	0
Yepez, Jesus, Boise *	.882	14	1	14	2	17	2
Zamzow, Brett, Spokane	.882	14	6	9	2	17	0

LEAGUE CHAMPIONS

Year	Team	Pct.
1901—	Portland	.675
1902—	Butte	.608
1903—	Butte	.578
1904—	Boise	.625
1905—	Vancouver	.586
	Everett *	.667
1906—	Tacoma	.600
1907—	Aberdeen	.625
1908—	Vancouver	.578
1909—	Seattle	.653
1910—	Spokane	.596
1911—	Vancouver	.628
1912—	Seattle	.600
1913—	Vancouver	.600
1914—	Vancouver	.632
1915—	Seattle	.564
1916—	Spokane	.622
1917—	Great Falls	.592
1918—	Seattle	.588
1919—	Seattle	.590
1920—	Victoria	.600
1921—	Yakima	.710
	Yakima	.660
1922—	Calgary‡	.600
1923-36—	Did not operate.	
1937—	Wenatchee	.603
	Tacoma*	.627
1938—	Yakima	.583
	Bellingham (2nd)†	.511
1939—	Wenatchee	.601
	Tacoma (2nd)†	.533
1940—	Spokane	.587
	Tacoma (4th)†	.500
1941—	Spokane	.669
1942—	Vancouver	.594
1943-45—	Did not operate.	
1946—	Wenatchee	.622
1947—	Vancouver	.566
1948—	Spokane	.614
1949—	Yakima	.660
	Vancouver (2nd)†	.615
1950—	Yakima	.613
1951—	Spokane	.655
1952—	Victoria	.631
1953—	Salem	.635
	Spokane*	.590
1954—	Vancouver*	.636
	Lewiston	.629
1955—	Salem	.646
	Eugene*	.639
1956—	Yakima	.691
	Yakima	.619
1957—	Eugene	.576
	Wenatchee*	.647
1958—	Lewiston	.621
	Yakima*	.594
1959—	Salem	.623
	Yakima*	.563
1960—	Yakima	.638
	Yakima	.562
1961—	Lewiston*	.621
	Yakima	.600
1962—	Wenatchee*	.574
	Tri-City	.580
1963—	Lewiston	.594
	Yakima*	.613
1964—	Eugene	.636
	Yakima*	.611
1965—	Lewiston	.667

Year	Team	Pct.
	Tri-City*	.681
1966—	Tri-City	.679
1967—	Medford	.607
1968—	Tri-City	.600
1969—	Rogue Valley	.633
1970—	Lewiston§	.538
	Coos Bay-No. Bend	.563
1971—	Tri-City§	.625
	Bend	.538
1972—	Lewiston§	.675
	Walla Walla	.513
1973—	Walla Walla∞	.638
	Portland	.563
1974—	Bellingham	.619
	Eugene▲	.571
1975—	Portland	.545
	Eugene◆	.684
1976—	Portland	.556
	Walla Walla◆	.639
1977—	Bellingham■	.618
	Portland	.667
1978—	Grays Harbor▼	.671
	Eugene	.514
1979—	Central Oregon◆	.606
	Walla Walla	.571
1980—	Bellingham*	.643
	Eugene*	.529
1981—	Medford◆	.600
	Bellingham	.557
1982—	Medford	.757
	Salem◆	.486
1983—	Medford††	.735
	Bellingham	.588
1984—	Tri-Cities††	.622
	Medford	.608
1985—	Everett††	.541
	Eugene	.541
1986—	Bellingham††	.608
	Eugene	.608
1987—	Spokane▲	.711
	Everett	.653
1988—	Southern Oregon	.605
	Spokane◆	.553
1989—	Southern Oregon	.600
	Spokane◆	.547
1990—	Boise	.697
	Spokane◆	.645
1991—	Boise◆	.658
	Yakima	.579
1992—	Bellingham◆	.566
	Bend	.566
1993—	Bellingham	.579
	Boise◆	.539
1994—	Yakima	.645
	Boise◆	.579
1995—	Boise◆	.640
	Bellingham	.566
1996—	Eugene	.645
	Yakima§	.526
1997—	Boise	.671
	Portland◆	.579
1998—	Spokane	.618
	Boise	.618
	Salem-Keizer◆	.566
1999—	Spokane◆	.579
2000—	Yakima◆	.539
	Boise	.539
2001—	Boise	.693
	Salem-Keizer◆	.671
2002—	Boise▲	.645
2003—	Spokane▲	.658
2004—	Boise▲	.553
2005—	Spokane▲	.487

*Won split-season playoff. †Won four-club playoff. ‡League disbanded June 18. §League divided into Northern and Southern divisions, declared champion under league rules. ∞League divided into Eastern and Western divisions, declared champion under league rules. ▲League divided into Eastern and Western divisions; won two-team playoff. ◆League divided into North and South divisions; won two-team playoff. ■League divided into Affiliate and Independent divisions; won two-team playoff. ▼Declared league champion after winning one-game playoff. Balance of playoff canceled due to rain and wet grounds. *Declared co-champion after winning one game. Balance of playoff canceled due to rain and wet grounds. ††League divided into Washington and Oregon divisions; won two-team playoff. (NOTE—Known as Pacific Northwest League 1901-02, Pacific National League 1903-04, Northwestern League 1905-18, Pacific Coast International League 1919-22 and Western International League 1937-54.)

APPALACHIAN LEAGUE

LEAGUE OFFICE

President
Lee Landers
Address
283 Deerchase Circle
Statesville, NC 28625
Phone
704-873-5300

Teams (affiliation)
Bluefield Orioles (Orioles)
Bristol White Sox (White Sox)
Burlington Indians (Indians)
Danville Braves (Braves)
Elizabethton Twins (Twins)
Greeneville Astros (Astros)

Johnson City Cardinals (Cardinals)
Kingsport Mets (Mets)
Princeton Devil Rays (Devil Rays)
Pulaski Blue Jays (Blue Jays)

2005 FINAL STANDINGS

EASTERN DIVISION

Team	W	L	T	Pct.	GB
Danville Braves	47	20	-	.701	-
Princeton Devil Rays	34	31	-	.523	12
Pulaski Blue Jays	34	33	-	.507	13
Bluefield Orioles	31	36	-	.463	16
Burlington Indians	25	43	-	.368	22.5

WESTERN DIVISION

Team	W	L	T	Pct.	GB
Elizabethton Twins	48	19	-	.716	-
Bristol Sox	30	36	-	.455	17.5
Greeneville Astros	29	37	-	.439	18.5
Johnson City Cardinals	28	39	-	.418	20
Kingsport Mets	28	40	-	.412	2.5

COMPOSITE

CLUB (AFFILIATE), ABBREV	ELI	DAN	PRI	PUL	BLU	BRI	GRE	JCY	KIN	BUR	W	L	PCT	GB
Elizabethton (Twins), ELI		2	5	6	3	7	8	5	7	5	48	19	.716	-
Danville (Braves,) DAN	4	...	4	7	7	5	4	6	4	6	47	20	.701	1.0
Princeton (Devil Rays), PRI	1	5	...	5	6	3	3	2	5	4	34	31	.523	13.0
Pulaski (Blue Jays), PUL	0	2	4	...	6	4	3	4	5	6	34	33	.507	14.0
Bluefield (Orioles), BLU	2	2	5	3	...	5	3	3	3	5	31	36	.463	17.0
Bristol (White Sox), BRI	2	1	2	3	1	...	5	6	5	5	30	36	.455	17.5
Greeneville (Astros), GRE	3	1	2	3	3	4	...	6	3	4	29	37	.439	18.5
Johnson City (Cardinals), JCY	4	0	3	2	3	3	3	...	5	5	28	39	.418	20.0
Kingsport (Mets), KIN	2	2	1	1	3	4	6	6	...	3	28	40	.412	20.5
Burlington (Indians), BUR	1	5	5	3	4	1	2	1	3	...	25	43	.368	23.5

Major league affiliations in parentheses.

PLAYOFFS: Finals: Elizabethton defeated Danville, two games to one.

REGULAR-SEASON ATTENDANCE: Greeneville, 49,963. Pulaski, 24,770. Danville, 37,064. Johnson City, 24,338. Princeton, 26,477. Burlington, 37,673. Kingsport, 36,962. Bluefield, 27,420. Bristol, 20,868. Elizabethton, 25,949. League total, 311,484. Postseason (3 games), 3,101.

MANAGERS: Greeneville, Russ Nixon. Pulaski, Dave Pano. Danville, Paul Runge. Johnson City, Tommy Kidwell. Princeton, Jamie Nelson. Burlington, Sean McNally (through July 16), Lee May Jr. (July 17 through August 27) and Brad Komminsk (August 28 through end of season). Kingsport, Jesse Levis. Bluefield, Jesus Alfaro. Bristol, Jerry Hairston. Elizabethton, Ray Smith.

ALL-STAR TEAM: 1B-Charles Hiser, Burlington. 2B-Ovandy Suero, Danville. 3B-Eric Campbell, Danville. SS-Stuart Musslewhite, Bluefield. UIF-Matthew Anderson, Kingsport. OF-Jacob Butler, Pulaski. OF-Aaron Cunningham, Bristol. OF-Christopher Cunningham, Princeton. UOF-Joshua Flores, Greeneville. C-Maximiliano Ramirez, Danville. DH-Christian Acosta, Bristol. RHP-Jairo Cuevas, Danville. LHP-Alexander Smit, Elizabethton. Relief Pitcher-Robert Findlay, Princeton. Players of the Year-Eric Campbell, Danville, and Maximiliano Ramirez, Danville. Pitcher of the Year-Jairo Cuevas, Danville. Manager of the Year-Ray Smith, Elizabethton.

2005 BATTING

TEAM

Team	G	TPA	AB	R	H	TB	2B	3B	HR	RBI	SH	SF	HP	BB	IBB	SO	SB	CS	GDP	LOB	ShO	Avg.	OBP	Slg.
Danville	67	2625	2322	427	659	1068	149	22	72	371	25	26	35	217	9	520	95	38	38	997	3	.284	.350	.460
Elizabethton	67	2491	2228	353	624	941	105	13	62	302	8	14	47	192	5	460	46	29	47	1010	2	.280	.348	.422
Princeton	66	2499	2174	347	586	885	117	10	54	307	16	14	51	244	10	559	76	46	55	1021	1	.270	.355	.407
Bluefield	67	2525	2264	368	603	947	122	15	64	326	20	22	29	189	10	566	81	14	35	977	1	.266	.328	.418
Pulaski	67	2564	2237	354	584	922	130	20	56	318	15	23	30	259	5	563	46	22	57	982	2	.261	.342	.412
Greeneville	66	2522	2271	342	586	875	98	28	45	300	8	13	42	186	6	546	81	29	31	1016	4	.258	.324	.385
Johnson City	67	2450	2167	351	557	873	117	20	53	297	6	31	43	203	4	514	82	28	54	942	2	.257	.329	.403
Bristol	66	2554	2255	318	574	843	137	12	36	281	27	16	56	199	7	577	49	20	39	1078	5	.255	.328	.374
Kingsport	68	2564	2295	339	584	857	114	9	47	291	19	14	43	193	1	512	77	31	58	996	6	.254	.322	.373
Burlington	68	2510	2207	297	502	754	93	15	43	260	11	16	32	244	8	559	58	19	37	1016	4	.227	.311	.342

INDIVIDUAL

TOP QUALIFIERS FOR BATTING CHAMPIONSHIP

Minimum 184 plate appearances. *Lefthanded batter. †Switch-hitter.

Player, Team	G	TPA	AB	R	H	TB	2B	3B	HR	RBI	SH	SF	HP	BB	IBB	SO	SB	CS	GDP	Avg.	OBP	Slg.
Aqueron, Rene, Bluefield *	56	187	163	35	66	95	15	1	4	32	0	2	4	17	2	24	9	3	4	.405	.468	.583
Ramirez, Maximiliano, Danville	63	278	239	45	83	126	19	0	8	47	0	4	4	31	2	41	1	2	5	.347	.424	.527
Cunningham, Christopher, Princeton	59	264	222	42	73	109	13	1	7	40	1	0	7	34	1	55	6	3	6	.329	.433	.491
Davis, Quentin, Danville *	49	220	201	44	65	87	9	2	3	36	0	1	4	14	1	26	8	4	1	.323	.377	.433
Cunningham, Aaron, Bristol	56	255	222	41	70	99	10	2	5	25	0	3	14	16	0	45	6	5	3	.315	.392	.446
Anderson, Matthew, Kingsport *	47	190	169	27	53	76	8	0	5	30	0	2	4	15	0	22	0	3	7	.314	.379	.450
Acosta, Christian, Bristol	65	259	220	40	69	104	20	0	5	41	1	2	7	29	0	48	0	2	6	.314	.407	.473
Campbell, Eric, Danville	66	298	262	77	82	166	26	2	18	64	0	4	4	28	3	64	15	4	4	.313	.383	.634

Player, Team	G	TPA	AB	R	H	TB	2B	3B	HR	RBI	SH	SF	HP	BB	IBB	SO	SB	CS	GDP	Avg.	OBP	Slg.
Welker, Kris, Bristol	54	226	198	31	60	85	16	0	3	29	4	1	6	17	2	34	2	1	4	.303	.374	.429
Franko, Paul, Pulaski	49	209	176	29	53	91	14	0	8	44	0	4	4	25	1	43	0	1	6	.301	.392	.517
Musslewhite, Stuart, Bluefield	57	236	223	36	67	109	18	0	8	36	0	2	0	11	2	33	4	1	4	.300	.331	.489
Rodriguez, Manuel, Danville *	65	267	250	34	75	122	19	2	8	47	0	5	0	12	1	69	1	1	6	.300	.326	.488
Suero, Ovandy, Danville †	60	272	247	53	74	107	5	8	4	17	6	2	3	14	0	54	46	11	2	.300	.342	.433
Jaspe, Jonathan, Pulaski †	47	191	174	29	52	75	12	1	3	31	0	3	0	14	1	30	1	0	5	.299	.346	.431
Rasmus, Colby, Johnson City *	62	244	216	47	64	111	16	5	7	27	1	3	3	21	2	73	13	3	0	.296	.362	.514
Carter, Charles, Johnson City	59	221	180	33	53	85	9	4	5	32	0	7	1	33	0	29	12	2	3	.294	.394	.472
Tucker, Jonathan, Bluefield	59	238	213	39	62	84	13	3	1	24	0	4	2	19	0	22	13	1	3	.291	.349	.394
Butler, Jacob, Pulaski	55	238	200	42	58	118	16	1	14	52	1	4	2	31	1	60	1	2	6	.290	.384	.590
Gonzalez, Jesus, Pulaski	46	194	180	25	52	92	14	1	8	28	0	2	1	11	0	42	0	0	3	.289	.330	.511
Ortiz, Yancarlos, Elizabethton †	49	211	187	30	54	58	4	0	0	17	1	1	3	19	0	38	10	5	1	.289	.362	.310
Devins, Matthew, Princeton	57	239	202	34	58	89	13	0	6	33	1	1	9	26	1	26	12	1	4	.287	.391	.441

DEPARTMENTAL LEADERS: G—Campbell, 66. AB—Campbell, 262. R—Campbell, 77. H—Flores and Ramirez, 83. TB—Campbell, 166. 2B—Campbell, 26. 3B—Suero, 8. HR—Campbell, 18. RBI—Campbell, 64. SH—Arnold, 8. SF—Carter, 7. HP—Cunningham, 14. BB—Kalter, 45. IBB—three players with 3. SO—De Leon, 75. SB—Suero, 46. CS—Suero, 11. GIDP—Moore and Oliveros, 8. OBP—Aqueron, .468. Slg.—Campbell, .634.

ALL PLAYERS

*Lefthanded batter. †Switch-hitter.

Player, Team	G	TPA	AB	R	H	TB	2B	3B	HR	RBI	SH	SF	HP	BB	IBB	SO	SB	CS	GDP	Avg.	OBP	Slg.
Abreu, Miguel, Bluefield	43	128	115	24	26	49	5	3	4	15	2	1	8	0	0	24	9	0	1	.226	.278	.426
Acosta, Christian, Bristol	65	259	220	40	69	104	20	0	5	41	1	2	7	29	0	48	0	2	6	.314	.407	.473
Acosta, Leonardo, Bristol	56	178	159	15	30	40	8	1	0	15	6	3	2	8	1	41	4	0	5	.189	.233	.252
Aguilar, Heliezer, Pulaski	41	158	146	21	44	57	10	0	1	18	4	1	2	5	0	16	7	1	5	.301	.331	.390
Anderson, Bryan, Johnson City *	51	176	154	28	51	79	8	1	6	36	1	5	1	15	1	29	6	1	3	.331	.383	.513
Anderson, Matthew, Kingsport *	47	190	169	27	53	76	8	0	5	30	0	2	4	15	0	22	0	3	7	.314	.379	.450
Andrews, Robert, Bluefield	27	109	98	19	27	46	4	3	3	15	0	1	1	9	3	23	9	0	1	.276	.339	.469
Andrus, Elvis, Danville	6	22	18	3	5	6	1	0	0	1	0	0	0	4	0	4	1	0	0	.278	.409	.333
Aqueron, Rene, Bluefield *	56	187	163	35	66	95	15	1	4	32	0	2	4	17	2	24	9	3	4	.405	.468	.583
Ard, Alfred, Burlington	50	182	162	25	37	52	4	4	1	17	0	0	5	15	0	38	10	2	2	.228	.313	.321
Arnal, Cristo, Burlington	43	176	157	21	35	39	2	1	0	13	1	3	1	14	0	30	7	0	1	.223	.286	.248
Arnold, William, Danville †	51	195	171	20	46	61	9	0	2	16	8	2	0	14	0	38	7	2	4	.269	.321	.357
Arratia, Jilmer, Elizabethton	28	104	100	9	27	33	1	1	1	12	2	1	0	1	0	21	0	0	2	.270	.275	.330
Austin, Parris, Kingsport	13	55	49	7	18	28	5	1	1	9	1	1	1	3	1	12	4	1	2	.367	.407	.571
Avila, Angel, Bluefield	30	105	97	12	26	40	5	0	3	14	2	0	0	6	0	31	2	1	2	.268	.311	.412
Badger, Graig, Pulaski	44	170	144	28	42	56	8	3	0	19	5	0	3	18	0	24	6	2	3	.292	.382	.389
Barksdale, James, Danville	10	36	35	4	6	6	0	0	0	2	0	0	0	1	0	15	0	0	2	.171	.194	.171
Batista, Franklin, Bristol	41	75	63	7	13	18	3	1	0	3	0	1	2	9	0	24	3	3	0	.206	.320	.286
Bensko, Dustin, Elizabethton	38	139	122	21	33	58	7	0	6	18	0	2	3	11	0	33	0	0	4	.270	.341	.475
Beras, Alexis, Kingsport	1	0	0	0	0	0	0	0	0	0	0	0	0	0	…	0	0	0	0	…	…	…
Bethel, Ryan, Princeton †	33	146	115	25	41	55	12	1	0	17	2	2	2	25	1	19	3	1	4	.357	.472	.478
Betsill, Matthew, Elizabethton †	45	167	148	24	41	54	5	1	2	19	0	1	0	18	0	34	4	2	5	.277	.359	.365
Brown, Kyle, Kingsport	15	57	43	16	12	16	4	0	0	4	0	0	3	11	0	10	12	0	0	.279	.456	.372
Butler, Jacob, Pulaski	55	238	200	42	58	118	16	1	14	52	1	4	2	31	1	60	1	2	6	.290	.384	.590
Campbell, Eric, Danville	66	298	262	77	82	166	26	2	18	64	0	4	4	28	3	64	15	4	4	.313	.383	.634
Campbell, Ryan, Johnson City	1	0	0	0	0	0	0	0	0	0	0	0	0	0	0	0	0	0	0	…	…	…
Carter, Charles, Johnson City	59	221	180	33	53	85	9	4	5	32	0	7	1	33	0	29	12	2	3	.294	.394	.472
Carter, Vernon, Bristol	65	263	233	33	66	113	17	0	10	37	2	2	8	17	0	64	2	1	4	.283	.350	.485
Castro, Jose, Kingsport †	8	17	14	1	4	4	0	0	0	1	0	0	1	2	0	1	0	1	1	.286	.412	.286
Causey, Marcos, Bristol	43	127	119	10	26	27	1	0	0	6	1	0	3	4	0	32	1	1	0	.218	.262	.227
Chacin, Steward, Johnson City	37	85	83	13	25	33	6	1	0	9	0	0	0	2	0	16	2	0	4	.301	.318	.398
Chavez, Jose, Burlington †	13	55	51	4	7	9	2	0	0	6	0	1	0	3	0	13	0	0	1	.137	.182	.176
Chmiel, Paul, Bluefield *	24	85	75	13	15	25	4	0	2	10	0	1	1	8	0	19	1	1	1	.200	.282	.333
Clark, John, Burlington	25	104	92	14	23	33	4	0	2	14	1	0	1	10	0	24	0	0	3	.250	.330	.359
Colon, Kevin, Princeton	30	113	94	12	21	22	1	0	0	9	6	0	2	11	0	17	3	5	1	.223	.318	.234
Combs, Weldon, Bristol	30	69	68	3	16	21	5	0	0	10	1	0	0	0	0	21	0	0	0	.235	.235	.309
Cordero, Octavio, Pulaski *	39	134	114	23	27	33	3	0	1	5	2	1	0	17	0	31	11	1	3	.237	.333	.289
Coronado, Jose, Kingsport †	39	172	139	24	37	47	5	1	1	8	7	0	4	22	0	27	6	4	2	.266	.382	.338
Cortez, Martin, Bristol *	1	0	0	0	0	0	0	0	0	0	0	0	0	0	…	0	0	0	0	…	…	…
Cruz, Elvis, Kingsport	38	118	108	14	16	32	4	0	4	16	0	0	0	10	0	29	0	0	1	.148	.220	.296
Cummins, Daniel, Kingsport	2	9	9	3	2	6	1	0	1	3	0	0	0	0	0	0	0	0	0	.222	.222	.667
Cunningham, Aaron, Bristol	56	255	222	41	70	99	10	2	5	25	0	3	14	16	0	45	6	5	3	.315	.392	.446
Cunningham, Christopher, Princeton	59	264	222	42	73	109	13	1	7	40	1	0	7	34	1	55	6	3	6	.329	.433	.491
Davis, Quentin, Danville *	49	220	201	44	65	87	9	2	3	36	0	1	4	14	1	26	8	4	1	.323	.377	.433
de la Rosa, Jairo, Princeton	17	64	63	8	17	27	5	1	1	6	0	0	0	1	0	11	6	4	2	.270	.281	.429
De La Rosa, Jose, Johnson City	1	0	0	0	0	0	0	0	0	0	0	0	0	0	0	0	0	0	0	…	…	…
De Leon, Epifanio, Princeton	50	202	185	23	44	73	9	1	6	22	0	1	5	11	0	75	2	1	5	.238	.297	.395
De Leon, Evandy, Burlington	18	78	67	14	13	28	3	0	4	9	0	0	2	9	0	18	4	0	0	.194	.308	.418
Denham, Jason, Burlington *	46	172	147	13	29	35	4	1	0	13	1	2	0	22	0	43	5	0	1	.197	.298	.238
Desmond, Geoffrey, Johnson City	41	123	109	15	23	43	9	1	3	15	0	2	1	11	0	29	3	1	2	.211	.285	.394
Devins, Matthew, Princeton	57	239	202	34	58	89	13	0	6	33	1	1	9	26	1	26	12	1	4	.287	.391	.441
Drennen, John, Burlington *	51	195	168	24	40	73	7	1	8	29	1	3	5	18	1	37	6	3	7	.238	.325	.435
Edwards, Ronald, Princeton	3	6	6	0	0	0	0	0	0	0	0	0	0	0	0	4	0	0	0	.000	.000	.000
Escobar, Jose, Danville	8	36	30	9	12	22	2	1	2	8	0	1	0	5	0	8	1	0	1	.400	.472	.733
Evans, Nicholas, Kingsport	15	68	64	11	22	47	7	0	6	22	0	0	0	4	1	17	1	0	1	.344	.382	.734
Fields, Matthew, Princeton	45	191	177	29	45	79	10	0	8	35	0	1	3	10	1	65	1	1	5	.254	.304	.446
Fitzgerald, Kevin, Johnson City	1	0	0	0	0	0	0	0	0	0	0	0	0	0	0	0	0	0	0	…	…	…
Franko, Paul, Pulaski	49	209	176	29	53	91	14	0	8	44	0	4	4	25	1	43	0	1	6	.301	.392	.517
Garcia, Julio Cesar, Burlington †	18	48	42	5	8	9	1	0	0	2	0	1	1	4	0	12	1	0	1	.190	.271	.214

Player, Team	G	TPA	AB	R	H	TB	2B	3B	HR	RBI	SH	SF	HP	BB	IBB	SO	SB	CS	GDP	Avg.	OBP	Slg.
Garcia, Santo, Bristol †	34	93	85	7	13	25	4	1	2	8	1	0	3	4	0	35	1	2	1	.153	.217	.294
Gardenhire, Toby, Elizabethton	30	113	100	10	20	23	3	0	0	5	1	0	4	8	1	21	2	1	3	.200	.286	.230
Garner, Brandon, Johnson City	35	100	94	13	17	22	2	0	1	5	1	0	0	5	0	30	0	1	4	.181	.222	.234
Gonzalez, Gregory, Kingsport *	33	138	126	26	45	57	8	2	0	7	2	0	2	8	0	13	15	6	3	.357	.404	.452
Gonzalez, Jesus, Pulaski	46	194	180	25	52	92	14	1	8	28	0	2	1	11	0	42	0	0	3	.289	.330	.511
Gonzalez, Steve, Johnson City	37	115	100	8	19	25	3	0	1	6	0	2	1	12	0	31	2	0	1	.190	.278	.250
Guerra, Junior, Danville	37	121	115	6	30	49	10	0	3	18	0	1	2	3	0	22	0	0	1	.261	.289	.426
Gutierrez, Christopher, Pulaski	43	168	148	15	35	52	9	1	2	20	0	1	4	15	0	26	2	1	3	.236	.321	.351
Hatch, Anthony, Pulaski *	41	139	128	16	35	65	11	2	5	26	0	0	2	9	0	30	0	1	3	.273	.331	.508
Henry, Sean, Kingsport	42	179	149	24	38	62	7	1	5	31	2	4	2	22	0	43	15	1	0	.255	.350	.416
Hiser, Charles, Burlington	38	155	135	29	44	96	15	2	11	36	0	1	1	18	1	43	1	2	3	.326	.406	.711
Holmes, Justin, Burlington	17	53	44	4	7	8	1	0	0	5	0	0	2	7	0	11	0	0	1	.159	.302	.182
Howell, Samuel, Bluefield	10	33	31	5	6	10	1	0	1	1	0	0	0	2	0	9	0	0	1	.194	.242	.323
Huches, Leonardo, Bluefield	30	81	76	5	13	16	3	0	0	5	1	0	0	4	0	26	0	0	2	.171	.213	.211
Infante, Jansy, Burlington †	37	150	139	19	26	30	2	1	0	8	0	0	0	11	0	27	6	2	3	.187	.247	.216
Irvin, Blair, Princeton *	7	12	11	1	1	1	0	0	0	0	0	0	0	1	0	4	0	0	1	.091	.167	.091
Jaspe, Jonathan, Pulaski †	47	191	174	29	52	75	12	1	3	31	0	3	0	14	1	30	1	0	5	.299	.346	.431
Jones, Brandon, Danville *	2	8	7	0	2	2	0	0	0	1	0	0	0	1	0	0	0	0	0	.286	.375	.286
Jones, Daryl, Johnson City *	61	212	182	36	38	52	6	1	2	10	0	2	13	15	0	41	10	4	6	.209	.311	.286
Jones, Larry, Elizabethton	36	126	108	20	31	45	9	1	1	12	0	0	4	14	0	30	4	2	2	.287	.389	.417
Kaaihue, Isaiah, Danville	5	16	16	4	7	16	3	0	2	3	0	0	0	0	0	5	0	0	0	.438	.438	1.000
Kalin, Travis, Elizabethton	30	109	98	14	26	41	2	2	3	13	0	0	1	10	0	34	3	1	0	.265	.339	.418
Kalter, Zachary, Pulaski *	58	261	209	49	56	82	9	7	1	17	2	2	3	45	2	33	17	7	6	.268	.402	.392
Kitch, Denver, Bluefield	37	126	115	17	30	48	8	2	2	16	4	0	1	6	0	32	1	1	4	.261	.303	.417
Kotch, Kevin, Bluefield *	37	121	108	15	17	27	4	0	2	11	1	0	2	10	0	35	1	1	1	.157	.242	.250
Lachapel, Alex, Bristol †	33	69	54	6	8	10	2	0	0	2	1	0	0	14	0	29	1	1	2	.148	.324	.185
Lagreid, Thomas, Princeton	50	171	150	20	43	51	2	0	2	11	1	0	1	19	0	30	7	3	5	.287	.371	.340
Land, Joshua, Elizabethton *	24	78	72	9	22	31	7	1	0	10	0	1	2	3	0	18	0	2	0	.306	.346	.431
Lietz, Todd, Kingsport	11	41	40	6	7	7	0	0	0	2	0	0	1	0	0	6	0	1	1	.175	.195	.175
Lis, Erik, Elizabethton *	49	180	168	29	53	97	12	1	10	41	0	1	2	9	2	35	0	0	2	.315	.356	.577
Looze, Christopher, Pulaski *	25	84	78	10	9	21	3	0	3	7	0	0	1	5	0	26	0	1	2	.115	.179	.269
Lopez, Andrew, Princeton	34	140	120	21	39	65	10	2	4	21	1	2	6	11	1	40	1	1	1	.325	.403	.542
Lopez, Christian, Johnson City	36	86	74	7	15	16	1	0	0	7	0	1	1	10	0	31	2	1	0	.203	.302	.216
Manuel, Anthony, Kingsport	36	134	114	18	28	34	3	0	1	11	3	1	4	12	0	17	1	2	2	.246	.336	.298
Marte, German, Kingsport	2	0	0	0	0	0	0	0	0	0	...	0	0	0	...	0	0	0	0	...	...	...
Martinez, Christopher, Pulaski *	23	67	56	5	9	17	2	0	2	4	0	1	3	7	0	28	0	1	1	.161	.284	.304
Martinez, Gilberto, Bluefield †	43	130	115	13	27	30	3	0	0	12	6	1	1	7	0	40	3	1	1	.235	.282	.261
Martinez, Joan, Kingsport †	37	136	129	15	30	50	3	1	5	20	1	1	2	3	0	36	0	1	5	.233	.259	.388
Martinez, Jose, Johnson City	55	174	150	28	45	75	8	2	6	31	1	1	2	20	0	15	9	2	5	.300	.387	.500
Mateo, Jose, Kingsport	37	147	126	20	34	53	7	0	4	19	1	1	1	18	0	31	5	4	4	.270	.363	.421
Matthews, William, Princeton †	15	40	38	3	2	3	1	0	0	2	0	1	0	1	0	18	0	1	1	.053	.075	.079
Matulia, John, Princeton *	27	121	105	19	38	54	6	2	2	15	2	0	0	14	2	18	8	10	1	.362	.437	.514
McCormick, Michael, Princeton	32	127	111	15	28	49	10	1	3	16	0	1	4	11	0	31	3	3	4	.252	.339	.441
McCraw, Sean, Kingsport *	32	115	101	8	22	26	1	0	1	7	0	0	4	10	0	27	0	0	3	.218	.313	.257
Mikrut, Jon, Johnson City	33	99	93	10	20	42	7	0	5	11	1	0	1	4	1	16	1	1	1	.215	.255	.452
Moffitt, Andrew, Bluefield	24	97	84	17	28	57	6	1	7	18	0	0	2	11	1	21	4	1	0	.333	.423	.679
Montero, Juan, Kingsport	19	76	70	8	11	18	1	0	2	6	1	0	2	3	0	30	1	1	1	.157	.213	.257
Moore, Michael, Elizabethton	36	135	123	20	38	53	6	0	3	13	1	0	1	9	0	19	2	2	8	.309	.361	.431
Morgan, Joshua, Bristol	62	260	229	36	55	80	18	2	1	19	1	1	3	26	0	60	7	0	4	.240	.324	.349
Morris, Adam, Johnson City	30	115	99	15	21	34	7	0	2	14	0	0	1	15	0	25	3	2	5	.212	.322	.343
Musslewhite, Stuart, Bluefield *	57	236	223	36	67	109	18	0	8	36	0	2	0	11	2	33	4	1	4	.300	.331	.489
Nieves, Javier, Pulaski	7	8	7	0	0	0	0	0	0	0	0	0	1	0	0	3	0	0	0	.000	.125	.000
Oliveros, Riky, Kingsport	56	227	210	22	60	84	12	0	4	31	0	2	3	12	0	38	4	1	8	.286	.330	.400
Ortiz, Yancarlos, Elizabethton †	49	211	187	30	54	58	4	0	0	17	1	1	3	19	0	38	10	5	1	.289	.362	.310
Ovalle, Edward, Elizabethton	65	273	239	44	68	104	13	1	7	27	0	0	9	25	0	49	6	3	3	.285	.374	.435
Owens, Malcolm, Johnson City	38	109	93	12	20	25	2	0	1	8	0	0	6	10	0	21	7	5	2	.215	.330	.269
Owings, John, Danville	33	128	116	27	34	82	8	2	12	31	1	0	5	6	0	31	1	2	2	.293	.354	.707
Pacheco, Joel, Bluefield	35	145	140	16	38	57	4	0	5	16	0	0	1	4	0	31	4	0	5	.271	.297	.407
Palmer, Cody, Johnson City	9	31	27	3	9	17	2	0	2	9	0	0	1	3	0	5	2	1	1	.333	.419	.630
Parker, Carnell, Princeton *	20	41	37	6	8	11	3	0	0	2	1	0	0	3	0	13	8	1	1	.216	.275	.297
Petrucci, Nicholas, Burlington	58	234	211	28	52	86	8	1	8	29	1	2	3	17	2	69	3	2	1	.246	.309	.408
Piazza, Thomas, Kingsport *	19	62	60	3	9	11	2	0	0	2	0	0	0	2	0	25	0	0	3	.150	.177	.183
Pickerell, Steven, Princeton	22	48	35	9	9	15	3	0	1	7	0	1	2	10	0	8	0	0	1	.257	.438	.429
Picornell, Carlos, Danville †	22	74	57	16	12	14	2	0	0	4	4	1	1	11	0	10	5	1	0	.211	.343	.246
Pope, Kieron, Bluefield	41	165	149	23	34	54	3	1	5	22	0	1	7	8	0	62	5	0	1	.228	.297	.362
Portes, Juan, Elizabethton	64	275	245	40	70	121	13	1	12	39	0	4	4	22	0	43	6	3	3	.286	.349	.494
Preston, Timothy, Johnson City	29	66	63	7	13	23	2	1	2	10	0	0	1	2	0	17	2	1	2	.206	.242	.365
Puente, Juan, Bluefield	14	45	39	5	12	15	3	0	0	6	0	0	1	5	0	12	0	0	0	.308	.400	.385
Pujols, Wilfrido, Johnson City	27	67	63	5	9	11	2	0	0	4	0	0	2	2	0	31	0	0	1	.143	.194	.175
Quinonez, Rudolph, Danville	1	1	0	0	0	0	0	0	0	0	0	0	0	0	0	0	0	0	0	...	...	...
Quintana, Alberto, Pulaski	26	86	78	11	22	30	4	2	0	11	0	1	0	7	0	15	1	1	1	.282	.337	.385
Ramirez, Maximiliano, Danville	63	278	239	45	83	126	19	0	8	47	0	4	4	31	2	41	1	2	5	.347	.424	.527
Rasmus, Colby, Johnson City *	62	244	216	47	64	111	16	5	7	27	1	3	3	21	2	73	13	3	0	.296	.362	.514
Regan, Christopher, Princeton *	19	59	56	4	13	16	3	0	0	5	0	0	1	2	0	14	0	1	2	.232	.271	.286
Richards, Glen, Danville	1	0	0	0	0	0	0	0	0	0	0	0	0	0	0	0	0	0	0	...	...	...
Richardson, Sean, Elizabethton	28	104	94	14	28	53	4	0	7	21	0	1	1	8	0	20	0	2	3	.298	.356	.564
Roberts, Joshua, Burlington *	50	182	156	18	33	50	7	2	2	15	0	1	5	20	1	44	3	1	2	.212	.319	.321
Robinson, Mark, Elizabethton *	61	254	229	31	56	81	7	3	4	29	0	2	5	18	1	35	7	4	7	.245	.311	.354
Rodriguez, Manuel, Danville †	65	267	250	34	75	122	19	2	8	47	0	5	0	12	1	69	1	1	6	.300	.326	.488
Romak, James, Danville	34	145	124	25	34	67	10	1	7	27	1	1	5	14	1	38	2	1	4	.274	.368	.540

Player, Team	G	TPA	AB	R	H	TB	2B	3B	HR	RBI	SH	SF	HP	BB	IBB	SO	SB	CS	GDP	Avg.	OBP	Slg.
Romero, Niuman, Burlington †	63	257	218	33	60	82	12	2	2	29	3	1	4	31	1	45	6	6	5	.275	.374	.376
Roth, Randy, Johnson City	35	133	119	27	39	75	13	1	7	27	0	4	4	6	0	24	3	1	5	.328	.368	.630
Royster, Ryan, Princeton	51	203	187	30	46	90	8	0	12	37	0	1	2	13	1	48	6	0	5	.246	.300	.481
Sanchez, Salvador, Bristol	64	268	246	38	64	95	17	1	4	30	3	0	2	17	3	62	14	2	4	.260	.313	.386
Sandes, Jorge, Pulaski †	31	119	100	17	25	41	3	2	3	11	0	0	3	16	0	25	0	2	5	.250	.370	.410
Santana, Luis, Kingsport	14	40	39	4	8	14	1	1	1	4	0	0	0	1	0	6	1	0	0	.205	.225	.359
Santana, Yury, Kingsport	12	41	37	7	9	15	6	0	0	5	1	0	1	2	0	11	0	0	2	.243	.300	.405
Santos, Jose, Danville	51	211	180	31	41	62	9	3	2	25	2	0	3	26	0	39	5	5	3	.228	.335	.344
Shafer, Dustin, Bristol	24	64	61	5	11	12	1	0	0	12	0	1	0	2	0	8	1	0	0	.180	.203	.197
Shehan, Jonathan, Danville	15	48	38	2	6	8	2	0	0	2	1	0	3	6	0	9	0	0	1	.158	.319	.211
Silva, Yohan, Danville †	64	249	216	27	45	65	15	1	1	22	1	4	1	27	1	51	3	5	2	.208	.294	.301
Skorupski, John, Johnson City	22	76	73	6	19	31	7	1	1	11	0	1	0	2	0	22	2	0	2	.260	.276	.425
Snyder, Brandon, Bluefield	44	180	144	26	39	71	8	0	8	35	1	6	1	28	2	36	7	2	2	.271	.380	.493
Solano, Donovan, Johnson City	45	164	145	27	38	42	4	0	0	11	1	1	3	14	0	22	3	2	6	.262	.337	.290
Soto, Leance, Pulaski	42	151	137	11	21	38	5	0	4	10	1	1	0	12	0	69	0	0	1	.153	.220	.277
Spilman, Ryan, Burlington	37	129	113	7	22	29	4	0	1	10	2	0	0	14	1	27	0	0	4	.195	.283	.257
Stone, Wesley, Pulaski	43	187	162	23	44	54	7	0	1	15	0	2	1	22	0	62	0	1	4	.272	.358	.333
Suero, Ovandy, Danville †	60	272	247	53	74	107	5	8	4	17	6	2	3	14	0	54	46	11	2	.300	.342	.433
Swain, Michael, Bristol *	55	195	166	29	43	74	11	4	4	28	1	1	3	24	1	53	0	0	0	.259	.361	.446
Tavares, Reymundo, Bristol	45	153	132	17	30	40	4	0	2	16	5	1	3	12	0	21	7	2	6	.227	.304	.303
Tavarez, Argenis, Burlington †	21	73	65	10	13	16	3	0	0	2	1 ·	0	0	7	0	13	4	0	0	.200	.278	.246
Thiel, Emile, Elizabethton	9	25	21	2	5	5	0	0	0	1	0	0	1	3	0	10	0	0	2	.238	.360	.238
Tintor, Eli, Elizabethton	40	150	139	20	39	57	6	0	4	18	0	1	4	6	1	26	0	1	2	.281	.327	.410
Tolleson, Steven, Elizabethton	16	73	56	18	18	32	6	1	2	8	3	0	3	11	0	4	2	1	2	.321	.457	.571
Tucker, Jonathan, Bluefield	59	238	213	39	62	84	13	3	1	24	0	4	2	19	0	22	13	1	3	.291	.349	.394
Turner, Clifton, Bluefield	7	27	26	6	8	13	2	0	1	1	0	0	0	1	0	10	2	0	1	.308	.333	.500
Van Slyke, A.J., Johnson City *	13	54	50	11	19	32	3	2	2	14	0	2	1	1	0	7	0	0	1	.380	.389	.640
Vasquez, Enrique, Burlington	31	101	93	7	19	28	3	0	2	10	0	0	1	7	0	23	0	0	2	.204	.267	.301
Vick, Hunter, Princeton †	49	197	166	34	39	43	4	0	0	16	1	2	4	24	0	35	7	9	2	.235	.342	.259
Wabick, David, Kingsport *	45	182	165	27	50	59	9	0	0	20	0	0	3	14	0	25	0	0	4	.303	.368	.358
Wargo, Cody, Bluefield	5	16	12	1	2	2	0	0	0	3	0	1	0	3	0	4	0	0	1	.167	.313	.167
Weglarz, Nicholas, Burlington *	41	166	147	22	34	51	11	0	2	13	0	1	1	17	1	42	2	1	0	.231	.313	.347
Welker, Kris, Bristol	54	226	198	31	60	85	16	0	3	29	4	1	6	17	2	34	2	1	4	.303	.374	.429
Wells, Cory, Kingsport	51	189	177	26	40	65	13	0	4	18	0	1	2	9	0	51	5	4	7	.226	.270	.367
Werman, Kyle, Kingsport †	11	39	34	5	4	5	1	0	0	1	0	0	2	3	0	6	1	0	2	.118	.231	.147
Wiens, Logan, Danville	32	115	94	12	21	33	4	1	2	13	0	1	2	18	2	28	3	1	3	.223	.357	.351
Winterling, Paul, Bluefield	47	153	132	30	37	66	9	1	6	23	0	1	2	18	0	37	7	0	0	.280	.373	.500
Wyrick, Joshua, Kingsport *	39	132	123	17	25	41	6	2	2	14	0	1	1	7	1	29	6	0	0	.203	.250	.333
Yeme, Leonel, Bluefield *	36	93	88	9	18	28	4	0	2	10	3	0	1	1	0	25	0	1	0	.205	.222	.318

GRAND SLAMS—B. Anderson, M. Anderson, E. Lis, J. Martinez, 2 each; J. Butler, E. Campbell, B. Clark, K. Clemens, Q. Davis, S. Henry, P. Hiser, E. Iorg, S. Musslewhite, J. Pacheco, L. Soto, 1 each.

AWARDED FIRST BASE ON CATCHER'S INTERFERENCE—R. Aqueron (E. Tintor); D. Bensko (E. Vasquez); C. Carter (R. Spilman); E. Iorg (T. Lagreid); C. Moore (J. Guerra); R. Reed (J. Martinez).

2005 PITCHING

TEAM

Team	W	L	Pct.	ERA	G	CG	ShO	Sv.	IP	H	TBF	R	ER	HR	SH	SF	HB	BB	IBB	SO	WP	Bk.
Elizabethton	48	19	.716	3.30	67	2	8	24	566.2	473	2344	246	208	42	11	13	28	170	2	612	63	2
Danville	47	20	.701	3.45	67	0	4	22	600.2	526	2522	284	230	40	15	19	20	230	10	514	62	5
Princeton	34	31	.523	4.00	65	1	3	17	558.2	580	2463	326	248	49	19	23	41	190	2	551	55	4
Pulaski	34	33	.507	4.30	67	0	2	14	586	634	2572	369	280	76	11	16	35	189	2	540	60	9
Bristol	30	36	.455	4.51	66	0	3	13	574.1	610	2543	350	288	51	17	16	45	190	21	516	38	9
Burlington	25	43	.368	4.52	68	2	3	5	569.2	603	2480	353	286	59	15	15	44	172	2	492	47	2
Kingsport	28	40	.412	4.68	68	2	1	13	584	634	2629	378	304	46	18	34	47	219	10	456	60	3
Bluefield	31	36	.463	4.73	67	0	3	17	564.2	573	2583	367	297	54	14	17	57	274	12	641	84	3
Greeneville	29	37	.439	4.86	66	0	5	14	568.2	583	2558	364	307	42	25	20	44	236	4	553	59	4
Johnson City	28	39	.418	5.97	67	1	1	18	559.2	643	2610	459	371	73	10	16	47	256	2	501	52	3

INDIVIDUAL

TOP QUALIFIERS FOR EARNED-RUN AVERAGE TITLE

Minimum 54 innings. *Lefthanded pitcher.

Pitcher, Team	W	L	Pct.	ERA	G	GS	CG	ShO	GF	Sv.	IP	H	TBF	R	ER	HR	SH	SF	HB	BB	IBB	SO	WP	Bk.
Hawes, Adam, Elizabethton	4	0	1.000	1.53	14	9	1	1	3	1	59.0	38	229	13	10	2	1	2	3	16	0	68	4	0
Cuevas, Jairo, Danville	6	1	.857	1.95	12	10	0	0	0	0	55.1	35	220	20	12	3	1	2	1	22	0	69	3	1
Litsch, Jesse, Pulaski	5	1	.833	2.74	11	11	0	0	0	0	65.2	51	255	22	20	6	0	0	4	10	0	67	2	1
Blackford, Todd, Danville	5	3	.625	3.17	12	12	0	0	0	0	59.2	48	246	24	21	2	1	2	3	22	3	30	6	0
Perez, Wilfrido, Bluefield *	3	4	.429	3.26	12	12	0	0	0	0	58.0	54	252	30	21	4	2	0	2	27	1	75	5	0
Valdez, Luis, Burlington	3	6	.333	3.54	13	13	1	0	0	0	61.0	64	254	31	24	8	1	3	3	12	0	59	5	0
Cayton, Jason, Princeton	3	2	.600	3.65	12	11	0	0	0	0	56.2	62	251	32	23	2	1	0	7	16	0	55	5	0
Pino, Yohan, Elizabethton	9	2	.818	3.72	12	12	1	0	0	0	67.2	68	283	31	28	3	0	1	2	13	0	64	3	0
Viola, Frank, Bristol	5	2	.714	3.84	13	12	0	0	0	0	70.1	74	307	35	30	2	3	3	8	20	1	59	3	0
Simmons, Jeramy, Kingsport	1	5	.167	4.26	13	12	0	0	0	0	57.0	58	247	39	27	5	1	2	1	15	0	47	8	0
Schmidt, Kyle, Bluefield	5	3	.625	4.50	13	13	0	0	0	0	70.0	77	314	37	35	6	1	0	6	26	0	76	8	0
Sosa, Oswaldo, Elizabethton	6	5	.545	4.95	12	11	0	0	0	0	56.1	59	244	37	31	4	1	0	0	21	0	40	10	1
Williamson, Logan, Bristol *	3	7	.300	5.03	13	12	0	0	0	1	59.0	64	269	41	33	6	0	0	5	21	1	60	3	1
Mateo, Francisco, Pulaski	1	7	.125	5.14	12	12	0	0	0	0	56.0	72	256	41	32	9	0	3	1	21	0	38	5	1

Pitcher, Team	W	L	Pct.	ERA	G	GS	CG	ShO	GF	Sv.	IP	H	TBF	R	ER	HR	SH	SF	HB	BB	IBB	SO	WP	Bk.
Walker, Matthew, Princeton	2	3	.400	5.31	13	12	0	0	1	1	57.2	63	257	39	34	2	1	4	1	22	0	71	8	0
Lane, Matthew, Johnson City	2	6	.250	5.37	13	13	0	0	0	0	55.1	68	255	40	33	7	0	0	1	22	1	51	7	0
Frias, Jusef, Kingsport	1	5	.167	6.99	13	13	0	0	0	0	55.1	70	267	44	43	3	2	6	11	24	0	43	7	1

DEPARTMENTAL LEADERS: W—Pino, 9. L—four pitchers tied with 7. Pct.—Hawes, 1.000. G—Lahey and Fitzgerald, 26. GS—eight pitchers tied with 13. CG—eight pitchers tied with 1. ShO—four pitchers tied with 1. GF—Lahey, 26. Sv.—Lahey, 15. Sv.—Findlay, 15. IP—Viola, 70.1. H—Schmidt, 77. TBF—Schmidt, 315. R—Gonzalez, 49. ER—Frias, 43. HR—Wice, 15. SAC—four pitchers tied with 4. SF—Frias, 6. HB—Frias, 11. BB—DeNaball, 38. IBB—Squires and Johnson, 4. SO—Smit, 86. WP—Spoone and Muro, 11. BK—Winn, 4.

ALL PITCHERS

*Lefthanded pitcher.

Pitcher, Team	W	L	Pct.	ERA	G	GS	CG	ShO	GF	Sv.	IP	H	TBF	R	ER	HR	SH	SF	HB	BB	IBB	SO	WP	Bk.
Acosta, Manuel, Danville	0	0	.000	3.00	3	2	0	0	0	0	6.0	3	19	2	2	0	1	0	0	1	0	8	2	0
Aguirre, Wilfreddy, Pulaski *	1	4	.200	5.51	9	9	0	0	0	0	32.2	38	154	25	20	1	0	1	3	16	0	23	6	2
Anderson, Devin, Danville *	4	1	.800	2.49	13	6	0	0	2	0	50.2	36	199	15	14	5	2	1	1	15	0	38	2	0
Arizmendi, Daniel, Kingsport *	4	4	.500	4.63	17	7	1	1	3	1	44.2	62	206	26	23	4	2	1	2	17	0	35	6	0
Baker, Brian, Princeton	6	2	.750	2.60	17	0	0	0	4	0	27.2	22	108	12	8	4	4	3	1	6	0	33	0	1
Banks, Demetrius, Bristol *	0	0	.000	0.00	2	1	0	0	0	0	3.2	2	16	0	0	0	0	0	0	3	0	4	2	0
Barone, Daniel, Johnson City	0	0	.000	9.00	1	0	0	0	0	0	1.0	1	4	1	1	1	0	0	0	0	0	1	0	0
Bastardo, Alberto, Bluefield *	4	1	.800	4.04	14	7	0	0	3	3	42.1	40	183	23	19	4	1	1	5	13	1	58	5	0
Benson, Shane, Pulaski	6	3	.667	5.52	16	6	0	0	5	1	44.0	57	199	30	27	7	0	1	3	10	1	39	10	0
Beras, Alexis, Kingsport	1	2	.333	5.73	19	0	0	0	6	0	33.0	30	145	22	21	3	1	4	2	17	0	32	8	0
Bigley, Dennis, Pulaski	1	2	.333	5.40	16	8	0	0	0	0	46.2	58	210	40	28	10	1	2	5	15	0	42	2	0
Blackford, Todd, Danville	5	3	.625	3.17	12	12	0	0	0	0	59.2	48	246	24	21	2	1	2	3	22	3	30	6	0
Borne, James, Johnson City *	1	0	1.000	2.74	15	0	0	0	3	0	23.0	20	98	10	7	1	0	2	1	8	0	18	0	0
Brooks, Richard, Bristol	0	2	.000	2.89	5	5	0	0	0	0	18.2	15	75	7	6	2	0	0	2	4	0	25	1	0
Bullock, Tyler, Danville	1	0	1.000	3.60	14	0	0	0	8	3	20.0	13	84	8	8	1	0	2	1	10	0	14	2	0
Byrnes, Scott, Pulaski	2	2	.500	5.85	21	0	0	0	16	3	32.1	46	156	30	21	4	2	2	1	13	1	36	3	0
Camacho, Gustavo, Bluefield	0	2	.000	4.78	16	0	0	0	7	1	32.0	36	155	27	17	6	0	0	3	13	2	17	5	0
Campbell, Ryan, Johnson City	4	2	.667	6.33	20	0	0	0	7	1	27.0	20	124	19	19	2	0	1	3	24	0	43	0	0
Castillo, Jonathan, Kingsport	2	3	.400	2.04	11	11	1	0	0	0	53.0	42	215	17	12	3	2	0	2	16	0	41	2	0
Cayton, Jason, Princeton	3	2	.600	3.65	12	11	0	0	0	0	56.2	62	251	32	23	2	1	0	7	16	0	55	5	0
Chacin, Steward, Johnson City	0	0	.000	6.75	4	0	0	0	3	0	2.2	5	13	3	2	1	0	0	0	1	0	3	0	0
Chamberlin, Bryce, Bluefield	0	0	.000	5.40	2	2	0	0	0	0	5.0	4	22	3	3	0	0	1	1	3	0	6	3	0
Childress, Dustin, Kingsport *	1	5	.167	6.98	16	6	0	0	1	0	40.0	50	183	34	31	3	4	5	2	17	2	34	1	0
Cho, Jung Ji, Danville	4	2	.667	0.94	7	3	0	0	1	0	28.2	22	110	4	3	0	0	1	0	6	0	35	3	1
Cortes, Daniel, Bristol	1	4	.200	5.17	15	7	0	0	3	0	38.1	44	171	23	22	2	0	2	4	13	1	38	3	0
Cortez, Martin, Bristol *	1	1	.500	6.35	17	1	0	0	6	0	28.1	36	134	24	20	5	1	1	3	10	2	26	3	1
Cruz, Wilander, Burlington	2	1	.667	4.88	15	0	0	0	5	0	24.0	24	109	17	13	3	1	0	3	11	0	22	1	0
Cuevas, Jairo, Danville	6	1	.857	1.95	12	10	0	0	0	0	55.1	35	220	20	12	3	1	2	1	22	0	69	3	1
Day, Timothy, Bristol	4	0	1.000	3.16	17	0	0	0	12	3	31.1	27	127	14	11	3	1	0	2	6	1	33	1	0
De La Rosa, Jose, Johnson City	0	1	.000	8.20	15	0	0	0	7	0	18.2	26	93	21	17	4	0	0	1	8	0	10	1	0
Delgadillo, Hector, Pulaski	5	3	.625	3.55	18	5	0	0	3	1	50.2	54	213	27	20	8	1	0	5	9	0	49	7	0
Demme, Asher, Danville	1	0	1.000	3.76	12	8	0	0	3	2	52.2	48	217	30	22	3	4	3	5	18	1	35	3	0
DeNaball, Fernando, Bluefield	2	3	.400	6.41	14	12	0	0	0	0	53.1	56	254	42	38	9	3	1	4	38	0	59	8	0
Dixon, Ryan, Johnson City	1	2	.333	2.81	15	2	0	0	2	0	25.2	21	114	10	8	3	2	0	2	16	0	23	5	0
Duensing, Brian, Elizabethton *	4	3	.571	2.32	12	9	0	0	0	0	50.1	49	214	19	13	4	1	1	0	16	0	55	6	0
Dupas, Gregory, Princeton	3	1	.750	3.55	14	3	0	0	1	0	38.0	38	165	24	15	3	1	1	2	13	0	27	5	1
Eberhardt, Peter, Pulaski	0	0	.000	0.90	6	0	0	0	3	1	10.0	6	38	1	1	0	0	0	0	2	0	8	0	0
Eichelberger, Jared, Kingsport	0	1	.000	5.96	17	1	0	0	4	0	25.2	30	136	24	17	5	0	2	9	17	3	18	2	1
Erbe, Brandon, Bluefield	1	1	.500	3.09	11	3	0	0	1	1	23.1	8	92	10	8	1	0	0	4	10	0	48	1	0
Evans, Raleigh, Bristol *	0	1	.000	3.38	13	0	0	0	4	1	21.1	25	90	10	8	3	1	0	0	3	1	17	2	1
Falk, Matthew, Princeton	1	1	.500	3.65	6	1	0	0	0	0	12.1	8	51	6	5	1	0	0	1	6	0	14	1	0
Falkenbach, Thomas, Pulaski	1	0	1.000	1.38	10	0	0	0	8	2	13.0	13	54	4	2	0	1	0	1	2	0	10	2	0
Farrell, Jarrod, Princeton	4	3	.571	3.23	16	0	0	0	1	0	39.0	47	169	17	14	3	1	1	5	5	0	26	0	0
Findlay, Robert, Princeton	3	1	.750	1.88	22	0	0	0	21	15	24.0	15	94	5	5	0	1	1	0	7	0	34	5	0
Fines, Donald, Princeton	2	3	.400	5.29	11	6	0	0	1	0	32.1	40	149	29	19	4	0	1	1	11	0	29	1	0
Finocchi, Michael, Burlington	0	2	.000	3.14	18	0	0	0	9	1	28.2	32	123	15	10	0	2	0	1	5	1	22	1	0
Fitzgerald, Kevin, Johnson City	2	4	.333	8.04	26	0	0	0	18	12	28.0	37	130	26	25	5	0	3	1	7	0	21	1	0
Foster, Matthew, Pulaski *	0	0	.000	2.45	2	0	0	0	0	0	3.2	4	18	5	1	0	1	0	0	5	0	0	1	0
Frias, Jusef, Kingsport	1	5	.167	6.99	13	13	0	0	0	0	55.1	70	267	44	43	3	2	6	11	24	0	43	7	1
Frontz, Neal, Princeton	1	4	.200	3.83	14	10	0	0	1	0	47.0	59	215	34	20	7	1	1	6	12	0	42	0	0
Furrow, Jason, Bluefield *	0	1	.000	8.56	15	0	0	0	6	0	27.1	51	134	29	26	6	0	2	2	5	0	21	2	1
Gabino, Armando, Elizabethton	1	2	.333	8.10	17	3	0	0	1	0	30.0	45	151	28	27	7	1	0	6	12	0	23	7	0
Garceau, Shaun, Johnson City	2	7	.222	7.66	12	12	1	1	0	0	44.2	55	212	47	38	7	1	0	3	23	0	42	4	1
Garza, Matthew, Elizabethton	1	1	.500	3.66	4	4	0	0	0	0	19.2	14	77	10	8	3	1	0	1	6	0	25	2	0
Gault, Joe, Elizabethton	2	0	1.000	5.94	15	0	0	0	8	0	16.2	17	74	11	11	2	1	2	3	6	0	8	9	0
Gehring, Ryan, Elizabethton *	1	0	1.000	3.00	17	0	0	0	7	0	30.0	23	126	11	10	3	1	1	1	16	0	31	0	0
Gonzalez, Jose, Kingsport	2	4	.333	7.13	13	12	0	0	0	0	53.0	62	251	49	42	6	0	5	7	29	0	35	9	1
Gonzalez, Reidier, Pulaski	2	0	1.000	1.63	7	6	0	0	0	0	27.2	26	115	9	5	0	1	0	2	6	0	24	1	0
Grijalva, Jonathon, Pulaski	0	1	.000	3.77	7	0	0	0	2	0	14.1	14	57	7	6	2	0	0	0	2	0	18	0	1
Guerrero, Alberto, Johnson City	2	0	1.000	9.22	17	0	0	0	3	0	27.1	49	144	32	28	1	0	0	2	12	0	26	3	0
Gustavo, Luis, Bluefield	2	4	.333	11.16	14	7	0	0	2	0	25.0	34	133	37	31	2	0	3	1	22	2	45	7	0
Gutierrez, Santiago de Jesus, Bristol *	1	0	1.000	4.50	13	0	0	0	7	0	12.0	10	57	8	6	1	0	0	1	6	1	3	1	1
Hahn, Cory, Pulaski	2	1	.667	1.41	18	0	0	0	8	0	32.0	24	132	11	5	1	0	2	2	10	0	38	6	0
Hanson, Mark, Burlington	1	2	.333	4.94	5	2	0	0	0	0	23.2	32	108	16	13	2	2	0	7	3	0	16	2	0
Harrington, Jake, Kingsport	1	0	1.000	7.20	6	0	0	0	1	0	10.0	18	52	12	8	0	0	0	2	5	0	6	2	0
Harris, Joshua, Burlington	1	4	.200	10.80	16	0	0	0	11	0	20.0	36	112	32	24	5	1	0	1	13	0	15	7	0
Harrison, Benjamin, Pulaski *	3	1	.750	3.82	19	0	0	0	8	2	35.1	30	148	17	15	1	0	2	0	6	0	45	3	0
Hawes, Adam, Elizabethton	4	0	1.000	1.53	14	9	1	1	3	1	59.0	38	229	13	10	2	1	2	3	16	0	68	4	0
Heil, Ryan, Kingsport	4	4	.500	4.44	19	0	0	0	8	3	26.1	35	123	21	13	1	1	2	1	7	0	17	4	0
Hellickson, Jeremy, Princeton	0	0	.000	6.00	4	0	0	0	1	0	6.0	6	27	4	4	1	0	0	1	1	0	11	0	0
Hendricks, Donavon, Danville *	1	2	.333	6.99	17	0	0	0	6	0	28.1	41	133	27	22	3	0	1	2	13	0	25	1	0
Herron, Tyler, Johnson City	0	3	.000	5.62	13	13	0	0	0	0	49.2	47	224	35	31	11	0	0	5	27	0	49	2	1
Hicks, Christopher, Burlington *	2	4	.333	4.02	13	13	0	0	0	0	53.2	46	222	31	24	3	1	1	3	21	0	61	4	0
Hooks, Ashley, Johnson City	1	1	.500	5.68	16	0	0	0	2	0	25.1	34	121	21	16	4	1	0	2	8	0	24	2	0
Horner, Mark, Bluefield *	5	6	.455	3.34	18	1	0	0	11	2	35.0	35	151	17	13	3	3	2	1	10	0	30	5	0

Pitcher, Team	W	L	Pct.	ERA	G	GS	CG	ShO	GF	Sv.	IP	H	TBF	R	ER	HR	SH	SF	HB	BB	IBB	SO	WP	Bk.
Jackson, Drew, Danville *	3	1	.750	4.02	12	0	0	0	2	0	15.2	16	68	7	7	0	1	1	0	9	1	13	0	0
Jean, Jacob, Bristol *	3	4	.429	6.56	16	8	0	0	1	1	48.0	63	224	46	35	5	2	3	2	20	2	40	3	0
Johnson, Bryan, Danville *	3	4	.429	2.20	20	0	0	0	11	4	32.2	26	142	15	8	1	1	1	0	17	4	27	5	0
Kelly, Christopher, Princeton	1	1	.500	3.94	16	1	0	0	10	0	16.0	18	77	11	7	0	3	1	2	10	0	14	1	0
Kite, Josh, Burlington *	0	0	.000	0.82	9	0	0	0	5	0	11.0	8	46	2	1	0	0	0	0	7	0	11	0	0
Koons, David, Kingsport	4	2	.667	3.46	24	0	0	0	11	2	39.0	38	163	15	15	2	3	0	2	9	2	25	3	0
Lahey, Timothy, Elizabethton	0	1	.000	3.55	26	0	0	0	26	15	25.1	21	111	13	10	0	0	1	3	8	1	30	1	0
Lane, Matthew, Johnson City	2	6	.250	5.37	13	13	0	0	0	0	55.1	68	255	40	33	7	0	0	1	22	1	51	7	0
Leach, Tyler, Johnson City	3	3	.500	6.31	10	8	0	0	0	0	35.2	47	167	32	25	5	2	0	3	13	0	29	4	1
Limas, Alejandro, Princeton	0	0	.000	4.88	13	0	0	0	3	0	27.2	22	118	19	15	8	1	1	1	14	0	26	6	1
Litsch, Jesse, Pulaski	5	1	.833	2.74	11	11	0	0	0	0	65.2	51	255	22	20	6	0	0	4	10	0	67	2	1
Lonsberry, Daniel, Bluefield	0	1	.000	2.25	20	1	0	0	11	7	32.0	28	137	11	8	2	0	3	2	11	2	40	3	0
Lubrano, Paul, Burlington *	2	1	.667	1.91	16	1	0	0	7	1	33.0	19	120	8	7	2	0	1	2	6	0	31	3	0
Marte, German, Kingsport	3	2	.600	2.91	21	3	0	0	15	4	43.1	29	166	16	14	1	1	0	1	12	1	53	2	0
Mateo, Francisco, Pulaski *	1	7	.125	5.14	12	12	0	0	0	0	56.0	72	256	41	32	9	0	3	1	21	0	38	5	1
Meacham, Cory, Johnson City	0	0	.000	9.00	2	0	0	0	0	0	2.0	4	11	2	2	1	0	0	0	1	0	2	0	0
Mercedes, Gerson, Burlington	2	2	.500	3.13	16	0	0	0	5	2	37.1	35	149	14	13	2	1	0	1	4	0	38	1	0
Mikrut, Jon, Johnson City	0	0	.000	0.00	2	0	0	0	0	0	3.0	1	11	0	0	0	0	0	0	0	0	5	0	0
Minor, Zachary, Bluefield *	0	0	.000	9.72	8	0	0	0	5	0	8.1	13	51	9	9	3	0	0	2	11	0	8	3	0
Montero, Joanniel, Burlington	0	3	.000	12.86	4	4	0	0	0	0	14.0	26	72	22	20	5	1	2	0	8	0	5	2	0
Moore, Jeffrey, Bluefield	1	2	.333	2.08	17	2	0	0	4	1	43.1	39	182	14	10	2	1	0	8	8	1	52	7	0
Morffe, Edgar, Burlington	0	0	.000	19.80	4	0	0	0	0	0	5.0	10	32	11	11	3	0	1	1	4	0	6	0	0
Morlan, Eduardo, Elizabethton	2	0	1.000	0.82	4	4	0	0	0	0	22.0	6	81	2	2	0	1	0	4	6	0	30	3	0
Morse, Ryan, Elizabethton	0	1	.000	5.24	12	3	0	0	0	0	22.1	27	106	14	13	1	1	4	1	12	0	18	3	1
Mullins, Ryan, Elizabethton *	3	0	1.000	2.18	11	11	0	0	0	0	53.2	34	203	16	13	4	1	1	2	13	0	60	4	0
Muro, Joseph, Princeton	0	0	.000	8.04	14	0	0	0	3	0	15.2	21	86	15	14	2	0	0	3	18	0	22	11	0
Nagy, Brett, Princeton	2	1	.667	2.59	18	0	0	0	6	1	24.1	20	99	10	7	2	2	1	2	9	1	20	2	0
Navaroli, Michael, Princeton	0	1	.000	2.25	6	0	0	0	3	0	8.0	4	29	2	2	1	0	0	0	1	0	5	0	0
Nix, Michael, Danville	1	0	1.000	0.00	5	0	0	0	4	0	6.0	1	21	0	0	0	0	0	0	2	0	11	0	0
Oakes, Gerard, Danville	0	0	.000	18.00	2	0	0	0	0	0	2.0	3	12	4	4	0	0	0	1	3	0	3	2	0
Parish, Brian, Johnson City	0	1	.000	23.62	4	0	0	0	1	0	2.2	8	19	10	7	1	1	0	1	2	0	1	2	0
Pendarvis, Chad, Princeton *	1	3	.250	6.75	11	3	0	0	3	0	16.0	21	72	13	12	3	0	1	0	5	0	12	0	0
Perdomo, Javier, Kingsport	1	1	.500	6.69	22	0	0	0	7	0	39.0	56	190	34	29	5	0	3	3	15	1	19	1	0
Perez, Rafael, Pulaski *	2	1	.667	6.66	18	0	0	0	6	2	25.2	26	125	21	19	2	2	0	3	23	0	27	3	2
Perez, Wilfrido, Bluefield *	3	4	.429	3.26	12	12	0	0	0	0	58.0	54	252	30	21	4	2	0	2	27	1	75	5	0
Phillips, David, Johnson City	1	0	1.000	5.02	12	0	0	0	4	1	14.1	17	69	12	8	0	0	0	1	8	0	19	4	0
Pino, Yohan, Elizabethton	9	2	.818	3.72	12	12	1	0	0	0	67.2	68	283	31	28	3	0	1	2	13	0	64	3	0
Pinto, Julio, Burlington	3	0	1.000	2.52	16	0	0	0	5	0	39.1	27	152	12	11	2	1	0	5	7	0	38	2	0
Powell, John, Johnson City	3	3	.500	6.87	12	3	0	0	1	0	38.0	40	184	40	29	5	0	2	5	24	0	27	3	0
Powers, Daniel, Elizabethton	3	3	.500	2.53	22	0	0	0	10	4	42.2	30	175	18	12	1	2	2	1	20	1	47	6	0
Pry, Jeffrey, Burlington	1	1	.500	5.87	15	0	0	0	7	0	23.0	28	109	15	15	4	2	0	0	14	1	24	2	0
Pudewell, Nathanial, Danville	1	1	.500	12.15	3	1	0	0	0	0	6.2	13	32	10	9	2	0	0	0	0	0	3	0	0
Quaglieri, William, Kingsport	0	0	.000	0.00	1	0	0	0	0	0	2.0	1	9	1	0	0	0	0	0	0	0	1	0	0
Quinonez, Rudolph, Danville	1	0	1.000	2.60	24	0	0	0	20	10	27.2	17	108	11	8	5	1	0	0	8	1	40	5	0
Reinoso, Ezemir, Pulaski	2	1	.667	5.20	17	0	0	0	3	0	27.2	35	125	18	16	4	0	1	2	10	0	20	1	0
Reyes, Joseph, Danville *	3	0	1.000	3.53	9	8	0	0	0	0	43.1	37	169	18	17	3	1	1	0	6	0	27	2	1
Rice, Jason, Bristol	3	2	.600	4.70	18	7	0	0	3	0	44.0	40	194	23	23	2	2	0	3	25	0	40	1	0
Richards, Glen, Danville *	1	0	1.000	1.93	10	0	0	0	3	0	14.0	7	54	4	3	0	0	0	0	5	0	15	2	0
Riera, Jorge, Burlington	3	2	.600	3.10	13	6	0	0	1	0	52.1	45	214	21	18	2	0	2	3	19	0	38	7	0
Rivas, Carlos, Danville *	4	1	.800	4.24	13	10	0	0	1	1	51.0	49	221	28	24	7	0	2	1	25	0	33	6	0
Rodriguez, Derek, Bristol	1	3	.250	3.82	11	6	0	0	3	0	35.1	35	148	19	15	2	0	0	4	7	1	36	2	0
Rosario, Eduardo, Danville *	1	1	.500	3.38	11	2	0	0	0	0	29.1	33	135	13	11	1	1	1	2	20	0	26	7	2
Rulon, Benjamin, Princeton *	2	2	.500	5.33	8	5	0	0	0	0	25.1	34	116	16	15	0	1	2	2	7	0	24	3	0
Russell, Stephen, Danville	1	1	.500	4.05	2	1	0	0	0	0	6.2	7	28	3	3	1	0	0	0	2	0	5	1	0
Sabo, Timothy, Bristol	3	2	.600	3.38	16	0	0	0	4	2	29.1	24	129	14	11	0	1	1	1	18	1	33	5	0
Sadlowski, Kyle, Johnson City	1	1	.500	2.35	3	0	0	0	2	1	7.2	4	31	4	2	0	1	0	0	3	1	6	0	0
Sanchez, Ramon, Bristol	0	0	.000	3.00	2	2	0	0	0	0	9.0	10	42	5	3	1	1	1	2	2	0	9	1	0
Sanchez, Raymon, Pulaski *	0	2	.000	7.23	16	0	0	0	5	2	23.2	25	115	24	19	6	2	0	2	19	0	21	6	0
Santiago, Jose, Danville	0	0	.000	8.22	8	0	0	0	2	0	7.2	11	42	7	7	1	0	0	0	8	0	13	4	0
Schindling, Andrew, Bluefield	1	0	1.000	5.06	15	0	0	0	5	1	26.2	26	124	21	15	2	0	0	4	23	1	16	0	0
Schmidt, Kyle, Bluefield	5	3	.625	4.50	13	13	0	0	0	0	70.0	77	314	37	35	6	1	0	6	26	0	76	8	0
Schutt, Jason, Burlington	2	7	.222	6.53	12	11	1	0	0	0	51.0	73	230	45	37	11	0	1	2	9	0	27	2	0
Schwartz, Josh, Johnson City *	2	0	1.000	4.24	24	0	0	0	4	0	34.0	30	152	16	16	2	0	2	8	11	0	28	4	0
Serfass, Joseph, Kingsport	1	0	1.000	0.00	7	0	0	0	5	3	12.2	6	45	2	0	0	0	0	1	1	0	10	1	0
Simmons, Jeramy, Kingsport	1	5	.167	4.26	13	12	0	0	0	0	57.0	58	247	39	27	5	1	2	1	15	0	47	8	0
Slowey, Kevin, Elizabethton	0	0	.000	1.17	4	0	0	0	2	1	7.2	2	25	1	1	1	0	0	0	0	0	15	0	0
Smit, Alexander, Elizabethton *	6	1	.857	1.97	21	0	0	0	7	3	45.2	25	173	12	10	3	0	1	1	12	0	86	7	1
Smith, Carlton, Burlington	0	2	.000	4.76	9	9	0	0	0	0	28.1	30	124	16	15	3	0	1	3	5	0	25	1	0
Soriano, Alexander, Johnson City *	0	0	.000	9.64	5	0	0	0	1	0	4.2	8	27	7	5	2	0	0	2	3	0	7	1	0
Soriano, Julio, Bluefield	2	3	.400	4.46	12	3	0	0	2	0	34.1	31	160	23	17	0	2	2	6	23	0	44	4	0
Sosa, Oswaldo, Elizabethton	6	5	.545	4.95	12	11	0	0	0	0	56.1	59	244	37	31	4	1	0	0	21	0	40	10	1
Soto, Jesus, Burlington	0	0	.000	3.00	6	0	0	0	4	0	6.0	6	26	4	2	2	0	0	1	2	0	8	0	0
Spoone, Chorye, Bluefield	2	5	.286	8.03	15	3	0	0	6	0	24.2	27	116	25	22	3	0	2	2	13	0	27	11	1
Squires, Steven, Bristol	1	0	1.000	9.95	17	0	0	0	7	0	19.0	29	95	21	21	5	0	0	8	4	1	14	1	1
Stadanlick, Ryan, Bluefield	3	0	1.000	2.25	12	1	0	0	4	1	24.0	14	109	9	6	1	1	0	4	18	2	19	7	1
Stanley, Adam, Danville *	1	0	1.000	5.79	4	0	0	0	0	0	9.1	12	44	7	6	0	0	1	1	3	0	8	1	0
Storey, Timothy, Burlington *	1	4	.200	6.41	13	9	0	0	1	0	39.1	47	186	36	28	2	1	2	7	18	0	30	4	1
Sullivan, Daniel, Princeton	0	0	.000	3.46	11	0	0	0	5	0	13.0	8	54	6	5	2	1	0	0	8	1	18	0	0
Tisone, Nicholas, Danville	4	1	.800	3.05	17	3	0	0	4	2	38.1	38	157	17	13	1	1	0	1	7	0	30	3	0
Vais, Daniel, Elizabethton	6	1	.857	3.13	13	4	0	0	1	0	40.0	42	166	24	22	5	0	1	1	5	0	30	1	0
Valdez, Luis, Burlington	3	6	.333	3.54	13	13	1	0	0	0	61.0	64	254	31	24	8	1	3	3	12	0	59	5	0
Vargas, Albert, Burlington	2	0	1.000	1.42	10	0	0	0	6	0	19.0	15	75	5	3	0	1	1	1	4	0	16	3	1

ADVANCED ROOKIE *Appalachian League*

Pitcher, Team	W	L	Pct.	ERA	G	GS	CG	ShO	GF	Sv.	IP	H	TBF	R	ER	HR	SH	SF	HB	BB	IBB	SO	WP	Bk.
Viola, Frank, Bristol	5	2	.714	3.84	13	12	0	0	0	0	70.1	74	307	35	30	2	3	3	8	20	1	59	3	0
Walker, Matthew, Princeton	2	3	.400	5.31	13	12	0	0	1	1	57.2	63	257	39	34	2	1	4	1	22	0	71	8	0
Walters, Nichols, Bristol *	2	5	.286	3.44	20	0	0	0	3	1	34.0	34	142	23	13	6	2	0	1	8	2	26	1	1
Weagle, Matthew, Johnson City	1	3	.250	7.00	18	4	0	0	8	3	36.0	52	170	34	28	3	1	3	1	12	0	34	6	0
Wice, Joseph, Pulaski *	1	4	.200	5.40	10	10	0	0	0	0	45.0	55	191	37	27	15	0	2	1	10	0	35	2	2
Wiggins, Johnnie, Danville *	1	1	.500	10.00	5	1	0	0	0	0	9.0	10	45	10	10	1	0	0	1	8	0	6	2	0
Williamson, Logan, Bristol *	3	7	.300	5.03	13	12	0	0	1	1	59.0	64	269	41	33	6	0	5	21	1	60	3	0	
Wilson, Joshua, Johnson City	2	2	.500	4.22	12	12	0	0	0	0	53.1	49	227	37	25	7	1	3	5	23	0	32	3	0
Winn, Joseph, Bristol	2	2	.500	4.50	18	5	0	0	6	1	48.0	55	208	29	24	5	1	4	4	11	1	32	0	4
Wladyka, James, Kingsport	2	2	.500	1.98	18	3	0	0	5	0	50.0	47	212	22	11	5	1	4	1	18	1	40	4	0
Wlodarczyk, Michael, Princeton *	3	2	.600	2.54	10	10	1	1	0	0	49.2	45	200	18	14	3	0	1	5	7	0	50	4	0
Woodson, Alexander, Bristol *	1	0	1.000	2.55	16	0	0	0	6	3	24.2	23	98	8	7	1	2	1	3	5	2	21	5	0

COMBINATION SHUTOUTS: Bluefield (3) -- Perez-Schindling, Schmidt-Stadanlick, Erbe-Horner. Bristol (3) -- Viola-Williamson, Williamson-Jean, Winn-Woodson. Burlington (3) -- Hicks-Cruz-Lubrano-Mercedes, Valdez-Storey, Schutt-Pry-Cruz. Danville (4) -- Cuevas-Anderson, Rivas-Cho-Nix, Reyes-Anderson-Quinonez, Cho-Rivas. Elizabethton (7) -- Morlan-Lahey, Mullins-Duensing-Smit-Lahey, Garza-Hawes-Duensing-Lahey, Sosa-Smit, Duensing-Powers, Mullins-Smit, Duensing-Gault-Sosa-Gehring. Greeneville (5) -- James-Gervacio, Mitchell-Bass-Campos, Hirsh-Noel, Mitchell-Trinidad-Gervacio, James-Campos. Princeton (2) -- Rulon-Falk-Nagy-Findlay, Dupas-Muro-Hellickson-Pendarvis. Pulaski (2) -- Gonzalez-Sanchez-Byrnes, Delgadillo-Harrison-Eberhardt.

2005 FIELDING

TEAM

Team	G	PO	A	E	TC	DP	TP	PB	Pct.
Danville	67	1802	715	78	2595	67	0	18	.970
Elizabethton	67	1700	649	77	2426	44	0	12	.968
Burlington	68	1709	713	99	2521	74	0	19	.961
Pulaski	67	1758	772	102	2632	73	0	14	.961
Greeneville	66	1706	647	103	2456	43	0	23	.958
Johnson City	67	1679	701	108	2488	66	0	31	.957
Princeton	65	1676	695	117	2488	52	0	17	.953
Bluefield	67	1694	615	116	2425	52	0	30	.952
Bristol	66	1723	739	123	2585	51	0	15	.952
Kingsport	68	1752	718	127	2597	57	0	15	.951

INDIVIDUAL

FIRST BASEMEN

NOTE: All caps denotes fielding-percentage leader based on 34 games for catchers, 45 for all other non-pitchers and 54 innings for pitchers. *Throws lefthanded.

Player, Team	Pct.	G	PO	A	E	TC	DP
Bensko, Dustin, Elizabethton	.989	32	257	11	3	271	21
Carter, Charles, Johnson City	.991	15	102	7	1	110	14
Carter, Vernon, Bristol	.986	20	191	13	3	207	18
Chacin, Steward, Johnson City	1.000	13	58	3	0	61	3
Chmiel, Paul, Bluefield	.993	20	140	6	1	147	8
Clark, John, Burlington	.972	21	165	9	5	179	19
Combs, Weldon, Bristol	1.000	2	11	1	0	12	1
Desmond, Geoffrey, Johnson City	.989	35	243	15	3	261	22
Evans, Nicholas, Kingsport	1.000	11	116	7	0	123	7
Fields, Matthew, Princeton	.984	38	283	25	5	313	25
Franko, Paul, Pulaski	.989	38	352	14	4	370	31
Guerra, Junior, Danville	.909	2	7	3	1	11	2
Hatch, Anthony, Pulaski	.994	19	156	10	1	167	18
Hiser, Charles, Burlington	.987	34	285	13	4	302	31
Holmes, Justin, Burlington	1.000	1	10	1	0	11	2
Kaaihue, Isaiah, Danville	.973	5	34	2	1	37	5
Kotch, Kevin, Bluefield	.962	7	47	4	2	53	5
Lis, Erik, Elizabethton *	.991	41	324	18	3	345	21
Looze, Christopher, Pulaski *	1.000	16	123	8	0	131	16
Morgan, Joshua, Bristol	.995	45	388	22	2	412	27
Oliveros, Riky, Kingsport	.978	28	212	8	5	225	16
Pacheco, Joel, Bluefield	.979	32	226	12	5	243	25
Puente, Juan, Bluefield	.938	3	13	2	1	16	1
Roberts, Jordan, Bristol	.982	15	106	1	2	109	13
RODRIGUEZ, MANUEL, Danville *	.985	65	542	39	9	589	49
Royster, Ryan, Princeton	.895	4	15	2	2	19	1
Santos, Jose, Danville	1.000	1	1	0	0	1	1
Shafer, Dustin, Bristol	.960	4	24	0	1	25	1
Skorupski, John, Johnson City	.980	13	96	4	2	102	10
Van Slyke, A.J., Johnson City	.989	10	85	3	1	89	7
Wabick, David, Kingsport	1.000	33	264	6	0	270	21
Wiens, Logan, Princeton	.996	29	248	16	1	265	21
Winterling, Paul, Bluefield	.980	13	47	1	1	49	3

SECOND BASEMEN

Player, Team	Pct.	G	PO	A	E	TC	DP
Abreu, Miguel, Bluefield	.943	23	34	32	4	70	8
Acosta, Christian, Bristol	.957	11	19	26	2	47	3

Player, Team	Pct.	G	PO	A	E	TC	DP
Aqueron, Rene, Bluefield	1.000	9	11	19	0	30	5
Arnal, Cristo, Burlington	.980	41	84	114	4	202	33
Arnold, William, Danville	.947	5	6	12	1	19	4
Badger, Graig, Bluefield	.970	28	55	76	4	135	19
Batista, Franklin, Bristol	.918	25	26	41	6	73	8
Bethel, Ryan, Princeton	.968	15	21	39	2	62	4
Castro, Kevin, Kingsport	.966	6	13	15	1	29	4
Chacin, Steward, Johnson City	.983	17	27	31	1	59	11
Colon, Kevin, Princeton	.833	2	2	3	1	6	0
Garcia, Julio Cesar, Burlington	1.000	8	14	18	0	32	6
Gardenhire, Toby, Elizabethton	.955	12	14	28	2	44	3
Garner, Brandon, Johnson City	.927	18	35	41	6	82	8
Gutierrez, Christopher, Pulaski	1.000	3	3	8	0	11	1
Henry, Sean, Kingsport	.925	23	46	53	8	107	13
Holmes, Justin, Burlington	.875	6	2	12	2	16	1
Kalin, Travis, Elizabethton	.940	11	15	32	3	50	8
Kitch, Denver, Bluefield	1.000	1	0	2	0	2	0
Lopez, Christian, Johnson City	.914	20	18	35	5	58	11
Manuel, Anthony, Kingsport	.951	30	51	86	7	144	11
Martinez, Jose, Johnson City	.953	34	44	78	6	128	20
Matthews, William, Princeton	.953	14	15	26	2	43	7
Musselwhite, Stuart, Bluefield	.900	3	3	6	1	10	1
Picornell, Carlos, Danville	.960	5	13	11	1	25	3
Portes, Juan, Elizabethton	.955	43	64	126	9	199	19
Romero, Niuman, Burlington	.964	16	41	39	3	83	11
Santana, Yury, Kingsport	.750	1	1	2	1	4	0
Santos, Jose, Danville	.960	36	66	100	7	173	27
Shafer, Dustin, Bristol	1.000	3	3	3	0	6	0
Solano, Donovan, Johnson City	.875	3	3	4	1	8	0
Stone, Wesley, Pulaski	.948	38	65	117	10	192	23
Suero, Ovandy, Danville	.939	26	33	60	6	99	10
Swain, Michael, Bristol	.943	47	70	111	11	192	26
Tavares, Reymundo, Bristol	1.000	3	2	1	0	3	0
Tolleson, Steven, Elizabethton	1.000	1	1	0	0	1	0
TUCKER, JONATHAN, Bluefield	.947	48	79	101	10	190	24
Vick, Hunter, Princeton	.974	43	83	107	5	195	26
Werman, Kyle, Kingsport	.981	11	28	24	1	53	3
Winterling, Paul, Bluefield	...	1	0	0	0	0	0

THIRD BASEMEN

Player, Team	Pct.	G	PO	A	E	TC	DP
Acosta, Christian, Bristol	.863	29	13	75	14	102	5
Acosta, Leonardo, Bristol	1.000	2	0	4	0	4	0
Anderson, Matthew, Kingsport	.899	46	25	91	13	129	3
Aqueron, Rene, Bluefield	.870	30	13	34	7	54	0
Arnold, William, Danville	.909	4	1	9	1	11	1
Badger, Graig, Pulaski	.848	13	7	21	5	33	1
Batista, Franklin, Bristol	1.000	2	0	3	0	3	1
Bethel, Ryan, Princeton	.792	7	5	14	5	24	3
Betsill, Matthew, Elizabethton	.904	44	24	79	11	114	9
Butler, Jacob, Pulaski	...	1	0	0	0	0	0
CAMPBELL, ERIC, Danville	.938	65	38	114	10	162	12
Carter, Vernon, Bristol	.845	38	14	57	13	84	5
Chacin, Steward, Johnson City	.750	4	1	5	2	8	1
Cunningham, Christopher, Princeton	...	1	0	0	0	0	0
de la Rosa, Jairo, Princeton	.900	14	8	28	4	40	2
Devins, Matthew, Princeton	.911	16	13	28	4	45	3
Gardenhire, Toby, Elizabethton	1.000	7	2	14	0	16	2
Gutierrez, Christopher, Pulaski	.964	10	7	20	1	28	4

Appalachian League

ADVANCED ROOKIE

Player, Team	Pct.	G	PO	A	E	TC	DP
Hatch, Anthony, Pulaski	.857	9	6	12	3	21	2
Holmes, Justin, Burlington	.947	7	4	14	1	19	2
Kalin, Travis, Elizabethton	.833	17	11	29	8	48	1
Kitch, Denver, Bluefield	.857	20	10	32	7	49	0
Lietz, Todd, Kingsport	.900	4	4	5	1	10	2
Lopez, Christian, Johnson City	.750	10	2	7	3	12	0
Manuel, Anthony, Kingsport	1.000	7	4	14	0	18	2
Martinez, Gilberto, Bluefield	...	1	0	0	0	0	0
McCormick, Michael, Princeton	.864	29	16	60	12	88	5
Mikrut, Jon, Johnson City	.970	18	8	24	1	33	3
Morris, Adam, Johnson City	.932	27	19	50	5	74	4
Musslewhite, Stuart, Bluefield	.000	1	0	0	1	1	0
Oliveros, Riky, Kingsport	.889	10	9	15	3	27	2
Petrucci, Nicholas, Burlington	.907	49	35	102	14	151	17
Pickerell, Steven, Princeton	1.000	1	0	1	0	1	0
Romero, Niuman, Burlington	.976	15	8	32	1	41	1
Roth, Randy, Johnson City	.855	21	8	39	8	55	2
Santana, Yury, Kingsport	1.000	6	5	12	0	17	1
Snyder, Brandon, Bluefield	.700	9	3	4	3	10	1
Soto, Leance, Pulaski	.788	41	24	65	24	113	8
Swain, Michael, Bristol	.500	2	1	0	1	2	0
Thiel, Emile, Bluefield	1.000	7	4	4	0	8	1
Tucker, Jonathan, Bluefield	.842	11	9	23	6	38	2

SHORTSTOPS

Player, Team	Pct.	G	PO	A	E	TC	DP
Abreu, Miguel, Bluefield	.800	3	4	4	2	10	1
Acosta, Christian, Bristol	.866	17	18	40	9	67	3
Acosta, Leonardo, Bristol	.919	54	68	160	20	248	29
Andrus, Elvis, Danville	1.000	5	9	11	0	20	2
Arnold, William, Danville	.952	43	73	143	11	227	28
Badger, Graig, Pulaski	.909	2	4	6	1	11	2
Barksdale, James, Danville	1.000	1	1	0	0	1	0
Batista, Franklin, Bristol	.600	11	1	8	6	15	2
Bethel, Ryan, Princeton	.968	7	9	21	1	31	3
Carter, Vernon, Bristol	1.000	1	1	0	0	1	0
Chacin, Steward, Johnson City	1.000	3	2	1	0	3	1
Chavez, Jose, Burlington	.939	8	8	23	2	33	1
Colon, Kevin, Princeton	.915	28	42	77	11	130	13
Coronado, Jose, Kingsport	.898	39	45	122	19	186	21
Devins, Matthew, Princeton	.921	34	38	90	11	139	16
Escobar, Yunel, Danville	.911	8	14	27	4	45	6
Garcia, Julio Cesar, Burlington	.926	8	7	18	2	27	1
Gardenhire, Toby, Elizabethton	.938	9	9	21	2	32	2
Garner, Brandon, Johnson City	.769	15	10	20	9	39	4
Gonzalez, Jesus, Pulaski	.939	43	45	155	13	213	22
Gutierrez, Christopher, Pulaski	.964	22	28	79	4	111	19
Henry, Sean, Kingsport	.920	19	35	57	8	100	9
Holmes, Justin, Burlington	1.000	1	0	1	0	1	0
Infante, Jansy, Burlington	.917	33	49	105	14	168	17
Kitch, Denver, Bluefield	.959	14	23	47	3	73	8
Lietz, Todd, Kingsport	.806	7	10	19	7	36	5
Lopez, Christian, Johnson City	1.000	1	1	1	0	2	1
Martinez, Jose, Johnson City	.972	23	30	74	3	107	13
Musslewhite, Stuart, Bluefield	.917	50	51	137	17	205	29
ORTIZ, YANCARLOS, Elizabethton	.972	47	59	116	5	180	20
Romero, Niuman, Burlington	.962	22	35	66	4	105	21
Santana, Yury, Kingsport	1.000	7	10	17	0	27	3
Santos, Jose, Danville	.938	14	23	53	5	81	8
Shafer, Dustin, Bristol	...	1	0	0	0	0	0
Solano, Donovan, Johnson City	.919	44	55	126	16	197	32
Swain, Michael, Bristol	1.000	2	0	1	0	1	0
Tolleson, Steven, Elizabethton	.918	11	15	30	4	49	6
Tucker, Jonathan, Bluefield	1.000	4	7	11	0	18	2
Vick, Hunter, Princeton	1.000	2	2	4	0	6	0

OUTFIELDERS

Player, Team	Pct.	G	PO	A	E	TC	DP
Abreu, Miguel, Bluefield	.920	19	22	1	2	25	0
Aguilar, Heliezer, Pulaski	.920	39	41	5	4	50	0
Anderson, Bryan, Johnson City	...	1	0	0	0	0	0
Andrews, Robert, Bluefield	.947	23	35	1	2	38	0
Aqueron, Rene, Bluefield	1.000	1	3	0	0	3	0
Ard, Alfred, Burlington	.964	46	80	1	3	84	0
Arratia, Jilmer, Elizabethton	1.000	24	22	1	0	23	0
Austin, Parris, Kingsport	.889	13	24	0	3	27	0
Avila, Angel, Bluefield	.964	29	48	5	2	55	2
Badger, Graig, Pulaski	...	1	0	0	0	0	0
Batista, Franklin, Bristol	1.000	1	1	0	0	1	0
Brown, Kyle, Kingsport	1.000	12	22	2	0	24	0

Player, Team	Pct.	G	PO	A	E	TC	DP
BUTLER, JACOB, Pulaski	1.000	51	96	7	0	103	2
Carter, Charles, Johnson City	.970	48	61	3	2	66	0
Causey, Marcos, Bristol	.963	36	49	3	2	54	0
Chacin, Steward, Johnson City	1.000	2	1	0	0	1	0
Cordero, Octavio, Pulaski *	.961	36	71	3	3	77	1
Cruz, Elvis, Kingsport	.875	27	40	2	6	48	2
Cunningham, Aaron, Bristol	.986	52	67	3	1	71	1
Cunningham, Christopher, Princeton	.926	40	45	5	4	54	1
Davis, Quentin, Danville	.979	47	90	3	2	95	1
De Leon, Epifanio, Princeton	.887	44	62	1	8	71	0
De Leon, Evandy, Burlington	1.000	15	15	2	0	17	0
Denham, Jason, Burlington *	.985	43	62	4	1	67	2
Desmond, Geoffrey, Johnson City	...	1	0	0	0	0	0
Drennen, John, Burlington *	.962	50	99	3	4	106	2
Garcia, Santo, Bristol *	1.000	32	49	0	0	49	0
Gonzalez, Gregory, Kingsport *	.988	32	77	2	1	80	0
Howell, Samuel, Bluefield	1.000	9	12	1	0	13	0
Irvin, Blair, Princeton	.833	6	10	0	2	12	0
Jaspe, Jonathan, Pulaski	...	1	0	0	0	0	0
Jones, Brandon, Danville	1.000	2	2	1	0	3	0
Jones, Daryl, Johnson City *	.938	58	70	6	5	81	1
Jones, Larry, Elizabethton	.934	35	52	5	4	61	1
Kalter, Zachary, Pulaski	.956	56	79	8	4	91	1
Lachapel, Alex, Bristol	.875	23	18	3	3	24	0
Land, Joshua, Elizabethton *	1.000	14	10	0	0	10	0
Lis, Erik, Elizabethton *	...	1	0	0	0	0	0
Lopez, Andrew, Princeton	.945	33	51	1	3	55	0
Martinez, Gilberto, Bluefield	.891	42	48	1	6	55	0
Mateo, Jose, Kingsport	.946	34	64	6	4	74	3
Matulia, John, Princeton *	.948	24	53	2	3	58	1
Moffitt, Andrew, Bluefield	.935	20	28	1	2	31	0
Montero, Juan, Kingsport	1.000	19	42	3	0	45	1
Morgan, Joshua, Bristol	.913	13	21	0	2	23	0
Musslewhite, Stuart, Bluefield	...	1	0	0	0	0	0
Ovalle, Edward, Elizabethton	.981	65	98	3	2	103	0
Owens, Malcolm, Johnson City	.880	32	21	1	3	25	0
Owings, John, Danville	.982	31	54	2	1	57	0
Parker, Carnell, Princeton *	1.000	9	13	0	0	13	0
Picornell, Carlos, Danville	.909	8	10	0	1	11	0
Pope, Kieron, Bluefield	.983	36	56	1	1	58	1
Portes, Juan, Elizabethton	1.000	13	11	0	0	11	0
Preston, Timothy, Johnson City	1.000	23	19	1	0	20	0
Pujols, Wilfrido, Johnson City	.778	12	7	0	2	9	0
Rasmus, Colby, Johnson City *	.971	62	128	4	4	136	2
Roberts, Joshua, Burlington	1.000	15	18	1	0	19	0
Robinson, Mark, Elizabethton	.952	57	78	2	4	84	0
Romak, James, Danville	.982	34	51	3	1	55	2
Roth, Randy, Johnson City	1.000	2	3	0	0	3	0
Royster, Ryan, Princeton	.932	46	55	0	4	59	0
Sanchez, Salvador, Bristol	.950	63	110	5	6	121	1
Sandes, Jorge, Pulaski	.846	25	29	4	6	39	0
Shafer, Dustin, Bristol	1.000	12	8	1	0	9	0
Silva, Yohan, Danville	.982	64	156	4	3	163	1
Suero, Ovandy, Danville	1.000	24	37	2	0	39	1
Tavarez, Argenis, Burlington	1.000	1	2	0	0	2	0
Tucker, Jonathan, Bluefield	...	1	0	0	0	0	0
Turner, Clifton, Bluefield	1.000	4	6	1	0	7	0
Vick, Hunter, Princeton	1.000	7	10	1	0	11	0
Weglarz, Nicholas, Burlington *	.932	40	54	1	4	59	0
Wells, Cory, Johnson City	.952	47	93	7	5	105	3
Winterling, Paul, Bluefield	1.000	28	31	3	0	34	2
Wyrick, Joshua, Kingsport *	.927	33	37	1	3	41	1
Yeme, Leonel, Bluefield *	.816	30	31	0	7	38	0

CATCHERS

Player, Team	Pct.	G	PO	A	E	TC	DP
Anderson, Bryan, Johnson City	.989	40	258	19	3	280	1
Barksdale, James, Danville	1.000	2	13	0	0	13	0
Chacin, Steward, Johnson City	1.000	1	1	1	0	2	0
Combs, Weldon, Bristol	1.000	10	34	1	0	35	0
Cummins, Daniel, Kingsport	.929	2	11	2	1	14	1
Gonzalez, Steve, Johnson City	.982	31	203	21	4	228	1
Guerra, Junior, Danville	.987	33	204	19	3	226	2
Huches, Leonardo, Bluefield	.991	29	197	17	2	216	2
Jaspe, Jonathan, Pulaski	.981	42	321	34	7	362	4
Kotch, Kevin, Bluefield	.983	18	168	7	3	178	1
Lagreid, Thomas, Princeton	.984	50	380	38	7	425	2
Lietz, Todd, Kingsport	...	1	0	0	0	0	0
Martinez, Christopher, Pulaski	1.000	14	66	5	0	71	0
Martinez, Joan, Kingsport	.984	25	170	18	3	191	1

Player, Team	Pct.	G	PO	A	E	TC	DP
McCraw, Sean, Kingsport	.983	25	153	23	3	179	8
Moore, Michael, Elizabethton	.993	30	269	12	2	283	1
Nieves, Javier, Pulaski	.875	6	22	6	4	32	1
Palmer, Cody, Johnson City	1.000	4	24	1	0	25	0
Piazza, Thomas, Kingsport	.917	9	49	6	5	60	1
Pickerell, Steven, Princeton	.978	17	77	14	2	93	0
Puente, Juan, Bluefield	1.000	9	53	2	0	55	0
Quintana, Alberto, Danville	.993	16	125	14	1	140	2
Ramirez, Maximiliano, Danville	.996	29	206	16	1	223	2
Regan, Christopher, Princeton	.981	14	90	13	2	105	1
Richardson, Sean, Elizabethton	.985	24	183	14	3	200	0
Roberts, Joshua, Burlington	.965	7	52	3	2	57	0
Santana, Luis, Kingsport	.975	14	71	7	2	80	0
Shehan, Jonathan, Danville	.990	14	92	7	1	100	1
Snyder, Brandon, Bluefield	.995	22	181	21	1	203	0
Spilman, Ryan, Burlington	.979	36	253	26	6	285	3
Tavares, Reymundo, Bristol	.988	30	222	19	3	244	0
Tavarez, Argenis, Burlington	.984	12	60	2	1	63	1
Tintor, Eli, Elizabethton	.970	17	151	11	5	167	1
Vasquez, Enrique, Burlington	.961	24	134	15	6	155	1
Wargo, Cody, Bluefield	1.000	4	31	2	0	33	1
WELKER, KRIS, Bristol	.993	36	262	34	2	298	4

PITCHERS

Player, Team	Pct.	G	PO	A	E	TC	DP
Acosta, Manuel, Danville	1.000	3	1	1	0	2	0
Aguirre, Wilfreddy, Pulaski *	1.000	9	3	4	0	7	1
Anderson, Devin, Danville *	.889	13	1	7	1	9	0
Arizmendi, Daniel, Kingsport *	.750	17	0	6	2	8	0
Baker, Brian, Princeton	.889	17	1	7	1	9	0
Banks, Demetrius, Bristol *	1.000	2	0	1	0	1	0
Barone, Daniel, Johnson City	...	1	0	0	0	0	0
Bastardo, Alberto, Bluefield *	.600	14	0	3	2	5	0
Benson, Shane, Pulaski	.900	16	0	9	1	10	0
Beras, Alexis, Kingsport	1.000	19	3	1	0	4	2
Bigley, Dennis, Pulaski	1.000	16	1	7	0	8	0
Blackford, Todd, Danville	1.000	12	3	8	0	11	0
Borne, James, Johnson City *	.000	15	0	0	1	1	0
Brooks, Richard, Bristol	1.000	5	1	2	0	3	0
Bullock, Tyler, Danville	1.000	14	0	1	0	1	0
Byrnes, Scott, Pulaski	1.000	21	2	4	0	6	0
Camacho, Gustavo, Bluefield	.714	16	2	3	2	7	0
Campbell, Ryan, Johnson City	1.000	20	3	5	0	8	0
Castillo, Jonathan, Kingsport	1.000	11	4	9	0	13	0
Cayton, Jason, Princeton	.750	12	2	4	2	8	0
Chacin, Steward, Johnson City	...	4	0	0	0	0	0
Chamberlin, Bryce, Bluefield	1.000	2	1	0	0	1	0
Childress, Dustin, Kingsport *	1.000	16	0	5	0	5	0
Cho, Jung Ji, Danville	1.000	7	0	4	0	4	1
Cortes, Daniel, Bristol	1.000	15	1	7	0	8	0
Cortez, Martin, Bristol *	.857	17	1	5	1	7	0
Cruz, Wilander, Burlington	.600	15	1	2	2	5	0
Cuevas, Jairo, Danville	.875	12	3	4	1	8	0
Day, Timothy, Bristol	1.000	17	1	12	0	13	2
De La Rosa, Jose, Johnson City	1.000	15	1	4	0	5	1
Delgadillo, Hector, Pulaski	1.000	18	0	7	0	7	1
Demme, Asher, Danville	.923	12	3	9	1	13	0
DeNaball, Fernando, Bluefield	.857	14	1	5	1	7	0
Dixon, Ryan, Johnson City	.833	15	1	4	1	6	0
Duensing, Brian, Elizabethton *	1.000	12	3	12	0	15	0
Dupas, Gregory, Princeton	.600	14	1	2	2	5	1
Eberhardt, Peter, Pulaski	1.000	6	0	2	0	2	0
Eichelberger, Jared, Kingsport	.000	17	0	0	2	2	0
Erbe, Brandon, Bluefield	1.000	11	0	2	0	2	0
Evans, Raleigh, Bristol *	1.000	13	1	3	0	4	0
Falk, Matthew, Princeton	1.000	6	1	2	0	3	0
Falkenbach, Thomas, Pulaski	1.000	10	0	3	0	3	0
Farrell, Jarrod, Princeton	.923	16	3	9	1	13	2
Findlay, Robert, Princeton	.800	22	2	2	1	5	0
Fines, Donald, Princeton	.800	11	2	6	2	10	0
Finocchi, Michael, Burlington	.444	18	0	4	5	9	0
Fitzgerald, Kevin, Johnson City	1.000	26	1	4	0	5	0
Foster, Matthew, Pulaski *	1.000	2	0	3	0	3	0
Frias, Jusef, Kingsport	.833	13	2	13	3	18	0
Frontz, Neal, Princeton	1.000	14	0	8	0	8	0
Furrow, Jason, Bluefield *	1.000	15	1	3	0	4	1
Gabino, Armando, Elizabethton	1.000	17	1	5	0	6	0
Garceau, Shaun, Johnson City	.667	12	1	5	3	9	1
Garza, Matthew, Elizabethton	1.000	4	2	2	0	4	0
Gault, Joe, Elizabethton	.800	15	1	3	1	5	0
Gehring, Ryan, Elizabethton *	.889	17	0	8	1	9	0
Gonzalez, Jose, Kingsport	.889	13	3	5	1	9	0
Gonzalez, Reidier, Pulaski	1.000	7	1	5	0	6	0
Grijalva, Jonathon, Pulaski	1.000	7	2	1	0	3	0
Guerrero, Alberto, Johnson City	1.000	17	3	5	0	8	0
Gustavo, Luis, Bluefield	...	14	0	0	0	0	0
Gutierrez, Santiago de Jesus, Bristol *	1.000	13	0	1	0	1	0
Hahn, Cory, Pulaski	1.000	18	4	8	0	12	2
Hanson, Mark, Burlington	1.000	5	3	6	0	9	0
Harrington, Jake, Kingsport	.667	6	0	2	1	3	0
Harris, Joshua, Burlington	.750	16	1	5	2	8	0
Harrison, Benjamin, Pulaski *	1.000	19	3	2	0	5	0
Hawes, Adam, Elizabethton	.875	14	2	5	1	8	0
Heil, Ryan, Kingsport	.889	19	2	6	1	9	0
Hellickson, Jeremy, Princeton	.500	4	0	1	1	2	0
Hendricks, Donavon, Danville *	1.000	17	2	10	0	12	2
Herron, Tyler, Johnson City	.889	13	3	5	1	9	0
Hicks, Christopher, Burlington *	.909	13	1	9	1	11	0
Hooks, Ashley, Johnson City	1.000	16	6	2	0	8	0
Horner, Mark, Bluefield *	.800	18	0	4	1	5	0
Jackson, Drew, Danville *	1.000	12	1	2	0	3	0
Jean, Jacob, Bristol *	1.000	16	3	5	0	8	0
Johnson, Bryan, Danville *	1.000	20	1	2	0	3	0
Kelly, Christopher, Princeton	1.000	16	1	3	0	4	0
Kite, Josh, Burlington *	1.000	9	0	3	0	3	0
Koons, David, Kingsport	1.000	24	1	10	0	11	0
Lahey, Timothy, Elizabethton	1.000	26	3	9	0	12	1
Lane, Matthew, Johnson City	.889	13	1	7	1	9	0
Leach, Tyler, Johnson City	1.000	10	2	7	0	9	1
Limas, Alejandro, Princeton	.800	13	0	4	1	5	1
Litsch, Jesse, Pulaski	.958	11	11	12	1	24	2
Lonsberry, Daniel, Bluefield	.857	20	3	3	1	7	1
Lubrano, Paul, Burlington *	1.000	16	1	11	0	12	1
Marte, German, Kingsport	.857	21	1	5	1	7	0
MATEO, FRANCISCO, Pulaski *	1.000	12	6	14	0	20	0
Meacham, Cory, Johnson City	...	2	0	0	0	0	0
Mercedes, Gerson, Burlington	.875	16	3	4	1	8	1
Mikrut, Jon, Johnson City	1.000	2	1	1	0	2	0
Minor, Zachary, Bluefield *	...	8	0	0	0	0	0
Montero, Joanniel, Burlington	1.000	4	0	2	0	2	0
Moore, Jeffrey, Bluefield	.750	17	1	5	2	8	0
Morffe, Edgar, Burlington	.000	4	0	0	1	1	0
Morlan, Eduardo, Elizabethton	.714	4	1	4	2	7	0
Morse, Ryan, Princeton *	1.000	12	0	4	0	4	0
Mullins, Ryan, Elizabethton *	1.000	11	4	8	0	12	0
Muro, Andrew, Danville	...	14	0	0	0	0	0
Nagy, Brett, Princeton	.714	18	3	2	2	7	1
Navaroli, Michael, Princeton	1.000	6	3	0	0	3	0
Nix, Michael, Danville	...	5	0	0	0	0	0
Oakes, Gerard, Danville	...	2	0	0	0	0	0
Parish, Brian, Johnson City	1.000	4	0	1	0	1	0
Pendarvis, Chad, Princeton *	1.000	11	1	6	0	7	1
Perdomo, Javier, Kingsport	.889	22	2	6	1	9	3
Perez, Rafael, Pulaski *	.800	18	0	4	1	5	0
Perez, Wilfrido, Bluefield *	.933	12	1	13	1	15	1
Phillips, David, Johnson City	.500	12	1	0	1	2	0
Pino, Yohan, Elizabethton	1.000	12	1	7	0	8	0
Pinto, Julio, Burlington	.923	16	4	8	1	13	1
Powell, John, Johnson City	.917	12	6	5	1	12	0
Powers, Daniel, Elizabethton	.909	22	3	7	1	11	0
Pry, Jeffrey, Burlington	1.000	15	1	1	0	2	0
Pudewell, Nathanial, Danville	1.000	3	0	1	0	1	0
Quaglieri, William, Kingsport	...	1	0	0	0	0	0
Quinonez, Rudolph, Danville	.667	24	0	2	1	3	0
Reinoso, Ezemir, Pulaski	1.000	17	0	2	0	2	1
Reyes, Joseph, Danville *	.857	9	2	4	1	7	0
Rice, Jason, Bristol	.600	18	1	5	4	10	1
Richards, Glen, Danville *	.667	10	0	2	1	3	0
Riera, Jorge, Burlington	1.000	13	4	8	0	12	0
Rivas, Carlos, Danville *	.909	13	4	6	1	11	1
Rodriguez, Derek, Bristol	1.000	11	5	3	0	8	1
Rosario, Eduardo, Danville *	1.000	11	2	7	0	9	0
Rulon, Benjamin, Princeton *	1.000	8	2	8	0	10	0
Russell, Stephen, Danville	...	2	0	0	0	0	0
Sabo, Timothy, Bristol	1.000	16	4	7	0	11	1
Sadlowski, Kyle, Johnson City	1.000	3	0	1	0	1	0
Sanchez, Ramon, Bristol	.500	2	0	1	1	2	0
Sanchez, Raymon, Pulaski *	1.000	16	0	3	0	3	0
Santiago, Jose, Danville	1.000	8	0	1	0	1	0
Schindling, Andrew, Bluefield	.917	15	4	7	1	12	1

Player, Team	Pct.	G	PO	A	E	TC	DP
Schmidt, Kyle, Bluefield	.750	13	2	4	2	8	0
Schutt, Jason, Burlington	1.000	12	5	5	0	10	1
Schwartz, Josh, Johnson City *	.909	24	0	10	1	11	0
Serfass, Joseph, Kingsport	1.000	7	0	4	0	4	0
Simmons, Jeramy, Kingsport	.733	13	3	8	4	15	0
Slowey, Kevin, Elizabethton	1.000	4	0	1	0	1	0
Smit, Alexander, Elizabethton *	.857	21	0	6	1	7	0
Smith, Carlton, Burlington	1.000	9	1	2	0	3	0
Soriano, Alexander, Johnson City *	...	5	0	0	0	0	0
Soriano, Julio, Bluefield	.750	12	0	6	2	8	0
SOSA, OSWALDO, Elizabethton	1.000	12	5	15	0	20	0
Soto, Jesus, Burlington	1.000	6	0	1	0	1	0
Spoone, Chorye, Bluefield	.889	15	2	6	1	9	0
Squires, Steven, Bristol	1.000	17	0	4	0	4	0
Stadanlick, Ryan, Bluefield	.889	12	2	6	1	9	0
Stanley, Adam, Danville *	1.000	4	0	1	0	1	0
Storey, Michael, Burlington *	1.000	13	2	7	0	9	0
Sullivan, Daniel, Princeton	.750	11	1	2	1	4	0
Tisone, Nicholas, Danville	.833	17	3	2	1	6	1
Vais, Daniel, Elizabethton	1.000	13	5	5	0	10	1
Valdez, Luis, Burlington	.857	13	0	6	1	7	0
Vargas, Albert, Burlington	1.000	10	0	3	0	3	0
Viola, Frank, Bristol	.889	13	4	12	2	18	0
Walker, Matthew, Princeton	.800	13	5	3	2	10	0
Walters, Nichols, Bristol *	.750	20	3	12	5	20	0
Weagle, Matthew, Johnson City	1.000	18	0	3	0	3	0
Wice, Joseph, Pulaski	1.000	10	0	5	0	5	0
Wiggins, Johnnie, Danville *	1.000	5	0	1	0	1	0
Williamson, Logan, Bristol *	.818	13	1	8	2	11	0
Wilson, Joshua, Johnson City	.867	12	6	7	2	15	1
Winn, Joseph, Bristol	.929	18	2	11	1	14	0
Wladyka, James, Kingsport	.857	18	0	6	1	7	0
Wlodarczyk, Michael, Princeton *	1.000	10	2	6	0	8	0
Woodson, Alexander, Bristol *	1.000	16	4	5	0	9	0

LEAGUE CHAMPIONS

Year	Team	Pct.
1921—	Greenville	.608
	Johnson City*	.627
1922—	Bristol	.557
1923—	Knoxville	.635
1924—	Knoxville*	.642
	Bristol	.607
1925—	Greenville	.667
1926-36—	Did not operate.	
1937—	Elizabethton	.559
	Pennington Gap*	.580
1938—	Elizabethton	.664
	Greenville (3rd)†	.571
1939—	Elizabethton‡	.597
1940—	Johnson City§	.726
	Elizabethton	.750
1941—	Johnson City	.614
	Elizabethton*	.661
1942—	Bristol	.667
	Bristol∞	.660
1943—	Bristol	.755
	Bristol▲	.617
1944—	Kingsport‡	.575
1945—	Kingsport‡	.670
1946—	New River‡	.675
1947—	Pulaski	.648
	New River (3rd)†	.516
1948—	Pulaski‡	.680
1949—	Bluefield‡	.721
1950—	Bluefield	.600
	Bluefield◆	.745
1951—	Kingsport‡	.659
1952—	Johnson City	.595
	Welch (3rd)†	.509
1953—	Welch*	.705
	Johnson City	.672
1954—	Bluefield‡	.619
1955—	Salem■	.689
1956—	Did not operate.	
1957—	Bluefield	.701
1958—	Johnson City	.662
1959—	Morristown	.603
1960—	Wytheville	.614
1961—	Middlesboro	.591
1962—	Bluefield	.671
1963—	Bluefield	.652
1964—	Johnson City	.662
1965—	Salem	.614
1966—	Marion	.623
1967—	Bluefield	.627
1968—	Marion	.583
1969—	Pulaski▼	.576
	Johnson City	.544
1970—	Bluefield	.638
1971—	Bluefield▼	.609
	Kingsport	.559
1972—	Bristol▼	.588
	Covington	.586
1973—	Kingsport	.757
1974—	Bristol▼	.754
	Bluefield	.536
1975—	Marion	.515
	Johnson City▼	.603
1976—	Johnson City▼	.714
	Bluefield	.600
1977—	Kingsport	.623
1978—	Elizabethton	.594
1979—	Paintsville	.800
1980—	Paintsville	.657
1981—	Paintsville	.657
1982—	Bluefield▼	.681
	Johnson City	.478
1983—	Paintsville	.653
1984—	Elizabethton*	.580
	Pulaski	.536
1985—	Bristol††	.638
1986—	Johnson City	.667
	Pulaski*	.621
1987—	Burlington*	.729
	Johnson City	.609
1988—	Kingsport*	.644
	Burlington	.529
1989—	Elizabethton*	.691
	Pulaski	.618
1990—	Elizabethton	.761
1991—	Pulaski*	.662
	Burlington	.597
1992—	Elizabethton	.742
	Bluefield*	.597
1993—	Burlington*	.647
	Elizabethton	.552
1994—	Princeton*	.621
	Johnson City	.618
1995—	Bluefield	.754
	Kingsport*	.727
1996—	Kingsport	.716
	Bluefield▼	.618
1997—	Pulaski	.632
	Bluefield*	.580
1998—	Bristol*	.636
	Princeton	.559
1999—	Pulaski	.696
	Martinsville*	.586
2000—	Elizabethton*	.719
2001—	Elizabethton	.651
	Bluefield*	.500
2002—	Bluefield	.662
	Bristol*	.632
2003—	Martinsville	.646
	Elizabethton*	.636
2004—	Danville	.621
	Greeneville*	.612
2005—	Danville	.701
	Elizabethton*	.716

*Won split-season playoff. †Won four-team playoff. ‡Won championship and four-team playoff. §Johnson City, first-half winner, won playoff involving six clubs. ∞Won both halves and defeated second-place Elizabethton in play-off. ▲Won both halves, but Erwin won four-team playoff. ◆Won both halves, but Bristol won two-club playoff. ■Salem and Johnson City declared playoff co-champions when weather forced cancellation of final series. ▼League was divided into Northern, Southern divisions; declared league champion based on highest won-lost percentage. *League was divided into divisions; won playoff. ††Bristol declared league champion based on regular-season record.

ADVANCED ROOKIE Appalachian League

PIONEER LEAGUE

President
Jim McCurdy
Address
P.O. Box 2564
Spokane, WA 99220
Phone
509-456-7615

Teams (affiliation)
Billings Mustangs (Reds)
Casper Rockies (Rockies)
Great Falls White Sox (White Sox)
Helena Brewers (Brewers)
Idaho Falls Chukars (Royals)

Missoula Osprey (Diamondbacks)
Ogden Raptors (Dodgers)
Orem Owlz (Angels)

2005 FINAL STANDINGS

FIRST HALF

NORTHERN DIVISION

Team	W	L	T	Pct.	GB
Helena Brewers	24	14	–	.632	–
Billings Mustangs	23	15	–	.605	1
Great Falls White Sox	15	23	–	.395	9
Missoula Osprey	13	25	–	.342	11

SOUTHERN DIVISION

Team	W	L	T	Pct.	GB
Ogden Raptors	22	16	–	.579	–
Casper Rockies	20	18	–	.526	2
Orem Owlz	18	20	–	.474	4
Idaho Falls Chukars	17	21	–	.447	5

SECOND HALF

NORTHERN DIVISION

Team	W	L	T	Pct.	GB
Helena Brewers	22	16	–	.579	–
Missoula Osprey	21	17	–	.553	1
Billings Mustangs	20	18	–	.526	2
Great Falls White Sox	17	21	–	.447	5

SOUTHERN DIVISION

Team	W	L	T	Pct.	GB
Orem Owlz	20	18	–	.526	–
Casper Rockies	18	20	–	.474	2
Idaho Falls Chukars	17	21	–	.447	3
Ogden Raptors	17	21	–	.447	3

COMPOSITE

CLUB (AFFILIATE), ABBREV	HEL	BIL	OGD	CAS	ORE	IDA	MIS	GRF	W	L	PCT	GB
Helena (Brewers), HEL		10	4	3	4	5	9	11	46	30	.605	–
Billings (Reds), BIL	6		3	3	5	5	10	11	43	33	.566	3.0
Ogden (Dodgers), OGD	3	...		7	9	10	3	3	39	37	.513	7.0
Casper (Rockies), CAS	4	3	9		8	8	1	5	38	38	.500	8.0
Orem (Angels), ORE	3	2	7	8		9	5	4	38	38	.500	8.0
Idaho Falls (Royals), IDA	2	3	6	8	7		4	4	34	42	.447	12.0
Missoula (D-backs), MIS	7	6	4	6	2	3	...	6	34	42	.447	12.0
Great Falls (White Sox), GRF	5	5	4	3	3	2	10	...	32	44	.421	14.0

Major league affiliations in parentheses.

PLAYOFFS: Semifinals: Helena defeated Billings, two games to none, and Orem defeated Ogden, two games to one. Finals: Orem defeated Helena, two games to none.

REGULAR-SEASON ATTENDANCE: Helena, 40,141. Idaho Falls, 65,313. Billings, 88,702. Missoula, 67,922. Orem, 76,784. Ogden, 131,371. Casper, 50,087. Great Falls, 96,012. League total, 616,332. Postseason (7 games), 11,793.

MANAGERS: Helena, Eddie Sedar. Idaho Falls, Brian Rupp. Billings, Rick Burleson. Missoula, Jim Presley. Orem, Tom Kotchman. Ogden, Juan Bustabad. Casper, P.J. Carey. Great Falls, John Orton.

ALL-STAR TEAM: 1B-David Sutherland, Ogden. 2B-Corey Wimberly, Casper. 3B-Russ Mitchell, Ogden. SS-Christopher McConnell, Idaho Falls. OF-Charlie Fermaint, Helena. OF-Brandon Roberts, Billings. OF-Ethien Santana, Idaho Falls. C-Angel Salome, Helena. DH-Francisco Hernandez, Great Falls. RHS-Chaz Roe, Casper. LHS-Gregory Smith, Missoula. Relief Pitcher-Andrew Johnston, Casper. Most Valuable Player-Angel Salome, Helena. Pitcher of the Year-Gregory Smith, Missoula. Manager of the Year-Paul Carey, Casper.

2005 BATTING

TEAM

Team	G	TPA	AB	R	H	TB	2B	3B	HR	RBI	SH	SF	HP	BB	IBB	SO	SB	CS	GDP	LOB	ShO	Avg.	OBP	Slg.
Helena	76	3161	2752	531	851	1303	167	18	83	461	26	32	50	300	11	567	112	37	73	1337	0	.309	.383	.473
Idaho Falls	76	3068	2611	482	748	1139	137	31	64	418	29	23	71	334	2	612	70	54	69	1230	5	.286	.379	.436
Casper	76	2978	2620	406	731	1076	136	19	57	352	22	23	57	256	4	680	124	74	41	1232	2	.279	.353	.411
Ogden	76	2997	2647	440	726	1103	139	8	74	381	18	22	51	259	6	544	75	34	57	1167	5	.274	.348	.417
Great Falls	76	2976	2608	387	708	1046	151	26	45	333	32	27	53	256	15	602	117	52	62	1180	4	.271	.345	.401
Orem	76	2996	2672	411	715	1095	146	27	60	366	25	17	44	238	7	725	81	42	38	1260	5	.268	.336	.410
Missoula	76	3014	2668	435	711	1071	161	20	53	377	12	15	75	244	6	633	74	57	50	1236	1	.266	.343	.401
Billings	76	2985	2560	427	661	1009	136	28	52	373	22	18	55	330	7	720	107	38	44	1272	2	.258	.353	.394

INDIVIDUAL

TOP QUALIFIERS FOR BATTING CHAMPIONSHIP

Minimum 205 plate appearances. *Lefthanded batter. †Switch-hitter.

Player, Team	G	TPA	AB	R	H	TB	2B	3B	HR	RBI	SH	SF	HP	BB	IBB	SO	SB	CS	GDP	Avg.	OBP	Slg.
Wimberly, Corey, Casper †	67	309	281	58	107	120	10	0	1	22	2	2	6	18	0	27	36	13	5	.381	.427	.427
Holmberg, Kenneth, Helena	59	248	207	40	77	129	16	0	12	51	6	3	3	29	3	34	2	2	4	.372	.450	.623

Player, Team	G	TPA	AB	R	H	TB	2B	3B	HR	RBI	SH	SF	HP	BB	IBB	SO	SB	CS	GDP	Avg.	OBP	Slg.
Hernandez, Francisco, Great Falls †	58	237	212	37	74	111	19	0	6	34	0	3	3	19	3	25	0	1	6	.349	.405	.524
Crew, Ryan, Helena	58	246	217	45	75	108	19	1	4	29	2	4	1	22	0	21	5	5	9	.346	.402	.498
Sutherland, David, Ogden *	66	287	247	44	83	112	13	2	4	47	0	2	4	34	2	27	4	1	4	.336	.422	.453
Ryal, Rusty, Missoula	72	326	294	59	98	146	22	4	6	46	1	2	15	14	1	47	11	3	7	.333	.391	.497
McConnell, Christopher, Idaho Falls	70	327	275	56	91	142	17	8	6	39	7	7	7	31	0	34	7	6	7	.331	.403	.516
Gamel, Mathew, Helena *	50	216	199	34	65	99	15	2	5	37	0	1	4	12	1	49	7	4	6	.327	.375	.497
Roberts, Brandon, Billings *	68	311	274	50	87	120	9	6	4	36	3	2	8	24	0	44	32	7	3	.318	.386	.438
Godwin, Adam, Ogden	55	222	197	38	61	78	12	1	1	21	4	4	5	12	1	32	12	7	1	.310	.358	.396
Tartaglia, Evan, Great Falls *	69	308	266	41	81	103	9	5	1	26	6	2	0	34	1	51	38	13	2	.305	.381	.387
Yost, Edgar, Helena	57	234	202	34	61	91	10	4	4	32	0	0	6	26	0	46	6	1	7	.302	.397	.450
Young, Eric, Casper †	63	264	219	48	66	96	7	7	3	25	4	2	4	35	0	52	25	10	4	.301	.404	.438
Bell, Michael, Helena	58	243	213	38	64	92	17	1	3	42	3	1	3	23	2	39	9	6	6	.300	.375	.432
Santana, Ethien, Idaho Falls *	63	285	240	51	72	99	8	5	3	29	5	0	7	33	1	54	20	17	2	.300	.400	.413
Mitchell, Russell, Ogden	69	303	270	54	78	138	19	1	13	54	1	2	4	26	1	52	3	3	14	.289	.358	.511
Roberts, Brandon, Billings *	63	238	204	40	58	99	14	0	9	39	1	3	2	28	1	64	3	0	3	.284	.371	.485
Richmond, Barry, Ogden *	66	268	232	29	66	95	14	0	5	30	0	4	1	31	0	55	12	4	5	.284	.366	.409
Cook, Christopher, Casper	50	219	187	29	53	108	10	0	15	46	0	9	4	19	0	59	0	2	4	.283	.347	.578
Crouch, Will, Missoula	58	251	202	43	57	100	19	0	8	37	0	0	10	39	0	54	6	5	5	.282	.422	.495

DEPARTMENTAL LEADERS: G—Ryal, 72. AB—Trumbo, 299. R—Ryal, 59. H—Wimberly, 107. TB—Ryal, 146. 2B—Morris and Trumbo, 23. 3B—McConnell, 8. HR—Cook, 15. RBI—Mitchell, 54. SH—McConnell, 7. SF—Cook, 9. HP—Ryal, 15. BB—Byrne, 42. IBB—Tribble, 5. SO—Garner, 105. SB—Tartaglia, 38. CS—Santana, 17. GIDP—Mitchell, 14. OBP—Holmberg, .450. Slg.—Holmberg, .623.

ALL PLAYERS

*Lefthanded batter. †Switch-hitter.

Player, Team	G	TPA	AB	R	H	TB	2B	3B	HR	RBI	SH	SF	HP	BB	IBB	SO	SB	CS	GDP	Avg.	OBP	Slg.
Acosta, Rolando, Great Falls	45	173	148	25	41	62	5	2	4	24	3	0	4	18	0	25	5	0	3	.277	.371	.419
Adkison, Blake, Idaho Falls	27	107	95	15	26	47	3	0	6	22	0	2	2	8	0	31	0	0	3	.274	.336	.495
Allen, Brandon, Great Falls *	66	273	231	41	61	109	11	2	11	42	0	3	7	32	3	69	7	5	7	.264	.366	.472
Allen, Trevor, Casper	31	137	122	23	47	74	12	0	5	33	0	3	3	9	1	34	5	3	2	.385	.431	.607
Alonso, John, Helena	9	34	31	6	10	18	2	0	2	5	0	0	0	3	0	10	1	0	1	.323	.382	.581
Apodaca, Juan, Helena	42	174	158	24	44	81	7	0	10	31	0	0	2	14	0	33	2	0	5	.278	.345	.513
Arias, Hector, Ogden	1	4	4	0	0	0	0	0	0	0	0	0	0	0	0	2	0	0	0	.000	.000	.000
Barber, Byron, Idaho Falls †	31	111	92	20	28	32	4	0	0	10	3	0	4	12	0	6	3	2	3	.304	.407	.348
Batten, Joseph, Missoula	23	62	52	11	9	14	2	0	1	10	1	0	1	8	0	11	1	2	1	.173	.295	.269
Belcher, Jordan, Billings	30	120	109	16	29	53	13	1	3	28	0	2	1	8	0	23	2	2	4	.266	.317	.486
Bell, Michael, Helena	58	243	213	38	64	92	17	1	3	42	3	1	3	23	2	39	9	6	6	.300	.375	.432
Berglund, Bret, Missoula	53	223	188	26	41	66	11	1	4	27	0	1	9	25	0	66	10	4	0	.218	.336	.351
Blevins, John, Helena *	12	46	39	6	13	15	2	0	0	5	0	1	0	6	0	3	1	0	1	.333	.413	.385
Blumenthal, Benjamin, Billings	29	102	92	13	18	27	3	0	2	11	1	0	1	8	0	39	0	1	2	.196	.267	.293
Blumenthal, Kyle, Casper *	60	252	214	32	59	93	14	1	6	42	1	0	0	37	0	45	4	3	4	.276	.382	.435
Brantley, Michael, Helena *	10	40	34	8	11	13	2	0	0	3	0	0	0	6	0	4	2	0	0	.324	.425	.382
Braun, Ryan, Helena	10	47	41	6	14	24	2	1	2	10	0	2	2	2	0	6	2	1	0	.341	.383	.585
Brooks, Parker, Ogden †	10	33	31	4	7	10	3	0	0	2	0	0	0	2	0	7	0	0	0	.226	.273	.323
Brownell, Jesse, Casper	31	109	93	14	20	33	4	0	3	9	2	0	3	11	0	39	3	3	1	.215	.318	.355
Bruce, Jay, Billings *	17	81	70	16	18	32	2	0	4	13	0	0	0	11	0	22	2	2	2	.257	.358	.457
Bustamante, Gerardo, Missoula	11	16	15	0	1	1	0	0	0	0	0	0	0	1	0	5	0	0	0	.067	.125	.067
Byrne, Bryan, Missoula *	64	266	221	39	59	88	15	1	4	36	0	0	3	42	2	50	3	4	5	.267	.391	.398
Cain, Lorenzo, Helena	6	28	24	4	5	5	0	0	0	1	0	0	3	1	0	6	0	0	1	.208	.321	.208
Camardese, Brandon, Billings	1	0	0	0	0	0	0	0	0	0	0	0	0	0	0	0	0	0	0	...	...	...
Castillo, Javier, Great Falls	52	204	178	24	39	51	7	1	1	20	3	1	6	16	0	43	5	2	5	.219	.303	.287
Chapman, Stephen, Helena *	54	197	167	25	45	74	9	1	6	25	3	3	3	20	0	38	10	3	2	.269	.352	.443
Ciriaco, Pedro, Missoula	69	268	254	28	61	84	9	4	2	31	3	2	2	7	0	50	7	2	3	.240	.264	.331
Colafemina, Joshua, Idaho Falls	49	176	151	30	36	49	8	1	1	17	5	1	2	17	0	20	12	1	3	.238	.322	.325
Cook, Christopher, Casper	50	219	187	29	53	108	10	0	15	46	0	9	4	19	0	59	0	2	4	.283	.347	.578
Crew, Ryan, Helena	58	246	217	45	75	108	19	1	4	29	2	4	1	22	0	21	5	5	9	.346	.402	.498
Crist, Justin, Ogden	16	59	56	9	13	17	1	0	1	7	0	0	0	3	0	5	2	1	0	.232	.271	.304
Crouch, Will, Missoula	58	251	202	43	57	100	19	0	8	37	0	0	10	39	0	54	6	5	5	.282	.422	.495
Cruz, Ricardo, Missoula	62	260	238	33	61	107	16	0	10	40	0	0	6	16	1	83	3	7	5	.256	.319	.450
DeCarlo, Michael, Missoula	42	151	132	22	31	49	9	0	3	19	1	1	5	12	0	32	1	2	4	.235	.320	.371
De Jesus, Ivan, Ogden	20	81	72	4	15	16	1	0	0	3	0	0	3	6	0	18	3	3	1	.208	.296	.222
De Jesus, Michael, Billings *	53	198	154	25	36	47	8	0	1	20	3	0	1	40	1	40	10	2	1	.234	.395	.305
Delgado, Ronny, Billings	6	26	21	4	6	10	1	0	1	5	0	0	2	3	0	6	1	0	0	.286	.423	.476
Denove, Christopher, Billings	49	169	138	28	36	53	8	0	3	23	2	0	6	23	1	29	2	1	3	.261	.389	.384
Diaz, Osvaldo, Missoula	63	273	252	35	68	106	18	1	6	38	1	3	3	14	1	63	1	4	6	.270	.313	.421
Dombek, Gregory, Casper	3	12	10	1	4	5	1	0	0	2	0	0	1	1	0	3	0	0	0	.400	.500	.500
Elder, Jake, Idaho Falls	40	136	111	22	32	45	7	0	2	10	1	0	8	16	0	14	2	3	2	.288	.415	.405
Emeterio, Oscar, Helena †	1	2	2	0	0	0	0	0	0	0	0	0	0	0	0	2	0	0	0	.000	.000	.000
Everett, Brady, Idaho Falls	29	127	108	24	39	64	8	1	5	21	0	0	6	13	0	16	0	2	2	.361	.457	.593
Eymann, Eric, Billings	34	126	113	16	27	44	4	2	3	12	0	0	2	11	1	33	2	0	0	.239	.317	.389
Feiner, Kevyn, Billings	3	10	10	2	1	1	0	0	0	1	0	0	0	0	0	3	0	0	0	.100	.100	.100
Feliz, Rainer, Billings	1	0	0	0	0	0	0	0	0	0	0	0	0	0	0	0	0	0	0	...	...	...
Fermaint, Charlie, Helena	31	149	129	46	47	96	9	2	12	32	1	4	0	15	0	28	11	2	3	.364	.419	.744
Ford, Darren, Helena	61	277	236	57	64	77	4	3	1	24	3	2	3	33	0	70	18	4	1	.271	.365	.326
Fowler, William, Casper	62	252	220	43	60	90	10	4	4	23	3	0	2	27	1	73	18	6	2	.273	.357	.409
Gallardo, Carlos, Helena *	28	76	68	10	15	24	6	0	1	7	1	0	2	5	0	15	0	0	3	.221	.293	.353
Gamel, Mathew, Helena *	50	216	199	34	65	99	15	2	5	37	0	1	4	12	1	49	7	4	6	.327	.375	.497
Garner, Robert, Casper †	66	284	265	34	69	122	21	1	10	48	0	2	8	9	1	105	2	8	3	.260	.303	.460
Getz, Christopher, Great Falls *	6	27	24	3	8	9	1	0	0	4	1	1	0	2	0	6	0	0	0	.333	.346	.375
Gil, Rotsen, Ogden †	12	45	43	5	7	16	3	0	2	4	0	1	0	2	0	10	0	0	1	.163	.200	.372
Godwin, Adam, Ogden	55	222	197	38	61	78	12	1	1	21	4	4	5	12	1	32	12	7	1	.310	.358	.396

ADVANCED ROOKIE *Pioneer League*

Player, Team	G	TPA	AB	R	H	TB	2B	3B	HR	RBI	SH	SF	HP	BB	IBB	SO	SB	CS	GDP	Avg.	OBP	Slg.
Griffin, Michael, Billings	13	47	38	12	10	16	0	0	2	4	0	0	4	5	0	6	1	0	0	.263	.404	.421
Guest, Dennis, Great Falls	67	268	230	21	53	64	11	0	0	21	5	5	1	27	0	33	5	2	9	.230	.308	.278
Hayes, Shawn, Idaho Falls *	17	65	56	6	12	16	4	0	0	8	0	1	0	8	0	21	3	1	1	.214	.308	.286
Hernandez, Francisco, Great Falls †	58	237	212	37	74	111	19	0	6	34	0	3	3	19	3	25	0	1	6	.349	.405	.524
Herrera, Brenan, Idaho Falls	29	141	122	25	31	47	8	1	2	17	1	0	4	14	0	27	0	0	6	.254	.350	.385
Holden, Joshua, Billings *	59	238	203	26	51	67	6	5	0	30	4	1	3	27	1	60	13	6	4	.251	.346	.330
Hollis, Eric, Great Falls	34	121	102	12	27	33	6	0	0	8	0	1	6	12	0	21	1	1	2	.265	.372	.324
Holmberg, Kenneth, Helena	59	248	207	40	77	129	16	0	12	51	6	3	3	29	3	34	2	2	4	.372	.450	.623
Howell, Jeffrey, Idaho Falls	39	167	136	29	47	61	9	1	1	17	0	2	0	29	0	36	1	2	5	.346	.455	.449
Jackson, Derry, Ogden	35	111	100	17	20	29	4	1	1	13	2	0	3	6	0	40	2	0	2	.200	.266	.290
Jansen, Kenley, Ogden †	3	12	11	2	2	3	1	0	0	1	0	0	0	1	0	5	0	0	1	.182	.250	.273
Jimenez, Jose, Helena	7	21	19	4	3	6	3	0	0	0	0	0	0	1	1	6	0	0	1	.158	.238	.316
Jirschele, Jeremy, Idaho Falls	16	62	53	8	10	10	0	0	0	4	0	1	3	5	0	16	0	0	4	.189	.290	.189
Johnson, Brandon, Great Falls *	61	234	212	30	59	82	13	2	2	20	3	0	3	16	0	45	19	5	3	.278	.338	.387
Johnson, Joshua, Idaho Falls †	37	160	129	20	31	50	5	4	2	26	3	1	2	25	0	25	3	0	7	.240	.369	.388
Justis, Shane, Ogden	36	126	110	20	30	47	7	2	2	15	1	1	5	9	0	17	3	3	2	.273	.352	.427
Katin, Brendan, Helena	33	136	114	30	44	74	6	0	8	26	0	2	3	17	1	25	3	1	3	.386	.471	.649
Lajara, Luis, Missoula *	11	25	22	2	4	7	0	0	1	4	0	0	0	3	0	6	0	1	0	.182	.280	.318
Landry, Michael, Great Falls *	20	64	52	10	12	21	3	0	2	8	0	0	4	8	0	20	1	1	1	.231	.375	.404
Langham, James, Billings	44	158	138	20	26	48	10	0	4	19	0	0	6	14	0	53	0	2	3	.188	.291	.348
Larsen, Andrew, Idaho Falls	64	265	229	41	62	93	6	2	7	31	2	1	7	26	0	43	10	3	8	.271	.361	.406
Lasso, Rick, Ogden	9	28	21	1	2	2	0	0	0	1	0	1	0	6	0	8	0	0	0	.095	.286	.095
Lewis, Kenneth, Billings *	59	207	172	23	41	54	6	2	1	15	4	1	1	29	1	60	14	5	2	.238	.350	.314
Locke, Andrew, Ogden	50	192	169	34	46	94	9	0	13	31	2	0	2	19	1	37	1	1	6	.272	.353	.556
Loupadiere, Maruis, Casper	25	94	84	12	22	26	4	0	0	5	2	0	3	5	1	11	3	4	1	.262	.326	.310
Mannon, Adam, Helena	22	68	59	10	14	28	2	0	4	9	0	0	0	9	1	23	3	0	3	.237	.338	.475
Mayora, Daniel, Casper	47	168	151	20	40	57	12	1	1	14	2	1	5	9	0	36	4	3	3	.265	.325	.377
McConnell, Christopher, Idaho Falls	70	327	275	56	91	142	17	8	6	39	7	7	7	31	0	34	7	6	7	.331	.403	.516
McDonald, James, Ogden *	28	94	83	12	19	24	3	1	0	8	1	0	1	9	0	25	3	0	1	.229	.312	.289
McKnight, Scott, Helena	40	146	128	16	31	41	8	1	0	14	3	4	2	9	0	25	3	0	3	.242	.294	.320
Melendez, Norman, Missoula	24	31	29	3	3	4	1	0	0	1	1	0	0	1	0	10	0	0	1	.103	.133	.138
Mena, Steve, Missoula	66	270	248	40	68	107	18	3	5	46	0	1	2	19	0	69	9	4	6	.274	.330	.431
Mitchell, Russell, Ogden	69	303	270	54	78	138	19	1	13	54	1	2	4	26	1	52	3	3	14	.289	.358	.511
Mooneyham, Jason, Ogden *	56	222	182	27	51	80	11	0	6	27	0	1	10	29	1	32	1	0	5	.280	.405	.440
Morris, James, Billings *	1	0	0	0	0	0	0	0	0	0	...	0	0	0	...	0	0	0	0	...	...	...
Mummy, Benjamin, Billings	44	175	148	25	31	48	10	2	1	14	0	0	7	20	0	47	4	2	2	.209	.331	.324
Nazario, Radames, Casper	56	209	182	24	41	48	5	1	0	12	4	0	4	19	0	40	7	4	4	.225	.312	.264
O'Neal, Charles, Billings	1	0	0	0	0	0	0	0	0	0	0	0	0	0	0	0	0	0	0	...	...	...
Opdyke, Bryan, Helena *	22	56	41	7	7	11	2	1	0	3	0	0	1	14	0	22	1	0	1	.171	.393	.268
Parejo, Freddy, Helena	33	145	124	20	42	48	3	0	1	19	2	1	9	9	0	21	12	3	2	.339	.420	.387
Pedroza, Sergio, Ogden *	12	54	46	13	23	36	1	0	4	18	0	0	2	6	0	8	4	0	0	.500	.574	.783
Peguero, Felix, Idaho Falls *	64	288	251	38	67	105	18	1	6	46	0	2	7	28	0	79	0	1	6	.267	.354	.418
Perez, Fernando, Idaho Falls	36	157	127	29	46	71	11	4	2	23	...	3	3	24	...	33	3	6	3	.362	.465	.559
Polanco, Armando, Casper	17	47	44	4	11	14	3	0	0	5	0	0	2	1	0	7	0	0	1	.250	.298	.318
Pujols, Kengshill, Ogden	32	98	87	7	17	25	2	0	2	11	0	1	2	8	0	25	0	1	2	.195	.276	.287
Reininger, Jarrett, Billings	48	201	177	24	54	83	12	1	5	35	0	1	0	23	0	41	4	3	3	.305	.383	.469
Richmond, Barry, Ogden *	66	268	232	29	66	95	14	0	5	30	0	4	1	31	0	55	12	4	5	.284	.366	.409
Rivera, Juan, Ogden †	41	191	171	27	43	51	5	0	1	16	2	2	2	14	0	32	9	7	2	.251	.312	.298
Roberts, Brandon, Ogden *	68	311	274	50	87	120	9	6	4	36	3	2	8	24	0	44	32	7	3	.318	.386	.438
Roberts, Brandon, Billings *	63	238	204	40	58	99	14	0	9	39	1	3	2	28	1	64	3	0	3	.284	.371	.485
Roberts, Daron, Great Falls	64	264	234	40	63	109	13	6	7	29	4	4	6	16	1	55	19	9	9	.269	.327	.466
Robinson, Trayvon, Ogden	8	23	23	2	5	8	0	0	1	2	0	0	0	0	0	9	0	0	1	.217	.217	.348
Rodriguez, Manuel Esteban, Great Falls	64	266	246	43	67	120	18	4	9	43	0	2	8	10	0	103	2	1	4	.272	.320	.488
Rodriguez, Mark, Billings	17	43	37	6	6	8	2	0	0	3	0	0	0	6	0	15	0	0	1	.162	.279	.216
Rodriguez, Ramon, Casper	29	107	92	8	23	30	4	0	1	9	1	2	3	9	0	16	1	1	4	.250	.330	.326
Roman, Edwin, Missoula †	21	78	63	13	15	24	1	1	2	5	1	1	11	2	0	22	5	5	0	.238	.364	.381
Ronda, Jose, Billings †	29	103	83	18	21	33	3	3	1	15	1	1	0	18	0	25	0	1	2	.253	.382	.398
Rosales, Adam, Billings	34	159	140	29	45	74	14	0	5	25	0	1	5	13	0	37	2	2	0	.321	.396	.529
Ryal, Rusty, Missoula	72	326	294	59	98	146	22	4	6	46	1	2	15	14	1	47	11	3	7	.333	.391	.497
Sabatini, Antonio, Idaho Falls	51	218	193	27	46	63	7	2	2	30	0	1	3	21	0	72	3	4	4	.238	.321	.326
Salome, Angel, Helena	37	175	159	34	66	107	17	0	8	50	0	0	1	15	3	16	6	2	6	.415	.469	.673
Sandoval, Mayker, Billings	59	245	218	33	58	90	11	6	3	28	3	5	6	13	1	65	15	2	7	.266	.318	.413
Santana, Ethien, Idaho Falls *	63	285	240	51	72	99	8	5	3	29	5	0	7	33	1	54	20	17	2	.300	.400	.413
Santiago, Jayson, Missoula *	35	130	122	20	31	44	3	2	2	11	1	0	1	6	0	29	8	0	2	.254	.295	.361
Sargent, Luke, Casper	9	33	29	4	8	11	0	0	1	4	0	1	0	3	0	9	0	0	1	.276	.333	.379
Schambough, Douglas, Idaho Falls	1	0	0	0	0	0	0	0	0	0	...	0	0	0	0	0	0	0	0	...	...	...
Schmidt, Jeffrey, Great Falls	42	154	143	13	37	53	13	0	1	15	2	0	2	7	0	43	4	3	2	.259	.303	.371
Septimo, Agustin, Helena *	36	134	121	27	38	58	3	1	5	16	1	2	1	9	0	22	10	2	4	.314	.361	.479
Sharp, Matthew, Great Falls *	25	96	84	9	18	26	6	1	0	8	0	0	0	12	2	22	1	1	3	.214	.313	.310
Soto, Jesus, Ogden †	63	286	254	57	71	105	16	0	6	28	5	4	2	21	0	44	13	1	4	.280	.335	.413
Steidl, Sam, Ogden *	8	33	26	4	5	6	1	0	0	3	0	0	0	7	0	3	1	1	0	.192	.364	.231
Strickland, Geoff, Casper †	36	134	123	13	28	39	5	3	0	7	0	0	0	11	0	34	6	7	3	.228	.291	.317
Suarez, Steven, Casper *	35	125	116	13	32	44	3	0	3	19	1	0	0	8	0	24	0	3	0	.276	.323	.379
Summers, Houston, Missoula	12	13	11	1	2	3	1	0	0	0	0	0	0	2	0	3	0	0	0	.182	.308	.273
Sutherland, David, Ogden *	66	287	247	44	83	112	13	2	4	47	0	2	4	34	2	27	4	1	4	.336	.422	.453
Taloa, Rick, Ogden	22	79	75	7	20	32	6	0	2	9	0	1	3	0	0	26	0	1	1	.267	.291	.427
Tartaglia, Evan, Great Falls *	69	308	266	41	81	103	9	5	1	26	6	2	0	34	1	51	38	13	2	.305	.381	.387
Terrell, Joshua, Missoula	6	20	17	0	5	6	1	0	0	1	0	0	0	3	0	7	1	0	0	.294	.400	.353
Thibault, Kiel, Idaho Falls	41	167	145	27	45	86	12	1	9	34	2	1	9	10	0	26	3	2	3	.310	.388	.593
Thomson, Gregory, Missoula *	49	221	200	29	54	73	10	3	1	20	0	3	6	12	1	43	5	8	2	.270	.326	.365

Player, Team	G	TPA	AB	R	H	TB	2B	3B	HR	RBI	SH	SF	HP	BB	IBB	SO	SB	CS	GDP	Avg.	OBP	Slg.
Tribble, Matthew, Great Falls *	65	287	246	38	68	93	16	3	1	31	5	5	3	28	5	45	8	7	6	.276	.351	.378
Tully, Travis, Missoula *	53	217	185	35	52	63	9	1	0	22	1	2	2	27	0	35	11	7	1	.281	.375	.341
Turner, Jase, Idaho Falls *	56	244	209	36	59	104	9	0	12	44	0	0	5	30	1	73	2	1	2	.282	.385	.498
Willcutt, Bradley, Helena	48	197	178	24	40	65	10	0	5	20	1	2	2	14	0	38	0	1	6	.225	.286	.365
Wimberly, Corey, Casper †	67	309	281	58	107	120	10	0	1	22	2	2	6	18	0	27	36	13	5	.381	.427	.427
Woody, Abraham, Billings	1	0	0	0	0	0	0	0	0	0	...	0	0	0	...	0	0	0	0	...	...	...
Yost, Edgar, Helena	57	234	202	34	61	91	10	4	4	32	0	0	6	26	0	46	6	1	7	.302	.397	.450
Young, Eric, Casper †	63	264	219	48	66	96	7	7	3	25	4	2	4	35	0	52	25	10	4	.301	.404	.438

GRAND SLAMS—K. Blumenthal, P. Ciriaco, J. Cowles, R. Cruz, J. Johnson, B. Katin, A. Locke, S. Mena, D. Morris, F. Peguero, K. Pujols, J. Roberts, E. Santana, K. Thibault, 1 each. AWARDED FIRST BASE ON CATCHER'S INTERFERENCE—S. Chapman (S. Suarez).

2005 PITCHING

TEAM

Team	W	L	Pct.	ERA	G	CG	ShO	Sv.	IP	H	TBF	R	ER	HR	SH	SF	HB	BB	IBB	SO	WP	Bk.
Orem	38	38	.500	4.16	76	0	5	13	679	706	2986	382	314	52	25	18	57	265	3	599	75	6
Helena	46	30	.605	4.30	76	0	4	24	679.2	700	2999	401	325	59	25	21	49	231	3	651	70	9
Billings	43	33	.566	4.42	76	0	3	25	664.1	697	2921	387	326	55	18	24	56	264	6	598	81	8
Great Falls	32	44	.421	4.56	76	0	2	14	672.2	708	3001	441	341	48	26	26	57	279	9	628	69	13
Ogden	39	37	.513	4.89	76	2	3	16	668.1	715	2991	432	363	67	20	18	52	305	5	669	88	6
Casper	38	38	.500	5.05	76	0	4	22	671.2	742	3059	475	377	70	25	22	57	291	16	624	86	9
Missoula	34	42	.447	5.59	76	0	2	20	677.1	761	3159	499	421	64	25	27	69	350	12	688	98	7
Idaho Falls	34	42	.447	5.68	76	0	1	19	664.1	822	3059	502	419	73	22	21	59	232	4	626	67	7

INDIVIDUAL

TOP QUALIFIERS FOR EARNED-RUN AVERAGE TITLE

Minimum 61 innings. *Lefthanded pitcher.

Pitcher, Team	W	L	Pct.	ERA	G	GS	CG	ShO	GF	Sv.	IP	H	TBF	R	ER	HR	SH	SF	HB	BB	IBB	SO	WP	Bk.
Leach, Brent, Ogden *	5	3	.625	2.43	14	13	1	0	0	0	66.2	53	267	21	18	4	2	0	5	29	0	77	4	0
Johnson, Thomas, Casper	3	2	.600	3.97	15	15	0	0	0	0	79.1	90	348	44	35	1	1	2	2	24	1	78	4	0
Moviel, Paul, Great Falls *	4	1	.800	4.04	15	15	0	0	0	0	78.0	89	335	40	35	3	1	3	5	20	0	72	8	0
Smith, Gregory, Missoula *	8	5	.615	4.15	16	14	0	0	0	0	82.1	69	324	40	38	8	2	2	5	18	2	100	6	0
Wade, Cory, Ogden	2	3	.400	4.35	16	11	1	0	0	0	72.1	81	303	42	35	12	3	1	5	19	0	60	3	0
Perez, Carlos, Great Falls	4	6	.400	4.38	16	10	0	0	1	0	61.2	67	269	39	30	7	3	3	3	22	0	40	9	1
Romanczuk, Mark, Missoula *	4	5	.444	4.55	13	13	0	0	0	0	61.1	70	273	37	31	6	7	2	6	17	1	59	4	1
Wooley, Robert, Helena	6	7	.462	4.70	18	13	0	0	3	1	74.2	86	331	48	39	7	2	2	6	20	0	69	8	0
Cupps, Anthony, Missoula	4	6	.400	5.05	15	12	0	0	0	0	67.2	76	295	48	38	6	4	1	5	29	1	54	6	4
Arias, Marlon, Ogden *	4	4	.500	5.48	14	14	0	0	0	0	70.2	81	319	53	43	11	0	4	1	27	0	73	9	4
Dipietro, Ryan, Idaho Falls *	1	6	.143	5.63	15	15	0	0	0	0	64.0	72	287	45	40	8	0	1	6	17	0	56	5	1
Morrison, Tyler, Helena	5	3	.625	5.78	17	12	0	0	2	0	67.0	91	302	51	43	7	3	2	2	14	0	63	12	0
Novoa, Yunior, Great Falls *	1	7	.125	7.32	15	13	0	0	2	0	62.2	83	292	58	51	11	5	4	4	28	1	44	5	3
Rodriguez, Aneury, Casper	3	4	.429	7.55	15	15	0	0	0	0	62.0	77	283	54	52	7	2	1	7	26	0	47	11	1

DEPARTMENTAL LEADERS: W—Smith, 8. L—Novoa and Wooley, 7. Pct.—Arredondo, 1.000. G—three pitchers tied with 30. GS—four pitchers tied with 15. CG—Leach and Wade, 1. GF—Johnston, 29. Sv.—Johnston, 18. IP—Smith, 82.1. H—Morrison, 91. TBF—Johnson, 349. R—Novoa, 58. ER—Rodriguez, 52. HR—Harkcom and Wade, 12. SAC—Romanczuk, 7. SF—three pitchers tied with 5. HB—Alvarez, 12. BB—Neighborgall, 45. IBB—four pitchers tied with 3. SO—Smith, 100. WP—Neighborgall, 23. BK—Cupps and Arias, 4.

ALL PITCHERS

*Lefthanded pitcher.

Pitcher, Team	W	L	Pct.	ERA	G	GS	CG	ShO	GF	Sv.	IP	H	TBF	R	ER	HR	SH	SF	HB	BB	IBB	SO	WP	Bk.
Alvarez, Mario, Ogden	3	3	.500	6.14	12	12	0	0	0	0	55.2	63	252	39	38	8	1	1	12	22	0	53	3	0
Arias, Marlon, Ogden *	4	4	.500	5.48	14	14	0	0	0	0	70.2	81	319	53	43	11	0	4	1	27	0	73	9	4
Baeza, Eduardo, Missoula	1	2	.333	2.25	25	0	0	0	13	3	40.0	31	159	12	10	1	1	0	0	13	1	50	4	1
Begnaud, Russell, Idaho Falls	2	4	.333	5.63	12	11	0	0	1	1	54.1	77	255	46	34	5	1	1	3	17	0	37	7	0
Beresford, Simon, Helena	1	1	.500	2.55	7	4	0	0	1	0	24.2	24	101	10	7	1	2	2	0	8	1	25	2	0
Bernal, Luis, Helena	1	1	.500	10.91	9	0	0	0	2	0	15.2	22	82	21	19	3	1	1	5	6	0	8	0	0
Binda, Byron, Casper	4	1	.800	4.60	21	0	0	0	4	0	31.1	39	146	24	16	5	0	2	4	12	1	38	4	0
Bongiovanni, Vincent, Missoula	0	2	.000	5.29	23	0	0	0	9	1	34.0	31	163	23	20	2	2	0	6	28	2	36	8	0
Brantley, Brandon, Idaho Falls	0	2	.000	7.11	18	7	0	0	4	0	50.2	70	243	44	40	8	1	2	7	24	0	47	7	0
Brennan, Chris, Great Falls *	0	0	.000	5.68	8	0	0	0	1	0	12.2	12	57	8	8	2	2	1	3	8	0	14	0	0
Breshears, Glenn, Helena	1	2	.333	4.50	12	0	0	0	8	3	16.0	15	78	8	8	1	1	0	3	11	0	21	3	0
Bulger, Kevin, Idaho Falls	0	1	.000	9.53	10	0	0	0	4	0	11.1	15	58	13	12	0	0	1	2	8	0	9	4	1
Camardese, Brandon, Billings *	1	1	.500	4.42	15	4	0	0	2	0	38.2	46	167	21	19	1	1	1	2	11	0	36	4	0
Carlson, Zane, Idaho Falls	0	0	.000	1.00	8	0	0	0	8	5	9.0	6	32	1	1	0	0	0	1	2	0	6	1	0
Casey, James, Great Falls	1	4	.200	5.71	22	0	0	0	7	0	34.2	32	166	24	22	3	2	3	5	32	3	39	6	1
Cedeno, Xavier, Casper *	1	3	.250	5.43	12	12	0	0	0	0	53.0	62	233	36	32	4	3	1	8	17	0	47	3	0
Chirino, Israel, Great Falls *	0	2	.000	11.25	10	0	0	0	2	0	12.0	18	73	20	15	0	1	2	0	16	1	14	8	0
Church, Lorenzo, Missoula	1	2	.333	5.58	20	0	0	0	2	0	40.1	53	204	31	25	3	0	5	6	26	2	48	7	0
Cromer, Bennett, Idaho Falls	7	3	.700	5.07	16	10	0	0	0	0	60.1	74	267	45	34	9	2	0	6	13	0	55	2	0
Cupps, Anthony, Missoula	4	6	.400	5.05	15	12	0	0	0	0	67.2	76	295	48	38	6	4	1	5	29	1	54	6	4
Davidson, Phillip, Idaho Falls	4	2	.667	6.75	9	5	0	0	1	0	34.2	46	162	27	26	3	1	2	1	14	2	29	1	0
Davis, Vincent, Missoula *	2	2	.500	3.16	16	0	0	0	5	1	25.2	24	113	12	9	2	0	0	2	15	1	28	2	0
De Los Santos, Riquy, Casper	2	3	.400	6.48	21	0	0	0	6	0	25.0	27	123	20	18	2	3	1	4	24	2	21	5	1
Dipietro, Ryan, Idaho Falls *	1	6	.143	5.63	15	15	0	0	0	0	64.0	72	287	45	40	8	0	1	6	17	0	56	5	1
Doyle, Travis, Great Falls	3	2	.600	4.68	13	4	0	0	4	0	32.2	40	152	23	17	2	0	2	3	10	0	33	1	0
Duda, Peter, Missoula	1	2	.333	10.80	19	1	0	0	6	0	31.2	49	180	44	38	9	0	2	10	31	0	29	7	0

ADVANCED ROOKIE Pioneer League

Pitcher, Team	W	L	Pct.	ERA	G	GS	CG	ShO	GF	Sv.	IP	H	TBF	R	ER	HR	SH	SF	HB	BB	IBB	SO	WP	Bk.
Durden, Brandon, Casper *	1	4	.200	6.02	12	11	0	0	0	0	49.1	72	238	42	33	7	4	3	3	23	3	49	5	0
Eckley, Jacob, Idaho Falls *	3	2	.600	7.18	21	0	0	0	11	3	31.1	49	151	31	25	3	3	1	0	8	0	25	3	0
Espinosa, Sandy, Casper	1	2	.333	4.64	21	0	0	0	6	0	33.0	32	154	23	17	3	2	3	5	22	0	30	7	1
Evans, Cody, Missoula	0	2	.000	9.23	20	3	0	0	3	0	40.0	68	214	44	41	4	2	5	4	25	0	27	7	0
Everly, Eric, Great Falls *	1	2	.333	3.12	8	8	0	0	0	0	43.1	41	185	26	15	1	6	2	5	17	1	35	0	1
Fabian, Robinson, Casper	1	3	.250	11.79	12	3	0	0	3	0	23.2	43	120	33	31	8	0	2	1	8	1	20	5	0
Feliz, Rainer, Billings	2	2	.500	7.12	16	2	0	0	4	1	30.1	43	140	30	24	2	1	4	2	12	0	17	3	0
Fisher, Charles, Billings	4	4	.500	4.19	15	8	0	0	1	1	53.2	56	235	30	25	3	0	2	5	19	0	45	3	0
Garcia, Eliszer, Idaho Falls *	2	2	.500	3.45	20	0	0	0	6	1	44.1	41	194	20	17	1	0	3	3	22	0	45	14	1
Garrison, Aaron, Billings	4	1	.800	3.41	8	4	0	0	0	0	29.0	23	117	12	11	1	1	0	2	6	0	24	4	0
Geiersbach, Kennth, Billings	3	4	.429	4.34	23	1	0	0	6	2	37.1	36	158	24	18	2	5	2	3	15	3	33	1	0
Goins, Mitchell, Idaho Falls	0	0	.000	8.72	8	0	0	0	0	0	21.2	35	103	22	21	4	1	0	2	4	0	12	2	1
Gomez de Segura, Matthew, Ogden	1	2	.333	6.57	17	0	0	0	10	1	24.2	31	129	22	18	2	0	1	4	24	1	19	5	0
Gonzalez, Rafael, Billings	3	0	1.000	3.43	11	6	0	0	1	1	42.0	36	182	18	16	7	1	0	5	23	0	37	4	1
Green, Matthew, Missoula	4	3	.571	5.55	15	12	0	0	2	0	60.0	77	278	41	37	6	1	3	5	26	0	59	7	0
Haltiwanger, Kevin, Billings	0	0	.000	6.43	3	2	0	0	1	0	7.0	10	37	8	5	0	0	1	1	4	0	7	2	0
Hammond, Steven, Helena *	1	0	1.000	1.06	4	2	0	0	0	0	17.0	13	65	5	2	1	1	1	1	0	0	23	0	0
Harkcom, James, Idaho Falls	3	5	.375	8.16	16	8	0	0	3	2	46.1	71	221	46	42	12	2	0	6	16	0	47	2	0
Hayes, Alvin, Ogden	2	1	.667	7.26	19	2	0	0	3	0	31.0	28	145	26	25	4	0	1	1	27	0	38	13	0
Henninger, David, Idaho Falls	5	1	.833	3.60	21	0	0	0	3	1	60.0	58	256	33	24	2	3	1	7	23	1	64	6	1
Hipke, Ross, Casper	1	1	.500	6.75	19	0	0	0	4	0	32.0	41	144	33	24	11	2	3	0	9	0	26	2	2
Hochgesang, Nathan, Ogden	1	2	.333	4.25	14	0	0	0	3	0	29.2	36	134	22	14	2	1	1	0	12	0	28	8	0
Horlacher, David, Ogden	0	0	.000	1.69	11	0	0	0	1	0	16.0	10	66	5	3	1	1	0	1	9	0	25	1	0
Inman, William, Helena	6	0	1.000	2.00	13	5	0	0	2	1	45.0	29	173	11	10	5	1	0	3	11	0	58	6	0
Jean, Christopher, Helena	0	0	.000	5.91	15	3	0	0	4	0	32.0	46	150	26	21	4	2	0	4	8	0	16	1	0
Johnson, Thomas, Casper	3	2	.600	3.97	15	15	0	0	0	0	79.1	90	348	44	35	1	1	2	2	24	1	78	4	0
Johnston, Andrew, Casper	1	2	.333	1.06	30	0	0	0	29	18	34.0	22	136	10	4	0	1	0	7	2	24	2	0
Julio, Donald, Missoula	3	2	.600	5.32	21	2	0	0	6	2	45.2	50	210	34	27	6	1	2	1	22	0	43	3	0
Kalkhof, Adam, Idaho Falls *	3	2	.600	4.31	19	0	0	0	7	1	39.2	44	176	21	19	4	1	2	1	12	0	52	2	1
Klusman, James, Ogden	4	2	.667	3.09	20	0	0	0	8	0	32.0	35	138	16	11	1	2	1	1	10	1	24	0	0
Kniginyzky, Matthew, Idaho Falls	2	5	.286	4.66	21	0	0	0	15	5	29.0	35	141	22	15	0	3	2	4	13	1	40	4	0
Kretzschmar, Mathew, Helena	0	0	.000	5.55	8	4	0	0	2	0	24.1	28	110	15	15	3	0	2	11	0	23	3	1
Krise, Kristopher, Ogden	0	4	.000	7.90	15	4	0	0	6	0	35.1	51	170	40	31	8	1	2	0	14	1	28	2	1
Lanier, Thomas, Billings	0	0	.000	6.23	5	0	0	0	2	0	4.1	8	26	4	3	1	0	1	4	0	3	1	0
Laureano, Wilfrido, Helena	0	0	.000	3.29	14	1	0	0	4	0	27.1	24	118	10	10	2	0	0	1	13	0	36	3	2
Leach, Brent, Ogden *	5	3	.625	2.43	14	13	1	0	0	0	66.2	53	267	21	18	4	2	0	5	29	0	77	4	0
Lecure, Samuel, Billings	5	1	.833	3.27	13	6	0	0	0	0	41.1	43	175	18	15	2	1	0	2	15	0	44	2	1
Lemon, Nickolas, Great Falls	3	4	.429	2.63	30	0	0	0	15	3	41.0	30	168	17	12	1	2	0	3	18	0	46	5	1
Lluberes, Rafael, Helena *	4	4	.500	6.00	16	8	0	0	2	2	48.0	55	217	39	32	4	1	5	3	19	0	27	1	2
Logan, Boone, Great Falls *	1	1	.500	3.31	21	0	0	0	5	2	35.1	34	141	15	13	1	0	1	2	13	0	29	4	0
Louis, Joshua, Helena	1	2	.333	5.64	17	0	0	0	6	5	30.1	38	138	23	19	3	2	0	2	8	0	28	5	0
Malave, Ronny, Helena	4	0	1.000	1.91	14	0	0	0	4	1	28.1	25	114	11	6	0	3	1	11	0	16	1	0
Mannon, Adam, Helena	0	0	.000	36.00	1	0	0	0	1	0	1.0	3	7	4	4	1	0	0	0	1	0	1	0	0
Manzueta, Radhames, Casper	0	4	.000	8.78	4	4	0	0	0	0	13.1	25	76	22	13	1	0	0	3	8	0	13	2	0
Marion, William, Helena	4	3	.571	5.90	17	10	0	0	4	1	58.0	57	276	47	38	9	0	2	7	36	0	49	9	1
Marshall, Jay, Great Falls *	2	0	1.000	2.70	29	0	0	0	16	6	43.1	35	174	20	13	3	0	1	3	7	0	43	1	0
McCleland, Bruce, Idaho Falls	0	0	.000	17.18	3	0	0	0	2	0	3.2	7	18	7	7	1	0	0	0	3	0	1	0	0
McDonald, James, Ogden	0	0	.000	1.50	4	0	0	0	0	0	6.0	4	26	3	1	0	0	0	1	2	0	9	0	0
Meloan, Jonathan, Ogden	0	2	.000	3.69	16	6	0	0	5	1	39.0	30	165	16	16	4	1	2	2	18	0	54	6	1
Metzger, Jason, Casper *	6	1	.857	5.13	22	4	0	0	1	0	47.1	50	201	29	27	7	3	2	3	13	0	40	4	2
Miller, Derek, Helena *	1	1	.500	2.75	9	6	0	0	1	1	36.0	31	142	16	11	4	1	1	0	4	0	35	0	0
Morris, James, Billings *	1	1	.500	6.88	17	0	0	0	12	0	17.0	20	82	14	13	3	0	0	3	13	0	14	5	0
Morrison, Tyler, Helena	5	3	.625	5.78	17	12	0	0	2	0	67.0	91	302	51	43	7	3	2	2	14	0	63	12	0
Moviel, Paul, Great Falls	4	1	.800	4.04	15	15	0	0	0	0	78.0	89	335	40	35	3	1	3	5	20	0	72	8	0
Nachreiner, Matthew, Great Falls	4	3	.571	6.55	22	0	0	0	6	1	33.0	39	163	31	24	1	0	1	3	23	2	31	7	0
Neighborgall, Jason, Missoula	1	2	.333	11.12	15	7	0	0	1	0	22.2	21	142	40	28	1	0	3	5	45	0	29	23	0
Nicoll, Christopher, Idaho Falls	0	3	.000	3.62	7	7	0	0	0	0	27.1	26	115	14	11	4	1	0	2	9	0	34	0	0
Nippert, Dustin, Missoula	1	1	.500	6.56	15	3	0	0	4	0	35.2	44	166	27	26	4	0	0	3	12	0	35	4	0
Novoa, Yunior, Great Falls *	1	7	.125	7.32	15	13	0	0	2	0	62.2	83	292	58	51	11	5	4	4	28	1	44	5	3
Obispo, Jose, Ogden	0	0	.000	8.53	6	0	0	0	2	0	6.1	8	38	6	6	0	0	0	0	5	0	6	5	0
Ondrusek, Logan, Billings	1	6	.143	6.02	15	9	0	0	1	0	55.1	72	255	49	37	9	2	1	6	19	0	46	10	0
O'Neal, Charles, Billings *	0	1	.000	6.20	17	2	0	0	3	0	24.2	31	117	17	17	1	0	2	0	17	0	17	6	0
Paredes, Ramon, Ogden *	1	1	.500	7.59	3	1	0	0	0	0	10.2	12	49	10	9	2	0	1	1	7	0	6	3	0
Parillo, Brandon, Helena *	2	1	.667	2.14	12	0	0	0	5	1	21.0	18	92	10	5	0	1	1	4	9	0	19	2	0
Pena, Luis, Great Falls	0	1	.000	6.75	18	0	0	0	6	0	33.1	44	168	32	25	5	0	2	6	22	1	25	6	2
Penn, Michael, Idaho Falls	0	1	.000	5.06	5	5	0	0	0	0	21.1	23	87	13	12	2	0	1	0	4	0	20	2	0
Perez, Carlos, Great Falls	4	6	.400	4.38	16	10	0	0	1	0	61.2	67	269	39	30	7	3	3	3	22	0	40	9	1
Pfeiffer, David, Ogden *	7	3	.700	5.63	15	7	0	0	4	1	56.0	62	239	42	35	4	3	1	3	14	0	47	2	0
Pichardo, Manuel, Casper	1	0	1.000	5.34	23	0	0	0	4	0	32.0	37	151	29	19	5	1	1	4	18	0	29	10	0
Pohlman, Daniel, Missoula	2	4	.333	3.63	27	3	0	0	22	13	44.2	41	197	24	18	2	3	1	6	21	2	48	3	0
Pratt, Jordan, Ogden	2	2	.500	3.25	14	0	0	0	2	0	27.2	24	122	12	10	0	1	1	5	14	0	35	11	0
Ramirez, Miguel, Ogden	0	0	.000	2.31	7	0	0	0	1	0	11.2	9	46	3	3	2	1	0	0	3	1	21	0	0
Renkert, Dane, Helena	2	1	.667	2.70	15	0	0	0	4	2	26.2	22	118	11	8	0	0	2	12	0	34	5	1
Rice, Jason, Great Falls	0	0	.000	10.38	2	0	0	0	0	0	4.1	6	22	6	5	0	0	1	5	0	4	1	0
Richard, Clayton, Great Falls *	2	1	.667	2.85	10	9	0	0	0	0	41.0	37	168	19	13	2	1	1	12	0	39	0	1
Roberts, Kevin, Helena	1	2	.333	2.82	8	3	0	0	2	0	22.1	19	94	8	7	0	2	0	0	8	0	34	2	1
Rodriguez, Aneury, Casper	3	4	.429	7.55	15	15	0	0	0	0	62.0	77	283	54	52	7	2	1	7	26	0	47	11	1
Rodriguez, Mark, Billings	0	0	.000	0.00	1	0	0	0	0	0	1.0	0	4	0	0	0	0	0	0	0	0	1	0	0
Rodriguez, Noe, Great Falls *	2	5	.286	4.50	13	10	0	0	0	0	58.0	60	255	38	29	4	0	1	4	20	0	71	7	2
Roe, Chaz, Casper	5	2	.714	4.17	12	12	0	0	0	0	49.2	31	220	25	23	2	0	1	6	36	0	55	8	0

Pitcher, Team	W	L	Pct.	ERA	G	GS	CG	ShO	GF	Sv.	IP	H	TBF	R	ER	HR	SH	SF	HB	BB	IBB	SO	WP	Bk.
Rojas, Jose A., Billings	2	4	.333	5.90	22	4	0	0	10	4	39.2	41	176	27	26	7	1	4	5	22	0	34	9	1
Romanczuk, Mark, Missoula *	4	5	.444	4.55	13	13	0	0	0	0	61.1	70	273	37	31	6	7	2	6	17	1	59	4	1
Rote, Ryan, Great Falls	3	3	.500	3.52	12	0	0	0	11	2	15.1	13	65	10	6	0	2	0	3	6	0	19	1	1
Ruthven, Sean, Casper	2	1	.667	3.58	18	0	0	0	6	1	27.2	25	120	20	11	5	1	0	1	11	2	35	7	0
Ryan, Patrick, Helena	0	0	.000	3.15	17	0	0	0	9	1	20.0	19	83	9	7	1	1	0	0	6	1	20	3	0
Sanchez, Rafael, Casper	2	1	.667	3.24	13	0	0	0	1	0	16.2	15	72	7	6	0	1	0	1	7	1	18	2	0
Sanchez, Ramon (Perez), Missoula	2	2	.500	5.71	9	6	0	0	0	0	34.2	39	155	26	22	4	2	1	3	14	0	37	4	1
Santiago, Mario, Idaho Falls	0	3	.000	6.61	10	8	0	0	0	0	32.2	39	164	34	24	3	2	2	7	20	0	20	4	0
Schambough, Douglas, Idaho Falls	0	0	.000	2.70	7	0	0	0	3	0	6.2	7	29	2	2	1	0	0	0	3	0	9	0	0
Smith, Gregory, Missoula *	8	5	.615	4.15	16	14	0	0	0	0	82.1	69	324	40	38	8	2	2	5	18	2	100	6	0
Stevens, Jeffrey, Billings	4	4	.500	2.98	13	8	0	0	1	0	54.1	44	222	20	18	4	0	2	5	15	0	58	1	0
Strickland, Brett, Casper	4	3	.571	1.43	30	0	0	0	10	3	44.0	34	181	11	7	0	1	0	1	16	3	45	3	2
Stumm, Jason, Great Falls	0	1	.000	5.06	3	0	0	0	0	0	5.1	10	26	7	3	1	1	0	0	0	0	4	0	0
Thatcher, Joeseph, Helena *	2	0	1.000	3.52	6	0	0	0	6	2	7.2	8	33	3	3	1	0	0	1	1	0	10	0	0
Thomas, Eric, Helena	0	1	.000	2.53	3	2	0	0	0	0	10.2	6	40	5	3	0	1	0	2	2	0	7	1	1
Torres, Carlos, Great Falls	1	1	.500	2.88	5	5	0	0	0	0	25.0	18	96	8	8	1	1	0	0	8	0	26	0	0
Trammell, Travis, Idaho Falls	2	0	1.000	7.31	15	0	0	0	6	0	16.0	27	78	16	13	3	1	2	0	3	0	16	0	1
Troncoso, Ramon, Ogden	6	2	.750	3.68	29	0	0	0	27	13	36.2	40	166	19	15	0	1	2	8	12	1	30	4	0
Ursin, Damian, Billings	1	0	1.000	2.00	3	1	0	0	1	0	9.0	9	38	2	2	1	0	0	0	5	1	7	3	0
Valiquette, Philippe-Alexandre, Billings *	2	1	.667	6.43	7	3	0	0	0	0	21.0	23	89	16	15	1	1	0	0	10	0	18	6	2
Vecchio, Jason, Billings	0	2	.000	5.06	5	0	0	0	3	1	5.1	5	24	4	3	1	0	0	1	2	0	8	0	0
Venas, Miliade, Missoula	0	0	.000	10.64	8	0	0	0	3	0	11.0	18	61	16	13	0	0	0	2	8	0	6	3	0
Wachman, Robert, Billings	3	1	.750	4.58	16	5	0	0	1	0	53.0	60	240	33	27	3	2	3	8	19	1	54	9	2
Wade, Cory, Ogden	2	3	.400	4.35	16	11	1	0	0	0	72.1	81	303	42	35	12	3	1	5	19	0	60	3	0
Webb, Lindsay, Casper	0	1	.000	5.40	15	0	0	0	6	0	18.1	20	87	13	11	2	0	0	4	10	0	9	2	0
Welch, David, Helena *	4	1	.800	2.77	12	3	0	0	4	3	26.0	21	110	10	8	2	2	1	0	12	1	29	3	0
White, Cody, Ogden *	1	3	.250	6.92	17	6	0	0	2	0	40.1	59	197	35	31	2	2	2	0	27	0	36	9	0
Wilson, David, Billings *	2	0	1.000	4.41	13	7	0	0	3	1	49.0	48	200	25	24	5	1	1	1	14	0	35	5	1
Wood, Travis, Billings *	2	0	1.000	1.82	6	4	0	0	0	0	24.2	15	103	6	5	0	1	0	4	13	0	22	2	0
Woody, Abraham, Billings	3	0	1.000	2.03	25	0	0	0	24	14	26.2	28	116	9	6	1	0	1	0	5	1	38	1	0
Wooley, Robert, Helena	6	7	.462	4.70	18	13	0	0	3	1	74.2	86	331	48	39	7	2	2	6	20	0	69	8	0

COMBINATION SHUTOUTS: Billings (3) -- Fisher-Rojas, Gonzalez-Garrison-Morris, Lecure-Geiersbach. Casper (4) -- Rodriguez-Binda-Ruthven-Strickland, Roe-Johnston, Johnson-Strickland, Roe-Metzger-Strickland-Johnston. Great Falls (2) -- Richard-Chirino-Rote, Moviel-Nachreiner-Marshall. Helena (4) -- Miller-Laureano-Bernal, Wooley-Renkert, Beresford-Breshears-Welch-Laureano, Beresford-Welch-Laureano-Malave. Idaho Falls (1) -- Cromer-Harkcom. Missoula (2) -- Smith-Baeza-Davis, Smith-Nippert-Pohlman. Ogden (3) -- Alvarez-Wade-Pratt-Klusman, Leach-Wade-Gomez de Segura, Leach-Ramirez. Orem (5) -- Whittington-Hawkins-Sullivan-Lynch, Arredondo-Morillo-Cruz Chavez, Hawkins-Cruz Chavez, Marek-Hill-Lynch, Hawkins-Pete-Lynch.

NO-HIT GAMES: Beresford (3 innings), Breshears (2.1 innings), Welch (1.2 innings) and Laureano (2 innings), Helena, defeated Billings, 11-0, August 5.

2005 FIELDING

TEAM

Team	G	PO	A	E	TC	DP	TP	PB	Pct.
Orem	76	2037	914	110	3061	74	0	23	.964
Billings	76	1993	829	110	2932	82	0	20	.962
Ogden	76	2004	863	114	2981	69	0	24	.962
Missoula	76	2032	816	122	2970	73	0	23	.959
Helena	76	2039	808	126	2973	51	0	21	.958
Idaho Falls	76	1993	825	127	2945	68	0	25	.957
Casper	76	2015	914	139	3068	82	0	34	.955
Great Falls	76	2018	926	166	3110	80	0	19	.947

INDIVIDUAL

FIRST BASEMEN

NOTE: All caps denotes fielding-percentage leader based on 38 games for catchers, 51 for all other non-pitchers and 61 innings for pitchers. *Throws lefthanded.

Player, Team	Pct.	G	PO	A	E	TC	DP
Adkison, Blake, Idaho Falls	.979	20	174	11	4	189	15
Allen, Brandon, Great Falls	.973	51	461	41	14	516	44
Alonso, John, Helena	.976	5	38	2	1	41	2
Berglund, Bret, Casper	.971	6	65	3	2	70	1
Blumenthal, Kyle, Casper	.983	29	272	18	5	295	30
BYRNE, BRYAN, Missoula	.990	57	455	30	5	490	43
Cook, Christopher, Casper	.969	38	348	28	12	388	32
Crouch, Will, Missoula	1.000	1	8	0	0	8	0
Diaz, Osvaldo, Missoula	.963	3	24	2	1	27	5
Everett, Brady, Idaho Falls	1.000	8	80	4	0	84	10
Gallardo, Carlos, Helena *	.992	26	121	8	1	130	7
Gamel, Mathew, Helena	.964	3	27	0	1	28	1
Herrera, Brenan, Idaho Falls	1.000	2	17	1	0	18	0
Howell, Jeffrey, Idaho Falls	1.000	2	5	1	0	6	0
Langham, James, Billings	.972	9	65	5	2	72	10
Mena, Steve, Missoula	.987	16	139	10	2	151	14
Mooneyhan, Jason, Ogden *	.995	22	171	20	1	192	17
Mummy, Benjamin, Billings	.997	44	351	37	1	389	40
Roberts, Brandon, Billings	.967	28	222	16	8	246	18
Rodriguez, Manuel Esteban, Great Falls	.966	20	162	9	6	177	19
Rodriguez, Mark, Billings	1.000	1	12	0	0	12	0

Player, Team	Pct.	G	PO	A	E	TC	DP
Ronda, Jose, Billings	1.000	2	9	1	0	10	0
Schmidt, Jeffrey, Great Falls	.986	7	69	4	1	74	1
Sharp, Matthew, Great Falls	1.000	4	29	4	0	33	6
Suarez, Steven, Casper	.977	5	39	3	1	43	6
Sutherland, David, Ogden *	.989	45	417	25	5	447	34
Taloa, Rick, Ogden	.974	11	70	6	2	78	10
Terrell, Joshua, Missoula	1.000	1	0	1	0	1	0
Turner, Jase, Idaho Falls	.984	48	400	22	7	429	31
Willcutt, Bradley, Helena	1.000	9	67	7	0	74	10
Yost, Edgar, Helena	.988	48	393	33	5	431	27

SECOND BASEMEN

Player, Team	Pct.	G	PO	A	E	TC	DP
Acosta, Rolando, Great Falls	.953	13	17	24	2	43	5
Batten, Joseph, Missoula	.908	20	36	43	8	87	12
Brooks, Parker, Ogden	.857	8	11	13	4	28	1
Castillo, Javier, Great Falls	1.000	1	0	1	0	1	0
Colafemina, Joshua, Idaho Falls	.973	16	23	48	2	73	9
Crew, Ryan, Helena	.929	3	6	7	1	14	0
Crist, Justin, Ogden	1.000	4	7	8	0	15	3
CRUZ, RICARDO, Missoula	.960	54	96	145	10	251	31
De Jesus, Michael, Billings	.978	40	72	105	4	181	28
Getz, Christopher, Great Falls	1.000	1	1	4	0	5	1
Guest, Dennis, Great Falls	.946	62	125	190	18	333	49
Holmberg, Kenneth, Helena	.977	49	81	130	5	216	20
Jirschele, Jeremy, Idaho Falls	.938	4	6	9	1	16	3
Johnson, Brandon, Great Falls	1.000	4	5	13	0	18	1
Johnson, Joshua, Idaho Falls	.957	37	85	93	8	186	23
Justis, Shane, Ogden	.955	10	13	29	2	44	3
Lasso, Yoni, Billings	...	1	0	0	0	0	0
McKnight, Scott, Helena	.894	22	33	43	9	85	4
Polanco, Armando, Casper	1.000	4	5	11	0	16	3
Ryal, Rusty, Missoula	.959	12	18	29	2	49	11
Sandoval, Mayker, Billings	.932	45	75	116	14	205	24
Septimo, Agustin, Helena	.923	12	26	34	5	65	7
Soto, Jesus, Ogden	.949	61	102	180	15	297	41
Wimberly, Corey, Casper	.944	22	25	77	6	108	17
Young, Eric, Casper	.930	56	111	182	22	315	39

THIRD BASEMEN

Player, Team	Pct.	G	PO	A	E	TC	DP
Bell, Michael, Helena	.865	22	14	31	7	52	1
Berglund, Bret, Casper	1.000	3	2	11	0	13	2

Player, Team	Pct.	G	PO	A	E	TC	DP
Braun, Ryan, Helena	.933	6	2	12	1	15	1
Castillo, Javier, Great Falls	.333	1	0	1	2	3	0
Colafemina, Joshua, Idaho Falls	.845	20	14	46	11	71	3
Cook, Christopher, Casper	1.000	1	2	0	0	2	0
Crew, Ryan, Helena	.857	6	0	6	1	7	0
Crist, Justin, Ogden	.750	2	0	3	1	4	1
Cruz, Ricardo, Missoula	.000	2	0	0	1	1	0
De Jesus, Michael, Billings	1.000	1	0	1	0	1	0
Delgado, Ronny, Billings	.938	4	7	8	1	16	1
Gamel, Mathew, Helena	.851	41	15	65	14	94	4
Griffin, Michael, Helena	1.000	3	3	7	0	10	2
Guest, Dennis, Great Falls	.500	1	0	1	1	2	0
Hayes, Shawn, Idaho Falls	1.000	10	7	9	0	16	0
Herrera, Brenan, Idaho Falls	.871	22	17	37	8	62	5
Hollis, Eric, Great Falls	.000	1	0	0	1	1	0
Holmberg, Kenneth, Helena	...	1	0	0	0	0	0
Jimenez, Jose, Helena	.900	7	3	15	2	20	1
Jirschele, Jeremy, Idaho Falls	.980	13	12	38	1	51	3
Johnson, Brandon, Great Falls	.802	54	30	112	35	177	8
Justis, Shane, Ogden	.727	10	2	6	3	11	0
Mayora, Daniel, Casper	.881	32	23	51	10	84	2
Mena, Steve, Missoula	.857	17	9	27	6	42	1
Mitchell, Russell, Ogden	.933	66	52	130	13	195	12
Polanco, Armando, Casper	.848	13	3	25	5	33	3
Reininger, Jarrett, Billings	.922	45	27	79	9	115	10
Rodriguez, Manuel Esteban, Great Falls	1.000	1	0	1	0	1	0
Ronda, Jose, Billings	.780	20	9	30	11	50	2
RYAL, RUSTY, Missoula	.953	61	48	115	8	171	13
Sandoval, Mayker, Billings	.842	9	5	11	3	19	0
Schmidt, Jeffrey, Great Falls	.920	25	27	42	6	75	6
Septimo, Agustin, Helena	1.000	3	4	3	0	7	0
Strickland, Geoff, Casper	1.000	5	4	12	0	16	0
Wimberly, Corey, Casper	.889	33	25	55	10	90	6
Garner, Robert, Casper	.950	49	72	4	4	80	0
Godwin, Adam, Ogden	.962	51	75	1	3	79	0
Holden, Joshua, Billings *	.986	53	70	2	1	73	1
Jackson, Derry, Ogden	.951	30	54	4	3	61	1
Johnson, Brandon, Great Falls	1.000	3	1	0	0	1	0
Katin, Brendan, Helena	.957	28	45	0	2	47	0
Lajara, Luis, Missoula *	.909	11	8	2	1	11	0
Langham, James, Billings	.946	26	32	3	2	37	1
Larsen, Andrew, Idaho Falls	.935	59	96	5	7	108	1
Lewis, Kenneth, Billings *	.934	53	55	2	4	61	2
Locke, Andrew, Ogden	.985	48	66	1	1	68	0
Loupadiere, Maruis, Casper	.967	24	28	1	1	30	0
Mannon, Adam, Helena	1.000	10	10	1	0	11	0
McDonald, James, Ogden	1.000	26	29	3	0	32	1
Melendez, Norman, Missoula	1.000	20	12	1	0	13	0
Mena, Steve, Missoula	.964	22	25	2	1	28	0
Parejo, Freddy, Helena	.945	33	66	3	4	73	0
Pedroza, Sergio, Ogden	.850	12	16	1	3	20	0
Peguero, Felix, Idaho Falls	.931	46	77	4	6	87	0
Pujols, Kengshill, Ogden	...	1	0	0	0	0	0
Richmond, Barry, Ogden *	.963	61	95	10	4	109	3
Roberts, Brandon, Billings	.983	63	113	4	2	119	1
Roberts, Daron, Great Falls	.969	62	88	5	3	96	2
Robinson, Trayvon, Ogden	1.000	6	13	0	0	13	0
Rodriguez, Manuel Esteban, Great Falls	.929	40	39	0	3	42	0
Roman, Edwin, Missoula	.957	19	22	0	1	23	0
Sabatini, Antonio, Idaho Falls *	.951	43	53	5	3	61	1
Santana, Ethien, Idaho Falls *	.962	60	100	2	4	106	0
Santiago, Jayson, Missoula *	.933	33	55	1	4	60	0
Schmidt, Jeffrey, Great Falls	1.000	8	5	1	0	6	1
Septimo, Agustin, Helena	1.000	12	16	2	0	18	1
Steidl, Sam, Ogden *	1.000	8	10	2	0	12	0
TARTAGLIA, EVAN, Great Falls *	.991	66	106	5	1	112	0
Thomson, Gregory, Missoula *	.976	42	78	4	2	84	2
Tribble, Matthew, Great Falls *	.905	63	82	4	9	95	0
Tully, Travis, Missoula *	.987	50	72	4	1	77	0
Yost, Edgar, Helena	1.000	4	4	0	0	4	0

SHORTSTOPS

Player, Team	Pct.	G	PO	A	E	TC	DP
Acosta, Rolando, Great Falls	.904	31	51	109	17	177	25
Bell, Michael, Helena	.933	32	48	92	10	150	16
Castillo, Javier, Great Falls	.922	43	60	130	16	206	19
Ciriaco, Pedro, Missoula	.899	69	105	199	34	338	39
Colafemina, Joshua, Idaho Falls	.944	10	10	24	2	36	4
Crew, Ryan, Helena	.927	35	37	103	11	151	6
Crist, Justin, Ogden	.955	9	15	27	2	44	6
Cruz, Ricardo, Missoula	.877	12	16	34	7	57	9
De Jesus, Ivan, Ogden	.913	17	24	39	6	69	7
De Jesus, Michael, Billings	1.000	7	5	3	0	8	2
Eymann, Eric, Billings	.925	30	53	83	11	147	20
Feiner, Kevyn, Billings	.800	3	2	6	2	10	1
Getz, Christopher, Great Falls	.909	5	8	12	2	22	6
Guest, Dennis, Great Falls	...	2	0	0	0	0	0
Hayes, Shawn, Idaho Falls	1.000	3	2	6	0	8	0
Justis, Shane, Ogden	.981	13	21	31	1	53	10
Lasso, Yoni, Billings	.974	8	13	24	1	38	3
Mayora, Daniel, Casper	.883	15	15	38	7	60	8
McConnell, Christopher, Idaho Falls	.929	66	114	187	23	324	36
McKnight, Scott, Helena	.896	20	23	37	7	67	10
NAZARIO, RADAMES, Casper	.940	56	87	178	17	282	41
Rivera, Juan, Ogden	.922	41	60	130	16	206	24
Rosales, Adam, Billings	.983	33	62	115	3	180	29
Wimberly, Corey, Casper	.885	12	18	28	6	52	5

OUTFIELDERS

Player, Team	Pct.	G	PO	A	E	TC	DP
Allen, Trevor, Casper	.951	31	37	2	2	41	1
Barber, Byron, Idaho Falls	.969	30	28	3	1	32	0
Belcher, Jordan, Billings	.979	29	43	3	1	47	1
Berglund, Bret, Casper	.957	44	60	6	3	69	1
Brantley, Michael, Helena *	.917	9	11	0	1	12	0
Brownell, Jesse, Casper	.970	30	29	3	1	33	0
Bruce, Jay, Billings *	.951	14	35	4	2	41	1
Cain, Lorenzo, Helena	1.000	3	5	1	0	6	0
Chapman, Stephen, Helena *	.961	51	71	3	3	77	1
Crew, Ryan, Helena	1.000	19	22	2	0	24	1
Crouch, Will, Missoula	.938	19	28	2	2	32	1
De Jesus, Michael, Billings	...	1	0	0	0	0	0
Diaz, Osvaldo, Missoula	.967	42	56	2	2	60	0
Fermaint, Charlie, Helena	.951	30	56	2	3	61	1
Ford, Darren, Helena	.979	60	92	2	2	96	0
Fowler, William, Casper	.965	59	108	3	4	115	1

CATCHERS

Player, Team	Pct.	G	PO	A	E	TC	DP
Apodaca, Juan, Ogden	.976	38	296	32	8	336	4
Blevins, John, Helena	1.000	11	83	12	0	95	0
Blumenthal, Benjamin, Billings	.978	28	195	32	5	232	2
Blumenthal, Kyle, Casper	.993	16	116	25	1	142	0
Bustamante, Gerardo, Missoula	1.000	7	18	1	0	19	0
DeCarlo, Michael, Missoula	.987	41	327	42	5	374	2
Denove, Christopher, Billings	.976	47	333	39	9	381	5
Dombek, Gregory, Casper	1.000	2	16	3	0	19	0
Elder, Jake, Missoula	.983	39	313	26	6	345	3
Everett, Brady, Idaho Falls	.972	9	63	7	2	72	0
Gil, Rotsen, Ogden	.961	12	85	13	4	102	0
HERNANDEZ, FRANCISCO, Great Falls	.989	39	296	57	4	357	5
Hollis, Eric, Great Falls	.979	29	220	18	5	243	2
Howell, Jeffrey, Idaho Falls	.986	33	253	31	4	288	1
Jansen, Kenley, Ogden	1.000	3	32	3	0	35	0
Landry, Michael, Great Falls *	1.000	3	17	2	0	19	0
Opdyke, Bryan, Helena	.992	22	110	10	1	121	0
Pujols, Kengshill, Ogden	.989	30	236	40	3	279	2
Rodriguez, Mark, Billings	.978	15	83	5	2	90	2
Rodriguez, Ramon, Casper	.983	29	213	20	4	237	2
Salome, Angel, Helena	.935	20	146	12	11	169	1
Sargent, Luke, Casper	1.000	9	62	10	0	72	0
Sharp, Matthew, Great Falls	.969	13	83	11	3	97	0
Suarez, Steven, Casper	.991	24	184	27	2	213	4
Summers, Houston, Missoula	1.000	6	26	0	0	26	0
Thibault, Kiel, Idaho Falls	.980	35	282	55	7	344	7
Willcutt, Bradley, Helena	.989	38	316	29	4	349	1

PITCHERS

Player, Team	Pct.	G	PO	A	E	TC	DP
Alvarez, Mario, Ogden	.818	12	2	7	2	11	1
Arias, Marlon, Ogden *	.714	14	1	4	2	7	1
Baeza, Eduardo, Missoula	1.000	25	0	7	0	7	0
Begnaud, Russell, Idaho Falls	1.000	12	3	11	0	14	0
Beresford, Simon, Helena	1.000	7	3	3	0	6	1
Bernal, Luis, Helena	1.000	9	1	1	0	2	0
Binda, Byron, Casper	.714	21	3	2	2	7	1
Bongiovanni, Vincent, Missoula	.833	23	2	3	1	6	1
Brantley, Brandon, Idaho Falls	1.000	18	5	7	0	12	1
Brennan, Chris, Great Falls *	.833	8	1	4	1	6	0

Player, Team	Pct.	G	PO	A	E	TC	DP
Breshears, Glenn, Helena	.667	12	1	3	2	6	0
Bulger, Kevin, Idaho Falls	1.000	10	0	1	0	1	0
Camardese, Brandon, Billings *	.900	15	4	5	1	10	0
Carlson, Zane, Idaho Falls	1.000	8	0	1	0	1	0
Casey, James, Great Falls	.857	22	1	5	1	7	2
Cedeno, Xavier, Casper *	.933	12	4	10	1	15	2
Chirino, Israel, Great Falls *	.667	10	0	2	1	3	0
Church, Lorenzo, Missoula	.889	20	1	7	1	9	0
Cromer, Bennett, Idaho Falls	.875	16	1	6	1	8	0
Cupps, Anthony, Missoula	.941	15	5	11	1	17	0
Davidson, Phillip, Idaho Falls	1.000	9	3	2	0	5	0
Davis, Vincent, Missoula *	.889	16	1	7	1	9	0
De Los Santos, Riquy, Casper	1.000	21	1	2	0	3	0
Dipietro, Ryan, Idaho Falls *	.800	15	1	3	1	5	0
Doyle, Travis, Great Falls *	1.000	13	1	1	0	2	0
Duda, Peter, Missoula	1.000	19	0	4	0	4	1
Durden, Brandon, Casper *	.917	12	1	10	1	12	1
Eckley, Jacob, Idaho Falls *	1.000	21	1	4	0	5	0
Espinosa, Sandy, Casper	.889	21	4	4	1	9	0
Evans, Cody, Missoula	.875	20	3	4	1	8	0
Everly, Eric, Great Falls *	.857	8	2	10	2	14	1
Fabian, Robinson, Casper	1.000	12	0	2	0	2	0
Feliz, Rainer, Billings	1.000	16	1	1	0	2	0
Fisher, Charles, Billings	.933	15	4	10	1	15	0
Garcia, Eliszer, Idaho Falls *	1.000	20	3	1	0	4	0
Garrison, Aaron, Billings	.833	8	1	4	1	6	0
Geiersbach, Kennth, Billings	1.000	23	5	7	0	12	0
Goins, Mitchell, Idaho Falls	1.000	8	1	7	0	8	0
Gomez de Segura, Matthew, Ogden	.600	17	2	1	2	5	0
Gonzalez, Rafael, Billings	.750	11	2	7	3	12	0
Green, Matthew, Missoula	1.000	15	6	5	0	11	0
Haltiwanger, Kevin, Billings	1.000	3	1	1	0	2	0
Hammond, Steven, Helena *	.667	4	0	2	1	3	0
Harkcom, James, Idaho Falls	1.000	16	1	5	0	6	0
Hayes, Alvin, Ogden	1.000	19	2	2	0	4	1
Henninger, David, Idaho Falls	.762	21	6	10	5	21	0
Hipke, Ross, Casper	1.000	19	3	4	0	7	0
Hochgesang, Nathan, Ogden	1.000	14	2	4	0	6	0
Horlacher, David, Ogden	1.000	11	1	1	0	2	0
Inman, William, Helena	.900	13	1	8	1	10	0
Jean, Christopher, Helena	1.000	15	3	5	0	8	0
Johnson, Thomas, Casper	.963	15	8	18	1	27	1
Johnston, Andrew, Casper	.857	30	0	6	1	7	1
Julio, Donald, Missoula	.625	21	1	4	3	8	0
Kalkhof, Adam, Idaho Falls *	.500	19	0	3	3	6	0
Klusman, James, Ogden	.889	20	1	7	1	9	0
Kniginyzky, Matthew, Idaho Falls	.833	21	2	8	2	12	1
Kretzschmar, Mathew, Helena	.875	8	1	6	1	8	0
Krise, Kristopher, Casper	1.000	15	4	4	0	8	0
Lanier, Thomas, Billings	1.000	5	1	0	0	1	0
Laureano, Wilfrido, Helena	1.000	14	1	3	0	4	0
Leach, Brent, Ogden *	.962	14	2	23	1	26	1
Lecure, Samuel, Billings	1.000	13	1	8	0	9	1
Lemon, Nickolas, Great Falls	.800	30	2	6	2	10	0
Lluberes, Rafael, Helena *	.941	16	4	12	1	17	1
Logan, Boone, Great Falls *	.933	21	1	13	1	15	0
Louis, Joshua, Helena	.833	17	0	5	1	6	0
Malave, Ronny, Helena	.750	14	3	3	2	8	0
Mannon, Adam, Helena	...	1	0	0	0	0	0
Manzueta, Radhames, Casper	.750	4	0	3	1	4	0
Marion, William, Helena	.600	17	1	2	2	5	0
Marshall, Jay, Great Falls *	.875	29	5	9	2	16	1
McCleland, Bruce, Idaho Falls	1.000	3	0	2	0	2	0
McDonald, James, Ogden	...	4	0	0	0	0	0
Meloan, Jonathan, Ogden	1.000	16	2	6	0	8	1
Metzger, Jason, Casper *	1.000	22	3	4	0	7	0
Miller, Derek, Helena *	.900	9	3	6	1	10	0
Morris, James, Billings *	1.000	17	1	1	0	2	0
Morrison, Tyler, Helena	.938	17	8	7	1	16	0
MOVIEL, PAUL, Great Falls	1.000	15	5	10	0	15	2
Nachreiner, Matthew, Great Falls	.889	22	4	4	1	9	0
Neighborgall, Jason, Missoula	.833	15	3	2	1	6	0
Nicoll, Christopher, Idaho Falls	1.000	7	1	2	0	3	0
Nippert, Dustin, Missoula	.900	15	4	5	1	10	0
Novoa, Yunior, Great Falls *	.857	15	1	11	2	14	0
Obispo, Jose, Ogden	1.000	6	1	0	0	1	0
Ondrusek, Logan, Billings	.778	15	4	3	2	9	0
O'Neal, Charles, Billings	1.000	17	0	4	0	4	0
Paredes, Ramon, Ogden *	1.000	3	0	2	0	2	0
Parillo, Brandon, Helena *	1.000	12	1	6	0	7	0
Pena, Luis, Great Falls	.889	18	2	6	1	9	1
Penn, Michael, Idaho Falls	1.000	5	0	3	0	3	1
Perez, Carlos, Great Falls *	.944	16	1	16	1	18	1
Pfeiffer, David, Ogden *	1.000	15	1	10	0	11	0
Pichardo, Manuel, Casper	1.000	23	3	2	0	5	0
Pohlman, Daniel, Missoula	1.000	27	6	3	0	9	1
Pratt, Jordan, Ogden	1.000	14	3	3	0	6	0
Ramirez, Miguel, Ogden	.000	7	0	0	1	1	0
Renkert, Dane, Helena	1.000	15	1	7	0	8	0
Rice, Jason, Great Falls	1.000	2	2	0	0	2	0
Richard, Clayton, Great Falls *	.818	10	3	6	2	11	0
Roberts, Kevin, Helena	1.000	8	2	5	0	7	0
Rodriguez, Aneury, Casper	.923	15	4	8	1	13	0
Rodriguez, Mark, Billings	...	1	0	0	0	0	0
Rodriguez, Noe, Great Falls *	1.000	13	2	10	0	12	0
Roe, Chaz, Casper	.875	12	3	4	1	8	0
Rojas, Jose A., Billings	1.000	22	6	5	0	11	1
Romanczuk, Mark, Missoula *	1.000	13	2	8	0	10	0
Rote, Ryan, Great Falls	1.000	12	1	4	0	5	0
Ruthven, Sean, Casper	.800	18	4	4	2	10	0
Ryan, Patrick, Helena	1.000	17	2	4	0	6	1
Sanchez, Rafael, Casper	.750	13	1	2	1	4	0
Sanchez, Ramon (Perez), Missoula	.800	9	1	3	1	5	0
Santiago, Mario, Idaho Falls	1.000	10	2	5	0	7	0
Schambough, Douglas, Idaho Falls	1.000	7	0	1	0	1	0
Smith, Gregory, Missoula *	.923	16	3	21	2	26	2
Stevens, Jeffrey, Billings	.917	13	5	6	1	12	0
Strickland, Brett, Casper	1.000	30	4	5	0	9	0
Stumm, Jason, Great Falls	1.000	3	0	1	0	1	0
Thatcher, Joeseph, Helena *	1.000	6	1	4	0	5	0
Thomas, Eric, Helena	1.000	3	2	2	0	4	0
Torres, Carlos, Great Falls	1.000	5	2	7	0	9	0
Trammell, Travis, Idaho Falls	1.000	15	2	2	0	4	0
Troncoso, Ramon, Ogden	.857	29	1	11	2	14	0
Ursin, Damian, Billings	1.000	3	0	1	0	1	0
Valiquette, Philippe-Alexandre, Billings *	1.000	7	0	3	0	3	0
Vecchio, Jason, Billings	...	5	0	0	0	0	0
Venas, Miliade, Missoula	...	8	0	0	0	0	0
Wachman, Robert, Billings	.875	16	2	5	1	8	0
Wade, Cory, Ogden	.947	16	5	13	1	19	1
Webb, Lindsay, Casper	.000	15	0	0	1	1	0
Welch, David, Helena *	1.000	12	4	3	0	7	0
White, Cody, Ogden *	.833	17	2	8	2	12	0
Wilson, David, Billings *	.917	13	3	8	1	12	2
Wood, Travis, Billings *	1.000	6	1	4	0	5	0
Woody, Abraham, Billings	.833	25	0	5	1	6	0
Wooley, Robert, Helena	.900	18	5	4	1	10	1

LEAGUE CHAMPIONS

Year	Team	Pct.
1939—	Twin Falls*	.581
1940—	Salt Lake City	.608
	Ogden (4th)*	.492
1941—	Boise	.623
	Ogden (2nd)*	.598
1942—	Pocatello†	.690
	Boise	.683
1943-44-45—	Did not operate.	
1946—	Twin Falls‡	.585
	Salt Lake City†	.585
1947—	Salt Lake City	.618
	Twin Falls†	.600
1948—	Pocatello	.611
	Twin Falls (2nd)*	.595
1949—	Twin Falls	.624
	Pocatello (3rd)*	.595
1950—	Pocatello	.635
	Billings (3rd)*	.571
1951—	Salt Lake City	.618
	Great Falls (3rd)*	.559
1952—	Pocatello	.595
	Idaho Falls (2nd)*	.573
1953—	Ogden	.679
	Salt Lake City (4th)*	.527
1954—	Salt Lake City	.595
	Great Falls (4th)*	.530
1955—	Boise	.588
	Magic Valley (4th)*	.489
1956—	Boise	.561
1957—	Salt Lake City	.650
	Billings†	.582
1958—	Great Falls	.582
	Boise†	.615

ADVANCED ROOKIE Pioneer League

Year	Team	Pct.
1959—	Boise	.633
	Billings (2nd)*	.523
1960—	Boise†	.686
	Idaho Falls	.650
1961—	Boise	.638
	Great Falls*	.571
1962—	Boise§	.565
	Billings†	.706
1963—	Idaho Falls	.702
	Magic Valley†	.643
1964—	Treasure Valley	.615
1965—	Treasure Valley	.530
1966—	Ogden	.591
1967—	Ogden	.621
1968—	Ogden	.609
1969—	Ogden	.620
1970—	Idaho Falls	.629
1971—	Great Falls	.643
1972—	Billings	.694
1973—	Billings	.629
1974—	Idaho Falls	.569
1975—	Great Falls	.577
1976—	Great Falls	.577
1977—	Lethbridge	.629
1978—	Billings∞	.735
1979—	Helena	.623
	Lethbridge▲	.559
1980—	Lethbridge▲	.743
	Billings	.629

Year	Team	Pct.
1981—	Calgary	.657
	Butte▲	.557
1982—	Medicine Hat▲	.629
	Idaho Falls	.600
1983—	Billings▲	.614
	Calgary	.600
1984—	Billings	.691
	Helena▲	.647
1985—	Great Falls	.771
	Salt Lake City▲	.657
1986—	Salt Lake City◆	.643
	Great Falls	.571
1987—	Salt Lake City◆	.700
	Helena	.657
1988—	Great Falls◆	.754
	Butte	.629
1989—	Great Falls◆	.791
	Butte	.621
1990—	Great Falls◆	.706
	Salt Lake	.618
1991—	Salt Lake City◆	.700
	Great Falls	.657
1992—	Salt Lake	.697
	Billings◆	.697
1993—	Billings◆	.653
	Helena	.589
1994—	Billings◆	.694
	Helena	.611
1995—	Billings	.710

Year	Team	Pct.
	Helena■	.690
1996—	Helena■	.597
	Ogden	.583
1997—	Great Falls	.556
	Billings■	.549
1998—	Medicine Hat	.622
	Idaho Falls■	.618
1999—	Idaho Falls	.640
	Missoula■	.592
2000—	Idaho Falls■	.608
2001—	Provo	.697
	Billings■	.613
2002—	Great Falls■	.627
2003—	Billings■	.539
2004—	Provo■	.579
2005—	Orem■	.500

*Won four-club playoff. †Won split-season playoff. ‡Ended first half in tie with Salt Lake City and won one-game playoff. §Ended first half in tie with Billings and Great Falls and won playoff. ∞Billings (first place) defeated Idaho Falls (second place) in first place-second place playoff. ▲League divided into Northern and Southern divisions; won two-club playoff. ◆Won two-club playoff. ■League divided into Northern and Southern divisions; won four-club playoff.

ARIZONA LEAGUE

LEAGUE OFFICE

President/treasurer
Bob Richmond
Address
P.O. Box 1645
Boise, ID 83701
Phone
208-429-1511

Teams*
Angels
Athletics
Brewers
Cubs
Giants
Padres

Mariners
Rangers
Royals

*Teams play their games in Mesa, Peoria, Phoenix, Scottsdale and Surprise, Ariz.

2005 FINAL STANDINGS

FIRST HALF

Team	W	L	T	Pct.	GB
Giants	21	7	-	.750	-
Royals	19	9	-	.679	2
Angels	15	13	-	.536	6
Padres	15	13	-	.536	6
Athletics	13	15	-	.464	8
Rangers	12	16	-	.429	9
Brewers	11	17	-	.393	10
Cubs	10	18	-	.357	11
Mariners	10	18	-	.357	11

SECOND HALF

Team	W	L	T	Pct.	GB
Giants	18	10	-	.643	-
Athletics	17	11	-	.607	1
Mariners	17	11	-	.607	1
Rangers	15	13	-	.536	3
Royals	15	13	-	.536	3
Padres	14	14	-	.500	4
Brewers	11	17	-	.393	7
Angels	10	18	-	.357	8
Cubs	9	19	-	.321	9

COMPOSITE

CLUB (AFFILIATE), ABBREV	GIA	ROY	ATH	PAD	MAR	RAN	ANG	BRE	CUB	W	L	PCT	GB
Giants (Giants),GIA		3	5	2	5	5	6	6	7	39	17	.696	-
Royals (Royals),ROY	4	...	4	3	3	4	6	4	6	34	22	.607	5.0
Athletics (Athletics),ATH	2	3	...	4	5	4	3	5	4	30	26	.536	9.0
Padres (Padres),PAD	5	4	3	...	2	3	3	5	4	29	27	.518	10.0
Mariners (Mariners),MAR	2	4	2	5	...	5	2	4	3	27	29	.482	12.0
Rangers (Rangers),RAN	2	3	3	4	2	...	4	3	6	27	29	.482	12.0
Angels (Angels),ANG	1	1	4	4	5	3	...	3	4	25	31	.446	14.0
Brewers (Brewers),BRE	1	3	2	2	3	4	4	...	3	22	34	.393	17.0
Cubs (Cubs),CUB	0	1	3	3	4	1	3	4	...	19	37	.339	20.0

Club names are major league affiliations.
Games played in Mesa, Peoria, Phoenix and Tucson.
PLAYOFFS: The Giants won both halves of the season to win league championship.
MANAGERS: Angels, Brian Harper. Athletics, Reuben Escalera. Brewers, Mike Guerrero. Cubs, Steve McFarland. Giants, Bert Hunter. Mariners, Dana Williams. Padres, Carlos Lezcano. Rangers, Pedro Lopez. Royals, Lloyd Simmons.
ALL-STAR TEAM: 1B-Andrew Hargrove, Mariners. 2B-Valentino Arce, Royals. 3B-Jose Jimenez, Brewers. SS-Jeffrey Bianchi, Royals. OF-Lorenzo Cain, Brewers. OF-Ariel Nunez, Giants. OF-Antoan Richardson, Giants. C-Luany Sanchez, Padres. DH-Kyle Blanks, Padres. RHP-Thomas Mendoza, Angels. LHP-Harold Williams, Mariners. RHR-Ernesto Frieri, Padres. LHR-Bradley Beck, Angels. Most Valuable Player-Lorenzo Cain, Brewers. Manager of the Year-Ruben Escalera, Athletics.

2005 BATTING

TEAM

Team	G	TPA	AB	R	H	TB	2B	3B	HR	RBI	SH	SF	HP	BB	IBB	SO	SB	CS	GDP	LOB	ShO	Avg.	OBP	Slg.
Mariners	56	2283	1989	364	580	855	106	32	35	318	11	20	56	206	2	489	53	34	37	957	0	.292	.371	.430
Giants	56	2221	1865	328	531	700	80	22	15	270	44	25	60	223	4	483	137	33	40	976	0	.285	.375	.375
Royals	56	2235	1933	356	549	825	93	39	35	320	12	20	44	226	1	483	84	54	33	883	1	.284	.368	.427
Brewers	56	2234	2022	311	571	786	98	30	19	265	20	13	25	153	2	457	59	32	37	897	1	.282	.338	.389
Padres	56	2288	2037	311	569	803	115	22	25	264	21	21	43	165	7	490	72	31	41	941	2	.279	.343	.394
Cubs	56	2214	1973	280	543	721	101	25	9	238	24	23	25	168	2	429	69	39	37	883	3	.275	.336	.365
Rangers	56	2228	1912	299	518	714	85	27	19	256	5	30	42	239	5	441	115	39	44	934	1	.271	.359	.373
Angels	56	2071	1847	259	465	672	98	26	19	229	6	15	28	174	0	531	75	35	35	735	4	.252	.323	.364
Athletics	56	2181	1837	300	439	632	76	30	19	249	19	22	55	246	4	487	79	44	37	842	3	.239	.343	.344

INDIVIDUAL

TOP QUALIFIERS FOR BATTING CHAMPIONSHIP
Minimum 151 plate appearances. *Lefthanded batter. †Switch-hitter.

Player, Team	G	TPA	AB	R	H	TB	2B	3B	HR	RBI	SH	SF	HP	BB	IBB	SO	SB	CS	GDP	Avg.	OBP	Slg.
Nunez, Ariel, Arizona Giants	46	179	150	30	55	67	4	4	0	21	4	0	7	18	0	43	28	6	3	.367	.457	.447
Cain, Lorenzo, Arizona Brewers	50	233	205	45	73	116	18	5	5	37	0	3	4	20	0	32	12	3	7	.356	.418	.566
Diaz, Javis, Arizona Padres *	39	168	145	22	51	74	5	6	2	24	1	2	3	17	1	30	19	5	1	.352	.425	.510
Brantley, Michael, Arizona Brewers *	44	201	173	34	60	65	3	1	0	19	4	0	2	22	0	13	14	5	2	.347	.426	.376
Arce, Valentino, Arizona Royals	47	191	170	37	57	70	10	0	1	21	1	0	13	7	0	17	7	5	1	.335	.405	.412
Lewis, Deryck, Arizona Cubs	45	198	174	37	56	80	14	5	0	27	1	4	2	17	0	23	3	3	6	.322	.381	.460
Richardson, Antoan, Arizona Giants †	53	252	193	45	62	73	4	2	1	10	7	0	8	44	1	43	40	6	1	.321	.465	.378
Guzman, Juan, Arizona Mariners †	35	167	153	30	49	61	5	2	1	24	1	0	2	11	0	19	6	4	1	.320	.373	.399

Player, Team	G	TPA	AB	R	H	TB	2B	3B	HR	RBI	SH	SF	HP	BB	IBB	SO	SB	CS	GDP	Avg.	OBP	Slg.
Mehl, Truan, Arizona Rangers *	54	238	203	38	65	85	14	3	0	33	0	4	5	26	0	50	27	8	3	.320	.403	.419
Valiente, Roberto, Arizona Rangers	45	178	155	27	49	60	3	1	2	27	1	3	2	17	0	37	14	4	3	.316	.384	.387
Hargrove, Andrew, Arizona Mariners	39	180	137	33	43	66	12	1	3	25	1	2	9	31	0	44	2	0	1	.314	.464	.482
Duarte, Jose, Arizona Royals	47	206	178	33	55	83	7	6	3	36	0	3	0	25	0	32	11	7	3	.309	.388	.466
Sanchez, Luany, Arizona Mariners	43	179	169	27	51	71	15	1	1	26	1	2	0	7	1	23	1	3	9	.302	.326	.420
Canzler, Russell, Arizona Cubs	49	188	157	22	47	67	11	3	1	20	2	4	1	24	1	41	1	5	4	.299	.387	.427
Blanks, Kyle, Arizona Padres	48	200	164	33	49	82	10	1	7	30	0	1	10	25	3	49	3	1	3	.299	.420	.500
Jimenez, Jose, Arizona Brewers	47	205	187	26	56	82	14	3	2	33	0	0	2	16	0	38	2	0	6	.299	.361	.439
Yoho, Nathan, Arizona Brewers *	40	185	168	31	50	71	5	5	2	29	0	3	3	11	0	25	6	1	2	.298	.346	.423
Episcopo, Ryan, Arizona Cubs *	46	197	168	30	50	65	7	1	2	26	1	3	0	25	0	48	7	3	2	.298	.383	.387
Alvarado, Ramon, Arizona Athletics	48	204	169	37	50	84	10	3	6	32	0	1	11	23	0	36	9	4	1	.296	.412	.497
Dickerson, Joseph, Arizona Royals *	56	245	214	27	63	105	12	9	4	40	0	3	1	27	1	46	9	12	1	.294	.371	.491
Davies, Joshua, Arizona Angels	44	165	157	19	46	63	11	0	2	23	0	1	1	6	0	30	5	6	5	.293	.321	.401

DEPARTMENTAL LEADERS: W—Frieri and Oliveros, 7. L—Franco Jr. and Poveda, 6. Pct.—Frieri and Oliveros, .875. G—Sanchez, 24. GS—Oliveros, 14. CG—three pitchers tied with 1. GF—Parejo, 17. Sv.—Thomson, 7. IP—Jimenez, 79.1. H—Jimenez, 95. TBF—Jimenez, 346. R—Rasner, 57. ER—Rasner, 44. HR—Jolliff and Rasner, 6. SAC—Bonilla, 5. SF—Rasner, 8. HB—Pawelek, 9. BB—Mercedes, 34. IBB—Ledezm and Fernandez, 3. SO—Espinoza, 78. WP—Pawelek, 13. BK—Lugo and Rivas, 6.

ALL PLAYERS

*Lefthanded batter. †Switch-hitter.

Player, Team	G	TPA	AB	R	H	TB	2B	3B	HR	RBI	SH	SF	HP	BB	IBB	SO	SB	CS	GDP	Avg.	OBP	Slg.
Acha, John, Arizona Giants	40	148	124	20	35	45	6	2	0	21	1	4	5	14	0	32	4	1	3	.282	.367	.363
Aguilar, Abraham, Arizona Padres	22	104	94	15	28	38	5	1	1	12	3	0	0	7	0	15	5	3	1	.298	.347	.404
Alonso, John, Arizona Brewers	15	56	48	5	14	21	4	0	1	6	0	1	0	7	1	17	0	0	1	.292	.375	.438
Alvarado, Ramon, Arizona Athletics	48	204	169	37	50	84	10	3	6	32	0	1	11	23	0	36	9	4	1	.296	.412	.497
Anderson, Ronnie, Arizona Rangers	47	213	185	32	53	58	5	0	0	14	1	3	4	20	0	46	18	9	6	.286	.363	.314
Angoma, Ruben, Arizona Brewers	8	23	22	5	6	8	2	0	0	3	0	0	0	1	0	5	1	0	1	.273	.304	.364
Arce, Valentino, Arizona Royals	47	191	170	37	57	70	10	0	1	21	1	0	13	7	0	17	7	5	1	.335	.405	.412
Aughey, Jon, Arizona Royals	13	39	30	8	4	11	1	0	2	3	0	0	2	7	0	14	1	0	0	.133	.333	.367
Auty, Timothy, Arizona Mariners	29	125	108	24	38	56	14	2	0	22	0	2	1	14	0	17	1	1	4	.352	.424	.519
Avila, Carlos, Arizona Royals	17	64	57	5	14	19	2	0	1	7	4	0	1	2	0	16	3	0	0	.246	.283	.333
Ayala, Angel, Arizona Brewers *	12	41	34	1	5	7	2	0	0	4	0	0	0	7	0	9	1	1	1	.147	.293	.206
Backman II, Walter, Arizona Rangers *	35	144	118	16	25	40	3	3	2	13	0	1	3	22	1	44	1	0	2	.212	.347	.339
Baez, Sammy, Arizona Cubs	41	157	150	13	32	38	4	1	0	10	1	0	1	5	0	26	3	2	2	.213	.242	.253
Bambino, Richard, Arizona Angels	16	42	39	5	7	9	2	0	0	6	1	1	1	0	0	9	0	0	0	.179	.195	.231
Bianchi, Jeffrey, Arizona Royals	28	122	98	29	40	73	7	4	6	30	0	5	3	16	0	22	5	2	2	.408	.484	.745
Blanc, Jhonathan, Arizona Brewers	29	88	83	8	18	22	2	1	0	5	2	0	1	2	0	21	1	3	2	.217	.244	.265
Blanco, Andres, Arizona Royals †	7	28	25	6	8	15	1	0	2	9	1	0	1	1	0	7	1	2	0	.320	.370	.600
Blanks, Kyle, Arizona Padres	48	200	164	33	49	82	10	1	7	30	0	1	10	25	3	49	3	1	3	.299	.420	.500
Bocachica, Hiram, Arizona Athletics	4	12	12	1	1	2	1	0	0	1	0	0	0	0	0	3	0	0	0	.083	.083	.167
Bone, Kyle, Arizona Giants	2	3	2	0	0	0	0	0	0	0	0	0	0	1	0	2	0	0	0	.000	.333	.000
Bonilla, Lecury, Arizona Mariners	34	146	125	22	31	48	3	4	2	22	3	5	3	10	0	40	1	2	2	.248	.308	.384
Borg, Hector, Arizona Giants †	46	206	169	28	43	51	4	2	0	24	10	2	5	20	1	23	8	3	6	.254	.347	.302
Boudreaux, Ross, Arizona Royals	27	101	81	24	21	34	7	0	2	13	0	0	6	14	0	25	1	0	0	.259	.406	.420
Bradford Jr., Samuel, Arizona Royals †	8	40	37	8	10	21	2	3	1	8	0	1	1	1	0	14	0	1	0	.270	.300	.568
Brantley, Michael, Arizona Brewers *	44	201	173	34	60	65	3	1	0	19	4	0	2	22	0	13	14	5	2	.347	.426	.376
Brown, Randy, Arizona Cubs	52	209	189	27	52	70	8	5	0	26	1	1	7	11	0	34	8	7	4	.275	.337	.370
Buller, Dayton, Arizona Giants	14	48	37	8	13	18	2	0	1	10	0	2	4	5	1	8	0	1	0	.351	.458	.486
Cain, Lorenzo, Arizona Brewers	50	233	205	45	73	116	18	5	5	37	0	3	4	20	0	32	12	3	7	.356	.418	.566
Canzler, Russell, Arizona Cubs	49	188	157	22	47	67	11	3	1	20	2	4	1	24	1	41	1	5	4	.299	.387	.427
Carter, Yusuf, Arizona Cubs †	11	40	38	6	10	15	2	0	1	8	0	1	0	1	0	14	1	0	0	.263	.275	.395
Carvajal, Aneuris, Arizona Rangers	32	124	110	14	25	33	3	1	1	12	1	4	2	7	0	24	2	1	4	.227	.276	.300
Chang, Raymond, Arizona Padres	15	56	48	9	8	10	2	0	0	4	0	1	1	5	0	12	0	0	0	.167	.255	.208
Cividanes, Emmanuel, Arizona Giants *	31	89	81	12	28	38	8	1	0	17	1	0	0	7	0	20	6	0	2	.346	.398	.469
Cleland, Clinton, Arizona Padres	25	104	93	14	30	40	10	0	0	8	2	2	2	5	0	18	0	2	4	.323	.363	.430
Copeland, Benjamin, Arizona Giants *	18	71	60	16	20	31	4	2	1	14	0	1	1	5	0	14	2	0	2	.333	.388	.517
Crabtree, Benjamin, Arizona Rangers	6	23	22	2	5	5	0	0	0	4	0	1	0	0	0	3	0	0	0	.227	.217	.227
Crafort, Willy, Arizona Padres	38	159	145	19	36	56	10	2	2	19	2	4	0	8	0	52	2	0	2	.248	.280	.386
Crouch, Nikolaus, Arizona Cubs	46	199	168	20	48	67	13	0	2	25	1	3	8	19	0	51	0	0	3	.286	.379	.399
Davies, Joshua, Arizona Angels	44	165	157	19	46	63	11	0	2	23	0	1	1	6	0	30	5	6	5	.293	.321	.401
Defendis, John, Arizona Cubs *	18	81	76	13	24	30	4	1	0	13	0	1	1	4	0	5	2	1	0	.316	.346	.395
De La Cruz, Angel, Arizona Rangers	1	1	1	0	0	0	0	0	0	0	0	0	0	0	0	0	0	0	0	.000	.000	.000
De La Cruz, Fredy, Arizona Brewers	28	114	106	15	28	45	2	0	5	20	1	1	2	4	0	26	0	1	1	.264	.301	.425
Delarosa, Anderson, Arizona Brewers	37	151	137	21	34	44	7	0	1	11	0	2	0	12	1	34	4	1	3	.248	.305	.321
Dennis III, Bernard, Arizona Brewers	25	81	71	8	21	27	6	0	0	6	2	0	1	7	0	16	1	2	1	.296	.367	.380
Desouza, Daniel, Arizona Giants *	16	53	44	8	10	12	2	0	0	2	1	0	0	8	1	10	1	1	2	.227	.346	.273
Diaz, Javis, Arizona Padres *	39	168	145	22	51	74	5	6	2	24	1	2	3	17	1	30	19	5	1	.352	.425	.510
Diaz, Matt, Arizona Royals	3	13	13	2	6	8	2	0	0	2	0	0	0	0	0	2	0	1	1	.462	.462	.615
Dickerson, Joseph, Arizona Royals *	56	245	214	27	63	105	12	9	4	40	0	3	1	27	1	46	9	12	1	.294	.371	.491
Disla, Lisandro, Arizona Giants	8	35	33	6	14	22	3	1	1	12	1	0	0	1	0	4	0	0	0	.424	.441	.667
Dixon, Kent, Arizona Mariners	19	74	67	8	15	22	4	0	1	8	1	0	2	4	0	19	2	0	3	.224	.288	.328
Dominguez, Jeffrey, Arizona Mariners †	33	140	125	17	30	36	4	1	0	11	2	2	1	10	0	35	8	1	1	.240	.297	.288
Doscher, Nicholas, Arizona Royals	17	63	48	13	7	8	1	0	0	4	0	0	0	15	0	10	2	0	4	.146	.349	.167
Duarte, Jose, Arizona Royals	47	206	178	33	55	83	7	6	3	36	0	3	0	25	0	32	11	7	3	.309	.388	.466
Eastley, Tyler, Arizona Mariners *	3	14	12	4	8	12	1	0	1	4	0	0	0	2	0	1	0	0	0	.667	.714	1.000
Edwards, Harold, Arizona Angels *	27	97	81	19	23	40	4	2	3	12	0	2	12	0	0	26	2	4	1	.284	.381	.494
Emeterio, Oscar, Arizona Brewers †	30	91	85	17	16	26	4	3	0	6	2	0	0	4	0	28	2	1	1	.188	.225	.306
Episcopo, Ryan, Arizona Cubs *	46	197	168	30	50	65	7	1	2	26	1	3	0	25	0	48	7	3	2	.298	.383	.387
Farina, Peter, Arizona Cubs	9	20	18	1	6	6	0	0	0	5	0	0	0	2	0	2	0	0	0	.333	.400	.333
Festa, Anthony, Arizona Brewers *	12	50	43	11	19	33	5	3	1	10	1	0	1	5	1	0	1	0	0	.442	.510	.767
Fuller, Cody, Arizona Angels	19	80	62	14	13	22	3	0	2	7	0	0	1	5	10	0	12	5	3	0	.210	.375	.355

Player, Team	G	TPA	AB	R	H	TB	2B	3B	HR	RBI	SH	SF	HP	BB	IBB	SO	SB	CS	GDP	Avg.	OBP	Slg.
Garciaparra, Nomar, Arizona Cubs	2	5	5	0	1	1	0	0	0	0	0	0	0	0	0	1	0	0	0	.200	.200	.200
Garth, Ronald, Arizona Mariners	27	128	112	23	40	69	10	5	3	15	0	1	8	7	0	17	3	2	2	.357	.430	.616
Gergel, Kevin, Arizona Mariners *	36	146	133	28	42	70	9	2	5	27	0	0	4	9	0	36	1	1	1	.316	.377	.526
Gill, Ernest, Arizona Padres	37	144	124	17	29	49	8	0	4	16	1	0	5	14	0	44	0	0	6	.234	.336	.395
Gomez, Mauro, Arizona Rangers	4	17	13	5	5	10	2	0	1	4	0	1	0	3	0	2	0	0	1	.385	.471	.769
Gonzalez, Jarol, Arizona Padres	42	163	150	19	35	42	5	1	0	14	4	2	3	4	0	33	5	2	1	.233	.264	.280
Gonzalez, Oscar, Arizona Royals	55	225	197	40	56	83	5	5	4	31	0	2	4	22	0	68	17	5	4	.284	.364	.421
Graterol, Oswaldo, Arizona Mariners	30	130	110	22	38	51	3	2	2	25	0	0	1	19	1	28	7	5	1	.345	.446	.464
Gregorio, Tom, Arizona Angels	4	13	12	1	2	2	0	0	0	1	0	0	1	0	0	3	0	0	0	.167	.231	.167
Groth, Bradley, Arizona Giants	22	79	62	10	14	16	0	1	0	5	0	2	2	13	0	15	5	1	6	.226	.367	.258
Gunther, Barry, Arizona Giants †	11	34	30	3	8	9	1	0	0	4	0	0	1	3	0	5	0	0	0	.267	.353	.300
Gutierrez, Henry, Arizona Giants	20	77	65	8	17	24	1	0	2	10	0	1	3	8	0	6	3	0	1	.262	.364	.369
Guzman, Juan, Arizona Mariners †	35	167	153	30	49	61	5	2	1	24	1	0	2	11	0	19	6	4	1	.320	.373	.399
Halman, Gregory, Arizona Mariners	26	103	89	17	23	40	2	3	3	11	0	1	3	10	0	19	1	3	5	.258	.350	.449
Hargrove, Andrew, Arizona Mariners	39	180	137	33	43	66	12	1	3	25	1	2	9	31	0	44	2	0	1	.314	.464	.482
Harper, Grant, Arizona Angels	32	121	113	8	27	37	5	1	1	6	0	0	3	5	0	31	0	1	3	.239	.289	.327
Harris, Steven, Arizona Cubs	22	100	94	12	31	37	4	1	0	14	3	0	0	3	0	16	1	1	1	.330	.351	.394
Hawke, Matthew, Arizona Rangers *	19	91	70	17	27	47	6	1	4	17	0	2	0	19	2	5	3	0	0	.386	.505	.671
Haynes, Nathan, Arizona Giants *	7	19	16	4	4	9	1	2	0	1	0	0	0	3	0	3	3	0	0	.250	.368	.563
Heckman, John, Arizona Mariners	10	43	36	8	10	11	1	0	0	4	0	1	0	6	0	1	2	0	0	.278	.372	.306
Heredia, Valerio, Arizona Cubs †	18	68	61	7	14	18	2	1	0	5	3	0	1	3	0	18	7	3	0	.230	.277	.295
Hernandez, Eddy, Arizona Mariners *	23	97	87	14	31	48	3	1	4	18	0	0	0	10	0	19	0	2	2	.356	.423	.552
Hernandez, Jairo, Arizona Mariners	7	29	24	4	8	16	2	0	2	3	0	0	0	5	1	8	0	0	0	.333	.448	.667
Hernandez, Samuel, Arizona Athletics	39	137	114	19	25	29	2	1	0	14	1	1	4	17	0	29	4	5	2	.219	.338	.254
Howard, Joshua, Arizona Padres *	23	110	96	21	34	44	6	2	0	14	1	2	1	10	1	15	12	2	1	.354	.413	.458
Hudson, Robert, Arizona Mariners	2	9	9	3	0	0	0	0	0	0	0	0	0	0	0	1	0	0	1	.000	.000	.000
Infante, Jefferson, Arizona Royals	16	35	28	6	8	17	3	0	2	7	0	0	2	5	0	12	0	1	0	.286	.429	.607
Infante, Larry, Arizona Angels †	36	139	119	17	27	42	4	1	3	13	2	0	1	16	0	22	5	3	2	.227	.324	.353
Ingold, Benjamin, Arizona Athletics	54	246	207	31	56	74	9	3	1	31	1	4	3	31	0	44	4	4	5	.271	.367	.357
Jacobo, Erwin, Arizona Mariners	17	67	56	10	10	11	1	0	0	9	0	0	2	9	0	23	1	2	4	.179	.313	.196
Jacobsen, Bucky, Arizona Mariners	4	18	13	1	4	7	3	0	0	3	0	0	1	4	0	4	0	0	0	.308	.500	.538
Janeway, Rich, Arizona Giants *	48	195	160	29	37	53	6	2	2	28	2	5	4	24	0	30	5	2	1	.231	.337	.331
Jimenez, Herman, Arizona Brewers	16	54	51	6	11	12	1	0	0	8	1	0	0	2	0	11	0	1	0	.216	.245	.235
Jimenez, Jose, Arizona Brewers	47	205	187	26	56	82	14	3	2	33	0	0	2	16	0	38	2	0	6	.299	.361	.439
Johnson, Joshua, Arizona Royals †	28	139	112	24	29	44	8	2	1	16	2	1	1	23	0	24	7	1	2	.259	.387	.393
Johnson, Tyler, Arizona Angels	47	184	166	23	44	65	10	1	3	23	0	2	3	13	0	64	9	3	4	.265	.326	.392
Johnston, Dylan, Arizona Cubs *	13	50	44	4	8	10	2	0	0	5	0	0	0	6	0	24	0	3	0	.182	.280	.227
Johnston, Trey, Arizona Padres	20	69	53	11	16	27	5	0	2	10	0	0	5	11	0	18	0	3	0	.302	.464	.509
Killian, William, Arizona Padres *	32	119	115	6	33	45	8	2	0	10	0	2	0	3	0	28	4	1	3	.287	.300	.391
King, Lisandro, Arizona Giants	16	52	43	2	14	15	1	0	0	6	2	1	2	4	0	12	2	0	2	.326	.400	.349
Klug, Michael, Arizona Athletics	29	124	88	19	16	25	4	1	1	13	1	1	5	29	0	29	14	5	2	.182	.407	.284
Laird, Gerald, Arizona Rangers	8	29	26	4	5	11	2	2	0	3	0	0	1	2	0	2	1	0	1	.192	.276	.423
Leblanc, Joshua, Arizona Angels *	2	9	9	1	1	2	1	0	0	2	0	0	0	0	0	4	1	0	1	.111	.111	.222
Leclercq, Lenny, Arizona Brewers	38	109	97	21	26	37	2	3	1	11	2	1	0	9	0	41	6	1	0	.268	.327	.381
Ledbetter, Curtis, Arizona Mariners	34	133	122	22	38	61	9	1	4	21	1	0	0	10	0	44	2	0	0	.311	.364	.500
Lewis, Deryck, Arizona Cubs	45	198	174	37	56	80	14	5	0	27	1	4	2	17	0	23	3	3	6	.322	.381	.460
Liriano, Victor, Arizona Cubs *	3	13	12	2	5	8	1	1	0	1	0	0	0	1	0	4	0	0	1	.417	.462	.667
Liverpool, Marquise, Arizona Mariners	30	111	94	24	28	33	5	0	0	10	1	1	6	9	0	23	10	3	1	.298	.391	.351
Lobaton, Jose, Arizona Padres †	5	20	14	2	5	7	2	0	0	2	0	0	0	6	0	4	1	0	0	.357	.550	.500
Long, Wesley, Arizona Athletics	16	71	58	13	16	20	1	0	1	7	0	2	2	9	0	12	3	0	0	.276	.380	.345
Lopez, Pedro, Arizona Royals †	46	184	166	28	46	58	6	3	0	27	2	1	3	12	0	39	4	6	1	.277	.335	.349
Lowen, John, Arizona Royals *	18	50	46	4	7	9	2	0	0	3	0	0	1	3	0	18	0	2	2	.152	.220	.196
Luster, Jeremiah, Arizona Giants	12	41	36	1	2	2	0	0	0	0	1	0	0	4	0	14	1	0	1	.056	.150	.056
Maldonado, Martin, Arizona Angels	27	91	86	6	22	24	2	0	0	10	1	1	1	2	0	9	0	0	3	.256	.278	.279
Maldonado, Pedro, Arizona Athletics	30	107	87	18	22	33	7	2	0	7	0	0	3	17	1	30	2	1	4	.253	.393	.379
Maroul, David, Arizona Giants	8	31	29	6	10	18	5	0	1	5	0	1	0	1	0	7	0	0	0	.345	.355	.621
Marrero, Oscar, Arizona Royals †	21	63	57	6	14	14	0	0	0	5	0	0	0	6	0	11	0	0	2	.246	.317	.246
Martinez, Alberto, Arizona Rangers	6	20	15	1	1	1	0	0	0	1	0	1	0	4	0	3	1	0	0	.067	.250	.067
Martinez, Frank, Arizona Athletics †	35	146	117	28	24	33	6	0	1	7	2	0	3	24	0	39	3	2	1	.205	.354	.282
Matos, Willie, Arizona Royals	45	166	148	18	36	51	7	1	2	18	2	2	0	14	0	54	0	3	4	.243	.305	.345
Matranga, Dave, Arizona Angels	3	10	10	0	0	0	0	0	0	0	0	0	0	0	0	6	0	0	0	.000	.000	.000
McCarthy, Greg, Arizona Giants	18	55	51	7	17	27	4	0	2	11	0	2	1	1	0	8	1	1	0	.333	.345	.529
McKnight, Scott, Arizona Brewers *	11	46	40	7	11	11	0	0	0	4	1	0	1	4	0	8	1	1	0	.275	.356	.275
McPherson, Dallas, Arizona Angels *	3	9	9	1	2	5	1	1	0	2	0	0	0	0	0	5	0	0	0	.222	.222	.556
Medina, Fernando, Arizona Athletics	38	139	126	12	19	32	2	4	1	12	2	0	2	8	0	52	4	2	5	.151	.213	.254
Mehl, Truan, Arizona Rangers *	54	238	203	38	65	85	14	3	0	33	0	4	5	26	0	50	27	8	3	.320	.403	.419
Mejia, Harold, Arizona Brewers	44	169	163	19	38	55	11	3	0	12	3	0	1	2	0	54	2	2	4	.233	.247	.337
Mendez, Ramiro, Arizona Athletics	13	54	51	7	14	19	3	1	0	6	0	0	0	3	0	12	1	0	2	.275	.315	.373
Mercedes, Mario, Arizona Cubs	34	92	84	12	25	31	3	0	1	11	1	1	1	5	0	5	1	2	5	.298	.341	.369
Merloni, Lou, Arizona Angels	6	17	15	3	5	6	1	0	0	2	0	0	0	2	0	2	0	0	0	.333	.412	.400
Moore, Jerome, Arizona Angels *	34	124	110	15	25	30	3	1	0	11	2	0	1	11	0	46	12	6	3	.227	.303	.273
Morales, Carlos, Arizona Athletics	52	224	192	22	49	64	8	2	1	28	0	1	8	23	1	52	4	4	4	.255	.357	.333
Morel, Alvi, Arizona Royals *	46	148	131	23	41	65	6	6	2	23	0	1	1	15	0	32	15	4	5	.313	.385	.496
Morgan, Justin, Arizona Cubs	30	73	68	6	15	19	4	0	0	7	0	0	1	4	0	20	0	0	2	.221	.274	.279
Mount, Ryan, Arizona Angels *	29	123	102	15	22	34	7	1	1	17	0	3	1	17	0	31	4	1	2	.216	.325	.333
Muyco, Dionisio, Arizona Cubs	1	2	2	0	1	2	1	0	0	0	0	0	0	0	0	0	0	0	0	.500	.500	1.000
Napoli, Joe, Arizona Rangers	36	136	120	12	26	38	3	3	1	16	0	2	1	13	0	27	0	2	3	.217	.294	.317
Nelson, Jonathan, Arizona Mariners	3	14	11	2	3	5	0	1	0	3	0	1	1	1	0	3	0	0	0	.273	.357	.455
Nickeas, Michael, Arizona Rangers	6	25	21	2	6	10	1	0	1	6	0	0	1	3	0	4	0	0	1	.286	.400	.476
Nieves, Abel, Arizona Angels	23	81	66	17	18	21	3	0	0	7	0	0	2	13	0	19	3	0	2	.273	.407	.318

Player, Team	G	TPA	AB	R	H	TB	2B	3B	HR	RBI	SH	SF	HP	BB	IBB	SO	SB	CS	GDP	Avg.	OBP	Slg.
Nunez, Ariel, Arizona Giants	46	179	150	30	55	67	4	4	0	21	4	0	7	18	0	43	28	6	3	.367	.457	.447
Palencia, Isaac, Arizona Brewers	22	79	70	10	28	32	4	0	0	11	0	0	3	6	0	13	2	3	2	.400	.468	.457
Parejo, Miguel, Arizona Brewers	1	0	0	0	0	0	0	0	0	0	...	0	0	0	...	0	0	0	0	...	...	...
Parker, David, Arizona Padres	44	185	160	24	35	39	2	1	0	15	3	0	6	16	0	31	5	3	4	.219	.313	.244
Parraz, Ezekiel, Arizona Athletics	12	55	46	7	13	22	1	1	2	10	0	2	2	5	0	6	3	2	0	.283	.364	.478
Peralta, Felix, Arizona Royals	35	143	128	21	36	55	6	2	3	25	0	2	5	8	0	33	1	2	1	.281	.343	.430
Perez, Hector, Arizona Giants	22	66	57	11	15	17	2	0	0	7	1	0	1	7	0	22	2	1	2	.263	.354	.298
Perez, Josue, Arizona Rangers †	3	7	7	1	1	2	1	0	0	1	0	0	0	0	0	1	0	0	1	.143	.143	.286
Phillips, Patrick, Arizona Angels	49	195	182	25	53	74	6	6	1	24	0	2	2	9	0	53	13	5	0	.291	.328	.407
Pina, Manuel, Arizona Rangers	27	101	85	13	21	26	3	1	0	10	0	1	8	7	1	12	2	0	4	.247	.356	.306
Piper-Jordan, Andre, Arizona Athletics	52	238	201	44	49	76	10	7	1	24	6	5	5	21	1	55	19	10	4	.244	.323	.378
Pressley, Ryan, Arizona Angels †	23	66	60	5	8	11	0	0	1	6	0	0	0	6	0	28	1	0	0	.133	.212	.183
Prettyman, Ronald, Arizona Mariners *	5	25	22	4	4	4	0	0	0	3	0	0	0	3	0	3	2	0	0	.182	.280	.182
Prosise, Nicholas, Arizona Mariners	29	111	100	9	24	33	9	0	0	14	0	1	3	7	0	18	0	3	3	.240	.306	.330
Pruitt, David, Arizona Angels	1	1	1	0	0	0	0	0	0	0	0	0	0	0	0	0	0	0	1	.000	.000	.000
Quinlan, Robb, Arizona Angels	4	15	12	3	3	5	2	0	0	3	0	1	0	2	0	3	1	0	0	.250	.333	.417
Reynolds, Kyle, Arizona Cubs *	1	5	5	0	0	0	0	0	0	0	0	0	0	0	0	1	0	0	0	.000	.000	.000
Richardson, Antoan, Arizona Giants †	53	252	193	45	62	73	4	2	1	10	7	0	8	44	1	43	40	6	1	.321	.465	.378
Rivera, Anthony, Arizona Cubs	3	12	12	2	4	4	0	0	0	1	0	0	0	0	0	2	0	0	0	.333	.333	.333
Rivera, Julio, Arizona Athletics	12	41	36	2	6	8	2	0	0	5	0	1	0	3	0	15	0	0	0	.167	.225	.222
Rivera, Luis, Arizona Angels	42	149	132	25	37	54	9	4	0	15	0	0	1	16	0	43	8	2	3	.280	.362	.409
Rivera, Luis, Arizona Cubs	27	114	103	15	29	34	5	0	0	9	2	0	3	6	0	15	9	2	2	.282	.339	.330
Rojas, Nestor, Arizona Giants	29	84	73	11	17	20	1	1	0	10	4	1	1	5	0	15	3	1	2	.233	.288	.274
Rosendo, Gustavo, Arizona Athletics	34	131	118	13	29	32	3	0	0	9	1	0	3	9	0	18	1	1	6	.246	.315	.271
Ruiz, Donato, Arizona Mariners	29	125	114	16	30	44	1	2	3	18	1	1	7	1	0	26	2	0	5	.263	.309	.386
Ryan, Matthew, Arizona Angels *	45	182	165	26	43	68	12	2	3	22	0	0	0	17	0	46	3	0	2	.261	.330	.412
Saavedra, Jonathan, Arizona Royals *	5	10	6	2	1	3	0	1	0	0	0	0	0	4	0	1	0	1	0	.167	.500	.500
Sales, Darrell, Arizona Angels	31	120	103	15	29	45	9	2	1	11	0	1	2	14	0	31	2	1	2	.282	.375	.437
Sanchez, Alex, Arizona Giants *	4	14	10	5	6	7	1	0	0	2	0	0	1	3	0	1	1	0	0	.600	.714	.700
Sanchez, Luany, Arizona Padres	43	179	169	27	51	71	15	1	1	26	1	2	0	7	1	23	1	3	9	.302	.326	.420
Santoro, Michael, Arizona Giants	14	42	38	5	9	18	4	1	1	8	0	0	1	3	0	11	0	1	1	.237	.310	.474
Schoop, Sharlon, Arizona Giants	48	196	169	29	43	50	4	0	1	19	7	1	5	14	0	18	10	4	4	.254	.328	.296
Seara, David, Arizona Cubs	34	120	106	10	24	38	9	1	1	7	3	1	0	9	0	16	6	1	0	.226	.284	.358
Serrano, Eduard, Arizona Cubs †	47	204	180	30	45	60	4	4	1	13	5	3	0	16	1	43	19	5	1	.250	.307	.333
Silva, Johan, Arizona Angels *	10	38	36	2	8	13	3	1	0	2	0	0	1	1	0	8	1	0	1	.222	.263	.361
Smith, John, Arizona Padres	21	93	84	13	30	46	7	0	3	18	0	1	0	8	0	23	1	2	1	.357	.409	.548
Smith, Matthew, Arizona Rangers *	35	148	128	20	31	36	3	1	0	10	0	2	0	18	0	25	8	3	1	.242	.331	.281
Snyder, Brian, Arizona Athletics	1	2	1	1	0	0	0	0	0	0	0	0	0	1	0	1	0	0	0	.000	.500	.000
Stanfield, James, Arizona Brewers	30	96	83	4	20	24	1	0	1	13	0	2	2	9	0	18	1	1	1	.241	.323	.289
Stanton, Christopher, Arizona Giants	33	152	133	24	38	58	12	1	2	23	2	2	8	7	0	23	12	4	1	.286	.353	.436
Steiner, Chad, Arizona Padres	35	144	137	21	38	45	7	0	0	13	1	1	0	5	0	23	3	0	4	.277	.301	.328
Sutton III, Donald, Arizona Athletics	8	28	25	2	8	10	2	0	0	4	0	1	0	2	0	10	0	0	0	.320	.357	.400
Thayer, Matthew, Arizona Padres	3	11	8	1	3	3	0	0	0	1	0	0	1	2	0	0	1	1	0	.375	.545	.375
Thomas-Dotson, Josh, Arizona Padres *	19	59	53	4	10	13	0	0	1	5	0	1	1	3	0	30	1	0	0	.189	.241	.245
Torres, Jose, Arizona Rangers	48	195	169	29	43	72	11	0	6	26	0	1	6	19	1	50	6	2	8	.254	.349	.426
Turner, Timothy, Arizona Padres	28	136	126	20	29	42	4	3	1	11	2	0	1	7	1	33	5	3	0	.230	.276	.333
Valdez, Alexander, Arizona Athletics	51	222	189	24	42	69	5	5	4	39	5	3	4	21	1	44	8	4	1	.222	.309	.365
Valichka, Brian, Arizona Rangers	19	69	62	4	13	18	5	0	0	8	0	1	2	4	0	15	2	1	1	.210	.275	.290
Valiente, Roberto, Arizona Rangers	45	178	155	27	49	60	3	1	2	27	1	3	2	17	0	37	14	4	3	.316	.384	.387
Vallejo, Jose, Arizona Rangers	52	230	203	28	59	73	7	2	1	15	2	1	5	19	0	49	18	5	2	.291	.364	.360
Venable, William, Arizona Padres *	15	65	59	13	19	30	4	2	1	12	0	0	4	2	0	9	4	0	1	.322	.385	.508
Vicioso, Osvaldo, Arizona Brewers †	43	162	156	17	37	48	5	3	0	17	1	0	0	5	0	44	2	5	2	.237	.261	.308
Westphal, Joshua, Arizona Cubs	5	20	19	4	7	9	0	1	0	3	0	0	0	1	0	6	1	1	0	.368	.400	.474
Whittleman, John, Arizona Rangers *	51	229	190	31	53	81	12	8	0	35	0	2	2	35	0	42	11	4	3	.279	.393	.426
Wick, Olin, Arizona Cubs †	26	47	40	7	9	12	3	0	0	4	1	0	0	6	0	14	0	0	1	.225	.326	.300
Yan, Ruddy, Arizona Rangers †	2	10	9	3	5	8	1	1	0	1	0	0	0	1	0	0	1	0	0	.556	.600	.889
Yoho, Nathan, Arizona Brewers *	40	185	168	31	50	71	5	5	2	29	0	3	3	11	0	25	6	1	2	.298	.346	.423
Zorn, Dean, Arizona Mariners †	24	108	93	11	23	30	3	2	0	10	0	1	1	13	0	28	2	4	0	.247	.343	.323

GRAND SLAMS—R. Alvarado, V. Arce, J. Diaz, J. Dickerson, O. Graterol, C. Ledbetter, A. Morel, D. Ruiz, C. Smith, J. Vallejo, 1 each.

AWARDED FIRST BASE ON CATCHER'S INTERFERENCE—B. Copeland 4 (I. Palencia, M. Mercedes, M. Pina, P. Maldonado); L. Cain (G. Rosendo); R. Chang (G. Rosendo); L. Infante (B. Killian); F. Medina (T. Johnston); J. Rivera (O. Wick); D. Ruiz (I. Palencia); D. Seara (L. Sanchez).

2005 PITCHING

TEAM

Team	W	L	Pct.	ERA	G	CG	ShO	Sv.	IP	H	TBF	R	ER	HR	SH	SF	HB	BB	IBB	SO	WP	Bk.
Giants	39	17	.696	2.93	56	0	2	17	492	441	2060	212	160	22	18	12	32	161	4	522	38	6
Angels	25	31	.446	4.23	56	1	0	14	482.2	496	2121	276	227	20	17	17	42	162	0	513	48	7
Royals	34	22	.607	4.31	56	0	4	18	495	550	2188	284	237	19	18	12	42	162	1	445	42	2
Padres	29	27	.518	4.46	56	1	1	9	511	500	2273	300	253	27	18	24	49	254	3	460	58	6
Cubs	19	37	.339	4.50	56	0	2	7	500	522	2229	317	250	19	17	23	40	207	8	464	56	4
Athletics	30	26	.536	4.56	56	1	1	12	499.2	536	2206	317	253	16	21	20	49	171	1	426	54	12
Mariners	27	29	.482	4.88	56	0	1	6	492.1	556	2241	358	267	18	23	28	35	220	1	438	47	4
Rangers	27	29	.482	4.90	56	0	3	11	498	567	2255	344	271	25	11	22	38	197	0	503	49	10
Brewers	22	34	.393	5.79	56	0	1	11	499	599	2382	400	321	29	19	31	51	266	9	425	55	32

INDIVIDUAL

TOP QUALIFIERS FOR EARNED-RUN AVERAGE TITLE

Minimum 45 innings. *Lefthanded pitcher.

Pitcher, Team	W	L	Pct.	ERA	G	GS	CG	ShO	GF	Sv.	IP	H	TBF	R	ER	HR	SH	SF	HB	BB	IBB	SO	WP	Bk.
Frieri, Ernesto, Arizona Padres	7	1	.875	1.17	17	5	0	0	5	0	46.1	21	186	7	6	0	1	0	4	29	0	59	2	1
Mendoza, Thomas, Arizona Angels	3	3	.500	1.55	13	4	0	0	2	0	52.1	42	204	14	9	1	1	0	1	13	0	56	2	0

Pitcher, Team	W	L	Pct.	ERA	G	GS	CG	ShO	GF	Sv.	IP	H	TBF	R	ER	HR	SH	SF	HB	BB	IBB	SO	WP	Bk.
Williams, Harold, Arizona Mariners *..	2	2	.500	2.30	10	6	0	0	0	0	47.0	38	192	16	12	2	1	0	2	16	0	44	6	0
Oliveros, Rayner, Arizona Royals........	7	1	.875	2.39	14	14	0	0	0	0	75.1	73	298	26	20	1	2	2	3	5	0	48	3	0
Fisher, Brent, Arizona Royals *	5	2	.714	3.04	13	8	0	0	4	1	50.1	48	211	20	17	2	1	1	4	13	0	69	3	0
Kirkman, Michael, Arizona Rangers *	3	1	.750	3.44	14	9	0	0	1	0	52.1	51	226	28	20	0	1	1	1	19	0	58	3	0
Franco Jr., Thomas, Arizona Athletics	5	6	.455	3.66	14	8	1	0	1	0	64.0	76	275	34	26	1	4	2	4	15	0	51	8	1
Espinoza, Gustavo, Arizona Angels *..	5	3	.625	3.84	13	12	0	0	0	0	70.1	72	295	36	30	3	0	1	2	12	0	78	5	0
Jimenez, Juan, Arizona Padres..........	4	4	.500	3.86	13	13	0	0	0	0	79.1	95	345	45	34	5	0	5	2	18	0	67	3	0
Phillips, Zachary, Arizona Rangers * ..	1	3	.250	3.93	14	11	0	0	0	0	50.1	52	216	26	22	3	0	0	3	13	0	73	2	0
Pina, Jose, Arizona Cubs	3	5	.375	4.78	14	11	0	0	1	0	52.2	59	231	34	28	4	1	3	7	14	0	37	7	0
Arredondo, Felipe, Arizona Angels......	2	5	.286	5.03	14	7	0	0	0	0	59.0	63	255	38	33	3	2	1	6	13	0	62	7	0
Lugo, Jose, Arizona Athletics *	2	3	.400	5.23	15	5	0	0	2	0	53.1	57	234	42	31	0	2	3	4	18	0	44	2	6
Cassevah, Robert, Arizona Angels......	2	5	.286	5.40	15	4	0	0	2	0	45.0	57	201	28	27	2	3	1	7	14	0	27	2	0
Torres, Luis, Arizona Athletics............	2	4	.333	5.50	14	3	0	0	1	0	52.1	63	230	35	32	1	3	4	5	12	0	29	3	1
Poveda, Omar, Arizona Rangers	2	6	.250	5.71	14	9	0	0	2	0	52.0	64	227	38	33	1	0	3	2	12	0	56	1	2
Raglione, Paul, Arizona Royals	3	4	.429	5.94	13	7	0	0	1	1	47.0	66	221	40	31	4	2	0	4	18	0	37	3	0
Rojas, Cesar, Arizona Padres	2	4	.333	6.75	13	11	0	0	0	0	49.1	48	228	41	37	1	1	5	7	32	0	33	8	0
Langille, Craig, Arizona Brewers........	2	3	.400	6.84	14	5	0	0	1	0	50.0	80	239	46	38	2	3	6	5	14	1	20	3	4
Abreu, Juan, Arizona Royals..............	2	5	.286	6.88	14	13	0	0	0	0	52.1	72	257	49	40	4	2	4	6	27	0	52	10	0
Marquez, Miguel, Arizona Mariners ..	2	2	.500	7.38	12	5	0	0	0	0	50.0	70	242	54	41	3	1	2	4	22	0	49	11	0

DEPARTMENTAL LEADERS: W—Frieri and Oliveros, 7 each; L—Franco Jr. and Poveda, 6 each; Pct.—Frieri and Oliveros, .875 each; G—Sanchez, 24; GS—Oliveros, 14; CG—Three pitchers tied with 1; GF—Parejo, 17; Sv.—Thomson, 7; IP—Jimenez, 79.1; H—Jimenez, 95; TBF—Jimenez, 346; R—Rasner, 57; ER—Rasner, 44; HR—Jolliff and Rasner, 6 each; SAC—Bonilla, 5; SF—Rasner, 8; HB—Pawelek, 9; BB—Mercedes, 34; IBB—Ledezm and Fernandez, 3 each; SO—Espinoza, 78; WP—Pawelek, 13; BK—Lugo and Rivas, 6 each.

ALL PITCHERS

*Lefthanded pitcher.

Pitcher, Team	W	L	Pct.	ERA	G	GS	CG	ShO	GF	Sv.	IP	H	TBF	R	ER	HR	SH	SF	HB	BB	IBB	SO	WP	Bk.
Abbott, Justin, Arizona Rangers	1	0	1.000	3.38	10	0	0	0	7	3	16.0	15	61	6	6	1	1	0	0	2	0	11	1	0
Abreu, Juan, Arizona Royals..............	2	5	.286	6.88	14	13	0	0	0	0	52.1	72	257	49	40	4	2	4	6	27	0	52	10	0
Acevedo, Danielin, Arizona Athletics ..	0	0	.000	6.00	2	1	0	0	0	0	3.0	3	12	2	2	0	0	0	0	0	0	1	0	0
Acosta, Kelyn, Arizona Giants	0	0	.000	9.00	2	0	0	0	0	0	3.0	5	13	3	3	0	1	0	1	0	0	1	1	1
Adenhart, Nicholas, Arizona Angels ..	2	3	.400	3.68	13	12	1	0	0	0	44.0	39	189	26	18	0	3	2	4	24	0	52	3	1
Aldridge, Richard, Arizona Angels......	0	0	.000	1.00	7	0	0	0	2	0	9.0	6	39	1	1	0	0	0	1	7	0	19	2	0
Alliston, Joshua, Arizona Brewers......	0	1	.000	2.25	4	2	0	0	0	0	4.0	3	16	1	1	0	0	0	1	0	0	3	0	0
Anderson, Ryan, Arizona Brewers * ..	0	0	.000	7.36	3	3	0	0	0	0	3.2	4	16	4	3	0	0	0	1	1	0	6	1	0
Arnold, Mitchell Scott, Arizona Angels	0	0	.000	1.59	6	0	0	0	1	1	5.2	3	24	1	1	0	0	0	2	1	0	10	0	1
Arredondo, Felipe, Arizona Angels......	2	5	.286	5.03	14	7	0	0	0	0	59.0	63	255	38	33	3	2	1	6	13	0	62	7	0
Atchison, Scott, Arizona Mariners......	0	0	.000	5.40	4	3	0	0	0	0	5.0	7	23	3	3	0	0	0	1	1	0	9	0	0
Avery, Matthew, Arizona Cubs	0	0	.000	10.80	1	1	0	0	0	0	1.2	2	10	2	2	0	0	0	2	2	0	1	0	0
Baca, Daniel, Arizona Padres	1	2	.333	3.54	12	0	0	0	5	0	20.1	21	84	8	8	1	2	0	2	3	0	23	3	0
Baena, Orlando, Arizona Padres	1	0	1.000	5.56	6	0	0	0	3	0	11.1	11	52	7	7	0	0	0	0	8	0	10	2	0
Bannister, Brett, Arizona Mariners	0	0	.000	2.25	2	1	0	0	0	0	4.0	4	17	4	1	1	0	0	0	0	0	5	0	0
Barrera, Enrique, Arizona Royals	1	1	.500	4.73	19	0	0	0	12	6	26.2	33	127	15	14	1	1	0	4	9	0	23	3	1
Bauer, Richard, Arizona Giants	1	0	1.000	0.00	6	0	0	0	3	0	8.1	3	28	0	0	0	1	0	2	0	0	12	1	0
Beck, Bradley, Arizona Angels *	2	3	.400	1.91	20	0	0	0	5	0	28.1	23	108	9	6	1	1	0	2	4	0	32	0	1
Bell, Trevor, Arizona Angels................	0	0	.000	4.50	4	4	0	0	0	0	8.0	10	37	4	4	0	1	1	1	3	0	7	1	0
Beltre, Jose, Arizona Brewers............	0	1	.000	7.20	13	6	0	0	0	0	35.0	49	177	33	28	0	3	2	4	21	0	50	3	2
Benoit, Joaquin, Arizona Rangers......	0	0	.000	0.00	1	1	0	0	0	0	2.0	0	6	0	0	0	0	0	0	1	0	4	0	0
Blanc, Jhonathan, Arizona Brewers ..	0	0	.000	0.00	2	0	0	0	1	0	1.2	0	7	0	0	0	0	0	1	2	0	2	1	0
Bonilla, Toma, Arizona Mariners	0	4	.000	6.00	15	1	0	0	3	0	33.0	36	152	29	22	2	5	2	4	19	0	30	1	1
Bradford, Chad, Arizona Athletics	0	0	.000	0.00	3	3	0	0	0	0	3.0	3	11	0	0	0	0	0	0	0	0	2	0	0
Brinson, Morgan, Arizona Giants........	0	0	.000	21.21	8	0	0	0	0	0	4.2	7	37	15	11	1	0	0	3	14	0	5	7	0
Bronder, Stephen, Arizona Cubs	1	1	.500	3.80	6	0	0	0	1	0	21.1	26	93	9	9	0	4	1	0	9	1	9	1	0
Bunch, Kevin, Arizona Athletics	2	0	1.000	2.70	5	0	0	0	1	1	10.0	6	38	3	3	1	0	0	1	3	0	11	2	0
Burcie, Jarrad, Arizona Rangers	1	1	.500	2.13	8	0	0	0	6	0	12.2	7	49	5	3	1	1	0	1	5	0	10	2	0
Byrd, Taylor, Arizona Rangers	0	0	.000	3.00	2	0	0	0	0	0	3.0	4	12	1	1	0	0	0	0	0	0	4	0	0
Cabeza, Manuel, Arizona Giants	2	1	.667	3.24	11	5	0	0	2	1	33.1	29	146	15	12	3	0	0	4	14	0	33	2	0
Callahan, Ryan, Arizona Giants *........	0	1	.000	2.03	11	0	0	0	3	0	13.1	14	56	4	3	0	0	1	0	6	1	16	0	0
Campillo, Jorge, Arizona Mariners	0	2	.000	5.73	4	4	0	0	0	0	11.0	18	52	11	7	0	0	1	0	2	0	10	0	0
Campusano, Edward, Arizona Cubs *	0	0	.000	0.00	1	1	0	0	0	0	2.0	1	8	0	0	0	0	0	0	0	0	2	0	0
Cassevah, Robert, Arizona Angels......	2	5	.286	5.40	15	4	0	0	2	0	45.0	57	201	28	27	2	3	1	7	14	0	27	2	0
Castillo, Julio, Arizona Cubs	1	1	.500	5.57	7	2	0	0	0	0	21.0	29	98	16	13	0	0	0	1	12	0	8	4	0
Cepeda, Benigno, Arizona Giants	0	0	.000	8.10	5	0	0	0	0	0	6.2	10	35	7	6	0	0	0	0	3	0	10	1	1
Cespedes, Carlos, Arizona Brewers ..	0	0	.000	8.49	10	0	0	0	3	0	11.2	18	71	21	11	1	0	1	1	13	0	15	3	1
Chambers, Ryan, Arizona Cubs *	0	1	.000	2.08	5	0	0	0	3	0	8.2	4	31	2	2	0	0	0	0	1	0	9	0	0
Chourio, Jesus, Arizona Brewers	1	3	.250	6.82	14	0	0	0	6	0	30.1	33	144	25	23	1	1	3	1	23	1	24	3	3
Clayton, Patrick, Arizona Padres........	5	3	.625	8.03	16	0	0	0	4	0	24.2	20	118	22	22	1	1	1	3	31	1	33	6	2
Cody, Buck, Arizona Giants *	0	0	.000	5.40	2	0	0	0	0	0	1.2	3	9	2	1	0	0	0	0	0	0	0	0	0
Coffey, Andrew, Arizona Royals *	0	0	.000	8.82	12	0	0	0	3	0	16.1	28	88	17	16	0	2	1	1	16	1	16	3	0
Colon, Juan, Arizona Mariners	0	0	.000	3.86	12	0	0	0	12	2	16.1	16	79	8	7	0	0	2	4	9	0	23	4	0
Cordero, Julian, Arizona Rangers *....	1	0	1.000	4.32	12	0	0	0	3	1	25.0	32	115	19	12	3	0	1	1	13	0	21	2	1
Crabtree, Tim, Arizona Rangers	0	2	.000	5.00	5	5	0	0	0	0	9.0	13	36	5	5	0	0	0	0	0	0	4	0	0
Crews, Jordan, Arizona Cubs	1	2	.333	3.21	11	0	0	0	10	3	14.0	9	56	9	5	1	1	2	0	3	1	15	1	0
Daigle, Richard, Arizona Padres	0	0	.000	3.60	6	5	0	0	0	0	25.0	27	108	12	10	0	0	2	3	10	0	12	1	0
Davidson, Phillip, Arizona Royals	3	1	.750	2.40	9	3	0	0	4	1	30.0	22	126	10	8	0	0	1	7	11	0	29	1	0
Deal, Scott, Arizona Athletics	1	2	.333	4.97	9	7	0	0	0	0	25.1	34	118	17	14	2	0	2	4	12	0	19	2	0
Decker, Chad, Arizona Padres *	1	0	1.000	6.75	13	0	0	0	2	0	14.2	16	75	12	11	1	0	0	6	12	0	15	4	0
De La Rosa, Carlos, Arizona Giants *	1	1	.500	2.57	11	5	0	0	4	3	35.0	32	142	11	10	2	1	1	3	11	0	32	2	1
De la vara, Gilbert, Arizona Royals * ..	4	1	.800	2.33	16	1	0	0	9	3	38.2	31	154	10	10	2	0	0	4	13	0	43	1	0
De Montigny, Mathieu, Arizona Padres	0	0	.000	0.00	1	0	0	0	0	0	1.0	0	4	0	0	0	0	0	0	1	0	0	0	0

Pitcher, Team	W	L	Pct.	ERA	G	GS	CG	ShO	GF	Sv.	IP	H	TBF	R	ER	HR	SH	SF	HB	BB	IBB	SO	WP	Bk.
Diaz, Amalio, Arizona Angels	4	2	.667	4.31	19	0	0	0	10	4	31.1	34	140	21	15	2	1	4	2	9	0	28	4	1
Dorman, Richard, Arizona Mariners	0	0	.000	5.40	4	3	0	0	0	0	10.0	7	43	6	6	0	1	0	0	5	0	20	2	0
Emeterio, Oscar, Arizona Brewers	0	0	.000	3.38	3	0	0	0	3	0	2.2	3	13	1	1	1	0	0	0	2	0	1	1	0
Espinoza, Gustavo, Arizona Angels *	5	3	.625	3.84	13	12	0	0	0	0	70.1	72	295	36	30	3	0	1	2	12	0	78	5	0
Eusebio, Keith, Arizona Athletics	1	2	.333	5.40	14	2	0	0	7	1	30.0	36	138	24	18	3	4	3	4	12	0	17	4	1
Farnum, Matthew, Arizona Rangers	0	1	.000	6.75	1	1	0	0	0	0	1.1	1	6	2	1	0	0	0	0	0	0	2	0	0
Farrach, Juan, Arizona Giants *	0	0	.000	6.43	8	0	0	0	0	0	7.0	9	30	6	5	1	2	0	0	2	0	5	0	0
Fermin, Jorge, Arizona Brewers	0	0	.000	9.82	2	0	0	0	0	0	3.2	8	24	6	4	2	0	0	0	2	0	2	1	0
Fernandez, Armando, Arizona Cubs	1	2	.333	8.03	17	2	0	0	6	1	24.2	36	116	23	22	1	2	1	1	11	3	23	4	0
Fisher, Brent, Arizona Royals *	5	2	.714	3.04	13	8	0	0	4	1	50.1	48	211	20	17	2	1	1	4	13	0	69	3	0
Fogelson, Scott, Arizona Padres *	1	0	1.000	3.08	5	3	1	0	0	0	26.1	17	98	12	9	2	2	2	0	9	0	21	1	0
Foor, Erik, Arizona Cubs	0	4	.000	4.95	16	0	0	0	9	1	20.0	17	89	15	11	1	2	1	0	18	2	20	2	0
Francisco, Alfredo, Arizona Cubs	2	3	.400	3.89	12	5	0	0	0	0	41.2	40	179	23	18	1	0	1	3	16	0	37	0	1
Franco Jr., Thomas, Arizona Athletics	5	6	.455	3.66	14	8	1	0	1	0	64.0	76	275	34	26	1	4	2	4	15	0	51	8	1
Frieri, Ernesto, Arizona Padres	7	1	.875	1.17	17	5	0	0	5	0	46.1	21	186	7	6	0	1	0	4	29	0	59	2	1
Fritz, Benjamin, Arizona Athletics	0	0	.000	0.00	4	4	0	0	0	0	11.0	3	38	1	0	0	0	0	1	3	0	9	0	0
Funk, Shane, Arizona Rangers	0	1	.000	7.86	9	3	0	0	2	0	26.1	35	126	26	23	3	1	1	3	12	0	28	4	0
Fyvie, Daniel, Arizona Athletics	0	0	.000	1.80	3	3	0	0	0	0	5.0	4	21	1	1	0	0	0	0	2	0	3	1	0
Gamboa, Felix, Arizona Angels	1	0	1.000	7.04	4	0	0	0	2	1	7.2	8	41	7	6	1	0	1	2	5	0	10	1	0
Garcia, Jose, Arizona Brewers	1	2	.333	6.00	12	5	0	0	0	0	30.0	27	142	28	20	3	1	2	8	16	1	23	4	2
Garrett, Troy, Arizona Royals	2	2	.500	5.01	13	0	0	0	7	1	23.1	25	97	14	13	2	3	0	2	7	0	21	0	0
Garrison, Stevenson, Arizona Brewers *	2	2	.500	2.86	11	4	0	0	2	2	34.2	39	136	13	11	0	2	1	0	5	0	28	5	0
Giles, Joshua, Arizona Rangers	1	0	1.000	8.44	5	0	0	0	4	0	10.2	15	55	11	10	1	0	0	3	5	0	13	2	0
Gill, Ernest, Arizona Padres	0	0	.000	0.00	1	0	0	0	1	0	1.0	1	3	0	0	0	0	0	0	0	0	0	0	0
Gomez, Josue, Arizona Giants *	2	0	1.000	2.65	11	6	0	0	3	2	34.0	27	143	16	10	2	0	1	2	19	0	37	1	1
Gonzalez, Miguel, Arizona Angels	1	0	1.000	0.00	3	0	0	0	1	0	4.0	0	12	0	0	0	0	0	0	0	0	7	0	0
Gornati, Thomas, Arizona Giants	6	0	1.000	1.30	11	5	0	0	3	0	41.2	32	162	6	6	1	1	0	3	8	1	44	2	0
Grace, Robert, Arizona Giants	6	1	.857	2.85	11	6	0	0	2	0	41.0	37	163	17	13	2	0	1	3	9	0	33	1	0
Granados, Ivan, Arizona Athletics *	1	0	1.000	0.00	1	0	0	0	0	0	4.1	2	16	1	0	0	0	0	0	1	0	7	0	0
Greenhouse, Michael, Arizona Cubs *	0	3	.000	3.31	19	0	0	0	6	1	32.2	32	141	16	12	3	0	3	3	11	0	32	3	0
Griffin, Daniel, Arizona Giants	0	0	.000	0.75	4	4	0	0	0	0	12.0	9	48	2	1	0	0	0	0	6	0	20	0	0
Grogan, John, Arizona Giants *	2	0	1.000	1.65	12	0	0	0	3	0	16.1	12	60	4	3	0	3	2	0	5	1	13	0	0
Guerrero, Carlos, Arizona Cubs *	0	0	.000	21.60	4	1	0	0	0	0	3.1	10	26	8	8	1	0	1	2	6	0	3	0	0
Guzman, Angel, Arizona Cubs	0	0	.000	1.50	4	4	0	0	0	0	12.0	10	48	3	2	0	0	0	1	1	0	17	0	0
Guzman, Julio, Arizona Brewers *	1	1	.500	9.33	8	3	0	0	0	0	18.1	22	90	19	19	3	0	1	1	15	0	18	2	2
Herrera, Pedro, Arizona Angels	2	0	1.000	6.00	16	0	0	0	9	5	24.0	29	115	17	16	1	0	1	2	15	0	17	7	1
Howell, Chris, Arizona Angels	0	1	.000	6.30	9	0	0	0	3	0	10.0	10	45	7	7	0	0	0	1	5	0	8	0	1
Huang, Chia An, Arizona Mariners	2	3	.400	6.96	11	7	0	0	0	0	32.1	46	158	30	25	2	0	4	1	17	0	21	4	0
Hussey, John, Arizona Padres	1	3	.250	6.44	9	9	0	0	0	0	36.1	38	160	30	26	2	2	2	7	13	0	31	4	0
Inman, William, Arizona Brewers	0	0	.000	0.00	1	0	0	0	0	0	2.0	0	7	0	0	0	0	0	0	1	0	1	0	0
Italiano, Thomas, Arizona Athletics	1	2	.333	6.75	8	3	0	0	0	0	18.2	20	87	17	14	0	0	0	4	8	0	27	6	0
Jackson, Brett, Arizona Cubs	1	0	1.000	5.91	4	1	0	0	1	0	10.2	11	47	7	7	0	0	0	0	6	0	9	3	2
Jaimes, Jose, Arizona Rangers	2	1	.667	9.60	10	0	0	0	4	1	15.0	20	77	20	16	0	2	1	3	10	0	17	4	0
James, Brandon, Arizona Rangers	3	1	.750	3.45	13	0	0	0	7	0	31.1	26	137	13	12	1	1	2	2	14	0	30	4	0
James, Mark, Arizona Brewers	1	3	.250	10.50	9	4	0	0	0	0	18.0	26	99	23	21	2	0	2	2	18	0	14	2	1
Javier, Alfredo, Arizona Padres	0	1	.000	9.00	11	0	0	0	2	0	16.0	25	85	20	16	1	1	1	2	13	0	10	6	0
Jepsen, Kevin, Arizona Angels	0	1	.000	5.52	7	7	0	0	0	0	14.2	8	67	10	9	1	0	0	3	11	0	17	4	1
Jimenez, Juan, Arizona Padres	4	4	.500	3.86	13	13	0	0	0	0	79.1	95	345	45	34	5	0	5	2	18	0	67	3	0
Joaquin, Waldis, Arizona Giants	1	1	.500	3.64	10	5	0	0	3	1	29.2	28	128	17	12	1	1	1	1	10	0	37	1	1
Jolliff, David, Arizona Padres	0	2	.000	6.21	10	4	0	0	0	0	29.0	42	144	26	20	6	2	1	5	11	0	23	6	1
Joseph, Alfred, Arizona Cubs	0	0	.000	0.00	1	0	0	0	0	0	0.1	0	4	2	0	0	0	0	0	2	0	0	0	0
Kafka, Ari, Arizona Mariners	0	1	.000	4.73	8	0	0	0	1	0	13.1	13	62	9	7	0	2	1	0	11	0	14	2	0
Kahn, Stephen, Arizona Mariners	0	0	.000	0.00	1	0	0	0	0	0	1.0	1	4	0	0	0	0	0	0	1	0	1	0	0
Kappel, Brian, Arizona Mariners	2	1	.667	0.00	5	0	0	0	1	0	7.1	7	33	8	0	1	0	0	1	2	0	9	0	0
Kay, Joshua, Arizona Athletics	0	1	.000	3.38	16	0	0	0	12	5	18.2	17	76	7	7	0	1	0	4	3	1	24	1	0
Kintzler, Brandon, Arizona Padres	2	0	1.000	4.09	8	0	0	0	6	1	11.0	15	53	5	5	2	1	0	0	4	1	17	1	0
Kirkman, Michael, Arizona Rangers *	3	1	.750	3.44	14	9	0	0	1	0	52.1	51	226	28	20	0	1	1	1	19	0	58	3	0
Komine, Shane, Arizona Athletics	0	1	.000	9.72	4	4	0	0	0	0	8.1	10	43	10	9	0	0	1	1	7	0	11	1	2
Krawiec, Aaron, Arizona Cubs *	0	0	.000	8.10	2	0	0	0	0	0	3.1	5	16	3	3	0	0	0	0	1	0	1	0	0
Kretzschmar, Mathew, Arizona Brewers	1	0	1.000	2.45	7	0	0	0	2	2	18.1	20	79	6	5	1	1	1	1	5	0	19	1	1
Labasta, William, Arizona Brewers	2	2	.500	5.09	14	0	0	0	6	0	23.0	21	113	19	13	3	1	1	3	21	1	14	4	2
Lamont, Tyrone, Arizona Mariners	1	2	.333	4.65	16	0	0	0	3	0	31.0	27	128	19	16	1	0	2	0	9	0	30	3	2
Langille, Craig, Arizona Brewers	2	3	.400	6.84	14	5	0	0	1	0	50.0	80	239	46	38	2	3	6	5	14	1	20	3	4
Lansford, Jared, Arizona Athletics	0	1	.000	1.27	7	6	0	0	0	0	21.1	16	80	4	3	0	1	0	1	5	0	20	0	0
Ledezma, Alirio, Arizona Brewers	3	3	.500	3.89	20	1	0	0	12	4	41.2	41	184	23	18	2	3	3	3	19	3	37	3	1
Lefort, Michael, Arizona Cubs	0	1	.000	15.19	6	0	0	0	1	0	5.1	7	30	10	9	0	2	0	3	6	0	1	2	0
Lopez, Aleurys, Arizona Cubs *	2	1	.667	2.95	10	0	0	0	4	0	21.1	23	98	10	7	0	0	1	1	9	1	29	0	0
Luces, Victor, Arizona Athletics	3	1	.750	3.86	9	0	0	0	1	0	21.0	21	91	10	9	0	1	0	3	10	0	20	5	0
Lugo, Jose, Arizona Athletics *	2	3	.400	5.23	15	5	0	0	2	0	53.1	57	234	42	31	0	2	3	4	18	0	44	2	6
Lumry, Rufus, Arizona Mariners *	2	1	.667	6.66	16	0	0	0	2	0	25.2	34	118	21	19	0	2	4	2	15	0	7	0	0
Lussier, Paul, Arizona Giants	1	1	.500	3.05	11	5	0	0	1	0	38.1	40	156	14	13	4	0	1	2	6	0	32	2	0
Marinez, Yeyser, Arizona Rangers	0	0	.000	2.40	8	0	0	0	3	1	15.0	9	66	6	4	0	0	0	4	16	0	15	3	0
Marquez, Miguel, Arizona Mariners	2	2	.500	7.38	12	5	0	0	0	0	50.0	70	242	54	41	3	1	2	4	22	0	49	11	0
Marte, Jose, Arizona Rangers	3	1	.750	4.09	15	1	0	0	4	2	33.0	36	159	21	15	1	1	2	3	20	0	36	5	1
Martinez, Gregorio, Arizona Giants	4	2	.667	1.99	11	5	0	0	4	2	40.2	25	155	11	9	2	1	1	1	9	0	46	3	0
Martinez, Jesus, Arizona Athletics	0	0	.000	0.00	1	0	0	0	0	0	1.0	2	4	0	0	0	0	0	0	0	0	0	0	0
Martis, Shairon, Arizona Giants	2	1	.667	1.85	11	5	0	0	4	1	34.0	28	134	10	7	1	3	0	1	9	0	50	3	0

Pitcher, Team	W	L	Pct.	ERA	G	GS	CG	ShO	GF	Sv.	IP	H	TBF	R	ER	HR	SH	SF	HB	BB	IBB	SO	WP	Bk.
McBeth, Marcus, Arizona Athletics	1	0	1.000	0.90	8	0	0	0	8	4	10.0	5	39	2	1	1	2	0	0	5	0	13	0	0
McGovern, Ryan, Arizona Giants *	1	1	.500	5.73	11	0	0	0	2	0	11.0	14	53	9	7	0	0	0	1	6	0	10	1	0
Mendoza, Thomas, Arizona Angels	3	3	.500	1.55	13	4	0	0	2	0	52.1	42	204	14	9	1	1	0	1	13	0	56	2	0
Mercedes, Roque, Arizona Brewers ..	2	3	.400	6.60	14	8	0	0	0	0	43.2	53	223	42	32	5	0	2	7	34	0	45	4	4
Miller, Ryan, Arizona Brewers	0	0	.000	4.50	2	2	0	0	0	0	2.0	3	9	1	1	0	0	0	0	0	0	0	0	0
Moore, Tyrell, Arizona Cubs *	0	0	.000	27.00	3	0	0	0	0	0	3.0	13	23	9	9	1	0	0	0	2	0	4	2	0
Morales, Angelo, Arizona Royals	3	2	.600	4.26	10	10	0	0	0	0	44.1	53	190	29	21	1	2	2	2	6	0	32	4	0
Morla, Wandy, Arizona Rangers	0	0	.000	27.00	1	0	0	0	0	0	1.0	2	7	3	3	0	0	1	0	2	0	1	1	0
Nageotte, Clint, Arizona Mariners	0	0	.000	0.00	1	1	0	0	0	0	3.0	0	9	0	0	0	0	0	0	0	0	6	0	0
Nesmith, Travis, Arizona Giants *	0	0	.000	3.60	4	0	0	0	1	0	5.0	6	23	2	2	0	0	0	0	2	0	3	0	0
Nevarez, Matthew, Arizona Rangers ..	2	1	.667	1.61	10	3	0	0	0	0	28.0	18	112	7	5	1	0	0	1	13	0	24	2	0
Nieto, Christopher, Arizona Giants * ..	2	2	.500	1.26	8	3	0	0	3	0	28.2	22	117	8	4	1	0	1	0	6	0	38	3	0
Noboa, Leandro, Arizona Athletics	0	0	.000	8.78	12	0	0	0	5	0	13.1	24	76	23	13	2	0	1	4	7	0	4	2	0
Nottingham, Shawn, Arizona Mariners *	0	0	.000	2.25	3	3	0	0	0	0	4.0	3	15	1	1	0	0	0	0	0	0	6	0	0
Oliveros, Rayner, Arizona Royals	7	1	.875	2.39	14	14	0	0	0	0	75.1	73	298	26	20	1	2	2	3	5	0	48	3	0
Olore, Kevin, Arizona Mariners	0	1	.000	6.00	5	3	0	0	0	0	6.0	7	27	4	4	0	0	0	0	3	0	9	0	0
Paewai, Peter, Arizona Padres	1	2	.333	3.77	7	6	0	0	1	0	28.2	25	125	15	12	3	0	1	2	25	0	15	2	0
Paganetti, William, Arizona Cubs	2	0	1.000	1.08	5	0	0	0	0	0	8.1	4	34	1	1	0	0	0	2	3	0	7	2	0
Parejo, Miguel, Arizona Brewers	3	4	.429	4.33	19	0	0	0	17	2	35.1	41	164	22	17	1	1	2	5	17	1	24	5	2
Parillo, Brandon, Arizona Brewers * ..	1	2	.333	2.00	6	3	0	0	0	0	18.0	5	71	6	4	0	0	0	0	10	0	22	2	0
Pawelek, Mark, Arizona Cubs *	0	3	.000	2.72	14	13	0	0	0	0	43.0	25	180	18	13	0	0	3	9	21	0	56	13	0
Peacock, Dylan, Arizona Angels	1	1	.500	7.71	15	0	0	0	7	0	18.2	30	94	20	16	0	2	0	2	8	0	24	1	0
Pena, Francisco, Arizona Athletics	4	0	1.000	3.00	14	0	0	0	10	0	27.0	26	115	12	9	0	0	1	2	8	0	29	3	0
Pena, Matthew, Arizona Royals *	1	1	.500	4.55	13	0	0	0	6	4	31.2	39	144	19	16	0	1	1	2	10	0	20	3	0
Perez, Roberto, Arizona Rangers	1	0	1.000	3.00	2	1	0	0	1	0	3.0	2	11	1	1	0	1	0	0	2	0	3	0	0
Periard, Alexandre, Arizona Brewers ..	0	1	.000	5.08	11	4	0	0	1	1	28.1	43	133	23	16	1	2	2	1	10	0	22	4	1
Petke, Timothy, Arizona Angels	0	1	.000	11.81	5	0	0	0	0	0	5.1	9	28	7	7	1	0	1	1	2	0	4	1	0
Phelps, Michael, Arizona Cubs	0	0	.000	0.00	1	0	0	0	0	0	0.2	0	2	0	0	0	0	0	0	0	0	2	0	0
Phillips, Zachary, Arizona Rangers * ..	1	3	.250	3.93	14	11	0	0	0	0	50.1	52	216	26	22	3	0	0	3	13	0	73	2	0
Piekarz, Joseph, Arizona Athletics * ..	0	0	.000	0.00	1	0	0	0	1	0	1.0	0	4	0	0	0	0	0	0	1	0	0	0	0
Pina, Jose, Arizona Cubs	3	5	.375	4.78	14	11	0	0	1	0	52.2	59	231	34	28	4	1	3	7	14	0	37	7	0
Posey, Micah, Arizona Angels *	0	0	.000	6.14	4	4	0	0	0	0	7.1	13	42	7	5	1	0	1	1	2	0	9	2	0
Pote, Lou, Arizona Rangers	0	0	.000	9.00	1	0	0	0	0	0	1.0	2	8	1	1	0	0	0	0	3	0	0	0	0
Poveda, Omar, Arizona Rangers	2	6	.250	5.71	14	9	0	0	2	0	52.0	64	227	38	33	1	0	3	2	12	0	56	1	2
Prinz, Bret, Arizona Angels	0	1	.000	12.00	2	2	0	0	0	0	3.0	5	17	5	4	1	0	0	0	2	0	6	1	0
Raglione, Paul, Arizona Royals	3	4	.429	5.94	13	7	0	0	1	1	47.0	66	221	40	31	4	2	0	4	18	0	37	3	0
Ramirez, Froilan, Arizona Giants	2	2	.500	13.50	8	0	0	0	0	0	7.1	9	40	12	11	1	0	0	2	9	0	9	3	0
Rasner, Jacob, Arizona Rangers	1	5	.167	8.37	14	10	0	0	0	0	47.1	79	241	57	44	6	1	8	7	15	0	31	10	0
Rayborn, Justin, Arizona Cubs	2	1	.667	2.08	13	0	0	0	5	1	26.0	17	94	8	6	0	2	0	0	4	0	37	0	0
Rea, Anthony, Arizona Athletics	1	2	.333	7.36	11	0	0	0	3	1	25.2	40	122	26	21	1	0	1	0	8	0	21	2	0
Regilio, Nick, Arizona Rangers	0	0	.000	9.00	1	1	0	0	0	0	1.0	2	5	1	1	0	0	0	0	0	0	0	0	0
Rice, Tim, Arizona Royals *	0	0	.000	5.25	7	0	0	0	3	0	12.0	11	52	8	7	0	0	0	1	7	0	14	1	1
Riley, Matt, Arizona Rangers *	0	0	.000	0.00	1	0	0	0	0	0	0.2	0	2	0	0	0	0	0	0	0	0	2	0	0
Rivas, Amaury, Arizona Brewers	2	3	.400	6.91	14	6	0	0	1	0	41.2	56	195	36	32	1	1	2	5	16	1	34	3	6
Rodriguez, William, Arizona Rangers *	0	2	.000	6.00	9	0	0	0	8	2	15.0	21	73	13	10	1	0	0	0	8	0	15	0	2
Rojas, Cesar, Arizona Padres	2	4	.333	6.75	13	11	0	0	0	0	49.1	48	228	41	37	1	1	5	7	32	0	33	8	0
Romero, Robert, Arizona Angels	0	0	.000	2.70	7	0	0	0	5	3	6.2	7	26	3	2	1	1	0	1	0	0	8	1	0
Rosebrock, Warren, Arizona Rangers	3	1	.750	4.85	5	0	0	0	1	0	13.0	15	53	8	7	1	0	1	0	3	0	11	0	0
Sanchez, Julio, Arizona Padres	2	3	.400	4.28	24	0	0	0	14	4	40.0	33	182	22	19	0	2	2	5	27	0	32	8	2
Santana, Felin, Arizona Cubs	1	1	.500	4.50	6	3	0	0	0	0	24.0	36	110	15	12	1	0	1	0	4	0	13	1	1
Santiago, Mario, Arizona Royals	0	1	.000	18.00	2	0	0	0	0	0	2.0	6	13	4	4	0	0	0	2	0	0	1	0	0
Schwab, Daniel, Arizona Mariners * ..	0	2	.000	6.30	6	0	0	0	3	0	10.0	15	54	11	7	1	1	2	2	12	0	4	3	0
Sharpe, Steven, Arizona Athletics	4	0	1.000	2.66	9	4	0	0	2	0	44.0	31	177	18	13	1	2	1	5	16	0	40	10	1
Shaver, Ryan, Arizona Giants	3	2	.600	3.18	9	2	0	0	1	0	22.2	24	94	12	8	0	2	2	2	4	0	24	3	0
Sherrill, George, Arizona Mariners * ..	0	0	.000	0.00	3	2	0	0	0	0	4.0	0	12	0	0	0	0	0	0	0	0	5	0	0
Sokoll, John, Arizona Royals *	1	0	1.000	4.63	13	0	0	0	3	1	23.1	24	103	15	12	1	0	0	0	8	0	23	4	0
Soto, Estelin, Arizona Mariners *	2	3	.400	7.28	17	0	0	0	12	1	29.2	41	145	31	24	0	3	4	5	15	1	25	4	1
Stanton, Travis, Arizona Angels	0	0	.000	0.00	2	0	0	0	1	0	1.2	3	8	0	0	0	0	0	0	0	0	2	0	0
Stitt, Brian, Arizona Mariners	1	0	1.000	6.00	4	2	0	0	0	0	6.0	13	29	4	4	0	1	0	0	1	0	5	0	0
Sullivan, Bradley, Arizona Athletics	0	1	.000	9.26	3	3	0	0	0	0	11.2	17	59	13	12	1	0	0	0	6	0	10	0	0
Sullivan, John, Arizona Mariners	3	0	1.000	2.92	16	0	0	0	9	2	24.2	28	104	12	8	1	1	1	2	6	0	23	0	0
Suriel, Jose, Arizona Mariners *	2	0	1.000	3.67	15	0	0	0	6	0	27.0	26	118	17	11	0	2	1	1	12	0	11	0	0
Taylor, David, Arizona Cubs *	0	0	.000	0.00	2	2	0	0	0	0	4.0	2	16	0	0	0	0	0	0	2	0	5	1	0
Taylor, Scott, Arizona Cubs	0	3	.000	6.89	6	6	0	0	0	0	15.2	21	75	14	12	0	0	1	0	7	0	13	2	0
Terry, Jason, Arizona Cubs *	0	1	.000	6.41	14	0	0	0	5	0	19.2	24	89	16	14	3	2	1	1	12	0	17	3	0
Thomley, Morrow, Arizona Cubs	0	0	.000	12.15	7	0	0	0	2	0	6.2	13	48	17	9	0	0	2	0	11	0	4	1	0
Thomson, Jordan, Arizona Giants	2	0	1.000	2.77	13	0	0	0	13	7	13.0	13	54	7	4	0	2	0	1	2	1	9	1	1
Tichota, Clay, Arizona Athletics	2	0	1.000	8.10	9	0	0	0	1	0	16.2	20	78	15	15	2	1	1	2	9	0	14	2	0
Torres, Luis, Arizona Athletics	2	4	.333	5.50	14	3	0	0	1	0	52.1	63	230	35	32	1	3	4	5	12	0	29	3	1
Touchet, Daniel, Arizona Rangers	1	1	.500	10.13	6	0	0	0	2	1	10.2	29	61	16	12	1	1	1	1	0	0	14	0	1
Trifolio, Nelson, Arizona Royals	2	1	.667	3.32	12	0	0	0	4	0	21.2	19	89	8	8	1	2	0	0	12	0	17	3	0
Uhlmansiek, Steven, Arizona Mariners *	0	0	.000	3.78	10	8	0	0	0	0	16.2	15	75	11	7	2	1	2	2	10	0	9	0	0
Underwood, Chad, Arizona Cubs	2	1	.667	2.10	15	0	0	0	2	0	34.1	29	138	13	8	0	1	1	1	6	0	30	2	0
Upwood, Jacob, Arizona Padres *	0	0	.000	2.45	4	0	0	0	0	0	3.2	2	14	1	1	0	1	0	0	1	0	1	0	0
Vandel, Geoff, Arizona Padres *	1	1	.500	0.43	11	0	0	0	5	1	21.0	12	80	2	1	0	1	1	1	5	0	32	1	0
Varnell, Grant, Arizona Padres	0	1	.000	3.12	14	0	0	0	7	3	26.0	31	108	13	9	2	1	1	0	2	1	26	0	0
Veal, Donald, Arizona Cubs *	0	1	.000	5.06	4	3	0	0	0	0	10.2	8	45	6	6	2	0	0	1	5	0	14	2	0

Pitcher, Team	W	L	Pct.	ERA	G	GS	CG	ShO	GF	Sv.	IP	H	TBF	R	ER	HR	SH	SF	HB	BB	IBB	SO	WP	Bk.
Vega, Marwin, Arizona Mariners	4	2	.667	4.73	9	3	0	0	1	1	32.1	34	144	22	17	0	2	0	3	18	0	30	4	0
Ventura, Robert, Arizona Giants	0	0	.000	0.00	1	0	0	0	0	0	0.1	1	3	0	0	0	0	0	0	1	0	0	0	0
Vera, Edwin, Arizona Rangers	1	1	.500	3.54	7	0	0	0	1	0	20.1	15	87	10	8	0	0	0	3	9	0	18	2	3
Villar, Nathanael, Arizona Brewers	0	0	.000	13.50	1	0	0	0	1	0	1.1	4	9	2	2	0	0	0	1	1	0	1	0	0
Volquez, Edison, Arizona Rangers	0	0	.000	0.00	1	1	0	0	0	0	2.0	2	9	0	0	0	0	0	0	0	0	2	1	0
Walk, Mitchell, Arizona Giants *	1	1	.500	2.70	3	0	0	0	1	0	3.1	2	13	2	1	0	0	0	0	0	0	3	0	0
West, James, Arizona Angels	0	2	.000	3.71	14	0	0	0	5	0	26.2	25	117	15	11	1	2	3	1	12	0	30	4	0
Williams, Harold, Arizona Mariners *	2	2	.500	2.30	10	6	0	0	0	0	47.0	38	192	16	12	2	1	0	2	16	0	44	6	0
Williamson, Scott, Arizona Cubs	0	2	.000	2.45	4	1	0	0	0	0	7.1	7	35	8	2	0	0	0	2	2	0	9	0	0
Zapata, Juan Riguelmy, Arizona Mariners	4	3	.571	3.86	15	4	0	0	3	0	42.0	50	183	27	18	2	0	0	1	14	0	33	3	0

COMBINATION SHUTOUTS: AZL Athletics (1) -- Franco Jr.-Torres-Eusebio. AZL Brewers (1) -- Guzman-Mercedes-Parejo. AZL Cubs (2) -- Pina-Williamson-Underwood-Chambers, Santana-Rayborn-Crews. AZL Giants (2) -- Grace-McGovern-De La Rosa, Martinez-Shaver-Martis. AZL Mariners (1) -- Uhlmansiek-Kahn-Bonilla-Lamont-Colon. AZL Padres (1) -- Paewai-Frieri-Sanchez. AZL Rangers (3) -- Kirkman-Nevarez-Marinez, Volquez-Phillips-Marte, Kirkman-Nevarez-Abbott. AZL Royals (4) –Oliveros-Barrera, Morales-Sokoll-Barrera, Fisher-Pena-Barrera, De la vara-Sokoll.

2005 FIELDING

TEAM

Team	G	PO	A	E	TC	DP	TP	PB	Pct.
Royals	56	1485	634	75	2194	50	0	10	.966
Giants	56	1476	639	87	2202	42	0	23	.960
Padres	56	1533	658	91	2282	63	0	22	.960
Rangers	56	1494	647	94	2235	51	0	19	.958
Cubs	56	1500	645	106	2251	55	0	11	.953
Athletics	56	1499	645	111	2255	58	0	17	.951
Mariners	56	1477	628	108	2213	46	0	23	.951
Angels	56	1448	515	105	2068	33	0	21	.949
Brewers	56	1497	650	122	2269	57	0	15	.946

INDIVIDUAL

FIRST BASEMEN

NOTE: All caps denotes fielding-percentage leader based on 28 games for catchers, 37 for all other non-pitchers and 45 innings for pitchers. *Throws lefthanded.

Player, Team	Pct.	G	PO	A	E	TC	DP
Acha, John, Arizona Giants	1.000	4	16	1	0	17	0
Alonso, John, Arizona Brewers	.958	14	108	6	5	119	9
Ayala, Angel, Arizona Brewers	.936	10	70	3	5	78	12
Backman II, Walter, Arizona Rangers	.980	35	322	13	7	342	27
BLANKS, KYLE, Arizona Padres	.997	40	365	18	1	384	41
Borg, Hector, Arizona Giants	1.000	1	7	0	0	7	0
Canzler, Russell, Arizona Cubs	.984	41	343	21	6	370	31
Crouch, Nikolaus, Arizona Cubs	.981	17	144	13	3	160	18
Davies, Joshua, Arizona Angels	1.000	2	2	1	0	3	0
De La Cruz, Fredy, Arizona Brewers	.951	5	37	2	2	41	5
Dixon, Kent, Arizona Mariners	.667	1	2	0	1	3	0
Festa, Anthony, Arizona Brewers	.981	11	99	3	2	104	9
Gergel, Kevin, Arizona Mariners	.987	11	70	7	1	78	7
Gill, Ernest, Arizona Padres	.981	18	142	13	3	158	12
Hargrove, Andrew, Arizona Mariners *	.984	34	284	20	5	309	24
Harper, Grant, Arizona Angels	...	1	0	0	0	0	0
Hawke, Matthew, Arizona Rangers *	.995	19	174	14	1	189	15
Hernandez, Samuel, Arizona Athletics	1.000	2	1	0	0	1	0
Ingold, Benjamin, Arizona Athletics	.995	19	180	7	1	188	15
Jacobo, Erwin, Arizona Mariners	.947	5	33	3	2	38	5
Janeway, Rich, Arizona Giants	.992	30	235	12	2	249	20
Jimenez, Herman, Arizona Brewers	.969	7	58	5	2	65	5
Jimenez, Jose, Arizona Brewers	.917	1	9	2	1	12	0
Johnson, Tyler, Arizona Angels	1.000	1	1	0	0	1	0
Leclercq, Lenny, Arizona Brewers	.976	18	112	9	3	124	9
Ledbetter, Curtis, Arizona Mariners	.944	7	64	4	4	72	5
Maldonado, Pedro, Arizona Athletics	1.000	1	6	2	0	8	2
Marrero, Oscar, Arizona Royals	.970	20	155	5	5	165	10
Matos, Willie, Arizona Royals	.985	44	366	19	6	391	36
Morales, Carlos, Arizona Athletics	.985	24	186	11	3	200	21
Napoli, Joe, Arizona Rangers	1.000	3	22	2	0	24	0
Palencia, Isaac, Arizona Brewers	1.000	1	8	0	0	8	0
Pressley, Ryan, Arizona Angels	.938	12	72	4	5	81	7
Quinlan, Robb, Arizona Angels	1.000	1	3	0	0	3	0
Rivera, Julio, Arizona Athletics	...	1	0	0	0	0	0
Rosendo, Gustavo, Arizona Athletics	1.000	10	78	6	0	84	10
Ryan, Matthew, Arizona Angels *	.979	42	311	17	7	335	16
Sales, Darrell, Arizona Angels	1.000	6	40	2	0	42	5
Sanchez, Luany, Arizona Padres	1.000	3	8	1	0	9	1
Santoro, Michael, Arizona Giants	.000	1	0	0	1	1	0
Seara, David, Arizona Cubs	1.000	1	2	0	0	2	0
Smith, John, Arizona Padres	1.000	2	12	1	0	13	3
Stanton, Christopher, Arizona Giants	.989	26	251	18	3	272	16
Steiner, Chad, Arizona Padres	1.000	1	0	1	0	1	0
Sutton III, Donald, Arizona Athletics	.986	8	64	4	1	69	4
Wick, Olin, Arizona Cubs	1.000	1	1	0	0	1	1

SECOND BASEMEN

Player, Team	Pct.	G	PO	A	E	TC	DP
Acha, John, Arizona Giants	.920	7	14	9	2	25	3
Aguilar, Abraham, Arizona Padres	.929	10	26	26	4	56	7
Arce, Valentino, Arizona Royals	1.000	23	42	50	0	92	9
Avila, Carlos, Arizona Royals	.950	13	22	35	3	60	4
Baez, Sammy, Arizona Cubs	.667	1	1	1	1	3	1
Borg, Hector, Arizona Giants	.968	36	62	87	5	154	18
Chang, Raymond, Arizona Padres	.957	3	9	13	1	23	3
Cleland, Clinton, Arizona Padres	.889	3	7	9	2	18	3
Davies, Joshua, Arizona Angels	.852	9	8	15	4	27	2
De La Cruz, Fredy, Arizona Brewers	...	1	0	0	0	0	0
Dominguez, Jeffrey, Arizona Mariners	.941	3	8	8	1	17	2
Eastley, Tyler, Arizona Mariners	1.000	3	5	7	0	12	1
Emeterio, Oscar, Arizona Brewers	.979	11	13	34	1	48	3
Garth, Ronald, Arizona Mariners	.976	20	38	45	2	85	13
Groth, Bradley, Arizona Giants	.934	17	16	41	4	61	10
Guzman, Juan, Arizona Mariners	.942	32	86	76	10	172	15
Hernandez, Samuel, Arizona Athletics	.950	29	57	94	8	159	14
Hudson, Robert, Arizona Mariners	1.000	1	2	2	0	4	0
Infante, Larry, Arizona Angels	.966	19	37	48	3	88	9
Jimenez, Jose, Arizona Brewers	...	1	0	0	0	0	0
Johnson, Joshua, Arizona Royals	.959	24	60	80	6	146	19
King, Lisandro, Arizona Giants	1.000	3	6	4	0	10	0
Klug, Michael, Arizona Athletics	.984	23	47	76	2	125	20
Leclercq, Lenny, Arizona Brewers	.938	9	19	26	3	48	4
Lopez, Pedro, Arizona Royals	.882	3	6	9	2	17	2
Lowen, John, Arizona Royals	...	1	0	0	0	0	0
Matranga, Dave, Arizona Angels	...	1	0	0	0	0	0
McKnight, Scott, Arizona Brewers	.861	6	9	22	5	36	2
Mount, Ryan, Arizona Angels	.958	8	15	8	1	24	2
Nieves, Abel, Arizona Angels	.909	15	17	23	4	44	3
PARKER, DAVID, Arizona Padres	.966	42	83	144	8	235	33
Phillips, Patrick, Arizona Angels	.833	5	3	7	2	12	1
Rivera, Luis, Arizona Cubs	1.000	1	1	3	0	4	1
Schoop, Sharlon, Arizona Giants	.000	1	0	0	1	1	0
Seara, David, Arizona Cubs	.947	19	20	51	4	75	5
Serrano, Eduard, Arizona Cubs	.928	40	75	106	14	195	25
Silva, Johan, Arizona Angels	1.000	5	5	12	0	17	0
Smith, Matthew, Arizona Rangers	.867	5	5	8	2	15	0
Stanton, Christopher, Arizona Giants	1.000	1	1	2	0	3	0
Valdez, Alexander, Arizona Athletics	.964	5	11	16	1	28	3
Vallejo, Jose, Arizona Rangers	.959	52	115	187	13	315	38
Vicioso, Osvaldo, Arizona Brewers	.958	35	79	104	8	191	32

THIRD BASEMEN

Player, Team	Pct.	G	PO	A	E	TC	DP
Acha, John, Arizona Giants	.851	27	13	44	10	67	1
Aguilar, Abraham, Arizona Padres	1.000	1	1	4	0	5	0
Alonso, John, Arizona Brewers	1.000	1	0	4	0	4	1
Arce, Valentino, Arizona Royals	.881	26	12	40	7	59	1
Aughey, Jon, Arizona Royals	.952	13	7	13	1	21	0
Backman II, Walter, Arizona Rangers	1.000	1	1	3	0	4	0
Baez, Sammy, Arizona Cubs	.833	5	3	7	2	12	0
Bonilla, Leury, Arizona Mariners	.903	31	23	61	9	93	4
Borg, Hector, Arizona Giants	1.000	1	0	3	0	3	0
Cleland, Clinton, Arizona Padres	.875	17	12	30	6	48	4

Player, Team	Pct.	G	PO	A	E	TC	DP
Crouch, Nikolaus, Arizona Cubs	.800	18	10	30	10	50	1
Davies, Joshua, Arizona Angels	.789	27	9	36	12	57	0
De La Cruz, Fredy, Arizona Brewers	.947	15	11	25	2	38	2
Disla, Lisandro, Arizona Giants	.909	8	6	14	2	22	0
Dominguez, Jeffrey, Arizona Mariners	.778	4	2	5	2	9	0
Festa, Anthony, Arizona Brewers	1.000	1	0	2	0	2	0
Garth, Ronald, Arizona Mariners	.889	7	7	17	3	27	1
Gomez, Mauro, Arizona Rangers	.769	4	3	7	3	13	1
Heckman, John, Arizona Mariners	.968	10	3	27	1	31	4
Heredia, Valerio, Arizona Cubs	.894	16	12	30	5	47	6
Infante, Larry, Arizona Angels	1.000	9	2	9	0	11	0
Ingold, Benjamin, Arizona Athletics	.843	18	9	34	8	51	3
Jacobo, Erwin, Arizona Mariners	1.000	1	2	0	0	2	0
Jimenez, Herman, Arizona Brewers	.900	2	1	8	1	10	2
Jimenez, Jose, Arizona Brewers	.911	35	33	69	10	112	12
Johnston, Trey, Arizona Padres	.773	7	5	12	5	22	0
King, Lisandro, Arizona Giants	.800	10	9	15	6	30	0
Lopez, Pedro, Arizona Royals	.855	25	11	48	10	69	3
Luster, Jeremiah, Arizona Giants	.842	8	1	15	3	19	1
Maroul, David, Arizona Giants	.947	7	6	12	1	19	2
Martinez, Alberto, Arizona Rangers	1.000	2	0	1	0	1	0
Matranga, Dave, Arizona Angels	1.000	1	1	1	0	2	0
McPherson, Dallas, Arizona Angels	1.000	3	0	6	0	6	0
Mejia, Harold, Arizona Brewers	1.000	2	2	6	0	8	0
Merloni, Lou, Arizona Angels	1.000	4	1	9	0	10	0
Nieves, Abel, Arizona Angels	1.000	2	0	2	0	2	0
Phillips, Patrick, Arizona Angels	.783	9	5	13	5	23	0
Prettyman, Ronald, Arizona Mariners	.833	5	3	7	2	12	0
Quinlan, Robb, Arizona Angels	...	1	0	0	0	0	0
Rivera, Anthony, Arizona Cubs	.750	1	1	2	1	4	0
Rivera, Luis, Arizona Cubs	.912	18	11	41	5	57	4
Sales, Darrell, Arizona Angels	.769	9	6	14	6	26	0
Seara, David, Arizona Cubs	.600	2	2	1	2	5	0
Silva, Johan, Arizona Angels	.938	4	3	12	1	16	1
Smith, Matthew, Arizona Rangers	.929	5	4	9	1	14	1
Steiner, David, Arizona Padres	.908	33	17	62	8	87	10
VALDEZ, ALEXANDER, Arizona Athletics	.892	38	33	83	14	130	10
Vicioso, Osvaldo, Arizona Brewers	.714	3	1	4	2	7	0
Whittleman, John, Arizona Rangers	.883	47	29	77	14	120	9

SHORTSTOPS

Player, Team	Pct.	G	PO	A	E	TC	DP
Aguilar, Abraham, Arizona Padres	.962	11	13	38	2	53	5
Arce, Valentino, Arizona Royals	1.000	2	2	2	0	4	0
Avila, Carlos, Arizona Royals	.960	5	13	11	1	25	4
Baez, Sammy, Arizona Cubs	.945	35	57	115	10	182	23
Bianchi, Jeffrey, Arizona Royals	.972	26	34	104	4	142	23
Blanco, Andres, Arizona Royals	.889	6	5	19	3	27	0
Bonilla, Leury, Arizona Mariners	.962	3	8	17	1	26	4
Borg, Hector, Arizona Angels	.912	9	9	22	3	34	4
Carvajal, Aneuris, Arizona Rangers	.901	32	26	102	14	142	9
Chang, Raymond, Arizona Padres	.979	11	15	31	1	47	8
Cleland, Clinton, Arizona Padres	.769	2	4	6	3	13	1
Davies, Joshua, Arizona Angels	.852	5	10	13	4	27	2
De La Cruz, Fredy, Arizona Brewers	1.000	1	2	3	0	5	1
Dominguez, Jeffrey, Arizona Mariners	.903	26	43	88	14	145	12
Garciaparra, Nomar, Arizona Cubs	1.000	2	2	4	0	6	2
Gonzalez, Jarol, Arizona Padres	.920	36	49	111	14	174	19
Guzman, Juan, Arizona Mariners	1.000	3	2	12	0	14	3
Hernandez, Samuel, Arizona Athletics	.857	3	5	7	2	14	2
Hudson, Robert, Arizona Mariners	.600	1	0	3	2	5	0
Infante, Larry, Arizona Angels	.913	6	9	12	2	23	1
Ingold, Benjamin, Arizona Athletics	.938	6	12	18	2	32	3
Jimenez, Herman, Arizona Brewers	.929	3	3	10	1	14	2
Jimenez, Jose, Arizona Brewers	.929	8	17	22	3	42	4
Johnson, Joshua, Arizona Royals	1.000	6	9	16	0	25	1
Johnston, Dylan, Arizona Cubs	.907	11	16	33	5	54	4
King, Lisandro, Arizona Giants	...	1	0	0	0	0	0
Leclercq, Lenny, Arizona Brewers	1.000	1	0	1	0	1	0
Lopez, Pedro, Arizona Royals	.959	20	21	50	3	74	13
Luster, Jeremiah, Arizona Giants	1.000	1	2	1	0	3	0
Maroul, David, Arizona Giants	1.000	1	2	4	0	6	0
Martinez, Frank, Arizona Athletics	.937	35	47	116	11	174	20
Matranga, Dave, Arizona Angels	1.000	1	0	1	0	1	0
McKnight, Scott, Arizona Brewers	.962	5	9	16	1	26	3
Mejia, Harold, Arizona Brewers	.869	41	44	109	23	176	19
Morel, Alvi, Arizona Royals *	1.000	1	0	1	0	1	0
Mount, Ryan, Arizona Angels	.907	17	11	28	4	43	3
Nieves, Abel, Arizona Angels	.941	5	13	19	2	34	4
Parraz, Ezekiel, Arizona Athletics	.934	12	21	36	4	61	8

Player, Team	Pct.	G	PO	A	E	TC	DP
Phillips, Patrick, Arizona Angels	.950	27	27	68	5	100	14
Rivera, Anthony, Arizona Cubs	1.000	2	2	4	0	6	1
Rivera, Luis, Arizona Cubs	.980	9	17	31	1	49	7
SCHOOP, SHARLON, Arizona Giants	.971	46	72	162	7	241	28
Seara, David, Arizona Cubs	...	1	0	0	0	0	0
Smith, Matthew, Arizona Rangers	.957	27	31	81	5	117	14
Vicioso, Osvaldo, Arizona Brewers	1.000	4	5	7	0	12	0
Zorn, Dean, Arizona Mariners	.939	24	43	65	7	115	11

OUTFIELDERS

Player, Team	Pct.	G	PO	A	E	TC	DP
Alvarado, Ramon, Arizona Athletics	.974	45	70	5	2	77	3
Anderson, Ronnie, Arizona Rangers	.939	45	57	5	4	66	3
Auty, Timothy, Arizona Mariners	.967	29	53	5	2	60	0
Blanc, Jhonathan, Arizona Brewers	.979	21	43	4	1	48	1
Blanks, Kyle, Arizona Padres	...	2	0	0	0	0	0
Bocachica, Hiram, Arizona Athletics	...	2	0	0	0	0	0
Bradford Jr., Samuel, Arizona Mariners	1.000	8	17	0	0	17	0
Brantley, Michael, Arizona Brewers *	.966	42	81	3	3	87	2
Brown, Randy, Arizona Cubs	.939	48	84	9	6	99	1
Cain, Lorenzo, Arizona Brewers	.987	41	71	5	1	77	0
Cividanes, Emmanuel, Arizona Giants *	.913	25	18	3	2	23	0
Copeland, Benjamin, Arizona Giants *	.950	14	18	1	1	20	0
Crafort, Willy, Arizona Padres	.947	38	49	5	3	57	3
Davies, Joshua, Arizona Angels	1.000	3	3	0	0	3	0
Defendis, John, Arizona Cubs	1.000	13	33	2	0	35	0
De La Cruz, Angel, Arizona Rangers	...	1	0	0	0	0	0
Delarosa, Anderson, Arizona Brewers	.983	31	52	5	1	58	1
Desouza, Daniel, Arizona Giants *	.880	16	20	2	3	25	0
Diaz, Javis, Arizona Giants *	.917	38	53	2	5	60	1
Diaz, Matt, Arizona Royals	1.000	2	2	0	0	2	0
Dickerson, Joseph, Arizona Royals *	.976	51	79	4	2	85	1
Duarte, Jose, Arizona Royals	.969	45	57	6	2	65	0
Edwards, Harold, Arizona Angels	.933	8	12	2	1	15	0
Emeterio, Oscar, Arizona Brewers	1.000	4	5	1	0	6	1
Episcopo, Ryan, Arizona Cubs	.982	40	54	2	1	57	0
Fuller, Cody, Arizona Angels	.968	19	29	1	1	31	0
Gill, Ernest, Arizona Padres	1.000	14	20	2	0	22	1
Gonzalez, Oscar, Arizona Royals	.954	51	60	2	3	65	0
Graterol, Oswaldo, Arizona Mariners	.981	28	48	3	1	52	0
Gutierrez, Henry, Arizona Giants	...	1	0	0	0	0	0
Halman, Gregory, Arizona Mariners	.941	25	31	1	2	34	0
Harper, Grant, Arizona Angels	.826	15	18	1	4	23	1
Harris, Steven, Arizona Cubs	.972	22	32	3	1	36	2
Haynes, Nathan, Arizona Angels *	1.000	7	2	0	0	2	0
Hernandez, Eddy, Arizona Mariners *	.946	22	33	2	2	37	0
Hernandez, Jairo, Arizona Mariners	1.000	3	5	0	0	5	0
Hernandez, Juan, Arizona Athletics	1.000	1	1	0	0	1	0
Howard, Joshua, Arizona Padres *	1.000	23	42	1	0	43	1
Janeway, Rich, Arizona Giants	.867	9	11	2	2	15	0
Jimenez, Herman, Arizona Brewers	1.000	1	1	0	0	1	0
Johnson, Tyler, Arizona Angels	.949	43	72	2	4	78	1
Klug, Michael, Arizona Athletics	...	1	0	0	0	0	0
Leblanc, Joshua, Arizona Angels	1.000	2	10	0	0	10	0
Leclercq, Lenny, Arizona Brewers	1.000	2	4	0	0	4	0
LEWIS, DERYCK, Arizona Cubs	1.000	38	51	5	0	56	2
Liriano, Victor, Arizona Cubs *	1.000	3	7	1	0	8	0
Liverpool, Marquise, Arizona Mariners	.921	27	32	3	3	38	1
Luster, Jeremiah, Arizona Giants	1.000	1	2	1	0	3	0
Medina, Fernando, Arizona Athletics	.962	36	49	2	2	53	0
Mehl, Truan, Arizona Rangers	.964	54	70	10	3	83	2
Mendez, Ramiro, Arizona Athletics	.867	10	24	2	4	30	0
Moore, Jerome, Arizona Angels	.952	33	59	0	3	62	0
Morales, Carlos, Arizona Athletics	.886	31	37	2	5	44	0
Morel, Alvi, Arizona Royals *	.971	27	34	0	1	35	0
Napoli, Joe, Arizona Padres	.929	21	25	1	2	28	0
Nelson, Jonathan, Arizona Mariners	1.000	1	1	0	0	1	0
Nunez, Ariel, Arizona Giants	.947	45	68	4	4	76	1
Peralta, Felix, Arizona Royals	.875	6	6	1	1	8	1
Perez, Hector, Arizona Giants	.500	2	1	0	1	2	0
Perez, Josue, Arizona Rangers	1.000	3	2	0	0	2	0
Piper-Jordan, Andre, Arizona Athletics	.943	51	113	2	7	122	1
Richardson, Antoan, Arizona Giants	.970	53	91	6	3	100	3
Rivera, Luis, Arizona Angels	.986	38	69	2	1	72	0
Ruiz, Donato, Arizona Mariners	.958	29	63	6	3	72	0
Ryan, Matthew, Arizona Angels *	...	1	0	0	0	0	0
Sales, Darrell, Arizona Angels	1.000	12	16	1	0	17	0
Sanchez, Alex, Arizona Giants *	.667	4	2	0	1	3	0
Santoro, Michael, Arizona Giants	.857	7	6	0	1	7	0
Seara, David, Arizona Cubs	1.000	5	8	1	0	9	0

Player, Team	Pct.	G	PO	A	E	TC	DP
Smith, John, Arizona Padres	.952	11	17	3	1	21	0
Stanton, Christopher, Arizona Giants	1.000	4	4	0	0	4	0
Steiner, Chad, Arizona Padres	...	1	0	0	0	0	0
Thayer, Matthew, Arizona Padres *	1.000	3	7	0	0	7	0
Thomas-Dotson, Josh, Arizona Padres *	1.000	5	1	0	0	1	0
Torres, Jose, Arizona Rangers	1.000	25	31	0	0	31	0
Turner, Timothy, Arizona Padres *	.989	28	82	4	1	87	2
Valiente, Roberto, Arizona Rangers	.957	30	39	5	2	46	2
Venable, William, Arizona Padres *	1.000	15	18	1	0	19	1
Westphal, Joshua, Arizona Cubs	1.000	5	12	1	0	13	0
Yan, Ruddy, Arizona Rangers	1.000	2	7	0	0	7	0
Yoho, Nathan, Arizona Brewers	.961	37	46	3	2	51	1

CATCHERS

Player, Team	Pct.	G	PO	A	E	TC	DP
Angoma, Ruben, Arizona Brewers	.982	8	47	7	1	55	0
Bambino, Richard, Arizona Angels	.968	16	114	7	4	125	0
Bone, Kyle, Arizona Giants	1.000	2	9	0	0	9	0
Boudreaux, Ross, Arizona Royals	.975	25	210	22	6	238	1
Buller, Dayton, Arizona Giants	1.000	9	70	11	0	81	1
Carter, Yusuf, Arizona Cubs	1.000	4	22	3	0	25	0
Crabtree, Benjamin, Arizona Rangers	.958	4	22	1	1	24	0
Delarosa, Anderson, Arizona Brewers	1.000	3	3	1	0	4	0
Dennis III, Bernard, Arizona Brewers	.958	25	138	21	7	166	2
Dixon, Kent, Arizona Mariners	.953	18	123	18	7	148	0
Doscher, Nicholas, Arizona Royals	.984	17	114	7	2	123	1
Edwards, Harold, Arizona Angels	.970	19	179	12	6	197	0
Farina, Peter, Arizona Cubs	.957	9	40	4	2	46	1
Gergel, Kevin, Arizona Mariners	.991	14	98	10	1	109	2
Gregorio, Tom, Arizona Angels	1.000	4	20	2	0	22	0
Gunther, Barry, Arizona Giants	1.000	10	39	8	0	47	1
Gutierrez, Henry, Arizona Giants	.979	15	122	20	3	145	0
Infante, Jefferson, Arizona Royals	1.000	16	57	7	0	64	0
Jacobo, Erwin, Arizona Mariners	1.000	2	3	0	0	3	0
Johnston, Trey, Arizona Padres	.960	8	22	2	1	25	0
Killian, William, Arizona Padres	.977	24	145	22	4	171	1
Laird, Gerald, Arizona Rangers	1.000	5	28	5	0	33	0
Ledbetter, Curtis, Arizona Mariners	.948	10	47	8	3	58	0
Lobaton, Jose, Arizona Padres	.955	3	19	2	1	22	0
Lowen, John, Arizona Royals	.978	14	76	14	2	92	0
Maldonado, Martin, Arizona Angels	.988	26	220	32	3	255	3
Maldonado, Pedro, Arizona Athletics	.971	27	179	23	6	208	0
Martinez, Alberto, Arizona Rangers	.923	4	31	5	3	39	1
McCarthy, Greg, Arizona Giants	.966	17	98	14	4	116	0
Mercedes, Mario, Arizona Cubs	.973	32	160	17	5	182	1
MORGAN, JUSTIN, Arizona Cubs	.984	29	170	13	3	186	2
Muyco, Dionisio, Arizona Cubs	1.000	1	4	2	0	6	0
Nickeas, Michael, Arizona Rangers	1.000	6	52	7	0	59	0
Palencia, Isaac, Arizona Brewers	.926	11	54	9	5	68	0
Pina, Manuel, Arizona Rangers	.969	26	186	30	7	223	2
Prosise, Nicholas, Arizona Mariners	.980	26	170	25	4	199	1
Pruitt, David, Arizona Angels	1.000	1	1	0	0	1	0
Rivera, Julio, Arizona Athletics	.939	10	68	9	5	82	2
Rojas, Nestor, Arizona Giants	1.000	25	147	33	0	180	1
Rosendo, Gustavo, Arizona Athletics	.967	25	177	26	7	210	1
Sanchez, Luany, Arizona Padres	.984	32	271	31	5	307	1
Stanfield, James, Arizona Brewers	.981	29	177	26	4	207	1
Valichka, Brian, Arizona Rangers	.995	19	182	15	1	198	2
Wick, Olin, Arizona Cubs	.976	23	75	5	2	82	0

PITCHERS

Player, Team	Pct.	G	PO	A	E	TC	DP
Abbott, Justin, Arizona Rangers	1.000	10	1	3	0	4	0
Abreu, Juan, Arizona Royals	.900	14	4	5	1	10	0
Acevedo, Danielin, Arizona Athletics	...	2	0	0	0	0	0
Acosta, Kelyn, Arizona Giants	1.000	2	1	1	0	2	0
Adenhart, Nicholas, Arizona Angels	.750	13	2	4	2	8	0
Aldridge, Richard, Arizona Angels	1.000	7	1	2	0	3	0
Alliston, Joshua, Arizona Angels	1.000	4	1	0	0	1	0
Anderson, Ryan, Arizona Brewers *	...	3	0	0	0	0	0
Arnold, Mitchell Scott, Arizona Angels	.000	6	0	0	1	1	0
Arredondo, Felipe, Arizona Angels	.875	14	3	11	2	16	1
Atchison, Scott, Arizona Mariners	1.000	4	0	1	0	1	0
Avery, Matthew, Arizona Cubs	1.000	1	1	1	0	2	1
Baca, Daniel, Arizona Padres	1.000	12	1	5	0	6	0
Baena, Orlando, Arizona Padres	1.000	6	1	0	0	1	0
Bannister, Brett, Arizona Mariners	...	2	0	0	0	0	0
Barrera, Enrique, Arizona Royals	1.000	19	1	2	0	3	0
Bauer, Richard, Arizona Giants	1.000	6	1	0	0	1	0
Beck, Bradley, Arizona Angels *	.846	20	1	10	2	13	0

Player, Team	Pct.	G	PO	A	E	TC	DP
Bell, Trevor, Arizona Angels	.500	4	1	0	1	2	0
Beltre, Jose, Arizona Brewers	.857	13	0	6	1	7	0
Benoit, Joaquin, Arizona Rangers	...	1	0	0	0	0	0
Blanc, Jhonathan, Arizona Brewers	...	2	0	0	0	0	0
Bonilla, Toma, Arizona Mariners	.929	15	3	10	1	14	0
Bradford, Chad, Arizona Athletics	...	3	0	0	0	0	0
Brinson, Morgan, Arizona Giants	1.000	8	1	0	0	1	0
Bronder, Stephen, Arizona Cubs	1.000	6	2	4	0	6	0
Bunch, Kevin, Arizona Athletics	1.000	5	0	1	0	1	0
Burcie, Jarrad, Arizona Rangers	1.000	8	1	3	0	4	0
Byrd, Taylor, Arizona Rangers	...	2	0	0	0	0	0
Cabeza, Manuel, Arizona Giants	.833	11	2	3	1	6	0
Callahan, Ryan, Arizona Giants *	1.000	11	0	4	0	4	0
Campillo, Jorge, Arizona Mariners	1.000	4	1	1	0	2	0
Campusano, Edward, Arizona Cubs *	...	1	0	0	0	0	0
Cassevah, Robert, Arizona Angels	.857	15	0	6	1	7	1
Castillo, Julio, Arizona Cubs	.600	7	0	3	2	5	0
Cepeda, Benigno, Arizona Giants	1.000	5	0	1	0	1	0
Cespedes, Carlos, Arizona Brewers	.333	10	1	0	2	3	0
Chambers, Ryan, Arizona Cubs *	...	5	0	0	0	0	0
Chourio, Jesus, Arizona Brewers	.778	14	2	5	2	9	0
Clayton, Patrick, Arizona Royals *	.714	16	1	4	2	7	1
Cody, Buck, Arizona Giants *	...	2	0	0	0	0	0
Coffey, Andrew, Arizona Royals *	1.000	12	3	3	0	6	0
Colon, Juan, Arizona Mariners	1.000	12	2	0	0	2	0
Cordero, Julian, Arizona Rangers *	1.000	12	1	4	0	5	1
Crabtree, Tim, Arizona Rangers	1.000	5	1	0	0	1	0
Crews, Jordan, Arizona Cubs	1.000	11	0	4	0	4	0
Daigle, Richard, Arizona Padres	1.000	6	0	1	0	1	0
Davidson, Phillip, Arizona Royals	1.000	9	3	2	0	5	0
Deal, Scott, Arizona Athletics	.833	9	1	4	1	6	0
Decker, Chad, Arizona Padres *	1.000	13	0	2	0	2	0
De La Rosa, Carlos, Arizona Giants *	.929	11	2	11	1	14	0
De la vara, Gilbert, Arizona Royals *	1.000	16	4	8	0	12	2
De Montigny, Mathieu, Arizona Padres	...	1	0	0	0	0	0
Diaz, Amalio, Arizona Angels	1.000	19	2	5	0	7	0
Dorman, Richard, Arizona Mariners	1.000	4	0	2	0	2	0
Emeterio, Oscar, Arizona Brewers	...	3	0	0	0	0	0
Espinoza, Gustavo, Arizona Angels *	1.000	13	1	10	0	11	1
Eusebio, Keith, Arizona Athletics	.800	14	1	3	1	5	1
Farnum, Matthew, Arizona Rangers	...	1	0	0	0	0	0
Farrach, Juan, Arizona Giants *	.667	8	0	2	1	3	0
Fermin, Jorge, Arizona Brewers	...	2	0	0	0	0	0
Fernandez, Armando, Arizona Cubs	1.000	17	2	6	0	8	0
Fisher, Brent, Arizona Royals *	.778	13	2	5	2	9	0
Fogelson, Scott, Arizona Padres *	1.000	5	0	4	0	4	0
Foor, Erik, Arizona Cubs	1.000	16	1	1	0	2	0
Francisco, Alfredo, Arizona Cubs	.778	12	3	4	2	9	0
Franco Jr., Thomas, Arizona Athletics	.889	14	2	6	1	9	0
Frieri, Ernesto, Arizona Padres	1.000	17	2	5	0	7	0
Fritz, Benjamin, Arizona Athletics	1.000	4	1	1	0	2	0
Funk, Shane, Arizona Rangers	.833	9	2	3	1	6	0
Fyvie, Daniel, Arizona Athletics	...	3	0	0	0	0	0
Gamboa, Felix, Arizona Angels	...	4	0	0	0	0	0
Garcia, Jose, Arizona Brewers	.714	12	2	3	2	7	0
Garrett, Troy, Arizona Royals	1.000	13	0	3	0	3	0
Garrison, Stevenson, Arizona Brewers *	1.000	11	0	5	0	5	1
Giles, Joshua, Arizona Rangers	1.000	5	1	2	0	3	1
Gill, Ernest, Arizona Padres	1.000	1	1	1	0	2	1
Gomez, Josue, Arizona Giants *	1.000	11	2	4	0	6	0
Gonzalez, Miguel, Arizona Angels	1.000	3	0	1	0	1	0
Gornati, Thomas, Arizona Giants	.667	11	0	2	1	3	0
Grace, Robert, Arizona Giants	.900	11	2	7	1	10	0
Granados, Ivan, Arizona Athletics *	...	1	0	0	0	0	0
Greenhouse, Michael, Arizona Cubs *	.750	19	0	3	1	4	0
Griffin, Daniel, Arizona Giants	1.000	4	1	1	0	2	0
Grogan, John, Arizona Giants *	1.000	12	1	1	0	2	0
Guerrero, Carlos, Arizona Cubs *	1.000	4	0	2	0	2	0
Guzman, Angel, Arizona Cubs	1.000	4	0	1	0	1	0
Guzman, Julio, Arizona Brewers *	...	8	0	0	0	0	0
Herrera, Pedro, Arizona Angels	1.000	16	0	5	0	5	0
Howell, Chris, Arizona Angels	1.000	9	1	2	0	3	0
Huang, Chia An, Arizona Mariners	1.000	11	1	5	0	6	1
Hussey, John, Arizona Padres	.750	9	0	6	2	8	0
Inman, William, Arizona Padres	...	8	0	0	0	0	0
Italiano, Thomas, Arizona Athletics	.750	8	2	1	1	4	0
Jackson, Brett, Arizona Cubs	1.000	4	1	3	0	4	0
Jaimes, Jose, Arizona Rangers	1.000	10	1	0	0	1	0
James, Brandon, Arizona Rangers	1.000	13	3	3	0	6	0
James, Mark, Arizona Brewers	.750	9	3	3	2	8	0

Player, Team	Pct.	G	PO	A	E	TC	DP
Javier, Alfredo, Arizona Padres	.667	11	0	2	1	3	0
Jepsen, Kevin, Arizona Angels	1.000	7	0	4	0	4	0
Jimenez, Juan, Arizona Padres	.933	13	5	9	1	15	0
Joaquin, Waldis, Arizona Giants	.500	10	1	0	1	2	0
Jolliff, David, Arizona Padres	1.000	10	0	3	0	3	1
Joseph, Alfred, Arizona Cubs	...	1	0	0	0	0	0
Kafka, Ari, Arizona Mariners	.750	8	0	3	1	4	0
Kahn, Stephen, Arizona Mariners	...	1	0	0	0	0	0
Kappel, Brian, Arizona Mariners	1.000	5	0	1	0	1	0
Kay, Joshua, Arizona Athletics	1.000	16	0	3	0	3	0
Kintzler, Brandon, Arizona Padres	...	8	0	0	0	0	0
Kirkman, Michael, Arizona Rangers *	.750	14	2	4	2	8	0
Komine, Shane, Arizona Athletics	.333	4	0	1	2	3	0
Krawiec, Aaron, Arizona Cubs *	...	2	0	0	0	0	0
Kretzschmar, Mathew, Arizona Brewers	1.000	7	0	1	0	1	0
Labasta, William, Arizona Brewers	1.000	14	2	1	0	3	0
Lamont, Tyrone, Arizona Mariners	1.000	16	1	4	0	5	0
Langille, Craig, Arizona Brewers	.929	14	6	7	1	14	0
Lansford, Jared, Arizona Athletics	1.000	7	1	7	0	8	1
Ledezma, Alirio, Arizona Brewers	.833	20	1	4	1	6	0
Lefort, Michael, Arizona Cubs	1.000	6	0	4	0	4	0
Lopez, Aleurys, Arizona Cubs *	1.000	10	1	2	0	3	0
Luces, Victor, Arizona Athletics	1.000	9	0	2	0	2	0
Lugo, Jose, Arizona Athletics *	.933	15	5	9	1	15	0
Lumry, Rufus, Arizona Mariners *	.833	16	2	3	1	6	0
Lussier, Paul, Arizona Giants	.800	11	1	7	2	10	1
Marinez, Yeyser, Arizona Rangers	1.000	8	0	2	0	2	0
Marquez, Miguel, Arizona Mariners	1.000	12	1	3	0	4	1
Marte, Jose, Arizona Rangers	.600	15	0	6	4	10	0
Martinez, Gregorio, Arizona Giants	.917	11	2	9	1	12	2
Martinez, Jesus, Arizona Athletics	...	1	0	0	0	0	0
Martis, Shairon, Arizona Giants	1.000	11	0	6	0	6	0
McBeth, Marcus, Arizona Athletics	.500	8	0	1	1	2	0
McGovern, Ryan, Arizona Giants *	1.000	11	1	4	0	5	2
Mendoza, Thomas, Arizona Angels	1.000	13	3	3	0	6	0
Mercedes, Roque, Arizona Brewers	.778	14	1	6	2	9	0
Miller, Ryan, Arizona Brewers	...	2	0	0	0	0	0
Moore, Tyrell, Arizona Cubs *	1.000	3	1	1	0	2	0
Morales, Angelo, Arizona Royals	1.000	10	1	6	0	7	0
Morla, Wandy, Arizona Rangers	...	1	0	0	0	0	0
Nageotte, Clint, Arizona Mariners	...	1	0	0	0	0	0
Nesmith, Travis, Arizona Giants *	...	4	0	0	0	0	0
Nevarez, Matthew, Arizona Rangers	.727	10	0	8	3	11	0
Nieto, Christopher, Arizona Giants *	.500	8	0	1	1	2	0
Noboa, Leandro, Arizona Athletics	1.000	12	1	1	0	2	0
Nottingham, Shawn, Arizona Mariners *	...	3	0	0	0	0	0
OLIVEROS, RAYNER, Arizona Royals	1.000	14	2	12	0	14	1
Olore, Kevin, Arizona Mariners	...	5	0	0	0	0	0
Paewai, Peter, Arizona Padres	.667	7	1	3	2	6	0
Paganetti, William, Arizona Cubs	1.000	5	2	0	0	2	0
Parejo, Miguel, Arizona Brewers	.857	19	3	3	1	7	0
Parillo, Brandon, Arizona Brewers *	1.000	6	2	4	0	6	0
Pawelek, Mark, Arizona Cubs *	.889	14	0	8	1	9	0
Peacock, Dylan, Arizona Angels	1.000	15	0	2	0	2	0
Pena, Francisco, Arizona Athletics	.500	14	0	1	1	2	0
Pena, Matthew, Arizona Royals *	1.000	13	0	8	0	8	1
Perez, Roberto, Arizona Angels	1.000	2	0	1	0	1	0
Periard, Alexandre, Arizona Brewers	.857	11	0	6	1	7	0
Petke, Timothy, Arizona Angels	1.000	5	0	2	0	2	0
Phelps, Michael, Arizona Cubs	...	1	0	0	0	0	0
Phillips, Zachary, Arizona Rangers *	1.000	14	1	7	0	8	0
Piekarz, Joseph, Arizona Athletics *	...	1	0	0	0	0	0
Pina, Jose, Arizona Cubs	.773	14	4	13	5	22	0
Posey, Micah, Arizona Angels *	.000	4	0	0	1	1	0
Pote, Lou, Arizona Rangers	...	1	0	0	0	0	0
Poveda, Omar, Arizona Rangers	.857	14	2	4	1	7	0
Prinz, Bret, Arizona Angels	.500	2	0	1	1	2	0
Raglione, Paul, Arizona Royals	.923	13	3	9	1	13	0
Ramirez, Froilan, Arizona Giants	...	8	0	0	0	0	0
Rasner, Jacob, Arizona Rangers	1.000	14	5	6	0	11	0
Rayborn, Justin, Arizona Cubs	.750	13	2	1	1	4	0
Rea, Anthony, Arizona Athletics	.667	11	1	3	2	6	0
Regilio, Nick, Arizona Rangers	1.000	1	1	0	0	1	0
Rice, Tim, Arizona Royals *	.667	7	0	2	1	3	0
Riley, Matt, Arizona Rangers *	...	1	0	0	0	0	0
Rivas, Amaury, Arizona Brewers	.846	14	2	9	2	13	0
Rodriguez, William, Arizona Rangers *	1.000	13	0	1	0	1	0
Rojas, Cesar, Arizona Padres	.600	13	0	3	2	5	2
Romero, Robert, Arizona Angels	1.000	7	0	1	0	1	0
Rosebrock, Warren, Arizona Rangers	1.000	5	1	1	0	2	0
Sanchez, Julio, Arizona Padres	.818	24	1	8	2	11	0
Santana, Felin, Arizona Padres	.714	6	1	4	2	7	0
Santiago, Mario, Arizona Royals	...	2	0	0	0	0	0
Schwab, Daniel, Arizona Mariners	1.000	6	1	2	0	3	0
Sharpe, Steven, Arizona Athletics	.778	9	6	8	4	18	2
Shaver, Ryan, Arizona Giants	.800	9	2	2	1	5	0
Sherrill, George, Arizona Mariners *	1.000	3	0	1	0	1	0
Sokoll, John, Arizona Royals *	1.000	13	1	2	0	3	0
Soto, Estelin, Arizona Mariners *	.900	17	2	7	1	10	1
Stanton, Travis, Arizona Angels	1.000	2	0	1	0	1	0
Stitt, Brian, Arizona Mariners	...	4	0	0	0	0	0
Sullivan, Bradley, Arizona Athletics	1.000	3	1	2	0	3	1
Sullivan, John, Arizona Mariners	1.000	16	0	2	0	2	0
Suriel, Jose, Arizona Mariners *	.900	15	2	7	1	10	1
Taylor, David, Arizona Cubs *	...	2	0	0	0	0	0
Taylor, Scott, Arizona Cubs	1.000	6	1	1	0	2	0
Terry, Jason, Arizona Cubs *	1.000	14	2	7	0	9	3
Thomley, Morrow, Arizona Cubs	.667	7	0	2	1	3	0
Thomson, Jordan, Arizona Giants	.500	13	0	1	1	2	0
Tichota, Clay, Arizona Athletics	1.000	9	0	3	0	3	0
Torres, Luis, Arizona Athletics	.900	14	2	7	1	10	1
Touchet, Daniel, Arizona Rangers	1.000	6	1	0	0	1	0
Trifolio, Nelson, Arizona Royals	1.000	12	1	2	0	3	0
Uhlmansiek, Steven, Arizona Mariners *	.636	10	2	5	4	11	0
Underwood, Chad, Arizona Cubs	1.000	15	4	6	0	10	0
Upwood, Jacob, Arizona Padres *	1.000	4	0	1	0	1	0
Vandel, Geoff, Arizona Padres *	1.000	11	0	4	0	4	0
Varnell, Grant, Arizona Padres	1.000	14	6	2	0	8	0
Veal, Donald, Arizona Padres *	.333	4	0	1	2	3	0
Vega, Marwin, Arizona Mariners	.714	9	1	4	2	7	0
Ventura, Robert, Arizona Giants	...	1	0	0	0	0	0
Vera, Edwin, Arizona Brewers	1.000	7	6	1	0	7	0
Villar, Nathanael, Arizona Brewers	...	1	0	0	0	0	0
Volquez, Edison, Arizona Rangers	...	1	0	0	0	0	0
Walk, Mitchell, Arizona Angels *	1.000	3	0	1	0	1	0
West, James, Arizona Angels	1.000	14	0	3	0	3	0
Williams, Harold, Arizona Mariners *	.923	10	3	9	1	13	0
Williamson, Scott, Arizona Cubs	1.000	4	0	2	0	2	0
Zapata, Juan Riguelmy, Arizona Mariners	.857	15	3	3	1	7	1

LEAGUE CHAMPIONS

Year	Team	Pct.	Year	Team	Pct.	Year	Team	Pct.
1988	Peoria Brewers	.690	1994	Chandler Cardinals	.607	2000	Mariners	.709
1989	Peoria Brewers	.732	1995	Scottsdale A's	.661	2001	Athletics	.625
1990	Peoria Brewers	.679	1996	Padres	.643	2002	Cubs	.625
1991	Scottsdale A's	.650	1997	Cubs	.618	2003	Royals-1	.633
1992	Scottsdale A's	.607	1998	Rockies	.750	2004	Giants	.655
1993	Scottsdale A's	.636	1999	Athletics	.696	2005	Giants	.696

GULF COAST LEAGUE

LEAGUE OFFICE

President
Tom Saffell
Address
1503 Clower Creek Dr., H-262
Sarasota, FL 34231
Phone
941-966-6407

Teams*
Braves
Dodgers
Marlins
Mets
Nationals
Phillies
Pirates
Reds
Red Sox
Tigers

Twins
Yankees

*Teams play their games in Bradenton, Clearwater, Fort Myers, Jupiter, Lakeland, Melbourne, Orlando, Port St. Lucie, Sarasota, Tampa and Vero Beach.

2005 FINAL STANDINGS

EASTERN DIVISION

Team	W	L	T	Pct.	GB
Mets	37	16	-	.698	-
Dodgers	25	29	-	.463	12.5
Marlins	24	30	-	.444	13.5
Nationals	21	32	-	.396	16

NORTHERN DIVISION

Team	W	L	T	Pct.	GB
Yankees	33	20	-	.623	-
Phillies	24	27	-	.471	8
Braves	24	28	-	.462	8.5
Tigers	24	30	-	.444	9.5

SOUTHERN DIVISION

Team	W	L	T	Pct.	GB
Red Sox	30	24	-	.556	-
Pirates	28	26	-	.519	2
Twins	28	26	-	.519	2
Reds	22	32	-	.407	8

COMPOSITE

CLUB (AFFILIATE), ABBREV	MTS	YAN	RSX	PIR	TWI	PHL	DGR	BRA	MRL	TIG	RDS	NAT	W	L	PCT	GB
Mets (Mets), MTS	-	-	-	-	-	-	9	-	14	-	-	14	37	16	.698	-
Yankees (Yankees), YAN	-	-	-	-	-	11	-	10	-	12	-	-	33	20	.623	4.0
Red Sox (Red Sox), RSX	-	-	-	11	6	-	-	-	-	-	13	-	30	24	.556	7.5
Pirates (Pirates), PIR	-	7	-	-	11	-	-	-	-	-	10	-	28	26	.519	9.5
Twins (Twins), TWI	-	12	7	-	-	-	-	-	-	-	9	-	28	26	.519	9.5
Phillies (Phillies), PHL	6	-	-	-	-	-	-	8	-	10	-	-	24	27	.471	12.0
Dodgers (Dodgers), DGR	9	-	-	-	-	-	-	-	6	-	-	10	25	29	.463	12.5
Braves (Braves), BRA	8	-	-	-	-	8	-	-	-	8	-	-	24	28	.462	12.5
Marlins (Marlins), MRL	4	-	-	-	-	-	12	-	-	-	-	8	24	30	.444	13.5
Tigers (Tigers), TIG	6	-	-	-	-	8	-	10	-	-	-	-	24	30	.444	13.5
Reds (Reds), RDS	-	-	5	8	9	-	-	-	-	-	-	8	22	32	.407	15.5
Nationals (Nationals), NAT	3	-	-	-	-	-	8	-	10	-	-	-	21	32	.396	16.0

Club names are major league affiliations.

PLAYOFFS: Semifinals: Yankees defeated Red Sox in a one-game playoff. Finals: Yankees defeated Mets, two games to none.

MANAGERS: Braves, Luis Ortiz. Dodgers, Luis Salazar. Nationals, Wendell Kim. Marlins, Edwin Rogers. Mets, Gary Carter. Phillies, Jim Morrison. Pirates, Jeff Livesey. Red Sox, Ralph Treuel. Reds, Luis Aguayo. Tigers, Kevin Bradshaw. Twins, Nelson Prada. Yankees, Oscar Acosta.

ALL-STAR TEAM: 1B-Eduardo Perez, Dodgers. 2B-Cooper Osteen, Phillies. 3B-Greg Creek, Braves. SS-Emmanuel Garcia, Mets. OF-Francisco Guzman, Nationals. OF-Matthew Kutler, Marlins. OF-Jose Tabata, Yankees. C-Yasmil Bucce, Mets. SP-Jacob Ruckle, Mets. Relief Pitcher-David Williams, Braves. Manager of the Year-Gary Carter, Mets.

2005 BATTING

TEAM

Team	G	TPA	AB	R	H	TB	2B	3B	HR	RBI	SH	SF	HP	BB	IBB	SO	SB	CS	GDP	LOB	ShO	Avg.	OBP	Slg.
Mets	53	2125	1801	326	517	735	78	19	34	281	32	15	50	226	1	437	64	17	36	906	1	.287	.379	.408
Dodgers	54	2059	1807	285	511	702	88	17	23	255	18	20	40	171	2	338	39	31	50	824	2	.283	.354	.388
Yankees	53	1986	1728	294	462	649	90	17	21	247	5	23	43	185	2	316	82	28	29	795	2	.267	.349	.376
Pirates	54	2073	1844	279	477	680	94	17	25	232	9	20	28	172	1	334	55	21	39	809	2	.259	.328	.369
Marlins	54	2008	1778	223	459	634	101	10	18	192	20	12	40	158	3	395	29	26	41	853	7	.258	.330	.357
Red Sox	54	2064	1818	244	468	656	96	10	24	213	11	15	37	183	0	357	37	27	53	854	3	.257	.335	.361
Phillies	51	1886	1663	244	417	585	82	10	22	203	13	12	22	183	0	367	92	39	32	717	2	.251	.327	.352
Nationals	54	2033	1798	207	448	632	82	9	28	178	18	8	34	174	3	454	16	9	44	915	3	.249	.326	.352
Twins	54	2005	1713	290	419	591	65	16	25	241	34	22	38	198	1	401	86	41	24	769	3	.245	.332	.345
Braves	52	1876	1694	204	414	618	78	12	34	181	5	18	32	127	0	349	35	26	38	672	1	.244	.306	.365
Tigers	54	1958	1776	228	417	637	71	19	37	205	10	11	28	133	0	475	60	16	37	754	3	.235	.297	.359
Reds	54	1970	1715	223	399	576	94	10	21	197	20	15	42	177	2	491	29	30	33	767	6	.233	.317	.336

INDIVIDUAL

TOP QUALIFIERS FOR BATTING CHAMPIONSHIP

Minimum 162 plate appearances. *Lefthanded batter. †Switch-hitter.

Player, Team	G	TPA	AB	R	H	TB	2B	3B	HR	RBI	SH	SF	HP	BB	IBB	SO	SB	CS	GDP	Avg.	OBP	Slg.
Perez, Eduardo, Gulf Coast Dodgers †	48	197	179	35	63	99	16	1	6	37	2	0	4	12	0	26	4	0	6	.352	.405	.553
Guzman, Francisco, Gulf Coast Nationals	40	169	154	20	53	80	6	0	7	24	0	1	8	5	0	20	0	0	3	.344	.393	.519

Player, Team	G	TPA	AB	R	H	TB	2B	3B	HR	RBI	SH	SF	HP	BB	IBB	SO	SB	CS	GDP	Avg.	OBP	Slg.
Garcia, Emmanuel, Gulf Coast Mets *	45	212	186	43	63	76	7	0	2	30	1	1	3	21	0	36	17	1	3	.339	.412	.409
Kutler, Matthew, Gulf Coast Marlins *	44	187	169	27	57	74	14	0	1	25	2	1	2	13	0	24	8	3	5	.337	.389	.438
Sojo, Richard, Gulf Coast Twins............	43	165	148	36	47	68	11	5	0	15	0	0	4	13	0	32	11	7	2	.318	.388	.459
Bell, Joshua, Gulf Coast Dodgers †	45	178	157	26	50	62	7	1	1	21	0	0	1	20	1	33	5	2	2	.318	.399	.395
Bell, Billy, Gulf Coast Red Sox *.........	43	179	164	18	52	75	13	2	2	27	0	2	3	10	0	14	2	4	6	.317	.363	.457
Tabata, Jose, Gulf Coast Yankees	44	173	156	30	49	65	5	1	3	25	0	0	2	15	1	14	22	6	3	.314	.382	.417
Rodriguez, Wilkin, Gulf Coast Tigers *	44	184	164	23	51	64	7	0	2	17	4	0	2	14	0	25	14	5	1	.311	.372	.390
Fermin, Angel, Gulf Coast Yankees	44	173	154	35	47	81	17	1	5	32	0	3	8	7	0	27	2	1	1	.305	.360	.526
Jackson, Austin, Gulf Coast Yankees	40	171	148	32	45	60	11	2	0	14	0	4	1	18	0	26	11	2	4	.304	.374	.405
McCutchen, Andrew, Gulf Coast Pirates ..	45	192	158	36	47	68	9	3	2	30	0	2	3	29	0	24	13	1	3	.297	.411	.430
Andrus, Elvis, Gulf Coast Braves	46	191	166	26	49	66	6	1	3	20	0	2	4	19	0	28	7	4	1	.295	.377	.398
Contreras, Junior, Gulf Coast Mets	46	177	148	28	43	74	7	0	8	31	0	1	2	26	0	49	1	1	2	.291	.401	.500
Rodriguez, Jesus, Gulf Coast Marlins	45	176	168	16	48	64	10	0	2	17	0	0	3	5	0	17	2	2	5	.286	.318	.381
Gil, Jose, Gulf Coast Yankees †	41	162	140	21	39	53	11	0	1	20	0	2	1	19	0	18	1	1	3	.279	.364	.379
Kelly, Paul, Gulf Coast Twins	40	165	137	16	38	50	6	0	2	20	6	3	5	14	0	36	3	5	1	.277	.358	.365
Loyola, Maiko, Gulf Coast Pirates	41	179	164	32	45	61	4	3	2	14	2	0	0	13	1	32	10	2	0	.274	.328	.372
De La Rossa, Wilkins, Gulf Coast Yankees *	49	211	185	32	50	66	12	2	0	30	0	2	3	21	0	25	7	2	3	.270	.351	.357
Castro, Jonathan, Gulf Coast Nationals † ..	47	211	186	29	50	67	13	2	0	10	4	1	4	16	0	53	4	4	5	.269	.338	.360
Monk, Brandon, Gulf Coast Marlins	46	171	156	19	42	61	10	0	3	18	1	1	4	9	0	16	0	1	5	.269	.324	.391

DEPARTMENTAL LEADERS: G—De La Rossa and Schafer, 49. AB—Castro and Garcia, 186. R—Garcia, 43. H—Garcia and Perez, 63. TB—Perez, 99. 2B—Fermin, 17. 3B—Spath, 7. HR—Reyes, 9. RBI—Perez, 37. SH—Batista and Valdez, 7. SF—Roman, 5. HP—Colon and Pino, 10. BB—Schemmel, 30. IBB—Ellington and Pahuta, 2. SO—Wells, 59. SB—Tabata, 22. CS—Hernandez, 8. GIDP—Ventura, 9. OBP—Garcia, .412. Slg.—Perez, .553.

ALL PLAYERS

*Lefthanded batter. †Switch-hitter.

Player, Team	G	TPA	AB	R	H	TB	2B	3B	HR	RBI	SH	SF	HP	BB	IBB	SO	SB	CS	GDP	Avg.	OBP	Slg.
Abellera, Joseph, Gulf Coast Twins	22	58	56	3	10	11	1	0	0	5	1	0	1	0	0	9	0	0	2	.179	.193	.196
Adduci, James, Gulf Coast Marlins *	11	40	37	3	14	19	3	1	0	7	0	0	0	3	0	5	1	0	0	.378	.425	.514
Aguilar, Jose, Gulf Coast Reds............	33	126	112	20	27	40	6	2	1	14	1	2	1	10	0	31	3	0	0	.241	.304	.357
Agustin, Juan, Gulf Coast Marlins	31	116	104	15	28	39	6	1	1	9	3	0	2	7	0	24	2	1	2	.269	.327	.375
Allen, Cody, Gulf Coast Marlins	45	161	139	16	31	44	8	1	1	10	0		3	19	0	48	1	2	5	.223	.329	.317
Alvarez, Jean Carlos, Gulf Coast Nationals	25	111	93	14	17	31	8	0	2	6	0	0	3	15	0	41	0	1	1	.183	.315	.333
Andrus, Elvis, Gulf Coast Braves	46	191	166	26	49	66	6	1	3	20	0	2	4	19	0	28	7	4	1	.295	.377	.398
Arambarris, Manuel, Gulf Coast Red Sox ..	26	94	85	11	21	28	7	0	0	9	0	0	2	7	0	11	1	1	4	.247	.319	.329
Arias, Claudio, Gulf Coast Red Sox	4	19	19	5	7	16	0	0	3	6	0	0	0	0	0	3	1	0	0	.368	.368	.842
Arnedo, Rolando, Gulf Coast Nationals ..	15	65	55	6	12	12	0	0	0	3	1	1	3	5	0	10	0	0	3	.218	.313	.218
Austin, Parris, Gulf Coast Mets	29	94	87	20	25	31	3	0	1	8	1	1	1	4	0	18	8	1	1	.287	.323	.356
Ayres, Mitchell, Gulf Coast Dodgers *	16	37	32	6	8	8	0	0	0	4	0	0	0	5	0	7	1	0	0	.250	.351	.250
Baez, Welinson, Gulf Coast Phillies	15	55	45	6	12	24	4	1	2	6	0	0	2	8	1	14	1	0	1	.267	.400	.533
Barnes, Larry, Gulf Coast Marlins *	3	11	9	1	3	4	1	0	0	3	0	0	1	1	0	0	0	0	1	.333	.455	.444
Barrientos, Miguel, Gulf Coast Twins * ...	18	51	44	3	7	8	1	0	0	7	1	1	0	5	0	4	1	1	2	.159	.240	.182
Batista, Norberto, Gulf Coast Marlins.....	24	101	71	12	13	16	3	0	0	5	7	2	3	18	0	10	0	0	0	.183	.362	.225
Bautista, Pedruin, Gulf Coast Tigers	36	129	122	15	28	42	7	2	1	21	1	2	1	3	0	30	6	2	3	.230	.250	.344
Bell, Billy, Gulf Coast Red Sox *.........	43	179	164	18	52	75	13	2	2	27	0	2	3	10	0	14	2	4	6	.317	.363	.457
Bell, Joshua, Gulf Coast Dodgers †	45	178	157	26	50	62	7	1	1	21	0	0	1	20	1	33	5	2	2	.318	.399	.395
Berg, Daniel, Gulf Coast Twins	28	104	88	13	14	18	1	0	0	8	2	1	5	8	0	20	4	4	3	.159	.265	.205
Bernard, Miguel, Gulf Coast Braves.......	10	32	28	3	9	13	1	0	1	6	0	1	0	3	0	2	1	1	0	.321	.375	.464
Berry, Vince, Gulf Coast Tigers	37	106	101	14	25	30	3	1	0	5	0	0	4	1	0	20	5	2	0	.248	.283	.297
Billingslea, Courtney, Gulf Coast Mets	33	136	116	16	27	49	5	1	5	17	4	1	5	10	0	48	2	1	1	.233	.318	.422
Bladergroen, Ian, Gulf Coast Red Sox * ..	5	21	18	4	8	14	1	1	1	6	0	0	0	3	0	3	0	0	1	.444	.524	.778
Blanton, John, Gulf Coast Phillies	7	26	23	4	5	6	1	0	0	5	0	0	0	3	1	5	2	0	1	.217	.308	.261
Blaquiere, Jean Luc, Gulf Coast Mets	21	59	52	6	11	15	1	0	1	7	0	0	1	6	0	17	0	0	1	.212	.305	.288
Brea, Manuel, Gulf Coast Tigers	40	111	104	6	18	23	1	2	0	5	0	1	0	6	0	39	5	1	0	.173	.216	.221
Brezeale, Daniel, Gulf Coast Braves	5	19	18	2	5	7	2	0	0	2	0	0	0	1	0	5	0	0	1	.278	.316	.389
Britton, Phillip, Gulf Coast Braves	18	44	39	3	9	13	1	0	1	2	0	0	3	2	0	7	0	0	2	.231	.318	.333
Broadway, Larry, Gulf Coast Nationals * ..	8	36	28	3	12	20	5	0	1	4	1	0	0	7	0	3	0	0	0	.429	.543	.714
Brooks, Parker, Gulf Coast Dodgers †	15	35	27	7	6	6	0	0	0	2	1	0	1	5	0	3	2	0	2	.222	.364	.222
Brown, Dustin, Gulf Coast Red Sox	6	22	18	3	4	5	1	0	0	3	0	0	0	4	0	2	0	0	0	.222	.364	.278
Brown, Jeremy, Gulf Coast Dodgers	29	119	101	17	25	36	1	2	2	12	0	2	5	11	0	23	2	5	4	.248	.345	.356
Bruce, Jay, Gulf Coast Reds *	37	136	122	29	33	61	9	2	5	25	0	2	1	11	0	31	4	6	2	.270	.331	.500
Bucce, Yasmil, Gulf Coast Mets	34	123	98	14	33	42	6	0	1	17	0	1	5	19	0	21	1	0	2	.337	.463	.429
Buck, Juan, Gulf Coast Reds	14	40	39	2	4	4	0	0	0	3	0	0	0	1	0	23	0	0	0	.103	.125	.103
Cabrera, Gerardo, Gulf Coast Reds	32	112	95	10	27	47	7	2	3	13	1	1	1	14	0	24	2	4	2	.284	.378	.495
Cain, Gregory, Gulf Coast Mets	30	122	94	13	19	29	5	1	1	11	2	2	4	20	0	39	7	3	0	.202	.358	.309
Cairo, Miguel, Gulf Coast Mets	3	13	13	3	4	5	1	0	0	0	0	0	0	0	0	0	0	0	0	.308	.308	.385
Camarena, Jose, Gulf Coast Braves †	22	76	68	6	19	28	4	1	1	8	0	0	1	7	0	14	1	1	3	.279	.355	.412
Cambero, Alberto, Gulf Coast Phillies † ..	28	100	89	13	17	20	3	0	0	8	0	1	1	9	0	31	9	1	1	.191	.273	.225
Carmona, Eliazar, Gulf Coast Braves	34	84	77	10	16	17	1	0	0	4	2	0	1	4	0	12	4	1	1	.208	.256	.221
Carroll, Mark, Gulf Coast Yankees	4	12	8	0	2	2	0	0	0	0	0	0	0	2	0	1	0	0	0	.250	.455	.250
Castro, Jonathan, Gulf Coast Nationals † ..	47	211	186	29	50	67	13	2	0	10	4	1	4	16	0	53	4	4	5	.269	.338	.360
Castro, Jose, Gulf Coast Mets †	31	133	116	15	34	44	3	2	1	10	5	0	6	6	0	39	2	0	5	.293	.359	.379
Cedron, Jhon, Gulf Coast Pirates	21	63	54	10	11	14	0	0	1	7	0	1	1	7	0	10	5	0	1	.204	.302	.259
Cervelli, Francisco, Gulf Coast Yankees † ..	24	70	58	10	11	16	2	0	1	9	0	2	2	8	0	13	1	0	0	.190	.300	.276
Cheesman, Aaron, Gulf Coast Tigers	31	108	89	17	31	45	9	1	1	16	2	1	2	14	0	9	3	2	2	.348	.443	.506
Ciaramella, Matthew, Gulf Coast Red Sox †	11	48	44	3	9	10	1	0	0	5	1	0	0	3	0	8	0	1	1	.205	.250	.227
Ciriaco, Audy, Gulf Coast Tigers..........	40	164	152	20	38	64	5	4	3	23	0	1		10	0	46	5	1	7	.250	.299	.421
Clark, Howie, Gulf Coast Pirates *	8	30	27	7	13	18	3	1	0	4	0	0	0	3	0	2	0	0	0	.481	.533	.667
Colon, Angel, Gulf Coast Reds	47	173	145	21	37	52	12	0	1	24	0	3	10	15	0	41	0	2	3	.255	.358	.359
Connor, Wesley, Gulf Coast Twins †	27	73	65	13	16	25	2	2	1	8	3	1	0	4	0	13	5	1	0	.246	.286	.385

ROOKIE Gulf Coast League

Player, Team	G	TPA	AB	R	H	TB	2B	3B	HR	RBI	SH	SF	HP	BB	IBB	SO	SB	CS	GDP	Avg.	OBP	Slg.
Contreras, Junior, Gulf Coast Mets	46	177	148	28	43	74	7	0	8	31	0	1	2	26	0	49	1	1	2	.291	.401	.500
Coronado, Jose, Gulf Coast Mets †	11	50	47	9	19	22	1	1	0	4	1	0	1	1	0	9	1	1	0	.404	.429	.468
Cortez, Jose, Gulf Coast Phillies †	1	2	2	0	0	0	0	0	0	0	0	0	0	0	0	1	0	0	0	.000	.000	.000
Cotto, Pedro, Gulf Coast Tigers *	13	48	46	5	9	11	0	1	0	1	0	0	0	2	0	2	0	1	1	.196	.229	.239
Creek, Gregory, Gulf Coast Braves *	41	154	143	21	46	64	10	1	2	14	0	0	0	11	0	22	0	0	3	.322	.370	.448
Creswell, Charles, Gulf Coast Phillies *	23	72	68	5	12	18	3	0	1	1	0	0	0	4	0	25	2	2	0	.176	.222	.265
Cronkhite, Ian, Gulf Coast Red Sox *	6	24	23	6	10	20	3	2	1	6	0	0	0	1	0	2	1	0	0	.435	.458	.870
Cuevas, Phillip, Gulf Coast Phillies	22	66	60	9	10	11	1	0	0	3	1	0	0	5	0	22	2	2	0	.167	.231	.183
Cummins, Daniel, Gulf Coast Mets	32	117	107	21	35	48	8	1	1	19	3	0	1	5	0	24	0	1	1	.327	.363	.449
Dasni, Chales, Gulf Coast Dodgers	1	4	4	1	1	3	0	1	0	0	0	0	0	0	0	0	0	0	0	.250	.250	.750
Dean, Joshua, Gulf Coast Twins *	34	122	106	21	36	43	4	0	1	20	0	0	1	15	0	9	5	1	2	.340	.426	.406
De Jesus, Ivan, Gulf Coast Dodgers	33	132	121	18	41	46	5	0	0	11	1	0	0	10	0	22	8	2	2	.339	.389	.380
De La Cruz, Jason, Gulf Coast Tigers	33	120	110	11	19	27	2	0	2	15	0	0	3	7	0	40	0	0	3	.173	.242	.245
De la Cruz, Jorge, Gulf Coast Nationals	10	35	32	4	9	13	1	0	1	3	1	0	0	2	0	11	0	0	0	.281	.324	.406
De La Rossa, Wilkins, Gulf Coast Yankees *	49	211	185	32	50	66	12	2	0	30	0	2	3	21	0	25	7	2	3	.270	.351	.357
Delaughter, Ryan, Gulf Coast Nationals	33	135	125	18	31	54	3	1	6	21	0	0	4	6	0	39	1	0	3	.248	.304	.432
De Leon, Santo, Gulf Coast Tigers	33	121	117	15	28	48	6	1	4	19	0	2	1	1	0	22	0	0	0	.239	.248	.410
Delgado, Juan, Gulf Coast Twins †	27	76	72	8	7	17	2	1	2	5	1	1	0	2	0	28	3	1	0	.097	.120	.236
Delgado, Ronny, Gulf Coast Reds	38	144	116	13	36	55	8	1	3	16	1	2	3	22	0	41	0	1	2	.310	.427	.474
de San Miguel, Allan, Gulf Coast Twins	23	62	54	9	11	17	3	0	1	11	1	0	4	3	0	14	1	2	2	.204	.295	.315
de Vrieze, Jeffrey, Gulf Coast Marlins	30	74	67	8	12	18	3	0	1	8	0	1	1	5	0	30	0	0	4	.179	.243	.269
Disla, Bienvenido, Gulf Coast Braves †	22	58	48	3	7	10	1	1	0	2	0	0	0	10	0	19	1	0	0	.146	.293	.208
Dunn, Michael, Gulf Coast Yankees *	24	74	62	4	12	18	2	2	0	9	0	3	1	8	0	16	0	1	0	.194	.284	.290
Durant, Michael, Gulf Coast Phillies	39	146	126	21	24	46	4	0	6	22	0	0	4	16	0	56	3	0	6	.190	.301	.365
Dyson, Colie, Gulf Coast Dodgers *	2	8	7	0	0	0	0	0	0	0	0	0	0	1	0	2	0	0	0	.000	.125	.000
Egan, Jonathan, Gulf Coast Red Sox	35	150	126	19	28	37	6	0	1	15	0	1	2	21	0	29	0	1	5	.222	.340	.294
Ellington, Matthew, Gulf Coast Marlins *	21	88	79	12	25	44	8	1	3	13	0	1	3	5	2	12	0	0	3	.316	.375	.557
Engel, Reid, Gulf Coast Red Sox *	27	117	103	9	24	34	2	1	2	8	2	0	1	11	0	36	2	2	1	.233	.313	.330
Enriquez, Andre, Gulf Coast Nationals	1	1	1	0	0	0	0	0	0	0	0	0	0	0	0	0	0	0	0	.000	.000	.000
Eymann, Eric, Gulf Coast Reds	1	4	3	1	1	2	1	0	0	0	0	0	1	0	0	1	0	0	0	.333	.500	.667
Feiner, Kevyn, Gulf Coast Reds	25	102	96	15	24	27	3	0	0	7	0	0	2	4	0	12	2	0	3	.250	.294	.281
Fermin, Angel, Gulf Coast Yankees	44	173	154	35	47	81	17	1	5	32	0	3	8	7	0	27	2	1	1	.305	.360	.526
Figuereo, Johan, Gulf Coast Nationals	47	190	174	16	45	60	9	0	2	16	0	0	3	13	0	32	1	0	3	.259	.321	.345
Fletcher, Simon, Gulf Coast Twins	21	74	60	8	12	17	2	0	1	4	3	0	1	10	0	22	6	1	0	.200	.324	.283
Flores, Angel, Gulf Coast Tigers	15	36	27	3	3	4	1	0	0	1	1	1	0	7	0	7	0	0	1	.111	.286	.148
Frazee, Joseph, Gulf Coast Phillies *	30	110	92	13	24	33	7	1	0	9	1	0	1	16	0	16	5	4	1	.261	.376	.359
Fulse, Sheldon, Gulf Coast Red Sox †	4	15	11	3	1	2	1	0	0	1	0	0	1	3	0	2	0	0	0	.091	.333	.182
Garcia, Emmanuel, Gulf Coast Mets *	45	212	186	43	63	76	7	0	2	30	1	1	3	21	0	36	17	1	3	.339	.412	.409
Garcia, Jesus, Gulf Coast Red Sox	32	121	106	12	28	39	5	0	2	12	0	4	1	10	0	19	1	0	4	.264	.322	.368
Garcia, Steven, Gulf Coast Braves	23	60	52	7	12	17	2	0	1	4	0	0	2	6	0	7	0	0	2	.231	.333	.327
Garcia, Yosanddy, Gulf Coast Dodgers	41	143	120	12	21	33	4	1	2	10	2	3	2	16	0	47	1	0	4	.175	.277	.275
Garrett, Matt, Gulf Coast Reds	23	78	66	3	11	12	1	0	0	1	2	0	2	7	0	31	0	1	2	.167	.267	.182
German, Agustin, Gulf Coast Nationals	29	119	106	13	21	28	4	0	1	9	1	1	2	9	0	28	0	0	2	.198	.271	.264
Gil, Jose, Gulf Coast Yankees †	41	162	140	21	39	53	11	0	1	20	0	2	1	19	0	18	1	1	3	.279	.364	.379
Gilbert, Archie, Gulf Coast Red Sox	24	83	73	9	16	19	3	0	0	7	1	1	6	2	0	10	0	0	1	.219	.293	.260
Gonzalez, Adolfo, Gulf Coast Dodgers †	37	136	119	18	34	45	7	2	0	15	3	1	6	7	0	9	2	2	5	.286	.353	.378
Gonzalez, Angel R., Gulf Coast Pirates †	19	88	84	9	23	34	4	2	1	8	0	0	2	2	0	23	4	5	1	.274	.307	.405
Gonzalez, Julio, Gulf Coast Reds	30	102	85	12	18	27	6	0	1	8	3	0	2	12	0	22	3	3	1	.212	.323	.318
Granadillo, Antonio, Gulf Coast Red Sox †	14	64	52	9	14	20	3	0	1	9	0	0	1	11	0	10	0	1	1	.269	.406	.385
Greenwood, Jared, Gulf Coast Yankees *	12	43	36	3	10	13	1	1	0	6	0	0	1	6	0	12	0	0	0	.278	.395	.361
Griffin, Trevion, Gulf Coast Braves	31	111	99	14	16	21	3	1	0	5	0	2	3	7	0	11	6	2	2	.162	.234	.212
Gutierrez, Eloy, Gulf Coast Dodgers †	41	142	119	19	32	41	4	1	1	19	1	1	5	15	0	26	2	6	1	.269	.371	.345
Guzman, Agustin, Gulf Coast Tigers	28	100	86	10	17	29	6	0	2	12	2	2	1	9	0	24	5	2	0	.198	.276	.337
Guzman, Francisco, Gulf Coast Nationals	40	169	154	20	53	80	6	0	7	24	0	1	8	5	0	20	0	0	3	.344	.393	.519
Guzman, Jose, Gulf Coast Dodgers	2	9	8	1	1	1	0	0	0	2	0	0	0	1	0	5	0	0	0	.125	.222	.125
Hall, Michael, Gulf Coast Red Sox *	9	33	27	4	7	8	1	0	0	1	0	0	1	5	0	10	0	0	0	.259	.394	.296
Haupt, Christopher, Gulf Coast Marlins	21	48	40	2	2	2	0	0	0	1	0	0	2	6	0	18	0	0	0	.050	.208	.050
Hayes, Brett, Gulf Coast Marlins	3	12	12	2	5	6	1	0	0	2	0	0	0	0	0	2	0	1	0	.417	.417	.500
Henry, Carl, Gulf Coast Yankees	48	204	181	32	45	69	9	3	3	17	0	0	6	17	0	39	17	4	0	.249	.333	.381
Hernandez, Diory, Gulf Coast Braves	7	28	28	5	10	14	1	0	1	4	0	0	0	0	0	2	0	2	3	.357	.357	.500
Hernandez, Fidel, Gulf Coast Phillies	35	130	123	16	32	35	3	0	0	14	1	2	1	3	0	12	10	8	1	.260	.279	.285
Hernandez, Habelito, Gulf Coast Reds	5	20	19	2	6	9	0	0	1	3	0	0	0	1	0	2	1	0	0	.316	.350	.474
Hernandez, Luis, Gulf Coast Braves †	1	4	4	1	1	4	0	0	1	1	0	0	0	0	0	2	0	0	0	.250	.250	1.000
Hodges, Scott, Gulf Coast Nationals *	2	7	7	0	0	0	0	0	0	0	0	0	0	0	0	2	0	0	0	.000	.000	.000
Honey, Raymond, Gulf Coast Reds	25	91	84	15	17	30	5	1	2	9	2	0	2	3	0	26	1	3	1	.202	.247	.357
Hurst, Jason, Gulf Coast Red Sox	32	123	103	18	24	37	4	0	3	20	0	2	4	14	0	19	2	0	3	.233	.341	.359
Igsema, Victor, Gulf Coast Pirates	38	151	131	21	31	44	10	0	1	15	0	0	4	16	0	40	3	0	1	.237	.338	.336
Jackson, Austin, Gulf Coast Yankees	40	171	148	32	45	60	11	2	0	14	0	4	1	18	0	26	11	2	4	.304	.374	.405
Jansen, Kenley, Gulf Coast Dodgers †	34	111	102	16	31	45	9	1	1	18	1	1	0	6	0	19	1	0	6	.304	.339	.441
Japa, Rolando, Gulf Coast Yankees	1	2	2	0	0	0	0	0	0	0	0	0	0	0	0	1	0	0	0	.000	.000	.000
Johnson, Deryck, Gulf Coast Nationals *	7	28	27	0	5	6	1	0	0	2	0	0	0	1	0	7	1	1	1	.185	.214	.222
Johnson, Taylor, Gulf Coast Reds *	39	139	117	10	26	39	10	0	1	17	2	1	1	18	1	26	3	1	3	.222	.328	.333
Johnson, Tod, Gulf Coast Reds *	1	4	4	0	0	0	0	0	0	0	0	0	0	0	0	1	0	0	0	.000	.000	.000
Jones, Brandon, Gulf Coast Braves *	2	8	8	0	1	1	0	0	0	2	0	0	0	0	0	2	0	1	0	.125	.125	.125
Jones, Michael, Gulf Coast Reds	27	105	99	9	20	27	4	0	1	5	0	0	2	4	0	37	1	0	1	.202	.248	.273
Jones, Michael, Gulf Coast Red Sox *	31	122	108	13	33	48	9	0	2	15	0	0	4	10	0	18	0	1	6	.306	.385	.444
Kaaihue, Isaiah, Gulf Coast Braves	40	148	127	18	36	66	8	2	6	22	0	4	2	15	0	38	0	0	4	.283	.358	.520
Kelly, Paul, Gulf Coast Twins	40	165	137	16	38	50	6	0	2	20	6	3	5	14	0	36	3	5	1	.277	.358	.365
Kennelly, Timothy, Gulf Coast Phillies	38	135	112	15	33	47	11	0	1	15	0	0	2	21	0	16	3	1	4	.295	.415	.420
Knowles, Marion, Gulf Coast Twins	36	138	121	16	30	39	4	1	1	17	0	0	0	17	1	30	3	1	2	.248	.341	.322

Player, Team	G	TPA	AB	R	H	TB	2B	3B	HR	RBI	SH	SF	HP	BB	IBB	SO	SB	CS	GDP	Avg.	OBP	Slg.
Kuhaulua, Kaulana, Gulf Coast Twins......	3	7	5	0	0	0	0	0	0	0	0	0	0	2	0	3	0	0	0	.000	.286	.000
Kutler, Matthew, Gulf Coast Marlins *	44	187	169	27	57	74	14	0	1	25	2	1	2	13	0	24	8	3	5	.337	.389	.438
Laboy, Albert, Gulf Coast Pirates	30	121	111	15	21	27	3	0	1	13	1	1	3	5	0	14	5	0	5	.189	.242	.243
Lafountain, Jason, Gulf Coast Yankees †	19	61	49	9	9	10	1	0	0	5	0	0	0	12	0	5	0	0	3	.184	.344	.204
Lane, Richard, Gulf Coast Nationals *	7	26	23	6	9	9	0	0	0	1	0	0	1	2	0	4	0	0	0	.391	.462	.391
Larish, Jeffrey, Gulf Coast Tigers *	6	24	18	1	4	5	1	0	0	4	0	1	1	4	0	5	0	1	0	.222	.375	.278
Lasso, Yoni, Gulf Coast Reds..................	23	86	73	8	17	22	5	0	0	13	0	1	2	10	0	22	0	0	3	.233	.337	.301
Lerud, Steven, Gulf Coast Pirates *........	18	74	60	13	16	27	3	1	2	15	0	4	3	7	0	13	0	0	1	.267	.351	.450
Lewis, Kenneth, Gulf Coast Reds *	2	8	7	2	2	2	0	0	0	0	0	0	0	1	0	0	1	0	0	.286	.375	.286
Linares, Emilio, Gulf Coast Red Sox †	36	120	108	16	25	35	7	0	1	8	2	1	0	9	0	35	1	2	2	.231	.288	.324
Linares, Miguel, Gulf Coast Tigers..........	37	145	136	18	38	56	7	1	3	12	1	0	1	7	0	34	5	0	5	.279	.319	.412
Lipsey, Carl, Gulf Coast Red Sox	7	30	26	5	4	4	0	0	0	4	0	0	0	4	0	7	0	1	0	.154	.267	.154
Little, Mark, Gulf Coast Marlins.............	2	4	4	2	2	8	0	0	2	6	0	0	0	0	0	1	0	0	0	.500	.500	2.000
Lowrance, Marvin, Gulf Coast Nationals *	8	31	28	4	9	16	1	0	2	9	0	0	0	3	0	2	0	0	0	.321	.387	.571
Loyola, Maiko, Gulf Coast Pirates	41	179	164	32	45	61	4	3	2	14	2	0	0	13	1	32	10	2	0	.274	.328	.372
Luque, William, Gulf Coast Twins............	33	109	90	21	29	34	1	2	0	11	3	2	4	10	0	16	13	4	1	.322	.406	.378
Lysaught, Michael, Gulf Coast Twins	23	82	72	17	18	28	5	1	1	10	2	0	0	8	0	26	3	1	0	.250	.325	.389
Made, Kelington, Gulf Coast Pirates	14	42	41	3	6	11	0	1	1	2	0	0	0	1	0	5	0	0	0	.146	.167	.268
Maldonado, Brahiam, Gulf Coast Mets ..	33	139	117	23	30	42	7	1	1	21	1	2	2	17	1	36	8	1	1	.256	.355	.359
Malec, Christopher, Gulf Coast Yankees †	21	83	73	16	28	35	4	0	1	14	0	1	1	7	1	4	1	1	1	.384	.439	.479
Mancebo, Melvin, Gulf Coast Nationals..	25	92	88	4	24	39	6	0	3	12	0	0	1	3	1	25	0	0	1	.273	.304	.443
Mann, Schuyler, Gulf Coast Yankees	5	11	9	1	3	3	0	0	0	0	0	0	1	1	0	0	0	0	0	.333	.455	.333
Mansolino, Anthony, Gulf Coast Pirates ..	42	179	165	21	40	63	10	2	3	21	0	2	1	11	0	20	0	3	7	.242	.291	.382
Marcial, Robert, Gulf Coast Braves	24	27	26	4	5	7	2	0	0	1	0	1	0	0	0	5	0	1	0	.192	.185	.269
Martinez, Jonathan, Gulf Coast Nationals †	38	156	124	17	24	29	3	1	0	7	5	1	0	26	0	22	6	2	4	.194	.331	.234
Mateo, Jose, Gulf Coast Mets	21	75	59	13	16	25	3	0	2	10	2	2	1	11	0	9	5	1	2	.271	.384	.424
Matsui, Kazuo, Gulf Coast Mets †	3	11	9	3	4	7	0	0	1	3	0	0	1	1	0	3	0	0	0	.444	.545	.778
Mauer, Donald, Gulf Coast Twins...........	2	8	6	0	2	2	0	0	0	0	0	0	0	2	0	0	1	0	0	.333	.500	.333
McCutchen, Andrew, Gulf Coast Pirates	45	192	158	36	47	68	9	3	2	30	0	2	3	29	0	24	13	1	3	.297	.411	.430
Medero-Stullz, Carlos, Gulf Coast Dodgers	31	111	99	11	31	42	5	0	2	18	1	2	1	8	0	10	0	0	3	.313	.364	.424
Mejia, Ernesto, Gulf Coast Braves	44	166	157	21	35	60	4	0	7	22	0	1	5	3	0	42	0	1	3	.223	.259	.382
Mesa, Juan, Gulf Coast Pirates	12	34	32	3	5	9	1	0	1	2	0	0	0	2	0	13	0	0	1	.156	.206	.281
Mesa, Maikol, Gulf Coast Reds	20	72	68	9	17	21	2	1	0	6	2	0	1	1	0	12	1	3	2	.250	.271	.309
Messner, Nathan, Gulf Coast Marlins......	5	23	20	6	6	7	1	0	0	5	0	0	1	2	0	5	0	0	0	.300	.391	.350
Miaso, Curt, Gulf Coast Phillies	42	159	140	28	34	52	6	0	4	24	0	1	0	18	0	34	13	2	1	.243	.327	.371
Mientkiewicz, Doug, Gulf Coast Mets * ..	4	14	10	2	5	9	1	0	1	5	0	0	0	4	0	1	0	0	0	.500	.643	.900
Miller, Cole, Gulf Coast Tigers	24	57	55	3	10	13	3	0	0	2	0	1	0	1	0	22	1	0	0	.182	.193	.236
Mitchell, Derrick, Gulf Coast Phillies	21	85	75	14	16	23	4	0	1	9	1	2	2	5	0	27	1	1	2	.213	.274	.307
Monk, Brandon, Gulf Coast Braves	46	171	156	19	42	61	10	0	3	18	1	1	4	9	0	16	0	1	5	.269	.324	.391
Montero, Juan, Gulf Coast Mets	20	81	73	9	19	26	5	1	0	12	4	1	1	2	0	27	2	1	3	.260	.286	.356
Mora, Jesus, Gulf Coast Dodgers	31	119	106	20	28	41	4	3	1	10	1	2	5	5	0	14	0	2	3	.264	.322	.387
Morales, Douglas, Gulf Coast Phillies * ..	37	131	113	21	34	45	6	1	1	10	0	0	4	14	0	21	12	4	3	.301	.397	.398
Moreno, Junior, Gulf Coast Red Sox	4	13	12	2	1	4	0	0	1	1	0	0	1	0	0	2	0	0	1	.083	.154	.333
Mortimer, Steve, Gulf Coast Nationals *..	5	16	14	0	3	4	1	0	0	0	0	0	0	2	0	7	0	0	1	.214	.313	.286
Mosby, Robert, Gulf Coast Reds	3	12	11	2	2	2	0	0	0	1	0	0	0	1	0	3	0	0	0	.182	.250	.182
Mota, Juan, Gulf Coast Braves	18	33	28	2	6	9	1	1	0	2	0	0	1	4	0	9	1	0	2	.214	.333	.321
Munoz, David, Gulf Coast Pirates †	23	75	65	10	15	22	4	0	1	5	1	0	0	9	0	13	0	2	1	.231	.324	.338
Naughton, Joel, Gulf Coast Phillies *......	29	97	91	12	25	31	3	0	1	11	0	0	0	5	0	7	1	1	1	.275	.313	.341
Nunez, Jose Miguel2, Gulf Coast Dodgers	36	119	99	13	22	30	5	0	1	16	0	3	0	17	0	15	1	0	2	.222	.328	.303
Nunez, Luis, Gulf Coast Yankees	42	139	126	16	29	36	3	2	0	23	4	3	0	6	0	15	2	3	2	.230	.259	.286
Nunez, Runi, Gulf Coast Reds	3	4	4	1	0	0	0	0	0	0	0	0	0	0	0	0	0	0	0	.000	.000	.000
Oakes, Gerard, Gulf Coast Braves *........	1	0	0	0	0	0	0	0	0	0	...	0	0	0	...	0	0	0	0	...	...	...
Ochoa, Blake, Gulf Coast Marlins	37	133	115	10	32	47	9	0	2	17	0	0	6	12	0	20	0	1	5	.278	.376	.409
Ogando, Cristian, Gulf Coast Nationals ..	38	154	136	18	40	45	3	1	0	13	4	0	2	12	0	24	2	0	5	.294	.360	.331
Osteen, Cooper, Gulf Coast Phillies †......	35	128	105	17	38	52	7	2	1	15	6	0	2	14	0	9	11	5	0	.362	.446	.495
Ott, Louis, Gulf Coast Tigers †................	32	122	108	16	25	31	2	2	0	8	0	0	3	11	0	27	6	1	6	.231	.320	.287
Padgett, Nathan, Gulf Coast Marlins	35	124	110	13	25	36	6	1	1	11	4	1	2	7	0	20	2	1	0	.227	.283	.327
Pahuta, Timothy, Gulf Coast Nationals *	38	155	133	13	31	50	8	1	3	20	1	2	2	17	2	35	0	1	5	.233	.325	.376
Palacios, Rodolfo, Gulf Coast Twins........	2	4	3	0	0	0	0	0	0	0	0	0	0	1	0	0	0	0	0	.000	.250	.000
Parliament, Adam, Gulf Coast Braves	46	170	157	15	37	55	6	0	4	16	0	1	2	10	0	44	0	1	2	.236	.288	.350
Paterson, Thomas, Gulf Coast Phillies *..	34	123	112	10	24	30	2	2	0	11	1	2	0	8	0	18	12	2	2	.214	.262	.268
Paul, Matthew, Gulf Coast Dodgers........	24	70	65	5	16	19	3	0	0	8	3	0	1	1	0	9	0	1	1	.246	.269	.292
Peabody, John, Gulf Coast Pirates.........	25	97	84	9	19	30	4	2	1	7	0	0	1	12	0	24	1	1	2	.226	.330	.357
Peacock, Brian, Gulf Coast Nationals......	42	179	160	18	35	47	6	3	0	12	0	1	1	17	0	49	1	0	4	.219	.296	.294
Pena, Hannsel, Gulf Coast Reds	24	65	55	7	6	7	1	0	0	2	0	1	4	5	0	30	1	1	0	.109	.231	.127
Peralta, Alexander, Gulf Coast Pirates	29	119	110	16	37	51	8	0	2	18	1	1	1	6	0	14	0	2	4	.336	.373	.464
Perez, Eduardo, Gulf Coast Dodgers †....	48	197	179	35	63	99	16	1	6	37	2	0	4	12	0	26	4	0	6	.352	.405	.553
Perez, Joel, Gulf Coast Yankees	42	147	124	17	30	53	4	2	5	25	0	2	4	17	0	40	3	2	2	.242	.347	.427
Perez, Melvin, Gulf Coast Nationals †	27	77	67	3	13	16	3	0	0	5	0	0	0	10	0	24	0	0	3	.194	.299	.239
Perez, Smelin, Gulf Coast Pirates †........	34	147	132	22	37	50	7	0	2	13	1	2	0	12	0	19	8	3	1	.280	.336	.379
Phillips, Nathan, Gulf Coast Yankees † ..	33	126	114	16	30	38	5	0	1	11	0	1	1	10	0	38	2	2	3	.263	.325	.333
Picart, Gregory, Gulf Coast Pirates †	26	115	103	17	31	48	10	2	1	8	2	0	1	9	0	14	6	2	2	.301	.363	.466
Pino, Wilmer, Gulf Coast Yankees	35	124	103	20	23	31	3	1	1	7	0	0	10	11	0	21	12	3	4	.223	.355	.301
Prady, Ricky, Gulf Coast Twins *	10	39	34	4	7	14	2	1	1	5	0	0	4	1	0	11	1	1	0	.206	.308	.412
Prasch, Edward, Gulf Coast Pirates *......	15	62	53	9	16	18	2	0	0	6	0	0	0	9	0	12	0	0	0	.302	.403	.340
Quintana, Estevan, Gulf Coast Reds	20	73	61	6	13	17	2	1	0	7	0	1	2	9	0	18	1	0	4	.213	.329	.279
Rafael, Manuel, Gulf Coast Red Sox †....	35	144	129	13	28	34	6	0	0	12	0	1	1	13	0	21	2	2	5	.217	.292	.264
Ramos, Luis, Gulf Coast Marlins *..........	23	66	60	9	16	21	3	1	0	6	1	0	0	5	0	18	0	3	1	.267	.323	.350
Reyes, Angel, Gulf Coast Tigers.............	44	166	151	23	34	69	8	0	9	25	0	0	1	14	0	48	2	0	5	.225	.295	.457
Rios, Daniel, Gulf Coast Pirates *	32	120	104	11	19	23	4	0	0	15	0	1	3	12	0	19	0	0	1	.183	.283	.221

Player, Team	G	TPA	AB	R	H	TB	2B	3B	HR	RBI	SH	SF	HP	BB	IBB	SO	SB	CS	GDP	Avg.	OBP	Slg.
Rivadeneira, Deivis, Gulf Coast Braves †	33	92	83	6	16	21	3	1	0	7	1	2	2	4	0	13	1	4	0	.193	.242	.253
Roa, Lonny, Gulf Coast Reds	15	44	38	3	8	10	2	0	0	4	0	1	0	5	0	16	0	1	1	.211	.295	.263
Roberson, Colin, Gulf Coast Marlins	48	191	180	15	40	56	8	1	2	16	0	1	0	10	0	56	5	3	3	.222	.262	.311
Robinson, Trayvon, Gulf Coast Dodgers	40	126	115	19	34	54	7	2	3	15	0	0	3	8	0	25	6	4	2	.296	.357	.470
Rodriguez, Jesus, Gulf Coast Marlins	45	176	168	16	48	64	10	0	2	17	0	0	3	5	0	17	2	2	5	.286	.318	.381
Rodriguez, Mark, Gulf Coast Reds	5	18	13	1	1	1	0	0	0	1	1	0	0	4	0	6	2	0	0	.077	.294	.077
Rodriguez, Wilkin, Gulf Coast Tigers *	44	184	164	23	51	64	7	0	2	17	4	0	2	14	0	25	14	5	1	.311	.372	.390
Rogers, Jose, Gulf Coast Reds	19	68	60	8	12	12	0	0	0	3	2	0	1	5	0	15	2	1	0	.200	.273	.200
Rojo, Billy Garrison, Gulf Coast Reds	24	84	73	11	20	32	6	0	2	11	3	0	3	5	0	14	1	3	0	.274	.346	.438
Roman, Willman, Gulf Coast Pirates	31	124	110	12	30	46	7	0	3	23	0	5	4	5	0	15	1	0	4	.273	.315	.418
Rumbos, Javier, Gulf Coast Reds	20	60	50	3	14	18	4	0	0	7	0	0	1	9	1	6	0	0	3	.280	.400	.360
Sanchez, Henry, Gulf Coast Twins	21	80	70	8	16	24	2	0	2	11	0	2	1	7	0	28	0	0	2	.229	.300	.343
Sanchez, Ricardo, Gulf Coast Red Sox	18	57	47	4	10	17	5	1	0	5	0	0	2	8	0	17	0	2	0	.213	.351	.362
Sandoval, Daniel, Gulf Coast Tigers	30	111	105	14	33	49	4	0	4	14	0	0	1	5	0	16	0	0	2	.314	.351	.467
Santa, Moises, Gulf Coast Red Sox	30	115	110	15	34	44	4	0	2	9	0	0	1	4	0	16	5	2	3	.309	.339	.400
Santana, Carlos, Gulf Coast Dodgers †	32	97	78	14	23	32	4	1	1	14	0	2	1	16	1	8	0	2	2	.295	.412	.410
Santana, Richard, Gulf Coast Red Sox	40	163	145	23	37	51	9	1	1	15	3	0	4	11	0	28	7	5	2	.255	.325	.352
Santiesteban, Danny, Gulf Coast Twins	21	85	75	16	23	48	5	1	6	24	0	2	1	7	0	19	1	0	1	.307	.365	.640
Sapp, Steven, Gulf Coast Dodgers	21	71	64	12	20	23	3	0	0	8	1	1	2	3	0	16	0	2	1	.313	.357	.359
Schafer, Jordan, Gulf Coast Braves *	49	200	182	18	37	64	12	3	3	19	1	3	1	13	0	49	13	6	4	.203	.256	.352
Schemmel, Jonathan, Gulf Coast Mets	34	141	101	22	35	44	5	2	0	20	4	2	4	30	0	16	2	0	2	.347	.504	.436
Segovia, Luis, Gulf Coast Red Sox †	45	187	161	20	43	55	5	2	1	15	3	2	2	19	0	35	12	2	5	.267	.348	.342
Shaw, Buck, Gulf Coast Phillies *	29	113	102	9	22	36	4	2	2	16	0	4	0	7	1	15	0	2	3	.216	.257	.353
Silverio, Rigoberto, Gulf Coast Marlins †	34	156	139	24	42	54	5	2	1	9	1	0	1	15	0	21	5	5	4	.302	.374	.388
Simmons, Lyndsey, Gulf Coast Nationals *	3	11	10	0	1	1	0	0	0	1	0	0	0	1	0	2	0	0	0	.100	.182	.100
Skelton, James, Gulf Coast Tigers *	17	47	33	6	6	7	1	0	0	1	1	0	0	13	0	9	0	0	0	.182	.413	.212
Smolarski, Freddy, Gulf Coast Marlins	28	100	93	10	26	34	5	0	1	11	0	2	2	3	0	14	1	1	1	.280	.310	.366
Sojo, Richard, Gulf Coast Twins	43	165	148	36	47	68	11	5	0	15	0	0	4	13	0	32	11	7	2	.318	.388	.459
Soto, Auddy, Gulf Coast Nationals	8	26	24	1	4	5	1	0	0	0	0	0	0	2	0	14	0	0	0	.167	.231	.208
Spath, Matthew, Gulf Coast Mets	29	101	86	18	20	36	2	7	0	11	1	0	1	13	0	28	3	2	1	.233	.340	.419
Suarez, Gabriel, Gulf Coast Nationals	1	3	3	0	0	0	0	0	0	0	0	0	0	0	0	0	0	0	0	.000	.000	.000
Tabata, Jose, Gulf Coast Yankees	44	173	156	30	49	65	5	1	3	25	0	0	2	15	1	14	22	6	3	.314	.382	.417
Tejada, Abraham, Gulf Coast Marlins	25	78	70	7	7	9	2	0	0	4	2	0	1	5	0	30	2	1	1	.100	.171	.129
Thole, Joshua, Gulf Coast Mets	35	130	104	14	28	35	2	1	1	12	2	0	4	20	0	11	1	1	2	.269	.406	.337
Thompson, Andrew, Gulf Coast Twins *	35	136	109	22	28	40	4	1	2	20	1	2	2	22	0	22	6	4	1	.257	.385	.367
Valdez, Odannys, Gulf Coast Twins †	39	146	114	22	25	30	2	0	1	14	7	3	1	21	0	19	15	2	2	.219	.338	.263
Van Slyke, Scott, Gulf Coast Dodgers	24	95	85	15	24	36	4	1	2	15	1	2	3	4	0	19	4	3	4	.282	.330	.424
Ventura, Leivi, Gulf Coast Mets	46	194	175	34	46	75	6	1	7	33	1	1	7	10	0	35	4	2	9	.263	.326	.429
Verley, Brandon, Gulf Coast Marlins *	8	25	20	2	4	6	0	1	0	2	0	1	1	3	1	6	0	0	0	.200	.320	.300
Walk, John, Gulf Coast Pirates	6	21	18	2	4	4	0	0	0	3	0	1	1	1	0	3	1	0	3	.222	.286	.222
Wallace, James, Gulf Coast Mets	1	3	3	0	1	1	0	0	0	0	0	0	0	0	0	1	0	0	0	.333	.333	.333
Webb, Justin, Gulf Coast Marlins	24	94	72	11	21	26	5	0	0	5	0	2	6	14	0	14	0	1	2	.292	.436	.361
Wells, Casper, Gulf Coast Tigers	45	167	141	25	31	65	9	5	5	20	0	0	8	18	0	59	6	0	3	.220	.341	.461
Westfield, Antonio, Gulf Coast Pirates	12	40	38	1	11	12	1	0	0	3	1	0	0	1	0	6	0	0	0	.289	.308	.316
Williams, Jermaine, Gulf Coast Phillies	30	100	96	14	24	31	4	0	1	8	0	0	1	3	0	29	2	2	3	.250	.280	.323
Wilson, John, Gulf Coast Twins	26	100	83	18	19	25	3	0	1	13	1	2	0	14	0	22	3	3	0	.229	.333	.301
Woodard, Johnny, Gulf Coast Twins *	6	19	17	3	4	6	0	1	0	2	0	0	0	2	0	3	0	0	0	.235	.316	.353
Yersich, Gregory, Gulf Coast Twins	31	102	84	13	20	27	4	0	1	11	2	2	4	10	0	15	1	2	1	.238	.340	.321

GRAND SLAMS—D. Berg, S. De Leon, J. Hurst, B. Maldonado, J. Perez, C. Roberson, L. Ventura, C. Wells, 1 each.

AWARDED FIRST BASE ON CATCHER'S INTERFERENCE—A. Cambero (J. Gil); D. Cummins (A. German); A. Fermin (J. Mota); M. Garrett (J. Egan); E. Gutierrez (A. Soto); F. Guzman (F. Smolarski); K. Jansen (A. Soto); C. Malec (S. Garcia); J. Naughton (D. Sandoval); C. Osteen (D. Sandoval); B. Parker (A. German).

2005 PITCHING

TEAM

Team	W	L	Pct.	ERA	G	CG	ShO	Sv.	IP	H	TBF	R	ER	HR	SH	SF	HB	BB	IBB	SO	WP	Bk.
Red Sox	30	24	.556	3.03	54	0	5	19	478.2	373	1970	213	161	25	22	13	27	155	0	433	37	8
Yankees	33	20	.623	3.14	53	0	2	13	447	392	1858	201	156	29	11	10	19	140	2	428	37	6
Marlins	24	30	.444	3.40	54	0	2	15	463	463	2008	232	175	22	22	17	35	166	3	427	55	6
Phillies	24	27	.471	3.76	51	0	1	9	438.1	449	1855	219	183	27	9	10	30	100	1	343	39	8
Mets	37	16	.698	4.03	53	0	4	12	462.1	460	1997	248	207	26	16	9	35	153	2	395	44	2
Twins	28	26	.519	4.03	54	1	3	18	460.1	480	2057	257	206	19	16	16	57	190	3	367	52	1
Pirates	28	26	.519	4.04	54	2	3	9	468.1	457	2041	277	210	35	18	21	28	176	0	386	47	3
Braves	24	26	.462	4.05	52	0	4	13	446.2	427	1924	258	201	25	8	16	20	173	0	396	39	8
Reds	22	32	.407	4.18	54	0	2	13	457	453	2044	289	212	16	18	22	33	209	1	397	52	8
Tigers	24	30	.444	4.52	54	0	1	17	464	442	2069	292	233	33	5	28	56	205	2	340	75	3
Dodgers	25	29	.463	4.55	54	0	5	12	464.1	491	2100	273	235	31	22	14	41	208	4	411	63	4
Nationals	21	32	.396	4.61	53	1	2	8	462.1	521	2120	288	237	24	28	15	53	202	0	391	49	5

INDIVIDUAL

TOP QUALIFIERS FOR EARNED-RUN AVERAGE TITLE

Minimum 48 innings. *Lefthanded pitcher.

Pitcher, Team	W	L	Pct.	ERA	G	GS	CG	ShO	GF	Sv.	IP	H	TBF	R	ER	HR	SH	SF	HB	BB	IBB	SO	WP	Bk.
Herman, Jason, Gulf Coast Pirates	3	3	.500	1.93	11	9	0	0	2	1	51.1	43	199	13	11	3	1	0	0	7	0	37	3	0
Manuel, Robert, Gulf Coast Mets	8	1	.889	2.06	12	5	0	0	4	0	56.2	55	226	19	13	2	2	1	1	4	0	49	1	0
Francisco, Bartolo, Gulf Coast Nationals	2	4	.333	2.08	10	5	0	0	2	0	52.0	55	224	26	12	2	2	2	4	13	0	29	4	1
Ruckle, Jacob, Gulf Coast Mets	8	1	.889	2.10	11	8	0	0	1	0	55.2	49	227	20	13	2	1	2	3	10	0	33	2	0

Pitcher, Team	W	L	Pct.	ERA	G	GS	CG	ShO	GF	Sv.	IP	H	TBF	R	ER	HR	SH	SF	HB	BB	IBB	SO	WP	Bk.
Cox, Timothy, Gulf Coast Red Sox * ..	3	1	.750	2.19	11	5	0	0	2	1	49.1	36	192	17	12	3	2	0	0	7	0	56	1	0
German, Yulkin, Gulf Coast Red Sox *	2	1	.667	2.57	11	8	0	0	0	0	49.0	33	204	19	14	1	1	0	3	29	0	56	6	0
Perks, Matthew, Gulf Coast Nationals	4	2	.667	2.83	12	8	1	0	3	2	60.1	51	241	22	19	2	5	4	6	17	0	41	4	0
Castillo, Jose, Gulf Coast Twins	4	4	.500	3.00	11	9	0	0	0	0	48.0	50	210	27	16	0	1	2	4	19	0	27	4	0
Gil, Luis, Gulf Coast Tigers	3	3	.500	3.04	9	8	0	0	1	0	53.1	42	212	24	18	1	1	2	2	12	0	47	3	1
Suero, Nicolas, Gulf Coast Pirates	5	5	.500	3.28	11	8	0	0	1	0	57.2	72	255	37	21	4	3	4	3	10	0	35	1	0
Castro, Julio Cesar, Gulf Coast Pirates	4	3	.571	3.38	13	7	1	0	5	3	53.1	45	208	23	20	4	1	2	0	11	0	47	2	0
Garcia, Edgar, Gulf Coast Phillies	4	4	.500	3.56	10	10	0	0	0	0	55.2	63	239	26	22	4	0	3	1	13	0	42	6	0
Garcia, Ramon, Gulf Coast Tigers *....	5	3	.625	3.65	10	10	0	0	0	0	56.2	53	233	27	23	4	0	3	2	14	0	25	9	1
Burnett, Alex, Gulf Coast Twins.........	4	2	.667	4.10	13	8	0	0	2	0	48.1	50	211	25	22	6	1	3	7	14	1	33	1	0
McConnell, Brandon, Gulf Coast Twins	5	4	.556	4.14	11	11	1	0	0	0	63.0	76	277	33	29	4	1	1	9	12	0	39	3	0
Pichardo, Kelvin, Gulf Coast Phillies ..	3	2	.600	4.17	10	9	0	0	1	0	54.0	59	223	28	25	4	0	0	4	3	0	37	6	1
Engles, Terrence, Gulf Coast Nationals	2	3	.400	4.28	12	9	0	0	1	0	54.2	56	233	33	26	2	3	1	3	15	0	45	5	0
Harrison, Ryan, Gulf Coast Nationals	3	3	.500	4.66	11	4	0	0	4	1	48.1	58	212	27	25	4	7	1	2	15	0	34	0	0
Wise, Brendan, Gulf Coast Tigers	2	4	.333	4.87	10	10	0	0	0	0	57.1	60	248	39	31	6	1	2	13	9	1	35	3	0

DEPARTMENTAL LEADERS: W—Manuel and Ruckle, 8. L—Newman, 6. Pct.—Ruckle and Manuel, .889. G—Craig, 21. GS—McConnell, 11. CG—four pitchers tied with 1. ShO—Jacobsen, 1. GF—Craig, 20. Sv.—Craig, 10. IP—McConnell, 63. H—McConnell, 76. TBF—McConnell, 278. R—Ozuna and Wise, 39. ER—Dasni, 37. HR—Caraballo, 7. SAC—Harrison, 7. SF—Cramer, 5. HB—Wise, 13. BB—Beattie, 30. IBB—Bahr, 2. SO—Cox and German, 56. WP—Ozuna, 18. BK—Cueto, 4.

ALL PITCHERS

*Lefthanded pitcher.

Pitcher, Team	W	L	Pct.	ERA	G	GS	CG	ShO	GF	Sv.	IP	H	TBF	R	ER	HR	SH	SF	HB	BB	IBB	SO	WP	Bk.
Acors, Matthew, Gulf Coast Pirates....	2	0	1.000	1.98	7	0	0	0	1	0	13.2	8	57	7	3	1	0	0	1	7	0	8	2	0
Acosta, Jorge, Gulf Coast Braves *	0	1	.000	5.11	9	0	0	0	3	0	12.1	12	54	7	7	4	0	0	1	5	0	16	1	0
Adames, Geovanny, Gulf Coast Reds	0	0	.000	0.96	9	0	0	0	8	3	9.1	5	37	1	1	0	0	1	1	3	0	9	2	0
Albury, James, Gulf Coast Red Sox....	2	2	.500	4.83	10	7	0	0	0	0	31.2	29	137	21	17	4	0	1	0	13	0	22	0	0
Alvarez, Basilio, Gulf Coast Pirates	1	1	.500	8.10	2	1	0	0	0	0	6.2	8	29	6	6	0	0	0	0	1	0	5	0	0
Alvarez, Juan, Gulf Coast Phillies	1	2	.333	5.23	11	0	0	0	5	0	20.2	23	88	13	12	1	1	0	1	4	1	18	2	0
Amador, Anderson, Gulf Coast Yankees	2	0	1.000	3.00	7	1	0	0	1	0	12.0	11	49	4	4	2	0	1	1	5	0	9	1	0
Appell, Josh, Gulf Coast Mets *	3	0	1.000	4.91	11	0	0	0	8	1	18.1	7	77	10	10	1	0	1	2	14	0	24	3	0
Arias, Keily, Gulf Coast Pirates *	3	2	.600	4.23	16	1	0	0	6	1	27.2	28	118	15	13	3	2	1	5	8	0	22	1	1
Averill, Erik, Gulf Coast Tigers *	1	2	.333	1.59	6	3	0	0	0	0	22.2	12	88	6	4	0	1	1	3	7	0	18	1	0
Avery, James, Gulf Coast Reds..........	0	1	.000	2.12	6	5	0	0	0	0	17.0	16	70	7	4	0	1	0	0	3	0	18	3	0
Bahr, Jesse, Gulf Coast Yankees *	1	1	.500	4.32	14	0	0	0	12	5	16.2	17	69	9	8	0	2	0	0	5	2	13	1	0
Barb, Andrew, Gulf Coast Phillies	0	2	.000	3.27	2	2	0	0	0	0	11.0	11	44	6	4	0	0	0	0	0	0	16	2	0
Battista, Michael, Gulf Coast Mets	1	0	1.000	6.16	10	0	0	0	2	0	19.0	26	86	15	13	3	0	0	1	3	0	15	3	0
Beattie, Eric, Gulf Coast Tigers	0	1	.000	20.25	10	1	0	0	2	0	10.2	10	75	25	24	0	0	3	6	30	0	6	15	0
Berger, Garrett, Gulf Coast Tigers	0	0	.000	11.32	7	0	0	0	0	0	10.1	9	73	18	13	0	0	0	6	27	0	11	12	0
Blasdell, Jared, Gulf Coast Phillies	0	0	.000	6.00	2	0	0	0	0	0	3.0	2	11	2	2	2	0	0	0	1	0	4	0	0
Blue, William, Gulf Coast Red Sox......	0	0	.000	21.00	4	1	0	0	0	0	3.0	3	21	8	7	1	1	0	0	9	0	2	5	0
Boehringer, Brian, Gulf Coast Yankees	0	0	.000	0.00	1	1	0	0	0	0	1.0	0	3	0	0	0	0	0	0	0	0	1	0	0
Borrell, Daniel, Gulf Coast Yankees *	0	0	.000	1.50	3	3	0	0	0	0	12.0	12	50	3	2	0	0	1	2	2	0	12	0	0
Bowden, Michael, Gulf Coast Red Sox	1	0	1.000	0.00	4	2	0	0	0	0	6.0	4	25	0	0	0	1	0	0	4	0	10	0	0
Bowie, Micah, Gulf Coast Nationals *	1	0	1.000	1.08	7	2	0	0	1	0	8.1	9	34	1	1	0	1	0	2	1	0	12	1	0
Brito, Jose, Gulf Coast Reds *...........	1	0	1.000	10.13	11	0	0	0	3	0	13.1	15	67	16	15	1	0	0	0	12	0	15	3	0
Broadway, Michael, Gulf Coast Braves	1	2	.333	5.40	7	3	0	0	0	0	21.2	30	99	18	13	3	0	1	1	8	0	12	3	0
Brown, Jared, Gulf Coast Pirates *	1	0	1.000	6.75	7	0	0	0	1	0	12.0	15	57	9	9	1	0	0	0	8	0	12	3	0
Bryant, Patrick, Gulf Coast Twins	1	3	.250	6.44	13	6	0	0	2	1	36.1	38	175	31	26	1	1	4	10	22	0	25	9	0
Burgos, Jose, Gulf Coast Twins	0	0	.000	6.64	15	0	0	0	9	2	20.1	29	96	17	15	0	1	1	1	7	0	5	5	1
Burnett, Alex, Gulf Coast Twins..........	4	2	.667	4.10	13	8	0	0	2	0	48.1	50	211	25	22	6	1	3	7	14	1	33	1	0
Byrd, Darren, Gulf Coast Phillies........	3	1	.750	2.66	9	8	0	0	0	0	44.0	36	176	14	13	1	0	0	2	10	0	24	1	0
Cabrera, Domingo, Gulf Coast Yankees *	4	1	.800	2.30	11	2	0	0	1	1	31.1	23	128	12	8	2	1	0	0	9	0	37	0	2
Cabrera, Henry, Gulf Coast Red Sox ..	2	2	.500	3.67	7	2	0	0	0	0	27.0	18	107	13	11	5	0	0	1	8	0	27	0	0
Candelario, Eddie, Gulf Coast Pirates	0	0	.000	3.00	1	1	0	0	0	0	3.0	6	13	1	1	0	0	0	0	1	0	1	0	0
Caraballo, Jesse, Gulf Coast Tigers....	1	3	.250	5.23	12	5	0	0	1	0	43.0	49	187	26	25	7	0	1	3	13	0	26	11	0
Carlyle, Buddy, Gulf Coast Dodgers ..	0	0	.000	3.00	1	1	0	0	0	0	3.0	3	11	1	1	0	0	0	0	0	0	1	0	0
Carrasco, Carlos, Gulf Coast Phillies..	0	0	.000	1.80	2	2	0	0	0	0	5.0	3	20	1	1	0	0	0	2	1	0	2	0	1
Carter, Andrew, Gulf Coast Yankees ..	2	1	.667	3.92	11	1	0	0	4	0	20.2	19	88	12	9	1	0	0	1	5	0	19	0	0
Castillo, Arismendy, Gulf Coast Dodgers	3	2	.600	4.19	12	4	0	0	2	0	38.2	37	178	26	18	0	2	2	4	24	0	41	9	1
Castillo, Francisco, Gulf Coast Yankees	3	1	.750	1.76	12	5	0	0	1	0	41.0	25	165	13	8	1	1	1	3	14	0	34	5	0
Castillo, Jose, Gulf Coast Twins	4	4	.500	3.00	11	9	0	0	0	0	48.0	50	210	27	16	0	1	2	4	19	0	27	4	0
Castor, Parrish, Gulf Coast Marlins *..	4	2	.667	2.93	15	2	0	0	2	0	40.0	36	167	14	13	4	3	1	1	15	0	40	4	1
Castro, Julio Cesar, Gulf Coast Pirates	4	3	.571	3.38	13	7	1	0	5	3	53.1	45	208	23	20	4	1	2	0	11	0	47	2	0
Castro, Yeliar, Gulf Coast Braves........	0	2	.000	9.82	5	2	0	0	0	0	11.0	13	54	12	12	3	0	0	1	12	0	6	2	0
Cerezo, Hector, Gulf Coast Nationals *	0	1	.000	2.08	4	1	0	0	1	1	8.2	8	33	2	2	1	1	0	0	2	0	8	0	0
Clapp, Bradley, Gulf Coast Pirates	1	2	.333	4.28	9	9	0	0	0	0	33.2	25	149	20	16	0	1	3	1	25	0	35	7	0
Cofield, Kyle, Gulf Coast Braves	0	0	.000	7.31	10	0	0	0	4	2	16.0	16	70	15	13	0	0	1	0	6	0	15	2	0
Colina, Ederson, Gulf Coast Pirates *	2	1	.667	8.25	9	0	0	0	3	0	12.0	13	64	17	11	1	1	2	1	13	0	13	3	0
Concepcion, Alexander, Gulf Coast Phillies	0	0	.000	4.91	7	0	0	0	2	0	11.0	9	50	7	6	0	0	1	2	7	0	20	1	2
Cook, Steven, Gulf Coast Nationals....	0	2	.000	3.00	3	3	0	0	0	0	6.0	5	23	3	2	0	1	0	0	0	0	5	0	0
Cordero, Jose, Gulf Coast Twins........	0	2	.000	2.25	12	0	0	0	4	1	24.0	24	101	9	6	0	2	0	2	10	1	20	4	0
Covington, Marcus, Gulf Coast Braves	1	1	.500	8.18	10	0	0	0	3	1	11.0	14	56	10	10	0	0	0	0	9	0	12	2	1
Cox, Timothy, Gulf Coast Red Sox * ..	3	1	.750	2.19	11	5	0	0	2	1	49.1	36	192	17	12	3	2	0	0	7	0	56	1	0
Craig, Aaron, Gulf Coast Twins	1	3	.250	3.97	21	0	0	0	20	10	22.2	20	102	12	10	2	1	1	5	7	1	23	2	0
Cramer, Terrence, Gulf Coast Pirates	1	0	1.000	2.96	18	0	0	0	12	1	24.1	23	102	11	8	0	3	5	0	10	0	21	1	1
Crawford, Nathan, Gulf Coast Twins ..	0	0	.000	5.09	14	0	0	0	4	1	23.0	25	110	15	13	0	0	1	4	15	0	16	5	0
Cruz, Reymond, Gulf Coast Phillies.....	3	4	.429	4.00	9	8	0	0	1	0	45.0	49	188	26	20	3	1	3	3	7	0	43	7	1
Cruz, Rhiner, Gulf Coast Tigers	1	0	1.000	4.50	14	0	0	0	8	1	28.0	35	135	15	14	5	0	1	5	12	0	23	4	0
Cueto, Johnny, Gulf Coast Reds	2	2	.500	5.02	13	6	0	0	4	1	43.0	49	189	31	24	2	2	4	5	8	0	38	1	4

Pitcher, Team	W	L	Pct.	ERA	G	GS	CG	ShO	GF	Sv.	IP	H	TBF	R	ER	HR	SH	SF	HB	BB	IBB	SO	WP	Bk.
Dasni, Chales, Gulf Coast Dodgers	1	5	.167	7.35	12	6	0	0	1	0	45.1	52	216	38	37	5	1	0	9	23	0	41	7	0
De La Cruz, Jose, Gulf Coast Marlins	1	0	1.000	1.56	17	0	0	0	13	6	17.1	14	74	4	3	0	0	0	1	9	0	24	4	0
De Los Santos, Armado, Gulf Coast Nationals	0	0	.000	13.50	1	0	0	0	0	0	0.2	2	7	3	1	0	0	0	1	1	0	1	1	0
Diaz, Jose, Gulf Coast Dodgers	0	0	.000	4.50	2	1	0	0	0	0	2.0	1	7	1	1	1	0	0	0	0	0	2	0	0
Diaz, Wilfredo, Gulf Coast Dodgers *	1	2	.333	3.67	13	1	0	0	1	0	27.0	27	122	15	11	2	2	1	2	11	0	22	2	0
Dillard, Johnny, Gulf Coast Reds	1	1	.500	4.32	13	0	0	0	10	4	16.2	21	81	12	8	0	0	4	1	9	0	15	3	1
Dominguez, Kelvin, Gulf Coast Dodgers *	0	0	.000	0.00	2	0	0	0	1	0	1.2	1	8	0	0	0	0	0	0	1	0	2	0	0
Duff, Grant, Gulf Coast Yankees	0	1	.000	6.48	4	2	0	0	0	0	8.1	7	40	12	6	1	0	0	0	8	0	9	2	0
Durkin, Matthew, Gulf Coast Mets	0	0	.000	0.00	1	1	0	0	0	0	3.0	2	10	0	0	0	0	0	0	0	0	4	0	0
Eager, Blake, Gulf Coast Mets	0	0	.000	5.79	2	2	0	0	0	0	4.2	6	20	3	3	0	1	0	0	0	0	4	0	0
Edlich, Kyle, Gulf Coast Twins *	4	2	.667	1.70	10	9	0	0	0	0	47.2	42	193	13	9	1	1	0	5	15	0	53	5	0
Engles, Terrence, Gulf Coast Nationals	2	3	.400	4.28	12	9	0	0	1	0	54.2	56	233	33	26	2	3	1	3	15	0	45	5	0
Enriquez, Andre, Gulf Coast Nationals	0	0	.000	0.87	7	0	0	0	4	1	10.1	11	43	2	1	0	0	0	1	2	0	10	2	0
Evangelista, Antonio, Gulf Coast Nationals	0	0	.000	2.57	4	0	0	0	1	0	7.0	8	36	4	2	0	0	0	1	6	0	8	0	0
Everitt, Keaton, Gulf Coast Yankees	3	0	1.000	3.19	8	3	0	0	1	0	31.0	30	123	15	11	2	0	0	0	7	0	28	5	0
Everts, Clinton, Gulf Coast Nationals	0	1	.000	3.38	7	7	0	0	0	0	16.0	18	77	9	6	0	0	0	2	8	0	15	1	0
Fernandes, Kyle, Gulf Coast Red Sox *	2	3	.400	3.59	11	7	0	0	0	0	42.2	35	171	19	17	1	1	1	4	10	0	47	3	2
Figueroa, Jorge, Gulf Coast Mets	0	1	.000	4.13	15	0	0	0	8	3	24.0	26	104	12	11	0	0	2	0	11	0	24	6	1
Flores, Adalberto, Gulf Coast Marlins	2	2	.500	2.59	13	1	0	0	1	0	31.1	33	135	17	9	1	0	0	2	6	0	21	1	1
Flores, Juan, Gulf Coast Dodgers *	1	1	.500	5.24	15	0	0	0	7	0	22.1	26	109	15	13	2	0	2	4	16	0	19	7	0
Francisco, Bartolo, Gulf Coast Nationals	2	4	.333	2.08	10	5	0	0	2	0	52.0	55	224	26	12	2	2	2	4	13	0	29	4	1
French, Lucas, Gulf Coast Tigers *	1	0	1.000	7.59	2	2	0	0	0	0	10.2	16	47	10	9	3	0	0	0	0	0	9	1	0
Frias, Juan, Gulf Coast Reds *	0	0	.000	3.75	3	2	0	0	1	0	12.0	13	50	6	5	1	1	1	2	3	0	8	2	0
Frias, Junior, Gulf Coast Red Sox	0	0	.000	0.00	1	1	0	0	0	0	1.0	0	3	0	0	0	0	0	0	0	0	2	0	0
Galbizo, Rafael, Gulf Coast Marlins	3	0	1.000	2.45	12	0	0	0	7	3	25.2	27	103	7	7	0	1	0	1	8	1	23	1	1
Garces, Rich, Gulf Coast Red Sox	0	0	.000	3.00	3	3	0	0	0	0	3.0	1	10	1	1	1	0	0	0	0	0	4	0	0
Garcia, Christian, Gulf Coast Yankees	0	0	.000	4.50	2	1	0	0	0	0	6.0	4	25	4	3	0	0	0	0	5	0	7	0	0
Garcia, Edgar, Gulf Coast Phillies	4	4	.500	3.56	10	10	0	0	0	0	55.2	63	239	26	22	4	0	3	1	13	0	42	6	0
Garcia, Jose, Gulf Coast Marlins	0	0	.000	0.00	1	1	0	0	0	0	2.0	1	7	0	0	0	1	0	0	1	0	3	0	0
Garcia, Ramon, Gulf Coast Tigers *	5	3	.625	3.65	10	10	0	0	0	0	56.2	53	233	27	23	4	0	3	2	14	0	25	9	1
Garmon, Ryan, Gulf Coast Reds *	0	3	.000	4.97	9	1	0	0	0	0	12.2	14	60	13	7	0	0	0	2	6	0	5	1	0
Garrison, Kale, Gulf Coast Dodgers *	0	0	.000	7.59	5	4	0	0	0	0	10.2	19	50	9	9	1	0	0	1	1	0	13	0	0
Garza, Rodolfo, Gulf Coast Nationals	0	1	.000	7.15	3	0	0	0	2	0	11.1	19	58	12	9	2	0	1	2	4	0	9	1	0
Gazo, Lenin, Gulf Coast Phillies	2	3	.400	2.81	11	2	0	0	6	2	32.0	23	128	14	10	1	0	1	2	9	0	16	3	0
Gearhart, Kalen, Gulf Coast Dodgers	1	2	.333	3.09	14	1	0	0	7	0	23.1	19	95	8	8	3	1	1	0	8	1	19	0	0
German, Yulkin, Gulf Coast Red Sox *	2	1	.667	2.57	11	8	0	0	0	0	49.0	33	204	19	14	1	1	0	3	29	0	56	6	0
Gil, Luis, Gulf Coast Tigers	3	3	.500	3.04	9	8	0	0	1	0	53.1	42	212	24	18	1	1	2	2	12	0	47	3	1
Gomez, Abel, Gulf Coast Yankees *	1	0	1.000	6.28	4	3	0	0	0	0	14.1	15	64	13	10	3	0	0	2	5	0	20	2	0
Gonzalez, Alexander, Gulf Coast Red Sox	2	2	.500	3.04	18	0	0	0	16	7	26.2	15	106	12	9	2	4	1	3	12	0	21	2	1
Gonzalez, Raul, Gulf Coast Braves	0	2	.000	3.06	6	4	0	0	0	0	17.2	16	69	8	6	2	1	1	1	3	0	14	0	0
Gooch, Tyler, Gulf Coast Phillies	0	0	.000	3.00	5	1	0	0	1	0	9.0	8	36	3	3	1	2	0	0	3	0	8	1	0
Gracesqui, Franklyn, Gulf Coast Marlins *	0	0	.000	0.00	3	1	0	0	1	1	3.0	1	12	1	0	0	0	0	0	2	0	5	0	0
Gray, Matthew, Gulf Coast Reds *	0	1	.000	11.45	10	0	0	0	2	0	11.0	9	65	17	14	0	0	1	0	21	0	4	2	0
Hakey, Patrick, Gulf Coast Mets	1	2	.333	14.63	6	0	0	0	2	0	8.0	12	53	14	13	0	2	0	5	14	1	6	4	0
Haldis, Jonathan, Gulf Coast Dodgers	0	1	.000	1.96	12	0	0	0	5	3	18.1	11	70	5	4	0	1	1	0	4	0	5	1	0
Haltiwanger, Kevin, Gulf Coast Reds	2	4	.333	1.83	13	3	0	0	3	2	39.1	28	158	10	8	2	3	0	4	17	1	30	4	0
Hampton, Mike, Gulf Coast Braves *	0	0	.000	0.00	1	1	0	0	0	0	5.0	6	20	0	0	0	0	0	0	0	0	4	0	0
Hansen, Craig, Gulf Coast Red Sox	1	0	1.000	0.00	2	1	0	0	0	0	3.0	2	11	0	0	0	0	0	0	0	0	4	0	0
Harrington, Jake, Gulf Coast Mets	1	2	.333	4.85	9	3	0	0	2	0	26.0	27	114	19	14	1	2	0	1	12	0	14	2	0
Harrison, Ryan, Gulf Coast Nationals	3	3	.500	4.66	11	4	0	0	4	1	48.1	58	212	27	25	4	7	1	2	15	0	34	0	0
Herbort, Ryan, Gulf Coast Pirates	0	1	.000	1.98	4	2	0	0	1	0	13.2	9	55	6	3	1	1	0	3	5	0	7	1	0
Herman, Jason, Gulf Coast Pirates	3	3	.500	1.93	11	9	0	0	2	1	51.1	43	199	13	11	3	1	0	0	7	0	37	3	0
Hernandez, Bladimil, Gulf Coast Pirates	0	1	.000	6.20	8	5	0	0	0	0	24.2	31	119	23	17	3	0	2	3	13	0	19	3	0
Hernandez, Danny, Gulf Coast Twins	1	1	.500	5.48	13	2	0	0	2	0	21.1	18	103	16	13	0	0	1	7	17	0	19	3	0
Hinchman, Grady, Gulf Coast Mets *	2	1	.667	1.85	14	0	0	0	11	5	24.1	18	100	6	5	1	4	1	1	12	1	38	5	0
Hirota, Rodrigo, Gulf Coast Mets	3	3	.500	5.34	8	4	0	0	1	0	32.0	35	135	19	19	2	1	0	4	6	0	21	1	1
Hobdy, Christopher, Gulf Coast Dodgers	0	1	.000	20.25	5	1	0	0	0	0	5.1	14	35	12	12	1	0	0	0	6	0	4	0	0
Holdzkom, Lincoln, Gulf Coast Marlins	0	0	.000	2.25	3	0	0	0	1	0	4.0	5	17	3	1	0	1	0	0	1	0	6	0	0
Holquin, Steven, Gulf Coast Mets	2	1	.667	6.85	11	2	0	0	4	1	22.1	28	103	23	17	2	2	0	2	6	0	11	2	0
Howington, Ty, Gulf Coast Reds *	0	0	.000	3.60	3	3	0	0	0	0	5.0	4	21	2	2	0	0	0	1	1	0	4	1	0
Huddy, Kyle, Gulf Coast Reds	3	5	.375	4.38	13	4	0	0	0	0	37.0	34	167	28	18	1	2	3	3	25	0	39	6	0
Jacobsen, Landon, Gulf Coast Pirates	3	1	.750	3.72	5	5	1	1	0	0	19.1	13	83	9	8	0	1	0	3	9	0	26	1	0
James, Jimmy, Gulf Coast Red Sox	2	1	.667	2.54	7	5	0	0	0	0	28.1	23	113	12	8	3	2	0	0	6	0	13	0	1
Japa, Rolando, Gulf Coast Yankees	2	3	.400	3.50	12	5	0	0	2	0	36.0	33	161	21	14	3	1	2	3	19	0	41	5	0
Jarrett, Jason, Gulf Coast Marlins	0	0	.000	3.12	9	0	0	0	8	2	8.2	10	43	8	3	0	0	0	2	3	0	7	3	0
Jefferson, John, Gulf Coast Red Sox	0	1	.000	9.53	4	0	0	0	1	0	5.2	8	25	6	6	0	1	1	0	2	0	2	1	0
Jimenez, Santos, Gulf Coast Reds	0	0	.000	0.00	5	0	0	0	1	0	4.2	5	22	3	0	0	0	0	0	2	0	6	0	0
Johnson, Anthony, Gulf Coast Nationals	0	0	.000	4.50	4	0	0	0	1	0	8.0	6	35	4	4	0	0	1	2	8	0	9	0	1
Johnson, Steven, Gulf Coast Dodgers	0	2	.000	9.53	6	3	0	0	0	0	11.1	18	58	12	12	1	1	0	4	4	0	14	1	1
Johnson, Tod, Gulf Coast Reds *	1	0	1.000	1.42	9	0	0	0	3	1	12.2	8	51	4	2	1	0	0	2	4	0	8	0	1
Jones, Beau, Gulf Coast Braves *	3	2	.600	3.86	8	7	0	0	0	0	35.0	25	139	15	15	0	3	1	4	16	0	41	3	2
Jones, Blake, Gulf Coast Marlins	0	0	.000	1.13	6	0	0	0	0	0	8.0	6	30	2	1	0	1	0	0	2	0	11	0	0
Jones, Christopher, Gulf Coast Red Sox	0	1	.000	0.00	1	1	0	0	0	0	1.2	3	11	4	0	0	0	1	1	0	0	1	1	0
Joseph, Jacob, Gulf Coast Mets	0	0	.000	1.80	4	2	0	0	1	0	5.0	4	19	1	1	1	0	0	0	0	0	4	0	0
Jostock, William, Gulf Coast Mets	1	0	1.000	4.87	9	0	0	0	1	0	20.1	22	87	13	11	1	0	1	3	7	0	18	2	0
Katz, Jeffrey, Gulf Coast Braves	2	0	1.000	9.64	9	0	0	0	0	0	14.0	21	79	16	15	0	0	1	2	14	0	14	1	2
Kelly, Mark, Gulf Coast Phillies	2	1	.667	3.27	13	0	0	0	6	1	22.0	22	98	10	8	0	0	0	2	6	0	28	1	1
Kroenke, Zachary, Gulf Coast Yankees *	0	1	.000	4.50	1	1	0	0	0	0	2.0	4	10	2	1	0	0	0	0	0	0	2	1	0
Lambert, Bryan, Gulf Coast Nationals	3	1	.750	1.54	10	1	0	0	8	1	23.1	21	96	5	4	1	2	0	4	5	0	16	1	0
Lanier, Thomas, Gulf Coast Reds	1	2	.333	3.33	10	3	0	0	3	0	27.0	19	113	14	10	1	0	1	1	13	0	18	6	0

Pitcher, Team	W	L	Pct.	ERA	G	GS	CG	ShO	GF	Sv.	IP	H	TBF	R	ER	HR	SH	SF	HB	BB	IBB	SO	WP	Bk.
Lawrence, Horace, Gulf Coast Mets *	0	0	.000	7.94	5	0	0	0	2	1	5.2	8	30	6	5	2	0	0	4	0	5	2	0
Lewis, Jonathan, Gulf Coast Marlins	1	0	1.000	2.25	3	0	0	0	1	0	4.0	2	15	1	1	1	0	0	0	2	0	8	1	0
Linares, Remos Eugenio, Gulf Coast Red Sox	1	1	.500	2.31	13	0	0	0	7	3	23.1	19	98	7	6	1	2	1	2	9	0	20	4	0
Lindeen, Scott, Gulf Coast Marlins	0	1	.000	3.64	15	1	0	0	6	3	29.2	34	125	14	12	1	0	0	3	8	0	25	5	0
Linder, Matthew, Gulf Coast Phillies	2	1	.667	8.16	12	0	0	0	6	1	14.1	19	64	14	13	2	2	0	0	4	0	10	0	0
Long, Nicholas, Gulf Coast Nationals	0	0	.000	4.50	2	1	0	0	0	0	2.0	2	9	1	1	1	0	0	0	1	0	1	0	0
Looney, Marshal, Gulf Coast Dodgers *	0	1	.000	5.79	3	2	0	0	0	0	4.2	8	23	6	3	1	0	0	0	4	0	4	0	0
Lorenzo, Pedro, Gulf Coast Dodgers	0	0	.000	10.12	1	0	0	0	0	0	2.2	3	15	3	3	0	0	0	2	3	0	0	0	0
Lugo, Chris, Gulf Coast Nationals	2	1	.667	2.20	5	3	0	0	1	0	28.2	25	121	8	7	0	1	0	3	11	0	24	0	0
Lyman, Jeffrey, Gulf Coast Braves	0	3	.000	4.24	8	7	0	0	0	0	34.0	41	153	27	16	2	2	3	4	7	0	28	2	0
Lyons, Thomas, Gulf Coast Tigers	1	2	.333	3.45	7	3	0	0	1	0	15.2	13	76	17	6	2	0	1	3	11	0	13	4	0
Manuel, Robert, Gulf Coast Mets	8	1	.889	2.06	12	5	0	0	4	0	56.2	55	226	19	13	2	2	1	1	4	0	49	1	0
Marte, Enmanuel, Gulf Coast Pirates *	1	0	1.000	1.86	10	0	0	0	2	0	19.1	16	78	4	4	1	0	0	0	4	0	18	4	1
Martinez, Yoffri, Gulf Coast Pirates	0	1	.000	5.23	14	0	0	0	5	0	20.2	22	95	16	12	3	1	0	0	13	0	14	1	0
Mateo, Marcos, Gulf Coast Reds	2	3	.400	4.30	13	4	0	0	6	0	44.0	54	189	26	21	2	3	1	3	10	0	23	7	0
Mavroulis, Coby, Gulf Coast Nationals *	2	3	.400	5.04	9	3	0	0	0	0	25.0	30	115	16	14	2	1	0	3	12	0	29	3	0
McConnell, Brandon, Gulf Coast Twins	5	4	.556	4.14	11	11	1	0	0	0	63.0	76	277	33	29	4	1	1	9	12	0	39	3	0
McDade, Neal, Gulf Coast Pirates	0	0	.000	0.00	1	0	0	0	1	0	1.0	0	5	2	0	0	0	0	1	0	0	1	1	0
McEnaney, Alex, Gulf Coast Phillies	0	0	.000	5.56	10	0	0	0	4	1	11.1	16	53	8	7	2	0	0	2	1	0	6	1	0
McIntyre, Robert, Gulf Coast Mets	4	2	.667	4.54	11	6	0	0	2	0	41.2	44	185	21	21	1	1	0	6	18	0	38	4	0
Medina, Josvic, Gulf Coast Mets	1	0	1.000	2.70	8	0	0	0	2	0	16.2	12	71	7	5	2	0	1	3	8	0	9	2	0
Megrew, Michael, Gulf Coast Dodgers *	0	0	.000	5.40	3	3	0	0	0	0	5.0	4	21	3	3	0	1	0	1	4	0	8	1	0
Mejias, Jose Angel, Gulf Coast Phillies	0	3	.000	3.32	15	0	0	0	11	3	19.0	22	85	12	7	1	1	0	4	5	0	12	2	1
Mendez, Deivi, Gulf Coast Yankees	0	0	.000	9.00	1	0	0	0	0	0	1.0	2	5	1	1	0	0	0	0	0	0	2	0	0
Mendez, Jesus, Gulf Coast Yankees	3	2	.600	4.50	12	0	0	0	4	0	16.0	19	69	9	8	1	0	1	4	1	0	12	2	0
Mendoza, Ramiro, Gulf Coast Yankees	0	0	.000	0.00	2	2	0	0	0	0	5.0	3	19	1	0	0	0	0	0	1	0	3	0	0
Mercedes, Manuel, Gulf Coast Nationals	1	3	.250	8.27	7	0	0	0	4	0	16.1	18	85	17	15	0	1	0	5	14	0	14	2	0
Meyers, Ryan, Gulf Coast Mets	0	0	.000	5.84	5	4	0	0	0	0	12.1	13	55	9	8	2	0	0	1	6	0	12	1	0
Miller, Greg, Gulf Coast Dodgers *	0	0	.000	2.25	4	3	0	0	0	0	12.0	7	48	5	3	0	0	0	4	0	0	14	4	0
Mitchinson, Scott, Gulf Coast Phillies	0	0	.000	0.00	1	1	0	0	0	0	3.0	1	10	0	0	0	0	0	0	0	0	4	0	0
Mlotkowski, Michael, Gulf Coast Yankees	0	0	.000	6.00	1	1	0	0	0	0	3.0	4	14	2	2	0	0	0	1	0	0	2	0	0
Molleken, Dustin, Gulf Coast Pirates	0	4	.000	7.20	9	5	0	0	1	0	30.0	34	141	29	24	5	2	2	3	16	0	22	7	0
Montan, Miguel, Gulf Coast Yankees	1	2	.333	3.52	12	0	0	0	9	3	15.1	18	64	6	6	3	1	1	0	4	0	13	1	0
Morales, Jorge, Gulf Coast Yankees	1	1	.500	2.30	11	0	0	0	6	3	15.2	11	60	4	4	1	0	1	1	5	0	17	2	0
Moya, Luis, Gulf Coast Reds	0	1	.000	1.23	3	1	0	0	0	0	7.1	10	35	6	1	0	1	0	2	0	0	5	3	0
Muniz, Carlos, Gulf Coast Mets	0	1	.000	16.20	2	0	0	0	1	0	1.2	6	11	4	3	0	0	0	0	0	0	1	0	0
Naatjes, Darin, Gulf Coast Phillies	0	0	.000	0.00	1	0	0	0	0	0	2.0	1	8	0	0	0	0	0	0	1	0	2	0	0
Napolitan, Phillip, Gulf Coast Tigers	0	0	.000	0.00	1	0	0	0	0	0	1.0	0	4	0	0	0	0	0	0	1	0	2	0	0
Nelson, Brad, Gulf Coast Braves	0	0	.000	0.00	1	0	0	0	1	1	1.0	0	4	0	0	0	0	0	0	1	0	1	0	0
Newman, Brandon, Gulf Coast Reds *	2	6	.250	4.89	13	8	0	0	1	0	46.0	62	209	38	25	1	2	1	1	13	0	26	0	0
Niese, Jonathon, Gulf Coast Mets *	1	0	1.000	3.65	7	5	0	0	0	0	24.2	23	105	10	10	1	0	1	0	10	0	24	2	0
Norrito, Giuseppe, Gulf Coast Dodgers	2	1	.667	2.48	11	1	0	0	10	3	29.0	30	122	12	8	2	0	1	0	9	0	21	2	0
Oakes, Gerard, Gulf Coast Braves	0	0	.000	0.00	3	0	0	0	1	0	5.0	6	26	4	0	0	0	0	5	0	1	0	0
Obispo, Jose, Gulf Coast Dodgers	0	0	.000	14.73	2	1	0	0	0	0	3.2	7	21	7	6	0	1	1	2	2	0	3	1	0
Olivo, Haysdersman, Gulf Coast Marlins	0	0	.000	3.77	14	0	0	0	3	0	14.1	10	69	9	6	1	0	0	2	15	0	6	4	1
Olson, Matthew, Gulf Coast Phillies	3	3	.500	3.07	9	8	0	0	0	0	41.0	43	169	15	14	2	1	0	4	12	0	27	2	0
Omana, Edgar, Gulf Coast Yankees *	1	0	1.000	1.59	9	0	0	0	4	0	11.1	8	47	2	2	0	1	0	8	0	17	1	0
Ortiz, Jose Francisco, Gulf Coast Red Sox	3	1	.750	3.82	14	0	0	0	2	1	35.1	24	145	18	15	1	3	2	17	0	39	3	2
Ozuna, Cruzito, Gulf Coast Nationals	0	3	.000	14.77	10	2	0	0	2	0	21.1	46	128	39	35	2	1	1	6	20	0	20	18	3
Pahucki, David, Gulf Coast Red Sox	0	0	.000	27.00	1	1	0	0	0	0	0.2	5	2	2	0	0	0	2	0	1	1	0
Paredes, Ramon, Gulf Coast Dodgers *	6	0	1.000	2.34	9	6	0	0	0	0	42.1	36	174	12	11	2	2	0	2	10	0	39	4	0
Paris, Gary, Gulf Coast Dodgers *	2	2	.500	5.03	14	3	0	0	1	0	34.0	36	151	21	19	0	5	2	2	20	1	40	8	0
Patton, Walter, Gulf Coast Twins	3	1	.750	7.43	17	1	0	0	2	0	23.0	25	112	20	19	0	3	2	1	24	0	20	5	0
Paulk, Robert, Gulf Coast Mets	0	0	.000	0.00	1	1	0	0	0	0	3.0	4	12	2	0	0	0	0	0	0	1	0	0
Pavano, Carl, Gulf Coast Yankees	0	0	.000	1.80	1	1	0	0	0	0	5.0	2	17	2	1	1	1	0	0	0	5	0	0
Pello, Brandon, Gulf Coast Dodgers	0	1	.000	2.31	7	0	0	0	1	0	11.2	9	44	5	3	1	0	0	0	2	0	6	2	0
Peralta, Yader, Gulf Coast Red Sox	2	3	.400	3.94	17	0	0	0	13	4	29.2	33	125	16	13	0	0	1	5	5	0	21	3	0
Perdomo, Orlando, Gulf Coast Tigers	3	2	.600	2.65	17	5	0	0	11	7	37.1	25	160	14	11	0	3	3	19	1	39	1	0
Perks, Matthew, Gulf Coast Phillies	4	2	.667	2.83	12	8	1	0	3	2	60.1	51	241	22	19	2	5	4	6	17	0	41	4	0
Phillips, Ryan, Gulf Coast Red Sox *	0	0	.000	0.00	1	0	0	0	0	0	0.2	0	2	0	0	0	0	0	0	0	0	1	0	1
Phillips, William, Gulf Coast Red Sox	0	1	.000	4.15	9	0	0	0	5	0	17.1	16	69	10	8	0	4	1	1	7	0	14	0	1
Pichardo, Eduardo, Gulf Coast Nationals	0	1	.000	22.09	8	0	0	0	4	0	7.1	17	60	18	18	2	0	2	2	19	0	7	3	0
Pichardo, Kelvin, Gulf Coast Phillies	3	2	.600	4.17	10	9	0	0	1	0	54.0	59	223	28	25	4	0	0	4	3	0	37	6	1
Pie, Esequier, Gulf Coast Marlins	1	5	.167	5.13	12	8	0	0	0	0	40.1	44	194	27	23	3	2	1	5	27	1	36	7	1
Pinango, Miguel, Gulf Coast Mets	0	0	.000	0.00	1	1	0	0	0	0	4.0	3	14	0	0	0	0	0	0	0	0	4	0	0
Plexico, Gerald, Gulf Coast Nationals *	0	0	.000	3.60	3	3	0	0	0	0	5.0	3	17	2	2	2	0	0	0	1	0	3	0	0
Plummer, Jarod, Gulf Coast Dodgers	0	0	.000	4.50	1	1	0	0	0	0	4.0	4	16	2	2	0	0	1	0	0	0	2	1	0
Powell, Jay, Gulf Coast Braves	0	0	.000	4.50	2	2	0	0	0	0	2.0	4	11	2	1	0	0	0	1	1	0	1	0	0
Powers, Joseph, Gulf Coast Reds	0	0	.000	0.00	1	1	0	0	0	0	1.2	1	7	0	0	0	0	0	0	1	0	1	1	0
Prieto, Victor, Gulf Coast Red Sox	0	1	.000	27.00	1	0	0	0	0	0	0.1	0	2	1	1	0	0	0	0	0	0	1	1	0
Quaglieri, William, Gulf Coast Mets	0	0	.000	9.00	1	0	0	0	0	0	1.0	2	4	1	1	0	0	0	0	0	0	2	1	0
Quintana, Eduardo, Gulf Coast Dodgers	1	1	.500	6.29	15	3	0	0	1	0	34.1	51	165	25	24	4	2	2	4	18	1	24	5	0
Ramirez, Emmanuel, Gulf Coast Pirates	0	1	.000	5.56	8	0	0	0	1	0	11.1	13	51	7	7	1	0	0	2	0	14	1	0
Ramirez, Miguel, Gulf Coast Dodgers	0	1	.000	1.64	15	0	0	0	12	5	22.0	20	85	4	4	0	2	0	0	4	0	22	2	0
Rasowsky, Avi, Gulf Coast Marlins *	1	2	.333	2.66	6	1	0	0	0	0	20.1	22	81	8	6	1	1	1	2	0	18	1	0
Raulinaitis, Christopher, Gulf Coast Phillies	0	1	.000	5.57	12	0	0	0	5	0	21.0	29	95	17	13	2	1	2	1	4	0	15	3	1
Rayo, Pedro, Gulf Coast Braves	1	1	.500	1.50	11	2	0	0	6	1	30.0	18	114	6	5	2	0	0	2	8	0	28	1	0

Pitcher, Team	W	L	Pct.	ERA	G	GS	CG	ShO	GF	Sv.	IP	H	TBF	R	ER	HR	SH	SF	HB	BB	IBB	SO	WP	Bk.
Reina, Dimas, Gulf Coast Dodgers	0	0	.000	0.00	1	1	0	0	0	0	2.0	0	6	0	0	0	0	0	0	0	0	2	0	0
Reyes, Joseph, Gulf Coast Braves *	0	1	.000	1.69	3	2	0	0	0	0	5.1	6	23	2	1	0	0	0	0	1	0	6	0	0
Richmond, Jamie, Gulf Coast Braves	2	0	1.000	3.09	8	0	0	0	2	0	11.2	7	42	4	4	0	0	1	0	2	0	12	0	0
Riggan, Jerrod, Gulf Coast Mets	1	0	1.000	0.00	6	3	0	0	0	0	7.0	3	27	1	0	0	0	0	0	3	0	11	1	0
Rios, Cristian, Gulf Coast Reds *	0	1	.000	9.58	8	0	0	0	4	0	10.1	14	58	13	11	1	0	2	0	11	0	8	2	0
Rios, Travis, Gulf Coast Red Sox	1	0	1.000	0.00	4	0	0	0	2	1	5.2	2	19	0	0	0	0	0	0	0	0	10	0	0
Robertson, Nash, Gulf Coast Pirates	0	0	.000	5.00	6	0	0	0	1	0	9.0	10	41	7	5	1	1	0	1	3	0	9	3	0
Rodriguez, Orlando, Gulf Coast Dodgers *	0	0	.000	0.00	1	1	0	0	0	0	1.0	1	4	0	0	0	0	0	0	0	0	2	0	0
Ruckle, Jacob, Gulf Coast Mets	8	1	.889	2.10	11	8	0	0	1	0	55.2	49	227	20	13	2	1	2	3	10	0	33	2	0
Rudrude, Brett, Gulf Coast Red Sox	0	1	.000	2.70	4	4	0	0	0	0	6.2	4	26	3	2	0	0	0	0	2	0	8	0	0
Rueger, Bryan, Gulf Coast Yankees *	1	0	1.000	0.00	4	0	0	0	0	0	6.0	3	22	0	0	0	0	0	0	0	0	6	0	0
Rusch, Matthew, Gulf Coast Tigers	1	3	.250	3.06	7	6	0	0	1	1	35.1	35	149	18	12	2	1	3	5	2	0	16	1	0
Russell, Stephen, Gulf Coast Braves	0	0	.000	2.89	3	0	0	0	1	0	9.1	8	42	8	3	0	0	1	0	5	0	9	4	1
Ruzic, Dushan, Gulf Coast Marlins	2	2	.500	6.41	17	0	0	0	6	0	26.2	31	128	21	19	1	1	3	5	12	1	24	6	0
Salas, Joseph, Gulf Coast Pirates *	0	0	.000	0.75	9	0	0	0	8	3	12.0	10	50	4	1	0	0	0	1	3	0	13	1	0
Sanchez, Romulo, Gulf Coast Pirates	1	0	1.000	1.80	2	1	0	0	0	0	10.0	7	38	2	2	1	0	0	0	4	0	7	0	0
Sanfler, Miguel, Gulf Coast Dodgers *	5	3	.625	3.79	13	3	0	0	1	0	40.1	40	189	23	17	4	0	0	4	25	0	41	5	1
Santiago, Jose, Gulf Coast Braves	0	0	.000	6.48	6	0	0	0	0	0	8.1	6	43	8	6	1	0	1	0	10	0	9	4	0
Santos, Adriano, Gulf Coast Tigers	1	3	.250	4.13	20	0	0	0	13	5	28.1	31	129	15	13	1	0	1	2	15	0	30	1	0
Schoenbachler, Jeffrey, Gulf Coast Twins *	2	2	.500	3.97	9	8	0	0	0	0	45.1	50	200	28	20	3	1	0	1	15	0	45	5	0
Schroder, Christopher, Gulf Coast Nationals	0	0	.000	9.00	1	0	0	0	0	0	1.0	2	5	1	1	0	0	0	0	0	0	3	0	0
Segovia, Omar, Gulf Coast Reds *	0	1	.000	3.07	6	4	0	0	0	0	14.2	13	66	5	5	0	0	0	1	8	0	23	0	0
Selenes, Josue, Gulf Coast Yankees	3	2	.600	5.19	12	3	0	0	2	1	26.0	26	110	16	15	1	1	1	0	10	0	22	2	0
Shaffer, Jared, Gulf Coast Braves	3	5	.375	5.40	9	5	0	0	2	0	36.2	41	167	30	22	2	0	2	0	15	0	31	6	1
Sierra, Waldy, Gulf Coast Tigers	2	2	.500	9.27	12	1	0	0	5	0	22.1	25	117	27	23	1	1	2	3	22	0	13	8	0
Smiley, Wesley, Gulf Coast Reds	2	0	1.000	5.47	14	2	0	0	3	2	26.1	30	119	18	16	2	0	1	2	13	0	28	4	0
Smith, Christopher, Gulf Coast Red Sox	0	0	.000	0.00	1	1	0	0	0	0	3.0	0	10	0	0	0	0	0	0	0	0	4	0	0
Soto, Auddy, Gulf Coast Nationals	0	0	.000	36.00	1	0	0	0	1	0	1.0	1	9	4	4	0	0	1	0	5	0	2	0	0
Soto, Edgar, Gulf Coast Yankees *	0	2	.000	4.24	8	6	0	0	0	0	23.1	21	99	12	11	1	1	0	1	9	0	26	2	2
Sparks, Terrance, Gulf Coast Reds *	3	1	.750	4.50	12	0	0	0	2	0	18.0	12	84	13	9	1	1	2	1	17	0	13	2	2
Stanley, Adam, Gulf Coast Braves *	1	0	1.000	0.00	4	0	0	0	0	0	7.2	6	31	1	0	0	0	0	0	0	0	9	1	1
Stewart, Clayton, Gulf Coast Phillies	0	0	.000	0.00	2	0	0	0	2	0	2.0	1	8	0	0	0	0	0	0	0	0	1	0	0
Suero, Nicolas, Gulf Coast Pirates	5	5	.500	3.28	11	8	0	0	1	0	57.2	72	255	37	21	4	3	4	3	10	0	35	1	0
Tabeek, Kyle, Gulf Coast Red Sox	1	0	1.000	1.56	8	0	0	0	3	1	17.1	12	63	3	3	0	0	0	1	1	0	17	2	0
Taylor, Rhys, Gulf Coast Red Sox	2	2	.500	1.49	11	5	0	0	0	0	36.1	28	145	13	6	1	2	2	2	7	0	15	2	0
Tejada, Jonathan, Gulf Coast Braves	2	2	.500	4.37	8	6	0	0	0	0	35.0	34	147	19	17	4	0	1	0	11	0	35	3	0
Tejeda, Ferdin, Gulf Coast Yankees	2	0	1.000	1.80	7	1	0	0	1	0	15.0	12	59	3	3	1	0	1	0	3	0	15	1	1
Thompson, Aaron, Gulf Coast Marlins *	2	4	.333	4.50	8	8	0	0	0	0	32.0	42	144	20	16	1	1	1	0	10	0	41	4	0
Thompson, Michael, Gulf Coast Braves	1	0	1.000	0.64	12	1	0	0	5	1	14.0	8	54	1	1	0	0	0	1	5	0	11	0	0
Towery, Kenneth, Gulf Coast Red Sox	3	0	1.000	1.48	12	0	0	0	2	1	24.1	24	102	8	4	1	0	0	2	5	0	16	2	0
Treanor, Bryan, Gulf Coast Marlins	1	0	1.000	7.20	5	0	0	0	0	0	5.0	6	25	6	4	0	0	1	2	2	0	1	2	0
Trejo, Miguel, Gulf Coast Tigers	2	1	.667	2.08	19	0	0	0	9	3	26.0	20	105	7	6	1	0	3	0	10	0	24	1	1
Tucker, Ryan, Gulf Coast Marlins	3	3	.500	3.69	8	7	0	0	0	0	31.2	35	131	13	13	0	6	2	2	16	0	23	3	0
Urena, Jose, Gulf Coast Nationals *	1	2	.333	6.23	13	1	0	0	7	1	30.1	34	140	21	21	0	1	1	3	19	0	33	1	0
Valenzuela, Sergio, Gulf Coast Braves	1	4	.200	3.60	8	7	0	0	0	0	35.0	35	142	16	14	1	0	1	2	4	0	16	0	0
Velazquez, Juan, Gulf Coast Yankees	1	0	1.000	1.96	10	0	0	0	4	0	18.1	10	72	5	4	0	1	0	1	7	0	12	3	0
Villalona, Guillermo, Gulf Coast Yankees	0	1	.000	3.32	7	5	0	0	0	0	21.2	21	86	9	8	3	0	0	1	5	0	19	1	1
Volstad, Christopher, Gulf Coast Marlins	1	1	.500	2.33	6	6	0	0	0	0	27.0	25	110	14	7	1	1	1	2	4	0	26	1	0
Waldie, Andrew, Gulf Coast Phillies	1	0	1.000	2.19	8	0	0	0	1	1	12.1	9	53	3	3	1	0	0	0	9	0	8	1	0
Walk, John, Gulf Coast Pirates	0	0	.000	36.00	1	0	0	0	1	0	2.0	6	16	9	8	2	0	0	0	3	0	0	1	0
Wall, Joshua, Gulf Coast Dodgers	1	3	.250	3.86	5	4	0	0	0	0	14.0	13	61	8	6	2	1	0	0	8	0	5	1	1
Ward, Joshua, Gulf Coast Braves	1	0	1.000	2.25	12	0	0	0	4	0	16.0	17	67	6	4	0	0	0	0	5	0	9	1	0
Warren, Jesse, Gulf Coast Braves *	2	0	1.000	7.62	10	0	0	0	3	0	13.0	13	58	11	11	1	1	0	0	9	0	11	3	0
Watkins, Michael, Gulf Coast Nationals	0	1	.000	4.82	5	0	0	0	4	1	9.1	16	47	8	5	1	1	0	1	3	0	13	2	0
Watts, Joey, Gulf Coast Tigers *	0	1	.000	1.69	5	0	0	0	1	0	5.1	7	24	4	1	0	0	2	0	1	0	3	0	0
West, Sean, Gulf Coast Marlins *	2	3	.400	2.35	9	8	0	0	1	0	38.1	33	157	12	10	2	0	3	3	7	0	40	2	1
Williams, David, Gulf Coast Braves	0	1	.000	0.47	13	0	0	0	10	7	19.0	8	67	1	1	0	0	1	0	4	0	25	0	0
Williams, Joseph, Gulf Coast Mets *	0	0	.000	0.00	3	3	0	0	0	0	8.0	8	34	0	0	0	0	0	1	3	0	7	0	0
Williams, Matthew, Gulf Coast Twins	3	2	.600	1.93	20	0	0	0	8	3	37.1	33	151	11	8	2	3	0	1	13	0	42	1	0
Wilson, Brandon, Gulf Coast Mets	0	1	.000	5.71	4	3	0	0	1	1	17.1	17	72	13	11	2	0	0	0	2	0	17	0	0
Wilson, David, Gulf Coast Braves *	2	0	1.000	0.79	9	0	0	0	7	0	11.1	5	44	3	1	0	0	0	0	5	0	11	0	0
Winters, Kyle, Gulf Coast Marlins	0	4	.000	3.64	11	10	0	0	0	0	42.0	37	174	26	17	4	3	3	3	12	0	33	4	0
Wise, Brendan, Gulf Coast Tigers	2	4	.333	4.87	10	10	0	0	0	0	57.1	60	248	39	31	6	1	2	13	9	1	35	3	0
Wood, Travis, Gulf Coast Reds *	0	0	.000	0.75	8	7	0	0	0	0	24.0	13	91	3	2	0	2	0	1	7	0	45	0	0
Wordekemper, Eric, Gulf Coast Yankees	2	0	1.000	2.12	9	5	0	0	1	0	29.2	28	115	7	7	2	0	0	2	1	0	24	0	0
Wright, Jaret, Gulf Coast Yankees	0	1	.000	7.71	1	1	0	0	0	0	2.1	4	13	2	2	0	0	0	0	2	0	3	0	0
Wright, Matthew, Gulf Coast Braves	1	1	.500	3.12	3	3	0	0	0	0	8.2	11	39	8	3	0	1	0	0	2	0	9	0	0
Young, Terrell, Gulf Coast Reds	2	0	1.000	6.75	3	0	0	0	0	0	4.0	4	17	3	3	0	0	0	0	2	0	6	0	0
Zuleta, Howar, Gulf Coast Dodgers	1	0	1.000	0.00	2	0	0	0	0	0	4.1	3	18	0	0	0	0	0	0	3	1	1	2	0

COMBINATION SHUTOUTS: GCL Braves (4) -- Valenzuela-Cofield-Williams, Thompson-Castro-Broadway-Oakes, Tejada-Covington, Wright-Jones-Ward-Williams. GCL Dodgers (5) -- Quintana-Paredes-Dominguez-Gearhart, Paredes-Gearhart-Ramirez, Paredes-Haldis-Ramirez, Garrison-Sanfler-Haldis-Ramirez, Gearhart-Dasni-Flores-Quintana. GCL Marlins (2) -- Tucker-Castor-Olivo, Pie-Castor-Ruzic-Lindeen. GCL Mets (4) -- Pinango-Riggan-Wilson, Williams-Riggan-Manuel, McIntyre-Jostock-Appell, McIntyre-Medina-Hinchman. GCL Nationals (2) -- Engles-Mercedes, Perks-Cerezo. GCL Phillies (1) -- Cruz-Alvarez-Mejias. GCL Pirates (2) -- Jacobsen-Herman, Herman-Marte-Colina-Martinez. GCL Red Sox (5) -- German-Rios-Gonzalez, Albury-Towery, Albury-Peralta, Garces-Fernandes-Towery-Peralta, German-Ortiz-Gonzalez. GCL Reds (2) -- Wood-Johnson-Huddy-Smiley, Huddy-Brito-Smiley-Dillard. GCL Tigers (1) -- Garcia-Watts-Trejo-Perdomo. GCL Twins (3) -- Edlich-Williams-Patton-Burgos, Castillo-Craig, Castillo-Williams-Hernandez. GCL Yankees (2) -- Wordekemper-Rueger-Cabrera, Soto-Everitt-Morales.

NO-HIT GAMES: Jacobsen, Pirates, defeated Twins, 5-0, July 28.

TEAM

Team	G	PO	A	E	TC	DP	TP	PB	Pct.
Dodgers	54	1393	520	65	1978	55	0	15	.967
Mets	53	1387	550	67	2004	59	0	8	.967
Marlins	54	1389	585	71	2045	50	0	18	.965
Red Sox	54	1436	575	76	2087	36	0	18	.964
Nationals	53	1389	605	77	2071	45	0	11	.963
Pirates	54	1405	630	80	2115	55	0	16	.962
Twins	54	1383	573	78	2034	51	0	16	.962
Phillies	51	1315	552	75	1942	48	0	15	.961
Yankees	53	1341	530	75	1946	53	0	8	.961
Braves	52	1340	519	81	1940	34	0	18	.958
Tigers	54	1392	618	94	2104	42	1	13	.955
Reds	54	1371	551	104	2026	57	0	16	.949

INDIVIDUAL

FIRST BASEMEN

NOTE: All caps denotes fielding-percentage leader based on 30 games for catchers, 40 for all other non-pitchers and 48 innings for pitchers. *Throws lefthanded.

Player, Team	Pct.	G	PO	A	E	TC	DP
Abellera, Joseph, Gulf Coast Twins	1.000	11	43	4	0	47	7
Adduci, James, Gulf Coast Marlins *	.979	5	45	1	1	47	4
Arambarris, Manuel, Gulf Coast Red Sox	.984	23	176	11	3	190	10
Ayres, Mitchell, Gulf Coast Dodgers	1.000	1	3	0	0	3	2
Barnes, Larry, Gulf Coast Marlins *	1.000	1	7	0	0	7	1
Bladergroen, Ian, Gulf Coast Red Sox *	1.000	5	43	3	0	46	1
Brezeale, Daniel, Gulf Coast Braves	1.000	1	11	1	0	12	0
Broadway, Larry, Gulf Coast Nationals *	1.000	7	44	8	0	52	5
Bucce, Yasmil, Gulf Coast Mets	1.000	1	9	0	0	9	2
Cain, Gregory, Gulf Coast Mets	.833	1	5	0	1	6	1
Camarena, Jose, Gulf Coast Braves	1.000	10	88	5	0	93	6
Clark, Howie, Gulf Coast Pirates	1.000	1	7	1	0	8	1
Colon, Angel, Gulf Coast Reds	.989	20	168	7	2	177	21
Contreras, Junior, Gulf Coast Mets	.986	33	279	12	4	295	35
Creek, Gregory, Gulf Coast Braves	1.000	4	27	3	0	30	1
Cummins, Daniel, Gulf Coast Mets	1.000	4	16	0	0	16	2
Dasni, Chales, Gulf Coast Dodgers	1.000	1	5	0	0	5	1
Dean, Joshua, Gulf Coast Twins	.969	19	147	10	5	162	9
De Leon, Santo, Gulf Coast Tigers	.992	14	107	13	1	121	7
de Vrieze, Jeffrey, Gulf Coast Marlins	.957	6	43	1	2	46	1
Dunn, Michael, Gulf Coast Yankees *	1.000	5	45	4	0	49	3
Durant, Michael, Gulf Coast Phillies	.994	36	315	21	2	338	28
Dyson, Colie, Gulf Coast Dodgers *	1.000	1	7	1	0	8	0
Ellington, Matthew, Gulf Coast Marlins *	.994	20	157	10	1	168	19
FERMIN, ANGEL, Gulf Coast Yankees	.976	43	330	31	9	370	39
Garcia, Jesus, Gulf Coast Red Sox	1.000	6	45	4	0	49	3
German, Agustin, Gulf Coast Nationals	.875	1	6	1	1	8	0
Gil, Jose, Gulf Coast Yankees	.941	2	14	2	1	17	2
Gonzalez, Adolfo, Gulf Coast Dodgers	1.000	10	46	3	0	49	4
Greenwood, Jared, Gulf Coast Yankees	1.000	6	35	3	0	38	2
Gutierrez, Eloy, Gulf Coast Dodgers	...	1	0	0	0	0	0
Jansen, Kenley, Gulf Coast Dodgers	1.000	6	49	1	0	50	4
Johnson, Taylor, Gulf Coast Reds *	.973	35	264	26	8	298	25
Johnson, Tod, Gulf Coast Reds *	1.000	1	11	1	0	12	2
Jones, Michael, Gulf Coast Red Sox	.983	20	163	12	3	178	13
Kaaihue, Isaiah, Gulf Coast Braves	.983	39	330	15	6	351	23
Knowles, Marion, Gulf Coast Twins	.982	14	101	6	2	109	10
Lane, Richard, Gulf Coast Nationals *	.960	6	47	1	2	50	1
Larish, Jeffrey, Gulf Coast Tigers	1.000	3	34	2	0	36	0
Linares, Emilio, Gulf Coast Red Sox	1.000	2	35	3	0	38	2
Maldonado, Brahiam, Gulf Coast Twins	1.000	1	2	0	0	2	0
Martinez, Jonathan, Gulf Coast Nationals	1.000	1	5	2	0	7	0
Messner, Nathan, Gulf Coast Nationals	.967	3	26	3	1	30	1
Mientkiewicz, Doug, Gulf Coast Mets	1.000	3	26	3	0	29	1
Miller, Cole, Gulf Coast Tigers	.957	9	66	1	3	70	3
Morales, Douglas, Gulf Coast Phillies *	1.000	3	20	0	0	20	0
Moreno, Junior, Gulf Coast Red Sox	1.000	2	12	0	0	12	1
Mortimer, Steve, Gulf Coast Nationals *	.950	3	19	0	1	20	4
Mosby, Robert, Gulf Coast Twins	1.000	1	10	3	0	13	1
Nunez, Jose Miguel2, Gulf Coast Dodgers	.988	36	237	13	3	253	29
Ochoa, Blake, Gulf Coast Marlins	.985	19	125	4	2	131	12
Padgett, Nathan, Gulf Coast Marlins	1.000	2	18	2	0	20	3
Pahuta, Timothy, Gulf Coast Nationals	.986	32	270	22	4	296	27
Peabody, John, Gulf Coast Pirates	.991	24	218	8	2	228	22

Player, Team	Pct.	G	PO	A	E	TC	DP
Perez, Eduardo, Gulf Coast Dodgers	1.000	11	70	4	0	74	12
Perez, Melvin, Gulf Coast Nationals	.944	7	50	1	3	54	5
Phillips, Nathan, Gulf Coast Yankees	1.000	2	11	1	0	12	2
Ramos, Luis, Gulf Coast Marlins	1.000	1	3	0	0	3	0
Reyes, Angel, Gulf Coast Tigers	.994	35	291	19	2	312	26
Rios, Daniel, Gulf Coast Pirates *	.997	32	281	20	1	302	23
Rivadeneira, Deivis, Gulf Coast Marlins	1.000	1	5	0	0	5	1
Rodriguez, Jesus, Gulf Coast Marlins	.952	2	18	2	1	21	1
Sanchez, Henry, Gulf Coast Twins	.984	15	120	5	2	127	16
Shaw, Buck, Gulf Coast Phillies	.984	17	118	5	2	125	10
Thole, Joshua, Gulf Coast Mets	.993	21	131	7	1	139	14
Wilson, John, Gulf Coast Twins	1.000	1	8	0	0	8	0
Woodard, Johnny, Gulf Coast Twins	.956	6	41	2	2	45	1

SECOND BASEMEN

Player, Team	Pct.	G	PO	A	E	TC	DP
Andrus, Elvis, Gulf Coast Braves	...	1	0	0	0	0	0
Batista, Norberto, Gulf Coast Marlins	1.000	3	7	9	0	16	3
Bautista, Pedruin, Gulf Coast Tigers	.951	35	74	100	9	183	22
Berg, Daniel, Gulf Coast Twins	.917	11	25	19	4	48	5
Brooks, Parker, Gulf Coast Dodgers	.968	8	13	17	1	31	6
Cairo, Miguel, Gulf Coast Mets	1.000	2	4	7	0	11	2
Cambero, Alberto, Gulf Coast Phillies	.967	20	44	43	3	90	13
Carroll, Mark, Gulf Coast Yankees	.000	1	0	0	1	1	0
CASTRO, JONATHAN, Gulf Coast Nationals	.974	45	113	111	6	230	24
Castro, Jose, Gulf Coast Mets	.988	19	36	47	1	84	17
Cuevas, Phillip, Gulf Coast Phillies	.951	20	27	51	4	82	7
Cummins, Daniel, Gulf Coast Mets	.667	1	0	2	1	3	0
Disla, Bienvenido, Gulf Coast Braves	1.000	3	2	4	0	6	1
Feiner, Kevyn, Gulf Coast Reds	.939	8	23	23	3	49	9
Garcia, Emmanuel, Gulf Coast Mets	.960	6	9	15	1	25	6
Garcia, Yosanddy, Gulf Coast Dodgers	.951	15	29	48	4	81	11
Gonzalez, Adolfo, Gulf Coast Dodgers	.975	27	52	67	3	122	20
Granadillo, Antonio, Gulf Coast Red Sox	1.000	12	15	34	0	49	8
Guzman, Agustin, Gulf Coast Tigers	.948	21	37	54	5	96	8
Hernandez, Fidel, Gulf Coast Pirates	1.000	6	10	10	0	20	2
Lafountain, Jason, Gulf Coast Yankees	1.000	1	1	1	0	2	0
Lasso, Yoni, Gulf Coast Reds	1.000	14	17	41	0	58	9
Linares, Emilio, Gulf Coast Red Sox	.959	17	32	38	3	73	9
Lipsey, Carl, Gulf Coast Red Sox	1.000	1	2	0	0	2	0
Luque, William, Gulf Coast Twins	1.000	3	0	2	0	2	0
Lysaught, Michael, Gulf Coast Twins	1.000	14	35	36	0	71	10
Malec, Christopher, Gulf Coast Yankees	.960	19	24	48	3	75	11
Marcial, Robert, Gulf Coast Braves	1.000	13	9	14	0	23	4
Martinez, Jonathan, Gulf Coast Nationals	.955	9	14	28	2	44	6
Matsui, Kazuo, Gulf Coast Mets	1.000	2	2	7	0	9	2
Mauer, Donald, Gulf Coast Twins	1.000	2	4	3	0	7	1
Mesa, Maikol, Gulf Coast Reds	...	1	0	0	0	0	0
Monk, Brandon, Gulf Coast Braves	.936	41	59	73	9	141	15
Nunez, Luis, Gulf Coast Yankees	.938	7	15	15	2	32	5
Osteen, Cooper, Gulf Coast Phillies	1.000	17	24	38	0	62	10
Padgett, Nathan, Gulf Coast Marlins	1.000	6	18	18	0	36	6
Paul, Matthew, Gulf Coast Dodgers	.977	13	19	23	1	43	3
Peralta, Alexander, Gulf Coast Pirates	.960	21	42	53	4	99	17
Perez, Melvin, Gulf Coast Nationals	...	1	0	0	0	0	0
Perez, Smelin, Gulf Coast Pirates	.971	22	38	64	3	105	11
Picart, Gregory, Gulf Coast Pirates	.973	14	26	46	2	74	7
Pino, Wilmer, Gulf Coast Yankees	.957	30	35	77	5	117	18
Rafael, Manuel, Gulf Coast Red Sox	1.000	1	2	1	0	3	0
Rivadeneira, Deivis, Gulf Coast Braves	1.000	14	15	21	0	36	5
Robinson, Trayvon, Gulf Coast Dodgers	...	1	0	0	0	0	0
Rodriguez, Jesus, Gulf Coast Marlins	.972	9	18	17	1	36	6
Rogers, Jose, Gulf Coast Reds	.925	16	35	39	6	80	10
Rojo, Billy Garrison, Gulf Coast Reds	.935	23	47	54	7	108	14
Santana, Carlos, Gulf Coast Dodgers	1.000	2	1	4	0	5	0
Santana, Richard, Gulf Coast Red Sox	.941	21	30	65	6	101	10
Schemmel, Jonathan, Gulf Coast Mets	.936	27	45	72	8	125	17
Segovia, Luis, Gulf Coast Red Sox	.966	6	11	17	1	29	3
Silverio, Rigoberto, Gulf Coast Reds	.967	30	77	69	5	151	22
Thompson, Andrew, Gulf Coast Twins	.982	19	49	58	2	109	18
Valdez, Odannys, Gulf Coast Twins	.981	10	22	29	1	52	5
Webb, Justin, Gulf Coast Marlins	.980	9	21	28	1	50	3

THIRD BASEMEN

Player, Team	Pct.	G	PO	A	E	TC	DP
Abellera, Joseph, Gulf Coast Twins	.920	8	9	14	2	25	2
Allen, Cody, Gulf Coast Marlins	.804	15	9	28	9	46	4

Player, Team	Pct.	G	PO	A	E	TC	DP
Arambarris, Manuel, Gulf Coast Red Sox	.727	2	2	6	3	11	0
Baez, Welinson, Gulf Coast Phillies	.957	9	9	13	1	23	0
Bell, Joshua, Gulf Coast Dodgers	.917	26	17	27	4	48	3
Berg, Daniel, Gulf Coast Twins	.788	12	8	18	7	33	2
Blanton, John, Gulf Coast Phillies	.917	6	8	14	2	24	3
Brezeale, Daniel, Gulf Coast Braves	1.000	4	4	6	0	10	0
Cambero, Alberto, Gulf Coast Phillies	.000	1	0	0	1	1	0
Ciriaco, Audy, Gulf Coast Tigers	1.000	1	0	3	0	3	1
Clark, Howie, Gulf Coast Pirates	.750	1	1	2	1	4	1
Colon, Angel, Gulf Coast Reds	.889	18	12	20	4	36	4
Creek, Gregory, Gulf Coast Braves	.908	37	26	63	9	98	12
Cummins, Daniel, Gulf Coast Mets	.909	10	8	22	3	33	3
De Leon, Santo, Gulf Coast Tigers	.915	16	7	36	4	47	4
Delgado, Juan, Gulf Coast Twins	.944	14	5	29	2	36	2
Delgado, Ronny, Gulf Coast Reds	.854	36	13	57	12	82	8
de Vrieze, Jeffrey, Gulf Coast Marlins	1.000	1	0	1	0	1	0
Disla, Bienvenido, Gulf Coast Dodgers	.935	12	5	24	2	31	1
Dunn, Michael, Gulf Coast Yankees *	.000	1	0	0	1	1	0
FIGUEREO, JOHAN, Gulf Coast Nationals	.934	45	38	90	9	137	5
Garcia, Jesus, Gulf Coast Red Sox	1.000	2	3	2	0	5	0
Granadillo, Antonio, Gulf Coast Red Sox	.000	1	0	0	1	1	0
Haupt, Christopher, Gulf Coast Marlins	...	1	0	0	0	0	0
Hernandez, Fidel, Gulf Coast Dodgers	1.000	4	2	8	0	10	0
Hernandez, Habelito, Gulf Coast Reds	1.000	1	1	2	0	3	1
Hodges, Scott, Gulf Coast Nationals	1.000	2	3	6	0	9	0
Johnson, Taylor, Gulf Coast Red Sox *	...	1	0	0	0	0	0
Kelly, Paul, Gulf Coast Twins	.969	9	9	22	1	32	4
Kennelly, Timothy, Gulf Coast Phillies	.935	34	18	68	6	92	8
Kuhaulua, Kaulana, Gulf Coast Twins	...	1	0	0	0	0	0
Lafountain, Jason, Gulf Coast Yankees	.862	12	5	20	4	29	5
Lasso, Yoni, Gulf Coast Reds	1.000	4	0	9	0	9	1
Linares, Emilio, Gulf Coast Red Sox	.692	16	5	22	12	39	1
Linares, Miguel, Gulf Coast Tigers	.980	27	32	64	2	98	7
Luque, William, Gulf Coast Twins	.846	11	6	16	4	26	0
Lysaught, Michael, Gulf Coast Twins	.923	5	5	7	1	13	1
Malec, Christopher, Gulf Coast Yankees	1.000	1	0	1	0	1	0
Mansolino, Anthony, Gulf Coast Pirates	.927	39	24	103	10	137	9
Nunez, Luis, Gulf Coast Yankees	.887	15	14	33	6	53	6
Osteen, Cooper, Gulf Coast Phillies	.923	8	3	9	1	13	0
Ott, Louis, Gulf Coast Tigers	.833	13	3	32	7	42	2
Padgett, Nathan, Gulf Coast Marlins	.958	8	4	19	1	24	2
Peralta, Alexander, Gulf Coast Pirates	.778	3	1	6	2	9	1
Perez, Eduardo, Gulf Coast Dodgers	.965	21	18	37	2	57	2
Perez, Melvin, Gulf Coast Nationals	.935	12	8	21	2	31	0
Phillips, Nathan, Gulf Coast Yankees	.833	29	16	29	9	54	1
Picart, Gregory, Gulf Coast Pirates	1.000	4	4	10	0	14	0
Pino, Wilmer, Gulf Coast Yankees	...	1	0	0	0	0	0
Prasch, Edward, Gulf Coast Pirates	.871	9	9	18	4	31	0
Rafael, Manuel, Gulf Coast Red Sox	.894	34	24	69	11	104	4
Ramos, Luis, Gulf Coast Marlins	1.000	1	2	0	0	2	0
Rivadeneira, Deivis, Gulf Coast Braves	1.000	7	3	7	0	10	0
Rodriguez, Jesus, Gulf Coast Marlins	.947	33	23	67	5	95	3
Santana, Carlos, Gulf Coast Dodgers	.956	14	16	27	2	45	4
Santana, Richard, Gulf Coast Red Sox	1.000	1	0	2	0	2	0
Santiesteban, Danny, Gulf Coast Twins	1.000	1	0	1	0	1	0
Schemmel, Jonathan, Gulf Coast Mets	1.000	2	1	7	0	8	1
Tejada, Abraham, Gulf Coast Marlins	...	1	0	0	0	0	0
Ventura, Leivi, Gulf Coast Mets	.925	44	35	89	10	134	9
Webb, Justin, Gulf Coast Marlins	1.000	1	0	2	0	2	0

Player, Team	Pct.	G	PO	A	E	TC	DP
Garcia, Emmanuel, Gulf Coast Mets	.940	36	48	93	9	150	19
Garcia, Yosanddy, Gulf Coast Dodgers	.844	24	32	49	15	96	14
Gonzalez, Adolfo, Gulf Coast Dodgers	.857	2	1	5	1	7	0
Gonzalez, Angel R., Gulf Coast Pirates	.913	19	21	63	8	92	17
Henry, Carl, Gulf Coast Yankees	.938	39	59	106	11	176	27
Hernandez, Diory, Gulf Coast Braves	.938	4	3	12	1	16	1
Hernandez, Fidel, Gulf Coast Phillies	.930	27	35	72	8	115	11
Hernandez, Luis, Gulf Coast Braves	.750	1	1	2	1	4	0
Honey, Raymond, Gulf Coast Reds	.926	23	39	73	9	121	19
Jones, Michael, Gulf Coast Reds	.822	22	24	59	18	101	10
Kelly, Paul, Gulf Coast Twins	.975	29	52	102	4	158	19
Kuhaulua, Kaulana, Gulf Coast Twins	.857	2	1	5	1	7	1
Lafountain, Jason, Gulf Coast Yankees	1.000	1	0	1	0	1	0
Lasso, Yoni, Gulf Coast Reds	.913	3	9	12	2	23	2
Linares, Miguel, Gulf Coast Tigers	.932	8	10	31	3	44	3
Luque, William, Gulf Coast Twins	.963	13	19	33	2	54	6
Marcial, Robert, Gulf Coast Braves	1.000	3	2	0	0	2	0
Martinez, Jonathan, Gulf Coast Nationals	.903	28	47	65	12	124	17
Mitchell, Derrick, Gulf Coast Phillies	.862	21	37	69	17	123	16
Munoz, David, Gulf Coast Pirates	.904	19	18	57	8	83	6
Nunez, Luis, Gulf Coast Yankees	.968	17	19	41	2	62	9
Osteen, Cooper, Gulf Coast Phillies	.727	6	3	5	3	11	0
Ott, Louis, Gulf Coast Tigers	.914	10	9	23	3	35	4
Padgett, Nathan, Gulf Coast Marlins	.941	15	12	52	4	68	8
Perez, Smelin, Gulf Coast Nationals	.902	11	17	38	6	61	8
Picart, Gregory, Gulf Coast Pirates	.944	8	12	22	2	36	5
Rivadeneira, Deivis, Gulf Coast Braves	.955	10	15	27	2	44	2
Santana, Richard, Gulf Coast Red Sox	.931	17	26	41	5	72	6
Segovia, Luis, Gulf Coast Red Sox	.943	39	54	112	10	176	20
Silverio, Rigoberto, Gulf Coast Marlins	.750	1	1	2	1	4	0
Suarez, Gabriel, Gulf Coast Nationals	1.000	1	0	1	0	1	0
Tejada, Abraham, Gulf Coast Marlins	.864	15	9	29	6	44	5
Thompson, Andrew, Gulf Coast Twins	.842	10	10	22	6	38	7
Webb, Justin, Gulf Coast Marlins	.939	6	11	20	2	33	5

OUTFIELDERS

Player, Team	Pct.	G	PO	A	E	TC	DP
Adducci, James, Gulf Coast Marlins *	1.000	5	8	0	0	8	0
Aguilar, Jose, Gulf Coast Reds	.977	32	42	1	1	44	0
Agustin, Juan, Gulf Coast Marlins	1.000	30	56	2	0	58	0
Allen, Cody, Gulf Coast Marlins	.931	21	23	4	2	29	1
Arias, Claudio, Gulf Coast Red Sox	1.000	3	5	0	0	5	0
Arnedo, Rolando, Gulf Coast Nationals	.960	15	22	2	1	25	0
Austin, Parris, Gulf Coast Mets	.944	26	31	3	2	36	1
Batista, Norberto, Gulf Coast Marlins	...	1	0	0	0	0	0
Bell, Billy, Gulf Coast Red Sox	.952	37	58	2	3	63	1
Berg, Daniel, Gulf Coast Twins	1.000	1	1	0	0	1	0
Berry, Vince, Gulf Coast Tigers	.978	33	42	2	1	45	1
Billingslea, Courtney, Gulf Coast Mets	.975	30	37	2	1	40	0
Brea, Manuel, Gulf Coast Tigers	.921	37	75	7	7	89	2
Brown, Dustin, Gulf Coast Red Sox	1.000	2	3	0	0	3	0
Brown, Jeremy, Gulf Coast Dodgers	1.000	28	62	1	0	63	0
Bruce, Jay, Gulf Coast Reds *	.962	27	48	2	2	52	1
Buck, Juan, Gulf Coast Reds	.889	7	8	0	1	9	0
Cabrera, Gerardo, Gulf Coast Mets	.976	31	40	1	1	42	0
Cain, Gregory, Gulf Coast Mets	1.000	23	50	0	0	50	0
Camarena, Jose, Gulf Coast Braves	1.000	2	3	0	0	3	0
Carmona, Eliazar, Gulf Coast Braves	.943	32	46	4	3	53	1
Carroll, Mark, Gulf Coast Yankees	1.000	3	1	0	0	1	0
Cedron, Jhon, Gulf Coast Pirates	1.000	21	28	2	0	30	1
Cervelli, Francisco, Gulf Coast Yankees	...	1	0	0	0	0	0
Ciaramella, Matthew, Gulf Coast Red Sox * .	.950	9	19	0	1	20	0
Clark, Howie, Gulf Coast Pirates	1.000	3	4	0	0	4	0
Connor, Wesley, Gulf Coast Nationals	.946	23	33	2	2	37	0
Cotto, Pedro, Gulf Coast Tigers *	1.000	11	12	2	0	14	0
Cronkhite, Ian, Gulf Coast Red Sox *	1.000	5	13	1	0	14	0
Cummins, Daniel, Gulf Coast Mets	1.000	1	0	1	0	1	0
De La Cruz, Jason, Gulf Coast Tigers	.921	28	33	2	3	38	0
De La Rossa, Wilkins, Gulf Coast Yankees *.	.961	48	92	7	4	103	2
Delaughter, Ryan, Gulf Coast Nationals	.956	27	40	3	2	45	0
Delgado, Juan, Gulf Coast Twins	1.000	1	1	0	0	1	0
Dunn, Michael, Gulf Coast Yankees *	1.000	12	17	2	0	19	0
Engel, Reid, Gulf Coast Red Sox	.941	24	48	0	3	51	0
Fermin, Angel, Gulf Coast Yankees	1.000	2	1	0	0	1	0
Fletcher, Simon, Gulf Coast Twins	.939	21	30	1	2	33	0
Frazee, Joseph, Gulf Coast Phillies	1.000	30	41	3	0	44	0
Fulse, Sheldon, Gulf Coast Red Sox	1.000	3	4	0	0	4	0
Garrett, Matt, Gulf Coast Reds	.977	23	42	0	1	43	0
Gilbert, Archie, Gulf Coast Red Sox	1.000	22	37	1	0	38	0
Griffin, Trevion, Gulf Coast Braves	.957	30	44	0	2	46	0

SHORTSTOPS

Player, Team	Pct.	G	PO	A	E	TC	DP
Alvarez, Jean Carlos, Gulf Coast Nationals ..	.905	24	34	71	11	116	12
Andrus, Elvis, Gulf Coast Braves	.925	40	63	98	13	174	16
Baez, Welinson, Gulf Coast Phillies	.857	2	1	5	1	7	1
Batista, Norberto, Gulf Coast Marlins	.961	21	33	66	4	103	15
Bell, Joshua, Gulf Coast Dodgers	1.000	1	0	1	0	1	0
Brooks, Parker, Gulf Coast Dodgers	.667	4	1	1	1	3	1
Cambero, Alberto, Gulf Coast Phillies	.846	5	6	5	2	13	3
Castro, Jonathan, Gulf Coast Nationals	.889	1	5	3	1	9	1
Castro, Jose, Gulf Coast Mets	.962	12	21	29	2	52	6
Ciriaco, Audy, Gulf Coast Tigers	.901	38	56	99	17	172	17
Coronado, Jose, Gulf Coast Mets	1.000	8	18	20	0	38	6
Creek, Gregory, Gulf Coast Braves	1.000	1	0	1	0	1	0
Cummins, Daniel, Gulf Coast Mets	...	1	0	0	0	0	0
De Jesus, Ivan, Gulf Coast Dodgers	.914	33	45	82	12	139	19
Delgado, Juan, Gulf Coast Twins	.857	5	7	5	2	14	1
Eymann, Eric, Gulf Coast Reds	1.000	1	0	2	0	2	0
Feiner, Kevyn, Gulf Coast Reds	.914	7	16	16	3	35	5
Figuereo, Johan, Gulf Coast Nationals	1.000	1	1	0	0	1	0

Player, Team	Pct.	G	PO	A	E	TC	DP
Gutierrez, Eloy, Gulf Coast Dodgers	.984	36	60	3	1	64	2
Guzman, Francisco, Gulf Coast Nationals	.950	40	74	2	4	80	1
Guzman, Jose, Gulf Coast Dodgers	.667	2	2	0	1	3	0
Hall, Michael, Gulf Coast Red Sox *	1.000	7	6	0	0	6	0
Haupt, Christopher, Gulf Coast Marlins	...	1	0	0	0	0	0
Hurst, Jason, Gulf Coast Red Sox	1.000	29	46	3	0	49	0
Igsema, Victor, Gulf Coast Pirates	.969	38	59	4	2	65	2
Jackson, Austin, Gulf Coast Yankees	1.000	35	61	2	0	63	0
Jansen, Kenley, Gulf Coast Dodgers	1.000	1	1	0	0	1	0
Johnson, Deryck, Gulf Coast Nationals *	1.000	7	10	0	0	10	0
Johnson, Taylor, Gulf Coast Reds *	...	1	0	0	0	0	0
Jones, Brandon, Gulf Coast Braves	1.000	2	3	0	0	3	0
Jones, Marion, Gulf Coast Red Sox	1.000	7	7	0	0	7	0
Knowles, Marion, Gulf Coast Twins	.917	15	21	1	2	24	0
Kutler, Matthew, Gulf Coast Marlins *	.969	41	56	7	2	65	2
Laboy, Albert, Gulf Coast Pirates	1.000	7	11	0	0	11	0
Lewis, Kenneth, Gulf Coast Reds *	...	2	0	0	0	0	0
Little, Mark, Gulf Coast Marlins	1.000	2	2	0	0	2	0
Lowrance, Marvin, Gulf Coast Nationals *	1.000	8	7	1	0	8	0
Loyola, Maiko, Gulf Coast Pirates	.970	41	64	1	2	67	0
Lysaught, Michael, Gulf Coast Twins	...	1	0	0	0	0	0
Maldonado, Brahiam, Gulf Coast Mets	.946	28	49	4	3	56	0
Mancebo, Melvin, Gulf Coast Nationals	.975	23	33	6	1	40	0
Marcial, Robert, Gulf Coast Braves	1.000	1	1	0	0	1	0
Mateo, Jose, Gulf Coast Mets	.947	19	36	0	2	38	1
McCutchen, Andrew, Gulf Coast Pirates	.964	43	74	6	3	83	4
Mejia, Ernesto, Gulf Coast Braves	.964	18	25	2	1	28	0
Mesa, Juan, Gulf Coast Pirates	.889	12	16	0	2	18	0
Mesa, Maikol, Gulf Coast Reds	.968	17	29	1	1	31	0
MIASO, CURT, Gulf Coast Phillies	1.000	42	75	3	0	78	1
Montero, Juan, Gulf Coast Mets	.931	16	25	2	2	29	0
Mora, Jesus, Gulf Coast Dodgers	1.000	30	44	4	0	48	2
Morales, Douglas, Gulf Coast Phillies *	.982	34	50	5	1	56	2
Mortimer, Steve, Gulf Coast Nationals *	1.000	1	1	1	0	2	0
Nunez, Luis, Gulf Coast Yankees	1.000	2	1	0	0	1	0
Nunez, Runi, Gulf Coast Reds	...	3	0	0	0	0	0
Ogando, Cristian, Gulf Coast Nationals	1.000	38	61	4	0	65	3
Pahuta, Timothy, Gulf Coast Nationals	...	1	0	0	0	0	0
Parliament, Adam, Gulf Coast Braves	.973	45	68	5	2	75	0
Paterson, Thomas, Gulf Coast Phillies *	.975	34	69	8	2	79	0
Peacock, Brian, Gulf Coast Nationals	1.000	3	6	1	0	7	0
Pena, Hannsel, Gulf Coast Reds	.900	21	34	2	4	40	0
Perez, Joel, Gulf Coast Yankees	1.000	30	46	2	0	48	1
Perez, Melvin, Gulf Coast Nationals	1.000	5	2	0	0	2	0
Prady, Ricky, Gulf Coast Twins	1.000	7	6	0	0	6	0
Quintana, Estevan, Gulf Coast Reds	1.000	14	19	0	0	19	0
Ramos, Luis, Gulf Coast Marlins	1.000	18	17	1	0	18	1
Rivadeneira, Deivis, Gulf Coast Braves	1.000	1	1	0	0	1	0
ROBERSON, COLIN, Gulf Coast Marlins	1.000	47	74	10	0	84	2
Robinson, Trayvon, Gulf Coast Dodgers	.969	35	58	5	2	65	1
Rodriguez, Wilkin, Gulf Coast Tigers *	.987	39	76	1	1	78	1
Sanchez, Ricardo, Gulf Coast Red Sox	1.000	1	1	0	0	1	0
Santa, Moises, Gulf Coast Red Sox	1.000	29	51	2	0	53	0
Santana, Carlos, Gulf Coast Dodgers	1.000	7	8	0	0	8	0
Santiesteban, Danny, Gulf Coast Twins	1.000	19	36	2	0	38	0
Sapp, Steven, Gulf Coast Dodgers	1.000	21	32	1	0	33	0
Schafer, Jordan, Gulf Coast Braves *	.966	47	82	3	3	88	0
Sojo, Richard, Gulf Coast Twins	.961	41	68	6	3	77	1
Spath, Matthew, Gulf Coast Mets	.978	27	44	0	1	45	0
Tabata, Jose, Gulf Coast Yankees	.959	41	43	4	2	49	0
Valdez, Odannys, Gulf Coast Twins	1.000	26	42	0	0	42	0
Van Slyke, Scott, Gulf Coast Dodgers	1.000	22	36	3	0	39	0
Verley, Brandon, Gulf Coast Marlins *	1.000	8	5	1	0	6	0
Webb, Justin, Gulf Coast Marlins	...	1	0	0	0	0	0
Wells, Casper, Gulf Coast Tigers	.959	39	69	2	3	74	0
Westfield, Antonio, Gulf Coast Pirates	.929	10	25	1	2	28	0
Williams, Jermaine, Gulf Coast Phillies	.944	29	32	2	2	36	1
Wilson, John, Gulf Coast Twins	.943	22	32	1	2	35	0

CATCHERS

Player, Team	Pct.	G	PO	A	E	TC	DP
Ayres, Mitchell, Gulf Coast Dodgers	.983	14	54	4	1	59	1
Barrientos, Miguel, Gulf Coast Twins	.984	11	51	10	1	62	0
Bernard, Miguel, Gulf Coast Braves	.982	9	46	8	1	55	0
Blaquiere, Jean Luc, Gulf Coast Mets	.980	20	87	11	2	100	1
Britton, Phillip, Gulf Coast Braves	.990	16	89	12	1	102	0
Brown, Dustin, Gulf Coast Red Sox	1.000	2	7	1	0	8	0
Bucce, Yasmil, Gulf Coast Mets	.977	29	191	21	5	217	1
Camarena, Jose, Gulf Coast Braves	1.000	10	47	8	0	55	0
Cervelli, Francisco, Gulf Coast Yankees	.986	21	127	18	2	147	0

Player, Team	Pct.	G	PO	A	E	TC	DP
Cheesman, Aaron, Gulf Coast Phillies	.974	18	98	13	3	114	3
Cortez, Jose, Gulf Coast Phillies	1.000	1	7	1	0	8	0
Creswell, Charles, Gulf Coast Phillies	.966	17	103	12	4	119	0
Cummins, Daniel, Gulf Coast Mets	1.000	12	76	5	0	81	0
de San Miguel, Allan, Gulf Coast Twins	1.000	23	139	24	0	163	3
de Vrieze, Jeffrey, Gulf Coast Marlins	1.000	15	70	8	0	78	0
Egan, Jonathan, Gulf Coast Red Sox	.995	23	184	22	1	207	1
Flores, Angel, Gulf Coast Tigers	.985	14	55	9	1	65	0
Garcia, Jesus, Gulf Coast Red Sox	.994	22	161	19	1	181	3
Garcia, Steven, Gulf Coast Braves	.962	22	137	15	6	158	0
German, Agustin, Gulf Coast Nationals	.974	19	158	27	5	190	3
GIL, JOSE, Gulf Coast Yankees	.990	35	259	31	3	293	1
Gonzalez, Julio, Gulf Coast Reds	.982	30	194	28	4	226	1
Greenwood, Jared, Gulf Coast Yankees	1.000	4	24	3	0	27	0
Haupt, Christopher, Gulf Coast Marlins	.976	12	38	3	1	42	0
Hayes, Brett, Gulf Coast Marlins	1.000	2	15	0	0	15	0
Jansen, Kenley, Gulf Coast Dodgers	1.000	28	181	13	0	194	1
Kennelly, Timothy, Gulf Coast Phillies	1.000	1	1	0	0	1	0
Lafountain, Jason, Gulf Coast Yankees	1.000	2	8	0	0	8	0
Lerud, Steven, Gulf Coast Pirates	.992	15	108	15	1	124	1
Made, Kelington, Gulf Coast Pirates	.974	13	67	8	2	77	2
Mancebo, Melvin, Gulf Coast Nationals	1.000	1	1	0	0	1	0
Mann, Schuyler, Gulf Coast Yankees	...	1	0	0	0	0	0
Marcial, Robert, Gulf Coast Braves	1.000	1	3	1	0	4	0
Medero-Stullz, Carlos, Gulf Coast Dodgers	.995	28	170	21	1	192	0
Miller, Cole, Gulf Coast Tigers	.963	15	46	6	2	54	2
Moreno, Junior, Gulf Coast Red Sox	1.000	1	5	0	0	5	0
Mota, Juan, Gulf Coast Braves	.962	18	59	16	3	78	0
Naughton, Joel, Gulf Coast Phillies	.981	27	134	24	3	161	2
Ochoa, Blake, Gulf Coast Marlins	.992	16	108	14	1	123	0
Palacios, Rodolfo, Gulf Coast Twins	1.000	2	5	1	0	6	0
Peacock, Brian, Gulf Coast Nationals	.991	28	182	27	2	211	0
Roa, Lonny, Gulf Coast Reds	.969	15	92	2	3	97	1
Rodriguez, Mark, Gulf Coast Reds	1.000	5	37	5	0	42	1
Roman, Willman, Gulf Coast Pirates	1.000	26	170	15	0	185	1
Rumbos, Javier, Gulf Coast Reds	.976	11	76	5	2	83	0
Sanchez, Ricardo, Gulf Coast Red Sox	.977	11	74	12	2	88	0
Sandoval, Daniel, Gulf Coast Tigers	.958	26	151	31	8	190	0
Santana, Carlos, Gulf Coast Dodgers	1.000	3	3	1	0	4	0
Simmons, Lyndsey, Gulf Coast Nationals	1.000	2	13	2	0	15	0
Skelton, James, Gulf Coast Tigers	.978	16	74	15	2	91	0
Smolarski, Freddy, Gulf Coast Marlins	.955	22	157	12	8	177	3
Soto, Auddy, Gulf Coast Nationals	.917	6	39	5	4	48	0
Thole, Joshua, Gulf Coast Mets	.980	7	42	6	1	49	0
Walk, John, Gulf Coast Pirates	.943	6	32	1	2	35	0
Webb, Justin, Gulf Coast Marlins	1.000	7	45	2	0	47	0
Yersich, Gregory, Gulf Coast Twins	.975	31	174	24	5	203	2

PITCHERS

Player, Team	Pct.	G	PO	A	E	TC	DP
Acors, Matthew, Gulf Coast Pirates	1.000	7	1	0	0	1	0
Acosta, Jorge, Gulf Coast Braves *	1.000	9	0	1	0	1	0
Adames, Geovanny, Gulf Coast Reds	1.000	9	2	0	0	2	0
Albury, James, Gulf Coast Red Sox	.875	10	4	3	1	8	0
Alvarez, Basilio, Gulf Coast Pirates	1.000	2	1	0	0	1	0
Alvarez, Juan, Gulf Coast Phillies	1.000	11	0	3	0	3	0
Amador, Anderson, Gulf Coast Yankees	...	7	0	0	0	0	0
Appell, Josh, Gulf Coast Mets *	1.000	11	1	0	0	1	0
Arias, Keily, Gulf Coast Pirates *	.750	16	0	3	1	4	0
Averill, Erik, Gulf Coast Tigers *	1.000	6	1	5	0	6	0
Avery, James, Gulf Coast Reds	1.000	6	1	2	0	3	0
Bahr, Jesse, Gulf Coast Yankees *	1.000	14	0	4	0	4	0
Barb, Andrew, Gulf Coast Phillies	1.000	2	0	2	0	2	0
Battista, Michael, Gulf Coast Mets	1.000	10	1	2	0	3	0
Beattie, Eric, Gulf Coast Tigers	.750	10	1	2	1	4	0
Berger, Garrett, Gulf Coast Tigers	1.000	7	2	2	0	4	0
Blasdell, Jared, Gulf Coast Phillies	1.000	2	1	0	0	1	0
Blue, William, Gulf Coast Red Sox	1.000	4	0	2	0	2	0
Boehringer, Brian, Gulf Coast Yankees	...	1	0	0	0	0	0
Borrell, Daniel, Gulf Coast Yankees *	1.000	3	3	0	0	3	0
Bowden, Michael, Gulf Coast Red Sox	1.000	4	0	2	0	2	0
Bowie, Micah, Gulf Coast Nationals *	1.000	7	1	2	0	3	0
Brito, Jose, Gulf Coast Reds *	...	11	0	0	0	0	0
Broadway, Michael, Gulf Coast Braves	.500	7	0	3	3	6	0
Brown, Jared, Gulf Coast Pirates *	1.000	7	2	0	0	2	0
Bryant, Patrick, Gulf Coast Twins	1.000	13	0	5	0	5	0
Burgos, Jose, Gulf Coast Twins	1.000	15	1	1	0	2	0
Burnett, Alex, Gulf Coast Twins	1.000	13	2	4	0	6	0
Byrd, Darren, Gulf Coast Phillies	.900	9	4	5	1	10	0

Player, Team	Pct.	G	PO	A	E	TC	DP
Cabrera, Domingo, Gulf Coast Yankees *	.909	11	4	6	1	11	0
Cabrera, Henry, Gulf Coast Red Sox	1.000	7	3	2	0	5	0
Candelario, Eddie, Gulf Coast Pirates	...	1	0	0	0	0	0
Caraballo, Jesse, Gulf Coast Tigers	.889	12	5	3	1	9	0
Carlyle, Buddy, Gulf Coast Dodgers	1.000	1	1	0	0	1	0
Carrasco, Carlos, Gulf Coast Phillies	1.000	2	0	1	0	1	0
Carter, Andrew, Gulf Coast Yankees	1.000	11	3	1	0	4	1
Castillo, Arismendy, Gulf Coast Dodgers	.778	12	2	5	2	9	0
Castillo, Francisco, Gulf Coast Yankees	.818	12	4	5	2	11	0
Castillo, Jose, Gulf Coast Twins	.917	11	5	6	1	12	1
Castor, Parrish, Gulf Coast Marlins *	1.000	15	3	6	0	9	0
Castro, Julio Cesar, Gulf Coast Pirates	.933	13	3	11	1	15	1
Castro, Yeliar, Gulf Coast Braves	...	5	0	0	0	0	0
Cerezo, Hector, Gulf Coast Nationals *	1.000	4	1	2	0	3	1
Clapp, Bradley, Gulf Coast Pirates	1.000	9	3	7	0	10	0
Cofield, Kyle, Gulf Coast Braves	1.000	10	1	0	0	1	0
Colina, Ederson, Gulf Coast Pirates *	1.000	9	0	4	0	4	0
Concepcion, Alexander, Gulf Coast Phillies	...	7	0	0	0	0	0
Cook, Steven, Gulf Coast Nationals	1.000	3	0	2	0	2	0
Cordero, Jose, Gulf Coast Twins	1.000	12	2	5	0	7	1
Covington, Marcus, Gulf Coast Braves	.667	10	0	2	1	3	0
Cox, Timothy, Gulf Coast Red Sox *	1.000	11	1	6	0	7	0
Craig, Aaron, Gulf Coast Twins	.833	21	1	4	1	6	0
Cramer, Terrence, Gulf Coast Pirates	.833	18	2	3	1	6	0
Crawford, Nathan, Gulf Coast Twins	.750	14	0	3	1	4	0
Cruz, Reymond, Gulf Coast Phillies	.667	9	1	3	2	6	0
Cruz, Rhiner, Gulf Coast Tigers	1.000	14	1	6	0	7	0
Cueto, Johnny, Gulf Coast Reds	.889	13	2	6	1	9	0
Dasni, Chales, Gulf Coast Dodgers	.800	12	2	2	1	5	0
De La Cruz, Jose, Gulf Coast Marlins	1.000	17	2	1	0	3	0
De Los Santos, Armado, Gulf Coast Nationals	...	1	0	0	0	0	0
Diaz, Jose, Gulf Coast Dodgers	1.000	2	1	0	0	1	0
Diaz, Wilfredo, Gulf Coast Dodgers *	.833	13	1	4	1	6	0
Dillard, Johnny, Gulf Coast Reds	1.000	13	0	3	0	3	0
Dominguez, Kelvin, Gulf Coast Dodgers *	...	2	0	0	0	0	0
Duff, Grant, Gulf Coast Yankees	.500	4	0	1	1	2	0
Durkin, Matthew, Gulf Coast Mets	...	1	0	0	0	0	0
Eager, Blake, Gulf Coast Mets	1.000	2	1	1	0	2	0
Edlich, Kyle, Gulf Coast Twins *	.818	10	0	9	2	11	0
Engles, Terrence, Gulf Coast Nationals	.950	12	6	13	1	20	0
Enriquez, Andre, Gulf Coast Nationals	1.000	7	0	1	0	1	0
Evangelista, Antonio, Gulf Coast Nationals	...	4	0	0	0	0	0
Everitt, Keaton, Gulf Coast Yankees	1.000	8	2	1	0	3	0
Everts, Clinton, Gulf Coast Nationals	1.000	7	1	1	0	2	0
Fernandes, Kyle, Gulf Coast Red Sox *	1.000	11	2	8	0	10	0
Figueroa, Jorge, Gulf Coast Mets	1.000	15	2	2	0	4	0
Flores, Adalberto, Gulf Coast Marlins	.600	13	0	3	2	5	0
Flores, Juan, Gulf Coast Dodgers *	1.000	15	0	4	0	4	0
Francisco, Bartolo, Gulf Coast Nationals	.947	10	5	13	1	19	0
French, Lucas, Gulf Coast Tigers *	.500	2	0	1	1	2	0
Frias, Juan, Gulf Coast Reds *	1.000	3	0	3	0	3	0
Frias, Junior, Gulf Coast Red Sox	...	1	0	0	0	0	0
Galbizo, Rafael, Gulf Coast Marlins	1.000	12	1	2	0	3	0
Garces, Rich, Gulf Coast Red Sox	1.000	3	1	0	0	1	0
Garcia, Christian, Gulf Coast Yankees	.000	2	0	0	1	1	0
Garcia, Edgar, Gulf Coast Phillies	1.000	10	2	5	0	7	0
Garcia, Jose, Gulf Coast Marlins	1.000	1	0	1	0	1	0
Garcia, Ramon, Gulf Coast Tigers *	1.000	10	3	7	0	10	0
Garmon, Ryan, Gulf Coast Reds *	.333	9	1	0	2	3	0
Garrison, Kale, Gulf Coast Dodgers *	1.000	5	1	0	0	1	0
Garza, Rodolfo, Gulf Coast Nationals	1.000	3	0	3	0	3	0
Gazo, Lenin, Gulf Coast Phillies	.857	11	1	5	1	7	0
Gearhart, Kalen, Gulf Coast Dodgers	1.000	14	0	2	0	2	0
German, Yulkin, Gulf Coast Red Sox *	1.000	11	5	5	0	10	0
Gil, Luis, Gulf Coast Tigers	1.000	9	5	10	0	15	1
Gomez, Abel, Gulf Coast Yankees *	.750	4	3	0	1	4	0
Gonzalez, Alexander, Gulf Coast Red Sox	1.000	18	0	6	0	6	0
Gonzalez, Raul, Gulf Coast Braves	1.000	6	1	2	0	3	0
Gooch, Tyler, Gulf Coast Phillies	1.000	5	0	2	0	2	0
Gracesqui, Franklyn, Gulf Coast Marlins *	...	3	0	0	0	0	0
Gray, Matthew, Gulf Coast Reds *	1.000	10	1	1	0	2	0
Hakey, Patrick, Gulf Coast Mets	1.000	6	0	3	0	3	0
Haldis, Jonathan, Gulf Coast Dodgers	1.000	12	2	2	0	4	0
Haltiwanger, Kevin, Gulf Coast Reds	1.000	13	3	5	0	8	0
Hampton, Mike, Gulf Coast Braves *	...	1	0	0	0	0	0
Hansen, Craig, Gulf Coast Red Sox	...	2	0	0	0	0	0
Harrington, Jake, Gulf Coast Mets	1.000	9	3	5	0	8	0
Harrison, Ryan, Gulf Coast Nationals	1.000	11	6	10	0	16	0
Herbort, Ryan, Gulf Coast Pirates	1.000	4	0	3	0	3	0
Herman, Jason, Gulf Coast Pirates	.867	11	5	8	2	15	1
Hernandez, Bladimil, Gulf Coast Pirates	.833	8	1	4	1	6	0
Hernandez, Danny, Gulf Coast Twins	1.000	13	1	1	0	2	0
Hinchman, Grady, Gulf Coast Mets *	1.000	14	1	6	0	7	0
Hirota, Rodrigo, Gulf Coast Mets	.923	8	2	10	1	13	0
Hobdy, Christopher, Gulf Coast Dodgers	...	5	0	0	0	0	0
Holdzkom, Lincoln, Gulf Coast Marlins	1.000	3	0	1	0	1	0
Holquin, Steven, Gulf Coast Mets	.667	11	2	2	2	6	0
Howington, Ty, Gulf Coast Reds *	...	3	0	0	0	0	0
Huddy, Kyle, Gulf Coast Reds	.833	13	1	4	1	6	0
Jacobsen, Landon, Gulf Coast Pirates	1.000	5	1	3	0	4	1
James, Jimmy, Gulf Coast Red Sox	.875	7	4	3	1	8	0
Japa, Rolando, Gulf Coast Yankees	.857	12	2	4	1	7	0
Jarrett, Jason, Gulf Coast Marlins	.750	9	0	3	1	4	0
Jefferson, John, Gulf Coast Red Sox	...	4	0	0	0	0	0
Jimenez, Santos, Gulf Coast Reds	...	5	0	0	0	0	0
Johnson, Anthony, Gulf Coast Nationals	1.000	4	0	1	0	1	0
Johnson, Steven, Gulf Coast Dodgers	1.000	6	0	2	0	2	0
Johnson, Tod, Gulf Coast Reds *	1.000	9	0	3	0	3	0
Jones, Beau, Gulf Coast Braves *	.882	8	3	12	2	17	0
Jones, Blake, Gulf Coast Marlins	1.000	6	0	1	0	1	0
Jones, Christopher, Gulf Coast Red Sox	...	1	0	0	0	0	0
Joseph, Jacob, Gulf Coast Mets	1.000	4	0	1	0	1	0
Jostock, William, Gulf Coast Mets	1.000	9	2	7	0	9	1
Katz, Jeffrey, Gulf Coast Braves	1.000	9	1	0	0	1	0
Kelly, Mark, Gulf Coast Phillies	1.000	13	2	1	0	3	0
Kroenke, Zachary, Gulf Coast Yankees *	.000	1	0	0	1	1	0
Lambert, Bryan, Gulf Coast Nationals	1.000	10	1	6	0	7	0
Lanier, Thomas, Gulf Coast Reds	1.000	10	2	3	0	5	0
Lawrence, Horace, Gulf Coast Mets *	...	5	0	0	0	0	0
Lewis, Jonathan, Gulf Coast Marlins	1.000	3	0	1	0	1	0
Linares, Remos Eugenio, Gulf Coast Red Sox.	1.000	13	1	2	0	3	0
Lindeen, Scott, Gulf Coast Marlins	.875	15	1	6	1	8	0
Linder, Matthew, Gulf Coast Phillies	.500	12	0	1	1	2	0
Long, Nicholas, Gulf Coast Nationals	...	2	0	0	0	0	0
Looney, Marshal, Gulf Coast Dodgers *	...	3	0	0	0	0	0
Lorenzo, Pedro, Gulf Coast Dodgers	...	1	0	0	0	0	0
Lugo, Chris, Gulf Coast Nationals	1.000	5	2	10	0	12	3
Lyman, Jeffrey, Gulf Coast Braves	.700	8	1	6	3	10	0
Lyons, Thomas, Gulf Coast Tigers	.800	7	2	2	1	5	0
Manuel, Robert, Gulf Coast Mets	1.000	12	3	4	0	7	0
Marte, Enmanuel, Gulf Coast Pirates *	.667	10	0	2	1	3	0
Martinez, Yoffri, Gulf Coast Pirates	1.000	14	1	1	0	2	0
Mateo, Marcos, Gulf Coast Reds	.929	13	3	10	1	14	0
Mavroulis, Coby, Gulf Coast Nationals *	.875	9	1	6	1	8	0
McConnell, Brandon, Gulf Coast Twins	.727	11	1	7	3	11	0
McDade, Neal, Gulf Coast Pirates	...	1	0	0	0	0	0
McEnaney, Alex, Gulf Coast Phillies	1.000	10	1	3	0	4	0
McIntyre, Robert, Gulf Coast Mets	1.000	11	1	6	0	7	0
Medina, Josvic, Gulf Coast Mets	.000	8	0	1	1	1	0
Megrew, Michael, Gulf Coast Dodgers *	1.000	3	0	1	0	1	0
Mejias, Jose Angel, Gulf Coast Phillies	.833	15	1	4	1	6	1
Mendez, Deivi, Gulf Coast Yankees	...	1	0	0	0	0	0
Mendez, Jesus, Gulf Coast Yankees	1.000	12	1	0	0	1	0
Mendoza, Ramiro, Gulf Coast Yankees	1.000	2	1	0	0	1	0
Mercedes, Manuel, Gulf Coast Nationals	1.000	7	1	2	0	3	0
Meyers, Ryan, Gulf Coast Mets	1.000	5	1	1	0	2	0
Miller, Greg, Gulf Coast Dodgers *	1.000	4	1	0	0	1	0
Mitchinson, Scott, Gulf Coast Phillies	...	1	0	0	0	0	0
Mlotkowski, Michael, Gulf Coast Yankees	1.000	1	2	0	0	2	0
Molleken, Dustin, Gulf Coast Pirates	.750	9	1	2	1	4	0
Montan, Miguel, Gulf Coast Yankees	1.000	12	0	3	0	3	0
Morales, Jorge, Gulf Coast Yankees	1.000	11	0	2	0	2	0
Moya, Luis, Gulf Coast Reds	1.000	3	1	1	0	2	0
Muniz, Carlos, Gulf Coast Mets	...	2	0	0	0	0	0
Naatjes, Darin, Gulf Coast Phillies	...	1	0	0	0	0	0
Napolitan, Phillip, Gulf Coast Tigers	...	1	0	0	0	0	0
Nelson, Brad, Gulf Coast Braves	...	1	0	0	0	0	0
Newman, Brandon, Gulf Coast Reds *	.846	13	2	9	2	13	0
Niese, Jonathon, Gulf Coast Mets *	1.000	7	0	2	0	2	0
Norrito, Giuseppe, Gulf Coast Dodgers	.750	11	0	3	1	4	0
Oakes, Gerard, Gulf Coast Braves	1.000	3	2	0	0	2	0
Obispo, Jose, Gulf Coast Dodgers	.000	2	0	0	1	1	0
Olivo, Haysdersman, Gulf Coast Marlins	1.000	14	3	1	0	4	0
Olson, Matthew, Gulf Coast Phillies	1.000	9	6	2	0	8	0
Omana, Edgar, Gulf Coast Yankees *	1.000	9	0	1	0	1	0
Ortiz, Jose Francisco, Gulf Coast Red Sox *.	1.000	14	4	5	0	9	0
Ozuna, Cruzito, Gulf Coast Nationals	.750	10	0	3	1	4	0
Pahucki, David, Gulf Coast Red Sox	...	1	0	0	0	0	0
Paredes, Ramon, Gulf Coast Dodgers *	1.000	9	3	10	0	13	1
Paris, Gary, Gulf Coast Dodgers *	.833	14	2	3	1	6	0

Player, Team	Pct.	G	PO	A	E	TC	DP
Patton, Walter, Gulf Coast Twins	.800	17	1	3	1	5	0
Paulk, Robert, Gulf Coast Mets	.500	1	0	2	2	4	1
Pavano, Carl, Gulf Coast Yankees	1.000	1	0	2	0	2	0
Pello, Brandon, Gulf Coast Marlins	1.000	7	0	2	0	2	0
Peralta, Yader, Gulf Coast Red Sox	.875	17	1	6	1	8	0
Perdomo, Orlando, Gulf Coast Tigers	.750	17	1	2	1	4	0
PERKS, MATTHEW, Gulf Coast Nationals	1.000	12	9	12	0	21	0
Phillips, Ryan, Gulf Coast Red Sox *	...	1	0	0	0	0	0
Phillips, William, Gulf Coast Red Sox	.714	9	0	5	2	7	1
Pichardo, Eduardo, Gulf Coast Nationals	...	8	0	0	0	0	0
Pichardo, Kelvin, Gulf Coast Phillies	.875	10	3	4	1	8	1
Pie, Esequier, Gulf Coast Marlins	.900	12	3	6	1	10	0
Pinango, Miguel, Gulf Coast Mets	1.000	1	0	1	0	1	0
Plexico, Gerald, Gulf Coast Nationals *	1.000	3	0	2	0	2	0
Plummer, Jarod, Gulf Coast Dodgers	...	1	0	0	0	0	0
Powell, Jay, Gulf Coast Braves	1.000	2	0	1	0	1	0
Powers, Joseph, Gulf Coast Reds	...	1	0	0	0	0	0
Prieto, Victor, Gulf Coast Red Sox	...	1	0	0	0	0	0
Quaglieri, William, Gulf Coast Mets	...	1	0	0	0	0	0
Quintana, Eduardo, Gulf Coast Dodgers	1.000	15	1	5	0	6	0
Ramirez, Emmanuel, Gulf Coast Pirates	1.000	8	0	1	0	1	1
Ramirez, Miguel, Gulf Coast Dodgers	1.000	15	1	1	0	2	0
Rasowsky, Avi, Gulf Coast Marlins *	1.000	6	0	3	0	3	0
Raulinaitis, Christopher, Gulf Coast Phillies..	1.000	12	2	1	0	3	1
Rayo, Pedro, Gulf Coast Braves	.750	11	0	3	1	4	0
Reina, Dimas, Gulf Coast Dodgers	...	1	0	0	0	0	0
Reyes, Joseph, Gulf Coast Braves *	1.000	3	0	1	0	1	0
Richmond, Jamie, Gulf Coast Braves	...	8	0	0	0	0	0
Riggan, Jerrod, Gulf Coast Mets	...	6	0	0	0	0	0
Rios, Cristian, Gulf Coast Reds *	.500	8	0	1	1	2	0
Rios, Travis, Gulf Coast Red Sox	1.000	4	0	1	0	1	0
Robertson, Nash, Gulf Coast Pirates	1.000	6	1	4	0	5	0
Rodriguez, Orlando, Gulf Coast Dodgers * ...	...	1	0	0	0	0	0
Ruckle, Jacob, Gulf Coast Mets	1.000	11	4	6	0	10	0
Rudrude, Brett, Gulf Coast Red Sox	1.000	4	0	1	0	1	0
Rueger, Bryan, Gulf Coast Yankees *	1.000	4	1	0	0	1	0
Rusch, Matthew, Gulf Coast Tigers	.714	7	1	4	2	7	0
Russell, Stephen, Gulf Coast Braves	.500	3	1	0	1	2	0
Ruzic, Dushan, Gulf Coast Marlins	.917	17	6	5	1	12	0
Salas, Joseph, Gulf Coast Pirates	.750	9	2	1	1	4	0
Sanchez, Romulo, Gulf Coast Pirates	1.000	2	1	1	0	2	0
Sanfler, Miguel, Gulf Coast Dodgers *	.700	13	1	6	3	10	0
Santiago, Jose, Gulf Coast Braves	.667	6	1	1	1	3	0
Santos, Adriano, Gulf Coast Tigers	1.000	20	1	5	0	6	0
Schoenbachler, Jeffrey, Gulf Coast Twins *..	.800	9	2	2	1	5	0
Schroder, Christopher, Gulf Coast Nationals.	...	1	0	0	0	0	0
Segovia, Omar, Gulf Coast Reds *	...	6	0	0	0	0	0

Player, Team	Pct.	G	PO	A	E	TC	DP
Selenes, Josue, Gulf Coast Yankees	1.000	12	2	1	0	3	0
Shaffer, Jared, Gulf Coast Braves	.909	9	1	9	1	11	0
Sierra, Waldy, Gulf Coast Tigers	.778	12	3	4	2	9	1
Smiley, Wesley, Gulf Coast Reds	1.000	14	0	2	0	2	0
Smith, Christopher, Gulf Coast Red Sox	...	1	0	0	0	0	0
Soto, Auddy, Gulf Coast Nationals	...	1	0	0	0	0	0
Soto, Edgar, Gulf Coast Yankees *	1.000	8	1	2	0	3	0
Sparks, Terrance, Gulf Coast Reds *	.600	12	1	2	2	5	1
Stanley, Adam, Gulf Coast Braves *	...	4	0	0	0	0	0
Stewart, Clayton, Gulf Coast Phillies	1.000	2	1	0	0	1	0
Suero, Nicolas, Gulf Coast Pirates	.846	11	3	8	2	13	0
Tabeek, Kyle, Gulf Coast Red Sox	1.000	8	0	1	0	1	0
Taylor, Rhys, Gulf Coast Red Sox	.857	11	0	6	1	7	0
Tejada, Jonathan, Gulf Coast Braves	1.000	8	1	7	0	8	1
Tejeda, Ferdin, Gulf Coast Yankees	1.000	7	1	3	0	4	0
Thompson, Aaron, Gulf Coast Marlins *	.333	8	1	0	2	3	0
Thompson, Michael, Gulf Coast Braves	1.000	12	0	3	0	3	0
Towery, Kenneth, Gulf Coast Red Sox	.875	12	1	6	1	8	0
Treanor, Bryan, Gulf Coast Marlins	1.000	5	0	1	0	1	0
Trejo, Miguel, Gulf Coast Tigers	.667	19	1	1	1	3	0
Tucker, Ryan, Gulf Coast Marlins	1.000	8	0	7	0	7	0
Urena, Jose, Gulf Coast Nationals *	1.000	13	1	2	0	3	0
Valenzuela, Sergio, Gulf Coast Braves	.917	8	1	10	1	12	0
Velazquez, Juan, Gulf Coast Yankees	.833	10	2	3	1	6	0
Villalona, Guillermo, Gulf Coast Yankees	.875	7	3	4	1	8	0
Volstad, Christopher, Gulf Coast Marlins	.833	6	2	3	1	6	0
Waldie, Andrew, Gulf Coast Phillies	1.000	8	0	3	0	3	0
Walk, John, Gulf Coast Pirates	...	1	0	0	0	0	0
Wall, Joshua, Gulf Coast Dodgers	1.000	5	1	4	0	5	0
Ward, Joshua, Gulf Coast Braves	.750	12	1	2	1	4	0
Warren, Jesse, Gulf Coast Braves *	1.000	10	1	1	0	2	0
Watkins, Michael, Gulf Coast Nationals	1.000	5	1	2	0	3	0
Watts, Joey, Gulf Coast Tigers *	1.000	5	0	2	0	2	0
West, Sean, Gulf Coast Marlins *	1.000	9	1	9	0	10	0
Williams, David, Gulf Coast Braves	.800	13	2	2	1	5	0
Williams, Joseph, Gulf Coast Mets *	1.000	3	0	1	0	1	0
Williams, Matthew, Gulf Coast Twins	.833	20	2	3	1	6	0
Wilson, Brandon, Gulf Coast Mets	.500	4	0	1	1	2	0
Wilson, David, Gulf Coast Braves *	...	9	0	0	0	0	0
Winters, Kyle, Gulf Coast Marlins	.933	11	5	9	1	15	1
Wise, Brendan, Gulf Coast Tigers	1.000	10	6	8	0	14	0
Wood, Travis, Gulf Coast Reds *	1.000	8	1	5	0	6	0
Wordekemper, Eric, Gulf Coast Yankees	1.000	9	3	4	0	7	1
Wright, Jaret, Gulf Coast Yankees	1.000	1	0	1	0	1	0
Wright, Matthew, Gulf Coast Braves	1.000	3	0	3	0	3	0
Young, Terrell, Gulf Coast Reds	...	3	0	0	0	0	0
Zuleta, Howar, Gulf Coast Dodgers	1.000	2	1	0	0	1	0

LEAGUE CHAMPIONS

Year	Team	Pct.
1964—	Sarasota Braves	.610
1965—	Bradenton Astros	.632
1966—	New York AL	.667
1967—	Kansas City	.614
1968—	Oakland	.650
1969—	Montreal	.585
1970—	Chicago AL	.600
1971—	Kansas City	.755
1972—	Chicago NL*	.651
	Kansas City*	.651
1973—	Texas	.732
1974—	Chicago NL	.702
1975—	Texas	.774
1976—	Texas	.704
1977—	Chicago AL	.731
1978—	Texas	.600
1979—	Houston	.635
1980—	Kansas City-Blue	.635
1981—	Kansas City-Gold	.688
1982—	New York AL	.667
1983—	Texas	.645
	Los Angeles†	.617
1984—	White Sox	.651
	Rangers†	.571
1985—	Yankees§	.705
	Rangers	.532
1986—	Reds	.548
	Dodgers†	.541
1987—	Dodgers†	.683

Year	Team	Pct.
	Royals	.635
1988—	Yankees†	.714
	Royals	.619
1989—	Yankees‡	.651
	Dodgers	.635
1990—	Expos	.635
	Dodgers‡	.603
1991—	Orioles	.593
	Expos∞	.533
1992—	Royals∞	.695
	Expos	.593
1993—	Rangers▲	.667
	Astros	.593
1994—	Royals◆	.797
	Astros	.695
1995—	Royals■	.649
	Tigers	.579
1996—	Yankees◆	.638
	Rangers	.617
1997—	Mets▼	.700
	Rangers	.567
1998—	Marlins	.633
	Rangers▲	.567
1999—	Mets◆	.650
2000—	Rangers◆	.679
2001—	Dodgers	.683
	Yankees◆	.583
2002—	Phillies◆	.650
2003—	Braves◆	.633

Year	Team	Pct.
2004—	Yankees◆	.610
2005—	Yankees◆	.623

*Declared co-champions; no playoff. †League divided into Northern and Southern divisions; won one-game playoff for league championship. ‡League divided into Northern and Southern divisions; won best-of-three playoff for league championship. §Yankees declared champion based on winning percentage when one-game playoff against Rangers was rained out. ∞League divided into Northern, Southern and Central divisions; won best-of-three playoff for league championship. ▲League divided into Eastern, Central and Western divisions; won three-team playoff. ◆League divided into Eastern, Northern and Southern divisions; won three-team playoff. ■League divided into Eastern, Northern, Northwest and Southwest divisions; won four-team playoff. ▼League divided into Eastern, Western and Northwest divisions; won four-club playoff. (Note—Known as Sarasota Rookie League in 1964 and Florida Rookie League in 1965.)

MINOR LEAGUE INDEX

TEAMS AND CITIES